Rob. P9-DTE-791

THE CRITICAL TRADITION

Classic Texts and Contemporary Trends

THE CRITICAL TRADITION

Classic Texts and Contemporary Trends

Second Edition

Edited by

David H. Richter

Queens College
of the City University of New York

BEDFORD BOOKS ☙ BOSTON

For Bedford Books
President and Publisher: Charles H. Christensen
General Manager and Associate Publisher: Joan E. Feinberg
Managing Editor: Elizabeth M. Schaaf
Developmental Editor: Katherine A. Retan
Production Editor: Julie Sullivan
Copyeditor: Marie Salter
Cover Design: Richard Emery Design, Inc.

Library of Congress Catalog Card Number: 97–74970

Copyright © 1998 by Bedford Books
A Division of St. Martin's Press, Inc.

All rights reserved. No part of this book may be reproduced, stored in a retrieval system, or transmitted in any form or by any means, electronic, mechanical, photocopying, recording, or otherwise, except as may be expressly permitted by the applicable copyright statutes or in writing by the Publisher.
Manufactured in the United States of America.

2 1 0 9 8
f e d c b

For information, write: Bedford Books, 75 Arlington Street, Boston, MA 02116
(617–426–7440)

ISBN: 0–312–10106–6

Acknowledgments

Theodor Adorno, from *Minima Moralia: Reflections from a Damaged Life* by Theodor Adorno. Translated by E. F. N. Jephcott. Copyright © 1974 by Verso / NLB. Reprinted by permission of the publisher.

Dante Alighieri, "Letter to Can Grande della Scala." Reprinted from *Literary Criticism of Dante Alighieri*, translated and edited by Robert S. Haller, by permission of the University of Nebraska Press. Copyright © 1973 by the University of Nebraska Press.

Aristotle, *Poetics*, reprinted from *Aristotle's Poetics: A Translation and Commentary for Students of Literature*, by Leon Golden and O. B. Hardison, Jr., by permission of the publisher, University Press of Florida.

Nancy Armstrong, "Some Call It Fiction: On the Politics of Domesticity," from *The Other Perspective in Gender and Culture: Rewriting Women and the Symbolic*, ed. Juliet Flower MacConnell. Copyright © 1990 by Columbia University Press. Reprinted with permission of the publisher.

Erich Auerbach, "Odysseus' Scar," from *Mimesis* by Erich Auerbach. Copyright © 1953 renewed 1981 by Princeton University Press. Reprinted by permission of Princeton University Press.

Mikhail Bakhtin, "Discourse in Dostoevsky," from *Problems of Dostoevsky's Poetics* by Mikhail Bakhtin, translated by Caryl Emerson, published by the University of Minnesota Press, Minneapolis. Copyright © 1984 by the University of Minnesota. Reprinted by permission. Excerpt from "Discourse in the Novel," from *The Dialogic Imagination: Four Essays* by M. M. Bakhtin, edited by Michael Holquist, translated by Caryl Emerson and Michael Holquist, Copyright © 1981. By permission of the University of Texas Press.

Roland Barthes, "From Work to Text," from *Image — Music — Text* by Roland Barthes. Copyright © 1977 by Roland Barthes by permission of Hill and Wang, a division of Farrar, Straus and Giroux and by permission of the Estate of Roland Barthes.

Acknowledgments and copyrights are continued at the back of the book on pages 1615–1618, which constitute an extension of the copyright page. It is a violation of the law to reproduce these selections by any means whatsoever without the written permission of the copyright holder.

Preface

The "canon of theory" introduces into the institutional context of literary pedagogy (the graduate seminar) a syllabus whose symptomatic function is to signify precisely methodological "rigor," rather than the taste or discrimination which for so long determined the ideological protocols of literary criticism. . . . Those authors or texts designated as "theoretical" are now increasingly capable of being introduced to students in traditional routinized forms, even by means of anthologies.

— JOHN GUILLORY, *Cultural Capital* (1993)

THE FIRST WAVE

In the late 1960s, when I started teaching, literary criticism was primarily an arcane subspecialty of historical research, in which scholars quarreled about Philip Sidney's distinction between "poesy" and "poetry" or the relative influence of Horace and Longinus on Samuel Johnson. My own interest in literary theory as an ongoing as well as a historic concern, stimulated by University of Chicago professors Wayne Booth and Sheldon Sacks, Norman Maclean and Richard McKeon, then seemed a harmless oddity to most of my colleagues at Queens College. One of them, since guilty of a metacritical book himself, warned me authoritatively over lunch that I was wasting my time with theory because there was no future in it.

By then, of course, a revolution had already begun that would end by making critical theory the roiling pivot-point of the profession of letters, the one topic the fans of Philip Roth and the devotees of Lady Mary Wroth might have in common. The turbulence and clash of ideas had begun decades before on the Continent, but those of us in the provinces, who read French and German haltingly and Russian not at all, did not experience the explosion of theory until the mid-1970s, as structuralism and semiotics, deconstruction, Lacanian psychology, Althusserian Marxism, Russian formalism, phenomenology, and reception theory rode successive waves into our awareness. A profession that a few years before had been hacking out dozens of progressively less plausible ways of misreading *The Turn of the Screw* was now lit up with a rush of ideas, a dozen disparate systems with enormous philosophical reach and scope, many of which were capable of informing and channeling the social imperatives of women and minorities who were seeking a theoretical manifestation of their need for greater freedom and power. To academics like me, the sense of liberation was palpable, and one felt like echoing Wordsworth's sentiments about a much more significant revolution two hundred years past: "Great it was in that dawn to be alive/But to be young was very heaven." The first edition of *The Critical Tradition* was conceived in the rush of that era, as a tool to help my own students and those like them all over North America, many innocent of philosophy of any sort, take tentative steps toward joining the magnificent conversation going on about them. Its aim was not merely to provide an anthology of contemporary theory, with examples of all the latest trends, but a book that could locate and present the sources of the new theory within Western intellectual history going back to Plato.

The revolution was, after all, reshaping our sense of intellectual history, forcing us to broaden our horizons. Anglo-American feminist theory, like that of Elaine Showalter and Sandra Gilbert, needed to be understood against the backdrop of Germaine de Staël, Virginia Woolf, Simone de Beauvoir, and other forebears who had served either as sources of inspiration or as antagonists. Understanding Derrida required a familiarity not only with the theories of structuralism and semiotics against which he had reacted, but with the work of such philosophers as Plato, Kant, Hegel, Nietzsche, and Heidegger, some of whom were comparative strangers to traditional literary criticism courses. With the waning of the hegemony of New Critical explication as the "normal" mode of practical criticism, the differences between the various New Critics like Allen Tate, John Crowe Ransom, and Cleanth Brooks no longer seemed as profound as they once had, and the New Criticism came to be characterized as a trend within the larger formalist movement of the earlier part of the twentieth century that also comprehended such disparate theorists as Victor Shklovsky and R. S. Crane. An entire tradition of rhetorical theory going back to classical times, whose centrality had depended on that of the New Criticism, was displaced. But original thinkers like Kenneth Burke, who had once been seen within the context of New Criticism, now assumed unique places in the pantheon.

THE SECOND WAVE: PRACTICES AND PIDGINS

Intellectual revolutions too have their Thermidors, and not long after *The Critical Tradition* appeared in 1989, it began to become clear that the era of Grand Theory was coming to an end. There was no longer to be arriving every year a rediscovered thinker with the impact of Bakhtin, nor a new theory with the impact of deconstruction: Theory had moved into a period of consolidation, in which it was being used not for its own sake but to make possible a new sort of encounter with a text or a series of related texts. New critical practices emergent since the beginning of the revolution, engaged in "gender studies," "new historicism," and, broadest of all, "cultural studies," began to dominate the graduate and undergraduate study of literature.

The new practices were based on theory and were incomprehensible in isolation from their theoretical origins. Genuinely coming to terms with the new historicist methodology involved reading abstract texts: not only practitioners like Stephen Greenblatt and Jerome McGann but theorists like Clifford Geertz and Hayden White and Michel Foucault. And to do things properly, one would have to read not only Clifford Geertz on the semiotics of culture but Max Weber and Émile Durkheim and Claude Lévi-Strauss; not only Hayden White on the tropics of history but Jacques Derrida and Ludwig Wittgenstein; not only Michel Foucault on the archaeology of power and knowledge, but Martin Heidegger and the later Nietzsche. The bases for gender studies and cultural studies were even wider and more diverse.

The process of consolidating and simplifying the elaborate and difficult Grand Theories into workable critical practices involved creating a pidgin, in much the same way people of different nationalities manage to communicate across language barriers by forming a lingua franca for trade and barter during interludes between hostilities. The development of this critical pidgin was encouraged by the way American universities avoided the creation of "schools" of like-minded thinkers such as those found on the Continent and instead filled positions so as to create the greatest possible diversity. English departments that had acquired a Lacanian or a reception theorist to be au courant did not feel the need for a breeding pair. This tendency to isolate individuals using particular theoretical vocabularies from one another had the consequence that, while practitioners of a given school could use their chosen critical language in all its purity in their own classrooms and at conferences of initiates, they had to find some common ground in talking with their colleagues. The result was a carnival of jostling jargons, in which purity of rhetoric took second place to the pragmatics of discourse. A gender theorist like Judith Butler could derive her notions about sex and society from Foucault, but her rhetorical ploys might be taken straight out of Derrida, and never mind that the two Frenchmen might otherwise be strange bedfellows. In the long run, one was less likely to talk like a feminist or a Marxist or a deconstructionist than like a combination of all three at once.

If all this has given literary studies a sense of common purpose that it has lacked since the hegemony of the New Criticism, there are also some potentially disturbing consequences. One problem is that pidgins are defective languages that suppress the more complex features of the individual languages that compose them. Critical pidgins frequently adopt terms without adopting the philosophies that generated them. When we try to say something for ourselves without fully understanding how each set of ideas from which we have borrowed works, the result is often gobbledygook composed of different and irreconcilable terminologies. One often reads "theory-damaged" discourse that sounds plausible but really makes no sense, like the following: "Bakhtin's reading of the process of self-realization is the opposite of Lacan's. If for Lacan there is an inevitable dismemberment of a total self, for Bakhtin there is a continual movement toward a self that is never total but always capable of further realization." It would take a long time to explain everything that is wrong with this formulation, though one might begin with the fact that in Lacan there is no "total self" to be dismembered except as an Imaginary construct. The main problem lies not in such details but in the unexamined assumption that Bakhtin's and Lacan's uses of the word "self" have enough in common to allow them to be juxtaposed in this way.

Muddle is one unfortunate result of our reliance on critical pidgins, but there may be a worse one. Many of our students may be absorbing the results of gender studies, new historicism, and cultural studies without coming to terms with the subtle theories that inform these approaches. For them, there is a danger that the pidgin will become a creole: a linguistic hybrid that is cut off from its origins in separate schools of thought and that suppresses the tacit implications of their ideas. Once this happens, the next generation of the theory-damaged will have no refuge from the internal contradictions of a hybrid discourse formed from some elements that aspire to be "scientific" and empirical, like Saussurean linguistics, and others that are deeply hostile to science and to positivism, like Foucauldian theory; some elements that are humanistic and pluralistic, like the work of Habermas, and others that, like the work of Derrida, are profoundly distrustful of any relics of the Enlightenment. So while a centralization of critical practices may have been desperately needed to correct the excesses of the era of Grand Theory, an understanding of theory is more desperately needed than ever to correct the incoherence of an eclectic critical practice.

YET ANOTHER CRITICAL TRADITION

It was against this understanding of our current moment in the history of literary criticism and theory that I began revising *The Critical Tradition.* In this age of pidgins and practices, there seemed to be less need than a decade ago to provide examples of literary theories in action, applied to particular texts. (There are also a good many excellent texts on the market, including the series edited by Ross Murfin for Bedford Books, which collect or commission Marxist, feminist, psychoanalytic, and other readings of a wide variety of literary materials.) It seemed more urgent to present the range of ideas and methods currently operating within critical modes: Terry Eagleton as well as Fredric Jameson in Marxist Criticism, Julia Kristeva as well as Peter Brooks in Psychoanalytic Theory. And there was an urgent need to present in their complexity the roots of the new practices: Two new chapters have been included, one on gender studies and queer theory, and one on the new historicism and cultural studies. (Post-colonial theory, slighted in the first edition, appears within the chapter on cultural studies.)

The volume, as before, is organized in two parts. Part I, Classic Texts, presents a history of criticism through fifty-eight selections by forty-four major critics from Plato through Susan Sontag. In this edition, new selections appear by Christine de Pisan, Aphra Behn, Germaine de Staël, Oscar Wilde, Sigmund Freud, Martin Heidegger, Erich Auerbach, and Hans-Georg Gadamer. In addition, essays by Karl Marx, Sigmund Freud, Carl Gustav Jung, Virginia Woolf, Edmund Wilson, F. R. Leavis, Jean-Paul Sartre, Simone de Beauvoir, Mikhail Bakhtin, and Northrop Frye, which had appeared in the first edition under one or another of the contemporary headings, have been repositioned, I think more suitably, as "classic texts."

Part II, Contemporary Trends, contains sixty-two essays. It is divided into nine chapters, as in the first edition, but the new arrangement of critical theories better reflects their current status and affiliations. In the first edition, for example, deconstruction was uneasily married to Foucault and other poststructuralist modes of criticism. In this edition, it is linked more aptly with structuralism and semiotics, as theories of languages and sign systems that continue to be essential for the understanding of current literary and cultural study but which are no longer widely being practiced purely as ends in themselves. (While gender theorists, for example, often employ deconstruction as a way of destabilizing binary thinking about sexual identities and practices, the vogue of publishing deconstructive readings of particular literary texts seems to have passed.) The chapter on psychoanalytic theory is more tightly focused on various forms of neo-Freudianism now that Freud, Jung, and Frye have been moved to Part I. What in the first edition had been a single "feminism" chapter has been split into two chapters, one on Anglo-American feminism of the 1970s and early 1980s, a project whose practices continue today, and the other on gender studies and queer theory, whose practitioners are interested in problematizing the very notions of sex and gender. The new historicism and cultural studies, casually mentioned in the introduction to Poststructuralism in the first edition, now have an extensive chapter presenting the theoretical roots of these practices. Finally, the "Issue under Debate" section has been replaced by a new chapter that explicitly combines the arguments within the canon wars with theories about multiculturalism and the politics of literature.

Other changes were made with an eye to the incoming mail. The survey of readers indicated a general aversion to the free translation of Horace's *Ars Poetica* I had chosen for the first edition, and a new translation by Smith Palmer Bovie has been substituted. A fuller and more accurate translation of the selections by Germaine de Staël, by Vivian Folkenflik, has been used now that it is available. I sought in vain for a new translation of Yuri Tynyanov's important contribution to the theory of literary history, and was forced to content myself with a more careful and elaborate annotation than usual to clarify his meanings for readers innocent both of Russian and of Russian literature. And there are dozens of other changes that users of the first edition will notice, including new essays by familiar authors as well as new exemplars of familiar modes of theory. All in all, over a third of the selections and editorial materials in the second edition of *The Critical Tradition* are new and, I hope, enormously improved.

"THE DULL DUTY OF AN EDITOR"

Because the critical tradition contains such varied ideas in such complex relationships, extensive apparatus — what Alexander Pope disdained as "dull duty" — has been provided to make the works collected here easier to assimilate. *The Critical Tradition* begins with an introduction that explores the ways in which theorists have tried to chart the terrain of criticism. This introduction describes the ineluctable fourfold classification of critical theories from M. H. Abrams's *The Mirror and the Lamp,* evaluates the powers and limitations of the Abrams map, its general biases and unspoken assumptions, and then discusses three other ways of mapping critical tasks and methods.

In Part I of *The Critical Tradition,* each reading is prefaced with an extensive headnote that places the text within the context of the author's life and works, explores the key issues of each reading and its relationship with other readings, and occasionally analyzes troublesome twists in the argumentation. For the readings by contemporary academic theorists and critics composing Part II, the biographical headnotes before each selection are necessarily briefer, but each of the nine chapters is prefaced by a substantial introduction. These introductions, addressed to the serious reader, cover the origins, the general approach, and the variations in theory and practice of each of the eight movements, and provide equivalent coverage for the issue under debate. Individual readings are analyzed primarily to mark out their place within larger critical trends. The introductions try to navigate between the Scylla of commentary that expresses only the prejudices of the editor and the Charybdis of neutralist mumbling addressed to nobody and expressing nothing. The intent was to provide an even-handed overview of each critical movement or issue showing both its powers and its limitations. Finally, following the headnotes to Part I and the introductions to Part II, selected bibliographies direct the interested reader to further works by and about the authors and their critical approaches. The texts in both parts are annotated to save the reader's time in tracking down allusions, to highlight the cross-references between one text and another, and to fill in the argument where the text has been abridged.

Although Part II sorts sixty-two selections into nine "schools" and "debates," it need hardly be said that even centrally placed "members" of a "school" swear no allegiance to its doctrines; despite the "fallacies" and "heresies" of the New Critics, there were no recorded excommunications. The problem is that some theorists bridge categories, as is becoming more and more usual these days. Pierre Bourdieu, one of the theoretical lights of cultural studies, is a Marxist sociologist, while the formalist Wayne Booth has written much reader-response criticism. Michel Foucault, influential everywhere these days, rightly appears in three chapters of the book, as a poststructuralist, as an influence on the new historicism, and as a gender theorist. Therefore, an additional table of contents that places theorists in alternative categories has been provided for Part II. The book concludes with an index to proper names and major critical terms, which, together with the cross-references in the annotations, should aid the reader in understanding the shifting skeins of influence upon which the critical tradition is built. "Let us now be told no more," as Samuel Johnson said with both weariness and pride, "of 'the dull duty of an editor.'"

ACKNOWLEDGMENTS

Although the title page might suggest a solo performance, no book the size and complexity of *The Critical Tradition* can be created alone. At every stage, from the initial impulse to produce the book to the final corrections in this revised edition, I have depended on the assistance and collaboration of colleagues within academia and publishing. At Bedford Books, first and foremost were Chuck Christensen and Joan Feinberg, who believed in the project and made it happen in the first place. Steve Scipione developed the first edition and worked out the myriad details that made it the teaching text it became, and Kathy Retan masterminded the adventurous revision that reshaped the book for the needs of the twenty-first century. The voluminous and candid dialogue between us (often grumpy on my side) gave me necessary perspective on my flippant prejudices and deep convictions and helped me recognize the difference between them. Aron Keesbury, Kathy's assistant, handled numerous details that came to my attention only when he caught and corrected my own errors and inadvertancies. For both editions, Elizabeth Schaaf headed the production crew that turned messy masses of manuscript into aesthetically pleasing objects, and Julie Sullivan undertook the unenviable task for the revision of threading a mass of new material with what was retained from the first edition, keeping continuity and consistency in the project. Having done it myself for the first edition, I am in a better position than most authors to appreciate the exhausting and intricate negotiations heroically performed by Margaret Hyre in procuring permissions for the revised edition.

I am also thankful to the literary critics, theorists, and teachers of literary theory who, during the development of one or both editions, have provided helpful suggestions and pointed comments on the choice of contents and editorial materials. They include Raymond L. Baubles, Jr., of Western Connecticut State University; Michael Beard of the University of North Dakota; Kathryn N. Benzel of the University of Nebraska, Kearney; Theron Britt of the University of Memphis; Suzanne L. Bunkers of Mankato State University; William E. Cain of Wellesley College; Joseph J. Colavito of the University of Arizona; Frederick Crews of the University of California, Berkeley; Robert Denham of Roanoke College; Bernard Duyfhuizen of the University of Wisconsin, Eau Claire; Neil Easterbrook of Texas Christian University; Lee Erickson of Marshall University; Thomas Ferraro of Duke University; Daniel Fineman of Occidental College; Jane Fisher of Canisius College; Peter Fitz of the University of Baltimore; Elizabeth Flynn of Michigan Technological University; Steven Goldsmith of the University of California, Berkeley; Stephen Greenblatt of the University of California, Berkeley; Marshall Gregory of Butler University; Susan Gubar of Indiana University, Bloomington; David Halliburton of Stanford University; Michael Hancher of the University of Minnesota; James Hans of Wake Forest University; Barbara Leah Harmon of Wellesley College; Frank Hoffman of Susquehanna University; Norman N. Holland of the University of Florida; John R. Holmes of the Franciscan University of Steubenville; Michael C. Jordan of the University of St. Thomas; William Kenney of Manhattan College; Mark Koch of St. Mary's College; Augustus M. Kolich of St. Xavier University; Page R. Laws of Norfolk State University; L. B. Lebim of Lock Haven University; Mary Libertin of Shippensburg University of Pennsylvania; Lawrence Lipking of Northwestern University; Zhang Longxi of the University of California, Riverside; Kathleen Lundeen of Western Washington University; Steven Mailloux of the University of California, Irvine; Bruce Martin of Drake University; Felix Martínez-Bonati of Columbia University; Bill McCarron of East Texas State University; Janet McNew of Illinois Wesleyan University; Michael Meyer of the University of Connecticut, Storrs; Nancy K. Miller of the Graduate Center, City University of New York; Michael Murrin of the University of Chicago; James W. Newcomb of Memphis State University; Eric W. Nye of the University of Wyoming; Charles O'Neill of St. Thomas Aquinas College; Edward O'Shea of the State University of New York, Oswego; Mary Poovey of New York University; Catherine Rainwater of St. Edward's University; Herman Rapaport of Wayne State University; James A. W. Rembert of The Citadel; Michael Karl Ritchie of Arkansas Tech University;

Thomas M. Rivers of the University of Southern Indiana; John G. Roberts of the University of Rochester; Michel Sexson of Montana State University; William Sheidley of the University of Southern Colorado; Elaine Showalter of Princeton University; Anne B. Simpson of California State Polytechnic University, Pomona; Barbara Herrnstein Smith of Duke University; Mark Trevor Smith of Southwest Missouri State University; James Sosnoski of Miami University; Patricia Meyer Spacks of the University of Virginia; Susan Suleiman of Harvard University; James Sullivan of California State University at Los Angeles; John Sykes of Wingate College; Brook Thomas of the University of California, Irvine; Jane Tompkins of Duke University; David Wagenknecht of Boston University; David Willbern of the State University of New York, Buffalo; and Clarisse Zimra of Southern Illinois University, Carbondale. While all these scholars and teachers have influenced the book's form and content, I would like to single out for particular mention James Phelan of Ohio State University, who read the entire manuscript of the first edition, whose perceptive commentary helped me to clarify and rethink my entrenched opinions, and whose unfailing tact and generosity of spirit made his suggestions easy to take.

In addition to these participants in formal reviewing procedures, the table of contents and sections of the manuscript were read by friends whose formal or casual suggestions I have shamelessly incorporated. These include Don Bialostosky of Penn State; Brian Corman of the University of Toronto (who told me all about Aphra); Bob Folkenflik of the University of California, Irvine; Susan K. Harris and William J. Harris of Penn State; Donald McQuade of the University of California, Berkeley; Laura Wadenpfuhl of Auburn University (who never spared me); and my colleagues at Queens College and/or the Graduate Center of the City University of New York: Barbara Bowen (who talked about gender and cultural studies with me), Nancy Comley (who has read everything), Bill Kelly, Steve Kruger (who put me straight about queer theory), Rich McCoy, Charles Molesworth, Tony O'Brien, Michael Sargent (who explained the *querelle*), Barbara Shollar, Joe Wittreich, and Susan Zimmerman. I would also like to thank my graduate assistant Gregory Erickson for his help with headnote research and manuscript preparation. My research for the second edition was carried out at the British Library, the Mina Rees Library at the CUNY Graduate Center, the New York Public Library, the Rosenthal Library of Queens College, and, hey, over the Internet. The index was produced and compiled on my own little Dell computer, and you don't want to know.

In closing, I recall those who taught me literary theory at the University of Chicago, including Wayne Booth, Norman Maclean, and Elder Olson, in whose criticism courses I sat with varying degrees of comprehension. At times I hear also the ghostly voices of R. S. Crane and Richard McKeon, and of Shelly Sacks, who taught me the uses of theory. From the thousands of students in the undergraduate and graduate literary criticism courses I have taught at Queens College over the last twenty-five years, I have learned what was clear and what opaque about the theoretical texts we studied together. I have tried to put some of that knowledge to work in this book, but I plan to continue learning from them.

The first edition of *The Critical Tradition* was dedicated to my son Gabriel, the boy I love, who will thank me, I hope, for not finding anything cute and embarrassing to say about him during his adolescence. The second edition is instead dedicated to a dear friend, a fine teacher, a brilliant scholar: Ralph Wilson Rader, of the University of California, Berkeley, whose lucid analysis of literary form and the historical institutions through which it operates to shape our culture has been the strongest single influence on my own recent work. May his exciting work in progress quickly follow this book into the patiently waiting world.

Contents

INTRODUCTION

Everybody . . . would be willing to admit, as a general proposition, that the critical faculty is lower than the inventive. But is it true that criticism is really, in itself, a baneful and injurious employment?

— MATTHEW ARNOLD, *The Function of Criticism at the Present Time* (1864)

What if criticism is a science as well as an art?

— NORTHROP FRYE, "The Function of Criticism at the Present Time" (1949)

Criticism is not literature, and the pleasure of criticism is not the pleasure of literature. . . . But experience suggests that the two pleasures go together, and the pleasure of criticism makes literature and its pleasure the more readily accessible.

— LIONEL TRILLING, Preface to *Literary Criticism: An Introductory Reader* (1970)

The movement to open the literary canon to works by minority authors has been paralleled in the last twenty-five years by an opening of the canon in another direction: The emergence of theory in the 1960s breached the disciplinary fortifications between literary texts and texts derived from other discourses, such as the linguistic, the psychoanalytic, the philosophical. These texts are sufficiently well identified now to constitute what may be called the "canon of theory."

— JOHN GUILLORY, *Cultural Capital* (1993)

In the Socratic dialogues of the early fourth century B.C., Plato raised skeptical questions about the value of art and literature that have provoked responses from artists and philosophers from Aristotle's day to our own. In striving to rescue poetry from the exile to which Socrates had condemned it, the defenders of literature have had to recast the questions Plato answered with such assurance. We are still asking the same questions today: What is the nature of the work of art? What are its sources in the artist, in the literary scene, in the society for which it is produced? What are its properties, uses, powers, and value? How is the nature of literature circumscribed by the properties of language itself, by the gender of the writer or the reader, by the intrinsic limitations of the human mind? What are literature's effects on individuals and on communities? Questions like these remain at the heart of the critical tradition. They have inspired an ongoing conversation that is continually modified by new voices from different cultural matrices, which join in with other critical languages, other norms, other views of the world.

The proliferation in the past three decades of new critical theories and practices is a sign that the inquiring and speculative spirit of that critical tradition is thriving as never before. But the very abundance of voices and vocabularies can be intimidating to the newcomer seeking to enter the conversation. The discussion that follows is intended as a guide to some of the various maps of the critical terrain and to various ways in which ideas about the nature of literature and the tasks of criticism have been organized. Learning this terrain is the surest way to take one's own bearings and find one's own voice.

MAPPING CRITICAL THEORIES: THE TRADITIONAL CLASSIFICATION

In his influential treatise on romantic views of art, *The Mirror and the Lamp* (1953), the literary historian M. H. Abrams distinguished between four different types of literary theories, and the map he drew is still valuable as a place to start thinking about the history of criticism.

Historically, the first type, the *mimetic* theories of classical antiquity, focused on the relationship between the outside world and the work of art. These theories posited that poetry could best be understood as an imitation, a representation, a copy of the physical world.

The second type, the *rhetorical,* emphasized the relationship between the work of art and its audience — either how the literary work should be formed to please and instruct its audience, or what that audience should be like in order to appreciate literature correctly. These theories held that to attain its proper effect, the poem must be shaped by both the poet's innate talent and the rules of art. Such theories, most popular during the later classical period, the Middle Ages, and the Renaissance, began to decline toward the end of the eighteenth century.

The third type, called *expressive* by Abrams, stressed the relationship between the work of art and the artist, particularly the special faculties of mind and soul that the artist brings to the act of creation. These theories proliferated during the late eighteenth and most of the nineteenth centuries.[1]

The fourth type, which developed around the beginning of the twentieth century, played down the connections of the work of art with the exterior world, the audience, and the artist. These *formal* theories stressed the purely aesthetic relationship between the parts of a work of literature, analyzing its "themes" or "motifs" as if a literary text were a form of classical music or an abstract painting, and strove for a quasi-scientific objectivity. Such theories probably prevail today, since thousands of

[1] Although it is possible to specify when mimetic, rhetorical, and expressive theories flourished, it must be understood that all three continue to be influential. Even when theory is not progressing along certain lines, the old questions are asked of new texts. Thus the movie reviewer who wonders whether *Braveheart* accurately depicts battle conditions in medieval Scotland is as much a mimetic critic as Aristotle.

teachers and scholars who might deny allegiance to any theory actually adhere to formalist principles. In their explicit claims to possessing the highest truth about literature, however, formal theories now face a great deal of competition.

One version of the Abrams map might look like Figure 1. The world of criticism is not as clear or as neat as this diagram suggests. Abrams himself points out that a label such as "mimetic" or "expressive" indicates only the primary orientation of a theory: "Any reasonable theory takes account of all four elements." A mimetic theorist (such as Aristotle) might have much to say about how works of art affect an audience or about the artist, but his views often derive directly from his mimetic principles. When Aristotle suggests in *Poetics,* Chapter 4, for example, that poets of noble character took up the art of tragedy and those of baser character created comedy, his rationale is that nobler poets are better able to understand and then to imitate in poetic language the noble characters of tragedy. In this sense, Aristotle's mimetic orientation comes through even when he takes up the problem of poetic creativity.

Abrams's notion of critical orientation helps us to distinguish the disparate rationales behind the same piece of conventional wisdom. A mimetic critic, for instance, might enjoin an aspiring poet to observe human nature well, the more accurately to imitate human actions in his poetry. A rhetorical critic might advise the poet in the very same words, but in order to prompt the poet to discover what pleases the various classes and age groups that comprise his audience. As the notes to Part One of this collection show, the various dicta of Plato and Aristotle, shorn of their mimetic logic, reappear in the works of rhetorical, expressive, and objective critics to bolster markedly different arguments.

Each of these four orientations covers a great deal of ground, and the fact that two critics are both mimetic in orientation does not guarantee that they agree. Quite

Figure 1

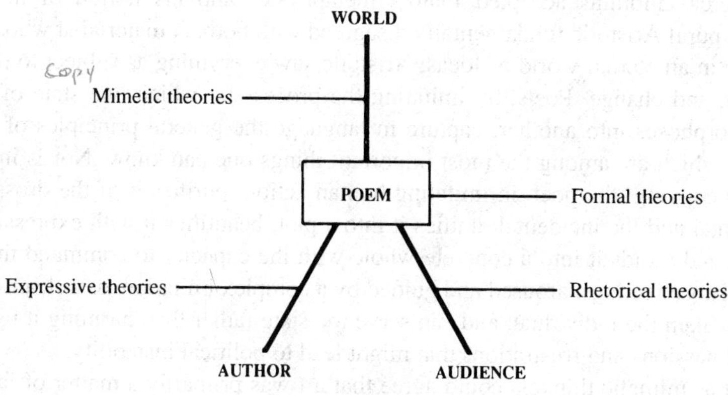

the contrary: whereas critics with different principles merely tend to miss each other's points, those who share a theoretical orientation are likely to clash in an interesting and violent way. A brief consideration of Plato, (p. 17) Aristotle (p. 38), and Plotinus (p. 108), three of the more influential mimetic critics, can reveal how some of these disagreements take shape.

DIFFERENCES WITHIN THEORETICAL ORIENTATIONS

Plato's view of art derives from a complicated metaphysics and a relatively simple notion of imitation. Imitation, for Plato, is the creation of an *eidolon.* The artist makes an "image" — a degraded copy — of the external world, which is analogous to the image formed in a mirror (it lasts longer than a mirror image, but, not being eternal, the difference is not significant). Plato's worldview is *idealist,* which means that he takes the material world, the world of the senses, to be a copy of an eternal world of Ideas. Works of art, in their turn, are copies of material things, and hence copies of copies. For Plato, art is therefore an activity inferior to artisanship — the making of useful objects — first, because art copies rather than creates a material object, and second, because an artist needs only the knowledge of the appearances of things, not of their real nature. Plato also worried that imitation might weaken the individual spirit by arousing passion and corrupt the body politic through its distance from the truth.

Six centuries later, the Neoplatonic philosopher Plotinus developed a mimetic theory of art that generally conformed with that of Plato but drew vastly different conclusions about the value of art. In the idealism of Plotinus, although imitation is still basically copying, the artist imitates not the material world but the Ideas themselves. A sculptor carving a statue of Zeus makes not a marble copy of a flesh-and-blood man but a representation of what Power and Majesty might be like if those concepts could become visible. The Idea of Beauty resides within the artist, shaping his conceptions as it shapes all beauty in nature. For Plotinus, the artist is superior to the artisan because Beauty, the Idea informing the artist's craft, is higher than Utility, which informs that of the artisan.

Whereas Plotinus accepted Plato's metaphysics and his notion of imitation, Plato's pupil Aristotle fundamentally disagreed with both. A materialist who did not believe in an eternal world of Ideas, Aristotle saw everything as subject to process, growth, and change. Poets, by imitating the process by which one state of affairs metamorphoses into another, capture in language the general principles of human action, which are among the most important things one can know. Nor is imitation merely copying: the poet, in imitating human action, purifies it of the dross of the accidental and the incidental, unifies it into a plot, beautifies it with expressive language, and molds it into a concrete whole with the capacity to command the emotions. Those feelings, aroused and guided by a complex imitation, can cleanse rather than weaken the individual, and can serve the state rather than harming it by draining off passions and frustrations that might lead to political instability.

Just as mimetic thinkers could agree that art was primarily a matter of imitation but differ about what the world was like, what aspect of that world the artists imitated, and what sort of process imitation actually was, so rhetorical theorists also had their differences about the ends and means of artistic production. The main question for them was how to construct a work of art so that it would affect an audience properly. Horace (p. 65), one of the earliest and most influential of the rhetorical theorists, thought that poems should "either delight, or instruct, or if possible accomplish both ends at once," but later critics subtly redrew his specifications. For moralists like Dante (p. 119) or Samuel Johnson (p. 218), the more significant purpose was instruction, delight being merely a means to that didactic end. Others, Sir Philip Sidney (p. 131) and John Dryden (p. 160), gave delight a more equal role. Although many theorists took "delight" and "instruction" as general and indivisible qualities to be sought in poetry, others elaborately classified the arts according to the varieties of pleasure and benefit that should reside in each.

And for which audience should the poet write? Horace's audience is apparently limited to the upper classes — the *senatores* and *equites* of the early Roman Empire. Dryden's debaters in *Essay of Dramatic Poesy* posit national audiences with specific national characteristics. Sidney assumes a universal contemporary audience (although that universe may be implicitly restricted to gentlemen). And in Samuel Johnson's analysis, Shakespeare's greatness inheres in affecting people of other countries and later eras. In the eighteenth century, when the question of taste had become an important one in literary theory, Horace's problem, the adaptation of work to audience, had, in effect, been inverted. For critics like David Hume (p. 239), the most important issue was not how poems should be shaped to please audiences but why some members of the audience were better adapted to appreciate the arts than others.

In similar fashion, expressive theorists concurred that art manifested the artist's sensibility even as they disputed the source of that sensibility. Many nineteenth-century Romantics agreed that the key faculty was the imagination — although they differed sharply on how that faculty worked. Later expressive theorists found the source of poetry in the artist's *un*conscious mind. For one group of psychological critics, the followers of Sigmund Freud (p. 481), a poem, like a dream, was the imagined fulfillment of an individual artist's unconscious wish; for another group, the followers of Carl Gustav Jung (p. 504), all art evinced archetypal imagery common to the entire human race. For critics like Northrop Frye (p. 641), the artist expresses the "dream of mankind," which is contained not in the collective unconscious but in a literary tradition that speaks through us all. For sociohistorical critics, followers of Karl Marx (p. 385) or Hippolyte Taine, artists inadvertently expressed the ideologies of their times, conveying their understanding of the world in ways determined by their position within the class struggle and their moment in history.

In the twentieth century, formalists have differed about both what sort of form should be sought and where it could be found. The "New Critics" discovered form in a dialectical thrust and counterthrust of themes; neo-Aristotelians in a complex linkage of plot, language, technique, and purpose; and structuralists and semioticians in repeated patterns of language. And just as in the eighteenth century, there is a split between those critics investigating the various principles of form within literature and those exploring the reader's capacity to discover form or to *supply* it when it is not to be found.

These variations and developments within major critical orientations seem to embody the behavior of biological organisms that proliferate to fill up a new ecological niche. Once a mode like *expressive* criticism had become established, it was almost inevitable that every aspect of the poet's psyche, conscious and unconscious, would be held up to scrutiny as a source of the creative spirit. A more difficult question is why changes in critical orientation occur — why mimetic criticism gave way to rhetorical or rhetorical to expressive.

Such epochs seem to be analogous to scientific revolutions, described by Thomas Kuhn in *The Structure of Scientific Revolutions* (1962). Over one or two generations, the previous "paradigm," a vast structure of assumptions, principles, and methods, gives way and is replaced by another for a variety of reasons — new facts that need explaining, new theories that cannot be reconciled with the present paradigm, a scientific community that has lost intellectual cohesion over its basic principles. The causes of such "revolutions" in critical tradition, where Kuhn's model is less exact, might include the creation of new literary works and styles, shifts in the canon (the informal list of the literature of the past that is held to be significant), developments in the other arts, in philosophy, and in other humanistic disciplines, and changes in politics and society.

CHANGES IN THEORETICAL PARADIGMS

The first critical revolution was the displacement of the Sophists, who saw literature as essentially a function of language, by Plato and his doctrine of imitation. Because the writings of the Sophists have largely failed to survive, too little is known about that revolution to hazard any explanation of Plato's triumph.

The second major change, from mimetic to rhetorical criticism, might have developed partly from a misreading of Aristotle's *Poetics,* a document of enormous authority, if one more respected than understood. (Critics quoted — or misquoted — Aristotle while ignoring his central ideas, methods, and principles as late as the age of Dryden and Johnson.) Though the *Poetics* view art as the imitation of human action, the product is not a simple copy. It differs from the natural process it represents in its form, its material (language instead of action itself), its technique, and its purpose. These four "causes," as Aristotle termed them, all contribute equally in defining the special character of a particular work of art. But one of them — purpose — is, so to speak, more equal than the rest, since it largely dictates the others. Purpose, for Aristotle, refers to the *potential* capacity of a work to move human beings in a certain way, not its *actual* effect on an audience.

One can easily imagine, however, how internal *purpose* could be altered to external *effect,* and how the four-cause structure of Aristotelian imitation might be simplified to the means/end argument we find in Horace. There were surely external reasons as well. The development in late republican Rome of a publishing industry (using hand-copying), serving a far-flung and disparate literary audience, may have fostered a critical scene different from that of post-Periclean Athens, where the poet's audience was the tight-knit coterie within the polis.

The revolution from rhetorical to expressive criticism may also have been partly the result of social change. The reading public grew enormously in the eighteenth century as formerly illiterate classes became avid consumers of literature. The new cadres of less-educated readers made *taste* an issue in criticism as it had never been before. As theorists investigating taste examined the inner experience of readers, they found that the faculties behind good taste, the capacities that made ideal readers — delicate imagination, good sense, wide experience — were the same as those that made the best poets. Creation and appreciation were more closely allied than one might have supposed, for the audience passively reenacted what the poets had actively created. Poetic creativity was therefore a refined but not a mysterious process: It could be investigated and understood.

The twentieth-century shift from expressive to formal criticism was not a total revolution: Biographical, psychological, sociological, and myth criticism continued to develop alongside the several varieties of formalism. But in a sense, formalism grew out of the *exhaustion* of expressive criticism. Literature, once thought to grow organically from the artistic imagination, which, as Samuel Taylor Coleridge (p. 321) said, was "coexistent with the conscious will," was increasingly seen as deriving from forces beyond the artist's control (milieu, class, unconscious drives, the collective unconscious). The poet appeared to be less an agent and more a mere catalyst in the act of creation,[2] while at the same time, poetry, like music, painting, and sculpture, became increasingly abstract. And in the demotic twentieth century, audience reaction has seemed an even less plausible guide to art than in the eighteenth. The eighteenth-century split between refined and popular art, which had been partially repaired during the Victorian era, re-emerged in the 1890s to become an ongoing fixture of twentieth-century culture.

As a result, criticism was left with almost nowhere to go. With the principle of imitation stymied by the vogue of abstraction, the fashion of the impersonal artist nullifying the Romantic appeal to expression, and the fragmented and unreliable audience undermining rhetorical criticism, the only avenue left was an appeal to pure form. These developments seem to have been felt all over Europe and America after World War I, and they culminated in a variety of formalist movements: Russian formalism, structuralism, the New Criticism, neo-Aristotelianism. Another factor, exterior to art and criticism, was the development of the modern university within which departments of literature, structured like those of the natural and social sciences, may have sought for a comparably "objective" and "scientific" mode of literary study, which the varieties of formalism could supply.[3]

During the most recent revolution, which began in the years since Abrams drew up his map, many literary theorists have viewed literature as the free play of signifiers. Words — the signifiers — have thus been detached from their meanings —

[2]The cult of impersonality in poetry and of the poet as the catalyst will be found in the criticism of T. S. Eliot (p. 495), one of the founders of the New Criticism.

[3]Cf. Richard Ohmann, *English in America* (New York: Oxford University Press, 1976), and Gerald Graff, *Professing Literature: An Institutional History* (Chicago: University of Chicago Press, 1987).

the signified. Instead of testifying to the truth and beauty of the world, instead of expressing the personality (or impersonality) of the author, instead of delighting and instructing its audience, instead of presenting an abstract aesthetic form, language now only expresses the circularity of meaning, contemplates only itself. The text is no longer the poem isolated in the center of the diagram. Rather textuality — the condition of inscription within language — is implicated in all our knowledge of the world, of reading, of expression. History is no longer the inferior of poetry, as Aristotle thought, nor its master, as Karl Marx suggested. History cannot even be opposed to poetry, for both of them are equally texts; they may be seen as discursive practices, modes of power/knowledge that need to be analyzed using the rules of the new historicism and cultural studies. Thus we have returned full circle to the position of the Sophists, for whom everything was ruled by the art of rhetoric. A key question for the future of theory is whether the key topics of textuality, language, and discursive practice will remain at the center of critical study, or whether some new revolution may not lurk over the horizon.

OTHER MAPS

The discussion has stayed within the context of Abrams's map of the spectrum of critical theory, which is useful as far as it goes. But maps have a way of reducing the number of dimensions, inevitably distorting even as they clarify the actual landscape.

The points of Abrams's compass should not be taken as natural, self-evident, or unquestionable. Like any other theoretical construct, Abrams's map includes areas of blindness as well as insight, and its limitations derive from its unstated assumptions. By differentiating between "rhetorical" and "objective" theories, for example, Abrams seems to presume that the text can have a meaning apart from what it means to its readers. In practice, however, many formalist critics have relied heavily for their analysis on what an "ideal" or "potential" reader would make of the text. Nor can Abrams's map comfortably accommodate forms of criticism (Marxist and otherwise) that view the text, author, and reader as determined, collectively or separately, by the processes of history. (Abrams may think that an author expresses his or her age, but while this will do for some forms of historical criticism, it will not adequately characterize neo-Marxist criticism, the new historicism, or cultural studies.

Another limitation of the Abrams map — or at least of how many readers have employed it — is the specious linearity it imposes upon the history of criticism. It seems to imply that mimetic thought was confined to classical antiquity and that everyone shifted from rhetorical to expressive criticism around the end of the eighteenth century. Not only did rhetorical criticism continue to be practiced throughout the nineteenth and twentieth centuries, but (as Robert Marsh has shown) one essential pattern of Romantic criticism flourished during what is typically considered the neoclassical period. The prestige of the Abrams map should not mask the importance of other theorists and critics (like James "Hermes" Harris, or Walter Scott) whose work challenges its implicit notion of historical succession.

One way of transcending the limitations of the Abrams map is by formulating other maps whose limitations are different. The Abrams map groups literary theories in terms of the critical *principle* on which each rests. Both R. S. Crane (p. 765) and Norman Friedman have, at different times, constructed a different sort of map to clarify the interrelationships of critical *tasks* and the variety of approaches to a given literary work. The form of these maps is not a group of adjacent territories but a series of concentric circles, with the work itself in the middle. A single composite map combining the essential features of both might look something like Figure 2.

This map is one way of visualizing the relationship of various modes of literary interpretation to one another. Its bias is its suggestion that a poem is determined most intimately by the requirements of form, both its own organic shape and the institutional shapes that culture bequeaths to art. (For example, the terseness of a

Figure 2

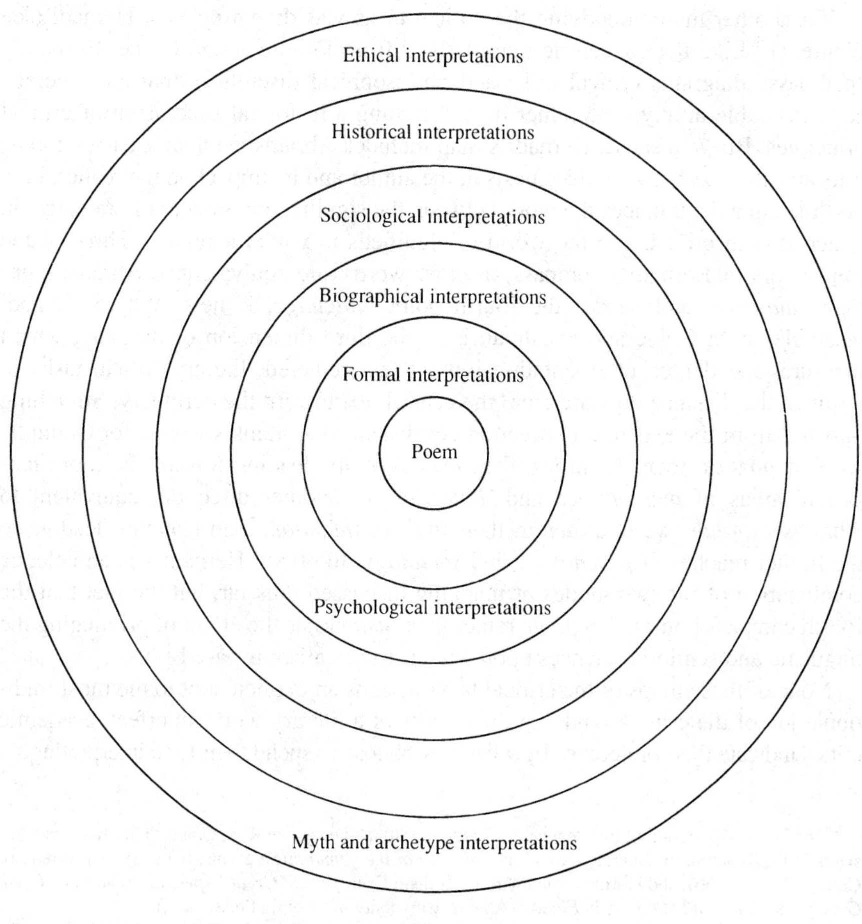

sonnet — its fourteen-line structure — is a formal issue.) Overdetermination is always a distinct possibility, but as long as form accounts adequately for an aspect of a given work, no explanation need be sought elsewhere.

But when form is exhausted, one must turn to the poet himself, both to his conscious life (biographical interpretation) and his unconscious fantasies and defenses (psychological interpretation). The circle is broader here, too, because what biographical and psychological interpretation reveals will cover the whole of the artist's work. Still broader modes of interpretation, sociological and historical, will link that work with others written by authors of the same class in the same era — or explain the differences in works written from different class perspectives and at different times. Broadest of all (and hence least explanatory of any given work) are interpretations based on human universals. One such universal is the collective unconscious of Carl Gustav Jung, whose *archetypes* are said to run through all imaginative literature and art. Another is the ethical wisdom that can give works of literature long-term significance across cultural boundaries.[4]

Yet another map embodying the critical tasks was drawn by Paul Hernadi (see Figure 3).[5] Like the concentric map derived from Friedman and Crane, Hernadi's "compass" diagrams critical tasks and philosophical disciplines that are theoretically available at any time rather than sketching a historical succession of critical principles. But in a sense, Hernadi's map includes Abrams's. On an east-west axis, it locates the text between its genesis in the author and its impact on the reader; on a north-south axis, it places the work between the signification system of language, in which it is inscribed, and the world of signifieds to which it relates. Three of the four points of Hernadi's compass, in other words, are equivalent to Abrams's *author, audience,* and *world;* the fourth point, *language,* is new. Where Hernadi resembles both Crane and Friedman is in the third dimension of the map, which measures the degree of orientation toward text-centered, literary-critical tasks in terms of the distance outward from the central *text* toward the periphery. Stretching outward from the text in the direction equivalent to Abrams's *world,* for example, we find *poetics,* then *thematics,* then *mythography,* leading toward the more tangential areas of *metaphysics* and *dialectics.* In another direction, equivalent to Abrams's *author,* we find *tactics,* then *study of intention,* then *genetics,* leading to the farther reaches of *psychology* and *sociology.* In effect, Hernadi's is an eclectic combination of the two modes of mapping discussed thus far, but the fact that the fourth compass point is *language* rather than *history* has the effect of privileging the linguistic and semiotic sciences upon which structuralism is based.

None of these maps of the critical tasks assigns an explicit spot to the most traditional job of the critic — judging the *quality* of a literary work. In effect, academic critics indicate their preference by what they choose to spend their time interpreting —

[4]For further discussion of this "concentric" map of critical theory, see R. S. Crane, "Questions and Answers in the Teaching of Literary Texts," in *The Idea of the Humanities,* 2 vols. (Chicago: University of Chicago Press, 1966); and Norman Friedman, "Pluralism Exemplified: *Great Expectations* and *The Great Gatsby,*" in *Form and Meaning in Fiction* (Athens: University of Georgia Press, 1975).

[5]This map appears in Paul Hernadi's "Literary Theory: A Compass for Critics," *Critical Inquiry* 3 (1976): 382.

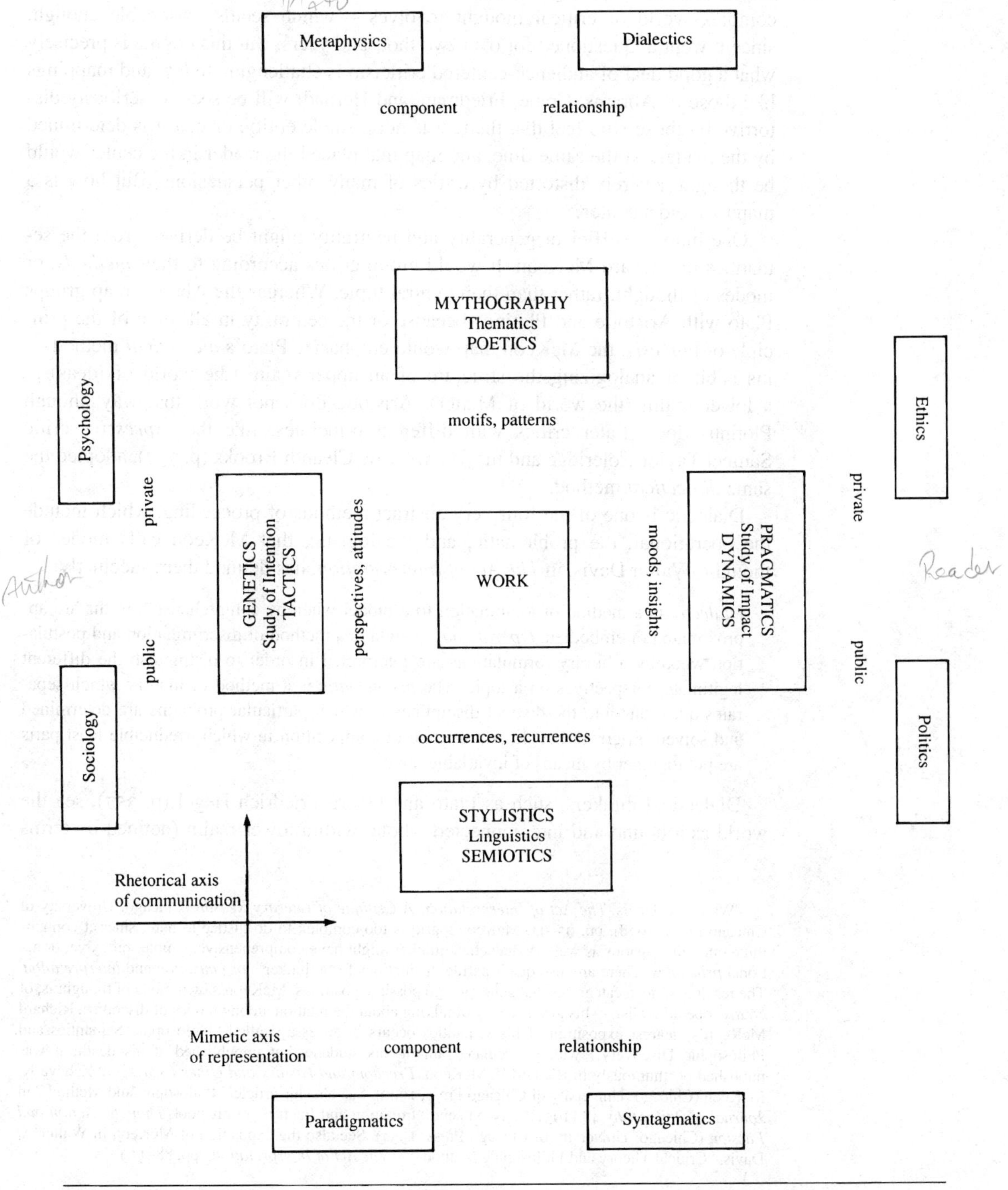

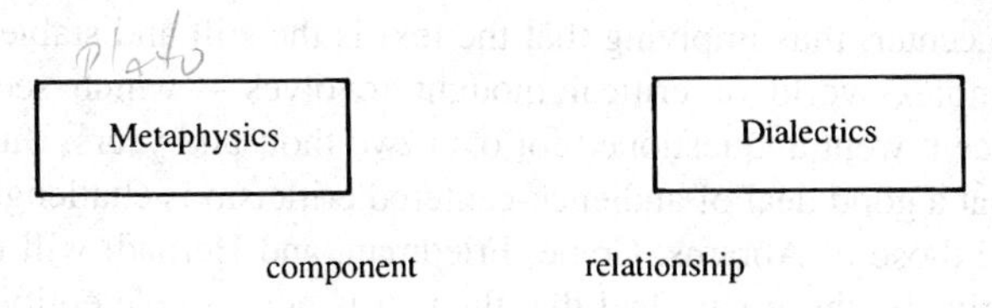

Metaphysics
Dialectics
component
relationship
MYTHOGRAPHY
Thematics
POETICS
Psychology
Ethics
motifs, patterns
private
GENETICS
Study of Intention
TACTICS
perspectives, attitudes
WORK
moods, insights
PRAGMATICS
Study of Impact
DYNAMICS
private
public
public
Sociology
Politics
occurrences, recurrences
STYLISTICS
Linguistics
SEMIOTICS
Rhetorical axis
of communication
Mimetic axis
of representation
component
relationship
Paradigmatics
Syntagmatics

Figure 3

although this implicit procedure is currently being questioned in a wide-ranging debate over the literary canon. And all three maps, it will be noted, place the work in the center, thus implying that the text is the still and stable point around which the complex world of critical thought revolves — which seems reasonable enough, since it went unquestioned for over two thousand years. But this dogma is precisely what a good deal of audience-centered criticism is challenging today, and mappings like those of Abrams, Crane, Friedman, and Hernadi will be seen as seriously distortive by those who feel that the text is not a stable entity, or that it is determined by the reader. At the same time, any map that placed the reader in the center would be thought severely distorted by critics of many other persuasions. But how is a map to avoid a center?

One map of sufficient generality and neutrality might be derived from the semantics of Richard McKeon. It would group critics according to their *methods,* or modes of thought, rather than their central topic. Whereas the Abrams map groups Plato with Aristotle and Plotinus because of the centrality in all three of the principle of *mimesis,* the McKeon map would emphasize Plato's *dialectical* method — his habit of analogizing the structure of an upper realm (the world of Ideas) to a lower realm (the world of Matter). Aristotle does not work that way, though Plotinus does. Later critics with different principles, like the *expressive* critic Samuel Taylor Coleridge and the *formal* critic Cleanth Brooks (p. 757), adopted the same *dialectical* method.

Dialectic is one of the four very abstract methods of proceeding, which include the operational, the problematic, and the logistic, that McKeon calls modes of thought. Walter Davis, in *The Act of Interpretation,* has defined them succinctly:

> *Dialectic* is a method of assimilation to a model whereby comprehensive truths are approximated or embodied. *Operational* thought is a method of discrimination and postulation whereby arbitrary formulations are interpreted in order to distinguish the different legitimate perspectives on a topic. The *problematic* is a method of inquiry which separates questions into the distinct disciplines in which particular problems are determined and solved. *Logistic* thought is a method of composition in which irreducible least parts are put together by means of invariable laws.[6]

Dialectical thinkers, such as Plato and Georg Friedrich Hegel (p. 357), see the world as a bound and interconnected whole, with a lower realm (defined by terms

[6]Walter A. Davis, *The Act of Interpretation: A Critique of Literary Reason* (Chicago: University of Chicago Press, 1978), pp. 93–94. McKeon's grid is too complex to do justice to here, since it contains three other dimensions as well: A dialectical thinker might have comprehensive, simple, reflexive, or actional *principles.* There are also quadripartite distinctions for a thinker's *organization* and *interpretation.* The result is sixteen categories that generate 256 possible positions. McKeon's own mode of thought is, of course, operationalist — his grid is a way of talking about the relation among modes of discourse. Richard McKeon's clearest exposition of his semantics occurs in an essay called "Philosophic Semantics and Philosophic Discovery," widely circulated among his students but unpublished at his death; it was published posthumously in Richard P. McKeon, *Freedom and History and Other Essays,* ed. Zahava K. McKeon (Chicago: University of Chicago Press, 1990). See also his article, "Philosophy and Method," in *Journal of Philosophy* 48 (1951): 653–81; and "Imitation and Poetry," in his book *Thought, Action and Passion* (Chicago: University of Chicago Press, 1954). See also the exposition of McKeon in Walter A. Davis, "Critical Theory and Philosophic Method," in *The Act of Interpretation,* pp. 88–119.

like "becoming" or mere "consciousness") and an upper realm (that of "being" or "self-consciousness"). Such a pattern runs through all of reality, and each aspect of life — religion, politics, ethics, aesthetics — can be analyzed in the same way using analogous terms.

But where dialectical thought is intrinsically interdisciplinary, problematic thought is discipline-bound. Problematic thinkers, such as Aristotle and John Dewey, see the world as containing a number of irreconcilable things, and therefore find no single method that will answer all questions, no single set of terms that can be used to grapple with all problems. The initial task of problematic thinking is to separate disciplines according to their scope, determining their bounds and establishing a method of inquiry according to the nature of the discipline itself.

Like dialectical thinkers, operational thinkers take a holistic view of the universe, but for them, the whole is determined not by the nature of things but by the way people view them and talk about them. There is no higher realm of being or truth: The way people see things is all there is. The role of operational thought, in Cicero or in Kenneth Burke (p. 581), is to clarify discourse, to reduce the ambiguities that arise from using common language to describe disparate perspectives.

Like problematic thinkers, logistic thinkers avoid the holistic; but unlike them, they have a single method, which is associated with but not limited to modern science: breaking down phenomena into their least parts and then discovering the laws by which those parts are interrelated. This method is clearest in sciences like chemistry and physics, which are concerned with particles and forces, but a logistic approach has also been made to politics (by Niccolò Machiavelli), ethics (by René Descartes and Thomas Hobbes), and social structure (by Claude Lévi-Strauss, p. 835).

Applied to literature, dialectical thought often takes poetry to be a mode of thinking, while problematic thought often takes it to be a mode of making. Operational thought considers literature as one of many forms of discourse; logistic thought considers literature as data in its scientific analysis of the parts of a text, confident that parts make up a whole. Another map might be created, in other words, gathering *dialectical* thinkers (like Plato, Plotinus, Coleridge, and Hegel) into one group, *problematic* thinkers (like Aristotle) into another, *logistic* thinkers (like Freud or Lévi-Strauss) into a third, and *operational* thinkers (like Alexander Pope, p. 206, and Kenneth Burke) into a fourth. This map would be more historically complicated than Abrams's since competing modes of thought would operate within a given age, but it would suggest some important linkages across the centuries that should not be ignored.[7]

It is useful to be able to refer to four maps rather than one, but in the long run, all maps are inadequate and none is wholly innocent. That is, any map, no matter how

[7]Applied to the critical revolution of the past three decades, the McKeon map might suggest that operational thought, hitherto one element among many, moved into the vanguard, as once dialectical Marxists began (after Louis Althusser) to consider history as a text rather than a force, as once logistical psychoanalysts began (after Jacques Lacan) to think of the unconscious as a mode of discourse rather than a hidden space. Similarly, the Derridean revolution consists, as Paul de Man has explicitly stated, in the displacement of grammar (in Ferdinand de Saussure's logistical approach) by rhetoric.

apparently objective and pluralistic, is certain to contain implicit assumptions congenial to some theorists and anathema to others. Maps are like Ludwig Wittgenstein's ladder in the *Tractatus Logico-Philosophicus* (1922): We can climb only with their assistance, but once we have ascended, we throw them to the ground. Once we outgrow the maps we are given, we learn to do without them or make our own.

Traditional literature courses typically impose a method and an order on the disparate texts of one period or one author. In contrast, a course in critical theory will often call into question the very myths of order the traditions of culture have handed down. The study of critical theory tends to raise the ultimate questions about literature and its relation to life without establishing an ultimate order, because the clash of one principle, one method, one logic with another cannot be evaded. To the extent that these oppositions are genuinely understood, we are unlikely to end by resolving their differences into a tidy and harmonious chorus. We can, however, set the voices at play, engage them in contrapuntal dialogue with each other, and enter that dialogue ourselves. And in discoursing with some of the most probing minds that have trained their gaze upon literature, we become participants in an ancient and exalted conversation.

Part One

CLASSIC TEXTS IN LITERARY CRITICISM

Plato

ca. 427–347 B.C.

"All of Western philosophy is but a footnote to Plato," Alfred North Whitehead once said, and it is true in the sense that most of the historically significant issues with which philosophy has been concerned — the nature of being, the question of how we know things, the purposes of right action, the structure of an ordered society, the meaning of love and beauty — were issues that he raised. Later philosophers, including Plato's great pupil, Aristotle, have disagreed not only with his results but also with his ways of setting up the questions, and their argument with Plato makes up much of the history of thought. Nor have later thinkers always merely disagreed with and revised Plato: Century after century has witnessed a renaissance of his system of thought, most notably in the Neoplatonists of the second century A.D., the Cambridge Platonists of the latter seventeenth century, and the idealists of the romantic movement. Later thinkers, including Plotinus (p. 108), Sidney (p. 131), and Shelley (p. 337), directly take up Plato's challenge, but his shadow falls, as Whitehead said, over all of Western thought.

For contemporary readers the most difficult concept in Plato's thought is his *idealism* — the doctrine of a permanent realm of eternal Forms that shape our mutable material world. In a philosophy class students might be asked to contrast the "Idea of the Desk" — the concept of a thing to write on that also holds one's papers — with the physical object in the classroom. The former is timeless and pure, while the latter is time-bound: It came into being, exists for a time, will soon vanish. Nor is the material desk a *perfect* desk: Its very materiality precludes it. Presumably, the Idea of the Desk must have preceded the material desk and caused it, in effect, to be created. A carpenter who is not merely copying an existing desk must be working from some inner awareness of this Idea.

This approach is a time-honored way of introducing Plato's ideas, but it tends to lead our thought downward, to wondering, for example, whether there is a Platonic Idea of a pencil-shaving or of manure. Actually, despite their vulgarity, these are perfectly sound Platonic questions. The usual solution is to assume that formless things — mud, sawdust, and so on — have no Forms because they are in fact formless matter. The real problem is that the explanation removes Plato's ideas from common human thought. Few of us are acquainted, other than in theory, with the ideas of things like desks. Nor is it apparent at first glance that the Idea of a Desk is a higher or better thing than a material desk; it is certainly much harder to do one's work on.

It may be more helpful to think of a geometry class, where one operates with perfect circles, right angles, and parallel lines, and where one learns to prove theorems — or eternal truths — about them. It is understood that the diagrams drawn to illustrate the theorems, however neatly done, are imperfect representations of the lines and angles of the theorem. Here, on a mathematical level, one is working with the Ideal and the Material, and it is the Ideal — the proof, not the diagram — which counts. This may be why the door to Plato's school, the Academy, had a warning on it: "Let no one ignorant of geometry enter here." The mathematics prerequisite, so to speak, had a good reason: Those who had already wrestled with the Idea of the Right Triangle in proving the Pythagorean theorem were prepared to understand the higher ideas of Truth, Goodness, and Beauty that Plato believed shape all human knowledge, right action, artistic endeavor, and love.

Plato developed his idealism in reaction against the notions of the Sophists. They have a poor reputation today — the word *sophistry* testifies to that — but the original Sophists were not a set of quibblers but a diverse group of teachers of what we would now call rhetoric and composition, the language arts. Some of the major Sophists, like Gorgias and Lysias, are known today because Plato used them as debating opponents for his spokesman, Socrates. The Sophists claimed that their science of language could lead to the knowledge of truth and virtue. Against this, Plato thought it dangerous to suppose that the highest realities — Truth, Goodness, and Beauty — had the flickering impermanence of human words, and his world of ideas may derive from his fear that, like language, even matter could be shaped to cheat and deceive.

Because Plato mistrusted writing, he did not set down his philosophy in the usual form of a set of treatises but rather in dialogues.[1] Their liveliness and depth remain unequalled, but their form creates problems of both interpretation (at times we may wonder whether Socrates is being serious or ironic, at other times whether he *always* speaks directly for Plato) and consistency (a position held in one dialogue may be renounced in another). Both issues emerge in the *Republic,* Book X, and in *Ion.*

REPUBLIC, BOOK X

Book X is the most influential discussion of art in the Platonic canon. Its central thesis — that poets have no place in Plato's perfect state save as writers of hymns to the gods and songs in praise of great leaders — has stung devotees of the arts for the last two thousand years.

Book X is at the end of the *Republic,* the longest of the dialogues, which opens with the issue of whether Might makes Right. This harsh question leads Socrates and his two friends to consider the question, What is Justice? Socrates's hypothesis is that Justice is knowing one's place and performing its duties — but how can one know and act properly in the Athenian polis? This question leads Socrates to fashion a model state, a republic governed by a natural elite of guardians, in which it would be possible, as it is not in Athens, to understand one's place and its duties. But how should the guardians be educated to rule? They must learn a great many other things, but at the center of their training is philosophy. And it is in answering *this* question — of what does philosophy consist? — that Socrates presents his hierarchical portrait of the physical and mental universe: the myth of the divided line. In simplified form, the diagram Socrates draws looks like this:

[1]Indeed, in the Seventh Letter, Plato claims that he never wrote his philosophy down at all, because it could not be written down. The usual interpretation of this claim is that the published dialogues represent philosophy *in action* rather than as doctrine; another possibility is that Plato meant the dialogues to *stimulate* philosophy — to cause *us* to philosophize — by reasoning and arguing with their positions.

MODES OF BEING	MODES OF MENTAL ACTIVITY
Ideas	Knowing
Mathematical Forms	Understanding
Material Things	Opinion
Images	Conjecture

The first horizontal line separates the eternal world of true Being from the world of Becoming, the material things that are begotten, born, and die. The vertical line separates modes of existence from the modes of thought appropriate to them. For Plato the word *know* applies only to Ideas, but about material animals, plants, and human artifacts we can at best hold correct opinions, and with respect to mere images we can only hazard guesses.

In this context, the discussion of art in Book X is logically sound. First of all, Plato identifies art as imitation, positing that what artists do (as they have claimed in the centuries before and after Plato) is hold the mirror up to nature: They copy the appearances of men, animals, and objects in the physical world. But if this is the case, then the artistic object is merely an image, slightly but not more meaningfully permanent than a reflection in a pool of water. And the intelligence that went into its creation need involve nothing more than conjecture. (Notice that Socrates is not being redundant when he twice proves the inferiority of art: The first time he proves the inferiority of the *mode of being* of art; the second, its inferiority as a *mode of mental activity.*) As a result, art cannot be justified as an activity worthy in its own right. The poets may stay as servants of the state if they teach piety and virtue, but the pleasures of art are condemned as inherently corrupting to citizens and guardians alike.

ION

Much of the *Ion* is reasonably consistent with the *Republic,* and a good deal more entertaining if we allow ourselves to enjoy the spectacle of Socrates exposing the vanity and pretensions of the none-too-bright performer for whom the dialogue is named. (The moment when Ion declares that he is the greatest general in Athens as well as its greatest rhapsode is made richer if one remembers that at the purported time of the discourse, Athens was fighting for its survival in the Pelopennesian War.) Here, as in the *Republic,* Socrates exposes the inferiority of art as a way of knowing.

Where *Ion* differs from the *Republic* is in the suggestion contained in the image of the magnet as a metaphor of divine inspiration. Just as a magnet attracts iron and passes that attraction along, so the muse inspires the artist, who inspires the interpreter, who inspires the audience. The chain runs from the god to Homer to Ion to the applauding citizens. If this view of art is true, then it is divine, not inferior stuff.

Reconciling this notion of art with the contrary position in *Republic,* Book X, has been attempted in a number of different ways. One way is to suppose that Plato changed his mind, but that would mean trying to discover which, the *Ion* or the *Republic,* is the later dialogue (we have only conjectural datings) and deciding whether his first or second thoughts were the more trustworthy.

Another possibility is to suppose that the *Ion* is an essentially ironic (as well as humorous) dialogue, and that Socrates does not seriously respect inspiration. The Greek word translated as "inspiration" is *enthousiasmós,* and its literal meaning is closer to "demonic possession" than to the English derivative "enthusiasm." It is hard to believe that the rationalistic Plato could commend such a state. But on the other side, Socrates *does* praise such an experience elsewhere, in the *Phaedrus,* the principal dialogue on love and beauty, where poetry finds its place along with prophecy and love as forms of divine madness, the gods' most precious gifts to humanity. There Socrates claims that the state of *enthousiasmós* allows a dim but gripping memory of the Ideas, the eternal Forms of Truth, Goodness, and Beauty, which the soul experienced directly prior to its incarnation. This doctrine is narrated as a myth, but it is surely not ironic in context.

Perhaps most plausibly, the discrepancies between *Ion* and *Republic* may be ascribed to their different contexts. In *Republic* Socrates is imagining a perfect state, one that must be designed to run without benefit of chance, luck, or divine intervention. Its rulers must therefore act rightly out of permanently dependable knowledge, not occasional inspiration. In the *Ion* Socrates is discoursing about the actual world, where poets may be generally foolish and ignorant, but can sometimes be heard to speak holy truths in tongues given them by the gods.

Selected Bibliography

Cavarnos, Constantine. *Plato's Theory of Fine Art.* Athens: Astir, 1973.

Else, Gerald F. *Plato and Aristotle on Poetry.* Chapel Hill: University of North Carolina Press, 1986.

Fortenbaugh, William W. and Lewis Ayres, eds. *The Passionate Intellect: The Transformation of the Classical Traditions.* New Brunswick: Rutgers University Press, 1995.

Friedländer, Paul. *Plato.* New York: Pantheon, 1958–69.

Gadamer, Hans-Georg. "Plato und die Dichter." In *Platos Dialektische Ethik und andere Studien.* Hamburg: F. Meiner, 1968.

Gebauer, Gunter. *Mimesis: Culture—Art—Society.* Berkeley: University of California Press, 1995.

Greene, William Chase. "Plato's View of Poetry." *Harvard Studies in Classical Philology* 29 (1918): 1–75.

Grube, G. M. A. *Plato's Thought.* London: Methuen, 1935.

Gulley, Norman. *Plato's Theory of Knowledge.* London: Methuen, 1962.

Havelock, Eric. *Preface to Plato.* Cambridge: Harvard University Press, 1963.

Lodge, Rupert C. *Plato's Theory of Art.* New York: Humanities Press, 1953.

Murdoch, Iris. *The Fire and the Sun: Why Plato Banished the Artists.* Oxford: Clarendon Press, 1972.

Nightingale, Andrea Wilson. *Genres in Dialogue: Plato and the Construct of Philosophy.* Cambridge: Cambridge University Press, 1996.
Oates, Whitney J. *Plato's View of Art.* New York: Scribner, 1972.
Partee, Morriss Henry. *Plato's Poetics: The Authority of Beauty.* Salt Lake City: University of Utah Press, 1981.
Shorey, Paul. *What Plato Said.* Chicago: University of Chicago Press, 1933.
Sinaiko, Herman J. *Love, Knowledge and Discourse in Plato.* Chicago: University of Chicago Press, 1965.
Taylor, A. E. *Plato.* 1929; Ann Arbor: University of Michigan Press, 1960.

Republic, Book X

Of the many excellences which I perceive in the order of our State, there is none which upon reflection pleases me better than the rule about poetry.

To what do you refer?

To our refusal to admit the imitative kind of poetry, for it certainly ought not to be received; as I see far more clearly now that the parts of the soul have been distinguished.

What do you mean?

Speaking in confidence, for you will not denounce me to the tragedians and the rest of the imitative tribe, all poetical imitations are ruinous to the understanding of the hearers, unless as an antidote they possess the knowledge of the true nature of the originals.

Explain the purport of your remark.

Well, I will tell you, although I have always from my earliest youth had an awe and love of Homer which even now makes the words falter on my lips, for he seems to be the great captain and teacher of the whole of that noble tragic company; but a man is not to be reverenced more than the truth, and therefore I will speak out.

Very good, he said.

Listen to me then, or rather, answer me.

Put your question.

Can you give me a general definition of imitation? for I really do not myself understand what it professes to be.

A likely thing, then, that I should know.

Translated by Benjamin Jowett. The speakers are Socrates and Glaucon.

There would be nothing strange in that, for the duller eye may often see a thing sooner than the keener.

Very true, he said; but in your presence, even if I had any faint notion, I could not muster courage to utter it. Will you inquire yourself?

Well then, shall we begin the inquiry at this point, following our usual method: Whenever a number of individuals have a common name, we assume that there is one corresponding idea or form: — do you understand me?

I do.

Let us take, for our present purpose, any instance of such a group; there are beds and tables in the world — many of each, are there not?

Yes.

But there are only two ideas or forms of such furniture — one the idea of a bed, the other of a table.

True.

And the maker of either of them makes a bed or he makes a table for our use, in accordance with the idea — that is our way of speaking in this and similar instances — but no artificer makes the idea itself: how could he?

Impossible.

And there is another artificer — I should like to know what you would say of him.

Who is he?

One who is the maker of all the works of all other workmen.

What an extraordinary man!

Wait a little, and there will be more reason for your saying so. For this is the craftsman who is able to make not only furniture of every kind, but all that grows out of the earth, and all living creatures, himself included; and besides these he can make earth and sky and the gods, and all the things which are in heaven or in the realm of Hades under the earth.

He must be a wizard and no mistake.

Oh! you are incredulous, are you? Do you mean that there is no such maker or creator, or that in one sense there might be a maker of all these things but in another not? Do you see that there is a way in which you could make them all yourself?

And what way is this? he asked.

An easy way enough; or rather, there are many ways in which the feat might be quickly and easily accomplished, none quicker than that of turning a mirror round and round — you would soon enough make the sun and the heavens, and the earth and yourself, and other animals and plants, and furniture and all the other things of which we were just now speaking, in the mirror.

Yes, he said; but they would be appearances only.

Very good, I said, you are coming to the point now. And the painter too is, as I conceive, just such another — a creator of appearances, is he not?

Of course.

But then I suppose you will say that what he creates is untrue. And yet there is a sense in which the painter also creates a bed? Is there not?

Yes, he said, but here again, an appearance only.

And what of the maker of the bed? Were you not saying that he too makes, not the idea which according to our view is the real object denoted by the word bed, but only a particular bed?

Yes, I did.

Then if he does not make a real object he cannot make what *is,* but only some semblance of existence; and if anyone were to say that the work of the maker of the bed, or of any other workman, has real existence, he could hardly be supposed to be speaking the truth.

Not, at least, he replied, in the view of those who make a business of these discussions.

No wonder, then, that his work too is an indistinct expression of truth.

No wonder.

Suppose now that by the light of the examples just offered we inquire who this imitator is?

If you please.

Well then, here we find three beds: one existing in nature, which is made by God, as I think that we may say — for no one else can be the maker?

No one, I think.

There is another which is the work of the carpenter?

Yes.

And the work of the painter is a third?

Yes.

Beds, then, are of three kinds, and there are three artists who superintend them: God, the maker of the bed, and the painter?

Yes, there are three of them.

God, whether from choice or from necessity, made one bed in nature and one only; two or more such beds neither ever have been nor ever will be made by God.

Why is that?

Because even if He had made but two, a third would still appear behind them of which they again both possessed the form, and that would be the real bed and not the two others.

Very true, he said.

God knew this, I suppose, and He desired to be the real maker of a real bed, not a kind of bed, and therefore He created a bed which is essentially and by nature one only.

So it seems.

Shall we, then, speak of Him as the natural author or maker of the bed?

Yes, he replied; inasmuch as by the natural process of creation, He is the author of this and of all other things.

And what shall we say of the carpenter — is not he also the maker of a bed?

Yes.

But would you call the painter an artificer and maker?

Certainly not.

Yet if he is not the maker, what is he in relation to the bed?

I think, he said, that we may fairly designate him as the imitator of that which the others make.

Good, I said; then you call him whose product is third in the descent from nature, an imitator?

Certainly, he said.

And so if the tragic poet is an imitator, he too is thrice removed from the king and from the truth; and so are all other imitators.

That appears to be so.

Then about the imitator we are agreed. And what about the painter? — Do you think he tries to imitate in each case that which originally exists in nature, or only the creation of artificers?

The latter.

As they are or as they appear? you have still to determine this.

What do you mean?

I mean to ask whether a bed really becomes different when it is seen from different points of view, obliquely or directly or from any other point of view? Or does it simply appear different, without being really so? And the same of all things.

Yes, he said, the difference is only apparent.

Now let me ask you another question: Which is the art of painting designed to be — an imitation of things as they are, or as they appear — of appearance or of reality?

Of appearance, he said.

Then the imitator is a long way off the truth, and can reproduce all things because he lightly touches on a small part of them, and that part an image. For example: A painter will paint a cobbler, carpenter, or any other artisan, though he knows nothing of their arts; and, if he is a good painter, he may deceive children or simple persons when he shows them his picture of a carpenter from a distance, and they will fancy that they are looking at a real carpenter.

Certainly.

And surely, my friend, this is how we should regard all such claims: Whenever any one informs us that he has found a man who knows all the arts, and all things else that anybody knows, and every single thing with a higher degree of accuracy than any other man — whoever tells us this, I think that we can only retort that he is a simple creature who seems to have been deceived by some wizard or imitator whom he met, and whom he thought all-knowing, because he himself was unable to analyze the nature of knowledge and ignorance and imitation.

Most true.

And next, I said, we have to consider tragedy and its leader, Homer; for we hear some persons saying that these poets know all the arts; and all things human; where virtue and vice are concerned, and indeed all divine things too; because the good poet cannot compose well unless he knows his subject, and he who has not this knowledge can never be a poet. We ought to consider whether here also there may not be a similar illusion. Perhaps they may have come across imitators and been deceived by them; they may not have remembered when they saw their works that these were thrice removed from the truth, and could easily be made without any knowledge of the truth, because they are appearances only and not realities? Or, after all, they may be in the right, and good poets do really know the things about which they seem to the many to speak so well?

The question, he said, should by all means be considered.

Now do you suppose that if a person were able to make the original as well as the image, he would seriously devote himself to the image-making branch? Would he allow imitation to be the ruling principle of his life, as if he had nothing higher in him?

I should say not.

But the real artist, who had real knowledge of those things which he chose also to imitate, would be interested in realities and not in imitations; and would desire to leave as memorials of himself works many and fair; and, instead of being the author of encomiums, he would prefer to be the theme of them.

Yes, he said, that would be to him a source of much greater honor and profit.

Now let us refrain, I said, from calling Homer or any other poet to account regarding those arts to which his poems incidentally refer: We will not ask them, in case any poet has been a doctor and not a mere imitator of medical parlance, to show what patients have been restored to health by a poet, ancient or modern, as they were by Asclepius; or what disciples in medicine a poet has left behind him, like the Asclepiads. Nor shall we press the same question upon them about the other arts. But we have a right to know respecting warfare, strategy, the administration of States, and the education of man, which are the chiefest and noblest subjects of his poems, and we may fairly ask him about them. "Friend Homer," then we say to him, "if you are only in the second remove from truth in what you say of virtue, and not in the third — not an image maker, that is, by our definition, an imitator — and if you are able to discern what pursuits make men better or worse in private or public life, tell us what State was ever better governed by your help? The good order of Lacedaemon is due to Lycurgus, and many other cities great and small have been similarly benefited by others; but who says that you have been a good legislator to them and have done them any good? Italy and Sicily boast of Charondas, and there is Solon who is renowned among us; but what city has anything to say about you?" Is there any city which he might name?

I think not, said Glaucon; not even the Homerids themselves pretend that he was a legislator.

Well, but is there any war on record which was carried on successfully owing to his leadership or counsel?

There is not.

Or is there anything comparable to those clever improvements in the arts, or in other operations, which are said to have been due to men of practical genius such as Thales the Milesian or Anacharsis the Scythian?

There is absolutely nothing of the kind.

But, if Homer never did any public service, was he privately a guide or teacher of any? Had he in his lifetime friends who loved to associate with him, and who handed down to posterity a Homeric way of life, such as was established by Pythagoras who was especially beloved for this reason and whose followers are to this day conspicuous among others by what they term the Pythagorean way of life?

Nothing of the kind is recorded of him. For surely, Socrates, Creophylus, the companion of Homer, that child of flesh, whose name always makes us laugh, might be more justly ridiculed for his want of breeding, if what is said is true, that Homer was greatly neglected by him in his own day when he was alive?

Yes, I replied, that is the tradition. But can you imagine, Glaucon, that if Homer had really been able to educate and improve mankind — if he had been capable of knowledge and not been a mere imitator — can you imagine, I say, that he would not have attracted many followers, and been honored and loved by them? Protagoras of Abdera, and Prodicus of Ceos, and a host of others, have only to whisper to their contemporaries: "You will never be able to manage either your own house or your own State until you appoint us to be your ministers of education" — and this ingenious device of theirs has such an effect in making men love them that their companions all but carry them about on their shoulders. And is it conceivable that the contemporaries of Homer, or again of Hesiod, would have allowed either of them to go about as rhapsodists, if they had really been able to help mankind forward in virtue? Would they not have been as unwilling to part with them as with gold, and have compelled them to stay at home with them? Or, if the master would not stay, then the disciples would have followed him about everywhere, until they had got education enough?

Yes, Socrates, that, I think, is quite true.

Then must we not infer that all these poetical individuals, beginning with Homer, are only imitators, who copy images of virtue and the other themes of their poetry, but have no contact with the truth? The poet is like a painter who, as we have already observed, will make a likeness of a cobbler though he understands nothing of cobbling; and his picture is good enough for those who know no more than he does, and judge only by colors and figures.

Quite so.

In like manner the poet with his words and phrases[1] may be said to lay on the colors of the several arts, himself understanding their nature only enough to imitate them; and other people, who are as ignorant as he is, and judge only from his words, imagine that if he speaks of cobbling, or of military tactics, or of anything else, in meter and harmony and rhythm, he speaks very well — such is the sweet influence which melody and rhythm by nature have. For I am sure that you know what a poor appearance the works of poets make when stripped of the colors which art puts

[1]Or, "with his nouns and verbs." [Tr.]

upon them, and recited in simple prose. You have seen some examples?

Yes, he said.

They are like faces which were never really beautiful, but only blooming, seen when the bloom of youth has passed away from them?

Exactly.

Come now, and observe this point: The imitator or maker of the image knows nothing, we have said, of true existence; he knows appearances only. Am I not right?

Yes.

Then let us have a clear understanding, and not be satisfied with half an explanation.

Proceed.

Of the painter we say that he will paint reins, and he will paint a bit?

Yes.

And the worker in leather and brass will make them?

Certainly.

But does the painter know the right form of the bit and reins? Nay, hardly even the workers in brass and leather who make them; only the horseman who knows how to use them — he knows their right form.

Most true.

And may we not say the same of all things?

What?

That there are three arts which are concerned with all things: one which uses, another which makes, a third which imitates them?

Yes.

And the excellence and beauty and rightness of every structure, animate or inanimate, and of every action of man, is relative solely to the use for which nature or the artist has intended them.

True.

Then beyond doubt it is the user who has the greatest experience of them, and he must report to the maker the good or bad qualities which develop themselves in use; for example, the flute player will tell the flute maker which of his flutes is satisfactory to the performer; he will tell him how he ought to make them, and the other will attend to his instructions?

Of course.

So the one pronounces with knowledge about the goodness and badness of flutes, while the other, confiding in him, will make them accordingly?

True.

The instrument is the same, but about the excellence or badness of it the maker will possess a correct belief, since he associates with one who knows, and is compelled to hear what he has to say; whereas the user will have knowledge?

True.

But will the imitator have either? Will he know from use whether or not that which he paints is correct or beautiful? or will he have right opinion from being compelled to associate with another who knows and gives him instructions about what he should paint?

Neither.

Then an imitator will no more have true opinion than he will have knowledge about the goodness or badness of his models?

I suppose not.

The imitative poet will be in a brilliant state of intelligence about the theme of his poetry?

Nay, very much the reverse.

And still he will go on imitating without knowing what makes a thing good or bad, and may be expected therefore to imitate only that which appears to be good to the ignorant multitude?

Just so.

Thus far then we are pretty well agreed that the imitator has no knowledge worth mentioning of what he imitates. Imitation is only a kind of play or sport, and the tragic poets, whether they write in iambic or in heroic verse,[2] are imitators in the highest degree?

Very true.

And now tell me, I conjure you — this imitation is concerned with an object which is thrice removed from the truth?

Certainly.

And what kind of faculty in man is that to which imitation makes its special appeal?

What do you mean?

I will explain: The same body does not appear equal to our sight when seen near and when seen at a distance?

True.

[2]Dramatists wrote in iambic verse and epic poets in dactylic hexameters — "heroic" verse. [Ed.]

And the same objects appear straight when looked at out of the water, and crooked when in the water; and the concave becomes convex, owing to the illusion about colors to which the sight is liable. Thus every sort of confusion is revealed within us; and this is that weakness of the human mind on which the art of painting in light and shadow, the art of conjuring, and many other ingenious devices impose, having an effect upon us like magic.

True.

And the arts of measuring and numbering and weighing come to the rescue of the human understanding — there is the beauty of them — with the result that the apparent greater or less, or more or heavier, no longer have the mastery over us, but give way before the power of calculation and measuring and weighing?

Most true.

And this, surely, must be the work of the calculating and rational principle in the soul?

To be sure.

And often when this principle measures and certifies that some things are equal, or that some are greater or less than others, it is, at the same time, contradicted by the appearance which the objects present?

True.

But did we not say that such a contradiction is impossible — the same faculty cannot have contrary opinions at the same time about the same thing?

We did; and rightly.

Then that part of the soul which has an opinion contrary to measure can hardly be the same with that which has an opinion in accordance with measure?

True.

And the part of the soul which trusts to measure and calculation is likely to be the better one?

Certainly.

And therefore that which is opposed to this is probably an inferior principle in our nature?

No doubt.

This was the conclusion at which I was seeking to arrive when I said that painting or drawing, and imitation in general, are engaged upon productions which are far removed from truth, and are also the companions and friends and associates of a principle within us which is equally removed from reason, and that they have no true or healthy aim.

Exactly.

The imitative art is an inferior who from intercourse with an inferior has inferior offspring.

Very true.

And is this confined to the sight only, or does it extend to the hearing also, relating in fact to what we term poetry?

Probably the same would be true of poetry.

Do not rely, I said, on a probability derived from the analogy of painting; but let us once more go directly to that faculty of the mind with which imitative poetry has converse, and see whether it is good or bad.

By all means.

We may state the question thus: Imitation imitates the actions of men, whether voluntary or involuntary, on which, as they imagine, a good or bad result has ensued, and they rejoice or sorrow accordingly. Is there anything more?

No, there is nothing else.

But in all this variety of circumstances is the man at unity with himself — or rather, as in the instance of sight there was confusion and opposition in his opinions about the same things, so here also is there not strife and inconsistency in his life? Though I need hardly raise the question again, for I remember that all this has been already admitted; and the soul has been acknowledged by us to be full of these and ten thousand similar oppositions occurring at the same moment?

And we were right, he said.

Yes, I said, thus far we were right; but there was an omission which must now be supplied.

What was the omission?

Were we not saying that a good man, who has the misfortune to lose his son or anything else which is most dear to him, will bear the loss with more equanimity than another?

Yes, indeed.

But will he have no sorrow, or shall we say that although he cannot help sorrowing, he will moderate his sorrow?

The latter, he said, is the truer statement.

Tell me: will he be more likely to struggle and hold out against his sorrow when he is seen by his equals, or when he is alone in a deserted place?

The fact of being seen will make a great difference, he said.

When he is by himself he will not mind saying many things which he would be ashamed of anyone hearing, and also doing many things which he would not care to be seen doing?

True.

And doubtless it is the law and reason in him which bids him resist; while it is the affliction itself which is urging him to indulge his sorrow?

True.

But when a man is drawn in two opposite directions, to and from the same object, this, as we affirm, necessarily implies two distinct principles in him?

Certainly.

One of them is ready to follow the guidance of the law?

How do you mean?

The law would say that to be patient under calamity is best, and that we should not give way to impatience, as the good and evil in such things are not clear, and nothing is gained by impatience; also, because no human thing is of serious importance, and grief stands in the way of that which at the moment is most required.

What is most required? he asked.

That we should take counsel about what has happened, and when the dice have been thrown, according to their fall, order our affairs in the way which reason deems best; not, like children who have had a fall, keeping hold of the part struck and wasting time in setting up a howl, but always accustoming the soul forthwith to apply a remedy, raising up that which is sickly and fallen, banishing the cry of sorrow by the healing art.

Yes, he said, that is the true way of meeting the attacks of fortune.

Well then, I said, the higher principle is ready to follow this suggestion of reason?

Clearly.

But the other principle, which inclines us to recollection of our troubles and to lamentation, and can never have enough of them, we may call irrational, useless, and cowardly?

Indeed, we may.

Now does not the principle which is thus inclined to complaint, furnish a great variety of materials for imitation? Whereas the wise and calm temperament, being always nearly equable, is not easy to imitate or to appreciate when imitated, especially at a public festival when a promiscuous crowd is assembled in a theater. For the feeling represented is one to which they are strangers.

Certainly.

Then the imitative poet who aims at being popular is not by nature made, nor is his art intended, to please or to affect the rational principle in the soul; but he will appeal rather to the lachrymose and fitful temper, which is easily imitated?

Clearly.

And now we may fairly take him and place him by the side of the painter, for he is like him in two ways: first, inasmuch as his creations have an inferior degree of truth — in this, I say, he is like him; and he is also like him in being the associate of an inferior part of the soul; and this is enough to show that we shall be right in refusing to admit him into a State which is to be well ordered, because he awakens and nourishes this part of the soul, and by strengthening it impairs the reason. As in a city when the evil are permitted to wield power and the finer men are put out of the way, so in the soul of each man, as we shall maintain, the imitative poet implants an evil constitution, for he indulges the irrational nature which has no discernment of greater and less, but thinks the same thing at one time great and at another small — he is an imitator of images and is very far removed from the truth.

Exactly.

But we have not yet brought forward the heaviest count in our accusation: The power which poetry has of harming even the good (and there are very few who are not harmed) is surely an awful thing?

Yes, certainly, if the effect is what you say.

Hear and judge: The best of us, as I conceive, when we listen to a passage of Homer or one of the tragedians, in which he represents some hero who is drawling out his sorrows in a long oration, or singing, and smiting his breast — the best of us, you know, delight in giving way to sympathy, and are in raptures at the excellence of the poet who stirs our feelings most.

Yes, of course I know.

But when any sorrow of our own happens to us, then you may observe that we pride ourselves on the opposite quality — we would fain be quiet and patient; this is considered the manly part, and the other which delighted us in the recitation is now deemed to be the part of a woman.

Very true, he said.

Now can we be right in praising and admiring another who is doing that which any one of us would abominate and be ashamed of in his own person?

No, he said, that is certainly not reasonable.

Nay, I said, quite reasonable from one point of view.

What point of view?

If you consider, I said, that when in misfortune we feel a natural hunger and desire to relieve our sorrow by weeping and lamentation, and that this very feeling which is starved and suppressed in our own calamities is satisfied and delighted by the poets; the better nature in each of us, not having been sufficiently trained by reason or habit, allows the sympathetic element to break loose because the sorrow is another's; and the spectator fancies that there can be no disgrace to himself in praising and pitying anyone who, while professing to be a brave man, gives way to untimely lamentation; he thinks that the pleasure is a gain, and is far from wishing to lose it by rejection of the whole poem. Few persons ever reflect, as I should imagine, that the contagion must pass from others to themselves. For the pity which has been nourished and strengthened in the misfortunes of others is with difficulty repressed in our own.

How very true!

And does not the same hold also of the ridiculous? There are jests which you would be ashamed to make yourself, and yet on the comic stage, or indeed in private, when you hear them, you are greatly amused by them, and are not at all disgusted at their unseemliness; the case of pity is repeated; there is a principle in human nature which is disposed to raise a laugh, and this, which you once restrained by reason because you were afraid of being thought a buffoon, is now let out again; and having stimulated the risible faculty at the theater, you are betrayed unconsciously to yourself into playing the comic poet at home.

Quite true, he said.

And the same may be said of lust and anger and all the other affections, of desire and pain and pleasure, which are held to be inseparable from every action — in all of them poetry has a like effect; it feeds and waters the passions instead of drying them up; she lets them rule, although they ought to be controlled if mankind are ever to increase in happiness and virtue.

I cannot deny it.

Therefore, Glaucon, I said, whenever you meet with any of the eulogists of Homer declaring that he has been the educator of Hellas, and that he is profitable for education and for the ordering of human things, and that you should take him up again and again and get to know him and regulate your whole life according to him, we may love and honor those who say these things — they are excellent people, as far as their lights extend; and we are ready to acknowledge that Homer is the greatest of poets and first of tragedy writers; but we must remain firm in our conviction that hymns to the gods and praises of famous men are the only poetry which ought to be admitted into our State. For if you go beyond this and allow the honeyed Muse to enter, either in epic or lyric verse, not law and the reason of mankind, which by common consent have ever been deemed best, but pleasure and pain will be the rulers in our State.

That is most true, he said.

And now since we have reverted to the subject of poetry, let this our defense serve to show the reasonableness of our former judgment in sending away out of our State an art having the tendencies which we have described; for reason constrained us. But that she may not impute to us any harshness or want of politeness, let us tell her that there is an ancient quarrel between philosophy and poetry; of which there are many proofs, such as the saying of "the yelping hound howling at her lord," or of one "mighty in the vain talk of fools," and "the mob of sages circumventing Zeus," and the "subtle thinkers who are beggars after all,"[3] and there are innumerable other signs of ancient enmity between them. Notwithstanding this, let us assure the poetry which aims at

[3]Socrates is alluding to various proverbs, otherwise unknown, denigrating both poets and philosophers. [Ed.]

pleasure, and the art of imitation, that if she will only prove her title to exist in a well-ordered State we shall be delighted to receive her — we are very conscious of her charms; but it would not be right on that account to betray the truth. I dare say, Glaucon, that you are as much charmed by her as I am, especially when she appears in Homer?

Yes, indeed, I am greatly charmed.

Shall I propose, then, that she be allowed to return from exile, but upon this condition only — that she make a defense of herself in some lyrical or other meter?

Certainly.

And we may further grant to those of her defenders who are lovers of poetry and yet not poets the permission to speak in prose on her behalf: let them show not only that she is pleasant but also useful to States and to human life, and we will listen in a kindly spirit; for we shall surely be the gainers if this can be proved, that there is a use in poetry as well as a delight?

Certainly, he said, we shall be the gainers.

If her defense fails, then, my dear friend, like other persons who are enamored of something, but put a restraint upon themselves when they think their desires are opposed to their interests, so too must we after the manner of lovers give her up, though not without a struggle. We too are inspired by that love of such poetry which the education of noble States has implanted in us, and therefore we shall be glad if she appears at her best and truest; but so long as she is unable to make good her defense, this argument of ours shall be a charm to us, which we will repeat to ourselves while we listen to her strains; that we may not fall away into the childish love of her which captivates the many. At all events we are well aware that poetry, such as we have described, is not to be regarded seriously as attaining to the truth; and he who listens to her, fearing for the safety of the city which is within him, should be on his guard against her seductions and make our words his law.

Yes, he said, I quite agree with you.

Yes, I said, my dear Glaucon, for great is the issue at stake, greater than appears, whether a man is to be good or bad. And what will any one be profited if under the influence of honor or money or power, aye, or under the excitement of poetry, he neglect justice and virtue?

Yes, he said; I have been convinced by the argument, as I believe that anyone else would have been.

Ion

SOCRATES: Welcome, Ion! And whence come you now to pay us a visit? From your home in Ephesus?

ION: No, Socrates, I come from Epidaurus and the festival of Asclepius.[1]

SOCRATES: What! Do the citizens of Epidaurus, in honoring the god, have a contest between rhapsodes[2] too?

ION: Indeed they do. They have every sort of musical competition.

SOCRATES: So? And did you compete? And how did you succeed?

ION: We carried off first prize, Socrates.

SOCRATES: Well done! See to it, now, that we win the Panathenaea also.

ION: It shall be so, God willing.

SOCRATES: I must say, Ion, I am often envious of you rhapsodists in your profession. Your art requires of you always to go in fine array, and look as beautiful as you can, and meanwhile you must be conversant with many excellent poets, and especially with Homer, the best and most divine of all. You have to understand his thought, and not merely learn his lines. It is an enviable lot! In fact, one never could be a rhapsode if one did not comprehend the utterances of the poet,

Translated by Lane Cooper.

[1]Greek god of medicine; his festival, like that of other minor divinities connected with Apollo, was the occasion for artistic performances and competitions. [Ed.]

[2]Professionals who delivered recitations of poetry, especially of Homer and the other epic poets. [Ed.]

for the rhapsode must become an interpreter of the poet's thought to those who listen, and to do this well is quite impossible unless one knows just what the poet is saying. All that, of course, will excite one's envy.

ION: What you say is true, Socrates; to me, at all events, this aspect of the art has given the most concern. And I judge that I, of all men, have the finest things to say on Homer, that neither Metrodorus of Lampsacus, nor Stesimbrotus of Thasos, nor Glaucon, nor anyone else who ever lived, had so many reflections, or such fine ones, to present on Homer as have I.

SOCRATES: That is pleasant news, Ion, for obviously you will not begrudge me a display of your talent.

ION: Not at all. And, Socrates, it really is worthwhile to hear how well I have embellished Homer. In my opinion I deserve to be crowned with a wreath of gold by the Homeridae.[3]

SOCRATES: Another time I shall find leisure to hear your recitation. At the moment do but answer me so far. Are you skilled in Homer only, or in Hesiod and Archilochus as well?

ION: No, only in regard to Homer; to me that seems enough.

SOCRATES: Is there any point on which both Homer and Hesiod say the same thing?

ION: Indeed, I think so; there are many cases of it.

SOCRATES: In those cases, then, would you interpret what Homer says better than what Hesiod says?

ION: In the cases where they say the same, Socrates, I should do equally well with both.

SOCRATES: But what about the cases where they do not say the same? For example, take the art of divination; Homer and Hesiod both speak of it.

ION: Quite so.

SOCRATES: Well then, where they say the same on the art of divination, and where they differ on it, would you interpret better what these two poets say, or would one of the diviners, one of the good ones, do so?

ION: One of the diviners.

[3]A group of poets who claimed descent from Homer, or more generally in this case, the admirers of Homer. [Ed.]

SOCRATES: But suppose you were a diviner. If you were competent to explain the passages where they agree, would you not be competent to explain as well the passages where they differ?

ION: Manifestly, yes.

SOCRATES: How is it, then, that you are skilled in Homer, but not in Hesiod or the other poets? Does Homer treat of matters different from those that all the other poets treat of? Wasn't his subject mainly war, and hasn't he discussed the mutual relations of men good and bad, or the general run as well as special craftsmen, the relations of the gods to one another and to men, as they forgather, the phenomena of the heavens and occurrences in the underworld, and the birth of gods and heroes? Are not these the subjects Homer dealt with in his poetry?

ION: What you say is true, Socrates.

SOCRATES: And what about the other poets? Haven't they dealt with these same themes?

ION: Yes, but, Socrates, not in the same way.

SOCRATES: How so? In a worse way than he?

ION: Far worse.

SOCRATES: He in a better way?

ION: Better indeed, I warrant you.

SOCRATES: Well now, Ion darling, tell me. When several persons are discussing number, and one of them talks better than the rest, there will be someone who distinguishes the good speaker?

ION: I agree.

SOCRATES: It will be the same one who distinguishes those who are speaking badly, or will it be another?

ION: No doubt the same.

SOCRATES: And this will be the one who knows the art of numbers?

ION: Yes.

SOCRATES: Tell me. When several are discussing diet, and what foods are wholesome, and one of them speaks better than the rest, will a given person see the excellence of the best speaker, and another the inferiority of the worst, or will the same man distinguish both?

ION: Obviously, I think, the same.

SOCRATES: Who is he? What is he called?

ION: The doctor.

SOCRATES: We may therefore generalize, and say: When several persons are discussing a given subject, the man who can distinguish the one who is talking well on it, and the one who is talking badly, will always be the same. Or, if he does not recognize the one who is talking badly, then, clearly, neither will he recognize the one who is talking well, granted that the subject is the same.

ION: That is so.

SOCRATES: Then the same man will be skilled with respect to both?

ION: Yes.

SOCRATES: Now you assert that Homer and the other poets, among them Hesiod and Archilochus, all treat of the same subjects, yet not all in the same fashion, but the one speaks well, and the rest of them speak worse.

ION: And what I say is true.

SOCRATES: Then you, if you can recognize the poet who speaks well, could also recognize the poets who speak worse, and see that they speak worse.

ION: So it seems.

SOCRATES: Well then, my best of friends, when we say that Ion has equal skill in Homer and all other poets, we shall not be mistaken. It must be so, since you yourself admit that the same man will be competent to judge of all who speak of the same matters, and that the poets virtually all deal with the same subjects.

ION: Then what can be the reason, Socrates, for my behavior? When anyone discusses any other poet, I pay no attention, and can offer no remark of any value. I frankly doze. But whenever anyone mentions Homer, immediately I am awake, attentive, and full of things to say.

SOCRATES: The riddle is not hard to solve, my friend. No, it is plain to everyone that not from art and knowledge comes your power to speak concerning Homer. If it were art that gave you power, then you could speak about all the other poets as well. There is an art of poetry as a whole? Am I not right?

ION: Yes.

SOCRATES: And is not the case the same with any other art you please, when you take it as a whole? The same method of inquiry holds for all the arts? Do you want some explanation, Ion, of what I mean by that?

ION: Yes, Socrates, upon my word I do. It gives me joy to listen to you wise men.

SOCRATES: I only wish you were right in saying that, Ion. But "wise men"! That means you, the rhapsodists and actors, and the men whose poems you chant, while I have nothing else to tell besides the truth, after the fashion of the ordinary man. For example, take the question I just now asked you. Observe what a trivial and commonplace remark it was that I uttered, something anyone might know, when I said that the inquiry is the same whenever one takes an art in its entirety. Let us reason the matter out. There is an art of painting taken as a whole?

ION: Yes.

SOCRATES: And there are and have been many painters, good and bad?

ION: Yes indeed.

SOCRATES: Now, take Polygnotus, son of Aglaophon. Have you ever seen a man with the skill to point out what is good and what is not in the works of Polygnotus, but without the power to do so in the works of other painters? A man who, when anybody shows the works of other painters, dozes off, is at a loss, has nothing to suggest, but when he has to express a judgment on one particular painter, say Polygnotus or anyone else you choose, wakes up, and is attentive, and is full of things to say?

ION: No, on my oath, I never saw the like.

SOCRATES: Or, again, take sculpture. Have you ever seen a man with the skill to judge the finer works of Daedalus, son of Metion, or of Epeus, son of Panopeus, or of Theodorus of Samos, or the works of any other single sculptor, but, confronted by the works of other sculptors, is at a loss, and dozes off, without a thing to say?

ION: No, on my oath, I never saw one.

SOCRATES: Yet further, as I think, the same is true of playing on the flute, and on the harp, and singing to the harp, and rhapsody. You never saw a man with the skill to judge of Olympus, of Thamyras, or of Orpheus, or of Phemius, the rhapsodist at Ithaca, but is at a loss, has no remark to make concerning Ion the Ephesian, and his success or failure in reciting.

ION: On that I cannot contradict you, Socrates. But of this thing I am conscious, that I excel all men in speaking about Homer, and on him have much to say, and that everybody else avers I do it well, but on the other poets I do not. Well then, see what that means.

SOCRATES: I do see, Ion, and in fact will proceed to show you what to my mind it betokens. As I just now said, this gift you have of speaking well on Homer is not an art; it is a power divine, impelling you like the power in the stone Euripides called the magnet, which most call "stone of Heraclea." This stone does not simply attract the iron rings, just by themselves; it also imparts to the rings a force enabling them to do the same thing as the stone itself, that is, to attract another ring, so that sometimes a chain is formed, quite a long one, of iron rings, suspended from one another. For all of them, however, their power depends upon that loadstone. Just so the Muse. She first makes men inspired, and then through these inspired ones others share in the enthusiasm, and a chain is formed, for the epic poets, all the good ones, have their excellence, not from art, but are inspired, possessed, and thus they utter all these admirable poems. So is it also with the good lyric poets; as the worshiping Corybantes[4] are not in their senses when they dance, so the lyric poets are not in their senses when they make these lovely lyric poems. No, when once they launch into harmony and rhythm, they are seized with the Bacchic transport, and are possessed — as the bacchants, when possessed, draw milk and honey from the rivers, but not when in their senses. So the spirit of the lyric poet works, according to their own report. For the poets tell us, don't they, that the melodies they bring us are gathered from rills that run with honey, out of glens and gardens of the Muses, and they bring them as the bees do honey, flying like the bees? And what they say is true, for a poet is a light and winged thing, and holy, and never able to compose until he has become inspired, and is beside himself, and reason is no longer in him. So long as he has this in his possession, no man is able to make poetry or to chant in prophecy. Therefore, since their making is not by art, when they utter many things and fine about the deeds of men, just as you do about Homer, but is by lot divine — therefore each is able to do well only that to which the Muse has impelled him — one to make dithyrambs, another panegyric odes, another choral songs, another epic poems, another iambs. In all the rest, each one of them is poor, for not by art do they utter these, but by power divine, since if it were by art that they knew how to treat one subject finely, they would know how to deal with all the others too. Herein lies the reason why the deity has bereft them of their senses, and uses them as ministers, along with soothsayers and godly seers; it is in order that we listeners may know that it is not they who utter these precious revelations while their mind is not within them, but that it is the god himself who speaks, and through them becomes articulate to us. The most convincing evidence of this statement is offered by Tynnichus of Chalcis. He never composed a single poem worth recalling, save the song of praise which everyone repeats, wellnigh the finest of all lyrical poems, and absolutely what he called it, an "Invention of the Muses." By this example above all, it seems to me, the god would show us, lest we doubt, that these lovely poems are not of man or human workmanship, but are divine and from the gods, and that the poets are nothing but interpreters of the gods, each one possessed by the divinity to whom he is in bondage. And to prove this, the deity on purpose sang the loveliest of all lyrics through the most miserable poet. Isn't it so, Ion? Don't you think that I am right?[5]

ION: You are indeed, I vow! Socrates, your words in some way touch my very soul, and it does seem to me that by dispensation from above good poets convey to us these utterances of the gods.

SOCRATES: Well, and you rhapsodists, again, interpret the utterances of the poets?

ION: There also you are right.

SOCRATES: Accordingly, you are interpreters of interpreters?

ION: Undeniably.

SOCRATES: Wait now, Ion; tell me this. And answer frankly what I ask you. Suppose you are

[4]Female worshippers of Dionysus whose rites drove them to frenzy; cf. Euripides's *The Bacchae*. [Ed.]

[5]In the preceding speech, the language spoken by Socrates takes on the rhythms of the dithyramb — the traditional hymn to Dionysus — as though he himself were in an inspired state. [Ed.]

reciting epic poetry well, and thrill the spectators most deeply. You are chanting, say, the story of Odysseus as he leaped up to the dais, unmasked himself to the suitors, and poured the arrows out before his feet, or of Achilles rushing upon Hector, or one of the pitiful passages, about Andromache, or Hecuba, or Priam. When you chant these, are you in your senses? Or are you carried out of yourself, and does not your soul in an ecstasy conceive herself to be engaged in the actions you relate, whether they are in Ithaca, or Troy, or wherever the story puts them?

ION: How vivid, Socrates, you make your proof for me! I will tell you frankly that whenever I recite a tale of pity, my eyes are filled with tears, and when it is one of horror or dismay, my hair stands up on end with fear, and my heart goes leaping.

SOCRATES: Well now, Ion, what are we to say of a man like that? There he is, at a sacrifice or festival, got up in holiday attire, adorned with golden chaplets, and he weeps, though he has lost nothing of his finery. Or he recoils with fear, standing in the presence of more than twenty thousand friendly people, though nobody is stripping him or doing him damage. Shall we say that the man is in his senses?

ION: Never, Socrates, upon my word. That is strictly true.

SOCRATES: Now then, are you aware that you produce the same effects in most of the spectators too?

ION: Yes, indeed, I know it very well. As I look down at them from the stage above, I see them, every time, weeping, casting terrible glances, stricken with amazement at the deeds recounted. In fact, I have to give them very close attention, for if I set them weeping, I myself shall laugh when I get my money, but if they laugh, it is I who have to weep at losing it.

SOCRATES: Well, do you see that the spectator is the last of the rings I spoke of, which receive their force from one another by virtue of the loadstone? You, the rhapsodist and actor, are the middle ring, and the first one is the poet himself. But it is the deity who, through all the series, draws the spirit of men wherever he desires, transmitting the attractive force from one into another. And so, as from the loadstone, a mighty chain hangs down, of choric dancers, masters of the chorus, undermasters, obliquely fastened to the rings which are suspended from the Muse. One poet is suspended from one Muse, another from another; we call it being "possessed," but the fact is much the same, since he is *held.* And from these primary rings, the poets, others are in turn suspended, some attached to this one, some to that, and are filled with inspiration, some by Orpheus, others by Musaeus. But the majority are possessed and held by Homer, and, Ion, you are one of these, and are possessed by Homer. And whenever anyone chants the work of any other poet, you fall asleep, and haven't a thing to say, but when anybody gives tongue to a strain of this one, you are awake at once, your spirit dances, and you have much to say, for not by art or science do you say of Homer what you say, but by dispensation from above and by divine possession. So the worshiping Corybantes have a lively feeling for that strain alone which is of the deity by whom they are possessed, and for that melody are well supplied with attitudes and utterances, and heed no others. And so it is with you, Ion. When anyone mentions Homer, you are ready, but about the other poets you are at a loss. You ask me why you are ready about Homer and not about the rest. Because it is not by art but by lot divine that you are eloquent in praise of Homer.

ION: Well put, I grant you, Socrates. And yet I should be much surprised if by your argument you succeeded in convincing me that I am possessed or mad when I praise Homer. Nor do I think that you yourself would find me so if you heard me speaking upon Homer.

SOCRATES: And indeed I wish to hear you, but not until you have answered me as follows. On what point in Homer do you speak well? Not on all points, I take it.

ION: I assure you, Socrates, I do it on every point, without exception.

SOCRATES: Yet not, I fancy, on those matters of which you happen to be ignorant, but Homer tells of?

ION: And the matters Homer tells of, and I do not know, what are they?

SOCRATES: Why, does not Homer in many passages speak of arts, and have much to say about them? About driving a chariot, for instance; if I can recollect the lines, I'll repeat them to you.

ION: No, let me do it, for I know them.

SOCRATES: Then recite for me what Nestor says to Antilochus, his son, where he warns him to be careful at the turning post, in the lay of the horse race in honor of Patroclus.

ION:

> Thyself lean slightly in the burnished car
> To the left of them, then call upon the off horse
> With goad and voice; with hand give him free rein.
> And at the post let the near horse come so close
> That the nave of the well-wrought wheel shall
> seem
> To graze the stone. Which yet beware to strike![6]

SOCRATES: That will do. Now, Ion, in these lines, which will be more capable of judging whether Homer speaks aright or not, a doctor or a charioteer?

ION: The charioteer, do doubt.

SOCRATES: Because that is his art, or for some other reason?

ION: No, because it is his art.

SOCRATES: Each separate art, then, has had assigned to it by the deity the power of knowing a particular occupation? I take it that what we know by the pilot's art we do not know by the art of medicine as well.

ION: No indeed.

SOCRATES: And what we know by medical art we do not know by the builder's art as well.

ION: No indeed.

SOCRATES: Well, and so it is with all the arts? What we know by one of them, we do not know by another? But before you answer that, just tell me this. Do you allow a distinction between arts? One differs from another?

ION: Yes.

SOCRATES: Now with me the mark of differentiation is that one art means the knowledge of one kind of thing, another art the knowledge of another, and so I give them their respective names. Do you do that?

ION: Yes.

SOCRATES: If they meant simply knowledge of the same things, why should we distinguish one art from another? Why call them different, when both would give us the same knowledge? For example, take these fingers. I know that there are five of them, and you know the same as I about them. Suppose I asked you if we knew this same matter, you and I, by the same art, that of arithmetic, or by different arts. I fancy you would hold that we knew it by the same?

ION: Yes.

SOCRATES: Then tell me now what just a little while ago I was on the point of asking you. Does that seem true to you of all the arts — that, necessarily, the same art makes us know the same, another art not the same, but, if it really is another art, it must make us know something else?

ION: That is my opinion, Socrates.

SOCRATES: Well then, if one does not possess a given art, one will not be capable of rightly knowing what belongs to it in word or action?

ION: That is true.

SOCRATES: Then, in the lines which you recited, which will have the better knowledge whether Homer speaks aright or not, you or a charioteer?

ION: The charioteer.

SOCRATES: Doubtless because you are a rhapsode, and not a charioteer?

ION: Yes.

SOCRATES: The rhapsode's art is different from the charioteer's?

ION: Yes.

SOCRATES: If it is another art, then, it is a knowledge also about other matters.

ION: Yes.

SOCRATES: Now what about the passage in which Homer tells how Hecamede, Nestor's concubine, gave the wounded Machaon the broth to drink? The passage runs something like this:

> She grated goat's-milk cheese in Pramnian wine,
> With brazen grater, adding onion as a relish to the
> brew.[7]

On the question whether Homer here speaks properly or not, is it for the art of the physician, or the rhapsode's art, to discriminate aright?

ION: The art of the physician.

[6] *Iliad* 23:335. [Tr.]

[7] *Iliad* 11:639–40. [Tr.]

SOCRATES: What of this? The passage in which Homer says:

She plunged to the bottom like a leaden sinker
Which, mounted on the horntip from a field ox,
Speeds its way bringing mischief to voracious fish.[8]

What shall we say? Is it rather for the art of fishing, or the rhapsode's art, to decide on what the verses mean, and whether they are good or not?

ION: Obviously, Socrates, it is for the art of fishing.

SOCRATES: Reflect now. Suppose that you were questioning, and asked me, "Now, Socrates, you find it is for these several arts to judge in Homer, severally, what appertains to each of them. Come then, pick me out the passages concerning the diviner, and the diviner's art, the kind of things that appertain to him, regarding which he must be able to discern whether the poetry is good or bad?" Observe how easily and truly I can answer you. The poet does, in fact, treat of this matter in the *Odyssey* too — for example, when a scion of Melampus, the diviner Theoclymenus, says to the wooers:

Ah, wretched men, what bane is this ye suffer? Shrouded in night
Are your heads and your faces and your limbs below,
And kindled is the voice of wailing, and cheeks are wet with tears.
And the porch is full of ghosts; the hall is full of them,
Hastening hellward beneath the gloom, and the sun
Has perished out of heaven, and an evil mist infolds the world.[9]

And he treats of it in many places in the *Iliad* — for instance, in the lay of the battle at the wall. There he says:

For, as they were eager to pass over, a bird approached them,
An eagle of lofty flight, skirting the host on the left,
And in its talons bearing a monstrous blood-red serpent,
Still alive and struggling; nor had it yet forgot the joy of battle.
Writhing back, it smote the bird that held it, upon the breast
Beside the neck, and the bird did cast it from him,
In the agony of pain, to the earth,
And dropped it in the middle of the throng.
And, with a cry, himself went flying on the gusty wind.[10]

These passages, I contend, and others like them, appertain to the diviner to examine and to judge.

ION: And, Socrates, you are right.

SOCRATES: And you are right too, Ion, when you say so. Come now, you do for me what I have done for you. From both the *Odyssey* and *Iliad* I picked out for you the passages belonging to the doctor, the diviner, and the fisherman; now you likewise, since you are better versed than I in Homer, pick out for me the sort of passages, Ion, that concern the rhapsode and the rhapsode's art, the passages it befits the rhapsode, above all other men, to examine and to judge.

ION: *All* passages, Socrates, is what I say.

SOCRATES: Surely, Ion, you don't mean *all!* Are you really so forgetful? Indeed, it would ill become a man who is a rhapsode to forget.

ION: Why? What am I forgetting?

SOCRATES: Don't you remember how you stated that the art of the rhapsode was different from the charioteer's?

ION: I remember.

SOCRATES: Well, and you admitted also that, being different, it had another field of knowledge?

ION: Yes.

SOCRATES: Well then, by your own account the art of rhapsody will not know everything, nor the rhapsode either.

ION: The exceptions, Socrates, are doubtless only such matters as that.

SOCRATES: In "such matters" you must include approximately all the other arts. Well, as the rhapsode does not know the subject matter of them all, what sort of matters *will* he know?

ION: The kind of thing, I judge, that a man would say, and a woman would say, and a slave and a free man, a subject and a ruler — the suitable thing for each.

[8]*Iliad* 24:80–82. [Tr.]

[9]*Odyssey* 20:351–56. [Tr.]

[10]*Iliad* 12:200–08. [Tr.]

SOCRATES: You mean, the rhapsode will know better what the ruler of a ship in a storm at sea should say than will the pilot?

ION: No, in that case the pilot will know better.

SOCRATES: But suppose it is the ruler of a sick man. Will the rhapsode know better what the ruler should say than will the doctor?

ION: No, not in that case, either.

SOCRATES: But you say, "the kind of speech that suits a slave."

ION: Yes.

SOCRATES: You mean, for instance, if the slave is a cowherd, it is not he who will know what one should say to quiet angry cattle, but the rhapsode?

ION: Surely not.

SOCRATES: Well, "the kind of speech that suits a woman" — one who spins — about the working up of wool?

ION: No.

SOCRATES: Well, the rhapsodist will know "the kind of speech that suits a man" — a general exhorting his soldiers?

ION: Yes! that is the sort of thing the rhapsodist will know.

SOCRATES: What! Is the rhapsode's art the general's?

ION: At all events I ought to know the kind of speech a general should make.

SOCRATES: Indeed, you doubtless have the talents of a general, Ion! And suppose you happened to have skill in horsemanship, along with skill in playing on the lyre, you would know when horses were well or badly ridden, but if I asked you, "By which art, Ion, do you know that horses are well managed — is it because you are a horseman, or because you play the lyre?" What answer would you give me?

ION: I should say, "It is by my skill as horseman."

SOCRATES: Then, too, if you were picking out good players on the lyre, you would admit that you discerned them by your art in playing the lyre, and not by your art as horseman?

ION: Yes.

SOCRATES: But when you know of military matters, do you know them because you are competent as a general, or as a rhapsode?

ION: I cannot see a bit of difference.

SOCRATES: What, no difference, you say? You mean to call the art of the rhapsode and the art of the general a single art, or two?

ION: To me, there is a single art.

SOCRATES: And so, whoever is an able rhapsode is going to be an able general as well?

ION: Unquestionably, Socrates.

SOCRATES: And then, whoever happens to be an able general is an able rhapsode too.

ION: No, I do not think that holds.

SOCRATES: But you thing the other does? That whoever is an able rhapsode is an able general too?

ION: Absolutely!

SOCRATES: Well, and you are the ablest rhapsodist in Greece?

ION: Yes, Socrates, by far.

SOCRATES: And the ablest general, Ion? The ablest one in Greece?

ION: You may be sure of it, for, Socrates, I learned this also out of Homer.

SOCRATES: Then, Ion, how in heaven's name is this? You are at once the ablest general and ablest rhapsodist among the Greeks, and yet you go about Greece performing as a rhapsode, but not as general. What think you? The Greeks are in great need of a rhapsode adorned with a wreath of gold, and do not need a general at all?[11]

ION: It is because my native city, Socrates, is under your dominion, and your military rule, and has no need whatever of a general. As for yours and Lacedaemon, neither would choose me for general; you think yourselves sufficient to yourselves.

SOCRATES: Excellent Ion, you know who Apollodorus is, of Cyzicus, don't you?

ION: What might he be?

SOCRATES: The man whom the Athenians at various times have chosen for their general, although he is an alien. The same is true of Phanosthenes of Andros, and Heraclides of Clazomenae, also aliens, who nevertheless, when they had shown their competence, were raised to the generalship by the city, and put in other high positions. And Ion of Ephesus, will she not elect him

[11]The dialogue occurs during the Peloponnesian War, which Athens eventually lost to Sparta. [Ed.]

general, and accord him honors, if his worth becomes apparent? Why, you inhabitants of Ephesus are originally Athenians, are you not, and Ephesus is a city inferior to none? But the fact is, Ion, that if you are right, if it really is by art and knowledge that you are able to praise Homer, then you do me wrong. You assure me that you have much fine knowledge about Homer, and you keep offering to display it, but you are deceiving me. Far from giving the display, you will not even tell me what subject it is on which you are so able, though all this while I have been entreating you to tell. No, you are just like Proteus; you twist and turn, this way and that, assuming every shape, until finally you elude my grasp and reveal yourself as a general. And all in order not to show how skilled you are in the lore concerning Homer! So if you are an artist, and, as I said just now, if you only promised me a display on Homer in order to deceive me, then you are at fault. But if you are not an artist, if by lot divine you are possessed by Homer, and so, knowing nothing, speak many things and fine about the poet, just as I said you did, then you do no wrong. Choose, therefore, how you will be called by us, whether we shall take you for a man unjust, or for a man divine.

ION: The difference, Socrates, is great. It is far lovelier to be deemed divine.

SOCRATES: This lovelier title, Ion, shall be yours, to be in our minds divine, and not an artist, in praising Homer.

Aristotle

384–322 B.C.

Unlike his teacher Plato, who was a native-born Athenian aristocrat, Aristotle was a *metic* — a foreigner with a green card, as it were — the son of a doctor from Thrace. Aristotle's origins may help explain why Plato's idealism had so little ultimate appeal for him. As a skilled biologist from Macedonia, an impoverished military state, Aristotle may have been loath to dismiss physical reality as an illusion. Certainly for Aristotle the universal *processes* of nature, the eternal laws of change, were not mere signs of the mutable, inferior character of the world of Becoming compared with the unalterable world of Ideas. They possessed immense significance.

Aristotle spent many years in Plato's Academy, learning its philosophy and its methods of argumentation, but his own school, the Lyceum, rejected Plato's idealism in favor of a materialism that investigated every aspect of the physical world. If Plato is the father of Western philosophy, Aristotle is the father of most of the sciences. Although Aristotle was often wildly wrong about details (Galileo's disproof of his speculations on gravity is the most famous instance), his systematizing of thought made science as we know it possible.

Aristotle's immense philosophical output may be divided into treatises on three types of science: the *theoretical* sciences, like logic or physics, which aimed at improving thought itself — one's general ideas on a particular subject; the *practical* sciences, like ethics and politics, whose goal lay in the realm of human action; and the *productive* sciences, like rhetoric and poetics, whose purpose was in making something. Here already, one can see a major difference from Plato, whose *Republic* combined speculation on metaphysics, ethics, politics, music, poetry, and much else. For Plato, thought was *holistic:* all was ultimately One and could be known through one dialectical method. For Aristotle, the world was not One but Many, and investigating it meant adapting one's methods and principles to the subject under consideration. This is the *problematic* method, and it is rare in the history of philosophy, where most thinkers have preferred universal dialectic to institutionalized improvisation. At the same time, Aristotle's mode of organization has clearly prevailed over Plato's in the structure of the modern university, where specialized departments of physics, psychology, literature, and music pursue their disparate disciplines by different methodologies.

Textual scholars believe the *Poetics* to be what is technically termed an *esoteric* treatise — it was circulated privately, within the Lyceum — rather than an *exoteric* one meant for general publication. It can be compared to teacher's lecture notes, brief and pointed, but meant to be filled out with further examples and arguments during presentation. Where the text seems dogmatic or disconnected or downright obscure, we should be tolerant — this was not the form in which Aristotle's students received it. There are other sources of obscurity, of course, the usual gaps that appear in transmitting and translating a verbal text more than two thousand years old. In Chapter 6, for example, Aristotle tells us that he will speak of comedy later,

KATHARSIS

One of the most controversial passages in the *Poetics* is contained in the passage on the final cause of tragedy: The play, "through incidents arousing pity and fear effects their *katharsis*."[4] But what does *katharsis* mean and what is "katharted"? Three possible translations of *katharsis* are "clarification," "purification," and "purgation"; and what is clarified, purified, or purged must be either the "incidents" or the emotions of "pity and fear."

According to the classical scholar Leon Golden, *katharsis* means "clarification," and it is the tragic *incidents* that are clarified: The process of poetic imitation, by stripping all accident and contingency from the tragic fall of the noble protagonist, reveals as clearly as possible how such things can happen. Tragedy here has an educative function. The "purification" theory, which has a long history beginning with the Renaissance theorists Lodovico Castelvetro and Francesco Robortello, suggests that tragedy has the function of tempering (or hardening) the emotions by revealing to the audience the proper objects of pity and fear.

The oldest theory holds that *katharsis* means "purgation," the violent driving-out of the emotions of pity and fear. This theory is supported by the only other instance in which Aristotle uses *katharsis* in the context of the arts, in a passage from the *Politics:*

> Music should be studied . . . for the sake of . . . many benefits . . . [one of which is] purgation (the word purgation we use at present without any explanation, but when hereafter we speak of poetry we will treat the subject with more precision). For feelings such as pity and fear, or, again, enthusiasm, exist very strongly in some souls, and have more or less influence over all. Some persons fall into a religious frenzy, whom we see . . . when they have used the sacred melodies, restored as though they had found healing and purgation. Those who are influenced by pity or fear, and every emotional nature, must have a like experience, and others in so far as each is susceptible to such emotions, and all are in a manner purged and their souls lightened and delighted. (*Politics* 1341^{b} 35 to 1342^{a} 15)

Aristotle thought that the *Poetics* would clarify the *Politics* rather than the other way around, but the context of this passage is clear enough: Unpleasant feelings may be relieved through music or poetry. When the experience is over, the soul is "lightened and delighted." After seeing a performance of *Oedipus the King* or *King Lear,* spectators are no longer gripped by pity and fear; rather they are exhausted, cleansed, emptied of emotion. The primary meaning of the word *katharsis,* preserved in the English cognate "cathartic," is the action of a powerful laxative. A doctor's son, Aristotle perhaps could not resist using a familiar medical metaphor for the experience.

Selected Bibliography

Belfiore, Elizabeth. *Tragic Pleasures: Aristotle on Art and Emotion.* Princeton: Princeton University Press, 1992.

Butcher, S. H. *Aristotle's Theory of Poetry and Fine Art.* New York: Macmillan, 1902.

[4]Editor's literal translation.

Cooper, Lane. *The Poetics of Aristotle: Its Meaning and Influence.* 1923; New York: Cooper Square, 1963.

Else, Gerald F. *Aristotle's Poetics: The Argument.* Cambridge: Harvard University Press, 1957.

———. *Plato and Aristotle on Poetry.* Chapel Hill: University of North Carolina Press, 1986.

Fergusson, Francis. "On the *Poetics.*" *Tulane Drama Review* 4 (1960): 23–32.

House, Humphrey. *The Poetics of Aristotle in England.* London: R. Hart-Davis, 1956.

Lucas, F. L. *Tragedy: Serious Drama in Relation to Aristotle's Poetics.* New York: Macmillan, 1958.

Modrak, Deborah. *Aristotle: The Power of Perception.* Chicago: University of Chicago Press, 1987.

Olson, Elder. *Aristotle's Poetics and English Literature.* Chicago: University of Chicago Press, 1965.

———. "The Poetic Method of Aristotle: Its Powers and Limitations." In *On Value Judgments in the Arts and Other Essays.* Chicago: University of Chicago Press, 1976.

Rorty, Amelie Oksenberg, ed. *Essays on Aristotle's Poetics.* Princeton: Princeton University Press, 1992.

Poetics

I

Let us discuss the art of poetry, itself, and its species, describing the character of each of them, and how it is necessary to construct plots if the poetic composition is to be successful and, furthermore, the number and kind of parts to be found in the poetic work, and as many other matters as are relevant. Let us follow the order of nature, beginning with first principles.

Now epic poetry, tragedy, comedy, dithyrambic poetry, and most forms of flute and lyre playing all happen to be, in general, imitations, but they differ from each other in three ways: either because the imitation is carried on by different means or because it is concerned with different kinds of objects or because it is presented, not in the same, but in a different manner.

For just as some artists imitate many different objects by using color and form to represent them (some through art, others only through habit), other artists imitate through sound, as indeed, in the arts mentioned above; for all these accomplish imitation through rhythm and speech and harmony, making use of these elements separately or in combination. Flute playing and lyre playing, for example, use harmony and rhythm alone; and this would also be true of any other arts (for example, the art of playing the shepherd's pipe) that are similar in character to these. Dancers imitate by using rhythm without harmony, since they imitate characters, emotions, and actions by rhythms that are arranged into dance-figures.

The art that imitates by words alone, in prose and in verse, and in the latter case, either combines various meters or makes use of only one, has been nameless up to the present time. For we cannot assign a common name to the mimes of Sophron and Xenarchus and the Socratic dialogues; nor would we have a name for such an imitation if someone should accomplish it through trimeters or elegiacs or some other such meter, except that the public at large by joining the term "poet" to a meter gives writers such names as "elegiac poets" and "epic poets." Here the public classifies all those who write in meter as poets and completely misses the point that the

Translated by Leon Golden.

capacity to produce an imitation is the essential characteristic of the poet. The public is even accustomed to apply the name "poet" to those who publish a medical or scientific treatise in verse, although Homer has nothing at all in common with Empedocles except the meter. It is just to call Homer a poet, but we must consider Empedocles a physicist rather than a poet.

And in the same way, if anyone should create an imitation by combining all the meters as Chairemon did when he wrote *The Centaur,* a rhapsody composed by the use of all the meters, he must also be designated a poet. Concerning these matters let us accept the distinctions we have just made.

There are some arts that use all the means that have been discussed, namely, rhythm and song and meter, as in the writing of dithyrambs and nomic poetry[1] and in tragedy and comedy. A difference is apparent here in that some arts use all the various elements at the same time, whereas others use them separately. These, then, are what I call the differences in the artistic means through which the imitation is accomplished.

2

Artists imitate men involved in action and these must either be noble or base since human character regularly conforms to these distinctions, all of us being different in character because of some quality of goodness or evil. From this it follows that the objects imitated are either better than or worse than or like the norm. We find confirmation of this observation in the practice of our painters. For Polygnotus represents men as better, Pauson as worse, and Dionysius as like the norm.[2] It is clear that each of the above-mentioned forms of imitation will manifest differences of this type and will be different through its choosing, in this way, a different kind of object to imitate. Even in dancing, flute-playing, and lyre-playing it is possible for these differences to exist, and they are seen also in prose, and in verse that does not make use of musical accompaniment, as is shown by the fact that Cleophon represents men like the norm, Homer as better, and both Hegemon the Thasian (who was the first writer of parodies) and Nicochares, the author of the *Deiliad,* as worse.[3] The same situation is found in dithyrambic and nomic poetry,[4] as we see in the way Timotheus and Philoxenus handled the Cyclops theme.[5] It is through the same distinction in objects that we differentiate comedy from tragedy, for the former takes as its goal the representation of men as worse, the latter as better, than the norm.

3

There is, finally, a third factor by which we distinguish imitations, and that is the manner in which the artist represents the various types of object. For, using the same means and imitating the same kinds of object, it is possible for the poet on different occasions to narrate the story (either speaking in the person of one of his characters as Homer does or in his own person without changing roles)[6] or to have the imitators performing and acting out the entire story.

[1]The dithyramb was originally a choral ode sung in honor of Dionysus, whereas nomic poetry was originally concerned with texts taken from the epic and was presented with a flute or lyre accompaniment. [Tr.]

[2]Polygnotus was one of the great painters of the fifth century B.C. Neither Pauson nor Dionysius are identified with certainty. [Tr.]

[3]Not much is known about the poets other than Homer mentioned here. Cleophon was a dramatic or epic writer; a small fragment of a parody of Hegemon of Thasos is preserved in Athenaeus; we have no further certain information about Nicochares. [Tr.]

[4]There is a lacuna in the text at this point where the name of another writer of nomic poetry was probably mentioned. [Tr.]

[5]Timotheus was a dithyrambic poet who lived in Miletus from 450 to 360 B.C.; Philoxenus was a dithyrambic poet who lived in Cythera from 436 to 380 B.C. [Tr.]

[6]The translation given of this phrase is based on the traditional text, which has been accepted by Butcher, Hardy, and Kassel. On philosophical and linguistic grounds, Bywater prefers to emend the text of the passage so that it reads as follows: "Given both the same means and the same kind of object for imitation, one may either (1) speak at one moment in narrative and at another in an assumed character, as Homer does; or (2) one may remain the same throughout, without any such change; or (3) the imitators may represent the whole story dramatically, as though they were actually doing the things described." [Tr.]

As we said at the beginning, imitations are to be distinguished under these three headings: means, object, and manner. Thus, in one way, Sophocles is the same kind of imitative artist as Homer, since they both imitate noble men; but in another sense, he resembles Aristophanes, since they both imitate characters as acting and dramatizing the incidents of the story. It is from this, some tell us, that these latter kinds of imitations are called "dramas" because they present characters who "dramatize" the incidents of the plot.

By the way, it is also for this reason that the Dorians claim to be the originators of both tragedy and comedy. The Megarians — both those in Megara itself, who assert that comedy arose when democracy was established among them, and those Megarians in Sicily, who point out that their poet Epicharmus far antedates Chionides and Magnes[7] — claim to have originated comedy; in addition, some of the Dorians in the Peloponnesus claim to be the originators of tragedy. As proof of their contentions, they cite the technical terms they use for these art forms; for they say that they call the towns around their city *komai,* but that the Athenians call their towns *demoi.* By this they argue that the root of the name "comedian" is not derived from *komazein* [the word for "reveling"] but from *komai* [their word for the towns] that the comic artists visited in their wanderings after they had been driven in disgrace from the city. In support of their claim to be the originators of "drama," they point out that the word for "doing" is *dran* in their dialect, whereas Athenians use the word *prattein* for this concept.

Concerning the number and kind of distinctions that characterize "imitations," let us accept what has been said above.

4

Speaking generally, the origin of the art of poetry is to be found in two natural causes. For the process of imitation is natural to mankind from childhood on: Man is differentiated from other animals because he is the most imitative of them, and he learns his first lessons through imitation, and we observe that all men find pleasure in imitations. The proof of this point is what actually happens in life. For there are some things that distress us when we see them in reality, but the most accurate representations of these same things we view with pleasure — as, for example, the forms of the most despised animals and of corpses. The cause of this is that the act of learning is not only most pleasant to philosophers but, in a similar way, to other men as well, only they have an abbreviated share in this pleasure. Thus men find pleasure in viewing representations because it turns out that they learn and infer what each thing is — for example, that this particular object is that kind of object; since if one has not happened to see the object previously, he will not find any pleasure in the imitation qua imitation but rather in the workmanship or coloring or something similar.

Since imitation is given to us by nature, as are harmony and rhythm (for it is apparent that meters are parts of the rhythms), men, having been naturally endowed with these gifts from the beginning and then developing them gradually, for the most part, finally created the art of poetry from their early improvisations.

Poetry then diverged in the directions of the natural dispositions of the poets. Writers of greater dignity imitated the noble actions of noble heroes; the less dignified sort of writers imitated the actions of inferior men, at first writing invectives as the former writers wrote hymns and encomia. We know of no "invective" by poets before Homer, although it is probable that there were many who wrote such poems; but it is possible to attribute them to authors who came after Homer — for example, the *Margites* of Homer himself, and other such poems. In these poems, the fitting meter came to light, the one that now bears the name "iambic" [i.e., invective] because it was originally used by men to satirize each other. Thus, of our earliest writers, some were heroic and some iambic poets. And just as Homer was especially the poet of noble actions (for he not only handled these well but he also made his imitations dramatic), so also he first

[7]Not much is known, beyond what Aristotle tells us in the *Poetics,* about these three comic writers who lived in the early part of the fifth century B.C. [Tr.]

traced out the form of comedy by dramatically presenting not invective but the ridiculous. For his *Margites* has the same relation to comedy as the *Iliad* and *Odyssey* have to tragedy. But when tragedy and comedy began to appear, poets were attracted to each type of poetry according to their individual natures, one group becoming writers of comedies in place of iambics, and the other, writers of tragedies instead of epics because these genres were of greater importance and more admired than the others.

Now then, the consideration of whether or not tragedy is by now sufficiently developed in its formal elements, judged both in regard to its essential nature and in regard to its public performances, belongs to another discussion. What is relevant is that it arose, at first, as an improvisation (both tragedy and comedy are similar in this respect) on the part of those who led the dithyrambs, just as comedy arose from those who led the phallic songs that even now are still customary in many of our cities. Tragedy, undergoing many changes (since our poets were developing aspects of it as they emerged), gradually progressed until it attained the fulfillment of its own nature. Aeschylus was the first to increase the number of actors from one to two; he also reduced the role of the chorus and made the dialogue the major element in the play. Sophocles increased the number of actors to three and introduced scene painting. Then tragedy acquired its magnitude. Thus by developing away from a satyr-play of short plots and absurd diction, tragedy achieved, late in its history, a dignified level. Then the iambic meter took the place of the tetrameter. For the poets first used the trochaic tetrameter because their poetry was satyric and very closely associated with dance; but when dialogue was introduced, nature itself discovered the appropriate meter. For the iambic is the most conversational of the meters — as we see from the fact that we speak many iambs when talking to each other, but few [dactylic] hexameters, and only when departing from conversational tone. Moreover, the number of episodes was increased. As to the other elements by which, we are told, tragedy was embellished, we must consider them as having been mentioned by us. For it would probably be an enormous task to go through each of these elements one by one.

5

As we have said, comedy is an imitation of baser men. These are characterized not by every kind of vice but specifically by "the ridiculous," which is a subdivision of the category of "deformity." What we mean by "the ridiculous" is some error or ugliness that is painless and has no harmful effects. The example that comes immediately to mind is the comic mask, which is ugly and distorted but causes no pain.

Now then, the successive changes in the history of tragedy and the men who brought them about have been recorded; but the analogous information about the history of comedy is lacking because the genre was not treated, at the beginning, as a serious art form. It was only recently that the archons began to grant choruses to the comic poets; until then, the performers were all volunteers. And it was only after comedy had attained some recognizable form that we began to have a record of those designated as "comic poets." Who introduced masks or prologues, who established the number of actors, and many other matters of this type, are unknown. The creation of plots came first from Sicily, where it is attributed to Epicharmus and Phormis; and it was first Crates among the Athenian poets who departed from iambic [or invective] poetry and began to write speeches and plots of a more universal nature.

Now epic poetry follows the same pattern as tragedy insofar as it is the imitation of noble subjects presented in an elevated meter. But epic differs from tragedy in that it uses a single meter, and its manner of presentation is narrative. And further, there is a difference in length. For tragedy attempts, as far as possible, to remain within one circuit of the sun or, at least, not depart from this by much. Epic poetry, however, has no limit in regard to time, and differs from tragedy in this respect; although at first the poets proceeded in tragedy in the same way as they did in epic. Some of the parts of a poem are common to both tragedy and epic, and some belong to tragedy alone. Therefore, whoever can judge what is good and bad in tragedy can also do this in regard to epic. For whatever parts epic poetry has, these are also found in tragedy; but, as we have said, not all of the parts of tragedy are found in epic poetry.

6

We shall speak about the form of imitation that is associated with hexameter verse and about comedy later.[8] Let us now discuss tragedy, bringing together the definition of its essence that has emerged from what we have already said. Tragedy is, then, an imitation of a noble and complete action, having the proper magnitude;[9] it employs language that has been artistically enhanced by each of the kinds of linguistic adornment, applied separately in the various parts of the play; it is presented in dramatic, not narrative form, and achieves, through the representation of pitiable and fearful incidents, the catharsis of such pitiable and fearful incidents. I mean by "language that has been artistically enhanced," that which is accompanied by rhythm and harmony and song; and by the phrase "each of the kinds of linguistic adornment applied separately in the various parts of the play," I mean that some parts are accomplished by meter alone and others, in turn, through song.

And since [in drama] agents accomplish the imitation by acting the story out, it follows, first of all, that the arrangement of the spectacle should be, of necessity, some part of the tragedy as would be melody and diction, also; for these are the means through which the agents accomplish the imitation. I mean by diction the act, itself, of making metrical compositions, and by melody, what is completely obvious. Since the imitation is of an action and is accomplished by certain agents, the sort of men these agents are is necessarily dependent upon their "character" and "thought." It is, indeed, on the basis of these two considerations that we designate the quality of actions, because the two natural causes of human action are thought and character. It is also in regard to these that the lives of all turn out well or poorly. For this reason we say that tragic plot is an imitation of action.

Now I mean by the plot the arrangement of the incidents, and by character that element in accordance with which we say that agents are of a certain type; and by thought I mean that which is found in whatever things men say when they prove a point or, it may be, express a general truth. It is necessary, therefore, that tragedy as a whole have six parts in accordance with which, as a genre, it achieves its particular quality. These parts are plot, character, diction, thought, spectacle, and melody. Two of these parts come from the means by which the imitation is carried out; one from the manner of its presentation, and three from the objects of the imitation. Beyond these parts there is nothing left to mention. Not a few poets, so to speak, employ these parts; for indeed, every drama [theoretically] has spectacle, character, plot, diction, song, and thought.

The most important of these parts is the arrangement of the incidents; for tragedy is not an imitation of men, per se, but of human action and life and happiness and misery. Both happiness and misery consist in a kind of action; and the end of life is some action, not some quality.[10] Now according to their characters men have certain qualities; but according to their actions they are happy or the opposite. Poets do not, therefore, create action in order to imitate character; but character is included on account of the action. Thus the end of tragedy is the presentation of the individual incidents and of the plot; and the end is, of course, the most significant thing of

[8]Aristotle discusses the epic in Chs. 23 and 24, but the section of the *Poetics* dealing with comedy seems to have been written but lost. Various Aristotelian scholars (including Lane Cooper and Elder Olson) have attempted to reconstruct what a poetics of comedy would be like. [Ed.]

[9]There is no word in the Greek text for "proper," but I have followed the practice of several other translators who add a modifier to the term "magnitude" where it is logically warranted. The term "representation" has also been added to the final clause of this sentence because of Aristotle's insistence that the pleasure of tragedy is achieved *through imitation* (Ch. 14, ll. 18–19). See L. Golden, "Catharsis," *TAPA* 93 (1962): 58. [Tr.]

[10]The text is corrupt here. The translation follows an emendation suggested by Vahlen and accepted by Bywater and Hardy. [Tr.]

all. Furthermore, without action tragedy would be impossible, but without character it would still be possible. This point is illustrated both by the fact that the tragedies of many of our modern poets are characterless, and by the fact that many poets, in general, experience this difficulty. Also, to take an example from our painters, Zeuxis illustrates the point when compared to Polygnotus; for Polygnotus is good at incorporating character into his painting, but the work of Zeuxis shows no real characterization at all. Furthermore, if someone arranges a series of speeches that show character and are well-constructed in diction and thought, he will not, by this alone, achieve the end of tragedy; but far more will this be accomplished by the tragedy that employs these elements rather inadequately but, nevertheless, has a satisfactory plot and arrangement of incidents. In addition to the arguments already given, the most important factors by means of which tragedy exerts an influence on the soul are parts of the plot, the reversal, and the recognition. We have further proof of our view of the importance of plot in the fact that those who attempt to write tragedies are able to perfect diction and character before the construction of the incidents, as we see, for example, in nearly all of our early poets.

The first principle, then, and to speak figuratively, the soul of tragedy, is the plot; and second in importance is character. A closely corresponding situation exists in painting. For if someone should paint by applying the most beautiful colors, but without reference to an overall plan, he would not please us as much as if he had outlined the figure in black and white. Tragedy, then, is an imitation of an action; and it is, on account of this, an imitation of men acting.

Thought is the third part of tragedy and is the ability to say whatever is pertinent and fitting to the occasion, which, in reference to the composition of speeches, is the essential function of the arts of politics and rhetoric. As proof of this we point out that our earlier poets made their characters speak like statesmen, and our contemporary poets make them speak like rhetoricians. Now character is that part of tragedy which shows an individual's purpose by indicating, in circumstances where it is not clear, what sort of things he chooses or rejects. Therefore those speeches do not manifest character in which there is absolutely nothing that the speaker chooses or rejects. Thought we find in those speeches in which men show that something is or is not, or utter some universal proposition.

The fourth literary part is diction, and I mean by diction, as has already been said, the expression of thoughts through language which, indeed, is the same whether in verse or prose.

Of the remaining parts, melody is the greatest of the linguistic adornments; and spectacle, to be sure, attracts our attention but is the least essential part of the art of poetry. For the power of tragedy is felt even without a dramatic performance and actors. Furthermore, for the realization of spectacle, the art of the costume designer is more effective than that of the poet.

7

Now that we have defined these terms, let us discuss what kind of process the arrangement of incidents must be, since this is the first and most important element of tragedy. We have posited that tragedy is the imitation of a complete and whole action having a proper magnitude. For it is possible for something to be a whole and yet not have any considerable magnitude. To be a whole is to have a beginning and a middle and an end. By a "beginning" I mean that which is itself not, by necessity, after anything else but after which something naturally is or develops. By an "end" I mean exactly the opposite: that which is naturally after something else, either necessarily or customarily, but after which there is nothing else. By a "middle" I mean that which is itself after something else and which has something else after it. It is necessary, therefore, that well-constructed plots not begin by chance, anywhere, nor end anywhere, but that they conform to the distinctions that have been made above.

Furthermore, for beauty to exist, both in regard to a living being and in regard to any object that is composed of separate parts, not only must there be a proper arrangement of the component elements, but the object must also be of a magnitude that is not fortuitous. For beauty is determined by magnitude and order; therefore, neither would a very small animal be beautiful (for one's view of the animal is not clear, taking place, as it does, in an almost unperceived length of time), nor is a very large animal beautiful (for then one's view does not occur all at once, but, rather, the unity and wholeness of the animal are lost to the viewer's sight as would happen, for example, if we should come across an animal a thousand miles in length). So that just as it is necessary in regard to bodies and animals for there to be a proper magnitude — and this is the length that can easily be perceived at a glance — thus, also, there must be a proper length in regard to plots, and this is one that can be easily taken in by the memory. The limit of length in regard to the dramatic contests and in terms of the physical viewing of the performance is not a matter related to the art of poetry. For if it were necessary for a hundred tragedies to be played, they would be presented by timing them with water clocks as we are told happened on some occasions in the past. The limit, however, that is set in regard to magnitude by the very nature of the subject itself is that whatever is longer (provided it remains quite clear) is always more beautiful. To give a general rule, we say that whatever length is required for a change to occur from bad fortune to good or from good fortune to bad through a series of incidents that are in accordance with probability or necessity, is a sufficient limit of magnitude.

8

A plot is a unity not, as some think, merely if it is concerned with one individual, for in some of the many and infinitely varied things that happen to any one person, there is no unity. Thus, we must assert, there are many actions in the life of a single person from which no overall unity of action emerges. For this reason all those poets seem to have erred who have written a *Heracleid* and a *Theseid* and other poems of this type; for they think that since Heracles was one person it is appropriate for his story to be one story. But Homer, just as he was superior in other respects, also seems to have seen this point well, whether through his technical skill or his native talent, since in making the *Odyssey* he did not include all the things that ever happened to Odysseus. (For example, it happened that Odysseus was wounded on Parnassus and that he feigned madness at the time of the call to arms; but between these two events there is no necessary or probable relation.) Homer, rather, organized the *Odyssey* around one action of the type we have been speaking about and did the same with the *Iliad*. Necessarily, then, just as in other forms of imitation, one imitation is of one thing, so also, a plot, since it is an imitation of an action, must be an imitation of an action that is one and whole. Moreover, it is necessary that the parts of the action be put together in such a way that if any one part is transposed or removed, the whole will be disordered and disunified. For that whose presence or absence has no evident effect is not part of the whole.

9

It is apparent from what we have said that it is not the function of the poet to narrate events that have actually happened, but rather, events such as might occur and have the capability of occurring in accordance with the laws of probability or necessity. For the historian and the poet do not differ by their writing in prose or verse (the works of Herodotus might be put into verse but they would, nonetheless, remain a form of history both in their metrical and prose versions). The difference, rather, lies in the fact that the historian narrates events that have actually happened, whereas the poet writes about things as they might possibly occur. Poetry, therefore, is more philosophical and more significant than history, for poetry is more concerned with the universal, and history more with the individual. By the universal I mean what sort of man turns out to say or do what sort of thing according to probability or necessity — this being the goal poetry aims at, although it gives individual names to the characters whose actions are imitated. By the individual I mean a statement telling, for example, "what Alcibiades did or experienced."

Now then, this point has already been made clear in regard to comedy; for the comic poets, once they have constructed the plot through probable incidents, assign any names that happen to occur to them, and they do not follow the procedure of the iambic poets who write about specific individuals. In regard to tragedy, however, our poets cling to the names of the heroes of the past on the principle that whatever is clearly capable of happening is readily believable. We cannot be sure that whatever has not yet happened is possible; but it is apparent that whatever has happened is also capable of happening for, if it were not, it could not have occurred. Nevertheless in some tragedies one or two of the names are well known and the rest have been invented for the occasion; in others not even one is well known, for example, Agathon's *Antheus,*[11] since in this play both the incidents and the names have been invented, and nonetheless they please us. Thus we must not seek to cling exclusively to the stories that have been handed down and about which our tragedies are usually written. It would be absurd, indeed, to do this since the well-known plots are known only to a few, but nevertheless please everyone. It is clear then from these considerations that it is necessary for the poet to be more the poet of his plots than of his meters, insofar as he is a poet because he is an imitator and imitates human actions. If the poet happens to write about things that have actually occurred, he is no less the poet for that. For nothing prevents some of the things that have actually occurred from belonging to the class of the probable or possible, and it is in regard to this aspect that he is the poet of them.

Of the simple plots and actions the episodic are the worst; and I mean by episodic a plot in which the episodes follow each other without regard for the laws of probability or necessity. Such plots are constructed by the inferior poets because of their own inadequacies, and by the good poets because of the actors. For since they are writing plays that are to be entered in contests (and so stretch the plot beyond its capacity) they are frequently forced to distort the sequence of action.

Since the imitation is not only a complete action but is also of fearful and pitiable incidents, we must note that these are intensified when they occur unexpectedly, yet because of one another. For there is more of the marvelous in them if they occur this way than if they occurred spontaneously and by chance. Even in regard to coincidences, those seem to be most astonishing that appear to have some design associated with them. We have an example of this in the story of the statue of Mitys in Argos killing the man who caused Mitys' death by falling upon him as he was a spectator at a festival.[12] The occurrence of such an event, we feel, is not without meaning and thus we must consider plots that incorporate incidents of this type to be superior ones.

10

Plots are divided into the simple and the complex, for the actions of which the plots are imitations are naturally of this character. An action that is, as has been defined, continuous and unified I call simple when its change of fortune arises without reversal and recognition, and complex when its change of fortune arises through recognition or reversal or both. Now these aspects of the plot must develop directly from the construction of the plot itself, so that they occur from prior events either out of necessity or according to the laws of probability. For it makes quite a difference whether they occur *because* of those events or merely *after* them.

11

Reversal is the change of fortune in the action of the play to the opposite state of affairs, just as has been said; and this change, we argue, should be in accordance with probability and necessity. Thus, in the *Oedipus* the messenger comes to cheer Oedipus and to remove his fears in regard to his mother; but by showing him who he actually is he accomplishes the very opposite effect. And in *Lynceus,* Lynceus is being led away to die and Danaus is following to kill him; but it turns

[11]Agathon was a late fifth-century B.C. tragic poet whose work has not survived except in fragments. He appears, prominently, in Plato's *Symposium.* [Tr.]

[12]I have followed Butcher's, Hardy's, and Bywater's interpretation of this passage. Others, however, understand the phrase to mean "when he was looking at the statue." [Tr.]

out, because of the action that has taken place, that Danaus dies and Lynceus is saved. Recognition, as the same indicates, is a change from ignorance to knowledge, bringing about either a state of friendship or one of hostility on the part of those who have been marked out for good fortune or bad. The most effective recognition is one that occurs together with reversal, for example, as in the *Oedipus*. There are also other kinds of recognition for, indeed, what we have said happens, in a way, in regard to inanimate things, even things of a very causal kind; and it is possible, further, to "recognize" whether someone has or has not done something. But the type of recognition that is especially a part of the plot and the action is the one that has been mentioned. For such a recognition and reversal will evoke pity or fear, and we have defined tragedy as an imitation of actions of this type; and furthermore, happiness and misery will appear in circumstances of this type. Since this kind of recognition is of persons, some recognitions that belong to this class will merely involve the identification of one person by another when the identity of the second person is clear; on other occasions it will be necessary for there to be a recognition on the part of both parties: for example, Iphigenia is recognized by Orestes from her sending of the letter; but it is necessary that there be another recognition of him on her part.

Now then, these are two parts of the plot, reversal and recognition, and there is also a third part, suffering. Of these, reversal and recognition have been discussed; the incident of suffering results from destructive or painful action such as death on the stage, scenes of very great pain, the infliction of wounds, and the like.

12

The parts of tragedy that we must view as formal elements we have discussed previously; looking at the quantitative aspect of tragedy and the parts into which it is divided in this regard, the following are the distinctions to be made: prologue, episode, exode, and the choral part, which is divided into parode and stasimon. These are commonly found in all plays, but only in a few are found songs from the stage and *kommoi*. The prologue is the complete section of a tragedy before the parode of the chorus; an episode is the complete section of a tragedy between complete choric songs; the exode is the complete section of a tragedy after which there is no song of the chorus. Of the choral part, the parode is the entire first speech of the chorus, the stasimon is a song of the chorus without anapests and trochees, and a *kommos* is a lament sung in common by the chorus and the actors. The parts of tragedy that we must view as formal elements we have discussed previously; the above distinctions have been made concerning the quantitative aspects of tragedy, and the parts into which it is divided in this regard.

13

What goals poets must aim at, which difficulties they must be wary of when constructing their plots, and how the proper function of tragedy is accomplished are matters we should discuss after the remarks that have just been made.

Since the plots of the best tragedies must be complex, not simple, and the plot of a tragedy must be an imitation of pitiable and fearful incidents (for this is the specific nature of the imitation under discussion), it is clear, first of all, that unqualifiedly good human beings must not appear to fall from good fortune to bad; for that is neither pitiable nor fearful; it is, rather, repellent. Nor must an extremely evil man appear to move from bad fortune to good fortune for that is the most untragic situation of all because it has none of the necessary requirements of tragedy; it both violates our human sympathy and contains nothing of the pitiable or fearful in it. Furthermore, a villainous man should not appear to fall from good fortune to bad. For, although such a plot would be in accordance with our human sympathy, it would not contain the necessary elements of pity and fear; for pity is aroused by someone who undeservedly falls into misfortune, and fear is evoked by our recognizing that it is someone like ourselves who encounters this misfortune (pity, as I say, arising for the former reason, fear for the latter). Therefore the emotional effect of the situation just mentioned will be neither pitiable nor fearful. What is left, after our considerations, is someone in between these extremes. This would be a person who is neither perfect in virtue and justice, nor one who falls into misfortune through vice and depravity; but rather, one who succumbs through some miscalculation. He must also be a person who enjoys great reputation and good fortune, such as Oedipus, Thyestes, and other illustrious men from similar families. It is necessary, furthermore, for the well-constructed plot to have a single rather than a double construction, as some urge, and to illustrate a change of fortune not from bad fortune to good but, rather, the very opposite, from good fortune to bad, and for this to take place not because of depravity but through some great miscalculation on the part of the type of person we have described (or a better rather than a worse one).

A sign of our point is found in what actually happens in the theater. For initially, our poets accepted any chance plots; but now the best tragedies are constructed about a few families, for example, about Alcmaeon, Oedipus, Orestes, Meleager, Thyestes, Telephon, and any others who were destined to experience, or to commit, terrifying acts. For as we have indicated, artistically considered, the best tragedy arises from this kind of plot. Therefore, those critics make the very mistake that we have been discussing who blame Euripides because he handles the material in his tragedies in this way, and because many of his plots end in misfortune. For this is, indeed, the correct procedure, as we have said. The very great proof of this is that on the stage and in the dramatic contests such plays appear to be the most tragic, if they are properly worked out; and Euripides, even if in other matters he does not manage things well, nevertheless appears to be the most tragic of the poets. The second ranking plot, one that is called first by some, has a double structure of events, as in the *Odyssey,* ending in opposite ways for the better and worse characters. It seems to be first on account of the inadequacy of the audience. For our poets trail along writing to please the tastes of the audience. But this double structure of events involves a pleasure that is not an appropriate pleasure of tragedy but rather of comedy. For in comedy, whoever are the greatest enemies in the story — for example, Orestes and Aegisthus — becoming friends at the end, go off together, and no one is killed by anyone.

14

Pity and fear can arise from the spectacle and also from the very structure of the plot, which is the superior way and shows the better poet. The poet should construct the plot so that even if the action is not performed before spectators, one who merely hears the incidents that have occurred both shudders and feels pity from the way they turn out. That is what anyone who hears the plot of the *Oedipus* would experience. The achievement of this effect through the spectacle does not have much to do with poetic art and really belongs to the business of producing the play. Those who use the spectacle to create not the fearful but only the monstrous have no share in the creation of tragedy; for we should not seek every pleasure from tragedy but only the one proper to it.

Since the poet should provide pleasure from pity and fear through imitation, it is apparent that this function must be worked into the incidents. Let us try to understand what type of occurrences appear to be terrifying and pitiable. It is, indeed, necessary that any such action occur either between those who are friends or enemies to each other, or between those who have no relationship, whatsoever, to each other. If an enemy takes such an action against an enemy, there is nothing pitiable in the performance of the act or in the intention to perform it, except the suffering itself. Nor would there be anything pitiable if neither party had any relationship with the other. But whenever the tragic incidents occur in situations involving strong ties of affection — for example, if a brother kills or intends to kill a brother or a son a father or a mother a son or a son a mother or commits some equally terrible act — there will be something pitiable. These situations, then, are the ones to be sought. Now, it is not possible for a poet to alter completely the traditional stories. I mean, for example, the given fact that Clytemnestra dies at the hands of Orestes, and Eriphyle at the hands of Alcmaeon; but it is necessary for the poet to be inventive and skillful in adapting the stories that have been handed down. Let us define more clearly what we mean by the skillful adaptation of a story. It is possible for the action to occur, as our early poets handled it, with the characters knowing and understanding what they are doing, as indeed Euripides makes Medea kill her children. It is also possible to have the deed done with those who accomplish the terrible deed in ignorance of the identity of their victim, only later recognizing the relationship as in Sophocles' *Oedipus*. The incident, here, is outside the plot, but we find an example of such an incident in the play itself, in the action of Astydamas's *Alcmaeon* or of Telegonus in the *Wounded Odysseus;*[13] and there is further a third type in addition to these that involves someone who intends to commit some fatal act through ignorance of his relationship to another person but recognizes this relationship before doing it. Beyond these possibilities, there is no other way to have an action take place. For it is necessary either to do the deed or not and either knowingly or in ignorance.

Of these possibilities, the case in which one knowingly is about to do the deed and does not is the worst; for it is repellent and not tragic because it lacks the element of suffering. Therefore, no one handles a situation this way, except rarely; for example, in the *Antigone,* Haemon is made to act in this way toward Creon. To do the deed knowingly is the next best way. Better than this is the case where one does the deed in ignorance and after he has done it recognizes his relationship to the other person. For the repellent aspect is not present, and the recognition is startling. But the most effective is the final type, for example, in the *Cresphontes,* where Merope is going to kill her son and does not, but, on the contrary, recognizes him, and in the *Iphigenia,* where a sister is involved in a similar situation with a brother, and in the *Helle,* where a son who is about to surrender his mother recognizes her.[14]

[13]Astydamas was a fourth-century B.C. poet; the *Wounded Odysseus* may have been a play by Sophocles. [Tr.]

[14]The *Cresphontes* and the *Iphigenia,* the former no longer extant, are plays by Euripides. We have no further information concerning the *Helle.* [Tr.]

It is for this reason that, as we have said previously, tragedies are concerned with a few families. For proceeding not by art, but by trial and error, poets learned how to produce the appropriate effect in their plots. They are compelled, therefore, to return time and again to that number of families in which these terrifying events have occurred. We have now spoken sufficiently about the construction of the incidents and of what type the plot must be.

15

In regard to character, there are four points to be aimed at. First and foremost, character should be good. If a speech or action has some choice connected with it, it will manifest character, as has been said, and the character will be good if the choice is good. Goodness is possible for each class of individuals. For, both a woman and a slave have their particular virtues even though the former of these is inferior to a man, and the latter is completely ignoble.[15] Second, character must be appropriate. For it is possible for a person to be manly in terms of character, but it is not appropriate for a woman to exhibit either this quality or the intellectual cleverness that is associated with men. The third point about character is that it should be like reality, for this is different from making character virtuous and making it appropriate, as we have defined these terms. The fourth aspect of character is consistency. For even if it is an inconsistent character who is the subject of the imitation (I refer to the model that suggested the kind of character being imitated), it is nevertheless necessary for him to be consistently inconsistent. We have an example of unnecessarily debased character in the figure of Menelaus in the *Orestes,* of unsuitable and inap-

[15]Aristotle's word for "good" here, *chrēstēn,* means "valuable" rather than "noble." Aristotle is distinguishing between the intrinsic value of personages (he considered women and slaves to be inferior beings) and the instrumental value of their ethical choices to the drama in which they figure. Aristotle's point is that character must serve the ends of the drama, and that *motiveless* choice, which has no effect on the action — like Menelaus's cowardice in Euripides' *Orestes* — is to be avoided. [Ed.]

propriate character in the lament of Odysseus in the *Scylla* and the speech of Melanippe, and of inconsistency of character in *Iphigenia at Aulis* where the heroine's role as a suppliant does not fit in with her character as it develops later in the play.

In character, as in the construction of the incidents, we must always seek for either the necessary or the probable, so that a given type of person says or does certain kinds of things, and one event follows another according to necessity or probability. Thus, it is apparent that the resolutions of the plots should also occur through the plot itself and not by means of the deus ex machina, as in the *Medea,* and also in regard to the events surrounding the department of the fleet in the *Iliad.* The deus ex machina must be reserved for the events that lie outside the plot, either those that happened before it that are not capable of being known by men, or those that occur after that need to be announced and spoken of beforehand. For we grant to the gods the power of seeing all things. There should, then, be nothing improbable in the action; but if this is impossible, it should be outside the plot as, for example, in Sophocles' *Oedipus.*

Because tragedy is an imitation of the nobler sort of men it is necessary for poets to imitate good portrait painters. For even though they reproduce the specific characteristics of their subjects and represent them faithfully, they also paint them better than they are. Thus, also, the poet imitating men who are prone to anger or who are indifferent or who are disposed in other such ways in regard to character makes them good as well, even though they have such characteristics, just as Agathon[16] and Homer portray Achilles.

It is necessary to pay close attention to these matters and, in addition, to those that pertain to the effects upon an audience that follow necessarily from the nature of the art of poetry. For, indeed, it is possible frequently to make mistakes in regard to these. We have spoken sufficiently about these matters in our published works.

[16] I have followed Butcher, Hardy, and Bywater in reading the name of the tragic poet here. Other scholars accept a manuscript reading of the word meaning "good." [Tr.]

16

What we mean by "recognition" we have indicated previously. Of the kinds of recognition that occur, there is one, first of all, that is least artistic, which poets mainly use through the poverty of their inspiration. This is the form of recognition that is achieved through external signs; some of these are birthmarks, for example, "the spearhead which the Earth-born are accustomed to bear," or the "stars" such as Carcinus wrote about in his *Thyestes.* Then there are characteristics that we acquire after birth. Of these some are found on the body, for example, scars; and others are external to the body, such as necklaces, and as another example, the ark through which the recognition is accomplished in the *Tyro.* It is also possible to employ these recognitions in better and worse ways; for example, Odysseus was recognized through his scar in one way by the nurse and in another way by the swineherds. Now those recognitions are less artistic that depend on signs as proof, as well as all that are similar to these; but those that derive from the reversal of action, as in the Bath Scene of the *Odyssey,* are better.

In second place come those recognitions that have been contrived for the occasion by the poet and are therefore inartistic. For example, the way Orestes in the *Iphigenia* makes known that he is Orestes; for Iphigenia made herself known through the letter, but he himself says what the poet wishes him to say but not what the plot requires. Therefore this type of recognition is rather close to the error that has already been mentioned; for it would have been just as possible for him to carry tokens with him. Another example of this type of recognition is the use of the "voice of the shuttle" in the *Tereus* of Sophocles.

The third type arises from our being stimulated by something that we see to remember an event that has an emotional significance for us. This type of recognition occurs in the *Cyprioe* of Dicaeogenes where the sight of the painting brings forth tears, and also in the story of Alcinous where Odysseus hears the lyre player and, reminded of his past fortunes, weeps; in both instances, it was by their emotional reactions that the characters were recognized.

The fourth type of recognition occurs through reasoning, for example, in the *Choëphoroe* it is achieved by the deduction: Someone like me has come; there is no one resembling me except Orestes; he, therefore, has come. Another recognition of this type was suggested by Polyidus the Sophist in regard to Iphigenia; for it was reasonable for Orestes to infer that, since his sister was sacrificed, he was also going to be sacrificed. Again, in the *Tydeus* of Theodectes, the deduction is made that he who had come to find a son was, himself, to perish. Another example is in the *Phinidae* where the women, when they had seen the place, inferred their destiny: that since they had been exposed there, they were fated to die there.

There is also a type of composite recognition from false reasoning on the part of another character,[17] for example, in the story of Odysseus, the False Messenger; for he said that he would know the bow that he had not seen, but it is false reasoning to suppose through this that he *would* recognize it again (as if he had seen it before).[18]

The best recognition is the one that arises from the incidents themselves, striking us, as they do, with astonishment through the very probability of their occurrence as, for example, in the action of the *Oedipus* of Sophocles and in the *Iphigenia,* where it is reasonable for the heroine to wish to dispatch a letter. Such recognitions alone are accomplished without contrived signs and necklaces. The second-best type of recognition is the one that is achieved by reasoning.

17

In constructing plots and working them out with diction, the poet must keep the action as much as possible before his eyes. For by visualizing the events as distinctly as he can, just as if he were present at their actual occurrence, he will discover what is fitting for his purpose, and there will be the least chance of incongruities escaping his notice. A sign of this is found in the criticism that is made of Carcinus. For Amphiarus is coming back from the temple, a point that would have escaped the audience's notice if it had not actually seen it; and on the stage, the play failed because the audience was annoyed at this incongruity.[19]

As much as is possible the poet should also work out the action with gestures. For, given poets of the same natural abilities, those are most persuasive who are involved in the emotions they imitate; for example, one who is distressed conveys distress, and one who is enraged conveys anger most truly. Therefore, the art of poetry is more a matter for the well-endowed poet than for the frenzied one. For poets marked by the former characteristic can easily change character, whereas those of the latter type are possessed.

In regard to arguments, both those that already are in existence and those he himself invents, the poet should first put them down in universal form and then extend them by adding episodes. I mean that the poet should take a general view of the action of the play, like, for example, the following general view of the *Iphigenia:* A young girl had been sacrificed and had disappeared in a way that was obscure to the sacrificers. She settled in another country in which it was the custom to sacrifice strangers to the goddess, and she came to hold the priesthood for this sacrifice. Later, it turned out that the brother of the priestess came to this country (the fact that the god, for some reason, commanded him to come is outside the argument; the purpose of his coming is outside of the plot). When he came he was seized, and on the point of being sacrificed he made himself known, either as Euripides handled the situation or as Polyidus arranged it, by his saying, in a very reasonable way, that not only had it been necessary for his sister to be sacrificed but also for him; and from this came his deliverance. After this, when the names have already been as-

[17]I have followed Bywater in accepting an emendation meaning "another" in place of the manuscript reading "audience" followed by Kassel and Hardy. [Tr.]

[18]In this passage, Bywater notes that, "both text and interpretation here are in the highest degree doubtful." I have followed his interpretation of this difficult passage. Except for the *Choëphoroe,* we do not have any information about the plays mentioned in the previous paragraph. [Tr.]

[19]Carcinus was a fifth-century B.C. tragic poet; nothing further is known of the play mentioned here. [Tr.]

signed, it is necessary to complete the episodes. The episodes must be appropriate, as, for example, the madness of Orestes through which he was captured and his deliverance through purification.

In drama, the episodes are short, but epic achieves its length by means of them. For the argument of the *Odyssey* is not long: A certain man is away from home for many years, closely watched by Poseidon but otherwise completely alone. His family at home continually faces a situation where his possessions are being squandered by the suitors who plot against his son. Storm-driven, he arrives home and, having made certain people acquainted with him, he attacks the suitors and, while destroying his enemies, is himself saved. This is the essence of the story; everything else is episode.

18

In every tragedy, we find both the complication and the resolution of the action. Frequently some matters outside the action together with some within it comprise the complication, and the rest of the play consists of the resolution. By complication I mean that part of the play from the beginning up to the first point at which the change occurs to good or to bad fortune. By resolution I mean the part of the play from the beginning of the change in fortune to the end of the play. For example, in the *Lynceus* of Theodectes, the complication comprises everything done before the action of the play begins and the seizing of the child, and, in turn, of the parents; the resolution comprises all that happens from the accusation of murder to the end of the play.[20]

There are four kinds of tragedy (for that number of parts has been mentioned): the complex, which consists wholly in reversal and recognition; the tragedies of suffering, for example, the *Ajaxes* and *Ixions* that have been written; the tragedies of character, for example, the *Phthiotian Women* and the *Peleus*.[21] And a fourth type [the tragedy of spectacle], for example, is *The Daughters of Phorcis* and *Prometheus*[22] and those plays that take place in Hades. Now it is necessary to attempt, as much as possible, to include all elements in the play, but if that is not possible, then as many as possible and certainly the most important ones. This is especially so now, indeed, when the public unjustly criticizes our poets. For although there have been poets who were outstanding in regard to each kind of tragedy, the public now demands that one man be superior to the particular virtue of each of his predecessors.

It is correct to speak of a tragedy as different from or similar to another one on the basis of its plot more than anything else: that is, in regard to an action having the same complication and resolution. Many poets are skillful in constructing their complications, but their resolutions are poor. It is, however, necessary for both elements to be mastered.

The poet, as has frequently been said, must remember not to make a tragedy out of an epic body of incidents (by which I mean a multiple plot), [as would be the case], for example, if someone should construct a plot out of the entire *Iliad*. For, there, because of the length, the parts take on the appropriate magnitude, but the same plot used in the drama turns out quite contrary to one's expectations. A sign of this is that so many as have written about the entire destruction of Troy (and not of sections of it, as Euripides) or about the entire story of Niobe (and not just a part, as Aeschylus) either completely fail on stage or do badly, since even Agathon failed for this reason alone. But in their reversals and in their simple plots, these poets aim with marvelous accuracy at the effects that they wish for: that is, whatever is tragic and touches our human sympathy. This occurs whenever a clever but evil person is deceived, as Sisyphus, or a brave but

[20]The text is in dispute here. Bywater, following a suggestion of Susemihl, translates the passage 1456^{a}, 7–10, at this point in the text. Butcher, Hardy, and Kassel retain the traditional reading that I have followed in my translation. [Tr.]

[21]*The Phthiotian Women* and *Peleus*, neither now extant, were probably written by Sophocles. The *Lynceus*, mentioned above and at l. 9 in Ch. 11, is also no longer extant. [Tr.]

[22]*The Daughters of Phorcis* and *Prometheus* are both by Aeschylus; Bywater identifies them as lost satyr-plays and does not connect the latter play with the famous *Prometheus Bound*. [Tr.]

unjust man is defeated. Such an event is probable, as Agathon says, because it is probable for many things to occur contrary to probability.

It is necessary to consider the chorus as one of the actors and as an integral part of the drama; its involvement in the action should not be in Euripides' manner but in Sophocles'. In the hands of our later poets, the songs included in the play are no more a part of that particular plot than they are of any other tragedy. They have been sung, therefore, as inserted pieces from the time Agathon first introduced this practice. And yet what difference does it make whether one sings an inserted song or adopts a speech or a whole episode from one play into another?

19

We have already spoken about other matters; it remains for us to discuss diction and thought. Concerning thought, let it be taken as given what we have written in the *Rhetoric,* for this is more appropriately a subject of that discipline. All those matters pertain to thought that must be presented through speech; and they may be subdivided into proof and refutation and the production of emotional effect, for example, pity or fear or anger or other similar emotions. Indications of the importance or insignificance of anything also fall under this heading. It is clear that we must employ thought also in actions in the same ways [as in speech] whenever we aim at the representation of the pitiable, the terrible, the significant, or the probable, with the exception of this one difference — that the effects arise in the case of the incidents without verbal explanation, whereas in the speech they are produced by the speaker and arise because of the speech. For what would be the function of the speaker if something should appear in the way that is required without being dependent on the speech?

Concerning diction one kind of study involves the forms of diction that are investigated by the art of elocution and are the concern of the individual who considers this his guiding art, for example, what a command is and what a prayer is, what a statement is, and threat and question and answer and any other such matters. For in regard to the knowledge or ignorance of these matters, no censure worth taking seriously can be made against the art of poetry. Why should any one accept as an error Protagoras's censure of Homer on the grounds that when he said, "Sing, O goddess, of the wrath . . ." he gave a command, although he really wished to utter a prayer. For Protagoras says to order someone to do something or not is a command. Let us, therefore, disregard such a consideration as being a principle of some other art, not the art of poetry.

20

The following parts comprise the entire scope of diction: letter, syllable, connective, noun, verb, inflection, and sentence. A letter is an indivisible sound; not every such sound is a letter, however, but only one from which a compound sound can be constructed. For I would call none of the individual sounds uttered by wild animals letters. The subdivisions of this category of "letters" are vowel, semivowel, and mute. A vowel is a sound that is audible without the contact of any of the physical structures of the mouth,[23] a semivowel is a sound that is audible with the contact of some of the physical structures of the mouth, for example, the *S* and *R* sounds; and a mute is a letter produced by the contact of the physical structures of the mouth, but inaudible in itself, although it becomes audible when it is accompanied by letters that are sounded, for example, the *G* and *D* sounds. These letters differ in the positions taken by the mouth to produce them, in the places in the mouth where they are produced, in aspiration and smoothness, in being long or short and, furthermore, in having an acute, grave, or middle [circumflex] pitch accent. The detailed investigation concerning these matters belongs to the study of metrics.

A syllable is a nonsignificant sound constructed from a mute and a vowel. For, indeed, *GR* without an *A* is a syllable and also with it, for

[23]I have followed Butcher and Hardy in seeing this passage as a reference to the physical means of producing speech. Bywater disputes this interpretation and argues that the ambiguous term *prosbole* does not refer to the impact of the physical structures of the mouth but to the addition of one letter to another. [Tr.]

example, *GRA*. However, it is the business of the art of metrics also to investigate distinctions in this area.[24]

A connective is a nonsignificant sound that neither hinders nor promotes the creation of one significant sound from many sounds and that it is not appropriate to place at the beginning of a speech that stands independently, for example, *men, dē, toi, de.* Or it is a nonsignificant sound that is naturally able to make one significant sound from a number of sounds, for example, *amphi, peri,* and others like them. There is also a kind of connective that is a nonsignificant sound that shows the beginning, end, or division of a sentence and that may naturally be placed at either end or in the middle of a sentence.

A noun is a compound significant sound, not indicating time, no part of which is significant by itself. For in compound nouns we do not consider each part of the compound as being significant in itself; for example, in the name "Theodore" the root *dor* [gift] has no significance.

A verb is a compound significant sound indicating time, no part of which is significant by itself in the same way as has been indicated in regard to nouns. For "man" or "white" do not tell us anything about "when"; but "he goes" or "he has gone" indicate the present and the past.

Inflection is a characteristic of a noun or verb signifying the genitive or dative relation, or other similar ones, or indicating the singular or plural, that is, man or men, or is concerned with matters that fall under the art of elocution, for example, questions and commands; for the phrases, "Did he go?" or "Go!" involve inflections of the verb in regard to these categories.

A speech is a compound, significant sound some of whose parts are significant by themselves. For not every speech is composed of verbs and nouns but it is possible to have a speech without verbs (for example, the definition of man). However, part of the speech will always have some significance, for example, "Cleon" in the phrase "Cleon walks." A speech is a unity in two ways. Either it signifies one thing or it is a unity through the joining together of many speeches. For example, the *Iliad* is a unity by the process of joining together many speeches, and the definition of man by signifying one thing.

[24]The passage that begins here is corrupt and contains many difficulties of interpretation. [Tr.]

21

Nouns are either simple, by which I mean constructed solely from nonsignificant elements, for example *gē* [earth], or compound. This latter category is divided into nouns that are constructed from both significant and nonsignificant elements (except that neither element is significant within the compound word itself) and nouns that are composed solely out of significant elements. Nouns may also be made up of three, four, or more parts, for example, many of the words in the Massilian vocabulary, such as Hermocaicoxanthus. . . .[25]

Every word is either standard, or is a strange word, or is a metaphor, or is ornamental, or is a coined word, or is lengthened, or contracted, or is altered in some way. I mean by standard, words that everyone uses, and by a strange word, one that foreigners use. Thus, it is apparent, the same word can be both strange and ordinary but not, of course, to the same persons. The word *sigunon* [spear] is ordinary for the Cyprians and strange to us.

Metaphor is the transference of a name from the object to which it has a natural application; this transference can take place from genus to species or species to genus or from species to species or by analogy. I mean by "from genus to species," for example, "This ship of mine stands there." For to lie at anchor is a species of standing. An example of the transference from species to genus, "Odysseus has truly accomplished a myriad of noble deeds." For a myriad is the equivalent of "many," for which the poet now substitutes this term. An example of the transference from species to species is "having drawn off life with a sword" and also "having cut with unyielding bronze." For here to draw off is to cut and to cut is called to draw off, for both are subdivisions of "taking away."

[25]There is a lacuna in the text here. Some editors accept Diel's conjecture, "praying to father Zeus," as the completion of this line. [Tr.]

I mean by "transference by analogy" the situation that occurs whenever a second element is related to a first as a fourth is to a third. For the poet will then use the fourth in place of the second or the second in place of the fourth, and sometimes poets add the reference to which the transferred term applies. I mean, for example, that a cup is related to Dionysus as a shield is to Ares. The poet will, therefore, speak of the cup as the shield of Dionysus and the shield as the cup of Ares. The same situation occurs in regard to the relation of old age to life and evening to day. A poet will say that evening is the old age of day, or however Empedocles expressed it, and that old age is the evening of life or the sunset of life. In some situations, there is no regular name in use to cover the analogous relation, but nevertheless the related elements will be spoken of by analogy; for example, to scatter seed is to sow, but the scattering of the sun's rays has no name. But the act of sowing in regard to grain bears an analogous relation to the sun's dispersing of its rays, and so we have the phrase "sowing the god-created fire."

It is also possible to use metaphor in a different way by applying the transferred epithet and then denying some aspect that is proper to it — for example, if one should call the shield not the cup of Ares but the wineless cup.[26] A coined word is one that is not in use among foreigners but is the invention of the poet. There seem to be some words of this type, for example, horns [*kerata*] called "sprouters" [*ernuges*], and a priest [*iereus*] called "supplicator" [*arētēr*].

A word may be lengthened or contracted. It is lengthened if it makes use of a longer vowel than is usual for it, or a syllable is inserted in it; and it is contracted if any element is removed from it. An example of lengthening is *poleōs* to *polēos* and *Pēleidou* to *Pēlēiadeō;* an example of contraction is *krī* and *dō* and *ops* in *"mia ginetai amphoterōn ops."*

A word is altered whenever a poet utilizes part of the regular name for the object he is describing and invents part anew, for example, in the phrase *"deksiteron kata mazon"* the use of *deksiteron* in place of *deksion*.[27]

Nouns are subdivided into masculine, feminine, and neuter. Those are masculine that end in nu, rho, and sigma and in the two letters psi and ksi that are constructed in combination with sigma. Those nouns are feminine that end in the vowels that are always long, the eta and omega, and that end (in regard to the vowels subject to lengthening) in the lengthened alpha. Thus it turns out that there are an equal number of terminations for masculine and feminine nouns since psi and ksi are subdivisions of sigma. No noun ends in a mute nor in a short vowel. Only three end in iota, *meli, kommi, peperi,* and five end in upsilon. Neuter nouns end in these vowels and in nu and sigma.

22

Diction achieves its characteristic virtue in being clear but not mean. The clearest style results from the use of standard words; but it is also mean, as can be seen in the poetry of Cleophon and Sthenelus. A really distinguished style varies ordinary diction through the employment of unusual words. By unusual I mean strange words and metaphor and lengthened words and everything that goes beyond ordinary diction. But if someone should write exclusively in such forms the result would either be a riddle or a barbarism. A riddle will result if someone writes exclusively in metaphor; and a barbarism will result if there is an exclusive use of strange words. For it is in the nature of a riddle for one to speak of a situation that actually exists in an impossible way. Now it is not possible to do this by the combination of strange words; but it can be done by metaphor, for example, "I saw a man who welded bronze on another man by fire," and other metaphors like this. A statement constructed exclusively from strange words is a barbarism.

It is therefore necessary to use a combination of all these forms. The employment of strange words and metaphor and ornamental words and

[26]Editors have noted that a definition of the term "ornamental word" belongs in the text at this point, although it is missing from the manuscripts. [Tr.]

[27]The phrase quoted comes from the *Iliad* 5:393 and means "at her right breast." Two words meaning "right" are quoted to illustrate Aristotle's point here. [Tr.]

the other forms of speech that have been mentioned will prevent the diction from being ordinary and mean; and the use of normal speech will keep the diction clear. The lengthening and contraction of words and alterations in them contribute in no small measure to the diction's clarity and its elevation above ordinary diction. For because such words are different they will prevent the diction from being ordinary through their contrast with the ordinary expression; and because they have a share in the customary word, they will keep the diction clear.

Thus, the criticism is not well-taken on the part of those who censure this way of using language and who mock the poet, as the elder Euclid did, on the grounds that it is easy to write poetry if you are allowed to lengthen forms as much as you want; Euclid composed a satiric verse in the very words he used, *Epicharēn eidon Marathōnade badizonta* and *ouk an g'eramenos ton ekeinou elleboron.*[28]

Now then, the employment of the technique of lengthening in excess is ridiculous, and moderation is a quality that is commonly needed in all aspects of diction. For, indeed, if one employs metaphors and strange words and other forms in an inappropriate way and with intended absurdity, he can also accomplish the same effect. When the ordinary words are inserted in the verse, it can be seen how great a difference the appropriate use of lengthening makes in epic poetry. If someone should also change the strange words and metaphors and other forms to ordinary words, he would see the truth of what we have said. For example, Aeschylus and Euripides wrote the same iambic line, but Euripides changed one word and instead of using a standard one employed a strange one; his line thus has an elegance to it, whereas the other is mean. For Aeschylus wrote in his *Philoctetes:*

> *phagediana hē mou sarkas esthiei podos*
> [this cancerous sore eats the flesh of my leg].

Euripides in place of "eats" substitutes *thoinatai* [feasts upon]. A similar situation would occur in the line

> *nun de m'eōn oligos te kai outidanos kai aeikēs*[29]

if someone should substitute the ordinary words

> *nun de m'eōn mikros te kai asthenikos kai aeidēs*

or if we changed the line

> *diphron aeikelion katatheis oligēn te trapezan*[30]

to

> *diphron moxtherōn katatheis mikran te trapezan*

or for *ēiones booōsin,* we substituted *ēiones krazousin.*[31] Furthermore, Ariphrades mocked the tragedians because no one would use their style in conversation; for example, the word order *dōmatōn apo* in place of *apo dōmatōn,* and the word *sethen,* and the phrase *egō de nin,* and the word order *Achilleōs peri* in place of *peri Achilleōs,* and many other similar expressions. For he missed the point that the virtue of all these expressions is that they create an unusual element in the diction by their not being in ordinary speech.

It is a matter of great importance to use each of the forms mentioned in a fitting way, as well as compound words and strange ones, but by far the most important matter is to have skill in the use of metaphor. This skill alone it is not possible to obtain from another, and it is, in itself, a sign of genius. For the ability to construct good metaphors implies the ability to see essential similarities.

In regard to words, compounds are especially suitable for dithyrambs, strange words for heroic verse, and metaphors for iambic verse; in heroic verse all the forms mentioned are serviceable; but in iambic verse, because as much as possible it imitates conversation, only those words are appropriate that might be used in prose.

[28] This passage offers a number of difficulties in text and interpretation. The essential point is that the prosaic lines quoted can be technically turned into verse if enough licenses are allowed. The first phrase may be translated "I saw Epichares going to Marathon." The text of the second phrase is corrupt and does not have a clear meaning as it stands. [Tr.]

[29] A passage quoted from *Odyssey* 9:515, meaning "someone small, worthless, and unseemly." [Tr.]

[30] A passage quoted from *Odyssey* 20:259, meaning "having set down [for him] an unseemly chair and a small table." [Tr.]

[31] A passage quoted from *Iliad* 17:265, meaning "the shores cry out." [Tr.]

Of this nature are standard words, metaphors, and ornamental words.

Now, then, concerning tragedy and the imitation that is carried out in action, let what has been said suffice.

23

Concerning that form of verse imitation that is narrative, it is necessary to construct the plot as in tragedy in a dramatic fashion, and concerning a single action that is whole and complete (having a beginning, middle, and end) so that, like a single integrated organism, it achieves the pleasure natural to it.

The composition of incidents should not be similar to that found in our histories, in which it is necessary to show not one action but one period of time and as many things as happened in this time, whether they concern one man or many, and whether or not each of these things is related to the others. For just as there occurred in the same period of time a sea battle at Salamis and a battle with the Carthaginians in Sicily, but these did not at all lead to a common goal, thus also in the sequence of time, occasionally one event happens after another without there being a common goal to join them.

However, almost all the poets commit this error. Also in this, then, Homer would appear to be of exceptional skill in relation to other poets, as we have already said, since he did not attempt to write about the complete war, although it had a beginning and end; for that would have been a very large subject and could not have been taken in easily in a single view; or even if its magnitude were moderate, the story still would be tangled because of the diversity of incidents. But note how although treating only one part of the war, he also introduces many of the other episodes in the war, for example, the catalogue of ships and others, by which he gives variety to his poem. Others write about one man and about one period and one action with diverse parts, for example, the poet who wrote the *Cypria* and the *Little Iliad*. Therefore from the *Iliad* and *Odyssey* one or two tragedies apiece are constructed; but from the *Cypria* many tragedies are constructed and from the *Little Iliad* eight, for example, *The Award of the Arms, Philoctetes, Neoptolemus, Eurypylus, The Beggar, The Laconian Woman, The Sack of Troy, The Return Voyage,* and a *Sinon,* and a *Women of Troy.*[32]

24

Moreover, it is necessary for epic poetry to exhibit the same characteristic forms as tragedy; for it is either simple or complex, displays character or suffering, and is composed of the same parts, with the exception of song and spectacle. In epic, there is also a necessity for reversals, recognitions, and the depiction of suffering. Here too, thought and diction must be handled with skill. Homer used all these elements first and in a proper way. For each of his poems is well constructed; the *Iliad* is simple and exhibits suffering, whereas the *Odyssey* is complex (for there is recognition throughout) and shows character. In addition to these matters, Homer outstrips all others in diction and thought.

Epic differs from tragedy in regard to the length of the plot, and the meter. The sufficient limit of length has been mentioned, for we have noted that it must be possible to take in the plot's beginning and end in one view. This would occur if the plots were shorter than those of the old epics but would extend to the length of the number of tragedies that are designated for one performance. For the purpose of extending its length, epic poetry has a very great capacity that is specifically its own, since it is not possible in tragedy to imitate many simultaneous lines of action but only that performed by the actors on the stage. But because of the narrative quality of epic it is possible to depict many simultaneous lines of action that, if appropriate, become the means of increasing the poem's scope. This has an advantage in regard to the elegance of the poem and in regard to varying the interest of the audience and for constructing a diverse sequence of episodes. For the rapid overloading of tragedies with the same kind of incident is what makes tragedies fail.

[32]Butcher and Kassel bracket the names of the last two plays as being later additions to the original text of the *Poetics*. [Tr.]

The heroic meter has been found appropriate to epic through practical experience. If someone should write a narrative imitation in another meter, or in a combination of meters, we would feel it to be inappropriate. For the heroic is the stateliest and most dignified meter, and therefore it is especially receptive to strange words and metaphors, for narrative poetry in this regard is exceptional among the forms of imitation; the iambic and the trochaic tetrameter are expressive of motion, the latter being a dance meter and the former displaying the quality of action. Furthermore, it makes a very strange impression if someone combines these meters as Chairemon did. Therefore, no one has written a long poem in a meter other than the heroic; but, as we said, nature herself teaches us to choose the appropriate meter.

Homer deserves praise for many qualities and, especially, because alone of the poets he is not ignorant of the requirements of his craft. For it is necessary for the poet himself to speak in his own person in the poem as little as possible, because he is not fulfilling his function as an imitator when he appears in this way. Now the other poets are themselves active performers throughout the poem, and they perform their imitative function infrequently and in regard to only a few objects. Homer, on the other hand, when he has made a brief prelude immediately brings in a man or woman or some other character; and all his figures are expressive of character, and none lacks it.

Now then, it is necessary in tragedy to create the marvelous, but the epic admits, even more, of the irrational, on which the marvelous especially depends, because the audience does not see the person acting. The whole business of the pursuit of Hector would appear ridiculous on the stage with some men standing about and not pursuing and Achilles nodding at them to keep them back; but in the narrative description of epic, this absurdity escapes notice.

The marvelous is pleasant, and the proof of this is that everyone embellishes the stories he tells as if he were adding something pleasant to his narration. Homer has especially taught others how it is necessary to lie, and this is through the employment of false reasoning. For whenever one event occurs or comes into existence and is naturally accompanied by a second event, men think that whenever this second event is present the first one must also have occurred or have come into existence. This, however, is a fallacy. Therefore, if the first event mentioned is false but there is another event that must occur or come into existence when the first event occurs, we feel compelled to join the two events in our thought. For our mind, through knowing that the second event is true, falsely reasons that the first event must have occurred or have come into existence also. There is an example of this type of fallacy in the Bath Scene in the *Odyssey.*

The use of impossible probabilities is preferable to that of unpersuasive possibilities. We must not construct plots from irrational elements, and we should especially attempt not to have anything irrational at all in them; but if this is not possible, the irrational should be outside the plot (as in Oedipus's ignorance of how Laius died); it should not be in the drama itself, as occurs in the *Electra* concerning those who bring news of the Pythian games, or in the *Mysians,* concerning the man who has come from Tegea to Mysia without speaking. To say that without the use of such incidents the plot would have been ruined is ridiculous. For it is necessary, right from the beginning, not to construct such plots.

If the poet takes such a plot and if it appears to admit of a more probable treatment, the situation is also absurd,[33] since it is clear that even the improbable elements in the *Odyssey* concerning the casting ashore of Odysseus would not be bearable if a poor poet had written them. Here the poet conceals the absurdity by making it pleasing through his other skillful techniques. It is necessary to intensify the diction only in those parts of the poem that lack action and are unexpressive of character and thought. For too brilliant a diction conceals character and thought.

[33]Butcher and Hardy, following a different punctuation of the text, interpret this passage to mean that it is possible to admit some element of the irrational to the plot; others feel that the Greek text does not make adequate sense as it stands. I have followed Bywater's punctuation and interpretation of this passage. [Tr.]

25

Concerning the number and character of the problems that lead to censure in poetry and the ways in which this censure must be met, the following considerations would be apparent to those who study the question. Since the poet is an imitator, like a painter or any maker of likenesses, he must carry out his imitations on all occasions in one of three possible ways. Thus, he must imitate the things that were in the past, or are now, or that people say and think to be or those things that ought to be. The poet presents his imitation in standard diction, as well as in strange words and metaphors and in many variations of diction, for we grant this license to poets. In addition to this, there is not the same standard of correctness for politics and poetry, nor for any other art and poetry. In regard to poetry itself, two categories of error are possible, one essential, and one accidental. For if the poet chose to imitate but imitated incorrectly through lack of ability,[34] the error is an essential one; but if he erred by choosing an incorrect representation of the object (for example, representing a horse putting forward both right hooves) or made a technical error, for example, in regard to medicine or any other art, or introduced impossibilities of any sort, the mistake is an accidental, not an essential, one.

As a result, we must meet the criticisms of the problems encountered in poetry by taking these points into consideration. First, in regard to the problems that are related to the essential nature of art: if impossibilities have been represented, an error has been made; but it may be permissible to do this if the representation supports the goal of the imitation (for the goal of an imitation has been discussed) and if it makes the section in which it occurs, or another part of the poem, more striking. An example of such a situation is the pursuit of Hector in the *Iliad*. If, indeed, the goal of the imitation admits of attainment as well, or better, when sought in accordance with technical requirements, then it is incorrect to introduce the impossible. For, if it is at all feasible, no error should be committed at all. Further, we must ascertain whether an error originates from an essential or an accidental aspect of the art. For it is a less important matter if the artist does not know that a hind does not have horns than if he is unskillful in imitating one. In addition, the criticism that a work of art is not a truthful representation can be met by the argument that it represents the situation as it should be. For example, Sophocles said that he himself created characters such as should exist, whereas Euripides created ones such as actually do exist. If neither of the above is the case, the criticism must be met by reference to men's opinions, for example, in the myths that are told about the gods. For, perhaps, they do not describe a situation that is better than actuality, nor a true one, but they are what Xenophanes said of them — in accordance, at any rate, with men's opinions. Perhaps the situation described by the artist is not better than actuality but was one that actually existed in the past, for example, the description of the arms that goes, "The spears were standing upright on their butt spikes"; for once this was customary, as it is now among the Illyrians. Now to judge the nobility or ignobility of any statement made or act performed by anyone, we must not only make an investigation into the thing itself that has been said or done, considering whether it is noble or ignoble, but we must also consider the one who does the act or says the words in regard to whom, when, by what means, and for what purpose he speaks or acts — for example, whether the object is to achieve a greater good or to avoid a greater evil.

We must meet some kinds of criticism by considering the diction, for example, by reference to the use of a strange word, as in the phrase, *ourēas men prōton.*[35] The word *oureas* here could cause some difficulty because perhaps the poet does not mean mules but guards. Dolon's statement, "I who was badly formed,"[36] has a similar difficulty involved in it; for he does not mean that he was misshapen in body but that he was ugly, because the Cretans use *eueidēs* [of fair form] to denote "handsome." A difficulty might arise in the phrase "mix the drink purer,"[37]

[34]There is a lacuna in the text here that I have filled by translating Bywater's suggested reading, *hēmarte de di'*. [Tr.]

[35]Quoted from *Iliad* 1:50. The phrase means "first of all, the mules." [Tr.]

[36]Quoted from *Iliad* 10:316. [Tr.]

[37]Quoted from *Iliad* 11:202. [Tr.]

which does not mean stronger, as if for drunkards, but faster. Difficulties arise in thoughts that are expressed in metaphors, for example, "All the gods and men slept the entire night through," which is said at the same time as "When truly he turned his gaze upon the Trojan plain, and hears the sound of flutes and pipes." "All" is used here metaphorically in place of "many," since "all" is some division of "many." The phrase "alone, she has no share"[38] shows a similar use of metaphor, since the best-known one is "alone." A problem may arise from the use of accent; Hippias the Thasian solved such a problem in the phrase, *didomen de oi* and similarly, in the phrase, *to men hoi katapythetai ombrō.*[39] Some difficulties are solved through punctuation, for example, in Empedocles' statement that "Suddenly things became mortal that had previously learned to be immortal and things unmixed before mixed."[40] Some problems are solved by reference to ambiguities, for example, "more than two-thirds of night has departed" because "more" is ambiguous here.[41] Some difficulties are met by reference to customary usages in our language. Thus, we call "wine" the mixture of water and wine; and it is with the same justification that the poet writes of "a greave of newly wrought tin"; and iron workers are called *chalkeas,* literally, copper smiths; and it is for this reason that Ganymede is called the wine pourer of Zeus, although the gods do not drink wine. This would also be justified through metaphor.

Whenever a word seems to signify something contradictory, we must consider how many different meanings it might have in the passage quoted; for example, in the phrase "the bronze spear was held there," we must consider how many different senses of "to be held" are possible, whether by taking it in this way or that one might best understand it. The procedure is opposite to the one that Glaucon mentions in which people make an unreasonable prior assumption and, having themselves made their decree, they draw their conclusions, and then criticize the poet as if he had said whatever they think he has said if it is opposed to their thoughts. We have had this experience in regard to discussion of the character Icarius.[42] People assume that he was a Spartan; but then it appears ridiculous that Telemachus did not meet him in Sparta when he visited there. Perhaps the situation is as the Cephallenians would have it, for they say that Odysseus married amongst them and that there was an Icadius involved, but no Icarius. Thus, it is probable that the difficulty has arisen through a mistake.

Speaking generally, the impossible must be justified in regard to the requirements of poetry, or in regard to what is better than actuality, or what, in the opinion of men, is held to be true. In regard to the art of poetry, we must prefer a persuasive impossibility to an unpersuasive possibility. Perhaps it is impossible[43] for the kind of men Zeuxis painted to exist; but they illustrate what is better than the actual. For whatever is a model must express superior qualities. The irrational must be justified in regard to what men say and also on the grounds that it is, sometimes, not at all irrational. For it is reasonable that some things occur contrary to reason.

We must consider contradictions in the same way as the refutation of arguments is carried on: that is, with reference to whether the same object is involved, and in the same relationship, and in the same sense, so that the poet, indeed, has contradicted himself in regard to what he himself says or what a sensible person might assume. There is justifiable censure for the presence of irrationality and depravity where, there being no necessity for them, the poet makes no use of them, as Euripides' handling of Aegeus in the

[38]Quoted from *Iliad* 18:489. [Tr.]

[39]The problem here is that words that are spelled the same way, when given different accents, change their meaning. In the first phrase quoted, *didomen* can be either a present indicative or an infinitive used as an imperative, depending on the way in which it is accented; in the second phrase, *ou* can be either a relative pronoun or a negative adverb, depending on the way in which it is accented. [Tr.]

[40]The problem treated here is the effect that punctuation has on the meaning of a sentence. Thus, by means of different punctuations the word "before" in Empedocles' statement could be referred either to the phrase that precedes it, "things unmixed," or to the word that follows it, "mixed." [Tr.]

[41]The word "more" has a form in Greek that can also be translated as "full." [Tr.]

[42]In Homer, Icarius is Penelope's father. [Tr.]

[43]Translating *kai ei adunaton,* suggested by Vahlen to fill a lacuna in the text at this point. [Tr.]

Medea (in regard to the irrational) or in the same poet's treatment of the character of Menelaus in the *Orestes* (in regard to depravity). Criticisms of poetry, then, derive from five sources: either that the action is impossible or that it is irrational or that it is morally harmful or that it is contradictory or that it contains technical errors. The answers to these criticisms must be sought from the solutions, twelve in number, that we have discussed.

26

The problem of whether epic or tragedy is the better type of imitation might be raised. For if whatever is less common is better, that art would be superior that is directed at the more discriminating audience; and it is very clear that the art that imitates every detail is common. For on the grounds that the audience does not see the point unless they themselves add something, the actors make quite a commotion; for example, the poorer sort of flute players roll about the stage if they must imitate a discus throw and drag their leader about if they are playing the *Scylla.* Now tragedy is considered to be of the same character that our older actors attribute to their successors; for, indeed, Mynescus called Callippides an ape on the grounds of overacting, and such an opinion was also held about Pindarus. As these two types of actor are related to each other, so the whole art of tragedy is thought to be related to epic by some people, who then conclude that epic is oriented toward a reasonable audience that does not at all require gestures, but that tragedy is disposed toward a less sophisticated audience. If, then, tragedy is directed toward a more common audience, it would be clear that it is the inferior art form.

Now then, first, this accusation is made against the art of acting, not poetry, since it is possible to overdo gestures both in epic recitations as Sosistratus did, and in song competitions as Mnasitheus the Opuntian did. Then, too, not every movement is to be rejected, if dancing indeed is not to be condemned, but only the movements of the ignoble, a point that was criticized in Callippides and now in others, since, it was charged, they were not representing freeborn women. Further, tragedy even without action achieves its function just as epic does; for its character is apparent simply through reading. If, then, tragedy is better in other respects, this defect is not essential to it. We argue, next, that it *is* better since it contains all of the elements that epic has (for it is even possible to use epic meter in tragedy) and, further, it has no small share in music and in spectacle, through which pleasure is very distinctly evoked. Tragedy also provides a vivid experience in reading as well as in actual performance. Further, in tragedy the goal of the imitation is achieved in a shorter length of time (for a more compact action is more pleasant than one that is much diluted). I mean, for example, the situation that would occur if someone should put Sophocles' *Oedipus* into an epic as long as the *Iliad.* Further, the imitation of an epic story is less unified than that of tragedy (a proof of this is that a number of tragedies can be derived from any one epic). So that if epic poets write a story with a single plot, that plot is either presented briefly and appears to lack full development, or, if it follows the accustomed length of epic, it has a watered-down quality (I mean, for example, if the epic should be composed of very many actions in the same way as the *Iliad* and *Odyssey* have many such elements that also have magnitude in themselves). And yet these poems are constructed in the best possible way and are, as much as possible, the imitations of a single action.

If, then, tragedy is superior in all these areas and, further, in accomplishing its artistic effect (for it is necessary that these genres create not any chance pleasure, but the one that has been discussed as proper to them), it is apparent that tragedy, since it is better at attaining its end, is superior to epic.

Now then, we have expressed our view of tragedy and epic, both in general, and in their various species, and of the number and differences in their parts, as well as of some of the causes of their effectiveness or ineffectiveness, and the criticisms that can be directed against them, and the ways in which these criticisms must be answered. . . .[44]

[44]One of our manuscripts, Riccardianus 46, continues the text briefly at this point. The continuation seems to read, "Now as to iambic poetry and comedy. . . ." [Tr.]

Horace

65–8 B.C.

Quintus Horatius Flaccus was the son of a freed slave but received an excellent education in the private academies of Rome. Following the assassination of Julius Caesar, Horace fought in the ill-fated army of Marcus Brutus but was allowed to return to Rome at the amnesty. He served for a time as a clerk in government offices, but his talent as a poet and satirist came to the attention of Virgil, who introduced him to the renowned Roman patron Maecenas. Maecenas provided Horace with encouragement and money, and ultimately, the farm in the Sabine hills to which he retired.

The *Ars Poetica (The Art of Poetry),* also known as the *Epistle to the Pisos,* was composed as a letter of advice in verse to the two sons of Lucius Calpurnius Piso, both of whom had poetic ambitions. Because it is a verse letter, it lacks the careful composition and exhaustive organization of a treatise on the art of poetry; Horace's aim was to blend witty reminders and sage maxims in an entertaining way.

Like Pope's *Essay on Criticism,* (p. 208), the *Ars Poetica* contains dozens of lines and phrases that passed into the Latin language (and to an extent into English) as proverbs or catch phrases. We still speak of "purple patches" in prose, a phrase Horace coined. *Bonus dormitat Homerus* is the familiar "even Homer sometimes nods." *Parturiunt montes, nascetur ridiculus mus* (the mountains labor, giving birth to a ridiculous mouse) has become an adage for any pretentious activity. (The meaning of some of Horace's maxims has become garbled over the years: *Ut pictura poesis* [a poem is like a picture] was Horace's way of saying that some poems repay close scrutiny while others appeal through their broad outlines; it has been misinterpreted to suggest that Horace saw spatial form in poetry.)

To a reader expecting system, the organization of the *Ars Poetica* can be baffling. It is traditionally divided into three parts: lines 1–41 of the Latin original are on *poesis* or subject matter; lines 42–294 on *poema* or technique; and lines 295–476 on *poeta* or the poet. But in fact, Horace's wildfire ideas always outrace any system or organization that can be devised, and the reader should be prepared for rapid and unexpected transitions from one topic to another.

In the Middle Ages and the Renaissance, the *Ars Poetica* was often regarded as a commentary on Aristotle's *Poetics.* Though undoubtedly Horace had read Aristotle and occasionally echoes some of his remarks, the two thinkers have little in common. Where Aristotle suggests that tragedy uses iambic meter because it is closest to natural human speech, Horace offers two other rationales: literary tradition and the fact that iambics are better able to drown out a noisy and inattentive audience. Aristotle's explanation derives from his principle of *mimesis,* Horace's from his understanding of the expectations and the physical boisterousness of the *audience.*

Although Horace pays lip service to *mimesis* from time to time, what is really important to him is audience response. The poet should stick to traditional subjects, he tells us, but treat them in a new way. Poetic language should be novel, but not too novel — and the only way of judging the mean here is by closely observing the audience and the literary marketplace. Regardless of his innate genius, the poet must learn his art, especially the conventions that guide his audience in their expectations. Some of these, like the use of iambics in drama, may be more than mere conventions: They may reflect enduring aspects of human nature. Others, like Horace's dictum that a tragedy should have neither more nor less than five acts, were pure formalities. From Horace's point of view, such a distinction makes no difference, and indeed, he does not differentiate between rules and conventions. All alike need to be observed if the poet is to succeed in gaining a hearing from a fastidious and often captiously critical audience.

At the center of the *Ars Poetica* is Horace's statement of the ultimate aim of poetry: *aut prodesse aut delectare,* to teach or to delight — or both if possible, because the poet's audience, made up of diverse types, will require both: the *equites,* the knightly class, insist upon amusement, while the *senatores* want profitable lessons. The poet must understand their demands — and even those of the middle classes, the "roast-beans-and-chestnuts crowd" who applaud what is simple and exciting.

Like Aristotle, Horace assumes that different genres have their proper subject matter, technical devices, and effects; for example, that tragedy will concern dire events, be written in the highest style, and cause the audience to weep. But while for Aristotle, genres come into existence as if by the laws of nature and are scientifically comprehensible as emergent outgrowths of natural human impulses, for Horace genres do not have to make sense: They are just *there*. They exist, by accident as far as he is concerned, as predefined parts of the literary scene into which the poet comes, and the poet learns their rules as any prudent traveler in a strange country would learn the laws.

Unlike Plato and Aristotle, Horace is very much the worldly philosopher, and it is possible to misunderstand and cheapen the values by which he operates. Though Horace tells us that the successful author's book "will bring in money for Sosius and Son" — the Roman family that ran an operation copying manuscripts much in demand — he is not a prostitute producing verses to order. It is not vulgar commercial success Horace worships. For Horace, the author's reward is not money but fame. His ambition is to be read and praised, his terror to be ignored or laughed at. For Horace the poet was not a private man, but a public servant, like a successful statesman or ruler; both wore their laurels with pride, and their rewards came from the same public source.

Selected Bibliography

Brink, C. O. *Horace on Poetry*. Cambridge: Cambridge University Press, 1963.

D'Alton, J. F. *Horace and His Age*. London: Longmans Green, 1917.

Dettmer, Helena. *Horace: A Study in Structure*. Hildesheim and New York: Olms-Weidmann, 1983.

Freudenberg, Kirk. *The Walking Muse: Horace on the Theory of Satire*. Princeton: Princeton University Press, 1993.

Frischer, Bernard. *Shifting Paradigms: New Approaches to Horace's* Ars Poetica. Atlanta, Georgia: Scholars Press, 1991.

Goad, Caroline. *Horace in the English Literature of the Eighteenth Century*. New Haven: Yale University Press, 1918.

Hack, R. K. "The Doctrine of Literary Forms." *Harvard Studies in Classical Philology* 27 (1916): 1–65.

Hardison, O. B., and Leon Golden, eds. *Horace for Students of Literature: The* Ars Poetica *and Its Tradition*. Gainesville: University Press of Florida, 1995.

Herrick, Marvin T. *The Fusion of Horatian and Aristotelian Literary Criticism*. Urbana: University of Illinois Press, 1946.

Perrot, Jacques. *Horace*. New York: New York University Press, 1964.

Showerman, Grant. *Horace and His Influence*. London: Longmans Green, 1922.

Stack, Frank. *Pope and Horace: Studies in Imitation*. Cambridge and New York: Cambridge University Press, 1985.

West, David. *Reading Horace*. Edinburgh: Edinburgh University Press, 1967.

Wood, Allen G. *Literary Satire and Theory: A Study of Horace, Boileau, and Pope*. New York: Garland, 1985.

The Art of Poetry

Humano capiti cervicem pictor equinam

Suppose you'd been asked to come for a private view
Of a painting wherein the artist had chosen to join
To a human head the neck of a horse, and gone on
To collect some odds and ends of arms and legs
And plaster the surface with feathers of differing colors,
So that what began as a lovely woman at the top
Tapered off into a slimy, discolored fish —
Could you keep from laughing, my friends? Believe me, dear Pisos,
Paintings like these look a lot like the book of a writer
Whose weird conceptions are just like a sick man's dreams,
So that neither the head nor the foot can be made to apply
To a single uniform shape. "But painters and poets
Have always been equally free to try anything."
We writers know that, and insist that such license be ours,
And in turn extend it to others — but not to the extent
Of mating the mild with the wild, so that snakes are paired
With birds, and tigers with lambs.
To works that begin
On a stately note and promise more grandeur to come
A couple of colorful patches are artfully stitched
To shimmer and shine, some sequins like these, for instance,
When the altar or grove of Diana, or perhaps it's a rainbow,
Or the Rhine is being described: "The sinuous stream
Rustles daintily, tastefully, on midst the sylvan scene."
But you put it in just the wrong place! You draw cypress trees
Particularly well? But you're paid to hit off the likeness
Of the desperate sailor swimming away from his shipwreck!
This thing began as a wine jar: how come it comes
Off the wheel at last as a milk jug? Make what you want,
So long as it's one and the same, complete and entire.

O father, and sons who deserve a father like yours,
We poets are too often tricked into trying to achieve
A particular kind of perfection: I studiously try
To be brief, and become obscure; I try to be smooth,
And my vigor and force disappear; another assures us
Of something big which turns out to be merely pompous.
Another one crawls on the ground because he's too safe,
Too much afraid of the storm. The poet who strives
To vary his single subject in wonderful ways
Paints dolphins in woods and foaming boars on the waves.
Avoiding mistakes, if awkwardly done, leads to error.
Nearby the gladiators' school there's a craftsman who molds
In bronze with special skill the lifelike shapes
Of fingernails and straying strands of hair,
But the whole result of his work is much less happy:
He can't represent the figure complete and entire.
If I were to try to cast a good piece of writing,
I'd no more prefer to be like this fellow than live
With my nose at an angle, no matter how much admired
I was for my coal-black hair and coal-black eyes.

Take up a subject equal to your strength, O writers,
And mull over well what loads your shoulders will bear,
And what they will not. The man who chooses a subject
He can really manage won't be at a loss for the words
Or the logical order they go in. As for order itself,
Its power and charm consist, if I'm not mistaken,
In saying just then what ought to be said at that point,
Putting some things off, leaving others out, for the present:
The author of the promised work must choose and discard.

In weaving your words, make use of care and good taste:

Translated by Smith Palmer Bovie.

You've done it right, if a clever connection of phrases
Makes a good old word look new. If you have to
display
Some recondite matter in brand-new terms, you can
forge
Words never heard in the pre-tunic days of Cethegus;
License is given, on condition that you use it with
care.
New-fashioned words, just coined, will soon gain
currency,
If derived from a Grecian source, *and* in small
amounts.
Will the Roman refuse the license to Vergil and
Varius
And grant it to Plautus and Caecilius?[1] And why
should I
Be refused the right to put in my bit, if I can,
When the language of Ennius and Cato enriched the
speech
Of our native land and produced some new terms for
things?
It has always been granted, and always will be, to
produce
Words stamped with the date of the present. As trees
change their leaves
When each year comes to its end, and the first fall
first,
So the oldest words die first and the newborn thrive
In the manner of youth, and enjoy life. All that we are
And have is in debt to death, as are all our
projects:[2]
The Portus Julius where Neptune is at home on the
land
And protects our ships from his storms — a princely
achievement;
The Pontine marshes, inhabitable only for boats
And plagues in the past, but now a food-bearing land
That feels the weight of the plow and feeds nearby
towns;
The straightening-out of the Tiber that used to wreak
havoc

[1]Horace's point is that Plautus and Caecilius, a century earlier, had made new Latin words out of good Greek ones, but his contemporaries Virgil and Varius were being criticized for the same artistic license. [Ed.]

[2]The creation of a sheltered harbor at Ostia, the draining of the Pontine marshes, and the straightening of the Tiber were three of Augustus's great civic achievements. [Ed.]

On fields of grain but has now learned to mend its
ways —
All these projects, whatever men make, will perish,
And the fame and dignity of speech are equally
mortal.
Much that has once dropped out will be born again,
And much of our language now held in high repute
Will fall to the ground if UTILITY so decrees,
With which rests the final decision, the ultimate
standard,
The legal existence, of speech.
Homer has showed us
The meter to use to describe sad wars and great deeds
Of kings and princes. The uneven couplet that joined
One verse to another was first adapted to grief,
But elegy easily turned into epigrammatic
Couplets expressive of thanks for prayers
answered.
Who wrote these first little couplets? The critics are
STILL
Disputing the subject; the case is still on the books.
Fury equipped Archilochus[3] with his iambics:
The foot slipped into the comic sock as neatly
As into the tragic boot, so dramatists used it
To make their dialogue heard, even over the noise
The audience was making — the rhythm of
purposeful action.
The muse entrusted to lyric verse the accounts
Of gods and the children of gods, of a winning boxer,
Of a prize-winning race horse, the laments of young
lads in love,
The intoxicating freedom of wine. If I can't observe
These distinctions of form and tone, do I really
deserve
To be hailed as a poet? Why, from a false sense of
shame,
Do I prefer being ignorant to learning? A good comic
sequence
Just won't submit to treatment in the meters of
tragedy.
Likewise, Thyestes' feast[4] resents being told
In strains more nearly like those that comedy needs
In the vein of everyday life. Let each of the styles
Be assigned to the places most proper for it to
maintain.

[3]Greek satiric poet of the sixth century B.C. [Ed.]

[4]As an act of revenge, Atreus served a feast to his brother Thyestes, consisting of Thyestes' own children. [Ed.]

Of course, now and then even comedy raises her voice:
Angry old Chremes swells up like a supersorehead;
And the Tragedy of Telephus, the Plight of Peleus, stoop
To the muse of prose for words of grief when, poor
Or exiled, either hero discards the bombast
That jars on our ears and his wordsafootandahalflong,
To let his lament wing its way to the hearer's heart.

It isn't enough for poems to be things of beauty:
Let them STUN the hearer and lead his heart where they will.
A man's face is wreathed in smiles when he sees someone smile;
It twists when he sees someone cry; if you expect *me*
To burst into tears, you have to feel sorrow yourself.
Then your woes will fasten on me, O Telephus, Peleus;
If you speak incongruous lines, I'll snooze or I'll giggle.
Touching words most become the sorrowful countenance,
Blistering threats the enraged, playful remarks
The cheerful, suitably dignified speech the severe.
For nature first forms us, deep in our hearts, to respond
To the changing guise of our fortunes; she makes us take heart
Or drives us wild or bends us down to the ground
And let us writhe over inconsolable grief;
Then she brings these emotions out by using the tongue
To interpret them. If a speaker's words don't accord
With his fortunes, the Roman knights and those wretched wights
Who bought only standing room will both rock the house
With uproarious laughter. It will make a great deal of difference
Who's speaking: a god or a hero, a wise old man,
Or a fervent fellow in the flower of youth, or a matron,
A *powerful* matron, a busy old nurse, or a merchant,
A wandering merchant, or a man who farms the green field,
Or the Colchian or Assyrian type, or a man bred at Thebes,
A man bred at Argos.
You should either stick to tradition
Or invent a consistent plot. If you bring back Achilles,
Have him say how laws don't apply to him, have prowess
Prevail over status, make him ruthless, impatient and fierce,
And ANGRY! Let Medea be wild, inconquerably so,
Ino tearful, Io "lost"; let Ixion
Go back on his word; let Orestes be sadly depressed.
If it's something as yet untried you put on the stage
And you dare construct a new character, you must keep
To the end the same sort of person you started out with,
And make your portrayal consistent.
It's hard to write
Of familiar concerns in a new and original way.
You're better off telling the story of Troy in five acts
Than being the first to foist something new and untried
On the world. In the public domain you'll have private rights
If you keep from loitering around the most common places
And from dawdling on the easiest path, and take pains to refrain
From translating faithfully word for word, and don't leap
Right down the close-scooped well of the source you draw on,
Precluded by shame or the laws of your task from lifting
Your foot up over the edge. And don't begin
As the Cyclic poet once did: "And now I shall sing
Of the fortune of Priam and famous war of that king."
What could issue from the mouth that made such an opening?
Mountains will labor, a funny little mouse will be born.
To take on less is a much more sensible labor:

> "Tell me, O Muse, of the man who, after Troy fell,
> Came to know well all manner of cities and men."[5]

[5]The opening lines of Homer's *Odyssey*. [Ed.]

This writer plans to send up not smoke from the flames
But light from the smoke, to deliver some marvelous events:
Antiphates' giants, Scylla, Charybdis, the Cyclops.
Diomedes' return is not traced back to begin
With Meleager's death. The Trojan War doesn't start
With the egg of the twins.[6] He is eager to get to the point
And hurries the reader along to the middle of things,
As if they were already known, and simply leaves out
Whatever he thinks he can't bring off shining and clear,
And devises so well, intermingling the true and the false,
That the middle part fits with the first, the last with the middle.

Now hear what I and the rest of your listeners expect
If you want them to sit there and wait till the curtain comes down
And the cantor intones "*vos plaudite*[7] . . . now is the time."
Make careful note of the way each age group behaves,
And apply the right tone to their changeable natures and years.
The child who by now knows how to reel off his words,
And plant his feet squarely beneath him, likes most of all
To play with his friends; he flies into rage like a flash
And forgets it equally fast, and changes every hour.
The beardless youth, finally free of his guardian,
Rejoices in horse and hounds and the sun-drenched grass
Of the Campus Martius: he is putty in your hands to mold
To evil courses, resentful of warning advisers;
Slow to provide for his needs but recklessly fast
To spend his money, enthusiastic, intense,
But quick to transfer his affections. As his interests change,
The man is seen in the manly style of his life:
He looks for wealth and for friends, is a slave to success,
Is wary of making a move he will soon be concerned
To undo. A great many troubles harass the old man,
Either because he keeps on trying for gain
And yet won't touch what he has, worried and afraid
To use it, or perhaps because in all that he does
He's slow and phlegmatic, and keeps postponing his pleasures,
Conscious of the rainy days he should be prepared for,
"Difficult," always complaining, ready to praise
The good old days when he was a boy and reprove
And disapprove of the young. As the years come along,
They bring along much that is fine; as they disappear,
They take many fine things away. In portraying our roles,
We will dwell on the matters best suited and best attached
To the age in question, and not let the old men's parts
Be assigned to a youth or the manly parts to a boy.

The events are either enacted on stage or described
As having occurred. But things entrusted to the ear
Impress our minds less vividly than what is exposed
To our trustworthy eyes so that a viewer informs himself
Of precisely what happened. Still, you are not to show
On stage what ought to take place backstage: remove
From our eyes the substance of things an eloquent messenger
Will soon be ready to state in person. Medea
Must not butcher her boys in front of the people;
Unspeakable Atreus should not cook up human flesh
Before our eyes, nor should Procne change into a bird,
Or Cadmus into a snake. Whatsoever such stuff
You *show* me, I won't believe it, I'll simply detest it.

The play that expects to be asked for another performance
Once it's been given, should be just five acts long,
No more, no less. A god must not intervene
Unless the action tangles itself in such knots

[6]Meleager, Diomedes' uncle, died before he was born. Helen of Troy was born from one of Leda's eggs; her twin brothers Castor and Polydeukes were born from the other. [Ed.]

[7]"Applaud." [Ed.]

That only a divine deliverer can work the denouement;
A fourth actor should not try to come forward to speak.[8]

The chorus should be handled as one of the actors and play
An important part, singing between episodes
What advances the plot and fits in well with the action.
Let it favor the good and offer them friendly advice,
Control the wrathful and develop a fondness for soothing
With quiet words the fearful in heart. Let it praise plain living,
The blessings of justice, the laws, and the doors left open
By Peace. Let the chorus respect the secrets it's told.
Let it pray to the gods, devoutly imploring that fortune
Return to the unhappy low and depart from the proud.

The present-day brass-bound flute produces a tone
That rivals the trumpet's, unlike the primitive pipe,
With its thin, clear tone and one or two stops, warbling woodnotes
To give the chorus the pitch, and provide an accompaniment —
A sound that could nevertheless carry in the uncrowded halls
When virtuous, decent, well-behaved folk came together.
But after a victorious people began to acquire
More land, and surround their cities with larger walls,
And drink to the Genius in broad daylight without shame,
More license entered the rhythms and modes of the music.
How could these rough country types be expected to judge,
Just off from work, mixed in with the city crowd,
The uncouth sitting next to the wealthy? And so the flute player
Added movement and gesture to the primitive style
And fluttered his robe as he strutted around the stage.
New notes increased the restricted range of the lyre,
And unrestrained wit produced a new form of eloquence,
So that even the thought, which had been such a fine detective
Of useful clues and prophet of future events,
Now resembled the unclear, ambiguous dictates of Delphi.

The writer who vied for the paltry prize of a goat
With tragic song, soon bared shaggy satyrs to view
On the stage, coarsely probing for laughs without losing dignity —
Some pleasant device and novel attraction like this
Being all that could make the spectator stay on and watch
After having fulfilled the ritual rites of the occasion,
And drunk a good bit, and been freed from the normal restraints.
But those laughing, bantering satyrs will have to be told
To transform the mood from the grave to the gay with some care
And not let a god or a hero, previously seen
Coming out from his palace clad in royal crimson and gold,
Move into a dingy shack and a low way of talking
Or, avoiding the depths, climb too fantastically high.
For tragedy, not condescending to mouth low lines,
Joins the satyrs but briefly, and not without some hesitation,
Like a matron commanded to dance on a festive occasion.
I assure you, good Pisos, if I write a satyr play,
I will not use only commonplace nouns and verbs
Or "plain words," nor try to depart from the tragic tone
To the point where it makes no difference whether Davus is speaking
With maudlin Pythias (who's just swiped some dough from old Simo)
Or Silenus, tutor and guide to his heavenly ward.[9]

[8]Latin and Greek plays had more than three characters, but by convention, no more than three speaking actors in addition to the chorus were allowed on stage at the same time. See Aristotle's *Poetics*, Ch. 4. [Ed.]

[9]Davus outwits Simo in Terence's *Andria;* Pythias is a character from his *Eunuchus;* Silenus was the tutor of the god Bacchus. [Ed.]

I shall set my sights on familiar things: anyone
Will think he can do as well but will soon find he can't
When he tries it and sweats and strains to bring it off.
The order and inner coherence and careful connection
Are what make your writing take hold: your major
success
Consists in mastering the language that is common to
all.
I incline to believe that when fauns trot in from the
woods,
They ought not to act as if they were reared in the
gutter
And virtually lived in the Forum, with citified ways
And prettified lays like those of young-bloods-about-
town,
Or resort to indecent remarks and crack dirty jokes.
The better-class patrons may take offense (the
freeborn,
The knights, the wealthy) and refuse to award the
crown,
As it were, unwilling to see in a favorable light
What the roast-beans-and-chestnuts[10] crowd find so
entertaining.

A short syllable followed by a long is of course an
iambus.
It moves along fast, so a verse consisting of six
Full-fledged iambic stresses has come to be known
As iambic trimeter. But recently, to come to our ears
More slowly and solemnly, father Iambus adopted
A firm-footed son, the spondee. Affable and kind
Though he was, the iambus did not admit the young
man
On equal terms into this partnership, but reserved
The second and fourth foot all for himself. This
iambus
Appears but rarely in the "fine old" trimeters of
Accius,
And the spondaic stress in the lines which Ennius
heavily
Launched on the stage is a sign of hasty production
Or a fault to be chalked up to careless ignorance of
style.
Not every critic can spot the lines that don't quite
scan right,

[10]Snacks sold outside Roman theaters. [Ed.]

And Roman poets have been granted too much
indulgence.
Shall I therefore run wild and write without any
restrictions
Or consider that everyone is bound to see my
mistakes
And cautiously keep well within the bounds of
indulgence?
I may have avoided the fault without rating praise.
Thumb through your Greek examples by day and by
night!
Your ancestors praised both the wit and rhythms of
Plautus?
For admiring both of these things they were *too*
tolerant,
Not to say dense, if you and I can distinguish
A crudeness in phrasing from lapidary strength of
wit,
And catch the legitimate beat with our fingers and
ears.

Thespis is said to have discovered the unknown style
Of the tragic muse, and to have carted his plays
about,
With actors singing the lines and performing the
parts,
Their faces smeared with a paste concocted from
wine lees —
So they trudged around in road shows, reveling in
tragedy.
Aeschylus thought up the masks and distinctive
costumes;
He built the first stage on a platform of several small
boards
And taught his actors a lofty manner of speech
And a stately, high-booted stride. These tragic arts
Were succeeded by Old Comedy, whose many good
points
Should be noted. From freedom that form declined
into license
And fell upon violent ways that required regulation.
The law was obeyed and the chorus then lapsed into
silence,
Deprived of its right to insult and abuse its victims.

Our Roman poets have left no style untried
And have not been the least deserving when they
have dared

To desert the traces of Greece and dwell on affairs
Originating here among us, on our native designs,
Whether tragic or comic. Latium would be as
triumphant
In language as in character and military might
If a single one of her poets could endure the effort
And time-consuming, slow discipline of the file.
Oh, descendants of Numa, turn your backs on the
poem
Which many a day and many a diligent erasure
Have not corrected, which a sensitive, newly-pared
nail
Has not run over and checked, at the least, ten times.

Because Democritus held that *genius was all*
And the miserable practice of art far inferior to it,
And denied that sensible poets rated a place
On Helicon's heights,[11] most poets neglect their
appearance —
They won't cut their nails or their beards, they won't
take a bath,
They wander off somewhere alone. For surely the
name
And the fame of the poet will attach itself to that
dome
Which has never entrusted itself to the shears of
Licinus,[12]
Which trips for treatment to three times as many
psychiatrists
As even Switzerland harbors have failed to set
straight.[13]
What a fool am I to purge myself of my bile
Seasonably, every spring! If I'd only refrained,
I'd be unsurpassed as a poet. But perhaps it's not
worth it
To lose your head and then write verses instead,

[11]Helicon was the mountain sacred to the Muses. [Ed.]

[12]A well-known Roman barber. [Ed.]

[13]Psychiatrists . . . Switzerland: The translator here indulges in an anachronism to avoid a complicated explanation. The geographical reference in Horace's Latin is not to Switzerland but to Antycra, a town famous for producing black hellebore, a poisonous plant that, in legend, was used by the physician Melampus to cure the madness of three daughters of the King of Argos. Horace's general point is that poets, supposed to be men of genius, affect to be both uncouth and mad. [Ed.]

So I'll play the whetstone's part, giving edge to the
steel,
Without being able to cut. And though I write
nothing,
I'll point out the writer's mission and function and
show
Him where his best material lies and what
Nurtures and shapes the poet, what best accords
With his role, what worst, where the right path goes,
and the wrong.

The principal source of all good writing is wisdom.
The Socratic pages will offer you ample material,
And with the matter in hand, the words will be quick
to follow.
A man who has learned what is owing to country and
friends,
The love that is due a parent, a brother, a guest,
What the role of a judge or senator chiefly requires,
What part is played by the general sent off to war,
Will surely know how to write the appropriate lines
For each of his players. I will bid the intelligent
student
Of the imitative art to look to the model of life
And see how men act, to bring his speeches alive.
At times a play of no particular merit,
Artistically lacking in strength and smoothness of
finish
But with vivid examples of character drawn true to
life,
Will please the audience and hold their attention
better
Than tuneful trifles and verses empty of thought.

To the Greeks the muse gave genius, the Greeks she
endowed
With eloquent speech and greed for nothing but
praise.
Our Roman lads learn arithmetic and divide
The unit into its hundreds. "The Son of
Albinus —
You here today? All right, your turn to recite!
Subtract a twelfth from five-twelfths, and what have
you left?
Come on, Albinus Minus — don't think so hard!"
"One-third, Sir." "Fine! You'll keep track of your
money, you will.
Now take that original sum and add on a twelfth.

How much?" "One-half." When once the corrosive concern
For petty cash has tainted our minds, can we hope to write poems
To be oiled with cedar and kept in smooth cypress cases?

Poets would either delight or enlighten the reader,
Or say what is both amusing and really worth using.
But when you instruct, be brief, so the mind can clearly
Perceive and firmly retain. When the mind is full,
Everything else that you say just trickles away.
Fictions that border on truth will generate pleasure,
So your play is not to expect automatic assent
To whatever comes into its head, nor to draw forth a child
Still alive from Lamia's stomach after she's dined.
Our elders will chase off the stage what is merely delightful;
Our young bloods will pass up the works that merely make sense.
He wins every vote who combines the sweet and the useful,
Charming the reader and warning him equally well.
This book will bring in money for Sosius and Son,
Booksellers, travel across the sea, and extend
Its author's fame a long distance into the future.

There still may be some oversights, and we may be willing
To overlook them, for the string won't always play back
What the hand had in mind: quite often you ask for a flat
And get back a sharp. You brandish your bow at the target,
But the arrow won't always fly home. If happy effects
Figure more, I won't take offense at the few bad spots
Which either carelessness let slip onto the page
Or human nature took too little pains to avert.
And what's the truth here? If a slave who copies out books
Keeps making the same mistake no matter how often
He's warned, he can't be excused; if a harpist keeps striking
The same wrong note, he'll be laughed at. I would reserve
The role of Choerilus for poets who strike something *good*[14]
Two or three times in the course of a largely flawed work,
Which makes me laugh as a matter of sheer amazement.
Good Homer sometimes nods, which gives me a jerk —
But sleep may well worm its way into any long work!

A poem is much like a painting: one will please more
If you see it close up, another if seen from a distance;
One prefers being viewed in the shade, while the other
Prefers being seen in broad daylight and doesn't shrink back
From the piercing glance of the critic. One pleased once;
The other will always please, though it's called for ten times.

Let me say to the older of you two boys, and remind
You to take it to heart, no matter how wise you may be
And well directed to the right by your father's voice:
The doctrine of the mean does not correctly apply
To all things, but rather to a few quite definite matters.
The average lawyer, consultant or trial attorney,
May lack Messalla's delivery, may not know as much
As Aulus Cascellius, and still be of no little worth.
But men and gods and booksellers WON'T PUT UP
WITH SECOND-RATE POETS. If the orchestra playing at dinner
Is all out of tune, if the ointment offered each guest
Is lumpy, if sour Sardinian honey is served
With the poppy seeds, the party is spoiled all the more;
It could have gone on perfectly, simply without them.
So a poem, designed and destined to afford the soul

[14]Choerilus was an epic poet of the fourth century B.C. who was offered a piece of gold by Alexander the Great for every *good* verse celebrating his victories. He died poor. [Ed.]

Genuine pleasure, if it falls somewhat short of the top,
Sinks right down to the bottom. If a man can't play,
He avoids the weapons drill going on in the Campus.
And if he can't handle the ball or discus or hoop,
He stands off, lest he provoke the justified laughter
Of spectators crowded around and forming the circle.
But someone who doesn't know how dares fashion verses.
Why not? He's free, freeborn, in fact, and his income
Is rated at a knightly sum, has a fine reputation.

But you, my dear fellow, will refrain from speaking or acting
Without Minerva's consent? That shows good judgment
And a sound attitude. If you ever do write something, though,
Be sure to expose it to such ears as Tarpa the Censor's,
And your father's, and mine. Then put the parchment away
For a good nine years! What you haven't yet published
You can always destroy, but once a word is let go,
It can't be called back.
When primitive men roamed the forests,
Orpheus, the sacred interpreter of heavenly will,
Turned them away from killing and living like beasts
And hence is said to have tamed wild lions and tigers.
Amphion is said, as founder of the city of Thebes,
To have moved the stones and led them wherever he wished
By the sound of his lyre and the winning appeal of his voice.
This was the wisdom of former times: to distinguish
Public from private concerns and sacred from common,
To forbid impromptu liaisons and make rules for marriage,
To build towns and carve out the laws on pillars of wood.
The poets who taught by expressing these things were acclaimed:
They and their works were considered divine. After them,
Tyrtaeus and Homer won wide renown by sharpening
Masculine minds to a warlike pitch with their poems.
Oracles were uttered in song, and a way of life
Pointed out, along gnomic lines. The favor of kings
Was courted in verse, and festival joy was found
As the suitable end to periods of long, hard work —
Lest you make excuses for Apollo, the god of song,
Or the muse so skilled with the lyre.
The question is raised
Whether nature or art makes a poem deserving of praise.
I fail to see what good either learning can be
Which is not veined with natural wealth or primitive genius.
Each needs the other's help and friendly alliance.
The racer who wants to win has learned, as a boy,
To strain and train, shiver and sweat, stay away
From women and wine. The flute player who gets to play
At the Pythian games has long since studied and shuddered
In the presence of his teacher. Today, it's enough just to say:
"I PEN these marvelous POEMS — I'm a Creative Person.
The last one's a dirty shirt. I won't get left back,
Admitting I just don't know what I've never yet learned."

Like the auctioneer who collects a crowd for a sale,
The poet with property or money put out in loans
Is ordering flatterers to make a profit from him.
But when he can serve a nice little dinner for friends,
Or put up the bail for a poor man who's not a good risk,
Or rescue one held in the gloomy grip of the law,
I'll marvel if the lucky man can always distinguish the false friend from the true.
And if you have given,
Or intend to give, a present to someone, don't take him
To hear, still glowing with joy, some verses you've written.
He'll shout out "Fine! Oh, *excellent!* How superb!"
Go pale at the sombre parts, even squeeze out a drop
Of dew from his friendly eyes, and pound on the ground
With his foot to keep time, and dance a bit for sheer joy.

Just as hired mourners often behave much better at
funerals
Than those sincerely bereaved, so the man who
pretends
Makes more perpetual emotion than your honest
admirer.
Kings are said to ply with drink after drink
And put through the ordeal by wine the man they
would test
As worthy of the royal friendship. And if you would
write,
Don't ever forget: there's a motive concealed in the
fox.

If you read something out to Quintilius,[15] he'd usually say,
"You could straighten out *this,* or *that.*" And if, after
trying
Two or three times with no luck, you'd said you
could *not*
Improve on the passage, he'd tell you to strike it right
out
And hand back to the anvil those verses that came out
so bent,
To be hammered into shape once again. Then, if you
preferred
Standing by your mistake to changing it, he'd waste
not a word
Or an ounce of energy more, and not interfere
With your loving, alone and unrivaled, yourself and
your work.
The fair-minded, thoughtful man will reproach the
verses
That come out spineless and flat, find fault with the
clumsy
And rhythmically harsh; with a straight black stroke
of the pen
He will line out disorganized parts; your elegant
effects
He will simply cut out; he will force you to let in
more light
On the dark passages, point out ambiguous phrasing,
And note what ought to be changed, a real Richard
Bentley,[16]
Who won't stop to say, "But why should I harass a
friend
With these minor repairs?" These minor repairs will
create
A major disaster, once that friend is exposed
To a hostile reception and unfriendly jeers in public.

The mad poet only makes sensible people avoid him
And fear to touch him, as if he were plagued by the
itch
Or the royal disease of jaundice (yellow as gold
And worth a king's ransom to cure) or St. Vitus'
dance
Or lunatic frenzy. Kids chase after and taunt him.
With his head held high, he strolls off belching his
lines,
And then if he falls down a well or into a pit —
Like a fowler whose eyes are steadily trained on the
merles —
He may yell long and loud for help: "To the rescue!
This way,
Fellow citizens!" None will care to come pull him
out.
And if someone *should have* the urge to lend him a
hand
And let down a rope, I will say, "But how do you
know
He hasn't intentionally thrown himself in and *doesn't*
Want to be saved?" and then I will tell of the death
Of the Sicilian poet. Because Empedocles wished
To be thought an immortal god, he leaped into Etna,
This cool customer, to his fiery fate. We are left
To conclude that poetic justice or poetic license
Includes suicide. To save some person from death
Against his will is just as wrong as to kill him.
This isn't the first time it's happened, and if he's
pulled out,
He will not necessarily be made over into a man

[15]A Roman critic of the second century B.C.; Horace is using the name to denote some man of taste. [Ed.]

[16]Another anachronism by the translator. Bentley (1662–1742) was a British critic who corrected Pope's translation of Homer. Horace's Latin refers to Aristarchus of Samothrace (220–143 B.C.), who wrote scholarly commentary on Homer. [Ed.]

And put aside his desire for a memorable end.

It's not quite clear what drove him to write, in the first place —
Did he sprinkle his well-wrought urine on ancestral ashes?
Or blasphemously joggle the ground at some sacred spot?
At any rate, he's got it bad; and, bold as a bear,
If he's strong enough to have smashed in the fretwork of bars
That kept him confined to his cage, he's on a rampage,
Stampeding unlearned and learned alike, in his rage
To recite. Once he's caught you, he'll hang on with all his might;
The leech just clings to your skin and never gives in
Until bloated with blood; *he'll* never run out of breath
But will read you and read you and read you and read you to death.

Longinus

First Century A.D.

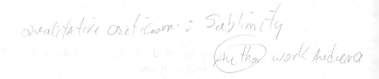

One of the most controversial aspects of "On the Sublime" has been its authorship. The oldest manuscript, from the tenth century, calls the author "Dionysius Longinus." The name is too apt to be true. Each of its two halves belongs to a great Greco-Roman philosopher, Dionysius of Halicarnassus (who wrote under Augustus Caesar) and Cassius Longinus (who died nearly three centuries later, in A.D. 273). But neither of these men is a plausible candidate to have written "On the Sublime." The literary opinions of Longinus are inconsistent with those of Dionysius, while Cassius Longinus, who wrote during the most brutally chaotic period of the Empire, is unlikely to have penned Chapter 44, which discusses the causes of literary decline in an era of universal peace.

The style and historical allusions suggest a date during the quiet reigns of Nerva and Trajan, toward the end of the first century. The quotation in Chapter 9 from the Old Testament book of Genesis would be an extraordinary allusion for a pagan author to make, and it has been suggested that Longinus may have been either a Hellenized Jew (perhaps of the circle of Philo Judaeus[1]) or a Greek with Jewish connections.

Unlike Plato, who concerned himself with common features of artistic works in general, Longinus is interested in a special quality, sublimity or elevation, which is possessed by some works but not others. Unlike Aristotle, whose poetics dealt with the particular characteristics of different literary forms, Longinus's sublimity is a quality that transcends generic boundaries. It can be found in drama or epic or lyric — or even in rhetoric or history or theology. Longinus's approach might be called "qualitative criticism," and it constitutes the third enduring method of literary theory, with descendants from Burke to Bakhtin. "On the Sublime" is related in one sense to the rhetorical criticism of Horace and others — its principal topics seem to be author, work, and audience — but where Horace differentiated between a high, a middle, and a low style, Longinus is concerned only with the first. And Longinus is far more methodical in exploring his more limited subject than Horace.

The argument of "On the Sublime" can be easily outlined. In Chapters 1 and 2 Longinus defines the Sublime as that quality within a discourse that produces "not persuasion but transport" (*ekstasis*) within the audience. He then questions whether there is such an art — whether it is purely a matter of inspiration or whether there are basic principles at work. Much of the actual argument itself has been lost, but from the rest of the essay, which presents five components of the art, it is clear on which side Longinus comes down. In Chapters 3 through 7, Longinus discusses the traps that lie on all sides of the target, those faults in literature that result from trying for the sublime and missing the mark. There are faults of commission, such as

[1]Philo may be the "philosopher" in Ch. 44 whom Longinus attempts to confute.

trying too hard (bombast, pedantry, hysteria), and there are faults of omission, such as frigidity of tone.

In Chapter 8, Longinus outlines the remainder of his essay, which successively treats the five sources (beyond language itself) of the Sublime. First are high thoughts (Chapters 9–15) and second, strong passions (not included but promised in a separate treatise), both of which are innate within the artist. Next are rhetorical figures (Chapters 16–29), then noble diction (Chapters 30–38 and 43), and finally, elevated composition (Chapters 39–42), all of which are the product of art and must be learned.

Just as important as Longinus's systematic method is the clarity and vigor with which he pursues it. He always has an apt quotation ready to exemplify a literary fault or grace, and for a judicial critic, there is nothing mean-spirited about his tone or temper.

Longinus's treatise "On the Sublime" was not influential in its own time. Its importance dates only from the Renaissance; it was published by Francesco Robortello in 1554 and translated by Nicolas Boileau in 1674. Soon thereafter it became common property, and poet-critics like John Dryden drew upon its central issues. During the eighteenth century, the Sublime was considered to be of great significance in opposition to the beautiful (a dichotomy treated by Edmund Burke, Immanuel Kant, and many others), and Longinus's brilliance as a critic was much appreciated. In his *Essay on Criticism,* Alexander Pope conveys the typical Augustan sentiments about the author of "On the Sublime":

> Thee, bold Longinus! all the Nine inspire,
> And bless their critic with a poet's fire:
> An ardent judge, who, zealous in his trust,
> With warmth gives sentence, yet is always just;
> Whose own example strengthens all his laws;
> And is himself that great Sublime he draws.

But Longinus was more admired than imitated in the eighteenth century — except on one occasion by Pope, who wrote a travesty of "On the Sublime" in "The Art of Sinking in Poetry," explaining (with delicious examples from contemporary works) the sources of the quality of Bathos. In the nineteenth century, his overt influence and reputation declined somewhat, perhaps owing to his antidemocratic political beliefs, but his method of qualitative criticism was paradoxically revived in thinkers like Matthew Arnold (*The Study of Poetry*), Walter Pater, and most recently Mikhail Bakhtin.

Selected Bibliography

Apfel, Henrietta Veit. *Literary Quotation and Allusion in Demetrius' Peri hermeneias and Longinus' Peri hypsos.* New York: Columbia University Library, 1935.

Ashfield, Andrew, and Peter De Bolla. *The Sublime: A Reader.* Cambridge: Cambridge University Press, 1993.

Brody, Jules. *Boileau and Longinus.* Geneva: Droz, 1953.

Davidson, Hugh M. "The Literary Arts of Longinus and Boileau." In *Studies in Seventeenth-Century French Literature,* ed. Jean Demonest. Ithaca: Cornell University Press, 1962.

Fuhrmann, Manfred. *Die Dichtungstheorie der Antike.* Darmstadt: Wissenschaftliche Buchgesellschaft, 1993.
Henn, T. R. *Longinus and English Criticism.* Cambridge: Cambridge University Press, 1934.
Marin, Demetrio St. *Bibliography of the Essay on the Sublime.* N.p. 1967.
Olson, Elder. "The Argument of Longinus's *On the Sublime.*" In *On Value Judgments in the Arts and Other Essays.* Chicago: University of Chicago Press, 1976.
Rosenberg, Alfred. *Longinus in England.* Berlin: Meyer und Müller, 1937.
Russell, D. A., ed. *"Longinus" on the Sublime.* Oxford: Clarendon Press, 1964.

On the Sublime

1

You will remember, my dear Postumius Terentianus, that when we examined together the treatise of Caecilius on the Sublime, we found that it fell below the dignity of the whole subject, while it failed signally to grasp the essential points, and conveyed to its readers but little of that practical help which it should be a writer's principal aim to give. In every systematic treatise two things are required. The first is a statement of the subject; the other, which although second in order ranks higher in importance, is an indication of the methods by which we may attain our end. Now Caecilius seeks to show the nature of the sublime by countless instances as though our ignorance demanded it, but the consideration of the means whereby we may succeed in raising our own capacities to a certain pitch of elevation he has, strangely enough, omitted as unnecessary. 2. However, it may be that the man ought not so much to be blamed for his shortcomings as praised for his happy thought and his enthusiasm. But since you have urged me, in my turn, to write a brief essay on the sublime for your special gratification, let us consider whether the views I have formed contain anything which will be of use to public men. You will yourself, my friend, in accordance with your nature and with what is fitting, join me in appraising each detail with the utmost regard for truth; for he answered well who, when asked in what qualities we resemble the gods, declared that we do so in benevolence and truth. 3. As I am writing to you, my good friend, who are well versed in literary studies, I feel almost absolved from the necessity of premising at any length that sublimity is a certain distinction and excellence in expression, and that it is from no other source than this that the greatest poets and writers have derived their eminence and gained an immortality of renown. 4. The effect of elevated language upon an audience is not persuasion but transport. At every time and in every way imposing speech, with the spell it throws over us, prevails over that which aims at persuasion and gratification. Our persuasions we can usually control, but the influences of the sublime bring power and irresistible might to bear, and reign supreme over every hearer. Similarly, we see skill in invention, and due order and arrangement of matter, emerging as the hard-won result not of one thing nor of two, but of the whole texture of the composition, whereas Sublimity flashing forth at the right moment scatters everything before it like a thunderbolt, and at once displays the power of the orator in all its plenitude. But enough; for these reflections, and others like them, you can, I know well, my dear Terentianus, yourself suggest from your own experience.

Translated by W. Rhys Roberts.

2

First of all, we must raise the question whether there is such a thing as an art of the sublime or lofty. Some hold that those are entirely in error who would bring such matters under the precepts of art. A lofty tone, says one, is innate, and does not come by teaching; nature is the only art that can compass it. Works of nature are, they think, made worse and altogether feebler when wizened by the rules of art. 2. But I maintain that this will be found to be otherwise if it be observed that, while nature as a rule is free and independent in matters of passion and elevation, yet is she wont not to act at random and utterly without system. Further, nature is the original and vital underlying principle in all cases, but system can define limits and fitting seasons, and can also contribute the safest rules for use and practice. Moreover, the expression of the sublime is more exposed to danger when it goes its own way without the guidance of knowledge — when it is suffered to be unstable and unballasted — when it is left at the mercy of mere momentum and ignorant audacity. It is true that it often needs the spur, but it is also true that it often needs the curb. 3. Demosthenes expresses the view, with regard to human life in general, that good fortune is the greatest of blessings, while good counsel, which occupies the second place, is hardly inferior in importance, since its absence contributes inevitably to the ruin of the former. This we may apply to diction, nature occupying the position of good fortune, art that of good counsel. Most important of all, we must remember that the very fact that there are some elements of expression which are in the hands of nature alone, can be learnt from no other source than art. If, I say, the critic of those who desire to learn were to turn these matters over in his mind, he would no longer, it seems to me, regard the discussion of the subject as superfluous or useless. . . .

3

Quell they the oven's far-flung splendour-glow!
Ha, let me but one hearth-abider mark —
One flame-wreath torrent-like I'll whirl on high;
I'll burn the roof, to cinders shrivel it —
Nay, now my chant is not of noble strain.[1]

[1]Aeschylus, *Oreithia.* [Ed.]

Such things are not tragic but pseudo-tragic — "flame-wreaths," and "belching to the sky," and Boreas represented as a "flute-player," and all the rest of it. They are turbid in expression and confused in imagery rather than the product of intensity, and each one of them, if examined in the light of day, sinks little by little from the terrible into the contemptible. But since even in tragedy, which is in its very nature stately and prone to bombast, tasteless tumidity is unpardonable, still less, I presume, will it harmonize with the narration of fact. 2. And this is the ground on which the phrases of Gorgias of Leontini are ridiculed when he describes Xerxes as the "Zeus of the Persians" and vultures as "living tombs." So is it with some of the expressions of Callisthenes which are not sublime but high-flown, and still more with those of Cleitarchus, for the man is frivolous and blows, as Sophocles has it,

On pigmy hautboys: mouthpiece have they none.

Other examples will be found in Amphicrates and Hegesias and Matris, for often when these writers seem to themselves to be inspired they are in no true frenzy but are simply trifling. 3. Altogether, tumidity seems particularly hard to avoid. The explanation is that all who aim at elevation are so anxious to escape the reproach of being weak and dry that they are carried, as by some strange law of nature, into the opposite extreme. They put their trust in the maxim that "failure in a great attempt is at least a noble error." 4. But evil are the swellings, both in the body and in diction, which are inflated and unreal, and threaten us with the reverse of our aim; for nothing, say they, is drier than a man who has the dropsy. While tumidity desires to transcend the limits of the sublime, the defect which is termed puerility is the direct antithesis of elevation, for it is utterly low and mean and in real truth the most ignoble vice of style. What, then, is this puerility? Clearly, a pedant's thoughts, which begin in learned trifling and end in frigidity. Men slip into this kind of error because, while they aim at the uncommon and elaborate and most of all at the attractive, they drift unawares into the tawdry and affected. 5. A third, and closely allied, kind of defect in matters of passion is that which Theodorus used to call *parenthyrsus.* By this is meant unseasonable and empty passion, where no passion is required, or immoderate, where moderation is needed. For men are often carried away, as if by intoxication, into displays of emotion which are not caused by the nature of the subject, but are purely personal and wearisome. In consequence they seem to hearers who are in no wise affected to act in an ungainly way. And no wonder; for they are beside themselves, while their hearers are not. But the question of the passions we reserve for separate treatment.

4

Of the second fault of which we have spoken — frigidity — Timaeus supplies many examples. Timaeus was a writer of considerable general ability, who occasionally showed that he was not incapable of elevation of style. He was learned and ingenious, but very prone to criticize the faults of others while blind to his own. Through his passion for continually starting novel notions, he often fell into the merest childishness. 2. I will set down one or two examples only of his manner, since the greater number have been already appropriated by Caecilius. In the course of a eulogy on Alexander the Great, he describes him as "the man who gained possession of the whole of Asia in fewer years than it took Isocrates to write his *Panegyric* urging war against the Persians." Strange indeed is the comparison of the man of Macedon with the rhetorician. How plain it is, Timaeus, that the Lacedaemonians, thus judged, were far interior to Isocrates in prowess, for they spent thirty years in the conquest of Messene, whereas he composed his *Panegyric* in ten. 3. Consider again the way in which he speaks of the Athenians who were captured in Sicily. "They were punished because they had acted impiously towards Hermes and mutilated his images, and the infliction of punishment was chiefly due to Hermocrates the son of Hermon, who was descended, in the paternal line, from the outraged god." I am surprised, beloved Terentianus, that he does not write with regard to the despot Dionysius that "Dion and Heracleides deprived him of his sovereignty because he had acted impiously towards Zeus and Heracles." 4. But why speak of Timaeus when even those heroes of literature, Xenophon and Plato, though trained in the school of Socrates, nevertheless sometimes forget themselves for the sake of such paltry pleasantries? Xenophon writes in the *Polity of the Lacedaemonians:* "You would find it harder to hear their voice than that of busts of marble, harder to deflect their gaze than that of statues of bronze; you would deem them more modest than the very maidens in their eyes."[2]

It was worthy of an Amphicrates and not of a Xenophon to call the pupils of our eyes "modest maidens." Good heavens, how strange it is that the pupils of the whole company should be believed to be modest notwithstanding the common saying that the shamelessness of individuals is indicated by nothing so much as the eyes! "Thou sot, that hast the eyes of a dog," as Homer has it.[3] 5. Timaeus, however, has not left even this piece of frigidity to Xenophon, but clutches it as though it were hid treasure. At all events, after saying of Agathocles that he abducted his cousin, who had been given in marriage to another man, from the midst of the nuptial rites, he asks, "Who could have done this had he not had wantons, in place of maidens, in his eyes?" 6. Yes, and Plato (usually so divine) when he means simply *tablets* says, "They shall write and preserve *cypress memorials* in the temples."[4]

And again, "As touching walls, Megillus, I should hold with Sparta that they be suffered to lie asleep in the earth and not summoned to arise."[5] The expression of Herodotus to the effect that beautiful women are "eye-smarts" is not much better.[6] This, however, may be condoned in some degree since those who use this particular phrase in his narrative are barbarians and in their cups, but not even in the mouths of such characters is it well that an author should suffer, in the judgment of posterity, from an unseemly exhibition of triviality.

[2]Xenophon, *On the Government of the Lacedaimonians* 3:5. [Tr.]

[3]Homer, *Iliad* 1:225. [Tr.]

[4]Plato, *Laws* 5:741c. [Tr.]

[5]Plato, *Laws* 6:778d [Tr.]

[6]Herodotus, *History* 5:18. [Tr.]

5

All these ugly and parasitical growths arise in literature from a single cause, that pursuit of novelty in the expression of ideas which may be regarded as the fashionable craze of the day. Our defects usually spring, for the most part, from the same sources as our good points. Hence, while beauties of expression and touches of sublimity, and charming elegances withal, are favorable to effective composition, yet these very things are the elements and foundation, not only of success, but also of the contrary. Something of the kind is true also of variations and hyperboles and the use of the plural number, and we shall show subsequently the dangers to which these seem severally to be exposed. It is necessary now to seek and to suggest means by which we may avoid the defects which attend the steps of the sublime.

6

The best means would be, my friend, to gain, first of all, clear knowledge and appreciation of the true sublime. The enterprise is, however, an arduous one. For the judgment of style is the last and crowning fruit of long experience. Nonetheless, if I must speak in the way of precept, it is not impossible perhaps to acquire discrimination in these matters by attention to some such hints as those which follow.

7

You must know, my dear friend, that it is with the sublime as in the common life of man. In life nothing can be considered great which it is held great to despise. For instance, riches, honors, distinctions, sovereignties, and all other things which possess in abundance the external trappings of the stage, will not seem, to a man of sense, to be supreme blessings, since the very contempt of them is reckoned good in no small degree, and in any case those who could have them, but are high-souled enough to disdain them, are more admired than those who have them. So also in the case of sublimity in poems and prose writings, we must consider whether some supposed examples have not simply the appearance of elevation with many idle accretions, so that when analyzed they are found to be mere vanity — objects which a noble nature will rather despise than admire. 2. For, as if instinctively, our soul is uplifted by the true sublime; it takes a proud flight, and is filled with joy and vaunting, as though it had itself produced what it has heard. 3. When therefore, a thing is heard repeatedly by a man of intelligence, who is well versed in literature, and its effect is not to dispose the soul to high thoughts, and it does not leave in the mind more food for reflection than the words seem to convey, but falls, if examined carefully through and through, into disesteem, it cannot rank as true sublimity because it does not survive a first hearing. For that is really great which bears a repeated examination, and which it is difficult or rather impossible to withstand, and the memory of which is strong and hard to efface. 4. In general, consider those examples of sublimity to be fine and genuine which please all and always. For when men of different pursuits, lives, ambitions, ages, languages, hold identical views on one and the same subject, then that verdict which results, so to speak, from a concert of discordant elements makes our faith in the object of admiration strong and unassailable.

8

There are, it may be said, five principal sources of elevated language. Beneath these five varieties there lies, as though it were a common foundation, the gift of discourse, which is indispensable. First and most important is the power of forming great conceptions, as we have elsewhere explained in our remarks on Xenophon. Secondly, there is vehement and inspired passion. These two components of the sublime are for the most part innate. Those which remain are partly the product of art. The due formation of figures deals with two sorts of figures, first those of thought and secondly those of expression. Next there is noble diction, which in turn comprises choice of words, and use of metaphors, and elaboration of language. The fifth cause of elevation — one which is the fitting conclusion of all that have preceded it — is dignified and elevated composition. Come now, let us consider what is involved in each of these varieties, with this one remark by way of preface, that Caecilius has omitted some of the five divisions, for example, that of passion. 2. Surely he is quite mistaken if he does so on the ground that these two, sublimity and passion, are a unity, and if it seems to him that they are by nature one and inseparable. For some passions are found which are far removed from sublimity and are of a low order, such as pity, grief and fear; and on the other hand there are many examples of the sublime which are independent of passion, such as the daring words of Homer with regard to the Aloadae, to take one out of numberless instances,

> Yea, Ossa in fury they strove to upheave on Olympus on high,
> With forest-clad Pelion above, that thence they might step to the sky.[7]

And so of the words which follow with still greater force:

> Ay, and the deed had they done.

3. Among the orators, too, eulogies and ceremonial and occasional addresses contain on every side examples of dignity and elevation, but are for the most part void of passion. This is the reason why passionate speakers are the worst eulogists, and why, on the other hand, those who are apt in encomium are the least passionate. 4. If, on the other hand, Caecilius thought that passion never contributes at all to sublimity, and if it was for this reason that he did not deem it worthy of mention, he is altogether deluded. I would affirm with confidence that there is no tone so lofty as that of genuine passion, in its right place, when it bursts out in a wild gust of mad enthusiasm and as it were fills the speaker's words with frenzy.

9

Now the first of the conditions mentioned, namely elevation of mind, holds the foremost rank among them all. We must, therefore, in this case also, although we have to do rather with an endowment than with an acquirement, nurture our souls (as far as that is possible) to thoughts sublime, and make them always pregnant, so to say, with noble inspiration. 2. In what way, you may ask, is this to be done? Elsewhere I have written as follows: "Sublimity is the echo of a great soul." Hence also a bare idea, by itself and without a spoken word, sometimes excites admiration just because of the greatness of soul implied. Thus the silence of Ajax in the Underworld is great and more sublime than words.[8] 3. First, then, it is absolutely necessary to indicate the source of this elevation, namely, that the truly eloquent must be free from low and ignoble thoughts. For it is not possible that men with mean and servile ideas and aims prevailing throughout their lives should produce anything that is admirable and worthy of immortality. Great accents we expect to fall from the lips of those whose thoughts are deep and grave. 4. Thus it is that stately speech comes naturally to the proudest spirits. [You will remember the answer of] Alexander to Parmenio when he said "For my part I had been well content."[9] . . .

. . . the distance from earth to heaven; and this might well be considered the measure of Homer no less than of Strife. 5. How unlike to this the expression which is used of Sorrow by Hesiod, if indeed the *Shield* is to be attributed to Hesiod:

> Rheum from her nostrils was trickling.[10]

The image he has suggested is not terrible but rather loathsome. Contrast the way in which Homer magnifies the higher powers:

> And far as a man with his eyes through the sea-line haze may discern,
> On a cliff as he sitteth and gazeth away o'er the wine-dark deep,
> So far at a bound do the loud-neighing steeds of the Deathless leap.[11]

He makes the vastness of the world the measure of their leap. The sublimity is so overpowering as naturally to prompt the exclamation that if the divine steeds were to leap thus twice in succession

[7]Homer, *Odyssey* 11:315–16. [Tr.]

[8]Homer, *Odyssey* 11:543. [Tr.]

[9]From Arrian's *Anabasis of Alexander*. A lacuna in the manuscript follows. [Ed.]

[10]Hesiod, *The Shield of Heracles*, 267. [Tr.]

[11]Homer, *Iliad* 5:770–72. [Tr.]

they would pass beyond the confines of the world. 6. How transcendent also are the images in the Battle of the Gods:

> Far round wide heaven and Olympus echoed his clarion of thunder;
> And Hades, king of the realm of shadows, quaked thereunder.
> And he sprang from his throne, and he cried aloud in the dread of his heart
> Lest o'er him earth-shaker Poseidon should cleave the ground apart,
> And revealed to Immortals and mortals should stand those awful abodes,
> Those mansions ghastly and grim, abhorred of the very Gods.[12]

You see, my friend, how the earth is torn from its foundations, Tartarus itself is laid bare, the whole world is upturned and parted asunder, and all things together — heaven and hell, things mortal and things immortal — share in the conflict and the perils of that battle!

7. But although these things are awe-inspiring, yet from another point of view, if they be not taken allegorically, they are altogether impious, and violate our sense of what is fitting. Homer seems to me, in his legends of wounds suffered by the gods, and of their feuds, reprisals, tears, bonds, and all their manifold passions, to have made, as far as lay within his power, gods of the men concerned in the Siege of Troy, and men of the gods. But whereas we mortals have death as the destined haven of our ills if our lot is miserable, he portrays the gods as immortal not only in nature but also in misfortune. 8. Much superior to the passages respecting the Battle of the Gods are those which represent the divine nature as it really is — pure and great and undefiled; for example, what is said of Poseidon in a passage fully treated by many before ourselves:

> Her far-stretching ridges, her forest-trees, quaked in dismay,
> And her peaks, and the Trojans' town, and the ships of Achaia's array,
> Beneath his immortal feet, as onward Poseidon strode.
> Then over the surges he drave: leapt sporting before the God
> Sea-beasts that uprose all around from the depths, for their king they knew,
> And for rapture the sea was disparted, and onward the car-steeds flew.[13]

9. Similarly, the legislator of the Jews, no ordinary man, having formed and expressed a worthy conception of the might of the Godhead, writes at the very beginning of his Laws, "God said," — what? "Let there be light, and there was light; let there be land, and there was land."[14] 10. Perhaps I shall not seem tedious, my friend, if I bring forward one passage more from Homer — this time with regard to the concerns of *men* — in order to show that he is wont himself to enter into the sublime actions of his heroes. In his poem the battle of the Greeks is suddenly veiled by mist and baffling night. Then Ajax, at his wits' end, cries:

> Zeus, Father, yet save thou Achaia's sons from beneath the gloom,
> And make clear day, and vouchsafe unto us with our eyes to see!
> So it be but in light, destroy us![15]

That is the true attitude of an Ajax. He does not pray for life, for such a petition would have ill beseemed a hero. But since in the hopeless darkness he can turn his valor to no noble end, he chafes at his slackness in the fray and craves the boon of immediate light, resolved to find a death worthy of his bravery, even though Zeus should fight in the ranks against him. 11. In truth, Homer in these cases shares the full inspiration of the combat, and it is neither more nor less than true of the poet himself that

> Mad rageth he as Arês the shaker of spears, or as mad flames leap
> Wild-wasting from hill unto hill in the folds of a forest deep,
> And the foam-froth fringeth his lips.[16]

[12]Homer, *Iliad* 20:61–65. [Tr.]

[13]Homer, *Iliad* 13:18–19, 27–29. The second line belongs at the beginning of the last quotation; it is *Iliad* 20:60. [Ed.]

[14]Genesis 1:3, slightly misquoted. [Ed.]

[15]Homer, *Iliad* 17:645–47. [Tr.]

[16]Homer, *Iliad* 15:605–7. [Tr.]

He shows, however, in the Odyssey (and this further observation deserves attention on many grounds) that, when a great genius is declining, the special token of old age is the love of marvelous tales. 12. It is clear from many indications that the Odyssey was his second subject. A special proof is the fact that he introduces in that poem remnants of the adventures before Ilium as episodes, so to say, of the Trojan War. And indeed, he there renders a tribute of mourning and lamentation to his heroes as though he were carrying out a long-cherished purpose. In fact, the Odyssey is simply an epilogue to the Iliad:

> There lieth Ajax the warrior wight, Achilles is
> there,
> There is Patroclus, whose words had weight as a
> God he were;
> There lieth mine own dear son.[17]

13. It is for the same reason, I suppose, that he has made the whole structure of the Iliad, which was written at the height of his inspiration, full of action and conflict, while the Odyssey for the most part consists of narrative, as is characteristic of old age. Accordingly, in the Odyssey Homer may be likened to a sinking sun, whose grandeur remains without its intensity. He does not in the Odyssey maintain so high a pitch as in those poems of Ilium. His sublimities are not evenly sustained and free from the liability to sink; there is not the same profusion of accumulated passions, nor the supple and oratorical style, packed with images drawn from real life. You seem to see henceforth the ebb and flow of greatness, and a fancy roving in the fabulous and incredible, as though the ocean were withdrawing into itself and were being laid bare within its own confines. 14. In saying this I have not forgotten the tempests in the Odyssey and the story of the Cyclops and the like. If I speak of old age, it is nevertheless the old age of Homer. The fabulous element, however, prevails throughout this poem over the real. The object of this digression has been, as I said, to show how easily great natures in their decline are sometimes diverted into absurdity, as in the incident of the wine-skin and of the men who were fed like swine by Circe (*whining porkers*, as Zoilus called them), and of Zeus like a nestling nurtured by the doves, and of the hero who was without food for ten days upon the wreck, and of the incredible tale of the slaying of the suitors.[18] For what else can we term these things than veritable dreams of Zeus? 15. These observations with regard to the Odyssey should be made for another reason — in order that you may know that the genius of great poets and prose-writers, as their passion declines, finds its final expression in the delineation of character. For such are the details which Homer gives, with an eye to characterization, of life in the home of Odysseus; they form as it were a comedy of manners.

[17]Homer, *Odyssey* 3:109–11. [Tr.]

10

Let us next consider whether we can point to anything further that contributes to sublimity of style. Now, there inhere in all things by nature certain constituents which are part and parcel of their substance. It must needs be, therefore, that we shall find one source of the sublime in the systematic selection of the most important elements, and the power of forming, by their mutual combination, what may be called one body. The former process attracts the hearer by the choice of the ideas, the latter by the aggregation of those chosen. For instance, Sappho everywhere chooses the emotions that attend delirious passion from its accompaniments in actual life. Wherein does she demonstrate her supreme excellence? In the skill with which she selects and binds together the most striking and vehement circumstances of passion:

> 2. Peer of Gods he seemeth to me, the blissful
> Man who sits and gazes at thee before him,
> Close beside thee sits, and in silence hears thee
> Silverly speaking,
> Laughing love's low laughter. Oh this, this only
> Stirs the troubled heart in my breast to tremble!

[18]Five incidents from the *Odyssey*. The Cyclops at 9:192; Aiolos's wineskin at 10:17; the metamorphosis at 10:237; Zeus's doves at 12:62; Odysseus's fast at 12:447; the slaying of the suitors at 22:79–380. [Ed.]

For should I but see thee a little moment,
Straight is my voice hushed;
Yea, my tongue is broken, and through and through me
'Neath the flesh impalpable fire runs tingling;
Nothing see mine eyes, and a noise of roaring
Waves in my ear sounds;
Sweat runs down in rivers, a tremor seizes
All my limbs, and paler than grass in autumn,
Caught by pains of menacing death, I falter,
Lost in the love-trance.

3. Are you not amazed how at one instant she summons, as though they were all alien from herself and dispersed, soul, body, ears, tongue, eyes, color? Uniting contradictions, she is, at one and the same time, hot and cold, in her senses and out of her mind, for she is either terrified or at the point of death. The effect desired is that not one passion only should be seen in her, but a concourse of the passions. All such things occur in the case of lovers, but it is, as I said, the selection of the most striking of them and their combination into a single whole that has produced the singular excellence of the passage. In the same way Homer, when describing tempests, picks out the most appalling circumstances. 4. The author of the *Arimaspeia* thinks to inspire awe in the following way:

A marvel exceeding great is this withal to my soul —
Men dwell on the water afar from the land, where deep seas roll.
Wretches are they, for they reap but a harvest of travail and pain,
Their eyes on the stars ever dwell, while their hearts abide in the main.
Often, I ween, to the Gods are their hands upraised on high,
And with hearts in misery heavenward-lifted in prayer do they cry.

It is clear, I imagine, to everybody that there is more elegance than terror in these words. 5. But what says Homer? Let one instance be quoted from among many:

And he burst on them like as a wave swift-rushing beneath black clouds,
Heaved huge by the winds, bursts down on a ship, and the wild foam shrouds
From the stem to the stern her hull, and the storm-blast's terrible breath
Roars in the sail, and the heart of the shipmen shuddereth
In fear, for that scantly upborne are they now from the clutches of death.[19]

6. Aratus has attempted to convert this same expression to his own use:

And a slender plank averteth their death.

Only, he has made it trivial and neat instead of terrible. Furthermore, he has put bounds to the danger by saying *A plank keeps off death.* After all, it *does* keep it off. Homer, however, does not for one moment set a limit to the terror of the scene, but draws a vivid picture of men continually in peril of their lives, and often within an ace of perishing with each successive wave. Moreover, he has in the words ὑπὲκ θανάτοιο, forced into union, by a kind of unnatural compulsion, prepositions not usually compounded.[20] He has thus tortured his line into the similitude of the impending calamity, and by the constriction of the verse has excellently figured the disaster, and almost stamped upon the expression the very form and pressure of the danger, ὑπὲκ θανάτοιο φέρονται. 7. This is true also of Archilochus in his account of the shipwreck, and of Demosthenes in the passage which begins "It was evening," where he describes the bringing of the news.[21] The salient points they selected, one might say, according to merit and massed them together, inserting in the midst nothing frivolous, mean, or trivial. For these faults mar the effect of the whole, just as though they introduced chinks or fissures into stately and coordered edifices, whose walls are compacted by their reciprocal adjustment.

II

An allied excellence to those already set forth is that which is termed *amplification.* This figure is employed when the narrative or the course of a

[19]Homer, *Iliad* 15:624–28. [Tr.]

[20]The point is that Homer has created an unusual compound word — *hypek,* out of *hyper* ("up") and *ek* ("out of"): "up out of death." [Ed.]

[21]Demosthenes, *On the Crown,* 169. [Tr.]

forensic argument admits, from section to section, of many starting points and many pauses, and elevated expressions follow, one after the other, in an unbroken succession and in an ascending order. 2. And this may be effected either by way of the rhetorical treatment of commonplaces, or by way of intensification (whether events or arguments are to be strongly presented), or by the orderly arrangement of facts or of passions; indeed, there are innumerable kinds of amplification. Only, the orator must in every case remember that none of these methods by itself, apart from sublimity, forms a complete whole, unless indeed where pity is to be excited or an opponent to be disparaged. In all other cases of amplification, if you take away the sublime, you will remove as it were the soul from the body. For the vigor of the amplification at once loses its intensity and its substance when not resting on a firm basis of the sublime. 3. Clearness, however, demands that we should define concisely how our present precepts differ from the point under consideration a moment ago, namely the marking-out of the most striking conceptions and the unification of them; and wherein, generally, the sublime differs from amplification.

12

Now the definition given by the writers on rhetoric does not satisfy me. Amplification is, say they, discourse which invests the subject with grandeur. This definition, however, would surely apply in equal measure to sublimity and passion and figurative language, since they too invest the discourse with a certain degree of grandeur. The point of distinction between them seems to me to be that sublimity consists in elevation, while amplification embraces a multitude of details. Consequently, sublimity is often comprised in a single thought, while amplification is universally associated with a certain magnitude and abundance. 2. Amplification (to sum the matter up in a general way) is an aggregation of all the constituent parts and topics of a subject, lending strength to the argument by dwelling upon it, and differing herein from proof that, while the latter demonstrates the matter under investigation. . . .

With his vast riches Plato swells, like some sea, into a greatness which expands on every side. 3. Wherefore it is, I suppose, that the orator in his utterance shows, as one who appeals more to the passions, all the glow of a fiery spirit. Plato, on the other hand, firm-planted in his pride and magnificent stateliness, cannot indeed be accused of coldness, but he has not the same vehemence. 4. And it is in these same respects, my dear friend Terentianus, that it seems to me (supposing always that we Greeks are allowed to have an opinion upon the point) that Cicero differs from Demosthenes in elevated passages. For the latter is characterized by sublimity which is for the most part rugged, Cicero by profusion. Our orator,[22] owing to the fact that in his vehemence — aye, and in his speed, power and intensity — he can as it were consume by fire and carry away all before him, may be compared to a thunderbolt or flash of lightning. Cicero, on the other hand, it seems to me, after the manner of a widespread conflagration, rolls on with all-devouring flames, having within him an ample and abiding store of fire, distributed now at this point now at that, and fed by an unceasing succession. 5. This, however, you will be better able to decide; but the great opportunity of Demosthenes' high-pitched elevation comes where intense utterance and vehement passion are in question, and in passages in which the audience is to be utterly enthralled. The profusion of Cicero is in place where the hearer must be flooded with words, for it is appropriate to the treatment of commonplaces, and to perorations for the most part and digressions, and to all descriptive and declamatory passages, and to writings on history and natural science, and to many other departments of literature.

13

To return from my digression. Although Plato thus flows on with noiseless stream, he is nonetheless elevated. You know this because you have read the *Republic* and are familiar with his

[22]Demosthenes. He is "our" orator because Longinus is a Greek writing to a Roman. [Ed.]

manner. "Those," says he, "who are destitute of wisdom and goodness and are ever present at carousals and the like are carried on the downward path, it seems, and wander thus throughout their life. They never look upwards to the truth, nor do they lift their heads, nor enjoy any pure and lasting pleasure, but like cattle they have their eyes ever cast downwards and bent upon the ground and upon their feeding-places, and they graze and grow fat and breed, and through their insatiate desire of these delights they kick and butt with horns and hoofs of iron and kill one another in their greed."[23]

2. This writer shows us, if only we were willing to pay him heed, that another way (beyond anything we have mentioned) leads to the sublime. And what, and what manner of way, may that be? It is the imitation and emulation of previous great poets and writers. And let this, my dear friend, be an aim to which we steadfastly apply ourselves. For many men are carried away by the spirit of others as if inspired, just as it is related of the Pythian priestess when she approaches the tripod, where there is a rift in the ground which (they say) exhales divine vapor. By heavenly power thus communicated she is impregnated and straightway delivers oracles in virtue of the afflatus. Similarly from the great natures of the men of old there are borne in upon the souls of those who emulate them (as from sacred caves) what we may describe as *effluences,* so that even those who seem little likely to be possessed are thereby inspired and succumb to the spell of the others' greatness. 3. Was Herodotus alone a devoted imitator of Homer? No, Stesichorus even before his time, and Archilochus, and above all Plato, who from the great Homeric source drew to himself innumerable tributary streams. And perhaps we should have found it necessary to prove this, point by point, had not Ammonius and his followers selected and recorded the particulars. 4. This proceeding is not plagiarism; it is like taking an impression from beautiful forms or figures or other works of art. And it seems to me that there would not have been so fine a bloom of perfection on Plato's philosophical doctrines, and that he would not in many cases have found his way to poetical subject matter and modes of expression, unless he had with all his heart and mind struggled with Homer for the primacy, entering the lists like a young champion matched against the man whom all admire, and showing perhaps too much love of contention and breaking a lance with him as it were, but deriving some profit from the contest nonetheless. For, as Hesiod says, "This strife is good for mortals."[24] And in truth that struggle for the crown of glory is noble and best deserves the victory in which even to be worsted by one's predecessors brings no discredit.

14

Accordingly it is well that we ourselves also, when elaborating anything which requires lofty expression and elevated conception, should shape some idea in our minds as to how perchance Homer would have said this very thing, or how it would have been raised to the sublime by Plato or Demosthenes or by the historian Thucydides. For those personages, presenting themselves to us and inflaming our ardor and as it were illumining our path, will carry our minds in a mysterious way to the high standards of sublimity which are imaged within us. 2. Still more effectual will it be to suggest this question to our thoughts, "What sort of hearing would Homer, had he been present, or Demosthenes have given to this or that when said by me, or how would they have been affected by the other?" For the ordeal is indeed a severe one, if we presuppose such a tribunal and theater for our own utterances, and imagine that we are undergoing a scrutiny of our writings before these great heroes, acting as judges and witnesses. 3. A greater incentive still will be supplied if you add the question, "In what spirit will each succeeding age listen to me who have written thus?" But if one shrinks from the very thought of uttering aught that may transcend the term of his own life and time, the conceptions of his mind must necessarily be incomplete, blind, and as it were untimely born, since they are by no

[23]Plato, *Republic* 9:586a. [Tr.]

[24]Hesiod, *Works and Days,* 24. [Tr.]

means brought to the perfection needed to ensure a futurity of fame.

15

Images, moreover, contribute greatly, my young friend, to dignity, elevation, and power as a pleader. In this sense some call them mental representations. In a general way the name of *image* or *imagination* is applied to every idea of the mind, in whatever form it presents itself, which gives birth to speech. But at the present day the word is predominantly used in cases where, carried away by enthusiasm and passion, you think you see what you describe, and you place it before the eyes of your hearers. 2. Further, you will be aware of the fact that an image has one purpose with the orators and another with the poets, and that the design of the poetical image is enthrallment, of the rhetorical — vivid description. Both, however, seek to stir the passions and the emotions.

> Mother — 'beseech thee, hark not thou on me
> Yon maidens gory-eyed and snaky-haired!
> Lo there — lo there! — they are nigh — they leap on me![25]

And:

> Ah! she will slay me! whither can I fly?[26]

In these scenes the poet himself saw Furies, and the image in his mind he almost compelled his audience also to behold. 3. Now, Euripides is most assiduous in giving the utmost tragic effect to these two emotions — fits of love and madness. Herein he succeeds more, perhaps, than in any other respect, although he is daring enough to invade all the other regions of the imagination. Notwithstanding that he is by nature anything but elevated, he forces his own genius, in many passages, to tragic heights, and everywhere in the matter of sublimity it is true of him (to adopt Homer's words) that

> The tail of him scourgeth his ribs and his flanks to left and to right,
> And he lasheth himself into frenzy, and spurreth him on to the fight.[27]

4. When the Sun hands the reins to Phaethon, he says

> "Thou, driving, trespass not on Libya's sky,
> Whose heat, by dews untempered, else shall split
> Thy car asunder."

And after that,

> "Speed onward toward the Pleiads seven thy course."
> Thus far the boy heard; then he snatched the reins:
> He lashed the flanks of that wing-wafted team;
> Loosed rein; and they through folds of cloudland soared.
> Hard after on a fiery star his sire
> Rode, counselling his son — "Ho! thither drive!
> Hither thy car turn — hither!"

Would you not say that the soul of the writer enters the chariot at the same moment as Phaethon and shares in his dangers and in the rapid flight of his steeds? For it could never have conceived such a picture had it not been borne in no less swift career on that journey through the heavens. The same is true of the words which Euripides attributes to his Cassandra:

> O chariot-loving Trojans.

5. Aeschylus, too, ventures on images of a most heroic stamp. An example will be found in his *Seven Against Thebes,* where he says

> For seven heroes, squadron-captains fierce,
> Over a black-rimmed shield have slain a bull,
> And, dipping in the bull's blood each his hand,
> By Ares and Enyo, and by Panic
> Lover of blood, have sworn.[28]

In mutual fealty they devoted themselves by that joint oath to a relentless doom. Sometimes, however, he introduces ideas that are rough-hewn and uncouth and harsh; and Euripides, when stirred by the spirit of emulation, comes perilously near the same fault, even in spite of his own natural bent. 6. Thus in Aeschylus the palace of Lycur-

[25]Euripides, *Orestes,* 255–57. [Tr.]

[26]Euripides, *Iphigeneia in Tauris,* 291. [Tr.] The three following quotations are from lost plays. [Ed.]

[27]Homer, *Iliad* 20:170–71. [Tr.]

[28]Aeschylus, *Seven Against Thebes,* 42–46. [Tr.] The following quotation is from a lost play. [Ed.]

gus at the coming of Dionysus is strangely represented as *possessed:*

> A frenzy thrills the hall; the roofs are bacchant
> With ecstasy:

an idea which Euripides has echoed, in other words, it is true, and with some abatement of its crudity, where he says:

> The whole mount shared their bacchic ecstasy.[29]

7. Magnificent are the images which Sophocles has conceived of the death of Oedipus, who makes ready his burial amid the portents of the sky.[30] Magnificent, too, is the passage where the Greeks are on the point of sailing away and Achilles appears above his tomb to those who are putting out to sea — a scene which I doubt whether anyone has depicted more vividly than Simonides. But it is impossible to cite all the examples that present themselves. 8. It is no doubt true that those which are found in the poets contain, as I said, a tendency to exaggeration in the way of the fabulous and that they transcend in every way the credible, but in oratorical imagery the best feature is always its reality and truth. Whenever the form of a speech is poetical and fabulous and breaks into every kind of impossibility, such digressions have a strange and alien air. For example, the clever orators forsooth of our day, like the tragedians, see Furies, and — fine fellows that they are — cannot even understand that Orestes when he cries

> Unhand me — of mine Haunting Fiends thou
> art —
> Dost grip my waist to hurl me into hell![31]

has these fancies because he is mad. 9. What, then, can oratorical imagery effect? Well, it is able in many ways to infuse vehemence and passion into spoken words, while more particularly when it is combined with the argumentative passages it not only persuades the hearer but actually makes him its slave. Here is an example. "Why, if at this very moment," says Demosthenes, "a loud cry were to be heard in front of the courts, and we were told that the prison-house lies open and the prisoners are in full flight, no one, whether he be old or young, is so heedless as not to lend aid to the utmost of his power; aye, and if anyone came forward and said that yonder stands the man who let them go, the offender would be promptly put to death without a hearing."[32] 10. In the same way, too, Hyperides on being accused, after he had proposed the liberation of the slaves subsequently to the great defeat, said "This proposal was framed, not by the orator, but by the battle of Chaeroneia." The speaker has here at one and the same time followed a train of reasoning and indulged a flight of imagination. He has, therefore, passed the bounds of mere persuasion by the boldness of his conception. 11. By a sort of natural law in all such matters we always attend to whatever possesses superior force; whence it is that we are drawn away from demonstration pure and simple to any startling image within whose dazzling brilliancy the argument lies concealed. And it is not unreasonable that we should be affected in this way, for when two things are brought together, the more powerful always attracts to itself the virtue of the weaker. 12. It will be enough to have said this much with regard to examples of the sublime in thought, when produced by greatness of soul, imitation, or imagery.

16

Here, however, in due order comes the place assigned to Figures; for they, if handled in the proper manner, will contribute, as I have said, in no mean degree to sublimity. But since to treat thoroughly of them all at the present moment would be a great, or rather an endless task, we will now, with the object of proving our proposition, run over a few only of those which produce elevation of diction. 2. Demosthenes is bringing forward a reasoned vindication of his public policy. What was the natural way of treating the subject? It was this. "You were not wrong, you who engaged in the struggle for the freedom of Greece. You have domestic warrant for it. For

[29]Euripides, *The Bacchae,* 726. [Tr.]
[30]Sophocles, *Oedipus at Colonus,* 1586. [Tr.]
[31]Euripides, *Orestes,* 264–65. [Tr.]
[32]Demosthenes, *Contra Timocrates,* 208. [Tr.]

the warriors of Marathon did no wrong, nor they of Salamis, nor they of Plataea."[33] When, however, as though suddenly inspired by heaven and as it were frenzied by the god of Prophecy, he utters his famous oath by the champions of Greece ("assuredly ye did no wrong; I swear it by those who at Marathon stood in the forefront of the danger"), in the public view by this one Figure of Adjuration, which I here term *Apostrophe,* he deifies his ancestors. He brings home the thought that we ought to swear by those who have thus nobly died as we swear by gods, and he fills the mind of the judges with the high spirit of those who there bore the brunt of the danger, and he has transformed the natural course of the argument into transcendent sublimity and passion and that secure belief which rests upon strange and prodigious oaths. He instills into the minds of his hearers the conviction — which acts as a medicine and an antidote — that they should, uplifted by these eulogies, feel no less proud of the fight against Philip than of the triumph at Marathon and Salamis. By all these means he carries his hearers clean away with him through the employment of a single figure. 3. It is said, indeed, that the germ of the oath is found in Eupolis:

For, by the fight I won at Marathon,
No one shall vex my soul and rue it not.

But it is not sublime to swear by a person in any chance way; the sublimity depends upon the place and the manner and the circumstances and the motive. Now in the passage of Eupolis there is nothing but the mere oath, addressed to the Athenians when still prosperous and in no need of comfort. Furthermore, the poet in his oath has not made divinities of the men in order so to create in his hearers a worthy conception of their valor, but he has wandered away from those who stood in the forefront of the danger to an inanimate thing — the fight. In Demosthenes the oath is framed for vanquished men, with the intention that Chaeroneia should no longer appear a failure to the Athenians. He gives them at one and the same time, as I remarked, a demonstration that they have done no wrong, an example, the sure evidence of oaths, a eulogy, an exhortation. 4. And since the orator was likely to be confronted with the objection, "You are speaking of the *defeat* which has attended your administration, and yet you swear by *victories,*" in what follows he consequently measures even individual words, and chooses them unerringly, showing that even in the revels of the imagination sobriety is required. "Those," he says, "who stood in the forefront of the danger at Marathon, and those who fought by sea at Salamis and Artemisium, and those who stood in the ranks at Plataea." Nowhere does he use the word "conquered," but at every turn he has evaded any indication of the result, since it was fortunate and the opposite of what happened at Chaeroneia. So he at once rushes forward and carries his hearer off his feet. "All of whom," says he, "were accorded a public burial by the state, Aeschines, and not *the successful only.*"

[33]Demosthenes, *On the Crown,* 208. [Tr.]

17

I ought not, my dear friend, to omit at this point an observation of my own, which shall be most concisely stated. It is that, by a sort of natural law, figures bring support to the sublime, and on their part derive support in turn from it in a wonderful degree. Where and how, I will explain. The cunning use of figures is peculiarly subject to suspicion, and produces an impression of ambush, plot, fallacy. This is so when the plea is addressed to a judge with absolute powers, and particularly to despots, kings, and leaders in positions of superiority. Such a one at once feels resentment if, like a foolish boy, he is tricked by the paltry figures of the oratorical craftsman. Construing the fallacy into a personal affront, sometimes he becomes quite wild with rage, or if he controls his anger, steels himself utterly against persuasive words. Wherefore a figure is at its best when the very fact that it is a figure escapes attention. 2. Accordingly, sublimity and passion form an antidote and a wonderful help against the mistrust which attends upon the use of figures. The art which craftily employs them lies hid and escapes all future suspicion, when once it has been associated with beauty and sublimity. A sufficient proof is the passage already adduced, "By the men of Marathon I swear." By what means has the orator here concealed the figure? Clearly, by the very excess of light. For just as all dim lights are extinguished in the blaze of the sun, so do the artifices of rhetoric fade from view when bathed in the pervading splendor of sublimity. 3. Something like this happens also in the art of painting. For although light and shade, as depicted in colors, lie side by side upon the same surface, light nevertheless meets the vision first, and not only stands out, but also seems far nearer. So also with the manifestations of passion and the sublime in literature. They lie nearer to our minds through a sort of natural kinship and through their own radiance, and always strike our attention before the figures, whose art they throw into the shade and as it were keep in concealment.

18

But what are we next to say of questions and interrogations? Is it not precisely by the visualizing qualities of these figures that Demosthenes strives to make his speeches far more effective and impressive? "Pray tell me — tell me, you sir — do you wish to go about and inquire of one another, Is there any news? Why, what greater news could there be than this, that a Macedonian is subduing Greece? Is Philip dead? No; but he is ill. Dead or ill, what difference to you? Should anything happen to him, you will speedily create another Philip." Again he says, "Let us sail against Macedonia. Where shall we find a landing-place? someone asks. The war itself will discover the weak places in Philip's position."[34] All this, if stated plainly and directly, would have been altogether weaker. As it is, the excitement, and the rapid play of question and answer, and the plan of meeting his own objections as though they were urged by another, have by the help of the figure made the language used not only more elevated but also more convincing. 2. For an exhibition of passion has a greater effect when it seems not to be studied by the speaker himself but to be inspired by the occasion; and questions asked and answered by oneself simulate a natural outburst of passion. For just as those who are interrogated by others experience a sudden excitement and answer the inquiry incisively and with the utmost candor, so the figure of question and answer leads the hearer to suppose that each deliberate thought is struck out and uttered on the spur of the moment, and thus beguiles his reason. We may further quote that passage of Herodotus which is regarded as one of the most elevated: "If thus. . . ."

[34]Demosthenes, *Philippics* 1:10, 44. [Tr.]

19

The words issue forth without connecting links and are poured out as it were, almost outstripping the speaker himself. "Locking their shields," says Xenophon, "they thrust fought slew fell."[35] 2. And so with the words of Eurylochus:

> We passed, as thou badst, Odysseus, midst twilight of oak-trees round.
> There amidst of the forest-glens a beautiful palace we found.[36]

For the lines detached from one another, but nonetheless hurried along, produce the impression of an agitation which interposes obstacles and at the same time adds impetuosity. This result Homer has produced by the omission of conjunctions.

20

A powerful effect usually attends the union of figures for a common object, when two or three mingle together as it were in partnership, and contribute a fund of strength, persuasiveness, beauty. Thus, in the speech against Meidias, examples will be found of *asyndeton,* interwoven with instances of *anaphora* and *diatyposis.*[37] "For the smiter can do many things (some of which the sufferer cannot even describe to another) by attitude, by look, by voice."[38] 2. Then,

[35]Xenophon, *Hellenica* 4:3, 19. [Tr.]

[36]Homer, *Odyssey* 10:251–52. [Tr.]

[37]Asyndeton is the omission of conjunctions between clauses; anaphora the repetition of words beginning clauses or sentences; diatyposis is vivid description. [Tr.]

[38]Demosthenes, *Against Meidias,* 72. [Tr.]

in order that the narrative may not, as it advances, continue in the same groove (for continuance betokens tranquillity, while passion — the transport and commotion of the soul — sets order at defiance) straightway he hurries off to other *Asyndeta* and *Repetitions*. "By attitude, by look, by voice, when he acts with insolence, when he acts like an enemy, when he smites with his fists, when he smites you like a slave." By these words the orator produces the same effect as the assailant — he strikes the mind of the judges by the swift succession of blow on blow. 3. Starting from this point again, as suddenly as a gust of wind, he makes another attack. "When smitten with blows of fists," he says, "when smitten upon the cheek. These things stir the blood, these drive men beyond themselves, when unused to insult. No one can, in describing them, convey a notion of the indignity they imply." So he maintains throughout, though with continual variation, the essential character of the *Repetitions* and *Asyndeta*. In this way, with him, order is disorderly, and on the other hand, disorder contains a certain element of order.

21

Come now, add, if you please, in these cases connecting particles after the fashion of the followers of Isocrates. Furthermore, this fact too must not be overlooked that the smiter may do many things, first by attitude, then by look, then again by the mere voice. You will feel, if you transcribe the passage in this orderly fashion, that the rugged impetuosity of passion, once you make it smooth and equable by adding the copulatives, falls pointless and immediately loses all its fire. 2. Just as the binding of the limbs of runners deprives them of their power of rapid motion, so also passion, when shackled by connecting links and other appendages, chafes at the restriction, for it loses the freedom of its advance and its rapid emission as though from an engine of war.

22

Hyperbata, or *inversions,* must be placed under the same category. They are departures in the order of expressions or ideas from the natural sequence; and they bear, it may be said, the very stamp and impress of vehement emotion. Just as those who are really moved by anger, or fear, or indignation, or jealousy, or any other emotion (for the passions are many and countless, and none can give their number), at times turn aside, and when they have taken one thing as their subject often leap to another, foisting in the midst some irrelevant matter, and then again wheel round to their original theme, and driven by their vehemence, as by a veering wind, now this way now that with rapid changes, transform their expressions, their thoughts, the order suggested by a natural sequence, into numberless variations of every kind; so also among the best writers it is by means of *hyperbaton* that imitation approaches the effects of nature. For art is perfect when it seems to be nature, and nature hits the mark when she contains art hidden within her. We may illustrate by the words of Dionysius of Phocaea in Herodotus. "Our fortunes lie on a razor's edge, men of Ionia; for freedom or for bondage, and that the bondage of runaway slaves. Now, therefore, if you choose to submit to hardships you will have toil for the moment, but you will be able to overcome your foes."[39] 2. Here the natural order would have been: "Men of Ionia, now is the time for you to meet hardships; for our fortunes lie on a razor's edge." But the speaker postpones the words "Men of Ionia." He starts at once with the danger of the situation, as though in such imminent peril he had no time at all to address his hearers. Moreover, he inverts the order of ideas. For instead of saying that they ought to endure hardships, which is the real object of his exhortation, he first assigns the reason because of which they ought to endure hardships, in the words "our fortunes lie on a razor's edge." The result is that what he says seems not to be premeditated but to be prompted by the necessities of the moment. 3. In a still higher degree Thucydides is most bold and skillful in disjoining from one another by means of transpositions things that are by nature intimately united and indivisible. Demosthenes is not so masterful as Thucydides, but of all writers he most abounds in

[39]Herodotus, *History* 6:11. [Tr.]

this kind of figure, and through his use of hyperbata makes a great impression of vehemence, yes and of unpremeditated speech, and moreover draws his hearers with him into all the perils of his long inversions. 4. For he will often leave in suspense the thought which he has begun to express, and meanwhile he will heap, into a position seemingly alien and unnatural, one thing upon another parenthetically and from any external source whatsoever, throwing his hearer into alarm lest the whole structure of his words should fall to pieces, and compelling him in anxious sympathy to share the peril of the speaker; and then unexpectedly, after a long interval, he adds the long-awaited conclusion at the right place, namely the end, and produces a far greater effect by this very use, so bold and hazardous, of hyperbaton. Examples may be spared because of their abundance.

23

The figures which are termed *polyptota* — accumulations, and variations, and climaxes — are excellent weapons of public oratory, as you are aware, and contribute to elegance and to every form of sublimity and passion. Again, how greatly do changes of cases, tenses, persons, numbers, genders, diversify and enliven exposition. 2. Where the use of numbers is concerned, I would point out that style is not adorned only or chiefly by those words which are, as far as their forms go, in the singular but in meaning are, when examined, found to be plural: as in the lines

A countless crowd forthright
Far-ranged along the beaches were clamoring
"Thunny in sight!"

The fact is more worthy of observation that in certain cases the use of the plural (for the singular) falls on the ear with still more imposing effect and impresses us by the very sense of multitude which the number conveys. 3. Such are the words of Oedipus in Sophocles:

O nuptials, nuptials,
Ye gendered me, and, having gendered, brought
To light the selfsame seed, and so revealed
Sires, brothers, sons, in one — all kindred blood! —
Brides, mothers, wives, in one! — yea, whatso deeds
Most shameful among humankind are done.[40]

The whole enumeration can be summed up in a single proper name — on the one side Oedipus, on the other Jocasta. Nonetheless, the expansion of the number into the plural helps to pluralize the misfortunes as well. There is a similar instance of multiplication in the line:

Forth Hectors and Sarpedons marching came,

and in that passage of Plato concerning the Athenians which we have quoted elsewhere. 4. "For no Pelopes, nor Cadmi, nor Aegypti and Danai, nor the rest of the crowd of born foreigners dwell with us, but ours is the land of pure Greeks, free from foreign admixture," etc.[41] For naturally a theme seems more imposing to the ear when proper names are thus added, one upon the other, in troops. But this must only be done in cases in which the subject admits of amplification or redundancy or exaggeration or passion — one or more of these — since we all know that a richly caparisoned style is extremely pretentious.

24

Further (to take the converse case) particulars which are combined from the plural into the singular are sometimes most elevated in appearance. "Thereafter," says Demosthenes, "all Peloponnesus was at variance."[42] "And when Phrynichus had brought out a play entitled the *Capture of Miletus*, the whole theater burst into tears."[43] For the compression of the number from multiplicity into unity gives more fully the feeling of a single body. 2. In both cases the explanation of the elegance of expression is, I think, the same. Where the words are singular, to make them plural is the mark of unlooked-for passion; and where they are plural, the rounding of a number of things into a fine-sounding singular is surprising owing to the converse change.

[40]Sophocles, *Oedipus the King*, 1403–7. [Tr.]
[41]Plato, *Menexinus*, 245d. [Tr.]
[42]Demosthenes, *On the Crown*, 18. [Tr.]
[43]Herodotus, *History* 6:21. [Tr.]

25

If you introduce things which are past as present and now taking place, you will make your story no longer a narration but an actuality. Xenophon furnishes an illustration. "A man," says he, "has fallen under Cyrus's horse, and being trampled strikes the horse with his sword in the belly. He rears and unseats Cyrus, who falls."[44] This construction is specially characteristic of Thucydides.

26

In like manner the interchange of persons produces a vivid impression, and often makes the hearer feel that he is moving in the midst of perils:

> Thou hadst said that with toil unspent, and all unwasted of limb,
> They closed in the grapple of war, so fiercely they rushed to the fray;[45]

and the line of Aratus.

> Never in that month launch thou forth amid lashing seas.

2. So also Herodotus: "From the city of Elephantine thou shalt sail upwards, and then shalt come to a level plain; and after crossing this tract, thou shalt embark upon another vessel and sail for two days, and then shalt thou come to a great city whose name is Meroe."[46] Do you observe, my friend, how he leads you in imagination through the region and makes you *see* what you hear? All such cases of direct personal address place the hearer on the very scene of action. 3. So it is when you seem to be speaking, not to all and sundry, but to a single individual:

> But Tydeides — thou wouldst not have known him, for whom that hero fought.[47]

You will make your hearer more excited and more attentive, and full of active participation, if you keep him on the alert by words addressed to himself.

27

There is further the case in which a writer, when relating something about a person, suddenly breaks off and converts himself into that selfsame person. This species of figure is a kind of outburst of passion:

> Then with a far-ringing shout to the Trojans Hector cried,
> Bidding them rush on the ships, bidding leave the spoils blood-dyed —
> And whomso I mark from the galleys aloof on the farther side,
> I will surely devise his death.[48]

The poet assigns the task of narration, as is fit, to himself, but the abrupt threat he suddenly, with no note of warning, attributes to the angered chief. It would have been frigid had he inserted the words, "Hector said so and so." As it is, the swift transition of the narrative has outstripped the swift transitions of the narrator. 2. Accordingly this figure should be used by preference when a sharp crisis does not suffer the writer to tarry but constrains him to pass at once from one person to another. An example will be found in Hecataeus: "Ceyx treated the matter gravely, and straightway bade the descendants of Heracles depart; for I am not able to succor you. In order, therefore, that ye may not perish yourselves and injure me, get you gone to some other country." 3. Demosthenes in dealing with Aristogeiton has, somewhat differently, employed this variation of person to betoken the quick play of emotion. "And will none of you," he asks, "be found to be stirred by loathing or even by anger at the violent deeds of this vile and shameless fellow, who — you whose license of speech, most abandoned of men, is not confined by barriers nor by doors, which might perchance be opened!"[49] With the sense thus incomplete, he suddenly breaks off and in his anger almost tears asunder a single expression into two persons — "he who, O thou

[44]Xenophon, *Cyropaedia* 7.i:37. [Tr.]
[45]Homer, *Iliad* 15:697–98. [Tr.]
[46]Herodotus, *History* 2:29. [Tr.]
[47]Homer, *Iliad* 5:85. [Tr.]
[48]Homer, *Iliad* 15:346–49. [Tr.]
[49]Demosthenes, *Contra Aristogeitus* 1:27. [Tr.]

most abandoned!" Thus, although he has turned aside his address and seems to have left Aristogeiton, yet through passion he directs it upon him with far greater force. 4. Similarly with the words of Penelope:

Herald, with what behest art thou come from the suitor-band?
To give to the maids of Odysseus the godlike their command
To forsake their labors, and yonder for them the banquet to lay?
I would that of all their wooing this were the latest day,
That this were the end of your banquets, your uttermost revelling-hour,
Ye that assemble together and all our substance devour,
The wise Telemachus' sore, as though ye never had heard,
In the days overpast of your childhood, your fathers' praising word,
How good Odysseus was.[50]

28

As to whether or not periphrasis contributes to the sublime, no one, I think, will hesitate. For just as in music the so-called accompaniments bring out the charm of the melody, so also periphrasis often harmonizes with the normal expression and adds greatly to its beauty, especially if it has a quality which is not inflated and dissonant but pleasantly tempered. 2. Plato will furnish an instance in proof at the opening of his Funeral Oration. "In truth they have gained from us their rightful tribute, in the enjoyment of which they proceed along their destined path, escorted by their country publicly, and privately each by his kinsmen."[51] Death he calls "their destined path," and the tribute of accustomed rites he calls "being escorted publicly by their fatherland." Is it in a slight degree only that he has magnified the conception by the use of these words? Has he not rather, starting with unadorned diction, made it musical, and shed over it like a harmony the melodious rhythm which comes from periphrasis? 3. And Xenophon says, "You regard toil as the guide to a joyous life. You have garnered in your souls the goodliest of all possessions and the fittest for warriors. For you rejoice in praise more than in all else."[52] In using, instead of "you are willing to toil," the words "you deem toil the guide to a joyous life," and in expanding the rest of the sentence in like manner, he has annexed to his eulogy a lofty idea. 4. And so with that inimitable phrase of Herodotus: "The goddess afflicted with an unsexing malady those Scythians who had pillaged the temple."[53]

29

A hazardous business, however, eminently hazardous is periphrasis, unless it be handled with discrimination; otherwise it speedily falls flat, with its odor of empty talk and its swelling amplitude. This is the reason why Plato (who is always strong in figurative language, and at times unseasonably so) is taunted because in his *Laws* he says that "neither gold nor silver treasure should be allowed to establish itself and abide in the city."[54] The critic says that, if he had been forbidding the possession of cattle, he would obviously have spoken of ovine and bovine treasure. 2. But our parenthetical disquisition with regard to the use of figures as bearing upon the sublime has run to sufficient length, my dear Terentianus; for all these things lend additional passion and animation to style, and passion is as intimately allied with sublimity as sketches of character with entertainment.

30

Since, however, it is the case that, in discourse, thought and diction are for the most part developed one through the other, come let us proceed to consider any branches of the subject of diction which have so far been neglected. Now it is, no doubt, superfluous to dilate to those who know it well upon the fact that the choice of proper and

[50]Homer, *Odyssey* 4:681–89. [Tr.]
[51]Plato, *Menexinus,* 236d. [Tr.]
[52]Xenophon, *Cyropaedia* 1:v. 12. [Tr.]
[53]Herodotus, *History* 1:105. [Tr.]
[54]Plato, *Laws,* 801b. [Tr.]

striking words wonderfully attracts and enthralls the hearer, and that such a choice is the leading ambition of all orators and writers, since it is the direct agency which ensures the presence in writings, as upon the fairest statues, of the perfection of grandeur, beauty, mellowness, dignity, force, power, and any other high qualities there may be, and breathes into dead things a kind of living voice. All this it is, I say, needless to mention, for beautiful words are in very truth the peculiar light of thought. 2. It may, however, be pointed out that stately language is not to be used everywhere, since to invest petty affairs with great and high-sounding names would seem just like putting a full-sized tragic mask upon an infant boy. But in poetry and. . . .

31

. . . full of vigor and racy; and so is Anacreon's line, "That Thracian mare no longer do I heed." In this way, too, that original expression of Theopompus merits praise. Owing to the correspondence between word and thing it seems to me to be highly expressive; and yet Caecilius for some unexplained reason finds fault with it. "Philip," says Theopompus, "had a genius for *stomaching* things." Now a homely expression of this kind is sometimes much more telling than elegant language, for it is understood at once since it is drawn from common life, and the fact that it is familiar makes it only the more convincing. So the words "stomaching things" are used most strikingly of a man who, for the sake of attaining his own ends, patiently and with cheerfulness endures things shameful and vile. 2. So with the words of Herodotus. "Cleomenes," he says, "went mad, and with a small sword cut the flesh of his own body into strips, until he slew himself by making mincemeat of his entire person." And, "Pythes fought on shipboard, until he was utterly hacked to pieces."[55] These phrases graze the very edge of vulgarity, but they are saved from vulgarity by their expressiveness.

[55]Herodotus, *History* 6:75; 7:181. [Tr.]

32

Further, with regard to the number of metaphors to be employed, Caecilius seems to assent to the view of those who lay it down that not more than two, or at the most three, should be ranged together in the same passage. Demosthenes is, in fact, the standard in this as in other matters. The proper time for using metaphors is when the passions roll like a torrent and sweep a multitude of them down their resistless flood. 2. "Men," says he, "who are vile flatterers, who have maimed their own fatherlands each one of them, who have toasted away their liberty first to Philip and now to Alexander, who measure happiness by their belly and their lowest desires, and who have overthrown that liberty and that freedom from despotic mastery which to the Greeks of an earlier time were the rules and standards of good."[56] Here the orator's wrath against the traitors throws a veil over the number of the tropes. 3. In the same spirit, Aristotle and Theophrastus point out that the following phrases serve to soften bold metaphors — "as if," and "as it were," and "if one may so say," and "if one may venture such an expression"; for the qualifying words mitigate, they say, the audacity of expression. 4. I accept that view, but still for number and boldness of metaphors I maintain, as I said in dealing with figures, that strong and timely passion and noble sublimity are the appropriate palliatives. For it is the nature of the passions, in their vehement rush, to sweep and thrust everything before them, or rather to demand hazardous turns as altogether indispensable. They do not allow the hearer leisure to criticize the number of the metaphors because he is carried away by the fervor of the speaker. 5. Moreover, in the treatment of commonplaces and in descriptions there is nothing so impressive as a number of tropes following close one upon the other. It is by this means that in Xenophon the anatomy of the human tabernacle is magnificently depicted, and still more divinely in Plato. Plato says that its head is a citadel; in the midst, between the head and the breast, is built the neck like some

[56]Demosthenes, *On the Crown,* 296. [Tr.]

isthmus. The vertebrae, he says, are fixed beneath like pivots. Pleasure is a bait which tempts men to ill, the tongue the test of taste; the heart is the knot of the veins and the wellspring of the blood that courses round impetuously, and it is stationed in the guardhouse of the body. The passages by which the blood races this way and that he names alleys. He says that the gods, contriving succor for the beating of the heart (which takes place when dangers are expected, and when wrath excites it, since it then reaches a fiery heat), have implanted the lungs, which are soft and bloodless and have pores within, to serve as a buffer, in order that the heart may, when its inward wrath boils over, beat against a yielding substance and so escape injury. The seat of the desires he compared to the women's apartments in a house, that of anger to the men's. The spleen he called the napkin of the inward parts, whence it is filled with secretions and grows to a great and festering bulk. After this, the gods canopied the whole with flesh, putting forward the flesh as a defense against injuries from without, as though it were a hair-cushion. The blood he called the fodder of the flesh. "In order to promote nutrition," he continues, "they irrigated the body, cutting conduits as in gardens, in order that, with the body forming a set of tiny channels, the streams of the veins might flow as from a never-failing source." When the end comes, he says that the cables of the soul are loosed like those of a ship, and she is allowed to go free.[57] 6. Examples of a similar nature are to be found in a never-ending series. But those indicated are enough to show that figurative language possesses great natural power, and that metaphors contribute to the sublime; and at the same time that it is impassioned and descriptive passages which rejoice in them to the greatest extent. 7. It is obvious, however, even though I do not dwell upon it, that the use of tropes, like all other beauties of expression, is apt to lead to excess. On this score Plato himself is much criticized, since he is often carried away by a sort of frenzy of words into strong and harsh metaphors and into inflated allegory. "For it is not readily observed," he says, "that a city ought to be mixed like a bowl, in which the mad wine seethes when it has been poured in, though when chastened by another god who is sober, falling thus into noble company, it makes a good and temperate drink."[58] For to call water "a sober god," and mixing "chastening," is — the critics say — the language of a poet, and one who is in truth far from sober. 8. Fastening upon such defects, however, Caecilius ventured, in his writings in praise of Lysias, to make the assertion that Lysias was altogether superior to Plato. In so doing he gave way to two blind impulses of passion. Loving Lysias better even than himself, he nevertheless hates Plato more perfectly than he loves Lysias. In fact, he is carried away by the spirit of contention, and even his premises are not, as he thought, admitted. For he prefers the orator as faultless and immaculate to Plato as one who has often made mistakes. But the truth is not of this nature, nor anything like it.

33

Come, now, let us take some writer who is really immaculate and beyond reproach. Is it not worthwhile, on this very point, to raise the general question whether we ought to give the preference, in poems and prose writings, to grandeur with some attendant faults, or to success which is moderate but altogether sound and free from error? Aye, and further, whether a greater number of excellences, or excellences higher in quality, would in literature rightly bear away the palm? For these are inquiries appropriate to a treatise on the sublime, and they imperatively demand a settlement. 2. For my part, I am well aware that lofty genius is far removed from flawlessness; for invariable accuracy incurs the risk of pettiness, and in the sublime, as in great fortunes, there must be something which is overlooked. It may be necessarily the case that low and average natures remain as a rule free from failing and in greater safety because they never run a risk or seek to scale the heights, while great endowments prove insecure because of their very greatness. 3. In the second place, I am not igno-

[57]Plato, *Timaeus*, 65c–85b. [Tr.]

[58]Plato, *Laws*, 773c. [Tr.]

rant that it naturally happens that the worse side of human character is always the more easily recognized, and that the memory of errors remains indelible, while that of excellences quickly dies away. 4. I have myself noted not a few errors on the part of Homer and other writers of the greatest distinction, and the slips they have made afford me anything but pleasure. Still I do not term them willful errors, but rather oversights of a random and casual kind, due to neglect and introduced with all the heedlessness of genius. Consequently I do not waver in my view that excellences higher in quality, even if not sustained throughout, should always on a comparison be voted the first place, because of their sheer elevation of spirit if for no other reason. Granted that Apollonius in his *Argonautica* shows himself a poet who does not trip, and that in his pastorals Theocritus is, except in a few externals, most happy, would you not, for all that, choose to be Homer rather than Apollonius? 5. Again: does Eratosthenes in the *Erigone* (a little poem which is altogether free from flaw) show himself a greater poet than Archilochus with the rich and disorderly abundance which follows in his train and with that outburst of the divine spirit within him which it is difficult to bring under the rules of law? Once more: in lyric poetry would you prefer to be Bacchylides rather than Pindar? And in tragedy to be Ion of Chios rather than — Sophocles? It is true that Bacchylides and Ion are faultless and entirely elegant writers of the polished school, while Pindar and Sophocles, although at times they burn everything before them as it were in their swift career, are often extinguished unaccountably and fail most lamentably. But would anyone in his senses regard all the compositions of Ion put together as an equivalent for the single play of the *Oedipus*?

34

If successful writing were to be estimated by number of merits and not by the true criterion, thus judged Hyperides would be altogether superior to Demosthenes. For he has a greater variety of accents than Demosthenes and a greater number of excellences, and like the pentathlete he falls just below the top in every branch. In all the contests he has to resign the first place to his rivals, while he maintains that place as against all ordinary persons. 2. Now Hyperides not only imitates all the strong points of Demosthenes with the exception of his composition, but he has embraced in a singular degree the excellences and graces of Lysias as well. For he talks with simplicity, where it is required, and does not adopt like Demosthenes one unvarying tone in all his utterances. He possesses the gift of characterization in a sweet and pleasant form and with a touch of piquancy. There are innumerable signs of wit in him — the most polished raillery, high-bred ease, supple skill in the contests of irony, jests not tasteless or rude after the well-known Attic manner but naturally suggested by the subject, clever ridicule, much comic power, biting satire with well-directed fun, and what may be termed an inimitable charm investing the whole. He is excellently fitted by nature to excite pity; in narrating a fable he is facile, and with his pliant spirit he is also most easily turned toward a digression (as for instance in his rather poetical presentation of the story of Leto), while he has treated his Funeral Oration in the epideictic vein with probably unequalled success. 3. Demosthenes, on the other hand, is not an apt delineator of character, he is not facile, he is anything but pliant or epideictic, he is comparatively lacking in the entire list of excellences just given. Where he forces himself to be jocular and pleasant, he does not excite laughter but rather becomes the subject of it, and when he wishes to approach the region of charm, he is all the farther removed from it. If he had attempted to write the short speech about Phryne or about Athenogenes, he would have all the more commended Hyperides to our regard. 4. The good points of the latter, however, many though they be, are wanting in elevation; they are the staid utterances of a sober-hearted man and leave the hearer unmoved, no one feeling terror when he reads Hyperides. But Demosthenes draws — as from a store — excellences allied to the highest sublimity and perfected to the utmost, the tone of lofty speech, living passions, copiousness, readiness, speed (where it is legitimate), and that power and vehemence of his which forbid approach. Having, I say, absorbed bodily within himself these mighty gifts which we may deem heaven-sent (for it would not be right to term them *human*), he thus with the noble qualities which are his own routs all comers even where the qualities he does not possess are concerned, and overpowers with thunder and with lightning the orators of every age. One could sooner face with unflinching eyes a descending thunderbolt than meet with steady gaze his bursts of passion in their swift succession.

35

But in the case of Plato and Lysias there is, as I said, a further point of difference. For not only in the degree of his excellences, but also in their number, Lysias is much inferior to Plato; and at the same time he surpasses him in his faults still more than he falls below him in his excellences. 2. What fact, then, was before the eyes of those superhuman writers who, aiming at everything that was highest in composition, contemned an all-pervading accuracy? This besides many other things, that Nature has appointed us men to be no base or ignoble animals; but when she ushers us into life and into the vast universe as into some great assembly, to be as it were spectators of the mighty whole and the keenest aspirants for honor, forthwith she implants in our souls the unconquerable love of whatever is elevated and more divine than we. 3. Wherefore not even the entire universe suffices for the thought and contemplation within the reach of the human mind, but our imaginations often pass beyond the bounds of space, and if we survey our life on every side and see how much more it everywhere abounds in what is striking, and great, and beautiful, we shall soon discern the purpose of our birth. 4. This is why, by a sort of natural impulse, we admire not the small streams, useful and pellucid though they be, but the Nile, the Danube or the Rhine, and still more the Ocean. Nor do we view the tiny flame of our own kindling (guarded in lasting purity as its light ever is) with greater awe than the celestial fires though they are often shrouded in darkness; nor do we deem it a greater marvel than the craters of Etna, whose eruptions throw up stones from its depths and great masses of rock, and at times pour forth rivers of that pure and unmixed subterranean fire. 5. In all such matters we may say that what is useful or necessary men regard as commonplace, while they reserve their admiration for that which is astounding.

36

Now as regards the manifestations of the sublime in literature, in which grandeur is never, as it sometimes is in nature, found apart from utility and advantage, it is fitting to observe at once that, though writers of this magnitude are far removed from faultlessness, they nonetheless all rise above what is mortal; that all other qualities prove their possessors to be men, but sublimity raises them near the majesty of God; and that, while immunity from errors relieves from censure, it is grandeur that excites admiration. 2. What need to add thereto that each of these supreme authors often redeems all his failures by a single sublime and happy touch, and (most important of all) that if one were to pick out and mass together the blunders of Homer, Demosthenes, Plato, and all the rest of the greatest writers, they would be found to be a very small part, nay an infinitesimal fraction, of the triumphs which those heroes achieve on every hand? This is the reason why the judgment of all posterity — a verdict which envy itself cannot convict of perversity — has brought and offered those meeds of victory which up to this day it guards intact and seems likely still to preserve,

> Long as earth's waters shall flow, and her tall trees burgeon and bloom.

3. In reply, however, to the writer who maintains that the faulty Colossus is not superior to the Spearman of Polycleitus, it is obvious to remark among many other things that in art the utmost exactitude is admired, grandeur in the works of nature; and that it is by nature that man is a being gifted with speech. In statues likeness to man is the quality required; in discourse we demand, as I said, that which transcends the human. 4. Nevertheless — and the counsel about to be given reverts to the beginning of our memoir — since freedom from failings is for the most part the successful result of art, and excellence (though it may be unevenly sustained) the result of sublim-

ity, the employment of art is in every way a fitting aid to nature; for it is the conjunction of the two which tends to ensure perfection.

Such are the decisions to which we have felt bound to come with regard to the questions proposed; but let every man cherish the view which pleases him best.

37

Closely related to Metaphors (for we must return to our point) are comparisons and similes, differing only in this respect. . . .

38

. . . such Hyperboles as: "unless you carry your brains trodden down in your heels."[59] It is necessary, therefore, to know where to fix the limit in each case; for an occasional overshooting of the mark ruins the hyperbole, and such expressions, when strained too much, lose their tension, and sometimes swing round and produce the contrary effect. 2. Isocrates, for example, fell into unaccountable puerility owing to the ambition which made him desire to describe everything with a touch of amplification. The theme of his *Panegyric* is that Athens surpasses Lacedaemon in benefits conferred upon Greece, and yet at the very outset of his speech he uses these words: "Further, language has such capacity that it is possible thereby to debase things lofty and invest things small with grandeur, and to express old things in a new way, and to discourse in ancient fashion about what has newly happened."[60] "Do you then, Isocrates," it may be asked, "mean in that way to interchange the facts of Lacedaemonian and Athenian history?" For in his eulogy of language he has, we may say, published to his hearers a preamble warning them to distrust himself. 3. Perhaps, then, as we said in dealing with figures generally, those hyperboles are best in which the very fact that they are hyperboles escapes attention. This happens when, through stress of strong emotion, they are uttered in connection with some great crisis, as is done by Thucydides in the case of those who perished in Sicily. "The Syracusans," he says, "came down to the water's edge and began the slaughter of those chiefly who were in the river, and the water at once became polluted, but nonetheless it was swallowed although muddy and mixed with blood, and to most it was still worth fighting for."[61] That a draught of blood and mud should still be worth fighting for, is rendered credible by the intensity of the emotion at a great crisis. 4. So with the passage in which Herodotus tells of those who fell at Thermopylae. "On this spot," he says, "the barbarians buried them as they defended themselves with daggers — those of them who had daggers still left — and with hands and mouths."[62] Here you may be inclined to protest against the expressions "fight with their very mouths" against men in armor, and "being buried" with darts. At the same time the narrative carries conviction; for the event does not seem to be introduced for the sake of the hyperbole, but the hyperbole to spring naturally from the event. 5. For (as I never cease to say) the deeds and passions which verge on transport are a sufficient lenitive and remedy for every audacity of speech. This is the reason why the quips of comedy, although they may be carried to the extreme of absurdity, are plausible because they are so amusing. For instance,

> Smaller his field was than a Spartan letter.

For mirth, too, is an emotion, an emotion which has its root in pleasure. 6. Hyperboles are employed in describing things small as well as great, since exaggeration is the common element in both cases. And, in a sense, ridicule is an amplification of the paltriness of things.

39

The fifth of those elements contributing to the sublime which we mentioned, my excellent friend, at the beginning, still remains to be dealt with, namely the arrangement of the words in a certain order. In regard to this, having already in two treaties sufficiently stated such results as our

[59]Demosthenes (?), *On Halonesius,* 45. [Tr.]
[60]Isocrates, *Panegyric,* 8. [Tr.]

[61]Thucydides, *Peloponnesian War* 7:84. [Tr.]
[62]Herodotus, *History* 7:225. [Tr.]

inquiry could compass, we will add, for the purpose of our present undertaking, only what is absolutely essential, namely the fact that harmonious arrangement is not only a natural source of persuasion and pleasure among men but also a wonderful instrument of lofty utterance and of passion. 2. For does not the flute instill certain emotions into its hearers and as it were make them beside themselves and full of frenzy, and supplying a rhythmical movement constrain the listener to move rhythmically in accordance therewith and to conform himself to the melody, although he may be utterly ignorant of music? Yes, and the tones of the harp, although in themselves they signify nothing at all, often cast a wonderful spell, as you know, over an audience by means of the variations of sounds, by their pulsation against one another, and by their mingling in concert. 3. And yet these are mere semblances and spurious copies of persuasion, not (as I have said) genuine activities of human nature. Are we not, then, to hold that composition (being a harmony of that language which is implanted by nature in man and which appeals not to the hearing only but to the soul itself), since it calls forth manifold shapes of words, thoughts, deeds, beauty, melody, all of them born at our birth and growing with our growth, and since by means of the blending and variation of its own tones it seeks to introduce into the minds of those who are present the emotion which affects the speaker, and since it always brings the audience to share in it and by the building of phrase upon phrase raises a sublime and harmonious structure are we not, I say, to hold that harmony by these selfsame means allures us and invariably disposes us to stateliness and dignity and elevation and every emotion which it contains within itself, gaining absolute mastery over our minds? But it is folly to dispute concerning matters which are generally admitted, since experience is proof sufficient. 4. An example of a conception which is usually thought sublime and is really admirable is that which Demosthenes associates with the decree: "This decree caused the danger which then beset the city to pass by just as a cloud."[63] But it owes its happy sound no less to the harmony than to the thought itself. For the thought is expressed throughout in dactylic rhythms, and these are most noble and productive of sublimity; and therefore it is that they constitute the heroic, the finest meter that we know. For if you derange the words of the sentence and transpose them in whatever way you will, as for example "This decree just as a cloud caused the danger of the time to pass by"; nay, if you cut off a single syllable only and say "caused to pass by as a cloud," you will perceive to what an extent harmony is in unison with sublimity. For the very words "just as a cloud" begin with a long rhythm, which consists of four metrical beats; but if one syllable is cut off and we read "as a cloud," we immediately maim the sublimity by the abbreviation. Conversely, if you elongate the word and write "caused to pass by just as if a cloud," it means the same thing, but no longer falls with the same effect upon the ear, inasmuch as the abrupt grandeur of the passage loses its energy and tension through the lengthening of the concluding syllables.

[63]Demosthenes, *On the Crown,* 188. [Tr.]

40

Among the chief causes of the sublime in speech, as in the structure of the human body, is the collocation of members, a single one of which if severed from another possesses in itself nothing remarkable, but all united together make a full and perfect organism. So the constituents of grandeur, when separated from one another, carry with them sublimity in distraction this way and that, but when formed into a body by association and when further encircled in a chain of harmony they become sonorous by their very rotundity; and in periods sublimity is, as it were, a contribution made by a multitude. 2. We have, however, sufficiently shown that many writers and poets who possess no natural sublimity and are perhaps even wanting in elevation have nevertheless, although employing for the most part common and popular words with no striking associations of their own, by merely joining and fitting these together, secured dignity and distinction and the appearance of freedom from meanness. Instances will be furnished by Philistus among many others, by Aristophanes in certain passages, by Euripides in most. 3. In the last-mentioned author, Heracles, after the scene in which he slays his children, uses the words:

> Full-fraught am I with woes — no space for more.[64]

The expression is a most ordinary one, but it has gained elevation through the aptness of the structure of the line. If you shape the sentence in a different way, you will see this plainly, the fact being that Euripides is a poet in virtue of his power of composition rather than of his invention. 4. In the passage which describes Dirce torn away by the bull:

> Whitherso'er he turned
> Swift wheeling round, he haled and hurled withal
> Dame, rock, oak, intershifted ceaselessly,

the conception itself is a fine one, but it has been rendered more forcible by the fact that the harmony is not hurried or carried as it were on rollers, but the words act as buttresses for one another and find support in the pauses, and issue finally in a well-grounded sublimity.

41

There is nothing in the sphere of the sublime that is so lowering as broken and agitated movement of language, such as is characteristic of pyrrhics and trochees and dichorees, which fall altogether to the level of dance-music.[65] For all overrhythmical writing is at once felt to be affected and finical and wholly lacking in passion owing to the monotony of its superficial polish. 2. And the worst of it all is that, just as petty lays draw their hearer away from the point and compel his attention to themselves, so also overrhythmical style does not communicate the feeling of the words but simply the feeling of the rhythm. Sometimes, indeed, the listeners knowing beforehand the due terminations stamp their feet in time with the speaker, and as in a dance give the right step in anticipation. 3. In like manner those words are destitute of sublimity which lie too close together, and are cut up into short and tiny syllables, and are held together as if with wooden bolts by sheer inequality and ruggedness.

42

Further, excessive concision of expression tends to lower the sublime, since grandeur is marred when the thought is brought into too narrow a compass. Let this be understood not of proper compression, but of what is absolutely petty and cut into segments. For concision curtails the sense, but brevity goes straight to the mark. It is plain that, vice versa, prolixities are frigid, for so is everything that resorts to unseasonable length.

43

Triviality of expression is also apt to disfigure sublimity. In Herodotus, for example, the tempest is described with marvelous effect in all its details, but the passage surely contains some words below the dignity of the subject. The following may serve as an instance — "when the sea seethed."[66] The word "seethed" detracts greatly from the sublimity because it is an ill-sounding one. Further, "the wind," he says, "grew fagged," and those who clung to the spars met "an unpleasant end."[67] The expression "grew fagged" is lacking in dignity, being vulgar; and the word "unpleasant" is inappropriate to so great a disaster. 2. Similarly, when Theopompus had dressed out in marvelous fashion the descent of the Persian king upon Egypt, he spoilt the whole by some petty words. "For which of the cities (he says) or which of the tribes in Asia did not send envoys to the Great King? Which of the products of the earth or of the achievements of art was not, in all its beauty or preciousness, brought as an offering to his presence? Consider the multitude of costly coverlets and mantles, in purple or white

[64]Euripides, *Heracles*, 1245. [Tr.] The subsequent passage is from a lost play. [Ed.]

[65]A pyrrhic foot was made up of two short syllables; a trochee was a long syllable followed by a short; a dichoric foot had four syllables arranged long-short-long-short. These variants on the nobler dactyls and iambs were thought to lower the tone. [Ed.]

[66]Herodotus, *History* 7:188. [Tr.]

[67]Herodotus, *History* 7:191; 8:13. [Tr.]

or embroidery; the multitude of pavilions of gold furnished with all things useful; the multitude, too, of tapestries and costly couches. Further, gold and silver plate richly wrought, and goblets and mixing bowls, some of which you might have seen set with precious stones, and others finished with care and at great price. In addition to all this, countless myriads of Greek and barbaric weapons, and beasts of burden beyond all reckoning and victims fattened for slaughter, and many bushels of condiments, and many bags and sacks and sheets of papyrus and all other useful things, and an equal number of pieces of salted flesh from all manner of victims, so that the piles of them were so great that those who were approaching from a distance took them to be hills and eminences confronting them." 3. He runs off from the more elevated to the more lowly, whereas he should, on the contrary, have risen higher and higher. With his wonderful description of the whole outfit he mixes bags and condiments and sacks, and conveys the impression of a confectioner's shop! For just as if, in the case of those very adornments, between the golden vessels and the jeweled mixing bowls and the silver plate and the pavilions of pure gold and the goblets, a man were to bring and set in the midst paltry bags and sacks, the proceeding would have been offensive to the eye, so do such words when introduced out of season constitute deformities and as it were blots on the diction. 4. He might have described the scene in broad outline just as he says that hills blocked their way, and with regard to the preparations generally have spoken of "wagons and camels and the multitude of beasts of burden carrying everything that ministers to the luxury and enjoyment of the table," or have used some such expression as "piles of all manner of grain and things which conduce preeminently to good cookery and comfort of body," or if he must necessarily put it in so uncompromising a way, he might have said that "all the dainties of cooks and caterers were there." 5. In lofty passages we ought not to descend to sordid and contemptible language unless constrained by some overpowering necessity, but it is fitting that we should use words worthy of the subject and imitate nature the artificer of man, for she has not placed in full view our grosser parts or the means of purging our frame, but has hidden them away as far as was possible, and as Xenophon says, has put their channels in the remotest background, so as not to sully the beauty of the entire creature. 6. But enough; there is no need to enumerate, one by one, the things which produce triviality. For since we have previously indicated those qualities which render style noble and lofty, it is evident that their opposites will for the most part make it low and base.

44

It remains however (as I will not hesitate to add, in recognition of your love of knowledge) to clear up, my dear Terentianus, a question which a certain philosopher has recently mooted. "I wonder," he says, "as no doubt do many others, how it happens that in our time there are men who have the gift of persuasion to the utmost extent, and are well fitted for public life, and are keen and ready, and particularly rich in all the charms of language, yet there no longer arise really lofty and transcendent natures unless quite exceptionally. So great and worldwide a dearth of high utterance attends our age." 2. "Can it be," he continued, "that we are to accept the trite explanation that democracy is the kind nursing-mother of genius, and that literary power may be said to share its rise and fall with democracy and democracy alone? For freedom, it is said, has power to feed the imaginations of the lofty-minded and to inspire hope, and where it prevails there spreads abroad the eagerness of mutual rivalry and the emulous pursuit of the foremost place. 3. Moreover, owing to the prizes which are open to all under popular government, the mental excellences of the orator are continually exercised and sharpened, and as it were rubbed bright, and shine forth (as it is natural they should) with all the freedom which inspires the doings of the state. Today," he went on, "we seem in our boyhood to learn the lessons of a righteous servitude, being all but enswathed in its customs and observances, when our thoughts are yet young and tender, and never tasting the fairest and most productive source of eloquence (by which," he added, "I mean freedom), so that we emerge in no other guise than that of sublime flatterers."

4. This is the reason, he maintained, why no slave ever becomes an orator, although all other faculties may belong to menials. In the slave there immediately burst out signs of fettered liberty of speech, of the dungeon as it were, of a man habituated to buffetings. 5. "For the day of slavery," as Homer has it, "takes away half our manhood."[68] "Just as," he proceeded, "the cages (if what I hear is true) in which are kept the Pygmies, commonly called *nani,* not only hinder the growth of the creatures confined within them, but actually attenuate them through the bonds which beset their bodies, so one has aptly termed all servitude (though it be most righteous) the cage of the soul and a public prisonhouse." 6. I answered him thus: "It is easy, my good sir, and characteristic of human nature, to find fault with the age in which one lives. But consider whether it may not be true that it is not the world's peace that ruins great natures, but far rather this war illimitable which holds our desires in its grasp, aye, and further still those passions which occupy as with troops our present age and utterly harry and plunder it. For the love of money (a disease from which we all now suffer sorely) and the love of pleasure make us their thralls, or rather, as one may say, drown us body and soul in the depths, the love of riches being a malady which makes men petty, and the love of pleasure one which makes them most ignoble. 7. On reflection I cannot discover how it is possible for us, if we value boundless wealth so highly, or (to speak more truly) deify it, to avoid allowing the entrance into our souls of the evils which are inseparable from it. For vast and unchecked wealth is accompanied, in close conjunction and step for step as they say, by extravagance, and as soon as the former opens the gates of cities and houses, the latter immediately enters and abides. And when time has passed the pair build nests in the lives of men, as the wise say, and quickly give themselves to the rearing of offspring, and breed ostentation, and vanity, and luxury, no spurious progeny of theirs, but only too legitimate. If these children of wealth are permitted to come to maturity, straightway they beget in the soul inexorable masters — insolence, and lawlessness, and shamelessness. 8. This must necessarily happen, and men will no longer lift up their eyes or have any further regard for fame, but the ruin of such lives will gradually reach its complete consummation and sublimities of soul fade and wither away and become contemptible, when men are lost in admiration of their own mortal parts and omit to exalt that which is immortal. 9. For a man who has once accepted a bribe for a judicial decision cannot be an unbiased and upright judge of what is just and honorable (since to the man who is venal his own interests must seem honorable and just), and the same is true where the entire life of each of us is ordered by bribes, and huntings after the death of others, and the laying of ambushes for legacies, while gain from any and every source we purchase — each one of us — at the price of life itself, being the slaves of pleasure. In an age which is ravaged by plagues so sore, is it possible for us to imagine that there is still left an unbiased and incorruptible judge of works that are great and likely to reach posterity, or is it not rather the case that all are influenced in their decisions by the passion for gain? 10. Nay, it is perhaps better for men like ourselves to be ruled than to be free, since our appetites, if let loose without restraint upon our neighbors like beasts from a cage, would set the world on fire with deeds of evil. 11. Summing up, I maintained that among the banes of the natures which our age produces must be reckoned that half-heartedness in which the life of all of us with few exceptions is passed, for we do not labor or exert ourselves except for the sake of praise and pleasure, never for those solid benefits which are a worthy object of our own efforts and the respect of others. 12. But " 'tis best to leave these riddles unresolved,"[69] and to proceed to what next presents itself, namely the subject of the Passions, about which I previously undertook to write in a separate treatise. These form, as it seems to me, a material part of discourse generally and of the Sublime itself. . . .

[68]Homer, *Odyssey* 17:322. [Tr.]

[69]Euripides, *Electra,* 379. [Tr.]

Plotinus

204?–270 A.D.

Plotinus, the greatest of the Neoplatonists, was born of Roman parents in the Egyptian city of Lycopolis. To one who has read Plato, Plotinus's ideas will be alternately familiar and strange. What is familiar is his metaphysics, the structure of the universe. Like Plato, Plotinus posits an Ideal world (which he calls *ekei,* "There") as the paradigm for the physical world here below. What is strange is encountering these ideas unaccompanied by the classical clarity of Plato. Like other Neoplatonists Plotinus derives not only from Plato but also from the Gnostics of Alexandria and the Eastern Mystery cults of Dionysus or Mithras. He gives the impression of an improbable combination of Plato and Zen: This is inaccurate historically, but there is an oriental flavor to his thought.

Plotinus's thought is based on the higher Ideas, which he views in a complex hierarchy. At the top is The One, the principle of existence itself, Plotinus's God-term. The One gives rise to the Intellectual-Principle, by which things are knowable and differentiable; the Intellectual-Principle is the basis of beauty in the universe. Similarly the Intellectual-Principle gives rise to the All-Soul, which is the paradigm for consciousness here below. In his treatise "On the Intellectual Beauty," Plotinus explains that the Greek gods Ouranos, Kronos, and Zeus are myths of these three basic Ideas, though the Ideas give birth one to the other not through temporal but through logical priority. Below the All-Soul is the Nature-Principle, and it is this that gives rise to matter in all its diverse forms.

Plotinus is not primarily an aesthetician, and when he discusses art, he generally thinks first about painting and sculpture rather than about poetry. Nevertheless, his ideas are a useful adjunct to Plato's because, unlike Plato, Plotinus is basically sympathetic to art. For Plotinus as for Plato, the artist imitates but does not *necessarily* copy the things of this world. The artist may represent his grasp of an Idea within the medium of his art: "Thus Phidias wrought the [Olympian] *Zeus* upon no model among things of sense but by apprehending what form Zeus must take if he chose to become manifest to sight." Art at its best can be a way of knowing the Ideas. In fact, it is the artist's grasp of higher things that lends quality to his or her work.

This does not mean, however, that the artist should be a mathematician or a philosopher, for art does not derive from reason. Like Benedetto Croce at the beginning of the twentieth century, Plotinus insists that the work of art exists primarily as the intuition of the artist and is known prior to reason. (Plotinus calls it "one totality . . . a unity working out into detail . . . a distinct image, . . . not an aggregate of discursive reasoning and detailed willing.") Beauty exists in its highest degree only There, in lesser degree as the intuition within the soul of the artist, and in still lesser degree ("insofar as it has subdued the resistance of the material") in the concrete and physical work the artist makes. But even natural beauty is primarily a quality of soul: Even beautiful women, Plotinus suggests, are beautiful only insofar as their flesh projects a beautiful spirit.

The most mystical part of "On the Intellectual Beauty" is found in sections 10 and 11, where Plotinus discusses a series of spiritual exercises that help to bring the world of There within the self. Thus, he says, "a man filled with a god — possessed by Apollo or by one of the Muses — need no longer look outside for his vision of the divine being; it is but finding the strength to see divinity within." In the *Ion* Plato discussed *enthousiasmós,* or inspiration, as a form of possession given to favored mortals; for Plotinus this mystical state of unity with the Divine lies within the reach of everyone.

In the first stage of mystical union, the Divine invades the subject as a glorified self-image. In its final stages, the self fades out completely as the subject becomes completely identified with divine power and will. This process may suggest why egoism and temperament are so often found in the incomplete artist, and why the most supreme creators — Shakespeare, Rembrandt, Mozart — seem to show in their art not mere personality but rather a transcendent objectivity and clarity.

Selected Bibliography

Armstrong, A. H. *The Architecture of the Intelligible Universe in the Philosophy of Plotinus.* Cambridge: Cambridge University Press, 1940.

Asti Vera, Carlos. *Arte y realidad en la estetica de Plotino.* San Antonio de Padua: Ediciones Castaneda, 1978.

Atkinson, M. J. *A Commentary on Plotinus.* New York: Oxford University Press, 1983.

Bishop, Donald. *Mysticism and the Mystical Experience.* Selinsgrove, PA: Susquehanna University Press, 1995.

Blumenthal, H. J. *Plotinus's Psychology: His Doctrines of the Embodied Soul.* The Hague: Nijhoff, 1971.

Deck, John N. *Nature, Contemplation and the One.* Toronto: University of Toronto Press, 1967.

Gerson, Lloyd. *Cambridge Companion to Plotinus.* Cambridge: Cambridge University Press, 1996.

Harris, R. Baines. *The Structure of Being: A Neoplatonic Approach.* Norfolk: International Society for Neoplatonic Studies, 1982.

Inge, William R. *The Philosophy of Plotinus.* 1918; Hamden, Conn.: Greenwood, 1968.

Mead, G. R. S. *The Spiritual World of Plotinus.* London: Quest, 1920.

O'Daly, Gerard. *Plotinus's Philosophy of the Self.* New York: Barnes and Noble, 1973.

Underhill, Evelyn. "The Mysticism of Plotinus." *Quarterly Review* 231 (1919): 479–97.

Wallis, R. T. *Neoplatonism.* London: Duckworth, 1995.

On the Intellectual Beauty

1

It is a principle with us that one who has attained to the vision of the Intellectual Beauty and grasped the beauty of the Authentic Intellect will be able also to come to understand the Father and Transcendent of that Divine Being. It concerns us, then, to try to see and say, for ourselves and as far as such matters may be told, how the Beauty of the divine Intellect and of the Intellectual Kosmos may be revealed to contemplation.

Let us go to the realm of magnitudes: Suppose two blocks of stone lying side by side: one is unpatterned, quite untouched by art; the other has been minutely wrought by the craftsman's hands into some statue of god or man, a Grace or a Muse, or if a human being, not a portrait but a creation in which the sculptor's art has concentrated all loveliness.

Now it must be seen that the stone thus brought under the artist's hand to the beauty of form is beautiful not as stone — for so the crude block would be as pleasant — but in virtue of the form or idea introduced by the art. This form is not in the material; it is in the designer before ever it enters the stone; and the artificer holds it not by his equipment of eyes and hands but by his participation in his art. The beauty, therefore, exists in a far higher state in the art; for it does not come over integrally into the work; that original beauty is not transferred; what comes over is a derivative and a minor: and even that shows itself upon the statue not integrally and with entire realization of intention but only insofar as it has subdued the resistance of the material.

Art, then, creating in the image of its own nature and content, and working by the Idea or Reason-Principle of the beautiful object it is to produce, must itself be beautiful in a far higher and purer degree since it is the seat and source of that beauty, indwelling in the art, which must naturally be more complete than any comeliness of the external. In the degree in which the beauty is diffused by entering into matter, it is so much the weaker than that concentrated in unity; everything that reaches outwards is the less for it, strength less strong, heat less hot, every power less potent, and so beauty less beautiful.

Then again every prime cause must be, within itself, more powerful than its effect can be: the musical does not derive from an unmusical source but from music; and so the art exhibited in the material work derives from an art yet higher.

Still the arts are not to be slighted on the ground that they create by imitation of natural objects; for, to begin with, these natural objects are themselves imitations; then we must recognize that they give no bare reproduction of the thing seen but go back to the Ideas from which Nature itself derives, and, furthermore, that much of their work is all their own; they are holders of beauty and add where nature is lacking. Thus Phidias wrought the Zeus upon no model among things of sense but by apprehending what form Zeus must take if he chose to become manifest to sight.[1]

2

But let us leave the arts and consider those works produced by Nature and admitted to be naturally beautiful which the creations of art are charged with imitating, all reasoning life and unreasoning things alike, but especially the consummate among them, where the moulder and maker has subdued the material and given the form he desired. Now what is the beauty here?[2] It has nothing to do with the blood or the menstrual process: either there is also a color and form apart from all this or there is nothing unless sheer ugliness or (at best) a bare recipient, as it were the mere Matter of beauty.

Translated by Stephen McKenna.

[1]Here Plotinus distinguishes his position from Plato's in the *Republic,* where the artist was said to imitate material objects, not ideas. [Ed.]

[2]Plotinus continues his argument that Beauty resides in ideal form rather than in matter or in the process of origin. [Ed.]

Whence shone forth the beauty of Helen, battle-sought; or of all those women like in loveliness to Aphrodite; or of Aphrodite herself; or of any human being that has been perfect in beauty; or of any of these gods manifest to sight, or unseen but carrying what would be beauty if we saw?

In all these is it not the Idea, something of that realm but communicated to the produced from within the producer just as in works of art, we held, it is communicated from the arts to their creations? Now we can surely not believe that, while the made thing and the Idea thus impressed upon Matter are beautiful, yet the Idea not so alloyed but resting still with the creator — the Idea primal, immaterial, firmly a unity — is not Beauty.

If material extension were in itself the ground of beauty, then the creating principle, being without extension, could not be beautiful: but beauty cannot be made to depend upon magnitude since, whether in a large object or a small, the one Idea equally moves and forms the mind by its inherent power. A further indication is that as long as the object remains outside us we know nothing of it; it affects us by entry; but only as an Idea can it enter through the eyes which are not of scope to take an extended mass: we are, no doubt, simultaneously possessed of the magnitude which, however, we take in not as mass but by an elaboration upon the presented form.

Then again the principle producing the beauty must be, itself, ugly, neutral or beautiful: ugly, it could not produce the opposite; neutral, why should its product be the one rather than the other? The Nature, then, which creates things so lovely must be itself of a far earlier beauty; we, undisciplined in discernment of the inward, knowing nothing of it, run after the outer, never understanding that it is the inner which stirs us; we are in the case of one who sees his own reflection but not realizing whence it comes goes in pursuit of it.

But that the thing we are pursuing is something different and that the beauty is not in the concrete object is manifest from the beauty there is in matters of study, in conduct and custom; briefly in soul or mind. And it is precisely here that the greater beauty lies, perceived whenever you look to the wisdom in a man and delight in it, not wasting attention on the face, which may be hideous, but passing all appearance by and catching only at the inner comeliness, the truly personal; if you are still unmoved and cannot acknowledge beauty under such conditions, then looking to your own inner being you will find no beauty to delight you and it will be futile in that state to seek the greater vision, for you will be questing it through the ugly and impure.

This is why such matters are not spoken of to everyone; you, if you are conscious of beauty within, remember.

3

Thus there is in the Nature-Principle itself an Ideal archetype of the beauty that is found in material forms and, of that archetype again, the still more beautiful archetype in Soul, source of that in Nature. In the proficient soul this is brighter and of more advanced loveliness: adorning the soul and bringing to it a light from that greater light which is beauty primally, its immediate presence sets the soul reflecting upon the quality of this prior, and archetype which has no such entries, and is present nowhere but remains in itself alone, and thus is not even to be called a Reason-Principle but is the creative source of the very first Reason-Principle, which is the Beauty to which Soul serves as Matter.

This prior, then, is the Intellectual-Principle, the veritable, abiding and not fluctuant since not taking intellectual quality from outside itself. By what image thus, can we represent it? We have nowhere to go but to what is less. Only from itself can we take an image of it; that is, there can be no representation of it, except in the sense that we represent gold by some portion of gold — purified, either actually or mentally, if it be impure — insisting at the same time that this is not the total thing gold, but merely the particular gold of a particular parcel. In the same way we learn in this matter from the purified Intellect in ourselves or, if you like, from the gods and the glory of the Intellect in them.

For assuredly all the gods are august and beautiful in a beauty beyond our speech. And what makes them so? Intellect; and especially Intellect operating within them (the divine sun and stars) to visibility. It is not through the loveliness of their corporeal forms: even those that have body are not gods by that beauty; it is in virtue of Intellect that they, too, are gods, and as gods beautiful. They do not veer between wisdom and folly: in the immunity of Intellect unmoving and pure, they are wise always, all-knowing, taking cognizance not of the human but of their own being and of all that lies within the contemplation of Intellect. Those of them whose dwelling is in the heavens are ever in this meditation — what task prevents them? — and from afar they look, too, into that further heaven by a lifting of the head. The Gods belonging to that higher Heaven itself, they whose station is upon it and in it, see and know in virtue of their omnipresence to it. For all There is heaven; earth is heaven, and sea heaven; and animal and plant and man; all is the heavenly content of that heaven: and the Gods in it, despising neither men nor anything else that is there where all is of the heavenly order, traverse all that country and all space in peace.

4

To "live at ease" is There;[3] and to these divine beings verity is mother and nurse, existence and sustenance; all that is not of process but of authentic being they see, and themselves in all: for all is transparent, nothing dark, nothing resistant; everything being is lucid to every other in breadth and depth; light runs through light. And each of them contains all within itself, and at the same time sees all in every other, so that everywhere there is all, and all is all and each all, and infinite the glory. Each of them is great; the small is great; the sun, There, is all the stars; and every star, again, is all the stars and sun. While some one manner of being is dominant in each, all are mirrored in every other.

Movement There is pure (as self-caused) for the moving principle is not a separate thing to complicate it as it speeds.

So, too, Repose is not troubled, for there is no admixture of the unstable; and the Beauty is all beauty since it is not merely resident (as an attribute or addition) in some beautiful object. Each There walks upon no alien soul; its place is its essential self; and, as each moves, so to speak, toward what is Above, it is attended by the very ground from which it starts: there is no distinguishing between the Being and the Place; all is Intellect, the Principle and the ground on which it stands, alike. Thus we might think that our visible sky (the ground or place of the stars), lit, as it is, produces the light which reaches us from it, though of course this is really produced by the stars (as it were, by the Principles of light alone not also by the ground as the analogy would require).

In our realm all is part rising from part and nothing can be more than partial; but There each being is an eternal product of a whole and is at once a whole and an individual manifesting as part but, to the keen vision There, known for the whole it is.

The myth of Lynceus seeing into the very deeps of the earth tells us of those eyes in the divine. No weariness overtakes this vision which yet brings no such satiety as would call for its ending; for there never was a void to be filled so that, with the fullness and the attainment of purpose, the sense of sufficiency be induced: nor is there any such incongruity within the divine that one Being there could be repulsive to another: and of course all There are unchangeable. This absence of satisfaction means only a satisfaction leading to no distaste for that which produces it; to see is to look the more, since for them to continue in the contemplation of an infinite self and of infinite objects is but to acquiesce in the bidding of their nature.

Life, pure, is never a burden; how then could there be weariness There where the living is most noble? That very life is wisdom, not a wisdom built up by reasonings but complete from the beginning, suffering no lack which could set it inquiring, a wisdom primal, unborrowed, not something added to the Being, but its very essence. No wisdom, thus, is greater; this is the authentic knowing, assessor to the divine Intellect as projected into manifestation simultaneously with it; thus, in the symbolic saying, Justice is assessor to Zeus.

[3]Just as "There" is Plotinus's term for the transcendent realm within and beyond matter, "Here" or "our realm" is the world of matter and time. [Ed.]

(Perfect wisdom) for all the Principles of this order, dwelling There, are as it were visible images projected from themselves, so that all becomes an object of contemplation to contemplators immeasurably blessed. The greatness and power of the wisdom There we may know from this, that it embraces all the real Beings, and has made all and all follow it, and yet that it is itself those beings, which sprang into being with it, so that all is one and the essence There is wisdom. If we have failed to understand, it is that we have thought of knowledge as a mass of theorems and an accumulation of propositions, though that is false even for our sciences of the sense-realm. But in case this should be questioned, we may leave our own sciences for the present, and deal with the knowing in the Supreme at which Plato glances where he speaks of "that knowledge which is not a stranger in something strange to it"—though in what sense, he leaves us to examine and declare, if we boast ourselves worthy of the discussion. This is probably our best starting point.

5

All that comes to be, work of nature or of craft, some wisdom has made: everywhere a wisdom presides at a making.

No doubt the wisdom of the artist may be the guide of the work; it is sufficient explanation of the wisdom exhibited in the arts; but the artist himself goes back, after all, to that wisdom in Nature which is embodied in himself; and this is not a wisdom built up of theorems but one totality, not a wisdom consisting of manifold detail coordinated into a unity but rather a unity working out into detail.

Now, if we could think of this as the primal wisdom, we need look no further, since, at that, we have discovered a principle which is neither a derivative nor a "stranger in something strange to it." But if we are told that, while this Reason-Principle is in Nature, yet Nature itself is its source, we ask how Nature came to possess it; and, if Nature derived it from some other source, we ask what that other source may be; if, on the contrary, the principle is self-sprung, we need look no further: but if (as we assume) we are referred to the Intellectual-Principle, we must make clear whether the Intellectual-Principle engendered the wisdom: if we learn that it did, we ask whence: if from itself, then inevitably, it is itself Wisdom.

The true Wisdom, then (found to be identical with the Intellectual-Principle) is Real Being; and Real Being is Wisdom; it is wisdom that gives value to Real Being; and Being is Real in virtue of its origin in wisdom. It follows that all forms of existence not possessing wisdom are, indeed, Beings in right of the wisdom which went to their forming, but, as not in themselves possessing it, are not Real Beings.

We cannot therefore think that the divine Beings of that sphere, or the other supremely blessed There, need look to our apparatus of science: all of that realm (the very Beings themselves), all is noble image, such images as we may conceive to lie within the soul of the wise—but There not as inscription but as authentic existence. The ancients had this is mind when they declared the Ideas to be Beings, Essentials.

6

Similarly, as it seems to me, the wise of Egypt—whether in precise knowledge or by a prompting of nature—indicated the truth where, in their effort toward philosophical statement, they left aside the writing forms that take in the detail of words and sentences—those characters that represent sounds and convey the propositions of reasoning—and drew pictures instead, engraving in the temple inscriptions a separate image for every separate item: thus they exhibited the mode in which the Supreme goes forth.

For each manifestation of knowledge and wisdom is a distinct image, an object in itself, an immediate unity, not an aggregate of discursive reasoning and detailed willing. Later, from this wisdom in unity there appears, in another form of being, an image, already less compact, which announces the original in an outward stage and seeks the causes by which things are such that the wonder rises how a generated world can be so excellent.

For one who knows must declare his wonder that this Wisdom, while not itself containing the causes by which Being exists and takes such excellence, yet imparts them to the entities produced in Being's realm. This excellence, whose necessity is scarcely or not at all manifest to search, exists, if we could but find it out, before all searching and reasoning.

What I say may be considered in one chief thing, and thence applied to all the particular entities.

7

Consider the universe: we are agreed that its existence and its nature come to it from beyond itself; are we, now, to imagine that its maker first thought it out in detail — the earth, and its necessary situation in the middle; water and, again, its position as lying upon the earth; all the other elements and objects up to the sky in due place and order; living beings with their appropriate forms as we know them, their inner organs and their outer limbs — and that having thus appointed every item beforehand, he then set about the execution?

Such designing was not even possible; how could the plan for a universe come to one that had never looked outward? Nor could he work on material gathered from elsewhere as our craftsmen do, using hands and tools; feet and hands are of the later order.

One way, only, remains: all things must exist in something else; of that prior — since there is no obstacle, all being continuous within the realm of reality — there has suddenly appeared a sign, an image, whether given forth directly or through the ministry of soul or of some phase of soul, matters nothing for the moment: thus the entire aggregate of existence springs from the divine world, in greater beauty There because There unmingled but mingled here.

From the beginning to end all is gripped by the Forms of the Intellectual Realm: Matter itself is held by the Ideas of the elements and to these Ideas are added other Ideas and others again, so that it is hard to work down to crude Matter beneath all that sheathing of Idea. Indeed since Matter itself is, in its degree, an Idea — the lowest — all this universe is Idea and there is nothing that is not Idea as the archetype was. And all is made silently, since nothing had part in the making but Being and Idea — a further reason why creation went without toil. The Exemplar was the Idea of an All, and so an All must come into being.

Thus nothing stood in the way of the Idea, and even now it dominates, despite all the clash of things: the creation is not hindered on its way even now; it stands firm in virtue of being All. To me, moreover, it seems that if we ourselves were archetypes, Ideas, veritable Being, and the Idea with which we construct here were our veritable Essence, then our creative power too would toillessly effect its purpose: as man now stands, he does not produce in his work a true image of himself: become man, he has ceased to be the All; ceasing to be man — we read — "he soars aloft and administers the Kosmos entire"; restored to the All he is maker of the All.

But — to our immediate purpose — it is possible to give a reason why the earth is set in the midst and why it is round and why the ecliptic runs precisely as it does, but, looking to the creating principle, we cannot say that because this was the way, therefore things were so planned: we can say only that because the All is what it is, therefore there is a total of good; the causing principle, we might put it, reached the conclusion before all formal reasoning and not from any premises, not by sequence or plan but before either, since all of that order is later, all reason, demonstration, persuasion.

Since there is a Source, all the created must spring from it and in accordance with it; and we are rightly told not to go seeking the causes impelling a Source to produce, especially when this is the perfectly sufficient Source and identical with the Term: a Source which is Source and Term must be the All-Unity, complete in itself.

8

This then is Beauty primally: it is entire and omnipresent as an entirety; and therefore in none of its parts or members lacking in beauty; beautiful thus beyond denial. Certainly it cannot be anything (be, for example, Beauty) without being wholly that thing; it can be nothing which it is to possess partially or in which it utterly fails (and therefore it must entirely be Beauty entire).

If this principle were not beautiful, what other could be? Its prior does not deign to be beautiful; that which is the first to manifest itself — Form and object of vision to the intellect — cannot but be lovely to see. It is to indicate this that Plato, drawing on something well within our observation, represents the Creator as approving the work he has achieved: the intention is to make us feel the lovable beauty of the autotype and of the Divine Idea; for to admire a representation is to admire the original upon which it was made.

It is not surprising if we fail to recognize what is passing within us: lovers, and those in general that admire beauty here, do not stay to reflect that it is to be traced, as of course it must be, to the Beauty There. That the admiration of the Demiurge is to be referred to the Ideal Exemplar is deliberately made evident by the rest of the passage: "He admired; and determined to bring the work into still closer likeness with the Exemplar": he makes us feel the magnificent beauty of the Exemplar by telling us that the Beauty sprung from this world is, itself, a copy from That.[4]

And indeed if the divine did not exist, the transcendently beautiful, in a beauty beyond all thought, what could be lovelier than the things we see? Certainly no reproach can rightly be brought against this world save only that it is not That.

9

Let us, then, make a mental picture of our universe: each member shall remain what it is, distinctly apart; yet all is to form, as far as possible, a complete unity so that whatever comes into view shall show as if it were the surface of the orb over all, bringing immediately with it the vision, on the one plane, of the sun and of all the stars with earth and sea and all living things as if exhibited upon a transparent globe.

Bring this vision actually before your sight, so that there shall be in your mind the gleaming representation of a sphere, a picture holding all the things of the universe moving or in repose or (as in reality) some at rest, some in motion. Keep this sphere before you, and from it image another, a sphere stripped of magnitude and of spatial differences; cast out your inborn sense of Matter, taking care not merely to attenuate it: call on God, maker of the sphere whose image you now hold, and pray Him to enter. And may He come bringing His own Universe with all the Gods that dwell in it — He who is the one God and all the gods, where each is all, blending into a unity, distinct in powers but all one god in virtue of that one divine power of many facets.

More truly, this is the one God who is all the gods; for, in the coming to be of all those, this, the one, has suffered no diminishing. He and all have one existence, while each again is distinct. It is distinction by state without interval: there is no outward form to set one here and another there and to prevent any from being an entire identity; yet there is no sharing of parts from one to another. Nor is each of those divine wholes a power in fragment, a power totaling to the sum of the measurable segments: the divine is one all-power, reaching out to infinity, powerful to infinity: and so great is God that his very members are infinites. What place can be named to which He does not reach?

Great, too, is this firmament of ours and all the powers constellated within it, but it would be greater still, unspeakably, but that there is inbound in it something of the petty power of body; no doubt the powers of fire and other bodily substances might themselves be thought very great, but in fact, it is through their failure in the true power that we see them burning, destroying, wearing things away, and slaving toward the production of life; they destroy because they are themselves in process of destruction, and they produce because they belong to the realm of the produced.

The power in that other world has merely Being and Beauty of Being. Beauty without Being could not be, nor Being voided of Beauty: abandoned of Beauty, Being loses something of its essence. Being is desirable because it is identical with Beauty; and Beauty is loved because it is Being. How then can we debate which is the cause of the other, where the nature is one? The very figment of Being needs some imposed image of Beauty to make it possible, and even to ensure its existence; it exists to the degree in which it has taken some share in the beauty of Idea; and the more deeply it has drawn on this,

[4]The Demiurge is the creator of the world in Plato's *Timaeus*, 40. [Ed.]

the less imperfect it is, precisely because the nature which is essentially the beautiful has entered into it the more intimately.

10

This is why Zeus, although the oldest of the gods and their sovereign, advances first (in the Phaidros myth) toward that vision, followed by gods and demigods and such souls as are of strength to see.[5] That Being appears before them from some unseen place and rising loftily over them pours its light upon all things, so that all gleams in its radiance; it upholds some beings, and they see; the lower are dazzled and turn away, unfit to gaze upon that sun, the trouble falling the more heavily on those most remote.

Of those looking upon that Being and its content, and able to see, all take something but not all the same vision always: intently gazing, one sees the fount and principle of Justice, another is filled with the sight of Moral Wisdom, the original of that quality as found, sometimes at least, among men, copied by them in their degree from the divine virtue which, covering all the expanse, so to speak, of the Intellectual Realm is seen, last attainment of all, by those who have known already many splendid visions.

The gods see, each singly and all as one. So, too, the souls; they see all There in right of being sprung, themselves, of that universe and therefore including all from beginning to end and having their existence There if only by that phase which belongs inherently to the Divine, though often too they are There entire, those of them that have not incurred separation.

This vision Zeus takes and it is for such of us, also, as share his love and appropriate our part in the Beauty There, the final object of all seeing, the entire beauty upon all things; for all There sheds radiance, and floods those that have found their way thither so that they too become beautiful; thus it will often happen that men climbing heights where the soil has taken a yellow glow will themselves appear so, borrowing color from the place on which they move. The color flowering on that other height we speak of is Beauty; or rather all There is light and beauty, through and through, for the beauty is no mere bloom upon the surface.

To those that do not see entire, the immediate impression is alone taken into account; but those drunken with this wine, filled with the nectar, all their soul penetrated by this beauty, cannot remain mere gazers: no longer is there a spectator outside gazing on an outside spectacle; the cleareyed hold the vision within themselves, though, for the most part, they have no idea that it is within but look toward it as to something beyond them and see it is an object of vision caught by the direction of the will.

All that one sees as a spectacle is still external; one must bring the vision within and see no longer in that mode of separation but as we know ourselves; thus a man filled with a god — possessed by Apollo or by one of the Muses — need no longer look outside for his vision of the divine being; it is but finding the strength to see divinity within.[6]

11

Similarly any one, unable to see himself, but possessed by that God, has but to bring that divine-within before his consciousness and at once he sees an image of himself, himself lifted to a better beauty: now let him ignore that image, lovely though it is, and sink into a perfect self-identity, no such separation remaining; at once he forms a multiple unity with the God silently present; in the degree of his power and will, the two become one; should he turn back to the former duality, still he is pure and remains very near to the God; he has but to look again and the same presence is there.

This conversion brings gain: at the first stage, that of separation, a man is aware of self; but retreating inward, he becomes possessor of all; he puts sense away behind him in dread of the separated life and becomes one in the Divine; if he plans to see in separation, he sets himself outside.

The novice must hold himself constantly under some image of the Divine Being and seek

[5]This is part of the myth of the soul in Plato's *Phaedrus*, 246e. [Ed.]

[6]Here Plotinus gives a very different account of inspiration than Plato in the *Ion:* the source of *enthousiasmós* is within, not outside the poet. [Ed.]

in the light of a clear conception; knowing thus, in a deep conviction, whither he is going — into what a sublimity he penetrates — he must give himself forthwith to the inner and, radiant with the Divine Intellections (with which he is now one), be no longer the seer, but, as that place has made him, the seen.

Still, we will be told, one cannot be in beauty and yet fail to see it. The very contrary: to see the divine as something external is to be outside of it; to become it is to be most truly in beauty: since sight deals with the external, there can here be no vision unless in the sense of identification with the object.

And this identification amounts to a self-knowing, a self-consciousness, guarded by the fear of losing the self in the desire of a too wide awareness.

It must be remembered that sensations of the ugly and evil impress us more violently than those of what is agreeable and yet leave less knowledge as the residue of the shock: sickness makes the rougher mark, but health, tranquilly present, explains itself better; it takes the first place, it is the natural thing, it belongs to our being; illness is alien, unnatural and thus makes itself felt by its very incongruity, while the other conditions are native and we take no notice. Such being our nature, we are most completely aware of ourselves when we are most completely identified with the object of our knowledge.

This is why in that other sphere, when we are deepest in that knowledge by intellection, we are aware of none; we are expecting some impression on sense, which has nothing to report since it has seen nothing and never could in that order see anything. The unbelieving element is sense; it is the other, the Intellectual-Principle, that sees; and if this too doubted, it could not even credit its own existence, for it can never stand away and with bodily eyes apprehend itself as a visible object.

12

We have told how this vision is to be procured, whether by the mode of separation or in identity: now, seen in either way, what does it give to report?

The vision has been of God in travail of a beautiful offspring, God engendering a universe within himself in a painless labor and — rejoiced in what he has brought into being, proud of his children — keeping all closely by Him, for the pleasure He has in his radiance and in theirs.

Of this offspring — all beautiful, but most beautiful those that have remained within — only one has become manifest without; from him (Zeus, sovereign over the visible universe) the youngest born, we may gather, as from some image, the greatness of the Father and of the Brothers that remain within the Father's house.

Still the manifested God cannot think that he has come forth in vain from the father; for through him another universe has arisen, beautiful as the image of beauty, and it could not be lawful that Beauty and Being should fail of a beautiful image.

This second Kosmos at every point copies the archetype: it has life and being in copy, and has beauty as springing from that diviner world. In its character of image it holds, too, that divine perpetuity without which it would only at times be truly representative and sometimes fail like a construction of art; for every image whose existence lies in the nature of things must stand during the entire existence of the archetype.

Hence it is false to put an end to the visible sphere as long as the Intellectual endures, or to found it upon a decision taken by its maker at some given moment.

That teaching shirks the penetration of such a making as is here involved: it fails to see that as long as the Supreme is radiant there can be no failing of its sequel but, that existing, all exists. And — since the necessity of conveying our meaning compels such terms — the Supreme has existed forever and forever will exist.

13

The God fettered (as in the Kronos Myth) to an unchanging identity leaves the ordering of this universe to his son (to Zeus), for it could not be in his character to neglect his rule within the divine sphere, and, as though sated with the Authentic-Beauty, seek a lordship too recent and too poor for his might. Ignoring this lower world,

Kronos (Intellectual-Principle) claims for his own father (Ouranios, the Absolute, or One) with all the upward-tending between them: and he counts all that tends to the inferior, beginning from his son (Zeus, the All-Soul), as ranking beneath him. Thus he holds a midposition determined on the one side by the differentiation implied in the severance from the very highest and, on the other, by that which keeps him apart from the link between himself and the lower: he stands between a greater father and an inferior son. But since that father is too lofty to be thought of under the name of Beauty, the second God remains the primally beautiful.[7]

[7]Plotinus presents the traditional succession of the Greek gods — Ouranos, Kronos, and Zeus — as an allegory of the philosophical relationship between the One, the Intellectual-Principle, and the All-Soul, which generates the Nature-Principle. The transcendent idea of Intellectual Beauty thus mediates between the incomprehensible One and the forms of beauty we can apprehend in matter. [Ed.]

Soul also has beauty, but is less beautiful than Intellect as being its image and therefore, though beautiful in nature, taking increase of beauty by looking to that original. Since then the All-Soul — to use the more familiar term — since Aphrodite herself is so beautiful, what name can we give to that other? If Soul is so lovely in its own right, of what quality must that prior be? And since its being is derived, what must that power be from which the Soul takes the double beauty, the borrowed and the inherent?

We ourselves possess beauty when we are true to our own being; our ugliness is in going over to another order; our self-knowledge, that is to say, is our beauty; in self-ignorance we are ugly.

Thus beauty is of the Divine and comes Thence only.

Do these considerations suffice to a clear understanding of the Intellectual Sphere or must we make yet another attempt by another road?

Dante Alighieri

1265–1321

Dante Alighieri was born in Florence, the son of Alighiero Alighieri of the lesser nobility. His mother died when Dante was quite young, and his father, whom Dante mentions seldom and then only formally, remarried and produced a large second family. Dante was well educated, probably by the Franciscans; his rhetoric tutor was Brunetto Latini. Around 1285, Dante married Gemma Donati, by whom he had two sons and two daughters. Gemma's influence on his life pales, however, beside the radiance of another Florentine noblewoman, Bice Portinari, whom Dante dubbed "Beatrice," the bringer of blessing. Dante's contacts with Beatrice (who married Simone dei Bardi) were undoubtedly few and platonic in the years before her death in 1290, but she became his lifelong Muse and his guide through Paradise in the *Commedia.*

Although Dante experimented with verse in his twenties (under the influence of the poet Guido Cavalcanti), his life was devoted to public affairs: He fought in 1289 in the battle of Campaldino, spoke in the Florentine assembly, and became one of the six priors of Florence. While Dante was away from Florence on a diplomatic mission in 1300, factional warfare broke out; a rival party came to power and convicted Dante in absentia of graft and corruption in office. Under sentence of death if he returned, Dante spent the rest of his life abroad, where he learned "how salt is the bread of exile and how steep the stairs of another." Except for the *Vita Nuova,* which was written in Florence in 1292, most of Dante's works are the product of his exile, including the *Convivio* ("The Banquet," 1304–08), the *De Monarchia* (1308), and his masterpiece the *Commedia* (1306–14) — "Divina" was added by its readers. Dante's literary life was spent wandering between Verona (where his patrons included Can Grande della Scala) and other intellectual centers such as Bologna and Paris. He finally settled in Ravenna, where he died in 1321.

Dante's letter to Can Grande is the most familiar exposition of medieval semiotic theory; the ideas are not original with Dante, but have a long and distinguished history. In the sixth century, St. Augustine had claimed in *Of the Value of Belief* that the Old Testament was to be interpreted as "history, etiology, analogy, and allegory." During the Middle Ages, the Hebrew bible was interpreted not only as the literal history of the Israelites, but as prefiguring events in the life of Christ. And in the thirteenth century, St. Thomas Aquinas's *Summa Theologica* had codified this mode of interpreting scripture:

> That first signification whereby words signify things belongs to the first sense, the historical. . . . That signification whereby things signified by words have themselves also a signification is called the spiritual sense. . . . Now this spiritual sense has a threefold division. . . . So far as the things of the Old Law signify the things of the New Law, there is the allegorical sense. . . . So far as the things done in Christ . . . are signs of what we ought to do, there is the moral sense. . . . But so far as they signify what relates to eternal glory, there is the anagogical sense.

Dante's principal innovation, if indeed it is an innovation, is in applying these principles of symbolic meaning to something other than sacred scripture — to his

Commedia, a poetical work written in the "vulgar" language of common speech. Some medievalists (the followers of D. W. Robertson) have suggested that this multivalent mode of reading was part of the freight of medieval literacy, and that even apparently secular texts (like Chaucer's *Canterbury Tales,* or Boccaccio's *Decameron*) were automatically read in this manner. Whether this was actually the case is controversial, but certainly with the coming of the Renaissance, this mode of reading began to fade away, and the notion that all literature was potentially ambiguous — indeed, that the mark of literature was ambiguity and multiplicity of interpretation — would not return until Northrop Frye (p. 641) and William Empson (p. 735) in the middle of the twentieth century.

Selected Bibliography

Alighieri, Dante. *The Divine Comedy.* Translated and with a commentary by Charles S. Singleton. Princeton: Princeton University Press, 1970–75.

Dunbar, Helen Flanders. *Symbolism in Medieval Thought.* New Haven: Yale University Press, 1929.

Hollander, Robert. *Allegory in Dante's Commedia.* Princeton: Princeton University Press, 1969.

Kirkpatrick, Robin. *Dante's Paradiso and the Limitations of Modern Criticism: A Study of Style and Poetic Theory.* Cambridge: Cambridge University Press, 1978.

Pietrobono, Luigi. "L'epistola a Can Grande." *Giornale dantesco* 4 (1939): 3–51.

Saley, John V. *Dante and the English Romantics.* New York: Columbia University Library, 1960.

Singleton, Charles S. *Dante Studies.* 2 vols. Cambridge: Harvard University Press, 1954–58.

Tock, J. F. *L'etterno piacer: Aesthetic Ideas in Dante.* Oxford: Clarendon Press, 1984.

Toynbee, Paget Jackson. *Dante in English Literature from Chaucer to Cary.* 2 vols. London: Methuen, 1909.

From the *Letter to Can Grande della Scala*

5. As the Philosopher says in the second book of the *Metaphysics,* "As a thing is with respect to being, so it is with respect to truth";[1] and the reason for this is that the truth concerning a thing, which consists in the truth as its subject, is the perfect image of the thing as it is. And so, of all things which have being, some are such that they have absolute being in themselves, others such that their being is dependent upon a relationship with something else: they exist at the same time with something which is their correlative, as is the case with father and son, master and servant, double and half, the whole and the parts, and many other such things. Because such things depend for their being upon another thing, it follows that their truth would depend upon the truth of the other; not knowing the "half," its "double" could not be understood, and so with the other cases.

Translated by Robert S. Haller.

[1]Aristotle, *Metaphysics* 2.1 [Tr.]

6. Therefore, if one should wish to present an introduction to a part of a work, it is necessary to present some conception of the whole work of which it is a part. For this reason I, who wish to present something in the form of an introduction to the above-mentioned part of the whole *Comedy,*[2] have decided to preface it with some discussion of the whole work, in order to make the approach to the part easier and more complete. There are six questions, then, which should be asked at the beginning about any doctrinal work: what is its subject, its form, its agent, its end, the title of the book, and its branch of philosophy. In three cases the answers to these questions will be different for the part of the work I propose to give you than for the whole, that is, in the cases of its subject, form, and title, while in the other three, as will be clear upon inspection, they will be the same. Thus these first three should be specifically asked in a discussion of the whole work, after which the way will be clear for an introduction to the part. Let us, then, ask the last three questions not only about the whole but also about the offered part itself.

7. For the clarification of what I am going to say, then, it should be understood that there is not just a single sense in this work: it might rather be called *polysemous,* that is, having several senses. For the first sense is that which is contained in the letter, while there is another which is contained in what is signified by the letter. The first is called literal, while the second is called allegorical, or moral or anagogical. And in order to make this manner of treatment clear, it can be applied to the following verses: "When Israel went out of Egypt, the house of Jacob from a barbarous people, Judea was made his sanctuary, Israel his dominion."[3] Now if we look at the letter alone, what is signified to us is the departure of the sons of Israel from Egypt during the time of Moses; if at the allegory, what is signified to us is our redemption through Christ; if at the moral sense, what is signified to us is the conversion of the soul from the sorrow and misery of sin to the state of grace; if at the anagogical, what is signified to us is the departure of the sanctified soul from bondage to the corruption of this world into the freedom of eternal glory. And although these mystical senses are called by various names, they may all be called allegorical, since they are all different from the literal or historical. For allegory is derived from the Greek *alleon,* which means in Latin *alienus* ("belonging to another") or *diversus* ("different").

8. This being established, it is clear that the subject about which these two senses play must also be twofold. And thus it should first be noted what the subject of the work is when taken according to the letter, and then what its subject is when understood allegorically. The subject of the whole work, then, taken literally, is the state of souls after death, understood in a simple sense; for the movement of the whole work turns upon this and about this. If on the other hand the work is taken allegorically, the subject is man, in the exercise of his free will, earning or becoming liable to the rewards or punishments of justice.

9. And the form is twofold: the form of the treatise and the form of the treatment. The form of the treatise is threefold, according to its three kinds of divisions. The first division is that which divides the whole work into three canticles. The second is that which divides each canticle into cantos. The third, that which divides the cantos into rhymed units. The form or manner of treatment is poetic, fictive, descriptive, digressive, and transumptive, and it as well consists in definition, division, proof, refutation, and the giving of examples.

10. The title of the work is, "Here begins the Comedy of Dante Alighieri, a Florentine by birth but not in character." To understand the title, it must be known that comedy is derived from *comos,* "a village," and from *oda,* "a song," so that a comedy is, so to speak, "a rustic song." Comedy, then, is a certain genre of poetic narrative differing from all others. For it differs from tragedy in its matter, in that tragedy is tranquil and conducive to wonder at the beginning, but foul and conducive to horror at the end, or catastrophe, for which reason it is derived from *tragos,* meaning "goat," and *oda,* making it, as it were, a "goat song," that is, foul as a goat is foul. This is evident in Seneca's tragedies. Comedy,

[2]His *Divine Comedy.* [Ed.]

[3]Psalm 113:1–2 (114:1–2 in the King James version). [Tr.]

on the other hand, introduces a situation of adversity, but ends its matter in prosperity, as is evident in Terence's comedies. And for this reason some writers have the custom of saying in their salutations, by way of greeting, "a tragic beginning and a comic ending to you." And, as well, they differ in their manner of speaking. Tragedy uses an elevated and sublime style, while comedy uses an unstudied and low style, which is what Horace implies in the *Art of Poetry* where he allows comic writers occasionally to speak like the tragic, and also the reverse of this:

> Yet sometimes even comedy elevates its voice,
> and angry Chremes rages in swelling tones;
> and in tragedy Telephus and Peleus often lament
> in prosaic speeches. . . .[4]

So from this it should be clear why the present work is called the *Comedy*. For, if we consider the matter, it is, at the beginning, that is, in Hell, foul and conducive to horror, but at the end, in Paradise, prosperous, conducive to pleasure, and welcome. And if we consider the manner of speaking, it is unstudied and low, since its speech is the vernacular, in which even women communicate. There are, besides these, other genres of poetic narrative, such as pastoral verse, elegy, satire, and the hymn of thanksgiving, as could also be gathered from Horace in his *Art of Poetry*. But there is no purpose to discussing these at this time.

11. Now it can be explained in what manner the part I have offered you may be assigned a subject. For if the subject of the whole work, on the literal level, is the state of souls after death, in an absolute, not in a restricted sense, then the subject of this part is the same state, but restricted to the state of blessed souls after death. And if the subject of the whole work, considered allegorically, is man, through exercise of free will, earning or becoming liable to the rewards or punishments of justice, then it is evident that the subject in this part is restricted to man's becoming eligible, to the extent he has earned them, for the rewards of justice.

12. And in the same manner the form of this part follows from the form ascribed to the whole. For if the form of the whole treatise is threefold, then the form in this part is twofold, that is, the division into cantos and into rhymed units. This part could not have the first division as its form, since this part itself is [a product] of the first division.

13. The title of the book also follows; for while the title of the whole book is, as was said earlier, "Here begins the Comedy, etc.," the title of this part is, "Here begins the third canticle of Dante's *Comedy*, etc., which is called *Paradise*."

14. Having settled these three questions, where the answer was different for the part than for the whole, it remains to deal with the other three, where the answers will not be different for either the part or the whole. The agent, then, in the whole and in the part, is he who has been mentioned above; and he is clearly so throughout.

15. The end of the whole and of the part could be multiple, that is, both immediate and ultimate. But, without going into details, it can be briefly stated that the end of the whole as of the part is to remove those living in this life from the state of misery and to lead them to the state of happiness.

16. The branch of philosophy which determines the procedure of the work as a whole and in this part is moral philosophy, or ethics, inasmuch as the whole and this part have been conceived for the sake of practical results, not for the sake of speculation. So even if some parts or passages are treated in the manner of speculative philosophy, this is not for the sake of the theory, but for a practical purpose, following that principle which the Philosopher advances in the second book of the *Metaphysics*, that "practical men sometimes speculate about things in their particular and temporal relations."[5]

[4]Horace, *Art of Poetry*, 93–96. [Tr.] See Horace, p. 70. [Ed.]

[5]Aristotle, *Metaphysics* 2.1. [Ed.]

Christine de Pisan

1365–ca. 1431

Christine de Pisan, one of the most remarkable literary women of the Middle Ages, was born in Venice, daughter of civil councillor Tommaso di Benvenuto da Pizzano, a citizen of both scientific and medical accomplishments. Shortly after Christine's birth, Tommaso became Court Astrologer to Charles V of France, a position he held until Charles's death in 1380. During the quarrelsome regency at the time of the minority of Charles VI, Tommaso's salary and perquisites were cut, the family's fortunes declined, and, after a long illness, he died around 1385. Meanwhile, however, Christine had received a literary education at court that would have been unusual for a nobleman of the time, much less a woman.[1] This was owing to her father's encouragement, but over her mother's protests; as Christine put it in *The City of Ladies* (1405), "Your father, who was a great scientist and philosopher, did not believe that women were worth less by knowing science; rather . . . he took great pleasure from seeing your inclination to learning. The feminine opinion of your mother, however, who worked to keep you busy with spinning and silly girlishness . . . was the major obstacle" (II.37.4).[2] In 1380, Christine was married — apparently happily — to a rising young courtier from Picardy, Estienne de Castel, notary to the King, by whom she had three children, including at least one son and one daughter who survived into adulthood. Estienne, traveling with the court to Beauvais, died during an epidemic in 1390, leaving Christine to deal with the responsibility of her mother and three children while Estienne's inheritance was tied up in legal disputes. She had to go to work, and the work she chose was literature. For more than two decades starting around 1393, Christine was what today would be called a professional writer, working in most of the dominant prose and poetical genres of her day: lyric and narrative poetry, penitential psalms and proverbs, biography and history, literary criticism; as well she produced a courtesy manual and even an essay on military strategy compiled from classical authors. She tended to give her personal slant to conventional forms: Her poem on the mutability of fortune, for example, in addition to giving well-known cases of historical figures raised and then thrown down by Fortune's Wheel, presents her own life as a case in point.

Christine was an exceptionally successful writer. Her patrons included King Charles VI of France, for whom she wrote a biography of his father, Louis the dauphin; Charles King of Navarre; Jean duc de Berry; and Charles the Bold and Jean Sans Peur, dukes of Burgundy; and she was invited to the courts of London and Milan. Her works were translated into English, Italian, and other vernacular

[1]Christine wrote exclusively in the French vernacular, but must have known how to read Latin in order to participate in the fifteenth-century debate known as the *Querelle de la Rose*, from which the following selection is taken.

[2]Christine de Pisan. *The Book of the City of Ladies*. Translated and with an introduction by Earl Jeffrey Richards (New York: Persea, 1982), II.37.4.

languages, and she carefully supervised, as few vernacular writers had done, the illumination of her manuscripts. Christine seems to have fallen silent around the time of the Burgundian massacres at Paris in 1418, and she is thought to have secluded herself in her daughter's convent, St. Louis de Poissy. But she emerged once more to write *La Ditié de Jehanne d'Arc* (1429), the only celebratory poem on Joan of Arc written in Joan's lifetime. After this there is only silence, and it is supposed that Christine died at Poissy around 1431.

The *Querelle de la Rose,* a literary debate that took place in the opening years of the fifteenth century, pitted Christine and her powerful ally Jean Gerson, the chancellor of the University of Paris, against the humanist royal secretaries Gontier and Pierre Col and Jean de Montreuil, provost of Lille, in a moralistic attack on the literary quality and effect of the *Roman de la Rose,* one of the masterworks of the Middle Ages. Enormously influential on Chaucer and his contemporaries, the *Roman de la Rose* (or *Romance of the Rose*), is an allegorical love poem begun around 1225 by Guillaume de Lorris and completed and augmented around 1275 by Jean de Meun, which describes the ultimately successful quest of a lover for the mystical and fleshly Rose. As usual, time has been on the side of the *Rose*'s defenders, rather than the moralists, and it may not be easy to understand what so disturbed Christine and Gerson. Christine seems to view her society as spiritually adrift and to attribute this lack of standards in part to the popularity of attractive but immoral literature. As E. J. Richards puts it, "The French court was left to its own devices during the frequent spells of insanity which plagued Charles VI. Charles' queen, Isabella of Bavaria, led a licentious and frivolous existence. Not surprisingly, Christine and Gerson connected the immorality of their day with the popularity of the *Rose*."[3]

For Christine, the *Rose* was also threatening because it reinforced the dominant misogyny of the Middle Ages, representing women as unchaste objects of desire. Men get away with such misrepresentation, Christine says, because they own the pen and thus "can tell endless tales and keep the best parts for themselves" with impunity; "my answer is that women did not write these books. . . . They know they stand wrongfully accused. If women had written these books, I know full well the matter would have been handled differently." Christine finds the *Rose* shameful, not merely for its sexual frankness, but for the manners and morals it attributes to women.

In her later, more explicitly feminist treatise, *The Book of the City of Ladies,* written as an antidote to Ovid's *Remedia amoris* and to Boccaccio's stories in *De mulieribus claris,* Christine sets forth representations of admirable women from the present as well as legendary times, middle-class dames as well as noblewomen and queens. The treatise is not merely a defense of women against the standard masculine accusations, but a reinscription of femininity suggesting that standard male virtues — including learning, bravery, leadership, and magnanimity — are not limited to men at all, that women have been capable of them in the past and would be so more frequently were their opportunities less limited by restrictive social roles.

[3]From E. J. Richards's introduction to *The Book of the City of Ladies* (New York: Persea, 1982), pp. 31–32.

By the end of her life, Christine found her vision of the ideal woman embodied in Joan of Arc, whom she represented as a chaste but heroic girl whose courage and fortitude could lead France to secular and spiritual salvation.

Selected Bibliography

Baird, Joseph L. and John R. Kane, eds. *La Querelle de la Rose: Letters and Documents.* Chapel Hill: North Carolina Studies in Romance Languages and Literatures, 1978.

Christine de Pisan. *Oeuvres Poetiques,* ed. Maurice Roy. 3 vols. 1886; New York: Johnson Reprint Corporation, 1965.

———. *The Book of the City of Ladies.* Translated and with an introduction by Earl Jeffrey Richards. New York: Persea, 1982.

Kelly, F. Douglas. "Reflections on the Role of Christine de Pisan as a Feminist Writer." *Sub-Stance* 2 (1972): 63–71.

McLeod, Enid. *The Order of the Rose: The Life and Ideas of Christine de Pizan.* Totowa, NJ: Rowman and Littlefield, 1976.

Quilligan, Maureen. *The Allegory of Female Authority: Christine de Pizan's Cité de Dames.* Ithaca: Cornell University Press, 1991.

Willard, Charity Cannon. *Christine de Pizan: Her Life and Works.* New York: Persea, 1984.

Yenal, Edith. *Christine de Pisan: A Bibliography.* Metuchen, NJ: Scarecrow Press, 1989.

From the *Querelle de la Rose*

To the very competent and wise person, Master John,[1] Secretary of the King our Lord and Provost of Lisle.

Reverence, honor, and due respect to you, Lord Provost of Lisle, esteemed Master, sage in morals, lover of knowledge, steeped in learning, and expert in rhetoric; from me, Christine de Pisan, a woman weak in understanding and inadequate in learning — for which things may your sagacity not hold in scorn the smallness of my reasons; rather may it take into account my feminine weakness. It has pleased you out of your goodness (for which I say thanks) to send me a small treatise expressed in fine language and true-seeming reasons. Your treatise was written, as I gather from your own words, to oppose critics of certain parts of the *Roman de la Rose,* to give firm support to the work, and to approve it and its authors, and in particular Meun.[2] Having read and considered your letter and having understood it, within the limits of my ability, I disagreed with your remarks and shared the opinion of the learned man to whom your letter was addressed. Therefore, although your letter was not addressed to me and did not require a reply, nevertheless I wish to say, to divulge, and to maintain openly that (saving your good grace) you are in grave error to give such lavish and unjustified praise to Meun's book — one which could better be called plain idleness[3] than useful work, in my judgment. You severely criticize his opponents and say, "that a great thing is therein to be under-

Translated by Joseph L. Baird and John R. Kane.

[1]Christine writes "Jehan Johannes," which was a frequent designation for Jean de Montreuil. [Trs.]

[2]Montreuil's original treatise, the first document in the debate known as *La Querelle de la Rose,* has been lost. [Ed.]

[3]Christine's word here is *oisiueté.* Is this not a half-amused allusion to Lady *Oiseuse,* keeper of the wicket gate of the garden in the *Roman de la Rose*? Not only is the garden to be condemned, *because* it is kept by Lady Idleness, but also the entire romance, which, for all the effort and industry that went into it, is mere trifling "idleness." [Trs.]

stood," "that what a third party says gives a better testimony," "has constructed and erected through great study and at great length." Yet may my daring to repudiate and find fault with an author so worthy and so subtle not seem presumption in me. Rather, take heed of the firm conviction which has moved me to oppose some opinions contained in your letter. In truth, a mere assertion not justified by law can be re-argued without prejudice. I am not, I confess, learned nor schooled in the subtle language, which would make my arguments dazzling, a language which you indeed can display with a fine array of carefully polished words. Nevertheless, I will not hesitate to express my opinion bluntly in the vernacular, although I may not be able to express myself elegantly.

But why did I say before that Meun's work could best be called idleness? Certainly, it seems to me that any trivial thing, even though it is treated, composed, and accomplished with great labor and difficulty, can be called idle, or worse than idle, insofar as evil follows from it. Yet because of the great and widespread fame of the said romance, I had long desired to read it, and once I had gained the knowledge to understand subtle matters somewhat, I did read and consider it at length, to the best of my ability. It is true that the subject matter did not please me in certain parts and so I skipped over it as quickly as a cock over hot embers; therefore, I have not read it in every detail. Nevertheless, some things have remained in my memory which my judgment strongly condemned, and still cannot approve, despite the contrary praise of other people. It is quite true that my small understanding finds great prettiness there; in some parts, he expresses himself very well indeed, using beautiful terms and graceful leonine rhyme. He could not have treated his subject more subtly or more skillfully. But I agree with the opinion (which you clearly oppose, it seems to me) that he speaks too dishonorably in some parts of the *Roman de la Rose,* even when he speaks through the character he calls Reason, who names the secret members plainly by name. You, in fact, support Meun and say that such frankness is perfectly reasonable, maintaining that in the things God has made there is no ugliness, and consequently no need to eschew their names. To this I say and confess that truly God created all things pure and clean coming from himself and that in the State of Innocence it would not have been wrong to name them; but by the pollution of sin man became impure, and his original sin has remained with us, as Holy Scripture testifies. I can make this clear by a comparison: God made Lucifer beautiful above all the angels and gave him a very solemn and beautiful name, but then Lucifer was reduced by his sin to horrible ugliness; whereupon, the name, albeit very beautiful in itself, now, because of the impression of the person, creates horror in those who hear it.

Further, you point out that Jesus Christ calls the women sinners *meretrix,*[4] etc. But I can explain to you why he called them by that name, because the name *meretrix* is not particularly dishonorable to utter considering the vileness of the thing named, and, in fact, it could have been more basely said even in Latin. Thus should modesty be respected when speaking publicly of things about which Nature herself is ashamed. Saving your reverence and the author's, I say that you commit great wrong against the noble virtue of modesty, which by its nature bridles indecency and dishonorable conduct in words and deeds. Holy Scripture makes clear in many places that this is a great wrong, outside the range of decent conduct and good morals. Moreover, I affirm that the indecent name should not be avoided by substituting the word "relics" for it. I suggest to you that the name does not make the thing dishonorable, but the thing, the name. Therefore, in my humble opinion, one should speak about such matters soberly and only when necessary, as in certain particular cases, such as sickness or other genuine need. Just as our first parents hid their private parts instinctively, so ought we to do in deed and in word.

Further, I cannot be silent about a subject that so displeases me: that the function of Reason, whom he even calls the daughter of God, should be to propound such a dictum as the one I found in the chapter where Reason says to the Lover, "In the amorous war, it is better to deceive than

[4]See Matthew XXI.31–32; Luke XV.30. [Trs.] *Meretrix* is Latin for prostitute. [Ed.]

to be deceived." And truly, Master Jean de Meun, I dare say that Reason denied her heavenly father in that teaching, for He taught an utterly different doctrine. If you hold one of these two to be better than the other, it would follow that both are good, and this cannot be. I hold a contrary opinion: it is far less evil, clearly, to be deceived than to deceive.

Further, let us consider the subject matter or choice of words, which many people find reprehensible. Dear Lord! What horrible stuff! What an affront to honor! What reprehensible teachings recorded in the chapter about the Old Woman! In God's name, what can one find there but sophistical exhortations filled with ugliness and things horrible to recall? Ha, you who have beautiful daughters! If you really want to introduce them to the honorable life, give them, give them, I say, this book so that they may learn from the *Roman de la Rose* ways to distinguish Good from Evil — what am I saying! — rather Evil from Good! To what purpose or to what profit is it that the hearers of this book have their ears assailed by so much sinfulness?

Then, in the chapter about Jealousy, my God, what great good can be observed there! What need to record the dishonorable things and the shameful words, which are common enough in the mouths of the unfortunate people impassioned by this sickness! What good example or preparation for life could this be? And the wickedness which is there recorded of women! Many people attempt to excuse him by saying that it is the Jealous Man who speaks and that in truth Meun does no more than God himself did when He spoke through the mouth of Jeremiah! But whatever lying additions he may have made, he certainly could not have rendered worse or abased the condition of women more! Ha! When I remember the deceits, the hypocrisies, and the conduct dissembled within marriage and outside it, which one can find in this book — certainly, I consider these to be beautiful and edifying tales for one to hear!

Further, what great marvels does the character that he calls Genius the priest say! Surely, the works of Nature would have completely fallen into disuse long since, if he had not so greatly recommended them! But, my God, who could show or convince me what profit there is in the great argument full of vituperation that he calls a sermon (as if to deride holy preaching), which, he says, Genius delivers? It contains too many dishonorable things, names, sophistical words, fanning the flames of those secrets of Nature which ought to be left tacit and not named. Moreover, the "sermon" is superfluous, for a work which is of the very order of Nature cannot, obviously, fail. If it were not so, then it would be good for the maintenance of human generation to invent and say exciting and inflaming words and terms in order to stimulate man to continue that work.

Yet the author does more, if I remember well; for the life of me I can't understand to what purpose. For in the said sermon he adduces, as a comparison, paradise and its joys. He says truly enough that the virtuous will go to that place, but he concludes that everyone, men and women alike, should know how to perform and exercise the functions of Nature; nor in this does he make any exception of law, as if he wished to say, and indeed says plainly, that they will all be saved. And by this it appears that he wishes to maintain that the sin of lechery is nothing, rather a virtue, which is error and against the law of God. Ha! what seed and what doctrine! What great good can come of it! I believe that many have left the world because of it and entered religion, or become hermits because of that holy message, or come out of the evil life and been saved by such exhortation! Certainly (I dare say it, no matter whom it offends), this never came from anywhere but a heart corrupted and abandoned to dissolution and vice, which can be cause of great sin and unbecoming conduct.

And again, for God's sake, let us look a little further to see what profit there can possibly be in his excessive, impetuous, and most untruthful criticism and denigration of women as exceedingly wicked creatures! He declares that their conduct is filled with all manner of perversity, with which condemnations, even with all the give and take among his characters, he cannot fully gorge himself. For if you wish to tell me that the Jealous Man does this as a man overcome by passion, I fail to see how he fulfills the teaching of Genius, for Genius so fully recommends and exhorts men to bed them and to perform the act which he praises so highly. And this Genius, more than any of the characters, makes great attacks on women, saying, in fact, "Flee, flee, flee from the deadly serpent."[5] Then he declares that men should pursue them unremittingly. Here is a glaring contradiction, evilly intended: to order men to flee what he wishes them to pursue, and to pursue what he wishes them to flee. But since women are so perverse, he ought not to command men to approach them at all. For he who fears a problem ought to eschew it. And it is for this reason that he so strongly forbids a man to tell his secret to a woman, who is so eager to know it (as he records), although I simply do not know where the devil he found so much nonsense and so many useless words, which are there laid out by a long process. But I pray all those who truly hold this teaching authentic and put so much faith in it, that they kindly tell me how many men they have seen accused, killed, hanged, and publicly rebuked by the accusations of their women? I think you will find them few and far between. Nevertheless, it would be good and praiseworthy counsel for a man to keep his affairs to himself for the greatest security, for he who does so is rich above all men. Indeed, not long ago I heard tell of a man who was accused and hanged on account of having revealed himself to a friend whom he trusted. But I think that few have come before a judge with accusations or complaints of such horrible evil, such disloyalties, and such wickedness which he says women know how to commit so maliciously and underhandedly. It is indeed secret when nobody sees it. As I have said previously on this subject in my work called "L'Epistre au Dieu d'Amours," where are those countries and kingdoms which have been ruined by the great evils of women? If it be not presumptuous, let us speak of the great crimes that one can attribute to even the worst and most deceitful of women. What do they do? In what ways do they deceive you? If they ask you for money from your purse, which they cannot get from you by a ruse or cannot take themselves, do not give it to them if you do not wish to. And if you say that they have made a fool of you, don't let them. Do they go into your house to woo, pursue, or rape you? It would be good to know how they deceive you. And, besides, he speaks superficially and wrongly about married women who deceive their husbands in this way, for he could know nothing of the married state by experience, and therefore he spoke of it only in generalities. I do not understand what good purpose this can serve or what good can come of it, save to impede the good and peace that is in marriage, and to render the husbands who hear so much babbling and extravagance (if they believe such things) suspicious and less affectionate toward their wives. God, what exhortation! How profitable it is! But truly since he blamed all women in general, I am constrained to believe that he never had acquaintance of, or regular contact with, any honorable or virtuous woman. But by having resort to many dissolute women of evil life (as lechers commonly do), he thought, or feigned to know, that all women were of that kind; for he had known no others. And if he had blamed only the dishonorable ones and counseled men to flee them, it would have been a good and just teaching. But no, without exception he accuses them all. But if, beyond all the bounds of reason, the author took it upon himself to accuse or judge them without justification, the ones accused ought not to be blamed for it. Rather, he should be blamed who carried his argument to the point where it was simply not true, since the contrary is so obvious. For if he and all his henchmen had sworn it in this matter (let no one take offense), there have been, there are, and there will be more virtuous women, more honorable, better bred, and even more learned, and from whom more great good has come forth into the world than ever did from his person. Similarly, there have been women well schooled in worldly conduct and virtuous morals, and many who have effected a reconciliation with their husbands and have borne their concerns and their secrets and their passions calmly and discreetly, despite the fact that their husbands were crude and brutish toward them. One finds proof enough of this in the Bible and in other ancient histories, women such as Sarah, Rebeccah, Esther, Judith,

[5]Cf. Vergil, *Bucolica,* III.92–93. [Trs.]

and many others. And even in our own time we have seen in France many virtuous women, great ladies and others of our ladies of France: the holy devout Queen Jeanne; Queen Blanche; the Duchess of Orleans, daughter of the King of France; the Duchess of Anjou, who is now called Queen of Sicily; and many others — all of whom had such great beauty, chastity, honor, and wisdom. And also women of lesser rank, like Madame de la Ferté, wife of Monsieur Pierre de Craon, who did much that was praiseworthy; besides many others, whom I pass over for lack of time.

And do not believe or let anyone else think, dear Sir, that I have written this defense, out of feminine bias, merely because I am a woman. For, assuredly, my motive is simply to uphold the pure truth, since I know by experience that the truth is completely contrary to those things I am denying. And it is precisely because I am a woman that I can speak better in this matter than one who has not had the experience, since he speaks only by conjecture and by chance. But above all these things, pray let us consider what the aim of the aforementioned treatise is; for as the proverb says, "By the intent a case is concluded." Thus may be seen and noted what can be profitable in that excessively horrible and shameful conclusion.[6] I call it shameful and so very dishonorable that I dare say that nobody who loves virtue and honor will hear it without being totally confounded by shame and abomination at hearing described, expressed, and distorted in dishonorable fictions what modesty and reason should restrain well-bred folk from even thinking about. Yet, further, I dare say that even the goliards[7] would have been horrified to read or hear it in public, in decent places, and before people whom they would have considered virtuous. But who could praise a work which can be neither read nor quoted at the table of queens, of princesses, and of worthy women, who would surely, on hearing it, be constrained to cover their blushing faces?

And if you wish to excuse him by saying that by means of a pretty novelty it pleases him to put the purpose of love through such figures, I answer you that in this work he tells us nothing new. Does one not know how men normally behave with women? If he had told us something about bears or lions or birds or other strange creatures, this would have been matter for laughing on account of the fable, but there is no novelty in this that he tells us. And certainly it could have been done more pleasantly, far more agreeably and by means of more courteous terms, a method which would have been more pleasing to handsome and decent lovers and to every other virtuous person.

Thus, without being more prolix, although a great deal more could be said, and said better, I do not know how, according to my small capacity and weak judgment, to consider this book useful in any way. But it seems so very manifest to me that a great labor was expended on it which produced nothing of value, although my judgment concedes that Master Jean de Meun was a very great, learned, and eloquent clerk. But he would have been able to produce so much better a work, more profitable, and of higher sentiment, if he had applied himself to it, and that he did not do so is great loss. I suppose, however, that perhaps the great carnality with which he was filled caused him to abandon himself to desire rather than to the good of his soul, for by one's actions generally the inclinations are known. Notwithstanding, I do not condemn the *Roman de la Rose* entirely, for it does indeed contain some good things, and its style is poetically pleasing, but therein lies the greater peril, for the more authentic the good the more faith one puts in the evil. And in this way many learned men have sometimes sown great errors by intermingling good and evil and by covering the errors over with truth and virtue. Thus if his priest Genius can say, "Flee, flee woman, the evil serpent hidden in the grass"; I can say, "Flee, flee the malice concealed in the shadow of goodness and virtue."

Therefore, I say this in conclusion to you, dear Sir, and to all your allies who praise this work so

[6]Christine refers here, of course, to the thinly veiled description of the sexual act which concludes the *Roman de la Rose*. [Trs.]

[7]The goliards were satiric poets of the thirteenth and fourteenth centuries. [Ed.]

highly and make so much of it that you dare and presume to minimize almost all other works by comparison — I say that it does not merit such praise (saving your good grace) and that you do great wrong to the more deserving works. For a work without usefulness, contributing nothing to the general or personal good (even though we concede it to be delightful, the fruit of great work and labor), in no way deserves praise. And as in former times the triumphant Romans would not attribute praise or honor to anything if it was not to the utility of the Republic, let us look to their example to see whether we can crown this Romance. But having considered the aforementioned things and numerous others we have touched on, I consider it more fitting to bury it in fire than to crown it with laurel, although you call it a mirror of good living and, for men of all classes, an example of good social conduct and of the wise, moral life. But to the contrary (saving your grace) I call it an exhortation to vice, a comfort to dissolute life, a doctrine full of deception, the way to damnation, a public defamer, the cause of suspicion and misbelieving, the shame of many people, and possibly the occasion of heresy. But I know well that you will excuse it by replying to me that therein he enjoins man to do the good but to eschew the evil. But my reasoning is better, for I can show that there is no point in reminding human nature, which is naturally inclined to evil, that it limps on one foot, in the hope that it will then walk straighter. Do you wish to speak of all the good which can be found in this book? Certainly, far more virtuous things, eloquently expressed, closer to the truth, and more profitable to the decorous and moral life can be found in many other books — books written by certain philosophers and by teachers of our faith, like Aristotle, Seneca, St. Paul, St. Augustine, and others, as you well know. For these testify and teach how to pursue virtue and flee vice more clearly and plainly than Master Jean de Meun has ever been able to do. But such teachings are not usually heard or remembered by fleshly men. They are like the thirsty invalid who, when the doctor permits him to drink, does so gladly and excessively, for the lust for drinking leads him to believe that now it will do him no harm.[8] If by God's grace you were restored to the light and purity of a clear conscience, freed from the stain and pollution of sin or any sinful intent, and purged by the prick of contrition which reveals the secrets of conscience and condemns self-will — and may God grant it to you and to all others — then you would be more receptive to truth and thus would make a different judgment of the *Rose;* perhaps you would wish that you had never seen it. So much suffices. And may it not be imputed to me as folly, arrogance, or presumption, that I, a woman, should dare to reproach and call into question so subtle an author, and to diminish the stature of his work, when he alone, a man, has dared to undertake to defame and blame without exception an entire sex.

[8]The passage is somewhat difficult to translate, because the comparison contains only its first term and is not completely worked out. Cf. Ovid, *Amores,* III.iv.18. [Trs.]

Sir Philip Sidney

1554–1586

As a skilled courtier, scholar, soldier, and poet, Philip Sidney was the pattern of the English Renaissance gentleman. After attending Shrewsbury School and Christ Church College at Oxford, and making a grand tour of the continent, he established himself at Elizabeth's court, where he joined the faction led by one of the Queen's favorites, his uncle Robert Dudley, Earl of Leicester. Sidney ended his short life as military governor in Flanders during the Dutch wars. His heroic death at the battle of Zutphen was the stuff of legend: Sidney is said to have courteously declined water and medical attention in favor of a lowlier fellow soldier, a deed that made him a model of the chivalric ideal. But notwithstanding his nobility of birth and spirit, Sidney's unique talents and personality would have procured him success and fame. His *Arcadia* (1593), a romance alternating prose with poetry, established a tradition for the English pastoral; it was a best-seller for over two centuries and was crucial to the development of the English novel. And his *Apology for Poetry,* written in 1583 and published in 1595, was the first significant piece of literary criticism in the English language. (The essay is also known as *The Defence of Poetry,* the title of a slightly earlier version.)

The occasion of *An Apology for Poetry* was to refute *The Schoole of Abuse* (1579), a moralistic attack on poetry written by Puritan minister Stephen Gosson and dedicated (without leave) to Sidney himself. In constructing his *apologia* — Greek for a legal defense — Sidney addressed himself less to Gosson than to Plato, whose *Republic* provides most of the ammunition the Puritan divine expended against poetry. Sidney's *Apology* is structured according to the principles of medieval rhetoric like a good legal brief, with an introduction that draws the reader into the case while offering reassurance of the ethical rightness of the speaker, a central argumentative section, a set of answers to objections, and a glowing peroration. The contemporary reader must have patience, however, with the slow Senecan amble of Sidney's sentences. They were formed before muscularity became the mainstay of English prose. The reader who gets lost will be glad of another characteristic of Renaissance prose: Sidney signals all his transitions with a rapid and elegant summary of the preceding section.

Sidney opens the systematic section of the *Apology* with a definition of poetry, which he calls "an art of imitation, for so Aristotle termeth it in his word *mimesis,* that is to say, a representing, counterfeiting, or figuring forth. . . ." The definition suggests an affinity with Aristotle that is more apparent than real, for Sidney concludes with the Horatian phrase ". . . with this end, to teach and delight." Like many Renaissance theorists, Sidney appeals to mimesis not because it is a crucial principle, but in order to set limits to his subject. He wants to differentiate that class of poetry he will discuss, fictions based on human action, from hymns and psalms on the one hand and philosophy or history or natural science written in verse on the other. The distinction is needed: The two latter types of poetry were not under attack as were fictions. But the end, "to teach and delight," is the pivotal phrase.

Sidney's world, like Plato's, is structured hierarchically and holistically. Like Plato also, he sees the sciences and arts all directed to a single end, "the mistress-knowledge, by the Greeks called *architectonike*, which stands . . . in the knowledge of a man's self, in the ethic and politic consideration, with the end of well doing and not of well knowing only." Horsemanship — the art Sidney begins his *Apology* by mentioning — is no end in itself but serves the art of the soldier, just as the soldier's art serves the statesman's; the ultimate goal is right action.

The arts are judged by their distance from that architectonic goal: the closer, the higher. Thus divinity, Sidney concedes, must be the highest of the sciences, and with this no merely earthly art, including poetry, can compete. It is only against the other major sublunary disciplines — law, history, and philosophy — that Sidney pits the poets. Which of these arts will best serve to make men better? Once the question is so phrased, poetry excels. For law at best keeps us from evil: Its function is not to make us good. Ethical philosophy will help us with the moral distinctions, but philosophy, although it teaches us what virtue is, will not *move* us to virtuous action. History occasionally teaches sound moral lessons — yet just as often its examples are immoral: how the evil triumphed or the virtuous were slain. Only poetry always provides poetic justice to move us to virtuous action, and by the pleasure it gives, move us to go on reading it. Poetry does not merely teach and delight; for Sidney it delights *in order to* teach.

Sidney's aesthetic principle, then, is Horatian, while his metaphysics owes much to Plato. Because of this, whenever he quotes and glosses Aristotle, he subtly alters and distorts his meaning. On page 142, for instance, Sidney argues for the poets and against the claims of history by quoting *Poetics,* Chapter 9, that "poetry is *philosophoteron* and *spoudaioteron,* that is to say, it is more philosophical and more studiously serious than history. . . . because poesy dealeth with *katholou,* that is to say, with the universal consideration, and the history with *kathekaston,* the particular. . . ." The quotation is accurate as far as it goes, but within the same paragraph, Sidney loses track of the distinction between the universal and the particular, substituting one more consistent with his basic Platonism between the *ideal* and the *real.* ("But if the question be . . . whether it be better to have it set down as it should be, or as it was, then certainly is more doctrinable [instructive] the feigned Cyrus in Xenophon than the true Cyrus in Justin. . . .")

The central argument in Sidney is based on poetry's "works and parts" — Elizabethan English for its *effects* and *genres.* After he has shown the superiority of poetry to law, history, and philosophy, he reviews the major genres of poetry to show that they are all instructive, or at least not injurious.

That done, Sidney runs through Gosson's four major objections to poetry in *The Schoole of Abuse.* The first, that there are more fruitful arts than poetry, his main argument has already disposed of. The second is an objection to fiction in general: that poets by the very nature of their trade must be liars. Here Sidney claims benefit of poetic license: that "the poet nothing affirmeth"; fictions are not asserted or received as verifiable truth and therefore can never deceive, as the statements of the historian or the scientist might.

The third objection, that "poetry abuseth man's wit," Sidney turns on its head. He admits that immoral poetry and fictions exist, but these constitute an abuse of the art, not a reflection of its deepest nature. In fact, the possible damage poetry may do, if its ends are perverted, is a reflection of poetry's importance — just as the improper use of the art of medicine will lead to illness and death. The fourth, that the poets were banished from Plato's republic, Sidney refutes with arguments ad hominem — that Plato, as a philosopher, was naturally in competition with the poets. While Sidney also expresses shock at Plato's frank discussions of homoerotic love (in the *Phaedrus* and the *Symposium*), in truth he wants Plato on his side, not on Gosson's, and his most serious argument here is that Plato banished poetry not because it was evil in its nature but only to avoid its possible abuses — such as the teaching of falsehoods about the nature of God. He thus assimilates the last objection to the previous one.

For many, the most interesting section of the *Apology for Poetry* is Sidney's digression on the arts in contemporary England, which he considered to be in a bad way. Applying the strict standards of Renaissance poetics to home-grown English verse and drama, Sidney finds most of his fellow poets admirable for their natural genius but lamentably ignorant about the rules and regulations that Horatian aesthetics had down the centuries evolved for literary art. Several of Sidney's accusations about the English theater — its neglect of the three unities of time, place, and action; mixing of comic scenes into tragedy, polluting genres that ought to be kept pure; indecorous portrayal of violence on the stage — will be debated nearly a century later in Dryden's *An Essay of Dramatic Poesy* (p. 163) and laid to rest after another century in Johnson's "Preface to *Shakespeare*" (p. 224). What Sidney thought to be immutable laws of art came to be seen, more and more, as mere conventions, useful in their day but no longer valid.

Sidney and his strictures on the artist's need for study and practice may seem pedantic unless we remember what was always before the well-traveled Sidney's eyes: how recently England had emerged from provincial barbarism into the sunlight of Elizabethan courtliness, and how much the English still needed to learn from the older cultures of Europe and the classical world. If these are the broad outlines of the *Apology,* this critical work repays close study as well. An undergraduate in one of my recent classes, Janet Strunk, noted that the word "poesy" itself switches gender in the course of the essay, and with the aid of a computer file of the essay we were able to confirm that, seven times referred to as "he" in the earlier sections of the essay, "poesy" becomes a "she" for Sidney three times toward its end.[1] Is this abstract gender-bending one more aspect of the Elizabethan fascination with cross-dressing, with which Sidney himself plays in the *Arcadia*? Or is it simply the argumentative context that dictates gender here? At the outset of the essay, poetry is portrayed as engaged in a contest to prove its excellence and virtue against rival

[1]For example, "But I list not to defend poesy with the help of her underling historiography" (p. 153); "Sweet Poesy, that hath anciently had kings . . . not only to favor poets, but to be poets; and of our nearer times can present for her patrons a Robert, king of Sicily . . ." (p. 153); "[drama] like an unmannerly daughter showing a bad education, causeth her mother poesy's honesty to be called in question" (p. 156). In the early part of the *Apology,* we often get sentences like this: "Nay truly, though I yield that poesy may not only be abused, but that, being abused, by the reason of his sweet charming force, it can do more hurt than any other army of words" (p. 150).

sciences like philosophy and history, and, like a participant in one of the formal Elizabethan tournaments, must be gendered masculine. By the end of the essay, though, poesy has become not the contender but what is contended for, the prize for which England's writers strive against those of other nations, the feminine reward of masculine valor. Such hidden metaphors remind us, if we needed such reminding, that the *Apology* was written by the Elizabethan age's foremost lyric poet, who could not help bringing his talents and wit into everything he did.

Selected Bibliography

Devereux, James A. "The Meaning of Delight in Sidney's Defense of Poesy." *Studies in the Literary Imagination* 15 (1982): 85–97.

Levao, Ronald. *Renaissance Minds and Their Fictions: Cusanus, Sidney, Shakespeare.* Berkeley: University of California Press, 1985.

Mason, H. A. "An Introduction to Literary Criticism by Way of Sidney's Apologie for Poetrie." *Cambridge Quarterly* 12, no. 2–3 (1984): 79–173.

McCoy, Richard C. *Sir Philip Sidney: Rebellion in Arcadia.* New Brunswick: Rutgers University Press, 1979.

Myrick, Kenneth Orne. *Sir Philip Sidney as a Literary Craftsman.* Cambridge: Harvard University Press, 1935.

Robinson, Forrest Glen. *The Shape of Things Known: Sidney's Apology in Its Philosophical Tradition.* Cambridge: Harvard University Press, 1972.

Spingarn, J. E. *A History of Literary Criticism in the Renaissance.* New York: Columbia University Press, 1912.

Stump, Donald V. "Sidney's Concept of Tragedy in the Apology and the Arcadia." *Studies in Philology* 79 (1982): 78–99.

Ulreich, John C., Jr. "Poets Only Deliver: Sidney's Conception of Mimesis." *Studies in the Literary Imagination* 15 (1982): 67–84.

Weiner, Andrew D. *Sir Philip Sidney and the Poetics of Protestantism.* Minneapolis: University of Minnesota Press, 1978.

An Apology for Poetry

When the right virtuous Edward Wotton and I were at the Emperor's Court together, we gave ourselves to learn horsemanship of John Pietro Pugliano, one that with great commendation had the place of an esquire in his stable. And he, according to the fertileness of the Italian wit, did not only afford us the demonstration of his practice, but sought to enrich our minds with the contemplations there which he thought most precious. But with none I remember mine ears were at any time more loaden, than when (either angered with slow payment, or moved with our learnerlike admiration) he exercised his speech in the praise of his faculty. He said soldiers were the noblest estate of mankind, and horsemen the noblest of soldiers. He said they were the masters of war and ornaments of peace; speedy goers and strong abiders; triumphers both in camps and courts. Nay, to so unbelieved a point he proceeded, as that no earthly thing bred such wonder to a prince as to be a good horseman. Skill of government was but a *pedenteria*[1] in comparison. Then would he add certain praises, by telling what a peerless beast a horse was, the only serviceable courtier without flattery, the beast of most beauty, faithfulness, courage, and such more, that, if I had not been a piece of a logician before I came to him, I think he would have persuaded me to have wished myself a horse. But thus much at least with his no few words he drove into me, that self-love is better than any gilding to make that seem gorgeous wherein ourselves are parties. Wherein, if Pugliano's strong affection and weak arguments will not satisfy you, I will give you a nearer example of myself, who (I know not by what mischance) in these my not old years and idlest times having slipped into the title of a poet, am provoked to say something unto you in the defense of that my unelected vocation, which if I handle with more good will than good reasons, bear with me, since the scholar is to be pardoned that followeth the steps of his master. And yet I must say that, as I have just cause to make a pitiful defense of poor Poetry, which from almost the highest estimation of learning is fallen to be the laughingstock of children, so have I need to bring some more available proofs, since the former is by no man barred of his deserved credit, the silly latter hath had even the names of philosophers used to the defacing of it, with great danger of civil war among the Muses.

And first, truly, to all them that professing learning inveigh against poetry may justly be objected, that they go very near to ungratefulness, to seek to deface that which, in the noblest nations and languages that are known, hath been the first light-giver to ignorance, and first nurse, whose milk by little and little enabled them to feed afterwards of tougher knowledges. And will they now play the hedgehog that, being received into the den, drove out his host, or rather the vipers, that with their birth kill their parents? Let learned Greece in any of her manifold sciences be able to show me one book before Musaeus, Homer, and Hesiod, all three nothing else but poets. Nay, let any history be brought that can say any writers were there before them, if they were not men of the same skill, as Orpheus, Linus, and some other are named, who, having been the first of that country that made pens deliverers of their knowledge to their posterity, may justly challenge to be called their fathers in learning, for not only in time they had this priority (although in itself antiquity be venerable) but went before them, as causes to draw with their charming sweetness the wild untamed wits to an admiration of knowledge, so, as Amphion was said to move stones with his poetry to build Thebes, and Orpheus to be listened to by beasts — indeed stony and beastly people.[2] So among the Romans were Livius Andronicus, and Ennius. So in the Italian language the first that made it aspire to be a treasure-house of science were the poets Dante, Boccaccio, and Petrarch. So in our English were Gower and Chaucer.

After whom, encouraged and delighted with their excellent foregoing, others have followed, to beautify our mother tongue, as well in the same kind as in other arts. This did so notably show itself that the philosophers of Greece durst not a long time appear to the world but under the masks of poets. So Thales, Empedocles, and Parmenides sang their natural philosophy in verses; so did Pythagoras and Phocylides their moral counsels; so did Tyrtaeus in war matters, and Solon in matters of policy: or rather, they, being poets, did exercise their delightful vein in those points of highest knowledge, which before them lay hid to the world. For that wise Solon was directly a poet it is manifest, having written in verse the notable fable of the Atlantic Island, which was continued by Plato.

And truly, even Plato, whosoever well considereth shall find that in the body of his work, though the inside and strength were philosophy, the skin as it were and beauty depended most of poetry: for all standeth upon dialogues, wherein he feigneth many honest burgesses of Athens to speak of such matters, that, if they had been set on the rack, they would never have confessed them, besides his poetical describing the circumstances of their meetings, as the well ordering of

[1]Pedantry: useless book-learning. [Ed.]

[2]Sidney's notion of poetry's power derives from Horace's *Art of Poetry*. See p. 76. [Ed.]

a banquet, the delicacy of a walk, with interlacing mere tales, as Gyges' ring, and others, which who knoweth not to be flowers of poetry did never walk into Apollo's garden.[3]

And even historiographers (although their lips sound of things done, and verity be written in their foreheads) have been glad to borrow both fashion and perchance weight of poets. So Herodotus entitled his history by the name of the nine Muses;[4] and both he and all the rest that followed him either stole or usurped of poetry their passionate describing of passions, the many particularities of battles, which no man could affirm, or, if that be denied me, long orations put in the mouths of great kinds and captains, which it is certain they never pronounced. So that, truly, neither philosopher nor historiographer could at the first have entered into the gates of popular judgments, if they had not taken a great passport of poetry, which in all nations at this day, where learning flourisheth not, is plain to be seen, in all which they have some feeling of poetry. In Turkey, besides their lawgiving divines, they have no other writers but poets. In our neighbor country Ireland, where truly learning goeth very bare, yet are their poets held in a devout reverence. Even among the most barbarous and simple Indians where no writing is, yet have they their poets, who make and sing songs, which they call *areytos,* both of their ancestors' deeds and praises of their gods — a sufficient probability that, if ever learning come among them, it must be by having their hard dull wits softened and sharpened with the sweet delights of poetry. For until they find a pleasure in the exercises of the mind, great promises of much knowledge will little persuade them that know not the fruits of knowledge. In Wales, the true remnant of the ancient Britons, as there are good authorities to show the long time they had poets, which they called bards, so through all the conquests of Romans, Saxons, Danes, and Normans, some of whom did seek to ruin all memory of learning from among them, yet do their poets, even to this day, last; so as it is not more notable in soon beginning than in long continuing. But since the authors of most of our sciences were the Romans, and before them the Greeks, let us a little stand upon their authorities, but even so far as to see what names they have given unto this now scorned skill.

Among the Romans a poet was called *vates,* which is as much as a diviner, foreseer, or prophet, as by his conjoined words *vaticinium* and *vaticinari* is manifest: so heavenly a title did that excellent people bestow upon this heart-ravishing knowledge. And so far were they carried into the admiration thereof, that they thought in the chanceable hitting upon any such verses great foretokens of their following fortunes were placed. Whereupon grew the word of *sortes Virgilianae*[5] when, by sudden opening Virgil's book, they lighted upon any verse of his making: whereof the histories of the emperors' lives are full, as of Albinus, the governor of our island, who in his childhood met with this verse, *"Arma amens capio nec sat rationis in armis"*;[6] and in his age performed it: which, although it were a very vain and godless superstition, as also it was to think that spirits were commanded by such verses — whereupon this word charms, derived of *carmina,*[7] "cometh" — so yet serveth it to show the great reverence those wits were held in. And altogether not without ground, since both the Oracles of Delphos and Sibylla's prophecies were wholly delivered in verses. For that same exquisite observing of number and measure in words, and that high flying liberty of conceit proper to the poet, did seem to have some divine force in it.

And may not I presume a little further, to show the reasonableness of this word *vates,* and say that the holy David's Psalms are a divine poem? If I do, I shall not do it without the testimony of great learned men, both ancient and modern. But even the name Psalms will speak for me, which, being interpreted, is nothing but

[3]The myth of Gyges' ring appears in *Republic,* Book II, and other myths appear in other dialogues; Plato also occasionally writes prose that modulates into dithyrambic verse, as in the *Ion* and the *Phaedrus.* [Ed.]

[4]Each of the nine books of Herodotus's *History* is titled with the name of one of the Muses. [Ed.]

[5]The Virgilian lots: a method of fortune-telling using a random passage from the *Aeneid.* [Ed.]

[6]"Insane, I seize my weapons; there's no sense in weapons. . . ." *Aeneid* 2:314. [Ed.]

[7]Songs. [Ed.]

"songs"; then that it is fully written in meter, as all learned Hebricians agree, although the rules be not yet fully found; lastly and principally, his handling his prophecy, which is merely poetical. For what else is the awaking his musical instruments, the often and free changing of persons, his notable *prosopopeias,*[8] when he maketh you, as it were, see God coming in his majesty, his telling of the beasts' joyfulness, and hills' leaping, but a heavenly poesy, wherein almost he showeth himself a passionate lover of that unspeakable and everlasting beauty to be seen by the eyes of the mind, only cleared by faith? But truly now having named him, I fear me I seem to profane that holy name, applying it to poetry, which is among us thrown down to so ridiculous an estimation. But they that with quiet judgments will look a little deeper into it, shall find the end and working of it such, as, being rightly applied, deserveth not to be scourged out of the church of God.

But now, let us see how the Greeks named it, and how they deemed of it. The Greeks called him "a poet" which name hath, as the most excellent, gone through other languages. It cometh of this word *poiein,* which is "to make": wherein, I know not whether by luck or wisdom, we Englishmen have met with the Greeks in calling him a *maker:* which name, how high and incomparable a title it is, I had rather were known by marking the scope of other sciences than by my partial allegation.

There is no art delivered to mankind that hath not the works of nature for his principal object, without which they could not consist, and on which they so depend, as they become actors and players, as it were, of what nature will have set forth. So doth the astronomer look upon the stars, and, by that he seeth, setteth down what order nature hath taken therein. So do the geometrician and arithmetician in their diverse sorts of quantities. So doth the musician in times tell you which by nature agree, which not. The natural philosopher thereon hath his name, and the moral philosopher standeth upon the natural virtues, vices, and passions of man; and "follow nature" (saith he) "therein, and thou shalt not err." The lawyer saith what men have determined; the historian what men have done. The grammarian speaketh only of the rules of speech; and the rhetorician and logician, considering what in nature will soonest prove and persuade, thereon give artificial rules, which still are compassed within the circle of a question according to the proposed matter. The physician weigheth the nature of a man's body, and the nature of things helpful or hurtful unto it. And the metaphysic, though it be in the second and abstract notions, and therefore be counted supernatural, yet doth he indeed build upon the depth of nature. Only the poet, disdaining to be tied to any such subjection, lifted up with the vigor of his own invention, doth grow in effect another nature, in making things either better than nature bringeth forth, or, quite anew, forms such as never were in nature, as the Heroes, Demigods, Cyclopes, Chimeras, Furies, and such like: so as he goeth hand in hand with nature, not enclosed within the narrow warrant of her gifts, but freely ranging only within the zodiac of his own wit.

Nature never set forth the earth in so rich tapestry as divers poets have done — neither with pleasant rivers, fruitful trees, sweet-smelling flowers, nor whatsoever else may make the too much loved earth more lovely. Her world is brazen, the poets only deliver a golden. But let those things alone, and go to man — for whom as the other things are, so it seemeth in him her uttermost cunning is employed — and know whether she have brought forth so true a lover as Theagenes, so constant a friend as Pylades, so valiant a man as Orlando, so right a prince as Xenophon's Cyrus, so excellent a man every way as Virgil's Aeneas. Neither let this be jestingly conceived, because the works of the one be essential, the other in imitation or fiction; for any understanding knoweth the skill of the artificer standeth in that idea or foreconceit of the work, and not in the work itself. And that the poet hath that idea is manifest, by delivering them forth in such excellency as he hath imagined them. Which delivering forth also is not wholly imaginative, as we are wont to say by them that build castles in the air: but so far substantially it worketh, not only to make a Cyrus, which had been but a particular excellency, as nature might have done, but to bestow a Cyrus upon the world,

[8]Personifications. [Ed.]

to make many Cyruses, if they will learn aright why and how that maker made him.

Neither let it be deemed too saucy a comparison to balance the highest point of man's wit with the efficacy of nature; but rather give right honor to the heavenly Maker of that maker, who, having made man to his own likeness, set him beyond and over all the works of that second nature: which in nothing he showeth so much as in poetry, when with the force of a divine breath he bringeth things forth far surpassing her doings, with no small argument to the incredulous of that first accursed fall of Adam, since our erected wit maketh us know what perfection is, and yet our infected will keepeth us from reaching unto it. But these arguments will by few be understood, and by fewer granted. Thus much (I hope) will be given me, that the Greeks with some probability of reason gave him the name above all names of learning. Now let us go to a more ordinary opening of him, that the truth may be more palpable: and so I hope, though we get not so unmatched a praise as the etymology of his names will grant, yet his very description, which no man will deny, shall not justly be barred from a principal commendation.

Poesy therefore is an art of imitation, for so Aristotle termeth it in his word *mimesis,*[9] that is to say, a representing, counterfeiting, or figuring forth — to speak metaphorically, a speaking picture; with this end, to teach and delight.[10] Of this have been three several kinds. The chief, both in antiquity and excellency, were they that did imitate the inconceivable excellencies of God. Such were David in his Psalms; Solomon in his Song of Songs, in his Ecclesiastes, and Proverbs; Moses and Deborah in their Hymns; and the writer of Job, which, beside other, the learned Emanuel Tremellius and Franciscus Junius do entitle the poetical part of the Scripture. Against these none will speak that hath the Holy Ghost in due holy reverence.

In this kind, though in a full wrong divinity, were Orpheus, Amphion, Homer in his *Hymns,* and many other, both Greeks and Romans, and this poesy must be used by whosoever will follow St. James's counsel in singing psalms when they are merry, and I know is used with the fruit of comfort by some, when, in sorrowful pangs of their death-bringing sins, they find the consolation of the never-leaving goodness.

The second kind is of them that deal with matters, philosophical: either moral, as Tyrtaeus, Phocylides, and Cato; or natural, as Lucretius and Virgil's *Georgics;* or astronomical, as Manilius and Pontanus; or historical, as Lucan; which who mislike, the fault is in their judgments quite out of taste, and not in the sweet food of sweetly uttered knowledge. But because this second sort is wrapped within the fold of the proposed subject, and takes not the course of his own invention, whether they properly be poets or no let grammarians dispute; and go to the third, indeed right poets, of whom chiefly this question ariseth, betwixt whom and these second is such a kind of difference as betwixt the meaner sort of painters, who counterfeit only such faces as are set before them, and the more excellent, who, having no law but wit, bestow that in colors upon you which is fittest for the eye to see, as the constant though lamenting look of Lucretia, when she punished in herself another's fault.

Wherein he painteth not Lucretia whom he never saw, but painteth the outward beauty of such a virtue. For these third be they which most properly do imitate to teach and delight, and to imitate borrow nothing of what is, hath been, or shall be; but range, only reined with learned discretion, into the divine consideration of what may be, and should be. These be they that, as the first and most noble sort may justly be termed *vates,* so these are waited on in the excellentest languages and best understandings, with the foredescribed name of poets; for these indeed do merely make to imitate, and imitate both to delight and teach, and delight to move men to take that goodness in hand, which without delight they would fly as from a stranger, and teach, to make them know that goodness whereunto they are moved: which being the noblest scope to which ever any learning was directed, yet want there not idle tongues to bark at them. These be subdivided into sundry more special denominations. The most notable be the heroic, lyric, tragic, comic, satiric, iambic, elegiac, pastoral, and certain others, some of these

[9]Aristotle, *Poetics,* Ch. I; see p. 42. [Ed.]
[10]Horace, *Art of Poetry;* see p. 75. [Ed.]

being termed according to the matter they deal with, some by the sorts of verses they liked best to write in; for indeed the greatest part of poets have appareled their poetical inventions in that numbrous kind of writing which is called verse — indeed but appareled, verse being but an ornament and no cause to poetry, since there have been many most excellent poets that never versified, and now swarm many versifiers that need never answer to the name of poets. For Xenophon, who did imitate so excellently as to give us *effigiem iusti imperii,* "the portraiture of a just empire," under name of Cyrus (as Cicero saith of him), made therein an absolute heroical poem.[11]

So did Heliodorus in his sugared invention of that picture of love in *Theagenes and Chariclea;* and yet both these writ in prose: which I speak to show that it is not rhyming and versing that maketh a poet — no more than a long gown maketh an advocate, who though he pleaded in armor should be an advocate and no soldier.[12] But it is that feigning notable images of virtues, vices, or what else, with that delightful teaching, which must be the right describing note to know a poet by, although indeed the senate of poets hath chosen verse as their fittest raiment, meaning, as in matter they passed all in all, so in manner to go beyond them — not speaking (table talk fashion or like men in a dream) words as they chanceably fall from the mouth, but peising[13] each syllable of each word by just proportion according to the dignity of the subject.

Now therefore it shall not be amiss first to weigh this latter sort of poetry by his works, and then by his parts,[14] and, if in neither of these anatomies he be condemnable, I hope we shall obtain a more favorable sentence. This purifying of wit, this enriching of memory, enabling of judgment, and enlarging of conceit, which commonly we call learning, under what name soever it come forth, or to what immediate end soever it be directed, the final end is to lead and draw us to as high a perfection as our degenerate souls, made worse by their clayey lodgings, can be capable of. This, according to the inclination of the man, bred many formed impressions. For some that thought this felicity principally to be gotten by knowledge and no knowledge to be so high and heavenly as acquaintance with the stars, gave themselves to astronomy; others, persuading themselves to be demigods if they knew the causes of things, became natural and supernatural philosophers; some an admirable delight drew to music; and some the certainty of demonstration to the mathematics. But all, one and other, having this scope — to know, and by knowledge to lift up the mind from the dungeon of the body to the enjoying his own divine essence. But when by the balance of experience it was found that the astronomer looking to the stars might fall into a ditch, that the inquiring philosopher might be blind in himself, and the mathematician might draw forth a straight line with a crooked heart, then, lo, did proof, the overruler of opinions, make manifest that all these are but serving sciences, which, as they have each a private end in themselves, so yet are they all directed to the highest end of the mistress-knowledge, by the Greeks called *architectonike,*[15] which stands (as I think) in the knowledge of a man's self, in the ethic and politic consideration, with the end of well doing and not of well knowing only — even as the saddler's next end is to make a good saddle, but his farther end to serve a nobler faculty, which is horsemanship; so the horseman's to soldiery, and the soldier not only to have the skill, but to perform the practice of a soldier. So that, the ending end of all earthly learning being virtuous action, those skills, that most serve to bring forth that, have a most just title to be princes over all the rest. Wherein we can show the poet's nobleness, by setting him before his other competitors, among whom as principal challengers step forth the moral philosophers, whom, me thinketh, I see coming towards me with a sullen gravity, as though they could not abide vice by daylight, rudely clothed for to witness outwardly their contempt of outward things,

[11]Sidney is praising Xenophon's *Cyropaedia,* or *Education of Cyrus.* [Ed.]

[12]Cf. Aristotle, *Poetics,* Ch. 9; see p. 48. [Ed.]

[13]Weighing, evaluating. [Ed.]

[14]"Works" and "parts" are, in modern English, effects and genres. [Ed.]

[15]In Aristotle, the controlling principle of something. For Sidney, the ultimate end of knowledge is the Greek ideal of *sophrosyne:* self-knowledge and self-mastery. [Ed.]

with books in their hands against glory, whereto they set their names, sophistically speaking against subtlety, and angry with any man in whom they see the foul fault of anger. These men casting largesse as they go of definitions, divisions, and distinctions, with a scornful interrogative do soberly ask whether it be possible to find any path so ready to lead a man to virtue as that which teacheth what virtue is — and teacheth it not only by delivering forth his very being, his causes, and effects, but also by making known his enemy, vice (which must be destroyed), and his cumbersome servant, passion (which must be mastered), by showing the generalities that containeth it, and the specialties that are derived from it; lastly, by plain setting down, how it extendeth itself out of the limits of a man's own little world to the government of families, and maintaining of public societies.

The historian scarcely giveth leisure to the moralist to say so much, but that he, laden with old mouse-eaten records, authorizing himself (for the most part) upon other histories, whose greatest authorities are built upon the notable foundation of hearsay; having much ado to accord differing writers and to pick truth out of partiality; better acquainted with a thousand years ago than with the present age, and yet better knowing how this world goeth than how his own wit runneth; curious for antiquities and inquisitive of novelties; a wonder to young folks and a tyrant in table talk, denieth, in a great chafe, that any man for teaching of virtue, and virtuous actions, is comparable to him. "I am '*lux vitae, temporum magistra, vita memoriae, nuntia vetustatis,*'" &c.[16]

The philosopher (saith he)

> teacheth a dispurative virtue, but I do an active. His virtue is excellent in the dangerless Academy of Plato, but mine showeth forth her honorable face in the battles of Marathon, Pharsalia, Poitiers, and Agincourt. He teacheth virtue by certain abstract considerations, but I only bid you follow the footing of them that have gone before you. Old-aged experience goeth beyond the fine-witted philosopher, but I give the experience of many ages. Lastly, if he make the song book, I put the learner's hand to the lute; and if he be the guide, I am the light.

Then would he allege you innumerable examples, conferring story by story, how much the wisest senators and princes have been directed by the credit of history, as Brutus, Alphonsus of Aragon, and who not, if need be? At length the long line of their disputation maketh a point in this, that the one giveth the precept, and the other the example.

Now, whom shall we find (since the question standeth for the highest form in the school of learning) to be moderator? Truly, as me seemeth, the poet; and if not a moderator, even the man that ought to carry the title from them both, and much more from all other serving sciences. Therefore compare we the poet with the historian, and with the moral philosopher; and, if he go beyond them both, no other human skill can match him. For as for the Divine, with all reverence it is ever to be excepted, not only for having his scope as far beyond any of these as eternity exceedeth a moment, but even for passing each of these in themselves.

And for the lawyer, though Jus be the daughter of justice, and justice the chief of virtues, yet because he seeketh to make men good rather *formidine poenae* than *virtutis amore,*[17] or, to say righter, doth not endeavor to make men good, but that their evil hurt not others, having no care, so he be a good citizen, how bad a man he be: therefore, as our wickedness maketh him necessary, and necessity maketh him honorable, so is he not in the deepest truth to stand in rank with these who all endeavor to take naughtiness away, and plant goodness even in the secretest cabinet of our souls. And these four are all that any way deal in that consideration of men's manners, which being the supreme knowledge, they that best breed it deserve the best commendation.

The philosopher therefore and the historian are they which would win the goal, the one by precept, the other by example. But both, not having both, do both halt. For the philosopher, setting down with thorny argument the bare rule, is so hard of utterance, and so misty to be con-

[16]"The light of life, the master of the times, the life of memory, the messenger of antiquity." Cicero, *On Oratory* 2.9:36. [Ed.]

[17]Rather through fear of punishment than through love of virtue. [Ed.]

ceived, that one that hath no other guide but his shall wade in him till he be old before he shall find sufficient cause to be honest. For his knowledge standeth so upon the abstract and general, that happy is that man who may understand him, and more happy that can apply what he doth understand.

On the other side, the historian, wanting the precept, is so tied, not to what should be but to what is, to the particular truth of things and not to the general reason of things, that his example draweth no necessary consequence, and therefore a less fruitful doctrine.

Now doth the peerless poet perform both: for whatsoever the philosopher saith should be done, he giveth a perfect picture of it in someone by whom he presupposeth it was done; so as he coupleth the general notion with the particular example. A perfect picture I say, for he yieldeth to the powers of the mind an image of that whereof the philosopher bestoweth but a wordish description: which doth neither strike, pierce, nor possess the sight of the soul so much as that other doth.

For as in outward things, to a man that had never seen an elephant or a rhinoceros, who should tell him most exquisitely all their shapes, color, bigness, and particular marks, or of a gorgeous palace the architecture, with declaring the full beauties might well make the hearer able to repeat, as it were by rote, all he had heard, yet should never satisfy his inward conceits with being witness to itself of a true lively knowledge: but the same man, as soon as he might see those beasts well painted, or the house well in model, should straightways grow, without need of any description, to a judicial comprehending of them: so no doubt the philosopher with his learned definition — be it of virtue, vices, matters of public policy or private government — replenisheth the memory with many infallible grounds of wisdom, which, notwithstanding, lie dark before the imaginative and judging power, if they be not illuminated or figured forth by the speaking picture of poesy.

Tully[18] taketh much pains, and many times not without poetical helps, to make us know the force love of our country hath in us. Let us but hear old Anchises speaking in the midst of Troy's flames, or see Ulysses in the fullness of all Calypso's delights bewail his absence from barren and beggarly Ithaca. Anger, the Stoics say, was a short madness: let but Sophocles bring you Ajax on a stage, killing and whipping sheep and oxen, thinking them the army of Greeks, with their chieftains Agamemnon and Menelaus, and tell me if you have not a more familiar insight into anger than finding in the schoolmen his genus and difference. See whether wisdom and temperance in Ulysses and Diomedes, valor in Achilles, friendship in Nisus and Euryalus, even to an ignorant man carry not an apparent shining, and, contrarily, the remorse of conscience in Oedipus, the soon repenting pride of Agamemnon, the self-devouring cruelty in his father Atreus, the violence of ambition in the two Theban brothers, the sour-sweetness of revenge in Medea, and, to fall lower, the Terentian Gnatho and our Chaucer's Pandar so expressed that we now use their names to signify their trades; and finally, all virtues, vices, and passions so in their own natural seats laid to the view, that we seem not to hear of them, but clearly to see through them. But even in the most excellent determination of goodness, what philosopher's counsel can so readily direct a prince, as the feigned Cyrus in Xenophon; or a virtuous man in all fortunes, as Aeneas in Virgil; or a whole commonwealth, as the way of Sir Thomas More's *Utopia*? I say the way, because where Sir Thomas More erred, it was the fault of the man and not of the poet, for that way of patterning a commonwealth was most absolute, though he perchance hath not so absolutely performed it. For the question is, whether the feigned image of poesy or the regular instruction of philosophy hath the more force in teaching: wherein if the philosophers have more rightly showed themselves philosophers than the poets have attained to the high top of their profession, as in truth, *"mediocribus esse poetis, / Non dii, non homines, non concessere columnae"*;[19] it is, I say again, not the fault of the art, but that by few men that art can be accomplished.

Certainly, even our Saviour Christ could as well have given the moral commonplaces of

[18] Cicero. [Ed.]

[19] "But men and gods and booksellers won't put up / With second-rate poets." Horace, *Art of Poetry;* see p. 75. [Ed.]

uncharitableness and humbleness as the divine narration of Dives and Lazarus; or of disobedience and mercy, as that heavenly discourse of the lost child and the gracious father; but that his through-searching wisdom knew the estate of Dives burning in hell, and of Lazarus being in Abraham's bosom, would more constantly (as it were) inhabit both the memory and judgment. Truly, for myself, meseems I see before my eyes the lost child's disdainful prodigality, turned to envy a swine's dinner: which by the learned divines are thought not historical acts, but instructing parables. For conclusion, I say the philosopher teacheth, but he teacheth obscurely, so as the learned only can understand him; that is to say, he teacheth them that are already taught. But the poet is the food for the tenderest stomachs, the poet is indeed the right popular philosopher, whereof Aesop's tales give good proof: whose pretty allegories, stealing under the formal tales of beasts, make many, more beastly than beasts, begin to hear the sound of virtue from these dumb speakers.

But now may it be alleged that, if this imagining of matters be so fit for the imagination, then must the historian needs surpass, who bringeth you images of true matters, such as indeed were done, and not such as fantastically or falsely may be suggested to have been done. Truly, Aristotle himself, in his discourse of poesy, plainly determineth this question, saying that poetry is *philosophoteron* and *spoudaioteron,* that is to say, it is more philosophical and more studiously serious than history. His reason is, because poesy dealeth with *katholou,* that is to say, with the universal consideration, and the history with *kathekaston,* the particular: "now," saith he, "the universal weighs what is fit to be said or done, either in likelihood or necessity (which the poesy considereth in his imposed names), and the particular only marks whether Alcibiades did, or suffered, this or that."[20] Thus far Aristotle: which reason of his (as all his) is most full of reason. For indeed, if the question were whether it were better to have a particular act truly or falsely set down, there is no doubt which is to be chosen, no more than whether you had rather have Vespasian's picture right as he was, or at the painter's pleasure nothing resembling. But if the question be for your own use and learning, whether it be better to have it set down as it should be, or as it was, then certainly is more doctrinable the feigned Cyrus in Xenophon than the true Cyrus in Justin, and the feigned Aeneas in Virgil than the right Aeneas in Dares Phrygius.[21]

As to a lady that desired to fashion her countenance to the best grace, a painter should more benefit her to portrait a most sweet face, writing Canidia upon it, than to paint Canidia as she was, who, Horace sweareth, was foul and ill favored.

If the poet do his part aright, he will show you in Tantalus, Atreus, and such like, nothing that is not to be shunned; in Cyrus, Aeneas, Ulysses, each thing to be followed; where the historian, bound to tell things as things were, cannot be liberal (without he will be poetical) of a perfect pattern, but, as in Alexander or Scipio himself, show doings, some to be liked, some to be misliked. And then how will you discern what to follow but by your own discretion, which you had without reading Quintus Curtius? And whereas a man may say, though in universal consideration of doctrine the poet prevaileth, yet that the history, in his saying such a thing was done, doth warrant a man more in that he shall follow.

The answer is manifest: that if he stand upon that *was* — as if he should argue, because it rained yesterday, therefore it should rain today — then indeed it hath some advantage to a gross conceit; but if he know an example only informs a conjectured likelihood, and so go by reason, the poet doth so far exceed him, as he is to frame his example to that which is most reasonable, be it in warlike, politic, or private matters; where the historian in his bare *was* hath many times that which we call fortune to overrule the best wisdom. Many times he must tell events whereof he can yield no cause: or, if he do, it must be poetical. For that a feigned example hath as much force to

[20]Aristotle, *Poetics,* Ch. 9; see p. 48. [Ed.]

[21]A slippage of terms characteristic of Sidney has just occurred. Aristotle's distinction between the universal and the particular has just become a distinction between the ideal and the real, which will support Sidney's defense of the moral function of poetry. [Ed.]

teach as a true example (for as for to move, it is clear, since the feigned may be tuned to the highest key of passion), let us take one example wherein a poet and a historian do concur.

Herodotus and Justin do both testify that Zopyrus, King Darius's faithful servant, seeing his master long resisted by the rebellious Babylonians, feigned himself in extreme disgrace of his king: for verifying of which, he caused his own nose and ears to be cut off, and so flying to the Babylonians, was received, and for his known valor so far credited, that he did find means to deliver them over to Darius. Much like matter doth Livy record of Tarquinius and his son. Xenophon excellently feigneth such another stratagem performed by Abradates in Cyrus's behalf. Now would I fain know, if occasion be presented unto you to serve your prince by such an honest dissimulation, why you do not as well learn it of Xenophon's fiction as of the other's verity — and truly so much the better, as you shall save your nose by the bargain; for Abradates did not counterfeit so far. So then the best of the historian is subject to the poet; for whatsoever action, or faction, whatsoever counsel, policy, or war stratagem the historian is bound to recite, that may the poet (if he list) with his imitation make his own, beautifying it both for further teaching, and more delighting, as it pleaseth him, having all, from Dante's heaven to his hell, under the authority of his pen. Which if I be asked what poets have done so, as I might well name some, yet say I, and say again, I speak of the art, and not of the artificer.

Now, to that which commonly is attributed to the praise of histories, in respect of the notable learning is gotten by marking the success, as though therein a man should see virtue exalted and vice punished — truly that commendation is peculiar to poetry, and far off from history. For indeed poetry ever setteth virtue so out in her best colors, making Fortune her well-waiting handmaid, that one must needs be enamored of her. Well may you see Ulysses in a storm, and in other hard plights; but they are but exercises of patience and magnanimity, to make them shine the more in the near-following prosperity. And of the contrary part, if evil men come to the stage, they ever go out (as the tragedy writer answered to one that misliked the show of such persons) so manacled as they little animate folks to follow them. But the historian, being captived to the truth of a foolish world, is many times a terror from well doing, and an encouragement to unbridled wickedness.

For see we not valiant Miltiades rot in his fetters: the just Phocion and the accomplished Socrates put to death like traitors; the cruel Severus live prosperously; the excellent Severus miserably murdered; Sylla and Marius dying in their beds; Pompey and Cicero slain then when they would have thought exile a happiness?

See we not virtuous Cato driven to kill himself, and rebel Caesar so advanced that his name yet, after 1,600 years, lasteth in the highest honor? And mark but even Caesar's own words of the forenamed Sylla (who in that only did honestly, to put down his dishonest tyranny). *Literas nescivit,*[22] as if want of learning caused him to do well. He meant it not by poetry, which, not content with earthly plagues, deviseth new punishments in hell for tyrants, nor yet by philosophy, which teacheth *Occidendos esse;*[23] but no doubt by skill in history, for that indeed can afford your Cypselus, Periander, Phalaris, Dionysius, and I know not how many more of the same kennel, that speed well enough to their abominable injustice or usurpation. I conclude, therefore, that he excelleth history, not only in furnishing the mind with knowledge, but in setting it forward to that which deserveth to be called and accounted good: which setting forward, and moving to well doing, indeed setteth the laurel crown upon the poet as victorious, not only of the historian, but over the philosopher, howsoever in teaching it may be questionable.

For suppose it be granted (that which I suppose with great reason may be denied) that the philosopher, in respect of his methodical proceeding, doth teach more perfectly than the poet, yet do I think that no man is so much *philophilosophos*[24] as to compare the philosopher, in moving, with the poet.

And that moving is of a higher degree than teaching, it may by this appear, that it is well-

[22]He did not know literature. [Ed.]
[23]They must be put to death. [Ed.]
[24]A lover of philosophy. [Ed.]

nigh the cause and the effect of teaching. For who will be taught, if he be not moved with desire to be taught, and what so much good doth that teaching bring forth (I speak still of moral doctrine) as that it moveth one to do that which it doth teach? For, as Aristotle saith, it is not *gnosis* but *praxis*[25] must be the fruit. And how *praxis* cannot be, without being moved to practice, it is no hard matter to consider.

The philosopher showeth you the way, he informeth you of the particularities, as well of the tediousness of the way, as of the pleasant lodging you shall have when your journey is ended, as of the many by-turnings that may divert you from your way. But this is to no man but to him that will read him, and read him with attentive studious painfulness; which constant desire whosoever hath in him, hath already passed half the hardness of the way, and therefore is beholding to the philosopher but for the other half. Nay truly, learned men have learnedly thought that where once reason hath so much over-mastered passion as that the mind hath a free desire to do well, the inward light each mind hath in itself is as good as a philosopher's book; seeing in nature we know it is well to do well, and what is well and what is evil, although not in the words of art which philosophers bestow upon us. For out of natural conceit the philosophers drew it; but to be moved to do that which we know, or to be moved with desire to know, *Hoc opus, hic labor est.*[26]

Now therein of all sciences (I speak still of human, and according to the humane conceits) is our poet the monarch. For he doth not only show the way, but giveth so sweet a prospect into the way, as will entice any man to enter into it. Nay, he doth, as if your journey should lie through a fair vineyard, at the first give you a cluster of grapes, that, full of that taste, you may long to pass further. He beginneth not with obscure definitions, which must blur the margent[27] with interpretations, and load the memory with doubtfulness; but he cometh to you with words set in delightful proportion, either accompanied with, or prepared for, the well-enchanting skill of music; and with a tale forsooth he cometh unto you, with a tale which holdeth children from play, and old men from the chimney corner. And, pretending no more, doth intend the winning of the mind with wickedness to virtue: even as the child is often brought to take most wholesome things by hiding them in such other as have a pleasant taste: which, if one should begin to tell them the nature of aloes or rhubarb they should receive, would sooner take their physic at their ears than at their mouth. So is it in men (most of which are childish in the best things, till they be cradled in their graves): glad they will be to hear the tales of Hercules, Achilles, Cyrus, and Aeneas; and, hearing them, must needs hear the right description of wisdom, valor, and justice; which, if they had been barely, that is to say philosophically, set out, they would swear they be brought to school again.

That imitation whereof poetry is, hath the most conveniency to nature of all other, insomuch that, as Aristotle saith, those things which in themselves are horrible, as cruel battles, unnatural monsters, are made in poetical imitation delightful. Truly, I have known men, that even with reading *Amadis de Gaule* (which God knoweth wanteth much of a perfect poesy) have found their hearts moved to the exercise of courtesy, liberality, and especially courage.

Who readeth Aeneas carrying old Anchises on his back, that wisheth not it were his fortune to perform so excellent an act? Whom do not the words of Turnus move, the tale of Turnus having planted his image in the imagination?— "*Fugientem haec terra videbit? / Usque adeone mori miserum est?*"[28] Where the philosophers, as they scorn to delight, so must they be content little to move, saving wrangling whether virtue be the chief or the only good, whether the contemplative or the active life do excel: which Plato and Boethius well knew, and therefore made Mistress Philosophy very often borrow the masking raiment of Poesy. For even those hardhearted

[25]Not abstract knowledge but action. [Ed.]

[26]"That is the labor, that is the task." Virgil, *Aeneid* 6: 129. [Ed.]

[27]The margins of the page, where the notes to a text were then placed. [Ed.]

[28]"And shall the land see me fleeing? And after all, is death so sad a thing?" *Aeneid* 12:645–46. [Ed.]

evil men who think virtue a school name, and know no other good but *indulgere genio,*[29] and therefore despise the austere admonitions of the philosopher, and feel not the inward reason they stand upon, yet will be content to be delighted — which is all the good fellow poet seemeth to promise — and so steal to see the form of goodness, which seen they cannot but love ere themselves be aware, as if they took a medicine of cherries. Infinite proofs of the strange effects of his poetical invention might be alleged; only two shall serve, which are so often remembered as I think all men know them.

The one of Menenius Agrippa, who, when the whole people of Rome had resolutely divided themselves from the Senate, with apparent show of utter ruin, though he were (for that time) an excellent orator, came not among them upon trust of figurative speeches or cunning insinuations, and much less with farfetched maxims of philosophy, which (especially if they were Platonic) they must have learned geometry before they could well have conceived; but forsooth he behaves himself like a homely and familiar poet. He telleth them a tale, that there was a time when all the parts of the body made a mutinous conspiracy against the belly, which they thought devoured the fruits of each other's labor: they concluded they would let so unprofitable a spender starve. In the end, to be short (for the tale is notorious, and as notorious that it was a tale), with punishing the belly they plagued themselves. This applied by him wrought such effect in the people, as I never read that ever words brought forth but then so sudden and so good an alteration; for upon reasonable conditions a perfect reconcilement ensured. The other is of Nathan the Prophet, who, when the holy David had so far forsaken God as to confirm adultery with murder, when he was to do the tenderest office of a friend, in laying his own shame before his eyes, sent by God to call again so chosen a servant, how doth he it but by telling of a man whose beloved lamb was ungratefully taken from his bosom? — the application most divinely true, but the discourse itself feigned. Which made David (I speak of the second and instrumental cause) as in a glass to see his own filthiness, as that heavenly Psalm of Mercy well testifieth.

By these, therefore, examples and reasons, I think it may be manifest that the poet, with that same hand of delight, doth draw the mind more effectually than any other art doth: and so a conclusion not unfitly ensueth, that, as virtue is the most excellent resting place for all worldly learning to make his end of, so poetry, being the most familiar to teach it, and most princely to move towards it, in the most excellent work is the most excellent workman. But I am content not only to decipher him by his works (although works in commendation or dispraise must ever hold an high authority), but more narrowly will examine his parts: so that, as in a man, though all together may carry a presence full of majesty and beauty, perchance in some one defectious piece we may find a blemish. Now in his parts, kinds, or species (as you list to term them), it is to be noted that some poesies have coupled together two or three kinds, as tragical and comical, whereupon is risen the tragicomical. Some, in the like manner, have mingled prose and verse, as Sannazzaro and Boethius. Some have mingled matters heroical and pastoral. But that cometh all to one in this question, for, if severed they be good, the conjunction cannot be hurtful. Therefore, perchance forgetting some, and leaving some as needless to be remembered, it shall not be amiss in a word to cite the special kinds, to see what faults may be found in the right use of them.

Is it then the pastoral poem which is misliked? For perchance where the hedge is lowest they will soonest leap over. Is the poor pipe disdained, which sometime out of Melibaeus's mouth can show the misery of people under hard lords or ravening soldiers, and again, by Tityrus, what blessedness is derived to them that lie lowest from the goodness of them that sit highest; sometimes, under the pretty tales of wolves and sheep, can include the whole considerations of wrongdoing and patience; sometimes show that contention for trifles can get but a trifling victory; where perchance a man may see that even Alexander and Darius, when they strave who should be cock of this world's dunghill, the

[29]To indulge one's nature. [Ed.]

benefit they got was that the afterlivers may say, *"Haec memini et victum frustra contendere Thirsin: / Ex illo Coridon, Coridon est tempore nobis"* ?[30]

Or is it the lamenting elegiac, which in a kind heart would move rather pity than blame, who bewails with the great philosopher Heraclitus the weakness of mankind and the wretchedness of the world; who surely is to be praised, either for compassionate accompanying just causes of lamentation, or for rightly pointing out how weak be the passions of woefulness? Is it the bitter but wholesome iambic, which rubs the galled mind, in making shame the trumpet of villainy with bold and open crying out against naughtiness? Or the satiric, who *"omne vafer vitium ridenti tangit amico"*;[31] who sportingly never leaveth until he make a man laugh at folly, and, at length ashamed, to laugh at himself, which he cannot avoid, without avoiding the folly; who, while *"circum praecordia ludit,"*[32] giveth us to feel how many headaches a passionate life bringeth us to; how, when all is done, *"est Ulubris animus si nos non deficit aequus?"*[33]

No, perchance it is the comic, whom naughty play-makers and stage-keepers have justly made odious. To the argument of abuse I will answer after. Only thus much now is to be said, that the comedy is an imitation of the common errors of our life, which he representeth in the most ridiculous and scornful sort that may be, so as it is impossible that any beholder can be content to be such a one.

Now, as in geometry the oblique must be known as well as the right, and in arithmetic the odd as well as the even, so in the actions of our life who seeth not the filthiness of evil wanteth a great foil to perceive the beauty of virtue. This doth the comedy handle so in our private and domestical matters, as with hearing it we get as it were an experience, what is to be looked for of a niggardly Demea, of a crafty Davus, of a flattering Gnatho, of a vainglorious Thraso; and not only to know what effects are to be expected, but to know who be such, by the signifying badge given them by the comedian. And little reason hath any man to say that men learn evil by seeing it so set out; since, as I said before, there is no man living but, by the force truth hath in nature, no sooner seeth these men play their parts, but wisheth them in *pistrinum;*[34] although perchance the sack of his own faults lie so behind his back that he seeth not himself dance the same measure; whereto yet nothing can more open his eyes than to find his own actions contemptibly set forth. So that the right use of comedy will (I think) by nobody be blamed, and much less of the high and excellent tragedy, that openeth the greatest wounds, and showeth forth the ulcers that are covered with tissue; that maketh kings fear to be tyrants, and tyrants manifest their tyrannical humors; that, with stirring the affects of admiration and commiseration, teacheth the uncertainty of this world, and upon how weak foundations gilden roofs are builded; that maketh us know, *"Qui sceptra saevus duro imperio regit, / Timet timentes, metus in auctorem redit."*[35]

But how much it can move, Plutarch yieldeth a notable testimony of the abominable tyrant Alexander Pheraeus, from whose eyes a tragedy, well made and represented, drew abundance of tears, who, without all pity, had murdered infinite numbers, and some of his own blood, so as he, that was not ashamed to make matters for tragedies, yet could not resist the sweet violence of a tragedy.

And if it wrought no further good in him, it was that he, in despite of himself, withdrew himself from hearkening to that which might mollify his hardened heart. But it is not the tragedy they do mislike; for it were too absurd to cast out so excellent a representation of whatsoever is most worthy to be learned. Is it the lyric that most displeaseth, who with his tuned lyre, and well-

[30]"I remember those things, and that conquered Thyrsis strove in vain; Since then Corydon is for us Corydon." Virgil, *Eclogues* 7:69–70. [Ed.]

[31]"The rogue touches every vice while making his friend laugh." Persius, *Satires* 1:116–17. [Ed.]

[32]"He plays about the heartstrings." From the passage above. [Ed.]

[33]"Happiness is to be found, even in Ulubrae [a dead city], so long as we don't lose our sense of proportion." Horace, *Epistles* I.11:30. [Ed.]

[34]A treadmill for slaves. [Ed.]

[35]"The savage ruler who wields the sceptre with a hard hand / Fears the timid, and thus fear returns to its author." Seneca, *Oedipus*, 705–06. [Ed.]

accorded voice, giveth praise, the reward of virtue, to virtuous acts, who gives moral precepts, and natural problems, who sometimes raiseth up his voice to the height of the heavens, in singing the lauds of the immortal God? Certainly, I must confess my own barbarousness, I never heard the old song of Percy and Douglas that I found not my heart moved more than with a trumpet; and yet is it sung but by some blind crowder, with no rougher voice than rude style; which, being so evil appareled in the dust and cobwebs of that uncivil age, what would it work, trimmed in the gorgeous eloquence of Pindar? In Hungary I have seen it the manner at all feasts, and other such meetings, to have songs of their ancestors' valor; which that right soldierlike nation think the chiefest kindlers of brave courage. The incomparable Lacedaemonians did not only carry that kind of music ever with them to the field, but even at home, as such songs were made, so were they all content to be the singers of them, when the lusty men were to tell what they did, the old men what they had done, and the young men what they would do. And where a man may say that Pindar many times praiseth highly victories of small moment, matters rather of sport than virtue; as it may be answered, it was the fault of the poet, and not of the poetry, so indeed the chief fault was in the time and custom of the Greeks, who set those toys at so high a price that Philip of Macedon reckoned a horse race won at Olympus among his three fearful felicities. But as the inimitable Pindar often did, so is that kind most capable and most fit to awake the thoughts from the sleep of idleness, to embrace honorable enterprises.

There rests the heroical, whose very name (I think) should daunt all backbiters; for by what conceit can a tongue be directed to speak evil of that which draweth with it no less champions than Achilles, Cyrus, Aeneas, Turnus, Tydeus, and Rinaldo? Who doth not only teach and move to a truth, but teacheth and moveth to the most high and excellent truth; who maketh magnanimity and justice shine throughout all misty fearfulness and foggy desires; who, if the saying of Plato and Tully be true, that who could see virtue would be wonderfully ravished with the love of her beauty — this man sets her out to make her more lovely in her holiday apparel, to the eye of any that will deign not to disdain until they understand. But if anything be already said in the defense of sweet Poetry, all concurreth to the maintaining the heroical, which is not only a kind, but the best and most accomplished kind of poetry.[36] For as the image of each action stirreth and instructeth the mind, so the lofty image of such worthies most inflameth the mind with desire to be worthy, and informs with counsel how to be worthy. Only let Aeneas be worn in the tablet of your memory, how he governeth himself in the ruin of his country, in the preserving his old father, and carrying away his religious ceremonies, in obeying the god's commandment to leave Dido, though not only all passionate kindness, but even the human consideration of virtuous gratefulness, would have craved other of him; how in storms, how in sports, how in war, how in peace, how a fugitive, how victorious, how besieged, how besieging, how to strangers, how to allies, how to enemies, how to his own; lastly, how in his inward self, and how in his outward government, and I think, in a mind not prejudiced with a prejudicating humor, he will be found in excellency fruitful, yea, even as Horace saith, *"melius Chrysippo et Crantore."*[37]

But truly I imagine it falleth out with these poet-whippers, as with some good women, who often are sick, but in faith they cannot tell where. So the name of poetry is odious to them, but neither his cause nor effects, neither the sum that contains him nor the particularities descending from him, give any fast handle to their carping dispraise.

Since then poetry is of all human learning the most ancient and of most fatherly antiquity, as from whence other learnings have taken their beginnings; since it is so universal that no learned nation doth despise it, nor no barbarous nation is without it; since both Roman and Greek gave divine names unto it, the one of *prophesying,* the

[36]It was characteristic of Renaissance criticism to favor epic over tragedy — unlike Aristotle, who in *Poetics,* Ch. 26, had favored the concise tragedy over the full-blown epic. [Ed.]

[37]"Better than Chrysippus and Crantor." Horace, *Epistles* I.2:4. Horace claims that Homer teaches virtue better than the above-mentioned two philosophers. [Ed.]

other of *making,* and that indeed that name of *making* is fit for him, considering that whereas other arts retain themselves within their subject, and receive, as it were, their being from it, the poet only bringeth his own stuff, and doth not learn a conceit out of a matter, but maketh matter for a conceit; since neither his description nor his end containeth any evil, the thing described cannot be evil; since his effects be so good as to teach goodness and to delight the learners; since therein (namely in moral doctrine, the chief of all knowledges) he doth not only far pass the historian, but, for instructing, is well-nigh comparable to the philosopher, and, for moving, leaves him behind him; since the Holy Scripture (wherein there is no uncleanness) hath whole parts in it poetical, and that even our Saviour Christ vouchsafed to use the flowers of it; since all his kinds are not only in their united forms but in their severed dissections fully commendable; I think (and think I think rightly) the laurel crown appointed for triumphing captains doth worthily (of all other learnings) honor the poet's triumph. But because we have ears as well as tongues, and that the lightest reasons that may be will seem to weigh greatly, if nothing be put in the counterbalance, let us hear, and, as well as we can, ponder, what objections may be made against this art, which may be worthy either of yielding or answering.

First, truly I note not only in these *mysomousoi,* "poet-haters," but in all that kind of people who seek a praise by dispraising others, that they do prodigally spend a great many wandering words in quips and scoffs, carping and taunting at each thing, which, by stirring the spleen, may stay the brain from a thorough beholding the worthiness of the subject.

Those kind of objections, as they are full of very idle easiness, since there is nothing of so sacred a majesty but that an itching tongue may rub itself upon it, so deserve they no other answer, but, instead of laughing at the jest, to laugh at the jester. We know a playing wit can praise the discretion of an ass, the comfortableness of being in debt, and the jolly commodity of being sick of the plague. So of the contrary side, if we will turn Ovid's verse, *"Ut lateat virtus proximitate mali,"* that "good lie hid in nearness of the evil," Agrippa will be as merry in showing the vanity of science as Erasmus was in commending of folly. Neither shall any man or matter escape some touch of these smiling railers. But for Erasmus and Agrippa, they had another foundation than the superficial part would promise. Marry, these other pleasant faultfinders, who will correct the verb before they understand the noun, and confute others' knowledge before they confirm their own, I would have them only remember that scoffing cometh not of wisdom; so as the best title in true English they get with their merriments is to be called good fools, for so have our grave forefathers ever termed that humorous kind of jesters. But that which giveth greatest scope to their scorning humors is rhyming and versing. It is already said (and, as I think truly said) it is not rhyming and versing that maketh poesy. One may be a poet without versing, and a versifier without poetry. But yet presuppose it were inseparable (as indeed it seemeth Scaliger judgeth) truly it were an inseparable commendation.[38] For if *oratio* next to *ratio,* "speech" next to "reason," be the greatest gift bestowed upon mortality, that cannot be praiseless which doth most polish that blessing of speech; which considers each word, not only (as a man may say) by his forcible quality, but by his best measured quantity, carrying even in themselves a harmony (without, perchance, number, measure, order, proportion be in our time grown odious). But lay aside the just praise it hath, by being the only fit speech for music (music, I say, the most divine striker of the senses), thus much is undoubtedly true, that if reading be foolish without remembering, memory being the only treasurer of knowledge, those words which are fittest for memory are likewise most convenient for knowledge.

Now, that verse far exceedeth prose in the knitting up of the memory, the reason is manifest — the words (besides their delight, which hath a great affinity to memory) being so set as one word cannot be lost but the whole work fails; which accuseth itself, calleth the remembrance back to itself, and so most strongly confirmeth it.

[38]In his *Poetics,* Julius Caesar Scaliger claimed that what the poet made was verses; Aristotle identified the poet's primary product as the imitation of a human action. [Ed.]

Besides, one word so, as it were, begetting another, as, be it in rhyme or measured verse, by the former a man shall have a near guess to the follower: lastly, even they that have taught the art of memory have showed nothing so apt for it as a certain room divided into many places well and thoroughly known. Now, that hath the verse in effect perfectly, every word having his natural seat, which seat must needs make the words remembered. But what needeth more in a thing so known to all men? Who is it that ever was a scholar that doth not carry away some verses of Virgil, Horace, or Cato, which in his youth he learned, and even to his old age serve him for hourly lessons? But the fitness it hath for memory is notably proved by all delivery of arts: wherein for the most part, from grammar to logic, mathematic, physic, and the rest, the rules chiefly necessary to be borne away are compiled in verses. So that, verse being in itself sweet and orderly, and being best for memory, the only handle of knowledge, it must be in jest that any man can speak against it. Now then go we to the most important imputations laid to the poor poets. For aught I can yet learn, they are these. First, that there being many other more fruitful knowledges, a man might better spend his time in them than in this. Secondly, that it is the mother of lies. Thirdly, that it is the nurse of abuse, infecting us with many pestilent desires, with a siren's sweetness drawing the mind to the serpent's tale of sinful fancy — and herein, especially, comedies give the largest field to ear (as Chaucer saith) — how both in other nations and in ours, before poets did soften us, we were full of courage, given to martial exercises, the pillars of manlike liberty, and not lulled asleep in shady idleness with poets' pastimes. And lastly, and chiefly, they cry out with an open mouth, as if they outshot Robin Hood, that Plato banished them out of his commonwealth.[39] Truly, this is much, if there be much truth in it. First, to the first, that a man might better spend his time is a reason indeed: but it doth (as they say) but *petere principium:*[40] for if it be, as I affirm, that no learning is so good as that which teacheth and moveth to virtue, and that none can both teach and move thereto so much as poetry, then is the conclusion manifest that ink and paper cannot be to a more profitable purpose employed. And certainly, though a man should grant their first assumption, it should follow (methinks) very unwillingly, that good is not good because better is better. But I still and utterly deny that there is sprung out of earth a more fruitful knowledge. To the second therefore, that they should be the principal liars, I answer paradoxically, but truly, I think truly, that of all writers under the sun the poet is the least liar, and, though he would, as a poet can scarcely be a liar. The astronomer, with his cousin the geometrician, can hardly escape, when they take upon them to measure the height of the stars.

How often, think you, do the physicians lie, when they aver things good for sicknesses, which afterwards send Charon a great number of souls drowned in a potion before they come to his ferry? And no less of the rest, which take upon them to affirm. Now, for the poet, he nothing affirms, and therefore never lieth. For, as I take it, to lie is to affirm that to be true which is false; so as the other artists, and especially the historian, affirming many things, can, in the cloudy knowledge of mankind, hardly escape from many lies. But the poet (as I said before) never affirmeth. The poet never maketh any circles about your imagination, to conjure you to believe for true what he writes. He citeth not authorities of other histories, but even for his entry calleth the sweet Muses to inspire into him a good invention; in truth, no laboring to tell you what is, or is not, but what should or should not be. And therefore, though he recount things not true, yet because he telleth them not for true, he lieth not — without we will say that Nathan lied in his speech, before alleged, to David; which as a wicked man durst scarce say, so think I none so simple would say that Aesop lied in the tales of his beasts: for who thinks that Aesop writ it for actually true were well worthy to have his name chronicled among the beasts he writeth of.

What child is there that, coming to a play, and seeing *Thebes* written in great letters upon an old door, doth believe that it is Thebes? If then a man

[39]Plato, *Republic,* see pp. 28–29. [Ed.]

[40]To beg the question — assume what one needs to prove. [Ed.]

can arrive, at that child's age, to know that the poets' persons and doings are but pictures what should be, and not stories what have been, they will never give the lie to things not affirmatively but allegorically and figuratively written. And therefore, as in history, looking for truth, they go away full fraught with falsehood, so in poesy, looking for fiction, they shall use the narration but as an imaginative ground plot of a profitable invention.

But hereto is replied, that the poets give names to men they write of, which argueth a conceit of an actual truth, and so, not being true, proves a falsehood. And doth the lawyer lie then, when under the names of John a Stile and John a Noakes he puts his case? But that is easily answered. Their naming of men is but to make their picture the more lively, and not to build any history; painting men, they cannot leave men nameless. We see we cannot play at chess but that we must give names to our chessmen; and yet, methinks, he were a very partial champion of truth that would say we lied for giving a piece of wood the reverend title of a bishop. The poet nameth Cyrus or Aeneas no other way than to show what men of their fames, fortunes, and estates should do.

Their third is, how much it abuseth men's wit, training it to wanton sinfulness and lustful love: for indeed that is the principal, if not the only, abuse I can hear alleged. They say the comedies rather teach than reprehend amorous conceits. They say the lyric is larded with passionate sonnets, the elegiac weeps the want of his mistress, and that even to the heroical Cupid hath ambitiously climbed. Alas, Love, I would thou couldst as well defend thyself as thou canst offend others. I would those on whom thou dost attend could either put thee away, or yield good reason why they keep thee. But grant love of beauty to be a beastly fault (although it be very hard, since only man, and no beast, hath that gift to discern beauty); grant that lovely name of Love to deserve all hateful reproaches (although even some of my masters the philosophers spent a good deal of their lamp-oil in setting forth the excellency of it); grant, I say, whatsoever they will have granted; that not only love, but lust, but vanity, but (if they list) scurrility, possesseth many leaves of the poets' books: yet think I, when this is granted, they will find their sentence may with good manners put the last words foremost, and not say that poetry abuseth man's wit, but that man's wit abuseth poetry.

For I will not deny but that man's wit may make poesy, which should be *eikastike,* which some learned have defined, "figuring forth good things," to be *phantastike,* which doth, contrariwise, infect the fancy with unworthy objects, as the painter, that should give to the eye either some excellent perspective, or some fine picture, fit for building or fortification, or containing in it some notable example, as Abraham sacrificing his son Isaac, Judith killing Holofernes, David fighting with Goliath, may leave those, and please an ill-pleased eye with wanton shows of better hidden matters. But what, shall the abuse of a thing make the right use odious? Nay truly, though I yield that poesy may not only be abused, but that being abused, by the reason of his sweet charming force, it can do more hurt than any other army of words, yet shall it be so far from concluding that the abuse should give reproach to the abused, that contrariwise it is a good reason, that whatsoever, being abused, doth most harm, being rightly used (and upon the right use each thing conceiveth his title), doth most good.

Do we not see the skill of physic (the best rampire[41] to our often-assaulted bodies), being abused, teach poison, the most violent destroyer? Doth not knowledge of law, whose end is to even and right all things, being abused, grow the crooked fosterer of horrible injuries? Doth not (to go to the highest) God's word abused breed heresy, and his name abused become blasphemy? Truly, a needle cannot do much hurt, and as truly (with leave of ladies be it spoken) it cannot do much good. With a sword thou mayest kill thy father, and with a sword thou mayest defend thy prince and country. So that, as in their calling poets the fathers of lies they say nothing, so in this their argument of abuse they prove the commendation.

They allege herewith, that before poets began to be in price our nation hath set their heart's de-

[41]Rampart, defense. [Ed.]

light upon action, and not upon imagination, rather doing things worthy to be written, than writing things fit to be done. What that before-time was, I think scarcely Sphinx can tell, since no memory is so ancient that hath the precedence of poetry. And certain it is that, in our plainest homeliness, yet never was the Albion nation without poetry. Marry, this argument, though it be leveled against poetry, yet is it indeed a chain-shot against all learning, or bookishness, as they commonly term it. Of such mind were certain Goths, of whom it is written that, having in the spoil of a famous city taken a fair library, one hangman, belike, fit to execute the fruits of their wits, who had murdered a great number of bodies, would have set fire to it. "No," said another very gravely, "take heed what you do, for while they are busy about these toys, we shall with more leisure conquer their countries."

This indeed is the ordinary doctrine of ignorance, and many words sometimes I have heard spent in it: but because this reason is generally against all learning, as well as poetry, or rather, all learning but poetry; because it were too large a digression to handle, or at least too superfluous (since it is manifest that all government of action is to be gotten by knowledge, and knowledge best by gathering many knowledges, which is reading), I only, with Horace, to him that is of that opinion, *"iubeo stultum esse libenter"*;[42] for as for poetry itself, it is the freest from this objection. For poetry is the companion of the camps.

I dare undertake, Orlando Furioso, or honest King Arthur, will never displease a soldier: but the quiddity of *ens* and *prima materia*[43] will hardly agree with a corselet. And therefore, as I said in the beginning, even Turks and Tartars are delighted with poets. Homer, a Greek, flourished before Greece flourished. And if to a slight conjecture a conjecture may be opposed, truly it may seem, that, as by him their learned men took almost their first light of knowledge, so their active men received their first motions of courage. Only Alexander's example may serve, who by Plutarch is accounted of such virtue, that fortune was not his guide but his footstool; whose acts speak for him, though Plutarch did not — indeed the Phoenix of warlike princes. This Alexander left his schoolmaster, living Aristotle, behind him, but took dead Homer with him. He put the philosopher Callisthenes to death for his seeming philosophical, indeed mutinous, stubbornness, but the chief thing he ever was heard to wish for was that Homer had been alive. He well found he received more bravery of mind by the pattern of Achilles than by hearing the definition of fortitude: and therefore, if Cato misliked Fulvius for carrying Ennius with him to the field, it may be answered that, if Cato misliked it, the noble Fulvius liked it, or else he had not done it: for it was not the excellent Cato Uticensis (whose authority I would much more have reverenced), but it was the former, in truth a bitter punisher of faults, but else a man that had never well sacrificed to the Graces. He misliked and cried out upon all Greek learning, and yet, being eighty years old, began to learn it, belike fearing that Pluto understood not Latin. Indeed, the Roman laws allowed no person to be carried to the wars but he that was in the soldier's roll, and therefore, though Cato misliked his unmustered persons, he misliked not his work. And if he had, Scipio Nasica, judged by common consent the best Roman, loved him. Both the other Scipio brothers, who had by their virtues no less surnames than of Asia and Afric, so loved him that they caused his body to be buried in their sepulcher. So as Cato's authority being but against his person, and that answered with so far greater than himself, is herein of no validity. But now indeed my burden is great; now Plato's name is laid upon me, whom, I must confess, of all philosophers I have ever esteemed most worthy of reverence, and with great reason, since of all philosophers he is the most poetical. Yet if he will defile the fountain out of which his flowing streams have proceeded, let us boldly examine with what reasons he did it. First truly, a man might maliciously object that Plato, being a philosopher, was a natural enemy of poets. For indeed, after the philosophers had picked out of the sweet mysteries of poetry the right discerning true points of knowledge, they forthwith, putting it in method, and making a school art of that

[42]"I ask him to be a fool as much as he likes." Horace, *Satires* I.1:63. [Ed.]

[43]The whatness of being and primal matter. Sidney uses scholastic terms here. [Ed.]

which the poets did only teach by a divine delightfulness, beginning to spurn at their guides, like ungrateful 'prentices, were not content to set up shops for themselves, but sought by all means to discredit their masters; which by the force of delight being barred them, the less they could overthrow them, the more they hated them. For indeed, they found for Homer seven cities strove who should have him for their citizen; where many cities banished philosophers as not fit members to live among them. For only repeating certain of Euripides' verses, many Athenians had their lives saved of the Syracusians, when the Athenians themselves thought many philosophers unworthy to live.

Certain poets, as Simonides and Pindarus, had so prevailed with Hiero the First, that of a tyrant they made him a just king; where Plato could do so little with Dionysius, that he himself of a philosopher was made a slave. But who should do thus, I confess, should require the objections made against poets with like cavillation against philosophers; as likewise one should do that should bid one read *Phaedrus* or *Symposium* in Plato, or the discourse of love in Plutarch, and see whether any poet do authorize abominable filthiness, as they do. Again, a man might ask out of what commonwealth Plato did banish them. In sooth, thence where he himself alloweth community of women. So as belike this banishment grew not for effeminate wantonness, since little should poetical sonnets be hurtful when a man might have what woman he listed. But I honor philosophical instructions, and bless the wits which bred them: so as they be not abused, which is likewise stretched to poetry.

St. Paul himself, who yet, for the credit of poets, allegeth twice two poets, and one of them by the name of a prophet, setteth a watchword upon philosophy — indeed upon the abuse. So doth Plato upon the abuse, not upon poetry. Plato found fault that the poets of his time filled the world with wrong opinions of the gods, making light tales of that unspotted essence, and therefore would not have the youth depraved with such opinions. Herein may much be said; let this suffice: the poets did not induce such opinions, but did imitate those opinions already induced. For all the Greek stories can well testify that the very religion of that time stood upon many and many-fashioned gods, not taught so by the poets, but followed according to their nature of imitation. Who list may read in Plutarch the discourses of Isis and Osiris, of the cause why oracles ceased, of the divine providence, and see whether the theology of that nation stood not upon such dreams which the poets indeed superstitiously observed, and truly (since they had not the light of Christ) did much better in it than the philosophers, who, shaking off superstition, brought in atheism. Plato therefore (whose authority I had much rather justly construe than unjustly resist) meant not in general of poets, in those words of which Julius Scaliger saith, *"Qua authoritate barbari quidam atque hispidi abuti velint ad poetas e republica exigendos"*;[44] but only meant to drive out those wrong opinions of the Deity (whereof now, without further law, Christianity hath taken away all the hurtful belief), perchance (as he thought) nourished by the then esteemed poets. And a man need go no further than to Plato himself to know his meaning: who, in his dialogue called *Ion,* giveth high and rightly divine commendation to poetry. So as Plato, banishing the abuse, not the thing, not banishing it, but giving due honor unto it, shall be our patron and not our adversary. For indeed I had much rather (since truly I may do it) show their mistaking of Plato (under whose lion's skin they would make an asslike braying against poesy) than go about to overthrow his authority; whom, the wiser a man is, the more just cause he shall find to have in admiration; especially since he attributeth unto poesy more than myself do, namely, to be a very inspiring of a divine force, far above man's wit, as in the afore-named dialogue is apparent.

Of the other side, who would show the honors have been by the best sort of judgments granted them, a whole sea of examples would present themselves: Alexanders, Caesars, Scipios, all favorers of poets; Laelius, called the Roman Socrates, himself a poet, so as part of *Heautontimorumenos*[45] in Terence was supposed to be

[44]"Barbarous and rude men would abuse this authority to drive poets out of the republic." Scaliger, *Poetics* 1:2. [Ed.]

[45]*The Self-Tormentor*. [Ed.]

made by him, and even the Greek Socrates, whom Apollo confirmed to be the only wise man, is said to have spent part of his old time in putting Aesop's fables into verses. And therefore, full evil should it become his scholar Plato to put such words in his master's mouth against poets. But what need more? Aristotle writes the *Art of Poesy:* and why, if it should not be written? Plutarch teacheth the use to be gathered of them, and how, if they should not be read? And who reads Plutarch's either history or philosophy, shall find he trimmeth both their garments with guards of poesy. But I list not to defend poesy with the help of her underling historiography. Let it suffice that it is a fit soil for praise to dwell upon; and what dispraise may set upon it, is either easily overcome, or transformed into just commendation. So that, since the excellencies of it may be so easily and so justly confirmed, and the low-creeping objections so soon trodden down; it not being an art of lies, but of true doctrine; not of effeminateness, but of notable stirring of courage; not of abusing man's wit, but of strengthening man's wit; not banished, but honored by Plato; let us rather plant more laurels for to engarland our poets' heads (which honor of being laureate, as besides them only triumphant captains wear, is a sufficient authority to show the price they ought to be had in) than suffer the ill-favoring breath of such wrongspeakers once to blow upon the clear springs of poesy.

But since I have run so long a career in this matter, methinks, before I give my pen a full stop, it shall be but a little more lost time to inquire why England (the mother of excellent minds) should be grown so hard a stepmother to poets, who certainly in wit ought to pass all other, since all only proceedeth from their wit, being indeed makers of themselves, not takers of others. How can I but exclaim, *"Musa, mihi causas memora, quo numine laeso!"*[46] Sweet Poesy, that hath anciently had kings, emperors, senators, great captains, such as, besides a thousand others, David, Adrian, Sophocles, Germanicus, not only to favor poets, but to be poets; and of our nearer times can present for her patrons a Robert, king of Sicily, the great King Francis of France, King James of Scotland; such cardinals as Bembus and Bibbiena: such famous preachers and teachers as Beza and Melancthon; so learned philosophers as Fracastorius and Scaliger; so great orators as Pontanus and Muretus; so piercing wits as George Buchanan; so grave counselors as, besides many, but before all, that Hospital of France, than whom (I think) that realm never brought forth a more accomplished judgment, more firmly builded upon virtue — I say, these, with numbers of others, not only to read others' poesies, but to poetize for others' reading — that poesy, thus embraced in all other places, should only find in our time a hard welcome in England, I think the very earth lamenteth it, and therefore decketh our soil with fewer laurels than it was accustomed. For heretofore poets have in England also flourished, and, which is to be noted, even in those times when the trumpet of Mars did sound loudest. And now that an overfaint quietness should seem to strew the house for poets, they are almost in as good reputation as the mountebanks at Venice. Truly even that, as of the one side it giveth great praise to poesy, which like Venus (but to better purpose) hath rather be troubled in the net with Mars than enjoy the homely quiet of Vulcan; so serves it for a piece of a reason why they are less grateful to idle England, which now can scarce endure the pain of a pen. Upon this necessarily followeth, that base men with servile wits undertake it, who think it enough if they can be rewarded of the printer. And so as Epaminondas is said, with the honor of his virtue, to have made an office, by his exercising it, which before was contemptible, to become highly respected, so these, no more but setting their names to it, by their own disgracefulness disgrace the most graceful poesy. For now, as if all the Muses were got with child, to bring forth bastard poets, without any commission they do post over the banks of Helicon, till they make the readers more weary than posthorses, while, in the meantime, they, *"queis meliore luto finxit praecordia Titan,"*[47] are better content to suppress the outflowing of their wit,

[46] "Tell me the reason, Muse: what was the injury to her divinity?" Virgil, *Aeneid* I:8. [Ed.]

[47] "Whom the Titan has formed out of finer clay." Juvenal, *Satires* 14:35. [Ed.]

than, by publishing them, to be accounted knights of the same order. But I that, before ever I durst aspire unto the dignity, am admitted into the company of the paper-blurrers, do find the very true cause of our wanting estimation is want of desert, taking upon us to be poets in despite of Pallas. Now, wherein we want desert were a thankworthy labor to express: but if I knew, I should have mended myself. But I, as I never desired the title, so have I neglected the means to come by it. Only, overmastered by some thoughts, I yielded an inky tribute unto them. Marry, they that delight in poesy itself should seek to know what they do, and how they do, and, especially, look themselves in an unflattering glass of reason, if they be inclinable unto it. For poesy must not be drawn by the ears; it must be gently led, or rather it must lead; which was partly the cause that made the ancient-learned affirm it was a divine gift, and no human skill; since all other knowledges lie ready for any that hath strength of wit; a poet no industry can make, if his own genius be not carried unto it; and therefore is it an old proverb, *Orator fit, poeta nascitur*.[48] Yet confess I always that as the fertilest ground must be manured, so must the highest-flying wit have a Daedalus to guide him. that Daedalus, they say, both in this and in other, hath three wings to bear itself up into the air of due commendation: that is, art, imitation, and exercise. But these, neither artificial rules nor imitative patterns, we much cumber ourselves withal. Exercise indeed we do, but that very forebackwardly: for where we should exercise to know, we exercise as having known: and so is our brain delivered of much matter which never was begotten by knowledge. For, there being two principal parts — matter to be expressed by words and words to express the matter — in neither we use art or imitation rightly. Our matter is *quodlibet*[49] indeed, though wrongly performing Ovid's verse, "*Quicquid conabar dicere, versus erat*":[50] never marshaling it into an assured rank, that almost the readers cannot tell where to find themselves.

Chaucer, undoubtedly, did excellently in his *Troilus and Cressida;* of whom, truly, I know not whether to marvel more, either that he in that misty time could see so clearly, or that we in this clear age walk so stumblingly after him. Yet had he great wants, fit to be forgiven in so reverent antiquity. I account the *Mirror of Magistrates* meetly furnished of beautiful parts, and in the Earl of Surrey's *Lyrics* many things tasting of a noble birth, and worthy of a noble mind. The *Shepherd's Calendar* hath much poetry in his eclogues, indeed worthy the reading, if I be not deceived. That same framing of his style to an old rustic language I dare not allow, since neither Theocritus in Greek, Virgil in Latin, nor Sannazzaro in Italian did affect it. Besides these, do I not remember to have seen but few (to speak boldly) printed, that have poetical sinews in them: for proof whereof, let but most of the verses be put in prose, and then ask the meaning; and it will be found that one verse did but beget another, without ordering at the first what should be at the last; which becomes a confused mass of words, with a tingling sound of rhyme, barely accompanied with reason.

Our tragedies and comedies (not without cause cried out against), observing rules neither of honest civility nor of skillful poetry, excepting *Gorboduc* (again, I say, of those that I have seen), which notwithstanding, as it is full of stately speeches and well-sounding phrases, climbing to the height of Seneca's style, and as full of notable morality, which it doth most delightfully teach, and so obtain the very end of poesy, yet in truth it is very defectious in the circumstances, which grieveth me, because it might not remain as an exact model of all tragedies. For it is faulty both in place and time, the two necessary companions of all corporal actions.[51] For where the stage should always represent but one place, and the uttermost time presupposed in it should be, both by Aristotle's precept and common reason, but one day, there is both many days, and many places, inartificially[52] imagined. But if it be so in *Gorboduc,* how much more in all the rest, where

[48]The orator is made; the poet is born. [Ed.]

[49]An impromptu performance. [Ed.]

[50]"Whatever I tried to say was verse." Ovid, *Tristia* IV. 10:26. [Ed.]

[51]*Gorboduc* fails to satisfy the unities of place and time, which Sidney ascribes to Aristotle. [Ed.]

[52]Unartistically. [Ed.]

you shall have Asia of the one side, and Afric of the other, and so many other underkingdoms, that the player, when he cometh in, must ever begin with telling where he is, or else the tale will not be conceived? Now ye shall have three ladies walk to gather flowers and then we must believe the stage to be a garden. By and by we hear news of shipwreck in the same place, and then we are to blame if we accept it not for a rock.

Upon the back of that comes out a hideous monster, with fire and smoke, and then the miserable beholders are bound to take it for a cave. While in the meantime two armies fly in, represented with four swords and bucklers, and then what hard heart will not receive it for a pitched field? Now, of time they are much more liberal, for ordinary it is that two young princes fall in love. After many traverses, she is got with child, delivered of a fair boy; he is lost, groweth a man, falls in love, and is ready to get another child; and all this in two hours' space: which, how absurd it is in sense, even sense may imagine, and art hath taught, and all ancient examples justified, and, at this day, the ordinary players in Italy will not err in. Yet will some bring in an example of *Eunuchus*[53] in Terence, that containeth matter of two days, yet far short of twenty years. True it is, and so was it to be played in two days, and so fitted to the time it set forth. And though Plautus hath in one place done amiss, let us hit with him, and not miss with him. But they will say, How then shall we set forth a story, which containeth both many places and many times? And do they not know that a tragedy is tied to the laws of poesy, and not of history; not bound to follow the story, but, having liberty, either to feign a quite new matter, or to frame the history to the most tragical conveniency? Again, many things may be told which cannot be showed, if they know the difference betwixt reporting and representing. As, for example, I may speak (though I am here) of Peru, and in speech digress from that to the description of Calicut; but in action I cannot represent it without Pacolet's horse. And so was the manner the ancients took, by some nuncius[54] to recount things done in former time or other place. Lastly, if they will represent an history, they must not (as Horace saith) begin *ab ovo*,[55] but they must come to the principal point of that one action which they will represent. By example this will be best expressed. I have a story of young Polydorus, delivered for safety's sake, with great riches, by his father Priam to Polymnestor, king of Thrace, in the Trojan war time. He, after some years, hearing the overthrow of Priam, for to make the treasure his own, murdereth the child. The body of the child is taken up by Hecuba. She, the same day, findeth a slight to be revenged most cruelly of the tyrant. Where now would one of our tragedy writers begin, but with the delivery of the child? Then should he sail over into Thrace, and so spend I know not how many years, and travel numbers of places. But where doth Euripides? Even with the finding of the body, leaving the rest to be told by the spirit of Polydorus. This need no further to be enlarged; the dullest wit may conceive it. But besides these gross absurdities, how all their plays be neither right tragedies, nor right comedies, mingling kings and clowns, not because the matter so carrieth it, but thrust in clowns by head and shoulders, to play a part in majestical matters, with neither decency nor discretion, so as neither the admiration and commiseration, nor the right sportfulness, is by their mongrel tragicomedy obtained. I know Apuleius did somewhat so, but that is a thing recounted with space of time, not represented in one moment: and I know the ancients have one or two examples of tragicomedies, as Plautus hath *Amphitrio*. But, if we mark them well, we shall find that they never, or very daintily, match hornpipes and funerals. So falleth it out that, having indeed no right comedy, in that comical part of our tragedy we have nothing but scurrility, unworthy of any chaste ears, or some extreme show of doltishness, indeed fit to lift up a loud laughter, and nothing else: where the whole tract of a comedy should be full of delight, as the tragedy should be still maintained in a well-raised admiration. But our comedians think there is no delight without laughter; which is

[53]Actually the *Self-Tormentor*, not the *Eunuch*. [Ed.]
[54]Messenger. [Ed.]

[55]"From the egg"; Horace praises Homer for not beginning his tale of the Trojan war with the egg from which Helen was hatched. See the *Art of Poetry*, p. 71. [Ed.]

very wrong, for though laughter may come with delight, yet cometh it not of delight, as though delight should be the cause of laughter; but well may one thing breed both together. Nay, rather in themselves they have, as it were, a kind of contrariety: for delight we scarcely do but in things that have a conveniency to ourselves or to the general nature: laughter almost ever cometh of things most disproportioned to ourselves and nature. Delight hath a joy in it, either permanent or present. Laughter hath only a scornful tickling.

For example, we are ravished with delight to see a fair woman, and yet are far from being moved to laughter. We laugh at deformed creatures, wherein certainly we cannot delight. We delight in good chances, we laugh at mischances; we delight to hear the happiness of our friends, or country, at which he were worthy to be laughed at that would laugh. We shall, contrarily, laugh sometimes to find a matter quite mistaken and go down the hill against the bias, in the mouth of some such men, as for the respect of them one shall be heartily sorry, yet he cannot choose but laugh; and so is rather pained than delighted with laughter. Yet deny I not but that they may go well together. For as in Alexander's picture well set out we delight without laughter, and in twenty mad antics we laugh without delight, so in Hercules, painted with his great beard and furious countenance, in woman's attire, spinning at Omphale's commandment, it breedeth both delight and laughter. For the representing of so strange a power in love procureth delight: and the scornfulness of the action stirreth laughter. But I speak to this purpose, that all the end of the comical part be not upon such scornful matters as stirreth laughter only, but, mixed with it, that delightful teaching which is the end of poesy. And the great fault even in that point of laughter, and forbidden plainly by Aristotle, is that they stir laughter in sinful things, which are rather execrable than ridiculous; or in miserable, which are rather to be pitied than scorned.[56] For what is it to make folks gape at a wretched beggar, or a beggarly clown; or, against the law of hospitality, to jest at strangers, because they speak not English so well as we do? What do we learn, since it is certain *"Nil habet infelix paupertas durius in se, / Quam quod ridiculos homines facit"?*[57] But rather a busy loving courtier, a heartless threatening Thraso, a self-wise–seeming schoolmaster, an awry-transformed traveler — these if we saw walk in stage names, which we play naturally, therein were delightful laughter, and teaching delightfulness: as in the other, the tragedies of Buchanan do justly bring forth a divine admiration. But I have lavished out too many words of this play matter. I do it because, as they are excelling parts of poesy, so is there none so much used in England, and none can be more pitifully abused; which, like an unmannerly daughter showing a bad education, causeth her mother poesy's honesty to be called in question. Other sorts of poetry almost have we none, but that lyrical kind of songs and sonnets: which, Lord, if he gave us so good minds, how well it might be employed, and with how heavenly fruit, both private and public, in singing the praises of the immortal beauty, the immortal goodness of that God who giveth us hands to write and wits to conceive; of which we might well want words, but never matter; of which we could turn our eyes to nothing, but we should ever have new budding occasions. But truly many of such writings as come under the banner of unresistible love, if I were a mistress, would never persuade me they were in love; so coldly they apply fiery speeches, as men that had rather read lovers' writings, and so caught up certain swelling phrases (which hang together like a man which once told me the wind was at northwest, and by south, because he would be sure to name winds enough), than that in truth they feel those passions, which easily (as I think) may be betrayed by that same forcibleness or *energia* (as the Greeks call it) of the writer. But let this be a sufficient though short note, that we miss the right use of the material point of poesy.

Now, for the outside of it, which is words, or (as I may term it) diction, it is even well worse. So is that honey-flowing matron eloquence appareled, or rather disguised, in a courtesanlike painted affectation: one time with so farfetched

[56]Sidney may be thinking of Ch. 5 of the *Poetics,* but this is not Aristotle's point there. [Ed.]

[57]"The worst thing about poverty is that it makes people ridiculous." Juvenal, *Satires* 2:152–53. [Ed.]

words, they may seem monsters, but must seem strangers, to any poor Englishman; another time, with coursing of a letter, as if they were bound to follow the method of a dictionary; another time, with figures and flowers, extremely winter-starved. But I would this fault were only peculiar to versifiers, and had not as large possession among prose-printers, and (which is to be marveled) among many scholars, and (which is to be pitied) among some preachers. Truly I could wish, if at least I might be so bold to wish in a thing beyond the reach of my capacity, the diligent imitators of Tully and Demosthenes (most worthy to be imitated) did not so much keep Nizolian paper books of their figures and phrases, as by attentive translation (as it were) devour them whole, and make them wholly theirs. For now they cast sugar and spice upon every dish that is served to the table, like those Indians, not content to wear earrings at the fit and natural place of the ears, but they will thrust jewels through their nose and lips, because they will be sure to be fine.

Tully, when he was to drive out Catiline, as it were with a thunderbolt of eloquence, often used that figure of repetition, *"Vivit. Vivit? Imo in Senatum venit,"* &c.[58] Indeed, inflamed with a well-grounded rage, he would have his words (as it were) double out of his mouth, and so do that artificially which we see men do in choler naturally. And we, having noted the grace of those words, hale them in sometime to a familiar epistle, when it were too much choler to be choleric. Now for similitudes in certain printed discourses, I think all herberists, all stories of beasts, fowls, and fishes are rifled up, that they come in multitudes to wait upon any of our conceits; which certainly is as absurd a surfeit to the ears as is possible: for the force of a similitude not being to prove anything to a contrary disputer, but only to explain to a willing hearer; when that is done, the rest is a most tedious prattling, rather overswaying the memory from the purpose whereto they were applied, than any whit informing the judgment, already either satisfied, or by similitudes not to be satisfied. For my part, I do not doubt, when Antonius and Crassus, the great forefathers of Cicero in eloquence, the one (as Cicero testifieth of them) pretended not to know art, the other not to set by it, because with a plain sensibleness they might win credit of popular ears; which credit is the nearest step to persuasion; which persuasion is the chief mark of oratory — I do not doubt (I say) that but they used these knacks very sparingly; which, who doth generally use, any man may see doth dance to his own music; and so be noted by the audience more careful to speak curiously than to speak truly.

Undoubtedly (at least to my opinion undoubtedly) I have found in divers small-learned courtiers a more sound style than in some professors of learning: of which I can guess no other cause, but that the courtier, following that which by practice he findeth fittest to nature, therein (though he know it not) doth according to art, though not by art: where the other, using art to show art, and not to hide art (as in these cases he should do), flieth from nature, and indeed abuseth art.

But what? Methinks I deserve to be pounded for straying from poetry to oratory: but both have such an affinity in this wordish consideration, that I think this digression will make my meaning receive the fuller understanding — which is not to take upon me to teach poets how they should do, but only, finding myself sick among the rest, to show some one or two spots of the common infection grown among the most part of writers: that, acknowledging ourselves somewhat awry, we may bend to the right use both of matter and manner; whereto our language giveth us great occasion, being indeed capable of any excellent exercising of it. I know some will say it is a mingled language. And why not so much the better, taking the best of both the other? Another will say it wanteth grammar. Nay truly, it hath that praise, that it wanteth grammar: for grammar it might have, but it needs it not; being so easy of itself, and so void of those cumbersome differences of cases, genders, moods, and tenses, which I think was a piece of the Tower of Babylon's curse, that a man should be put to school to learn his mother tongue. But for the uttering sweetly and properly the conceits of the mind, which is the end of speech, that hath it equally

[58]"He lives. Does he live? He even comes into the Senate." [Ed.]

with any other tongue in the world: and is particularly happy in compositions of two or three words together, near the Greek, far beyond the Latin: which is one of the greatest beauties can be in a language.

Now, of versifying there are two sorts, the one ancient, the other modern: the ancient marked the quantity of each syllable, and according to that framed his verse; the modern observing only number (with some regard of the accent), the chief life of it standeth in that like sounding of the words, which we call rhyme. Whether of these be the most excellent, would bear many speeches. The ancient (no doubt) more fit for music, both words and tune observing quantity, and more fit lively to express divers passions, by the low and lofty sound of the well-weighed syllable. The latter likewise, with his rhyme, striketh a certain music to the ear: and, in fine, since it doth delight, though by another way, it obtains the same purpose: there being in either sweetness, and wanting in neither majesty. Truly the English, before any other vulgar language I know, is fit for both sorts: for, for the ancient, the Italian is so full of vowels that it must ever be cumbered with elisions; the Dutch so, of the other side, with consonants, that they cannot yield the sweet sliding fit for a verse; the French, in his whole language, hath not one word that hath his accent in the last syllable saving two, called *antepenultima;* and little more hath the Spanish: and, therefore, very gracelessly may they use dactyls. The English is subject to none of these defects.

Now, for the rhyme, though we do not observe quantity, yet we observe the accent very precisely: which other languages either cannot do, or will not do so absolutely. That *caesura,* or breathing place in the midst of the verse, neither Italian nor Spanish have, the French, and we, never almost fail of. Lastly, even the very rhyme itself the Italian cannot put in the last syllable, by the French named the "masculine rhyme," but still in the next to the last, which the French call the "female," or the next before that, which the Italians term *sdrucciola.* The example of the former is *buono:suono,* of the *sdrucciola, femina: semina.* The French, of the other side, hath both the male, as *bon:son,* and the female, as *plaise:taise,* but the *sdrucciola* he hath not: where the English hath all three, as *due:true, father:rather, motion:potion,* with much more which might be said, but that I find already the triflingness of this discourse is much too much enlarged. So that since the ever-praise-worthy poesy is full of virtue-breeding delightfulness, and void of no gift that ought to be in the noble name of learning; since the blames laid against it are either false or feeble; since the cause why it is not esteemed in England is the fault of poet-apes, not poets; since, lastly, our tongue is most fit to honor poesy, and to be honored by poesy; I conjure you all that have had the evil luck to read this ink-wasting toy of mine, even in the name of the nine Muses, no more to scorn the sacred mysteries of poesy, no more to laugh at the name of *poets,* as though they were next inheritors to fools, no more to jest at the reverent title of a *rhymer;* but to believe, with Aristotle, that they were the ancient treasurers of the Grecians' divinity; to believe, with Bembus,[59] that they were first bringers-in of all civility; to believe, with Scaliger, that no philosopher's precepts can sooner make you an honest man than the reading of Virgil; to believe, with Clauserus, the translator of Cornutus, that it pleased the heavenly Deity, by Hesiod and Homer, under the veil of fables, to give us all knowledge, logic, rhetoric, philosophy, natural and moral, and *Quid non?;*[60] to believe, with me, that there are many mysteries contained in poetry, which of purpose were written darkly, lest by profane wits it should be abused; to believe, with Landino, that they are so beloved of the gods that whatsoever they write proceeds of a divine fury; lastly, to believe themselves, when they tell you they will make you immortal by their verses.

Thus doing, your name shall flourish in the printers' shops; thus doing, you shall be of kin to many a poetical preface; thus doing, you shall be most fair, most rich, most wise, most all; you shall dwell upon superlatives. Thus doing, though you be *"libertino patre natus,"* you shall suddenly grow *"Herculea proles," "si quid mea*

[59]Pietro Bembo (1470–1547), Italian scholar and critic. [Ed.]

[60]What not? [Ed.]

carmina possunt."[61] Thus doing, your soul shall be placed with Dante's Beatrix, or Virgil's Anchises. But if (fie of such a but) you be born so near the dull-making cataract of Nilus that you cannot hear the planetlike music of poetry, if you have so earth-creeping a mind that it cannot lift itself up to look to the sky of poetry, or rather, by a certain rustical disdain, will become such a mome as to be a momus of poetry; then, though I will not wish unto you the ass's ears of Midas, nor to be driven by a poet's verses (as Bubonax was) to hang himself, nor to be rhymed to death, as is said to be done in Ireland; yet thus much curse I must send you, in the behalf of all poets, that while you live, you live in love, and never get favor for lacking skill of a sonnet, and, when you die, your memory die from the earth for want of an epitaph.

[61]"Thus doing, though you be 'the son of a freed slave,' you shall suddenly grow 'Herculean offspring,' 'if my poems can do anything.'" The quotations are from Horace, Ovid, and Virgil. [Ed.]

John Dryden

1631–1700

Best known as the poet laureate of Charles II and James II, and as the satirical author of *Mac Flecknoe* (1682) and the political allegory *Absalom and Achitophel* (1681), Dryden was also one of the most successful of the Restoration dramatists, famous for comedies like *Marriage à-la-Mode* (1673); for tragedies like *All for Love* (1678); and for operatic melodramas, now long out of fashion, called "heroic plays." *An Essay of Dramatic Poesy* (1668) derives from Dryden's practical experience in all areas of the theater.

The *Essay* is neither a Platonic dialogue nor a treatise, but rather a formal debate on the drama among four speakers: Crites, Eugenius, Lisideius, and Neander. Although no one supposes that any such debate actually took place, the speakers have traditionally been identified with contemporary personages. Crites, whose name suggests his captiously critical air, may be Sir Robert Howard, Dryden's brother-in-law and sometime collaborator, with whom Dryden had publicly quarreled over the issue of rhyme in drama. Eugenius, which means "well-born," is probably Charles Sackville, Lord Buckhurst, Dryden's patron before his laureateship and an eminent Cavalier poet in his own right. Lisideius is Sir Charles Sedley (the name is a Latinized anagram of Sedley). And Neander (Greek for "new man") is Dryden himself, of middle-class origins. By using the debate form, Dryden gives the other side equal time (or nearly) but manages to reserve some of the best arguments for himself.

Like Jonathan Swift's *Battle of the Books*, the *Essay of Dramatic Poesy* might be thought of as one volley of the international controversy in the late seventeenth century over the relative value of the ancient and modern writers. Conservative thinkers like Swift felt that the ancients — Homer, Virgil, Juvenal — could never be surpassed, while others, enthusiastic about the advances in learning since the Renaissance, felt that by building upon the foundations of the past, the present might progress beyond it. ("Dwarfs who stand on the shoulders of giants may see farther than the giants themselves," said Isaac Newton, Dryden's contemporary and fellow Modern.) This context helps explain the debate between Crites and Eugenius on the merits of classical and modern drama.

But there was another even more topical concern. The London theaters, closed for twenty years during the Civil War and the Protectorate of Cromwell, had reopened only six years before, in 1662. The drama was beginning to revive, but the traditions of the Elizabethan and Jacobean stage had lapsed during the interregnum. It remained to be seen on what model the English stage would return. Would the new drama be built on the native Tudor-Stuart model and look to Shakespeare, Jonson, and Fletcher as exemplars? Or would the English stage imitate Racine and Corneille, who had created the elegant but rather formal drama of France, where Charles II and his cavaliers had spent most of the interregnum?

Underlying these topical concerns are a set of more abstract issues that divided Renaissance and neoclassical critics. One was the status of the so-called Three Unities of Time, Place, and Action, a set of rules for drama supposedly derived from Aristotle and Horace.[1] Under Unity of Time, it was claimed that the plot of a drama might take up no more than a single day from the first incident to the last; ideally, according to Pierre Corneille, the plot of a drama should last no longer than the dramatic representation itself — two hours or so. Under Unity of Place, it was asserted that the plot should be laid in a single city, ideally in a single room. Unity of Action meant that everything in a drama should further a single plot and that subplots, like that of Gloucester and his sons in *King Lear,* were to be avoided.

A second issue was that of generic integrity: comedy and tragedy were considered mutually exclusive, and characters and speeches appropriate to the one would not be appropriate to the other. The gravediggers in *Hamlet* or Iago's bawdy jokes in *Othello* would thus be inappropriate. A third issue was that of decorum: All acts of violence, especially deaths, should be performed offstage and revealed to the audience through narration. These matters were arguably a part of both Greek and Roman dramatic practice, though only Horace comments on them.

As the debate is joined between Crites and Eugenius, and between Lisideius and Neander, the reader is forced to dwell on an all-subsuming question: What is the status of the Three Unities, Generic Integrity, and Stage Decorum? Are they rules of art that hold for the ages or are they merely artistic conventions? Beyond this there is the further question: If there is no real difference between conventions and rules, then how do artistic styles change? If conventions may be irresponsibly disregarded, how can art function without them?

An Essay of Dramatic Poesy, like Aristotle's *Poetics,* hinges on a definition, this time of a *play,* which Lisideius defines as "a just and lively image of human nature, representing its passions and humours, and the changes of fortune to which it is subject; for the delight and instruction of mankind." The derivation from Horace and the *Ars Poetica* appears clearly in the last clause. Crites objects that the definition is "*a genere et fine,*" that it states only general class and purpose, implying that it is too broad, since it could serve as a definition of a novel or poem as well.

Crites is correct but has missed the main ambiguity in the definition: The combatants have differing interpretations of the key words "just" and "lively." For Crites, an image is "just" when it has been constructed according to correct rules; for Neander, when it gives a faithful impression of the original. For Lisideius, "lively" takes its older meaning of *lifelike;* for Neander it means something more like *spirited.*

Another confusion seems to arise over just what "mankind" is: While some of the debaters seem to be absolutists, Neander is a critical relativist who feels that the

[1]Unity of Action is the only unity that is taken directly and unequivocally from Aristotle's *Poetics* (Ch. 8). Unity of Time may derive from one passage in *Poetics,* Ch. 5 ("Tragedy endeavors as far as possible to confine itself to a single revolution of the sun or to exceed this but slightly"), which is contradicted by another passage in *Poetics,* Ch. 7 ("The proper magnitude is comprised within such limits that the sequence of events, according to the law of probability or necessity, will admit of a change from bad fortune to good or from good to bad"). Unity of Place does not appear in Aristotle or Horace, but one could claim that it follows as a corollary from the Unities of Time and Action: A single action occurring within a single day could not possibly, in the days before automobiles and airplanes, take place over a very widespread area.

French and the English will be delighted and instructed by very different sorts of things. This is not to suggest that the debaters are quarreling over the meaning of terms; on the contrary their apparent unanimity on the definition masks genuine disagreements over what drama ought to be.

In the final debate, Crites and Neander square off directly over the use of rhymed verse in the drama, with Crites attacking the practice and Neander defending it. In this section, Neander concedes half his ground by admitting the inappropriateness of rhyme in comedy. (In fact, Dryden was later to recant his position and write his tragedies, including the popular *All for Love,* in blank verse.) Here as elsewhere, however, Neander applies his audience-centered criteria, arguing that rhyme may be used in tragic drama if it is used well and thereby gains the acceptance of the public, while Crites puts forth a pseudo-mimetic argument that the characters of a drama may not speak poetry since their counterparts in real life spoke prose.[2]

For many readers, the most fascinating section of the *Essay of Dramatic Poesy* is Neander's comparative discussion of Shakespeare, Jonson, and Fletcher, and his explication of Jonson's *Epicoene, or The Silent Woman.* Abstract argument recedes as a major poet responds to his great exemplars. It is interesting to see how tastes have changed — that Shakespeare was not so certainly the greatest of the Elizabethan dramatists in Dryden's day as he is today. It is also enlightening to watch the principles of rhetorical criticism applied by a sensitive critic, who was also his age's most versatile practicing playwright.

Selected Bibliography

Bredvold, Louis I. *The Intellectual Milieu of John Dryden.* Ann Arbor: University of Michigan Press, 1934.

Cole, Elmer Joseph. *The Consistency of John Dryden's Literary Criticism in Theory and Practice.* Albuquerque: New Mexico University Press, 1970.

Eliot, T. S. *John Dryden: The Poet, the Dramatist, the Critic; Three Essays.* New York: Haskell House, 1966.

Hume, Robert D. *Dryden's Criticism.* Ithaca: Cornell University Press, 1970.

Huntley, Frank Livingstone. *On Dryden's Essay of Dramatic Poesy.* Ann Arbor: University of Michigan Press, 1951.

Mishra, J. B. *John Dryden: His Theory and Practice of Drama.* New Delhi: Bahri Publications, 1978.

Pechter, Edward. *Dryden's Classical Theory of Literature.* London and New York: Cambridge University Press, 1975.

Trowbridge, Hoyt. "The Place of Rules in Dryden's Criticism." *Modern Philology* 44 (1946): 84–96.

Watson, George. *John Dryden: Of Dramatic Poesy and Other Critical Essays.* 2 vols. London: J. Dent, 1962.

[2]Neither Aristotle nor Horace had so argued, certainly, and it is not clear where such literal-minded mimesis would stop. Should the characters in *Julius Caesar* have spoken in Latin because their historical originals did?

An Essay of Dramatic Poesy

It was that memorable day,[1] in the first summer of the late war, when our Navy engaged the Dutch: a day wherein the two most mighty and best appointed fleets which any age had ever seen, disputed the command of the greater half of the globe, the commerce of nations, and the riches of the universe. While these vast floating bodies, on either side, moved against each other in parallel lines, and our countrymen, under the happy conduct of his Royal Highness,[2] went breaking, by little and little, into the line of the enemies, the noise of the cannon from both navies reached our ears about the City; so that all men, being alarmed with it, and in a dreadful suspense of the event, which they knew was then deciding, every one went following the sound as his fancy led him; and leaving the town almost empty, some took towards the Park, some cross the river, others down it; all seeking the noise in the depth of silence.

Amongst the rest, it was the fortune of Eugenius, Crites, Lisideius and Neander,[3] to be in company together: three of them persons whom their wit and quality have made known to all the town: and whom I have chose to hide under these borrowed names, that they may not suffer by so ill a relation as I am going to make of their discourse.

Taking then a barge which a servant of Lisideius had provided for them, they made haste to shoot the bridge, and left behind them that great fall of waters which hindered them from hearing what they desired: after which, having disengaged themselves from many vessels which rode at anchor in the Thames, and almost blocked up the passage towards Greenwich, they ordered the watermen to let fall their oars more gently; and then every one favouring his own curiosity with a strict silence, it was not long ere they perceived the air to break about them like the noise of distant thunder, or of swallows in a chimney: those little undulations of sound, though almost vanishing before they reached them, yet still seeming to retain somewhat of their first horror which they had betwixt the fleets: after they had attentively listened till such time as the sound by little and little went from them; Eugenius lifting up his head, and taking notice of it, was the first who congratulated to the rest that happy omen of our nation's victory: adding, that we had but this to desire in confirmation of it, that we might hear no more of that noise which was now leaving the English coast. When the rest had concurred in the same opinion, Crites, a person of a sharp judgment, and somewhat too delicate a taste in wit, which the world have mistaken in him for ill nature, said, smiling to us, that if the concernment of this battle had not been so exceeding great, he could scarce have wished the victory at the price he knew he must pay for it, in being subject to the reading and hearing of so many ill verses as he was sure would be made on that subject. Adding, that no argument could scape some of those eternal rhymers, who watch a battle with more diligence than the ravens and birds of prey; and the worst of them surest to be first in upon the quarry, while the better able, either out of modesty writ not at all, or set that due value upon their poems, as to let them be often desired and long expected! There are some of those impertinent people of whom you speak, answered Lisideius, who to my knowledge are already so provided, either way, that they can produce not only a panegyric upon the victory, but, if need be, a funeral elegy on the Duke: wherein after they have crowned his valour with many laurels, they will at last deplore the odds under which he fell, concluding that his courage deserved a better destiny. All the company smiled at the conceit of Lisideius; but Crites, more eager than before, began to make particular exceptions against some writers, and said the public magistrate ought to send betimes

[1]June 3, 1665. [Ed.]

[2]James, Duke of York, the Lord Admiral, afterward James II. [Ed.]

[3]For the traditional ascriptions of these names, see p. 160. [Ed.]

to forbid them; and that it concerned the peace and quiet of all honest people, that ill poets should be as well silenced as seditious preachers. In my opinion, replied Eugenius, you pursue your point too far; for as to my own particular, I am so great a lover of poesy, that I could wish them all rewarded who attempt but to do well, at least I would not have them worse used than one of their brethren was by Sylla the dictator: *Quem in concione vidimus* (says Tully) *cum ei libellum malus poeta de populo subjecisset, quod epigramma in eum fecisset tantummodo alternis versibus longiusculis, statim ex iis rebus quas tunc vendebat jubere ei praemium tribui, sub ea conditione ne quid postea scriberet.*[4] I could wish with all my heart, replied Crites; that many whom we know were as bountifully thanked upon the same condition, that they would never trouble us again. For amongst others, I have a mortal apprehension of two poets, whom this victory with the help of both her wings will never be able to escape;[5] 'tis easy to guess whom you intend, said Lisideius, and without naming them, I ask you if one of them does not perpetually pay us with clenches[6] upon words and a certain clownish kind of raillery? If now and then he does not offer at a catachresis[7] or Clevelandism, wresting and torturing a word into another meaning: in fine, if he be not one of those whom the French would call *un mauvais buffon;* one who is so much a well-willer to the satire, that he intends at least, to spare no man; and though he cannot strike a blow to hurt any, yet he ought to be punished for the malice of the action; as our witches are justly hanged because they think themselves to be such: and suffer deservedly for believing they did mischief, because they meant it. You have described him, said Crites, so exactly, that I am afraid to come after you with my other extremity of poetry: he is one of those who having had some advantage of education and converse, knows better than the other what a poet should be, but puts it into practice more unluckily than any man; his style and matter are everywhere alike; he is the most calm, peaceable writer you ever read: he never disquiets your passions with the least concernment, but still leaves you in as even a temper as he found you; he is a very Leveller in poetry, he creeps along with ten little words in every line,[8] and helps out his numbers with *For to,* and *Unto,* and all the pretty expletives he can find, till he drags them to the end of another line; while the sense is left tired half way behind it: he doubly starves all his verses, first for want of thought, and then of expression; his poetry neither has wit in it, nor seems to have it; like him in Martial.

Pauper videri Cinna vult, et est pauper:[9]

He affects plainness, to cover his want of imagination: when he writes the serious way, the highest flight of his fancy is some miserable antithesis, or seeming contradiction; and in the comic he is still reaching at some thin conceit, the ghost of a jest, and that too flies before him, never to be caught; these swallows which we see before us on the Thames, are the just resemblance of his wit: you may observe how near the water they stoop, how many proffers they make to dip, and yet how seldom they touch it: and when they do, 'tis but the surface: they skim over it but to catch a gnat, and then mount into the air and leave it. Well gentlemen, said Eugenius, you may speak your pleasure of these authors; but though I and some few more about the town may give you a peaceable hearing, yet assure yourselves, there are multitudes who would think you malicious and them injured: especially him whom you first described; he is the very

[4]"We have seen how, at a public meeting, when a bad poet among the people offered him an epigram made on himself, written in limping elegiacs, Sulla ordered that he be paid a reward from the booty on sale, provided that he never write again." Cicero, *Pro Archia Poeta* 10:25. [Ed.]

[5]It has been conjectured that Dryden's two poets were Richard Wild and Richard Flecknoe, respectively, who wrote on the battle. But the poets' faults seem to correspond to the two criteria of value in the subsequent definition of a play: The former poet's language fails to be just; the latter's, to be lively. [Ed.]

[6]Puns. [Ed.]

[7]Abuse of language. John Cleveland (1613–58) tortured language in this way. [Ed.]

[8]Cf. Pope, *An Essay on Criticism:* "And ten low words oft creep in one dull line." [Ed.]

[9]"Cinna wishes to seem poor — and he is poor." Martial, *Epigrams* 8:19. [Ed.]

Withers[10] of the City: they have bought more editions of his works than would serve to lay under all their pies at the Lord Mayor's Christmas. When his famous poem first came out in the year 1660, I have seen them reading it in the midst of change-time; nay so vehement they were at it, that they lost their bargain by the candles' ends: but what will you say, if he has been received amongst great persons; I can assure you he is, this day, the envy of one, who is lord in the art of quibbling; and who does not take it well, that any man should intrude so far into his province. All I would wish, replied Crites, is, that they who love his writings, may still admire him, and his fellow poet, *qui Bavium non odit,*[11] etc. is curse sufficient. And farther, added Lisideius, I believe there is no man who writes well, but would think he had hard measure, if their admirers should praise anything of his: *Nam quos contemnimus eorum quoque laudes contemnimus.*[12] There are so few who write well in this age, said Crites, that methinks any praises should be welcome; they neither rise to the dignity of the last age, nor to any of the Ancients; and we may cry out of the writers of this time, with more reason than Petronius of his, *Pace vestra liceat dixisse, primi omnium eloquentiam perdidistis:*[13] you have debauched the true old poetry so far, that nature, which is the soul of it, is not in any of your writings.

If your quarrel (said Eugenius) to those who now write, be grounded only on your reverence to antiquity, there is no man more ready to adore those great Greeks and Romans than I am: but on the other side, I cannot think so contemptibly of the age in which I live or so dishonourably of my own country, as not to judge we equal the Ancients in most kinds of poesy, and in some surpass them; neither know I any reason why I may not be as zealous for the reputation of our age, as we find the Ancients themselves were in reference to those who lived before them. For you hear your Horace saying,

> Indignor quidquam reprehendi, non quia crasse compositum, illepideve putetur, sed quia nuper.

And after,

> Si meliora dies, ut vina, poemata reddit,
> scire velim pretium chartis quotus arroget
> annus?[14]

But I see I am engaging in a wide dispute, where the arguments are not like to reach close on either side; for poesy is of so large an extent, and so many both of the Ancients and Moderns have done well in all kinds of it, that in citing one against the other, we shall take up more time this evening, than each man's occasions will allow him: therefore I would ask Crites to what part of poesy he would confine his arguments, and whether he would defend the general cause of the Ancients against the Moderns, or oppose any age of the Moderns against this of ours?[15]

Crites a little while considering upon this demand, told Eugenius that if he pleased, he would limit their dispute to Dramatic Poesy; in which he thought it not difficult to prove, either that the Ancients were superior to the Moderns, or the last age to this of ours.

Eugenius was somewhat surprised, when he heard Crites make choice of the subject; for aught I see, said he, I have undertaken a harder province than I imagined; for though I never judged the plays of the Greek or Roman poets comparable to ours; yet on the other side those we now see acted, come short of many which were written in the last age: but my comfort is if we are overcome, it will be only by our own countrymen: and if we yield to them in this one part of poesy, we more surpass them in all the other; for in the epic or lyric way it will be hard

[10] "George Withers (1588–1667) was a Puritan poet. [Ed.]

[11] "Let whoever does not hate Bavius [love your songs, Maevius]." Virgil, *Eclogues* 3:90. [Ed.]

[12] "We despise the praise of those whom we despise." [Ed.]

[13] "If you will allow me to say so, you have killed the old eloquence." Petronius, *Satyricon,* 2. [Ed.]

[14] "I get angry when something is attacked, not for being course or clumsy, but for being new." and "If like wine, poems improve with age, how many years does it take for a poem to be ripe?" Horace, *Epistles* II.1:76–177 and 34–35. [Ed.]

[15] The periods in dispute are classical and modern literature — a traditional argument known as the *querelle des anciens et des modernes* — and within the modern age, the Elizabethan era and the contemporary period. [Ed.]

for them to show us one such amongst them, as we have many now living, or who lately were. They can produce nothing so courtly writ, or which expresses so much the conversation of a gentleman, as Sir John Suckling; nothing so even, sweet, and flowing as Mr. Waller, nothing so majestic, so correct as Sir John Denham; nothing so elevated, so copious, and full of spirit, as Mr. Cowley; as for the Italian, French, and Spanish plays, I can make it evident, that those who now write, surpass them; and that the drama is wholly ours.

All of them were thus far of Eugenius' opinion, that the sweetness of English verse was never understood or practised by our fathers. Even Crites himself did not much oppose it: and every one was willing to acknowledge how much our poesy is improved, by the happiness of some writers yet living; who first taught us to mould our thoughts into easy and significant words, to retrench the superfluities of expression, and to make our rhyme so properly a part of the verse, that it should never mislead the sense, but itself be led and governed by it.

Eugenius was going to continue this discourse, when Lisideius told him that it was necessary, before they proceeded further, to take a standing measure of their controversy; for how was it possible to be decided who writ the best plays, before we know what a play should be? but, this once agreed on by both parties, each might have recourse to it, either to prove his own advantages, or to discover the failings of his adversary.

He had no sooner said this, but all desired the favour of him to give the definition of a play; and they were the more importunate, because neither Aristotle, nor Horace, nor any other, who had writ of that subject, had ever done it.

Lisideius, after some modest denials, at last confessed he had a rude notion of it; indeed rather a description than a definition, but which served to guide him in his private thoughts, when he was to make a judgement of what others writ: that he conceived a play ought to be, a just and lively image of human nature, representing its passions and humours, and the changes of fortune to which it is subject; for the delight and instruction of mankind.

This definition, though Crites raised a logical objection against it; that it was only *a genere et fine,*[16] and so not altogether perfect; was yet well received by the rest: and after they had given order to the watermen to turn their barge, and row softly, that they might take the cool of the evening in their return, Crites, being desired by the company to begin, spoke on behalf of the Ancients, in this manner:

If confidence presage a victory, Eugenius, in his own opinion, has already triumphed over the Ancients. Nothing seems more easy to him, than to overcome those whom it is our greatest praise to have imitated well: for we do not only build upon their foundations; but by their models. Dramatic poesy had time enough, reckoning from Thespis (who first invented it) to Aristophanes, to be born, to grow up, and to flourish in maturity. It has been observed of arts and sciences, that in one and the same century they have arrived to great perfection; and no wonder, since every age has a kind of universal genius, which inclines those that live in it to some particular studies: the work then being pushed on by many hands, must of necessity go forward.

Is it not evident, in these last hundred years (when the study of philosophy[17] has been the business of all the virtuosi in Christendom) that almost a new nature has been revealed to us? that more errors of the school have been detected, more useful experiments in philosophy have been made, more noble secrets in optics, medicine, anatomy, astronomy, discovered, than in all those credulous and doting ages from Aristotle to us? so true it is that nothing spreads more fast than science, when rightly and generally cultivated.

Add to this the more than common emulation that was in those times of writing well; which though it be found in all ages and all persons that pretend to the same reputation; yet poesy being then in more esteem than now it is, had greater

[16]"By genus and end": Crites is complaining that the definition is not restrictive enough, since it will serve to define poetry and prose fiction as well as drama. In fact, the problem is that the meaning of central terms — "just," "lively," and "representing" — is slippery. [Ed.]

[17]Natural philosophy; science. [Ed.]

honours decreed to the professors of it; and consequently the rivalship was more high between them; they had judges ordained to decide their merit, and prizes to reward it: and historians have been diligent to record of Aeschylus, Euripides, Sophocles, Lycophron, and the rest of them, both who they were that vanquished in these wars of the theatre, and how often they were crowned: while the Asian kings, and Grecian commonwealths scarce afforded them a nobler subject than the unmanly luxuries of a debauched court, or giddy intrigues of a factious city. *Alit aemulatio ingenia* (says Paterculus) *et nunc invidia, nunc admiratio incitationem accendit:* Emulation is the spur of wit, and sometimes envy, sometimes admiration quickens our endeavours.[18]

But now since the rewards of honour are taken away, that virtuous emulation is turned into direct malice; yet so slothful, that it contents itself to condemn and cry down others, without attempting to do better. 'Tis a reputation too unprofitable, to take the necessary pains for it; yet wishing they had it, that desire is incitement enough to hinder others from it. And this, in short, Eugenius, is the reason, why you have now so few good poets; and so many severe judges. Certainly, to imitate the Ancients well, much labour and long study is required: which pains, I have already shown, our poets would want encouragement to take, if yet they had ability to go through the work. Those Ancients have been faithful imitators and wise observers of that nature which is so torn and ill represented in our plays; they have handed down to us a perfect resemblance of her; which we, like ill copiers, neglecting to look on, have rendered monstrous, and disfigured. But, that you may know how much you are indebted to those your masters, and be ashamed to have so ill requited them, I must remember you that all the rules by which we practise the drama at this day, (either such as relate to the justness and symmetry of the plot; or the episodical ornaments, such as descriptions, narrations, and other beauties, which are not essential to the play) were delivered to us from the observations which Aristotle made, of those poets, who either lived before him, or were his contemporaries: we have added nothing of our own, except we have the confidence to say our wit is better; of which none boast in this our age, but such as understand not theirs. Of that book which Aristotle has left us περι τῆς Ποιητικῆς[19] Horace's *Art of Poetry* is an excellent comment, and, I believe, restores to us that second book of his concerning comedy, which is wanting in him.

Out of these two have been extracted the famous rules which the French call, *Des Trois Unités,* or, the three unities, which ought to be observed in every regular play; namely, of time, place, and action.[20]

The unity of time they comprehend in twenty-four hours, the compass of a natural day; or as near it as can be contrived. And the reason of it is obvious to every one; that the time of the feigned action, or fable of the play, should be proportioned as near as can be to the duration of that time in which it is represented; since therefore all plays are acted on the theatre in a space of time much within the compass of twenty-four hours, that play is to be thought the nearest imitation of nature, whose plot or action is confined within that time; and, by the same rule which concludes this general proportion of time, it follows, that all the parts of it are (as near as may be) to be equally sub-divided; namely, that one act take not up the supposed time of half a day, which is out of proportion to the rest, since the other four are then to be straitened within the compass of the remaining half. For it is unnatural that one act, which being spoke or written, is not longer than the rest, should be supposed longer by the audience. 'Tis therefore the poet's duty, to take care that no act should be imagined to exceed the time in which it is represented on the stage; and that the intervals and inequalities of time be supposed to fall out between the acts.

[18]Velleius Paterculus, in the *Historia Romana* 1:17. [Ed.]

[19]The *Poetics.* [Ed.]

[20]The unity of Place is not explicitly mentioned in the *Poetics,* but it is implied by the constraints of the unities of Time and Action. If a tragedy "is confined to one revolution of the sun" then its single action cannot occur at widely separated places, given the limits of premodern transportation. But while Aristotle treats the unity of action as an essential matter of art, he treats the limitations of time in tragedy as a stage convention, with the length of plays regulated by such extraneous matters as dramatic competitions. [Ed.]

This rule of time how well it has been observed by the Ancients, most of their plays will witness. You see them in their tragedies (wherein to follow this rule, is certainly most difficult) from the very beginning of their plays, falling close into that part of the story which they intend for the action or principal object of it; leaving the former part to be delivered by narration: so that they set the audience, as it were, at the post where the race is to be concluded: and, saving them the tedious expectation of seeing the poet set out and ride the beginning of the course, they suffer you not to behold him, till he is in sight of the goal, and just upon you.

For the second unity, which is that of place, the Ancients meant by it, that the scene ought to be continued through the play, in the same place where it was laid in the beginning: for the stage, on which it is represented, being but one and the same place, it is unnatural to conceive it many; and those far distant from one another. I will not deny but by the variation of painted scenes, the fancy (which in these cases will contribute to its own deceit) may sometimes imagine it several places, with some appearance of probability; yet it still carries the greater likelihood of truth, if those places be supposed so near each other, as in the same town or city; which may all be comprehended under the larger denomination of one place: for a greater distance will bear no proportion to the shortness of time, which is allotted in the acting, to pass from one of them to another; for the observation of this, next to the Ancients, the French are to be most commended. They tie themselves so strictly to the unity of place, that you never see in any of their plays, a scene changed in the middle of an act: if the act begins in a garden, a street, or chamber, 'tis ended in the same place; and that you may know it to be the same, the stage is so supplied with persons that it is never empty all the time: he who enters second has business with him who was on before; and before the second quits the stage, a third appears who has business with him.

This Corneille[21] calls *La liaison des scènes,* the continuity or joining of the scenes; and 'tis a good mark of a well contrived play when all the persons are known to each other, and every one of them has some affairs with all the rest.

As for the third unity, which is that of action, the Ancients meant no other by it than what the logicians do by their Finis, the end or scope of any action: that which is the first in intention, and last in execution. Now the poet is to aim at one great and complete action, to the carrying on of which all things in his play, even the very obstacles, are to be subservient; and the reason of this is as evident as any of the former.

For two actions equally laboured and driven on by the writer, would destroy the unity of the poem; it would be no longer one play, but two: not but that there may be many actions in a play, as Ben Jonson has observed in his *Discoveries;* but they must be all subservient to the great one, which our language happily expresses in the name of under-plots: such as in Terence's *Eunuch* is the difference and reconcilement of Thais and Phaedria, which is not the chief business of the play, but promotes the marriage of Charea and Chremes's sister, principally intended by the poet. There ought to be but one action, says Corneille, that is one complete action which leaves the mind of the audience in a full repose. But this cannot be brought to pass but by many other imperfect actions which conduce to it, and hold the audience in a delightful suspense of what will be.

If by these rules (to omit many other drawn from the precepts and practice of the Ancients) we should judge our modern plays, 'tis probable, that few of them would endure the trial. That which should be the business of a day, takes up in some of them an age; instead of one action they are the epitomes of a man's life; and for one spot of ground (which the stage should represent) we are sometimes in more countries than the map can show us.

But if we will allow the Ancients to have contrived well, we must acknowledge them to have written better; questionless we are deprived of a great stock of wit in the loss of Menander among the Greek poets, and of Caecilius, Affranius, and Varius, among the Romans: we may guess at Menander's excellency by the plays of Terence, who translated some of them: and yet wanted so

[21]In the *Discours des trois unités* (1660). [Ed.]

much of him that he was called by C. Caesar the half-Menander; and may judge of Varius, by the testimonies of Horace, Martial, and Velleius Paterculus. 'Tis probable that these, could they be recovered, would decide the controversy; but so long as Aristophanes and Plautus are extant; while the tragedies of Euripides, Sophocles, and Seneca are in our hands, I can never see one of those plays which are now written, but it increases my admiration of the Ancients; and yet I must acknowledge further, that to admire them as we ought, we should understand them better than we do. Doubtless many things appear flat to us, the wit of which depended on some custom or story which never came to our knowledge, or perhaps on some criticism in their language, which being so long dead, and only remaining in their books, 'tis not possible they should make us understand perfectly. To read Macrobius, explaining the propriety and elegancy of many words in Virgil, which I had before passed over without consideration, as common things, is enough to assure me that I ought to think the same of Terence; and that in the purity of his style (which Tully so much valued that he ever carried his works about him) there is yet left in him great room for admiration, if I knew but where to place it. In the mean time I must desire you to take notice, that the greatest man of the last age (Ben Jonson) was willing to give place to them in all things. He was not only a professed imitator of Horace, but a learned plagiary of all the others. You track him everywhere in their snow. If Horace, Lucan, Petronius Arbiter, Seneca, and Juvenal, had their own from him, there are few serious thoughts which are new in him. You will pardon me therefore if I presume he loved their fashion when he wore their clothes. But since I have otherwise a great veneration for him, and you, Eugenius, prefer him above all other poets, I will use no farther argument to you than his example. I will produce before you Father Ben, dressed in all the ornaments and colours of the Ancients, you will need no other guide to our party if you follow him; and whether you consider the bad plays of our age, or regard the good plays of the last, both the best and worst of the modern poets will equally instruct you to admire the Ancients.

Crites had no sooner left speaking, but Eugenius, who had waited with some impatience for it, thus began:

I have observed in your speech that the former part of it is convincing as to what the Moderns have profited by the rules of the Ancients, but in the latter you are careful to conceal how much they have excelled them. We own all the helps we have from them, and want neither veneration nor gratitude while we acknowledge that to overcome them we must make use of the advantages we have received from them; but to these assistances we have joined our own industry; for (had we sat down with a dull imitation of them) we might then have lost somewhat of the old perfection, but never acquired any that was new. We draw not therefore after their lines, but those of nature; and having the life before us, besides the experience of all they knew, it is no wonder if we hit some airs and features which they have missed. I deny not what you urge of arts and sciences, that they have flourished in some ages more than others; but your instance in philosophy makes for me; for if natural causes be more known now than in the time of Aristotle, because more studied, it follows that poesy and other arts may with the same pains arrive still nearer to perfection, and, that granted, it will rest for you to prove that they wrought more perfect images of human life than we; which, seeing in your discourse you have avoided to make good, it shall now be my task to show you some part of their defects, and some few excellencies of the Moderns; and I think there is none among us can imagine I do it enviously, or with purpose to detract from them; for what interest of fame or profit can the living lose by the reputation of the dead? On the other side, it is a great truth which Velleius Paterculus affirms, *Audita visis libentius laudamus; et praesentia invidia, praeterita admiratione prosequimur; et his nos obrui, illis instrui credimus:*[22] That praise or censure is certainly the most sincere which unbribed posterity shall give us.

[22]"We praise more freely what we have heard about than what we have seen; we view the present with envy and the past with admiration; and we believe we are injured by the present and taught by the past." *Historia Romana* 2:92. [Ed.]

Be pleased then in the first place to take notice, that the Greek poesy, which Crites has affirmed to have arrived to perfection in the reign of the Old Comedy,[23] was so far from it, that the distinction of it into acts was not known to them; or if it were, it is yet so darkly delivered to us that we cannot make it out.

All we know of it is from the singing of their chorus, and that too is so uncertain that in some of their plays we have reason to conjecture they sung more than five times. Aristotle indeed divides the integral parts of a play into four.[24] First, the protasis or entrance, which gives light only to the characters of the persons, and proceeds very little into any part of the action: secondly, the epitasis, or working up of the plot where the play grows warmer; the design or action of it is drawing on, and you see something promising that it will come to pass: thirdly, the catastasis, called by the Romans, status, the height, and full growth of the play: we may call it properly the counterturn, which destroys that expectation, embroils the action in new difficulties, and leaves you far distant from that hope in which it found you, as you may have observed in a violent stream resisted by a narrow passage: it runs round to an eddy, and carries back the waters with more swiftness than it brought them on. Lastly, the catastrophe, which the Grecians called λύσις, the French *le dénouement,* and we the discovery or unravelling of the plot: there you see all things settling again upon their first foundations, and the obstacles which hindered the design or action of the play once removed, it ends with that resemblance of truth and nature, that the audience are satisfied with the conduct of it. Thus this great man delivered to us the image of a play, and I must confess it is so lively that from thence much light has been derived to the forming it more perfectly into acts and scenes; but what poet first limited to five the number of the acts I know not; only we see it so firmly established in the time of Horace, that he gives it for a rule in comedy; *Neu brevior quinto, neu sit productior actu:*[25] So that you see the Grecians cannot be said to have consummated this art; writing rather by entrances than by acts, and having rather a general indigested notion of a play, than knowing how and where to bestow the particular graces of it.

But since the Spaniards at this day allow but three acts, which they call *jornadas,* to a play, and the Italians in many of theirs follow them, when I condemn the Ancients, I declare it is not altogether because they have not five acts to every play, but because they have not confined themselves to one certain number; 'tis building an house without a model: and when they succeeded in such undertakings, they ought to have sacrificed to Fortune, not to the Muses.

Next, for the plot, which Aristotle called τὸ μῦθος, and often τῶν πραγμάτων σύνθεσις,[26] and from him the Romans *fabula,* it has already been judiciously observed by a late writer, that in their tragedies it was only some tale derived from Thebes or Troy, or at least something that happened in those two ages; which was worn so threadbare by the pens of all the epic poets, and even by tradition itself of the talkative Greeklings (as Ben Jonson calls them) that before it came upon the stage, it was already known to all the audience: and the people so soon as ever they heard the name of Oedipus, knew as well as the poet, that he had killed his father by a mistake, and committed incest with his mother, before the play; that they were now to hear of a great plague, an oracle, and the ghost of Laius: so that they sat with a yawning kind of expectation, till he was to come with his eyes pulled out, and speak a hundred or more verses in a tragic tone, in complaint of his misfortunes. But one Oedipus, Hercules, or Medea, had been tolerable; poor people they scaped not so good cheap: they had still the *chapon bouillé*[27] set before them, till their appetites were cloyed with the same dish,

[23]The time of Aristophanes. [Ed.]

[24]Aristotle's discussion of the quantitative parts of tragedy occurs in *Poetics,* Ch. 12, where he differentiates the prologue, episode, exode, and choral ode. Later, in Ch. 18, he divides the play into the complication and the denouement. Neither of these corresponds to Eugenius's distinctions here. [Ed.]

[25]"The play that expects to be asked for another performance / Once it's been given, should be just five acts long." Horace, *Art of Poetry,* 189; see p. 71. [Ed.]

[26]The synthesis of the actions. [Ed.]

[27]Boiled capon. [Ed.]

and the novelty being gone, the pleasure vanished: so that one main end of dramatic poesy in its definition, which was to cause delight, was of consequence destroyed.

In their comedies, the Romans generally borrowed their plots from the Greek poets; and theirs was commonly a little girl stolen or wandered from her parents, brought back unknown to the city, there got with child by some lewd young fellow; who, by the help of his servant, cheats his father, and when her time comes, to cry *Juno Lucina fer opem;*[28] one or other sees a little box or cabinet which was carried away with her, and so discovers her to her friends, if some God do not prevent it, by coming down in a machine,[29] and taking the thanks of it to himself.

By the plot you may guess much of the characters of the persons. An old father who would willingly before he dies see his son well married; his debauched son, kind in his nature to his mistress, but miserably in want of money; a servant or slave, who has so much wit to strike in with him, and help to dupe his father, a braggadochio captain, a parasite, and a lady of pleasure.

As for the poor honest maid, on whom the story is built, and who ought to be one of the principal actors in the play, she is commonly a mute in it. She has the breeding of the old Elizabeth way, which was for maids to be seen and not to be heard; and it is enough you know she is willing to be married, when the fifth act requires it.

These are plots built after the Italian mode of houses, you see through them all at once; the characters are indeed the imitations of nature, but so narrow as if they had imitated only an eye or an hand, and did not dare to venture on the lines of a face, or the proportion of a body.

But in how straight a compass soever they have bounded their plots and characters, we will pass it by, if they have regularly pursued them, and perfectly observed those three unities of time, place, and action: the knowledge of which you say is derived to us from them. But in the first place give me leave to tell you, that the unity of place, however it might be practised by them, was never any of their rules. We neither find it in Aristotle, Horace, or any who have written of it, till in our age the French poets first made it a precept of the stage.[30] The unity of time, even Terence himself (who was the best and most regular of them) has neglected. His *Heautontimoroumenos* or *Self-Punisher* takes up visibly two days; says Scaliger, the two first acts concluding the first day, the three last the day ensuing; and Euripides, in tying himself to one day, has committed an absurdity never to be forgiven him: for in one of his tragedies he has made Theseus go from Athens to Thebes, which was about forty English miles, under the walls of it to give battle, and appear victorious in the next act; and yet from the time of his departure to the return of the Nuntius, who gives the relation of his victory, Aethra and the chorus have but thirty-six verses; which is not for every mile a verse.

The like error is as evident in Terence's *Eunuch,* when Laches, the old man, enters by mistake into the house of Thais, where betwixt his exit and the entrance of Pythias, who comes to give ample relation of the disorders he has raised within, Parmeno who was left upon the stage, has not above five lines to speak: *C'est bien employer un temps si court,*[31] says the French poet, who furnished me with one of the observations; and almost all their tragedies will afford us examples of the like nature.

'Tis true, they have kept the continuity, or as you called it, *liaison des scènes* somewhat better: two do not perpetually come in together, talk and go out together; and other two succeed them, and do the same throughout the act, which the English call by the name of single scenes; but the reason is, because they have seldom above two or three scenes, properly so called, in every act; for it is to be accounted a new scene, not only every time the stage is empty, but every person who enters, though to others, makes it so; because he introduces a new business. Now the

[28]"Juno goddess of childbirth, help me!" Terence, *Andria* 3.1.15. [Ed.]

[29]The *deus ex machina* of Horace's stricture. [Ed.]

[30]Eugenius forgets that the quintessentially English Philip Sidney condemns *Gorboduc* as "faulty in both place and time." See p. 154. [Ed.]

[31]"It's a good use of so short a time." Here and elsewhere, Dryden is paraphrasing Corneille's *Discours des trois unités.* [Ed.]

plots of their plays being narrow, and the persons few, one of their acts was written in a less compass than one of our well wrought scenes, and yet they are often deficient even in this. To go no further than Terence, you find in the *Eunuch* Antipho entering single in the midst of the third act, after Chremes and Pythias were gone off. In the same play you have likewise Dorias beginning the fourth act alone; and after she has made a relation of what was done at the soldiers' entertainment (which by the way was very inartificial) because she was presumed to speak directly to the audience, and to acquaint them with what was necessary to be known, but yet should have been so contrived by the poet as to have been told by persons of the drama to one another (and so by them to have come to the knowledge of the people) she quits the stage, and Phaedria enters next, alone likewise. He also give you an account of himself, and of his returning from the country, in monologue, to which unnatural way of narration Terence is subject in all his plays: In his *Adelphi* or Brothers, Syrus and Demea enter; after the scene was broken by the departure of Sostrata, Geta and Canthara; and indeed you can scarce look into any of his comedies, where you will not presently discover the same interruption.

But as they have failed both in laying of their plots, and in the management, swerving from the rules of their own art, by misrepresenting nature to us, in which they have ill-satisfied one intention of a play, which was delight, so in the instructive part they have erred worse: instead of punishing vice and rewarding virtue, they have often shown a prosperous wickedness, and an unhappy piety. They have set before us a bloody image of revenge in *Medea,* and given her dragons to convey her safe from punishment. A Priam and Astyanax murdered, and Cassandra ravished, and the lust and murder ending in the victory of him who acted them. In short, there is no indecorum in any of our modern plays, which if I would excuse, I could not shadow with some authority from the Ancients.

And one farther note of them let me leave you. Tragedies and comedies were not writ then as they are now, promiscuously, by the same person; but he who found his genius bending to the one, never attempted the other way. This is so plain, that I need not instance to you, that Aristophanes, Plautus, Terence, never any of them writ a tragedy; Aeschylus, Euripides, Sophocles, and Seneca, never meddled with comedy: the sock and buskin were not worn by the same poet: having then so much care to excel in one kind, very little is to be pardoned them if they miscarried in it; and this would lead me to the consideration of their wit, had not Crites given me sufficient warning not to be too bold in my judgement of it; because the languages being dead, and many of the customs and little accidents on which it depended, lost to us, we are not competent judges of it. But though I grant that here and there we may miss the application of a proverb or a custom, yet a thing well said will be wit in all languages; and though it may lose something in the translation, yet to him who reads it in the original, 'tis still the same; he has an idea of its excellency, though it cannot pass from his mind into any other expression or words than those in which he finds it. When Phaedria, in the *Eunuch,* had a command from his mistress to be absent two days; and encouraging himself to go through with it, said; *Tandem ego non illa caream, si opus sit, vel totum triduum?* Parmeno to mock the softness of his master, lifting up his hands and eyes, cries out as it were in admiration; *Hui! universum triduum!*[32] the elegancy of which *universum,* though it cannot be rendered in our language, yet leaves an impression on our souls: but this happens seldom in him, in Plautus oftener; who is infinitely too bold in his metaphors and coining words; out of which many times his wit is nothing, which questionless was one reason why Horace falls upon him so severely in those verses:

> Sed proavi nostri Plautinos et numeros, et
> laudavere sales, nimium patienter utrumque
> ne dicam stolide.[33]

[32]"But cannot I manage to do without her, if I have to, for three whole days. . . . Alas, three entire days!" Terence, *Eunuch* 2.1.17–18. [Ed.]

[33]"Your ancestors praised both the wit and rhythms of Plautus? / For admiring both of these things they were *too* tolerant, / Not to say dense, if you and I can distinguish / A crudeness in phrasing from lapidary strength of wit . . ." Horace, *Art of Poetry,* 270–72; see p. 73. [Ed.]

For Horace himself was cautious to obtrude a new word on his readers, and makes custom and common use the best measure of receiving it into our writings.

> Multa renascentur quae nunc cecidere, cadentque
> quae nunc sunt in honore vocabula, si volet usus,
> quem penes, arbitrium est, et jus, et norma
> loquendi.[34]

The not observing this rule is that which the world has blamed in our satirist Cleveland; to express a thing hard and unnaturally, is his new way of elocution. 'Tis true, no poet but may sometimes use a catachresis, Virgil does it;

> Mistaque ridenti colocasia fundet acantho.

In his Eclogue of Pollio, and in his 7th *Æneid.*

> Mirantur et undae,
> miratur nemus, insuetum fulgentia longe,
> scuta virum fluvio, pictasque, innare carinas.

And Ovid once so modestly, that he asks leave to do it;

> Si verbo audacia detur
> haud metuam summi dixisse Palatia coeli.[35]

Calling the court of Jupiter by the name of Augustus's palace, though in another place he is more bold, where he says, *et longas visent capitolia pompas.*[36] But to do this always, and never be able to write a line without it, though it may be admired by some few pedants, will not pass upon those who know that wit is best conveyed to us in the most easy language; and is most to be admired when a great thought comes dressed in words so commonly received that it is understood by the meanest apprehensions, as the best meat is the most easily digested: but we cannot read a verse of Cleveland's without making a face at it, as if every word were a pill to swallow. He gives us many times a hard nut to break our teeth, without a kernel for our pains. So that there is this difference between his satires and Doctor Donne's, that the one gives us deep thoughts in common language, though rough cadence; the other gives us common thoughts in abstruse words: 'tis true, in some places his wit is independent of his words, as in that of the *Rebel Scot:*

> Had Cain been Scot God would have changed his
> doom;
> Not forced him wander, but confined him home,

Si sic omnia dixisset![37] This is wit in all languages: 'tis like Mercury, never to be lost or killed; and so that other:

> For beauty like white-powder makes no noise,
> And yet the silent hypocrite destroys.

You see the last line is highly metaphorical, but it is so soft and gentle that it does not shock us as we read it.

But, to return from whence I have digressed, to the consideration of the Ancients' writing and their wit, (of which by this time you will grant us in some measure to be fit judges,) though I see many excellent thoughts in Seneca, yet he, of them who had a genius most proper for the stage, was Ovid; he had a way of writing so fit to stir up a pleasing admiration and concernment, which are the objects of a tragedy, and to show the various movements of a soul combating between two different passions, that, had he lived in our age, or in his own could have writ with our advantages, no man but must have yielded to him; and therefore I am confident the *Medea* is none of his; for, though I esteem it for the gravity and sententiousness of it, which he himself concludes to be suitable to a tragedy, *Omne genus scripti gravitate tragaedia vincit,*[38] yet it moves not my

[34]"All these projects, whatever men make, will perish, / And the fame and dignity of speech are equally mortal. / Much that has once dropped out will be born again, / And much of our language now held in high repute / Will fall to the ground if utility so decrees, / With which rests the final decision, the ultimate standard, / The legal existence, of speech." Horace, *Art of Poetry,* 70–72; see p. 69. [Ed.]

[35]"The Egyptian bean, mixed with smiling acanthus, will flourish." (Virgil, *Eclogues* 4:20); "The waves and the woods wonder, shocked by the men's shining shields and by the painted ships." (Virgil, *Aeneid* 8:91–93); "If I were bold, I would not hesitate to call it the Palace of Heaven" (Ovid, *Metamorphoses* 1:175–76). [Ed.]

[36]"And Capitols view the long processions." Ovid, *Metamorphoses* 1:561. [Ed.]

[37]"If only he had always spoken thus!" [Ed.]

[38]"Tragedy surpasses in gravity all other kinds of writing." Ovid, *Tristia* 2:381. [Ed.]

soul enough to judge that he, who in the epic way wrote things so near the drama, as the story of Myrrha, of Caunus and Biblis, and the rest, should stir up no more concernment where he most endeavoured it. The masterpiece of Seneca I hold to be that scene in the *Troades,* where Ulysses is seeking for Astyanax to kill him. There you see the tenderness of a mother, so represented in Andromache, that it raises compassion to a high degree in the reader, and bears the nearest resemblance of anything in the tragedies of the Ancients, to the excellent scenes of passion in Shakespeare, or in Fletcher. For love-scenes you will find few among them, their tragic poets dealt not with that soft passion, but with lust, cruelty, revenge, ambition, and those bloody actions they produced; which were more capable of raising horror than compassion in an audience: leaving love untouched, whose gentleness would have tempered them, which is the most frequent of all the passions, and which being the private concernment of every person, is soothed by viewing its own image in a public entertainment.

Among their comedies, we find a scene or two of tenderness, and that where you would least expect it, in Plautus; but to speak generally, their lovers say little, when they see each other, but *anima mea, vita mea;* ζωὴ καὶ ψυχή,[39] as the women in Juvenal's time used to cry out in the fury of their kindness. Any sudden gust of passion (as an ecstasy of love in an unexpected meeting) cannot better be expressed than in a word and a sigh, breaking one another. Nature is dumb on such occasions, and to make her speak, would be to represent her unlike herself. But there are a thousand other concernments of lovers, as jealousies, complaints, contrivances and the like, where not to open their minds at large to each other, were to be wanting to their own love, and to the expectation of the audience who watch the movements of their minds, as much as the changes of their fortunes. For the imaging of the first is properly the work of a poet, the latter he borrows from the historian.

Eugenius was proceeding in that part to his discourse, when Crites interrupted him. I see, said he, Eugenius and I are never like to have this question decided betwixt us; for he maintains the Moderns have acquired a new perfection in writing; I can only grant they have altered the mode of it. Homer described his heroes men of great appetites, lovers of beef broiled upon the coals, and good fellows; contrary to the practice of the French romances, whose heroes neither eat, nor drink, nor sleep, for love. Virgil makes Aeneas a bold avower of his won virtues,

> Sum pius Aeneas fama super aethera notus;[40]

which in the civility of our poets is the character of a fanfaron or Hector: for with us the knight takes occasion to walk out, or sleep, to avoid the vanity of telling his own story, which the trusty squire is ever to perform for him. So in their love scenes, of which Eugenius spoke last, the Ancients were more hearty, we more talkative: they writ love as it was then the mode to make it, and I will grant thus much to Eugenius, that perhaps one of their poets, had he lived in our age,

> Si foret hoc nostrum fato delapsus in aevum,[41]

(as Horace says of Lucilius) he had altered many things; not that they were not natural before, but that he might accommodate himself to the age in which he lived; yet in the mean time we are not to conclude anything rashly against those great men, but preserve to them the dignity of masters, and give that honour to their memories, *(Quos libitina sacravit*[42];) part of which we expect may be paid to us in future times.

This moderation of Crites, as it was pleasing to all the company, so it put an end to that dispute; which, Eugenius, who seemed to have the better of the argument, would urge no farther: but Lisideius after he had acknowledged himself of Eugenius's opinion concerning the Ancients, yet told him he had forborne, till his discourse were ended, to ask him why he preferred the English plays above those of other nations? and whether

[39]"My soul, my life, life and soul." Cf. Juvenal, *Satires* 6:195. [Ed.]

[40]"I am pious Aeneas, renowned above the heavens." Virgil, *Aeneid* 1:378–89. [Ed.]

[41]"If Fate had dropped him into this era of ours." Horace, *Satires* I.9:68. [Ed.]

[42]"Whom the Goddess of funerals has sanctified." Horace, *Epistles* II.1:9. [Ed.]

we ought not to submit our stage to the exactness of our next neighbours?

Though, said Eugenius, I am at all times ready to defend the honour of my country against the French, and to maintain, we are as well able to vanquish them with our pens as our ancestors have been with their swords, yet, if you please, added he, looking upon Neander, I will commit this cause to my friend's management; his opinion of our plays is the same with mine: and besides, there is no reason, that Crites and I, who have now left the stage, should re-enter so suddenly upon it; which is against the laws of comedy.

If the question had been stated, replied Lisideius, who had writ best, the French or English forty years ago, I should have been of your opinion, and adjudged the honour to our own nation; but since that time (said he, turning towards Neander) we have been so long together bad Englishmen, that we had not leisure to be good poets; Beaumont, Fletcher, and Jonson (who were only capable of bringing us to that degree of perfection which we have) were just then leaving the world; as if in an age of so much horror, wit and those milder studies of humanity, had no farther business among us. But the Muses, who ever follow peace, went to plant in another country; it was then, that the great Cardinal of Richelieu began to take them into his protection; and that, by his encouragement, Corneille and some other Frenchmen reformed their theatre, (which before was as much below ours as it now surpasses it and the rest of Europe); but because Crites, in his discourse for the Ancients, has prevented me, by observing many rules of the stage, which the Moderns have borrowed from them, I shall only, in short, demand of you, whether you are not convinced that of all nations the French have best observed them? In the unity of time you find them so scrupulous, that it yet remains a dispute among their poets, whether the artificial day of twelve hours more or less, be not meant by Aristotle, rather than the natural one of twenty-four; and consequently whether all plays ought not to be reduced into that compass? This I can testify, that in all their dramas writ within these last twenty years and upwards, I have not observed any that have extended the time to thirty hours: in the unity of place they are full as scrupulous, for many of their critics limit it to that very spot of ground where the play is supposed to begin; none of them exceed the compass of the same town or city.

The unity of action in all their plays is yet more conspicuous, for they do not burden them with under-plots, as the English do, which is the reason why many scenes of our tragi-comedies carry on a design that is nothing of kin to the main plot; and that we see two distinct webs in a play, like those in ill-wrought stuffs; and two actions, that is, two plays carried on together, to the confounding of the audience, who, before they are warm in their concernments for one part, are diverted to another; and by that means espouse the interest of neither. From hence likewise it arises that the one half of our actors are not known to the other. They keep their distances as if they were Montagues and Capulets, and seldom begin an acquaintance till the last scene of the fifth act, when they are all to meet upon the stage. There is no theatre in the world has anything so absurd as the English tragi-comedy, 'tis a drama of our own invention, and the fashion of it is enough to proclaim it so; here a course of mirth, there another of sadness and passion; and a third of honour, and a duel. Thus in two hours and a half we run through all the fits of Bedlam. The French afford you as much variety on the same day, but they do it not so unseasonably, or *mal à propos* as we. Our poets present you the play and the farce together, and our stages still retain somewhat of the original civility of the Red Bull;

> Atque ursum et pugiles media inter carmina poscunt.[43]

The end of tragedies or serious plays, says Aristotle, is to beget admiration, compassion, or concernment;[44] but are not mirth and compassion things incompatible? and is it not evident that the poet must of necessity destroy the former by intermingling of the latter? that is, he must ruin the

[43]"They ask for a bear and boxers in the middle of the play." Horace, *Epistles* II.1:185–86. [Ed.]

[44]Aristotle mentions pity and fear, which may correspond to "compassion" and "concernment." [Ed.]

sole end and object of his tragedy to introduce somewhat that is forced in to it; and is not of the body of it. Would you not think that physician mad, who having prescribed a purge, should immediately order you to take restringents?

But to leave our plays, and return to theirs, I have noted one great advantage they have had in the plotting of their tragedies; that is, they are always grounded upon some known history: according to that of Horace, *ex noto fictum carmen sequar*[45]; and in that they have so imitated the Ancients, that they have surpassed them. For the Ancients, as was observed before, took for the foundation of their plays some poetical fiction, such as under that consideration could move but little concernment in the audience, because they already knew the event of it. But the French goes farther;

> Atque ita mentitur; sic veris falsa remiscet,
> primo ne medium, medio ne discrepet imum.[46]

He so interweaves truth with probable fiction, that he puts a pleasing fallacy upon us; mends the intrigues of fate, and dispenses with the severity of history, to reward that virtue which has been rendered to us there unfortunate. Sometimes the story has left the success so doubtful, that the writer is free, by the privilege of a poet, to take that which of two or more relations will best suit with his design. As for example, in the death of Cyrus, whom Justin and some others report to have perished in the Scythian war, but Xenophon affirms to have died in his bed of extreme old age. Nay more, when the event is past dispute, even then we are willing to be deceived, and the poet, if he contrives it with appearance of truth, has all the audience of his party; at least during the time his play is acting: so naturally we are kind to virtue, when our own interest is not in question, that we take it up as the general concernment of mankind. On the other side, if you consider the historical plays of Shakespeare, they are rather so many chronicles of kings, or the business many times of thirty or forty years, cramped into a representation of two hours and an half, which is not to imitate or paint nature, but rather to draw her in miniature, to take her in little, to look upon her through the wrong end of a perspective, and receive her images not only much less, but infinitely more imperfect than the life: this, instead of making a play delightful, renders it ridiculous.

> Quodcumque ostendis mihi sic, incredulus odi.[47]

For the spirit of man cannot be satisfied but with truth, or at least verisimility; and a poem is to contain, if not τὰ ἔτυμα, yet ἐτύμοισιν ὁμοῖα,[48] as one of the Greek poets has expressed it.

Another thing in which the French differ from us and from the Spaniards, is that they do not embarrass, or cumber themselves with too much plot: they only represent so much of a story as will constitute one whole and great action sufficient for a play; we, who undertake more, do but multiply adventures; which, not being produced from one another, as effects from causes, but barely following, constitute many actions in the drama, and consequently make it many plays.

But by pursuing closely one argument, which is not cloyed with many turns, the French have gained more liberty for verse, in which they write: they have leisure to dwell on a subject which deserves it; and to represent the passions (which we have acknowledged to be the poet's work) without being hurried from one thing to another, as we are in the plays of Calderón, which we have seen lately upon our theatres, under the name of Spanish plots.[49] I have taken notice but of one tragedy of ours, whose plot has that uniformity and unity of design in it which I have commended in the French; and that is *Rollo,* or rather, under the name of *Rollo,* the story of Bassianus and Geta in Herodian; there indeed the plot is neither large nor intricate, but just enough to fill the minds of

[45]"I shall set my sights on familiar things." Horace, *Art of Poetry,* 240; see p. 73. [Ed.]

[46]". . . and simply leaves out / Whatever he thinks he can't bring off shining and clear, / And devises so well, intermingling the true and the false. / That the middle part fits with the first, the last with the middle." Horace, *Art of Poetry,* 151–52; see p. 71. [Ed.]

[47]"Whatsoever such stuff / You *show* me, I won't believe it, I'll simply detest it." Horace, *Art of Poetry,* 188; see p. 71. [Ed.]

[48]"The truth"; "things like the truth." Homer, *Odyssey* 19:203. [Ed.]

[49]Dryden himself was to adapt Calderón in *An Evening's Love* (1668). [Ed.]

the audience, not to cloy them. Besides, you see it founded upon the truth of history, only the time of the action is not reducible to the strictness of the rules; and you see in some places a little farce mingled, which is below the dignity of the other parts; and in this all our poets are extremely peccant, even Ben Jonson himself in *Sejanus* and *Catiline* has given us this oleo of a play: this unnatural mixture of comedy and tragedy, which to me sounds just as ridiculously as the history of David with the merry humours of Golia. In *Sejanus* you may take notice of the scene betwixt Livia and the physician, which is a pleasant satire upon the artificial helps of beauty. In *Catiline* you may see the parliament of women; the little envies of them to one another; and all that passes betwixt Curio and Fulvia, scenes admirable in their kind, but of an ill mingle with the rest.

But I return again to the French writers who, as I have said, do not burden themselves too much with plot, which has been reproached to them by an ingenious person of our nation as a fault, for he says they commonly make but one person considerable in a play; they dwell on him, and his concernments, while the rest of the persons are only subservient to set him off. If he intends this by it, that there is one person in the play who is of greater dignity than the rest, he must tax, not only theirs, but those of the Ancients, and which he would be loth to do, the best of ours; for 'tis impossible but that one person must be more conspicuous in it than any other, and consequently the greatest share in the action must devolve on him. We see it so in the management of all affairs; even in the most equal aristocracy, the balance cannot be so justly poised, but someone will be superior to the rest, either in parts, fortune, interest, or the consideration of some glorious exploit, which will reduce the greatest part of business into his hands.

But, if he would have us to imagine that in exalting one character the rest of them are neglected, and that all of them have not some share or other in the action of the play, I desire him to produce any of Corneille's tragedies, wherein every person (like so many servants in a well governed family) has not some employment, and who is not necessary to the carrying on of the plot, or at least to your understanding it.

There are indeed some protatic[50] persons in the Ancients, whom they make use of in their plays, either to hear, or give the relation: but the French avoid this with great address, making their narrations only to, or by such, who are some way interested in the main design. And now I am speaking of relations, I cannot take a fitter opportunity to add this in favour of the French, that they often use them with better judgement and more *à propos* than the English do. Not that I commend narrations in general, but there are two sorts of them; one of those things which are antecedent to the play, and are related to make the conduct of it more clear to us, but, 'tis a fault to choose such subjects for the stage as will force us on that rock; because we see they are seldom listened to by the audience, and that is many times the ruin of the play: for, being once let pass without attention, the audience can never recover themselves to understand the plot; and indeed it is somewhat unreasonable that they should be put to so much trouble as, that to comprehend what passes in their sight, they must have recourse to what was done, perhaps, ten or twenty years ago.

But there is another sort of relations, that is, of things happening in the action of the play, and supposed to be done behind the scenes, and this is many times both convenient and beautiful: for, by it the French avoid the tumult, to which we are subject in England, by representing duels, battles, and the like, which renders our stage too like the theatres where they fight prizes. For what is more ridiculous than to represent an army with a drum and five men behind it; all which, the hero of the other side is to drive in before him, or to see a duel fought, and one slain with two or three thrusts of the foil, which we know are so blunted, that we might give a man an hour to kill another in good earnest with them.

I have observed that in all our tragedies, the audience cannot forbear laughing when the actors are to die; 'tis the most comic part of the whole play. All passions may be lively[51] represented on the stage, if to the well-writing of them

[50]Introductory: like the Watchman in Aeschylus's *Agamemnon*. [Ed.]

[51]In a lifelike manner. [Ed.]

the actor supplies a good commanded voice, and limbs that move easily, and without stiffness; but there are many actions which can never be imitated to a just height: dying especially is a thing which none but a Roman gladiator could naturally perform on the stage when he did not imitate or represent, but do it; and therefore it is better to omit the representation of it.

The words of a good writer which describe it lively, will make a deeper impression of belief in us than all the actor can insinuate into us, when he seems to fall dead before us; as a poet in the description of a beautiful garden, or a meadow, will please our imagination more than the place itself can please our sight. When we see death represented we are convinced it is but fiction; but when we hear it related, our eyes (the strongest witnesses) are wanting, which might have undeceived us; and we are all willing to favour the sleight when the poet does not too grossly impose on us. They therefore who imagine these relations would make no concernment in the audience, are deceived, by confounding them with the other, which are of things antecedent to the play; those are made often in cold blood (as I may say) to the audience; but these are warmed with our concernments, which were before awakened in the play. What the philosophers say of motion, that, when it is once begun, it continues of itself, and will do so to eternity without some stop put to it,[52] is clearly true on this occasion; the soul being already moved with the characters and fortunes of those imaginary persons, continues going of its own accord, and we are no more weary to hear what becomes of them when they are not on the stage, than we are to listen to the news of an absent mistress. But it is objected, that if one part of the play may be related, then why not all? I answer, some parts of the action are more fit to be represented, some to be related. Corneille says judiciously, that the poet is not obliged to expose to view all particular actions which conduce to the principal: he ought to select such of them to be seen which will appear with the greatest beauty, either by the magnificence of the show, or the vehemence of passions which they produce, or some other charm which they have in them, and let the rest arrive to the audience by narration. 'Tis a great mistake in us to believe the French present no part of the action on the stage: every alteration or crossing of a design, every new sprung passion, and turn of it, is a part of the action, and much the noblest, except we conceive nothing to be action till the players come to blows; as if the painting of the hero's mind were not more properly the poet's work than the strength of his body. Nor does this anything contradict the opinion of Horace, where he tells us,

> Segnius irritant animos demissa per aurem,
> quam quae sunt oculis subjecta fidelibus. —

For he says immediately after,

> Non tamen intus
> digna geri promes in scenam, multaque tolles
> ex oculis, quae mox narret facundia praesens.

Among which many he recounts some.

> Nec pueros coram populo Medea trucidet,
> aut in avem Progne mutetur, Cadmus in anguem,
> etc.[53]

That is, those actions which by reason of their cruelty will cause aversion in us, or by reason of their impossibility unbelief, ought either wholly to be avoided by a poet, or only delivered by narration. To which, we may have leave to add such as to avoid tumult, (as was before hinted) or to reduce the plot into a more reasonable compass of time, or for defect of beauty in them, are rather to be related than presented to the eye. Examples of all these kinds are frequent, not only among all the Ancients, but in the best received of our En-

[52]Dryden is not quoting Newton's first law of motion before it was announced; he is probably echoing Descartes's *Principia Philosophiae,* which had just been translated into English. [Ed.]

[53]"But things entrusted to the ear / Impress our minds less vividly than what is exposed / To our trustworthy eyes so that a viewer informs himself / Of precisely what happened. Still, you are not to show / On stage what ought to take place backstage: remove / From our eyes the substance of things . . . / Medea / must not butcher her boys in front of the people; / Unspeakable Atreus should not cook up human flesh / Before our eyes, nor should Procne change into a bird, / Or Cadmus into a snake." Horace, *Art of Poetry,* 180–87; see p. 71. [Ed.]

glish poets. We find Ben Jonson using them in his *Magnetic Lady,* where one comes out from dinner, and relates the quarrels and disorders of it to save the indecent appearance of them on the stage, and to abbreviate the story: and this in express imitation of Terence, who had done the same before him in his *Eunuch,* where Pythius makes the like relation of what had happened within at the soldiers' entertainment. The relations likewise of Sejanus's death, and the prodigies before it are remarkable; the one of which was hid from sight to avoid the horror and tumult of the representation; the other to shun the introducing of things impossible to be believed. In that excellent play, *The King and No King,* Fletcher goes yet farther; for the whole unravelling of the plot is done by narration in the fifth act, after the manner of the Ancients; and it moves great concernment in the audience, though it be only a relation of what was done many years before the play. I could multiply other instances, but these are sufficient to prove that there is no error in choosing a subject which requires this sort of narrations; in the ill-management of them, there may.

But I find I have been too long in this discourse since the French have many other excellencies not common to us; as that you never see any of their plays end with a conversion, or simple change of will, which is the ordinary way which our poets use to end theirs. It shows little art in the conclusion of a dramatic poem, which they who have hindered the felicity during the four acts, desist from it in the fifth without some powerful cause to take them off their design; and though I deny not but such reasons may be found, yet it is a path that is cautiously to be trod, and the poet is to be sure he convinces the audience that the motive is strong enough. As for example, the conversion of the usurer in *The Scornful Lady,* seems to me a little forced; for being a usurer, which implies a lover of money to the highest degree of covetousness (and such the poet has represented him) the account he gives for the sudden change is that he has been duped by the wild young fellow, which in reason might render him more wary another time, and make him punish himself with harder fare and coarser clothes to get up again what he had lost: but that he should look on it as a judgement, and so repent, we may expect to hear in a sermon, but I should never endure it in a play.

I pass by this; neither will I insist on the care they take, that no person after his first entrance shall ever appear, but the business which brings him upon the stage shall be evident: which rule if observed, must needs render all the events in the play more natural; for there you see the probability of every accident, in the cause that produced it; and that which appears chance in the play will seem so reasonable to you, that you will there find it almost necessary; so that in the exit of the actor you have a clear account of his purpose and design in the next entrance: (though, if the scene be well wrought, the event will commonly deceive you) for there is nothing so absurd, says Corneille, as for an actor to leave the stage, only because he has no more to say.

I should now speak of the beauty of their rhyme, and the just reason I have to prefer that way of writing in tragedies before ours in blank verse; but because it is partly received by us, and therefore not altogether peculiar to them, I will say no more of it in relation to their plays. For our own I doubt not but it will exceedingly beautify them, and I can see but one reason why it should not generally obtain, that is, because our poets write so ill in it. This indeed may prove a more prevailing argument than all others which are used to destroy it, and therefore I am only troubled when great and judicious poets, and those who are acknowledged such, have writ or spoke against it; as for others they are to be answered by that one sentence of an ancient author.

> Sed ut primo ad consequendos eos quos priores ducimus accendimur, itaubi aut praeteriri, aut aequari eos posse desperavimus, studium cum spesenescit: quod, scilicet, assequi non potest, sequi desinit; praeteritoque eo in quo eminere non possumus, aliquid in quo nitamur conquirimus.[54]

[54]"At first we burn to excel those whom we think our leaders, but when we despair of surpassing them or even equalling them, our enthusiasm weakens with our hope; when it cannot overtake, it ceases to follow; putting away what we cannot excel in, we seek another outlet for our efforts." Velleius Paterculus, *Historia Romana* I:17. [Ed.]

Lisideius concluded in this manner; and Neander after a little pause thus answered him.

I shall grant Lisideius, without much dispute, a great part of what he has urged against us; for I acknowledge that the French contrive their plots more regularly, and observe the laws of comedy, and decorum of the stage (to speak generally) with more exactness than the English. Farther, I deny not but he has taxed us justly in some irregularities of ours which he has mentioned; yet, after all, I am of opinion that neither our faults nor their virtues are considerable enough to place them above us.

For the lively imitation of nature being in the definition of a play, those which best fulfill that law ought to be esteemed superior to the others. 'Tis true, those beauties of the French poesy are such as will raise perfection higher where it is, but are not sufficient to give it where it is not: they are indeed the beauties of a statue, but not of a man, because not animated with the soul of poesy, which is imitation of humour and passions: and this Lisideius himself, or any other, however biased to their party, cannot but acknowledge, if he will either compare the humours of our comedies, or the characters of our serious plays with theirs. He who will look upon theirs which have been written till these last ten years or thereabouts, will find it an hard matter to pick out two or three passable humours amongst them. Corneille himself, their arch-poet, what has he produced except *The Liar,* and you know how it was cried up in France; but when it came upon the English stage, though well translated, and that part of Dorant acted to so much advantage as I am confident it never received in its own country, the most favourable to it would not put it in competition with many of Fletcher's or Ben Jonson's. In the rest of Corneille's comedies you have little humour; he tells you himself his way is first to show two lovers in good intelligence with each other; in the working up of the play to embroil them by some mistake, and in the latter end to clear it, and reconcile them.

But of late years Molière, the younger Corneille, Quinault, and some others, have been imitating afar off the quick turns and graces of the English stage. They have mixed their serious plays with mirth, like our tragi-comedies, since the death of Cardinal Richelieu, which Lisideius and many others not observing, have commended that in them for a virtue which they themselves no longer practise. Most of their new plays are like some of ours, derived from the Spanish novels. There is scarce one of them without a veil, and a trusty Diego,[55] who drolls much after the rate of the *Adventures.* But their humours, if I may grace them with that name, are so thin sown that never above one of them comes up in any play. I dare take upon me to find more variety of them in some one play of Ben Jonson's than in all theirs together: as he who has seen the *Alchemist, The Silent Woman,* or *Bartholomew Fair,* cannot but acknowledge with me.

I grant the French have performed what was possible on the ground-work of the Spanish plays; what was pleasant before, they have made regular; but there is not above one good play to be writ on all those plots; they are too much alike to please often, which we need not the experience of our own stage to justify. As for their new way of mingling mirth with serious plot, I do not with Lisideius condemn the thing, though I cannot approve their manner of doing it. He tell us we cannot so speedily recollect ourselves after a scene of great passion and concernment, as to pass to another of mirth and humour, and to enjoy it with any relish: but why should he imagine the soul of man more heavy than his senses? Does not the eye pass from an unpleasant object to a pleasant in a much shorter time than is required to this? and does not the unpleasantness of the first commend the beauty of the latter? The old rule of logic might have convinced him, that contraries when placed near, set off each other. A continued gravity keeps the spirit too much bent; we must refresh it sometimes, as we bait in a journey, that we may go on with greater ease. A scene of mirth mixed with tragedy has the same effect upon us which our music has betwixt the acts, which we find a relief to us from the best plots and language of the stage, if the discourses have been long. I must therefore have stronger arguments ere I am convinced, that compassion

[55]Neander is alluding to a comic servant, Diego, in Samuel Tuke's *Adventures of Five Hours.* [Ed.]

and mirth in the same subject destroy each other, and in the mean time cannot but conclude, to the honour of our nation, that we have invented, increased and perfected a more pleasant way of writing for the stage than was ever known to the Ancients or Moderns of any nation, which is tragi-comedy.

And this leads me to wonder why Lisideius and many others should cry up the barrenness of the French plots above the variety and copiousness of the English. Their plots are single, they carry on one design which is pushed forward by all the actors, every scene in the play contributing and moving towards it. Our plays besides the main design, have under-plots or by-concernments, of less considerable persons, and intrigues, which are carried on with the motion of the main plot: as they say the orb of the fixed stars, and those of the planets, though they have motions of their own, are whirled about by the motion of the *primum mobile,* in which they are contained: that similitude expresses much of the English stage, for if contrary motions may be found in nature to agree; if a planet can go east and west at the same time, one way by virtue of his own motion, the other by the force of the first mover, it will not be difficult to imagine how the underplot, which is only different, not contrary to the great design, may naturally be conducted along with it.

Eugenius[56] has already shown us, from the confession of the French poets, that the unity of action is sufficiently preserved if all the imperfect actions of the play are conducing to the main design: but when those petty intrigues of a play are so ill ordered, that they have no coherence with the other, I must grant that Lisideius has reason to tax that want of due connexion; for coordination in a play is as dangerous and unnatural as in a state. In the mean time he must acknowledge our variety, if well ordered, will afford a greater pleasure to the audience.

As for his other argument, that by pursuing one single theme they gain an advantage to express and work up the passions, I wish any example he could bring from them would make it good: for I confess their verses are to me the coldest I have ever read. Neither indeed is it possible for them, in the way they take, so to express passion, as that the effects of it should appear in the concernment of an audience, their speeches being so many declamations, which tire us with the length; so that instead of persuading us to grieve for their imaginary heroes, we are concerned for our own trouble, as we are in tedious visits of bad company; we are in pain till they are gone. When the French stage came to be reformed by Cardinal Richelieu, those long harangues were introduced, to comply with the gravity of a churchman. Look upon the *Cinna* and the *Pompey,* they are not so properly to be called plays, as long discourses of reason of state: and *Polyeucte* in matters of religion is as solemn as the long stops upon our organs. Since that time it is grown into a custom, and their actors speak by the hourglass, like our parsons; nay, they account it the grace of their parts, and think themselves disparaged by the poet, if they may not twice or thrice in a play entertain the audience with a speech of an hundred lines. I deny not but this may suit well enough with the French; for as we, who are a more sullen people, come to be diverted at our plays; so they who are of an airy and gay temper come thither to make themselves more serious. And this I conceive to be one reason why comedies are more pleasing to us, and tragedies to them. But to speak generally, it cannot be denied that short speeches, and replies are more apt to move the passions, and beget concernment in us than the other: for it is unnatural for any one in a gust of passion to speak long together, or for another in the same condition, to suffer him, without interruption. Grief and passion are like floods raised in little brooks by a sudden rain; they are quickly up, and if the concernment be poured unexpectedly in upon us, it overflows us. But a long sober shower gives them leisure to run out as they came in, without troubling the ordinary current. As for comedy, repartee is one of its chiefest graces; the greatest pleasure of the audience is a chase of wit kept up on both sides, and swiftly managed. And this our forefathers, if not we, have had in Fletcher's plays, to a much higher degree of per-

[56]Crites; see p. 168. [Ed.]

fection than the French poets can, reasonably, hope to reach.

There is another part of Lisideius's discourse, in which he has rather excused our neighbours than commended them; that is, for aiming only to make one person considerable in their plays. 'Tis very true what he has urged, that one character in all plays, even without the poet's care, will have advantage of all the others; and that the design of the whole drama will chiefly depend on it. But this hinders not that there may be more shining characters in the play: many persons of a second magnitude, nay, some so very near, so almost equal to the first, that greatness may be opposed to greatness, and all the persons be made considerable, not only by their quality, but their action. 'Tis evident that the more the persons are, the greater will be the variety of the plot. If then the parts are managed so regularly that the beauty of the whole be kept entire, and that the variety become not a perplexed and confused mass of accidents, you will find it infinitely pleasing to be led in a labyrinth of design, where you see some of your way before you, yet discern not the end till you arrive at it. And that all this is practicable, I can produce for examples many of our English plays: as *The Maid's Tragedy, The Alchemist, The Silent Woman:* I was going to have named *The Fox,* but that the unity of design seems not exactly observed in it; for there appear two actions in the play; the first naturally ending with the fourth act; the second forced from it in the fifth: which yet is the less to be condemned in him, because the disguise of Volpone, though it suited not with his character as a crafty or covetous person, agreed well enough with that of a voluptuary: and by it the poet gained the end at which he aimed, the punishment of vice, and the reward of virtue, both which that disguise produced. So that to judge equally of it, it was an excellent fifth act, but not so naturally proceeding from the former.

But to leave this, and pass to the latter part of Lisideius's discourse, which concerns relations, I must acknowledge with him, that the French have reason to hide that part of the action which would occasion too much tumult on the stage, and to choose rather to have it made known by narration to the audience. Farther I think it very convenient, for the reasons he has given, that all incredible actions were removed; but, whether custom has so insinuated itself into our countrymen, or nature has so formed them to fierceness, I know not; but they will scarcely suffer combats and other objects of horror to be taken from them. And indeed, the indecency of tumults is all which can be objected against fighting. For why may not our imagination as well suffer itself to be deluded with the probability of it, as with any other thing in the play? For my part, I can with as great ease persuade myself that the blows are given in good earnest, as I can, that they who strike them are kings or princes, or those persons which they represent. For objects of incredibility I would be satisfied from Lisideius, whether we have any so removed from all appearance of truth as are those of Corneille's *Andromède*? A play which has been frequented the most of any he has writ? If the Perseus, or the son of an heathen god, the Pegasus and the monster were not capable to choke a strong belief, let him blame any representation of ours hereafter. Those indeed were objects of delight; yet the reason is the same as to the probability: for he makes it not a ballet or masque, but a play, which is to resemble truth. But for death, that it ought not to be represented, I have besides the arguments alleged by Lisideius, the authority of Ben Jonson, who has forborne it in his tragedies; for both the death of Sejanus and Catiline are related: though in the latter I cannot but observe one irregularity of that great poet: he has removed the scene in the same act, from Rome to Catiline's army, and from thence again to Rome; and besides, has allowed a very inconsiderable time, after Catiline's speech, for the striking of the battle, and the return of Petreius, who is to relate the event of it to the Senate: which I should not animadvert on him, who was otherwise a painful observer of τὸ πρέπον, or the decorum of the stage, if he had not used extreme severity in his judgement on the incomparable Shakespeare for the same fault. To conclude on this subject of relations, if we are to be blamed for showing too much of the action, the French are as faulty for discovering too little of it: a mean betwixt both should be observed by every judicious writer, so as the audience may neither be left unsatisfied by not seeing what is beautiful, or shocked by beholding what is either incredible or indecent. I hope I have already proved in this discourse, that though we are not altogether so punctual as the French, in observing the laws of comedy; yet our errors are so few and little, and those things wherein we excel them so considerable, that we ought of right to be preferred before them. But what will Lisideius say if they themselves acknowledge they are too strictly bounded by those laws, for breaking which he has blamed the English? I will allege Corneille's words, as I find them in the end of his Discourse of the three unities; *Il est facile aux speculatifs d'estre sevères,* etc. ''Tis easy for speculative persons to judge severely; but if they would produce to public view ten or twelve pieces of this nature, they would perhaps give more latitude to the rules than I have done, when by experience they had known how much we are limited and constrained by them, and how many beauties of the stage they banished from it.' To illustrate a little what he has said; by their servile observations of the unities of time and place, and integrity of scenes, they have brought on themselves that dearth of plot, and narrowness of imagination, which may be observed in all their plays. How many beautiful accidents might naturally happen in two or three days, which cannot arrive with any probability in the compass of twenty-four hours? There is time to be allowed also for maturity of design, which amongst great and prudent persons, such as are often represented in tragedy, cannot, with any likelihood of truth, be brought to pass at so short a warning. Farther, by tying themselves strictly to the unity of place, and unbroken scenes, they are forced many times to omit some beauties which cannot be shown where the act began; but might, if the scene were interrupted, and the stage cleared for the persons to enter in another place; and therefore the French poets are often forced upon absurdities: for if the act begins in a chamber, all the persons in the play must have some business or other to come thither, or else they are not to be shown that act, and sometimes their characters are very unfitting to appear there; as, suppose it were the king's bedchamber, yet the meanest man in the tragedy must come and dispatch his business there, rather than in the lobby or courtyard, (which is fitter for him) for fear the stage should be cleared, and the scenes broken. Many times they fall by it into a greater inconvenience; for they keep their scenes unbroken, and yet change the place; as in one of their newest plays where the act begins in the street. There a gentleman is to meet his friend; he sees him with his man, coming out from his father's house; they talk together, and the first goes out: the second, who is a lover, has made an appointment with his mistress; she appears at the window, and then we are to imagine the scene lies under it. This gentleman is called away, and leaves his servant with his mistress: presently her father is heard from within; the young lady is afraid the servingman should be discovered, and thrusts him into a place of safety, which is supposed to be her closet. After this, the father enters to the daughter, and now the scene is in a house: for he is seeking from one room to another for this poor Philipin, or French Diego, who is heard from within, drolling and breaking many a miserable conceit on the subject of his sad condition. In this ridiculous manner the play goes forward, the stage being never empty all the while: so that the street, the window, the two houses, and the closet, are made to walk about, and the persons to stand still. Now what, I beseech you, is more easy than to write a regular French play, or more difficult than to write an irregular English one, like those of Fletcher, or of Shakespeare?

If they content themselves as Corneille did, with some flat design, which, like an ill riddle, is found out ere it be half proposed, such plots we can make every way regular as easily as they: but whenever they endeavour to rise to any quick turns and counterturns of plot, as some of them have attempted, since Corneille's plays have been less in vogue, you see they write as irregularly as we, though they cover it more speciously. Hence the reason is perspicuous, why no French plays, when translated, have, or ever can, succeed on the English stage. For, if you consider the plots, our own are fuller of variety; if the writing, ours are more quick and fuller of spirit: and therefore 'tis a strange mistake in those who decry the way of writing plays in verse, as if the English therein imitated the French. We have borrowed nothing from them; our plots are weaved in English looms: we endeavour therein to follow the variety and greatness of characters which are derived to us from Shakespeare and Fletcher. The copiousness and well-knitting of the intrigues we have from Jonson, and for the verse itself we have English precedents of elder date than any of Corneille's plays (not to name our old comedies before Shakespeare, which were all writ in verse of six feet, or Alexandrines, such as the French now use). I can show in Shakespeare, many scenes of rhyme together, and the like in Ben Jonson's tragedies: in *Catiline* and *Sejanus* sometimes thirty or forty lines; I mean besides the chorus, or the monologues, which by the way, showed Ben no enemy to this way of writing, especially if you read his *Sad Shepherd,* which goes sometimes on rhyme, sometimes on blank verse, like an horse who eases himself on trot and amble. You find him likewise commending Fletcher's pastoral of *The Faithful Shepherdess;* which is for the most part rhyme, though not refined to that purity to which it hath since been brought. And these examples are enough to clear us from a servile imitation of the French.

But to return whence I have digressed, I dare boldly affirm these two things of the English drama: first, that we have many plays of ours as regular as any of theirs; and which, besides, have more variety of plot and characters: and secondly, that in most of the irregular plays of Shakespeare or Fletcher (for Ben Jonson's are for the most part regular) there is a more masculine fancy and greater spirit in the writing, than there is in any of the French. I could produce even in Shakespeare's and Fletcher's works, some plays which are almost exactly formed; as *The Merry Wives of Windsor,* and *The Scornful Lady:* but because (generally speaking) Shakespeare, who writ first, did not perfectly observe the laws of comedy, and Fletcher, who came nearer to perfection, yet through carelessness made many faults, I will take the pattern of a perfect play from Ben Jonson, who was a careful and learned observer of the dramatic laws, and from all his comedies I shall select *The Silent Woman;* of which I will make a short examen, according to those rules which the French observe.

As Neander was beginning to examine *The Silent Woman,* Eugenius, earnestly regarding him; I beseech you, Neander, said he, gratify the company and me in particular so far, as before you speak of the play, to give us a character of the author; and tell us frankly your opinion, whether you do not think all writers, both French and English, ought to give place to him?

I fear, replied Neander, that in obeying your commands I shall draw some envy on myself. Besides, in performing them, it will be first necessary to speak somewhat of Shakespeare and Fletcher, his rivals in poesy, and one of them, in my opinion, at least is equal, perhaps his superior.

To begin with Shakespeare; he was the man who of all modern, and perhaps ancient poets, had the largest and most comprehensive soul. All the images of nature were still present to him, and he drew them not laboriously, but luckily: when he describes anything, you more than see it, you feel it too. Those who accuse him to have wanted learning, give him the greater commendation: he was naturally learned; he needed not the spectacles of books to read nature; he looked inwards, and found her there. I cannot say he is everywhere alike; were he so, I should do him injury to compare him with the greatest of mankind. He is many times flat, insipid; his comic wit degenerating into clenches, his serious swelling into bombast. But he is always great, when some great occasion is presented to him: no man can say he ever had a fit subject for his wit, and did not then raise himself as high above the rest of poets.

> Quantum lenta solent inter viburna cupressi.[57]

The consideration of this made Mr. Hales of Eton say that there was no subject of which any poet ever writ, but he would produce it much better done in Shakespeare; and however others are now generally preferred before him, yet the age wherein he lived, which had contemporaries with him, Fletcher and Jonson, never equalled them to him in their esteem. And in the last king's Court,

[57] "As cypresses usually do among bending osiers." Virgil, *Eclogues* 1:25. [Ed.]

when Ben's reputation was at highest, Sir John Suckling, and with him the greater part of the courtiers, set our Shakespeare far above him.

Beaumont and Fletcher of whom I am next to speak, had with the advantage of Shakespeare's wit, which was their precedent, great natural gifts, improved by study, Beaumont especially being so accurate a judge of plays, that Ben Jonson while he lived, submitted all his writings to his censure, and 'tis thought, used his judgement in correcting, if not contriving all his plots. What value he had for him, appears by the verse he writ to him; and therefore I need speak no farther of it. The first play that brought Fletcher and him in esteem was their *Philaster,* for before that, they had written two or three very unsuccessfully: as the like is reported of Ben Jonson, before he writ *Every Man in His Humour*. Their plots were generally more regular than Shakespeare's, especially those which were made before Beaumont's death; and they understood and imitated the conversation of gentlemen much better; whose wild debaucheries, and quickness of wit in repartees, no poet before them could paint as they have done. Humour which Ben Jonson derived from particular persons, they made it not their business to describe. They represented all the passions very lively, but above all, love. I am apt to believe the English language in them arrived to its highest perfection; what words have since been taken in, are rather superfluous than ornamental. Their plays are now the most pleasant and frequent entertainments of the stage, two of theirs being acted through the year for one of Shakespeare's or Jonson's: the reason is, because there is a certain gaiety in their comedies, and pathos in their more serious plays, which suits generally with all men's humours. Shakespeare's language is likewise a little obsolete, and Ben Jonson's wit comes short of theirs.

As for Jonson, to whose character I am now arrived, if we look upon him while he was himself, (for his last plays were but his dotages) I think him the most learned and judicious writer which any theatre ever had. He was a most severe judge of himself as well as others. One cannot say he wanted wit, but rather that he was frugal of it. In his works you find little to retrench or alter. Wit and language, and humour also in some measure we had before him; but something of art was wanting to the drama till he came. He managed his strength to more advantage than any who preceded him. You seldom find him making love in any of his scenes, or endeavouring to move the passions; his genius was too sullen and saturnine to do it gracefully, especially when he knew he came after those who had performed both to such an height. Humour was his proper sphere, and in that he delighted most to represent mechanic[58] people. He was deeply conversant in the Ancients, both Greek and Latin, and he borrowed boldly from them. There is scarce a poet or historian among the Roman authors of those times whom he has not translated in *Sejanus* and *Catiline*. But he has done his robberies so openly, that one may see he fears not to be taxed by any law. He invades authors like a monarch, and what would be theft in other poets, is only victory in him. With the spoils of these writers he so represents old Rome to us, in its rites, ceremonies and customs, that if one of their poets had written either of his tragedies, we had seen less of it than in him. If there was any fault in his language, 'twas that he weaved it too closely and laboriously, in his comedies especially: perhaps too, he did a little too much Romanize our tongue, leaving the words which he translated almost as much Latin as he found them: wherein though he learnedly followed their language, he did not enough comply with the idiom of ours. If I would compare him with Shakespeare, I must acknowledge him the more correct poet, but Shakespeare the greater wit. Shakespeare was the Homer, or father of our dramatic poets; Jonson was the Virgil, the pattern of elaborate writing. I admire him, but I love Shakespeare. To conclude of him, as he has given us the most correct plays, so in the precepts which he has laid down in his *Discoveries,* we have as many and profitable rules for perfecting the stage as any wherewith the French can furnish us.

Having thus spoken of the author, I proceed to the examination of his comedy, *The Silent Woman.*

[58]Low, vulgar. [Ed.]

EXAMEN OF *THE SILENT WOMAN*

To begin first with the length of the action, it is so far from exceeding the compass of a natural day, that it takes not up an artificial one. 'Tis all included in the limits of three hours and an half, which is no more than is required for the presentment on the stage. A beauty perhaps not much observed; if it had, we should not have looked on the Spanish translation of *Five Hours* with so much wonder. The scene of it is laid in London; the latitude of place is almost as little as you can imagine, for it lies all within the compass of two houses, and after the first act, in one.[59] The continuity of scenes is observed more than in any of our plays, except his own *Fox* and *Alchemist.* They are not broken above twice or thrice at most in the whole comedy, and in the two best of Corneille's plays, the *Cid* and *Cinna,* they are interrupted once. The action of the play is entirely one; the end or aim of which is the settling Morose's estate on Dauphine. The intrigue of it is the greatest and most noble of any pure unmixed comedy in any language: you see in it many persons of various characters and humours, and all delightful; as first, Morose, or an old man, to whom all noise but his own talking is offensive. Some who would be thought critics, say this humour of his is forced: but to remove that objection, we may consider him first to be naturally of a delicate hearing, as many are to whom all sharp sounds are unpleasant; and secondly, we may attribute much of it to the peevishness of his age, or the wayward authority of an old man in his own house, where he may make himself obeyed; and to this the poet seems to allude in his name, Morose. Beside this, I am assured from divers persons, that Ben Jonson was actually acquainted with such a man, one altogether as ridiculous as he is here represented. Others say it is not enough to find one man of such an humour; it must be common to more, and the more common the more natural. To prove this, they instance in the best of comical characters, Falstaff. There are many men resembling him; old, fat, merry, cowardly, drunken, amorous, vain, and lying. But to convince these people, I need but tell them, that humour is the ridiculous extravagance of conversation, wherein one man differs from all others. If then it be common, or communicated to many, how differs it from other men's? or what indeed causes it to be ridiculous so much as the singularity of it? As for Falstaff, he is not properly one humour, but a miscellany of humours or images, drawn from so many several men; that wherein he is singular is his wit, or those things he says, *praeter expectatum,* unexpected by the audience; his quick evasions when you imagine him surprised, which as they are extremely diverting of themselves, so receive a great addition from his person; for the very sight of such an unwieldy old debauched fellow is a comedy alone. And here having a place so proper for it, I cannot but enlarge somewhat upon this subject of humour into which I am fallen. The Ancients had little of it in their comedies; for the τὸ γελοῖον,[60] of the Old Comedy, of which Aristophanes was chief, was not so much to imitate a man, as to make the people laugh at some odd conceit, which had commonly somewhat of unnatural or obscene in it. Thus when you see Socrates brought upon the stage you are not to imagine him made ridiculous by the imitation of his actions, but rather by making him perform something very unlike himself, something so childish and absurd, as by comparing it with the gravity of the true Socrates, makes a ridiculous object for the spectators. In their New Comedy which succeeded, the poets sought indeed to express the ἦθος, as in their tragedies the πάθος of mankind.[61] But this ἦθος contained only the general characters of men and manners; as old men, lovers, serving-men, courtesans, parasites, and such other persons as we see in their comedies; all which they made alike: that is, one old man or father; one lover, one courtesan so like another, as if the first of them had begot the rest of every sort: *ex homine hunc natum dicas.*[62] The same custom they observed likewise in their

[59]There are actually six different locations, and the action of the play takes up more than twelve hours, or more than an "artificial" day. [Ed.]

[60]The ridiculous. [Ed.]

[61]*Ethos* in Aristotle is "character": *pathos* is "suffering" — in particular the tragic deed. [Ed.]

[62]"You'd say the spit and image." Terence, *Eunuch,* 460. [Ed.]

tragedies. As for the French, though they have the word *humeur* among them, yet they have small use of it in their comedies, or farces; they being but ill imitations of the *ridiculum,* or that which stirred up laughter in the Old Comedy. But among the English 'tis otherwise, whereby humour is meant some extravagant habit, passion, or affection, particular (as I said before) to some one person, by the oddness of which, he is immediately distinguished from the rest of men; which being lively and naturally represented, most frequently begets that malicious pleasure in the audience which is testified by laughter, as all things which are deviations from customs are ever the aptest to produce it, though by the way this laughter is only accidental, as the person represented is fantastic or bizarre. But pleasure is essential to it, as the imitation of what is natural. The description of these humours, drawn from the knowledge and observation of particular persons, was the peculiar genius and talent of Ben Jonson; to whose play I now return.

Besides Morose, there are at least nine or ten different characters and humours in *The Silent Woman,* all which persons have several concernments of their own, yet are all used by the poet, to the conducting of the main design of perfection. I shall not waste time in commending the writing of this play, but I will give you my opinion, that there is more wit and acuteness of fancy in it than in any of Ben Jonson's. Besides, that he has here described the conversation of gentlemen in the persons of Truewit, and his friends, with more gaiety, air and freedom, than in the rest of his comedies. For the contrivance of the plot, 'tis extreme elaborate, and yet withal easy; for the λύσις, or untying of it, 'tis so admirable, that when it is done, no one of the audience would think the poet could have missed it; and yet it was concealed so much before the last scene, that any other way would sooner have entered into your thoughts. But I dare not take upon me to commend the fabric of it, because it is altogether so full of art, that I must unravel every scene in it to commend it as I ought. And this excellent contrivance is still the more to be admired, because 'tis comedy where the persons are only of common rank, and their business private, not elevated by passions or high concernments as in serious plays. Here everyone is a proper judge of all he sees; nothing is represented but that with which he daily converses: so that by consequence all faults lie open to discovery, and few are pardonable. 'Tis this which Horace has judiciously observed:

> Creditur ex medio quia res arcessit habere
> sudoris minimum, sed habet Comedia tanto
> plus oneris, quanto veniae minus. — [63]

But our poet, who was not ignorant of these difficulties, has made use of all advantages, as he who designs a large leap takes his rise from the highest ground. One of these advantages is that which Corneille has laid down as the greatest which can arrive to any poem, and which he himself could never compass above thrice in all his plays, viz., the making choice of some signal and long-expected day, whereon the action of the play is to depend. This day was that designed by Dauphine for the settling of his uncle's estate upon him; which to compass he contrives to marry him. That the marriage had been plotted by him long beforehand is made evident by what he tells Truewit in the second act, that in one moment he had destroyed what he had been raising many months.

There is another artifice of the poet, which I cannot here omit, because by the frequent practice of it in his comedies, he has left it to us almost as a rule, that is, when he has any character or humour wherein he would show a *coup de maistre,* or his highest skill; he recommends it to your observation by a pleasant description of it before the person first appears. Thus, in *Bartholomew Fair* he gives you the pictures of Numps and Cokes, and in this those of Daw, Lafoole, Morose, and the Collegiate Ladies; all which you hear described before you see them. So that before they come upon the stage you have a longing expectation of them, which prepares you to receive them favourably; and when they are there, even from their first appearance you are so far acquainted with them, that nothing of their humour is lost to you.

[63]"One might think that Comedy takes less work because its matter comes from daily life, but it takes more because less allowance is made." Horace, *Epistles* II.1:168–70. [Ed.]

I will observe yet one thing further of this admirable plot; the business of it rises in every act. The second is greater than the first, the third than the second, and so forward to the fifth. There too you see, till the very last scene, new difficulties arising to obstruct the action of the play; and when the audience is brought into despair that the business can naturally be effected, then, and not before, the discovery is made. But that the poet might entertain you with more variety all this while, he reserves some new characters to show you, which he opens not till the second and third act. In the second Morose, Daw, the Barber and Otter; in the third the Collegiate Ladies, all which he moves afterwards in by-walks, or under-plots, as diversions to the main design, lest it should grow tedious, though they are still naturally joined with it, and somewhere or other subservient to it. Thus, like a skilful chess-player, by little and little he draws out his men, and makes his pawns of use to his greater persons.

If this comedy, and some others of his, were translated into French prose (which would now be no wonder to them, since Molière has lately given them plays out of verse which have not displeased them) I believe the controversy would soon be decided betwixt the two nations, even making them the judges. But we need not call our heroes to our aid. Be it spoken to the honour of the English, our nation can never want in any age such who are able to dispute the empire of wit with any people in the universe. And though the fury of a civil war, and power, for twenty years together, abandoned to a barbarous race of men, enemies of all good learning, had buried the muses under the ruins of monarchy, yet with the restoration of our happiness, we see revived poesy lifting up its head, and already shaking off the rubbish which lay so heavy on it. We have seen since his majesty's return, many dramatic poems which yield not to those of any foreign nation, and which deserve all laurels but the English. I will set aside flattery and envy. It cannot be denied but we have had some little blemish either in the plot or writing of all those plays which have been made within these seven years: (and perhaps there is no nation in the world so quick to discern them, or so difficult to pardon them, as ours:) yet if we can persuade ourselves to use the candour of that poet, who (though the most severe of critics) has left us this caution by which to moderate our censures;

> — Ubi plura nitent in carmine non ego paucis offendar maculis.[64]

If in consideration of their many and great beauties, we can wink at some slight, and little imperfections; if we, I say, can be thus equal to ourselves, I ask no favour from the French. And if I do not venture upon any particular judgement of our late plays, 'tis out of the consideration which an ancient writer gives me; *Vivorum, ut magna admiratio, ita censura difficilis:* betwixt the extremes of admiration and malice, 'tis hard to judge uprightly of the living. Only I think it may be permitted me to say, that as it is no lessening to us to yield to some plays, and those not many of our own nation in the last age, so can it be no addition to pronounce of our present poets that they have far surpassed all the Ancients, and the modern writers of other countries.

This, my Lord, was the substance of what was then spoke on that occasion; and Lisideius, I think, was going to reply, when he was prevented thus by Crites: "I am confident," said he, "that the most material things that can be said have been already urged on either side; if they have not, I must beg of Lisideius that he will defer his answer till another time: for I confess I have a joint quarrel to you both, because you have concluded, without any reason given for it, that rhyme is proper for the stage. I will not dispute how ancient it hath been among us to write this way; perhaps our ancestors knew no better till Shakespeare's time. I will grant it was not altogether left by him, and that Fletcher and Ben Jonson used it frequently in their Pastorals, and sometimes in other plays. Farther, I will not argue whether we received it originally from our own countrymen, or from the French; for that is an inquiry of as little benefit, as theirs who, in the midst of the great Plague, were not so solicitous to provide against it as to know whether we had it from the malignity of our own air, or by trans-

[64]"If happy effects / Figure more, I won't take offense at the few bad spots." Horace, *Art of Poetry,* 352; see p. 75. [Ed.]

portation from Holland. I have therefore only to affirm, that it is not allowable in serious plays; for comedies, I find you already concluding with me. To prove this, I might satisfy myself to tell you, how much in vain it is for you to strive against the stream of the people's inclination; the greatest part of which are prepossessed so much with those excellent plays of Shakespeare, Fletcher, and Ben Jonson, which have been written out of rhyme, that except you could bring them such as were written better in it, and those too by persons of equal reputation with them, it will be impossible for you to gain your cause with them, who will still be judges. This it is to which, in fine, all your reasons must submit. The unanimous consent of an audience is so powerful, that even Julius Cæsar (as Macrobius reports of him), when he was perpetual dictator, was not able to balance it on the other side. But when Laberius, a Roman Knight, at his request contended in the Mime with another poet, he was forced to cry out, *Etiam favente me victus es, Laberi.*[65] But I will not on this occasion take the advantage of the greater number, but only urge such reasons against rhyme, as I find in the writings of those who have argued for the other way. First then, I am of opinion, that rhyme is unnatural in a play, because dialogue there is presented as the effect of sudden thought: for a play is the imitation of Nature; and since no man without premeditation speaks in rhyme, neither ought he to do it on the stage. This hinders not but the fancy may be there elevated to an higher pitch of thought than it is in ordinary discourse; for there is a probability that men of excellent and quick parts may speak noble things *ex tempore:* but those thoughts are never fettered with the numbers or sound of verse without study, and therefore it cannot be but unnatural to present the most free way of speaking in that which is the most constrained. For this reason, says Aristotle, 'tis best to write tragedy in that kind of verse which is the least such, or which is nearest prose: and this amongst the Ancients was the iambic, and with us is blank verse, or the measure of verse kept exactly without rhyme. These numbers therefore are fittest for a play; the others for a paper of verses, or a poem; blank verse being as much below them, as rhyme is improper for the Drama. And if it be objected that neither are blank verses made *ex tempore,* yet, as nearest nature, they are still to be preferred. But there are two particular exceptions, which many besides myself have had to verse; by which it will appear yet more plainly how improper it is in plays. And the first of them is grounded on that very reason for which some have commended rhyme; they say, the quickness of repartees in argumentative scenes receives an ornament from verse. Now what is more unreasonable than to imagine that a man should not only light upon the wit, but the rhyme too, upon the sudden? This nicking of him who spoke before both in sound and measure, is so great an happiness, that you must at least suppose the persons of your play to be born poets: *Arcades omnes, et cantare pares, et respondere parati:*[66] they must have arrived to the degree of *quicquid conabar dicere;*[67] to make verses almost whether they will or no. If they are any thing below this, it will look rather like the design of two, than the answer of one: it will appear that your actors hold intelligence together; that they perform their tricks like fortune-tellers, by confederacy. The hand of art will be too visible in it, against that maxim of all professions, *Ars est celare artem,* that it is the greatest perfection of art to keep itself undiscovered. Nor will it serve you to object, that however you manage it, 'tis still known to be a play; and, consequently, the dialogue of two persons understood to be the labour of one poet. For a play is still an imitation of Nature; we know we are to be deceived, and we desire to be so; but no man ever was deceived but with a probability of truth; for who will suffer a gross lie to be fastened on him? Thus we sufficiently understand, that the scenes which represent cities and countries to us are not really such, but only painted on boards and canvas; but shall that excuse the ill painture or designment of them? Nay, rather ought they not to be laboured with so much the more diligence and exactness,

[65]"Even with me favoring you, you are beaten, Laberius." Macrobius, *Saturnalia* 2:7. [Ed.]

[66]"All Arcadians, prepared to sing and to respond." Virgil, *Eclogues* 7:4–5. [Ed.]

[67]"To say whatever I tried to say." [Ed.]

to help the imagination? since the mind of man does naturally tend to, and seek after truth; and therefore the nearer any thing comes to the imitation of it, the more it pleases.

"Thus, you see, your rhyme is uncapable of expressing the greatest thoughts naturally, and the lowest it cannot with any grace: for what is more unbefitting the majesty of verse, than to call a servant, or bid a door be shut in rhyme? And yet this miserable necessity you are forced upon. But verse, you say, circumscribes a quick and luxuriant fancy, which would extend itself too far on every subject, did not the labour which is required to well-turned and polished rhyme, set bounds to it. Yet this argument, if granted, would only prove that we may write better in verse, but not more naturally. Neither is it able to evince that; for he who wants judgement to confine his fancy in blank verse, may want it as much in rhyme: and he who has it will avoid errors in both kinds. Latin verse was as great a confinement to the imagination of those poets, as rhyme to ours; and yet you find Ovid saying too much on every subject. *Nescivit* (says Seneca) *quod bene cessit relinquere:*[68] of which he gives you one famous instance in his description of the deluge:

> *Omnia pontus erat, deerant quoque litora ponto.*
> Now all was sea, nor had that sea a shore.

Thus Ovid's fancy was not limited by verse, and Virgil needed not verse to have bounded his.

"In our own language we see Ben Jonson confining himself to what ought to be said, even in the liberty of blank verse; and yet Corneille, the most judicious of the French poets, is still varying the same sense an hundred ways, and dwelling eternally on the same subject, though confined by rhyme. Some other exceptions I have to verse; but being these I have named are for the most part already public, I conceive it reasonable they should first be answered."

"It concerns me less than any," said Neander (seeing he had ended), "to reply to this discourse; because when I should have proved that verse may be natural in plays, yet I should always be ready to confess, that those which I have written in this kind come short of that perfection which is required. Yet since you are pleased I should undertake this province, I will do it, though with all imaginable respect and deference, both to that person from whom you have borrowed your strongest arguments, and to whose judgement, when I have said all, I finally submit. But before I proceed to answer your objections, I must first remember you, that I exclude all Comedy from my defence; and next that I deny not but blank verse may be also used; and content myself only to assert, that in serious plays where the subject and characters are great, and the plot unmixed with mirth, which might allay or divert these concernments which are produced, rhyme is there as natural and more effectual than blank verse.

"And now having laid down this as a foundation, to begin with Crites, I must crave leave to tell him, that some of his arguments against rhyme reach no farther than, from the faults or defects of ill rhyme, to conclude against the use of it in general. May not I conclude against blank verse by the same reason? If the words of some poets who write in it, are either ill chosen, or ill placed, which makes not only rhyme, but all kind of verse in any language unnatural, shall I, for their vicious affectation, condemn those excellent lines of Fletcher, which are written in that kind? Is there any thing in rhyme more constrained than this line in blank verse, *I heaven invoke, and strong resistance make?* where you see both the clauses are placed unnaturally, that is, contrary to the common way of speaking, and that without the excuse of a rhyme to cause it: yet you would think me very ridiculous, if I should accuse the stubbornness of blank verse for this, and not rather the stiffness of the poet. Therefore, Crites, you must either prove that words, though well chosen, and duly placed, yet render not rhyme natural in itself; or that, however natural and easy the rhyme may be, yet it is not proper for a play. If you insist on the former part, I would ask you, what other conditions are required to make rhyme natural in itself, besides an election of apt words, and a right disposing of

[68]"He does not know when to leave well enough alone." Marcus Seneca, spoken of Ovid, in *Controversiae.* But the quotation and praise of the line from Ovid's *Metamorphoses* is by Lucius Seneca in *Quaestiones Naturales.* [Ed.]

them? For the due choice of your words expresses your sense naturally, and the due placing them adapts the rhyme to it. If you object that one verse may be made for the sake of another, though both the words and rhyme be apt, I answer, it cannot possibly so fall out; for either there is a dependence of sense betwixt the first line and the second, or there is none: if there be that connection, then in the natural position of the words the latter line must of necessity flow from the former, if there be no dependence, yet still the due ordering of words makes the last line as natural in itself as the other: so that the necessity of a rhyme never forces any but bad or lazy writers to say what they would not otherwise. 'Tis true, there is both care and art required to write in verse. A good poet never concludes upon the first line, till he has sought out such a rhyme as may fit the sense, already prepared to heighten the second: many times the close of the sense falls into the middle of the next verse, or farther off, and he may often prevail himself of the same advantages in English which Virgil had in Latin; he may break off in the hemistich,[69] and begin another line. Indeed, the not observing these two last things, makes plays which are writ in verse so tedious: for though, most commonly, the sense is to be confined to the couplet, yet nothing that does *perpetuo tenore fluere,* run in the same channel, can please always. 'Tis like the murmuring of a stream, which not varying in the fall, causes at first attention, at last drowsiness. Variety of cadences is the best rule; the greatest help to the actors, and refreshment to the audience.

"If then verse may be made natural in itself, how becomes it improper to a play? You say the stage is the representation of Nature, and no man in ordinary conversation speaks in rhyme. But you foresaw when you said this, that it might be answered — neither does any man speak in blank verse, or in measure without rhyme. Therefore you concluded, that which is nearest Nature is still to be preferred. But you took no notice that rhyme might be made as natural as blank verse, by the well placing of the words, &c. All the difference between them, when they are both correct, is, the sound in one, which the other wants; and if so, the sweetness of it, and all the advantage resulting from it, which are handled in the Preface to *The Rival Ladies,*[70] will yet stand good. As for that place of Aristotle, where he says, plays should be writ in that kind of verse which is nearest prose, it makes little for you; blank verse being properly but measured prose. Now measure alone, in any modern language, does not constitute verse; those of the Ancients in Greek and Latin consisted in quantity of words, and a determinate number of feet. But when, by the inundation of the Goths and Vandals into Italy, new languages were brought in, and barbarously mingled with the Latin, of which the Italian, Spanish, French, and ours (made out of them and the Teutonic) are dialects, a new way of poesy was practised; new, I say, in those countries, for in all probability it was that of the conquerors in their own nations. This new way consisted in measure or number of feet, and rhyme; the sweetness of rhyme, and observation of accent, supplying the place of quantity in words, which could neither exactly be observed by those Barbarians, who knew not the rules of it, neither was it suitable to their tongues, as it had been to the Greek and Latin. No man is tied in modern poesy to observe any farther rule in the feet of his verse, but that they be dissyllables; whether spondee, trochee, or iambic, it matters not; only he is obliged to rhyme. Neither do the Spanish, French, Italian, or Germans, acknowledge at all, or very rarely, any such kind of poesy as blank verse amongst them. Therefore, at most 'tis but a poetic prose, a *sermo pedestris;* and as such, most fit for comedies, where I acknowledge rhyme to be improper. Farther; as to that quotation of Aristotle, our couplet verses may be rendered as near prose as blank verse itself, by using those advantages I lately named, as breaks in a hemistich, or running the sense into another line, thereby making art and order appear as loose and free as nature: or not tying ourselves to couplets strictly, we may use the benefit of the Pindaric way practised

[69]Halfway through the hexameter verse. [Ed.]

[70]Dryden's *The Rival Ladies* (1664) was partly in rhyme; his preface had defended the practice. [Ed.]

in *The Siege of Rhodes;*[71] where the numbers vary, and the rhyme is disposed carelessly, and far from often chiming. Neither is that other advantage of the Ancients to be despised, of changing the kind of verse when they please, with the change of the scene, or some new entrance; for they confine not themselves always to iambics, but extend their liberty to all lyric numbers, and sometimes even to hexameter. But I need not go so far to prove that rhyme, as it succeeds to all other offices of Greek and Latin verse, so especially to this of plays, since the custom of all nations at this day confirms it, all the French, Italian, and Spanish tragedies are generally writ in it; and sure the universal consent of the most civilized parts of the world ought in this, as it doth in other customs, to include the rest.

"But perhaps you may tell me, I have proposed such a way to make rhyme natural, and consequently proper to plays, as is unpracticable; and that I shall scarce find six or eight lines together in any play, where the words are so placed and chosen as is required to make it natural. I answer, no poet need constrain himself at all times to it. It is enough he makes it his general rule; for I deny not but sometimes there may be a greatness in placing the words otherwise; and sometimes they may sound better, sometimes also the variety itself is excuse enough. But if, for the most part, the words be placed as they are in the negligence of prose, it is sufficient to denominate the way practicable; for we esteem that to be such, which in the trial oftener succeeds than misses. And thus far you may find the practice made good in many plays: where you do not, remember still, that if you cannot find six natural rhymes together, it will be as hard for you to produce as many lines in blank verse, even among the greatest of our poets, against which I cannot make some reasonable exception.

"And this, Sir, calls to my remembrance the beginning of your discourse, where you told us we should never find the audience favourable to this kind of writing, till we could produce as good plays in rhyme, as Ben Jonson, Fletcher, and Shakespeare, had writ out of it. But it is to raise envy to the living, to compare them with the dead. They are honoured, and almost adored by us, as they deserve; neither do I know any so presumptuous of themselves as to contend with them. Yet give me leave to say thus much, without injury to their ashes; that not only we shall never equal them, but they could never equal themselves, were they to rise and write again. We acknowledge them our fathers in wit; but they have ruined their estates themselves, before they came to their children's hands. There is scarce an humour, a character, or any kind of plot, which they have not blown upon. All comes sullied or wasted to us: and were they to entertain this age, they could not make so plenteous treatments out of such decayed fortunes. This therefore will be a good argument to us, either not to write at all, or to attempt some other way. There is no bays to be expected in their walks: *tentanda via est, qua me quoque possum tollere humo.*[72]

"This way of writing in verse they have only left free to us; our age is arrived to a perfection in it, which they never knew; and which (if we may guess by what of theirs we have seen in verse, as *The Faithful Shepherdess,* and *Sad Shepherd)*[73] 'tis probable they never could have reached. For the genius of every age is different; and though ours excel in this, I deny not but that to imitate Nature in that perfection which they did in prose, is a greater commendation than to write in verse exactly. As for what you have added, that the people are not generally inclined to like this way; if it were true, it would be no wonder, that betwixt the shaking off an old habit, and the introducing of a new, there should be difficulty. Do we not see them stick to Hopkins's and Sternhold's psalms, and forsake those of David, I mean Sandys his translation of them? If by the people you understand the multitude, οἱ πολλοί, 'tis no matter what they think; they are sometimes in the right, sometimes in the wrong: their judgement is a mere lottery. *Est ubi plebs recte*

[71]An operatic entertainment (1656) by Sir William Davenant, prototype of the Restoration heroic play and influenced by Abraham Cowley's pindarics. [Ed.]

[72]"I too must find a way to raise myself from the earth." Virgil, *Georgics* 3:8–9. [Ed.]

[73]By Beaumont and Fletcher, and Ben Jonson, respectively. [Ed.]

putat, est ubi peccat.[74] Horace says it of the vulgar, judging poesy. But if you mean the mixed audience of the populace and the noblesse, I dare confidently affirm that a great part of the latter sort are already favourable to verse; and that no serious plays written since the King's return have been more kindly received by them, than *The Siege of Rhodes,* the *Mustapha, The Indian Queen,* and *Indian Emperor.*[75]

"But I come now to the inference of your first argument. You said the dialogue of plays is presented as the effect of sudden thought, but no man speaks suddenly, or *ex tempore,* in rhyme; and you inferred from thence, that rhyme, which you acknowledge to be proper to epic poesy, cannot equally be proper to dramatic, unless we could suppose all men born so much more than poets, that verses should be made in them, not by them.

"It has been formerly urged by you, and confessed by me, that since no man spoke any kind of verse *ex tempore,* that which was nearest Nature was to be preferred. I answer you, therefore, by distinguishing betwixt what is nearest to the nature of Comedy, which is the imitation of common persons and ordinary speaking, and what is nearest the nature of a serious play: this last is indeed the representation of Nature, but 'tis Nature wrought up to an higher pitch. The plot, the characters, the wit, the passions, the descriptions, are all exalted above the level of common converse, as high as the imagination of the poet can carry them, with proportion to verisimility. Tragedy, we know, is wont to image to us the minds and fortunes of noble persons, and to portray these exactly; heroic rhyme is nearest Nature, as being the noblest kind of modern verse.

Indignatur enim privatis et prope socco
Dignis carminibus narrari cœna Thyestæ,[76]

says Horace: and in another place,

Effutire leves indigna tragœdia versus.[77]

Blank verse is acknowledged to be too low for a poem, nay more, for a paper of verses; but if too low for an ordinary sonnet, how much more for Tragedy, which is by Aristotle, in the dispute betwixt the epic poesy and the dramatic, for many reasons he there alleges, ranked above it?

"But setting this defence aside, your argument is almost as strong against the use of rhyme in poems as in plays; for the epic way is every where interlaced with dialogue, or discoursive scenes; and therefore you must either grant rhyme to be improper there, which is contrary to your assertion, or admit it into plays by the same title which you have given it to poems. For though Tragedy be justly preferred above the other, yet there is a great affinity between them, as may easily be discovered in that definition of a play which Lisideius gave us. The *genus* of them is the same, a just and lively image of human nature, in its actions, passions, and traverses of fortune: so is the end, namely, for the delight and benefit of mankind. The characters and persons are still the same, viz. the greatest of both sorts; only the manner of acquainting us with those actions, passions, and fortunes, is different. Tragedy performs it *viva voce,* or by action, in dialogue; wherein it excels the Epic Poem, which does it chiefly by narration, and therefore is not so lively an image of human nature. However, the agreement betwixt them is such, that if rhyme be proper for one, it must be for the other. Verse, 'tis true, is not the effect of sudden thought; but this hinders not that sudden thought may be represented in verse, since those thoughts are such as must be higher than Nature can raise them without premeditation, especially to a continuance of them, even out of verse; and consequently you cannot imagine them to have been sudden either in the poet or in the actors. A play, as I have said, to be like Nature, is to be set above it; as statues which are placed on high are

[74] "Sometimes the people are right and sometimes wrong." Horace, *Epistles* 2.1:63. [Ed.]

[75] *Mustapha* (1665) was by Roger Boyle, Earl of Orrery; *The Indian Queen* (1664) by Dryden and Sir Robert Howard; *The Indian Emperor* (1665) by Dryden. [Ed.]

[76] "Thyestes' feast resents being told / In strains more nearly like those that comedy needs." Horace, *Art of Poetry,* 90–91; see p. 69. [Ed.]

[77] "if I write a satyr play, / I will not use only commonplace nouns and verbs." Horace, *Art of Poetry,* 231; see p. 72. [Ed.]

made greater than the life, that they may descend to the sight in their just proportion.

"Perhaps I have insisted too long on this objection; but the clearing of it will make my stay shorter on the rest. You tell us, Crites, that rhyme appears most unnatural in repartees, or short replies: when he who answers, it being presumed he knew not what the other would say, yet makes up that part of the verse which was left incomplete, and supplies both the sound and measure of it. This, you say, looks rather like the confederacy of two, than the answer of one.

"This, I confess, is an objection which is in every one's mouth, who loves not rhyme: but suppose, I beseech you, the repartee were made only in blank verse, might not part of the same argument be turned against you? for the measure is as often supplied there, as it is in rhyme; the latter half of the hemistich as commonly made up, or a second line subjoined as a reply to the former; which any one leaf in Jonson's plays will sufficiently clear to you. You will often find in the Greek tragedians, and in Seneca, that when a scene grows up into the warmth of repartees, which is the close fighting of it, the latter part of the trimeter is supplied by him who answers; and yet it was never observed as a fault in them by any of the ancient or modern critics. The case is the same in our verse, as it was in theirs; rhyme to us being in lieu of quantity to them. But if no latitude is to be allowed a poet, you take from him not only his licence of *quidlibet audendi*,[78] but you tie him up in a straiter compass than you would a philosopher. This is indeed *Musas colere severiores*.[79] You would have him follow Nature, but he must follow her on foot; you have dismounted him from his Pegasus. But you tell us, this supplying the last half of a verse, or adjoining a whole second to the former, looks more like the design of two, than the answer of one. Supposing we acknowledge it: how comes this confederacy to be more displeasing to you, than in a dance which is well contrived? You see there the united design of many persons to make up one figure: after they have separated themselves in many petty divisions, they rejoin one by one into a gross: the confederacy is plain amongst them, for chance could never produce any thing so beautiful; and yet there is nothing in it, that shocks your sight. I acknowledge the hand of art appears in repartee, as of necessity it must in all kinds of verse. But there is also the quick and poynant brevity of it (which is an high imitation of Nature in those sudden gusts of passion) to mingle with it; and this, joined with the cadency and sweetness of the rhyme, leaves nothing in the soul of the hearer to desire. 'Tis an art which appears; but it appears only like the shadowings of painture, which being to cause the rounding of it, cannot be absent; but while that is considered, they are lost: so while we attend to the other beauties of the matter, the care and labour of the rhyme is carried from us, or at least drowned in its own sweetness, as bees are sometimes buried in their honey. When a poet has found the repartee, the last perfection he can add to it, is to put it into verse. However good the thought may be, however apt the words in which 'tis couched, yet he finds himself at a little unrest, while rhyme is wanting: he cannot leave it till that comes naturally, and then is at ease, and sits down contented.

"From replies, which are the most elevated thoughts of verse, you pass to the most mean ones, those which are common with the lowest of household conversation. In these, you say, the majesty of verse suffers. You instance in the calling of a servant, or commanding a door to be shut, in rhyme. This, Crites, is a good observation of yours, but no argument; for it proves no more but that such thoughts should be waived, as often as may be, by the address of the poet. But suppose they are necessary in the places where he uses them, yet there is no need to put them into rhyme. He may place them in the beginning of a verse, and break it off, as unfit, when so debased, for any other use; or granting the worst, that they require more room than the hemistich will allow, yet still there is a choice to be made of the best words, and least vulgar (provided they be apt) to express such thoughts. Many have blamed rhyme in general, for this fault, when the poet with a little care might have redressed it. But they do it with no more justice, than if En-

[78]"Daring anything." Horace, *Art of Poetry*, 10. [Ed.]

[79]"To worship the stricter muses." Martial, *Epigrams* 9.11:17. [Ed.]

glish Poesy should be made ridiculous for the sake of the Water Poet's rhymes.[80] Our language is noble, full, and significant; and I know not why he who is master of it may not clothe ordinary things in it as decently as the Latin, if he use the same diligence in his choice of words. *Delectus verborum origo est eloquentiae.*[81] It was the saying of Julius Cæsar, one so curious in his, that none of them can be changed but for a worse. One would think, *unlock the door,* was a thing as vulgar as could be spoken; and yet Seneca could make it sound high and lofty in his Latin:

Reserate clusos regii postes laris.[82]
Set wide the palace gates.

"But I turn from this exception, both because it happens not above twice or thrice in any play that those vulgar thoughts are used; and then too, were there no other apology to be made, yet the necessity of them which is alike in all kind of writing, may excuse them. Besides that the great eagerness and precipitation with which they are spoken makes us rather mind the substance than the dress; that for which they are spoken, rather than what is spoken. For they are always the effect of some hasty concernment, and something of consequence depends on them.

"Thus, Crites, I have endeavoured to answer your objections; it remains only that I should vindicate an argument for verse, which you have gone about to overthrow. It had formerly been said, that the easiness of blank verse renders the poet too luxuriant, but that the labour of rhyme bounds and circumscribes an overfruitful fancy; the sense there being commonly confined to the couplet, and the words so ordered that the rhyme naturally follows them, not they the rhyme. To this you answered, that it was no argument to the question in hand; for the dispute was not which way a man may write best, but which is most proper for the subject on which he writes.

"First, give me leave, Sir, to remember you, that the argument against which you raised this objection, was only secondary: it was built on this hypothesis, that to write in verse was proper for serious plays. Which supposition being granted (as it was briefly made out in that discourse, by showing how verse might be made natural), it asserted, that this way of writing was an help to the poet's judgement, by putting bounds to a wild overflowing fancy. I think, therefore, it will not be hard for me to make good what it was to prove. But you add, that were this let pass, yet he who wants judgement in the liberty of his fancy, may as well show the defect of it when he is confined to verse; for he who has judgement will avoid errors, and he who has it not, will commit them in all kinds of writing.

"This argument, as you have taken it from a most acute person,[83] so I confess it carries much weight in it: but by using the word judgement here indefinitely, you seem to have put a fallacy upon us. I grant, he who has judgement, that is, so profound, so strong, so infallible a judgement, that he needs no helps to keep it always poised and upright, will commit no faults either in rhyme or out of it. And on the other extreme, he who has a judgement so weak and crazed that no helps can correct or amend it, shall write scurvily out of rhyme, and worse in it. But the first of these judgements is no where to be found, and the latter is not fit to write at all. To speak therefore of judgement as it is in the best poets; they who have the greatest proportion of it, want other helps than from it, within. As for example, you would be loth to say, that he who was endued with a sound judgement had no need of History, Geography, or Moral Philosophy, to write correctly. Judgement is indeed the master-workman in a play; but he requires many subordinate hands, many tools to his assistance. And verse I affirm to be one of these; 'tis a rule and line by which he keeps his building compact and even, which otherwise lawless imagination would raise either irregularly or loosely. At least, if the poet commits errors with this help, he would make greater and more without it: 'tis, in short, a slow and painful, but the surest kind of working. Ovid, whom you accuse for luxuriancy in verse, had

[80]John Taylor (1580–1653), boatman on the Thames and facetious poet. [Ed.]

[81]"Choice of words is the fount of eloquence." Cicero, *Brutus* 72:253, misquoted. [Ed.]

[82]Seneca, *Hippolytus,* 863. [Ed.]

[83]From Sir Robert Howard's preface to *Four New Plays* (1665). [Ed.]

perhaps been farther guilty of it, had he writ in prose. And for your instance of Ben Jonson, who, you say, writ exactly without the help of rhyme; you are to remember, 'tis only an aid to a luxuriant fancy, which his was not: as he did not want imagination, so none ever said he had much to spare. Neither was verse then refined so much to be an help to that age, as it is to ours. Thus then the second thoughts being usually the best, as receiving the maturest digestion from judgement, and the last and most mature product of those thoughts being artful and laboured verse, it may well be inferred, that verse is a great help to a luxuriant fancy; and this is what that argument which you opposed was to evince."

Neander was pursuing this discourse so eagerly, that Eugenius had called to him twice or thrice, ere he took notice that the barge stood still, and that they were at the foot of Somerset Stairs, where they had appointed it to land. The company were all sorry to separate so soon, though a great part of the evening was already spent; and stood a while looking back on the water, which the moon-beams played upon, and made it appear like floating quick-silver: at last they went up through a crowd of French people, who were merrily dancing in the open air, and nothing concerned for the noise of guns which had alarmed the town that afternoon. Walking thence together to the Piazze, they parted there; Eugenius and Lisideius to some pleasant appointment they had made, and Crites and Neander to their several lodgings.

Aphra Behn

1640?–1689

Aphra Behn is considered the first Englishwoman to have lived by her pen, but her birthplace and maiden name and many of the facts of her life are still either cloaked in darkness or subjects of controversy. One theory has it that she was born Aphra Johnson, daughter of the barber Bartholomew Johnson of the cathedral town of Canterbury, and that she came by her education through the aristocratic Colepeper family when her mother became wet nurse to one of its children. Another is that she was the "Ayfara" born the same year to John and Amy Amis (of unknown occupation) in Wye. And it is generally agreed that she traveled at some time between 1658 and 1663 to Surinam (now the independent country of Suriname) on the north equatorial coast of South America, which until its loss to the Dutch in 1665 had been a British colony. She stayed in Surinam at the plantation of the governor-general, Lord Willoughby, and there collected the factual background for her most famous narrative, *Oroonoko, or The Royal Slave* (published 1688), including the names and personal habits of the ruling gentry. She apparently brought back to England a cloak of feathers of native manufacture, which was used as a costume in a Dryden play. Yet there is no evidence that her father, like that of the narrator of *Oroonoko,* had been appointed lieutenant-governor of the colony.

On her return to England (she said she was eighteen but may have been somewhat older), she married a merchant of Dutch extraction named Behn, and she was known by that name from then on. Behn himself does not appear in her later writings, and some have surmised that he may have died or separated from Aphra before 1666. She had, along with her verbal ability and skill at intrigue, a connection to the government through the theatrical producer Thomas Killigrew. As a result of his recommendation, Aphra Behn had a personal interview with Charles II and was sent by Charles's foreign minister, Lord Arlington, to spy for England in Antwerp. Behn brought back and transmitted intelligence gathered by others about Admiral de Wit's plans to assault English vessels in their harbors at the outset of the Second Dutch War (1665–67). Her information might have been valuable had it been credited. It was disregarded, however, and Behn found herself seriously in debt because she wrongly believed that the Crown would pay the expenses she incurred in its service. In the late 1660s, Behn was jailed in debtor's prison, but she was soon bailed out, and began her literary career as a playwright around 1670.

Her plays, mainly comedies of intrigue like those of George Etherege and William Wycherley, were performed primarily by Killigrew's "King's Company" during the next two decades. Behn kept herself very busy, as was required in an age when the playwright's "royalties" were the receipts from the third night's performance and irregular "author's nights" thereafter — a risky business when many plays did not run even three nights. At least thirteen of her plays were produced between 1670 and 1687. Her works for the theater include *The Forced Marriage* (1670); *The Dutch Lover* (1673); *Abdelazar;* or, *The Moor's Revenge* (1676); *The Rover*; or, *The Banished Cavalier, Part I* (1677); *Sir Patient Fancy* (1678); *The*

Feign'd Courtesans; or, *A Night's Intrigue* (1679); *The Roundheads;* or, *The Good Old Cause* (1681); *The Rover, Part II* (1681); *The City Heiress;* or, *Sir Timothy Treat-all* (1682); *The Lucky Chance;* or, *An Alderman's Bargain* (ca. 1686); and *The Widow Ranter,* the first British play set in America (published posthumously in 1690).

Though some of Behn's plays have been successfully revived, as in recent London productions of *The Rover* and *The Lucky Chance,* today Behn is better known as an innovator in prose fiction who created the "factual fictions" that Daniel Defoe was later to bring to greater perfection. The narrative of *Oroonoko, or The Royal Slave* is filled with the sort of gritty, concrete details that suggest the narrator was an eyewitness to real happenings. Its ideology is equally surprising for its day: *Oroonoko* is intensely anti-imperialistic, attacking the base venality and cruelty of the European colonists and settlers. Indeed, the novel was instrumental in establishing the convention of the "noble savage," which dominated Western culture in the era of Rousseau. On the other hand, *Oroonoko* was not in any sense (as it has frequently been called) an antislavery novel. The novel takes the institution of slavery for granted; its African hero himself captures and sells others into slavery, and resents only that he, a prince, has been tricked into bondage. Behn's other stories and novels include *Love Letters Between a Noble-Man and His Sister* (1684), a reconstruction of the scandal surrounding a Whig lord who had eloped with his sister-in-law; and *The Fair Jilt* (1688), based upon an incident Behn observed in The Hague in the 1660s. Behn also published her *Poems on Several Occasions* in 1684. Behn's health began to fail in the early 1680s and she died in 1689, the year of the Glorious Revolution; she is buried in Westminster Abbey.

Behn's Preface to *The Lucky Chance* focuses on the charges of obscenity laid against her by envious fellow poets who, she claims, maliciously wish to tear down anything of quality that would threaten the success of their own plays. Her witty response deflates the hypocrisy of her fellow wits, but it is also interesting as an illustration of how an individual text was attacked and defended in an age when literature was considered a form of rhetoric, thus having an immediate relation with the audience. When every member of an audience is a qualified judge, but community standards are not really univocal or agreed upon, where stretching the permissible limits of a genre gains an enthusiastic audience until "going over the top" loses it, the successful dramatist is caught between the Scylla of recurrent moral outrage and the Charybdis of an audience's craving for the new.

Behn's rhetoric, despite the unfamiliar language in which it is couched, should remind us of twentieth-century issues. Like a Hollywood director accused of bringing sex or violence to a new level of offensiveness in a film, Behn insists that the outrageousness of her text is essentially that of the genre within which it works, that comedies of intrigue require offstage extramarital sex. Behn maintains that the much-criticized moment in the play where "Mr. Leigh opens his *Night Gown,* when he comes into the Bride-chamber," was an actor's improvisation, rather than her own stage direction. She also argues that *The Lucky Chance* was previewed and judged (given perhaps the equivalent of today's PG-13 rating) by the most authoritative persons, including the "rating board" of Davenant, L'Estrange, and Killigrew, and, in case their masculine sensibilities might be expected to be a bit coarse, that it was vetted before publication by "several Ladys of very great Quality, and unquestioned Fame," who considered it harmless fun. Equally modern is Behn's claim that, as a woman writer, she has been singled out for attacks on the decency of her plays, and that similar scrutiny is not accorded to equally outrageous texts by her male contemporaries — such as *Limberham* by poet laureate John Dryden. Behn's feminist successors would hardly be in agreement with Behn's claim that "the poet in me" is "my Masculine Part": but they would surely be sympathetic to her plea that women competing with men be judged by the same standards.

Behn seems more intensely feminist in the Preface to her quarto edition of *The Dutch Lover* (1673), where she takes on the "phlegmatick, white, ill-favour'd, wretched Fop" who complained on opening night "that they were to expect a woful Play, God damn him, for it was a woman's." Like her near-contemporary, Mary Astell, Behn presumes that women are "as capable of knowledge, of whatever sort" as men, if granted the same access to education. But given the male audience for her plays, she does not argue this directly, stressing instead that education is hardly a playwright's first requirement. The "immortal Shakespeare" had no more learning himself "than often falls to women's share," and even the more educated Ben Jonson "was no such Rabbi neither." Those who most overestimate the poet's need for learning are often, she suggests, those who have absorbed the least education themselves. Given that native genius and invention are more important than learning and the rules of art, there is little bar to women excelling in the arts: ". . . except our most unimitable Laureat [John Dryden] 201. . . I know of none that write . . . but that a woman may well hope to reach their greatest heights," says Behn. If in those words she was immodestly thinking of herself, as one may suspect, most of today's readers would agree that Behn achieved those heights.

Selected Bibliography

Chibka, Robert L. "'Oh! Do Not Fear a Woman's Invention': Truth, Falsehood and Fiction in Aphra Behn's *Oroonoko*." *Texas Studies in Literature and Language* 30 (1988): 510–37.

Duffy, Maureen. *The Passionate Shepherdess: Aphra Behn, 1640–1689*. London: Cape, 1977.

Goreau, Angeline. *Reconstructing Aphra: A Social Biography of Aphra Behn*. New York: Dial Press, 1980.

Huttner, Heidi, ed. *Rereading Aphra Behn: History, Theory and Criticism*. Charlottesville: University Press of Virginia, 1993.

O'Donnell, Mary Ann. "Tory Wit and Unconventional Woman: Aphra Behn." In *Women Writers of the Seventeenth Century,* eds. Katharina M. Wilson and Frank J. Warnke. Athens: University of Ohio Press, 1989, pp. 349–72.

Todd, Janet, ed. *Aphra Behn Studies*. New York and London: Cambridge University Press, 1996.

An Epistle to the Reader from *The Dutch Lover*

Good, Sweet, Honey, Sugar-Candied READER,

Which I think is more than anyone has called you yet, I must have a word or two with you before you do advance into the Treatise; but 'tis not to beg your pardon for diverting you from your affairs, by such an idle Pamphlet as this is, for I presume you have not much to do and therefore are to be obliged to me for keeping you from worse employment, and if you have a better you may get you gone about your business: but if you will misspend your Time, pray lay the fault upon yourself; for I have dealt pretty fairly in the matter, told you in the Title Page what you are to expect within. Indeed, had I hung a sign of the Immortality of the Soul, of the Mystery of Godliness, or of Ecclesiastical Policie, and then had treated you with Indiscerpibility and Essential Spissitude (words, which though I am no competent Judge of, for want of Languages, yet I fancy strongly ought to mean just nothing) with a company of Apocryphal midnight Tales cull'd out of the choicest Insignificant Authors; If I had only proved in Folio that Appolonius was a naughty knave, or had presented you with two or three of the worst principles transcrib'd out of the peremptory and ill-natur'd (though prettily ingenious) Doctor of Malmsbury undigested and ill-manag'd by a silly, saucy, ignorant, impertinent, ill educated Chaplain I were then indeed sufficiently in fault; but having inscrib'd Comedy on the beginning of my Book, you may guess pretty near what penny-worths you are like to have, and ware your money and your time accordingly. I would not yet be understood to lessen the dignity of Playes, for surely they deserve a place among the middle if not the better sort of Books; for I have heard the most of that which bears the name of Learning, and which has abused such quantities of Ink and Paper, and continually employs so many ignorant, unhappy souls for ten, twelve, twenty years in the University (who yet poor wretches think they are doing something all the while) as Logick etc. and several other things (that shall be nameless lest I misspell them) are much more absolutely nothing than the errantest Play that e'er was writ. Take notice, Reader, I do not assert this purely upon my own knowledge, but I think I have known it very fully prov'd, both sides being fairly heard, and even some ingenious opposers of it most abominably baffl'd in the Argument: Some of which I have got so perfectly by rote, that if this were a proper place for it, I am apt to think myself could almost make it clear; and as I would not undervalue Poetry, so neither am I altogether of their judgement who believe no wisdom in the world beyond it. I have often heard indeed (and read) how much the World was anciently oblig'd to it for most of that which they call'd Science, which my want of letters makes me less assured of than others happily may be: but I have heard some wise men say that no considerable part of useful knowledge was this way communicated, and on the other way, that it hath serv'd to propogate so many idle superstitions, as all the benefits it hath or can be guilty of, can never make sufficient amends for; which unaided by the unlucky charms of Poetry, could never have possest a thinking Creature such as man. However true this is, I am myself well able to affirm that none of all our English Poets, and least the Dramatique (so I think you call them) can be justly charg'd with too great reformation of men's minds or manners, and for that I may appeal to general experiment, if those who are the most assiduous Disciples of the Stage, do not make the fondest and the lewdest Crew about this Town; for if you should unhappily converse them through the year, you will not find one Dram of sense amongst a Club of them, unless you will allow for such a little Link-Boy's[1] Ribaldry thick larded with unseasonable oaths & impudent defiance of God, and all things

[1]A boy hired to carry a "link" (a torch made of tow dipped in pitch) to light his employer through the otherwise unlit streets. As observers of the nocturnal habits of the dissipated men and women of Charles II's London, link-boys could be expected to have seen everything and to have a street-wise sense of humor about it all. [Ed.]

serious; and that at such a senseless damn'd unthinking rate, as, if 'twere well distributed, would spoil near half the Apothecaries trade, and save the sober people of the Town the charge of Vomits; And it was smartly said (how prudently I cannot tell) by a late learned Doctor, who, though himself no great asserter of a Deity, (as you'll believe by that which follows) yet was observed to be continually persuading of this sort of men (if I for once may call them so) of the necessity and truth of our Religion; and being ask'd how he came to bestir himself so much this way, made answer that it was because their ignorance and indiscreet debauch made them a scandal to the profession of Atheism. And for their wisdom and design I never knew it reach beyond the invention of some notable expedient, for the speedier ridding them of their Estate, (a devilish clog to Wit and Parts), than other grouling Mortals know, or battering half-a-dozen fair new Windows in a Morning after their debauch, whilst the dull unjantee[2] Rascal they belong to is fast asleep. But I'll proceed no farther in their character, because that miracle of Wit (in spite of Academick frippery) the mighty Echard[3] hath already done it to my satisfaction; and whoever undertakes a Supplement to anything he hath discourst, had better for their reputation be doing nothing.

Besides this Theam is worn too thread-bare by the whiffling would-be Wits of the Town, and of both the stone-blind-eyes of the Kingdom. And therefore to return to that which I before was speaking of, I will have leave to say that in my judgement the increasing number of our latter Plays have not done much more towards the amending of men's Morals, or their Wit, than hath the frequent Preaching, which this last age hath been pester'd with, (indeed without all Controversie they have done less harm) nor can I once imagine what temptation anyone can have to expect it from them; for sure I am no Play was ever writ with that design. If you consider Tragedy, you'll find their best of Characters unlikely patterns for a wise man to pursue: For he that is the Knight of the Play, no sublunary feats must serve his Dulcinea; for if he can't bestrid the Moon, he'll ne'er make good his business to the end, and if he chance to be offended, he must without considering right or wrong confound all things he meets, and put you half-a-score likely tall fellows into each pocket; and truly if he come not something near this Pitch I think the Tragedy's not worth a farthing; for Playes were certainly intended for the exercising of men's passions not their understandings, and he is infinitely far from wise that will bestow one moment's meditation on such things: And as for Comedie, the finest folks you meet with there are still unfitter for your imitation, for though within a leaf or two of the Prologue, you are told that they are people of Wit, good Humour, good Manners, and all that: yet if the Authors did not kindly add their proper names, you'd never know them by their Characters; for whatsoe'er's the matter, it hath happen'd so spightfully in several Playes, which have been prettie well received of late, that even those persons that were meant to be the ingenious Censors of the Play, have either prov'd the most debauch'd, or most unwittie people in the Company: nor is this error very lamentable, since as I take it Comedie was never meant, either for a converting or a conforming Ordinance: In short, I think a Play the best divertisement that wise men have: but I do also think them nothing so who do discourse as formallie about the rules of it, as if 'twere the grand affair of humane life. This being my opinion of Plays, I studied only to make this as entertaining as I could, which whether I have been successful in, my gentle Reader, you may for your shilling judge. To tell you my thoughts of it, were to little purpose, for were they very ill, you may be sure I would not have expos'd it; nor did I so till I had first consulted most of those who have a reputation for judgement of this kind; who were at least so civil (if not kind) to it as did encourage me to venture it upon the Stage, and in the Press: Nor did I take their single word for it, but us'd their reasons as a confirmation of my own.

Indeed that day 'twas Acted first, there comes me into the Pit, a long, lither, phlegmatick, white, ill-favour'd, wretched Fop, an Officer in Mas-

[2]Variant of "unjaunty," characterizing the stay-at-home sleepers, as opposed to the hellraisers battering their windows at dawn. [Ed.]

[3]Probably Laurence Echard, author of a contemporary *History of England*. [Ed.]

querade newly transported with a Scarf & Feather out of France, a sorry Animal that has nought else to shield it from the uttermost contempt of all mankind, but that respect which we afford to Rats and Toads, which though we do not well allow to live, yet when considered as a part of God's Creation, we make honourable mention of them. A thing, Reader — but no more of such a Smelt: This thing, I tell ye, opening that which serves it for a mouth, out issued such a noise as this to those that sate about it, that they were to expect a woful Play, God damn him, for it was a woman's. Now how this came about I am not sure, but I suppose he brought it piping hot from some who had with him the reputation of a villanous Wit: for Creatures of his size of sense talk without all imagination, such scraps as they pick up from other folks. I would not for a world be taken arguing with such a propertie as this; but if I thought there were a man of any tolerable parts, who could upon mature deliberation distinguish well his right hand from his left, and justly state the difference between the number of sixteen and two, yet had this prejudice upon him; I would take a little pains to make him know how much he errs. For waving the examination why women having equal education with men, were not as capable of knowledge, of whatsoever sort as well as they: I'll only say as I have touch'd before, that Plays have no great room for that which is men's great advantage over women, that is Learning; We all well know that the immortal Shakespeare's Plays (who was not guilty of much more of this than often falls to women's share) have better pleas'd the World than Johnson's works, though by the way 'tis said that Benjamin was no such Rabbi neither, for I am inform'd that his Learning was but Grammar high; (sufficient indeed to rob poor Salust of his best orations) and it hath been observ'd that they are apt to admire him most confoundedly, who have just such a scantling of it as he had; and I have seen a man the most severe of Johnson's Sect, sit with his Hat remov'd less than a hair's breadth from one sullen posture for almost three hours at *The Alchymist;* who at that excellent Play of *Harry the Fourth* (which yet I hope is far enough from Farce) hath very hardly kept his Doublet whole; but affectation hath always had a greater share both in the action and discourse of men than truth and judgement have; and for our Modern ones, except our most unimitable Laureat, I dare to say I know of none that write at such a formidable rate, but that a woman may well hope to reach their greatest heights. Then for their musty rules of Unity, and God knows what besides, if they meant anything, they are enough intelligible and as practible by a woman; but really methinks they that disturb their heads with any other rule of Playes besides the making them pleasant, and avoiding of scurrility, might much better be employed in studying how to improve men's too imperfect knowledge of that ancient English Game which hight long Laurence:[4] And if Comedy should be the picture of ridiculous mankind I wonder anyone should think it such a sturdy task, whilst we are furnish'd with such precious Originals as him I lately told you of; if at least that Character do not dwindle into Farce, and so become too mean an entertainment for those persons who are us'd to think. Reader, I have a complaint or two to make to you and I have done; Know then that this Play was hugely injur'd in the Acting, for 'twas done so imperfectly as never any was before, which did more harm to this than it could have done to any of another sort; the Plot being busie (though I think not intricate) and so requiring a continual attention, which being interrupted by the intolerable negligence of some that acted in it, must needs much spoil the beauty on't. My Dutch Lover spoke but little of what I intended for him, but supplied it with a great deal of idle stuff, which I was wholly unacquainted with until I had heard it first from him; so that Jack-pudding ever us'd to do: which though I knew before, I gave him yet the Part, because I knew him so acceptable to

[4]Janet Todd's new edition of Aphra Behn's works defines a "Long Lawrence" as an instrument marked with signs about three inches long like a short ruler or totem with eight sides. Each side had a different set of markings of strokes, zigzags, and crosses. The ancient English game with the same name was played (particularly at Christmas), by rolling the Long Lawrence; each player would win or lose pins or tokens according to which side came up. The name itself may have come from the marks on the instrument, which resembled the bars of a gridiron, on which St. Lawrence was martyred. Todd cites Alice Bertha Gomme, *The Traditional Games of England, Scotland, and Ireland* (1894). [Ed.]

most o'th' lighter Periwigs about the Town, and he indeed did vex me so, I could almost be angry: Yet, but Reader, you remember, I suppose, a fusty piece of Latine[5] that has past from hand to hand this thousand years they say (and how much longer I can't tell) in favour of the dead. I intended him a habit much more notably ridiculous, which if ever it be important was so here, for many of the Scenes in the three last Acts depended upon the mistakes of the Colonel for Haunce, which the ill-favour'd likeness of their Habits is suppos'd to cause. Lastly my Epilogue was promis'd me by a Person who had surely made it good, if any, but he failing of his word, deput'd one, who has made it as you see, and to make out your penyworth you have it here. The Prologue is by misfortune lost. Now, Reader, I have eas'd my mind of all I had to say, and so sans farther complyment, Adieu.

[5]The "fusty bit of Latine . . . in favour of the dead" is probably the proverb "De mortuis nil nisi bonum": Of the dead speak nothing but good. The application is to Edward Angel, the actor who played the male lead in *The Dutch Lover* and whose ad-libbing of lines and vulgar stage business caused the scandal Behn is discussing: Angel had died in the interval between the production and publication of the play. [Ed.]

Preface to *The Lucky Chance*

The little Obligation I have to some of the witty Sparks and Poets of the Town, has put me on a Vindication of this Comedy from those Censures that Malice, and ill Nature have thrown upon it, tho in vain: The Poets I heartily excuse, since there is a sort of Self-Interest in their Malice, which I shou'd rather call a witty Way they have in this Age, of Railing at every thing they find with pain successful, and never to shew good Nature and speak well of any thing; but when they are sure 'tis damn'd, then they afford it that worse Scandal, their Pity. And nothing makes them so thorough-stitcht an Enemy as a full Third Day,[1] that's Crime enough to load it with all manner of Infamy; and when they can no other way prevail with the Town, they charge it with the old never failing Scandal — That 'tis not fit for the Ladys: As if (if it were as they falsly give it out) the Ladys were oblig'd to hear Indecencys only from their Pens and Plays and some of them have ventur'd to treat 'em as Coursely as 'twas possible, without the least Reproach from them; and in some of their most Celebrated Plays have entertained 'em with things, that if I should here strip from their Wit and Occasion that conducts 'em in and makes them proper, their fair Cheeks would perhaps wear a natural Colour at the reading them: yet are never taken Notice of, because a Man writ them, and they may hear that from them they blush at from a Woman — But I make a Challenge to any Person of common Sense and Reason — that is not wilfully bent on ill Nature, and will in spight of Sense wrest a double *Entendre* from every thing, lying upon the Catch for a Jest or a Quibble, like a Rook for a Cully;[2] but any unprejudic'd Person that knows not the Author, to read any of my Comedy's and compare 'em with others of this Age, and if they find one Word that can offend the chastest Ear, I will submit to all their peevish Cavills; but Right or Wrong they must be Criminal because a Woman's; condemning them without having the Christian Charity, to examine whether it be guilty or not, with reading, comparing, or thinking; the Ladies taking up any Scandal on Trust from some conceited Sparks, who will in spight of Nature be Wits and *Beaus;* then scatter it for Authentick all over the Town and Court, poysoning of others Judgements with their false Notions, condemning it to worse than Death, Loss of Fame. And to fortifie their Detraction, charge me with all the Plays that have ever been offensive; though I wish with all their Faults I had been the Author of some of those they have honour'd me with.

[1]Restoration playwrights were paid not by a fixed royalty but by the receipts of the third night of the production (and other subsequently declared author's nights). When a play did not run a full three days, the author received nothing. [Ed.]

[2]Like a cheat for his victim. [Ed.]

For the farther Justification of this Play; it being a Comedy of Intrigue Dr. *Davenant* out of Respect to the Commands he had from Court, to take great Care that no Indecency should be in Plays, sent for it and nicely look't it over, putting out anything he but imagin'd the Criticks would play with. After that, Sir *Roger L'Estrange* read it and licens'd it, and found no such Faults as 'tis charg'd with: Then Mr. *Killigrew*, who more severe than any, from the strict Order he had, perus'd it with great Circumspection; and lastly the Master Players, who you will I hope in some Measure esteem Judges of Decency and their own Interest, having been so many Years Prentice to the Trade of Judging.

I say, after all these Supervisors the Ladys may be convinc'd, they left nothing that could offend, and the Men of their unjust Reflections on so many Judges of Wit and Decencys. When it happens that I challenge any one, to point me out the least Expression of what some have made their Discourse, they cry, *That Mr. Leigh opens his Night Gown, when he comes into the Bride-chamber;* if he do, which is a Jest of his own making, and which I never saw, I hope he has his Cloaths on underneath? And if so, where is the Indecency? I have seen in that admirable Play of *Oedipus,*[3] the Gown open'd wide, and the Man shown in his Drawers and Waist coat, and never thought it an Offence before. Another crys, *Why we know not what they mean, when the Man takes a Woman off the Stage, and another is thereby cuckolded;* is that any more than you see in the most Celebrated of your Plays? as the *City Politicks*,[4] the *Lady Mayoress*, and the *Old Lawyers Wife,* who goes with a Man she never saw before, and comes out again the joyfull'st Woman alive, for having made her Husband a Cuckold with such Dexterity, and yet I see nothing unnatural nor obscene: 'tis proper for the Characters. So in that lucky Play of the *London Cuckolds*, not to recite Particulars. And in that good Comedy of *Sir Courtly Nice*, the *Taylor to the young Lady* — in the fam'd Sir *Fopling Dorimont* and *Bellinda*, see the very Words — in *Valentinian*, see the Scene between the *Court Bawds*. And *Valentinian* all loose and ruffld a Moment after the Rape, and all this you see without Scandal, and a thousand others The *Moor of Venice* in many places. The *Maids Tragedy* — see the Scene of undressing the Bride, and between the *King* and *Amintor,* and after between the *King* and *Evadne* — All these I Name as some of the best Plays I know; If I should repeat the Words exprest in these Scenes I mention, I might justly be charg'd with course ill Manners, and very little Modesty, and yet they so naturally fall into the places they are designed for, and so are proper for the Business, that there is not the least Fault to be found with them; though I say those things in any of mine wou'd damn the whole Peice, and alarm the Town. Had I a Day or two's time, as I have scarce so many Hours to write this in (the Play, being all printed off and the Press waiting,) I would sum up all your Beloved Plays, and all the Things in them that are past with such Silence by; because written by Men: such Masculine Strokes in me, must not be allow'd. I must conclude those Women (if there be any such) greater Critics in that sort of Conversation than my self, who find any of that sort in mine, or any thing that can justly be reproach't. But 'tis in vain by dint of Reason or Comparison to convince the obstinate Criticks, whose Business is to find Fault, if not by a loose and gross Imagination to create them, for they must either find the Jest, or make it; and those of this sort fall to my share, they find Faults of another kind for the Men Writers. And this one thing I will venture to say, though against my Nature, because it has a Vanity in it: That had the Plays I have writ come forth under any Mans Name, and never known to have been mine; I appeal to all unbyast Judges of Sense, if they had not said that Person had made as many good

[3]This would have to be the John Dryden / Nathaniel Lee version of 1679, based on Seneca, not the original play by Sophocles. In Act 2, scene 1, there is a stage direction: "Oedipus enters walking asleep in his shirt." This was not a joke or funny business, merely sleepwear of the day. Behn cites it for her own purpose, to ridicule the idea that an actor appearing without his coat must be obscene. [Ed.]

[4]Behn refers to several plays in this passage. *City Politicks:* a comedy by John Crowne (1683). *The London Cuckolds:* a comedy by Edward Ravenscroft (1682). *Sir Courtly Nice:* a comedy by John Crowne (1685). *Sir Fopling:* Behn alludes to *The Man of Mode, or Sir Fopling Flutter*, a classic Restoration comedy by George Etherege (1676). *Valentinian:* a tragedy by John Fletcher (performed 1610–14, published 1647). *The Moor of Venice:* the subtitle of Shakespeare's *Othello* (1602–4). *The Maid's Tragedy:* a tragedy by Francis Beaumont and John Fletcher (1610–11). [Ed.]

Comedies, as any one Man that has writ in our Age; but a Devil on't the Woman damns the Poet.

Ladies, for its further Justification to you, be pleas'd to know, that the first Copy of this Play was read by several Ladys of very great Quality, and unquestioned Fame, and received their most favourable Opinion, not one charging it with the Crime, that some have been pleas'd to find in the Acting. Other Ladys who saw it more than once, whose Quality and Vertue can sufficiently justifie any thing they design to favour, were pleas'd to say, they found an Entertainment in it very far from scandalous; and for the Generality of the Town, I found by my Receipts it was not thought so Criminal. However, that shall not be an Incouragement to me to trouble the Criticks with new Occasion of affronting me, for endeavouring at least to divert; and at this rate, both the few Poets that are left, and the Players who toil in vain will be weary of their Trade.

I cannot omit to tell you, that a Wit of the Town, a Friend of mine at *Wills* Coffee House, the first Night of the Play, cry'd it down as much as in him lay, who before had read it and assured me he never saw a prettier Comedy. So complaisant one pestilent Wit will be to another, and in the full Cry make his Noise too; but since 'tis to the witty Few I speak, I hope the better Judges will take no Offence, to whom I am oblig'd for better Judgments; and those I hope will be so kind to me, knowing my Conversation not at all addicted to the Indecencys alledged, that I would much less practice it in a Play, that must stand the Test of the censoring World. And I must want common Sense, and all the Degrees of good Manners, renouncing my Fame, all Modesty and Interest for a silly Sawcy fruitless Jest, to make Fools laugh, and Women blush, and wise Men asham'd; My self all the while, if I had been guilty of this Crime charg'd to me, remaining the only stupid, insensible. Is this likely, is this reasonable to be believ'd by any body, but the wilfully blind? All I ask, is the Priviledge for my Masculine Part the Poet in me, (if any such you will allow me) to tread in those successful Paths my Predecessors have so long thriv'd in, to take those Measures that both the Ancient and Modern Writers have set me, and by which they have pleas'd the World so well: If I must not, because of my Sex, have this Freedom, but that you will usurp all to your selves; I lay down my Quill, and you shall hear no more of me, no not so much as to make Comparisons, because I will be kinder to my Brothers of the Pen, than they have been to a defenceless Woman; for I am not content to write for a Third day only. I value Fame as much as if I had been born a *Hero;* and if you rob me of that, I can retire from the ungrateful World, and scorn its fickle Favours.

Alexander Pope

1688–1744

Born into a Roman Catholic family in the year the last Catholic monarch of England, James II, was forced to abdicate his throne, Alexander Pope was legally barred from a university education and from many careers. From his wet nurse he caught a severe case of spinal tuberculosis, which left him dwarfed, twisted, and delicate of constitution. Nevertheless, with the private education provided by his father, a well-to-do merchant of London just retired to Windsor Forest, Pope crafted himself into the prodigy and soon into the poet of eighteenth-century England, its laureate in all but name. His translations of the *Iliad* and the *Odyssey* (1720 and 1725) not only made him a fortune in royalties, they set the poetic standard for the age; his *Essay on Man* (1733) became its optimistic and rationalistic creed. What has best survived, however, are his satires, delicate fantasies like *The Rape of the Lock* (1714), or vitriolic diatribes like *An Epistle to Dr. Arbuthnot* (1735) and the *Dunciad* (1728–43).

The *Essay on Criticism*, published in 1711 and written possibly as early as 1707, belongs to Pope's earliest years, when he "lisp'd in numbers, and the numbers came." It would be astonishing for any nineteen-year-old, however learned, to make an original contribution to literary theory, and in fact, the *Essay on Criticism* is original only in that it is addressed to critics rather than to poets. But since Pope considered it the critic's first duty to endeavor to comprehend fully and disinterestedly the poem's form, matter, and end, the *Essay* easily and often shifts its focus from qualities of criticism to qualities of poetry. Pope's central ideas are the standard poetic notions of the Augustan Age, drawn from a variety of classical and Renaissance sources — from Horace and Quintilian to Boileau and Dryden — but these well-worn truths he imbues with a clarity and brilliance of expression.

The central and recurring image of the *Essay on Criticism* is that of the eternal war between critics, who judge according to a rigid system of regulations, and poets, hemmed in by such rules and longing to soar. By and large, although Pope presents the poets' perspective, he sides with the critics. While he insists that "Some beauties yet no precepts can declare / For there's a happiness as well as care," and admits that poets can through genius "snatch a grace beyond the reach of art," he also warns them that remorseless criticism will justly clip their wings should they depart from the precedent of the rules and practices of the ancients. The critics come in for a lashing in Part II, where they are attacked for partial readings, partial both in the sense that their praise and blame depend on the congruence of their party politics with that of the poet, and in the sense that they take only a single aspect of a poem into account without understanding its end or how it relates to the chosen means. Pope's demonstrations of prosody and imagery here have become classic citations.

Pope's tendency to use his central terms in a variety of related but distinct ways can be confusing. "Nature" is sometimes used to signify the objective world of creation and other times to mean human nature or the instinctual basis of our humanity.

"Art" can be opposed to "Nature" in any of the following senses: It can be the world of human invention, as opposed to that of divine creation; it can be technique and craft, as opposed to creative instinct; it can be the rules behind a skill, as opposed to the skill itself; it can be (as in its usual modern meaning) the class of objects created by human intelligence and creativity. "Wit" is even more ambiguous than "Art" and "Nature" and can partake of either realm: It may mean "sense" or "intelligence" or "verbal facility" or "genius" or "creative power," or it may signify a person with any of these qualities — or just an educated person in general. These shifts, which are not announced, can create an immense and bewildering compression of meaning. When Pope claims that nature is "at once the source, and end, and test of Art," he may be using both Nature and Art in three different senses. Context is a guide here, and fortunately, the context is enhanced by Pope's tendency to repeat each of his ideas at least once before moving on to the next.

What may be more problematic for the reader is Pope's tendency to draw a distinction only to collapse it later on. Like Sidney, Pope suggests that the poet requires natural genius, a knowledge of the rules of art, and an education based on the classics to provide models for imitation. But art and nature, creation and imitation, turn out to be false dichotomies. The rules of art remain "Nature still, but Nature methodiz'd"; Virgil discovers that imitating Nature and imitating Homer are "the same." Pope in 1711 is content to leave such contradictions unresolved as poetic paradoxes; in later hands, like those of David Hume and Immanuel Kant, these issues will recur as evidence of inward mental structures common to humanity.

Selected Bibliography

Empson, William. "'Wit' in the *Essay on Criticism.*" *Hudson Review* 2 (1950): 559–77.

Fenner, Arthur, Jr. "The Unity of Pope's *Essay on Criticism.*" *Philological Quarterly* 39 (1960): 435–56.

Griffin, Dustin. *Alexander Pope: The Poet in the Poems.* Princeton: Princeton University Press, 1978.

Hooker, E. N. "Pope on Wit: The Essay on Criticism." *Hudson Review* 2 (1950): 84–100.

Stack, Frank. *Pope and Horace: Studies in Imitation.* Cambridge and New York: Cambridge University Press, 1985.

Warren, Austin. *Pope as Critic and Humanist.* Princeton: Princeton University Press, 1929.

Wood, Allen G. *Literary Satire and Theory: A Study of Horace, Boileau, and Pope.* New York: Garland, 1985.

An Essay on Criticism

— Si quid novisti rectius istis,
Candidus imperti; si non, his utere mecum.[1]

PART I

'Tis hard to say, if greater want of skill
Appear in writing or in judging ill;
But of the two less dangerous is the offense
To tire our patience than mislead our sense.
Some few in that, but numbers err in this,
Ten censure wrong for one who writes amiss;
A fool might once himself alone expose,
Now one in verse makes many more in prose.
'Tis with our judgments as our watches, none
Go just alike, yet each believes his own.
In poets as true genius is but rare,
True taste as seldom is the critic's share;
Both must alike from Heaven derive their light,
These born to judge, as well as those to write.
Let such teach others who themselves excel,
And censure freely who have written well.
Authors are partial to their wit,[2] 'tis true.
But are not critics to their judgment too?
Yet if we look more closely, we shall find
Most have the seeds of judgment in their mind:
Nature affords at least a glimmering light;
The lines, though touched but faintly, are drawn right.
But as the slightest sketch, if justly traced,
Is by ill coloring but the more disgraced,
So by false learning is good sense defaced:
Some are bewildered in the maze of schools,[3]
And some made coxcombs Nature meant but fools.
In search of wit these lose their common sense,
And then turn critics in their own defense:
Each burns alike, who can, or cannot write,
Or with a rival's or an eunuch's spite.
All fools have still an itching to deride,
And fain would be upon the laughing side.

[1]"If you know better maxims, impart them to me; if not, use these with me." Horace, *Epistles* 6:1. [Ed.]
[2]Artistic genius. [Ed.]
[3]Scholastic learning. [Ed.]

If Maevius[4] scribble in Apollo's spite,
There are who judge still worse than he can write.
Some have at first for wits, then poets passed,
Turned critics next, and proved plain fools at last.
Some neither can for wits nor critics pass,
As heavy mules are neither horse nor ass.
Those half-learn'd witlings, numerous in our isle,
As half-formed insects on the banks of Nile;[5]
Unfinished things, one knows not what to call,
Their generation's so equivocal:
To tell[6] them would a hundred tongues require,
Or one vain wit's, that might a hundred tire.
But you who seek to give and merit fame,
And justly bear a critic's noble name,
Be sure yourself and your own reach to know,
How far your genius, taste, and learning go;
Launch not beyond your depth, but be discreet,
And mark that point where sense and dullness meet.
Nature to all things fixed the limits fit,
And wisely curbed proud man's pretending wit.
As on the land while here the ocean gains,
In other parts it leaves wide sandy plains;
Thus in the soul while memory prevails,
The solid power of understanding fails;
Where beams of warm imagination play,
The memory's soft figures melt away.
One Science[7] only will one genius fit,
So vast is art, so narrow human wit.[8]
Not only bounded to peculiar arts,
But oft in those confined to single parts.
Like kings we lose the conquests gained before,
By vain ambition still to make them more;
Each might his several province well command,
Would all but stoop to what they understand.

[4]A legendarily bad poet, known only through contemptuous references by both Virgil and Horace. [Ed.]
[5]Insects were supposed to be spontaneously generated by river mud and other similar matter. [Ed.]
[6]Count. [Ed.]
[7]Branch of knowledge. [Ed.]
[8]Here, mental power. [Ed.]

First follow Nature, and your judgment frame
By her just standard, which is still the same;
Unerring Nature, still divinely bright,
One clear, unchanged, and universal light,
Life, force, and beauty must to all impart,
At once the source, and end, and test of art.
Art from that fund each just supply provides,
Works without show, and without pomp presides.
In some fair body thus the informing soul
With spirits feeds, with vigor fills the whole,
Each motion guides, and every nerve sustains;
Itself unseen, but in the effects remains.
Some, to whom Heaven in wit has been profuse,
Want as much more to turn it to its use;
For wit[9] and judgment often are at strife,
Though meant each other's aid, like man and wife.
'Tis more to guide than spur the Muse's steed,[10]
Restrain his fury than provoke his speed;
The wingéd courser, like a generous horse,
Shows most true mettle when you check his course.
Those rules of old discovered, not devised,
Are Nature still, but Nature methodized;
Nature, like liberty, is but restrained
By the same laws which first herself ordained.
Hear how learn'd Greece her useful rules indites,
When to repress and when indulge our flights:
High on Parnassus'[11] top her sons she showed,
And pointed out those arduous paths they trod;
Held from afar, aloft, the immortal prize,
And urged the rest by equal steps to rise.
Just precepts thus from great examples given,
She drew from them what they derived from Heaven.
The generous critic fanned the poet's fire,
And taught the world with reason to admire.
Then criticism the Muse's handmaid proved,
To dress her charms, and make her more beloved:
But following wits from that intention strayed,
Who could not win the mistress, wooed the maid;
Against the poets their own arms they turned,
Sure to hate most the men from whom they learned.
So modern 'pothecaries, taught the art
By doctors' bills to play the doctor's part,
Bold in the practice of mistaken rules,
Prescribe, apply, and call their masters fools.[12]
Some on the leaves of ancient authors prey,
Nor time nor moths e'er spoiled so much as they.
Some dryly plain, without invention's aid,
Write dull receipts[13] how poems may be made.
These leave the sense their learning to display,
And those explain the meaning quite away.
You then whose judgment the right course would steer,
Know well each ancient's proper character;
His fable, subject, scope in every page;
Religion, country, genius of his age:
Without all these at once before your eyes,
Cavil you may, but never criticize.
Be Homer's works your study and delight,
Read them by day, and meditate by night;
Thence form your judgment, thence your maxims bring,
And trace the Muses upward to their spring.
Still with itself compared, his text peruse;
And let your comment be the Mantuan Muse.[14]
When first young Maro in his boundless mind
A work to outlast immortal Rome designed,
Perhaps he seemed above the critic's law,
And but from Nature's fountains scorned to draw;
But when to examine every part he came,
Nature and Homer were, he found, the same.
Convinced, amazed, he checks the bold design,
And rules as strict his labored work confine
As if the Stagirite[15] o'erlooked each line.
Learn hence for ancient rules a just esteem;
To copy Nature is to copy them.
Some beauties yet no precepts can declare,
For there's a happiness as well as care.[16]

[9]Here, imagination. [Ed.]

[10]Pegasus, the winged horse associated with the Muses. [Ed.]

[11]Hill where the Muses gathered. [Ed.]

[12]Pope refers to a contemporary dispute between doctors and druggists, who were invading each other's territories. [Ed.]

[13]Recipes. [Ed.]

[14]Virgil, born in Mantua: his last name, mentioned in the next line, was Maro. [Ed.]

[15]Aristotle, born in Stagira. [Ed.]

[16]Beauty that transcends the taking of pains. [Ed.]

Music resembles poetry, in each
Are nameless graces which no methods teach,
And which a master hand alone can reach.
If, where the rules not far enough extend
(Since rules were made but to promote their end)
Some lucky license answers to the full
The intent proposed, that license is a rule.
Thus Pegasus, a nearer way to take,
May boldly deviate from the common track.
From vulgar bounds with brave disorder part,
And snatch a grace beyond the reach of art,
Which without passing through the judgment,
gains
The heart, and all its end at once attains.
In prospects thus, some objects please our eyes,
Which out of Nature's common order rise,
The shapeless rock, or hanging precipice.
Great wits sometimes may gloriously offend,
And rise to faults true critics dare not mend;
But though the ancients thus their rules invade
(As kings dispense with laws themselves have
made)
Moderns, beware! or if you must offend
Against the precept, ne'er transgress its end;
Let it be seldom, and compelled by need;
And have at least their precedent to plead.
The critic else proceeds without remorse,
Seizes your fame, and puts his laws in force.
I know there are, to whose presumptuous
thoughts
Those freer beauties, even in them, seem faults.
Some figures monstrous and misshaped appear,
Considered singly, or beheld too near,
Which, but proportioned to their light or place,
Due distance reconciles to form and grace.[17]
A prudent chief not always must display
His powers in equal ranks and fair array,
But with the occasion and the place comply,
Conceal his force, nay seem sometimes to fly.
Those oft are stratagems which errors seem,
Nor is it Homer nods, but we that dream.[18]

[17]Pope alludes to the "ut pictura poesis" passage in Horace's *Art of Poetry,* which stresses that some poems, like some paintings, need to be looked at from afar, not scrutinized in detail. [Ed.]

[18]Where Horace claims in the *Art of Poetry* to be "indignant even when it is the great Homer who falls asleep on the job," Pope suggests that the critic rather than the poet may be at fault. [Ed.]

Still green with bays each ancient altar stands
Above the reach of sacrilegious hands,
Secure from flames, from envy's fiercer rage,
Destructive war, and all-involving age.
See, from each clime the learn'd their incense
bring!
Here in all tongues consenting paeans ring!
In praise so just let every voice be joined,
And fill the general chorus of mankind.
Hail, bards triumphant! born in happier days,
Immortal heirs of universal praise!
Whose honors with increase of ages grow,
As streams roll down, enlarging as they flow;
Nations unborn your mighty names shall sound,
And worlds applaud that must not yet be found!
Oh, may some spark of your celestial fire,
The last, the meanest of your sons inspire
(That on weak wings, from far, pursues your
flights,
Glows while he reads, but trembles as he writes)
To teach vain wits a science little known,
To admire superior sense, and doubt their own!

PART II

Of all the causes which conspire to blind
Man's erring judgment, and misguide the mind,
What the weak head with strongest bias rules,
Is pride, the never-failing vice of fools.
Whatever Nature has in worth denied,
She gives in large recruits of needful pride;
For as in bodies, thus in souls, we find
What wants in blood and spirits swelled with
wind:
Pride, where wit fails, steps in to our defense,
And fills up all the mighty void of sense.
If once right reason drives that cloud away,
Truth breaks upon us with resistless day.
Trust not yourself: but your defects to know,
Make use of every friend — and every foe.
A little learning is a dangerous thing;
Drink deep, or taste not the Pierian spring.[19]
There shallow draughts intoxicate the brain,
And drinking largely sobers us again.
Fired at first sight with what the Muse imparts,
In fearless youth we tempt the heights of arts,

[19]Pieria, near Mt. Olympus, was sacred to the Muses. [Ed.]

While from the bounded level of our mind
Short views we take, nor see the lengths behind;
But more advanced, behold with strange surprise
New distant scenes of endless science rise!
So pleased at first the towering Alps we try,
Mount o'er the vales, and seem to tread the sky,
The eternal snows appear already past,
And the first clouds and mountains seem the last;
But, those attained, we tremble to survey
The growing labors of the lengthened way,
The increasing prospect tires our wandering eyes,
Hills peep o'er hills, and Alps on Alps arise!
A perfect judge will read each work of wit
With the same spirit that its author writ:
Survey the whole, nor seek slight faults to find
Where Nature moves, and rapture warms the mind;
Nor lose, for that malignant dull delight,
The generous pleasure to be charmed with wit.
But in such lays as neither ebb nor flow,
Correctly cold, and regularly low,
That, shunning faults, one quiet tenor keep,
We cannot blame indeed — but we may sleep.
In wit, as nature, what affects our hearts
Is not the exactness of peculiar parts;
'Tis not a lip, or eye, we beauty call,
But the joint force and full result of all.
Thus when we view some well-proportioned dome[20]
(The world's just wonder, and even thine, O Rome!),
No single parts unequally surprise,
All comes united to the admiring eyes:
No monstrous height, or breadth, or length appear;
The whole at once is bold and regular.
Whoever thinks a faultless piece to see,
Thinks what ne'er was, nor is, nor e'er shall be.
In every work regard the writer's end,
Since none can compass more than they intend;
And if the means be just, the conduct true,
Applause, in spite of trivial faults, is due.
As men of breeding, sometimes men of wit,
To avoid great errors must the less commit,
Neglect the rules each verbal critic lays,
For not to know some trifles is a praise.

[20]Of St. Peter's Basilica. [Ed.]

Most critics, fond of some subservient art,
Still make the whole depend upon a part:
They talk of principles, but notions prize,
And all to one loved folly sacrifice.
Once on a time La Mancha's knight,[21] they say,
A certain bard encountering on the way,
Discoursed in terms as just, with looks as sage,
As e'er could Dennis,[22] of the Grecian stage;
Concluding all were desperate sots and fools
Who durst depart from Aristotle's rules.
Our author, happy in a judge so nice,
Produced his play, and begged the knight's advice;
Made him observe the subject and the plot,
The manners, passions, unities; what not?
All which exact to rule were brought about,
Were but a combat in the lists left out.
"What! leave the combat out?" exclaims the knight.
"Yes, or we must renounce the Stagirite."
"Not so, by Heaven!" he answers in a rage,
"Knights, squires, and steeds must enter on the stage."
"So vast a throng the stage can ne'er contain."
"Then build a new, or act it in a plain."
Thus critics of less judgment than caprice,
Curious,[23] not knowing, not exact, but nice,
Form short ideas, and offend in arts
(As most in manners), by a love to parts.
Some to conceit[24] alone their taste confine,
And glittering thoughts struck out at every line;
Pleased with a work where nothing's just or fit,
One glaring chaos and wild heap of wit.
Poets, like painters, thus unskilled to trace
The naked nature and the living grace,
With gold and jewels cover every part,
And hide with ornaments their want of art.
True wit is Nature to advantage dressed,
What oft was thought, but ne'er so well expressed;

[21]Don Quixote. The episode is not in Cervantes but in a sequel written under the name of Alonzo Fernandez de Avellaneda and translated into English around 1705. [Ed.]

[22]John Dennis (1657–1734), a playwright and critic who had argued for the application of classical rules to the English stage. [Ed.]

[23]Pedantically careful; "nice" in the same line means "overrefined." [Ed.]

[24]Figures of speech. [Ed.]

Something whose truth convinced at sight we find,
That gives us back the image of our mind.
As shades more sweetly recommend the light,
So modest plainness sets off sprightly wit;
For works may have more wit than does them good,
As bodies perish through excess of blood.
Others for language all their care express,
And value books, as women men, for dress.
Their praise is still — the style is excellent;
The sense they humbly take upon contént.[25]
Words are like leaves; and where they most abound,
Much fruit of sense beneath is rarely found.
False eloquence, like the prismatic glass,
Its gaudy colors spreads on every place;
The face of Nature we no more survey,
All glares alike, without distinction gay.
But true expression, like the unchanging sun,
Clears and improves whate'er it shines upon;
It gilds all objects, but it alters none.
Expression is the dress of thought, and still
Appears more decent as more suitable.
A vile conceit in pompous words expressed
Is like a clown in regal purple dressed:
For different styles with different subjects sort,
As several garbs with country, town, and court.
Some by old words to fame have made pretense,
Ancients in phrase, mere moderns in their sense.
Such labored nothings, in so strange a style,
Amaze the unlearn'd, and make the learned smile;
Unlucky as Fungoso[26] in the play,
These sparks with awkward vanity display
What the fine gentleman wore yesterday;
And but so mimic ancient wits at best,
As apes our grandsires in their doublets dressed.
In words as fashions the same rule will hold,
Alike fantastic if too new or old:
Be not the first by whom the new are tried,
Nor yet the last to lay the old aside.
But most by numbers[27] judge a poet's song,
And smooth or rough with them is right or wrong.
In the bright Muse though thousand charms conspire,
Her voice is all these tuneful fools admire,
Who haunt Parnassus but to please their ear,
Not mend their minds; as some to church repair,
Not for the doctrine, but the music there.
These equal syllables alone require,
Though oft the ear the open vowels tire,
While expletives their feeble aid do join,
And ten low words oft creep in one dull line:
While they ring round the same unvaried chimes,
With sure returns of still expected rhymes;
Where'er you find "the cooling western breeze,"
In the next line, it "whispers through the trees";
If crystal streams "with pleasing murmurs creep,"
The reader's threatened (not in vain) with "sleep";
Then, at the last and only couplet fraught
With some unmeaning thing they call a thought,
A needless Alexandrine[28] ends the song
That, like a wounded snake, drags its slow length along.
Leave such to tune their own dull rhymes, and know
What's roundly smooth or languishingly slow;
And praise the easy vigor of a line
Where Denham's strength and Waller's sweetness join.
True ease in writing comes from art, not chance,
As those move easiest who have learned to dance.
'Tis not enough no harshness gives offense,
The sound must seem an echo to the sense.
Soft is the strain when Zephyr gently blows,
And the smooth stream in smoother numbers flows;
But when loud surges lash the sounding shore,
The hoarse, rough verse should like the torrent roar.
When Ajax strives some rock's vast weight to throw,
The line too labors, and the words move slow;
Not so when swift Camilla[29] scours the plain,

[25]On faith. [Ed.]

[26]A character in Ben Jonson's *Every Man out of His Humour* (1599). [Ed.]

[27]Prosody. [Ed.]

[28]Line of iambic hexameter, usually broken in the middle. [Ed.]

[29]Camilla was an Amazonian warrior allied to Turnus in Virgil's *Aeneid.* [Ed.]

Flies o'er the unbending corn, and skims along
the main.
Hear how Timotheus'[30] varied lays surprise,
And bid alternate passions fall and rise!
While at each change the son of Libyan Jove
Now burns with glory, and then melts with love;
Now his fierce eyes with sparkling fury glow,
Now sighs steal out, and tears begin to flow:
Persians and Greeks like turns of nature found
And the world's victor stood subdued by sound!
The power of music all our hearts allow,
And what Timotheus was is Dryden now.
Avoid extremes; and shun the fault of such
Who still are pleased too little or too much.
At every trifle scorn to take offense:
That always shows great pride, or little sense.
Those heads, as stomachs, are not sure the best,
Which nauseate all, and nothing can digest.
Yet let not each gay turn thy rapture move;
For fools admire, but men of sense approve:
As things seem large which we through mists de-
scry,
Dullness is ever apt to magnify.
Some foreign writers, some our own despise;
The ancients only, or the moderns prize.
Thus wit, like faith, by each man is applied
To one small sect, and all are damned beside.
Meanly they seek the blessing to confine,
And force that sun but on a part to shine,
Which not alone the southern wit sublimes,
But ripens spirits in cold northern climes;
Which from the first has shone on ages past,
Enlights the present, and shall warm the last;
Though each may feel increases and decays,
And see now clearer and now darker days.
Regard not then if wit be old or new,
But blame the false and value still the true.
Some ne'er advance a judgment of their own,
But catch the spreading notion of the town;
They reason and conclude by precedent,
And own stale nonsense which they ne'er invent.
Some judge of authors' names, not works, and
then
Nor praise nor blame the writings, but the men.

[30]Pope retells the story of Dryden's *Alexander's Feast:* how Alexander the Great's bard, Timotheus, was able to subdue the conqueror of the world through his art. The "son of Libyan Jove" is Alexander, who claimed descent from Ammon after conquering Egypt. [Ed.]

Of all this servile herd the worst is he
That in proud dullness joins with quality,
A constant critic at the great man's board,
To fetch and carry nonsense for my lord.
What woeful stuff this madrigal would be
In some starved hackney sonneteer or me!
But let a lord once own the happy lines,
How the wit brightens! how the style refines!
Before his sacred name flies every fault,
And each exalted stanza teems with thought!
The vulgar thus through imitation err;
As oft the learn'd by being singular;
So much they scorn the crowd, that if the throng
By chance go right, they purposely go wrong.
So schismatics the plain believers quit,
And are but damned for having too much wit.
Some praise at morning what they blame at
night,
But always think the last opinion right.
A Muse by these is like a mistress used,
This hour she's idolized, the next abused;
While their weak heads like towns unfortified,
'Twixt sense and nonsense daily change their
side.
Ask them the cause; they're wiser still, they say;
And still tomorrow's wiser than today.
We think our fathers fools, so wise we grow;
Our wiser sons, no doubt, will think us so.
Once school divines[31] this zealous isle o'er-
spread;
Who knew most sentences was deepest read.
Faith, Gospel, all seemed made to be disputed,
And none had sense enough to be confuted.
Scotists and Thomists now in peace remain
Amidst their kindred cobwebs in Duck Lane.[32]
If faith itself has different dresses worn,
What wonder modes in wit should take their
turn?
Oft, leaving what is natural and fit,
The current folly proves the ready wit;
And authors think their reputation safe,
Which lives as long as fools are pleased to laugh.
Some valuing those of their own side or mind,
Still make themselves the measure of mankind:
Fondly[33] we think we honor merit then,

[31]Scholastic theologians. [Ed.]
[32]Street of used bookstores. [Ed.]
[33]Foolishly. [Ed.]

When we but praise ourselves in other men.
Parties in wit attend on those of state,
And public faction doubles private hate.
Pride, Malice, Folly against Dryden rose,
In various shapes of parsons, critics, beaux;
But sense survived, when merry jests were past;
For rising merit will buoy up at last.
Might he return and bless once more our eyes,
New Blackmores and new Milbourns must
arise.[34]
Nay, should great Homer lift his awful head,
Zoilus[35] again would start up from the dead.
Envy will merit, as its shade, pursue,
But like a shadow, proves the substance true;
For envied wit, like Sol eclipsed, makes known
The opposing body's grossness, not its own.
When first that sun too powerful beams displays,
It draws up vapors which obscure its rays;
But even those clouds at last adorn its way,
Reflect new glories, and augment the day.
Be thou the first true merit to befriend;
His praise is lost who stays till all commend.
Short is the date, alas! of modern rhymes,
And 'tis but just to let them live betimes.
No longer now that golden age appears,
When patriarch wits survived a thousand years:
Now length of fame (our second life) is lost,
And bare threescore is all even that can boast;
Our sons their fathers' failing language see,
And such as Chaucer is shall Dryden be.[36]
So when the faithful pencil has designed
Some bright idea of the master's mind,
Where a new world leaps out at his command,
And ready Nature waits upon his hand;
When the ripe colors soften and unite,
And sweetly melt into just shade and light;
When mellowing years their full perfection give,
And each bold figure just begins to live,
The treacherous colors the fair art betray,
And all the bright creation fades away!
Unhappy wit, like most mistaken things,
Atones not for that envy which it brings.

[34]Richard Blackmore had attacked Dryden's dramas, Luke Milbourn his translation of the *Aeneid*. [Ed.]

[35]Zoilus was a severe critic of Homer of the fourth century B.C. [Ed.]

[36]The Middle English in which Chaucer wrote had become unintelligible by Pope's time. [Ed.]

In youth alone its empty praise we boast,
But soon the short-lived vanity is lost;
Like some fair flower the early spring supplies,
That gaily blooms, but even in blooming dies,
What is this wit, which must our cares employ?
The owner's wife, that other men enjoy;
Then most our trouble still when most admired,
And still the more we give, the more required;
Whose fame with pains we guard, but lose with
ease,
Sure some to vex, but never all to please;
'Tis what the vicious fear, the virtuous shun,
By fools 'tis hated, and by knaves undone!
If wit so much from ignorance undergo,
Ah, let not learning too commence its foe!
Of old those met rewards who could excel,
And such were praised who but endeavored well;
Though triumphs were to generals only due,
Crowns were reserved to grace the soldiers too.
Now they who reach Parnassus' lofty crown
Employ their pains to spurn some others down;
And while self-love each jealous writer rules,
Contending wits become the sport of fools;
But still the worst with most regret commend,
For each ill author is as bad a friend.
To what base ends, and by what abject ways,
Are mortals urged through sacred[37] lust of
praise!
Ah, ne'er so dire a thirst of glory boast,
Nor in the critic let the man be lost!
Good nature and good sense must ever join;
To err is human, to forgive divine.
But if in noble minds some dregs remain
Nor yet purged off, of spleen and sour disdain,
Discharge that rage on more provoking crimes,
Nor fear a dearth in these flagitious[38] times.
No pardon vile obscenity should find,
Though wit and art conspire to move your mind;
But dullness with obscenity must prove
As shameful sure as impotence in love.
In the fat age of pleasure, wealth, and ease
Sprung the rank weed, and thrived with large in-
crease:
When love was all an easy monarch's[39] care,
Seldom at council, never in a war;

[37]Accursed. [Ed.]

[38]Wicked. [Ed.]

[39]Charles II (reigned 1660–85). [Ed.]

Jilts[40] ruled the state, and statesmen farces writ;
Nay, wits had pensions, and young lords had wit;
The fair sat panting at a courtier's play,
And not a mask[41] went unimproved away;
The modest fan was lifted up no more,
And virgins smiled at what they blushed before.
The following license of a foreign reign[42]
Did all the dregs of bold Socinus drain;
Then unbelieving priests reformed the nation,
And taught more pleasant methods of salvation;
Where Heaven's free subjects might their rights dispute,
Lest God himself should seem too absolute;
Pulpits their sacred satire learned to spare,
And Vice admired to find a flatterer there!
Encouraged thus, wit's Titans braved the skies,
And the press groaned with licensed blasphemies.
These monsters, critics! with your darts engage,
Here point your thunder, and exhaust your rage!
Yet shun their fault, who, scandalously nice,
Will needs mistake an author into vice;
All seems infected that the infected spy,
As all looks yellow to the jaundiced eye.

PART III

Learn then what morals Critics ought to show,
For 'tis but half a judge's task to know.
'Tis not enough Taste, Judgment, Learning join;
In all you speak let Truth and Candour shine;
That not alone what to your Sense is due
All may allow, but seek your friendship too.
Be silent always when you doubt your Sense,
And speak, tho' sure, with seeming diffidence.
Some positive persisting fops we know,
Who if once wrong will needs be always so;
But you with pleasure own your errors past,
And make each day a critique on the last.
'Tis not enough your counsel still be true;
Blunt truths more mischief than nice falsehoods do.
Men must be taught as if you taught them not,
And things unknown proposed as things forgot.
Without good breeding truth is disapprov'd;
That only makes superior Sense belov'd.
Be niggards of advice on no pretence,
For the worst avarice is that of Sense.
With mean complacence ne'er betray your trust,
Nor be so civil as to prove unjust.
Fear not the anger of the wise to raise;
Those best can bear reproof who merit praise.
'Twere well might critics still this freedom take,
But Appius[43] reddens at each word you speak,
And stares tremendous, with a threat'ning eye,
Like some fierce tyrant in old tapestry.
Fear most to tax an honourable fool,
Whose right it is, uncensured to be dull:
Such without Wit, are poets when they please,
As without Learning they can take degrees.[44]
Leave dangerous truths to unsuccessful satires,
And flattery to fulsome dedicators;
Whom, when they praise, the world believes no more
Than when they promise to give scribbling o'er.
'Tis best sometimes your censure to restrain,
And charitably let the dull be vain;
Your silence there is better than your spite,
For who can rail so long as they can write?
Still humming on their drowsy course they keep,
And lash'd so long, like tops, are lash'd asleep.
False steps but help them to renew the race,
As, after stumbling, jades will mend their pace.
What crowds of these, impenitently bold,
In sounds and jingling syllables grown old,
Still run on poets, in a raging vein,
Ev'n to the dregs and squeezings of the brain,
Strain out the last dull dropping of their sense,
And rhyme with all the rage of impotence!
Such shameless bards we have; and yet 'tis true
There are as mad abandon'd critics too.
The bookful blockhead ignorantly read,
With loads of learned lumber in his head,
With his own tongue still edifies his ears,
And always list'ning to himself appears.

[40]Charles's mistresses. [Ed.]

[41]Women wearing a vizard mask, whose concealment allowed one to behave immorally without scandal. [Ed.]

[42]The reign of William III (1689–1701), who came from Holland. Socinus, in the next line, was the name of two Renaissance Italian theologians whose doctrines denied the divinity of Christ and the efficacy of the Atonement. [Ed.]

[43]See n. 22. Dennis wrote an unsuccessful play, *Appius and Virginia* (1709). [Ed.]

[44]Sons of peers were allowed to take degrees at Oxford and Cambridge without meeting the usual requirements. [Ed.]

All books he reads, and all he reads assails,
From Dryden's Fables down to Durfey's Tales.[45]
With him most authors steal their works, or buy;
Garth did not write his own Dispensary.[46]
Name a new play, and he's the poet's friend;
Nay, show'd his faults — but when would poets mend?
No place so sacred from such fops is barr'd,
Nor is Paul's church more safe than Paul's churchyard:[47]
Nay, fly to altars, there they'll talk you dead;
For fools rush in where angels fear to tread.
Distrustful sense with modest caution speaks,
It still looks home, and short excursions makes;
But rattling nonsense in full volleys breaks
And never shock'd, and never turn'd aside,
Bursts out, resistless, with a thund'ring tide.

But where's the man who counsel can bestow,
Still pleas'd to teach, and yet not proud to know?
Unbiass'd or by favour or by spite;
Not dully prepossess'd nor blindly right;
Tho' learn'd, well bred, and tho' well bred sincere;
Modestly bold, and humanly severe;
Who to a friend his faults can freely show,
And gladly praise the merit of a foe;
Bless'd with a taste exact, yet unconfin'd,
A knowledge both of books and humankind;
Gen'rous converse; a soul exempt from pride;
And love to praise, with reason on his side?
Such once were critics; such the happy few
Athens and Rome in better ages knew.
The mighty Stagyrite first left the shore,
Spread all his sails, and durst the deeps explore;
He steer'd securely, and discover'd far,
Led by the light of the Mæonian star.[48]
Poets, a race long unconfin'd and free,
Still fond and proud of savage liberty,
Receiv'd his laws, and stood convinc'd 'twas fit
Who conquer'd Nature should preside o'er Wit.

Horace still charms with graceful negligence,
And without method talks us into sense;
Will, like a friend, familiarly convey
The truest notions in the easiest way.
He who, supreme in judgment as in wit,
Might boldly censure as he boldly writ,
Yet judg'd with coolness, though he sung with fire;
His precepts teach but what his works inspire.
Our critics take a contrary extreme,
They judge with fury, but they write with phlegm;
Nor suffers Horace more in wrong translations
By Wits, than Critics in as wrong quotations.
See Dionysius[49] Homer's thoughts refine,
And call new beauties forth from ev'ry line!
Fancy and art in gay Petronius[50] please,
The Scholar's learning with the courtier's ease.

In grave Quintilian's[51] copious work we find
The justest rules and clearest method join'd.
Thus useful arms in magazines we place,
All ranged in order, and disposed with grace;
But less to please the eye then arm the hand,
Still fit for use, and ready at command.

Thee, bold Longinus! all the Nine[52] inspire,
And bless their critic with a poet's fire:
An ardent judge, who, zealous in his trust,
With warmth gives sentence, yet is always just;
Whose own example strengthens all his laws,
And is himself that great sublime he draws.

Thus long succeeding critics justly reign'd,
License repress'd, and useful laws ordain'd:
Learning and Rome alike in empire grew,
And arts still follow'd where her eagles flew;
From the same foes at last both felt their doom,
And the same age saw learning fall and Rome.
With tyranny then superstition join'd,
As that the body, this enslaved the mind;
Much was believ'd, but little understood,
And to be dull was construed to be good;
A second deluge learning thus o'errun,
And the monks finish'd what the Goths begun.

At length Erasmus, that great injur'd name,
(The glory of the priesthood and the shame!)

[45]Thomas Durfey (1653–1723), author of popular songs, tales, plays, and other entertainments. [Ed.]

[46]Samuel Garth (1661–1719), physician-poet who wrote a didactic poem called "The Dispensary." [Ed.]

[47]Where booksellers plied their trade. [Ed.]

[48]Homer, whose birthplace, according to tradition, was Maeonia. [Ed.]

[49]Dionysius of Halicarnassus (first century B.C.), literary critic and historian. [Ed.]

[50]Petronius Arbiter (?–65 A.D.), author of the *Satyricon*. [Ed.]

[51]Quintilian (35–95), rhetorician and author of *Institutio Oratoria*. [Ed.]

[52]The nine Muses. [Ed.]

Stemm'd the wild torrent of a barb'rous age,
And drove those holy Vandals off the stage.
But see! each Muse in Leo's[53] golden days
Starts from her trance, and trims her wither'd bays.
Rome's ancient genius, o'er its ruins spread,
Shakes off the dust, and rears his rev'rend head.
Then sculpture and her sister arts revive;
Stones leap'd to form, and rocks began to live;
With sweeter notes each rising temple rung;
A Raphael painted and a Vida[54] sung:
Immortal Vida! on whose honour'd brow
The poet's bays and critic's ivy grow:
Cremona now shall ever boast thy name,
As next in place to Mantua,[55] next in fame!
But soon by impious arms from Latium chased,
Their ancient bounds the banish'd Muses pass'd;
Thence arts o'er all the northern world advance,
But critic learning flourish'd most in France;
The rules a nation born to serve obeys,
And Boileau[56] still in right of Horace sways.
But we, brave Britons, foreign laws despised,
And kept unconquer'd and uncivilized;
Fierce for the liberties of wit, and bold,
We still defied the Romans, as of old.
Yet some there were, among the sounder few
Of those who less presumed and better knew,
Who durst assert the juster ancient cause,
And here restor'd Wit's fundamental laws.
Such was the Muse whose rules and practice tell
"Nature's chief masterpiece is writing well."[57]
Such was Roscommon,[58] not more learn'd than good,
With manners gen'rous as his noble blood;
To him the wit of Greece and Rome was known,
And every author's merit but his own.
Such late was Walsh[59] — the Muse's judge and friend,
Who justly knew to blame or to commend;
To failings mild but zealous for desert,
The clearest head, and the sincerest heart.
This humble praise, lamented Shade! receive;
This praise at least a grateful Muse may give:
The Muse whose early voice you taught to sing,
Prescribed her heights, and pruned her tender wing,
(Her guide now lost), no more attempts to rise,
But in low numbers short excursions tries;
Content if hence th' unlearn'd their wants may view,
The learn'd reflect on what before they knew;
Careless of censure, nor too fond of fame;
Still pleas'd to praise, yet not afraid to blame;
Averse alike to flatter or offend;
Not free from faults, nor yet too vain to mend.

[53]Leo X, originally Giovanni de' Medici (1475–1521), whose pontificate was "golden" from the artistic commissions given out. [Ed.]

[54]Marco Girolamo Vida (1480–1566), Italian critic, poet, and author of *De arte poetica*. [Ed.]

[55]Birthplace of Virgil. [Ed.]

[56]Nicolas Boileau-Despréaux (1636–1711), French poet and critic, whose *Art poétique* is one of the sources of Pope's ideas. [Ed.]

[57]From Buckingham's "Essay on Poetry." [Ed.]

[58]Wentworth Dillon, Earl of Roscommon (1633–85), poet, critic, and translator of Horace. [Ed.]

[59]William Walsh (1663–1708), Pope's friend, who had advised the young poet that he could make his mark by striving for correctness. [Ed.]

Samuel Johnson

1709–1784

Samuel Johnson, the "Great Cham of Literature," is the magisterial personality that dominates the late eighteenth century in England with his insistent moralism, his unflappable common sense, and his tragic vision of life. The only son of a provincial book dealer, whose formal education came to an end after an impecunious year at Oxford, Johnson made himself into the most broadly learned man of his age.

He arrived in London in 1737, just around the time the system of patrician patronage (which had supported John Dryden so well) was giving way to the one familiar today, in which authors bargain with publishers for their material support. In his thirties, Johnson joined the army of hack writers who eked out their living by producing for the Grub Street booksellers the journalism, travel books, occasional essays, translations, and histories for which the new middle-class reading public hankered. From 1747 to 1755, in sickness and sorrow, Johnson labored virtually alone on his massive *Dictionary of the English Language;* its appearance made Johnson's reputation, became the standard dictionary for over half a century, and helped to standardize the chaotic English tongue. He wrote major works in every important literary genre of his age: They include satirical poems like "London" (1739) and "The Vanity of Human Wishes" (1749); the fable *Rasselas* (1759); the tragedy *Irene* (1749); weekly essays for *The Rambler* (1750–52), *The Adventurer* (1753–54), and *The Idler* (1758–60); an authoritative edition of Shakespeare (1763); and a massive series of biographical and critical essays, *Lives of the Poets*, on all the significant English writers of the seventeenth and eighteenth centuries (1779–81).

Johnson's criticism, like that of Sidney and Dryden and most of his own contemporaries, derives its principles from Horace: He conceives of the literary work as a piece of rhetoric to be judged by the impact it makes upon the audience. But those trying to place Johnson within the broad spectrum of rhetorical criticism should note that he takes the didactic purpose of literature far more seriously than either Horace or Dryden, and that his insistence on the universal character of poetry differentiates him from such Platonizing critics as Sidney.

"The end of writing is to instruct; the end of poetry is to instruct by pleasing," he declared in his Preface to *Shakespeare*, and this *locus classicus* dominates the rest of his theory. Didacticism is surely the keynote in his essay on the novel in *The Rambler*, No. 4 (1750). While Johnson admits that literature should imitate life, and that the novel is therefore an improvement over the romance, he sees no reason why writers should not be selective about what aspects of life they choose to imitate. The plots of novels should end with poetic justice, and in presenting characters, novelists should strive to exhibit "the most perfect idea of virtue" in their heroes, not to present characters at once fascinating and deeply flawed. The date of the essay suggests that Johnson may have been reacting specifically to Fielding's *Tom Jones* (1749) and its scapegrace hero, but the viewpoint he presents is not topical, and it was one with which his entire age was in sympathy.

If the aim of poetry is "to instruct by pleasing," then we might inquire how that is brought about. The answer, also found in the Preface to *Shakespeare*, runs briefly thus: "Nothing can please many, and please long, but just representations of general nature." Poetry must be deeply true to life, not because art is a matter of imitation, but because the truth of accurate representation holds us longer than any artful fancy could: "The pleasures of sudden wonder are soon exhausted, and the mind can only repose on the stability of truth."

Precisely what Johnson means by "general nature" is glossed in *Rasselas*, Chapter 10, where Imlac tells the Prince that "the business of the poet . . . is to examine, not the individual, but the species; to remark general properties and large appearances: he does not number the streaks of the tulip. . . . He . . . must neglect the minuter discriminations, which one may have remarked, and another have neglected, for those characteristics which are alike obvious to vigilance and carelessness." Johnson's insistence on the universality of poetry is very similar to Aristotle's, but his point is Horatian: If the literary work is to please a universal audience it must deal broadly with the world we all know, not with special issues of interest to a few.

From Johnson's universalizing perspective, the old topics of rhetorical criticism — the three unities, generic integrity, decorum of the stage — finally recede to the status of mere conventions, and conventions that were not those of Shakespeare's era. With all due reverence to the venerable antiquity of these doctrines, Johnson refutes their assumptions so thoroughly that it becomes difficult to see how they influenced so many for so long. At every point, Johnson insists that "there is always an appeal open from criticism to nature," and the old dogmas wither in the brutal spotlight of Johnson's common sense. The unities of time and place, he says, derive from "the supposed necessity of making the drama credible"; but in fact, no one in the audience believes for an instant that the things happening on stage are actually occurring. The audience's enjoyment indeed depends upon their sense that they are watching fiction. Critics have claimed that by mixing comic with tragic scenes, the passions are interrupted and the drama is deprived of emotional force. This reasoning, Johnson insinuates, is "so specious [attractive] that it is received as true even by those who in daily experience feel it to be false." To critics who object to the apparent indecorum of Shakespeare presenting King Claudius of Denmark as a drunkard, Johnson scoffs that "these are the petty cavils of petty minds."

Those who are accustomed to believe that Shakespeare could do no wrong may be surprised by Johnson's strictly judicial appraisal of the bard's faults and virtues. Johnson's didactic streak, in fact, is offended by Shakespeare's amorality, and Shakespeare's greatness is rescued only by his surpassing universality and trueness to life. In his stray judgments on Shakespeare, however, Johnson can be very shrewd — as when he states that Shakespeare's "tragedy seems to be skill, his comedy to be instinct."

The pleasures of reading Johnson's criticism are not merely intellectual. In his hands criticism becomes literature, delighting as well as instructing, and the source of the pleasure is Johnson's unique personality. We value his wisdom as much as his learning, and his tragic vision as much as his ebullient combativeness. He speaks of readers "willing to be thought wicked, if they may be allowed to be wits," and of writers who "are willing to hope from posterity what the present age refuses, and flatter themselves that the regard which is yet denied by envy, will be at last bestowed by time." He refers to the way "the common satiety of life sends us all in quest" of fantastic but worthless novelties; and reminds us that love "is only one of many passions, and . . . has no great influence upon the sum of life." It is then that we sense the presence of the very human sage who felt so deeply "The Vanity of Human Wishes."

Selected Bibliography

Bate, Walter Jackson. *The Achievement of Samuel Johnson.* Chicago: University of Chicago Press, 1978.

Battersby, James L. *Rational Praise and Natural Lamentation: Johnson, Lycidas and Principles of Criticism.* Rutherford, NJ: Fairleigh Dickinson University Press, 1980.

Damrosch, Leopold. *The Uses of Johnson's Criticism.* Charlottesville: University Press of Virginia, 1976.

Fussell, Paul. *Samuel Johnson and the Life of Writing.* New York: Norton, 1986.

Hagstrum, Jean H. *Samuel Johnson's Literary Criticism.* 1952; Chicago: University of Chicago Press, 1967.

Jenkins, Ralph Eugene. *Some Sources of Samuel Johnson's Literary Criticism.* Austin: University of Texas Press, 1969.

Keast, W. R. "Theoretical Foundations of Johnson's Criticism." In *Critics and Criticism: Ancient and Modern,* ed. R. S. Crane. Chicago: University of Chicago Press, 1952.

Stock, R. D. *Samuel Johnson and Neoclassical Dramatic Theory: The Literary Content of the "Preface to Shakespeare."* Lincoln: University of Nebraska Press, 1973.

The Rambler, No. 4

Simul et jucunda et idonea dicere vitæ.
—HORACE, *Ars Poetica,* 334

And join both profit and delight in one — CREECH

The works of fiction, with which the present generation seems more particularly delighted, are such as exhibit life in its true state, diversified only by accidents that daily happen in the world, and influenced by passions and qualities which are really to be found in conversing with mankind.

This kind of writing may be termed not improperly the comedy of romance, and is to be conducted nearly by the rules of comic poetry. Its province is to bring about natural events by easy means, and to keep up curiosity without the help of wonder: it is therefore precluded from the machines and expedients of the heroic romance, and can neither employ giants to snatch away a lady from the nuptial rites, nor knights to bring her back from captivity; it can neither bewilder its personages in deserts, nor lodge them in imaginary castles.

I remember a remark made by Scaliger[1] upon Pontanus, that all his writings are filled with the same images; and that if you take from him his lilies and his roses, his satyrs and his dryads, he will have nothing left that can be called poetry. In like manner almost all the fictions of the last

[1]Julius Caesar Scaliger, *Poetics* 5:4. [Ed.]

age will vanish, if you deprive them of a hermit and a wood, a battle and a shipwreck.

Why this wild strain of imagination found reception so long in polite and learned ages, it is not easy to conceive; but we cannot wonder that while readers could be procured, the authors were willing to continue it; for when a man had by practice gained some fluency of language, he had no further care than to retire to his closet, let loose his invention, and heat his mind with incredibilities; a book was thus produced without fear of criticism, without the toil of study, without knowledge of nature, or acquaintance with life.

The task of our present writers is very different; it requires, together with that learning which is to be gained from books, that experience which can never be attained by solitary diligence, but must arise from general converse and accurate observation of the living world. Their performances have, as Horace expresses it, *plus oneris quantum veniæ minus*, little indulgence, and therefore more difficulty.[2] They are engaged in portraits of which every one knows the original, and can detect any deviation from exactness of resemblance. Other writings are safe, except from the malice of learning, but these are in danger from every common reader; as the slipper ill executed was censured by a shoemaker who happened to stop in his way at the Venus of Apelles.[3]

But the fear of not being approved as just copiers of human manners, is not the most important concern that an author of this sort ought to have before him. These books are written chiefly to the young, the ignorant, and the idle, to whom they serve as lectures of conduct, and introductions into life. They are the entertainment of minds unfurnished with ideas, and therefore easily susceptible of impressions; not fixed by principles, and therefore easily following the current of fancy; not informed by experience, and consequently open to every false suggestion and partial account.

That the highest degree of reverence should be paid to youth, and that nothing indecent should be suffered to approach their eyes or ears, are precepts extorted by sense and virtue from an ancient writer, by no means eminent for chastity of thought. The same kind, though not the same degree, of caution, is required in every thing which is laid before them, to secure them from unjust prejudices, perverse opinions, and incongruous combinations of images.

In the romances formerly written, every transaction and sentiment was so remote from all that passes among men, that the reader was in very little danger of making any applications to himself; the virtues and crimes were equally beyond his sphere of activity; and he amused himself with heroes and with traitors, deliverers and persecutors, as with beings of another species, whose actions were regulated upon motives of their own, and who had neither faults nor excellencies in common with himself.

But when an adventurer is levelled with the rest of the world, and acts in such scenes of the universal drama, as may be the lot of any other man; young spectators fix their eyes upon him with closer attention, and hope, by observing his behaviour and success, to regulate their own practices, when they shall be engaged in the like part.

For this reason these familiar histories may perhaps be made of greater use than the solemnities of professed morality, and convey the knowledge of vice and virtue with more efficacy than axioms and definitions. But if the power of example is so great as to take possession of the memory by a kind of violence, and produce effects almost without the intervention of the will, care ought to be taken, that, when the choice is unrestrained, the best examples only should be exhibited; and that which is likely to operate so strongly, should not be mischievous or uncertain in its effects.

The chief advantage which these fictions have over real life is, that their authors are at liberty, though not to invent, yet to select objects, and to cull from the mass of mankind, those individuals upon which the attention ought most to be employed; as a diamond, though it cannot be made, may be polished by art, and placed in such a situation, as to display that lustre which before was buried among common stones.

[2]Horace, *Epistles* II.1:70. [Ed.]
[3]Pliny, *Natural History* 35:84–85. [Ed.]

It is justly considered as the greatest excellency of art, to imitate nature; but it is necessary to distinguish those parts of nature, which are most proper for imitation: greater care is still required in representing life, which is so often discoloured by passion, or deformed by wickedness. If the world be promiscuously described, I cannot see of what use it can be to read the account; or why it may not be as safe to turn the eye immediately upon mankind as upon a mirror which shows all that presents itself without discrimination.

It is therefore not a sufficient vindication of a character, that it is drawn as it appears; for many characters ought never to be drawn: nor of a narrative, that the train of events is agreeable to observation and experience; for that observation which is called knowledge of the world, will be found much more frequently to make men cunning than good. The purpose of these writings is surely not only to show mankind, but to provide that they may be seen hereafter with less hazard; to teach the means of avoiding the snares which are laid by Treachery for Innocence, without infusing any wish for that superiority with which the betrayer flatters his vanity; to give the power of counteracting fraud, without the temptation to practise it; to initiate youth by mock encounters in the art of necessary defence, and to increase prudence without impairing virtue.

Many writers, for the sake of following nature, so mingle good and bad qualities in their principal personages, that they are both equally conspicuous; and as we accompany them through their adventures with delight, and are led by degrees to interest ourselves in their favour, we lose the abhorrence of their faults, because they do not hinder our pleasure, or, perhaps, regard them with some kindness, for being united with so much merit.

There have been men indeed splendidly wicked, whose endowments threw a brightness on their crimes, and whom scarce any villainy made perfectly detestable, because they never could be wholly divested of their excellencies; but such have been in all ages the great corrupters of the world, and their resemblance ought no more to be preserved, than the art of murdering without pain.

Some have advanced, without due attention to the consequences of this notion, that certain virtues have their correspondent faults, and therefore that to exhibit either apart is to deviate from probability. Thus men are observed by Swift to be "grateful in the same degree as they are resentful." This principle, with others of the same kind, supposes man to act from a brute impulse, and pursue a certain degree of inclination, without any choice of the object; for, otherwise, though it should be allowed that gratitude and resentment arise from the same constitution of the passions, it follows not that they will be equally indulged when reason is consulted; yet, unless that consequence be admitted, this sagacious maxim becomes an empty sound, without any relation to practice or to life.

Nor is it evident, that even the first motions to these effects are always in the same proportion. For pride, which produces quickness of resentment, will obstruct gratitude, by unwillingness to admit that inferiority which obligation implies; and it is very unlikely that he who cannot think he receives a favour, will acknowledge or repay it.

It is of the utmost importance to mankind, that positions of this tendency should be laid open and confuted; for while men consider good and evil as springing from the same root, they will spare the one for the sake of the other, and in judging, if not of others at least of themselves, will be apt to estimate their virtues by their vices. To this fatal error all those will contribute, who confound the colours of right and wrong, and instead of helping to settle their boundaries, mix them with so much art, that no common mind is able to disunite them.

In narratives where historical veracity has no place, I cannot discover why there should not be exhibited the most perfect idea of virtue; of virtue not angelical, nor above probability, for what we cannot credit, we shall never imitate, but the highest and purest that humanity can reach, which, exercised in such trials as the various revolutions of things shall bring upon it, may, by conquering some calamities, and enduring others, teach us what we may hope, and what we can perform. Vice, for vice is necessary to be shown, should always disgust; nor should the graces of gaiety, or the dignity of courage, be so united with it, as to reconcile it to the mind. Wherever it appears, it should raise hatred by the malignity of its practices, and contempt by the meanness of its stratagems: for while it is supported by either parts or spirit, it will be seldom heartily abhorred. The Roman tyrant was content to be hated, if he was but feared; and there are thousands of the readers of romances willing to be thought wicked, if they may be allowed to be wits. It is therefore to be steadily inculcated, that virtue is the highest proof of understanding, and the only solid basis of greatness; and that vice is the natural consequence of narrow thoughts; that it begins in mistake, and ends in ignominy.

Rasselas, Chapter 10

IMLAC'S HISTORY CONTINUED

"Wherever I went, I found that Poetry was considered as the highest learning, and regarded with a veneration somewhat approaching to that which man would pay to the Angelick Nature. And it yet fills me with wonder, that, in almost all countries, the most ancient poets are considered as the best: whether it be that every other kind of knowledge is an acquisition gradually attained, and poetry is a gift conferred at once; or that the first poetry of every nation surprised them as a novelty, and retained the credit by consent which it received by accident at first: or whether the province of poetry is to describe Nature and Passion, which are always the same, and the first writers took possession of the most striking objects for description, and the most probable occurrences for fiction, and left nothing to those that followed them, but transcription of the same events, and new combinations of the same images. Whatever be the reason, it is commonly observed that the early writers are in possession of nature, and their followers of art: that the first excel in strength and invention, and the latter in elegance and refinement.

"I was desirous to add my name to this illustrious fraternity. I read all the poets of Persia and Arabia, and was able to repeat by memory the volumes that are suspended in the mosque of Mecca. But I soon found that no man was ever great by imitation. My desire of excellence impelled me to transfer my attention to nature and to life. Nature was to be my subject, and men to be my auditors: I could never describe what I had not seen: I could not hope to move those with delight of terrour, whose interests and opinions I did not understand.

"Being now resolved to be a poet, I saw every thing with a new purpose; my sphere of attention was suddenly magnified: no kind of knowledge was to be overlooked. I ranged mountains and deserts for images and resemblances, and pictured upon my mind every tree of the forest and flower of the valley. I observed with equal care the crags of the rock and the pinnacles of the palace. Sometimes I wandered along the mazes of the rivulet, and sometimes watched the changes of the summer clouds. To a poet nothing can be useless. Whatever is beautiful, and whatever is dreadful, must be familiar to his imagination: he must be conversant with all that is awfully vast or elegantly little. The plants of the garden, the animals of the wood, the minerals of the earth, and meteors of the sky, must all concur to store his mind with inexhaustible variety: for every idea is useful for the inforcement or decoration of moral or religious truth; and he, who knows most, will have most power of diversifying his scenes, and of gratifying his reader with remote allusions and unexpected instruction.

"All the appearances of nature I was therefore careful to study, and every country which I have surveyed has contributed something to my poetical powers."

"In so wide a survey, said the prince, you must surely have left much unobserved. I have lived, till now, within the circuit of these mountains, and yet cannot walk abroad without the sight of something which I had never beheld before, or never heeded."

"The business of a poet, said Imlac, is to examine, not the individual, but the species; to remark general properties and large appearances: he does not number the streaks of the tulip, or describe the different shades in the verdure of the forest. He is to exhibit in his portraits of nature such prominent and striking features, as recal the original to every mind; and must neglect the minuter discriminations, which one may have remarked, and another have neglected, for those characteristicks which are alike obvious to vigilance and carelessness.

"But the knowledge of nature is only half the task of a poet; he must be acquainted likewise with all the modes of life. His character requires that he estimate the happiness and misery of every condition; observe the power of all the passions in all their combinations, and trace the changes of the human mind as they are modified by various institutions and accidental influences of climate or custom, from the spriteliness of infancy to the despondence of decrepitude. He must divest himself of the prejudices of his age or country; he must consider right and wrong in their abstracted and invariable state; he must disregard present laws and opinions, and rise to general and transcendental truths, which will always be the same: he must therefore content himself with the slow progress of his name; contemn the applause of his own time, and commit his claims to the justice of posterity. He must write as the interpreter of nature, and the legislator of mankind, and consider himself as presiding over the thoughts and manners of successive generations; as a being superiour to time and place. His labour is not yet at an end: he must know many languages and many sciences; and, that his stile may be worthy of his thoughts, must, by incessant practice, familiarize to himself every delicacy of speech and grace of harmony."

From *Preface to Shakespeare*

That praises are without reason lavished on the dead, and that the honours due only to excellence are paid to antiquity, is a complaint likely to be always continued by those, who, being able to add nothing to truth, hope for eminence from the heresies of paradox; or those, who, being forced by disappointment upon consolatory expedients, are willing to hope from posterity what the present age refuses, and flatter themselves that the regard which is yet denied by envy, will be at last bestowed by time.

Antiquity, like every other quality that attracts the notice of mankind, has undoubtedly votaries that reverence it, not from reason, but from prejudice. Some seem to admire indiscriminately whatever has been long preserved, without considering that time has sometimes cooperated with chance; all perhaps are more willing to honour past than present excellence; and the mind contemplates genius through the shades of age, as the eye surveys the sun through artificial opacity. The great contention of criticism is to find the faults of the moderns, and the beauties of the ancients. While an author is yet living we estimate his powers by his worst performance, and when he is dead we rate them by his best.

To works, however, of which the excellence is not absolute and definite, but gradual and comparative; to works not raised upon principles demonstrative and scientific, but appealing wholly to observation and experience, no other test can be applied than length of duration and continuance of esteem. What mankind have long possessed they have often examined and compared, and if they persist to value the possession, it is because frequent comparisons have confirmed opinion in its favour. As among the works of nature no man can properly call a river deep or a mountain high, without the knowledge of many mountains and many rivers; so in the productions of genius, nothing can be styled excellent till it has been compared with other works of the same kind. Demonstration immediately displays its power, and has nothing to hope or fear from the flux of years; but works tentative and experimental must be estimated by their proportion to the general and collective ability of man, as it is discovered in a long succession of endeavours. Of the first building that was raised, it might be with certainty determined that it was round or square, but whether it was spacious or lofty must have been referred to time. The Pythagorean scale of numbers was at once discovered to be perfect; but the poems of Homer we yet know not to transcend the common limits of human intelligence, but by remarking, that nation after nation, and century after century, has been able to do little more than transpose his incidents, new name his characters, and paraphrase his sentiments.

The reverence due to writings that have long subsisted arises therefore not from any credulous confidence in the superior wisdom of past ages, or gloomy persuasion of the degeneracy of mankind, but is the consequence of acknowledged and indubitable positions, that what has been longest known has been most considered, and what is most considered is best understood.

The Poet, of whose works I have undertaken the revision, may now begin to assume the dignity of an ancient, and claim the privilege of established fame and prescriptive veneration. He has long outlived his century, the term commonly fixed as the test of literary merit. Whatever advantages he might once derive from personal allusions, local customs, or temporary opinions, have for many years been lost; and every topic of merriment or motive of sorrow, which the modes of artificial life afforded him, now only obscure the scenes which they once illuminated. The effects of favour and competition are at an end; the tradition of his friendships and his enmities has perished; his works support no opinion with arguments, nor supply any faction with invectives; they can neither indulge vanity nor gratify malignity, but are read without any other reason than the desire of pleasure, and are therefore praised only as pleasure is obtained; yet, thus unassisted by interest or passion, they have passed through variations of taste and changes of manners, and, as they devolved from one generation to another, have received new honours at every transmission.

But because human judgement, though it be gradually gaining upon certainty, never becomes infallible; and approbation, though long continued, may yet be only the approbation of prejudice or fashion; it is proper to inquire, by what peculiarities of excellence Shakespeare has gained and kept the favour of his countrymen.

Nothing can please many, and please long, but just representations of general nature. Particular manners can be known to few, and therefore few only can judge how nearly they are copied. The irregular combinations of fanciful invention may delight a while, by that novelty of which the common satiety of life sends us all in quest; but the pleasures of sudden wonder are soon exhausted, and the mind can only repose on the stability of truth.

Shakespeare is above all writers, at least above all modern writers, the poet of nature; the poet that holds up to his readers a faithful mirror of manners and of life. His characters are not modified by the customs of particular places, unpractised by the rest of the world; by the peculiarities of studies or professions, which can operate but upon small numbers; or by the accidents of transient fashions or temporary opinions: they are the genuine progeny of common humanity, such as the world will always supply, and observation will always find. His persons act and speak by the influence of those general passions and principles by which all minds are agitated, and the whole system of life is continued in motion. In the writings of other poets a character is too often an individual; in those of Shakespeare it is commonly a species.

It is from this wide extension of design that so much instruction is derived. It is this which fills the plays of Shakespeare with practical axioms and domestic wisdom. It was said of Euripides, that every verse was a precept; and it may be said of Shakespeare, that from his works may be collected a system of civil and economical prudence. Yet his real power is not shown in the splendour of particular passages, but by the progress of his fable, and the tenor of his dialogue; and he that tries to recommend him by select quotations, will succeed like the pedant in *Hierocles*, who, when he offered his house to sale, carried a brick in his pocket as a specimen.

It will not easily be imagined how much Shakespeare excels in accommodating his sentiments to real life, but by comparing him with other authors. It was observed of the ancient schools of declamation, that the more diligently they were frequented, the more was the student disqualified for the world, because he found nothing there which he should ever meet in any other place. The same remark may be applied to every stage but that of Shakespeare. The theatre, when it is under any other direction, is peopled by such characters as were never seen conversing in a language which was never heard, upon topics which will never arise in the commerce of mankind. But the dialogue of this author is often so evidently determined by the incident which produces it, and is pursued with so much ease and simplicity, that it seems scarcely to claim the merit of fiction, but to have been gleaned by diligent selection out of common conversation, and common occurrences.

Upon every other stage the universal agent is love, by whose power all good and evil is distributed, and every action quickened or retarded. To bring a lover, a lady and a rival into the fable; to entangle them in contradictory obligations, perplex them with oppositions of interest, and harass them with violence of desires inconsistent with each other; to make them meet in rapture and part in agony; to fill their mouths with hyperbolical joy and outrageous sorrow; to distress them as nothing human ever was distressed; to deliver them as nothing human ever was delivered, is the business of a modern dramatist. For this probability is violated, life is misrepresented, and language is depraved. But love is only one of many passions, and as it has no great influence upon the sum of life, it has little operation in the dramas of a poet, who caught his ideas from the living world, and exhibited only what he saw before him. He knew, that any other passion, as it was regular or exorbitant, was a cause of happiness or calamity.

Characters thus ample and general were not easily discriminated and preserved, yet perhaps no poet ever kept his personages more distinct from each other. I will not say with Pope[1] that every speech may be assigned to the proper speaker, because many speeches there are which have nothing characteristical; but perhaps, though some may be equally adapted to every person, it will be difficult to find any that can be properly transferred from the present possessor to another claimant. The choice is right, when there is reason for choice.

Other dramatists can only gain attention by hyperbolical or aggravated characters, by fabulous and unexampled excellence or depravity, as the writers of barbarous romances invigorated the reader by a giant and a dwarf; and he that should form his expectations of human affairs from the play, or from the tale, would be equally deceived. Shakespeare has no heroes; his scenes are occupied only by men, who act and speak as the reader thinks that he should himself have spoken or acted on the same occasion. Even where the agency is supernatural the dialogue is level with life. Other writers disguise the most natural passions and most frequent incidents; so that he who contemplates them in the book will not know them in the world; Shakespeare approximates the remote, and familiarizes the wonderful; the event which he represents will not happen, but if it were possible, its effects would probably be such as he has assigned; and it may be said, that he has not only shown human nature as it acts in real exigencies, but as it would be found in trials, to which it cannot be exposed.

This therefore is the praise of Shakespeare, that his drama is the mirror of life; that he who has mazed his imagination, in following the phantoms which other writers raise up before him, may here be cured of his delirious ecstasies, by reading human sentiment in human language;

[1]In Pope's preface to his 1725 edition of Shakespeare. [Ed.]

by scenes from which a hermit may estimate the transactions of the world, and a confessor predict the progress of the passions.

His adherence to general nature has exposed him to the censure of critics, who form their judgements upon narrower principles. Dennis and Rhymer think his Romans not sufficiently Roman; and Voltaire censures his kings as not completely royal.[2] Dennis is offended, that Menenius, a senator of Rome, should play the buffoon; and Voltaire perhaps thinks decency violated when the Danish usurper is represented as a drunkard. But Shakespeare always makes nature predominate over accident; and if he preserves the essential character, is not very careful of distinctions superinduced and adventitious. His story requires Romans or kings, but he thinks only on men. He knew that Rome, like every other city, had men of all dispositions; and wanting a buffoon, he went into the senate-house for that which the senate-house would certainly have afforded him. He was inclined to show a usurper and a murderer not only odious but despicable; he therefore added drunkenness to his other qualities, knowing that kings love wine like other men, and that wine exerts its natural power upon kings. These are the petty cavils of petty minds; a poet overlooks the casual distinction of country and condition, as a painter, satisfied with the figure, neglects the drapery.

The censure which he has incurred by mixing comic and tragic scenes, as it extends to all his works, deserves more consideration. Let the fact be first stated, and then examined.

Shakespeare's plays are not in the rigorous and critical sense either tragedies or comedies, but compositions of a distinct kind; exhibiting the real state of sublunary nature, which partakes of good and evil, joy and sorrow, mingled with endless variety of proportion and innumerable modes of combination; and expressing the course of the world, in which the loss of one is the gain of another; in which, at the same time, the reveller is hasting to his wine, and the mourner burying his friend; in which the malignity of one is sometimes defeated by the frolic of another; and many mischiefs and many benefits are done and hindered without design.

Out of this chaos of mingled purposes and casualties the ancient poets, according to the laws which custom had prescribed, selected some the crimes of men, and some their absurdities; some the momentous vicissitudes of life, and some the lighter occurrences; some the terrors of distress, and some the gaieties of prosperity. Thus rose the two modes of imitation, known by the names of *tragedy* and *comedy*, compositions intended to promote different ends by contrary means, and considered as so little allied, that I do not recollect among the Greeks or Romans a single writer who attempted both.

Shakespeare has united the powers of exciting laughter and sorrow not only in one mind but in one composition. Almost all his plays are divided between serious and ludicrous characters, and, in the successive evolutions of the design, sometimes produce seriousness and sorrow, and sometimes levity and laughter.

That this is a practice contrary to the rules of criticism will be readily allowed; but there is always an appeal open from criticism to nature. The end of writing is to instruct; the end of poetry is to instruct by pleasing. That the mingled drama may convey all the instruction of tragedy or comedy cannot be denied, because it includes both in its alternations of exhibition, and approaches nearer than either to the appearance of life, by showing how great machinations and slender designs may promote or obviate one another, and the high and the low co-operate in the general system by unavoidable concatenation.

It is objected, that by this change of scenes the passions are interrupted in their progression, and that the principal event, being not advanced by a due gradation of preparatory incidents, wants at last the power to move, which constitutes the perfection of dramatic poetry. This reasoning is so specious, that it is received as true even by those who in daily experience feel it to be false. The interchanges of mingled scenes seldom fail

[2]Johnson refers to John Dennis's *Essay on the Genius and Writings of Shakespeare* (1713); Thomas Rymer's *A Short View of Tragedy* (1692); and Voltaire's *Dissertation sur la tragédie ancienne et moderne* (1749) and *Appel à toutes les nations de l'Europe* (1761). [Ed.]

to produce the intended vicissitudes of passion. Fiction cannot move so much, but that the attention may be easily transferred; and though it must be allowed that pleasing melancholy be sometimes interrupted by unwelcome levity, yet let it be considered likewise, that melancholy is often not pleasing, and that the disturbance of one man may be the relief of another; that different auditors have different habitudes; and that, upon the whole, all pleasure consists in variety.

The players, who in their edition[3] divided our author's works into comedies, histories, and tragedies, seem not to have distinguished the three kinds, by any very exact or definite ideas.

An action which ended happily to the principal persons, however serious or distressful through its intermediate incidents, in their opinion constituted a comedy. This idea of a comedy continued long amongst us, and plays were written, which, by changing the catastrophe, were tragedies today and comedies tomorrow.

Tragedy was not in those times a poem of more general dignity or elevation than comedy; it required only a calamitous conclusion, with which the common criticism of that age was satisfied, whatever lighter pleasure it afforded in its progress.

History was a series of actions, with no other than chronological succession, independent on each other, and without any tendency to introduce or regulate the conclusion. It is not always very nicely distinguished from tragedy. There is not much nearer approach to unity of action in the tragedy of *Antony and Cleopatra*, than in the history of *Richard the Second*. But a history might be continued through many plays; as it had no plan, it had no limits.

Through all these denominations of the drama, Shakespeare's mode of composition is the same; an interchange of seriousness and merriment, by which the mind is softened at one time, and exhilarated at another. But whatever be his purpose, whether to gladden or depress, or to conduct the story, without vehemence or emotion, through tracts of easy and familiar dialogue, he never fails to attain his purpose; as he commands us, we laugh or mourn, or sit silent with quiet expectation, in tranquillity without indifference.

When Shakespeare's plan is understood, most of the criticisms of Rhymer and Voltaire vanish away. The play of *Hamlet* is opened, without impropriety, by two sentinels; Iago bellows at Brabantio's window, without injury to the scheme of the play, though in terms which a modern audience would not easily endure; the character of Polonius is seasonable and useful; and the gravediggers themselves may be heard with applause.

Shakespeare engaged in the dramatic poetry with the world open before him; the rules of the ancients were yet known to few; the public judgement was unformed; he had no example of such fame as might force him upon imitation, nor critics of such authority as might restrain his extravagance. He therefore indulged his natural disposition, and his disposition, as Rhymer has remarked, led him to comedy. In tragedy he often writes with great appearance of toil and study, what is written at last with little felicity; but in his comic scenes, he seems to produce without labour, what no labour can improve. In tragedy he is always struggling after some occasion to be comic, but in comedy he seems to repose, or to luxuriate, as in a mode of thinking congenial to his nature. In his tragic scenes there is always something wanting, but his comedy often surpasses expectation or desire. His comedy pleases by the thoughts and the language, and his tragedy for the greater part by incident and action. His tragedy seems to be skill, his comedy to be instinct.

The force of his comic scenes has suffered little diminution from the changes made by a century and a half, in manners or in words. As his personages act upon principles arising from genuine passion, very little modified by particular forms, their pleasures and vexations are communicable to all times and to all places; they are natural, and therefore durable; the adventitious peculiarities of personal habits, are only superficial dies, bright and pleasing for a little while, yet soon fading to a dim tinct, without any remains of former lustre; but the discriminations of true passion are the colours of nature; they pervade the whole mass, and can only perish with the

[3]John Heminges and Henry Condell, who edited the First Folio in 1623. [Ed.]

body that exhibits them. The accidental compositions of heterogeneous modes are dissolved by the chance which combined them; but the uniform simplicity of primitive qualities neither admits increase, nor suffers decay. The sand heaped by one flood is scattered by another, but the rock always continues in its place. The stream of time, which is continually washing the dissoluble fabrics of other poets, passes without injury by the adamant of Shakespeare.

If there be, what I believe there is, in every nation, a style which never becomes obsolete, a certain mode of phraseology so consonant and congenial to the analogy and principles of its respective language as to remain settled and unaltered; this style is probably to be sought in the common intercourse of life, among those who speak only to be understood, without ambition of elegance. The polite are always catching modish innovations, and the learned depart from established forms of speech, in hope of finding or making better; those who wish for distinction forsake the vulgar, when the vulgar is right; but there is a conversation above grossness and below refinement, where propriety resides, and where this poet seems to have gathered his comic dialogue. He is therefore more agreeable to the ears of the present age than any other author equally remote, and among his other excellencies deserves to be studied as one of the original masters of our language.

These observations are to be considered not as unexceptionably constant, but as containing general and predominant truth. Shakespeare's familiar dialogue is affirmed to be smooth and clear, yet not wholly without ruggedness or difficulty; as a country may be eminently fruitful, though it has spots unfit for cultivation. His characters are praised as natural, though their sentiments are sometimes forced, and their actions improbable; as the earth upon the whole is spherical, though its surface is varied with protuberances and cavities.

Shakespeare with his excellencies has likewise faults, and faults sufficient to obscure and overwhelm any other merit. I shall show them in the proportion in which they appear to me, without envious malignity or superstitious veneration. No question can be more innocently discussed than a dead poet's pretensions to renown; and little regard is due to that bigotry which sets candour higher than truth.

His first defect is that to which may be imputed most of the evil in books or in men. He sacrifices virtue to convenience, and is so much more careful to please than to instruct, that he seems to write without any moral purpose. From his writings indeed a system of social duty may be selected, for he that thinks reasonably must think morally; but his precepts and axioms drop casually from him; he makes no just distribution of good or evil, nor is always careful to show in the virtuous a disapprobation of the wicked; he carries his persons indifferently through right and wrong, and at the close dismisses them without further care, and leaves their examples to operate by chance. This fault the barbarity of his age cannot extenuate; for it is always a writer's duty to make the world better, and justice is a virtue independent on time or place.

The plots are often so loosely formed, that a very slight consideration may improve them, and so carelessly pursued, that he seems not always fully to comprehend his own design. He omits opportunities of instructing or delighting which the train of his story seems to force upon him, and apparently rejects those exhibitions which would be more affecting, for the sake of those which are more easy.

It may be observed, that in many of his plays the latter part is evidently neglected. When he found himself near the end of his work, and in view of his reward, he shortened the labour to snatch the profit. He therefore remits his efforts where he should most vigorously exert them, and his catastrophe is improbably produced or imperfectly represented.

He had no regard to distinction of time or place, but gives to one age or nation, without scruple, the customs, institutions, and opinions of another, at the expense not only of likelihood, but of possibility. These faults Pope has endeavoured, with more zeal than judgement, to transfer to his imagined interpolators. We need not wonder to find Hector quoting Aristotle,[4] when we

[4]In *Troilus and Cressida,* II.ii:166–67. [Ed.]

see the loves of Theseus and Hippolyta combined with the Gothic mythology of fairies. Shakespeare, indeed, was not the only violator of chronology, for in the same age Sidney, who wanted not the advantages of learning, has, in his *Arcadia*, confounded the pastoral with the feudal times, the days of innocence, quiet and security, with those of turbulence, violence, and adventure.

In his comic scenes he is seldom very successful, when he engages his characters in reciprocations of smartness and contests of sarcasm; their jests are commonly gross, and their pleasantry licentious; neither his gentlemen nor his ladies have much delicacy, nor are sufficiently distinguished from his clowns by any appearance of refined manners. Whether he represented the real conversation of his time is not easy to determine; the reign of Elizabeth is commonly supposed to have been a time of stateliness, formality and reserve; yet perhaps the relaxations of that severity were not very elegant. There must, however, have been always some modes of gaiety preferable to others, and a writer ought to choose the best.

In tragedy his performance seems constantly to be worse, as his labour is more. The effusions of passion which exigence forces out are for the most part striking and energetic; but whenever he solicits his invention, or strains his faculties, the offspring of his throes is tumour, meanness, tediousness, and obscurity.

In narration he affects a disproportionate pomp of diction, and a wearisome train of circumlocution, and tells the incident imperfectly in many words, which might have been more plainly delivered in few. Narration in dramatic poetry is naturally tedious, as it is unanimated and inactive, and obstructs the progress of the action; it should therefore always be rapid, and enlivened by frequent interruption. Shakespeare found it an encumbrance, and instead of lightening it by brevity, endeavoured to recommend it by dignity and splendour.

His declamations or set speeches are commonly cold and weak, for his power was the power of nature; when he endeavoured, like other tragic writers, to catch opportunities of amplification, and instead of inquiring what the occasion demanded, to show how much his stores of knowledge could supply, he seldom escapes without the pity or resentment of his reader.

It is incident to him to be now and then entangled with an unwieldy sentiment, which he cannot well express, and will not reject; he struggles with it a while, and if it continues stubborn, comprises it in words such as occur, and leaves it to be disentangled and evolved by those who have more leisure to bestow upon it.

Not that always where the language is intricate the thought is subtle, or the image always great where the line is bulky; the equality of words to things is very often neglected, and trivial sentiments and vulgar ideas disappoint the attention, to which they are recommended by sonorous epithets and swelling figures.

But the admirers of this great poet have never less reason to indulge their hopes of supreme excellence, than when he seems fully resolved to sink them in dejection, and mollify them with tender emotions by the fall of greatness, the danger of innocence, or the crosses of love. He is not long soft and pathetic without some idle conceit, or contemptible equivocation. He no sooner begins to move, than he counteracts himself; and terror and pity, as they are rising in the mind, are checked and blasted by sudden frigidity.

A quibble is to Shakespeare, what luminous vapours are to the traveller; he follows it at all adventures, it is sure to lead him out of his way, and sure to engulf him in the mire. It has some malignant power over his mind, and its fascinations are irresistible. Whatever be the dignity or profundity of his disquisition, whether he be enlarging knowledge or exalting affection, whether he be amusing attention with incidents, or enhancing it in suspense, let but a quibble spring up before him, and he leaves his work unfinished. A quibble is the golden apple for which he will always turn aside from his career, or stoop from his elevation. A quibble, poor and barren as it is, gave him such delight, that he was content to purchase it, by the sacrifice of reason, propriety and truth. A quibble was to him the fatal Cleopatra for which he lost the world, and was content to lose it.

It will be thought strange, that, in enumerating the defects of this writer, I have not yet mentioned his neglect of the unities; his violation of those laws which have been instituted and established by the joint authority of poets and of critics.

For his other deviations from the art of writing, I resign him to critical justice, without making any other demand in his favour, than that which must be indulged to all human excellence; that his virtues be rated with his failings: but, from the censure which his irregularity may bring upon him, I shall, with due reverence to that learning which I must oppose, adventure to try how I can defend him.

His histories, being neither tragedies nor comedies, are not subject to any of their laws; nothing more is necessary to all the praise which they expect, than that the changes of action be so prepared as to be understood, that the incidents be various and affecting, and the characters consistent, natural and distinct. No other unity is intended, and therefore none is to be sought.

In his other works he has well enough preserved the unity of action. He has not, indeed, an intrigue regularly perplexed and regularly unravelled; he does not endeavour to hide his design only to discover it, for this is seldom the order of real events, and Shakespeare is the poet of nature: but his plan has commonly what Aristotle requires, a beginning, a middle, and an end;[5] one event is concatenated with another, and the conclusion follows by easy consequence. There are perhaps some incidents that might be spared, as in other poets there is much talk that only fills up time upon the stage; but the general system makes gradual advances, and the end of the play is the end of expectation.

To the unities of time and place he has shown no regard, and perhaps a nearer view of the principles on which they stand will diminish their value, and withdraw from them the veneration which, from the time of Corneille,[6] they have very generally received, by discovering that they have given more trouble to the poet, than pleasure to the auditor.

[5]Aristotle, *Poetics*, Ch. 7; see p. 47. [Ed.]

[6]Pierre Corneille's *Discours des trois unités* was published in 1660. For other discussions of the three unities, see the selections from Sidney and Dryden. [Ed.]

The necessity of observing the unities of time and place arises from the supposed necessity of making the drama credible. The critics hold it impossible, that an action of months or years can be possibly believed to pass in three hours; or that the spectator can suppose himself to sit in the theatre, while ambassadors go and return between distant kings, while armies are levied and towns besieged, while an exile wanders and returns, or till he whom they saw courting his mistress, shall lament the untimely fall of his son. The mind revolts from evident falsehood, and fiction loses its force when it departs from the resemblance of reality.

From the narrow limitation of time necessarily arises the contraction of place. The spectator, who knows that he saw the first act at Alexandria, cannot suppose that he sees the next at Rome, at a distance to which not the dragons of Medea could, in so short a time, have transported him; he knows with certainty that he has not changed his place; and he knows that place cannot change itself; that what was a house cannot become a plain; that what was Thebes can never be Persepolis.

Such is the triumphant language with which a critic exults over the misery of an irregular poet, and exults commonly without resistance or reply. It is time therefore to tell him, by the authority of Shakespeare, that he assumes, as an unquestionable principle, a position which, while his breath is forming it into words, his understanding pronounces to be false. It is false, that any representation is mistaken for reality; that any dramatic fable in its materiality was ever credible, or, for a single moment, was ever credited.

The objection arising from the impossibility of passing the first hour at Alexandria, and the next at Rome, supposes, that when the play opens, the spectator really imagines himself at Alexandria, and believes that his walk to the theatre has been a voyage to Egypt, and that he lives in the days of Antony and Cleopatra. Surely he that imagines this may imagine more. He that can take the stage at one time for the palace of the Ptolemies, may take it in half an hour for the promontory of Actium. Delusion, if delusion be admitted, has no certain limitation; if the spectator can be once persuaded, that his old acquaintance are Alexander and Caesar, that a room illuminated with candles is the plain of Pharsalia, or the bank of Granicus, he is in a state of elevation above the reach of reason, or of truth, and from the heights of empyrean poetry, may despise the circumscriptions of terrestrial nature. There is no reason why a mind thus wandering in ecstasy should count the clock, or why an hour should not be a century in that calenture[7] of the brains that can make the stage a field.

The truth is, that the spectators are always in their senses, and know, from the first act to the last, that the stage is only a stage, and that the players are only players. They came to hear a certain number of lines recited with just gesture and elegant modulation. The lines relate to some action, and an action must be in some place; but the different actions that complete a story may be in places very remote from each other; and where is the absurdity of allowing that space to represent first Athens, and then Sicily, which was always known to be neither Sicily nor Athens, but a modern theatre?

By supposition, as place is introduced time may be extended; the time required by the fable elapses for the most part between the acts; for, of so much of the action as is represented, the real and poetical duration is the same. If, in the first act, preparations for war against Mithridates are represented to be made in Rome, the event of the war may without absurdity, be represented, in the catastrophe, as happening in Pontus; we know that there is neither war, nor preparation for war; we know that we are neither in Rome nor Pontus; that neither Mithridates nor Lucullus are before us. The drama exhibits successive imitations of successive actions, and why may not the second imitation represent an action that happened years after the first; if it be so connected with it, that nothing but time can be supposed to intervene. Time is, of all modes of existence, most obsequious to the imagination; a lapse of years is as easily conceived as a passage of hours. In contemplation we easily contract the time of real actions, and therefore willingly permit it to be contracted when we only see their imitation.

It will be asked, how the drama moves, if it is not credited. It is credited with all the credit due to a drama. It is credited, whenever it moves, as a just picture of a real original; as representing to the auditor what he would himself feel, if he were to do or suffer what is there feigned to be suffered or to be done. The reflection that strikes the heart is not, that the evils before us are real evils, but that they are evils to which we ourselves may be exposed. If there be any fallacy, it is not that we fancy the players, but that we fancy ourselves unhappy for a moment; but we rather lament the possibility than suppose the presence of misery, as a mother weeps over her babe, when she remembers that death may take it from her. The delight of tragedy proceeds from our consciousness of fiction; if we thought murders and treasons real, they would please no more.

Imitations produce pain or pleasure, not because they are mistaken for realities, but because they bring realities to mind. When the imagination is recreated by a painted landscape, the trees are not supposed capable to give us shade, or the fountains coolness; but we consider, how we should be pleased with such fountains playing beside us, and such woods waving over us. We are agitated in reading the history of *Henry the Fifth*, yet no man takes his book for the field of Agincourt. A dramatic exhibition is a book recited with concomitants that increase or diminish its effect. Familiar comedy is often more powerful in the theatre, than on the page; imperial tragedy is always less. The humour of Petruchio may be heightened by grimace; but what voice or what gesture can hope to add dignity or force to the soliloquy of Cato?

A play read, affects the mind like a play acted. It is therefore evident, that the action is not supposed to be real, and it follows that between the acts a longer or shorter time may be allowed to pass, and that no more account of space or duration is to be taken by the auditor of a drama, than by the reader of a narrative, before whom may pass in an hour the life of a hero, or the revolutions of an empire.

Whether Shakespeare knew the unities, and rejected them by design, or deviated from them by happy ignorance, it is, I think, impossible to decide, and useless to inquire. We may reason-

[7]Fever. [Ed.]

ably suppose, that, when he rose to notice, he did not want the counsels and admonitions of scholars and critics, and that he at last deliberately persisted in a practice, which he might have begun by chance. As nothing is essential to the fable, but unity of action, and as the unities of time and place arise evidently from false assumptions, and, by circumscribing the extent of the drama, lessen its variety, I cannot think it much to be lamented, that they were not known by him, or not observed: nor, if such another poet could arise, should I very vehemently reproach him, that his first act passed at Venice, and his next in Cyprus. Such violations of rules merely positive, become the comprehensive genius of Shakespeare, and such censures are suitable to the minute and slender criticism of Voltaire:

> Non usque adeo permiscuit imis
> Longus summa dies, ut non, si voce Metelli
> Serventur leges, malint a Cæsare tolli.[8]

Yet when I speak thus slightly of dramatic rules, I cannot but recollect how much wit and learning may be produced against me; before such authorities I am afraid to stand, not that I think the present question one of those that are to be decided by mere authority, but because it is to be suspected, that these precepts have not been so easily received but for better reasons than I have yet been able to find. The result of my inquiries, in which it would be ludicrous to boast of impartiality, is, that the unities of time and place are not essential to a just drama, that though they may sometimes conduce to pleasure, they are always to be sacrificed to the nobler beauties of variety and instruction; and that a play, written with nice observation of critical rules, is to be contemplated as an elaborate curiosity, as the product of superfluous and ostentatious art, by which is shown, rather what is possible, than what is necessary.

He that, without diminution of any other excellence, shall preserve all the unities unbroken, deserves the like applause with the architect, who shall display all the orders of architecture in a citadel, without any deduction from its strength; but the principal beauty of a citadel is to exclude the enemy; and the greatest graces of a play, are to copy nature and instruct life.

Perhaps, what I have here not dogmatically but deliberately written, may recall the principles of the drama to a new examination. I am almost frightened at my own temerity; and when I estimate the fame and the strength of those that maintain the contrary opinion, am ready to sink down in reverential silence; as Æneas withdrew from the defence of Troy, when he saw Neptune shaking the wall, and Juno heading the besiegers.[9]

Those whom my arguments cannot persuade to give their approbation to the judgement of Shakespeare, will easily, if they consider the condition of his life, make some allowance for his ignorance.

Every man's performances, to be rightly estimated, must be compared with the state of the age in which he lived, and with his own particular opportunities; and though to the reader a book be not worse or better for the circumstances of the author, yet as there is always a silent reference of human works to human abilities, and as the inquiry, how far man may extend his designs, or how high he may rate his native force, is of far greater dignity than in what rank we shall place any particular performance, curiosity is always busy to discover the instruments, as well as to survey the workmanship, to know how much is to be ascribed to original powers, and how much to casual and adventitious help. The palaces of Peru or Mexico were certainly mean and incommodious habitations, if compared to the houses of European monarchs; yet who could forbear to view them with astonishment, who remembered that they were built without the use of iron?

The English nation, in the time of Shakespeare, was yet struggling to emerge from barbarity. The philology of Italy had been transplanted hither in the reign of Henry the Eighth; and the learned languages had been successfully cultivated by Lilly, Linacre and More; by Pole,

[8]"So long a time has not passed that the laws themselves would not prefer to be broken by Caesar than supported by Metellus." Lucan, *Pharsalia* 3:138–40. [Ed.]

[9]Virgil, *Aeneid* 2:610–15. [Ed.]

Cheke, and Gardiner; and afterwards by Smith, Clerk, Haddon, and Ascham.[10] Greek was now taught to boys in the principal schools; and those who united elegance with learning, read, with great diligence, the Italian and Spanish poets. But literature was yet confined to professed scholars, or to men and women of high rank. The public was gross and dark; and to be able to read and write, was an accomplishment still valued for its rarity.

Nations, like individuals, have their infancy. A people newly awakened to literary curiosity, being yet unacquainted with the true state of things, knows not how to judge of that which is proposed as its resemblance. Whatever is remote from common appearance is always welcome to vulgar, as to childish credulity; and of a country unenlightened by learning, the whole people is the vulgar. The study of those who then aspired to plebeian learning was laid out upon adventures, giants, dragons, and enchantments. *The Death of Arthur*[11] was the favourite volume.

The mind, which has feasted on the luxurious wonders of fiction, has no taste of the insipidity of truth. A play which imitated only the common occurrences of the world, would upon the admirers of *Palmerin* and *Guy of Warwick*, have made little impression; he that wrote for such an audience was under the necessity of looking round for strange events and fabulous transactions, and that incredibility, by which maturer knowledge is offended, was the chief recommendation of writings, to unskilful curiosity.

Our author's plots are generally borrowed from novels, and it is reasonable to suppose, that he chose the most popular, such as were read by many, and related by more; for his audience could not have followed him through the intricacies of the drama, had they not held the thread of the story in their hands.

The stories, which we now find only in remoter authors, were in his time accessible and familiar. The fable of *As You Like It*, which is supposed to be copied from Chaucer's *Gamelyn*,[12] was a little pamphlet of those times; and old Mr. Cibber[13] remembered the tale of *Hamlet* in plain English prose, which the critics have now to seek in *Saxo Grammaticus*.[14]

His English histories he took from English chronicles and English ballads; and as the ancient writers were made known to his countrymen by versions, they supplied him with new subjects; he dilated some of Plutarch's lives into plays, when they had been translated by North.[15]

His plots, whether historical or fabulous, are always crowded with incidents, by which the attention of a rude people was more easily caught than by sentiment or argumentation; and such is the power of the marvellous even over those who despise it, that every man finds his mind more strongly seized by the tragedies of Shakespeare than of any other writer; others please us by particular speeches, but he always makes us anxious for the event, and has perhaps excelled all but Homer in securing the first purpose of a writer, by exciting restless and unquenchable curiosity, and compelling him that reads his work to read it through.

The shows and bustle with which his plays abound, have the same original. As knowledge advances, pleasure passes from the eye to the ear, but returns, as it declines, from the ear to the eye. Those to whom our author's labours were exhibited had more skill in pomps or processions than in poetical language, and perhaps wanted some visible and discriminated events, as comments on the dialogue. He knew how he should most please; and whether his practice is more agreeable to nature, or whether his example has preju-

[10]Johnson's honor roll of Renaissance humanists includes William Lily, the author of a Latin grammar; Thomas Linacre, a Greek scholar; Thomas More, author of *Utopia* and other Latin works; Reginald Pole and Stephen Gardiner, scholar-statesmen who served Henry VIII and Mary Tudor; Sir John Cheke, who taught Greek at Cambridge; Sir Thomas Smith and Walter Haddon, who taught at Cambridge; John Clerk, who was Wolsey's chaplain; and Roger Ascham, who was tutor to Elizabeth and the author of *Toxophilus*. [Ed.]

[11]Sir Thomas Malory's *Morte D'Arthur*. [Ed.]

[12]A tale once attributed to Chaucer. [Ed.]

[13]Colley Cibber (1671–1757). The book referred to is *History of Hamblet* published in 1608, too late to be the source of Shakespeare's play. [Ed.]

[14]Saxo Grammaticus's *Historia Danica* (1514). [Ed.]

[15]In 1579. [Ed.]

diced the nation, we still find that on our stage something must be done as well as said, and inactive declamation is very coldly heard, however musical or elegant, passionate or sublime.

Voltaire expresses his wonder, that our author's extravagances are endured by a nation, which has seen the tragedy of *Cato*. Let him be answered, that Addison speaks the language of poets, and Shakespeare, of men. We find in *Cato* innumerable beauties which enamour us of its author, but we see nothing that acquaints us with human sentiments or human actions; we place it with the fairest and the noblest progeny which judgement propagates by conjunction with learning, but *Othello* is the vigorous and vivacious offspring of observation impregnated by genius. *Cato* affords a splendid exhibition of artificial and fictitious manners, and delivers just and noble sentiments, in diction easy, elevated and harmonious, but its hopes and fears communicate no vibration to the heart; the composition refers us only to the writer; we pronounce the name of *Cato*, but we think on Addison.

The work of a correct and regular writer is a garden accurately formed and diligently planted, varied with shades, and scented with flowers; the composition of Shakespeare is a forest, in which oaks extend their branches, and pines tower in the air, interspersed sometimes with weeds and brambles, and sometimes giving shelter to myrtles and to roses; filling the eye with awful pomp, and gratifying the mind with endless diversity. Other poets display cabinets of precious rarities, minutely finished, wrought into shape, and polished unto brightness. Shakespeare opens a mine which contains gold and diamonds in unexhaustible plenty, though clouded by incrustations, debased by impurities, and mingled with a mass of meaner minerals.

It has been much disputed, whether Shakespeare owed his excellence to his own native force, or whether he had the common helps of scholastic education, the precepts of critical science, and the examples of ancient authors.

There has always prevailed a tradition, that Shakespeare wanted learning, that he had no regular education, nor much skill in the dead languages. Jonson, his friend, affirms, that "he had small Latin, and no Greek";[16] who, besides that he had no imaginable temptation to falsehood, wrote at a time when the character and acquisitions of Shakespeare were known to multitudes. His evidence ought therefore to decide the controversy, unless some testimony of equal force could be opposed.

Some have imagined, that they have discovered deep learning in many imitations of old writers; but the examples which I have known urged, were drawn from books translated in his time; or were such easy coincidences of thought, as will happen to all who consider the same subjects; or such remarks on life or axioms of morality as float in conversation, and are transmitted through the world in proverbial sentences.

I have found it remarked, that, in this important sentence, "Go before, I'll follow," we read a translation of, *I prae, sequar*. I have been told, that when Caliban, after a pleasing dream, says, "I cry'd to sleep again," the author imitates Anacreon, who had, like every other man, the same wish on the same occasion.

There are a few passages which may pass for imitations, but so few, that the exception only confirms the rule; he obtained them from accidental quotations, or by oral communication, and as he used what he had, would have used more if he had obtained it.

The *Comedy of Errors* is confessedly taken from the *Menæchmi* of Plautus; from the only play of Plautus which was then in English.[17] What can be more probable, than that he who copied that, would have copied more; but that those which were not translated were inaccessible?

Whether he knew the modern languages is uncertain. That his plays have some French scenes proves but little; he might easily procure them to be written, and probably, even though he had known the language in the common degree, he could not have written it without assistance. In the story of *Romeo and Juliet* he is observed to have followed the English translation, where it

[16]In the verses prefaced to the First Folio. [Ed.]

[17]The 1595 translation of *Menaechmi* by W. W. probably postdates Shakespeare's *Comedy of Errors*. [Ed.]

deviates from the Italian; but this on the other part proves nothing against his knowledge of the original. He was to copy, not what he knew himself, but what was known to his audience.

It is most likely that he had learned Latin sufficiently to make him acquainted with construction, but that he never advanced to an easy perusal of the Roman authors. Concerning his skill in modern languages, I can find no sufficient ground of determination; but as no imitations of French or Italian authors have been discovered, though the Italian poetry was then high in esteem, I am inclined to believe, that he read little more than English, and chose for his fables only such tales as he found translated.

That much knowledge is scattered over his works is very justly observed by Pope, but it is often such knowledge as books did not supply. He that will understand Shakespeare, must not be content to study him in the closet, he must look for his meaning sometimes among the sports of the field, and sometimes among the manufactures of the shop.

There is however proof enough that he was a very diligent reader, nor was our language then so indigent of books, but that he might very liberally indulge his curiosity without excursion into foreign literature. Many of the Roman authors were translated, and some of the Greek; the reformation had filled the kingdom with theological learning; most of the topics of human disquisition had found English writers; and poetry had been cultivated, not only with diligence, but success. This was a stock of knowledge sufficient for a mind so capable of appropriating and improving it.

But the greater part of his excellence was the product of his own genius. He found the English stage in a state of the utmost rudeness; no essays either in tragedy or comedy had appeared, from which it could be discovered to what degree of delight either one or other might be carried. Neither character nor dialogue were yet understood. Shakespeare may be truly said to have introduced them both amongst us, and in some of his happier scenes to have carried them both to the utmost height.

By what gradations of improvement he proceeded, is not easily known; for the chronology of his works is yet unsettled. Rowe is of opinion, that

> perhaps we are not to look for his beginning, like those of other writers, in his least perfect works; art had so little, and nature so large a share in what he did, that for ought I know, [says he] the performances of his youth, as they were the most vigorous, were the best.[18]

But the power of nature is only the power of using to any certain purpose the materials which diligence procures, or opportunity supplies. Nature gives no man knowledge, and when images are collected by study and experience, can only assist in combining or applying them. Shakespeare, however favoured by nature, could impart only what he had learned; and as he must increase his ideas, like other mortals, by gradual acquisition, he, like them, grew wiser as he grew older, could display life better, as he knew it more, and instruct with more efficacy, as he was himself more amply instructed.

There is a vigilance of observation and accuracy of distinction which books and precepts cannot confer; from this almost all original and native excellence proceeds. Shakespeare must have looked upon mankind with perspicacity, in the highest degree curious and attentive. Other writers borrow their characters from preceding writers, and diversify them only by the accidental appendages of present manners; the dress is a little varied, but the body is the same. Our author had both matter and form to provide; for except the characters of Chaucer, to whom I think he is not much indebted, there were no writers in English, and perhaps not many in other modern languages, which showed life in its native colours.

The contest about the original benevolence or malignity of man had not yet commenced. Speculation had not yet attempted to analyse the mind, to trace the passions to their sources, to unfold the seminal principles of vice and virtue, or sound the depths of the heart for the motives of action. All those inquiries, which from that time that human nature became the fashionable study, have been made sometimes with nice discern-

[18]Nicholas Rowe, *Some Account of the Life &c of Mr. William Shakespeare* (1709). [Ed.]

ment, but often with idle sublety, were yet unattempted. The tales, with which the infancy of learning was satisfied, exhibited only the superficial appearances of action, related the events but omitted the causes, and were formed for such as delighted in wonders rather than in truth. Mankind was not then to be studied in the closet; he that would know the world, was under the necessity of gleaning his own remarks, by mingling as he could in its business and amusements.

Boyle congratulated himself upon his high birth, because it favoured his curiosity, by facilitating his access. Shakespeare had no such advantage; he came to London a needy adventurer, and lived for a time by very mean employments. Many works of genius and learning have been performed in states of life, that appear very little favourable to thought or to inquiry; so many, that he who considers them is inclined to think that he sees enterprise and perseverance predominating over all external agency, and bidding help and hindrance vanish before them. The genius of Shakespeare was not to be depressed by the weight of poverty, not limited by the narrow conversation to which men in want are inevitably condemned; the incumbrances of his fortune were shaken from his mind, "as dewdrops from a lion's mane."[19]

Though he had so many difficulties to encounter, and so little assistance to surmount them, he has been able to obtain an exact knowledge of many modes of life, and many casts of native dispositions; to vary them with great multiplicity; to mark them by nice distinctions; and to show them in full view by proper combinations. In this part of his performances he had none to imitate, but has himself been imitated by all succeeding writers; and it may be doubted, whether from all his successors more maxims of theoretical knowledge, or more rules of practical prudence, can be collected, than he alone has given to his country.

Nor was his attention confined to the actions of men; he was an exact surveyor of the inanimate world; his descriptions have always some peculiarities, gathered by contemplating things as they really exist. It may be observed, that the oldest poets of many nations preserve their reputation, and that the following generations of wit, after a short celebrity, sink into oblivion. The first, whoever they be, must take their sentiments and descriptions immediately from knowledge; the resemblance is therefore just, their descriptions are verified by every eye, and their sentiments acknowledged by every breast. Those whom their fame invites to the same studies, copy partly them, and partly nature, till the books of one age gain such authority, as to stand in the place of nature to another, and imitation, always deviating a little, becomes at last capricious and casual. Shakespeare, whether life or nature be his subject, shows plainly, that he has seen with his own eyes; he gives the image which he receives, not weakened or distorted by the intervention of any other mind; the ignorant feel his representations to be just, and the learned see that they are complete.

Perhaps it would not be easy to find any author, except Homer, who invented so much as Shakespeare, who so much advanced the studies which he cultivated, or effused so much novelty upon his age or country. The form, the characters, the language, and the shows of the English drama are his. He seems, says Dennis,

> to have been the very original of our *English* tragical harmony, that is, the harmony of blank verse, diversified often by dissyllable and trissyllable terminations. For the diversity distinguishes it from heroic harmony, and by bringing it nearer to common use makes it more proper to gain attention, and more fit for action and dialogue. Such verse we make when we are writing prose; we make such verse in common conversation.[20]

I know not whether this praise is rigorously just. The dissyllable termination, which the critic rightly appropriates to the drama, is to be found, though, I think, not in *Gorboduc* which is confessedly before our author; yet in *Hieronimo*,[21] of which the date is not certain, but which there is reason to believe at least as old as his earliest plays. This however is certain, that he is the first who taught either tragedy or comedy to please,

[19]*Troilus and Cressida,* III.iii.224. [Ed.]

[20]In *Essay on the Genius and Writings of Shakespeare,* II:4–5. [Ed.]

[21]Thomas Kyd's *Spanish Tragedy* (1592). [Ed.]

there being no theatrical piece of any older writer, of which the name is known, except to antiquaries and collectors of books, which are sought because they are scarce, and would not have been scarce, had they been much esteemed.

To him we must ascribe the praise, unless Spenser may divide it with him, of having first discovered to how much smoothness and harmony the English language could be softened. He has speeches, perhaps sometimes scenes, which have all the delicacy of Rowe, without his effeminacy. He endeavours indeed commonly to strike by the force and vigour of his dialogue, but he never executes his purpose better, than when he tries to soothe by softness.

Yet it must be at last confessed that as we owe every thing to him, he owes something to us; that, if much of his praise is paid by perception and judgement, much is likewise given by custom and veneration. We fix our eyes upon his graces, and turn them from his deformities, and endure in him what we should in another loathe or despise. If we endured without praising, respect for the father of our drama might excuse us; but I have seen, in the book of some modern critic, a collection of anomalies, which show that he has corrupted language by every mode of depravation, but which his admirer has accumulated as a monument of honour.

He has scenes of undoubted and perpetual excellence, but perhaps not one play, which, if it were now exhibited as the work of a contemporary writer, would be heard to the conclusion. I am indeed far from thinking, that his works were wrought to his own ideas of perfection; when they were such as would satisfy the audience, they satisfied the writer. It is seldom that authors, though more studious of fame than Shakespeare, rise much above the standard of their own age; to add a little to what is best will always be sufficient for present praise, and those who find themselves exalted into fame, are willing to credit their encomiasts, and to spare the labour of contending with themselves.

It does not appear, that Shakespeare thought his works worthy of posterity, that he levied any ideal tribute upon future times, or had any further prospect, than of present popularity and present profit. When his plays had been acted, his hope was at an end; he solicited no addition of honour from the reader. He therefore made no scruple to repeat the same jests in many dialogues, or to entangle different plots by the same knot of perplexity, which may be at least forgiven him, by those who recollect, that of Congreve's four comedies, two are concluded by a marriage in a mask, by a deception, which perhaps never happened, and which, whether likely or not, he did not invent.[22]

So careless was this great poet of future fame, that, though he retired to ease and plenty, while he was yet little "declined into the vale of years,"[23] before he could be disgusted with fatigue, or disabled by infirmity, he made no collection of his works, nor desired to rescue those that had been already published from the depravations that obscured them, or secure to the rest a better destiny, by giving them to the world in their genuine state.

[22]*The Old Bachelor* and *Love for Love*. [Ed.]
[23]*Othello*, III.iii.269–70. [Ed.]

David Hume

1711–1776

David Hume was one of the major figures of the Scottish Enlightenment, a group of skeptical, empiricist thinkers that also included the economist Adam Smith and the political philosophers Adam Ferguson and Francis Hutcheson. Hume's earliest work, the *Treatise of Human Nature* (1739), upon its appearance, as Hume put it, "fell dead-born from the press." It is, however, the centerpiece of all the philosopher's thought: His more successful later works, the *Enquiry Concerning Human Understanding* (1748), the *Enquiry Concerning the Principles of Morals* (1752), and his political essays all find their origin here.

Hume's last published work, the posthumous *Dialogues on Natural Religion* (1779), was a brilliantly ironic dramatic performance in which the skeptical Philo — a character identifiable with Hume himself — defeats two opponents, one propounding the mysteries of revealed religion, the other a deistical "natural religion" of the sort found in Pope's *Essay on Man*. In his private life, Hume was an infidel and an atheist. James Boswell, Samuel Johnson's biographer, was present at Hume's death, and he reports that the philosopher died calmly and quietly without any belief in God or in the comforts of religion. This was something remarkable in his time: When the pious Johnson heard Boswell tell of this, he scoffed and refused to believe it.

Hume wrote few essays on the principles of art and aesthetics, except where they intersected his central interest in the workings of the human mind. The essay *Of the Standard of Taste* (published in 1757 as part of *Four Dissertations*) is an attempt to refine the century's growing interest in the psychology of the audience's response to literature and the other arts. (This is Horatian rhetorical criticism stood on its head: Instead of discussing the qualities poems should have, given the characteristics of an audience, the aestheticians of taste discuss the qualities that readers should possess, given a body of classic literature.) Hume, in other words, is interested in the same issue as Pope in his *Essay on Criticism:* What makes a good reader? But where Pope simply assumes that one reader or critic's assessment of a work of art can be rationally said to be better than another's, Hume subjects such questions to strict philosophical scrutiny.

The first twelve paragraphs of Hume's essay are written in his most subtle style and repay close examination. Hume begins by separating "taste" from "opinion." We hold opinions upon matters of fact; we have taste with regard to the arts. Furthermore, when we differ in our opinions, it is likely to be over generalities rather than particulars. (For example, two people might disagree over whether the United States ought to be called a democracy or a republic, though they might agree entirely about how laws are made and carried out.) When our sentiments differ on a matter of taste, however, according to Hume we tend to agree on the generalities but disagree over how to apply them. We will agree, for example, that elegance is a virtue in writing and coldness a fault; but the work you are damning for its chilliness of spirit, I may be applauding for its elegant form.

So far, so good. But now Hume embarks upon what looks like a digression into moral questions. "Those who found morality on sentiment more than on reason" (and Hume is one of these) tend to link up ethics with aesthetics here as an area in which we agree on our general principles but disagree on particular cases. We may agree that courage is a virtue and that rashness and cowardice are vices, but whether an individual act was courageous or rash may depend on who is doing the labeling.

The purpose of the digression becomes clear in the sixth paragraph: "It is natural for us to seek a standard of taste; a rule by which the various sentiments of men may be reconciled. . . ." In the field of ethics the need for a standard is obvious; indeed, societies set up massive institutions, courts of law and equity, to make sure that there is a clear standard of conduct, to reconcile our moral sentiments or, at least, to decide in favor of one sentiment and against another. And so it must be in aesthetics: We would seek a standard of taste — if such a standard is possible.

But *is* it possible? We all know the proverb *de gustibus non est disputandum:* there is no disputing about tastes. The argument for this position, which Hume endeavors to refute, runs as follows. Opinions and judgments are objective: They refer to something outside themselves and can thus be proven right or wrong. If a person looks at a painting and guesses that it measures three feet by five, we can take a tape measure and discover whether the guess is right or wrong. But sentiments are different. A sentiment is subjective: It states a relation between the perceiving subject and an object outside. The relation exists in the human consciousness, and we cannot second-guess it from outside. If a man looks at a painting and experiences it as beautiful, he cannot be wrong. If another man looks at the same painting and experiences it as ugly, he too is right. Beauty, as the saying goes, lies in the eye of the beholder. If the beholders disagree, there exists no intersubjective standard that can mediate between them, no standard of taste.

The obvious way out of this would be to deny that beauty is merely subjective. If beauty were a quality within things themselves, then it would be possible in principle to compare two works of art objectively. (Plato, for instance, takes Beauty to be an Idea in which any work of art or nature participates to greater or lesser extent. For Plato there is clearly an objective standard of taste.) But Hume has already foreclosed this escape by claiming that sentiments of taste are essentially different from opinions on matters of fact. Any standard of taste will have to be a subjective standard.

Hume's first step toward such a solution is to point out that wide and varied as our disagreements on taste are, they are not so wide as they look. We may differ as to whether Shakespeare or Milton is the greater poet, but we don't differ over whether Shakespeare's sonnets are greater than the jingles in greeting cards. We may differ as to whether Rembrandt is greater than Michelangelo, yet we don't differ over whether a Rembrandt is more beautiful than a lump of mud. When two geniuses are at nearly the same level, we find it difficult to adjudicate their respective claims; if anybody defended the superiority of the greeting-card lyric or the lump of mud, we would assume he or she was either not being serious or not to be taken seriously. But to do this is to assume the existence of a standard of taste that is capable of making at least the coarsest of judgments.

Hume also appeals to the existence of rules of art. Whatever their value, such rules are not provable a priori, like a mathematical theorem. They are empirical rules, codifications of the "experience and . . . observation of the common sentiments of human nature." We cannot deny that such common sentiments exist; otherwise, how would we account for the way classic works of art have moved humanity from generation to generation? But the key point is that such "common sentiments" exist because there is a definable "human nature." Humankind, despite our wide variation, is cut to a pattern, and so a norm can be defined. There are thus "general principles of approbation and blame" deriving from the "operations of the mind. Some particular forms or qualities, from the original structures of the internal fabric [of the brain], are calculated to please, and others displease; and if they fail of their effect in any particular instance, it is from some apparent defect or imperfection in the organ."

In effect Hume's aesthetic norm is like the norm of human vision. The norm is a standard of perfection for the organism, but it is not the average: Most of us do not have 20/20 vision, and most of us do not possess the standard of taste. And just as we would defer, in our attempts to read a distant sign, to someone with better vision, we should defer in our sentiments to those closer to the standard of taste.

From the thirteenth through the twenty-second paragraph, Hume attempts to define the qualities that the man of taste needs and the corresponding defects that keep most of us from attaining perfect aesthetic vision. He concludes that the man who combines exquisite sensitivity with freedom from prejudice, long experience, the habit of comparison, and massive good sense is the rare character who will embody the standard of taste.

But how does one find such a character and how does one tell a true claimant to the standard of taste from an imposter? We would seem to be back in the same skeptical swamp where we started. But though problems still remain, we have in fact advanced in some real way. For the issue of whether A or B is in accord with the existing standard of taste is now a factual question, not one of judgment. And critic X can be compared with critic Y in terms of the five qualities that Hume finds make good readers. For instance, a sensitive reader will see subtleties in a poem that a less sensitive reader will ignore unless they are pointed out. And experience, freedom from prejudice, and general good sense are reasonably objectifiable qualities. Good critics, like good artists, make themselves known to us by appealing to what is best in our common human nature.

The penultimate section of Hume's essay suggests areas where the writ of the standard fails to run, places where the differing sentiments of men may *not* be reconcilable. One area is the generation gap. As Hume says, "At twenty, Ovid may be the favorite author; Horace at forty; and perhaps Tacitus at fifty." A second moot area is nationality. Though they may understand the nature of his greatness, few Americans can take the unaffected pleasure in reading Racine that the French can — nor do the French ever seem to comprehend what the English-speaking world sees in Shakespeare.

The final question Hume takes up is that of the factors by which the passage of time alters our perspectives on literature. Some changes, like advances in science or a shift in the dominant religion, cause no problems. We take no less pleasure in Homer because his scientific ideas have been superseded or because his characters worship pagan gods. On the other hand, changes in morality from his time to ours may be problematic. The brutality of Achilles and the casual way Odysseus breaks his oaths for personal advantage may affront our modern sensibilities — and Hume thinks we would not be wrong to be upset. The other manifestation that can upset the otherwise tolerant Hume is religious superstition; he objects to Catholic propaganda in Racine and Corneille, and even more to the easy mixture of the religious and the secular in medieval authors like Boccaccio and Petrarch. These are not the most important sections of *The Standard of Taste* but it is interesting to see what made Hume the infidel wince.

Selected Bibliography

Brunet, Olivier. *Philosophie et esthetique chez David Hume*. Paris: A.-G. Nizet, 1965.

Brunius, Teddy. *David Hume on Criticism*. Stockholm: Almqvist and Wiksell, 1952.

Mall, Ram Adhar. *Naturalism and Criticism*. The Hague: Nijhoff, 1975.

Mossner, E. C. *The Life of David Hume*. Edinburgh: Nelson, 1954.

Murphy, Richard T. *Hume and Husserl: Towards Radical Subjectivism*. The Hague and Boston: M. Nijhoff, 1980.

Smith, N. K. *The Philosophy of David Hume*. London: Macmillan, 1941.

Wilbanks, Jan. *Hume's Theory of Imagination*. The Hague: Mouton, 1968.

Of the Standard of Taste

The great variety of taste, as well as of opinion, which prevails in the world, is too obvious not to have fallen under everyone's observation. Men of the most confined knowledge are able to remark a difference of taste in the narrow circle of their acquaintance, even where the persons have been educated under the same government, and have early imbibed the same prejudices. But those, who can enlarge their view to contemplate distant nations and remote ages, are still more surprised at the great inconsistence and contrariety. We are apt to call barbarous whatever departs widely from our own taste and apprehension: but soon find the epithet of reproach retorted on us. And the highest arrogance and self-conceit is at last startled, on observing an equal assurance on all sides, and scruples, amidst such a contest of sentiment, to pronounce positively in its own favor.

As this variety of taste is obvious to the most careless inquirer; so will it be found, on examination, to be still greater in reality than in appearance. The sentiments of men often differ with regard to beauty and deformity of all kinds, even while their general discourse is the same. There are certain terms in every language, which import blame, and others praise; and all men, who use the same tongue, must agree in their application of them. Every voice is united in applauding elegance, propriety, simplicity, spirit in writing; and in blaming fustian, affectation, coldness, and a false brilliancy: but when critics come to particulars, this seeming unanimity vanishes; and it is found, that they had affixed a very different meaning to their expressions. In all matters of opinion and science, the case is opposite: The difference among men is there oftener found to lie in generals than in particulars; and to be less in reality than in appearance. An explanation of the terms commonly ends the controversy; and the disputants are surprised to find, that they had been quarreling, while at bottom they agreed in their judgment.

Those who found morality on sentiment, more than on reason are inclined to comprehend ethics under the former observation, and to maintain, that, in all questions, which regard conduct and manners, the difference among men is really greater than at first sight it appears. It is indeed obvious that writers of all nations and all ages concur in applauding justice, humanity, magnanimity, prudence, veracity; and in blaming the opposite qualities. Even poets and other authors, whose compositions are chiefly calculated to please the imagination, are yet found, from Homer down to Fénelon,[1] to inculcate the same moral precepts, and to bestow their applause and blame on the same virtues and vices. This great unanimity is usually ascribed to the influence of plain reason; which, in all these cases, maintains similar sentiments in all men, and prevents those controversies, to which the abstract sciences are so much exposed. So far as the unanimity is real, this account may be admitted as satisfactory: but we must also allow that some part of the seeming harmony in morals may be accounted for from the very nature of language. The word *virtue*, with its equivalent in every tongue, implies praise; as that of *vice* does blame: And no one, without the most obvious and grossest impropriety, could affix reproach to a term, which in general acceptation is understood in a good sense; or bestow applause, where the idiom requires disapprobation. Homer's general precepts, where he delivers any such, will never be controverted; but it is obvious, that, when he draws particular pictures of manners, and represents heroism in Achilles and prudence in Ulysses, he intermixes a much greater degree of ferocity in the former, and of cunning and fraud in the latter, than Fénelon would admit of. The sage Ulysses in the Greek poet seems to delight in lies and fictions, and often employs them without any necessity or even advantage: But his more scrupulous son, in the French epic writer, exposes himself to the most imminent perils, rather than depart from the most exact line of truth and veracity.

The admirers and followers of the Alcoran[2] insist on the excellent moral precepts interspersed throughout that wild and absurd performance. But it is to be supposed, that the Arabic words, which correspond to the English, equity, justice, temperance, meekness, charity, were such as, from the constant use of that tongue, must always be taken in a good sense; and it would have argued the greatest ignorance, not of morals, but of language, to have mentioned them with any epithets, besides those of applause and approbation. But would we know, whether the pretended prophet had really attained a just sentiment of morals? Let us attend to his narration; and we shall soon find, that he bestows praise on such instances of treachery, inhumanity, cruelty, revenge, bigotry, as are utterly incompatible with civilized society. No steady rule of right seems there to be attained to; and every action is blamed or praised, so far only as it is beneficial or hurtful to the true believers.

The merit of delivering true general precepts in ethics is indeed very small. Whoever recommends any moral virtues, really does no more than is implied in the terms themselves. That people, who invented the word *charity*, and used it in a good sense, inculcated more clearly and much more efficaciously, the precept, "be charitable," than any pretended legislator or prophet, who should insert such a maxim in his writings. Of all expressions, those, which, together with their other meaning, imply a degree either of blame or approbation, are the least liable to be perverted or mistaken.

It is natural for us to seek a standard of taste; a rule by which the various sentiments of men may be reconciled; at least, a decision afforded, confirming one sentiment, and condemning another.

There is a species of philosophy, which cuts off all hope of success in such an attempt, and represents the impossibility of ever attaining any standard of taste. The difference, it is said, is very wide between judgment and sentiment. All

[1]François de Salignac de la Mothe Fénelon, who wrote a novel, *Telemaque* (1699) as a continuation of Book 4 of Homer's *Odyssey*. [Ed.]

[2]The Koran. [Ed.]

sentiment is right; because sentiment has a reference to nothing beyond itself, and is always real, wherever a man is conscious of it. But all determinations of the understanding are not right; because they have a reference to something beyond themselves, to wit, real matter of fact; and are not always conformable to that standard. Among a thousand different opinions which different men may entertain of the same subject, there is one, and but one, that is just and true; and the only difficulty is to fix and ascertain it. On the contrary, a thousand different sentiments, excited by the same object, are all right: because no sentiment represents what is really in the object. It only marks a certain conformity or relation between the object and the organs or faculties of the mind; and if that conformity did not really exist, the sentiment could never possibly have being. Beauty is no quality in things themselves: it exists merely in the mind which contemplates them; and each mind perceives a different beauty. One person may even perceive deformity, where another is sensible of beauty; and every individual ought to acquiesce in his own sentiment, without pretending to regulate those of others. To seek the real beauty, or real deformity, is as fruitless an inquiry, as to pretend to ascertain the real sweet or real bitter. According to the disposition of the organs, the same object may be both sweet and bitter; and the proverb has justly determined it to be fruitless to dispute concerning tastes. It is very natural, and even quite necessary, to extend this axiom to mental, as well as bodily taste; and thus common sense, which is so often at variance with philosophy, especially with the skeptical kind, is found, in one instance at least, to agree in pronouncing the same decision.

But though this axiom, by passing into a proverb, seems to have attained the sanction of common sense; there is certainly a species of common sense which opposes it, at least serves to modify and restrain it. Whoever would assert an equality of genius and elegance between Ogilby[3] and Milton, or Bunyan and Addison, would be thought to defend no less an extravagance, than if he had maintained a molehill to be as high as Tenerife,[4] or a pond as extensive as the ocean. Though there may be found persons, who give the preference to the former authors, no one pays attention to such a taste; and we pronounce without scruple the sentiment of these pretended critics to be absurd and ridiculous. The principle of the natural equality of tastes is then totally forgot, and while we admit it on some occasions, where the objects seem near an equality, it appears an extravagant paradox, or rather a palpable absurdity, where objects so disproportioned are compared together.

It is evident that none of the rules of composition are fixed by reasoning *a priori,* or can be esteemed abstract conclusions of the understanding, from comparing those habitudes and relations of ideas, which are eternal and immutable. Their foundation is the same with that of all the practical sciences, experience; nor are they anything but general observations, concerning what has been universally found to please in all countries and in all ages. Many of the beauties of poetry and even of eloquence are founded on falsehood and fiction, on hyperboles, metaphors, and an abuse or perversion of terms from their natural meaning. To check the sallies of the imagination, and to reduce every expression to geometrical truth and exactness, would be the most contrary to the laws of criticism; because it would produce a work, which, by universal experience, has been found the most insipid and disagreeable. But though poetry can never submit to exact truth, it must be confined by rules of art, discovered to the author either by genius or observation. If some negligent or irregular writers have pleased, they have not pleased by their transgressions of rule or order, but in spite of these transgressions: They have possessed other beauties, which were conformable to just criticism; and the force of these beauties has been able to overpower censure, and give the mind a satisfaction superior to

[3]John Ogilby (1600–1676), a Scottish poet who, like Milton, but less successfully, tried his hand at epic. In Hume's day the comparison of Bunyan with Addison was as clear as that of Ogilby with Milton: The former in both pairings was considered a far inferior popular writer. Two hundred years later, Hume's preference for Addison seems less self-explanatory. [Ed.]

[4]A mountain in the Canary Islands. [Ed.]

the disgust arising from the blemishes. Ariosto[5] pleases; but not by his monstrous and improbable fictions, by his bizarre mixture of the serious and comic styles, by the want of coherence in his stories, or by the continual interruptions of his narration. He charms by the force and clearness of his expression, by the readiness and variety of his inventions, and by his natural pictures of the passions, especially those of the gay and amorous kind: And however his faults may diminish our satisfaction, they are not able entirely to destroy it. Did our pleasure really arise from those parts of his poem, which we denominate faults, this would be no objection to criticism in general: It would only be an objection to those particular rules of criticism, which would establish such circumstances to be faults, and would represent them as universally blamable. If they are found to please, they cannot be faults; let the pleasure, which they produce, be ever so unexpected and unaccountable.

But though all the general rules of art are founded only on experience and on the observation of the common sentiments of human nature, we must not imagine, that, on every occasion, the feelings of men will be conformable to these rules. Those finer emotions of the mind are of a very tender and delicate nature, and require the concurrence of many favorable circumstances to make them play with facility and exactness, according to their general and established principles. The least exterior hindrance to such small springs, or the least internal disorder, disturbs their motion, and confounds the operation of the whole machine. When we would make an experiment of this nature, and would try the force of any beauty or deformity, we must choose with care a proper time and place, and bring the fancy to a suitable situation and disposition. A perfect serenity of mind, a recollection of thought, a due attention to the object; if any of these circumstances be wanting, our experiment will be fallacious, and we shall be unable to judge of the catholic and universal beauty. The relation, which nature has placed between the form and the sentiment, will at least be more obscure; and it will require greater accuracy to trace and discern it. We shall be able to ascertain its influence not so much from the operation of each particular beauty, as from the durable admiration, which attends those works, that have survived all the caprices of mode and fashion, all the mistakes of ignorance and envy.

The same Homer, who pleased at Athens and Rome two thousand years ago, is still admired at Paris and at London. All the changes of climate, government, religion, and language, have not been able to obscure his glory. Authority or prejudice may give a temporary vogue to a bad poet or orator; but his reputation will never be durable or general. When his compositions are examined by posterity or by foreigners, the enchantment is dissipated, and his faults appear in their true colors. On the contrary, a real genius, the longer his works endure, and the more wide they are spread, the more sincere is the admiration which he meets with. Envy and jealousy have too much place in a narrow circle; and even familiar acquaintance with his person may diminish the applause due to his performances: but when these obstructions are removed, the beauties, which are naturally fitted to excite agreeable sentiments, immediately display their energy; and while the world endures, they maintain their authority over the minds of men.

It appears then, that, amidst all the variety and caprice of taste, there are certain general principles of approbation or blame, whose influence a careful eye may trace in all operations of the mind. Some particular forms or qualities, from the original structures of the internal fabric, are calculated to please, and others displease; and if they fail of their effect in any particular instance, it is from some apparent defect or imperfection in the organ. A man in a fever would not insist on his palate as able to decide concerning flavors; nor would one, affected with the jaundice, pretend to give a verdict with regard to colors. In each creature, there is a sound and defective state; and the former alone can be supposed to afford us a true standard of taste and sentiment. If, in the sound state of the organ, there be an entire or a considerable uniformity of sentiment among men, we may thence derive an idea of the perfect beauty; in like manner as the appearance of ob-

[5]Ludovico Ariosto was the author of the fanciful epic, *Orlando Furioso* (1516). [Ed.]

jects in daylight, to the eye of a man in health, is denominated their true and real color, even while color is allowed to be merely a phantasm of the senses.

Many and frequent are the defects in the internal organs which prevent or weaken the influence of those general principles, on which depends our sentiment of beauty or deformity. Though some objects, by the structure of the mind, be naturally calculated to give pleasure, it is not to be expected, that in every individual the pleasure will be equally felt. Particular incidents and situations occur, which either throw a false light on the objects, or hinder the true from conveying to the imagination the proper sentiment and perception.

One obvious cause, why many feel not the proper sentiment of beauty, is the want of that delicacy of imagination, which is requisite to convey a sensibility of those finer emotions. This delicacy everyone pretends to: everyone talks of it; and would reduce every kind of taste or sentiment to its standard. But as our intention in this essay is to mingle some light of the understanding with the feeling of sentiment, it will be proper to give a more accurate definition of delicacy, than has hitherto been attempted. And not to draw our philosophy from too profound a source, we shall have recourse to a noted story in *Don Quixote*.

"It is with good reason," says Sancho to the squire with the great nose, "that I pretend to have a judgment in wine: this is a quality hereditary in our family. Two of my kinsmen were once called to give their opinion of a hogshead, which was supposed to be excellent, being old and of a good vintage. One of them tastes it; considers it; and after mature reflection pronounces the wine to be good, were it not for a small taste of leather, which he perceived in it. The other, after using the same precautions, gives also his verdict in favor of the wine; but with the reserve of a taste of iron, which he could easily distinguish. You cannot imagine how much they were both ridiculed for their judgment. But who laughed in the end? On emptying the hogshead, there was found at the bottom, an old key with a leathern thong tied to it."

The great resemblance between mental and bodily taste will easily teach us to apply this story. Though it be certain that beauty and deformity, more than sweet and bitter, are not qualities in objects, but belong entirely to the sentiment, internal or external; it must be allowed, that there are certain qualities in objects, which are fitted by nature to produce those particular feelings. Now as these qualities may be found in a small degree, or may be mixed and confounded with each other, it often happens, that the taste is not affected with such minute qualities, or is not able to distinguish all the particular flavors, amidst the disorder, in which they are presented. Where the organs are so fine, as to allow nothing to escape them; and at the same time so exact as to perceive every ingredient in the composition: this we call delicacy of taste, where we employ these terms in the literal or metaphorical sense. Here then the general rules of beauty are of use; being drawn from established models, and from the observation of what pleases or displeases, when presented singly and in a high degree: and if the same qualities, in a continued composition and in a smaller degree, affect not the organs with a sensible delight or uneasiness, we exclude the person from all pretensions to this delicacy. To produce these general rules or avowed patterns of composition is like finding the key with the leathern thong; which justified the verdict of Sancho's kinsmen, and confounded those pretended judges who had condemned them. Though the hogshead had never been emptied, the taste of the one was still equally delicate, and that of the other equally dull and languid: but it would have been more difficult to have proved the superiority of the former, to the conviction of every bystander. In like manner, though the beauties of writing had never been methodized, or reduced to general principles; though no excellent models had ever been acknowledged; the different degrees of taste would still have subsisted, and the judgment of one man been preferable to that of another; but it would not have been so easy to silence the bad critic, who might always insist upon his particular sentiment, and refuse to submit to his antagonist. But when we show him an avowed principle of art; when we illustrate this principle by examples, whose operation, from his own particular taste, he acknowledges to be conformable to the principle; when we prove, that the same principle may be applied to the present case, where he did not perceive or feel its influence: he must conclude, upon the whole, that the fault lies in himself, and that he wants the delicacy, which is requisite to make him sensible of every beauty and every blemish, in any composition or discourse.

It is acknowledged to be the perfection of every sense or faculty, to perceive with exactness its most minute objects, and allow nothing to escape its notice and observation. The smaller the objects are, which become sensible to the eye, the finer is that organ, and the more elaborate its make and composition. A good palate is not tried by strong flavors; but by a mixture of small ingredients, where we are still sensible of each part, notwithstanding its minuteness and its confusion with the rest. In like manner, a quick and acute perception of beauty and deformity must be the perfection of our mental taste; nor can a man be satisfied with himself while he suspects, that any excellence or blemish in a discourse has passed him unobserved. In this case, the perfection of the man, and the perfection of the sense or feeling, are found to be united. A very delicate palate, on many occasions, may be a great inconvenience both to a man himself and to his friends: but a delicate taste of wit or beauty must always be a desirable quality; because it is the source of all the finest and most innocent enjoyments, of which human nature is susceptible. In this decision the sentiments of all mankind are agreed. Wherever you can ascertain a delicacy of taste, it is sure to meet with approbation; and the best way of ascertaining it is to appeal to those models and principles, which have been established by the uniform consent and experience of nations and ages.

But though there be naturally a wide difference in point of delicacy between one person and another, nothing tends further to increase and improve this talent, than practice in a particular art, and the frequent survey or contemplation of a particular species of beauty. When objects of any kind are first presented to the eye or imagination, the sentiment, which attends them, is obscure and confused; and the mind is, in a great measure, incapable of pronouncing concerning their merits or defects. The taste cannot perceive the several excellences of the performance; much less distinguish the particular character of each excellency, and ascertain its quality and degree. If it pronounce the whole in general to be beautiful or deformed, it is the utmost that can be expected; and even this judgment, a person, so unpracticed, will be apt to deliver with great hesitation and reserve. But allow him to acquire experience in those objects, his feeling becomes more exact and nice: he not only perceives the beauties and defects of each part, but marks the distinguishing species of each quality, and assigns it suitable praise or blame. A clear and distinct sentiment attends him through the whole survey of the objects; and he discerns that very degree and kind of approbation or displeasure, which each part is naturally fitted to produce. The mist dissipates, which seemed formerly to hang over the object: the organ acquires greater perfection in its operations; and can pronounce, without danger of mistake, concerning the merits of every performance. In a word, the same address and dexterity, which practice gives to the execution of any work, is also acquired by the same means, in the judging of it.

So advantageous is practice to the discernment of beauty, that, before we can give judgment on any work of importance, it will even be requisite, that that very individual performance be more than once perused by us, and be surveyed in different lights with attention and deliberation. There is a flutter or hurry of thought which attends the first perusal of any piece, and which confounds the genuine sentiment of beauty. The relation of the parts is not discerned: the true characters of style are little distinguished: the several perfections and defects seem wrapped up in a species of confusion, and present themselves indistinctly to the imagination. Not to mention, that there is a species of beauty, which, as it is florid and superficial, pleases at first; but being found incompatible with a just expression either of reason or passion, soon palls upon the taste, and is then rejected with disdain, at least rated at much lower value.

It is impossible to continue in the practice of contemplating any order of beauty, without being frequently obliged to form comparisons between the several species and degrees of excellence, and estimating their proportion to each other. A man, who has had no opportunity of comparing the different kinds of beauty, is indeed totally unqualified to pronounce an opinion with regard to any object presented to him. By comparison alone we fix the epithets of praise or blame, and learn how to assign the due degree of each. The coarsest daubing contains a certain luster of colors and exactness of imitation, which are so far beauties, and would affect the mind of a peasant or Indian with the highest admiration. The most vulgar ballads are not entirely destitute of harmony or nature; and none but a person, familiarized to superior beauties, would pronounce their numbers harsh, or narration uninteresting. A great inferiority of beauty gives pain to a person conversant in the highest excellence of the kind, and is for that reason pronounced a deformity: as the most finished object, with which we are acquainted, is naturally supposed to have reached the pinnacle of perfection, and to be entitled to the highest applause. One accustomed to see, and examine, and weigh the several performances, admired in different ages and nations, can only rate the merits of a work exhibited to his view, and assign its proper rank among the productions of genius.

But to enable a critic the more fully to execute this undertaking, he must preserve his mind free from all prejudice, and allow nothing to enter into his consideration, but the very object which is submitted to his examination. We may observe, that every work of art, in order to produce its due effect on the mind, must be surveyed in a certain point of view, and cannot be fully relished by persons, whose situation, real or imaginary, is not conformable to that which is required by the performance. An orator addresses himself to a particular audience, and must have a regard to their particular genius, interest, opinions, passions, and prejudices; otherwise he hopes in vain to govern their resolutions, and inflame their affections. Should they even have entertained some prepossessions against him, however unreasonable, he must not overlook this disadvantage; but, before he enters upon the subject, must endeavor to conciliate their affection, and acquire their good graces. A critic of a different age or nation, who should peruse this discourse, must have all these circumstances in his eye, and must place himself in the same situation as the audience, in order to form a true judgment of the oration. In like manner, when any work is addressed to the public, though I should have a friendship or enmity with the author, I must depart from this situation; and considering myself as a man in general, forget, if possible, my individual being and my peculiar circumstances. A person influenced by prejudice, complies not with this condition; but obstinately maintains his natural position, without placing himself in that point of view, which the performance supposes. If the work be addressed to persons of a different age or nation, he makes no allowance for their peculiar views and prejudices; but, full of the manners of his own age and country, rashly condemns what seemed admirable in the eyes of those for whom alone the discourse was calculated. If the work be executed for the public, he never sufficiently enlarges his comprehension, or forgets his interest as a friend or enemy, as a rival or commentator. By this means, his sentiments are perverted; nor have the same beauties and blemishes the same influence upon him, as if he had imposed a proper violence on his imagination, and had forgotten himself for a moment. So far his taste evidently departs from the true standard; and of consequence loses all credit and authority.

It is well known, that in all questions, submitted to the understanding, prejudice is destructive of sound judgment, and perverts all operations of the intellectual faculties; it is no less contrary to good taste; nor has it less influence to corrupt our sentiment of beauty. It belongs to good sense to check its influence in both cases; and in this respect, as well as in many others, reason, if not an essential part of taste, is at least requisite to the operations of this latter faculty. In all the nobler productions of genius, there is a mutual relation and correspondence of parts; nor can either the beauties or blemishes be perceived by him, whose thought is not capacious enough to comprehend all those parts, and compare them with each other, in order to perceive the consistence and uniformity of the whole. Every work of art has also a certain end or purpose, for which it is calculated; and is to be deemed more or less perfect, as it is more or less fitted to attain this end. The object of eloquence is to persuade, of history to instruct, of poetry to please by means of the passions and the imagination. These ends we must carry constantly in our view, when we peruse any performance; and we must be able to judge how far the means employed are adapted to their respective purposes. Besides every kind of composition, even the most poetical, is nothing but a chain of propositions and reasonings; not always, indeed, the justest and most exact, but still plausible and specious, however disguised by the coloring of the imagination. The persons introduced in tragedy and epic poetry, must be represented as reasoning, and thinking, and concluding, and acting, suitably to their character and circumstances; and without judgment, as well as taste and invention, a poet can never hope to succeed in so delicate an undertaking. Not to mention, that the same excellence of faculties which contributes to the improvement of reason, the same clearness of conception, the same exactness of distinction, the same vivacity of apprehension, are essential to the operations of true taste, and are its infallible concomitants. It seldom, or never happens, that a man of sense, who has experience in any art, cannot judge of its beauty; and it is no less rare to meet with a man who has a just taste without a sound understanding.

Thus, though the principles of taste be universal, and, nearly, if not entirely the same in all men; yet few are qualified to give judgment on any work of art, or establish their own sentiment as the standard of beauty. The organs of internal sensation are seldom so perfect as to allow the general principles their full play, and produce a feeling correspondent to those principles. They either labor under some defect, or are vitiated by some disorder; and by that means, excite a sentiment, which may be pronounced erroneous. When the critic has no delicacy, he judges without any distinction, and is only affected by the grosser and more palpable qualities of the object: the finer touches pass unnoticed and disregarded. Where he is not aided by practice, his verdict is attended with confusion and hesitation. Where no comparison has been employed, the most frivolous beauties, such as rather merit the name of defects, are the objects of his admiration. Where he lies under the influence of prejudice, all his natural sentiments are perverted. Where good sense is wanting, he is not qualified to discern the beauties of design and reasoning, which are the highest and most excellent. Under some or other of these imperfections, the generality of men labor; and hence a true judge in the finer arts is observed, even during the most polished ages, to be so rare a character: strong sense, united to delicate sentiment, improved by practice, perfected by comparison, and cleared of all prejudice, can alone entitle critics to this valuable character; and the joint verdict of such, wherever they are to be found, is the true standard of taste and beauty.

But where are such critics to be found? By what marks are they to be known? How distinguish them from pretenders? These questions are embarrassing; and seem to throw us back into the same uncertainty, from which, during the course of this essay, we have endeavored to extricate ourselves.

But if we consider the matter aright, these are questions of fact, not of sentiment. Whether any particular person be endowed with good sense and a delicate imagination, free from prejudice, may often be the subject of dispute, and be liable to great discussion and inquiry: But that such a character is valuable and estimable will be agreed in by all mankind. Where these doubts occur, men can do no more than in other disputable questions, which are submitted to the understanding: they must produce the best arguments, that their invention suggests to them; they must acknowledge a true and decisive standard to exist somewhere, to wit, real existence and matter of fact; and they must have indulgence to such as differ from them in their appeals to this standard. It is sufficient for our present purpose, if we have proved, that the taste of all individuals is not upon an equal footing, and that some men in general, however difficult to be particularly pitched upon, will be acknowledged by universal sentiment to have a preference above others.

But in reality the difficulty of finding, even in particulars, the standard of taste, is not so great as it is represented. Though in speculation, we may readily avow a certain criterion in science and deny it in sentiment, the matter is found in practice to be much more hard to ascertain in the former case than in the latter. Theories of abstract philosophy, systems of profound theology, have prevailed during one age: in a successive period, these have been universally exploded: their absurdity has been detected: other theories and systems have supplied their place, which again gave place to their successors: and nothing has been experienced more liable to the revolutions of chance and fashion than these pretended decisions of science. The case is not the same with beauties of eloquence and poetry. Just expressions of passion and nature are sure, after a little time, to gain public applause, which they maintain forever. Aristotle, and Plato, and Epicurus, and Descartes, may successively yield to each other: but Terence and Virgil maintain a universal, undisputed empire over the minds of men. The abstract philosophy of Cicero has lost its credit: the vehemence of his oratory is still the object of our admiration.

Though men of delicate taste be rare, they are easily to be distinguished in society, by the soundness of their understanding and the superiority of their faculties above the rest of mankind. The ascendant, which they acquire, gives a prevalence to that lively approbation, with which they receive any productions of genius, and renders it generally predominant. Many men, when left to themselves, have but a faint and dubious perception of beauty, who yet are capable of relishing any fine stroke, which is pointed out to them. Every convert to the admiration of the real poet or orator is the cause of some new conversion. And though prejudices may prevail for a time, they never unite in celebrating any rival to the true genius, but yield at last to the force of nature and just sentiment. Thus, though a civilized nation may easily be mistaken in the choice of their admired philosopher, they never have been found long to err, in their affection for a favorite epic or tragic author.

But notwithstanding all our endeavors to fix a standard of taste, and reconcile the discordant apprehensions of men, there still remain two sources of variation, which are not sufficient indeed to confound all the boundaries of beauty and deformity, but will often serve to produce a difference in the degrees of our approbation or blame. The one is the different humors of particular men; the other, the particular manners and opinions of our age and country. The general principles of taste are uniform in human nature: where men vary in their judgments, some defect or perversion in the faculties may commonly be remarked; proceeding either from prejudice, from want of practice, or want of delicacy; and there is just reason for approving one taste, and condemning another. But where there is such a diversity in the internal frame or external situation as is entirely blameless on both sides, and leaves no room to give one the preference above the other; in that case a certain degree of diversity in judgment is unavoidable, and we seek in vain for a standard, by which we can reconcile the contrary sentiments.

A young man, whose passions are warm, will be more sensibly touched with amorous and tender images, than a man more advanced in years, who takes pleasure in wise, philosophical reflections concerning the conduct of life and moderation of the passions. At twenty, Ovid may be the favorite author; Horace at forty; and perhaps Tacitus at fifty. Vainly would we, in such cases, endeavor to enter into the sentiments of others, and divest ourselves of those propensities, which are natural to us. We choose our favorite author as we do our friend, from a conformity of humor and disposition. Mirth or passion, sentiment or reflection; whichever of these most predominates in our temper, it give us a peculiar sympathy with the writer who resembles us.

One person is more pleased with the sublime; another with the tender; a third with raillery. One has a strong sensibility to blemishes, and is extremely studious of correctness: another has a more lively feeling of beauties, and pardons twenty absurdities and defects for one elevated or pathetic stroke. The ear of this man is entirely turned toward conciseness and energy; that man is delighted with a copious, rich, and harmonious expression. Simplicity is affected by one; ornament by another. Comedy, tragedy, satire, odes, have each its partisans, who prefer that particular species of writing to all others. It is plainly an error in a critic, to confine his approbation to one species or style of writing, and condemn all the rest. But it is almost impossible not to feel a predilection for that which suits our particular turn and disposition. Such preferences are innocent and unavoidable, and can never reasonably be the object of dispute, because there is no standard, by which they can be decided.

For a like reason, we are more pleased, in the course of our reading, with pictures and characters, that resemble objects which are found in our own age or country, than with those which describe a different set of customs. It is not without some effort, that we reconcile ourselves to the simplicity of ancient manners, and behold princesses carrying water from the spring, and kings and heroes dressing their own victuals. We may allow in general, that the representation of such manners is no fault in the author, nor deformity in the piece; but we are not so sensibly touched with them. For this reason, comedy is not easily transferred from one age or nation to another. A Frenchman or Englishman is not pleased with the *Andria* of Terence, or *Clitia* of Machiavel; where the fine lady, upon whom all the play turns, never once appears to the spectators, but is always kept behind the scenes, suitably to the reserved humor of the ancient Greeks and modern Italians. A man of learning and reflection can make allowance for these peculiarities of manners; but a common audience can never divest themselves so far of their usual ideas and sentiments, as to relish pictures which in no wise resemble them.

But here there occurs a reflection, which may, perhaps, be useful in examining the celebrated controversy concerning ancient and modern learning; where we often find the one side excusing any seeming absurdity in the ancients from the manners of the age, and the other refusing to admit this excuse, or at least, admitting it only as an apology for the author, not for the performance. In my opinion, the proper boundaries in this subject have seldom been fixed between the contending parties. Where any innocent peculiarities of manners are represented, such as those above mentioned, they ought certainly to be admitted; and a man, who is shocked with them, gives an evident proof of false delicacy and refinement. The poet's monument more durable than brass must fall to the ground like common brick or clay, were men to make no allowance for the continual revolutions of manners and customs, and would admit of nothing but what was suitable to the prevailing fashion. Must we throw aside the pictures of our ancestors, because of their ruffs and farthingales? But where the ideas of morality and decency alter from one age to another, and where vicious manners are described, without being marked with the proper characters of blame and disapprobation; this must be allowed to disfigure the poem, and to be a real deformity. I cannot, nor is it proper I should, enter into such sentiments; and however I may excuse the poet, on account of the manners of his age, I never can relish the composition. The want of humanity and of decency, so conspicuous in the characters drawn by several of the ancient poets, even sometimes by Homer and the Greek tragedians, diminishes considerably the merit of their noble performances, and gives modern authors an advantage over them. We are not interested in the fortunes and sentiments of such rough heroes: we are displeased to find the limits of vice and virtue so much confounded: and whatever indulgence we may give to the writer on account of his prejudices, we cannot prevail on ourselves to enter into his sentiments, or bear an affection to characters, which we plainly discover to be blamable.

The case is not the same with moral principles, as with speculative opinions of any kind. These are in continual flux and revolution. The son embraces a different system from the father. Nay, there scarcely is any man, who can boast of great constance and uniformity in this particular. Whatever speculative errors may be found in the polite writings of any age or country, they detract but little from the value of those compositions. There needs but a certain turn of thought or imagination to make us enter into all the opinions, which then prevailed, and relish the sentiments or conclusions derived from them. But a very violent effort is requisite to change our judgment of manners, and excite sentiments of approbation or blame, love or hatred, different from those to which the mind from long custom has been familiarized. And where a man is confident of the rectitude of that moral standard, by which he judges, he is justly jealous of it, and will not pervert the sentiments of his heart for a moment, in complaisance to any writer whatsoever.

Of all speculative errors, those, which regard religion, are the most excusable in compositions of genius; nor is it ever permitted to judge of the civility or wisdom of any people, or even of single persons, by the grossness or refinement of their theological principles. The same good sense, that directs men in the ordinary occurrences of life, is not harkened to in religious matters, which are supposed to be placed altogether above the cognizance of human reason. On this account, all the absurdities of the pagan system of theology must be overlooked by every critic, who would pretend to form a just notion of ancient poetry; and our posterity, in their turn, must have the same indulgence to their forefathers. No religious principles can ever be imputed as a fault to any poet, while they remain merely principles, and take no such strong possession of his heart, as to lay him under the imputation of bigotry or superstition. Where that happens, they confound the sentiments of morality, and alter the natural boundaries of vice and virtue. They are therefore eternal blemishes, according to the principle above mentioned; nor are the prejudices and false opinions of the age sufficient to justify them.

It is essential to the Roman Catholic religion to inspire a violent hatred of every other worship, and to represent all pagans, Mahometans, and heretics as the objects of divine wrath and vengeance. Such sentiments, though they are in reality very blamable, are considered as virtues by the zealots of that communion, and are represented in their tragedies and epic poems as a kind of divine heroism. This bigotry has disfigured two very fine tragedies of the French theater, *Polyeucte* and *Athalie;*[6] where an intemperate zeal for particular modes of worship is set off with all the pomp imaginable, and forms the predominant character of the heroes. "What is this," says the sublime Joad to Josabet, finding her in discourse with Mathan, the priest of Baal, "does the daughter of David speak to this traitor? Are you not afraid, lest the earth should open and pour forth flames to devour you both? Or lest these holy walls should fall and crush you together? What is his purpose? Why comes that enemy of God hither to poison the air, which we breathe, with his horrid presence?" Such sentiments are received with great applause on the theater of Paris; but at London the spectators would be full as much pleased to hear Achilles tell Agamemnon, that he was a dog in his forehead, and a deer in his heart, or Jupiter threaten Juno with a sound drubbing, if she will not be quiet.

Religious principles are also a blemish in any polite composition, when they rise up to superstition, and intrude themselves into every sentiment, however remote from any connection with religion. It is no excuse for the poet, that the customs of his country had burthened life with so many religious ceremonies and observances, that no part of it was exempt from that yoke. It must forever be ridiculous in Petrarch to compare his mistress Laura, to Jesus Christ. Nor is it less ridiculous in that agreeable libertine, Boccace, very seriously to give thanks to God Almighty and the ladies, for their assistance in defending him against his enemies.

[6]Plays by Corneille and Racine, respectively. The dialogue Hume quotes is from the latter. [Ed.]

Immanuel Kant

1724–1804

It is an irony of the history of philosophy that the most revolutionary thinker of the eighteenth century, an unwitting founder of the romantic movement, should have lived a life whose restriction and regularity were the stuff of legend. Immanuel Kant, son of a saddlemaker, was born and educated in the Prussian seaport of Königsberg, became professor of philosophy at the university, and died without traveling more than forty miles from his birthplace. His self-discipline was so stringent and his routine so invariable that Königsbergers reputedly set their watches by him: He was awakened daily at five A.M., read for two hours, lectured to his students for two hours, wrote for two hours, and then went to a restaurant for his midday meal, where, at the height of his fame, crowds of strangers would gather to see and hear him.

Kant began his career as a scientist rather than a metaphysician (his collected works include treatises on earthquakes and lunar volcanos), and he may have turned to philosophy to determine for himself the boundaries between the physical questions that may result in positive knowledge and the moral and aesthetic questions that can only produce further speculation.

In his *Critique of Pure Reason* (1781), Kant shifted the entire basis of our understanding of perception by showing how the mind, previously considered a passive receptor of objective sense data, instead actively *creates* the sensual world of which we are conscious. But because each mind has essentially the same equipment and performs the same operations, and because these creative operations occur prior to consciousness, we are able — in fact, we are forced — to experience the world of the senses as though it were objectively present. This theory of the mind has had immense influence on critical theory. (See the headnote for Samuel Taylor Coleridge on p. 315 for a fuller discussion of Kant's theory of perception.) In his *Critique of Judgment* (1790), Kant takes a similar tack. Just as the sensual world is the product of our subjective mental processes rather than of objective features, so our judgments of beauty are also subjective. The beauty of a work of art or a natural landscape exists nowhere but in the eye of the beholder. Yet because of their special qualities, aesthetic judgments seem to have an objective character and to reflect universal rather than individual concerns.

Kant has an unenviable reputation as one of the most perversely difficult of philosophers. His language tends to be abstract, it is true, but he proceeds slowly and delights in giving examples. The major problem readers often have with the *Critique of Judgment* involves their misunderstanding of the exact nature of the questions Kant is trying to answer. He is not trying, as Plato might have done, to define the essence of Beauty, since for him, such essences have no meaning. Nor is he concerned, as Aristotle was, to note what features good works of art have in common. His interest is in the mind, not in the object: He is more of a psychologist than a metaphysician. His overriding question might be paraphrased as follows: When a person looks at a flower or listens to a symphony and experiences it as beautiful, what propositions does that moment of aesthetic judgment strictly entail? When someone looks at Velasquez's *Las Meninas* and exclaims in aesthetic delight, what mental experience is implicit in that exclamation? Kant analyzes that mental experience in a vigorous and systematic way, by running it through his list of categories (Quality, Quantity, Relation, Modality).

The first issue is Quality: What sort of mental process underlies the judgment that a work of art or of nature is beautiful? Here Kant distinguishes beauty from two other types of judgments, those of utility and ethical goodness. Something is useful when it is good for an individual (though it may not benefit anybody else); ethically good things — virtuous actions — are universally beneficial, since it is to each person's collective advantage that everyone act justly. But to judge something as beautiful is to approve of it *freely,* without considering individual or collective interests. (Obviously some works of art — like a Frank Lloyd Wright house — can be functional as well as beautiful, but the judgment of beauty, strictly speaking, has nothing to do with function.) Personal satisfaction in a thing of beauty, therefore, is entirely *disinterested.*

The second issue is Quantity. Some judgments we make — that something is *pleasant,* for example — are *singular:* We apply them purely as individuals. Someone might enjoy raspberries but without any sense that others should agree; if a friend says he detests raspberries, a rational reaction is "All the more for me!" Other judgments are *universal:* We apply them as individuals but with a sense that our judgment holds for all humankind. Ethical judgments are universal in this sense. If we are morally outraged at, for example, the Iranian persecution of the Baha'i faith, our judgment is combined with a sense that everyone ought to agree with us. According to Kant, the judgment of taste is *universal,* like moral judgments, not *singular,* like the judgment that something is pleasant; for to judge a thing as beautiful is also to *impute* that judgment implicitly to everyone else. Kant is not saying that aesthetic judgments are *in practice* universal, that everyone in fact agrees about what is and is not beautiful; he knew as well as Hume that human tastes differ enormously. His point is only that the *disinterested* quality of our sense of beauty makes us feel that, since there is nothing peculiar about us or our situation, everyone similarly placed ought to make the same judgment.

The third issue in the judgment of taste has to do with the "relations of purposes" inherent in it, which is the closest Kant comes to talking about the nature of beauty. His contemporaries had proposed that beauty was a matter of simple charm (Winckelmann) or the contemplation of perfection (Wolff). Kant disagreed: For him the central experience in a beautiful object is the form of "purposiveness without purpose" (*Zweckmässigkeit ohne Zweck*). That is, works of art and natural beauty evince relationships of parts to whole or means to end that are *like* artifacts that have purposes. The intricacy of the interaction of themes in a Bach fugue or the pattern of petals in a chrysanthemum is like the patterned intricacy of a precisely tooled machine; but the machine is made to serve another end — an exterior purpose — while the formal purposiveness in the fugue or the flower is an end in itself. However, Kant is never talking about what is objectively *in* the object we find beautiful. He is talking about the psychological experience of judgment and this sense of purposiveness-without-purpose as something that takes hold within us.

Kant's thesis under his final category, Modality, seems to follow from all that has gone before: Taste is an *exemplary* judgment. By this Kant means that our aesthetic feelings do not seem to be merely random; rather, they feel as though they were the *necessary* consequence of a rule, but one we cannot state. Our sense of beauty seems to be formed prior to conceptual knowledge, and its basis seems to be common sense. As a result, there can be (indeed, must be) disagreements about taste. But, as the proverb states, there cannot be *disputations* about taste, since there are no general, a priori principles to which we can rationally appeal.

In the second book, Kant takes up another common topic of late eighteenth-century aesthetics: the differences between the beautiful and the sublime. Consistently, Kant's interest is in psychological processes rather than in realities; he is less concerned to explain what things we consider sublime than to help us understand the motions of the mind when we experience it. Motion is important here, for the sublime is psychologically *dynamic,* while the beautiful is a matter of restful contemplation.

The movement of the mind that constitutes the sublime resembles one or the other of two mental acts: cognition or desire. But herein lies the paradox. We judge something to be sublime precisely when cognition fails — when in looking up into the starry sky, for instance, we experience a height, or depth, or magnitude that defies reason or is beyond our power to comprehend. On the other hand, it may be that the principles of rational desire are overthrown. When we contemplate something horrible and dangerous, like rocky cliffs or a storm at sea, and yet manage to stifle the imaginative desire to flee, we also experience the sublime. This means that the sublime depends on human reason, with its attendant limitations. An angelic or divine mind could experience the beautiful, as Kant defines it, but an omnipotent and omniscient God could not find his own handiwork sublime.

In Section 49, near the end of the *Critique of Judgment,* Kant shifts his interest from the (chiefly) eighteenth-century issue of *taste* to the quintessentially romantic issue of *genius,* from the psychological qualities involved in the reception of beauty to those involved in its creation.[1] His discussion is not developed at great length or in detail, but one can see in it many of the ideas that later German critics, such as Schiller, were to take up and that students of German philosophy, such as Coleridge, were to import into the English tradition.

Here we begin with Kant's presentation of the imagination as the primary mental faculty in genius, and one that is primarily *creative and intuitive* rather than *rational and cognitive*. The imagination indulges in the free play of spirit, breaking the laws that bind rational thought (though it follows laws of its own) and "creating another

[1]Kant here also shifts his attention away from the beauty of nature to that of art. Where Hume's essay on taste had taken the response of the spectator to *art* (especially poetry) as the typical moment of aesthetic judgment, Kant instead presented taste as the response to nature ("flowers," he says, "are typical free beauties"). Perhaps this is because in nature the forms of animals, plants, and landscapes seem clearly ends in themselves and our response to them almost unconditioned by social motives.

nature . . . out of the material that actual nature gives it." Genius consists of the ability to seize and make concrete this free play of spirit and then to embody it in a material that will make it universally communicable. In this final process, the imagination must work unfettered yet somehow under the control of the understanding. This enables the creator to get *outside* the creative process in order to assess the product of the imagination as it would appear to the spirit of another. Artists must therefore be at once creators and consumers: They must approach their creations from the outside, via their faculty of taste, to shape and mold them into proper form.

But on the other side, the consumer of art must also be, potentially, at least, a producer, because the product of the artist's free play is what Kant calls an *aesthetical idea.* Unlike a *rational idea,* an aesthetical idea calls up the faculty of cognition only to defeat it by employing more thought in the representation than we can clearly grasp. To comprehend aesthetical ideas embodied in a poem or painting requires the free play of the listener's or viewer's imagination as well.

In a sense, however, Kant had appealed to this free play of the spirit even in the earlier sections of the *Critique of Judgment* — particularly when he defined beauty as a product of the subjective sense of purposiveness (rational structure) cut loose from purpose itself. How could it be anything but a free play of the mind, untrammeled by the usually utilitarian (or ethical) notions of purpose, that could succeed in thus divorcing form from goal.

Selected Bibliography

Cassirer, H. W. *Commentary on Kant's Critique of Judgment.* London: Methuen, 1938.

Cohen, Ted, and Paul Guyer, eds. *Essays in Kant's Aesthetics.* Chicago: University of Chicago Press, 1982.

Coleman, Francis X. J. *The Harmony of Reason: A Study in Kant's Aesthetics.* Pittsburgh: University of Pittsburgh Press, 1974.

Crawford, Donald W. *Kant's Aesthetic Theory.* Madison: University of Wisconsin Press, 1974.

Guyer, Paul. *Kant and the Claims of Taste.* Cambridge: Harvard University Press, 1979.

Jaspers, Karl. *Kant.* Munich: R. Piper, 1975.

McCloskey, Mary A. *Kant's Aesthetic.* Basingstoke, Hampshire: Macmillan, 1987.

Richardson, Robert Allan. *Aesthetics and Freedom: A Critique of Kant's Analysis of Beauty.* New Haven: Yale University Press, 1969.

Rogerson, Kenneth F. *Kant's Aesthetics: The Roles of Form and Expression.* Lanham, MD: University Press of America, 1986.

Schaper, Eva. *Studies in Kant's Aesthetics.* Edinburgh: University of Edinburgh Press, 1979.

Zimmerman, R. L. "Kant: The Aesthetic Judgment." *Journal of Aesthetics and Art Criticism* 21 (1963): 333–44.

From *Critique of Judgment*

First Book. Analytic of the Beautiful

FIRST MOMENT. OF THE JUDGMENT OF TASTE,[1] ACCORDING TO QUALITY

1. The Judgment of Taste Is Aesthetical

In order to distinguish whether anything is beautiful or not, we refer the representation, not by the understanding to the object for cognition, but by the imagination (perhaps in conjunction with the understanding) to the subject and its feeling of pleasure or pain. The judgment of taste is therefore not a judgment of cognition, and is consequently not logical but aesthetical, by which we understand that whose determining ground can be *no other than subjective*. Every reference of representations, even that of sensations, may be objective (and then it signifies the real element of an empirical representation), save only the reference to the feeling of pleasure and pain, by which nothing in the object is signified, but through which there is a feeling in the subject as it is affected by the representation.

To apprehend a regular, purposive building by means of one's cognitive faculty (whether in a clear or a confused way of representation) is something quite different from being conscious of this representation as connected with the sensation of satisfaction. Here the representation is altogether referred to the subject and to its feeling of life, under the name of the feeling of pleasure or pain. This establishes a quite separate faculty of distinction and of judgment, adding nothing to cognition, but only comparing the given representation in the subject with the whole faculty of representations, of which the mind is conscious in the feeling of its state. Given representations in a judgment can be empirical (consequently, aesthetical); but the judgment which is formed by means of them is logical, provided they are referred in the judgment to the object. Conversely, if the given representations are rational, but are referred in a judgment simply to the subject (to its feeling), the judgment is so far always aesthetical.

2. The Satisfaction Which Determines the Judgment of Taste Is Disinterested

The satisfaction which we combine with the representation of the existence of an object is called "interest." Such satisfaction always has reference to the faculty of desire, either as its determining ground or as necessarily connected with its determining ground. Now when the question is if a thing is beautiful, we do not want to know whether anything depends or can depend on the existence of the thing, either for myself or for anyone else, but how we judge it by mere observation (intuition or reflection). If anyone asks me if I find that palace beautiful which I see before me, I may answer: I do not like things of that kind which are made merely to be stared at. Or I can answer like that Iroquois Sachem, who was pleased in Paris by nothing more than by the cook shops. Or again, after the manner of Rousseau, I may rebuke the vanity of the great who waste the sweat of the people on such superfluous things. In fine, I could easily convince myself that if I found myself on an uninhabited island without the hope of ever again coming among men, and could conjure up just such a splendid building by my mere wish, I should not even give myself the trouble if I had a sufficiently comfortable hut. This may all be admitted and approved, but we are not now talking of this. We wish only to know if this mere representation of the object is accompanied in me with satisfaction, however indifferent I may be as

Translated by J. H. Bernard.

[1]The definition of "taste" which is laid down here is that it is the faculty of judging of the beautiful. But the analysis of judgments of taste must show what is required in order to call an object beautiful. The moments to which this judgment has regard in its reflection I have sought in accordance with the guidance of the logical functions of judgment (for in a judgment of taste a reference to the understanding is always involved). I have considered the moment of quality first because the aesthetical judgment upon the beautiful first pays attention to it. [Au.]

regards the existence of the object of this representation. We easily see that, in saying it is *beautiful* and in showing that I have taste, I am concerned, not with that in which I depend on the existence of the object, but with that which I make out of this representation in myself. Everyone must admit that a judgment about beauty, in which the least interest mingles, is very partial and is not a pure judgment of taste. We must not be in the least prejudiced in favor of the existence of the things, but be quite indifferent in this respect, in order to play the judge in things of taste.

We cannot, however, better elucidate this proposition, which is of capital importance, than by contrasting the pure disinterested[2] satisfaction in judgments of taste with that which is bound up with an interest, especially if we can at the same time be certain that there are no other kinds of interest than those which are to be now specified.

3. *The Satisfaction in the Pleasant Is Bound Up with Interest*

That which pleases the senses in sensation is "pleasant." Here the opportunity presents itself of censuring a very common confusion of the double sense which the word "sensation" can have, and of calling attention to it. All satisfaction (it is said or thought) is itself sensation (of a pleasure). Consequently everything that pleases is pleasant because it pleases (and according to its different degrees or its relations to other pleasant sensations it is *agreeable, lovely, delightful, enjoyable,* etc.). But if this be admitted, then impressions of sense which determine the inclination, fundamental propositions of reason which determine the will, mere reflective forms of intuition which determine the judgment, are quite the same as regards the effect upon the feeling of pleasure. For this would be pleasantness in the sensation of one's state; and since in the end all the operations of our faculties must issue in the practical and unite in it as their goal, we could suppose no other way of estimating things and their worth than that which consists in the gratification that they promise. It is of no consequence at all how this is attained, and since then the choice of means alone could make a difference, men could indeed blame one another for stupidity and indiscretion, but never for baseness and wickedness. For thus they all, each according to his own way of seeing things, seek one goal, that is, gratification.

If a determination of the feeling of pleasure or pain is called sensation, this expression signifies something quite different from what I mean when I call the representation of a thing (by sense, as a receptivity belonging to the cognitive faculty) sensation. For in the latter case the representation is referred to the object, in the former simply to the subject, and is available for no cognition whatever, not even for that by which the subject *cognizes* itself.

In the above elucidation we understand by the word "sensation" an objective representation of sense; and, in order to avoid misinterpretation, we shall call that which must always remain merely subjective and can constitute absolutely no representation of an object by the ordinary term "feeling." The green color of the meadows belongs to *objective* sensation, as a perception of an object of sense; the pleasantness of this belongs to *subjective* sensation by which no object is represented, i.e., to feeling, by which the object is considered as an object of satisfaction (which does not furnish a cognition of it).

Now that a judgment about an object by which I describe it as pleasant expresses an interest in it, is plain from the fact that by sensation it excites a desire for objects of that kind; consequently the satisfaction presupposes, not the mere judgment about it, but the relation of its existence to my state, so far as this is affected by such an object. Hence we do not merely say of the pleasant, *it pleases,* but, *it gratifies.* I give to it no mere assent, but inclination is aroused by it; and in the case of what is pleasant in the most lively fashion there is no judgment at all upon the character of the object, for those persons who always lay themselves out for enjoyment (for that is the word describing intense gratification) would fain dispense with all judgment.

[2]A judgment upon an object of satisfaction may be quite *disinterested,* but yet very *interesting,* i.e., not based upon an interest, but bringing an interest with it; of this kind are all pure moral judgments. Judgments of taste, however, do not in themselves establish any interest. Only in society is it *interesting* to have taste; the reason of this will be shown in the sequel. [Au.]

[good
useful
good in itself

4. The Satisfaction in the Good Is Bound Up with Interest

Whatever by means of reason pleases through the mere concept is *good*. That which pleases only as a means we call *good for something* (the useful), but that which pleases for itself is *good in itself*. In both there is always involved the concept of a purpose, and consequently the relation of reason to the (at least possible) volition, and thus a satisfaction in the *presence* of an object or an action, i.e., some kind of interest.

In order to find anything good, I must always know what sort of a thing the object ought to be, i.e., I must have a concept of it. But there is no need of this to find a thing beautiful. Flowers, free delineations, outlines intertwined with one another without design and called conventional foliage, have no meaning, depend on no definite concept, and yet they please. The satisfaction in the beautiful must depend on the reflection upon an object, leading to any concept (however indefinite), and it is thus distinguished from the pleasant, which rests entirely upon sensation.

It is true, the pleasant seems in many cases to be the same as the good. Thus people are accustomed to say that all gratification (especially if it lasts) is good in itself, which is very much the same as to say that lasting pleasure and the good are the same. But we can soon see that this is merely a confusion of words, for the concepts which properly belong to these expressions can in no way be interchanged. The pleasant, which, as such, represents the object simply in relation to sense, must first be brought by the concept of a purpose under principles of reason, in order to call it good, as an object of the will. But that there is involved a quite different relation to satisfaction in calling that which gratifies at the same time *good* may be seen from the fact that, in the case of the good, the question always is whether it is mediately or immediately good (useful or good in itself); but on the contrary in the case of the pleasant, there can be no question about this at all, for the word always signifies something which pleases immediately. (The same is applicable to what I call beautiful.)

Even in common speech men distinguish the pleasant from the good. Of a dish which stimulates the taste by spices and other condiments we say unhesitatingly that it is pleasant, though it is at the same time admitted not to be good; for though it immediately *delights* the senses, yet mediately, i.e., considered by reason which looks to the after results, it displeases. Even in the judging of health we may notice this distinction. It is immediately pleasant to everyone possessing it (at least negatively, i.e., as the absence of all bodily pains). But in order to say that it is good, it must be considered by reason with reference to purposes, viz., that it is a state which makes us fit for all our business. Finally, in respect of happiness, everyone believes himself entitled to describe the greatest sum of the pleasantness of life (as regards both their number and their duration) as a true, even as the highest, good. However, reason is opposed to this. Pleasantness is enjoyment. And if we were concerned with this alone, it would be foolish to be scrupulous as regards the means which procure it for us, or to care whether it is obtained passively by the bounty of nature or by our own activity and work. But reason can never be persuaded that the existence of a man who merely lives for *enjoyment* (however busy he may be in this point of view) has a worth in itself, even if he at the same time is conducive as a means to the best enjoyment of others and shares in all their gratifications by sympathy. Only what he does, without reference to enjoyment, in full freedom and independently of what nature can procure for him passively, gives an absolute worth to his presence in the world as the existence of a person; and happiness, with the whole abundance of its pleasures, is far from being an unconditioned good.[3]

However, notwithstanding all this difference between the pleasant and the good, they both agree in this that they are always bound up with an interest in their object; so are not only the pleasant (§ 3), and the mediate good (the useful) which is pleasing as a means toward pleasantness

[3]An obligation to enjoyment is a manifest absurdity. Thus the obligation to all actions which have merely enjoyment for their aim can only be a pretended one, however spiritually it may be conceived (or decked out), even if it is a mystical, or so-called heavenly, enjoyment. [Au.]

somewhere, but also that which is good absolutely and in every aspect, viz., moral good, which brings with it the highest interest. For the good is the object of will (i.e., of a faculty of desire determined by reason). But to wish for something and to have a satisfaction in its existence, i.e., to take an interest in it, are identical.

5. Comparison of the Three Specifically Different Kinds of Satisfaction

The pleasant and the good have both a reference to the faculty of desire, and they bring with them, the former a satisfaction pathologically conditioned (by impulses, *stimuli*), the latter a pure practical satisfaction which is determined not merely by the representation of the object but also by the represented connection of the subject with the existence of the object. It is not merely the object that pleases, but also its existence. On the other hand, the judgment of taste is merely *contemplative;* i.e., it is a judgment which, indifferent as regards the existence of an object, compares its character with the feeling of pleasure and pain. But this contemplation itself is not directed to concepts; for the judgment of taste is not a cognitive judgment (either theoretical or practical), and thus is not *based* on concepts, nor has it concepts as its *purpose*.

The pleasant, the beautiful, and the good designate then three different relations of representations to the feeling of pleasure and pain, in reference to which we distinguish from one another objects or methods of representing them. And the expressions corresponding to each, by which we mark our complacency in them, are not the same. That which *gratifies* a man is called *pleasant;* that which merely *pleases* him is *beautiful;* that which is *esteemed* or *approved* by him, i.e., that to which he accords an objective worth, is *good.* Pleasantness concerns irrational animals also, but beauty only concerns men, i.e., animal, but still rational, beings — not merely *qua* rational (e.g., spirits), but *qua* animal also — and the good concerns every rational being in general. This is a proposition which can only be completely established and explained in the sequel. We may say that, of all these three kinds of satisfaction, that of taste in the beautiful is alone a disinterested and *free* satisfaction; for no interest, either of sense or of reason, here forces our assent. Hence we may say of satisfaction that it is related in the three aforesaid cases to *inclination,* to *favor,* or to *respect.* Now *favor* is the only free satisfaction. An object of inclination and one that is proposed to our desire by a law of reason leave us no freedom in forming for ourselves anywhere an object of pleasure. All interest presupposes or generates a want, and, as the determining ground of assent, it leaves the judgment about the object no longer free.

As regards the interest of inclination in the case of the pleasant, everyone says that hunger is the best sauce, and everything that is eatable is relished by people with a healthy appetite; and thus a satisfaction of this sort shows no choice directed by taste. It is only when the want is appeased that we can distinguish which of many men has or has not taste. In the same way there may be manners (conduct) without virtue, politeness without good will, decorum without modesty, etc. For where the moral law speaks there is no longer, objectively, a free choice as regards what is to be done; and to display taste in its fulfillment (or in judging of another's fulfillment of it) is something quite different from manifesting the moral attitude of thought. For this involves a command and generates a want, while moral taste only plays with the objects of satisfaction, without attaching itself to one of them.

Explanation of the Beautiful Resulting from the First Moment

Taste is the faculty of judging of an object or a method of representing it by an *entirely disinterested* satisfaction or dissatisfaction. The object of such satisfaction is called *beautiful.*[4]

[4]Ueberweg points out (*History of Philosophy, II,* 528, English translation) that Mendelssohn had already called attention to the disinterestedness of our satisfaction in the beautiful. "It appears," says Mendelssohn, "to be a particular mark of the beautiful, that it is contemplated with quiet satisfaction, that it pleases, even though it be not in our possession, and even though we be never so far removed from the desire to put it to our use." But, of course, as Ueberweg remarks, Kant's conception of disinterestedness extends far beyond the idea of merely not desiring to possess the object. [Tr.]

SECOND MOMENT. OF THE JUDGMENT OF TASTE, ACCORDING TO QUANTITY

6. The Beautiful Is That Which Apart from Concepts Is Represented as the Object of a Universal Satisfaction

This explanation of the beautiful can be derived from the preceding explanation of it as the object of an entirely disinterested satisfaction. For the fact of which everyone is conscious, that the satisfaction is for him quite disinterested, implies in his judgment a ground of satisfaction for all men. For since it does not rest on any inclination of the subject (nor upon any other premeditated interest), but since the person who judges feels himself quite *free* as regards the satisfaction which he attaches to the object, he cannot find the ground of this satisfaction in any private conditions connected with his own subject, and hence it must be regarded as grounded on what he can presuppose in every other person. Consequently he must believe that he has reason for attributing a similar satisfaction to everyone. He will therefore speak of the beautiful as if beauty were a characteristic of the object and the judgment logical (constituting a cognition of the object by means of concepts of it), although it is only aesthetical and involves merely a reference of the representation of the object to the subject. For it has this similarity to a logical judgment that we can presuppose its validity for all men. But this universality cannot arise from concepts; for from concepts there is no transition to the feeling of pleasure or pain (except in pure practical laws, which bring an interest with them such as is not bound up with the pure judgment of taste). Consequently the judgment of taste, accompanied with the consciousness of separation from all interest, must claim validity for every man, without this universality depending on objects. That is, there must be bound up with it a title to subjective universality.

7. Comparison of the Beautiful with the Pleasant and the Good by Means of the Above Characteristic

As regards the pleasant, everyone is content that his judgment, which he bases upon private feeling and by which he says of an object that it pleases him, should be limited merely to his own person. Thus he is quite contented that if he says, "Canary wine is pleasant," another man may correct his expression and remind him that he ought to say, "It is pleasant *to me*." And this is the case not only as regards the taste of the tongue, the palate, and the throat, but for whatever is pleasant to anyone's eyes and ears. To one, violet color is soft and lovely; to another, it is washed out and dead. One man likes the tone of wind instruments, another that of strings. To strive here with the design of reproving as incorrect another man's judgment which is different from our own, as if the judgments were logically opposed, would be folly. As regards the pleasant, therefore, the fundamental proposition is valid: *Everyone has his own taste* (the taste of sense).

The case is quite different with the beautiful. It would (on the contrary) be laughable if a man who imagined anything to his own taste thought to justify himself by saying: "The object (the house we see, the coat that person wears, the concert we hear, the poem submitted to our judgment) is beautiful *for me*." For he must not call it *beautiful* if it merely pleases him. Many things may have for him charm and pleasantness — no one troubles himself at that — but if he gives out anything as beautiful, he supposes in others the same satisfaction; he judges not merely for himself, but for everyone, and speaks of beauty as if it were a property of things. Hence he says "the *thing* is beautiful"; and he does not count on the agreement of others with this his judgment of satisfaction, because he has found this agreement several times before, but he *demands* it of them. He blames them if they judge otherwise and he denies them taste, which he nevertheless requires from them. Here, then, we cannot say that each man has his own particular taste. For this would be as much as to say that there is no taste whatever, i.e., no aesthetical judgment which can make a rightful claim upon everyone's assent.

At the same time we find as regards the pleasant that there is an agreement among men in their judgments upon it in regard to which we deny taste to some and attribute it to others, by this not meaning one of our organic senses, but a faculty of judging in respect of the pleasant generally. Thus we say of a man who knows how to entertain his guests with pleasures (of enjoyment for all the senses), so that they are all pleased, "he has taste." But here the universality is only taken comparatively; and there emerge rules which are only *general* (like all empirical ones), and not *universal,* which latter the judgment of taste upon the beautiful undertakes or lays claim to. It is a judgment in reference to sociability, so far as this rests on empirical rules. In respect of the good it is true that judgments make rightful claim to validity for everyone; but the good is represented only *by means of a concept* as the object of a universal satisfaction, which is the case neither with the pleasant nor with the beautiful.

8. The Universality of the Satisfaction Is Represented in a Judgment of Taste Only as Subjective

This particular determination of the universality of an aesthetical judgment, which is to be met with in a judgment of taste, is noteworthy, not indeed for the logician, but for the transcendental philosopher. It requires no small trouble to discover its origin, but we thus detect a property of our cognitive faculty which without this analysis would remain unknown.

First, we must be fully convinced of the fact that in a judgment of taste (about the beautiful) the satisfaction in the object is imputed to *everyone,* without being based on a concept (for then it would be the good). Further, this claim to universal validity so essentially belongs to a judgment by which we describe anything as *beautiful* that, if this were not thought in it, it would never come into our thoughts to use the expression at all, but everything which pleases without a concept would be counted as pleasant. In respect of the latter, everyone has his own opinion; and no one assumes in another agreement with his judgment of taste, which is always the case in a judgment of taste about beauty. I may call the first the taste of sense, the second the taste of reflection, so far as the first lays down mere private judgments and the second judgments supposed to be generally valid (public), but in both cases aesthetical (not practical) judgments about an object merely in respect of the relation of its representation to the feeling of pleasure and pain. Now here is something strange. As regards the taste of sense, not only does experience show that its judgment (of pleasure or pain connected with anything) is not valid universally, but everyone is content not to impute agreement with it to others (although actually there is often found a very extended concurrence in these judgments). On the other hand, the taste of reflection has its claim to the universal validity of its judgments (about the beautiful) rejected often enough, as experience teaches, although it may find it possible (as it actually does) to represent judgments which can demand this universal agreement. In fact it imputes this to everyone for each of its judgments of taste, without the persons that judge disputing as to the possibility of such a claim, although in particular cases they cannot agree as to the correct application of this faculty.

Here we must, in the first place, remark that a universality which does not rest on concepts of objects (not even on empirical ones) is not logical but aesthetical; i.e., it involves no objective quantity of the judgment, but only that which is subjective. For this I use the expression *general validity,* which signifies the validity of the reference of a representation, not to the cognitive faculty, but to the feeling of pleasure and pain for every subject. (We can avail ourselves also of the same expression for the logical quantity of the judgment, if only we prefix "objective" to "universal validity," to distinguish it from that which is merely subjective and aesthetical.)

A judgment with *objective universal validity* is also always valid subjectively; i.e., if the judgment holds for everything contained under a given concept, it holds also for everyone who represents an object by means of this concept. But from a *subjective universal validity,* i.e., aesthetical and resting on no concept, we cannot infer that which is logical because that kind of judgment does not extend to the object. But, therefore, the aesthetical universality which is ascribed to a judgment must be of a particular kind, because it does not unite the predicate of beauty with the concept of the object, considered in its whole logical sphere, and yet extends it to the whole sphere of judging persons.

In respect of logical quantity, all judgments of taste are *singular* judgments. For because I must refer the object immediately to my feeling of pleasure and pain, and that not by means of concepts, they cannot have the quantity of objective generally valid judgments. Nevertheless, if the singular representation of the object of the judgment of taste, in accordance with the conditions determining the latter, were transformed by comparison into a concept, a logically universal judgment could result therefrom. E.g., I describe by a judgment of taste the rose that I see as beautiful. But the judgment which results from the comparison of several singular judgments, "Roses in general are beautiful," is no longer described simply as aesthetical, but as a logical judgment based on an aesthetical one. Again the judgment, "The rose is pleasant" (to use) is, although aesthetical and singular, not a judgment of taste but of sense. It is distinguished from the former by the fact that the judgment of taste carries with it an *aesthetic quantity* of universality, i.e., of validity for everyone, which cannot be found in a judgment about the pleasant. It is only judgments about the good which, although they also determine satisfaction in an object, have logical and not merely aesthetical universality, for they are valid of the object as cognitive of it, and thus are valid for everyone.

If we judge objects merely according to concepts, then all representation of beauty is lost. Thus there can be no rule according to which anyone is to be forced to recognize anything as beautiful. We cannot press [upon others] by the aid of any reasons or fundamental propositions our judgment that a coat, a house, or a flower is beautiful. People wish to submit the object to their own eyes, as if the satisfaction in it depended on sensation; and yet, if we then call the object beautiful, we believe that we speak with a universal voice, and we claim the assent of everyone, although on the contrary all private sensation can only decide for the observer himself and his satisfaction.

We may see now that in the judgment of taste nothing is postulated but such a *universal voice,* in respect of the satisfaction without the intervention of concepts, and thus the *possibility* of an aesthetical judgment that can, at the same time, be regarded as valid for everyone. The judgment of taste itself does not *postulate* the agreement of everyone (for that can only be done by a logically universal judgment because it can adduce reasons); it only *imputes* this agreement to everyone, as a case of the rule in respect of which it expects, not confirmation by concepts, but assent from others. The universal voice is, therefore, only an idea (we do not yet inquire upon what it rests). It may be uncertain whether or not the man who believes that he is laying down a judgment of taste is, as a matter of fact, judging in conformity with that idea; but that he refers his judgment thereto, and consequently that it is intended to be a judgment of taste, he announces by the expression "beauty." He can be quite certain of this for himself by the mere consciousness of the separating off everything belonging to the pleasant and the good from the satisfaction which is left; and this is all for which he promises himself the agreement of everyone — a claim which would be justifiable under these conditions, provided only he did not often make mistakes, and thus lay down an erroneous judgment of taste. . . .

Explanation of the Beautiful
Resulting from the Second Moment

The *beautiful* is that which pleases universally without requiring a concept.

THIRD MOMENT. OF JUDGMENTS OF TASTE, ACCORDING TO THE RELATION OF THE PURPOSES WHICH ARE BROUGHT INTO CONSIDERATION IN THEM

10. Of Purposiveness in General

If we wish to explain what a purpose is according to its transcendental determinations (without presupposing anything empirical like the feeling of pleasure), we say that the purpose is the object of a concept, insofar as the concept is regarded as the cause of the object (the real ground of its possibility); and the causality of a *concept* in respect of its *object* is its purposiveness (*forma finalis*). Where then not merely the cognition of an object but the object itself (its form and existence) is thought as an effect only possible by means of the concept of this latter, there we think a purpose. The representation of the effect is here the determining ground of its cause and precedes it. The consciousness of the causality of a representation, for *maintaining* the subject in the same state, may here generally denote what we call pleasure; while on the other hand pain is that representation which contains the ground of the determination of the state of representations into their opposite of restraining or removing them.[5]

The faculty of desire, so far as it is determinable to act only through concepts, i.e., in conformity with the representation of a purpose, would be the will. But an object, or a state of mind, or even an action is called purposive, although its possibility does not necessarily presuppose the representation of a purpose, merely because its possibility can be explained and conceived by us only so far as we assume for its ground a causality according to purposes, i.e., in accordance with a will which has regulated it according to the representation of a certain rule. There can be, then, purposiveness without purpose, so far as we do not place the causes of this form in a will, but yet can only make the explanation of its possibility intelligible to ourselves by deriving it from a will. Again, we are not always forced to regard what we observe (in respect of its possibility) from the point of view of reason. Thus we can at least observe a purposiveness according to form, without basing it on a purpose (as the material of the *nexus finalis*), and remark it in objects, although only by reflection.

11. The Judgment of Taste Has Nothing at Its Basis but the Form of the Purposiveness of an Object (or of Its Mode of Representation)

Every purpose, if it be regarded as a ground of satisfaction, always carries with it an interest — as the determining ground of the judgment — about the object of pleasure. Therefore no subjective purpose can lie at the basis of the judgment of taste. But also the judgment of taste can be determined by no representation of an objective purpose, i.e., of the possibility of the object itself in accordance with principles of purposive combination, and consequently by no concept of the good, because it is an aesthetical and not a cognitive judgment. It therefore has to do with no *concept* of the character and internal or external possibility of the object by means of this or that cause, but merely with the relation of the representative powers to one another, so far as they are determined by a representation.

Now this relation in the determination of an object as beautiful is bound up with the feeling of pleasure, which is declared by the judgment of taste to be valid for everyone; hence a pleasantness merely accompanying the representation can as little contain the determining ground of the judgment as the representation of the perfection of the object and the concept of the good can. Therefore it can be nothing else than the subjective purposiveness in the representation of an object without any purpose (either objective or subjective), and thus it is the mere form of purposiveness in the representation by which an object is *given* to us, so far as we are conscious of it, which constitutes the satisfaction that we without a concept judge to be universally communicable; and, consequently, this is the determining ground of the judgment of taste.

12. The Judgment of Taste Rests on **A Priori** *Grounds*

To establish *a priori* the connection of the feeling of a pleasure or pain as an effect, with any representation whatever (sensation or concept) as its cause, is absolutely impossible, for that would be a particular causal relation which (with objects of experience) can always only be cognized *a posteriori* and through the medium of experience itself. We actually have, indeed, in the *Critique of Practical Reason,* derived from universal moral concepts *a priori* the feeling of respect (as a special and peculiar modification of feeling which will not strictly correspond either to the pleasure or the pain that we get from empirical objects). But there we could go beyond the bounds of experience and call in a causality which rested on a

[5]Mr. Herbert Spencer expresses much more concisely what Kant has in his mind here. "Pleasure . . . is a feeling which we seek to bring into consciousness and retain there; pain is . . . a feeling which we seek to get out of consciousness and to keep out." *Principles of Psychology,* 125. [Tr.]

supersensible attribute of the subject, viz., freedom. And even there, properly speaking, it was not this *feeling* which we derived from the idea of the moral as cause, but merely the determination of the will. But the state of mind which accompanies any determination of the will is in itself a feeling of pleasure and identical with it, and therefore does not follow from it as its effect. This last must only be assumed if the concept of the moral as a good precedes the determination of the will by the law, for in that case the pleasure that is bound up with the concept could not be derived from it as from a mere cognition.

Now the case is similar with the pleasure in aesthetical judgments, only that here it is merely contemplative and does not bring about an interest in the object, while on the other hand in the moral judgment it is practical.[6] The consciousness of the mere formal purposiveness in the play of the subject's cognitive powers, in a representation through which an object is given, is the pleasure itself, because it contains a determining ground of the activity of the subject in respect of the excitement of its cognitive powers, and therefore an inner causality (which is purposive) in respect of cognition in general, without however being limited to any definite cognition, and consequently contains a mere form of the subjective purposiveness of a representation in an aesthetical judgment. This pleasure is in no way practical, neither like that arising from the pathological ground of pleasantness, nor that from the intellectual ground of the presented good. But yet it involves causality, viz., of *maintaining* without further design the state of the representation itself and the occupation of the cognitive powers. We *linger* over the contemplation of the beautiful because this contemplation strengthens and reproduces itself, which is analogous to (though not of the same kind as) that lingering which takes place when a physical charm in the representation of the object repeatedly arouses the attention, the mind being passive. . . .

[6]Cf. *Metaphysic of Morals,* Introduction I. "The pleasure which is necessarily bound up with the desire (of the object whose representation affects feeling) may be called *practical* pleasure, whether it be cause or effect of the desire. On the contrary, the pleasure which is not necessarily bound up with the desire of the object, and which, therefore, is at bottom not a pleasure in the existence of the object of the representation, but clings to the representation only, may be called mere contemplative pleasure or *passive satisfaction.* The feeling of the latter kind of pleasure we call *taste.*" [Tr.]

16. The Judgment of Taste, by Which an Object Is Declared to Be Beautiful Under the Condition of a Definite Concept, Is Not Pure

There are two kinds of beauty: free beauty (*pulchritudo vaga*), or merely dependent beauty (*pulchritudo adhaerens*). The first presupposes no concept of what the object ought to be; the second does presuppose such a concept and the perfection of the object in accordance therewith. The first is called the (self-subsistent) beauty of this or that thing; the second, as dependent upon a concept (conditioned beauty), is ascribed to objects which come under the concept of a particular purpose.

Flowers are free natural beauties. Hardly anyone but a botanist knows what sort of a thing a flower ought to be; and even he, though recognizing in the flower the reproductive organ of the plant, pays no regard to this natural purpose if he is passing judgment on the flower by taste. There is, then, at the basis of this judgment no perfection of any kind, no internal purposiveness, to which the collection of the manifold is referred. Many birds (such as the parrot, the hummingbird, the bird of paradise) and many seashells are beauties in themselves, which do not belong to any object determined in respect of its purpose by concepts, but please freely and in themselves. So also delineations *à la grecque,* foliage for borders or wall papers, mean nothing in themselves; they represent nothing — no object under a definite concept — and are free beauties. We can refer to the same class what are called in music phantasies (i.e., pieces without any theme), and in fact all music without words.

In the judging of a free beauty (according to the mere form), the judgment of taste is pure. There is presupposed no concept of any purpose which the manifold of the given object is to serve, and which therefore is to be represented in it. By such a concept the freedom of the imagination which disports itself in the contemplation of the figure would be only limited.

But human beauty (i.e., of a man, a woman, or a child), the beauty of a horse, or a building (be it church, palace, arsenal, or summer house), presupposes a concept of the purpose which determines what the thing is to be, and consequently a concept of its perfection; it is therefore adherent beauty. Now as the combination of the pleasant (in sensation) with beauty, which properly is only concerned with form, is a hindrance to the purity of the judgment of taste, so also is its purity injured by the combination with beauty of the good (viz., that manifold which is good for the thing itself in accordance with its purpose).

We could add much to a building which would immediately please the eye if only it were not to be a church. We could adorn a figure with all kinds of spirals and light but regular lines, as the New Zealanders do with their tattooing, if only it were not the figure of a human being. And again this could have much finer features and a more pleasing and gentle cast of countenance provided it were not intended to represent a man, much less a warrior.

Now the satisfaction in the manifold of a thing in reference to the internal purpose which determines its possibility is a satisfaction grounded on a concept; but the satisfaction in beauty is such as presupposes no concept, but is immediately bound up with the representation through which the object is given (not through which it is thought). If now the judgment of taste in respect of the beauty of a thing is made dependent on the purpose in its manifold, like a judgment of reason, and thus limited, it is no longer a free and pure judgment of taste.

It is true that taste gains by this combination of aesthetical with intellectual satisfaction, inasmuch as it becomes fixed; and though it is not universal, yet in respect to certain purposively determined objects it becomes possible to prescribe rules for it. These, however, are not rules of taste, but merely rules for the unification of taste with reason, i.e., of the beautiful with the good, by which the former becomes available as an instrument of design in respect of the latter. Thus the tone of mind which is self-maintaining and of subjective universal validity is subordinated to the way of thinking which can be maintained only by painful resolve, but is of objective universal validity. Properly speaking, however, perfection gains nothing by beauty, or beauty by perfection; but when we compare the representation by which an object is given to us with the object (as regards what it ought to be) by means of a concept, we cannot avoid considering along with it the sensation in the subject. And thus when both states of mind are in harmony our *whole faculty* of representative power gains.

A judgment of taste, then, in respect of an object with a definite internal purpose, can only be pure if either the person judging has no concept of this purpose or else abstracts from it in his judgment. Such a person, although forming an accurate judgment of taste in judging of the object as free beauty, would yet by another who considers the beauty in it only as a dependent attribute (who looks to the purpose of the object) be blamed and accused of false taste, although both are right in their own way — the one in reference to what he has before his eyes, the other in reference to what he has in his thought. By means of this distinction we can settle many disputes about beauty between judges of taste, by showing that the one is speaking of free, the other of dependent, beauty — that the first is making a pure, the second an applied, judgment of taste. . . .

Explanation of the Beautiful Derived from This Third Moment

Beauty is the form of the *purposiveness* of an object, so far as this is perceived in it *without any representation of a purpose*.[7]

[7]It might be objected to this explanation that there are things in which we see a purposive form without cognizing any purpose in them, like the stone implements often gotten from old sepulchral tumuli with a hole in them, as if for a handle. These, although they plainly indicate by their shape a purposiveness of which we do not know the purpose, are nevertheless not described as beautiful. But if we regard a thing as a work of art, that is enough to make us admit that its shape has reference to some design and definite purpose. And hence there is no immediate satisfaction in the contemplation of it. On the other hand a flower, e.g., a tulip, is regarded as beautiful, because in perceiving it we find a certain purposiveness which, in our judgment, is referred to no purpose at all. [Au.]

FOURTH MOMENT. OF THE JUDGMENT OF TASTE, ACCORDING TO THE MODALITY OF THE SATISFACTION IN THE OBJECT

18. What the Modality in a Judgment of Taste Is

I can say of every representation that it is at least *possible* that (as a cognition) it should be bound up with a pleasure. Of a representation that I call *pleasant* I say that it *actually* excites pleasure in me. But the *beautiful* we think as having a *necessary* reference to satisfaction. Now this necessity is of a peculiar kind. It is not a theoretical objective necessity, in which case it would be cognized *a priori* that everyone *will feel* this satisfaction in the object called beautiful by me. It is not a practical necessity, in which case, by concepts of a pure rational will serving as a rule for freely acting beings, the satisfaction is the necessary result of an objective law and only indicates that we absolutely (without any further design) ought to act in a certain way. But the necessity which is thought in an aesthetical judgment can only be called exemplary, i.e., a necessity of the assent of *all* to a judgment which is regarded as the example of a universal rule that we cannot state. Since an aesthetical judgment is not an objective cognitive judgment, this necessity cannot be derived from definite concepts and is therefore not apodictic. Still less can it be inferred from the universality of experience (of a complete agreement of judgments as to the beauty of a certain object). For not only would experience hardly furnish sufficiently numerous vouchers for this, but also, on empirical judgments, we can base no concept of the necessity of these judgments.

19. The Subjective Necessity, Which We Ascribe to the Judgment of Taste, Is Conditioned

The judgment of taste requires the agreement of everyone, and he who describes anything as beautiful claims that everyone *ought* to give his approval to the object in question and also describe it as beautiful. The *ought* in the aesthetical judgment is therefore pronounced in accordance with all the data which are required for judging, and yet is only conditioned. We ask for the agreement of everyone else, because we have for it a ground that is common to all; and we could count on this agreement, provided we were always sure that the case was correctly subsumed under that ground as rule of assent.

20. The Condition of Necessity Which a Judgment of Taste Asserts Is the Idea of a Common Sense

If judgments of taste (like cognitive judgments) had a definite objective principle, then the person who lays them down in accordance with this latter would claim an unconditioned necessity for his judgment. If they were devoid of all principle, like those of the mere taste of sense, we would not allow them in thought any necessity whatever. Hence they must have a subjective principle which determines what pleases or displeases only by feeling and not by concepts, but yet with universal validity. But such a principle could only be regarded as a *common sense,* which is essentially different from common understanding which people sometimes call common sense (*sensus communis*); for the latter does not judge by feeling but always by concepts, although ordinarily only as by obscurely represented principles.

Hence it is only under the presupposition that there is a common sense (by which we do not understand an external sense, but the effect resulting from the free play of our cognitive powers) — it is only under this presupposition, I say, that the judgment of taste can be laid down. . . .

Explanation of the Beautiful Resulting from the Fourth Moment

The *beautiful* is that which without any concept is cognized as the object of a *necessary* satisfaction.

GENERAL REMARK ON THE FIRST SECTION OF THE ANALYTIC

If we seek the result of the preceding analysis, we find that everything runs up into this concept of taste — that it is a faculty for judging an object in reference to the imagination's *free conformity to law*. Now, if in the judgment of taste the imagination must be considered in its freedom, it is in the first place not regarded as reproductive, as it is subject to the laws of association, but as productive and spontaneous (as the author of arbitrary forms of possible intuition). And although in the apprehension of a given object of sense it is tied to a definite form of this object and so far has no free play (such as that of poetry), yet it may readily be conceived that the object can furnish it with such a form containing a collection of the manifold as the imagination itself, if it were left free, would project in accordance with the *conformity to law of the understanding* in general. But that the *imaginative power* should be *free* and yet *of itself conformed to law,* i.e., bringing autonomy with it, is a contradiction. The understanding alone gives the law. If, however, the imagination is compelled to proceed according to a definite law, its product in respect of form is determined by concepts as to what it ought to be. But then, as is above shown, the satisfaction is not that in the beautiful, but in the good (in perfection, at any rate in mere formal perfection), and the judgment is not a judgment of taste. Hence it is a conformity to law without a law; and a subjective agreement of the imagination and understanding — without such an objective agreement as there is when the representation is referred to a definite concept of an object — can subsist along with the free conformity to law of the understanding (which is also called purposiveness without purpose) and with the peculiar feature of a judgment of taste.

Now geometrically regular figures, such as a circle, a square, a cube, etc., are commonly adduced by critics of taste as the simplest and most indisputable examples of beauty, and yet they are called regular because we can only represent them by regarding them as mere presentations of a definite concept which prescribes the rule of the figure (according to which alone it is possible). One of these two must be wrong, either that judgment of the critic which ascribes beauty to the said figures, or ours which regards purposiveness apart from a concept as requisite for beauty.

Hardly anyone will say that a man must have taste in order that he should find more satisfaction in a circle than in a scrawled outline, in an equilateral and equiangular quadrilateral than in which is oblique, irregular, and as it were deformed, for this belongs to the ordinary understanding and is not taste at all. Where, e.g., our design is to judge of the size of an area or to make intelligible the relation of the parts of it, when divided, to one another and to the whole, then regular figures and those of the simplest kind are needed, and the satisfaction does not rest immediately on the aspect of the figure, but on its availability for all kinds of possible designs. A room whose walls form oblique angles, or a parterre of this kind, even every violation of symmetry in the figure of animals (e.g., being one-eyed), of buildings, or of flower beds, displeases because it contradicts the purpose of the thing, not only practically in respect of a definite use of it, but also when we pass judgment on it as regards any possible design. This is not the case in the judgment of taste, which when pure combines satisfaction or dissatisfaction — without any reference to its use or to a purpose — with the mere *consideration* of the object.

The regularity which leads to the concept of an object is indeed the indispensable condition (*conditio sine qua non*) for grasping the object in a single representation and determining the manifold in its form. This determination is a purpose in respect of cognition, and in reference to this it is always bound up with satisfaction (which accompanies the execution of every, even problematical, design). There is here, however, merely the approval of the solution satisfying a problem, and not a free and indefinite purposive entertainment of the mental powers with what we call beautiful, where the understanding is at the service of imagination, and not *vice versa.*

In a thing that is only possible by means of design — a building, or even an animal — the regularity consisting in symmetry must express the unity of the intuition that accompanies the concept of purpose, and this regularity belongs to cognition. But where only a free play of the representative powers (under the condition, however, that the understanding is to suffer no shock thereby) is to be kept up, in pleasure gardens, room decorations, all kinds of tasteful furniture, etc., regularity that shows constraint is avoided as much as possible. Thus in the English taste in gardens or in bizarre taste in furniture, the freedom of the imagination is pushed almost near to the grotesque, and in this separation from every constraint of rule we have the case where taste can display its greatest perfection in the enterprises of the imagination.

All stiff regularity (such as approximates to mathematical regularity) has something in it repugnant to taste; for our entertainment in the contemplation of it lasts for no length of time, but it rather, insofar as it has not expressly in view cognition or a definite practical purpose, produces weariness. On the other hand, that with which imagination can play in an unstudied and purposive manner is always new to us, and one does not get tired of looking at it. Marsden, in his description of Sumatra, makes the remark that the free beauties of nature surround the spectator everywhere and thus lose their attraction for him.[8] On the other hand, a pepper garden, where the stakes on which this plant twines itself form parallel rows, had much attractiveness for him if he met with it in the middle of a forest. And he hence infers that wild beauty, apparently irregular, only pleases as a variation from the regular beauty of which one has seen enough. But he need only have made the experiment of spending one day in a pepper garden to have been convinced that, if the understanding has put itself in accordance with the order that it always needs by means of regularity, the object will not entertain for long — nay, rather it will impose a burdensome constraint upon the imagination. On the other hand, nature, which there is prodigal in its variety even to luxuriance, that is subjected to no constraint of artificial rules, can supply constant food for taste. Even the song of birds, which we can bring under no musical rule, seems to have more freedom, and therefore more for taste, than a song of a human being which is produced in accordance with all the rules of music; for we very much sooner weary of the latter if it is repeated often and at length. Here, however, we probably confuse our participation in the mirth of a little creature that we love with the beauty of its song, for if this were exactly imitated by man (as sometimes the notes of the nightingale are), it would seem to our ear quite devoid of taste.

Again, beautiful objects are to be distinguished from beautiful views of objects (which often on account of their distance cannot be more clearly cognized). In the latter case taste appears, not so much in what the imagination *apprehends* in this field, as in the impulse it thus gets to *fiction,* i.e., in the peculiar fancies with which the mind entertains itself, while it is continually being aroused by the variety which strikes the eye. An illustration is afforded, e.g., by the sight of the changing shapes of a fire on the hearth or of a rippling brook; neither of these has beauty, but they bring with them a charm for the imagination because they entertain it in free play.

Second Book. Analytic of the Sublime

23. Transition from the Faculty Which Judges of the Beautiful to That Which Judges of the Sublime

The beautiful and the sublime agree in this that both please in themselves. Further, neither presupposes a judgment of sense nor a judgment logically determined, but a judgment of reflection. Consequently the satisfaction belonging to them does not depend on a sensation, as in the case of the pleasant, nor on a definite concept, as in the case of the good; but it is nevertheless referred to concepts, although indeterminate ones. And so the satisfaction is connected with the mere presentation of the object or with the faculty of presentation, so that in the case of a given intuition this faculty or the imagination is considered as in agreement with the *faculty of concepts* of understanding or reason, regarded as promoting these latter. Hence both kinds of judgments are *singular,* and yet announce themselves as universally valid for every subject; although they lay claim merely to the feeling of pleasure, and not to any cognition of the object.

But there are also remarkable differences between the two. The beautiful in nature is connected with the form of the object, which consists in having definite boundaries. The sublime, on the other hand, is to be found in a formless

[8] W. Marsden, *The History of Sumatra* (London, 1783), p. 113. [Tr.]

object, so far as in it or by occasion of it *boundlessness* is represented, and yet its totality is also present to thought. Thus the beautiful seems to be regarded as the presentation of an indefinite concept of understanding, the sublime as that of a like concept of reason. Therefore the satisfaction in the one case is bound up with the representation of *quality,* in the other with that of *quantity.* And the latter satisfaction is quite different in kind from the former, for the beautiful directly brings with it a feeling of the furtherance of life, and thus is compatible with charms and with the play of the imagination. But the feeling of the sublime is a pleasure that arises only indirectly; viz., it is produced by the feeling of a momentary checking of the vital powers and a consequent stronger outflow of them, so that it seems to be regarded as emotion — not play, but earnest in the exercise of the imagination. Hence it is incompatible with physical charm; and as the mind is not merely attracted by the object but is ever being alternately repelled, the satisfaction in the sublime does not so much involve a positive pleasure as admiration or respect, which rather deserves to be called negative pleasure.

But the inner and most important distinction between the sublime and beautiful is, certainly, as follows. (Hence, as we are entitled to do, we only bring under consideration in the first instance the sublime in natural objects, for the sublime of art is always limited by the conditions of agreement with nature.) Natural beauty (which is independent) brings with it a purposiveness in its form by which the object seems to be, as it were, preadapted to our judgment, and thus constitutes in itself an object of satisfaction. On the other hand, that which excites in us, without any reasoning about it, but in the mere apprehension of it, the feeling of the sublime may appear, as regards its form, to violate purpose in respect of the judgment, to be unsuited to our presentative faculty, and as it were to do violence to the imagination; and yet it is judged to be only the more sublime.

Now we may see from this that, in general, we express ourselves incorrectly if we call any *object of nature* sublime, although we can quite correctly call many objects of nature beautiful. For how can that be marked by an expression of approval which is apprehended in itself as being a violation of purpose? All that we can say is that the object is fit for the presentation of a sublimity which can be found in the mind, for no sensible form can contain the sublime properly so-called. This concerns only ideas of the reason which, although no adequate presentation is possible for them, by this inadequateness that admits of sensible presentation are aroused and summoned into the mind. Thus the wide ocean, disturbed by the storm, cannot be called sublime. Its aspect is horrible; and the mind must be already filled with manifold ideas if it is to be determined by such an intuition to a feeling itself sublime, as it is incited to abandon sensibility and to busy itself with ideas that involve higher purposiveness.

Independent natural beauty discovers to us a technique of nature which represents it as a system in accordance with laws, the principle of which we do not find in the whole of our faculty of understanding. That principle is the principle of purposiveness, in respect of the use of our judgment in regard to phenomena, which requires that these must not be judged as merely belonging to nature in its purposeless mechanism, but also as belonging to something analogous to art. It therefore actually extends, not indeed our cognition of natural objects, but our concept of nature, which is now not regarded as mere mechanism but as art. This leads to profound investigations as to the possibility of such a form. But in what we are accustomed to call sublime there is nothing at all that leads to particular objective principles and forms of nature corresponding to them; so far from it that, for the most part, nature excites the ideas of the sublime in its chaos or in its wildest and most irregular disorder and desolation, provided size and might are perceived. Hence, we see that the concept of the sublime is not nearly so important or rich in consequences as the concept of the beautiful; and that, in general, it displays nothing purposive in nature itself, but only in that possible use of our intuitions of it by which there is produced in us a feeling of a purposiveness quite independent of nature. We must seek a ground external to ourselves for the beautiful of nature, but seek it for the sublime merely in ourselves and in our attitude of thought, which introduces sublimity into the representation of nature. This is a very needful preliminary remark, which quite separates the ideas of the sublime from that of a purposiveness of *nature* and makes the theory of the sublime a mere appendix to the aesthetical judging of that purposiveness, because by means of it no particular form is represented in nature, but there is only developed a purposive use which the imagination makes of its representation.

24. Of the Divisions of an Investigation into the Feeling of the Sublime

As regards the division of the moments of the aesthetical judging of objects in reference to the feeling of the sublime, the Analytic can proceed according to the same principle as was adopted in the analysis of judgments of taste. For as an act of the aesthetical reflective judgment, the satisfaction in the sublime must be represented just as in the case of the beautiful — according to *quantity* as universally valid, according to *quality* as devoid of *interest,* according to *relation* as subjective purposiveness, and according to *modality* as necessary. And so the method here will not diverge from that of the preceding section, unless indeed we count it a difference that in the case where the aesthetical judgment is concerned with the form of the object we began with the investigation of its quality, but here, in view of the formlessness which may belong to what we call sublime, we will begin with quantity, as the first moment of the aesthetical judgment as to the sublime. The reason for this may be seen from the preceding paragraph.

But the analysis of the sublime involves a division not needed in the case of the beautiful, viz., a division into the *mathematically* and the *dynamically sublime.*

For the feeling of the sublime brings with it as its characteristic feature a *movement* of the mind bound up with the judging of the object, while in the case of the beautiful taste presupposes and maintains the mind in *restful* contemplation. Now this movement ought to be judged as subjectively purposive (because the sublime pleases us), and thus it is referred through the imagination either to the *faculty of cognition* or *of desire.* In either reference the purposiveness of the given representation ought to be judged only in respect of this *faculty* (without purpose or interest), but in the first case, it is ascribed to the object as a *mathematical* determination of the imagination, in the second as *dynamical.* And hence we have this twofold way of representing the sublime.

A. OF THE MATHEMATICALLY SUBLIME

25. Explanation of the Term Sublime

We call that *sublime* which is *absolutely great.* But to be great and to be a great something are quite different concepts (*magnitudo* and *quantitas*). In like manner to say simply (*simpliciter*) that anything is *great* is quite different from saying that it is *absolutely great* (*absolute, non comparative magnum*). The latter is *what is great beyond all comparison.* What now is meant by the expression that anything is great or small or of medium size? It is not a pure concept of understanding that is thus signified; still less is it an intuition of sense; and just as little is it a concept of reason, because it brings with it no principle of cognition. It must therefore be a concept of judgment or derived from one, and a subjective purposiveness of the representation in reference to the judgment must lie at its basis. That anything is a magnitude (*quantum*) may be cognized from the thing itself, without many comparisons of it with other things, viz., if there is a multiplicity of the homogeneous constituting one thing. But to cognize *how great* it is always requires some other magnitude as a measure. But because the judging of magnitude depends, not merely on multiplicity (number), but also on the magnitude of the unit (the measure), and since, to judge of the magnitude of this latter again requires another as measure with which it may be compared, we see that the determination of the magnitude of phenomena can supply no absolute concept whatever of magnitude, but only a comparative one.

If now I say simply that anything is great, it appears that I have no comparison in view, at least none with an objective measure, because it is thus not determined at all how great the object is. But although the standard of comparison is merely subjective, yet the judgment nonetheless claims universal assent; "this man is beautiful" and "he is tall" are judgments, not limited merely to the judging subject, but, like theoretical judgments, demanding the assent of everyone.

In a judgment by which anything is designated simply as great, it is not merely meant that the object has a magnitude, but that this magnitude is superior to that of many other objects of the same kind, without, however, any exact determination of this superiority. Thus there is always at the basis of our judgment a standard which we assume as the same for everyone; this, however, is not available for any logical (mathematically definite) judging of magnitude, but only for aesthetical judging of the same, because it is a merely subjective standard lying at the basis of the reflective judgment upon magnitude. It may be empirical, as, e.g., the average size of the men known to us, of animals of a certain kind, trees, houses, mountains, etc. Or it may be a standard given *a priori* which, through the defects of the judging subject, is limited by the subjective conditions of presentation *in concreto,* as, e.g., in the practical sphere, the greatness of a certain virtue or of the public liberty and justice in a country, or, in the theoretical sphere, the greatness of the accuracy or the inaccuracy of an observation or measurement that has been made, etc.

Here it is remarkable that, although we have no interest whatever in an object — i.e., its existence is indifferent to us — yet its mere size, even if it is considered as formless, may bring a satisfaction with it that is universally communicable and that consequently involves the consciousness of a subjective purposiveness in the use of our cognitive faculty. This is not indeed a satisfaction in the object (because it may be formless), as in the case of the beautiful, in which the reflective judgment finds itself purposively determined in reference to cognition in general, but a satisfaction in the extension of the imagination by itself.

If (under the above limitation) we say simply of an object "it is great," this is no mathematically definite judgment, but a mere judgment of reflection upon the representation of it, which is subjectively purposive for a certain use of our cognitive powers in the estimation of magnitude; and we always then bind up with the representation a kind of respect, as also a kind of contempt, for what we simply call "small." Further, the judging of things as great or small extends to everything, even to all their characteristics; thus we describe beauty as great or small. The reason of this is to be sought in the fact that whatever we present in intuition according to the precept of the judgment (and thus represent aesthetically) is always a phenomenon, and thus a quantum.

But if we call anything, not only great, but absolutely great in every point of view (great beyond all comparison), i.e., sublime, we soon see that it is not permissible to seek for an adequate standard of this outside itself, but merely in itself. It is a magnitude which is like itself alone. It follows hence that the sublime is not to be sought in the things of nature, but only in our ideas; but in which of them it lies must be reserved for the "Deduction."

The foregoing explanation can be thus expressed: *The sublime is that in comparison with which everything else is small.* Here we easily see that nothing can be given in nature, however great it is judged by us to be, which could not, if considered in another relation, be reduced to the infinitely small; and conversely there is nothing so small which does not admit of extension by our imagination to the greatness of a world if compared with still smaller standards. Telescopes have furnished us with abundant material for making the first remark, microscopes for the second. Nothing, therefore, which can be an object of the senses is, considered on this basis, to be called sublime. But because there is in our imagination a striving toward infinite progress and in our reason a claim for absolute totality, regarded as a real idea, therefore this very inadequateness for that idea in our faculty for estimating the magnitude of things of sense excites in us the feeling of a supersensible faculty. And it is not the object of sense, but the use which the judgment naturally makes of certain objects on behalf of this latter feeling that is absolutely great, and in comparison every other use is small. Consequently it is the state of mind produced by a certain representation with which the reflective judgment is occupied, and not the object, that is to be called sublime.

We can therefore append to the preceding formulas explaining the sublime this other: *The sublime is that, the mere ability to think which shows a faculty of the mind surpassing every standard of sense. . . .*

27. *Of the Quality of the Satisfaction in Our Judgments upon the Sublime*

The feeling of our incapacity to attain to an idea *which is a law for us* is *respect.* Now the idea of the comprehension of every phenomenon that can be given us in the intuition of a whole is an idea prescribed to us by a law of reason, which recognizes no other measure, definite, valid of everyone, and invariable, than the absolute whole. But our imagination, even in its greatest efforts, in respect of that comprehension which we expect from it of a given object in a whole of intuition (and thus with reference to the presentation of the idea of reason) exhibits its own limits and inadequacy, although at the same time it shows that its destination is to make itself adequate to this idea regarded as a law. Therefore the feeling of the sublime in nature is respect for our own destination, which, by a certain subreption, we attribute to an object of nature (conversion of respect for the idea of humanity in our own subject into respect for the object). This makes intuitively evident the superiority of the rational determination of our cognitive faculties to the greatest faculty of our sensibility.

The feeling of the sublime is therefore a feeling of pain arising from the want of accordance between the aesthetical estimation of magnitude formed by the imagination and the estimation of the same formed by reason. There is at the same time a pleasure thus excited, arising from the correspondence with rational ideas of this very judgment of the inadequacy of our greatest faculty of sense, in so far as it is a law for us to strive after these ideas. In fact it is for us a law (of reason) and belongs to our destination to estimate as small, in comparison with ideas of reason, everything which nature, regarded as an object of sense, contains that is great for us; and that which arouses in us the feeling of this supersensible destination agrees with that law. Now the greatest effort of the imagination in the presentation of the unit for the estimation of magnitude indicates a reference to something *absolutely great,* and consequently a reference to the law of reason, which bids us take this alone as our highest measure of magnitude. Therefore the inner perception of the inadequacy of all sensible standards for rational estimation of magnitude indicates a correspondence with rational laws; it involves a pain, which arouses in us the feeling of our supersensible destination, according to which it is purposive and therefore pleasurable to find every standard of sensibility inadequate to the ideas of understanding.

The mind feels itself *moved* in the representation of the sublime in nature, while in aesthetical judgments about the beautiful it is in *restful* contemplation. This movement may (especially in its beginning) be compared to a vibration, i.e., to a quickly alternating attraction toward, and repulsion from, the same object. The transcendent (toward which the imagination is impelled in its apprehension of intuition) is for the imagination like an abyss in which it fears to lose itself; but for the rational idea of the supersensible it is not transcendent, but in conformity with law to bring about such an effort of the imagination, and consequently here there is the same amount of attraction as there was of repulsion for the mere sensibility. But the judgment itself always remains in this case only aesthetical, because, without having any determinate concept of the object at its basis, it merely represents the subjective play of the mental powers (imagination and reason) as harmonious through their very contrast. For just as imagination and *understanding,* in judging of the beautiful, generate a subjective purposiveness of the mental powers by means of their harmony, so in this case imagination and *reason* do so by means of their conflict. That is, they bring about a feeling that we possess pure self-subsistent reason, or a faculty for the estimation of magnitude, whose superiority can be made intuitively evident only by the inadequacy of that faculty imagination which is itself unbounded in the presentation of magnitudes (of sensible objects).

The measurement of a space (regarded as apprehension) is at the same time a description of it, and thus an objective movement in the act of imagination and a progress. On the other hand, the comprehension of the manifold in the unity — not of thought but of intuition — and consequently the comprehension of the successively apprehended elements in one glance is a regress which annihilates the condition of time in this progress of the imagination and makes *coexistence* intuitible. It is therefore (since the time series is a condition of the internal sense and of an intuition) and subjective movement of the imagination, by which it does violence to the internal sense; this must be the more noticeable, the greater the quantum in which the imagination comprehends in one intuition. The effort, therefore, to receive in one single intuition a measure for magnitude that requires a considerable time to apprehend is a kind of representation which, subjectively considered, is contrary to purpose; but objectively, as requisite for the estimation of magnitude, it is purposive. Thus that very violence which is done to the subject through the imagination is judged as purposive *in reference to the whole determination* of the mind.

The *quality* of the feeling of the sublime is that it is a feeling of pain in reference to the faculty by which we judge aesthetically of an object, which pain, however, is represented at the same time as purposive. This is possible through the fact that the very incapacity in question discovers the consciousness of an unlimited faculty of the same subject, and that the mind can only judge of the latter aesthetically by means of the former.

In the logical estimation of magnitude, the impossibility of ever arriving at absolute totality, by means of the progress of the measurement of things of the sensible world in time and space, was cognized as objective, i.e., as an impossibility of *thinking* the infinite as entirely given, and not as merely subjective or that there was only an incapacity to *grasp* it. For there we have not to do with the degree of comprehension in an intuition, regarded as a measure, but everything depends on a concept of number. But in aesthetical estimation of magnitude, the concept of number must disappear or be changed, and the comprehension of the imagination in reference to the unit of measure (thus avoiding the concepts of a law of the successive production of concepts of magnitude) is alone purposive for it. If now a magnitude almost reaches the limit of our faculty of comprehension in an intuition, and yet the imagination is invited by means of numerical magnitudes (in respect of which we are conscious that our faculty is unbounded) to aesthetical comprehension in a greater unit, then we mentally feel ourselves confined aesthetically within bounds. But nevertheless the pain in regard to the necessary extension of the imagination for accordance with that which is unbounded in our faculty of reason, viz., the idea of the absolute whole, and consequently the very unpurposiveness of the faculty of imagination for rational ideas and the arousing of them, are represented as purposive. Thus it is that the aesthetical judgment itself is subjectively purposive for the reason as the source of ideas, i.e., as the source of an intellectual comprehension for which all aesthetical comprehension is small, and there accompanies the reception of an object as sublime a pleasure, which is only possible through the medium of a pain.

B. OF THE DYNAMICALLY SUBLIME IN NATURE

28. Of Nature Regarded as Might

Might is that which is superior to great hindrances. It is called *dominion* if it is superior to the resistance of that which itself possesses might. Nature, considered in an aesthetical judgment as might that has no dominion over us, is *dynamically sublime*.

If nature is to be judged by us as dynamically sublime, it must be represented as exciting fear (although it is not true conversely that every object which excites fear is regarded in our aesthetical judgment as sublime). For in aesthetical judgments (without the aid of concepts) superiority to hindrances can only be judged according to the greatness of the resistance. Now that which we are driven to resist is an evil and, if we do not find our faculties a match for it, is an object of fear. Hence nature can be regarded by the aesthetical judgment as might, and consequently as dynamically sublime, only so far as it is considered an object of fear.

But we can regard an object as *fearful* without being afraid *of* it, viz., if we judge of it in such a way that we merely *think* a case in which we would wish to resist it and yet in which all resistance would be altogether vain. Thus the virtuous man fears God without being afraid of Him, because to wish to resist Him and His commandments he thinks is a case that *he* need not apprehend. But in every such case that he thinks as not impossible, he cognizes Him as fearful.

He who fears can form no judgment about the sublime in nature, just as he who is seduced by inclination and appetite can form no judgment about the beautiful. The former flies from the sight of an object which inspires him with awe, and it is impossible to find satisfaction in a terror that is seriously felt. Hence the pleasurableness arising from the cessation of an uneasiness is *a state of joy*. But this, on account of the deliverance from danger which is involved, is a state of joy when conjoined with the resolve that we shall no more be exposed to the danger; we cannot willingly look back upon our sensations of danger, much less seek the occasion for them again.

Bold, overhanging, and as it were threatening rocks; clouds piled up in the sky, moving with lightning flashes and thunder peals; volcanoes in all their violence of destruction; hurricanes with their track of devastation; the boundless ocean in a state of tumult; the lofty waterfall of a mighty river, and such like — these exhibit our faculty of resistance as insignificantly small in comparison with their might. But the sight of them is the more attractive, the more fearful it is, provided only that we are in security; and we willingly call these objects sublime, because they raise the energies of the soul above their accustomed height and discover in us a faculty of resistance of a quite different kind, which gives us courage to measure ourselves against the apparent almightiness of nature.

Now, in the immensity of nature and in the insufficiency of our faculties to take in a standard proportionate to the aesthetical estimation of the magnitude of its *realm,* we find our own limitation, although at the same time in our rational faculty we find a different, nonsensuous standard, which has that infinity itself under it as a unity, in comparison with which everything in nature is small, and thus in our mind we find a superiority to nature even in its immensity. And so also the irresistibility of its might, while making us recognize our own physical impotence, considered as beings of nature, discloses to us a faculty of judging independently of and a superiority over nature, on which is based a kind of self-preservation entirely different from that which can be attacked and brought into danger by external nature. Thus humanity in our person remains unhumiliated, though the individual might have to submit to this dominion. In this way nature is not judged to be sublime in our aesthetical judgments insofar as it excites fear, but because it calls up that power in us (which is not nature) of regarding as small the things about which we are solicitous (goods, health, and life), and of regarding its might (to which we are no doubt subjected in respect of these things) as nevertheless without any dominion over us and our personality to which we must bow where our highest fundamental propositions, and their assertion or abandonment, are concerned. Therefore nature is here called sublime merely because it elevates the imagination to a presentation of those cases in which the mind can make felt the proper sublimity of its destination, in comparison with nature itself.

This estimation of ourselves loses nothing through the fact that we might regard ourselves as safe in order to feel this inspiriting satisfaction and that hence, as there is no seriousness in the danger, there might be also (as might seem to be the case) just as little seriousness in the sublimity of our spiritual faculty. For the satisfaction here concerns only the *destination* of our faculty which discloses itself in such a case, so far as the tendency to this destination lies in our nature, while its development and exercise remain incumbent and obligatory. And in this there is truth and reality, however conscious the man may be of his present actual powerfulness, when he turns his reflection to it.

No doubt this principle seems to be too farfetched and too subtly reasoned, and consequently seems to go beyond the scope of an aesthetical judgment; but observation of men proves the opposite and shows that it may lie at the root of the most ordinary judgments, although we are not always conscious of it. For what is that which is, even to the savage, an object of the greatest admiration? It is a man who shrinks from nothing, who fears nothing, and therefore does not yield to danger, but rather goes to face it vigorously with the most complete deliberation. Even in the most highly civilized state this peculiar veneration for the soldier remains, though only under the condition that he exhibit all the virtues of peace, gentleness, compassion, and even a becoming care for his own person; because even by these it is recognized that his mind is unsubdued by danger. Hence whatever disputes there may be about the superiority of the respect which is to be accorded them, in the comparison of a statesman and a general, the aesthetical judgment decides for the latter. War itself, if it is carried on with order and with a sacred respect for the rights of citizens, has something sublime in it, and makes the disposition of the people who carry it on thus only the more sublime, the more numerous are the dangers to which they are exposed and in respect of which they behave with courage. On the other hand, a long peace generally brings about a predominant commercial spirit and, along with it, low selfishness, cowardice, and effeminacy, and debases the disposition of the people.

It appears to conflict with this solution of the concept of sublime, so far as sublimity is ascribed to might, that we are accustomed to represent God as presenting Himself in His wrath and yet in His sublimity, in the tempest, the storm, the earthquake, etc.; and that it would be foolish and criminal to imagine a superiority of our minds over these works of His and, as it seems, even over the designs of such might. Hence it would appear that no feeling of the sublimity of our own nature, but rather subjection, abasement, and a feeling of complete powerlessness, is a fitting state of mind in the presence of such an object; and this is generally bound up with the idea of it during natural phenomena of this kind. In religion in general, prostration, adoration with bent head, with contrite, anxious demeanor and voice, seems to be the only fitting behavior in presence of the Godhead, and hence most peoples have adopted and still observe it. But this state of mind is far from being necessarily bound up with the idea of the *sublimity* of a religion and its object. The man who is actually afraid, because he finds reasons for fear in himself, while conscious by his culpable disposition of offending against a might whose will is irresistible and at the same time just, is not in the frame of mind for admiring the divine greatness. For this a mood of calm contemplation and a quiet free judgment are needed. Only if he is conscious of an upright disposition pleasing to God do those operations of might serve to awaken in him the idea of the sublimity of this Being, for then he recognizes in himself a sublimity of disposition conformable to His will; and thus he is raised above the fear of such operations of nature, which he no longer regards as outbursts of His wrath. Even humility, in the shape of a stern judgment upon his own faults — which otherwise, with a consciousness of good intentions, could be easily palliated from the frailty of human nature — is a sublime state of mind, consisting in a voluntary subjection of himself to the pain of remorse, in order that the causes of this may be gradually removed. In this way religion is essentially distinguished from superstition. The latter establishes in the mind, not reverence for the sublime, but fear and apprehension of the all-powerful Being to whose will the terrified man sees himself subject, without according Him any high esteem. From this nothing can arise but a seeking of favor and flattery, instead of a religion which consists in a good life.[9]

Sublimity, therefore, does not reside in anything of nature, but only in our mind, in so far as we can become conscious that we are superior to nature within, and therefore also to nature without us (so far as it influences us). Everything that excites this feeling in us, e.g., the *might* of nature which calls forth our forces, is called then (although improperly) sublime. Only by supposing this idea in ourselves and in reference to it are we capable of attaining to the idea of the sublimity of that Being which produces respect in us, not

[9]In the *Philosophical Theory of Religion,* Pt. I (Abbott's trans., p. 360), Kant, as here, divides "all religions into two classes — *favor-seeking* religion (mere worship) and *moral* religion, that is, the religion *of a good life*"; and he concludes that "amongst all the public religions that have ever existed the Christian alone is moral." [Tr.]

merely by the might that it displays in nature, but rather by means of the faculty which resides in us of judging it fearlessly and of regarding our destination as sublime in respect of it. . . .

49. Of the Faculties of the Mind That Constitute Genius

We say of certain products of which we expect that they should at least in part appear as beautiful art, they are without *spirit,*[10] although we find nothing to blame in them on the score of taste. A poem may be very neat and elegant, but without spirit. A history may be exact and well arranged, but without spirit. A festal discourse may be solid and at the same time elaborate, but without spirit. Conversation is often not devoid of entertainment, but it is without spirit; even of a woman we say that she is pretty, an agreeable talker, and courteous, but without spirit. What then do we mean by spirit?

Spirit, in an aesthetical sense, is the name given to the animating principle of the mind. But that by means of which this principle animates the soul, the material which it applies to that purpose, is what puts the mental powers purposively into swing, i.e., into such a play as maintains itself and strengthens the mental powers in their exercise.

Now I maintain that this principle is no other than the faculty of presenting *aesthetical ideas.* And by an aesthetical idea I understand that representation of the imagination which occasions much thought, without however any definite thought, i.e., any *concept,* being capable of being adequate to it; it consequently cannot be completely compassed and made intelligible by language. We easily see that it is the counterpart (pendant) of a *rational idea,* which conversely is a concept to which no *intuition* (or representation of the imagination) can be adequate.

The imagination (as a productive faculty of cognition) is very powerful in creating another nature, as it were, out of the material that actual nature gives it. We entertain ourselves with it when experience becomes too commonplace, and by it we remold experience, always indeed in accordance with analogical laws, but yet also in accordance with principles which occupy a higher place in reason (laws, too, which are just as natural to us as those by which understanding comprehends empirical nature). Thus we feel our freedom from the law of association (which attaches to the empirical employment of imagination), so that the material supplied to us by nature in accordance with this law can be worked up into something different which surpasses nature.

Such representations of the imagination we may call *ideas,* partly because they at least strive after something which lies beyond the bounds of experience and so seek to approximate to a presentation of concepts of reason (intellectual ideas), thus giving to the latter the appearance of objective reality, but especially because no concept can be fully adequate to them as internal intuitions. The poet ventures to realize to sense,[11] rational ideas of invisible beings, the kingdom of the blessed, hell, eternity, creation, etc.; or even if he deals with things of which there are examples in experience — e.g., death, envy and all vices, also love, fame, and the like — he tries, by means of imagination, which emulates the play of reason in its quests after a maximum, to go beyond the limits of experience and to present them to sense with a completeness of which there is no example in nature. This is properly speaking the art of the poet, in which the faculty of aesthetical ideas can manifest itself in its entire strength. But this faculty, considered in itself, is properly only a talent (of the imagination).

If now we place under a concept a representation of the imagination belonging to its presentation, but which occasions in itself more thought than can ever be comprehended in a definite concept and which consequently aesthetically enlarges the concept itself in an unbounded fashion, the imagination is here creative, and it brings the faculty of intellectual ideas (the reason) into movement; i.e., by a representation more thought (which indeed belongs to the concept of the object) is occasioned than can in it be grasped or made clear.

[10]In English we would rather say "without soul," but I prefer to translate "*Geist*" consistently by "spirit," to avoid the confusion of it with "*Seele.*" [Tr.]

[11]Ventures to make real for the senses. [Ed.]

Those forms which do not constitute the presentation of a given concept itself but only, as approximate representations of the imagination, express the consequences bound up with it and its relationship to other concepts, are called (aesthetical) *attributes* of an object whose concept as a rational idea cannot be adequately presented. Thus Jupiter's eagle with the lightning in its claws is an attribute of the mighty king of heaven, as the peacock is of his magnificent queen. They do not, like *logical attributes,* represent what lies in our concepts of the sublimity and majesty of creation, but something different, which gives occasion to the imagination to spread itself over a number of kindred representations that arouse more thought than can be expressed in a concept determined by words. They furnish an *aesthetical idea,* which for that rational idea takes the place of logical presentation; and thus, as their proper office, they enliven the mind by opening out to it the prospect into an illimitable field of kindred representations. But beautiful art does this not only in the case of painting or sculpture (in which the term "attribute" is commonly employed); poetry and rhetoric also get the spirit that animates their works simply from the aesthetical attributes of the object, which accompany the logical and stimulate the imagination, so that it thinks more by their aid, although in an undeveloped way, than could be comprehended in a concept and therefore in a definite form of words. For the sake of brevity, I must limit myself to a few examples only.

When the great King in one of his poems expresses himself as follows:

Oui, finissons sans trouble et mourons sans regrets,
En laissant l'univers comblé de nos bienfaits.
Ainsi l'astre du jour au bout de sa carriere,
Répand sur l'horizon une douce lumière;
Et les derniers rayons qu'il darde dans les airs,
Sont les derniers soupirs qu'il donne à l'univers;[12]

he quickens his rational idea of a cosmopolitan disposition at the end of life by an attribute which the imagination (in remembering all the pleasures of a beautiful summer day that are recalled at its close by a serene evening) associates with that representation, and which excites a number of sensations and secondary representations for which no expression is found. On the other hand, an intellectual concept may serve conversely as an attribute for a representation of sense, and so can quicken this latter by means of the idea of the supersensible, but only by the aesthetical element, that subjectively attaches to the concept of the latter, being here employed. Thus, for example, a certain poet says, in his description of a beautiful morning:

The sun arose
As calm from virtue springs.

The consciousness of virtue, if we substitute it in our thoughts for a virtuous man, diffuses in the mind a multitude of sublime and restful feelings, and a boundless prospect of a joyful future, to which no expression that is measured by a definite concept completely attains.[13]

In a word, the aesthetical idea is a representation of the imagination associated with a given concept, which is bound up with such a multiplicity of partial representations in its free employment that for it no expression marking a definite concept can be found; and such a representation, therefore, adds to a concept much ineffable thought, the feeling of which quickens the cognitive faculties, and with language, which is the mere letter, binds up spirit also.

[12]"Yes, let us end without sadness and let us die without regrets, in leaving the world filled with our good deeds. So the day-star, at the end of its course, sheds a gentle light on the horizon; and the last rays that it darts into the air are the last sighs which it gives to the world." [Ed.] Barni quotes these lines as occurring in one of Frederick the Great's French poems: "Epitre au maréchal Keith, sur les vaines terreurs de la mort et les frayeurs d'une autre vie" [Letter to Marshal Keith on the Pointless Terror of Death and Fears of Another Life]; but I have not been able to verify his reference. Kant here translates them into German. [Tr.]

[13]Perhaps nothing more sublime was ever said and no sublimer thought ever expressed than the famous inscription on the Temple of Isis (Mother Nature): "I am all that is and that was and that shall be, and no mortal hath lifted my veil." Segner availed himself of this idea in a *suggestive* vignette prefixed to his *Natural Philosophy,* in order to inspire beforehand the pupil whom he was about to lead into that temple with a holy awe, which should dispose his mind to serious attention. [Au.] J. A. de Segner (1704–1777) was Professor of Natural Philosophy at Göttingen and the author of several scientific works of repute. [Tr.]

The mental powers, therefore, whose union (in a certain relation) constitutes genius are imagination and understanding. In the employment of the imagination for cognition, it submits to the constraint of the understanding and is subject to the limitation of being conformable to the concept of the latter. On the contrary, in an aesthetical point of view it is free to furnish unsought, over and above that agreement with a concept, abundance of undeveloped material for the understanding, to which the understanding paid no regard in its concept but which it applies, though not objectively for cognition, yet subjectively to quicken the cognitive powers and therefore also indirectly to cognitions. Thus genius properly consists in the happy relation between these faculties, which no science can teach and no industry can learn, by which ideas are found for a given concept; and, on the other hand, we thus find for these ideas the expression by means of which the subjective state of mind brought about by them, as an accompaniment of the concept, can be communicated to others. The latter talent is, properly speaking, what is called spirit; for to express the ineffable element in the state of mind implied by a certain representation and to make it universally communicable — whether the expression be in speech or painting or statuary — this requires a faculty of seizing the quickly passing play of imagination and of unifying it in a concept (which is even on that account original and discloses a new rule that could not have been inferred from any preceding principles of examples) that can be communicated without any constraint of rules.

If, after this analysis, we look back to the explanation given above of what is called *genius*, we find: first, that it is a talent for art, not for science, in which clearly known rules must go beforehand and determine the procedure. Secondly, as an artistic talent it presupposes a definite concept of the product as the purpose, and therefore understanding; but it also presupposes a representation (although an indeterminate one) of the material, i.e., of the intuition, for the presentment of this concept, and, therefore a relation between the imagination and the understanding. Thirdly, it shows itself, not so much in the accomplishment of the proposed purpose in a presentment of a definite concept, as in the enunciation or expression of aesthetical ideas which contain abundant material for that very design; and consequently it represents the imagination as free from all guidance of rules and yet as purposive in reference to the presentment of the given concept. Finally, in the fourth place, the unsought, undesigned subjective purposiveness in the free accordance of the imagination with the legality of the understanding presupposes such a proportion and disposition of these faculties as no following of rules, whether of science or of mechanical imitation, can bring about, but which only the nature of the subject can produce.

In accordance with these suppositions, genius is the examplary originality of the natural gifts of a subject in the *free* employment of his cognitive faculties. In this way the product of a genius (as regards what is to be ascribed to genius and not to possible learning or schooling) is an example, not to be imitated (for then that which in it is genius and constitutes the spirit of the work would be lost), but to be followed by another genius, whom it awakens to a feeling of his own originality and whom it stirs so to exercise his art in freedom from the constraint of rules, that thereby a new rule is gained for art; and thus his talent shows itself to be exemplary. But because a genius is a favorite of nature and must be regarded by us as a rare phenomenon, his example produces for other good heads a school, i.e., a methodical system of teaching according to rules, so far as these can be derived from the peculiarities of the products of his spirit. For such persons beautiful art is so far imitation, to which nature through the medium of a genius supplied the rule.

But this imitation becomes a mere *aping* if the scholar *copies* everything down to the deformities, which the genius must have let pass only because he could not well remove them without weakening his idea. This mental characteristic is meritorious only in the case of a genius. A certain *audacity* in expression — and in general many a departure from common rules — becomes him well, but it is in no way worthy of imitation; it always remains a fault in itself which we must seek to remove, though the genius is, as it were, privileged to commit it, because the inimitable rush of his spirit would suffer from overanxious carefulness. *Mannerism* is another kind of aping, viz., of mere *peculiarity* (originality) in general, by which a man separates himself as far as possible from imitators, without however possessing the talent to be at the same time *exemplary*. There are indeed in general two ways (*modi*) in which such a man may put together his notions of expressing himself; the one is called a *manner* (*modus aestheticus*), the other a *method* (*modus logicus*). They differ in this, that the former has no other standard than the *feeling* of unity in the presentment, but the latter follows definite *principles;* hence the former alone avails for beautiful art. But an artistic product is said to show *mannerism* only when the exposition of the artist's idea is *founded* on its very singularity and is not made appropriate to the idea itself. The ostentatious (*précieux*), contorted, and affected manner adopted to differentiate oneself from ordinary persons (though devoid of spirit) is like the behavior of a man of whom we say that he hears himself talk, or who stands and moves about as if he were on a stage in order to be stared at; this always betrays a bungler.

Germaine de Staël

1766–1817

Born into a society that even today seems to exclude women systematically from many cultural and intellectual pursuits, Anne-Louise-Germaine Necker, Baronne de Staël-Holstein was the first French woman to become a writer of international importance. She was well placed to do so as the daughter of Jacques Necker, the Swiss banker and financier who was finance minister to Louis XVI from 1776 to 1781 and again at the fateful calling of the Estates General in 1788. Her mother, Suzanne Curchod, was an intellectual in her own right, a clergyman's daughter to whom the historian Edward Gibbon had in his youth been engaged.

Germaine de Staël's *Essay on Fictions* dates from 1795, just after her return from exile in England, and its primary examples — Richardson and Fielding — are taken from English literature rather than from that of her native country. The ideas in the essay, like much written during this period, represent an awkward transitional phase between Enlightenment and Romantic thinking. Parts of the essay sound like an apology for fiction in line with Sidney's *Apology for Poetry* by insisting upon the greater power of the novel over history to make a sustained moral impression upon us. He is not mentioned by name, but her primary antagonist seems to be Samuel Johnson, for although she adroitly concedes what she must, she parries his major attacks in *The Rambler,* No. 4, on the immorality of fiction.

Instead of agreeing that the subject proper to art is general nature, she insists upon the importance of *nuance,* the specific and particular emotional quality within events that makes them real for us. (The reality achieved by the elaboration of details does not, on the other hand, strike her as artistically interesting.) Even more directly she defends the object of Johnson's odium, Fielding's *Tom Jones,* for possessing "the most general moral of any novel" geared "to show the uncertainty of judgments founded on appearances, proving the superiority of natural and what we may call involuntary virtues over reputations based on mere respect for exteral etiquette."

If Germaine de Staël defends Fielding as a moral educator — which would be Sidney's or Dryden's or Johnson's criterion as well — her ethical values, and specifically her preference for nature and instinct over social convention, bring her closer to being the first spokeswoman for Romanticism. If, like a woman of the Enlightenment salons, she spoke for Truth, she also felt, like the major Romantics, that the highest truth was that of feeling and that such a truth needed nurturing. She defended the growing literature of passionate eloquence, from Pope's "Eloisa to Abelard" to Goethe's *Werther,* as serving a significant function in reconciling especially gifted individuals — sensitive, passionate, and isolated from society — to their place in the world. A generation later, Shelley, who was born the year de Staël published her essay on fiction, would term these sensitive beings — whose passions are Aeolian harps on which the world plays — the "unacknowledged legislators of the world."

De Staël's last important piece of literary criticism, *On Literature Considered in Relation to Social Institutions* (1800), is, theoretically speaking, her most ambitious work, breaking ground that would later be explored by Hyppolite Taine and Karl Marx. If, as her translator Vivian Folkenflik suggests, the book helped establish the Romantic canon, it went beyond the Romantic view of literature as the verbal product of special psychological traits like fancy, imagination, and genius. For de Staël, literature, however fantastic, is a product of the society within which artists produce and audiences enjoy creations, and it takes its form from geography, history, and politics, which shape the "manners" out of which art springs. De Staël's sense of manners is not a matter of mere politenesses and grace, like knowing which fork to use when picking up your smoked salmon. For de Staël, manners are the way connections are formed in a society, how influence works, how the powerful are constrained, and whose voice counts and with whom: The notion of manners is similar to what Foucault, in a more extensive context, calls "power/knowledge" (see the introduction to New Historicism and Cultural Studies, p. 1208).

De Staël's assessment of French literature since the Revolution is subtly balanced for a returned emigrée: She understands the overrefinement of the French court of the ancien régime, and the way in which many artistic talents were lost on an audience that demanded not merely wit, but wit of a sort that could be learned only by thorough familiarity with the conventions of that court. But she also recognizes that, in breaking through all the rules that had bound polite society, the republican revolution in politics had produced a vulgarity that was even more brutal. The satire that had restrained the powerful under Louis XVI had lost its force under the corrupt *Directoire*.[1]

In Section 2.4 of *On Literature* ("On Women Writers," reproduced here), de Staël views the republican revolution from her own particular perspective. A small clique of intelligent refined women — including her own mother, Mme. Necker — had set the intellectual and moral tone for the court under Louis XVI; incapable of holding public office themselves, their disinterested judgment of the capability and honesty of courtiers and ministers carried weight. With the destruction of the discursive practices of the old régime, however, women had no place at all, belonging "neither to the natural nor the social order." Not despite but because of the democratic institutions being established, the intelligent and creative woman had become an object of hatred to men and of indifference to her fellow women. De Staël hoped that a French republic would eventually foster equality of education between men and women, correcting this injustice, but, from our perspective it is not clear whether two centuries of democracy have entirely changed how both men and women respond to the exceptional woman.

Selected Bibliography

Andrews, Wayne. *Germaine: A Portrait of Madame de Staël.* New York: Atheneum, 1963.

Duffy, Bella. *Madame de Staël.* Boston: Roberts Brothers, 1887.

Folkenflik, Vivian, ed. and trans. *An Extraordinary Woman: Selected Writings of Germaine de Staël.* New York: Columbia University Press, 1987.

[1]The five-man executive body that ruled France from the collapse of the Revolutionary government in 1795 to the consulate of Napoleon (1799).

Forsberg, Roberta. *Madame de Staël and the English*. New York: Astra Books, 1967.
Gutwirth, Madelyn. *Madame de Staël, Novelist: The Emergence of the Artist as Woman*. Urbana: University of Illinois Press, 1978.
Luppé, Robert de. *Les Idées littéraires de Madame de Staël et l'heritage des lumières*. Paris: J. Vrin, 1969.
Postgate, Helen B. Smith. *Madame de Staël*. New York: Twayne, 1968.
Van Tieghem, Paul, ed. *De la littérature, considérée dans ses rapports avec les institutions sociales. Edition critique*. 3 vols. Geneva: Droz, 1959.
Winegarten, Renee. *Madame de Staël*. Leamington Spa, Eng., and Dover, NH: Berg, 1985.

Essay on Fictions

INTRODUCTION

Man's most valuable faculty is his imagination. Human life seems so little designed for happiness that we need the help of a few creations, a few images, a lucky choice of memories to muster some sparse pleasure on this earth and struggle against the pain of all our destinies — not by philosophical force, but by the more efficient force of distraction. The dangers of imagination have been discussed a good deal, but there is no point in looking up what impotent mediocrity and strict reason have said on this topic over and over again. The human race is not about to give up being stimulated, and anyone who has the gift of appealing to people's emotions is even less likely to give up the success promised by such talent. The number of necessary and evident truths is limited; it will never be enough for the human mind or heart. The highest honor may well go to those who discover such truths, but the authors of books producing sweet emotions or illusions have also done useful work for humanity. Metaphysical precision cannot be applied to man's affections and remain compatible with his nature. Beginnings are all we have on this earth — there is no limit. Virtue is actual and real, but happiness floats in space; anyone who tries to examine happiness inappropriately will destroy it, as we dissolve the brilliant images of the mist if we walk straight through them. And yet the advantage of fictions is not the pleasure they bring.

Translated by Vivian Folkenflik.

If fictions please nothing but the eye, they do nothing but amuse; but if they touch our hearts, they can have a great influence on all our moral ideas. This talent may be the most powerful way there is of controlling behavior and enlightening the mind. Man has only two distinct faculties: reason and imagination. All the others, even feeling, are simply results or combinations of these two. The realm of fiction, like that of imagination, is therefore vast. Fictions do not find obstacles in passions: they make use of them. Philosophy may be the invisible power in control of fictions, but if she is the first to show herself, she will destroy all their magic.

When I talk about fictions, I will therefore be considering them from two perspectives of content and charm: this kind of writing may contain pleasure without useful purpose, but never vice versa. Fictions are meant to attract us; the more moral or philosophical the result one is trying to achieve, the more they have to be decked out with things to move us, leading us to the goal without advance warning. In mythological fictions I will consider only the poet's talent; these fictions could well be examined in the light of their religious influence, but such a point of view is absolutely foreign to my subject. I will be discussing the writings of the ancients according to the impression they create in our times, so my concern must be with their literary talent rather than their religious beliefs.

Fictions can be divided into three groups: (1) marvelous and allegorical fictions, (2) historical fictions, (3) fictions in which everything is both invented and imitated, where nothing is true and everything is likely.

This topic should really be discussed in an extensive treatise including most existing literary works and involving thoughts on almost every topic, since the complete exposition of any one idea is connected to the whole chain of ideas. But I am only trying to prove that the most useful kind of fiction will be novels taking life as it is, with delicacy, eloquence, depth, and morality, and I have excluded everything irrelevant to that goal from this essay.[1] . . .

III

The third and last part of this essay must deal with the usefulness of natural fictions, as I call them, where everything is both invented and imitated, so that nothing is true but everything looks true to life. Tragedies with completely imaginary subjects will not be included here; they portray a more lofty nature, an extraordinary situation at an extraordinary level. The verisimilitude of such plays depends on events that are extremely rare, and morally applicable to very few people. Comedies and other dramas are in the theater what novels are to other fiction: their plots are taken from private life and natural circumstances. However, the conventions of the theater deprive us of the commentary which gives examples of reflections their individuality. Dramas are allowed to choose their characters among people other than kings and heroes, but they can show only broadly defined situations, because there is no time for nuance. And life is not concentrated like that — does not happen in contrasts — is not really theatrical in the way plays have to be written. Dramatic art has different effects, advantages, and means which might well be discussed separately, but I think only the modern novel is capable of achieving the constant, accurate usefulness we can get from the picture of our ordinary, habitual feelings. People usually make a separate case of what they call philosophical novels; all novels should be philosophical, as they should all have a moral goal. Perhaps, however, we are not guided so inevitably toward this moral goal when all the episodes narrated are focused on one principal idea, exempting the author from all probability in the way one situation follows another. Each chapter then becomes a kind of allegory — its events are only there to illustrate the maxim at the end. The novels *Candide, Zadig,* and *Memnon,* while delightful in other respects, would be much more useful if they were not marvelous, if they offered an example instead of an emblem and if, as I say, the whole story did not have to relate to the same goal.[2] Such novels are at the same disadvantage as teachers: children never believe them, because they make everything that happens relate to the lesson at hand. Children unconsciously know already that there is less regularity than that in real life. Events are also invented in novels like Richardson's and Fielding's, where the author is trying to keep close to life by following with great accuracy the stages, developments, and inconsistencies of human history, and the way the results of experience always come down to the morality of actions and the advantages of virtue, nonetheless. In these novels, however, the feelings are so natural that the reader often believes he is being spoken to directly, with no artifice but the tactfulness of changing the names.

The art of novel-writing does not have the reputation it deserves because of a throng of bad writers overwhelming us with their colorless productions; in this genre, perfection may require the greatest genius, but mediocrity is well within everyone's grasp. This infinite number of colorless novels has almost used up the passion portrayed in them; one is terrified of finding the slightest resemblance in one's own life to the situations they describe. It has taken the very greatest masters to bring this genre back again, despite the writers who have degraded it. And others

[1]I have read several chapters of a book called *The Spirit of Religions,* by M. Benjamin Constant, which offers some extremely ingenious insights into this whole question. The world of letters and philosophers ought to insist that the author of so great a work finish it and publish it. [Au.] Later published as *The Origin, Forms, and Development of Religion* (1824–1831). Benjamin Constant de Rebecque (1767–1830), known today chiefly for his autobiographical love story *Adolphe,* was the longtime companion of Mme. de Staël, and the father of her daughter Albertine. They collaborated on writing and on plans for the political reform of France. [Tr.]

[2]Tales by Voltaire: *Zadig* was published in 1747, *Memnon* in 1749, *Candide* in 1759. [Tr.]

have dragged it even lower by including disgusting scenes of vice. Despite the fact that fiction's main advantage is to gather around man everything in nature that might be useful to him as a lesson or model, some writers supposed we might have some kind of use for these detestable paintings of evil habits. As if such fictions could ever leave a heart that rejected them in the same state of purity as a heart that had never known them! The novel as we conceive of it, however — as we have a few examples of it — is one of the most beautiful creations of the human mind, and one of the most influential on individual morality, which is what ultimately determines the morality of the public.

There is a very good reason why public opinion does not have enough respect for the writing of good novels, however. This is because novels are considered to be exclusively devoted to the portrayal of love — the most violent, universal, and true passion of them all, but also the passion which inspires no interest at any other time of life than youth, since youth is all it influences. We may well believe that all deep and tender feelings belong to the nature of love, and that hearts which have neither known nor pardoned love cannot feel enthusiasm in friendship, devotion in misery, worship of one's parents, passion for one's children. One can feel respect for one's duties, but no delight or self-surrender in their accomplishment, if one has not loved with all the strength of one's soul, ceasing to be one's self to live entirely in another. The destiny of women and the happiness of men who are not called upon to govern empires often depend for the rest of their lives on the role they gave to the influence of love in their youth. Nevertheless, when people reach a certain age, they completely forget the impression love made on them. Their character changes; they devote themselves to other goals, other passions; and these new interests are what we should extend the subjects of novels to include. A new career would then be open to authors who have the talent to paint all the emotions of the human heart, and are able to use their intimate knowledge of it to involve us. Ambition, pride, greed, vanity could be the primary topic of novels which would have situations as varied as those arising from love, and fresher plots. Will people object that such a tableau of men's passions exists in history, and that we should look for it there? History does not reach the lives of private men, feelings and characters that do not result in public events. History does not act on you with sustained moral interest. Reality often fails to make an effect; and the commentary needed to make a lasting impression would stop the essential quick narrative pace, and give dramatic form to a work that should have a very different sort of merit. And the moral of history can never be completely clear. This may be because one cannot always show with any degree of certainty the inner feelings that punish the wicked in their prosperity and reward the virtuous in their misery, or perhaps because man's destiny is not completed in this life. Practical morality is founded on the advantages of virtue, but the reading of history does not always put it in the limelight.

Great historians (especially Tacitus) do try to attach some moral to every event they relate, making us envy the dying Germanicus, and hate Tiberius at the pinnacle of his grandeur.[3] But they can still portray only those feelings certified by facts. What stays with us from a reading of history is more likely to be the influence of talent, the brilliance of glory, the advantages of power, than the quiet, subtle, gentle morality which is the basis of individual happiness and the relationship between individuals. Everyone would think me ridiculous if I said I set no value on history, and that I preferred fictions — as if fictions did not arise from experience, and as if the delicate nuances shown in novels did not come from the philosophical results and mother-ideas presented by the great panorama of public events! However, the morality of history only exists in bulk. History gives constant results by means of the recurrence of a certain number of chances: its lessons apply to nations, not individuals. Its examples always fit nations, because if one considers them in a general way they are invariable; but it never explains the exceptions. These exceptions can seduce each man as an individual; the exceptional circumstances consecrated by history leave vast empty spaces into

[3]See Tacitus' *Annales*, 2.72; books I and 2. [Tr.]

which the miseries and wrongs that make up most private destinies could easily fall. On the other hand, novels can paint characters and feeling with such force and detail that they make more of an impression of hatred for vice and love for virtue than any other kind of reading. The morality of novels belongs more to the development of the internal emotions of the soul than to the events they relate. We do not draw a useful lesson from whatever arbitrary circumstance the author invents as punishment for the crime; what leaves its indelible mark on us comes from the truthful rendition of the scenes, the gradual process or sequence of wrongdoing, the enthusiasm for sacrifices, the sympathy for misfortune. Everything is so true to life in such novels that we have no trouble persuading ourselves that everything could happen just this way — not past history, but often, it seems, the history of the future.

Novels give a false idea of mankind, it has been said. This is true of bad novels, as it is true of paintings which imitate nature badly. When novels are good, however, nothing gives such an intimate knowledge of the human heart as these portrayals of the various circumstances of private life and the impressions they inspire. Nothing gives so much play to reflection, which finds much more to discover in details than in generalities. Memoirs would be able to do this if their only subjects were not, as in history, famous men and public events. If most men had the wit and good faith to give a truthful, clear account of what they had experienced in the course of their lives, novels would be useless — but even these sincere narratives would not have all the advantages of novels. We would still have to add a kind of dramatic effect to the truth; not deforming it, but condensing it to set it off. This is the art of the painter: far from distorting objects, it represents them in a way that makes them more immediately apprehended. Nature sometimes shows us things all on the same level, eliminating any contrasts; if we copy her too slavishly we become incapable of portraying her. The most truthful account is always an imitative truth: as a tableau, it demands a harmony of its own. However remarkable a true story may be for its nuances, feelings, and characters, it cannot interest us without the talent necessary for the composition of fiction. But despite our admiration for the genius that lets us penetrate the recesses of the human heart, it is impossible to bear all those minute details with which even the most famous novels are burdened. The author thinks they add to the picture's verisimilitude, blind to the fact that anything that slows down the interest destroys the only truth fiction has: the impression it produces. To put everything that happens in a room onstage is to destroy theatrical illusion completely. Novels have dramatic conventions also: the only thing necessary in an invention is what adds to the effect one is creating. If a glance, a movement, or an unnoticed circumstance helps paint a character or develop our understanding of a feeling, the simpler the means, the greater the merit in catching it — but a scrupulously detailed account of an ordinary event diminishes verisimilitude instead of increasing it. Thrown back on a positive notion of what is true by the kind of details that belong only to truth, you soon break out of the illusion, weary of being unable to find either the instruction of history or the interest of a novel.

The greatest power of fiction is its talent to touch us; almost all moral truths can be made tangible if they are shown in action. Virtue has so much influence on human happiness or misery that one can make most of life's situations depend on it. Some severe philosophers condemn all emotions, wanting moral authority to rule by a simple statement of moral duty. Nothing is less suited to human nature. Virtue must be brought to life if she is to fight the passions with any chance of winning; a sort of exaltation must be aroused for us to find any charm in sacrifice; misfortune must be embellished for us to prefer it to the great charm of guilty enticement; and the touching fictions which incite the soul to generous feelings make it unconsciously engage itself in a promise that it would be ashamed to retract in similar circumstances. But the more real power there is in fiction's talent for touching us, the more important it becomes to widen its influence to the passions of all ages, and the duties of all situations. The primary subject of novels is love, and characters who have nothing to do with it are present only as accessories. It would be possible to find a host of new subjects if one followed a different plan. *Tom Jones* has the most general moral of any novel: love appears in it as only one of many means of showing the philosophical result. The real aim of *Tom Jones* is to show the uncertainty of judgments founded on appearances, proving the superiority of natural and what we may call involuntary virtues over reputations based on mere respect for external etiquette. And this is one of the most useful, most deservedly famous of all novels. *Caleb Williams,* by Mr. Godwin, is a recent novel which, despite some tedious passages and oversights, seems to give a good idea of this inexhaustible genre.[4] Love plays no part in this fiction; the only motives for the action are the hero's unbridled passion for the world's respect and Caleb's overpowering curiosity, leading him to discover whether or not Falkland deserves the esteem he enjoys. We read this story with all the absorption inspired by romantic interest and the reflection commanded by the most philosophical tableau.

Some successful fictions do give pictures of life unrelated to love: several *Moral Tales* of Marmontel, a few chapters of *Sentimental Journey,* various anecdotes from the *Spectator* and other books on morality, some pieces taken from German literature, whose superiority is growing every day.[5] There is still, however, no new Richardson devoting himself to paint men's other passions in a novel completely exploring the progress and consequences of these passions. The success of such a work would come from the truth of its characters, the force of its contrasts and the energy of its situations, rather than from that feeling which is so easy to paint, so quick to arouse interest, pleasing women by what it makes them remember even if it cannot attract them by the greatness or novelty of the scenes it presents. What beautiful things we would find in the Lovelace of ambition![6] What philosophical developments, if we were eager to explain and analyze all the passions, as novels have already done for love! Let no one object that books on morality are enough to teach us a knowledge of our duties; such books cannot possibly go into all the nuances of delicacy, or detail the myriad resources of the passions. We can glean a morality purer and higher from novels than from any didactic work on virtue; didactic works are so dry that they have to be too indulgent. Maxims have to be generally applicable, so they never achieve that heroic delicacy we may offer as a model but cannot reasonably impose as a duty. Where is the moralist who could say: "If your whole family wants you to marry a detestable man, and you are prompted by their persecution to give a few signs of the most innocent interest to the man you find attractive, you are going to bring death and dishonor upon yourself"? This, however, is the plot of *Clarissa;* this is what we read with admiration, without a word of protest to the author who touches us and holds us captive. What moralist would claim that it is better to abandon oneself to deep despair, the sort of despair that threatens life and disturbs the mind, rather than marry the most virtuous man in the world if his religion is different from your own? Well, we need not approve of the superstitious opinions of *Clementina,* but love struggling against a scruple of conscience and duty winning out over passion are a sight that moves and touches even loose-principled people who would have rejected such a conclusion disdainfully if it had been a maxim preceding the tableau instead of an effect that followed it.[7] In novels of a less sublime genre, there are so many subtle rules for women's conduct! We could support this opinion by quoting from masterpieces like *The Princess of Clèves, The Count of Comminge, Paul and Virginia, Cecilia,* most of the writings of Madame Riccoboni, *Caroline,* whose charm is felt by everyone, the touching episode of Caliste, the letters of Camilla, in which the mistakes of a woman and

[4]William Godwin published *Caleb Williams* in 1794. [Tr.]

[5]Jean-François Marmontel, *Moral Tales* (1761, 1789–1792); Laurence Sterne, *A Sentimental Journey* (1768); Joseph Addison and Richard Steele, *The Spectator* (1711–12). [Tr.]

[6]Lovelace is the hero-villain of Richardson's *Clarissa* (1748). [Tr.]

[7]Clementina is the Italian woman who renounces the eponymous hero of Richardson's *Sir Charles Grandison* (1754), enabling him to marry Harriet Byron. Prévost's translation retains Richardson's title, but Mme. de Staël sees Clementina as primary. For the influence of this character on Corinne, see Ellen Moers, *Literary Women* (Garden City, N.Y.: Doubleday, 1977), p. 306. [Tr.]

their miserable consequences give a more moral and severe picture than the spectacle of virtue itself, and many other French, English, and German works.[8] Novels have the right to offer the severest morality without revolting our hearts; they have captured feeling, the only thing that can successfully plead for indulgence. Pity for misfortune or interest in passion often win the struggle against books of morality, but good novels have the art of putting this emotion itself on their side and using it for their own ends.

There is still one serious objection to love stories: that they paint love in such a way as to arouse it, and that there are moments in life when this danger wins out over every kind of advantage. This drawback could not exist in novels about any other human passion, however. By recognizing the most fleeting symptoms of a dangerous inclination from the very beginning, one could turn oneself as well as others away from it. Ambition, pride, and avarice often exist without the least consciousness on the part of those they rule. Love feeds on the portrait of its own feelings, but the best way to fight the other passions is to make them be recognized. If the features, tricks, means, and results of these passions were as fully shown and popularized by novels as the history of love, society would have more trustworthy rules and more scrupulous principles about all the transactions of life. Even if purely philosophical writings could predict and detail all the nuances of actions, as do novels, dramatic morality would still have the great advantage of arousing indignant impulses, an exaltation of soul, a sweet melancholy — the various effects of fictional situations, and a sort of supplement to existence. This impression resembles the one we have of real facts we might have witnessed, but it is less distracting for the mind than the incoherent panorama of events around us, because it is always directed toward a single goal. Finally, there are men over whom duty has no influence, and who could still be preserved from crime by developing within them the ability to be moved. Characters capable of adopting humanity only with the help of such a faculty of emotion, the physical pleasure of the soul, would naturally not deserve much respect; nevertheless, if the effect of these touching fictions became widespread enough among the people, it might give us some assurance that we would no longer have in our country those beings whose character poses the most incomprehensible moral problem that has ever existed. The gradual steps from the known to the unknown stop well before we reach any understanding of the emotions which rule the executioners of France. Neither events nor books can have developed in them the least trace of humanity, the memory of a single sensation of pity, any mobility within the mind itself for them to remain capable of that constant cruelty, so foreign to all the impulses of nature — a cruelty which has given mankind its first limitless concept, the complete idea of crime.

There are writings whose principal merit is the eloquence of passion, such as the "Epistle of Abelard" by Pope, *Werther,* the *Portuguese Letters,* and especially *The New Héloïse.*[9] The aim of such works is often moral, but what remains with us more than anything else is the absolute power of the heart. We cannot classify such novels. Every century has one soul and one genius capable of achieving this — it cannot be a genre, it cannot be a goal. Who would want to proscribe these miracles of the word, these deep impressions which satisfy all the emotions of the passionate? Readers enthusiastic about such talent are very few in number; these works always do their admirers good. Let ardent, sensitive souls admire them; they cannot make their language understood by anyone else. The feelings that disturb such beings are rarely understood; con-

[8]All these works are novels. *The Princess of Clèves* is by Mme. de La Fayette (1678); *The Count of Comminge* is by Mme. de Tencin (1735); *Paul and Virginia* is by Jacques-Henri Bernadin de Saint-Pierre (1787); *Cecilia* (1782) and *Camilla* (1796) are by Fanny Burney; Marie-Jeanne Riccoboni wrote a number of novels in the mid-eighteenth century. *Caroline* is probably *Caroline de Lichtfield,* by Isabelle de Montolieu (1785). Isabelle de Charrière, later Constant's intimate friend, wrote *Caliste* (1787). [Tr.]

[9]Alexander Pope's poem "Eloisa to Abelard" (1717); Johann Wolfgang von Goethe's *The Sorrows of Young Werther* (1774); *The Portuguese Letters,* said to have been written by a Portuguese nun to her lover, but probably written by the translator, Gabriel-Joseph de Guilleragues (1669); Jean-Jacques Rousseau's *Julie, or The New Héloïse* (1761). All of these are epistolary fictions. [Tr.]

stantly condemned, they would believe themselves alone in the world, they would soon hate their own nature for isolating them, if a few passionate, melancholy works did not make them hear a voice in the desert of life, letting them find in solitude a few rays of the happiness that escapes them in the middle of society. The pleasure of retreat is refreshing after the vain attempts of disappointed hope; far from this unfortunate creature, the entire universe may be in motion, but such eloquent, tender writing stays near him as his most faithful friend, the one who understands him best. Yes, a book must be right if it offers even one day's distraction from pain; it helps the best of men. Of course there are also sorrows that come from one's own character flaws, but so many of them come from superiority of mind or sensitivity of heart! and there are so many that would be easier to bear if one had fewer good qualities! I respect the suffering heart, even when it is unknown to me; I take pleasure in fictions whose only effect might be to comfort this heart by capturing its interest. In this life, which we pass through rather than feel, the distributor of the only real happiness of which human nature is capable would be someone who distracts man from himself and others, suspending the action of the passions by substituting independent pleasures for them — if the influence of his talent could only last.

On Women Writers

Unhappiness is like the black mountain of Bember, at the edge of the blazing kingdom of Lahor. As long as you are climbing it, you see nothing ahead of you but sterile rocks; but once you are at the peak, heaven is at your head, and at your feet the kingdom of Cashmere.

— *The Indian Hut,* by BERNADIN DE SAINT-PIERRE[1]

The existence of women in society is still uncertain in many ways. A desire to please excites their minds; reason recommends obscurity; and their triumphs and failures are equally and completely arbitrary.

I believe a day will come when philosophical legislators will give serious attention to the education of women, to the laws protecting them, to the duties which should be imposed on them, to the happiness which can be guaranteed them. At present, however, most women belong neither to the natural nor to the social order. What succeeds for some women is the ruin of others; their good points may do them harm, their faults may prove useful. One minute they are everything, the next nothing. Their destiny resembles that of freedmen under the emperors: if they try to gain any influence, this unofficial power is called criminal, while if they remain slaves their destiny is crushed.

It would no doubt be generally preferable for women to devote themselves entirely to the domestic virtues, but the peculiar thing about men's judgments of women is that they are much likelier to forgive women for neglecting these duties than for attracting attention by unusual talent. Men are quite willing to tolerate women's degradation of the heart, so long as it is accompanied by mediocrity of mind. The best behavior in the world can scarcely obtain forgiveness for real superiority.

I am now going to discuss the various causes of this peculiar phenomenon, beginning with the condition of women writers in monarchies, then in republics. I am interested in the differences these political situations make in the destinies of women who set their minds upon literary celebrity; I will then consider more generally the sort of happiness fame can promise these women.

In monarchies, women have ridicule to fear; in republics, hatred.

In a monarchy, the sense of the right and proper is so acute that any unusual act or impulse

[1]A novel published in 1790. [Tr.]

to change one's situation looks ridiculous right away. Anything your rank or position forces you to do finds a thousand admirers; everything you invent spontaneously, with no obligation, is judged severely and in advance. The jealousy natural to all men calms down only if you can apologize for success under cover of some obligation. Unless you cover fame itself with the excuse of your situation and practical interests, if people think your only motive is a need to distinguish yourself, you will annoy those whom ambition is leading in the same direction as yourself.

Men can always hide their vanity or their craving for applause under the appearance or reality of stronger, nobler passions; but women who write are generally assumed to be primarily inspired by a wish to show off their wit. As a result, the public is very reluctant to grant its approval, and the public's sense that women cannot do without this approval is precisely what tempts it to deny it. In every walk of life, as soon as a man sees your obvious need of him, his feelings for you almost always cool down. A woman publishing a book makes herself so dependent on public opinion that those who mete it out make her harshly aware of their power.

These general causes, acting more or less uniformly in all countries, are reinforced by various circumstances peculiar to the French monarchy. The spirit of chivalry, still lingering on in France, was opposed in some respects to the overeager cultivation of letters even by men; it must have aroused all the more dislike for women concentrating on literary studies and turning their thoughts away from their primary concern, the sentiments of the heart. The niceties of the code of honor might well make men averse from submitting themselves to the motley criticism attracted by publicity. How much more must they have disliked seeing the creatures entrusted to their protection — their wives, sisters, daughters — running the gauntlet of public criticism, or even giving the public the right to make a habit of talking about them!

Great talent could triumph over all these considerations, but it was still hard for women to bear reputations as authors nobly, simultaneously combining them with the independence of high rank and keeping up the dignity, grace, ease, and unself-consciousness that were supposed to distinguish their habitual style and manners.

Women were certainly allowed to sacrifice household occupations to a love of society and its pleasures; serious study, however, was condemned as pedantic. If from the very first moment one did not rise above the teasing which went on from all sides, this teasing would end by discouraging talent and poisoning the well of confidence and exaltation.

Some of these disadvantages are not found in republics, especially if one of the goals of the republic is the encouragement of enlightenment. It might perhaps be natural for literature to become women's portion in such a state, and for men to devote themselves entirely to higher philosophy.

The education of women has always followed the spirit of the constitutions established in free countries. In Sparta, women were accustomed to the exercises of war; in Rome, they were expected to have austere and patriotic virtues. If we want the moving principle of the French Republic to be the emulation of enlightenment and philosophy, it is only reasonable to encourage women to cultivate their minds, so that men can talk with them about ideas that would hold their interest.

Nevertheless, ever since the Revolution men have deemed it politically and morally useful to reduce women to a state of the most absurd mediocrity. They have addressed women only in a wretched language with no more delicacy than wit. Women have no longer any motive to develop their minds. This has been no improvement in manners or morality. By limiting the scope of ideas we have not succeeded in bringing back the simplicity of primitive life: the only result of less wit has been less delicacy, less respect for public opinion, fewer ways to endure solitude. And this applies to everything else in the current intellectual climate too: people invariably think that enlightenment is the cause of whatever is going wrong, and they want to make up for it by making reason go backward. Either morality is a false concept, or the more enlightened we are the more attached to morality we become.

If Frenchmen could give their wives all the virtues of Englishwomen, including retiring habits and a taste for solitude, they would do very well to prefer such virtues to the gifts of brilliant wit. All the French will manage to do this way, however, is to make their women read nothing, know nothing, and become incapable of carrying on a conversation with an interesting idea, or an apt expression, or eloquent language. Far from being kept at home by this happy ignorance, Frenchwomen unable to direct their children's education would become less fond of them. Society would become more necessary to these women — and also more dangerous, because no one could talk to them of anything but love, and this love would not even have the delicacy that can stand in for morality.

If such an attempt to make women completely insipid and frivolous ever succeeded, there would be several important losses to national morality and happiness. Women would have fewer ways to calm men's furious passions. They would no longer have any useful influence over opinion — and women are the ones at the heart of everything relating to humanity, generosity, delicacy. Women are the only human beings outside the realm of political interest and the career of ambition, able to pour scorn on base actions, point out ingratitude, and honor even disgrace if that disgrace is caused by noble sentiments. The opinion of society would no longer have any power over men's actions at all if there were no women left in France enlightened enough to make their judgments count, and imposing enough to inspire genuine respect.

I firmly believe that under the ancien régime, when opinion exerted such wholesome authority, this authority was the work of women distinguished by character and wit. Their eloquence was often quoted when they were inspired by some generous scheme or defending the unfortunate; if the expression of some sentiment demanded courage because it would offend those in power.

These are the same women who gave the strongest possible proofs of devotion and energy during the course of the Revolution.

Men in France will never be republican enough to manage without the independence and pride that comes naturally to women. Women may indeed have had too much influence on public affairs under the ancien régime; but they are no less dangerous when bereft of enlightenment, and therefore of reason. Their influence then turns to an inordinate craving for luxury, undiscerning choices, indelicate recommendations. Such women debase the men they love, instead of exalting them. And is the state the better off for it? Should the very limited risk of meeting a woman whose superiority is out of line with the destiny of her sex deprive the republic of France's reputation for the art of pleasing and living in society? Without any women, society can be neither agreeable nor amusing; with women bereft of wit, or the kind of conversational grace which requires the best education, society is spoiled rather than embellished. Such women introduce a kind of idiotic chatter and cliquish gossip into the conversation, alienating all the superior men and reducing brilliant Parisian gatherings to young men with nothing to do and young women with nothing to say.

We can find disadvantages to everything in life. There are probably disadvantages to women's superiority — and to men's; to the vanity of clever people; to the ambition of heroes; to the imprudence of kind hearts, the irritability of independent minds, the recklessness of courage, and so forth. But does that mean we should use all our energy to fight natural gifts, and direct our social institutions toward humbling our abilities? It is hardly as if there were some guarantee that such degradation would promote familial or governmental authority. Women without the wit for conversation or writing are usually just that much more skillful at escaping their duties. Unenlightened countries may not understand how to be free, but they are able to change their masters with some frequency.

Enlightening, teaching, and perfecting women together with men on the national and individual level: this must be the secret for the achievement of every reasonable goal, as well as the establishment of any permanent social or political relationships.

The only reason to fear women's wit would be some sort of scrupulous anxiety about their happiness. And indeed, by developing their rational minds one might well be enlightening them as to the misfortunes often connected with their fate; but that same reasoning would apply to the effect of enlightenment on the happiness of the human race in general, a question which seems to me to have been decided once and for all.

If the situation of women in civil society is so imperfect, what we must work toward is the improvement of their lot, not the degradation of their minds. For women to pay attention to the development of mind and reason would promote both enlightenment and the happiness of society in general. The cultivated education they deserve could have only one really unfortunate result: if some few of them were to acquire abilities distinguished enough to make them hungry for glory. Even this risk, however, would do society no harm, and would only be unfortunate for the very limited number of women whom nature might dedicate to the torture of useless superiority.

And if there were to be some woman seduced by intellectual celebrity and insistent on achieving it! How easy it would be to divert her, if she were caught in time! She could be shown the dreadful destiny to which she was on the verge of committing herself. Examine the social order, she would be told; you will soon see it up in arms against any woman trying to raise herself to the height of masculine reputation.

As soon as any woman is pointed out as a person of distinction, the general public is prejudiced against her. The common people judge according to a few common rules which can be followed without taking any risks. Whatever goes beyond the habitual immediately offends people who consider daily routine the safeguard of mediocrity. A superior man is enough to startle them; a superior woman, straying even farther from the beaten track, must surprise and annoy them even more. A distinguished man almost always has some important career as his field of action, so his talents may turn out to be useful to the interests of even those who least value the delights of the mind. The man of genius may become a man of power, so envious and silly people humor him. But a clever woman is only called upon to offer them new ideas of lofty sentiments, about which they could not care less; her celebrity seems to them much ado about nothing.

Even glory can be a source of reproach to a woman, because it contrasts with her natural destiny. Strict virtue condemns the celebrity even of something which is good in itself, because it damages the perfection of modesty. Men of wit are so astounded by the existence of women rivals that they cannot judge them with either an adversary's generosity or a protector's indulgence. This is a new kind of combat, in which men follow the laws of neither kindness nor honor.

Suppose, as a crowning misfortune, a woman were to acquire celebrity in a time of political dissension. People would think her influence unbounded, even if she had no influence at all; accuse her of all her friends' actions; and hate her for everything she loved. It is far preferable to attack a defenseless target than a dangerous one.

Nothing lends itself more quickly to vague assumptions than the dubious life of a woman with a famous name and an obscure career. An empty-witted man may inspire ridicule, a man of bad character may drop under the weight of contempt, a mediocre man may be cast aside — but everyone would much rather attack the unknown power they call a woman. When the plans of the ancients did not work out, they used to convince themselves that fate had thwarted them. Our modern vanity also prefers to attribute its failures to secret causes instead of to itself; in time of need, what stands in for fatality is the supposed power of famous women.

Women have no way to show the truth, no way to throw light on their lives. The public hears the lie; only their intimate friends can judge the truth. What real way is there for a woman to disprove slanderous accusations? A man who had been slandered lets his actions answer the universe, saying, "My life is a witness: it too must be heard."[2] But where can a woman find any such witness? A few private virtues, hidden favors, feelings locked into the narrow circle of her situation, writings which may make her known in places where she does not live, in times when she will no longer exist.

A man can refute calumny in his work itself, but self-defense is an additional handicap for women. For a woman to justify herself is a new

[2]"Ma vie est un témoin qu'il faut entendre aussi." Mme. de Staël may be quoting an alexandrine from French classical drama. [Tr.]

topic for gossip. Women feel there is something pure and delicate in their nature, quickly withered by the very gaze of the public. Wit, talent, passion in the soul may make them emerge from this mist which should always be surrounding them, but they will always yearn for it as their true refuge.

However distinguished women may be, the sight of ill will makes them tremble. Courageous in misfortune, they are cowards against dislike; thought uplifts them, but their character is still weak and sensitive. Most women whose superior abilities make them want renown are like Erminia dressed in armor.[3] Warriors see the helmet, the lance, the bright plume of feathers, and think they are up against strength, so they attack with violence; with the very first blows, they have struck at the heart.

Such injustices can not only spoil a woman's happiness and peace of mind, but also alienate even the most important objects of her affection. Who can be sure that a libelous portrayal will not strike at the truth of memory? Who knows whether or not slanderers, having wreaked havoc with life, will rob death itself of the tender, regretful feelings that should be associated with the memory of a beloved woman?

So far I have portrayed only the unfairness of men: but what about the threat of injustice from other women? Do not women secretly arouse the malevolence of men? Do women ever form an alliance with a famous woman, sustaining her, defending her, supporting her faltering steps?

And that is still not all. Public opinion seems to release men from every duty toward a recognizably superior woman. Men can be ungrateful to her, unfaithful, even wicked, without making public opinion responsible for avenging her. "Is she not an extraordinary woman?" That says it all; she is abandoned to her own strength, and left to struggle with misery. She lacks both the sympathy inspired by a woman and the power protecting a man. Like the pariahs of India, such a woman parades her peculiar existence among classes she cannot belong to, which consider her as destined to exist on her own, the object of curiosity and perhaps a little envy: what she deserves, in fact, is pity.

[3]In *Tasso's Jerusalem Delivered* (1581), the princess Erminia wears borrowed armor to seek her love Tancred in the Christian camp. [Tr.]

Friedrich von Schiller

1759–1805

Friedrich von Schiller, who chafed at being thought the *second* greatest poet, dramatist, and thinker of the early phase of the German Romantic Movement, was the son of an army doctor who had risen to the rank of captain and married the daughter of an innkeeper. He was educated through the patronage of the Duke of Württemberg at his military school and trained in his father's career of military medicine. While still in school he published lyric poetry, and at eighteen he wrote his most romantic tragedy, *Die Räuber* (published in 1781 and performed the next year). Despite the fame *Die Räuber* brought him, Schiller's artistic career took a long time to become established; his patron disapproved of and discouraged his literary ambitions, the more so as his drama became infected with liberal politics.

Schiller escaped to another province and wrote the domestic tragedy *Kabale und Liebe* (1784) and the political drama *Don Carlos* (1787), plays that are familiar to operagoers from Verdi's *Luisa Miller* and *Don Carlo.* For most of the 1780s Schiller worked in provincial capitals like Mannheim and Dresden without securing a satisfactory position. At Weimar in 1787, however, he turned from the drama of Spanish politics — in *Don Carlos* — to its history, and began a study of the Dutch struggle against Spanish rule in the sixteenth century and the subsequent Thirty Years' War that destroyed the Spanish Empire. As a result, he won the patronage of the Duchess of Weimar and Goethe's recommendation to a professorship, and was able to marry Charlotte von Lengefeld.

In the 1790s, Schiller moved from history to philosophy, absorbing the then new theories of Immanuel Kant and turning his hand to the aesthetic questions that Kant's *Critique of Judgment* had raised. His criticism includes *On Tragic Art* (1792), *Letters on Aesthetic Development* (1795), and *On Naive and Sentimental Poetry* (published in the journal *Die Horen* in 1795–96 and collected in 1800).

Following his work on poetic theory, Schiller returned to its practice, and in the late 1790s published his major ballads. At the end of his life, however, he went back to his first love, the theater, writing a series of grandly tragic plays that developed out of his studies of the past and out of his political vision of a free society. Drawing on his history of the Thirty Years' War, Schiller developed a trilogy about the upstart General Wallenstein (1798–99), which he followed with *The Maid of Orleans* (1801), *The Bride of Messina* (1803), and *Wilhelm Tell* (1804). In chronic ill-health for the last several decades of his life, Schiller died at Weimar in 1805.

Schiller's motivation for writing *On Naive and Sentimental Poetry* is closely linked to his ambivalent feelings — a combination of envy and admiration — about his great contemporary, Goethe. Schiller was struck by how different he was from Goethe: He wrote with painful hesitations, Goethe with ease; he was chronically ill, Goethe vigorous; he was from the middle classes and social encounters were difficult for him, while Goethe had an aristocrat's easy manners. Since Goethe was evidently a great master of letters, what was Schiller? In a letter to his friend Wilhelm von Humboldt, Schiller said: "We shall be differently categorized, but in my most courageous moments I am convinced that our categories will not be subordinated to one another, but instead will be jointly assimilated to a higher ideal concept of the species." So long as Schiller thought of human nature as one thing, as Kant's notions in the *Critique of Judgment* would incline one to do, either he or Goethe would have to be the closer to its ideal, but the dichotomy he sees between the *naive* and the *sentimental* implicitly allowed both poets to be supreme, each in his category: Goethe as the type of the naive genius, Schiller himself as the type of the sentimental.

The central distinction between naive and sentimental poetry turns on the poet's basic temperament, and the relation of that temperament to nature, which was regarded by Schiller as an ideal. The naive poets (Schiller's chief examples are Homer and Shakespeare) *are* nature itself: Their character is that of a child, with a child's sweetness and simplicity, and with a child's cruelty.

> The childlike character that the genius imposes upon his works he likewise displays in his private life and morals. He is *chaste,* for this nature always is; but he is not *prudish,* for only decadence is prudish. He is *intelligent,* for nature can never be otherwise; but he is not *cunning,* for only art can be so. He is *true* to his characters and his inclinations, but not so much because he possesses principles as because nature, despite all fluctuations, always returns to its former state. . . . He is *modest,* . . . because genius always remains a mystery to itself, but he is not fearful because he does not know the dangers of the path he travels. The genres of naive poetry are the classic genres of epic, tragedy, and comedy.

If the naive poets *are* nature, the sentimental poets, in contrast, *love* nature — love it as something they feel they lack, as something that complements their character. The genres of sentimental poetry take shape from the poet's response to this lack. If the sentimental poet takes up the subject of the world as it is, alienated from nature, the real contrary to the ideal, then the poetry will be some form of *satire* — *punitive* (like that of Juvenal or Swift) if the poet "dwells in the realm of the will," conscious of the need to make things better; or *playful* (like that of Horace and Sterne) if the poet dwells in the "realm of the understanding," where the world's problems can be contemplated without battling over them.

On the other hand, the poet may write about the ideal rather than the real; the result is *elegiac* poetry. The true *elegy* is produced when the subject is the ideal of the past compared with the fallen present. (Here Schiller's primary example is the German poet Klopstock, but he also mentions James Thomson's *The Seasons* and Edward Young's *Night Thoughts* — a masterpiece of the English "graveyard school"). Or the poet may produce an *idyll* (as in Rousseau's *Julie, or the New Héloïse*) if the ideal is presented *as though* it were contemporary.

Since both the naive and the sentimental have associated temperaments and genres, it is possible for a sentimental master to work in a naive genre (as Virgil's and Milton's work in the epic demonstrates). Goethe is analyzed here as the reverse case, a naive genius taking up (in *The Sorrows of Young Werther* and *Wilhelm Meister's Apprenticeship*) sentimental themes and genres: "fanatically unhappy love, sensitivity to nature, feeling for religion . . . the gloomy, formless, melancholic Ossianic world." "This task," Schiller concedes, "appears to be completely new and of quite unique difficulty, for in the ancient and naive world a *theme* of this kind did not occur, whereas in the modern the *poet* would be lacking." Goethe's subject — Werther — is "a personality who embraces the ideal with burning feeling and abandons actuality in order to contend with an insubstantial infinitude, who seeks continuously outside himself for that which he destroys within himself, to whom only his dreams are real." He himself is of all modern poets the most child-like and naive, the "least removed from the sensuous truth of things."

Schiller's ideas in *On Naive and Sentimental Poetry* spring from those of Kant but have a tendency to bring a historical dimension into idealist aesthetics, as the poet's work responds to his age and synthesizes its approach to the eternal nature from which all springs. As such, he is one of the links between the thinking of Kant and the later trends in German idealism that culminate in Hegel.

Selected Bibliography

Grossmann, Walter. "The Idea of Cultural Evolution in Schiller's *Aesthetic Education*." *Germanic Review* 34 (1959): 39–49.

Hermand, Jost. "Schillers Abhandlung über naive und sentimentalische Dichtung im Lichte der deutschen Popularphilosophie der 18. Jahrhunderts." *PMLA* 79 (1964): 428–41.

Jones, Michael T. "Twilight of the Gods: The Greeks in Schiller and Lukács." *Germanic Review* 59 (1984): 49–56.

Lloyd, Tom. "Madame Roland and Schiller's Aesthetics." *Prose Studies* 9 (1986): 39–53.

Lukács, Georg. "Schillers Theorie der modernen Literatur." In *Goethe und Seinen Zeit.* Bern: A. Francke, 1947.

Miller, R. D. *A Study of Schiller's 'Letters on the Aesthetic Education of Man.'* Harrogate, Eng.: Duchy, 1986.

Schaper, Eva. "Towards the Aesthetic: A Journey with Friedrich Schiller." *British Journal of Aesthetics* 25 (1985): 153–68.

Sharpe, Leslie. "Schiller's Fragment 'Tragödie und Komödie.'" *Modern Language Review* 81 (1986): 116–17.

Wilm, Emil Carl. *The Philosophy of Schiller in Its Historic Relations.* Boston: Luce and Co., 1912.

From *On Naive and Sentimental Poetry*

The poet, I said either *is* nature or he will *seek* her. The former is the naive, the latter the sentimental poet.

The poetic spirit is immortal and inalienable in mankind, it cannot be lost except together with humanity or with the capacity for it. For even if man should separate himself by the freedom of his fantasy and his understanding from the simplicity, truth and necessity of nature, yet not only does the way back to her remain open always, but also a powerful and ineradicable impulse, the moral, drives him ceaselessly back to her, and it is precisely with this impulse that the poetic faculty stands in the most intimate relationship.

Translated by Julius Elias.

Even now, nature is the sole flame at which the poetic spirit nourishes itself; from her alone it draws its whole power, to her alone it speaks even in the artificial man entoiled by civilization. All other modes of expression are alien to the poetic spirit; hence, generally speaking, all so-called works of wit are quite misnamed poetic; although, for long, misled by the reputation of French literature, we have mistaken them as such. It is still nature, I say, even now in the artificial condition of civilization, in virtue of which the poetic spirit is powerful; but now it stands in quite another relation to nature.

So long as man is pure — not, of course, crude — nature, he functions as an undivided sensuous unity and as a unifying whole. Sense and reason, passive and active faculties, are not separated in their activities, still less do they stand in conflict with one another. His perceptions are not the formless play of chance, his thoughts not the empty play of the faculty of representation; the former proceed out of the law of *necessity,* the latter out of *actuality*. Once man has passed into the state of civilization and art has laid her hand upon him, that *sensuous* harmony in his is withdrawn, and he can now express himself only as a *moral* unity, i.e., as striving after unity. The correspondence between his feeling and thought which in his first condition *actually* took place, exists now only *ideally;* it is no longer within him, but outside of him, as an idea still to be realized, no longer as a fact in his life. If one now applies the notion of poetry, which is nothing but *giving mankind its most complete possible expression,* to both conditions, the result in the earlier state of natural simplicity is the completest possible *imitation of actuality* — at that stage man still functions with all his powers simultaneously as a harmonious unity and hence the whole of his nature is expressed completely in actuality; whereas now, in the state of civilization where that harmonious cooperation of his whole nature is only an idea, it is the elevation of actuality to the ideal or, amounting to the same thing, the *representation of the ideal,* that makes for the poet. And these two are likewise the only possible modes in which poetic genius can express itself at all. They are, as one can see, extremely different from one another, but there is a higher concept under which both can be subsumed, and there should be no surprise if this concept should coincide with the idea of humanity.

This is not the place further to pursue these thoughts, which can only be expounded in full measure in a separate disquisition. But anyone who is capable of making a comparison, based on the spirit and not just on the accidental forms, between ancient and modern poets,[1] will be able readily to convince himself of the truth of the matter. The former move us by nature, by sensuous truth, by living presence; the latter by ideas.

This path taken by the modern poets is, moreover, that along which man in general, the individual as well as the race, must pass. Nature sets him at one with himself, art divides and cleaves him in two, through the ideal he returns to unity. But because the ideal is an infinitude to which he never attains, the civilized man can never become perfect in *his* own wise, while the natural man can in his. He must therefore fall infinitely short of the latter in perfection, if one heeds only the relation in which each stands to his species and to his maximum capacity. But if one compares the species with one another, it becomes evident that the goal to which man in civilization *strives* is infinitely preferable to that which he *attains* in nature. For the one obtains its value by the absolute achievement of a finite, the other by approximation to an infinite greatness. But only the latter possesses *degrees* and displays a *progress,* hence the relative worth of a man who is involved in civilization is in general never determinable, even though the same man considered as an individual necessarily finds himself at a disadvantage compared with one in whom nature functions in her utter perfection. But insofar as the ultimate object of mankind is not otherwise to be attained than by that progress, and

[1]It is perhaps not superfluous to remark that if here the new poets are set over against the ancients, the difference of manner rather than of time is to be understood. We possess in modern times, even most recently, naive works of poetry in all classes, even if no longer of the purest kind and, among the old Latin, even among the Greek poets, there is no lack of sentimental ones. Not only in the same poet, even in the same work one often encounters both species combined, as, for example, in *The Sorrows of Young Werther,* and such creations will always produce the greater effects. [Au.]

man cannot progress other than by civilizing himself and hence passing over into the first category, there cannot therefore be any question to which of the two the advantage accrues with reference to that ultimate object.

The very same as has been said of the two different forms of humanity can likewise be applied to those species of poet corresponding to them.

Perhaps on this account one should not compare ancient with modern — naive with sentimental — poets either at all, or only by reference to some higher concept common to both (there is in fact such a concept). For clearly, if one has first abstracted the concept of those species one-sidedly from the ancient poets, nothing is easier, but nothing also more trivial, than to depreciate the moderns by comparison. If one calls poetry only that which in every age has affected simple nature uniformly, the result cannot be other than to deny the modern poets their title just where they achieve their most characteristic and sublimest beauty, since precisely here they speak only to the adherent of civilization and have nothing to say to simple nature.[2] Anyone whose temperament is not already prepared to pass beyond actuality into the realm of ideas will find the richest content empty appearance, and the loftiest flights of the poet exaggeration. It would not occur to a reasonable person to want to compare any modern with Homer where Homer excels, and it sounds ridiculous enough to find Milton or Klopstock honored with the title of a modern Homer. But just as little could any ancient poet, and least of all Homer, support the comparison with a modern poet in those aspects which most characteristically distinguish him. The former, I might put it, is powerful through the art of finitude; the latter by the art of the infinite.

And for the very reason that the strength of the ancient artist (for what has been said here of the poet can, allowing for self-evident qualifications, be extended to apply to the fine arts generally) subsists in finitude, the great advantage arises which the plastic art of antiquity maintains over that of modern times, and in general the unequal value relationship in which the modern art of poetry and modern plastic art stand to both species of art in antiquity. A work addressed to the eye can achieve perfection only in finitude; a work addressed to the imagination can achieve it also through the infinite. In plastic art works the modern is little aided by his superiority in ideas; here he is obliged to *determine in space in the most precise way* the representation of his imagination and hence to compete with the ancient artists in precisely that quality in which they indisputably excel. In poetic works it is otherwise, and even if the ancient poets are victorious too in the simplicity of forms and in whatever is sensuously representable and *corporeal,* the modern can nonetheless leave them behind in richness of material in whatever is insusceptible of representation and ineffable, in a word, in whatever in the work of art is called *spirit*.

Since the naive poet only follows simple nature and feeling, and limits himself solely to imitation of actuality, he can have only a single relationship to his subject and in *this* respect there is for him no choice in his treatment. The varied impression of naive poetry depends (provided that one puts out of mind everything which in it belongs to the content, and considers that impression only as the pure product of the poetic treatment), it depends, I say, solely upon the various degrees of one and the same mode of feeling; even the variety of external forms cannot effect any alteration in the quality of that aesthetic impression. The form may be lyric or epic, dramatic or narrative: We can indeed be moved to a weaker or stronger degree, but (as soon as the matter is abstracted) never heterogeneously. Our feeling is uniformly the same, entirely composed of *one* element, so that we cannot differentiate within it. Even the difference of language and era

[2]Molière, as a naive poet, is said to have left it in every case to the opinion of his chambermaid what should stand or fall in his comedies; it might also be wished that the masters of the French buskin had occasionally tried the same experiment with their tragedies. But I would not advise that a similar experiment be undertaken with Klopstock's *Odes,* with the finest passages in the *Messiade,* in *Paradise Lost,* in *Nathan the Wise,* or in many other pieces. Yet what am I saying? — the test has really been undertaken, and Molière's chambermaid chops logic back and forth in our critical literature, philosophical and belletristic journals and travel accounts, on poetry, art and the like, as easily, if in poorer taste, on German soil than on French, as only becomes the servants' hall of German literature. [Au.]

changes nothing in this regard, for just this pure unity of its origin and of its effect is a characteristic of naive poetry.

The case is quite otherwise with the sentimental poet. He *reflects* upon the impression that objects make upon him, and only in that reflection is the emotion grounded which he himself experiences and which he excites in us. The object here is referred to an idea and his poetic power is based solely upon this referral. The sentimental poet is thus always involved with two conflicting representations and perceptions — with actuality as a limit and with his idea as infinitude; and the mixed feelings that he excites will always testify to this dual source.[3] Since in this case there is a plurality of principles it depends which of the two will *predominate* in the perception of the poet and in his representation, and hence a variation in the treatment is possible. For now the question arises whether he will tend more toward actuality or toward the ideal — whether he will realize the former as an object of antipathy or the latter as an object of sympathy. His presentation will, therefore, be either *satirical* or it will be (in a broader connotation of the word which will become clearer later) *elegiac;* every sentimental poet will adhere to one of these two modes of perception.

[3]Anyone who observes the impression that naive poetry makes on him and is able to separate from it that part which is due to the content will find this impression always joyous, always pure, always serene, even in the case of very pathetic objects; with sentimental poetry it will always be somewhat solemn and intense. This is because with naive accounts, regardless of their subject matter, we always rejoice in our imagination in the truth, in the living presence of the object, and seek nothing further beyond these; whereas with the sentimental we have to reconcile the representation of imagination with an idea of reason and hence always fluctuate between two different conditions. [Au.]

William Wordsworth

1770–1850

William Wordsworth was born in Cockermouth, Cumberlandshire, the son of an attorney who was steward to a noble lord, and raised in the Lake District in northwest England among hills and lakes and their rustic inhabitants and sojourners, whom he would celebrate in his poetry. Though orphaned at thirteen, Wordsworth managed to attend St. John's College, Cambridge. Taking his degree in 1791, Wordsworth spent a year on the Continent absorbing the sights and the spirit of the French Revolution in its most idealistic phase. On his return to England, Wordsworth wrote *Descriptive Sketches* and met an admirer of that volume, Samuel Taylor Coleridge, who was to be a major poetical and intellectual influence. Together, Wordsworth and Coleridge (mostly Wordsworth) wrote *Lyrical Ballads* (1798), the premier volume of English Romanticism. Although the critics were harsh ("This will never do," Francis Jeffrey began in his notorious attack), the public was not, and a second edition was published in 1800, to which Wordsworth contributed a preface, his single major piece of literary criticism, reprinted here.[1]

Most of Wordsworth's best poetry was written in a single decade, 1797–1807; during this period he wrote not only *Lyrical Ballads* but *Poems in Two Volumes* (1807), including the "Intimations of Immortality" Ode, and *The Prelude* (1805, published 1850). By his forties, when he published *The Excursion* (1814), he was in decline, though he continued to write long into his eighth decade. In old age he had become an institution, and Queen Victoria appointed him poet laureate in 1843.

The Preface to *Lyrical Ballad*s is a transitional work between the rhetorical/mimetic literary theory of the eighteenth century and the expressive theories of the nineteenth. As an argument it is at odds with itself. Part of the confusion derives from Wordsworth's revisions: Most of the original 1800 version of the Preface adheres to a mode of thought (though not, of course, a thesis) that Samuel Johnson would readily have understood, while the 1802 version and subsequent editions ally the essay with later expressive theories of literature.

The occasion of the Preface was Wordsworth's desire to defend two of the revolutionary aspects of *Lyrical Ballads*: their use of a plain style and their rustic subject matter. He does so by attacking the poetic diction of the latter eighteenth century as artificial and meaningless. His memorable analysis of Thomas Gray's "Sonnet on the Death of Mr. Richard West" demonstrates how little of that brief poem actually functions in making its elegiac impression.

When he discusses the subject and style of *Lyrical Ballads,* however, Wordsworth calls on the values the eighteenth century already revered. Why did he choose to write about "low and rustic life"? Because there "the essential passions of the heart find a better soil in which they can attain their maturity, are under less restraint," and

[1]Reprinted here is the 1802 version of the Preface to *Lyrical Ballads,* which includes the "What is a poet?" section, among other revisions.

because "the manners of rural life . . . are most easily comprehended; and are more durable." This recalls Johnson's dictum that the poet who wishes to become a classic should choose to imitate "general nature" rather than topical but evanescent manners. Why did Wordsworth choose to write in the plain style, and what is the role of the reader? "I have proposed to myself to imitate, and, as far as is possible, to adopt the very language of men. . . . to keep my reader in the company of flesh and blood, persuaded that by so doing I shall interest him." At the same time, he hopes to "enlighten the understanding" of the reader and "strengthen and purify" his affections. It sounds as if Wordsworth, however revolutionary his style and subject matter, were defending his poetic practice in the most traditional terms as an attempt to "please many and please long" by providing "just representations of general nature."

Wordsworth thus far seems to be claiming that in *Lyrical Ballads* he was imitating the manners, passions, and actions of rustic Englishmen for the delight and instruction of his audience, but the sections added in 1802 suggest a very different approach to poetry: That poetry is created less by representing what is in the outside world than by attending to the voice within. These passages focus on the poet and the genesis of poetry. But once he had defined poetry as "the spontaneous overflow of powerful feelings," it becomes necessary to explain how the feelings of his preferred humble rustics, such as Goody Blake and Harry Gill, can overflow from a university-educated son of a country lawyer. Wordsworth's solution is to posit for the poet a special internal makeup. The poet is "endued with more lively sensibility, more enthusiasm and tenderness . . . a greater knowledge of human nature, and a more comprehensive soul, than are supposed to be common among mankind." Most important, the poet can express "those thoughts and feelings which," voluntarily or not, "arise in him without immediate external excitement." At times the poet can "let himself slip into an entire delusion, and even confound and identify his own feelings with" those of the people he describes. The poet is thus able to internalize something he has seen and experienced and call it up in himself as though he were participating in it.

As he discusses the process of poetic imagination and composition, Wordsworth erodes the mimetic/rhetorical framework with which he has begun by claiming that the feeling will not be precisely the same when it is imaginatively "recollected in tranquillity" as in immediate experience: It will be purified, on the one hand, but it will "fall short" of reality on the other. The validity of the feeling the poet conveys therefore is not measurable by its accuracy, as a mimetic theory would suggest; it must be measured by a subjective, internal measure: The poet's "faith that no words, which *his* fancy or imagination can suggest, will be to be compared with those which are the emanations of reality and truth."

Wordsworth's theories of poetic diction would be criticized by his friend Coleridge (in *Biographia Literaria,* Ch. 17), his theory of poetic process and imagination refined and replaced by more sophisticated versions, and his vision of the high status and purposes of poetry superseded by the celestial ascending rhetoric of Shelley. But in the Preface to *Lyrical Ballads* Wordsworth created the first and one of the most lasting apologies for the Romantic Movement in poetry and for the expressive theory of literature that underpinned its other beliefs.

Selected Bibliography

Barstow, Marjorie Latta. *Wordsworth's Theory of Poetic Diction*. New Haven: Yale University Press, 1917.

Hirsch, E. D. *Wordsworth and Schelling*. New Haven: Yale University Press, 1960.

Jackson, Wallace. *The Probable and the Marvelous: Blake, Wordsworth and the Eighteenth-Century Critical Tradition*. Athens: University of Georgia Press, 1978.

Jones, Henry John Franklin. *The Egotistical Sublime: A History of Wordsworth's Imagination*. London: Chatto and Windus, 1960.

Knapp, Steven. *Personification and the Sublime: Milton to Coleridge*. Cambridge: Harvard University Press, 1985.

Peacock, M. L., Jr. *Critical Opinions of William Wordsworth*. Baltimore: Johns Hopkins University Press, 1950.

Smith, Nowell C., ed. *Wordsworth's Literary Criticism*. Bristol, Eng.: Bristol Classical Press, 1980.

Thorpe, C. D. "The Imagination: Coleridge versus Wordsworth." *Philological Quarterly* 18 (1939): 1–18.

Wlecke, Albert O. *Wordsworth and the Sublime*. Berkeley: University of California Press, 1973.

Preface to *Lyrical Ballads*

The first volume of these poems has already been submitted to general perusal. It was published, as an experiment, which, I hoped, might be of some use to ascertain, how far, by fitting to metrical arrangement a selection of the real language of men in a state of vivid sensation, that sort of pleasure and that quantity of pleasure may be imparted, which a poet may rationally endeavour to impart.

I had formed no very inaccurate estimate of the probable effect of those poems: I flattered myself that they who should be pleased with them would read them with more than common pleasure: and, on the other hand, I was well aware, that by those who should dislike them they would be read with more than common dislike. The result has differed from my expectation in this only, that I have pleased a greater number, than I ventured to hope I should please.

For the sake of variety, and from a consciousness of my own weakness, I was induced to request the assistance of a friend, who furnished me with the poems of the *Ancient Mariner*, the "Foster-Mother's Tale," the *Nightingale*, and the poem entitled *Love*. I should not, however, have requested this assistance, had I not believed that the poems of my friend would in a great measure have the same tendency as my own, and that, though there would be found a difference, there would be found no discordance in the colours of our style; as our opinions on the subject of poetry do almost entirely coincide.

Several of my friends are anxious for the success of these poems from a belief, that, if the views with which they were composed were indeed realized, a class of poetry would be produced, well adapted to interest mankind permanently, and not unimportant in the multiplicity, and in the quality of its moral relations: and on this account they have advised me to prefix a systematic defence of the theory, upon which the poems were written. But I was unwilling to undertake the task, because I knew that on this occasion the reader would look coldly upon my arguments, since I might be suspected of having been principally influenced by the selfish and foolish hope of *reasoning* him into an approbation of these particular poems: and I was still more unwilling to undertake the task, because, adequately to display my opinions, and fully to enforce my arguments, would require a space wholly disproportionate to the nature of a preface. For to treat the subject with the clearness and coherence, of which I believe it susceptible, it would be necessary to give a full account of the present state of the public taste in this country, and to determine how far this taste is healthy or depraved; which, again, could not be determined, without pointing out, in what manner language and the human mind act and react on each other, and without retracing the revolutions, not of literature alone, but likewise of society itself. I have therefore altogether declined to enter regularly upon this defence; yet I am sensible, that there would be some impropriety in abruptly obtruding upon the public, without a few words of introduction, poems so materially different from those, upon which general approbation is at present bestowed.

It is supposed, that by the act of writing in verse an author makes a formal engagement that he will gratify certain known habits of association; that he not only thus apprizes the reader that certain classes of ideas and expressions will be found in his book, but that others will be carefully excluded. This exponent or symbol held forth by metrical language must in different eras of literature have excited very different expectations: for example, in the age of Catullus, Terence, and Lucretius and that of Statius or Claudian; and in our own country, in the age of Shakespeare and Beaumont and Fletcher, and that of Donne and Cowley, or Dryden, or Pope. I will not take upon me to determine the exact import of the promise which by the act of writing in verse an author, in the present day, makes to his reader; but I am certain, it will appear to many persons that I have not fulfilled the terms of an engagement thus voluntarily contracted. They who have been accustomed to the gaudiness and inane phraseology of many modern writers, if they persist in reading this book to its conclusion, will, no doubt, frequently have to struggle with feelings of strangeness and awkwardness: they will look round for poetry, and will be induced to inquire by what species of courtesy these attempts can be permitted to assume that title. I hope therefore the reader will not censure me, if I attempt to state what I have proposed to myself to perform; and also (as far as the limits of a preface will permit), to explain some of the chief reasons which have determined me in the choice of my purpose: that at least he may be spared any unpleasant feeling of disappointment, and that I myself may be protected from the most dishonourable accusation which can be brought against an author, namely, that of an indolence which prevents him from endeavouring to ascertain what is his duty, or, when his duty is ascertained, prevents him from performing it.

The principal object, then, which I proposed to myself in these poems was to choose incidents and situations from common life and to relate or describe them, throughout, as far as was possible, in a selection of language really used by men; and, at the same time, to throw over them a certain colouring of imagination, whereby ordinary things should be presented to the mind in an unusual way; and, further, and above all, to make these incidents and situations interesting by tracing in them, truly though not ostentatiously, the primary laws of our nature: chiefly, as far as regards the manner in which we associate ideas in a state of excitement. Low and rustic life was generally chosen, because in that condition, the essential passions of the heart find a better soil in which they can attain their maturity, are less under restraint, and speak a plainer and more emphatic language; because in that condition of life our elementary feelings co-exist in a state of greater simplicity, and, consequently, may be more accurately contemplated, and more forcibly communicated; because the manners of rural life germinate from those elementary feelings; and, from the necessary character of rural occupations, are most easily comprehended; and are more durable; and lastly, because in that condition the passions of men are incorporated with the beautiful and permanent forms of nature. The language, too, of these men is adopted (purified indeed from what appear to be its real defects, from all lasting and rational causes of dislike or disgust) because such men hourly communicate with the best objects from which the best part of language is originally derived; and because, from their rank in society and the sameness and narrow circle of their intercourse, being less under the influence of social vanity they convey their feelings and notions in simple and unelaborated expressions. Accordingly, such a language, arising out of repeated experience and regular feelings, is a more permanent, and a far more philosophical language, than that which is frequently substituted for it by poets, who think that they are conferring honour upon themselves and their art, in proportion as they separate themselves from the sympathies of men, and indulge in arbitrary and capricious habits of expression, in order to furnish food for fickle tastes, and fickle appetites, of their own creation.

I cannot, however, be insensible of the present outcry against the triviality and meanness both of thought and language, which some of my contemporaries have occasionally introduced into their metrical compositions; and I acknowledge, that this defect, where it exists, is more dishonourable to the writer's own character than false refinement or arbitrary innovation, though I should contend at the same time that it is far less pernicious in the sum of its consequences. From such verses the poems in these volumes will be found distinguished at least by one mark of difference, that each of them has a worthy *purpose*. Not that I mean to say, that I always began to write with a distinct purpose formally conceived; but I believe that my habits of meditation have so formed my feelings, as that my descriptions of such objects as strongly excite those feelings, will be found to carry along with them a *purpose*. If in this opinion I am mistaken, I can have little right to the name of a poet. For all good poetry is the spontaneous overflow of powerful feelings: but though this be true, poems to which any value can be attached, were never produced on any variety of subjects but by a man, who being possessed of more than usual organic sensibility, had also thought long and deeply. For our continued influxes of feeling are modified and directed by our thoughts, which are indeed the representatives of all our past feelings; and, as by contemplating the relation of these general representatives to each other we discover what is really important to men, so, by the repetition and continuance of this act, our feelings will be connected with important subjects, till at length, if we be originally possessed of much sensibility, such habits of mind will be produced, that, by obeying blindly and mechanically the impulses of those habits, we shall describe objects, and utter sentiments, of such a nature and in such connection with each other, that the understanding of the being to whom we address ourselves, if he be in a healthful state of association, must necessarily be in some degree enlightened, and his affections ameliorated.

I have said that each of these poems has a purpose. I have also informed my reader what this purpose will be found principally to be: namely to illustrate the manner in which our feelings and ideas are associated in a state of excitement. But, speaking in language somewhat more appropriate, it is to follow the fluxes and refluxes of the mind when agitated by the great and simple affections of our nature. This object I have endeavoured in these short essays to attain by various means; by tracing the maternal passion through many of its more subtle windings, as in the poems of the *Idiot Boy* and the *Mad Mother;* by accompanying the last struggles of a human being, at the approach of death, cleaving in solitude to life and society, as in the poem of the "Forsaken Indian"; by showing, as in the stanzas entitled "We Are Seven," the perplexity and obscurity which in childhood attend our notion of death, or rather our utter inability to admit that notion; or by displaying the strength of fraternal, or to speak more philosophically, of moral attachment when early associated with the great and beautiful objects of nature, as in *The Brothers;* or, as in the incident of "Simon Lee," by placing my reader in the way of receiving from ordinary moral sensations another and more salutary impression than we are accustomed to receive from them. It has also been part of my general purpose to attempt to sketch characters under the influence of less impassioned feelings, as in the "Two April Mornings," "The Fountain," "The Old Man Travelling," "The Two Thieves," etc. characters of which the elements are simple, belonging rather to nature than to manners, such as exist now, and will probably always exist, and which from their constitution may be distinctly and profitably contemplated. I will not abuse the indulgence of my reader by dwelling longer upon this subject; but it is proper that I should mention one other circumstance which distinguishes these poems from the popular poetry of the day; it is this, that the feeling therein developed gives importance to the action and situation, and not the action and situation to the feeling. My meaning will be rendered perfectly intelligible by referring my reader to the poems entitled "Poor Susan" and the "Childless Father," particularly to the last stanza of the latter poem.

I will not suffer a sense of false modesty to prevent me from asserting, that I point my reader's attention to this mark of distinction, far less for the sake of these particular poems than from the general importance of the subject. The subject is indeed important! For the human mind is capable of being excited without the application of gross and violent stimulants; and he must have a very faint perception of its beauty and dignity who does not know this, and who does not further know, that one being is elevated above another, in proportion as he possesses this capability. It has therefore appeared to me, that to endeavour to produce or enlarge this capability is one of the best services in which, at any period, a writer can be engaged; but this service, excellent at all times, is especially so at the present day. For a multitude of causes, unknown to former times, are now acting with a combined force to blunt the discriminating powers of the mind, and unfitting it for all voluntary exertion to reduce it to a state of almost savage torpor. The most effective of these causes are the great national events which are daily taking place, and the increasing accumulation of men in cities, where the uniformity of their occupations produces a craving for extraordinary incident, which the rapid communication of intelligence hourly gratifies.[1] To this tendency of life and manners the literature and theatrical exhibitions of the country have conformed themselves. The invaluable works of our elder writers, I had almost said the works of Shakespeare and Milton, are driven into neglect by frantic novels, sickly and stupid German tragedies, and deluges of idle and extravagant stories in verse.[2] — When I think upon this degrading thirst after outrageous stimulation, I am almost ashamed to have spoken of the feeble effort with which I have endeavoured to counteract it; and, reflecting upon the magnitude of the general evil, I should be oppressed with no dishonourable melancholy, had I not a deep impression of certain inherent and indestructible qualities of the human mind, and likewise of certain powers in the great and permanent objects that act upon it which are equally inherent and indestructible; and did I not further add to this impression a belief, that the time is approaching when the evil will be systematically opposed, by men of greater powers, and with far more distinguished success.

Having dwelt thus long on the subjects and aim of these poems, I shall request the reader's permission to apprize him of a few circumstances relating to their *style,* in order, among other reasons, that I may not be censured for not having performed what I never attempted. The reader will find that personifications of abstract ideas rarely occur in these volumes; and, I hope, are utterly rejected as an ordinary device to elevate the style, and raise it above prose. I have proposed to myself to imitate, and, as far as is possible, to adopt the very language of men; and assuredly such personifications do not make any natural or regular part of that language. They are, indeed, a figure of speech occasionally prompted by passion, and I have made use of them as such; but I have endeavoured utterly to reject them as a mechanical device of style, or as a family language which writers in metre seem to lay claim to by prescription. I have wished to keep my reader in the company of flesh and blood, persuaded that by so doing I shall interest him. I am, however, well aware that others who pursue a different track may interest him likewise; I do not interfere with their claim, I only wish to prefer a different claim of my own. There will also be found in these volumes little of what is usually called poetic diction; I have taken as much pains to avoid it as others ordinarily take to produce it; this I have done for the reason already alleged, to bring my language near to the language of men, and further, because the pleasure which I have proposed to myself to impart is of a kind very different from that which is supposed by many persons

[1]Wordsworth refers to the French Revolution and the war between England and France that followed. [Ed.]

[2]Wordsworth alludes to the vogue of the Gothic novel, which lasted from the early 1790s until about 1825. [Ed.]

to be the proper object of poetry. I do not know how without being culpably particular I can give my reader a more exact notion of the style in which I wished these poems to be written than by informing him that I have at all times endeavoured to look steadily at my subject, consequently, I hope that there is in these poems little falsehood of description, and that my ideas are expressed in language fitted to their respective importance. Something I must have gained by this practice, as it is friendly to one property of all good poetry, namely, good sense; but it has necessarily cut me off from a large portion of phrases and figures of speech which from father to son have long been regarded as the common inheritance of poets. I also have thought it expedient to restrict myself still further, having abstained from the use of many expressions, in themselves proper and beautiful, but which have been foolishly repeated by bad poets, till such feelings of disgust are connected with them as it is scarcely possible by any art of association to overpower.

If in a poem there should be found a series of lines, or even a single line, in which the language, though naturally arranged and according to the strict laws of metre, does not differ from that of prose, there is a numerous class of critics, who, when they stumble upon these prosaisms as they call them, imagine that they have made a notable discovery, and exult over the poet as over a man ignorant of his own profession. Now these men would establish a canon of criticism which the reader will conclude he must utterly reject, if he wishes to be pleased with these volumes. And it would be a most easy task to prove to him, that not only the language of a large portion of every good poem, even of the most elevated character, must necessarily, except with reference to the metre, in no respect differ from that of good prose, but likewise that some of the most interesting parts of the best poems will be found to be strictly the language of prose, when prose is well written. The truth of this assertion might be demonstrated by innumerable passages from almost all the poetical writings, even of Milton himself. I have not space for much quotation; but, to illustrate the subject in a general manner, I will here adduce a short composition of Gray, who was at the head of those who by their reasonings have attempted to widen the space of separation betwixt prose and metrical composition, and was more than any other man curiously elaborate in the structure of his own poetic diction.

In vain to me the smiling mornings shine,
And reddening Phoebus lifts his golden fire:
The birds in vain their amorous descant join,
Or cheerful fields resume their green attire:
These ears alas! for other notes repine;
A different object do these eyes require;
My lonely anguish melts no heart but mine;
And in my breast the imperfect joys expire;
Yet Morning smiles the busy race to cheer,
And new-born pleasure brings to happier men;
The fields to all their wonted tribute bear;
To warm their little loves the birds complain.
I fruitless mourn to him that cannot hear
And weep the more because I weep in vain.[3]

It will easily be perceived that the only part of this sonnet which is of any value is the lines printed in italics: it is equally obvious, that, except in the rhyme, and in the use of the single word "fruitless" for fruitlessly, which is so far a defect, the language of these lines does in no respect differ from that of prose.

By the foregoing quotation I have shown that the language of prose may yet be well adapted to poetry; and I have previously asserted that a large portion of the language of every good poem can in no respect differ from that of good prose. I will go further. I do not doubt that it may be safely affirmed, that there neither is, nor can be, any essential difference between the language of prose and metrical composition. We are fond of tracing the resemblance between poetry and painting, and, accordingly, we call them sisters: but where shall we find bonds of connection sufficiently strict to typify the affinity betwixt metrical and prose composition? They both speak by and to the same organs; the bodies in which both of them are clothed may be said to be of the same substance, their affections are kindred and almost identical, not necessarily differing even in de-

[3]Thomas Gray, "Sonnet on the Death of Richard West." [Ed.]

gree; poetry[4] sheds no tears "such as Angels weep," but natural and human tears; she can boast of no celestial ichor that distinguishes her vital juices from those of prose; the same human blood circulates through the veins of them both.

If it be affirmed that rhyme and metrical arrangement of themselves constitute a distinction which overturns what I have been saying on the strict affinity of metrical language with that of prose, and paves the way for other artificial distinctions which the mind voluntarily admits, I answer that the language of such poetry as I am recommending is, as far as is possible, a selection of the language really spoken by men; that this selection, wherever it is made with true taste and feeling, will of itself form a distinction far greater than would at first be imagined, and will entirely separate the composition from the vulgarity and meanness of ordinary life; and, if metre be superadded thereto, I believe that a dissimilitude will be produced altogether sufficient for the gratification of a rational mind. What other distinction would we have? Whence is it to come? And where is it to exist? Not, surely, where the poet speaks through the mouths of his characters: it cannot be necessary here, either for elevation of style, or any of its supposed ornaments: for, if the poet's subject be judiciously chosen, it will naturally, and upon fit occasion, lead him to passions the language of which, if selected truly and judiciously, must necessarily be dignified and variegated, and alive with metaphors and figures. I forbear to speak of an incongruity which would shock the intelligent reader, should the poet interweave any foreign splendour of his own with that which the passion naturally suggests: it is sufficient to say that such addition is unnecessary. And, surely, it is more probable that those passages, which with propriety abound with metaphors and figures, will have their due effect, if, upon other occasions where the passions are of a milder character, the style also be subdued and temperate.

But, as the pleasure which I hope to give by the poems I now present to the reader must depend entirely on just notions upon this subject, and, as it is in itself of the highest importance to our taste and moral feelings, I cannot content myself with these detached remarks. And if, in what I am about to say, it shall appear to some that my labour is unnecessary, and that I am like a man fighting a battle without enemies, I would remind such persons, that, whatever may be the language outwardly holden by men, a practical faith in the opinions which I am wishing to establish is almost unknown. If my conclusions are admitted, and carried as far as they must be carried if admitted at all, our judgments concerning the works of the greatest poets both ancient and modern will be far different from what they are at present, both when we praise, and when we censure: and our moral feelings influencing, and influenced by these judgments will, I believe, be corrected and purified.

Taking up the subject, then, upon general grounds, I ask what is meant by the word poet? What is a poet? To whom does he address himself? And what language is to be expected from him? He is a man speaking to men: a man, it is true, endued with more lively sensibility, more enthusiasm and tenderness, who has a greater knowledge of human nature, and a more comprehensive soul, than are supposed to be common among mankind; a man pleased with his own passions and volitions, and who rejoices more than other men in the spirit of life that is in him; delighting to contemplate similar volitions and passions as manifested in the goings-on of the universe, and habitually impelled to create them where he does not find them. To these qualities he has added a disposition to be affected more than other men by absent things as if they were present; an ability of conjuring up in himself passions, which are indeed far from being the same as those produced by real events, yet (especially in those parts of the general sympathy which are pleasing and delightful) do more nearly resemble the passions produced by real events, than any thing which, from the motions of their own

[4]I here use the word "poetry" (though against my own judgment) as opposed to the word prose, and synonymous with metrical composition. But much confusion has been introduced into criticism by this contradistinction of poetry and prose, instead of the more philosophical one of poetry and matter of fact, or science. The only strict antithesis to prose is metre; nor is this, in truth, a *strict* antithesis, because lines and passages of metre so naturally occur in writing prose, that it would be scarcely possible to avoid them, even were it desirable. [Au.]

minds merely, other men are accustomed to feel in themselves; whence, and from practice, he has acquired a greater readiness and power in expressing what he thinks and feels, and especially those thoughts and feelings which, by his own choice, or from the structure of his own mind, arise in him without immediate external excitement.

But, whatever portion of this faculty we may suppose even the greatest poet to possess, there cannot be a doubt but that the language which it will suggest to him, must, in liveliness and truth, fall far short of that which is uttered by men in real life, under the actual pressure of those passions, certain shadows of which the poet thus produces, or feels to be produced, in himself. However exalted a notion we would wish to cherish of the character of a poet, it is obvious, that, while he describes and imitates passions, his situation is altogether slavish and mechanical, compared with the freedom and power of real and substantial action and suffering. So that it will be the wish of the poet to bring his feelings near to those of the persons whose feelings he describes, nay, for short spaces of time perhaps, to let himself slip into an entire delusion, and even confound and identify his own feelings with theirs; modifying only the language which is thus suggested to him, by a consideration that he describes for a particular purpose, that of giving pleasure. Here, then, he will apply the principle on which I have so much insisted, namely, that of selection; on this he will depend for removing what would otherwise be painful or disgusting in the passion; he will feel that there is no necessity to trick out or to elevate nature: and, the more industriously he applies this principle, the deeper will be his faith that no words, which *his* fancy or imagination can suggest, will be to be compared with those which are the emanations of reality and truth.

But it may be said by those who do not object to the general spirit of these remarks, that, as it is impossible for the poet to produce upon all occasions language as exquisitely fitted for the passion as that which the real passion itself suggests, it is proper that he should consider himself as in the situation of a translator, who deems himself justified when he substitutes excellences of another kind for those which are unattainable by him; and endeavours occasionally to surpass his original, in order to make some amends for the general inferiority to which he feels that he must submit. But this would be to encourage idleness and unmanly despair. Further, it is the language of men who speak of what they do not understand; who talk of poetry as of a matter of amusement and idle pleasure; who will converse with us as gravely about a *taste* for poetry, as they express it, as if it were a thing as indifferent as a taste for rope-dancing, or frontiniac or sherry. Aristotle, I have been told, hath said, that poetry is the most philosophic of all writing:[5] it is so: its object is truth, not individual and local, but general, and operative; not standing upon external testimony, but carried alive into the heart by passion; truth which is its own testimony, which gives strength and divinity to the tribunal to which it appeals, and receives them from the same tribunal. Poetry is the image of man and nature. The obstacles which stand in the way of the fidelity of the biographer and historian, and of their consequent utility, are incalculably greater than those which are to be encountered by the poet who has an adequate notion of the dignity of his art. The poet writes under one restriction only, namely, that of the necessity of giving immediate pleasure to a human being possessed of that information which may be expected from him, not as a lawyer, a physician, a mariner, an astronomer or a natural philosopher, but as a man. Except this one restriction, there is no object standing between the poet and the image of things; between this, and the biographer and historian there are a thousand.

Nor let this necessity of producing immediate pleasure be considered as a degradation of the poet's art. It is far otherwise. It is an acknowledgment of the beauty of the universe, an acknowledgment the more sincere because it is not formal, but indirect; it is a task light and easy to him who looks at the world in the spirit of love: further, it is a homage paid to the native and naked dignity of man, to the grand elementary principle of pleasure, by which he knows, and feels, and

[5]Aristotle, *Poetics,* Ch. 9. One notes that Wordsworth misquotes Artistotle by hearsay. [Ed.]

lives, and moves. We have no sympathy but what is propagated by pleasure: I would not be misunderstood; but wherever we sympathize with pain it will be found that the sympathy is produced and carried on by subtle combinations with pleasure. We have no knowledge, that is, no general principles drawn from the contemplation of particular facts, but what has been built up by pleasure, and exists in us by pleasure alone. The man of science, the chemist and mathematician, whatever difficulties and disgusts they may have had to struggle with, know and feel this. However painful may be the objects with which the anatomist's knowledge is connected, he feels that his knowledge is pleasure; and where he has no pleasure he has no knowledge. What then does the poet? He considers man and the objects that surround him as acting and reacting upon each other, so as to produce an infinite complexity of pain and pleasure; he considers man in his own nature and in his ordinary life as contemplating this with a certain quantity of immediate knowledge, with certain convictions, intuitions, and deductions which by habit become of the nature of intuitions; he considers him as looking upon this complex scene of ideas and sensations, and finding every where objects that immediately excite in him sympathies which, from the necessities of his nature, are accompanied by an overbalance of enjoyment.

To this knowledge which all men carry about with them, and to these sympathies in which without any other discipline than that of our daily life we are fitted to take delight, the poet principally directs his attention. He considers man and nature as essentially adapted to each other, and the mind of man as naturally the mirror of the fairest and most interesting qualities of nature. And thus the poet, prompted by this feeling of pleasure which accompanies him through the whole course of his studies, converses with general nature with affections akin to those, which, through labour and length of time, the man of science has raised up in himself, by conversing with those particular parts of nature which are the objects of his studies. The knowledge both of the poet and the man of science is pleasure; but the knowledge of the one cleaves to us as a necessary part of our existence, our natural and unalienable inheritance; the other is a personal and individual acquisition, slow to come to us, and by no habitual and direct sympathy connecting us with our fellow-beings. The man of science seeks truth as a remote and unknown benefactor; he cherishes and loves it in his solitude: the poet, singing a song in which all human beings join with him, rejoices in the presence of truth as our visible friend and hourly companion. Poetry is the breath and finer spirit of all knowledge; it is the impassioned expression which is in the countenance of all science. Emphatically may it be said of the poet, as Shakespeare hath said of man, "that he looks before and after." He is the rock of defence of human nature; an upholder and preserver, carrying every where with him relationship and love. In spite of difference of soil and climate, of language and manners, of laws and customs, in spite of things silently gone out of mind and things violently destroyed, the poet binds together by passion and knowledge the vast empire of human society, as it is spread over the whole earth, and over all time. The objects of the poet's thoughts are every where; though the eyes and senses of man are, it is true, his favourite guides, yet he will follow wheresoever he can find an atmosphere of sensation in which to move his wings. Poetry is the first and last of all knowledge — it is as immortal as the heart of man. If the labours of men of science should ever create any material revolution, direct or indirect, in our condition, and in the impressions which we habitually receive, the poet will sleep then no more than at present, but he will be ready to follow the steps of the man of science, not only in those general indirect effects, but he will be at his side, carrying sensation into the midst of the objects of the science itself. The remotest discoveries of the chemist, the botanist, or mineralogist, will be as proper objects of the poet's art as any upon which it can be employed, if the time should ever come when these things shall be familiar to us, and the relations under which they are contemplated by the followers of these respective sciences shall be manifestly and palpably material to us as enjoying and suffering beings. If the time should ever come when what is now called science, thus familiarized to men, shall be ready to put on, as it were, a form of flesh and blood, the poet will lend his divine spirit to aid the transfiguration, and will welcome the being thus produced, as a dear and genuine inmate of the household of man. — It is not, then, to be supposed that any one, who holds that sublime notion of poetry which I have attempted to convey, will break in upon the sanctity and truth of his pictures by transitory and accidental ornaments, and endeavour to excite admiration of himself by arts, the necessity of which must manifestly depend upon the assumed meanness of his subject.

What I have thus far said applies to poetry in general; but especially to those parts of composition where the poet speaks through the mouths of his characters; and upon this point it appears to have such weight that I will conclude, there are few persons, of good sense, who would not allow that the dramatic parts of composition are defective, in proportion as they deviate from the real language of nature, and are coloured by a diction of the poet's own, either peculiar to him as an individual poet, or belonging simply to poets in general, to a body of men who, from the circumstance of their compositions being in metre, it is expected will employ a particular language.

It is not, then, in the dramatic parts of composition that we look for this distinction of language; but still it may be proper and necessary where the poet speaks to us in his own person and character. To this I answer by referring my reader to the description which I have before given of a poet. Among the qualities which I have enumerated as principally conducing to form a poet, is implied nothing differing in kind from other men, but only in degree. The sum of what I have there said is, that the poet is chiefly distinguished from other men by a greater promptness to think and feel without immediate external excitement, and a greater power in expressing such thoughts and feelings as are produced in him in that manner. But these passions and thoughts and feelings are the general passions and thoughts and feelings of men. And with what are they connected? Undoubtedly with our moral sentiments and animal sensations, and with the causes which excite these; with the operations of the elements and the appearances of the visible universe; with storm and sunshine, with the revolutions of the seasons, with cold and heat, with loss of friends and kindred, with injuries and resentments, gratitude and hope, with fear and sorrow. These, and the like, are the sensations and objects which the poet describes, as they are the sensations of other men, and the objects which interest them. The poet thinks and feels in the spirit of the passions of men. How, then, can his language differ in any material degree from that of all other men who feel vividly and see clearly? It might be *proved* that it is impossible. But supposing that this were not the case, the poet might then be allowed to use a peculiar language, when expressing his feelings for his own gratification, or that of men like himself. But poets do not write for poets alone, but for men. Unless therefore we are advocates for that admiration which depends upon ignorance, and that pleasure which arises from hearing what we do not understand, the poet must descend from this supposed height, and, in order to excite rational sympathy, he must express himself as other men express themselves. To this it may be added, that while he is only selecting from the real language of men, or, which amounts to the same thing, composing accurately in the spirit of such selection, he is treading upon safe ground, and we know what we are to expect from him. Our feelings are the same with respect to metre; for, as it may be proper to remind the reader, the distinction of metre is regular and uniform, and not like that which is produced by what is usually called poetic diction, arbitrary, and subject to infinite caprices upon which no calculation whatever can be made. In the one case, the reader is utterly at the mercy of the poet respecting what imagery or diction he may choose to connect with the passion, whereas, in the other, the metre obeys certain laws, to which the poet and reader both willingly submit because they are certain, and because no interference is made by them with the passion but such as the concurring testimony of ages has shown to heighten and improve the pleasure which co-exists with it.

It will now be proper to answer an obvious question, namely, why, professing these opinions, have I written in verse? To this, in addition to such answer as is included in what I have already said, I reply in the first place, because, however I may have restricted myself, there is still left open to me what confessedly constitutes the most valuable object of all writing whether in prose or verse, the great and universal passions of men, the most general and interesting of their occupations, and the entire world of nature, from which I am at liberty to supply myself with endless combinations of forms and imagery. Now, supposing for a moment that whatever is interesting in these objects may be as vividly described in prose, why am I to be condemned, if to such description I have endeavoured to superadd the charm which, by the consent of all nations, is acknowledged to exist in metrical language? To this, by such as are unconvinced by what I have already said, it may be answered, that a very small part of the pleasure given by poetry depends upon the metre, and that it is injudicious to write in metre, unless it be accompanied with the other artificial distinctions of style with which metre is usually accompanied, and that by such deviation more will be lost from the shock which will be thereby given to the reader's associations, than will be counterbalanced by any pleasure which he can derive from the general power of numbers. In answer to those who still contend for the necessity of accompanying metre with certain appropriate colours of style in order to the accomplishment of its appropriate end, and who also, in my opinion, greatly underrate the power of metre in itself, it might perhaps, as far as relates to these poems, have been almost sufficient to observe, that poems are extant, written upon more humble subjects, and in a more naked and simple style than I have aimed at, which poems have continued to give pleasure from generation to generation. Now, if nakedness and simplicity be a defect, the fact here mentioned affords a strong presumption that poems somewhat less naked and simple are capable of affording pleasure at the present day; and, what I wished *chiefly* to attempt, at present, was to justify myself for having written under the impression of this belief.

But I might point out various causes why, when the style is manly, and the subject of some importance, words metrically arranged will long continue to impart such a pleasure to mankind as he who is sensible of the extent of that pleasure will be desirous to impart. The end of poetry is to produce excitement in co-existence with an overbalance of pleasure. Now, by the supposition, excitement is an unusual and irregular state of the mind; ideas and feelings do not in that state succeed each other in accustomed order. But, if the words by which this excitement is produced are in themselves powerful, or the images and feelings have an undue proportion of pain connected with them, there is some danger that the excitement may be carried beyond its proper bounds. Now the co-presence of something regular, something to which the mind has been accustomed in various moods and in a less excited state, cannot but have great efficacy in tempering and restraining the passion by an inter-texture of ordinary feeling, and of feeling not strictly and necessarily connected with the passion. This is unquestionably true, and hence, though the opinion will at first appear paradoxical, from the tendency of metre to divest language in a certain degree of its reality, and thus to throw a sort of half consciousness of unsubstantial existence over the whole composition, there can be little doubt but that more pathetic situations and sentiments, that is, those which have a greater proportion of pain connected with them, may be endured in metrical composition, especially in rhyme, than in prose. The metre of the old ballads is very artless; yet they contain many passages which would illustrate this opinion, and, I hope, if the following poems be attentively perused, similar instances will be found in them. This opinion may be further illustrated by appealing to the reader's own experience of the reluctance with which he comes to the reperusal of the distressful parts of *Clarissa Harlowe*, or the *Gamester*.[6] While Shakespeare's writings, in the most pathetic scenes, never act upon us as pathetic beyond the bounds of pleasure — an effect which, in a much greater degree than might at first be imagined, is to be ascribed to small, but continual and regular impulses of pleasurable surprise from the metrical arrangement. — On the other hand (what it must be allowed will much more frequently happen) if the poet's words should be incommensurate with the passion, and inadequate to raise the

[6]Samuel Richardson's *Clarissa* (1747–48) and Edward Moore's *The Gamester* (1753). [Ed.]

reader to a height of desirable excitement, then, (unless the poet's choice of his metre has been grossly injudicious) in the feelings of pleasure which the reader has been accustomed to connect with metre in general, and in the feeling, whether cheerful or melancholy, which he has been accustomed to connect with that particular movement of metre, there will be found something which will greatly contribute to impart passion to the words, and to effect the complex end which the poet proposes to himself.

If I had undertaken a systematic defence of the theory upon which these poems are written, it would have been my duty to develop the various causes upon which the pleasure received from metrical language depends. Among the chief of these causes is to be reckoned a principle which must be well known to those who have made any of the arts the object of accurate reflection; I mean the pleasure which the mind derives from the perception of similitude in dissimilitude. This principle is the great spring of the activity of our minds, and their chief feeder. From this principle the direction of the sexual appetite, and all the passions connected with it take their origin: it is the life of our ordinary conversation; and upon the accuracy with which similitude in dissimilitude, and dissimilitude in similitude are perceived, depend our taste and our moral feelings. It would not have been a useless employment to have applied this principle to the consideration of metre, and to have shown that metre is hence enabled to afford much pleasure, and to have pointed out in what manner that pleasure is produced. But my limits will not permit me to enter upon this subject, and I must content myself with a general summary.

I have said that poetry is the spontaneous overflow of powerful feelings: it takes its origin from emotion recollected in tranquillity: the emotion is contemplated till by a species of reaction the tranquillity gradually disappears, and an emotion, kindred to that which was before the subject of contemplation, is gradually produced, and does itself actually exist in the mind. In this mood successful composition generally begins, and in a mood similar to this it is carried on; but the emotion, of whatever kind and in whatever degree, from various causes is qualified by various pleasures, so that in describing any passions whatsoever, which are voluntarily described, the mind will upon the whole be in a state of enjoyment. Now, if nature be thus cautious in preserving in a state of enjoyment a being thus employed, the poet ought to profit by the lesson thus held forth to him, and ought especially to take care, that whatever passions he communicates to his reader, those passions, if his reader's mind be sound and vigorous, should always be accompanied with an overbalance of pleasure. Now the music of harmonious metrical language, the sense of difficulty overcome, and the blind association of pleasure which has been previously received from works of rhyme or metre of the same or similar construction, an indistinct perception perpetually renewed of language closely resembling that of real life, and yet, in the circumstance of metre, differing from it so widely, all these imperceptibly make up a complex feeling of delight, which is of the most important use in tempering the painful feeling which will always be found intermingled with powerful descriptions of the deeper passions. This effect is always produced in pathetic and impassioned poetry; while, in lighter compositions, the ease and gracefulness with which the poet manages his numbers are themselves confessedly a principal source of the gratification of the reader. I might perhaps include all which it is *necessary* to say upon this subject by affirming, what few persons will deny, that, of two descriptions, either of passions, manners, or characters, each of them equally well executed, the one in prose and the other in verse, the verse will be read a hundred times where the prose is read once. We see that Pope by the power of verse alone, has contrived to render the plainest common sense interesting, and even frequently to invest it with the appearance of passion. In consequence of these convictions I related in metre the tale of *Goody Blake and Harry Gill,* which is one of the rudest of this collection. I wished to draw attention to the truth that the power of the human imagination is sufficient to produce such changes even in our physical nature as might almost appear miraculous. The truth is an important one; the fact (for it is a *fact*) is a valuable illustration of it. And I have the satisfaction of knowing that it has been communicated to many hundreds of people who would never have heard of it, had it not been narrated as a ballad, and in a more impressive metre than is usual in ballads.

Having thus explained a few of the reasons why I have written in verse, and why I have chosen subjects from common life, and endeavoured to bring my language near to the real language of men, if I have been too minute in pleading my own cause, I have at the same time been treating a subject of general interest; and it is for this reason that I request the reader's permission to add a few words with reference solely to these particular poems, and to some defects which will probably be found in them. I am sensible that my associations must have sometimes been particular instead of general, and that, consequently, giving to things a false importance, sometimes from diseased impulses I may have written upon unworthy subjects; but I am less apprehensive on this account, than that my language may frequently have suffered from those arbitrary connexions of feelings and ideas with particular words and phrases, from which no man can altogether protect himself. Hence I have no doubt, that, in some instances, feelings even of the ludicrous may be given to my readers by expressions which appeared to me tender and pathetic. Such faulty expressions, were I convinced they were faulty at present, and that they must necessarily continue to be so, I would willingly take all reasonable pains to correct. But it is dangerous to make these alterations on the simple authority of a few individuals, or even of certain classes of men; for where the understanding of an author is not convinced, or his feelings altered, this cannot be done without great injury to himself: for his own feelings are his stay and support, and, if he sets them aside in one instance, he may be induced to repeat this act till his mind loses all confidence in itself, and becomes utterly debilitated. To this it may be added, that the reader ought never to forget that he is himself exposed to the same errors as the poet, and perhaps in a much greater degree: for there can be no presumption in saying, that it is not probable he will be so well acquainted with the various stages of meaning through which words have passed, or with the fickleness or stability of the relations of particular ideas to each other; and above all, since he is so much less interested in the subject, he may decide lightly and carelessly.

Long as I have detained my reader, I hope he will permit me to caution him against a mode of false criticism which has been applied to poetry in which the language closely resembles that of life and nature. Such verses have been triumphed over in parodies of which Dr. Johnson's stanza is a fair specimen.

> I put my hat upon my head,
> And walked into the Strand,
> And there I met another man
> Whose hat was in his hand.

Immediately under these lines I will place one of the most justly admired stanzas of the "Babes in the Wood."

> These pretty Babes with hand in hand
> Went wandering up and down;
> But never more they saw the Man
> Approaching from the Town.

In both these stanzas the words, and the order of the words, in no respect differ from the most unimpassioned conversation. There are words in both, for example, "the Strand," and "the Town," connected with none but the most familiar ideas; yet the one stanza we admit as admirable, and the other as a fair example of the superlatively contemptible. Whence arises this difference? Not from the metre, not from the language, not from the order of the words; but the *matter* expressed in Dr. Johnson's stanza is contemptible. The proper method of treating trivial and simple verses to which Dr. Johnson's stanza would be a fair parallelism is not to say, this is a bad kind of poetry, or this is not poetry; but this wants sense; it is neither interesting in itself, nor can *lead* to any thing interesting; the images neither originate in that sane state of feeling which arises out of thought, nor can excite thought or feeling in the reader. This is the only sensible manner of dealing with such verses: Why trouble yourself about the species till you have previously decided upon the genus? Why take pains to prove that an ape is not a Newton when it is self-evident that he is not a man?

I have one request to make of my reader, which is, that in judging these poems he would decide by his own feelings genuinely, and not by reflection upon what will probably be the judgment of others. How common is it to hear a person say, "I myself do not object to this style of composition or this or that expression, but to such and such classes of people it will appear mean or ludicrous." This mode of criticism, so destructive of all sound unadulterated judgment, is almost universal: I have therefore to request, that the reader would abide independently by his own feelings, and that if he finds himself affected he would not suffer such conjectures to interfere with his pleasure.

If an author by any single composition has impressed us with respect for his talents, it is useful to consider this as affording a presumption, that, on other occasions where we have been displeased, he nevertheless may not have written ill or absurdly; and, further, to give him so much credit for this one composition as may induce us to review what has displeased us with more care than we should otherwise have bestowed upon it. This is not only an act of justice, but in our decisions upon poetry especially, may conduce in a high degree to the improvement of our own taste: for an *accurate* taste in poetry and in all the other arts, as Sir Joshua Reynolds has observed,[7] is an *acquired* talent, which can only be produced by thought and a long continued intercourse with the best models of composition. This is mentioned, not with so ridiculous a purpose as to prevent the most inexperienced reader from judging for himself (I have already said that I wish him to judge for himself), but merely to temper the rashness of decision, and to suggest, that, if poetry be a subject on which much time has not been bestowed, the judgment may be erroneous; and that in many cases it necessarily will be so.

I know that nothing would have so effectually contributed to further the end which I have in view as to have shown of what kind the pleasure is, and how that pleasure is produced, which is confessedly produced by metrical composition essentially different from that which I have here endeavoured to recommend: for the reader will say that he has been pleased by such composition; and what can I do more for him? The power of any art is limited; and he will suspect, that, if I propose to furnish him with new friends, it is only upon condition of his abandoning his old friends. Besides, as I have said, the reader is himself conscious of the pleasure which he has received from such composition, composition to which he has peculiarly attached the endearing name of poetry; and all men feel an habitual gratitude, and something of an honourable bigotry for the objects which have long continued to please them: we not only wish to be pleased, but to be pleased in that particular way in which we have been accustomed to be pleased. There is a host of arguments on these feelings; and I should be the less able to combat them successfully, as I am willing to allow, that, in order entirely to enjoy the poetry which I am recommending, it would be necessary to give up much of what is ordinarily enjoyed. But, would my limits have permitted me to point out how this pleasure is produced, I might have removed many obstacles, and assisted my reader in perceiving that the powers of language are not so limited as he may suppose; and that it is possible that poetry may give other enjoyments, of a purer, more lasting, and more exquisite nature. This part of my subject I have not altogether neglected; but it has been less my present aim to prove, that the interest excited by some other kinds of poetry is less vivid, and less worthy of the nobler powers of the mind, than to offer reasons for presuming, that, if the object which I have proposed to myself were adequately attained, a species of poetry would be produced, which is genuine poetry; in its nature well adapted to interest mankind permanently, and likewise important in the multiplicity and quality of its moral relations.

From what has been said, and from a perusal of the poems, the reader will be able clearly to perceive the object which I have proposed to myself: he will determine how far I have attained this object; and, what is a much more important question, whether it be worth attaining; and upon the decision of these two questions will rest my claim to the approbation of the public.

[7]Wordsworth refers to Joshua Reynolds's *Discourses* on art, probably a passage in Discourse 12 (*Works,* 2:95). [Ed.]

Samuel Taylor Coleridge

1772–1834

Coleridge's father, a parson in rural Devonshire, died when his son was nine years old. Thereafter Coleridge was educated at Christ's Hospital school as a charity student and then at Jesus College, Cambridge, which he left in 1794 without a degree. He became involved with Robert Southey's protosocialist pantisocracy scheme and in 1795 married Southey's sister-in-law, Sara Fricker, with whom he was deeply unhappy. That same year he was introduced to William Wordsworth, and the two "lake poets" collaborated on the seminal Romantic work of *Lyrical Ballads* (1798), in which Coleridge published "The Rime of the Ancient Mariner." Although he had experimented with opium as early as 1797, Coleridge did not become fully addicted until 1803 and remained so until 1816, when Dr. James Gillman attempted, with some success, to wean him gradually from the drug. Coleridge published *Christabel and Other Poems,* including the title poem "Christabel" and "Kubla Khan," in 1816, and his critical testament, *Biographia Literaria,* in 1817. The latter, together with some of Coleridge's Shakespeare lectures, comprises some of the richest critical theory the English Romantic Movement produced.

Coleridge based his ideas about the nature of imagination and art on his reading in the late 1790s of Kant and Kant's student Schelling. To understand fully what Coleridge intends in the *Biographia Literaria* requires a short detour into the history of the philosophy of mind.

KANT AND THE MIND

Immanuel Kant's most difficult and important work is probably the *Critique of Pure Reason,* in which his central concern is the way the mind operates. Since we are necessarily unaware of many of the operations of the mind, Kant is forced to focus on the most fleeting of our sensations; in fact he must generate a large-scale set of abstract notions in order to account for the mental output of which we are aware. The debate about mind that Kant joined in the eighteenth century was in some ways much like the debate in post–World War II psychology between the behaviorists and the mentalists.

Nearly a century before Kant, John Locke, in the *Essay Concerning Human Understanding* (1690), had attempted to establish the ultimate behaviorist position. Locke posited that the mind is a *tabula rasa,* a blank slate upon which experience writes. All ideas are derived from two sources: sense experience and the ability of the mind to contemplate itself. Locke tried to show that one could explain the most complex notions of the mind as aggregations of simple ideas. All the mind has to be able to do, by and large, is to place current sensations in memory and recall them on demand, to form simple ideas by associating and comparing current with past sense data, and to be able to associate and compare the simple ideas that result to build up more complex ones. In Locke's notion, the mind is like a computer with data inputs (the senses), an information storage/retrieval system, and some very simple programs, endlessly iterated, to process and compare the data.

Locke's picture of the mind as a simple machine influenced the thought of the entire eighteenth century (the novelist Laurence Sterne based *Tristram Shandy* on the workings and misworkings of Lockean associationism). But over the course of the century, Locke's system came to seem less and less adequate to account for the world as we know it. One problem was that Locke's philosophy assumed a sharp distinction between the inner world of mind and the outer world of matter. But since, as the philosopher George Berkeley argued, we know the world of matter only through mind, skeptics might doubt the very existence of the material world.

Another problem (raised by David Hume) concerned causality, surely the most important of the simple ideas by which we make sense of the phenomenal world. When we say that event A caused event B, we minimally mean that A is included in the ground of being of B. But when we see (on a billiard table, for example) the red ball hit the white ball (A) and the white ball move into the pocket (B), it is not clear that we know this much. What we know is that two events show spatial contiguity (the balls touched) and temporal succession (B followed A). But spatial contiguity and temporal succession do not add up to causality. If a baseball player were to scratch his nose and then hit a home run, would the scratching be thought the *cause* of the homer? Hume suggested that we attribute causality only where we have seen consistency of behavior. Only if there were a pattern in which nose-scratching led to home runs would we say that the former caused the latter; only on the basis of long experience with billiard balls do we say that the motion of the red ball causes that of the white. But this adds only subjective mental habit to the objective spatiotemporal contact we had before, and we seem just as far as ever from what we mean by cause.

Berkeley questioned the existence of the physical world that provides Locke's sense data and experience, and Hume raised doubts about whether the behavioristic mind Locke had assumed could effectually process its data in the way we know it does. The problem, it was becoming clear, was that the human mind had to be more complicated in its workings than Locke had thought. In fact, in order to account for what the mind can do, Kant was forced to attribute a great many more features of our sense of reality to the subjective mind.

For Kant, the external world consists of *noumena,* things whose existence we have to assume but about which we can form no clear idea. As the noumena impinge upon our senses, the mind actively (not passively as Locke claimed) processes the data into "representations." First the datum is marked with our identity — as *ours.* Then it is labeled for space and time — which for Kant were features of mind rather than of matter. Then it is run through the Kantian categories of the understanding and marked for quality, quantity, substance, relation, and so on. The noumena enter the mind; what emerges is phenomena, the world as it appears to us. For Kant, then, the phenomenal world is not *given;* it is *created* by us at every conscious moment through the processing system he calls the productive imagination. Since all minds contain the same mechanisms, we all perceive phenomena consistently and in roughly the same ways: The features of the outside world appear objectively real to us, although they are largely produced by the subjective workings of the mind.

COLERIDGE ON THE IMAGINATION

The above is a more elaborate explanation of what Coleridge is trying to say in a single enigmatic sentence of Chapter 13 of the *Biographia Literaria.* "The primary IMAGINATION I hold to be the living Power and prime Agent of all human Perception, and as a repetition in the finite mind of the eternal act of creation in the infinite I AM." What Kant had called the productive imagination, Coleridge renamed the primary: that mental faculty by which we create the world of our perceptions at each moment of consciousness. Just as God created the *noumena,* man creates the *phenomena.*

If the primary imagination is responsible for perception, the *secondary* imagination is responsible for art. It is, Coleridge says, "an echo" of the primary, and like an echo it is similar to but weaker than what it echoes. Like the primary imagination, it is a creative faculty, but even when the imagination operates it may not wholly displace the phenomenal world. Unlike the primary imagination, the power of the secondary imagination varies from individual to individual. Where the primary imagination creates the perceptual world without our desiring it, the secondary is "co-existing with," and at least partially responsive to, "the conscious will." It operates by dissolving, diffusing, dissipating the perceptual world and creating another world in its place — or at least minimally reshaping the perceptual world into a more idealized and unified picture. The more complete the process of dissolution and recreation, the more fantastic the art form produced; the less complete, the more realistic. Coleridge has thus accounted for the differences between his poetry and that of his friend Wordsworth.

At the end of Chapter 13, Coleridge differentiates between fancy and imagination. Imagination — the secondary imagination described above — is a fully creative activity that, in effect, produces a new perceptual world. Fancy, on the other hand, is an inferior activity, since it operates entirely within the usual perceptual world; it is an activity describable in purely Lockean terms as the willful conjunction of ideas that are normally distinct (like placing an elephant's head on the body of a camel).

COLERIDGE ON POEMS AND POETRY

In Chapter 14 Coleridge differentiates between *poem* and *poetry* — which are almost but not quite related as product is to process. The procedure by which Coleridge defines "poem" is laborious but not entirely lucid. The confusion largely stems from an internal conflict. On the one hand Coleridge wants to evaluate as he defines, to define the *legitimate* as opposed to the *mere* poem; on the other hand, he also knows well that the word *poem* is generally used to apply to any composition in verse — good, bad, or indifferent. In trying to have it both ways, Coleridge muddies his argument. First, he grudgingly concedes that mere rhyming mnemonics "may be given the name of poem." But the real process of definition is more involved.

In Coleridge's definition there are two criteria: "object" or purpose and "superficial form." A poem has as its immediate purpose "pleasure not truth" and is thus differentiated from history or science. And it is written in verse: rhyme or meter or both conjointly. In effect, Coleridge specifies the following outline for major genres of poetry and prose:

	IMMEDIATE OBJECT	
	PLEASURE	TRUTH
SUPERFICIAL FORM:		
RHYME AND/OR METER	Poem	Mnemonic
PROSE	Novel	History or science

This outline seems mechanical enough — but then Coleridge asks a revealing question: If we turned a work of prose fiction into verse, would that make it a poem? The superficial answer would be "yes," but Coleridge says it would not: "Nothing can permanently please, which does not contain in itself the reason why it is so, and not otherwise." In a genuine poem, the linguistic and ideological content justifies the "perpetual and distinct attention to each part" that meter excites in us. A novel versified might look like a poem, but it would be dreadful in effect, since its texture would not be tightly woven enough to bear up under the sort of attention we would give it *as verse*. In legitimate poems, on the other hand, form and content, structure and texture, are interconnected: They are designed to stand the intense scrutiny that meter provokes.

The broad principle to which Coleridge appeals is that of *organic form;* he discusses it at greater length in "Shakespeare's Judgment Equal to His Genius," where he contrasts the merely mechanical form that it is possible to impose upon materials with the organic form that grows out of the nature of the materials themselves. The "superficial" form in a genuine poem is, in fact, not superficial at all: It is an integral part of the poem's design.

Having defined "poem," Coleridge turns to "poetry," which to him is not a collective term for poems but an independent category. Poetry, he says, may be written in prose rather than in verse; and it may occur in works whose immediate object is truth rather than pleasure. More positively, his definition of poetry has "been in part anticipated in [some of the remarks] on the Fancy and Imagination": Less coyly, poetry is the verbal product of the "poetic genius" — the secondary imagination as defined in Chapter 13.

Long poems, Coleridge asserts, cannot be all poetry; conversely, much that is poetry is not in the form of a poem. In fact, so disparate are the two definitions that one might wonder why there needs to be *any* poetry whatever in the poem. The definitions only appear to be disconnected, however. What links them is Coleridge's concept of "organic form." If organic form is implicit in his definition of "poem," it is even more obvious that the distinction between organic and mechanical form is essentially that between imagination and fancy. Organicism is an essential characteristic of the workings of the secondary imagination in recreating an idealized, unified, and coherent fictive universe.

Selected Bibliography

Barth, J. Robert. *The Symbolic Imagination: Coleridge and the Romantic Tradition.* Princeton: Princeton University Press, 1977.

Christensen, Jerome. *Coleridge's Blessed Machine of Language.* Ithaca: Cornell University Press, 1981.

Corrigan, Timothy. *Coleridge, Language and Criticism.* Athens: University of Georgia Press, 1982.

Fogle, R. H. *The Idea of Coleridge's Criticism.* Berkeley: University of California Press, 1962.

Hamilton, Paul. *Coleridge's Poetics.* Oxford: Blackwell, 1983.

Harding, Anthony John. *Coleridge and the Inspired Word.* Kingston, Ont.: McGill-Queen's University Press, 1985.

Marks, Emerson. *Coleridge on the Language of Verse.* Princeton: Princeton University Press, 1981.

McKenzie, Gordon. *Organic Unity in Coleridge.* Berkeley: University of California Press, 1939.

Read, Herbert Edward. *Coleridge as a Critic.* London: Faber and Faber, 1949.

Richards, Ivor Armstrong. *Coleridge on Imagination,* 3rd ed. London: Routledge and Kegan Paul, 1962.

Sharma, L. S. *Coleridge: His Contribution to English Criticism.* New Delhi: Arnold-Heinemann, 1981.

Thorpe, C. D. "Coleridge as Aesthetician and Critic." *Journal of the History of Ideas* 1 (1944): 387–414.

Shakespeare's Judgment Equal to His Genius

The object which I was proceeding to attain in my last lecture was to prove that independently of his peculiar merits, which are hereafter to be developed, Shakespeare appears, from his poems alone, apart from his great works, to have possessed all the conditions of a true poet, and by this proof to do away, as far as may [be] in my power, the popular notion that he was a great dramatist by a sort of instinct, immortal in his own despite, and sinking below men of second- or third-rate character when he attempted aught beside the drama — even as bees construct their cells and manufacture their honey to admirable perfection, but would in vain attempt to build a nest. Now this mode of reconciling a compelled sense of inferiority with a feeling of pride, began in a few pedants, who having read that Sophocles was the great model of tragedy, and Aristotle the infallible dictator, and finding that the *Lear, Hamlet, Othello,* and the rest, were neither in imitation of Sophocles, nor in obedience to Aristotle — and not having (with one or two excep-

"Shakespeare's Judgment" was delivered as a lecture, probably around 1808. The text is compiled from Coleridge's notebooks. [Ed.]

tions) the courage to affirm that the delight which their country received from generation to generation, in defiance of the alterations of circumstances and habits, was wholly groundless — it was a happy medium and refuge, to talk of Shakespeare as a sort of beautiful *lusus naturae,*[1] a delightful monster, — wild, indeed, without taste or judgment, but like the inspired idiots so much venerated in the East, uttering, amid the strangest follies, the sublimest truths. In nine places out of ten in which I find his awful name mentioned, it is with some epithet of "wild," "irregular," "pure child of nature," etc., etc., etc. If all this be true, we must submit to it; tho' to a thinking mind it cannot but be painful to find any excellence, merely human, thrown out of all human analogy, and thereby leaving us neither rules for imitation, nor motives to imitate. But if false, it is a dangerous falsehood; for it affords a refuge to secret self-conceit, — enables a vain man at once to escape his reader's indignation by general swoln panegyrics on Shakespeare, merely by his *ipse dixit*[2] to treat what he has not intellect enough to comprehend, or soul to feel, as contemptible, without assigning any reason, or referring his opinion to any demonstrated principle; and so has left Shakespeare as a sort of Tartarian Dalai Lama, adored indeed, and his very excrescences prized as relics, but with no authority, no real influence. I grieve that every late voluminous edition of his works would enable me to substantiate the present charge with a variety of facts one tenth of which would of themselves exhaust the time allotted to me. Every critic, who has or has not made a collection of black letter books — in itself a useful and respectable amusement — puts on the seven-league boots of self-opinion and strides at once from an illustrator into a supreme judge, and blind and deaf, fills his three-ounce phial at the waters of Niagara — and determines positively the greatness of the cataract to be neither more nor less than his three-ounce phial has been able to receive.

Not only a multitude of individuals but even whole nations [are] so enslaved to the habits of their education and immediate circumstances as not to judge disinterestedly even on those subjects, the very pleasure from which consists in their disinterestedness — subjects of taste and *belles lettres.* Instead of deciding concerning their own modes and customs by any rule of reason, nothing appears natural, becoming, or beautiful but what coincides with the accidents of their education. In this narrow circle individuals may attain exquisite discrimination, as the French critics have in their own literature, but a true critic can no man be without placing himself on some central point in which he can command the whole; i.e., some general rule, which, [as] founded in reason, or faculties common to all men, must therefore apply to all men.

This will not produce despotism, but on the contrary true tolerance. He will indeed require, as the spirit and substance of a work, something true in human nature, and independent of circumstances; but in the mode of applying it, he will estimate genius and judgement according to the felicity with which this imperishable soul has clothed and adapted itself to the age, place, and existing manners.

The error is reversing this by considering the circumstances as perpetual, to the neglect of the animating power.

The subject of the present lecture is no less than a question submitted to your understandings, emancipated from national prejudice: Are the plays of *Shakespeare* works of rude uncultivated genius, in which the splendor of the parts compensates, if aught can compensate, for the barbarous shapelessness and irregularity of the whole? To which not only the French critics, but even his own English admirers, say [yes]. Or is the form equally admirable with the matter, the judgment of the great poet not less deserving of our wonder than his genius? Or to repeat the question in other words, is Shakespeare a great dynamic poet on account only of those beauties and excellencies which he possesses in common with the ancients, but with diminished claims to our love and honor to the full extent of his difference from them? Or are these very differences additional proofs of poetic wisdom, at once results and symbols of living power as contrasted with lifeless mechanism, of

[1]Freak of nature. [Ed.]
[2]Authority. [Ed.]

free and rival originality as contradistinguished from servile imitation, or more accurately, [from] a blind copying of effects instead of a true imitation of the essential principles? Imagine not I am about to oppose genius to rules. No! the comparative value of these rules is the very cause to be tried. The spirit of poetry, like all other living powers, must of necessity circumscribe itself by rules, were it only to unite power with beauty. It must embody in order to reveal itself; but a living body is of necessity an organized one, — and what is organization, but the connection of parts to a whole, so that each part is at once end and means! This is no discovery of criticism; it is a necessity of the human mind — and all nations have felt and obeyed it, in the invention of metre and measured sounds as the vehicle and involucrum of poetry, itself a fellow-growth from the same life, even as the bark is to the tree.

No work of true genius dare want its appropriate form; neither indeed is there any danger of this. As it must not, so neither can it, be lawless! For it is even this that constitutes its genius — the power of acting creatively under laws of its own origination. How then comes it that not only single Zoili,[3] but whole nations have combined in unhesitating condemnation of our great dramatist, as a sort of African nature, fertile in beautiful monsters, as a wild heath where islands of fertility look greener from the surrounding waste, where the loveliest plants now shine out among unsightly weeds and now are choked by their parasitic growth, so intertwined that we cannot disentangle the weed without snapping the flower. In this statement I have had no reference to the vulgar abuse of Voltaire, save as far as his charges are coincident with the decisions of his commentators and (so they tell you) his almost idolatrous admirers. The true ground of the mistake, as has been well remarked by a continental critic,[4] lies in the confounding mechanical regularity with organic form. The form is mechanic when on any given material we impress a predetermined form, not necessarily arising out of the properties of the material, as when to a mass of wet clay we give whatever shape we wish it to retain when hardened. The organic form, on the other hand, is innate; it shapes as it develops itself from within, and the fullness of its development is one and the same with the perfection of its outward form. Such is the life, such the form. Nature, the prime genial artist, inexhaustible in diverse powers, is equally inexhaustible in forms. Each exterior is the physiognomy of the being within, its true image reflected and thrown out from the concave mirror. And even such is the appropriate excellence of her chosen poet, of our own Shakespeare, himself a nature humanized, a genial understanding directing self-consciously a power and an implicit wisdom deeper than consciousness.

[3]Zoilus was a captious critic of Homer around the fourth century B.C. [Ed.]

[4]August Wilhelm von Schlegel, from whose writings many of Coleridge's ideas derive. [Ed.]

From *Biographia Literaria*

From Chapter 13

The IMAGINATION then, I consider either as primary, or secondary. The primary IMAGINATION I hold to be the living Power and prime Agent of all human Perception, and as a repetition in the finite mind of the eternal act of creation in the infinite I AM. The secondary Imagination I consider as an echo of the former, coexisting with the conscious will, yet still as identical with the primary in the *kind* of its agency, and differing only in *degree,* and in the *mode* of its operation. It dissolves, diffuses, dissipates, in order to recreate; or where this process is rendered impossible, yet still at all events it struggles to idealize and to unify. It is essentially *vital,* even as all objects (*as* objects) are essentially fixed and dead.

FANCY, on the contrary, has no other counters to play with, but fixities and definites. The Fancy is indeed no other than a mode of Memory emancipated from the order of time and space; while it is blended with, and modified by that empirical phenomenon of the will, which we express by the word CHOICE. But equally with the ordinary memory the Fancy must receive all its materials ready made from the law of association.

Chapter 14

Occasion of the Lyrical Ballads, and the objects originally proposed — Preface to the second edition — The ensuing controversy, its causes and acrimony — Philosophic definitions of a poem and poetry with scholia.

During the first year that Mr. Wordsworth and I were neighbours,[1] our conversations turned frequently on the two cardinal points of poetry, the power of exciting the sympathy of the reader by a faithful adherence to the truth of nature, and the power of giving the interest of novelty by the modifying colors of imagination. The sudden charm, which accidents of light and shade, which moon-light or sun-set diffused over a known and familiar landscape, appeared to represent the practicability of combining both. These are the poetry of nature. The thought suggested itself (to which of us I do not recollect) that a series of poems might be composed of two sorts. In the one, the incidents and agents were to be, in part at least, supernatural; and the excellence aimed at was to consist in the interesting of the affections by the dramatic truth of such emotions, as would naturally accompany such situations, supposing them real. And real in *this* sense they have been to every human being who, from whatever source of delusion, has at any time believed himself under supernatural agency. For the second class, subjects were to be chosen from ordinary life; the characters and incidents were to be such, as will be found in every village and its vicinity, where there is a meditative and feeling mind to seek after them, or to notice them, when they present themselves.

In this idea originated the plan of the "Lyrical Ballads"; in which it was agreed, that my endeavours should be directed to persons and characters supernatural, or at least romantic; yet so as to transfer from our inward nature a human interest and a semblance of truth sufficient to procure for these shadows of imagination that willing suspension of disbelief for the moment, which constitutes poetic faith. Mr. Wordsworth, on the other hand, was to propose to himself as his object, to give the charm of novelty to things of every day, and to excite a feeling analogous to the supernatural, by awakening the mind's attention from the lethargy of custom, and directing it to the loveliness and the wonders of the world before us; an inexhaustible treasure, but for which, in consequence of the film of familiarity and selfish solicitude we have eyes, yet see not, ears that hear not, and hearts that neither feel nor understand.

With this view I wrote "The Ancient Mariner," and was preparing among other poems, "The Dark Ladie," and the "Christabel," in which I should have more nearly realized my ideal, than I had done in my first attempt. But Mr. Wordsworth's industry had proved so much more successful, and the number of his poems so much greater, that my compositions, instead of forming a balance, appeared rather an interpolation of heterogeneous matter. Mr. Wordsworth added two or three poems written in his own character, in the impassioned, lofty, and sustained diction, which is characteristic of his genius. In this form the "Lyrical Ballads" were published; and were presented by him, as an *experiment,* whether subjects, which from their nature rejected the usual ornaments and extra-colloquial style of poems in general, might not be so managed in the language of ordinary life as to produce the pleasureable interest, which it is the peculiar business of poetry to impart. To the second edition he added a preface of considerable length; in which, notwithstanding some passages of apparently a contrary import, he was understood to contend for the extension of this style to poetry of all kinds, and to reject as vicious and indefensible all phrases and forms of style that were not included in what he

[1]In 1797. [Ed.]

(unfortunately, I think, adopting an equivocal expression) called the language of *real* life. From this preface, prefixed to poems in which it was impossible to deny the presence of original genius, however mistaken its direction might be deemed, arose the whole long-continued controversy. For from the conjunction of perceived power with supposed heresy I explain the inveteracy and in some instances, I grieve to say, the acrimonious passions, with which the controversy has been conducted by the assailants.

Had Mr. Wordsworth's poems been the silly, the childish things, which they were for a long time described as being; had they been really distinguished from the compositions of other poets merely by meanness of language and inanity of thought; had they indeed contained nothing more than what is found in the parodies and pretended imitations of them; they must have sunk at once, a dead weight, into the slough of oblivion, and have dragged the preface along with them. But year after year increased the number of Mr. Wordsworth's admirers. They were found too not in the lower classes of the reading public, but chiefly among young men of strong sensibility and meditative minds; and their admiration (inflamed perhaps in some degree by opposition) was distinguished by its intensity, I might almost say, by its *religious* fervor. These facts, and the intellectual energy of the author, which was more or less consciously felt, where it was outwardly and even boisterously denied, meeting with sentiments of aversion to his opinions, and of alarm at their consequences, produced an eddy of criticism, which would of itself have borne up the poems by the violence, with which it whirled them round and round. With many parts of this preface, in the sense attributed to them, and which the words undoubtedly seem to authorize, I never concurred; but on the contrary objected to them as erroneous in principle, and as contradictory (in appearance at least) both to other parts of the same preface, and to the author's own practice in the greater number of the poems themselves. Mr. Wordsworth in his recent collection has, I find, degraded this prefatory disquisition to the end of his second volume, to be read or not at the reader's choice. But he has not, as far as I can discover, announced any change in his poetic creed. At all events, considering it as the source of a controversy, in which I have been honored more than I deserve by the frequent conjunction of my name with his, I think it expedient to declare once for all, in what points I coincide with his opinions, and in what points I altogether differ. But in order to render myself intelligible I must previously, in as few words as possible, explain my ideas, first, of a POEM; and secondly, of POETRY itself, in *kind,* and in *essence*.

The office of philosophical *disquisition* consists in just *distinction;* while it is the privilege of the philosopher to preserve himself constantly aware, that distinction is not division. In order to obtain adequate notions of any truth, we must intellectually separate its distinguishable parts; and this is the technical *process* of philosophy. But having so done, we must then restore them in our conceptions to the unity, in which they actually co-exist; and this is the *result* of philosophy. A poem contains the same elements as a prose composition; the difference therefore must consist in a different combination of them, in consequence of a different object being proposed. According to the difference of the object will be the difference of the combination. It is possible, that the object may be merely to facilitate the recollection of any given facts or observations by artificial arrangement; and the composition will be a poem, merely because it is distinguished from prose by metre, or by rhyme, or by both conjointly. In this, the lowest sense, a man might attribute the name of a poem to the well-known enumeration of the days in the several months;

> Thirty days hath September,
> April, June, and November, &c.

and others of the same class and purpose. And as a particular pleasure is found in anticipating the recurrence of sounds and quantities, all compositions that have this charm superadded, whatever be their contents, *may* be entitled poems.

So much for the superficial *form.* A difference of object and contents supplies an additional ground of distinction. The immediate purpose may be the communication of truths; either of truth absolute and demonstrable, as in works of science; or of facts experienced and recorded, as in history. Pleasure, and that of the highest and most permanent kind, may *result* from the *attainment* of the end; but it is not itself the immediate end. In other works the communication of pleasure may be the immediate purpose; and though truth, either moral or intellectual, ought to be the *ultimate* end, yet this will distinguish the character of the author, not the class to which the work belongs. Blest indeed is that state of society, in which the immediate purpose would be baffled by the perversion of the proper ultimate end; in which no charm of diction or imagery could exempt the Bathyllus even of an Anacreon, or the Alexis of Virgil, from disgust and aversion![2]

But the communication of pleasure may be the immediate object of a work not metrically composed; and that object may have been in a high degree attained, as in novels and romances. Would then the mere superaddition of metre, with or without rhyme, entitle *these* to the name of poems? The answer is, that nothing can permanently please, which does not contain in itself the reason why it is so, and not otherwise. If metre be superadded, all other parts must be made consonant with it. They must be such, as to justify the perpetual and distinct attention to each part, which an exact correspondent recurrence of accent and sound are calculated to excite. The final definition then, so deduced, may be thus worded. A poem is that species of composition, which is opposed to works of science, by proposing for its *immediate* object pleasure, not truth; and from all other species (having *this* object in common with it) it is discriminated by proposing to itself such delight from the *whole,* as is compatible with a distinct gratification from each component *part*.

Controversy is not seldom excited in consequence of the disputants attaching each a different meaning to the same word; and in few instances has this been more striking, than in disputes concerning the present subject. If a man chooses to call every composition a poem, which is rhyme, or measure, or both, I must leave his opinion uncontroverted. The distinction is at least competent to characterize the writer's intention. If it were subjoined, that the whole is likewise entertaining or affecting, as a tale, or as a series of interesting reflections, I of course admit this as another fit ingredient of a poem, and an additional merit. But if the definition sought for be that of a *legitimate* poem, I answer, it must be one, the parts of which mutually support and explain each other; all in their proportion harmonizing with, and supporting the purpose and known influences of metrical arrangement. The philosophic critics of all ages coincide with the ultimate judgement of all countries, in equally denying the praises of a just poem, on the one hand, to a series of striking lines or distiches, each of which, absorbing the whole attention of the reader to itself, disjoins it from its context, and makes it a separate whole, instead of an harmonizing part; and on the other hand, to an unsustained composition, from which the reader collects rapidly the general result, unattracted by the component parts. The reader should be carried forward, not merely or chiefly by the mechanical impulse of curiosity, or by a restless desire to arrive at the final solution; but by the pleasureable activity of mind excited by the attractions of the journey itself. Like the motion of a serpent, which the Egyptians made the emblem of intellectual power; or like the path of sound through the air; at every step he pauses and half recedes, and from the retrogressive movement collects the force which again carries him onward. "Præcipitandus est *liber* spiritus," says Petronius Arbiter most happily.[3] The epithet, *liber,* here balances the preceding verb; and it is not easy to conceive more meaning condensed in fewer words.

But if this should be admitted as a satisfactory character of a poem, we have still to seek for a definition of poetry. The writings of PLATO, and Bishop TAYLOR, and the "Theoria Sacra" of BURNET, furnish undeniable proofs that poetry of the highest kind may exist without metre, and even without the contra-distinguishing objects of a poem. The first chapter of Isaiah (indeed a very large portion of the whole book) is poetry in the most emphatic sense; yet it would be not less irrational than strange to assert, that pleasure, and not truth, was the immediate object of the

[2]Anacreon's Ode 29 to Bathyllus, and Virgil's *Eclogue* 2. [Ed.]

[3]"The free spirit must be hurried onward." Petronius, *Satyricon,* 118. [Ed.]

prophet. In short, whatever *specific* import we attach to the word, poetry, there will be found involved in it, as a necessary consequence, that a poem of any length neither can be, nor ought to be, all poetry. Yet if an harmonious whole is to be produced, the remaining parts must be preserved *in keeping* with the poetry; and this can be no otherwise effected than by such a studied selection and artificial arrangement, as will partake of *one,* though not a *peculiar* property of poetry. And this again can be no other than the property of exciting a more continuous and equal attention than the language of prose aims at, whether colloquial or written.

My own conclusions on the nature of poetry, in the strictest use of the word, have been in part anticipated in the preceding disquisition on the fancy and imagination. What is poetry? is so nearly the same question with, what is a poet? that the answer to the one is involved in the solution of the other. For it is a distinction resulting from the poetic genius itself, which sustains and modifies the images, thoughts, and emotions of the poet's own mind.

The poet, described in *ideal* perfection, brings the whole soul of man into activity, with the subordination of its faculties to each other, according to their relative worth and dignity. He diffuses a tone and spirit of unity, that blends, and (as it were) *fuses,* each into each, by that synthetic and magical power, to which we have exclusively appropriated the name of imagination. This power, first put in action by the will and understanding, and retained under their irremissive, though gentle and unnoticed, controul (*laxis effertur habenis*)[4] reveals itself in the balance or reconciliation of opposite or discordant qualities: of sameness, with difference; of the general, with the concrete; the idea, with the image; the individual, with the representative; the sense of novelty and freshness, with old and familiar objects; a more than usual state of emotion, with more than usual order; judgement ever awake and steady self-possession, with enthusiasm and feeling profound or vehement; and while it blends and harmonizes the natural and the artificial, still subordinates art to nature; the manner to the matter; and our admiration of the poet to our sympathy with the poetry. "Doubtless," as Sir John Davies observes of the soul (and his words may with slight alteration be applied, and even more appropriately, to the poetic IMAGINATION)

Doubtless this could not be, but that she turns
 Bodies to spirit by sublimation strange,
As fire converts to fire the things it burns,
 As we our food into our nature change.

From their gross matter she abstracts their forms,
 And draws a kind of quintessence from things;
Which to her proper nature she transforms,
 To bear them light on her celestial wings.

Thus does she, when from individual states
 She doth abstract the universal kinds;
Which then re-clothed in divers names and fates
 Steal access through our senses to our minds.[5]

Finally, GOOD SENSE is the BODY of poetic genius, FANCY its DRAPERY, MOTION its LIFE, and IMAGINATION the SOUL that is everywhere, and in each; and forms all into one graceful and intelligent whole.

Chapter 17

Examination of the tenets peculiar to Mr. Wordsworth—Rustic life (above all, low *and rustic life) especially unfavorable to the formation of a human diction—The* best *parts of language the product of philosophers, not of clowns or shepherds—Poetry essentially ideal and generic—The language of Milton as much the language of* real *life, yea, incomparably more so than that of the cottager.*

As far then as Mr. Wordsworth in his preface contended, and most ably contended, for a reformation in our poetic diction, as far as he has evinced the truth of passion, and the *dramatic* propriety of those figures and metaphors in the original poets, which, stripped of their justifying reasons, and converted into mere artifices of connection or ornament, constitute the characteristic falsity in the poetic style of the moderns; and as far as he has, with equal acuteness and clearness,

[4]"Carried on with slackened reins." Petrarch, *Epistola Barbato Sulmonensi,* 39. [Ed.]

[5]Sir John Davies, *Nosce Teipsum: Of the Soule of Man and the Immortality Thereof,* 4:11–13. [Ed.]

pointed out the process by which this change was effected, and the resemblances between that state into which the reader's mind is thrown by the pleasureable confusion of thought from an unaccustomed train of words and images; and that state which is induced by the natural language of empassioned feeling; he undertook a useful task, and deserves all praise, both for the attempt and for the execution. The provocations to this remonstrance in behalf of truth and nature were still of perpetual recurrence before and after the publications of this preface. I cannot likewise but add, that the comparison of such poems of merit, as have been given to the public within the last ten or twelve years, with the majority of those produced previously to the appearance of that preface, leave no doubt on my mind, that Mr. Wordsworth is fully justified in believing his efforts to have been by no means ineffectual. Not only in the verses of those who have professed their admiration of his genius, but even of those who have distinguished themselves by hostility to his theory, and depreciation of his writings, are the impressions of his principles plainly visible. It is possible, that with these principles others may have been blended, which are not equally evident; and some which are unsteady and subvertible from the narrowness or imperfection of their basis. But it is more than possible, that these errors of defect or exaggeration, by kindling and feeding the controversy may have conduced not only to the wider propagation of the accompanying truths, but that, by their frequent presentation to the mind in an excited state, they may have won for them a more permanent and practical result. A man will borrow a part from his opponent the more easily, if he feels himself justified in continuing to reject a part. While there remain important points in which he can still feel himself in the right, in which he still finds firm footing for continued resistance, he will gradually adopt those opinions, which were the least remote from his own convictions, as not less congruous with his own theory than with that which he reprobates. In like manner with a kind of instinctive prudence, he will abandon by little and little his weakest posts, till at length he seems to forget that they had ever belonged to him, or affects to consider them at most as accidental and "petty annexments," the removal of which leaves the citadel unhurt and unendangered.

My own differences from certain supposed parts of Mr. Wordsworth's theory ground themselves on the assumption, that his words had been rightly interpreted, as purporting that the proper diction for poetry in general consists altogether in a language taken, with due expectations, from the mouths of men in real life, a language which actually constitutes the natural conversation of men under the influence of natural feelings. My objection is, first, that in *any* sense this rule is applicable only to *certain* classes of poetry; secondly, that even to these classes it is not applicable, except in such a sense, as hath never by any one (as far as I know or have read) been denied or doubted; and lastly, that as far as, and in that degree in which it is *practicable,* yet as a *rule* it is useless, if not injurious, and therefore either need not, or ought not to be practised. The poet informs his reader, that he had generally chosen *low and rustic* life; but not *as* low and rustic, or in order to repeat that pleasure of doubtful moral effect, which persons of elevated rank and of superior refinement oftentimes derive from a happy *imitation* of the rude unpolished manners and discourse of their inferiors. For the pleasure so derived may be traced to three exciting causes. The first is the naturalness, in *fact,* of the things represented. The second is the apparent naturalness of the *representation,* as raised and qualified by an imperceptible infusion of the author's own knowledge and talent, which infusion does, indeed, constitute it an *imitation* as distinguished from a mere *copy.* The third cause may be found in the reader's conscious feeling of his superiority awakened by the contrast presented to him; even as for the same purpose the kings and great barons of yore retained sometimes *actual* clowns and fools, but more frequently shrewd and witty fellows in that *character.* These, however, were not Mr. Wordsworth's objects. *He* chose low and rustic life, "because in that condition the essential passions of the heart find a better soil, in which they can attain their maturity, are less under restraint, and speak a plainer and more emphatic language; because in that condition of life our elementary feelings coexist in a state of greater simplicity, and consequently may be more accurately contemplated, and more forcibly communicated; because the manners of rural life germinate from those elementary feelings; and from the necessary character of rural occupations are more easily comprehended, and are more durable; and lastly, because in that condition the passions of men are incorporated with the beautiful and permanent forms of nature."

Now it is clear to me, that in the most interesting of the poems, in which the author is more or less dramatic, as "the Brothers," "Michael," "Ruth," "the Mad Mother," &c., the persons introduced are by no means taken *from low or rustic life* in the common acceptation of those words; and it is not less clear, that the sentiments and language, as far as they can be conceived to have been really transferred from the minds and conversation of such persons, are attributable to causes and circumstances not necessarily connected with "their occupations and abode." The thoughts, feelings, language, and manners of the shepherd-farmers in the vales of Cumberland and Westmoreland, as far as they are actually adopted in those poems, may be accounted for from causes, which will and do produce the same results in *every* state of life, whether in town or country. As the two principal I rank that INDEPENDENCE, which raises a man above servitude, or daily toil for the profit of others, yet not above the necessity of industry and a frugal simplicity of domestic life; and the accompanying unambitious, but solid and religious, EDUCATION, which has rendered few books familiar, but the Bible, and the liturgy or hymn book. To this latter cause, indeed, which is so far *accidental,* that it is the blessing of particular countries and a particular age, not the product of particular places or employments, the poet owes the show of probability, that his personages might really feel, think, and talk with any tolerable resemblance to his representation. It is an excellent remark of Dr. Henry More's (Enthusiasmus triumphatus, Sec. 35), that "a man of confined education, but of good parts, by constant reading of the Bible will naturally form a more winning and commanding rhetoric than those that are learned; the intermixture of tongues and of artificial phrases debasing *their* style."

It is, moreover, to be considered that to the formation of healthy feelings, and a reflecting mind, *negations* involve impediments not less formidable than sophistication and vicious intermixture. I am convinced, that for the human soul to prosper in rustic life a certain vantage-ground is pre-requisite. It is not every man that is likely to be improved by a country life or by country labors. Education, or original sensibility, or both, must pre-exist, if the changes, forms, and incidents of nature are to prove a sufficient stimulant. And where these are not sufficient, the mind contracts and hardens by want of stimulants: and the man becomes selfish, sensual, gross, and hard-hearted. Let the management of the POOR LAWS in Liverpool, Manchester, or Bristol be compared with the ordinary dispensation of the poor rates in agricultural villages, where the *farmers* are the overseers and guardians of the poor. If my own experience had not been particularly unfortunate, as well as that of the many respectable country clergymen with whom I have conversed on the subject, the result would engender more than scepticism concerning the desireable influences of low and rustic life in and for itself. Whatever may be concluded on the other side, from the stronger local attachments and enterprising spirit of the Swiss, and other mountaineers, applies to a particular mode of pastoral life, under forms of property that permit and beget manners truly republican, not to rustic life in general, or to the absence of artificial cultivation. On the contrary the mountaineers, whose manners have been so often eulogized, are in general better educated and greater readers than men of equal rank elsewhere. But where this is not the case, as among the peasantry of North Wales, the ancient mountains, with all their terrors and all their glories, are pictures to the blind, and music to the deaf.

I should not have entered so much into detail upon this passage, but here seems to be the point, to which all the lines of difference converge as to their source and centre. (I mean, as far as, and in whatever respect, my poetic creed *does* differ from the doctrines promulged in this preface.) I adopt with full faith the principle of Aristotle, that poetry as poetry is essentially[6] *ideal,* that it avoids and excludes all *accident;* that its apparent individualities of rank, character, or occupation must be *representative* of a class; and that the *persons* of poetry must be clothed with *generic* attributes, with the *common* attributes of the class: not with such as one gifted individual might *possibly* possess, but such as from his situation it is most probable before-hand that he *would* possess. If my premises are right and my deductions legitimate, it follows that there can be no *poetic* medium between the swains of Theocritus and those of an imaginary golden age.

The characters of the vicar and the shepherd-mariner in the poem of "The Brothers," that of the shepherd of Greenhead Ghyll in the "Michael," have all the verisimilitude and representative quality, that the purposes of poetry can require. They are persons of a known and abiding class, and their manners and sentiments the natural product of circumstances common to the class. Take "Michael" for instance:

An old man stout of heart, and strong of limb:
His bodily frame had been from youth to age
Of an unusual strength: his mind was keen,
Intense, and frugal, apt for all affairs,
And in his shepherd's calling he was prompt
And watchful more than ordinary men.
Hence he had learnt the meaning of all winds,
Of blasts of every tone; and oftentimes
When others heeded not, he heard the South
Make subterraneous music, like the noise
Of bagpipers on distant Highland hills.
The shepherd, at such warning, of his flock
Bethought him, and he to himself would say,
The winds are now devising work for me!
And truly at all times the storm, that drives
The traveller to a shelter, summon'd him
Up to the mountains. He had been alone
Amid the heart of many thousand mists,
That came to him and left him on the heights.
So liv'd he, till his eightieth year was pass'd.
And grossly that man errs, who should suppose
That the green vallies, and the streams and rocks,
Were things indifferent to the shepherd's thoughts.
Fields, where with chearful spirits he had breath'd
The common air; the hills, which he so oft
Had climb'd with vigorous steps; which had impress'd
So many incidents upon his mind
Of hardship, skill or courage, joy or fear;
Which, like a book, preserved the memory
Of the dumb animals, whom he had sav'd,
Had fed or shelter'd, linking to such acts,
So grateful in themselves, the certainty
Of honorable gain; these fields, these hills
Which were his living being, even more
Than his own blood — what could they less? had laid
Strong hold on his affections, were to him
A pleasureable feeling of blind love,
The pleasure which there is in life itself.

On the other hand, in the poems which are pitched at a lower note, as the "Harry Gill," "Idiot Boy," the *feelings* are those of human nature in general; though the poet has judiciously laid the *scene* in the country, in order to place *himself* in the vicinity of interesting images, without the necessity of ascribing a sentimental

[6]Say not that I am recommending abstractions; for these class-characteristics which constitute the instructiveness of a character, are so modified and particularized in each person of the Shakespearean Drama, that life itself does not excite more distinctly that sense of individuality which belongs to real existence. Paradoxical as it may sound, one of the essential properties of Geometry is not less essential to dramatic excellence; and Aristotle has accordingly required of the poet an involution of the universal in the individual. The chief differences are, that in Geometry it is the universal truth, which is uppermost in the consciousness; in poetry the individual form, in which the truth is clothed. With the ancients, and not less with the elder dramatists of England and France, both comedy and tragedy were considered as kinds of poetry. They neither sought in comedy to make us laugh merely; much less to make us laugh by wry faces, accidents of jargon, *slang* phrases for the day, or the clothing of common-place morals drawn from the shops or mechanic occupations of their characters. Nor did they condescend in tragedy to wheedle away the applause of the spectators, by representing before them facsimiles of their own mean selves in all their existing meanness, or to work on the sluggish sympathies by a pathos not a whit more respectable than the maudlin tears of drunkenness. Their tragic scenes were meant to *affect* us indeed; but yet within the bounds of pleasure, and in union with the activity both of our understanding and imagination. They wished to transport the mind to a sense of its possible greatness, and to implant the germs of that greatness, during the temporary oblivion of the worthless "thing we are," and of the peculiar state in which each man *happens* to be, suspending our individual recollections and lulling them to sleep amid the music of nobler thoughts.

FRIEND, Pages 251, 252. [Au.]

perception of their beauty to the persons of his drama. In the "Idiot Boy," indeed, the mother's character is not so much a real and native product of a "situation where the essential passions of the heart find a better soil, in which they can attain their maturity and speak a plainer and more emphatic language," as it is an impersonation of an instinct abandoned by judgement. Hence the two following charges seem to me not wholly groundless: at least, they are the only plausible objections, which I have heard to that fine poem. The one is, that the author has not, in the poem itself, taken sufficient care to preclude from the reader's fancy the disgusting images of *ordinary morbid idiocy,* which yet it was by no means his intention to represent. He has even by the "burr, burr, burr," uncounteracted by any preceding description of the boy's beauty, assisted in recalling them. The other is, that the idiocy of the *boy* is so evenly balanced by the folly of the *mother*, as to present to the general reader rather a laughable burlesque on he blindness of anile dotage, than an analytic display of maternal affection in its ordinary workings.

In the "Thorn" the poet himself acknowledges in a note the necessity of an introductory poem, in which he should have portrayed the character of the person from whom the words of the poem are supposed to proceed: a superstitious man moderately imaginative, of slow faculties and deep feelings, "a captain of a small trading vessel, for example, who, being past the middle age of life, had retired upon an annuity, or small independent income, to some village or country town of which he was not a native, or in which he had not been accustomed to live. Such men having nothing to do become credulous and talkative from indolence." But in a poem, still more in a lyric poem (and the Nurse in Shakespeare's *Romeo and Juliet* alone prevents me from extending the remark even to dramatic *poetry,* if indeed the Nurse itself can be deemed altogether a case in point) it is not possible to imitate truly a dull and garrulous discourser, without repeating the effects of dullness and garrulity. However this may be, I dare assert, that the parts (and these form the far larger portion of the whole) which might as well or still better have proceeded from the poet's own imagination, and have been spoken in his own character, are those which have given, and which will continue to give, universal delight; and that the passages exclusively appropriate to the supposed narrator, such as the late couplet of the third stanza;[7] the seven last lines of the tenth;[8] and the five

[7]"I've measured it from side to side;
'Tis three feet long, and two feet wide." [Au.]

[8]"Nay, rack your brain — 'tis all in vain,
I'll tell you every thing I know;
But to the Thorn, and to the Pond
Which is a little step beyond,
I wish that you would go:
Perhaps when you are at the place,
You something of her tale may trace.

I'll give you the best help I can:
Before you up the mountain go,
Up to the dreary mountain-top,
I'll tell you all I know.
'Tis now some two-and-twenty years
Since she (her name is Martha Ray)
Gave, with a maiden's true good will,
Her company to Stephen Hill;
And she was blithe and gay,
And she was happy, happy still
Whene'er she thought of Stephen Hill.

And they had fix'd the wedding-day,
The morning that must wed them both;
But Stephen to another maid
Had sworn another oath;
And, with this other maid, to church
Unthinking Stephen went —
Poor Martha! on that woeful day
A pang of pitiless dismay
Into her soul was sent;
A fire was kindled in her breast,
Which might not burn itself to rest.

They say, full six months after this,
While yet the summer leaves were green,
She to the mountain-top would go,
And there was often seen.
'Tis said a child was in her womb,
As now to any eye was plain;
She was with child, and she was mad;
Yet often she was sober sad
From her exceeding pain.
Oh me! ten thousand times I'd rather
That he had died, that cruel father!

. . . .

Last Christmas when we talked of this,
Old farmer Simpson did maintain,
That in her womb the infant wrought
About its mother's heart, and brought
Her senses back again:
And, when at last her time drew near,
Her looks were calm, her senses clear.

following stanzas, with the exception of the four admirable lines at the commencement of the fourteenth, are felt by many unprejudiced and unsophisticated hearts, as sudden and unpleasant sinkings from the height to which the poet had previously lifted them, and to which he again re-elevates both himself and his reader.

If then I am compelled to doubt the theory, by which the choice of *characters* was to be directed, not only *a priori,* from grounds of reason, but both from the few instances in which the poet himself *need* be supposed to have been governed by it, and from the comparative inferiority of those instances; still more must I hesitate in my assent to the sentence which immediately follows the former citation; and which I can neither admit as particular fact, or as general rule. "The language too of these men is adopted (purified indeed from what appear to be its real defects, from all lasting and rational causes of dislike or disgust) because such men hourly communicate with the best objects from which the best part of language is originally derived; and because, from their rank in society and the sameness and narrow circle of their intercourse, being less under the action of social vanity, they convey their feelings and notions in simple and unelaborated expressions." To this I reply; that a rustic's language, purified from all provincialism and grossness, and so far reconstructed as to be made consistent with the rules of grammar (which are in essence no other than the laws of universal logic, applied to psychological materials) will not differ from the language of any other man of common-sense, however learned or refined he may be, except as far as the notions, which the rustic has to convey, are fewer and more indiscriminate. This will become still clearer, if we add the consideration (equally important though less obvious) that the rustic, from the more imperfect developement of his faculties, and from the lower state of their cultivation, aims almost solely to convey *insulated facts,* either those of his scanty experience or his traditional belief; while the educated man chiefly seeks to discover and express those *connections* of things, or those relative *bearings* of fact to fact, from which some more or less general law is deducible. For *facts* are valuable to a wise man, chiefly as they lead to the discovery of the indwelling *law,* which is the true *being* of things, the sole solution of their modes of existence, and in the knowledge of which consists our dignity and our power.

As little can I agree with the assertion, that from the objects with which the rustic hourly communicates the best part of language is formed. For first, if to communicate with an object implies such an acquaintance with it, as renders it capable of being discriminately reflected on; the distinct knowledge of an uneducated rustic would furnish a very scanty vocabulary. The few things, and modes of action, requisite for his bodily conveniences, would alone be individualized; while all the rest of nature would be expressed by a small number of confused general terms. Secondly, I deny that the words and combinations of words derived from the objects, with which the rustic is familiar, whether with distinct or confused knowledge, can be justly said to form the *best* part of language. It is more than probable, that many classes of the brute creation possess discriminating sounds, by which they can convey to each other notices of such objects as concern their food, shelter, or safety. Yet we hesitate to call the aggregate of such sounds a language, otherwise than metaphorically. The best part of human language, properly so called, is derived from reflection on the acts of the mind itself. It is formed by a voluntary appropriation of fixed symbols to internal acts, to processes and results of imagination, the greater part of which have no place in the consciousness of uneducated man; though in civilized society, by imitation and passive remembrance of what they hear from their religious instructors and other superiors, the most uneducated share in the harvest which they neither sowed or reaped. If the history of the phrases

No more I know, I wish I did,
And I would tell it all to you:
For what became of this poor child
There's none that ever knew:
And if a child was born or no,
There's no one that could ever tell;
And if 'twas born alive or dead,
There's no one knows, as I have said:
But some remember well,
That Martha Ray about this time
Would up the mountain often climb." [Au.]

in hourly currency among our peasants were traced, a person not previously aware of the fact would be surprised at finding so large a number, which three or four centuries ago were the exclusive property of the universities and the schools; and, at the commencement of the Reformation, had been transferred from the school to the pulpit, and thus gradually passed into common life. The extreme difficulty, and often the impossibility, of finding words for the simplest moral and intellectual processes in the languages of uncivilized tribes has proved perhaps the weightiest obstacle to the progress of our most zealous and adroit missionaries. Yet these tribes are surrounded by the same nature as our peasants are; but in still more impressive forms; and they are, moreover, obliged to *particularize* many more of them. When, therefore, Mr. Wordsworth adds, "accordingly, such a language" (meaning, as before, the language of rustic life purified from provincialism) "arising out of repeated experience and regular feelings, is a more permanent, and a far more philosophical language, than that which is frequently substituted for it by poets, who think they are conferring honor upon themselves and their art in proportion as they indulge in arbitrary and capricious habits of expression:" it may be answered, that the language, which he has in view, can be attributed to rustics with no greater right, than the style of Hooker or Bacon to Tom Brown or Sir Roger L'Estrange.[9] Doubtless, if what is peculiar to each were omitted in each, the result must needs be the same. Further, that the poet, who uses an illogical diction, or a style fitted to excite only the low and changeable pleasure of wonder by means of groundless novelty, substitutes a language of *folly* and *vanity,* not for that of the *rustic,* but for that of *good sense* and *natural feeling.*

Here let me be permitted to remind the reader, that the positions, which I controvert, are contained in the sentences — "*a selection of the* REAL *language of men;*" — "*the language of these men*" (i.e., men in low and rustic life) "*I propose to myself to imitate, and, as far as is possible, to adopt the very language of men.*" "*Between the language of prose and that of metrical composition, there neither is, nor can be any essential difference.*" It is against these exclusively that my opposition is directed.

I object, in the very first instance, to an equivocation in the use of the word "real." Every man's language varies, according to the extent of his knowledge, the activity of his faculties, and the depth or quickness of his feelings. Every man's language has, first, its *individualities;* secondly, the common properties of the *class* to which he belongs; and thirdly, words and phrases of *universal* use. The language of Hooker, Bacon, Bishop Taylor, and Burke differs from the common language of the learned class only by the superior number and novelty of the thoughts and relations which they had to convey. The language of Algernon Sidney differs not at all from that, which every well-educated gentleman would wish to write, and (with due allowances for the undeliberateness, and less connected train, of thinking natural and proper to conversation) such as he would wish to talk. Neither one nor the other differ half so much from the general language of cultivated society, as the language of Mr. Wordsworth's homeliest composition differs from that of a common peasant. For "real" therefore, we must substitute *ordinary,* or *lingua communis.* And this, we have proved, is no more to be found in the phraseology of low and rustic life than in that of any other class. Omit the peculiarities of each, and the result of course must be common to all. And assuredly the omissions and changes to be made in the language of rustics, before it could be transferred to any species of poem, except the drama or other professed imitation, are at least as numerous and weighty, as would be required in adapting to the same purpose the ordinary language of tradesmen and manufacturers. Not to mention, that the language so highly extolled by Mr. Wordsworth varies in every county, nay in every village, according to the accidental character of the clergyman, the existence or non-existence of schools; or even, perhaps, as the exciseman, publican, or barber, happen to be, or not to be, zealous politi-

[9]Richard Hooker was the sixteenth-century author of *Ecclesiastical Polity;* Francis Bacon wrote philosophy and essays at the beginning of the seventeenth century. Tom Brown and Roger L'Estrange were popular writers of the late seventeenth and early eighteenth centuries. [Ed.]

cians, and readers of the weekly newspaper *pro bono publico.*[10] Anterior to cultivation, the lingua communis of every country, as Dante has well observed, exists every where in parts, and no where as a whole.

Neither is the case rendered at all more tenable by the addition of the words, *in a state of excitement.* For the nature of a man's words, where he is strongly affected by joy, grief, or anger, must necessarily depend on the number and quality of the general truths, conceptions and images, and of the words expressing them, with which his mind had been previously stored. For the property of passion is not to *create;* but to set in increased activity. At least, whatever new connections of thoughts or images, or (which is equally, if not more than equally, the appropriate effect of strong excitement) whatever generalizations of truth or experience, the heat of passion may produce; yet the terms of their conveyance must have pre-existed in his former conversations, and are only collected and crowded together by the unusual stimulation. It is indeed very possible to adopt in a poem the unmeaning repetitions, habitual phrases, and other blank counters, which an unfurnished or confused understanding interposes at short intervals, in order to keep hold of his subject, which is still slipping from him, and to give him time for recollection; or in mere aid of vacancy, as in the scanty companies of a country stage the same player pops backwards and forwards, in order to prevent the appearance of empty spaces, in the procession of Macbeth, or Henry VIIIth. But what assistance to the poet, or ornament to the poem, these can supply, I am at a loss to conjecture. Nothing assuredly can differ either in origin or in mode widely from the *apparent* tautologies of intense and turbulent feeling, in which the passion is greater and of longer endurance than to be exhausted or satisfied by a single representation of the image or incident exciting it. Such repetitions I admit to be a beauty of the highest kind; as illustrated by Mr. Wordsworth himself from the song of Deborah. "*At her feet he bowed, he fell, he lay down; at her feet he bowed, he fell; where he bowed, there he fell down dead.*"[11]

[10]For the public good. [Ed.]

[11]Judges 5:27. [Ed.]

John Keats

1795–1821

John Keats was born in London, the son of a livery stableman who had married the stable-owner's daughter. He was educated in a private school at Enfield by Charles Cowden Clarke, later a friend to many of the second generation of Romantic poets, who encouraged Keats's love of reading and writing. Orphaned at fourteen with his mother's capital tied up in a chancery suit, Keats was apprenticed by his guardian to an apothecary-surgeon, and he studied medicine at Guy's Hospital in London until he was twenty-one. In London, Keats met Leigh Hunt, who gathered him into a politically radical circle of artists that included the poet Percy Bysshe Shelley, the essayist William Hazlitt, and the painter Benjamin Haydon. As soon as he was of age, Keats abandoned the medical profession to become a poet.

Keats's first books, *Poems* (1817) and *Endymion* (1818), were attacked, mainly by conservative enemies of Hunt. Stimulated more by his own scrutiny than by outside criticism, Keats refined his style and in 1819 wrote "The Eve of St. Agnes," "Lamia," the six Odes (on Psyche, Indolence, the Nightingale, the Grecian Urn, Melancholy, and Autumn), and "La Belle Dame sans Merci" — the quintessential lyrics of English Romanticism. In that year Keats also knew he was racing the clock: He had returned from a walking tour in the autumn of 1818 with an ulcerated throat and had enough medical training to foresee his own death from tuberculosis. Keats worked furiously at his fragmentary epic, *The Fall of Hyperion,* but in February 1820 he began to cough up blood and had serious hemorrhages later in the spring. That summer he left for the milder climate of Rome, but it was already too late. He died there on February 23, 1821, and is buried in the Protestant Cemetery.

Keats wrote no developed body of critical theory; his ideas — picked up from the intellectual atmosphere of the Romantics and completely unstructured by schools — appear as brilliant fragments in his personal letters to friends.

The letter to Benjamin Bailey reflects Keats's most idealistic phase. In it, Keats asserts that the product of the sensual intuition seems superior to the product of the rational intellect, and that what the imagination produces and records as Beauty is not illusion but "truth" — an authentic reality — "whether it existed before or not" in the material sense. Keats's first example of the authenticity of imagination — Adam's dream — comes from *Paradise Lost,* and seems to be a merely literary manifestation. But his second, when he asks Bailey to recall the way imagination reconstitutes the content of an old memory from a tiny stimulus, yet recaptures it more beautifully than it actually occurred, has become a major touchstone of Romantic aesthetics.

The same is true of the letter to his brothers George and Thomas Keats. Here we find Keats's classic definition of *negative capability:* "when man is capable of being in uncertainties, Mysteries, doubts, without any irritable reaching after fact & reason." The meaning of the phrase is clear enough, but its significance takes some teasing out from the context. Keats begins by contrasting two painful but beautiful works of art: Benjamin West's painting, *Death on the Pale Horse* and Shakespeare's *King Lear*. Keats is only moderately pleased by the former, which lacks the intensity of Shakespeare's tragedy. The intensity of *Lear* seems to come from the "depth of speculation excited" in the audience that contemplates it. Shakespeare's work presents a vision of the pain and evil of life without attempting to comprehend and explain it; its raw presentation demands the intellectual and emotional participation of the viewer. But the West picture has already been processed through the artist's mind, and thus leaves less for the audience to do. Shakespeare possesses immense negative capability; West and the poet Coleridge (in the example at the end of the letter) are artists of a different kind. Keats's idea here may connect with Schiller's distinction between "naive" and "sentimental" writers; the naive Shakespeare presents the emotional object directly for the reader's consideration, whereas the sentimental West presents it filtered through his own private consciousness.

Selected Bibliography

Bate, Walter Jackson. *Negative Capability*. Cambridge: Harvard University Press, 1939.

Ende, Stuart A. *Keats and the Sublime*. New Haven: Yale University Press, 1976.

Sharp, Ronald A. *Keats, Skepticism, and the Religion of Beauty*. Athens: University of Georgia Press, 1979.

Tate, Priscilla Weston. *From Innocence through Experience: Keats's Myth of the Poet*. Salzburg: Institut für Englische Sprache und Literatur, 1974.

Thekla, Sister. *The Disinterested Heart: The Philosophy of John Keats*. Newport Pagnell, Eng.: Greek Orthodox Monastery of the Assumption, 1973.

Thorpe, Clarence Dewitt. *The Mind of John Keats*. New York: Oxford University Press, 1926.

From a *Letter to Benjamin Bailey*

[November 22, 1817]

My dear Bailey,

. . . O I wish I was as certain of the end of all your troubles as that of your momentary start about the authenticity of the Imagination. I am certain of nothing but of the holiness of the Heart's affections and the truth of Imagination — What the imagination seizes as Beauty must be truth[1] — whether it existed before or not — for I have the same Idea of all our Passions as of Love they are all in their sublime, creative of essential Beauty — In a Word, you may know my favorite Speculation by my first Book and the little song I sent in my last[2] — which is a representation from the fancy of the probable mode of operating in these Matters — The Imagination may be compared to Adam's dream[3] — he awoke and found it truth. I am the more zealous in this affair, because I have never yet been able to perceive how any thing can be known for truth by consequitive reasoning — and yet it must be — Can it be that even the greatest Philosopher ever arrived at his goal without putting aside numerous objections — However it may be, O for a Life of Sensations rather than of Thoughts! It is "a Vision in the

[1]Cf. the last two lines of "Ode on a Grecian Urn": in both cases, "truth" seems to mean something like "authentic reality" rather than "verifiable fact." [Ed.]

[2]"O Sorrow" from *Endymion*. [Ed.]

[3]Milton, *Paradise Lost*, 8:460–90. [Ed.]

form of Youth" a Shadow of reality to come — and this consideration has further convinced me for it has come as auxiliary to another favorite Speculation of mine, that we shall enjoy ourselves here after by having what we called happiness on Earth repeated in a finer tone and so repeated — And yet such a fate can only befall those who delight in sensation rather than hunger as you do after Truth — Adam's dream will do here and seems to be a conviction that Imagination and its empyreal reflection is the same as human Life and its spiritual repetition. But as I was saying — the simple imaginative Mind may have its rewards in the repetition of its own silent Working coming continually on the spirit with a fine suddenness — to compare great things with small — have you never by being surprised with an old Melody — in a delicious place — by a delicious voice, felt over again your very speculations and surmises at the time it first operated on your soul — do you not remember forming to yourself the singer's face more beautiful than it was possible and yet with the elevation of the Moment you did not think so — even then you were mounted on the Wings of Imagination so high — that the Prototype must be here after — that delicious face you will see — What a time! I am continually running away from the subject — sure this cannot be exactly the case with a complex Mind — one that is imaginative and at the same time careful of its fruits — who would exist partly on sensation partly on thought — to whom it is necessary that years should bring the philosophic Mind[4] — such an one I consider your's and therefore it is necessary to your eternal Happiness that you not only drink this old Wine of Heaven which I shall call the redigestion of our most ethereal Musings on Earth; but also increase in knowledge and know all things. I am glad to hear you are in a fair Way for Easter — you will soon get through your unpleasant reading and then! — but the world is full of troubles and I have not much reason to think myself pesterd with many — I think Jane or Marianne[5] has a better opinion of me than I deserve — for really and truly I do not think my Brothers illness connected with mine — you know more of the real Cause than they do — nor have I any chance of being rack'd as you have been — you perhaps at one time thought there was such a thing as Worldly Happiness to be arrived at, at certain periods of time marked out — you have of necessity from your disposition been thus led away — I scarcely remember counting upon any Happiness — I look not for it if it be not in the present hour — nothing startles me beyond the Moment. The setting sun will always set me to rights — or if a Sparrow come before my Window I take part in its existince and pick about the Gravel. The first thing that strikes me on hearing a Misfortune having befalled another is this. Well it cannot be helped. — he will have the pleasure of trying the resources of his spirit, and I beg now my dear Bailey that hereafter should you observe anything cold in me not to put it to the account of heartlessness but abstraction — for I assure you I sometimes feel not the influence of a Passion or Affection during a whole week — and so long this sometimes continues I begin to suspect myself and the genuiness of my feelings at other times — thinking them a few barren Tragedy-tears. . . .

Your affectionate friend
John Keats —

[4]Keats is quoting Wordsworth's "Intimations of Immortality" ode. [Ed.]

[5]Jane and Marianne Reynolds, friends of Keats. [Ed.]

From a *Letter to George and Thomas Keats*

[December 21, 27 (?), 1817]

My dear Brothers

I must crave your pardon for not having written ere this. . . . I spent Friday evening with Wells[1] & went the next morning to see *Death on the Pale horse*. It is a wonderful picture, when West's age[2] is considered; But there is nothing to be intense upon; no women one feels mad to kiss; no face swelling into reality. The excellence of every Art is its intensity, capable of making all disagreeables evaporate, from their being in close relationship with Beauty & Truth — Examine King Lear & you will find this exemplified throughout; but in this picture we have unpleasantness without any momentous depth of speculation excited, in which to buy its repulsiveness — The picture is larger than Christ rejected — I dined with Haydon[3] the sunday after you left, & had a very pleasant day, I dined too (for I have been out too much lately) with Horace Smith & met his two Brothers with Hill & Kingston & one Du Bois,[4] they only served to convince me, how superior humour is to wit in respect to enjoyment — These men say things which make one start, without making one feel, they are all alike; their manners are alike; they all know fashionables; they have a mannerism in their very eating & drinking, in their mere handling a Decanter — They talked of Kean[5] & his low company — Would I were with that company instead of yours said I to myself! I know such like acquaintance will never do for me & yet I am going to Reynolds, on wednesday — Brown & Dilke[6] walked with me & back from the Christmas pantomime. I had not a dispute but a disquisition with Dilke, on various subjects; several things dovetailed in my mind, & at once it struck me, what quality went to form a Man of Achievement especially in Literature & which Shakespeare possessed so enormously — I mean *Negative Capability*, that is when man is capable of being in uncertainties, Mysteries, doubts, without any irritable reaching after fact & reason — Coleridge, for instance, would let go by a fine isolated verisimilitude caught from the Penetralium[7] of mystery, from being incapable of remaining content with half knowledge. This pursued through Volumes would perhaps take us no further than this, that with a great poet the sense of Beauty overcomes every other consideration, or rather obliterates all consideration.

Shelley's poem[8] is out & there are words about its being objected too, as much as Queen Mab was. Poor Shelley I think he has his Quota of good qualities, in sooth la!! Write soon to your most sincere friend & affectionate Brother

John

[1]Charles Wells, who had gone to school with Thomas Keats. [Ed.]

[2]Benjamin West (1738–1820) was seventy-nine when he painted *Death on the Pale Horse*. [Ed.]

[3]Benjamin Haydon, a painter who was a good friend of Keats. [Ed.]

[4]Literary figures of the day. [Ed.]

[5]Edmund Kean, the Shakespearean actor. [Ed.]

[6]John Hamilton Reynolds, Charles Armitage Brown, and Charles Wentworth Dilke were literary friends of Keats. [Ed.]

[7]Inner sanctum. [Ed.]

[8]*Laon and Cythna* (1817). [Ed.]

Percy Bysshe Shelley

1792–1822

The most radical English poet since Milton, Percy Bysshe Shelley wrote in proud rebellion against his conservative and aristocratic roots: His grandfather was a landowning baronet, his father a member of Parliament. Shelley was educated at Eton and Oxford, from which he was sent down at the age of eighteen for publishing a tract advocating atheism. In London, he came under the influence of the philosopher William Godwin, whose *Political Justice* questioned the foundations of the English state. Though already married to Harriet Westbrook, Shelley fell in love with Godwin's daughter Mary, and in 1814 eloped with her to France; they were able to marry only after Harriet's suicide, in 1816. In financial straits and anathematized by the British public for his political opinions as well as his sexual immorality, Shelley moved to Italy the next year. There he wrote his most impressive works: *Prometheus Unbound* (1819), *The Masque of Anarchy* (1819), *Epipsychidion* (1821), and *Adonais* (1821). He had just embarked on his most ambitious poem, *The Triumph of Life,* when he drowned in July of 1822 in a boating accident in the Gulf of Spezia.

Like Sir Philip Sidney's *An Apology for Poetry,* Shelley's *A Defence of Poetry* (written in 1821, though not published until 1840) is a reply to Plato's attacks on mimetic art in *Republic,* Book X. It should not be surprising that in the period after Kant and his successors, Shelley's riposte would depend on the notion of mental faculties and their powers. He thus begins the *Defence* with the parallel dialectical oppositions of *tò logizeín* and *tò poieîn,* reason and imagination, analysis and synthesis. His purpose is to refute Plato's attack on the mimetic artist as inferior to the artisan in knowledge and understanding by insisting that the poetic faculty is equal and complementary to logical reason.

The reader who scans *A Defence of Poetry* in search of a systematic approach to Romantic critical theory, however, will be disappointed. Although the essay begins austerely enough with what appears to be a set of logical distinctions, philosophical rigor is soon abandoned. Indeed, some readers may find Shelley's prose disjointed and contradictory, apparently unplanned in organization, at times almost incoherent. But if we set aside system and rigor and attend instead to Shelley's ideals and imagery, the essay yields an inspiring vision, rather like that at the conclusion of *Adonais,* of how the Romantic poets saw themselves and the place of poetry in human society. Perhaps the first and third sections of *A Defence of Poetry* (pp. 339–43 and 353–56) should be read as we read a lyric, through key metaphors.

The first of these metaphors likens the mind to an Aeolian lyre, struck to melody by the wind of its "external and internal impressions." Shelley develops this metaphor further: The mind produces not just melody but harmony as well, and the spontaneous song of the child is an expression of delight in this harmony, an effect the child prolongs by recalling its cause. It is here, deep in human nature, that Shelley locates the impulse to produce art, for poetry is nothing but the adult analogy to this process.

Toward the end of the *Defence,* in discussing the haphazard nature of poetic inspiration Shelley likens the mind of the poet to "a fading coal which some invisible influence, like an inconstant wind, awakens to transitory brightness." Again, the external world is like a wind, forcible but insubstantial, while the mind is like a physical object that can make light or heat or melody. Perhaps nothing suggests Shelley's deep affinity to Plato more than this; it is as if the mind and its ideas are real while the external physical world is not.

Shelley is most Platonic in opposition to his master. Where Plato ejected the poets from his Republic, Shelley makes them its masters, calling them "the unacknowledged legislators of the World." He begins with the idea that "every original language near to its source is in itself the chaos of a cyclic [i.e., epic] poem." We might think of poetry as a special use of language that arranges a harmony between sound and meaning, but all language does that. Whoever creates any new word or names any unnamed feature of the sensual world is, in effect, a poet. Language is everywhere a network of living, dying, and dead metaphors, statements of the likenesses between one aspect of experience and another. We talk of "the iron curtain," we play the game of "cat's cradle": Both are poetic metaphors. And language embalms metaphors in its etymologies: At one time the verb *transgress* literally signified "straying from the herd." In shaping language, the poets — these innovators of language, who are not necessarily identical with the canonized poets from Homer to Shelley himself — have in effect shaped human thought, and thus molded society and human relations.

But it is not enough for Shelley to find a poetic act somewhere behind any use of language. He claims that poetry, in any age removed from the primitive *source* of language, recaptures for humanity, by metaphor and harmony, the immediacy of life and experience, an immediacy that is lost by the use of logical, analytical thought and language. For Shelley, the world is veiled from human participation by dead thought and language, and it is the poets alone who are able to penetrate and "lift the veil from the hidden beauty of the world."

In the course of this argument the words *poetry* and *poet* shift their ground away from pure aesthetics. A poet is anyone who can synthesize a vision of the world and express that apprehended synthesis in language. Thus the great philosophers, Plato among them, are revealed to be nothing other than poets. And conversely, since poets' visions are necessarily of the eternal truths of the human spirit, Shakespeare, Dante, and Milton must be seen as "philosophers of the very loftiest power."

The development of these general ideas is interrupted by a long middle section (pp. 343–53), which was inspired less by Plato than by "The Four Ages of Poetry" (1820), a pamphlet by Shelley's friend, the satirist Thomas Love Peacock. Perhaps influenced by the Italian philosopher Giambattista Vico, Peacock posited a cyclical theory of the history of Western civilization: Both history and poetry had by then gone through two cycles with four phases in each.

Each cycle begins with an "age of iron," like the archaic period or the Middle Ages, when the poet is essentially a bard paid to flatter in verse the exploits of military chieftains. There follows an "age of gold," a tough but harmonious civilization, like Periclean Athens or Elizabethan England, which produces the finest poetry, the

Homers and the Shakespeares. From then on, however, the increasing encroachment of scientific knowledge limits the scope of poetry. There arrives an "age of silver," a polished and classicizing civilization that gives rise to the Virgils and the Miltons and Popes. Finally comes the decadence of the "age of brass," in which poetry is mere nostalgic archaism, like the later Roman Empire — or the English Romantic period. At last, the destruction of civilization itself — the fall of the Roman Empire in the first cycle — puts an end to the decay and allows a new age of iron to begin. The bulk of *A Defence of Poetry* is a reply to Peacock's attack on Romantics and Romanticism, which takes the form of a progressive (rather than a cyclical) theory of history and of the poetry that grew up alongside (and in Shelley's view helped to form) political institutions.

Selected Bibliography

Bloom, Harold. *Shelley's Mythmaking.* New Haven: Yale University Press, 1959.

Damm, Robert F. *A Tale of Human Power: Art and Life in Shelley's Poetic Theory.* Oxford, OH: Miami University Press, 1970.

Grabo, C. H. *The Magic Plant: The Growth of Shelley's Thought.* Chapel Hill: University of North Carolina Press, 1936.

Notopoulos, J. A. *The Platonism of Shelley.* Durham: Duke University Press, 1949.

Schulze, Earl J. *Shelley's Theory of Poetry: A Reappraisal.* The Hague: Mouton, 1966.

Shawcross, John, ed. *Shelley's Literary and Philosophical Criticism.* London: H. Frowde, 1909.

Solve, Melvin T. *Shelley: His Theory of Poetry.* Chicago: University of Chicago Press, 1927.

A Defence of Poetry

or Remarks Suggested by an Essay Entitled "The Four Ages of Poetry"

According to one mode of regarding those two classes of mental action, which are called reason and imagination, the former may be considered as mind contemplating the relations borne by one thought to another, however produced; and the latter, as mind acting upon those thoughts so as to colour them with its own light, and composing from them, as from elements, other thoughts, each containing within itself the principle of its own integrity. The one is the τὸ ποιειν,[1] or the principle of synthesis, and has for its objects those forms which are common to universal nature and existence itself; the other is the τὸ λογιζειν,[2] or principle of analysis, and its action regards the relations of things, simply as relations; considering thoughts, not in their integral unity, but as the algebraical representations which conduct to certain general results. Reason is the enumeration of quantities already known; imagination is the perception of the value of those quantities, both separately and as a whole. Reason respects the differences, and imagination the similitudes of things. Reason is to Imagination as the instrument to the agent, as the body to the spirit, as the shadow to the substance.

[1]Making. [Ed.]

[2]Reasoning. [Ed.]

Poetry, in a general sense, may be defined to be "the expression of the Imagination": and poetry is connate with the origin of man. Man is an instrument over which a series of external and internal impressions are driven, like the alternations of an ever-changing wind over an Æolian lyre, which move it by their motion to ever-changing melody. But there is a principle within the human being, and perhaps within all sentient beings, which acts otherwise than in the lyre, and produces not melody alone, but harmony, by an internal adjustment of the sounds or motions thus excited to the impressions which excite them. It is as if the lyre could accommodate its chords to the motions of that which strikes them, in a determined proportion of sound; even as the musician can accommodate his voice to the sound of the lyre. A child at play by itself will express its delight by its voice and motions; and every inflexion of tone and every gesture will bear exact relation to a corresponding antitype in the pleasurable impressions which awakened it; it will be the reflected image of that impression; and as the lyre trembles and sounds after the wind has died away, so the child seeks, by prolonging in its voice and motions the duration of the effect, to prolong also a consciousness of the cause. In relation to the objects which delight a child, these expressions are what poetry is to higher objects. The savage (for the savage is to ages what the child is to years) expresses the emotions produced in him by surrounding objects in a similar manner; and language and gesture, together with plastic or pictorial imitation, become the image of the combined effect of those objects, and of his apprehension of them. Man in society, with all his passions and his pleasures, next becomes the object of the passions and pleasures of man; an additional class of emotions produces an augmented treasure of expressions; and language, gesture, and the imitative arts, become at once the representation and the medium, the pencil and the picture, the chisel and the statue, the chord and the harmony. The social sympathies, or those laws from which as from its elements society results, begin to develope themselves from the moment that two human beings coexist; the future is contained within the present as the plant within the seed; and equality, diversity, unity, contrast, mutual dependence, become the principles alone capable of affording the motives according to which the will of a social being is determined to action, inasmuch as he is social; and constitute pleasure in sensation, virtue in sentiment, beauty in art, truth in reasoning, and love in the intercourse of kind. Hence men, even in the infancy of society, observe a certain order in their words and actions, distinct from that of the objects and the impressions represented by them, all expression being subject to the laws of that from which it proceeds. But let us dismiss those more general considerations which might involve an enquiry into the principles of society itself, and restrict our view to the manner in which the imagination is expressed upon its forms.

In the youth of the world, men dance and sing and imitate natural objects, observing in these actions, as in all others, a certain rhythm or order. And, although all men observe a similar, they observe not the same order, in the motions of the dance, in the melody of the song, in the combinations of language, in the series of their imitations of natural objects. For there is a certain order or rhythm belonging to each of these classes of mimetic representation, from which the hearer and the spectator receive an intenser and purer pleasure than from any other: the sense of an approximation to this order has been called taste, by modern writers. Every man in the infancy of art, observes an order which approximates more or less closely to that from which this highest delight results: but the diversity is not sufficiently marked, as that its gradations should be sensible, except in those instances where the predominance of this faculty of approximation to the beautiful (for so we may be permitted to name the relation between this highest pleasure and its cause) is very great. Those in whom it exists in excess are poets, in the most universal sense of the word; and the pleasure resulting from the manner in which they express the influence of society or nature upon their own minds, communicates itself to others, and gathers a sort of reduplication from that community. Their language is vitally metaphorical; that is, it marks the before unapprehended relations of things, and perpetuates their apprehension, until the words which represent them, become through time signs for portions or classes of thoughts instead of pictures of integral thoughts; and then if no new poets should arise to create afresh the associations which have been thus disorganized, language will be dead to all the nobler purposes of human intercourse. These similitudes or relations are finely said by Lord Bacon to be "the same footsteps of nature impressed upon the various subjects of the world"[3] — and he considers the faculty which perceives them as the storehouse of axioms common to all knowledge. In the infancy of society every author is necessarily a poet, because language itself is poetry; and to be a poet is to apprehend the true and the beautiful, in a word the good which exists in the relation, subsisting, first between existence and perception, and secondly between perception and expression. Every original language near to its source is in itself the chaos of a cyclic poem: the copiousness of lexicography and the distinctions of grammar are the works of a later age, and are merely the catalogue and the form of the creations of Poetry.

But Poets, or those who imagine and express this indestructible order, are not only the authors of language and of music, of the dance and architecture and statuary and painting: they are the institutors of laws, and the founders of civil society and the inventors of the arts of life and the teachers, who draw into a certain propinquity with the beautiful and the true that partial apprehension of the agencies of the invisible world which is called religion. Hence all original religions are allegorical, or susceptible of allegory, and like Janus have a double face of false and true. Poets, according to the circumstances of the age and nation in which they appeared, were called in the earlier epochs of the world legislators or prophets: a poet essentially comprises and unites both these characters.[4] For he not only beholds intensely the present as it is, and discovers those laws according to which present things ought to be ordered, but he beholds the future in the present, and his thoughts are the germs of the flower and the fruit of latest time. Not that I assert poets to be prophets in the gross sense of the word, or that they can foretell the form as surely as they foreknow the spirit of events: such is the pretence of superstition which would make poetry an attribute of prophecy, rather than prophecy an attribute of poetry. A Poet participates in the eternal, the infinite, and the one; as far as relates to his conceptions, time and place and number are not. The grammatical forms which express the moods of time, and the difference of persons and the distinction of place are convertible with respect to the highest poetry without injuring it as poetry, and the choruses of Æschylus, and the book of Job, and Dante's Paradise would afford, more than any other writings, examples of this fact, if the limits of this essay did not forbid citation. The creations of sculpture, painting, and music, are illustrations still more decisive.

Language, colour, form, and religious and civil habits of action are all the instruments and materials of poetry; they may be called poetry by that figure of speech which considers the effect as a synonime of the cause. But poetry in a more restricted sense expresses those arrangements of language, and especially metrical language, which are created by that imperial faculty, whose throne is curtained within the invisible nature of man. And this springs from the nature itself of language, which is a more direct representation of the actions and passions of our internal being, and is susceptible of more various and delicate combinations, than colour, form, or motion, and is more plastic and obedient to the controul of that faculty of which it is the creation. For language is arbitrarily produced by the Imagination and has relation to thoughts alone; but all other materials, instruments and conditions of art, have relations among each other, which limit and interpose between conception and expression. The former is as a mirror which reflects, the latter as a cloud which enfeebles, the light of which both are mediums of communication. Hence the fame of sculptors, painters and musicians, although the intrinsic powers of the great masters of these arts, may yield in no degree to that of those who have employed language as the hieroglyphic of their thoughts, has never equalled that of poets in the restricted sense of the term; as two performers of equal skill will produce unequal effects from a

[3]Francis Bacon, *The Advancement of Learning*. 3:1. [Ed.]
[4]Cf. Philip Sidney, *An Apology for Poetry;* see p. 136. [Ed.]

guitar and a harp. The fame of legislators and founders of religions, so long as their institutions last, alone seems to exceed that of poets in the restricted sense; but it can scarcely be a question whether, if we deduct the celebrity which their flattery of the gross opinions of the vulgar usually conciliates, together with that which belonged to them in their higher character of poets, any excess will remain.

We have thus circumscribed the meaning of the word Poetry within the limits of that art which is the most familiar and the most perfect expression of the faculty itself. It is necessary however to make the circle still narrower, and to determine the distinction between measured and unmeasured language; for the popular division into prose and verse is inadmissible in accurate philosophy.

Sounds as well as thoughts have relation both between each other and towards that which they represent, and a perception of the order of those relations has always been found connected with a perception of the order of the relations of thoughts. Hence the language of poets has ever affected a certain uniform and harmonious recurrence of sound, without which it were not poetry, and which is scarcely less indispensable to the communication of its influence, than the words themselves, without reference to that peculiar order. Hence the vanity of translation; it were as wise to cast a violet into a crucible that you might discover the formal principle of its colour and odour, as seek to transfuse from one language into another the creations of a poet. The plant must spring again from its seed or it will bear no flower — and this is the burthen of the curse of Babel.

An observation of the regular mode of the recurrence of this harmony in the language of poetical minds, together with its relation to music, produced metre, or a certain system of traditional forms of harmony of language. Yet it is by no means essential that a poet should accommodate his language to this traditional form, so that the harmony which is its spirit, be observed. The practise is indeed convenient and popular, and to be preferred, especially in such composition as includes much form and action: but every great poet must inevitably innovate upon the example of his predecessors in the exact structure of his peculiar versification. The distinction between poets and prose writers is a vulgar error. The distinction between philosophers and poets has been anticipated. Plato was essentially a poet — the truth and splendour of his imagery and the melody of his language is the most intense that it is possible to conceive. He rejected the measure of the epic, dramatic, and lyrical forms, because he sought to kindle a harmony in thoughts divested of shape and action, and he forbore to invent any regular plan of rhythm which would include, under determinate forms, the varied pauses of his style. Cicero sought to imitate the cadence of his periods but with little success. Lord Bacon was a poet.[5] His language has a sweet and majestic rhythm, which satisfies the sense, no less than the almost superhuman wisdom of his philosophy satisfies the intellect; it is a strain which distends, and then bursts the circumference of the hearer's mind, and pours itself forth together with it into the universal element with which it has perpetual sympathy. All the authors of revolutions in opinion are not only necessarily poets as they are inventors, nor even as their words unveil the permanent analogy of things by images which participate in the life of truth; but as their periods are harmonious and rhythmical and contain in themselves the elements of verse; being the echo of the eternal music. Nor are those supreme poets, who have employed traditional forms of rhythm on account of the form and action of their subjects, less capable of perceiving and teaching the truth of things, than those who have omitted that form. Shakespeare, Dante and Milton (to confine ourselves to modern writers) are philosophers of the very loftiest power.

A poem is the very image of life expressed in its eternal truth. There is this difference between a story and a poem, that a story is a catalogue of detached facts, which have no other bond of connexion than time, place, circumstance, cause and effect; the other is the creation of actions according to the unchangeable forms of human nature, as existing in the mind of the creator, which is it-

[5]See the *Filium Labyrinthi* and the *Essay on Death* particularly. [Au.]

self the image of all other minds. The one is partial, and applies only to a definite period of time, and a certain combination of events which can never again recur; the other is universal, and contains within itself the germ of a relation to whatever motives or actions have place in the possible varieties of human nature. Time, which destroys the beauty and the use of the story of particular facts, stript of the poetry which should invest them, augments that of Poetry, and for ever developes new and wonderful applications of the eternal truth which it contains. Hence epitomes have been called the moths of just history; they eat out the poetry of it. The story of particular facts is as a mirror which obscures and distorts that which should be beautiful: Poetry is a mirror which makes beautiful that which is distorted.

The parts of a composition may be poetical, without the composition as a whole being a poem. A single sentence may be considered as a whole though it be found in a series of unassimilated portions; a single word even may be a spark of inextinguishable thought. And thus all the great historians, Herodotus, Plutarch, Livy, were poets; and although the plan of these writers, especially that of Livy, restrained them from developing this faculty in its highest degree, they make copious and ample amends for their subjection, by filling all the interstices of their subjects with living images.

Having determined what is poetry, and who are poets, let us proceed to estimate its effects upon society.

Poetry is ever accompanied with pleasure: all spirits on which it falls, open themselves to receive the wisdom which is mingled with its delight. In the infancy of the world, neither poets themselves nor their auditors are fully aware of the excellence of poetry: for it acts in a divine and unapprehended manner, beyond and above consciousness; and it is reserved for future generations to contemplate and measure the mighty cause and effect in all the strength and splendour of their union. Even in modern times, no living poet ever arrived at the fulness of his fame; the jury which sits in judgement upon a poet, belonging as he does to all time, must be composed of his peers: it must be impanelled by Time from the selectest of the wise of many generations. A Poet is a nightingale, who sits in darkness and sings to cheer its own solitude with sweet sounds; his auditors are as men entranced by the melody of an unseen musician, who feel that they are moved and softened, yet know not whence or why. The poems of Homer and his contemporaries were the delight of infant Greece; they were the elements of that social system which is the column upon which all succeeding civilization has reposed. Homer embodied the ideal perfection of his age in human character; nor can we doubt that those who read his verses were awakened to an ambition of becoming like to Achilles, Hector and Ulysses: the truth and beauty of friendship, patriotism and persevering devotion to an object, were unveiled to the depths in these immortal creations: the sentiments of the auditors must have been refined and enlarged by a sympathy with such great and lovely impersonations, until from admiring they imitated, and from imitation they identified themselves with the objects of their admiration. Nor let it be objected, that these characters are remote from moral perfection, and that they can by no means be considered as edifying patterns for general imitation. Every epoch under names more or less specious has deified its peculiar errors; Revenge is the naked Idol of the worship of a semi-barbarous age; and Self-deceit is the veiled Image of unknown evil before which luxury and satiety lie prostrate. But a poet considers the vices of his contemporaries as the temporary dress in which his creations must be arrayed, and which cover without concealing the eternal proportions of their beauty. An epic or dramatic personage is understood to wear them around his soul, as he may the antient armour or the modern uniform around his body; whilst it is easy to conceive a dress more graceful than either. The beauty of the internal nature cannot be so far concealed by its accidental vesture, but that the spirit of its form shall communicate itself to the very disguise, and indicate the shape it hides from the manner in which it is worn. A majestic form and graceful motions will express themselves through the most barbarous and tasteless costume. Few poets of the highest class have chosen to exhibit the beauty of their conceptions in its naked truth and splendour; and it is doubtful whether the alloy of costume, habit, etc., be not necessary to temper this planetary music for mortal ears.

The whole objection however of the immortality of poetry rests upon a misconception of the manner in which poetry acts to produce the moral improvement of man. Ethical science arranges the elements which poetry has created, and propounds schemes and proposes examples of civil and domestic life: nor is it for want of admirable doctrines that men hate, and despise, and censure, and deceive, and subjugate one another. But Poetry acts in another and diviner manner. It awakens and enlarges the mind itself by rendering it the receptacle of a thousand unapprehended combinations of thought. Poetry lifts the veil from the hidden beauty of the world, and makes familiar objects be as if they were not familiar; it reproduces all that it represents, and the impersonations clothed in its Elysian light stand thenceforward in the minds of those who have once contemplated them, as memorials of that gentle and exalted content which extends itself over all thoughts and actions with which it coexists. The great secret of morals is Love; or a going out of our own nature, and an identification of ourselves with the beautiful which exists in thought, action, or person, not our own. A man, to be greatly good, must imagine intensely and comprehensively; he must put himself in the place of another and of many others; the pains and pleasures of his species must become his own. The great instrument of moral good is the imagination; and poetry administers to the effect by acting upon the cause. Poetry enlarges the circumference of the imagination by replenishing it with thoughts of ever new delight, which have the power of attracting and assimilating of their own nature all other thoughts, and which form new intervals and interstices whose void for ever craves fresh food. Poetry strengthens that faculty which is the organ of the moral nature of man, in the same manner as exercise strengthens a limb. A Poet therefore would do ill to embody his own conceptions of right and wrong, which are usually those of his place and time, in his poetical creations, which participate in neither. By this assumption of the inferior office of interpreting the effect, in which perhaps after all he might acquit himself but imperfectly, he would resign the glory in a participation in the cause. There was little danger that Homer, or any of the eternal poets, should have so far misunderstood themselves as to have abdicated this throne of their widest dominion. Those in whom the poetical faculty, though great, is less intense, as Euripides, Lucan, Tasso, Spenser, have frequently affected a moral aim, and the effect of their poetry is diminished in exact proportion to the degree in which they compel us to advert to this purpose.

Homer and the cyclic poets were followed at a certain interval by the dramatic and lyrical Poets of Athens, who flourished contemporaneously with all that is most perfect in the kindred expressions of the poetical faculty; architecture, painting, music, the dance, sculpture, philosophy, and we may add the forms of civil life. For although the scheme of Athenian society was deformed by many imperfections which the poetry existing in Chivalry and Christianity have erased from the habits and institutions of modern Europe; yet never at any other period has so much energy, beauty, and virtue, been developed; never was blind strength and stubborn form so disciplined and rendered subject to the will of man, or that will less repugnant to the dictates of the beautiful and the true, as during the century which preceded the death of Socrates. Of no other epoch in the history of our species have we records and fragments stamped so visibly with the image of the divinity in man. But it is Poetry alone, in form, in action, or in language, which has rendered this epoch memorable above all others, and the storehouse of examples to everlasting time. For written poetry existed at that epoch simultaneously with the other arts, and it is an idle enquiry to demand which gave and which received the light, which all as from a common focus have scattered over the darkest periods of succeeding time. We know no more of cause and effect than a constant conjunction of events: Poetry is ever found to coexist with whatever other arts contribute to the happiness and perfection of man. I appeal to what has already been established to distinguish between the cause and the effect.

It was at the period here adverted to, that the Drama had its birth; and however a succeeding writer may have equalled or surpassed those few great specimens of the Athenian drama which have been preserved to us, it is indisputable that the art itself never was understood or practised according to the true philosophy of it, as at Athens. For the Athenians employed language, action, music, painting, the dance, and religious institutions, to produce a common effect in the representation of the highest idealisms of passion and of power; each division in the art was made perfect in its kind by artists of the most consummate skill, and was disciplined into a beautiful proportion and unity one towards another. On the modern stage a few only of the elements capable of expressing the image of the poet's conception are employed at once. We have tragedy without music and dancing; and music and dancing without the highest impersonations of which they are the fit accompaniment, and both without religion and solemnity. Religious institution has indeed been usually banished from the stage. Our system of divesting the actor's face of a mask, on which the many expressions appropriated to his dramatic character might be moulded into one permanent and unchanging expression, is favourable only to a partial and inharmonious effect; it is fit for nothing but a monologue, where all the attention may be directed to some great master of ideal mimicry. The modern practice of blending comedy with tragedy, though liable to great abuse in point of practise, is undoubtedly an extension of the dramatic circle; but the comedy should be as in King Lear, universal, ideal, and sublime. It is perhaps the intervention of this principle which determines the balance in favour of King Lear against the Œdipus Tyrannus or the Agamemnon, or, if you will the trilogies with which they are connected;[6] unless the intense power of the choral poetry, especially that of the latter, should be considered as restoring the equilibrium. King Lear, if it can sustain this comparison, may be judged to be the most perfect specimen of the dramatic art existing in the world; in spite of the narrow conditions to which the poet was subjected by the ignorance of the philosophy of the Drama which has prevailed in modern Europe. Calderón in his religious Autos[7] has attempted to fulfil some of the high conditions of dramatic representation neglected by Shakespeare; such as the establishing a relation between the drama and religion, and the accommodating them to music and dancing; but he omits the observation of conditions still more important, and more is lost than gained by a substitution of the rigidly-defined and ever-repeated idealisms of a distorted superstition for the living impersonations of the truth of human passion.

But we digress. — The Author of the Four Ages of Poetry[8] has prudently omitted to dispute on the effect of the Drama upon life and manners. For, if I know the knight by the device of his shield, I have only to inscribe Philoctetes or Agamemnon or Othello[9] upon mine to put to flight the giant sophisms which have enchanted him, as the mirror of intolerable light, though on the arm of one of the weakest of the Paladins, could blind and scatter whole armies of necromancers and pagans. The connexion of scenic exhibitions with the improvement or corruption of the manners of men, has been universally recognized: in other words, the presence or absence of poetry in its most perfect and universal form has been found to be connected with good and evil in conduct and habit. The corruption which has been imputed to the drama as an effect, begins, when the poetry employed in its constitution ends: I appeal to the history of manners whether the periods of the growth of the one and the decline of the other have not corresponded with an exactness equal to any other example of moral cause and effect.

The drama at Athens, or wheresoever else it may have approached to its perfection, coexisted with the moral and intellectual greatness of the age. The tragedies of the Athenian poets are as mirrors in which the spectator beholds himself, under a thin disguise of circumstance, stript of all but that ideal perfection and energy which every one feels to be the internal type of all that he

[6]The *Agamemnon* by Aeschylus is the first play of the *Oresteia* trilogy. Sophocles' *Oedipus Tyrannos* is not part of an extant trilogy, though he wrote plays connected with the Oedipus story twenty years earlier *(Antigone)* and twenty years later *(Oedipus at Colonus)*. [Ed.]

[7]The *autos* of the Spanish dramatist Calderón (1600–1681) were short religious allegorical dramas. [Ed.]

[8]Shelley's friend, Thomas Love Peacock (1785–1866). [Ed.]

[9]Tragic protagonists of Sophocles, Aeschylus, and Shakespeare, respectively. [Ed.]

loves, admires, and would become. The imagination is enlarged by a sympathy with pains and passions so mighty, that they distend in their conception the capacity of that by which they are conceived; the good affections are strengthened by pity, indignation, terror and sorrow; and an exalted calm is prolonged from the satiety of this high exercise of them into the tumult of familiar life; even crime is disarmed of half its horror and all its contagion by being represented as the fatal consequence of the unfathomable agencies of nature; error is thus divested of its wilfulness; men can no longer cherish it as the creation of their choice. In a drama of the highest order there is little food for censure or hatred; it teaches rather self-knowledge and self-respect. Neither the eye nor the mind can see itself, unless reflected upon that which it resembles. The drama, so long as it continues to express poetry, is as a prismatic and many-sided mirror, which collects the brightest rays of human nature and divides and reproduces them from the simplicity of these elementary forms, and touches them with majesty and beauty, and multiplies all that it reflects, and endows it with the power of propagating its like wherever it may fall.

But in periods of the decay of social life, the drama sympathizes with that decay. Tragedy becomes a cold imitation of the form of the great masterpieces of antiquity, divested of all harmonious accompaniment of the kindred arts; and often the very form misunderstood: or a weak attempt to teach certain doctrines, which the writer considers as moral truths; and which are usually no more than specious flatteries of some gross vice or weakness with which the author in common with his auditors are infected. Hence what has been called the classical and domestic drama. Addison's "Cato" is a specimen of the one; and would it were not superfluous to cite examples of the other! To such purposes Poetry cannot be made subservient. Poetry is a sword of lightning, ever unsheathed, which consumes the scabbard that would contain it. And thus we observe that all dramatic writings of this nature are unimaginative in a singular degree; they affect sentiment and passion: which, divested of imagination, are other names for caprice and appetite. The period in our own history of the grossest degradation of the drama is the reign of Charles II when all forms in which poetry had been accustomed to be expressed became hymns to the triumph of kingly power over liberty and virtue. Milton stood alone illuminating an age unworthy of him. At such periods the calculating principle pervades all the forms of dramatic exhibition, and poetry ceases to be expressed upon them. Comedy loses its ideal universality: wit succeeds to humour; we laugh from self-complacency and triumph instead of pleasure; malignity, sarcasm and contempt, succeed to sympathetic merriment; we hardly laugh, but we smile. Obscenity, which is ever blasphemy against the divine beauty in life, becomes, from the very veil which it assumes, more active if less disgusting: it is a monster for which the corruption of society for ever brings forth new food, which it devours in secret.

The drama being that form under which a greater number of modes of expression of poetry are susceptible of being combined than any other, the connexion of poetry and social good is more observable in the drama than in whatever other form: and it is indisputable that the highest perfection of human society has ever corresponded with the highest dramatic excellence; and that the corruption or the extinction of the drama in a nation where it has once flourished, is a mark of a corruption of manners, and an extinction of the energies which sustain the soul of social life. But, as Machiavelli says of political institutions, that life may be preserved and renewed, if men should arise capable of bringing back the drama to its principles. And this is true with respect to poetry in its most extended sense: all language, institution and form, require not only to be produced but to be sustained: the office and character of a poet participates in the divine nature as regards providence, no less than as regards creation.

Civil war, the spoils of Asia, and the fatal predominance first of the Macedonian, and then of the Roman arms were so many symbols of the extinction or suspension of the creative faculty in Greece. The bucolic writers, who found patronage under the lettered tyrants of Sicily and Egypt, were the latest representatives of its most glorious reign. Their poetry is intensely melodious; like the odour of the tuberose, it overcomes and sickens the spirit with excess of sweetness;

whilst the poetry of the preceding age was as a meadow-gale of June which mingles the fragrance of all the flowers of the field, and adds a quickening and harmonizing spirit of its own which endows the sense with a power of sustaining its extreme delight. The bucolic and erotic delicacy in written poetry is correlative with that softness in statuary, music, and the kindred arts, and even in manners and institutions which distinguished the epoch to which we now refer. Nor is it the poetical faculty itself, or any misapplication of it, to which this want of harmony is to be imputed. An equal sensibility to the influence of the senses and the affections is to be found in the writings of Homer and Sophocles: the former especially has clothed sensual and pathetic images with irresistible attractions. Their superiority over these succeeding writers consists in the presence of those thoughts which belong to the inner faculties of our nature, not in the absence of those which are connected with the external; their incomparable perfection consists in an harmony of the union of all. It is not what the erotic writers have, but what they have not, in which their imperfection consists. It is not inasmuch as they were Poets, but inasmuch as they were not Poets, that they can be considered with any plausibility as connected with the corruption of their age. Had that corruption availed so as to extinguish in them the sensibility to pleasure, passion and natural scenery, which is imputed to them as an imperfection, the last triumph of evil would have been achieved. For the end of social corruption is to destroy all sensibility to pleasure; and therefore it is corruption. It begins at the imagination and the intellect as at the core, and distributes itself thence as a paralyzing venom, through the affections into the very appetites, until all become a torpid mass in which sense hardly survives. At the approach of such a period, Poetry ever addresses itself to those faculties which are the last to be destroyed, and its voice is heard, like the footsteps of Astræa, departing from the world.[10] Poetry ever communicates all the pleasure which men are capable of receiving: it is ever still the light of life; the source of whatever of beautiful, or generous, or true can have place in an evil time. It will readily be confessed that those among the luxurious citizens of Syracuse and Alexandria who were delighted with the poems of Theocritus, were less cold, cruel and sensual than the remnant of their tribe. But corruption must have utterly destroyed the fabric of human society before Poetry can ever cease. The sacred links of that chain have never been entirely disjoined, which descending through the minds of many men is attached to those great minds, whence as from a magnet the invisible effluence is sent forth, which at once connects, animates and sustains the life of all. It is the faculty which contains within itself the seeds at once of its own and of social renovation. And let us not circumscribe the effects of the bucolic and erotic poetry within the limits of the sensibility of those to whom it was addressed. They may have perceived the beauty of those immortal compositions, simply as fragments and isolated portions: those who are more finely organized, or born in a happier age, may recognize them as episodes to that great poem, which all poets, like the cooperating thoughts of one great mind, have built up since the beginning of the world.

The same revolutions within a narrower sphere had place in antient Rome; but the actions and forms of its social life never seem to have been perfectly saturated with the poetical element. The Romans appear to have considered the Greeks as the selectest treasuries of the selectest forms of manners and of nature, and to have abstained from creating in measured language, sculpture, music or architecture, anything which might bear a particular relation to their own condition, whilst it should bear a general one to the universal constitution of the world. But we judge from partial evidence; and we judge perhaps partially. Ennius, Varro, Pacuvius, and Accius, all great poets, have been lost. Lucretius is in the highest, and Virgil in a very high sense, a creator. The chosen delicacy of the expressions of the latter is as a mist of light which conceals from us the intense and exceeding truth of his conceptions of nature. Livy is instinct with poetry. Yet Horace, Catullus, Ovid, and generally the other great writers of the Virgilian age, saw man and nature in the mirror of Greece. The institutions

[10]Astraea was the goddess of justice who fled Earth for Heaven once the reign of Zeus began. [Ed.]

also and the religion of Rome were less poetical than those of Greece, as the shadow is less vivid than the substance. Hence poetry in Rome, seemed to follow rather than accompany the perfection of political and domestic society. The true Poetry of Rome lived in its institutions; for whatever of beautiful, true and majestic they contained could have sprung only from the faculty which creates the order in which they consist. The life of Camillus, the death of Regulus; the expectation of the Senators, in their godlike state, of the victorious Gauls; the refusal of the Republic to make peace with Hannibal after the battle of Cannae, were not the consequences of a refined calculation of the probable personal advantage to result from such a rhythm and order in the shews of life, to those who were at once the poets and the actors of these immortal dramas. The imagination beholding the beauty of this order, created it out of itself according to its own idea: the consequence was empire, and the reward ever-living fame. These things are not the less poetry, *quia carent vate sacro.*[11] They are the episodes of the cyclic poem written by Time upon the memories of men. The Past, like an inspired rhapsodist, fills the theatre of everlasting generations with their harmony.

At length the antient system of religion and manners had fulfilled the circle of its revolution. And the world would have fallen into utter anarchy and darkness, but that there were found poets among the authors of the Christian and Chivalric systems of manners and religion, who created forms of opinion and action never before conceived; which, copied into the imaginations of men, became as generals to the bewildered armies of their thoughts. It is foreign to the present purpose to touch upon the evil produced by these systems: except that we protest, on the ground of the principles already established, that no portion of it can be imputed to the poetry they contain.

It is probable that the astonishing poetry of Moses, Job, David, Solomon and Isaiah had produced a great effect upon the mind of Jesus and his disciples. The scattered fragments preserved to us by the biographers of this extraordinary person, are all instinct with the most vivid poetry. But his doctrines seem to have been quickly distorted. At a certain period after the prevalence of a system of opinions founded upon those promulgated by him, the three forms into which Plato had distributed the faculties of mind underwent a sort of apotheosis, and became the object of the worship of the civilized world. Here it is to be confessed that "Light seems to thicken," and

> The crow makes wing to the rooky wood,
> Good things of day begin to droop and drowze,
> And night's black agents to their preys do rouze.[12]

But mark how beautiful an order has sprung from the dust and blood of this fierce chaos! how the World, as from a resurrection, balancing itself on the golden wings of knowledge and of hope, has reassumed its yet unwearied flight into the Heaven of time. Listen to the music, unheard by outward ears, which is as a ceaseless and invisible wind, nourishing its everlasting course with strength and swiftness.

The poetry in the doctrines of Jesus Christ, and the mythology and institutions of the Celtic[13] conquerors of the Roman empire, outlived the darkness and the convulsions connected with their growth and victory, and blended themselves into a new fabric of manners and opinion. It is an error to impute the ignorance of the dark ages to the Christian doctrines or the predominance of the Celtic nations. Whatever of evil their agencies may have contained sprung from the extinction of the poetical principle, connected with the progress of despotism and superstition. Men, from causes too intricate to be here discussed, had become insensible and selfish: their own will had become feeble, and yet they were its slaves, and thence the slaves of the will of others: lust, fear, avarice, cruelty and fraud, characterised a race amongst whom no one was to be found capable of *creating* in form, language, or institu-

[11]"Because they lack a sacred prophet/poet." Horace, *Odes* IV.9:28. [Ed.]

[12]Shakespeare, *Macbeth,* III.ii.50–53. [Ed.]

[13]Shelley uses "Celtic" to refer to Germanic tribes (like those Caesar fought), not the aboriginal inhabitants of the British Isles. [Ed.]

tion. The moral anomalies of such a state of society are not justly to be charged upon any class of events immediately connected with them, and those events are most entitled to our approbation which could dissolve it most expeditiously. It is unfortunate for those who cannot distinguish words from thoughts, that many of these anomalies have been incorporated into our popular religion.

It was not until the eleventh century that the effects of the poetry of the Christian and Chivalric systems began to manifest themselves. The principle of equality had been discovered and applied by Plato in his Republic, as the theoretical rule of the mode in which the materials of pleasure and of power produced by the common skill and labour of human beings ought to be distributed among them. The limitations of this rule were asserted by him to be determined only by the sensibility of each, or the utility to result to all. Plato, following the doctrines of Timæus and Pythagoras, taught also a moral and intellectual system of doctrine comprehending at once the past, the present, and the future condition of man. Jesus Christ divulged the sacred and eternal truths contained in these views to mankind, and Christianity, in its abstract purity, became the exoteric expression of the esoteric doctrines of the poetry and wisdom of antiquity. The incorporation of the Celtic nations with the exhausted population of the South, impressed upon it the figure of the poetry existing in their mythology and institutions. The result was a sum of the action and reaction of all the causes included in it; for it may be assumed as a maxim that no nation or religion can supersede any other without incorporating into itself a portion of that which it supersedes. The abolition of personal and domestic slavery, and the emancipation of women from a great part of the degrading restraints of antiquity were among the consequences of these events.

The abolition of personal slavery is the basis of the highest political hope that it can enter into the mind of man to conceive. The freedom of women produced the poetry of sexual love. Love became a religion, the idols of whose worship were ever present. It was as if the statues of Apollo and the Muses had been endowed with life and motion and had walked forth among their worshippers; so that earth became peopled by the inhabitants of a diviner world. The familiar appearance and proceedings of life became wonderful and heavenly; and a paradise was created as out of the wrecks of Eden. And as this creation itself is poetry, so its creators were poets; and language was the instrument of their art: "Galeotto fù il libro, e chi lo scrisse."[14] The Provençal Trouveurs, or inventors, preceded Petrarch, whose verses are as spells, which unseal the inmost enchanted fountains of the delight which is in the grief of Love. It is impossible to feel them without becoming a portion of that beauty which we contemplate: it were superfluous to explain how the gentleness and the elevation of mind connected with these sacred emotions can render men more amiable, more generous, and wise, and lift them out of the dull vapours of the little world of self. Dante understood the secret things of love even more than Petrarch. His *Vita Nuova* is an inexhaustible fountain of purity of sentiment and language: it is the idealized history of that period, and those intervals of his life which were dedicated to love. His apotheosis of Beatrice in Paradise and the gradations of his own love and her loveliness, by which as by steps he feigns himself to have ascended to the throne of the Supreme Cause, is the most glorious imagination of modern poetry. The acutest critics have justly reversed the judgement of the vulgar, and the order of the great acts of the "Divine Drama," in the measure of the admiration which they accord to the Hell, Purgatory and Paradise. The latter is a perpetual hymn of everlasting love. Love, which found a worthy poet in Plato alone of all the antients, has been celebrated by a chorus of the greatest writers of the renovated world; and the music has penetrated the caverns of society, and its echoes still

[14] "That book was a Galeotto [legend of Sir Galahad], and so was he that wrote it." Dante, *Inferno* 5:137. The quotation is spoken by Francesca di Rimini, an adulterous wife Dante meets in Hell, who recounts how her affair with Paolo Malatesta began over a book of chivalric romance. Galahad introduced his uncle Lancelot to Queen Guinevere and so began their adulterous liaison; hence "Galeotto" in Italian can mean a go-between. [Ed.]

drown the dissonance of arms and superstition. At successive intervals, Ariosto, Tasso, Shakespeare, Spenser, Calderón, Rousseau, and the great writers of our own age, have celebrated the dominion of love, planting as it were trophies in the human mind of that sublimest victory over sensuality and force. The true relation borne to each other by the sexes into which human kind is distributed has become less misunderstood; and if the error which confounded diversity with inequality of the powers of the two sexes has become partially recognized in the opinions and institutions of modern Europe, we owe this great benefit to the worship of which Chivalry was the law, and poets the prophets.

The poetry of Dante may be considered as the bridge thrown over the stream of time, which unites the modern and antient world. The distorted notions of invisible things which Dante and his rival Milton have idealized, are merely the mask and the mantle in which these great poets walk through eternity enveloped and disguised. It is a difficult question to determine how far they were conscious of the distinction which must have subsisted in their minds between their own creeds and that of the people. Dante at least appears to wish to mark the full extent of it by placing Riphæus, whom Virgil calls *justissimus unus,* in Paradise[15] and observing a most heretical caprice in his distribution of rewards and punishments. And Milton's poem contains within itself a philosophical refutation of that system of which, by a strange and natural antithesis, it has been a chief popular support. Nothing can exceed the energy and magnificence of the character of Satan as expressed in Paradise Lost. It is a mistake to suppose that he could ever have been intended for the popular personification of evil. Implacable hate, patient cunning, and a sleepless refinement of device to inflict the extremest anguish on an enemy, these things are evil; and although venial in a slave are not to be forgiven in a tyrant; although redeemed by much that ennobles his defeat in one subdued, are marked by all that dishonours his conquest in the victor. Milton's Devil as a moral being is as far superior to his God as one who perseveres in some purpose which he has conceived to be excellent in spite of adversity and torture, is to one who in the cold security of undoubted triumph inflicts the most horrible revenge upon his enemy, not from any mistaken notion of inducing him to repent of a perseverance in enmity, but with the alleged design of exasperating him to deserve new torments. Milton has so far violated the popular creed (if this shall be judged to be a violation) as to have alleged no superiority of moral virtue to his God over his Devil. And this bold neglect of a direct moral purpose is the most decisive proof of the supremacy of Milton's genius. He mingled as it were the elements of human nature, as colours upon a single pallet, and arranged them into the composition of his great picture according to the laws of epic truth; that is, according to the laws of that principle by which a series of actions of the external universe and of intelligent and ethical beings is calculated to excite the sympathy of succeeding generations of mankind. The Divina Commedia and Paradise Lost have conferred upon modern mythology a systematic form; and when change and time shall have added one more superstition to the mass of those which have arisen and decayed upon the earth, commentators will be learnedly employed in elucidating the religion of ancestral Europe, only not utterly forgotten because it will have been stamped with the eternity of genius.

Homer was the first, and Dante the second epic poet: that is, the second poet the series of whose creations bore a defined and intelligible relation to the knowledge, and sentiment, and religion, and political conditions of the age in which he lived, and of the ages which followed it, developing itself in correspondence with their developement. For Lucretius had limed the wings of his swift spirit in the dregs of the sensible world; and Virgil, with a modesty which ill became his genius, had affected the fame of an imitator even whilst he created anew all that he copied; and none among the flock of mock-birds, though their notes were sweet, Apollonius Rhodius, Quintus Calaber Smyrnaeus, Nonnus, Lucan, Statius, or Claudian, have sought even to fulfil a single condition of epic truth. Milton was

[15]"The one who is most just." Virgil, *Aeneid* 2:426. Dante finds him, to his surprise (since he was a pagan), in Paradise (*Paradiso* 20:67–69). [Ed.]

the third Epic Poet. For if the title of epic in its highest sense be refused to the Æneid, still less can it be conceded to the Orlando Furioso, the Gerusalemme Liberata, the Lusiad, or the Fairy Queen.

Dante and Milton were both deeply penetrated with the antient religion of the civilized world; and its spirit exists in their poetry probably in the same proportion as its forms survived in the unreformed worship of modern Europe. The one preceded and the other followed the Reformation at almost equal intervals. Dante was the first religious reformer, and Luther surpassed him rather in the rudeness and acrimony, than in the boldness of his censures of papal usurpation. Dante was the first awakener of entranced Europe; he created a language in itself music and persuasion out of a chaos of inharmonious barbarisms. He was the congregator of those great spirits who presided over the resurrection of learning; the Lucifer[16] of that starry flock which in the thirteenth century shone forth from republican Italy, as from a heaven, into the darkness of the benighted world. His very words are instinct with spirit; each is as a spark, a burning atom of inextinguishable thought; and many yet lie covered in the ashes of their birth, and pregnant with a lightning which has yet found no conductor. All high poetry is infinite; it is as the first acorn, which contained all oaks potentially. Veil after veil may be undrawn, and the inmost naked beauty of the meaning never exposed. A great Poem is a fountain for ever overflowing with the waters of wisdom and delight; and after one person and one age has exhausted all its divine effluence which their peculiar relations enable them to share, another and yet another succeeds, and new relations are ever developed, the source of an unforeseen and an unconceived delight.

The age immediately succeeding to that of Dante, Petrarch, and Boccaccio, was characterized by a revival of painting, sculpture, music, and architecture. Chaucer caught the sacred inspiration, and the superstructure of English literature is based upon the materials of Italian invention.

[16]Shelley intends here the literal sense of "bearer of light." [Ed.]

But let us not be betrayed from a defence into a critical history of Poetry and its influence on Society. Be it enough to have pointed out the effects of poets, in the large and true sense of the word, upon their own and all succeeding times and to revert to the partial instances cited as illustrations of an opinion the reverse of that attempted to be established in the Four Ages of Poetry.

But poets have been challenged to resign the civic crown to reasoners and mechanists on another plea. It is admitted that the exercise of the imagination is most delightful, but it is alleged that of reason is more useful. Let us examine as the grounds of this distinction, what is here meant by Utility. Pleasure or good in a general sense, is that which the consciousness of a sensitive and intelligent being seeks, and in which when found it acquiesces. There are two kinds of pleasure, one durable, universal, and permanent; the other transitory and particular. Utility may either express the means of producing the former or the latter. In the former sense, whatever strengthens and purifies the affections, enlarges the imagination, and adds spirit to sense, is useful. But the meaning in which the Author of the Four Ages of Poetry seems to have employed the word utility is the narrower one of banishing the importunity of the wants of our animal nature, the surrounding men with security of life, the dispersing the grosser delusions of superstition, and the conciliating such a degree of mutual forbearance among men as may consist with the motives of personal advantage.

Undoubtedly the promoters of utility in this limited sense, have their appointed office in society. They follow the footsteps of poets, and copy the sketches of their creations into the book of common life. They make space, and give time. Their exertions are of the highest value so long as they confine their administration of the concerns of the inferior powers of our nature within the limits due to the superior ones. But whilst the sceptic destroys gross superstitions, let him spare to deface, as some of the French writers have defaced, the eternal truths charactered upon the imaginations of men. Whilst the mechanist abridges, and the political œconomist combines, labour, let them beware that their speculations, for want of correspondence with those first principles which belong to the imagination, do not tend, as they have in modern England, to exasperate at once the extremes of luxury and want. They have exemplified the saying, "To him that hath, more shall be given; and from him that hath not, the little that he hath shall be taken away."[17] The rich have become richer, and the poor have become poorer; and the vessel of the state is driven between the Scylla and Charybdis of anarchy and despotism. Such are the effects which must ever flow from an unmitigated exercise of the calculating faculty.

It is difficult to define pleasure in its highest sense; the definition involving a number of apparent paradoxes. For, from an inexplicable defect of harmony in the constitution of human nature, the pain of the inferior is frequently connected with the pleasures of the superior portions of our being. Sorrow, terror, anguish, despair itself are often the chosen expressions of an approximation to the highest good. Our sympathy in tragic fiction depends on this principle; tragedy delights by affording a shadow of the pleasure which exists in pain. This is the source also of the melancholy which is inseparable from the sweetest melody. The pleasure that is in sorrow is sweeter than the pleasure of pleasure itself. And hence the saying, "It is better to go to the house of mourning, than to the house of mirth."[18] Not that this highest species of pleasure is necessarily linked with pain. The delight of love and friendship, the extacy of the admiration of nature, the joy of the perception and still more of the creation of poetry is often wholly unalloyed.

The production and assurance of pleasure in this highest sense is true utility. Those who produce and preserve this pleasure are Poets or poetical philosophers.

The exertions of Locke, Hume, Gibbon, Voltaire, Rousseau,[19] and their disciples, in favour of oppressed and deluded humanity, are entitled to the gratitude of mankind. Yet it is easy to calculate the degree of moral and intellectual improvement which the world would have exhibited, had they never lived. A little more nonsense would have been talked for a century or two; and perhaps a few more men, women, and children, burnt as heretics. We might not at this moment have been congratulating each other on the abolition of the Inquisition in Spain. But it exceeds all imagination to conceive what would have been the moral condition of the world if neither Dante, Petrarch, Boccaccio, Chaucer, Shakespeare, Calderón, Lord Bacon, nor Milton, had ever existed; if Raphael and Michael Angelo had never been born; if the Hebrew poetry had never been translated; if a revival of the study of Greek literature had never taken place; if no monuments of antient sculpture had been handed down to us; and if the poetry of the religion of the antient world had been extinguished together with its belief. The human mind could never, except by the intervention of these excitements, have been awakened to the invention of the grosser sciences, and that application of analytical reasoning to the aberrations of society, which it is now attempted to exalt over the direct expression of the inventive and creative faculty itself.

We have more moral, political and historical wisdom, than we know how to reduce into practise; we have more scientific and œconomical knowledge than can be accommodated to the just distribution of the produce which it multiplies. The poetry in these systems of thought, is concealed by the accumulation of facts and calculating processes. There is no want of knowledge respecting what is wisest and best in morals, government, and political œconomy, or at least, what is wiser and better than what men now practise and endure. But we let "*I dare not* wait upon *I would,* like the poor cat i' the adage."[20] We want the creative faculty to imagine that which we know; we want the generous impulse to act that which we imagine; we want the poetry of life: our calculations have outrun conception; we have eaten more than we can digest. The cultivation of those sciences which have enlarged the limits of the empire of man over the external

[17]Matthew 25:29. [Ed.]

[18]Ecclesiastes 7:2. [Ed.]

[19]I follow the classification adopted by the author of the Four Ages of Poetry. But Rousseau was essentially a poet. The others, even Voltaire, were mere reasoners. [Au.]

[20]Shakespeare, *Macbeth,* I.vii:44–45. [Ed.]

world, has, for want of the poetical faculty, proportionally circumscribed those of the internal world; and man, having enslaved the elements, remains himself a slave. To what but a cultivation of the mechanical arts in a degree disproportioned to the presence of the creative faculty, which is the basis of all knowledge, is to be attributed the abuse of all invention for abridging and combining labour, to the exasperation of the inequality of mankind? From what other cause has it arisen that the discoveries which should have lightened, have added a weight to the curse imposed on Adam? Poetry, and the principle of Self, of which money is the visible incarnation, are the God and the Mammon of the world.

The functions of the poetical faculty are twofold; by one it creates new materials of knowledge, and power and pleasure; by the other it engenders in the mind a desire to reproduce and arrange them according to a certain rhythm and order which may be called the beautiful and the good. The cultivation of poetry is never more to be desired than at periods when, from an excess of the selfish and calculating principle, the accumulation of the materials of external life exceed the quantity of the power of assimilating them to the internal laws of human nature. The body has then become too unwieldy for that which animates it.

Poetry is indeed something divine. It is at once the centre and circumference of knowledge; it is that which comprehends all science, and that to which all science must be referred. It is at the same time the root and blossom of all other systems of thought: it is that from which all spring, and that which adorns all; and that which, if blighted, denies the fruit and the seed, and withholds from the barren world the nourishment and the succession of the scions of the tree of life. It is the perfect and consummate surface and bloom of things; it is as the odour and the colour of the rose to the texture of the elements which compose it, as the form and the splendour of unfaded beauty to the secrets of anatomy and corruption. What were Virtue, Love, Patriotism, Friendship &c. — what were the scenery of this beautiful Universe which we inhabit — what were our consolations on this side of the grave — and what were our aspirations beyond it — if Poetry did not ascend to bring light and fire from those eternal regions where the owl-winged faculty of calculation dare not ever soar? Poetry is not like reasoning, a power to be exerted according to the determination of the will. A man cannot say, "I will compose poetry." The greatest poet even cannot say it: for the mind in creation is as a fading coal which some invisible influence, like an inconstant wind, awakens to transitory brightness: this power arises from within, like the colour of a flower which fades and changes as it is developed, and the conscious portions of our natures are unprophetic either of its approach or its departure. Could this influence be durable in its original purity and force, it is impossible to predict the greatness of the results: but when composition begins, inspiration is already on the decline, and the most glorious poetry that has ever been communicated to the world is probably a feeble shadow of the original conception of the poet. I appeal to the greatest Poets of the present day, whether it be not an error to assert that the finest passages of poetry are produced by labour and study. The toil and the delay recommended by critics can be justly interpreted to mean no more than a careful observation of the inspired moments, and an artificial connexion of the spaces between their suggestions by the intertexture of conventional expressions; a necessity only imposed by a limitedness of the poetical faculty itself. For Milton conceived the Paradise Lost as a whole before he executed it in portions. We have his own authority also for the Muse having "dictated" to him the "unpremeditated song,"[21] and let this be an answer to those who would allege the fifty-six various readings of the first line of the Orlando Furioso. Compositions so produced are to poetry what mosaic is to painting. This instinct and intuition of the poetical faculty is still more observable in the plastic and pictorial arts: a great statue or picture grows under the power of the artist as a child in the mother's womb, and the very mind which directs the hands in formation is incapable of accounting to itself for the origin, the gradations, or the media of the process.

[21]Milton, *Paradise Lost,* 9:21–24. [Ed.]

Poetry is the record of the best and happiest moments of the happiest and best minds. We are aware of evanescent visitations of thought and feeling sometimes associated with place or person, sometimes regarding our own mind alone, and always arising unforeseen and departing unbidden, but elevating and delightful beyond all expression: so that even in the desire and the regret they leave, there cannot but be pleasure, participating as it does in the nature of its object. It is as it were the interpenetration of a diviner nature through our own; but its footsteps are like those of a wind over a sea, which the coming calm erases, and whose traces remain only as on the wrinkled sand which paves it. These and corresponding conditions of being are experienced principally by those of the most delicate sensibility and the most enlarged imagination; and the state of mind produced by them is at war with every base desire. The enthusiasm of virtue, love, patriotism, and friendship is essentially linked with these emotions; and whilst they last, self appears as what it is, an atom to a Universe. Poets are not only subject to these experiences as spirits of the most refined organization, but they can colour all that they combine with the evanescent hues of this etherial world; a word, a trait in the representation of a scene or a passion, will touch the enchanted chord, and reanimate, in those who have ever experienced these emotions, the sleeping, the cold, the buried image of the past. Poetry thus makes immortal all that is best and most beautiful in the world; it arrests the vanishing apparitions which haunt the interlunations of life, and veiling them or in language or in form sends them forth among mankind, bearing sweet news of kindred joy to those with whom their sisters abide — abide, because there is no portal of expression from the caverns of the spirit which they inhabit into the universe of things. Poetry redeems from decay the visitations of the divinity in man.

Poetry turns all things to loveliness; it exalts the beauty of that which is most beautiful, and it adds beauty to that which is most deformed: it marries exultation and horror, grief and pleasure, eternity and change; it subdues to union under its light yoke all irreconcilable things. It transmutes all that it touches, and every form moving within the radiance of its presence is changed by wondrous sympathy to an incarnation of the spirit which it breathes; its secret alchemy turns to potable gold the poisonous waters which flow from death through life; it strips the veil of familiarity from the world, and lays bare the naked and sleeping beauty which is the spirit of its forms.

All things exist as they are perceived: at least in relation to the percipient. "The mind is its own place, and of itself can make a heaven of hell, a hell of heaven."[22] But poetry defeats the curse which binds us to be subjected to the accident of surrounding impressions. And whether it spreads its own figured curtain or withdraws life's dark veil from before the scene of things, it equally creates for us a being within our being. It makes us the inhabitants of a world to which the familiar world is a chaos. It reproduces the common universe of which we are portions and percipients, and it purges from our inward sight the film of familiarity which obscures from us the wonder of our being. It compels us to feel that which we perceive, and to imagine that which we know. It creates anew the universe after it has been annihilated in our minds by the recurrence of impressions blunted by reiteration. It justifies that bold and true word of Tasso — *Non merita nome di creatore, se non Iddio ed il Poeta.*[23]

A Poet, as he is the author to others of the highest wisdom, pleasure, virtue and glory, so he ought personally to be the happiest, the best, the wisest, and the most illustrious of men. As to his glory, let Time be challenged to declare whether the fame of any other institutor of human life be comparable to that of a poet. That he is the wisest, the happiest, and the best, inasmuch as he is a poet, is equally incontrovertible: the greatest poets have been men of the most spotless virtue, of the most consummate prudence, and, if we could look into the interior of their lives, the most fortunate of men: and the exceptions, as they regard those who possessed the poetic faculty in a high yet inferior degree, will be found on consideration to confirm rather than destroy the rule. Let us for a moment stoop to the arbitra-

[22]Milton, *Paradise Lost,* 1:254–55. [Ed.]

[23]"Nobody merits the title of Creator save God and the Poet." The line is quoted thus in Serassi's *Life of Torquato Tasso.* [Ed.]

tion of popular breath, and usurping and uniting in our own persons the incompatible characters of accuser, witness, judge and executioner, let us decide without trial, testimony, or form, that certain motives of those who are "there sitting where we dare not soar"[24] are reprehensible. Let us assume that Homer was a drunkard, that Virgil was a flatterer, that Horace was a coward, that Tasso was a madman, that Lord Bacon was a peculator, that Raphael was a libertine, that Spenser was a poet laureate.[25] It is inconsistent with this division of our subject to cite living poets, but Posterity has done ample justice to the great names now referred to. Their errors have been weighed and found to have been dust in the balance: if their sins "were as scarlet, they are now white as snow"; they have been washed in the blood of the mediator and the redeemer Time. Observe in what a ludicrous chaos the imputations of real or fictitious crime have been confused in the contemporary calumnies against poetry and poets; consider how little is, as it appears — or appears, as it is; look to your own motives, and judge not, lest ye be judged.

Poetry, as has been said, in this respect differs from logic, that it is not subject to the controul of the active powers of the mind, and that its birth and recurrence has no necessary connexion with consciousness or will. It is presumptuous to determine that these are the necessary conditions of all mental causation, when mental effects are experienced insusceptible of being referred to them. The frequent recurrence of the poetical power, it is obvious to suppose, may produce in the mind an habit or order and harmony correlative with its own nature and with its effects upon other minds. But in the intervals of inspiration, and they may be frequent without being durable, a poet becomes a man, and is abandoned to the sudden reflux of the influences under which others habitually live. But as he is more delicately organized than other men, and sensible to pain and pleasure, both his own and that of others, in a degree unknown to them, he will avoid the one and pursue the other with an ardour proportioned to this difference. And he renders himself obnoxious to calumny, when he neglects to observe the circumstances under which these objects of universal pursuit and flight have disguised themselves in one another's garments.

But there is nothing necessarily evil in this error, and thus cruelty, envy, revenge, avarice, and the passions purely evil, have never formed any portion of the popular imputations on the lives of poets.

I have thought it most favourable to the cause of truth to set down these remarks according to the order in which they were suggested to my mind by a consideration of the subject itself, instead of following that of the treatise that excited me to make them public. Thus although devoid of the formality of a polemical reply; if the view they contain be just, they will be found to involve a refutation of the Four Ages of Poetry, so far at least as regards the first division of the subject. I can readily conjecture what should have moved the gall of the learned and intelligent author of that paper; I confess myself like him unwilling to be stunned by the Theseids of the hoarse Codri of the day. Bavius and Mævius undoubtedly are, as they ever were, insufferable persons.[26] But it belongs to a philosophical critic to distinguish rather than confound.

The first part of these remarks has related to Poetry in its elements and principles; and it has been shewn, as well as the narrow limits assigned them would permit, that what is called poetry, in a restricted sense, has a common source with all other forms of order and of beauty according to which the materials of human life are susceptible of being arranged, and which is poetry in an universal sense.

The second part will have for its object an application of these principles to the present state of the cultivation of Poetry, and a defence of the attempt to idealize the modern forms of manners and opinion, and compel them into a subordination to the imaginative and creative faculty.[27] For

[24]Milton, *Paradise Lost,* 4:829. [Ed.]

[25]Poet laureate may seem an odd member of this sequence, unless we remember that the current laureate was Robert Southey, a personal and political enemy of Shelley's. [Ed.]

[26]Codrus, Bavius, and Maevius are traditional examples of bad poets cited by Juvenal, Horace, and Virgil. [Ed.]

[27]The "second part" was never written. [Ed.]

the literature of England, an energetic developement of which has ever preceded or accompanied a great and free developement of the national will, has arisen as it were from a new birth. In spite of the low-thoughted envy which would undervalue contemporary merit, our own will be a memorable age in intellectual achievements, and we live among such philosophers and poets as surpass beyond comparison any who have appeared since the last national struggle for civil and religious liberty. The most unfailing herald, companion, and follower of the awakening of a great people to work a beneficial change in opinion or institution, is Poetry. At such periods there is an accumulation of the power of communicating and receiving intense and impassioned conceptions respecting man and nature. The persons in whom this power resides, may often, as far as regards many portions of their nature, have little apparent correspondence with that spirit of good of which they are the ministers. But even whilst they deny and abjure, they are yet compelled to serve, the Power which is seated upon the throne of their own soul. It is impossible to read the compositions of the most celebrated writers of the present day without being startled with the electric life which burns within their words. They measure the circumference and sound the depths of human nature with a comprehensive and all-penetrating spirit, and they are themselves perhaps the most sincerely astonished at its manifestations, for it is less their spirit than the spirit of the age. Poets are the hierophants of an unapprehended inspiration, the mirrors of the gigantic shadows which futurity casts upon the present, the words which express what they understand not; the trumpets which sing to battle, and feel not what they inspire: the influence which is moved not, but moves. Poets are the unacknowledged legislators of the World.

Georg Wilhelm Friedrich Hegel

1770–1831

The central philosopher of modern nationalism was born the son of a civil servant in Stuttgart. Hegel is not known to have been a remarkable child. As a boy he played cards, learned to take snuff, and made a vast, painstakingly arranged collection of clippings and extracts from sources as varied as the classics and local newspapers. Hegel studied theology at Tübingen University without having much interest in it or, for that matter, much commitment to the mystical content of Christianity. After taking his Ph.D., he wrote (in advance of the demythologizer David Friedrich Strauss) a biography of Jesus, which considers him not as the son of God but as a human professor of ethics and religion whose contribution was to restore to Judaism the classical harmony between God and Man. Two friends from Tübingen assisted Hegel's early career: The poet Friedrich Hölderlin helped him to good posts as a private tutor, and the philosopher Friedrich von Schelling got him a course of lectures at the university at Jena.

There, in the first years of the nineteenth century, he developed his central ideas about mind, art, and the state. These years were dominated by the epoch-making figure of Napoleon, who carved the map of Europe with his sword, and whom Hegel saw as one of the "world-historical individuals" — his term for people who embodied the spirit of an age, and whose greatness came from the confluence of their private wills with the ineluctable movement of history. When Napoleon took Jena in a great battle in 1806, Hegel's sympathies were with the emperor rather than with the German states, which he saw as desperately in need of the same political reform and consolidation, through blood and iron, that the Revolution and Napoleon had given France. His political ideas became the watchwords of the second German Reich, of Bismarck and the Hohenzollern emperors.

But the battle — and the decade of war — had made Jena an uncomfortable place for the philosopher. Despite the publication of his revolutionary *Phenomenology of Spirit* (1807), Hegel was nearly bankrupt. He edited a newspaper and then took a post in Nuremberg as rector of a secondary school, the Aegidien-Gymnasium. There, at forty-two, he married a local girl of nineteen, who bore him two sons and with whom he had a happy and affectionate relationship.

Hegel continued his work at Nuremberg and, on the publication of his *Logic* (1812–16), was offered three secure professorships. Hegel went first to Heidelberg, where he brought out his *Encyclopaedia of the Philosophical Sciences* (1817). The following year, he accepted the chair of philosophy in Berlin, where he published his essay on *Philosophy of Right* (1821) as a guide to the burgeoning Prussian state and where he taught for the rest of his life.

By the late 1820s, Hegel had become the founder of a school of philosophy with a host of disciples and imitators. He was decorated by the king of Prussia and made rector of his university. Then in 1831, at the height of his fame, he died suddenly during a cholera epidemic. His death expanded rather than erased his influence, however. Most of his major works were derived from his class lectures at Berlin, and many of them were compiled after his death from his notes and those of his students. These works were issued in nineteen volumes between 1832 and 1847; they include *The Philosophy of History, The Philosophy of Religion,* and *Aesthetics.* The selection that follows is taken from the *Introduction to the Philosophy of Art.* This was originally published posthumously in 1835 as the manuscript notes to Hegel's lectures on aesthetics. The lectures themselves were originally given in 1820, but were revised in 1823, 1826, and 1829.

Hegel's philosophy in its broadest sense presents the metamorphoses of the Spirit of the World from the beginning of history, when Man differentiated himself from the rest of Nature, to modern times. *The Phenomenology of Spirit* describes this evolution of mind from its most primitive stage, mere consciousness of an outside world, through the intermediate stages of consciousness-of-self, reason, spirit, and religion, to the ultimate realm of Absolute Knowledge.

Like Plato, Hegel is a holistic thinker. His later treatises on various subjects, like his posthumous lectures on politics, religion, and art, did not constitute a departure from the philosophy of mind in *The Phenomenology.* Rather, they showed how the spiritual evolution described in *The Phenomenology* had worked itself out in different areas of human experience. In each area, Hegel regarded the primitive oriental mode as engaged with substance at the expense of spirit, the intermediate classic mode as characterized by a harmony between body and spirit, and the modern mode as the culminating triumph of spirit over substance.

In politics, for example, Hegel saw the spiritual metamorphosis as the historical development of freedom. Politics originated in the alienation of man from nature, which required taming by collective action. The first solution was the patriarchal family, where all power and right are invested in the father, and the father is free to kill his wife or children if they disobey him. In the oriental world, patriarchal power was collectivized in the despotism of the ruler, who was a father to his subjects. In the empires of China and Persia, only one man was free: the emperor. This patriarchal form of government gave way to the democracy and aristocracy of Greece and Rome, where a whole class of people could be free, but whose freedom was based on the subjugation of slaves and foreigners. In the postclassical age — what Hegel called the German World — he foresaw the day when all men could be free, not as patriarchs or oriental despots or slave-owning aristocrats, but as mutual participants in an orderly freedom under law as subjects of an enlightened monarch.

In terms of religion, Hegel saw the faiths of the Orient — of China and India — as spiritually coherent with their despotic politics. The ancestor worship of China is its most obvious and direct manifestation. The later Confucian notion that the emperor rules under the mandate of T'ien, or Heaven, is only a slight deviation, since it reifies the magical forces of nature as operating through that individual. The Indian religions, Hinduism and Buddhism, represent the opposite reaction. Religion is a quietistic escape, through reincarnation and nirvana, from a despotism that, left intact on earth, is ignored as irrelevant or devalued as Maya (Illusion). Judaism too created a patriarchal God (like that of China) who was viewed as existing behind and transcending Nature (like the deities of India).

For Hegel the Greek religion was the next stage. Where the Orientals had portrayed spirit overwhelmed by substance, the Greeks found a balance between the two. Their gods were anthropomorphic and human in their spiritual nature as well as in their physical forms. Having humanized the gods that lurked behind natural phenomena, the Greeks were free to trust nature. This confidence allowed them to develop a politics of trust in themselves rather than one of subjection to a semi-divine despot. Christianity, the religion of the modern world, tips the balance from substance toward spirit. It combines the patriarchal despot inherited from Judaism (God the Creator) with an anthropomorphic deity (Jesus); but it adds the Holy Spirit, who incarnates the divine in the spirit of each man and ends the divorce of man from nature.

Each of these historical transformations is mediated by Hegel's "transcendental dialectic" — a well-known feature of his reasoning usually summarized by the triad of thesis, antithesis, and synthesis. An aspect of life becomes a thesis when it is abstracted from the background of nature and made into an absolute. Each Absolute calls into being its Other, the antithesis, which it negates and which in turn negates it. At length the conflict is mediated by a higher transcendent being that can resolve the negations and contradictions. The Judaic god, for example, is absolutized as God the Creator. He is thus defined by, and in opposition to, his creation, nature, including man, and is therefore outside nature and time, inhuman and incomprehensible. At the same time, nature and man are defined as barren of the divine. Thesis and antithesis negate each other. The synthesis mediating and transcending these negations was provided in Christianity through God the Son, who is human and natural as well as divine. Hegel's dialectic was later adopted by Karl Marx, who used it to support a materialistic theory of economics and society rather than an idealist approach to spiritual evolution.

Hegel's ideas on art must be seen in the context of both his dialectical method and his thinking on the histories of politics and religion, for in *The Phenomenology,* art is an aspect of religion (and vice versa) rather than a separate spiritual mode, and the collective expression of a society rather than of an individual voice. Although he was generally a follower of Kant's idealism, Hegel rejected Kant's aesthetic with its basis in natural beauty and its insistence on the purposelessness of the beautiful object. For Hegel, nature is beautiful only by analogy with art, and art is supremely useful to man, not as mere pleasure but for "its ability to represent in *sensuous form* even the highest ideas, bringing them thus nearer to . . . the senses, and to feeling." In the long run, perhaps in the last stage of human evolution toward absolute knowledge, art would be superseded by the more direct apprehension of ideas through philosophy. But far from being deceptive, as Plato thought, art serves to free "the true meaning of appearances from the show and deception of this bad and transient world."

If art is "the sensuous form of the idea," then it has two distinct ways of evolving: in the history of its forms — the modes of substance the idea inhabits — and through the history of the spirit itself. The latter gives Hegel his distinction between symbolic, classic, and romantic art. Each has its defects and virtues. Symbolic art (we should call it allegorical art) is typically the art of the oriental world, where substance is present in abundance but where the "spiritual idea has not yet found its adequate form." It can convey the sublime, as the pyramids do, although it has a spiritual quality that excludes the human, or it can merely degenerate into the grotesque. In classical art, as in Greek religion and politics, substance and spirit exist in full harmony in sculptures that express spiritual ideas "through the bodily form of man." But classic art, although perfect in its way, is limited to the contemplation of the merely human. Only romantic art can portray the greater spirituality of the divine. Here, though, the spirit outruns substance, giving the audience the sense of a meaning that extends beyond the power of matter to convey it.

In a second classification of artistic genres and forms, Hegel discusses the particular arts, categorizing them according to their relation to these movements of historical evolution. Architecture, the most massively physical of the arts, whose products dwarf the spectator, is clearly linked with the symbolic art of the oriental world while sculpture is obviously linked with the classic world. The romantic arts of the modern world are painting, music, and poetry, for they owe the least to substance and the most to spirit. Painting, like sculpture, is graphic, but a painting imposes a subjective point of view that sculpture — designed to be viewed in the round — cannot. And painting can represent whatever can be imagined — thoughts and feelings as well as plastic forms. Music is even more spiritual since it is insubstantial, but it still requires players and performance. Poetry alone is totally free of the requirements of substance.

Elsewhere, Hegel classifies poetic forms, viewing epic as the most objective and lyric as the most subjective of the poetic arts, and drama as the synthesis of the two. Like Aristotle, Hegel regarded tragedy as the highest of the arts, particularly because he felt that, at its best (as in Sophocles' *Antigone*), the tragic agon could be viewed not as a material struggle but as a battle for primacy between two ideas — an example of Hegel's own vision of spiritual evolution through the conflict of thesis and antithesis.

Selected Bibliography

Bungay, Stephen. *Beauty and Truth: A Study of Hegel's Aesthetics.* Oxford and New York: Oxford University Press, 1984.

Horn, András. *Kunst und Freiheit: Eine kritische Interpretation der Hegelische Asthetik.* The Hague: Martinus Nijhoff, 1969.

Kaminsky, Jack. *Hegel on Art: An Interpretation of Hegel's Aesthetics.* Albany: State University of New York Press, 1962.

Kaufmann, Walter. *Hegel: Reinterpretation, Texts, and Commentary.* Garden City, NY: Doubleday, 1965.

Kedney, John Steinfort. *Hegel's Aesthetics: A Critical Exposition.* Chicago: B. C. Griggs, 1892.

Knox, Israel. *The Aesthetic Theories of Kant, Hegel and Schopenhauer.* New York: Columbia University Press, 1936.

Stace, W. T. *The Philosophy of Hegel.* London: Macmillan, 1924.

Steinkraus, W., K. L. Schmitz, and J. O'Malley, eds. *Art and Logic in Hegel's Philosophy.* Atlantic Highlands, NJ: Humanities Press, 1980.

Sussman, Henry. *The Hegelian Aftermath: Readings in Hegel, Kierkegaard, Freud, Proust, and James.* Baltimore: Johns Hopkins University Press, 1982.

Teyssèdre, Bernard. *L'esthétique de Hegel.* Paris: Presses Universitaires de France, 1958.

Introduction to the Philosophy of Art

THE MEANING OF ART

The appropriate expression for our subject is the Philosophy of Art, or, more precisely, the Philosophy of Fine Arts. By this expression we wish to exclude the beauty of nature. In common life we are in the habit of speaking of beautiful color, a beautiful sky, a beautiful river, beautiful flowers, beautiful animals, and beautiful human beings. But quite aside from the question, which we wish not to discuss here, how far beauty may be predicated of such objects, or how far natural beauty may be placed side by side with artistic beauty, we must begin by maintaining that artistic beauty is higher than the beauty of nature. For the beauty of art is beauty born — and born again — of the spirit. And as spirit and its products stand higher than nature and its phenomena, by so much the beauty that resides in art is superior to the beauty of nature.

To say that spirit and artistic beauty stand higher than natural beauty, is to say very little, for "higher" is a very indefinite expression, which states the difference between them as quantitative and external. The "higher" quality of spirit and of artistic beauty does not at all stand in a merely relative position to nature. Spirit only is the true essence and content of the world, so that whatever is beautiful is truly beautiful only when it partakes of this higher essence and is produced by it. In this sense natural beauty appears only as a reflection of the beauty that belongs to spirit; it is an imperfect and incomplete expression of the spiritual substance.

Confining ourselves to artistic beauty, we must first consider certain difficulties. The first that suggests itself is the question whether art is at all worthy of a philosophic treatment. To be sure, art and beauty pervade, like a kindly genius, all the affairs of life, and joyously adorn all its inner and outer phases, softening the gravity and the burden of actual existence, furnishing pleasure for idle moments, and, where it can accomplish nothing positive, driving evil away by occupying its place. Yet, although art wins its way everywhere with its pleasing forms, from the crude adornment of the savages to the splendour of the temple with its marvellous wealth of decoration, art itself appears to fall outside the real aims of life. And though the creations of art cannot be said to be directly disadvantageous to the serious purposes of life, nay, on occasion actually further them by holding evil at bay, on the whole, art belongs to the relaxation and leisure of the mind, while the substantial interests of life demand its exertion. At any rate, such a view renders art a superfluity, though the tender and emotional influence which is wrought upon the mind by occupation with art is not thought necessarily detrimental, because effeminate.

There are others, again, who, though acknowledging art to be a luxury, have thought it necessary to defend it by pointing to the practical necessities of the fine arts and to the relation they bear to morality and piety. Very serious aims have been ascribed to art. Art has been recommended as a mediator between reason and sensuousness, between inclination and duty, as the reconcilor of all these elements constantly warring with one another. But it must be said that, by making art serve two masters, it is not rendered thereby more worthy of a philosophic treatment. Instead of being an end in itself, art is degraded into a means of appealing to higher aims, on the one hand, and to frivolity and idleness on the other.

Art considered as means offers another difficulty which springs from its form. Granting that art can be subordinated to serious aims and that the results which it thus produces will be significant, still the means used by art is deception, for beauty is appearance, its form is its life; and one must admit that a true and real purpose should not be achieved through deception. Even

Translated by Joseph Loewenberg.

if a good end is thus, now and then, attained by art its success is rather limited, and even then deception cannot be recommended as a worthy means; for the means should be adequate to the dignity of the end, and truth can be produced by truth alone and not by deception and semblance.

It may thus appear as if art were not worthy of philosophic consideration because it is supposed to be merely a pleasing pastime; even when it pursues more serious aims it does not correspond with their nature. On the whole, it is conceived to serve both grave and light interests, achieving its results by means of deception and semblance.

As for the worthiness of art to be philosophically considered, it is indeed true that art can be used as a casual amusement, furnishing enjoyment and pleasure, decorating our surroundings, lending grace to the external conditions of life, and giving prominence to other objects through ornamentation. Art thus employed is indeed not an independent or free, but rather a subservient art. That art might serve other purposes and still retain its pleasure-giving function, is a relation which it has in common with thought. For science, too, in the hands of the servile understanding is used for finite ends and accidental means, and is thus not self-sufficient, but is determined by outer objects and circumstances. On the other hand, science can emancipate itself from such service and can rise in free independence to the pursuit of truth, in which the realization of its own aims is its proper function.

Art is not genuine art until it has thus liberated itself. It fulfils its highest task when it has joined the same sphere with religion and philosophy and has become a certain mode of bringing to consciousness and expression the divine meaning of things, the deepest interests of mankind, and the most universal truths of the spirit. Into works of art the nations have wrought their most profound ideas and aspirations. Fine Art often constitutes the key, and with many nations it is the only key, to an understanding of their wisdom and religion. This character art has in common with religion and philosophy. Art's peculiar feature, however, consists in its ability to represent in *sensuous form* even the highest ideas, bringing them thus nearer to the character of natural phenomena, to the senses, and to feeling. It is the height of a supra-sensuous world into which *thought* reaches, but it always appears to immediate consciousness and to present experience as an alien *beyond.* Through the power of philosophic thinking we are able to soar above what is merely *here,* above sensuous and finite experience. But spirit can heal the breach between the supra-sensuous and the sensuous brought on by its own advance; it produces out of itself the world of fine art as the first reconciling medium between what is merely external, sensuous, and transient, and the world of pure thought, between nature with its finite reality and the infinite freedom of philosophic reason.

Concerning the unworthiness of art because of its character as appearance and deception, it must be admitted that such criticism would not be without justice, if appearance could be said to be equivalent to falsehood and thus to something that ought not to be. Appearance is essential to reality; truth could not be, did it not shine through appearance. Therefore not appearance in general can be objected to, but merely the particular kind of appearance through which art seeks to portray truth. To charge the appearance in which art chooses to embody its ideas as deception, receives meaning only by comparison with the external world of phenomena and its immediate materiality, as well as with the inner world of sensations and feelings. To these two worlds we are wont, in our empirical work-a-day life, to attribute the value of actuality, reality, and truth, in contrast to art, which is supposed to be lacking such reality and truth. But, in fact, it is just the whole sphere of the empirical inner and outer world that is not the world of true reality; indeed it may be called a mere show and a cruel deception in a far stricter sense than in the case of art. Only beyond the immediacy of sense and of external objects is genuine reality to be found. Truly real is but the fundamental essence and the underlying substance of nature and of spirit, and the universal element in nature and in spirit is precisely what art accentuates and makes visible. This essence of reality appears also in the common outer and inner world, but it appears in the form of a chaos of contingencies, distorted by the immediateness of sense perception, and by the capriciousness and conditions, events, characters, etc. Art frees the true meaning of appearances from the show and deception of this bad and transient world, and invests it with a higher reality and a more genuine being than the things of ordinary life.

THE CONTENT AND IDEAL OF ART

The content of art is spiritual, and its form is sensuous; both sides art has to reconcile into a united whole. The first requirement is that the content, which art is to represent, must be worthy of artistic representation; otherwise we obtain only a bad unity, since a content not capable of artistic treatment is made to take on an artistic form, and a matter prosaic in itself is forced into a form quite opposed to its inherent nature.

The second requirement demands of the content of art that it shall be no abstraction. By this is not meant that it must be concrete, as the sensuous is alleged to be concrete in contrast to everything spiritual and intellectual. For everything that is genuinely true, in the realm of thought as well as in the domain of nature, is concrete, and has, in spite of universality, nevertheless, a particular and subjective character. By saying, for example, that God is simply One, the Supreme Being as such, we express thereby nothing but a lifeless abstraction of an understanding devoid of reason. Such a God, as indeed he is not conceived in his concrete truth, can furnish no content for art, least of all for plastic art. Thus the Jews and the Turks have not been able to represent their God, who is still more abstract, in the positive manner in which the Christians have represented theirs. For in Christianity God is conceived in his truth, and therefore concrete, as a person, as a subject, and, more precisely still, as Spirit. What he is as spirit appears to the religious consciousness as a Trinity of persons, which at the same time is One. Here the essence of God is the reconciled unity of universality and particularity, such unity alone being concrete. Hence, as a content in order to be true must be concrete in this sense, art demands the same concreteness; because a mere abstract idea, or an abstract universal, cannot manifest itself in a particular and sensuous unified form.

If a true and therefore concrete content is to have its adequate sensuous form and shape, this sensuous form must — this being the third requirement — also be something individual, completely concrete, and one. The nature of concreteness belonging to both the content and the representation of art, is precisely the point in which both can coincide and correspond to each other. The natural shape of the human body, for example, is a sensuous concrete object, which is perfectly adequate to represent the spiritual in its concreteness; the view should therefore be abandoned that an existing object from the external world is accidentally chosen by art to express a spiritual idea. Art does not seize upon this or that form either because it simply finds it or because it can find no other, but the concrete spiritual content itself carries with it the element of external, real, yes, even sensuous, representation. And this is the reason why a sensuous concrete object, which bears the impress of an essentially spiritual content, addresses itself to the inner eye; the outward shape whereby the content is rendered visible and imaginable aims at an existence only in our heart and mind. For this reason alone are content and artistic shape harmoniously wrought. The mere sensuously concrete external nature as such has not this purpose for its only origin. The gay and variegated plumage of the birds shines unseen, and their song dies away unheard; the torch-thistle which blossoms only for a night withers without having been admired in the wilds of southern forests; and these forests, groves of the most beautiful and luxuriant vegetation, with the most odorous and fragrant perfumes, perish and waste, no more enjoyed. The work of art is not so unconsciously self-immersed, but it is essentially a question, an address to the responsive soul, an appeal to the heart and to the mind.

Although the sensuous form in which art clothes its content is not accidental, yet it is not the highest form whereby the spiritually concrete may be grasped. A higher mode than representation through a sensuous form, is thought. True and rational thinking, though in a relative sense abstract, must not be one-sided, but concrete. How far a definite content can be adequately treated by art and how far it needs, according to its nature, a higher and more spiritual form, is a distinction which we see at once, if, for example, the Greek gods are compared with God as conceived in accordance with Christian notions. The Greek god is not abstract but individual, closely related to the natural human form. The Christian God is also a concrete personality, but he is purely spiritual, and can be known only as spirit and in spirit. His sphere of existence is therefore essentially inner knowledge, and not the outer natural shape through which he can be represented but imperfectly and not in the whole depth of his essence.

But the task of art is to represent a spiritual idea to direct contemplation in sensuous form, and not in the form of thought or of pure spirituality. The value and dignity of such representation lies in the correspondence and unity of the two sides, of the spiritual content and its sensuous embodiment, so that the perfection and excellency of art must depend upon the grade of inner harmony and union with which the spiritual idea and the sensuous form interpenetrate.

The requirement of the conformity of spiritual idea and sensuous form might at first be interpreted as meaning that any idea whatever would suffice, so long as the concrete form represented this idea and no other. Such a view, however, would confound the ideal of art with mere correctness, which consists in the expression of any meaning in its appropriate form. The artistic ideal is not to be thus understood. For any content whatever is capable, according to the standard of its own nature, of adequate representation, but yet it does not for that reason lay claim to artistic beauty in the ideal sense. Judged by the standard of ideal beauty, even such correct representation will be defective. In this connection we may remark that the defects of a work of art are not to be considered simply as always due to the incapacity of the artist; defectiveness of form has also its root in defectiveness of content. Thus, for instance, the Chinese, Indians, Egyptians, in their artistic objects, their representations of the gods, and their idols, adhered to formlessness, or to a vague and inarticulate form, and were not able to arrive at genuine beauty, because their mythological ideas, the content and conception of their works of art, were as yet vague and obscure. The more perfect in form works of art are, the more profound is the inner truth of their content and thought. And it is not merely a question of the greater or lesser skill with which the objects of external nature are studied and copied, for, in certain stages of artistic consciousness and artistic activity, the misrepresentation and distortion of natural objects are not unintentional technical inexpertness and incapacity, but conscious alteration, which depends upon the content that is in consciousness, and is, in fact, demanded by it. We may thus speak of imperfect art, which, in its own proper sphere, may be quite perfect both technically and in other respects. When compared with the highest idea and ideal of art, it is indeed defective. In the highest art alone are the idea and its representation in perfect congruity, because the sensuous form of the idea is in itself the adequate form, and because the content, which that form embodies, is itself a genuine content.

The higher truth of art consists, then, in the spiritual having attained a sensuous form adequate to its essence. And this also furnishes the principle of division for the philosophy of art. For the Spirit, before it wins the true notion or meaning of its absolute essence, has to develop through a series of stages which constitute its very life. To this universal evolution there corresponds a development of the phases of art, under the form of which the Spirit — as artist — attains to a comprehension of its own meaning.

This evolution within the spirit of art has two sides. The development is, in the first place, a spiritual and universal one, insofar as a gradual series of definite conceptions of the universe — of nature, man, and God — finds artistic representation. In the second place, this universal development of art, embodying itself in sensuous form, determines definite modes of artistic expression and a totality of necessary distinctions within the sphere of art. These constitute the particular arts.

We have now to consider three definite relations of the spiritual idea to its sensuous expression.

SYMBOLIC ART

Art begins when the spiritual idea, being itself still indefinite and obscure and ill-comprehended, is made the content of artistic forms. As indefinite, it does not yet have that individuality which the artistic ideal demands; its abstractness and one-sidedness thus render its shape defective and whimsical. The first form of art is therefore rather a mere search after plasticity than a capacity of true representation. The spiritual idea has not yet found its adequate form, but is still engaged in striving and struggling after it. This form we may, in general, call the *symbolic* form of art; in such form the abstract idea assumes a shape in natural sensuous matter which is foreign to it; with this foreign matter the artistic creation begins, from which, however, it seems unable to free itself. The objects of external nature are reproduced unchanged, but at the same time the meaning of the spiritual idea is attached to them. They thus receive the vocation of expressing it, and must be interpreted as if the spiritual idea were actually present in them. It is indeed true that natural objects possess an aspect which makes them capable of representing a universal meaning, but in symbolic art a complete correspondence is not yet possible. In it the correspondence is confined to an abstract quality, as when, for example, a lion is meant to stand for strength.

This abstract relation brings also to consciousness the foreignness of the spiritual idea to natural phenomena. And the spiritual idea, having no other reality to express its essence, expatiates in all these natural shapes, seeks itself in their unrest and disproportion, but finds them inadequate to it. It then exaggerates these natural phenomena and shapes them into the huge and the boundless. The spiritual idea revels in them, as it were, seethes and ferments in them, does violence to them, distorts and disfigures them into grotesque shapes, and endeavors by the diversity, hugeness, and splendor of such forms to raise the natural phenomena to the spiritual level. For here it is the spiritual idea which is more or less vague and nonplastic, while the objects of nature have a thoroughly definite form.

The incongruity of the two elements to each other makes the relation of the spiritual idea to objective reality a negative one. The spiritual as a wholly inner element and as the universal substance of all things, is conceived unsatisfied with all externality, and in its *sublimity* it triumphs over the abundance of unsuitable forms. In this conception of sublimity the natural objects and the human shapes are accepted and left unaltered, but at the same time recognized as inadequate to their own inner meaning; it is this inner meaning which is glorified far and above every worldly content.

These elements constitute, in general, the character of the primitive artistic pantheism of the Orient, which either invests even the lowest objects with absolute significance, or forces all phenomena with violence to assume the expression of its world-view. This art becomes therefore bizarre, grotesque, and without taste, or it represents the infinite substance in its abstract freedom turning away with disdain from the illusory and perishing mass of appearances. Thus the meaning can never be completely molded into the expression, and, notwithstanding all the aspiration and effort, the incongruity between the spiritual idea and the sensuous form remains insuperable. This is, then, the first form of art — symbolic art with its endless quest, its inner struggle, its sphinxlike mystery, and its sublimity.

CLASSICAL ART

In the second form of art, which we wish to designate as the *classical,* the double defect of symbolic art is removed. The symbolic form is imperfect, because the spiritual meaning which it seeks to convey enters into consciousness in but an abstract and vague manner, and thus the congruity between meaning and form must always remain defective and therefore abstract. This double aspect disappears in the classical type of art; in it we find the free and adequate embodiment of the spiritual idea in the form most suitable to it, and with it meaning and expression are in perfect accord. It is classical art, therefore, which first affords the creation and contemplation of the completed ideal, realizing it as a real fact in the world.

But the congruity of idea and reality in classical art must not be taken in the formal sense of the agreement of a content with its external form; otherwise every photograph of nature, every picture of a countenance, landscape, flower, scene, etc., which constitutes the aim of a representation, would, through the conformity of content and form, be at once classical. The peculiarity of classical art, on the contrary, consists in its content being itself a concrete idea, and, as such, a concrete spiritual idea, for only the spiritual is a truly classical content. For a worthy object of such a content, Nature must be consulted as to whether she contains anything to which a spiritual attribute really belongs. It must be the World-Spirit itself that *invented* the proper form for the concrete spiritual ideal; the subjective mind — in this case the spirit of art — has only *found* it, and given it natural plastic existence in accordance with free individual spirituality. The form in which the idea, as spiritual and individual, clothes itself when revealed as a temporal phenomenon, is the *human form.* To be sure, personification and anthropomorphism have frequently been decried as a degradation of the spiritual; but art, insofar as its task is to bring before direct contemplation the spiritual in sensuous form, must advance to such anthropomorphism, for only in its body can mind appear in an adequately sensuous fashion. The migration of souls[1] is, in this respect, an abstract notion, and physiology should make it one of its fundamental principles that life has necessarily, in its evolution, to advance to the human shape as the only sensuous phenomenon appropriate to the mind.

The human body as portrayed by classical art is not represented in its mere physical existence, but solely as the natural and sensuous form and garb of mind; it is therefore divested of all the defects that belong to the merely sensuous and of all the finite contingencies that appertain to the phenomenal. But if the form must be thus purified in order to express the appropriate content, and, furthermore, if the conformity of meaning and expression is to be complete, the content which is the spiritual idea must be perfectly capable of being expressed through the bodily form of man, without projecting into another sphere beyond the physical and sensuous representation. The result is that Spirit is characterized as a particular form of mind, namely, as human mind, and not as simply absolute and eternal; but the absolute and eternal Spirit must be able to reveal and express itself in a manner far more spiritual.

This latter point brings to light the defect of classical art, which demands its dissolution and its transition to a third and higher form, to wit, the *romantic* form of art.

ROMANTIC ART

The romantic form of art destroys the unity of the spiritual idea and its sensuous form, and goes back, though on a higher level, to the difference and opposition of the two, which symbolic art left unreconciled. The classical form of art attained, indeed, the highest degree of perfection which the sensuous process of art was capable of realizing; and, if it shows any defects, the defects are those of art itself, due to the limitation of its sphere. This limitation has its root in the general attempt of art to represent in sensuous concrete form the infinite and universal Spirit, and in the attempt of the classical type of art to blend so completely spiritual and sensuous existence that the two appear in mutual conformity. But in such a fusion of the spiritual and sensuous aspects Spirit cannot be portrayed according to its true essence, for the true essence of Spirit is its infinite subjectivity; and its absolute internal meaning does not lend itself to a full and free expression in the confinement of the bodily form as its only appropriate existence.

Now, romantic art dissolves the inseparable unity which is the ideal of the classical type, because it has won a content which goes beyond the classical form of art and its mode of expression. This content — if familiar ideas may be recalled — coincides with what Christianity declares to be true of God as Spirit, in distinction to the Greek belief in gods which constitutes the essential and appropriate subject for classical art. The concrete content of Hellenic art implies the unity of the human and divine nature, a unity which, just because it is merely *implied* and *immediate,* permits of a representation in an immediately

[1]Hegel means the transmigration of souls into the bodies of other animals; this notion is "abstract" because it presumes that the soul has an ideal reality that allows it to be put into any earthly envelope. [Ed.]

visible and sensuous mold. The Greek god is the object of naïve contemplation and sensuous imagination; his shape is, therefore, the bodily shape of man; the circle of his power and his essence is individual and confined. To man the Greek god appears as a being and a power with whom he may *feel* a kinship and unity, but this kinship and unity are not reflected upon or raised into definite knowledge. The higher stage is the *knowledge* of this unconscious unity, which underlies the classical form of art and which it has rendered capable of complete plastic embodiment. The elevation of what is unconscious and implied into self-conscious knowledge brings about an enormous difference; it is the infinite difference which, for example, separates man from the animal. Man is an animal, but, even in his animal functions, does not rest satisfied with the potential and the unconscious as the animal does, but becomes conscious of them, reflects upon them, and raises them — as, for instance, the process of digestion — into self-conscious science. And it is thus that man breaks through the boundary of his merely immediate and unconscious existence, so that, just because he knows himself to be animal, he ceases in virtue of such knowledge to be animal, and, through such self-knowledge only, can characterize himself as mind or spirit.

If in the manner just described the unity of the human and divine nature is raised from an *immediate* to a *conscious* unity, the true mold for the reality of this content is no longer the sensuous, immediate existence of the spiritual, the bodily frame of man, but self-conscious and internal contemplation. For this reason Christianity, in depicting God as Spirit — not as particularized individual mind, but as absolute and universal Spirit — retires from the sensuousness of imagination into the sphere of inner being, and makes this, and not the bodily form, the material and mold of its content; and thus the unity of the human and divine nature is a conscious unity, capable of realization only by spiritual knowledge. The new content, won by this unity, is not dependent upon sensuous representation; it is now exempt from such immediate existence. In this way, however, romantic art becomes art which transcends itself, carrying on this process of self-transcendence within its own artistic sphere and artistic form.

Briefly stated, the essence of romantic art consists in the artistic object being the free, concrete, spiritual idea itself, which is revealed in its spirituality to the inner, and not the outer, eye. In conformity with such a content, art can, in a sense, not work for sensuous perception, but must aim at the inner mood, which completely fuses with its object, at the most subjective inner shrine, at the heart, the feeling, which, as spiritual feeling, longs for freedom within itself and seeks and finds reconciliation only within the inner recesses of the spirit. This *inner* world is the content of romantic art, and as such an inner life, or as its reflection, it must seek embodiment. The inner life thus triumphs over the outer world — indeed, so triumphs over it that the outer world itself is made to proclaim its victory, through which the sensuous appearance sinks into worthlessness.

On the other hand, the romantic type of art, like every other, needs an external mode of expression. But the spiritual has now retired from the outer mode into itself, and the sensuous externality of form assumes again, as it did in symbolic art, an insignificant and transient character. The subjective, finite mind and will, the particularity and caprice of the individual, of character, action or of incident and plot, assume likewise the character they had in symbolic art. The external side of things is surrendered to accident and committed to the excesses of the imagination, whose caprice now mirrors existence as it is, now chooses to distort the objects of the outer world into a bizarre and grotesque medley, for the external form no longer possesses a meaning and significance, as in classical art, on its own account and for its own sake. Feeling is now everything. It finds its artistic reflection, not in the world of external things and their forms, but in its own expression; and in every incident and accident of life, in every misfortune, grief, and even crime, feeling preserves or regains its healing power of reconciliation.

Hence, the indifference, incongruity, and antagonism of spiritual idea and sensuous form, the characteristics of symbolic art, reappear in the romantic type, but with this essential difference. In the romantic realm, the spiritual idea, to whose defectiveness was due the defective forms of symbolic art, now reveals itself in its perfection within mind and feeling. It is by virtue of the higher perfection of the idea that it shuns any adequate union with an external form, since it can seek and attain its true reality and expression best within itself.

This, in general terms, is the character of the symbolic, classical, and romantic forms of art, which stand for the three relations of the spiritual idea to its expression in the realm of art. They consist in the aspiration after, and the attainment and transcendence of, the ideal as the true idea of beauty.

THE PARTICULAR ARTS

But, now, there inhere in the idea of beauty different modifications which art translates into sensuous forms. And we find a fundamental principle by which the several particular arts may be arranged and defined — that is, the species of art contain in themselves the same essential differences which we have found in the three general types of art. External objectivity, moreover, into which these types are molded by means of a sensuous and particular material, renders them independent and separate means of realizing different artistic functions, as far as each type finds its definite character in some one definite external material whose mode of portrayal determines its adequate realization.[2] Furthermore, the general types of art correspond to the several particular arts, so that they (the particular arts) belong each of them *specifically* to *one* of the general types of art. It is these particular arts which give adequate and artistic external being to the general types.

ARCHITECTURE

The first of the particular arts with which, according to their fundamental principle, we have to begin, is architecture. Its task consists in so shaping external inorganic nature that it becomes homogeneous with mind, as an artistic outer world. The material of architecture is matter itself in its immediate externality as a heavy mass subject to mechanical laws, and its forms remain the forms of inorganic nature, but are merely arranged and ordered in accordance with the abstract rules of the understanding, the rules of symmetry. But in such material and in such forms the ideal as concrete spirituality cannot be realized; the reality which is represented in them remains, therefore, alien to the spiritual idea, as something external which it has not penetrated or with which it has but a remote and abstract relation. Hence the fundamental type of architecture is the *symbolical* form of art. For it is architecture that paves the way, as it were, for the adequate realization of the God, toiling and wrestling in his service with external nature, and seeking to extricate it from the chaos of finitude, and the abortiveness of chance. By this means it levels a space for the God, frames his external surroundings, and builds him his temple as the place for inner contemplation and for reflection upon the eternal objects of the spirit. It raises an enclosure around those gathered together, as a defense against the threatening of the wind, against rain, the thunderstorm, and wild beasts, and reveals the will to assemble, though externally, yet in accordance with the artistic form. A meaning such as this, the art of architecture is able to mold into its material and its forms with more or less success, according as the determinate nature of the content which it seeks to embody is more significant or more trivial, more concrete or more abstract, more deeply rooted within its inner being or more dim and superficial. Indeed, it may even advance so far as to endeavor to create for such meaning an adequate artistic expression with its material and forms, but in such an attempt it has already overstepped the bounds of its own sphere, and inclines towards sculpture, the higher phase of art. For the limit of architecture lies precisely in this, that it refers to the spiritual as an internal essence in contrast with the external forms of its art, and thus whatever is en-

[2]Hegel's point is that while the art forms of architecture, sculpture, and poetry have intrinsic correspondences with the symbolic, the classical, and the romantic modalities of art, respectively, there nevertheless exist classical and romantic forms of architecture, symbolic and romantic forms of sculpture, symbolic and classical forms of poetry. [Ed.]

dowed with mind and spirit must be indicated as something other than itself.

SCULPTURE

Architecture, however, has purified the inorganic external world, has given it symmetric order, has impressed upon it the seal of mind, and the temple of the God, the house of his community, stands ready. Into this temple now enters the God himself. The lightning-flash of individuality strikes the inert mass, permeates it, and a form no longer merely symmetrical, but infinite and spiritual, concentrates and molds its adequate bodily shape. This is the task of sculpture. Inasmuch as in it the inner spiritual element, which architecture can no more than hint at, completely abides with the sensuous form and its external matter, and as both sides are so merged into each other that neither predominates, sculpture has the *classical* form of art as its fundamental type. In fact, the sensuous realm itself can command no expression which could not be that of the spiritual sphere, just as, conversely, no spiritual content can attain perfect plasticity in sculpture which is incapable of being adequately presented to perception in bodily form. It is sculpture which arrests for our vision the spirit in its bodily frame, in immediate unity with it, and in an attitude of peace and repose; and the form in turn is animated by the content of spiritual individuality. Therefore the external sensuous matter is here not wrought, either according to its mechanical quality alone, as heavy mass, or in forms peculiar to inorganic nature, or as indifferent to color, etc., but in ideal forms of the human shape, and in the whole of the spatial dimensions. In this last respect sculpture should be credited with having first revealed the inner and spiritual essence in its eternal repose and essential self-possession. To such repose and unity with itself corresponds only that external element which itself persists in unity and repose. Such an element is the form taken in its abstract spatiality. The spirit which sculpture represents is that which is solid in itself, not variously broken up in the play of contingencies and passions; nor does its external form admit of the portrayal of such a manifold play, but it holds to this one side only, to the abstraction of space in the totality of its dimensions.

THE DEVELOPMENT OF THE ROMANTIC ARTS

After architecture has built the temple and the hand of sculpture has placed inside it the statue of the God, then this sensuously visible God faces in the spacious halls of his house the *community*. The community is the spiritual, self-reflecting element in this sensuous realm, it is the animating subjectivity and inner life. A new principle of art begins with it. Both the content of art and the medium which embodies it in outward form now demand particularization, individualization, and the subjective mode of expressing these. The solid unity which the God possesses in sculpture breaks up into the plurality of inner individual lives, whose unity is not sensuous, but essentially ideal.

And now God comes to assume the aspect which makes him truly spiritual. As a hither-and-thither, as an alteration between the unity within himself and his realization in subjective knowledge and individual consciousness, as well as in the common and unified life of the man individuals, he is genuinely Spirit — the Spirit in his community. In his community God is released from the abstractness of a mysterious self-identity, as well as from the naïve imprisonment in a bodily shape, in which he is represented by sculpture. Here he is exalted into spirituality, subjectivity, and knowledge. For this reason the higher content of art is now this spirituality in its absolute form. But since what chiefly reveals itself in this stage is not the serene repose of God in himself, but rather his appearance, his being, and his manifestation to others, the objects of artistic representation are now the most varied subjective expressions of life and activity for their own sake, as human passions, deeds, events, and, in general, the wide range of human feeling, will, and resignation. In accordance with this content, the sensuous element must differentiate and show itself adequate to the expression of subjective feeling. Such different media are furnished by color, by the musical sound, and finally by the sound as the mere indication of inner intuitions and ideas; and thus as different forms of realizing the spiritual content of art by means of these media we obtain painting, music, and poetry. The sensuous media employed in these arts being individualized and in their essence recognized as ideal, they correspond most effectively to the spiritual content of art, and the union between spiritual meaning and sensuous expression develops, therefore, into greater intimacy than was possible in the case of architecture and sculpture. This intimate unity, however, is due wholly to the subjective side.

Leaving, then, the symbolic spirit and architecture and the classical ideal of sculpture behind, these new arts in which form and content are raised to an ideal level borrow their type from the *romantic* form of art, whose mode of expression they are most eminently fitted to voice. They form, however, a totality of arts, because the romantic type is the most concrete in itself.

PAINTING

The first art in this totality, which is akin to sculpture, is painting. The material which it uses for its content and for the sensuous expression of that content is visibility as such, in so far as it is individualized, viz., specified as color. To be sure, the media employed in architecture and sculpture are also visible and colored, but they are not, as in painting, visibility as such, not the simple light which contrasts itself with darkness and in combination with it becomes color. This visibility as a subjective and ideal attribute, requires neither, like architecture, the abstract mechanical form of mass which we find in heavy matter, nor, like sculpture, the three dimensions of sensuous space, even though in concentrated and organic plasticity, but the visibility which appertains to painting has its differences on a more ideal level, in the particular kind of color; and thus painting frees art from the sensuous completeness in space peculiar to material things only, by confining itself to a plane surface.

On the other hand, the content also gains in varied particularization. Whatever can find room in the human heart, as emotion, idea, and purpose, whatever it is able to frame into a deed, all this variety of material can constitute the many-colored content of painting. The whole range of particular existence, from the highest aspirations of the mind down to the most isolated objects of nature, can obtain a place in this art. For even finite nature, in its particular scenes and aspects, can here appear, if only some allusion to a spiritual element makes it akin to thought and feeling.

MUSIC

The second art in which the romantic form finds realization, on still a higher level than in painting, is music. Its material, though still sensuous, advances to a deeper subjectivity and greater specification. The idealization of the sensuous, music brings about by negating space. In music the indifferent extension of space whose appearance painting admits and consciously imitates is concentrated and idealized into a single point. But in the form of a motion and tremor of the material body within itself, this single point becomes a concrete and active process within the idealization of matter. Such an incipient ideality of matter which no longer appears under the spatial form, but as temporal ideality, is sound — the sensuous acknowledged as ideal, whose abstract visibility is transformed into audibility. Sound, as it were, exempts the ideal from its absorption in matter.

This earliest animation and inspiration of matter furnishes the medium for the inner and intimate life of the spirit, as yet on an indefinite level; it is through the tones of music that the heart pours out its whole scale of feelings and passions. Thus as sculpture constitutes the central point between architecture and the arts of romantic subjectivity, so music forms the center of the romantic arts, and represents the point of transition between abstract spatial sensuousness, which belongs to painting, and the abstract spirituality of poetry. Within itself music has, like architecture, an abstract quantitative relation, as a contrast to its inward and emotional quality; it also has as its basis a permanent law to which the tones with their combinations and successions must conform.[3]

POETRY

For the third and most spiritual expression of the romantic form of art, we must look to poetry. Its characteristic peculiarity lies in the power with which it subjugates to the mind and to its ideas the sensuous element from which music and painting began to set art free. For sound, the one external medium of which poetry avails itself, is in it no longer a feeling of the tone itself, but is a sign which is, by itself, meaningless. This sign, moreover, is a sign of an idea which has become concrete, and not merely of indefinite feeling and of its *nuances* and grades. By this means the tone becomes the *word,* an articulate voice, whose function it is to indicate thoughts and ideas. The negative point to which music had advanced now reveals itself in poetry as the completely concrete point, as the spirit or the self-consciousness of the individual, which spontaneously unites the infinite space of its ideas with the time-element of sound. But this sensuous element which, in music, was still in immediate union with inner feelings and moods, is, in poetry, divorced from the content of consciousness, for in poetry the mind determines this content on its own account and for the sake of its ideas, and while it employs sound to express them, yet sound itself is reduced to a symbol without value or meaning. From this point of view sound may just as well be considered a mere letter, for the audible, like the visible, is now relegated to a mere suggestion of mind. Thus the genuine mode of poetic representation is the inner perception and the poetic imagination itself. And since all types of art share in this mode, poetry runs through them all, and develops itself independently in each. Poetry, then, is the universal art of the spirit which has attained inner freedom, and which does not depend for its realization upon external sensuous matter, but expatiates only in the inner space and inner time of the ideas and feelings. But just in this, its highest phase, art oversteps the bounds of its own sphere by abandoning the harmoniously sensuous mode of portraying the spirit and by passing from the poetry of imagination into the prose of thought.

SUMMARY

Such, then, is the organic totality of the several arts; the external art of architecture, the objective art of sculpture, and the subjective arts of painting, music, and poetry. The higher principle from which these are derived we have found in the types of art, the symbolic, the classical, and the romantic, which form the universal phases of the idea of beauty itself. Thus symbolic art finds its most adequate reality and most perfect application in architecture, in which it is self-complete, and is not yet reduced, so to speak, to the inorganic medium for another art. The classical form of art, on the other hand, attains its most complete realization in sculpture, while it accepts architecture only as forming an enclosure round its products and is as yet not capable of developing painting and music as absolute expressions of its meaning. The romantic type of art, finally, seizes upon painting, music, and poetry as its essential and adequate modes of expression. Poetry, however, is in conformity with all types of the beautiful and extends over them all, because its characteristic element is the aesthetic imagination, and imagination is necessary for every product of art, to whatever type it may belong.

Thus what the particular arts realize in individual artistic creations are, according to the philosophic conception, simply the universal types of the self-unfolding idea of beauty. Out of the external realization of this idea arises the wide Pantheon of art, whose architect and builder is the self-developing spirit of beauty, for the completion of which, however, the history of the world will require its evolution of countless ages.

[3]Hegel refers to the mathematical basis of the diatonic scale and the laws of harmony and counterpoint that derive from it. [Ed.]

Ralph Waldo Emerson

1803–1882

Emerson was the son of a Unitarian minister of Boston; he was educated at Boston Latin School and Harvard University and, after a brief and unhappy stint as a schoolmaster, returned to Cambridge to attend Harvard Divinity School. In 1826 he was licensed to preach and in 1829 was ordained as minister of the Second Church of Boston, where Cotton Mather had preached over a century before. In the same year he married Ellen Tucker, a young heiress who died of tuberculosis within sixteen months, leaving Emerson a widower with a legacy of over a thousand dollars a year and no pressing need to earn a living.

In the watershed year 1832, Emerson resigned his position at the Second Church because he had ceased to believe in the validity of the sacrament of the Lord's Supper and could no longer administer it. He embarked on an extended European tour, where he met the poets Wordsworth and Coleridge, and (most important for his intellectual development) Thomas Carlyle, who was to publicize Emerson in Britain and in return was publicized by Emerson in America.

In 1834, Emerson settled in the village of Concord, Massachusetts, where he married Lydia Jackson and began the quiet and orderly intellectual life that would continue for nearly fifty years. Although he believed in the theory that hard manual labor should be combined with scholarship, he found that work in the fields sapped his energies for his study. He also tried vegetarianism for a while but gave it up, since it seemed to be doing him no particular good. He wrote sermons at his farm and delivered them in enormously popular lectures on tours of Boston and the Northeast.

His first work, *Nature* (1836), though influenced by the mystical theology of Emmanuel Swedenborg, was essentially an American restatement of the idealistic and pantheist philosophy of Carlyle's *Sartor Resartus* (1834). It became the unofficial bible of the "Symposium"— an informal and occasional gathering of the American Transcendentalists, who included Bronson Alcott, Margaret Fuller, and Henry David Thoreau. His lectures appeared in print as *Essays* (1841), *Essays,* Second Series (1844), *Representative Men* (1850), and *The Conduct of Life* (1860). Like most Unitarians, Emerson was antislavery, as his journals of the 1850s reveal, but he steered clear of the abolitionist movement until it was too late for him to influence its course. After the Civil War, his writing declined as his once-prodigious memory began to fail, and the Sage of Concord gradually sank into senility at least a decade before his death.

"The Poet" is from Emerson's second series of *Essays,* and like many of his effusions, it preaches rather than analyzes its topic. "The Poet" quickly expands from its ostensible subject to include many of Emerson's central ideas, which strongly resemble the mystical views of Plotinus. Where Plotinus's god-term was "The One," Emerson's is the "Over-Soul," a pantheistic spiritual entity wherein everything living is united, the ultimate source of truth, goodness, and beauty. The universe itself, in its materiality, is merely a physical symbol, an emblem, of the Over-Soul. And the parts are as the whole: Each element in the material world is symbolic of spiritual truths.

Hence the centrality of the poet to Emerson's metaphysic, for the poet is, when working at full power, the individual who can transcend individuality, who through the professional manipulation of symbols and figures understands best the highest truths about the relationship between matter and spirit, which are to each other as the signifier is to the signified. Emerson consistently deals with poetry, as it was understood by Kant and Coleridge, as the product of the creative imagination. In this sense, any great spiritual thinker is a poet. Emerson's poet is not, however, the maker of *poems,* linguistic forms in measured language. His essay embodies instead, even more than Shelley's "Defence of Poetry," a heaven-ascending compendium of romantic ideas about the poet as idealist.

Selected Bibliography

Foerster, Norman. *American Criticism: A Study in Literary Theory from Poe to the Present.* 1928; New York: Russell and Russell, 1962.

Hopkins, Vivian C. *Spires of Form: A Study of Emerson's Aesthetic Theory.* New York: Russell and Russell, 1965.

Matthiessen, F. O. *American Renaissance: Art and Expression in the Age of Emerson and Whitman.* New York: Oxford University Press, 1941.

Maulsby, David Lee. *Emerson: His Contribution to Literature.* Folcroft, PA: Folcroft Library Editions, 1973.

Michaud, Régis. *L'esthétique d'Emerson: La nature, l'art, l'histoire.* Paris: F. Alcan, 1927.

Paul, Sherman. *Emerson's Angle of Vision.* Cambridge: Harvard University Press, 1952.

Porte, Joel. *Representative Man: Emerson in His Time.* New York: Oxford University Press, 1979.

Van Leer, David. *Emerson's Epistemology: The Argument of the Essays.* New York: Cambridge University Press, 1976.

Yoder, R. A. *Emerson and the Orphic Poet in America.* Berkeley: University of California Press, 1978.

The Poet

A moody child and wildly wise
Pursued the game with joyful eyes,
Which chose, like meteors, their way,
And rived the dark with private ray:
They overleapt the horizon's edge,
Searched with Apollo's privilege;
Through man, and woman, and sea, and star
Saw the dance of nature forward far;
Through worlds, and races, and terms, and times
Saw musical order, and pairing rhymes.[1]

Olympian bards who sung
Divine ideas below,
Which always find us young,
And always keep us so.[2]

Those who are esteemed umpires of taste are often persons who have acquired some knowledge of admired pictures or sculptures, and have an inclination for whatever is elegant; but if you inquire whether they are beautiful souls, and whether their own acts are like fair pictures, you

[1]From Emerson's poem, "The Poet." [Ed.]

[2]From Emerson's "Ode to Beauty," lines 61–64. [Ed.]

learn that they are selfish and sensual. Their cultivation is local, as if you should rub a log of dry wood in one spot to produce fire, all the rest remaining cold. Their knowledge of the fine arts is some study of rules and particulars, or some limited judgment of color or form, which is exercised for amusement or for show. It is a proof of the shallowness of the doctrine of beauty as it lies in the minds of our amateurs, that men seem to have lost the perception of the instant dependence of form upon soul. There is no doctrine of forms in our philosophy. We were put into our bodies, as fire is put into a pan to be carried about; but there is no accurate adjustment between the spirit and the organ, much less is the latter the germination of the former. So in regard to other forms, the intellectual men do not believe in any essential dependence of the material world on thought and volition. Theologians think it a pretty air-castle to talk of the spiritual meaning of a ship or a cloud, of a city or a contract, but they prefer to come again to the solid ground of historical evidence; and even the poets are contented with a civil and conformed manner of living, and to write poems from the fancy, at a safe distance from their own experience. But the highest minds of the world have never ceased to explore the double meaning, or shall I say the quadruple or the centuple of much more manifold meaning, of every sensuous fact; Orpheus, Empedocles, Heraclitus, Plato, Plutarch, Dante, Swedenborg, and the masters of sculpture, picture and poetry. For we are not pans and barrows, nor even porters of the fire and torch-bearers, but children of the fire, made of it, and only the same divinity transmuted and at two or three removes, when we know least about it. And this hidden truth, that the fountains whence all this river of Time and its creatures floweth are intrinsically ideal and beautiful, draws us to the consideration of the nature and functions of the Poet, or the man of Beauty; to the means and materials he uses, and to the general aspect of the art in the present time.

The breadth of the problem is great, for the poet is representative. He stands among partial men for the complete man, and apprises us not of his wealth, but of the common wealth. The young man reveres men of genius, because, to speak truly, they are more himself than he is. They receive of the soul as he also receives, but they more. Nature enhances her beauty, to the eye of loving men, from their belief that the poet is beholding her shows at the same time. He is isolated among his contemporaries by truth and by his art, but with this consolation in his pursuits, that they will draw all men sooner or later. For all men live by truth and stand in need of expression. In love, in art, in avarice, in politics, in labor, in games, we study to utter our painful secret. The man is only half himself, the other half is his expression.

Notwithstanding this necessity to be published, adequate expression is rare. I know not how it is that we need an interpreter, but the great majority of men seem to be minors, who have not yet come into possession of their own, or mutes, who cannot report the conversation they have had with nature. There is no man who does not anticipate a supersensual utility in the sun and stars, earth and water. These stand and wait to render him a peculiar service. But there is some obstruction or some excess of phlegm in our constitution, which does not suffer them to yield the due effect. Too feeble fall the impressions of nature on us to make us artists. Every touch should thrill. Every man should be so much an artist that he could report in conversation what had befallen him. Yet, in our experience, the rays or appulses have sufficient force to arrive at the senses, but not enough to reach the quick and compel the reproduction of themselves in speech. The poet is the person in whom these powers are in balance, the man without impediment, who sees and handles that which others dream of, traverses the whole scale of experience, and is representative of man, in virtue of being the largest power to receive and to impart.

For the universe has three children, born at one time, which reappear under different names in every system of thought, whether they be called cause, operation and effect; or, more poetically, Jove, Pluto, Neptune; or, theologically, the Father, the Spirit and the Son; but which we will call here the Knower, the Doer and the Sayer. These stand respectively for the love of truth, for the love of good, and for the love of beauty. These three are equal. Each is that which he is, essentially, so that he cannot be surmounted or analyzed, and each of these three has the power of the others latent in him and his own, patent.

The poet is the sayer, the namer, and represents beauty. He is a sovereign, and stands on the center. For the world is not painted or adorned, but is from the beginning beautiful; and God has not made some beautiful things, but Beauty is the creator of the universe. Therefore the poet is not any permissive potentate, but is emperor in his own right. Criticism is infested with a cant of materialism, which assumes that manual skill and activity is the first merit of all men, and disparages such as say and do not, overlooking the fact that some men, namely poets, are natural sayers, sent into the world to the end of expression, and confounds them with those whose province is action but who quit it to imitate the sayers. But Homer's words are as costly and admirable to Homer as Agamemnon's victories are to Agamemnon. The poet does not wait for the hero or the sage, but, as they act and think primarily, so he writes primarily what will and must be spoken, reckoning the others, though primaries also, yet, in respect to him, secondaries and servants; as sitters or models in the studio of a painter, or as assistants who bring building-materials to an architect.

For poetry was all written before time was, and whenever we are so finely organized that we can penetrate into that region where the air is music, we hear those primal warblings and attempt to write them down, but we lose ever and anon a word or a verse and substitute something of our own, and thus miswrite the poem. The men of more delicate ear write down these cadences more faithfully, and these transcripts, though imperfect, become the songs of the nations. For nature is as truly beautiful as it is good, or as it is reasonable, and must as much appear as it must be done, or be known. Words and deeds are quite indifferent modes of the divine energy. Words are also actions, and actions are a kind of words.

The sign and credentials of the poet are that he announces that which no man foretold. He is the true and only doctor; he knows and tells; he is the only teller of news, for he was present and privy to the appearance which he describes. He is a beholder of ideas and an utterer of the necessary and causal. For we do not speak now of men of poetical talents, or of industry and skill in meter, but of the true poet. I took part in a conversation the other day concerning a recent writer of lyrics, a man of subtle mind, whose head appeared to be a music-box of delicate tunes and rhythms, and whose skill and command of language we could not sufficiently praise. But when the question arose whether he was not only a lyrist but a poet, we were obliged to confess that he is plainly a contemporary, not an eternal man. He does not stand out of our low limitations, like a Chimborazo[3] under the line, running up from a torrid base through all the climates of the globe, with belts of the herbage of every latitude on its high and mottled sides; but this genius is the landscape-garden of a modern house, adorned with fountains and statues, with well-bred men and women standing and sitting in the walks and terraces. We hear, through all the varied music, the ground-tone of conventional life. Our poets are men of talents who sing, and not the children of music. The argument is secondary, the finish of the verses is primary.

For it is not meters, but a meter-making argument that makes a poem, — a thought so passionate and alive that like the spirit of a plant or an animal it has an architecture of its own, and adorns nature with a new thing. The thought and the form are equal in the order of time, but in the order of genesis the thought is prior to the form. The poet has a new thought; he has a whole new experience to unfold; he will tell us how it was with him, and all men will be the richer in his fortune. For the experience of each new age requires a new confession, and the world seems always waiting for its poet. I remember when I was young how much I was moved one morning by tidings that genius had appeared in a youth who sat near me at table. He had left his work and gone rambling none knew whither, and had written hundreds of lines, but could not tell whether that which was in him was therein told; he could tell nothing but that all was changed, — man, beast, heaven, earth and sea. How gladly we listened! how credulous! Society seemed to be

[3]A mountain in Ecuador, near the equator ("under the line"). [Ed.]

compromised. We sat in the aurora of a sunrise which was to put out all the stars. Boston seemed to be at twice the distance it had the night before, or was much farther than that. Rome, — what was Rome? Plutarch and Shakespeare were in the yellow leaf, and Homer no more should be heard of. It is much to know that poetry has been written this very day, under this very roof, by your side. What! that wonderful spirit has not expired! These stony moments are still sparkling and animated! I had fancied that the oracles were all silent, and nature had spent her fires; and behold! all night, from every pore, these fine auroras have been streaming. Every one has some interest in the advent of the poet, and no one knows how much it may concern him. We know that the secret of the world is profound, but who or what shall be our intepreter, we know not. A mountain ramble, a new style of face, a new person, may put the key into our hands. Of course the value of genius to us is in the veracity of its report. Talent may frolic and juggle; genius realizes and adds. Mankind in good earnest have availed so far in understanding themselves and their work, that the foremost watchman on the peak announces his news. It is the truest word ever spoken, and the phrase will be the fittest, most musical, and the unerring voice of the world for that time.

All that we call sacred history attests that the birth of a poet is the principal event in chronology. Man, never so often deceived, still watches for the arrival of a brother who can hold him steady to a truth until he has made it his own. With what joy I begin to read a poem which I confide in as an inspiration! And now my chains are to be broken; I shall mount above these clouds and opaque airs in which I live, — opaque, though they seem transparent, — and from the heaven of truth I shall see and comprehend my relations. That will reconcile me to life and renovate nature, to see trifles animated by a tendency, and to know what I am doing. Life will no more be a noise; now I shall see men and women, and know the signs by which they may be discerned from fools and satans. This day shall be better than my birthday: then I became an animal; now I am invited into the science of the real. Such is the hope, but the fruition is postponed. Oftener it falls that this winged man, who will carry me into the heaven, whirls me into mists, then leaps and frisks about with me as it were from cloud to cloud, still affirming that he is bound heavenward; and I, being myself a novice, am slow in perceiving that he does not know the way into the heavens, and is merely bent that I should admire his skill to rise like a fowl or a flying fish, a little way from the ground or the water; but the all-piercing, all-feeding and ocular air of heaven that man shall never inhabit. I tumble down again soon into my old nooks, and lead the life of exaggerations as before, and have lost my faith in the possibility of any guide who can lead me thither where I would be.

But, leaving these victims of vanity, let us, with new hope, observe how nature, by worthier impulses, has insured the poet's fidelity to his office of announcement and affirming, namely by the beauty of things, which becomes a new and higher beauty when expressed. Nature offers all her creatures to him as a picture-language. Being used as a type, a second wonderful value appears in the object, far better than its old value; as the carpenter's stretched cord, if you hold your ear close enough, is musical in the breeze. "Things more excellent than every image," says Iamblichus,[4] "are expressed through images." Things admit of being used as symbols because nature is a symbol, in the whole, and in every part. Every line we can draw in the sand has expression; and there is no body without its spirit or genius. All form is an effect of character; all condition, of the quality of the life; all harmony, of health; and for this reason a perception of beauty should be sympathetic, or proper only to the good. The beautiful rests on the foundations of the necessary. The soul makes the body, as the wise Spenser teaches: —

> So every spirit, as it is more pure,
> And hath in it the more of heavenly light,
> So it the fairer body doth procure
> To habit in, and it more fairly dight,
> With cheerful grace and amiable sight.
> For, of the soul, the body form doth take,
> For soul is form, and doth the body make.[5]

[4]Iamblichus was a fourth-century Neoplatonist. [Ed.]

[5]Edmund Spenser, "An Hymne in Honour of Beautie," 19:127–34. [Ed.]

Here we find ourselves suddenly not in a critical speculation but in a holy place, and should go very warily and reverently. We stand before the secret of the world, there where Being passes into Appearance and Unity into Variety.

The Universe is the externization of the soul. Wherever the life is, that bursts into appearance around it. Our science is sensual, and therefore superficial. The earth and the heavenly bodies, physics and chemistry, we sensually treat, as if they were self-existent; but these are the retinue of that Being we have. "The mighty heaven," said Proclus, "exhibits, in its transfigurations, clear images of the splendor of intellectual perceptions; being moved in conjunction with the unapparent periods of intellectual natures."[6] Therefore science always goes abreast with the just elevation of the man, keeping step with religion and metaphysics; or the state of science is an index of our self-knowledge. Since every thing in nature answers to a moral power, if any phenomenon remains brute and dark it is because the corresponding faculty in the observer is not yet active.

No wonder then, if these waters be so deep, that we hover over them with a religious regard. The beauty of the fable proves the importance of the sense; to the poet, and to all others; or, if you please, every man is so far a poet as to be susceptible of these enchantments of nature; for all men have the thoughts whereof the universe is the celebration. I find that the fascination resides in the symbol. Who loves nature? Who does not? It is only poets, and men of leisure and cultivation, who live with her? No; but also hunters, farmers, grooms and butchers, though they express their affection in their choice of life and not in their choice of words. The writer wonders what the coachman or the hunter values in riding, in horses and dogs. It is not superficial qualities. When you talk with him he holds these at as slight a rate as you. His worship is sympathetic; he has no definitions, but he is commanded in nature by the living power which he feels to be there present. No imitation or playing of these things would content him; he loves the earnest of the north wind, of rain, of stone and wood and iron. A beauty not explicable is dearer than a beauty which we can see to the end of. It is nature the symbol, nature certifying the supernatural, body overflowed by life which he worships with coarse but sincere rites.

The inwardness and mystery of this attachment drive men of every class to the use of emblems. The schools of poets and philosophers are not more intoxicated with their symbols than the populace with theirs. In our political parties, compute the power of badges and emblems. See the great ball which they roll from Baltimore to Bunker Hill! In the political processions, Lowell goes in a loom, and Lynn in a shoe, and Salem in a ship. Witness the cider-barrel, the log-cabin, the hickory-stick, the palmetto, and all the cognizances of party. See the power of national emblems. Some stars, lilies, leopards, a crescent, a lion, an eagle, or other figure which came into credit God knows how, on an old rag of bunting, blowing in the wind on a fort at the ends of the earth, shall make the blood tingle under the rudest or the most conventional exterior. The people fancy they hate poetry, and they are all poets and mystics!

Beyond the universality of the symbolic language we are apprised of the divineness of this superior use of things, whereby the world is a temple whose walls are covered with emblems, pictures and commandments of the Deity, — in this, that there is no fact in nature which does not carry the whole sense of nature; and the distinctions which we make in events and in affairs, of low and high, honest and base, disappear when nature is used as a symbol. Thought makes everything fit for use. The vocabulary of an omniscient man would embrace words and images excluded from polite conversation. What would be base, or even obscene, to the obscene, becomes illustrious, spoken in a new connection of thought. The piety of the Hebrew prophets purges their grossness. The circumcision is an example of the power of poetry to raise the low and offensive. Small and mean things serve as well as great symbols. The meaner the type by which a law is expressed, the more pungent it is, and the more lasting in the memories of men; just as we choose the smallest box or case in which

[6]Proclus was a fifth-century Neoplatonist. [Ed.]

any needful utensil can be carried. Bare lists of words are found suggestive to an imaginative and excited mind, as it is related of Lord Chatham that he was accustomed to read in Bailey's Dictionary when he was preparing to speak in Parliament. The poorest experience is rich enough for all the purposes of expressing thought. Why covet a knowledge of new facts? Day and night, house and garden, a few books, a few actions, serve us as well as would all trades and all spectacles. We are far from having exhausted the significance of the few symbols we use. We can come to use them yet with a terrible simplicity. It does not need that a poem should be long. Every word was once a poem. Every new relation is a new word. Also we use defects and deformities to a sacred purpose, so expressing our sense that the evils of the world are such only to the evil eye. In the old mythology, mythologists observe, defects are ascribed to divine natures, as lameness to Vulcan, blindness to Cupid, and the like, — to signify exuberances.

For as it is dislocation and detachment from the life of God that makes things ugly, the poet, who re-attaches things to nature and the Whole, — re-attaching even artificial things and violation of nature, to nature, by a deeper insight, — disposes very easily of the most disagreeable facts. Readers of poetry see the factory-village and the railway, and fancy that the poetry of the landscape is broken up by these; for these works of art are not yet consecrated in their reading; but the poet sees them fall within the great Order not less than the beehive or the spider's geometrical web. Nature adopts them very fast into her vital circles, and the gliding train of cars she loves like her own. Besides, in a centered mind, it signifies nothing how many mechanical inventions you exhibit. Though you add millions, and never so surprising, the fact of mechanics has not gained a grain's weight. The spiritual fact remains unalterable, by many or by few particulars; as no mountain is of any appreciable height to break the curve of the sphere. A shrewd country-boy goes to the city for the first time, and the complacent citizen is not satisfied with his little wonder. It is not that he does not see all the fine houses and know that he never saw such before, but he disposes of them as easily as the poet finds place for the railway. The chief value of the new fact is to enhance the great and constant fact of Life, which can dwarf any and every circumstance, and to which the belt of wampum and the commerce of America are alike.

The world being thus put under the mind for verb and noun, the poet is he who can articulate it. For though life is great, and fascinates and absorbs; and though all men are intelligent of the symbols through which it is named; yet they cannot originally use them. We are symbols and inhabit symbols; workmen, work, and tools, words and things, birth and death, all are emblems but we sympathize with the symbols, and being infatuated with the economical uses of things, we do not know that they are thoughts. The poet, by an ulterior intellectual perception, gives them a power which makes their old use forgotten, and puts eyes and a tongue into every dumb and inanimate object. He perceives the independence of the thought on the symbol, the stability of the thought, the accidency and fugacity of the symbol. As the eyes of Lyncaeus were said to see through the earth, so the poet turns the world to glass, and shows us all things in their right series and procession. For through that better perception he stands one step nearer to things, and sees the flowing or metamorphosis; perceives that thought is multiform; that within the form of every creature is a force compelling it to ascend into a higher form; and following with his eyes the life, uses the forms which express that life, and so his speech flows with the flowing of nature. All the facts of the animal economy, sex, nutriment, gestation, birth, growth, are symbols of the passage of the world into the soul of man, to suffer there a change and reappear a new and higher fact. He uses forms according to the life, and not according to the form. This is true science. The poet alone knows astronomy, chemistry, vegetation and animation, for he does not stop at these facts, but employs them as signs. He knows why the plain or meadow or space was strown with these flowers we call suns and moons and stars; why the great deep is adorned with animals, with men, and gods; for in every word he speaks he rides on them as the horses of thought.

By virtue of this science the poet is the Namer or Language-maker, naming things sometimes after their appearance, sometimes after their essence, and giving to every one its own name and not another's, thereby rejoicing the intellect, which delights in detachment or boundary. The poets made all the words, and therefore language is the archives of history, and, if we must say it, a sort of tomb of the muses. For though the origin of most of our words is forgotten, each word was at first a stroke of genius, and obtained currency because for the moment it symbolized the world to the first speaker and to the hearer. The etymologist finds the deadest word to have been once a brilliant picture. Language is fossil poetry. As the limestone of the continent consists of infinite masses of the shells of animalcules, so language is made up of images or tropes, which now, in their secondary use, have long ceased to remind us of their poetic origin. But the poet names the thing because he sees it, or comes one step nearer to it than any other. This expression or naming is not art, but a second nature, grown out of the first, as a leaf out of a tree. What we call nature is a certain self-regulated motion or change; and nature does all things by her own hands, and does not leave another to baptize her but baptizes herself; and this through the metamorphosis again. I remember that a certain poet[7] described it to me thus: —

> Genius is the activity which repairs the decays of things, whether wholly or partly of a material and finite kind. Nature, through all her kingdoms, insures herself. Nobody cares for planting the poor fungus; so she shakes down from the gills of one agaric countless spores, any one of which, being preserved, transmits new billions of spores tomorrow or next day. The new agaric of this hour has a chance which the old one had not. This atom of seed is thrown into a new place, not subject to the accidents which destroyed its parent two rods off. She makes a man; and having brought him to ripe age, she will no longer run the risk of losing this wonder at a blow, but she detaches from him a new self, that the kind may be safe from accidents to which the individual is exposed. So when the soul of the poet has come to ripeness of thought, she detaches and sends away from it its poems or songs, — a fearless, sleepless, deathless progeny, which is not exposed to the accidents of the weary kingdom of time; a fearless, vivacious offspring, clad with wings (such was the virtue of the soul out of which they came) which carry them fast and far, and infix them irrecoverably into the hearts of men. These wings are the beauty of a poet's soul. The songs, thus flying immortal from their mortal parent, are pursued by clamorous flights of censures, which swarm in far greater numbers and threaten to devour them; but these last are not winged. At the end of a very short leap they fall plump down and rot, having received from the souls out of which they came no beautiful wings. But the melodies of the poet ascend and leap and pierce into the deeps of infinite time.

So far the bard taught me, using his freer speech. But nature has a higher end, in the production of new individuals, than security, namely *ascension,* or the passage of the soul into higher forms. I knew in my younger days the sculptor who made the statue of the youth which stands in the public garden. He was, as I remember, unable to tell directly what made him happy or unhappy, but by wonderful indirections he could tell. He rose one day, according to his habit, before the dawn, and saw the morning break, grand as the eternity out of which it came, and for many days after, he strove to express this tranquillity, and lo! his chisel had fashioned out of marble the form of a beautiful youth, Phosphorus,[8] whose aspect is such that it is said all persons who look on it become silent. The poet also resigns himself to his mood, and that thought which agitated him is expressed, but *alter idem,*[9] in a manner totally new. The expression is organic, or the new type which things themselves take when liberated. As, in the sun, objects paint their images on the retina of the eye, so they, sharing the aspiration of the whole universe, tend to paint a far more delicate copy of their essence in his mind. Like the metamorphosis of things into higher organic forms is their change into melodies. Over everything stands its daemon or soul, and, as the form of the

[7]The following passage is Emerson's own adaptation of Plato's *Phaedrus.* [Ed.]

[8]The morning star. [Ed.]

[9]The same thing in another way. [Ed.]

thing is reflected by the eye, so the soul of the thing is reflected by a melody. The sea, the mountain-ridge, Niagara, and every flower-bed, pre-exist, or super-exist, in precantations, which sail like odors in the air, and when any man goes by with an ear sufficiently fine, he overhears them and endeavors to write down the notes without diluting or depraving them. And herein is the legitimation of criticism, in the mind's faith that the poems are a corrupt version of some text in nature with which they ought to be made to tally. A rhyme in one of our sonnets should not be less pleasing than the iterated nodes of a seashell, or the resembling difference of a group of flowers. The pairing of the birds is an idyl, not tedious as our idyls are; a tempest is a rough ode, without falsehood or rant; a summer, with its harvest sown, reaped and stored, is an epic song, subordinating how many admirably executed parts. Why should not the symmetry and truth that modulate these, glide into our spirits, and we participate the invention of nature?

This insight, which expresses itself by what is called Imagination, is a very high sort of seeing, which does not come by study, but by the intellect being where and what it sees; by sharing the path or circuit of things through forms, and so making them translucid to others. The path of things is silent. Will they suffer a speaker to go with them? A spy they will not suffer; a lover, a poet, is the transcendency of their own nature, — him they will suffer. The condition of true naming, on the poet's part, is his resigning himself to the divine *aura* which breathes through forms, and accompanying that.

It is a secret which every intellectual man quickly learns, that beyond the energy of his possessed and conscious intellect he is capable of a new energy (as of an intellect doubled on itself), by abandonment to the nature of things; that beside his privacy of power as an individual man, there is a great public power on which he can draw, by unlocking, at all risks, his human doors, and suffering the ethereal tides to roll and circulate through him; then he is caught up into the life of the Universe, his speech is thunder, his thought is law, and his words are universally intelligible as the plants and animals. The poet knows that he speaks adequately then only when he speaks somewhat wildly, or "with the flower of the mind"; not with the intellect used as an organ, but with the intellect released from all service and suffered to take its direction from its celestial life; or as the ancients were wont to express themselves, not with intellect alone but with the intellect inebriated by nectar. As the traveler who has lost his way throws his reins on his horse's neck and trusts to the instinct of the animal to find his road, so must we do with the divine animal who carries us through this world. For if in any manner we can stimulate this instinct, new passages are opened for us into nature; the mind flows into and through things hardest and highest, and the metamorphosis is possible.

This is the reason why bards love wine, mead, narcotics, coffee, tea, opium, the fumes of sandalwood and tobacco, or whatever other procurers of animal exhilaration. All men avail themselves of such means as they can, to add this extraordinary power to their normal powers; and to this end they prize conversation, music, pictures, sculpture, dancing, theaters, traveling, war, mobs, fires, gaming, politics, or love, or science, or animal intoxication, — which are several coarser or finer *quasi*-mechanical substitutes for the true nectar, which is the ravishment of the intellect by coming nearer to the fact. These are auxiliaries to the centrifugal tendency of a man, to his passage out into free space, and they help him to escape the custody of that body in which he is pent up, and of that jail-yard of individual relations in which he is enclosed. Hence a great number of such as were professionally expressers of Beauty, as painters, poets, musicians and actors, have been more than others wont to lead a life of pleasure and indulgence; all but the few who received the true nectar; and, as it was a spurious mode of attaining freedom, as it was an emancipation not into the heavens but into the freedom of baser places, they were punished for that advantage they won, by a dissipation and deterioration. But never can any advantage be taken of nature by a trick. The spirit of the world, the great calm presence of the Creator, comes not forth to the sorceries of opium or of wine. The sublime vision comes to the pure and simple soul in a clean and chaste body. That is not an inspiration, which we owe to narcotics, but some counterfeit excitement and fury. Milton says that the lyric poet may drink wine and live generously, but the epic poet, he who shall sing of the gods and their descent unto men, must drink water out of a wooden bowl. For poetry is not "Devil's wine," but God's wine. It is with this as it is with toys. We fill the hands and nurseries of our children with all manner of dolls, drums and horses; withdrawing their eyes from the plain face and sufficing objects of nature, the sun and moon, the animals, the water and stones, which should be their toys. So the poet's habit of living should be set on a key so low that the common influences should delight him. His cheerfulness should be the gift of the sunlight; the air should suffice for his inspiration, and he should be tipsy with water. That spirit which suffices quiet hearts, which seems to come forth to such from every dry knoll of sere grass, from every pine stump and half-imbedded stone on which the dull March sun shines, comes forth to the poor and hungry, and such as are of simple taste. If thou fill thy brain with Boston and New York, with fashion and covetousness, and wilt stimulate thy jaded senses with wine and French coffee, thou shalt find no radiance of wisdom in the lonely waste of the pine woods.

If the imagination intoxicates the poet, it is not inactive in other men. The metamorphosis excites in the beholder an emotion of joy. The use of symbols has a certain power of emancipation and exhilaration for all men. We seem to be touched by a wand which makes us dance and run about happily, like children. We are like persons who come out of a cave or cellar into the open air. This is the effect on us of tropes, fables, oracles and all poetic forms. Poets are thus liberating gods. Men have really got a new sense, and found within their world another world, or nest of worlds; for, the metamorphosis once seen, we divine that it does not stop. I will not now consider how much this makes the charm of algebra and the mathematics, which also have their tropes, but it is felt in every definition; as when Aristotle defines *space* to be an immovable vessel in which things are contained; — or when Plato defines a *line* to be a flowing point; or *figure* to be bound of solid; and many the like. What a joyful sense of freedom we have when Vitruvius announces the old opinion of artists that no architect can build any house well who does not know something of anatomy. When Socrates, in Charmides, tells us that the soul is cured of its maladies by certain incantations, and that these incantations are beautiful reasons, from which temperance is generated in souls; when Plato calls the world an animal, and Timaeus affirms that the plants also are animals; or affirms a man to be a heavenly tree, growing with his root, which is his head, upward; and, as George Chapman, following him, writes,

> So in our tree of man, whose nervie root
> Springs in his top; —

when Orpheus speaks of hoariness as "that white flower which marks extreme old age"; when Proclus calls the universe the statue of the intellect; when Chaucer, in his praise of "Gentilesse," compares good blood in mean condition to fire, which, though carried to the darkest house betwixt this and the mount of Caucasus, will yet hold its natural office and burn as bright as if twenty thousand men did it behold; when John saw, in the Apocalypse, the ruin of the world through evil, and the stars fall from heaven as the fig tree casteth her untimely fruit; when Aesop reports the whole catalogue of common daily relations through the masquerade of birds and beasts; — we take the cheerful hint of the immortality of our essence and its versatile habit and escapes, as when the gypsies say of themselves "it is in vain to hang them, they cannot die."

The poets are thus liberating gods. The ancient British bards had for the title of their order, "Those who are free throughout the world." They are free, and they make free. An imaginative book renders as much more service at first, by stimulating us through its tropes, than afterward when we arrive at the precise sense of the author. I think nothing is of any value in books excepting the transcendental and extraordinary. If a man is inflamed and carried away by his thought, to that degree that he forgets the authors and the public and heeds only this one dream which holds him like an insanity, let me read his paper, and you may have all the arguments and histories and criticism. All the value which attaches to

Pythagoras, Paracelsus, Cornelius Agrippa, Cardan, Kepler, Swedenborg, Schelling, Oken, or any other who introduces questionable facts into his cosmogony, as angels, devils, magic, astrology, palmistry, mesmerism, and so on, is the certificate we have of departure from routine, and that here is a new witness. That also is the best success in conversation, the magic of liberty, which puts the world like a ball in our hands. How cheap even the liberty then seems; how mean to study, when an emotion communicates to the intellect the power to sap and upheave nature; how great the perspective! nations, times, systems, enter and disappear like threads in tapestry of large figure and many colors; dream delivers us to dream, and while the drunkenness lasts we will sell our bed, our philosophy, our religion, in our opulence.

There is good reason why we should prize this liberation. The fate of the poor shepherd, who, blinded and lost in the snowstorm, perishes in a drift within a few feet of his cottage door, is an emblem of the state of man. On the brink of the waters of life and truth, we are miserably dying. The inaccessibleness of every thought but that we are in, is wonderful. What if you come near to it; you are as remote when you are nearest as when you are farthest. Every thought is also a prison; every heaven is also a prison. Therefore we love the poet, the inventor, who in any form, whether in an ode or in an action or in looks and behavior, has yielded us a new thought. He unlocks our chains and admits us to a new scene.

This emancipation is dear to all men, and the power to impart it, as it must come from greater depth and scope of thought, is a measure of intellect. Therefore all books of the imagination endure, all which ascend to that truth that the writer sees nature beneath him, and uses it as his exponent. Every verse or sentence possessing this virtue will take care of its own immortality. The religions of the world are the ejaculations of a few imaginative men.

But the quality of the imagination is to flow, and not to freeze. The poet did not stop at the color or the form, but read their meaning; neither may he rest in this meaning, but he makes the same objects exponents of his new thought. Here is the difference betwixt the poet and the mystic, that the last nails a symbol to one sense, which was a true sense for a moment, but soon becomes old and false. For all symbols are fluxional; all language is vehicular and transitive, and is good, as ferries and horses are, for conveyance, not as farms and houses are, for homestead. Mysticism consists in the mistake of an accidental and individual symbol for an universal one. The morning-redness happens to be the favorite meteor to the eyes of Jacob Behmen,[10] and comes to stand to him for truth and faith; and, he believes, should stand for the same realities to every reader. But the first reader prefers as naturally the symbol of a mother and child, or a gardener and his bulb, or a jeweler polishing a gem. Either of these, or of a myriad more, are equally good to the person to whom they are significant. Only they must be held lightly, and be very willingly translated into the equivalent terms which others use. And the mystic must be steadily told, — All that you say is just as true without the tedious use of that symbol as with it. Let us have a little algebra, instead of this trite rhetoric, — universal signs, instead of these village symbols, — and we shall both be gainers. The history of hierarchies seems to show that all religious error consisted in making the symbol too stark and solid, and was at last nothing but an excess of the organ of language.

Swedenborg, of all men in the recent ages, stands eminently for the translator of nature into thought. I do not know the man in history to whom things stood so uniformly for words. Before him the metamorphosis continually plays. Everything on which his eye rests, obeys the impulses of moral nature. The figs become grapes whilst he eats them. When some of his angels affirmed a truth, the laurel twig which they held blossomed in their hands. The noise which at a distance appeared like gnashing and thumping, on coming nearer was found to be the voice of disputants. The men in one of his visions, seen in heavenly light, appeared like dragons, and seemed in darkness; but to each other they appeared as men, and when the light from heaven shone into their cabin, they complained of the

[10]Emerson probably means German mystic Jakob Böhme (1575–1624). [Ed.]

darkness, and were compelled to shut the window that they might see.

There was this perception in him which makes the poet or seer an object of awe and terror, namely that the same man or society of men may wear one aspect to themselves and their companions, and a different aspect to higher intelligences. Certain priests, whom he describes as conversing very learnedly together, appeared to the children who were at some distance, like dead horses; and many the like misappearances. And instantly the mind inquires whether these fishes under the bridge, yonder oxen in the pasture, those dogs in the yard, are immutably fishes, oxen and dogs, or only so appear to me, and perchance to themselves appear upright men; and whether I appear as a man to all eyes. The Brahmins and Pythagoras propounded the same question, and if any poet has witnessed the transformation he doubtless found it in harmony with various experiences. We have all seen changes as considerable in wheat and caterpillars. He is the poet and shall draw us with love and terror, who sees through the flowing vest the firm nature, and can declare it.

I look in vain for the poet whom I describe. We do not with sufficient plainness or sufficient profoundness address ourselves to life, nor dare we chaunt our own times and social circumstance. If we filled the day with bravery, we should not shrink from celebrating it. Time and nature yield us many gifts, but not yet the timely man, the new religion, the reconciler, whom all things await. Dante's praise is that he dared to write his autobiography in colossal cipher, or into universality. We have had no genius in America, with tyrannous eye, which knew the value of our incomparable materials, and saw, in the barbarism and materialism of the times, another carnival of the same gods whose picture he so much admires in Homer; then in the Middle Age; then in Calvinism. Banks and tariffs, the newspaper and caucus, Methodism and Unitarianism, are flat and dull to dull people, but rest on the same foundations of wonder as the town of Troy and the temple of Delphi, and are as swiftly passing away. Our log-rolling, our stumps and their politics, our fisheries, our Negroes and Indians, our boasts and our repudiations, the wrath of rogues and the pusillanimity of honest men, the northern trade, the southern planting, the western clearing, Oregon and Texas, are yet unsung. Yet America is a poem in our eyes; its ample geography dazzles the imagination, and it will not wait long for meters. If I have not found that excellent combination of gifts in my countrymen which I seek, neither could I aid myself to fix the idea of the poet by reading now and then in Chalmers's collection of five centuries of English poets. These are wits more than poets, though there have been poets among them. But when we adhere to the ideal of the poets, we have our difficulties even with Milton and Homer. Milton is too literary, and Homer too literal and historical.

But I am not wise enough for a national criticism, and must use the old largeness a little longer, to discharge my errand from the muse to the poet concerning his art.

Art is the path of the creator to his work. The paths or methods are ideal and eternal, though few men ever see them; not the artist himself for years, or for a lifetime, unless he come into the conditions. The painter, the sculptor, the composer, the epic rhapsodist, the orator, all partake one desire, namely to express themselves symmetrically and abundantly, not dwarfishly and fragmentarily. They found or put themselves in certain conditions, as, the painter and sculptor before some impressive human figures; the orator into the assembly of the people; and the others in such scenes as each has found exciting to his intellect; and each presently feels the new desire. He hears a voice, he sees a beckoning. Then he is apprised, with wonder, what herds of daemons hem him in. He can no more rest; he says, with the old painter, "By God it is in me and must go forth of me." He pursues a beauty, half seen, which flies before him. The poet pours out verses in every solitude. Most of the things he says are conventional, no doubt; but by and by he says something which is original and beautiful. That charms him. He would say nothing else but such things. In our way of talking we say "That is yours, this is mine"; but the poet knows well that it is not his; that it is as strange and beautiful to him as to you; he would fain hear the like eloquence at length. Once having tasted this immortal ichor, he cannot have enough of it, and as an admirable creative power exists in these intellections, it is of the last importance that these things get spoken. What a little of all we know is said! What drops of all the sea of our science are baled up! and by what accident it is that these are exposed, when so many secrets sleep in nature! Hence the necessity of speech and song; hence these throbs and heart-beatings in the orator, at the door of the assembly, to the end namely that thought may be ejaculated as Logos, or Word.

Doubt not, O poet, but persist. Say "It is in me, and shall out." Stand there, balked and dumb, stuttering and stammering, hissed and hooted, stand and strive, until at last rage draw out of thee that *dream*-power which every night shows thee is thine own; a power transcending all limit and privacy, and by virtue of which a man is the conductor of the whole river of electricity. Nothing walks, or creeps, or grows, or exists, which must not in turn arise and walk before him as exponent of his meaning. Comes he to that power, his genius is no longer exhaustible. All the creatures by pairs and by tribes pour into his mind as into a Noah's ark, to come forth again to people a new world. This is like the stock of air for our respiration or for the combustion of our fireplace; not a measure of gallons, but the entire atmosphere if wanted. And therefore the rich poets, as Homer, Chaucer, Shakespeare, and Raphael, have obviously no limits to their works except the limits of their lifetime, and resemble a mirror carried through the street, ready to render an image of every created thing.

O poet! a new nobility is conferred in groves and pastures, and not in castles or by the sword-blade any longer. The conditions are hard, but equal. Thou shalt leave the world, and know the muse only. Thou shalt not know any longer the times, customs, graces, politics, or opinions of men, but shall take all from the muse. For the time of towns is tolled from the world by funereal chimes, but in nature the universal hours are counted by succeeding tribes of animals and plants, and by growth of joy on joy. God wills also that thou abdicate a manifold and duplex life, and that thou be content that others speak for thee. Others shall be thy gentlemen and shall represent all courtesy and wordly life for thee; others shall do the great and resounding actions also. Thou shalt lie close hid with nature, and canst not be afforded to the Capitol or the Exchange. The world is full of renunciations and apprenticeships, and this is thine; thou must pass for a fool and a churl for a long season. This is the screen and sheath in which Pan has protected his well-beloved flower, and thou shalt be known only to thine own, and they shall console thee with tenderest love. And thou shalt not be able to rehearse the names of thy friends in thy verse, for an old shame before the holy ideal. And this is the reward; that the ideal shall be real to thee, and the impressions of the actual world shall fall like summer rain, copious, but not troublesome to thy invulnerable essence. Thou shalt have the whole land for thy park and manor, the sea for thy bath and navigation, without tax and without envy; the woods and the rivers thou shalt own, and thou shalt possess that wherein others are only tenants and boarders. Thou true land-lord! sea-lord! air-lord! Wherever snow falls or water flows, or birds fly, wherever day and night meet in twilight, wherever the blue heaven is hung by clouds or sown with stars, wherever are forms with transparent boundaries, wherever are outlets into celestial space, wherever is danger, and awe, and love, — there is Beauty, plenteous as rain, shed for thee, and though thou shouldst walk the world over, thou shalt not be able to find a condition inopportune or ignoble.

Karl Marx

1818–1883

Karl Marx, the chief philosopher and theorist of modern socialism, was born into a comfortable middle-class home in Trier, Germany. The son of a lawyer who converted from Judaism to Lutheranism, Marx studied law at Bonn and Berlin before turning to philosophy and taking his Ph.D. at Jena in 1841. He became editor of the *Rheinische Zeitung* in 1842, but his calls for radical reform led to its suppression in 1843. That same year he emigrated to Paris, where he began his lifelong partnership with Friedrich Engels, committed himself to socialism, and commenced his study of the works of the classical economists. Within a year he was expelled from France for his radical views, and he settled for the next three years in Brussels.

Marx's evolving theories, although recorded in 1846, were not published until 1932, as *The German Ideology.* In 1847 he joined the Communist League and with Engels wrote *The Communist Manifesto,* which was published in 1848 just before revolution swept the continent. Exiled from most European centers, in 1849 Marx settled permanently in London to a life of poverty, chronic illness, and arduous, unflagging devotion to the cause of world communism. *A Contribution to the Critique of Political Economy* was published in 1859, and the next twelve years saw the founding of the First International Working Men's Council (1864) and the publication of both the first volume of his monumental *Capital* (1867) and *The Civil War in France* (1871), an analysis of the brutally suppressed Paris Commune of 1871. Marx's last years, clouded by ill-health and by the deaths of his eldest daughter and wife, were less precarious financially owing to the pension that Engels settled on him in 1869.

Marx is usually classified as a "dialectical materialist." Like his teacher Hegel, Marx believed that historical transformations occur through a *dialectic* of thesis, antithesis, and synthesis, whereby each historical force calls into being its Other so that the two opposites negate each other and ultimately give rise to a third force, which transcends this opposition (see the headnote for Hegel, p. 359). But while Hegel was an idealist who believed in spiritual forces that bend and transform the material world, Marx was a materialist who contended that "it is not the consciousness of men that determines their being, but, on the contrary, their social being that determines their consciousness."

Marx argues in *The German Ideology* that the ultimate moving force of human history is economics, or perhaps one should use the older and broader term "political economy," since in Marxist thought the engine of change is a fusion of political and social as well as economic issues. Each society lives by certain "forces of production" — the methods and techniques by which it produces food, clothing, shelter, and the other necessities of life — and by the "social relations of production" these methods create. In an economy based on sheep-raising, for example, the shepherds work alone and relate primarily to the flock owner, while an economy based on manufacturing demands a division of labor, which in turn requires elaborate patterns of cooperation among workers and a hierarchy of managers. These modes of production and their accompanying social relations are the foundation *(Grundlage)* of a culture.

Marx posited that major historical changes occur not as a result of spiritual contradictions, as Hegel had thought, but because of economic ones. (It is in this sense that, as the cliché puts it, Marx stood Hegel on his head.) Feudalism, for example, was a relatively stable system as long as it was based on local agriculture; but as trade began to generate wealth, feudal rulers became rich and powerful by taxing it and secured their power by giving their towns and traders maximum freedom of action. By so doing, they created two rival centers of power, the feudal countryside and the bourgeois city. In the city, the merchants and manufacturers formed cooperative social relationships with one another and recognized their mutual class interests, which were not always in harmony with those of the agricultural feudatories. It was inevitable that eventually the bourgeoisie of the tightly organized city would gain ascendancy over the feudal lords, who were unaccustomed to cooperation. Conflict between feudal lords and the middle classes broke out most violently in bourgeois revolutions, like the English Civil War in the 1640s and the French Revolution of the 1790s. Marx devoted most of his efforts to demonstrating that capitalism was developing the same sorts of internal contradictions as feudalism and to predicting the course of the proletarian revolution that would displace it.

If the material foundation of a culture is economic, the spiritual superstructure *(Überbau)* finds expression in the culture's *ideology*. Marx used the term *ideology* to denote the culture's collective consciousness of its own being — comprising all its elaborate codes of law, politics, religion, art, and philosophy. By and large, the ideology of a society will be consistent with and supportive of its dominant material basis. One would expect, for example, that a society whose economy is based on herds of livestock (like that of the Old Testament Hebrews) would erect a paternalistic monarchy and believe in a fatherly God of their own profession ("The Lord is my shepherd; I shall not want"). This does not mean that art always expresses only the sentiments of the dominant class. All the implicit contradictions and conflicts within the economic base are likely to find some sort of expression within the ideological superstructure. For example, the aspiration of the capitalist middle classes to equality with the great lords emerges in literature as early as Chaucer's *Canterbury Tales,* in the Merchant's sentiment that tradesmen too may possess "gentilesse." But the term *ideology* in Marx's usage often has the connotation of "false consciousness," a set of illusions fostered by the dominant class in order to ensure social stability — and its own continued dominance. Marx was notoriously hostile to religious visions of equality in heaven that defused the proletarian desire for greater equality here on earth. Literature too might be "the opium of the people" to the extent that vicarious participation in the struggles of upper–middle-class life would undermine the natural solidarity of the working classes. Indeed, merely representing the world as it is as a coherent social structure has the conservative force of making the present into an icon: It implies that, since things are thus, they cannot be otherwise.

Art and literature are therefore dependent ideological features of the dominant socioeconomic system, changing as the base changes but usually reflecting the values of the hegemonic class. In part, this is true for obvious economic reasons: Making art is one way of earning a living and those who create art must flatter, or at least not affront, their patrons, those in a position to pay for it. Note, for example, the aristocratic bias of Shakespeare's plays in a day when theaters were licensed by the Crown and theatrical companies were sponsored by courtiers, or the fact that genre painting depicting bourgeois interiors with stunning detail arose in seventeenth-century Dutch society, which was dominated by merchants.

But beyond conscious pandering, there is Marx's broader assumption that individuals can only think the thoughts that are thinkable in their society. If Shakespeare regarded Jack Cade (in *2 Henry VI*) or the plebeian rebels of *Coriolanus* as bringers of chaos, chances are no one else in Shakespeare's still-feudal society could imagine how a democratic commonwealth might function. Similarly, Dickens was able to understand and represent the immense human misery produced by the Industrial Revolution and the gospel of wealth, but he was unable to envision any solution for that misery, other than a change of heart from acquisitiveness to benevolence on the part of wealthy capitalists.

On the other hand, in artistic matters at least, individuals can continue to think thoughts that their society no longer considers thinkable. Why the art of the distant past, based on social and political relationships that have long been superseded, should still have such an intense effect upon later audiences, is a question that long troubled Marx and his followers. The immense appeal of Greek art to the German middle class (including Marx) is one of the more perplexing issues Marx treats in the selection from *Contribution to a Critique of Political Economy*. It is a problem he solves as a collective case of emotional nostalgia: Just as our sentimental attachment to our own personal childhood depends on the fact that we will never have to live it over again, so Greek art reflects the idyllic childhood of the human race. For Marx, the lucidity and force of Greek literature and sculpture are captivating precisely because the hard life, the meager diet, the tyrants, and the slaves that produced it are things we no longer have to endure.

Selected Bibliography

Ahearn, Edward. *Marx and Modern Fiction*. New Haven: Yale University Press, 1989.

Berlin, Isaiah. *Karl Marx: His Life and Environment*, 4th ed. New York: Oxford University Press, 1996.

Demetz, Peter. *Marx, Engels, and the Poets: Origins of Marxist Literary Criticism*. Chicago: University of Chicago Press, 1967.

Dowling, William P. *Jameson, Althusser, Marx: An Introduction to The Political Unconscious*. Ithaca: Cornell University Press, 1984.

Foucault, Michel. *Remarks on Marx*. London: Autonomedia, 1991.

Kedourie, Elie. *Lectures on Hegel and Marx*. London: Blackwell, 1991.

Lifshitz, Mikhail. *The Philosophy of Art of Karl Marx*, 1933; London: Plato Press, 1973.

Marx, Karl, and Friedrich Engels. *Marx and Engels on Literature and Art*. St. Louis: Telos Press, 1973.

Mazlish, Bruce. *The Meaning of Karl Marx*. New York: Oxford University Press, 1984.

Wilson, H. T. *Marx's Critical-Dialectical Procedure*. New York: Routledge, 1990.

Consciousness Derived from Material Conditions from *The German Ideology*

The premises from which we begin are not arbitrary ones, not dogmas, but real premises from which abstraction can only be made in the imagination. They are the real individuals, their activity, and the material conditions under which they live, both those which they find already existing and those produced by their activity. These premises can thus be verified in a purely empirical way.

The first premise of all human history is, of course, the existence of living human individuals. Thus the first fact to be established is the physical organization of these individuals and their consequent relation to the rest of nature. Of course, we cannot here go either into the actual physical nature of man, or into the natural conditions in which man finds himself — geological, orohydrographical, climatic, and so on. The writing of history must always set out from these natural bases and their modification in the course of history through the action of man.

Men can be distinguished from animals by consciousness, by religion, or anything else you like. They themselves begin to distinguish themselves from animals as soon as they begin to *produce* their means of subsistence, a step which is conditioned by their physical organization. By producing their means of subsistence men are indirectly producing their actual material life.

The way in which men produce their means of subsistence depends first of all on the nature of the actual means they find in existence and have to reproduce. This mode of production must not be considered simply as being the reproduction of the physical existence of the individuals. Rather it is a definite form of activity of these individuals, a definite form of expressing their life, a definite *mode of life* on their part. As individuals express their life, so they are. What they are, therefore, coincides with their production, both with *what* they produce and with *how* they produce. The nature of individuals thus depends on the material conditions determining their production.

This production only makes its appearance with the increase of population. In its turn this presupposes the intercourse of individuals with one another. The form of this intercourse is again determined by production.

The relations of different nations among themselves depend upon the extent to which each has developed its productive forces, the division of labor, and internal intercourse.[1] This statement is generally recognized. But not only the relation of one nation to others, but also the whole internal structure of the nation itself depends on the stage of development reached by its production and its internal and external intercourse. How far the productive forces of a nation are developed is shown most manifestly by the degree to which the division of labor has been carried. Each new productive force, insofar as it is not merely a quantitative extension of productive forces already known, (for instance, the bringing into cultivation of fresh land), brings about a further development of the division of labor.

The division of labor inside a nation leads at first to the separation of industrial and commercial from agricultural labor, and hence to the separation of town and country and a clash of interests between them. Its further development leads to the separation of commercial from industrial labor. At the same time through the division of labor there develop further, inside these various branches, various divisions among the individuals cooperating in definite kinds of labor. The relative position of these individual groups is determined by the methods employed in agriculture,

Translated by R. Pascal.

[1]Markets within the economy of the nation. [Ed.]

industry, and commerce (patriarchalism, slavery, estates, classes). These same conditions are to be seen (given a more developed intercourse) in the relations of different nations to one another.

The various stages of development in the division of labor are just so many different forms of ownership; i.e., the existing stage in the division of labor determines also the relations of individuals to one another with reference to the material, instrument, and product of labor.

The first form of ownership is tribal ownership. It corresponds to the undeveloped stage of production, at which a people lives by hunting and fishing, by the rearing of beasts or, in the highest stage, agriculture. In the latter case it presupposes a great mass of uncultivated stretches of land. The division of labor is at this stage still very elementary and is confined to a further extension of the natural division of labor imposed by the family. The social structure is therefore limited to an extension of the family; patriarchal family chieftains; below them the members of the tribe; finally slaves. The slavery latent in the family only develops gradually with the increase of population, the growth of wants, and with the extension of external relations, of war or of trade.

The second form is the ancient communal and State ownership which proceeds especially from the union of several tribes into a city by agreement or by conquest, and which is still accompanied by slavery. Beside communal ownership we already find movable, and later also immovable, private property developing, but as an abnormal form subordinate to communal ownership. It is only as a community that the citizens hold power over their laboring slaves, and on this account alone, therefore, they are bound to the form of communal ownership. It is the communal private property which compels the active citizens to remain in this natural form of association over against their slaves. For this reason the whole structure of society based on this communal ownership, and with it the power of the people, decays in the same measure as immovable private property evolves. The division of labor is already more developed. We already find the antagonism of town and country; later the antagonism between those states which represent town interests and those which represent country, and inside the towns themselves the antagonism between industry and maritime commerce. The class relation between citizens and slaves is now completely developed.

The whole interpretation of history appears to be contradicted by the fact of conquest. Up till now violence, war, pillage, rape, and slaughter, etc. have been accepted as the driving force of history. Here we must limit ourselves to the chief points and take therefore only a striking example — the destruction of an old civilization by a barbarous people and the resulting formation of an entirely new organization of society. (Rome and the barbarians; Feudalism and Gaul; the Byzantine Empire and the Turks.) With the conquering barbarian people war itself is still, as hinted above, a regular form of intercourse, which is the more eagerly exploited as the population increases, involving the necessity of new means of production to supersede the traditional and, for it, the only possible, crude mode of production. In Italy it was, however, otherwise. The concentration of landed property (caused not only by buying-up and indebtedness but also by inheritance, since loose living being rife and marriage rare, the old families died out and their possessions fell into the hands of a few) and its conversion into grazing-land (caused not only by economic forces still operative today but by the importation of plundered and tribute-corn and the resultant lack of demand for Italian corn) brought about the almost total disappearance of the free population. The very slaves died out again and again, and had constantly to be replaced by new ones. Slavery remained the basis of the whole productive system. The plebeians, mid-way between freemen and slaves, never succeeded in becoming more than a proletarian rabble. Rome indeed never became more than a city; its connection with the provinces was almost exclusively political and could therefore easily be broken again by political events.

With the development of private property, we find here for the first time the same conditions which we shall find again, only on a more extensive scale, with modern private property. On the one hand the concentration of private property, which began very early in Rome (as the Licinian agrarian law[2] proves), and proceeded very rapidly from the time of the civil wars and especially under the Emperors; on the other hand, coupled with this, the transformation of the plebeian small peasantry into a proletariat, which, however, owing to its intermediate position between propertied citizens and slaves, never achieved an independent development.

The third form of ownership is feudal or estate-property. If antiquity started out from the town and its little territory, the Middle Ages started out from the country. This different starting-point was determined by the sparseness of the population at that time, which was scattered over a large area and which received no large increase from the conquerors. In contrast to Greece and Rome, feudal development therefore extends over a much wider field, prepared by the Roman conquests and the spread of agriculture at first associated with it. The last centuries of the declining Roman Empire and its conquest by the barbarians destroyed a number of productive forces; agriculture had declined, industry had decayed for want of a market, trade had died out or been violently suspended, the rural and urban population had decreased. From these conditions and the mode of organizations of the conquest determined by them, feudal property developed under the influence of the Germanic military constitution. Like tribal and communal ownership, it is based on a community; but the directly producing class standing over against it is not, as in the case of the ancient community, the slaves, but the enserfed small peasantry. As soon as feudalism is fully developed, there also arises antagonism to the towns. The hierarchical system of land ownership, and the armed bodies of retainers associated with it, gave the nobility power over the serfs. This feudal organization was, just as much as the ancient communal ownership, an association against a subjected producing class; but the form of association and the relation to the direct producers were different because of the different conditions of production.

[2]A law dating to the early days of the Republic that prevented the dispersal of estates by providing that the eldest son inherited the landed property. [Ed.]

This feudal organization of land-ownership had its counterpart in the towns in the shape of corporative property, the feudal organization of trades. Here property consisted chiefly in the labor of each individual person. The necessity for association against the organized robber-nobility, the need for communal covered markets in an age when the industrialist was at the same time a merchant, the growing competition of the escaped serfs swarming into the rising towns, the feudal structure of the whole country: these combined to bring about the guilds. Further, the gradually accumulated capital of individual craftsmen and their stable numbers, as against the growing population, evolved the relation of journeyman and apprentice, which brought into being in the towns a hierarchy similar to that in the country.

Thus the chief form of property during the feudal epoch consisted on the one hand of landed property with serf-labor chained to it, and on the other of individual labor with small capital commanding the labor of journeymen. The organization of both was determined by the restricted conditions of production — the small-scale and primitive cultivation of the land, and the craft type of industry. There was little division of labor in the heyday of feudalism. Each land bore in itself the conflict of town and country and the division into estates was certainly strongly marked; but apart from the differentiation of princes, nobility, clergy, and peasants in the country, and masters, journeymen, apprentices, and soon also the rabble of casual laborers in the towns, no division of importance took place. In agriculture it was rendered difficult by the strip-system, beside which the cottage industry of the peasants themselves emerged as another factor. In industry there was no division of labor at all in the individual trades themselves, and very little between them. The separation of industry and commerce was found already in existence in older towns; in the newer it only developed later, when the towns entered into mutual relations.

The grouping of larger territories into feudal kingdoms was a necessity for the landed nobility as for the towns. The organization of the ruling class, the nobility, had, therefore, everywhere a monarch at its head.

The fact is, therefore, that definite individuals who are productively active in a definite way enter into these definite social and political relations. Empirical observation must in each separate instance bring out empirically, and without any mystification and speculation, the connection of the social and political structure with production. The social structure and the State are continually evolving out of the life-process of definite individuals, but of individuals, not as they may appear in their own or other people's imagination, but as they really are; i.e., as they are effective, produce materially, and are active under definite material limits, presuppositions, and conditions independent of their will.

The production of ideas, of conceptions, of consciousness, is at first directly interwoven with the material activity and the material intercourse of men, the language of real life. Conceiving, thinking, the mental intercourse of men, appear at this stage as the direct efflux of their material behavior. The same applies to mental production as expressed in the language of the politics, laws, morality, religion, metaphysics of a people. Men are the producers of their conceptions, ideas, etc. — real, active men, as they are conditioned by a definite development of their productive forces and of the intercourse corresponding to these, up to its furthest forms. Consciousness can never be anything else than conscious existence, and the existence of men is their actual life-process. If in all ideology men and their circumstances appear upside down as in a *camera obscura,*[3] this phenomenon arises just as much from their historical life-process as the inversion of objects on the retina does from their physical life-process.

[3]Marx refers to the fact that the lens of a camera inverts the image while projecting it onto the plate or film. [Ed.]

In direct contrast to German philosophy which descends from heaven to earth, here we ascend from earth to heaven. That is to say, we do not set out from what men say, imagine, conceive, nor from men as narrated, thought of, imagined, conceived, in order to arrive at men in the flesh. We set out from real, active men, and on the basis of their real life-process we demonstrate the development of the ideological reflexes and echoes of this life-process. The phantoms formed in the human brain are also, necessarily, sublimates of their material life-process, which is empirically verifiable and bound to material premises. Morality, religion, metaphysics, all the rest of ideology and their corresponding forms of consciousness, thus no longer retain the semblance of independence. They have no history, no development; but men, developing their material production and their material intercourse, alter, along with this their real existence, their thinking and the products of their thinking. Life is not determined by consciousness, but consciousness by life. In the first method of approach the starting point is consciousness taken as the living individual; in the second it is the real living individuals themselves, as they are in actual life, and consciousness is considered solely as *their* consciousness.

This method of approach is not devoid of premises. It starts out from the real premises and does not abandon them for a moment. Its premises are men, not in any fantastic isolation or abstract definition, but in their actual, empirically perceptible process of development under definite conditions. As soon as this active life-process is described, history ceases to be a collection of dead facts as it is with the empiricists (themselves still abstract), or an imagined activity of imagined subjects, as with the idealists.

On Greek Art in Its Time
from *A Contribution to the Critique of Political Economy*

THE MODE OF PRODUCTION OF MATERIAL LIFE DETERMINES THE SOCIAL, POLITICAL, AND INTELLECTUAL PROCESSES OF LIFE

In the social production which men carry on they enter into definite relations that are indispensable and independent of their will; these relations of production correspond to a definite stage of development of their material forces of production. The sum total of these relations of production constitutes the economic structure of society — the real foundation, on which rises a legal and political superstructure and to which correspond definite forms of social consciousness. The mode of production in material life determines the social, political, and intellectual life processes in general. It is not the consciousness of men that determines their being, but, on the contrary, their social being that determines their consciousness. At a certain stage of their development, the material forces of production in society come in conflict with the existing relations of production or — what is but a legal expression for the same thing — with the property relations within which they have been at work before. From forms of development of the forces of production these relations turn into their fetters. Then begins an epoch of social revolution. With the change of the economic foundation the entire immense superstructure is more or less rapidly transformed. In considering such transformations a distinction should always be made between the material transformation of the economic conditions of production which can be determined with the precision of natural science, and the legal, political, religious, aesthetic, or philosophic — in short, ideological — forms in which men become conscious of this conflict and fight it out. Just as our opinion of an individual is not based on what he thinks of himself, so can we not judge of such a period of transformation by its own consciousness, on the contrary this consciousness must be explained rather from the contradictions of material life, from the existing conflict between the social forces of production and the relations of production. No social order ever disappears before all the productive forces for which there is room in it have been developed; and new higher relations of production never appear before the material conditions of their existence have matured in the womb of the old society itself. Therefore, mankind always sets itself only such tasks as it can solve; since, looking at the matter more closely, we will always find that the task itself arises only when the material conditions necessary for its solution already exist or are at least in the process of formation. In broad outlines we can designate the Asiatic, the ancient, the feudal, and the modern bourgeois modes of production as so many epochs in the progress of the economic formation of society. The bourgeois relations of production are the last antagonistic form of the social process of production — antagonistic not in the sense of individual antagonism, but of one arising from the social conditions of life of the individuals; at the same time the productive forces developing in the womb of bourgeois society create the material conditions for the solution of that antagonism. This social formation constitutes, therefore, the closing chapter of the prehistoric stage of human society.

It is well known that certain periods of highest development of art stand in no direct connection with the general development of society, nor with the material basis and the skeleton structure of its organization. Witness the example of the Greeks as compared with the modern nations or even Shakespeare. As regards certain forms of art, as

Translated by Nahum Isaac Stone.

e.g., the epos, it is admitted that they can never be produced in the world-epoch making form as soon as art as such comes into existence; in other words, that in the domain of art certain important forms of it are possible only at a low stage of its development. If that be true of the mutual relations of different forms of art within the domain of art itself, it is far less surprising that the same is true of the relation of art as a whole to the general development of society. The difficulty lies only in the general formulation of these contradictions. No sooner are they specified than they are explained. Let us take for instance the relation of Greek art and of that of Shakespeare's time to our own. It is a well-known fact that Greek mythology was not only the arsenal of Greek art, but also the very ground from which it had sprung. Is the view of nature and of social relations which shaped Greek imagination and Greek [art] possible in the age of automatic machinery, and railways, and locomotives, and electric telegraphs? Where does Vulcan come in as against Roberts & Co.; Jupiter, as against the lightning rod; and Hermes, as against the Credit Mobilier?[1] All mythology masters and dominates and shapes the forces of nature in and through the imagination; hence it disappears as soon as man gains mastery over the forces of nature. What becomes of the Goddess Fame side by side with Printing House Square?[2] Greek art presupposes the existence of Greek mythology; i.e., that nature and even the form of society are wrought up in popular fancy in an unconsciously artistic fashion. That is its material. Not, however, any mythology taken at random, nor any accidental unconsciously artistic elaboration of nature (including under the latter all objects, hence [also] society). Egyptian mythology could never be the soil or womb which would give birth to Greek art. But in any event [there had to be] *a* mythology. In no event [could Greek art originate] in a society which excludes any mythological explanation of nature, any mythological attitude towards it and which requires from the artists an imagination free from mythology.

Looking at it from another side: is Achilles possible side by side with powder and lead? Or is the *Iliad* at all compatible with the printing press and steam press? Does not singing and reciting and the muses necessarily go out of existence with the appearance of the printer's bar, and do not, therefore, disappear the prerequisites of epic poetry?

But the difficulty is not in grasping the idea that Greek art and epos are bound up with certain forms of social development. It rather lies in understanding why they still constitute with us a source of aesthetic enjoyment and in certain respects prevail as the standard and model beyond attainment.

A man can not become a child again unless he becomes childish. But does he not enjoy the artless ways of the child and must he not strive to reproduce its truth on a higher plane? Is not the character of every epoch revived perfectly true to nature in child nature? Why should the social childhood of mankind, where it had obtained its most beautiful development, not exert an eternal charm as an age that will never return? There are ill-bred children and precocious children. Many of the ancient nations belong to the latter class. The Greeks were normal children. The charm their art has for us does not conflict with the primitive character of the social order from which it had sprung. It is rather the product of the latter, and is rather due to the fact that the unripe social conditions under which the art arose and under which alone it could appear can never return.

[1]Marx wittily compares ancient and modern institutions; Vulcan was the god of manufactures, while Roberts & Co. was a munitions maker; Jupiter controlled the lightning as now the lightning rod does; Hermes was the god of thieves, while the Credit Mobilier was a large financial institution. [Ed.]

[2]Where the London *Times* was printed. [Ed.]

Matthew Arnold

1822–1888

Matthew Arnold was born at Laleham, Middlesex, but in 1828 moved to Rugby, where his father Dr. Thomas Arnold, the sage and humane spirit of *Tom Brown's School Days,* had been appointed headmaster. Arnold went to Winchester, then to Rugby, to Balliol College of Oxford, and then to a fellowship at Oriel. In 1851 Arnold left academia, became an inspector of schools (a position he held for thirty-five years), and married Frances Lucy Wightman. His chief volumes of poetry were *Empedocles on Etna* (1852), *Poems* (1853), *Poems,* Second Series (1855), *Merope, a Tragedy* (1858), and *New Poems* (1867). His chief critical publications were *Essays in Criticism,* First Series (1865), *Culture and Anarchy* (1869), *Literature and Dogma* (1873), and *Essays in Criticism,* Second Series (1888). Arnold was elected professor of poetry at Oxford in 1857 and held the position for ten years. He died unexpectedly in 1888.

Some passages in Arnold's criticism have struck commentators as Aristotelian, notably a section from his preface to *Poems* (1853), which insists that human action, rather than the consciousness of the poet, is the true subject of poetry:

> What are the eternal objects of poetry, among all nations and at all times? They are actions; human actions; possessing an inherent interest in themselves, and which are to be communicated in an interesting manner by the art of the poet. Vainly will the latter imagine that he has everything in his power; that he can make an intrinsically inferior action . . . delightful . . . by his treatment of it. . . . I fearlessly assert that *Hermann and Dorothea, Childe Harold, Jocelyn, The Excursion,* leave the reader cold in comparison with the effect produced on him by the latter books of the *Iliad,* by the *Oresteia,* or by the episode of Dido. . . .

If to know and to cite Aristotle is to be Aristotelian, then Arnold was one of the most loyal Aristotelians the nineteenth century produced. Indeed, in both of the essays included here, Arnold quotes or alludes to *Poetics,* Chapter 9, that poetry is a higher thing than history, because poetry is *philosophoteron kai spoudaioteron,* the more philosophical and more nobly serious human activity.

But in fact, Arnold's conception of literature is far from the gist and method of the *Poetics.* For Aristotle the poem's only duty is to be good in the way of its kind, and he resolutely differentiated between the genres of poetry and between poetry and all other forms of creativity. Aristotle's sense of the discreteness of activities and the primacy of form over content — both intellectual and spiritual — would be totally foreign to Arnold's way of thinking. For Arnold, form as an issue in itself never comes up.

Even the word "criticism" in "The Function of Criticism at the Present Time" (1864) is far broader than *literary* criticism: It denominates literature itself as a "criticism of life." Literature and literary criticism alike engage in a comprehensive critique of the entire culture. And while Arnold seems at times to be discussing literature as such, art is never for art's sake: Literature is of interest to him primarily as an index to and a banner of the society that produced it. In this sense Arnold is as holistic a critic as Plato in *Republic,* Book X. In another sense, however, Arnold entirely inverts Plato, for he views art as one possible salvation for an inhumane society rather than as a potential source of pollution in a utopia. Instead of being, as in Plato, a distorting mirror of reality, art for Arnold is one way of increasing the accuracy of one's spiritual vision — and a corrective for the illusions of political propaganda.

In one passage of "The Function of Criticism," for example, Arnold quotes some of the dithyrambically optimistic oratory of contemporary parliamentarians Charles Adderley and John Arthur Roebuck, who viewed Victorian society as not merely perfectible but as nearly perfected. Arnold responds not with a quotation from the classics but rather with a sordid newspaper paragraph about a "shocking child murder" committed at Nottingham by a workhouse girl named Wragg. Arnold asks us to imagine "the workhouse, the dismal Mapperly hills . . . the gloom, the smoke, the cold, the strangled illegitimate child. . . . And the final touch, — short, bleak, and inhuman: *Wragg is in custody.*" The passage is astonishing in a work of literary criticism. In a way, though, it is the center of the essay. This quotation represents the lowest level at which literature — the imaginative recreation of human existence — can be "criticism of life": minimally, by ironically exploding the pretenses of current ideology. But criticism of life has other phases. At its best literature can reawaken in us a sense of what it would mean to be fully human — a reawakening that Arnold sensed was needed more than ever in his mechanical age.

Because of what literature is capable of at its best, Arnold is concerned that we recognize what is best and not mistake cheaper merchandise for the genuine article. This form of elitism inspired "The Study of Poetry" (1880) and its doctrine of "touchstones" — lines of poetry that supposedly characterize the highest flights of the human spirit. When we hear a line of poetry, Arnold recommends that we compare it immediately to those lines in literature that are most sublime: "*In la sua voluntade è nostra pace*" from Dante's *Paradiso,* or "Absent thee from felicity awhile" from *Hamlet.*

As a method of literary criticism, "touchstonery" had been exploded a century before, in Johnson's *Preface to Shakespeare:* "He that tries to recommend [Shakespeare] by select quotations, will succeed like the pedant in Hierocles, who, when he offered his house to sale, carried a brick in his pocket as a specimen." One problem with touchstonery is obvious: It valorizes the single, sublime line to the neglect of every other aspect of literature: plot, characterization, consistency of tone, originality of thought. Less obviously, perhaps, it devalues genres other than epic and tragedy. Within Arnold's essay itself it is clear that the comic genius of Chaucer must be placed below the soberer Milton, even below François Villon. The brilliant eighteenth-century wits who devoted themselves to satire and comedy fall, by Arnold's standard, below the salt.

While it would be hard to defend Arnold's touchstones as a mode of literary analysis, it is important to understand their historical significance as well as the general importance of the sublime in Arnold's thought. Arnold's age was also that of Charles Darwin and Herbert Spencer and David Friedrich Strauss. With science beginning to undermine the tenets of revealed religion, with philosophy becoming either too abstruse or too pragmatic to provide consolation and solace, Arnold felt that poetry could provide the new Word for which humanity was listening. "More and more," Arnold prophesies, "mankind will discover that we have to turn to poetry to interpret life for us, to console us, to sustain us. Without poetry, our science will appear incomplete; most of what now passes with us for religion and philosophy will be replaced by poetry." Culture would be grounded in literature, and Arnold was determined that if the culture was not to decline or vanish, that foundation would have to be revelatory of humanity's highest spiritual aspirations.

Arnold expected that the trends he saw would continue or accelerate, but as is usual with human affairs, this did not precisely happen. Revealed religion revived in the decade of Arnold's death, and the pendulum has swung back and forth several times since then. In a few regions of America, Darwinian evolution is on the defensive, at least in the public schools, and one might as easily fear the possibility that religion might subvert science in the popular mind. But what has come to pass in the last few decades — a culture grounded not in poetry but in television and dedicated not to the sublime but to the lowest common denominator — might well have been Arnold's worst nightmare.

Selected Bibliography

Boutellier, Victor N. *Imaginative Reason: The Continuity of Arnold's Critical Effort.* Bern: Franke, 1977.

Buckley, Vincent. *Poetry and Morality: Studies in the Criticism of Matthew Arnold, T. S. Eliot, and F. R. Leavis.* London: Chatto and Windus, 1959.

Carroll, Joseph. *The Cultural Theory of Matthew Arnold.* Berkeley: University of California Press, 1982.

Eells, John Shepard. *The Touchstones of Matthew Arnold.* New York: Bookman Associates, 1955.

Garrod, Heathcote William. *Poetry and the Criticism of Life.* New York: Russell and Russell, 1963.

Knickerbocker, William S. "Matthew Arnold's Theory of Poetry." *Sewanee Review* 33 (1925): 440–50.

Perkins, David. "Arnold and the Function of Literature." *ELH* 18 (1951): 287–309.

Stange, G. Robert. *Matthew Arnold: The Poet as Humanist.* Princeton: Princeton University Press, 1967.

Trilling, Lionel. *Matthew Arnold.* New York: Norton, 1939.

Wills, Anthony Aldwin. *Matthew Arnold's Literary and Religious Thought.* Stanford: Stanford University Press, 1968.

The Function of Criticism at the Present Time

Many objections have been made to a proposition which, in some remarks of mine on translating Homer, I ventured to put forth; a proposition about criticism, and its importance at the present day. I said: "Of the literature of France and Germany, as of the intellect of Europe in general, the main effort, for now many years, has been a critical effort; the endeavour, in all branches of knowledge, theology, philosophy, history, art, science, to see the object as in itself it really is." I added, that owing to the operation in English literature of certain causes, "almost the last thing for which one would come to English literature is just that very thing which now Europe most desires, — criticism"; and that the power and value of English literature was thereby impaired. More than one rejoinder declared that the importance I here assigned to criticism was excessive, and asserted the inherent superiority of the creative effort of the human spirit over its critical effort. And the other day, having been led by an excellent notice of Wordsworth[1] published in the *North British Review,* to turn again to his biography, I found, in the words of this great man, whom I, for one, must always listen to with the profoundest respect, a sentence passed on the critic's business, which seems to justify every possible disparagement of it. Wordsworth says in one of his letters:

> The writers in these publications [the Reviews], while they prosecute their inglorious employment, can not be supposed to be in a state of mind very favourable for being affected by the finer influences of a thing so pure as genuine poetry.[2]

And a trustworthy reporter of his conversation quotes a more elaborate judgment to the same effect:

> Wordsworth holds the critical power very low, infinitely lower than the inventive; and he said today that if the quantity of time consumed in writing critiques on the works of others were given to original composition, of whatever kind it might be, it would be much better employed; it would make a man find out sooner his own level, and it would do infinitely less mischief. A false or malicious criticism may do much injury to the minds of others, a stupid invention, either in prose or verse, is quite harmless.[3]

It is almost too much to expect of poor human nature, that a man capable of producing some effect in one line of literature, should, for the greater good of society, voluntarily doom himself to impotence and obscurity in another. Still less is this to be expected from men addicted to the composition of the "false or malicious criticism," of which Wordsworth speaks. However, everybody would admit that a false or malicious criticism had better never have been written. Everybody, too, would be willing to admit, as a general proposition, that the critical faculty is lower than the inventive. But is it true that criticism is really, in itself, a baneful and injurious employment; is it true that all time given to writing critiques on the works of others would be much better employed if it were given to original composition, of whatever kind this may be? Is it true that John-

[1]I cannot help thinking that a practice, common in England during the last century, and still followed in France, of printing a notice of this kind,—a notice by a competent critic,—to serve as an introduction to an eminent author's works, might be revived among us with advantage. To introduce all succeeding editions of Wordsworth, Mr. Sharp's notice (it is permitted, I hope, to mention his name) might, it seems to me, excellently serve; it is written from the point of view of an admirer, nay, of a disciple, and that is right; but then the disciple must be also, as in this case he is, a critic, a man of letters, not, as too often happens, some relation or friend with no qualification for his task except affection for his author. [Au.] J. C. Shairp's "Wordsworth: The Man and Poet" appeared in *North British Review* 61 (1864): 1–54. [Ed.]

[2]Letter of January 12, 1816, to Bernard Barton in *The Letters of William and Dorothy Wordsworth* (ed. Ernest de Selincourt, revised by Mary Moorman and Alan G. Hill), 3: 269. [Ed.]

[3]William Knight, *Life of William Wordsworth* (1889) 3: 438. [Ed.]

son had better have gone on producing more *Irenes* instead of writing his *Lives of the Poets;* nay, it is certain that Wordsworth himself was better employed in making his Ecclesiastical Sonnets than when he made his celebrated Preface, so full of criticism, and criticism of the works of others? Wordsworth was himself a great critic, and it is to be sincerely regretted that he has not left us more criticism; Goethe was one of the greatest of critics, and we may sincerely congratulate ourselves that he has left us so much criticism. Without wasting time over the exaggeration which Wordsworth's judgment on criticism clearly contains, or over an attempt to trace the causes, — not difficult I think to be traced, — which may have led Wordsworth to this exaggeration, a critic may with advantage seize an occasion for trying his own conscience, and for asking himself of what real service, at any given moment, the practice of criticism either is, or may be made, to his own mind and spirit, and to the minds and spirits of others.

The critical power is of lower rank than the creative. True; but in assenting to this proposition, one or two things are to be kept in mind. It is undeniable that the exercise of a creative power, that a free creative activity, is the highest function of man; it is proved to be so by man's finding in it his true happiness. But it is undeniable, also, that men may have the sense of exercising this free creative activity in other ways than in producing great works of literature or art; if it were not so, all but a very few men would be shut out from the true happiness of all men. They may have it in well-doing, they may have it in learning, they may have it even in criticizing. This is one thing to be kept in mind. Another is, that the exercise of the creative power in the production of great works of literature or art, however high this exercise of it may rank, is not at all epochs and under all conditions possible; and that therefore labour may be vainly spent in attempting it, which might with more fruit be used in preparing for it, in rendering it possible. This creative power works with elements, with materials; what if it has not those materials, those elements, ready for its use? In that case it must surely wait till they are ready. Now in literature, — I will limit myself to literature, for it is about literature that the question arises, — the elements with which the creative power works are ideas; the best ideas, on every matter which literature touches, current at the time. At any rate we may lay it down as certain that in modern literature no manifestation of the creative power not working with these can be very important or fruitful. And I say *current* at the time, not merely accessible at the time; for creative literary genius does not principally show itself in discovering new ideas; that is rather the business of the philosopher: the grand work of literary genius is a work of synthesis and exposition, not of analysis and discovery; its gift lies in the faculty of being happily inspired by a certain intellectual and spiritual atmosphere, by a certain order of ideas, when it finds itself in them; of dealing divinely with these ideas, presenting them in the most effective and attractive combinations, — making beautiful works with them, in short. But it must have the atmosphere, it must find itself amidst the order of ideas, in order to work freely; and these it is not so easy to command. This is why great creative epochs in literature are so rare; this is why there is so much that is unsatisfactory in the production of many men of real genius; because for the creation of a masterwork of literature two powers must concur, the power of the man and the power of the moment, and the man is not enough without the moment; the creative power has, for its happy exercise, appointed elements, and those elements are not in its own control.

Nay, they are more within the control of the critical power. It is the business of the critical power, as I said in the words already quoted, "in all branches of knowledge, theology, philosophy, history, art, science, to see the object as in itself it really is." Thus it tends, at last, to make an intellectual situation of which the creative power can profitably avail itself. It tends to establish an order of ideas, if not absolutely true, yet true by comparison with that which it displaces; to make the best ideas prevail. Presently these new ideas reach society, the touch of truth is the touch of life, and there is a stir and growth everywhere; out of this stir and growth come the creative epochs of literature.

Or, to narrow our range, and quit these considerations of the general march of genius and of society, considerations which are apt to become too abstract and impalpable, — everyone can see that a poet, for instance, ought to know life and the world before dealing with them in poetry; and life and the world being, in modern times, very complex things, the creation of a modern poet, to be worth much, implies a great critical effort behind it; else it must be a comparatively poor, barren, and short-lived affair. This is why Byron's poetry had so little endurance in it, and Goethe's so much; both Byron and Goethe had a great productive power, but Goethe's was nourished by a great critical effort providing the true materials for it, and Byron's was not; Goethe knew life and the world, the poet's necessary subjects, much more comprehensively and thoroughly than Byron. He knew a great deal more of them, and he knew them much more as they really are.

It has long seemed to me that the burst of creative activity in our literature, through the first quarter of this century, had about it, in fact, something premature; and that from this cause its productions are doomed, most of them, in spite of the sanguine hopes which accompanied and do still accompany them, to prove hardly more lasting than the productions of far less splendid epochs. And this prematureness comes from its having proceeded without having its proper data, without sufficient materials to work with. In other words, the English poetry of the first quarter of this century, with plenty of energy, plenty of creative force, did not know enough. This makes Byron so empty of matter, Shelley so incoherent, Wordsworth even, profound as he is, yet so wanting in completeness and variety. Wordsworth cared little for books, and disparaged Goethe. I admire Wordsworth, as he is, so much that I cannot wish him different; and it is vain, no doubt, to imagine such a man different from what he is, to suppose that he could have been different. But surely the one thing wanting to make Wordsworth an even greater poet than he is, — his thought richer, and his influence of wider application, — was that he should have read more books, among them, no doubt, those of that Goethe whom he disparaged without reading him.

But to speak of books and reading may easily lead to a misunderstanding here. It was not really books and reading that lacked to our poetry at this epoch; Shelley had plenty of reading, Coleridge had immense reading. Pindar and Sophocles — as we all say so glibly, and often with so little discernment of the real import of what we are saying — had not many books; Shakespeare was no deep reader. True; but in the Greece of Pindar and Sophocles, in the England of Shakespeare, the poet lived in a current of ideas in the highest degree animating and nourishing to the creative power; society was, in the fullest measure, permeated by fresh thought, intelligent and alive; and this state of things is the true basis for the creative power's exercise, — in this it finds its data, its materials, truly ready for its hand; all the books and reading in the world are only valuable as they are helps to this. Even when this does not actually exist, books and reading may enable a man to construct a kind of semblance of it in his own mind, a world of knowledge and intelligence in which he may live and work: this is by no means an equivalent, to the artist, for the nationally diffused life and thought of the epochs of Sophocles or Shakespeare, but, besides that it may be a means of preparation for such epochs, it does really constitute, if many share in it, a quickening and sustaining atmosphere of great value. Such an atmosphere the many-sided learning and the long and widely combined critical effort of Germany formed for Goethe, when he lived and worked. There was no national glow of life and thought there as in the Athens of Pericles, or the England of Elizabeth. That was the poet's weakness. But there was a sort of equivalent for it in the complete culture and unfettered thinking of a large body of Germans. That was his strength. In the England of the first quarter of this century, there was neither a national glow of life and thought, such as we had in the age of Elizabeth, nor yet a culture and a force of learning and criticism, such as were to be found in Germany. Therefore the creative power of poetry wanted, for success in the highest sense, materials and a basis; a thorough interpretation of the world was necessarily denied to it.

At first sight it seems strange that out of the immense stir of the French Revolution and its age should not have come a crop of works of genius equal to that which came out of the stir of the great productive time of Greece, or out of that of the Renascence, with its powerful episode the Reformation. But the truth is that the stir of the French Revolution took a character which essentially distinguished it from such movements as these. These were, in the main, disinterestedly intellectual and spiritual movements; movements in which the human spirit looked for its satisfaction in itself and in the increased play of its own activity: the French Revolution took a political, practical character. The movement which went on in France under the old régime, from 1700 to 1789, was far more really akin than that of the Revolution itself to the movement of the Renascence; the France of Voltaire and Rousseau told far more powerfully upon the mind of Europe than the France of the Revolution. Goethe reproached this last expressly with having "thrown quiet culture back."[4] Nay, and the true key to how much in our Byron, even in our Wordsworth, is this! — that they had their source in a great movement of feeling, not in a great movement of mind. The French Revolution, however, — that object of so much blind love and so much blind hatred, — found undoubtedly its motive-power in the intelligence of men and not in their practical sense; — this is what distinguishes it from the English Revolution of Charles the First's time; this is what makes it a more spiritual event than our Revolution, an event of much more powerful and worldwide interest, though practically less successful; — it appeals to an order of ideas which are universal, certain, permanent. 1789 asked of a thing, Is it rational? 1642 asked of a thing, Is it legal? Or, when it went furthest, Is it according to conscience? This is the English fashion; a fashion to be treated, within its own sphere, with the highest respect; for its success, within its own sphere, has been prodigious. But what is law in one place, is not law in another; what is law here today, is not law even here tomorrow; and as for conscience, what is binding on one man's conscience is not binding on another's; the old woman who threw her stool at the head of the surpliced minister in St. Giles's Church at Edinburgh[5] obeyed an impulse to which millions of the human race may be permitted to remain strangers. But the prescriptions of reason are absolute, unchanging, of universal validity; *to count by tens is the easiest way of counting,* — that is a proposition of which every one, from here to the Antipodes, feels the force; at least, I should say so, if we did not live in a country where it is not impossible that any morning we find a letter in *The Times* declaring that a decimal coinage is an absurdity.[6] That a whole nation should have been penetrated with an enthusiasm for pure reason, and with an ardent zeal for making its prescriptions triumph, is a very remarkable thing, when we consider how little of mind, or anything so worthy and quickening as mind, comes into the natives which alone, in general, impel great masses of men. In spite of the extravagant direction given to this enthusiasm, in spite of the crimes and follies in which it lost itself, the French Revolution derives from the force, truth, and universality of the ideas which took for its law, and from the passion with which it could inspire a multitude for these ideas, a unique and still living power; it is — it will probably long remain — the greatest, the most animating event in history. And, as no sincere passion for the things of the mind, even though it turns out in many respects an unfortunate passion, is ever quite thrown away and quite barren of good, France has reaped from hers one fruit — the natural and legitimate fruit, though not precisely the grand fruit she expected: she is the country in Europe where *the people* is most alive.

But the mania for giving an immediate political and practical application to all these fine ideas of the reason was fatal. Here an Englishman is in his element: on this theme we can all go on for hours. And all we are in the habit of saying on it has undoubtedly a great deal of truth. Ideas cannot be too much prized in and for themselves, cannot be too much lived with; but to transport them abruptly into the world of politics and practice, violently to revolutionize this world to their bidding, — that is quite another thing. There is the world of ideas and there is the world of practice; the French are often for suppressing the one

[4]In Goethe's "The Four Seasons: Spring." [Ed.]
[5]Jenny Geddes did this on July 23, 1637. [Ed.]

[6]A decimal coinage bill was introduced and withdrawn in 1863. [Ed.]

and the English the other; but neither is to be suppressed. A member of the House of Commons said to me the other day: "That a thing is an anomaly, I consider to be no objection to it whatever." I venture to think he was wrong; that a thing is an anomaly *is* an objection to it, but absolutely and in the sphere of ideas: it is not necessarily, under such and such circumstances, or at such and such a moment, an objection to it in the sphere of politics and practice. Joubert has said beautifully: "C'est la force et la droit qui règlent toutes choses dans le monde; la force en attendant le droit." (Force and right are the governors of this world; force till right is ready.)[7] *Force till right is ready;* and till right is ready, force, the existing order of things, is justified, is the legitimate ruler. But right is something moral, and implies inward recognition, free assent of the will; we are not ready for right, — *right,* so far as we are concerned, *is not ready,* — until we have attained this sense of seeing it and willing it. The way in which for us it may change and transform force, the existing order of things, and become, in its turn, the legitimate ruler of the world, should depend on the way in which, when our time comes, we see it and will it. Therefore for other people enamoured of their own newly discerned right, to attempt to impose it upon us as ours, and violently to substitute their right for our force, is an act of tyranny, and to be resisted. It sets at nought the second great half of our maxim, *force till right is ready.* This was the grand error of the French Revolution; and its movement of ideas, by quitting the intellectual sphere and rushing furiously into the political sphere, ran, indeed, a prodigious and memorable course, but produced no such intellectual fruit as the movement of ideas of the Renascence, and created, in opposition to itself, what I may call an *epoch of concentration.* The great force of that epoch of concentration was England; and the great voice of that epoch of concentration was Burke. It is the fashion to treat Burke's writings on the French Revolution as superannuated and conquered by the event; as the eloquent but unphilosophical tirades of bigotry and prejudice. I will not deny that they are often disfigured by the violence and passion of the moment, and that in some directions Burke's view was bounded, and his observation therefore at fault; but on the whole, and for those who can make the needful corrections, what distinguishes these writings is their profound, permanent, fruitful, philosophical truth; they contain the true philosophy of an epoch of concentration, dissipate the heavy atmosphere which its own nature is apt to engender round it, and make its resistance rational instead of mechanical.

But Burke is so great because, almost alone in England, he brings thought to bear upon politics, he saturates politics with thought; it is his accident that his ideas were at the service of an epoch of concentration, not of an epoch of expansion; it is his characteristic that he so lived by ideas, and had such a source of them welling up within him, that he could float even an epoch of concentration and English Tory politics with them. It does not hurt him that Dr. Price and the Liberals were enraged with him; it does not even hurt him that George the Third and the Tories were enchanted with him. His greatness is that he lived in a world which neither English Liberalism nor English Toryism is apt to enter; — the world of ideas, not the world of catchwords and party habits. So far is it from being really true of him that he "to party gave up what was meant for mankind," that at the very end of his fierce struggle with the French Revolution, after all his invectives against its false pretensions, hollowness, and madness, with his sincere conviction of its mischievousness, he can close a memorandum on the best means of combating it, some of the last pages he ever wrote, — the *Thoughts on French Affairs,* in December 1791, — with these striking words:

> The evil is stated, in my opinion, as it exists. The remedy must be where power, wisdom, and information, I hope, are more united with good intentions than they can be with me. I have done with this subject, I believe, for ever. It has given me many anxious moments for the last two years. *If a great change is to be made in human affairs, the minds of men will be fitted to it; the general opinions and feelings will draw that way. Every fear, every hope will forward it; and then they who persist in opposing this mighty current in human affairs, will appear rather to resist the decrees of*

[7]Jean Joubert, *Pensées* (1877), 2: 178. [Ed.]

Providence itself, than the mere designs of men. They will not be resolute and firm, but perverse and obstinate.

That return of Burke upon himself has always seemed to me one of the finest things in English literature, or indeed in any literature. That is what I call living by ideas; when one side of a question has long had your earnest support, when all your feelings are engaged, when you hear all round you no language but one, when your party talks this language like a steam-engine and can imagine no other, — still to be able to think, still to be irresistibly carried, if so it be, by the current of thought to the opposite side of the question, and, like Balaam, to be unable to speak anything *but what the Lord has put in your mouth.*[8] I know nothing more striking, and I must add that I know nothing more un-English.

For the Englishman in general is like my friend the Member of Parliament, and believes, point-blank, that for a thing to be an anomaly is absolutely no objection to it whatever. He is like the Lord Auckland of Burke's day, who, in a memorandum on the French Revolution, talks of "certain miscreants, assuming the name of philosophers, who have presumed themselves capable of establishing a new system of society." The Englishman has been called a political animal, and he values what is political and practical so much that ideas easily become objects of dislike in his eyes, and thinkers "miscreants," because ideas and thinkers have rashly meddled with politics and practice. This would be all very well if the dislike and neglect confined themselves to ideas transported out of their own sphere, and meddling rashly with practice; but they are inevitably extended to ideas as such, and to the whole life of intelligence; practice is everything, a free play of the mind is nothing. The notion of the free play of the mind upon all subjects being a pleasure in itself, being an object of desire, being an essential provider of elements without which a nation's spirit, whatever compensations it may have for them, must, in the long run, die of inanition, hardly enters into an Englishman's thoughts. It is noticeable that the word *curiosity,* which in other languages is used in a good sense, to mean, as a high and fine quality of man's nature, just this disinterested love of a free play of the mind on all subjects, for its own sake, — it is noticeable, I say, that this word has in our language no sense of the kind, no sense but a rather bad and disparaging one. But criticism, real criticism, is essentially the exercise of this very quality; it obeys an instinct prompting it to know the best that is known and thought in the world, irrespectively of practice, politics, and everything of the kind; and to value knowledge and thought as they approach this best, without the intrusion of any other considerations whatever. This is an instinct for which there is, I think, little original sympathy in the practical English nature, and what there was of it has undergone a long benumbing period of blight and suppression in the epoch of concentration which followed the French Revolution.

But epochs of concentration cannot well endure for ever; epochs of expansion, in the due course of things, follow them. Such an epoch of expansion seems to be opening in this country. In the first place all danger of a hostile forcible pressure of foreign ideas upon our practice has long disappeared; like the traveller in the fable, therefore, we begin to wear our cloak a little more loosely. Then, with a long peace, the ideas of Europe steal gradually and amicably in, and mingle, though in infinitesimally small quantities at a time, with our own notions. Then, too, in spite of all that is said about the absorbing and brutalizing influence of our passionate material progress, it seems to me indisputable that this progress is likely, though not certain, to lead in the end to an apparition of intellectual life; and that man, after he has made himself perfectly comfortable and has now to determine what to do with himself next, may begin to remember that he has a mind and that the mind may be made the source of great pleasure. I grant it is mainly the privilege of faith, at present, to discern this end to our railways, our business, and our fortune-making; but we shall see if, here as elsewhere, faith is not in the end the true prophet. Our ease, our travelling, and our unbounded liberty to hold just as hard and securely as we please to the practice to which our notions

[8]Numbers 22:38. [Ed.]

have given birth, all tend to beget an inclination to deal a little more freely with these notions themselves, to canvass them a little, to penetrate a little into their real nature. Flutterings of curiosity, in the foreign sense of the word, appear amongst us, and it is in these that criticism must look to find its account. Criticism first; a time of true creative activity, perhaps, — which, as I have said, must inevitably be preceded amongst us by a time of criticism, — hereafter, when criticism has done its work.

It is of the last importance that English criticism should clearly discern what rule for its course, in order to avail itself of the field now opening to it, and to produce fruit for the future, it ought to take. The rule may be summed up in one word, — *disinterestedness*. And how is criticism to show disinterestedness? By keeping aloof from practice; by resolutely following the law of its own nature, which is to be a free play of the mind on all subjects which it touches; by steadily refusing to lend itself to any of those ulterior, political, practical considerations about ideas which plenty of people will be sure to attach to them, which perhaps ought often to be attached to them, which in this country at any rate are certain to be attached to them quite sufficiently, but which criticism has really nothing to do with. Its business is, as I have said, simply to know the best that is known and thought in the world, and by in its turn making this known, to create a current of true and fresh ideas. Its business is to do this with inflexible honesty, with due ability; but its business is to do no more, and to leave alone all questions of practical consequences and applications, questions which will never fail to have due prominence given to them. Else criticism, besides being really false to its own nature, merely continues in the old rut which it has hitherto followed in this country, and will certainly miss the chance now given to it. For what is at present the bane of criticism in this country? It is that practical considerations cling to it and stifle it; it subserves interests not its own; our organs of criticism are organs of men and parties having practical ends to serve, and with them those practical ends are the first thing and the play of mind the second; so much play of mind as is compatible with the prosecution of those practical ends is all that is wanted. An organ like the *Revue des Deux Mondes,* having for its main function to understand and utter the best that is known and thought in the world, existing, it may be said, as just an organ for a free play of the mind, we have not; but we have the *Edinburgh Review,* existing as an organ of the old Whigs, and for as much play of the mind as may suit its being that; we have the *Quarterly Review,* existing as an organ of the Tories, and for as much play of mind as may suit its being that; we have the *British Quarterly Review,* existing as an organ of the political Dissenters, and for as much play of mind as may suit its being that; we have *The Times,* existing as an organ of the common, satisfied, well-to-do Englishman, and for as much play of mind as may suit its being that. And so on through all the various fractions, political and religious, of our society; every fraction has, as such, its organ of criticism, but the notions of combining all fractions in the common pleasure of a free disinterested play of mind meets with no favour. Directly this play of mind wants to have more scope, and to forget the pressure of practical considerations a little, it is checked, it is made to feel the chain; we saw this the other day in the extinction, so much to be regretted, of the *Home and Foreign Review;* perhaps in no organ of criticism in this country was there so much knowledge, so much play of mind; but these could not save it: the *Dublin Review* subordinates play of mind to the practical business of English and Irish Catholicism, and lives. It must needs be that men should act in sects and parties, that each of these sects and parties should have its organ, and should make this organ subserve the interests of its action; but it would be well, too, that there should be a criticism, not the minister of these interests, not their enemy, but absolutely and entirely independent of them. No other criticism will ever attain any real authority or make any real way towards its end, — the creating a current of true and fresh ideas.

It is because criticism has so little kept in the pure intellectual sphere, has so little detached itself from practice, has been so directly polemical and controversial, that it has so ill accomplished, in this country, its best spiritual work; which is to keep man from a self-satisfaction which is retarding and vulgarizing, to lead him towards perfection, by making his mind dwell upon what is excellent in itself, and the absolute beauty and fitness of things. A polemical practical criticism makes men blind even to the ideal imperfection of their practice, makes them willingly assert its ideal perfection, in order the better to secure it against attack; and clearly this is narrowing and baneful for them. If they were reassured on the practical side, speculative considerations of ideal perfection they might be brought to entertain, and their spiritual horizon would thus gradually widen. Mr. Adderley says to the Warwickshire farmers:

> Talk of the improvement of breed! Why, the race we ourselves represent, the men and women, the old Anglo-Saxon race, are the best breed in the whole world. . . . The absence of a too enervating climate, too unclouded skies, and a too luxurious nature, has produced so vigorous a race of people, and has rendered us so superior to all the world.

Mr. Roebuck says to the Sheffeld cutlers:

> I look around me and ask what is the state of England? Is not property safe? Is not every man able to say what he likes? Can you not walk from one end of England to the other in perfect security? I ask you whether, the world over or in past history, there is anything like it? Nothing. I pray that our unrivalled happiness may last.[9]

Now obviously there is a peril for poor human nature in words and thoughts of each exuberant self-satisfaction, until we find ourselves safe in the streets of the Celestial City.

> Das wenige verschwindet leicht dem Blicke
> Der vorwärts sieht, wie viel noch übrig
> bleibt —[10]

says Goethe; the little that is done seems nothing when we look forward and see how much we have yet to do. Clearly this is a better line of reflection for weak humanity, so long as it remains on this earthly field of labour and trial.

But neither Mr. Adderley nor Mr. Roebuck is by nature inaccessible to considerations of this sort. They only lose sight of them owing to the controversial life we all lead, and the practical form which all speculation takes with us. They have in view opponents whose aim is not ideal, but practical; and in their zeal to uphold their own practice against these innovators, they go so far as even to attribute to this practice an ideal perfection. Somebody has been wanting to introduce a six-pound franchise, or to abolish church-rates, or to collect agricultural statistics by force, or to diminish local self-government. How natural, in reply to such proposals, very likely improper or ill-timed, to go a little beyond the mark and to say stoutly: "Such a race of people as we stand, so superior to all the world! The old Anglo-Saxon race, the best breed in the whole world! I pray that our unrivalled happiness may last! I ask you whether, the world over or in past history, there is anything like it?" And so long as criticism answers this dithyramb by insisting that the old Anglo-Saxon race would be still more superior to all others if it had no church-rates, or that our unrivalled happiness would last yet longer with a six-pound franchise, so long will the strain, "The best breed in the whole world!" swell louder and louder, everything ideal and refining will be lost out of sight, and both the assailed and their critics will remain in a sphere, to say the truth, perfectly unvital, a sphere in which spiritual progression is impossible. But let criticism leave church-rates and the franchise alone, and in the most candid spirit, without a single lurking thought of practical innovation, confront with our dithyramb this paragraph on which I stumbled in a newspaper immediately after reading Mr. Roebuck:

> A shocking child murder has just been committed at Nottingham. A girl named Wragg left the workhouse there on Saturday morning with her young illegitimate child. The child was soon afterwards found dead on Mapperly Hills, having been strangled. Wragg is in custody.[11]

[9]These speeches were reported in the London *Times* on September 17, 1863, and August 19, 1864, respectively. [Ed.]

[10]Goethe, *Iphigenia on Tauris,* I.ii.91–92. [Ed.]

[11]The crime was committed on September 10, 1864. Elizabeth Wragg was sentenced to twenty years in prison in March of the following year. [Ed.]

Nothing but that; but, in juxtaposition with the absolute eulogies of Mr. Adderley and Mr. Roebuck, how eloquent, how suggestive are those few lines! "Our old Anglo-Saxon breed, the best in the whole world!" — how much that is harsh and ill-favoured there is in this best! *Wragg!* If we are to talk of ideal perfection, of "the best in the whole world," has anyone reflected what a touch of grossness in our race, what an original shortcoming in the more delicate spiritual perceptions, is shown by the natural growth amongst us of such hideous names, — Higginbottom, Stiggins, Bugg! In Ionia and Attica they were luckier in this respect than "the best race in the world"; by the Ilissus there was no Wragg, poor thing! And "our unrivalled happiness"; — what an element of grimness, bareness, and hideousness mixes with it and blurs it; the workhouse, the dismal Mapperly Hills, — how dismal those who have seen them will remember; — the gloom, the smoke, the cold, the strangled illegitimate child! "I ask you whether, the world over or in past history, there is anything like it?" Perhaps not, one is inclined to answer; but at any rate, in that case, the world is very much to be pitied. And the final touch, — short, bleak, and inhuman: *Wragg is in custody.* The sex lost in the confusion of our unrivalled happiness; or (shall I say?) the superfluous Christian name lopped off by the straightforward vigour of our old Anglo-Saxon breed! There is profit for the spirit in such contrasts as this; criticism serves the cause of perfection by establishing them. By eluding sterile conflict, by refusing to remain in the sphere where alone narrow and relative conceptions have any worth and validity, criticism may diminish its momentary importance, but only in this way has it a chance of gaining admittance for those wider and more perfect conceptions to which all its duty is really owed. Mr. Roebuck will have a poor opinion of an adversary who replies to his defiant songs of triumph only by murmuring under his breath, *Wragg is in custody;* but in no other way will these songs of triumph be induced gradually to moderate themselves, to get rid of what in them is excessive and offensive, and to fall into a softer and truer key.

It will be said that it is a very subtle and indirect action which I am thus prescribing for criticism, and that, by embracing in this manner the Indian virtue of detachment and abandoning the sphere of practical life, it condemns itself to a slow and obscure work. Slow and obscure it may be, but it is the only proper work of criticism. The mass of mankind will never have any ardent zeal for seeing things as they are; very inadequate ideas will always satisfy them. On these inadequate ideas reposes, and must repose, the general practice of the world. That is as much as saying that whoever sets himself to see things as they are will find himself one of a very small circle; but it is only by this small circle resolutely doing its own work that adequate ideas will ever get current at all. The rush and roar of practical life will always have a dizzying and attracting effect upon the most collected spectator, and tend to draw him into its vortex; most of all will this be the case where that life is so powerful as it is in England. But it is only by remaining collected, and refusing to lend himself to the point of view of the practical man, that the critic can do the practical man any service; and it is only by the greatest sincerity in pursuing his own course, and by at last convincing even the practical man of his sincerity, that he can escape misunderstandings which perpetually threaten him.

For the practical man is not apt for fine distinctions, and yet in these distinctions truth and the highest culture greatly find their account. But it is not easy to lead a practical man — unless you reassure him as to your practical intentions, you have no chance of leading him — to see that a thing which he has always been used to look at from one side only, which he greatly values, and which, looked at from that side, quite deserves, perhaps, all the prizing and admiring which he bestows upon it, — that this thing, looked at from another side, may appear much less beneficent and beautiful, and yet retain all its claims to our practical allegiance. Where shall we find language innocent enough, how shall we make the spotless purity of our intentions evident enough, to enable us to say to the political Englishman that the British Constitution itself, which, seen from the practical side, looks such a magnificent organ of progress and virtue, seen from the speculative side, — which its compromises, its love of facts, its horror of theory, its studied avoidance of clear thoughts, — that, seen from this side, our august Constitution sometimes looks, — forgive me, shade of Lord Somers! — a colossal machine for the manufacture of Philistines? How is Cobbett to say this and not be misunderstood, blackened as he is with the smoke of a lifelong conflict in the field of political practice? how is Mr. Carlyle to say it and not be misunderstood, after his furious raid into this field with his *Latter-day Pamphlets*? how is Mr. Ruskin, after his pugnacious political economy? I say, the critic must keep out of the region of immediate practice in the political, social, humanitarian sphere, if he wants to make a beginning for that more free speculative treatment of things, which may perhaps one day make its benefits felt even in this sphere, but in a natural and thence irresistible manner.

Do what he will, however, the critic will still remain exposed to frequent misunderstandings, and nowhere so much as in this country. For here people are particularly indisposed even to comprehend that without this free disinterested treatment of things, truth and the highest culture are out of the question. So immersed are they in practical life, so accustomed to take all their notions from this life and its processes, that they are apt to think that truth and culture themselves can be reached by the processes of this life, and that it is an impertinent singularity to think of reaching them in any other. "We are all *terrae filii,*"[12] cries their eloquent advocate; "all Philistines together. Away with the notion of proceeding by any other course than the course dear to the Philistines; let us have a social movement, let us organize and combine a party to pursue truth and new thought, let us call it *the liberal party,* and let us all stick to each other, and back each other up. Let us have no nonsense about independent criticism, and intellectual delicacy, and the few and the many. Don't let us trouble ourselves about foreign thought; we shall invent the whole thing for ourselves as we go along: if one of us speaks well, applaud him; if one of us speaks ill, applaud him too; we are all in the same movement, we are all liberals, we are all in pursuit of truth." In this way the pursuit of truth becomes really a social, practical, pleasurable affair, almost requiring a chairman, a secretary, and advertisements; with the excitement of an occasional scandal, with a little resistance to give the happy sense of difficulty overcome; but, in general, plenty of bustle and very little thought. To act is so easy, as Goethe says; to think is so hard! It is true that the critic has many temptations to go with the stream, to make one of the party movement, one of these *terrae filii;* it seems ungracious to refuse to be a *terrae filius,* when so many excellent people are; but the critic's duty is to refuse, or, if resistance is vain, at least to cry with Obermann: *Périssons en résistant.*[13]

How serious a matter it is to try and resist, I had ample opportunity of experiencing when I ventured some time ago to criticize the celebrated first volume of Bishop Colenso.[14] The echoes of the storm which was then raised I still, from time to time, hear grumbling round me. That storm arose out of a misunderstanding almost inevitable. It is a result of no little culture to attain to a clear perception that science and religion are two wholly different things; the multitude will for ever confuse them; but happily that is of no great real importance, for while the multitude imagines itself to live by its false science, it does really live by its true religion. Dr. Colenso, however, in his first volume did all he could to strengthen the confusion,[15] and to make

[12]Children of earth. [Ed.]

[13]"Let us perish while resisting." Étienne de Sénancour, *Obermann* (1804). [Ed.]

[14]So sincere is my dislike to all personal attack and controversy, that I abstain from reprinting, at this distance of time from the occasion which called them forth, the essays in which I criticized Dr. Colenso's book; I feel bound, however, after all that has passed, to make here a final declaration of my sincere impenitence for having published them. Nay, I cannot forbear repeating yet once more, for his benefit and that of his readers, this sentence from my original remarks upon him: *There is truth of science and truth of religion; truth of science does not become truth of religion till it is made religious.* And I will add; Let us have all the science there is from the men of science; from the men of religion let us have religion. [Au.] The essays in which Arnold criticized John William Colenso's *The Pentateuch and the Book of Judges Critically Examined* (1863) were "The Bishop and the Philosopher" and "Dr. Stanley's Lectures on the Jewish Church," published in 1863. [Ed.]

[15]It has been said I make it "a crime against literary criticism and the higher culture to attempt to inform the ignorant." Need I point out that the ignorant are not informed by being confirmed in a confusion? [Au.]

it dangerous. He did this with the best intentions, I freely admit, and with the most candid ignorance that this was the natural effect of what he was doing; but, says Joubert, "Ignorance, which in matters of morals extenuates the crime, is itself, in intellectual matters, a crime of the first order."[16] I criticized Bishop Colenso's speculative confusion. Immediately there was a cry raised: "What is this? here is a liberal attacking a liberal. Do not you belong to the movement? are not you a friend of truth? Is not Bishop Colenso in pursuit of truth? then speak with proper respect of his book. Dr. Stanley is another friend of truth, and you speak with proper respect of his book; why make these invidious differences? both books are excellent, admirable, liberal; Bishop Colenso's perhaps the most so, because it is the boldest, and will have the best practical consequences for the liberal cause. Do you want to encourage to the attack of a brother liberal his, and your, and our implacable enemies, the *Church and State Review* or the *Record,* — the High Church rhinoceros and the Evangelical hyaena? Be silent, therefore; or rather speak, speak as loud as ever you can, and go into ecstasies over the eighty and odd pigeons."

But criticism cannot follow this coarse and indiscriminate method. It is unfortunately possible for a man in pursuit of truth to write a book which reposes upon a false conception. Even the practical consequences of a book are to genuine criticism no recommendation of it, if the book is, in the highest sense, blundering. I see that a lady who herself, too, is in pursuit of truth, and who writes with great ability, but a little too much, perhaps, under the influence of the practical spirit of the English liberal movement, classes Bishop Colenso's book and M. Renan's[17] together, in her survey of the religious state of Europe, as facts of the same order, works, both of them, of "great importance"; "great ability, power, and skill"; Bishop Colenso's, perhaps, the most powerful; at least, Miss Cobbe[18] gives special expression to her gratitude that to Bishop Colenso "has been given the strength to grasp, and the courage to teach, truths of such deep import." In the same way, more than one popular writer has compared him to Luther. Now it is just this kind of false estimate which the critical spirit is, it seems to me, bound to resist. It is really the strongest possible proof of the low ebb at which, in England, the critical spirit is, that while the critical hit in the religious literature of Germany is Dr. Strauss's book,[19] in that of France M. Renan's book, the book of Bishop Colenso is the critical hit in the religious literature of England. Bishop Colenso's book reposes on a total misconception of the essential elements of the religious problem, as that problem is now presented for solution. To criticism, therefore, which seeks to have the best that is known and thought on this problem, it is, however well meant, of no importance whatever. Mr. Renan's book attempts a new synthesis of the elements furnished to us by the Four Gospels. It attempts, in my opinion, a synthesis, perhaps premature, perhaps impossible, certainly not successful. Up to the present time, at any rate, we must acquiesce in Fleury's sentence on such recastings of the Gospel story: *Quiconque s'imagine la pouvoir mieux écrire, ne l'entend pas.*[20] M. Renan had himself passed by anticipation a like sentence on his own work, when he said: "If a new presentation of the character of Jesus were offered to me, I would not have it; its very clearness would be, in my opinion, the best proof of its insufficiency." His friends may with perfect justice rejoin that at the sight of the Holy Land, and of the actual scene of the Gospel story, all the current of M. Renan's thoughts may have naturally changed, and a new casting of that story irresistibly suggested itself to him; and that this is just a case for applying Cicero's maxim: Change of mind is not inconsistency — *nemo doctus unquam mutationem consilii inconstantiam dixit esse.*[21] Nevertheless, for criticism, M. Renan's first thought must still be the truer one, as long as

[16]Joubert, *Pensées,* 2:311. [Ed.]

[17]Ernest Renan, *La Vie de Jesus* (1863). [Ed.]

[18]Frances Power Cobbe in *Broken Lights: An Inquiry into the Present Condition and Future Prospects of Religious Faith* (1864). [Ed.]

[19]David Friedrich Strauss's *Leben Jesus* (1835). [Ed.]

[20]"Whoever imagines himself able to write it better, does not understand it." Claude Fleury, *Ecclesiastical History* (1722). [Ed.]

[21]Cicero, *To Atticus* 16.17:3. [Ed.]

his new casting so fails more fully to commend itself, more fully (to use Coleridge's happy phrase about the Bible) to *find* us. Still M. Renan's attempt is, for criticism, of the most real interest and importance, since, with all its difficulty, a fresh synthesis of the New Testament *data,* — not a making war on them, in Voltaire's fashion, not a leaving them out of mind, in the world's fashion, but the putting a new construction upon them, the taking them from under the old, adoptive, traditional, unspiritual point of view and placing them under a new one, — is the very essence of the religious problem, as now presented; and only by efforts in this direction can it receive a solution.

Again, in the same spirit in which she judges Bishop Colenso, Miss Cobbe, like so many earnest liberals of our practical race, both here and in America, herself sets vigorously about a positive reconstruction of religion, about making a religion of the future out of hand, or at least setting about making it; we must not rest, she and they are always thinking and saying, in negative criticism, we must be creative and constructive; hence we have such works as her recent *Religious Duty,* and works still more considerable, perhaps, by others, which will be in everyone's mind. These works often have much ability; they often spring out of sincere convictions, and a sincere wish to do good; and they sometimes, perhaps, do good. Their fault is (if I may be permitted to say so) one which they have in common with the British College of Health, in the New Road. Everyone knows the British College of Health; it is that building with the lion and the statue of the Goddess Hygeia before it; at least I am sure about the lion, though I am not absolutely certain about the goddess Hygeia. This building does credit, perhaps, to the resources of Dr. Morrison and his disciples; but it falls a good deal short of one's idea of which a British College of Health ought to be. In England, where we hate public interference and love individual enterprise, we have a whole crop of places like the British College of Health; the grand name without the grand thing. Unluckily, creditable to individual enterprise as they are, they tend to impair our taste by making us forget what more grandiose, noble, or beautiful character properly belongs to a public institution. The same may be said of the religions of the future of Miss Cobbe and others. Creditable, like the British College of Health, to the resources of their authors, they yet tend to make us forget what more grandiose, noble, or beautiful character properly belongs to religious constructions. The historic religions, with all their faults, have had this; it certainly belongs to the religious sentiment, when it truly flowers, to have this; and we impoverish our spirit if we allow a religion of the future without it. What then is the duty of criticism here? To take the practical point of view, to applaud the liberal movement and all its works, — its New Road religions of the future into the bargain, — for their general utility's sake? By no means; but to be perpetually dissatisfied with these works, while they perpetually fall short of a high and perfect ideal.

For criticism, these are elementary laws; but they never can be popular, and in this country they have been very little followed, and one meets with immense obstacles in following them. That is a reason for asserting them again and again. Criticism must maintain its independence of the practical spirit and its aim. Even with well-meant efforts of the practical spirit it must express dissatisfaction, if in the sphere of the ideal they seem impoverishing and limiting. It must not hurry on to the goal because of its practical importance. It must be patient, and know how to wait; and flexible, and know how to attach itself to things and how to withdraw from them. It must be apt to study and praise elements that for the fulness of spiritual perfection are wanted, even though they belong to a power which in the practical sphere may be maleficent. It must be apt to discern the spiritual shortcomings or illusions of powers that in the practical sphere may be beneficent. And this without any notion of favouring or injuring, in the practical sphere, one power or the other; without any notion of playing off, in this sphere, one power against the other. When one looks, for instance, at the English Divorce Court, — an institution which perhaps has its practical conveniences, but which in the ideal sphere is so hideous; an institution which neither makes divorce impossible nor makes it decent, which allows a man to get rid of his wife, or a wife of her husband, but makes them drag one another first, for the public edification, through a mire of unutterable infamy, — when one looks at this charming institution, I say, with its crowded benches, its newspaper-reports, and its money-compensations, this institution in which the gross unregenerate British Philistine has indeed stamped an image of himself, — one may be permitted to find the marriage-theory of Catholicism refreshing and elevating. Or when Protestantism, in virtue of its supposed rational and intellectual origin, gives the law to criticism too magisterially, criticism may and must remind it that its pretensions, in this respect, are illusive and do it harm; that the Reformation was a moral rather than an intellectual event; that Luther's theory of grace no more exactly reflects the mind of the spirit than Bossuet's philosophy of history[22] reflects it; and that there is no more antecedent probability of the Bishop of Durham's stock of ideas being agreeable to perfect reason than of Pope Pius the Ninth's. But criticism will not on that account forget the achievements of Protestantism in the practical and moral sphere; nor that, even in the intellectual sphere, Protestantism, though in a blind and stumbling manner, carried forward the Renascence, while Catholicism threw itself violently across its path.

I lately heard a man of thought and energy[23] contrasting the want of ardour and movement which he now found amongst young men in this country with what he remembered in his own youth, twenty years ago. "What reformers we were then!" he exclaimed; "what a zeal we had! how we canvassed every institution in Church and State, and were prepared to remodel them all on first principles!" He was inclined to regret, as a spiritual flagging, the lull which he saw. I am disposed rather to regard it as a pause in which the turn to a new mode of spiritual progress is being accomplished; everything was long seen, by the young and ardent amongst us, in inseparable connection with politics and practical life; we have pretty well exhausted the benefits of seeing things in this connection, we have got all that can be got by so seeing them. Let us try a more disinterested mode of seeing them; let us betake ourselves more to the serener life of the mind and spirit. This life, too, may have its excesses and dangers; but they are not for us at present. Let us think of quietly enlarging our stock of true and fresh ideas, and not, as soon as we get an idea or half an idea, be running out with it into the street, and trying to make it rule there. Our ideas will, in the end, shape the world all the better for maturing a little. Perhaps in fifty years' time it will in the English House of Commons be an objection to an institution that it is an anomaly, and my friend the Member of Parliament will shudder in his grave. But let us in the meanwhile rather endeavour that in twenty years' time it may, in English literature, be an objection to a proposition that it is absurd. That will be a change so vast, that the imagination almost fails to grasp it. *Ab integro saeclorum nascitur ordo.*[24]

If I have insisted so much on the course which criticism must take where politics and religion are concerned, it is because, where these burning matters are in question, it is most likely to go astray. I have wished, above all, to insist on the attitude which criticism should adopt towards everything; on its right tone and temper of mind. Then comes the question as to the subject-matter which criticism should most seek. Here, in general, its course is determined for it by the idea which is the law of its being; the idea of a disinterested endeavour to learn and propagate the best that is known and thought in the world, and thus to establish a current of fresh and true ideas. By the very nature of things, as England is not all the world, much of the best that is known and thought in the world cannot be of English growth, must be foreign; by the nature of things, again, it is just this that we are least likely to know, while English thought is streaming in upon us from all sides, and takes excellent care that we shall not be ignorant of its existence; the English critic, there-

[22]Jacques-Bénigne Boussuet, *Discourse on Universal History* (1681). [Ed.]

[23]Charles Thomas Baring, Bishop of Durham (1861–79). [Ed.]

[24]"Order is born from the renewal of the ages." Virgil, *Eclogues* 4:5. [Ed.]

fore, must dwell much on foreign thought, and with particular heed on any part of it, which, while significant and fruitful in itself, is for any reason specially likely to escape him. Again, judging is often spoken of as the critic's one business, and so in some sense it is; but the judgment which almost insensibly forms itself in a fair and clear mind, along with fresh knowledge, is the valuable one; and thus knowledge, and ever fresh knowledge, must be the critic's great concern for himself; and it is by communicating fresh knowledge, and letting his own judgment pass along with it, — but insensibly, and in the second place not the first, as a sort of companion and clue, not as an abstract lawgiver, — that he will generally do most good to his readers. Sometimes, no doubt, for the sake of establishing an author's place in literature, and his relation to a central standard (and if this is not done, how are we to get at our *best in the world?*) criticism may have to deal with a subject-matter so familiar that fresh knowledge is out of the question, and then it must be all judgment; an enunciation and detailed application of principles. Here the great safeguard is never to let oneself become abstract, always to retain an intimate and lively consciousness of the truth of what one is saying, and, the moment this fails us, to be sure that something is wrong. Still, under all circumstances, this mere judgment and application of principles is, in itself, not the most satisfactory work to the critic; like mathematics, it is tautological, and cannot well give us, like fresh learning, the sense of creative activity.

But stop, someone will say; all this talk is of no practical use to us whatever; this criticism of yours is not what we have in our minds when we speak of criticism; when we speak of critics and criticism, we mean critics and criticism of the current English literature of the day; when you offer to tell criticism its function, it is to this criticism that we expect you to address yourself. I am sorry for it, for I am afraid I must disappoint these expectations. I am bound by my own definition of criticism: *a disinterested endeavour to learn and propagate the best that is known and thought in the world.* How much of current English literature comes into this "best that is known and thought in the world"? Not very much, I fear; certainly less, at this moment, than of the current literature of France or Germany. Well, then, am I to alter my definition of criticism, in order to meet the requirements of a number of practising English critics, who, after all, are free in their choice of a business? That would be making criticism lend itself just to one of those alien practical considerations, which, I have said, are so fatal to it. One may say, indeed, to those who have to deal with the mass — so much better disregarded — of current English literature, that they may at all events endeavour, in dealing with this, to try it, so far as they can, by the standard of the best that is known and thought in the world; one may say, that to get anywhere near this standard, every critic should try and possess one great literature, at least, besides his own; and the more unlike his own; the better. But, after all, the criticism I am really concerned with, — the criticism which alone can much help us for the future, the criticism which, throughout Europe, is at the present day meant, when so much stress is laid on the importance of criticism and the critical spirit, — is a criticism which regards Europe as being, for intellectual and spiritual purposes, one great confederation, bound to a joint action and working to a common result; and whose members have, for their proper outfit, a knowledge of Greek, Roman, and Eastern antiquity, and of one another. Special, local, and temporary advantages being put out of account, that modern nation will in the intellectual and spiritual sphere make most progress, which most thoroughly carries out this programme. And what is that but saying that we too, all of us, as individuals, the more thoroughly we carry it out, shall make the more progress?

There is so much inviting us! — what are we to take? what will nourish us in growth towards perfection? That is the question which, with the immense field of life and of literature lying before him, the critic has to answer; for himself first, and afterwards for others. In this idea of the critic's business the essays brought together in the following pages have had their origin; in this idea, widely different as are their subjects, they have, perhaps, their unity.

I conclude with what I said in the beginning: to have the sense of creative activity is the great happiness and the great proof of being alive, and it is not denied to criticism to have it; but then criticism must be sincere, simple, flexible, ardent, ever widening its knowledge. Then it may have, in no contemptible measure, joyful sense of creative activity; a sense which a man of insight and conscience will prefer to what he might derive from a poor, starved, fragmentary, inadequate creation. And at some epochs no other creation is possible.

Still, in full measure, the sense of creative activity belongs only to genuine creation; in literature we must never forget that. But what true man of letters ever can forget it? It is no such common matter for a gifted nature to come into possession of a current of true and living ideas, and to produce amidst the inspiration of them, that we are likely to underrate it. The epochs of Aeschylus and Shakespeare make us feel their pre-eminence. In an epoch like those is, no doubt, the true life of a literature; there is the promised land, towards which criticism can only beckon. That promised land it will not be ours to enter, and we shall die in the wilderness: but to have desired to enter it, to have saluted it from afar, is already, perhaps, the best distinction among contemporaries; it will certainly be the best title to esteem with posterity.

From *The Study of Poetry*

> The future of poetry is immense, because in poetry, where it is worthy of its high destinies, our race, as time goes on, will find an ever surer and surer stay. There is not a creed which is not shaken, not an accredited dogma which is not shown to be questionable, not a received tradition which does not threaten to dissolve. Our religion has materialized itself in the fact, in the supposed fact; it has attached its emotion to the fact, and now the fact is failing it. But for poetry the idea is everything; the rest is a world of illusion, of divine illusion. Poetry attaches its emotion to the idea; the idea *is* the fact. The strongest part of our religion today is its unconscious poetry.[1]

Let me be permitted to quote these words of my own, as uttering the thought which should, in my opinion, go with us and govern us in all our study of poetry. In the present work it is the course of one great contributory stream to the world-river of poetry that we are invited to follow. We are here invited to trace the stream of English poetry. But whether we set ourselves, as here, to follow only one of the several streams that make the mighty river of poetry, or whether we seek to know them all, our governing thought should be the same. We should conceive of poetry worthily, and more highly than it has been the custom to conceive of it. We should conceive of it as capable of higher uses, and called to higher destinies, than those which in general men have assigned to it hitherto. More and more mankind will discover that we have to turn to poetry to interpret life for us, to console us, to sustain us. Without poetry, our science will appear incomplete; and most of what now passes with us for religion and philosophy will be replaced by poetry. Science, I say, will appear incomplete without it. For finely and truly does Wordsworth call poetry "the impassioned expression which is in the countenance of all science"[2], and what is a countenance without its expression? Again, Wordsworth finely and truly calls poetry "the breath and finer spirit of all knowledge": our religion, parading evidences such as those on which the popular mind relies now; our philosophy, pluming itself on its reasonings about causation and finite and infinite being; what are they but the shadows and dreams and false shows of knowl-

[1]From the Introduction to *The Hundred Greatest Men* (1879). [Ed.]

[2]In "Preface to *Lyrical Ballads*"; see p. 309. [Ed.]

edge? The day will come when we shall wonder at ourselves for having trusted to them, for having taken them seriously; and the more we perceive their hollowness, the more we shall prize "the breath and finer spirit of knowledge" offered to us by poetry.

But if we conceive thus highly of the destinies of poetry, we must also set our standard for poetry high, since poetry, to be capable of fulfilling such high destinies, must be poetry of a high order of excellence. We must accustom ourselves to a high standard and to a strict judgment. Sainte-Beuve relates that Napoleon one day said, when somebody was spoken of in his presence as a charlatan: "Charlatan as much as you please; but where is there *not* charlatanism?" — "Yes," answers Sainte-Beuve, "in politics, in the art of governing mankind, that is perhaps true. But in the order of thought, in art, the glory, the eternal honour is that charlatanism shall find no entrance; herein lies the inviolableness of that noble portion of man's being." It is admirably said, and let us hold fast to it. In poetry, which is thought and art in one, it is the glory, the eternal honour, that charlatanism shall find no entrance; that this noble sphere be kept inviolate and inviolable. Charlatanism is for confusing or obliterating the distinctions between excellent and inferior, sound and unsound or only half-sound, true and untrue or only half-true. It is charlatanism, conscious or unconscious, whenever we confuse or obliterate these. And in poetry, more than anywhere else, it is unpermissible to confuse or obliterate them. For in poetry the distinction between excellent and inferior, sound and unsound or only half-sound, true and untrue or only half-true, is of paramount importance. It is of paramount importance because of the high destinies of poetry. In poetry, as a criticism of life under the conditions fixed for such a criticism by the laws of poetic truth and poetic beauty, the spirit of our race will find, we have said, as time goes on and as other helps fail, its consolation and stay. But the consolation and stay will be of power in proportion to the power of the criticism of life. And the criticism of life will be of power in proportion as the poetry conveying it is excellent rather than inferior, sound rather than unsound or half-sound, true rather than untrue or half-true.

The best poetry is what we want; the best poetry will be found to have a power of forming, sustaining, and delighting us, as nothing else can. A clearer, deeper sense of the best in poetry, and of the strength and joy to be drawn from it, is the most precious benefit which we can gather from a poetical collection such as the present. And yet in the very nature and conduct of such a collection there is inevitably something which tends to obscure in us the consciousness of what our benefit should be, and to distract us from the pursuit of it. We should therefore steadily set it before our minds at the outset, and should compel ourselves to revert constantly to the thought of it as we proceed.

Yes; constantly, in reading poetry, a sense for the best, the really excellent, and of the strength and joy to be drawn from it, should be present in our minds and should govern our estimate of what we read. But this real estimate, the only true one, is liable to be superseded, if we are not watchful, by two other kinds of estimate, the historic estimate and the personal estimate, both of which are fallacious. A poet or a poem may count to us historically, they may count to us on grounds personal to ourselves, and they may count to us really. They may count to us historically. The course of development of a nation's language, thought, and poetry, is profoundly interesting; and by regarding a poet's work as a stage in this course of development we may easily bring ourselves to make it of more importance as poetry than in itself it really is, we may come to use a language of quite exaggerated praise in criticizing it; in short, to overrate it. So arises in our poetic judgments the fallacy caused by the estimate which we may call historic. Then, again, a poet or a poem may count to us on grounds personal to ourselves. Our personal affinities, likings, and circumstances have great power to sway our estimates of this or that poet's work, and to make us attach more importance to it as poetry than in itself it really possesses, because to us it is, or has been, of high importance. Here also we overrate the object of our interest, and apply to it a language of praise which is quite exaggerated. And thus we get the source of a second fallacy in our poetic judgments — the fallacy caused by an estimate which we may call personal.

Both fallacies are natural. It is evident how naturally the study of the history and development of a poetry may incline a man to pause over reputations and works once conspicuous but now obscure, and to quarrel with a careless public for skipping, in obedience to mere tradition and habit, from one famous name or work in its natural poetry to another, ignorant of what it misses, and of the reason for keeping what it keeps, and of the whole process of growth in its poetry. The French have become diligent students of their own early poetry, which they long neglected; the study makes many of them dissatisfied with their so-called classical poetry, the court-tragedy of the seventeenth century, a poetry which Pellisson long ago reproached with its want of the true poetic stamp, with its *politesse stérile et rampante,* but which nevertheless has reigned in France as absolutely as if it had been the perfection of classical poetry indeed. The dissatisfaction is natural; yet a lively and accomplished critic, M.Charles d'Héricault, the editor of Clément Marot, goes too far when he says that "the cloud of glory playing round a classic is a mist as dangerous to the future of a literature as it is intolerable for the purposes of history." "It hinders," he goes on, "it hinders us from seeing more than one single point, the culminating and exceptional point; the summary, fictitious and arbitrary, of a thought and of a work. It substitutes a halo for a physiognomy, it puts a statue where there was once a man, and, hiding from us all trace of the labour, the attempts, the weaknesses, the failures, it claims not study but veneration; it does not show us how the thing is done, it imposes upon us a model. Above all, for the historian this creation of classic personages is inadmissible; for it withdraws the poet from his time, from his proper life, it breaks historical relationships, it blinds criticism by conventional admiration, and renders the investigation of literary origins unacceptable. It gives us a human personage no longer, but a God seated immovable amidst His perfect work, like Jupiter on Olympus; and hardly will it be possible for the young student, to whom such work is exhibited at such a distance from him, to believe that it did not issue ready made from that divine head."

All this is brilliantly and tellingly said, but we must plead for a distinction. Everything depends on the reality of a poet's classic character. If he is a dubious classic, let us sift him; if he is a false classic, let us explode him. But if he is a real classic, if his work belongs to the class of the very best (for this is the true and right meaning of the word *classic, classical*), then the great thing for us is to feel and enjoy his work as deeply as ever we can, and to appreciate the wide difference between it and all work which has not the same high character. This is what is salutary, this is what is formative; this is the great benefit to be got from the study of poetry. Everything which interferes with it, which hinders it, is injurious. True, we must read our classic with open eyes, and not with eyes blinded with superstition; we must perceive when his work comes short, when it drops out of the class of the very best, and we must rate it, in such cases, at its proper value. But the use of this negative criticism is not in itself, it is entirely in its enabling us to have a clearer sense and a deeper enjoyment of what is truly excellent. To trace the labour, the attempts, the weaknesses, the failures of a genuine classic, to acquaint oneself with his time and his life and his historical relationships, is mere literary dilettantism unless it has that clear sense and deeper enjoyment for its end. It may be said that the more we know about a classic the better we shall enjoy him; and, if we lived as long as Methuselah and had all of us heads of perfect clearness and wills of perfect steadfastness, this might be true in fact as it is plausible in theory. But the case here is much the same as the case with the Greek and Latin studies of our schooldays. The elaborate philological groundwork which we require them to lay is in theory an admirable preparation for appreciating the Greek and Latin authors worthily. The more thoroughly we lay the groundwork, the better we shall be able, it may be said, to enjoy the authors. True, if time were not so short, and schoolboys' wits not so soon tired and their power of attention exhausted;

only, as it is, the elaborate philological preparation goes on, but the authors are little known and less enjoyed. So with the investigator of "historic origins" in poetry. He ought to enjoy the true classic all the better for his investigations; he often is distracted from the enjoyment of the best, and with the less good he overbusies himself, and is prone to overrate it in proportion to the trouble which it has cost him.

The ideas of tracing historic origins and historical relationships cannot be absent from a compilation like the present. And naturally the poets to be exhibited in it will be assigned to those persons for exhibition who are known to prize them highly, rather than to those who have no special inclination towards them. Moreover, the very occupation with an author, and the business of exhibiting him, disposes us to affirm and amplify his importance. In the present work, therefore, we are sure of frequent temptation to adopt the historic estimate, or the personal estimate, and to forget the real estimate; which latter, nevertheless, we must employ if we are to make poetry yield us its full benefit. So high is that benefit, the benefit of clearly feeling and of deeply enjoying the really excellent, the truly classic in poetry, that we do well, I say, to set it fixedly before our minds as our object in studying poets and poetry, and to make the desire of attaining it the one principle to which, as the *Imitation*[3] says, whatever we may read or come to know, we always return. *Cum multa legeris et cognoveris, ad unum semper oportet redire principium.*

The historic estimate is likely in especial to affect our judgment and our language when we are dealing with ancient poets; the personal estimate when we are dealing with poets our contemporaries, or at any rate modern. The exaggerations due to the historic estimate are not in themselves, perhaps, of very much gravity. Their report hardly enters the general ear; probably they do not always impose even on the literary men who adopt them. But they lead to a dangerous abuse of language. So we hear Caedmon, amongst our own poets, compared to Milton. I have already noticed the enthusiasm of one accomplished French critic for "historic origins." Another eminent French critic, M. Vitet, comments upon that famous document of the early poetry of his nation, the *Chanson de Roland.* It is indeed a most interesting document. The *joculator* or *jongleur* Taillefer, who was with William the Conqueror's army at Hastings, marched before the Norman troops, so said the tradition, singing "of Charlemagne and of Roland and of Oliver, and of the vassals who died at Roncevaux"; and it is suggested that in the *Chanson de Roland* by one Turoldus or Théroulde, a poem preserved in a manuscript of the twelfth century in the Bodleian Library at Oxford, we have certainly the matter, perhaps even some of the words, of the chant which Taillefer sang. The poem has vigour and freshness; it is not without pathos. But M. Vitet is not satisfied with seeing in it a document of some poetic value, and of a very high historic and linguistic value; he sees in it a grand and beautiful work, a monument of epic genius. In its general design he finds the grandiose conception, in its details he finds the constant union of simplicity with greatness, which are the marks, he truly says, of the genuine epic, and distinguish it from the artificial epic of literary ages. One thinks of Homer; this is the sort of praise which is given to Homer, and justly given. Higher praise there cannot well be, and it is the praise due to epic poetry of the highest order only and to no other. Let us try, then, the *Chanson de Roland* at its best. Roland, mortally wounded, lays himself down under a pine-tree, with his face turned towards Spain and the enemy —

> De plusurs choses a remembrer li prist,
> De tantes teres cume li bers cunquist,
> De dulce France, des humes de sun lign,
> De Carlemagne sun seignor ki l'nurrit.[4]

That is primitive work, I repeat, with an undeniable poetic quality of its own. It deserves such praise, and such praise is sufficient for it. But now turn to Homer —

[3]Thomas à Kempis, *The Imitation of Christ.* [Ed.]

[4]"Then began he to call many things to remembrance, — all the lands which his valour conquered, and pleasant France, and the men of his lineage, and Charlemagne his liege lord who nourished him." — *Chanson de Roland,* iii.939–42. [Au.]

῝Ως φάτο· τοὺς δ' ἤδη κατέχεν φυσίζοος αἶα
ἐν Λακεδαίμονι αὖθι, φίλῃ ἐν πατρίδι γαίῃ.[5]

We are here in another world, another order of poetry altogether; here is rightly due such supreme praise as that which M. Vitet gives to the *Chanson de Roland*. If our words are to have any meaning, if our judgments are to have any solidity, we must not heap that supreme praise upon poetry of an order immeasurably inferior.

Indeed there can be no more useful help for discovering what poetry belongs to the class of the truly excellent, and can therefore do us most good, than to have always in one's mind lines and expressions of the great masters, and to apply them as a touchstone to other poetry. Of course we are not to require this other poetry to resemble them; it may be very dissimilar. But if we have any tact we shall find them, when we have lodged them well in our minds, an infallible touchstone for detecting the presence or absence of high poetic quality, and also the degree of this quality, in all other poetry which we may place beside them. Short passages, even single lines, will serve our turn quite sufficiently. Take the two lines which I have just quoted from Homer, the poet's comment on Helen's mention of her brothers; — or take his

ἆ δειλώ τί σφῶϊ δόμεν Πηλῆϊ ἄνακτι
θνητῷ; ὑμεῖς δ' ἐστόν ἀγήρω τ' ἀθανάτω τε.
ἦ ἵνα δυστήνοισι μετ' ἀνδράσιν ἄλγε'
ἔχητον;[6]

the address of Zeus to the horses of Peleus; — or take finally his

Καὶ σέ, γέρον, τὸ πρὶν μὲν ἀκούομεν ὄλβιον
εἶναι.[7]

the words of Achilles to Priam, a suppliant before him. Take that incomparable line and a half of Dante, Ugolino's tremendous words —

Io no piangeva; sì dentro impietrai.
Piangevan elli . . .[8]

take the lovely words of Beatrice to Virgil —

Io son fatta da Dio, sua mercè, tale,
Che la vostra miseria non mi tange,
Nè fiamma d' esto incendio non m' assale . . .[9]

take the simple, but perfect, single line —

In la sua volontade è nostra pace.[10]

Take of Shakespeare a line or two of Henry the Fourth's expostulation with sleep —

Wilt thou upon the high and giddy mast
Seal up the ship-boy's eyes, and rock his brains
In cradle of the rude imperious surge . . .[11]

and take, as well, Hamlet's dying request to Horatio —

If thou didst ever hold me in thy heart,
Absent thee from felicity awhile,
And in this harsh world draw thy breath in pain
To tell my story . . .[12]

Take of Milton that Miltonic passage —

Darken'd so, yet shone
Above them all the archangel; but his face
Deep scars of thunder had intrench'd, and care
Sat on his faded cheek . . .[13]

add two such lines as —

And courage never to submit or yield
And what is else not to be overcome . . .[14]

and finish with the exquisite close to the loss of Proserpine, the loss

[5]"So said she; they long since in Earth's soft arms were reposing,/There, in their own dear land, their fatherland, Lacedaemon." *Iliad,* iii. 243, 244 (translated by Dr. Hawtrey). [Au.]

[6]"Ah, unhappy pair, why gave we you to King Peleus, to a mortal? but ye are without old age, and immortal. Was it that with men born in misery ye might have sorrow?" — *Iliad,* xvii. 443–45. [Au.]

[7]"Nay, and thou too, old man, in former days wast, as we hear, happy." — *Iliad,* xxiv. 543. [Au.]

[8]"I wailed not, so of stone grew I within; — *they* wailed." — *Inferno,* xxxiii. 39, 40. [Au.]

[9]"Of such sort hath God, thanked be His mercy, made me, that your misery toucheth me not, neither doth the flame of this fire strike me." — *Inferno,* ii. 91–93. [Au.]

[10]"In His will is our peace." — *Paradiso,* iii. 85. [Au.]

[11]Shakespeare, *2 Henry IV,* III.i.18–20. [Ed.]

[12]Shakespeare, *Hamlet,* V.ii.357–60. [Ed.]

[13]Milton, *Paradise Lost,* 1:599–602. [Ed.]

[14]Milton, *Paradise Lost,* 1:108–9. [Ed.]

. . . which cost Ceres all that pain
To seek her through the world.[15]

These few lines, if we have tact and can use them, are enough even of themselves to keep clear and sound our judgments about poetry, to save us from fallacious estimates of it, to conduct us to a real estimate.

The specimens I have quoted differ widely from one another, but they have in common this: the possession of the very highest poetical quality. If we are thoroughly penetrated by their power, we shall find that we have acquired a sense enabling us, whatever poetry may be laid before us, to feel the degree in which a high poetical quality is present or wanting there. Critics give themselves great labour to draw out what in the abstract constitutes the characters of a high quality of poetry. It is much better simply to have recourse to concrete examples; — to take specimens of poetry of the high, the very highest quality, and to say: The characters of a high quality of poetry are what is expressed *there*. They are far better recognized by being felt in the verse of the master, than by being perused in the prose of the critic. Nevertheless if we are urgently pressed to give some critical account of them, we may safely, perhaps, venture on laying down, not indeed how and why the characters arise, but where and in what they arise. They are in the matter and substance of the poetry, and they are in its manner and style. Both of these, the substance and matter on the one hand, the style and manner on the other, have a mark, an accent, of high beauty, worth, and power. But if we are asked to define this mark and accent in the abstract, our answer must be: No, for we should thereby be darkening the question, not clearing it. The mark and accent are as given by the substance and matter of that poetry, by the style and manner of that poetry, and of all other poetry which is akin to it in quality.

Only one thing we may add as to the substance and matter of poetry, guiding ourselves by Aristotle's profound observation that the superiority of poetry over history consists in its possessing a higher truth and a higher seriousness (φιλοσοφώτερον καὶ σπουδαιότερον).[16] Let us add, therefore, to what we have said, this: that the substance and matter of the best poetry acquire their special character from possessing, in an eminent degree, truth and seriousness. We may add yet further, what is in itself evident, that to the style and manner of the best poetry their special character, their accent, is given by their diction, and, even yet more, by their movement. And though we distinguish between the two characters, the two accents, of superiority, yet they are nevertheless vitally connected one with the other. The superior character of truth and seriousness, in the matter and substance of the best poetry, is inseparable from the superiority of diction and movement marking its style and manner. The two superiorities are closely related, and are in steadfast proportion one to the other. So far as high poetic truth and seriousness are wanting to a poet's matter and substance, so far also, we may be sure, will a high poetic stamp of diction and movement be wanting to his style and manner. In proportion as this high stamp of diction and movement, again, is absent from a poet's style and manner, we shall find, also, that high poetic truth and seriousness are absent from his substance and matter.

So stated, these are but dry generalities; their whole force lies in their application. And I could wish every student of poetry to make the application of them for himself. Made by himself, the application would impress itself upon his mind far more deeply than if made by me. Neither will my limits allow me to make any full application of the generalities above propounded; but in the hope of bringing out, at any rate, some significance in them, and of establishing an important principle more firmly by their means, I will, in the space which remains to me, follow rapidly from the commencement the course of our English poetry with them in my view.

[15]Milton, *Paradise Lost*, 4:271–72. [Ed.]

[16]Aristotle, *Poetics*, Chapter 9. [Ed.]

Friedrich Nietzsche

1844–1900

Friedrich Wilhelm Nietzsche was born in 1844, the son of a Saxon pastor. He was educated at the universities of Bonn and Leipzig, took his degrees in philology, and was appointed professor at the University of Basel in 1869. The selection included here is from Nietzsche's first book, *The Birth of Tragedy from the Spirit of Music* (1872). *The Birth of Tragedy* is unusual among Nietzsche's works in having a sustained and coherent argument: In his later works, he intentionally became more and more aphoristic, conveying his thought in brief flashes and ironic hints. Because he died relatively young of complications from tertiary syphilis and because of nervous breakdowns in the decade before his death, some of his critics have suggested that he was incapable of sustained argument almost from the outset of his career. This is unfair to Nietzsche, who, like Plato, was in rebellion against the stultifying philosophical treatise. His aim was to stimulate thought in others, and for this he was willing to risk being misunderstood. As a result, he has been misunderstood as few philosophers ever have been. Nietzsche was neither nationalistic nor racist nor anti-Semitic, for example, so it is hideously ironic that less than a generation after his death, his ideas, perverted almost beyond recognition, were adopted as the pet philosophy of the Nazi regime.

If there is any central theme in Nietzsche's philosophy it is his opposition to the complacent Victorian faith in progress through a rationalistic reordering of society. He saw as basic to human nature darker motives (like the will-to-power) than his utilitarian contemporaries were willing to acknowledge, but he also saw the possibility of self-sacrifice and transcendence. These themes appear most strongly in his ecstatic tract, *Thus Spake Zarathustra* (1883–92), along with *The Joyful Wisdom* (1882) and *Beyond Good and Evil* (1886). Like Dostoevsky, Nietzsche was a reactionary whose insights into the obscene hunger of the human soul strikingly prefigured the discoveries of Freud.

APOLLO AND DIONYSUS

Nietzsche's essay begins with two opposed symbolic images: Apollo and Dionysus, dream and intoxication, plastic arts and music. The obvious question is why they should divide the aesthetic world between them. This dichotomy is best understood if we see Nietzsche as a follower — with many qualifications — of Arthur Schopenhauer. Schopenhauer's monumental treatise, *The World as Will and Idea* (1819), had posited that human life reverberates between the extremes of boredom and longing — most often the latter, given the competition among the many hungry wills inhabiting the universe. To be alive, Nietzsche agreed, was to be in a state of want: The image of Tantalus, forever groping at the desired food and drink beyond his grasp, was for Nietzsche an image of humankind. Existence was, in a word, tragic.

Nietzsche saw art as civilization's most effective means of coping with this tragedy of existence. Art works by taming dream and intoxication, two primitive methods of coping with the hungry will. In dream the hunger is satiated; in intoxication the self is obliterated. In dream (as Freud and many others had noted) we retreat into a fantasy world in which our desires are all fulfilled, as they cannot be in reality. In intoxication we do not lose our desires so much as we lose *ourselves:* When drunk, our sense of self — our awareness of an inside and an outside, of a consciousness differentiated from the Other — fades away as the ego is annihilated.

THE BIRTH, AND DEATH, AND REBIRTH, OF TRAGEDY

Most of Nietzsche's treatise is a historical essay on the development of Greek tragedy out of the religious ritual of Dionysus. It is startling to think that he developed this notion by an intuitive leap from a few hints in the classics, long before classical research established the religious origins and the ritual nature of the drama.

In the beginning was music, a chorus of dancing satyrs rhythmically, musically expressing their devotion to the god of intoxication, each Greek citizen losing his individuality within the satyr chorus. The choric dance then begins to include song, takes on language and, with it, the plastic images of Apollonian dream. For Nietzsche the essence of tragedy is now already present, before anything like a play exists, in the "Dionysiac chorus which again and again discharges itself in Apollonian images." Later still the god himself is impersonated by the choral leader, who becomes in effect the first actor. From here to the enactment of story and the addition of the second and third actors — to the drama of Aeschylus and Sophocles — it is only a short step: mere complications.

For Nietzsche, tragedy reaches its height with Aeschylus and Sophocles. Its essence in the fusion of Apollonian and Dionysiac impulses begins to be destroyed almost immediately thereafter. Nietzsche's villains are the individualism of Euripides and the rationalism of Socrates, which were consistent with the lyrics of Apollo but not with the music of Dionysus. Individualism and rationalism infected Greek civilization and the Roman and Western European civilizations that followed. Tragedy now began to explore the causes of the errors of highly placed individuals rather than expressing the essence of all human life. Even music itself began in the nineteenth century to become plastic and descriptive — Apollonian rather than Dionysian in character. This perversion of the tragic hit bottom, for Nietzsche, in the Italian opera.

The antidote for all this Nietzsche found in the music-dramas of Richard Wagner, who by 1871 had already written *Tristan und Isolde* and *Die Meistersinger* and had just produced *Das Rheingold* and *Die Walküre,* the first two segments of his massive cycle based on the *Nibelungenlied.* In Wagner's use of myth and universal types, and above all in his return of the leading role to the communal spirit of music rather than the individuation of the Apollonian image, Nietzsche saw the possibility for a rebirth of the healing qualities of art that had been lost when Greek tragedy declined. This enthusiasm with Wagner was to be short-lived. By the second edition of *The Birth of Tragedy,* Nietzsche had broken with Wagner, disgusted by his nationalism and the sickly spiritualism of his last opera, *Parsifal.* Nevertheless,

Nietzsche's aesthetic ideas, his notions about the place of the tragic in human life, remain profoundly moving.

Selected Bibliography

Danto, Arthur. *Nietzsche as a Philosopher.* New York: Macmillan, 1965.

Donadio, Stephen. *Nietzsche, Henry James, and the Artistic Will.* New York: Oxford University Press, 1976.

Gilman, Sander L. *Nietzschean Parody: An Introduction to Reading Nietzsche.* Bonn: Bouvier Verlag, 1976.

Jaspers, Karl. *Nietzsche: An Introduction to the Understanding of His Philosophical Activity.* Tucson: University of Arizona Press, 1965.

Kaufmann, Walter. *Nietzsche: Philosopher, Psychologist, Antichrist,* 3rd ed. Princeton: Princeton University Press, 1968.

Ludovici, Anthony. *Nietzsche and Art.* Boston: J. W. Luce, 1912.

Megill, Allan. *Prophets of Extremity: Nietzsche, Heidegger, Foucault, Derrida.* Berkeley: University of California Press, 1985.

Nehamas, Alexander. *Nietzsche: Life as Literature.* Cambridge: Harvard University Press, 1985.

Silk, M. S. *Nietzsche on Tragedy.* Cambridge and New York: Cambridge University Press, 1981.

From *The Birth of Tragedy from the Spirit of Music*

I

Much will have been gained for esthetics once we have succeeded in apprehending directly — rather than merely *ascertaining* — that art owes its continuous evolution to the Apollonian-Dionysiac duality, even as the propagation of the species depends on the duality of the sexes, their constant conflicts and periodic acts of reconciliation. I have borrowed my adjectives from the Greeks, who developed their mystical doctrines of art through plausible *embodiments,* not through purely conceptual means. It is by those two art-sponsoring deities, Apollo and Dionysos, that we are made to recognize the tremendous split, as regards both origins and objectives, between the plastic, Apollonian arts and the non-visual art of music inspired by Dionysos. The two creative tendencies developed alongside one another, usually in fierce opposition, each by its taunts forcing the other to more energetic production, both perpetuating in a discordant concord that agon[1] which the term *art* but feebly denominates: until at last, by the thaumaturgy of an Hellenic act of will, the pair accepted the yoke of marriage and, in this condition, begot Attic tragedy, which exhibits the salient features of both parents.

To reach a closer understanding of both these tendencies, let us begin by viewing them as the separate art realms of *dream* and *intoxication,* two physiological phenomena standing toward one another in much the same relationship as the Apollonian and Dionysiac. It was in a dream, according to Lucretius, that the marvelous gods and

Translated by Francis Golffing.

[1]Tragic struggle. [Ed.]

goddesses first presented themselves to the minds of men. That great sculptor, Phidias, beheld in a dream the entrancing bodies of more-than-human beings, and likewise, if anyone had asked the Greek poets about the mystery of poetic creation, they too would have referred him to dreams and instructed him much as Hans Sachs instructs us in *Die Meistersinger:*

> My friend, it is the poet's work
> Dreams to interpret and to mark.
> Believe me that man's true conceit
> In a dream becomes complete:
> All poetry we ever read
> Is but true dreams interpreted.[2]

The fair illusion of the dream sphere, in the production of which every man proves himself an accomplished artist, is a precondition not only of all plastic art, but even, as we shall see presently, of a wide range of poetry. Here we enjoy an immediate apprehension of form, all shapes speak to us directly, nothing seems indifferent or redundant. Despite the high intensity with which these dream realities exist for us, we still have a residual sensation that they are illusions; at least such has been my experience — and the frequency, not to say normality, of the experience is borne out in many passages of the poets. Men of philosophical disposition are known for their constant premonition that our everyday reality, too, is an illusion, hiding another, totally different kind of reality. It was Schopenhauer who considered the ability to view at certain times all men and things as mere phantoms or dream images to be the true mark of philosophic talent. The person who is responsive to the stimuli of art behaves toward the reality of dream much the way the philosopher behaves toward the reality of existence: he observes exactly and enjoys his observations, for it is by these images that he interprets life, by these processes that he rehearses it. Nor is it by pleasant images only that such plausible connections are made: the whole divine comedy of life, including its somber aspects, its sudden balkings, impish accidents, anxious expectations, moves past him, not quite like a shadow play — for it is he himself, after all, who lives and suffers through these scenes — yet never without giving a fleeting sense of illusion; and I imagine that many persons have reassured themselves amidst the perils of dream by calling out, "It is a dream! I want it to go on." I have even heard of people spinning out the causality of one and the same dream over three or more successive nights. All these facts clearly bear witness that our innermost being, the common substratum of humanity, experiences dreams with deep delight and a sense of real necessity. This deep and happy sense of the necessity of dream experiences was expressed by the Greeks in the image of Apollo. Apollo is at once the god of all plastic powers and the soothsaying god. He who is etymologically the "lucent" one, the god of light, reigns also over the fair illusion of our inner world of fantasy. The perfection of these conditions in contrast to our imperfectly understood waking reality, as well as our profound awareness of nature's healing powers during the interval of sleep and dream, furnishes a symbolic analogue to the soothsaying faculty and quite generally to the arts, which make life possible and worth living. But the image of Apollo must incorporate that thin line which the dream image may not cross, under penalty of becoming pathological, of imposing itself on us as crass reality: a discreet limitation, a freedom from all extravagant urges, the sapient tranquillity of the plastic god. His eye must be sunlike, in keeping with his origin. Even at those moments when he is angry and ill-tempered there lies upon him the consecration of fair illusion. In an eccentric way one might say of Apollo what Schopenhauer says, in the first part of *The World as Will and Idea,* of man caught in the veil of Maya:[3] "Even as on an immense, raging sea, assailed by huge wave crests, a man sits in a little rowboat trusting his frail craft, so, amidst the furious torments of this world, the individual sits tranquilly, supported by the *principium individuationis*[4] and relying on it." One might say that the unshakable

[2]Richard Wagner, *The Mastersingers of Nuremberg,* III.i.99–104. [Ed.]

[3]Illusion. [Ed.]

[4]"The principle of individuation": that which differentiates the Self from the Other, the ego from the outside world. [Ed.]

confidence in that principle has received its most magnificent expression in Apollo, and that Apollo himself may be regarded as the marvelous divine image of the *principium individuationis,* whose looks and gestures radiate the full delight, wisdom, and beauty of "illusion."

In the same context Schopenhauer has described for us the tremendous awe which seizes man when he suddenly begins to doubt the cognitive modes of experience, in other words, when in a given instance the law of causation seems to suspend itself. If we add to this awe the glorious transport which arises in man, even from the very depths of nature, at the shattering of the *principium individuationis,* then we are in a position to apprehend the essence of Dionysiac rapture, whose closest analogy is furnished by physical intoxication. Dionysiac stirrings arise either through the influence of those narcotic potions of which all primitive races speak in their hymns, or through the powerful approach of spring, which penetrates with joy the whole frame of nature. So stirred, the individual forgets himself completely. It is the same Dionysiac power which in medieval Germany drove ever increasing crowds of people singing and dancing from place to place; we recognize in these St. John's and St. Vitus' dancers the bacchic choruses of the Greeks, who had their precursors in Asia Minor and as far back as Babylon and the orgiastic Sacaea.[5] There are people who, either from lack of experience or out of sheer stupidity, turn away from such phenomena, and, strong in the sense of their own sanity, label them either mockingly or pityingly "endemic diseases." These benighted souls have no idea how cadaverous and ghostly their "sanity" appears as the intense throng of Dionysiac revelers sweeps past them.

Not only does the bond between man and man come to be forged once more by the magic of the Dionysiac rite, but nature itself, long alienated or subjugated, rises again to celebrate the reconciliation with her prodigal son, man. The earth offers its gifts voluntarily, and the savage beasts of mountain and desert approach in peace. The chariot of Dionysos is bedecked with flowers and garlands; panthers and tigers stride beneath his yoke. If one were to convert Beethoven's "Paean to Joy"[6] into a painting, and refuse to curb the imagination when that multitude prostrates itself reverently in the dust, one might form some apprehension of Dionysiac ritual. Now the slave emerges as a freeman; all the rigid, hostile walls which either necessity or despotism has erected between men are shattered. Now that the gospel of universal harmony is sounded, each individual becomes not only reconciled to his fellow but actually at one with him — as though the veil of Maya had been torn apart and there remained only shreds floating before the vision of mystical Oneness. Man now expresses himself through song and dance as the member of a higher community; he has forgotten how to walk, how to speak, and is on the brink of taking wing as he dances. Each of his gestures betokens enchantment; through him sounds a supernatural power, the same power which makes the animals speak and the earth render up milk and honey. He feels himself to be godlike and strides with the same elation and ecstasy as the gods he has seen in his dreams. No longer the *artist,* he has himself become a *work of art:* the productive power of the whole universe is now manifest in his transport, to the glorious satisfaction of the primordial One. The finest clay, the most precious marble — man — is here kneaded and hewn, and the chisel blows of the Dionysiac world artist are accompanied by the cry of the Eleusinian mystagogues: "Do you fall on your knees, multitudes, do you divine your creator?"[7]

III

In order to comprehend this we must take down the elaborate edifice of Apollonian culture stone by stone until we discover its foundations. At first the eye is struck by the marvelous shapes of the Olympian gods who stand upon its pediments, and whose exploits, in shining bas-relief,

[5]The Babylonian "day of the false king" — a kind of Saturnalia. [Ed.]

[6]The setting of Schiller's "Ode to Joy" takes up most of the final movement of the Ninth Symphony. [Ed.]

[7]The Eleusinian Mysteries were a cult devoted to the goddess Persephone which celebrated the coming of winter and the return of spring; the quotation is from Schiller's "Ode to Joy." [Ed.]

adorn its friezes. The fact that among them we find Apollo as one god among many, making no claim to a privileged position, should not mislead us. The same drive that found its most complete representation in Apollo generated the whole Olympian world, and in this sense we may consider Apollo the father of that world. But what was the radical need out of which that illustrious society of Olympian beings sprang?

Whoever approaches the Olympians with a different religion in his heart, seeking moral elevation, sanctity, spirituality, loving-kindness, will presently be forced to turn away from them in ill-humored disappointment. Nothing in these deities reminds us of asceticism, high intellect, or duty: we are confronted by luxuriant, triumphant *existence,* which deifies the good and the bad indifferently. And the beholder may find himself dismayed in the presence of such overflowing life and ask himself what potion these heady people must have drunk in order to behold, in whatever direction they looked, Helen laughing back at them, the beguiling image of their own existence. But we shall call out to this beholder, who had already turned his back: Don't go! Listen first to what the Greeks themselves have to say of this life, which spreads itself before you with such puzzling serenity. An old legend has it that King Midas hunted a long time in the woods for the wise Silenus, companion of Dionysos, without being able to catch him. When he had finally caught him the king asked him what he considered man's greatest good. The daemon remained sullen and uncommunicative until finally, forced by the king, he broke into a shrill laugh and spoke: "Ephemeral wretch, begotten by accident and toil, why do you force me to tell you what it would be your greatest boon not to hear? What would be best for you is quite beyond your reach: not to have been born, not to *be,* to be *nothing.* But the second best is to die soon."

What is the relation of the Olympian gods to this popular wisdom? It is that of the entranced vision of the martyr to his torment.

Now the Olympian magic mountain[8] opens itself before us, showing us its very roots. The Greeks were keenly aware of the terrors and horrors of existence; in order to be able to live at all they had to place before them the shining fantasy of the Olympians. Their tremendous distrust of the titanic forces of nature: *Moira,*[9] mercilessly enthroned beyond the knowable world; the vulture which fed upon the great philanthropist Prometheus; the terrible lot drawn by wise Oedipus; the curse on the house of Atreus which brought Orestes to the murder of his mother: that whole Panic[10] philosophy, in short, with its mythic examples, by which the gloomy Etruscans perished, the Greeks conquered — or at least hid from view — again and again by means of this artificial Olympus. In order to live at all the Greeks had to construct these deities. The Apollonian need for beauty had to develop the Olympian hierarchy of joy by slow degrees from the original titanic hierarchy of terror, as roses are seen to break from a thorny thicket. How else could life have been borne by a race so hypersensitive, so emotionally intense, so equipped for suffering? The same drive which called art into being as a completion and consummation of existence, and as a guarantee of further existence, gave rise also to the Olympian realm which acted as a transfiguring mirror to the Hellenic will. The gods justified human life by living it themselves — the only satisfactory theodicy[11] ever invented. To exist in the clear sunlight of such deities was now felt to be the highest good, and the only real grief suffered by Homeric man was inspired by the thought of leaving that sunlight, especially when the departure seemed imminent. Now it became possible to stand the wisdom of Silenus on its head and proclaim that it was the worst evil for man to die soon, and second worst for him to die at all. Such laments as arise now arise over short-lived Achilles, over the generations ephemeral as leaves, the decline of the heroic age. It is not unbecoming to even the greatest hero to yearn for an afterlife, though it be as a day laborer. So impetuously, during the Apollonian

[8]The Zauberberg was the mountain where Venus lived, to which the troubador Tannhäuser was attracted in the medieval legend. Nietzsche uses it as a symbol for a fantasy world. [Ed.]

[9]Destiny. [Ed.]

[10]Relating to Pan, the god of Nature. [Ed.]

[11]Explanation of divine activity. [Ed.]

phase, does man's will desire to remain on earth, so identified does he become with existence, that even his lament turns to a song of praise.

It should have become apparent by now that the harmony with nature which we late-comers regard with such nostalgia, and for which Schiller has coined the cant term *naïve,*[12] is by no means a simple and inevitable condition to be found at the gateway to every culture, a kind of paradise. Such a belief could have been endorsed only by a period for which Rousseau's Emile was an artist and Homer just such an artist nurtured in the bosom of nature. Whenever we encounter "naïveté" in art, we are face to face with the ripest fruit of Apollonian culture — which must always triumph first over titans, kill monsters, and overcome the somber contemplation of actuality, the intense susceptibility to suffering, by means of illusions strenuously and zestfully entertained. But how rare are the instances of true naïveté, of that complete identification with the beauty of appearance! It is this achievement which makes Homer so magnificent — Homer, who, as a single individual, stood to Apollonian popular culture in the same relation as the individual dream artist to the oneiric capacity of a race and of nature generally. The naïveté of Homer must be viewed as a complete victory of Apollonian illusion. Nature often uses illusions of this sort in order to accomplish its secret purposes. The true goal is covered over by a phantasm. We stretch out our hands to the latter, while nature, aided by our deception, attains the former. In the case of the Greeks it was the will wishing to behold itself in the work of art, in the transcendence of genius; but in order so to behold itself its creatures had first to view themselves as glorious, to transpose themselves to a higher sphere, without having that sphere of pure contemplation either challenge them or upbraid them with insufficiency. It was in that sphere of beauty that the Greeks saw the Olympians as their mirror images; it was by means of that esthetic mirror that the Greek will opposed suffering and the somber wisdom of suffering which always accompanies artistic talent. As a monument to its victory stands Homer, the naïve artist.

[12]See Schiller, "On Naive and Sentimental Poetry," p. 294. [Ed.]

IV

We can learn something about the naïve artist through the analogy of dream. We can imagine the dreamer as he calls out to himself, still caught in the illusion of his dream and without disturbing it, "This is a dream, and I want to go on dreaming," and we can infer, on the one hand, that he takes deep delight in the contemplation of his dream, and, on the other, that he must have forgotten the day, with its horrible importunity, so to enjoy his dream. Apollo, the interpreter of dreams, will furnish the clue to what is happening here. Although of the two halves of life — the waking and the dreaming — the former is generally considered not only the more important but the only one which is truly lived, I would, at the risk of sounding paradoxical, propose the opposite view. The more I have come to realize in nature those omnipotent formative tendencies and, with them, an intense longing for illusion, the more I feel inclined to the hypothesis that the original Oneness, the ground of Being, ever-suffering and contradictory, time and again has need of rapt vision and delightful illusion to redeem itself. Since we ourselves are the very stuff of such illusions, we must view ourselves as the truly nonexistent, that is to say, as a perpetual unfolding in time, space, and causality — what we label "empiric reality." But if, for the moment, we abstract from our own reality, viewing our empiric existence, as well as the existence of the world at large, as the *idea* of the original Oneness, produced anew each instant, then our dreams will appear to us as illusions of illusions, hence as a still higher form of satisfaction of the original desire for illusion. It is for this reason that the very core of nature takes such a deep delight in the naïve artist and the naïve work of art, which likewise is merely the illusion of an illusion. Raphael, himself one of those immortal "naïve" artists, in a symbolic canvas has illustrated that reduction of illusion to further illusion which is the original act of the naïve artist and at the same time of all Apollonian culture. In the lower half of his *Transfiguration,* through the figures of the possessed boy, the despairing bearers, the helpless, terrified disciples, we see a reflection of original pain, the sole ground of being: "illusion" here is a reflection of eternal contradiction, begetter of all things. From this illusion there rises, like the fragrance of ambrosia, a new illusory world, invisible to those enmeshed in the first: a radiant vision of pure delight, a rapt seeing through wide-open eyes. Here we have, in a great symbol of art, both the fair world of Apollo and its substratum, the terrible wisdom of Silenus, and we can comprehend intuitively how they mutually require one another. But Apollo appears to us once again as the apotheosis of the *principium individuationis,* in whom the eternal goad of the original Oneness, namely its redemption through illusion, accomplishes itself. With august gesture the god shows us how there is need for a whole world of torment in order for the individual to produce the redemptive vision and to sit quietly in his rocking rowboat in mid-sea, absorbed in contemplation.

If this apotheosis of individuation is to be read in normative terms, we may infer that there is one norm only: the individual — or, more precisely, the observance of the limits of the individual: *sophrosyne.* As a moral deity Apollo demands self-control from his people and, in order to observe such self-control, a knowledge of self. And so we find that the esthetic necessity of beauty is accompanied by the imperatives, "Know thyself," and "Nothing too much." Conversely, excess and *hubris* come to be regarded as the hostile spirits of the non-Apollonian sphere, hence as properties of the pre-Apollonian era — the age of Titans — and the extra-Apollonian world, that is to say the world of the barbarians. It was because of his Titanic love of man that Prometheus had to be devoured by vultures; it was because of his extravagant wisdom which succeeded in solving the riddle of the Sphinx that Oedipus had to be cast into a whirlpool of crime: in this fashion does the Delphic god interpret the Greek past.

The effects of the Dionysiac spirit struck the Apollonian Greeks as titanic and barbaric; yet they could not disguise from themselves the fact that they were essentially akin to those deposed Titans and heroes. They felt more than that: their whole existence, with its temperate beauty, rested upon a base of suffering and *knowledge* which had been hidden from them until the reinstatement of Dionysos uncovered it once more. And lo and behold! Apollo found it impossible to live without Dionysos. The elements of titanism and barbarism turned out to be quite as fundamental as the Apollonian element. And now let us imagine how the ecstatic sounds of the Dionysiac rites penetrated ever more enticingly into that artificially restrained and discreet world of illusion, how this clamor expressed the whole outrageous gamut of nature — delight, grief, knowledge — even to the most piercing cry; and then let us imagine how the Apollonian artist with his thin, monotonous harp music must have sounded beside the demoniac chant of the multitude! The muses presiding over the illusory arts paled before an art which enthusiastically told the truth, and the wisdom of Silenus cried "Woe!" against the serene Olympians. The individual, with his limits and moderations, forgot himself in the Dionysiac vortex and became oblivious to the laws of Apollo. Indiscreet extravagance revealed itself as truth, and contradiction, a delight born of pain, spoke out of the bosom of nature. Wherever the Dionysiac voice was heard, the Apollonian norm seemed suspended or destroyed. Yet it is equally true that, in those places where the first assault was withstood, the prestige and majesty of the Delphic god appeared more rigid and threatening than before. The only way I am able to view Doric art and the Doric state[13] is as a perpetual military encampment of the Apollonian forces. An art so defiantly austere, so ringed about with fortifications — an education so military and exacting — a polity so ruthlessly cruel — could endure only in a continual state of resistance against the titanic and barbaric menace of Dionysos.

Up to this point I have developed at some length a theme which was sounded at the beginning of this essay: how the Dionysiac and Apollonian elements, in a continuous chain of creations, and enhancing the other, dominated the Hellenic mind; how from the Iron Age, with its battles of Titans and its austere popular philoso-

[13]Sparta. [Ed.]

phy, there developed under the aegis of Apollo and Homeric world of beauty; how this "naïve" splendor was then absorbed once more by the Dionysiac torrent, and how, face to face, with this new power, the Apollonian code rigidified into the majesty of Doric art and contemplation. If the earlier phase of Greek history may justly be broken down into four major artistic epochs dramatizing the battle between the two hostile principles, then we must inquire further (lest Doric art appear to us as the acme and final goal of all these striving tendencies) what was the true end toward which that evolution moved. And our eyes will come to rest on the sublime and much lauded achievement of the dramatic dithyramb and Attic tragedy, as the common goal of both urges; whose mysterious marriage, after long discord, ennobled itself with such a child, at once Antigone and Cassandra.[14]

V

We are now approaching the central concern of our inquiry, which has as its aim an understanding of the Dionysiac-Apollonian spirit, or at least an intuitive comprehension of the mystery which made this conjunction possible. Our first question must be: where in the Greek world is the new seed first to be found which was later to develop into tragedy and the dramatic dithyramb? Greek antiquity gives us a pictorial clue when it represents in statues, on cameos, etc., Homer and Archilochus side by side as ancestors and torchbearers of Greek poetry, in the certainty that only these two are to be regarded as truly original minds, from whom a stream of fire flowed onto the entire later Greek world. Homer, the hoary dreamer, caught in utter abstraction, prototype of the Apollonian naïve artist, stares in amazement at the passionate head of Archilochus, soldierly servant of the Muses, knocked about by fortune. All that more recent esthetics has been able to add by way of interpretation is that here the "objective" artist is confronted by the first "subjective" artist. We find this interpretation of little use, since to us the subjective artist is simply the bad artist, and since we demand above all, in every genre and range of art, a triumph over subjectivity, deliverance from the self, the silencing of every personal will and desire; since, in fact, we cannot imagine the smallest genuine art work lacking objectivity and disinterested contemplation. For this reason our esthetic must first solve the following problem: how is the lyrical poet at all possible as artist — he who, according to the experience of all times, always says "I" and recites to us the entire chromatic scale of his passions and appetites? It is this Archilochus who most disturbs us, placed there beside Homer, with the stridor of his hate and mockery, the drunken outbursts of his desire. Isn't he — the first artist to be called subjective — for that reason the veritable nonartist? How, then, are we to explain the reverence in which he was held as a poet, the honor done him by the Delphic oracle, that seat of "objective" art, in a number of very curious sayings?

Schiller has thrown some light on his own manner of composition by a psychological observation which seems inexplicable to himself without, however, giving him pause. Schiller confessed that, prior to composing, he experienced not a logically connected series of images but rather a *musical mood*. "With me emotion is at the beginning without clear and definite ideas; those ideas do not arise until later on. A certain musical disposition of mind comes first, and after follows the poetical idea." If we enlarge on this, taking into account the most important phenomenon of ancient poetry, by which I mean that union — nay identity — everywhere considered natural, between musician and poet (alongside which our modern poetry appears as the statue of a god without a head), then we may, on the basis of the esthetics adumbrated earlier, explain the lyrical poet in the following manner. He is, first and foremost, a Dionysiac artist, become wholly identified with the original Oneness, its pain and contradiction, and producing a replica of that Oneness as music, if music may legitimately be seen as a repetition of the world; however, this music becomes visible to him again, as in a dream similitude, through the Apollonian dream influence. That reflection, without image or idea, or original pain in music, with its redemption

[14]The dutiful Antigone may represent the Apollonian principle, the possessed Cassandra the Dionysiac. [Ed.]

through illusion, now produces a second reflection as a single simile or example. The artist had abrogated his subjectivity earlier, during the Dionysiac phase: the image which now reveals to him his oneness with the heart of the world is a dream scene showing forth vividly, together with original pain, the original delight of illusion. The "I" thus sounds out of the depth of being; what recent writers on esthetics speak of as "subjectivity" is a mere figment. When Archilochus, the first lyric poet of the Greeks, hurls both his frantic love and his contempt at the daughters of Lycambes, it is not his own passion that we see dancing before us in an orgiastic frenzy: we see Dionysos and the maenads, we see the drunken reveler Archilochus, sunk down in sleep — as Euripides describes him for us in the *Bacchae,* asleep on a high mountain meadow, in the midday sun — and now Apollo approaches him and touches him with his laurel. The sleeper's enchantment through Dionysiac music now begins to emit sparks of imagery, poems which, at their point of highest evolution, will bear the name of tragedies and dramatic dithyrambs.

The sculptor, as well as his brother, the epic poet, is committed to the pure contemplation of images. The Dionysiac musician, himself imageless, is nothing but original pain and reverberation of the image. Out of this mystical process of un-selving, the poet's spirit feels a whole world of images and similitudes arise, which are quite different in hue, causality, and pace from the images of the sculptor or narrative poet. While the latter lives in those images and only in them, with joyful complacence, and never tires of scanning them down to the most minute features, while even the image of angry Achilles is no more for him than an *image* whose irate countenance he enjoys with a dreamer's delight in appearance — so that this mirror of appearance protects him from complete fusion with his characters — the lyrical poet, on the other hand, himself becomes his images, his images are objectified versions of himself. Being the active center of that world he may boldly speak in the first person, only his "I" is not that of the actual waking man, but the "I" dwelling, truly and eternally, in the ground of being. It is through the reflections of that "I" that the lyric poet beholds the ground of being. Let us imagine, next, how he views himself too among these reflections — as nongenius, that is, as his own subject matter, the whole teeming crowd of his passions and intentions directed toward a definite goal; and when it now appears as though the poet and the nonpoet joined to him were one, and as though the former were using the pronoun "I," we are able to see through this appearance, which has deceived those who have attached the label "subjective" to the lyrical poet. The man Archilochus, with his passionate loves and hates, is really only a vision of genius, a genius who is no longer merely Archilochus but the genius of the universe, expressing its pain through the similitude of Archilochus the man. Archilochus, on the other hand, the subjectively willing and desiring human being, can never be a poet. Nor is it at all necessary for the poet to see only the phenomenon of the man Archilochus before him as a reflection of Eternal Being: the world of tragedy shows us to what extent the vision of the poet can remove itself from the urgent, immediate phenomenon.

Schopenhauer, who was fully aware of the difficulties the lyrical poet creates for the speculative esthetician, thought that he had found a solution, which, however, I cannot endorse. It is true that he alone possessed the means, in his profound philosophy of music, for solving this problem; and I think I have honored his achievement in these pages, I hope in his own spirit. Yet in the first part of *The World as Will and Idea* he characterizes the essence of song as follows:

> The consciousness of the singer is filled with the subject of will, which is to say with his own willing. That willing may either be a released, satisfied willing (joy), or, as happens more commonly, an inhibited willing (sadness). In either case there is affect here: passion, violent commotion. At the same time, however, the singer is moved by the contemplation of nature surrounding him to experience himself as the subject of pure, unwilling ideation, and the unshakable tranquillity of that ideation becomes contrasted with the urgency of his willing, its limits, and its lacks. It is the experience of this contrast, or tug of war, which he expresses in his song. While we find ourselves in the lyrical condition, pure ideation approaches us, as it were, to deliver us from the urgencies of willing; we obey, yet obey for moments only. Again and

again our willing, our memory of personal objectives, distracts us from tranquil contemplation, while, conversely, the next scene of beauty we behold will yield us up once more to pure ideation. For this reason we find in song and in the lyrical mood a curious mixture of willing (our personal interest in *purposes*) and pure contemplation (whose subject matter is furnished by our surroundings); relations are sought and imagined between these two sets of experiences. Subjective mood — the affection of the will — communicates its color to the purely viewed surroundings, and vice versa. All authentic song reflects a state of mind mixed and divided in this manner.

Who can fail to perceive in this description that lyric poetry is presented as an art never completely realized, indeed a hybrid whose essence is made to consist in an uneasy mixture of will and contemplation, i.e., the esthetic and the nonesthetic conditions? We, on our part, maintain that the distinction between subjective and objective, which even Schopenhauer still uses as a sort of measuring stick to distinguish the arts, has no value whatever in esthetics; the reason being that the subject — the striving individual bent on furthering his egoistic purposes — can be thought of only as an enemy to art, never as its source. But to the extent that the subject is an artist he is already delivered from individual will and has become a medium through which the True Subject celebrates. His redemption in illusion. For better or worse, one thing should be quite obvious to all of us: the entire comedy of art is not played for our own sakes — for our betterment or education, say — nor can we consider ourselves the true originators of that art realm; while on the other hand we have every right to view ourselves as esthetic projections of the veritable creator and derive such dignity as we possess from our status as art works. Only as an esthetic product can the world be justified to all eternity — although our consciousness of our own significance does scarcely exceed the consciousness a painted soldier might have of the battle in which he takes part. Thus our whole knowledge of art is at bottom illusory, seeing that as mere *knowers* we can never be fused with that essential spirit, at the same time creator and spectator, who has prepared the comedy of art for his own edification. Only as the genius in the act of creation merges with the primal architect of the cosmos can he truly know something of the eternal essence of art. For in that condition he resembles the uncanny fairy tale image which is able to see itself by turning its eyes. He is at once subject and object, poet, actor, and audience.

XIV

Let us now imagine Socrates' great Cyclops' eye — that eye which never glowed with the artist's divine frenzy — turned upon tragedy. Bearing in mind that he was unable to look with any pleasure into the Dionysiac abysses, what could Socrates see in that tragic art which to Plato seemed noble and meritorious? Something quite abstruse and irrational, full of causes without effects and effects seemingly without causes, the whole texture so checkered that it must be repugnant to a sober disposition, while it might act as dangerous tinder to a sensitive and impressionable mind. We are told that the only genre of poetry Socrates really appreciated was the Aesopian fable. This he did with the same smiling complaisance with which honest Gellert sings the praise of poetry in his fable of the bee and the hen:

> I exemplify the use of poetry:
> To convey to those who are a bit backward
> The truth in a simile.[15]

The fact is that for Socrates tragic art failed even to "convey the truth," although it did address itself to those who were "a bit backward," which is to say to nonphilosophers: a double reason for leaving it alone.[16] Like Plato, he reckoned it among the beguiling arts which represent the agreeable, not the useful, and in consequence exhorted his followers to abstain from such unphilosophical stimulants. His success was such that the young tragic poet Plato burned all his writings in order to qualify as a student of Socrates. And while strong native genius might

[15]Christian Fürchtegott Gellert (1715–69), poet and novelist of the German Enlightenment; the quotation is from *Poems and Fables* (1746–48). [Ed.]

[16]Nietzsche alludes to Socrates' final assessment of poetry in Plato's *Republic*, Book X; see p. 28. [Ed.]

now and again manage to withstand the Socratic injunction, the power of the latter was still great enough to force poetry into entirely new channels.

A good example of this is Plato himself. Although he did not lag behind the naïve cynicism of his master in the condemnation of tragedy and of art in general, nevertheless his creative gifts forced him to develop an art form deeply akin to the existing form which he had repudiated. The main objection raised by Plato to the older art (that it was the imitation of an imitation and hence belonged to an even lower order of empiric reality) must not, at all costs, apply to the new genre; and so we see Plato intent on moving beyond reality and on rendering the idea which underlies it. By a detour Plato the thinker reached the very spot where Plato the poet had all along been at home, and from which Sophocles, and with him the whole poetic tradition of the past, protested such a change. Tragedy had assimilated to itself all the older poetic genres. In a somewhat eccentric sense the same thing can be claimed for the Platonic dialogue, which was a mixture of all the available styles and forms and hovered between narrative, lyric, drama, between prose and poetry, once again breaking through the old law of stylistic unity. The Cynic philosophers went even farther in that direction, seeking, by their utterly promiscuous style and constant alternation between verse and prose, to project their image of the "raving Socrates" in literature, as they sought to enact it in life. The Platonic dialogue was the lifeboat in which the shipwrecked older poetry saved itself, together with its numerous offspring. Crowded together in a narrow space, and timidly obeying their helmsman Socrates, they moved forward into a new era which never tired of looking at this fantastic spectacle. Plato has furnished for all posterity the pattern of a new art form, the novel, viewed as the Aesopian fable raised to its highest power; a form in which poetry played the same subordinate role with regard to dialectic philosophy as that same philosophy was to play for many centuries with regard to theology. This, then, was the new status of poetry, and it was Plato who, under the pressure of daemonic Socrates, had brought it about.

It is at this point that philosophical ideas begin to entwine themselves about art, forcing the latter to cling closely to the trunk of dialectic. The Apollonian tendency now appears disguised as logical schematism, just as we found in the case of Euripides a corresponding translation of the Dionysiac affect into a naturalistic one. Socrates, the dialectical hero of the Platonic drama, shows a close affinity to the Euripidean hero, who is compelled to justify his actions by proof and counterproof, and for that reason is often in danger of forfeiting our tragic compassion. For who among us can close his eyes to the optimistic element in the nature of dialectics, which sees a triumph in every syllogism and can breathe only in an atmosphere of cool, conscious clarity? Once that optimistic element had entered tragedy, it overgrew its Dionysiac regions and brought about their annihilation and, finally, the leap into genteel domestic drama. Consider the consequences of the Socratic maxims: "Virtue is knowledge; all sins arise from ignorance; only the virtuous are happy" — these three basic formulations of optimism spell the death of tragedy. The virtuous hero must henceforth be a dialectician; virtue and knowledge, belief and ethics, be necessarily and demonstrably connected; Aeschylus' transcendental concept of justice be reduced to the brash and shallow principle of poetic justice with its regular *deus ex machina*.

What is the view taken of the chorus in this new Socratic-optimistic stage world, and of the entire musical and Dionysiac foundation of tragedy? They are seen as accidental features, as reminders of the origin of tragedy, which can well be dispensed with — while we have in fact come to understand that the chorus is the cause of tragedy and the tragic spirit. Already in Sophocles we find some embarrassment with regard to the chorus, which suggests that the Dionysiac floor of tragedy is beginning to give way. Sophocles no longer dares to give the chorus the major role in the tragedy but treats it as almost on the same footing as the actors, as though it had been raised from the *orchestra* onto the *scene*. By so doing he necessarily destroyed its meaning, despite Aristotle's endorsement of this conception of the chorus. This shift in attitude, which Sophocles displayed not only in practice but also, we are told, in theory, was the first step toward the total disintegration of the chorus: a process whose rapid phases we can follow in Euripides, Agathon, and the New Comedy. Optimistic dialectics took up the whip of its syllogisms and drove music out of tragedy. It entirely destroyed the meaning of tragedy — which can be interpreted only as a concrete manifestation of Dionysiac conditions, music made visible, an ecstatic dream world.

Since we have discovered an anti-Dionysiac tendency antedating Socrates, its most brilliant exponent, we must now ask, "Toward what does a figure like Socrates point?" Faced with the evidence of the Platonic dialogues, we are certainly not entitled to see in Socrates merely an agent of disintegration. While it is clear that the immediate result of the Socratic strategy was the destruction of Dionysiac drama, we are forced, nevertheless, by the profundity of the Socratic experience to ask ourselves whether, in fact, art and Socratism are diametrically opposed to one another, whether there is really anything inherently impossible in the idea of a Socratic artist?

It appears that this despotic logician had from time to time a sense of void, loss, unfulfilled duty with regard to art. In prison he told his friends how, on several occasions, a voice had spoken to him in a dream, saying "Practice music, Socrates!"[17] Almost to the end he remained confident that his philosophy represented the highest art of the muses, and would not fully believe that a divinity meant to remind him of "common, popular music." Yet in order to unburden his conscience he finally agreed, in prison, to undertake that music which hitherto he had held in low esteem. In this frame of mind he composed a poem on Apollo and rendered several Aesopian fables in verse. What prompted him to these exercises was something very similar to that warning voice of his daimonion: an Apollonian perception that, like a barbarian king, he had failed to comprehend the nature of a divine effigy, and was in danger of offending his own god through ignorance. These words heard by Socrates in his dream are the only indication that he ever experienced any uneasiness about the limits of his logical universe. He may have asked himself: "Have I been too ready to view what was unintelligible to me as being devoid of meaning? Perhaps there is a realm of wisdom, after all, from which the logician is excluded? Perhaps art must be seen as the necessary complement of rational discourse?"

[17]In Plato's *Phaedo.* [Ed.]

XIX

The best way to characterize the core of Socratic culture is to call it the culture of the opera. It is in this area that Socratism has given an open account of its intentions — a rather surprising one when we compare the evolution of the opera with the abiding Apollonian and Dionysiac truths. First I want to remind the reader of the genesis of the *stilo rappresentativo*[18] and of recitative. How did it happen that this operatic music, so wholly external and incapable of reverence, was enthusiastically greeted by an epoch which, not so very long ago, had produced the inexpressibly noble and sacred music of Palestrina? Can anyone hold the luxury and frivolity of the Florentine court and the vanity of its dramatic singers responsible for the speed and intensity with which the vogue of opera spread? I can explain the passion for a semimusical declamation, at the same period and among the same people who had witnessed the grand architecture of Palestrina's harmonies (in the making of which the whole Christian Middle Ages had conspired), only by reference to an extra-artistic tendency. To the listener who desires to hear the words above the music corresponds the singer who speaks more than he sings, emphasizing the verbal pathos in a kind of half-song. By this emphasis he aids the understanding of the words and gets rid of the remaining half of music. There is a danger that now and again the music will preponderate, spoiling the pathos and clarity of his declamation, while conversely he is

[18]A term characterizing the opera created in the late sixteenth century by the Florentine musical society known as the *Camerata,* in which dramatic recitative alternates with florid arias expressing emotion. Operas in the current repertory written in the *stilo rappresentativo* include Monteverdi's *L'Incoronazione di Poppaea* and Purcell's *Dido and Aeneas.* [Ed.]

always under the temptation to discharge the music of his voice in a virtuoso manner. The pseudopoetic librettist furnishes him ample opportunity for this display in lyrical interjections, repetitions of words and phrases, etc., where the singer may give himself up to the purely musical element without consideration for the text. This constant alternation, so characteristic of the *stilo rappresentativo,* between emotionally charged, only partly sung declamation and wholly musical interjections, this rapid shift of focus between concept and imagination, on the one hand, and the musical response of the listener, on the other, is so completely unnatural, equally opposed to the Dionysiac and the Apollonian spirit, that one must conclude the origin of recitative to have lain outside any artistic instinct. Viewed in these terms, the recitative may be characterized as a mixture of epic and lyric declamation. And yet, since the components are so wholly disparate, the resulting combination is neither harmonious nor constant, but rather a superficial and mosaic-like conglutination, not without precedent in the realm of nature and experience. However, the inventors of recitative took a very different view of it. They, and their age with them, thought they had discovered the secret of ancient music, that secret which alone could account for the amazing feats of an Orpheus or an Amphion or, indeed, for Greek tragedy. They thought that by that novel style they had managed to resuscitate ancient Greek music in all its power; and, given the popular conception of the Homeric world as the primordial world, it was possible to embrace the illusion that one had at last returned to the paradisaical beginnings of mankind, in which music must have had that supreme purity, power, and innocence of which the pastoral poets wrote so movingly. Here we have touched the nerve center of opera, that genuinely modern genre. In it, art satisfies a strong need, but one that can hardly be called esthetic: a hankering for the idyll, a belief in the primordial existence of pure, artistically sensitive man. Recitative stood for the rediscovered language of that archetypal man, opera for the rediscovered country of that idyllic and heroically pure species, who in all their actions followed a natural artistic bent — who, no matter what they had to say, sang at least part of it, and who when their emotions were ever so little aroused burst into full song. It is irrelevant to our inquiry that the humanists of the time used the new image of the paradisaical artist to combat the old ecclesiastical notion of man as totally corrupt and damned; that opera thus represented the opposition dogma of man as essentially good, and furnished an antidote to that pessimism which, given the terrible instability of the epoch, naturally enlisted its strongest and most thoughtful minds. What matters here is our recognition that the peculiar attraction and thus the success of this new art form must be attributed to its satisfaction of a wholly unesthetic need: it was optimistic; it glorified man in himself; it conceived of man as originally good and full of talent. This principle of opera has by degrees become a menacing and rather appalling claim, against which we who are faced with present-day socialist movements cannot stop our ears. The "noble savage" demands his rights: what a paradisaical prospect!

There is still a further point in support of my contention that opera is built on the same principles as our Alexandrian culture. Opera is the product of the man of theory, the critical layman, not the artist. This constitutes one of the most disturbing facts in the entire history of art. Since the demand, coming from essentially unmusical people, was for a clear understanding of the words, a renascence of music could come about only through the discovery of a type of music in which the words lorded it over the counterpoint as a master over his servant. For were not the words nobler than the accompanying harmonic system, as the soul is nobler than the body? It was with precisely that unmusical clumsiness that the combinations of music, image, and word were treated in the beginning of opera, and in this spirit the first experiments in the new genre were carried out, even in the noble lay circles of Florence, by the poets and singers patronized by those circles. Inartistic man produces his own brand of art, precisely by virtue of his artistic impotence. Having not the faintest conception of the Dionysiac profundity of music, he transforms musical enjoyment into a rationalistic rhetoric of passion in the *stilo rappresentativo,* into a voluptuous indulgence of vocal virtuoso feats; lacking imagination, he must employ engineers and stage designers; being incapable of understanding the true nature of the artist, he invents an "artistic primitive" to suit his taste, i.e., a man who, when his passions are aroused, breaks into song and recites verses. He projects himself into a time when passion sufficed to produce songs and poems — as though mere emotion had ever been able to create art. There lies at the root of opera a fallacious conception of the artistic process, the idyllic belief that every sensitive man is at bottom an artist. In keeping with this belief, opera is the expression of dilettantism in art, dictating its rules with the cheerful optimism of the theorist.

If we were to combine the two tendencies conspiring at the creation of opera into one, we might speak of an idyllic tendency of opera. Here it would be well to refer back to Schiller's account. Nature and ideal, according to Schiller, are objects of grief when the former is felt to be lost, the latter to be beyond reach. But both may become objects of joy when they are represented as actual. Then the first will produce the elegy, in its strict sense, and the second the idyll, in its widest sense. I would like to point out at once the common feature of these two conceptions in the origin of opera: here the ideal is never viewed as unattained nor nature as lost. Rather, a primitive period in the history of man is imagined, in which he lay at the heart of nature and in this state of nature attained immediately the ideal of humanity through Edenic nobility and artistry. From this supposedly perfect primitive we are all said to derive; indeed, we are still his faithful replicas. All we need do in order to recognize ourselves in that primitive is to jettison some of our later achievements, such as our superfluous learning and excess culture. The educated man of the Renaissance used the operatic imitation of Greek tragedy to lead him back to that concord of nature and ideal, to an idyllic reality. He used ancient tragedy the way Dante used Virgil, to lead him to the gates of Paradise,[19] but from there on he went ahead on his own, moving from an imitation of the highest Greek art form to a "restitution of all things," to a re-creation of man's original art world. What confidence and bonhomie these bold enterprises betokened, arising as they did in the very heart of theoretical culture! The only explanation lies in the comforting belief of the day that "essential man" is the perennially virtuous operatic hero, the endlessly piping or singing shepherd, who, if he should ever by chance lose himself for a spell, would inevitably recover himself intact; in the optimism that rises like a perfumed, seductive cloud from the depths of Socratic contemplation.

Opera, then, does not wear the countenance of eternal grief but rather that of joy in an eternal reunion. It expresses the complacent delight in an idyllic reality, or such, at least, as can be viewed as real at any moment. Perhaps people will one day come to *realize* that this supposititious reality is at bottom no more than a fantastic and foolish trifling, which should make anyone who pits against it the immense seriousness of genuine nature and of the true origins of man exclaim in disgust: "Away with that phantom!" And yet it would be self-delusion to think that, trivial as it is, opera can be driven off with a shout, like an apparition. Whoever wants to destroy opera must gird himself for battle with that Alexandrian cheerfulness that has furnished opera its favorite conceptions and whose natural artistic expression it is. As for art proper, what possible benefit can it derive from a form whose origins lie altogether outside the esthetic realm, a form which from a semimoral sphere has trespassed on the domain of art and can only at rare moments deceive us as to its hybrid origin? What sap nourishes this operatic growth if not that of true art? Are we not right in supposing that its idyllic seductions and Alexandrian blandishments may sophisticate the highest, the truly serious task of art (to deliver the eye from the horror of night, to redeem us by virtue of the healing balm of illusion, from the spastic motions of the will) into an empty and frivolous amusement? What becomes of the enduring Apollonian and Dionysiac truths in such a mixture of styles as we find in the *stilo rappresentativo*; where music acts the part of the ser-

[19]In the *Divina Commedia* the pagan Virgil guided Dante through Hell and Purgatory, but handed him over to Beatrice at the gates of Paradise. [Ed.]

vant, the text that of the master; where music is likened to the body, the text to the soul; where the ultimate goal is at best a periphrastic tone painting, similar to that found in the new Attic dithyramb; where music has abrogated its true dignity as the Dionysiac mirror of the universe and seems content to be the slave of appearance, to imitate the play of phenomenal forms, and to stimulate an artificial delight by dallying with lines and proportions? To a careful observer this pernicious influence of opera on music recapitulates the general development of modern music. The optimism that presided at the birth of opera and of the society represented by opera has succeeded with frightening rapidity in divesting music of its grand Dionysiac meanings and stamping it with the trivial character in a *divertissement,*[20] a transformation only equaled in scope by that of Aeschylean man into jovial Alexandrian man.

If we have been justified in suggesting a connection between the disappearance of the Dionysiac spirit and the spectacular, yet hitherto unexplained, degeneration of the Greek species, with what high hopes must we greet the auspicious signs of the opposite development in our own era, namely the gradual reawakening of the Dionysiac spirit! The divine power of Heracles cannot languish for ever in the service of Omphale.[21] Out of the Dionysiac recesses of the German soul has sprung a power which has nothing in common with the presuppositions of Socratic culture and which that culture can neither explain nor justify. Quite the contrary, the culture sees it as something to be dreaded and abhorred, something infinitely potent and hostile. I refer to German music, in its mighty course from Bach to Beethoven, and from Beethoven to Wagner. How can the petty intellectualism of our day deal with this monster that has risen out of the infinite deeps? There is no formula to be found, in either the reservoir of operatic filigree and arabesque or the abacus of the fugue and contrapuntal dialectics, that will subdue this monster, make it stand and deliver. What a spectacle to see our estheticians beating the air with the butterfly nets of their pedantic slogans, in vain pursuit of that marvelously volatile musical genius, their movements sadly belying their standards of "eternal" beauty and grandeur! Look at these patrons of music for a moment at close range, as they repeat indefatigably: "Beauty! Beauty!" and judge for yourselves whether they really look like the beautiful darlings of nature, or whether it would not be more correct to say that they have assumed a disguise for their own coarseness, as esthetic pretext for their barren and jejune sensibilities — take the case of Otto Jahn.[22] But liars and prevaricators ought to watch their step in the area of German music. For amidst our degenerate culture music is the only pure and purifying flame, towards which and away from which all things move in a Heracleitean double motion.[23] All that is now called culture, education, civilization will one day have to appear before the incorruptible judge, Dionysos.

Let us now recall how the new German philosophy was nourished from the same sources, how Kant and Schopenhauer succeeded in destroying the complacent acquiescence of intellectual Socratism,[24] how by their labors an infinitely more profound and serious consideration of questions of ethics and art was made possible — a conceptualized form, in fact, of Dionysiac wisdom. To what does this miraculous union between German philosophy and music point if not to a new mode of existence, whose precise nature we can divine only with the aid of Greek analogies? For us, who stand on the watershed between two different modes of existence, the Greek example is still of inestimable value, since it embodies the violent transition to a classical, rationalistic form of suasion; only, we are living through the great phases of Hellenism in reverse

[20]Diversion. [Ed.]

[21]In the legend, in atonement for killing Iphitus, Heracles was forced to wear women's clothes and learn to spin at the direction of Queen Omphale. [Ed.]

[22]Otto Jahn (1813–69), a classicist and archeologist, was a contemporary of Neitzsche. [Ed.]

[23]Heracleitus, who believed that all matter was in flux, thought nevertheless that changes in one direction for one aspect of the universe were balanced by changes in the opposite direction for another. [Ed.]

[24]Nietzsche is suggesting that Kant and Schopenhauer made aesthetics a matter of pure intuition, replacing the rationalist aesthetics common since Horace. [Ed.]

order and seem at this very moment to be moving backward from the Alexandrian age into an age of tragedy. And we can't help feeling that the dawn of a new tragic age is for the German spirit only a return to itself, a blessed recovery of its true identity. For an unconscionably long time powerful forces from the outside have compelled the German spirit, which had vegetated in barbaric formlessness, to subserve their forms. But at long last the German spirit may stand before the other nations, free of the leading strings of Romance culture — provided that it continues to be able to learn from the nation from whom to learn at all is a high and rare thing, the Greeks. And was there ever a time when we needed these supreme teachers more urgently than now, as we witness the rebirth of tragedy and are in danger of not knowing either whence it comes or whither it goes?

Henry James

1843–1916

Born in America, partly formed by the French, and late in life naturalized a British subject, Henry James was a relentless experimentalist with technique and subject matter who brought a new sophistication to the art of fiction. His father, Henry James, Sr., an independently wealthy gentleman, was a philosopher and religious mystic who valued eccentricity in himself and in his offspring. Henry and his equally well-known elder brother, William, were educated at schools in England, France, Switzerland, and Germany as well as in their birthplace, New York City; their father believed that his sons could become themselves only by avoiding attachments to any master, school, place, or nation, and he also loathed the pragmatism and professionalism of the American educational system. The paradoxical result was that both Henry and William became ardent professionals — William a psychologist and philosopher, Henry a novelist and critic.

James began publishing stories in his twenties but did not find his true voice until he left America for good in 1875 to live in Paris and then settle in London. The fiction of his first period is often some variation on the "international theme" — the moral and spiritual gap between America and Europe. *The American* (1877), *Daisy Miller* (1878), and *Portrait of a Lady* (1881) made his reputation; today these works (especially the last) seem to mark a transition between the social chronicle of the nineteenth century and the twentieth-century novel of psychological realism. The novels of his middle years, like *The Princess Casamassima* (1886) and *The Tragic Muse* (1890), were less successful, and James's attempt to conquer the London stage with *Guy Domville* (1895) ended in disaster. James withdrew from London to the retirement of Lamb House in Rye, where he produced the three ambiguous and highly nuanced masterworks of his late period, *The Wings of the Dove* (1902), *The Ambassadors* (1903), and *The Golden Bowl* (1904). In the next decade, James turned from fiction to memoir, but the outbreak of World War I disturbed the quiet of his last years. As an expression of solidarity with the British cause during America's long neutrality, James applied for citizenship (granted in 1915) and worked at war relief, the exertions of which broke his own health. He died on February 26, 1916.

"The Art of Fiction" (1884) seems to promise a manual of techniques, but this is precisely what James is least willing to provide. The title in fact is not James's own but was taken from a lecture by Walter Besant, which proposed that "laws of fiction may be laid down and taught with as much precision and exactness as the laws of harmony, perspective, and proportion." While generously granting everything he can to Besant's claims, James — who had been trained as a painter — essentially disagrees that regulations and conventions in fiction comparable to those in painting and music could exist. "If there are exact sciences, there are also exact arts, and the grammar of painting is so much more definite that it makes the difference." And James might have said, *Vive la différence,* for most of the distinctions that had become current in the short history of the criticism of fiction struck him as mechanical and empty.

Even before the English novel existed as such, William Congreve in his preface to *Incognita* (1692) had contrasted the romance and the novel. Later critics differentiated novels of incident from novels of character. For James, these notions might make talking about the novel easier but would only make excellence in writing more difficult. "What is character," he asks, "but the determination of incident? What is incident but the illustration of character?" For James, the novel is intended to convey the felt impression of life — a seamless web of action and motive that could not be reduced to simple formulas. The only Besantine dictum James wholeheartedly endorses is the recommendation that the prospective novelist keep a notebook to record impressions.

Although James rejects all of Besant's particular recommendations, he agrees that fiction is indeed an art. Today, after Joyce and Woolf and James himself, this contention would seem to need no proof. But the Victorian novel had been created mainly by entertainers who made few claims for themselves and their trade, and the British public was used to retreating into three-volume narratives that guaranteed adventure and escape, a love story with a happy ending, and poetic justice for all. In "The Art of Fiction" James positions himself against this stultifying formula. He is also concerned to champion his own style of writing fiction, which was more subtle and inward than was common. More generally, however, he wants the novelist to have the freedom to experiment not just with subject matter and point of view but with moral issues that disturb and disquiet.

Since James sets himself squarely against the philistines, we might expect him, in the 1880s, to embrace either the naturalism of Émile Zola or the pure "art for art's sake" aestheticism of Walter Pater. In fact he enters neither camp. James holds to fairly traditional notions of realism; beauty of form is not to be pursued merely for its own sake but in the process of conveying a complex and authentic experience that rests on the contingencies of life. "Do not listen," he warns, "to those who would . . . persuade you that this heavenly messenger wings her way outside of life altogether, breathing a superfine air, and turning away her head from the truth of things." But at the same time, James does not, like Zola, expect the artist to present social conditions in a scientifically accurate way; he claimed, in fact, that Zola's deterministic philosophy "vitiated" his portraiture.

Ultimately, James's impatience with rules and formulas for fiction derives from a post-Romantic, expressive theory of art. "The deepest quality of a work of art will always be the quality of the mind of the producer. In proportion as that intelligence is fine will the novel . . . partake of the substance of beauty and truth." James's most heartfelt recommendation to the aspiring artist is not to watch his handling of point-of-view but to remain open to experience, to "be one of the people on whom nothing is lost." A fine intelligence will, he is confident, find or invent the techniques needed to realize the imagined vision, while a mechanical mind, using all the arts, will never produce something worthy of lasting fame.

Selected Bibliography

Beach, Joseph Warren. *The Method of Henry James.* Philadelphia: A. Saifer, 1954.

Cameron, J. M. "History, Realism, and the Work of Henry James." *English Studies in Canada* 10 (1984): 299–316.

Daugherty, Sarah B. *The Literary Criticism of Henry James.* Athens: Ohio University Press, 1981.

Edel, Leon. *The Prefaces of Henry James.* Paris: Jouvé, 1931.

Hughes, Herbert Leland. *Theory and Practice in Henry James.* Ann Arbor: Edwards Bros., 1926.

Jackson, Wendell P. "Theory of the Creative Process in the 'Prefaces' of Henry James." In *Amid Visions and Revisions: Poetry and Criticism on Literature and the Arts,* ed. Burney J. Hillis. Baltimore: Morgan State University Press, 1985, pp. 59–64.

James, Henry. *The Art of the Novel: Critical Prefaces.* Introduction by R. P. Blackmur. New York: Scribner, 1934.

Roberts, Morris. *Henry James's Criticism.* Cambridge: Harvard University Press, 1929.

Veeder, William. "Image as Argument: Henry James and the Style of Criticism." *Henry James Review* 6 (1985): 172–81.

The Art of Fiction

I should not have affixed so comprehensive a title to these few remarks, necessarily wanting in any completeness upon a subject the full consideration of which would carry us far, did I not seem to discover a pretext for my temerity in the interesting pamphlet lately published under this name by Mr. Walter Besant.[1] Mr. Besant's lecture at the Royal Institution — the original form of his pamphlet — appears to indicate that many persons are interested in the art of fiction, and are not indifferent to such remarks, as those who practice it may attempt to make about it. I am therefore anxious not to lose the benefit of this favorable association, and to edge in a few words under cover of the attention which Mr. Besant is sure to have excited. There is something very encouraging in his having put into form certain of his ideas on the mystery of story-telling.

It is a proof of life and curiosity — curiosity on the part of the brotherhood of novelists as well as on the part of their readers. Only a short time ago it might have been supposed that the English novel was not what the French call *discutable.* It had no air of having a theory, a conviction, a consciousness of itself behind it — of being the expression of an artistic faith, the result of choice and comparison. I do not say it was necessarily the worse for that; it would take much more courage than I possess to intimate that the form of the novel as Dickens and Thackeray (for instance) saw it had any taint of incompleteness. It was, however, *naïf* (if I may help myself out with another French word); and evidently if it be destined to suffer in any way for having lost its *naïveté* it has now an idea of making sure of the corresponding advantages. During the period I have alluded to there was a comfortable, good-humored feeling abroad that a novel is a novel, as a pudding is a pudding and that our only business with it could be to swallow it. But within a year or two, for some reason or other, there have been signs of returning animation — the era of discussion would appear to have been to a certain ex-

[1]Victorian man of letters (1836–1901). Besant's lecture on the art of fiction was delivered on April 25, 1884. [Ed.]

tent opened. Art lives upon discussion, upon experiment, upon curiosity, upon variety of attempt, upon the exchange of views and the comparison of standpoints; and there is a presumption that those times when no one has anything particular to say about it, and has no reason to give for practice or preference, though they may be times of honor, are not times of development — are times, possibly even, a little of dullness. The successful application of any art is a delightful spectacle, but the theory too is interesting; and though there is a great deal of the latter without the former I suspect there has never been a genuine success that has not had a latent core of conviction. Discussion, suggestion, formulation, these things are fertilizing when they are frank and sincere. Mr. Besant has set an excellent example in saying what he thinks, for his part, about the way in which fiction should be written, as well as about the way in which it should be published; for his view of the "art," carried on into an appendix, covers that too. Other laborers in the same field will doubtless take up the argument, they will give it the light of their experience, and the effect will surely be to make our interest in the novel a little more what it had for some time threatened to fail to be — a serious, active, inquiring interest, under protection of which this delightful study may, in moments of confidence, venture to say a little more what it thinks of itself.

It must take itself seriously for the public to take it so. The old superstition about fiction being "wicked"[2] has doubtless died out in England; but the spirit of it lingers in a certain oblique regard directed toward any story which does not more or less admit that it is only a joke. Even the most jocular novel feels in some degree the weight of the proscription that was formerly directed against literary levity: the jocularity does not always succeed in passing for orthodoxy. It is still expected, though perhaps people are ashamed to say it, that a production which is after all only a "make-believe" (for what else is a "story"?) shall be in some degree apologetic — shall renounce the pretension of attempting really to represent life. This, of course, any sensible, wide-awake story declines to do, for it quickly perceives that the tolerance granted to it on such a condition is only an attempt to stifle it disguised in the form of generosity. The old evangelical hostility to the novel, which was as explicit as it was narrow, and which regarded it as little less favorable to our immortal part than a stage play, was in reality far less insulting. The only reason for the existence of a novel is that it does attempt to represent life. When it relinquishes this attempt, the same attempt that we see on the canvas of the painter, it will have arrived at a very strange pass. It is not expected of the picture that it will make itself humble in order to be forgiven; and the analogy between the art of the painter and the art of novelist is, so far as I am able to see, complete. Their inspiration is the same, their process (allowing for the different quality of the vehicle) is the same, their success is the same. They may learn from each other, they may explain and sustain each other. Their cause is the same, and the honor of one is the honor of another. The Mahometans think a picture an unholy thing, but it is a long time since any Christian did, and it is therefore the more odd that in the Christian mind the traces (dissimulated though they may be) of a suspicion of the sister art should linger to this day. The only effectual way to lay it to rest is to emphasize the analogy to which I just alluded — to insist on the fact that as the picture is reality, so the novel is history. That is the only general description (which does it justice) that we may give of the novel. But history also is allowed to represent life; it is not, any more than painting, expected to apologize. The subject-matter of fiction is stored up likewise in documents and records, and if it will not give itself away, as they say in California, it must speak with assurance, with the tone of the historian. Certain accomplished novelists have a habit of giving themselves away which must often bring tears to the eyes of people who take their fiction seriously. I was lately struck, in reading over many pages of Anthony Trollope, with his want of discretion in this particular. In a digression, a parenthesis or an aside, he concedes to the reader that he and this

[2]Cf. Johnson's stricture in *The Rambler*, No. 4. See p. 220. [Ed.]

trusting friend are only "making believe." He admits that the events he narrates have not really happened, and that he can give his narrative any turn the reader may like best.[3] Such a betrayal of a sacred office seems to me, I confess, a terrible crime; it is what I mean by the attitude of apology, and it shocks me every whit as much in Trollope as it would have shocked me in Gibbon or Macaulay. It implies that the novelist is less occupied in looking for the truth (the truth, of course I mean, that he assumes, the premises that we grant him, whatever they may be) than the historian, and in doing so it deprives him at a stroke of all his standing room. To represent and illustrate the past, the actions of men, is the task of either writer, and the only difference that I can see is, in proportion as he succeeds, to the honor of the novelist, consisting as it does in his having more difficulty in collecting his evidence, which is so far from being purely literary. It seems to me to give him a great character, the fact that he has at once so much in common with the philosopher and the painter; this double analogy is a magnificent heritage.

It is of all this evidently that Mr. Besant is full when he insists upon the fact that fiction is one of the *fine* arts, deserving in its turn of all the honors and emoluments that have hitherto been reserved for the successful profession of music, poetry, painting, architecture. It is impossible to insist too much on so important a truth, and the place that Mr. Besant demands for the work of the novelist may be represented, a trifle less abstractly, by saying that he demands not only that it shall be reputed artistic, but that it shall be reputed very artistic indeed. It is excellent that he should have struck this note, for his doing so indicates that there was need of it, that his proposition may be to many people a novelty. One rubs one's eyes at the thought; but the rest of Mr. Besant's essay confirms the revelation. I suspect in truth that it would be possible to confirm it still further, and that one would not be far wrong in saying that in addition to the people to whom it has never occurred that a novel ought to be artistic, there are a great many others who, if this principle were urged upon them, would be filled with an indefinable mistrust. They would find it difficult to explain their repugnance, but it would operate strongly to put them on their guard. "Art," in our Protestant communities, where so many things have got so strangely twisted about, is supposed in certain circles to have some vaguely injurious effect upon those who make it an important consideration, who let it weigh in the balance. It is assumed to be opposed in some mysterious manner to morality, to amusement, to instruction. When it is embodied in the work of the painter (the sculptor is another affair!) you know what it is: it stands there before you, in the honesty of pink and green and a gilt frame; you can see the worst of it at a glance, and you can be on your guard. But when it is introduced into literature it becomes more insidious — there is danger of its hurting you before you know it. Literature should be either instructive or amusing, and there is in many minds an impression that these artistic preoccupations, the search for form, contribute to neither end, interfere indeed with both. They are too frivolous to be edifying, and too serious to be diverting; and they are moreover priggish and paradoxical and superfluous. That, I think, represents the manner in which the latent thought of many people who read novels as an exercise in skipping would explain itself if it were to become articulate. They would argue, of course, that a novel ought to be "good," but they would interpret this term in a fashion of their own, which indeed would vary considerably from one critic to another. One would say that being good means representing virtuous and aspiring characters, placed in prominent positions; another would say that it depends on a "happy ending," on a distribution at the last of prizes, pensions, husbands, wives, babies, millions, appended paragraphs, and cheerful remarks. Another still would say that it means being full of incident and movement, so that we shall wish to jump ahead, to see who was the mysterious stranger, and if the stolen will was ever found, and shall not be distracted from this pleasure by any tiresome analysis or "description." But they would all agree that

[3]James may be thinking about such addresses to the reader as the opening of Ch. 51 in *Barchester Towers*, where the narrator worries aloud about the difficulty of writing endings. [Ed.]

the "artistic" idea would spoil some of their fun. One would hold it accountable for all the description, another would see it revealed in the absence of sympathy. Its hostility to a happy ending would be evident, and it might even in some cases render any ending at all impossible. The "ending" of a novel is, for many persons, like that of a good dinner, a course of dessert and ices, and the artist in fiction is regarded as a sort of meddlesome doctor who forbids agreeable aftertastes. It is therefore true that this conception of Mr. Besant's of the novel as a superior form encounters not only a negative but a positive indifference. It matters little that as a work of art it should really be as little or as much of its essence to supply happy endings, sympathetic characters, and an objective tone, as if it were a work of mechanics: the association of ideas, however incongruous, might easily be too much for it if an eloquent voice were not sometimes raised to call attention to the fact that it is at once as free and as serious a branch of literature as any other.

Certainly this might sometimes be doubted in presence of the enormous number of works of fiction that appeal to the credulity of our generation, for it might easily seem that there could be no great character in a commodity so quickly and easily produced. It must be admitted that good novels are much compromised by bad ones, and that the field at large suffers discredit from overcrowding. I think, however, that this injury is only superficial, and that the superabundance of written fiction proves nothing against the principle itself. It has been vulgarized, like all other kinds of literature, like everything else today, and it has proved more than some kinds accessible to vulgarization. But there is as much difference as there ever was between a good novel and a bad one: the bad is swept with all the daubed canvases and spoiled marble into some unvisited limbo, or infinite rubbish-yard beneath the back-windows of the world, and the good subsists and emits its light and stimulates our desire for perfection. As I shall take the liberty of making but a single criticism of Mr. Besant, whose tone is so full of the love of his art, I may as well have done with it at once. He seems to me to mistake in attempting to say so definitely beforehand what sort of an affair the good novel will be. To indicate the danger of such an error as that has been the purpose of these few pages; to suggest that certain traditions on the subject, applied *a priori,* have already had much to answer for, and that the good health of an art which undertakes so immediately to reproduce life must demand that it be perfectly free. It lives upon exercise, and the very meaning of exercise is freedom. The only obligation to which in advance we may hold a novel, without incurring the accusation of being arbitrary, is that it be interesting. That general responsibility rests upon it, but it is the only one I can think of. The ways in which it is at liberty to accomplish this result (of interesting us) strike me as innumerable, and such as can only suffer from being marked out or fenced in by prescription. They are as various as the temperament of man, and they are successful in proportion as they reveal a particular mind, different from others. A novel is in its broadest definition a personal, a direct impression of life: that, to begin with, constitutes its value, which is greater or less according to the intensity of the impression. But there will be no intensity at all, and therefore no value, unless there is freedom to feel and say. The tracing of a line to be followed, of a tone to be taken, of a form to be filled out, is a limitation of that freedom and a suppression of the very thing that we are most curious about. The form, it seems to me, is to be appreciated after the fact: then the author's choice has been made, his standard has been indicated; then we can follow lines and directions and compare tones and resemblances. Then in a word we can enjoy one of the most charming of pleasures, we can estimate quality, we can apply the test of execution. The execution belongs to the author alone; it is what is most personal to him, and we measure him by that. The advantage, the luxury, as well as the torment and responsibility of the novelist, is that there is no limit to what he may attempt as an executant — no limit to his possible experiments, efforts, discoveries, successes. Here it is especially that he works, step by step, like his brother of the brush, of whom we may always say that he has painted his picture in a manner best known to himself. His manner is his secret, not necessarily a jealous one. He cannot disclose it as a general thing if he would; he would be at a loss to teach it to others. I say this with a due recollection of having insisted on the community of method of the artist who paints a picture and the artist who writes a novel. The painter *is* able to teach the rudiments of his practice, and it is possible, from the study of good work (granted the aptitude), both to learn how to paint and to learn how to write. Yet it remains true, without injury to the *rapprochement,* that the literary artists would be obliged to say to his pupil much more than the other, "Ah, well, you must do it as you can!" It is a question of degree, a matter of delicacy. If there are exact sciences, there are also exact arts, and the grammar of painting is so much more definite that it makes the difference.

I ought to add, however, that if Mr. Besant says at the beginning of his essay that the "laws of fiction may be laid down and taught with as much precision and exactness as the laws of harmony, perspective, and proportion," he mitigates what might appear to be an extravagance by applying his remark to "general" laws, and by expressing most of these rules in a manner with which it would certainly be unaccommodating to disagree. That the novelist must write from his experience, that his "characters must be real and such as might be met with in actual life"; that "a young lady brought up in a quiet country village should avoid descriptions of garrison life," and "a writer whose friends and personal experiences belong to the lower middle-class should carefully avoid introducing his characters into society"; that one should enter one's notes in a common-place book; that one's figures should be clear in outline; that making them clear by some trick of speech or of carriage is a bad method, and "describing them at length" is a worse one; that English Fiction should have a "conscious moral purpose"; that "it is almost impossible to estimate too highly the value of careful workmanship — that is, of style"; that "the most important point of all is the story," that "the story is everything": these are principles with most of which it is surely impossible not to sympathize. That remark about the lower middle-class writer and his knowing his place is perhaps rather chilling; but for the rest I should find it difficult to dissent from any one of these recommendations. At the same time, I should find it difficult positively to assent to them, with the exception, perhaps, of the injunction as to entering one's notes in a common-place book. They scarcely seem to me to have the quality that Mr. Besant attributes to the rules of the novelist — the "precision and exactness" of "the laws of harmony, perspective, and proportion." They are suggestive, they are even inspiring, but they are not exact, though they are doubtless as much so as the case admits of: which is a proof of that liberty of interpretation for which I just contended. For the value of these different injunctions — so beautiful and so vague — is wholly in the meaning one attaches to them. The characters, the situation, which strike one as real will be those that touch and interest one most, but the measure of reality is very difficult to fix. The reality of Don Quixote or of Mr. Micawber is a very delicate shade; it is a reality so colored by the author's vision that, vivid as it may be, one would hesitate to propose it as a model: one would expose one's self to some very embarrassing questions on the part of a pupil. It goes without saying that you will not write a good novel unless you possess the sense of reality; but it will be difficult to give you a recipe for calling that sense into being. Humanity is immense, and reality has a myriad forms; the most one can affirm is that some of the flowers of fiction have the odor of it, and others have not; as for telling you in advance how your nosegay should be composed, that is another affair. It is equally excellent and inconclusive to say that one must write from experience; to our supposititious aspirant such a declaration might savor of mockery. What kind of experience is intended, and where does it begin and end? Experience is never limited, and it is never complete; it is an immense sensibility, a kind of huge spider-web of the finest silken threads suspended in the chamber of consciousness, and catching every air-borne particle in its tissue. It is the very atmosphere of the mind; and when the mind is imaginative — much more when it happens to be that of a man of genius — it takes to itself the faintest hints of life, it converts the very pulses of the air into revelations. The young lady living in a village has only to be a damsel upon whom nothing is lost to make it quite unfair (as it seems to me) to declare to her that she shall have nothing to say about the military. Greater miracles have been seen than that, imagination assisting, she should speak the truth about some of these gentlemen. I remember an English novelist, a woman of genius, telling me that she was much commended for the impression she had managed to give in one of her tales of the nature and way of life of the French Protestant youth.[4] She had been asked where she learned so much about his recondite being, she had been congratulated on her peculiar opportunities. These opportunities consisted in her having once, in Paris, as she ascended a staircase, passed an open door where, in the household of a *pasteur,*[5] some of the young Protestants were seated at table round a finished meal. The glimpse made a picture; it lasted only a moment, but that moment was experience. She had got her direct personal impression, and she turned out her type. She knew what youth was, and what Protestantism; she also had the advantage of having seen what it was to be French, so that she converted these ideas into a concrete image and produced a reality. Above all, however, she was blessed with the faculty which when you give it an inch takes an ell, and which for the artist is a much greater source of strength than any accident of residence or of place in the social scale. The power to guess the unseen from the seen, to trace the implication of things, to judge the whole piece by the pattern, the condition of feeling life in general so completely that you are well on your way to knowing any particular corner of it — this cluster of gifts may almost be said to constitute experience, and they occur in country and in town, and in the most differing stages of education. If experience consists of impressions, it may be said that impressions *are* experience, just as (have we not seen it?) they are the very air we breathe. Therefore, if I should certainly say to a novice, "Write from experience and experience only," I should feel that this was rather a tantalizing monition if I were not careful immediately to add, "Try to be one of the people on whom nothing is lost!"

I am far from intending by this to minimize the importance of exactness — of truth of detail. One can speak best from one's own taste, and I may therefore venture to say that the air of reality (solidity of specification) seems to me to be the supreme virtue of a novel — the merit on which all its other merits (including that conscious moral purpose of which Mr. Besant speaks) helplessly and submissively depend. If it be not there they are all as nothing, and if these be there, they owe their effect to the success with which the author has produced the illusion of life. The cultivation of this success, the study of this exquisite process, form, to my taste, the beginning and the end of the art of the novelist. They are his inspiration, his despair, his reward, his torment, his delight. It is here in very truth that he competes with life; it is here that he competes with his brother the painter in *his* attempt to render the look of things, the look that conveys their meaning, to catch the color, the relief, the expression, the surface, the substance of the human spectacle. It is in regard to this that Mr. Besant is well inspired when he bids him take notes. He cannot possibly take too many, he cannot possibly take enough. All life solicits him, and to "render" the simplest surface, to produce the most momentary illusion is a very complicated business. His case would be easier, and the rule would be more exact, if Mr. Besant had been able to tell him what notes to take. But this, I fear, he can never learn in any manual; it is the business of his life. He has to take a great many in order to select a few, he has to work them up as he can, and even the guides and philosophers who might have most to say to him must leave him alone when it comes to the applications of precepts, as we leave the painter in communion with his palette. That his characters "must be clear in outline," as Mr. Besant says — he feels that down to his boots; but how he shall make them so is a secret between his good angel and himself. It would be absurdly simple if he could be taught that a great deal of "description" would make them so, or that on the contrary the absence of description and the cultivation of dialogue, or the absence of

[4]Probably *The Story of Elizabeth* by Anne Thackeray, Lady Ritchie. [Ed.]

[5]Minister. [Ed.]

dialogue and the multiplication of "incident," would rescue him from his difficulties. Nothing, for instance, is more possible than that he be of a turn of mind for which this odd, literal opposition of description and dialogue, incident and description, has little meaning and light. People often talk of these things as if they had a kind of internecine distinctness, instead of melting into each other at every breath, and being intimately associated parts of one general effort of expression. I cannot imagine composition existing in a series of blocks, nor conceive, in any novel worth discussing at all, of a passage of description that is not in its intention narrative, a passage of dialogue that is not in its intention descriptive, a touch of truth of any sort that does not partake of the nature of incident, or an incident that derives its interest from any other source than the general and only source of the success of a work of art — that of being illustrative. A novel is a living thing, all one and continuous, like any other organism, and in proportion as it lives will it be found. I think, that in each of the parts there is something of each of the other parts. The critic who over the close texture of a finished work shall pretend to trace a geography of items will mark some frontiers as artificial, I fear, as any that have been known to history. There is an old-fashioned distinction between the novel of character and the novel of incident which must have cost many a smile to the intending fabulist who was keen about his work. It appears to me as little to the point as the equally celebrated distinction between the novel and the romance — to answer as little to any reality. There are bad novels and good novels, as there are bad pictures and good pictures; but that is the only distinction in which I see any meaning, and I can as little imagine speaking of a novel of character as I can imagine speaking of a picture of character. When one says picture one says of character, when one says novel one says of incident, and the terms may be transposed at will. What is character but the determination of incident? What is incident but the illustration of character? What is either a picture or a novel that is *not* of character? What else do we seek in it and find in it? It is an incident for a woman to stand up with her hand resting on a table and look out at you in a certain way; or if it be not an incident I think it will be hard to say what it is. At the same time it is an expression of character. If you say you don't see it (character in *that — allons donc!*[6]), this is exactly what the artist who has reasons of his own for thinking he *does* see it undertakes to show you. When a young man makes up his mind that he has not faith enough after all to enter the church as he intended, that is an incident, though you may not hurry to the end of the chapter to see whether perhaps he doesn't change once more. I do not say that these are extraordinary or startling incidents. I do not pretend to estimate the degree of interest proceeding from them, for this will depend upon the skill of the painter. It sounds almost puerile to say that some incidents are intrinsically much more important than others, and I need not take this precaution after having professed my sympathy for the major ones in remarking that the only classification of the novel that I can understand is into that which has life and that which has it not.

The novel and the romance, the novel of incident and that of character — these clumsy separations appear to me to have been made by critics and readers for their own convenience, and to help them out of some of their occasional queer predicaments, but to have little reality or interest for the producer, from whose point of view it is of course that we are attempting to consider the art of fiction. The case is the same with another shadowy category which Mr. Besant apparently is disposed to set up — that of the "modern English novel"; unless indeed it be that in this matter he has fallen into an accidental confusion of standpoints. It is not quite clear whether he intends the remarks in which he alludes to it to be didactic or historical. It is as difficult to suppose a person intending to write a modern English as to suppose him writing an ancient English novel: that is a label which begs the question. One writes the novel, one paints the picture, of one's language and of one's time, and calling it modern English will not, alas! make the difficult task any easier. No more, unfortunately, will calling this or that work of one's fellow-artist a romance — unless it be, of course, simply for the pleasant-

[6]Get out of here! [Ed.]

ness of the thing, as for instance when Hawthorne gave this heading to his story of *Blithedale*. The French, who have brought the theory of fiction to remarkable completeness, have but one name for the novel, and have not attempted smaller things in it, that I can see, for that. I can think of no obligation to which the "romancer" would not be held equally with the novelist; the standard of execution is equally high for each. Of course it is of execution that we are talking — that being the only point of a novel that is open to contention. This is perhaps too often lost sight of, only to produce interminable confusions and cross-purposes. We must grant the artist his subject, his idea, his *donnée:*[7] our criticism is applied only to what he makes of it. Naturally I do not mean that we are bound to like it or find it interesting: in case we do not our course is perfectly simple — to let it alone. We may believe that of a certain idea even the most sincere novelist can make nothing at all, and the event may perfectly justify our belief; but the failure will have been a failure to execute, and it is in the execution that the fatal weakness is recorded. If we pretend to respect the artist at all, we must allow him his freedom of choice, in the face, in particular cases, of innumerable presumptions that the choice will not fructify. Art derives a considerable part of its beneficial exercise from flying in the face of presumptions, and some of the most interesting experiments of which it is capable are hidden in the bosom of common things. Gustave Flaubert has written a story about the devotion of a servant-girl to a parrot,[8] and the production, highly finished as it is, cannot on the whole be called a success. We are perfectly free to find it flat, but I think it might have been interesting; and I, for my part, am extremely glad he should have written it; it is a contribution to our knowledge of what can be done — or what cannot. Ivan Turgenev has written a tale about a deaf and dumb serf and a lap-dog,[9] and the thing is touching, loving, a little masterpiece. He struck the note of life where Gustave Flaubert missed it — he flew in the face of a presumption and achieved a victory.

Nothing, of course, will ever take the place of the good old fashion of "liking" a work of art or not liking it: the most improved criticism will not abolish that primitive, that ultimate test. I mention this to guard myself from the accusation of intimating that the idea, the subject, of a novel or a picture, does not matter. It matters, to my sense, in the highest degree, and if I might put up a prayer it would be that artists should select none but the richest. Some, as I have already hastened to admit, are much more remunerative than others, and it would be a world happily arranged in which persons intending to treat them should be exempt from confusions and mistakes. This fortunate condition will arrive only, I fear, on the same day that critics become purged from error. Meanwhile, I repeat, we do not judge the artist with fairness unless we say to him,

"Oh, I grant you your starting-point, because if I did not I should seem to prescribe to you, and heaven forbid I should take that responsibility. If I pretend to tell you what you must not take, you will call upon me to tell you then what you must take; in which case I shall be prettily caught. Moreover, it isn't till I have accepted your data that I can begin to measure you. I have the standard, the pitch; I have no right to tamper with your flute and then criticize your music. Of course I may not care for your idea at all; I may think it silly, or stale, or unclean; in which case I wash my hands of you altogether. I may content myself with believing that you will not have succeeded in being interesting, but I shall, of course, not attempt to demonstrate it, and you will be as indifferent to me as I am to you. I needn't remind you that there are all sorts of tastes: who can know it better? Some people, for excellent reasons, don't like to read about carpenters; others, for reasons even better, don't like to read about courtesans. Many object to Americans. Others (I believe they are mainly editors and publishers) won't look at Italians. Some readers don't like quiet subjects; others don't like bustling ones. Some enjoy a complete illusion, others the consciousness of large concessions. They choose their novels accordingly, and if they don't care

[7]What is given. [Ed.]
[8]*A Simple Heart.* [Ed.]
[9]*Mumu.* [Ed.]

about your idea they won't, *a fortiori,* care about your treatment."

So that it comes back very quickly, as I have said, to the liking: in spite of M. Zola, who reasons less powerfully than he represents, and who will not reconcile himself to this absoluteness of taste, thinking that there are certain things that people ought to like, and that they can be made to like. I am quite at a loss to imagine anything (at any rate in this matter of fiction) that people *ought* to like or to dislike. Selection will be sure to take care of itself, for it has a constant motive behind it. That motive is simply experience. As people feel life, so they will feel the art that is most closely related to it. This closeness of relation is what we should never forget in talking of the effort of the novel. Many people speak of it as a factitious, artificial form, a product of ingenuity, the business of which is to alter and arrange the things that surround us, to translate them into conventional, traditional moulds. This, however, is a view of the matter which carries us but a very short way, condemns the art to an eternal repetition of a few familiar *clichés,* cuts short its development, and leads us straight up to a dead wall. Catching the very note and trick, the strange irregular rhythm of life, that is the attempt whose strenuous force keeps Fiction upon her feet. In proportion as in what she offers us we see life *without* rearrangement do we feel that we are touching the truth; in proportion as we see it *with* rearrangement do we feel that we are being put off with a substitute, a compromise and convention. It is not uncommon to hear an extraordinary assurance of remark in regard to this matter of rearranging, which is often spoken of as if it were the last word of art. Mr. Besant seems to me in danger of falling into the great error with his rather unguarded talk about "selection." Art is essentially selection, but it is a selection whose main care is to be typical, to be inclusive. For many people art means rose-colored window-panes, and selection means picking a bouquet for Mrs. Grundy.[10] They will tell you glibly that artistic considerations have nothing to do with the disagreeable, with the ugly; they will rattle off shallow commonplaces about the province of art and the limits of art till you are moved to some wonder in return as to the province and the limits of ignorance. It appears to me that no one can ever have made a seriously artistic attempt without becoming conscious of an immense increase — a kind of revelation — of freedom. One perceives in that case — by the light of a heavenly ray — that the province of art is all life, all feeling, all observation, all vision. As Mr. Besant so justly intimates, it is all experience. That is a sufficient answer to those who maintain that it must not touch the sad things of life, who stick into its divine unconscious bosom little prohibitory inscriptions on the end of sticks, such as we see in public gardens — "It is forbidden to walk on the grass; it is forbidden to touch the flowers; it is not allowed to introduce dogs or to remain after dark; it is requested to keep to the right." The young aspirant in the line of fiction whom we continue to imagine will do nothing without taste, for in that case his freedom would be of little use to him; but the first advantage of his taste will be to reveal to him the absurdity of the little sticks and tickets. If he have taste, I must add, of course he will have ingenuity, and my disrespectful reference to that quality just now was not meant to imply that it is useless in fiction. But it is only a secondary aid; the first is a capacity of receiving straight impressions.

Mr. Besant has some remarks on the question of "the story" which I shall not attempt to criticize, though they seem to me to contain a singular ambiguity, because I do not think I understand them. I cannot see what is meant by talking as if there were a part of a novel which is the story and part of it which for mystical reasons is not — unless indeed the distinction be made in a sense in which it is difficult to suppose that any one should attempt to convey anything. "The story," if it represents anything, represents the subject, the idea, the *donnée* of the novel; and there is surely no "school" — Mr. Besant speaks of a school — which urges that a novel should be all treatment and no subject. There must assuredly be something to treat; every school is intimately conscious of that. This sense of the story being the idea, the starting-point, of the novel, is the only one that I see in which it can be spoken of as something different from its organic whole;

[10]Personification of prudery. [Ed.]

and since in proportion as the work is successful the idea permeates and penetrates it, informs and animates it, so that every word and every punctuation-point contribute directly to the expression, in that proportion do we lose our sense of the story being a blade which may be drawn more or less out of its sheath. The story and the novel, the idea and the form, are the needle and thread, and I never heard of a guild of tailors who recommended the use of the thread without the needle, or the needle without the thread. Mr. Besant is not the only critic who may be observed to have spoken as if there were certain things in life which constitute stories, and certain others which do not. I find the same odd implication in an entertaining article in the *Pall Mall Gazette,* devoted, as it happens, to Mr. Besant's lecture. "The story is the thing!" says this graceful writer, as if with a tone of opposition to some other idea. I should think it was, as every painter who, as the time for "sending in" his picture looms in the distance, finds himself still in quest of a subject — as every belated artist not fixed about his theme will heartily agree. There are some subjects which speak to us and others which do not, but he would be a clever man who should undertake to give a rule — an *index expurgatorius* — by which the story and the no-story should be known apart. It is impossible (to me at least) to imagine any such rule which shall not be altogether arbitrary. The writer in the *Pall Mall* opposes the delightful (as I suppose) novel of *Margot la Balafrée* to certain tales in which "Bostonian nymphs" appear to have "rejected English dukes for psychological reasons."[11] I am not acquainted with the romance just designated, and can scarcely forgive the *Pall Mall* critic for not mentioning the name of the author, but the title appears to refer to a lady who may have received a scar in some heroic adventure. I am inconsolable at not being acquainted with this episode, but am utterly at a loss to see why it is a story when the rejection (or acceptance) of a duke is not, and why a reason, psychological or other, is not a subject when a cicatrix is. They are all particles of the multitudinous life with which the novel deals, and surely no dogma which pretends to make it lawful to touch the one and unlawful to touch the other will stand for a moment on its feet. It is the special picture that must stand or fall, according as it seem to possess truth or to lack it. Mr. Besant does not, to my sense, light up the subject by intimating that a story must, under penalty of not being a story, consist of "adventures." Why of adventures more than of green spectacles? He mentions a category of impossible things, and among them he places "fiction without adventure." Why without adventure, more than without matrimony, or celibacy, or parturition, or cholera, or hydropathy, or Jansenism? This seems to me to bring the novel back to the hapless little *rôle* of being an artificial, ingenious thing — bring it down from its large, free character of an immense and exquisite correspondence with life. And what *is* adventure, when it comes to that and by what sign is the listening pupil to recognize it? It is an adventure — an immense one — for me to write this little article; and for a Bostonian nymph to reject an English duke is an adventure only less stirring, I should say, than for an English duke to be rejected by a Bostonian nymph. I see dramas within dramas in that, and innumerable points of view. A psychological reason is, to my imagination, an object adorably pictorial; to catch the tint of its complexion — I feel as if that idea might inspire one to Titianesque efforts. There are few things more exciting to me, in short, than a psychological reason, and yet, I protest, the novel seems to me the most magnificent form of art. I have just been reading, at the same time, the delightful story of *Treasure Island,* by Mr. Robert Louis Stevenson and, in a manner less consecutive, the last tale from M. Edmond de Goncourt, which is entitled *Chérie.* One of these works treats of murder, mysteries, islands of dreadful renown, hairbreadth escapes, miraculous coincidences and buried doubloons. The other treats of a little French girl who lived in a fine house in Paris, and died of wounded sensibility because no one would marry her. I call *Treasure Island* delightful, because it appears to me to have succeeded wonderfully in what it attempts; and I venture to bestow no epithet upon *Chérie,* which strikes me as having failed deplorably in what it

[11]Henry James's own *An International Episode* (1879). *Margot la Balafrée* (1884) is by Fortune de Boisgobey. [Ed.]

attempts — that is in tracing the development of the moral consciousness of a child. But one of these productions strikes me as exactly as much of a novel as the other, and as having a "story" quite as much. The moral consciousness of a child is as much a part of life as the islands of the Spanish Main, and the one sort of geography seems to me to have those "surprises" of which Mr. Besant speaks quite as much as the other. For myself (since it comes back in the last resort, as I say, to the preference of the individual), the picture of the child's experience has the advantage that I can at successive steps (an immense luxury, near to the "sensual pleasure" of which Mr. Besant's critic in the *Pall Mall* speaks) say Yes or No, as it may be, to what the artist puts before me. I have been a child in fact, but I have been on a quest for a buried treasure only in supposition, and it is a simple accident that with M. de Goncourt I should have for the most part to say No. With George Eliot, when she painted that country with a far other intelligence, I always said Yes.

The most interesting part of Mr. Besant's lecture is unfortunately the briefest passage — his very cursory allusion to the "conscious moral purpose" of the novel. Here again it is not very clear whether he be recording a fact or laying down a principle; it is a great pity that in the latter case he should not have developed his idea. This branch of the subject is of immense importance, and Mr. Besant's few words point to considerations of the widest reach, not to be lightly disposed of. He will have treated the art of fiction but superficially who is not prepared to go every inch of the way that these considerations will carry him. It is for this reason that at the beginning of these remarks I was careful to notify the reader that my reflections on so large a theme have no pretension to be exhaustive. Like Mr. Besant, I have left the question of the morality of the novel till the last, and at the last I find I have used up my space. It is a question surrounded with difficulties, as witness the very first that meets us, in the form of a definite question, on the threshold. Vagueness, in such a discussion, is fatal, and what is the meaning of your morality and your conscious moral purpose? Will you not define your terms and explain how (a novel being a picture) a picture can be either moral or immoral? You wish to paint a moral picture or carve a moral statue: will you not tell us how you would set about it? We are discussing the Art of Fiction; questions of art are questions (in the widest sense) of execution; questions of morality are quite another affair, and will you not let us see how it is that you find it so easy to mix them up? These things are so clear to Mr. Besant that he has deduced from them a law which he sees embodied in English Fiction, and which is "a truly admirable thing and a great cause for congratulation." It is a great cause for congratulation indeed when such thorny problems become as smooth as silk. I may add that in so far as Mr. Besant perceives that in point of fact English Fiction has addressed itself preponderantly to these delicate questions he will appear to many people to have made a vain discovery. They will have been positively struck, on the contrary, with the moral timidity of the usual English novelist; with his (or with her) aversion to face the difficulties with which on every side the treatment of reality bristles. He is apt to be extremely shy (whereas the picture that Mr. Besant draws is a picture of boldness), and the sign of his work, for the most part, is a cautious silence on certain subjects. In the English novel (by which of course I mean the American as well), more than in any other there is a traditional difference between that which people know and that which they agree to admit that they know, that which they see and that which they speak of, that which they feel to be a part of life and that which they allow to enter into literature. There is the great difference, in short, between what they talk of in conversation and what they talk of in print. The essence of moral energy is to survey the whole field, and I should directly reverse Mr. Besant's remark and say not that the English novel has a purpose, but that it has a diffidence. To what degree a purpose in a work of art is a source of corruption I shall not attempt to inquire; the one that seems to me least dangerous is the purpose of making a perfect work. As for our novel, I may say lastly on this score that as we find it in England today it strikes me as addressed in a large degree to "young people," and that this in itself constitutes a presumption that it will be rather shy. There are certain things which it is generally agreed not to discuss, not even to mention, before young people. That is very well, but the absence of discussion is not a symptom of the moral passion. The purpose of the English novel — "a truly admirable thing, and a great cause for congratulation" — strikes me therefore as rather negative.

There is one point at which the moral sense and the artistic sense lie very near together; that is in the light of the very obvious truth that the deepest quality of a work of art will always be the quality of the mind of the producer. In proportion as that intelligence is fine will the novel, the picture, the statue partake of the substance of beauty and truth. To be constituted of such elements is, to my vision, to have purpose enough. No good novel will ever proceed from a superficial mind; that seems to me an axiom which, for the artist in fiction, will cover all needful moral ground: If the youthful aspirant take it to heart it will illuminate for him many of the mysteries of "purpose." There are many other useful things that might be said to him, but I have come to the end of my article, and can only touch them as I pass. The critic in the *Pall Mall Gazette,* whom I have already quoted, draws attention to the danger, in speaking of the art of fiction, of generalizing. The danger that he has in mind is rather, I imagine, that of particularizing, for there are some comprehensive remarks which, in addition to those embodied in Mr. Besant's suggestive lecture, might without fear of misleading him be addressed to the ingenuous student. I should remind him first of the magnificence of the form that is open to him, which offers to sight so few restrictions and such innumerable opportunities. The other arts, in comparison, appear confined and hampered; the various conditions under which they are exercised are so rigid and definite. But the only condition that I can think of attaching to the composition of the novel is, as I have already said, that it be sincere. This freedom is a splendid privilege, and the first lesson of the young novelist is to learn to be worthy of it.

"Enjoy it as it deserves [I should say to him]; take possession of it, explore it to its utmost extent, publish it, rejoice in it. All life belongs to you, and do not listen either to those who would shut you up into corners of it and tell you that it is only here and there that art inhabits, or to those who would persuade you that this heavenly messenger wings her way outside of life altogether, breathing a superfine air, and turning away her head from the truth of things. There is no impression of life, no manner of seeing it and feeling it, to which the plan of the novelist may not offer a place; you have only to remember that talents so dissimilar as those of Alexandre Dumas and Jane Austen, Charles Dickens and Gustave Flaubert have worked in this field with equal glory. Do not think too much about optimism and pessimism; try and catch the color of life itself. In France today we see a prodigious effort (that of Émile Zola, to whose solid and serious work no explorer of the capacity of the novel can allude without respect), we see an extraordinary effort vitiated by a spirit of pessimism on a narrow basis. M. Zola is magnificent, but he strikes an English reader as ignorant; he has an air of working in the dark; if he had as much light as energy, his results would be of the highest value. As for the aberrations of a shallow optimism, the ground (of English fiction especially) is strewn with their brittle particles as with broken glass. If you must indulge in conclusions, let them have the taste of a wide knowledge. Remember that your first duty is to be as complete as possible — to make as perfect a work. Be generous and delicate and pursue the prize."

Oscar Wilde

1854–1900

Oscar Fingal O'Flahertie Wills Wilde was born in Dublin, the son of the surgeon Sir William Wilde and Jane Francesca Elgee, who wrote poetry under the name of "Speranza." Wilde was educated first at Trinity College, Dublin, and then at Magdalen College, Oxford. At Oxford he proclaimed himself a disciple of the art historians and critics John Ruskin and Walter Pater, and developed a reputation for eccentricity by wearing his hair long, dressing in velvet knee breeches, and collecting china, the aesthetic perfection of which he hoped to duplicate in himself. Wilde won the Newdigate prize for poetry in 1878 and published his first volume of verse in 1881. At twenty-seven, he was already a public figure, lampooned by W. S. Gilbert as the "aesthetic sham" Bunthorne in his comic opera *Patience* (1881), who suggests that to impress the ladies you should "walk down Piccadilly with a poppy or a lily in your med-i-ee-val hand." Wilde's successful response to public ridicule (still current a century later) was to take his notoriety on tour, lecturing in the United States on the gospel of "Art for Art's Sake" — a pure aestheticism that rejected the notion of art and aesthetics as morally uplifting or socially useful. His first play, *Vera, or The Nihilists,* was produced in New York during his 1882 lecture tour. Two years later he married Constance Lloyd, an Irish heiress, with whom he had two sons.

Wilde published a volume of fairy tales, *The Happy Prince,* in 1888, but his notoriety had a second blossoming with the publication of *The Picture of Dorian Gray* (1891), which was attacked viciously in the press for immorality. Although Wilde's preface insists on the independence of art from moral and social value, the story itself — a Victorian Gothic masterpiece — seems distinctly moral, indeed moralistic today, as an apologue explicating the difference between hedonism (a life lived for mere physical pleasure) and epicureanism (a life lived for spiritual intensity). The eternally beautiful hero, Dorian, is as horrifying a figure in his empty pursuit of pleasure as the portrait that graphically expresses the rotting of his soul. What probably upset the press more deeply than Wilde's philosophy were the unmistakable hints of homosexual feeling, the love that "dared not speak its name" in the 1890s, in his portrayal of the relationship between the Paterian epicure, Sir Henry Wotton, and the young hedonist, Dorian Gray. Partly despite his embattled character and partly because of it, Wilde's dramas of the 1890s, jewelled with witty and amoral epigrams, became the hits of the London stage: *Lady Windemere's Fan* (1892), *A Woman of No Importance* (1893), *An Ideal Husband* (1895), and *The Importance of Being Earnest* (1895) were successively and often simultaneously on show in the West End, while his tragedy, *Salomé* (1894), was being played in Paris with Sarah Bernhardt in the title role.

The crash came in 1895, just when Wilde was at the height of his popularity. Wilde had been publicly labeled a sodomite by the Marquess of Queensberry, the father of Wilde's younger lover Lord Alfred Douglas, and Wilde was forced by social pressure to sue Queensberry for libel. Queensberry defended the truth of his accusation and won the civil lawsuit. Wilde then faced criminal prosecution for immoral conduct; convicted, he received two years' imprisonment with hard labor in Reading Gaol. A wealthy darling of society when the scandal broke, he was bankrupt and abandoned when he was released from prison in 1898. He published his most effective poem, "The Ballad of Reading Gaol," after leaving prison, but both the theater and society — the two sites of his triumph — had shut their doors upon him forever. He left England for Paris, living under the name of Sebastian Melmoth, where he died of meningitis in 1900.

"The Decay of Lying" (1889) is Wilde's wittiest and freshest expression of the "art for art's sake" aesthetic that he had learned from Walter Pater. In this not-so-Platonic dialogue between two Victorian gentlemen, the earnest Cyril and the dandified Vivian, Wilde takes up the relationship between art and life, poetic and logical truth, that had been at the center of the aesthetics debate since Plato. With playful paradox and overstatement, Vivian, Wilde's raisonneur, offers up what is not at bottom a very extreme version of Aristotle's answer to Plato: that art has only extraneous and incidental relations to politics, morality, and other social spheres; that it is an autonomous human activity with its own means and ends whose products can be judged only by its own rules. Wilde's position may at times appear extreme, but he was arguing in a utilitarian age that often took the most literal realism and the strictest conformity with the morality of the community as the hallmarks of successful art. These tests were not merely those of the journalistic worshippers of Mrs. Grundy:[1] We see them as well in literary geniuses like Zola and Tolstoy. (See in this context Tolstoy, "What Is Art?" p. 472.)

But though an Aristotelian rather than a Platonist by inclination, Wilde sees a grander role for art than mere independence. Like Shelley, who calls poets "the unacknowledged legislators of the World," Wilde views the canonical works of art as a collective book of instruction not only on proper thought and feeling but even on the nature of existence. In a crucial section, Vivian attempts to prove that all life — even the life of nature itself — is merely an imitation of art. He argues that people model themselves and their behavior on literary characters, falling in love like Juliet or committing suicide like Goethe's Werther. Even the beautiful brown fogs of the London autumn are, according to Vivian, the product of Impressionist painters like Monet and Whistler.

Vivian's statements are extreme and his examples sometimes perverse, but his most profound point — often made in contemporary post-structuralist thought — is that nature is known to us only through culture, which frames it and makes it comprehensible. Since one culture differs from another primarily through its art, it is indeed art that instructs and defines our sense of the natural world. The fogs of London may have been made up materially of coke and coal smoke mixed with water vapor, but the sense of their peculiar beauty can be traced to the Impressionists' taste for the vague and indefinite. Longer ago, the two-point perspective introduced by Italian Renaissance painters of the late fifteenth century permanently transformed the human sense of space.

[1]Personification of prudery. [Ed.]

In "The Decay of Lying" Wilde's speakers draw their examples from painting, where the relation between art and human vision may be clearest, but elsewhere Wilde extends his argument to other artistic forms. Music changes the human idea of time and relation, and poetry and drama the psychological sense of the self in relation to the world. Wilde's aestheticism is not merely a product of the purple nineties; rather, his vision of art as transvaluing all values is reminiscent of his predecessor Nietzsche, while his sense of culture as constituting the ground of our experiencing of the world we inhabit seems to foreshadow the ideas of Heidegger.

Selected Bibliography

Behrendt, Patricia F. *Oscar Wilde: Eros and Aesthetics.* New York: St. Martin's Press, 1991.

Buckler, William E. "Wilde's 'Trumpet against the Gate of Dullness': 'The Decay of Lying.'" *English Literature in Transition* 33 (1990): 311–23.

Freedman, Jonathan, ed. *Oscar Wilde: A Collection of Critical Essays.* Englewood Cliffs, NJ: Prentice-Hall, 1995.

Gide, André. *Oscar Wilde: A Study.* New York: Gordon Press, 1975.

Hannon, Patrice. "Aesthetic Criticism, Useless Art." In *Critical Essays on Oscar Wilde,* ed. Regenia Gagnier. New York: G. K. Hall, 1991, pp. 186–201.

Murray, Isobel M. *Oscar Wilde.* New York: Oxford University Press, 1989.

Novitz, David. "Art, Life and Reality." *British Journal of Aesthetics* 30 (1990): 301–10.

Small, Ian. "Semiotics and Oscar Wilde's Accounts of Art." *British Journal of Aesthetics* 25 (1985): 50–56.

Wilde, Oscar. *The Artist as Critic: Critical Writings of Oscar Wilde,* ed. Richard Ellmann. Chicago: University of Chicago Press, 1968.

Zhang, Longxi. "The Critical Legacy of Oscar Wilde." In *Critical Essays on Oscar Wilde,* ed. Regenia Gagnier. New York: G. K. Hall, 1991, pp. 157–71.

The Decay of Lying

An observation

A Dialogue.
Persons: Cyril and Vivian.
Scene: the library of a country house in Nottinghamshire.

CYRIL (*coming in through the open window from the terrace*): My dear Vivian, don't coop yourself up all day in the library. It is a perfectly lovely afternoon. The air is exquisite. There is a mist upon the woods, like the purple bloom upon a plum. Let us go and lie on the grass, and smoke cigarettes, and enjoy Nature.

VIVIAN: Enjoy Nature! I am glad to say that I have entirely lost that faculty. People tell us that Art makes us love Nature more than we loved her before; that it reveals her secrets to us; and that after a careful study of Corot and Constable[1] we see things in her that had escaped our observation. My own experience is that the more we study Art, the less we care for Nature. What Art really reveals to us is Nature's lack of design, her curious crudities, her extraordinary monotony,

[1]Jean-Baptiste Camille Corot (1796–1875) and John Constable (1776–1837) were nineteenth-century landscape painters, French and British, respectively. [Ed.]

her absolutely unfinished condition. Nature has good intentions, of course, but, as Aristotle once said, she cannot carry them out. When I look at a landscape I cannot help seeing all its defects. It is fortunate for us, however, that Nature is so imperfect, as otherwise we should have had no art at all. Art is our spirited protest, our gallant attempt to teach Nature her proper place. As for the infinite variety of Nature, that is a pure myth. It is not to be found in Nature herself. It resides in the imagination, or fancy, or cultivated blindness of the man who looks at her.

CYRIL: Well, you need not look at the landscape. You can lie on the grass and smoke and talk.

VIVIAN: But Nature is so uncomfortable. Grass is hard and lumpy and damp, and full of dreadful black insects. Why, even Morris' poorest workman[2] could make you a more comfortable seat than the whole of Nature can. Nature pales before the furniture of "the street which from Oxford has borrowed its name,"[3] as the poet you love so much once vilely phrased it. I don't complain. If Nature had been comfortable, mankind would never have invented architecture, and I prefer houses to the open air. In a house we all feel of the proper proportions. Everything is subordinated to us, fashioned for our use and our pleasure. Egotism itself, which is so necessary to a proper sense of human dignity, is entirely the result of indoor life. Out of doors one becomes abstract and impersonal. One's individuality absolutely leaves one. And then Nature is so indifferent, so unappreciative. Whenever I am walking in the park here, I always feel that I am no more to her than the cattle that browse on the slope, or the burdock that blooms in the ditch. Nothing is more evident than that Nature hates Mind. Thinking is the most unhealthy thing in the world, and people die of it just as they die of any other disease. Fortunately, in England at any rate, thought is not catching. Our splendid physique as a people is entirely due to our national stupidity. I only hope we shall be able to keep this great historic bulwark of our happiness for many years to come; but I am afraid that we are beginning to be over-educated; at least everybody who is incapable of learning has taken to teaching — that is really what our enthusiasm for education has come to. In the meantime, you had better go back to your wearisome uncomfortable Nature, and leave me to correct my proofs.

CYRIL: Writing an article! That is not very consistent after what you have just said.

VIVIAN: Who wants to be consistent? The dullard and the doctrinaire, the tedious people who carry out their principles to the bitter end of action, to the *reductio ad absurdum* of practice. Not I. Like Emerson, I write over the door of my library the word "Whim." Besides, my article is really a most salutary and valuable warning. If it is attended to, there may be a new Renaissance of Art.

CYRIL: What is the subject?

VIVIAN: I intend to call it "The Decay of Lying: A Protest."

CYRIL: Lying! I should have thought that our politicians kept up that habit.

VIVIAN: I assure you that they do not. They never rise beyond the level of misrepresentation, and actually condescend to prove, to discuss, to argue. How different from the temper of the true liar, with his frank, fearless statements, his superb irresponsibility, his healthy, natural disdain of proof of any kind! After all, what is a fine lie? Simply that which is its own evidence. If a man is sufficiently unimaginative to produce evidence in support of a lie, he might just as well speak the truth at once. No, the politicians won't do. Something may, perhaps, be urged on behalf of the Bar.[4] The mantle of the Sophist has fallen on its members. Their feigned ardours and unreal rhetoric are delightful. They can make the worse appear the better cause, as though they were fresh from Leontine schools,[5] and have been known to wrest from reluctant juries triumphant

[2]The poet and painter William Morris (1834–96) also ran a very profitable business designing and manufacturing furniture and other household articles, starting in 1861. [Ed.]

[3]Oxford Street was in the late nineteenth century, as today, the middle-class shopping district of London. [Ed.]

[4]The legal profession. [Ed.]

[5]Wilde's reference is to the sixth-century theologian Leontius of Byzantium, known as the first scholastic philosopher, who adapted Aristotelian logic to theological problems. [Ed.]

verdicts of acquittal for their clients, even when those clients, as often happens, were clearly and unmistakeably innocent. But they are briefed by the prosaic, and are not ashamed to appeal to precedent. In spite of their endeavors, the truth will out. Newspapers, even, have degenerated. They may now be absolutely relied upon. One feels it as one wades through their columns. It is always the unreadable that occurs. I am afraid that there is not much to be said in favour of either the lawyer or the journalist. Besides, what I am pleading for is Lying in art. Shall I read you what I have written? It might do you a great deal of good.

CYRIL: Certainly, if you give me a cigarette. Thanks. By the way, what magazine do you intend it for?

VIVIAN: For the *Retrospective Review*. I think I told you that the elect had revived it.

CYRIL: Whom do you mean by "the elect"?

VIVIAN: Oh, The Tired Hedonists of course. It is a club to which I belong. We are supposed to wear faded roses in our button-holes when we meet, and to have a sort of cult for Domitian.[6] I am afraid you are not eligible. You are too fond of simple pleasures.

CYRIL: I should be black-balled on the ground of animal spirits, I suppose?

VIVIAN: Probably. Besides, you are a little too old. We don't admit anybody who is of the usual age.

CYRIL: Well, I should fancy you are all a good deal bored with each other.

VIVIAN: We are. That is one of the objects of the club. Now, if you promise not to interrupt too often, I will read you my article.

CYRIL: You will find me all attention.

VIVIAN (*reading in a very clear, musical voice*): "THE DECAY OF LYING: A PROTEST. — One of the chief causes that can be assigned for the curiously commonplace character of most of the literature of our age is undoubtedly the decay of Lying as an art, a science, and a social pleasure. The ancient historians gave us delightful fiction in the form of fact; the modern novelist presents us with dull facts under the guise of fiction. The Blue-Book[7] is rapidly becoming his ideal both for method and manner. He has his tedious '*document humain*,'[8] his miserable little '*coin de la création*,'[9] into which he peers with his microscope. He is to be found at the Librairie Nationale, or at the British Museum,[10] shamelessly reading up his subject. He has not even the courage of other people's ideas, but insists on going directly to life for everything, and ultimately, between encyclopædias and personal experience, he comes to the ground, having drawn his types from the family circle or from the weekly washerwoman, and having acquired an amount of useful information from which never, even in his most meditative moments, can he thoroughly free himself.

"The loss that results to literature in general from this false ideal of our time can hardly be overestimated. People have a careless way of talking about a 'born liar,' just as they talk about a 'born poet.' But in both cases they are wrong. Lying and poetry are arts — arts, as Plato[11] saw, not unconnected with each other — and they require the most careful study, the most disinterested devotion. Indeed, they have their technique, just as the more material arts of painting and sculpture have, their subtle secrets of form and colour, their craft-mysteries, their deliberate artistic methods. As one knows the poet by his fine music, so one can recognize the liar by his rich rhythmic utterance, and in neither case will the casual inspiration of the moment suffice. Here, as elsewhere, practice must precede perfection. But in modern days while the fashion of writing poetry has become far too common, and should, if possible, be discouraged, the fashion of lying has almost fallen into disrepute. Many a young man starts in life with a natural gift for exaggeration which, if nurtured in congenial and

[6]Roman emperor 81–96 A.D., known for his pathological cruelty and suspicion. [Ed.]

[7]The official reports of Parliament, which are issued in a dark blue paper cover, were often referred to as "Blue-Books" in the nineteenth century. [Ed.]

[8]"Story of human life." [Ed.]

[9]"Corner of existence." [Ed.]

[10]The Bibliotheque Nationale and British Museum are the national libraries of France and England, respectively. [Ed.]

[11]See introduction to Plato, p. 17. [Ed.]

sympathetic surroundings, or by the imitation of the best models, might grow into something really great and wonderful. But, as a rule, he comes to nothing. He either falls into careless habits of accuracy — "

CYRIL: My dear fellow!

VIVIAN: Please don't interrupt in the middle of a sentence. "He either falls into careless habits of accuracy, or takes to frequenting the society of the aged and the well-informed. Both things are equally fatal to his imagination, as indeed they would be fatal to the imagination of anybody, and in a short time he develops a morbid and unhealthy faculty of truth-telling, begins to verify all statements made in his presence, has no hesitation in contradicting people who are much younger than himself, and often ends by writing novels which are so like life that no one can possibly believe in their probability. This is no isolated instance that we are giving. It is simply one example out of many; and if something cannot be done to check, or at least to modify, our monstrous worship of facts, Art will become sterile, and Beauty will pass away from the land.

"Even Mr. Robert Louis Stevenson,[12] that delightful master of delicate and fanciful prose, is tainted with this modern vice, for we know positively no other name for it. There is such a thing as robbing a story of its reality by trying to make it too true, and *The Black Arrow* is so inartistic as not to contain a single anachronism to boast of, while the transformation of Dr. Jekyll reads dangerously like an experiment out of the *Lancet*. As for Mr. Rider Haggard, who really has, or had once, the makings of a perfectly magnificent liar, he is now so afraid of being suspected of genius that when he does tell us anything marvellous, he feels bound to invent a personal reminiscence, and to put it into a footnote as a kind of cowardly corroboration. Nor are our other novelists much better. Mr. Henry James writes fiction as if it were a painful duty, and wastes upon mean motives and imperceptible 'points of view' his neat literary style, his felicitous phrases, his swift and caustic satire. Mr. Hall Caine, it is true, aims at the grandiose, but then he writes at the top of his voice. He is so loud that one cannot hear what he says. Mr. James Payn is an adept in the art of concealing what is not worth finding. He hunts down the obvious with the enthusiasm of a short-sighted detective. As one turns over the pages, the suspense of the author becomes almost unbearable. The horses of Mr. William Black's phaeton do not soar towards the sun. They merely frighten the sky at evening into violent chromolithographic effects. On seeing them approach, the peasants take refuge in dialect. Mrs. Oliphant prattles pleasantly about curates, lawn-tennis parties, domesticity, and other wearisome things. Mr. Marion Crawford has immolated himself upon the altar of local colour. He is like the lady in the French comedy who keeps talking about 'le beau ciel d'Italie.'[13] Besides, he has fallen into a bad habit of uttering moral platitudes. He is always telling us that to be good is to be good, and that to be bad is to be wicked. At times he is almost edifying. *Robert Elsmere* is of course a masterpiece — a masterpiece of the 'genre ennuyeux,'[14] the one form of literature that the English people seem to thoroughly enjoy. A thoughtful young friend of ours once told us that it reminded him of the sort of conversation

[12]Vivian lists many of the most popular British fiction writers of the late nineteenth century, most of them nearly forgotten today. *The Black Arrow* (1888) is a historical romance by Robert Louis Stevenson (1850–94), which is implicitly being compared with the more anachronistic (and exciting) *Treasure Island* (1883) and *Kidnapped* (1886). Sir Henry Rider Haggard (1856–1925) wrote fantasy adventure stories set in exotic locations, like *King Solomon's Mines* (1885) and *She* (1887). For Henry James, see introduction to James, p. 434. Thomas Henry Hall Caine (1853–1931) wrote many sensational novels including *The Shadow of a Crime* (1885) and *The Scapegoat* (1891). James Payn (1830–98) published over a hundred novels including *By Proxy* (1878). William Black (1841–98) was a Scottish novelist known best for *A Daughter of Heth* (1872). Margaret Oliphant (1828–97) was a prolific journalist and novelist who is enjoying a revival today; her *Miss Marjoribanks* (1866) is currently in print. Francis Marion Crawford (1854–1909) was an American short story writer and novelist who set novels in exotic lands, basing the stories on the lives of people he met while traveling. *Robert Elsmere* (1888) is a novel by Mary Augusta (Mrs. Humphry) Ward (1851–1920); Wilde's special animus against this novel was that it represents the Oxford at which he had studied under Walter Pater. [Ed.]

[13]"The beautiful sky of Italy." [Ed.]

[14]"Boring kind." [Ed.]

that goes on at a meat tea in the house of a serious Nonconformist family, and we can quite believe it. Indeed it is only in England that such a book could be produced. England is the home of lost ideas. As for that great and daily increasing school of novelists for whom the sun always rises in the East-End,[15] the only thing that can be said about them is that they find life crude, and leave it raw.

"In France, though nothing so deliberately tedious as *Robert Elsmere* has been produced, things are not much better. M. Guy de Maupassant,[16] with his keen mordant irony and his hard vivid style, strips life of the few poor rags that still cover her, and shows us foul sore and festering wound. He writes lurid little tragedies in which everybody is ridiculous; bitter comedies at which one cannot laugh for very tears. M. Zola,[17] true to the lofty principle that he lays down in one of his pronunciamentos on literature, 'L'homme de génie n'a jamais d'esprit,'[18] is determined to show that, if he has not got genius, he can at least be dull. And how well he succeeds! He is not without power. Indeed at times, as in *Germinal,* there is something almost epic in his work. But his work is entirely wrong from beginning to end, and wrong not on the ground of morals, but on the ground of art. From any ethical standpoint it is just what it should be. The author is perfectly truthful, and describes things exactly as they happen. What more can any moralist desire? We have no sympathy at all with the moral indignation of our time against M. Zola. It is simply the indignation of Tartuffe[19] on being exposed. But from the standpoint of art, what can be said in favour of the author of *L'Assommoir, Nana,* and *Pot-Bouille*? Nothing. Mr. Ruskin once described the characters in George Eliot's novels as being like the sweepings of a Pentonville omnibus, but M. Zola's characters are much worse. They have their dreary vices, and their drearier virtues. The record of their lives is absolutely without interest. Who cares what happens to them? In literature we require distinction, charm, beauty, and imaginative power. We don't want to be harrowed and disgusted with an account of the doings of the lower orders. M. Daudet[20] is better. He has wit, a light touch, and an amusing style. But he has lately committed literary suicide. Nobody can possibly care for Delobelle with his 'Il faut lutter pour l'art,'[21] or for Valmajour with his eternal refrain about the nightingale, or for the poet in *Jack* with his 'mots cruels,'[22] now that we have learned from *Vingt Ans de ma Vie littéraire* that these characters were taken directly from life. To us they seem to have suddenly lost all their vitality, all the few qualities they ever possessed. The only real people are the people who never existed, and if a novelist is base enough to go to life for his personages he should at least pretend that they are creations, and not boast of them as copies. The justification of a character in a novel is not that other persons are what they are, but that the author is what he is. Otherwise the novel is not a work of art. As for M. Paul Bourget,[23] the master of the *roman psychologique,*[24] he commits the error of imagining that the men and women of modern life are capable of being infinitely analysed for an innumerable series of chapters. In point of fact what is interesting about people in good society — and M. Bourget rarely moves out of the Faubourg St. Germain,[25] except to come to London, — is the mask that each one of them wears, not the reality that lies behind the

[15]The area of London east of the commercial district contained the poorest neighborhoods. [Ed.]

[16]French writer (1850–93) famous for mordantly ironic short stories. [Ed.]

[17]Émile Zola (1840–1902), French author of dozens of naturalistic novels including *L'Assommoir* (*The Dram Shop,* 1877), *Nana* (1880), and *Pot-Bouille* (*The Stew,* 1882), which focused attention on the social problems of alcoholism, prostitution, and middle-class competitiveness, respectively. [Ed.]

[18]"The man of genius never has wit." [Ed.]

[19]Hypocritical anti-hero of Molière's comedy by the same name. [Ed.]

[20]Alphonse Daudet, French novelist and dramatist (1840–97), who wrote *Jack* in 1876. [Ed

[21]"One must struggle for the sake of art." [Ed.]

[22]"Cruel words." [Ed.]

[23]French psychological novelist (1852–1935) best known for *Le Disciple* (1889). [Ed.]

[24]"Psychological novel." [Ed.]

[25]The most fashionable and aristocratic neighborhood in late nineteenth-century Paris. [Ed.]

mask. It is a humiliating confession, but we are all of us made out of the same stuff. In Falstaff there is something of Hamlet, in Hamlet there is not a little of Falstaff. The fat knight has his moods of melancholy, and the young prince his moments of coarse humour. Where we differ from each other is purely in accidentals: in dress, manner, tone of voice, religious opinions, personal appearance, tricks of habit, and the like. The more one analyses people, the more all reasons for analysis disappear. Sooner or later one comes to that dreadful universal thing called human nature. Indeed, as any one who has ever worked among the poor knows only too well, the brotherhood of man is no mere poet's dream, it is a most depressing and humiliating reality; and if a writer insists upon analysing the upper classes, he might just as well write of match-girls and costermongers[26] at once." However, my dear Cyril, I will not detain you any further just here. I quite admit that modern novels have many good points. All I insist on is that, as a class, they are quite unreadable.

CYRIL: That is certainly a very grave qualification, but I must say that I think you are rather unfair in some of your strictures. I like *The Deemster,* and *The Daughter of Heth,* and *Le Disciple,* and *Mr. Isaacs,*[27] and as for *Robert Elsmere* I am quite devoted to it. Not that I can look upon it as a serious work. As a statement of the problems that confront the earnest Christian it is ridiculous a antiquated. It is simply Arnold's *Literature and Dogma* with the literature left out. It is as much behind the age as Paley's *Evidences,*[28] or Colenso's[29] method of Biblical exegesis. Nor could anything be less impressive than the unfortunate hero gravely heralding a dawn that rose long ago, and so completely missing its true significance that he proposes to carry on the business of the old firm under the new name. On the other hand, it contains several clever caricatures, and a heap of delightful quotations, and Green's philosophy very pleasantly sugars the somewhat bitter pill of the author's fiction. I also cannot help expressing my surprise that you have said nothing about the two novelists whom you are always reading, Balzac[30] and George Meredith.[31] Surely they are realists, both of them?

VIVIAN: Ah! Meredith! Who can define him? His style is chaos illumined by flashes of lightning. As a writer he has mastered everything except language: as a novelist he can do everything, except tell a story: as an artist he is everything, except articulate. Somebody in Shakespeare — Touchstone, I think — talks about a man who is always breaking his shins over his own wit, and it seems to me that this might serve as the basis for a criticism of Meredith's method. But whatever he is, he is not a realist. Or rather I would say that he is a child of realism who is not on speaking terms with his father. By deliberate choice he has made himself a romanticist. He has refused to bow the knee to Baal, and after all, even if the man's fine spirit did not revolt against the noisy assertions of realism, his style would be quite sufficient of itself to keep life at a respectful distance. By its means he has planted round his garden a hedge full of thorns, and red with wonderful roses. As for Balzac, he was a most remarkable combination of the artistic temperament with the scientific spirit. The latter he bequeathed to his disciples: the former was entirely his own. The difference between such a book as M. Zola's *L'Assommoir* and Balzac's *Illusions Perdues* is the difference between unimaginative realism and imaginative reality.

[26]People who peddle their wares out of street wagons. [Ed.]

[27]Cyril goes back up Vivian's list of losers: *The Deemster* is by Hall Caine, *The Daughter of Heth* by William Black, *Le Disciple* by Paul Bourget, *Mr. Isaacs* by Marion Crawford. [Ed.]

[28]William Paley (1743–1805), English theologian, published *Evidences of the Existence and Attributes of the Deity* in 1802. [Ed.]

[29]Bishop John William Colenso, author of *The Pentateuch and the Book of Judges Critically Examined* (1863), attacked by Arnold; see p. 406. [Ed.]

[30]Honoré de Balzac (1799–1850), French author of at least ninety-five novels forming a "Comédie Humaine" depicting life from the Revolution to the 1840s. [Ed.]

[31]English novelist (1828–1909), author of over a dozen novels of which *The Ordeal of Richard Feverel* (1859) and *The Egoist* (1879) are the best known. [Ed.]

"All Balzac's characters," said Baudelaire,[32] "are gifted with the same ardour of life that animated himself. All his fictions are as deeply coloured as dreams. Each mind is a weapon loaded to the muzzle with will. The very scullions have genius." A steady course of Balzac reduces our living friends to shadows, and our acquaintances to the shadows of shades. His characters have a kind of fervent fiery-coloured existence. They dominate us, and defy scepticism. One of the greatest tragedies of my life is the death of Lucien de Rubempré.[33] It is a grief from which I have never been able to completely rid myself. It haunts me in my moments of pleasure. I remember it when I laugh. But Balzac is no more a realist than Holbein[34] was. He created life, he did not copy it. I admit, however, that he set far too high a value on modernity of form, and that, consequently, there is no book of his that, as an artistic masterpiece, can rank with *Salammbô* or *Esmond,* or *The Cloister and the Hearth,* or the *Vicomte de Bragelonne*.[35]

CYRIL: Do you object to modernity of form, then?

VIVIAN: Yes. It is a huge price to pay for a very poor result. Pure modernity of form is always somewhat vulgarising. It cannot help being so. The public imagine that, because they are interested in their immediate surroundings, Art should be interested in them also, and should take them as her subject-matter. But the mere fact that they are interested in these things makes them unsuitable subjects for Art. The only beautiful things, as somebody once said, are the things that do not concern us. As long as a thing is useful or necessary to us, or affects us in any way, either for pain or for pleasure, or appeals strongly to our sympathies, or is a vital part of the environment in which we live, it is outside the proper sphere of art. To art's subject-matter we should be more or less indifferent. We should, at any rate, have no preferences, no prejudices, no partisan feeling of any kind. It is exactly because Hecuba is nothing to us that her sorrows are such an admirable motive for a tragedy. I do not know anything in the whole history of literature sadder than the artistic career of Charles Reade. He wrote one beautiful book, *The Cloister and the Hearth,* a book as much above *Romola* as *Romola* is above *Daniel Deronda,*[36] and wasted the rest of his life in a foolish attempt to be modern, to draw public attention to the state of our convict prisons, and the management of our private lunatic asylums. Charles Dickens was depressing enough in all conscience when he tried to arouse our sympathy for the victims of the poor-law administration;[37] but Charles Reade, an artist, a scholar, a man with a true sense of beauty, raging and roaring over the abuses of contemporary life like a common pamphleteer or a sensational journalist, is really a sight for the angels to weep over. Believe me, my dear Cyril, modernity of form and modernity of subject-matter are entirely and absolutely wrong. We have mistaken the common livery of the age for the vesture of the Muses, and spend our days in the sordid streets and hideous suburbs of our vile cities when we should be out on the hillside with Apollo. Certainly we are a degraded race, and have sold our birthright for a mess of facts.

CYRIL: There is something in what you say, and there is no doubt that whatever amusement

[32]Charles Baudelaire (1821–67), French poet and critic; the quotation is, however, from his friend Theophile Gautier (1811–72). [Ed.]

[33]Hero of Balzac's *Illusions perdues*. [Ed.]

[34]Hans Holbein the Younger (1497–1543), German portrait painter who sketched many of the nobles of Henry VIII's court. [Ed.]

[35]*Salammbô:* romantic historical novel set in the Orient (1863) by French novelist Gustave Flaubert (1821–80). *Esmond: The History of Henry Esmond* (1852), historical novel set in the early eighteenth century by English novelist William Makepeace Thackeray (1811–63). *The Cloister and the Hearth:* 1861 historical novel about the Dutch renaissance humanist Desiderius Erasmus by Charles Reade (1814–84). *Vicomte de Bragelonne:* third novel (1848–51) in the *Three Musketeers* trilogy by French novelist Alexandre Dumas the Elder (1802–70), best known for containing the final segment concerning the Man in the Iron Mask. [Ed.]

[36]Two novels by George Eliot (1819–80); *Romola* (1863) is a historical novel set in the late renaissance Florence of Savonarola; *Daniel Deronda* (1876) is set in contemporary England and deals with (among other things) the Jewish Question. [Ed.]

[37]The effects of the Poor Law of 1834 were illustrated in Dickens's *Oliver Twist* (1837–39). [Ed.]

we may find in reading a purely modern novel, we have rarely any artistic pleasure in re-reading it. And this is perhaps the best rough test of what is literature and what is not. If one cannot enjoy reading a book over and over again, there is no use reading it at all. But what do you say about the return to Life and Nature? This is the panacea that is always being recommended to us.

VIVIAN: I will read you what I say on that subject. The passage comes later on in the article, but I may as well give it to you now: —

"The popular cry of our time is 'Let us return to Life and Nature; they will recreate Art for us, and send the red blood coursing through her veins; they will shoe her feet with swiftness and make her hand strong.' But, alas! we are mistaken in our amiable and well-meaning efforts. Nature is always behind the age. And as for Life, she is the solvent that breaks up Art, the enemy that lays waste her house."

CYRIL: What do you mean by saying that Nature is always behind the age?

VIVIAN: Well, perhaps that is rather cryptic. What I mean is this. If we take Nature to mean natural simple instinct as opposed to self-conscious culture, the work produced under this influence is always old-fashioned, antiquated, and out of date. One touch of Nature may make the whole world kin,[38] but two touches of Nature will destroy any work of Art. If, on the other hand, we regard Nature as the collection of phenomena external to man, people only discover in her what they bring to her. She has no suggestions of her own. Wordsworth went to the lakes, but he was never a lake poet. He found in stones the sermons he had already hidden there. He went moralizing about the district, but his good work was produced when he returned, not to Nature but to poetry. Poetry gave him "Laodamia," and the fine sonnets, and the great Ode, such as it is. Nature gave him "Martha Ray" and "Peter Bell," and the address to Mr. Wilkinson's spade.

CYRIL: I think that view might be questioned. I am rather inclined to believe in the "impulse from a vernal wood,"[39] though of course the artistic value of such an impulse depends entirely on the kind of temperament that receives it, so that the return to Nature would come to mean simply the advance to a great personality. You would agree with that, I fancy. However, proceed with your article.

VIVIAN (*reading*): "Art begins with abstract decoration with purely imaginative and pleasurable work dealing with what is unreal and non-existent. This is the first stage. Then Life becomes fascinated with this new wonder, and asks to be admitted into the charmed circle. Art takes life as part of her rough material, recreates it, and refashions it in fresh forms, is absolutely indifferent to fact, invents, imagines, dreams, and keeps between herself and reality the impenetrable barrier of beautiful style, of decorative or ideal treatment. The third stage is when Life gets the upper hand, and drives Art out into the wilderness. This is the true decadence, and it is from this that we are now suffering.

"Take the case of the English drama. At first in the hands of the monks Dramatic Art was abstract, decorative, and mythological. Then she enlisted Life in her service, and using some of life's external forms, she created an entirely new race of beings, whose sorrows were more terrible than any sorrow man has ever felt, whose joys were keener than lover's joys, who had the rage of the Titans and the calm of the gods, who had monstrous and marvellous sins, monstrous and marvellous virtues. To them she gave a language different from that of actual use, a language full of resonant music and sweet rhythm, made stately by solemn cadence, or made delicate by fanciful rhyme, jewelled with wonderful words, and enriched with lofty diction. She clothed her children in strange raiment and gave them masks, and at her bidding the antique world rose from its marble tomb. A new Cæsar stalked through the streets of risen Rome, and with purple sail and flute-led oars another Cleopatra passed up the river to Antioch. Old myth and legend and dream took shape and substance. History was entirely re-written, and there was hardly one of the dramatists who did not recognize that the object of Art is not simple truth but complex beauty. In this they were perfectly right. Art itself is really a

[38]Shakespeare, *Troilus and Cressida*, III.iii.171. [Ed.]

[39]From Wordsworth's "The Tables Turned," line 21. [Ed.]

form of exaggeration; and selection, which is the very spirit of art, is nothing more than an intensified mode of over-emphasis.

"But Life soon shattered the perfection of the form. Even in Shakespeare we can see the beginning of the end. It shows itself by the gradual breaking up of the blank-verse in the later plays, by the predominance given to prose, and by the over-importance assigned to characterisation. The passages in Shakespeare — and they are many — where the language is uncouth, vulgar, exaggerated, fantastic, obscene even, are entirely due to Life calling for an echo of her own voice, and rejecting the intervention of beautiful style, through which alone should Life be suffered to find expression. Shakespeare is not by any means a flawless artist. He is too fond of going directly to life, and borrowing life's natural utterance. He forgets that when Art surrenders her imaginative medium she surrenders everything. Goethe says, somewhere —

> In der Beschränkung zeigt sich erst der Meister,

'It is in working within limits that the master reveals himself,' and the limitation, the very condition of any art is style. However, we need not linger any longer over Shakespeare's realism. *The Tempest* is the most perfect of palinodes.[40] All that we desired to point out was, that the magnificent work of the Elizabethan and Jacobean artists contained within itself the seeds of its own dissolution, and that, if it drew some of its strength from using life as rough material, it drew all its weakness from using life as an artistic method. As the inevitable result of this substitution of an imitative for a creative medium, this surrender of an imaginative form, we have the modern English melodrama. The characters in these plays talk on the stage exactly as they would talk off it; they have neither aspirations nor aspirates; they are taken directly from life and reproduce its vulgarity down to the smallest detail; they present the gait, manner, costume, and accent of real people; they would pass unnoticed in a third-class railway carriage. And yet how wearisome the plays are! They do not succeed in producing even that impression of reality at which they aim, and which is their only reason for existing. As a method, realism is a complete failure.

"What is true about drama and the novel is no less true about those arts that we call decorative arts. The whole history of these arts in Europe is the record of the struggle between Orientalism, with its frank rejection of imitation, its love of artistic convention, its dislike to the actual representation of any object in Nature, and our own imitative spirit. Wherever the former has been paramount, as in Byzantium, Sicily, and Spain, by actual contact, or in the rest of Europe by the influence of the Crusades, we have had beautiful and imaginative work in which the visible things of life are transmuted into artistic conventions, and the things that Life has not are invented and fashioned for her delight. But wherever we have returned to Life and Nature, our work has always become vulgar, common, and uninteresting. Modern tapestry, with its aërial effects, its elaborate perspective, its broad expanses of waste sky, its faithful and laborious realism, has no beauty whatsoever. The pictorial glass of Germany is absolutely detestable. We are beginning to weave possible carpets in England, but only because we have returned to the method and spirit of the East. Our rugs and carpets of twenty years ago, with their solemn depressing truths, their inane worship of Nature, their sordid reproductions of visible objects, have become, even to the Philistine, a source of laughter. A cultured Mahomedan once remarked to us, 'You Christians are so occupied in misinterpreting the fourth commandment that you have never thought of making an artistic application of the second.' He was perfectly right, and the whole truth of the matter is this: The proper school to learn art in is not Life but Art."

And now let me read you a passage which seems to me to settle the question very completely.

"It was not always thus. We need not say anything about the poets, for they, with the unfortunate exception of Mr. Wordsworth, have been really faithful to their high mission, and are universally recognized as being absolutely unre-

[40]A palinode is a poem that retracts the poet's previous work. [Ed.]

liable. But in the works of Herodotus,[41] who, in spite of the shallow and ungenerous attempts of modern sciolists to verify his history, may justly be called the 'Father of Lies'; in the published speeches of Cicero and the biographies of Suetonius; in Tacitus at his best; in Pliny's *Natural History*; in Hanno's *Periplus*; in all the early chronicles; in the Lives of the Saints; in Froissart and Sir Thomas Mallory; in the travels of Marco Polo; in Olaus Magnus, and Aldrovandus, and Conrad Lycosthenes, with his magnificent *Prodigiorum et Ostentorum Chronicon*; in the autobiography of Benvenuto Cellini; in the memoirs of Casanuova; in Defoe's *History of the Plague*; in Boswell's *Life of Johnson*; in Napoleon's despatches, and in the works of our own Carlyle, whose *French Revolution* is one of the most fascinating historical novels ever written, facts are either kept in their proper subordinate position, or else entirely excluded on the general ground of dulness. Now, everything is changed. Facts are not merely finding a footing-place in history, but they are usurping the domain of Fancy, and have invaded the kingdom of Romance. Their chilling touch is over everything. They are vulgarising mankind. The crude commercialism of America, its materialising spirit, its indifference to the poetical side of things, and its lack of imagination and of high unattainable ideals, are entirely due to that country having adopted for its national hero a man, who according to his own confession, was incapable of telling a lie, and it is not too much to say that the story of George Washington and the cherry-tree[42] has done more harm, and in a shorter space of time, than any other moral tale in the whole of literature."

CYRIL: My dear boy!

VIVIAN: I assure you it is the case, and the amusing part of the whole thing is that the story of the cherry-tree is an absolute myth. However, you must not think that I am too despondent about the artistic future either of America or of our own country. Listen to this: —

"That some change will take place before this century has drawn to its close we have no doubt whatsoever. Bored by the tedious and improving conversation of those who have neither the wit to exaggerate nor the genius to romance, tired of the intelligent person whose reminiscences are always based upon memory, whose statements are invariably limited by probability, who is at any time liable to be corroborated by the merest Philistine who happens to be present, Society sooner or later must return to its lost leader, the cultured and fascinating liar. Who he was who first, without ever having gone out to the rude chase, told the wondering cavemen at sunset how he had dragged the Megatherium from the purple darkness of its jasper cave, or slain the Mammoth in single combat and brought back its gilded tusks, we cannot tell, and not one of our modern anthropologists, for all their much-boasted science, has had the ordinary courage to tell us. Whatever was his name or race, he certainly was the true founder of social intercourse. For the aim of the liar is simply to charm, to delight, to give pleasure. He is the very basis of civilized society, and without him a dinner party, even at the mansions of the great, is as dull as a lecture at the Royal Society, or a debate at the Incorporated Authors, or one of Mr. Burnand's[43] farcical comedies.

"Nor will he be welcomed by society alone. Art, breaking from the prison-house of realism, will run to greet him, and will kiss his false, beautiful lips, knowing that he alone is in possession of the great secret of all her manifestations, the secret that Truth is entirely and absolutely a matter of style; while Life — poor, probable, uninteresting human life — tired of repeating herself for the benefit of Mr. Herbert Spencer,[44] scientific historians, and the compilers of statistics in general, will follow meekly after him, and try

[41]Vivian's list mixes imaginative histories from those of Herodotus, Greek historian of the fifth century B.C., to *The French Revolution* (1837) by Thomas Carlyle (1795–1881), with works of rhetoric, natural science, hagiography, historical novels (e.g., Defoe's 1722 *Journal of the Plague Year*). Sciolists are pedantic scholars. [Ed.]

[42]The fifth edition (1806) of Mason Locke Weems's *Life and Memorable Actions of George Washington* contained the fictionalized story about the cherry tree. [Ed.]

[43]Francis C. Burnand (knighted in 1910) was the editor of *Punch*. [Ed.]

[44]Spencer (1820–1903) developed theories that adapted Darwin's ideas about evolution through natural selection to societies. [Ed.]

to produce, in her own simple and untutored way, some of the marvels of which he talks.

"No doubt there will always be critics who, like a certain writer in the *Saturday Review,* will gravely censure the teller of fairy tales for his defective knowledge of natural history, who will measure imaginative work by their own lack of any imaginative faculty, and will hold up their inkstained hands in horror if some honest gentleman, who has never been farther than the yew-trees of his own garden, pens a fascinating book of travels like Sir John Mandeville,[45] or, like great Raleigh,[46] writes a whole history of the world, without knowing anything whatsoever about the past. To excuse themselves they will try and shelter under the shield of him who made Prospero the magician, and gave him Caliban and Ariel as his servants, who heard the Tritons blowing their horns round the coral reefs of the Enchanted Isle, and the fairies singing to each other in a wood near Athens, who led the phantom kings in dim procession across the misty Scottish heath, and hid Hecate in a cave with the weird sisters. They will call upon Shakespeare — they always do — and will quote that hackneyed passage about Art holding the mirror up to Nature, forgetting that this unfortunate aphorism is deliberately said by Hamlet in order to convince the bystanders of his absolute insanity in all art-matters."

CYRIL: Ahem! Another cigarette, please.

VIVIAN: My dear fellow, whatever you may say, it is merely a dramatic utterance, and no more represents Shakespeare's real views upon art than the speeches of Iago represent his real views upon morals. But let me get to the end of the passage:

"Art finds her own perfection within, and not outside of, herself. She is not to be judged by any external standard of resemblance. She is a veil, rather than a mirror. She has flowers that no forests know of, birds that no woodland possesses. She makes and unmakes many worlds, and can draw the moon from heaven with a scarlet thread. Hers are the 'forms more real than living man,' and hers the great archetypes of which things that have existence are but unfinished copies. Nature has, in her eyes, no laws, no uniformity. She can work miracles at her will, and when she calls monsters from the deep they come. She can bid the almond tree blossom in winter, and send the snow upon the ripe cornfield. At her word the frost lays its silver finger on the burning mouth of June, and the winged lions creep out from the hollows of the Lydian hills. The dryads peer from the thicket as she passes by, and the brown fauns smile strangely at her when she comes near them. She has hawk-faced gods that worship her, and the centaurs gallop at her side."

CYRIL: I like that. I can see it. Is that the end?

VIVIAN: No. There is one more passage, but it is purely practical. It simply suggests some methods by which we could revive this lost art of Lying.

CYRIL: Well, before you read it to me, I should like to ask you a question. What do you mean by saying that life, "poor, probable, uninteresting human life," will try to reproduce the marvels of art? I can quite understand your objection to art being treated as a mirror. You think it would reduce genius to the position of a cracked looking-glass. But you don't mean to say that you seriously believe that Life imitates Art, that Life in fact is the mirror, and Art the reality?

VIVIAN: Certainly I do. Paradox though it may seem — and paradoxes are always dangerous things — it is none the less true that Life imitates art far more than Art imitates life. We have all seen in our own day in England how a certain curious and fascinating type of beauty, invented and emphasised by two imaginative painters,[47] has so influenced Life that whenever one goes to a private view or to an artistic salon one sees, here the mystic eyes of Rossetti's dream, the long ivory throat, the strange square-cut jaw, the loosened shadowy hair that he so ardently loved,

[45]Sir John Mandeville (1300?–72) was the author of a book of *Travels* written in Norman French between 1357–71; it is a compilation of other travelers' tales into a single first-person narrative. [Ed.]

[46]Sir Walter Raleigh (1554–1618) wrote a *History of the World* (1614) while in prison. [Ed.]

[47]Vivian gives a list of paintings by the Pre-Raphaelite artist (and poet) Dante Gabriel Rossetti (1828–82). The other "imaginative painter" may be Sir Edward Coley Burne-Jones (1833–98). [Ed.]

there the sweet maidenhood of "The Golden Stair," the blossom-like mouth and weary loveliness of the "Laus Amoris," the passion-pale face of Andromeda, the thin hands and lithe beauty of the Vivien in "Merlin's Dream." And it has always been so. A great artist invents a type, and Life tries to copy it, to reproduce it in a popular form, like an enterprising publisher. Neither Holbein nor Vandyck found in England what they have given us. They brought their types with them, and Life with her keen imitative faculty set herself to supply the master with models. The Greeks, with their quick artistic instinct, understood this, and set in the bride's chamber the statue of Hermes or of Apollo, that she might bear children as lovely as the works of art that she looked at in her rapture or her pain. They knew that Life gains from Art not merely spirituality, depth of thought and feeling, soul-turmoil or soul-peace, but that she can form herself on the very lines and colours of art, and can reproduce the dignity of Pheidias as well as the grace of Praxiteles. Hence came their objection to realism. They disliked it on purely social grounds. They felt that it inevitably makes people ugly, and they were perfectly right. We try to improve the conditions of the race by means of good air, free sunlight, wholesome water, and hideous bare buildings for the better housing of the lower orders. But these things merely produce health, they do not produce beauty. For this, Art is required, and the true disciples of the great artist are not his studio-imitators, but those who become like his works of art, be they plastic as in the Greek days, or pictorial as in modern times; in a word, Life is Art's best, Art's only pupil.

As it is with the visible arts, so it is with literature. The most obvious and the vulgarest form in which this is shown is in the case of the silly boys who, after reading the adventures of Jack Sheppard or Dick Turpin,[48] pillage the stalls of unfortunate apple-women, break into sweet-shops at night, and alarm old gentlemen who are returning home from the city by leaping out on them in suburban lanes, with black masks and unloaded revolvers. This interesting phenomenon, which always occurs after the appearance of a new edition of either of the books I have alluded to, is usually attributed to the influence of literature on the imagination. But this is a mistake. The imagination is essentially creative and always seeks for a new form. The boy-burglar is simply the inevitable result of life's imitative instinct. He is Fact, occupied as Fact usually is, with trying to reproduce Fiction, and what we see in him is repeated on an extended scale throughout the whole of life. Schopenhauer has analyzed the pessimism that characterises modern thought, but Hamlet invented it. The world has become sad because a puppet was once melancholy. The Nihilist, that strange martyr who has no faith, who goes to the stake without enthusiasm, and dies for what he does not believe in, is a purely literary product. He was invented by Tourgénieff, and completed by Dostoieffski.[49] Robespierre came out of the pages of Rousseau as surely as the People's Palace rose out of the *débris* of a novel. Literature always anticipates life. It does not copy it, but moulds it to its purpose. The nineteenth century, as we know it, is largely an invention of Balzac. Our Luciens de Rubempré, our Rastignacs, and De Marsays made their first appearance on the stage of the *Comédie Humaine.* We are merely carrying out, with footnotes and unnecessary additions, the whim or fancy or creative vision of a great novelist. I once asked a lady, who knew Thackeray intimately, whether he had had any model for Becky Sharp. She told me that Becky was an invention, but that the idea of the character had been partly suggested by a governess who lived in the neighbourhood of Kensington Square, and was the companion of a very selfish and rich old woman. I inquired what became of the governess, and she replied that, oddly enough, some years after the appearance of *Vanity Fair,* she ran away with the nephew of the lady with whom she was living, and for a short time made a great splash in society, quite in Mrs. Rawdon Crawley's style, and entirely by Mrs. Rawdon

[48]Legendary British highwaymen of the eighteenth century. [Ed.]

[49]Nihilism was analyzed by Ivan Sergeievich Turgenev (1818–83) in *Fathers and Sons* (1862) and by Fyodor Mikhailovich Dostoevsky (1821–81) in *The Devils* (1871–72). [Ed.]

Crawley's methods. Ultimately she came to grief, disappeared to the Continent, and used to be occasionally seen at Monte Carlo and other gambling places. The noble gentleman from whom the same great sentimentalist drew Colonel Newcome died, a few months after *The Newcomes* had reached a fourth edition, with the word "Adsum" on his lips. Shortly after Mr. Stevenson published his curious psychological story of transformation, a friend of mine, called Mr. Hyde, was in the north of London, and being anxious to get to a railway station, took what he thought would be a short cut, lost his way, and found himself in a network of mean, evil-looking streets. Feeling rather nervous he began to walk extremely fast, when suddenly out of an archway ran a child right between his legs. It fell on the pavement, he tripped over it, and trampled upon it. Being of course very much frightened and a little hurt, it began to scream, and in a few seconds the whole street was full of rough people who came pouring out of the houses like ants. They surrounded him, and asked him his name. He was just about to give it when he suddenly remembered the opening incident in Mr. Stevenson's story. He was so filled with horror at having realized in his own person that terrible and well written scene, and at having done accidently, though in fact, what the Mr. Hyde of fiction had done with deliberate intent, that he ran away as hard as he could go. He was, however, very closely followed, and finally he took refuge in a surgery, the door of which happened to be open, where he explained to a young assistant, who happened to be there, exactly what had occurred. The humanitarian crowd were induced to go away on his giving them a small sum of money, and as soon as the coast was clear he left. As he passed out, the name on the brass doorplate of the surgery caught his eye. It was "Jekyll." At least it should have been.

Here the imitation, as far as it went, was of course accidental. In the following case the imitation was self-conscious. In the year 1879, just after I had left Oxford, I met at a reception at the house of one of the Foreign Ministers a woman of very curious exotic beauty. We became great friends, and were constantly together. And yet what interested me most in her was not her beauty, but her character, her entire vagueness of character. She seemed to have no personality at all, but simply the possibility of many types. Sometimes she would give herself up entirely to art, turn her drawing-room into a studio, and spend two or three days a week at picture-galleries or museums. Then she would take to attending race-meetings, wear the most horsey clothes, and talk about nothing but betting. She abandoned religion for mesmerism, mesmerism for politics, and politics for the melodramatic excitements of philanthropy. In fact, she was a kind of Proteus, and as much a failure in all her transformations as was that wondrous sea-god when Odysseus laid hold of him. One day a serial began in one of the French magazines. At that time I used to read serial stories, and I well remember the shock of surprise I felt when I came to the description of the heroine. She was so like my friend that I brought her the magazine, and she recognized herself in it immediately, and seemed fascinated by the resemblance. I should tell you, by the way, that the story was translated from some dead Russian writer, so that the author had not taken his type from my friend. Well, to put the matter briefly, some months afterwards I was in Venice, and finding the magazine in the reading-room of the hotel, I took it up casually to see what had become of the heroine. It was a most piteous tale, as the girl had ended by running away with a man absolutely inferior to her, not merely in social station, but in character and intellect also. I wrote to my friend that evening about my views on John Bellini,[50] and the admirable ices at Florio's, and the artistic value of gondolas, but added a postscript to the effect that her double in the story had behaved in a very silly manner. I don't know why I added that, but I remember I had a sort of dread over me that she might do the same thing. Before my letter had reached her, she had run away with a man who deserted her in six months. I saw her in 1884 in Paris, where she was living with her mother, and I asked her whether the story had had anything to

[50]"John" Bellini is Giovanni Bellini (1431–1515), Venetian artist and craftsman. [Ed.]

do with her action. She told me that she had felt an absolutely irresistible impulse to follow the heroine step by step in her strange and fatal progress, and that it was with a feeling of real terror that she had looked forward to the last few chapters of the story. When they appeared, it seemed to her that she was compelled to reproduce them in life, and she did so. It was a most clear example of this imitative instinct of which I was speaking, and an extremely tragic one.

However, I do not wish to dwell any further upon individual instances. Personal experience is a most vicious and limited circle. All that I desire to point out is the general principle that Life imitates Art far more than Art imitates Life, and I feel sure that if you think seriously about it you will find that it is true. Life holds the mirror up to Art, and either reproduces some strange type imagined by painter or sculptor, or realizes in fact what has been dreamed in fiction. Scientifically speaking, the basis of life — the energy of life, as Aristotle would call it — is simply the desire for expression, and Art is always presenting various forms through which this expression can be attained. Life seizes on them and uses them, even if they be to her own hurt. Young men have committed suicide because Rolla did so, have died by their own hand because by his own hand Werther died. Think of what we owe to the imitation of Christ, of what we owe to the imitation of Cæsar.

CYRIL: The theory is certainly a very curious one, but to make it complete you must show that Nature, no less than Life, is an imitation of Art. Are you prepared to prove that?

VIVIAN: My dear fellow, I am prepared to prove anything.

CYRIL: Nature follows the landscape painter then, and takes her effects from him?

VIVIAN: Certainly. Where, if not from the Impressionists, do we get those wonderful brown fogs that come creeping down our streets, blurring the gas-lamps and changing the houses into monstrous shadows? To whom, if not to them and their master, do we owe the lovely silver mists that brood over our river, and turn to faint forms of fading grace curved bridge and swaying barge? The extraordinary change that has taken place in the climate of London during the last ten years is entirely due to this particular school of Art. You smile. Consider the matter from a scientific or a metaphysical point of view, and you will find that I am right. For what is Nature? Nature is no great mother who has borne us. She is our creation. It is in our brain that she quickens to life. Things are because we see them, and what we see, and how we see it, depends on the Arts that have influenced us. To look at a thing is very different from seeing a thing. One does not see anything until one sees its beauty. Then, and then only, does it come into existence. At present, people see fogs, not because there are fogs, but because poets and painters have taught them the mysterious loveliness of such effects. There may have been fogs for centuries in London. I dare say there were. But no one saw them, and so we do not know anything about them. They did not exist till Art had invented them. Now, it must be admitted, fogs are carried to excess. They have become the mere mannerism of a clique,[51] and the exaggerated realism of their method gives dull people bronchitis. Where the cultured catch an effect, the uncultured catch cold. And so, let us be humane, and invite Art to turn her wonderful eyes elsewhere. She has done so already, indeed. That white quivering sunlight that one sees now in France, with its strange blotches of mauve, and its restless violet shadows, is her latest fancy, and, on the whole, Nature reproduces it quite admirably. Where she used to give us Corots and Daubignys, she gives us now exquisite Monets and entrancing Pissarros. Indeed there are moments, rare, it is true, but still to be observed from time to time, when Nature becomes absolutely modern. Of course she is not always to be relied upon. The fact is that she is in this unfortunate position. Art creates an incomparable and unique effect, and, having done so, passes on to other things. Nature, upon the other hand, forgetting that imitation can be made the sincerest form of insult, keeps on repeating this effect until we all become absolutely wearied of it. Nobody

[51]Wilde is gibing at his friend James Abbott McNeill Whistler (1834–1903), whose smoky paintings of London in fog began the fad of which he speaks. [Ed.]

of any real culture, for instance, ever talks now-a-days about the beauty of a sunset. Sunsets are quite old-fashioned. They belong to the time when Turner was the last note in art.[52] To admire them is a distinct sign of provincialism of temperament. Upon the other hand they go on. Yesterday evening Mrs. Arundel insisted on my going to the window, and looking at the glorious sky, as she called it. Of course I had to look at it. She is one of those absurdly pretty Philistines, to whom one can deny nothing. And what was it? It was simply a very second-rate Turner, a Turner of a bad period, with all the painter's worst faults exaggerated and overemphasized. Of course, I am quite ready to admit that Life very often commits the same error. She produces her false Renés and her sham Vautrins, just as Nature gives us, on one day a doubtful Cuyp,[53] and on another a more than questionable Rousseau. Still, Nature irritates one more when she does things of that kind. It seems so stupid, so obvious, so unnecessary. A false Vautrin might be delightful. A doubtful Cuyp is unbearable. However, I don't want to be too hard on Nature. I wish the Channel, especially at Hastings, did not look quite so often like a Henry Moore,[54] grey pearl with yellow lights, but then, when Art is more varied, Nature will, no doubt, be more varied also. That she imitates Art, I don't think even her worst enemy would deny now. It is the one thing that keeps her in touch with civilized man. But have I proved my theory to your satisfaction?

CYRIL: You have proved it to my dissatisfaction, which is better. But even admitting this strange imitative instinct in Life and Nature, surely you would acknowledge that Art expresses the temper of its age, the spirit of its time, the moral and social conditions that surround it, and under whose influence it is produced.

VIVIAN: Certainly not! Art never expresses anything but itself. This is the principle of my new æsthetics; and it is this, more than that vital connection between form and substance, on which Mr. Pater[55] dwells, that makes music the type of all the arts. Of course, nations and individuals, with that healthy natural vanity which is the secret of existence, are always under the impression that it is of them that the Muses are talking, always trying to find in the calm dignity of imaginative art some mirror of their own turbid passions, always forgetting that the singer of life is not Apollo, but Marsyas.[56] Remote from reality, and with her eyes turned away from the shadows of the cave,[57] Art reveals her own perfection, and the wondering crowd that watches the opening of the marvellous, many-petalled rose fancies that it is its own history that is being told to it, its own spirit that is finding expression in a new form. But it is not so. The highest art rejects the burden of the human spirit, and gains more from a new medium or a fresh material than she does from any enthusiasm for art, or from any lofty passion, or from any great awakening of the human consciousness. She develops purely on her own lines. She is not symbolic of any age. It is the ages that are her symbols.

Even those who hold that Art is representative of time and place and people, cannot help admitting that the more imitative an art is, the less it represents to us the spirit of its age. The evil faces of the Roman emperors look out at us from the foul porphyry and spotted jasper in which the realistic artists of the day delighted to work, and we fancy that in those cruel lips and heavy sensual jaws we can find the secret of the ruin of the Empire. But it was not so. The vices of Tiberius could not destroy that supreme civilization, any more than the virtues of the Antonines could save

[52]Joseph Mallord William Turner (1775–1851) was the last word in art in the 1840s. [Ed.]

[53]René is the eponymous hero of vicomte Francois René de Chateaubriand's novella (1805); Vautrin is the Napoleon of crime in several novels by Balzac, including *Le Père Goriot* (1835). Aelbert Cuyp (1620–91) was a Dutch painter of landscapes, often ones replete with recumbent cows. [Ed.]

[54]Not the English sculptor named Henry Moore, born 1898, after the publication of "The Decay of Lying," but an English landscape artist known for seascapes (1831–95). [Ed.]

[55]Walter Pater (1839–94) said that "all art aspires to the condition of music" in *Studies in the History of the Renaissance* (1873). [Ed.]

[56]In Greek legend, Marsyas was the satyr who invented the flute; beaten in a contest of music with Apollo, he was flayed to death by the god. [Ed.]

[57]See introduction to Plato, p. 17. [Ed.]

it. It fell for other, for less interesting reasons. The sibyls and prophets of the Sistine may indeed serve to interpret for some that new birth of the emancipated spirit that we call the Renaissance; but what do the drunken boors and brawling peasants of Dutch art tell us about the great soul of Holland? The more abstract, the more ideal an art is, the more it reveals to us the temper of its age. If we wish to understand a nation by means of its art, let us look at its architecture or its music.

CYRIL: I quite agree with you there. The spirit of an age may be best expressed in the abstract ideal arts, for the spirit itself is abstract and ideal. Upon the other hand, for the visible aspect of an age, for its look, as the phrase goes, we must of course go to the arts of imitation.

VIVIAN: I don't think so. After all, what the imitative arts really give us are merely the various styles of particular artists, or of certain schools of artists. Surely you don't imagine that the people of the Middle Ages bore any resemblance at all to the figures on mediæval stained glass, or in mediæval stone and wood carving, or on mediæval metal-work, or tapestries, or illuminated MSS.[58] They were probably very ordinary-looking people, with nothing grotesque, or remarkable, or fantastic in their appearance. The Middle Ages, as we know them in art, are simply a definite form of style, and there is no reason at all why an artist with this style should not be produced in the nineteenth century. No great artist ever sees things as they really are. If he did, he would cease to be an artist. Take an example from our own day. I know that you are fond of Japanese things. Now, do you really imagine that the Japanese people, as they are presented to us in art, have any existence? If you do, you have never understood Japanese art at all. The Japanese people are the deliberate self-conscious creation of certain individual artists. If you set a picture by Hokusai, or Hokkei, or any of the great native painters, beside a real Japanese gentleman or lady, you will see that there is not the slightest resemblance between them. The actual people who live in Japan are not unlike the general run of English people; that is to say, they are extremely commonplace, and have nothing curious or extraordinary about them. In fact the whole of Japan is a pure invention. There is no such country, there are no such people. One of our most charming painters went recently to the Land of the Chrysanthemum in the foolish hope of seeing the Japanese. All he saw, all he had the chance of painting, were a few lanterns and some fans. He was quite unable to discover the inhabitants, as his delightful exhibition at Messrs. Dowdeswell's Gallery showed only too well. He did not know that the Japanese people are, as I have said, simply a mode of style, an exquisite fancy of art. And so, if you desire to see a Japanese effect, you will not behave like a tourist and go to Tokio. On the contrary, you will stay at home, and steep yourself in the work of certain Japanese artists, and then, when you have absorbed the spirit of their style, and caught their imaginative manner of vision, you will go some afternoon and sit in the Park or stroll down Piccadilly, and if you cannot see an absolutely Japanese effect there, you will not see it anywhere. Or, to return again to the past, take as another instance the ancient Greeks. Do you think that Greek art ever tells us what the Greek people were like? Do you believe that the Athenian women were like the stately dignified figures of the Parthenon frieze, or like those marvellous goddesses who sat in the triangular pediments of the same building? If you judge from the art, they certainly were so. But read an authority, like Aristophanes for instance. You will find that the Athenian ladies laced tightly, wore high-heeled shoes, dyed their hair yellow, painted and rouged their faces, and were exactly like any silly fashionable or fallen creature of our own day. The fact is that we look back on the ages entirely through the medium of Art, and Art, very fortunately, has never once told us the truth.

CYRIL: But modern portraits by English painters, what of them? Surely they are like the people they pretend to represent?

VIVIAN: Quite so. They are so like them that a hundred years from now no one will believe in them. The only portraits in which one believes are portraits where there is very little of the sitter,

[58]Manuscripts. [Ed.]

and a very great deal of the artist. Holbein's drawings of the men and women of his time impress us with a sense of their absolute reality. But this is simply because Holbein compelled life to accept his conditions, to restrain itself within his limitations, to reproduce his type, and to appear as he wished it to appear. It is style that makes us believe in a thing — nothing but style. Most of our modern portrait painters are doomed to absolute oblivion. They never paint what they see. They paint what the public sees, and the public never sees anything.

CYRIL: Well, after that I think I should like to hear the end of your article.

VIVIAN: With pleasure. Whether it will do any good I really cannot say. Ours is certainly the dullest and most prosaic century possible. Why, even Sleep has played us false, and has closed up the gates of ivory, and opened the gates of horn.[59] The dreams of the great middle classes of this country, as recorded in Mr. Myers's[60] two bulky volumes on the subject and in the Transactions of the Psychical Society, are the most depressing things that I have ever read. There is not even a fine nightmare among them. They are commonplace, sordid, and tedious. As for the Church I cannot conceive anything better for the culture of a country than the presence in it of a body of men whose duty it is to believe in the supernatural, to perform daily miracles, and to keep alive that mythopœic faculty which is so essential for the imagination. But in the English Church a man succeeds, not through his capacity for belief, but through his capacity for disbelief. Ours is the only Church where the sceptic stands at the altar, and where St. Thomas is regarded as the ideal apostle.[61] Many a worthy clergyman, who passes his life in admirable works of kindly charity, lives and dies unnoticed and unknown; but it is sufficient for some shallow uneducated passman out of either University to get up in his pulpit and express his doubts about Noah's ark, or Balaam's ass, or Jonah and the whale, for half of London to flock to hear him, and to sit open-mouthed in rapt admiration at his superb intellect. The growth of common sense in the English Church is a thing very much to be regretted. It is really a degrading concession to a low form of realism. It is silly, too. It springs from an entire ignorance of psychology. Man can believe the impossible, but man can never believe the improbable. However, I must read the end of my article: —

"What we have to do, what at any rate it is our duty to do, is to revive this old art of Lying. Much of course may be done, in the way of educating the public, by amateurs in the domestic circle, at literary lunches, and at afternoon teas. But this is merely the light and graceful side of lying, such as was probably heard at Cretan dinner parties. There are many other forms. Lying for the sake of gaining some immediate personal advantage, for instance — lying with a moral purpose, as it is usually called — though of late it has been rather looked down upon, was extremely popular with the antique world. Athena laughs when Odysseus tells her 'his words of sly devising,' as Mr. William Morris phrases it, and the glory of mendacity illumines the pale brow of the stainless hero of Euripidean tragedy, and sets among the noble women of the past the young bride of one of Horace's most exquisite odes. Later on, what at first had been merely a natural instinct was elevated into a self-conscious science. Elaborate rules were laid down for the guidance of mankind, and an important school of literature grew up round the subject. Indeed, when one remembers the excellent philosophical treatise of Sanchez on the whole question, one cannot help regretting that no one has ever thought of publishing a cheap and condensed edition of the works of that great casuist. A short primer, 'When to Lie and How,' if brought out in an attractive and not too expensive a form, would no doubt command a large sale, and would prove of real practical service to many earnest and deep-thinking people. Lying for the sake of the

[59]In the *Iliad,* Book 2, Zeus sends true dreams to men through the gate of horn, false dreams through the gate of ivory. [Ed.]

[60]Frederic William Henry Myers (1843–1901), English essayist, was a member of the Society for Psychical Research, and published a two-volume study of dreams, *Phantasms of the Living* (1886). [Ed.]

[61]The disciple Thomas, seeing the risen Christ, wanted to touch his wounds to assure his senses that what he saw was real. [Ed.]

improvement of the young, which is the basis of home education, still lingers amongst us, and its advantages are so admirably set forth in the early books of Plato's *Republic*[62] that it is unnecessary to dwell upon them here. It is a mode of lying for which all good mothers have peculiar capabilities, but it is capable of still further development, and has been sadly overlooked by the School Board. Lying for the sake of a monthly salary is of course well known in Fleet Street,[63] and the profession of a political leader-writer[64] is not without its advantages. But it is said to be a somewhat dull occupation, and it certainly does not lead to much beyond a kind of ostentatious obscurity. The only form of lying that is absolutely beyond reproach is Lying for its own sake, and the highest development of this is, as we have already pointed out, Lying in Art. Just as those who do not love Plato more than Truth cannot pass beyond the threshold of the Academe, so those who do not love Beauty more than Truth never know the inmost shrine of Art. The solid stolid British intellect lies in the desert sands like the Sphinx in Flaubert's marvellous tale, and fantasy, *La Chimère,* dances round it, and calls to it with her false, flute-toned voice. It may not hear her now, but surely some day, when we are all bored to death with the commonplace character of modern fiction, it will hearken to her and try to borrow her wings.

"And when that day dawns, or sunset reddens how joyous we shall all be! Facts will be regarded as discreditable, Truth will be found mourning over her fetters, and Romance, with her temper of wonder, will return to the land. The very aspect of the world will change to our startled eyes. Out of the sea will rise Behemoth and Leviathan, and sail round the high-pooped galleys, as they do on the delightful maps of those ages when books on geography were actually readable. Dragons will wander about the waste places, and the phœnix will soar from her nest of fire into the air. We shall lay our hands upon the basilisk, and see the jewel in the toad's head. Champing his gilded oats, the Hippogriff will stand in our stalls, and over our heads will float the Blue Bird singing of beautiful and impossible things, of things that are lovely and that never happen, of things that are not and that should be. But before this comes to pass we must cultivate the lost art of Lying."

CYRIL: Then we must certainly cultivate it at once. But in order to avoid making any error I want you to tell me briefly the doctrines of the new æsthetics.

VIVIAN: Briefly, then, they are these. Art never expresses anything but itself. It has an independent life, just as Thought has, and develops purely on its own lines. It is not necessarily realistic in an age of realism, nor spiritual in an age of faith. So far from being the creation of its time, it is usually in direct opposition to it, and the only history that it preserves for us is the history of its own progress. Sometimes it returns upon its footsteps, and revives some antique form, as happened in the archaistic movement of late Greek Art, and in the pre-Raphaelite movement of our own day. At other times it entirely anticipates its age, and produces in one century work that it takes another century to understand, to appreciate, and to enjoy. In no case does it reproduce its age. To pass from the art of a time to the time itself is the great mistake that all historians commit.

The second doctrine is this. All bad art comes from returning to Life and Nature, and elevating them into ideals. Life and Nature may sometimes be used as part of Art's rough material, but before they are of any real service to art they must be translated into artistic conventions. The moment Art surrenders its imaginative medium it surrenders everything. As a method Realism is a complete failure, and the two things that every artist should avoid are modernity of form and modernity of subject-matter. To us, who live in the nineteenth century, any century is a suitable subject for art except our own. The only beautiful things are the things that do not concern us. It is, to have the pleasure of quoting myself, exactly

[62]Plato suggests that the education of children in the Republic should be suited to their age, small children taught morality through fictions and fables until they are old enough for philosophy. [Ed.]

[63]Fleet Street: Where London newspapers were published. [Ed.]

[64]Editorial writer. [Ed.]

because Hecuba is nothing to us that her sorrows are so suitable a motive for a tragedy.[65] Besides, it is only the modern that ever becomes old-fashioned. M. Zola sits down to give us a picture of the Second Empire. Who cares for the Second Empire now? It is out of date. Life goes faster than Realism, but Romanticism is always in front of Life.

The third doctrine is that Life imitates Art far more than Art imitates Life. This results not merely from Life's imitative instinct, but from the fact that the self-conscious aim of Life is to find expression, and that Art offers it certain beautiful forms through which it may realize that energy. It is a theory that has never been put forward before, but it is extremely fruitful, and throws an entirely new light upon the history of Art.

It follows, as a corollary from this, that external Nature also imitates Art. The only effects that she can show us are effects that we have already seen through poetry, or in paintings. This is the secret of Nature's charm, as well as the explanation of Nature's weakness.

The final revelation is that Lying, the telling of beautiful untrue things, is the proper aim of Art. But of this I think I have spoken at sufficient length. And now let us go out on the terrace, where "droops the milk-white peacock like a ghost," while the evening star "washes the dusk with silver." At twilight nature becomes a wonderfully suggestive effect, and is not without loveliness, though perhaps its chief use is to illustrate quotations from the poets. Come! We have talked long enough.

[65] Vivian alludes to Hamlet's line about the Player: "What's Hecuba to him or he to Hecuba / That he should weep for her?" Shakespeare, *Hamlet,* II.ii.593. [Ed.]

Leo Tolstoy

1828–1910

Born on his mother's estate of Yasnaya Polyana, Count Leo Nikolaievich Tolstoy was educated privately and at Kazan University. After a dissipated youth spent drinking and hunting in the country and womanizing in Moscow, Tolstoy began to question the meaning of life, leaving records of his self-examinations in a series of diaries that he kept to the end of his days. Partly with the intent of reforming himself, Tolstoy enlisted in the army in 1850, and it was during the boredom of guard duty in the Caucasus that he began to write autobiographical sketches, which were published starting in 1852. In 1856 he left the service and took two extended European tours; these had the paradoxical effect of confirming him in his essential Russianness.

In 1861 Tolstoy returned to Yasnaya Polyana, where he set up and ran a successful progressive school for his peasants, recently emancipated from serfdom. He married Sofia Behr the following year, published his first major novel, *The Cossacks,* in 1863, and began to plan out his great epic of Napoleonic Russia, *War and Peace,* which was finally completed in 1869. His more concentrated psychological tragedy, *Anna Karenina,* was published in 1877.

That year Tolstoy experienced a major spiritual crisis in which he desperately sought the ultimate basis of moral action. He found it in quietism, a doctrine of nonresistance to evil, and in the rejection of self-gratification in favor of social responsibility. These doctrines govern Tolstoy's later fiction, including his classic novella, *The Death of Ivan Ilych* (1886) and his underrated late novel, *Resurrection* (1899). This later fiction is more explicitly didactic than the fiction Tolstoy wrote prior to his conversion, but his penetrating observation of human nature and his natural gifts as a storyteller remain intact.

Tolstoy's morality required absolute truth, without any of the myths that underlie most popular religion, and his demythologizing of Christianity resulted in his excommunication by the Orthodox church. This, along with his renunciation of his private property (which was divided among his wife and thirteen children), may have been responsible for his being the first major czarist author to be fully accepted by the Soviets. He died at the age of eighty-two and was buried at Yasnaya Polyana.

What Is Art? may be, as Ernest J. Simmons, a scholar of Russian literature, has said, "the most immodest contribution to aesthetics ever written." Composed at white heat in 1897, it is the fruit of Tolstoy's speculations since the 1850s about the nature of art. Except for Tolstoy's biographers, few commentators have been charitable to *What Is Art?,* partly because Tolstoy himself is so dismissive of all previous aesthetic thought and partly because the conclusions to which he comes put most of the masterpieces of painting, music, and literature (including Tolstoy's own) into the vast category of bad art. In fact, Tolstoy's notions about art have an admirable consistency, and they are important if only because they voice a theory one needs to learn how to argue with.

Tolstoy begins by rejecting most of the central aesthetic principles of the nineteenth century. He is mystified by Hegel's idea that art is a necessary road to

Absolute Spirit, and equally mystified by philosophers' use of the idea of beauty. The various definitions of beauty either lead in a circle (e.g., "beauty is that which pleases without exciting desire") or culminate in the notion of taste, which is unsatisfactory because people's tastes differ, so that any aesthetic based on taste would have to be specific to a particular class, and hence, insufficiently universal. At this point, Tolstoy presents his own idea of art:

> To evoke in oneself a feeling that one has once experienced and having evoked it in oneself then by means of movements, lines, colors, sounds or forms expressed in words, so to transmit that feeling that others experience the same feeling — that is the activity of art.
>
> Art is a human activity consisting in this, that one man consciously by means of certain external signs, hands on to others feelings he has lived through, and that others are infected by these feelings and also experience them.
>
> Art is not, as the metaphysicians say, the manifestation of some mysterious Idea of beauty or God; it is not, as the aesthetic physiologists say, a game in which man lets off his excess of stored-up energy; it is not the expression of man's emotions by external signs; it is not the production of pleasing objects; and, above all, it is not pleasure; but it is a means of union among men joining them together in the same feelings, and indispensable for the life and progress towards well-being of individuals and humanity. (Ch. 5)

If art is a form of infection, then there are two criteria for value, one internal and the other external. The internal criterion is *efficacy:* the best art will be that which infects us most strongly, and this, Tolstoy said, depends upon "(1) the greater or lesser individuality of the feeling transmitted; (2) on the greater or lesser clearness with which the feeling is transmitted; (3) on the sincerity of the artist" (Ch. 15).

More significant to Tolstoy was the external criterion for quality of art: the subject matter, which would determine the specific feelings that were communicated. The better the feelings according to some criterion of value, the better the art. Tolstoy does not pause to justify which are the best feelings. He merely suggests that every society has what he calls a "religious ideal," which becomes the repository of its most cherished values. (Tolstoy emphatically does not mean the ideal of any specific *organized* religion, since he was inveterately hostile to all religious cults as coming between man and God.) This value system Tolstoy locates in "Christianity in its true meaning" — what is today called the Judeo-Christian tradition of human brotherhood.

Once he has located the values which art should infect us with, Tolstoy is forced to distinguish invidiously between the upper class art of his time, whose infectious feelings were those to which the upper class are devoted — pride, sensuality, and ennui — and universal art, which serves *"to unite men with God and with one another."*

Here he distinguishes once more between the "higher, positive" kind of true art, which actively transmits the message of human brotherhood (and he gives a list that includes Dickens's *A Christmas Carol* and Eliot's *Adam Bede*), and a "lower, negative kind," which conveys universal feelings, if not the feeling of universality (the list here includes *Don Quixote* and Molière's comedies).

Had Tolstoy stopped here, he might have found general agreement with his thesis, but he also felt compelled to point out the negative consequence of his theory, which is that most of the artistic works beloved of the intelligentsia are, in his terms, bad art. Shakespeare's plays, for example, in that his characters speak a language never spoken by normal people and unintelligible to the normal people of the present day, work to divide rather than unite humankind. The same would be true of music, like Beethoven's *Ninth Symphony,* since, regardless of its explicit message, the medium in which it is expressed is such as to be unintelligible to most people. (A simple folksong or a lullaby would for Tolstoy be considered better art.) If Tolstoy was brutal, he was also consistent enough to consign most of his own works to the dustbin: He repudiated *War and Peace* and *Anna Karenina* as bad art, and excepted from the general condemnation only two of his stories: "God Sees the Truth but Waits" and "A Captive in the Caucasus."

The difficulties with *What Is Art?* have less to do with consistency than with the theory's external plausibility and internal coherence. It is questionable, for instance, whether feelings of pride, sensuality, and ennui are found only among the upper classes or whether modern culture has not made them universal. Similarly, Tolstoy's assumption that a folksong is more universal than a Beethoven symphony needs to be examined: The folksong, like the symphony, is informed by a Western scale and strophic form that may not be intelligible to a different musical culture (Indonesians, for example, or Hopi Indians). On the other side, Tolstoy (who was not musical) tended to overestimate the amount of cultural training required to appreciate a symphony. Internally, there are difficulties with the "infection" theory that Tolstoy did not anticipate. For one thing, the criterion of *sincerity* of feeling is one that cannot be tested: We know what a work has communicated to us but cannot know whether it is the same thing the artist experienced or indeed whether the artist experienced anything at all. In fact, the central notion implicit in Tolstoy's infection metaphor — the idea that art instills identical feelings into its whole audience — is equally untestable, since we cannot cross-compare the feelings of everyone who has experienced and will experience a specific work. These problems do not devastate Tolstoy's theory: They are objections that can be answered. But it is interesting to note what different questions arise when a moral critique of art (begun by Plato) is couched, as Tolstoy's version is, in the post-Romantic aesthetic tradition that art is a form not of imitation but of self-expression.

Selected Bibliography

Bayley, John. *Tolstoy and the Novel.* London: Chatto and Windus, 1966.

Farrell, James T. *Literature and Morality.* New York: Vanguard Press, 1947.

Garrod, H. W. *Tolstoi's Theory of Art.* Oxford: Clarendon Press, 1935.

Jones, Malcolm, ed. *New Essays on Tolstoy.* Cambridge and New York: Cambridge University Press, 1978.

Macy, John A. "Tolstoi's Moral Theory of Art." *Century Magazine* 62 (1901): 298–307.

Maude, Aylmer. *Tolstoi on Art and Its Critics.* London: H. Milford, 1925.

Perosa, Sergio. "James, Tolstoy, and the Novel." *Revue de Littérature Comparée* 53 (1983): 359–68.

Steiner, George. *Tolstoy or Dostoevsky: An Essay in Contrast.* London: Faber and Faber, 1960.
Tolstoy, Lev Nikolaievich. *What Is Art?* Trans. Aylmer Maude. New York: T. Y. Crowell, 1898.
Troyat, Henri. *Tolstoy.* Garden City, NY: Doubleday, 1967.

From *What Is Art?*

How in the subject-matter of art are we to decide what is good and what is bad?

Art like speech is a means of communication and therefore of progress, that is, of the movement of humanity forward toward perfection. Speech renders accessible to men of the latest generations all the knowledge discovered by the experience and reflection both of preceding generations and of the best and foremost men of their own times; art renders accessible to men of the latest generations all the feelings experienced by their predecessors and also those felt by their best and foremost contemporaries. And as the evolution of knowledge proceeds by truer and more necessary knowledge dislodging and replacing what was mistaken and unnecessary, so the evolution of feeling proceeds by means of art — feelings less kind and less necessary for the well-being of mankind being replaced by others kinder and more needful for that end. That is the purpose of art. And speaking now of the feelings which are its subject-matter, the more art fulfills that purpose the better the art, and the less it fulfills it the worse the art.

The appraisement of feelings (that is, the recognition of one or other set of feelings as more or less good, more or less necessary for the well-being of mankind) is effected by the religious perception of the age.

In every period of history and in every human society there exists an understanding of the meaning of life, which represents the highest level to which men of that society have attained — an understanding indicating the highest good at which that society aims. This understanding is the religious perception of the given time and society. And this religious perception is always clearly expressed by a few advanced men and more or less vividly perceived by members of the society generally. Such a religious perception and its corresponding expression always exists in every society. If it appears to us that there is no religious perception in our society, this is not because there really is none, but only because we do not wish to see it. And we often wish not to see it because it exposes the fact that our life is inconsistent with that religious perception.

Religious perception in a society is like the direction of a flowing river. If the river flows at all it must have a direction. If a society lives, there must be a religious perception indicating the direction in which, more or less consciously, all its members tend.

And so there always has been, and is, a religious perception in every society. And it is by the standard of this religious perception that the feelings transmitted by art have always been appraised. It has always been only on the basis of this religious perception of their age, that men have chosen from amid the endlessly varied spheres of art that art which transmitted feelings making religious perception operative in actual life. And such art has always been highly valued and encouraged, while art transmitting feelings already outlived, flowing from the antiquated religious perceptions of a former age, has always been condemned and despised. All the rest of art transmitting those most diverse feelings by means of which people commune with one another was not condemned and was tolerated if only it did not transmit feelings contrary to religious perception. Thus for instance among the

Translated by Aylmer Maude.

Greeks, art transmitting feelings of beauty, strength, and courage (Hesiod, Homer, Phidias) was chosen, approved, and encouraged, while art transmitting feelings of rude sensuality, despondency, and effeminacy, was condemned and despised. Among the Jews, art transmitting feelings of devotion and submission to the God of the Hebrews and to His will (the epic of Genesis, the prophets, the Psalms) was chosen and encouraged, while art transmitting feelings of idolatry (the Golden Calf) was condemned and despised. All the rest of art — stories, songs, dances, ornamentation of houses, of utensils, and of clothes — which was not contrary to religious perception, was neither distinguished nor discussed. Thus as regards its subject matter has art always and everywhere been appraised and thus it should be appraised, for this attitude toward art proceeds from the fundamental characteristics of human nature, and those characteristics do not change.

I know that according to an opinion current in our times religion is a superstition humanity has outgrown, and it is therefore assumed that no such thing exists as a religious perception common to us all by which art in our time can be appraised. I know that this is the opinion current in the pseudo-cultured circles of today. People who do not acknowledge Christianity in its true meaning because it undermines their social privileges, and who therefore invent all kinds of philosophic and aesthetic theories to hide from themselves the meaninglessness and wrongfulness of their lives, cannot think otherwise. These people intentionally, or sometimes unintentionally, confuse the notion of a religious cult with the notion of religious perception, and think that by denying the cult they get rid of the perception. But even the very attacks on religion and the attempts to establish an idea of life contrary to the religious perception of our times, most clearly demonstrate the existence of a religious perception condemning the lives that are not in harmony with it.

If humanity progresses, that is, moves forward, there must inevitably be a guide to the direction of that movement. And religions have always furnished that guide. All history shows that the progress of humanity is accomplished no otherwise than under the guidance of religion. But if the race cannot progress without the guidance of religion — and progress is always going on, and consequently goes on also in our own times — then there must be a religion of our times. So that whether it pleases or displeases the so-called cultured people of to-day, they must admit the existence of religion — not of a religious cult, Catholic, Protestant or another, but of religious perception — which even in our times is the guide always present where there is any progress. And if a religious perception exists amongst us, then the feelings dealt with by our art should be appraised on the basis of that religious perception; and as has been the case always and everywhere, art transmitting feelings flowing from the religious perception of our time should be chosen from amid all the indifferent art, should be acknowledged, highly valued, and encouraged, while art running counter to that perception should be condemned and despised, and all the remaining, indifferent, art should neither be distinguished nor encouraged.

The religious perception of our time in its widest and most practical application is the consciousness that our well-being, both material and spiritual, individual and collective, temporal and eternal, lies in the growth of brotherhood among men — in their loving harmony with one another. This perception is not only expressed by Christ and all the best men of past ages, it is not only repeated in most varied forms and from most diverse sides by the best men of our times, but it already serves as a clue to all the complex labour of humanity, consisting as this labour does on the one hand in the destruction of physical and moral obstacles to the union of men, and on the other hand in establishing the principles common to all men which can and should unite them in one universal brotherhood. And it is on the basis of this perception that we should appraise all the phenomena of our life and among the rest our art also: choosing from all its realms and highly prizing and encouraging whatever transmits feelings flowing from this religious perception, rejecting whatever is contrary to it, and not attributing to the rest of art an importance that does not properly belong to it.

The chief mistake made by people of the upper classes at the time of the so-called Renaissance — a mistake we will still perpetuate — was not that they ceased to value and attach importance to religious art (people of that period could not attach importance to it because, like our own upper classes, they could not believe in what the majority considered to be religion), but their mistake was that they set up in place of the religious art that was lacking, an insignificant art which aimed merely at giving pleasure, that is, they began to choose, to value, and to encourage, in place of religious art, something which in any case did not deserve such esteem and encouragement.

One of the Fathers of the Church said that the great evil is not that men do not know God, but that they have set up instead of God, that which is not God. So also with art. The great misfortune of the people of the upper classes of our time is not so much that they are without a religious art as that, instead of a supreme religious art chosen from all the rest as being specially important and valuable, they have chosen a most insignificant and, usually, harmful art, which aims at pleasing certain people and which therefore, if only by its exclusive nature, stands in contradiction to that Christian principle of universal union which forms the religious perception of our time. Instead of religious art, an empty and often vicious art is set up, and this hides from men's notice the need of that true religious art which should be present in life to improve it.

It is true that art which satisfies the demands of the religious perception of our time is quite unlike former art, but notwithstanding this dissimilarity, to a man who does not intentionally hide the truth from himself, what forms the religious art of our age is very clear and definite. In former times when the highest religious perception united only some people (who even if they formed a large society were yet but one society among others — Jews, or Athenian or Roman citizens), the feelings transmitted by the art of that time flowed from a desire for the might, greatness, glory, and prosperity of that society, and the heroes of art might be people who contributed to that prosperity by strength, by craft, by fraud, or by cruelty (Ulysses, Jacob, David, Samson, Hercules, and all the heroes). But the religious perception of our times does not select any one society of men; on the contrary it demands the union of all — absolutely of all people without exception — and above every other virtue it sets brotherly love of all men. And therefore the feelings transmitted by the art of our time not only cannot coincide with the feelings transmitted by former art, but must run counter to them.

Christian, truly Christian, art has been so long in establishing itself, and has not yet established itself, just because the Christian religious perception was not one of those small steps by which humanity advances regularly, but was an enormous revolution which, if it has not already altered, must inevitably alter the entire conception of life of mankind, and consequently the whole internal organization of that life. It is true that the life of humanity, like that of an individual, moves regularly; but in that regular movement come, as it were, turning-points which sharply divide the preceding from the subsequent life. Christianity was such a turning-point; such at least it must appear to us who live by the Christian perception of life. Christian perception gave another, a new, direction to all human feelings, and therefore completely altered both the content and the significance of art. The Greeks could make use of Persian art and the Romans could use Greek art, or similarly, the Jews could use Egyptian art — the fundamental ideals were one and the same. Now the ideal was the greatness and prosperity of the Greeks, now that of the Romans. The same art was transferred to other conditions and served new nations. But the Christian ideal changed and reversed everything, so that, as the Gospel puts it, "That which was exalted among men has become an abomination in the sight of God."[1] The ideal is no longer the greatness of Pharaoh or of a Roman emperor, not the beauty of a Greek nor the wealth of Phœnicia, but humility, purity, compassion, love. The hero is no longer Dives, but Lazarus the beggar; not Mary Magdalene in the day of her beauty but in the day of her repentance; not those who acquire wealth but those who have abandoned it; not those who dwell in palaces but those who dwell in catacombs and huts; not those who rule over others, but those

[1]Luke 16:15. [Ed.]

who acknowledge no authority but God's. And the greatest work of art is no longer a cathedral of victory[2] with statues of conquerors, but the representation of a human soul so transformed by love that a man who is tormented and murdered, yet pities and loves his persecutors.

And the change is so great that men of the Christian world find it difficult to resist the inertia of the heathen art to which they have been accustomed all their lives. The subject matter of Christian religious art is so new to them, so unlike the subject matter of former art, that it seems to them as though Christian art were a denial of art, and they cling desperately to the old art. But this old art, having no longer in our day any source in religious perception, has lost its meaning, and we shall have to abandon it whether we wish to or not.

The essence of the Christian perception consists in the recognition by every man of his sonship to God and of the consequent union of men with God and with one another, as is said in the Gospel (John 17:21).[3] Therefore the subject matter of Christian art is of a kind that feeling can unite men with God and with one another.

The expression *unite men with God and with one another* may seem obscure to people accustomed to the misuse of these words that is so customary, but the words have a perfectly clear meaning nevertheless. They indicate that the Christian union of man (in contradiction to the partial, exclusive, union of only certain men) is that which unites all without exception.

Art, all art, has this characteristic, that it unites people. Every art causes those to whom the artist's feeling is transmitted to unite in soul with the artist and also with all who receive the same impression. But non-Christian art while uniting some people, makes that very union a cause of separation between these united people and others; so that union of this kind is often a source not merely of division but even of enmity towards others. Such is all patriotic art, with its anthems, poems, and monuments; such is all Church art, that is, the art of certain cults, with their images, statues, processions, and other local ceremonies. Such art is belated and non-Christian, uniting the people of one cult only to separate them yet more sharply from the members of other cults, and even to place them in relations of hostility to one another. Christian art is such only as tends to unite all without exception, either by evoking in them the perception that each man and all men stand in a like relation toward God and toward their neighbor, or by evoking in them identical feelings, which may even be the very simplest, provided that they are not repugnant to Christianity and are natural to every one without exception.

Good Christian art of our time may be unintelligible to people because of imperfections in its form or because men are inattentive to it, but it must be such that all men can experience the feelings it transmits. It must be the art not of some one group of people, or of one class, or of one nationality, or of one religious cult; that is, it must not transmit feelings accessible only to a man educated in a certain way, or only to an aristocrat, or a merchant, or only to a Russian, or a native of Japan, or a Roman Catholic, or a Buddhist, and so on, but it must transmit feelings accessible to every one. Only art of this kind can in our time be acknowledged to be good art, worthy of being chosen out from all the rest of art and encouraged.

Christian art, that is, the art of our time, should be catholic in the original meaning of the word, that is, universal, and therefore it should unite all men. And only two kinds of feeling unite all men: first, feelings flowing from a perception of our sonship to God and of the brotherhood of man; and next, the simple feelings of common life accessible to every one without exception — such as feelings of merriment, of pity, of cheerfulness, of tranquility, and so forth. Only these two kinds of feelings can now supply material for art good in its subject matter.

And the action of these two kinds of art apparently so dissimilar, is one and the same. The feelings flowing from the perception of our sonship to God and the brotherhood of man — such as a feeling of sureness in truth, devotion to the will

[2]There is in Moscow a magnificent cathedral of our Savior, erected to commemorate the defeat of the French in the war of 1812. [Tr.]

[3]"That they may all be one; even as thou, Father, art in me, and I in Thee, that they also may be in us." [Tr.]

of God, self-sacrifice, respect for and love of man — evoked by Christian religious perception; and the simplest feelings, such as a softened or a merry mood caused by a song or an amusing jest intelligible to every one, or by a touching story, or a drawing, or a little doll: both alike produce one and the same effect — the loving union of man with man. Sometimes people who are together, if not hostile to one another, are at least estranged in mood and feeling, till perhaps a story, a performance, a picture, or even a building, but oftenest of all music, unites them all as by an electric flash, and in place of their former isolation or even enmity they are conscious of union and mutual love. Each is glad that another feels what he feels; glad of the communion established not only between him and all present, but also with all now living who will yet share the same impression; and more than that, he feels the mysterious gladness of a communion which, reaching beyond the grave, unites us with all men of the past who have been moved by the same feelings and with all men of the future who will yet be touched by them. And this effect is produced both by religious art which transmits feelings of love of God and one's neighbour, and by universal art transmitting the very simplest feelings common to all men.

The art of our time should be appraised differently from former art chiefly in this, that the art of our time, that is, Christian art (basing itself on a religious perception which demands the union of man), excludes from the domain of art good in its subject matter, everything transmitting exclusive feelings which do not unite men but divide them. It relegates such work to the category of art that is bad in its subject matter; while on the other hand it includes in the category of art that is good in subject matter a section not formerly admitted as deserving of selection and respect, namely, universal art transmitting even the most trifling and simple feelings if only they are accessible to all men without exception, and therefore unite them. Such art cannot but be esteemed good in our time, for it attains the end which Christianity, the religious perception of our time, sets before humanity.

Christian art either evokes in men feelings which through love of God and of one's neighbor draw them to closer and ever closer union and make them ready for, and capable of, such union; or evokes in them feelings which show them that they are already united in the joys and sorrows of life. And therefore the Christian art of our time can be and is of two kinds: first, art transmitting feelings flowing from a religious perception of man's position in the world in relation to God and to his neighbor — religious art in the limited meaning of the term; and secondly, art transmitting the simplest feelings of common life, but such always as are accessible to all men in the whole world — the art of common life — the art of the people — universal art. Only these two kinds of art can be considered good art in our time.

The first, religious art — transmitting both positive feelings of love of God and one's neighbor, and negative feelings of indignation and horror at the violation of love — manifests itself chiefly in the form of words, and to some extent also in painting and sculpture: the second kind, universal art, transmitting feelings accessible to all, manifests itself in words, in painting, in sculpture, in dances, in architecture, and most of all in music.

If I were asked to give modern examples of each of these kinds of art, then as examples of the highest art flowing from love of God and man (both of the higher, positive, and of the lower, negative kind), in literature I should name *The Robbers* by Schiller; Victor Hugo's *Les Pauvres Gens* and *Les Misérables;* the novels and stories of Dickens — *The Tale of Two Cities, The Christmas Carol, The Chimes,* and others — *Uncle Tom's Cabin;* Dostoevsky's works — especially his *Memoirs from the House of Death* — and *Adam Bede* by George Eliot.

In modern painting, strange to say, works of this kind, directly transmitting the Christian feeling of love of God and of one's neighbor, are hardly to be found, especially among the works of the celebrated painters. There are plenty of pictures treating of the Gospel stories; these however, while depicting historical events with great wealth of detail, do not and cannot transmit religious feelings not possessed by their painters. There are many pictures treating of the personal feelings of various people, but of pictures representing great deeds of self-sacrifice and Christian love there are very few, and what there are are principally by artists who are not celebrated, and they are for the most part not pictures but merely sketches. Such for instance is the drawing by Kramskoy (worth many of his finished pictures), showing a drawing-room with a balcony past which troops are marching in triumph on their return from the war. On the balcony stands a wet-nurse holding a baby, and a boy. They are admiring the procession of the troops, but the mother, covering her face with a handkerchief, has fallen back on the sofa sobbing. Such also is the picture by Walter Langley to which I have already referred, and such again is a picture by the French artist Morlon, depicting a lifeboat hastening in a heavy storm to the relief of a steamer that is being wrecked. Approaching these in kind are pictures which represent the hard-working peasant with respect and love. Such are the pictures by Millet and particularly his drawing, *The Man with the Hoe,* also pictures in this style by Jules Breton, Lhermitte, Defregger, and others. As examples of pictures evoking indignation and horror at the violation of love of God and man, Gay's picture *Judgment* may serve, and also Leizen-Mayer's *Signing the Death Warrant.* But there are very few of this kind also. Anxiety about the technique and the beauty of the picture for the most part obscures the feeling. For instance, Gérôme's *Pollice Verso* expresses, not so much horror at what is being perpetrated as attraction by the beauty of the spectacle.[4]

To give examples from the modern art of our upper classes, of art of the second kind: good universal art, or even of the art of a whole people, is yet more difficult, especially in literature and music. If there are some works which by their inner contents might be assigned to this class (such as *Don Quixote,* Molière's comedies, *David Copperfield* and *The Pickwick Papers* by Dickens, Gogol's and Pushkin's tales, and some things of Maupassant's), these works for the most part — owing to the exceptional nature of the feelings they transmit, and the superfluity of special details of time and locality, and above all on account of the poverty of their subject matter in comparison with examples of universal ancient art (such, for instance, as the story of Joseph) — are comprehensible only to people of their own circle. That Joseph's brethren, being jealous of his father's affection, sell him to the merchants; that Potiphar's wife wishes to tempt the youth; that having attained to highest station he takes pity on his brothers, including Benjamin the favorite — these and all the rest are feelings accessible alike to a Russian peasant, a Chinese, an African, a child, or an old man, educated or uneducated; and it is all written with such restraint, is so free from any superfluous detail, that the story may be told to any circle and will be equally comprehensible and touching to everyone. But not such are the feelings of Don Quixote or of Molière's heroes (though Molière is perhaps the most universal, and therefore the most excellent, artist of modern times), nor of Pickwick and his friends. These feelings are not common to all men but very exceptional, and therefore to make them contagious the authors have surrounded them with abundant details of time and place. And this abundance of detail makes the stories difficult of comprehension to all who do not live within reach of the conditions described by the author.

The author of the novel of Joseph did not need to describe in detail, as would be done nowadays, the blood-stained coat of Joseph, the dwelling and dress of Jacob, the pose and attire of Potiphar's wife, and how adjusting the bracelet on her left arm she said, "Come to me," and so on, because the content of feeling in this novel is so strong that all details except the most essential — such as that Joseph went out into another room to weep — are superfluous and would only hinder the transmission of emotion. And therefore this novel is accessible to all men, touches people of all nations and classes young and old, and has lasted to our times and will yet last for thousands of years to come. But strip the best novels of our time of their details and what will remain?

It is therefore impossible in modern literature to indicate works fully satisfying the demands of universality. Such works as exist are to a great

[4]In this picture the spectators in the Roman Amphitheater are turning down their thumbs to show that they wish the vanquished gladiator to be killed. [Tr.]

extent spoilt by what is usually called "realism," but would be better termed "provincialism," in art.

In music the same occurs as in verbal art, and for similar reasons. In consequence of the poorness of the feeling they contain, the melodies of the modern composers are amazingly empty and insignificant. And to strengthen the impression produced by these empty melodies the new musicians pile complex modulations on each trivial melody, not only in their own national manner, but also in the way characteristic of their own exclusive circle and particular musical school. Melody — every melody — is free and may be understood of all men; but as soon as it is bound up with a particular harmony, it ceases to be accessible except to people trained to such harmony, and it becomes strange, not only to common men of another nationality, but to all who do not belong to the circle whose members have accustomed themselves to certain forms of harmonization. So that music, like poetry, travels in a vicious circle. Trivial and exclusive melodies, in order to make them attractive, are laden with harmonic, rhythmic, and orchestral complications and thus become yet more exclusive, and far from being universal are not even national, that is, they are not comprehensible to the whole people, but only to some people.

In music, besides marches and dances by various composers which satisfy the demands of universal art, one can indicate very few works of this class: Bach's famous violin *aria,* Chopin's nocturne in E flat major, and perhaps a dozen bits (not whole pieces, but parts) selected from the works of Haydn, Mozart, Schubert, Beethoven, and Chopin.[5]

Although in painting the same thing is repeated as in poetry and in music — namely, that in order to make them more interesting, works weak in conception are surrounded by minutely studied accessories of time and place which give them a temporary and local interest but make them less universal — still in painting more than in other spheres of art may be found works satisfying the demands of universal Christian art; that is to say, there are more works expressing feelings in which all men may participate.

In the arts of painting and sculpture, all pictures and statues in so-called genre style, representations of animals, landscapes, and caricatures with subjects comprehensible to every one, and also all kinds of ornaments, are universal in subject matter. Such productions in painting and sculpture are very numerous (for instance, china dolls), but for the most part such objects (for instance, ornaments of all kinds) are either not considered to be art or are considered to be art of low quality. In reality all such objects if only they transmit a true feeling experienced by the artist and comprehensible to every one (however insignificant it may seem to us to be), are works of real, good, Christian, art.

I fear it will here be urged against me that having denied that the conception of beauty can supply a standard for works of art, I contradict myself by acknowledging ornaments to be works of good art. The reproach is unjust, for the subject matter of all kinds of ornamentation consists not in the beauty but in the feeling (of admiration at, and delight in, the combination of lines and colors) which the artist has experienced and with which he infects the spectator. Art remains what it was and what it must be: nothing but the infection by one man of another or of others with the feelings experienced by the artist. Among these feelings is the feeling of delight at what pleases the sight. Objects pleasing the sight may be such as please a small or a large number of people, or such as please all men — and ornaments for the most part are of the latter kind. A landscape representing a very unusual view, or a genre picture

[5]While offering as examples of art those that seem to me best, I attach no special importance to my selection: for, besides being insufficiently informed in all branches of art, I belong to the class of people whose taste has been perverted by false training. And therefore my old, inured habits may cause me to err, and I may mistake for absolute merit the impression a work produced upon me in my youth. My only purpose in mentioning examples of works of this or that class is to make my meaning clearer and to show how, with my present views, I understand excellence in art in relation to its subject matter. I must moreover mention that I consign my own artistic productions to the category of bad art, excepting the story *God Sees the Truth but Waits,* which seeks a place in the first class, and *A Prisoner of the Caucasus,* which belongs to the second. [Au.]

of a special subject, may not please every one, but ornaments, from Yakútsk ornaments to Greek ones, are intelligible to every one and evoke a similar feeling of admiration in all, and therefore this despised kind of art should in Christian society be esteemed far above exceptional, pretentious, pictures and sculptures.

So that in relation to feelings conveyed, there are only two kinds of good Christian art, all the rest of art not comprised in these two divisions should be acknowledged to be bad art, deserving not to be encouraged but to be driven out, denied, and despised, as being art not uniting but dividing people. Such in literary art are all novels and poems which transmit ecclesiastical or patriotic feelings, and also exclusive feelings pertaining only to the class of the idle rich: such as aristocratic honor, satiety, spleen, pessimism, and refined and vicious feelings flowing from sex-love — quite incomprehensible to the great majority of mankind.

In painting we must similarly place in the class of bad art all ecclesiastical, patriotic, and exclusive pictures; all pictures representing the amusements and allurements of a rich and idle life; all so-called symbolic pictures in which the very meaning of the symbol is comprehensible only to those of a certain circle; and above all pictures with voluptuous subjects — all that odious female nudity which fills all the exhibitions and galleries. And to this class belongs almost all the chamber and opera music of our times — beginning especially with Beethoven (Schumann, Berlioz, Liszt, Wagner) — by its subject matter devoted to the expression of feelings accessible only to people who have developed in themselves an unhealthy nervous irritation evoked by this exclusive, artificial, and complex music.

"What! the *Ninth Symphony* not a good work of art!" I hear exclaimed by indignant voices.

And I reply: Most certainly it is not. All that I have written I have written with the sole purpose of finding a clear and reasonable criterion by which to judge the merits of works of art. And this criterion, coinciding with the indications of plain and sane sense, indubitably shows me that that symphony of Beethoven's is not a good work of art. Of course to people educated in the worship of certain productions and of their authors, to people whose taste has been perverted just by being educated in such a worship, the acknowledgment that such a celebrated work is bad, is amazing and strange. But how are we to escape the indications of reason and common sense?

Beethoven's *Ninth Symphony* is considered a great work of art. To verify its claim to be such I must first ask myself whether this work transmits the highest religious feeling? I reply in the negative, since music in itself cannot transmit those feelings; and therefore I ask myself next: Since this work does not belong to the highest kind of religious art, has it the other characteristic of the good art of our time — the quality of uniting all men in one common feeling — does it rank as Christian universal art? And again I have no option but to reply in the negative; for not only do I not see how the feelings transmitted by this work could unite people not specially trained to submit themselves to its complex hypnotism, but I am unable to imagine to myself a crowd of normal people who could understand anything of this long, confused, and artificial production, except short snatches which are lost in a sea of what is incomprehensible. And therefore, whether I like it or not, I am compelled to conclude that this work belongs to the rank of bad art. It is curious to note in this connexion, that attached to the end of this very symphony is a poem of Schiller's[6] which (though somewhat obscurely) expresses this very thought, namely that feeling (Schiller speaks only of the feeling of gladness) unites people and evokes love in them. But though this poem is sung at the end of the symphony, the music does not accord with the thought expressed in the verses; for the music is exclusive and does not unite all men, but unites only a few, dividing them off from the rest of mankind.

And just in this same way, in all branches of art, many and many works considered great by the upper classes of our society will have to be judged. By this one sure criterion we shall have to judge the celebrated *Divine Comedy* and

[6]The "Ode to Joy." [Ed.]

Jerusalem Delivered; and a great part of Shakespeare's and Goethe's work, and in painting every representation of miracles, including Raphael's *Transfiguration,* etc.

Whatever the work may be and however it may have been extolled, we have first to ask whether this work is one of real art, or a counterfeit. Having acknowledged, on the basis of the indication of its infectiousness even to a small class of people, that a certain production belongs to the realm of art, it is necessary on this basis to decide the next question. Does this work belong to the category of bad exclusive art opposed to religious perception, or of Christian art uniting people? And having acknowledged a work to belong to real Christian art, we must then, according to whether it transmits feelings flowing from love of God and man, or merely the simple feelings uniting all men, assign it a place in the ranks of religious art, or in those of universal art.

Only on the basis of such verification shall we find it possible to select from the whole mass of what in our society claims to be art, those works which form real, important, necessary, spiritual food, and to separate them from all the harmful and useless art and from the counterfeits of art which surround us. Only on the basis of such verification shall we be able to rid ourselves of the pernicious results of harmful art and avail ourselves of that beneficent action which is the purpose of true and good art, and which is indispensable for the spiritual life of man and of humanity.

Sigmund Freud

1856–1939

Sigmund Freud, the patriarch of psychoanalysis, was by no means primarily a literary critic, but his ideas have had a major influence on twentieth-century literary theory, and his influence has been as far-reaching on those who are outraged by his ideas as it has been on his disciples. (Freud's theory of the unconscious is given more complete exposition in the introduction to Psychoanalytic Theory in Part Two of this book, to which the reader is referred; see p. 1014.)

Freud was born in Moravia (now part of the Czech Republic) but lived most of his assiduous life in the imperial capital of Vienna, where he received his M.D. from the university in 1881. He studied under Charcot in Paris, and then with Josef Breuer in Vienna, where their collaborative investigations of the treatment of hysterical patients, though not well received by the rest of the profession, led Freud to devise his famed analytical technique, based on free association, to reveal the contents of the unconscious mind. Freud's epochal *The Interpretation of Dreams* (1900) and other ground-breaking studies met with much skeptical antagonism; nevertheless, by 1910 his fame had spread throughout Europe and had reached America.

A group calling itself "The International Psycho-Analytical Association" gathered around him, but by 1913 — the year Freud published *Totem and Taboo* — two of its most impressive members, Carl Jung and Alfred Adler, had resigned to form their own schools in protest against Freud's insistence on the primacy of infantile sexuality. During and after World War I, despite hardships that included agonizing jaw cancer, Freud continued to publish important work, notably *Beyond the Pleasure Principle* (1920) and *The Ego and the Id* (1923). His last year was spent in London, where he fled in 1938 after the Nazi invasion of Austria.

Freud's most important general discussion of art is "Creative Writers and Daydreaming"; it was delivered as a lecture in 1907 and published in 1908. Here Freud draws an analogy between nocturnal dreams, daytime fantasies, and the conscious constructions of literary artists, all of which he views as disguised versions of repressed wishes. Freud does not explain his method of dream-analysis fully in this brief essay (which had been contained in his earlier treatise, *The Interpretation of Dreams*), but the key to his explication is that what motivates the dream is the *pleasure principle,* in which one's unconscious desires are magically fulfilled. The unconscious wish for pleasure or power is the latent content of the dream. But the dream as it appears to the dreamer and is reported to the analyst consists of what Freud termed *manifest content* — it is a story that has, in effect, been censored by the defenses of the ego. One could say that latent content is to manifest content, as primary process (the basic urges and drives) is to secondary process (in which those urges and drives are shifted, filtered, sublimated, and altered into more socially acceptable forms). The analysis of a dream involves peeling back the ego-defenses that have distorted the wish in order to reveal the working of the primary process beneath.

Like nocturnal dreams, Freud believes, literature contains a latent and a manifest content. According to Freud, the primary process that lurks behind popular novels (for example, ranging from *The Godfather* to *The Bridges of Madison County*) obviously embodies the ambitious and erotic wishes to dominate others and to possess loved objects, wishes that formed during the Oedipal phase of childhood development. But those same drives underlie the greatest masterpieces, like *Emma* or *The Great Gatsby*. The differences between popular fiction and literature is not in the latent content but in the way the ego's defenses are marshalled. Freud suggests that "better" fiction contains the same Oedipal fantasies but that they are expressed in a form that is more carefully and elaborately defended. Because the form is less raw, the fantasy content is more acceptable to refined readers.

While Freud was once attacked by Jung (p. 504) for implying that the artist is sick, creating out of personal neurotic needs, it is now widely accepted that nearly all of us are at least slightly neurotic and that the artist's need to create comes not from any incapacitating lunacy but merely from a greater sensitivity to the lacks and dissatisfactions that plague us all. The primary objection to Freudian criticism of this sort is its insensitivity to aesthetic quality: Although Freud was personally deeply moved by art and literature, in his version of artistic creation, form itself enters the work of art merely as a sugar-coating that allows the reader to swallow the dose of fantasy more easily. Later analytic critics, like Peter Brooks, have tried to deal more constructively with this issue, although the function of artistic form remains one of the vexing questions within the psychoanalytic approach to literature. (See Brooks, p. 1033).

Freud also wrote papers analyzing specific literary texts. One of the most famous is "The Uncanny" (1919), in his discussion of E. T. A. Hoffmann's "The Sandman." In "The Theme of the Three Caskets" (1913), Freud analyzes the casket scene in Shakespeare's *The Merchant of Venice* and the division of the kingdom in *King Lear*. His wide-ranging discussion of these sequences — which structurally resemble such disparate stories as the Greek myth of Psyche, the French fairy tale of Cinderella, and an Estonian astral myth — leads him ultimately to the conclusion that the lead casket and the mute daughter are symbolic representations of the youngest of the Fates, Atropos, the goddess of Death. For Freud, these myths, fairy tales, and literary texts are all "created as a result of a discovery that warned man that he too is a part of nature and therefore subject to the immutable law of death." It was to hide this unwelcome truth that humanity constructed stories in which Love instead of Death is the reward of the third quiet sister. These stories thus obey the universal pleasure principle.

But some of the implications of "The Three Caskets" eventually led Freud to a different conclusion. After World War I, as a result of studying the recurrent dreams of shell-shocked veterans and the repetition-compulsions of other patients, Freud was to question the universality of the pleasure principle and to suggest, in *Beyond the Pleasure Principle* (1920), that there are some dreams (and thus some literary texts) that give voice to a drive other than libido — a true death wish — over which the dream work attempts to give the subject a greater sense of control. The function of tragedy for Freud thus shifts from a highly defended sort of wish-fulfillment to what he called the "Mithridatic" — a term coined from the ancient king of Persia who took small doses of poison as a way of immunizing himself against assassination. For the later Freud, tragedy becomes a way of acclimatizing and immunizing ourselves against the painful journey we all must eventually take.

Selected Bibliography

Bowie, Malcolm. *Psychoanalysis and the Future of Theory.* London: Blackwell, 1994.

Brenner, Charles. *An Elementary Textbook of Psychoanalysis.* New York: Anchor Books, 1974.

Freud, Sigmund. *The Standard Edition of the Complete Psychological Works.* 24 vols. London: Hogarth Press and the Institute for Psychoanalysis, 1940–68.

Gilman, Sander L., ed. *Introducing Psychoanalytic Theory.* New York: Brunner/Mazel, 1982.

Hoffman, Frederick J. *Freudianism and the Literary Mind.* New York: Greenwood, 1977.

Jones, Ernest. *Hamlet and Oedipus.* New York: Doubleday, 1949.

Kris, Ernst. *Psychoanalytic Exploration in Art.* New York: Schocken Books, 1962.

Thomas, Ronald R. *Dreams of Authority: Freud and the Fictions of the Unconscious.* Ithaca, NY: Cornell University Press.

Creative Writers and Daydreaming

We laymen have always been intensely curious to know — like the cardinal who put a similar question to Ariosto[1] — from what sources that strange being, the creative writer, draws his material, and how he manages to make such an impression on us with it and to arouse in us emotions of which, perhaps, we had not even thought ourselves capable. Our interest is only heightened the more by the fact that, if we ask him, the writer himself gives us no explanation, or none that is satisfactory; and it is not at all weakened by our knowledge that not even the clearest insight into the determinants of his choice of material and into the nature of the art of creating imaginative form will ever help to make creative writers of *us.*

If we could at least discover in ourselves or in people like ourselves an activity which was in some way akin to creative writing! An examination of it would then give us a hope of obtaining the beginnings of an explanation of the creative work of writers. And, indeed, there is some prospect of this being possible. After all, creative writers themselves like to lessen the distance between their kind and the common run of humanity; they so often assure us that every man is a poet at heart and that the last poet will not perish till the last man does.

Should we not look for the first traces of imaginative activity as early as in childhood? The child's best-loved and most intense occupation is with his play or games. Might we not say that every child at play behaves like a creative writer, in that he creates a world of his own, or, rather, rearranges the things of his world in a new way which pleases him? It would be wrong to think he does not take that world seriously; on the contrary, he takes his play very seriously and he expends large amounts of emotion on it. The opposite of play is not what is serious but what is real. In spite of all the emotion with which he cathects[2] his world of play, the child distin-

Translated by I. F. Grant-Duff.

[1]Ariosto dedicated the *Orlando Furioso* to Cardinal Ippolito d'Este, who said in response, "Where did you find so many stories?" [Au.]

[2]Cathexis is the investment of *libido* energy in an activity. [Ed.]

guishes it quite well from reality; and he likes to link his imagined objects and situations to the tangible and visible things of the real world. This linking is all that differentiates the child's "play" from "fantasying."

The creative writer does the same as the child at play. He creates a world of fantasy which he takes very seriously — that is, which he invests with large amounts of emotion — while separating it sharply from reality. Language has preserved this relationship between children's play and poetic creation. It gives the name of *Spiel* ["play"] to those forms of imaginative writing which require to be linked to tangible objects and which are capable of representation. It speaks of a *Lustspiel* or *Trauerspiel* ["comedy" or "tragedy"] and describes those who carry out the representation as *Schauspieler* ["players"]. The unreality of the writer's imaginative world, however, has very important consequences for the technique of his art; for many things which, if they were real, could give no enjoyment, can do so in the play of fantasy, and many excitements which, in themselves, are actually distressing, can become a source of pleasure for the hearers and spectators at the performance of a writer's work.

There is another consideration for the sake of which we will dwell a moment longer on this contrast between reality and play. When the child has grown up and has ceased to play, and after he has been laboring for decades to envisage the realities of life with proper seriousness, he may one day find himself in a mental situation which once more undoes the contrast between play and reality. As an adult he can look back on the intense seriousness with which he once carried on his games in childhood, and, by equating his ostensibly serious occupations of today with his childhood games, he can throw off the too heavy burden imposed on him by life and win the high yield of pleasure afforded by *humor*.

As people grow up, then, they cease to play, and they seem to give up the yield of pleasure which they gained from playing. But whoever understands the human mind knows that hardly anything is harder for a man than to give up a pleasure which he has once experienced. Actually, we can never give anything up; we only exchange one thing for another. What appears to be a renunciation is really the formation of a substitute or surrogate. In the same way, the growing child, when he stops playing, gives up nothing but the link with real objects; instead of *playing*, he now *fantasies*. He builds castles in the air and creates what are called *daydreams*. I believe that most people construct fantasies at times in their lives. This is a fact which has long been overlooked and whose importance has therefore not been sufficiently appreciated.

People's fantasies are less easy to observe than the play of children. The child, it is true, plays by himself or forms a closed psychical system with other children for the purposes of a game; but even though he may not play his game in front of the grown-ups, he does not, on the other hand, conceal it from them. The adult, on the contrary, is ashamed of his fantasies and hides them from other people. He cherishes his fantasies as his most intimate possessions, and as a rule he would rather confess his misdeeds than tell anyone his fantasies. It may come about that for that reason he believes he is the only person who invents such fantasies and has no idea that creations of this kind are widespread among other people. This difference in the behavior of a person who plays and a person who fantasies is accounted for by the motives of these two activities, which are nevertheless adjuncts to each other.

A child's play is determined by wishes: in point of fact by a single wish — one that helps in his upbringing — the wish to be big and grown up. He is always playing at being "grown up," and in his games he imitates what he knows about the lives of his elders. He has no reason to conceal this wish. With the adult, the case is different. On the one hand, he knows that he is expected not to go on playing or fantasying any longer, but to act in the real world; on the other hand, some of the wishes which give rise to his fantasies are of a kind which it is essential to conceal. Thus he is ashamed of his fantasies as being childish and as being unpermissible.

But, you will ask, if people make such a mystery of their fantasying, how is it that we know such a lot about it? Well, there is a class of human beings upon whom, not a god, indeed, but a stern goddess — Necessity — has allotted the task of telling what they suffer and what things give them happiness. These are the victims of nervous illness, who are obliged to tell their fantasies, among other things, to the doctor by whom they expect to be cured by mental treatment. This is our best source of knowledge, and we have since found good reason to suppose that our patients tell us nothing that we might not also hear from healthy people.

Let us make ourselves acquainted with a few of the characteristics of fantasying. We may lay it down that a happy person never fantasies, only an unsatisfied one. The motive forces of fantasies are unsatisfied wishes, and every single fantasy is the fulfillment of a wish, a correction of unsatisfying reality. These motivating wishes vary according to the sex, character, and circumstances of the person who is having the fantasy; but they fall naturally into two main groups. They are either ambitious wishes, which serve to elevate the subject's personality; or they are erotic ones. In young women the erotic wishes predominate almost exclusively, for their ambition is as a rule absorbed by erotic trends. In young men egoistic and ambitious wishes come to the fore clearly enough alongside of erotic ones. But we will not lay stress on the opposition between the two trends; we would rather emphasize the fact that they are often united. Just as, in many altarpieces, the portrait of the donor is to be seen in a corner of the picture, so, in the majority of ambitious fantasies, we can discover in some corner or other the lady for whom the creator of the fantasy performs all his heroic deeds and at whose feet all his triumphs are laid. Here, as you see, there are strong enough motives for concealment; the well-brought-up young woman is only allowed a minimum of erotic desire, and the young man has to learn to suppress the excess of self-regard which he brings with him from the spoilt days of his childhood, so that he may find his place in a society which is full of other individuals making equally strong demands.

We must not suppose that the products of this imaginative activity — the various fantasies, castles in the air and daydreams — are stereotyped or unalterable. On the contrary, they fit themselves into the subject's shifting impressions of life, change with every change in his situation, and receive from every fresh active impression what might be called a "date-mark." The relation of a fantasy to time is in general very important. We may say that it hovers, as it were, between three times — the three moments of time which our ideation involves. Mental work is linked to some current impression, some provoking occasion in the present which has been able to arouse one of the subject's major wishes. From there it harks back to a memory of an earlier experience (usually an infantile one) in which this wish was fulfilled; and it now creates a situation relating to the future which represents a fulfillment of the wish. What it thus creates is a daydream or fantasy, which carries about it traces of its origin from the occasion which provoked it and from the memory. Thus past, present, and future are strung together, as it were, on the thread of the wish that runs though them.

A very ordinary example may serve to make what I have said clear. Let us take the case of a poor orphan boy to whom you have given the address of some employer where he may perhaps find a job. On his way there he may indulge in a daydream appropriate to the situation from which it arises. The content of his fantasy will perhaps be something like this. He is given a job, finds favor with his new employer, makes himself indispensable in the business, is taken into his employer's family, marries the charming young daughter of the house, and then himself becomes a director of the business, first as his employer's partner and then as his successor. In this fantasy, the dreamer has regained what he possessed in his happy childhood — the protecting house, the loving parents, and the first objects of his affectionate feelings. You will see from this example the way in which the wish makes use of an occasion in the present to construct, on the pattern of the past, a picture of the future.

There is a great deal more that could be said about fantasies; but I will only allude as briefly as possible to certain points. If fantasies become overluxuriant and overpowerful, the conditions are laid for an onset of neurosis or psychosis. Fantasies, moreover, are the immediate mental precursors of the distressing symptoms complained of by our patients. Here a broad bypath branches off into pathology.

I cannot pass over the relation of fantasies to dreams. Our dreams at night are nothing else than fantasies like these, as we can demonstrate from the interpretation of dreams. Language, in its unrivaled wisdom, long ago decided the question of the essential nature of dreams by giving the name of *daydreams* to the airy creations of fantasy. If the meaning of our dreams usually remains obscure to us in spite of this pointer, it is because of the circumstance that at night there also arise in us wishes of which we are ashamed; these we must conceal from ourselves, and they have consequently been repressed, pushed into the unconscious. Repressed wishes of this sort and their derivatives are only allowed to come to expression in a very distorted form. When scientific work had succeeded in elucidating this factor of *dream distortion,* it was no longer difficult to recognize that night dreams are wish-fulfillments in just the same way as daydreams — the fantasies which we all know so well.

So much for fantasies. And now for the creative writer. May we really attempt to compare the imaginative writer with the "dreamer in broad daylight," and his creations with daydreams? Here we must begin by making an initial distinction. We must separate writers who, like the ancient authors of epics and tragedies, take over their material ready-made, from writers who seem to originate their own material. We will keep to the latter kind, and, for the purposes of our comparison, we will choose not the writers most highly esteemed by the critics, but the less pretentious authors of novels, romances, and short stories, who nevertheless have the widest and most eager circle of readers of both sexes. One feature above all cannot fail to strike us about the creations of these story-writers: each of them has a hero who is the center of interest, for whom the writer tries to win our sympathy by every possible means and whom he seems to place under the protection of a special providence. If, at the end of one chapter of my story, I leave the hero unconscious and bleeding from severe wounds, I am sure to find him at the beginning of the next being carefully nursed and on the way to recovery; and if the first volume closes with the ship he is in going down in a storm at sea, I am certain, at the opening of the second volume, to read of his miraculous rescue — a rescue without which the story could not proceed. The feeling of security with which I follow the hero through his perilous adventures is the same as the feeling with which a hero in real life throws himself into the water to save a drowning man or exposes himself to the enemy's fire in order to storm a battery. It is the true heroic feeling, which one of our best writers has expressed in an inimitable phrase: "Nothing can happen to *me*!" It seems to me, however, that through this revealing characteristic of invulnerability we can immediately recognize His Majesty the Ego, the hero alike of every daydream and of every story.

Other typical features of these egocentric stories point to the same kinship. The fact that all the women in the novel invariably fall in love with the hero can hardly be looked on as a portrayal of reality, but it is easily understood as a necessary constituent of a daydream. The same is true of the fact that the other characters in the story are sharply divided into good and bad, in defiance of the variety of human characters that are to be observed in real life. The "good" ones are the helpers, while the "bad" ones are the enemies and rivals, of the ego which has become the hero of the story.

We are perfectly aware that very many imaginative writings are far removed from the model of the naive daydream; and yet I cannot suppress the suspicion that even the most extreme deviations from that model could be linked with it through an uninterrupted series of transitional cases. It has struck me that in many of what are known as "psychological" novels only one person — once again the hero — is described from within. The author sits inside his mind, as it were, and looks at the other characters from outside. The psychological novel in general no doubt owes its special nature to the inclination of the modern writer to split up his ego, by self-observation, into many part-egos, and, in consequence, to personify the conflicting currents of his own mental life in several heroes. Certain novels, which might be described as "eccentric," seem to stand in quite special contrast to the types of the daydream. In these, the person who is introduced as the hero plays only a very small active part; he sees the actions and sufferings of other people pass before him like a spectator. Many of Zola's later works belong to this category. But I must point out that the psychological analysis of individuals who are not creative writers, and who diverge in some respects from the so-called norm, has shown us analogous variations of the daydream, in which the ego contents itself with the role of spectator.

If our comparison of the imaginative writer with the daydreamer, and of poetical creation with the daydream, is to be of any value, it must, above all, show itself in some way or other fruitful. Let us, for instance, try to apply to these authors' works the thesis we laid down earlier concerning the relation between fantasy and the three periods of time and the wish which runs through them; and, with its help, let us try to study the connections that exist between the life of the writer and his works. No one has known, as a rule, what expectations to frame in approaching this problem; and often the connection has been thought of in much too simple terms. In the light of the insight we have gained from fantasies, we ought to expect the following state of affairs. A strong experience in the present awakens in the creative writer a memory of an earlier experience (usually belonging to his childhood) from which there now proceeds a wish which finds its fulfillment in the creative work. The work itself exhibits elements of the recent provoking occasion as well as of the old memory.

Do not be alarmed at the complexity of this formula. I suspect that in fact it will prove to be too exiguous a pattern. Nevertheless, it may contain a first approach to the true state of affairs; and, from some experiments I have made, I am inclined to think that this way of looking at creative writings may turn out not unfruitful. You will not forget that the stress it lays on childhood memories in the writer's life — a stress which may perhaps seem puzzling — is ultimately derived from the assumption that a piece of creative writing, like a daydream, is a continuation of, and a substitute for, what was once the play of childhood.

We must not neglect, however, to go back to the kind of imaginative works which we have to recognize, not as original creations, but as the refashioning of ready-made and familiar material. Even here, the writer keeps a certain amount of independence, which can express itself in the choice of material and in changes in it which are often quite extensive. Insofar as the material is already at hand, however, it is derived from the popular treasure-house of myths, legends, and fairy tales. The study of constructions of folk psychology such as these is far from being complete, but it is extremely probable that myths, for instance, are distorted vestiges of the wishful fantasies of whole nations, the *secular dreams* of youthful humanity.

You will say that, although I have put the creative writer first in the title of my paper, I have told you far less about him than about fantasies. I am aware of that, and I must try to excuse it by pointing to the present state of our knowledge. All I have been able to do is to throw out some encouragements and suggestions which, starting from the study of fantasies, lead on to the problem of the writer's choice of his literary material. As for the other problem — by what means the creative writer achieves the emotional effects in us that are aroused by his creations — we have as yet not touched on it at all. But I should like at least to point out to you the path that leads from our discussion of fantasies to the problems of poetical effects.

You will remember how I have said that the daydreamer carefully conceals his fantasies from other people because he feels he has reasons for being ashamed of them. I should now add that even if he were to communicate them to us he could give us no pleasure by his disclosures. Such fantasies, when we learn them, repel us or at least leave us cold. But when a creative writer presents his plays to us or tells us what we are inclined to take to be his personal daydreams, we experience a great pleasure, and one which probably arises from the confluence of many sources. How the writer accomplishes this is his innermost secret; the essential *ars poetica*[3] lies in the technique of overcoming the feeling of repulsion in us which is undoubtedly connected with the barriers that rise between each single ego and the others. We can guess two of the methods used by this technique. The writer softens the character of

[3]Art of poetry. [Ed.]

his egoistic daydreams by altering and disguising it, and he bribes us by the purely formal — that is, aesthetic — yield of pleasure which he offers us in the presentation of his fantasies. We give the name of an *incentive bonus,* or a *forepleasure,* to a yield of pleasure such as this, which is offered to us so as to make possible the release of still greater pleasure arising from deeper psychical sources. In my opinion, all the aesthetic pleasure which a creative writer affords us has the character of a forepleasure of this kind, and our actual enjoyment of an imaginative work proceeds from a liberation of tensions in our minds. It may even be that not a little of this effect is due to the writer's enabling us thenceforward to enjoy our own daydreams without self-reproach or shame. This brings us to the threshold of new, interesting, and complicated inquiries; but also, at least for the moment, to the end of our discussion.

The Theme of the Three Caskets

I

Two scenes from Shakespeare, one from a comedy and the other from a tragedy, have lately given me occasion for setting and solving a little problem.

The former scene is the suitors' choice between the three caskets in *The Merchant of Venice.* The fair and wise Portia, at her father's bidding, is bound to take for her husband only that one among her suitors who chooses the right casket from among the three before him. The three caskets are of gold, silver and lead: the right one is that containing her portrait. Two suitors have already withdrawn, unsuccessful: they have chosen gold and silver. Bassanio, the third, elects for the lead; he thereby wins the bride, whose affection was already his before the trial of fortune. Each of the suitors had given reasons for his choice in a speech in which he praised the metal he preferred, while depreciating the other two. The most difficult task thus fell to the share of the third fortunate suitor; what he finds to say in glorification of lead as against gold and silver is but little and has a forced ring about it. If in psycho-analytic practice we were confronted with such a speech, we should suspect concealed motives behind the unsatisfying argument.

Shakespeare did not invent this oracle of choosing a casket; he took it from a tale in the *Gesta Romanorum,* in which a girl undertakes the same choice to win the son of the Emperor.[1] Here too the third metal, the lead, is the bringer of fortune. It is not hard to guess that we have here an ancient theme, which requires to be interpreted and traced back to its orgin. A preliminary conjecture about the meaning of this choice between gold, silver and lead is soon confirmed by a statement from E. Stucken,[2] who has made a study of the same material in far-reaching connections. He says, "The identity of the three suitors of Portia is clear from their choice: the Prince of Morocco chooses the gold casket: he is the sun; the Prince of Arragon chooses the silver casket: he is the moon; Bassanio chooses the leaden casket: he is the star youth." In support of this explanation he cites an episode from the Esthonian folk-epic "Kalewipoeg," in which the three suitors appear undisguisedly as the sun, moon and star youths ("the eldest son of the Pole star") and the bride again falls to the lot of the third.

Thus our little problem leads to an astral myth. The only pity is that with this explanation we have not got to the end of the matter. The question goes further, for we do not share the belief of many investigators that myths were read off direct from the heavens; we are more inclined to judge with Otto Rank[3] that they were projected

Translated by C. J. M. Hubback.

[1]G. Brandes, *William Shakespeare.* [Au.]

[2]*Astralmythen,* p. 655. [Au.]

[3]O. Rank, *Der Mythus von der Geburt des Helden,* p. 8 *et seq.* [Au.]

on to the heavens after having arisen quite otherwise under purely human conditions. Now our interest is in this human content.

Let us glance once more at our material. In the Esthonian epic, as in the tale from the *Gesta Romanorum,* the subject is the choice of a maiden among three suitors; in the scene from *The Merchant of Venice* apparently the subject is the same, but at the same time in this last something in the nature of an inversion of the idea makes its appearance: a man chooses between three — caskets. If we had to do with a dream, it would at once occur to us that caskets are also women, symbols of the essential thing in woman, and therefore of a woman herself, like boxes, large or small, baskets, and so on. If we let ourselves assume the same symbolic substitution in the story, then the casket scene in *The Merchant of Venice* really becomes the inversion we suspected. With one wave of the hand, such as usually only happens in fairy-tales, we have stripped the astral garment from our theme; and now we see that the subject is an idea from human life, a man's choice between three women.

This same content, however, is to be found in another scene of Shakespeare's, in one of his most powerfully moving dramas; this time not the choice of a bride, yet linked by many mysterious resemblances to the casket-choice in *The Merchant of Venice.* The old King Lear resolves to divide his kingdom while he yet lives among his three daughters, according to the love they each in turn express for him. The two elder ones, Goneril and Regan, exhaust themselves in asseverations and glorifications of their love for him, the third, Cordelia, refuses to join in these. He should have recognized the unassuming, speechless love of the third and rewarded it, but he misinterprets it, banishes Cordelia, and divides the kingdom between the other two, to his own and the general ruin. Is not this once more a scene of choosing between three women, of whom the youngest is the best, the supreme one?

There immediately occur to us other scenes from myth, folk-tale and literature, with the same situation as their content: the shepherd Paris has to choose between three goddesses, of whom he declares the third to be the fairest. Cinderella is another such youngest, and is preferred by the prince to the two elder sisters; Psyche in the tale of Apuleius is the youngest and fairest of three sisters; on the one hand, she becomes human and is revered as Aphrodite, on the other, she is treated by the goddess as Cinderella was treated by her stepmother and has to sort a heap of mixed seeds, which she accomplishes with the help of little creatures (doves for Cinderella, ants for Psyche).[4] Anyone who cared to look more closely into the material could undoubtedly discover other versions of the same idea in which the same essential features had been retained.

Let us content ourselves with Cordelia, Aphrodite, Cinderella and Psyche! The three women, of whom the third surpasses the other two, must surely be regarded as in some way alike if they are represented as sisters. It must not lead us astray if in *Lear* the three are the daughters of him who makes the choice; this means probably nothing more than that Lear has to be represented as an old man. An old man cannot very well choose between three women in any other way: thus they become his daughters.

But who are these three sisters and why must the choice fall on the third? If we could answer this question, we should be in possession of the solution we are seeking. We have once already availed ourselves of an application of psychoanalytic technique, in explaining the three caskets as symbolic of three women. If we have the courage to continue the process, we shall be setting foot on a path which leads us first to something unexpected and incomprehensible, but perhaps by a devious route to a goal.

It may strike us that this surpassing third one has in several instances certain peculiar qualities besides her beauty. They are qualities that seem to be tending towards some kind of unity; we certainly may not expect to find them equally well marked in every example. Cordelia masks her true self, becomes as unassuming as lead, she remains dumb, she "loves and is silent." Cinderella hides herself, so that she is not to be found. We may perhaps equate concealment and dumbness. These would of course be only two instances out

[4]I have to thank Dr. Otto Rank for calling my attention to these similarities. [Au.]

of the five we have picked out. But there is an intimation of the same thing to be found, curiously enough, in two other cases. We have decided to compare Cordelia, with her obstinate refusal, to lead. In Bassanio's short speech during the choice of the caskets these are his words of the lead — properly speaking, without any connection:

> Thy paleness moves me more than eloquence
> ("plainness," according to another reading)

Thus: Thy plainness moves me more than the blatant nature of the other two. Gold and silver are "loud"; lead is dumb, in effect like Cordelia, who "loves and is silent."[5]

In the ancient Greek tales of the Judgement of Paris, nothing is said of such a withholding of herself on the part of Aphrodite. Each of the three goddesses speaks to the youth and tries to win him by promises. But, curiously enough, in a quite modern handling of the same scene this characteristic of the third that has struck us makes its appearance again. In the libretto of Offenbach's *La Belle Hélène,* Paris, after telling of the solicitations of the other two goddesses, relates how Aphrodite bore herself in this contest for the prize of beauty:

> La troisième, ah! La troisième!
> La troisième ne dit rien,
> Elle eut le prix tout de même. . . .

If we decide to regard the peculiarities of our "third one" as concentrated in the "dumbness," then psycho-analysis has to say that dumbness is in dreams a familiar representation of death.[6]

More than ten years ago a highly intelligent man told me a dream which he wanted to look upon as proof of the telepathic nature of dreams. He saw an absent friend from whom he had received no news for a very long time, and reproached him warmly for his silence. The friend made no reply. It then proved that he had met his death by suicide about the time of the dream. Let us leave the problem of telepathy on one side: there seems to be no doubt that here the dumbness in the dream represents death. Concealment, disappearance from view, too, which the prince in the fairy-tale of Cinderella has to experience three times, is in dreams an unmistakable symbol of death; and no less so is a striking pallor, of which the paleness of the lead in one reading of Shakespeare's text reminds us.[7] The difficulty of translating these significations from the language of dreams into the mode of expression in the myth now occupying our attention is much lightened if we can show with any probability that dumbness must be interpreted as a sign of death in other productions that are not dreams.

I will single out at this point the ninth of Grimm's *Fairy Tales,* the one with the title "The Twelve Brothers." A king and a queen have twelve children, all boys. Thereupon the king says, "If the thirteenth child is a girl, the boys must die." In expectation of this birth he has twelve coffins made. The twelve sons flee with their mother's help into a secret wood, and swear death to every maiden they shall meet.

A girl-child is born, grows up, and learns one day from her mother that she had twelve brothers. She decides to seek them out, and finds the youngest in the wood; he recognizes her but wants to hide her on account of the brothers' oath. The sister says: "I will gladly die, if thereby I can save my twelve brothers." The brothers welcome her gladly, however, and she stays with them and looks after their house for them.

In a little garden near the house grow twelve lilies: the maiden plucks these to give one to each brother. At that moment the brothers are changed into ravens, and disappear, together with the house and garden. Ravens are spirit-birds, the killing of the twelve brothers by their sister is thus again represented by the plucking of the flowers, as at the beginning of the story by the coffins and the disappearance of the brothers. The maiden, who is once more ready to save her

[5]In Schlegel's translation this allusion is quite lost; indeed, changed into the opposite meaning: *Dein schlichtes Wesen spricht beredt mich an.* (Thy plainness speaks to me with eloquence.) [Au.]

[6]In Stekel's *Sprache des Traumes,* dumbness is also mentioned among the "death" symbols (p. 351). [Au.]

[7]Stekel, *loc. cit.* [Au.]

brothers from death, is now told that as a condition she is to be dumb for seven years, and not speak one single word. She submits to this test, by which she herself goes into danger, *i.e.* she herself dies for her brothers, as she promised before meeting with them. By remaining dumb she succeeds at last in delivering the ravens.

In the story of "The Six Swans" the brothers who are changed into birds are released in exactly the same way, *i.e.* restored to life by the dumbness of the sister. The maiden has taken the firm resolve to release her brothers, "an if it cost her life"; as the king's wife she again risks her own life because she will not relinquish her dumbness to defend herself against evil accusations.

Further proofs could undoubtedly be gathered from fairy-tales that dumbness is to be understood as representing death. If we follow these indications, then the third one of the sisters between whom the choice lies would be a dead woman. She may, however, be something else, namely, Death itself, the Goddess of Death. By virtue of a displacement that is not infrequent, the qualities that a deity imparts to men are ascribed to the deity himself. Such a displacement will astonish us least of all in relation to the Goddess of Death, since in modern thought and artistic representation, which would thus be anticipated in these stories, death itself is nothing but a dead man.

But if the third of the sisters is the Goddess of Death, we know the sisters. They are the Fates, the Moirae, the Parcae or the Norns, the third of whom is called Atropos, the inexorable.

II

Let us leave on one side for a while the task of inserting this new-found meaning into our myth, and let us hear what the mythologists have to say about the origin of and the part played by the Fates.[8]

[8]What follows is taken from Roscher's *Lexikon der griechischen und römischen Mythologie,* under the relevant headings. [Au.]

The earliest Greek mythology only knows one Μοῖρα, personifying the inevitable doom (in Homer). The further development of this one Moira into a group of three sisters — goddesses —, less often two, probably came about in connection with other divine figures to which the Moirae are clearly related: the Graces and the Horae, the Hours.

The Hours are originally goddesses of the waters of the sky, dispensing rain and dew, and of the clouds from which rain falls; and since these clouds are conceived of as a kind of web it comes about that these goddesses are looked on as spinners, a character that then became attached to the Moirae. In the sun-favoured Mediterranean lands it is the rain on which the fertility of the soil depends, and thus the Hours become the goddesses of vegetation. The beauty of flowers and the abundance of fruit is their doing, and man endows them plentifully with charming and graceful traits. They become the divine representatives of the Seasons, and possibly in this connection acquire their triple number, if the sacred nature of the number three is not sufficient explanation of this. For these ancient peoples at first distinguished only three seasons: winter, spring, summer. Autumn was only added in late Graeco-Roman times, after which four Hours were often represented in art.

The relation to time remained attached to the Hours: later they presided over the time of day, as at first over the periods of the year: at last their name came to be merely a designation for the period of sixty minutes (hour, *heure, ora*). The Norns of German mythology are akin to the Hours and the Moirae and exhibit this time-signification in their names. The nature of these deities could not fail, however, to be apprehended more profoundly in time, so that the essential thing about them was shifted until it came to consist of the abiding law at work in the passage of time: the Hours thus became guardians of the law of Nature, and of the divine order of things whereby the constant recurrence of the same things in unalterable succession in the natural world takes place.

This knowledge of nature reacted on the conception of human life. The nature-myth changed into a myth of human life: the weather-goddesses became goddesses of destiny. But this aspect of the Hours only found expression in the Moirae, who watch over the needful ordering of human life as inexorably as do the Hours over the regular order of nature. The implacable severity of this law, the affinity of it with death and ruin, avoided in the winsome figures of the Hours, was now stamped upon the Moirae, as though mankind had only perceived the full solemnity of natural law when he had to submit his own personality to its working.

The names of the three spinners have been interpreted significantly by mythologists. Lachesis, the name of the second, seems to mean "the accidental within the decrees of destiny"[9] — we might say "that which is experienced: — while Atropos means "the inevitable" — Death —, and then for Clotho there remains "the fateful tendencies each one of us brings into the world."

And now it is time to return to the idea contained in the choice between the three sisters, which we are endeavouring to interpret. It is with deep dissatisfaction that we find how unintelligible insertion of the new interpretation makes the situations we are considering and what contradictions of the apparent content then result. The third of the sisters should be the Goddess of Death, nay, Death itself; in the Judgement of Paris she is the Goddess of Love, in the tale of Apuleius one comparable to the goddess for her beauty, in *The Merchant of Venice* the fairest and wisest of women, in *Lear* the one faithful daughter. Can a contradiction be more complete? Yet perhaps close at hand there lies even this, improbable as it is — the acme of contradiction. It is certainly forthcoming if every time in this theme of ours there occurs a free choice between the women, and if the choice is thereupon to fall on death — that which no man chooses, to which by destiny alone man falls a victim.

However, contradictions of a certain kind, replacements by the exact opposite, offer no serious difficulty to analytic interpretation. We shall not this time take our stand on the fact that contraries are constantly represented by one and the same element in the modes of expression used by the unconscious, such as dreams. But we shall remember that there are forces in mental life tending to bring about replacement by the opposite, such as the so-called reaction-formation, and it is just in the discovery of such hidden forces that we look for the reward of our labours. The Moirae were created as a result of a recognition which warns man that he too is a part of nature and therefore subject to the immutable law of death. Against this subjection something in man was bound to struggle, for it is only with extreme unwillingness that he gives up his claim to an exceptional position. We know that man makes use of his imaginative faculty (phantasy) to satisfy those wishes that reality does not satisfy. So his imagination rebelled against the recognition of the truth embodied in the myth of the Moirae, and constructed instead the myth derived from it, in which the Goddess of Death was replaced by the Goddess of Love and by that which most resembles her in human shape. The third of the sisters is no longer Death, she is the fairest, best, most desirable and the most lovable among women. Nor was this substitution in any way difficult: it was prepared for by an ancient ambivalence, it fulfilled itself along the lines of an ancient context which could at that time not long have been forgotten. The Goddess of Love herself, who now took the place of the Goddess of Death, had once been identical with her. Even the Greek Aphrodite had not wholly relinquished her connection with the underworld, although she had long surrendered her rôle of goddess of that region to other divine shapes, to Persephone, or to the tri-form Artemis-Hecate. The great Mother-goddesses of the oriental peoples, however, all seem to have been both founts of being and destroyers; goddesses of life and of fertility, and death-goddesses. Thus the replacement by the wish-opposite of which we have spoken in our theme is built upon an ancient identity.

The same consideration answers the question how the episode of a choice came into the myth of the three sisters. A wished-for reversal is again found here. Choice stands in the place of necessity, of destiny. Thus man overcomes death,

[9]Roscher, after Preller-Robert's *Grieschische Mythologie*. [Au.]

which in thought he has acknowledged. No greater triumph of wish-fulfillment is conceivable. Just where in reality he obeys compulsion, he exercises choice; and that which he chooses is not a thing of horror, but the fairest and most desirable thing in life.

On a closer inspection we observe, to be sure, that the original myth is not so much disguised that traces of it do not show through and betray its presence. The free choice between the three sisters is, properly speaking, no free choice, for it must necessarily fall on the third if every kind of evil is not to come about, as in *Lear*. The fairest and the best, she who has stepped into the place of the Death-goddess, has kept certain characteristics that border on the uncanny, so that from them we might guess at what lay beneath.[10]

So far we have followed out the myth and its transformation, and trust that we have rightly indicated the hidden causes of this transformation. Now we may well be interested in the way in which the poet has made use of the idea. We gain the impression that in his mind a reduction to the original idea of the myth is going on, so that we once more perceive the original meaning containing all the power to move us that had been weakened by the distortion of the myth. It is by means of this undoing of the distortion and partial return to the original that the poet achieves his profound effect upon us.

To avoid misunderstandings, I wish to say that I have no intention of denying that the drama of *King Lear* inculcates the two prudent maxims: that one should not forgo one's possessions and privileges in one's lifetime and that one must guard against accepting flattery as genuine. These and similar warnings do undoubtedly arise from the play; but it seems to me quite impossible to explain the overpowering effect of *Lear* from the impression that such a train of thought would produce, or to assume that the poet's own creative instincts would not carry him further than the impulse to illustrate these maxims. Moreover, even though we are told that the poet's intention was to present the tragedy of ingratitude, the sting of which he probably felt in his own heart, and that the effect of the play depends on the purely formal element, its artistic trappings, it seems to me that this information cannot compete with the comprehension that dawns upon us after our study of the theme of a choice between the three sisters.

Lear is an old man. We said before that this is why the three sisters appear as his daughters. The paternal relationship, out of which so many fruitful dramatic situations might arise, is not turned to further account in the drama. But Lear is not only an old man; he is a dying man. The extraordinary project of dividing the inheritance thus loses its strangeness. The doomed man is nevertheless not willing to renounce the love of women; he insists on hearing how much he is loved. Let us now recall that most moving last scene, one of the culminating points reached in modern tragic drama: "Enter Lear with Cordelia dead in his arms." Cordelia is Death. Reverse the situation and it becomes intelligible and familiar to us — the Death-goddess bearing away the dead hero from the place of battle, like the Valkyr in German mythology. Eternal wisdom, in the garb of the primitive myth, bids the old man renounce love, choose death and make friends with the necessity of dying.

The poet brings us very near to the ancient idea by making the man who accomplishes the choice between the three sisters aged and dying. The regressive treatment he has thus undertaken with the myth, which was disguised by the reversal of the wish, allows its original meaning so far to appear that perhaps a superficial allegorical interpretation of the three female figures in the

[10]The Psyche of Apuleius' story has kept many traits that remind us of her kinship with death. Her wedding is celebrated like a funeral, she has to descend into the underworld, and afterwards sinks into a death-like sleep (Otto Rank).

On the significance of Psyche as goddess of the spring and as "Bride of Death," cf. A. Zinzow, *Psyche und Eros*.

In another of Grimm's Tales ("The Goose-girl at the Fountain") there is, as in "Cinderella," an alternation between the ugly and the beautiful aspect of the third sister, in which may be seen an indication of her double nature — before and after the substitution. This third one is repudiated by her father, after a test which nearly corresponds with that in *King Lear*. Like the other sisters, she has to say how dear she holds their father, and finds no expression for her love except the comparison of it with salt. (Kindly communicated by Dr. Hanns Sachs.) [Au.]

theme becomes possible as well. One might say that the three inevitable relations man has with woman are here represented: that with the mother who bears him, with the companion of his bed and board, and with the destroyer. Or it is the three forms taken on by the figure of the mother as life proceeds: the mother herself, the beloved who is chosen after her pattern, and finally the Mother Earth who receives him again. But it is in vain that the old man yearns after the love of woman as once he had it from his mother; the third of the Fates alone, the silent goddess of Death, will take him into her arms.

T. S. Eliot

1888–1965

Thomas Stearns Eliot, America's most influential literary expatriate since Henry James, was born in St. Louis, Missouri, where his father was a businessman and his mother a locally renowned poet. He was educated at private schools in St. Louis and in Milton, Massachusetts, before entering Harvard, where he studied with the philosophers Bertrand Russell and George Santayana (from whom he may have derived the idea of the "objective correlative"), and the literary critic Irving Babbitt, from whom he absorbed an inveterate hostility to Romanticism. Eliot graduated from Harvard College in 1909 and spent most of the next five years in England working toward a Ph.D. in philosophy. He actually wrote his dissertation, on the English neo-idealist F. H. Bradley, but never returned to take his final orals. In 1914, he accepted a traveling fellowship to the University of Marburg but was stranded in England by the outbreak of World War I, stayed at Merton College, Oxford, and gradually came to make England his home. In 1915 he married Vivien Haigh-Wood, a beautiful and intelligent woman whose infidelities, emotional demands, and nervous instability made home life a misery for him; he eventually left her in 1933, and they lived apart until her death fourteen years later.

Eliot's poetic career seems to have dated from a year spent in France (1910–11), where his encounter with the French symbolists, especially Jules Laforgue, helped him to find his own voice. His first volume, *Prufrock and Other Observations* (1917), was a major contribution to the Modernist movement in poetry, characterized by the combination of hard clear images, mysterious and transcendent symbols, and an almost classical restraint of subjective feeling. In *The Waste Land* (1922), Eliot produced Modernism's epic of decay: an elegy upon the desiccation and near-death of the poet's own spirit with an odd Buddhistic conclusion ambiguously suggesting the hope of renewal and rebirth. The poem, written rapidly while Eliot was recovering from a nervous breakdown in a Swiss sanatorium, was tightened drastically by his friend Ezra Pound. Eliot found a more conventional source of solace and hope in his conversion to Anglo-Catholicism in 1927. Later poems included *Journey of the Magi* (1927), *Ash Wednesday* (1930), *Old Possum's Book of Practical Cats* (1939; adapted by Andrew Lloyd Webber into *Cats,* an international theatrical success in the 1980s and 1990s), and *Four Quartets* (1943). Eliot was also a successful playwright whose dry, menacing dialogue influenced postwar dramatists such as Harold Pinter. *The Cocktail Party* (1950), his most successful play, made Eliot a good deal of money from both the London and New York productions, though *Murder in the Cathedral* (1935), a verse tragedy on St. Thomas à Becket, may be the most durable and interesting of his dramas.

While he was gaining his reputation as a poet and playwright, Eliot worked first as a teacher of French and Latin, then as a clerk at Lloyds Bank, until he was made an editor at the publishing firm of Faber and Faber — which also subsidized the *Criterion,* a little magazine Eliot edited, and in which he published much of his critical writing. Eliot's criticism has been attacked as dry and pedantic, but at the time it was highly influential. Theoretical pieces like "Tradition and the Individual Talent" (1917) were manifestos of literary Modernism. But Eliot may have been more important as a tastemaker than as a theorist: His essays on Jacobean playwrights such as Philip Massinger and Thomas Middleton helped put a vanished generation of English drama back on the stage, while those on the metaphysical poets heralded a revival of interest in such then-neglected names as John Donne and George Herbert and such virtually forgotten figures as Thomas Traherne and Lancelot Andrewes.

Most of Eliot's major poetry and criticism was written before the end of World War II, though it could be argued that his most pleasant days were spent after the war, as an honored elder statesman of letters. In 1948 he was awarded both the Nobel Prize for literature and the British Order of Merit. At the age of 69 he married his secretary, Valerie Fletcher, who shared his last happy years. He died in 1965 and was buried in East Coker, the Somerset village from which his ancestors had emigrated to America.

Eliot's literary theory does not appear in total in any single book. His most celebrated passages usually occur within an appreciation of an author or a text, and to put all of them together would require reprinting quite a number of different essays. His famous definition of an "objective correlative," so important for the development of the New Criticism, appears in an essay on *Hamlet:*

> The only way of expressing emotion in the form of art is by finding an "objective correlative"; in other words a set of objects, a situation, a chain of events which shall be the formula of that *particular* emotion; such that when the external facts, which must terminate in sensory experience, are given, the emotion is immediately evoked.[1]

His theory of the dissociation of sensibility comes in the course of an essay on the metaphysical poets:

> . . . Something . . . had happened to the mind of England between the time of Donne or Lord Herbert of Cherbury and the time of Tennyson and Browning; it is the difference between the intellectual poet and the reflective poet. Tennyson and Browning are poets, and they think; but they do not feel their thought as immediately as the odour of a rose. A thought to Donne was an experience; it modified his sensibility. When a poet's mind is perfectly equipped for its work, it is constantly amalgamating disparate experience; the ordinary man's experience is chaotic, irregular, fragmentary. The latter falls in love, or reads Spinoza, and these two experiences have nothing to do with each other, or with the noise of the typewriter or the smell of cooking; in the mind of the poet these experiences are always forming new wholes.[2]

In context, the first quotation is designed to explain what is special about *Hamlet* — it is a play that is problematic precisely because the external causes of feeling do not match the internal effects; the second is designed to explain the characteristic tone of seventeenth-century poetry to readers whose notions of the poetic

[1]T. S. Eliot, "Hamlet" (1919), in *Elizabethan Essays* (New York: Haskell House, 1964), p. 61.

[2]T. S. Eliot, "The Metaphysical Poets" (1921), in *Selected Prose of T. S. Eliot,* ed. Frank Kermode (New York: Harcourt, Brace and Jovanovich; Farrar, Straus and Giroux, 1975), p. 65.

have been corrupted, in Eliot's view, by the dissociation of sensibility that set in with Milton and Dryden. Both of these ideas, however, also have direct bearing on the poetics of the Modernism that Eliot practiced. The doctrine of the objective correlative would lead to the sort of imagism practiced by both Eliot and Pound in their earliest poems, while the Modernists, just as much as Donne, were interested in exploring a varied range of the sensibilities. In addition to the heart's feelings, Eliot went on, "one must look into the cerebral cortex, the nervous system, and the digestive tracts."

"Tradition and the Individual Talent" is much more openly a manifesto for Modernism. In a voice that vacillates between a leaderly "we" and a modest "I," Eliot is clearly calling for a new "programme" for the *métier* of poetry. If the essay is a relatively difficult one, it is because of the ambiguities at the heart of what Eliot means by his two central terms, "tradition," which the poet is asked to cultivate, and "personality," which the poet must sacrifice.

Many creative writers are wary of immersing themselves in the tradition of English and American poetry because they fear that their own voices are not strong enough for the encounter and are likely to be lost in the process. Eliot argues the opposite: that a poet cannot become himself, cannot understand his own place in time, his own modernness, without an understanding of the past. As a result, the historical sense is "indispensable to anyone who would continue to be a poet beyond his twenty-fifth year" — Keats's age when he died. It is easy to understand the value Eliot places on tradition and on the historical sense that allows the poet to contemplate the current significance of the past.

What seems a bit mystical, however, is Eliot's claim that there is an "ideal order" in literary tradition.

> The existing monuments form an ideal order among themselves, which is modified by the introduction of the new (the really new) work of art among them. The existing order is complete before the new work arrives; for order to persist after the supervention of novelty, the *whole* existing order must be, if ever so slightly, altered; and so the relations, proportions, values of each work of art toward the whole are readjusted; and this is conformity between the old and the new.

Since Eliot never makes clear what the basis of the "ideal order" is — how this order is *ordered* — it remains unclear how the order can be perfect and complete both before and after the introduction of a new work. Nor is it clear of what this order is composed. It is not merely an anthology of celebrated texts, the current canon, but Eliot does not discuss how far removed a work can be from current fashion and yet remain within the tradition or how far down into popular culture the tradition reaches.

The difficulty with the issue of personality is not fuzziness but the apparent contradictions with other Eliot criticism. In "Tradition" Eliot seems to be suggesting that art is, or at least ought to be, essentially impersonal: that the tradition writes itself, as it were, using the poet as a catalyst for converting emotion and thought into poetry. But in an essay on Philip Massinger in 1920, Eliot suggests that personality is necessary for high art: "Marlowe's and Jonson's comedies . . . were, as great literature is, the transformation of a personality into a personal work of art. . . . Massinger is not simply a smaller personality: his personality hardly exists. He did not, out of his own personality, build a world of art, as Shakespeare and Marlowe and Jonson built."[3]

A careful reading finds a paradox here, but no real self-contradiction. Eliot (like Proust in *Contre Sainte-Beuve*) repudiates the post-Romantic notion that the self an artist expresses is the habitual self one presents in society to intimates, friends, and acquaintances. He postulates another deeper self that is responsible for the artist's unique vision of reality, and that lends that vision authority and general truth. The former "personality" is what the artist escapes from into art; the latter is the source of that art. These two definitions of "personality," which incidentally correspond to the "you" and "I" in that schizoid lyric, "The Love Song of J. Alfred Prufrock," are what Eliot puns on throughout the last section of "Tradition and the Individual Talent."

Selected Bibliography

Allan, Mowbray, *T. S. Eliot's Impersonal Theory of Poetry*. Lewisburg, PA: Bucknell University Press, 1974.

Austin, Allen. *T. S. Eliot: The Literary and Social Criticism*. Bloomington: Indiana University Press, 1971.

Brombert, Victor. *The Criticism of T. S. Eliot*. New Haven: Yale University Press, 1949.

Freed, Lewis. *T. S. Eliot: Aesthetics and History*. La Salle, IL: Open Court, 1962.

Frye, Northrop. *T. S. Eliot*. New York: Grove Press, 1963.

Lee, Brian. *Theory and Personality: The Significance of T. S. Eliot's Criticism*. London: Athlone Press, 1979.

Lu, Fei-Pai. *T. S. Eliot: The Dialectical Structure of His Theory of Poetry*. Chicago: University of Chicago Press, 1966.

Lucy, Sean. *T. S. Eliot and the Idea of Tradition*. London: Cohen and West, 1960.

Matthiessen, F. O. *The Achievement of T. S. Eliot*. New York: Oxford University Press, 1947.

Menand, Louis. *Discovering Modernism: T. S. Eliot and His Context*. New York: Oxford University Press, 1987.

Spurr, David. *Conflicts in Consciousness: T. S. Eliot's Poetry and Criticism*. Urbana: University of Illinois Press, 1983.

[3]T. S. Eliot, "Philip Massinger" (1920), in *Elizabethan Essays*, p. 171.

Tradition and the Individual Talent

I

In English writing we seldom speak of tradition, though we occasionally apply its name in deploring its absence. We cannot refer to "the tradition" or to "a tradition"; at most, we employ the adjective in saying that the poetry of so-and-so is "traditional" or even "too traditional." Seldom, perhaps, does the word appear except in a phrase of censure. If otherwise, it is vaguely approbative, with the implication, as to the work approved, of some pleasing archaeological reconstruction. You can hardly make the word agreeable in English ears without this comfortable reference to the reassuring science of archaeology.

Certainly the word is not likely to appear in our appreciations of living or dead writers. Every nation, every race, has not only its own creative, but its own critical turn of mind; and is even more oblivious of the shortcomings and limitations of its critical habits than of those of its creative genius. We know, or think we know, from the enormous mass of critical writing that has appeared in the French language the critical method or habit of the French; we only conclude (we are such unconscious people) that the French are "more critical" than we, and sometimes even plume ourselves a little with the fact, as if the French were the less spontaneous. Perhaps they are; but we might remind ourselves that criticism is as inevitable as breathing, and that we should be none the worse for articulating what passes in our minds when we read a book and feel an emotion about it, for criticizing our own minds in their work of criticism. One of the facts that might come to light in this process is our tendency to insist, when we praise a poet, upon those aspects of his work in which he least resembles anyone else. In these aspects or parts of his work we pretend to find what is individual, what is the peculiar essence of the man. We dwell with satisfaction upon the poet's difference from his predecessors, especially his immediate predecessors; we endeavor to find something that can be isolated in order to be enjoyed. Whereas if we approach a poet without this prejudice we shall often find not only the best, but the most individual parts of his work may be those in which the dead poets, his ancestors, assert their immortality most vigorously. And I do not mean the impressionable period of adolescence, but the period of full maturity.

Yet if the only form of tradition, of handing down, consisted in following the ways of the immediate generation before us in a blind or timid adherence to its successes, "tradition" should positively be discouraged. We have seen many such simple currents soon lost in the sand; and novelty is better than repetition. Tradition is a matter of much wider significance. It cannot be inherited, and if you want it you must obtain it by great labor. It involves, in the first place, the historical sense, which we may call nearly indispensable to anyone who would continue to be a poet beyond his twenty-fifth year; and the historical sense involves a perception, not only of the pastness of the past, but of its presence; the historical sense compels a man to write not merely with his own generation in his bones, but with a feeling that the whole of the literature of Europe from Homer and within it the whole of the literature of his own country has a simultaneous existence and composes a simultaneous order. This historical sense, which is a sense of the timeless as well as of the temporal and of the timeless and of the temporal together, is what makes a writer traditional. And it is at the same time what makes a writer most acutely conscious of his place in time, of his own contemporaneity.

No poet, no artist of any art, has his complete meaning alone. His significance, his appreciation is the appreciation of his relation to the dead poets and artists. You cannot value him alone; you must set him, for contrast and comparison, among the dead. I mean this as a principle of aesthetic, not merely historical, criticism. The necessity that he shall conform, that he shall cohere, is not one-sided; what happens when a new work of art is created is something that happens simultaneously to all the works of art which preceded it. The existing monuments form an ideal order among themselves, which is modified by the introduction of the new (the really new) work of art among them. The existing order is complete before the new work arrives; for order to persist after the supervention of novelty, the whole existing order must be, if ever so slightly, altered; and so the relations, proportions, values of each work of art toward the whole are readjusted; and this is conformity between the old and the new. Whoever has approved this idea of order, of the form of European, of English literature will not find it preposterous that the past should be altered by the present as much as the present is directed by the past. And the poet who is aware of this will be aware of great difficulties and responsibilities.

In a peculiar sense he will be aware also that he must inevitably be judged by the standards of the past. I say judged, not amputated, by them; not judged to be as good as, or worse or better than, the dead; and certainly not judged by the canons of dead critics. It is a judgment, a comparison, in which two things are measured by each other. To conform merely would be for the new work not really to conform at all; it would not be new, and would therefore not be a work of art. And we do not quite say that the new is more valuable because it fits in; but its fitting in is a test of its value — a test, it is true, which can only be slowly and cautiously applied, for we are none of us infallible judges of conformity. We say: It appears to conform, and is perhaps individual, or it appears individual, and may conform; but we are hardly likely to find that it is one and not the other.

To proceed to a more intelligible exposition of the relation of the poet to the past: he can neither take the past as a lump, an indiscriminate bolus, nor can he form himself wholly on one or two private admirations, nor can he form himself wholly upon one preferred period. The first course is inadmissible, the second is an important experience of youth, and the third is a pleasant and highly desirable supplement. The poet must be very conscious of the main current, which does not at all flow invariably through the most distinguished reputations. He must be quite aware of the obvious fact that art never improves, but that the material of art is never quite the same. He must be aware that the mind of Europe — the mind of his own country — a mind which he learns in time to be much more important than his own private mind — is a mind which changes, and that this change is a development which abandons nothing en route, which does not superannuate either Shakespeare, or Homer, or the rock drawing of the Magdalenian draftsmen.[1] That this development, refinement perhaps, complication certainly, is not, from the point of view of the artist, any improvement. Perhaps not even an improvement from the point of view of the psychologist or not to the extent which we imagine; perhaps only in the end based upon a complication in economics and machinery. But the difference between the present and the past is that the conscious present is an awareness of the past in a way and to an extent which the past's awareness of itself cannot show.

Someone said: "The dead writers are remote from us because we *know* so much more than they did." Precisely, and they are that which we know.

I am alive to a usual objection to what is clearly part of my program for the métier of poetry. The objection is that the doctrine requires a ridiculous amount of erudition (pedantry), a claim which can be rejected by appeal to the lives of poets in any pantheon. It will even be affirmed that much learning deadens or perverts poetic sensibility. While, however, we persist in believing that a poet ought to know as much as will not encroach upon his necessary receptivity and necessary laziness, it is not desirable to confine knowledge to whatever can be put into a useful shape for examinations, drawing rooms, or the still more pretentious modes of publicity. Some can absorb knowledge, the more tardy must sweat for it. Shakespeare acquired more essential history from Plutarch than most men could from the whole British Museum. What is to be insisted upon is that the poet must develop or procure the consciousness of the past and that he should continue to develop this consciousness throughout his career.

What happens is a continual surrender of himself as he is at the moment to something which is more valuable. The progress of an artist is a continual self-sacrifice, a continual extinction of personality.

There remains to define this process of depersonalization and its relation to the sense of tradition. It is in this depersonalization that art may be said to approach the condition of science. I, therefore, invite you to consider, as a suggestive analogy, the action which takes place when a bit of finely filiated platinum is introduced into a chamber containing oxygen and sulfur dioxide.

II

Honest criticism and sensitive appreciation are directed not upon the poet but upon the poetry. If we attend to the confused cries of the newspaper critics and the susurrus of popular repetition that follows, we shall hear the names of poets in great

[1]The Cro-Magnon cave men. [Ed.]

numbers; if we seek not blue-book knowledge but the enjoyment of poetry, and ask for a poem, we shall seldom find it. I have tried to point out the importance of the relation of the poem to other poems by other authors, and suggested the conception of poetry as a living whole of all the poetry that has ever been written. The other aspect of this impersonal theory of poetry is the relation of the poem to its author. And I hinted, by an analogy, that the mind of the mature poet differs from that of the immature one not precisely in any valuation of "personality," not being necessarily more interesting, or having "more to say," but rather by being a more finely perfected medium in which special, or very varied, feelings are at liberty to enter into new combinations.

The analogy was that of the catalyst. When the two gases previously mentioned are mixed in the presence of a filament of platinum, they form sulfurous acid. This combination takes place only if the platinum is present; nevertheless the newly formed acid contains no trace of platinum, and the platinum itself is apparently unaffected; has remained inert, neutral, and unchanged. The mind of the poet is the shred of platinum. It may partly or exclusively operate upon the experience of the man himself; but, the more perfect the artist, the more completely separate in him will be the man who suffers and the mind which creates; the more perfectly will the mind digest and transmute the passions which are its material.

The experience, you will notice, the elements which enter the presence of the transforming catalyst, are of two kinds: emotions and feelings. The effect of a work of art upon the person who enjoys it is an experience different in kind from any experience not of art. It may be formed out of one emotion, or may be a combination of several; and various feelings, inhering for the writer in particular words of phrases or images, may be added to compose the final result. Or great poetry may be made without the direct use of any emotion whatever: composed out of feelings solely. Canto XV of the *Inferno* (Brunetto Latini) is a working up of the emotion evident in the situation; but the effect, though single as that of any work of art, is obtained by considerable complexity of detail. The last quatrain gives an image, a feeling attaching to an image, which "came," which did not develop simply out of what precedes, but which was probably in suspension in the poet's mind until the proper combination arrived for it to add itself to.[2] The poet's mind is in fact a receptacle for seizing and storing up numberless feelings, phrases, images, which remain there until all the particles which can unite to form a new compound are present together.

If you compare several representative passages of the greatest poetry you see how great is the variety of types of combination, and also how completely any semiethical criterion of "sublimity" misses the mark. For it is not the "greatness," the intensity, of the emotions, the components, but the intensity of the artistic process, the pressure, so to speak, under which the fusion takes place, that counts. The episode of Paolo and Francesca employs a definite emotion, but the intensity of the poetry is something quite different from whatever intensity in the supposed experience it may give the impression of. It is no more intense, furthermore, than Canto XXVI, the voyage of Ulysses, which has not the direct dependence upon an emotion. Great variety is possible in the process of transmutation of emotion: the murder of Agamemnon, or the agony of Othello, gives an artistic effect apparently closer to a possible original than the scenes from Dante. In the *Agamemnon,* the artistic emotion approximates to the emotion of an actual spectator; in *Othello* to the emotion of the protagonist himself. But the difference between art and the event is always absolute; the combination which is the murder of Agamemnon is probably as complex as that which is the voyage of Ulysses. In either case there has been a fusion of elements. The ode of Keats contains a number of feelings which have nothing particular to do with the nightingale, but which the nightingale, partly, perhaps, because of its attractive name, and partly because of its reputation, served to bring together.

The point of view which I am struggling to attack is perhaps related to the metaphysical theory

[2] "And seemed like one of those who over the flat / And open course in the fields beside Verona / Run for the green cloth; and he seemed, at that, / Not like a loser but like the winning runner." Dante, *Inferno* 15:121–24. [Ed.]

of the substantial unity of the soul: for my meaning is, that the poet has, not a "personality" to express, but a particular medium, which is only a medium and not a personality, in which impressions and experiences combine in peculiar and unexpected ways. Impressions and experiences which are important for the man may take no place in the poetry, and those which become important in the poetry may play quite a negligible part in the man, the personality.

I will quote a passage which is unfamiliar enough to be regarded with fresh attention in the light — or darkness — of these observations:

And now methinks I could e'en chide myself
For doting on her beauty, though her death
Shall be revenged after no common action.
Does the silkworm expend her yellow labors
For thee? For thee does she undo herself?
Are lordships sold to maintain ladyships
For the poor benefit of a bewildering minute?
Why does yon fellow falsify highways,
And put his life between the judge's lips,
To refine such a thing — keeps horse and men
To beat their valors for her? . . .[3]

In this passage (as is evident if it is taken in its context) there is a combination of positive and negative emotions: an intensely strong attraction toward beauty and an equally intense fascination by the ugliness which is contrasted with it and which destroys it. This balance of contrasted emotion is in the dramatic situation to which the speech is pertinent, but that situation alone is inadequate to it. This is, so to speak, the structural emotion, provided by the drama. But the whole effect, the dominant tone, is due to the fact that a number of floating feelings, having an affinity to this emotion by no means superficially evident, have combined with it to give us a new art emotion.

It is not in his personal emotions, the emotions provoked by particular events in his life, that the poet is in any way remarkable or interesting. His particular emotions may be simple, or crude, or flat. The emotion in his poetry will be a very complex thing, but not with the complexity of the emotions of people who have very complex or unusual emotions in life. One error, in fact, of eccentricity in poetry is to seek for new human emotions to express; and in this search for novelty in the wrong place it discovers the perverse. The business of the poet is not to find new emotions, but to use the ordinary ones and, in working them up into poetry, to express feelings which are not in actual emotions at all. And emotions which he has never experienced will serve his turn as well as those familiar to him. Consequently, we must believe that "emotion recollected in tranquility"[4] is an inexact formula. For it is neither emotion, nor recollection, nor, without distortion of meaning, tranquility. It is a concentration, and a new thing resulting from the concentration, of a very great number of experiences which to the practical and active person would not seem to be experiences at all; it is a concentration which does not happen consciously or of deliberation. These experiences are not "recollected," and they finally unite in an atmosphere which is "tranquil" only in that it is a passive attending upon the event. Of course this is not quite the whole story. There is a great deal, in the writing of poetry, which must be conscious and deliberate. In fact, the bad poet is usually unconscious where he ought to be conscious, and conscious where he ought to be unconscious. Both errors tend to make him "personal." Poetry is not a turning loose of emotion, but an escape from emotion; it is not the expression of personality, but an escape from personality. But, of course, only those who have personality and emotions know what it means to want to escape from these things.

III

ὁ δὲ νοῦς ἴσως Θειότερον τὶ καὶ ἀπαθές ἔστιν.[5]

This essay proposes to halt at the frontier of metaphysics or mysticism, and confine itself to such practical conclusions as can be applied by the responsible person interested in poetry. To divert interest from the poet to the poetry is a laud-

[3]Cyril Tourneur, *The Revenger's Tragedy,* III.iv. [Ed.]

[4]Eliot is quoting Wordsworth's Preface to *Lyrical Ballads;* see p. 312. [Ed.]

[5]"The mind may be too divine and therefore unimpassioned." Heracleitus. [Ed.]

able aim: for it would conduce to a juster estimation of actual poetry, good and bad. There are many people who appreciate the expression of sincere emotion in verse, and there is a smaller number of people who can appreciate technical excellence. But very few know when there is an expression of *significant* emotion, emotion which has its life in the poem and not in the history of the poet. The emotion of art is impersonal. And the poet cannot reach his impersonality without surrendering himself wholly to the work to be done. And he is not likely to know what is to be done unless he lives in what is not merely the present, but the present moment of the past, unless he is conscious; not of what is dead, but of what is already living.

Carl Gustav Jung

1875–1961

Carl Gustav Jung, the founder of analytic psychology, was born in Switzerland. The son of a philologist and pastor, from a clan of many clergymen, Jung turned his back on the ministry to pursue philosophical and medical interests. He studied at Basel (1895–1900) and Zürich, where he earned his M.D. in 1902 after working under Eugen Bleuler at the Burghölzli Psychiatric Clinic.

In 1907 Jung met Freud and quickly became the intellectual "son" for whom Freud had long been looking. But in an Oedipal struggle that Freud doubtless appreciated, Jung rapidly and thoroughly shook off his master to declare an independent vision of the mind involving less the cure of symptomatic neurosis than the pursuit of a lifelong task: the achievement of individuation, including the harmonious wholeness of conscious and unconscious. The close collaboration ended in 1912, a year after Jung became president of The International Psycho-Analytical Association, and the year when he published the clearly un-Freudian *The Psychology of the Unconscious.* In 1933 Jung became professor of psychology at the Federal Polytechnical University in Zürich, and in 1943 professor of medical psychology at the University of Basel. Immensely prolific, Jung revised and reissued much of his work. His important books include *The Psychology of Dementia* (1906), *Psychological Types* (1921), and *Psychology and Alchemy* (1944). "On the Relation of Analytical Psychology to Poetry" was delivered to a German learned society as a lecture in 1922 and published later that year. "The Principal Archetypes" is from *Aion: Researches into the Phenomenology of the Self* (1951), a late work that tidily summarizes many of Jung's key ideas.

Jung took from Freud the notion of a structured unconscious mind, but beyond this the differences between them are profound. In Jung, the unconscious of Freud's writings is termed the "personal unconscious"; it is but a "thin layer" under the conscious mind, relatively accessible by tricks of free association and parapraxis, and therefore not of supreme significance. More important is the "collective unconscious," or racial memory, through which the spirit of the whole human species manifests itself. This deeper layer of the unconscious is not accessible through the techniques of analysis; we understand its existence through our profound response to universal symbols that appear both in dreams and in our waking lives.

Jung developed the idea of a racial memory through his study of anthropology and comparative mythology, sciences that were beginning to show interesting results by the first decade of the century. Studies like James Frazer's *The Golden Bough* (1890) had revealed striking similarities between the myths and rituals of primitive peoples around the globe, peoples who seemed to be too distant to have influenced each other directly. Jung's hypothesis was that direct influence was unnecessary, that the similar mythologies were merely differing manifestations of structures deep in the human unconscious.

These structures Jung termed *archetypes;* they manifest themselves not only in myth and in dreams but in the finished art of cultures like our own in the form of symbols. Jung distinguished very strictly between the archetype itself, as a purely psychic structure, and its images: the representations the archetype takes within the symbolic fantasies created by the individual, and which then reappear in various forms in art and literature. (Later thinkers strongly influenced by Jung, such as Northrop Frye (see p. 641) and Claude Lévi-Strauss (see p. 835), use the term "archetype" for what Jung would have called the "archetypal image.")

The archetypes and their symbols take the shape of various aspects of the Self. On the surface of the Self is the *Mask,* the face we show to the outside world. Beneath this is the *Shadow,* a demonic image of evil that represents the side of the Self that we reject. Beneath this is the *Anima,* the feminine side of the male Self, and the *Animus,* the correspondingly masculine side of the female Self. (The Animus, for males, becomes an image of the Father.) For men, the Anima, the Great Mother, is characteristically split in the shadow of the Shadow into the nurturing Mother, the tempting Whore, and the destroying Crone. Women, in turn, split the Animus into a Protector, a Lover, and a Destroying Angel. Finally there is the image of the *Spirit,* symbolized by a wise old man or woman. The four principal archetypes — Shadow, Anima, Animus, and Spirit — make up what Jung called the *Syzygy:* a quaternion composing a whole, the unified self of which people are in search. That very search for unity can take the archetypal form of the Quest, in which the Self journeys to encounter the various elements that make it up, thereby forming the relationships that constitute its individuality. The quest itself often culminates in another archetype, the Night-Sea-Journey, a voyage from life through death to a new rebirth.

In Jungian analysis, the patient recapitulates his life and looks for the ways in which symbols of the above-mentioned archetypes have been embodied within its texture. Similarly, Jungian criticism is generally involved with a search for the embodiment of these symbols within particular works of art. The pleasures of Jungian criticism often come in noting the parallels between one work and another; how, for example, Cora and Alice in *The Last of the Mohicans,* Rebecca and Rowena in *Ivanhoe,* Becky Sharp and Amelia Sedley in *Vanity Fair,* and Eustacia and Thomasin in *The Return of the Native* can all be read as variations on the Dark Lady and the White Lady — split versions of the Anima. On the other hand, since the archetypes can be found in all powerful literature, Jungian criticism can become a relatively monotonous and predictable approach, harping invariably on the same chord, finding the basic motifs of the Quest, the Shadow, and the Night-Sea-Journey in every text.

Selected Bibliography

Bodkin, Maud. *Archetypal Patterns in Poetry.* London: Oxford University Press, 1934.

Jung, Carl Gustav. *Complete Works.* 17 vols. Eds. Herbert Read, Michael Fordham, and Gerhard Adler. New York: Pantheon, 1953–.

Knapp, Bettina L. *Music, Archetype and the Writer: A Jungian View.* University College: Pennsylvania State University Press, 1988.

Sugg, Richard, ed. *Jungian Literary Criticism.* Evanston, IL: Northwestern University Press, 1993.

Van Meurs, Jos. *Jungian Literary Criticism, 1920–1980: An Annotated Critical Bibliography of Works in English.* Metuchen, NJ: Scarecrow Press, 1988.

On the Relation of Analytical Psychology to Poetry

In spite of its difficulty, the task of discussing the relation of analytical psychology to poetry affords me a welcome opportunity to define my views on the much debated question of the relations between psychology and art in general. Although the two things cannot be compared, the close connections which undoubtedly exist between them call for investigation. These connections arise from the fact that the practice of art is a psychological activity and, as such, can be approached from a psychological angle. Considered in this light, art, like any other human activity deriving from psychic motives, is a proper subject for psychology. This statement, however, involves a very definite limitation of the psychological viewpoint when we come to apply it in practice. Only that aspect of art which consists in the process of artistic creation can be a subject for psychological study, but not that which constitutes its essential nature. The question of what art is in itself can never be answered by the psychologist, but must be approached from the side of aesthetics.

A similar distinction must be made in the realm of religion. A psychological approach is permissible only in regard to the emotions and symbols which constitute the phenomenology of religion, but which do not touch upon its essential nature. If the essence of religion and art could be explained, then both of them would become mere subdivisions of psychology. This is not to say that such violations of their nature have not been attempted. But those who are guilty of them obviously forget that a similar fate might easily befall psychology, since its intrinsic value and specific quality would be destroyed if it were regarded as a mere activity of the brain, and were relegated along with the endocrine functions to a subdivision of physiology. This too, as we know, has been attempted.

Art by its very nature is not science, and science by its very nature is not art; both these spheres of the mind have something in reserve that is peculiar to them and can be explained only in its own terms. Hence when we speak of the relation of psychology to art, we shall treat only of that aspect of art which can be submitted to psychological scrutiny without violating its nature. Whatever the psychologist has to say about art will be confined to the process of artistic creation and has nothing to do with its innermost essence. He can no more explain this than the intellect can describe or even understand the nature of feeling. Indeed, art and science would not exist as separate entities at all if the fundamental difference between them had not long since forced itself on the mind. The fact that artistic, scientific, and religious propensities still slumber peacefully together in the small child, or that with primitives the beginnings of art, science, and religion coalesce in the undifferentiated chaos of the magical mentality, or that no trace of "mind" can be found in the natural instincts of animals — all this does nothing to prove the existence of a unifying principle which alone would justify a reduction of the one to the other. For if we go so far back into the history of the mind that the distinctions between its various fields of activity become altogether invisible, we do not reach an underlying principle of their unity, but merely an earlier, undifferentiated state in which no separate activities yet exist. But the elementary state is not an explanatory principle that would allow us to draw conclusions as to the nature of later, more highly developed states, even though they must necessarily derive from it. A scientific attitude will always tend to overlook the peculiar nature of these more differentiated states in favor of their causal derivation, and will endeavor to subordinate them to a general but more elementary principle.

These theoretical reflections seem to me very much in place today, when we so often find that works of art, and particularly poetry, are interpreted precisely in this manner, by reducing them to more elementary states. Though the material he works with and its individual treatment can easily be traced back to the poet's personal rela-

Translated by R. F. C. Hull.

tions with his parents, this does not enable us to understand his poetry. The same reduction can be made in all sorts of other fields, and not least in the case of pathological disturbances. Neuroses and psychoses are likewise reducible to infantile relations with the parents, and so are a man's good and bad habits, his beliefs, peculiarities, passions, interests, and so forth. It can hardly be supposed that all these very different things must have exactly the same explanation, for otherwise we would be driven to the conclusion that they actually are the same thing. If a work of art is explained in the same way as a neurosis, then either the work of art is a neurosis or a neurosis is a work of art. This explanation is all very well as a play on words, but sound common sense rebels against putting a work of art on the same level as a neurosis. An analyst might, in an extreme case, view a neurosis as a work of art through the lens of his professional bias, but it would never occur to an intelligent layman to mistake a pathological phenomenon for art, in spite of the undeniable fact that a work of art arises from much the same psychological conditions as a neurosis. This is only natural, because certain of these conditions are present in every individual and, owing to the relative constancy of the human environment, are constantly the same, whether in the case of a nervous intellectual, a poet, or a normal human being. All have had parents, all have a father- or a mother-complex, all know about sex and therefore have certain common and typical human difficulties. One poet may be influenced more by his relation to his father, another by the tie to his mother, while a third shows unmistakable traces of sexual repression in his poetry. Since all this can be said equally well not only of every neurotic but of every normal human being, nothing specific is gained for the judgment of a work of art. At most our knowledge of its psychological antecedents will have been broadened and deepened.

The school of medical psychology inaugurated by Freud has undoubtedly encouraged the literary historian to bring certain peculiarities of a work of art into relations with the intimate, personal life of the poet. But this is nothing new in principle, for it has long been known that the scientific treatment of art will reveal the personal threads that the artist, intentionally or unintentionally, has woven into his work. The Freudian approach may, however, make possible a more exhaustive demonstration of the influences that reach back into earliest childhood and play their part in artistic creation. To this extent the psychoanalysis of art differs in no essential from the subtle psychological nuances of a penetrating literary analysis. The difference is at most a question of degree, though we may occasionally be surprised by indiscreet references to things which a rather more delicate touch might have passed over if only for reasons of tact. This lack of delicacy seems to be a professional peculiarity of the medical psychologist, and the temptation to draw daring conclusions easily leads to flagrant abuses. A slight whiff of scandal often lends spice to a biography, but a little more becomes a nasty inquisitiveness — bad taste masquerading as science. Our interest is insidiously deflected from the work of art and gets lost in the labyrinth of psychic determinants, the poet becomes a clinical case and, very likely, yet another addition to the curiosa of *psychopathia sexualis*.[1] But this means that the psychoanalysis of art has turned aside from its proper objective and strayed into a province that is as broad as mankind, that is not in the least specific to the artist and has even less relevance to his art.

This kind of analysis brings the work of art into the sphere of general human psychology, where many other things besides art have their origin. To explain art in these terms is just as great a platitude as the statement that "every artist is a narcissist." Every man who pursues his own goal is a "narcissist" — though one wonders how permissible it is to give such wide currency to a term specifically coined for the pathology of neurosis. The statement therefore amounts to nothing; it merely elicits the faint surprise of a bon mot. Since this kind of analysis is in no way concerned with the work of art itself, but strives like a mole to bury itself in the dirt as speedily as possible, it always ends up in the common earth that unites all mankind. Hence its explanations have the same tedious monotony as the recitals which one daily hears in the consulting room.

[1]Sexual psychopathology. [Ed.]

The reductive method of Freud is a purely medical one, and the treatment is directed at a pathological or otherwise unsuitable formation which has taken the place of the normal functioning. It must therefore be broken down, and the way cleared for healthy adaptation. In this case, reduction to the common human foundation is altogether appropriate. But when applied to a work of art it leads to the results I have described. It strips the work of art of its shimmering robes and exposes the nakedness and drabness of *Homo sapiens,* to which species the poet and artist also belong. The golden gleam of artistic creation — the original object of discussion — is extinguished as soon as we apply to it the same corrosive method which we use in analyzing the fantasies of hysteria. The results are no doubt very interesting and may perhaps have the same kind of scientific value as, for instance, a post-mortem examination of the brain of Nietzsche, which might conceivably show us the particular atypical form of paralysis from which he died. But what would this have to do with *Zarathustra?* Whatever its subterranean background may have been, is it not a whole world in itself, beyond the human, all-too-human imperfections, beyond the world of migraine and cerebral atrophy?

I have spoken of Freud's reductive method but have not stated in what that method consists. It is essentially a medical technique for investigating morbid psychic phenomena, and it is solely concerned with the ways and means of getting round or peering through the foreground of consciousness in order to reach the psychic background, or the unconscious. It is based on the assumption that the neurotic patient represses certain psychic contents because they are morally incompatible with his conscious values. It follows that the repressed contents must have correspondingly negative traits — infantile-sexual, obscene, or even criminal — which make them unacceptable to consciousness. Since no man is perfect, everyone must possess such a background whether he admits it or not. Hence it can always be exposed if only one uses the technique of interpretation worked out by Freud.

In the short space of a lecture I cannot, of course, enter into the details of the technique. A few hints must suffice. The unconscious background does not remain inactive, but betrays itself by its characteristic effects on the contents of consciousness. For example, it produces fantasies of a peculiar nature, which can easily be interpreted as sexual images. Or it produces characteristic disturbances of the conscious processes, which again can be reduced to repressed contents. A very important source for knowledge of the unconscious contents is provided by dreams, since these are direct products of the activity of the unconscious. The essential thing in Freud's reductive method is to collect all the clues pointing to the unconscious background, and then, through the analysis and interpretation of this material, to reconstruct the elementary instinctual processes. Those conscious contents which give us a clue to the unconscious background are incorrectly called *symbols* by Freud. They are not true symbols, however, since according to his theory they have merely the role of *signs* or *symptoms* of the subliminal processes. The true symbol differs essentially from this, and should be understood as an expression of an intuitive idea that cannot yet be formulated in any other or better way. When Plato, for instance, puts the whole problem of the theory of knowledge in his parable of the cave,[2] or when Christ expresses the idea of the Kingdom of Heaven in parables, these are genuine and true symbols, that is, attempts to express something for which no verbal concept yet exists. If we were to interpret Plato's metaphor in Freudian terms we would naturally arrive at the uterus, and would have proved that even a mind like Plato's was still stuck on a primitive level of infantile sexuality. But we would have completely overlooked what Plato actually created out of the primitive determinants of his philosophical ideas; we would have missed the essential point and merely discovered that he had infantile-sexual fantasies like any other mortal. Such a discovery could be of value only for a man who regarded Plato as superhuman, and who can now state with satisfaction that Plato too was an ordinary human being. But who would want to regard Plato as a god? Surely only one who is dominated by infantile fantasies and therefore possesses a neurotic mentality. For him

[2]In Plato, *Republic,* Book VII. [Ed.]

the reduction to common human truths is salutary on medical grounds, but this would have nothing whatever to do with the meaning of Plato's parable.

I have purposely dwelt on the application of medical psychoanalysis to works of art because I want to emphasize that the psychoanalytic method is at the same time an essential part of the Freudian doctrine. Freud himself by his rigid dogmatism has ensured that the method and the doctrine — in themselves two very different things — are regarded by the public as identical. Yet the method may be employed with beneficial results in medical cases without at the same time exalting it into a doctrine. And against this doctrine we are bound to raise vigorous objections. The assumptions it rests on are quite arbitrary. For example, neuroses are by no means exclusively caused by sexual repression, and the same holds true for psychoses. There is no foundation for saying that dreams merely contain repressed wishes whose moral incompatibility requires them to be disguised by a hypothetical dream-censor. The Freudian technique of interpretation, so far as it remains under the influence of its own one-sided and therefore erroneous hypotheses, displays a quite obvious bias.

In order to do justice to a work of art, analytical psychology must rid itself entirely of medical prejudice; for a work of art is not a disease, and consequently requires a different approach from the medical one. A doctor naturally has to seek out the causes of a disease in order to pull it up by the roots, but just as naturally the psychologist must adopt exactly the opposite attitude towards a work of art. Instead of investigating its typically human determinants, he will inquire first of all into its meaning, and will concern himself with its determinants only insofar as they enable him to understand it more fully. Personal causes have as much or as little to do with a work of art as the soil with the plant that springs from it. We can certainly learn to understand some of the plant's peculiarities by getting to know its habitat, and for the botanist this is an important part of his equipment. But nobody will maintain that everything essential has then been discovered about the plant itself. The personal orientation which the doctor needs when confronted with the question of etiology in medicine is quite out of place in dealing with a work of art, just because a work of art is not a human being, but is something suprapersonal. It is a thing and not a personality; hence it cannot be judged by personal criteria. Indeed, the special significance of a true work of art resides in the fact that it has escaped from the limitations of the personal and has soared beyond the personal concerns of its creator.

I must confess from my own experience that it is not at all easy for a doctor to lay aside his professional bias when considering a work of art and look at it with a mind cleared of the current biological causality. But I have come to learn that although a psychology with a purely biological orientation can explain a good deal about man in general, it cannot be applied to a work of art and still less to man as creator. A purely causalistic psychology is only able to reduce every human individual to a member of the species *Homo sapiens,* since its range is limited to what is transmitted by heredity or derived from other sources. But a work of art is not transmitted or derived — it is a creative reorganization of those very conditions to which a causalistic psychology must always reduce it. The plant is not a mere product of the soil; it is a living, self-contained process which in essence has nothing to do with the character of the soil. In the same way, the meaning and individual quality of a work of art inhere within it and not in its extrinsic determinants. One might almost describe it as a living being that uses man only as a nutrient medium, employing his capacities according to its own laws and shaping itself to the fulfillment of its own creative purpose.

But here I am anticipating somewhat, for I have in mind a particular type of art which I still have to introduce. Not every work of art originates in the way I have just described. There are literary works, prose as well as poetry, that spring wholly from the author's intention to produce a particular result. He submits his material to a definite treatment with a definite aim in view; he adds to it and subtracts from it, emphasizing one effect, toning down another, laying on a touch of color here, another there, all the time carefully considering the overall result and paying strict attention to the laws of form and style. He exercises the keenest judgment and chooses his words with complete freedom. His material is entirely subordinated to his artistic purpose; he wants to express this and nothing else. He is wholly at one with the creative process, no matter whether he has deliberately made himself its spearhead, as it were, or whether it has made him its instrument so completely that he has lost all consciousness of this fact. In either case, the artist is so identified with his work that his intentions and his faculties are indistinguishable from the act of creation itself. There is no need, I think, to give examples of this from the history of literature or from the testimony of the artists themselves.

Nor need I cite examples of the other class of works which flow more or less complete and perfect from the author's pen. They come as it were fully arrayed into the world, as Pallas Athene sprang from the head of Zeus. These works positively force themselves upon the author; his hand is seized, his pen writes things that his mind contemplates with amazement. The work brings with it its own form; anything he wants to add is rejected, and what he himself would like to reject is thrust back at him. While his conscious mind stands amazed and empty before this phenomenon, he is overwhelmed by a flood of thoughts and images which he never intended to create and which his own will could never have brought into being. Yet in spite of himself he is forced to admit that it is his own self speaking, his own inner nature revealing itself and uttering things which he would never have entrusted to his tongue. He can only obey the apparently alien impulse within him and follow where it leads, sensing that his work is greater than himself, and wields a power which is not his and which he cannot command. Here the artist is not identical with the process of creation; he is aware that he is subordinate to his work or stands outside it, as though he were a second person; or as though a person other than himself had fallen within the magic circle of an alien will.

So when we discuss the psychology of art, we must bear in mind these two entirely different modes of creation, for much that is of the greatest importance in judging a work of art depends on this distinction. It is one that had been sensed earlier by Schiller, who as we know attempted to classify it in his concept of the *sentimental* and the *naive*.[3] The psychologist would call "sentimental" art *introverted* and the "naive" kind *extraverted*. The introverted attitude is characterized by the subject's assertion of his conscious intentions and aims against the demands of the object, whereas the extraverted attitude is characterized by the subject's subordination to the demands which the object makes upon him. In my view, Schiller's plays and most of his poems give one a good idea of the introverted attitude: the material is mastered by the conscious intentions of the poet. The extraverted attitude is illustrated by the second part of *Faust:* here the material is distinguished by its refractoriness. A still more striking example is Nietzsche's *Zarathustra,* where the author himself observed how "one became two."

From what I have said, it will be apparent that a shift of psychological standpoint has taken place as soon as one speaks not of the poet as a person but of the creative process that moves him. When the focus of interest shifts to the latter, the poet comes into the picture only as a reacting subject. This is immediately evident in our second category of works, where the consciousness of the poet is not identical with the creative process. But in works of the first category the opposite appears to hold true. Here the poet appears to be the creative process itself, and to create of his own free will without the slightest feeling of compulsion. He may even be fully convinced of his freedom of action and refuse to admit that his work could be anything else than the expression of his will and ability.

Here we are faced with a question which we cannot answer from the testimony of the poets themselves. It is really a scientific problem that psychology alone can solve. As I hinted earlier, it might well be that the poet, while apparently creating out of himself and producing what he consciously intends, is nevertheless so carried away by the creative impulse that he is no longer aware of an "alien" will, just as the other type of poet is no longer aware of his own will speaking to him

[3]See Schiller, *On Naive and Sentimental Poetry,* p. 296. [Ed.]

in the apparently "alien" inspiration, although this is manifestly the voice of his own self. The poet's conviction that he is creating in absolute freedom would then be an illusion: he fancies he is swimming, but in reality an unseen current sweeps him along.

This is not by any means an academic question, but is supported by the evidence of analytical psychology. Researchers have shown that there are all sorts of ways in which the conscious mind is not only influenced by the unconscious but actually guided by it. Yet is there any evidence for the supposition that a poet, despite his self-awareness, may be taken captive by his work? The proof may be of two kinds, direct or indirect. Direct proof would be afforded by a poet who thinks he knows what he is saying but actually says more than he is aware of. Such cases are not uncommon. Indirect proof would be found in cases where behind the apparent free will of the poet there stands a higher imperative that renews its peremptory demands as soon as the poet voluntarily gives up his creative activity, or that produces psychic complications whenever his work has to be broken off against his will.

Analysis of artists consistently shows not only the strength of the creative impulse arising from the unconscious, but also its capricious and willful character. The biographies of great artists make it abundantly clear that the creative urge is often so imperious that it battens on their humanity and yokes everything to the service of the work, even at the cost of health and ordinary human happiness. The unborn work in the psyche of the artist is a force of nature that achieves its end either with tyrannical might or with the subtle cunning of nature herself, quite regardless of the personal fate of the man who is its vehicle. The creative urge lives and grows in him like a tree in the earth from which it draws its nourishment. We would do well, therefore, to think of the creative process as a living thing implanted in the human psyche. In the language of analytical psychology this living thing is an *autonomous complex.* It is a split-off portion of the psyche, which leads a life of its own outside the hierarchy of consciousness. Depending on its energy charge, it may appear either as a mere disturbance of conscious activities or as a supraordinate authority which can harness the ego to its purpose. Accordingly, the poet who identifies with the creative process would be one who acquiesces from the start when the unconscious imperative begins to function. But the other poet, who feels the creative force as something alien, is one who for various reasons cannot acquiesce and is thus caught unawares.

It might be expected that this difference in its origins would be perceptible in a work of art. For in the one case it is a conscious product shaped and designed to have the effect intended. But in the other we are dealing with an event originating in unconscious nature; with something that achieves its aim without the assistance of human consciousness, and often defies it by willfully insisting on its own form and effect. We would therefore expect that works belonging to the first class would nowhere overstep the limits of comprehension, that their effect would be bounded by the author's intention and would not extend beyond it. But with works of the other class we would have to be prepared for something suprapersonal that transcends our understanding to the same degree that the author's consciousness was in abeyance during the process of creation. We would expect a strangeness of form and content, thoughts that can only be apprehended intuitively, a language pregnant with meanings, and images that are true symbols because they are the best possible expressions for something unknown — bridges thrown out towards an unseen shore.

These criteria are, by and large, corroborated in practice. Whenever we are confronted with a work that was consciously planned and with material that was consciously selected, we find that it agrees with the first class of qualities, and in the other case with the second. The example we gave of Schiller's plays, on the one hand, and *Faust II* on the other, or better still *Zarathustra,* is an illustration of this. But I would not undertake to place the work of an unknown poet in either of these categories without first having examined rather closely his personal relations with his work. It is not enough to know whether the poet belongs to the introverted or to the extraverted type, since it is possible for either type to work with an introverted attitude at one time, and an extraverted attitude at another. This is particularly noticeable in the difference between Schiller's plays and his philosophical writings, between Goethe's perfectly formed poems and the obvious struggle with his material in *Faust II*, and between Nietzsche's well-turned aphorisms and the rushing torrent of *Zarathustra*. The same poet can adopt different attitudes to his work at different times, and on this depends the standard we have to apply.

The question, as we now see, is exceedingly complicated, and the complication grows even worse when we consider the case of the poet who identifies with the creative process. For should it turn out that the apparently conscious and purposeful manner of composition is a subjective illusion of the poet, then his work would possess symbolic qualities that are outside the range of his consciousness. They would only be more difficult to detect, because the reader as well would be unable to get beyond the bounds of the poet's consciousness which are fixed by the spirit of the time. There is no Archimedean point outside his world by which he could lift his time-bound consciousness off its hinges and recognize the symbols hidden in the poet's work. For a symbol is the intimation of a meaning beyond the level of our present powers of comprehension.

I raise this question only because I do not want my typological classification to limit the possible significance of works of art which apparently mean no more than what they say. But we have often found that a poet who has gone out of fashion is suddenly rediscovered. This happens when our conscious development has reached a higher level from which the poet can tell us something new. It was always present in his work but was hidden in a symbol, and only a renewal of the spirit of the time permits us to read its meaning. It needed to be looked at with fresher eyes, for the old ones see in it only what they were accustomed to see. Experiences of this kind should make us cautious, as they bear out my earlier argument. But works that are openly symbolic do not require this subtle approach; their pregnant language cries out at us that they mean more than they say. We can put our finger on the symbol at once, even though we may not be able to unriddle its meaning to our entire satisfaction. A symbol remains a perpetual challenge to our thoughts and feelings. That probably explains why a symbolic work is so stimulating, why it grips us so intensely, but also why it seldom affords us a purely aesthetic enjoyment. A work that is manifestly not symbolic appeals much more to our aesthetic sensibility because it is complete in itself and fulfills its purpose.

What then, you may ask, can analytical psychology contribute to our fundamental problem, which is the mystery of artistic creation? All that we have said so far has to do only with the psychological phenomenology of art. Since nobody can penetrate to the heart of nature, you will not expect psychology to do the impossible and offer a valid explanation of the secret of creativity. Like every other science, psychology has only a modest contribution to make towards a deeper understanding of the phenomena of life, and is no nearer than its sister sciences to absolute knowledge.

We have talked so much about the meaning of works of art that one can hardly suppress a doubt as to whether art really "means" anything at all. Perhaps art has no "meaning," at least not as we understand meaning. Perhaps it is like nature, which simply *is* and "means" nothing beyond that. Is "meaning" necessarily more than mere interpretation — an interpretation secreted into something by an intellect hungry for meaning? Art, it has been said, is beauty, and "a thing of beauty is a joy forever."[4] It needs no meaning, for meaning has nothing to do with art. Within the sphere of art, I must accept the truth of this statement. But when I speak of the relation of psychology to art we are outside its sphere, and it is impossible for us not to speculate. We must interpret, we must find meanings in things, otherwise we would be quite unable to think about them. We have to break down life and events, which are self-contained processes, into meanings, images, concepts, well knowing that in doing so we are getting further away from the living mystery. As long as we ourselves are caught up in the process of creation, we neither see nor understand; indeed we ought not to understand, for nothing is more injurious to immediate experience than cognition. But for the pur-

[4]Keats, "Endymion," I. [Ed.]

pose of cognitive understanding we must detach ourselves from the creative process and look at it from the outside; only then does it become an image that expresses what we are bound to call "meaning." What was a mere phenomenon before becomes something that in association with other phenomena has meaning, that has a definite role to play, serves certain ends, and exerts meaningful effects. And when we have seen all this we get the feeling of having understood and explained something. In this way we meet the demands of science.

When, a little earlier, we spoke of a work of art as a tree growing out of the nourishing soil, we might equally well have compared it to a child growing in the womb. But as all comparisons are lame, let us stick to the more precise terminology of science. You will remember that I described the nascent work in the psyche of the artists as an autonomous complex. By this we mean a psychic formation that remains subliminal until its energy-charge is sufficient to carry it over the threshold into consciousness. Its association with consciousness does not mean that it is assimilated, only that it is perceived; but it is not subject to conscious control, and can be neither inhibited nor voluntarily reproduced. Therein lies the autonomy of the complex: it appears and disappears in accordance with its own inherent tendencies, independently of the conscious will. The creative complex shares this peculiarity with every other autonomous complex. In this respect it offers an analogy with pathological processes, since these too are characterized by the presence of autonomous complexes, particularly in the case of mental disturbances. The divine frenzy of the artist comes perilously close to a pathological state, though the two things are not identical. The *tertium comparationis*[5] is the autonomous complex. But the presence of autonomous complexes is not in itself pathological, since normal people, too, fall temporarily or permanently under their domination. This fact is simply one of the normal peculiarities of the psyche, and for a man to be unaware of the existence of an autonomous complex merely betrays a high degree of unconsciousness. Every typical attitude that is to some extent differentiated shows a tendency to become an autonomous complex, and in most cases it actually does. Again, every instinct has more or less the character of an autonomous complex. In itself, therefore, an autonomous complex has nothing morbid about it; only when its manifestations are frequent and disturbing is it a symptom of illness.

How does an autonomous complex arise? For reasons which we cannot go into here, a hitherto unconscious portion of the psyche is thrown into activity, and gains ground by activating the adjacent areas of association. The energy needed for this is naturally drawn from consciousness — unless the latter happens to identify with the complex. But where this does not occur, the drain of energy produces what Janet calls an *abaissement du niveau mental*.[6] The intensity of conscious interests and activities gradually diminishes, leading either to apathy — a condition very common with artists — or to a regressive development of the conscious functions, that is, they revert to an infantile and archaic level and undergo something like a degeneration. The "inferior parts of the functions," as Janet calls them, push to the fore; the instinctual side of the personality prevails over the ethical, the infantile over the mature, and the unadapted over the adapted. This too is something we see in the lives of many artists. The autonomous complex thus develops by using the energy that has been withdrawn from the conscious control of the personality.

But in what does an autonomous *creative* complex consist? Of this we can know next to nothing so long as the artist's work affords us no insight into its foundations. The work presents us with a finished picture, and this picture is amenable to analysis only to the extent that we can recognize it as a symbol. But if we are unable to discover any symbolic value in it, we have merely established that, so far as we are concerned, it means no more than what it says, or to put it another way, that it *is* no more than what it *seems* to be. I used the word *seems* because our own bias may prevent a deeper appreciation of it.

[5]Third element; the "middle term" or common factor between two disparate things. [Ed.]

[6]Lowering of mental level. [Ed.]

At any rate we can find no incentive and no starting point for an analysis. But in the case of a symbolic work we should remember the dictum of Gerhard Hauptmann: "Poetry evokes out of words the resonance of the primordial word." The question we should ask, therefore, is: what primordial image lies behind the imagery of art?

This question needs a little elucidation. I am assuming that the work of art we propose to analyze, as well as being symbolic, has its source not in the *personal unconscious* of the poet, but in a sphere of unconscious mythology whose primordial images are the common heritage of mankind. I have called this sphere the *collective unconscious,* to distinguish it from the personal unconscious. The latter I regard as the sum total of all those psychic processes and contents which are capable of becoming conscious and often do, but are then suppressed because of their incompatibility and kept subliminal. Art receives tributaries from this sphere too, but muddy ones; and their predominance, far from making a work of art a symbol, merely turns it into a symptom. We can leave this kind of art without injury and without regret to the purgative methods employed by Freud.

In contrast to the personal unconscious, which is a relatively thin layer immediately below the threshold of consciousness, the collective unconscious shows no tendency to become conscious under normal conditions, nor can it be brought back to recollection by an analytical technique, since it was never repressed or forgotten. The collective unconscious is not to be thought of as a self-subsistent entity; it is no more than a potentiality handed down to us from primordial times in the specific form of mnemonic images or inherited in the anatomical structure of the brain. There are no inborn ideas, but there are inborn possibilities of ideas that set bounds to even the boldest fantasy and keep our fantasy activity within certain categories: *a priori* ideas, as it were, the existence of which cannot be ascertained except from their effects. They appear only in the shaped material of art as the regulative principles that shape it; that is to say, only by inferences drawn from the finished work can we reconstruct the age-old original of the primordial image.

The primordial image, or archetype, is a figure — be it a demon, a human being, or a process — that constantly recurs in the course of history and appears wherever creative fantasy is freely expressed. Essentially, therefore, it is a mythological figure. When we examine these images more closely, we find that they give form to countless typical experiences of our ancestors. They are, so to speak, the psychic residua of innumerable experiences of the same type. They present a picture of psychic life in the average, divided up and projected into the manifold figures of the mythological pantheon. But the mythological figures are themselves products of creative fantasy and still have to be translated into conceptual language. Only the beginnings of such a language exist, but once the necessary concepts are created they could give us an abstract, scientific understanding of the unconscious processes that lie at the roots of the primordial images. In each of these images there is a little piece of human psychology and human fate, a remnant of the joys and sorrows that have been repeated countless times in our ancestral history, and on the average follow ever the same course. It is like a deeply graven river-bed in the psyche, in which waters of life, instead of flowing along as before in a broad but shallow stream, suddenly swell into a mighty river. This happens whenever that particular set of circumstances is encountered which over long periods of time has helped to lay down the primordial image.

The moment when this mythological situation reappears is always characterized by a peculiar emotional intensity; it is as though chords in us were struck that had never resounded before, or as though forces whose existence we never suspected were unloosed. What makes the struggle for adaptation so laborious is the fact that we have constantly to be dealing with individual and atypical situations. So it is not surprising that when an archetypal situation occurs we suddenly feel an extraordinary sense of release, as though transported, or caught up by an overwhelming power. At such moments we are no longer individuals, but the race; the voice of all mankind resounds in us. The individual man cannot use his powers to the full unless he is aided by one of those collective representations we call ideals, which releases all the hidden forces of instinct that are inaccessible to his conscious will. The most effective ideals are always fairly obvious variants of an archetype, as is evident from the fact that they lend themselves to allegory. The ideal of the "mother country," for instance, is an obvious allegory of the mother, as is the "fatherland" of the father. Its power to stir us does not derive from the allegory, but from the symbolical value of our native land. The archetype here is the *participation mystique* of primitive man with the soil on which he dwells, and which contains the spirits of his ancestors.

The impact of an archetype, whether it takes the form of immediate experience or is expressed through the spoken word, stirs us because it summons up a voice that is stronger than our own. Whoever speaks in primordial images speaks with a thousand voices; he enthralls and overpowers, while at the same time he lifts the idea he is seeking to express out of the occasional and the transitory into the realm of the ever-enduring. He transmutes our personal destiny into the destiny of mankind, and evokes in us all those beneficent forces that ever and anon have enabled humanity to find a refuge from every peril and to outlive the longest night.

That is the secret of great art, and of its effect upon us. The creative process, so far as we are able to follow it at all, consists in the unconscious activation of an archetypal image, and in elaborating and shaping this image into the finished work. By giving it shape, the artist translates it into the language of the present, and so makes it possible for us to find our way back to the deepest springs of life. Therein lies the social significance of art: it is constantly at work educating the spirit of the age, conjuring up the forms in which the age is most lacking. The unsatisfied yearning of the artist reaches back to the primordial image in the unconscious which is best fitted to compensate the inadequacy and one-sidedness of the present. The artist seizes on this image, and in raising it from deepest unconsciousness he brings it into relation with conscious values, thereby transforming it until it can be accepted by the minds of his contemporaries according to their powers.

People and times, like individuals, have their own characteristic tendencies and attitudes. The very word *attitude* betrays the necessary bias that every marked tendency entails. Direction implies exclusion, and exclusion means that very many psychic elements that could play their part in life are denied the right to exist because they are incompatible with the general attitude. The normal man can follow the general trend without injury to himself; but the man who takes to the back streets and alleys because he cannot endure the broad highway will be the first to discover the psychic elements that are waiting to play their part in the life of the collective. Here the artist's relative lack of adaptation turns out to his advantage; it enables him to follow his own yearnings far from the beaten path, and to discover what it is that would meet the unconscious needs of his age. Thus, just as the onesidedness of the individual's conscious attitude is corrected by reactions from the unconscious, so art represents a process of self-regulation in the life of nations and epochs.

I am aware that in this lecture I have only been able to sketch out my views in the barest outline. But I hope that what I have been obliged to omit, that is to say their practical application to poetic works of art, has been furnished by your own thoughts, thus giving flesh and blood to my abstract intellectual frame.

The Principal Archetypes

THE EGO

Investigation of the psychology of the unconscious confronted me with facts which required the formulation of new concepts. One of these concepts is the *self*. The entity so denoted is not meant to take the place of the one that has always been known as the *ego*, but includes it in a supraordinate concept. We understand the ego as the complex factor to which all conscious contents are related. It forms, as it were, the center of the field of consciousness; and, insofar as this comprises the empirical personality, the ego is the subject of all personal acts of consciousness. The relation of a psychic content to the ego forms the criterion of its consciousness, for no content can be conscious unless it is represented to a subject.

With this definition we have described and delimited the *scope* of the subject. Theoretically, no limits can be set to the field of consciousness, since it is capable of indefinite extension. Empirically, however, it always finds its limit when it comes up against the *unknown*. This consists of everything we do not know, which, therefore, is not related to the ego as the center of the field of consciousness. The unknown falls into two groups of objects: those which are outside and can be experienced by the senses, and those which are inside and are experienced immediately. The first group comprises the unknown in the outer world; the second the unknown in the inner world. We call this latter territory the *unconscious*.

The ego, as a specific content of consciousness, is not a simple or elementary factor but a complex one which, as such, cannot be described exhaustively. Experience shows that it rests on two seemingly different bases: the *somatic* and the *psychic*. The somatic basis is inferred from the totality of endosomatic perceptions, which for their part are already of a psychic nature and are associated with the ego, and are therefore conscious. They are produced by endosomatic stimuli, only some of which cross the threshold of consciousness. A considerable proportion of these stimuli occur unconsciously, that is, subliminally. The fact that they are subliminal does not necessarily mean that their status is merely physiological, any more than this would be true of a psychic content. Sometimes they are capable of crossing the threshold, that is, of becoming perceptions. But there is no doubt that a large proportion of these endosomatic stimuli are simply incapable of consciousness and are so elementary that there is no reason to assign them a psychic nature — unless of course one favors the philosophical view that all life-processes are psychic anyway. The chief objection to this hardly demonstrable hypothesis is that it enlarges the concept of the psyche beyond all bounds and interprets the life-process in a way not absolutely warranted by the facts. Concepts that are too broad usually prove to be unsuitable instruments because they are too vague and nebulous. I have therefore suggested that the term "psychic" be used only where there is evidence of a will capable of modifying reflex or instinctual processes. Here I must refer the reader to my paper "On the Nature of the Psyche," where I have discussed this definition of the "psychic" at somewhat greater length.

The somatic basis of the ego consists, then, of conscious and unconscious factors. The same is true of the psychic basis: on the one hand the ego rests on the *total field of consciousness,* and on the other, on the *sum total of unconscious contents*. These fall into three groups: first, temporarily subliminal contents that can be reproduced voluntarily (memory); second, unconscious contents that cannot be reproduced voluntarily; third, contents that are not capable of becoming conscious at all. Group two can be inferred from the spontaneous irruption of subliminal contents into consciousness. Group three is hypothetical; it is a logical inference from the facts underlying group two. It contains contents which have *not yet* irrupted into consciousness, or which never will.

When I said that the ego "rests" on the total field of consciousness I do not mean that it *con-*

Translated by R. F. C. Hull.

sists of this. Were that so, it would be indistinguishable from the field of consciousness as a whole. The ego is only the latter's point of reference, grounded on and limited by the somatic factor described above.

Although its bases are in themselves relatively unknown and unconscious, the ego is a conscious factor par excellence. It is even acquired, empirically speaking, during the individual's lifetime. It seems to arise in the first place from the collision between the somatic factor and the environment, and, once established as a subject, it goes on developing from further collisions with the outer world and the inner.

Despite the unlimited extent of its bases, the ego is never more and never less than consciousness as a whole. As a conscious factor the ego could, theoretically at least, be described completely. But this would never amount to more than a picture of the *conscious personality;* all those features which are unknown or unconscious to the subject would be missing. A total picture would have to include these. But a total description of the personality is, even in theory, absolutely impossible, because the unconscious portion of it cannot be grasped cognitively. This unconscious portion, as experience has abundantly shown, is by no means unimportant. On the contrary, the most decisive qualities in a person are often unconscious and can be perceived only by others, or have to be laboriously discovered with outside help.

Clearly, then, the *personality as a total phenomenon* does not coincide with the ego, that is, with the conscious personality, but forms an entity that has to be distinguished from the ego. Naturally the need to do this is incumbent only on a psychology that reckons with the fact of the unconscious, but for such a psychology the distinction is of paramount importance. Even for jurisprudence it should be of some importance whether certain psychic facts are conscious or not — for instance, in adjudging the question of responsibility.

I have suggested calling the total personality which, though present, cannot be fully known, the *self.* The ego is, by definition, subordinate to the self and is related to it like a part to the whole. Inside the field of consciousness it has, as we say, free will. By this I do not mean anything philosophical, only the well-known psychological fact of "free choice," or rather the subjective feeling of freedom. But, just as our free will clashes with necessity in the outside world, so also it finds its limits outside the field of consciousness in the subjective inner world, where it comes into conflict with the facts of the self. And just as circumstances or outside events "happen" to us and limit our freedom, so the self acts upon the ego like an *objective occurrence* which free will can do very little to alter. It is, indeed, well known that the ego not only can do nothing against the self, but is sometimes actually assimilated by unconscious components of the personality that are in the process of development and is greatly altered by them.

It is, in the nature of the case, impossible to give any general description of the ego except a formal one. Any other mode of observation would have to take account of the *individuality* which attaches to the ego as one of its main characteristics. Although the numerous elements composing this complex factor are, in themselves, everywhere the same, they are infinitely varied as regards clarity, emotional coloring, and scope. The result of their combination — the ego — is therefore, so far as one can judge, individual and unique, and retains its identity up to a certain point. Its stability is relative, because far-reaching changes of personality can sometimes occur. Alterations of this kind need not always be pathological; they can also be developmental and hence fall within the scope of the normal.

Since it is the point of reference for the field of consciousness, the ego is the subject of all successful attempts at adaptation so far as these are achieved by the will. The ego therefore has a significant part to play in the psychic economy. Its position there is so important that there are good grounds for the prejudice that the ego is the center of the personality, and that the field of consciousness is the psyche *per se.* If we discount certain suggestive ideas in Leibniz, Kant, Schelling, and Schopenhauer, and the philosophical excursions of Carus and von Hartmann, it is only since the end of the nineteenth century that modern psychology, with its inductive methods, has discovered the foundations of consciousness and proved empirically the existence of a psyche outside consciousness. With this discovery the position of the ego, till then absolute, became relativized; that is to say, though it retains its quality as the center of the field of consciousness, it is questionable whether it is the center of the personality. It is part of the personality but not the whole of it. As I have said, it is simply impossible to estimate how large or how small its share is; how free or how dependent it is on the qualities of this "extra-conscious" psyche. We can only say that its freedom is limited and its dependence proved in ways that are often decisive. In my experience one would do well not to underestimate its dependence on the unconscious. Naturally there is no need to say this to persons who already overestimate the latter's importance. Some criterion for the right measure is afforded by the psychic consequences of a wrong estimate, a point to which we shall return later on.

We have seen that, from the standpoint of the psychology of consciousness, the unconscious can be divided into three groups of contents. But from the standpoint of the psychology of the personality a twofold division ensues: an "extra-conscious" psyche whose contents are *personal,* and an "extra-conscious" psyche whose contents are *impersonal* and *collective.* The first group comprises contents which are integral components of the individual personality and could therefore just as well be conscious; the second group forms, as it were, an omnipresent, unchanging, and everywhere identical *quality or substrate of the psyche per se.* This is, of course, no more than a hypothesis. But we are driven to it by the peculiar nature of the empirical material, not to mention the high probability that the general similarity of psychic processes in all individuals must be based on an equally general and impersonal principle that conforms to law, just as the instinct manifesting itself in the individual is only the partial manifestation of an instinctual substrate common to all men.

THE SHADOW

Whereas the contents of the personal unconscious are acquired during the individual's lifetime, the contents of the collective unconscious are invariably archetypes that were present from the beginning. Their relation to the instincts has been discussed elsewhere.[1] The archetypes most clearly characterized from the empirical point of view are those which have the most frequent and the most disturbing influence on the ego. These are the *shadow,* the *anima,* and the *animus.*[2] The most accessible of these, and the easiest to experience, is the shadow, for its nature can in large measure be inferred from the contents of the personal unconscious. The only exceptions to this rule are those rather rare cases where the positive qualities of the personality are repressed, and the ego in consequence plays an essentially negative or unfavorable role.

The shadow is a moral problem that challenges the whole ego-personality, for no one can become conscious of the shadow without considerable moral effort. To become conscious of it involves recognizing the dark aspects of the personality as present and real. This act is the essential condition for any kind of self-knowledge, and it therefore, as a rule, meets with considerable resistance. Indeed, self-knowledge as a psychotherapeutic measure frequently requires much painstaking work extending over a long period.

Closer examination of the dark characteristics — that is, the inferiorities constituting the shadow — reveals that they have an *emotional* nature, a kind of autonomy, and accordingly an obsessive or, better, possessive quality. Emotion, incidentally, is not an activity of the individual but something that happens to him. Affects occur usually where adaptation is weakest, and at the same time they reveal the reason for its weakness, namely a certain degree of inferiority and the existence of a lower level of personality. On this lower level with its uncontrolled or scarcely controlled emotions one behaves more or less like a primitive, who is not only the passive victim of his affects but also singularly incapable of moral judgment.

[1] "Instinct and the Unconscious" and "On the Nature of the Psyche," pars. 397ff. [Au.]

[2] The contents of this and the following chapter are taken from a lecture delivered to the Swiss Society for Practical Psychology, in Zurich, 1948. The material was first published in the *Wiener Zeitschrift für Nervenheilkunde und deren Genzgebiete* I (1948): 4. [Au.]

Although, with insight and good will, the shadow can to some extent be assimilated into the conscious personality, experience shows that there are certain features which offer the most obstinate resistance to moral control and prove almost impossible to influence. These resistances are usually bound up with *projections,* which are not recognized as such, and their recognition is a moral achievement beyond the ordinary. While some traits peculiar to the shadow can be recognized without too much difficulty as one's own personal qualities, in this case both insight and good will are unavailing because the cause of the emotion appears to lie, beyond all possibility of doubt, in the *other person.* No matter how obvious it may be to the neutral observer that it is a matter of projections, there is little hope that the subject will perceive this himself. He must be convinced that he throws a very long shadow before he is willing to withdraw his emotionally-toned projections from their object.

Let us suppose that a certain individual shows no inclination whatever to recognize his projections. The projection-making factor then has a free hand and can realize its object — if it has one — or bring about some other situation characteristic of its power. As we know, it is not the conscious subject but the unconscious which does the projecting. Hence one meets with projections, one does not make them. The effect of projection is to isolate the subject from his environment, since instead of a real relation to it there is now only an illusory one. Projections change the world into the replica of one's own unknown face. In the last analysis, therefore, they lead to an autoerotic or autistic condition in which one dreams a world whose reality remains forever unattainable. The resultant *sentiment d'incomplétude*[3] and the still worse feeling of sterility are in their turn explained by projection as the malevolence of the environment, and by means of this vicious circle the isolation is intensified. The more projections are thrust in between the subject and the environment, the harder it is for the ego to see through its illusions. A forty-five-year-old patient who had suffered from a compulsion neurosis since he was twenty and had become completely cut off from the world once said to me: "But I can never admit to myself that I've wasted the best twenty-five years of my life!"

It is often tragic to see how blatantly a man bungles his own life and the lives of others yet remains totally incapable of seeing how much the whole tragedy originates in himself, and how he continually feeds it and keeps it going. Not *consciously,* of course — for consciously he is engaged in bewailing and cursing a faithless world that recedes further and further into the distance. Rather, it is an unconscious factor which spins the illusions that veil his world. And what is being spun is a cocoon, which in the end will completely envelop him.

One might assume that projections like these, which are so very difficult if not impossible to dissolve, would belong to the realm of the shadow — that is, to the negative side of the personality. This assumption becomes untenable after a certain point, because the symbols that then appear no longer refer to the same but to the opposite sex, in a man's case to a woman and vice versa. The source of projections is no longer the shadow — which is always of the same sex as the subject — but a contrasexual figure. Here we meet the animus of a woman and the anima of a man, two corresponding archetypes whose autonomy and unconsciousness explain the stubbornness of their projections. Though the shadow is a motif as well known to mythology as anima and animus, it represents first and foremost the personal unconscious, and its content can therefore be made conscious without too much difficulty. In this it differs from anima and animus, for whereas the shadow can be seen through and recognized fairly easily, the anima and animus are much further away from consciousness and in normal circumstances are seldom if ever realized. With a little self-criticism one can see through the shadow — so far as its nature is personal. But when it appears as an archetype, one encounters the same difficulties as with anima and animus. In other words, it is quite within the bounds of possibility for a man to recognize the relative evil of his nature, but it is a rare and shattering experience for him to gaze into the face of absolute evil.

[3]Feeling of incompleteness. [Ed.]

What, then, is this projection-making factor? The East calls it the "Spinning Woman"[4] — Maya, who creates illusion by her dancing. Had we not long since known it from the symbolism of dreams, this hint from the Orient would put us on the right track: the enveloping, embracing, and devouring element points unmistakably to the mother,[5] that is, to the son's relation to the real mother, to her imago, and to the woman who is to become a mother for him. His Eros is passive like a child's; he hopes to be caught, sucked in, enveloped, and devoured. He seeks, as it were, the protecting, nourishing, charmed circle of the mother, the condition of the infant released from every care, in which the outside world bends over him and even forces happiness upon him. No wonder the real world vanishes from sight!

If this situation is dramatized, as the unconscious usually dramatizes it, then there appears before you on the psychological stage a man living regressively, seeking his childhood and his mother, fleeing from a cold cruel world which denies him understanding. Often a mother appears beside him who apparently shows not the slightest concern that her little son should become a man, but who, with tireless and self-immolating effort, neglects nothing that might hinder him from growing up and marrying. You behold the secret conspiracy between mother and son, and how each helps the other to betray life.

Where does the guilt lie? With the mother, or with the son? Probably with both. The unsatisfied longing of the son for life and the world ought to be taken seriously. There is in him a desire to touch reality, to embrace the earth and fructify the field of the world. But he makes no more than a series of fitful starts, for his initiative as well as his staying power are crippled by the secret memory that the world and happiness may be had as a gift — from the mother. The fragment of world which he, like every man, must encounter again and again is never quite the right one, since it does not fall into his lap, does not meet him half way, but remains resistant, has to be conquered, and submits only to force. It makes demands on the masculinity of a man, on his ardor, above all on his courage and resolution when it comes to throwing his whole being into the scales. For this he would need a faithless Eros, one capable of forgetting his mother and undergoing the pain of relinquishing the first love of his life. The mother, foreseeing this danger, has carefully inculcated into him the virtues of faithfulness, devotion, loyalty, so as to protect him from the moral disruption which is the risk of every life adventure. He has learnt these lessons only too well, and remains true to his mother. This naturally causes her the deepest anxiety (when, to her greater glory, he turns out to be a homosexual, for example) and at the same time affords her an unconscious satisfaction that is positively mythological. For, in the relationship now reigning between them, there is consummated the immemorial and most sacred archetype of the marriage of mother and son. What, after all, has commonplace reality to offer, with its registry offices, pay envelopes, and monthly rent, that could outweigh the mystic awe of the *hieros gamos?*[6] Or the star-crowned woman whom the dragon pursues, or the pious obscurities veiling the marriage of the Lamb?

This myth, better than any other, illustrates the nature of the collective unconscious. At this level the mother is both old and young, Demeter and Persephone, and the son is spouse and sleeping suckling rolled into one. The imperfections of real life, with its laborious adaptations and manifold disappointments, naturally cannot compete with such a state of indescribable fulfilment.

In the case of the son, the projection-making factor is identical with the mother-imago, and this is consequently taken to be the real mother. The projection can only be dissolved when the son sees that in the realm of his psyche there is an imago not only of the mother but of the

[4]Erwin Rousselle, "Seelische Führung im lebenden Taoismus," Pl. I, pp. 150, 170. Rousselle calls the spinning woman the "animal soul." There is a saying that runs, "The spinner sets in motion." I have defined the anima as a personification of the unconscious. [Au.]

[5]Here and in what follows, the word "mother" is not meant in the literal sense but as a symbol of everything that functions as a mother. [Au.]

[6]Sacred marriage. Jung's allusions are to the book of Revelation. [Ed.]

daughter, the sister, the beloved, the heavenly goddess, and the chthonic Baubo.[7] Every mother and every beloved is forced to become the carrier and embodiment of this omnipresent and ageless image, which corresponds to the deepest reality in a man. It belongs to him, this perilous image of Woman; she stands for the loyalty which in the interests of life he must sometimes forgo; she is the much needed compensation for the risks, struggles, sacrifices that all end in disappointment; she is the solace for all the bitterness of life. And, at the same time, she is the great illusionist, the seductress, who draws him into life with her Maya — and not only in life's reasonable and useful aspects, but into its frightful paradoxes and ambivalences where good and evil, success and ruin, hope and despair, counterbalance one another. Because she is his greatest danger she demands from a man his greatest, and if he has it in him she will receive it.

This image is "My Lady Soul," as Spitteler called her. I have suggested instead the term "anima," as indicating something specific, for which the expression "soul" is too general and too vague. The empirical reality summed up under the concept of the anima forms an extremely dramatic content of the unconscious. It is possible to describe this content in rational, scientific language, but in this way one entirely fails to express its living character. Therefore, in describing the living processes of the psyche, I deliberately and consciously give preference to a dramatic, mythological way of thinking and speaking, because this is not only more expressive but also more exact than an abstract scientific terminology, which is wont to toy with the notion that its theoretic formulations may one fine day be resolved into algebraic equations.

The projection-making factor is the anima, or rather the unconscious as represented by the anima. Whenever she appears, in dreams, visions, and fantasies, she takes on personified form, thus demonstrating that the factor she embodies possesses all the outstanding characteristics of a feminine being. She is not an invention of the conscious, but a spontaneous product of the unconscious. Nor is she a substitute figure for the mother. On the contrary, there is every likelihood that the numinous qualities which make the mother-imago so dangerously powerful derive from the collective archetype of the anima, which is incarnated anew in every male child.

Since the anima is an archetype that is found in men, it is reasonable to suppose that an equivalent archetype must be present in women; for just as the man is compensated by a feminine element, so woman is compensated by a masculine one. I do not, however, wish this argument to give the impression that these compensatory relationships were arrived at by deduction. On the contrary, long and varied experience was needed in order to grasp the nature of anima and animus empirically. Whatever we have to say about these archetypes, therefore, is either directly verifiable or at least rendered probable by the facts. At the same time, I am fully aware that we are discussing pioneer work which by its very nature can only be provisional.

Just as the mother seems to be the first carrier of the projection-making factor for the son, so is the father for the daughter. Practical experience of these relationships is made up of many individual cases presenting all kinds of variations on the same basic theme. A concise description of them can, therefore, be no more than schematic.

Woman is compensated by a masculine element and therefore her unconscious has, so to speak, a masculine imprint. This results in a considerable psychological difference between men and women, and accordingly I have called the projection-making factor in women the animus, which means mind or spirit. The animus corresponds to the paternal Logos[8] just as the anima corresponds to the maternal Eros.[9] But I do not wish or intend to give these two intuitive concepts too specific a definition. I use Eros and Logos merely as conceptual aids to describe the fact that woman's consciousness is characterized more by the connective quality of Eros than by the discrimination and cognition associated with Logos. In men, Eros, the function of relationship, is usually less developed than Logos. In women, on the

[7]The earth mother, symbol of the grave to which man goes. [Ed.]

[8]Reason. [Ed.]

[9]Love, desire. [Ed.]

other hand, Eros is an expression of their true nature, while their Logos is often only a regrettable accident. It gives rise to misunderstandings and annoying interpretations in the family circle and among friends. This is because it consists of *opinions* instead of reflections, and by opinions I mean *a priori* assumptions that lay claim to absolute truth. Such assumptions, as everyone knows, can be extremely irritating. As the animus is partial to argument, he can best be seen at work in disputes where both parties know they are right. Men can argue in a very womanish way, too, when they are anima-possessed and have thus been transformed into the animus of their own anima. With them the question becomes one of personal vanity and touchiness (as if they were females); with women it is a question of *power,* whether of truth or justice or some other "ism"— for the dressmaker and hairdresser have already taken care of their vanity. The "Father" (i.e., the sum of conventional opinions) always plays a great role in female argumentation. No matter how friendly and obliging a woman's Eros may be, no logic on earth can shake her if she is ridden by the animus. Often the man has the feeling— and he is not altogether wrong — that only seduction or a beating or rape would have the necessary power of persuasion. He is unaware that this highly dramatic situation would instantly come to a banal and unexciting end if he were to quit the field and let a second woman carry on the battle (his wife, for instance, if she herself is not the fiery war horse). This sound idea seldom or never occurs to him, because no man can converse with an animus for five minutes without becoming the victim of his own anima. Anyone who still had enough sense of humor to listen objectively to the ensuing dialogue would be staggered by the vast number of commonplaces, misapplied truisms, clichés from newspapers and novels, shop-soiled platitudes of every description interspersed with vulgar abuse and brain-splitting lack of logic. It is a dialogue which, irrespective of its participants, is repeated millions and millions of times in all the languages of the world and always remains essentially the same.

This singular fact is due to the following circumstance: when animus and anima meet, the animus draws his sword of power and the anima ejects her poison of illusion and seduction. The outcome need not always be negative, since the two are equally likely to fall in love (a special instance of love at first sight). The language of love is of astonishing uniformity, using the well-worn formulas with the utmost devotion and fidelity, so that once again the two partners find themselves in a banal collective situation. Yet they live in the illusion that they are related to one another in the most individual way.

In both its positive and its negative aspects the anima/animus relationship is always full of "animosity," i.e., it is emotional, and hence collective. Affects lower the level of the relationship and bring it closer to the common instinctual basis, which no longer has anything individual about it. Very often the relationship runs its course heedless of its human performers, who afterwards do not know what happened to them.

Whereas the cloud of "animosity" surrounding the man is composed chiefly of sentimentality and resentment, in woman it expresses itself in the form of opinionated views, interpretations, insinuations, and misconstructions, which all have the purpose (sometimes attained) of serving the relation between two human beings. The woman, like the man, becomes wrapped in a veil of illusions by her demon-familiar, and, as the daughter who alone understands her father (that is, is eternally right in everything), she is translated to the land of sheep, where she is put to graze by the shepherd of her soul, the animus.

Like the anima, the animus too has a positive aspect. Through the figure of the father he expresses not only conventional opinion but— equally — what we call "spirit," philosophical or religious ideas in particular, or rather the attitude resulting from them. Thus the animus is a psychopomp, a mediator between the conscious and the unconscious and a personification of the latter. Just as the anima becomes, through integration, the Eros of consciousness, so the animus becomes a Logos; and in the same way that the anima gives relationship and relatedness to a man's consciousness, the animus gives to woman's consciousness a capacity for reflection, deliberation, and self-knowledge.

The effect of anima and animus on the ego is in principle the same. This effect is extremely difficult to eliminate because, in the first place, it is uncommonly strong and immediately fills the ego-personality with an unshakable feeling of rightness and righteousness. In the second place, the cause of the effect is projected and appears to lie in objects and objective situations. Both these characteristics can, I believe, be traced back to the peculiarities of the archetype. For the archetype, of course, exists *a priori*. This may possibly explain the often totally irrational yet undisputed and indisputable existence of certain moods and opinions. Perhaps these are so notoriously difficult to influence because of the powerfully suggestive effect emanating from the archetype. Consciousness is fascinated by it, held captive, as if hypnotized. Very often the ego experiences a vague feeling of moral defeat and then behaves all the more defensively, defiantly, and self-righteously, thus setting up a vicious circle which only increases its feeling of inferiority. The bottom is then knocked out of the human relationship, for, like megalomania, a feeling of inferiority makes mutual recognition impossible, and without this there is no relationship.

As I said, it is easier to gain insight into the shadow than into the anima or animus. With the shadow, we have the advantage of being prepared in some sort by our education, which has always endeavored to convince people that they are not one-hundred-per-cent pure gold. So everyone immediately understands what is meant by "shadow," "inferior personality," etc. And if he has forgotten, his memory can easily be refreshed by a Sunday sermon, his wife, or the tax collector. With the anima and animus, however, things are by no means so simple. Firstly, there is no moral education in this respect, and secondly, most people are content to be self-righteous and prefer mutual vilification (if nothing worse!) to the recognition of their projections. Indeed, it seems a very natural state of affairs for men to have irrational moods and women irrational opinions. Presumably this situation is grounded on instinct and must remain as it is to ensure that the Empedoclean game of the hate and love of the elements shall continue for all eternity. Nature is conservative and does not easily allow her courses to be altered; she defends in the most stubborn way the inviolability of the preserves where anima and animus roam. Hence it is much more difficult to become conscious of one's anima/animus projections than to acknowledge one's shadow side. One has, of course, to overcome certain moral obstacles, such as vanity, ambition, conceit, resentment, etc., but in the case of projections all sorts of purely intellectual difficulties are added, quite apart from the contents of the projection which one simply doesn't know how to cope with. And on top of all this there arises a profound doubt as to whether one is not meddling too much with nature's business by prodding into consciousness things which it would have been better to leave asleep.

Although there are, in my experience, a fair number of people who can understand without special intellectual or moral difficulties what is meant by anima and animus, one finds very many more who have the greatest trouble in visualizing these empirical concepts as anything concrete. This shows that they fall a little outside the usual range of experience. They are unpopular precisely because they seem unfamiliar. The consequence is that they mobilize prejudice and become taboo like everything else that is unexpected.

So if we set it up as a kind of requirement that projections should be dissolved, because it is wholesomer that way and in every respect more advantageous, we are entering upon new ground. Up till now everybody has been convinced that the idea "my father," "my mother," etc., is nothing but a faithful reflection of the real parent, corresponding in every detail to the original, so that when someone says "my father" he means no more and no less than what his father is in reality. This is actually what he supposes he does mean, but a supposition of identity by no means brings that identity about. This is where the fallacy of the *enkekalymmenos* ('the veiled one') comes in.[10] If one includes in the psychological equation X's picture of his father, which he takes for the real father, the equation will not work out, because the unknown quantity he has introduced does not tally with reality. X has overlooked the fact that his

[10]The fallacy, which stems from Eubulides the Megarian, runs: "Can you recognize your father?" Yes. "Can you recognize this veiled one?" No. "This veiled one is your father. Hence you can recognize your father and not recognize him." [Au.]

idea of a person consists, in the first place, of the possibly very incomplete picture he has received of the real person and, in the second place, of the subjective modifications he has imposed upon this picture. X's idea of his father is a complex quantity for which the real father is only in part responsible, an indefinitely larger share falling to the son. So true is this that every time he criticizes or praises his father he is unconsciously hitting back at himself, thereby bringing about those psychic consequences that overtake people who habitually disparage or overpraise themselves. If, however, X carefully compares his reactions with reality, he stands a chance of noticing that he has miscalculated somewhere by not realizing long ago from his father's behavior that the picture he has of him is a false one. But as a rule X is convinced that he is right, and if anybody is wrong it must be the other fellow. Should X have a poorly developed Eros, he will be either indifferent to the inadequate relationship he has with his father or else annoyed by the inconsistency and general incomprehensibility of a father whose behavior never really corresponds to the picture X has of him. Therefore X thinks he has every right to feel hurt, misunderstood, and even betrayed.

One can imagine how desirable it would be in such cases to dissolve the projection. And there are always optimists who believe that the golden age can be ushered in simply by telling people the right way to go. But just let them try to explain to these people that they are acting like a dog chasing its own tail. To make a person see the shortcomings of his attitude considerably more than mere "telling" is needed, for more is involved than ordinary common sense can allow. What one is up against here is the kind of fateful misunderstanding which, under ordinary conditions, remains forever inaccessible to insight. It is rather like expecting the average respectable citizen to recognize himself as a criminal.

I mention all this just to illustrate the order of magnitude to which the anima/animus projections belong, and the moral and intellectual exertions that are needed to dissolve them. Not all the contents of the anima and animus are projected, however. Many of them appear spontaneously in dreams and so on, and many more can be made conscious through active imagination. In this way we find that thoughts, feelings, and affects are alive in us which we would never have believed possible. Naturally, possibilities of this sort seem utterly fantastic to anyone who has not experienced them himself, for a normal person "knows what he thinks." Such a childish attitude on the part of the "normal person" is simply the rule, so that no one without experience in this field can be expected to understand the real nature of anima and animus. With these reflections one gets into an entirely new world of psychological experience, provided of course that one succeeds in realizing it in practice. Those who do succeed can hardly fail to be impressed by all that the ego does not know and never has known. This increase in self-knowledge is still very rare nowadays and is usually paid for in advance with a neurosis, if not with something worse.

The autonomy of the collective unconscious expresses itself in the figures of anima and animus. They personify those of its contents which, when withdrawn from projection, can be integrated into consciousness. To this extent, both figures represent *functions* which filter the contents of the collective unconscious through to the conscious mind. They appear or behave as such, however, only so long as the tendencies of the conscious and unconscious do not diverge too greatly. Should any tension arise, these functions, harmless till then, confront the conscious mind in personified form and behave rather like systems split off from the personality, or like part souls. This comparison is inadequate in so far as nothing previously belonging to the ego-personality has split off from it; on the contrary, the two figures represent a disturbing accretion. The reason for their behaving in this way is that though the *contents* of anima and animus can be integrated they themselves cannot, since they are archetypes. As such they are the foundation stones of the psychic structure, which in its totality exceeds the limits of consciousness and therefore can never become the object of direct cognition. Though the effects of anima and animus can be made conscious, they themselves are factors transcending consciousness and beyond the reach of perception and volition. Hence they remain autonomous despite the integration of their contents, and for this reason they should be borne constantly in mind. This is extremely important from the therapeutic standpoint, because constant observation pays the unconscious a tribute that more or less guarantees its cooperation. The unconscious as we know can never be "done with" once and for all. It is, in fact, one of the most important tasks of psychic hygiene to pay continual attention to the symptomatology of unconscious contents and processes, for the good reason that the conscious mind is always in danger of becoming one-sided, of keeping to well-worn paths and getting stuck in blind alleys. The complementary and compensating function of the unconscious ensures that these dangers, which are especially great in neurosis, can in some measure be avoided. It is only under ideal conditions, when life is still simple and unconscious enough to follow the serpentine path of instinct without hesitation or misgiving, that the compensation works with entire success. The more civilized, the more unconscious and complicated a man is, the less he is able to follow his instincts. His complicated living conditions and the influence of his environment are so strong that they drown the quiet voice of nature. Opinions, beliefs, theories, and collective tendencies appear in its stead and back up all the aberrations of the conscious mind. Deliberate attention should then be given to the unconscious so that the compensation can set to work. Hence it is especially important to picture the archetypes of the unconscious not as a rushing phantasmagoria of fugitive images but as constant, autonomous factors, which indeed they are.

Both these archetypes, as practical experience shows, possess a fatality that can on occasion produce tragic results. They are quite literally the father and mother of all the disastrous entanglements of fate and have long been recognized as such by the whole world. Together they form a divine pair,[11] one of whom, in accordance with his Logos nature, is characterized by *pneuma* and *nous*,[12] rather like Hermes with his ever-shifting hues, while the other, in accordance with her Eros nature, wears the features of Aphrodite, Helen (Selene), Persephone, and Hecate. Both of them are unconscious powers, "gods" in fact, as the ancient world quite rightly conceived them to be. To call them by this name is to give them that central position in the scale of psychological values which has always been theirs whether consciously acknowledged or not; for their power grows in proportion to the degree that they remain unconscious. Those who do not see them are in their hands, just as typhus epidemic flourishes best when its source is undiscovered. Even in Christianity the divine syzygy has not become obsolete, but occupies the highest place as Christ and his bride the Church.[13] Parallels like these prove extremely helpful in our attempts to find the right criterion for gauging the significance of these two archetypes. What we can discover about them from the conscious side is so slight as to be almost imperceptible. It is only when we throw light into the dark depths of the psyche and explore the strange and tortuous paths of human fate that it gradually becomes clear to us how immense is the influence wielded by these two factors that complement our conscious life.

Recapitulating, I should like to emphasize that the integration of the shadow, or the realization of the personal unconscious, marks the first stage in the analytic process, and that without it a recognition of anima and animus is impossible. The shadow can be realized only through a relation to a partner, and anima and animus only through a relation to a partner of the opposite sex, because only in such a relation do their projections become operative. The recognition of the anima gives rise, in a man, to a triad, one third of which is transcendent: the masculine subject, the opposing feminine subject, and the transcendent anima. With a woman the situation

[11]Naturally this is not meant as a psychological definition, let alone a metaphysical one. As I pointed out in "The Relations between the Ego and the Unconscious" (pars. 296ff.), the syzygy consists of three elements: the femininity pertaining to the man and the masculinity pertaining to the woman; the experience which man has of woman and vice versa; and, finally, the masculine and feminine archetypal image. The first element can be integrated into the personality by the process of conscious realization, but the last one cannot. [Au.]

[12]Spirit and mind. [Ed.]

[13]"For the Scripture says, God made man male and female; the male is Christ, the female is the Church." — Second Epistle of Clement to the Corinthians, xiv, 2 (trans. by Lake, I, p. 151). In pictorial representations, Mary often takes the place of the Church. [Au.]

is reversed. The missing fourth element that would make the triad a quaternity is, in a man, the archetype of the Wise Old Man, which I have not discussed here, and in a woman the Chthonic Mother. These four constitute a half immanent and half transcendent quaternity, an archetype which I have called the *marriage quaternio*.[14] The marriage quaternio provides a schema not only for the self but also for the structure of primitive society with its cross-cousin marriage, marriage classes, and division of settlements into quarters. The self, on the other hand, is a God-image, or at least cannot be distinguished from one. Of this the early Christian spirit was not ignorant, otherwise Clement of Alexandria could never have said that he who knows himself knows God.

[14] "The Psychology of the Transference," pars. 425ff. [Au.]

Mikhail Bakhtin

1895–1975

Nearly lost to the world because of Soviet political turbulence in the first half of the century, the literary and aesthetic theories of the Russian polymath Mikhail Bakhtin have, in the past two decades, exerted a spellbinding and fertile power over critical imaginations in North America and Europe. Born in Orel, Russia, Bakhtin attended the universities in Odessa and St. Petersburg. In 1920 he moved to the cultural center Vitebsk and in 1924 back to St. Petersburg (then renamed Leningrad), where he worked at the Historical Institute and became part of an intellectual circle that opposed itself to the then-fashionable philosophy of the neo-Kantian Hermann Cohen.[1]

Bakhtin's magisterial *Problems of Dostoevsky's Poetics* appeared in 1929, but its impact was stifled when a Stalinist purge sent its author into internal exile, probably because of his connections with Russian Orthodox "Old-Believers." During the next six precarious years on the border of Siberia, Bakhtin wrote the seminal essay "Discourse in the Novel" (later printed as one of the four essays in *The Dialogic Imagination*) and a study of the German *Bildungsroman* that was thought lost when it disappeared from a publishing house during the German invasion; fragments of it have since been recovered and are being translated. On his return from exile in 1936, Bakhtin was offered a position at the Mordovia State Teachers' College (later University) at Saransk, where he taught until his retirement in 1961. In 1940, Bakhtin submitted a dissertation on Rabelais but was unable to defend it until after the war; when he did defend it in 1946, the dissertation's very originality worked against its acceptance. Its acceptance in 1951 and eventual publication in 1965 (as *Rabelais and His World*) lifted Bakhtin's ideas from obscurity and made them available to the international scholarly community. One important vector for the spread of his fame was Julia Kristeva, who incorporated Bakhtin's ideas about intertextuality into her early structuralist work. Meanwhile Bakhtin, in declining health from osteomyelitis, which had plagued him all his life, was able to move from Saransk to Moscow in 1969. At the end of his life he gathered around him a group of students that reportedly included the daughter of then-KGB director Yuri Andropov. At the center rather than the periphery of Russia, and no longer in danger of being purged for heterodox views, he was finally able to publish many of the seminal pieces on the philosophy of language and theory of literature that he had written fifty years before. He died in Moscow in 1975.

Given his views on the social construction of languages and the literary codes based on language, Mikhail Bakhtin has been claimed as both a Marxist and a formalist. Part of the difficulty in categorizing his work stems from the still-disputed question of Bakhtin's contribution to three books published in the late 1920s by

[1]Cohen, who worked at the University of Marburg, is almost unknown today; he is a significant figure in intellectual history, however, because his views inspired reaction by so many other literary/philosophical theorists, including Gadamer (see p. 676) and Heidegger (see p. 560).

members of his philosophical circle. Bakhtin's thought clearly informs *Marxism and the Study of Language* (1929–30) and *Freudianism: A Critical Sketch* (1927) by V. N. Vološinov, and *The Formal Method in Literary Scholarship* (1928) by P. N. Medvedev. Some scholars have argued that Bakhtin actually wrote these attacks on Freudian psychology and formalist literary theory, publishing them, for some reason, under the names of his friends. But more recent evidence suggests that these Marxist texts of the Bakhtin circle owe their orthodox slant and dialectical argumentation to their titular authors. Without these texts as part of his canon, Bakhtin can be seen as a highly individualistic theorist concerned with problems similar to the ones that engrossed Shklovsky (see p. 716) and other formalists, such as Yuri Tynyanov (see p. 727).

At the center of Bakhtin's ideas is the principle usually translated as *heteroglossia* (in the original Russian: *raznorecie,* literally "the word of another"): the notion that the meaning of language is socially determined, that utterances reflect social values and depend for their meaning on their relation to other utterances. The idea is a familiar one in the purely linguistic context of speech-act theory: An imperative sentence can be an order, a command, a request, a plea, or a prayer, depending on who is talking to whom. We could say that Bakhtin — who was working on these ideas many years before the speech-act theorists Austin and Searle — essentially directs our attention to the *pragmatics* of literary discourse. He differentiates sharply between *dialogical* discourse, which explicitly or tacitly acknowledges the language of the Other, the controlling presence of a social context; and *monological* discourse, which tries to have its say in a vacuum. What many English and American critics find worth emulating in Bakhtin's criticism is the extraordinary sensitivity with which he succeeds in locating the various nuances — the responses to internal and external pressures — that go into the creation of dialogical fictional discourse.

But Bakhtin does not merely analyze literary pragmatics neutrally; he loathes single-voiced authoritative discourse, the unquestionable word that comes from above to dictate meaning. For Bakhtin, monologism denies the existence and validity of the Other, assuming an auditor to whom one speaks without needing to listen. Instead, Bakhtin valorizes dialogism and the types of discourse he calls *double-voiced (dvugolosnöe slovo),* in which a single sentence will bring into dialogue two or more different languages. What Bakhtin calls languages can be idiolects — the individualized discourse of a particular person — or various sorts of dialects, communication styles, or jargons characteristic of particular social groups: trades, professions, classes, parties, generations. The shifting planes of intention that can occur whenever one language meets another in a single discourse permit an exhilaratingly chaotic freedom of expression. Bakhtin particularly loves the various forms of parody, which mediate comically between an audience and a known prior discourse.

Thus, purity and clarity of speech, with clear levels of discourse of the sort Aristotle and Horace recommended, earn no points from Bakhtin. They suggest to him a closed and stratified society without freedom of thought, devoted to "terror, dogmatism, reverence, and piety." What he values instead is the Rabelaisian carnivalization of literature: the sociolinguistic fun-fair where, as in the medieval festival or carnival, rulers and ruled mix on equal terms in a parodic rout devoted to "ambivalent laughter, blasphemy, the profanation of everything sacred, full of debasing and obscenities, familiar contact with everyone and everything."

Bakhtin consequently prefers the novel — in which dialogism is possible — over poetry, which is typically single-voiced.[2] And within the novel he contrasts the single-voiced Tolstoy, whose multifarious characters nonetheless always express the author's dogmas, with the double-voiced Dostoevsky, whose characters engage in genuine dialogue. The distinction has nothing to do with the use of conversational dialogue as such. Dialogue appears for Bakhtin even in the narrator's discourse and in characters' solo speeches (like that of the Underground Man) so long as the speaker's language bears perceptibly the imprint, the pressure, of the Other inside or outside the novel to whom it is addressed. Bakhtin's dialogism is the basis of a broader genre-criticism, which in turn is the basis for an innovative approach to the history of literature — but his notion of the languages competing within an individual's speech, the way one's discourse is at the same time the discourse of an Other, lies at the heart of his critical system.

The first selection reprinted here is from *Discourse in the Novel;* the second is from *Problems in Dostoevsky's Poetics.*

Selected Bibliography

Bakhtin, Mikhail. *Rabelais and His World.* Cambridge: MIT Press, 1968.

———. *The Dialogic Imagination: Four Essays.* Austin: University of Texas Press, 1981.

———. *Problems of Dostoevsky's Poetics.* Minneapolis: University of Minnesota Press, 1984.

———. *Speech Genres, and Other Essays.* Austin: University of Texas Press, 1987.

———. *Art and Answerability: Early Philosophical Essays.* Austin: University of Texas Press, 1990.

Clark, Katerina, and Michael Holquist. *Mikhail Bakhtin.* Cambridge: Belknap Press of Harvard University, 1984.

Emerson, Caryl. *Bakhtin Across the Disciplines.* Evanston, IL: Northwestern University Press, 1995.

Holquist, Michael. *Dialogism: Bakhtin and His World.* London and New York: Routledge, 1990.

Medvedev, P. N. *The Formal Method in Literary Scholarship.* Baltimore: Johns Hopkins University Press, 1978.

Morson, Gary. *Bakhtin: Essays and Dialogues on His Work.* Chicago: University of Chicago Press, 1986.

Richter, David. "Dialogism and Poetry." *Studies in the Literary Imagination* (Spring 1990): 3–27.

Todorov, Tzvetan. *Mikhail Bakhtin: The Dialogical Principle.* Minneapolis: University of Minnesota Press, 1985.

Vološinov, V. N. *Marxism and the Philosophy of Language.* Cambridge: Harvard University Press, 1986.

[2]Technically this is not a question of genre: As Bakhtin himself points out, there can be what he calls "novelized" forms within any genre. But historically the novel has lent itself to heteroglossia far more than lyric poetry has done.

From *Discourse in the Novel*

The Topic of the Speaking Person

Before, then, taking up the issue of the artistic representation of another's speech conceived as the image of a language, we should say something about the importance in extra-artistic areas of life and ideology of the topic of the speaking person and his discourse. While in the many forms available for transmitting another's speech outside the novel there is no defining concern for the images of a language, such forms are used in the novel for self-enrichment — but not before they are first transformed and subjected within it to the new holistic unity of the novel itself (and, conversely, novels have a powerful influence on the extra-artistic perception and transmission of another's discourse).

The topic of a speaking person has enormous importance in everyday life. In real life we hear speech about speakers and their discourse at every step. We can go so far as to say that in real life people talk most of all about what others talk about — they transmit, recall, weigh and pass judgment on other people's words, opinions, assertions, information; people are upset by others' words, or agree with them, contest them, refer to them and so forth. Were we to eavesdrop on snatches of raw dialogue in the street, in a crowd, in lines, in a foyer and so forth, we would hear how often the words "he says," "people say," "he said . . ." are repeated, and in the conversational hurly-burly of people in a crowd, everything often fuses into one big "he says . . . you say . . . I say. . . ." Reflect how enormous is the weight of "everyone says" and "it is said" in public opinion, public rumor, gossip, slander and so forth. One must also consider the psychological importance in our lives of what others say about us, and the importance, for us, of understanding and interpreting these words of others ("living hermeneutics").

The importance of this motif is in no way diminished in the higher and better-organized areas of everyday communication. Every conversation is full of transmissions and interpretations of other people's words. At every step one meets a "quotation" or a "reference" to something that a particular person said, a reference to "people say" or "everyone says," to the words of the person one is talking with, or to one's own previous words, to a newspaper, an official decree, a document, a book and so forth. The majority of our information and opinions is usually not communicated in direct form as our own, but with reference to some indefinite and general source: "I heard," "It's generally held that . . . ," "It is thought that . . ." and so forth. Take one of the most widespread occurrences in our everyday life, conversations about some official meeting: they are all constructed on the transmission, interpretation and evaluation of various kinds of verbal performance, resolutions, the rejected and accepted corrections that are made to them and so forth. Thus talk goes on about speaking people and their words everywhere — this motif returns again and again; it either accompanies the development of the other topics in everyday life, or directly governs speech as its leading theme.

Further examples of the significance of the topic of the speaking person in everyday life would be superfluous. We need only keep our ears open to the speech sounding everywhere around us to reach such a conclusion: in the everyday speech of any person living in society, no less than half (on the average) of all the words uttered by him will be someone else's words (consciously someone else's), transmitted with varying degrees of precision and impartiality (or more precisely, partiality).

It goes without saying that not all transmitted words belonging to someone else lend themselves, when fixed in writing, to enclosure in quotation marks. That degree of otherness and purity in another's word that in written speech would require quotation marks (as per the intention of the speaker himself, how he himself determines this degree of otherness) is required much less frequently in everyday speech.

Translated by Caryl Emerson and Michael Holquist.

Furthermore, syntactic means for formulating the transmitted speech of another are far from exhausted by the grammatical paradigms of direct and indirect discourse: the means for its incorporation, for its formulation and for indicating different degrees of shading are highly varied. This must be kept in mind if we are to make good our claim that of all words uttered in everyday life, no less than half belong to someone else.

The speaking person and his discourse are not, in everyday speech, subjects for artistic representation, but rather they are topics in the engaged transmission of practical information. For this reason everyday speech is not concerned with forms of representation, but only with means of *transmission.* These means, conceived both as a way to formulate verbally and stylistically another's speech and as a way to provide an interpretive frame, a tool for reconceptualization and re-accenting — from direct verbatim quotation in a verbal transmission to malicious and deliberately parodic distortion of another's word, slander — are highly varied.[1]

The following must be kept in mind: that the speech of another, once enclosed in a context, is — no matter how accurately transmitted — always subject to certain semantic changes. The context embracing another's word is responsible for its dialogizing background, whose influence can be very great. Given the appropriate methods for framing, one may bring about fundamental changes even in another's utterance accurately quoted. Any sly and ill-disposed polemicist knows very well which dialogizing backdrop he should bring to bear on the accurately quoted words of his opponent, in order to distort their sense. By manipulating the effects of context, it is very easy to emphasize the brute materiality of another's words, and to stimulate dialogic reactions associated with such "brute materiality"; thus it is, for instance, very easy to make even the most serious utterance comical. Another's discourse, when introduced into a speech context, enters the speech that frames it not in a mechanical bond but in a chemical union (on the semantic and emotionally expressive level); the degree of dialogized influence, one on the other, can be enormous. For this reason we cannot, when studying the various forms for transmitting another's speech, treat any of these forms in isolation from the means for its contextualized (dialogizing) framing — the one is indissolubly linked with the other. The formulation of another's speech as well as its framing (and the context can begin preparing for the introduction of another's speech far back in the text) both express the unitary act of dialogic interaction with that speech, a relation determining the entire nature of its transmission and all the changes in meaning and accent that take place in it during transmission.

The speaking person and his discourse in everyday speech, we have said, serves as a *subject* for the engaged, practical transmission of information, and not as a *means* of representation. As a matter of fact, all everyday forms for transmitting another's discourse, as well as the changes in discourse connected with those forms — from subtle nuances in meaning and emphasis to gross externalized distortions of the verbal composition — are defined by this practical engagement. But this emphasis on engaged discourse does not exclude certain aspects of representability. In order to assess and divine the real meaning of others' words in everyday life, the following are surely of decisive significance: *who* precisely is speaking, and under *what* concrete circumstances? When we attempt to understand and make assessments in everyday life, we do not separate discourse from the personality speaking it (as we can in the ideological realm), because the personality is so materially present to us. And the entire speaking situation is very important: who is present during it, with what expression or mimicry is it uttered, with what shades of intonation? During everyday verbal transmission of another's words, the entire complex of discourse as well as the personality of the speaker may be expressed and even played with (in the form of anything from an exact replication to a parodic ridiculing and exaggeration of gestures and intonations). This representation is always subordinated to the tasks of practical, en-

[1]There are different ways to falsify someone else's words while taking them to their furthest extreme, to reveal their *potential* content. Rhetoric, the art of argument, and "heuristics" explore this area somewhat. [Au.]

gaged transmission and is wholly determined by these tasks. This of course does not involve the artistic image of a speaking person and the artistic image of his discourse, and even less the image of a language. Nevertheless, everyday episodes involving the same person, when they become linked, already entail prose devices for the double-voiced and even double-languaged representation of another's words.

These conversations about speaking persons and others' words in everyday life do not go beyond the boundaries of the superficial aspects of discourse, the weight it carries in a specific situation; the deeper semantic and emotionally expressive levels of discourse do not enter the game. The topic of a speaking person takes on quite another significance in the ordinary ideological workings of our consciousness, in the process of assimilating our consciousness to the ideological world. The ideological becoming of a human being, in this view, is the process of selectively assimilating the words of others.

When verbal disciplines are taught in school, two basic modes are recognized for the appropriation and transmission — simultaneously — of another's words (a text, a rule, a model): "reciting by heart" and "retelling in one's own words." The latter mode poses on a small scale the task implicit in all prose stylistics: retelling a text in one's own words is to a certain extent a double-voiced narration of another's words, for indeed "one's own words" must not completely dilute the quality that makes another's words unique; a retelling in one's own words should have a mixed character, able when necessary to reproduce the style and expressions of the transmitted text. It is this second mode used in schools for transmitting another's discourse, "retelling in one's own words," that includes within it an entire series of forms for the appropriation while transmitting of another's words, depending upon the character of the text being appropriated and the pedagogical environment in which it is understood and evaluated.

The tendency to assimilate others' discourse takes on an even deeper and more basic significance in an individual's ideological becoming, in the most fundamental sense. Another's discourse performs here no longer as information, directions, rules, models and so forth — but strives rather to determine the very bases of our ideological interrelations with the world, the very basis of our behavior; it performs here as *authoritative discourse,* and as *internally persuasive discourse.*

Both the authority of discourse and its internal persuasiveness may be united in a single word — one that is *simultaneously* authoritative and internally persuasive — despite the profound differences between these two categories of alien discourse. But such unity is rarely a given — it happens more frequently that an individual's becoming, an ideological process, is characterized precisely by a sharp gap between these two categories: in one, the authoritative word (religious, political, moral; the word of a father, of adults and of teachers, etc.) that does not know internal persuasiveness; in the other the internally persuasive word that is denied all privilege, backed up by no authority at all, and is frequently not even acknowledged in society (not by public opinion, nor by scholarly norms, nor by criticism), not even in the legal code. The struggle and dialogic interrelationship of these categories of ideological discourse are what usually determine the history of an individual ideological consciousness.

The authoritative word demands that we acknowledge it, that we make it our own; it binds us, quite independent of any power it might have to persuade us internally; we encounter it with its authority already fused to it. The authoritative word is located in a distanced zone, organically connected with a past that is felt to be hierarchically higher. It is, so to speak, the word of the fathers. Its authority was already *acknowledged* in the past. It is a *prior* discourse. It is therefore not a question of choosing it from among other possible discourses that are its equal. It is given (it sounds) in lofty spheres, not those of familiar contact. Its language is a special (as it were, hieratic) language. It can be profaned. It is akin to taboo, i.e., a name that must not be taken in vain.

We cannot embark here on a survey of the many and varied types of authoritative discourse (for example, the authority of religious dogma, or of acknowledged scientific truth or of a currently fashionable book), nor can we survey different degrees of authoritativeness. For our purposes only formal features for the transmission and representation of authoritative discourse are important, those common to all types and degrees of such discourse.

The degree to which a word may be conjoined with authority — whether the authority is recognized by us or not — is what determines its specific demarcation and individuation in discourse; it requires a *distance* vis-à-vis itself (this distance may be valorized as positive or as negative, just as our attitude toward it may be sympathetic or hostile). Authoritative discourse may organize around itself great masses of other types of discourses (which interpret it, praise it, apply it in various ways), but the authoritative discourse itself does not merge with these (by means of, say, gradual transitions); it remains sharply demarcated, compact and inert: it demands, so to speak, not only quotation marks but a demarcation even more magisterial, a special script, for instance.[2] It is considerably more difficult to incorporate semantic changes into such a discourse, even with the help of a framing context: its semantic structure is static and dead, for it is fully complete, it has but a single meaning, the letter is fully sufficient to the sense and calcifies it.

It is not a free appropriation and assimilation of the word itself that authoritative discourse seeks to elicit from us; rather, it demands our unconditional allegiance. Therefore authoritative discourse permits no play with the context framing it, no play with its borders, no gradual and flexible transitions, no spontaneously creative stylizing variants on it. It enters our verbal consciousness as a compact and indivisible mass; one must either totally affirm it, or totally reject it. It is indissolubly fused with its authority — with political power, an institution, a person — and it stands and falls together with that authority. One cannot divide it up — agree with one part, accept but not completely another part, reject utterly a third part. Therefore the distance we ourselves observe vis-à-vis this authoritative discourse remains unchanged in all its projections: a playing with distances, with fusion and dissolution, with approach and retreat, is not here possible.

All these functions determine the uniqueness of authoritative discourse, both as a concrete means for formulating itself during transmission and as its distinctive means for being framed by contexts. The zone of the framing context must likewise be distanced — no familiar contact is possible here either. The one perceiving and understanding this discourse is a distant descendent; there can be no arguing with him.

These factors also determine the potential role of authoritative discourse in prose. Authoritative discourse can not be represented — it is only transmitted. Its inertia, its semantic finiteness and calcification, the degree to which it is hard-edged, a thing in its own right, the impermissibility of any free stylistic development in relation to it — all this renders the artistic representation of authoritative discourse impossible. Its role in the novel is insignificant. It is by its very nature incapable of being double-voiced; it cannot enter into hybrid constructions. If completely deprived of its authority it becomes simply an object, a *relic*, or *thing*. It enters the artistic context as an alien body, there is no space around it to play in, no contradictory emotions — it is not surrounded by an agitated and cacophonous dialogic life, and the context around it dies, words dry up. For this reason images of official-authoritative truth, images of virtue (of any sort: monastic, spiritual, bureaucratic, moral, etc.) have never been successful in the novel. It suffices to mention the hopeless attempts of Gogol and Dostoevsky in this regard.[3] For this reason the authoritative text always remains, in the novel, a dead quotation, something that falls out of the artistic context (for example, the evangelical texts in Tolstoy at the end of *Resurrection*).[4]

[2]Often the authoritative word is in fact a word spoken by another in a foreign language (cf. for example the phenomenon of foreign-language religious texts in most cultures). [Au.]

Latin mass
opposition to translation
vulgarization
vernacular

[3]Bakhtin refers to Gogol's and Dostoevsky's failed attempts to represent the ideal of holiness they believed in — such as Father Zossima in the latter's *Brothers Karamazov*. [Ed.]

[4]When analyzing a concrete example of authoritative discourse in a novel, it is necessary to keep in mind the fact that purely authoritative discourse may, in another epoch, be internally persuasive; this is especially true where ethics are concerned. [Au.]

Authoritative discourses may embody various contents: authority as such, or the authoritativeness of tradition, of generally acknowledged truths, of the official line and other similar authorities. These discourses may have a variety of zones (determined by the degree to which they are distanced from the zone of contact) with a variety of relations to the presumed listener or interpreter (the apperceptive background presumed by the discourse, the degree of reciprocation between the two and so forth).

In the history of literary language, there is a struggle constantly being waged to overcome the official line with its tendency to distance itself from the zone of contact, a struggle against various kinds and degrees of authority. In this process discourse gets drawn into the contact zone, which results in semantic and emotionally expressive (intonational) changes: there is a weakening and degradation of the capacity to generate metaphors, and discourse becomes more reified, more concrete, more filled with everyday elements and so forth. All of this has been studied by psychology, but not from the point of view of its verbal formulation in possible inner monologues of developing human beings, the monologue that lasts a whole life. What confronts us is the complex problem presented by forms capable of expressing such a (dialogized) monologue.

When someone else's ideological discourse is internally persuasive for us and acknowledged by us, entirely different possibilities open up. Such discourse is of decisive significance in the evolution of an individual consciousness: consciousness awakens to independent ideological life precisely in a world of alien discourses surrounding it, and from which it cannot initially separate itself; the process of distinguishing between one's own and another's discourse, between one's own and another's thought, is activated rather late in development. When thought begins to work in an independent, experimenting and discriminating way, what first occurs is a separation between internally persuasive discourse and authoritarian enforced discourse, along with a rejection of those congeries of discourses that do not matter to us, that do not touch us.

Internally persuasive discourse — as opposed to one that is externally authoritative — is, as it is affirmed through assimilation, tightly interwoven with "one's own word."[5] In the everyday rounds of our consciousness, the internally persuasive word is half ours and half someone else's. Its creativity and productiveness consist precisely in the fact that such a word awakens new and independent words, that it organizes masses of our words from within, and that it does not remain in an isolated and static condition. It is not so much interpreted by us as it is further, that is, freely, developed, applied to new material, new conditions; it enters into interanimating relationships with new contexts. More than that, it enters into an intense interaction, a *struggle* with other internally persuasive discourses. Our ideological development is just such an intense struggle within us for hegemony among various available verbal and ideological points of view, approaches, directions and values. The semantic structure of an internally persuasive discourse is *not finite,* it is *open;* in each of the new contexts that dialogize it, this discourse is able to reveal ever newer *ways to mean.*

The internally persuasive word is either a contemporary word, born in a zone of contact with unresolved contemporaneity, or else it is a word that has been reclaimed for contemporaneity; such a word relates to its descendents as well as to its contemporaries as if *both* were contemporaries; what is constitutive for it is a special conception of listeners, readers, perceivers. Every discourse presupposes a special conception of the listener, of his apperceptive background and the degree of his responsiveness; it presupposes a specific distance. All this is very important for coming to grips with the historical life of discourse. Ignoring such aspects and nuances leads to a reification of the word (and to a muffling of the dialogism native to it).

All of the above determine the methods for formulating internally persuasive discourse during its transmission, as well as methods for framing it in contexts. Such methods provide maximal interaction between another's word and its con-

[5]One's own discourse is gradually and slowly wrought out of others' words that have been acknowledged and assimilated, and the boundaries between the two are at first scarcely perceptible. [Au.]

text, for the dialogizing influence they have on each other, for the free and creative development of another's word, for a gradation of transitions. They serve to govern the play of boundaries, the distance between that point where the context begins to prepare for the introduction of another's word and the point where the word is actually introduced (its "theme" may sound in the text long before the appearance of the actual word). These methods account for other peculiarities as well, which also express the essence of the internally persuasive word, such as that word's semantic openness to us, its capacity for further creative life in the context of our ideological consciousness, its unfinishedness and the inexhaustibility of our further dialogic interaction with it. We have not yet learned from it all it might tell us; we can take it into new contexts, attach it to new material, put it in a new situation in order to wrest new answers from it, new insights into its meaning, and even wrest from it new words, of its *own* (since another's discourse, if productive, gives birth to a new word from us in response).

The means for formulating and framing internally persuasive discourse may be supple and dynamic to such an extent that this discourse may literally be *omnipresent* in the context, imparting to everything its own specific tones and from time to time breaking through to become a completely materialized thing, as another's word fully set off and demarcated (as happens in character zones). Such variants on the theme of another's discourse are widespread in all areas of creative ideological activity, and even in the narrowly scientific disciplines. Of such a sort is any gifted, creative exposition defining alien world views: such an exposition is always a free stylistic variation on another's discourse; it expounds another's thought in the style of that thought even while applying it to new material, to another way of posing the problem; it conducts experiments and gets solutions in the language of another's discourse.

In other less obvious instances we notice analogous phenomena. We have in mind first of all those instances of powerful influence exercised by another's discourse on a given author. When such influences are laid bare, the half-concealed life lived by another's discourse is revealed within the new context of the given author. When such an influence is deep and productive, there is no external imitation, no simple act of reproduction, but rather a further creative development of another's (more precisely, half-other) discourse in a new context and under new conditions.

In all these instances the important thing is not only forms for transmitting another's discourse, but the fact that in such forms there can always be found the embryonic beginnings of what is required for an artistic representation of another's discourse. A few changes in orientation and the internally persuasive word easily becomes an object of representation. For certain kinds of internally persuasive discourse can be fundamentally and organically fused with the image of a speaking person: ethical (discourse fused with the image of, let us say, a preacher), philosophical (discourse fused with the image of a wise man), sociopolitical (discourse fused with an image of a Leader). While creatively stylizing upon and experimenting with another's discourse, we attempt to guess, to imagine, how a person with authority might conduct himself in the given circumstances, the light he would cast on them with his discourse. In such experimental guesswork the image of the speaking person and his discourse become the object of creative, artistic imagination.[6]

This process — experimenting by turning persuasive discourse into speaking persons — becomes especially important in those cases where a struggle against such images has already begun, where someone is striving to liberate himself from the influence of such an image and its discourse by means of objectification, or is striving to expose the limitations of both image and discourse. The importance of struggling with another's discourse, its influence in the history of an individual's coming to ideological consciousness, is enormous. One's own discourse and one's own voice, although born of another or dynamically stimulated by another, will sooner or later begin to liberate themselves from the authority of the other's discourse. This process is

[6]In Plato, Socrates serves as just such an artistic image of the wise man and teacher, an image employed for the purposes of experiment. [Au.]

made more complex by the fact that a variety of alien voices enter into the struggle for influence within an individual's consciousness (just as they struggle with one another in surrounding social reality). All this creates fertile soil for experimentally objectifying another's discourse. A conversation with an internally persuasive word that one has begun to resist may continue, but it takes on another character: it is questioned, it is put in a new situation in order to expose its weak sides, to get a feel for its boundaries, to experience it physically as an object. For this reason stylizing discourse by attributing it to a person often becomes parodic, although not crudely parodic — since another's word, having been at an earlier stage internally persuasive, mounts a resistance to this process and frequently begins to sound with no parodic overtones at all. Novelistic images, profoundly double-voiced and double-languaged, are born in such a soil, seek to objectivize the struggle with all types of internally persuasive alien discourse that had at one time held sway over the author (of such a type, for instance, is Pushkin's Onegin or Lermontov's Pechorin).[7] At the heart of the *Prüfungsroman*[8] is the same kind of subjective struggle with internally persuasive, alien discourse, and just such a liberation from this discourse by turning it into an object. Another illustration of what we mean here is provided by the *Bildungsroman,*[9] but in such novels the maturation — a selecting, ideological process — is developed as a theme within the novel, whereas in the *Prüfungsroman* the subjectivity of the author himself remains outside the work.

The works of Dostoevsky, in such a view, can be seen to occupy an extraordinary and unique place. The acute and intense interaction of another's word is present in his novels in two ways. In the first place in his characters' language there is a profound and unresolved conflict with another's word on the level of lived experience ("another's word about me"), on the level of ethical life (another's judgment, recognition or nonrecognition by another) and finally on the level of ideology (the world views of characters understood as unresolved and unresolvable dialogue). What Dostoevsky's characters *say* constitutes an arena of never-ending struggle with others' words, in all realms of life and creative ideological activity. For this reason these utterances may serve as excellent models of the most varied forms for transmitting and framing another's discourse. In the second place, the works (the novels) in their entirety, taken as utterances of their *author,* are the same never-ending, internally unresolved dialogues among characters (seen as embodied points of view) and between the author himself and his characters; the characters' discourse is never entirely subsumed and remains free and open (as does the discourse of the author himself). In Dostoevsky's novels, the life experience of the characters and their discourse may be resolved as far as plot is concerned, but internally they remain incomplete and unresolved.[10]

The enormous significance of the motif of the speaking person is obvious in the realm of ethical and legal thought and discourse. The speaking person and his discourse is, in these areas, the major topic of thought and speech. All fundamental categories of ethical and legal inquiry and evaluation refer to speaking persons precisely as such: conscience (the "voice of conscience," the "inner word"), repentance (a free admission, a statement of wrongdoing by the person himself), truth and falsehood, being liable and not liable, the right to vote *[pravo golosa]* and so on. An independent, responsible and active discourse is *the* fundamental indicator of an ethical, legal and political human being. Challenges to this discourse, provocations of it, interpretations and assessments of it, the establishing of boundaries and forms for its activity (civil and political rights), the juxtaposing of various wills and discourses and so on — all these acts carry enormous weight in the realms of ethics and the law.

[7]The antiheroes, respectively, of *Eugene Onegin* and *A Hero for Our Time.* [Ed.]

[8]Novel of testing. [Ed.]

[9]Novel of education. [Ed.]

[10]Cf. our book *Problems of Dostoevsky's Art* [*Problemy tvorčestva Dostoevskogo*], Leningrad, 1929 (in its second and third editions, *Problems of Dostoevsky's Poetics* [*Problemy poetiki Dostoevskogo*], Moscow, 1963, Moscow, 1972). This book contains stylistic analyses of characters' utterances, revealing various forms of transmission and contextual framing. [Au.]

It is enough to point out the role played in narrowly judicial spheres by formulation, analysis and interpretation of testimony, declarations, contracts, various documents and other forms of others' utterances; finally, of course, there is legal hermeneutics.

All this calls for further study. Juridical (and ethical) techniques have been developed for dealing with the discourse of another [after it has been uttered], for establishing authenticity, for determining degrees of veracity and so forth (for example, the process of notarizing and other such techniques). But problems connected with the methods used for formulating such kinds of discourse — compositional, stylistic, semantic and other — have not as yet been properly posed.

The problem of *confession* in cases being investigated for trial (what has made it necessary and what provokes it) has so far been interpreted only at the level of laws, ethics and psychology. Dostoevsky provides a rich body of material for posing this language (of discourse): the problem of a thought, a desire, a motivation that is authentic — as in the case of Ivan Karamazov, for instance — and how these problems are exposed in words; the role of the other in formulating discourse, problems surrounding an inquest and so forth.

The speaking person and his discourse, as subject of thought and speech, is of course treated in the ethical and legal realms only insofar as it contributes to the specific interests of these disciplines. All methods for transmitting, formulating and framing another's discourse are made subordinate to such special interests and orientations. However, even there elements of an artistic representation of another's word are possible, especially in the ethical realm: for example, a representation of the struggle waged by the voice of conscience with other voices that sound in a man, the internal dialogism leading to repentance and so forth. Artistic prose, the novelistic element present in ethical tracts, especially in confessions, may be quite significant — for example, in Epictetus, Marcus Aurelius, Augustine and Petrarch we can detect the embryonic beginnings of the *Prüfungs-* and *Bildungsroman*.

Our motif carries even greater weight in the realm of religious thought and discourse (mythological, mystical and magical). The primary subject of this discourse is a being who speaks: a deity, a demon, a soothsayer, a prophet. Mythological thought does not, in general, acknowledge anything not alive or not responsive. Divining the will of a deity, of a demon (good or bad), interpreting signs of wrath or beneficence, tokens, indications and finally the transmission and interpretation of words directly spoken by a deity (revelation), or by his prophets, saints, soothsayers — all in all, the transmission and interpretation of the divinely inspired (as opposed to the profane) word are acts of religious thought and discourse having the greatest importance. All religious systems, even primitive ones, possess an enormous, highly specialized methodological apparatus (hermeneutics) for transmitting and interpreting various kinds of holy word.

The situation is somewhat different in the case of scientific thought. Here, the significance of discourse as such is comparatively weak. Mathematical and natural sciences do not acknowledge discourse as a subject in its own right. In scientific activity one must, of course, deal with another's discourse — the words of predecessors, the judgments of critics, majority opinion and so forth; one must deal with various forms for transmitting and interpreting another's word — struggle with an authoritative discourse, overcoming influences, polemics, references, quotations and so forth — but all this remains a mere operational necessity and does not affect the subject matter itself of the science, into whose composition the speaker and his discourse do not, of course, enter. The entire methodological apparatus of the mathematical and natural sciences is directed toward mastery over *mute objects, brute things,* that do not reveal themselves in words, that do not *comment on themselves.* Acquiring knowledge here is not connected with receiving and interpreting words or signs from the object itself under consideration.

In the humanities — as distinct from the natural and mathematical sciences — there arises the specific task of establishing, transmitting and interpreting the words of others (for example, the problem of sources in the methodology of the historical disciplines). And of course in the philological disciplines, the speaking person and his discourse is the fundamental object of investigation.

Philology has specific aims and approaches to its subject (the speaker and his discourse) that determine the ways it transmits and represents others' words (for example, discourse as an object of study in the history of language). However, within the limits of the humanities (and even of philology in the narrow sense) there is possible a twofold approach to another's word when it is treated as something we seek to understand.

The word can be perceived purely as an object (something that is, in its essence, a thing). It is perceived as such in the majority of the linguistic disciplines. In such a word-object even meaning becomes a thing: there can be no dialogic approach to such a word of the kind immanent to any deep and actual understanding. Understanding, so conceived, is inevitably abstract: it is completely separated from the living, ideological power of the word to mean — from its truth or falsity, its significance or insignificance, beauty or ugliness. Such a reified word-thing cannot be understood by attempts to penetrate its meaning dialogically: there can be no conversing with such a word.

In philology, however, a dialogic penetration into the word is obligatory (for indeed without it no sort of understanding is possible): dialogizing it opens up fresh aspects in the word (semantic aspects, in the broadest sense), which, since they were revealed by dialogic means, become more immediate to perception. Every step forward in our knowledge of the word is preceded by a "stage of genius" — *a sharpened dialogic relationship to the word* — that in turn uncovers fresh aspects within the word.

Precisely such an approach is needed, more concrete and that does not deflect discourse from its actual power to mean in real ideological life, an approach where objectivity of understanding is linked with dialogic vigor and a deeper penetration into discourse itself. No other approach is in fact possible in the area of poetics, or the history of literature (and in the history of ideologies in general) or to a considerable extent even in the philosophy of discourse: even the driest and flattest positivism in these disciplines cannot treat the word neutrally, as if it were a thing, but is obliged to initiate talk not only about words but in words, in order to penetrate their ideological meanings — which can only be grasped dialogically, and which include evaluation and response. The forms in which a dialogic understanding is transmitted and interpreted may, if the understanding is deep and vigorous, even come to have significant parallels with the double-voiced representations of another's discourse that we find in prose art. It should be noted that the novel always includes in itself the activity of coming to know another's word, a coming to knowledge whose process is represented in the novel.

Finally, a few words about the importance of our theme in the rhetorical genres. The speaker and his discourse is, indisputably, one of the most important subjects of rhetorical speech (and all other themes are inevitably implicated in the topic of discourse). In the rhetoric of the courts, for example, rhetorical discourse accuses or defends the subject of a trial, who is, of course, a speaker, and in so doing relies on his words, interprets them, polemicizes with them, creatively erecting *potential* discourses for the accused or for the defense (just such free creation of likely, but never actually uttered, words, sometimes whole speeches — "as he must have said" or "as he might have said" — was a device very widespread in ancient rhetoric); rhetorical discourse tries to outwit possible retorts to itself, it passes on and compiles the words of witnesses and so forth. In political rhetoric, for example, discourse can support some candidacy, represent the personality of a candidate, present and defend his point of view, his verbal statements, or in other cases protest against some decree, law, order, announcement, occasion — that is, protest against the specific verbal utterances toward which it is dialogically aimed.

Publicistic discourse also deals with the word itself and with the individual as its agent: it criticizes a speech, an article, a point of view; it polemicizes, exposes, ridicules and so forth. When it analyzes an act it uncovers its verbal motifs, the point of view in which it is grounded, it formulates such acts in words, providing them the appropriate emphases — ironic, indignant and so on. This does not mean, of course, that the rhetoric behind the word forgets that there are deeds, acts, a reality outside words. But such rhetoric has always to do with social man, whose most fundamental gestures are made meaningful ideologically through the word, or directly embodied in words.

The importance of another's speech as a subject in rhetoric is so great that the word frequently begins to cover over and substitute itself for reality; when this happens the word itself is diminished and becomes shallow. Rhetoric is often limited to purely verbal victories over the word; when this happens, rhetoric degenerates into a formalistic verbal play. But, we repeat, when discourse is torn from reality, it is fatal for the word itself as well: words grow sickly, lose semantic depth and flexibility, the capacity to expand and renew their meanings in new living contexts — they essentially die as discourse, for the signifying word lives beyond itself, that is, it lives by means of directing its purposiveness outward. The exclusive concentration on another's discourse as a subject does not, however, *in itself* inevitably indicate such a rupture between discourse and reality.

Rhetorical genres possess the most varied forms for transmitting another's speech, and for the most part these are intensely dialogized forms. Rhetoric relies heavily on the vivid reaccentuating of the words it transmits (often to the point of distorting them completely) that is accomplished by the appropriate framing context. Rhetorical genres provide rich material for studying a variety of forms for transmitting another's speech, the most varied means for formulating and framing such speech. Using rhetoric, even a representation of a speaker and his discourse of the sort one finds in prose art is possible — but the rhetorical double-voicedness of such images is usually not very deep: its roots do not extend to the dialogical essence of evolving language itself; it is not structured on authentic heteroglossia but on a mere diversity of voices; in most cases the double-voicedness of rhetoric is abstract and thus lends itself to formal, purely logical analysis of the ideas that are parceled out in voices, an analysis that then exhausts it. For this reason it is proper to speak of a distinctive *rhetorical* double-voicedness, or, put another way, to speak of the double-voiced rhetorical transmission of another's word (although it may involve some artistic aspects), in contrast to the double-voiced *representation* of another's word in the novel with its orientation toward the *image of a language*.

Such, then, is the importance of the speaker and his discourse as a topic in all areas of everyday, as well as verbal-ideological, life. It might be said, on the basis of our argument so far, that in the makeup of almost every utterance spoken by a social person — from a brief response in a casual dialogue to major verbal-ideological works (literary, scholarly and others) — a significant number of words can be identified that are implicitly or explicitly admitted as someone else's, and that are transmitted by a variety of different means. Within the arena of almost every utterance an intense interaction and struggle between one's own and another's word is being waged, a process in which they oppose or dialogically interanimate each other. The utterance so conceived is a considerably more complex and dynamic organism than it appears when construed simply as a thing that articulates the intention of the person uttering it, which is to see the utterance as a direct, single-voiced vehicle for expression.

That one of the main subjects of human speech is discourse itself has not up to now been sufficiently taken into consideration, nor has its crucial importance been appreciated. There has been no comprehensive philosophical grasp of all the ramifications of this fact. The specific nature of discourse as a topic of speech, one that requires the transmission and reprocessing of another's word, has not been understood: one may speak of another's discourse only with the help of that alien discourse itself, although in the process, it is true, the speaker introduces into the other's words his own intentions and highlights the context of those words in his own way. To speak of discourse as one might speak of any other subject, that is, thematically, without any dialogized transmission of it, is possible only when such discourse is utterly reified, a thing; it is possible, for example, to talk about the word in such a way in grammar, where it is precisely the dead, thing-like shell of the word that interests us.

From *Problems of Dostoevsky's Poetics*

The classification offered [in Table 1] is of course somewhat abstract in character. A concrete discourse may belong simultaneously to different varieties and even types. Moreover, interrelationships with another person's discourse in a concrete living context are of a dynamic and not a static character: the interrelationship of voices in discourse may change drastically, unidirectional words may turn into vari-directional ones, internal dialogization may become stronger or weaker, a passive type may be activized, and so forth.

"Notes from Underground" is a confessional *Ich-Erzählung*.[1] Originally the work was entitled "A Confession."[2] And it is in fact an authentic confession. Of course, "confession" is understood here not in the personal sense. The author's intention is refracted here, as in any *Ich-Erzählung;* this is not a personal document but a work of art.

In the confession of the Underground Man what strikes us first of all is its extreme and acute dialogization: there is literally not a single monologically firm, undissociated word. From the very first sentence the hero's speech has already begun to cringe and break under the influence of the anticipated words of another, with whom the hero, from the very first step, enters into the most intense internal polemic.

"I am a sick man . . . I am a spiteful man. I am an unpleasant man." Thus begins the confession. The ellipsis and the abrupt change of tone after it are significant. The hero began in a somewhat plaintive tone "I am a sick man," but was immediately enraged by that tone: it looked as if he were complaining and needed sympathy, as if he were seeking that sympathy in another person, as if he needed another person! And then there occurs an abrupt dialogic turnaround, one of those typical breaks in accent so characteristic of the whole style of the "Notes," as if the hero wants to say: You, perhaps, were led to believe from my first word that I am seeking your sympathy, so take this: I am a spiteful man. I am an unpleasant man!

Characteristic here is a gradual increase in negative tone (to spite the other) under the influence of the other's anticipated reaction. Such breaks in accent always lead to an accumulation of ever-intensifying abusive words or words that are, in any case, unflattering to the other person, as in this example:

> To live longer than forty years is bad manners; it is vulgar, immoral. Who does live beyond forty? Answer that, sincerely and honestly. I will tell you who: fools and worthless people do. I tell all old men that to their face, all those respectable old men, all those silver-haired and reverend old men! I tell the whole world that to its face. I have a right to say so, for I'll go on living to sixty myself. I'll live till seventy! Till eighty! Wait, let me catch my breath. [*SS* IV, 135; "Notes," Part One, 1]

In the opening words of the confession, this internal polemic with the other is concealed. But the other's words are present invisibly, determining the style of speech from within. Midway into the first paragraph, however, the polemic has already broken out into the open: the anticipated response of the other takes root in the narration, although, to be sure, still in a weakened form. "No, I refuse to treat it out of spite. You probably will not understand that. Well, but *I* understand it."

At the end of the third paragraph there is already a very characteristic anticipation of the other's reaction:

> Well, are you not imagining, gentlemen, that I am repenting for something now, that I am asking your forgiveness for something? I am sure you are imagining that. However, I assure you it does not matter to me if you are.

At the end of the next paragraph comes the above-quoted polemical attack against the "reverend old men." The following paragraph begins

Translated by Caryl Emerson.

[1]First-person narrative. [Ed.]

[2]"Notes from Underground" was originally announced by Dostoevsky under this title in "Time." [Au.]

Table 1

I. Direct, unmediated discourse directed exclusively toward its referential object, as an expression of the speaker's ultimate semantic authority	
II. Objectified discourse (discourse of a represented person)	
1. With a predominance of sociotypical determining factors 2. With a predominance of individually characteristic determining factors	Various degrees of objectification.
III. Discourse with an orientation toward someone else's discourse (double-voiced discourse)	
1. Unidirectional double-voiced discourse	
a. Stylization; b. Narrator's narration; c. Unobjectified discourse of a character who carries out (in part) the author's intentions; d. *Ich-Erzählung*	When objectification is reduced, these tend toward a fusion of voices, i.e., toward discourse of the first type.
2. Vari-directional double-voiced discourse	
a. Parody with all its nuances; b. Parodistic narration; c. Parodistic *Ich-Erzählung*; d. Discourse of a character who is parodically represented; e. Any transmission of someone else's words with a shift in accent	When objectification is reduced and the other's idea activated, these become internally dialogized and tend to disintegrate into two discourses (two voices) of the first type.
3. The active type (reflected discourse of another)	
a. Hidden internal polemic; b. Polemically colored autobiography and confession; c. Any discourse with a sideward glance at someone else's word; d. A rejoinder of a dialogue; e. Hidden dialogue	The other discourse exerts influence from without; diverse forms of interrelationship with another's discourse are possible here, as well as various degrees of deforming influence exerted by one discourse on the other.

directly with the anticipation of a response to the preceding paragraph:

> No doubt you think, gentlemen, that I want to amuse you. You are mistaken in that, too. I am not at all such a merry person as you imagine, or as you may imagine; however, if irritated by all this babble (and I can feel that you are irritated) you decide to ask me just who I am — then my answer is, I am a certain low-ranked civil servant.

The next paragraph again ends with an anticipated response:

> . . . I'll bet you think I am writing all this to show off, to be witty at the expense of men of action; and what is more, that out of ill-bred showing-off, I am clanking a sword, like my officer.

Later on such endings to paragraphs become more rare, but it remains true that all basic semantic sections of the work become sharper and more shrill near the end, in open anticipation of someone else's response.

Thus the entire style of the "Notes" is subject to the most powerful and all-determining influence of other people's words, which either act on speech covertly from within as in the beginning of the work, or which, as the anticipated response of another person, take root in the very fabric of speech, as in those above-quoted ending passages. The work does not contain a single word gravitating exclusively toward itself and its referential object; that is, there is not a single monologic word. We shall see that this intense relationship to another's consciousness in the Underground Man is complicated by an equally intense relationship to his own self. But first we shall make a brief structural analysis of this act of anticipating another's response.

Such anticipation is marked by one peculiar structural trait: it tends toward a vicious circle. The tendency of these anticipations can be reduced to a necessity to retain for oneself the final word. This final word must express the hero's full independence from the views and words of the other person, his complete indifference to the other's opinion and the other's evaluation. What he fears most of all is that people might think he is repenting before someone, that he is asking someone's forgiveness, that he is reconciling himself to someone else's judgment or evaluation, that his self-affirmation is somehow in need of affirmation and recognition by another. And it is in this direction that he anticipates the other's response. But precisely in this act of anticipating the other's response and in responding to it he again demonstrates to the other (and to himself) his own dependence on this other. He *fears* that the other might think he *fears* that other's opinion. But through this fear he immediately demonstrates his own dependence on the other's consciousness, his own inability to be at peace with his own definition of self. With his refutation, he confirms precisely what he wishes to refute, and he knows it. Hence the inescapable circle in which the hero's self-consciousness and discourse are trapped: "Well, are you not imagining, gentlemen, that I am repenting for something now? . . . I am sure you are imagining that. However, I assure you it does not matter to me if you are. . . ."

During that night out on the town, the Underground Man, insulted by his companions, wants to show them that he pays them no attention:

> I smiled contemptuously and walked up and down the other side of the room, opposite the sofa, along the wall, from the table to the stove and back again. I tried my very utmost to show them that I could do without them, and yet I purposely stomped with my boots, thumping with my heels. But it was all in vain. They paid no attention at all. [*SS* IV, 199; "Notes," Part Two, Ch. IV]

Meanwhile our underground hero recognizes all this perfectly well himself, and understands perfectly well the impossibility of escaping from that circle in which his attitude toward the other moves. Thanks to this attitude toward the other's consciousness, a peculiar *perpetuum mobile*[3] is achieved, made up of his internal polemic with another and with himself, an endless dialogue where one reply begets another, which begets a third, and so on to infinity, and all of this without any forward motion.

Here is an example of that inescapable *perpetuum mobile* of the dialogized self-consciousness:

> You will say that it is vulgar and base to drag all this [the hero's dreaming — M. B.] into public after all the tears and raptures I have myself admitted. But why is it base? Can you imagine that I am ashamed of it all, and that it was stupider than anything in your life, gentlemen? And I can assure you that some of these fancies were by no means badly composed. Not everything took place on the shores of Lake Como. And yet you are right — it really is vulgar and base. And what is most base of all is that I have now started to justify myself to you. And even more base than that is my making this remark now. But that's enough, or, after all, there will be no end to it; each step will be more base than the last. [*SS* IV, 181; "Notes," Part Two, Ch. II]

Before us is an example of a vicious circle of dialogue which can neither be finished nor finalized. The formal significance of such inescapable

[3]Perpetual motion. [Ed.]

dialogic oppositions in Dostoevsky's work is very great. But nowhere in his subsequent works does this opposition appear in such naked, abstractly precise, one could even say directly mathematical, form.[4]

As a result of the Underground Man's attitude toward the other's consciousness and its discourse — extraordinary dependence upon it and at the same time extreme hostility toward it and nonacceptance of its judgments — his narration takes on one highly essential artistic characteristic. This is a deliberate clumsiness of style, albeit subject to a certain artistic logic. His discourse does not flaunt itself and cannot flaunt itself, for there is not one before whom it can flaunt. It does not, after, all, gravitate naively toward itself and its referential object. It is addressed to another person and to the speaker himself (in his internal dialogue with himself). And in both of these directions it wants least of all to flaunt itself and be "artistic" in the usual sense of the word. In its attitude toward the other person it strives to be deliberately inelegant, to "spite" him and his tastes in all respects. But this discourse takes the same position even in regard to the speaker himself, for one's attitude toward oneself is inseparably interwoven with one's attitude toward another. Thus discourse is pointedly cynical, calculatedly cynical, yet also anguished. It strives to play the holy fool, for holy-foolishness is indeed a sort of form, a sort of aestheticism — but, as it were, in reverse.

As a result, the prosaic triteness of the portrayal of his inner life is carried to extreme limits. In its material, in its theme, the first part of "Notes from Underground" is lyrical. From a formal point of view, this is the same prose lyric of spiritual and emotional quest, of spiritual unfulfillment that we find, for example, in Turgenev's "Phantoms" or "Enough,"[5] or in any lyrical page from a confessional *Ich-Erzählung* or a page from *Werther*. But this is a peculiar sort of lyric, analogous to the lyrical expression of a toothache.

This expression of a toothache, oriented in an internally polemical way toward the listener and toward the sufferer, is spoken by the Underground Hero himself, and he speaks of it, of course, not by chance. He suggests eavesdropping on the groans of an "educated man of the nineteenth century" who suffers from a toothache, on the second or third day of his illness. He tries to expose the peculiar sensuality behind this whole cynical expression of pain, an expression intended for the "public":

> His moans become nasty, disgustingly spiteful, and go on for whole days and nights. And, after all, he himself knows that he does not benefit at all from his moans; he knows better than anyone that he is only lacerating and irritating himself and others in vain; he knows that even the audience for whom he is exerting himself and his whole family now listen to him with loathing, do not believe him for a second, and that deep down they understand that he could moan differently, more simply, without trills and flourishes, and that he is only indulging himself like that out of spite, out of malice. Well, sensuality exists precisely in all these consciousnesses and infamies. "It seems I am troubling you, I am lacerating your hearts, I am keeping everyone in the house awake. Well, stay awake then, you, too, feel every minute that I have a toothache. I am no longer the hero to you now that I tried to appear before, but simply a nasty person, a scoundrel. Well, let it be that way, then! I am very glad that you see through me. Is it nasty for you to hear my foul moans? Well, let it be nasty. Here I will let you have an even nastier flourish in a minute. . . ." [*SS* IV, 144; "Notes," Part One, Ch. IV]

Of course any implied comparison here between the structure of the Underground Man's confession and the expression of a toothache is on the level of parodic exaggeration, and in this sense is cynical. But the orientation of this expression of a toothache, with all its "trills and flourishes," nevertheless does, in its relation to the listener and to the speaker himself, reflect very accurately the orientation of discourse in a confession — although, we repeat, it reflects not objectively but in a taunting, parodically exag-

[4]This can be explained by the genetic similarities between "Notes from Underground" and Menippean satire. [Au.]

[5]"Phantoms," the least successful of Turgenev's several stories on the supernatural; "Enough" is one of Turgenev's periodic gestures of withdrawal, a sort of prose poem announcing to the public his disillusionment with life and art. Both pieces, and their author, are vigorously parodied by Dostoevsky in the character of Karmazinov in *The Possessed*. [Tr.]

gerating style, just as *The Double* reflected the internal speech of Golyadkin.

The destruction of one's own image in another's eyes, the sullying of that image in another's eyes as an ultimate desperate effort to free oneself from the power of the other's consciousness and to break through to one's self for the self alone — this, in fact, is the orientation of the Underground Man's entire confession. For this reason he makes his discourse about himself deliberately ugly. He wants to kill in himself any desire to appear the hero in others' eyes (and in his own): "I am no longer the hero to you now that I tried to appear before, but simply a nasty person, a scoundrel. . . ."

To accomplish this he must banish from his discourse all epic and lyrical tones, all "heroizing" tones; he must make his discourse *cynically* objective. A soberly objective definition of himself, without exaggeration or mockery, is impossible for a hero from the underground, because such a soberly prosaic definition would presuppose a word without a sideward glance, a word without a loophole; neither the one nor the other exist on his verbal palette. True, he is continually trying to break through to such a word, to break through to spiritual sobriety, but for him the path lies through cynicism and holy-foolishness. He has neither freed himself from the power of the other's consciousness nor admitted its power over him,[6] he is for now merely struggling with it, polemicizing with it maliciously, not able to accept it but also not able to reject it. In this striving to trample down his own image and his own discourse as they exist in and for the other person, one can hear not only the desire for sober self-definition, but also a desire to annoy the other person; and this forces him to overdo his sobriety, mockingly exaggerating it to the point of cynicism and holy-foolishness: "Is it nasty for you to hear my foul moans? Well, let it be nasty. Here I will let you have an even nastier flourish in a minute. . . ."

But the underground hero's word about himself is not only a word with a sideward glance; it is also, as we have said, a word with a loophole.

[6]According to Dostoevsky, such an admittance would also serve to calm down the discourse and purify it. [Au.]

The influence of the loophole on the style of his confession is so great that his style cannot be understood without a consideration of its formal activity. The word with a loophole has enormous significance in Dostoevsky's works in general, especially in the later works. And here we pass on to another aspect of the structure of "Notes from Underground": the hero's attitude toward his own self, which throughout the course of the entire work is interwoven and combined with his dialogue with another.

What, then, is this loophole of consciousness and of the word?

A loophole is the retention for oneself of the possibility for altering the ultimate, final meaning of one's own words. If a word retains such a loophole this must inevitably be reflected in its structure. This potential other meaning, that is, the loophole left open, accompanies the word like a shadow. Judged by its meaning alone, the word with a loophole should be an ultimate word and does present itself as such, but in fact it is only the penultimate word and places after itself only a conditional, not a final, period.

For example, the confessional self-definition with a loophole (the most widespread form in Dostoevsky) is, judging by its meaning, an ultimate word about oneself, a final definition of oneself, but in fact it is forever taking into account internally the responsive, contrary evaluation of oneself made by another. The hero who repents and condemns himself actually wants only to provoke praise and acceptance by another. Condemning himself, he wants and demands that the other person dispute this self-definition, and he leaves himself a loophole in case the other person should suddenly in fact agree with him, with his self-condemnation, and not make use of this privilege as the other.

Here is how the hero from the underground tells of his "literary" dreams:

> I, for instance, was triumphant over everyone; everyone, of course, lay in the dust and was *forced* to recognize my superiority *spontaneously,* and I forgave them all. I, a famous poet, and a courtier, fell in love; I inherited countless millions and immediately devoted them to humanity, and *at the same time I confessed before all the people my shameful deeds, which, of course, were not merely*

shameful, but contained an enormous amount of "the sublime and the beautiful," something in the Manfred[7] *style. Everyone would weep and kiss me (what idiots they would be if they did not),* while I would go barefoot and hungry preaching new ideas and fighting a victorious Austerlitz against the reactionaries. [*SS* IV, 181; "Notes," Part Two, Ch. II]

Here he ironically relates dreams of heroic deeds with a loophole, dreams of confession with a loophole. He casts a parodic light on these dreams. But his very next words betray the fact that his repentant confession of his dreams has its own loophole, too, and that he himself is prepared to find in these dreams and in his very confessing of them something, if not in the Manfred style, then at least in the realm of "the sublime and the beautiful," if anyone should happen to agree with him that the dreams are indeed base and vulgar: "You will say that it is vulgar and base to drag all this into public after all the tears and raptures I have myself admitted. But why is it base? Can you imagine that I am ashamed of it all, and that it was stupider than anything in your life, gentlemen? And I can assure you that some of these fancies were by no means badly composed. . . ."

And this passage, already cited by us above, is caught up in the vicious circle of self-consciousness with a sideward glance.

The loophole creates a special type of fictive ultimate word about oneself with an unclosed tone to it, obtrusively peering into the other's eyes and demanding from the other a sincere refutation. We shall see that the word with a loophole achieves especially sharp expression in Ippolit's[8] confession, but it is to one degree or another inherent in all the confessional self-utterances of Dostoevsky's heroes.[9] The loophole makes all the heroes' self-definitions unstable, the word in them has no hard and fast meaning, and at any moment, like a chameleon, it is ready to change its tone and its ultimate meaning.

The loophole makes the hero ambiguous and elusive even for himself. In order to break through to his self the hero must travel a very long road. The loophole profoundly distorts his attitude toward himself. The hero does not know whose opinion, whose statement is ultimately the final judgment on him: is it his own repentant and censuring judgment, or on the contrary is it another person's opinion that he desires and has compelled into being, an opinion that accepts and vindicates him? The image of Nastasya Filippovna,[10] for example, is built almost entirely on this motif alone. Considering herself guilty, a fallen woman, she simultaneously assumes that the other person, precisely as the other, is obliged to vindicate her and cannot consider her guilty. She genuinely quarrels with Myshkin, who vindicates her in everything, but she equally genuinely despises and rejects all those who agree with her self-condemnation and consider her a fallen woman. Ultimately Nastasya Filippovna does not know even her own final word on herself: does she really consider herself a fallen woman, or does she vindicate herself? Self-condemnation and self-vindication, divided between two voices — I condemn myself, another vindicates me — but anticipated by a single voice, create in that voice interruptions and an internal duality. An anticipated and obligatory vindication by the other merges with self-condemnation, and both tones begin to sound simultaneously in that voice, resulting in abrupt interruptions and sudden transitions. Such is the voice of Nastasya Filippovna, such is the style of her discourse. Her entire inner life (and, as we shall see, her outward life as well) is reduced to a search for herself and for her own undivided voice beneath the two voices that have made their home in her.

The Underground Man conducts the same sort of inescapable dialogue with himself that he conducts with the other person. He cannot merge completely with himself in a unified monologic voice simply by leaving the other's voice entirely outside himself (whatever that voice might be, without a loophole), for, as is the case with Golyadkin, his voice must also perform the function of surrogate for the other person. He cannot reach an agreement with himself, but neither can he stop talking with himself. The style of his discourse about himself is organically alien to the

[7]Demonic hero of Byron's dramatic poem. [Ed.]
[8]In *The Idiot.* [Ed.]
[9]Exceptions will be pointed out below. [Au.]

[10]In *The Idiot.* [Ed.]

period, alien to finalization, both in its separate aspects and as a whole. This is the style of internally endless speech which can be mechanically cut off but cannot be organically completed.

But precisely for that reason is Dostoevsky able to conclude his work in a way so organic and appropriate for the hero; he concludes it on precisely that which would foreground the tendency toward eternal endlessness embedded in his hero's notes.

> But enough; I don't want to write more from "underground."...
>
> The "notes" of this paradoxalist do not end here, however. He could not resist and continued them. But it also seems to me that we may stop here. [*SS* IV, 224; "Notes," Part Two, Ch. X]

In conclusion we will comment upon two additional characteristics of the Underground Man. Not only his discourse but his face too has its sideward glance, its loophole, and all the phenomena resulting from these. It is as if interference, voices interrupting one another, penetrate his entire body, depriving him of self-sufficiency and unambiguousness. The Underground Man hates his own face, because in it he senses the power of another person over him, the power of that other's evaluations and opinions. He himself looks on his own face with another's eyes, with the eyes of the other. And this alien glance interruptedly merges with his own glance and creates in him a peculiar hatred toward his own face:

> For instance, I hated my face; I thought it disgusting, and even suspected that there was something base in its expression and therefore every time I turned up at the office I painfully tried to behave as independently as possible so that I might not be suspected of being base, and to give my face as noble an expression as possible. "Let my face even be ugly," I thought, "but let it be noble, expressive, and above all, extremely intelligent." But I was absolutely and painfully certain that my face could never express those perfections; but what was worst of all, I thought it positively stupid-looking. And I would have been quite satisfied if I could have looked intelligent. In fact, I would even have put up with looking base if, at the same time, my face could have been thought terribly intelligent. [*SS* IV, 168; "Notes," Part Two, CH. I]

Just as he deliberately makes his discourse about himself unattractive, so is he made happy by the unattractiveness of his face:

> I happened to look at myself in the mirror. My harassed face struck me as extremely revolting, pale, spiteful, nasty, with disheveled hair. "No matter, I am glad of it," I thought; "I am glad that I shall seem revolting to her; I like that." [*SS* IV, 206; "Notes," Part Two, Ch. V]

This polemic with the other on the subject of himself is complicated in "Notes from Underground" by his polemic with the other on the subject of the world and society. The underground hero, in contrast to Devushkin and Golyadkin,[11] is an ideologist.

In his ideological discourse we can easily uncover the same phenomena that are present in his discourse about himself. His discourse about the world is both overtly and covertly polemical; it polemicizes not only with other people, with other ideologies, but also with the very subject of its thinking — with the world and its order. And in this discourse on the world there are two voices, as it were, sounding for him, among which he cannot find himself and his own world, because even the world he defines with a loophole. Just as his body has become an "interrupted" thing in his own eyes, so is the world, nature, society perceived by him as "interrupted." In each of his thoughts about them there is a battle of voices, evaluations, points of view. In everything he senses above all *someone else's will* predetermining him. It is within the framework of this alien will that he perceives the world order, nature with its mechanical necessity, the social order. His own thought is developed and structured as *the thought of someone personally insulted by the world order,* personally humiliated by its blind necessity. This imparts a profoundly intimate and passionate character to his ideological discourse, and permits it to become tightly interwoven with his discourse about himself. It seems (and such indeed was Dostoevsky's intent) that we are dealing here with a single discourse, and only by arriving at himself will the

[11]Makar Devushkin is the protagonist of Dostoevsky's first novel, *Poor Folk;* Golyadkin, of *The Double*. [Ed.]

hero arrive at his world. Discourse about the world, just like discourse about oneself, is profoundly dialogic: the hero casts an energetic reproach at the world order, even at the mechanical necessity of nature, as if he were talking not about the world but with the world. Of these peculiarities of ideological discourse we will speak below, when we take up the general issue of hero-ideologists and Ivan Karamazov in particular; in him these features are especially acute and clear-cut.

The discourse of the Underground Man is entirely a discourse-address. To speak, for him, means to address someone; to speak about himself means to address his own self with his own discourse; to speak about another person means to address that other person; to speak about the world means to address the world. But while speaking with himself, with another, with the world, he simultaneously addresses a third party as well: he squints his eyes to the side, toward the listener, the witness, the judge.[12] This simultaneous triple-directedness of his discourse and the fact that he does not acknowledge any object without addressing it is also responsible for the extraordinarily vivid, restless, agitated, and one might say, obtrusive nature of this discourse. It cannot be seen as a lyrical or epic discourse, calmly gravitating toward itself and its referential object; no, first and foremost one reacts to it, responds to it, is drawn into its game; it is capable of agitating and irritating, almost like the personal address of a living person. It destroys footlights, but not because of its concern for topical issues or for reasons that have any direct philosophical significance, but precisely because of that formal structure analyzed by us above.

The element of *address* is essential to every discourse in Dostoevsky, narrative discourse as well as the discourse of the hero. In Dostoevsky's world generally there is nothing merely thing-like, no mere matter, no object — there are only subjects. Therefore there is no word-judgment, no word about an object, no secondhand referential word — there is only the word as address, the word dialogically contacting another word, a word about a word addressed to a word.

[12]We recall the characterization that Dostoevsky himself gave to the hero's speech in "A Meek One": ". . . he either argues with himself or addresses some unseen listener, a judge as it were. However, it is always like that in real life." [Au.]

Virginia Woolf

1882–1941

The novelist and critic Virginia Woolf, one of the founders of literary modernism in fiction, was born in London. The daughter of the Victorian intellectual Sir Leslie Stephen, Woolf educated herself thoroughly using the resources of her father's library and friends. On her father's death in 1904, she moved to Gordon Square in the Bloomsbury neighborhood that houses the University of London and the British Museum. There she and her sister Vanessa gathered round them that coterie of artists and intellectuals that have become known as the "Bloomsbury Group." In 1912 she married the journalist and editor Leonard Woolf, and together in 1917 they founded the Hogarth Press, a small press distinguished for publishing not only her own work but that of authors such as D. H. Lawrence and T. S. Eliot, in addition to the English translations of Sigmund Freud. Woolf's early *The Voyage Out* (1915) and *Night and Day* (1919) prepared the way for her more ambitious, experimental *Jacob's Room* (1922) and the novels for which she is most admired, *Mrs. Dalloway* (1925), *To the Lighthouse* (1927), and *The Waves* (1931). Her other novels include *Orlando: A Biography* (1928), *The Years* (1937), and *Between the Acts* (1941). While Woolf was completing *Between the Acts* during the darkest days of World War II, it was expected that at any moment the German Wehrmacht would invade the Sussex coast not far from her home — an event Woolf knew would create incomprehensible havoc for England, her Jewish husband, and herself. The invasion never came off but at that time of crisis Woolf suffered a terrifying recurrence of the depression that had plagued her since childhood, and she drowned herself in the River Ouse.

While Woolf may be best known for her novels, she was also a prolific writer of critical essays, reviews, and autobiography: The complete edition of her essays will contain over one million words. Working rapidly for the journalistic deadlines of the weekly *Times Literary Supplement,* the *Nation and Athenaeum,* and T. S. Eliot's *Criterion,* Woolf took up in her writing individual authors, schools, and aspects of contemporary culture. Although her subjects were often dictated by journalistic assignment, she used them to explore her own central aesthetic beliefs about the bankruptcy of the realist literary tradition and the importance of what we today call *modernism.* This credo can be found in the two volumes of *The Common Reader* (1925 and 1932), in *The Death of the Moth* (1942), and in *Granite and Rainbow* (1958) published after her death. The selections below are taken from her well-known work of feminist theory, *A Room of One's Own* (1929).

Woolf takes her place in the world of literary criticism as both a modernist and a feminist, and as a feminist she is considerably more modern than her dates of birth and death might suggest. If the major feminist issues of the 1970s and 1980s were the critique of patriarchal culture and its attitudes toward women, the analysis of female creativity and the tradition of women's writing, and the analysis of *écriture féminine* (as French feminists termed the special quality of women's writing), the roots of all three can be found in Woolf's *A Room of One's Own.*

The most famous section of *A Room of One's Own* — a personal brief for women writers expanded from two lectures Woolf gave at Newnham and Girton Colleges — is that which traces the tragically wasted career of an imaginary "Shakespeare's sister," whose creativity and talent would have found no outlet in the society of the sixteenth century. This fictional history is the premise for a historical sketch of actual women writers and the difficulties they experienced in their work, from Aphra Behn, the first female dramatist to make a living by her pen, through the noble bluestockings of the eighteenth century, to the four major novelists of the nineteenth: Jane Austen, Emily and Charlotte Brontë, and George Eliot. In her manifesto, written in 1929, ten years after women received the vote and sixty-five years after the founding of the first women's college at Oxford, Woolf remains painfully conscious of the disparities that still exist between women and men. But she is convinced that the birth of a female Shakespeare, one with an "incandescent" spirit capable of unimpeded expression, is possible within the century — if the rest of her sisters work to prepare her way.

In the course of tracing the histories of women writers, Woolf touches on a great many issues taken up by later feminists. Her ironic commentary, set in the British Museum, on the way women have traditionally been defined and analyzed as inferiors by men previews the issues later raised by Simone de Beauvoir, Kate Millett, Mary Ellmann, and other images-of-women critics. Woolf's analysis of the women novelists of the nineteenth century — of how the adoption of a masculine prose by Charlotte Brontë and George Eliot hampered their expressiveness, and of how Austen succeeded in devising a feminine prose that allowed her to say what she needed to — anticipates current research on women's language and *écriture féminine.* And in her emphatic endorsement of Coleridge's claim that a great mind is androgynous, Woolf takes a stand on the most contested feminist question — whether there are distinct masculine and feminine modes of creativity — which would be attacked by critics like Showalter who are committed to the idea of a uniquely feminine poetics, and by French feminists such as Cixious and Irigaray exploring a more polymorphous sexuality (see pp. 1453 and 1466).

But, in her feminism, Woolf is also very much the modernist, convinced that the key role of the artist is to create a world whose validity stands independent of the testimony and personal life of the artist herself. Like Eliot's catalytic creator, Woolf's must be impersonal and detached, with the ego shaping a sensibility but not expressing a personality. This vision accounts for some of Woolf's judgments on her major predecessors, the women who made the nineteenth-century novel what it was. Austen's delicacy and disinterestedness wins the highest acclaim, as does Emily Brontë's masterly creation of a transcendent Yorkshire world of pure poetic imagination. In *Jane Eyre,* however, Woolf spots the telltale signs of Charlotte Brontë's rage:

> She left her story, to which her entire devotion was due, to attend to some personal grievance. She remembered that she had been starved of her proper due of experience — she had been made to stagnate in a parsonage mending stockings when she wanted to wander free over the world. Her imagination swerved from indignation and we feel it swerve. . . . The portrait of Rochester is drawn in the dark. We feel the influence of fear in it; just as

> we constantly feel an acidity which is the result of oppression, a buried suffering smouldering beneath her passion, a rancour which contracts those books, splendid as they are, with a spasm of pain.

As Woolf well understands, the root causes of Charlotte Brontë's aesthetic imperfections were social. It would take a miracle for any woman under the oppression of patriarchal society, deprived of the financial independence and quiet leisure that men often took for granted, to produce texts that transcend the creating self. Woolf closes her treatise by arguing that it will take the transformation of society, giving women the titular "room of one's own," to make a space where Shakespeare's future sisters can evolve.

Selected Bibliography

Bell, Quentin. *Virginia Woolf: A Biography.* New York: Harcourt, Brace and Jovanovich, 1972.

Hanson, Clare. *Virginia Woolf.* London: Macmillan, 1994.

King, James. *Virginia Woolf.* New York: Norton, 1995.

Majumdar, Robin. *Virginia Woolf: An Annotated Bibliography of Criticism.* New York: Garland, 1976.

Marcus, Jane. *Art and Anger: Reading Like a Woman.* Columbus: Ohio State University Press, 1988.

Marder, Herbert. *Feminism and Art: A Study of Virginia Woolf.* Chicago: University of Chicago Press, 1968.

Moi, Toril. *Sexual/Textual Politics: Feminist Literary Theory.* London: Methuen, 1985.

Newman, Herta. *Virginia Woolf and Mrs. Brown: Toward a Realism of Uncertainty.* New York: Garland, 1996.

Rosenbaum, S. P. *Women and Fiction: The Manuscript Versions of A Room of One's Own.* Oxford: Blackwell, 1992.

Rosenman, Ellen Bayuk. *A Room of One's Own: Women Writers and the Politics of Creativity.* New York: Twayne, 1995.

Woolf, Virginia. *A Room of One's Own.* New York: Harcourt Brace, 1929.

———. *Three Guineas.* New York: Harcourt Brace, 1938.

———. *The Essays of Virginia Woolf,* ed. Andrew McNeillie. London: Hogarth Press, 1986–.

Shakespeare's Sister from *A Room of One's Own*

Let me imagine, since facts are so hard to come by, what would have happened had Shakespeare had a wonderfully gifted sister, called Judith, let us say. Shakespeare himself went, very probably — his mother was an heiress — to the grammar school, where he may have learnt Latin — Ovid, Virgil and Horace — and the elements of grammar and logic. He was, it is well known, a wild boy who poached rabbits, perhaps shot a deer, and had, rather sooner than he should have done, to marry a woman in the neighborhood, who bore him a child rather quicker than was right. That escapade sent him to seek his fortune in London. He had, it seemed, a taste for the theatre; he began by holding horses at the stage door. Very soon he got work in the theatre, became a successful actor, and lived at the hub of the universe, meeting everybody, knowing everybody, practising his art on the boards, exercising his wits in the streets, and even getting access to the palace of the queen. Meanwhile his extraordinarily gifted sister, let us suppose, remained at home. She was as adventurous, as imaginative, as agog to see the world as he was. But she was not sent to school. She had no chance of learning grammar and logic, let alone of reading Horace and Virgil. She picked up a book now and then, one of her brother's perhaps, and read a few pages. But then her parents came in and told her to mend the stockings or mind the stew and not moon about with books and papers. They would have spoken sharply but kindly, for they were substantial people who knew the conditions of life for a woman and loved their daughter — indeed, more likely than not she was the apple of her father's eye. Perhaps she scribbled some pages up in an apple loft on the sly, but was careful to hide them or set fire to them. Soon, however, before she was out of her teens, she was to be betrothed to the son of a neighboring woolstapler. She cried out that marriage was hateful to her, and for that she was severely beaten by her father. Then he ceased to scold her. He begged her instead not to hurt him, not to shame him in this matter of her marriage. He would give her a chain of beads or a fine petticoat, he said; and there were tears in his eyes. How could she disobey him? How could she break his heart? The force of her own gift alone drove her to it. She made up a small parcel of her belongings, let herself down by a rope one summer's night and took the road to London. She was not seventeen. The birds that sang in the hedge were not more musical than she was. She had the quickest fancy, a gift like her brother's, for the tune of words. Like him, she had a taste for the theatre. She stood at the stage door; she wanted to act, she said. Men laughed in her face. The manager — a fat, loose-lipped man — guffawed. He bellowed something about poodles dancing and women acting — no woman, he said, could possibly be an actress. He hinted — you can imagine what. She could get no training in her craft. Could she even seek her dinner in a tavern or roam the streets at midnight? Yet her genius was for fiction and lusted to feed abundantly upon the lives of men and women and the study of their ways. At last — for she was very young, oddly like Shakespeare the poet in her face, with the same grey eyes and rounded brows — at last Nick Greene the actor-manager took pity on her; she found herself with child by that gentleman and so — who shall measure the heat and violence of the poet's heart when caught and tangled in a woman's body? — killed herself one winter's night and lies buried at some cross-roads where the omnibuses now stop outside the Elephant and Castle.[1]

That, more or less, is how the story would run, I think, if a woman in Shakespeare's day had had Shakespeare's genius. But for my part, I agree with the deceased bishop, if such he was — it is unthinkable that any woman in Shakespeare's

[1]Public square in London on the south bank of the Thames. [Ed.]

day should have had Shakespeare's genius. For genius like Shakespeare's is not born among labouring, uneducated, servile people. It was not born in England among the Saxons and the Britons. It is not born today among the working classes. How, then, could it have been born among women whose work began, according to Professor Trevelyan,[2] almost before they were out of the nursery, who were forced to it by their parents and held to it by all the power of law and custom? Yet genius of a sort must have existed among women as it must have existed among the working classes. Now and again an Emily Brontë or a Robert Burns blazes out and proves its presence. But certainly it never got itself on to paper. When, however, one reads of a witch being ducked, of a woman possessed by devils, of a wise women selling herbs, or even of a very remarkable man who had a mother, then I think we are on the track of a lost novelist, a suppressed poet, of some mute and inglorious Jane Austen, some Emily Brontë who dashed her brains out on the moor or mopped and mowed about the highways crazed with the torture that her gift had put her to. Indeed, I would venture to guess that Anon, who wrote so many poems without signing them, was often a woman. It was a woman Edward Fitzgerald, I think, suggested who made the ballads and the folk-songs, crooning them to her children, beguiling her spinning with them, or the length of the winter's night.

This may be true or it may be false — who can say? — but what is true in it, so it seemed to me, reviewing the story of Shakespeare's sister as I had made it, is that any woman born with a great gift in the sixteenth century would certainly have gone crazed, shot herself, or ended her days in some lonely cottage outside the village, half witch, half wizard, feared and mocked at. For it needs little skill in psychology to be sure that a highly gifted girl who had tried to use her gift for poetry would have been so thwarted and hindered by other people, so tortured and pulled asunder by her own contrary instincts, that she must have lost her health and sanity to a certainty. No girl could have walked to London and stood at a stage door and forced her way into the presence of actor-managers without doing herself a violence and suffering an anguish which may have been irrational — for chastity may be a fetish invented by certain societies for unknown reasons — but were none the less inevitable. Chastity had then, it has even now, a religious importance in a woman's life, and has so wrapped itself round with nerves and instincts that to cut it free and bring it to the light of day demands courage of the rarest. To have lived a free life in London in the sixteenth century would have meant for a woman who was poet and playwright a nervous stress and dilemma which might well have killed her. Had she survived, whatever she had written would have been twisted and deformed, issuing from a strained and morbid imagination. And undoubtedly, I thought, looking at the shelf where there are no plays by women, her work would have gone unsigned. That refuge she would have sought certainly. It was the relic of the sense of chastity that dictated anonymity to women even so late as the nineteenth century. Currer Bell, George Eliot, George Sand, all the victims of inner strife as their writings prove, sought ineffectively to veil themselves by using the name of a man. Thus they did homage to the convention, which if not implanted by the other sex was liberally encouraged by them (the chief glory of a woman is not to be talked of, said Pericles, himself a much-talked-of man), that publicity in women is detestable. Anonymity runs in their blood. The desire to be veiled still possesses them. They are not even now as concerned about the health of their fame as men are, and, speaking generally, will pass a tombstone or a signpost without feeling an irresistible desire to cut their names on it, as Alf, Bert or Chas. must do in obedience to their instinct, which murmurs if it sees a fine woman go by, or even a dog, Ce chien est à moi.[3] And, of course, it may not be a dog, I thought, remembering Parliament Square, the Sieges Allee[4] and other avenues; it may be a piece of land or a

[2]George Macaulay Trevelyan (1876–1962), Regius professor of modern history at Cambridge, author of *England in the Age of Wycliffe* (1899) and *British History in the Nineteenth Century* (1922). [Ed.]

[3]The dog is mine. [Ed.]

[4]Broad avenue in Berlin. [Ed.]

man with curly black hair. It is one of the great advantages of being a woman that one can pass even a very fine negress without wishing to make an Englishwoman of her.

That woman, then, who was born with a gift of poetry in the sixteenth century, was an unhappy woman, a woman at strife against herself. All the conditions of her life, all her own instincts, were hostile to the state of mind which is needed to set free whatever is in the brain. But what is the state of mind that is most propitious to the act of creation, I asked. Can one come by any notion of the state that furthers and makes possible that strange activity? Here I opened the volume containing the Tragedies of Shakespeare. What was Shakespeare's state of mind, for instance, when he wrote *Lear* and *Antony and Cleopatra*? It was certainly the state of mind most favourable to poetry that there has ever existed. But Shakespeare himself said nothing about it. We only know casually and by chance that he "never blotted a line." Nothing indeed was ever said by the artist himself about his state of mind until the eighteenth century perhaps. Rousseau perhaps began it. At any rate, by the nineteenth century self-consciousness had developed so far that it was the habit for men of letters to describe their minds in confessions and autobiographies. Their lives also were written, and their letters were printed after their deaths. Thus, though we do not know what Shakespeare went through when he wrote *Lear,* we do know what Carlyle went through when he wrote the *French Revolution;* what Flaubert went through when he wrote *Madame Bovary;* what Keats was going through when he tried to write poetry against the coming of death and the indifference of the world.

And one gathers from this enormous modern literature of confession and self-analysis that to write a work of genius is almost always a feat of prodigious difficulty. Everything is against the likelihood that it will come from the writer's mind whole and entire. Generally material circumstances are against it. Dogs will bark; people will interrupt; money must be made; health will break down. Further, accentuating all these difficulties and making them harder to bear is the world's notorious indifference. It does not ask people to write poems and novels and histories; it does not need them. It does not care whether Flaubert finds the right word or whether Carlyle scrupulously verifies this or that fact. Naturally, it will not pay for what it does not want. And so the writer, Keats, Flaubert, Carlyle, suffers, especially in the creative years of youth, every form of distraction and discouragement. A curse, a cry of agony, rises from those books of analysis and confession. "Mighty poets in their misery dead" — that is the burden of their song. If anything comes through in spite of all this, it is a miracle, and probably no book is born entire and uncrippled as it was conceived.

But for women, I thought, looking at the empty shelves, these difficulties were infinitely more formidable. In the first place, to have a room of her own, let alone a quiet room or a sound-proof room, was out of the question, unless her parents were exceptionally rich or very noble, even up to the beginning of the nineteenth century. Since her pin money, which depended on the good will of her father, was only enough to keep her clothed, she was debarred from such alleviations as came even to Keats or Tennyson or Carlyle, all poor men, from a walking tour, a little journey to France, from the separate lodging which, even if it were miserable enough, sheltered them from the claims and tyrannies of their families. Such material difficulties were formidable; but much worse were the immaterial. The indifference of the world which Keats and Flaubert and other men of genius have found so hard to bear was in her case not indifference but hostility. The world did not say to her as it said to them, Write if you choose; it makes no difference to me. The world said with a guffaw, Write? What's the good of your writing?

Austen–Brontë–Eliot from *A Room of One's Own*

Here, then, one had reached the early nineteenth century. And here, for the first time, I found several shelves given up entirely to the works of women. But why, I could not help asking, as I ran my eyes over them, were they, with very few exceptions, all novels? The original impulse was to poetry. The "supreme head of song" was a poetess. Both in France and in England the women poets precede the women novelists. Moreover, I thought, looking at the four famous names, what had George Eliot in common with Emily Brontë? Did not Charlotte Brontë fail entirely to understand Jane Austen? Save for the possibly relevant fact that not one of them had a child, four more incongruous characters could not have met together in a room — so much so that it is tempting to invent a meeting and a dialogue between them. Yet by some strange force they were all compelled, when they wrote, to write novels. Had it something to do with being born of the middle class, I asked; and with the fact, which Miss Emily Davies[1] a little later was so strikingly to demonstrate, that the middle-class family in the early nineteenth century was possessed only of a single sitting-room between them? If a woman wrote, she would have to write in the common sitting-room. And, as Miss Nightingale was so vehemently to complain, — "women never have an half hour . . . that they can call their own" — she was always interrupted. Still it would be easier to write prose and fiction there than to write poetry or a play. Less concentration is required. Jane Austen wrote like that to the end of her days. "How she was able to effect all this," her nephew writes in his Memoir, "is surprising, for she had no separate study to repair to, and most of the work must have been done in the general sitting-room, subject to all kinds of casual interruptions. She was careful that her occupation should not be suspected by servants or visitors or any persons beyond her own family party."[2] Jane Austen hid her manuscripts or covered them with a piece of blotting-paper. Then, again, all the literary training that a woman had in the early nineteenth century was training in the observation of character, in the analysis of emotion. Her sensibility had been educated for centuries by the influences of the common sitting-room. People's feelings were impressed on her; personal relations were always before her eyes. Therefore, when the middle-class woman took to writing, she naturally wrote novels, even though, as seems evident enough, two of the four famous women here named were not by nature novelists. Emily Brontë should have written poetic plays; the overflow of George Eliot's capacious mind should have spread itself when the creative impulse was spent upon history or biography. They wrote novels, however; one may even go further, I said, taking *Pride and Prejudice* from the shelf, and say that they wrote good novels. Without boasting or giving pain to the opposite sex, one may say that *Pride and Prejudice* is a good book. At any rate, one would not have been ashamed to have been caught in the act of writing *Pride and Prejudice*. Yet Jane Austen was glad that a hinge creaked, so that she might hide her manuscript before any one came in. To Jane Austen there was something discreditable in writing *Pride and Prejudice*. And, I wondered, would *Pride and Prejudice* have been a better novel if Jane Austen had not thought it necessary to hide her manuscript from visitors? I read a page or two to see; but I could not find any signs that her circumstances had harmed her work in the slightest. That, perhaps, was the chief miracle about it. Here was a woman about the year 1800 writing without hate, without bitterness, without fear, without protest, without

[1]Sarah Emily Davies (1830–1921), British feminist responsible for the admission of women to University College, London (1870) and the foundation of Girton College, Cambridge (1873). [Ed.]

[2]*Memoir of Jane Austen,* by her nephew, James Edward Austen-Leigh. [Au.]

preaching. That was how Shakespeare wrote, I thought, looking at *Antony and Cleopatra;* and when people compare Shakespeare and Jane Austen, they may mean that the minds of both had consumed all impediments; and for that reason we do not know Jane Austen and we do not know Shakespeare, and for that reason Jane Austen pervades every word that she wrote, and so does Shakespeare. If Jane Austen suffered in any way from her circumstances it was in the narrowness of life that was imposed upon her. It was impossible for a woman to go about alone. She never travelled; she never drove through London in an omnibus or had luncheon in a shop by herself. But perhaps it was the nature of Jane Austen not to want what she had not. Her gift and her circumstances matched each other completely. But I doubt whether that was true of Charlotte Brontë, I said, opening *Jane Eyre* and laying it beside *Pride and Prejudice.*

I opened it at chapter twelve and my eye was caught by the phrase, "Anybody may blame me who likes." What were they blaming Charlotte Brontë for, I wondered? And I read how Jane Eyre used to go up on the roof when Mrs. Fairfax was making jellies and looked over the fields at the distant view. And then she longed — and it was for this that they blamed her — that "then I longed for a power of vision which might overpass that limit; which might reach the busy world, towns, regions full of life I had heard of but never seen: that then I desired more of practical experience than I possessed; more of intercourse with my kind, of acquaintance with variety of character than was here within my reach. I valued what was good in Mrs. Fairfax, and what was good in Adèle; but I believed in the existence of other and more vivid kinds of goodness, and what I believed in I wished to behold.

"Who blames me? Many, no doubt, and I shall be called discontented. I could not help it: the restlessness was in my nature; it agitated me to pain sometimes. . . .

"It is vain to say human beings ought to be satisfied with tranquillity: they must have action; and they will make it if they cannot find it. Millions are condemned to a stiller doom than mine, and millions are in silent revolt against their lot. Nobody knows how many rebellions ferment in the masses of life which people earth. Women are supposed to be very calm generally: but women feel just as men feel; they need exercise for their faculties and a field for their efforts as much as their brothers do; they suffer from too rigid a restraint, too absolute a stagnation, precisely as men would suffer; and it is narrow-minded in their more privileged fellow-creatures to say that they ought to confine themselves to making puddings and knitting stockings, to playing on the piano and embroidering bags. It is thoughtless to condemn them, or laugh at them, if they seek to do more or learn more than custom has pronounced necessary for their sex.

"When thus alone I not unfrequently heard Grace Poole's laugh. . . ."

That is an awkward break, I thought. It is upsetting to come upon Grace Poole all of a sudden. The continuity is disturbed. One might say, I continued, laying the book down beside *Pride and Prejudice,* that the woman who wrote those pages had more genius in her than Jane Austen; but if one reads them over and marks that jerk in them, that indignation, one sees that she will never get her genius expressed whole and entire. Her books will be deformed and twisted. She will write in a rage where she should write calmly. She will write foolishly where she should write wisely. She will write of herself where she should write of her characters. She is at war with her lot. How could she help but die young, cramped and thwarted?

One could not but play for a moment with the thought of what might have happened if Charlotte Brontë had possessed say three hundred a year — but the foolish woman sold the copyright of her novels outright for fifteen hundred pounds; had somehow possessed more knowledge of the busy world, and towns and regions full of life; more practical experience, and intercourse with her kind and acquaintance with a variety of character. In those words she puts her finger exactly not only upon her own defects as a novelist but upon those of her sex at that time. She knew, no one better, how enormously her genius would have profited if it had not spent itself in solitary visions over distant fields; if experience and intercourse and travel had been granted her. But they were not granted; they were withheld; and we must accept the fact that all those good novels, *Villette, Emma, Wuthering Heights, Middlemarch,* were written by women without more experience of life than could enter the house of a respectable clergyman; written too in the common sitting-room of that respectable house and by women so poor that they could not afford to buy more than a few quires of paper at a time upon which to write *Wuthering Heights* or *Jane Eyre*. One of them, it is true, George Eliot, escaped after much tribulation, but only to a secluded villa in St. John's Wood. And there she settled down in the shadow of the world's disapproval. "I wish it to be understood," she wrote, "that I should never invite any one to come and see me who did not ask for the invitation"; for was she not living in sin with a married man and might not the sight of her damage the chastity of Mrs. Smith or whoever it might be that chanced to call? One must submit to the social convention, and be "cut off from what is called the world." At the same time, on the other side of Europe, there was a young man living freely with this gipsy or with that great lady; going to the wars; picking up unhindered and uncensored all that varied experience of human life which served him so splendidly later when he came to write his books. Had Tolstoy lived at the Priory in seclusion with a married lady "cut off from what is called the world," however edifying the moral lesson, he could scarcely, I thought, have written *War and Peace*.

But one could perhaps go a little deeper into the question of novel-writing and the effect of sex upon the novelist. If one shuts one's eyes and thinks of the novel as a whole, it would seem to be a creation owning a certain looking-glass likeness to life, though of course with simplifications and distortions innumerable. At any rate, it is a structure leaving a shape on the mind's eye, built now in squares, now pagoda shaped, now throwing out wings and arcades, now solidly compact and domed like the Cathedral of Saint Sofia at Constantinople. This shape, I thought, thinking back over certain famous novels, starts in one the kind of emotion that is appropriate to it. But that emotion at once blends itself with others, for the "shape" is not made by the relation of stone to stone, but by the relation of human being to human being. Thus a novel starts in us all sorts of antagonistic and opposed emotions. Life conflicts with something that is not life. Hence the difficulty of coming to any agreement about novels, and the immense sway that our private prejudices have upon us. On the one hand, we feel You — John the hero — must live, or I shall be in the depths of despair. On the other, we feel, Alas, John, you must die, because the shape of the book requires it. Life conflicts with something that is not life. Then since life it is in part, we judge it as life. James is the sort of man I most detest, one says. Or, This is a farrago of absurdity. I could never feel anything of the sort myself. The whole structure, it is obvious, thinking back on any famous novel, is one of infinite complexity, because it is thus made up of so many different judgments, of so many different kinds of emotion. The wonder is that any book so composed holds together for more than a year or two, or can possibly mean to the English reader what it means for the Russian or the Chinese. But they do hold together occasionally very remarkably. And what holds them together in these rare instances of survival (I was thinking of *War and Peace*) is something that one calls integrity, though it has nothing to do with paying one's bills or behaving honourably in an emergency. What one means by integrity, in the case of the novelist, is the conviction that he gives one that this is the truth. Yes, one feels, I should never have thought that this could be so; I have never known people behaving like that. But you have convinced me that so it is, so it happens. One holds every phrase, every scene to the light as one reads — for Nature seems, very oddly, to have provided us with an inner light by which to judge of the novelist's integrity or disintegrity. Or perhaps it is rather that Nature, in her most irrational mood, has traced in invisible ink on the walls of the mind a premonition which these great artists confirm; a sketch which only needs to be held to the fire of genius to become visible. When one so exposes it and sees it come to life one exclaims in rapture, But this is what I have always felt and known and desired! And one boils over with excitement, and, shutting the book even with a kind of reverence as if it were something very precious, a stand-by to return to as long as one lives, one puts it back on the shelf, I said, taking *War and Peace* and putting it back in its place. If, on the other hand, these poor sentences that one takes and tests rouse first a quick and eager response with their bright colouring and their dashing gestures but there they stop: something seems to check them in their development: or if they bring to light only a faint scribble in that corner and a blot over there, and nothing appears whole and entire, then one heaves a sigh of disappointment and says, Another failure. This novel has come to grief somewhere.

And for the most part, of course, novels do come to grief somewhere. The imagination falters under the enormous strain. The insight is confused; it can no longer distinguish between the true and false; it has no longer the strength to go on with the vast labour that calls at every moment for the use of so many different faculties. But how would all this be affected by the sex of the novelist, I wondered, looking at *Jane Eyre* and the others. Would the fact of her sex in any way interfere with the integrity of a woman novelist — that integrity which I take to be the backbone of the writer? Now, in the passages I have quoted from *Jane Eyre,* it is clear that anger was tampering with the integrity of Charlotte Brontë the novelist. She left her story, to which her entire devotion was due, to attend to some personal grievance. She remembered that she had been starved of her proper due of experience — she had been made to stagnate in a parsonage mending stockings when she wanted to wander free over the world. Her imagination swerved from indignation and we feel it swerve. But there were many more influences than anger tugging at her imagination and deflecting it from its path. Ignorance, for instance. The portrait of Rochester is drawn in the dark. We feel the influence of fear in it; just as we constantly feel an acidity which is the result of oppression, a buried suffering smouldering beneath her passion, a rancour which contracts those books, splendid as they are, with a spasm of pain.

And since a novel has this correspondence to real life, its values are to some extent those of real life. But it is obvious that the values of women differ very often from the values which have been made by the other sex; naturally, this is so. Yet it is the masculine values that prevail. Speaking crudely, football and sport are "important"; the worship of fashion, the buying of clothes "trivial." And these values are inevitably transferred from life to fiction. This is an important book, the critic assumes, because it deals with war. This is an insignificant book because it deals with the feelings of women in a drawing-room. A scene in a battlefield is more important than a scene in a shop — everywhere and much more subtly the difference of value persists. The whole structure, therefore, of the early nineteenth-century novel was raised, if one was a woman, by a mind which was slightly pulled from the straight, and made to alter its clear vision in deference to external authority. One has only to skim those old forgotten novels and listen to the tone of voice in which they were written to divine that the writer was meeting criticism; she was saying this by way of aggression, or that by way of conciliation. She was admitting that she was "only a woman," or protesting that she was "as good as a man." She met that criticism as her temperament dictated, with docility and diffidence, or with anger and emphasis. It does not matter which it was; she was thinking of something other than the thing itself. Down comes her book upon our heads. There was a flaw in the centre of it. And I thought of all the women's novels that lie scattered, like small pock-marked apples in an orchard, about the secondhand book shops of London. It was the flaw in the centre that had rotted them. She had altered her values in deference to the opinion of others.

But how impossible it must have been for them not to budge either to the right or to the left. What genius, what integrity it must have required in face of all that criticism, in the midst of that purely patriarchal society, to hold fast to the thing as they saw it without shrinking. Only Jane Austen did it and Emily Brontë. It is another feather, perhaps the finest, in their caps. They wrote as women write, not as men write. Of all the thousand women who wrote novels then, they alone entirely ignored the perpetual admonitions of the eternal pedagogue — write this, think that. They alone were deaf to that persistent voice, now grumbling, now patronising, now domineering, now grieved, now shocked, now angry, now avuncular, that voice which cannot let women alone, but must be at them, like some too conscientious governess, adjuring them, like Sir Egerton Brydges, to be refined; dragging even into the criticism of poetry criticism of sex;[3] admonishing them, if they would be good and win, as I suppose, some shiny prize, to keep within certain limits which the gentleman in question thinks suitable: ". . . female novelists should only aspire to excellence by courageously acknowledging the limitations of their sex."[4] That puts the matter in a nutshell, and when I tell you, rather to your surprise, that this sentence was written not in August 1828 but in August 1928, you will agree, I think, that however delightful it is to us now, it represents a vast body of opinion — I am not going to stir those old pools, I take only what chance has floated to my feet — that was far more vigorous and far more vocal a century ago. It would have needed a very stalwart young woman in 1828 to disregard all those snubs and chidings and promises of prizes. One must have been something of a firebrand to say to oneself, Oh, but they can't buy literature too. Literature is open to everybody. I refuse to allow you, Beadle though you are, to turn me off the grass. Lock up your libraries if you like; but there is no gate, no lock, no bolt that you can set upon the freedom of my mind.

But whatever effect discouragement and criticism had upon their writing — and I believe that they had a very great effect — that was unimportant compared with the other difficulty which faced them (I was still considering those early nineteenth-century novelists) when they came to set their thoughts on paper — that is that they had no tradition behind them, or one so short and partial that it was of little help. For we think back through our mothers if we are women. It is useless to go to the great men writers for help, however much one may go to them for pleasure. Lamb, Browne, Thackeray, Newman, Sterne, Dickens, De Quincey — whoever it may be — never helped a woman yet, though she may have learnt a few tricks of them and adapted them to her use. The weight, the pace, the stride of a man's mind are too unlike her own for her to lift anything substantial from him successfully. The ape is too distant to be sedulous. Perhaps the first thing she would find, setting pen to paper, was that there was no common sentence ready for her use. All the great novelists like Thackeray and Dickens and Balzac have written a natural prose, swift but not slovenly, expressive but not precious, taking their own tint without ceasing to be common property. They have based it on the sentence that was current at the time. The sentence that was current at the beginning of the nineteenth century ran something like this perhaps: "The grandeur of their works was an argument with them, not to stop short, but to proceed. They could have no higher excitement or satisfaction than in the exercise of their art and endless generations of truth and beauty. Success prompts to exertion; and habit facilitates success." That is a man's sentence; behind it one can see Johnson, Gibbon and the rest. It was a sentence that was unsuited for a woman's use. Charlotte Brontë, with all her splendid gift for prose, stumbled and fell with that clumsy weapon in her hands. George Eliot committed atrocities with it that beggar description. Jane Austen looked at it and laughed at it and devised a perfectly natural, shapely sentence proper for her own use and never departed from it. Thus, with less genius for writing than Charlotte Brontë, she got infinitely more said. Indeed, since freedom and fullness of expression are of the essence of the art, such a lack of tradition, such a scarcity and inadequacy of tools, must have told enormously upon the writing of women. Moreover, a book is not made of sentences laid end to end, but of sentences built, if an image helps, into arcades or domes. And this shape too has been made by men out of their own needs for their own uses. There is no reason to think that the form of the epic or of the poetic play suits a woman any more than the sentence suits her. But all the older forms of litera-

[3]"[She] has a metaphysical purpose, and that is a dangerous obsession, especially with a woman, for women rarely possess men's healthy love of rhetoric. It is a strange lack in the sex which is in other things more primitive and more materialistic." — *New Criterion,* June 1928. [Au.]

[4]"If, like the reporter, you believe that female novelists should only aspire to excellence by courageously acknowledging the limitations of their sex (Jane Austen [has] demonstrated how gracefully this gesture can be accomplished). . . ." — *Life and Letters,* August 1928. [Au.]

ture were hardened and set by the time she became a writer. The novel alone was young enough to be soft in her hands — another reason, perhaps, why she wrote novels. Yet who shall say that even now "the novel" (I give it inverted commas to mark my sense of the words' inadequacy), who shall say that even this most pliable of all forms is rightly shaped for her use? No doubt we shall find her knocking that into shape for herself when she has the free use of her limbs; and providing some new vehicle, not necessarily in verse, for the poetry in her. For it is the poetry that is still denied outlet. And I went on to ponder how a woman nowadays would write a poetic tragedy in five acts — would she use verse — would she not use prose rather?

Martin Heidegger

1889–1976

Martin Heidegger, born in Messkirch in the German province of Basel, was educated at the University of Freiburg where he studied under the phenomenologist Edmund Husserl. Heidegger began teaching at Freiburg in 1915, left to become a *privatdozent* at Marburg in 1923, and returned as professor of philosophy to Freiburg the year after the publication of his magnum opus, *Being and Time* (1927).

Briefly, *Being and Time* represents human beings as isolated individuals thrown helplessly into worlds not of their own making, who understand existence only through their interactions with the worlds they inhabit. This mode of existence Heidegger called *Dasein,* a coinage that is usually translated as "Being-There" or "Being-in-the-World." If our *Dasein* involves being endlessly distracted by the trivial everyday struggles within a mass society, human beings nevertheless are driven relentlessly to seek *Sein* (true Being), a transcendent state in which the meaning of life would be clarified. But this quest is by its very nature absurd. In Heidegger's philosophy, no romantic transcendence to the higher level of Being is possible: The best we can attain is an authentic (*eigentlich*) existence. Authenticity is predicated on three interlocking issues: (1) dread, the nauseating sense that our own death is the only thing indisputably our own; (2) conscience, the sense that while we cannot choose the world into which we are thrown, we can always choose how we act within it; and (3) history, the subjective sense of the relation of our personal destiny to the fate of the other human beings among whom we live.

If all this sounds a bit like the tenets of French existentialism, that is no accident: While studying in Berlin in 1933, Jean-Paul Sartre was immensely influenced by Heidegger's *Being and Time.* But for Heidegger, the relation of the individual to others making up the world was important in different ways than for Sartre. Heidegger was certain this relation was being destroyed by the fragmentation of modern life and emphasized each individual's need for a homeland and a folk culture with which to identify. He was thus attracted not to the internationalist and socialist Left in Germany, but to the reactionary parties of the Right who stressed the uniqueness of the German *Volk.*

When the National Socialists took power in Germany in 1933, Heidegger successfully campaigned to be made rector of the university, a position that he resigned ten months later when it became clear that the Nazis were merely using him and that his program to restructure the university was not going to be implemented. Heidegger continued to teach at the university and, during the later years of the Reich, increasingly distanced himself from Hitler's methods and goals, claiming after the war to have in effect created an "intellectual resistance" in his classes. While questions have been raised about precisely what damage Heidegger did in the service of Nazism to his Jewish and socialist colleagues, he was certainly, at least during 1933–34, not simply an opportunistic timeserver but an enthusiastic supporter of the Nazis' racial ideas and political program. Even after the fall of Hitler, Heidegger refused to apologize for his speeches and acts under the Nazi regime and unrepentently viewed the German people as a race of high destiny beset by two barbarian mass societies: the Soviet Union and the United States. He died in his home town of Messkirch in 1976.

Despite his political and racial views, Heidegger was — together with Ludwig Wittgenstein — one of the most important influences on twentieth-century philosophy. Curiously enough, those he has influenced most decisively have not been conservatives or reactionaries but have located their politics either on the radical Left (not only Jean-Paul Sartre but cultural theorist Michel Foucault) or the liberal Center (such as theologians Rudolf Bultmann, Karl Jaspers, and Paul Tillich; political philosopher Hannah Arendt; phenomenologist Hans-Georg Gadamer; and deconstructionist Jacques Derrida). Heidegger's radical critique of science and its rhetoric underlies the thought of philosophers of science Thomas S. Kuhn (*The Structure of Scientific Revolutions,* 1970) and Paul Feyerabend (*Against Method,* 1975). His principal message, on the nature of man and human experience and the vital role of language (including poetic language) in our understanding of the world, has inspired many who were deeply disgusted by his life and politics, and it continues to underlie much of contemporary criticism.

Heidegger's essay, "Hölderlin and the Essence of Poetry" (1936), uses touchstones within texts of the poet Friedrich Hölderlin (1770–1843) to develop the theory of poetry and language that he presents at greater length in "The Origin of the Work of Art" (1936). Here Hölderlin's Romantic lyrics, rediscovered early in the twentieth century, provide perfect "pointers" for the turns of Heidegger's thought because they combine an intense subjective inwardness with serene abstraction, like a combination of Shelley with Wallace Stevens. Heidegger is able to use phrases and lines from Hölderlin's poetry to convey some of the basic themes that he developed in *Being and Time* and never abandoned. For example, in a prose poem, Hölderlin's seemingly chance phrase, "but Man dwells in huts," reminds Heidegger of the alienation of our species from Nature. The need to make houses becomes, for Heidegger, a metaphor for the need to choose one's being, to determine with authenticity precisely who one is. But while the essay recapitulates many of the themes of *Being and Time,* Heidegger here seems more influenced by the later works of Nietzsche than by Husserl, his former teacher. It is aesthetics and language, rather than quotidian experience, that Heidegger portrays as the cornerstone on which the vision of life is built.

Heidegger viewed art as the bringing-into-being of something new, a new world. In part this means that a work of art opens new worlds to us in the usual sense, by exposing us to an aspect of human experience that we would not know otherwise. Some of us don't have access to a certain form of play of language, for example, till we experience the works of James Joyce or Vladimir Nabokov. But in part it means something more. When Heidegger asserts that "Poetry is the primitive language of a historical people," he is insisting on the way in which language itself can become a homeland. As a result of the work of the poet, Heidegger believes, art can function as the "homeland" that he felt mass culture was distancing us from; it can give back to us the beauty and truth of certain aspects of experience that modern culture treats as mere instrumentalities.

This may seem like a version of Romantic aesthetics — like Hegel's view of art as a bearer of truth, or Shelley's argument in the "Defence of Poetry" that "Poets are the unacknowledged legislators of the World" (see p. 356) — but Heidegger puts it this way: "The speech of the poet is establishment . . . in the sense of the firm basing of human existence on its foundation." In fact, Heidegger's formulation goes much farther than Hegel's or Shelley's. Those Romantic idealists view the Truth or Law borne by the work of art as an independent essence prior to all human thought, which is discovered by the spirit of the artist and then conveyed to mankind by means of the poem. But for Heidegger, there are no such essences prior to thinking. The truth *in* the work is the truth *of* the work; the truth happens when it comes into historical existence, in that contingent moment when the work is made, when the poem is written or the painting painted. And it "happens" again when we read or view and understand the poem or the painting.

At the center of the Hölderlin essay, Heidegger briefly takes up the question of Language: "Language is not a mere tool, one of the many which man possesses; on the contrary, it is only language that affords the very possibility of standing in the openness of the existent. Only where there is language, is there world. . . . Only where world predominates, is there history" (see pp. 565–566). These remarks about language as the ground-of-being of the truth that is poetry hint at something new, for they suggest that the most basic level of existence is no longer lonely *Dasein* (Being-in-the-World) but the collective conversation that forms human Language.

These hints are developed into major themes in Heidegger's later work, which, like Nietzsche's later work, grounds his vision of reality on aesthetics. In his later essays, including "Language" (1950), "A Dialogue on Language" (1953–54), and "The Way to Language" (1959), Language replaces *Dasein* as the bedrock from which the world is called into being; it is not *Dasein* that speaks to us but Language, whose mystical power of naming and showing calls the world into existence for us. In his essay, "Language," Heidegger insists that "We do not wish to ground language in something else that is not language itself."[1] And, in "The Nature of Language," Heidegger enigmatically follows out the implications of the poet Stefan Georg's line "Where word breaks off, no thing may be," and himself poetically suggests how language creates the universe we experience: "When the word is called the mouth's flower and its blossom, we hear the sound of language rising like the earth. From whence? From Saying in which it comes to pass that World is made to appear. The sound rings out in the resounding assembly call which, open to the Open, makes World appear in all things."[2] From here it is no distance at all to St. John's mystical vision of the Logos that is God.

[1]"Language." In *Poetry, Language and Thought,* p. 191.
[2]"The Nature of Language." In *On the Way to Language,* p. 101.

Selected Bibliography

Bourdieu, Pierre. *The Political Ontology of Martin Heidegger.* Stanford: Stanford University Press, 1991.

Davis, Walter A. *Inwardness and Existence: Subjectivity in Hegel, Heidegger, Marx, and Freud.* Madison: University of Wisconsin Press, 1989.

Foti, Veronique M. *Heidegger and the Poets: Poesis—Sophia—Techne.* New York: Humanities Press International, 1995.

Gadamer, Hans-Georg. *Heidegger's Ways.* Albany: State University of New York Press, 1994.

Heidegger, Martin. *Martin Heidegger: Existence and Being,* trans. Douglas Scott. Chicago: Henry Regnery, 1949.

———. *Being and Time,* trans. John Macquarrie and Edward Robinson, 1927. New York: Harper and Row, 1962.

———. *On the Way to Language,* trans. Peter D. Hertz. New York: Harper and Row, 1971.

———. *Poetry, Language and Thought,* trans. Albert Hofstadter. New York: Harper and Row, 1971.

Megill, Alan. *Prophets of Extremity: Nietzsche, Heidegger, Foucault, Derrida.* Berkeley: University of California Press, 1985.

Ott, Hugo. *Martin Heidegger: A Political Life.* New York: Basic Books, 1993.

Rorty, Richard. *Philosophical Papers: Essays on Heidegger and Others,* vol. 2. New York and London: Cambridge University Press, 1991.

Sass, Hans-Martin. *Martin Heidegger: Bibliography and Glossary.* Bowling Green, OH: Bowling Green University Press, 1982.

Spanos, William V. *Heidegger and Criticism: Retrieving the Cultural Politics of Destruction.* Minneapolis: University of Minnesota Press, 1993.

Wolin, Richard, ed. *The Heidegger Controversy: A Critical Reader.* Cambridge, MA: MIT Press, 1992.

Hölderlin and the Essence of Poetry

THE FIVE POINTERS

1. Writing poetry: "That most innocent of all occupations." (III, 377.)
2. "Therefore has language, most dangerous of possessions, been given to man . . . so that he may affirm what he is. . . ." (IV, 246.)
3. "Much has man learnt.
   Many of the heavenly ones has he named,
   Since we have been a conversation
   And have been able to hear from one another." (IV, 343.)
4. "But that which remains, is established by the poets." (IV, 63.)
5. "Full of merit, and yet poetically, dwells Man on this earth." (VI, 25.)

Why has Hölderlin's work been chosen for the purpose of showing the essence of poetry? Why not Homer or Sophocles, why not Virgil or Dante, why not Shakespeare or Goethe? The essence of poetry is realised in the works of these poets too, and more richly even, than in the creative work of Hölderlin, which breaks off so early and abruptly.

Translated by Douglas Scott.

This may be so. And yet Hölderlin has been chosen, and he alone. But generally speaking is it possible for the universal essence of poetry to be read off from the work of one single poet? Whatever is universal, that is to say, what is valid for many, can only be reached through a process of comparison. For this, one requires a sample containing the greatest possible diversity of poems and kinds of poetry. From this point of view Hölderlin's poetry is only one among many others. By itself it can in no way suffice as a criterion for determining the essence of poetry. Hence we fail in our purpose at the very outset. Certainly — so long as we take "essence of poetry" to mean what is gathered together into a universal concept, which is then valid in the same way for every poem. But this universal which thus applies equally to every particular, is always the indifferent, that essence which can never become essential.

Yet it is precisely this essential element of the essence that we are searching for — that which compels us to decide whether we are going to take poetry seriously and if so how, whether and to what extent we can bring with us the presuppositions necessary if we are to come under the sway of poetry.

Hölderlin has not been chosen because his work, one among many, realises the universal essence of poetry, but solely because Hölderlin's poetry was borne on by the poetic vocation to write expressly of the essence of poetry. For us Hölderlin is in a pre-eminent sense *the poet of the poet.* That is why he compels a decision.

But — to write about the poet, is this not a symptom of a perverted narcissism and at the same time a confession of inadequate richness of vision? To write about the poet, is that not a senseless exaggeration, something decadent and a blind alley?

The answer will be given in what follows. To be sure, the path by which we reach the answer is one of expediency. We cannot here, as would have to be done, expound separately each of Hölderlin's poems one after the other. Instead let us take only five pointers which the poet gave on the subject of poetry. The necessary order in these sayings and their inner connectedness ought to bring before our eyes the essential essence of poetry.

1

In a letter to his mother in January 1799, Hölderlin calls the writing of poetry "that most innocent of all occupations" (III, 377). To what extent is it the "most innocent"? Writing poetry appears in the modest guise of *play.* Unfettered, it invents its world of images and remains immersed in the realm of the imagined. This play thus avoids the seriousness of decisions, which always in one way or another create guilt. Hence writing poetry is completely harmless. And at the same time it is ineffectual; since it remains mere saying and speaking. It has nothing about it of action, which grasps hold directly of the real and alters it. Poetry is like a dream, and not reality; a playing with words, and not the seriousness of action. Poetry is harmless and ineffectual. For what can be less dangerous than mere speech? But in taking poetry to be the "most innocent of all occupations," we have not yet comprehended its essence. At any rate this gives us an indication of where we must look for it. Poetry creates its works in the realm and out of the "material" of language. What does Hölderlin say about language? Let us hear a second saying of the poet.

2

In a fragmentary sketch, dating from the same period (1800) as the letter just quoted, the poet says:

> But man dwells in huts and wraps himself in the bashful garment, since he is more fervent and more attentive too in watching over the spirit, as the priestess the divine flame; this is his understanding. And therefore he has been given arbitrariness, and to him, godlike, has been given higher power to command and to accomplish, and therefore has language, most dangerous of possessions, been given to man, so that creating, destroying, and perishing and returning to the ever-living, to the mistress and mother, he may affirm what he is — that he has inherited, learned from thee, thy most divine possession, all-preserving love. (IV, 246.)

Language, the field of the "most innocent of all occupations," is the "most dangerous of possessions." How can these two be reconciled? Let us put this question aside for the moment and consider the three preliminary questions:

1. Whose possession is language? 2. To what extent is it the most dangerous of possessions? 3. In what sense is it really a possession?

First of all we notice where this saying about language occurs: in the sketch for a poem which is to describe who man is, in contrast to the other beings of nature; mention is made of the rose, the swans, the stag in the forest (IV, 300 and 385). So, distinguishing plants from animals, the fragment begins: "But man dwells in huts."

And who then is man? He who must affirm what he is. To affirm means to declare; but at the same time it means: to give in the declaration a guarantee of what is declared. Man is *he* who he *is,* precisely in the affirmation of his own existence. This affirmation does not mean here an additional and supplementary expression of human existence, but it does in the process make plain the existence of man. But what must man affirm? That he belongs to the earth. This relation of belonging to consists in the fact that man is heir and learner in all things. But all these things are in conflict. That which keeps things apart in opposition and thus at the same time binds them together, is called by Hölderlin "intimacy." The affirmation of belonging to this intimacy occurs through the creation of a world and its ascent, and likewise through the destruction of a world and its decline. The affirmation of human existence and hence its essential consummation occurs through freedom of decision. This freedom lays hold of the necessary and places itself in the bonds of a supreme obligation. This bearing witness of belonging to all that is existent, becomes actual as history. In order that history may be possible, language has been given to man. It is one of man's possessions.

But to what extent is language the "most dangerous of possessions?" It is the danger of all dangers, because it creates initially the possibility of a danger. Danger is the threat to existence from what is existent. But now it is only by virtue of language at all that man is exposed to something manifest, which, *as* what is existent, afflicts and enflames man in his existence, and as what is non-existent deceives and disappoints. It is language which first creates the manifest conditions for menace and confusion to existence, and thus the possibility of the loss of existence, that is to say — danger. But language is not only the danger of dangers, but necessarily conceals in itself a continual danger for itself. Language has the task of making manifest in its work the existent, and of preserving it as such. In it, what is purest and what is most concealed, and likewise what is complex and ordinary, can be expressed in words. Even the essential word, if it is to be understood and so become a possession in common, must make itself ordinary. Accordingly it is remarked in another fragment of Hölderlin's: "Thou spokest to the Godhead, but this you have all forgotten, that the first-fruits are never for mortals, they belong to the gods. The fruit must become more ordinary, more everyday, and then it will be mortals' own." (IV, 238.) The pure and the ordinary are both equally something said. Hence the word as word never gives any direct guarantee as to whether it is an essential word or a counterfeit. On the contrary — an essential word often looks in its simplicity like an unessential one. And on the other hand that which is dressed up to look like the essential, is only something recited by heart or repeated. Therefore language must constantly present itself in an appearance which it itself attests, and hence endanger what is most characteristic of it, the genuine saying.

In what sense however is this most dangerous thing one of man's possessions? Language is his own property. It is at his disposal for the purpose of communicating his experiences, resolutions and moods. Language serves to give information. As a fit instrument for this, it is a "possession."[1] But the essence of language does not consist entirely in being a means of giving information. This definition does not touch its essential essence, but merely indicates an effect of its essence. Language is not a mere tool, one of the many which man possesses; on the contrary, it is only language that affords the very possibility of standing in the openness of the existent. Only where there is language, is there world, i.e., the perpetually altering circuit of decision and pro-

[1]The German word *"Gut,"* which has been translated throughout as "possession," also has the meaning of "a good thing"; it is thus related to the English word "goods" as in "goods and chattels." [Tr.]

duction, of action and responsibility, but also of commotion and arbitrariness, of decay and confusion. Only where world predominates, is there history. Language is a possession[2] in a more fundamental sense. It is good for the fact that (i.e., it affords a guarantee that) man can *exist* historically. Language is not a tool at his disposal, rather it is that event which disposes of the supreme possibility of human existence. We must first of all be certain of this essence of language, in order to comprehend truly the sphere of action of poetry and with it poetry itself. How does language become actual? In order to find the answer to this question, let us consider a third saying of Hölderlin's.

3

We come across this saying in a long and involved sketch for the unfinished poem which begins "Versöhnender, der du nimmergeglaubt . . ." (IV, 162ff. and 339ff.):

> Much has man learnt.
> Many of the heavenly ones has he named,
> Since we have been a conversation
> And have been able to hear from one another. (IV, 343.)

Let us first pick out from these lines the part which has a direct bearing on what we have said so far: "Since we have been a conversation . . ." We — mankind — are a conversation. The being of men is founded in language. But this only becomes actual in *conversation.* Nevertheless the latter is not merely a manner in which language is put into effect, rather it is only as conversation that language is essential. What we usually mean by language, namely, a stock of words and syntactical rules, is only a threshold of language. But now what is meant by "a conversation"? Plainly, the act of speaking with others about something. Then speaking also brings about the process of coming together. But Hölderlin says: "Since we have been a conversation and have been able to hear from one another." Being able to hear is not a mere consequence of speaking with one another, on the contrary it is rather pre-supposed in the latter process. But even the ability to hear is itself also adapted to the possibility of the word and makes use of it. The ability to speak and the ability to hear are equally fundamental. We are a conversation — and that means: we can hear from one another. We are a conversation, that always means at the same time: we are a *single* conversation. But the unity of a conversation consists in the fact that in the essential word there is always manifest that one and the same thing on which we agree, and on the basis of which we are united and so are essentially ourselves. Conversation and its unity support our existence.

But Hölderlin does not say simply: we are a conversation — but: "Since we have been a conversation . . ." Where the human faculty of speech is present and is exercised, that is not by itself sufficient for the essential actualisation of language — conversation. Since when have we been a conversation? Where there is to be a *single* conversation, the essential word must be constantly related to the one and the same. Without this relation an argument too is absolutely impossible. But the one and the same can only be manifest in the light of something perpetual and permanent. Yet permanence and perpetuity only appear when what persists and is present begins to shine. But that happens in the moment when time opens out and extends. After man has placed himself in the presence of something perpetual, then only can he expose himself to the changeable, to that which comes and goes; for only the persistent is changeable. Only after "ravenous time" has been riven into present, past and future, does the possibility arise of agreeing on something permanent. We have been a single conversation since the time when it "is time." Ever since time arose, we have *existed* historically. Both — existence as a *single* conversation and historical existence — are alike ancient, they belong together and are the same thing.

Since we have been a conversation — man has learnt much and named many of the heavenly ones. Since language really became actual as conversation, the gods have acquired names and a world has appeared. But again it should be noticed: the presence of the gods and the appearance of the world are not merely a consequence

[2]See note 1. [Tr.]

of the actualisation of language, they are contemporaneous with it. And this to the extent that it is precisely in the naming of the gods, and in the transmutation of the world into word, that the real conversation, which we ourselves are, consists.

But the gods can acquire a name only by addressing and, as it were, claiming us. The word which names the gods is always a response to such a claim. This response always springs from the responsibility of a destiny. It is in the process by which the gods bring our existence to language, that we enter the sphere of the decision as to whether we are to yield ourselves to the gods or withhold ourselves from them.

Only now can we appreciate in its entirety what is meant by: "Since we have been a conversation . . ." Since the gods have led us into conversation, since time has been time, ever since then the basis of our existence has been a conversation. The proposition that language is the supreme event of human existence has through it acquired its meaning and foundation.

But the question at once arises: how does this conversation, which we are, begin? Who accomplishes this naming of the gods? Who lays hold of something permanent in ravenous time and fixes it in the word? Hölderlin tells us with the sure simplicity of the poet. Let us hear a fourth saying.

4

This saying forms the conclusion of the poem "Remembrance" and runs:

> But that which remains, is established by the poets. (IV. 63.)

This saying throws light on our question about the essence of poetry. Poetry is the act of establishing by the word and in the word. What is established in this manner? The permanent. But can the permanent be established then? Is it not that which has always been present? No! Even the permanent must be fixed so that it will not be carried away, the simple must be wrested from confusion, proportion must be set before what lacks proportion. That which supports and dominates the existent in its entirety must become manifest. Being must be opened out, so that the existent may appear. But this very permanent is the transitory. "Thus, swiftly passing is everything heavenly; but not in vain." (IV, 163f.) But that this should remain, is "Entrusted to the poets as a care and a service" (IV, 145). The poet names the gods and names all things in that which they are. This naming does not consist merely in something already known being supplied with a name; it is rather that when the poet speaks the essential word, the existent is by this naming nominated as what it is. So it becomes known *as* existent. Poetry is the establishing of being by means of the word. Hence that which remains is never taken from the transitory. The simple can never be picked out immediately from the intricate. Proportion does not lie in what lacks proportion. We never find the foundation in what is bottomless. Being is never an existent. But, because the being and essence of things can never be calculated and derived from what is present, they must be freely created, laid down and given. Such a free act of giving is establishment.

But when the gods are named originally and the essence of things receives a name, so that things for the first time shine out, human existence is brought into a firm relation and given a basis. The speech of the poet is establishment not only in the sense of the free act of giving, but at the same time in the sense of the firm basing of human existence on its foundation.

If we conceive this essence of poetry as the establishing of being by means of the word, then we can have some inkling of the truth of that saying which Hölderlin spoke long after he had been received into the protection of the night of lunacy.

5

We find this fifth pointer in the long and at the same time monstrous poem which begins:

> In the lovely azure there flowers with its
> Metallic roof the church-tower. (VI, 24ff.)

Here Hölderlin says (line 32f.):

> Full of merit, and yet poetically, dwells
> Man on this earth.

What man works at and pursues is through his own endeavours earned and deserved. "Yet" — says Hölderlin in sharp antithesis, all this does not touch the essence of his sojourn on this earth, all this does not reach the foundation of human existence. The latter is fundamentally "poetic." But we now understand poetry as the inaugural naming of the gods and of the essence of things. To "dwell poetically" means: to stand in the presence of the gods and to be involved in the proximity of the essence of things. Existence is "poetical" in its fundamental aspect — which means at the same time: in so far as it is established (founded), it is not a recompense, but a gift.

Poetry is not merely an ornament accompanying existence, not merely a temporary enthusiasm or nothing but an interest and amusement. Poetry is the foundation which supports history, and therefore it is not a mere appearance of culture, and absolutely not the mere "expression" of a "culture-soul."

That our existence is fundamentally poetic, this cannot in the last resort mean that it is really only a harmless game. But does not Hölderlin himself, in the first pointer which we quoted, call poetry "That most innocent of all occupations?" How can this be reconciled with the essence of poetry as we are now revealing it? This brings us back to the question which we laid aside in the first instance. In now proceeding to answer this question, we will try at the same time to summarise and bring before the inner eye the essence of poetry and of the poet.

First of all it appeared that the field of action of poetry is language. Hence the essence of poetry must be understood through the essence of language. Afterwards it became clear that poetry is the inaugural naming of being and of the essence of all things — not just any speech, but that particular kind which for the first time brings into the open all that which we then discuss and deal with in everyday language. Hence poetry never takes language as a raw material ready to hand, rather it is poetry which first makes language possible. Poetry is the primitive language of a historical people. Therefore, in just the reverse manner, the essence of language must be understood through the essence of poetry.

The foundation of human existence is conversation, in which language does truly become actual. But primitive language is poetry, in which being is established. Yet language is the "most dangerous of possessions." Thus poetry is the most dangerous work — and at the same time the "most innocent of all occupations."

In fact — it is only if we combine these two definitions and conceive them as one, that we fully comprehend the essence of poetry.

But is poetry then truly the most dangerous work? In a letter to a friend, immediately before leaving on his last journey to France, Hölderlin writes:

> O Friend! The world lies before me brighter than it was, and more serious. I feel pleasure at how it moves onward, I feel pleasure when in summer "the ancient holy father with calm hand shakes lightnings of benediction out of the rosy clouds." For amongst all that I can perceive of God, this sign has become for me the chosen one. I used to be able to exult over a new truth, a better insight into that which is above us and around us, now I am frightened lest in the end it should happen with me as with Tantalus of old, who received more from the gods than he was able to digest. (V, 321.)

The poet is exposed to the divine lightnings. This is spoken of in the poem which we must recognise as the purest poetry about the essence of poetry, and which begins:

> When on festive days a countryman goes
> To gaze on his field, in the morning . . . (IV, 151ff.)

There, the last stanza says:

> Yet it behoves us, under the storms of God,
> Ye poets! with uncovered head to stand,
> With our own hand to grasp the very lightning-flash
> Paternal, and to pass, wrapped in song,
> The divine gift to the people.

And a year later, when he had returned to his mother's house, struck down with madness, Hölderlin wrote to the same friend, recalling his stay in France:

> The mighty element, the fire of heaven and the stillness of men, their life amid nature, and their limitation and contentment, have constantly seized

> me, and, as it is told of the heroes, I can truly say that I have been struck by Apollo. (V, 327.)

The excessive brightness has driven the poet into the dark. Is any further evidence necessary as to the extreme danger of his "occupation"? The very destiny itself of the poet tells everything. The passage in Hölderlin's "Empedocles" rings like a premonition:

> He, through whom the spirit speaks, must leave betimes. (III, 154.)

And nevertheless: poetry is the "most innocent of all occupations," Hölderlin writes to this effect in his letter, not only in order to spare his mother, but because he knows that this innocent fringe belongs to the essence of poetry, just as the valley does to the mountain; for how could this most dangerous work be carried on and preserved, if the poet were not "cast out" ("Empedocles" III, 191) from everyday life and protected *against* it by the apparent harmlessness of his occupation?

Poetry looks like a game and yet it is not. A game does indeed bring men together, but in such a way that each forgets himself in the process. In poetry on the other hand, man is reunited on the foundation of his existence. There he comes to rest; not indeed to the seeming rest of inactivity and emptiness of thought, but to that infinite state of rest in which all powers and relations are active (cf. the letter to his brother, dated 1st January, 1799. III, 368f.).

Poetry rouses the appearance of the unreal and of dream in the face of the palpable and clamorous reality, in which we believe ourselves at home. And yet in just the reverse manner, what the poet says and undertakes to be, is the real. So Panthea, with the clairvoyance of a friend, declares of "Empedocles" (III, 78):

> That he himself should be, is
> What is life, and the rest of us are dreams of it.

So in the very appearance of its outer fringe the essence of poetry seems to waver and yet stands firm. In fact it is itself essentially establishment — that is to say: an act of firm foundation.

Yet every inaugural act remains a free gift, and Hölderlin hears it said: "Let poets be free as swallows" (IV, 168). But this freedom is not undisciplined arbitrariness and capricious desire, but supreme necessity.

Poetry, as the act of establishing being, is subject to a *two-fold* control. In considering these integral laws we first grasp the essence entire.

The writing of poetry is the fundamental naming of the gods. But the poetic word only acquires its power of naming, when the gods themselves bring us to language. How do the gods speak?

> .... And signs to us from antiquity are the language of the gods. (IV, 135.)

The speech of the poet is the intercepting of these signs, in order to pass them on to his own people. This intercepting is an act of receiving and yet at the same time a fresh act of giving; for "in the first signs" the poet catches sight already of the completed message and in his word boldly presents what he has glimpsed, so as to tell in advance of the not-yet-fulfilled. So:

> ... the bold spirit, like an eagle
> Before the tempests, flies prophesying
> In the path of his advancing gods. (IV, 135.)

The establishment of being is bound to the signs of the gods. And at the same time the poetic word is only the interpretation of the "voice of the people." This is how Hölderlin names the sayings in which a people remembers that it belongs to the totality of all that exists. But often this voice grows dumb and weary. In general even it is not capable of saying of itself what is true, but has need of those who explain it. The poem which bears the title "Voice of the People," has been handed down to us in two versions. It is above all the concluding stanzas which are different, but the difference is such that they supplement one another. In the first version the ending runs:

> Because it is pious, I honour for love of the heavenly ones
> The people's voice, the tranquil,
> Yet for the sake of gods and men
> May it not always be tranquil too willingly! (IV, 141.)

And the second version is:

. . . and truly
Sayings are good, for they are a reminder
Of the Highest, yet something is also needed
To explain the holy sayings. (IV, 144.)

In this way the essence of poetry is joined on to the laws of the signs of the gods and of the voice of the people, laws which tend towards and away from each other. The poet himself stands between the former — the gods, and the latter — the people. He is one who has been cast out — out into that *Between,* between gods and men. But only and for the first time in this Between is it decided, who man is and where he is settling his existence. "Poetically, dwells man on this earth."

Unceasingly and ever more securely, out of the fullness of the images pressing about him and always more simply, did Hölderlin devote his poetic word to this realm of Between. And this compels us to say that he is the poet of the poet.

Can we continue now to suppose that Hölderlin is entangled in an empty and exaggerated narcissism due to inadequate richness of vision? Or must we recognize that this poet, from an excess of impetus, reaches out with poetic thought into the foundation and the midst of being. It is to *Hölderlin himself* that we must apply what he said of Oedipus in the late poem "In the lovely azure there flowers . . .":

King Oedipus has one
Eye too many perhaps. (VI, 26.)

Hölderlin writes poetry about the essence of poetry — but not in the sense of a timelessly valid concept. This essence of poetry belongs to a determined time. But not in such a way that it merely conforms to this time, as to one which is already in existence. It is that Hölderlin, in the act of establishing the essence of poetry, first determines a new time. It is the time of the gods that have fled *and* of the god that is coming. It is the time *of need,* because it lies under a double lack and a double Not: the No-more of the gods that have fled and the Not-yet of the god that is coming.

The essence of poetry, which Hölderlin establishes, is in the highest degree historical, because it anticipates a historical time; but as a historical essence it is the sole essential essence.

The time is needy and therefore its poet is extremely rich — so rich that he would often like to relax in thoughts of those that have been and in eager waiting for that which is coming and would like only to sleep in this apparent emptiness. But he holds his ground in the Nothing of this night. Whilst the poet remains thus by himself in the supreme isolation of his mission, he fashions truth, vicariously and therefore truly, for his people. The seventh stanza of the elegy "Bread and Wine" (IV, 123f.) tells of this. What it has only been possible to analyse here intellectually, is expressed there poetically.

But Friend! we come too late. The gods are alive, it is true,
But up there above one's head in another world.
Eternally they work there and seem to pay little heed
To whether we live, so attentive are the Heavenly Ones.
For a weak vessel cannot always receive them,
Only now and then does man endure divine abundance.
Life is a dream of them. But madness
Helps, like slumber and strengthens need and night,
Until heroes enough have grown in the iron cradle,
Hearts like, as before, to the Heavenly in power.
Thundering they come. Meanwhile it often seems
Better to sleep than to be thus without companions,
To wait thus, and in the meantime what to do and say
I know not, and what use are poets in a time of need?
But, thou sayest, they are like the wine-god's holy priests,
Who go from land to land in the holy night.

Edmund Wilson

1895–1972

In a career spanning fifty years, from 1920 to 1970, Edmund Wilson came to be widely recognized as one of the leading men of letters in the United States. Raised in genteel circumstances in Red Bank, New Jersey, the son of the state Attorney General, Wilson attended Princeton University, where he was a friend of F. Scott Fitzgerald and was inspired toward a career in letters by the legendary professor of French, Christian Gauss. Wilson served as a reporter for the *New York Sun* before enlisting in the U.S. Army, where he saw action in France during World War I. After the demobilization, he wrote for *Vanity Fair* before becoming the literary editor of *The New Republic* in 1926. Though Wilson was always primarily a critic of literature, he published a novel (*I Thought of Daisy,* 1929), a volume of linked stories (*Memoirs of Hecate County,* 1946), and five volumes of poetry.

It was the appearance of *Axel's Castle* in 1931 that established Wilson's reputation as a critic. His analysis of the function of symbolism in Yeats, Joyce, Proust, Eliot, and Stein and the debt of the twentieth-century writers to the French Symbolist poets, like Valéry and Rimbaud, showed American readers how to interpret the major modernist texts. Wilson wrote as a literary journalist throughout his life, and many of his books, including *The Triple Thinkers* (1938), *Classics and Commercials* (1950), and *The Bit Between My Teeth* (1965) are essentially compilations of his essays for publications like *The New Republic, The New Yorker,* and, at the end of his life, the *New York Review of Books.* These collections deal with a wide variety of texts: *The Triple Thinkers,* for example, takes up Pushkin, Flaubert, Housman, John Jay Chapman, Bernard Shaw, Ben Jonson, and Henry James. An essayist rather than a scholar, Wilson despised and condemned the postwar takeover of literary studies by the academic profession, which he saw as a recrudescence of medieval scholasticism. A late essay, *The Fruits of the MLA* (1968), bitterly attacks the professional critical editions of the American classics, which he felt intruded dryasdust scholarship between the responsive lay reader and the text. His own editions of F. Scott Fitzgerald's posthumous works, *The Last Tycoon* (1941) and *The Crack Up* (1945), are self-consciously self-effacing. Wilson himself was more stringently self-educated than most members of the academic profession. In addition to the French, German, Latin, and Greek that were the common property of educated professionals, Wilson taught himself enough Hebrew and Aramaic to have an educated opinion on the meaning and value of the Dead Sea Scrolls (expressed in *The Scrolls from the Dead Sea,* 1955, later revised as *Israel and the Dead Sea Scrolls,* 1978), and enough Russian to be able to bandy opinions with Vladimir Nabokov about the latter's edition/translation of Pushkin's *Eugene Onegin.* His range of reference was enormous: A minor work, *Red, Black, Blond and Olive* (1956), examines the civilizations of the Zuni Indians, Haiti, Soviet Russia, and Israel.

Wilson married four times; his third wife was the novelist and critic Mary McCarthy. His last years were enlivened by feuds not only with Nabokov and with the MLA but with the far more powerful U.S. Internal Revenue Service, which resented his failure — for principled reasons — to file income tax returns. He died in his mother's family home in Talcottsville, New York. Since his death, he has remained a major figure in the literary landscape because of the posthumous publication of his correspondence with Nabokov, his other letters, and his diaries and journals.

In "The Historical Interpretation of Literature," originally given as a lecture in 1941, and first published in a revised edition of *The Triple Thinkers* (1948), Wilson reacted against the "vulgar Marxism" of contemporary American critics like Granville Hicks, who graded writers on their attitude toward the proletariat's struggle for mastery over the forces of bourgeois capitalism. At the same time, he insisted that the change in material life in the millennia since Sappho and Sophocles requires every artist who does not want merely to reproduce previous masterpieces to reinterpret his or her contemporary culture as "a new set of phenomena which has never yet been mastered." In 1941 Wilson also published *The Wound and the Bow,* a collection of essays on various writers linked by his vision of Philoctetes as a metaphor for the artist in Western society. Philoctetes, the legendary Greek archer, possessed a bow without which Troy could not be taken, but he also had a festering wound which made him abhorrent to society. Wilson suggests that there is a necessary link between Philoctetes's bow and his wound, his godlike talent, and his horrifying curse. Artists too, Wilson suggests, are necessary to redeem their societies but their art comes out of wounds — neuroses — that often make them into social misfits and outcasts.

Although these two works are perhaps Wilson's best-known contributions to contemporary criticism, he can be categorized as neither Marxist nor Freudian. Literature was for Wilson a social text, but he had no dialectical method for analyzing the representations of ideology authors cannot help but create. Like the French literary historian Hippolyte Taine, Wilson read each text as a complex product of its author's life, origins, and times. Nor did Wilson's Freudianism go much beyond the parlor variety of analysis. He was, rather, a broadly learned journalist who saw the need to bring Continental European ideas to a profoundly provincial American audience. If we feel today that we *ought* to have read Kafka and Camus, Brecht and Mann, Dostoevsky and Gogol, whether we have actually done so or not, that is partly because of magisterial critics like Wilson, who assumed that these foreign objects should form part of the average American's furnished mind.

Selected Bibliography

Castronovo, David. *Edmund Wilson.* New York: Ungar, 1984.

Dabney, Lewis M. "Edmund Wilson and *The Wound and the Bow.*" *Sewanee Review* 91 (1983):155–65.

Day, Frank. *Edmund Wilson: A Reference Guide.* New York: Garland, 1990.

Douglas, George H. "Edmund Wilson: The Man of Letters as Journalist." *Journal of Popular Culture* 15 (1981):78–85.

Groth, Janet. *Edmund Wilson: A Critic for Our Time.* Athens: Ohio University Press, 1989.

Meyers, Jeffrey. *Edmund Wilson: A Biography.* New York: Houghton Mifflin, 1995.

Polan, Dana. "Last Intellectual, Lapsed Intellectual?: The Ends of Edmund Wilson." *Boundary* 2, 21 (1994):247–65.
Wilson, Edmund. *Axel's Castle,* 1931; New York: Scribner's, 1961.
———. *The Triple Thinkers,* 1938; New York: Oxford University Press, 1948.

The Historical Interpretation of Literature

I want to talk about the historical interpretation of literature — that is, about the interpretation of literature in its social, economic, and political aspects.

To begin with, it will be worthwhile to say something about the kind of criticism which seems to be furthest removed from this. There is a kind of comparative criticism which tends to be nonhistorical. The essays of T. S. Eliot, which have had such an immense influence in our time, are, for example, fundamentally nonhistorical. Eliot sees, or tries to see, the whole of literature, so far as he is acquainted with it, spread out before him under the aspect of eternity. He then compares the work of different periods and countries, and tries to draw from it general conclusions about what literature ought to be. He understands, of course, that our point of view in connection with literature changes, and he has what seems to me a very sound conception of the whole body of writing of the past as something to which new works are continually being added, and which is not thereby merely increased in bulk but modified as a whole — so that Sophocles is no longer precisely what he was for Aristotle, or Shakespeare what he was for Ben Jonson or for Dryden or for Dr. Johnson, on account of all the later literature that has intervened between them and us. Yet at every point of this continual accretion, the whole field may be surveyed, as it were, spread out before the critic.[1] The critic tries to see it as God might; he calls the books to a Day of Judgment. And, looking at things in this way, he may arrive at interesting and valuable conclusions which could hardly be reached by approaching them in any other way. Eliot was able to see, for example — what I believe had never been noticed before — that the French Symbolist poetry of the nineteenth century had certain fundamental resemblances to the English poetry of the age of Donne. Another kind of critic would draw certain historical conclusions from these purely esthetic findings, as the Russian D. S. Mirsky[2] did; but Eliot does not draw them.

Another example of this kind of nonhistorical criticism, in a somewhat different way and on a somewhat different plane, is the work of the late George Saintsbury. Saintsbury was a connoisseur of wines; he wrote an entertaining book on the subject.[3] And his attitude toward literature, too, was that of the connoisseur. He tastes the authors and tells you about the vintages; he distinguishes the qualities of the various wines. His palate was as fine as could be, and he possessed the great qualification that he knew how to take each book on its own terms without expecting it to be some other book and was thus in a position to appreciate a great variety of kinds of writing. He was a man of strong social prejudices and peculiarly intransigent political views, but, so far as it is humanly possible, he kept them out of his literary criticism. The result is one of the most agreeable and most comprehensive commentaries on literature that have ever been written in English. Most scholars who have read as much as Saintsbury do not have Saintsbury's discriminating taste. Here is a critic who has covered the whole ground like

[1]See Eliot, "Tradition and the Individual Talent," p. 498. [Ed.]

[2]Prince Dmitri Svyatopolk Mirsky, Russian literary historian (1890–?). [Ed.]

[3]*Notes on a Cellarbook* (1920), by George Saintsbury, English literary historian, professor at Edinburgh University (1845–1933). [Ed.]

any academic historian, yet whose account of it is not merely a chronology but a record of fastidious enjoyment. Since enjoyment is the only thing he is looking for, he does not need to know the causes of things, and the historical background of literature does not interest him very much.

There is, however, another tradition of criticism which dates from the beginning of the eighteenth century. In the year 1725, the Neapolitan philosopher Vico published *La Scienza Nuova,* a revolutionary work on the philosophy of history, in which he asserted for the first time that the social world was certainly the work of man, and attempted what is, so far as I know, the first social interpretation of a work of literature. This is what Vico says about Homer: "Homer composed the *Iliad* when Greece was young and consequently burning with sublime passions such as pride, anger, and vengeance — passions which cannot allow dissimulation and which consort with generosity; so that she then admired Achilles, the hero of force. But, grown old, he composed the *Odyssey,* at a time when the passions of Greece were already somewhat cooled by reflection, which is the mother of prudence — so that she now admired Ulysses, the hero of wisdom. Thus also, in Homer's youth, the Greek people liked cruelty, vituperation, savagery, fierceness, ferocity; whereas, when Homer was old, they were already enjoying the luxuries of Alcinoüs, the delights of Calypso, the pleasures of Circe, the songs of the sirens and the pastimes of the suitors, who went no further in aggression and combat than laying siege to the chaste Penelope — all of which practices would appear incompatible with the spirit of the earlier time. The divine Plato is so struck by this difficulty that, in order to solve it, he tells us that Homer had foreseen in inspired vision these dissolute, sickly and disgusting customs. But in this way he makes Homer out to have been but a foolish instructor for Greek civilization, since, however much he may condemn them, he is displaying for imitation these corrupt and decadent habits which were not to be adopted till long after the foundation of the nations of Greece, and accelerating the natural course which human events would take by spurring the Greeks on to corruption. Thus it is plain that the Homer of the *Iliad* must have preceded by many years the Homer who wrote the *Odyssey;* and it is plain that the former must belong to the northeastern part of Greece, since he celebrates the Trojan War, which took place in his part of the country, whereas the latter belongs to the southeastern part, since he celebrates Ulysses, who reigned there."

You see that Vico has here explained Homer in terms both of historical period and of geographical origin. The idea that human arts and institutions were to be studied and elucidated as the products of the geographical and climatic conditions in which the people who created them lived, and of the phase of their social development through which they were passing at the moment, made great progress during the eighteenth century. There are traces of it even in Dr. Johnson, that most orthodox and classical of critics — as, for example, when he accounts for certain characteristics of Shakespeare by the relative barbarity of the age in which he lived, pointing out, just as Vico had done, that "nations, like individuals, have their infancy."[4] And by the eighties of the eighteenth century Herder, in his *Ideas on the Philosophy of History,* was writing of poetry that it was a kind of "Proteus among the people, which is always changing its form in response to the languages, manners, and habits, to the temperaments and climates, nay even to the accents of different nations." He said — what could still seem startling even so late as that — that "language was not a divine communication, but something men had produced themselves."[5] In the lectures on the philosophy of history that Hegel delivered in Berlin in 1822–23, he discussed the national literatures as expressions of the societies which had produced them — societies which he conceived as great organisms continually transforming themselves under the influence of a succession of dominant ideas.

In the field of literary criticism, this historical point of view came to its first complete flower in the work of the French critic Taine, in the middle of the nineteenth century. The whole school of

[4]See Johnson, "Preface to Shakespeare," p. 234. [Ed.]

[5]Johann Gottfried von Herder (1744–1803), German aesthetician and philosopher; his *Ideas on the Philosophy of History of Humanity* came out in 1784–91. [Ed.]

historian-critics to which Taine belonged — Michelet, Renan, Sainte-Beuve — had been occupied in interpreting books in terms of their historical origins. But Taine was the first of these to attempt to apply such principles systematically and on a large scale in a work devoted exclusively to literature. In the Introduction to his *History of English Literature,* published in 1853, he made his famous pronouncement that works of literature were to be understood as the upshot of three interfusing factors: *the moment, the race and the milieu.* Taine thought he was a scientist and a mechanist, who was examining works of literature from the same point of view as the chemist's in experimenting with chemical compounds. But the difference between the critic and the chemist is that the critic cannot first combine his elements and then watch to see what they will do: he can only examine phenomena which have already taken place. The procedure that Taine actually follows is to pretend to set the stage for the experiment by describing the moment, the race and the milieu, and then to say: "Such a situation demands such and such a kind of writer." He now goes on to describe the kind of writer that the situation demands, and the reader finds himself at the end confronted with Shakespeare or Milton or Byron or whoever the great figure is — who turns out to prove the accuracy of Taine's prognosis by precisely living up to this description.

There was thus a certain element of imposture in Taine; but it was the rabbits he pulled out that saved him. If he had really been the mechanist that he thought he was, his work on literature would have had little value. The truth was that Taine loved literature for its own sake — he was at his best himself a brilliant artist — and he had very strong moral convictions which give his writing emotional power. His mind, to be sure, was an analytic one, and his analysis, though terribly oversimplified, does have an explanatory value. Yet his work was what we call creative. Whatever he may say about chemical experiments, it is evident when he writes of a great writer that the moment, the race and the milieu have combined, like the three sounds of the chord in Browning's poem about Abt Vogler, to produce not a fourth sound but a star.

To Taine's set of elements was added, dating from the middle of the century, a new element, the economic, which was introduced into the discussion of historical phenomena mainly by Marx and Engels. The non-Marxist critics themselves were at the time already taking into account the influence of the social classes. In his chapters on the Norman conquest of England, Taine shows that the difference between the literatures produced respectively by the Normans and by the Saxons was partly the difference between a ruling class, on the one hand, and a vanquished and repressed class, on the other. And Michelet, in his volume on the Regency, which was finished the same year that the *History of English Literature* appeared, studies the *Manon Lescaut* of the Abbé Prévost as a document representing the point of view of the small gentry before the French Revolution. But Marx and Engels derived the social classes from the way that people made or got their livings — from what they called the *methods of production;* and they tended to regard these economic processes as fundamental to civilization.

The Dialectical Materialism of Marx and Engels was not really so materialistic as it sounds. There was in it a large element of the Hegelian idealism that Marx and Engels thought they had got rid of. At no time did these two famous materialists take so mechanistic a view of things as Taine began by professing; and their theory of the relation of works of literature to what they called the *economic base* was a good deal less simple than Taine's theory of the moment, the race and the milieu. They thought that art, politics, religion, philosophy and literature belonged to what they called the *superstructure* of human activity; but they saw that the practitioners of these various professions tended also to constitute social groups, and that they were always pulling away from the kind of solidarity based on economic classes in order to establish a professional solidarity of their own. Furthermore, the activities of the superstructure could influence one another, and they could influence the economic base. It may be said of Marx and Engels in general that, contrary to the popular impression, they were tentative, confused and modest when it came down to philosophical first principles, where a materialist like Taine was cocksure. Marx once made an attempt to explain why the poems of Homer were so good when the society that produced them was from his point of view — that is, from the point of view of its industrial development — so primitive; and this gave him a good deal of trouble.[6] If we compare his discussion of this problem with Vico's discussion of Homer, we see that the explanation of literature in terms of a philosophy of social history is becoming, instead of simpler and easier, more difficult and more complex.

Marx and Engels were deeply imbued, moreover, with the German admiration for literature, which they had learned from the age of Goethe. It would never have occurred to either of them that *der Dichter*[7] was not one of the noblest and most beneficent of humankind. When Engels writes about Goethe, he presents him as a man equipped for "practical life," whose career was frustrated by the "misery" of the historical situation in Germany in his time, and reproaches him for allowing himself to lapse into the "cautious, smug, and narrow" philistinism of the class from which he came; but Engels regrets this, because it interfered with the development of the "mocking, defiant, world-despising genius," "der geniale Dichter," "der gewaltige Poet,"[8] of whom Engels would not even, he says, have asked that he should have been a political liberal if Goethe had not sacrificed to his bourgeois shrinkings his truer esthetic sense. And the great critics who were trained on Marx — Franz Mehring[9] and Bernard Shaw — had all this reverence for the priesthood of literature. Shaw deplores the absence of political philosophy and what he regards as the middle-class snobbery in Shakespeare; but he celebrates Shakespeare's poetry and his dramatic imagination almost as enthusiastically as Swinburne does, describing even those potboiling comedies, *Twelfth Night* and *As You Like It* — the themes of which seem to him most trashy — as "the Crown Jewels of English dramatic poetry." Such a critic may do more for a writer by showing him as a real man dealing with a real world at a definite moment of time than the impressionist critic of Swinburne's type who flourished in the same period of the late nineteenth century. The purely impressionist critic approaches the whole of literature as an exhibit of belletristic jewels, and he can only write a rhapsodic catalogue. But when Shaw turned his spotlight on Shakespeare as a figure in the Shavian drama of history, he invested him with a new interest as no other English critic had done.

The insistence that the man of letters should play a political role, the disparagement of works of art in comparison with political action, were thus originally no part of Marxism. They only became associated with it later. This happened by way of Russia, and it was due to special tendencies in that country that date from long before the Revolution or the promulgation of Marxism itself. In Russia there have been very good reasons why the political implications of literature should particularly occupy the critics. The art of Pushkin itself, with its marvelous power of implication, had certainly been partly created by the censorship of Nicholas I, and Pushkin set the tradition for most of the great Russian writers that followed him. Every play, every poem, every story, must be a parable of which the moral is *implied.* If it were stated, the censor would suppress the book as he tried to do with Pushkin's *Bronze Horseman,* where it was merely a question of the packed implications protruding a little too plainly. Right down through the writings of Chekhov and up almost to the Revolution, the imaginative literature of Russia presents the peculiar paradox of an art that is technically objective and yet charged with social messages. In Russia under the Tsar, it was inevitable that social criticism should lead to political conclusions, because the most urgent need from the point of view of any kind of improvement was to get rid of the tsarist regime. Even the neo-Christian moralist Tolstoy, who pretended to be non-political, was to exert a subversive influence, because his independent preaching was bound to embroil him with the Church, and the Church was an in-

[6]See Marx, "A Contribution to a Critique of Political Economy," p. 392. [Ed.]

[7]The literary writer. [Ed.]

[8]"The genial author, the powerful poet." [Ed.]

[9]Franz Mehring (1846–1919), social-democratic journalist, biographer of Marx, ally of Rosa Luxemburg and the Spartacists. [Ed.]

tegral part of the tsardom. Tolstoy's pamphlet called *What Is Art?,* in which he throws overboard Shakespeare and a large part of modern literature, including his own novels, in the interest of his intransigent morality, is the example which is most familiar to us of the moralizing Russian criticism;[10] but it was only the most sensational expression of a kind of approach which had been prevalent since Belinsky and Chernyshevsky in the early part of the century. The critics, who were usually journalists writing in exile or in a contraband press, were always tending to demand of the imaginative writers that they should dramatize bolder morals.

Even after the Revolution had destroyed the tsarist government, this state of things did not change. The old habits of censorship persisted in the new socialist society of the Soviets, which was necessarily made up of people who had been stamped by the die of the despotism. We meet here the peculiar phenomenon of a series of literary groups that attempt, one after the other, to obtain official recognition or to make themselves sufficiently powerful to establish themselves as arbiters of literature. Lenin and Trotsky and Lunacharsky had the sense to oppose these attempts: the comrade-dictators of Proletcult or Lev or Rapp[11] would certainly have been just as bad as the Count Benckendorff who made Pushkin miserable, and when the Stalin bureaucracy, after the death of Gorky, got control of this department as of everything else, they instituted a system of repression that made Benckendorff and Nicholas I look like Lorenzo de' Medici. In the meantime, Trotsky, who was the Commissar of War but himself a great political writer with an interest in belles-lettres, attempted, in 1924, apropos of one of these movements, to clarify the situation. He wrote a brilliant and valuable book called *Literature and Revolution,* in which he explained the aims of the government, analyzed the work of the Russian writers, and praised or rebuked the latter as they seemed to him in harmony or at odds with the former. Trotsky is intelligent, sympathetic; it is evident that he is really fond of literature and that he knows that a work of art does not fulfill its function in terms of the formulas of party propaganda. But Mayakovsky, the Soviet poet, whom Trotsky had praised with reservations, expressed himself in a famous joke when he was asked what he thought of Trotsky's book — a pun which implied that a Commissar turned critic was inevitably a Commissar still;[12] and what a foreigner cannot accept in Trotsky is his assumption that it is the duty of the government to take a hand in the direction of literature.

This point of view, indigenous to Russia, has been imported to other countries through the permeation of Communist influence. The Communist press and its literary followers have reflected the control of the Kremlin in all the phases through which it has passed, down to the wholesale imprisonment of Soviet writers which has been taking place since 1935. But it has never been a part of the American system that our Republican or Democratic administration should lay down a political line for the guidance of the national literature. A recent gesture in this direction on the part of Archibald MacLeish, who seems a little carried away by his position as Librarian of Congress, was anything but cordially received by serious American writers. So long as the United States remains happily a non-totalitarian country, we can very well do without this aspect of the historical criticism of literature.

Another element of a different order has, however, since Marx's time been added to the historical study of the origins of works of literature. I mean the psychoanalysis of Freud. This appears as an extension of something which had already got well started before, which had figured even in Johnson's *Lives of the Poets* and of which the great exponent had been Sainte-Beuve: the interpretation of works of literature in the light of the personalities behind them. But the Freudians made this interpretation more exact and more systematic. The great example of the psychoanalysis of an artist is Freud's own essay on

[10]See Tolstoy, "What is Art?" p. 472. [Ed.]

[11]RAPP was the Russian union of writers after the Bolshevik revolution; following the death of Lenin it became an instrument of oppression. [Ed.]

[12]**Первый блин лег наркомом,** The first pancake lies like a narkom (people's commissar) — a parody of the Russian saying, **Первый блин лег комом,** The first pancake lies like a lump. [Au.]

Leonardo da Vinci; but this has little critical interest: it is an attempt to construct a case history. One of the best examples I know of the application of Freudian analysis to literature is in Van Wyck Brooks's book, *The Ordeal of Mark Twain,* in which Mr. Brooks uses an incident of Mark Twain's boyhood as a key to his whole career. Mr. Brooks has since repudiated the method he resorted to here, on the ground that no one but an analyst can ever know enough about a writer to make a valid psychoanalytic diagnosis. This is true, and it is true of the method that it has led to bad results where the critic has built a Freudian mechanism out of very slender evidence, and then given us what is really merely a romance exploiting the supposed working of this mechanism, in place of an actual study that sticks close to the facts and the documents of the writer's life and work. But I believe that Van Wyck Brooks really had hold of something important when he fixed upon that childhood incident of which Mark Twain gave so vivid an account to his biographer — that scene at the deathbed of his father when his mother had made him promise that he would not break her heart. If it was not one of those crucial happenings that are supposed to determine the complexes of Freud, it has certainly a typical significance in relation to Mark Twain's whole psychology. The stories that people tell about their childhood are likely to be profoundly symbolic even when they have been partly or wholly made up in the light of later experience. And the attitudes, the compulsions, the emotional "patterns" that recur in the work of a writer are of great interest to the historical critic.

These attitudes and patterns are embedded in the community and the historical moment, and they may indicate its ideals and its diseases as the cell shows the condition of the tissue. The recent scientific experimentation in the combining of Freudian with Marxist method, and of psychoanalysis with anthropology, has had its parallel development in criticism. And there is thus another element added to our equipment for analyzing literary works, and the problem grows still more complex.

The analyst, however, is of course not concerned with the comparative values of his patients any more than the surgeon is. He cannot tell you why the neurotic Dostoevsky produces work of immense value to his fellows while another man with the same neurotic pattern would become a public menace. Freud himself emphatically states in his study of Leonardo that his method can make no attempt to account for Leonardo's genius. The problems of comparative artistic value still remain after we have given attention to the Freudian psychological factor just as they do after we have given attention to the Marxist economic factor and to the racial and geographical factors. No matter how thoroughly and searchingly we may have scrutinized works of literature from the historical and biographical points of view, we must be ready to attempt to estimate, in some such way as Saintsbury and Eliot do, the relative degrees of success attained by the products of the various periods and the various personalities. We must be able to tell good from bad, the first-rate from the second-rate. We shall not otherwise write literary criticism at all, but merely social or political history as reflected in literary texts, or psychological case histories from past eras, or, to take the historical point of view in its simplest and most academic form, merely chronologies of books that have been published.

And now how, in these matters of literary art, do we tell the good art from the bad? Norman Kemp Smith, the Kantian philosopher, whose courses I was fortunate enough to take at Princeton twenty-five years ago, used to tell us that this recognition was based primarily on an emotional reaction.[13] For purposes of practical criticism this is a safe assumption on which to proceed. It is possible to discriminate in a variety of ways the elements that in any given department go to make a successful work of literature. Different schools have at different times demanded different things of literature: *unity, symmetry, universality, originality, vision, inspiration, strangeness, suggestiveness, improving morality, socialist realism,* etc. But you could have any set of these qualities that any school of writing has called for and still not have a good play, a good novel, a

[13]See Kant, *Critique of Judgment,* p. 257. [Ed.]

good poem, a good history. If you identify the essence of good literature with any one of these elements or with any combination of them, you simply shift the emotional reaction to the recognition of the element or elements. Or if you add to your other demands the demand that the writer must have *talent,* you simply shift this recognition to the talent. Once people find some grounds of agreement in the coincidence of their emotional reactions to books, they may be able to discuss these elements profitably; but if they do not have this basic agreement, the discussion will make no sense.

But how, you may ask, can we identify this élite who know what they are talking about? Well, it can only be said of them that they are self-appointed and self-perpetuating, and that they will compel you to accept their authority. Impostors may try to put themselves over, but these quacks will not last. The implied position of the people who know about literature (as is also the case in every other art) is simply that they know what they know, and that they are determined to impose their opinions by main force of eloquence or assertion on the people who do not know. This is not a question, of course, of professional workers in literature — such as editors, professors and critics, who very often have no real understanding of the products with which they deal — but of readers of all kinds in all walks of life. There are moments when a first-rate writer, unrecognized or out of fashion with the official chalkers-up for the market, may find his support in the demand for his work of an appreciative cultivated public.

But what is the cause of this emotional reaction which is the critic's divining rod? This question has long been a subject of study by the branch of philosophy called esthetics, and it has recently been made a subject of scientific experimentation. Both these lines of inquiry are likely to be prejudiced in the eyes of the literary critic by the fact that the inquiries are sometimes conducted by persons who are obviously deficient in literary feeling or taste. Yet one should not deny the possibility that something of value might result from the speculations and explorations of men of acute minds who take as their primary data the esthetic emotions of other men.

Almost everybody interested in literature has tried to explain to himself the nature of these emotions that register our approval of artistic works; and I of course have my own explanation.

In my view, all our intellectual activity, in whatever field it takes place, is an attempt to give a meaning to our experience — that is, to make life more practicable; for by understanding things we make it easier to survive and get around them. The mathematician Euclid, working in a convention of abstractions, shows us relations between the distances of our unwieldy and cluttered-up environment upon which we are able to count. A drama of Sophocles also indicates relations between the various human impulses, which appear so confused and dangerous, and it brings out a certain justice of Fate — that is to say, of the way in which the interaction of these impulses is seen in the long run to work out — upon which we can also depend. The kinship, from this point of view, of the purposes of science and art appears very clearly in the case of the Greeks, because not only do both Euclid and Sophocles satisfy us by making patterns, but they make much the same kind of patterns. Euclid's *Elements* takes simple theorems and by a series of logical operations builds them up to a climax in the square on the hypotenuse. A typical drama of Sophocles develops in a similar way.

Some writers (as well as some scientists) have a different kind of explicit message beyond the reassurance implicit in the mere feat of understanding life or of molding the harmony of artistic form. Not content with such an achievement as that of Sophocles — who has one of his choruses tell us that it is better not to be born,[14] but who, by representing life as noble and based on law, makes its tragedy easier to bear — such writers attempt, like Plato, to think out and recommend a procedure for turning it into something better. But other departments of literature — lyric poetry such as Sappho's, for example — have *less* philosophical content than Sophocles. A lyric gives us nothing but a pattern imposed on the expression of a feeling; but this pattern of metrical quantities and of consonants and vowels

[14]In *Oedipus at Colonus.* [Ed.]

that balance has the effect of reducing the feeling, however unruly or painful it may seem when we experience it in the course of our lives, to something orderly, symmetrical, and pleasing; and it also relates this feeling to the more impressive scheme, works it into the larger texture, of the body of poetic art. The discord has been resolved, the anomaly subjected to discipline. And this control of his emotion by the poet has the effect at second-hand of making it easier for the reader to manage his own emotions. (Why certain sounds and rhythms gratify us more than others, and how they are connected with the themes and ideas that they are chosen as appropriate for conveying, are questions that may be passed on to the scientist.)

And this brings us back again to the historical point of view. The experience of mankind on the earth is always changing as man develops and has to deal with new combinations of elements; and the writer who is to be anything more than an echo of his predecessors must always find expression for something which has never yet been expressed, must master a new set of phenomena which has never yet been mastered. With each such victory of the human intellect, whether in history, in philosophy or in poetry, we experience a deep satisfaction: we have been cured of some ache of disorder, relieved of some oppressive burden of uncomprehended events.

This relief that brings the sense of power, and, with the sense of power, joy, is the positive emotion which tells us that we have encountered a first-rate piece of literature. But stay! you may at this point warn: are not people often solaced and exhilarated by literature of the trashiest kind? They are: crude and limited people do certainly feel some such emotion in connection with work that is limited and crude. The man who is more highly organized and has a wider intellectual range will feel it in connection with work that is finer and more complex. The difference between the emotion of the more highly organized man and the emotion of the less highly organized one is a matter of mere gradation. You sometimes discover books — the novels of John Steinbeck, for example — that seem to mark precisely the borderline between work that is definitely superior and work that is definitely bad. When I was speaking a little while back of the genuine connoisseurs who establish the standards of taste, I meant, of course, the people who can distinguish Grade A and who prefer it to the other grades.

Kenneth Burke

1897–1993

Kenneth Duva Burke was born on May 5, 1897, in Pittsburgh, where he was educated through high school. He attended college at Ohio State University in Columbus and Columbia University in New York but did not take a degree; this has been amply made up for by the number of universities — over a dozen at last count — that have awarded him honorary doctorates. Burke worked as a researcher for the Laura Spelman Rockefeller Foundation, as the music critic for *The Dial* and *The Nation,* and as an editor for government publications, but his chief occupation during his long life was that of itinerant scholar and critic. Burke took literally dozens of academic appointments at prestigious institutions but most of them, except for an eighteen-year appointment at Bennington College from 1943 to 1961, itself broken by visiting appointments elsewhere, were for a year or two. In addition to writing dozens of critical and philosophical books, Burke was a poet from his eighteenth year, and his first publication (*The White Oxen,* 1924) was a collection of short stories. Burke was married twice, to two sisters, and had three daughters by the first marriage and two sons by the second.

Burke, who was a quirky and individualistic thinker, has often and for understandable reasons been mischaracterized as a New Critic strongly influenced by Marx and Freud. Of the same generation as Brooks and Wimsatt, Burke was interested, like the New Critics, in the poem as a verbal creation, or as he put it himself, "a dance of attitudes"; and like most twentieth-century thinkers from Lionel Trilling to William Empson, he was also interested in the two most revolutionary thinkers of the later Victorian era. Nevertheless, Burke was more a philosopher than a literary critic as such, and his ideas, although primarily applied to literature and to prose texts, range far beyond our purposes here: his vision of language and literature as forms of symbolic action.

Perhaps we should begin at a very general level, with Burke's famous definition of Man. Burke conceived of man not as *homo sapiens* but as *homo symbolicus,* the only being capable of using (and therefore misusing) symbols. Man is therefore also the "inventor of the negative," since negation is a product only of symbol systems: Nature may not abhor a vacuum, but only language can explore the absence of something in a world that knows only presence. Man is also "separated from his natural condition by instruments of his own making," so conditioned by language and the social aspects of life that are created within and through language that even his physiology has changed from that of the arboreal apes from which he descended. Man is also "goaded by the spirit of hierarchy," a characteristically less pleasant way of saying "moved by a sense of order."

Finally, Burke likes to say that man is "rotten with perfection," in that our sense of order leads us to carry out our ideas to the nth degree, regardless of the consequences. One obvious instance is Hitler's idea of racial purity. Carried out to perfection, and with full negativity, using the power that rigidly enforced hierarchies give to a leader, the symbolic enactment leads to the horrors of the Holocaust.

Although Burke's theory suggests that humanity has a drive to "perfect" such ideas in such a way, a utopian strain in Burke hopes that the strife between contrary symbol-systems (like capitalism and communism) can be indefinitely confined, with all our help, to symbolic battles, rather than exploding in that final negativity, nuclear annihilation.

The idea of conflict confined to a symbolic agon, a struggle of words, brings us back to Burke and literature. Saying something is another way of doing something. Essentially, Burke assumes that human beings write literature, just as they do everything else, in an effort to achieve some personal goal. Writing is itself a drama. Authors are *agents* who *act* within a certain *scene* (their environment) by means of a certain *agency* (writing) to achieve a *purpose*. These five terms — agent, act, scene, agency, and purpose — make up the Burkean *pentad;* their "ratios," or the relationships between the terms, are crucial to his criticism. Authors do not merely write as an end in itself, nor do they write for secular reasons — to make money or achieve fame. Rather, they select their particular subjects, topics, conflicts, for reasons that go beyond the secular, usually the purgation of their own sense of sinfulness, which leads to a sense of redemption within their lives. As Burke says in "Literature as Equipment for Living," there is no room for such a thing as "pure literature" of the sort the New Critics wished to analyze. Works of art are "equipment for living," "strategies for selecting enemies and allies, for socializing losses, for warding off evil eye, for purification, propitiation, and desanctification, consolation and vengeance, admonition and exhortation, implicit commands or instructions of one sort or another."

As an example of how the poet may socialize a loss or give himself symbolic instructions, we could take Burke's analysis of Milton's "Lycidas" in *Attitudes toward History* (1937). While a New Critic like John Crowe Ransom considered "Lycidas" "a poem nearly anonymous" in its exquisite variants on the general themes of the pastoral elegy, Burke boldly commits the intentional fallacy, even takes the poem, with its evocation of the death and resurrection of a poet, as a personal prophecy. After writing "Lycidas," Burke claims,

> Milton travelled in 1638 and 1639. And for the next twenty years thereafter, with the exception of an occasional sonnet, he devoted all his energies to his polemic prose. These dates, coupled with the contents of the poem, would justify us in contending that "Lycidas" was the symbolic dying of his poetic self. . . . In "Lycidas" he testifies that he is holding his dead self in abeyance, and that it will rise again. . . . So the poet remained, for all his dying; and at the Restoration, after the political interregnum of Cromwell, he would be reborn. "Paradise Lost" is the fulfillment of his contract.[1]

Similarly, "The Rime of the Ancient Mariner" represents Coleridge's symbolic way of purging the guilt arising out of his failed marriage and his drug addiction, and of achieving an equally symbolic redemption. For Burke, the slain albatross can be equated with Sarah Coleridge, since they are "in the same equational cluster" — connected by similar imagery in "Mariner" and "The Aeolian Harp." Similarly, the

[1]Kenneth Burke, *Attitudes toward History,* 3rd ed. (Berkeley: University of California Press, 1984), p. 57.

watersnakes whom the mariner blesses as a part of nature connect with his drug addiction, which is referred to in a letter as "a scourge of ever restless, ever coiling and uncoiling serpents," while Coleridge feels "driven on from behind" — as the Mariner's ship is driven. In effect, Coleridge uses the poem to symbolically "bless" his drug addiction and "curse" his marriage — the scene of the poem itself involves a detained wedding-guest who misses the ceremony, and the poem ends by denigrating marriage in favor of the brotherhood of Nature and of humanity ("to walk together to the kirk, With a goodly company").

Not only may authors have their purgative/redemptive purposes, their societies also have them (and, we might add, the "affective" fallacy means as little to Burke as the "intentional" fallacy does). Burke's analysis of Shakespeare's *Coriolanus* in *Language as Symbolic Action* (1966) presents the hero of that play as the apotheosis of the aristocracy, with all the virtues and vices of the highborn — courage, pride, stoical fortitude, snobbery, family feeling — taken to the last extreme, "rotten with perfection," as Burke liked to put it. According to Burke, the action of the tragedy shapes everything toward the sacrifice of Coriolanus as a scapegoat — a symbolic destruction of the ultimate patrician enacted at a time when the strife between patrician and plebeian in English society was already becoming virulent, although it would not erupt into civil war for another three decades. The death of Coriolanus causes the reunification of Rome and symbolically allows the English Cavaliers and Roundheads, enemies-to-be, to join in unity in a purgative/redemptive experience.

Here and in the Milton example, Burke is characteristically cavalier in his use of the facts and delights in prophecy after-the-fact. One could pedantically object that Milton in 1637 could not have foreseen Cromwell and his secretaryship, that Coleridge was not fully addicted to laudanum at the time he wrote "The Ancient Mariner," that Shakespeare in 1609 could not have foreseen the Civil War. But the sort of conflict Burke is talking about always runs behind and above such facts: If Milton could not have predicted Cromwell, he certainly saw the conflict within himself between poetry and politics, and if Shakespeare could not have predicted the civil war that broke out twenty-five years after his death, he certainly understood the clash between classes within his own society. The same is true of Coleridge; even if one is not willing to claim (as Burke once did) that the poet was an *incipient* addict in 1796, there was surely a deep-seated and long-standing conflict in Coleridge between affections licensed by society (symbolized by the wedding in the poem) and affections that transcend and defy the social (like the Mariner's demonic bond with the watersnakes).

Burke's method of analyzing literature turns primarily on reducing the text to its scene of conflict, then viewing that conflict as symbolic of other conflicts within other scenes — within the poet's self, family, or society, including his or her relation with intellectual forebears or poetic rivals. The "scene" for which the poem is a grand metaphor can be psychological, economic, political, sociological, even theological. And as the example of Coleridge shows, Burke is willing to read other poems or letters onto the text under analysis. Everything is relevant.

If this allegorizing and psychologizing is utterly foreign to the formalist movements against which Burke defined his own poetics, he nevertheless resembles the

New Critics in his concern for symbol, language, and imagery. The notion that themes essentially reside in clusters of images, that the associations of primary terms determine their psychic meaning, is close to the New Critical method. Nevertheless, the freewheeling Burke went considerably further than the New Critics were ever comfortable with in his "joycings" — puns, usually scatological, that reduce the high-flown meaning of a passage to a physiological level. Burke's analysis of Keats's "Ode on a Grecian Urn" in *A Grammar of Motives* (1945), reprinted here, is relatively decorous, but in the later *A Rhetoric of Motives* (1950), the "urn" is joyced to "urine," while the final sentiment, "Beauty is truth, truth beauty," is joyced to "Body is turd, turd body." Burke is not being childishly dirty-minded here. His point is that, in any poem so concerned with transcendence, the poet tends to repress the earthly and bodily functions that are being transcended; but what is repressed returns in language that, in distorted form, conveys what the poet has been avoiding talking about. In Burke conflict is unavoidable and language always takes over — that much is certain.

Selected Bibliography

Frank, Armin Paul. *Kenneth Burke.* New York: Twayne, 1969.

Heath, Robert L. "Kenneth Burke's Break with Formalism." *Quarterly Journal of Speech* 70 (1984): 132–43.

———. *Realism and Relativism: A Perspective on Kenneth Burke.* GA: Mercer University Press, 1986.

Rueckert, William H. *The Rhetoric of Rebirth: A Study of the Literary Theory and Critical Practice of Kenneth Burke.* Ann Arbor: University Microfilms, 1957.

———. *Kenneth Burke and the Drama of Human Relations,* 2nd ed. Berkeley: University of California Press, 1982.

Southwell, Samuel B. *Kenneth Burke and Martin Heidegger, with a Note Against Deconstruction.* Gainesville: University Presses of Florida, 1987.

White, Hayden, and Margaret Brose, eds. *Representing Kenneth Burke.* Baltimore: Johns Hopkins University Press, 1982.

Symbolic Action in a Poem by Keats

We are here set to analyze the "Ode on a Grecian Urn" as a viaticum that leads, by a series of transformations, into the oracle, "Beauty is truth, truth beauty." We shall analyze the Ode "dramatistically," in terms of symbolic action.

To consider language as a means of *information* or *knowledge* is to consider it epistemologically, semantically, in terms of "science." To consider it as a mode of *action* is to consider it in terms of "poetry." For a poem is an act, the symbolic act of the poet who made it — an act of such a nature that, in surviving as a structure or object, it enables us as readers to re-enact it.

"Truth" being the essential word of knowledge (science) and "beauty" being the essential word of art or poetry, we might substitute accordingly. The oracle would then assert, "Poetry is science, science poetry." It would be particularly exhilarating to proclaim them one if there were a strong suspicion that they were at odds (as the assertion that "God's in his heaven, all's right with the world" is really a *counter*-assertion to doubts about God's existence and suspicions that much is wrong). It was the dialectical opposition between the "aesthetic" and the "practical," with "poetry" on one side and utility (business and applied science) on the other that was being ecstatically denied. The *relief* in this denial was grounded in the romantic philosophy itself, a philosophy which gave strong recognition to precisely the *contrast* between "beauty" and "truth."

Perhaps we might put it this way: If the oracle were to have been uttered in the first stanza of the poem rather than the last, its phrasing proper to that place would have been: "Beauty is *not* truth, truth *not* beauty." The five stanzas of successive transformation were necessary for the romantic philosophy of a romantic poet to transcend itself (raising its romanticism to a new order, or new dimension). An abolishing of romanticism through romanticism! (To transcend romanticism through romanticism is, when all is over, to restore in one way what is removed in another.)

But to the poem, step by step through the five stanzas.

As a "way in," we begin with the sweeping periodic sentence that, before the stanza is over, has swiftly but imperceptibly been transmuted in quality from the periodic to the breathless, a cross between interrogation and exclamation:

Thou still unravish'd bride of quietness,
Thou foster-child of silence and slow time,
Sylvan historian, who canst thus express
A flowery tale more sweetly than our rhyme:
What leaf-fring'd legend haunts about thy shape
Of deities or mortals, or of both,
In Tempe or the dales of Arcady?
What men or gods are these? What maidens loth?
What mad pursuit? What struggle to escape?
What pipes and timbrels? What wild ecstasy?

Even the last quick outcries retain somewhat the quality of the periodic structure with which the stanza began. The final line introduces the subject of "pipes and timbrels," which is developed and then surpassed in Stanza II:

Heard melodies are sweet, but those unheard
Are sweeter; therefore, ye soft pipes, play on;
Not to the sensual ear, but, more endear'd,
Pipe to the spirit ditties of no tone:
Fair youth, beneath the trees, thou canst not leave
Thy song, nor ever can those trees be bare;
Bold Lover, never, never canst thou kiss,
Though winning near the goal — yet, do not grieve;
She cannot fade, though thou hast not thy bliss,
Forever wilt thou love, and she be fair!

If we had only the first stanza of this Ode, and were speculating upon it from the standpoint of motivation, we could detect there tentative indications of two motivational levels. For the lines express a doubt whether the figures on the urn are "deities or mortals" — and the motives of gods are of a different order from the motives of men. This bare hint of such a possibility emerges with something of certainty in the second stanza's development of the "pipes and timbrels" theme. For we explicitly consider a contrast between body and mind (in the contrast between "heard melodies," addressed "to the sensual ear," and "ditties of no tone," addressed "to the spirit").

Also, of course, the notion of inaudible sound brings us into the region of the mystic oxymoron (the term in rhetoric for "the figure in which an epithet of a contrary significance is added to a word: e.g., *cruel kindness; laborious idleness*"). And it clearly suggests a concern with the level of motives-behind-motives, as with the paradox of the prime mover that is itself at rest, being the unmoved ground of all motion and action. Here the poet whose sounds are the richest in our language is mediating upon *absolute* sound, the *essence* of sound, which would be soundless as the prime mover is motionless, or as the "principle" of sweetness would not be sweet, having transcended sweetness, or as the sub-atomic particles of the sun are each, in their isolate purity, said to be devoid of temperature.

Contrast Keats's unheard melodies with those of Shelley:

Music, when soft voices die,
Vibrates in the memory —
Odours, when sweet violets sicken,
Live within the sense they quicken.

Rose leaves, when the rose is dead,
Are heaped for the beloved's bed;
And so thy thoughts, when thou art gone,
Love itself shall slumber on.[1]

Here the futuristic Shelley is anticipating retrospection; he is looking forward to looking back. The form of thought is naturalistic and temporalistic in terms of *past* and *future*. But the form of thought in Keats is mystical, in terms of an *eternal present*. The Ode is striving to move beyond the region of becoming into the realm of *being*. (This is another way of saying that we are here concerned with two levels of motivation.)

In the last four lines of the second stanza, the state of immediacy is conveyed by a development peculiarly Keatsian. I refer not simply to translation into terms of the erotic, but rather to a quality of *suspension* in the erotic imagery, defining an eternal prolongation of the state just prior to fulfilment — not exactly arrested ecstasy, but rather an arrested pre-ecstasy.[2]

Suppose that we had but this one poem by Keats, and knew nothing of its author or its period, so that we could treat it only in itself, as a series of internal transformations to be studied in their development from a certain point, and without reference to any motives outside the Ode. Under such conditions, I think, we should require no further observations to characterize (from the standpoint of symbolic action) the main argument in the second stanza. We might go on to make an infinity of observations about the details of the stanza; but as regards major deployments we should deem it enough to note that the theme of "pipes and timbrels" is developed by the use of mystic oxymoron, and then surpassed (or given a development-atop-the-development) by the stressing of erotic imagery (that had been ambiguously adumbrated in the references to "maidens loth" and "mad pursuit" of Stanza I). And we could note the quality of *incipience* in this imagery, its state of arrest not at fulfilment, but at the point just prior to fulfilment.

Add, now, our knowledge of the poem's place as an enactment in a particular cultural scene, and we likewise note in this second stanza a variant of the identification between death and sexual love that was so typical of nineteenth-century romanticism and was to attain its musical monument in the Wagnerian *Liebestod*.[3] On a purely dialectical basis, to die in love would be to be born to love (the lovers dying as individual identities that they might be transformed into a common identity). Adding historical factors, one can note the part that capitalist individualism plays in sharpening this consummation (since a property structure that heightens the sense of individual identity would thus make it more imperiously a "death" for the individual to take on the new identity made by a union of two). We can thus see why the love-death equation would be particularly representative of a romanticism that was the reflex of business.

Fortunately, the relation between private property and the love-death equation is attested on unimpeachable authority, concerning the effect of consumption and consummation in a "mutual flame":

So between them love did shine,
That the turtle saw his right
Flaming in the phoenix' sight;
Either was the other's mine.
Property was thus appall'd,
That the self was not the same;
Single nature's double name
Neither two nor one was called.[4]

The addition of fire to the equation, with its pun on sexual burning, moves us from purely dialectical considerations into psychological ones. In the lines of Shakespeare, fire is the third term, the ground term for the other two (the synthesis that ends the lovers' roles as thesis and antithesis). Less obviously, the same movement from the purely dialectical to the psychological is implicit in any imagery of a *dying* or a *falling* in

[1]Shelley's poem is titled "To———" in the *Posthumous Poems* of 1824. [Ed.]

[2]Mr. G. Wilson Knight, in *The Starlit Dome*, refers to "that recurring tendency in Keats to image a posed form, a stillness suggesting motion, what might be called a 'tiptoe' effect." [Au.]

[3]Love-death; the denouement of Wagner's *Tristan und Isolde* in which the lovers find their apotheosis in death. [Ed.]

[4]Shakespeare, "The Phoenix and the Turtle." [Ed.]

common, which when woven with sexual imagery signalizes a "transcendent" sexual consummation. The figure appears in a lover's compliment when Keats writes to Fanny Brawne, thus:

> I never knew before, what such a love as you have made me feel, was; I did not believe in it; my Fancy was afraid of it lest it should burn me up. But if you will fully love me, though there may be some fire, 'twill not be more than we can bear when moistened and bedewed with pleasures.

Our primary concern is to follow the transformations of the poem itself. But to understand its full nature as a symbolic act, we should use whatever knowledge is available. In the case of Keats, not only do we know the place of this poem in his work and its time, but also we have material to guide our speculations as regards correlations between poem and poet. I grant that such speculations interfere with the symmetry of criticism as a game. (Criticism as a game is best to watch, I guess, when one confines himself to the single unit, and reports on its movements like a radio commentator broadcasting the blow-by-blow description of a prizefight.) But linguistic analysis has opened up new possibilities in the correlating of producer and product — and these concerns have such important bearing upon matters of culture and conduct in general that no sheer conventions or ideals of criticism should be allowed to interfere with their development.

From what we know of Keats's illness, with the peculiar inclination to erotic imaginings that accompany its fever (as with the writings of D. H. Lawrence) we can glimpse a particular bodily motive expanding and intensifying the lyric state in Keats's case. Whatever the intense *activity* of his thoughts, there was the material *pathos* of his physical condition. Whatever transformations of mind or body he experienced, his illness was there as a kind of constitutional substrate, whereby all aspects of the illness would be imbued with their derivation from a common ground (the phthisic fever thus being at one with the phthisic chill, for whatever the clear contrast between fever and chill, they are but modes of the same illness, the common underlying substance).

The correlation between the state of agitation in the poems and the physical condition of the poet is made quite clear in the poignant letters Keats wrote during his last illness. In 1819 he complains that he is "scarcely content to write the best verses for the fever they leave behind." And he continues: "I want to compose without this fever." But a few months later he confesses, "I am recommended not even to read poetry, much less write it." Or: "I must say that for 6 Months before I was taken ill I had not passed a tranquil day. Either that gloom overspre[a]d me or I was suffering under some passionate feeling, or if I turn'd to versify that exacerbated the poison of either sensation." Keats was "like a sick eagle looking at the sky," as he wrote of his mortality in a kindred poem, "On Seeing the Elgin Marbles."

But though the poet's body was a *patient,* the poet's mind was an *agent.* Thus, as a practitioner of poetry, he could *use* his fever, even perhaps encouraging, though not deliberately, esthetic habits that, in making for the perfection of his lines, would exact payment in the ravages of his body (somewhat as Hart Crane could write poetry only by modes of living that made for the cessation of his poetry and so led to his dissolution).

Speaking of agents, patients, and action here, we might pause to glance back over the centuries thus: in the Aristotelian grammar of motives, action has its reciprocal in passion, hence *passion* is the property of a *patient.* But by the Christian paradox (which made the martyr's action identical with his passion, as the accounts of the martyrs were called both Acts and Passionals), *patience* is the property of a moral *agent.* And this Christian view, as secularized in the philosophy of romanticism, with its stress upon creativeness, leads us to the possibility of a bodily suffering redeemed by a poetic act.

In the third stanza, the central stanza of the Ode (hence properly the fulcrum of its swing) we see the two motives, the action and the passion, in the process of being separated. The possibility raised in the first stanza (which was dubious whether the level of motives was to be human or divine), and developed in the second stanza (which contrasts the "sensual" and the "spirit"), becomes definitive in Stanza III:

> Ah, happy, happy boughs! that cannot shed
>   Your leaves, nor ever bid the Spring adieu;
> And, happy melodist, unwearied,
>   For ever piping songs for ever new;
> More happy love! more happy, happy love!
>   For ever warm and still to be enjoy'd,
>   For ever panting, and for ever young;
> All breathing human passion far above,
>   That leaves a heart high-sorrowful and cloy'd,
>   A burning forehead, and a parching tongue.

The poem as a whole makes permanent, or fixes in a state of arrest, a peculiar agitation. But within this fixity, by the nature of poetry as a progressive medium, there must be development. Hence, the agitation that is maintained throughout (as a mood absolutized so that it fills the entire universe of discourse) will at the same time undergo internal transformations. In the third stanza, these are manifested as a clear division into two distinct and contrasted realms. There is a transcendental fever, which is felicitous, divinely above "all breathing human passion." And this "leaves" the other level, the level of earthly fever, "a burning forehead and a parching tongue." From the bodily fever, which is a passion, and malign, there has split off a spiritual activity, a wholly benign aspect of the total agitation.

Clearly, a movement has been finished. The poem must, if it is well-formed, take a new direction, growing out of and surpassing the curve that has by now been clearly established by the successive stages from "Is there the possibility of two motivational levels?" through "there are two motivational levels" to "the 'active' motivational level 'leaves' the 'passive' level."

Prophesying, with the inestimable advantage that goes with having looked ahead, what should we expect the new direction to be? First, let us survey the situation. Originally, before the two strands of the fever had been definitely drawn apart, the bodily passion could serve as the scene or ground of the spiritual action. But at the end of the third stanza, we abandon the level of bodily passion. The action is "far above" the passion, it "leaves" the fever. What then would this transcendent act require, to complete it?

It would require a scene of the same quality as itself. An act and a scene belong together. The nature of the one must be a fit with the nature of the other. (I like to call this the "scene-act ratio," or "dramatic ratio.") Hence, the act having now transcended its bodily setting, it will require, as its new setting, a transcendent scene. Hence, prophesying *post eventum,* we should ask that, in Stanza IV, the poem *embody* the transcendental act by endowing it with an appropriate scene.

The scene-act ratio involves a law of dramatic consistency whereby the quality of the act shares the quality of the scene in which it is enacted (the synecdochic relation of container and thing contained). Its grandest variant was in supernatural cosmogonies wherein mankind took on the attributes of gods by acting in cosmic scenes that were themselves imbued with the presence of godhead.[5]

Or we may discern the logic of the scene-act ratio behind the old controversy as to whether "God willed the good because it is good," or "the good is good because God willed it." This strictly theological controversy had political implications. But our primary concern here is with the *dramatistic* aspects of this controversy. For you will note that the whole issue centers in the problem of the *grounds* of God's creative act.

Since, from the purely dramatic point of view, every act requires a scene in which it takes place, we may note that one of the doctrines (that "God willed the good because it is good") is more symmetrical than the other. For by it, God's initial act of creation is itself given a ground, or scene (the objective existence of goodness, which was so real that God himself did not simply make it up, but acted in conformity with its nature when willing it to be the law of his creation). In the scholastic formulas taken over from Aristotle, God was defined as "pure act" (though this pure

[5]In an article by Leo Spitzer, "*Milieu* and *Ambiance:* An Essay in Historical Semantics" (September and December 1942 numbers of *Philosophy and Phenomenological Research*), one will find a wealth of material that can be read as illustrative of "dramatic ratio." [Au.]

act was in turn the ultimate ground or *scene* of human acting and willing). And from the standpoint of purely dramatic symmetry, it would be desirable to have some kind of "scene" even for God. This requirement is met, we are suggesting, in the doctrine that "God willed the good *because* it is good." For this word, "because," in assigning a reason for God's willing, gives us in principle a kind of scene, as we may discern in the pun of our word, "ground," itself, which indeterminately applies to either "place" or "cause."

If even theology thus responded to the pressure for dramatic symmetry by endowing God, as the transcendent act, with a transcendent scene of like quality, we should certainly expect to find analogous tactics in this Ode. For as we have noted that the romantic passion is the secular equivalent of the Christian passion, so we may recall Coleridge's notion that poetic action itself is a "dim analogue of Creation."[6] Keats in his way confronting the same dramatistic requirement that the theologians confronted in theirs, when he has arrived at his transcendent act at the end of Stanza III (that is, when the benign fever has split sway from the malign bodily counterpart, as a divorcing of spiritual action from sensual passion), he is ready in the next stanza for the imagining of a scene that would correspond in quality to the quality of the action as so transformed. His fourth stanza will concretize, or "materialize," the act, by dwelling upon its appropriate ground.

> Who are these coming to the sacrifice?
> To what green altar, O mysterious priest,
> Lead'st thou that heifer lowing at the skies,
> And all her silken flanks with garlands drest?
> What little town, by river or sea shore,
> Or mountain built with peaceful citadel,
> Is emptied of this folk, this pious morn?
> And, little town, thy streets for evermore
> Will silent be; and not a soul to tell
> Why thou art desolate, can e'er return.

It is a vision, as you prefer, of "death" or of "immortality." "Immortality," we might say, is the "good" word for "death," and must necessarily be conceived in terms of death (the necessity that Donne touches upon when he writes, " . . . but thinke that I / Am, by being dead, immortall"). This is why, when discussing the second stanza, I felt justified in speaking of the variations of the love-death equation, though the poem spoke not of love and *death,* but of love *for ever.* We have a deathy-deathless scene as the corresponding ground of our transcendent act. The Urn itself, as with the scene upon it, is not merely an immortal act in our present mortal scene; it was originally an immortal act in a mortal scene quite different. The imagery, of sacrifice, piety, silence, desolation, is that of communication with the immortal or the dead.[7]

Incidentally, we might note that the return to the use of rhetorical questions in the fourth stanza serves well, on a purely technical level, to keep our contact with the mood of the opening stanza, a music that now but vibrates in the memory. Indeed, one even gets the impression that the form of the rhetorical question had never been abandoned; that the poet's questings had been couched as questions throughout. This is tonal felicity at its best, and something much like unheard tonal felicity. For the actual persistence of the rhetorical questions through these stanzas would have been wearisome, whereas their return now gives us an inaudible variation, by making us feel that the exclamations in the second and

[6]Coleridge goes even further in *Biographia Literaria,* chapter 13; see p. 321. [Ed.]

[7]In imagery there is no negation, or disjunction. Logically, we can say, "this *or* that," "this, *not* that." In imagery we can but say "this *and* that," "this *with* that," "this-that," etc. Thus, imagistically considered, a commandment cannot be simply a proscription, but is also latently a provocation (a state of affairs that figures in the kind of stylistic scrupulosity and/or curiosity to which Gide's heroes have been particularly sensitive, as "thou shalt not . . . " becomes imaginatively transformed into "what would happen if . . . "). In the light of what we have said about the deathiness of immortality, and the relation between the erotic and the thought of a "dying," perhaps we might be justified in reading the last line of the great "Bright Star!" sonnet as naming states not simply alternative but also synonymous:

> And so live ever — or else swoon to death.

This use of the love-death equation is as startlingly paralleled in a letter to Fanny Brawne:

> I have two luxuries to brood over in my walks, your loveliness and the hour of my death. O that I could take possession of them both in the same moment. [Au.]

third stanzas had been questions, as the questions in the first stanza had been exclamations.

But though a lyric greatly profits by so strong a sense of continuousness, or perpetuity, I am trying to stress the fact that in the fourth stanza we *come upon* something. Indeed, this fourth stanza is related to the three foregoing stanzas quite as the sestet is related to the octave in Keats's sonnet, "On First Looking into Chapman's Homer":

Much have I travell'd in the realms of gold,
And many goodly states and kingdoms seen;
Round many western islands have I been
Which bards in fealty to Apollo hold.
Oft of one wide expanse had I been told
That deep-brow'd Homer ruled as his demesne;
Yet did I never breathe its pure serene
Till I heard Chapman speak out loud and bold:
Then felt I like some watcher of the skies
When a new planet swims into his ken;
Or like stout Cortez when with eagle eyes
He stared at the Pacific — and all his men
Look'd at each other with a wild surmise —
Silent, upon a peak in Darien.

I am suggesting that, just as the sestet in this sonnet, *comes upon a scene,* so it is with the fourth stanza of the Ode. In both likewise we end on the theme of silence; and is not the Ode's reference to the thing that "not a soul can tell" quite the same in quality as the sonnet's reference to a "wild surmise"?

Thus, with the Urn as viaticum (or rather, with the *poem* as viaticum, and *in the name* of the Urn), having symbolically enacted a kind of act that transcends our mortality, we round out the process by coming to dwell upon the transcendental ground of this act. The dead world of ancient Greece, as immortalized on an Urn surviving from that period, is the vessel of this deathy-deathless ambiguity. And we have gone dialectically from the "human" to the "divine" and thence to the "ground of the divine" (here tracing in poetic imagery the kind of "dramatistic" course we have considered, on the purely conceptual plane, in the theological speculations about the "grounds" for God's creative act). Necessarily, there must be certain inadequacies in the conception of this ground, precisely because of the fact that immortality can only be conceived in terms of death. Hence the reference to the "desolate" in a scene otherwise possessing the benignity of the eternal.

The imagery of pious sacrifice, besides its fitness for such thoughts of departure as when the spiritual act splits from the sensual pathos, suggests also a bond of communication between the levels (because of its immortal character in a mortal scene). And finally, the poem, in the name of the Urn, or under the aegis of the Urn, is such a bond. For we readers, by re-enacting it in the reading, use it as a viaticum to transport us into the quality of the scene which it depicts on its face (the scene containing as a fixity what the poem as act extends into a process). The scene *on* the Urn is really the scene *behind* the Urn; the Urn is literally the ground of this scene, but transcendentally the scene is the ground of the Urn. The Urn contains the scene out of which it arose.

We turn now to the closing stanza:

O Attic shape! Fair attitude! with brede
Of marble men, and maidens overwrought,
With forest branches and the trodden weed;
Thou, silent form, dost tease us out of thought
As doth eternity: Cold Pastoral!
When old age shall this generation waste,
Thou shalt remain, in midst of other woe
Than ours, a friend to man, to whom thou say'st,
"Beauty is truth, truth beauty," — that is all
Ye know on earth, and all ye need to know.

In the third stanza we were at a moment of heat, emphatically sharing an imagery of loves "panting" and "for ever warm" that was, in the transcendental order, companionate to "a burning forehead, and a parching tongue" in the order of the passions. But in the last stanza, as signalized in the marmorean utterance, "Cold Pastoral!" we have gone from transcendental fever to transcendental chill. Perhaps, were we to complete our exegesis, we should need reference to some physical step from phthisic chill, that we might detect here a final correlation between bodily passion and mental action. In any event we may note that, the mental action having departed from the bodily passion, the change from fever to chill is not a sufferance. For, as only the *benign* aspects of the fever had been left after the split, so it is a wholly benign chill on which the poem ends.[8]

I wonder whether anyone can read the reference to "brede of marble men and maidens overwrought" without thinking of "breed" for "brede" and "excited" for "overwrought." (Both expressions would thus merge notions of sexuality and craftsmanship, the erotic and the poetic.) As for the designating of the Urn as an "Attitude," it fits in admirably with our stress upon symbolic action. For an attitude is an arrested, or incipient *act* — not just an *object,* or *thing.*

Yeats, in *A Vision,* speaks of "the diagrams in Law's *Boehme,* where one lifts a paper to discover both the human entrails and the starry heavens." This equating of the deeply without and the deeply within (as also with Kant's famous remark) might well be remembered when we think of the sky that the "watcher" saw in Keats's sonnet. It is an internal sky, attained through meditations induced by the reading of a book. And so the oracle, whereby truth and beauty are proclaimed as one, would seem to derive from a profound inwardness.

Otherwise, without these introductory mysteries, "truth" and "beauty" were at odds. For whereas "beauty" had its fulfillment in romantic poetry, "truth" was coming to have its fulfillment in science, technological accuracy, accountancy, statistics, actuarial tables, and the like. Hence, without benefit of the rites which one enacts in a sympathetic reading of the Ode (rites that remove the discussion to a different level), the enjoyment of "beauty" would involve an esthetic kind of awareness radically in conflict with the kind of awareness deriving from the practical "truth." And as regards the tactics of the poem, this conflict would seem to be solved by "estheticizing" the true rather than by "verifying" the beautiful.

Earlier in our essay, we suggested reading "poetry" for "beauty" and "science" for "truth," with the oracle deriving its *liberating* quality from the fact that it is uttered at a time when the poem has taken us to a level where earthly contradictions do not operate. But we might also, in purely conceptual terms, attain a level where "poetry" and "science" cease to be at odds; namely: by translating the two terms into the "grammar" that lies behind them. That is: we could generalize the term "poetry" by widening it to the point where we could substitute for it the term "act." And we could widen "science" to the point where we could substitute "scene." Thus we have:

"beauty"	equals	"poetry"	equals	"act"
"truth"	equals	"science"	equals	"scene"

We would equate "beauty" with "act," because it is not merely a decorative thing, but an assertion, an affirmative, a creation, hence in the fullest sense an act. And we would equate "truth" or "science" with the "scenic" because science is a knowledge of *what is* — and *all that is* comprises the over-all universal *scene.* Our corresponding transcendence, then, got by "translation" into purely grammatical terms, would be: "Act is scene, scene act." We have got to this point by a kind of purely conceptual transformation that would correspond, I think, to the transformations of imagery leading to the oracle in the Ode.

"Act is scene, scene act." Unfortunately, I must break the symmetry a little. For poetry, as conceived in idealism (romanticism) could not quite be equated with *act,* but rather with *attitude.* For idealistic philosophies, with their stress upon the subjective, place primary stress upon the *agent* (the individual, ego, the will, etc.). It was medieval scholasticism that placed primary stress upon the *act.* And in the Ode the Urn (which is the vessel or representative of poetry) is called an "attitude," which is not outright an act, but an incipient or arrested act, a *state of mind,* the property of an *agent.* Keats, in calling the Urn an attitude, is *personifying* it. Or we might use the italicizing resources of dialectic by

[8]In a letter to Fanny Brawne, Keats touches upon the fever-chill contrast in a passage that also touches upon the love-death equation, though here the chill figures in an untransfigured state:

> I fear that I am too prudent for a dying kind of Lover. Yet, there is a great difference between going off in warm blood like Romeo; and making one's exit like a frog in a frost. [Au.]

saying that for Keats, beauty (poetry) was not so much "the *act* of an agent" as it was "the act of an *agent*."

Perhaps we can re-enforce this interpretation by examining kindred strategies in Yeats, whose poetry similarly derives from idealistic, romantic sources. Indeed, as we have noted elsewhere,[9] Yeats's vision of immortality in his Byzantium poems but carries one step further the Keatsian identification with the Grecian Urn:

> Once out of nature I shall never take
> My bodily form from any natural thing,
> But such a form as Grecian goldsmiths make
> Of hammered gold and gold enamelling . . .

Here certainly the poet envisions immortality as "esthetically" as Keats. For he will have immortality as a golden bird, a fabricated thing, a work of Grecian goldsmiths. Here we go in the same direction as the "overwrought" Urn, but farther along in that direction.

The ending of Yeats's poem, "Among School Children," helps us to make still clearer the idealistic stress upon agent:

> Labour is blossoming or dancing where
> The body is not bruised to pleasure soul,
> Nor beauty torn out of its own despair,
> Nor blear-eyed wisdom out of midnight oil.
> O chestnut tree, great rooted blossomer,
> Are you the leaf, the blossom or the bole?
> O body swayed to music, O brightening glance,
> How can we know the dancer from the dance?

Here the chestnut tree (as personified agent) is the ground of unity or continuity for all its scenic manifestations; and with the agent (dancer) is merged the act (dance). True, we seem to have here a commingling of act, scene, and agent, all three. Yet it is the *agent* that is "foremost among the equals." Both Yeats and Keats, of course, were much more "dramatistic" in their thinking than romantic poets generally, who usually center their efforts upon the translation of *scene* into terms of *agent* (as the materialistic science that was the dialectical counterpart of romantic idealism preferred conversely to translate *agent* into terms of *scene,* or in other words, to treat "consciousness" in terms of "matter," the "mental" in terms of the "physical," "people" in terms of "environment").

To review briefly: The poem begins with an ambiguous fever which in the course of the further development is "separated out," splitting into a bodily fever and a spiritual counterpart. The bodily passion is the malign aspect of the fever, the mental action its benign aspect. In the course of the development, the malign passion is transcended and the benign active partner, the intellectual exhilaration, takes over. At the beginning, where the two aspects were ambiguously one, the bodily passion would be the "scene" of the mental action (the "objective symptoms" of the body would be paralleled by the "subjective symptoms" of the mind, the bodily state thus being the other or ground of the mental state). But as the two become separated out, the mental action transcends the bodily passion. It becomes an act in its own right, making discoveries and assertions not grounded in the bodily passion. And this quality of action, in transcending the merely physical symptoms of the fever, would thus require a different ground or scene, one more suited in quality to the quality of the transcendent act.

The transcendent act is concretized, or "materialized," in the vision of the "immortal" scene, the reference in Stanza IV to the original scene of the Urn, the "heavenly" scene of the dead, or immortal, Greece (the scene in which the Urn was originally enacted and which is also fixed on its face). To indicate the internality of this vision, we referred to a passage in Yeats relating the "depths" of the sky without to the depths of the mind within; and we showed a similar pattern in Keats's account of the vision that followed his reading of Chapman's Homer. We suggested that the poet is here coming upon a new internal sky, through identification with the Urn as act, the same sky that he came upon through identification with the enactments of Chapman's translation.

This transcendent scene is the level at which the earthly laws of contradiction no longer prevail. Hence, in the terms of this scene, he can

[9]"On Motivation in Yeats" (*The Southern Review,* Winter 1942). [Au.]

proclaim the unity of truth and beauty (of science and art), a proclamation which he needs to make precisely because here was the basic split responsible for the romantic agitation (in both poetic and philosophic idealism). That is, it was gratifying to have the oracle proclaim the unity of poetry and science because the values of technology and business were causing them to be at odds. And from the perspective of a "higher level" (the perspective of a dead or immortal scene transcending the world of temporal contradictions) the split could be proclaimed once more a unity.

At this point, at this stage of exaltation, the fever has been replaced by chill. But the bodily passion has completely dropped out of account. All is now mental action. Hence, the chill (as in the ecstatic exclamation, "Cold Pastoral!") is proclaimed only in its benign aspect.

We may contrast this discussion with explanations such as a materialist of the Kretschmer school might offer. I refer to accounts of motivation that might treat disease as cause and poem as effect. In such accounts, the disease would not be "passive," but wholly active; and what we have called the mental action would be wholly passive, hardly more than an epiphenomenon, a mere symptom of the disease quite as are the fever and the chill themselves. Such accounts would give us no conception of the essential matter here, the intense linguistic activity.

Literature as Equipment for Living

Here I shall put down, as briefly as possible, a statement in behalf of what might be catalogued, with a fair degree of accuracy, as a *sociological* criticism of literature. Sociological criticism in itself is certainly not new. I shall here try to suggest what partially new elements or emphasis I think should be added to this old approach. And to make the "way in" as easy as possible, I shall begin with a discussion of proverbs.

I

Examine random specimens in *The Oxford Dictionary of English Proverbs.* You will note, I think, that there is no "pure" literature here. Everything is "medicine." Proverbs are designed for consolation or vengeance, for admonition or exhortation, for foretelling.

Or they name typical, recurrent situations. That is, people find a certain social relationship recurring so frequently that they must "have a word for it." The Eskimos have special names for many different kinds of snow (fifteen, if I remember rightly) because variations in the quality of snow greatly affect their living. Hence, they must "size up" snow much more accurately than we do. And the same is true of social phenomena. Social structures give rise to "type" situations, subtle subdivisions of the relationships involved in competitive and coöperative acts. Many proverbs seek to chart, in more or less homey and picturesque ways, these "type" situations. I submit that such naming is done, not for the sheer glory of the thing, but because of its bearing upon human welfare. A different name for snow implies a different kind of hunt. Some names for snow imply that one should not hunt at all. And similarly, the names for typical, recurrent social situations are not developed out of "disinterested curiosity," but because the names imply a command (what to expect, what to look out for).

To illustrate with a few representative examples:

Proverbs designed for consolation: "The sun does not shine on both sides of the hedge at once." "Think of ease, but work on." "Little troubles the eye, but far less the soul." "The worst luck now, the better another time." "The wind in one's face makes one wise." "He that hath lands hath quarrels." "He knows how to carry the dead cock home." "He is not poor that hath little, but he that desireth much."

For vengeance: "At length the fox is brought to the furrier." "Shod in the cradle, barefoot in the stubble." "Sue a beggar and get a louse." "The higher the ape goes, the more he shows his tail." "The moon does not heed the barking of dogs." "He measures another's corn by his own bushel." "He shuns the man who knows him well." "Fools tie knots and wise men loose them."

Proverbs that have to do with foretelling (the most obvious are those to do with the weather): "Sow peas and beans in the wane of the moon, Who soweth them sooner, he soweth too soon." "When the wind's in the north, the skilful fisher goes not forth." "When the sloe tree is as white as a sheet, sow your barley whether it be dry or wet." "When the sun sets bright and clear, An easterly wind you need not fear. When the sun sets in a bank, A westerly wind we shall not want."

In short: "Keep your weather eye open": be realistic about sizing up today's weather, because your accuracy has bearing upon tomorrow's weather. And forecast not only the meteorological weather, but also the social weather: "When the moon's in the full, then wit's in the wane." "Straws show which way the wind blows." "When the fish is caught, the net is laid aside." "Remove an old tree, and it will wither to death." "The wolf may lose his teeth, but never his nature." "He that bites on every weed must needs light on poison." "Whether the pitcher strikes the stone, or the stone the pitcher, it is bad for the pitcher." "Eagles catch no flies." "The more laws, the more offenders."

In this foretelling category we might also include the recipes for wise living, sometimes moral, sometimes technical: "First thrive, and then wive." "Think with the wise but talk with the vulgar." "When the fox preacheth, then beware your geese." "Venture a small fish to catch a great one." "Respect a man, he will do the more."

In the class of "typical, recurrent situations" we might put such proverbs and proverbial expressions as: "Sweet appears sour when we pay." "The treason is loved but the traitor is hated." "The wine in the bottle does not quench thirst." "The sun is never the worse for shining on a dunghill." "The lion kicked by an ass." "The lion's share." "To catch one napping." "To smell a rat." "To cool one's heels."

By all means, I do not wish to suggest that this is the only way in which the proverbs could be classified. For instance, I have listed in the "foretelling" group the proverb, "When the fox preacheth, then beware your geese." But it could obviously be "taken over" for vindictive purposes. Or consider a proverb like, "Virtue flies from the heart of a mercenary man." A poor man might obviously use it either to console himself for being poor (the implication being, "Because I am poor in money I am rich in virtue") or to strike at another (the implication being, "When he got money, what else could you expect of him but deterioration?"). In fact, we could even say that such symbolic vengeance would itself be an aspect of solace. And a proverb like "The sun is never the worse for shining on a dunghill" (which I have listed under "typical recurrent situations") might as well be put in the vindictive category.

The point of issue is not to find categories that "place" the proverbs once and for all. What I want is categories that suggest their active nature. Here is no "realism for its own sake." Here is realism for promise, admonition, solace, vengeance, foretelling, instruction, charting, all for the direct bearing that such acts have upon matters of welfare.

2

Step two: Why not extend such analysis of proverbs to encompass the whole field of literature? Could the most complex and sophisticated works of art legitimately be considered somewhat as "proverbs writ large"? Such leads, if held admissible, should help us to discover important facts about literary organization (thus satisfying the requirements of technical criticism). And the kind of observation from this perspective should apply beyond literature to life in general (thus helping to take literature out of its separate bin and give it a place in a general "sociological" picture).

The point of view might be phrased in this way: Proverbs are *strategies* for dealing with *situations.* In so far as situations are typical and recurrent in a given social structure, people develop names for them and strategies for handling them. Another name for strategies might be *attitudes.*

People have often commented on the fact that there are *contrary* proverbs. But I believe that the above approach to proverbs suggests a necessary modification of that comment. The apparent contradictions depend upon differences in *attitude,* involving a correspondingly different choice of *strategy.* Consider, for instance, the *apparently* opposite pair: "Repentance comes too late" and "Never too late to mend." The first is admonitory. It says in effect: "You'd better look out, or you'll get yourself too far into this business." The second is consolatory, saying in effect: "Buck up, old man, you can still pull out of this."

Some critics have quarreled with me about my selection of the word "strategy" as the name for this process. I have asked them to suggest an alternative term, so far without profit. The only one I can think of is "method." But if "strategy" errs in suggesting to some people an overly *conscious* procedure, "method" errs in suggesting an overly "*methodical*" one. Anyhow, let's look at the documents:

Concise Oxford Dictionary: "Strategy: Movement of an army or armies in a campaign, art of so moving or disposing troops or ships as to impose upon the enemy the place and time and conditions for fighting preferred by oneself" (from a Greek word that refers to the leading of an army).

New English Dictionary: "Strategy: The art of projecting and directing the larger military movements and operations of a campaign."

André Cheron, *Traité Complet d'Echecs: "On entend par stratégie les manoeuvres qui ont pour but la sortie et le bon arrangement des pièces."*[1]

[1]*Complete Treatise on Chess:* "Strategy signifies the maneuvers whose goal is attack and correct position." [Ed.]

Looking at these definitions, I gain courage. For surely, the most highly alembicated and sophisticated work of art, arising in complex civilizations, could be considered as designed to organize and command the army of one's thoughts and images, and to so organize them that one "imposes upon the enemy the time and place and conditions for fighting preferred by oneself." One seeks to "direct the larger movements and operations" in one's campaign of living. One "maneuvers," and the maneuvering is an "art."

Are not the final results one's "strategy"? One tries, as far as possible, to develop a strategy whereby one "can't lose." One tries to change the rules of the game until they fit his own necessities. Does the artist encounter disaster? He will "make capital" of it. If one is a victim of competition, for instance, if one is elbowed out, if one is willy-nilly more jockeyed against than jockeying, one can by the solace and vengeance of art convert this very "liability" into an "asset." One tries to fight on his own terms, developing a strategy for imposing the proper "time, place, and conditions."

But one must also, to develop a full strategy, be *realistic.* One must *size things up* properly. One cannot accurately know how things *will be,* what is promising and what is menacing, unless he accurately knows how things *are.* So the wise strategist will not be content with strategies of merely a self-gratifying sort. He will "keep his weather eye open." He will not too eagerly "read into" a scene an attitude that is irrelevant to it. He won't sit on the side of an active volcano and "see" it as a dormant plain.

Often, alas, he will. The great allurement in our present popular "inspirational literature," for instance, may be largely of this sort. It is a strategy for easy consolation. It "fills a need," since there is always a need for easy consolation— and in an era of confusion like our own the need is especially keen. So people are only too willing to "meet a man halfway" who will *play down* the realistic naming of our situation and *play up* such strategies as make solace cheap. However, I should propose a reservation here. We usually take it for granted that people who consume our current output of books on "How to Buy Friends and Bamboozle Oneself and Other People"[2] are reading as *students* who will attempt applying the recipes given. Nothing of the sort. *The reading of a book on the attaining of success is in itself the symbolic attaining of that success.* It is *while they read* that these readers are "succeeding." I'll wager that, in by far the great majority of cases, such readers make no serious attempt to apply the book's recipes. The lure of the book resides in the fact that the reader, while reading it, is then living in the aura of success. What he wants is *easy* success; and he gets it in symbolic form by the mere reading itself. To attempt applying such stuff in real life would be very difficult, full of many disillusioning problems.

Sometimes a different strategy may arise. The author may remain realistic, avoiding too easy a form of solace — yet he may get as far off the track in his own way. Forgetting that realism is an aspect for foretelling, he may take it as an end in itself. He is tempted to do this by two factors: (1) an *ill-digested* philosophy of science, leading him mistakenly to assume that "relentless" naturalistic "truthfulness" is a proper end in itself, and (2) a merely *competitive* desire to outstrip other writers by being "more realistic" than they. Works thus made "efficient" by tests of competition internal to the book trade are a kind of academicism not so named (the writer usually thinks of it as the *opposite* of academicism). Realism thus stepped up competitively might be distinguished from the proper sort by the name of "naturalism." As a way of "sizing things up," the naturalistic tradition tends to become as inaccurate as the "inspirational" strategy, though at the opposite extreme.

Anyhow, the main point is this: A work like *Madame Bovary* (or its homely American translation, *Babbitt*) is the strategic naming of a situation. It singles out a pattern of experience that is sufficiently representative of our social structure, that recurs sufficiently often *mutatis mutandis,* for people to "need a word for it" and to adopt an attitude towards it. Each work of art is the addition of a word to an informal dictionary (or, in the case of purely derivative artists, the addition of a subsidiary meaning to a word already given by some originating artist). As for *Madame Bovary,* the French critic Jules de Gaultier proposed to add it to our *formal* dictionary by coining the word "Bovarysme" and writing a whole book to say what he meant by it.

Mencken's book on *The American Language,* I hate to say, is splendid. I console myself with the reminder that Mencken didn't write it. Many millions of people wrote it, and Mencken was merely the amanuensis who took it down from their dictation. He found a true "vehicle" (that is, a book that could be greater than the author who wrote it). He gets the royalties, but the job was done by a collectivity. As you read that book, you see a people who were up against a new set of typical recurrent situations, situations typical of their business, their politics, their criminal organizations, their sports. Either there were no words for these in standard English, or people didn't know them, or they didn't "sound right." So a new vocabulary arose, to "give us a word for it." I see no reason for believing that Americans are unusually fertile in word-coinage. American slang was not developed out of some exceptional gift. It was developed out of the fact that new typical situations had arisen and people needed names for them. They had to "size things up." They had to console and strike, to promise and admonish. They had to describe for purposes of forecasting. And "slang" was the result. It is, by this analysis, simply *proverbs not so named,* a kind of "folk criticism."

3

With what, then, would "sociological criticism" along these lines be concerned? It would seek to codify the various strategies which artists have developed with relation to the naming of situations. In a sense, much of it would even be "timeless," for many of the "typical, recurrent situations" are not peculiar to our own civilization at all. The situations and strategies framed in Aesop's Fables, for instance, apply to human relations now just as fully as they applied in ancient Greece. They are, like philosophy, sufficiently "generalized" to extend far beyond the particular combination of events named by them

[2]Burke is parodying Dale Carnegie's *How to Make Friends and Influence People* in particular, but the genre of the self-help book continues to thrive today. [Ed.]

in any one instance. They name an "essence." Or, we could say that they are on a "high level of abstraction." One doesn't usually think of them as "abstract," since they are usually so concrete in their stylistic expression. But they invariably aim to discern the "general behind the particular" (which would suggest that they are good Goethe).

The attempt to treat literature from the standpoint of situations and strategies suggests a variant of Spengler's notion of the "contemporaneous." By "contemporaneity" he meant corresponding stages of different cultures. For instance, if modern New York is much like decadent Rome, then we are "contemporaneous" with decadent Rome, or with some corresponding decadent city among the Mayas, etc. It is in this sense that situations are "timeless," "non-historical," "contemporaneous." A given human relationship may be at one time named in terms of foxes and lions, if there are foxes and lions about; or it may now be named in terms of salesmanship, advertising, the tactics of politicians, etc. But beneath the change in particulars, we may often discern the naming of the one situation.

So sociological criticism, as here understood, would seek to assemble and codify this lore. It might occasionally lead us to outrage good taste, as we sometimes found exemplified in some great sermon or tragedy or abstruse work of philosophy the same strategy as we found exemplified in a dirty joke. At this point, we'd put the sermon and the dirty joke together, thus "grouping by situation" and showing the range of possible particularizations. In his exceptionally discerning essay, "A Critic's Job of Work," R. P. Blackmur says, "I think on the whole his (Burke's) method could be applied with equal fruitfulness to Shakespeare, Dashiell Hammett, or Marie Corelli."[3] When I got through wincing, I had to admit that Blackmur was right. This article is an attempt to say for the method what can be said. As a matter of fact, I'll go a step further and maintain: You can't properly put Marie Corelli and Shakespeare apart until you have first put them together. First genus, then differentia. The strategy in common is the genus. The *range* or *scale* or *spectrum* of particularizations is the differentia.

Anyhow, that's what I'm driving at. And that's why reviewers sometime find in my work "intuitive" leaps that are dubious as "science." They are not "leaps" at all. They are classifications, groupings, made on the basis of some strategic element common to the items grouped. They are neither more nor less "intuitive" than *any* grouping or classification of social events. Apples can be grouped with bananas as fruits, and they can be grouped with tennis balls as round. I am simply proposing, in the social sphere, a method of classification with reference to *strategies*.

The method has these things to be said in its favor: It gives definite insight into the organization of literary works; and it automatically breaks down the barriers erected about literature as a specialized pursuit. People can classify novels by reference to three kinds, eight kinds, seventeen kinds. It doesn't matter. Students patiently copy down the professor's classification and pass examinations on it, because the range of possible academic classifications is endless. Sociological classification, as herein suggested, would derive its relevance from the fact that it should apply both to works of art and to social situations outside of art.

It would, I admit, violate current pieties, break down current categories, and thereby "outrage good taste." But "good taste" has become *inert*. The classifications I am proposing would be *active*. I think that what we need is active categories.

These categories will lie on the bias across the categories of modern specialization. The new alignment will outrage in particular those persons who take the division of faculties in our universities to be an exact replica of the way in which God himself divided up the universe. We have had the Philosophy of Being; and we have had the Philosophy of Becoming. In typical contemporary specialization, we have been getting the Philosophy of the Bin. Each of these mental localities has had its own peculiar way of life, its

[3]Richard P. Blackmur, "A Critic's Job of Work" (1935), published in *Language as Gesture* (1952). [Ed.]

own values, even its own special idiom for seeing, thinking, and "proving." Among other things, a sociological approach should attempt to provide a reintegrative point of view, a broader empire of investigation encompassing the lot.

What would such sociological categories be like? They would consider works of art, I think, as strategies for selecting enemies and allies, for socializing losses, for warding off evil eye, for purification, propitiation, and desanctification, consolation and vengeance, admonition and exhortation, implicit commands or instructions of one sort or another. Art forms like "tragedy" or "comedy" or "satire" would be treated as *equipments for living,* that size up situations in various ways and in keeping with correspondingly various attitudes. The typical ingredients of such forms would be sought. Their relation to typical situations would be stressed. Their comparative values would be considered, with the intention of formulating a "strategy of strategies," the "overall" strategy obtained by inspection of the lot.

F. R. Leavis

1895–1978

Frank Raymond Leavis, a critic devoted to firm standards and implacable moralism, was born in Cambridge, England, and was educated there at the Perse School. Leavis survived his tenure as an ambulance bearer on the Western Front in World War I to become a lecturer at Emmanuel College, Cambridge, in 1925. He moved on to Downing College in 1932, where he was elected to a fellowship in 1936. He and his wife, the former Queenie Dorothy Roth, were the founding editors of *Scrutiny* (1932–53), a quarterly journal of criticism devoted to the advancement of their critical principles. Leavis retired from Downing College in 1962 to serve as a visiting professor of English at a number of universities, including those of York (1965–68), Wales (1969), and Bristol (1970). He received numerous honorary degrees, and in the year of his death was made a Companion of Honour.

It has been said that Leavis's early critical interest was in poetry (*New Bearings in English Poetry: A Study of the Contemporary Situation* [1932]; *Revaluation: Tradition and Development in English Poetry* [1936]) and that his later interest was in the novel (*The Great Tradition* [1948]; *D. H. Lawrence: Novelist* [1955]; *"Anna Karenina," and Other Essays* [1968]; *Dickens: The Novelist* [1971; with Q. D. Leavis]). But this generalization does not take into account his consistent preoccupation with criticism itself (*The Common Pursuit* [1952]) and with questions of teaching and the university (*Education and the University: A Sketch for an "English School"* [1943]; *Literature in Our Time and the University* [1969; based on the Clark Lectures of 1965]; *The Living Principle: "English" as a Discipline of Thought* [1975]). In fact one must go beyond these categories and see Leavis as one of the successors to Matthew Arnold in viewing literary study (as Arnold had viewed literature itself) as a form of the "criticism of life" that would pierce through the dominant ideology and allow a blind and mechanical age to know and redeem itself.

Like his German contemporary, Martin Heidegger, and like the American New Critics, Leavis viewed the world of the twentieth century as anomic and rudderless, drifting after World War I had destroyed any semblance of the old Victorian consensus. Although England, unlike Germany, had been victorious in the war, the aristocratic ideology of the military elite had been exposed as pernicious folly in the mud of the Flanders trenches. Organized religion, already in retreat in Arnold's day, failed to offer any coherent explanation for the disasters of the war, and the desperate hedonism of the 1920s testified both to the emptiness of modern life and the loss of faith in any of the codes that had regulated it. Leavis's messianic vision of literary studies was a response to this moment in history.

Was it possible for a small cadre of highly educated, deeply cultured individuals to counter the leveling forces of popular literature and middlebrow culture, to restore coherence to contemporary life? This was the mission Leavis and his students undertook. Together with his contemporaries at Cambridge, who included I. A. Richards and William Empson (see p. 735), Leavis set up literary studies as a way of understanding the evolution of modern life in all its complexity and established the prestige of the literary degree as one that fitted the bearer for the highest offices. As Terry Eagleton has put it, "In the early 1920s it was desperately unclear why English was worth studying at all; by the early 1930s it had become a question of why it was worth wasting your time on anything else. English was not only a subject worth pursuing, but *the* supremely civilizing pursuit, the spiritual essence of the social formation."[1] Before Leavis, professors of literature had been gifted aesthetes and dilettantes or pedantic philological pedagogues; after Leavis, it was the aim of the literary scholar to bring his research to bear on sociopolitical issues and the conduct of cultural life. He was to guard and give exposition to the literary and cultural tradition that united the nation. From the perspective of the 1990s, it seems clear that although Leavis's own values for analyzing literature may no longer be fashionable, his vision of what the profession of letters was all about has not changed. And in this sense he may be the most influential British critic of the century.

Just as Matthew Arnold had endorsed "touchstones" for determining which literary texts (or stanzas, or single lines) possessed the "high seriousness" that would make them suitable for altering the consciousness of Victorians in need of standards of quality, so too Leavis's program included a re-evaluation of the course of English literature. Leavis got rid of the previously standard practice of studying all the literary texts of a century, regardless of their tendency, and substituted a smaller and denser canon of works he approved of, ones that engaged "properly" with the essential social and cultural issues. Literary figures who were interested in form more than content, in the beauties of language rather than its ideological uses, were downgraded. The mellifluous Tennyson was not to be preferred to the harsh, difficult Hopkins. The clever self-referentiality and aestheticism of Joyce ranked far below the prophetic visions and cultural radicalism of D. H. Lawrence. The récherché medievalism of Spenser and the idiosyncratic religiosity of Milton devalued them beneath Donne and Marvell. While a few of these judgments — like that on Joyce — were ultimately ignored, Leavis's influence in forming the canon for English and American readers at midcentury was enormous.

It is in this context of moral judgment and cultural politics that we need to place the following selection, from the first chapter of the revised edition of *The Great Tradition* (1960), in which Leavis identifies the few novelists of whose vision of life he wholeheartedly approves. It is not easy, at times, to discern the precise criteria Leavis uses to make his selection. One conservative comedic novelist (Austen) might be a leader of the canon, while another (Fielding) might be beyond the pale. Leavis at first dismissed Dickens as a "mere entertainer"; later he accepted him into the Great Tradition. What seems to garner Leavis's basic approval is a certain core of psychological realism, which is one common denominator in Eliot, James, and Conrad, as long as it is not wrecked by playfulness (as in Trollope and Thackeray), or by a deep pessimism (as in Hardy or Ford Madox Ford). Leavis was once challenged by René Wellek to give some sort of general exposition to his criteria of

[1]Terry Eagleton, *Literary Theory: An Introduction* (Minneapolis: University of Minnesota Press, 1983), p. 31.

value, to move beyond judgment to some sort of *theory* — and he declined. Theory as we know it was neither his forte nor his business: He was one of the great magisterial figures — the Samuel Johnson of the twentieth century — and his refusal to theorize in this age of theory is one mark of his peculiar place in the critical tradition.

Selected Bibliography

Bell, Michael. *F. R. Leavis*. New York and London: Routledge, 1988.

Bilan, R. P. *The Literary Criticism of F. R. Leavis*. London: Cambridge University Press, 1979.

Cordner, Christopher. "F. R. Leavis and the Moral in Literature." In *On Literary Theory and Philosophy,* ed. Richard Freadman and Lloyd Reinhardt. New York: St. Martin's Press, 1991, pp. 60–81.

Gregor, Ian. "F. R. Leavis and The Great Tradition." *Sewanee Review* 93 (1985): 434–46.

Kinch, M. B., William Baker, and John Kimber. *F. R. Leavis and Q. D. Leavis: An Annotated Bibliography*. New York: Garland, 1989.

Robertson, P. J. *The Leavises on Fiction: A Historic Partnership*. New York: St. Martin's Press, 1981.

Samson, Anne. *F. R. Leavis*. Toronto: University of Toronto Press, 1992.

From *The Great Tradition*

. . . not dogmatically but deliberately . . .
— JOHNSON, *Preface to Shakespeare*

The great English novelists are Jane Austen, George Eliot, Henry James, and Joseph Conrad — to stop for the moment at that comparatively safe point in history. Since Jane Austen, for special reasons, needs to be studied at considerable length, I confine myself in this book to the last three. Critics have found me narrow, and I have no doubt that my opening proposition, whatever I may say to explain and justify it, will be adduced in reinforcement of their strictures. It passes as fact (in spite of the printed evidence) that I pronounced Milton negligible, dismiss "the Romantics," and hold that, since Donne, there is no poet we need bother about except Hopkins and Eliot. The view, I suppose, will be as confidently attributed to me that, except Jane Austen, George Eliot, James, and Conrad, there are no novelists in English worth reading.

The only way to escape misrepresentation is never to commit oneself to any critical judgment that makes an impact — that is, never to *say* anything. I still, however, think that the best way to promote profitable discussion is to be as clear as possible with oneself about what one sees and judges, to try and establish the essential discriminations in the given field of interest, and to state them as clearly as one can (for disagreement, if necessary). And it seems to me that in the field of fiction some challenging discriminations are very much called for; the field is so large and offers such insidious temptations to complacent confusions of judgment and to critical indolence. It is of the field of fiction belonging to Literature that I am thinking, and I am thinking in particular of the present vogue of the Victorian age. Trollope, Charlotte Yonge, Mrs. Gaskell, Wilkie Collins,

Charles Reade, Charles and Henry Kingsley, Marryat, Shorthouse[1] — one after another the minor novelists of that period are being commended to our attention, written up, and publicized by broadcast, and there is a marked tendency to suggest that they not only have various kinds of interest to offer but that they are living classics. (Are not they all in the literary histories?) There are Jane Austen, Mrs. Gaskell, Scott, "the Brontës,"[2] Dickens, Thackeray, George Eliot, Trollope, and so on, all, one gathers, classical novelists.

It is necessary to insist, then, that there are important distinctions to be made, and that far from all of the names in the literary histories really belong to the realm of significant creative achievement. And as a recall to a due sense of differences it is well to start by distinguishing the few really great — the major novelists who count in the same way as the major poets, in the sense that they not only change the possibilities of the art for practitioners and readers, but that they are significant in terms of the human awareness they promote; awareness of the possibilities of life.[3]

To insist on the pre-eminent few in this way is not to be indifferent to tradition; on the contrary, it is the way towards understanding what tradition is. "Tradition," of course, is a term with many forces — and often very little at all. There is a habit nowadays of suggesting that there is a tradition of "the English Novel," and that all that can be said of the tradition (that being its peculiarity) is that "the English Novel" can be anything you like. To distinguish the major novelists in the spirit proposed is to form a more useful idea of tradition (and to recognize that the conventionally established view of the past of English fiction needs to be drastically revised). It is in terms of the major novelists, those significant in the way suggested, that tradition, in any serious sense, has its significance.

To be important historically is not, of course, to be necessarily one of the significant few. Fielding deserves the place of importance given him in the literary histories, but he hasn't the kind of classical distinction we are also invited to credit him with. He is important not because he leads to Mr. J. B. Priestley but because he leads to Jane Austen, to appreciate whose distinction is to feel that life isn't long enough to permit of one's giving much time to Fielding or any to Mr. Priestley.

Fielding made Jane Austen possible by opening the central tradition of English fiction. In fact, to say that the English novel began with him is as reasonable as such propositions ever are. He completed the work begun by *The Tatler* and *The Spectator,* in the pages of which we see the drama turning into the novel — that this development should occur by way of journalism being in the natural course of things. To the art of presenting character and *mœurs*[4] learnt in that school (he

[1]The novelist who has not been revived is Disraeli. Yet, though he is not one of the great novelists, he is so alive and intelligent as to deserve permanent currency, at any rate in the trilogy *Coningsby, Sybil* and *Tancred:* his own interests as expressed in these books — the interests of a supremely intelligent politician who has a sociologist's understanding of civilization and its movement in his time — are so mature. [Au.]

[2]See Note: "The Brontës," [p. 607]. [Au.]

[3]Characteristic of the confusion I am contending against is the fashion (for which the responsibility seems to go back to Virginia Woolf and Mr. E. M. Forster) of talking of *Moll Flanders* as a "great novel." Defoe was a remarkable writer, but all that need be said about him as a novelist was said by Leslie Stephen in *Hours in a Library* (First Series). He made no pretension to practising the novelist's art, and matters little as an influence. In fact, the only influence that need be noted is that represented by the use made of him in the nineteen-twenties by the practitioners of the fantastic *conte* (or pseudo-moral fable) with its empty pretence of significance.

Associated with this use of Defoe is the use that was made in much the same *milieu* of Sterne, in whose irresponsible (and nasty) trifling, regarded as in some way extraordinarily significant and mature, was found a sanction for attributing value to other trifling.

The use of Bunyan by T. F. Powys is quite another matter. It is a mark of the genuine nature of Mr. Powys's creative gift (his work seems to me not to have had due recognition) that he has been able to achieve a kind of traditional relation to Bunyan — especially, of course, in *Mr. Weston's Good Wine.* Otherwise there is little that can be said with confidence about Bunyan as an influence. And yet we know him to have been for two centuries one of the most frequented of all classics, and in such a way that he counts immeasurably in the English-speaking consciousness. It is, perhaps, worth saying that his influence would tend strongly to reinforce the un-Flaubertian quality of the line of English classical fiction . . . as well as to co-operate with the Jonsonian tradition of morally significant typicality in characters. [Au.]

[4]Manners. [Ed.]

himself, before he became a novelist, was both playwright and periodical essayist) he joined a narrative habit the nature of which is sufficiently indicated by his own phrase, "comic epic in prose." That the eighteenth century, which hadn't much lively reading to choose from, but had much leisure, should have found *Tom Jones* exhilarating is not surprising; nor is it that Scott, and Coleridge, should have been able to give that work superlative praise. Standards are formed in comparison, and what opportunities had they for that? But the conventional talk about the "perfect construction" of *Tom Jones* (the late Hugh Walpole brought it out triumphantly and you may hear it in almost any course of lectures on "the English Novel") is absurd. There can't be subtlety of organization without richer matter to organize, and subtler interests, than Fielding has to offer. He is credited with range and variety and it is true that some episodes take place in the country and some in Town, some in the churchyard and some in the inn, some on the high-road and some in the bed-chamber, and so on. But we haven't to read a very large proportion of *Tom Jones* in order to discover the limits of the essential interests it has to offer us. Fielding's attitudes, and his concern with human nature, are simple, and not such as to produce an effect of anything but monotony (on a mind, that is, demanding more than external action) when exhibited at the length of an "epic in prose." What he *can* do appears to best advantage in *Joseph Andrews*. *Jonathan Wild,* with its famous irony, seem to me mere hobbledehoydom (much as one applauds the determination to explode the gangster-hero), and by *Amelia* Fielding has gone soft.

We all know that if we want a more inward interest it is to Richardson we must go. And there is more to be said for Johnson's preference, and his emphatic way of expressing it at Fielding's expense, than is generally recognized. Richardson's strength in the analysis of emotional and moral states is in any case a matter of common acceptance; and *Clarissa* is a really impressive work. But it's no use pretending that Richardson can ever be made a current classic again. The substance of interest that he too has to offer is in its own way extremely limited in range and variety, and the demand he makes on the reader's time is in proportion — and absolutely — so immense as to be found, in general, prohibitive (though I don't know that I wouldn't sooner read through again *Clarissa* than *A la recherche du temps perdu*). But we can understand well enough why his reputation and influence should have been so great throughout Europe; and his immediately relevant historical importance is plain: he too is a major fact in the background of Jane Austen.

The social gap between them was too wide, however, for his work to be usable by her directly: the more he tries to deal with ladies and gentlemen, the more immitigably vulgar he is. It was Fanny Burney who, by transposing him into educated life, made it possible for Jane Austen to absorb what he had to teach her. Here we have one of the important lines of English literary history — Richardson–Fanny Burney–Jane Austen. It is important because Jane Austen is one of the truly great writers, and herself a major fact in the background of other great writers. Not that Fanny Burney is the only other novelist who counts in her formation; she read all there was to read, and took all that was useful to her — which wasn't only lessons.[5] In fact, Jane Austen, in her indebtedness to others, provides an exceptionally illuminating study of the nature of originality, and she exemplifies beautifully the relations of "the individual talent" to tradition. If the influences bearing on her hadn't comprised something fairly to be called tradition she couldn't have found herself and her true direction; but her relation to tradition is a creative one. She not only makes tradition for those coming after, but her achievement has for us a retroactive effect: as we look back beyond her we see in what goes before, and see because of her, potentialities and significances brought out in such a way that, for us, she creates the tradition we see leading down to her. Her work, like the work of all great creative writers, gives a meaning to the past.[6]

[5]For the relation of Jane Austen to other writers see the essay by Q. D. Leavis, "A Critical Theory of Jane Austen's Writings," in *Scrutiny* 10, no. 1. [Au.]

[6]In the next four paragraphs, omitted here, Leavis discusses other critics who have seen the central tradition of the English novel beginning with Austen. [Ed.]

The great novelists in that tradition are all very much concerned with "form"; they are all very original technically, having turned their genius to the working out of their own appropriate methods and procedures. But the peculiar quality of their preoccupation with "form" may be brought out by a contrasting reference to Flaubert. Reviewing Thomas Mann's *Der Tod in Venedig,* D. H. Lawrence[7] adduces Flaubert as figuring to the world the "will of the writer to be greater than and undisputed lord over the stuff he writes." This attitude in art, as Lawrence points out, is indicative of an attitude in life — or towards life. Flaubert, he comments, "stood away from life as from a leprosy." For the later Aesthetic writers, who, in general, represent in a weak kind of way the attitude that Flaubert maintained with a perverse heroism, "form" and "style" are ends to be sought for themselves, and the chief preoccupation is with elaborating a beautiful style to apply to the chosen subject. There is George Moore, who in the best circles, I gather (from a distance), is still held to be among the very greatest masters of prose, though — I give my own limited experience for what it is worth — it is very hard to find an admirer who, being pressed, will lay his hand on his heart and swear he has read one of the "beautiful" novels through. "The novelist's problem is to evolve an orderly composition which is also a convincing picture of life" — this is the way an admirer of George Moore sees it. Lord David Cecil, attributing this way to Jane Austen, and crediting her with a superiority over George Eliot in "satisfying the rival claims of life and art," explains this superiority, we gather, by a freedom from moral preoccupations that he supposes her to enjoy. (George Eliot, he tells us, was a Puritan, and earnestly bent on instruction.)[8]

As a matter of fact, when we examine the formal perfection of *Emma,* we find that it can be appreciated only in terms of the moral preoccupations that characterize the novelist's peculiar interest in life. Those who suppose it to be an "aesthetic matter," a beauty of "composition" that is combined, miraculously, with "truth to life," can give no adequate reason for the view that *Emma* is a great novel, and no intelligent account of its perfection of form. It is in the same way true of the other great English novelists that their interest in their art gives them the opposite of an affinity with Pater and George Moore; it is, brought to an intense focus, an unusually developed interest in life. For, far from having anything of Flaubert's disgust or disdain or boredom, they are all distinguished by a vital capacity for experience, a kind of reverent openness before life, and a marked moral intensity.

It might be commented that what I have said of Jane Austen and her successors is only what can be said of any novelist of unqualified greatness. That is true. But there *is* — and this is the point — an English tradition, and these great classics of English fiction belong to it; a tradition that, in the talk about "creating characters" and "creating worlds," and the appreciation of Trollope and Mrs. Gaskell and Thackeray and Meredith and Hardy and Virginia Woolf, appears to go unrecognized. It is not merely that we have no Flaubert (and I hope I haven't seemed to suggest that a Flaubert is no more worth having than a George Moore). Positively, there is a continuity from Jane Austen. It is not for nothing that George Eliot admired her work profoundly, and wrote one of the earliest appreciations of it to be published. The writer whose intellectual weight and moral earnestness strike some critics as her handicap certainly saw in Jane Austen something more than an ideal contemporary of Lytton Strachey.[9] What one great original artist learns from another, whose genius and problems are necessarily very different, is the hardest kind of "influence" to define, even when we see it to have been

[7]D. H. Lawrence, *Phoenix: The Posthumous Papers of D. H. Lawrence* (London: Heinemann, 1936), p. 308. [Au.]

[8]She is a moralist and a highbrow, the two handicaps going together. "Her humour is less affected by her intellectual approach. Jokes, thank heaven, need not be instructive." — Lord David Cecil, *Early Victorian Novelists: Essays in Revaluation* (London: Constable, 1934), p. 299. [Au.]

[9]It is perhaps worth insisting that Peacock is more than that too. He is not at all in the same class as the Norman Douglas of *South Wind* and *They Went.* In his ironical treatment of contemporary society and civilization he is seriously applying serious standards, so that his books, which are obviously not novels in the same sense as Jane Austen's, have a permanent life as light reading — indefinitely rereadable — for minds with mature interests. [Au.]

of the profoundest importance. The obvious manifestation of influence is to be seen in this kind of passage:

> A little daily embroidery had been a constant element in Mrs. Transome's life; that soothing occupation of taking stitches to produce what neither she nor any one else wanted, was then the resource of many a well-born and unhappy woman.
>
> In short, he felt himself to be in love in the right place, and was ready to endure a great deal of predominance, which, after all, a man could always put down when he liked. Sir James had no idea that he should ever like to put down the predominance of this handsome girl, in whose cleverness he delighted. Why not? A man's mind — what there is of it — has always the advantage of being masculine, — as the smallest birch-tree is of a higher kind than the most soaring palm — and even his ignorance is of a sounder quality. Sir James might not have originated this estimate; but a kind Providence furnishes the limpest personality with a little gum or starch in the form of tradition.[10]

The kind of irony here is plainly akin to Jane Austen's — though it is characteristic enough of George Eliot; what she found was readily assimilated to her own needs. In Jane Austen herself the irony has a serious background, and is no mere display of "civilization." George Eliot wouldn't have been interested in it if she hadn't perceived its full significance — its relation to the essential moral interest offered by Jane Austen's art. And here we come to the profoundest kind of influence, that which is not manifested in likeness. One of the supreme debts one great writer can owe another is the realization of unlikeness (there is, of course, no significant unlikeness without the common concern — and the common seriousness of concern — with essential human issues). One way of putting the difference between George Eliot and the Trollopes whom we are invited to consider along with her is to say that she was capable of understanding Jane Austen's greatness and capable of learning from her. And except for Jane Austen there was no novelist to learn from — none whose work had any bearing on her own essential problems as a novelist.[11]

Is there no name later than Conrad's to be included in the great tradition? There is, I am convinced, one: D. H. Lawrence. Lawrence, in the English language, was the great genius of our time (I mean the age, or climatic phase, following Conrad's). It would be difficult to separate the novelist off for consideration, but it was in the novel that he committed himself to the hardest and most sustained creative labour, and he was, as a novelist, the representative of vital and significant development. He might, he has shown conclusively, have gone on writing novels with the kind of "character creation" and psychology that the conventional cultivated reader immediately appreciates — novels that demanded no unfamiliar effort of approach. He might — if his genius had let him. In nothing is the genius more manifest than in the way in which, after the great success — and *succès d'estime*[12] — of *Sons and Lovers* he gives up that mode and devotes himself to the exhausting toil of working out the new things, the developments, that as the highly conscious and intelligent servant of life he saw to be necessary. Writing to Edward Garnett of the work that was to become *Women in Love* he says: "It is *very* different from *Sons and Lovers:* written in another language almost. I shall be sorry if you don't like it, but am prepared. I shan't write in the same manner as *Sons and Lovers* again, I think — in that hard, violent style full of sensation and presentation."[13]

Describing at length what he is trying to do he says:

> You mustn't look in my novel for the old stable *ego* of the character. There is another *ego,* according to whose action the individual is unrecognizable, and passes through, as it were, allotropic

[10]The passages are from *Middlemarch.* [Ed.]

[11]In the next passage, omitted here, Leavis continues to trace the line of development and influence through Henry James and Joseph Conrad and to discuss why Dickens, though a "great genius," is not a stimulus to an "adult mind." [Ed.]

[12]Recognition. [Ed.]

[13]*The Letters of D. H. Lawrence,* ed. Aldous Huxley (London: Heinemann, 1934), p. 172. [Au.]

states which it needs a deeper sense than any we've been used to exercise, to discover are states of the same single radically unchanged element. (Like as diamond and coal are the same pure simple element of carbon. The ordinary novel would trace the history of the diamond — but I say, "Diamond, what! This is carbon." And my diamond might be coal or soot, and my theme is carbon.) You must not say my novel is shaky — it is not perfect, because I am not expert in what I want to do. But it is the real thing, say what you like. And I shall get my reception, if not now, then before long. Again I say, don't look for the development of the novel to follow the lines of certain characters: the characters fall into the form of some other rhythmic form, as when one draws a fiddle-bow across a fine tray delicately sanded, the sand takes lines unknown.[14]

He is a most daring and radical innovator in "form," method, technique. And his innovations and experiments are dictated by the most serious and urgent kind of interest in life. This is the spirit of it:

> Do you know Cassandra in Aeschylus and Homer? She is one of the world's great figures, and what the Greeks and Agamemnon did to her is symbolic of what mankind has done to her since — raped and despoiled her, to their own ruin. It is not your brain that you must trust to, nor your will — but to that fundamental pathetic faculty for receiving the hidden waves that come from the depths of life, and for transferring them to the unreceptive world. It is something which happens below the consciousness, and below the range of the will — it is something which is unrecognizable and frustrated and destroyed.[15]

It is a spirit that, for all the unlikeness, relates Lawrence closely to George Eliot.[16] He writes, again, to Edward Garnett:[17]

> You see — you tell me I am half a Frenchman and one-eighth a Cockney. But that isn't it. I have very often the vulgarity and disagreeableness of the common people, as you say Cockney, and I may be a Frenchman. But primarily I am a passionately religious man, and my novels must be written from the depth of my religious experience. That I must keep to, because I can only work like that. And my Cockneyism and commonness are only when the deep feeling doesn't find its way out, and a sort of jeer comes instead, and sentimentality and purplism. But you should see the religious, earnest, suffering man in me first, and then the flippant or common things after. Mrs. Garnett says I have no true nobility — with all my cleverness and charm. But that is not true. It is there, in spite of all the littlenesses and commonnesses.

It is this spirit, by virtue of which he can truly say that what he writes must be written from the depth of his religious experience, that makes him, in my opinion, so much more significant in relation to the past and future, so much more truly creative as a technical inventor, an innovator, a master of language, than James Joyce. I know that Mr. T. S. Eliot has found in Joyce's work something that recommends Joyce to him as positively religious in tendency (see *After Strange Gods*). But it seems plain to me that there is no organic principle determining, informing, and controlling into a vital whole, the elaborate analogical structure, the extraordinary variety of technical devices, the attempts at an exhaustive rendering of consciousness, for which *Ulysses* is remarkable, and which got it accepted by a cosmopolitan literary world as a new start. It is rather, I think, a dead end, or at least a pointer to disintegration — a view strengthened by Joyce's own development (for I think it significant and appropriate that *Work in Progress — Finnegans Wake,* as it became — should have engaged the interest of the inventor of Basic English).

It is true that we can point to the influence of Joyce in a line of writers to which there is no parallel issuing from Lawrence. But I find here further confirmation of my view. For I think that in these writers, in whom a regrettable (if minor) strain of Mr. Eliot's influence seems to me to join with that of Joyce, we have, insofar as we have anything significant, the wrong kind of reaction against liberal idealism.[18] I have in mind writers in whom Mr. Eliot has expressed an interest in

[14]*Letters,* p. 198. [Au.]

[15]*Letters,* p. 232. [Au.]

[16]*Letters,* p. 190. [Au.]

[17]Lawrence too has been called a Puritan. [Au.]

[18]See D. H. Lawrence's *Fantasia of the Unconscious,* especially Ch. XI. [Au.]

strongly favourable terms: Djuna Barnes of *Nightwood,* Henry Miller, Lawrence Durrell of *The Black Book.* In these writers — at any rate in the last two (and the first seems to me insignificant) — the spirit of what we are offered affects me as being essentially a desire, in Laurentian phrase, to "do dirt" on life. It seems to me important that one should, in all modesty, bear one's witness in these matters. "One must speak for life and growth, amid all this mass of destruction and disintegration."[19] This is Lawrence, and it is the spirit of all his work. It is the spirit of the originality that gives his novels their disconcerting quality, and gives them the significance of works of genius.

I am not contending that he isn't, as a novelist, open to a great deal of criticism, or that his achievement is as a whole satisfactory (the potentiality being what it was). He wrote his later books far too hurriedly. But I know from experience that it is far too easy to conclude that his very aim and intention condemned him to artistic unsatisfactoriness. I am thinking in particular of two books at which he worked very hard, and in which he developed his disconcertingly original interests and approaches — *The Rainbow* and *Women in Love.* Reread, they seem to me astonishing works of genius, and very much more largely successful than they did when I read them (say) fifteen years ago. I still think that *The Rainbow* doesn't build up sufficiently into a whole. But I shouldn't be quick to offer my criticism of *Women in Love,* being pretty sure that I should in any case have once more to convict myself of stupidity and habit-blindness on later rereading. And after these novels there comes, written, perhaps, with an ease earned by this hard work done, a large body of short stories and *nouvelles* that are as indubitably successful works of genius as any the world has to show.

[19]*The Letters of D. H. Lawrence,* p. 256. [Au.]

I have, then, given my hostages. What I think and judge I have stated as responsibly and clearly as I can. Jane Austen, George Eliot, Henry James, Conrad, and D. H. Lawrence: the great tradition of the English novel is *there.*

NOTE: "THE BRONTËS"

It is tempting to retort that there is only one Brontë. Actually, Charlotte, though claiming no part in the great line of English fiction (it is significant that she couldn't see why any value should be attached to Jane Austen), has a permanent interest of a minor kind. She had a remarkable talent that enabled her to do something first-hand and new in the rendering of personal experience, above all in *Villette.*

The genius, of course, was Emily. I have said nothing about *Wuthering Heights* because that astonishing work seems to me a kind of sport. It may, all the same, very well have had some influence of an essentially undetectable kind: she broke completely, and in the most challenging way, both with the Scott tradition that imposed on the novelist a romantic resolution of his themes, and with the tradition coming down from the eighteenth century that demanded a plane-mirror reflection of the surface of "real" life. Out of her a minor tradition comes, to which belongs, most notably, *The House with the Green Shutters.*

Lionel Trilling

1905–1975

Lionel Trilling was born in New York City, the son of David Trilling, a Jewish immigrant from Bialystok, Poland, who became a furrier and custom tailor, and Fannie Cohen Trilling, who grew up in London's East End and who imparted to her son a lifelong Anglophilia. Though a descendant of the Bialystoker Rabbi, Trilling was always ambivalent about his ethnic status: He identified himself as a Jew and wrote for periodicals like *Menorah Journal* and *Commentary,* but rather than priding himself on his roots, as did fellow New York intellectuals like Alfred Kazin, he aspired to assimilation within American culture. Trilling was educated at Columbia University, receiving his B.A. and M.A. degrees in 1925 and 1926. He went to the Midwest to teach for a year or so, then returned to Columbia for his doctorate, which was awarded in 1938; his dissertation on Matthew Arnold was published in 1939. The same year, at the insistence of Columbia president Nicholas Murray Butler, he was appointed assistant professor of English, the first Jew to hold faculty rank in that department. Trilling rose through the ranks quickly, reaching full professor in 1948 and a named chair in 1965. He retired from teaching in 1974 but continued part-time until just before his death the next year.

It was prophetic for Trilling's later career that his book on Arnold was an evaluation and an appreciation rather than a contribution to scholarship. Trilling continued to publish widely but substituted evaluative cultural criticism and belletristic writing (including a book of short stories and a novel, *The Middle of the Journey*) for the scholarly work most professors of English pursued. In his teaching he preferred undergraduates still learning the traditions of Western civilization to graduate students aspiring to standards of professional training in scholarship.

In his criticism, Trilling is allied with the cultural criticism of the group of radical New York intellectuals that included Edmund Wilson, Philip Rahv, Delmore Schwartz, Alfred Kazin, and Irving Howe, discussed later in this collection as American Marxists. But although Trilling was strongly influenced by Marx's examination of society, it would be going too far to label him a Marxist, even of the most fellow-traveler sort. While his criticism is neither formalistic nor New Critical but rather social and political, there is little sense of economic determinism or ideology, and he is clearly disillusioned with socialism, Stalin, Soviet Russia, and all the other panaceas of the 1930s. His political philosophy is that of liberalism as it would have been defined around 1950, when *The Liberal Imagination* appeared: greater equality of opportunity for minority groups and an end to intolerance; greater compassion for the poor, leading to a welfare state; greater internationalism of spirit, leading to an end to the cold war between West and East. But his political purpose in writing and in explicating the major texts of literature was precisely to prevent the oversimplification of liberal ideology. Trilling feared that the "ideas that can survive" the political process of organization, delegation, and bureaucracy "incline to be ideas of a certain . . . simplicity: they give up something of their largeness and modulation and complexity in order to survive." For Trilling, as for Arnold, literature was the "criticism of life." It was through literature — regardless of the political philosophy of the writer — that the ideas of the liberal persuasion were to be criticized, brought back to their "essential imagination of variousness and possibility, which implies the awareness of complexity and difficulty."[1]

Trilling was not a literary theorist but a critic, and deriving a literary theory from his work requires massive generalization. Much of Trilling's work took the form of essays devoted to the explication of particular texts: *The Liberal Imagination* is not a treatise but a collection of pieces, most originally published elsewhere, on Theodore Dreiser, Sherwood Anderson, Henry James, Freud, Rudyard Kipling, Tacitus, Twain, and others, as varied a group as one might wish. The essay reprinted here is perhaps the most theoretical piece Trilling ever wrote. It contemplates the central problem of the Arnoldian tradition to which he had attached himself, the relation between ideas and literature, the sense in which literature manifests ideas. The question is an old one — going back, like so many, to Plato — but it had been given renewed currency by the New Critics, then just beginning to attain hegemony, who asserted that poems do not "mean, but be," and that poetry makes not statements but pseudostatements.[2] The first half of Trilling's essay is a theoretical attack on T. S. Eliot's denigration of intellection, ideology, and personality in poetry, and on the charter of the New Critics as inscribed by René Wellek and Austin Warren's *Theory of Literature* (1949). Trilling was in fact willing to concede that "there is a large body of literature to which ideas, with their tendency to refer to action and effectiveness, are alien and inappropriate. But also much of literature wishes to give the sensations and to win the responses that are given and won by ideas, and it makes use of ideas to gain its effects, considering ideas — like people, sentiments, things and scenes — to be indispensable elements of human life." Trilling's response here would not have impressed the New Critics, who did not deny that literature could be thought of as referential. They had merely suggested that viewing literature as ideology denied to it its peculiarly literary qualities. But Trilling's point — that concentration on the aesthetic robs literature of its life within the world — is equally irrefutable.

The second half of the essay is less purely theoretical in scope; it concerns the relation between ideas and American literature, and the question of how intellectual power operates in the best American writers of the generation before World War II. Here Trilling argues that "in any extended work of literature, the aesthetic effect . . . depends in large degree upon intellectual power, upon the amount and recalcitrance of the material the mind works on, and upon the mind's success in mastering the large material." Mastery is not a function of ideology. In fact, Trilling seems to regard ideology as the enemy of literature in the sense that ideology generally remains unassimilated, a messianic or pessimistic prophecy

[1]Lionel Trilling, Introduction to *The Liberal Imagination* (New York: Macmillan, 1948), pp. xiv–xv.
[2]See the introduction to Formalisms, p. 707.

within what should be a coherent work of imagination. In exemplifying this point, Trilling contrasts Thomas Wolfe, John Dos Passos, and Eugene O'Neill — whom he sees as essentially passive intellectually, or ridden by their precommitments — with William Faulkner and Ernest Hemingway, who, he contends, have mastered their material without undue dependence on the pieties of religion or secular philosophy.

Trilling's ultimate problem, of course, is that the literature he respects most, that of the European moderns, was written by men whom he took to be "indifferent to, or even hostile to, the tradition of democratic liberalism as we know it. Yeats and Eliot, Proust and Joyce, Lawrence and Gide — these men do not seem to confirm us in the social and political ideals which we hold." Whatever we may think of these particular examples — and neither Proust nor Joyce took the reactionary side within their own societies — Trilling is faced with a very real problem for a liberal: The greatest writers are so often of a conservative bent. The tradition of "Tory wits" runs nearly unbroken from the late seventeenth century to the present. For Trilling, the remedy is the liberal imagination itself — if liberalism will use its imagination. A liberalism that produces "pellets of intellection or crystallizations of thought, precise and completed," will produce no literature worthy of the name; only if liberals think of ideas as "living things, inescapably connected with our wills and desires" will an "active literature" be realized from within this political framework, and the implicit conflict between liberal sentiments and reactionary wit be reconciled.

Selected Bibliography

Abel, Lionel. "Lionel Trilling and His Critics." *Commentary* 82 (1986): 56–63.

Boyers, Robert. *Lionel Trilling: Negative Capability and the Wisdom of Avoidance*. Columbia: University of Missouri Press, 1977.

Chace, William M. *Lionel Trilling: Criticism and Politics*. Stanford: Stanford University Press, 1980.

Dickstein, Morris. "Lionel Trilling and the Liberal Imagination." *Sewanee Review* 94 (1986): 323–34.

Krupnick, Mark. *Lionel Trilling and the Fate of Cultural Criticism*. Evanston, IL: Northwestern University Press, 1986.

Shoben, Edward Joseph. *Lionel Trilling*. New York: Ungar, 1981.

The Meaning of a Literary Idea

. . . Though no great minist'ring reason sorts
Out the dark mysteries of human souls
To clear conceiving: yet there ever rolls
A vast idea before me, and I glean
Therefrom my liberty . . .

KEATS, "Sleep and Poetry"

I

The question of the relation which should properly obtain between what we call creative literature and what we call ideas is a matter of insistent importance for modern criticism. It did not always make difficulties for the critic, and that it now makes so many is a fact which tells us much about our present relation to literature.

Ever since men began to think about poetry, they have conceived that there is a difference between the poet and the philosopher, a difference in method and in intention and in result. These differences I have no wish to deny. But a solidly established difference inevitably draws the fire of our question; it tempts us to inquire whether it is really essential or whether it is quite so settled and extreme as at first it seems. To this temptation I yield perhaps too easily, and very possibly as the result of an impercipience on my part — it may be that I see the difference with insufficient sharpness because I do not have a proper notion either of the matter of poetry or of the matter of philosophy. But whatever the reason, when I consider the respective products of the poetic and of the philosophic mind, although I see that they are by no means the same and although I can conceive that different processes, even different mental faculties, were at work to make them and to make them different, I cannot resist the impulse to put stress on their similarity and on their easy assimilation to each other.

Let me suggest some of the ways in which literature, by its very nature, is involved with ideas. I can be quite brief because what I say will not be new to you.

The most elementary thing to observe is that literature is of its nature involved with ideas because it deals with man in society, which is to say that it deals with formulations, valuations, and decisions, some of them implicit, others explicit. Every sentient organism *acts* on the principle that pleasure is to be preferred to pain, but man is the sole creature who formulates or exemplifies this as an idea and causes it to lead to other ideas. His consciousness of self abstracts this principle of action from his behavior and makes it the beginning of a process of intellection or a matter for tears and laughter. And this is but one of the innumerable assumptions or ideas that are the very stuff of literature.

This is self-evident and no one ever thinks of denying it. All that is ever denied is that literature is within its proper function in bringing these ideas to explicit consciousness, or ever gains by doing so. Thus, one of the matters of assumption in any society is the worth of men as compared with the worth of women; upon just such an assumption, more or less settled, much of the action of the *Oresteia* is based, and we don't in the least question the propriety of this — or not until it becomes the subject of open debate between Apollo and Athene, who, on the basis of an elaborate biological speculation, try to decide which is the less culpable, to kill your father or to kill your mother. At this point we, in our modern way, feel that in permitting the debate Aeschylus has made a great and rather silly mistake, that he has for the moment ceased to be *literary*. Yet what drama does not consist of the opposition of formulable ideas, what drama, indeed, is not likely to break into the explicit exposition and debate of these ideas?

This, as I say, is elementary. And scarcely less elementary is the observation that whenever we put two emotions into juxtaposition we have what we can properly call an idea. When Keats brings together, as he so often does, his emotions about love and his emotions about death, we have a very powerful idea and the source of consequent ideas. The force of such an idea depends upon the force of the two emotions which are brought to confront each other, and also, of course, upon the way the confrontation is contrived.

Then it can be said that the very form of a literary work, considered apart from its content, so far as that is possible, is in itself an idea. Whether we deal with syllogisms or poems, we deal with dialectic — with, that is, a developing series of statements. Or if the word "statements" seems to pre-judge the question so far as literature is concerned, let us say merely that we deal with a developing series — the important word is "developing." We judge the value of the development by judging the interest of its several stages and the propriety and the relevance of their connection among themselves. We make the judgment in terms of the implied purpose of the developing series.

Dialectic, in this sense, is just another word for form, and has for its purpose, in philosophy or in art, the leading of the mind to some conclusion. Greek drama, for example, is an arrangement of moral and emotional elements in such a way as to conduct the mind — "inevitably," as we like to say — to a certain affective condition. This condition is a quality of personal being which may be judged by the action it can be thought ultimately to lead to.

We take Aristotle to be a better critic of the drama than Plato because we perceive that Aristotle understood and Plato did not understand that the form of the drama was of itself an idea which controlled and brought to a particular issue the subordinate ideas it contained. The form of the drama *is* its idea, and its idea *is* its form. And form in those arts which we call abstract is no less an idea than is form in the representational arts. Governments nowadays are very simple and accurate in their perception of this — much more simple and accurate than are academic critics and aestheticians — and they are as quick to deal with the arts of "pure" form as they are to deal with ideas stated in discourse: it is as if totalitarian governments kept in mind what the rest of us tend to forget, that "idea" in one of its early significations exactly means form and was so used by many philosophers.

It is helpful to have this meaning before us when we come to consider that particular connection between literature and ideas which presents us with the greatest difficulty, the connection that involves highly elaborated ideas, or ideas as we have them in highly elaborated systems such as philosophy, or theology, or science. The modern feeling about this relationship is defined by two texts, both provided by T. S. Eliot. In his essay on Shakespeare Mr. Eliot says, "I can see no reason for believing that either Dante or Shakespeare did any thinking on his own. The people who think that Shakespeare thought are always people who are not engaged in writing poetry, but who are engaged in thinking, and we all like to think that great men were like ourselves."[1] And in his essay on Henry James Mr. Eliot makes the well-known remark that James had a mind so fine that no idea could violate it.

In both statements, as I believe, Mr. Eliot permits his impulse to spirited phrase to run away with him, yielding too much to what he conceives to be the didactic necessities of the moment, for he has it in mind to offer resistance to the nineteenth-century way of looking at poetry as a heuristic medium, as a communication of knowledge. This is a view which is well exemplified in a sentence of Carlyle's: "If called to define Shakespeare's faculty, I should say superiority of Intellect, and think I had included all in that." As between the two statements about Shakespeare's mental processes, I give my suffrage to Carlyle's as representing a more intelligible and a more available notion of intellect than Mr. Eliot's, but I think I understand what Mr. Eliot is trying to do with his — he is trying to rescue poetry from the kind of misinterpretation of Carlyle's view which was once more common than it is now; he is trying to save for poetry what is peculiar to it, and for systematic thought what is peculiar to it.

As for Mr. Eliot's statement about James and ideas, it is useful to us because it gives us a clue to what might be called the sociology of our question. "Henry James had a mind so fine that no idea could violate it." In the context "violate" is a strong word, yet we can grant that the mind of the poet is a sort of Clarissa Harlowe and that an idea is a sort of Colonel Lovelace, for it is a truism of contemporary thought that the whole nature of man stands in danger of being brutalized by the intellect, or at least by some one of its apparently accredited surrogates. A specter haunts our culture — it is that people will eventually be unable to say, "They fell in love and married," let alone understand the language of *Romeo and Juliet,* but will as a matter of course say, "Their libidinal impulses being reciprocal, they activated their individual erotic drives and integrated them within the same frame of reference."

Now this is not the language of abstract thought or of any kind of thought. It is the language of non-thought. But it is the language which is developing from the peculiar status which we in our culture have given to abstract thought. There can be no doubt whatever that it constitutes a threat to the emotions and thus to life itself.

The specter of what this sort of language suggests has haunted us since the end of the eigh-

[1]T. S. Eliot, "Shakespeare and the Stoicism of Seneca," *Selected Essays, 1917–32.* [Ed.]

teenth century. When he speaks of the mind being violated by an idea, Mr. Eliot, like the Romantics, is simply voicing his horror at the prospect of life being intellectualized out of all spontaneity and reality.

We are the people of the idea, and we rightly fear that the intellect will dry up the blood in our veins and wholly check the emotional and creative part of the mind. And although I said that the fear of the total sovereignty of the abstract intellect began in the Romantic period, we are of course touching here upon Pascal's opposition between two faculties of the mind, of which *l'esprit de finesse* has its heuristic powers no less the *l'esprit de géométrie,*[2] powers of discovery and knowledge which have a particular value for the establishment of man in society and the universe.

But to call ourselves the people of the idea is to flatter ourselves. We are rather the people of ideology, which is a very different thing. Ideology is not the product of thought; it is the habit or the ritual of showing respect for certain formulas to which, for various reasons having to do with emotional safety, we have very strong ties of whose meaning and consequences in actuality we have no clear understanding. The nature of ideology may in part be understood from its tendency to develop the sort of language I parodied, and scarcely parodied, a moment ago.

It is therefore no wonder that any critical theory that conceives itself to be at the service of the emotions, and of life itself, should turn a very strict and jealous gaze upon an intimate relationship between literature and ideas, for in our culture ideas tend to deteriorate into ideology. And indeed it is scarcely surprising that criticism, in its zeal to protect literature and life from the tyranny of the rational intellect, should misinterpret the relationship. Mr. Eliot, if we take him literally, does indeed misinterpret the relationship when he conceives of "thinking" in such a way that it must be denied to Shakespeare and Dante. It must puzzle us to know what thinking is if Shakespeare and Dante did not do it.

And it puzzles us to know what René Wellek and Austin Warren mean when in their admirable *Theory of Literature* they say that literature can make use of ideas only when ideas "cease to be ideas in the ordinary sense of concepts and become symbols, or even myths." I am not sure that the ordinary sense of *ideas* actually is *concepts,* or at any rate concepts of such abstractness that they do not arouse in us feelings and attitudes. And I take it that when we speak of the relationship of literature and ideas, the ideas we refer to are not those of mathematics or of symbolic logic, but only such ideas as can arouse and traditionally have aroused the feelings — the ideas, for example, of men's relation to one another and to the world. A poet's simple statement of a psychological fact recalls us to a proper simplicity about the nature of ideas. "Our continued influxes of feeling," said Wordsworth, "are modified and directed by our thoughts, which are indeed the representatives of all our past feelings."[3] The interflow between emotion and idea is a psychological fact which we do well to keep clearly in mind, together with the part that is played by desire, will, and imagination in philosophy as well as in literature. Mr. Eliot, and Mr. Wellek and Mr. Warren — and in general those critics who are zealous in the defense of the autonomy of poetry — prefer to forget the ground which is common to both emotion and thought; they presume ideas to be only the product of formal systems of philosophy, not remembering, at least on the occasion of their argument, that poets too have their effect in the world of thought. *L'esprit de finesse* is certainly not to be confused with *l'esprit de géométrie,* but neither — which is precisely the point of Pascal's having distinguished and named the two different qualities of mind — is it to be denied its powers of comprehension and formulation.

Mr. Wellek and Mr. Warren tell us that "the artist will be hampered by too much ideology[4] if it remains unassimilated." We note the tautology of the statement — for what else is "too much" ideology except ideology that *is* unassimilated? — not because we wish to take a disputatious ad-

[2]Spirit of delicacy; spirit of geometry. [Ed.]

[3]Preface to *Lyrical Ballads;* see p. 304. [Ed.]

[4]The word is used by Mr. Wellek and Mr. Warren, not in the pejorative sense in which I have earlier used it, but to mean simply a body of ideas. [Au.]

vantage over authors to whom we have reason to be grateful, but because the tautology suggests the uneasiness of the position it defends. We are speaking of art, which is an activity which defines itself exactly by its powers of assimilation and of which the essence is the just amount of any of its qualities or elements; of course too much or unassimilated ideology will "hamper" the artist, but so will too much of anything, so will too much metaphor: Coleridge tells us that in a long poem there can be too much *poetry*.[5] The theoretical question is simply being begged, out of an undue anxiety over the "purity" of literature, over its perfect literariness.

The authors of *Theory of Literature* are certainly right to question the "intellectualist misunderstanding of art" and the "confusions of the functions of art and philosophy" and to look for the flaws in the scholarly procedures which organize works of art according to their ideas and their affinities with philosophical systems. Yet on their own showing there has always been a conscious commerce between the poet and the philosopher, and not every poet has been violated by the ideas that have attracted him. The sexual metaphor is forced upon us, not only explicitly by Mr. Eliot but also implicitly by Mr. Wellek and Mr. Warren, who seem to think of ideas as masculine and gross and of art as feminine and pure, and who permit a union of the two sexes only when ideas give up their masculine, effective nature and "cease to be ideas in the ordinary sense and become symbols, or even myths." We naturally ask: symbols of what, myths about what? No anxious exercise of aesthetic theory can make the ideas of, say, Blake and Lawrence other than what they are intended to be — ideas relating to action and to moral judgment.

This anxiety lest the work of art be other than totally self-contained, this fear lest the reader make reference to something beyond the work itself, has its origin, as I have previously suggested, in the reaction from the earlier impulse — it goes far back beyond the nineteenth century — to show that art is justified in comparison with the effective activity of the systematic disciplines. It arises too from the strong contemporary wish to establish, in a world of unremitting action and effectiveness, the legitimacy of contemplation, which it is now no longer convenient to associate with the exercises of religion but which may be associated with the experiences of art. We will all do well to advance the cause of contemplation, to insist on the right to a haven from perpetual action and effectiveness. But we must not enforce our insistence by dealing with art as if it were a unitary thing, and by making reference only to its "purely" aesthetic element, requiring that every work of art serve our contemplation by being wholly self-contained and without relation to action. No doubt there is a large body of literature to which ideas, with their tendency to refer to action and effectiveness, are alien and inappropriate. But also much of literature wishes to give the sensations and to win the responses that are given and won by ideas, and it makes use of ideas to gain its effects, considering ideas — like people, sentiments, things, and scenes — to be indispensable elements of human life. Nor is the intention of this part of literature always an aesthetic one in the strict sense that Mr. Wellek and Mr. Warren have in mind; there is abundant evidence that the aesthetic upon which the critic sets primary store is to the poet himself frequently of only secondary importance.

We can grant that the province of poetry is one thing and the province of intellection another. But keeping the difference well in mind, we must yet see that systems of ideas have a particular quality which is much coveted as their chief effect — let us even say as their chief aesthetic effect — by at least certain kinds of literary works. Say what we will as critics and teachers trying to defend the province of art from the dogged tendency of our time to ideologize all things into grayness, say what we will about the "purely" literary, the purely aesthetic values, we as readers know that we demand of our literature some of the virtues which define a successful work of systematic thought. We want it to have — at least when it is appropriate for it to have, which is by no means infrequently — the author-

[5]Actually, he says that "a poem of any length neither can be, nor ought to be, all poetry." See *Biographia Literaria*, Ch. 14; p. 325 in this collection. [Ed.]

ity, the cogency, the completeness, the brilliance, the *hardness* of systematic thought.[6]

Of late years criticism has been much concerned to insist on the indirection and the symbolism of the language of poetry. I do not doubt that the language of poetry is very largely that of indirection and symbolism. But it is not only that. Poetry is closer to rhetoric than we today are willing to admit; syntax plays a greater part in it than our current theory grants, and syntax connects poetry with rational thought, for, as Hegel says, "grammar, in its extended and consistent form" — by which he means syntax — "is the work of thought, which makes its categories distinctly visible therein." And those poets of our time who make the greatest impress upon us are those who are most aware of rhetoric, which is to say, of the intellectual content of their work. Nor is the intellectual content of their work simply the inevitable effect produced by good intelligence turned to poetry; many of these poets — Yeats and Eliot himself come most immediately to mind — have been at great pains to develop consistent intellectual positions along with, and consonant with, their work in poetry.

The aesthetic effect of intellectual cogency, I am convinced, is not to be slighted. Let me give an example for what it is worth. Of recent weeks my mind has been much engaged by two statements, disparate in length and in genre, although as it happens they have related themes. One is a couplet of Yeats:

> We had fed the heart on fantasies,
> The heart's grown brutal from the fare.

[6]Mr. Wellek and Mr. Warren say something of the same sort, but only, as it were, in a concessive way: "Philosophy, ideological content, in its proper context, seems to enhance artistic value because it corroborates several important artistic values: those of complexity and coherence. . . . But it need not be so. The artist will be hampered by too much ideology if it remains unassimilated" (p. 122). Earlier (p. 27) they say: "Serious art implies a view of life which can be stated in philosophical terms, even in terms of systems. Between artistic coherence . . . and philosophic coherence there is some kind of correlation." They then hasten to distinguish between emotion and thinking, sensibility and intellection, etc., and to tell us that art is more complex than "propaganda." [Au.]

I am hard put to account for the force of the statement. It certainly does not lie in any metaphor, for only the dimmest sort of metaphor is to be detected. Nor does it lie in any special power of the verse. The statement has for me the pleasure of relevance and cogency, in part conveyed to me by the content, in part by the rhetoric. The other statement is Freud's short book, his last, *An Outline of Psychoanalysis,* which gives me a pleasure which is no doubt different from that given by Yeats's couplet, but which is also similar; it is the pleasure of listening to a strong, decisive, self-limiting voice uttering statements to which I can give assent. The pleasure I have in responding to Freud I find very difficult to distinguish from the pleasure which is involved in responding to a satisfactory work of art.

Intellectual assent in literature is not quite the same thing as agreement. We can take pleasure in literature where we do not agree, responding to the power or grace of a mind without admitting the rightness of its intention or conclusion — we can take our pleasure from an intellect's *cogency,* without making a final judgment on the correctness or adaptability of what it says.

II

And now I leave these general theoretical matters for a more particular concern — the relation of contemporary American literature to ideas. In order to come at this as directly as possible we might compare modern American prose literature — for American poetry is a different thing — with modern European literature. European literature of, say, the last thirty or forty years seems to me to be, in the sense in which I shall use the word, essentially an active literature. It does not, at its best, consent to be merely comprehended. It refuses to be understood as a "symptom" of its society, although of course it may be that, among other things. It does not submit to being taped. We as scholars and critics try to discover the source of its effective energy and of course we succeed in some degree. But inevitably we become aware that it happily exists beyond our powers of explanation, although not, certainly, beyond our powers of response.

Proust, Joyce, Lawrence, Kafka, Yeats, and Eliot himself do not allow us to finish with them; and the refusal is repeated by a great many European writers less large than these. With exceptions that I shall note, the same thing cannot be said of modern American literature. American literature seems to me essentially passive: our minds tend always to be made up about this or that American author, and we incline to speak of him, not merely incidentally but conclusively, in terms of his moment in history, of the conditions of the culture that "produced" him. Thus American literature as an academic subject is not so much a *subject* as an *object* of study: it does not, as a literature should, put the scrutinizer of it under scrutiny but, instead, leaves its students with a too comfortable sense of complete comprehension.

When we try to discover the root of this difference between European and American literature, we are led to the conclusion that it is the difference between the number and weight or force of the ideas which the two literatures embody or suggest. I do not mean that European literature makes use of, as American literature does not, the ideas of philosophy or theology or science. Kafka does not exemplify Kierkegaard, Proust does not dramatize Bergson. One way of putting the relationship of this literature to ideas is to say that the literature of contemporary Europe is in competition with philosophy, theology, and science, that it seeks to match them in comprehensiveness and power and seriousness.

This is not to say that the best of contemporary European literature makes upon us the effect of a rational system of thought. Quite the contrary, indeed; it is precisely its artistic power that we respond to, which I take in part to be its power of absorbing and disturbing us in secret ways. But this power it surely derives from its commerce, according to its own rules, with systematic ideas.

For in the great issues with which the mind has traditionally been concerned there is, I would submit, something *primitive* which is of the highest value to the literary artist. I know that it must seem a strange thing to say, for we are in the habit of thinking of systematic ideas as being of the very essence of the not-primitive, of the highly developed. No doubt they are: but they are at the same time the means by which a complex civilization keeps the primitive in mind and refers to it. Whence and whither, birth and death, fate, free will, and immortality — these are never far from systematic thought; and Freud's belief that the child's first inquiry — beyond which, really, the adult does not go in kind — is in effect a sexual one seems to me to have an empirical support from literature. The ultimate questions of conscious and rational thought about the nature of man and his destiny match easily in the literary mind with the dark *un*conscious and with the most primitive human relationships. Love, parenthood, incest, patricide: these are what the great ideas suggest to literature, these are the means by which they express themselves. I need but mention three great works of different ages to suggest how true this is: *Oedipus, Hamlet, The Brothers Karamazov*.

Ideas, if they are large enough and of a certain kind, are not only not hostile to the creative process, as some think, but are virtually inevitable to it. Intellectual power and emotional power go together. And if we can say, as I think we can, that contemporary American prose literature in general lacks emotional power, it is possible to explain the deficiency by reference to the intellectual weakness of American prose literature.

The situation in verse is different. Perhaps this is to be accounted for by the fact that the best of our poets are, as good poets usually are, scholars of their tradition. There is present to their minds the degree of intellectual power which poetry is traditionally expected to exert. Questions of form and questions of language seem of themselves to demand, or to create, an adequate subject matter; and a highly developed aesthetic implies a matter strong enough to support its energy. We have not a few poets who are subjects and not objects, who are active and not passive. One does not finish quickly, if at all, with the best work of, say, Cummings, Stevens, and Marianne Moore. This work is not exempt from our judgment, even from adverse judgment, but it is able to stay with a mature reader as a continuing element of his spiritual life. Of how many writers of prose fiction can we say anything like the same thing?

The topic which was originally proposed to me for this occasion and which I have taken the liberty of generalizing was the debt of four American writers to Freud and Spengler. The four writers were O'Neill, Dos Passos, Wolfe, and Faulkner. Of the first three how many can be continuing effective elements of our mental lives? I hope I shall never read Mr. Dos Passos without interest nor ever lose the warm though qualified respect that I feel for his work. But it is impossible for me to feel of this work that it is autonomous, that it goes on existing beyond our powers of explanation. As for Eugene O'Neill and Thomas Wolfe, I can respect the earnestness of their dedication, but I cannot think of having a living, reciprocal relation with what they have written. And I believe that is because these men, without intellectual capital of their own, don't owe a sufficient debt of ideas to anyone. Spengler is certainly not a great mind; at best he is but a considerable dramatist of the idea of world history and of, as it were, the natural history of cultures; and we can find him useful as a critic who summarizes the adverse views of our urban, naturalistic culture which many have held. Freud is a very great mind indeed. Without stopping to specify what actual influence of ideas was exerted by Spengler and Freud on O'Neill, Dos Passos, or Wolfe, or even to consider whether there was any influence at all, we can fairly assume that all are in something of the same ambiance. But if, in that ambiance, we want the sense of the actuality of doom — actuality being one of the qualities we expect of literature — surely we do better to seek it in Spengler himself than in any of the three literary artists, just as, if we want the sense of the human mystery, of tragedy truly conceived in the great terms of free will, necessity, and hope, surely we do far better to seek it directly in Freud himself than in these three literary men.

In any extended work of literature, the aesthetic effect, as I have said, depends in large degree upon intellectual power, upon the amount and recalcitrance of the material the mind works on, and upon the mind's success in mastering the large material. And it is exactly the lack of intellectual power that makes our three writers, after our first response of interest, so inadequate aesthetically. We have only to compare, say, Dos Passos's *USA* to a work of similar kind and intention, Flaubert's *L'Education Sentimentale,* to see that in Dos Passos's novel the matter encompassed is both less in amount and less in resistance than in Flaubert's; the energy of the encompassing mind is also less. Or we consider O'Neill's crude, dull notion of the unconscious and his merely elementary grasp of Freud's ideas about sex and we recognize the lamentable signs of a general inadequacy of mind. Or we ask what it is about Thomas Wolfe that always makes us uncomfortable with his talent, so that even his admirers deal with him not as a subject but as an object — an object which must be explained and accounted for — and we are forced to answer that it is the disproportion between the energy of his utterance and his power of mind. It is customary to say of Thomas Wolfe that he is an emotional writer. Perhaps: although it is probably not the most accurate way to describe a writer who could deal with but one single emotion; and we feel that it is a function of his unrelenting, tortured egoism that he could not submit his mind to the ideas that might have brought the variety and interest of order to the single, dull chaos of his powerful self-regard, for it is true that the intellect makes many emotions out of the primary egoistic one.

At this point it may be well to recall what our subject is. It is not merely the part that is played in literature by those ideas which may be derived from the study of systematic, theoretical works; it is the part that is played in literature by ideas in general. To be sure, the extreme and most difficult instance of the general relation of literature to ideas is the relation of literature to highly developed and formulated ideas; and because this is indeed so difficult a matter, and one so often misconceived, I have put a special emphasis upon it. But we do not present our subject adequately — we do not, indeed, represent the mind adequately — if we think of ideas only as being highly formulated. It will bring us back to the proper generality of our subject if I say that the two contemporary writers who hold out to me the possibility of a living reciprocal relationship with their work are Ernest Hemingway and William Faulkner — it will bring us back the more dramatically because Hemingway and Faulkner have insisted on their indifference to the conscious intellectual tradition of our time and have acquired the reputation of achieving their effects by means that have the least possible connection with any sort of intellectuality or even with intelligence.

In trying to explain a certain commendable quality which is to be found in the work of Hemingway and Faulkner — and a certain quality only, not a total and unquestionable literary virtue — we are not called upon by our subject to show that particular recognizable ideas of a certain force or weight are "used" in the work. Nor are we called upon to show that new ideas of a certain force and weight are "produced" by the work. All that we need to do is account for a certain aesthetic effect as being in some important part achieved by a mental process which is not different from the process by which discursive ideas are conceived, and which is to be judged by some of the criteria by which an idea is judged.

The aesthetic effect which I have in mind can be suggested by a word that I have used before — activity. We feel that Hemingway and Faulkner are intensely at work upon the recalcitrant stuff of life; when they are at their best they give us the sense that the amount and intensity of their activity are in a satisfying proportion to the recalcitrance of the material. And our pleasure in their activity is made the more secure because we have the distinct impression that the two novelists are not under any illusion that they have conquered the material upon which they direct their activity. The opposite is true of Dos Passos, O'Neill, and Wolfe; at each point of conclusion in their work we feel that *they* feel that they have said the last word, and we feel this even when they represent themselves, as O'Neill and Wolfe so often do, as puzzled and baffled by life. But of Hemingway and Faulkner we seldom have the sense that they have deceived themselves, that they have misrepresented to themselves the nature and the difficulty of the matter they work on. And we go on to make another intellectual judgment: we say that the matter they present, together with the degree of difficulty which they assume it to have, seems to be very cogent. This, we say, is to the point; this really has something to do with life as we live it; we cannot ignore it.

There is a traditional and aggressive rationalism that can understand thought only in its conscious, developed form and believes that the phrase "unconscious mind" is a meaningless contradiction in terms. Such a view, wrong as I think it is, has at least the usefulness of warning us that we must not call by the name of thought or idea all responses of the human organism whatever. But the extreme rationalist position ignores the simple fact that the life of reason, at least in its most extensive part, begins in the emotions. What comes into being when two contradictory emotions are made to confront each other and are required to have a relationship with each other is, as I have said, quite properly called an idea. Ideas may also be said to be generated in the opposition of ideals, and in the felt awareness of the impact of new circumstances upon old forms of feeling and estimation, in the response to the conflict between new exigencies and old pieties. And it can be said that a work will have what I have been calling cogency in the degree that the confronting emotions go deep, or in the degree that the old pieties are firmly held and the new exigencies strongly apprehended. In Hemingway's stories[7] a strongly charged piety toward the ideals and attachments of boyhood and the lusts of maturity is in conflict not only with the imagination of death but also with that imagination as it is peculiarly modified by the dark negation of the modern world. Faulkner as a Southerner of today, a man deeply implicated in the pieties of his tradition, is of course at the very heart of an exigent historical event which thrusts upon him the awareness of the inadequacy and wrongness of the very tradition he loves. In the work of both men the cogency is a function not of their conscious but of their unconscious minds. We can, if we admire Tolstoy and Dostoevsky, regret the deficiency of consciousness, blaming it for the inadequacy in both our American writers of the talent for generalization.[8] Yet it

[7]It is in the stories rather than in the novels that Hemingway is characteristic and at his best. [Au.]

[8]Although there is more impulse to generalization than is usually supposed. This is especially true of Faulkner, who has never subscribed to the contemporary belief that only concrete words have power and that only the representation of things and actions is dramatic. [Au.]

is to be remarked that the unconscious minds of both men have wisdom and humility about themselves. They seldom make the attempt at formulated solutions, they rest content with the "negative capability." And this negative capability, this willingness to remain in uncertainties, mysteries, and doubts, is not, as one tendency of modern feeling would suppose, an abdication of intellectual activity. Quite to the contrary, it is precisely an aspect of their intelligence, of their seeing the full force and complexity of their subject matter. And this we can understand the better when we observe how the unconscious minds of Dos Passos, O'Neill, and Wolfe do not possess humility and wisdom; nor are they fully active, as the intellectual histories of all three men show. A passivity on the part of Dos Passos before the idea of the total corruption of American civilization has issued in his later denial of the possibility of economic and social reform and in his virtually unqualified acceptance of the American status quo. A passivity on the part of O'Neill before the clichés of economic and metaphysical materialism issued in his later simplistic Catholicism. The passivity of Thomas Wolfe before all his experience led him to that characteristic *malice* toward the objects or partners of his experience which no admirer of his ever takes account of, and eventually to that simple affirmation, recorded in *You Can't Go Home Again,* that literature must become the agent of the immediate solution of all social problems and undertake the prompt eradication of human pain; and because his closest friend did not agree that this was a possible thing for literature to do, Wolfe terminated the friendship. These are men of whom it is proper to speak of their having been violated by ideas; but we must observe that it was an excess of intellectual passivity that invited the violence.

In speaking of Hemingway and Faulkner I have used the word "piety." It is a word that I have chosen with some care and despite the pejorative meanings that nowadays adhere to it, for I wished to avoid the word "religion," and piety is not religion, yet I wished too to have religion come to mind as it inevitably must when piety is mentioned. Carlyle says of Shakespeare that he was the product of medieval Catholicism, and implies that Catholicism *at the distance at which Shakespeare stood from it* had much to do with the power of Shakespeare's intellect. Allen Tate has developed in a more particular way an idea that has much in common with what Carlyle here implies. Loosely put, the idea is that religion in its decline leaves a detritus of pieties, of strong assumptions, which afford a particularly fortunate condition for certain kinds of literature; these pieties carry a strong charge of intellect, or perhaps it would be more accurate to say that they tend to stimulate the mind in a powerful way.

Religious emotions are singularly absent from Shakespeare and it does not seem possible to say of him that he was a religious man. Nor does it seem possible to say of the men of the great period of American literature in the nineteenth century that they were religious men. Hawthorne and Melville, for example, lived at a time when religion was in decline and they were not drawn to support it. But from religion they inherited a body of pieties, a body of issues, if you will, which engaged their hearts and their minds to the very bottom. Henry James was not a religious man and there is not the least point in the world in trying to make him out one. But you need not accept all the implications of Quentin Anderson's thesis that James allegorized his father's religious system to see that Mr. Anderson is right when he says that James was dealing, in his own way, with the questions that his father's system propounded.[9] This will indicate something of why James so catches our imagination today, and why we turn so eagerly again to Hawthorne and Melville.

The piety which descends from religion is not the only possible piety, as the case of Faulkner reminds us, and perhaps also the case of Hemingway. But we naturally mention first that piety which does descend from religion because it is most likely to have in it the quality of transcendence which, whether we admit it or no, we expect literature at its best to have.

The subject is extremely delicate and complex and I do no more than state it barely and crudely. But no matter how I state it, I am sure that you

[9]Cf. Quentin Anderson, *The American Henry James* (1957). [Ed.]

will see that what I am talking about leads us to the crucial issue of our literary culture.

I know that I will not be wrong if I assume that most of us here are in our social and political beliefs consciously liberal and democratic. And I know that I will not be wrong if I say that most of us, and in the degree of our commitment to literature and our familiarity with it, find that the contemporary authors we most wish to read and most wish to admire for their literary qualities demand of us a great agility and ingenuity in coping with their antagonism to our social and political ideals. For it is in general true that the modern European literature to which we can have an active, reciprocal relationship, which is the right relationship to have, has been written by men who are indifferent to, or even hostile to, the tradition of democratic liberalism as we know it. Yeats and Eliot, Proust and Joyce, Lawrence and Gide — these men do not seem to confirm us in the social and political ideals which we hold.

If we now turn and consider the contemporary literature of America, we see that whatever we can describe it as patently liberal and democratic, we must say that it is not of lasting interest. I do not say that the work which is written to conform to the liberal democratic tradition is of no value but only that we do not incline to return to it, we do not establish it in our minds and affections. Very likely we learn from it as citizens; and as citizen-scholars and citizen-critics we understand and explain it. But we do not live in an active reciprocal relation with it. The sense of largeness, of cogency, of the transcendence which largeness and cogency can give, the sense of being reached in our secret and primitive minds — this we virtually never get from the writers of the liberal democratic tradition at the present time.

And since liberal democracy inevitably generates a body of ideas, it must necessarily occur to us to ask why it is that these particular ideas have not infused with force and cogency the literature that embodies them. This question is the most important, the most fully challenging question in culture that at this moment we can ask.

The answer to it cannot of course even be begun here, and I shall be more than content if now it is merely accepted as a legitimate question. But there are one or two things that may be said about the answer, about the direction we must take to reach it in its proper form. We will not find it if we come to facile conclusions about the absence from our culture of the impressive ideas of traditional religion. I have myself referred to the historical fact that religion has been an effective means of transmitting or of generating ideas of a sort which I feel are necessary for the literary qualities we want, and to some this will no doubt mean that I believe religion to be a necessary condition of great literature. I do not believe that; and what is more, I consider it from many points of view an impropriety to try to guarantee literature by religious belief.

Nor will we find our answer if we look for it in the weakness of the liberal democratic ideas in themselves. It is by no means true that the inadequacy of the literature that connects itself with a body of ideas is the sign of the inadequacy of those ideas, although it is no doubt true that some ideas have less affinity with literature than others.

Our answer, I believe, will rather be found in a cultural fact — in the kind of relationship which we, or the writers who represent us, maintain toward the ideas we claim as ours, and in our habit of conceiving the nature of ideas in general. If we find that it is true of ourselves that we conceive ideas to be pellets of intellection or crystallizations of thought, precise and completed, and defined by their coherence and their procedural recommendations, then we shall have accounted for the kind of prose literature we have. And if we find that we do indeed have this habit, and if we continue in it, we can predict that our literature will continue much as it is. But if we are drawn to revise our habit of conceiving ideas in this way and learn instead to think of ideas as living things, inescapably connected with our wills and desires, as susceptible of growth and development by their very nature, as showing their life by their tendency to change, as being liable, by this very tendency, to deteriorate and become corrupt and to work harm, then we shall stand in a relation to ideas which makes an active literature possible.

Jean-Paul Sartre

1905–1980

As a philosopher, novelist, dramatist, and essayist, Jean-Paul Sartre is indelibly associated with existentialism, the ethical and humanistic movement that developed from the phenomenological thought of Edmund Husserl and Martin Heidegger (see p. 560). Sartre was born in Paris. His father died a year after his birth, and he was raised by his mother and his grandfather of the famous Schweitzer family in Paris and Meudon. He attended the prestigious Louis-le-Grand preparatory school and the Lycée Henri IV before training in philosophy at the École Normale Supérieure where he received his *agrégation* (postgraduate) degree in 1929, the same year as his lifelong companion, Simone de Beauvoir (see p. 635). He taught philosophy in various elite secondary schools until the outbreak of World War II in 1939. Caught in the German blitzkrieg, Sartre spent much of 1940–41 as a prisoner of war. When released, he joined the resistance and worked for the liberation of France as a journalist for underground publications. After the liberation of Paris in 1944, Sartre and de Beauvoir founded the prestigious literary and intellectual monthly, *Les Temps Modernes* (1945–).

Sartre's existential philosophy grew out of his year of postgraduate study at the Institut Français in Berlin in 1933, where he became fascinated with the ideas of Heidegger and Husserl, using them as a springboard for his own work. Several shorter treatises culminated in his monumental *Being and Nothingness* (*L'Être et le néant,* 1943), whose title plays off that of Heidegger's 1927 treatise, *Being and Time.* In *Being and Nothingness,* Sartre distinguishes between things, which exist purely in themselves and can be essentialized (the *en-soi*), and human beings (the *pour-soi*). As human beings we have no essence to which we aspire: Ever-changing, we are always free to make ourselves what we are, negating what we currently are and do in favor of some other mode of action and existence. Indeed one should not say that we *are*, but rather that we *become.* Our existence is contingent, unfixed, dependent on our interactions with an ever-changing environment. To live in the world, to "become" in freedom, we are forced to project ourselves into the void of nothingness, the as-yet-nonexistent future. Unlike things, we are conscious of our own mortality, of a future in which we will not exist. This negation and projection involves the rejection of one way of existing and the choice of another, a choice we can never evade. The responsibility for conscious choice of what we shall become at every moment of existence produces in the authentic individual the feeling of *angst,* or existential dread. So terrifying is our freedom and responsibility that we are constantly tempted by what Sartre calls bad faith (*mauvaise foi*), comforting lies by which we reassure ourselves that we have been merely formed by circumstance, that our choices are predetermined by psychic or social forces beyond our control.

If Sartre's name became a household word, unlike those of his teachers, it was largely because he presented his ideas not only in philosophical treatises but in novels, such as *Nausea (La Nausée,* 1938) and *The Roads to Freedom* trilogy (*Les Chemins de la liberté,* 1945–49). His preferred genre, possibly because he felt humanity expresses its nature best through action, was the drama, and successful plays like *The Flies (Les Mouches,* 1943), *No Exit (Huis Clos,* 1945), *Dirty Hands (Les Mains sales,* 1948), and *The Condemned of Altona (Les Sequestrés d'Altona,* 1959) made adherents of people who would have been unlikely to read through even ten pages of *Being and Nothingness.*

After World War II, Sartre's principal interests were politics and literary criticism. Sartre was by temperament a leftist but had steered clear of Soviet-style communism until after the end of the war. It was precisely when the revelations of Stalin's mass murders and other crimes were shocking and repelling once-loyal party members that Sartre announced he wanted to align himself with the Soviets. This announcement led to a break between Sartre and other French intellectuals, like Raymond Aron and Albert Camus. Sartre returned to his original stance of distance from Russian communism after the brutal Soviet invasion of Hungary in 1956. His *Critique of Dialectical Reason (Critique de la raison dialectique,* 1960) presents his liberal Marxist vision of social action.

In the last two decades of his life, Sartre produced a fragmented literary autobiography in *The Words (Les Mots,* 1964) and a body of sustained literary biography, including *Saint Genet (Saint-Genet: Comédien et martyre,* 1963) and a lengthy study of Flaubert, *The Family Idiot (L'Idiot de la famille,* 1971–72). His major contribution to literary theory is the short volume *What Is Literature? (Qu'est-ce que la litterature?,* 1947), which applies phenomenology and existentialism to questions of reading and writing but is also informed by Sartre's leftist social thought.

Toward the end of his life, Sartre fell further and further behind the shifts in French thought; he survived the height of his fame by about fifteen years, and Les Deux Magots, the left-bank cafe where he spent his afternoons, became a tourist site — and an intellectual backwater. Immediately after his death in 1980, his works went out of fashion with the intelligentsia and are only now returning to favor. In a sense, though, Sartre was never out of style in that his anti-essentialism — his insistence on absence and negation as the origin and bedrock of thought — profoundly influenced many later branches of French philosophy and psychology that reacted against his ideas, such as the neo-Freudianism of Jacques Lacan, the neo-Marxism of Louis Althusser, or the structuralism and poststructuralism of Roland Barthes and Jacques Derrida.

The Sartre of "Why Write?" elaborately considers the phenomenological position of the writer who creates from a deep sense of metaphysical absence. We who know that the physical world we animate with our perceptions will go on darkly after we are gone must write to make something that will survive us. We do this out of "the need of feeling that we are essential in relationship to the world." But writers are not alone with the rumblings of the void: The "world" we are essential to is that of the reader. But like Wolfgang Iser and Hans Robert Jauss of the school of Konstanz, who see the reader as performing the text (see the introduction to Reader-Response Criticism, p. 917), Sartre sees the reader as at least equally necessary to the writer. In the process of reading, which Sartre says synthesizes the processes of "perception and creation," the reader completes what the writer has begun, in a re-invention that "would be as new and as original an act as the first invention."

Collaboration between reader and writer, after all, can be viewed under different enabling metaphors, and the politics of Sartre's literary phenomenology is uniquely his own. His fellow phenomenologist George Poulet saw the writer as "colonizing" the consciousness of the reader, who becomes a "prey" by temporarily abdicating his selfhood and individuality to the direction of the writer. The consciousness of the text is "inbreathed" by the reader whose consciousness it annexes, almost like the *daimonion* of Plato, which inspires the reader through a sort of divine possession. Unlike Poulet, Sartre characterizes the relation of writer and reader as the camaraderie of equals, each cherishing the freedom of the other as guaranteeing and enhancing his own.[1]

It is true that no earthly government has ever given its citizens anything but relative freedom, as opposed to the absolute existential freedom that is the tragic possession of every human being. Yet since "the author writes in order to address himself to the freedom of readers," since "he requires it in order to make his work exist," the politics of literature is a serious business. Not only is it in writers' interest *as writers* to work for the freedom of their societies, Sartre believes it is impossible for genuine writers to continue writing for readers whose minds and wills are enslaved by a totalitarian government. His historical example was Drieu la Rochelle, a collaborationist writer who attempted to produce a periodical review during the Nazi occupation of France: "The first few months he reprimanded, rebuked, and lectured his countrymen. No one answered him because no one was free to do so. He became irritated; he no longer *felt* his readers. . . . Finally, he kept still, gagged by the silence of others."

Selected Bibliography

Dobson, Andrew. *Jean-Paul Sartre and the Politics of Reason: A Theory of History.* New York and London: Cambridge University Press, 1993.

Hayman, Ronald. *Sartre: A Biography.* New York: Carroll and Graf, 1991.

Jameson, Fredric. *Sartre: The Origins of a Style.* New York: Columbia University Press, 1984.

LaCapra, Dominick. *A Preface to Sartre.* Ithaca, NY: Cornell University Press, 1978.

McCulloch, Gregory. *Using Sartre: An Analytical Introduction to Early Sartrean Themes.* New York: Routledge, 1994.

Nordquist, Joan. *Jean-Paul Sartre: A Bibliography.* New York: Reference and Research Services, 1993.

Sartre, Jean-Paul. *What Is Literature?* New York: Philosophical Library, 1966.

———. *The Family Idiot: Gustave Flaubert, 1821–1857.* 5 vols. Trans. Carol Cosman. Chicago: University of Chicago Press, 1981–93.

———. *The Words.* New York: Random House, 1981.

Thody, Philip. *Jean-Paul Sartre.* New York: St. Martin's Press, 1992.

[1]Poulet feels that the abdication of the self is also the route to the fullest possible realization of the self. Similarly, Sartre sees reading as "a Passion, in the Christian sense of the word, that is, a freedom which resolutely puts itself into a state of passivity to obtain a transcendent effect by this sacrifice."

Why Write?

Each one has his reasons: for one, art is a flight; for another, a means of conquering. But one can flee into a hermitage, into madness, into death. One can conquer by arms. Why does it have to be *writing,* why does one have to manage his escapes and conquests by *writing*? Because, behind the various aims of authors, there is a deeper and more immediate choice which is common to all of us. We shall try to elucidate this choice, and we shall see whether it is not in the name of this very choice of writing that the engagement of writers must be required.

Each of our perceptions is accompanied by the consciousness that human reality is a "revealer," that is, it is through human reality that "there is" being, or, to put it differently, that man is the means by which things are manifested. It is our presence in the world which multiplies relations. It is we who set up a relationship between this tree and that bit of sky. Thanks to us, that star which has been dead for millennia, that quarter moon, and that dark river are disclosed in the unity of a landscape. It is the speed of our auto and our airplane which organizes the great masses of the earth. With each of our acts, the world reveals to us a new face. But, if we know that we are directors of being, we also know that we are not its producers. If we turn away from this landscape, it will sink back into its dark permanence. At least, it will sink back; there is no one mad enough to think that it is going to be annihilated. It is we who shall be annihilated, and the earth will remain in its lethargy until another consciousness comes along to awaken it. Thus, to our inner certainty of being "revealers" is added that of being inessential in relation to the thing revealed.

One of the chief motives of artistic creation is certainly the need of feeling that we are essential in relationship to the world. If I fix on canvas or in writing a certain aspect of the fields or the sea or a look on someone's face which I have disclosed, I am conscious of having produced them by condensing relationships, by introducing order where there was none, by imposing the unity of mind on the diversity of things. That is, I feel myself essential in relation to my creation. But this time it is the created object which escapes me; I can not reveal and produce at the same time. The creation becomes inessential in relation to the creative activity. First of all, even if it appears to others as definitive, the created object always seems to us in a state of suspension; we can always change this line, that shade, that word. Thus, it never *forces itself.* A novice painter asked his teacher, "When should I consider my painting finished?" And the teacher answered, "When you can look at it in amazement and say to yourself '*I'm* the one who did *that!*' "

Which amounts to saying "never." For it is virtually considering one's work with someone else's eyes and revealing what one has created. But it is self-evident that we are proportionally less conscious of the thing produced and more conscious of our productive activity. When it is a matter of pottery or carpentry, we work according to traditional norms, with tools whose usage is codified; it is Heidegger's famous "they" who are working with our hands. In this case, the result can seem to us sufficiently strange to preserve its objectivity in our eyes. But if we ourselves produce the rules of production, the measures, the criteria, and if our creative drive comes from the very depths of our heart, then we never find anything but ourselves in our work. It is we who have invented the laws by which we judge it. It is our history, our love, our gaiety that we recognize in it. Even if we should regard it without touching it any further, we never *receive* from it that gaiety or love. We put them into it. The results which we have obtained on canvas or paper never seem to us *objective.* We are too familiar with the processes of which they are the effects. These processes remain a subjective discovery; they are ourselves, our inspiration, our ruse, and when we seek to *perceive* our work, we create it again, we repeat mentally the operations which produced it; each of its aspects appears as

Translated by Bernard Frechtman.

a result. Thus, in the perception, the object is given as the essential thing and the subject as the inessential. The latter seeks essentiality in the creation and obtains it, but then it is the object which becomes the inessential.

This dialectic is nowhere more apparent than in the art of writing, for the literary object is a peculiar top which exists only in movement. To make it come into view a concrete act called reading is necessary, and it lasts only as long as this act can last. Beyond that, there are only black marks on paper. Now, the writer can not read what he writes, whereas the shoemaker can put on the shoes he has just made if they are his size, and the architect can live in the house he has built. In reading, one foresees; one waits. He foresees the end of the sentence, the following sentence, the next page. He waits for them to confirm or disappoint his foresights. The reading is composed of a host of hypotheses, of dreams followed by awakenings, of hopes and deceptions. Readers are always ahead of the sentence they are reading in a merely probable future which partly collapses and partly comes together in proportion as they progress, which withdraws from one page to the next and forms the moving horizon of the literary object. Without waiting, without a future, without ignorance, there is no objectivity.

Now the operation of writing involves an implicit quasi-reading which makes real reading impossible. When the words form under his pen, the author doubtless sees them, but he does not see them as the reader does, since he knows them before writing them down. The function of his gaze is not to reveal, by stroking them, the sleeping words which are waiting to be read, but to control the sketching of the signs. In short, it is a purely regulating mission, and the view before him reveals nothing except for slight slips of the pen. The writer neither foresees nor conjectures; he *projects*. It often happens that he awaits, as they say, the inspiration. But one does not wait for himself the way he waits for others. If he hesitates, he knows that the future is not made, that he himself is going to make it, and if he still does not know what is going to happen to his hero, that simply means that he has not thought about it, that he has not decided upon anything. The future is then a blank page, whereas the future of the reader is two hundred pages filled with words which separate him from the end. Thus, the writer meets everywhere only *his* knowledge, *his* will, *his* plans, in short, himself. He touches only his own subjectivity; the object he creates is out of reach; he does not create it *for himself*. If he rereads himself, it is already too late. The sentence will never quite be a thing in his eyes. He goes to the very limits of the subjective but without crossing it. He appreciates the effect of a touch, of an epigram, of a well-placed adjective, but it is the effect they will have on others. He can judge it, not feel it. Proust never discovered the homosexuality of Charlus, since he had decided upon it even before starting on his book. And if a day comes when the book takes on for its author a semblance of objectivity, it is that years have passed, that he has forgotten it, that its spirit is quite foreign to him, and doubtless he is no longer capable of writing it. This was the case with Rousseau when he reread the *Social Contract* at the end of his life.

Thus, it is not true that one writes for himself. That would be the worst blow. In projecting his emotions on paper, one barely manages to give them a languishing extension. The creative act is only an incomplete and abstract moment in the production of a work. If the author existed alone he would be able to write as much as he liked; the work as *object* would never see the light of day and he would either have to put down his pen or despair. But the operation of writing implies that of reading as its dialectical correlative and these two connected acts necessitate two distinct agents. It is the conjoint effort of author and reader which brings upon the scene that concrete and imaginary object which is the work of the mind. There is no art except for and by others.

Reading seems, in fact, to be the synthesis of perception and creation.[1] It supposes the essentiality of both the subject and the object. The object is essential because it is strictly transcendent, because it imposes its own structures, and be-

[1]The same is true in different degrees regarding the spectator's attitude before other works of art (paintings, symphonies, statues, etc.). [Au.]

cause one must wait for it and observe it; but the subject is also essential because it is required not only to disclose the object (that is, to make *there be* an object) but also so that this object might *be* (that is, to produce it). In a word, the reader is conscious of disclosing in creating, of creating by disclosing. In reality, it is not necessary to believe that reading is a mechanical operation and that signs make an impression upon him as light does on a photographic plate. If he is inattentive, tired, stupid, or thoughtless, most of the relations will escape him. He will never manage to "catch on" to the object (in the sense in which we see that fire "catches" or "doesn't catch"). He will draw some phrases out of the shadow, but they will seem to appear as random strokes. If he is at his best, he will project beyond the words a synthetic form, each phrase of which will be no more than a partial function: the "theme," the "subject," or the "meaning." Thus, from the very beginning, the meaning is no longer contained in the words, since it is he, on the contrary, who allows the signification of each of them to be understood; and the literary object, though realized *through* language, is never given *in* language. On the contrary, it is by nature a silence and an opponent of the word. In addition, the hundred thousand words aligned in a book can be read one by one so that the meaning of the work does not emerge. Nothing is accomplished if the reader does not put himself from the very beginning and almost without a guide at the height of this silence; if, in short, he does not invent it and does not then place there, and hold on to, the words and sentences which he awakens. And if I am told that it would be more fitting to call this operation a reinvention or a discovery, I shall answer that, first, such a reinvention would be as new and as original an act as the first invention. And, especially, when an object has never existed before, there can be no question of reinventing it or discovering it. For if the silence about which I am speaking is really the goal at which the author is aiming, he has, at least, never been familiar with it; his silence is subjective and anterior to language. It is the absence of words, the undifferentiated and lived silence of inspiration, which the word will then particularize, whereas the silence produced by the reader is an object. And at the very interior of this object there are more silences — which the author does not tell. It is a question of silences which are so particular that they could not retain any meaning outside of the object which the reading causes to appear. However, it is these which give it its density and its particular face.

To say that they are unexpressed is hardly the word; for they are precisely the inexpressible. And that is why one does not come upon them at any definite moment in the reading; they are everywhere and nowhere. The quality of the marvelous in *The Wanderer (Le Grand Meaulnes),* the grandiosity of *Armance,* the degree of realism and truth of Kafka's mythology, these are never given. The reader must invent them all in a continual exceeding of the written thing. To be sure, the author guides him, but all he does is guide him. The landmarks he sets up are separated by the void. The reader must unite them; he must go beyond them. In short, reading is directed creation.

On the one hand, the literary object has no other substance than the reader's subjectivity; Raskolnikov's waiting is my waiting which I lend him. Without this impatience of the reader he would remain only a collection of signs. His hatred of the police magistrate who questions him is my hatred which has been solicited and wheedled out of me by signs, and the police magistrate himself would not exist without the hatred I have for him via Raskolnikov. That is what animates him, it is his very flesh.

But on the other hand, the words are there like traps to arouse our feelings and to reflect them toward us. Each word is a path of transcendence; it shapes our feelings, names them, and attributes them to an imaginary personage who takes it upon himself to live them for us and who has no other substance than these borrowed passions; he confers objects, perspectives, and a horizon upon them.

Thus, for the reader, all is to do and all is already done; the work exists only at the exact level of his capacities; while he reads and creates, he knows that he can always go further in his reading, can always create more profoundly, and thus the work seems to him as inexhaustible and opaque as things. We would readily reconcile that "rational intuition" which Kant reserved to divine Reason with this absolute production of qualities, which, to the extent that they emanate from our subjectivity, congeal before our eyes into impermeable objectivities.

Since the creation can find its fulfillment only in reading, since the artist must entrust to another the job of carrying out what he has begun, since it is only through the consciousness of the reader that he can regard himself as essential to his work, all literary work is an appeal. To write is to make an appeal to the reader that he lead into objective existence the revelation which I have undertaken by means of language. And if it should be asked *to what* the writer is appealing, the answer is simple. As the sufficient reason for the appearance of the aesthetic object is never found either in the book (where we find merely solicitations to produce the object) or in the author's mind, and as his subjectivity, which he cannot get away from, cannot give a reason for the act of leading into objectivity, the appearance of the work of art is a new event which cannot *be explained* by anterior data. And since this directed creation is an absolute beginning, it is therefore brought about by the freedom of the reader, and by what is purest in that freedom. Thus, the writer appeals to the reader's freedom to collaborate in the production of his work.

It will doubtless be said that all tools address themselves to our freedom since they are the instruments of a possible action, and that the work of art is not unique in that. And it is true that the tool is the congealed outline of an operation. But it remains on the level of the hypothetical imperative. I may use a hammer to nail up a case or to hit my neighbor over the head. Insofar as I consider it in itself, it is not an appeal to my freedom; it does not put me face to face with it; rather, it aims at using it by substituting a set succession of traditional procedures for the free invention of means. The book does not serve my freedom; it requires it. Indeed, one cannot address himself to freedom as such by means of constraint, fascination, or entreaties. There is only one way of attaining it; first, by recognizing it, then, having confidence in it, and finally, requiring of it an act, an act in its own name, that is, in the name of the confidence that one brings to it.

Thus, the book is not, like the tool, a means for any end whatever; the end to which it offers itself is the reader's freedom. And the Kantian expression "finality without end"[2] seems to me quite inappropriate for designating the work of art. In fact, it implies that the aesthetic object presents only the appearance of a finality and is limited to soliciting the free and ordered play of the imagination. It forgets that the imagination of the spectator has not only a regulating function, but a constitutive one. It does not play; it is called upon to recompose the beautiful object beyond the traces left by the artist. The imagination can not revel in itself any more than can the other functions of the mind; it is always on the outside, always engaged in an enterprise. There would be finality without end if some object offered such a set ordering that it would lead us to suppose that it has one even though we can not ascribe one to it. By defining the beautiful in this way one can — and this is Kant's aim — liken the beauty of art to natural beauty, since a flower, for example, presents so much symmetry, such harmonious colors, and such regular curves, that one is immediately tempted to seek a finalist explanation for all these properties and to see them as just so many means at the disposal of an unknown end. But that is exactly the error. The beauty of nature is in no way comparable to that of art. The work of art *does not have* an end; there we agree with Kant. But the reason is that it is an end. The Kantian formula does not account for the appeal which resounds at the basis of each painting, each statue, each book. Kant believes that the work of art first exists as fact and that it is then seen. Whereas, it exists only if one *looks* at it and if it is first pure appeal, pure exigence to exist. It is not an instrument whose existence is manifest and whose end is undetermined. It presents itself as a task to be discharged; from the very beginning it places itself on the level of the categorical imperative. You are perfectly free to leave that book on the table. But if you open it, you assume responsibility for it. For freedom is not experienced by its enjoying its free subjective functioning, but in a creative act required by an impera-

[2]*Zweckmässigkeit ohne Zweck,* purposiveness without purpose. See Kant, p. 264. [Ed.]

tive. This absolute end, this imperative which is transcendent yet acquiesced in, which freedom itself adopts as its own, is what we call a value. The work of art is a value because it is an appeal.

If I appeal to my reader so that we may carry the enterprise which I have begun to a successful conclusion, it is self-evident that I consider him as a pure freedom, as an unconditioned activity; thus, in no case can I address myself to his passivity, that is, try to *affect* him, to communicate to him, from the very first, emotions of fear, desire, or anger. There are, doubtless, authors who concern themselves solely with arousing these emotions because they are foreseeable, manageable, and because they have at their disposal sure-fire means for provoking them. But it is also true that they are reproached for this kind of thing, as Euripides has been since antiquity because he had children appear on the stage. Freedom is alienated in the state of passion; it is abruptly engaged in partial enterprises; it loses sight of its task which is to produce an absolute end. And the book is no longer anything but a means for feeding hate or desire. The writer should not seek to *overwhelm;* otherwise he is in contradiction with himself; if he wishes to *make demands* he must propose only the task to be fulfilled. Hence, the character of pure presentation which appears essential to the work of art. The reader must be able to make a certain aesthetic withdrawal. This is what Gautier foolishly confused with "art for art's sake" and the Parnassians with the imperturbability of the artist. It is simply a matter of precaution, and Genet more justly calls it the author's politeness toward the reader. But that does not mean that the writer makes an appeal to some sort of abstract and conceptual freedom. One certainly creates the aesthetic object with feelings; if it is touching, it appears through our tears; if it is comic, it will be recognized by laughter. However, these feelings are of a particular kind. They have their origin in freedom; they are loaned. The belief which I accord the tale is freely assented to. It is a Passion, in the Christian sense of the word, that is, a freedom which resolutely puts itself into a state of passivity to obtain a certain transcendent effect by this sacrifice. The reader renders himself credulous; he descends into credulity which, though it ends by enclosing him like a dream, is at every moment conscious of being free. An effort is sometimes made to force the writer into this dilemma: "Either one believes in your story, and it is intolerable, or one does not believe in it, and it is ridiculous." But the argument is absurd because the characteristic of aesthetic consciousness is to be a belief by means of engagement, by oath, a belief sustained by fidelity to one's self and to the author, a perpetually renewed choice to believe. I can awaken at every moment, and I know it; but I do not want to; reading is a free dream. So that all feelings which are exacted on the basis of this imaginary belief are like particular modulations of my freedom. Far from absorbing or masking it, they are so many different ways it has chosen to reveal itself to itself. Raskolnikov, as I have said, would only be a shadow, without the mixture of repulsion and friendship which I feel for him and which makes him live. But, by a reversal which is the characteristic of the imaginary object, it is not his behavior which excites my indignation or esteem, but my indignation and esteem which give consistency and objectivity to his behavior. Thus, the reader's feelings are never dominated by the object, and as no external reality can condition them, they have their permanent source in freedom; that is, they are all generous — for I call a feeling generous which has its origin and its end in freedom. Thus, reading is an exercise in generosity, and what the writer requires of the reader is not the application of an abstract freedom but the gift of his whole person, with his passions, his prepossessions, his sympathies, his sexual temperament, and his scale of values. Only this person will give himself generously; freedom goes through and through him and comes to transform the darkest masses of his sensibility. And as activity has rendered itself passive in order for it better to create the object, vice-versa, passivity becomes an act; the man who is reading has raised himself to the highest degree. That is why we see people who are known for their toughness shed tears at the recital of imaginary misfortunes; for the moment they have become what they would have been if they had not spent their lives hiding their freedom from themselves.

Thus, the author writes in order to address himself to the freedom of readers, and he requires it in order to make his work exist. But he does not stop there; he also requires that they return this confidence which he has given them, that they recognize his creative freedom, and that they in turn solicit it by a symmetrical and inverse appeal. Here there appears the other dialectical paradox of reading; the more we experience our freedom, the more we recognize that of the other; the more he demands of us, the more we demand of him.

When I am enchanted with a landscape, I know very well that it is not I who create it, but I also know that without me the relations which are established before my eyes among the trees, the foliage, the earth, and the grass would not exist at all. I know that I can give no reason for the appearance of finality which I discover in the assortment of hues and in the harmony of the forms and movements created by the wind. Yet, it exists; there it is before my eyes, and I can make *there be* being only if being already *is*. But even if I believe in God, I can not establish any passage, unless it be purely verbal, between the divine, universal solicitude and the particular spectacle which I am considering. To say that He made the landscape in order to charm me or that He made me the kind of person who is pleased by it is to take a question for an answer. Is the marriage of this blue and that green deliberate? How can I know? The idea of a universal providence is no guarantee of any particular intention, especially in the case under consideration, since the green of the grass is explained by biological laws, specific constants, and geographical determinism, while the reason for the blue of the water is accounted for by the depth of the river, the nature of the soil and the swiftness of the current. The assorting of the shades, if it is willed, can only be something *thrown into the bargain;* it is the meeting of two causal series, that is to say, at first sight, a fact of chance. At best, the finality remains problematic. All the relations we establish remain hypotheses; no end is proposed to us in the manner of an imperative, since none is expressly revealed as having been willed by a creator. Thus, our freedom is never *called forth* by natural beauty. Or rather, there is an appearance of order in the ensemble of the foliage, the forms, and the movements, hence, the illusion of a calling forth which seems to solicit this freedom and which disappears immediately when one regards it. Hardly have we begun to run our eyes over this arrangement, than the call disappears; we remain alone, free to tie up one color with another or with a third, to set up a relationship between the tree and the water or the tree and the sky, or the tree, the water and the sky. My freedom becomes caprice. To the extent that I establish new relationships, I remove myself further from the illusory objectivity which solicits me. I *muse* about certain motifs which are vaguely outlined by the things; the natural reality is no longer anything but a pretext for musing. Or, in that case, because I have deeply regretted that this arrangement which was momentarily perceived was not offered to me by somebody and consequently is not *real,* the result is that I fix my dream, that I transpose it to canvas or in writing. Thus, I interpose myself between the finality without end which appears in the natural spectacles and the gaze of other men. I transmit it to them. It becomes human by this transmission. Art here is a ceremony of the *gift* and the gift alone brings about the metamorphosis. It is something like the transmission of titles and powers in the matriarchate where the mother does not possess the names, but is the indispensable intermediary between uncle and nephew. Since I have captured this illusion in flight, since I lay it out for other men and have disengaged it and rethought it for them, they can consider it with confidence. It has become intentional. As for me, I remain, to be sure, at the border of the subjective and the objective without ever being able to contemplate the objective ordonnance which I transmit.

The reader, on the contrary, progresses in security. However far he may go, the author has gone farther. Whatever connections he may establish among the different parts of the book — among the chapters or the words — he has a guarantee, namely, that they have been expressly willed. As Descartes says, he can even pretend that there is a secret order among parts which seem to have no connection. The creator has preceded him along the way, and the most beautiful disorders are effects of art, that is, again order. Reading is induction, interpolation, extrapolation, and the basis of these activities rests on the reader's will, as for a long time it was believed that that of scientific induction rested on the divine will. A gentle force accompanies us and supports us from the first page to the last. That does not mean that we fathom the artist's intentions easily. They constitute, as we have said, the object of conjectures, and there is an *experience* of the reader; but these conjectures are supported by the great certainty we have that the beauties which appear in the book are never accidental. In nature, the tree and the sky harmonize only by chance; if, on the contrary, in the novel, the protagonists find themselves in a *certain* tower, in a *certain* prison, if they stroll in a *certain* garden, it is a matter both of the restitution of independent causal series (the character had a certain state of mind which was due to a succession of psychological and social events; on the other hand, he betook himself to a determined place and the layout of the city required him to cross a certain park) and of the expression of a deeper finality, for the park came into existence only *in order to* harmonize with a certain state of mind, to express it by means of things or to put it into relief by a vivid contrast, and the state of mind itself was conceived in connection with the landscape. Here it is causality which is appearance and which might be called "causality without cause," and it is the finality which is the profound reality. But if I can thus in all confidence put the order of ends under the order of causes, it is because by opening the book I am asserting that the object has its source in human freedom.

If I were to suspect the artist of having written out of passion and in passion, my confidence would immediately vanish, for it would serve no purpose to have supported the order of causes by the order of ends. The latter would be supported in its turn by a psychic causality and the work of art would end by re-entering the chain of determinism. Certainly I do not deny when I am reading that the author may be impassioned, nor even that he might have conceived the first plan of his work under the sway of passion. But his decision to write supposes that he withdraws somewhat from his feelings, in short, that he has transformed his emotions into free emotions as I do mine while reading him; that is, that he is in an attitude of generosity.

Thus, reading is a pact of generosity between author and reader. Each one trusts the other; each one counts on the other, demands of the other as much as he demands of himself. For this confidence is itself generosity. Nothing can force the author to believe that his reader will use his freedom; nothing can force the reader to believe that the author has used his. Both of them make a free decision. There is then established a dialectical going-and-coming; when I read, I make demands; if my demands are met, what I am then reading provokes me to demand more of the author, which means to demand of the author that he demand more of me. And, vice-versa, the author's demand is that I carry my demands to the highest pitch. Thus, my freedom, by revealing itself, reveals the freedom of the other.

It matters little whether the aesthetic object is the product of "realistic" art (or supposedly such) or "formal" art. At any rate, the natural relations are inverted; that tree on the first plane of the Cézanne painting first appears as the product of a causal chain. But the causality is an illusion; it will doubtless remain as a proposition as long as we look at the painting, but it will be supported by a deep finality; if the tree is placed in such a way, it is because the rest of the painting *requires* that this form and those colors be placed on the first plane. Thus, through the phenomenal causality, our gaze attains finality as the deep structure of the object, and, beyond finality, it attains human freedom as its source and original basis. Vermeer's realism is carried so far that at first it might be thought to be photographic. But if one considers the splendor of his texture, the pink and velvety glory of his little brick walls, the blue thickness of a branch of woodbine, the glazed darkness of his vestibules, the orange-colored flesh of his faces which are as polished as the stone of holy-water basins, one suddenly feels, in the pleasure that he experiences, that the finality is not so much in the forms or colors as in his material imagination. It is the very substance and temper of the things which here give the forms their reason for being. With this realist we are perhaps closest to absolute creation, since it is in the very passivity of the matter that we meet the unfathomable freedom of man.

The work is never limited to the painted, sculpted, or narrated object. Just as one perceives things only against the background of the world, so the objects represented by art appear against the background of the universe. On the background of the adventures of Fabrice[3] are the Italy of 1820, Austria, France, the sky and stars which the Abbé Blanis consults, and finally the whole earth. If the painter presents us with a field or a vase of flowers, his paintings are windows which are open on the whole world. We follow the red path which is buried among the wheat much farther than Van Gogh has painted it, among other wheat fields, under other clouds, to the river which empties into the sea, and we extend to infinity, to the other end of the world, the deep finality which supports the existence of the field and the earth. So that, through the various objects which it produces or reproduces, the creative act aims at a total renewal of the world. Each painting, each book, is a recovery of the totality of being. Each of them presents this totality to the freedom of the spectator. For this is quite the final goal of art: to recover this world by giving it to be seen as it is, but as if it had its source in human freedom. But, since what the author creates takes on objective reality only in the eyes of the spectator, this recovery is consecrated by the ceremony of the spectacle — and particularly of reading. We are already in a better position to answer the question we raised a while ago: the writer chooses to appeal to the freedom of other men so that, by the reciprocal implications of their demands, they may readapt the totality of being to man and may again enclose the universe within man.

If we wish to go still further, we must bear in mind that the writer, like all other artists, aims at giving his reader a certain feeling that is customarily called aesthetic pleasure, and which I would very much rather call aesthetic joy, and that this feeling, when it appears, is a sign that the work is achieved. It is therefore fitting to examine it in the light of the preceding considerations. In effect, this joy, which is denied to the creator, insofar as he creates, becomes one with the aesthetic consciousness of the spectator, that is, in the case under consideration, of the reader. It is a complex feeling but one whose structures and condition are inseparable from one another. It is identical, at first, with the recognition of a transcendent and absolute end which, for a moment, suspends the utilitarian round of ends-means and means-ends,[4] that is, of an appeal or, what amounts to the same thing, of a value. And the positional consciousness which I take of this value is necessarily accompanied by the non-positional consciousness of my freedom, since my freedom is manifested to itself by a transcendent exigency. The recognition of freedom by itself is joy, but this structure of non-thetical consciousness implies another: since, in effect, reading is creation, my freedom does not only appear to itself as pure autonomy but as creative activity, that is, it is not limited to giving itself its own law but perceives itself as being constitutive of the object. It is on this level that the phenomenon specifically is manifested, that is, a creation wherein the created object is given *as object* to its creator. It is the sole case in which the creator gets any enjoyment out of the object he creates. And the word enjoyment which is applied to the positional consciousness of the work read indicates sufficiently that we are in the presence of an essential structure of aesthetic joy. This positional enjoyment is accompanied by the non-positional consciousness of being essential in relation to an object perceived as essential. I shall call this aspect of aesthetic consciousness the feeling of security; it is this which stamps the strongest aesthetic emotions with a sovereign calm. It has its origin in the authentication of a strict harmony between subjectivity and objectivity. As, on the other hand, the aesthetic object is properly the world insofar as it is aimed at through the imaginary, aesthetic joy accompanies the positional consciousness that the world is a value, that is, a task proposed to human freedom. I shall call this the aesthetic modification of the human project, for, as usual, the world appears as the horizon of our situation, as the infinite dis-

[3]In Stendhal's *Charterhouse of Parma* (1839). [Ed.]

[4]In *practical life* a means may be taken for an end as soon as one searches for it, and each end is revealed as a means of attaining another end. [Au.]

tance which separates us from ourselves, as the synthetic totality of the given, as the undifferentiated ensemble of obstacles and implements — but never as a demand addressed to our freedom. Thus, aesthetic joy proceeds to this level of the consciousness which I take of recovering and internalizing that which is non-ego par excellence, since I transform the given into an imperative and the fact into a value. The world is *my task,* that is, the essential and freely accepted function of my freedom is to make that unique and absolute object which is the universe come into being in an unconditioned movement. And, thirdly, the preceding structures imply a pact between human freedoms, for, on the one hand, reading is a confident and exacting recognition of the freedom of the writer, and, on the other hand, aesthetic pleasure, as it is itself experienced in the form of a value, involves an absolute exigence in regard to others; every man, insofar as he is a freedom, feels the same pleasure in reading the same work. Thus, all mankind is present in its highest freedom; it sustains the being of a world which is both *its* world and the "external" world. In aesthetic joy the positional consciousness is an *image-making* consciousness of the world in its totality both as being and having to be, both as totally ours and totally foreign, and the more ours as it is the more foreign. The nonpositional consciousness *really* envelops the harmonious totality of human freedoms insofar as it makes the object of a universal confidence and exigency.

To write is thus both to disclose the world and to offer it as a task to the generosity of the reader. It is to have recourse to the consciousness of others in order to make one's self be recognized as *essential* to the totality of being; it is to wish to live this essentiality by means of interposed persons; but, on the other hand, as the real world is revealed only by action, as one can feel himself in it only by exceeding it in order to change it, the novelist's universe would lack thickness if it were not discovered in a movement to transcend it. It has often been observed that an object in a story does not derive its density of existence from the number and length of the descriptions devoted to it, but from the complexity of its connections with the different characters. The more often the characters handle it, take it up, and put it down, in short, go beyond it toward their own ends, the more real will it appear. Thus, of the world of the novel, that is, the totality of men and things, we may say that in order for it to offer its maximum density the disclosure-creation by which the reader discovers it must also be an imaginary engagement in the action; in other words, the more disposed one is to change it, the more alive it will be. The error of realism has been to believe that the real reveals itself to contemplation, and that consequently one could draw an impartial picture of it. How could that be possible, since the very perception is partial, since by itself the naming is already a modification of the object? And how could the writer, who wants himself to be essential to this universe, want to be essential to the injustice which this universe comprehends? Yet, he must be; but if he accepts being the creator of injustices, it is in a movement which goes beyond them toward their abolition. As for me who reads, if I create and keep alive an unjust world, I can not help making myself responsible for it. And the author's whole art is bent on obliging me to *create* what he *discloses,* therefore to compromise myself. So both of us bear the responsibility for the universe. And precisely because this universe is supported by the joint effort of our two freedoms, and because the author, with me as medium, has attempted to integrate it into the human, it must appear truly *in itself,* in its very marrow, as being shot through and through with a freedom which has taken human freedom as its end, and if it is not really the city of ends that it ought to be, it must at least be a stage along the way; in a word, it must be a becoming and it must always be considered and presented not as a crushing mass which weighs us down, but from the point of view of its going beyond toward that city of ends. However bad and hopeless the humanity which it paints may be, the work must have an air of generosity. Not, of course, that this generosity is to be expressed by means of edifying discourses and virtuous characters; it must not even be premeditated, and it is quite true that fine sentiments to not make fine books. But it must be the very warp and woof of the book, the stuff out of which the people and things are cut; whatever the subject, a sort of essential lightness must appear everywhere and remind us that the work is never a natural datum, but an *exigence* and a *gift*. And if I am given this world with its injustices, it is not so that I might contemplate them coldly, but that I might animate them with my indignation, that I might disclose them and create them with their nature as injustices, that is, as abuses to be suppressed. Thus, the writer's universe will only reveal itself in all its depth to the examination, the admiration, and the indignation of the reader; and the generous love is a promise to maintain, and the generous indignation is a promise to change, and the admiration a promise to imitate; although literature is one thing and morality a quite different one, at the heart of the aesthetic imperative we discern the moral imperative. For, since the one who writes recognizes, by the very fact that he takes the trouble to write, the freedom of his readers, and since the one who reads, by the mere fact of his opening the book, recognizes the freedom of the writer, the work of art, from whichever side you approach it, is an act of confidence in the freedom of men. And since readers, like the author, recognize this freedom only to demand that it manifest itself, the work can be defined as an imaginary presentation of the world insofar as it demands human freedom. The result of which is that there is no "gloomy literature," since, however dark may be the colors in which one paints the world, he paints it only so that free men may feel their freedom as they face it. Thus, there are only good and bad novels. The bad novel aims to please by flattering, whereas the good one is an exigence and an act of faith. But above all, the unique point of view from which the author can present the world to those freedoms whose concurrence he wishes to bring about is that of a world to be impregnated always with more freedom. It would be inconceivable that this unleashing of generosity provoked by the writer could be used to authorize an injustice, and that the reader could enjoy his freedom while reading a work which approves or accepts or simply abstains from condemning the subjection of man by man. One can imagine a good novel being written by an American Negro even if hatred of the whites were spread all over it, because it is the freedom of his race that he demands through this hatred. And, as he invites me to assume the attitude of generosity, the moment I feel myself a pure freedom I can not bear to identify myself with a race of oppressors. Thus, I require of all freedoms that they demand the liberation of colored people against the white race and against myself insofar as I am a part of it, but nobody can suppose for a moment that it is possible to write a good novel in praise of anti-Semitism.[5] For, the moment I feel that my freedom is indissolubly linked with that of all other men, it can not be demanded of me that I use it to approve the enslavement of a part of these men. Thus, whether he is an essayist, a pamphleteer, a satirist, or a novelist, whether he speaks only of individual passions or whether he attacks the social order, the writer, a free man addressing free men, has only one subject — freedom.

Hence, any attempt to enslave his readers threatens him in his very art. A blacksmith can be affected by fascism in his life as a man, but not necessarily in his craft; a writer will be affected in both, and even more in his craft than in his life. I have seen writers, who before the war, called for fascism with all their hearts, smitten with sterility at the very moment when the Nazis were loading them with honors. I am thinking of Drieu la Rochelle in particular; he was mistaken, but he was sincere. He proved it. He had agreed to direct a Nazi-inspired review. The first few months he reprimanded, rebuked, and lectured his countrymen. No one answered him because no one was free to do so. He became irritated; he no longer *felt* his readers. He became more insistent, but no sign appeared to prove that he had been understood. No sign of hatred, nor of anger either; nothing. He seemed disoriented, the victim of a growing distress. He complained bitterly to the Germans. His articles had been superb;

[5]This last remark may arouse some readers. If so, I'd like to know a single good novel whose express purpose was to serve oppression, a single good novel which has been written against Jews, negroes, workers, or colonial people. "But if there isn't any, that's no reason why someone may not write one some day." But you then admit that you are an abstract theoretician. You, not I. For it is in the name of your abstract conception of art that you assert the possibility of a fact which has never come into being, whereas I limit myself to proposing an explanation for a recognized fact. [Au.]

they became shrill. The moment arrived when he struck his breast; no echo, except among the bought journalists whom he despised. He handed in his resignation, withdrew it, again spoke, still in the desert. Finally, he kept still, gagged by the silence of others. He had demanded the enslavement of others, but in his crazy mind he must have imagined that it was voluntary, that it was still free. It came; the man in him congratulated himself mightily, but the writer could not bear it. While this was going on, others, who, happily, were in the majority, understood that the freedom of writing implies the freedom of the citizen. One does not write for slaves. The art of prose is bound up with the only regime in which prose has meaning, democracy. When one is threatened, the other is too. And it is not enough to defend them with the pen. A day comes when the pen is forced to stop, and the writer must then take up arms. Thus, however you might have come to it, whatever the opinions you might have professed, literature throws you into battle. Writing is a certain way of wanting freedom; once you have begun, you are engaged, willy-nilly.

Engaged in what? Defending freedom? That's easy to say. Is it a matter of acting as guardian of ideal values like Benda's clerk before the betrayal,[6] or is it concrete, everyday freedom which must be protected by our taking sides in political and social struggles? The question is tied up with another one, one very simple in appearance but which nobody ever asks himself: "For whom does one write?"

[6]The reference here is to Julien Benda's *La Trahison des clercs,* translated into English as *The Treason of the Intellectuals.* [Tr.]

Simone de Beauvoir

1908–1986

Simone-Lucie-Ernestine-Marie-Bertrand de Beauvoir was born and raised in a middle-class Parisian household that discouraged her interest in matters intellectual, but she went on to obtain a prestigious *agrégation* (postgraduate) degree in philosophy at the Sorbonne in 1929 and to write the influential feminist treatise, *The Second Sex* (*Le Deuxième Sexe,* 1949). While she was preparing for her degree, she met Jean-Paul Sartre, who became her companion in a lifelong nonmarital union, though it was a partnership fraught with conflicts produced by, among other things, his persistent and pointed infidelities. They were also partners in the important intellectual journal *Les Temps Modernes,* a monthly that she and Sartre began in 1945 and that she continued to edit and review after Sartre's death in 1980.

After taking her *agré,* Beauvoir taught philosophy for thirteen years in various schools, then decided to make her living by her pen, publishing novels, essays, and travel literature. Most of her novels focus on themes of freedom, responsibility, and angst — giving concrete exposition to the issues highlighted in existentialism, the philosophy espoused by Beauvoir and Sartre. (For a fuller discussion of the background of existentialism, see the introductions to Heidegger, p. 560, and Sartre, p. 621.) Her first novel, *She Came to Stay (L'Invitée,* 1943), for example, focuses on the problems of conscience produced by conflicts within a close familial group. It also reflects the emotional upheaval in the Beauvoir-Sartre *ménage* caused by the prolonged stay of Olga Kosakiewicz, a young girl that Sartre had "adopted." Her second, *The Blood of Others (Le Sang des autres,* 1945) raises the issue of causes and consequences: Must a French resistance fighter consider himself responsible for the reprisals carried out by the Nazis? Her later novel, *The Mandarins (Les Mandarins,* 1954), a probing portrait of the French literary and intellectual establishment after World War II, won the Prix Goncourt, an award presented by that very establishment.

Beginning at the age of fifty, Beauvoir turned from philosophical fiction to autobiography and memoir. *Memoirs of a Dutiful Daughter (Mémoires d'une jeune fille rangée,* 1958) explores her youth and rebellion; *The Prime of Life (La Force de l'age,* 1960) and *The Force of Circumstance (La Force des choses,* 1963) continue her story into her middle age. As she grew older, Beauvoir concerned herself more and more with the problems of aging and dying, which she addressed in *A Very Easy Death (Une Morte très douce,* 1964), which focuses on the death of her mother; she wrote about Sartre's last illness and death in *Adieux: A Farewell to Sartre (La Cérémonies des adieux,* 1981).

Beauvoir's magnum opus, *The Second Sex,* is one of the most important texts for twentieth-century feminism, a broad and wide-ranging attempt to review and critique the social and psychological constructions that since the Bronze Age have defined "humanity" in terms of the capacities, ideologies, and desires of the male sex, and correspondingly have positioned women as protected — even at times worshipped — but inferior: "She is defined and differentiated with reference to man and not he with reference to her; she is the incidental, the inessential as opposed to the essential. He is the Subject, he is the Absolute — she is the Other."[1]

In terms of the existential philosophy that Beauvoir developed along with Jean-Paul Sartre, this "alterity" or Otherness means that a woman is implicitly defined as *en-soi* rather than *pour-soi:* a thing rather than a person, a means to some other end rather than an end-in-itself. If, as existentialist philosophy suggests, the freedom to define what one is through one's choices and acts is terrifyingly difficult to accept for men, Beauvoir argues that it is almost impossible for women, who internalize and help maintain a patriarchal belief that their essential nature is to exist for the sake of others.

For Beauvoir, the destiny of Woman to be the Other begins, though it does not end, with mammalian anatomy. Unlike the controlling female queens in bee and ant societies, or the choosy (and devouring) female arachnids, whose power depends on exteriorizing their reproductive maneuvers, the human female carries the fertilized ovum inside her — a growing being that is a part of her and yet not herself, a parasite whose significance to the survival of the species makes her body an object rather than a subject, something Other even to herself.[2] When at the dawn of history man began to till the soil, woman in her fecundity was like the Earth itself, and like the Earth was made to yield her harvest for his benefit.[3] The tool-making and tool-using capacity vested more significance in man's upper-body strength and less in woman's adaptivity and endurance. Once created, patriarchy required that property descend through the male line, which in turn demanded that virtuous women be passive, acquiescent, and above all chaste, to guarantee true genetic inheritance as strictly as possible in a species whose individuals can never truly know who their father is.

Beauvoir, like Hegel, sees the progress of civilization as bringing the individual closer and closer to the realization of his or her freedom, but she argues that while events like the French revolution liberated the masculine spirit from outmoded feudal social structures, the liberation of woman has been far slower in coming. She believes this is partly because women, however oppressed, are not a true class in Marx's sense: Restrictions on aristocratic women were imposed differently than on bourgeois or working-class women, and women could therefore gain no sense of common interest. The delay mainly results because women are epiphenomenal to the historically developing class struggle of men: Historical changes in women's status and choices — greater or less occupational or familial or sexual freedom — seem to depend not on what they want but on what men want of them.

In part III of *The Second Sex,* Beauvoir explores the ideological component of women's alterity: the way in which women are made to think of themselves as the Other, not by social rules or restrictions but by the myths through which societies

[1]Simone de Beauvoir, *The Second Sex* (New York: Random House, 1953), p. xix.

[2]Some contemporary feminists have been critical of Beauvoir's essentialization of female inferiority and of the implication of her argument that anatomy was always destiny.

[3]Beauvoir dismisses as "a myth" the theory of some anthropologists that an early Bronze-Age matriarchal society may have preceded the development of patriarchal society. The theory is based on texts like Aeschylus's *The Eumenides,* which presupposes that the patriarchal Olympian gods had recently displaced the rule of the female principles of Earth and Night.

construct the female consciousness. In "Myths: Of Women in Five Authors," Beauvoir exposes several myths that present women not as they are, but as projections of male needs, defined as whatever men need to complete themselves. These myths can be vulgar, as in Henri de Montherlant's casting of woman as mere "slimy" flesh with which man satiates himself sexually, or comparatively refined, as in D. H. Lawrence's vision of passive woman subordinating herself to the enabling transcendence of the Phallus. Or the myth can invert alterity, as in Paul Claudel's vision of woman as the holy channel through which the striving male soul may find the peace of God. Even Stendhal — who liked his women to have minds and hearts as well as bodies and souls, so that Beauvoir feels it is "a relief" to be able to talk about his complex and subtle creations — has his mythic woman. Stendhal's women — such as Madame de Rénal or la Sanseverina — are more complicated and intelligent than their male counterparts, but they are never the subject of the narrative in their own right: They are there as the Other to play their part in the maturation of the male subject, Julien Sorel or Fabrizio.[4]

The result of the construction of woman as an ideal, whatever her characteristics, Beauvoir argues, is to force women to choose between being a "woman" and being themselves. In her final section, she sees light at the end of the tunnel: In the dissatisfaction of contemporary men with the lack of womanliness of present-day women, Beauvoir senses that a parting of the ways has come and that the myth of femininity is not all-powerful. Her book itself gave a gigantic tug at that unstable ideological structure. Some present-day feminists would argue that it is necessary to go beyond Beauvoir's own dogmas, her own inherited essentialisms, such as the rigid dialectic between masculinity and femininity, but surely *The Second Sex* has a clear place on the map of today's feminist theory.

Selected Bibliography

Beauvoir, Simone de. *The Second Sex.* New York: Random House, 1953.

———. *All Said and Done.* New York: Marlowe, 1994.

Francis, Claude, and Fernande Gontier. *Simone de Beauvoir: A Life — A Love Story.* New York: St. Martin's Press, 1988.

Fullbrook, Kate, and Edward Fullbrook. *Simone de Beauvoir and Jean-Paul Sartre: The Remaking of the Twentieth-Century Legend.* New York: Basic Books, 1994.

Lundgren-Gothlin, Eva. *Sex and Existence: Simone de Beauvoir's* The Second Sex. Boston: University Press of New England, 1996.

Marks, Elaine, ed. *Critical Essays on Simone de Beauvoir.* Boston: G. K. Hall, 1987.

Moi, Toril. *Simone de Beauvoir: The Making of an Intellectual Woman.* London: Blackwell, 1994.

Simons, Margaret A., ed. *Feminist Interpretations of Simone de Beauvoir.* University Park: Pennsylvania State University Press, 1995.

[4]Beauvoir's observations concerning Stendhal's novels are similar to what James Phelan has more recently argued about *A Farewell to Arms* — that the essential sexism of Hemingway's novel resides less in how Catherine Barkley is characterized than in the fact that the novel is structured so that the central tragedy is not her death but Frederic Henry's having to go on living without her. It is his loss, not hers, that counts.

Myths: Of Women in Five Authors

It is to be seen from these examples that each separate writer reflects the great collective myths: we have seen woman as *flesh;* the flesh of the male is produced in the mother's body and recreated in the embraces of the woman in love. Thus woman is related to *nature,* she incarnates it: vale of blood, open rose, siren, the curve of a hill, she represents to man the fertile soil, the sap, the material beauty and the soul of the world. She can hold the keys to *poetry;* she can be *mediatrix* between this world and the beyond: grace or oracle, star or sorceress, she opens the door to the supernatural, the surreal. She is doomed to *immanence;* and through her passivity she bestows peace and harmony — but if she declines this role, she is seen forthwith as a praying mantis, an ogress. In any case she appears as the *privileged Other,* through whom the subject fulfills himself: one of the measures of man, his counterbalance, his salvation, his adventure, his happiness.

But these myths are very differently orchestrated by our authors. The *Other* is particularly defined according to the particular manner in which the *One* chooses to set himself up. Every man asserts his freedom and transcendence — but they do not all give these words the same sense. For Montherlant[1] transcendence is a situation: he is the transcendent, he soars in the sky of heroes; woman crouches on earth, beneath his feet; it amuses him to measure the distance that separates him from her; from time to time he raises her up to him, takes her, and then throws her back; never does he lower himself down to her realm of slimy shadows. Lawrence[2] places transcendence in the phallus; the phallus is life and power only by grace of woman; immanence is therefore good and necessary; the false hero who pretends to be above setting foot on earth, far from being a demigod, fails to attain man's estate. Woman is not to be scorned, she is deep richness, a warm spring; but she should give up all personal transcendence and confine herself to furthering that of her male. Claudel[3] asks her for the same devotion: for him, too, woman should maintain life while man extends its range through his activities; but for the Catholic all earthly affairs are immersed in vain immanence: the only transcendent is God; in the eyes of God the man in action and the woman who serves him are exactly equal; it is for each to surpass his or her earthly state: salvation is in all cases an autonomous enterprise. For Breton[4] the rank of the sexes is reversed; action and conscious thought, in which the male finds his transcendence, seem to Breton to constitute a silly mystification that gives rise to war, stupidity, bureaucracy, the negation of anything human; it is immanence, the pure, dark presence of the real, which is truth; true transcendence would be accomplished by a return to immanence. His attitude is the exact opposite of Montherlant's: the latter likes war because in war one gets rid of women; Breton venerates woman because she brings peace. Montherlant confuses mind and subjectivity — he refuses to accept the given universe; Breton thinks that mind is objectively present at the heart of the world; woman endangers Montherlant because she breaks his solitude; she is revelation for Breton because she tears him out of his subjectivity. As for Stendhal,[5] we have seen that for him woman hardly has a mystical value: he

Translated by H. M. Parshley.

[1]Henri de Montherlant (1896–1972), antifeminist author of *Les Jeune filles* (1936), *Pitié pour les femmes* (1936), *Le Démon du bien* (1937), and *Les Lepreuses* (1939). [Ed.]

[2]D. H. Lawrence (1885–1930), author of *Sons and Lovers* (1913) and *Women in Love* (1920); Beauvoir's later discussion of "Kate" and "Don Cipriano" refers to his novel, *The Plumed Serpent* (1926). [Ed.]

[3]Paul Claudel (1868–1955), poet and playwright, author of *L'Annonce faite à Marie* (1912) and *Le Soulier de satin* (1937), which contains the salvation of Rodrigue by Prouhèze that Beauvoir refers to later. [Ed.]

[4]André Breton (1896–1966), surrealist poet and novelist, author of *Nadja* (1928) and *L'Amour fou* (1937). [Ed.]

[5]Marie-Henri Beyle (1783–1842), psychological novelist who wrote as Stendhal; his works include *Le Rouge et le noir* (1830) and *La Chartreuse de Parme* (1839). [Ed.]

regards her as being, like man, a transcendent; for this humanist, free beings of both sexes fulfill themselves in their reciprocal relations; and for him it is enough if the *Other* be simply an other so that life may have what he calls "a pungent saltiness." He is not seeking a "stellar equilibrium," he is not fed on the bread of disgust; he is not looking for a miracle; he does not wish to be concerned with the cosmos or with poetry, but with free human beings.

More, Stendhal feels that he is himself a clear, free being. The others — and this is a most important point — pose as transcendents but feel themselves prisoners of a dark presence in their own hearts: they project this "unbreakable core of night" upon woman. Montherlant has an Adlerian complex, giving rise to his thick-witted bad faith: it is this tangle of pretensions and fears that he incarnates in woman; his disgust for her is what he dreads feeling for himself. He would trample underfoot, in woman, the always possible proof of his own insufficiency; he appeals to scorn to save him; and woman is the trench into which he throws all the monsters that haunt him. The life of Lawrence shows us that he suffered from an analogous though more purely sexual complex: in his works woman serves as a compensation myth, exalting a virility that the writer was none too sure of; when he describes Kate at Don Cipriano's feet, he feels as if he had won a male triumph over his wife, Frieda; nor does he permit his companion to raise any questions: if she were to oppose his aims he would doubtless lose confidence in them; her role is to reassure him. He asks of her peace, repose, faith, as Montherlant asks for certainty regarding his superiority: they demand what is missing in them. Claudel's lack is not that of self-confidence: if he is timid it is only in secret with God. Nor is there any trace of the battle of the sexes in his work. Man boldly assumes woman's weight; she is a possibility for temptation or for salvation. It would seem that for Breton man is true only through the mystery that is within him; it pleases him for Nadja to see that star toward which he moves and which is like "the heart of a heartless flower." In his dreams, his presentiments, the spontaneous flow of his stream of consciousness — in such activities, which escape the control of the will and the reason, he recognizes his true self; woman is the visible image of that veiled presence which is infinitely more essential than his conscious personality.

Stendhal is in tranquil agreement with himself; but he needs woman as she needs him in order to gather his diffuse existence into the unity of a single design and destiny: it is as though man reaches manhood for another; but still he needs to have the lending of the other's consciousness. Other males are too indifferent toward their fellows; only the loving woman opens her heart to her lover and shelters him there, wholly. Except for Claudel, who finds in God his preferred witness, all the writers we have considered expect that woman will cherish in them what Malraux[6] calls "this incomparable monster" known to themselves only. In cooperation or contest men face each other as generalized types. Montherlant is for his fellows a writer, Lawrence a doctrinaire, Breton a school principal, Stendhal a diplomat or man of wit; it is woman who reveals in one a magnificent and cruel prince, in another a disquieting faun, in this one a god or a sun or a being "black and cold as a man struck by lightning at the feet of the Sphinx,"[7] in the last a seducer, a charmer, a lover.

For each of them the ideal woman will be she who incarnates most exactly the *Other* capable of revealing him to himself. Montherlant, the solar spirit, seeks pure animality in her; Lawrence, the phallicist, asks her to sum up the feminine sex in general; Claudel defines her as a soul-sister; Breton cherishes Mélusine, rooted in nature, pinning his hope on the woman-child; Stendhal wants his mistress intelligent, cultivated, free in spirit and behavior: an equal. But the sole earthly destiny reserved for the equal, the woman-child, the soul-sister, the woman-sex, the woman-animal is always man! Whatever ego may seek himself through her, he can find himself only if she is willing to act as his crucible. She is required in every case to forget self and to love. Monther-

[6]André Malraux (1901–76), novelist and political figure; his works include *La Condition humaine* (1933) and *Les Voix du silence* (1951). [Ed.]

[7]Breton's *Nadja*. [Au.]

lant consents to have pity upon the woman who allows him to measure his virile potency; Lawrence addresses a burning hymn to the woman who gives up being herself for his sake; Claudel exalts the handmaid, the female servant, the devotee who submits to God in submitting to the male; Breton is in hopes of human salvation from woman because she is capable of total love for her child or her lover; and even in Stendhal the heroines are more moving than the masculine heroes because they give themselves to their passion with a more distraught violence; they help man fulfill his destiny, as Prouhèze contributes to the salvation of Rodrigue; in Stendhal's novels it often happens that they save their lovers from ruin, prison, or death. Feminine devotion is demanded as a duty by Montherlant and Lawrence; less arrogant, Claudel, Breton, and Stendhal admire it as a generous free choice; they wish for it without claiming to deserve it; but — except for the astounding Lamiel — all their works show that they expect from woman that altruism which Comte[8] admired in her and imposed upon her, and which according to him constituted a mark at once of flagrant inferiority and of an equivocal superiority.

We could multiply examples, but they would invariably lead us to the same conclusions. When he describes woman, each writer discloses his general ethics and the special idea he has of himself; and in her he often betrays also the gap between his world view and his egotistical dreams. The absence or insignificance of the feminine element throughout the work of an author is in its own way symptomatic; but that element is extremely important when it sums up in its totality all the aspects of the Other, as happens with Lawrence. It remains important when woman is viewed simply as an other but the writer is interested in the individual adventure of her life, as with Stendhal; it loses importance in an epoch such as ours when personal problems of the individual are of secondary interest. Woman, however, as the other still plays a role to the extent that, if only to transcend himself, each man still needs to learn more fully what he is.

[8]Auguste Comte (1798–1857), French philosopher and sociologist, author of *Système de politique positive* (1851–54). [Ed.]

Northrop Frye

1912–1991

In his native Canada, Northrop Frye's intellectual stature made him something of a national oracle and celebrity. In the world of literary theory and criticism, he was also a formidable and revered figure. Herman Northrop Frye was born in Sherbrooke, Quebec, received his B.A. from the University of Toronto in 1933, studied theology there at Emmanuel College, and was ordained a minister in 1936. He received an M.A. from Merton College, Oxford, in 1940. In 1948 he became a professor of English at Victoria College, Toronto; in 1959 principal of the college; and in 1967 he became the first University Professor at the University of Toronto. He wrote more than forty books, including *Fearful Symmetry* (1947), *Fables of Identity* (1963), *The Modern Century* (1967), *The Stubborn Structure* (1970), *The Critical Path* (1971), *The Secular Scripture* (1976), *The Great Code* (1982), and his last book, *Words with Power* (1990), which might be known as *The Great Code II*. His most celebrated work is *Anatomy of Criticism* (1957). "The Archetypes of Literature," first published in the *Kenyon Review* (vol. 8, 1951) and later reprinted in *Fables of Identity,* is, in Frye's words, "to some extent a summarized statement of the critical program" later expanded in *Anatomy of Criticism.*[1]

What is most distinctive about Northrop Frye's criticism is its metaphorical relationship to Jungian psychology. Frye was careful to disclaim any belief in a collective unconscious or racial memory, or the dependence of his literary theories upon any such belief. Indeed, Frye reads Jung only as one who has provided "a grammar of literary symbolism," as a textual critic rather than as a psychologist. Nevertheless, for Frye as for Jung, the power of literature comes out of its evocation of archetypes that have a permanent place in human life: the hero and the virgin, the witch and the magus, the quest and the journey, the open green world of the forest and the walled-off city.

But Frye sees mere mystification in Jung's notion that literature originates in a "collective unconscious" stored as racial memory within each individual. For Frye, literature originates in other literature, as stories are broken down into bits and reshaped into other stories. Many of these kernel structures of story arise naturally out of the cyclical patterns of life on a planet that spins circling the sun: The dualistic cycle of day and night, the sense of beginnings, maturation, ripeness, and death that come from the cycle of the agricultural seasons, and the slower parallel cycle that imitates the longer journey from birth to death that each individual and generation must follow. Each generation rewrites the stories of the past in ways that make sense for it, recycling a vast tradition over the ages. The great myths of the gods, created in the vast dream of mankind in an almost prehistoric past, are converted into legends of semidivine heroes, then into stories of people very much like ourselves.

[1]Northrop Frye, *Fables of Identity: Studies in Poetic Mythology* (New York: Harcourt Brace and World, 1963), p. 1.

Frye's "The Archetypes of Literature" (1951) promises in effect to go beyond the Jungian criticism of precursors such as Maud Bodkin by presenting not just fragmentary insights but the "ground plan of a systematic and comprehensive development of criticism." What Frye eventually delivered was the encyclopaedic and highly influential study *Anatomy of Criticism* (1957), in which the schema of archetypal criticism is elaborated much further into an exhaustive mapping of the possibilities of literary form and content. Frye begins with a theory of *modes,* describing five levels of narrative (myth, legend, high mimetic, low mimetic, and ironic), which correspond to the stature and degree of freedom of action of the protagonist. For example, the tragic myth of the dying god of nature might descend to a legend in Malory's *Morte d'Arthur,* a high mimetic epic in Tennyson's *Idylls of the King,* a low mimetic novel in T. H. White's *The Once and Future King,* and an ironic parody in the film *Monty Python and the Holy Grail.*

A second theory of *symbols* differentiates five methods of symbolic interpretation, not unlike Dante's theory of polysemy: (1) In the *literal* approach to the symbol, the very shape of the signifier becomes important; (2) in the *descriptive* phase, the signifier is related to its signified — its usual meaning; (3) in the *formal* phase, the signifier is related to other similar signifiers in patterns of imagery; (4) in the *archetypal* phase, the signifier is related to its ritual significance; and (5) in the *anagogic* phase, the signifier becomes a monad, a symbolic universe in itself, a function of the total dream of mankind.

A third theory of *myth* elaborates on the relationships between comedy, romance, tragedy, and irony discussed in "The Archetypes of Literature," and categorizes them as twenty-four distinct variants on the monomyth of the quest. And finally, the theory of *genres* creates a schema for locating the various forms of presentation — lyric, drama, epos, and fiction — and divides the category of fiction into the forms of novel, romance, confession, and anatomy. Taken together, the four essays that constitute *Anatomy of Criticism* construct a multidimensional space in which one may locate the position of any work of literature and its relationship to any other.

Frye's *Anatomy of Criticism* comes close to fleshing out T. S. Eliot's remark that "the works of literature form an ideal order among themselves." In this direction, Frye seems to reach out toward the Structuralists, who were just beginning work on the Continent. Nevertheless, what is most original about Frye is the practical use he made of the theories of Jung, which is evident in "The Archetypes of Literature."

Selected Bibliography

Adamson, Joseph. *Northrop Frye: A Visionary Life.* London: InBook, 1993.

Denham, Robert D. *Northrop Frye: An Enumerative Bibliography.* Metuchen, NJ: Scarecrow Press, 1974.

———. *Northrop Frye: An Annotated Bibliography of Primary and Secondary Sources.* Toronto: University of Toronto Press, 1987.

Frye, Northrop. *Anatomy of Criticism: Four Essays.* Princeton: Princeton University Press, 1957.

———. *The Great Code: The Bible in Literature.* New York: Harcourt, Brace and Jovanovich, 1983.

Hart, Jonathan. *Northrop Frye: The Theoretical Imagination.* New York and London: Routledge, 1994.

Lee, Alvin A., and Robert D. Denham, eds. *The Legacy of Northrop Frye.* Toronto: University of Toronto Press, 1994.

The Archetypes of Literature

I

Every organized body of knowledge can be learned progressively; and experience shows that there is also something progressive about the learning of literature. Our opening sentence has already got us into a semantic difficulty. Physics is an organized body of knowledge about nature, and a student of it says that he is learning physics, not that he is learning nature. Art, like nature, is the subject of a systematic study, and has to be distinguished from the study itself, which is criticism. It is therefore impossible to "learn literature": one learns about it in a certain way, but what one learns, transitively, is the criticism of literature. Similarly, the difficulty often felt in "teaching literature" arises from the fact that it cannot be done: the criticism of literature is all that can be directly taught. So while no one expects literature itself to behave like a science, there is surely no reason why criticism, as a systematic and organized study, should not be, at least partly, a science. Not a "pure" or "exact" science, perhaps, but these phrases form part of a nineteenth-century cosmology which is no longer with us. Criticism deals with the arts and may well be something of an art itself, but it does not follow that it must be unsystematic. If it is to be related to the sciences too, it does not follow that it must be deprived of the graces of culture.

Certainly criticism as we find it in learned journals and scholarly monographs has every characteristic of a science. Evidence is examined scientifically; previous authorities are used scientifically; fields are investigated scientifically; texts are edited scientifically. Prosody is scientific in structure; so is phonetics; so is philology. And yet in studying this kind of critical science the student becomes aware of a centrifugal movement carrying him away from literature. He finds that literature is the central division of the "humanities," flanked on one side by history and on the other by philosophy. Criticism so far ranks only as a subdivision of literature; and hence, for the systematic mental organization of the subject, the student has to turn to the conceptual framework of the historian for events, and to that of the philosopher for ideas. Even the more centrally placed critical sciences, such as textual editing, seem to be part of a "background" that recedes into history or some other nonliterary field. The thought suggests itself that the ancillary critical disciplines may be related to a central expanding pattern of systematic comprehension which has not yet been established, but which, if it were established, would prevent them from being centrifugal. If such a pattern exists, then criticism would be to art what philosophy is to wisdom and history to action.

Most of the central area of criticism is at present, and doubtless always will be, the area of commentary. But the commentators have little sense, unlike the researchers, of being contained within some sort of scientific discipline: they are chiefly engaged, in the words of the gospel hymn, in brightening the corner where they are. If we attempt to get a more comprehensive idea of what criticism is about, we find ourselves wandering over quaking bogs of generalities, judicious pronouncements of value, reflective comments, perorations to works of research, and other consequences of taking the large view. But this part of the critical field is so full of pseudo-propositions, sonorous nonsense that contains no truth and no falsehood, that it obviously exists only because criticism, like nature, prefers a waste space to an empty one.

The term "pseudo-proposition" may imply some sort of logical positivist attitude on my own part.[1] But I would not confuse the significant proposition with the factual one; nor should I consider it advisable to muddle the study of literature with a schizophrenic dichotomy between subjective-emotional and objective-descriptive aspects of meaning, considering that in order to produce any literary meaning at all one has to ignore this dichotomy. I say only that the principles by which one can distinguish a significant from a meaningless statement in criticism are not clearly defined. Our first step, therefore, is to recognize and get rid of meaningless criticism: that is, talking about literature in a way that cannot help to build up a systematic structure of knowledge. Casual value-judgments belong not to criticism but to the history of taste, and reflect, at best, only the social and psychological compulsions which prompted their utterance. All judgments in which the values are not based on literary experience but are sentimental or derived from religious or political prejudice may be regarded as casual. Sentimental judgments are usually based either on nonexistent categories or antitheses ("Shakespeare studied life, Milton books") or on a visceral reaction to the writer's personality. The literary chitchat which makes the reputations of poets boom and crash in an imaginary stock exchange[2] is pseudo-criticism. That wealthy investor Mr. Eliot, after dumping Milton on the market, is now buying him again; Donne has probably reached his peak and will begin to taper off; Tennyson may be in for a slight flutter but the Shelley stocks are still bearish. This sort of thing cannot be part of any systematic study, for a systematic study can only progress: whatever dithers or vacillates or reacts is merely leisure-class conversation.

We next meet a more serious group of critics who say: the foreground of criticism is the impact of literature on the reader. Let us, then, keep the study of literature centripetal, and base the learning process on a structural analysis of the literary work itself. The texture of any great work of art is complex and ambiguous, and in unravelling the complexities we may take in as much history and philosophy as we please, if the subject of our study remains at the center. If it does not, we may find that in our anxiety to write about literature we have forgotten how to read it.

The only weakness in this approach is that it is conceived primarily as the antithesis of centrifugal or "background" criticism, and so lands us in a somewhat unreal dilemma, like the conflict of internal and external relations in philosophy. Antitheses are usually resolved, not by picking one side and refuting the other, or by making eclectic choices between them, but by trying to get past the antithetical way of stating the problem. It is right that the first effort of critical apprehension should take the form of a rhetorical or structural analysis of a work of art. But a purely structural approach has the same limitation in criticism that it has in biology. In itself it is simply a discrete series of analyses based on the mere existence of the literary structure, without developing any explanation of how the structure came to be what it was and what its nearest relatives are. Structural analysis brings rhetoric back to criticism, but we need a new poetics as well, and the attempt to construct a new poetics out of rhetoric alone can hardly avoid a mere complication of rhetorical terms into a sterile jargon. I suggest that what is at present missing from literary criticism is a co-ordinating principle, a central hypothesis which, like the theory of evolution in biology, will see the phenomena it deals with as parts of a whole. Such a principle, though it would retain the centripetal perspective of structural analysis, would try to give the same perspective to other kinds of criticism too.

The first postulate of this hypothesis is the same as that of any science: the assumption of total coherence. The assumption refers to the science, not to what it deals with. A belief in an order of nature is an inference from the intelligibility of the natural sciences; and if the natural sciences ever completely demonstrated the order of nature they would presumably exhaust their subject. Criticism, as a science, is totally intelligible; literature, as the subject of a science, is, so

[1]Logical positivists, like Ludwig Wittgenstein in the *Tractatus* (1922), believe that many "philosophical" questions are actually meaningless. [Ed.]

[2]Shocking as the admission may be, I was not aware when I wrote this that the same figure had appeared in Mr. Eliot's own essay, "What Is Minor Poetry?" [Au.]

far as we know, an inexhaustible source of new critical discoveries, and would be even if new works of literature ceased to be written. If so, then the search for a limiting principle in literature in order to discourage the development of criticism is mistaken. The assertion that the critic should not look for more in a poem than the poet may safely be assumed to have been conscious of putting there is a common form of what may be called the fallacy of premature teleology. It corresponds to the assertion that a natural phenomenon is as it is because Providence in its inscrutable wisdom made it so.

Simple as the assumption appears, it takes a long time for a science to discover that it is in fact a totally intelligible body of knowledge. Until it makes this discovery it has not been born as an individual science, but remains an embryo within the body of some other subject. The birth of physics from "natural philosophy" and of sociology from "moral philosophy" will illustrate the process. It is also very approximately true that the modern sciences have developed in the order of their closeness to mathematics. Thus physics and astronomy assumed their modern form in the Renaissance, chemistry in the eighteenth century, biology in the nineteenth and the social sciences in the twentieth. If systematic criticism, then, is developing only in our day, the fact is at least not an anachronism.

We are now looking for classifying principles lying in an area between two points that we have fixed. The first of these is the preliminary effort of criticism, the structural analysis of the work of art. The second is the assumption that there is such a subject as criticism, and that it makes, or could make, complete sense. We may next proceed inductively from structural analysis, associating the data we collect and trying to see larger patterns in them. Or we may proceed deductively, with the consequences that follow from postulating the unity of criticism. It is clear, of course, that neither procedure will work indefinitely without correction from the other. Pure induction will get us lost in haphazard guessing; pure deduction will lead to inflexible and oversimplified pigeonholing. Let us now attempt a few tentative steps in each direction, beginning with the inductive one.

II

The unity of a work of art, the basis of structural analysis, has not been produced solely by the unconditioned will of the artist, for the artist is only its efficient cause:[3] it has form, and consequently a formal cause. The fact that revision is possible, that the poet makes changes not because he likes them better but because they are better, means that poems, like poets, are born and not made. The poet's task is to deliver the poem in as uninjured a state as possible, and if the poem is alive, it is equally anxious to be rid of him, and screams to be cut loose from his private memories and associations, his desire for self-expression, and all the other navel-strings and feeding tubes of his ego. The critic takes over where the poet leaves off, and criticism can hardly do without a kind of literary psychology connecting the poet with the poem. Part of this may be a psychological study of the poet, though this is useful chiefly in analyzing the failures in his expression, the things in him which are still attached to his work. More important is the fact that every poet has his private mythology, his own spectroscopic band or peculiar formation of symbols, of much of which he is quite unconscious. In works with characters of their own, such as dramas and novels, the same psychological analysis may be extended to the interplay of characters, though of course, literary psychology would analyze the behavior of such characters only in relation to literary convention.

There is still before us the problem of the formal cause of the poem, a problem deeply involved with the question of genres. We cannot say much about genres, for criticism does not know much about them. A good many critical efforts to grapple with such words as "novel" or "epic" are chiefly interesting as examples of the psychology of rumor. Two conceptions of the genre, however, are obviously fallacious, and as

[3]Here and later in this essay, Frye uses the Aristotelian terminology of the four causes (formal, material, efficient, and final) for the analysis of a manufactured object, but his use of the terminology is quite different from Aristotle's. For Aristotle, the material cause of a poem is language; for Frye, it is "the social conditions and cultural demands which produced it." [Ed.]

they are opposite extremes, the truth must lie somewhere between them. One is the pseudo-Platonic conception of genres as existing prior to and independently of creation, which confuses them with mere conventions of form like the sonnet. The other is that pseudobiological conception of them as evolving species which turns up in so many surveys of the "development" of this or that form.

We next inquire for the origin of the genre, and turn first of all to the social conditions and cultural demands which produced it — in other words to the material cause of the work of art. This leads us into literary history, which differs from ordinary history in that its containing categories, "Gothic," "Baroque," "Romantic," and the like are cultural categories, of little use to the ordinary historian. Most literary history does not get as far as these categories, but even so we know more about it than about most kinds of critical scholarship. The historian treats literature and philosophy historically; the philosopher treats history and literature philosophically; and the so-called history of ideas approach marks the beginning of an attempt to treat history and philosophy from the point of view of an autonomous criticism.

But still we feel that there is something missing. We say that every poet has his own peculiar formation of images. But when so many poets use so many of the same images, surely there are much bigger critical problems involved than biographical ones. As Mr. Auden's brilliant essay *The Enchafèd Flood* shows, an important symbol like the sea cannot remain within the poetry of Shelley or Keats or Coleridge: it is bound to expand over many poets into an archetypal symbol of literature. And if the genre has a historical origin, why does the genre of drama emerge from medieval religion in a way so strikingly similar to the way it emerged from Greek religion centuries before? This is a problem of structure rather than origin, and suggests that there may be archetypes of genres as well as of images.

It is clear that criticism cannot be systematic unless there is a quality in literature which enables it to be so, an order of words corresponding to the order of nature in the natural sciences. An archetype should be not only a unifying category of criticism, but itself a part of a total form, and it leads us at once to the question of what sort of total form criticism can see in literature. Our survey of critical techniques has taken us as far as literary history. Total literary history moves from the primitive to the sophisticated, and here we glimpse the possibility of seeing literature as a complication of a relatively restricted and simple group of formulas that can be studied in primitive culture. If so, then the search for archetypes is a kind of literary anthropology, concerned with the way that literature is informed by preliterary categories such as ritual, myth and folk tale. We next realize that the relation between these categories and literature is by no means purely one of descent, as we find them reappearing in the greatest classics — in fact there seems to be a general tendency on the part of great classics to revert to them. This coincides with a feeling that we have all had: that the study of mediocre works of art, however energetic, obstinately remains a random and peripheral form of critical experience, whereas the profound masterpiece seems to draw us to a point at which we can see an enormous number of converging patterns of significance. Here we begin to wonder if we cannot see literature, not only as complicating itself in time, but as spread out in conceptual space from some unseen center.

This inductive movement towards the archetype is a process of backing up, as it were, from structural analysis, as we back up from a painting if we want to see composition instead of brushwork. In the foreground of the grave-digger scene in *Hamlet,* for instance, is an intricate verbal texture, ranging from the puns of the first clown to the *danse macabre*[4] of the Yorick soliloquy, which we study in the printed text. One step back, and we are in the Wilson Knight and Spurgeon group of critics, listening to the steady rain of images of corruption and decay.[5] Here too, as the sense of the place of this scene in the

[4]Dance of the dead. [Ed.]

[5]Caroline Spurgeon and G. Wilson Knight, whose Shakespearean criticism involves the sorting of images into significant clusters. [Ed.]

whole play begins to dawn on us, we are in the network of psychological relationships which were the main interest of Bradley.[6] But after all, we say, we are forgetting the genre: *Hamlet* is a play, and an Elizabethan play. So we take another step back into the Stoll and Shaw group and see the scene conventionally as part of its dramatic context.[7] One step more, and we can begin to glimpse the archetype of the scene, as the hero's *Liebestod*[8] and first unequivocal declaration of his love, his struggle with Laertes and the sealing of his own fate, and the sudden sobering of his mood that marks the transition to the final scene, all take shape around a leap into and return from the grave that has so weirdly yawned open on the stage.

At each stage of understanding this scene we are dependent on a certain kind of scholarly organization. We need first an editor to clean up the text for us, then the rhetorician and philologist, then the literary psychologist. We cannot study the genre without the help of the literary social historian, the literary philosopher and the student of the "history of ideas," and for the archetype we need a literary anthropologist. But now that we have got our central pattern of criticism established, all these interests are seen as converging on literary criticism instead of receding from it into psychology and history and the rest. In particular, the literary anthropologist who chases the source of the Hamlet legend from the pre-Shakespeare play[9] to Saxo, and from Saxo to nature-myths, is not running away from Shakespeare: he is drawing closer to the archetypal form which Shakespeare recreated. A minor result of our new perspective is that contradictions among critics, and assertions that this and not that critical approach is the right one, show a remarkable tendency to dissolve into unreality. Let us now see what we can get from the deductive end.

III

Some arts move in time, like music; others are presented in space, like painting. In both cases the organizing principle is recurrence, which is called rhythm when it is temporal and pattern when it is spatial. Thus we speak of the rhythm of music and the pattern of painting; but later, to show off our sophistication, we may begin to speak of the rhythm of painting and the pattern of music. In other words, all arts may be conceived both temporally and spatially. The score of a musical composition may be studied all at once; a picture may be seen as the track of an intricate dance of the eye. Literature seems to be intermediate between music and painting: its words form rhythms which approach a musical sequence of sounds at one of its boundaries, and from patterns which approach the hieroglyphic or pictorial image at the other. The attempts to get as near to these boundaries as possible form the main body of what is called experimental writing. We may call the rhythm of literature the narrative, and the pattern, the simultaneous mental grasp of the verbal structure, the meaning or significance. We hear or listen to a narrative, but when we grasp a writer's total pattern we "see" what he means.

The criticism of literature is much more hampered by the representational fallacy than even the criticism of painting. That is why we are apt to think of narrative as a sequential representation of events in an outside "life," and of meaning as a reflection of some external "idea." Properly used as critical terms, an author's narrative is his linear movement; his meaning is the integrity of his completed form. Similarly an image is not merely a verbal replica of an external object, but any unit of a verbal structure seen as part of a total pattern or rhythm. Even the letters an author spells his words with form part of his imagery, though only in special cases (such as alliteration) would they call for critical notice. Narrative and meaning thus become respectively, to

[6]A. C. Bradley, in *Shakespearean Tragedy* (1904), discussed the relation of character and plot with great depth and subtlety. [Ed.]

[7]Elmer Edgar Stoll (1874–1950) was a historical critic of Shakespeare, author of *Shakespeare Studies* (1927) and *Art and Artifice in Shakespeare*, among many others. George Bernard Shaw, the playwright (1856–1950) wrote outrageous Shakespeare criticism, which has been collected by Edwin Wilson in *Shaw on Shakespeare* (1961). [Ed.]

[8]Love-death. [Ed.]

[9]The putative ur-*Hamlet* from which Shakespeare drew his plot. [Ed.]

borrow musical terms, the melodic and harmonic contexts of the imagery.

Rhythm, or recurrent movement, is deeply founded on the natural cycle, and everything in nature that we think of as having some analogy with works of art, like the flower or the bird's song, grows out of a profound synchronization between an organism and the rhythms of its environment, especially that of the solar year. With animals some expressions of synchronization, like the mating dances of birds, could almost be called rituals. But in human life a ritual seems to be something of a voluntary effort (hence the magical element in it) to recapture a lost rapport with the natural cycle. A farmer must harvest his crop at a certain time of year, but because this is involuntary, harvesting itself is not precisely a ritual. It is the deliberate expression of a will to synchronize human and natural energies at that time which produces the harvest songs, harvest sacrifices and harvest folk customs that we call rituals. In ritual, then, we may find the origin of narrative, a ritual being a temporal sequence of acts in which the conscious meaning or significance is latent: it can be seen by an observer, but is largely concealed from the participators themselves. The pull of ritual is toward pure narrative, which, if there could be such a thing, would be automatic and unconscious repetition. We should notice too the regular tendency of ritual to become encyclopedic. All the important recurrences in nature, the day, the phases of the moon, the seasons and solstices of the year, the crises of existence from birth to death, get rituals attached to them, and most of the higher religions are equipped with a definitive total body of rituals suggestive, if we may put it so, of the entire range of potentially significant actions in human life.

Patterns of imagery, on the other hand, or fragments of significance, are oracular in origin, and derive from the epiphanic moment, the flash of instantaneous comprehension with no direct reference to time, the importance of which is indicated by Cassirer in *Myth and Language*.[10] By the time we get them, in the form of proverbs, riddles, commandments, and etiological folk tales, there is already a considerable element of narrative in them. They too are encyclopedic in tendency, building up a total structure of significance, or doctrine, from random and empiric fragments. And just as pure narrative would be an unconscious act, so pure significance would be an incommunicable state of consciousness, for communication begins by constructing narrative.

The myth is the central informing power that gives archetypal significance to the ritual and archetypal narrative to the oracle. Hence the myth *is* the archetype, though it might be convenient to say myth only when referring to narrative, and archetype when speaking of significance. In the solar cycle of the day, the seasonal cycle of the year, and the organic cycle of human life, there is a single pattern of significance, out of which myth constructs a central narrative around a figure who is partly the sun, partly vegetative fertility and partly a god or archetypal human being. The crucial importance of this myth has been forced on literary critics by Jung and Frazer[11] in particular, but the several books now available on it are not always systematic in their approach, for which reason I supply the following table of its phases:

1. The dawn, spring, and birth phase. Myths of the birth of the hero, of revival and resurrection, of creation and (because the four phases are a cycle) of the defeat of the powers of darkness, winter and death. Subordinate characters: the father and the mother. The archetype of romance and of most dithyrambic and rhapsodic poetry.[12]

2. The zenith, summer, and marriage or triumph phase. Myths of apotheosis, of the sacred marriage, and of entering into Paradise. Subordinate characters: the companion and the bride. The archetype of comedy, pastoral, and idyll.

3. The sunset, autumn, and death phase. Myths of fall, of the dying god, of violent death

[10]Ernst Cassirer, neo-Kantian philosopher (1874–1945): *Myth and Language* (1925). [Ed.]

[11]Sir James Frazer, anthropologist, whose classic work, *The Golden Bough* (1890; 12-volume edition 1907–15), studied primitive myth in various cultures to argue the evolution of human thought from magic to religion and then to science. [Ed.]

[12]In *Anatomy of Criticism* (1957), Frye shifted romance to the summer season and comedy from summer to spring. [Ed.]

and sacrifice and of the isolation of the hero. Subordinate characters: the traitor and the siren. The archetype of tragedy and elegy.

4. The darkness, winter, and dissolution phase. Myths of the triumph of these powers; myths of floods and the return of chaos, of the defeat of the hero, and Götterdämmerung[13] myths. Subordinate characters: the ogre and the witch. The archetype of satire (see, for instance, the conclusion of *The Dunciad*).

The quest of the hero also tends to assimilate the oracular and random verbal structures, as we can see when we catch the chaos of local legends that results from prophetic epiphanies consolidating into a narrative mythology of departmental gods. In most of the higher religions this in turn has become the same central quest-myth that emerges from ritual, as the Messiah myth became the narrative structure of the oracles of Judaism. A local flood may beget a folk tale by accident, but a comparison of flood stories will show how quickly such tales become examples of the myth of dissolution. Finally, the tendency of both ritual and epiphany to become encyclopedic is realized in the definitive body of myth which constitutes the sacred scriptures of religions. These sacred scriptures are consequently the first documents that the literary critic has to study to gain a comprehensive view of his subject. After he has understood their structure, then he can descend from archetypes to genres, and see how the drama emerges from the ritual side of myth and lyric from the epiphanic or fragmented side, while the epic carries on the central encyclopedic structure.

Some words of caution and encouragement are necessary before literary criticism has clearly staked out its boundaries in these fields. It is part of the critic's business to show how all literary genres are derived from the quest-myth, but the derivation is a logical one within the science of criticism: the quest-myth will constitute the first chapter of whatever future handbooks of criticism may be written that will be based on enough organized critical knowledge to call themselves "introductions" or "outlines" and still be able to live up to their titles. It is only when we try to expound the derivation chronologically that we find ourselves writing pseudo-prehistorical fictions and theories of mythological contact. Again, because psychology and anthropology are more highly developed sciences, the critic who deals with this kind of material is bound to appear, for some time, a dilettante of those subjects. These two phases of criticism are largely undeveloped in comparison with literary history and rhetoric, the reason being the later development of the sciences they are related to. But the fascination which *The Golden Bough* and Jung's book on libido symbols have for literary critics is not based on dilettantism, but on the fact that these books are primarily studies in literary criticism, and very important ones.

In any case the critic who is studying the principles of literary form has a quite different interest from the psychologist's concern with states of mind or the anthropologist's with social institutions. For instance: the mental response to narrative is mainly passive; to significance mainly active. From this fact Ruth Benedict's *Patterns of Culture* develops a distinction between "Apollonian" cultures based on obedience to ritual and "Dionysiac" ones based on a tense exposure of the prophetic mind to epiphany. The critic would tend rather to note how popular literature which appeals to the inertia of the untrained mind puts a heavy emphasis on narrative values, whereas a sophisticated attempt to disrupt the connection between the poet and his environment produces the Rimbaud type of *illumination,* Joyce's solitary epiphanies, and Baudelaire's conception of nature as a source of oracles. Also how literature, as it develops from the primitive to the self-conscious, shows a gradual shift of the poet's attention from narrative to significant values, this shift of attention being the basis of Schiller's distinction between naive and sentimental poetry.[14]

The relation of criticism to religion, when they deal with the same documents, is more complicated. In criticism, as in history, the divine is always treated as a human artifact. God for the critic, whether he finds him in *Paradise Lost* or the Bible, is a character in a human story; and for

[13]Twilight of the gods. [Ed.]

[14]See Schiller, p. 296. [Ed.]

the critic all epiphanies are explained, not in terms of the riddle of a possessing god or devil, but as mental phenomena closely associated in their origin with dreams. This once established, it is then necessary to say that nothing in criticism or art compels the critic to take the attitude of ordinary waking consciousness towards the dream or the god. Art deals not with the real but with the conceivable; and criticism, though it will eventually have to have some theory of conceivability, can never be justified in trying to develop, much less assume, any theory of actuality. It is necessary to understand this before our next and final point can be made.

We have identified the central myth of literature, in its narrative aspect, with the quest-myth. Now if we wish to see this central myth as a pattern of meaning also, we have to start with the workings of the subconscious where the epiphany originates, in other words in the dream. The human cycle of waking and dreaming corresponds closely to the natural cycle of light and darkness, and it is perhaps in this correspondence that all imaginative life begins. The correspondence is largely an antithesis: it is in daylight that man is really in the power of darkness, a prey to frustration and weakness; it is in the darkness of nature that the "libido" or conquering heroic self awakes. Hence art, which Plato called a dream for awakened minds, seems to have as its final cause the resolution of the antithesis, the mingling of the sun and the hero, the realizing of a world in which the inner desire and the outward circumstance coincide. This is the same goal, of course, that the attempt to combine human and natural power in ritual has. The social function of the arts, therefore, seems to be closely connected with visualizing the goal of work in human life. So in terms of significance, the central myth of art must be the vision of the end of social effort, the innocent world of fulfilled desires, the free human society. Once this is understood, the integral place of criticism among the other social sciences, in interpreting and systematizing the vision of the artist, will be easier to see. It is at this point that we can see how religious conceptions of the final cause of human effort are as relevant as any others to criticism.

The importance of the god or hero in the myth lies in the fact that such characters, who are conceived in human likeness and yet have more power over nature, gradually build up the vision of an omnipotent personal community beyond an indifferent nature. It is this community which the hero regularly enters in his apotheosis. The world of this apotheosis thus begins to pull away from the rotary cycle of the quest in which all triumph is temporary. Hence if we look at the quest-myth as a pattern of imagery, we see the hero's quest first of all in terms of its fulfillment. This gives us our central pattern of archetypal images, the vision of innocence which sees the world in terms of total human intelligibility. It corresponds to, and is usually found in the form of, the vision of the unfallen world or heaven in religion. We may call it the comic vision of life, in contrast to the tragic vision, which sees the quest only in the form of its ordained cycle.

We conclude with a second table of contents, in which we shall attempt to set forth the central pattern of the comic and tragic visions. One essential principle of archetypal criticism is that the individual and the universal forms of an image are identical, the reasons being too complicated for us just now. We proceed according to the general plan of the game of Twenty Questions, or, if we prefer, of the Great Chain of Being:

1. In the comic vision the *human* world is a community, or a hero who represents the wish-fulfillment of the reader. The archetype of images of symposium, communion, order, friendship, and love. In the tragic vision the human world is a tyranny or anarchy, or an individual or isolated man, the leader with his back to his followers, the bullying giant of romance, the deserted or betrayed hero. Marriage or some equivalent consummation belongs to the comic vision; the harlot, witch, and other varieties of Jung's "terrible mother"[15] belongs to the tragic one. All divine, heroic, angelic, or other superhuman communities follow the human pattern.

2. In the comic vision the *animal* world is a community of domesticated animals, usually a

[15]The negative projection of the *anima*. See Jung, p. 520. [Ed.]

flock of sheep, or a lamb, or one of the gentler birds, usually a dove. The archetype of pastoral images. In the tragic vision the animal world is seen in terms of beasts and birds of prey, wolves, vultures, serpents, dragons, and the like.

3. In the comic vision the *vegetable* world is a garden, grove or park, or a tree of life, or a rose or lotus. The archetype of Arcadian images, such as that of Marvell's green world or of Shakespeare's forest comedies. In the tragic vision it is a sinister forest like the one in *Comus* or at the opening of the *Inferno,* or a heath or wilderness, or a tree of death.

4. In the comic vision the *mineral* world is a city, or one building or temple, or one stone, normally a glowing precious stone — in fact, the whole comic series, especially the tree, can be conceived as luminous or fiery. The archetype of geometrical images: the "starlit dome"[16] belongs here. In the tragic vision the mineral world is seen in terms of deserts, rocks and ruins, or of sinister geometrical images like the cross.

5. In the comic vision the *unformed* world is a river, traditionally fourfold, which influenced the Renaissance image of the temperate body with its four humors.[17] In the tragic vision this world usually becomes the sea, as the narrative myth of dissolution is so often a flood myth. The combination of the sea and beast images gives us the leviathan and similar water-monsters.

Obvious as this table looks, a great variety of poetic images and forms will be found to fit it. Yeats's "Sailing to Byzantium," to take a famous example of the comic vision at random, has the city, the tree, the bird, the community of sages, the geometrical gyre and the detachment from the cyclic world. It is, of course, only the general comic or tragic context that determines the interpretation of any symbol: this is obvious with relatively neutral archetypes like the island, which may be Prospero's island or Circe's.[18]

Our tables are, of course, not only elementary but grossly oversimplified, just as our inductive approach to the archetype was a mere hunch. The important point is not the deficiencies of either procedure, taken by itself, but the fact that, somewhere and somehow, the two are clearly going to meet in the middle. And if they do meet, the ground plan of a systematic and comprehensive development of criticism has been established.

[16]Yeats's image of inanimate perfection in "Byzantium." [Ed.]

[17]The four humors were blood, bile, choler, and phlegm. Frye's notion of a fourfold balance is similar to Jung's quaternion; see p. 526. [Ed.]

[18]In Shakespeare's *The Tempest* and Homer's *Odyssey,* respectively. [Ed.]

Erich Auerbach

1892–1957

Erich Auerbach was born in Berlin in 1892 and was educated in the law before becoming in 1929 a professor of Romance philology at the University of Marburg. Auerbach was of the generation of German humanists, including Leo Spitzer and Robert Curtius, that developed the fields of comparative literature and history of ideas. In 1936, the year his Marburg colleague Martin Heidegger became chancellor of the University, Auerbach emigrated to Turkey, teaching at the State University of Istanbul.

It was there, deprived of his research library and assistants, that he wrote essays ranging widely from Homer and the Bible to Proust and Woolf that were collected into *Mimesis: The Representation of Reality in Western Literature* (1946; introductory chapter is reprinted here). Auerbach suggests in the "Epilogue" to *Mimesis* that, while the book has unavoidable flaws resulting from his lack of access to books, journals, and even to reliable critical editions of the texts he discusses, he would not have been bold enough to write such a wide-ranging study had they been available to him: "If it had been possible for me to acquaint myself with all the work that has been done on so many subjects, I might never have reached the point of writing" (p. 557). After World War II, Auerbach came to the United States, where he held the Sterling Professorship of Romance Languages at Yale until his death in 1957.

Mimesis is often celebrated as a model of pure literary interpretation and exegesis — as opposed to the products of contemporary literary theory — and indeed it is hard not to wonder at the seeming ease with which Auerbach finds passages and performs analyses that illuminate how certain texts (including Petronius, Gregory of Tours, the Chanson Roland, Dante, Boccaccio, Rabelais, Montaigne, Goethe, Schiller, Balzac, Stendhal, Flaubert, and Zolà) purely express the ethos of their eras and cultures. Interestingly, the aim of Auerbach — to discover how discourse is defined by and evokes the cultures of the past — is precisely the aim of the New Historians and Cultural Studies proponents today.

Auerbach's literary-historical vision is far from the postmodern notions of Michel Foucault or Hayden White: It harkens back to the philosophies of Giambattista Vico and G. W. F. Hegel. Like Vico, Auerbach believes that history is not linear, but cyclical. In two different eras, classical Rome and neoclassical Europe, the culture had developed stratified style-systems, with very different languages for treating the "high," "middle," and "low" aspects of life. In both eras there had been a triumphant rebellion against the rigid distinctions of such systems marshalled in terms of a figural realism that incorporated the basest details in the service of the noblest and most significant narratives. Auerbach saw the revolt against the neoclassical ordering of literary styles at the beginning of the nineteenth century (which culminated in the novels of Balzac and Stendhal) not as a unique event but as a return of the rebellion against the classical ordering of styles made first by Augustine and, much later, by Dante.

Like Hegel, Auerbach believes this cyclical movement in history and culture is driven by the dialectical thrust of thesis and antithesis, which gives rise to a transcendent new synthesis. The *Odyssey* and the book of Genesis archetypally stand for the two different approaches to the representation of reality that Auerbach traces through nearly three millennia of history. For Auerbach, Homer presents reality as fixed and definite, lying on the surface, accessible through the selection of details used to sketch characters and events. In Homer past events not only shape the present situation, they also can be represented as present memory through the narrative vision. In the Bible, Auerbach believes, reality is implicit rather than explicit; the figural representation of the patriarchs and kings suggests that the interior truth of their histories is contained in a vision too vast to be expressed in words. Such figural vision therefore demands interpretation and exegesis, in which the individual event becomes iconic for a reality that recurs in later history and can only be fully contained in the mind of God. Auerbach returns to the contrast between Homer and the Bible in later chapters of *Mimesis,* as for example, when he contrasts the limited and static Roman narrative realism (exemplified by the layered details in the portrayal of Trimalchio's banquet in Petronius's *Satyricon*) with the richly implicit figural quality of the Gospels (where Peter's denials of Jesus demand engaged interpretation and complex exegesis precisely because they stand in themselves beyond any simple explanation). In still later chapters, Auerbach observes the recurrence of the same sorts of contrasts between the abstract or schematic and the figural modes of representation in different periods of literature up to that of high modernism. For example, Auerbach contrasts the abstract quality of medieval allegory (such as the *Roman de la Rose*) with the figural quality of Dante's vision of universal history in the *Commedia.* Or using examples from the later nineteenth century, Auerbach contrasts Zola's Petronian use of "low" detail in his *Rougon-Macquart* saga with the more figural treatment of humble life in the novels of Tolstoy and Dostoyevsky.

Auerbach's saga culminates in a discussion of Virginia Woolf's modernism that centers on a passage from *To the Lighthouse.* Auerbach sees Woolf's presentation of the rich meaning within the apparently insignificant moment as iconic of the beauty and goodness he envisions as emerging out of the horror of his own historical era:

> An economic and cultural leveling process is taking place. It is still a long way to a common life of mankind on earth, but the goal begins to be visible. And it is most concretely visible now in the unprejudiced, precise, interior and exterior representation of the random moment in the lives of different people. So the complicated process of dissolution which led to the fragmentation of the exterior action, to the reflection of consciousness, and to the stratification of time [as in Proust] seems to be tending toward a very simple solution (552–53).

This notion of literary modernism as the teleological endpoint of Old Testament realism is one testimony to the utopianism that underlies all of Auerbach's thought and that makes him such an attractive figure today.

Selected Bibliography

Auerbach, Erich. *Mimesis: The Representation of Reality in Western Literature.* Translated by Willard R. Trask. Princeton: Princeton University Press, 1953.

———. *Scenes from the Drama of European Literature: Six Essays.* New York: Meridian Books, 1959.

———. *Dante: Poet of the Secular World.* Translated by Ralph Manheim. Chicago: University of Chicago Press, 1961.

———. *Literary Language and Its Public in Late Latin Antiquity and in the Middle Ages.* Translated by Ralph Manheim. New York: Pantheon Books, 1965.

Bahti, Timothy. "Auerbach's *Mimesis:* Figural Structure and Historical Narrative." In *After Strange Texts,* ed. Gregory S. Jay and David L. Miller. Alabama University Press, 1985, pp. 125–48.

Bové, Paul. *Intellectuals in Power: A Genealogy of Critical Humanism.* New York: Columbia University Press, 1986.

Costa-Lima, Luiz. "Erich Auerbach: History and Metahistory." *New Literary History* 19 (1988): 467–99.

Damrosch, David. "Auerbach in Exile." *Comparative Literature* 47 (1995): 97–117.

Green, Geoffrey. *Literary Criticism and the Structures of History: Erich Auerbach and Leo Spitzer.* Lincoln: University of Nebraska Press, 1982.

Holquist, Michael. "The Last European: Erich Auerbach as Precursor in the History of Cultural Criticism." *Modern Language Quarterly* 54 (1993): 371–91.

Lerer, Seth, ed. *Literary History and the Challenge of Philology: The Legacy of Erich Auerbach.* Stanford: Stanford University Press, 1996.

Manheim, Ralph. "Bibliography of the Writings of Erich Auerbach." In *Literary Language and Its Public in Late Latin Antiquity and in the Middle Ages,* trans. Ralph Manheim. New York: Pantheon Books, 1965, pp. 343–68.

Odysseus' Scar

Readers of the *Odyssey* will remember the well-prepared and touching scene in book 19, when Odysseus has at last come home, the scene in which the old housekeeper Euryclea, who had been his nurse, recognizes him by a scar on his thigh. The stranger has won Penelope's good will; at his request she tells the housekeeper to wash his feet, which, in all old stories, is the first duty of hospitality toward a tired traveler. Euryclea busies herself fetching water and mixing cold with hot, meanwhile speaking sadly of her absent master, who is probably of the same age as the guest, and who perhaps, like the guest, is even now wandering somewhere, a stranger; and she remarks how astonishingly like him the guest looks. Meanwhile Odysseus, remembering his scar, moves back out of the light; he knows that, despite his efforts to hide his identity, Euryclea will now recognize him, but he wants at least to keep Penelope in ignorance. No sooner has the old woman touched the scar than, in her joyous surprise, she lets Odysseus' foot drop into the basin; the water spills over, she is about to cry out her joy; Odysseus restrains her with whispered threats and endearments; she recovers herself and conceals her emotion. Penelope, whose attention Athena's foresight had diverted from the incident, has observed nothing.

All this is scrupulously externalized and narrated in leisurely fashion. The two women express their feelings in copious direct discourse. Feelings though they are, with only a slight admixture of the most general considerations upon human destiny, the syntactical connection between part and part is perfectly clear, no contour is blurred. There is also room and time for or-

Translated by Willard R. Trask.

derly, perfectly well-articulated, uniformly illuminated descriptions of implements, ministrations, and gestures; even in the dramatic moment of recognition, Homer does not omit to tell the reader that it is with his right hand that Odysseus takes the old woman by the throat to keep her from speaking, at the same time that he draws her closer to him with his left. Clearly outlined, brightly and uniformly illuminated, men and things stand out in a realm where everything is visible; and not less clear — wholly expressed, orderly even in their ardor — are the feelings and thoughts of the persons involved.

In my account of the incident I have so far passed over a whole series of verses which interrupt it in the middle. There are more than seventy of these verses — while to the incident itself some forty are devoted before the interruption and some forty after it. The interruption, which comes just at the point when the housekeeper recognizes the scar — that is, at the moment of crisis — describes the origin of the scar, a hunting accident which occurred in Odysseus' boyhood, at a boar hunt, during the time of his visit to his grandfather Autolycus. This first affords an opportunity to inform the reader about Autolycus, his house, the precise degree of the kinship, his character, and, no less exhaustively than touchingly, his behavior after the birth of his grandson; then follows the visit of Odysseus, now grown to be a youth; the exchange of greetings, the banquet with which he is welcomed, sleep and waking, the early start for the hunt, the tracking of the beast, the struggle, Odysseus' being wounded by the boar's tusk, his recovery, his return to Ithaca, his parents' anxious questions — all is narrated, again with such a complete externalization of all the elements of the story and of their interconnections as to leave nothing in obscurity. Not until then does the narrator return to Penelope's chamber, not until then, the digression having run its course, does Euryclea, who had recognized the scar before the digression began, let Odysseus' foot fall back into the basin.

The first thought of a modern reader — that this is a device to increase suspense — is, if not wholly wrong, at least not the essential explanation of this Homeric procedure. For the element of suspense is very slight in the Homeric poems; nothing in their entire style is calculated to keep the reader or hearer breathless. The digressions are not meant to keep the reader in suspense, but rather to relax the tension. And this frequently occurs, as in the passage before us. The broadly narrated, charming, and subtly fashioned story of the hunt, with all its elegance and self-sufficiency, its wealth of idyllic pictures, seeks to win the reader over wholly to itself as long as he is hearing it, to make him forget what had just taken place during the foot-washing. But an episode that will increase suspense by retarding the action must be so constructed that it will not fill the present entirely, will not put the crisis, whose resolution is being awaited, entirely out of the reader's mind, and thereby destroy the mood of suspense; the crisis and the suspense must continue, must remain vibrant in the background. But Homer — and to this we shall have to return later — knows no background. What he narrates is for the time being the only present, and fills both the stage and the reader's mind completely. So it is with the passage before us. When the young Euryclea (vv. 401ff.) sets the infant Odysseus on his grandfather Autolycus' lap after the banquet, the aged Euryclea, who a few lines earlier had touched the wanderer's foot, has entirely vanished from the stage and from the reader's mind.

Goethe and Schiller, who, though not referring to this particular episode, exchanged letters in April 1797 on the subject of "the retarding element" in the Homeric poems in general, put it in direct opposition to the element of suspense — the latter word is not used, but is clearly implied when the "retarding" procedure is opposed, as something proper to epic, to tragic procedure (letters of April 19, 21, and 22). The "retarding element," the "going back and forth" by means of episodes, seems to me, too, in the Homeric poems, to be opposed to any tensional and suspensive striving toward a goal, and doubtless Schiller is right in regard to Homer when he says that what he gives us is "simply the quiet existence and operation of things in accordance with their natures"; Homer's goal is "already present in every point of his progress." But both Schiller and Goethe raise Homer's procedure to the level

Time expands

of a law for epic poetry in general, and Schiller's words quoted above are meant to be universally binding upon the epic poet, in contradistinction from the tragic. Yet in both modern and ancient times, there are important epic works which are composed throughout with no "retarding element" in this sense but, on the contrary, with suspense throughout, and which perpetually "rob us of our emotional freedom" — which power Schiller will grant only to the tragic poet. And besides it seems to me undemonstrable and improbable that this procedure of Homeric poetry was directed by aesthetic considerations or even by an aesthetic feeling of the sort postulated by Goethe and Schiller. The effect, to be sure, is precisely that which they describe, and is, furthermore, the actual source of the conception of epic which they themselves hold, and with them all writers decisively influenced by classical antiquity. But the true cause of the impression of "retardation" appears to me to lie elsewhere — namely, in the need of the Homeric style to leave nothing which it mentions half in darkness and unexternalized.

The excursus upon the origin of Odysseus' scar is not basically different from the many passages in which a newly introduced character, or even a newly appearing object or implement, though it be in the thick of a battle, is described as to its nature and origin; or in which, upon the appearance of a god, we are told where he last was, what he was doing there, and by what road he reached the scene; indeed, even the Homeric epithets seem to me in the final analysis to be traceable to the same need for an externalization of phenomena in terms perceptible to the senses. Here is the scar, which comes up in the course of the narrative; and Homer's feeling simply will not permit him to see it appear out of the darkness of an unilluminated past; it must be set in full light, and with it a portion of the hero's boyhood — just as, in the *Iliad,* when the first ship is already burning and the Myrmidons finally arm that they may hasten to help, there is still time not only for the wonderful simile of the wolf, not only for the order of the Myrmidon host, but also for a detailed account of the ancestry of several subordinate leaders (16, vv. 155ff.). To be sure, the aesthetic effect thus produced was soon noticed and thereafter consciously sought; but the more original cause must have lain in the basic impulse of the Homeric style: to represent phenomena in a fully externalized form, visible and palpable in all their parts, and completely fixed in their spatial and temporal relations. Nor do psychological processes receive any other treatment: here too nothing must remain hidden and unexpressed. With the utmost fullness, with an orderliness which even passion does not disturb, Homer's personages vent their inmost hearts in speech; what they do not say to others, they speak in their own minds, so that the reader is informed of it. Much that is terrible takes place in the Homeric poems, but it seldom takes place wordlessly: Polyphemus talks to Odysseus; Odysseus talks to the suitors when he begins to kill them; Hector and Achilles talk at length, before battle and after; and no speech is so filled with anger or scorn that the particles which express logical and grammatical connections are lacking or out of place. This last observation is true, of course, not only of speeches but of the presentation in general. The separate elements of a phenomenon are most clearly placed in relation to one another; a large number of conjunctions, adverbs, particles, and other syntactical tools, all clearly circumscribed and delicately differentiated in meaning, delimit persons, things, and portions of incidents in respect to one another, and at the same time bring them together in a continuous and ever flexible connection; like the separate phenomena themselves, their relationships — their temporal, local, causal, final, consecutive, comparative, concessive, antithetical, and conditional limitations — are brought to light in perfect fullness; so that a continuous rhythmic procession of phenomena passes by, and never is there a form left fragmentary or half-illuminated, never a lacuna, never a gap, never a glimpse of unplumbed depths.

And this procession of phenomena takes place in the foreground — that is, in a local and temporal present which is absolute. One might think that the many interpolations, the frequent moving back and forth, would create a sort of perspective in time and place; but the Homeric style never gives any such impression. The way in which any impression of perspective is avoided can be clearly observed in the procedure for introducing episodes, a syntactical construction with which every reader of Homer is familiar; it is used in the passage we are considering, but can also be found in cases when the episodes are much shorter. To the word scar (v. 393) there is first attached a relative clause ("which once long ago a boar . . ."), which enlarges into a voluminous syntactical parenthesis; into this an independent sentence unexpectedly intrudes (v. 396: "A god himself gave him . . ."), which quietly disentangles itself from syntactical subordination, until, with verse 399, an equally free syntactical treatment of the new content begins a new present which continues unchallenged until, with verse 467 ("The old woman now touched it . . ."), the scene which had been broken off is resumed. To be sure, in the case of such long episodes as the one we are considering, a purely syntactical connection with the principal theme would hardly have been possible; but a connection with it through perspective would have been all the easier had the content been arranged with that end in view; if, that is, the entire story of the scar had been presented as a recollection which awakens in Odysseus' mind at this particular moment. It would have been perfectly easy to do; the story of the scar had only to be inserted two verses earlier, at the first mention of the word scar, where the motifs "Odysseus" and "recollection" were already at hand. But any such subjectivistic-perspectivistic procedure, creating a foreground and background, resulting in the present lying open to the depths of the past, is entirely foreign to the Homeric style; the Homeric style knows only a foreground, only a uniformly illuminated, uniformly objective present. And so the excursus does not begin until two lines later, when Euryclea has discovered the scar — the possibility for a perspectivistic connection no longer exists, and the story of the wound becomes an independent and exclusive present.

The genius of the Homeric style becomes even more apparent when it is compared with an equally ancient and equally epic style from a different world of forms. I shall attempt this comparison with the account of the sacrifice of Isaac, a homogeneous narrative produced by the so-called Elohist. The King James version translates the opening as follows (Genesis 22:1): "And it came to pass after these things, that God did tempt Abraham, and said to him, Abraham! and he said, Behold, here I am." Even this opening startles us when we come to it from Homer. Where are the two speakers? We are not told. The reader, however, knows that they are not normally to be found together in one place on earth, that one of them, God, in order to speak to Abraham, must come from somewhere, must enter the earthly realm from some unknown heights or depths. Whence does he come, whence does he call to Abraham? We are not told. He does not come, like Zeus or Poseidon, from the Aethiopians, where he has been enjoying a sacrificial feast. Nor are we told anything of his reasons for tempting Abraham so terribly. He has not, like Zeus, discussed them in set speeches with other gods gathered in council; nor have the deliberations in his own heart been presented to us; unexpected and mysterious, he enters the scene from some unknown height or depth and calls: Abraham! It will at once be said that this is to be explained by the particular concept of God which the Jews held and which was wholly different from that of the Greeks. True enough — but this constitutes no objection. For how is the Jewish concept of God to be explained? Even their earlier God of the desert was not fixed in form and content, and was alone; his lack of form, his lack of local habitation, his singleness, was in the end not only maintained but developed even further in competition with the comparatively far more manifest gods of the surrounding Near Eastern world. The concept of God held by the Jews is less a cause than a symptom of their manner of comprehending and representing things.

This becomes still clearer if we now turn to the other person in the dialogue, to Abraham. Where is he? We do not know. He says, indeed: Here I am — but the Hebrew word means only something like "behold me," and in any case is not meant to indicate the actual place where Abraham is, but a moral position in respect to God, who has called to him — Here am I awaiting thy command. Where he is actually, whether in Beersheba or elsewhere, whether indoors or in the open air, is not stated; it does not interest the narrator, the reader is not informed; and what Abraham was doing when God called to him is left in the same obscurity. To realize the difference, consider Hermes' visit to Calypso, for example, where command, journey, arrival and reception of the visitor, situation and occupation of the person visited, are set forth in many verses; and even on occasions when gods appear suddenly and briefly, whether to help one of their favorites or to deceive or destroy some mortal whom they hate, their bodily forms, and usually the manner of their coming and going, are given in detail. Here, however, God appears without bodily form (yet he "appears"), coming from some unspecified place — we only hear his voice, and that utters nothing but a name, a name without an adjective, without a descriptive epithet for the person spoken to, such as is the rule in every Homeric address; and of Abraham too nothing is made perceptible except the words in which he answers God: *Hinne-ni,* Behold me here — with which, to be sure, a most touching gesture expressive of obedience and readiness is suggested, but it is left to the reader to visualize it. Moreover the two speakers are not on the same level: if we conceive of Abraham in the foreground, where it might be possible to picture him as prostrate or kneeling or bowing with outspread arms or gazing upward, God is not there too: Abraham's words and gestures are directed toward the depths of the picture or upward, but in any case the undetermined, dark place from which the voice comes to him is not in the foreground.

After this opening, God gives his command, and the story itself begins: everyone knows it; it unrolls with no episodes in a few independent sentences whose syntactical connection is of the most rudimentary sort. In this atmosphere it is unthinkable that an implement, a landscape through which the travelers passed, the serving-men, or the ass, should be described, that their origin or descent or material or appearance or usefulness should be set forth in terms of praise; they do not even admit an adjective: they are serving-men, ass, wood, and knife, and nothing else, without an epithet; they are there to serve the end which God has commanded; what in other respects they were, are, or will be, remains in darkness. A journey is made, because God has designated the place where the sacrifice is to be performed; but we are told nothing about the journey except that it took three days, and even that we are told in a mysterious way: Abraham and his followers rose "early in the morning" and "went unto" the place of which God had told him; on the third day he lifted up his eyes and saw the place from afar. That gesture is the only gesture, is indeed the only occurrence during the whole journey, of which we are told; and though its motivation lies in the fact that the place is elevated, its uniqueness still heightens the impression that the journey took place through a vacuum; it is as if, while he traveled on, Abraham had looked neither to the right nor to the left, had suppressed any sign of life in his followers and himself save only their footfalls.

Thus the journey is like a silent progress through the indeterminate and the contingent, a holding of the breath, a process which has no present, which is inserted, like a blank duration, between what has passed and what lies ahead, and which yet is measured: three days! Three such days positively demand the symbolic interpretation which they later received. They began "early in the morning." But at what time on the third day did Abraham lift up his eyes and see his goal? The text says nothing on the subject. Obviously not "late in the evening," for it seems that there was still time enough to climb the mountain and make the sacrifice. So "early in the morning" is given, not as an indication of time, but for the sake of its ethical significance; it is intended to express the resolution, the promptness, the punctual obedience of the sorely tried Abraham. Bitter to him is the early morning in which he saddles his ass, calls his serving-men and his son Isaac, and sets out; but he obeys, he walks on until the third day, then lifts up his eyes and sees the place. Whence he comes, we do not know, but the goal is clearly stated: Jeruel in the land of Moriah.[1] What place this is meant to indicate is

[1]The particular spot called "Jeruel" appears in the Bible only in 2 Chronicles 20:16 as the wilderness site of a battle between Jehoshaphat, King of Judah and the Moabites and Edomites; it is not mentioned by the narrator of Genesis. Perhaps Auerbach intends the name Abraham subsequently gives to the particular mountain on which the sacrifice was to have taken place, called יהוה יראה in Hebrew ("Jeho-

not clear — "Moriah" especially may be a later correction of some other word. But in any case the goal was given, and in any case it is a matter of some sacred spot which was to receive a particular consecration by being connected with Abraham's sacrifice. Just as little as "early in the morning" serves as a temporal indication does "Jeruel in the land of Moriah" serve as a geographical indication; and in both cases alike, the complementary indication is not given, for we know as little of the hour at which Abraham lifted up his eyes as we do of the place from which he set forth — Jeruel is significant not so much as the goal of an earthly journey, in its geographical relation to other places, as through its special election, through its relation to God, who designated it as the scene of the act, and therefore it must be named.

In the narrative itself, a third chief character appears: Isaac. While God and Abraham, the serving-men, the ass, and the implements are simply named, without mention of any qualities or any other sort of definition, Isaac once receives an appositive; God says, "Take Isaac, thine only son, whom thou lovest." But this is not a characterization of Isaac as a person, apart from his relation to his father and apart from the story; he may be handsome or ugly, intelligent or stupid, tall or short, pleasant or unpleasant — we are not told. Only what we need to know about him as a personage in the action, here and now, is illuminated, so that it may become apparent how terrible Abraham's temptation is, and that God is fully aware of it. By this example of the contrary, we see the significance of the descriptive adjectives and digressions of the Homeric poems; with their indications of the earlier and as it were absolute existence of the persons described, they prevent the reader from concentrating exclusively on a present crisis; even when the most terrible things are occurring, they prevent the establishment of an overwhelming suspense. But here, in the story of Abraham's sacrifice, the overwhelming suspense is present; what Schiller makes the goal of the tragic poet — to rob us of our emotional freedom, to turn our intellectual and spiritual powers (Schiller says "our activity") in one direction, to concentrate them there — is effected in this Biblical narrative, which certainly deserves the epithet epic.[2]

We find the same contrast if we compare the two uses of direct discourse. The personages speak in the Bible story too; but their speech does not serve, as does speech in Homer, to manifest, to externalize thoughts — on the contrary, it serves to indicate thoughts which remain unexpressed. God gives his command in direct discourse, but he leaves his motives and his purpose unexpressed; Abraham, receiving the command, says nothing and does what he has been told to do. The conversation between Abraham and Isaac on the way to the place of sacrifice is only an interruption of the heavy silence and makes it all the more burdensome. The two of them, Isaac carrying the wood and Abraham with fire and a knife, "went together." Hesitantly, Isaac ventures to ask about the ram, and Abraham gives the well-known answer. Then the text repeats: "So they went both of them together." Everything remains unexpressed.

It would be difficult, then, to imagine styles more contrasted than those of these two equally ancient and equally epic texts. On the one hand, externalized, uniformly illuminated phenomena, at a definite time and in a definite place, connected together without lacunae in a perpetual foreground; thoughts and feeling completely expressed; events taking place in leisurely fashion and with very little of suspense. On the other hand, the externalization of only so much of the phenomena as is necessary for the purpose of the narrative, all else left in obscurity; the decisive points of the narrative alone are emphasized, what lies between is nonexistent; time and place are undefined and call for interpretation; thoughts and feeling remain unexpressed, are only suggested by the silence and the fragmentary speeches; the whole, permeated with the most

vahjireh" in the Authorized Version), properly translated "the Lord will see." Auerbach's coinage reverses the order of the original Hebrew, putting a different version of the "God" morpheme (el) at the end, and the "see" morpheme (yr'h) at the beginning. [Ed.]

[2]Schiller's notions of tragedy are presented in "On Tragic Art" and "On the Pleasure We Derive from Tragic Representation," both 1792. [Ed.]

unrelieved suspense and directed toward a single goal (and to that extent far more of a unity), remains mysterious and "fraught with background."

I will discuss this term in some detail, lest it be misunderstood. I said above that the Homeric style was "of the foreground" because, despite much going back and forth, it yet causes what is momentarily being narrated to give the impression that it is the only present, pure and without perspective. A consideration of the Elohistic text teaches us that our term is capable of a broader and deeper application. It shows that even the separate personages can be represented as possessing "background"; God is always so represented in the Bible, for he is not comprehensible in his presence, as is Zeus; it is always only "something" of him that appears, he always extends into depths. But even the human beings in the Biblical stories have greater depths of time, fate, and consciousness than do the human beings in Homer; although they are nearly always caught up in an event engaging all their faculties, they are not so entirely immersed in its present that they do not remain continually conscious of what has happened to them earlier and elsewhere; their thoughts and feelings have more layers, are more entangled. Abraham's actions are explained not only by what is happening to him at the moment, nor yet only by his character (as Achilles' actions by his courage and his pride, and Odysseus' by his versatility and foresightedness), but by his previous history; he remembers, he is constantly conscious of, what God has promised him and what God has already accomplished for him — his soul is torn between desperate rebellion and hopeful expectation; his silent obedience is multilayered, has background. Such a problematic psychological situation as this is impossible for any of the Homeric heroes, whose destiny is clearly defined and who wake every morning as if it were the first day of their lives: their emotions, though strong, are simple and find expression instantly.

How fraught with background, in comparison, are characters like Saul and David! How entangled and stratified are such human relations as those between David and Absalom, between David and Joab! Any such "background" quality of the psychological situation as that which the story of Absalom's death and its sequel (II Samuel 18 and 19, by the so-called Jahvist) rather suggests than expresses, is unthinkable in Homer.[3] Here we are confronted not merely with the psychological processes of characters whose depth of background is veritably abysmal, but with a purely geographical background too. For David is absent from the battlefield; but the influence of his will and his feelings continues to operate, they affect even Joab in his rebellion and disregard for the consequences of his actions; in the magnificent scene with the two messengers, both the physical and psychological background is fully manifest, though the latter is never expressed. With this, compare, for example, how Achilles, who sends Patroclus first to scout and then into battle, loses almost all "presentness" so long as he is not physically present.[4] But the most important thing is the "multilayeredness" of the individual character; this is hardly to be met with in Homer, or at most in the form of a conscious hesitation between two possible courses of action; otherwise, in Homer, the complexity of the psychological life is shown only in the succession and alternation of emotions; whereas the Jewish writers are able to express the simultaneous existence of various layers of consciousness and the conflict between them.

The Homeric poems, then, though their intellectual, linguistic, and above all syntactical culture appears to be so much more highly devel-

[3]The love-hate relationship between Saul and David, the first king of Israel and his worthier successor, is represented throughout the second half of 1 Samuel. In 2 Samuel 13, David's son Absalom kills David's firstborn son Amnon, who had raped Absalom's sister Tamar; subsequently Absalom leads a palace revolt against David that all but succeeds in displacing him; in 2 Samuel 18 Absalom is killed after a battle on the orders of David's general, Joab. Joab himself, though essential to David's security throughout his reign, is often treated by his monarch with contempt, and in 1 Kings 2:5, the dying David advises his son and successor Solomon to have Joab put to death. Auerbach is probably mistaken when he says that 2 Samuel 18 is "by the so-called Jahvist": it is part of what is usually called the "Court History of David" now generally believed to have been written somewhat before the J document of the Pentateuch. [Ed.]

[4]Patroclus obtains Achilles's permission to return to the fighting and achieves both his battle success and his death wound at the hands of Hector in Book 16 of the Iliad. [Ed.]

oped, are yet comparatively simple in their picture of human beings; and no less so in their relation to the real life which they describe in general. Delight in physical existence is everything to them, and their highest aim is to make that delight perceptible to us. Between battles and passions, adventures and perils, they show us hunts, banquets, palaces and shepherds' cots, athletic contests and washing days — in order that we may see the heroes in their ordinary life, and seeing them so, may take pleasure in their manner of enjoying their savory present, a present which sends strong roots down into social usages, landscape, and daily life. And thus they bewitch us and ingratiate themselves to us until we live with them in the reality of their lives; so long as we are reading or hearing the poems, it does not matter whether we know that all this is only legend, "make-believe." The oft-repeated reproach that Homer is a liar takes nothing from his effectiveness, he does not need to base his story on historical reality, his reality is powerful enough in itself; it ensnares us, weaving its web around us, and that suffices him. And this "real" world into which we are lured, exists for itself, contains nothing but itself; the Homeric poems conceal nothing, they contain no teaching and no secret second meaning. Homer can be analyzed, as we have essayed to do here, but he cannot be interpreted. Later allegorizing trends have tried their arts of interpretation upon him, but to no avail. He resists any such treatment; the interpretations are forced and foreign, they do not crystallize into a unified doctrine. The general considerations which occasionally occur (in our episode, for example, v. 360: that in misfortune men age quickly) reveal a calm acceptance of the basic facts of human existence, but with no compulsion to brood over them, still less any passionate impulse either to rebel against them or to embrace them in an ecstasy of submission.

It is all very different in the Biblical stories. Their aim is not to bewitch the senses, and if nevertheless they produce lively sensory effects, it is only because the moral, religious, and psychological phenomena which are their sole concern are made concrete in the sensible matter of life. But their religious intent involves an absolute claim to historical truth. The story of Abraham and Isaac is not better established than the story of Odysseus, Penelope, and Euryclea; both are legendary. But the Biblical narrator, the Elohist, had to believe in the objective truth of the story of Abraham's sacrifice — the existence of the sacred ordinances of life rested upon the truth of this and similar stories.[5] He had to believe in it passionately; or else (as many rationalistic interpreters believed and perhaps still believe) he had to be a conscious liar — no harmless liar like Homer, who lied to give pleasure, but a political liar with a definite end in view, lying in the interest of a claim to absolute authority.

To me, the rationalistic interpretation seems psychologically absurd; but even if we take it into consideration, the relation of the Elohist to the truth of his story still remains a far more passionate and definite one than is Homer's relation. The Biblical narrator was obliged to write exactly what his belief in the truth of the tradition (or, from the rationalistic standpoint, his interest in the truth of it) demanded of him — in either case, his freedom in creative or representative imagination was severely limited; his activity was perforce reduced to composing an effective version of the pious tradition. What he produced, then, was not primarily oriented toward "realism" (if he succeeded in being realistic, it was merely a means, not an end); it was oriented toward truth. Woe to the man who did not believe it! One can perfectly well entertain historical doubts on the subject of the Trojan War or of Odysseus' wanderings, and still, when reading Homer, feel precisely the effects he sought to produce; but without believing in Abraham's sacrifice, it is possible to put the narrative of it to

[5]The "Elohist" is a term that is sometimes used for the author of the E document, an important strand of Biblical narrative within Genesis, Exodus, and Numbers, probably written during the 9th century B.C. in the northern kingdom of Israel. (The name comes from the fact that in this document the deity is referred to as Elohim, usually translated "God." By contrast, the earlier J document, probably created several generations earlier in the southern kingdom of Judah, generally refers to the deity using the unvocalized word YHWH, usually translated "the LORD.") Genesis 22, in which the story of the sacrifice of Isaac takes place, is generally considered to have been written by the Elohist, although there has apparently been some conflation of the E and J texts at this point, since at verses 11 and 14–16, the deity is called YHWH. [Ed.]

Monologic Discourse

the use for which it was written. Indeed, we must go even further. The Bible's claim to truth is not only far more urgent than Homer's, it is tyrannical — it excludes all other claims. The world of the Scripture stories is not satisfied with claiming to be a historically true reality — it insists that it is the only real world, is destined for autocracy. All other scenes, issues, and ordinances have no right to appear independently of it, and it is promised that all of them, the history of all mankind, will be given their due place within its frame, will be subordinated to it. The Scripture stories do not, like Homer's, court our favor, they do not flatter us that they may please us and enchant us — they seek to subject us, and if we refuse to be subjected we are rebels.

Let no one object that this goes too far, that not the stories, but the religious doctrine, raises the claim to absolute authority; because the stories are not, like Homer's, simply narrated "reality." Doctrine and promise are incarnate in them and inseparable from them; for that very reason they are fraught with "background" and mysterious, containing a second, concealed meaning. In the story of Isaac, it is not only God's intervention at the beginning and the end, but even the factual and psychological elements which come between, that are mysterious, merely touched upon, fraught with background; and therefore they require subtle investigation and interpretation, they demand them. Since so much in the story is dark and incomplete, and since the reader knows that God is a hidden God, his effort to interpret it constantly finds something new to feed upon. Doctrine and the search for enlightenment are inextricably connected with the physical side of the narrative — the latter being more than simple "reality"; indeed they are in constant danger of losing their own reality, as very soon happened when interpretation reached such proportions that the real vanished.

If the text of the Biblical narrative, then, is so greatly in need of interpretation on the basis of its own content, its claim to absolute authority forces it still further in the same direction. Far from seeking, like Homer, merely to make us forget our own reality for a few hours, it seeks to overcome our reality: we are to fit our own life into its world, feel ourselves to be elements in its structure of universal history. This becomes increasingly difficult the further our historical environment is removed from that of the Biblical books; and if these nevertheless maintain their claim to absolute authority, it is inevitable that they themselves be adapted through interpretative transformation. This was for a long time comparatively easy; as late as the European Middle Ages it was possible to represent Biblical events as ordinary phenomena of contemporary life, the methods of interpretation themselves forming the basis for such a treatment. But when, through too great a change in environment and through the awakening of a critical consciousness, this becomes impossible, the Biblical claim to absolute authority is jeopardized; the method of interpretation is scorned and rejected, the Biblical stories become ancient legends, and the doctrine they had contained, now dissevered from them, becomes a disembodied image.

As a result of this claim to absolute authority, the method of interpretation spread to traditions other than the Jewish. The Homeric poems present a definite complex of events whose boundaries in space and time are clearly delimited; before it, beside it, and after it, other complexes of events, which do not depend upon it, can be conceived without conflict and without difficulty. The Old Testament, on the other hand, presents universal history: it begins with the beginning of time, with the creation of the world, and will end with the Last Days, the fulfilling of the Covenant, with which the world will come to an end. Everything else that happens in the world can only be conceived as an element in this sequence; into it everything that is known about the world, or at least everything that touches upon the history of the Jews, must be fitted as an ingredient of the divine plan; and as this too became possible only by interpreting the new material as it poured in, the need for interpretation reaches out beyond the original Jewish-Israelitish realm of reality — for example to Assyrian, Babylonian, Persian, and Roman history; interpretation in a determined direction becomes a general method of comprehending reality; the new and strange world which now comes into view and which, in the form in which it presents itself, proves to be wholly unutilizable within the Jewish religious frame, must be so interpreted that it can find a place there. But this process nearly always also reacts upon the frame, which requires enlarging and modifying. The most striking piece of interpretation of this sort occurred in the first century of the Christian era, in consequence of Paul's mission to the Gentiles: Paul and the Church Fathers reinterpreted the entire Jewish tradition as a succession of figures prognosticating the appearance of Christ, and assigned the Roman Empire its proper place in the divine plan of salvation. Thus while, on the one hand, the reality of the Old Testament presents itself as complete truth with a claim to sole authority, on the other hand that very claim forces it to a constant interpretative change in its own content; for millennia it undergoes an incessant and active development with the life of man in Europe.

The claim of the Old Testament stories to represent universal history, their insistent relation — a relation constantly redefined by conflicts — to a single and hidden God, who yet shows himself and who guides universal history by promise and exaction, gives these stories an entirely different perspective from any the Homeric poems can possess. As a composition, the Old Testament is incomparably less unified than the Homeric poems, it is more obviously pieced together — but the various components all belong to one concept of universal history and its interpretation. If certain elements survived which did not immediately fit in, interpretation took care of them; and so the reader is at every moment aware of the universal religio-historical perspective which gives the individual stories their general meaning and purpose. The greater the separateness and horizontal disconnection of the stories and groups of stories in relation to one another, compared with the *Iliad* and the *Odyssey,* the stronger is their general vertical connection, which holds them all together and which is entirely lacking in Homer. Each of the great figures of the Old Testament, from Adam to the prophets, embodies a moment of this vertical connection. God chose and formed these men to the end of embodying his essence and will — yet choice and formation do not coincide, for the latter proceeds gradually, historically, during the earthly life of him upon whom the choice has fallen. How the process is accomplished, what terrible trials such a formation inflicts, can be seen from our story of Abraham's sacrifice. Herein lies the reason why the great figures of the Old Testament are so much more fully developed, so much more fraught with their own biographical past, so much more distinct as individuals, than are the Homeric heroes. Achilles and Odysseus are splendidly described in many well-ordered words, epithets cling to them, their emotions are constantly displayed in their words and deeds — but they have no development, and their life-histories are clearly set forth once and for all. So little are the Homeric heroes presented as developing or having developed, that most of them — Nestor, Agamemnon, Achilles — appear to be of an age fixed from the very first. Even Odysseus, in whose case the long lapse of time and the many events which occurred offer so much opportunity for biographical development, shows almost nothing of it. Odysseus on his return is exactly the same as he was when he left Ithaca two decades earlier. But what a road, what a fate, lie between the Jacob who cheated his father out of his blessing and the old man whose favorite son has been torn to pieces by a wild beast! — between David the harp player, persecuted by his lord's jealousy, and the old king, surrounded by violent intrigues, whom Abishag the Shunnamite warmed in his bed, and he knew her not![6] The old man, of whom we know how he has become what he is, is more of an individual than the young man; for it is only during the course of an eventful life that men are differentiated into full individuality; and it is this history of a personality which the Old Testament presents to us as the formation undergone by those whom God has chosen to be examples. Fraught with their development, sometimes even aged to the verge of dissolution, they show a distinct stamp of individuality entirely foreign to the

[6]Jacob cheats his brother Esau out of his father Isaac's blessing in Genesis 27; Jacob's favorite son Joseph is misrepresented by his older brothers as having been torn to pieces by a wild beast in Genesis 37:33. The jealous persecution of the youthful court musician David by King Saul begins in 1 Samuel 18 and ends only with Saul's life; the aged David's failure to carnally know his bedmate Abishag the Shunnamite is recounted in 1 Kings 1. [Ed.]

Homeric heroes. Time can touch the latter only outwardly, and even that change is brought to our observation as little as possible; whereas the stern hand of God is ever upon the Old Testament figures; he has not only made them once and for all and chosen them, but he continues to work upon them, bends them and kneads them, and, without destroying them in essence, produces from them forms which their youth gave no grounds for anticipating. The objection that the biographical element of the Old Testament often springs from the combination of several legendary personages does not apply; for this combination is a part of the development of the text. And how much wider is the pendulum swing of their lives than that of the Homeric heroes! For they are bearers of the divine will, and yet they are fallible, subject to misfortune and humiliation — and in the midst of misfortune and in their humiliation their acts and words reveal the transcendent majesty of God. There is hardly one of them who does not, like Adam, undergo the deepest humiliation — and hardly one who is not deemed worthy of God's personal intervention and personal inspiration. Humiliation and elevation go far deeper and far higher than in Homer, and they belong basically together. The poor beggar Odysseus is only masquerading, but Adam is really cast down, Jacob really a refugee, Joseph really in the pit and then a slave to be bought and sold. But their greatness, rising out of humiliation, is almost superhuman and an image of God's greatness. The reader clearly feels how the extent of the pendulum's swing is connected with the intensity of the personal history — precisely the most extreme circumstances, in which we are immeasurably forsaken and in despair, or immeasurably joyous and exalted, give us, if we survive them, a personal stamp which is recognized as the product of a rich existence, a rich development. And very often, indeed generally, this element of development gives the Old Testament stories a historical character, even when the subject is purely legendary and traditional.

Homer remains within the legendary with all his material, whereas the material of the Old Testament comes closer and closer to history as the narrative proceeds; in the stories of David the historical report predominates. Here too, much that is legendary still remains, as for example the story of David and Goliath; but much — and the most essential — consists in things which the narrators knew from their own experience or from firsthand testimony. Now the difference between legend and history is in most cases easily perceived by a reasonably experienced reader. It is a difficult matter, requiring careful historical and philological training, to distinguish the true from the synthetic or the biased in a historical presentation; but it is easy to separate the historical from the legendary in general. Their structure is different. Even where the legendary does not immediately betray itself by elements of the miraculous, by the repetition of well-known standard motives, typical patterns and themes, through neglect of clear details of time and place, and the like, it is generally quickly recognizable by its composition. It runs far too smoothly. All cross-currents, all friction, all that is casual, secondary to the main events and themes, everything unresolved, truncated, and uncertain, which confuses the clear progress of the action and the simple orientation of the actors, has disappeared. The historical event which we witness, or learn from the testimony of those who witnessed it, runs much more variously, contradictorily, and confusedly; not until it has produced results in a definite domain are we able, with their help, to classify it to a certain extent; and how often the order to which we think we have attained becomes doubtful again, how often we ask ourselves if the data before us have not led us to a far too simple classification of the original events! Legend arranges its material in a simple and straightforward way; it detaches it from its contemporary historical context, so that the latter will not confuse it; it knows only clearly outlined men who act from few and simple motives and the continuity of whose feelings and actions remains uninterrupted. In the legends of martyrs, for example, a stiff-necked and fanatical persecutor stands over against an equally stiff-necked and fanatical victim; and a situation so complicated — that is to say, so real and historical — as that in which the "persecutor" Pliny finds himself in his celebrated letter to Trajan on the subject of the Christians, is unfit for legend.[7] And that is still a comparatively simple case. Let the reader think of the history which we are ourselves witnessing; anyone who, for example, evaluates the behavior of individual men and groups of men at the time of the rise of National Socialism in Germany, or the behavior of individual peoples and states before and during the last war, will feel how difficult it is to represent historical themes in general, and how unfit they are for legend;[8] the historical comprises a great number of contradictory motives in each individual, a hesitation and ambiguous groping on the part of groups; only seldom (as in the last war) does a more or less plain situation, comparatively simple to describe, arise, and even such a situation is subject to division below the surface, is indeed almost constantly in danger of losing its simplicity; and the motives of all the interested parties are so complex that the slogans of propaganda can be composed only through the crudest simplification — with the result that friend and foe alike can often employ the same ones. To write history is so difficult that most historians are forced to make concessions to the technique of legend.

It is clear that a large part of the life of David as given in the Bible contains history and not legend. In Absalom's rebellion, for example, or in the scenes from David's last days, the contradictions and crossing of motives both in individuals and in the general action have become so concrete that it is impossible to doubt the historicity of the information conveyed. Now the men who composed the historical parts are often the same who edited the older legends too; their peculiar religious concept of man in history, which we have attempted to describe above, in no way led them to a legendary simplification of events; and so it is only natural that, in the legendary passages of the Old Testament, historical structure is frequently discernible — of course, not in the sense that the traditions are examined as to their credibility according to the methods of scientific criticism; but simply to the extent that the tendency to a smoothing down and harmonizing of events, to a simplification of motives, to a static definition of characters which avoids conflict, vacillation, and development, such as are natural to legendary structure, does not predominate in the Old Testament world of legend. Abraham, Jacob, or even Moses produces a more concrete, direct, and historical impression than the figures of the Homeric world — not because they are better described in terms of sense (the contrary is the case) but because the confused, contradictory multiplicity of events, the psychological and factual cross-purposes, which true history reveals, have not disappeared in the representation but still remain clearly perceptible. In the stories of David, the legendary, which only later scientific criticism makes recognizable as such, imperceptibly passes into the historical; and even in the legendary, the problem of the classification and interpretation of human history is already passionately apprehended — a problem which later shatters the framework of historical composition and completely overruns it with prophecy; thus the Old Testament, in so far as it is concerned with human events, ranges through all three domains: legend, historical reporting, and interpretative historical theology.

Connected with the matters just discussed is the fact that the Greek text seems more limited and more static in respect to the circle of personages involved in the action and to their political activity. In the recognition scene with which we began, there appears, aside from Odysseus and Penelope, the housekeeper Euryclea, a slave whom Odysseus' father Laertes had bought long before. She, like the swineherd Eumaeus, has

[7] The younger Pliny (Gaius Plinius Caecilius Secundus, A.D. 61–113), nephew of the more famous author of the *Natural History* who perished at the eruption of Pompeii, had been made governor of the province of Bithynia around 111 by the Roman emperor Trajan. During his fifteen months in office, Pliny was required to try persons accused of being Christians and execute those found guilty; inexperienced at this practice, he wrote to Trajan (*Epistola* 96) to confirm the emperor's approval of his course of action: pardoning those who denied or recanted, ignoring anonymous accusations, but sternly meting out the letter of the law to those who admitted their beliefs and refused to recant. [Ed.]

[8] The reader should be reminded that Auerbach was writing *Mimesis* while in self-imposed exile from his native Germany, which he had fled when the Nazis attempted to impose their ideology upon the University of Marburg, where he had taught. [Ed.]

spent her life in the service of Laertes' family; like Eumaeus, she is closely connected with their fate, she loves them and shares their interests and feelings. But she has no life of her own, no feelings of her own; she has only the life and feelings of her master. Eumaeus too, though he still remembers that he was born a freeman and indeed of a noble house (he was stolen as a boy), has, not only in fact but also in his own feeling, no longer a life of his own, he is entirely involved in the life of his masters. Yet these two characters are the only ones whom Homer brings to life who do not belong to the ruling class. Thus we become conscious of the fact that in the Homeric poems life is enacted only among the ruling class — others appear only in the role of servants to that class. The ruling class is still so strongly patriarchal, and still itself so involved in the daily activities of domestic life, that one is sometimes likely to forget their rank. But they are unmistakably a sort of feudal aristocracy, whose men divide their lives between war, hunting, marketplace councils, and feasting, while the women supervise the maids in the house. As a social picture, this world is completely stable; wars take place only between different groups of the ruling class; nothing ever pushes up from below. In the early stories of the Old Testament the patriarchal condition is dominant too, but since the people involved are individual nomadic or half-nomadic tribal leaders, the social picture gives a much less stable impression; class distinctions are not felt. As soon as the people completely emerges — that is, after the exodus from Egypt — its activity is always discernible, it is often in ferment, it frequently intervenes in events not only as a whole but also in separate groups and through the medium of separate individuals who come forward; the origins of prophecy seem to lie in the irrepressible politico-religious spontaneity of the people. We receive the impression that the movements emerging from the depths of the people of Israel-Judah must have been of a wholly different nature from those even of the later ancient democracies — of a different nature and far more elemental.

With the more profound historicity and the more profound social activity of the Old Testament text, there is connected yet another important distinction from Homer: namely, that a different conception of the elevated style and of the sublime is to be found here. Homer, of course, is not afraid to let the realism of daily life enter into the sublime and tragic; our episode of the scar is an example, we see how the quietly depicted, domestic scene of the foot-washing is incorporated into the pathetic and sublime action of Odysseus' homecoming. From the rule of the separation of styles which was later almost universally accepted and which specified that the realistic depiction of daily life was incompatible with the sublime and had a place only in comedy or, carefully stylized, in idyl — from any such rule Homer is still far removed. And yet he is closer to it than is the Old Testament. For the great and sublime events in the Homeric poems take place far more exclusively and unmistakably among the members of a ruling class; and these are far more untouched in their heroic elevation than are the Old Testament figures, who can fall much lower in dignity (consider, for example, Adam, Noah, David, Job); and finally, domestic realism, the representation of daily life, remains in Homer in the peaceful realm of the idyllic, whereas, from the very first, in the Old Testament stories, the sublime, tragic, and problematic take shape precisely in the domestic and commonplace: scenes such as those between Cain and Abel, between Noah and his sons, between Abraham, Sarah, and Hagar, between Rebekah, Jacob, and Esau, and so on, are inconceivable in the Homeric style. The entirely different ways of developing conflicts are enough to account for this. In the Old Testament stories the peace of daily life in the house, in the fields, and among the flocks, is undermined by jealousy over election and the promise of a blessing, and complications arise which would be utterly incomprehensible to the Homeric heroes. The latter must have palpable and clearly expressible reasons for their conflicts and enmities, and these work themselves out in free battles; whereas, with the former, the perpetually smouldering jealousy and the connection between the domestic and the spiritual, between the paternal blessing and the divine blessing, lead to daily life being permeated with the stuff of conflict, often with poison. The sublime influence of God here reaches so deeply into the everyday that the two realms of the sublime and the everyday are not only actually unseparated but basically inseparable.

We have compared these two texts, and, with them, the two kinds of style they embody, in order to reach a starting point for an investigation into the literary representation of reality in European culture. The two styles, in their opposition, represent basic types: on the one hand fully externalized description, uniform illumination, uninterrupted connection, free expression, all events in the foreground, displaying unmistakable meanings, few elements of historical development and of psychological perspective; on the other hand, certain parts brought into high relief, others left obscure, abruptness, suggestive influence of the unexpressed, "background" quality, multiplicity of meanings and the need for interpretation, universal-historical claims, development of the concept of the historically becoming, and preoccupation with the problematic.

Homer's realism is, of course, not to be equated with classical-antique realism in general; for the separation of styles, which did not develop until later, permitted no such leisurely and externalized description of everyday happenings; in tragedy especially there was no room for it; furthermore, Greek culture very soon encountered the phenomena of historical becoming and of the "multilayeredness" of the human problem, and dealt with them in its fashion; in Roman realism, finally, new and native concepts are added. We shall go into these later changes in the antique representation of reality when the occasion arises; on the whole, despite them, the basic tendencies of the Homeric style, which we have attempted to work out, remained effective and determinant down into late antiquity.

Since we are using the two styles, the Homeric and the Old Testament, as starting points, we have taken them as finished products, as they appear in the texts; we have disregarded everything that pertains to their origins, and thus have left untouched the question whether their peculiarities were theirs from the beginning or are to be referred wholly or in part to foreign influences. Within the limits of our purpose, a consideration of this question is not necessary; for it is in their full development, which they reached in early times, that the two styles exercised their determining influence upon the representation of reality in European literature.

Hans-Georg Gadamer

b. 1900

Hans-Georg Gadamer was born the son of a chemistry professor at the University of Breslau, the provincial capital of Silesia, which is now called Wroclow in Poland. Against his parents' wishes, Gadamer began to study philosophy at the University of Marburg. Studying under the Neo-Kantian philosophers Hermann Cohen[1] and Paul Natorp, Gadamer earned his doctorate at the age of twenty-two. He continued postgraduate work at Marburg and in 1923 came under the influence of Martin Heidegger, who had just arrived as a *privatdozent* and who remained Gadamer's friend for life.

Gadamer began teaching at Marburg in 1929 — around the time Heidegger left to take up the vacated chair of his teacher, Edmund Husserl — and was named professor of philosophy in 1937. In 1938 he moved to the University of Leipzig, where he stayed throughout the war years. He was appointed rector of the university in 1946 and helped rebuild after the damage caused by the war, but he left Leipzig (which was in the eastern sector) as the result of his growing dissatisfaction with and distrust of the communist government. In 1948 Gadamer went to Frankfurt and then to the University of Heidelberg, where he succeeded the theologian Karl Jaspers as chair of the department of philosophy, and where he trained the literary theorists Wolfgang Iser and Hans Robert Jauss, who founded a school of reader-response theory in Constanz.[2] Since retiring from Heidelberg in 1968, Gadamer has taught as a visiting professor all over the world, returning most often to Boston College.

The originality of Gadamer's thought, paradoxically enough, began when he came under the influence of Martin Heidegger. Heidegger, a student of the phenomenologist Edmund Husserl, was then working out the details of his major treatise, *Being and Time;* Gadamer adopted some of the same principles as Heidegger but developed them into what was primarily a theory of knowledge and interpretation, rather than a theory of being and action.

Gadamer's philosophical field is usually called "hermeneutics," from the Greek god Hermes who was associated with hidden writings, codes, and mysteries. Hermeneutics is a study of how people make interpretations out of encoded texts. The field dates back to the late eighteenth century when it was becoming clear that the most important text of all — the Judeo-Christian Bible — was a compilation of a number of sources by various authors who had quite disparate moral and literary intentions. It became quintessentially important for theologians, particularly Protestant theologians, to evaluate one interpretation or method of interpretation against

[1]The relatively unknown Cohen seems to have played an instrumental part in the formation of some of the most important literary and philosophical thinkers of the twentieth century, including not only Gadamer and Martin Heidegger, who studied with him, but also Mikhail Bakhtin, who learned of his work through a Petersburg friend, Matvey Kagan. Interestingly, Cohen's best students reacted *against* his idealism, producing theories of worldly knowledge and action that contradicted it.

[2]See the introduction to Reader-Response Criticism, p. 917.

another, in order to develop a sense of how and how far interpretations of texts could be trusted. Today, of course, hermeneutics is a major issue in relation to secular literary as well as biblical texts: The question of whether it is possible to achieve an "objective" interpretation of a particular literary text, or to develop criteria by which one interpretation can be preferred to another, remains very much with us today.

The title of Gadamer's treatise, from which the following selection is taken, is *Truth and Method* (1960). It is an ironic title, in a way, because "truth" and "method" are the key terms of scientific thought after Descartes: The objective and inductive scientific methods are seen as the way to objective truth. The question Gadamer asked was whether the "human sciences" (art and literature, but also history and cultural studies) should be modeled on the natural sciences — whether you could find or create a method that would lead to truth in any discipline. His answer came out of his sense of human experience and of art's place in that experience. Gadamer agreed with Heidegger that our sense of experience is structured by our placement in time, the place into which we are thrown. He postulated that art is by nature a sort of game that we play, a game whose rules we learn as we go along and that changes us as we play it. Given the shifting, contingent position of the observing subject, Gadamer concluded that the search for objective truth in aesthetic interpretation based upon a special hermeneutical method was a fool's errand. We could never know what a text meant. The best we could achieve was what he called an "effective-historical understanding."

Gadamer entered the debate over hermeneutics in reaction to the post-Kantian hermeneutic theories associated with Friedrich Schleiermacher (1778–1841) and Wilhelm Dilthey (1833–1911). Schleiermacher argued that the interpreter's job is to place himself in the position of the author, to project himself into the author's subjectivity, and in that way try to understand not only the author's intended meaning, but also meanings that may not have been present to the author's consciousness. Dilthey saw more clearly than Schleiermacher that historical change was involved in the problem of finding an author's meaning, that the reader had to seek out the mental structures authors create in accordance with the demands of their world-views, which are the world-views of their age. Both Schleiermacher and Dilthey argued that the business of the interpreter of texts is to clear his or her mind of the prejudices and the mental detritus of the present age, so as to be able to enter, with a clean mental slate, the world of the author. For Gadamer, such a clean slate — the "reading-degree-zero" that Dilthey postulated — can never exist, because one's consciousness is defined by, and therefore cannot get outside of, the culture one inhabits. Objective truth is therefore impossible. When one exists in a world, one automatically perceives that world — and its texts — through the "horizon" of meaning that the culture of the present moment provides. Whereas Gadamer's metaphor of the "horizon" suggests the limit of vision imposed by one's physical position in *space,* he argues that our mental horizons are limited not by space but by our position in *time*.

The keys to interpretation, for Gadamer, are the very prejudices through which one reads. The English word "prejudice" has a pejorative cast, summoning up thoughts of a kangaroo court that judges and condemns before it has heard the facts. But the German word Gadamer uses, "Vorurteilungen," literally "fore-understandings," has nothing of this juridical flavor. Gadamer claims that without the fore-understanding our prejudices provide it would be impossible to achieve any effective-historical understanding of the past. For Gadamer, the voices of tradition and authority that can be barriers to scientific discovery are, in the human sciences, a part of what constitutes us as historical beings living in a world of time.

Interpretive reading, then, is a dialogical activity for Gadamer, in which the meaning-horizon of the reader and the meaning-horizon of the text impinge upon each other. We do not need a special scientific "method": we are always already fusing our own horizon with that of the text. When we read a text whose origins go back in time, we are often surprised, "brought up short," by what it says and the way it says it. When this happens, we enter into a dialogue with the text, asking questions and receiving answers in ways that begin to blend what Gadamer calls the "horizons" of the text and the "horizons" of the reader. Part of what links these two horizons is the force of a community of readers, a "tradition" of interpretation whose authority is earned by the wisdom and insight of those who have helped to constitute it. The force of such tradition is not absolute, but it inevitably conditions the kinds of issues we can raise and the kinds of questions we can ask.

As a result of our interaction with the text, we as readers not only come to understand the text better, we also come to understand ourselves better, in that we become more conscious of the historical place from which we interpret. We use the tradition, and in using it we remake it as something new. Consequently, the "prejudices" or "fore-understandings" through which we interpret texts of the past are not a fixed set of ideas but are themselves constituted and altered by our use of them.

All this seems to suggest a rigid division between the "human sciences," where truth is the product of an inevitably subjective interaction between text and reader, and the "hard sciences," which depend upon an objective scientific method, where the observer has no influence on what he or she observes. But phenomenological approaches to science, such as that of Thomas J. Kuhn, have suggested that the vaunted objectivity of science is only an enabling myth, and that something like Gadamer's notion of "fore-understanding" — in the shape of the "paradigms" that define scientific problems and the methodologies of their investigation — plays exactly the same role within scientific discovery that it does in historical or literary interpretation.

Selected Bibliography

Devereaux, Mary. "Can Art Save Us? A Meditation on Gadamer." *Philosophy and Literature* 15 (1991): 59–73.

Gadamer, Hans-Georg. *Truth and Method,* 1960; London: Sheed and Ward, 1975.

Holub, Robert C. *Reception Theory: A Critical Introduction.* London: Methuen, 1984.

Ingram, David. "Hermeneutics and Truth." In *Hermeneutics and Praxis,* ed. Robert Hollinger. Notre Dame: University of Notre Dame Press, 1985, pp. 32–53.

Misgeld, Dieter. "On Gadamer's Hermeneutics." In *Hermeneutics and Praxis,* ed. Robert Hollinger. Notre Dame: University of Notre Dame Press, 1985, pp. 143–70.

Palmer, L.M. "Gadamer and the Enlightenment's 'Prejudice against All Prejudices.' " *Clio* 22 (1993): 369–82.

Silverman, Hugh J., ed. *Gadamer and Hermeneutics.* London and New York: Routledge, 1991.

Weinsheimer, Joel. *Gadamer's Hermeneutics: A Reading of Truth and Method.* New Haven: Yale University Press, 1985.

———. *Philosophical Hermeneutics and Literary Theory.* New Haven: Yale University Press, 1991.

The Elevation of the Historicality of Understanding to the Status of Hermeneutical Principle

(A) THE HERMENEUTIC CIRCLE AND THE PROBLEM OF PREJUDICES

(i) Heidegger's Disclosure of the Fore-Structure of Understanding

Heidegger went into the problems of historical hermeneutics and criticism only in order to develop from it, for the purposes of ontology, the fore-structure of understanding.[1] Contrariwise, our question is how hermeneutics, once freed from the ontological obstructions of the scientific concept of objectivity, can do justice to the historicality of understanding. The way in which hermeneutics has traditionally understood itself is based on its character as art or technique.[2] This is true even of Dilthey's extension of hermeneutics to become an organon of the human sciences. It may be asked whether there is such a thing as this art or technique of understanding — we shall come back to the point. But at any rate we may inquire into the consequences that Heidegger's fundamental derivation of the circular structure of understanding from the temporality of There-being has for the hermeneutics of the human sciences. These consequences do not need to be such that a theory is applied to practice and the latter now be performed differently, i.e., in a way that is technically correct. They could also consist in a correction (and purification of inadequate manners) of the way in which constantly exercised understanding understands itself — a procedure that would benefit the art of understanding at most only indirectly.

Hence we shall examine once more Heidegger's description of the hermeneutical circle in order to use, for our own purpose, the new fundamental significance acquired here by the circular structure. Heidegger writes: "It is not to be reduced to the level of a vicious circle, or even of a circle which is merely tolerated. In the circle is hidden a positive possibility of the most primordial kind of knowing. To be sure, we genuinely take hold of this possibility only when, in our interpretation, we have understood that our first, last and constant task is never to allow our fore-having, fore-sight, and fore-conception to be presented to us by fancies and popular conceptions, but rather to make the scientific theme secure by working out these fore-structures in terms of the things themselves." (*Being and Time*)

What Heidegger works out here is not primarily a demand on the practice of understanding, but is a description of the way in which interpretation through understanding is achieved. The point of Heidegger's hermeneutical thinking is not so much to prove that there is a circle as to show that this circle possesses an ontologically

Translated by Garrett Burden and John Cumming.

[1]Heidegger, *Being and Time,* p. 312ff. [Au.]

[2]Cf Schleiermacher's *Hermeneutik* (ed H. Kimmerle in *Abhandlungen der Heidelberger Akademie,* 1959, 2nd *Abhandlung*), which is explicitly committed to the old ideal of technique (p. 127, note: "I . . . hate it when theory does not go beyond nature and the bases of art, whose object it is.") [Au.]

positive significance. The description as such will be obvious to every interpreter who knows what he is about.[3] All correct interpretation must be on guard against arbitrary fancies and the limitations imposed by imperceptible habits of thought and direct its gaze "on the things themselves" (which, in the case of the literary critic, are meaningful texts, which themselves are again concerned with objects). It is clear that to let the object take over in this way is not a matter for the interpreter of a single decision, but is "the first, last and constant task." For it is necessary to keep one's gaze fixed on the thing throughout all the distractions that the interpreter will constantly experience in the process and which originate in himself. A person who is trying to understand a text is always performing an act of projecting. He projects before himself a meaning for the text as a whole as soon as some initial meaning emerges in the text. Again, the latter emerges only because he is reading the text with particular expectations in regard to a certain meaning. The working out of this fore-project, which is constantly revised in terms of what emerges as he penetrates into the meaning, is understanding what is there.

This description is, of course, a rough abbreviation of the whole. The process that Heidegger describes is that every revision of the fore-project is capable of projecting before itself a new project of meaning, that rival projects can emerge side by side until it becomes clearer what the unity of meaning is, that interpretation begins with fore-conceptions that are replaced by more suitable ones. This constant process of new projection is the movement of understanding and interpretation. A person who is trying to understand is exposed to distraction from fore-meanings that are not borne out by the things themselves. The working-out of appropriate projects, anticipatory in nature, to be confirmed "by the things" themselves, is the constant task of understanding. The only "objectivity" here is the confirmation of a fore-meaning in its being worked out. The only thing that characterizes the arbitrariness of inappropriate fore-meanings is that they come to nothing in the working-out. But understanding achieves its full potentiality only when the fore-meanings that it uses are not arbitrary. Thus it is quite right for the interpreter not to approach the text directly, relying solely on the fore-meaning at once available to him, but rather to examine explicitly the legitimacy, i.e., the origin and validity, of the fore-meanings present within him.

This fundamental requirement must be seen as the radicalization of a procedure that in fact we exercise whenever we understand anything. Every text presents the task of not simply employing unexamined our own linguistic usage — or in the case of a foreign language the usage that we are familiar with from writers or from daily intercourse. We regard our task as rather that of deriving our understanding of the text from the linguistic usage of the time of the author. The question is, of course, to what extent this general requirement can be fulfilled. In the field of semantics, in particular, we are confronted with the problem of the unconscious nature of our own use of language. How do we discover that there is a difference between our own customary usage and that of the text?

I think we must say that it is generally the experience of being pulled up short by the text. Either it does not yield any meaning or its meaning is not compatible with what we had expected. It is this that makes us take account of possible difference in usage. It is a general presupposition that can be questioned only in particular cases that someone who speaks the same language as I do uses the words in the sense familiar to me. The same thing is true in the case of a foreign language, i.e., that we all think we have a normal knowledge of it and assume this normal usage when we are reading a text.

What is true of the fore-meaning of usage, however, is equally true of the fore-meanings with regard to content with which we read texts, and which make up our fore-understanding. Here too we may ask how we can break the spell of our own notion that what is stated in a text will fit perfectly with my own meanings and expecta-

[3] Cf E. Staiger's description, which is in accord with that of Heidegger, in *Die Kunst der Interpretation,* p. 11ff. I do not however, agree that the work of a literary critic begins only "when we are in the situation of a contemporary reader." This is something we never are, and yet we are capable of understanding, although we can never achieve a definite "personal or temporal identity" with the author. [Au.]

tions. On the contrary, what another person tells me, whether in conversation, letter, book or whatever, is generally thought automatically to be his own and not my opinion; and it is this that I am to take note of without necessarily having to share it. But this presupposition is not something that makes understanding easier, but harder, in that the fore-meanings that determine my own understanding can go entirely unnoticed. If they give rise to misunderstandings, how can misunderstandings of a text be recognized at all if there is nothing else to contradict? How can a text be protected from misunderstanding from the start?

If we examine the situation more closely, however, we find that meanings cannot be understood in an arbitrary way. Just as we cannot continually misunderstand the use of a word without its affecting the meaning of the whole, so we cannot hold blindly to our own fore-meaning of the thing if we would understand the meaning of another. Of course this does not mean that when we listen to someone or read a book we must forget all our fore-meanings concerning the content, and all our own ideas. All that is asked is that we remain open to the meaning of the other person or of the text. But this openness always includes our placing the other meaning in a relation with the whole of our own meanings or ourselves in a relation to it. Now it is the case that meanings represent a fluid variety of possibilities (when compared with the agreement presented by a language and a vocabulary), but it is still not the case that within this variety of what can be thought, i.e., of what a reader can find meaningful and hence expect to find, everything is possible, and if a person fails to hear what the other person is really saying, he will not be able to place correctly what he has misunderstood within the range of his own various expectations of meaning. Thus there is a criterion here also. The hermeneutical task becomes automatically a questioning of things and is always in part determined by this. This places hermeneutical work on a firm basis. If a person is trying to understand something, he will not be able to rely from the start on his own chance previous ideas, missing as logically and stubbornly as possible the actual meaning of the text until the latter becomes so persistently audible that it breaks through the imagined understanding of it. Rather, a person trying to understand a text is prepared for it to tell him something. That is why a hermeneutically trained mind must be, from the start, sensitive to the text's quality of newness. But this kind of sensitivity involves neither "neutrality" in the matter of the object nor the extinction of one's self, but the conscious assimilation of one's own fore-meanings and prejudices. The important thing is to be aware of one's own bias, so that the text may present itself in all its newness and thus be able to assert its own truth against one's own fore-meanings.

When Heidegger showed that what we call the "reading of what is there" is the fore-structure of understanding, this was, phenomenologically, completely correct. He also showed by an example the task that arises from this. In *Being and Time* he gave a concrete example, in the question of being, of the general statement that was, for him, a hermeneutical problem.[4] In order to explain the hermeneutical situation of the question of being in regard to fore-having, fore-sight and fore-conception, he critically applied his question, directed at metaphysics, to important turning-points in the history of metaphysics. Here he was actually doing simply what the historical, hermeneutical consciousness requires in every case. Methodologically conscious understanding will be concerned not merely to form anticipatory ideas, but to make them conscious, so as to check them and thus acquire right understanding from the things themselves. This is what Heidegger means when he talks about "securing" our scientific theme by deriving our fore-having, fore-sight and fore-conceptions from the things themselves.

It is not, then, at all a case of safeguarding ourselves against the tradition that speaks out of the text but, on the contrary, to keep everything away that could hinder us in understanding it in terms of the thing. It is the tyranny of hidden prejudices that makes us deaf to the language that speaks to us in tradition. Heidegger's demonstration that the concept of consciousness in Descartes and of spirit in Hegel is still influenced by Greek substance-ontology, which sees being

[4] *Being and Time*, pp. 312ff. [Au.]

in terms of what is present and actual, undoubtedly goes beyond the self-understanding of modern metaphysics, yet not in an arbitrary, willful way, but on the basis of a fore-having that in fact makes this tradition intelligible by revealing the ontological premises of the concept of subjectivity. On the other hand, Heidegger discovers in Kant's critique of "dogmatic" metaphysics the idea of a metaphysics of the finite which is a challenge to his own ontological scheme. Thus he "secures" the scientific theme by framing it within the understanding of tradition and so putting it, in a sense, at risk. This is the concrete form of the historical consciousness that is involved in understanding.

This recognition that all understanding inevitably involves some prejudice gives the hermeneutical problem its real thrust. By the light of this insight it appears that historicism, despite its critique of rationalism and of natural law philosophy, is based on the modern enlightenment and unknowingly shares its prejudices. And there is one prejudice of the enlightenment that is essential to it: the fundamental prejudice of the enlightenment is the prejudice against prejudice itself, which deprives tradition of its power.

Historical analysis shows that it is not until the enlightenment that the concept of prejudice acquires the negative aspect we are familiar with. Actually "prejudice" means a judgment that is given before all the elements that determine a situation have been finally examined. In German legal terminology a "prejudice" is a provisional legal verdict before the final verdict is reached. For someone involved in a legal dispute, this kind of judgment against him affects his chances adversely. Accordingly, the French *préjudice,* as well as the Latin *praejudicium,* means simply "adverse effect," "disadvantage," "harm." But this negative sense is only a consecutive one. The negative consequence depends precisely on the positive validity, the value of the provisional decision as a prejudgment, which is that of any precedent.

Thus "prejudice" certainly does not mean a false judgment, but it is part of the idea that it can have a positive and a negative value. This is due clearly to the influence of the Latin *praejudicium.* There are such things as *préjugés légitimes.* This seems a long way from our current use of the word. The German *Vorurteil,* like English "prejudice" and even more than the French *préjugé,* seems to have become limited in its meaning, through the enlightenment and its critique of religion, and have the sense simply of an "unfounded judgment."[5] It is only its having a basis, a methodological justification (and not the fact that it may be actually correct) that gives a judgment its dignity. The lack of such a basis does not mean, for the enlightenment, that there might be other kinds of certainty, but rather that the judgment does not have any foundation in the facts themselves, i.e., that it is "unfounded." This is a conclusion only in the spirit of rationalism. It is the reason for the discrediting of prejudices and the claim by scientific knowledge completely to exclude them.

Modern science, in adopting this principle, is following the rule of Cartesian doubt of accepting nothing as certain which can in any way be doubted, and the idea of the method that adheres to this requirement. In our introductory observations we have already pointed out how difficult it is to harmonize the historical knowledge that helps to shape our historical consciousness with this ideal and how difficult it is, for that reason, for the modern concept of method to grasp its true nature. This is the place to turn these negative statements into positive ones. The concept of the "prejudice" is where we can make a beginning. . . .

(B) PREJUDICES AS CONDITIONS OF UNDERSTANDING

(ii) The Classical Example

It is a lot to ask of the self-understanding of the human sciences to detach itself, in the whole of its activity, from the model of the natural sciences and to regard the historical movement of

[5] Cf Leo Strauss, *Die Religionskritik Spinozas,* p. 163: "The word 'prejudice' is the most suitable expression for the great aim of the enlightenment, the desire for free, untrammeled verification; the *Vorurteil* is the unambiguous polemical correlate of the very ambiguous word 'freedom.' " [Au.]

whatever it is concerned with not simply as an impairment of its objectivity, but as something of positive value. There are, however, in the recent development of the human sciences points at which reflection could start that would really do justice to the problem. The naive methodologism of historical research no longer dominates the field alone. The progress of inquiry is no longer universally seen within the framework of the expansion or penetration into new fields or material, but instead as the attaining of a higher stage of reflection in the problem. Even where this happens, thinking is still teleological, in terms of the progress of research, in a way appropriate to the scientist. But a hermeneutical consciousness is gradually growing which is infusing the attitude of inquiry with a spirit of self-criticism; this is true, above all, of those human sciences that have the oldest tradition. Thus the study of classical antiquity, after it had worked over the whole extent of the available transmitted texts, continually applied itself again, with more subtle questions, to the old favorite objects of its study. This introduced something of an element of self-criticism, in that it reflected on what constituted the real merit of its favorite objects. The concept of the classical, that since Droysen's[6] discovery of Hellenism had reduced historical thinking to a mere stylistic concept, now acquired a new scientific legitimacy.

It requires hermeneutical reflection of some sophistication to discover how it is possible for a normative concept such as that of the classical to acquire or regain its scientific legitimacy. For it follows from the self-understanding of historical consciousness that all normative significance of the past is ultimately dissolved by the now sovereign historical reason. Only at the beginnings of historicism, as for example in Winckelmann's[7] epoch-making work, was the normative element still a real motive of historical research.

[6]Johann Gustav Droysen, German historian (1808–1884), author of celebrated histories of Alexander the Great (1833) and of Hellenism (1836–43). [Ed.]

[7]Johann Joachim Winckelmann, German archeologist (1717–1768), most famous for his *History of Ancient Art* (1764), which set up the ideal of Greek sculpture as noble simplicity and calm greatness. [Ed.]

The concept of classical antiquity and of the classical, such as dominated pedagogical thought in particular, since the days of German classicism, had both a normative and an historical side. A particular stage in the historical development of man was thought to have produced a mature and perfect formation of man. This combination of a normative and an historical meaning in the concept goes back to Herder.[8] But Hegel[9] still preserved this combination, even though he gave it another emphasis in terms of the history of philosophy. Classical art retained its special excellence for him through being seen as the "religion of art." Since this is a form of the spirit that is past, it is exemplary only in a qualified sense. The fact that it is a past art testifies to the "past" character of art in general. Hegel used this to justify systematically the historicization of the concept of the classical and introduced that process of development that finally made the classical into a descriptive stylistic concept that describes the brief harmony of measure and fullness that comes between archaic rigidity and baroque dissolution. Since it became part of the aesthetic vocabulary of historical studies, the concept of the classical has preserved the reference to a normative content only in an unacknowledged way.

It was indicative of the start of historical self-criticism when classical studies started to examine themselves after the first world war in relation to a new humanism, and hesitantly again brought out the combination of the normative and the historical elements in "the classical."[10] It proved, however, impossible (although the attempt was made) to interpret the concept of the classical that arose in antiquity and was operative in the canonization of certain writers as if it had

[8]Johann Gottfried von Herder, German philosopher and philologist of the Romantic era (1744–1803). His *Ideas toward a Philosophy of History* sets up an evolutionary theory of history that prefigures Darwin's notions of adaptation to environment and struggle for existence. [Ed.]

[9]See the introduction to Hegel, p. 357. [Ed.]

[10]The congress at Naumburg on the classical (1930), which was completely dominated by Werner Jaeger, is as much an example of this as the founding of the periodical *Die Antike*. Cf *Das Problem des Klassischen und die Antike* (1931). [Au.]

itself expressed the unity of a stylistic ideal.[11] On the contrary, the ancient concept was wholly ambiguous. When today we use "classic" as an historical stylistic concept that has a clear meaning by being set against what came before and after, this concept has become quite detached from the ancient one. The concept of the "classical" now signifies a period of time, the period of an historical development, but does not signify any suprahistorical value.

In fact, however, the normative element in the concept of the classical has never completely disappeared. It is still the basis of the idea of liberal education. The classicist is, rightly, not satisfied with simply applying to his texts the historical stylistic concept that has developed through the history of the plastic arts. The question that suggests itself, whether Homer is also "classical," shatters the historical stylistic category of the classical that is used in an analogy with the history of art — an instance of the fact that historical consciousness always includes more than it acknowledges of itself.

If we try to see what these implications mean, we might say that the classical is a truly historical category, precisely in that it is more than a concept of a period or an historical stylistic one and that yet it does not seek to be a suprahistorical concept of value. It does not refer to a quality that we assign to particular historical phenomena, but to a notable mode of "being historical," the historical process of preservation that, through the constant proving of itself, sets before us something that is true. It is not at all the case, as the historical mode of thought would have us believe, that the value judgment through which something is dubbed classical was in fact destroyed by historical reflection and its criticism of all teleological constructions of the process of history. The value judgment that is implicit in the concept of the classical gains, rather, through this criticism a new, real legitimacy. The classical is what resists historical criticism because its historical dominion, the binding power of its validity that is preserved and handed down, precedes all historical reflection and continues through it.

To take the key example of the blanket concept of "classical antiquity," it is, of course, unhistorical to devalue the hellenistic as an age of the decline and fall of classicism, and Droysen has rightly emphasized its importance and its place within the continuity of history for the birth and spread of christianity. But he would not have needed to undertake this historical apologetic if there had not always been a prejudice in favor of the classical and if the culture of humanism had not held on to "classical antiquity" and preserved it within Western culture as the heritage of the past. The classical is fundamentally something quite different from a descriptive concept used by an objectivizing historical consciousness. It is a historical reality to which historical consciousness belongs and is subordinate. What we call "classical" is something retrieved from the vicissitudes of changing time and its changing taste. It can be approached directly, not through that, as it were, electric touch that sometimes characterizes a contemporary work of art and in which the fulfillment of an apprehension of meaning that surpasses all conscious expectation is instantaneously experienced. Rather it is a consciousness of something enduring, of significance that cannot be lost and is independent of all the circumstances of time, in which we call something "classical" — a kind of timeless present that is contemporaneous with every other age.

So the first thing about the concept of the classical (and this is wholly true of both the ancient and the modern use of the word) is the normative sense. But insofar as this norm is related retrospectively to a past entity that fulfilled and embodied it, it always contains a temporal quality that articulates it historically. So it was not surprising that, with the rise of historical reflection in Germany which took as its standard the classicism of Winckelmann, an historical concept of a time or a period detached itself from what was regarded as classical in Winckelmann's sense and denoted a quite specific stylistic ideal and, in a historically descriptive way, also a time or period that fulfilled this ideal. From the distance of the Epigones, who set up the criterion, it becomes clear that this stylistic ideal was fulfilled

[11]Cf the legitimate criticism that A. Körte made of the Naumburg lecture by J. Stroux, in the *Berichte der Sächsischen Akademie der Wissenschaften* 86, 1934, and my note in *Gnomon* 11 (1935), p. 612f. [Au.]

at a particular past moment of the world's history. Accordingly, the concept of the classical came to be used in modern thought to describe the whole of "classical antiquity" when humanism proclaimed anew the exemplary nature of this antiquity. It was taking up an ancient usage, with some justification, for those ancient authors who were "discovered" by humanism were the same ones that, for the later period of antiquity, comprised the canon of classics.

They were preserved in the history of Western culture precisely because they became canonical as the writers of the "school." But it is easy to see how the historical stylistic concept was able to follow this usage. For although it is a normative consciousness that is behind this concept, it is still a retrospective element. It is an awareness of decline and distance that gives birth to the classical norm. It is not by accident that the concept of the classical and of classical style emerges in late periods. The *Dialogus* of Callimachus and Tacitus has been decisive in this connection.[12] But there is something else. Those authors who are regarded as classical are, as we know, always the representatives of particular literary genres. They were considered as the perfect fulfilment of the norm of that literary genre, an ideal that the retrospective view of literary criticism makes plain. If we now examine these norms of literary genres historically, i.e., if we consider their history, then the classical is seen as the concept of a stylistic phase, of a climax that articulates the history of the genre in terms of before and after. Insofar as the climactic points in the history of genres come largely within the same brief period of time, the classical, within the totality of the historical development of classical antiquity, refers to such a period and thus also becomes a concept denoting a period: this concept fuses with the stylistic one.

As this kind of historical stylistic concept, the concept of the classical is capable of being extended to any "development" to which an immanent telos gives unity. And in fact all cultures have high periods, in which a particular civilization is marked by special achievements in all fields. Thus the general value concept of the classical becomes, via its particular historical fulfilment, again a general historical stylistic concept.

Although this is an understandable development, the historicization of the concept also involves its uprooting, and that is why historical consciousness, when it started to engage in self-criticism, reinstated the normative element in the concept of the classical and the historical uniqueness of its fulfilment. Every "new humanism" shares, with the first and oldest, the awareness of being directly committed to its model which, as something past, is unattainable and yet present. Thus there culminates in the classical a general character of historical being, preservation amid the ruins of time. It is the general nature of tradition that only that of the past which is preserved offers the possibility of historical knowledge. The classical, however, as Hegel says, is "that which signifies itself and hence also interprets itself."[13] But that means ultimately that the classical is what is preserved precisely because it signifies and interprets itself: i.e., that which speaks in such a way that it is not a statement about what is past, a mere testimony to something that still needs to be interpreted, but says something to the present as if it were said specially to it. What we call "classical" does not first require the overcoming of historical distance, for in its own constant communication it does overcome it. The classical, then, is certainly "timeless," but this timelessness is a mode of historical being.

Of course this does not exclude the fact that works regarded as classical present tasks of historical understanding to a developed historical consciousness that is aware of the historical distance. It is not the aim of the historical consciousness to use the classical model in the direct

[12]Thus the *Dialogus de oratoribus,* rightly, received special attention in the Naumburg discussions on the classical. The reasons for the decline of rhetoric include the recognition of its former greatness, i.e., a normative awareness. B. Snell is correct when he points out that the historical stylistic concepts of "baroque," "archaic" etc all presuppose a relation to the normative concept of the classical and have only gradually lost their pejorative sense: "Wesen und Wirklichkeit des Menschen." *Festschrift für H. Plessner,* p. 333ff. [Au.] Callimachus was a Greek poet and grammarian who flourished around 250 B.C. Cornelius Tacitus, the great Roman historian (ca. 55–120), also wrote a *Dialogue on Orators* analyzing the causes of the decay of eloquence under the Roman empire. [Ed.]

[13]Hegel, *Ästhetik* II, 3. [Au.]

way of Palladio or Corneille,[14] but to know it as an historical phenomenon that can be understood solely in terms of its own time. But this understanding will always be more than the mere historical construction of the past "world" to which the work belongs. Our understanding will always include consciousness of our belonging to that world. And correlative to this is the fact that the work belongs to our world.

This is just what the word "classical" means, that the duration of the power of a work to speak directly is fundamentally unlimited.[15] However much the concept of the classical expresses distance and unattainability and is part of cultural awareness, the phrase "classical culture" still expresses something of the continuing validity of the classical. Cultural awareness manifests an element of ultimate community and sharing in the world out of which a classical work speaks.

This discussion of the concept of the classical does not lay claim to any independent significance, but serves only to evoke a general question, namely: Does this kind of historical fusion of the past with the present that characterizes what is classical, ultimately lie at the base of the whole historical attitude as its effective substratum? Whereas romantic hermeneutics had taken human nature as the unhistorical substratum of its theory of understanding and hence had freed the connatural interpreter from all historical limitations, the self-criticism of historical consciousness leads finally to seeing historical movement not only in process, but also in understanding itself. Understanding is not to be thought of so much as an action of one's subjectivity, but as the placing of oneself within a process of tradition, in which past and present are constantly fused. This is what must be expressed in hermeneutical theory, which is far too dominated by the idea of a process, a method.

[14]Andrea Palladio, Italian architect (1518–1580), produced an enormously influential four-volume folio on classical architecture that in the next century brought in the neoclassical style. Pierre Corneille, French playwright and critic (1606–1684), had a similarly classicizing impact on European drama. [Ed.]

[15]Friedrich Schlegel (*Fragmente*, Minor 20) draws the hermeneutical consequence: "A classical work of literature can never be completely understood. But those who are educated and educating themselves must always desire to learn more from it." [Au.]

(iii) The Hermeneutic Significance of Temporal Distance

Let us consider first how hermeneutics sets about its work. What follows for understanding from the hermeneutic condition of belonging to a tradition? We remember here the hermeneutical rule that we must understand the whole in terms of the detail and the detail in terms of the whole. This principle stems from ancient rhetoric, and modern hermeneutics has taken it and applied it to the art of understanding. It is a circular relationship in both cases. The anticipation of meaning in which the whole is envisaged becomes explicit understanding in that the parts, that are determined by the whole, themselves also determine this whole.

We know this from the learning of ancient languages. We learn that we must "construe" a sentence before we attempt to understand the individual parts of the sentence in their linguistic meaning. But this process of construing is itself already governed by an expectation of meaning that follows from the context of what has gone before. It is also necessary for this expected meaning to be adjusted if the text calls for it. This means, then, that the expectation changes and that the text acquires the unity of a meaning from another expected meaning. Thus the movement of understanding is constantly from the whole to the part and back to the whole. Our task is to extend in concentric circles the unity of the understood meaning. The harmony of all the details with the whole is the criterion of correct understanding. The failure to achieve this harmony means that understanding has failed.

Schleiermacher differentiated this hermeneutic circle of part and whole in both its objective and its subjective aspect. As the single word belongs within the total context of the sentence, so the single text belongs within the total context of a writer's work, and the latter within the whole of the particular literary genre or of literature. At the same time, however, the same text, as a manifestation of a creative moment, belongs to the whole of its author's inner life. Full understanding can take place only within this objective and subjective whole. Following this theory, Dilthey . . . is applying to the historical world what has always been a principle of all textual interpretation: namely, that a text must be understood in terms of itself.

The question is, however, whether this is an adequate account of the circular movement of understanding. Here we must go back to the result of our analysis of Schleiermacher's hermeneutics. We may set aside Schleiermacher's ideas on subjective interpretation. When we try to understand a text, we do not try to recapture the author's attitude of mind but, if this is the terminology we are to use, we try to recapture the perspective within which he has formed his views. But this means simply that we try to accept the objective validity of what he is saying. If we want to understand, we shall try to make his arguments even more cogent. This happens even in conversation, so how much truer is it of the understanding of what is written down that we are moving in a dimension of meaning that is intelligible in itself and as such offers no reason for going back to the subjectivity of the author. It is the task of hermeneutics to clarify this miracle of understanding, which is not a mysterious communion of souls, but a sharing of a common meaning.

But even the objective side of this circle, as Schleiermacher describes it, does not reach the heart of the matter. We have seen that the goal of all communication and understanding is agreement concerning the object. Hence the task of hermeneutics has always been to establish agreement where it had failed to come about or been disturbed in some way. The history of hermeneutics can offer a confirmation of this if, for example, we think of Augustine, who sought to relate the christian gospel to the old testament, or of early protestantism, which faced the same problem or, finally, the age of the enlightenment, when it is almost like a renunciation of agreement to seek to acquire "full understanding" of a text only by means of historical interpretation. It is something qualitatively new when romanticism and Schleiermacher ground a universal historical consciousness by no longer seeing the binding form of tradition, from which they come and in which they stand, as the firm foundation of all hermeneutical endeavor.

One of the immediate predecessors of Schleiermacher, Friedrich Ast,[16] still had a view of hermeneutical work that was markedly concerned with content, in that, for him, its purpose was to establish harmony between the world of classical antiquity and christianity, between a newly discovered genuine antiquity and the christian tradition. This is something new, in comparison with the enlightenment, in that this hermeneutics no longer accepts or rejects tradition in accord with the criterion of natural reason. But in its attempt to bring about a meaningful agreement between the two traditions to which it sees itself as belonging, this kind of hermeneutics is still pursuing the task of all preceding hermeneutics, namely to achieve in understanding agreement in content.

In going beyond the "particularity" of this reconciliation of the ancient classical world and christianity, Schleiermacher and, following him, nineteenth-century science, conceive the task of hermeneutics in a way that is formally universal. They were able to harmonize it with the natural sciences' ideal of objectivity, but only by ignoring the concentration of historical consciousness in hermeneutical theory.

Heidegger's description and existential account of the hermeneutic circle constitutes in contrast a decisive turning-point. The hermeneutic theory of the nineteenth century often spoke of the circular structure of understanding, but always within the framework of a formal relation of the part and the whole or its subjective reflex, the intuitive anticipation of the whole and its subsequent articulation in the parts. According to this theory, the circular movement of understanding runs backwards and forwards along the text and disappears when it is perfectly understood. This view of understanding culminated logically in Schleiermacher's theory of the divinatory act, by means of which one places oneself entirely within the writer's mind and from there resolves

[16]Georg Anton Friedrich Ast, German philosopher (1778–1841), was best known as an editor of Plato and a critic of the Platonic canon. [Ed.]

all that is strange and unusual about the text. As against this approach, Heidegger describes the circle in such a way that the understanding of the text remains permanently determined by the anticipatory movement of fore-understanding. The circle of the whole and the part is not dissolved in perfect understanding but, on the contrary, is most fully realized.

The circle, then, is not formal in nature, it is neither subjective nor objective, but describes understanding as the interplay of the movement of tradition and the movement of the interpreter. The anticipation of meaning that governs our understanding of a text is not an act of subjectivity, but proceeds from the communality that binds us to the tradition. But this is contained in our relation to tradition, in the constant process of education. Tradition is not simply a precondition into which we come, but we produce it ourselves, inasmuch as we understand, participate in the evolution of tradition and hence further determine it ourselves. Thus the circle of understanding is not a "methodological" circle, but describes an ontological structural element in understanding.

The significance of this circle, which is fundamental to all understanding, has a further hermeneutic consequence which I may call the "fore-conception of completion." But this, too, is obviously a formal condition of all understanding. It states that only what really constitutes a unity of meaning is intelligible. So when we read a text we always follow this complete presupposition of completion, and only when it proves inadequate, i.e., the text is not intelligible, do we start to doubt the transmitted text and seek to discover in what way it can be remedied. The rules of such textual criticism can be left aside, for the important thing to note is that their proper application cannot be detached from the understanding of the textual content.

The anticipation of completion that guides all our understanding is, then, always specific in content. Not only is an immanent unity of meaning guiding the reader assumed, but his understanding is likewise guided by the constant transcendent expectations of meaning which proceed from the relation to the truth of what is being said. Just as the recipient of a letter understands the news that it contains and first sees things with the eyes of the person who wrote the letter, i.e., considers what he writes as true, and is not trying to understand the alien meanings of the letter writer, so we understand texts that have been handed down to us on the basis of expectations of meaning which are drawn from our own anterior relation to the subject. And just as we believe the news reported by a correspondent because he was present or is better informed, we are fundamentally open to the possibility that the writer of a transmitted text is better informed than we are, with our previously formed meaning. It is only when the attempt to accept what he has said as true fails that we try to "understand" the text, psychologically or historically, as another's meaning.[17] The anticipation of completion, then, contains not only this formal element that a text should fully express its meaning, but also that what it says should be the whole truth.

We see here again that understanding means, primarily, to understand the content of what is said, and only secondarily to isolate and understand another's meaning as such. Hence the first of all hermeneutic requirements remains one's own fore-understanding, which proceeds from being concerned with the same subject. It is this that determines what unified meaning can be realized and hence the application of the anticipation of completion.[18]

[17]In a lecture on aesthetic judgment at a conference in Venice in 1958 I tried to show that it too, like historical judgment, is secondary in character and confirms the "anticipation of completion." (It appeared in the *Rivista di Estetica,* M A III, 1958, under the title "Zur Fragwürdigkeit des ästhetischen Bewusstseins"). [Au.]

[18]There is one exception to this anticipation of completion, namely the case of writing that is presenting something in disguise, e.g. a *roman à clef.* This presents one of the most difficult hermeneutical problems (cf the interesting remarks by Leo Strauss in *Persecution and the Art of Writing*). This exceptional hermeneutical case is of special significance, in that it goes beyond interpretation of meaning in the same way as when historical source criticism goes back behind the tradition. Although the task here is not an historical, but an hermeneutical one, it can be performed only by using understanding of the subject as a key to discover what is behind the disguise — just as in conversation we understand irony to the extent to which we are in agreement on the subject with

Thus the meaning of the connection with tradition, i.e., the element of tradition in our historical, hermeneutical attitude, is fulfilled in the fact that we share fundamental prejudices with tradition. Hermeneutics must start from the position that a person seeking to understand something has a relation to the object that comes into language in the transmitted text and has, or acquires, a connection with the tradition out of which the text speaks. On the other hand, hermeneutical consciousness is aware that it cannot be connected with this object in some self-evident, questioned way, as is the case with the unbroken stream of a tradition. There is a polarity of familiarity and strangeness on which hermeneutic work is based: only that this polarity is not to be seen, psychologically, with Schleiermacher, as the tension that conceals the mystery of individuality, but truly hermeneutically, i.e., in regard to what has been said: the language in which the text addresses us, the story that it tells us. Here too there is a tension. The place between strangeness and familiarity that a transmitted text has for us is that intermediate place between being an historically intended separate object and being part of a tradition. The true home of hermeneutics is in this intermediate area.

It follows from this intermediate position in which hermeneutics operates that its work is not to develop a procedure of understanding, but to clarify the conditions in which understanding takes place. But these conditions are not of the nature of a "procedure" or a method, which the interpreter must of himself bring to bear on the text, but rather they must be given. The prejudices and fore-meanings in the mind of the interpreter are not at his free disposal. He is not able to separate in advance the productive prejudices that make understanding possible from the prejudices that hinder understanding and lead to misunderstandings.

This separation, rather, must take place in the understanding itself, and hence hermeneutics must ask how it happens. But this means it must place in the foreground what has remained entirely peripheral in previous hermeneutics: temporal distance and its significance for understanding.

This point can be clarified by comparing it with the hermeneutic-theory of romanticism. We shall recall that the latter conceived understanding as the reproduction of an original production. Hence it was possible to say that one should be able to understand an author better than he understood himself. We examined the origin of this statement and its connection with the aesthetics of genius, but must now come back to it, as our present inquiry lends it a new importance.

That subsequent understanding is superior to the original production and hence can be described as superior understanding does not depend so much on the conscious realization that places him on the same level as the author (as Schleiermacher said), but denotes rather an inevitable difference between the interpreter and the author that is created by the historical distance between them. Every age has to understand a transmitted text in its own way, for the text is part of the whole of the tradition in which the age takes an objective interest and in which it seeks to understand itself. The real meaning of a text, as it speaks to the interpreter, does not depend on the contingencies of the author and whom he originally wrote for. It certainly is not identical with them, for it is always partly determined also by the historical situation of the interpreter and hence by the totality of the objective course of history. A writer like Chladenius, who does not yet see understanding in terms of history, is saying the same thing in a naive, ingenuous way when he says that an author does not need to know the real meaning of what he has written, and hence the interpreter can, and must, often understand more than he. But this is of fundamental importance. Not occasionally only, but always, the meaning of a text goes beyond its author. That is why understanding is not merely a reproductive, but always a productive attitude as well. Perhaps it is not correct to refer to this productive element in understanding as "superior understanding." For this phrase is, as we have shown, the application of a principle of criticism from

the other person. Thus the apparent exception confirms that understanding involves agreement. [Au.]

the age of the enlightenment on the basis of the aesthetics of genius. Understanding is not, in fact, superior understanding, neither in the sense of superior knowledge of the subject because of clearer ideas, nor in the sense of fundamental superiority that the conscious has over the unconscious nature of creation. It is enough to say that we understand in a different way, if we understand at all.

This concept of understanding undoubtedly breaks right out of the circle drawn by romantic hermeneutics. Because what we are now concerned with is not individuality and what it thinks, but the objective truth of what is said, a text is not understood as a mere expression of life, but taken seriously in its claim to truth. That this is what is meant by "understanding" was once self-evident (we need only recall Chladenius).

But this dimension of the hermeneutical problem was discredited by historical consciousness and the psychological turn that Schleiermacher gave to hermeneutics, and could only be regained when the impasses of historicism appeared and led finally to the new development inspired chiefly, in my opinion, by Heidegger. For the hermeneutic importance of temporal distance could be understood only as a result of the ontological direction that Heidegger gave to understanding as an "existential" and of his temporal interpretation of the mode of being of there-being.

Time is no longer primarily a gulf to be bridged, because it separates, but it is actually the supportive ground of process in which the present is rooted. Hence temporal distance is not something that must be overcome. This was, rather, the naive assumption of historicism, namely that we must set ourselves within the spirit of the age, and think with its ideas and its thoughts, not with our own, and thus advance towards historical objectivity. In fact the important thing is to recognize the distance in time as a positive and productive possibility of understanding. It is not a yawning abyss, but is filled with the continuity of custom and tradition, in the light of which all that is handed down presents itself to us. Here it is not too much to speak of a genuine productivity of process. Everyone knows that curious impotence of our judgment where the distance in time has not given us sure criteria. Thus the judgment of contemporary works of art is desperately uncertain for the scientific consciousness. Obviously we approach such creations with the prejudices we are not in control of, presuppositions that have too great an influence over us for us to know about them; these can give to contemporary creations an extra resonance that does not correspond to their true content and their true significance. Only when all their relations to the present time have faded away can their real nature appear, so that the understanding of what is said in them can claim to be authoritative and universal.

It is this experience that has led to the idea in historical studies that objective knowledge can be arrived at only when there has been a certain historical distance. It is true that what a thing has to say, its intrinsic content, first appears only after it is divorced from the fleeting circumstances of its actuality. The positive conditions of historical understanding include the self-contained quality of an historical event, which allows it to appear as a whole, and its distance from the opinions concerning its import with which the present is filled. The implicit prerequisite of the historical method, then, is that the permanent significance of something can first be known objectively only when it belongs within a self-contained context. In other words, when it is dead enough to have only historical interest. Only then does it seem possible to exclude the subjective involvement of the observer. This is, in fact, a paradox, the epistemological counterpart to the old moral problem of whether anyone can be called happy before his death. Just as Aristotle showed what a sharpening of the powers of human judgment this kind of problem can bring about,[19] so hermeneutical reflection cannot fail to find here a sharpening of the methodological self-consciousness of science. It is true that certain hermeneutic requirements are automatically fulfilled when a historical context has become of no more than historical interest. Certain sources of error are automatically excluded. But it is questionable whether this is the end of the

[19] *Eth Nic* I, 7. [Au.]

hermeneutical problem. Temporal distance has obviously another meaning than that of the quenching of our interest in the object. It lets the true meaning of the object emerge fully. But the discovery of the true meaning of a text or a work of art is never finished; it is in fact an infinite process. Not only are fresh sources of error constantly excluded, so that the true meaning has filtered out of it all kinds of things that obscure it, but there emerge continually new sources of understanding, which reveal unsuspected elements of meaning. The temporal distance which performs the filtering process is not a closed dimension, but is itself undergoing constant movement and extension. And with the negative side of the filtering process brought about by temporal distance there is also the positive side, namely the value it has for understanding. It not only lets those prejudices that are of a particular and limited nature die away, but causes those that bring about genuine understanding to emerge clearly as such.

It is only this temporal distance that can solve the really critical question of hermeneutics, namely of distinguishing the true prejudices, by which we understand, from the false ones by which we misunderstand. Hence the hermeneutically trained mind will also include historical consciousness. It will make conscious the prejudices governing our own understanding, so that the text, as another's meaning, can be isolated and valued on its own. The isolation of a prejudice clearly requires the suspension of its validity for us. For so long as our mind is influenced by a prejudice, we do not know and consider it as a judgment. How then are we able to isolate it? It is impossible to make ourselves aware of it while it is constantly operating unnoticed, but only when it is, so to speak, stimulated. The encounter with a text from the past can provide this stimulus. For what leads to understanding must be something that has already asserted itself in its own separate validity. Understanding begins, as we have already said above,[20] when something addresses us. This is the primary hermeneutical condition. We now know what this requires, namely the fundamental suspension of our own prejudices. But all suspension of judgments and hence, a fortiori, of prejudices, has logically the structure of a question.

The essence of the question is the opening up, and keeping open, of possibilities. If a prejudice becomes questionable, in view of what another or a text says to us, this does not mean that it is simply set aside and the other writing or the other person accepted as valid in its place. It shows, rather, the naiveté of historical objectivism to accept this disregarding of ourselves as what actually happens. In fact our own prejudice is properly brought into play through its being at risk. Only through its being given full play is it able to experience the other's claim to truth and make it possible for he himself to have full play.[21]

The naiveté of so called historicism consists in the fact that it does not undertake this reflection, and in trusting to its own methodological approach forgets its own historicality. We must here appeal from a badly understood historical thinking to one that can better perform the task of understanding. True historical thinking must take account of its own historicality. Only then will it not chase the phantom of an historical object which is the object of progressive research, but learn to see in the object the counterpart of itself and hence understand both. The true historical object is not an object at all, but the unity of the one and the other, a relationship in which exist both the reality of history and the reality of historical understanding. A proper hermeneutics would have to demonstrate the effectivity of history within understanding itself. I shall refer to this as "effective-history." Understanding is, essentially, an effective-historical relation.

(iv) The Principle of Effective-History

The fact that the interest of the historian is directed not only towards the historical phenomenon and the work that has been handed down but also, secondarily, towards their effect in history (which also includes the history of research) is regarded in general as a mere supplement to the

[20]See p. 680. [Ed.]

[21]In this passage the author plays on the German expressions *ins Spiel bringen, auf dem Spiele stehen* and *sich ausspielen.* [Tr.]

historical problematic that, from Hermann Grimm's *Raffael* to Gundolf and beyond, has given rise to many valuable insights. To this extent, effective-history is not new. But that this kind of effective-historical approach be required every time that a work of art or an element of the tradition is led from the twilight region between tradition and history to be seen clearly and openly in terms of its own meaning — this is a new demand (addressed not to research, but to methodological consciousness itself) that proceeds inevitably from the analysis of historical consciousness.

It is not, of course, a hermeneutical requirement in the sense of the traditional concept of hermeneutics. I am not saying that historical inquiry should develop this effective-historical problematic that would be something separate from that which is concerned directly with the understanding of the work. The requirement is of a more theoretical kind. Historical consciousness must become aware that in the apparent immediacy with which it approaches a work of art or a tradition, there is also contained, albeit unrecognized and hence not allowed for, this other element. If we are trying to understand a historical phenomenon from the historical distance that is characteristic of our hermeneutical situation, we are always subject to the effects of effective-history. It determines in advance both what seems to us worth inquiring about and what will appear as an object of investigation, and we more or less forget half of what is really there — in fact, we miss the whole truth of the phenomenon when we take its immediate appearance as the whole truth.

In our understanding, which we imagine is so straightforward, we find that, by following the criterion of intelligibility, the other presents himself so much in terms of our own selves that there is no longer a question of self and other. Historical objectivism, in appealing to its critical method, conceals the involvement of the historical consciousness itself in effective-history. By the method of its foundational criticism it does away with the arbitrariness of cosy re-creations of the past, but it preserves its good conscience by failing to recognize those presuppositions — certainly not arbitrary, but still fundamental — that govern its own approach to understanding, and hence falls short of reaching that truth which, despite the finite nature of our understanding, could be reached. In this, historical objectivism resembles statistics, which are such an excellent means of propaganda because they let facts speak and hence simulate an objectivity that in reality depends on the legitimacy of the questions asked.

We are not saying, then, that effective-history must be developed as a new independent discipline ancillary to the human sciences, but that we should learn to understand ourselves better and recognize that in all understanding, whether we are expressly aware of it or not, the power of this effective-history is at work. When a naive faith in scientific method ignores its existence, there can be an actual deformation of knowledge. We know it from the history of science as the irrefutable proof of something that is obviously false. But looking at the whole situation, we see that the power of effective-history does not depend on its being recognized. This, precisely, is the power of history over finite human consciousness, namely that it prevails even where faith in method leads one to deny one's own historicality. The demand that we should become conscious of this effective-history is pressing because it is necessary for scientific consciousness. But this does not mean that it can be fulfilled in an absolute way. That we should become completely aware of effective-history is just as hybrid a statement as when Hegel speaks of absolute knowledge, in which history would become completely transparent to itself and hence be raised to the level of a concept. Rather, effective-historical consciousness is an element in the act of understanding itself and, as we shall see, is already operative in the choice of the right question to ask.

Effective-historical consciousness is primarily consciousness of the hermeneutical situation. To acquire an awareness of a situation is, however, always a task of particular difficulty. The very idea of a situation means that we are not standing outside it and hence are unable to have any objective knowledge of it.[22] We are always within the situation, and to throw light on it is a task that

[22]The structure of the concept of situation has been illuminated chiefly by K. Jaspers (*Die geistige Situation der Zeit*) and Erich Rothacker. [Au.]

is never entirely completed. This is true also of the hermeneutic situation, i.e., the situation in which we find ourselves with regard to the tradition that we are trying to understand. The illumination of this situation — effective-historical reflection — can never be completely achieved, but this is not due to a lack in the reflection, but lies in the essence of the historical being which is ours. To exist historically means that knowledge of oneself can never be complete. All self-knowledge proceeds from what is historically pregiven, what we call, with Hegel, "substance," because it is the basis of all subjective meaning and attitude and hence both prescribes and limits every possibility of understanding any tradition whatsoever in terms of its unique historical quality. This almost defines the aim of philosophical hermeneutics: its task is to move back along the path of Hegel's phenomenology of mind until we discover in all that is subjective the substantiality that determines it.

Every finite present has its limitations. We define the concept of "situation" by saying that it represents a standpoint that limits the possibility of vision. Hence an essential part of the concept of situation is the concept of "horizon." The horizon is the range of vision that includes everything that can be seen from a particular vantage point. Applying this to the thinking mind, we speak of narrowness of horizon, of the possible expansion of horizon, of the opening up of new horizons etc. The word has been used in philosophy since Nietzsche and Husserl[23] to characterize the way in which thought is tied to its finite determination, and the nature of the law of the expansion of the range of vision. A person who has no horizon is a man who does not see far enough and hence overvalues what is nearest to him. Contrariwise, to have an horizon means not to be limited to what is nearest, but to be able to see beyond it. A person who has an horizon knows the relative significance of everything within this horizon, as near or far, great or small. Similarly, the working out of the hermeneutical situation means the achievement of the right horizon of inquiry for the questions evoked by the encounter with tradition.

In the sphere of historical understanding we also like to speak of horizons, especially when referring to the claim of historical consciousness to see the past in terms of its own being, not in terms of our contemporary criteria and prejudices, but within its own historical horizon. The task of historical understanding also involves acquiring the particular historical horizon, so that what we are seeking to understand can be seen in its true dimensions. If we fail to place ourselves in this way within the historical horizon out of which tradition speaks, we shall misunderstand the significance of what it has to say to us. To this extent it seems a legitimate hermeneutical requirement to place ourselves in the other situation in order to understand it. We may ask, however, whether this does not mean that we are failing in the understanding that is asked of us. The same is true of a conversation that we have with someone simply in order to get to know him, i.e., to discover his standpoint and his horizon. This is not a true conversation, in the sense that we are not seeking agreement concerning an object, but the specific contents of the conversation are only a means to get to know the horizon of the other person. Examples are oral examinations, or some kinds of conversation between doctor and patient. The historical consciousness is clearly doing something similar when it places itself within the situation of the past and hence is able to acquire the right historical horizon. Just as in a conversation, when we have discovered the standpoint and horizon of the other person, his ideas become intelligible, without our necessarily having to agree with him, the person who thinks historically comes to understand the meaning of what has been handed down, without necessarily agreeing with it, or seeing himself in it.

In both cases, in our understanding we have as it were, withdrawn from the situation of trying to reach agreement. He himself cannot be reached. By including from the beginning the other person's standpoint in what he is saying to us, we

[23]Edmund Husserl's notion of the horizon, Gadamer explains earlier, "is not a rigid frontier, but something that moves with one and invites one to advance further." This subjective horizon intentionality, "which constitutes the unity and flow of experience, is paralleled by an equally comprehensive horizon intentionality on the objective side." (*Truth and Method,* p. 217). [Ed.]

are making our own standpoint safely unattainable. We have seen, in considering the origin of historical thinking, that in fact it makes this ambiguous transition from means to ends, i.e., it makes an end of what is only a means. The text that is understood historically is forced to abandon its claim that it is uttering something true. We think we understand when we see the past from a historical standpoint, i.e., place ourselves in the historical situation and seek to reconstruct the historical horizon. In fact, however, we have given up the claim to find, in the past, any truth valid and intelligible for ourselves. Thus this acknowledgment of the otherness of the other, which makes him the object of objective knowledge, involves the fundamental suspension of his claim to truth.

The question is, however, whether this description really corresponds to the hermeneutical phenomenon. Are there, then, two different horizons here, the horizon in which the person seeking to understand lives, and the particular historical horizon within which he places himself? Is it a correct description of the art of historical understanding to say that we are learning to place ourselves within alien horizons? Are there such things as closed horizons, in this sense? We recall Nietzsche's complaint against historicism that it destroyed the horizon bounded by myth in which alone a culture is able to live.[24] Is the horizon of one's own present time ever closed in this way, and can a historical situation be imagined that has this kind of closed horizon?

Or is this a romantic reflection, a kind of Robinson Crusoe dream of the historical enlightenment, the fiction of an unattainable island, as artificial as Crusoe himself for the alleged primary phenomenon of the solus ipse? Just as the individual is never simply an individual, because he is always involved with others, so too the closed horizon that is supposed to enclose a culture is an abstraction. The historical movement of human life consists in the fact that it is never utterly bound to any one standpoint, and hence can never have a truly closed horizon. The horizon is, rather, something into which we move and that moves with us. Horizons change for a person who is moving. Thus the horizon of the past, out of which all human life lives and which exists in the form of tradition, is always in motion. It is not historical consciousness that first sets the surrounding horizon in motion. But in it this motion becomes aware of itself.

When our historical consciousness places itself within historical horizons, this does not entail passing into alien worlds unconnected in any way with our own, but together they constitute the one great horizon that moves from within and, beyond the frontiers of the present, embraces the historical depths of our self-consciousness. It is, in fact, a single horizon that embraces everything contained in historical consciousness. Our own past, and that other past towards which our historical consciousness is directed, help to shape this moving horizon out of which human life always lives, and which determines it as tradition.

Understanding of the past, then, undoubtedly requires an historical horizon. But it is not the case that we acquire this horizon by placing ourselves within a historical situation. Rather, we must always already have a horizon in order to be able to place ourselves within a situation. For what do we mean by "placing ourselves" in a situation? Certainly not just disregarding ourselves. This is necessary, of course, in that we must imagine the other situation. But into this other situation we must also bring ourselves. Only this fulfils the meaning of "placing ourselves." If we place ourselves in the situation of someone else, for example, then we shall understand him, ie become aware of the otherness, the indissoluble individuality of the other person, by placing ourselves in his position.

This placing of ourselves is not the empathy of one individual for another, nor is it the application to another person of our own criteria, but it always involves the attainment of a higher universality that overcomes, not only our own particularity, but also that of the other. The concept of the "horizon" suggests itself because it expresses the wide, superior vision that the person who is seeking to understand must have. To ac-

[24]Nietzsche, *Unzeitgemässe Betrachtungen* II, at the beginning. [Au.]

quire a horizon means that one learns to look beyond what is close at hand — not in order to look away from it, but to see it better within a larger whole and in truer proportion. It is not a correct description of historical consciousness to speak, with Nietzsche, of the many changing horizons into which it teaches us to place ourselves. If we disregard ourselves in this way, we have no historical horizon. Nietzsche's view that historical study is deleterious to life is not directed, in fact, against historical consciousness as such, but against the self-alienation that it undergoes when it regards the method of modern historical science as its own true nature. We have already pointed out that a truly historical consciousness always sees its own present in such a way that it sees itself, as it sees the historically other, within the right circumstances. It requires a special effort to acquire an historical horizon. We are always affected, in hope and fear, by what is nearest to us, and hence approach, under its influence, the testimony of the past. Hence it is constantly necessary to inhibit the overhasty assimilation of the past to our own expectations of meaning. Only then will we be able to listen to the past in a way that enables it to make its own meaning heard.

We have shown above that this is a process of distinguishing. Let us consider what this idea of distinguishing involves. It is always reciprocal. Whatever is being distinguished must be distinguished from something which, in turn, must be distinguished from it. Thus all distinguishing also makes visible that from which something is distinguished. We have described this above as the operation of prejudices. We started by saying that a hermeneutical situation is determined by the prejudices that we bring with us. They constitute, then, the horizon of a particular present, for they represent that beyond which it is impossible to see. But now it is important to avoid the error of thinking that it is a fixed set of opinions and evaluations that determine and limit the horizon of the present, and that the otherness of the past can be distinguished from it as from a fixed ground.

In fact the horizon of the present is being continually formed, in that we have continually to test all our prejudices. An important part of this testing is the encounter with the past and the understanding of the tradition from which we come. Hence the horizon of the present cannot be formed without the past. There is no more an isolated horizon of the present than there are historical horizons. Understanding, rather, is always the fusion of these horizons which we imagine to exist by themselves. We know the power of this kind of fusion chiefly from earlier times and their naive attitude to themselves and their origin. In a tradition this process of fusion is continually going on, for there old and new continually grow together to make something of living value, without either being explicitly distinguished from the other.

If, however, there is no such thing as these horizons that are distinguished from one another, why do we speak of the fusion of horizons and not simply of the formation of the one horizon, whose bounds are set in the depths of tradition? To ask the question means that we are recognizing the special nature of the situation in which understanding becomes a scientific task, and that it is necessary to work out this situation as a hermeneutical situation. Every encounter with tradition that takes place within historical consciousness involves the experience of the tension between the text and the present. The hermeneutic task consists in not covering up this tension by attempting a naive assimilation but consciously bringing it out. This is why it is part of the hermeneutic approach to project an historical horizon that is different from the horizon of the present. Historical consciousness is aware of its own otherness and hence distinguishes the horizon of tradition from its own. On the other hand, it is itself, as we are trying to show, only something laid over a continuing tradition, and hence it immediately recombines what it has distinguished in order, in the unity of the historical horizon that it thus acquires, to become again one with itself.

The projecting of the historical horizon, then, is only a phase in the process of understanding, and does not become solidified into the self-alienation of a past consciousness, but is overtaken by our own present horizon of understanding. In the process of understanding there takes place a real fusing of horizons, which means that as the historical horizon is projected, it is simultaneously removed. We described the conscious act of this fusion as the task of the effective-historical consciousness. Although this task had been obscured by aesthetic historical positivism in the train of romantic hermeneutics, it is, in fact, the central problem of hermeneutics. It is the problem of application that exists in all understanding.

Susan Sontag

b. 1933 d. 2004

Susan Sontag was born in New York City but raised in Tucson, Arizona, and in Los Angeles. She began her college work at the University of California, Berkeley, but transferred to the University of Chicago, where she received her B.A. in philosophy in 1951, at the age of eighteen. She did graduate work in English and philosophy at Harvard, where she received her M.A., and further graduate study at Oxford and the Sorbonne. Sontag has taught at Harvard, the University of Connecticut, Rutgers, and Columbia, but has supported herself mainly through her books and periodical essays.

Though she resists being classified "primarily as an essayist," Sontag is usually regarded nevertheless as a literary and cultural critic, her two novels, shorter fiction, and screenplays notwithstanding. Like Lionel Trilling, Sontag seems to function as a cultural barometer. Her fiction, like his, seems to be generated by her cultural observations and critical ideas. But where Trilling was primarily concerned with demonstrating the continuity of the present with the past, Sontag — writing from the sixties to the present, rather than in the forties and fifties — has always appeared less concerned with the traditions than with the discontinuities of contemporary life.

One of Sontag's major roles, at the outset of her career at least, was as a conduit between America and Europe of avant-garde ideas and personalities. Theorists like Walter Benjamin and Roland Barthes, now canonical, were almost unknown in the United States when they were recommended by Sontag in 1964 as writers who "reveal the sensuous surface of art without mucking about in it" in Section 8 of "Against Interpretation." In other essays in the early 1960s, she called attention on this side of the Atlantic to writers like Nathalie Sarraute, Antonin Artaud, and Alain Robbe-Grillet.

But Sontag is not a typical literary critic. She does not wish to analyze and interpret a series of standard texts so much as to discuss the conditions for their appearance, and the cultural assumptions that underlie their production and their reception. The subjects that have most appealed to her are the marginal areas of art, which sketch in the boundaries of a culture and its perceptions: the "camp" sensibility, the pornographic imagination, illness as metaphor, and photography as an art form. Despite the variety of topics, Sontag's work, according to Susan Jeffords, "is of a piece. . . . No matter what form they take, Sontag asks the same questions — about the construction and resolution of identity, about manipulation and violence as a basis for social and aesthetic encounters, about the structure and function of cultural interpretation, about the inspiration of those outside accepted social boundaries — hoping that new answers will appear as a byproduct of new form. It is paradigmatic of Sontag's position as a modernist that they do not." Although she is not a reader-response critic in any of the usual senses of the term (see the introduction to Reader-Response Criticism, p. 917), Sontag is most strongly engaged by the question of how readers process texts, and by the cultural uses to which literature is put. This is the central concern in "Against Interpretation."

The core of the essay is the three short sentences in Section 5: "Real art has the capacity to make us nervous. By reducing the work of art to its content and then interpreting *that,* one tames the work of art. Interpretation makes art manageable, comfortable." Interpretation, for Sontag, is a vicious and cowardly form of translation, in which the work of art is stripped of its sensuous life and reduced to a bare statement, which is then processed through the categories of the various schools of criticism (Marxist, Freudian, Christian) into a message that is inevitably familiar, indeed always already known. Appreciative and analytical criticism — not the nasty judgmental kind — has thus become the most deadly enemy of art.

The reaction to "Against Interpretation" was predictably fierce, and not merely from the Freudians and Marxists whose oxen were explicitly gored. Representatives of the New Criticism, then enjoying its hegemony, objected that they had been making Sontag's point for her all along (in such essays as Cleanth Brooks's "The Heresy of Paraphrase"). In fact, Sontag's strictures would apply equally against the New Critics, who, while granting lip service to the primacy of form, had always treated poetry as a general statement (or pseudostatement) about the world, albeit an especially complex sort of statement, riffed by paradox, irony, ambiguity, and other tropes. In New Critical terminology, theme is a part of form — and thus Sontag's dichotomy of "form" and "content" might mislead one to think she favored that school of exegesis. In fact, for Sontag any *translation* of the text into other terms is a betrayal of that text, and the *thematization* of any text always reduces it to a subartistic level.

Since "Against Interpretation" was published, there have been at least a few faltering steps toward exploring the "erotics of art" Sontag mentions. In particular, much recent psychoanalytic theory (like that of Peter Brooks) have dropped the old dichotomy between latent and manifest content and attempted to discuss the form of the text as something other than a nicely wrapped container for fantasy and defense. Some new historicist and cultural critics have moved beyond the representative quality and the political tendency of the text. Nevertheless, since translation and thematization have always been the mainstay of academic criticism, Sontag could be certain to find, in the pages of almost every scholarly journal today, specimens of the same destructive, spiritually impoverished interpretation she rejects.

Selected Bibliography

Brooks, Peter. "Death of/as Metaphor." *Partisan Review* 46 (1979): 438–44.

Jeffords, Susan. "Susan Sontag." *Modern American Critics Since 1955*, ed. Gregory Jay. Detroit: Bruccoli-Clark-Layman, 1988.

Phillips, William. "Radical Styles." *Partisan Review* 36 (1969): 388–400.

Roudiez, Leon S. "Susan Sontag: Against the Ideological Grain." *World Literature Today* 57 (1983): 219–23.

Rubin, Louis D., Jr. "Susan Sontag and the Camp Followers." *Sewanee Review* 82 (1974): 503–10.

Shaw, Peter. "Two Afterthoughts on Susan Sontag." *Encounter* 58/59 (1982): 38–40.

Against Interpretation

Content is a glimpse of something, an encounter like a flash. It's very tiny — very tiny, content.

— WILLEM DE KOONING, in an interview

It is only shallow people who do not judge by appearances. The mystery of the world is the visible, not the invisible.

— OSCAR WILDE, in a letter

1

The earliest *experience* of art must have been that it was incantatory, magical; art was an instrument of ritual. (Cf. the paintings in the caves at Lascaux, Altamira, Niaux, La Pasiega, etc.) The earliest *theory* of art, that of the Greek philosophers, proposed that art was mimesis, imitation of reality.

It is at this point that the peculiar question of the *value* of art arose. For the mimetic theory, by its very terms, challenges art to justify itself.

Plato, who proposed the theory, seems to have done so in order to rule that the value of art is dubious. Since he considered ordinary material things as themselves mimetic objects, imitations of transcendent forms or structures, even the best painting of a bed would be only an "imitation of an imitation." For Plato, art is neither particularly useful (the painting of a bed is no good to sleep on), nor, in the strict sense, true. And Aristotle's arguments in defense of art do not really challenge Plato's view that all art is an elaborate *trompe l'oeil*,[1] and therefore a lie. But he does dispute Plato's idea that art is useless. Lie or no, art has a certain value according to Aristotle because it is a form of therapy. Art is useful, after all, Aristotle counters, medicinally useful in that it arouses and purges dangerous emotions.[2]

In Plato and Aristotle, the mimetic theory of art goes hand in hand with the assumption that art is always figurative. But advocates of the mimetic theory need not close their eyes to decorative and abstract art. The fallacy that art is necessarily a "realism" can be modified or scrapped without ever moving outside the problems delimited by the mimetic theory.

The fact is, all Western consciousness of and reflection upon art have remained within the confines staked out by the Greek theory of art as mimesis or representation. It is through this theory that art as such — above and beyond given works of art — becomes problematic, in need of defense. And it is the defense of art which gives birth to the odd vision by which something we have learned to call "form" is separated off from something we have learned to call "content," and to the well-intentioned move which makes content essential and form accessory.

Even in modern times, when most artists and critics have discarded the theory of art as representation of an outer reality in favor of the theory of art as subjective expression, the main feature of the mimetic theory persists. Whether we conceive of the work of art on the model of a picture (art as a picture of reality) or on the model of a statement (art as the statement of the artist), content still comes first. The content may have changed. It may now be less figurative, less lucidly realistic. But it is still assumed that a work of art *is* its content. Or, as it's usually put today, that a work of art by definition says something. ("What X is saying is . . . ," "What X is trying to say is . . . ," "What X said is . . ." etc., etc.)

2

None of us can ever retrieve that innocence before all theory when art knew no need to justify itself, when one did not ask of a work of art what it *said* because one knew (or thought one knew) what it *did*. From now to the end of consciousness, we are stuck with the task of defending art. We can only quarrel with one or another means of defense. Indeed, we have an obligation to overthrow any means of defending and justifying art which becomes particularly obtuse or onerous or insensitive to contemporary needs and practice.

[1]Deception of the eye. [Ed.]

[2]Sontag conflates Aristotle's *Poetics* with the reference to *katharsis* in the *Politics*, quoted in the introduction to Aristotle; see p. 41. [Ed.]

This is the case, today, with the very idea of content itself. Whatever it may have been in the past, the idea of content is today mainly a hindrance, a nuisance, a subtle or not so subtle philistinism.

Though the actual developments in many arts may seem to be leading us away from the idea that a work of art is primarily its content, the idea still exerts an extraordinary hegemony. I want to suggest that this is because the idea is now perpetuated in the guise of a certain way of encountering works of art thoroughly ingrained among most people who take any of the arts seriously. What the overemphasis on the idea of content entails is the perennial, never consummated project of *interpretation.* And, conversely, it is the habit of approaching works of art in order to *interpret* them that sustains the fancy that there really is such a thing as the content of a work of art.

3

Of course, I don't mean interpretation in the broadest sense, the sense in which Nietzsche (rightly) says, "There are no facts, only interpretations." By interpretation, I mean here a conscious act of the mind which illustrates a certain code, certain "rules" of interpretation.

Directed to art, interpretation means plucking a set of elements (the X, the Y, the Z, and so forth) from the whole work. The task of interpretation is virtually one of translation. The interpreter says, Look, don't you see that X is really — or, really means — A? That Y is really B? That Z is really C?

What situation could prompt this curious project for transforming a text? History gives us the materials for an answer. Interpretation first appears in the culture of late classical antiquity, when the power and credibility of myth had been broken by the "realistic" view of the world introduced by scientific enlightenment. Once the question that haunts post-mythic consciousness — that of the *seemliness* of religious symbols — had been asked, the ancient texts were, in their pristine form, no longer acceptable. Then interpretation was summoned, to reconcile the ancient texts to "modern" demands. Thus, the Stoics, to accord with their view that the gods had to be moral, allegorized away the rude features of Zeus and his boisterous clan in Homer's epics. What Homer really designated by the adultery of Zeus with Leto, they explained, was the union between power and wisdom. In the same vein, Philo of Alexandria interpreted the literal historical narratives of the Hebrew Bible as spiritual paradigms. The story of the exodus from Egypt, the wandering in the desert for forty years, and the entry into the promised land, said Philo, was really an allegory of the individual soul's emancipation, tribulations, and final deliverance.[3] Interpretation thus presupposes a discrepancy between the clear meaning of the text and the demands of (later) readers. It seeks to resolve that discrepancy. The situation is that for some reason a text has become unacceptable; yet it cannot be discarded. Interpretation is a radical strategy for conserving an old text, which is thought too precious to repudiate, by revamping it. The interpreter, without actually erasing or rewriting the text, *is* altering it. But he can't admit to doing this. He claims to be only making it intelligible, by disclosing its true meaning. However far the interpreters alter the text (another notorious example is the Rabbinic and Christian "spiritual" interpretations of the clearly erotic Song of Songs), they must claim to be reading off a sense that is already there.

Interpretation in our own time, however, is even more complex. For the contemporary zeal for the project of interpretation is often prompted not by piety toward the troublesome text (which may conceal an aggression), but by an open aggressiveness, an overt contempt for appearances. The old style of interpretation was insistent, but respectful; it erected another meaning on top of the literal one. The modern style of interpretation excavates, and as it excavates, destroys; it digs "behind" the text, to find a sub-text which is the true one. The most celebrated and influential modern doctrines, those of Marx and Freud, actually amount to elaborate systems of hermeneutics, aggressive and impious theories of interpretation. All observable phenomena are bracketed, in Freud's phrase, as *manifest content*. This manifest content must be probed and pushed aside to

[3]Dante's redaction of Philo's system appears in his letter to Can Grande della Scala, p. 120. [Ed.]

find the true meaning — the *latent content* — beneath.[4] For Marx, social events like revolutions and wars; for Freud, the events of individual lives (like neurotic symptoms and slips of the tongue) as well as texts (like a dream or a work of art) — all are treated as occasions for interpretation. According to Marx and Freud, these events only *seem* to be intelligible. Actually, they have no meaning without interpretation. To understand *is* to interpret. And to interpret is to restate the phenomenon, in effect to find an equivalent for it.

Thus, interpretation is not (as most people assume) an absolute value, a gesture of mind situated in some timeless realm of capabilities. Interpretation must itself be evaluated, within a historical view of human consciousness. In some cultural contexts, interpretation is a liberating act. It is a means of revising, of transvaluing, of escaping the dead past. In other cultural contexts, it is reactionary, impertinent, cowardly, stifling.

4

Today is such a time, when the project of interpretation is largely reactionary, stifling. Like the fumes of the automobile and of heavy industry which befoul the urban atmosphere, the effusion of interpretations of art today poisons our sensibilities. In a culture whose already classical dilemma is the hypertrophy of the intellect at the expense of energy and sensual capability, interpretation is the revenge of the intellect upon art.

Even more. It is the revenge of the intellect upon the world. To interpret is to impoverish, to deplete the world — in order to set up a shadow world of "meanings." It is to turn *the* world into *this* world. ("This world"! As if there were any other.)

The world, our world, is depleted, impoverished enough. Away with all duplicates of it, until we again experience more immediately what we have.

[4]See the introduction to Psychoanalytic Theory, p. 1014. [Ed.]

5

In most modern instances, interpretation amounts to the philistine refusal to leave the work of art alone. Real art has the capacity to make us nervous. By reducing the work of art to its content and then interpreting *that,* one tames the work of art. Interpretation makes art manageable, comfortable.

This philistinism of interpretation is more rife in literature than in any other art. For decades now, literary critics have understood it to be their task to translate the elements of the poem or play or novel or story into something else. Sometimes a writer will be so uneasy before the naked power of his art that he will install within the work itself — albeit with a little shyness, a touch of the good taste of irony — the clear and explicit interpretation of it. Thomas Mann is an example of such an overcooperative author. In the case of more stubborn authors, the critic is only too happy to perform the job.

The work of Kafka, for example, has been subjected to a mass ravishment by no less than three armies of interpreters. Those who read Kafka as a social allegory see case studies of the frustrations and insanity of modern bureaucracy and its ultimate issuance in the totalitarian state. Those who read Kafka as a psychoanalytic allegory see desperate revelations of Kafka's fear of his father, his castration anxieties, his sense of his own impotence, his thralldom to his dreams. Those who read Kafka as a religious allegory explain that K. in *The Castle* is trying to gain access to heaven, that Joseph K. in *The Trial* is being judged by the inexorable and mysterious justice of God. . . . Another *oeuvre* that has attracted interpreters like leeches is that of Samuel Beckett. Beckett's delicate dramas of the withdrawn consciousness — pared down to essentials, cut off, often represented as physically immobilized — are read as a statement about modern man's alienation from meaning or from God, or as an allegory of psychopathology.

Proust, Joyce, Faulkner, Rilke, Lawrence, Gide . . . one could go on citing author after author; the list is endless of those around whom thick encrustations of interpretation have taken hold. But it should be noted that interpretation is not simply the compliment that mediocrity pays to genius. It is, indeed, *the* modern way of understanding something, and is applied to works of every quality. Thus, in the notes that Elia Kazan published on his production of *A Streetcar Named Desire,* it becomes clear that, in order to direct the play, Kazan had to discover that Stanley Kowalski represented the sensual and vengeful barbarism that was engulfing our culture, while Blanche Du Bois was Western civilization, poetry, delicate apparel, dim lighting, refined feelings and all, though a little the worse for wear to be sure. Tennessee Williams's forceful psychological melodrama now became intelligible: it was *about* something, about the decline of Western civilization. Apparently, were it to go on being a play about a handsome brute named Stanley Kowalski and a faded mangy belle named Blanche Du Bois, it would not be manageable.

6

It doesn't matter whether artists intend, or don't intend, for their works to be interpreted. Perhaps Tennessee Williams thinks *Streetcar* is about what Kazan thinks it to be about. It may be that Cocteau in *The Blood of a Poet* and in *Orpheus* wanted the elaborate readings which have been given these films, in terms of Freudian symbolism and social critique. But the merit of these works certainly lies elsewhere than in their "meanings." Indeed, it is precisely to the extent that Williams's plays and Cocteau's films do suggest these portentous meanings that they are defective, false, contrived, lacking in conviction.

From interviews, it appears that Resnais and Robbe-Grillet consciously designed *Last Year at Marienbad* to accommodate a multiplicity of equally plausible interpretations. But the temptation to interpret *Marienbad* should be resisted. What matters in *Marienbad* is the pure, untranslatable, sensuous immediacy of some of its images, and its rigorous if narrow solutions to certain problems of cinematic form.

Again, Ingmar Bergman may have meant the tank rumbling down the empty night street in *The Silence* as a phallic symbol. But if he did, it was a foolish thought. ("Never trust the teller, trust the tale," said Lawrence.) Taken as a brute object, as an immediate sensory equivalent for the mysterious abrupt armored happenings going on inside the hotel, that sequence with the tank is the most striking moment in the film. Those who reach for a Freudian interpretation of the tank are only expressing their lack of response to what is there on the screen.

It is always the case that interpretation of this type indicates a dissatisfaction (conscious or unconscious) with the work, a wish to replace it by something else.

Interpretation, based on the highly dubious theory that a work of art is composed of items of content, violates art. It makes art into an article for use, for arrangement into a mental scheme of categories.

7

Interpretation does not, of course, always prevail. In fact, a great deal of today's art may be understood as motivated by a flight from interpretation. To avoid interpretation, art may become parody. Or it may become abstract. Or it may become ("merely") decorative. Or it may become non-art.

The flight from interpretation seems particularly a feature of modern painting. Abstract painting is the attempt to have, in the ordinary sense, no content; since there is no content, there can be no interpretation. Pop Art works by the opposite means to the same result; using a content so blatant, so "what it is," it, too, ends by being uninterpretable.

A great deal of modern poetry as well, starting from the great experiments of French poetry (including the movement that is misleadingly called Symbolism) to put silence into poems and to reinstate the *magic* of the word, has escaped from the rough grip of interpretation. The most recent revolution in contemporary taste in poetry — the revolution that has deposed Eliot and elevated Pound — represents a turning away from content in poetry in the old sense, an impatience with what made modern poetry prey to the zeal of interpreters.

I am speaking mainly of the situation in America, of course. Interpretation runs rampant here in those arts with a feeble and negligible avant-garde: fiction and the drama. Most American novelists and playwrights are really either journalists or gentlemen sociologists and psychologists. They are writing the literary equivalent of program music. And so rudimentary, uninspired, and stagnant has been the sense of what might be done with *form* in fiction and drama that even when the content isn't simply information, news, it is still peculiarly visible, handier, more exposed. To the extent that novels and plays (in America), unlike poetry and painting and music, don't reflect any interesting concern with changes in their form, these arts remain prone to assault by interpretation.

But programmatic avant-gardism — which has meant, mostly, experiments with form at the expense of content — is not the only defense against the infestation of art by interpretations. At least, I hope not. For this would be to commit art to being perpetually on the run. (It also perpetuates the very distinction between form and content which is, ultimately, an illusion.) Ideally, it is possible to elude the interpreters in another way, by making works of art whose surface is so unified and clean, whose momentum is so rapid, whose address is so direct that the work can be . . . just what it is. Is this possible now? It does happen in films, I believe. This is why cinema is the most alive, the most exciting, the most important of all art forms right now. Perhaps the way one tells how alive a particular art form is, is by the latitude it gives for making mistakes in it, and still being good. For example, a few of the films of Bergman — though crammed with lame messages about the modern spirit, thereby inviting interpretations — still triumph over the pretentious intentions of their director. In *Winter Light* and *The Silence,* the beauty and visual sophistication of the images subvert before our eyes the callow pseudo-intellectuality of the story and some of the dialogue. (The most remarkable instance of this sort of discrepancy is the work of D. W. Griffith.) In good films, there is always a directness that entirely frees us from the itch to interpret. Many old Hollywood films, like those of Cukor, Walsh, Hawks, and countless other directors, have this liberating anti-symbolic quality, no less than the best work of the new European directors, like Truffaut's *Shoot the Piano Player* and *Jules and Jim,* Godard's *Breathless* and *Vivre Sa Vie,* Antonioni's *L'Avventura,* and Olmi's *The Fiancés.*

The fact that films have not been overrun by interpreters is in part due simply to the newness of cinema as an art. It also owes to the happy accident that films for such a long time were just movies; in other words, that they were understood to be part of mass, as opposed to high, culture, and were left alone by most people with minds. Then, too, there is always something other than content in the cinema to grab hold of, for those who want to analyze. For the cinema, unlike the novel, possesses a vocabulary of forms — the explicit, complex, and discussable technology of camera movements, cutting, and composition of the frame that goes into the making of a film.

8

What kind of criticism, of commentary on the arts, is desirable today? For I am not saying that works of art are ineffable, that they cannot be described or paraphrased. They can be. The question is how. What would criticism look like that would serve the work of art, not usurp its place?

What is needed, first, is more attention to form in art. If excessive stress on *content* provokes the arrogance of interpretation, more extended and more thorough descriptions of *form* would silence. What is needed is a vocabulary — a descriptive, rather than prescriptive, vocabulary — for forms.[5] The best criticism, and it is uncommon, is of this sort that dissolves considerations of content into those of form. On film, drama, and painting respectively, I can think of Erwin Panofsky's essay, "Style and Medium in the Motion Pictures," Northrop Frye's essay "A Conspectus of Dramatic Genres," Pierre Francastel's

[5]One of the difficulties is that our idea of form is spatial (the Greek metaphors for form are all derived from notions of space). This is why we have a more ready vocabulary of forms for the spatial than for the temporal arts. The exception among the temporal arts, of course, is the drama; perhaps this is because the drama is a narrative (i.e., temporal) form that extends itself visually and pictorially, upon a stage. . . . What we don't have yet is a poetics of the novel, any clear notion of the forms of narration. Perhaps film criticism will be the occasion of a breakthrough here, since films are primarily a visual form, yet they are also a subdivision of literature. [Au.]

essay "The Destruction of a Plastic Space." Roland Barthes's book *On Racine* and his two essays on Robbe-Grillet are examples of formal analysis applied to the work of a single author. (The best essays in Erich Auerbach's *Mimesis,* like "The Scar of Odysseus," are also of this type.) An example of formal analysis applied simultaneously to genre and author is Walter Benjamin's essay, "The Story Teller: Reflections on the Works of Nicolai Leskov."

Equally valuable would be acts of criticism which would supply a really accurate, sharp, loving description of the appearance of a work of art. This seems even harder to do than formal analysis. Some of Manny Farber's film criticism, Dorothy Van Ghent's essay "The Dickens World: A View from Todgers'," Randall Jarrell's essay on Walt Whitman are among the rare examples of what I mean. These are essays which reveal the sensuous surface of art without mucking about in it.

9

Transparence is the highest, most liberating value in art — and in criticism — today. Transparence means experiencing the luminousness of the thing in itself, of things being what they are. This is the greatness of, for example, the films of Bresson and Ozu and Renoir's *The Rules of the Game.*

Once upon a time (say, for Dante), it must have been a revolutionary and creative move to design works of art so that they might be experienced on several levels. Now it is not. It reinforces the principle of redundancy that is the principal affliction of modern life.

Once upon a time (a time when high art was scarce), it must have been a revolutionary and creative move to interpret works of art. Now it is not. What we decidedly do not need now is further to assimilate Art into Thought, or (worse yet) Art into Culture.

Interpretation takes the sensory experience of the work of art for granted, and proceeds from there. This cannot be taken for granted, now. Think of the sheer multiplication of works of art available to every one of us, superadded to the conflicting tastes and odors and sights of the urban environment that bombard our senses. Ours is a culture based on excess, on overproduction; the result is a steady loss of sharpness in our sensory experience. All the conditions of modern life — its material plenitude, its sheer crowdedness — conjoin to dull our sensory faculties. And it is in the light of the condition of our senses, our capacities (rather than those of another age), that the task of the critic must be assessed.

What is important now is to recover our senses. We must learn to *see* more, to *hear* more, to *feel* more.

Our task is not to find the maximum amount of content in a work of art, much less to squeeze more content out of the work than is already there. Our task is to cut back content so that we can see the thing at all.

The aim of all commentary on art now should be to make works of art — and, by analogy, our own experience — more, rather than less, real to us. The function of criticism should be to show *how it is what it is,* even *that it is what it is,* rather than to show *what it means.*

10

In place of a hermeneutics we need an erotics of art.

Part Two

CONTEMPORARY TRENDS IN LITERARY CRITICISM

1

FORMALISMS: RUSSIAN FORMALISM, NEW CRITICISM, NEO-ARISTOTELIANISM

Habitualization devours works, clothes, furniture, one's wife, and the fear of war. . . . And art exists that one may recover the sensation of life; it exists to make one feel things, to make the stone stony. *The purpose of art is to impart the sensation of things as they are perceived and not as they are known.*
— VICTOR SHKLOVSKY

Finding its proper symbol, defined and refined by the participating metaphors, the theme becomes a part of the reality in which we live — an insight, rooted in and growing out of concrete experience, many-sided, three-dimensional.
— CLEANTH BROOKS

There are many questions that Aristotle's approach will not answer: questions about the spirit of tragedy throughout the ages, questions about how to rise from despair to faith, questions about how to use art to attack your enemies. . . . But you know there is no better cure for despair than rousing yourself and joining a great artist in his particular creative acts; there is no better proof of nobility than seeing a bit of it really work in a great piece of art; there is no more satisfactory proof of the existence of the good, the true and the beautiful than experiencing their fusion in the unique, particular achievement of a story. . . .
— WAYNE C. BOOTH

The three movements discussed here cover a vast amount of geographical ground (centered in Moscow, in London and Nashville, and in Chicago), and they have flourished over a long stretch of the present century, from just after World War I to the present day. Whether the theoretical territories inhabited by the formalists are seen as vast or confined depends on whether one looks at the positive ideas they have espoused or at their oppositions. All three versions of formalism proposed an "intrinsic" criticism that defined and addressed the specifically literary qualities in the text, and all three began in reaction to various forms of "extrinsic" criticism that viewed the text as either the product of social and historical forces or a document making an ethical statement. But no two of the three agreed on precisely what made a text "literary," what qualities of form, language, or content differentiated it from nonliterary discourse, or what the significance of literature was for humanity. There are major discrepancies among these three movements, as one might expect, but the divergences *within* each movement are almost as striking.

RUSSIAN FORMALISM

Of the three movements, Russian formalism had the briefest flowering. It originated in Moscow in 1915 with a group of linguists and stylisticians known as OPOYAZ (Society for the Study of Poetic Language), grew for about a decade in postrevolutionary Russia, and as a movement was finally eliminated for political reasons by Joseph Stalin and his henchman Andrey Zhdanov around 1930. Most of its members either formally recanted (as did Victor Shklovsky) or emigrated (like Roman Jakobson). Their publications, suppressed in the USSR, were lost to the West until Victor Erlich's pioneering study *Russian Formalism: History—Doctrine* (1955) and Tzvetan Todorov's 1965 translation of the formalists into French. Nevertheless, the ultimate influence of the formalists was considerable. Roman Jakobson carried their ideas west, first to the Prague Linguistic Circle (which included Jan Mukařovský), and then to Paris, where he and Claude Lévi-Strauss helped create the structuralist movement that flourished from the early 1960s.

The origins of Russian formalism and the New Criticism show some interesting parallels, largely because the two movements developed in opposition to the same two mainstream forms of contemporary criticism. On the one hand they rejected the historicism of academic criticism, which was seen as a tedious investigation of the circumstances of poetic creation pursued in the absence of any coherent notion of poetics itself. On the other, they despised the liberal "social criticism" of reformers who wished to use literature as a means of cultural progress. What the moralist Paul Elmer More was to the New Critics, nineteenth-century socialist critics like Vissarion Belinsky, Nikolay Chernyshevsky, and Nikolay Dobrolyubov were to the Russian formalists.

Serious divergences occurred, however. The New Critics were essentially allied with the imagist poets (including T. E. Hulme, T. S. Eliot, and Ezra Pound), who viewed poetry as a means of communicating, through image and symbol, what could not be said in prose. The poetics of the New Critics centered in semantics, and set the critic the task of decoding the text by explicating its tropes. The systems of individual New Critics largely differed over which of the principal figures of speech or thought — such as metaphor, irony, and ambiguity — was chosen as the master trope.

The Russian formalists began by refining but ultimately rejecting the work of a nineteenth-century philologist who might be seen as a prototype New Critic. Alexander Potebnya viewed imagery as the master trope distinguishing poetry from prose, which he regarded as two distinct ways of knowing the world. This theory was embraced by the symbolist poets (like Andrey Bely and Dmitry Merezhkovsky), who looked to art to produce a mystical form of knowledge. Potebnya was as much an exemplar as he was an opponent of the formalists; he had been concerned about the line dividing the literary from the nonliterary (an issue about which the social critics cared little), and he had defined literariness as a function of language, a point of view the formalists were also to embrace.

Potebnya is chiefly known today, however, through the attack on his ideas in Victor Shklovsky's manifesto of formalism, "Art as Technique," which takes issue with the narrowness of Potebnya's conception of art in elevating metaphor and symbolism, imagery, or any single trope to master status. From Shklovsky's perspective, the central difficulty with Potebnya's conception of poetry was its obsession with semantics, with the notion that the things poetry had to express were mystically different from those of prose. For Shklovsky, the chief function of art is not to lead us to a knowledge above and beyond the world but to restore our capacity to see a world to which use and habit have blinded us. "As perception becomes habitual, it becomes automatic," says Shklovsky, "and art exists that one may recover the sensation of life . . . of things as they are perceived and not as they are known." By its use of unaccustomed language, art makes the world strange again, so that we can see it with the freshness of a child. *Ostranenie* (defamiliarization), the concept at the center of Shklovsky's poetics, is an inversion of Samuel Johnson's notion that art "approximates the remote and familiarizes the wonderful."

The concept of defamiliarization is central to the formalist project, but the term can be used in different ways at different levels of approach to the literary object. At the most basic level of discourse, the formalists analyzed sentences taken from literary texts to see how they estranged reality as a purely aesthetic end in itself. But at the higher level where discourse becomes social, the formalists saw texts' representations of reality as a technique for defamiliarizing the social ideas of the dominant culture, and thus for challenging our automatic acceptance of these ideas. They would say, for example, that an apparently naive and incoherent narrative voice (like that of Gogol's *The Nose*) functions so as to expose the cruelty and hypocrisy of the social ideas of the time.

At a still higher and more abstract level, the formalists, as Tony Bennett has put it, "were concerned with the formal mechanisms whereby literary works tended to reveal or make strange the systems of coherence imposed on reality by the codes and conventions of other, usually earlier literary forms."[1] For example, Shklovsky's essay on *Tristram Shandy* (1921) distinguishes between *fabula* (or story), that is, the temporal-causal sequence of narrated events that comprise the raw materials of the work, and *sjuzet* (or plot), the way in which these raw materials are formally manipulated, in order to argue that *Tristram Shandy,* as Bennett puts it, "is told in such a way as to limit and reveal the narrative conventions of the time. . . ."

The distinction between *fabula* and *sjuzet* owes a great deal to another nineteenth-century forebear of the formalists, the academic literary historian Alexander Veselovsky. Around 1906, Veselovsky evolved a poetics of "motifs," in which the literary work is dissected into its smallest irreducible components, and plot is seen as a complex cluster of story-motifs, ordered, altered, and rearranged by art; Veselovsky thought that shifting motifs correlated with changes in cultural attitudes. The formalists predictably disagreed with his version of historical determinism but adopted Veselovsky's techniques of thematic analysis, as exemplified by Boris Tomashevsky's "Thematics" (1925) and Vladimir Propp's *The Morphology of the Folk-Tale* (1928).

[1]Tony Bennett, *Formalism and Marxism* (London: Methuen, 1979), p. 23.

In effect, the formalists viewed literature as a mode of construction. Poetry was defined by its use of poetic language, fiction as the craft of manipulating story materials by narrative technique. What was not a matter of construction, such as the origins and the cultural meaning of a literary work, was not specifically literary, and was therefore dismissed as not a true part of poetics. The difficulty with such a view, as one historian of formalism has suggested, is that "it does not permit us to evaluate" individual texts. "But the OPOYAZ members never introduced the problems of evaluation into their system."[2]

If Shklovsky established the principal issues governing the literary qualities of texts, Roman Jakobson most succinctly defined the poetic in what would today be called semiotic fashion: as a special use of language. Poetry was "an utterance oriented toward the mode of expression"; in poetry "a word is perceived as a word and not merely as a proxy for the denoted object or an outburst of emotion. . . . Words and their arrangement . . . their outward and inward form acquire weight and value of their own."[3]

At the outset, the Russian formalists talked as though it were the emotive quality of poetry that differentiated it from common language, but a *semantic* feature of that sort was bound to seem unsatisfactory in the long run; obviously some expressions of feeling are poetic and some are not, while a great deal of what is clearly poetry is not primarily emotional expression. Besides, emotion was a sort of content, and with such a discriminant, the formalists would have been entrapped in the notion of an external form enclosing a crude content. Jakobson's idea made it possible to drop entirely the notion of a separable content and to view poetic form as that which integrates the raw material of language into a shaped structure. Jakobson's sense of form as a dynamic shaping process thus resembles the Aristotelian *eidos;* as we shall see, it has more in common with the Chicago neo-Aristotelians' notions of form than that of the New Critics.

If the idea of the literary was the important feature of Russian formalism, nevertheless literary history — or literary evolution, as it is called in the Tynyanov selection — rapidly became one of the main concerns of the school. For the formalists, the older modes of literary history were essentially inadequate because they had never established any strong sense of what made a particular text into literature in a given age: Without any systematic notion of the literary, the only causal mechanisms available were what Boris Eikhenbaum called "the naive theory of 'inheritance' and 'influence' and hence naive biographism based on individual psychology."[4]

The formalists believed that at any given moment a national literature was not a collection of individual works but a system of genres. As Tynyanov puts it, "It is clear that in literature there is no such thing as a separate work, but that the separate work belongs to the system of literature, correlates with it in genre and style . . . that

[2]Krystyna Pomorska, "Russian Formalism in Retrospect," in *Readings in Russian Poetics,* ed. Ladislaw Matejka and Krystyna Pomorska (Cambridge: MIT Press, 1971), p. 275.

[3]Victor Erlich, *Russian Formalism: History — Doctrine* (The Hague: Mouton, 1963), p. 183.

[4]Boris Mikhailovich Eikhenbaum, "Literature and Literary Life," in *Moi Vramennik* (Leningrad, 1929): 52.

a work has a function in the literary system of a given period."[5] Any synchronous study would reveal that the system is hierarchical — that one genre dominates at any given time — and that the genres tend to exist in dialectical relations with one another. In mid-eighteenth-century England, for example, the highest honors were given to poetry in general over prose genres, and to philosophical poetry (Pope's "Essay on Man," Johnson's "The Vanity of Human Wishes") over satirical poetry (Pope's *Dunciad,* Johnson's "London"), and satirical over pastoral and elegiac.

In discussing the movement of systems, the dethroning of one dominant genre by another, the formalists were quite clear that difference was more important than similarity. The succession of genres was not a clear line of influence, with one dominant passing on the position to another within its range of filiation, but rather of divergence. Shklovsky uses the following metaphor: "When literary schools change, the succession passes not from father to son, but from uncle to nephew." His point is that the dominant school of one era is not an obviously predictable development of the dominant school of the former era.

Yuri Tynyanov's sense of the motor behind formal succession is that as a genre becomes dominant within an era, it develops a system of conventions — plot devices, character types, tropes of language — that can be thought of as characteristic of the genre. The genre, as a dominant, then attracts more and more writers to it, and the writers attracted become less and less creative and more and more imitative. Seeking new sources of originality, the genre expands to fill as much territory as it can, as any successful organism expands to fill as many niches as possible in its potential habitat. Furthermore, because of its prevalence, the genre becomes coarsened: The effects that worked before have become familiar, and it is necessary to deliver stronger sensations to provide the same literary impact. As the genre expands, then, it is held together essentially by its conventions; it thus becomes automatized (and this, as Shklovsky had said, is the mark of the nonliterary). A genre that has reached this point thus becomes ripe for being toppled from the dominant position: A new genre becomes dominant, and the process begins again within the new dominant. Tynyanov's process, presented in "On Literary Evolution," expounds a motor for literary history that stands in compelling contrast with the Marxist view that literature responds to exterior social and economic change.

THE NEW CRITICISM

The Russian formalists were Underground Men, whose ideas were absent from the critical dialogue of the West until the 1960s. The New Criticism, to the contrary, is one of the more conspicuous success stories of the century, and if the movement is centered somewhat less coherently than the others, that may have been one of the principal reasons for its popularity, because the New Criticism is associated less with a body of theoretical doctrine about the nature of language and poetry than with a method of critical exegesis and explication.

[5]Yuri Tynyanov, "Oda kak oratorskii zhanr," *Poetika* 3 (1927), 48–86, quoted in Ann Shukman, "A Glossary of Russian Formalism," *Poetica: Russian Poetics in Translation* 4 (1977): 41.

The name "New Criticism" seems to have been bestowed by John Crowe Ransom in a 1941 book of that title, which examines the work of I. A. Richards and William Empson, T. S. Eliot, Yvor Winters, and the philosopher Charles W. Morris. The most important New Critics include this group, Ransom himself, and his fellow Southern "fugitive" writers Allen Tate, Cleanth Brooks, and Robert Penn Warren. Other important theorists associated with the movement include René Wellek, R. P. Blackmur, Robert B. Heilman, Austin Warren, and Murray Krieger. After this point it is hard to tell where to stop, since by the 1950s the New Critical method of poetic explication had come to dominate the teaching of literature in England and America, and most working literary critics had been touched by it in one way or another. One should look to I. A. Richards and T. S. Eliot as the primary founders of this method, the former through his philosophical theories and the latter through his critical practice and tastes.

Like the Russian formalists, Richards was mainly concerned with what differentiated poetry from common language. For him the issue was principally referentiality. Richards held that in common language we make statements that refer to matters of fact, whereas in poetry we make pseudostatements that may appear to be referential but in fact are not. Statements made in poetry cannot be verified; their function is affective rather than cognitive. A poem arouses and allays feelings through the dance of conflicting attitudes stimulated by its complex language. Such an aesthetic moment shakes up the reader's established responses to real life by stimulating the reader's experience of a sense of harmony established among opposing impulses. The form of the poem consists of these stimuli and responses within an ideal reader. (Richards's notion of poetry is at bottom a more behavioristic version of Coleridge, who held that the imagination operates by reconciling opposing qualities into an ideal unity of form.) Richards was primarily a theorist; the critical practice inherent in his ideas was taken over by his student, William Empson. Empson's *Seven Types of Ambiguity* (1930) was an attempt to establish the ways in which texts create, through ambiguity, a multiplicity of meanings, which stimulate the reader to see their harmonious reconciliation. Since it would be possible using any good dictionary to find dozens of possible meanings for the words in a short poem and thousands of possible combinations of these meanings, Empson was attacked for employing a method that, when used mechanically, would produce an inchoate cloud of possible interpretations for any text. Empson was in fact sensitive to the issue of literary intentionality and the question of how the many possible constituents of meaning coalesce into a single complex and moving idea; his epilogue to *Seven Types of Ambiguity* discusses the limits to ambiguity and the relation between audience response and authorial intent.

Two decades later, the most rigorous of the American New Critics, including Ransom and Wimsatt, would reject the reader-oriented formulation of Richards and Empson: The "affective fallacy" would insist that the form of a poem is not to be identified with the psychological process undergone by its audience. (Since this process is likely to differ in various readers, it would leave the form at best indeterminate and at worst under the control of the audience.) But purged of its affective slant, this view of form as an interplay of feelings and attitudes, like the interwoven themes of music, was to prove persuasive and fertile.

T. S. Eliot was also to lend ideas to the New Criticism. In "Tradition and the Individual Talent" Eliot spoke of literature as an "ideal order," a tradition which exists not successively in history but is somehow present simultaneously as it exerts influence upon the newly created work. (See Eliot's essay, p. 498.) This viewpoint had justified the breach between the New Criticism and the historical scholarship that had dominated the academy. In "Hamlet and His Problems," Eliot also presented the "objective correlative," the idea of one-to-one correspondence between the images in a poem and the feelings for which the image is supposed to be the formula. Given this correspondence, poetry could have emotive significance, but its themes could be discussed *objectively* in a more concrete explication of the poem's emotional content. Although these were influential ideas, Eliot was perhaps even more influential in his tastes, which valorized the poets and playwrights of the English Renaissance over the Augustans, Romantics, and Victorians who had dominated the canon, and in his critical practice, which lucidly explicated the poetry of Donne and the plays of Middleton as though they were his contemporaries.

Despite the efforts of René Wellek to give the New Criticism a pedigree in Kantian aesthetics, its development from the late 1930s on was primarily as a critical practice rather than a set of theoretical doctrines. The general theory was simply that literature was a special kind of language and that practical criticism reflects and is constrained by that principle. The most influential ideological statements tended to explain what criticism should not do, rather than what it should. Pride of place should be given to a pair of papers by William K. Wimsatt and Monroe C. Beardsley defending new critical practice against a series of "fallacies": One was "The Affective Fallacy" (1949), which rejected the notion that the poem could be defined in terms of the internal experiences of actual readers (although the New Critics, without precisely admitting to it, tended to analyze poetry in terms of the response of *ideal* readers).

Even more influential was "The Intentional Fallacy" (1946), which, consistent with Eliot's assertion of the impersonality of poetry in "Tradition and the Individual Talent," attacks the notion of the work of art as the essentially private product of the internal experience of a particular individual. The poem is defined as a public text, and its meaning by what the public norms of language allow it to mean. The text's aesthetic success or failure must be judged in those terms alone. Within its original context, the intentional fallacy was a convincing refutation of Crocean idealism, which would have located the aesthetic object in the author's lyrical intuition, and of the old historicism, which referred the meaning of the text to the circumstances of its genesis and its historical context. The intent of the intentional fallacy was to liberate the reader: Thereafter, the only apparatus one needed to read Chaucer and Shakespeare was a good text and a historical dictionary. But the ultimate effect of anti-intentionalism was to foster the irresponsible interpretation of texts, a search for originality of reading without regard to the creator's probable purposes.

There were other fallacies and heresies: the *fallacy of imitative form* attempted to cut the text off from the world it supposedly represented in order to purify the New Criticism of the mimetic principle, as it had already been purified of the expressive and affective ones. The *fallacy of neoclassic species* was aimed at R. S. Crane and the Chicago critics, whose formal theories located the text within an open system of genres. The *biographical heresy* was aimed at those who would identify the speaker of the poem with its author. In general, these treatises aimed to isolate the text as a "verbal icon" (to use Wimsatt's phrase) whose form was to be found entirely within itself.

As various historians of critical theory have pointed out, the creators of this version of formalism may have had ulterior reasons for purifying the text. Many of the American New Critics were from the South, a depressed region that during and after World War II had been undergoing a social and economic revolution, which had displaced traditional values and culture. As the Marxist Terry Eagleton puts it, the New Criticism "was the ideology of an uprooted, defensive intelligentsia who reinvented in literature what they could not find in reality. Poetry was the new religion, a nostalgic haven from the alienations of industrial capitalism."[6] Poetry was not only viewed as a force opposing the crassness and secularization of modern life, but as the location of the spiritual values these critics held dear. As Cleanth Brooks once confessed, "it is no accident that so many of the [New Critics] have gone on, either to avow an orthodox religious position or else to affirm the possibility and necessity for metaphysics as a science."[7] Brooks's associates at the *Kenyon Review,* including critics like John Crowe Ransom and Allen Tate, felt that "the whole effort of the literary imagination is toward a kind of incarnation of reality in language."[8]

We can see this quasi-religious impulse in the theories of John Crowe Ransom, who sought in poetry something larger than aesthetic form, something that in *The World's Body* (1941) he had called "ontological": a capturing of the *body* of experience. And in criticism he was seeking a way of helping the reader recapture that essence:

> The poet perpetuates in his poem an order of existence which in actual life is constantly crumbling beneath his touch. . . . For each poem even, ideally, there is distinguishable a logical object or universal, but at the same time a tissue of irrelevance from which it does not really emerge. The critic has to take the poem apart, or analyze it, for the sake of uncovering these features. With all the finesse possible, it is rude and patchy business. . . . But without it there could hardly be much understanding of the value of poetry, or of the natural history behind any adult poem.[9]

For Ransom, poetry is defined by the interplay between structure and texture. Like prose, poetry has a determinate meaning (or logical structure), but in the case of poetry the determinate meaning is deformed by (among other things) the pressure of versification. The necessity of finding rhymes and rhythmic form results in an admixture of what he calls "indeterminate meaning," which may be a mere dross of

[6]Terry Eagleton, *Literary Criticism: An Introduction* (Minneapolis: University of Minnesota Press, 1983), p. 47.

[7]"Metaphor and the Function of Criticism," in *Spiritual Problems in Contemporary Literature,* ed. S. R. Hooper (New York: Harper Torchbooks, 1957), p. 134.

[8]Allen Tate, quoted in Michael Millgate, "An Interview with Allen Tate," *Shenandoah* 12 (1961): 31.

[9]John Crowe Ransom, *The World's Body* (New York: Scribner's, 1938): 348–49.

verbiage that testifies to the human process of creation or may include wonderful, shockingly brilliant novelties that contribute to poetic texture.

Although there was considerable agreement on the principles of art and on the technique of literary explication that was the critic's "job of work," each New Critic developed a slightly different terminology for discussing the issues. For Cleanth Brooks, the terms equivalent to Ransom's structure and texture would be the "paraphrasable content" of a poem (which he equates with its "rational or logical structure") and its "essential structure." In "The Heresy of Paraphrase" (1947) (another heresy!), Brooks insists that the poem not only cannot be equated with its paraphrasable content, but that the content should not be seen as an inner core wrapped about in an exterior form consisting of metrical language. Harking back to Richards, in *The Well Wrought Urn* (1947) Brooks instead defines the "essential structure" of the poem as being like that of

> architecture or painting: it is a pattern of resolved stresses. Or, to move closer still . . . the structure of a poem resembles that of a ballet or musical composition. It is a pattern of resolutions and balances and harmonizations developed through a temporal scheme.[10]

The thematic criticism of the New Critics tended to operate by finding within the texture of the poem oppositions and conflicts that were resolved into a harmonious balance. The principal mediator of this resolution was poetic language, specifically the capacity of language to carry multiple meanings that could disclose hidden conflicts and tensions at the outset of the poem and converge into a harmonious balance at the end. For I. A. Richards's pupil William Empson, the proper term for this polysemic capacity of language was *ambiguity,* of which he distinguished and elaborately discussed seven distinct types. The American New Critics preferred to locate individual master tropes (or figures of speech) that would serve as the center for their discourse. For Cleanth Brooks, the master tropes were *paradox* and *irony*, the latter defined not in its strict sense — saying the opposite of what is intended — but very broadly, as occurring whenever a statement is undercut or qualified by its context. Similarly, for Allen Tate the chief issue in poetry was the "*tension* between two opposing forces." Although the criticism of Robert Penn Warren flirted with irony, his usual master trope, like that of R. P. Blackmur, was the literary *symbol.* For Robert B. Heilman, the principal issue was the *image,* and it was through the conflict of opposing clusters of images that eventual resolution was achieved. For Murray Krieger, as for the Russian formalists, the master trope was *metaphor.* These divergences were more apparent than real, for each of these literary figures of speech and of thought was in practice broadened from its usual definition to potentially include all the others as well.

What may seem strange, especially given the contrary example of the Russian formalists, is that despite the New Critical emphasis on poetic language, none of the major theorists had any interest in contemporary discoveries in linguistics and semiotics; in fact they disdained "professionalism" in the study of language. This disdain

[10]Cleanth Brooks, "The Heresy of Paraphrase" in *The Well Wrought Urn: Studies in the Structure of Poetry* (New York: Harcourt, Brace and World, 1947): p. 203.

may have been held over from the amateur's stance that the New Critics cultivated, a stance opposed to the professionalism of historical scholarship, against which the movement had originally defined itself.

As we have noted, the dominance of the New Critical thematic explication was nearly absolute through the 1960s. Even today the critical practice of many American teachers of literature owes a great deal to Cleanth Brooks and William Empson. But as a theory, the New Criticism has few current defenders, and its vitality has suffered more than one might gather by counting its remaining devotees. Nevertheless, while the New Criticism has been supplanted by a variety of other interpretive modes, these modes have been forced to define themselves against a once-dominant New Critical tradition, and in this negative sense the New Criticism still lives.

Its more important surviving legacy is the cult of the interpretation and reinterpretation of texts that makes up so much of the critic's professional life. John Crowe Ransom had begun by noting that for the poem to capture the world's body, the critic must recapture it for the common reader. The New Criticism redefined the professoriate as the priesthood of twentieth-century humanism, making the verbal icon accessible to the laity. The critic's proper job of work was the decoding of a text whose surface meaning, however evident to the average reader, is seen as insufficient. The journals and little magazines accordingly filled with interpretations, but eventually the very success of the New Critical methods bred failure. By the 1960s it had spawned an insistent hunger for reinterpretation of canonical texts (or at least for the books and articles upon which professional academic success depends). And eventually the New Criticism, within its formal strictures of fallacies and heresies, could provide for this demand only by more farfetched decodings. But if New Critical theory has been jettisoned in favor of readings based on Marxist, feminist, or deconstructionist literary theories, the view of literature as a mystery to which the critic alone has the key survives. The profession has not so readily relinquished the verbal icon.

NEO-ARISTOTELIANISM

Just as the New Criticism arose out of the New South, neo-Aristotelianism grew out of the innovative Hutchins curriculum at the University of Chicago, which replaced the traditional lecture system with a program of the close study of the "Great Books of the Western Tradition." Moved by the general intellectual ferment of the time and galvanized by the philosophical semantics of Richard McKeon, the historical scholar R. S. Crane came out in 1935 against teaching literature to undergraduates through its purely historical origins and in favor of a new approach using textual explication and aesthetics.[11] As chairman of the English department, Crane was able to hire over the next decade a number of humanists who assisted him in developing a critical theory and practice that has become known as neo-Aristotelianism or

[11]R. S. Crane, "History versus Criticism in the Study of Literature" (1935), reprinted in *The Idea of the Humanities* (Chicago: University of Chicago Press, 1967), vol. 2, pp. 3–24.

Chicago criticism; this group included Elder Olson, Norman Maclean, and W. R. Keast, in addition to McKeon and Crane himself.

Though Crane had placed himself on the side of the New Critics on the issue of history vs. criticism, he and his group were scornful of New Critical theories of literature, which they considered reductive, simplistic, and a serious distortion of the nature of literature and language. As a result, the 1940s and 1950s saw an acrimonious debate in the pages of scholarly journals and little magazines, intemperate on both sides, between Crane's group and such New Critics as Brooks, Wimsatt, Warren, and Heilman. By 1960, when the dust had settled, the New Critics held the field, primarily because their critical methods, propagated in successful textbooks like *Understanding Poetry* (1938), had revolutionized undergraduate and even secondary-school training in literature across America. The textual explications of the Chicago school, in contrast, were confined primarily to scholarly books and learned journals. And the neo-Aristotelian method of analyzing literature was a more complex approach, which did not lend itself to popularization. On the other hand, the New Criticism succeeded at the cost of ideological stagnation, while neo-Aristotelianism developed a second generation of critics (including Wayne C. Booth, Sheldon Sacks, Ralph Rader, Robert Marsh, Norman Friedman, Mary Doyle Springer, and Austin Wright) and a third generation (including Don Bialostosky, Brian Corman, Walter Davis, Barbara Foley, Elizabeth Langland, James Phelan, Peter Rabinowitz, and Adena Rosmarin), all of whom are endeavoring to revise, extend, and adapt Crane's ideas to new projects.

Aristotle's concept of *mimesis,* or imitation, is not central to Chicago criticism. The crucial Aristotelian concepts are from the *Metaphysics* rather than the *Poetics;* they include the *eidos,* or "shaping form," and the *synolon,* or "concrete whole" of formed matter, found in nature or manufactured by art. The *synolon* is analyzed in terms of its formal, material, efficient, and final causes. Poetic works of art are *synola* in which plot, character, and thought (the formal cause) give shape to language (the material cause) using various techniques or devices of disclosure (the efficient cause) to create an object with the power to affect a reader in various ways (the final cause).

The "concrete whole" is matter shaped by form to be "inherently meaningful and beautiful."[12] The work's power comes from the inferred sense of the whole, not from the parts; in fact our sense of the whole *as a pattern* is what governs the perceived meaning of the parts. Language, however crucial to our perception of the form, does not define poetic form as it did for the New Critics: It is only a means — and not even the most important one — to an end. Not even plot, which was so crucial for Crane's notions of form, is wholly decisive. Although our sense of the whole takes shape through our experience of the parts, we revise our sense of the parts through our growing sense of the whole to which they contribute. And while the powers of some literary works may require temporary or permanent

[12]Ralph Rader, "Defoe, Richardson, Joyce, and the Concept of Form in Fiction," in *Autobiography, Biography and the Novel* (Los Angeles: Clark Memorial Library, 1973), p. 29.

ambiguities, many merely *potential* ambiguities within a text are cleared up by this shaping process.

R. S. Crane viewed Aristotle primarily as the founder of a positivistic and "differential" method (one opposed to Plato's idealistic and synthesizing method). In tragedy the final cause, the *dynamis,* is the catharsis of pity and fear, and Aristotle judges various Attic tragedies by how well their various elements are designed, the ultimate criterion being their capacity to effect the tragic *dynamis.* Crane wanted to extend the systematic approach of the *Poetics* to other genres with different powers, which different structures of plot, character, thought, language, and technique were designed to serve.

In practice, Crane's genres were based primarily upon the formal and the final causes, and the efficient and material causes were unofficially relegated to relatively subordinate roles. And despite claims of empiricism, his literary classes are those of a proto-structuralist and derive from a large number of structural predicates, many of which Crane outlines in "The Concept of Plot and the Plot of *Tom Jones*" (1952). For example, the protagonist may be of either better, worse, or the same moral quality as the reader, and this moral nature may be either static or capable of moving from one to another of these levels; the protagonist's fate may be either fortunate or unfortunate, in greater or lesser degree, in the short run or the long run; the protagonist may be responsible for this fate, or it may be the result of chance, fate, fortune, providence, or historical necessity; the plot as a whole may turn on a change in the protagonist's circumstances, moral character, or way of thinking; the text as a whole may be an imitation of human action (mimetic) or of an argument (didactic); and so on. The interplay of these predicates would generate hundreds, perhaps thousands of distinct genres.

While other genre critics (like Northrop Frye) felt the need to map literature as a field, for the Chicago critics, genres had a different purpose. They functioned as multiple models to which the critic might look in creating strong hypotheses about the specific texts under analysis, hypotheses leading to predictions that might (like scientific hypotheses) be verified or falsified by the text itself or by features of its creation or reception. The openness and pluralism of the genre system served to make it less likely that the critic would have to distort the text to make it fit a single procrustean model. The aim was a method similar to that of science, where conjectures are tested and refuted, and false leads eliminated, until the best explanation is found. Indeed, the critical aims of the Chicago school included the attainment of power through the successful search for objective truth. They were displaced scientists, unlike most of the New Critics, whose motivations, by their own accounts, were more like those of disappointed priests seeking in literature for a new Word to replace the one the world had lost.

Crane's genres are ideal forms, and his theory succeeded best with masterpieces like *Macbeth* and *Tom Jones,* in which a complex plot and a great variety of characters have been marshalled to the service of a single end. His approach was less effective with mixed forms like *The Vicar of Wakefield* or *Moby-Dick,* or with partial failures like Fielding's *Amelia,* in which the author failed at integrating didactic materials into a mimetic plot, and extraformal intentions were realized at the expense of the reader's emotional affect. The second generation of neo-Aristotelians, especially Wayne Booth and Ralph Rader, were to explore more adequately how architectonic notions of form could be reconciled with the multifarious intentions of authors and with the institutional shapes that culture bequeaths to literature.

Another difference between the first generation of Chicago critics and their successors is in their attitude toward literary autonomy. Despite Crane's attacks on the New Critics, he accepted the autonomy of the literary text:

> What is held constant is the whole complex of accidental causes of variation in poetry that depend on the talents, characters, educations, and intentions of individual authors, the opinions and tastes of the audiences they address, the state of the language in their time, and all the other external factors which affect their choice of materials and conventions in particular works. The provisional exclusion of these is necessary if the analysis is to be concentrated upon the internal causes which account for the peculiar construction and effect of any poem qua artistic whole.[13]

The exclusion of the extrinsic is a tactical gesture more than a statement of the *nature* of literature, but it may nevertheless have seriously distorted Crane's readings of poetry. In particular, the notion of autonomy long blinded the Chicago critics to fundamental differences between many forms of lyric poetry and other literary modes such as drama and fiction. With the author excluded, the lyric "I" had to be viewed as an externalized speaker, the principal character in a tiny agon that could be analyzed according to the same terms Crane had used for prose fiction and theatrical drama. This externalized speaker is seen as either "moved in a certain way by his situation" or "acting in a certain manner in relation to it" or as "deliberating morally in a certain frame of mind." Thus, lyric poems, like plays and novels, have something analogous to a plot, in fact have plots of thought, action, or character.

This sort of analysis works best in poems in which the "I" is indeed a dramatic character, felt as Other to the poet, as in Browning's "My Last Duchess." But as Ralph Rader has pointed out, in the majority of poems in the Western tradition the poet is immanent within the poem; that is, as a condition of reading them, a reader recognizes the speaker's voice as a projection, displaced or immediate, of the poet's. It is not a mere "accidental cause of variation" but integral to the nature of lyric poetry that readers for the last two hundred years have viewed the words of "Elegy in a Country Churchyard" as the expression of one Thomas Gray rather than of a nameless, fully externalized "virtuous, sensitive, and ambitious young man of humble birth," as Crane was forced to see him.[14] And as Rader was to show in "Defoe, Richardson, Joyce, and the Concept of Form in the Novel" (1973), the author may be immanently present within the form of the text in fiction as well as in

[13] R. S. Crane, Introduction to *Critics and Criticism: Ancient and Modern* (Chicago: University of Chicago Press, 1952), p. 20.

[14] The New Critics had also banished authorial intention and spoke of an autonomous speaker within the poem, but for their mode of thematic analysis it made little practical difference whether the thematic focus was ascribed to the author or his creation. Given Crane's emphasis on character and action, the separation of speaker/actor from poet seemed considerably more artificial. In fact, there is no reason within Crane's system to insist upon such a rigid textual autonomy, and the poet/character relation in all its variations can be compassed under the aegis of Aristotle's efficient cause.

poetry. From the other side, the rhetorical criticism of Wayne C. Booth was to show that the reader was also immanently present within the form of the text, and how one is as manipulated by the subtle and indirect techniques of modern fiction as by the direct appeals of eighteenth-century narrative.

The most abstract feature of the Chicago critics' contribution to literary theory, and perhaps its least controversial, is their commitment to pluralism. Crane's version of pluralism begins with the premise that criticism is not a field like biochemistry, which slowly advances along a single front according to a common set of factual and methodological assumptions — what the philosopher of science Thomas Kuhn was later to call a paradigm. Criticism is instead "a collection of distinct and more or less incommensurable 'frameworks' or 'languages'" differing widely in "matters of assumed principle, definition and method."[15] Each of these "languages" has its own intrinsic powers and limitations, and certain areas of insight — questions it can pose and answer — while remaining blind to other, equally significant issues. Each separate mode of criticism should therefore be considered an instrument, a tool useful for one or more specific purposes but ill-adapted to a great many others. For all his investment in neo-Aristotelianism, Crane felt that there were questions it could not answer.

> It is a method not at all suited, as is criticism in the grand line of Longinus, Coleridge, and Matthew Arnold, to the definition and appreciation of those general qualities of writing — mirroring the souls of writers — for the sake of which most of us read or at any rate return to what we have read. It is a method that necessarily abstracts from history. . . . It is a method, above all, that completely fails, because of its essentially differentiating character, to give us insights into the larger moral and political values of literature or into any of the other organic relations with human nature and human experience in which literature is involved.[16]

Crane embraced pluralism as a way of coping with the diversity of critical languages that had begun, even by midcentury, to generate terminological squabbles and to make it difficult for literary scholars to understand one another. Later Chicago critics have advanced Crane's commitment to pluralism.

Booth's "Pluralism and Its Rivals" (1970) is an affirmation of Crane's vision of critical systems as a collection of instruments, or tools, each with areas of blindness and insight. Written at a time of radical protest during the late 1960s at the University of Chicago, when deep divisions existed both between and within the faculty and the student body, and when political divisions were making well-intentioned scholars skeptical not merely of the arguments but of the facts presented by their opponents, Booth's lecture stands as a ringing defense of the complexities of rational inquiry. His argument tacitly appeals to a distinction made by philosopher Stephen Pepper between "data" (facts that logically precede all interpretation, that would have to be explained by any critical mode) and "danda" (elements within a text that become facts only within a specific interpretive mode). That Hamlet in

[15]R. S. Crane, *The Languages of Criticism and the Structure of Poetry* (Toronto: University of Toronto Press, 1953), p. 13.

[16]Crane, p. 192.

Shakespeare's tragedy is Claudius's nephew would be "data"; that Hamlet's relationship to his uncle is deeply ambivalent owing to his Oedipal struggle with his father would be "danda" viable only within a Freudian critique.

This was not, however, where Booth's vision of pluralism ended. In *Critical Understanding* (1979), Booth was to inquire more searchingly into exactly where the dividing line between data and danda lay, and to embrace the notion that some ways of "overstanding" a text (viewing it in the light of a prior ideological commitment) might be as vital to an engaged critical discourse as the ways of "understanding" it. Where the Booth of 1969 offhandedly rejects a feminist view of "Araby" as tangential to the author's vision and the story's concerns (p. 794), the Booth of 1979 is receptive to this sort of ideological reading.

Booth, Sacks, and Rader, of the second generation of Neo-Aristotelians, had moved away from Crane's notion of the concrete whole to a more rhetorical view of texts as embodying complex, sometimes contradictory, authorial intentions. In *Narrative as Rhetoric* (1996), James Phelan, of the third generation, represents a further move — away from the author as the controlling principle of the text toward a more free-floating view of literary meaning as determined by complex "recursive relationships among authorial agency, textual phenomena, and reader response." Like Booth with "Araby," Phelan presents his own "transactional" interpretation of Katherine Anne Porter's "Magic," together with a rival, deconstructive interpretation, as a way of showing what is at stake when we take up different modes of critical practice. But Phelan's primary engagement in "Reading the Spells of Porter's 'Magic'," the introductory chapter of *Narrative as Rhetoric,* is not with deconstruction but with a more sophisticated version of the radical skepticism Booth attacks in "Pluralism and Its Rivals." Phelan's arch-rival is the pragmatic theory of discourse associated with Stanley Fish (see p. 976) that claims all interpretations are merely different ways of writing the tales we read. If Fish is right, there is nothing at stake in choosing between the deconstructive and the transactional reading of "Magic." Phelan's own rhetoric tries to convince us that Fish's vision does not account for the world in which we live and to which we respond. Phelan portrays a world that can contain progressive dialogue rather than only debates in Babel.

Selected Bibliography

Antczak, Frederick J., ed. *Rhetoric and Pluralism: Legacies of Wayne Booth.* Columbus: Ohio State University Press, 1995.

Bann, Stephen, and John E. Bowlt, eds. *Russian Formalism: A Collection of Articles and Texts in Translation.* New York: Barnes and Noble, 1973.

Bennett, Tony. *Formalism and Marxism.* London: Methuen, 1979.

Blackmur, R. P. *Language as Gesture.* New York: Harcourt, Brace and World, 1952.

———. *The Lion and the Honeycomb.* New York: Harcourt, Brace and World, 1955.

———. *New Criticism in the United States.* Tokyo: Kenkyusha, 1959.

Booth, Wayne C. *The Rhetoric of Fiction.* Chicago: University of Chicago Press, 1961; 2nd edition, 1983.

———. *A Rhetoric of Irony.* Chicago: University of Chicago Press, 1974.

———. *Critical Understanding: The Powers and Limits of Pluralism.* Chicago: University of Chicago Press, 1979.

———. *The Company We Keep: An Ethics of Fiction.* Berkeley and Los Angeles: University of California Press, 1988.

Brooks, Cleanth, and Robert Penn Warren. *Understanding Poetry.* New York: Henry Holt, 1938.

———. *Modern Poetry and the Tradition.* Chapel Hill: University of North Carolina Press, 1939.

———. *The Well Wrought Urn: Studies in the Structure of Poetry.* New York: Reynal and Hitchcock, 1947.

Crane, Ronald Salmon. *Critics and Criticism: Ancient and Modern.* Chicago: University of Chicago Press, 1952.

———. *The Languages of Criticism and the Structure of Poetry.* Toronto: University of Toronto Press, 1953.

———. *The Idea of the Humanities, and Other Essays.* 2 vols. Chicago: University of Chicago Press, 1967.

Davis, Walter A. *The Act of Interpretation: A Critique of Literary Reason.* Chicago: University of Chicago Press, 1978.

Eikhenbaum, Boris Mikhailovich. *O. Henry and the Theory of the Short Story.* Ann Arbor: Dept. of Slavic Languages and Literatures of the University of Michigan, 1968.

———. *Lermontov: A Study in Literary-Historical Evaluation.* Ann Arbor: Ardis, 1981.

Eliot, Thomas Stearns. *The Sacred Wood: Essays on Poetry and Criticism.* London: Methuen, 1920.

———. *For Lancelot Andrewes.* London: Faber and Gwyer, 1928.

———. *The Use of Poetry and the Use of Criticism.* London: Faber and Faber, 1933.

Empson, William. *Seven Types of Ambiguity.* London: Chatto & Windus, 1930.

Erlich, Victor. *Russian Formalism: History — Doctrine.* The Hague: Mouton, 1955.

Foley, Barbara. *Telling the Truth: The Theory and Practice of Documentary Fiction.* Ithaca: Cornell University Press, 1986.

Friedman, Norman. *Form and Meaning in Fiction.* Athens: University of Georgia Press, 1975.

Gorman, David. "A Bibliography of Russian Formalism in English." *Style* 26 (1992): 554–76.

Jakobson, Roman. *Selected Writings.* 7 vols. The Hague: Mouton, 1962.

———. *The Framework of Language.* Ann Arbor: Graduate School of the University of Michigan, 1980.

Jancovich, Mark. *The Cultural Politics of the New Criticism.* Cambridge: Cambridge University Press, 1992.

Krieger, Murray. *The New Apologists for Poetry.* Minneapolis: University of Minnesota Press, 1956.

Langland, Elizabeth. *Society in the Novel.* Chapel Hill: University of North Carolina Press, 1984.

Lemon, Lee T., and Marion J. Reis, eds. *Russian Formalist Criticism: Four Essays.* Lincoln: University of Nebraska Press, 1965.

Matejka, Ladislav, and Krystyna Pomorska, eds. *Readings in Russian Poetics.* Cambridge: MIT Press, 1971.

Murphy, Richard J. "Russian Formalism and German Reception Theory: A Reconsideration: Continuities in the Methodologies of Victor Shklovsky and Wolfgang Iser." *Germano-Slavica* 6 (1990): 339–49.

Olson, Elder. *The Poetry of Dylan Thomas.* Chicago: University of Chicago Press, 1954.
———. *Tragedy and the Theory of Drama.* Chicago: University of Chicago Press, 1962.
———. *The Theory of Comedy.* Bloomington: Indiana University Press, 1975.
———. *On Value Judgments in the Arts.* Chicago: University of Chicago Press, 1976.
Phelan, James. *Worlds from Words: A Theory of Language in Fiction.* Chicago: University of Chicago Press, 1981.
———. *Reading People, Reading Plots.* Chicago: University of Chicago Press, 1991.
———. *Narrative as Rhetoric.* Columbus: Ohio State University Press, 1996.
———, and Peter J. Rabinowitz, eds. *Understanding Narrative.* Columbus: Ohio State University Press, 1994.
Propp, Vladimir. *Theory and History of Folklore.* Minneapolis: University of Minnesota Press, 1984.
Rader, Ralph. "Defoe, Richardson, Joyce, and the Concept of Form in the Novel." In *Autobiography, Biography and the Novel.* Los Angeles: William Andrews Clark Memorial Library, 1973.
———. "The Concept of Genre and Eighteenth-Century Studies." In *New Approaches to Eighteenth Century Literature: Selected Papers from the English Institute,* ed. Philip Harth. New York: Columbia University Press, 1974.
———. "Fact, Theory and Literary Explanation." *Critical Inquiry* 1 (1974): 245–72.
———. "The Dramatic Monologue and Related Lyric Forms." *Critical Inquiry* 3 (1976): 131–51.
———. "The Literary-Theoretical Contribution of Sheldon Sacks." *Critical Inquiry* 6 (1979): 183–92.
———. "Literary Constructs: Experience and Explanation." *Poetics* 18 (1989): 337–53.
———. "The Emergence of the Novel in England: Genre in History vs. History of Genre." *Narrative* 1 (1993): 69–83.
Ransom, John Crowe. *The World's Body.* New York: Scribner's, 1938.
———. *The New Criticism.* Norfolk, CT: New Directions, 1941.
———. *Poems and Essays.* New York: Vintage, 1955.
Richards, I. A. *Principles of Literary Criticism.* New York: Harcourt Brace Jovanovich, 1924.
Richter, David H. *Fable's End: Completeness and Closure in Rhetorical Fiction.* Chicago: University of Chicago Press, 1974.
———. "The Second Flight of the Phoenix: Neo-Aristotelianism Since Crane." *The Eighteenth Century: Theory and Interpretation* 23 (1982): 27–48.
Rosmarin, Adena. *The Power of Genre.* Minneapolis: University of Minnesota Press, 1985.
Sacks, Sheldon. *Fiction and the Shape of Belief.* Berkeley: University of California Press, 1964.
———. "Golden Birds and Dying Generations." *Comparative Literature Studies* 6 (1969): 274–91.
———. "*Clarissa* and the Tragic Traditions." In *Studies in Eighteenth-Century Culture,* ed. Harold E. Pagliaro. Cleveland: Case Western Reserve University Press, 1972, pp. 195–221.
Schneider, Anna-Dorothea. *Literaturkritik und Bildungspolitik: R. S. Crane, die Chicago (Neo-Aristotelian) Critics und die University of Chicago.* Heidelberg: 1994.
Shklovsky, Victor Borisovich. *Works.* Moscow: Khudozh' Lit'ra, 1973–4.
Springer, Mary Doyle. *Forms of the Modern Novella.* Chicago: University of Chicago Press, 1976.
Spurlin, William J., and Michael Fischer, eds. *The New Criticism and Contemporary Literary Theory: Connections and Continuities.* New York: Garland, 1995.

Steiner, Peter. *Russian Formalism: A Meta-Poetics.* Ithaca: Cornell University Press, 1984.

Striedter, Jurij. *Literary Structure, Evolution, and Value: Russian Formalism and Czech Structuralism Reconsidered.* Cambridge: Harvard University Press, 1989.

Tate, Allen. *Reactionary Essays on Poetry and Ideas.* New York: Scribner's, 1936.

———. *Reason in Madness: Critical Essays.* New York: G. P. Putnam, 1941.

Thompson, Ewa Majewska. *Russian Formalism and Anglo-American New Criticism: A Comparative Study.* Hawthorne, NY: Mouton, 1971.

Tynyanov, Yuri. *The Problem of Verse Language.* Ann Arbor: Ardis, 1981.

Vygotsky, L. S. *Mind in Society: The Development of Higher Psychological Processes.* Cambridge: Harvard University Press, 1978.

Warren, Austin. *Rage for Order: Essays in Criticism.* Ann Arbor: University of Michigan Press, 1948.

Wellek, René, and Austin Warren. *Theory of Literature.* New York: Harcourt, Brace and World, 1949.

———. *A History of Modern Criticism 1759–1950.* 6 vols. New Haven: Yale University Press, 1955–87.

Willingham, John R. "The New Criticism: Then and Now." In *Contemporary Literary Theory,* ed. Douglas Atkins and Janice Morrow. Amherst: University of Massachusetts Press, 1989, pp. 24–41.

———. *Concepts of Criticism.* New Haven: Yale University Press, 1963.

Wimsatt, William K. *The Verbal Icon: Studies in the Meaning of Poetry.* Lexington: University Press of Kentucky, 1954.

———. *Hateful Contraries: Studies in Literature and Criticism.* Lexington: University Press of Kentucky, 1965.

———, and Cleanth Brooks. *Literary Criticism: A Short History.* New York: Alfred A. Knopf, 1957.

Victor Shklovsky

1893–1984

The versatile Russian man of letters Victor Shklovsky was born the son of a teacher in Petersburg and studied at the university there. An outspoken founding member of the Russian literary society OPOYAZ, Shklovsky wrote one of the central theoretical statements of the formalist school ("Art as Technique," 1917) and his ideas were singled out for special denunciation by Leon Trotsky. Problems with the Bolsheviks prompted his emigration in 1921, but he returned two years later. Within a few years, after the publication of The Theory of Prose *(1925), he backed away from the politically risky business of theorizing and took up other pursuits, particularly film criticism, screenwriting, and historical fiction. He wrote books on Tolstoy (1928), Mayakovsky (1940), and Dostoevsky (1957), and is also remembered for his autobiographical account of the revolutionary years,* A Sentimental Journal: Memoirs 1917–1922 *(1923). Ultimately, Shklovsky came to be considered an honored member of the Soviet literary establishment.*

Art as Technique

"Art is thinking in images." This maxim, which even high school students parrot, is nevertheless the starting point for the erudite philologist who is beginning to put together some kind of systematic literary theory. The idea, originated in part by Potebnya, has spread. "Without imagery there is no art, and in particular no poetry," Potebnya writes.[1] And elsewhere, "Poetry, as well as prose, is first and foremost a special way of thinking and knowing."[2]

Poetry is a special way of thinking; it is, precisely, a way of thinking in images, a way which permits what is generally called "economy of mental effort," a way which makes for "a sensation of the relative ease of the process." Aesthetic feeling is the reaction to this economy. This is how the academician Ovsyaniko-Kulikovsky,[3] who undoubtedly read the works of Potebnya attentively, almost certainly understood and faithfully summarized the ideas of his teacher. Potebnya and his numerous disciples consider poetry a special kind of thinking — thinking by means of images; they feel that the purpose of imagery is to help channel various objects and activities into groups and to clarify the unknown by means of the known. Or, as Potebnya wrote:

> The relationship of the image to what is being clarified is that: (a) the image is the fixed predicate of that which undergoes change — the unchanging means of attracting what is perceived as changeable. . . . (b) the image is far clearer and simpler than what it clarifies.[4]

In other words:

> Since the purpose of imagery is to remind us, by approximation, of those meanings for which the image stands, and since, apart from this, imagery is unnecessary for thought, we must be more familiar with the image than with what it clarifies.[5]

It would be instructive to try to apply this principle to Tyutchev's comparison of summer lightning to deaf and dumb demons or to Gogol's comparison of the sky to the garment of God.[6]

"Without imagery there is no art" — "Art is thinking in images." These maxims have led to far-fetched interpretations of individual works of art. Attempts have been made to evaluate even music, architecture, and lyric poetry as imagistic thought. After a quarter of a century of such attempts Ovsyaniko-Kulikovsky finally had to assign lyric poetry, architecture, and music to a special category of imageless art and to define them as lyric arts appealing directly to the emotions. And thus he admitted an enormous area of art which is not a mode of thought. A part of this area, lyric poetry (narrowly considered), is quite like the visual arts; it is also verbal. But, much more important, visual art passes quite imperceptibly into nonvisual art; yet our perceptions of both are similar.

Nevertheless, the definition "Art is thinking in images," which means (I omit the usual middle terms of the argument) that art is the making of symbols, has survived the downfall of the theory which supported it. It survives chiefly in the wake of Symbolism, especially among the theorists of the Symbolist movement.

Many still believe, then, that thinking in images — thinking, in specific scenes of "roads and landscape" and "furrows and boundaries"[7] — is

Translated by Lee T. Lemon and Marion Reis.

[1]Alexander Potebnya, *Iz zapisok po teorii slovesnosti* [*Notes on the Theory of Language*] (Kharkov, 1905), p. 83. [Au.]

[2]Ibid., p. 97. [Au.]

[3]Dmitry Ovsyaniko-Kulikovsky (1835–1920), a leading Russian scholar, was an early contributor to Marxist periodicals and a literary conservative, antagonistic towards the deliberately meaningless poems of the Futurists. [Tr.]

[4]Potebnya, *Iz zapisok po teorii slovesnosti,* p. 314. [Au.]

[5]Ibid., p. 291. [Au.]

[6]Fyodor Tyutchev (1803–1873), a poet, and Nicholas Gogol (1809–1852), a master of prose fiction and satire, are mentioned here because their bold use of imagery cannot be accounted for by Potebnya's theory. Shklovsky is arguing that writers frequently gain their effects by comparing the commonplace to the exceptional rather than vice versa. [Tr.]

[7]This is an allusion to Vyacheslav Ivanov's *Borozdy i*

the chief characteristic of poetry. Consequently, they should have expected the history of "imagistic art," as they call it, to consist of a history of changes in imagery. But we find that images change little; from century to century, from nation to nation, from poet to poet, they flow on without changing. Images belong to no one: they are "the Lord's." The more you understand an age, the more convinced you become that the images a given poet used and which you thought his own were taken almost unchanged from another poet. The works of poets are classified or grouped according to the new techniques that poets discover and share, and according to their arrangement and development of the resources of language; poets are much more concerned with arranging images than with creating them. Images are given to poets; the ability to remember them is far more important than the ability to create them.

Imagistic thought does not, in any case, include all the aspects of art nor even all the aspects of verbal art. A change in imagery is not essential to the development of poetry. We know that frequently an expression is thought to be poetic, to be created for aesthetic pleasure, although actually it was created without such intent — e.g., Annensky's opinion that the Slavic languages are especially poetic and Andrey Bely's ecstasy over the technique of placing adjectives after nouns, a technique used by eighteenth-century Russian poets. Bely joyfully accepts the technique as something artistic, or more exactly, as intended, if we consider intention as art. Actually, this reversal of the usual adjective-noun order is a peculiarity of the language (which had been influenced by Church Slavonic). Thus a work may be (1) intended as prosaic and accepted as poetic, or (2) intended as poetic and accepted as prosaic. This suggests that the artistry attributed to a given work results from the way we perceive it. By "works of art," in the narrow sense, we mean works created by special techniques designed to make the works as obviously artistic as possible.

mezhi [Furrows and Boundaries] (Moscow, 1916), a major statement of Symbolist theory. [Tr.]

Potebnya's conclusion, which can be formulated "poetry equals imagery," gave rise to the whole theory that "imagery equals symbolism," that the image may serve as the invariable predicate of various subjects. (This conclusion, because it expressed ideas similar to the theories of the Symbolists, intrigued some of their leading representatives — Andrey Bely, Merezhkovsky and his "eternal companions" — and, in fact, formed the basis of the theory of Symbolism.) The conclusion stems partly from the fact that Potebnya did not distinguish between the language of poetry and the language of prose. Consequently, he ignored the fact that there are two aspects of imagery: imagery as a practical means of thinking, as a means of placing objects within categories; and imagery as poetic, as a means of reinforcing an impression. I shall clarify with an example. I want to attract the attention of a young child who is eating bread and butter and getting the butter on her fingers. I call, "Hey, butterfingers!" This is a figure of speech, a clearly prosaic trope. Now a different example. The child is playing with my glasses and drops them. I call, "Hey, butterfingers!"[8] This figure of speech is a poetic trope. (In the first example, "butterfingers" is metonymic; in the second, metaphoric — but this is not what I want to stress.)

Poetic imagery is a means of creating the strongest possible impression. As a method it is, depending upon its purpose, neither more nor less effective than other poetic techniques; it is neither more nor less effective than ordinary or negative parallelism, comparison, repetition, balanced structure, hyperbole, the commonly accepted rhetorical figures, and all those methods which emphasize the emotional effect of an expression (including words or even articulated sounds.)[9] But poetic imagery only externally re-

[8]The Russian text involves a play on the word for "hat," colloquial for "clod," "duffer," etc. [Tr.]

[9]Shklovsky is here doing two things of major theoretical importance: (1) he argues that different techniques serve a single function, and that (2) no single technique is all-important. The second permits the formalists to be concerned with any and all literary devices; the first permits them to discuss the devices from a single consistent theoretical position. [Tr.]

sembles either the stock imagery of fables and ballads or thinking in images — e.g., the example in Ovsyaniko-Kulikovsky's *Language and Art* in which a little girl calls a ball a little watermelon. Poetic imagery is but one of the devices of poetic language. Prose imagery is a means of abstraction: a little watermelon instead of a lampshade, or a little watermelon instead of a head, is only the abstraction of one of the object's characteristics, that of roundness. It is no different from saying that the head and the melon are both round. This is what is meant, but it has nothing to do with poetry.

The law of the economy of creative effort is also generally accepted. [Herbert] Spencer wrote:

> On seeking for some clue to the law underlying these current maxims, we may see shadowed forth in many of them, the importance of economizing the reader's or the hearer's attention. To so present ideas that they may be apprehended with the least possible mental effort, is the desideratum towards which most of the rules above quoted point. . . . Hence, carrying out the metaphor that language is the vehicle of thought, there seems reason to think that in all cases the friction and inertia of the vehicle deduct from its efficiency; and that in composition, the chief, if not the sole thing to be done, is to reduce this friction and inertia to the smallest possible amount.[10]

And R[ichard] Avenarius:

> If a soul possess inexhaustible strength, then, of course, it would be indifferent to how much might be spent from this inexhaustible source; only the necessarily expended time would be important. But since its forces are limited, one is led to expect that the soul hastens to carry out the apperceptive process as expediently as possible — that is, with comparatively the least expenditure of energy, and, hence, with comparatively the best result.

Petrazhitsky, with only one reference to the general law of mental effort, rejects [William] James's theory of the physical basis of emotion, a theory which contradicts his own. Even Alexander Veselovsky acknowledged the principle of the economy of creative effort, a theory especially appealing in the study of rhythm, and agreed with Spencer: "A satisfactory style is precisely that style which delivers the greatest amount of thought in the fewest words." And Andrey Bely, despite the fact that in his better pages he gave numerous examples of "roughened" rhythm[11] and (particularly in the examples from Baratynsky) showed the difficulties inherent in poetic epithets, also thought it necessary to speak of the law of the economy of creative effort in his book[12] — a heroic effort to create a theory of art based on unverified facts from antiquated sources, on his vast knowledge of the techniques of poetic creativity, and on Krayevich's high school physics text.

These ideas about the economy of energy, as well as about the law and aim of creativity, are perhaps true in their application to "practical" language; they were, however, extended to poetic language. Hence they do not distinguish properly between the laws of practical language and the laws of poetic language. The fact that Japanese poetry has sounds not found in conversational Japanese was hardly the first factual indication of the differences between poetic and everyday language. Leo Jakubinsky has observed that the law of the dissimilation of liquid sounds does not apply to poetic language.[13] This suggested to him that poetic language tolerated the admission of hard-to-pronounce conglomerations of similar sounds. In his article, one of the first examples of scientific criticism, he indicates inductively, the contrast (I shall say more about this point later) between the laws of poetic language and the laws of practical language.[14]

[10]Herbert Spencer, *The Philosophy of Style* (Humboldt Library, vol. 34, New York, 1882), pp. 2–3. [Au.] Shklovsky's quoted reference, in Russian, preserves the idea of the original but shortens it. [Tr.]

[11]The Russian *zatrudyonny* means "made difficult." The suggestion is that poems with "easy" or smooth rhythms slip by unnoticed; poems that are difficult or "roughened" force the reader to attend to them. [Tr.]

[12]*Simvolizm*, probably. [Tr.]

[13]Leo Jakubinsky, "O zvukakh poeticheskovo yazyka" ["On the Sounds of Poetic Language"], *Sborniki* I (1916): 38. [Au.]

[14]Leo Jakubinsky, "Skopleniye odinakovykh plavnykh v prakticheskom i poeticheskom yazykakh" ["The Accumulation of Identical Liquids in Practical and Poetic Language"], *Sborniki* II (1917): 13–21. [Au.]

We must, then, speak about the laws of expenditure and economy in poetic language not on the basis of an analogy with prose, but on the basis of the laws of poetic language.

If we start to examine the general laws of perception, we see that as perception becomes habitual, it becomes automatic. Thus, for example, all of our habits retreat into the area of the unconsciously automatic; if one remembers the sensations of holding a pen or of speaking in a foreign language for the first time and compares that with his feeling at performing the action for the ten thousandth time, he will agree with us. Such habituation explains the principles by which, in ordinary speech, we leave phrases unfinished and words half expressed. In this process, ideally realized in algebra, things are replaced by symbols. Complete words are not expressed in rapid speech; their initial sounds are barely perceived. Alexander Pogodin offers the example of a boy considering the sentence "The Swiss mountains are beautiful" in the form of a series of letters: T, *S, m, a, b.*[15]

This characteristic of thought not only suggests the method of algebra, but even prompts the choice of symbols (letters, especially initial letters). By this "algebraic" method of thought we apprehend objects only as shapes with imprecise extensions; we do not see them in their entirety but rather recognize them by their main characteristics. We see the object as though it were enveloped in a sack. We know what it is by its configuration, but we see only its silhouette. The object, perceived thus in the manner of prose perception, fades and does not leave even a first impression; ultimately even the essence of what it was is forgotten. Such perception explains why we fail to hear the prose word in its entirety (see Leo Jakubinsky's article[16]) and, hence, why (along with other slips of the tongue) we fail to pronounce it. The process of "algebrization," the over-automatization of an object, permits the greatest economy of perceptive effort. Either objects are assigned only one proper feature — a number, for example — or else they function as though by formula and do not even appear in cognition:

> I was cleaning a room and, meandering about, approached the divan and couldn't remember whether or not I had dusted it. Since these movements are habitual and unconscious, I could not remember and felt that it was impossible to remember — so that if I had dusted it and forgot — that is, had acted unconsciously, then it was the same as if I had not. If some conscious person had been watching, then the fact could be established. If, however, no one was looking, or looking on unconsciously, if the whole complex lives of many people go on unconsciously, then such lives are as if they had never been.[17]

And so life is reckoned as nothing. Habitualization devours works, clothes, furniture, one's wife, and the fear of war. "If the whole complex lives of many people go on unconsciously, then such lives are as if they had never been." And art exists that one may recover the sensation of life; it exists to make one feel things, to make the stone *stony*. The purpose of art is to impart the sensation of things as they are perceived and not as they are known. The technique of art is to make objects "unfamiliar," to make forms difficult, to increase the difficulty and length of perception because the process of perception is an aesthetic end in itself and must be prolonged. *Art is a way of experiencing the artfulness of an object; the object is not important.*

The range of poetic (artistic) work extends from the sensory to the cognitive, from poetry to prose, from the concrete to the abstract: from Cervantes's Don Quixote — scholastic and poor nobleman, half consciously bearing his humiliation in the court of the duke — to the broad but empty Don Quixote of Turgenev; from Charlemagne to the name "king" [in Russian "Charles" and "king" obviously derive from the same root, *korol*]. The meaning of a work broadens to the extent that artfulness and artistry diminish; thus a fable symbolizes more than a poem, and a

[15]Alexander Pogodoin, *Yazyk, kak tvorchestvo [Language as Art]* (Kharkov, 1931), p. 42. [Au.] The original sentence was in French, "*Les montaignes de la Suisse sont belles,*" with the appropriate initials. [Tr.]

[16]Jakubinsky, *Sborniki* I (1916). [Au.]

[17]Leo Tolstoy's *Diary,* entry dated February 29, 1897. [Au.] The date is transcribed incorrectly; it should read March 1, 1897. [Tr.]

proverb more than a fable. Consequently, the least self-contradictory part of Potebnya's theory is his treatment of the fable, which, from his point of view, he investigated thoroughly. But since his theory did not provide for "expressive" works of art, he could not finish his book. As we know, *Notes on the Theory of Literature* was published in 1905, thirteen years after Potebnya's death. Potebnya himself completed only the section on the fable.[18]

After we see an object several times, we begin to recognize it. The object is in front of us and we know about it, but we do not see it[19] — hence we cannot say anything significant about it. Art removes objects from the automatism of perception in several ways. Here I want to illustrate a way used repeatedly by Leo Tolstoy, that writer who, for Merezhkovsky at least, seems to present things as if he himself saw them, saw them in their entirety, and did not alter them.

Tolstoy makes the familiar seem strange by not naming the familiar object. He describes an object as if he were seeing it for the first time, an event as if it were happening for the first time. In describing something he avoids the accepted names of its parts and instead names corresponding parts of other objects. For example, in "Shame" Tolstoy "defamiliarizes" the idea of flogging in this way: "to strip people who have broken the law, to hurl them to the floor, and to rap on their bottoms with switches," and, after a few lines, "to lash about on the naked buttocks." Then he remarks:

> Just why precisely this stupid, savage means of causing pain and not any other — why not prick the shoulders or any part of the body with needles, squeeze the hands or the feet in a vise, or anything like that?

I apologize for this harsh example, but it is typical of Tolstoy's way of pricking the conscience. The familiar act of flogging is made unfamiliar both by the description and by the proposal to change its form without changing its nature. Tolstoy uses this technique of "defamiliarization" constantly. The narrator of "Kholstomer," for example, is a horse, and it is the horse's point of view (rather than a person's) that makes the content of the story seem unfamiliar. Here is how the horse regards the institution of private property:

> I understood well what they said about whipping and Christianity. But then I was absolutely in the dark. What's the meaning of "his own," "his colt"? From these phrases I saw that people thought there was some sort of connection between me and the stable. At the time I simply could not understand the connection. Only much later, when they separated me from the other horses, did I begin to understand. But even then I simply could not see what it meant when they called me "man's property." The words "my horse" referred to me, a living horse, and seemed as strange to me as the words "my land," "my air," "my water."
>
> But the words made a strong impression on me. I thought about them constantly, and only after the most diverse experiences with people did I understand, finally, what they meant. They meant this: In life people are guided by words, not by deeds. It's not so much that they love the possibility of doing or not doing something as it is the possibility of speaking with words, agreed on among themselves, about various topics. Such are the words "my" and "mine," which they apply to different things, creatures, objects, and even to land, people, and horses. They agree that only one may say "mine" about this, that, or the other thing. And the one who says "mine" about the greatest number of things is, according to the game which they've agreed to among themselves, the one they consider the most happy. I don't know the point of all this, but it's true. For a long time I tried to explain it to myself in terms of some kind of real gain, but I had to reject that explanation because it was wrong.
>
> Many of those, for instance, who called me their own never rode on me — although others did. And so with those who fed me. Then again, the coachman, the veterinarians, and the outsiders in general treated me kindly, yet those who called me their own did not. In due time, having widened the scope of my observations, I satisfied myself that the notion "my," not only in relation to us horses, has no other basis than a narrow human instinct which is called a sense of or right to private property. A man says "this house is mine" and never lives in it; he only worries about its construction and upkeep. A merchant says "my shop," "my dry goods shop,"

[18]Alexander Potebnya, *Iz lektsy po teorii slovesnosti* [Lectures on the Theory of Language] (Kharkov, 1914). [Au.]

[19]Victor Shklovsky, *Voskresheniye slova [The Resurrection of the Word]* (Petersburg, 1914). [Au.]

for instance, and does not even wear clothes made from the better cloth he keeps in his own shop.

There are people who call a tract of land their own, but they never set eyes on it and never take a stroll on it. There are people who call others their own, yet never see them. And the whole relationship between them is that the so-called "owners" treat the others unjustly.

There are people who call women their own, or their "wives," but their women live with other men. And people strive not for the good in life, but for goods they can call their own.

I am now convinced that this is the essential difference between people and ourselves. And therefore, not even considering the other ways in which we are superior, but considering just this one virtue, we can bravely claim to stand higher than men on the ladder of living creatures. The actions of men, at least those with whom I have had dealings, are guided by *words* — ours, by deeds.

The horse is killed before the end of the story, but the manner of the narrative, its technique, does not change:

> Much later they put Serpukhovsky's body, which had experienced the world, which had eaten and drunk, into the ground. They could profitably send neither his hide, nor his flesh, nor his bones anywhere.
>
> But since his dead body, which had gone about in the world for twenty years, was a great burden to everyone, its burial was only a superfluous embarrassment for the people. For a long time no one had needed him; for a long time he had been a burden on all. But nevertheless, the dead who buried the dead found it necessary to dress this bloated body, which immediately began to rot, in a good uniform and good boots; to lay it in a good new coffin with new tassels at the four corners, then to place this new coffin in another of lead and ship it to Moscow; there to exhume ancient bones and at just that spot, to hide this putrefying body, swarming with maggots, in its new uniform and clean boots, and to cover it over completely with dirt.

Thus we see that at the end of the story Tolstoy continues to use the technique even though the motivation for it [the reason for its use] is gone.

In *War and Peace* Tolstoy uses the same technique in describing whole battles as if battles were something new. These descriptions are too long to quote; it would be necessary to extract a considerable part of the four-volume novel. But Tolstoy uses the same method in describing the drawing room and the theater:

> The middle of the stage consisted of flat boards; by the sides stood painted pictures representing trees, and at the back a linen cloth was stretched down to the floor boards. Maidens in red bodices and white skirts sat on the middle of the stage. One, very fat, in a white silk dress, sat apart on a narrow bench to which a green pasteboard box was glued from behind. They were all singing something. When they had finished, the maiden in white approached the prompter's box. A man in silk with tight-fitting pants on his fat legs approached her with a plume and began to sing and spread his arms in dismay. The man in the tight pants finished his song alone; then the girl sang. After that both remained silent as the music resounded; and the man, obviously waiting to begin singing his part with her again, began to run his fingers over the hand of the girl in the white dress. They finished their song together, and everyone in the theater began to clap and shout. But the men and women on stage, who represented lovers, start to bow, smiling and raising their hands.
>
> In the second act there were pictures representing monuments and openings in the linen cloth representing the moonlight, and they raised lamp shades on a frame. As the musicians started to play the bass horn and counter-bass, a large number of people in black mantles poured onto the stage from right and left. The people, with something like daggers in their hands, started to wave their arms. Then still more people came running out and began to drag away the maiden who had been wearing a white dress but who now wore one of sky blue. They did not drag her off immediately, but sang with her for a long time before dragging her away. Three times they struck on something metallic behind the side scenes, and everyone got down on his knees and began to chant a prayer. Several times all of this activity was interrupted by enthusiastic shouts from the spectators.

The third act is described:

> . . . But suddenly a storm blew up. Chromatic scales and chords of diminished sevenths were heard in the orchestra. Everyone ran about and again they dragged one of the bystanders behind the scenes as the curtain fell.

In the fourth act, "There was some sort of devil who sang, waving his hands, until the boards were moved out from under him and he dropped down."[20]

In *Resurrection* Tolstoy describes the city and the court in the same way; he uses a similar technique in "Kreutzer Sonata" when he describes marriage — "Why, if people have an affinity of souls, must they sleep together?" But he did not defamiliarize only those things he sneered at:

> Pierre stood up from his new comrades and made his way between the campfires to the other side of the road where, it seemed, the captive soldiers were held. He wanted to talk with them. The French sentry stopped him on the road and ordered him to return. Pierre did so, but not to the campfire, not to his comrades, but to an abandoned, unharnessed carriage. On the ground, near the wheel of the carriage, he sat cross-legged in the Turkish fashion, and lowered his head. He sat motionless for a long time, thinking. More than an hour passed. No one disturbed him. Suddenly he burst out laughing with his robust, good natured laugh — so loudly that the men near him looked around, surprised at his conspicuously strange laughter.
>
> "Ha, ha, ha," laughed Pierre. And he began to talk to himself. "The soldier didn't allow me to pass. They caught me, barred me. Me — me — my immortal soul. Ha, ha, ha," he laughed with tears starting in his eyes.
>
> Pierre glanced at the sky, into the depths of the departing, playing stars. "And all this is mine, all this is in me, and all this is I," thought Pierre. "And all this they caught and put in a planked enclosure." He smiled and went off to his comrades to lie down to sleep.[21]

Anyone who knows Tolstoy can find several hundred such passages in his work. His method of seeing things out of their normal context is also apparent in his last works. Tolstoy described the dogmas and rituals he attacked as if they were unfamiliar, substituting everyday meanings for the customarily religious meanings of the words common in church ritual. Many persons were painfully wounded; they considered it blasphemy to present as strange and monstrous what they accepted as sacred. Their reaction was due chiefly to the technique through which Tolstoy perceived and reported his environment. And after turning to what he had long avoided, Tolstoy found that his perceptions had unsettled his faith.

The technique of defamiliarization is not Tolstoy's alone. I cited Tolstoy because his work is generally known.

Now, having explained the nature of this technique, let us try to determine the approximate limits of its application. I personally feel that defamiliarization is found almost everywhere form is found. In other words, the difference between Potebnya's point of view and ours is this: An image is not a permanent referent for those mutable complexities of life which are revealed through it; its purpose is not to make us perceive meaning, but to create a special perception of the object — *it creates a "vision" of the object instead of serving as a means for knowing it.*

The purpose of imagery in erotic art can be studied even more accurately; an erotic object is usually presented as if it were seen for the first time. Gogol, in "Christmas Eve," provides the following example:

> Here he approached her more closely, coughed, smiled at her, touched her plump, bare arm with his fingers, and expressed himself in a way that showed both his cunning and his conceit.
>
> "And what is this you have, magnificent Solokha?" and having said this, he jumped back a little.
>
> "What? An arm, Osip Nikiforovich!" she answered.
>
> "Hmm, an arm! *He, he, he!*" said the secretary cordially, satisfied with his beginning. He wandered about the room.
>
> "And what is this you have, dearest Solokha?" he said in the same way, having approached her again and grasped her lightly by the neck, and in the very same way he jumped back.
>
> "As if you don't see, Osip Nikiforovich!" answered Solokha, "a neck, and on my neck a necklace."
>
> "Hmm! On the neck a necklace! *He, he, he!*" and the secretary again wandered about the room, rubbing his hands.
>
> "And what is this you have, incomparable Solokha?" . . . It is not known to what the secretary would stretch his longer fingers now.

[20]The Tolstoy and Gogol translations are ours. The passage occurs in Vol. II, Part 8, Chap. 9 of the edition of *War and Peace* published in Boston by the Dana Estes Co. in 1904–1912. [Tr.]

[21]Leo Tolstoy, *War and Peace,* IV, Part 13. Chap. 14. [Tr.]

And Knut Hamsun has the following in *Hunger:* "Two white prodigies appeared from beneath her blouse."

Erotic subjects may also be presented figuratively with the obvious purpose of leading us away from their "recognition." Hence sexual organs are referred to in terms of lock and key,[22] or quilting tools,[23] or bow and arrow, or rings and marlinspikes, as in the legend of Stavyor, in which a married man does not recognize his wife, who is disguised as a warrior. She proposes a riddle:

"Remember, Stavyor, do you recall
How we little ones walked to and fro in the street?
You and I together sometimes played with a marlinspike —
You had a silver marlinspike,
But I had a gilded ring?
I found myself at it just now and then,
But you fell in with it ever and always."
Says Stavyor, son of Godinovich,
"What! I didn't play with you at marlinspikes!"
Then Vasilisa Mikulichna: "So he says.
Do you remember, Stavyor, do you recall,
Now must you know, you and I together learned to read and write;
Mine was an ink-well of silver,
And yours a pen of gold?
But I just moistened it a little now and then,
And I just moistened it ever and always."[24]

In a different version of the legend we find a key to the riddle:

Here the formidable envoy Vasilyushka
Raised her skirts to the very navel,
And then the young Stavyor, son of Godinovich,
Recognized her gilded ring. . . .[25]

But defamiliarization is not only a technique of the erotic riddle — a technique of euphemism — it is also the basis and point of all riddles. Every riddle pretends to show its subject either by words which specify or describe it but which, during the telling, do not seem applicable (the type: "black and white and 'red' — read — all over") or by means of odd but imitative sounds ("'Twas brillig, and the slithy toves / Did gyre and gimble in the wabe").[26]

Even erotic images not intended as riddles are defamiliarized ("boobies," "tarts," "piece," etc.). In popular imagery there is generally something equivalent to "trampling the grass" and "breaking the guelder-rose." The technique of defamiliarization is absolutely clear in the widespread image — a motif of erotic affectation — in which a bear and other wild beasts (or a devil, with a different reason for nonrecognition) do not recognize a man.[27]

The lack of recognition in the following tale is quite typical:

A peasant was plowing a field with a piebald mare. A bear approached him and asked, "Uncle, what's made this mare piebald for you?"

"I did the piebalding myself."

"But how?"

"Let me, and I'll do the same for you."

The bear agreed. The peasant tied his feet together with a rope, took the ploughshare from the two-wheeled plough, heated it on the fire, and applied it to his flanks. He made the bear piebald by scorching his fur down to the hide with the hot ploughshare. The man untied the bear, which went off and lay down under a tree.

A magpie flew at the peasant to pick at the meat on his shirt. He caught her and broke one of her legs. The magpie flew off to perch in the same tree under which the bear was lying. Then, after the magpie, a horsefly landed on the mare, sat down, and began to bite. The peasant caught the fly, took

[22][Dmitry] Savodnikov, *Zagadki russkovo naroda* [*Riddles of the Russian People*] (St. Petersburg, 1901), Nos. 102–107. [Au.]

[23]Ibid., Nos. 588–591. [Au.]

[24]A. E. Gruzinsky, ed., *Pesni, sobrannye P*[*avel*] *N. Rybnikovym* [*Songs Collected by P. N. Rybnikov*] (Moscow, 1909–1910), No. 30. [Au.]

[25]Ibid., No. 171.

[26]We have supplied familiar English examples in place of Shklovsky's word-play. Shklovsky is saying that we create words with no referents or with ambiguous referents in order to force attention to the objects represented by the similar-sounding words. By making the reader go through the extra step of interpreting the nonsense word, the writer prevents an automatic response. A toad is a toad, but "tove" forces one to pause and think about the beast. [Tr.]

[27]E. R. Romanov, "Besstrashny barin" *Velikorusskiye skazki* (Zapiski Imperskovo Russkovo Geograficheskovo Obschestva, XLII, No. 52). Belorussky sbornik, "Spravyadlivy soldat" ["The Intrepid Gentleman," *Great Russian Tales* (Notes of the Imperial Russian Geographical Society, XLII, No. 52). White Russian Anthology, "The Upright Soldier" (1886–1912).] [Au.]

a stick, shoved it up its rear, and let it go. The fly went to the tree where the bear and the magpie were. There all three sat.

The peasant's wife came to bring his dinner to the field. The man and his wife finished their dinner in the fresh air, and he began to wrestle with her on the ground.

The bear saw this and said to the magpie and the fly, "Holy priests! The peasant wants to piebald someone again."

The magpie said, "No, he wants to break someone's legs."

The fly said, "No, he wants to shove a stick up someone's rump."[28]

The similarity of technique here and in Tolstoy's "Kholstomer," is, I think, obvious.

Quite often in literature the sexual act itself is defamiliarized; for example, the *Decameron* refers to "scraping out a barrel," "catching nightingales," "gay wool-beating work" (the last is not developed in the plot). Defamiliarization is often used in describing the sexual organs.

A whole series of plots is based on such a lack of recognition; for example, in Afanasyev's *Intimate Tales* the entire story of "The Shy Mistress" is based on the fact that an object is not called by its proper name — or, in other words, on a game of nonrecognition. So too in Onchukov's "Spotted Petticoats," tale no. 525, and also in "The Bear and the Hare" from *Intimate Tales,* in which the bear and the hare make a "wound."

Such constructions as "the pestle and the mortar," or "Old Nick and the infernal regions" *(Decameron),* are also examples of the technique of defamiliarization. And in my article on plot construction I write about defamiliarization in psychological parallelism. Here, then, I repeat that the perception of disharmony in a harmonious context is important in parallelism. The purpose of parallelism, like the general purpose of imagery, is to transfer the usual perception of an object into the sphere of a new perception — that is, to make a unique semantic modification.

In studying poetic speech in its phonetic and lexical structure as well as in its characteristic distribution of words and in the characteristic thought structures compounded from the words, we find everywhere the artistic trademark — that is, we find material obviously created to remove the automatism of perception; the author's purpose is to create the vision which results from that deautomatized perception. A work is created "artistically" so that its perception is impeded and the greatest possible effect is produced through the slowness of the perception. As a result of this lingering, the object is perceived not in its extension in space, but, so to speak, in its continuity. Thus "poetic language" gives satisfaction. According to Aristotle, poetic language must appear strange and wonderful; and, in fact, it is often actually foreign: the Sumerian used by the Assyrians, the Latin of Europe during the Middle Ages, the Arabisms of the Persians, the Old Bulgarian of Russian literature, or the elevated, almost literary language of folk songs. The common archaisms of poetic language, the intricacy of the sweet new style [*dolce stil nuovo*],[29] the obscure style of the language of Arnaut Daniel with the "roughened" [*harte*] forms *which make pronunciation difficult* — these are used in much the same way. Leo Jakubinsky has demonstrated the principle of phonetic "roughening" of poetic language in the particular case of the repetition of identical sounds. The language of poetry is, then, a difficult, roughened, impeded language. In a few special instances the language of poetry approximates the language of prose, but this does not violate the principle of "roughened" form.

Her sister was called Tatyana.
For the first time we shall
Wilfully brighten the delicate
Pages of a novel with such a name.[30]

wrote Pushkin. The usual poetic language of Pushkin's contemporaries was the elegant style of Derzhavin; but Pushkin's style, because it seemed trivial then, was unexpectedly difficult for them. We should remember the consternation of Pushkin's contemporaries over the vulgarity of his expressions. He used the popular language

[28]D[mitry] S. Zelenin, *Velikorusskiye skazki Permskoy gubernii [Great Russian Tales of the Permian Province* (St. Petersburg, 1913)], No. 70. [Au.]

[29]Dante, *Purgatorio,* 24:56. Dante refers to the new lyric style of his contemporaries. [Tr.]

[30]Alexander Pushkin, *Eugene Onegin,* I.ii.24. [Ed.]

as a special device for prolonging attention, just as his contemporaries generally used Russian words in their usually French speech (see Tolstoy's examples in *War and Peace*).

Just now a still more characteristic phenomenon is under way. Russian literary language, which was originally foreign to Russia, has so permeated the language of the people that it has blended with their conversation. On the other hand, literature has now begun to show a tendency towards the use of dialects (Remizov, Klyuyev, Essenin, and others,[31] so unequal in talent and so alike in language, are intentionally provincial) and of barbarisms (which gave rise to the Severyanin group[32]). And currently Maxim Gorky is changing his diction from the old literary language to the new literary colloquialism of Leskov.[33] Ordinary speech and literary language have thereby changed places (see the work of Vyacheslav Ivanov and many others). And finally, a strong tendency, led by Khlebnikov, to create a new and properly poetic language has emerged. In the light of these developments we can define poetry as *attenuated, tortuous* speech. Poetic speech is *formed speech.* Prose is ordinary speech — economical, easy, proper; the goddess of prose [*dea prosae*] is a goddess of the accurate, facile type, of the "direct" expression of a child. I shall discuss roughened form and retardation as the general *law* of art at greater length in an article on plot construction.[34]

Nevertheless, the position of those who urge the idea of economy of artistic energy as something which exists in and even distinguishes poetic language seems, at first glance, tenable for the problem of rhythm. Spencer's description of rhythm would seem to be absolutely incontestable:

> Just as the body in receiving a series of varying concussions, must keep the muscles ready to meet the most violent of them, as not knowing when such may come: so, the mind in receiving unarranged articulations, must keep its perspectives active enough to recognize the least easily caught sounds. And as, if the concussions recur in definite order, the body may husband its forces by adjusting the resistance needful for each concussion; so, if the syllables be rhythmically arranged, the mind may economize its energies by anticipating the attention required for each syllable.[35]

This apparently conclusive observation suffers from the common fallacy, the confusion of the laws of poetic and prosaic language. In *The Philosophy of Style* Spencer failed utterly to distinguish between them. But rhythm may have two functions. The rhythm of prose, or of a work song like "Dubinushka," permits the members of the work crew to do their necessary "groaning together" and also eases the work by making it automatic. And, in fact, it is easier to march with music than without it, and to march during an animated conversation is even easier, for the walking is done unconsciously. Thus the rhythm of prose is an important automatizing element; the rhythm of poetry is not. There is "order" in art, yet not a single column of a Greek temple stands exactly in its proper order; poetic rhythm is similarly disordered rhythm. Attempts to systematize the irregularities have been made, and such attempts are part of the current problem in the theory of rhythm. It is obvious that the systematization will not work, for in reality the problem is not one of complicating the rhythm but of disordering the rhythm — a disordering which cannot be predicted. Should the disordering of rhythm become a convention, it would be ineffective as a device for the roughening of language. But I will not discuss rhythm in more detail since I intend to write a book about it.[36]

[31]Alexey Remizov (1877–1957) is best known as a novelist and satirist; Nicholas Klyuyev (1885–1937) and Sergey Essenin (1895–1925) were "peasant poets." All three were noted for their faithful reproduction of Russian dialects and colloquial language. [Tr.]

[32]A group noted for its opulent and sensuous verse style. [Tr.]

[33]Nicholas Leskov (1831–1895), novelist and short story writer, helped popularize the *skaz*, or yarn, and hence, because of the part dialect peculiarities play in the *skaz*, also altered Russian literary language. [Tr.]

[34]Shklovsky is probably referring to his *Razvyortyvaniye syuzheta* [*Plot Development*] (Petrograd, 1291). [Tr.]

[35]Spencer, p. 169. Again the Russian text is shortened from Spencer's original. [Tr.]

[36]We have been unable to discover the book Shklovsky promised. [Tr.]

Yuri Tynyanov

1894–1943

The Russian scholar, novelist, and literary critic Yuri Tynyanov was born in the town of Rezhitsa in the province of Vitebsk. Like Victor Shklovsky, a fellow member of the Society for the Study of Poetic Language (OPOYAZ), Tynyanov studied at the University of Petersburg, and like Shklovsky he eventually moved away from theorizing in the wake of official disapproval of formalist ideas. From 1921 to 1930 he was a lecturer in Russian poetry at the Petrograd State Institute of Art History. His early works, notably on Pushkin (1926) and Dostoevsky and Gogol (1921), are considered to be remarkable both for their dexterous scholarship and for the boldness of their interpretations. An important theoretical statement, "On Literary Evolution," appeared in 1927, but because Soviet hostility to formalism was on the rise, Tynyanov prudently turned mainly to writing historical fiction. Illness and premature death prevented him from finishing the huge novel about Pushkin he began writing in 1936.

On Literary Evolution

1

Within the cultural disciplines literary history still retains the status of a colonial territory. On the one hand, individualistic psychologism dominates it to a significant extent, particularly in the West, unjustifiably replacing the problem of literature with the question of the author's psychology, while the problem of literary evolution becomes the problem of the genesis of literary phenomena. On the other hand, a simplified causal approach to a literary order leads to a sharp break between the literary order itself and the point of observation, which always turns out to be the major but also the most remote social orders. The organization of a closed literary order and the examination of the evolution within it sometimes collides with the neighboring cultural, behavioral, and social orders in the broad sense. Thus such an effort is doomed to incompleteness. The theory of value in literary investigation has brought about the danger of studying major but isolated works and has changed the history of literature into a *history of generals*.[1] The blind rejection of a history of generals has in turn caused an interest in the study of mass literature, but no clear theoretical awareness of how to study it or what the nature of its significance is.

Finally, the relationship between the history of literature and living contemporary literatures — a relationship useful and very necessary to science — is not always necessary and useful to the development of literature. The representatives of literature are ready to view the history of literature as the codification of certain traditional norms and laws and to confuse the historical character of a literary phenomenon with "historicism." As a result of this conflict, there has arisen an attempt to study isolated works and the laws of their construction on an extrahistorical plane, resulting in the abolition of the history of literature.

2

In order to become finally a science, the history of literature must claim reliability. All of its ter-

Translated by C. A. Luplow.

[1]Generals as opposed to sergeants or privates. Tynyanov is speaking of literary histories, like Ian Watt's *The Rise of the Novel,* that throw the entire burden of history on certain world-historic writers and texts (Defoe, Richardson, Fielding) in a genre that was both crowded with lesser figures and undeniably more complex. [Ed.]

minology, and first of all the very term, "the history of literature," must be reconsidered. The term proves to be extremely broad, covering both the material history of belles lettres, the history of verbal art, and the history of writing in general. It is also pretentious, since "the history of literature" considers itself a priori a discipline ready to enter into "the history of culture" as a system equipped with a scientific methodology. As yet it has no right to such a claim.

Meanwhile, the historical investigations of literature fall into at least two main types, depending on the points of observation: the investigation of the genesis of literary phenomena, and the investigation of the evolution of a literary order, that is, of literary changeability.

The point of view determines not only the significance but also the nature of the phenomenon being studied. In the investigation of literary evolution, the moment of genesis has its own significance and character, which are obviously not the same as in the investigation of the genesis per se.

Furthermore, the study of literary evolution or changeability must reject the theories of naive evaluation, which result from the confusion of points of observation, in which evaluation is carried over from one epoch or system into another.[2] At the same time, evaluation itself must be freed from its subjective coloring, and the "value" of a given literary phenomenon must be considered as having an "evolutionary significance and character."

The same must also apply to such concepts as "epigonism," "dilettantism," or "mass literature," which are for now evaluative concepts.[3]

Tradition, the basic concept of the established history of literature, has proved to be an unjustifiable abstraction of one or more of the literary elements of a given system within which they occupy the same plane and play the same role. They are equated with the like elements of another system in which they are on a different plane, thus they are brought into a seemingly unified, fictitiously integrated system.

The main concept for literary evolution is the *mutation* of systems, and thus the problem of "traditions" is transferred onto another plane.

3

Before this basic problem can be analyzed, it must be agreed that a literary work is a system, as is literature itself. Only after this basic agreement has been established is it possible to create a literary science which does not superficially examine diverse phenomena but studies them closely. In this way the problem of the role of contiguous

[2]Tynyanov's point here is that texts that are highly valued in the historian's era may have been virtually unknown to contemporaries (and vice versa), tempting the historian to ascribe historical consequences to a particular text that may not have been influential at the time. [Ed.]

[3]One need only examine the mass literature of the 1820s and 1830s to be convinced of their colossal evolutionary difference. In the 1830s, years of the automatization of preceding traditions, years of work on dusty literary material, "dilettantism" suddenly received a tremendous evolutionary significance. It is from dilettantism, from the atmosphere of "verse notes written on the margins of books," that a new phenomenon emerged — Tyutchev, who transformed poetic language and genres by his intimate intonations. The relationship of social conventions to literature, which seems to be its degeneration from an evaluative point of view, transforms the literary system. In the 1820s, the years of the "masters" and the creation of new poetic genres, dilettantism and mass literature were called "graphomania." The poets, who from the point of view of evolutionary significance were the leading figures of the 1830s, appeared to be determined as the "dilettantes" (Tyutchev, Polezhaev) or the "epigones" and "pupils" (Lermontov) in their struggle with the preceding norms. In the period of the 1820s, however, even the secondary poets appeared like leading masters; note, for example, the universality and grandioseness of the genres used by such mass poets as Olin. It is clear that the evolutionary significance of such phenomena as dilettantism or epigonism is different from period to period. Supercilious, evaluative treatment of these phenomena is the heritage of the old history of literature. [Au.] Here again, Tynyanov is talking about the difference between how a literary movement appears to its contemporaries and what its effect may have been in enabling future developments in art. A more familiar example might be the vogue of primitivism in poetry in the 1760s, which produced forgeries like MacPherson's *Ossian* poems and Thomas Percy's *Reliques of English Poesy* (which included ballads *written* as well as collected by Percy and his friends). These texts were condemned as phony, simple-minded trash by contemporaries like Samuel Johnson. But the movement had a "social" as well as a literary significance in the production of the sense of "nationality," and it eventuated in literary experimentation with "lyrical ballads" by Wordsworth and Coleridge. [Ed.]

systems in literary evolution is actually posited instead of being rejected.

The analysis of the separate elements of a work, such as the composition, style, rhythm, and syntax in prose, and the rhythm and semantics in poetry, provides sufficient evidence that these elements, within certain limits, can be abstracted as a *working hypothesis,* although they are interrelated and interacting. The study of rhythm in poetry and prose was bound to show that the role of a given element is different in different systems.

The interrelationship of each element with every other in a literary work and with the whole literary system as well may be called the constructional *function* of the given element.

On close examination, such a function proves to be a complex concept. An element is on the one hand interrelated with similar elements in other works in other systems, and on the other hand it is interrelated with different elements within the same work. The former may be termed the *auto-function* and the latter, the *syn-function.*

Thus, for example, the lexicon of a given work is interrelated with both the whole literary lexicon and the general lexicon of the language, as well as with other elements of that given work. These two components or functions operate simultaneously but are not of equal relevance.

The function of archaisms, for example, depends wholly on the system within which they are used. In Lomonosov's system, in which lexical coloring plays a dominant role, such archaisms function as "elevated" word usage. They are used for their lexical association with Church Slavic. In Tyutchev's work archaisms have a different function. In some instances they are abstract, as in the pair: *fontan-vodomet* [fountain-spout]. An interesting example is the usage of archaisms in an ironical function: "*Pušek grom i musikija*" [Thunder of guns and musicke] is used by a poet who otherwise employs a word such as *musikijskij* [musicall] in a completely different function. The auto-function, although it is not decisive, makes the existence of the syn-function possible and at the same time conditions it. Thus up to the time of Tyutchev, in the eighteenth and nineteenth centuries, there existed an extensive parodic literature in which archaisms had a parodic function. But the semantic and intonational system of the given work finally determines the function of a given expression, in this case determining the word usage to be "ironic" rather than "elevated."[4]

It is incorrect to isolate the elements from one system outside their constructional function and to correlate them with other systems.

4

Is the so-called "immanent" study of a work as a system possible without comparing it with the general literary system? Such an isolated study of a literary work is equivalent to abstracting isolated elements and examining them outside their work. Such abstracting is continuously applied to contemporary works and may be successful in literary criticism, since the interrelationship of a contemporary work with contemporary literature is in advance an established, although concealed, fact. (The interrelationship of a work with other works by the same author, its relationship to genre, and so on, belong here.)

Even in contemporary literature, however, isolated study is impossible. The very existence of a fact *as literary* depends on its differential quality, that is, on its interrelationship with both literary and extraliterary orders. Thus, its existence depends on its function. What in one epoch would be a literary fact would in another be a common matter of social communication, and vice versa, depending on the whole literary system in which the given fact appears.

Thus the friendly letter of Derzhavin is a social fact. The friendly letter of the Karamzhin and Pushkin epoch is a literary fact. Thus one has the literariness of memories and diaries in one system and their extraliterariness in another.

We cannot be certain of the structure of a work if it is studied in isolation.

Finally, the auto-function, that is, the interrelationship of an element with similar elements in

[4]Likewise with the second generation of English Romantics: Archaisms in Keats, such as the "fragrant zone" and "elfin grot" of "La Belle Dame sans Merci" (1819), are usually meant to be elevated language, while those in Byron, like "the far mountains wax a little hoary" from *Don Juan,* published the same year, are usually parodic of an outmoded poetic diction. [Ed.]

other systems, conditions the syn-function, that is, the constructional function of the element.

Thus, whether or not an element is "effaced" is important. But what is the effacement of a line, meter, plot structure, and so on? What, in other words, is the "automatization" of one or another element?

The following is an example from linguistics. When the referential meaning of a word is effaced, that word becomes the expression of a relationship, a connection, and thus it becomes an auxiliary word. In other words, its function changes. The same is true of the "automatization" of a literary element. It does not disappear. Its function simply changes, and it becomes auxiliary. If the meter of a poem is "effaced," then the other signs of verse and the other elements of the work become more important in its place, and the meter takes on other functions.[5]

Thus the short feuilleton[6] verse of the newspaper uses mainly effaced, banal meters which have long been rejected by poetry. No one would read it as a "poem" related to "poetry." Here the effaced meter is a means of attaching feuilleton material from everyday life to literature. Meter thus has an auxiliary function, which is completely different from its function in a poetic work. This also applies to parody in the verse feuilleton. Parody is viable only in so far as what is being parodied is still alive. What literary significance can the thousandth parody of Lermontov's "When the gold cornfield sways . . ." or Pushkin's "The Prophet" have today? The verse feuilleton, however, uses such parody constantly. Here again we have the same phenomenon: the function of parody has become auxiliary, as it serves to apply extraliterary facts to literature.

In a work in which the so-called plot is effaced, the story carries out different functions than in a work in which it is not effaced. The story might be used merely to motivate style or as a strategy for developing the material. Crudely speaking, from our vantage point in a particular literary system, we would be inclined to reduce nature descriptions in old novels to an auxiliary role, to the role of making transitions or retardation; therefore we would almost ignore them, although from the vantage point of a different literary system we would be forced to consider nature descriptions as the main, dominant element. In other words, there are situations in which the story simply provides the motivation for the treatment of "static descriptions."

5

The more difficult and less studied question of literary genres can be resolved in the same way. The novel, which seems to be an integral genre that has developed in and of itself over the centuries, turns out to be not an integral whole but a variable. Its material changes from one literary system to another, as does its method of introducing extraliterary language materials into literature. Even the features of the genre evolve. The genres of the "short story" and the "novella" were defined by different features in the system of the twenties to forties than they are in our time, as is obvious from their very names. We tend to name genres according to secondary features or, crudely speaking, by size. For us the labels, short story, novella, and novel, are adequate only to define the quantity of printed pages. This proves not so much the "automatization" of genres in our literary system as the fact that we define genres by other features. The size of a thing, the quantity of verbal material, is not an indifferent feature; we cannot, however, define the genre of a work if it is isolated from the system. For example, what was called an ode in the 1820s or by Fet was so labeled on the basis of features different from those used to define an ode in Lomonosov's time.

Consequently, we may conclude that the study of isolated genres outside the features characteristic of the genre system with which they are related is impossible. The historical novel of Tolstoy is not related to the historical novel of

[5]For example, the meter of Robert Browning's "My Last Duchess" is heroic couplets, but the lines are so enjambed that the regular meter and rhyme can seldom be heard in reading. This enhances the dramatic qualities of the poem (our attention to character and setting), but it also suggests the presence of a voice behind the Duke's words (Browning's) judging his language and behavior. Thus, what is effaced (meter and rhyme) loses its usual function (beautifying the language) but takes on another function. [Ed.]

[6]Popular or kitsch art; literally a "notebook." [Ed.]

Zagoskin, but to the prose of his contemporaries.[7]

6

Strictly speaking, one cannot study literary phenomena outside of their interrelationships. Such, for example, is the problem of prose and poetry. We tacitly consider metrical prose to be prose, and nonmetrical free verse to be poetry, without considering the fact that in another literary system we would thus be placed in a difficult position. The point is that prose and poetry are interrelated and that there is a mutually shared function of prose and poetry. (Note the interrelationship of prose and poetry in their respective development, as established by Boris Eichenbaum.)

The function of poetry in a particular literary system was fulfilled by the formal element of meter; but prose displays differentiation and develops, and so does poetry. The differentiation of one interrelated type leads to, or better, is connected with, the differentiation of another interrelated type. Thus metrical prose arises, as in the works of Andrey Bely. This is connected with the transfer of the verse function in poetry from meter onto other features which are in part secondary and resultant.[8] Such features may be rhythm, used as the feature of verse units, a particular syntax or particular lexicon, and so on. The function of prose with regard to verse remains, but the formal elements fulfilling this function are different. In the course of centuries the further evolution of forms may consolidate the function of verse with regard to prose, transfer it onto a whole series of other features, or it may infringe upon it and make it unessential. And just as in contemporary literature the interrelationship of genres is hardly essential and is established according to secondary signs, so a period may come in which it will be unessential whether a work is written in prose or poetry.

7

The evolutionary relationship of function and formal elements is a completely uninvestigated problem. An example is given above of how the evolution of forms results in a change of function. There are also many examples of how a form with an undetermined function creates or defines a new one, and there are also others in which a function seeks its own form. I will give an example in which both occurred together.

In the archaist trend of the 1820s the function of the combined elevated and folk verse epos arises. *The interrelationship of literature with the social order led to the large verse form.* But there were no formal elements, and the demands of the social system turned out to be unequal to the demands of literature. Then the search for formal elements began. In 1824 Katenin advocated the octave[9] as the formal element of the poetic epopea.[10] The passionate quarrels concerning the seemingly innocent octave were appropriate to the tragic "orphanhood" of function without form. The epos of the archaists failed. Six years later Shevyrev and Pushkin used the form in a different function: to break with the whole iambic tetrameter epos and create a new, "debased" (as opposed to "elevated"), prosaicized epos, such as Pushkin's *Little House in Kolomna.*

The relationship between form and function is not accidental. The comparable combination of a particular lexicon with a particular meter by Katenin and then twenty or thirty years later by Nekrasov, who probably did not know about Katenin, was not accidental.

The variability of the functions of a given formal element, the rise of some new function of a formal element, and the attaching of a formal element to a function are all important problems of literary evolution; but there is no room to study or resolve these problems here. I would like to

[7]Zagoskin was a Russian imitator of Walter Scott, with a heroic and romantic view of history that Tolstoy's historical novels (like *War and Peace*) were at pains to demolish. [Ed.]

[8]Similar features appear in English and American literature around the same time as Andrey Bely (1880–1934), modernist author of *Petersburg* (1922); rhythmical prose appears in Gertrude Stein and James Joyce in an era when meter and rhythm are ceasing to be the hallmarks of poetry. [Ed.]

[9]*Ottava rima,* the stanza used by Byron in *Don Juan.* [Ed.]

[10]Narrative poetry. [Ed.]

say only that the whole problem of literature as a system demands further investigation.

8

The assumption that the interrelationship of literary phenomena occurs when a work enters into a synchronic literary system and there "acquires" a function is not entirely correct. The very concept of a continuously evolving synchronic system is contradictory. A literary system is first of all a *system of the functions of the literary order which are in continual interrelationship with other orders.* Systems change in their composition, but the differentiation of human activities remains. The evolution of literature, as of other cultural systems, does not coincide either in tempo or in character with the systems with which it is interrelated. This is owing to the specificity of the material with which it is concerned. The evolution of the structural function occurs rapidly; the evolution of the literary function occurs over epochs; and the evolution of the functions of a whole literary system in relation to neighboring systems occurs over centuries.

9

Since a system is not an equal interaction of all elements but places a group of elements in the foreground — the "dominant" — and thus involves the deformation of the remaining elements, a work enters into literature and takes on its own literary function through this dominant. Thus we correlate poems with the verse category, not with the prose category, not on the basis of all their characteristics, but only of some of them. The same is true concerning genres. We relate a novel to "the novel" on the basis of its size and the nature of its plot development, while at one time it was distinguished by the presence of a love intrigue.[11]

Another interesting fact from an evolutionary point of view is the following. A work is correlated with a particular literary system depending on its deviation, its "difference" as compared with the literary system with which it is confronted. Thus, for example, the unusually sharp argument among the critics of the 1820s over the genre of the Pushkin narrative poem arose because the Pushkin genre was a combined, mixed, new genre without a ready-made "name." The sharper the divergence or differentiation from a particular literary system, the more that system from which the derivation occurs is accentuated. Thus, free verse emphasized the verse principle of *nonmetrical* features, while Sterne's novel[12] emphasized the compositional principle of *nonplot* features (Shklovsky). The following is an analogy from linguistics: "The variability of the word stem makes it the center of maximum expressiveness and thus extricates it from the net of prefixes which do not change" (Vendryes).

10

What constitutes the interrelationship of literature with neighboring orders? What, moreover, are these neighboring orders? The answer is obvious: social conventions.

Yet, in order to solve the problem of the interrelationship of literature with social conventions, the question must be posited: *how and by what means* are social conventions interrelated with literature? Social conventions are by nature many-sided and complex, and only the function of all their aspects is specific in it. Social conventions are correlated with literature first of all in its verbal aspect. This interrelationship is realized through language. That is, literature in relation to social conventions has a verbal function.

We use the term "orientation." It denotes approximately the "creative intention of the author." Yet it happens that "the intention may be good, but the fulfillment bad." Furthermore, the author's intention can only be a catalyst. In using a specific literary material, the author may yield to it, thus departing from his first intention. Thus Griboedov's *Wit Works Woe* was supposed to be "elevated" and even "grandiose," according to the author's terminology. But instead it turned

[11]Samuel Johnson's *Dictionary* defines "novel" as "a short tale, generally of love." [Ed.]

[12]*Tristram Shandy.* [Ed.]

out to be a political publicistic comedy of the archaist school. *Eugene Onegin* was first meant to be a "satiric narrative poem" in which the author would be "brimming over with bitterness." However, while working on the fourth chapter, Pushkin had already said, "Where is my satire? There's not a trace of it in *Eugene Onegin.*"

The structural function, that is, the interrelationship of elements within a work, changes the "author's intention" into a catalyst, but does nothing more. "Creative freedom" thus becomes an optimistic slogan which does not correspond to reality, but yields instead to the slogan "creative necessity."

The literary function, that is, the interrelationship of a work with the literary order, completes the whole thing. If we eliminate the teleological, goal-oriented allusion, the "intention," from the word "orientation," what happens? The "orientation" of a literary work then proves to be its verbal function, its interrelationship with the social conventions.

The "orientation" of the Lomonosov ode, its verbal function, is oratorical. The word is oriented on *pronunciation.* And to carry further the associations with actual life, the orientation is on declamation in the large palace hall. By the time of Karamzin, the ode was literarily "worn out." The "orientation" had died out or narrowed down in significance and had been transferred onto other forms related to life. Congratulatory odes, as well as others, became "uniform verses," i.e., what are purely real-life phenomena. Ready-made literary genres did not exist. Everyday verbal communication took their place. The verbal function, or orientation, was seeking its forms and found them in the romance, the joking play with rhymes, *bouts rimés,*[13] charades, and so on. And here the moment of genesis, the presence of certain forms of everyday speech, received evolutionary significance. These speech phenomena were found in the salon of Karamzin's epoch. And the salon, a fact of everyday life, at this time became a literary fact. In this way the forms of social life acquired a literary function.[14]

Similarly, the semantics of the intimate domestic circle always exists, but in particular periods it takes on a literary function. Such, too, is the application of *accidental results.* The rough drafts of Pushkin's verse programs and the drafts of his "scenarios" became his finished prose. This is possible only through the evolution of a whole system — through the evolution of its orientation.

An analogy from our own time of the struggle between two orientations is seen in the mass orientation of Mayakovsky's poetry ("the ode") in competition with the romance, chamber-style orientation of Esenin ("the elegy").

II

The verbal function must also be taken into consideration in dealing with the problem of the reverse expansion of literature into actual life. The *literary personality,* or the *author's personality,* or at various times the *hero,* becomes the verbal orientation of literature. And from there it enters into real life. Such are the lyric heroes of Byron in relationship to his "literary personality," i.e., to the personality which came to life for the readers of his poems and which was thus transferred into life. Such is the "literary personality" of Heine, which is far removed from the real biographical Heine. In given periods, biography becomes oral, apocryphal literature. This happens naturally, in connection with the speech orientation of a given system. Thus, one has Pushkin, Tolstoy, Blok, Mayakovsky, and Esenin as opposed to the absence of a literary personality in Leskov, Turgenev, Fet, Maykov, Gumilev, and others. This corresponds to the absence of a speech orientation on "the literary personality." Obviously, special real-life conditions are necessary for the expansion of literature into life.[15]

[13]Rhyming games. [Ed.]

[14]Whitman's free verse rhythms, similarly, owed much to the rhythms of pulpit oratory, while much of contemporary American poetry is flavored with the spritzing humor of stand-up comedy or the pseudo-intimate revelations of talk shows. [Ed.]

[15]British and American writers with "literary personality" in Tynyanov's sense would include Dickens (as opposed to Trollope), Hemingway (as opposed to Woolf), and Frost (as opposed to Stevens). The issue is not the writer's quality but the impress of his or her life upon the culture. [Ed.]

12

Such is the immediate social function of literature. It can be established and investigated only through the study of closely related conditions, without the forcible incorporation of remote, though major, causal orders.

Finally, the concept of the "orientation" of a speech function is applicable to a literary order but not to an individual work. A separate work must be related to a literary order before one can talk about its orientation. The law of large numbers does not apply to small numbers. In establishing the distant causal orders for separate works and authors, we study not the evolution of literature but its modification, not how literature changes and evolves in correlation with other orders, but how neighboring orders deform it. This problem too is worth studying, but on a completely different plane.

The direct study of the author's psychology and the construction of a causal "bridge" from the author's environment, daily life, and class to his works is particularly fruitless. The erotic poetry of Batyushkov[16] resulted from his work on the poetic language — note his speech, "On the Influence of Light Poetry on Language" — and Vyazemsky[17] refused to seek its genesis in Batyushkov's psychology. The poet, Polonsky, who was never a theoretician but who as a poet and master of his craft understood this, wrote of Benediktov,

> It is very possible that the severity of nature, the forests, the fields . . . influenced the impressionable soul of the child and future poet, but how did they influence it? This is a difficult question, and no one will resolve it without straining the point. It is not nature, which is the same for everyone, that plays the major role here.

Sudden changes in artists which are unexplainable in terms of their personal changes are typical. Such are the sudden changes in Derzhavin and Nekrasov, in whose youth "elevated" poetry went side by side with "low" satiric poetry, but later under objective conditions were merged, thus creating new phenomena. Clearly, the problem here is not one of individual psychological conditions, but of objective, evolving functions of the literary order in relation to the adjacent social order.

13

It is therefore necessary to reexamine one of the most complex problems of literary evolution, the problem of "influence." There are deep psychological and personal influences which are not reflected on the literary level at all, as with Chadaev and Pushkin. There are influences which modify and deform literature without having any evolutionary significance, as with Mikhailovsky and Gleb Uspensky. Yet what is most striking of all is the fact that you can have an extrinsic indication of an influence where no such influence has occurred. I have already cited the examples of Katenin and Nekrasov. There are other examples as well. The South American tribes created the myth of Prometheus without the influence of classical mythology. These facts point to a convergence or coincidence. They have proved to be so significant that they completely obscure the psychological approach to the problem of influence and make chronology ("Who said it first?") unessential. "Influence" can occur at such a time and in such a direction as literary conditions permit. In the case of functional coincidence, whatever influences him provides the artist with elements which permit the development and strengthening of the function. If there is no such "influence," then an analogous function may result in analogous formal elements without any influence.[18]

[16]Konstantin Nikolaievich Batyushkov (1787–1855), poet who imitated the erotic verse of Tibullus and other Latin poets. [Ed.]

[17]Pyotr Andreievich Vyazemsky (1792–1878), poet and critic of Pushkin's circle. [Ed.]

[18]An example of Tynyanov's notion of structural similarity without influence might be the simplicity of poetic forms and language, the use of symbolism, and the avoidance of oratory in both William Blake and Emily Dickinson, despite the fact that Dickinson never read Blake. [Ed.]

14

It is now time to pose the problem of the main term with which literary history operates, namely, "tradition." If we agree that evolution is the change in interrelationships between the elements of a system — between functions and formal elements — then evolution may be seen as the "mutations" of systems. These changes vary from epoch to epoch, occurring sometimes slowly, sometimes rapidly. They do not entail the sudden and complete renovation or the replacement of formal elements, but rather the *new function of these formal elements.* Thus the very comparison of certain literary phenomena must be made on the basis of functions, not only forms. Seemingly dissimilar phenomena of diverse functional systems may be similar in function, and vice versa.[19] The problem is obscured here by the fact that each literary movement in a given period seeks its supporting point in the preceding systems. This is what may be called "traditionalism."

Thus, perhaps, the functions of Pushkin's prose are closer to the functions of Tolstoy's prose than the functions of Pushkin's verse are to those of his imitators in the 1830s or those of Maykov.

[19]The different functions of apparently similar phenomena might be exemplified in the historical perspective of the Gothic novel of the 1790s (where the medieval English setting of Radcliffe's *Castles of Athlin and Dunbayne,* for example, primarily produces an exoticism of setting where anything can happen) and the historical perspective of novels of the 1820s (where Scott's *Waverley* or *Ivanhoe,* for example, are concerned about the impact of historical movements on individuals), or the historical perspective of novels of the 1890s (where Stevenson's historical novels, like *Kidnapped,* present a nostalgia for a simpler and more heroic time). [Ed.]

15

To summarize, the study of literary evolution is possible only in relation to literature as a system, interrelated with other systems and conditioned by them. Investigation must go from constructional function to literary function; from literary function to verbal function. It must clarify the problem of the evolutionary interaction of functions and forms. The study of evolution must move from the literary system to the nearest correlated systems, not the distant, even though major, systems. In this way the prime significance of major social factors is not at all discarded. Rather, it must be elucidated to its full extent through the problem of the evolution of literature. This is in contrast to the establishment of the direct "influence" of major social factors, which replaces the study of *evolution* of literature with the study of the *modification* of literary works — that is to say, of their deformation.

William Empson

1906–1984

The enfant terrible *who turned I. A. Richards's complex psychological theories about emotion and literature into a reproducible critical practice was born in Howden, in the East Riding of Yorkshire, and educated at Winchester College. His highest earned degree was a B.A. in mathematics, awarded by Magdalene College, Cambridge, in 1929. After taking his examinations in mathematics, Empson switched over to English, attaching himself to Richards, who was director of studies at Magdalene. According to Richards's own recollections, Empson had been taken with the "interpretive games" that Laura Riding and Robert Graves had been playing with an unpunctuated version of Shakespeare's Sonnet 129, and suggested that the variety of meanings they had found could probably be discovered in any poetry. Richards encouraged him to work this out as a research project and, within a fortnight, Empson had produced the central core of* Seven Types of Ambiguity *(1930), which takes the uncertainties about construing the meaning of words, tropes, and grammatical structures as the mark of poetic discourse. Empson's later work would complicate this position:* Some Versions of Pastoral *(1935) viewed the literary text as the product of psychological and social motives as well as verbal tropes, and* The Structure of Complex Words *(1951) presented a more refined notion of grammar and meaning than had directed his classic early study. Empson was also a poet whose* Collected Poems *was published in 1949.*

Empson's academic career was largely spent in the far east. In 1931, he went to Japan to take the chair in English at Bunrika Daigaku in Tokyo, then to a professorship at Peking National University in 1937. When war broke out, Empson returned to England, working for the BBC (British Broadcasting Company) from 1940 to 1946 but later returned to his professorship in the Chinese capital from 1947 to 1952. In 1953, Empson came back to England to take the professorship of English at Sheffield University, where he remained to the end of his career. He was awarded honorary doctorates in literature by the University of East Anglia and the University of Bristol and was knighted in 1979.

Epilogue to *Seven Types of Ambiguity*[1]

I must devote a final chapter to some remarks about what I have been doing; about the conditions under which ambiguity is proper, about the degree to which the understanding of it is of immediate importance, and about the way in which it is apprehended.

For the first of these the preface to *Oxford Poetry,* 1927, stated an opposition very clearly; that there is a "logical conflict, between the denotary and the connotatory sense of words; between, that is to say, an asceticism tending to kill language by stripping words of all association and a hedonism tending to kill language by dissipating their sense under a multiplicity of associations." The methods I have been using seem to assume that all poetical language is debauched into associations to any required degree; I ought at this point to pay decent homage to the opposing power.

Evidently all the subsidiary meanings must be relevant, because anything (phrase, sentence, or poem) meant to be considered as a unit must be unitary, must stand for a single order of the mind. In complicated situations this unity is threatened; you are thinking of several things, or one thing as it is shown by several things, or one thing in several ways. A sort of unity may be given by the knowledge of a scheme on which all the things occur; so that the scheme itself becomes the one thing which is being considered. More generally one may say that if an ambiguity is to be unitary there must be "forces" holding its elements together, and I ought then, in considering ambiguities, to have discussed what the forces were, whether they were adequate. But the situation here is like the situation in my first chapter, about

[1]Empson's seven types of ambiguity run from tropes that one might hardly notice to ones of which the reader (and writer) cannot help being aware. They are arranged from the least to the greatest logical or grammatical disorder and are described thus in his analytical table of contents: (1) "when a detail is effective in several ways at once"; (2) "when two or more alternative meanings are fully resolved into one"; (3) "when two apparently unconnected meanings are given simultaneously"; (4) "when the alternative meanings combine to make clear a complicated state of mind in the author"; (5) "a fortunate confusion, as when the author is discovering his idea in the act of writing"; (6) "when what is said is contradictory or irrelevant and the reader is forced to invent interpretations"; (7) "full contradiction, marking a division in the author's mind" (pp. v–vi). [Ed.]

rhythm; it is hard to show in detail how the rhythm acts, and one can arrive at the same result by showing the effects of the rhythm upon the meaning of the words.

Some sort of parallel may be found in the way logical connectives (the statement of logical form in addition to logical content) are usually unnecessary and often misleading, because too simple. Omitting an adjective one would need "therefore," stressing the adjective "although"; both logical connections are implied if the sentences are just put one after another. In the same way, people are accustomed to judge automatically the forces that hold together a variety of ideas; they feel they know about the forces, if they have analysed the ideas; many forces, indeed, are covertly included within ideas; and so of the two elements, each of which defines the other, it is much easier to find words for the ideas than for the forces. Most of the ambiguities I have considered here seem to me beautiful; I consider, then, that I have shown by example, in showing the nature of the ambiguity, the nature of the forces which are adequate to hold it together. It would seem very artificial to do it the other way round, and very tedious to do it both ways at once.[2] I wish only, then, to say here that such vaguely imagined "forces" are essential to the totality of a poem, and that they cannot be discussed in terms of ambiguity, because they are complementary to it. But by discussing ambiguity, a great deal may be made clear about them. In particular, if there is contradiction, it must imply tension; the more prominent the contradiction, the greater the tension; in some way other than by the contradiction, the tension must be conveyed, and must be sustained.

An ambiguity, then, is not satisfying in itself, nor is it, considered as a device on its own, a thing to be attempted; it must in each case arise from, and be justified by, the peculiar requirements of the situation. On the other hand, it is a thing which the more interesting and valuable situations are more likely to justify. Thus the practice of "trying not to be ambiguous" has a great deal to be said for it, and I suppose was followed by most of the poets I have considered. It is likely to lead to results more direct, more communicable, and hence more durable; it is a necessary safeguard against being ambiguous without proper occasion, and it leads to more serious ambiguities when such occasions arise. But, of course, the phrase "trying not to be ambiguous" is itself very indefinite and treacherous; it involves problems of all kinds as to what a poet can try to do, how much of his activity he is conscious of, and how much of his activity he could become conscious of if he tried. I believe that the methods I have been describing are very useful to critics, but certainly they leave a poet in a difficult position. Even in prose the belief in them is liable to produce a sort of doctrinaire sluttishness; one is tempted to set down a muddle in the hope that it will convey the meaning more immediately.

As for the immediate importance of the study of ambiguity, it would be easy enough to take up an alarmist attitude, and say that the English language needs nursing by the analyst very badly indeed. Always rich and dishevelled, it is fast becoming very rich and dishevelled; always without adequate devices for showing the syntax intended, it is fast throwing away the few devices it had; it is growing liable to mean more things, and less willing to stop and exclude the other possible meanings. A brief study of novels will show that English, as spoken by educated people, has simplified its grammar during the last century to an extraordinary degree. People sometimes say that words are now used as flat counters, in a way which ignores their delicacy; that English is coming to use fewer of its words, and those more crudely. But this journalist flatness does not mean that the words have simple meanings, only that the word is used, as at a distance, to stand for a vague and complicated mass of ideas and systems which the journalist has no time to apprehend. The sciences might be expected to diminish the ambiguity of the language, both because of their tradition of clarity and because much of their jargon has, if not only one meaning, at any rate only one setting and point of view. But such

[2]I was claiming here a purity I had failed to attain. Many of the analyses in the book are, I should say, convincing, if at all, through consideration of forces known to be at work in the poet's mind, not by the verbal details used in illustration of them. However, this doesn't affect the theoretical distinction. [Au.]

words are not in general use; they only act as a further disturbing influence on the words used already. English is becoming an aggregate of vocabularies only loosely in connection with one another, which yet have many words in common, so that there is much danger of accidental ambiguity, and you have to bear firmly in mind the small clique for whom the author is writing. It is to combat this that so much recent writing has been determinedly unintelligible from any but the precise point of view intended.

Of the increasing vagueness, compactness, and lack of logical distinctions in English, the most obvious example is the newspaper headline. I remember a very fine one that went

ITALIAN ASSASSIN BOMB PLOT DISASTER.

Here we have the English language used as a Chinese system of flat key-words, given particular meaning by noun-adjectives in apposition, or perhaps rather as an agglutinative system, one word one sentence, like Esquimo. I am told that American headlines, however mysterious, are usually sentences; the English method is more complete. *Bomb* and *plot*, you notice, can be either nouns or verbs, and would take kindly to being adjectives, not that they are anything so definite here. One thinks at first that there are two words or sentences, and a semicolon has been left out as in telegrams: "I will tell you for your penny about the Italian Assassin and the well-known Bomb Plot Disaster"; but the *assassin*, as far as I remember, was actually not an *Italian; Italian* refers to the whole aggregate, and its noun, if any, is *disaster*. Perhaps, by being so far separated from its noun, it gives the impression that the other words, too, are somehow connected with *Italy;* that *bombs*, *plots*, and *disasters* belong both to government and rebel in those parts; perhaps *Italian Assassin* is not wholly separate in one's mind from the injured Mussolini. This extended use of the adjective acts as a sort of syncopation, which gives energy and excitement to the rhythm, rather like the effect of putting two caesuras into a line; but, of course, the main rhythm conveys: "This is a particularly exciting sort of disaster, the assassin-bomb-plot type they have in Italy," and there is a single chief stress on *bomb*.

Evidently this is a very effective piece of writing, quite apart from the fact that it conveys its point in a form short enough for large type. It conveys it with a compactness which gives the mind several notions at one glance of the eye, with a unity like that of metaphor, with a force like that of its own favourite *bombs*. Nor can I feel that it will be a *disaster* if other forms of English literature adopt this fundamental mode of statement, so interesting to the logician; it is possible that a clear analysis of the possible modes of statement, and a fluid use of grammar which sets out to combine them as sharply as possible into the effect intended, may yet give back something of the Elizabethan energy to what is at present a rather exhausted language. The grammatical sentence is not the only form of statement in modern English, and I want to suggest that the machinery I have been using upon poetry is going to become increasingly necessary if we are to keep the language under control.

I am not sure that I have been approaching this matter with an adequate skeleton of metaphysics. For instance, Mr. Richards distinguishes a poem into Sense, Feeling, Tone, and Intention; you may say an interpretation is not being done properly (if the analyst has conquered the country, still he is not ruling it) unless these four are separated out into sub-headings and the shades of grammar that convey the contents of each sub-heading are then listed in turn. But the process of apprehension, both of the poem and of its analysis, is not at all like reading a list; one wants as far as clarity will allow to say things in the form in which they will be remembered when properly digested. People remember a complex notion as a sort of feeling that involves facts and judgments; one cannot give or state the feeling directly, any more than the feeling of being able to ride a bicycle; it is the result of a capacity, though it might be acquired perhaps by reading a list. But to state the fact and the judgment (the thought and the feeling) separately, as two different relevant matters, is a bad way of suggesting how they are combined; it makes the reader apprehend as two things what he must, in fact, apprehend as one thing. Detailed analysis of this kind might be excellent as psychology, but it would hardly be literary criticism; it would start much further back;

and a mere reader of the poem would have to read a great deal of it to get the information he wanted.

This notion of unity is of peculiar importance; not only, though chiefly, in poetry, but in all literature and most conversation. One may remember, rather as a comparison than as an explanation, what Pavlov found in the brains of his dogs; that stimulation of a particular region produced inhibition, almost immediately, over regions in the neighbourhood, and at the region itself a moment later. Thus to say a thing in two parts is different in incalculable ways from saying it as a unit; Coleridge says somewhere that the mind insists on having a single word for a single mental operation, and will use an inadequate word rather than two adequate ones. When you are holding a variety of things in your mind, or using for a single matter a variety of intellectual machinery, the only way of applying all your criteria is to apply them simultaneously; the only way of forcing the reader to grasp your total meaning is to arrange that he can only feel satisfied if he is bearing all the elements in mind at the moment of conviction; the only way of not giving something heterogeneous is to give something which is at every point a compound.

My third heading is more important, as to the way in which ambiguity is apprehended. I have continually employed a method of analysis which jumps the gap between two ways of thinking; which produces a possible set of alternative meanings with some ingenuity, and then says it is grasped in the pre-consciousness of the reader by a native effort of the mind. This must seem very dubious; but then the facts about the apprehension of poetry are in any case very extraordinary. Such an assumption is best judged by the way it works in detail; I shall only try here to make it seem plausible.

We think not in words but in directed phrases, and yet in accepting a syntax there is a preliminary stage of uncertainty; "the grammar may be of such or such a kind; the words are able to be connected in this way or in that." Words are seen as already in a grammar rather as letters are seen as already in a word, but one is much more prepared to have been wrong about the grammar than about the word. Under some drugs that make things jump about you see any particular thing moving or placed elsewhere in proportion as it is likely to move or be placed elsewhere, in proportion to a sort of coefficient of mobility which you have already given it as part of your apprehension. In the same way, a plausible grammar is picked up at the same time as the words it orders, but with a probability attached to it, and the less probable alternatives, ready, if necessary, to take its place, are in some way present at the back of your mind.

In poetry much stress is laid on such alternatives; "getting to know" a poet is largely the business of learning to control them. And as, to take another coefficient which the eye attaches to things, as you have an impression of a thing's distance away, which can hardly ever be detached from the pure visual sensation, and when it is so detached leaves your eye disconcerted (if what you took for a wall turns out to be the sea, you at first see nothing, perhaps are for a short time puzzled as with a blur, and then see differently), so the reading of a new poet, or of any poetry at all, fills many readers with a sense of mere embarrassment and discomfort, like that of not knowing, and wanting to know, whether it is a wall or the sea.

It is these faint and separate judgments of probability which unite, as if with an explosion, to "make sense" and accept the main meaning of a connection of phrases; and the reaction, though rapid, is not as immediate as one is liable to believe. Also, as in a chemical reaction, there will have been reverse or subsidiary reactions, or small damped explosions, or slow widespread reactions, not giving out much heat, going on concurrently, and the final result may be complicated by preliminary stages in the main process, or after-effects from the products of the reaction. As a rule, all that you recognise as in your mind is the one final association of meanings which seems sufficiently rewarding to be the answer — "now I have understood *that*"; it is only at intervals that the strangeness of the process can be observed. I remember once clearly seeing a word so as to understand it, and, at the same time, hearing myself imagine that I had read its opposite. In the same way, there is a preliminary stage in reading poetry when the grammar is still being settled, and the words have not all been given their due weight; you have a broad impression of what it is all about, but there are various incidental impressions wandering about in your mind; these may not be part of the final meaning arrived at by the judgment, but tend to be fixed in it as part of its colour. In the same way, there is a preliminary stage in writing poetry, when not all the grammar, but the grammar at crucial points of contact between different ideas, is liable to be often changed. There is a trivial but typical example of this in the two versions of the Crashaw *Hymn for the Circumcision of our Lord.*[3]

All the purple pride of *Laces*,
The crimson curtaines of thy bed;
Guild thee not with so sweet graces;
Nor set thee in so rich a red. (1646)

All the purple pride that *laces*
The crimson curtains of thy bed,
Guilds thee not in so sweet graces
Nor setts thee in so rich a red. (1652)

I have assumed that much could be extracted from the fact that one syntax rather than another was selected for a poetical statement; this example shows the limitations of such a method. For, clearly, the verse is altered very little by these quite considerable changes in the grammar; it would be easy in a rapid reading to think they had been the same. It does not make much difference whether *laces* the noun or the verb is used, because, though their meaning is different, each reminds the reader of the other. So for the corresponding change in *guild*, it does not matter whether this is said to be done by the *pride* or by the upholstery which expresses it; whichever syntax is chosen, the reader thinks of the *guilding* as done, in their respective ways, by both. Thus each of these versions includes the other among its possibilities; probably there is a stage for most readers when they have not yet noticed which syntax is, in fact, used. This example of the complexity of the absorption of grammar in poetry may be convincing because so simple; it shows, by the way, what I have said already, that a poetical effect is not easily disturbed by altering a few words.

One should also consider, not merely whether this generalising of the grammar at first occurs, but how scrupulously it is cleaned away; how far, then, an attention to it will be profitable. Clearly, the critical principles of the author and of the public he is writing for will decide this to a considerable degree, and one has to bear them in mind in deciding whether a particular ambiguity is part of the total effect intended. (This is hardly a solemn warning, because they have to be borne in mind in any case.) Thus it is fair to hold the seventeenth century responsible for most of its ambiguities, because its taste seems to have been curiously free from such critical principles as interpose a judgment before the experience of accepting the poetry is completed. On the other hand, it would often be unprofitable to insist on the ambiguities of Pope, because he expected his readers to prune their minds of any early disorder as carefully as he had pruned his own. My eighteenth-century examples, therefore, have to depend on variations of grammar the authors would have thought trivial, puns which they had intended and thought intelligible, and variations of sense which spring from an effective superficiality in their thought. But, in the same way, one must often ignore ambiguities in the seventeenth century, because they would be irrelevant to the total effect intended and so were not absorbed.

Ben Jonson's most famous poem[4] gives a puzzling example of this:

Drink to me only with thine eyes,
And I will pledge with mine;
Or leave a kiss but in the cup
And I'll not look for wine.
The thirst that from the soul doth rise
Doth ask a drink divine;
But might I of Jove's nectar sup
I would not change for thine.

The last two lines say the opposite of what is meant; I must take some credit for not putting this well-known case into the seventh type of ambiguity.[5] But one has already decided from the

[3]Richard Crashaw (1612?–1649), poet, and author of *Steps to the Temple* (1646). [Ed.]

[4]"Song: To Celia" (1616). [Ed.]

[5]The last two lines, unlike the rest, are not a translation; so one can't settle the question that way. [Au.]

rest of the verse that a simple lyrism is intended; there are no other two-faced implications of any plausibility, and the word *but*, after all, admits of only one form for the antithesis. This is not to say that the last two lines are an accident, and should be altered; you may feel it gives a touching completeness to his fervour that he feels so sure no one will misunderstand him. And indeed, you may take the matter more seriously, so as to regard these lines as a true statement of two opposites. You may say that the irrelevant meaning was one to which Jonson was much better accustomed; that he may have been echoing, for the purposes of lyrism, some phrase he had used already at the Mermaid,[6] to express poetical rather than amorous ambition; that he might then not notice till too late about the grammar; that in this sort of lyric, whose business it is to be wholehearted to an exhausting degree, a man would naturally draw on any generous enthusiasm he had already phrased to himself warmly; and that, at any rate, the lines are a true hyperbole, since Jonson did very seriously feel the *thirst* of the *soul* for the divine draught of poetry. All this may be true, and these facts very interesting to the biographer, but they have nothing to do with the enjoyment of the poem. Of course, such a distinction is hard to draw, and those who enjoy poems must in part be biographers, but this extreme example may serve to make clear that it is not all significant ambiguities which are relevant, that I am talking less about the minds of poets than about the mode of action of poetry.

This seems an important point, because I am treating the act of communication as something very extraordinary, so that the next step would be to lose faith in it altogether. It might seem more reasonable, when dealing with obscure alternatives of syntax, to abandon the claim that you are explaining a thing communicated, to say either that you are showing what happened in the author's mind (this should interest the biographer) or what was likely to happen in a reader's mind (this should interest the poet). This might be more tidy, but, like many forms of doubt, it would itself claim to know too much; the rules as to what is conveyable are so much more mysterious even than the rules governing the effects of ambiguity, whether on the reader or the author, that it is better to talk about both parties at once, and be thankful if what you say is true about either.

The problem as to belief in poetry might well be mentioned here; as to whether it is necessary to share the opinions of the poet if you are to understand his sensibility. Very often it is necessary to believe them in a behaviouristic sense; you have to be well enough habituated to them to be able to imagine their consequences; thus you have to be a person who is liable to act as if they were true. Certainly, if this is so, it becomes puzzling that we should be able to enjoy so many poets. The explanation seems to be that in the last few generations literary people have been trained socially to pick up hints at once about people's opinions, and to accept them, while in the company of their owners, with as little fuss as possible; I might say, putting this more strongly, that in the present state of indecision of the cultured world people do, in fact, hold all the beliefs, however contradictory, that turn up in poetry, in the sense that they are liable to use them all in coming to decisions. It is for reasons of this sort that the habit of reading a wide variety of different sorts of poetry, which has, after all, only recently been contracted by any public as a whole, gives to the act of appreciation a puzzling complexity, tends to make people less sure of their own minds, and makes it necessary to be able to fall back on some intelligible process of interpretation. Thus one finds it hard, in reading some passages of Keats, to realise that they were long enjoyed empirically, without the theoretical reassurance now given by the psycho-analysts; the same applies to the "anthropological" writings of mystics, like those lines from Crashaw in my last chapter.[7]

[6]Tavern frequented by actors and literary men. [Ed.]

[7]The lines to which Empson alludes are from Crashaw's meditation on Luke xi, "Blessed by the paps that thou hast sucked":

Suppose he had been Tabled at thy Teates,
Thy hunger feeles not what he eates:
Hee'l have his Teat e're long (a bloody one)
The Mother then must suck the Son. [Ed.]

One's situation here is very like that of the visualiser who cannot imagine enjoying poetry without seeing the pictures on which he relies; any intellectual framework that seems relevant is very encouraging (as one sees from the cocksureness of the scientists) whether it actually "explains" anything or not; if you feel that your reactions *could* be put into a rational scheme that you can roughly imagine, you become willing, for instance, to abandon yourself to the ecstasies of the Romantic Movement, with a much lower threshold of necessary excitement, with much less fear for your critical self-respect. Thus it is very greatly to the credit of the eighteenth century that it accepted Shakespeare; indeed Dr. Johnson was much more sure that his humour was first-rate (nobody wants to feel a joke could be explained) than that his methods of rousing the more far-reaching sentiments of tragedy were to be admitted.[8] The same machinery of reassurance, I suppose, is sought for in my use of phrases like "outside the focus of consciousness," without very definite support from psychological theory. To give a reassurance of this kind, indeed, is the main function of criticism.

Many people who would admit that there is a great deal of ambiguity in poetry, and that it is important, will consider that I have gone on piling up ambiguities on to particular cases till the "whole thing" becomes absurd; "you can't expect us to believe all that." I have, in fact, been as complete as I could in cases that seemed to deserve it, and considered whether each of the details was reasonable, not whether the result was reasonable as a whole. For these analytical methods are usually employed casually and piecemeal, with an implication that the critic has shown tact by going no further; if they are flung together into a heap they make, I think, rather a different impression, and this at any rate is a test to which it is proper that they should be subjected. If the reader has found me expounding the obvious and accepted at tedious length, he must remember that English literary critics have been so unwilling to appear niggling and lacking in soul that upon these small technical points the obvious, even the accepted, has been said culpably seldom.

This attitude, however, can be justified; the position of a literary critic is far more a social than a scientific one. There is no question of dealing finally with the matter, because, in so far as people are always reading an author, he is always being read differently. It is the business of the critic to extract for his public what it wants; to organise, what he may indeed create, the taste of his period. So that literature, in so far as it is a living matter, demands a sense, not so much of what is really there, as of what is necessary to carry a particular situation "off." Detailed explanation, in the literary as in the social field, calls up a reaction of suspicion; "*Why* is he wasting our time, nagging us about this thing, when everybody knows it is all right? What good will it do?" In the same way, the analyst must be humbled by that story about Proust asking his duchesses why and how they came into a drawing-room like duchesses; they could not tell him, and the only result was to make them laugh when they saw him come into a drawing-room himself. It does not even satisfy the understanding to stop living in order to understand.

This social comparison or derivation may be worked out in some detail, and involves the problems of my first chapter. Thus the relation of Meaning to Pure Sound is very closely paralleled by the relation of Character to Looks; this may serve to show how very completely one may have to behave, in practice, as if the theory of Pure Sound was true. The fundamental source of pleasure about Looks is an apprehension of Character; a change in one's knowledge of the Character alters (by altering the elements selected) one's apprehension of the Looks. The Beauty resides in the Sound and the Looks; but these, being aesthetic constructions, are largely distillations (solutions into forms immediately conceivable) from the Meaning and the Character.

As to say that the Meaning (rather than the Sound) is what matters about poetry, so it seems very intellectual and puritanical to say that Character (rather than Looks) is what matters about people; in both cases those who do so can save the phenomena by invoking first pre-conscious and then instinctive modes of apprehension; in

[8]See Samuel Johnson, "Preface to Shakespeare," p. 228. [Ed.]

both cases they are using, for the satisfaction of the mind, words belonging to the more intelligible part of a scale about the whole scale. And both involve the intellectual fallacy that regards the mind as something otherwise passive that collects propositions; or the assumption that truth is valuable in the abstract rather than as something digested so as to be useful. In both cases one can partly get over this by saying that it is less the Meaning that matters than "what it means to you," that it is less the Character itself that is apprehended than its possible relations with your own. And, of course, in both cases, the distinction which I am teasing so pitilessly is largely a verbal one which most people regard as indifferent; some one may say he reads Swinburne for the Sound and George Herbert for the Meaning, but he would not eagerly deny that he reads them both for Meaning conveyed in different ways; a business man engaging a secretary may feel a distinction between Looks and Character, but he would not find it absurd to call this a distinction between two sorts of character estimated in terms of Looks.

A reader may have regarded this parallel as a kind of theoretical joke; if so, it will have been misleading, because as a joke it involves a moral element and depends on an ambiguity. In both cases there is a noble-naughty scale (corresponding in part to the power of the thing to survive analysis if it could be analysed), and also an intellectual-instinctive scale (corresponding in part to the ease or difficulty with which such analysis could be performed); in both cases it is a naive intellectualism or Puritanism which mixes the two scales up together. I must confess it is not very far from this fallacy to make the assumption in the first bracket; to say, as I did in my first chapter, that only bad poems are hurt by analysis. There is no necessary reason why this should be true, and it is worth noticing an important class of readers for whom it is not.

Many works of art give their public a sort of relief and strength, because they are independent of the moral code which their public accepts and is dependent on; relief, by fantasy gratification; strength, because it gives you a sort of equilibrium within your boundaries to have been taken outside them, however secretly, because you know your own boundaries better when you have seen them from both sides. Such works give a valuable imaginative experience, and such a public cannot afford to have them analysed; the Crashaw poems in my last chapter may be examples of this state of things. And I suspect that the parallel of personal with poetical beauty still holds good; that there are some excellent people who rightly admire their neighbour's Looks, for valid reasons of Character, which they would find shocking if they could understand them.

Under these rather special circumstances one should try to prevent people from having to analyse their reactions, with all the tact at one's disposal; nor are they so special as might appear. The object of life, after all, is not to understand things, but to maintain one's defences and equilibrium and live as well as one can; it is not only maiden aunts who are placed like this. And one must remember (since I am saying the best I can for the enemy) that, as a first approximation, or a general direction, to people who really do not know how to read poetry, the dogma of Pure Sound often acts as a recipe for aesthetic receptiveness, and may be necessary.

So that to defend analysis in general one has to appeal to the self-esteem of the readers of the analysis, and assume that they possess a quality that is at present much respected. They must possess a fair amount of equilibrium or fairly strong defences; they must have the power first of reacting to a poem sensitively and definitely (one may call that feminine) and then, having fixed the reaction, properly stained, on a slide, they must be able to turn the microscope on to it with a certain indifference and without smudging it with their fingers; they must be able to prevent their new feelings of the same sort from interfering with the process of understanding the original ones (one may call that "masculine") and have enough detachment not to mind what their sources of satisfaction may turn out to be. ("Fixed" in the last sentence is a metaphor from printing snapshots; on second thoughts, it is better than the microscopical one, because after all a microscope is not available.) This quality is admired at present because it gives one a certain power of dealing with anything that may turn out to be true; and people have come to feel that that may be absolutely anything. I do not say that this power is of unique value; it tends to prevent the sensibility from having its proper irrigating and fertilising effect upon the person as a whole; a medieval sensibility may have been more total and satisfying than a modern one. But it is widely and reasonably felt that those people are better able to deal with our present difficulties whose defences are strong enough for them to be able to afford to understand things; nor can I conceal my sympathy with those who want to understand as many things as possible, and to hang those consequences which cannot be foreseen.

After this statement of preference I must return to what I have just called its fallacy, and discuss whether the scientific idea of truth is relevant to poetry at all. I have been trying to analyse verses which a great variety of critics have enjoyed but only described in terms of their effects; thus I have claimed to show how a properly-qualified mind works when it reads the verses, how those properly-qualified minds have worked which have not at all understood their own working. It would be tempting, then, to say I was concerned with science rather than with beauty; to treat poetry as a branch of applied psychology. But, so far as poetry can be regarded altogether dispassionately, so far as it is an external object for examination, it is dead poetry and not worth examining; further, so far as a critic has made himself dispassionate about it, so far as he has repressed sympathy in favour of curiosity, he has made himself incapable of examining it.

This is not simply the old difficulty about what subjects can be treated by the scientific method; at least, it is here more difficult. For instance, one might apply the above argument to medicine; "those bodies which can rightly be regarded dispassionately are not worth curing." This may not seem very convincing, but it has been argued; it is the root of the objection to vivisection, and made the Russian Orthodox Church forbid the use of medical textbooks. However, there are, on the face of it, two ways of dealing with bodies; what is found as truth from bodies not considered valuable is found to work as goodness upon bodies that are so considered; and, even more important, the same body can effectively be considered both ways at once; certainly there are difficulties such as appear in the doctor's objections to psycho-analysis, but the separation is possible. But poetry is not like bodies, because the act of knowing is itself an act of sympathising; unless you are enjoying the poetry you cannot create it, as poetry, in your mind. The scientific idea of truth is that the mind, otherwise passive, collects propositions about the outside world; the application of scientific ideas to poetry is interesting because it reduces that idea of truth (much more intimately than elsewhere) to a self-contradiction.

The human situation is oddly riddled with these antinomies, and, when they seem completely solved by intuition, there is not much object in separating them out; thus I have a vague impression that Proust has listed a great many reasons why it is impossible to be happy, but, in the course of being happy, one finds it difficult to remember them. Still, it seems proper here to consider how intuition *ought* to solve this antinomy, to say how the analysis of poetry can be useful, and indeed what it can be.

On the face of it, there are two sorts of literary critic, the appreciative and the analytical; the difficulty is that they have all got to be both. An appreciator produces literary effects similar to the one he is appreciating, and sees to it, perhaps by using longer and plainer language, or by concentrating on one element of a combination, that his version is more intelligible than the original to the readers he has in mind. Having been shown what to look for, they are intended to go back to the original and find it there for themselves. Parodies are appreciative criticisms in this sense, and much of Proust reads like the work of a superb appreciative critic upon a novel which has unfortunately not survived. The analyst is not a teacher in this way; he assumes that something has been conveyed to the reader by the work under consideration, and sets out to explain, in terms of the rest of the reader's experience, why the work has had the effect on him that is assumed. As an analyst he is not repeating the effect; he may even be preventing it from happening again. Now, evidently the appreciator has got to be an analyst, because the only way to say a complicated thing more simply is to separate it into its parts and say each of them in turn. The analyst has also got to be an appreciator; because he must convince the reader that he knows what he is talking about (that he has had the experience which is in question); because he must be able to show the reader which of the separate parts of the experience he is talking about, after he has separated them; and because he must coax the reader into seeing that the cause he names does, in fact, produce the effect which is experienced; otherwise they will not seem to have anything to do with each other. On the other hand, once the analyst has abandoned himself to being also an appreciator, he can never be sure that he has explained anything; if he seems to have explained something, it may be because he has managed to do the same unexplained thing over again. Thus, in finding several words to convey the mode of action of a single word in a poem, I do not, of course, claim that the new words are any more simple in their action than the old one; a word is of the nature of an organism, or of the nature of the part of an organism; not by a small series of propositions, but by a new piece of writing, must one sharpen a reader's apprehension of the way it is being used. And yet it is precisely the nature of a "piece of writing" which is supposed to be undergoing analysis.

Mention of Sir Richard Paget's tongue-gestures,[9] in my first chapter, led to an alarming notion; that it was no use trying to say how a poem came to take effect as it did because one could not say how much of the effect was being produced by sound-effects, such as belong to the nature of language and have not yet been explained in sufficient detail. The answer is that such an explanation as I have attempted need not be complete because of the nature of its process; it should imply, by its own writing, both how much of the effect is produced by the one device explained and how much is left as at present inexplicable.

The process, then, must be that of alternating between, or playing off against one another, these two sorts of criticism. When you have made a quotation, you must first show the reader how you feel about it, by metaphor, implication, devices of sound, or anything else that will work; on the other hand, when you wish to make a critical remark, to explain *why* your quotation takes effect as it does, you must state your result as plainly (in as transferable, intellectually handy terms) as you can. You may say that this distinction is false, because in practice one must do both at once, but I think it is useful; one can apply it, for instance, to that problem about how much one is to say the obvious which always seems to hamper the analytical critic.

Certainly, in appreciative criticism, where you are trying to show the reader how you feel about a poetical effect, it is important not to tease him; it is annoying to read platitudes in such work because they interfere with the process, which is essentially that of repeating the original effect, in a plainer form. But in an analysis, whose object is to show the modes of action of a poetical effect, the author may safely insist on the obvious because the reader feels willing that the process should be complete. Indeed, it is then as arrogant in the author to hint at a subtlety as to explain it too fully; firstly, because he implies that those who do not know it already are not worth his notice; secondly, because he assumes that there is no more to know. For some readers may take the subtlety in question for granted, so they will think the hint must refer to something still more subtle.

Not to explain oneself at length in such a case is a snobbery in the author and excites an opposing snobbery in the reader; it is a distressing and common feature of modern aesthetics, due much more to disorientation and a forlorn sense that the matter is inexplicable (it is no use appealing to the reason of ordinary people, one has got to keep up one's dignity) than to any unfortunate qualities in the aestheticians. That is one of the reasons why the cult of irrationalism is such a bore; analytical is more cheerful than apprecia-

[9] Paget's theory is that the sound of a word is thought to be "appropriate" to its meaning whenever what happens in the mouth during pronunciation produces an experience that connects with meaning. For example, when articulating the word "wee" the tongue moves from a position close to the teeth and palate to one even closer, creating a "wee" space within one's mouth. [Ed.]

tive criticism (both, of course, must be present) precisely because there is less need to agonise over these questions of tone.

It may be said that the business of analysis is to progress from poetical to prosaic, from intuitive to intellectual, knowledge; evidently these are just the same sort of opposites, in that each assumes the other is also there. But the idea of this doublet certainly enshrines some of the advantages of analysis, and it may be as well to show how I have been using it. You may know what it will be satisfying to do for the moment; precisely how you are feeling; how to express the thing conceived clearly, but alone, in your mind. That, in its appreciation of, and dependence on, the immediate object or state of mind, is poetical knowledge. (It is true that poetry is largely the perception of the relations between several such things, but then it is the relations which are known poetically.) You may, on the other hand, be able to put the object known into a field of similar objects, in some order, so that it has some degree of balance and safety; you may know several ways of getting to the thing, other things like it but different, enough of its ingredients and the way they are put together to retain control over the situation if some are missing or if the conditions are altered; the thing can be said to your neighbours, and has enough valencies in your mind for it to be connected with a variety of other things into a variety of different classes. That, from its administrative point of view, from its desire to put the thing known into a coherent structure, is prosaic knowledge. Thus a poetical word is a thing conceived in itself and includes all its meanings; a prosaic word is flat and useful and might have been used differently.

One cannot conceive observation except in terms of comparison, or comparison except as based on recognition; immediate knowledge and past experience presuppose one another; thus the question in any particular case must be largely as to what is uppermost in your mind. But this way of using the word-pair at least gives one an answer against those who say that analysis is bad for poetry; it often happens that, for historical reasons or what not, one can no longer appreciate a thing directly by poetical knowledge, and yet can rediscover it in a more controlled form by prosaic knowledge.

But even if we abandon the oppositions between thought and feeling, and attend to the intellectual notion of explanation, the situation is not much more encouraging. It is a matter of luck whether or not you have in your language or your supply of intellectual operations anything which, for a particular problem, will be of use; and this may be true even in a field of known limitation, for instance, it is a matter of luck whether you can find a construction in Euclidean geometry (it would remain so even if you always could); whereas in Analytical geometry there will always be a way of setting about the proof of a proposition, if it is a recognisably geometrical one, but it is a matter of luck whether or not it is too complicated for human patience. And it is only by chance that these two matters of chance will work out the same in a particular case. Things temporarily or permanently inexplicable are not, therefore, to be thought of as essentially different from things that can be explained in some terms you happen to have at your disposal; nor can you have reason to think them likely to be different unless there is a great deal about the inexplicable things that you already know. Explanations of literary matters, to elaborate a perhaps rather trivial analogy, involving as they do much apparently random invention, are more like Pure than Analytical geometry, and, if you cannot think of a construction, that may show that you would be wise to use a different set of methods, but cannot show the problem is of a new kind.

I have been insisting on this because it seems important that people should believe that such explanations are possible, even if they have never yet been performed; but the analogy is useful in another way, through giving the notion of a construction. Continually, in order to paraphrase a piece of verse, it is necessary to drag in some quite irrelevant conceptions; thus I have often been puzzled by finding it necessary to go and look things up in order to find machinery to express distinctions that were already in my mind; indeed, this is involved in the very notion of that activity, for how else would one know what to look up? Such machinery is necessary, partly so as to look as if you knew what you were talking about, partly as a matter of 'style,' and partly from the basic assumption of prose that all the parts of speech must have some meaning. (These three give the same idea with increasing generality.) Otherwise, one would be continually stating relations between unknown or indefinite objects, or only stating something *about* such relations, themselves unknown and indefinite, in a way which probably reflects accurately the nature of your statement, but to which only the pure mathematician is accustomed. So that many of my explanations may be demonstrably wrong, and yet efficient for their purpose, and *vice versa*.

The notion of a construction also shows the dangers of the process it describes. With a moderate intellectual apparatus one should be able to draw irrelevant distinctions without limit, and even those that are of linguistic interest need not be of interest to a reader of the poem. When a poem refers simply and unambiguously to a field it is usually possible to plant a hedge across the field, and say triumphantly that two contiguous fields were being described by an ambiguity. This may be of some use in that it shows the field to have extension, but one must not suppose that there is anything in a right apprehension of the field which corresponds to one's own hedge. Thus I think my seven types form an immediately useful set of distinctions, but to a more serious analysis they would probably appear trivial and hardly to be distinguished from one another. I call them useful, not merely as a means of stringing examples, but because, in complicated matters, any distinction between cases, however irrelevant, may serve to heighten one's consciousness of the cases themselves.

Since, however, I admit that the analysis of a poem can only be a long way of saying what is said anyhow by the poem it analyses, that it does not show how the devices it describes can be invented or used, that it gives no source of information about them which can replace that of normal sensibility, and that it is only tolerable in so far as it is in some way useful, I suppose I ought, in conclusion, to say what use I think it can be. It need not be any. Normal sensibility is a tissue of what has been conscious theory made habitual and returned to the pre-conscious, and, therefore, conscious theory may make an addition to sensibility even though it draws no (or no true) conclusion, formulates no general theory, in the scientific sense, which reconciles and makes quickly available the results which it describes. Such an advance in the machinery of description makes a reader feel stronger about his appreciations, more reliably able to distinguish the private or accidental from the critically important or repeatable, more confident of the reality (that is, the transferability) of his experiences; adds, in short, in the mind of the reader to the things there to be described, whether or not it makes those particular things more describable. What is needed for literary satisfaction is not, "this is beautiful because of such and such a theory," but "this is all right; I am feeling correctly about this; I know the kind of way in which it is meant to be affecting me."

Of course, this distinction is not new, but it needs repeating; indeed, one often finds the surrealist type of critic saying that poetry would have been just the same if no criticism had ever been written. So Pope, for instance, would have written just the same if he had had no critical dogmas. Now it is unwise to say blankly that a theorist is talking nonsense (for instance, it is no use saying that all men are *not* equal) because he may consciously be making a paradox to imply a larger truth; thus, even here, there would be a little truth in saying that Pope could afford to forget his dogmas, so deeply had they become part of his sensibility. And certainly one is again faced with the problem about the hen and the egg; the dogma produces the sensibility, but it must itself have been produced by it. But to say that the dogma does not influence the sensibility is absurd. People only say it when they are trying to put the sensibility in a peculiar state of control over the dogma. The conflict between the scientific and aesthetic points of view, between which I have been trying to arbitrate, gives them a reason; people feel uncertain as to what sort of validity a critical dogma can have, how far one ought to be trying to be independent of one's own age, how far one ought to be trying to be independent of one's own preferences, and do not want their sensibility to be justified by reasons because they are afraid that once they start reasoning they will fall into the wrong point of view. Another such cause, arising out of this, has been mentioned already; it is only recently that the public, as a whole, has come to admire a great variety of different styles of poetry, requiring a great variety of critical dogmas, simultaneously, so as to need not so much a single habit for the reading of poetry as a sort of understanding which enables one to jump neatly from one style to another. This produces a sort of anxious watchfulness over the feelings excited by poetry; it is important not to forget what sort of poetry this is and so allow oneself to have the wrong feelings.

For such reasons, then, it is necessary for us to protect our sensibility against critical dogma, but it is just because of this that the reassurance given by some machinery for analysis has become so necessary in its turn. Thus I suppose that all present-day readers of poetry would agree that some modern poets are charlatans, though different people would attach this floating suspicion to different poets; but they have no positive machinery, such as Dr. Johnson thought he had, to a great extent rightly, by which such a fact could be proved. It is not that such machinery is unknown so much as that it is unpopular; people feel that, because it must always be inadequate, it must always be unfair. The result is a certain lack of positive satisfaction in the reading of any poetry; doubt becomes a permanent background of the mind, both as to whether the thing is being interpreted rightly and as to whether, if it is, one ought to allow oneself to feel pleased. Evidently, in the lack of any machinery of analysis, such as can be thought moderately reliable, to decide whether one's attitude is right, this leads to a sterility of emotion such as makes it hardly worth while to read the poetry at all. It is not surprising, then, that this age should need, if not really an explanation of any one sort of poetry, still the general assurance which comes of a belief that all sorts of poetry may be conceived as explicable.

I should claim, then, that for those who find this book contains novelties, it will make poetry more beautiful, without their ever having to remember the novelties, or endeavour to apply them. It seems a sufficient apology for many niggling pages.

W. K. Wimsatt and

1907–1975

Monroe C. Beardsley

1915–1985

Of the three important essays on which W. K. Wimsatt and Monroe C. Beardsley collaborated, "The Intentional Fallacy" (1946) is probably the most celebrated. The premier heresy hunter among the New Critics, William Kurtz Wimsatt was born in Washington, D.C., and educated at Georgetown University and at Yale, where he took his Ph.D. in 1939 and taught until his death. Yale published his dissertation, The Prose Style of Samuel Johnson, *in 1941. In addition to other works on Samuel Johnson and Alexander Pope, Wimsatt is also the author of* The Verbal Icon *(1954),* Literary Criticism: A Short History *(with Cleanth Brooks, 1957),* Hateful Contraries *(1965), and* The Day of the Leopards *(1976), a bitter response to contemporary trends in life and letters. Wimsatt argued for a "tensional" criticism that would avoid the intentional, affective, genetic, and stylistic "fallacies." Like Shelley, he found the value of poetry in its mystical incarnation, through metaphor, of relations and connections within reality. The formalist aesthetician Monroe Curtis Beardsley was born in Bridgeport, Connecticut, and educated at Yale (B.A., 1936; Ph.D., 1939). He taught philosophy there before moving on to Mt. Holyoke College (1944–46), Swarthmore College (1947–69), and finally Temple University. Beardsley's books include* Aesthetics from Classical Greece to the Present *(1966),* Aesthetic Inquiry *(1967), and* The Possibility of Criticism *(1970). The text of "The Intentional Fallacy" is taken from the version reprinted in* The Verbal Icon.

The Intentional Fallacy

I

The claim of the author's "intention" upon the critic's judgment has been challenged in a number of recent discussions, notably in the debate entitled *The Personal Heresy*, between Professors Lewis and Tillyard. But it seems doubtful if this claim and most of its romantic corollaries are as yet subject to any widespread questioning. The present writers, in a short article entitled "Intention" for a *Dictionary*[1] of literary criticism, raised the issue but were unable to pursue its implications at any length. We argued that the design or intention of the author is neither available nor desirable as a standard for judging the success of a work of literary art, and it seems to us that this is a principle which goes deep into some differences in the history of critical attitudes. It is a principle which accepted or rejected points to the polar opposites of classical "imitation" and romantic expression. It entails many specific truths about inspiration, authenticity, biography, literary history and scholarship, and about some trends of contemporary poetry, especially its allusiveness. There is hardly a problem of literary criticism in which the critic's approach will not be qualified by his view of "intention."

"Intention," as we shall use the term, corresponds to *what he intended* in a formula which more or less explicitly has had wide acceptance. "In order to judge the poet's performance, we must know *what he intended*." Intention is design or plan in the author's mind. Intention has obvious affinities for the author's attitude toward his work, the way he felt, what made him write.

We begin our discussion with a series of propositions summarized and abstracted to a degree where they seem to us axiomatic.

1. A poem does not come into existence by accident. The words of a poem, as Professor Stoll has remarked, come out of a head, not out of a hat. Yet to insist on the designing intellect as a *cause* of a poem is not to grant the design or intention as a *standard* by which the critic is to judge the worth of the poet's performance.

2. One must ask how a critic expects to get an answer to the question about intention. How is he to find out what the poet tried to do? If the poet succeeded in doing it, then the poem itself shows what he was trying to do. And if the poet did not succeed, then the poem is not adequate evidence, and the critic must go outside the poem — for evidence of an intention that did not become effective in the poem. "Only one *caveat* must be borne in mind," says an eminent intentionalist[2] in a moment when his theory repudiates itself; "the poet's aim must be judged at the moment of the creative act, that is to say, by the art of the poem itself."

3. Judging a poem is like judging a pudding or a machine. One demands that it work. It is only because an artifact works that we infer the intention of an artificer. "A poem should not mean but be."[3] A poem can *be* only through its

[1]*Dictionary of World Literature*, ed. Joseph T. Shipley (New York, 1942), pp. 326–29. [Au.]

[2]J. E. Spingarn, "The New Criticism," in *Criticism in America* (New York, 1924), pp. 24–25. [Au.]

[3]Archibald MacLeish in "Ars Poetica." [Ed.]

meaning — since its medium is words — yet it *is*, simply *is*, in the sense that we have no excuse for inquiring what part is intended or meant. Poetry is a feat of style by which a complex of meaning is handled all at once. Poetry succeeds because all or most of what is said or implied is relevant; what is irrelevant has been excluded, like lumps from pudding and "bugs" from machinery. In this respect poetry differs from practical messages, which are successful if and only if we correctly infer the intention. They are more abstract than poetry.

4. The meaning of a poem may certainly be a personal one, in the sense that a poem expresses a personality or state of soul rather than a physical object like an apple. But even a short lyric poem is dramatic, the response of a speaker (no matter how abstractly conceived) to a situation (no matter how universalized). We ought to impute the thoughts and attitudes of the poem immediately to the dramatic *speaker*, and if to the author at all, only by an act of biographical inference.

5. There is a sense in which an author, by revision, may better achieve his original intention. But it is a very abstract sense. He intended to write a better work, or a better work of a certain kind, and now has done it. But it follows that his former concrete intention was not his intention. "He's the man we were in search of, that's true," says Hardy's rustic constable, "and yet he's not the man we were in search of. For the man we were in search of was not the man we wanted."

"Is not a critic," asks Professor Stoll, "a judge, who does not explore his own consciousness, but determines the author's meaning or intention, as if the poem were a will, a contract, or the constitution? The poem is not the critic's own." He has accurately diagnosed two forms of irresponsibility, one of which he prefers. Our view is yet different. The poem is not the critic's own and not the author's (it is detached from the author at birth and goes about the world beyond his power to intend about it or control it). The poem belongs to the public. It is embodied in language, the peculiar possession of the public, and it is about the human being, an object of public knowledge. What is said about the poem is subject to the same scrutiny as any statement in linguistics or in the general science of psychology.

A critic of our *Dictionary* article, Ananda K. Coomaraswamy, has argued[4] that there are two kinds of inquiry about a work of art: (1) whether the artist achieved his intentions; (2) whether the work of art "ought ever to have been undertaken at all" and so "whether it is worth preserving." Number (2), Coomaraswamy maintains, is not "criticism of any work of art *qua* work of art," but is rather moral criticism; number (1) is artistic criticism. But we maintain that (2) need not be moral criticism: that there is another way of deciding whether works of art are worth preserving and whether, in a sense, they "ought" to have been undertaken, and this is the way of objective criticism of works of art as such, the way which enables us to distinguish between a skillful murder and a skillful poem. A skillful murder is an example which Coomaraswamy uses, and in his system the difference between the murder and the poem is simply a "moral" one, not an "artistic" one, since each if carried out according to plan is "artistically" successful. We maintain that (2) is an inquiry of more worth than (1), and since (2) and not (1) is capable of distinguishing poetry from murder, the name "artistic criticism" is properly given to (2).

II

It is not so much a historical statement as a definition to say that the intentional fallacy is a romantic one. When a rhetorician of the first century A.D. writes: "Sublimity is the echo of a great soul," or when he tells us that "Homer enters into the sublime actions of his heroes" and "shares the full inspiration of the combat," we shall not be surprised to find this rhetorician considered as a distant harbinger of romanticism and greeted in the warmest terms by Saintsbury.[5] One may wish to argue whether Longinus should be called ro-

[4]Ananda K. Coomaraswamy, "Intention," in *American Bookman* 1 (1944), pp. 41–48. [Au.]

[5]The rhetorician is Longinus; see "On the Sublime," p. 81. [Ed.]

mantic, but there can hardly be a doubt that in one important way he is.

Goethe's three questions for "constructive criticism" are "What did the author set out to do? Was his plan reasonable and sensible, and how far did he succeed in carrying it out?" If one leaves out the middle question, one has in effect the system of Croce — the culmination and crowning philosophic expression of romanticism. The beautiful is the successful intuition-expression, and the ugly is the unsuccessful; the intuition or private part of art is *the* aesthetic fact, and the medium or public part is not the subject of aesthetic at all.

> The Madonna of Cimabue is still in the Church of Santa Maria Novella; but does she speak to the visitor of to-day as to the Florentines of the thirteenth century?
>
> *Historical interpretation* labours . . . to reintegrate in us the psychological conditions which have changed in the course of history. It . . . enables us to see a work of art (a physical object) as its *author saw it* in the moment of production.[6]

The first italics are Croce's, the second ours. The upshot of Croce's system is an ambiguous emphasis on history. With such passages as a point of departure a critic may write a nice analysis of the meaning or "spirit" of a play by Shakespeare or Corneille — a process that involves close historical study but remains aesthetic criticism — or he may, with equal plausibility, produce an essay in sociology, biography, or other kinds of non-aesthetic history.

III

> I went to the poets; tragic, dithyrambic, and all sorts. . . . I took them some of the most elaborate passages in their own writings, and asked what was the meaning of them. . . . Will you believe me? . . . there is hardly a person present who would not have talked better about their poetry than they did themselves. Then I knew that not by wisdom do poets write poetry, but by a sort of genius and inspiration.[7]

That reiterated mistrust of the poets which we hear from Socrates may have been part of a rigorously ascetic view in which we hardly wish to participate, yet Plato's Socrates saw a truth about the poetic mind which the world no longer commonly sees — so much criticism, and that the most inspirational and most affectionately remembered, has proceeded from the poets themselves.

Certainly the poets have had something to say that the critic and professor could not say; their message has been more exciting: that poetry should come as naturally as leaves to a tree, that poetry is the lava of the imagination, or that it is emotion recollected in tranquillity. But it is necessary that we realize the character and authority of such testimony. There is only a fine shade of difference between such expressions and a kind of earnest advice that authors often give. Thus Edward Young, Carlyle, Walter Pater:

> I know two golden rules from *ethics,* which are no less golden in *Composition,* than in life. 1. *Know thyself;* 2dly, *Reverence thyself.*
>
> This is the grand secret for finding readers and retaining them: let him who would move and convince others, be first moved and convinced himself. Horace's rule, *Si vis me flere*, is applicable in a wider sense than the literal one. To every poet, to every writer, we might say: Be true, if you would be believed.
>
> Truth! there can be no merit, no craft at all, without that. And further, all beauty is in the long run only *fineness* of truth, or what we call expression, the finer accommodation of speech to that vision within.

And Housman's little handbook to the poetic mind yields this illustration:

> Having drunk a pint of beer at luncheon — beer is a sedative to the brain, and my afternoons are the least intellectual portion of my life — I would go out for a walk of two or three hours. As I went along, thinking of nothing in particular, only look-

[6]It is true that Croce himself in his *Ariosto, Shakespeare and Corneille* (London, 1920), chap. 7, "The Practical Personality and the Poetical Personality," and in his *Defense of Poetry* (Oxford, 1933), p. 24, and elsewhere, early and late, has delivered telling attacks on emotive geneticism, but the main drive of the *Aesthetic* is surely toward a kind of cognitive intentionalism. [Au.]

[7]From the *Apology.* [Ed.]

ing at things around me and following the progress of the seasons, there would flow into my mind, with sudden and unaccountable emotion, sometimes a line or two of verse, sometimes a whole stanza at once.

This is the logical terminus of the series already quoted. Here is a confession of how poems were written which would do as a definition of poetry just as well as "emotion recollected in tranquillity" — and which the young poet might equally well take to heart as a practical rule. Drink a pint of beer, relax, go walking, think on nothing in particular, look at things, surrender yourself to yourself, search for the truth in your own soul, listen to the sound of your own inside voice, discover and express the *vraie vérité*.[8]

It is probably true that all this is excellent advice for poets. The young imagination fired by Wordsworth and Carlyle is probably closer to the verge of producing a poem than the mind of the student who has been sobered by Aristotle or Richards. The art of inspiring poets, or at least of inciting something like poetry in young persons, has probably gone further in our day than ever before. Books of creative writing such as those issued from the Lincoln School are interesting evidence of what a child can do.[9] All this, however, would appear to belong to an art separate from criticism — to a psychological discipline, a system of self-development, a yoga, which the young poet perhaps does well to notice, but which is something different from the public art of evaluating poems.

Coleridge and Arnold were better critics than most poets have been, and if the critical tendency dried up the poetry in Arnold and perhaps in Coleridge, it is not inconsistent with our argument, which is that judgment of poems is different from the art of producing them. Coleridge has given us the classic "anodyne" story, and tells what he can about the genesis of a poem which he calls "psychological curiosity," but his definitions of poetry and of the poetic quality "imagination" are to be found elsewhere and in quite other terms.

It would be convenient if the passwords of the intentional school, "sincerity," "fidelity," "spontaneity," "authenticity," "genuineness," "originality," could be equated with the terms such as "integrity," "relevance," "unity," "function," "maturity," "subtlety," "adequacy," and other more precise terms of evaluation — in short, if "expression" always meant aesthetic achievement. But this is not so.

"Aesthetic" art, says Professor Curt Ducasse, an ingenious theorist of expression, is the conscious objectification of feelings, in which an intrinsic part is the critical moment. The artist corrects the objectification when it is not adequate. But this may mean that the earlier attempt was not successful in objectifying the self, or "it may also mean that it was a successful objectification of a self which, when it confronted us clearly, we disowned and repudiated in favor of another."[10] What is the standard by which we disown or accept the self? Professor Ducasse does not say. Whatever it may be, however, this standard is an element in the definition of art which will not reduce to terms of objectification. The evaluation of the work of art remains public; the work is measured against something outside the author.

IV

There is criticism of poetry and there is author psychology, which when applied to the present or future takes the form of inspirational promotion; but author psychology can be historical, too, and then we have literary biography, a legitimate and attractive study in itself, one approach, as Professor Tillyard would argue, to personality, the poem being only a parallel approach. Certainly it need not be with a derogatory purpose that one points out personal studies, as distinct from po-

[8]True truth. [Ed.]

[9]See Hughes Mearns, *Creative Youth* (Garden City, 1925), esp. pp. 10, 27–29. The technique of inspiring poems has apparently been outdone more recently by the study of inspiration in successful poets and other artists. See, for instance, Rosamond E. M. Harding, *An Anatomy of Inspiration* (Cambridge, 1940); Julius Portnoy, *A Psychology of Art Creation* (Philadelphia, 1942); Rudolf Arnheim and others, *Poets at Work* (New York, 1947); Phyllis Bartlett, *Poems in Process* (New York, 1951); Brewster Ghiselin (ed.), *The Creative Process: A Symposium* (Berkeley and Los Angeles, 1952). [Au.]

[10]Curt Ducasse, *The Philosophy of Art* (New York, 1929), p. 116. [Au.]

etic studies, in the realm of literary scholarship. Yet there is danger of confusing personal and poetic studies; and there is the fault of writing the personal as if it were poetic.

There is a difference between internal and external evidence for the meaning of a poem. And the paradox is only verbal and superficial that what is (1) internal is also public: it is discovered through the semantics and syntax of a poem, through our habitual knowledge of the language, through grammars, dictionaries, and all the literature which is the source of dictionaries, in general through all that makes a language and culture; while what is (2) external is private or idiosyncratic; not a part of the work as a linguistic fact: it consists of revelations (in journals, for example, or letters or reported conversations) about how or why the poet wrote the poem — to what lady, while sitting on what lawn, or at the death of what friend or brother. There is (3) an intermediate kind of evidence about the character of the author or about private or semiprivate meanings attached to words or topics by an author or by a coterie of which he is a member. The meaning of words is the history of words, and the biography of an author, his use of a word, and the associations which the word had for *him*, are part of the word's history and meaning.[11] But the three types of evidence, especially (2) and (3), shade into one another so subtly that it is not always easy to draw a line between examples, and hence arises the difficulty for criticism. The use of biographical evidence need not involve intentionalism, because while it may be evidence of what the author intended, it may also be evidence of the meaning of his words and the dramatic character of his utterance. On the other hand, it may not be all this. And a critic who is concerned with evidence of type (1) and moderately with that of type (3) will in the long run produce a different sort of comment from that of the critic who is concerned with (2) and with (3) where it shades into (2).

The whole glittering parade of Professor Lowes's *Road to Xanadu*, for instance, runs along the border between types (2) and (3) or boldly traverses the romantic region of (2). "'Kubla Khan,'" says Professor Lowes, "is the fabric of a vision, but every image that rose up in its weaving had passed that way before. And it would seem that there is nothing haphazard or fortuitous in their return." This is not quite clear — not even when Professor Lowes explains that there were clusters of associations, like hooked atoms, which were drawn into complex relation with other clusters in the deep well of Coleridge's memory, and which then coalesced and issued forth as poems. If there was nothing "haphazard or fortuitous" in the way the images returned to the surface, that may mean (1) that Coleridge could not produce what he did not have, that he was limited in his creation by what he had read or otherwise experienced, or (2) that having received certain clusters of associations, he was bound to return them in just the way he did, and that the value of the poem may be described in terms of the experiences on which he had to draw. The latter pair of propositions (a sort of Hartleyan associationism which Coleridge himself repudiated in the *Biographia*) may not be assented to. There were certainly other combinations, other poems, worse or better, that might have been written by men who had read Bartram and Purchas and Bruce and Milton. And this will be true no matter how many times we are able to add to the brilliant complex of Coleridge's reading. In certain flourishes (such as the sentence we have quoted) and in chapter headings like "The Shaping Spirit," "The Magical Synthesis," "Imagination Creatrix," it may be that Professor Lowes pretends to say more about the actual poems than he does. There is a certain deceptive variation in these fancy chapter titles; one expects to pass on to a new stage in the argument, and one finds — more and more sources, more and more about "the streamy nature of association."[12]

"Wohin der Weg?" quotes Professor Lowes for the motto of his book. "Kein Weg! Ins Unbe-

[11]And the history of words *after* a poem is written may contribute meanings which if relevant to the original pattern should not be ruled out by a scruple about intention. [Au.]

[12]Chaps. 8, "The Pattern," and 16, "The Known and Familiar Landscape," will be found of most help to the student of the poem. [Au.]

tretene."[13] Precisely because the way is *unbetreten*, we should say, it leads away from the poem. Bartram's *Travels* contains a good deal of the history of certain words and of certain romantic Floridian conceptions that appear in "Kubla Khan." And a good deal of that history has passed and was then passing into the very stuff of our language. Perhaps a person who has read Bartram appreciates the poem more than one who has not. Or, by looking up the vocabulary of "Kubla Khan" in the *Oxford English Dictionary*, or by reading some of the other books there quoted, a person may know the poem better. But it would seem to pertain little to the poem to know that *Coleridge* had read Bartram. There is a gross body of life, of sensory and mental experience, which lies behind and in some sense causes every poem, but can never be and need not be known in the verbal and hence intellectual composition which is the poem. For all the objects of our manifold experience, for every unity, there is an action of the mind which cuts off roots, melts away context — or indeed we should never have objects or ideas or anything to talk about.

It is probable that there is nothing in Professor Lowes's vast book which could detract from anyone's appreciation of either *The Ancient Mariner* or "Kubla Khan." We next present a case where preoccupation with evidence of type (3) has gone so far as to distort a critic's view of a poem (yet a case not so obvious as those that abound in our critical journals).

In a well known poem by John Donne[14] appears this quatrain:

> Moving of th' earth brings harmes and feares,
> Men reckon what it did and meant,
> But trepidation of the spheares,
> Though greater farre, is innocent.

A recent critic in an elaborate treatment of Donne's learning has written of this quatrain as follows:

> He touches the emotional pulse of the situation by a skillful allusion to the new and the old astronomy. . . . Of the new astronomy, the "moving of the earth" is the most radical principle; of the old, the "trepidation of the spheres" is the motion of the greatest complexity. . . . The poet must exhort his love to quietness and calm upon his departure; and for this purpose the figure based upon the latter motion (trepidation), long absorbed into the traditional astronomy, fittingly suggests the tension of the moment without arousing the "harmes and feares" implicit in the figure of the moving earth.[15]

The argument is plausible and rests on a well substantiated thesis that Donne was deeply interested in the new astronomy and its repercussions in the theological realm. In various works Donne shows his familiarity with Kepler's *De Stella Nova*, with Galileo's *Siderius Nuncius*, with William Gilbert's *De Magnete*, and with Clavius's commentary on the *De Sphaera* of Sacrobosco. He refers to the new science in his Sermon at Paul's Cross and in a letter to Sir Henry Goodyer. In *The First Anniversary* he says the "new philosophy calls all in doubt." In the *Elegy on Prince Henry* he says that the "least moving of the center" makes "the world to shake."

It is difficult to answer argument like this, and impossible to answer it with evidence of like nature. There is no reason why Donne might not have written a stanza in which the two kinds of celestial motion stood for two sorts of emotion at parting. And if we become full of astronomical ideas and see Donne only against the background of the new science, we may believe that he did. But the text itself remains to be dealt with, the analyzable vehicle of a complicated metaphor. And one may observe: (1) that the movement of the earth according to the Copernican theory is a celestial motion, smooth and regular, and while it might cause religious or philosophic fears, it could not be associated with the crudity and earthiness of the kind of commotion which the speaker in the poem wishes to discourage; (2) that there is another moving of the earth, an earthquake, which has just these qualities and is to be associated with the tear-floods and sigh-tempests of the second stanza of the poem;

[13]Goethe: "Whither leads the road? No road! Into the untraveled." [Ed.]

[14]"A Valediction, Forbidding Mourning." [Ed.]

[15]Charles M. Coffin, *John Donne and the New Philosophy* (New York, 1927), pp. 97–98. [Au.]

(3) that "trepidation" is an appropriate opposite of earthquake, because each is a shaking or vibratory motion; and "trepidation of the spheres" is "greater far" than an earthquake, but not much greater (if two such motions can be compared as to greatness) than the annual motion of the earth; (4) that reckoning what it "did and meant" shows that the event has passed, like an earthquake, not like the incessant celestial movement of the earth. Perhaps a knowledge of Donne's interest in the new science may add another shade of meaning, an overtone to the stanza in question, though to say even this runs against the words. To make the geocentric and heliocentric antithesis the core of the metaphor is to disregard the English language, to prefer private evidence to public, external to internal.

V

If the distinction between kinds of evidence has implications for the historical critic, it has them no less for the contemporary poet and his critic. Or, since every rule for a poet is but another side of a judgment by a critic, and since the past is the realm of the scholar and critic, and the future and present that of the poet and the critical leaders of taste, we may say that the problems arising in literary scholarship from the intentional fallacy are matched by others which arise in the world of progressive experiment.

The question of "allusiveness," for example, as acutely posed by the poetry of Eliot, is certainly one where a false judgment is likely to involve the intentional fallacy. The frequency and depth of literary allusion in the poetry of Eliot and others has driven so many in pursuit of full meanings to the *Golden Bough* and the Elizabethan drama that it has become a kind of commonplace to suppose that we do not know what a poet means unless we have traced him in his reading — a supposition redolent with intentional implications. The stand taken by F. O. Matthiessen is a sound one and partially forestalls the difficulty.

> If one reads these lines with an attentive ear and is sensitive to their sudden shifts in movement, the contrast between the actual Thames and the idealized vision of it during an age before it flowed through a megalopolis is sharply conveyed by that movement itself, whether or not one recognizes the refrain to be from Spenser.

Eliot's allusions work when we know them — and to a great extent even when we do not know them, through their suggestive power.

But sometimes we find allusions supported by notes, and it is a nice question whether the notes function more as guides to send us where we may be educated, or more as indications in themselves about the character of the allusions. "Nearly everything of importance . . . that is apposite to an appreciation of 'The Waste Land,'" writes Matthiessen of Miss Weston's book,[16] "has been incorporated into the structure of the poem itself, or into Eliot's Notes." And with such an admission it may begin to appear that it would not much matter if Eliot invented his sources (as Sir Walter Scott invented chapter epigraphs from "old plays" and "anonymous" authors, or as Coleridge wrote marginal glosses for *The Ancient Mariner*). Allusions to Dante, Webster, Marvell, or Baudelaire doubtless gain something because these writers existed, but it is doubtful whether the same can be said for an allusion to an obscure Elizabethan:

> The sound of horns and motors, which shall bring
> Sweeney to Mrs. Porter in the spring.

"Cf. Day, *Parliament of Bees:*" says Eliot,

> When of a sudden, listening, you shall hear,
> A noise of horns and hunting, which shall bring
> Actaeon to Diana in the spring,
> Where all shall see her naked skin.

The irony is completed by the quotation itself; had Eliot, as is quite conceivable, composed these lines to furnish his own background, there would be no loss of validity. The conviction may grow as one reads Eliot's next note: "I do not know the origin of the ballad from which these lines are taken: it was reported to me from Sydney, Australia." The important word in this note — on Mrs. Porter and her daughter who washed

[16]Jessie Weston's *From Ritual to Romance* (1920), an influence on *The Waste Land*. [Ed.]

their feet in soda water — is "ballad." And if one should feel from the lines themselves their "ballad" quality, there would be little need for the note. Ultimately, the inquiry must focus on the integrity of such notes as parts of the poem, for where they constitute special information about the meaning of phrases in the poem, they ought to be subject to the same scrutiny as any of the other words in which it is written. Matthiessen believes that notes were the price Eliot "had to pay in order to avoid what he would have considered muffling the energy of his poem by extended connecting links in the text itself." But it may be questioned whether the notes and the need for them are not equally muffling. F. W. Bateson has plausibly argued that Tennyson's "The Sailor Boy" would be better if half the stanzas were omitted, and the best versions of ballads like "Sir Patrick Spens" owe their power to the very audacity with which the minstrel has taken for granted the story upon which he comments. What then if a poet finds he cannot take so much for granted in a more recondite context and rather than write informatively, supplies notes? It can be said in favor of this plan that at least the notes do not pretend to be dramatic, as they would if written in verse. On the other hand, the notes may look like unassimilated material lying loose beside the poem, necessary for the meaning of the verbal symbol, but not integrated, so that the symbol stands incomplete.

We mean to suggest by the above analysis that whereas notes tend to seem to justify themselves as external indexes to the author's *intention*, yet they ought to be judged like any other parts of a composition (verbal arrangement special to a particular context), and when so judged their reality as parts of the poem, or their imaginative integration with the rest of the poem, may come into question. Matthiessen, for instance, sees that Eliot's titles for poems and his epigraphs are informative apparatus, like the notes. But while he is worried by some of the notes and thinks that Eliot "appears to be mocking himself for writing the note at the same time that he wants to convey something by it," Matthiessen believes that the "device" of epigraphs "is not at all open to the objection of not being sufficiently structural." "The *intention*," he says, "is to enable the poet to secure a condensed expression in the poem itself." "In each case the epigraph is *designed* to form an integral part of the effect of the poem." And Eliot himself, in his notes, has justified his poetic practice in terms of intention.

> The Hanged Man, a member of the traditional pack, fits my purpose in two ways: because he is associated in my mind with the Hanged God of Frazer, and because I associate him with the hooded figure in the passage of the disciples to Emmaus in Part V. . . . The man with Three Staves (an authentic member of the Tarot pack) I associate, quite arbitrarily, with the Fisher King himself.

And perhaps he is to be taken more seriously here, when off guard in a note, than when in his Norton Lectures he comments on the difficulty of saying what a poem means and adds playfully that he thinks of prefixing to a second edition of *Ash Wednesday* some lines from *Don Juan:*

> I don't pretend that I quite understand
> My own meaning when I would be *very* fine;
> But the fact is that I have nothing planned
> Unless it were to be a moment merry.

If Eliot and other contemporary poets have any characteristic fault, it may be in *planning* too much.

Allusiveness in poetry is one of several critical issues by which we have illustrated the more abstract issue of intentionalism, but it may be for today the most important illustration. As a poetic practice allusiveness would appear to be in some recent poems an extreme corollary of the romantic intentionalist assumption, and as a critical issue it challenges and brings to light in a special way the basic premise of intentionalism. The following instance from the poetry of Eliot may serve to epitomize the practical implications of what we have been saying. In Eliot's "Love Song of J. Alfred Prufrock," toward the end, occurs the line: "I have heard the mermaids singing, each to each," and this bears a certain resemblance to a line in a Song by John Donne, "Teach me to heare Mermaides singing," so that for the reader acquainted to a certain degree with Donne's poetry, the critical question arises: Is Eliot's line an allusion to Donne's? Is Prufrock thinking about Donne? Is Eliot thinking about Donne? We suggest that there are two radically different ways of looking for an answer to this question. There is (1) the way of poetic analysis and exegesis, which inquires whether it makes any sense if Eliot-Prufrock *is* thinking about Donne. In an earlier part of the poem, when Prufrock asks, "Would it have been worth while, . . . To have squeezed the universe into a ball," his words take half their sadness and irony from certain energetic and passionate lines of Marvell "To His Coy Mistress." But the exegetical inquirer may wonder whether mermaids considered as "strange sights" (to hear them is in Donne's poem analogous to getting with child a mandrake root) have much to do with Prufrock's mermaids, which seem to be symbols of romance and dynamism, and which incidentally have literary authentication, if they need it, in a line of a sonnet by Gérard de Nerval. This method of inquiry may lead to the conclusion that the given resemblance between Eliot and Donne is without significance and is better not thought of, or the method may have the disadvantage of providing no certain conclusion. Nevertheless, we submit that this is the true and objective way of criticism, as contrasted to what the very uncertainty of exegesis might tempt a second kind of critic to undertake: (2) the way of biographical or genetic inquiry, in which, taking advantage of the fact that Eliot is still alive, and in the spirit of a man who would settle a bet, the critic writes to Eliot and asks what he meant, or if he had Donne in mind. We shall not here weigh the probabilities — whether Eliot would answer that he meant nothing at all, had nothing at all in mind — a sufficiently good answer to such a question — or in an unguarded moment might furnish a clear and, within its limits, irrefutable answer. Our point is that such an answer to such an inquiry would have nothing to do with the poem "Prufrock"; it would not be a critical inquiry. Critical inquiries, unlike bets, are not settled in this way. Critical inquiries are not settled by consulting the oracle.

Cleanth Brooks

1906–1994

To many minds, Cleanth Brooks is the archetypal New Critic, the man whose catch phrases, critical studies, and college textbooks epitomized New Critical ideas, practice, and pedagogy. Brooks was born in Kentucky, educated at Vanderbilt, Tulane, and Oxford (where he was a Rhodes scholar), and began his teaching career at Louisiana State University in 1932. From 1935 to 1942, Brooks and the poet Robert Penn Warren edited The Southern Review, *which promulgated the New Critical program; the two later collaborated on* Understanding Poetry *(1938) and* Understanding Fiction *(1943), textbooks which further advanced the New Critical cause. The year 1947 saw the publication of Brooks's classic of criticism,* The Well Wrought Urn, *and the beginning of his career at Yale, where he became a professor emeritus of rhetoric thirteen years later. Brooks's other works include two studies of William Faulkner (1963 and 1978),* Modern Poetry and the Tradition *(1939),* Literary Criticism: A Short History *(1957) with W. K. Wimsatt, and* A Shaping Joy: Studies in the Writer's Craft *(1972). "Irony as a Principle of Structure," from* Literary Opinion in America *(1951), edited by M. D. Zabel, is a revision of an article that first appeared in the February 1948 issue of* College English.

Irony as a Principle of Structure

One can sum up modern poetic technique by calling it the rediscovery of metaphor and the full commitment to metaphor. The poet can legitimately step out into the universal only by first going through the narrow door of the particular. The poet does not select an abstract theme and then embellish it with concrete details. On the contrary, he must establish the details, must abide by the details, and through his realization of the details attain to whatever general meaning he can attain. The meaning must issue from the particulars; it must not seem to be arbitrarily forced upon the particulars. Thus, our conventional habits of language have to be reversed when we come to deal with poetry. For here it is the tail that wags the dog. Better still, here it is the tail of the kite — the tail that makes the kite fly — the tail that renders the kite more than a frame of paper blown crazily down the wind.

The tail of the kite, it is true, seems to negate the kite's function: it weights down something made to rise; and in the same way, the concrete particulars with which the poet loads himself seem to deny the universal to which he aspires. The poet wants to "say" something. Why, then, doesn't he say it directly and forthrightly? Why is he willing to say it only through his metaphors? Through his metaphors, he risks saying it partially and obscurely, and risks not saying it at all. But the risk must be taken, for direct statement leads to abstraction and threatens to take us out of poetry altogether.

The commitment to metaphor thus implies, with respect to general theme, a principle of indirection. With respect to particular images and statements, it implies a principle of organic relationship. That is, the poem is not a collection of beautiful or "poetic" images. If there really existed objects which were somehow intrinsically "poetic," still the mere assemblage of these would not give us a poem. For in that case, one might arrange bouquets of these poetic images and thus create poems by formula. But the elements of a poem are related to each other, not as blossoms juxtaposed in a bouquet, but as the blossoms are related to the other parts of a growing plant. The beauty of the poem is the flowering of the whole plant, and needs the stalk, the leaf, and the hidden roots.

If this figure seems somewhat highflown, let us borrow an analogy from another art: the poem is like a little drama. The total effect proceeds from all the elements in the drama, and in a good poem, as in a good drama, there is no waste motion and there are no superfluous parts.

In coming to see that the parts of a poem are related to each other organically, and related to the total theme indirectly, we have come to see the importance of *context.* The memorable verses in poetry — even those which seem somehow intrinsically "poetic" — show on inspection that they derive their poetic quality from their relation to a particular context. We may, it is true, be tempted to say that Shakespeare's "Ripeness is all" is poetic because it is a sublime thought, or because it possesses simple eloquence; but that is to forget the context in which the passage appears. The proof that this is so becomes obvious when we contemplate such unpoetic lines as "vitality is all," "serenity is all," "maturity is all," — statements whose philosophical import in the abstract is about as defensible as that of "ripeness is all." Indeed, the commonplace word "never" repeated five times becomes one of the most poignant lines in *Lear,* but it becomes so because of the supporting context. Even the "meaning" of any particular item is modified by the context. For what is said is said in a particular situation and by a particular dramatic character.

The last instances adduced can be most properly regarded as instances of "loading" from the context. The context endows the particular word or image or statement with significance. Images so charged become symbols; statements so charged become dramatic utterances. But there is another way in which to look at the impact of the context upon the part. The part is modified by the pressure of the context.

Now the *obvious* warping of a statement by the context we characterize as "ironical." To take the simplest instance, we say "this is a fine state of affairs," and in certain contexts the statement means quite the opposite of what it purports to say literally. This is sarcasm, the most obvious kind of irony. Here a complete reversal of meaning is effected: effected by the context, and pointed, probably, by the tone of voice. But the modification can be most important even though it falls far short of sarcastic reversal, and it need not be underlined by the tone of voice at all. The tone of irony can be effected by the skillful disposition of the context. Gray's *Elegy* will furnish an obvious example:

> Can storied urn or animated bust
> Back to its mansion call the fleeting breath?
> Can Honour's voice provoke the silent dust,
> Or Flatt'ry soothe the dull cold ear of death?

In its context, the question is obviously rhetorical. The answer has been implied in the characterization of the breath as fleeting and of the ear of death as dull and cold. The form is that of a question, but the manner in which the question has been asked shows that it is no true question at all.

These are obvious instances of irony, and even on this level, much more poetry is ironical than the reader may be disposed to think. Many of Hardy's poems and nearly all of Housman's, for example, reveal irony quite as definite and overt as this. Lest these examples, however, seem to specialize irony in the direction of the sardonic, the reader ought to be reminded that irony, even in its obvious and conventionally recognized forms, comprises a wide variety of modes: tragic irony, self-irony, playful, arch, mocking, or gentle irony, etc. The body of poetry which may be said to contain irony in the ordinary senses of the term stretches from *Lear,* on the one hand, to "Cupid and Campaspe Played," on the other.

What indeed would be a statement wholly devoid of an ironic potential — a statement that did not show any qualification of the context? One is forced to offer statements like "Two plus two equals four," or "The square on the hypotenuse of a right triangle is equal to the sum of the squares on the two sides." The meaning of these statements is unqualified by any context; if they are true, they are equally true in any possible context.[1] These statements are properly abstract, and their terms are pure denotations. (If "two" or "four" actually happened to have connotations for the fancifully minded, the connotations would be quite irrelevant: they do not participate in the meaningful structure of the statement.)

But connotations are important in poetry and do enter significantly into the structure of meaning which is the poem. Moreover, I should claim also — as a corollary of the foregoing proposition — that poems never contain abstract statements. That is, any "statement" made in the poem bears the pressure of the context and has its meaning modified by the context. In other words, the statements made — including those which appear to be philosophical generalizations — are to be read as if they were speeches in a drama. Their relevance, their propriety, their rhetorical force, even their meaning, cannot be divorced from the context in which they are imbedded.

The principle I state may seem a very obvious one, but I think that it is nonetheless very important. It may throw some light upon the importance of the term *irony* in modern criticism. As one who has certainly tended to overuse the term *irony* and perhaps, on occasion, has abused the term, I am closely concerned here. But I want to make quite clear what that concern is: it is not to justify the term *irony* as such, but rather to indicate why modern critics are so often tempted to use it. We have doubtless stretched the term too much, but it has been almost the only term available by which to point to a general and important aspect of poetry.

Consider this example: The speaker in Matthew Arnold's "Dover Beach" states that the

[1]This is not to say, of course, that such statements are not related to a particular "universe of discourse." They are indeed, as are all statements of whatever kind. But I distinguish here between "context" and "universe of discourse." "Two plus two equals four" is not dependent on a special dramatic context in the way in which a "statement" made in a poem is. Compare "two plus two equals four" and the same "statement" as contained in Housman's poem:

> — To think that two and two are four
> And neither five nor three
> The heart of man has long been sore
> And long 'tis like to be. [Au.]

world, "which seems to lie before us like a land of dreams . . . hath really neither joy nor love nor light. . . ." For some readers the statement will seem an obvious truism. (The hero of a typical Hemingway short story or novel, for example, will say this, though of course in a rather different idiom.) For other readers, however, the statement will seem false, or at least highly questionable. In any case, if we try to "prove" the proposition, we shall raise some very perplexing metaphysical questions, and in doing so, we shall certainly also move away from the problems of the poem and, finally, from a justification of the poem. For the lines are to be justified in the poem in terms of the context: the speaker is standing beside his loved one, looking out of the window on the calm sea, listening to the long withdrawing roar of the ebbing tide, and aware of the beautiful delusion of moonlight which "blanches" the whole scene. The "truth" of the statement, and of the poem itself, in which it is imbedded, will be validated, not by a majority report of the association of sociologists, or a committee of physical scientists, or of a congress of metaphysicians who are willing to stamp the statement as proved. How is the statement to be validated? We shall probably not be able to do better than to apply T. S. Eliot's test: does the statement seem to be that which the mind of the reader can accept as coherent, mature, and founded on the facts of experience? But when we raise such a question, we are driven to consider the poem as drama. We raise such further questions as these: Does the speaker seem carried away with his own emotions? Does he seem to oversimplify the situation? Or does he, on the other hand, seem to have won to a kind of detachment and objectivity? In other words, we are forced to raise the question as to whether the statement grows properly out of a context; whether it acknowledges the pressures of the context; whether it is "ironical" — or merely callow, glib, and sentimental.

I have suggested elsewhere that the poem which meets Eliot's test comes to the same thing as I. A. Richards's "poetry of synthesis" — that is, a poetry which does not leave out what is apparently hostile to its dominant tone, and which, because it is able to fuse the irrelevant and discordant, has come to terms with itself and is invulnerable to irony.[2] Irony, then, in this further sense, is not only an acknowledgment of the pressures of a context. Invulnerability to irony is the stability of a context in which the internal pressures balance and mutually support each other. The stability is like that of the arch: the very forces which are calculated to drag the stones to the ground actually provide the principle of support — a principle in which thrust and counterthrust become the means of stability.

In many poems the pressures of the context emerge in obvious ironies. Marvell's "To His Coy Mistress" or Raleigh's "Nymph's Reply" or even Gray's "Elegy" reveal themselves as ironical, even to readers who use irony strictly in the conventional sense.

But can other poems be subsumed under this general principle, and do they show a comparable basic structure? The test case would seem to be presented by the lyric, and particularly the simple lyric. Consider, for example, one of Shakespeare's songs:

> Who is Silvia: what is she
>   That all our swains commend her?
> Holy, fair, and wise is she;
>   The heavens such grace did lend her,
> That she might admired be.
> Is she kind as she is fair?
>   For beauty lives with kindness.
> Love doth to her eyes repair,
>   To help him of his blindness,
> And, being help'd, inhabits there.
> Then to Silvia let us sing,
>   That Silvia is excelling;
> She excels each mortal thing
>   Upon the dull earth dwelling:
> To her let us garlands bring.

On one level the song attempts to answer the question "Who is Silvia?" and the answer given makes her something of an angel and something of a goddess. She excels each mortal thing "Upon the dull earth dwelling." Silvia herself, of course, dwells upon that dull earth, though it is presumably her own brightness which makes it dull by comparison. (The dull earth, for example,

[2]See I. A. Richards, *Principles of Literary Criticism* (New York: Harcourt Brace Jovanovich, 1924), pp. 774ff. [Ed.]

yields bright garlands which the swains are bringing to her.) Why does she excel each mortal thing? Because of her virtues ("Holy, fair, and wise is she"), and these are a celestial gift. She is heaven's darling ("The heavens such grace did lend her").

Grace, I suppose, refers to grace of movement, and some readers will insist that we leave it at that. But since Silvia's other virtues include holiness and wisdom, and since her grace has been lent from above, I do not think that we can quite shut out the theological overtones. Shakespeare's audience would have found it even more difficult to do so. At any rate, it is interesting to see what happens if we are aware of these overtones. We get a delightful richness, and we also get something very close to irony.

The motive for the bestowal of grace — that she might admired be — is oddly untheological. But what follows is odder still, for the love that "doth to her eyes repair" is not, as we might expect, Christian "charity" but the little pagan god Cupid ("Love doth to her eyes repair, / To help him of his blindness.") But if Cupid lives in her eyes, then the second line of the stanza takes on another layer of meaning. "For beauty lives with kindness" becomes not merely a kind of charming platitude — actually often denied in human experience. (The Petrarchan lover, for example, as Shakespeare well knew, frequently found a beautiful and *cruel* mistress.) The second line, in this context, means also that the love god lives with the kind Silvia, and indeed has taken these eyes that sparkle with kindness for his own.

Is the mixture of pagan myth and Christian theology, then, an unthinking confusion into which the poet has blundered, or is it something wittily combined? It is certainly not a confusion, and if blundered into unconsciously, it is a happy mistake. But I do not mean to press the issue of the poet's self-consciousness (and with it, the implication of a kind of playful irony). Suffice it to say that the song is charming and delightful, and that the mingling of elements is proper to a poem which is a deft and light-fingered attempt to suggest the quality of divinity with which lovers perennially endow maidens who are finally mortal. The touch is light, there is a lyric grace, but the tone is complex, nonetheless.

I shall be prepared, however, to have this last example thrown out of court since Shakespeare, for all his universality, was a contemporary of the metaphysical poets, and may have incorporated more of their ironic complexity than is necessary or normal. One can draw more innocent and therefore more convincing examples from Wordsworth's Lucy poems.

She dwelt among the untrodden ways
  Beside the springs of Dove,
A maid whom there were none to praise
  And very few to love;

A violet by a mossy stone
  Half hidden from the eye!
Fair as a star, when only one
  Is shining in the sky.

She lived unknown, and few could know
  When Lucy ceased to be;
But she is in her grave, and, oh,
  The difference to me.

Which is Lucy really like — the violet or the star? The context in general seems to support the violet comparison. The violet, beautiful but almost unnoticed, already half hidden from the eye, is now, as the poem ends, completely hidden in its grave, with none but the poet to grieve for its loss. The star comparison may seem only vaguely relevant — a conventional and here a somewhat anomalous compliment. Actually, it is not difficult to justify the star comparison: to her lover's eyes, she is the solitary star. She has no rivals, nor would the idea of rivalry, in her unself-conscious simplicity, occur to her.

The violet and the star thus balance each other and between themselves define the situation: Lucy was, from the viewpoint of the great world, unnoticed, shy, modest, and half hidden from the eye, but from the standpoint of her lover, she is the single star, completely dominating that world, not arrogantly like the sun, but sweetly and modestly, like the star. The implicit contrast is that so often developed ironically by John Donne in his poems where the lovers, who amount to nothing in the eyes of the world, become, in their own eyes, each the other's world — as in "The Good-Morrow," where their love makes "one little room an everywhere," or as in "The Canonization," where the lovers drive into the mirrors of each other's eyes the "towns, countries, courts" — which make up the great world; and thus find that world in themselves. It is easy to imagine how Donne would have exploited the contrast between the violet and the star, accentuating it, developing the irony, showing how the violet was really like its antithesis, the star, etc.

Now one does not want to enter an Act of Uniformity against the poets. Wordsworth is entitled to his method of simple juxtaposition with no underscoring of the ironical contrast. But it is worth noting that the contrast with its ironic potential is there in his poem. It is there in nearly all of Wordsworth's successful lyrics. It is certainly to be found in "A slumber did my spirit seal."

> A slumber did my spirit seal;
>   I had no human fears:
> She seemed a thing that could not feel
>   The touch of earthly years.
>
> No motion has she now, no force;
>   She neither hears nor sees,
> Rolled round in earth's diurnal course,
>   With rocks, and stones, and trees.

The lover's insensitivity to the claims of mortality is interpreted as a lethargy of spirit — a strange slumber. Thus the "human fears" that he lacked are apparently the fears normal to human beings. But the phrase has a certain pliability. It could mean fears *for* the loved one as a mortal human being; and the lines that follow tend to warp the phrase in this direction: it does not occur to the lover that he needs to fear for one who cannot be touched by "earthly years." We need not ague that Wordsworth is consciously using a witty device, a purposed ambiguity; nor need we conclude that he is confused. It is enough to see that Wordsworth has developed, quite "normally," let us say, a context calculated to pull "human fears" in opposed directions, and that the slightest pressure of attention on the part of the reader precipitates an ironical effect.

As we move into the second stanza, the potential irony almost becomes overt. If the slumber has sealed the lover's spirit, a slumber, immersed in which he thought it impossible that his loved one could perish, so too a slumber has now definitely sealed *her* spirit: "No motion has she now, no force; / She neither hears nor sees." It is evident that it is her unnatural slumber that has waked him out of his. It is curious to speculate on what Donne or Marvell would have made of this.

Wordsworth, however, still does not choose to exploit the contrast as such. Instead, he attempts to suggest something of the lover's agonized shock at the loved one's present lack of motion — of his response to her utter and horrible inertness. And how shall he suggest this? He chooses to suggest it, not by saying that she lies as quiet as marble or as a lump of clay; on the contrary, he attempts to suggest it by imagining her in violent motion — violent, but imposed motion, the same motion indeed which the very stones share, whirled about as they are in earth's diurnal course. Why does the image convey so powerfully the sense of something inert and helpless? Part of the effect, of course, resides in the fact that a dead lifelessness is suggested more sharply by an object's being whirled about by something else than by an image of the object in repose. But there are other matters which are at work here: the sense of the girl's falling back into the clutter of things, companioned by things chained like a tree to one particular spot, or by things completely inanimate, like rocks and stones. Here, of course, the concluding figure leans upon the suggestion made in the first stanza, that the girl once seemed something not subject to earthly limitations at all. But surely, the image of the whirl itself is important in its suggestion of something meaningless — motion that mechanically repeats itself. And there is one further element: the girl, who to her lover seemed a thing that could not feel the touch of earthly years, is caught up helplessly into the empty whirl of the earth which measures and makes time. She is touched by and held by earthly time in its most powerful and horrible image. The last figure thus seems to me to summarize the poem — to offer to almost every facet of meaning suggested in the earlier lines a concurring and resolving image which meets and accepts and reduces each item to its place in the total unity.

Wordsworth, as we have observed above, does not choose to point up specifically the ironical contrast between the speaker's former slumber and the loved one's present slumber. But there is one ironical contrast which he does stress: this is the contrast between the two senses in which the girl becomes insulated against the "touch of earthly years." In the first stanza, she "could not feel / The touch of earthly years" because she seemed divine and immortal. But in the second stanza, now in her grave, she still does not "feel the touch of earthly years," for, like the rocks and stones, she feels nothing at all. It is true that Wordsworth does not repeat the verb "feels"; instead he writes "She neither *hears* nor *sees*." But the contrast, though not commented upon directly by any device of verbal wit, is there nonetheless, and is bound to make itself felt in any sensitive reading of the poem. The statement of the first stanza has been literally realized in the second, but its meaning has been ironically reversed.

Ought we, then, to apply the term *ironical* to Wordsworth's poem? Not necessarily. I am trying to account for my temptation to call such a poem ironical — not to justify my yielding to the temptation — least of all to insist that others so transgress. Moreover, Wordsworth's poem seems to be admirable, and I entertain no notion that it might have been more admirable still had John Donne written it rather than William Wordsworth. I shall be content if I can make a much more modest point: namely, that since both Wordsworth and Donne are poets, their work has at basis a similar structure, and that the dynamic structure — the pattern of thrust and counterthrust — which we associate with Donne has its counterpart in Wordsworth. In the work of both men, the relation between part and part is organic, which means that each part modifies and is modified by the whole.

Yet to intimate that there are potential ironies in Wordsworth's lyric may seem to distort it. After all, is it not simple and spontaneous? With these terms we encounter two of the critical catchwords of the nineteenth century, even as *ironical* is in danger of becoming a catchword of our own period. Are the terms *simple* and *ironical* mutually exclusive? What after all do we mean by *simple* or by *spontaneous*? We may mean that the poem came to the poet easily and even spontaneously: very complex poems may — indeed have — come just this way. Or the poem may seem in its effect on the reader a simple and spontaneous utterance: some poems of great complexity possess this quality. What is likely to cause trouble here is the intrusion of a special theory of composition. It is fairly represented as an intrusion since a theory as to how a poem is written is being allowed to dictate to us how the poem is to be read. There is no harm in thinking of Wordsworth's poem as simple and spontaneous unless these terms deny complexities that actually exist in the poem, and unless they justify us in reading the poem with only half our minds. A slumber ought not to seal the *reader's* spirit as he reads this poem, or any other poem.

I have argued that irony, taken as the acknowledgment of the pressures of context, is to be found in poetry of every period and even in simple lyrical poetry. But in the poetry of our own time, this pressure reveals itself strikingly. A great deal of modern poetry does use irony as its special and perhaps its characteristic strategy. For this there are reasons, and compelling reasons. To cite only a few of these reasons: there is the breakdown of a common symbolism; there is the general scepticism as to universals; not least important, there is the depletion and corruption of the very language itself, by advertising and by the mass-produced arts of radio, the moving picture, and pulp fiction. The modern poet has the task of rehabilitating a tired and drained language so that it can convey meanings once more with force and with exactitude. This task of qualifying and modifying language is perennial; but it is imposed on the modern poet as a special burden. Those critics who attribute the use of ironic techniques to the poet's own bloodless sophistication and tired scepticism would be better advised to refer these vices to his potential readers, a public corrupted by Hollywood and the Book of the Month Club. For the modern poet is not addressing simple primitives but a public sophisticated by commercial art.

At any rate, to the honor of the modern poet be it said that he has frequently succeeded in using his ironic techniques to win through to clarity and passion. Randall Jarrell's "Eighth Air Force" represents a success of this sort.

If, in an odd angle of the hutment,
A puppy laps the water from a can
Of flowers, and the drunk sergeant shaving
Whistles *O Paradiso!* — shall I say that man
Is not as men have said: a wolf to man?

The other murderers troop in yawning;
Three of them play Pitch, one sleeps, and one
Lies counting missions, lies there sweating
Till even his heart beats: One; One; One.
O murderers! . . . Still, this is how it's done:

This is a war. . . . But since these play, before they die,
Like puppies with their puppy; since, a man,
I did as these have done, but did not die —
I will content the people as I can
And give up these to them: Behold the man!

I have suffered, in a dream, because of him,
Many things; for this last saviour, man,
I have lied as I lie now. But what is lying?
Men wash their hands, in blood, as best they can:
I find no fault in this just man.

There are no superfluous parts, no dead or empty details. The airmen in their hutment are casual enough and honest enough to be convincing. The raw building is domesticated: there are the flowers in water from which the mascot, a puppy, laps. There is the drunken sergeant, whistling an opera aria as he shaves. These "murderers," as the poet is casually to call the airmen in the next stanza, display a touching regard for the human values. How, then, can one say that man is a wolf to man, since these men "play before they die, like puppies with their puppy." But the casual presence of the puppy in the hutment allows us to take the stanza both ways, for the dog is a kind of tamed and domesticated wolf, and his presence may prove on the contrary that the hutment is the wolf den. After all, the timber wolf plays with its puppies.

The second stanza takes the theme to a perfectly explicit conclusion. If three of the men play pitch, and one is asleep, at least one man is awake and counts himself and his companions murderers. But his unvoiced cry "O murderers" is met, countered, and dismissed with the next two lines: ". . . Still this is how it's done: / This is a war. . . ."

The note of casuistry and cynical apology prepares for a brilliant and rich resolving image, the image of Pontius Pilate, which is announced specifically in the third stanza:

I will content the people as I can
And give up these to them: behold the man!

Yet if Pilate, as he is first presented, is a jesting Pilate, who asks "What is truth?" it is a bitter and grieving Pilate who concludes the poem. It is the integrity of Man himself that is at stake. Is man a cruel animal, a wolf, or is he the last savior, the Christ of our secular religion of humanity?

The Pontius Pilate metaphor, as the poet uses it, becomes a device for tremendous concentration. For the speaker (presumably the young airman who cried "O murderers") is himself the confessed murderer under judgment, and also the Pilate who judges, and, at least as a representative of man, the savior whom the mob would condemn. He is even Pilate's better nature, his wife, for the lines "I have suffered, in a dream, because of him, / Many things" is merely a rearrangement of *Matthew* 27:19, the speech of Pilate's wife to her husband. But this last item is more than a reminiscence of the scriptural scene. It reinforces the speaker's present dilemma. The modern has had high hopes for man; are the hopes merely a dream? Is man incorrigible, merely a cruel beast? The speaker's present torture springs from that hope and from his reluctance to dismiss it as an empty dream. This Pilate is even harder-pressed than was the Roman magistrate. For he must convince himself of this last savior's innocence. But he has lied for him before. He will lie for him now.

Men wash their hands in blood, as best they can:
I find no fault in this just man.

What is the meaning of "Men wash their hands in blood, as best they can"? It can mean: Since my own hands are bloody, I have no right to condemn the rest. It can mean: I know that man can love justice, even though his hands are bloody, for there is blood on mine. It can mean: Men are essentially decent: they try to keep their hands clean even if they have only blood in which to wash them.

None of these meanings cancels out the others. All are relevant, and each meaning contributes to the total meaning. Indeed, there is not a facet of significance which does not receive illumination from the figure.

Some of Jarrell's weaker poems seem weak to me because they lean too heavily upon this concept of the goodness of man. In some of them, his approach to the theme is too direct. But in this poem, the affirmation of man's essential justness by a Pilate who contents the people as he washes his hands in blood seems to me to supply every qualification that is required. The sense of self-guilt, the yearning to believe in man's justness, the knowledge of the difficulty of so believing — all work to render accurately and dramatically the total situation.

It is easy at this point to misapprehend the function of irony. We can say that Jarrell's irony pares his theme down to acceptable dimensions. The theme of man's goodness has here been so qualified that the poet himself does not really believe in it. But this is not what I am trying to say. We do not ask a poet to bring his poem into line with our personal beliefs — still less to flatter our personal beliefs. What we do ask is that the poem dramatize the situation so accurately, so honestly, with such fidelity to the total situation that it is no longer a question of our beliefs, but of our participation in the poetic experience. At his best, Jarrell manages to bring us, by an act of imagination, to the most penetrating insight. Participating in that insight, we doubtless become better citizens. (One of the "uses" of poetry, I should agree, is to make us better citizens.) But poetry is not the eloquent rendition of the citizen's creed. It is not even the accurate rendition of his creed. Poetry must carry us beyond the abstract creed into the very matrix out of which, and from which, our creeds are abstracted. That is what "The Eighth Air Force" does. That is what, I am convinced, all good poetry does.

For the theme in a genuine poem does not confront us as abstraction — that is, as one man's generalization from the relevant particulars. Finding its proper symbol, defined and refined by the participating metaphors, the theme becomes a part of the reality in which we live — an insight, rooted in and growing out of concrete experience, many-sided, three-dimensional. Even the resistance to generalization has its part in this process — even the drag of the particulars away from the universal — even the tension of opposing themes — play their parts. The kite properly loaded, tension maintained along the kite string, rises steadily *against* the thrust of the wind.

R. S. Crane

1886–1967

Ronald Salmon Crane was the leader and moving spirit of the Chicago School of neo-Aristotelian criticism, one of the two major formalist movements in America. Crane was born in Michigan, took his A.B. from the University of Michigan, Ann Arbor (1908), and his doctorate at the University of Pennsylvania (1911). In 1911 he started teaching at Northwestern University in Illinois, then moved on in 1924 to the University of Chicago, where he became full professor in 1925 and head of the English department in 1935. Crane's interest in literary theory and his notion that criticism, rather than historical scholarship, was the preferred mode of teaching literature, began in the 1930s during the implementation of the innovative Hutchins curriculum. Crane's publications are primarily academic articles dense with thought, rather than critical books; the best and farthest reaching of his articles were collected in two volumes as The Idea of the Humanities and Other Essays Critical and Historical

(1967). His only theoretical treatise (from which this selection is taken) is The Languages of Criticism and the Structure of Poetry *(1953).*

Toward a More Adequate Criticism of Poetic Structure

II

It is not a question of regarding the *Poetics,* in Mr. Blackmur's phrase, as a "sacred book"[1] and certainly not of looking upon ourselves, in any exclusive sense, as forming an "Aristotelian" or "Neo-Aristotelian" school. It would be a desirable thing, indeed, if we could do away with "schools" in criticism as they have been done away with in most of the disciplines in which learning as distinguished from doctrine has been advanced. But our loyalty at any rate should be to problems rather than to ancient masters; and if it happens that we have problems for which Aristotle can give us the means, or some of the means, of solution, we should be prepared to benefit from his initiative in precisely the same way as many of our contemporaries have benefited from the more recent initiatives of Coleridge, Richards, Frazer, and Freud without necessarily becoming disciples of any of these men. And it is not difficult to see what there is in Aristotle, or what we can develop out of him, that is immediately pertinent to the problem of poetic structure in the particular form in which I have defined it at the beginning of this lecture.

I should put first in the list the conception of poetic works as "concrete wholes." Now anything is a concrete whole, as I have said before, the unity of which can be adequately stated only by saying that it "is such and such a form embodied in this or that matter, or such and such a matter with this or that form; so that its shape and structure must be included in our description" as well as that out of which it is constituted or made. And of the two natures which must join in any such whole, or in our account of it, "the formal nature is of greater importance than the material nature" inasmuch as the "form" of any individual object, such as a man or a couch, is the principle or cause "by reason of which the matter is some definite thing."[2] In spite of the now somewhat unfamiliar language in which the conception is stated in Aristotle, the underlying insight is one that we can easily translate into the terms of common experience. I take, for instance, a piece of modelling clay. There are many things which I cannot do with it — of which, as Aristotle would say, it cannot be the matter; but on the other hand the potentialities it does hold out, within these limits, are indefinite in number: I can make of it, if I wish, a geographical globe, with all its continents indicated, or the model of a house, or the bust of a sinister-looking man, and so on through a vast range of similar possibilities that is bounded only by my invention and skill. In any of these realizations the thing I make remains a thing of clay, having all the permanent characteristics of such a thing; but it remains this only in a partial sense; in itself, as a particular object to which we may respond practically or aesthetically, it is at the same time something else — a globe, a house, a sinister-looking man; and any description we may give of it, though it must obviously specify its clayness — that is, its material nature — would be of no use to anybody unless it also specified the definite kind of thing into which the clay has been shaped — that is, its formal nature. And the latter is clearly more important than the former since it is what accounts, in any particular case, for the clay being handled thus and not otherwise and for our response

[1]*Hudson Review* 3 (1951): 297. [Au.]

[2]*On the Parts of Animals* i.1.640^{b}25–29; *Metaphysics* vii.17.1041^{b}5–8. [Au.]

being of such and such a quality rather than any other.

It is not difficult to see how the conception fits the work of the poet or of any other writer. Here is a speech in a famous novel:

> "Ah, my poor dear child, the truth is, that in London it is always a sickly season. Nobody is healthy in London — nobody can be. It is a dreadful thing to have you forced to live there; so far off! and the air so bad!"

Taken in isolation, this may be described simply as an expression of regret that the person addressed has to live in London, based on the commonplace thought that the air of London, as compared with the air of the country, is far from healthy. The speech, we may say, is made out of this matter; but it is a matter, obviously, that permits of a variety of particular uses: it might be a speech in an idyll, or in a satire, or in a moral epistle in the manner of Cowper; and in each case its formal nature and hence our response would be different. It is actually, of course, a speech by Mr. Woodhouse in *Emma;* and when it is so read, in its position in the dialogue of Chapter 12 and in the light of what we have already seen of Emma's father, it assumes the nature of a characteristic comic act, wherein the most important thing is not the commonplace thought itself, but the excessive and inappropriate emotion, at the prospect of Isabella's coming departure for home, which this is made to express, and which is the formal principle shaping the matter of the speech into a definite, though not self-contained, artistic unit capable of directing our thoughts in a particular way.

Or here again is a whole poem, the material nature of which is comprised of the following sequence of happenings:

> A young Italian duke, influenced by his idle companions, dismisses the wise counsellor his father had recommended to him, refuses the advice of his fiancée, and devotes himself to a life of private pleasure and neglect of public duty. A Turkish corsair takes advantage of this situation to storm the Duke's castle and to reduce him and all his court to slavery; and the Duke falls into despair when he learns that his fiancée is destined for the conqueror's harem. She, however, deceives the corsair into giving her a delay of three days and a chance to speak to her lover. She uses this time to rouse the Duke to repentance for his past errors and to work out with him a plan whereby he and his father's counsellor will attempt a rescue before the three days are up. The plan succeeds; the Duke and his friends overcome the corsair's troops and make him prisoner. The Duke's false companions then demand that the Turk be executed; but the Duke, grateful for the lesson his captivity has taught him, responds by banishing them and allowing the corsair to depart unharmed; whereupon he marries his fiancée and resolves to rule more wisely in the future.

As an action this is clearly not without some form, being a coherent and complete chain of possible events, to which we are likely to respond by taking sides with the Duke and the girl against their captors. I am sure, however, that anyone who reads *The Duke of Benevento* for the first time after hearing my summary will think that I have given a very indefinite account of what happens in Sir John Henry Moore's poem and hence misled him completely as to the poem's distinctive nature and effect. He will probably be prepared to read a vaguely tragicomic romance or drama of a kind common enough in the 1770s; what he will actually find is a short piece of 204 lines beginning as follows:

> I hate the prologue to a story
> Worse than the tuning of a fiddle,
>   Squeaking and dinning;
> Hang order and connection,
> I love to dash into the middle;
>   Exclusive of the fame and glory,
> There is a comfort on reflection
>   To think you've done with the beginning.
>
> And so at supper one fine night,
>   Hearing a cry of Alla, Alla,
> The Prince was damnably confounded,
>   And in a fright,
> But more so when he saw himself surrounded
> By fifty Turks; and at their head the fierce Abdalla,
>
> And then he look'd a little grave
> To find himself become a slave, . . .

And so on consistently to the end, in a rapidly narrated episode of which the formal nature is the kind of anti-romantic comedy clearly foreshadowed in these lines — a form that is only potentially in the story of the poem (since this could yield several other forms) and is created out of it, partly indeed by Moore's pre-Byronic language and manner of narration, but also, as a reading of the whole poem will show, by the notably unheroic qualities of character and thought which he gives to his hero and heroine, with the result that we are unable to take their predicament any more tragically than they themselves do.

It can be seen from these illustrations how different is such a conception of the internal relations of form and matter in a "concrete whole" from the later and much commoner analytic in which form or art is set over against content or subject-matter in one or another of the many ways we have already illustrated. A poem, on the view of its structure suggested by Aristotle, is not a composite of *res* and *verba*[3] but a certain matter formed in a certain way or a certain form imposed upon or wrought out of a certain matter. The two are inseparable aspects of the same individual thing, though they are clearly distinct analytically as principles or causes, and though, of the two, the formal nature is necessarily the more important as long as our concern is with the poem as a concrete object. On the one hand, we do not cease to talk about the matter of a poem when we examine its formal structure, and, on the other hand, there is a sense in which nothing in a completed poem, or any distinguishable part thereof, is matter or content merely, in relation to which something else is form. In a well-made poem, everything is formed, and hence rendered poetic (whatever it may have been in itself), by virtue simply of being made to do something definite in the poem or to produce a definitely definable effect, however local, which the same materials of language, thought, character-traits, or actions would be incapable of in abstraction from the poem, or the context in the poem, in which they appear. We are not speaking poetically but only materially of anything in a poem, therefore, when we abstract it from its function or effect in the poem; we speak poetically, or formally, only when we add to a description of the thing in terms of its constituent elements (for example, the content of a metaphor or the events of a plot) an indication of the definite quality it possesses or of that in the poem for the sake of which it is there. In an absolute sense, then, nothing in a successful poem is nonformal or nonpoetic; but it is also true that structure of any kind necessarily implies a subordination of some parts to others; and in this relative sense we may intelligibly say of one formed element of a poem that it is material to something else in the same poem, the existence and specific effectiveness of which it makes possible. We may thus speak of the words of a poem as the material basis of the thought they express, although the words also have form as being ordered in sentences and rhythms; and similarly we may speak of thought as the matter of character, of character and thought in words as the matter of action or emotion, and so on up to but not including the overall form which synthesizes all these subordinate elements, formally effective in themselves, into a continuous poetic whole. Or we can reverse the order of consideration, and ask what matter of action, character, and thought a poem requires if its plot or lyric structure is to be formally of a certain kind, or what kind of character a speech ought to suggest if it is to serve adequately its function in a scene, or what selection and arrangement of words will render best or most economically a given state of mind.

Here then is an intelligible, universally applicable, and analytically powerful conception of the basic structural relations in poems which we can take over from Aristotle without committing ourselves to the total philosophy in which it was evolved. We can also take over, in the second place, the method of investigation and reasoning which he found appropriate to structures of this kind. The conception and the method, indeed, can hardly be divorced. For if we are to consider poetic works, in practical criticism, from the point of view of their concrete wholeness, then our central problem is to make their elements and subordinate structures causally intelligible in the light of their respective organizing forms. This can be done, however, only by means of general concepts embodying answers to two major questions relative to such kinds of poetry as we may be interested in: first, what different forms can go

[3]Subject-matter and language. [Ed.]

with what different matters, and, second, what parts, and what constructions of each of them, are necessary to the achievement of any given form. But these, it is obvious, are questions of fact, the answers to which can never be given by any "abstract" method but must depend upon inquiries of an *a posteriori* type which move inductively (in Aristotle's sense of induction) from particulars to the universals they embody and from ends or forms thus defined, by hypothetical necessity to the essential conditions of their realization in poetic matter. The method, of course, is not Aristotelian in any unique sense, but no one has shown as fully as he did how it may be applied to poetics or how completely it depends, in this application, upon an adequate knowledge of literary history.

The method is factual, but it is not indifferent to values; and the third thing we can learn from Aristotle is a manner of considering questions of better and worse in poetry which is likewise appropriate to the conception of poems as concrete wholes organized by formal principles. As things made by and for men, poems, as I have said before, can have a great variety of uses and be judged not improperly in terms of many different criteria, moral, political, intellectual, grammatical, rhetorical, historical. To judge them as poems, however, is to judge them in their distinctive aspects as wholes of certain kinds, in the light of the assumption that the poet's end — the end which makes him a poet — is simply the perfecting of the poem as a beautiful or intrinsically excellent thing. I do not mean by this that poems are ever perfected in an absolute sense. We need not quarrel with R. G. Collingwood when he remarks, in his *Autobiography,* that as a boy living in a household of artists he "learned to think of a picture not as a finished product exposed for the admiration of virtuosi, but as the visible record, lying about the house, of an attempt to solve a definite problem in painting, so far as the attempt has gone." "I learned," he adds, "what some critics and aestheticians never know to the end of their lives, that no 'work of art' is ever finished, so that in that sense of the phrase there is no such thing as a 'work of art' at all. Work ceases upon the picture or manuscript, not because it is finished, but because sending-in day is at hand, or because the printer is clamorous for copy, or because 'I am sick of working at this thing' or 'I can't see what more I can do to it.' "[4] This is sound sense, which critics and aestheticians ought to learn if they do not know it; but it is clearly not incompatible with the assumption that what a poet seeks to do, as a poet, is to make as good a work poetically speaking as he can; and this goodness, we can surely agree with Aristotle, must always consist in a mean between doing too much and not doing enough in his invention and handling of all its parts. The criterion, again, is not an absolute one; the mean in art, as in morals, is a relative mean, which has to be determined in adjustment to the particular necessities and possibilities of the form the artist is trying to achieve. And just as the poet can know these only by trial and error plus reflection upon the general conditions of his art and on what other poets have been able to do, so the critic can know them, and the ends to which they are relative, only by similar *ex post facto* means. He must therefore leave to other critics with less strictly "poetic" preoccupations the task of formulating criteria for poetry on the basis of general "abstract" principles; his business is to take the point of view of the poet and his problems and to judge what he has done, as sympathetically as possible, in terms of what must and what might be done *given* the distinctive form, new or old, which the poet is trying to work out of his materials.[5] And here, once more, the procedure of Aristotle can be of use.

We can still profit, moreover, not merely from these general features of his approach — all of them relevant also to other than critical problems — but likewise from many of the more particular applications of his method in the *Poetics,* including, first of all, the fundamental distinction, on which the whole treatise is based, between poetry which is "imitation" and poetry which is not.[6] The former, for Aristotle, is poetry in the most distinctive sense, since its principles are not the

[4] *An Autobiography,* p. 2. [Au.]

[5] On the kind of criticism which refuses to grant to an artist the "subject" he has chosen, see the remarks of Henry James in his preface to *The Portrait of a Lady.* [Au.]

[6] See Aristotle's *Poetics* and the note (p. 40) that clarifies the accidental relation in Aristotle between imitation and poetry. [Ed.]

principles of any other art; but to insist on this is not to question the possibility of discussing as "poetry" other kinds of works of which the materials and devices, though not the forms, are those of poems in the stricter meaning of the word; the difference is not one of relative dignity or value but purely of constructive principle, and hence of the kinds of hypotheses and terms that are required, respectively, for the analysis and judgment of works belonging to each. The distinction, as Aristotle understood it, has played no important part in the subsequent history of criticism. A class of "didactic" poems has, it is true, been more or less constantly recognized, but the differentiation between these and other poems has most often been made in terms of purpose, content, and technique rather than of matter and form, a "didactic" poem being distinguished sometimes as one in which the end of instruction is more prominent than that of delight, sometimes as one that uses or springs from or appeals to the reason rather than the imagination, sometimes as one that relies mainly on precepts instead of fictions and images or that uses direct rather than indirect means of expression. This breakdown of the original distinction was natural enough in the periods of criticism in which the ends of poetry were defined broadly as instruction and pleasure, and it is still natural in a period, such as our own, when the great preoccupation is with "meaning" and with poetry as a special kind of language for expressing special modes of signification. In both periods, although some classes of poems have been set apart as "didactic" in a peculiar and frequently pejorative sense, all poetry, or all poetry except that which can be described as "entertainment" merely, has tended to assume an essentially didactic character and function. The prevalence nowadays of "thematic analysis" as a method of discussion applicable to all poetic works that can be taken seriously at all is a clear sign of this, as is also the currency of "archetypal" analogies.[7] The result, however, has been to banish from criticism, or to confuse beyond clear recognition, a distinction which has as much validity now as when it was first made and which has not been supplanted by any of the later distinctions, since these all rest on quite different bases of principle. The distinction is simply between works, on the one hand, in which the formal nature is constituted of some particular human activity or state of feeling qualified morally and emotionally in a certain way, the beautiful rendering of this in words being the sufficient end of the poet's effort, and works, on the other hand (like the *Divine Comedy, Absalom and Achitophel, Don Juan, 1984*, etc.), in which the material nature is "poetic" in the sense that it is made up of parts similar to those of imitative poems and the formal nature is constituted of some particular thesis, intellectual or practical, relative to some general human interest, the artful elaboration and enforcement of this by whatever means are available and appropriate being the sufficient end of the poet's effort. Great and serious works can be and have been written on either of these basic principles of construction, but the principles themselves, it must be evident, are sharply distinct, and the difference is bound to be reflected, in innumerable subtle as well as obvious ways, in everything that poets have to do or can do in the two major kinds. To continue to neglect the distinction, therefore, is merely to deprive ourselves unnecessarily of an analytical device — however hard to apply in particular cases — which can only serve, when intelligently used, to introduce greater exactness into our critical descriptions and greater fairness into our critical judgments.

Of the many other distinctions and concepts in the *Poetics* which are still valid and useful — at least for the kind of discussion of poetic structure we now have in mind — nearly all are limited, in their strict applicability, to imitative works. For any inquiry into such forms we cannot neglect, to begin with, the all-important distinctions of object, means, manner, and *dynamis*[8] upon which the definition of tragedy in Chapter 6 is based. They are, as I have tried to show in the second lecture, the essential and basic determinants of the structure of any species of imitative works when these

[7]Crane alludes to the New Criticism, such as that of Cleanth Brooks, p. 757, and to archetypal criticism, such as that of Northrop Frye, p. 641. [Ed.]

[8]Power: Aristotle's general term for the end or final cause of a poetic genre. [Ed.]

are viewed as concrete wholes, for we can conceive adequately of such a whole only when we consider as precisely as possible what kind of human experience is being imitated, by the use of what possibilities of the poetic medium, through what mode of representation, and for the sake of evoking and resolving what particular sequence of expectations and emotions relative to the successive parts of the imitated object. It is always some definite combination of these four things that defines, for the imitative writer, the necessities and possibilities of any work he may have in hand; for what he must and can do at any point will differ widely according as he is imitating a character, a state of passion, or an action, and if an action (with character, thought, and passion inevitably involved), whether one of which the central figures are men and women morally better than we are, or like ourselves, or in some sense worse; and according as he is doing this in verse of a certain kind or in prose or in some joining of the two; and according as he is doing it in a narrative or a dramatic or a mixed manner; and according, finally, as he is shaping his incidents and characters and their thoughts and feelings, his language, and his technique of representation (whatever it may be) so as to give us, let us say, the peculiar kind of comic pleasure we get from *Tom Jones* or that we get from *The Alchemist* or, to add still another possible nuance of comic effect, from *Volpone.* These, then, are indispensable distinctions for the critic who wishes to grasp the principles of construction and the consequences thereof in any imitative work; and he will be sacrificing some of the precision of analysis possible to him if he fails to take them all into consideration as independent variables — if he talks, for instance, about the plot of a novel or the pattern of images in a lyric poem without specifying the emotional "working or power" which is its controlling form, or if, in dealing with any kind of imitative work, he neglects to distinguish clearly between the "things" being imitated, upon which the *dynamis* primarily depends, and the expedients of representational manner by which the writer has sought to clarify or maximize their peculiar effect.[9]

There remains, lastly, the detailed analytic of imitative forms which is represented in the *Poetics* by the chapters on tragedy and epic. I need not repeat what I have said in the second lecture about Aristotle's distinctive conceptions — which have largely vanished from later criticism — of plot, character, thought, and diction — or about the relationships of causal subordination in which these "parts" are made to stand to one another in the tragic and epic structures, so that the last three (together with music and spectacle in tragedy), while being capable of form themselves, have the status of necessary material conditions of the plot, which, in the most specific sense of the synthesis of things done and said in a work as determined to a certain "working or power," is the principal part or controlling form of the whole. I have said why this analysis seems to me sound, given the assumptions on which it is based and its limited applicability to works of which the subjects are actions of the more or less extended sort Aristotle here had in mind. We can therefore still use it, and the many constituent definitions and distinctions it involves, in the criticism of the larger poetic forms; and we can profit particularly, I think, from the discussion of tragic plot-form in Chapter 13, not only because it gives us a clue to the structure of many later "tragic" works (this plot-form is clearly the formula, for example, of *Othello,* though not quite of *Macbeth,* and certainly not of *Richard III*) but also, and chiefly, because it suggests the four general questions we have to ask ourselves about any work having a plot as its principle of construction if we are to see clearly what problems its writer faced in composing it: as to precisely what the change is, from what it starts and to what it moves; in what kind of man it takes place; by reason of what causes in the man's thoughts and actions or outside him; and with what succession of emotional effects in the representation.

[9]Cf. Olson, in Crane, *Critics and Criticism,* pp. 71 ff., 562–63. With the remarkable development, in modern literature, of elaborate representational means for making effective relatively simple or universalized plots, the problem of distinguishing the two is sometimes a delicate one; there has been a good deal of confusion, consequently, in some of the discussions of works like *Ulysses, A Passage to India,* and Hemingway's "The Killers." [Au.]

III

We should be merely "Aristotelians," however, rather than independent scholars were we to remain content with what we can thus extract from Aristotle for present-day critical use; and we should be able to deal only crudely and inadequately with a great many of the most interesting structural problems raised by modern works. We need therefore to push the Aristotelian type of theoretical analysis far beyond the point where Aristotle himself left off, and this in several different directions.

There are, to begin with, the many nonimitative species of poetry or imaginative literature with which the *Poetics* does not deal at all. A large number of these have been roughly distinguished in the nomenclature and theories of subsequent criticism under such heads as: philosophical poems, moral essays, epigrams, treatises in verse, occasional poems; Horatian satires, Juvenalian satires, Varronian or Menippean satires; allegories, apologues, fables, parables, exempla, thesis or propaganda dramas and novels. But though a vast deal of critical and historical discussion has been devoted to these forms, we have as yet only fragments and beginnings of a usable inductive analytic of their structural principles as distinguished from their material conventions.[10]

Again, there are all the shorter imitative forms, most of them later in origin or artistic development than Aristotle, which we commonly group together as lyric poems; much of the best criticism of these has been concerned either with their techniques and fixed conventional patterns or with a dialectical search for the qualities of subject-matter and expression which are thought to differentiate lyric poetry, as a homogeneous type, from other poetic kinds.[11] What we need to have, therefore, is a comprehensive study, free from "abstract" assumptions, of the existing species of such poems in terms both of the different "proper pleasures" achievable in them and of the widely variant material structures in which the pleasures may inhere. Lyrics, it is plain, do not have plots, but any successful lyric obviously has something analogous to a plot in the sense of a specific form which synthesizes into a definite emotional whole what is said or done in the poem and conditions the necessities and probabilities which the poet must embody somehow in his lines; and the nature of this formal principle — whether it is, for example, a man in an evolving state of passion interpreted for him by his thought (as in the "Ode to a Nightingale") or a man adjusting himself voluntarily to an emotionally significant discovery about his life (as in the "Ode on Intimations of Immortality") — has to be grasped with some precision if we are to be able to speak appropriately and adequately about the poem's construction in all its parts and the degree of its artistic success. And here too most of the necessary analytical work still remains to be done.

We are much better off, thanks to Aristotle, with respect to the full-length imitative forms of narrative and drama; but even in this field of theory there are many important outstanding questions. Except for one suggestive paragraph in Chapter 5 on the general nature of the ridiculous, the *Poetics* as we have it is silent on comedy; and although there is much to be learned from the innumerable later discussions, especially since the eighteenth century, the insights these make available still have to be translated out of the rhetorical and psychological languages in which they are, for the most part, embodied into the more consistently "poetic" language we are committed to using. That there are a good many distinguishable comic plot-forms, both in drama and in narrative, must be evident to every one; but as to what they are, and what different artistic necessities and possibilities each of them involves, we have as yet, I think, only rather vague general notions; and the problem has not been greatly advanced by the traditional classifications into comedy of intrigue, comedy of manners, comedy of character, and so on. The same thing is true of the many intermediate forms between comedy in the stricter sense and tragedy proper: of tragicomedy, for example, or the "serious" and "tender" comedy which emerged in the eighteenth century, or the kind of domestic novel which Jane Austen wrote in *Pride and Prejudice*, *Mansfield Park*, and *Persuasion*, or the adventure ro-

[10]Cf. Norman Maclean, in Crane, *Critics and Criticism*, pp. 408 ff. [Au.]

[11]Cf. Norman Maclean, ibid., pp. 408 ff. [Au.]

mance in its earlier as well as its contemporary forms, or even the detective novel, much as has been written about the "poetics" of that. Nor is tragedy itself in much better case. What the *Poetics* gives us is an analytic of only one among the many plot-forms which the critical opinion as well as the common sense of later times has thought proper to call "tragic"; and it is one of the unfortunate results of the respect which Aristotle has always commanded that critics have tended to blur the distinctive principles of construction and effect, or to impair the artistic integrity, of these "non-Aristotelian" tragic forms in their eagerness to bring them in some fashion under his definition. We need therefore a fresh attempt at analysis, by the same method but in more appropriate terms, for such plot-forms, among others, as are represented severally by *Richard III* and *The Duchess of Malfi*,[12] by *The Orphan*, by *The Brothers Karamazov*, and by *A Passage to India*.

It is not merely of the forms of drama and narrative, however, that we require a better theory but also of many of their characteristic structural devices. We still tend to think of plot in its material aspects in the limited terms in which it is treated in the *Poetics* on the basis of the somewhat elementary practice of the Greeks, with the result that when we have to deal with works that combine in various ways two or many lines of action or concern themselves primarily not with external actions but with changes in thought and feeling or with the slow development or degeneration of moral character or with the fortunes of groups rather than of individuals, we often fall into the confusion which has led many modern critics to reject the concept of plot altogether. This is clearly no solution, but the remedy can be only a more comprehensive and discriminating induction of possible dramatic and narrative structures than Aristotle was able to provide. And there is also the complex question of how plots of whatever kind, or their equivalents in other forms, have to be or can be represented in words — the question, in short, of imitative manner in a sense that goes beyond, while still depending upon, Aristotle's distinction of the three manners in his third chapter. Of all the topics I have mentioned, this is perhaps the one on which the largest body of precise and useful observation has been accumulated, by all those critics from the Renaissance to our day who have devoted themselves to the "techniques" first of the drama and epic and then of the novel, short-story, and lyric. Even here, however, much remains to be done; and one of the chief requisites, I think, is a clearer posing of the whole problem in such a way as to correlate the many devices of manner which these critics have discriminated, as well as others that have escaped them, with the distinguishable functions which manner has to serve with respect to form. I have touched upon some of these functions in the second lecture, and I will add only the suggestion that there are likely to be, in all richly developed imitative works, incidents, characters, speeches, and images which are not parts of the plot-form but must be viewed by the critic as elements of "thought" in a sense akin to but distinct from that intended by Aristotle in Chapters 6 and 19. We may treat as "thought" of this kind anything permitting of inference in a poetic work, over and above the direct working of the imitated object, that functions as a device, vis-à-vis the audience, for disclosing or hinting at relevant traits of character or situation, awakening or directing expectations, conditioning states of mind, emphasizing essential issues, suggesting in what light something is to be viewed, or, more broadly still, setting the action or some part of it in a larger context of ideas or analogies so that it may come to seem, in its universal implications for human beings, not simply the particular and untypical action it might otherwise be taken to be. Every novelist or dramatist — or lyric poet, for that matter — who reflects on his own work will understand what this means; but the conception has still to become widely recognized among critics, or it surely would have been applied long since to such things as the apparently superfluous episodes and characters and the recurrent general words and patterns of images in Shakespeare — the dialectic of "Nature" in *King Lear*, for instance — concerning which most recent writers have thought it

[12]One of my former students, Mr. Richard Levin, is completing a study of the plot-forms of these and other similar works in Renaissance English drama. [Au.]

necessary to offer much more profound explanations.

It would be well, finally, if we could carry our method of inductive and causal analysis into some of the larger questions of theory — common to both imitative and nonimitative poetry — to which these writers and other contemporary critics have given special prominence: we could profit greatly, for example, from a re-examination, in our distinctive language, of poetic images, of the elements and functions of diction in poetry, of the various modes and uses of symbols, and of the structural characteristics of myths.

We need not wait, however, for the completion of these possible studies before beginning to use such theory of poetic forms as we now possess in the service of practical criticism. There is after all a close mutual interdependence, in the method we are considering, between theoretical analysis and the investigation of particular works; and as our attempts at application become more numerous and more varied in their objects, so will our grasp of the necessary general distinctions and principles tend to improve.

IV

In these attempts, as should be clear from what I have said, we shall be making a pretty complete break with the tradition of practical criticism discussed in the last two lectures — a tradition in which it has always been necessary, before individual works of poetic art can be analysed or judged, to conceive of poetry as a homogeneous whole and to define its nature in some kind of dialectical relation to other modes of discourse and thought. We shall not need, for our purposes, to commit ourselves to any of the numerous and apparently inconsistent theories of poetry, tragedy, lyric, or the like, based on such a presupposition, which this tradition has developed. We shall not need to worry, as so many contemporaries have done, about how poetry differs from science or prose, or about what its mission is in the modern world. We shall not need to decide in advance of our studies of poems whether poetry in general is best defined as a kind of language or a kind of subject-matter; whether its end is pleasure or some species of knowledge or practical good; whether its proper domain includes all the kinds of imaginative writing or only some of these; whether it is most closely akin to rhetoric and dialectic or to ritual, myth, or dream; or whether it is or is not a separable element in prose fiction and drama. Nor shall we need to assume that all good poems have "themes" or that poetic expression is always indirect, metaphorical, and symbolic. Not merely would such speculative commitments be useless to us, given our empirical starting-point, but they would be fatal, in proportion as we allowed our analyses to be directed by them, to our very effort, since they would inevitably blind us to all those aspects of our problem which our particular doctrine of poetry failed to take into account.

I do not mean that we shall not have to make some assumptions of our own, but only that these need not and ought not to be particularized assumptions about the intrinsic nature and necessary structure of our objects considered as a unitary class of things. We shall have to assume that any poetic work, like any other production of human art, has, or rather is, a definite structure of some kind which is determined immediately by its writer's intuition of a form to be achieved in its materials by the right use of his medium, and, furthermore, that we can arrive at some understanding of what this form actually is and use our understanding as a principle in the analysis and criticism of the work. We shall have to come to some agreement, moreover, as to what we will mean by "poetic works"; but here again the fewer specifications we impose on ourselves in advance the better. It will be sufficient for all our purposes if we begin, simply, by taking as "poems" or "works of literary art" all those kinds of productions which have been commonly called such at different times, but without any supposition that, because these have the same name, they are all "poems" or "works of literary art" in the same fundamental structural sense — that the art necessary to write *The Divine Comedy* or *The Faerie Queene* is the same art, when viewed in terms of its peculiar principles of form, as the art which enabled Shakespeare to write *King Lear* and *Othello*. And for such productions we shall need to assume, in addition, only one common characteristic: that they are all works which, in one degree or another, justify critical consideration primarily for their own sake, as artistic structures, rather than merely for the sake of the knowledge or wisdom they express or the practical utility we may derive from them, though either or both of these other values may be importantly involved in any particular case.

The problem of structure, for any individual work of this kind, is the problem — to give it its most general statement — of how the material nature of the work is related to its formal nature, when we understand by form that principle, or complex of principles, which gives to the subject-matter the power it has to affect our opinions and emotions in a certain definite way such as would not have been possible had the synthesizing principle been of a different kind. The question, as I have said, is primarily one of fact and cause; and it is answered, for a given work, when we have made as intelligible as we can the fashion in which its material elements of whatever kind — words, images, symbols, thoughts, character-traits, incidents, devices of representation — are made to function in relation to a formal whole which we can warrantably assert was the actual final cause of its composition. By "actual final cause" I mean simply a cause without the assumption of which, as somehow effective in the writing, the observable characteristics of the parts, their presence in the poem, their arrangement and proportioning, and their interconnections cannot be adequately understood. In discovering what this shaping principle is in any work we must make use of such evidence as there may be concerning the history of its conception and writing, including any statements the writer may have made about his intentions. Our task, however, is not to explain the writer's activity but the result thereof; our problem is not psychological but artistic; and hence the causes that centrally concern us are the internal causes of which the only sufficient evidence is the work itself as a completed product. What we want to know is not the actual process but the actual rationale of the poem's construction in terms of the poetic problems the writer faced and the reasons which determined his solutions. And in looking for these we shall assume that if the poem holds together as an intelligibly effective whole, in which a certain form is realized in a certain matter which never before had this form, the result can be understood fully only by supposing that such and such problems were involved and were solved by the writer in accordance with reasons which, in part at least, we can state; and this clearly does not commit us to holding that the problems and reasons we uncover in our analysis, as necessarily implied by the completed poem, must have presented themselves to the writer explicitly as such in a continuous movement of self-conscious deliberation; it will be sufficient if we can show that the poem could hardly have been written as it is or have the effect it does on our minds had the writer not done, somehow or at some time, what these particular problems and reasons dictate.

We can never, of course, know such things directly, but only by inference from the consequences of the conceived form, whether of the whole or of any of its parts, in the details of the completed work; and there can be no such inference except by way of hypotheses which both imply and are implied by the observable traits of the work. There are, however, hypotheses and hypotheses, and the character of those we shall have to make is determined by the nature of our problem. We propose to consider poems as unique existent things the structural principles of which are to be discovered, rather than as embodiments of general truths about the structure of poetry already adequately known. Hence our procedure must be the reverse of that procedure by way of preferred paradigms or models of structure which we have seen to be so characteristic of contemporary practical criticism. Our task is not to show the reflection in poems of complex or "ironical" attitudes, interactions of prose and poetry or of logical structure and irrelevant texture, patterns of ritual drama, or basic mythical themes, on the assumption that if the poem is a good poem it will inevitably have whichever of these or other similarly derived general structures we happen to be interested in finding examples of; it is rather the task of making formal sense out of any poetic work before us on the assumption that it may in fact be a work for whose peculiar principles of structure there are nowhere any usable parallels either in literary theory or in our experience of other works. The hypotheses we have to make, therefore, will not be of the fixed and accredited kind which scientists employ only when their problem is not to find out something still unknown but to "demonstrate" a classic experiment to beginners, but rather of the tentative kind — to be modified or rejected altogether at the dictation of the facts — which are the proper means to any serious inductive inquiry. They will be particular working hypotheses for the investigation of the structures of individual poems, not general hypotheses about such things as poetry or "poetic drama" in which the specific nature of the individual structures to be examined is already assumed.

We must also distinguish between critical hypotheses in the strict sense and interpretative hypotheses concerning the details of literary works in their material aspects. It is not one of our presuppositions that "form" in poetry is "meaning"; we should hold, rather, that meaning is something involved in poems as a necessary, but not sufficient, condition of the existence in them of poetic form, and hence that the recovery of meaning is an essential prerequisite to the discovery of form though not in itself such a discovery. Before we can understand a poem as an artistic structure we must understand it as a grammatical structure made up of successive words, sentences, paragraphs, and speeches which give us both meanings in the ordinary sense of that term and signs from which we may infer what the speakers, whether characters or narrators, are like and what they are thinking, feeling, or doing. The great temptation for critics who are not trained and practising scholars is to take this understanding for granted or to think that it may easily be obtained at second hand by consulting the work of scholars. This is an illusion, just as it is an illusion in scholars to suppose that they can see, without training in criticism, all the problems which their distinctive methods are fitted to solve. The ideal would be that all critics should be scholars and all scholars critics; but, although there ought to be the closest correlation of the two functions in practice, they are nevertheless distinct in nature and in the kinds of hypotheses to which they lead. The hypotheses of interpretation are concerned with the meanings and implications in texts that result from their writers' expressive intentions in setting down particular sequences. Such meanings and implications, indeed, are forms, of which words and sentences are the matter; but they are forms of a kind that can appear in any sort of discourse, however unpoetic. They are to be interpreted by resolving the forms into the elements which poems share with the common speech or writing and the common thought and experience of the times when they were written; and this requires the use of techniques and principles quite different from any that poetic theory can afford: the techniques and principles of historical grammar, of the analysis and history of ideas, of the history of literary conventions, manners, and so on, and the still more general techniques and principles, seldom methodized, by which we construe characters and actions in everyday life.

The hypotheses of criticism, on the contrary, are concerned with the shaping principles, peculiar to the poetic arts, which account in any work for the power of its grammatical materials, in the particular ordering given to these, to move our opinions and feelings in such-and-such a way. They will be of two sorts according as the questions to which they are answers relate to the principles by which poetic works have been constructed as wholes of certain definite kinds or to the reasons which connect a particular part of a given work, directly or indirectly, with such a principle by way of the poetic problems it set for the writer at this point. And there can be no good practical criticism in this mode in which both sorts are not present; for although the primary business of the critic is with the particulars of any work he studies down to its minuter details of diction and rhythm, he can never exhibit the artistic problems involved in these or find other than extra-poetic reasons for their solutions without the guidance of an explicit definition of the formal whole which they have made possible.

A single work will suffice to illustrate both kinds of critical hypotheses as well as the relation between them, and I will begin by considering what idea of the governing form of *Macbeth* appears to accord best with the facts of that play and the sequence of emotions it arouses in us. I need not say again why it seems to me futile to look for an adequate structural formula for *Macbeth* in any of the more "imaginative" directions commonly taken by recent criticism; I shall assume, therefore, without argument, that we have to do, not with a lyric "statement of evil" or an allegory of the workings of sin in the soul and the state or a metaphysical myth of destruction followed by recreation or a morality play with individualized characters rather than types, but simply with an imitative tragic drama based on historical materials. To call it an imitative tragic drama, however, does not carry us very far; it merely limits roughly the range of possible forms we have to consider. Among these are the contrasting plot-forms embodied respectively in *Othello* and in *Richard III:* the first a tragic plot-form in the classic sense of Aristotle's analysis in *Poetics* 13; the second a plot-form which Aristotle rejected as non-tragic but which appealed strongly to tragic poets in the Renaissance — a form of serious action designed to arouse moral indignation for the deliberately unjust and seemingly prospering acts of the protagonist and moral satisfaction at his subsequent ruin. The plot-form of *Macbeth* clearly involves elements which assimilate it now to the one and now to the other of both these kinds. The action of the play is twofold, and one of its aspects is the punitive action of Malcolm, Macduff, and their friends which in the end brings about the protagonist's downfall and death. The characters here are all good men, whom Macbeth has unforgivably wronged, and their cause is the unqualifiedly just cause of freeing Scotland from a bloody tyrant and restoring the rightful line of kings. All this is made clear in the representation not only directly through the speeches and acts of the avengers but indirectly by those wonderfully vivid devices of imagery and general thought in which modern critics have found the central value and meaning of the play as a whole; and our responses, when this part of the action is before us, are such as are clearly dictated by the immediate events and the poetic commentary: we desire, that is, the complete success of the counter-action and this as speedily as possible before Macbeth can commit further horrors. We desire this, however — and that is what at once takes the plot-form out of the merely retributive class — not only for the sake of humanity and Scotland but also for the sake of Macbeth himself. For what most sharply distinguishes our view of Macbeth from that of his victims and enemies is that, whereas they see him from the outside only, we see him also, throughout the other action of the play — the major action — from the inside, as he sees himself; and what we see thus is a moral spectacle the emotional quality of which, for the impartial observer, is not too far removed from the tragic *dynamis* specified in the *Poetics.* This is not to say that the main action of *Macbeth* is not significantly different, in several respects, from the kind of tragic action which Aristotle envisages. The change is not merely from good to bad fortune, but from a good state of character to a state in which the hero is almost, but not quite, transformed into a monster; and the tragic act which initiates the change, and still more the subsequent unjust acts which this entails, are acts done — unlike Othello's killing of Desdemona — in full knowledge of their moral character. We cannot, therefore, state the form of this action in strictly Aristotelian terms, but the form is none the less one that involves, like tragedy in Aristotle's sense, the arousal and catharsis of painful emotions for, and not merely with respect to, the protagonist — emotions for which the terms pity and fear are not entirely inapplicable.

Any adequate hypothesis about the structure of *Macbeth,* then, would have to take both of these sets of facts into account. For both of the views we are given of the hero are true: he is in fact, in terms of the nature and objective consequences of his deeds, what Macduff and Malcolm say he is throughout Acts IV and V, but he is also — and the form of the play is really the interaction of the two views in our opinions and emotions — what we ourselves see him to be as we witness the workings of his mind before the murder of Duncan, then after the murder, and finally when, at the end, all his illusions and hopes gone, he faces Macduff. He is one who commits monstrous deeds without becoming wholly a monster, since his knowledge of the right principle is never altogether obscured, though it is almost so in Act IV. We can understand such a person and hence feel fear and pity of a kind for him because he is only doing upon a grander scale and with deeper guilt and more terrifying consequences for himself and others what we can, without too much difficulty, imagine ourselves doing, however less extremely, in circumstances generally similar. For the essential story of *Macbeth* is that of a man, not naturally depraved, who has fallen under the compulsive power of an imagined better state for himself which he can attain only by acting contrary to his normal habits and feelings; who attains this state and then finds that he must continue to act thus, and even worse, in order to hold on to what he has got; who persists and becomes progressively hardened morally in the process; and who then, ultimately, when the once alluring good is about to be taken away from him, faces the loss in terms of what is left of his original character. It is something like this moral universal that underlies, I think, and gives emotional form to the main action of *Macbeth.* It is a form that turns upon the difference between what seemingly advantageous crime appears to be in advance to a basically good but incontinent man and what its moral consequences for such a man inevitably are; and the catharsis is effected not merely by the man's deserved overthrow but by his own inner suffering and by his discovery, before it is too late, of what he had not known before he began to act. If we are normal human beings we must abhor his crimes; yet we cannot completely abhor but must rather pity the man himself, and even when he seems most the monster (as Macbeth does in Act IV) we must still wish for such an outcome as will be best, under the circumstances, not merely for Scotland but for him.

But if this, or something close to it, is indeed the complex emotional structure intended in *Macbeth,* then we have a basis for defining with some precision the various problems of incident, character, thought, imagery, diction, and representation which confronted Shakespeare in writing the play, and hence a starting-point for discussing, in detail, the rationale of its parts.[13]

[13]See, in addition to what follows, Wayne C. Booth, *Journal of General Education* 6 (1951): 21–25. For a somewhat similar discussion of an episode in *King Lear,* cf. Maclean, in *Critics and Criticism,* pp. 595–615. [Au.]

Consider — to take only one instance — the final scene. In the light of the obvious consequences of the form I have attributed to the play as a whole, it is not difficult to state what the main problems at this point are. If the catharsis of the tragedy is to be complete, we must be made to feel both that Macbeth is being killed in a just cause and that his state of mind and the circumstances of his death are such as befit a man who, for all his crimes, has not altogether lost our pity and goodwill. We are of course prepared for this double response by all that has gone before, and, most immediately, in the earlier scenes of Act V, by the fresh glimpses we are given of the motivation of the avengers and by Macbeth's soliloquies. But it will clearly be better if the dual effect can be sustained until the very end; and this requires, on the one hand, that we should be vividly reminded once more of Macbeth's crimes and the justified hatred they have caused and of the prospect of a new and better time which his death holds out for Scotland, and, on the other hand, that we should be allowed to take satisfaction, at last, in the manner in which Macbeth himself behaves. The artistic triumph of the scene lies in the completeness with which both problems are solved: the first in the words and actions of Macduff, the speeches about young Siward, and Malcolm's closing address; the second by a variety of devices, both of invention and of representation, the appropriateness of which to the needed effect can be seen if we ask what we would not want Macbeth to do at this moment. We want him to be killed, as I have said, for his sake no less than that of Scotland; but we would not want him either to seek out Macduff or to flee the encounter when it comes or to "play the Roman fool"; we would not want him to show no recognition of the wrongs he has done Macduff or, when his last trust in the witches has gone, to continue to show fear or to yield or to fight with savage animosity; and he is made to do none of these things, but rather the contraries of all of them, so that he acts in the end as the Macbeth whose praises we have heard in the second scene of the play. And I would suggest that the carthartic effect of these words and acts is reinforced indirectly, in the representation, by the analogy we can hardly help drawing between his conduct now and the earlier conduct of young Siward, for of Macbeth too it can be said that "he parted well and paid his score"; the implication of this analogy is surely one of the functions, though not the only one, which the lines about Siward are intended to serve.

Such are the kinds of hypotheses we shall need to make if we are to have critical knowledge of the shaping principles of poetic works or of the artistic reasons governing the character and interrelation of their parts. They are working suppositions which, as I have said, both imply and are implied by the particulars of the works for which they are constructed; and they can never be made well by any critic who is not naturally sensitive to such particulars and in the habit of observing them closely. These, however, though indispensable, are not sufficient conditions. It never happens in any inquiry into matters of fact that the particulars we observe determine their own meaning automatically; the concrete or the individual is never intelligible except through the general and the abstract; and if we are to allow the facts to speak for themselves, we must in some fashion supply them with a language in which to talk. Hypotheses, in short, are not made out of nothing, but presuppose on the part of the inquirer who forms them a systematic body of concepts relative to the subject-matter with which he is dealing. The critic who proposes to explore hypothetically the structures of individual poems is in the same predicament; he must bring to his task, inescapably, general ideas about poetic structure, or he can never construct a workable hypothesis about the structure of any poem.

Hence the crucial importance for the practical critic of poetic forms, in the sense we are now giving to this term, of the kind of analytic of poetry which was outlined earlier in this lecture. From the point of view of the criticism of individual poems, the concepts and distinctions involved in that analytic differ from those which most contemporary critics have been content to use: they supply, not a unified set of terms for constituting structural patterns in poems (like Mr. Heilman's formula for "poetic drama" or the theories that make all good poetry a species of "ironical" or "paradoxical" structure), but a great variety of terms designating distinct and alternative principles, devices, and functions in poetry from which the critic need select only such combinations as appear to be relevant to the poems he is examining. What he thus acquires are not hypotheses ready formed but elements out of which he may form such hypotheses as the facts of his poems seem to warrant — in short, knowledge of structural possibilities only, resting on inductive inquiry into the principles poets have actually used in building poems and hence expanding with the development and progressive differentiation of poetry itself, so that he brings to the discussion of individual poems merely conceptual materials for framing pertinent questions about them without any predetermination of the substance of his answers, much as a physician uses the alternatives given him by medical theory in diagnosing symptoms in one of his patients. In the other mode of criticism the relation of theory to a particular poem is the relation of a previously selected idea or pattern of structure to its embodiment or reflection in a given work; here the relation is one of many known possibilities of structural patterning in poetry to the actualization in the poem examined of some one or more of these.

A critic using the first type of theory might argue somewhat as follows, for example, about the structure of Gray's *Elegy*. We must assume, he might say, the language of poetry being what it is, that the principle of structure in any good poem is a principle of balancing and harmonizing discrepant connotations, attitudes, and meanings; we must look therefore for a structure of this kind in Gray's poem or be content to relegate it to an inferior class of poetry; and our quest, indeed, is not in vain, for when we examine the text in the light of our general hypothesis of "ironical" structure, we quickly find that all the details of the *Elegy* can be subsumed under the theme of a continuous contrast of two modes of burial — in the church itself and in the churchyard — in which, as in all good poetry, opposing meanings are finally resolved.[14] A critic, however, whose theory was of the second type, would proceed in

[14]Cleanth Brooks, *The Well Wrought Urn,* pp. 96–113. [Au.]

an altogether different way. He would have no favourite hypothesis of structure as such, but would know merely that among short poems which, like the *Elegy,* evoke in us serious emotions, the shaping principle may be of several essentially distinct types, each of them generating distinct artistic problems for the poet; and he would use this knowledge as a basis for asking himself some such questions as these: Is what happens in the *Elegy* best explained by supposing, as the other critic has clearly done, that the poem is intended to be read as an emotionalized argument in verse (whether about modes of burial or something else), the personal qualities of the speaker and the setting of his meditation being simply devices for enforcing the unifying dialectic? Or is the poem better read — better, that is, with respect to the actual shaping principle of its construction — as an imitative lyric? And if it is this latter kind of structure, is the form one in which the speaker is conceived as being merely moved in a certain way by his situation (as in Gray's "Ode on a Distant Prospect of Eton College"), or as acting in a certain manner in relation to it (as in Marvell's "To His Coy Mistress"), or as deliberating morally in a certain state of mind on what is for him a serious issue in life? Weighing these possibilities (which give us perhaps the major forms which short serious imitative poems can have), our second critic would probably conclude that it is the last possibility which best explains both the constructed matter and the arrangement of the *Elegy* and the peculiar quality of the emotions which Gray's words and rhythms arouse in us. He might then describe the *Elegy* as an imitative lyric of moral choice rather than of action or of mood, representing a situation in which a virtuous, sensitive, and ambitious young man of undistinguished birth confronts the possibility of his death while still to "Fortune and to Fame unknown," and eventually, after much disturbance of mind (hinted at in the Swain's description of him), reconciles himself to his probable fate by reflecting that none of the rewards of successful ambition can "sooth the dull cold ear of Death," which comes as inevitably to the great as to the obscure; that a life passed "far from the madding crowd's ignoble strife," though circumscribing the exercise of virtue and talent, may yet be a means of preserving innocence; and that he can at any rate look forward to — what all men desire as a minimum — living on in the memory of at least one friend, while his merits and frailties alike repose "in trembling hope" on the bosom of his Father and his God. Something like this, I think (pedantic as any brief statement of it must sound), is the answer our second critic would give; but the point is that in arriving at it he would be using his theory of possible principles of structure in short poems simply to furnish him with the distinctions he needs if he is not to substitute a structure of his own for the structure Gray achieved.

The more extensive and discriminating such general knowledge, therefore, the better the critic's hypotheses are likely to be. But it is also the nature of this kind of theoretical knowledge to be always inadequate, though in varying degrees, to the particulars we use it to illuminate. We can never know in advance all the possibilities, and we can never, consequently, form a hypothesis about a work of any artistic complexity or even about many simpler works without making a shorter or longer inductive leap from the words and sentences before us to the peculiar combination of universals which define their poetic form. And that is why, in this mode of criticism, we can make no separation except analytically between theory and application, the latter being possible only if the former already exists at least up to a certain point and the former being constantly refined and enlarged as we proceed with the latter.

Application, however, is our main problem here, and its success depends upon the extent to which the universal terms of our hypotheses and the perceived and felt particulars of the texts for which they are constructed can be made to fit together. The general conditions are two: first, our ability to keep our explanatory formulae fluid and to submit them to constant revisions in principle or in detail before we transform them into conclusions; and, second, our willingness to use systematically what has been called "the method of multiple working hypotheses."[15] We have to

[15]By T. C. Chamberlin, in a paper with this title, first published in *Science,* Old Series, 15 (1890): 92–96; reprinted in

remember, that is, that the value of a hypothesis is always relative, not merely to the facts it is intended to explain, but to all the other variant hypotheses which the same facts might suggest if only we gave them a chance; that the best hypothesis is simply the best among several possible hypotheses, relevant to the same work or problem, with which we have actually compared it; and that unless we make such comparisons a regular part of our procedure, we always court the danger of missing either slightly or altogether what our author was really attempting to do.

There are also, in addition to these very general rules, several more particular criteria. Our aim is an explanation and judgment of poetic works in terms of their structural causes; hence, in the first place, the necessity of so framing our hypotheses that they are not descriptive formulae merely but clearly imply practical artistic consequences, in what the writers must or cannot or might well do in the act of writing, for the details of the works they are being used to explain; that is the character, for example, of Aristotle's definition of tragic plot-form in *Poetics* 13, and I have tried to impart a similar character to the statements above about *Macbeth*. The ideal is to have a central principle of explanation that will enable us to see precisely the functional relations between all the particular problems a writer has attempted to solve and the form of his work as a whole, even though we may have to conclude, in some cases, that the relation is a very tenuous one. In the second place, our aim is an explanation and judgment in terms adapted as closely as possible to the peculiar structure and power of the work before us; hence the necessity of trying to go beyond formulae that imply the work as a whole or any of its parts only generically; as when, for instance, we neglect to distinguish between the different material structures possible in lyrics and treat a particular lyric without regard to such distinctions, or as when we discuss a work like Jane Austen's *Emma* merely as a comedy, failing to see how little this can tell us about its distinctive comic construction. In the third place, we aspire to completeness of explanation; and this means that in framing a hypothesis about any work we must consider everything in the text as significant evidence that involves in any way a free choice on the writer's part between possible alternative things to be done with his materials or ways of doing them at any point. The hypothesis must therefore be complex rather than simple; it must recognize that the same parts may have different functions, including that of mere adornment; and, above all, it cannot be arrived at by giving a privileged position, on *a priori* grounds, to a particular variety of signs of artistic intention, in a complex work, to the exclusion of other and often conflicting signs of the same thing. This last is conspicuously the error of those interpreters of *Macbeth* who have inferred the central form of that play chiefly from the thought and imagery that serve to emphasize the "unnatural" character of the hero's crimes and the inevitability of a just retribution, without attempting to correlate with this the many signs, both in the construction of the plot and in its extraordinarily artful representation, of the distinctive moral quality of Macbeth's actions when these are seen from the inside. There will always be incompleteness in any hypothesis, moreover, or in any criticism that follows its use, that leaves out of account, as one of the crucial facts, the peculiar sequence of emotions we feel when we read the work unbiased by critical doctrine; for, as we have seen, the most important thing about any poetic production is the characteristic power it has to affect us in this definite way rather than that. Completeness, however, is impossible without coherence; hence our hypotheses, in the fourth place, must aim at a maximum of internal unity, on the assumption that, although many works are episodic and although many predominantly imitative works, for example, also have didactic or topical parts, this can best be seen if we begin by presuming that literary artists usually aim at creating wholes.

The only proof there can be of a hypothesis about any particular thing lies in its power of completeness and coherence of explanation within the limits of the data it makes significant — and this always relatively to the other hy-

the *Journal of Geology* 39 (1931): 155–65. The "method of multiple working hypotheses" is contrasted with "the method of the ruling theory" and "the method of the working hypothesis." [Au.]

potheses pertinent to the same data with which it has been compared. We must be guided, however, in choosing among alternative hypotheses, by a further criterion — the classic criterion of economy: that that hypothesis is the best, other things being equal, which requires the fewest supplementary hypotheses to make it work or which entails the least amount of explaining away; it is no recommendation, thus, for Mr. [L. C.] Knight's interpretation of *Macbeth* that he has to say of the emotion aroused in most readers as well as in [A. C.] Bradley by Macbeth's soliloquies in Act V, that this is mere conventional 'sympathy for the hero.'" which ought not to be allowed to distort that dialectical system of values in the play that is for him "the pattern of the whole."[16] And we must be careful, further, not to construe our "data" in too narrow a sense and so be satisfied with hypotheses that clearly conflict with facts external to the works we are considering but relevant nevertheless to their interpretation; I mean not only such particular evidences as we can often find of writers' intentions — for example, Coleridge's statements about the kind of poem he designed *The Rime of the Ancient Mariner* to be — but also such general probabilities with respect to the works of a given period or genre or with respect to poetic works of any kind or age as are supplied by either our historical knowledge or our common sense. It is not likely, for instance, that a Shakespearean tragedy intended for the popular stage should really have a kind of basic structure which practising playwrights of any time would find it difficult or impossible to make effective for their audiences. Nor is it ever a sensible thing in a critic to cultivate indifference to common opinion about the works he is discussing. The opinion may be wrong or, as often happens, it may need to be corrected and refined; but in such conflicts — at least when they involve the larger aspects and effects of works — the burden of proof is on him. For the secrets of art are not, like the secrets of nature, things lying deeply hid, inaccessible to the perception and understanding of all who have not mastered the special techniques their discovery requires. The critic does, indeed, need special techniques, but for the sake of building upon common sense apprehensions of his objects, not of supplanting these; and few things have done greater harm to the practice and repute of literary criticism in recent times than the assumption that its discoveries, like those of the physical sciences, must gain in importance and plausibility as they become more and more paradoxical in the ancient sense of that word: as if — to adapt a sharp saying of Professor Frank Knight about social studies — now that everybody is agreed that natural phenomena are not like works of art, the business of criticism must be to show that works of art are like natural phenomena.

It remains, finally, to consider the bearing of all this on judgments of poetic value. And the first thing to observe is that, if our hypothesis concerning the shaping principle of any work is adequate, it will give us a basis for saying with some precision (as my example of Act V of *Macbeth* will perhaps suggest) what are the necessities which such a form imposes on any artist whose aim is its successful realization in his materials. Some of them will be necessities common to all self-contained poetic works of no matter what kind, such as the necessity, if the parts are to cohere, of devices for effecting continuity from beginning through middle to end; others will be more and more specific necessities determined by the nature of the form we assume to have been intended, such as the necessity, if a comic effect like that of *Tom Jones* is to be obtained, of keeping the ridiculous mistakes of the hero from obscuring the sympathetic traits that make us wish him ultimate good fortune. These will all be consequences inferable from our basic definition of the form, and our primary task will be to trace them, in detail, throughout the particulars of the work at all its levels from plot or lyric situation down to the imagery and words. A kind of judgment of value will thus emerge in the very process of our analysis: if the writer has indeed done, somehow, all the essential things he would need to do on the assumption that he is actually writing the kind of work we have defined, then to that extent the work is good, or at least not artistically bad; and we should have to use very little rhetoric in addition to make this clear. But this is

[16]"How Many Children Had Lady Macbeth?" in *Explorations,* p. 36. [Ed.]

only half of the problem, for it is true of most mediocre writers that they usually do, in some fashion, a great part or all of the things their particular forms require, but do little more besides. The crucial question, therefore, concerns not so much the necessities of the assumed form as its possibilities. What is it that the writer might have done, over and above the minimum requirements of this task, which he has not done, or what is it that we have not expected him to do which he has yet triumphantly accomplished? These are the things our analyses ought peculiarly to attend to if they are to be adequate to their objects.

The possible in this sense, as distinguished from the necessary, is that which tends to perfect — to warrant praise of a positive rather than a merely negative kind. We can know it in two ways: by having our minds stored with memories of what both the most and the least perfect of artists have done when confronted with similar problems of invention, representation, and writing; and by considering theoretically the conditions under which any particular effect aimed at in a given work might be better or worse achieved — by asking, for instance, what would in general make a predicament like that of Tom Jones on the discovery of his first affair with Molly seem most completely comic, and then discussing the episode, as it is actually developed by Fielding, in these terms. Both methods are comparative, but the comparisons, if they are not to result in unfair impositions on the writer whose work we are considering, must take account of the fact that the desirable or admirable in literature is never something absolute but is always relative, in any given part of a work, to the requirements of the overall form and to the function of the part as only one part along with many others: forgetting this, we should make the mistake of Mr. Joyce Cary's critic and demand neatness where clumsiness is what "belongs," vividness and particularity where faintness and generality are needed, doing more than is done when this would be doing too much.

The judgments of value we should thus be trying to make would for this reason always be judgments in kind, grounded on a prior definition of the writer's problems as problems peculiar, at least in their concrete determination, to the formal nature of the work he is writing. They would also be judgments in terms of intentions — what is it that the writer aimed to do here and how well has he succeeded in doing it? — but the intentions we should take as principles would not be those, except accidentally, which the writer had stated explicitly before or after writing or those which can be defined for the writer by saying that he must have intended to write this work because this is what he has written. The common objections to criticism based on "intention" in either of these senses are unanswerable. They do not hold, however, when we identify intention with the hypothesized form of a poetic work and then consider how fully what we know of the necessities and possibilities of this form are achieved in the work, on the assumption that, if the work shows any serious concern with art at all, the writer must have wished or been willing to be judged in this way. There is nothing unfair to the writer in such an approach, inasmuch as we are not engaged in a judicial process of bringing his work under a previously formulated general theory of literary value but in a free inquiry whose aim is simply the discovery of those values in his work — among them, we always hope, unprecedented values — which he has been able to put there. They will always be values incident to the relation between the form of the work and its matter at all of its structural levels; and it will be appropriate to interpret what we find in terms of a distinction between three classes of works considered from this point of view: works that are well conceived as wholes but contain few parts the formal excellence of which remains in our memory or invites us to another reading; works that are rich in local virtues but have only a loose or tenuous overall form; and works that satisfy Coleridge's criterion for a poem, that it aims at "the production of as much immediate pleasure in parts, as is compatible with the largest sum of pleasure in the whole."[17] These last are the few relatively perfect productions in the various literary kinds, and as between the other two we shall naturally prefer the second to the first.

[17] *Coleridge's Shakespearean Criticism,* ed. T. M. Raysor (London, 1930), II, 66–67; cf. *Biographia Literaria,* II, 9–10. [Au.]

VI

When all this is said, however, it is still true that what I have been talking about in this lecture is only one out of many possible legitimate approaches to the question of poetic structure, not to speak of the innumerable other questions with which critics can profitably concern themselves. I should not want to leave the impression, therefore, that I think it the only mode of criticism seriously worth cultivation at the present time by either teachers of literature or critics, but simply that its development, along with the others, might have many fruitful consequences for our teaching and criticism generally. What distinguishes it from the other modes is its preoccupation with the immediate constructive problems of writers in the making of individual works and with the artistic reasoning necessarily involved in their successful solution; and its great claim to consideration is that it can deal with these matters more precisely and adequately, and with a more complete reliance on the canons of inductive inquiry, unhampered by doctrinal preconceptions, than any of the other existing critical languages. It can give us, consequently, a body of primary literary facts about literary works, in their aspect as concrete wholes, in the light of which we can judge the relevance and validity — or see the precise bearing — of such observations and statements of value as result from the application to the same works of other critical principles and procedures: if the structural principles of *Macbeth* or of Gray's *Elegy* are actually what we have taken them to be, then whatever else may be truly said about these same works, in answer to other questions or in the context of other ways of reasoning about them, must obviously be capable of being brought into harmony with this prior factual knowledge of the distinctive how and why of their construction. Here is something, therefore, which critics who prefer a more generalizing or a more speculative approach to literary works can hardly neglect if they wish to be responsible students of literature rather than merely rhetoricians bent on exploiting favorite theses at any cost. For though it is true enough, for example, that what writers do is conditioned by their personal lives and complexes, their social circumstances, and their literary traditions, there is always a risk that exclusive explanations of literary peculiarities in terms of such remoter causes will collapse and seem absurd as soon as we consider, for any work to which they have been applied, what are the immediate artistic exigencies which its writer faced because of his choice of form or manner in this particular work.[18] These exigencies can never be safely disregarded so long as the genetic relation between art and its sources and materials in life remains the very indirect relation we know it is; and it is perhaps not the least of the utilities to be found in the criticism of forms that its cultivation, in a context of the many other kinds of critical inquiry, would help to keep critics of all schools constantly reminded of their existence and importance.

But the other kinds ought to be there. Of the truth about literature, no critical language can ever have a monopoly or even a distant approach to one; and there are obviously many things which the language I have been speaking of cannot do. It is a method not at all suited, as is criticism in the grand line of Longinus, Coleridge, and Matthew Arnold, to the definition and appreciation of those general qualities of writing —

[18]An instance in point, verging on caricature of the fault I speak of in the text, is a recent discussion of the character of Jane Austen's Darcy. Why, the critic asks, "is he, among the major figures in *Pride and Prejudice,* the only one disturbingly derived and wooden?" And the answer, in terms of his psychoanalytical thesis, is given at once, without any consideration of the great difficulties that must have arisen, for the novelist, from the role which Darcy had to play in the first part of the plot and from the fact that the choice of point of view prevented even later any direct or sustained disclosure of his unspoken thought: "The reason seems to be the same as that which *compelled* Jane Austen to falsify her tone and commentary concerning Wickham's seductions and to supply Elinor and Marianne Dashwood with such nonentities for husbands. The socially unmanageable, the personally involving aspects of sex, Jane Austen *can* no longer treat with irony, nor *can* she as yet treat them straightforwardly. Darcy is the hero, he is the potential lover of a complex young woman much like the author herself; and as such Jane Austen *cannot* animate him with emotion, or with her characteristic informing irony. She borrows him from a book; and, though she alters and illuminates everything else, she *can* do nothing more with him than fit him functionally into the plot." Marvin Mudrick, *Jane Austen: Irony as Defense and Discovery,* p. 117; italics mine. [Au.]

mirroring the souls of writers — for the sake of which most of us read or at any rate return to what we have read. It is a method that necessarily abstracts from history and hence requires to be supplemented by other very different procedures if we are to replace the works we study in the circumstances and temper of their times and see them as expressions and forces as well as objects of art. It is a method, above all, that completely fails, because of its essentially differentiating character, to give us insights into the larger moral and political values of literature or into any of the other organic relations with human nature and human experience in which literature is involved. And yet who will say that these are not as compelling considerations for criticism as anything comprised in the problem of poetic structure as we have been discussing it in these lectures? The moral is surely that we ought to have at our command, collectively at least, as many different critical methods as there are distinguishable major aspects in the construction, appreciation, and use of literary works. The multiplicity of critical languages is therefore something not to be deplored but rather rejoiced in, as making possible a fuller exploration of our subject in its total extent than we could otherwise attain; and for my part I have as fond a regard for Longinus and for the masters of historical criticism as I have for Aristotle, and as strong a conviction of their continuing utility. Nor will there ever cease to be employment for criticism of the less rigorous or more imaginative types — in directing attention to aspects of poems which only a new model or analogy can bring into view, in formulating and promoting new ideals of poetic excellence or new poetic styles, in suggesting to poets unrealized possibilities in subject-matter and language, in relating poetry, for readers, to large non-poetic human contexts of emotion and meaning, in keeping the life of poetry and of taste from declining into orthodoxy and routine.

The best hope for criticism in the future, indeed, lies in the perpetuation of this multiplicity; nothing could be more damaging than the practical success of any effort to define authoritatively the frontiers and problems of our subject or to assign to each of its variant languages a determinate place in a single hierarchy of critical modes. Better far than that the chaos of schools and splinter parties we have with us now! But there need be no such choice; for the great obstacle to advance in criticism is not the existence of independent groups of critics each pursuing separate interests, but the spirit of exclusive dogmatism which keeps them from learning what they might from one another; and for that the only effective remedy, I think, is to take to heart the two lessons which the persistence throughout history of many distinct critical languages ought to teach us. The first is the lesson of self-knowledge: we can attempt to become more clearly aware than we have usually been of just what it is that we ourselves are doing — and why — when we make critical statements of any kind, and at the same time try to extend that clarity, in as intellectually sympathetic a way as possible, to the statements of other critics, and especially to those that appear to be most inconsistent with our own. And it will be all the easier to attain this self-understanding, with its natural discouragements to doctrinal prejudice, if we also learn the second lesson, and come habitually to think of the various critical languages of the past and present, including our own, no longer as rival attempts to foreclose the "real" or "only profitable" truth about poetry, so that we have to choose among them as we choose among religious dogmas or political causes, but simply as tools of our trade — as so many distinct conceptual and logical means, each with its peculiar capacities and limitations, for solving truly the many distinct kinds of problems which poetry, in its magnificent variety of aspects, presents to our view.[19]

[19]I have discussed some of the practical consequences of this view in an essay, to be published soon, entitled, "Questions and Answers in the Teaching of Literature." [Au.] "Questions and Answers" is reprinted in Crane's *The Idea of the Humanities* (1967). [Ed.]

Wayne C. Booth

b. 1921

Wayne Clayson Booth has been the most effective teacher — in the most far-reaching sense — of the Chicago neo-Aristotelians. Booth was born in 1921 in American Fork, Utah, and educated at Brigham Young University and — after serving in the infantry during World War II — at the University of Chicago, where he received his Ph.D. in 1950. He taught at Haverford and Earlham Colleges before returning to Chicago as Pullman Professor of English in 1962. He served as president of the Modern Language Association in 1982. Booth's enormous influence on the way we talk about narrative began with the publication of The Rhetoric of Fiction *(1961; 2nd edition, 1983), which adapted Aristotelian theory to consider the reader and the ways in which literary texts themselves shape the audience they require. His controversial thirteenth chapter questioned the moral impact of certain narrative techniques. Booth promised an "ethics of fiction" to clarify his ideas and delivered it, nearly thirty years later, in* The Company We Keep *(1988). Booth's other books include* A Rhetoric of Irony *(1974),* Modern Dogma and the Rhetoric of Assent *(1974),* Critical Understanding: The Powers and Limits of Pluralism *(1979),* The Vocation of a Teacher: Rhetorical Occasions *(1988), and* The Art of Growing Older: Writers on Living and Aging *(1992). Now retired from the University of Chicago, Booth is currently at work on a rhetoric of religious discourse. Booth has also been the object of study, in* Rhetoric and Pluralism, *edited by Fred Antczak (1995). "Pluralism and Its Rivals" was originally given as a talk before undergraduate humanities students in 1969; it was first published in* Now Don't Try to Reason With Me: Essays and Ironies for a Credulous Age *(1970).*

Pluralism and Its Rivals[1]

Everyone here today has just lived through a scandalous period in the university's history. No doubt each of us would describe the scandal differently, but for the purposes of this course perhaps the most humiliating side to the affair has been the way in which so many faculty and students have, as the old-fashioned expression goes, lost their heads. I have sometimes felt, during the past six weeks, as if I were surrounded by colleagues, old and young, who were deliberately repudiating all they ever knew about trying to use their heads. I'm sure that you can think of plenty of examples of blind, uncritical, even stupid credulity. Haven't you encountered a fantastic amount of just plain gullibility lately? But now ask yourselves honestly: weren't the examples you just thought of committed by people who were not on your side, whatever that was? Am I right? The uncritical distortions that strike me most are usually committed by my enemies. I am not so impressed by the follies of my friends, and when the unscholarly credulity is exhibited by myself, it becomes for some reason excusable, even in the rare case when I am forced to admit that I *have* been credulous. My enemies are *gullible,* if they are not actually liars; the average man (committing exactly the same offense) is *uncritical;* my friends are sometimes inclined, quite forgivably, to *leap before they look;* and I — I am so loyal to my own noble principles that I occasionally, just once in a blue moon, overlook a minor fact or two.

[1]Final lecture to Liberal Arts I, winter 1969. Students had read works of Aristotle, Plato, Freud, and Nietzsche earlier in the academic quarter. A sixteen-day sit-in occurred in February. [Au.]

But let me give you two examples, one from each "side," as we have tragically learned to say. A faculty member said to me two Saturdays ago, "Have you heard that 'they' have threatened again to destroy the university?" "No, I haven't." "Well, Professor X told me that they've issued a new set of demands, saying that if we don't meet the demands by Tuesday, they'll burn the place down, or something like that." A few moments later another faculty member told me the same thing, also derived from Professor X. The source of this rumor was that mocking phrase in the leaflet, "will in and of itself constitute grounds for further militant action"! Example two: On the second day of the sit-in, when the students opposing it were trying to hold a meeting in Mandel Hall, a student asked to make an announcement: "I've just learned from one of the marshalls [of the students in the building] that the Ellis Avenue exit has been closed, and that men who look like they're dressed in Chicago city police uniforms are stationed inside." A gasp went through the audience and many students left in excitement. The young man then came down into the hall, sat down beside me, and whispered, "Mr. Booth, is that true, what I just said?"

These two examples of intellectual irresponsibility, not to say lack of integrity, could be multiplied indefinitely. Too many of us have behaved as if we had never come within miles of any educational institution, let alone one that prides itself on a tradition of aggressive critical-mindedness, or that offers a course like Liberal Arts I that is supposed to deal with the arts of inquiry, argument, and proof, and with such questions as "What is a fact?"

So, it is a scandal. Or it would be, if we had a climate of opinion, here and elsewhere, in which acts of criminal credulity were taken as seriously as they ought to be. But we live in a credulous age and country. We live in a time when hundreds, perhaps thousands of people in Chicago can be convinced that President Kennedy is still alive by a letter read over the radio by a disk jockey; a country in which Attorney General Garrison can get away with his antics without providing as yet one shred of solid evidence; a country in which millions of citizens, apparently, believe that flying saucers come from outer space, while few of those citizens will bother to read Condon's scientific report on the subject; a country, in short, in which there is a credibility gap far greater than the cliché usually suggests: the real credibility gap is between conclusions and reasons for conclusions. You and I are members of a public that is increasingly a nonpublic, in Dewey's terms, not because we expect to be deceived by each other — though that would be bad enough — but because increasingly we don't even care whether we *are* deceived. Every man, in this newly levelled egalopolis, is entitled to his own brand of nonsense, and woe unto the elitist who demands evidence. I asked Mr. Lemke what he thought would happen on campus if a forceful speaker argued that he had seen the prophet Elijah return to earth in a chariot of fire. "He would find many followers," Lemke said, and I could not tell — perhaps he himself could not precisely tell — whether he was joking or not.

The scandal of the past six weeks has been that the university has entered the uncritical, credulous world with a vengeance — that too many of us have too often forgotten the special responsibilities that fall on any man who would like to claim that there is some connection between his opinions and actions, on the one hand, and defensible principles or demonstrable facts, on the other.

But what connection should it be? Isn't the very lesson we learn as we scramble our way through Aristotle, Plato, Freud, and Nietzsche, that there are many different connections, depending on who you are and what you want to do? And if that is so, who is to tell us that this or that statement, whether of fact or of principle or of connections between them and conclusions, is right or wrong? You pays your money and you takes your choice.

Since I've been adopting a moralizing tone so far, let me continue with it and say that to me it is an intellectual disaster of a very serious kind if any student of Liberal Arts I comes to the end of the year believing that there is no such thing as an error of fact, or that every man's intellectual structure is as good as every other man's, or that there is, finally, no such thing as validity or truth. I can't begin to show, in my remaining time, why I think this is such an enormous disaster when it occurs — and it does occur — but I do want to try, as I continue my sermon, to wrestle with the problems that give rise to this disaster. The catastrophe of total skepticism would not occur — especially it would not occur with very good students — if there were not some plausibility about it; indeed, it is part of the purpose of this course to dramatize and make real the reasons for skepticism about many of our beliefs. An educated man *must* be skeptical, and in one sense skeptical about everything; when he stops being skeptical, he stops thinking and is no longer an educated man. We believe this — and it is therefore not surprising that the kind of catastrophe I have described sometimes occurs. The alternatives to thoroughgoing skepticism are mainly two, and they can be approached best by taking any subject and seeing what kinds of things we can say about it.[2]

I

Suppose we take the short story I asked you all to read ("Araby," by James Joyce) and play with it for awhile, trying to discover to what degree it is a "hard object," as it were, that determines what we say about it, and to what extent it is malleable — a different object depending on who looks at it.

The complete skeptic or relativist will say, of course, that what "Araby" seems to be it in fact is. And my first point about the story is an obvious and important one, namely that there is a hard resistant core of fact about "Araby" that will test what anyone wants to say about it, regardless of his system or perspective. This core we might call precritical, because it consists of all the elements that everyone will admit to, once his attention is called to them. Some of these matters are entirely obvious and not worth mentioning except to make the point I'm making now: the title, for example, is "Araby," not "A Piece of James Joyce's Soul" or "Disestablishmentarianism in Dublin." The books that the first-person narrator finds in the priest's belongings include a novel by Walter Scott and a detective story, not the works of Thomas Aquinas or the New Testament. The coin that the narrator holds "tightly in my hand" is a florin, and a florin is worth two shillings, not five or ten; the uncle is an uncle, not a father; and so on. Anyone whose reading of the story is clearly based on contradictions of these facts, simple as they are, rules himself out of court. A truly committed skeptic may want to say that to him a florin is really a crushed bluebird, held tightly in the boy's hand, or that the word *uncle* really stands for paternal grandfather. To maintain the full skeptical position that "everything depends on your point of view," he must be willing to contradict or reject any fact I advance as self-evident. Yet if he does reject florin *as florin* he rules himself out of any further productive discussion of the story. Everyone he talks with will know that he is wrong, as soon as he looks at the page and sees the word *florin*.

When the sum of such facts is totted up, for any story, it makes a pretty big sum. It includes not just the obvious facts mentioned so far, but everything that all readers, regardless of their critical presuppositions, can be presumed to admit to, once their attention is called to it. Only less obvious than florin is, in this story, the whole sequence of actions performed by the narrator and the other characters. It is true that as soon as I describe any *selection* from these actions, I am beginning to impose my own special views. But my imposition is strictly limited, at this stage, by whether what I say can be checked by *any* observer.

The objective test is as strict here as it can ever be in any laboratory; either I have seen what is on the page or I have not. Admitting, then, that my *choice* of details is to some degree mine and not easily demonstrated to be Joyce's, let me describe some of the precritical facts that seem to

[2]The four logical possibilities when we are faced with rival claims to truth are: one will prove right and the others all wrong (dogmatism); all must be untenable, known in advance to be so because truth is unobtainable (skepticism); each will prove partly right and partly wrong (eclecticism); more than one (but not all) will prove true, when looked at closely, yielding a plurality of truths (pluralism).What looks like a fifth possibility — all will prove true — is in fact no real alternative; if all possible statements about a subject are equally true, then truth has become meaningless and we must end in the second position, complete skepticism. For this lecture I have simplified the four possibilities, taken from Elder Olson, by telescoping skepticism and eclecticism. [Au.]

me undeniable about this story: A narrator remembers from his boyhood (age unspecified) a house he moved to, with his aunt and uncle. What he mainly remembers about the house, besides the remaining belongings of the priest who died in the back-drawing room, is his vision of "Mangan's sister," unnamed — as he saw her, as he imagined her, as she spoke to him about a bazaar, as she looked when he promised to bring her something from the bazaar. Then he remembers his impatience to get to the bazaar, his uncle's drunken forgetfulness about his need for money, his belated trip to the bazaar, his arrival too late to enjoy anything or to buy anything even if he had had enough money left. And he remembers his emotional reaction to all this: "Gazing up into the darkness I saw myself as a creature driven and derided by vanity; and my eyes burned with anguish and anger."

This sequence is by no means exhaustive of what every genuine reader will see in this story. One could expand it until one had in effect recopied the whole story, because, at the factual level, it turns out that every sentence, every word, could be prefaced with "*It is a fact that* Joyce shows his narrator remembering that ——— (fill in the blank)." If we did a careful reconstruction of the facts of the story in this sense, we would have performed a first-level, commonsensical, noncritical reading of it. Such a reading would be complete only when we were reasonably sure that we had reconstructed each word and phrase in the meaning or meanings most probable in Joyce's time: Café Chantant, salver, third-class carriage, "some Freemason affair," fib, and so on.

Now, of course, it is true that even while we have been reconstructing the facts, our minds have been busy putting the so-called facts together to make inferred patterns; even the inferential process whereby you and I take a word like *f-l-o-r-i-n* and constitute the fact of two shillings, which is twenty-four pence, which means, according to the arithmetic of the story, that the boy has spent two-thirds of his cash by the time he has paid the fourpence for the tram and a shilling to get into the bazaar — even this process is elaborate indeed, and it may require some of us to use a dictionary. But we are still at the unquestionably factual level for all that, because we can say, without the shadow of a doubt, that any reader who constitutes the facts differently — arguing, say, that two pennies plus sixpence is not one-third of a florin, the boy's original cash-in-pocket, or that he really may have had lots of additional cash hidden away somewhere, for all we know — any such reader can be shown to have ignored the words on the page.

Perhaps some of you may wonder at this point why I make such a big issue out of what is, after all, quite obvious. But I ask you to remember where we began, and how far we now are from the skeptic's statement that what you see in a story is true for you if it's true for you. We have already found a supply of literally hundreds, perhaps thousands, of statements about this story that are demonstrably factual or nonfactual, and not one of them would be denied by *any* critic writing from any system — if we could get his attention long enough to have him come with us and look at the words on the page. I must admit, sorrowfully, that many publishing critics do *not* stop long enough to see what is written; I would guess that more than half of the literary criticism published would not be published if the authors took proper care with this simple, precritical, task — a task that earlier critics called the grammatical task: recovering the meanings at the indisputable level.

II

It is only now, presuming ourselves to have restored all of the words and phrases to their public meanings at the time the story was written, that we begin the task of criticism. And it is only now that we can say with any clarity that our systematic biases begin to enter inescapably. When we stop asking what are the facts about florins or about the literal description of this or that episode in the story and begin to ask, what *is* this story, as a larger fact in itself, we begin to constitute the facts according to our intellectual perspectives. Each perspective can yield its results without distorting what I have so far called the facts; yet it will seem to yield a different set of facts from those yielded by any other perspective. In speaking of perspectives, I am of course using a metaphor, comparing the various modes of asking questions about the soul or about art with visual slants. I think it is a useful metaphor, because it dramatizes for us how a particular procedure can be limited and still be true in its own lights.

Einstein somewhere illustrates the difference between classical physics and relativity physics by talking of a cone and of the variety of fixed perspectives a man can have of a cone. If he is directly above it, looking down, he will see a circle, and if he cannot shift from his fixed perspective, he'll think that he has the true view of the cone. If he is directly to one side, he'll see a triangle, and he'll be convinced that the object *is* a triangle. From another angle he'll see an ellipse joined to a triangle. And so on. Einstein sees the physicist as approaching nature with an inevitably limited perspective; it is as if he and the cone were fixed, so that he cannot shift about, add up perspectives, and finally say, "Oh, yes, now I see *it all,* it is a *cone,* not a circle, not a triangle, not an ellipse."

I am suggesting that our views of "Araby," like our views of nature in Einstein's analogy, are permanently doomed to partiality. Each view may still be, in its own terms, completely valid, subject to rigorous tests imposed both by limits of malleability (as it were) of the subject viewed and by the standards-of-viewing proper to the chosen perspective. But it will be only one of many possible views, no one of them easily tested from any *other* perspective; in fact, each may appear wrong to anyone proceeding from any of the other perspectives.

To pursue this line further would lead us into a philosophical discussion of theories of truth — the so-called correspondence theory, the pragmatic theory of Dewey, and so on. I'd prefer now to turn for the rest of our time to "Araby" and to questions about its nature and purpose. What *is* "Araby"? How do we interpret it? What is it for? Why is it made? What does it tell us? Any one question already moves us in the direction of a type of interpretation, but we can run quickly through some alternatives, in order to illustrate how different perspectives will yield different "Arabys," without our having to say either that any old statement about "Araby" is as good as any other statement, or that we must choose one as true and reject all the others as false.

III

What is "Araby"? Why, clearly, "Araby" is an imitation or representation of a character in action, as reported by himself as an older person, long after the action occurs. Unlike the action of tragedy, the action here has no magnitude to speak of — it is a mere week, or at most a few weeks, in the life of a mere boy, and what happens to him is in itself seemingly trivial. The narrative manner (moving now from the *formal* to the *efficient* cause) is in a way more complicated than the action imitated, because the manner of telling chosen by the older speaker reflects a constant ironic light over the actions of the boy. The style (the "means," the *material* cause) is "embellished" systematically to heighten the variations of manner, sometimes revealing the tonal judgment of the maturer narrator, sometimes revealing the characteristic expressions of the boy. The story is designed (now moving to the *final* cause) to yield a special mixture of sympathy and ironic amusement.[3]

Continuing as Aristotelians, we can note that the effect of the story is due more to the manner of telling and the diction than to any inherent effect of the incidents themselves. If the story were told in a neutral tone, one could never guess, as one can with a neutral telling of a tragic plot, what effect is intended: a young boy, living with his aunt and uncle, decides that he loves a neighbor girl; he promises to bring her a present from a bazaar, but because of circumstances beyond his control, he is unable to do so, and he ends in momentary "anguish and anger." Such material could be made into comedy, farce, burlesque, pathos, romance. But the author has chosen to heighten a mixture of sympathy and ironic criticism: the boy is made essentially sympathetic by showing everything through his vision (no special sympathetic characteristics are offered or needed), and the implied criticism of his imma-

[3]Booth uses Aristotelian terms here; see the Introduction to Aristotle, p. 38. [Ed.]

ture romanticism is thus kept under friendly control.

For such a story one needs only the generalized sympathy and tolerant amusement that everyone feels for a suffering young romantic, a young boy who chooses his books on the basis of the yellowness of the pages; a young boy who is so much in love with love that he crouches in the dark, clasping his hands together and murmuring "O, love! O love!"; a young boy whose "body was like a harp and her words and gestures were like fingers running upon the wires." Such a young man is laughable and lovable at the same time. The first third of the story establishes him in his *blind* romanticism, in the *blind* alley, looking through the *blind,* thankful that he can see so little, with his senses *veiled* — the very opposite, incidentally, of the condition that Joyce thought characterized the true artist. Then we have the only conversation with the vaguely described, unnamed, uncharacterized girl, with the promise to bring something from the fair. The rest of the story is made up of two pages of helpless grappling with the vivid and disappointing realities of the boy's very unromantic existence; in contrast to the vague romanticisms of the opening, we see harsh detail after detail of his real world, and we then see him go to the fair, with both his cash and the evening rapidly disappearing, with the very real and threatening young lady at the bazaar stall humiliating him, and with his final realization: "Gazing up into the darkness I saw myself as a creature driven and derided by vanity [and we know that this is true enough] and my eyes burned with anguish and anger [and we know that this is excessive, romantic, adolescent, if you will, and temporary]." We do not feel anguish and anger with him; the revelation of his nature and of the tightly knit episode has given us the pleasure proper to the spectacle of such pain. There is no catharsis, of course, because we need none, having felt no deep pangs of emotion.

Once we have seen the basic structure of the story in this way, we can go on to see how skillfully Joyce has heightened his effects. A full analysis of these strokes would require at least an hour; I call your attention now only to one touch not previously mentioned: the repetition, within a page, of the key memory of the girl's romanticized appearance: "The light from the lamp opposite our door caught the white curve of her neck, lit up her hair that rested there, and, falling, lit up the hand upon the railing. It fell over one side of her dress and caught the white border of a petticoat, just visible as she stood at ease." It could be *any* girl, and a page later we read, "I may have stood there for an hour, [leaning his forehead against the cool glass] seeing nothing but the brown-clad figure cast by my imagination, touched discreetly by the lamplight at the curved neck, at the hand upon the railings and at the border below the dress." Again it is all abstractly romantic. The repetition is obviously chosen with great care, like every other detail. In this story of how the boy encounters a moment of reality through the haze of youthful romanticism, every choice contributes beautifully, in ways specifiable though not spelled out here, to the pleasure of the whole.

IV

What is "Araby"? Why, clearly, "Araby" is an imitation of a human passion, the passion of youthful romanticism, in a form that is calculated to make us sympathize with a young man who gives himself over wholly to self-indulgence in his infatuation. Though it is clear to a mature reader that the author himself does not see the world as does his young hero, it is equally obvious, in the words of our master, Plato, that this is the kind of art that will corrupt the minds of all readers who do not "possess as an antidote a knowledge of its real nature." The reader is, in fact, seduced into seeing everything through the immature eyes of the boy; as we travel through the story with him, we are required, by the terms of the story as presented, to scoff at the decent lives of normal citizens ("The other houses of the street, conscious of decent lives within them, gazed at one another with brown imperturbable faces"), and to scorn a priest because of his misguided charity. ("He had been a very charitable priest; in his will he had left all his money to institutions and the furniture of his house to his sister".) Note also that we are required to assume by this bit of satire that institutions are impersonal and thus really unworthy objects of charity as compared to one's personal relatives; if we are subtle readers, we are then required to indulge in the petty pleasure of laughing at a well-meaning but ignorant boy; if we are not subtle readers, we are sure to fall into the trap of palpitating with him in his romantic haze. Whether we read subtly or not, we are required to wallow with him in his anger and impatience with his drunken uncle, and to grovel with him as he is driven, according to his own final judgment, by vanity and anguish and anger. All in all, the deeper we go into the story the more we "water" and "harrow" our pettier emotions.

But there is something deeper here. Joyce has taken a major step, as in other early stories, toward the totally distorted view of man and his proper ends which has dominated modern literature in recent decades. In his hands we approach the view that all of man's aspirations are ridiculous, that every hero is a nonhero, that life is a drab collection of realities that contrast with ideals which are absurd. In Joyce's world there is never any redeeming depth of meaning, never any grace to give significance to the petty lives portrayed. If we now find ourselves, in the last third of this battered century, unable to conceive of any genuinely heroic action, any finally defensible ideals, any value worth pursuing with courage and wisdom and a passion for decency, it is in part because Joyce and others following him have given us a literature of pettiness: Joyce gives us the illusion that to be snubbed by a bazaar clerk when you have only eightpence in your pocket is a significant disaster — and in doing so, he has helped to take true significance from the world of literature. His story is "an imitation of a phantasm, not of the truth"; if nobody in 1969 has any inclination to *think* about justice and victimization, if we all automatically respond with quick-triggered emotions *against* institutions and *for* any character presented as a victim, it is in part because our souls have been schooled by such brilliantly produced and essentially debasing literature. "The part of us that leads us to dwell in memory on our suffering and impels us to lamentations, and cannot get enough of that sort of thing, is the irrational and idle part of us, the associate of cowardice," and it is the part that this story caters to.

V

What is "Araby"? Why, clearly, "Araby" is an expression of the author's deepest anxieties and drives, in the form of a quest for peace in the circle of the womb. Joyce's lifelong battle for freedom from the bonds of church, of politics, of family, and of his own fears is dramatized in story after story; here it is given almost perfect expression in his passionate drive to leave the harsh realities of his adoptive home and enter the mysterious adult world of sexual freedom. The boy is from the beginning deeply troubled by sexual fantasies, though he does not see them for what they are. He is consciously obsessed with Mangan's sister and what he calls her "figure"; even her name is "like a summons" to what he calls euphemistically "all my foolish blood." His body is like a harp, he says, and her words and gestures were "like fingers running upon wires." He sees her, significantly enough, as a *chalice* which he bears through the market place, yet this holy sublimation of the sexual organ is quite openly tainted for the boy with the detail of the "white border of the petticoat," mentioned twice. The desirability of escape to the fantasy-world of Araby grows upon him, and he finally, having abandoned the essentially masturbatory inaction of chanting "O love! O love!" begins to act. He takes a *train* — though a slow moving one — which in a few moments brings him to the lighted dial of a *clock*. He cannot at first find an *entrance* into the "big hall *girdled* . . . by a gallery," most of it in darkness. In a sequence that is surprisingly Kafkaesque, he enters the vast dark hall and finds there a young lady who rebuffs him; instead of the safety and joy he had expected, he is forced to linger "before her stall, though I knew my stay was useless, to make my interest *in her wares* seem the more real." Trapped by the closed dome instead of liberated by it, he gazes up into the darkness and sees himself in all his frustrated impotence, the quest for release unsuccessful. But of course Joyce has managed to achieve for *himself* some release, as our master,

Freud, has taught us to expect of all artists: the release of a mythic projection of his own entrapment.

VI

What is "Araby"? Why, obviously, it is a manifestation of what happened to the Apollonian and Dionysiac spirits in literature at the beginning of the twentieth century. Though the spirit of tragedy remained buried, Joyce found a new way "to parade the images of life before us" and "to incite us to seize their ideational essence."[4] Joyce knew that if he could fix the reality of any deeply felt moment in a verbal form wrought "for its aesthetic value alone," if he could realize the intensely perceived moment, however seemingly trivial in itself, he would have freed the spirits of his readers from any concern about practical effect, about the ethical qualities of his characters or his art, and have led them into an aesthetic domain. He would have made, in other words, a literary work that was strictly analogous to music. For Joyce, a work of verbal art should display the same subtle fusion of image and concept, of individuality and universality, that music displays. It is no accident that Joyce called his poems chamber music, and it is also no accident that he called some of his literary vignettes epiphanies — for him they were moments when a divine truth was revealed in the concrete individuality of things. The "metaphysical delight" of such verbal music is a translation of "instinctive Dionysiac wisdom" — all the world of practical and illusory longings shown by the young hero — into Apollonian images, creating a fusion which can then be said to have "justified the world by transforming it into an aesthetic phenomenon." Though the result is never, in Joyce, anything spectacular enough to be called a rebirth of tragedy, it is a rebirth, from the spirit of music, of "the essential metaphysical activity of man."

[4]Now I am quoting from Nietzsche, of course. [Au.] See Nietzsche, From *The Birth of Tragedy from the Spirit of Music,* p. 419. [Ed.]

VII

Any of you who have really got hold of Freud or Nietzsche will have been made uneasy, I suspect, by my last two sections. I assure you that I am uneasy about them too. But at the moment I'm not so much troubled by the pseudocritics I have created as I am by all the other voices I hear in the wings, demanding to be heard on the subject of what "Araby" is. Marx is here to claim that "Araby" is *really* a portrait of decadent middle-class values, drawn by an aesthete who, despite his clever indictment of the bourgeois boy and his absurdly class-ridden quest, never managed to shake off his allegiance to the romantic individualism of the artist. Another economist, considerably cruder but just as insistent, shouts that "Araby" is really a commercial object, written to be bought and sold. A literary historian enters with a bullhorn to say that "Araby" is really, along with the other stories in this volume, a crucial moment in the history of narrative technique; the subtle variations of point-of-view throughout the volume show the first signs of the full flowering of technical exploration which Joyce, above all modern novelists, brought into fiction from poetry and drama. A cultural historian says that "Araby" is really a major moment in the development of attacks on romanticism as the twentieth century began; the sardonic portrait of the empty-headed young lover could not have been painted in England before this period. A rhetorical critic sees "Araby" as an obvious piece of persuasion designed to manipulate a twentieth-century audience in a certain way. While it uses what looks like an imitation of an action, it is really best explained as a series of strokes shrewdly calculated to hit us where we live. Notice, for example, the first sentence: "North Richmond Street, being blind," — note that! — "was a quiet street except at the hour when the Christian Brothers' School *set the boys free.*" A sociologist jumps in to say that "Araby" is really one of the most interesting signs of change in the nature of literary audiences just before World War I. Though Joyce always talked as if he were writing for an audience of one, his story shares with the work of many other young writers of the time — Virginia Woolf and

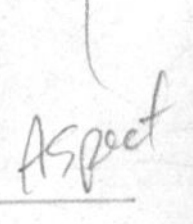

E. M. Forster, for example — a confident sense that a special audience had developed that did not require blatant Dickensian effects of plot or sentiment; Joyce could by now anticipate a reader who would catch the most delicate nuances, and who would at the same time respond more to subtle criticisms of sentiment than to sentimental appeals. It was in fact this audience that was to become, in some respects, the most important influence on twentieth-century culture: the bright young men and women of London and Paris whom Ortega y Gasset[5] refers to ten years later, in *The Dehumanization of Art,* who look for an art that "avoids living forms," who demand that "a work of art be *nothing but* a work of art," that it be "play," that it be "ironical," and that it avoid sham and aspire "to scrupulous portrayals of reality."

VIII

And so they rush in, view after view after view. Every conceivable field of inquiry, past and future, will have *some* view of "Araby," and though they will not all claim that their view is the essential view, they will all define the work as a different fact or set of facts, depending on their purposes. And many of them *will* insist that their view is the essential view, that "Araby" really *is* this or that, even though it obviously falls into the clutches of men who try to make it into other things.

Yes, but what is it *really?* Well, clearly, it is — . Now, if I finished that sentence, I would be a fraud, because my lecture should have demonstrated by now that "Araby," despite its commonsensical core of fact, is not an entity that defines itself aside from the purposes and views — more or less conscious and systematic — of those who do the defining. "Araby" is not only what Joyce made but what other men make of it; each of us constitutes our own "Araby." To return to Einstein's cone, it is as if none of us had ever seen a cone except from one or another perspective. Many of us are inclined to be dogmatists and think that our view — say, "This is a circle" or "This is a triangle" — is *the* view. Some of us are relativists or skeptics, who say that it doesn't matter what view you take of the cone, since all views are false. And what I am working toward as the concluding section of this lecture is a kind of pluralism — the notion that every reality, every subject, can be and will be validly grasped in more than one way depending on the purposes and intellectual systems of the viewers; there is a plurality of valid philosophies, of valid approaches to literature, of valid political philosophies, of valid pictures of the soul, of valid views of the nature and function of art. To understand what this means for your relation to intellectual pursuits will take you many years — unless you are a lot brighter than most of us. But there are at least two things it does *not* mean.

First, it does not mean that *every* view is valid, or that there are not differences of validity or usefulness among different views. If I call a cone a tragedy, because it really is a figure that tried to make it as a sphere and failed, I will have nothing to contribute to myself or fellow investigators except a feeble joke. If I say that "Araby" is really a trumpet-blast in the eternal battle for women's rights (just think about that poor anonymous girl, dressed in brown, her petticoat showing, ignored by the world, failing to receive her present — a great silent heroine!) I have so clearly allowed my intellectual system (feminism) to impose itself blindly on the world, that all validity is gone. And even among more plausible views of the story, it is often easy to show that some are inherently flimsy or impoverished while others are more fruitful and liberating. (To say what I have just said is possible, of course, only within intellectual systems that value liberation above confinement, or richness of view over poverty, which is another way of saying that these things are very complicated.)

To discuss how one chooses among the more plausible modes of viewing would take more than another lecture. But let me just assert in one more way that though complicated such choices are not ultimately beyond us. In fact we make them successfully all the time, as our purposes, both practical and intellectual, dictate. Shall I deal with "Araby" as Aristotle or as Freud would suggest? The choice will depend on what ques-

[5]José Ortega y Gasset (1883–1935), Spanish philosopher who wrote *La deshumanización del arte* in 1925. [Ed.]

tions I want to answer. Do I want to know how "Araby" is put together, what makes it a functioning whole? Freud tells me very little, and what he tells me is so general that it will apply to most other stories equally well. Do I want to understand the secret sources of Joyce's creative energy? The *Poetics* could not be more irrelevant to my query. Do I want to know both? Then I must learn how to pursue both, and I'll probably find that I cannot do them both at the same time. At best they'll be two separable parts of my lecture, or my book, or my life — and what's more, I'll probably find that I'll do one or the other badly. Few men have the temperament or the intellectual flexibility to operate with more than one or two intellectual systems, except in different periods of their lives — and then usually after painful conversion experiences.

But this brings us to the second point. Pluralism does not mean that one is tongue-tied in the face of sloppy work *within any perspective*. I have given today illustrations that show how choice of a valid system does not guarantee valid statements. My Aristotelian analysis, though incomplete, was moving in the direction of a more or less adequate account of "Araby" as a *made object*. My Platonic analysis, though less nearly complete, was similarly a sympathetic and more or less serious reconstruction of what is to me a plausible though unpopular view of the morality of this story. But my Freudian description was feeble and even at points satirical, and my Nietzsche was a job performed by the lowliest *Untermensch*[6] imaginable. None of my analyses committed the fault, so far as I know, of violating the commonsense factual encounter with the story with which I began today, so my present judgment is not made as a judgment of factual error. It is made, once the elementary level is passed, on the basis of *adequacy to the possibilities of the particular system,* when held up against *the potentialities offered to that system by the particular piece of reality examined.*

A man is lucky if he learns to use even one intellectual mode well. He is luckier if he can master more than one. He is luckiest of all, I suppose, if he can invent a new road to truth that proves fruitful to other men, or can elaborate or extend an already existing one. Many roads lead toward the heart of the city, but no one is allowed to go all the way: nobody ever looks on truth bare. Or if he does — and many mystics claim to — he will find that when he tries to report back to us ordinary mortals, his report will fall into one or another of the very limited intellectual modes available, and it will thus fail to catch more than a fraction of what is, we all must believe, *really there*.

IX

Let me conclude with a summary of the four forms of behavior that I would consider scandalous if I saw them exhibited in any kind of controversy among graduates of Liberal Arts I. The first is our uncritical behavior of the past two weeks: it is credulity, gullibility, readiness to be intellectually seduced by the latest comer or loudest shouter without checking the facts. The second disaster would be two of you quarrelling together about whether Freud or Aristotle "is right." This is the disaster of dogmatism, and it can be exhibited only by men who have not yet discovered that systems answering different questions for different purposes using different methods cannot be placed in direct opposition. The third scandal would be any one of you deciding to refuse credence to *any* view because "they all cancel each other out." Since such skepticism about all systems is intolerable, those who espouse it almost always move quickly to one or another form of dogmatism, usually a highly solipsistic and self-destructive kind: if none of the great philosophies is true, then anything I come up with that happens to appeal to me is as good as anything else. From this point of view it is no accident, as the Marxists used to say, that the current student generation, more threatened than earlier generations by plausible reasons for skepticism, seems to flit from dogmatism to dogmatism. I know a recent graduate of Princeton who has moved in four years from a form of scientism through Freudianism, Marxism, and Maoism to espousing the so-called philosophy of Ayn

[6]Booth's playful reversal of Nietzsche's *Übermensch* (superman). [Ed.]

Rand.[7] I'm afraid he'll be a prime candidate for any openly fascistic movement that promises him some sort of final intellectual peace in a dogma imposed by an elite — and the reason is simply that he has never yet paused long enough on any one system to make it work for him.

[7]Ayn Rand (1905–1982) wrote novels such as *The Fountainhead* (1943), advocating "enlightened self-interest" as preferable to altruism. [Ed.]

While I would not quite claim that a fortunate exposure as a freshman to my lecture on pluralism would have saved him, a full exposure to any one of the great philosophical positions might have. But I stress the tentativeness of "might." The recent behavior of some of my colleagues, old and young, who I had thought were committed to thinking things through, has shaken my confidence that anything will save universities as a place where real intellectual differences can be freely and honestly pursued.

James Phelan

b. 1951

James Phelan was born in Flushing, New York, in 1951 and educated at Boston College and at the University of Chicago, where he completed his doctorate in English in 1977. Since that year he has taught in the English department at Ohio State University, where he currently serves as Chair. Rather than orienting his work around the texts of a given historical period, Phelan typically gravitates toward theoretical issues or problems and pursues them in texts from different periods. He has written about style in Worlds from Words: A Theory of Language in Fiction *(1981), about character and narrative progression in* Reading People, Reading Plots *(1989), and, most recently, about voice, homodiegetic narration, and audiences in* Narrative as Rhetoric *(1996), from which the following selection is taken. He has also published the autobiographical* Beyond the Tenure Track: Fifteen Months in the Life of an English Professor *(1991) and has edited* Reading Narrative: Form, Ethics, Ideology *(1989),* Understanding Narrative *(1994, with Peter J. Rabinowitz), and* The Adventures of Huckleberry Finn: Case Study in Critical Controversy *(1995, with Gerald Graff). The editor of the journal* Narrative, *Phelan is currently working on a study of narrative dynamics.*

Narrative as Rhetoric: Reading the Spells of Porter's "Magic"

READING A NARRATIVE OF RHETORIC

What does it mean to treat narrative as rhetoric? Although this question, a natural way to begin a book entitled *Narrative as Rhetoric,* tempts me to deliver a long, theoretical disquisition on authors, readers, narrative techniques, structures, conventions, and the concept of rhetoric, I will spare you that and opt for illustration by offering a rhetorical reading of a particular narrative. The narrative I choose is a narrative *of* rhetoric, that is, a narrative whose central event is the telling of a story, Katherine Anne Porter's "Magic."[1]

[1]Porter's "Magic" was published in 1930. [Ed.]

And, Madame Blanchard, believe that I am happy to be here with you and your family because it is so serene, everything, and before this I worked for a long time in a fancy house — maybe you don't know what is a fancy house? Naturally . . . everyone must have heard sometime or other. Well, Madame, I work always where there is work to be had, and so in this place I worked very hard all hours, and saw too many things, things you wouldn't believe, and I wouldn't think of telling you, only maybe it will rest you while I brush your hair. You'll excuse me too but I could not help hearing you say to the laundress maybe someone had bewitched your linens, they fall away so fast in the wash. Well, there was a girl there in that house, poor thing, thin, but well-liked by all the men who called, and you understand she could not get along with the woman who ran the house. They quarreled, the madam cheated her on her checks: you know, the girl got a check, a brass one, every time, and at the week's end she gave those back to the madam, yes, that was the way, and got her percentage, a very small little of her earnings: it is a business, you see, like any other — and the madam used to pretend the girl had given back only so many checks, you see, and really she had given many more, but after they were out of her hands, what could she do? So she would say, I will get out of this place, and curse and cry. Then the madam would hit her over the head. She always hit people over the head with bottles, it was the way she fought. My good heavens, Madame Blanchard, what confusion there would be sometimes with a girl running raving downstairs, and the madam pulling her back by the hair and smashing a bottle on her forehead.

It was nearly always about the money, the girls got in debt so, and if they wished to go they could not without paying every sou manqué. The madam had full understanding with the police; the girls must come back with them or go to the jails. Well, they always came back with the policemen or with another kind of man friend of the madam: she could make men work for her too, but she paid them very well for all, let me tell you: and so the girls stayed on unless they were sick; if so, if they got too sick she sent them away again.

Madame Blanchard said, "You are pulling a little here," and eased a strand of hair: "and then what?"

Pardon — but this girl, there was a true hatred between her and the madam. She would say many times, I make more money than anybody else in the house, and every week were scenes. So at last she said one morning, Now I will leave this place, and she took out forty dollars from under her pillow and said, Here's your money! The madam began to shout, Where did you get all that, you ———? and accused her of robbing the men who came to visit her. The girl said, Keep your hands off or I'll brain you: and at that the madam took hold of her shoulders, and began to lift her knee and kick this girl most terribly in the stomach, and even in her most secret place, Madame Blanchard, and then she beat her in the face with a bottle, and the girl fell back again into her room where I was making clean. I helped her to the bed, and she sat there holding her sides with her head hanging down, and when she got up again there was blood everywhere she had sat. So then the madam came in once more and screamed, Now you can get out, you are no good for me any more: I don't repeat all, you understand it is too much. But she took all the money she could find, and at the door she gave the girl a great push in the back with her knee, so that she fell again in the street, and then got up and went away with the dress barely on her.

After this the men who knew this girl kept saying, Where is Ninette? And they kept asking this in the next days, so that the madam could not say any longer, I put her out because she is a thief. No, she began to see she was wrong to send this Ninette away, and then she said, She will be back in a few days, don't trouble yourself.

And now, Madame Blanchard, if you wish to hear, I come to the strange part, the thing recalled to me when you said your linens were bewitched. For the cook in that place was a woman, colored like myself, like myself with much French blood just the same, like myself living always among people who worked spells. But she had a very hard heart, she helped the madam in everything, she liked to watch all that happened, and she gave away tales on the girls. The madam trusted her above everything, and she said, Well, where can I find that slut? because she had gone altogether out of Basin Street before the madam began to ask the police to bring her again. Well, the cook said, I know a charm that works here in New Orleans, colored women do it to bring back their men: in seven days they come again very happy to stay and they cannot say why: even your enemy will come back to you believing you are his friend. It is a New Orleans charm for sure, for certain, they say it does not work even across the river. . . . And then they did it just as the cook said. They took the chamber pot of this girl from under her bed, and in it they mixed with water and milk all the relics of her they found there: the hair from her brush, and the face powder from the puff, and even little bits of her nails they found about the edges of the carpet where she sat by habit to cut her finger- and toenails; and they dipped the sheets with her blood into the water, and all the time the cook said something over it in a low voice; I could not hear all, but at last she said to the madam, Now spit in it: and the madam spat, and the cook said, When she comes back she will be dirt under your feet.

Madame Blanchard closed her perfume bottle with a thin click: "Yes, and then?"

Then in seven nights the girl came back and she looked very sick, the same clothes and all, but happy to be there. One of the men said, Welcome home, Ninette! and when she started to speak to the madam, the madam said, Shut up and get upstairs and dress yourself. So Ninette, this girl, she said, I'll be down in just a minute. And after that she lived there quietly.

In saying that "Magic" is a narrative of rhetoric, I want to call attention, first, to the rhetorical dimensions of the maid's action: she is *telling a particular story to a particular audience in a particular situation for, presumably, a particular purpose.* I want to call attention, second, to the parallel between the maid's action and Porter's: the particular story that Porter is telling is the maid's telling of Ninette's story. In analyzing these parallel acts of telling, I want to focus on teller, technique, story, situation, audience, and purpose: all the elements that help determine the shape and effect of the story.

By approaching both the maid's telling and Porter's telling as parallel rhetorical acts, we can recognize a crucial element of its construction that may not initially jump out during a first reading: "Magic" is a narrative with three interrelated levels. These are (1) the inner level, narrated by the maid: the story of Ninette, the madam, and the cook; I shall refer to this level as Ninette's story; (2) the middle level, narrated by the heterodiegetic narrator,[2] who appears only twice: the report of the maid's telling Ninette's story to Madame Blanchard; I shall refer to this level as the maid's story; and (3) the outer level, constructed and designed by Porter as implied author: the largely covert communication from Porter to her audiences, implied and real, of the narrator telling the maid's story of Ninette's story; I shall refer to this level as Porter's story.

In looking first at the technique of "Magic," notice that, rather than calling attention to the three different levels, Porter's presentation blurs the borders between them, especially the border between Ninette's story and the maid's story. Porter starts in the midst of things and does not even use quotation marks for the maid's story (*And* Madame Blanchard, I am happy to be here [emphasis mine]); furthermore, she has the heterodiegetic narrator speak only after Ninette's story is well under way and, as noted above, only twice in the whole story — and each time very briefly. As a result, Porter elides the difference between Ninette's story and the maid's story — or perhaps, better, she foregrounds Ninette's story and backgrounds the maid's. Given this technique, it is not surprising that, as Helen Leath has noted,[3] many critics focus on Ninette to the exclusion of the maid. Surely, one effect of the technique is to engage us strongly in the horrors of Ninette's story.

Indeed, as we attend to those horrors, we also recognize the major disparity between the maid's version of Ninette's story and Porter's: in Porter's version Ninette is not defeated by the cook's magic spell but rather by the social forces lined up against her. Ninette returns to the fancy house looking sick and wearing the same clothes because she has had no money to live on and has not been able to find another way to support herself. Ninette's story in Porter's version is not about magic but rather about failed rebellion and victory for the oppressive madam and her support system of police and well-off men.

This first act of seeing beneath the surface of Ninette's story quickly moves us into the next,

[2]In the narratological terminology of Gérard Genette, any narrator positioned external to the frame of the story is said to be "heterodiegetic"; ones inside the frame of the story are "homodiegetic"; ones telling their own story are "autodiegetic." [Ed.]

[3]Helen Leath, "Washing the Dirty Linen in Private: An Analysis of Katherine Anne Porter's 'Magic,'" *Conference of College Teachers of English Studies* (September 1985): 50–53. [Ed.]

richer area of the rhetorical exchange, that involving the ways that Ninette's story, the maid's story, and Porter's story intersect. As soon as we infer that Porter does not expect us to believe in magic, we are inclined to ask whether the maid does — and whether the maid expects Madame Blanchard to. The answers are not immediately obvious, but merely posing these questions highlights the fact that the maid seizes upon the pretext of Madame Blanchard's remark about her laundry being bewitched to tell Ninette's story. This recognition in turn prompts the questions that form the interpretive crux of "Magic": what are the maid's motivations for telling Ninette's story, what does she hope to achieve by telling it, and does she achieve any of her goals? In short, what rhetorical purposes does the maid want her narration to serve, and does it achieve those purposes?

Porter's technique of eliding the first two levels of the narrative suggests that the answer can be found in parallels and contrasts between them. Porter provides many. First, there are the two madams. Though they move in different social spheres, both are powerful women — they have money, authority, employees. At the same time, their power itself depends on a larger patriarchal structure: the madam provides a service to the men of New Orleans, and when they complain about Ninette's absence, the madam responds; Madame Blanchard's wealth and comfort depend, to some extent at least, on her marriage to M. Blanchard. Second, there are the maid and Ninette: they are both subservient employees of a madam. Third, and most strongly, there are the maid and the cook: both have "mixed racial blood"; both have lived always among people who work spells; both like to watch all that happens; both apparently like to tell tales.

All these parallels help us answer the questions about the maid's rhetorical purposes, though we have a multitude of possibilities rather than any single answer. The maid may be giving Madame Blanchard a warning: If you do not treat me well, I will, like Ninette, oppose you — and because I am like the cook, I will be more successful in my opposition than she. The maid may be trying to ingratiate herself, saying in effect, "Like the cook, I am willing to help my Madame in all things." Or the maid may be signifying on Madame Blanchard's remark that the sheets are bewitched in order to scare Madame Blanchard: Like the cook, I can do powerful magic; if you think those sheets are bewitched, you ain't seen nothin' yet.

Because the end of the maid's story coincides with the end of Ninette's, we cannot know which is her primary purpose and we do not know whether she has achieved it. But the two appearances of the heterodiegetic narrator and the two interjections by Madame Blanchard do direct our attention in specific ways. The power struggle between employer and employee that defines Ninette's story seems to be very much the subtext of the maid's story. It is when the maid is telling about the madam's general ill-treatment of her employees that the maid pulls Madame Blanchard's hair: a quiet assertion of the maid's power even as she is serving her mistress. Madame Blanchard reasserts control by gently stopping the hair pulling, but she also reveals that she has been caught by the power of the maid's storytelling: she asks the rapt audience's perpetual question, "And then what?" In the second appearance, just after the maid recounts the cook's spell, the heterodiegetic narrator calls attention to Madame Blanchard's closing her perfume bottle "with a thin click." Since Ninette's madam asserted her power over her employees by beating them with bottles, Madame Blanchard's clicking her own perfume bottle shut at this moment suggests that she feels some need to remind herself — and the maid — of her power. But, like the first interruption of the maid's telling, this one also ends with Madame Blanchard asking the engaged audience's question: "Yes, and then?"[4]

More generally, the more we look at the interaction of Ninette's story, the maid's story, and Porter's story, the more it seems that Porter wants us to view the maid's telling of Ninette's story as the prime example of the maid's magic.

[4]It is perhaps especially significant that this second request comes as a spontaneous interruption to the maid's story: so caught up is Madame Blanchard in the narrative that her impatience to learn what happened next paradoxically leads her to slow down the progress of the narration by her expression of interest in having it move to the next stage. [Au.]

Like the cook, the maid casts a spell. By calling her story "Magic," Porter makes the same claim for herself: just as the maid seeks to catch Madame Blanchard in the spell of Ninette's story, so too does Porter want to catch us up in her telling of the maid's story.

In this way, the rhetorical exchanges in which we participate as we read and interpret Ninette's story, the maid's story, and Porter's story eventually lead us to reflect on the power of narrative. We do not know exactly what the effect of the maid's telling on Madame Blanchard will be, but the clues about the subtext of power relations and the evidence of Madame Blanchard's being caught by the maid's spell strongly suggest that it will have some effect. And the effect of this conclusion on us is to reinforce our sense of the magic of narrative and to take pleasure in our consenting to Porter's spell. In this respect, the open-endedness of the story is all to the good. The more interpretations we find of the maid, her motive, her story, and its likely effect, the more we are both drawn into her world and made cognizant of the magical power of narrative.

CONCEPTS OF RHETORIC: DECONSTRUCTION, PRAGMATISM, COMMUNICATION

There is more to say about the concrete particularities of "Magic," and I will return to them shortly, but I turn now to consider the theoretical principles I have been using to discuss the story so far. First, the phrase "narrative as rhetoric" means something more than that narrative uses rhetoric or has a rhetorical dimension. It means instead that narrative is not just story but also action, *the telling of a story by someone to someone on some occasion for some purpose.*[5] Furthermore, as the analysis of "Magic" indicates, this basic configuration of teller-story-situation-audience-purpose is at least doubled in most narrative: there is the narrator's telling the story to his or her audience and then the author's telling of the narrator's telling to the author's audience. Consequently, the narrator's telling is part of the author's construction of the whole narrative, and in that sense, what is a matter of the telling at one level becomes a matter of the told at the next. Before exploring the details of this rhetorical configuration, I would like to highlight some of its key assumptions and emphases by comparing the general approach with the ones that follow from two other widely circulating conceptions of rhetoric: deconstruction and pragmatism.[6]

I call deconstruction's conception of rhetoric "widely circulating" with full knowledge that deconstruction's heyday has passed and that most critics and theorists are currently more concerned with reinventing historical criticism and merging literary with cultural studies in ways that foreground the politics and ideology of both cultural and critical texts. I engage deconstruction here because its *legacy* is so influential: it is to deconstruction that we owe the wide acceptance of the principles that language is inherently unstable, that there is no transcendental anchor to textual meanings, and that textual meanings are more likely to be at odds with one another than not. Like most other contemporary theorists, I acknowledge the value of these deconstructionist principles for complicating our understandings of language, textuality, and interpretation. At the same time, however, I find these views less compelling than many other critics do, and although I

[5]For more on this definition see Barbara Herrnstein Smith and the reply by Seymour Chatman. [Au.] See Barbara Herrnstein Smith, "Narrative Vision, Narrative Theorists." *Critical Inquiry* 7 (1980): 213–36; and Seymour Chatman, "Response to Barbara Herrnstein Smith." *Critical Inquiry* 7 (1981): 802–09. [Ed.]

[6]*Deconstruction* by now is a term whose meaning has widened considerably as it has been disseminated through our culture. It is not only Derridean philosophers and critics who deconstruct but also television personalities and sportswriters — indeed, anyone who questions anything is liable to be called a deconstructor. Within the realm of theory, to deconstruct sometimes now means to demystify or to show that what we thought was natural and immutable is actually constructed and changeable as well as to show how a given logic, when read rigorously, undermines itself. I am concerned with this last meaning of the term not only because I think it is closer to what was originally seen as radical in deconstruction but also because it is the one that bears most closely upon deconstruction's attention to rhetoric. [Au.] See Structuralism, Semiotics, and Deconstruction, p. 818. [Ed.]

am not interested in trying to repudiate deconstruction, I do want, first, to show how the principles of my approach to narrative as rhetoric differ from deconstruction's and, second, to suggest that, despite appearances, deconstruction does not invalidate or otherwise supplant those principles.[7]

I call pragmatism's conception of rhetoric a widely circulating one because, through the efforts of Stanley Fish and Richard Rorty, this conception has come to be seen as part and parcel of poststructuralist antifoundationalism.[8] Again, my efforts here are less to argue either for or against pragmatism as a philosophical position than to locate my approach to narrative as rhetoric in relation to it — and, more specifically, to make a space for that approach in the contemporary critical landscape.

Paul de Man's famous essay "Semiology and Rhetoric" illustrates the fundamental emphasis of deconstruction's approach to rhetoric: a rigorous reading of language as a system of tropes and a rigorous analysis of the logic implied by the tropes of any text. De Man argues that the grammar and rhetoric of texts frequently diverge, but efforts to decide whether one should be privileged over the other are doomed to failure precisely because there is no decisive evidence in the text. He brilliantly illustrates this logic of deconstruction in his tour de force reading of an interchange from the 1970s television show *All in the Family.* When Edith Bunker asks her husband, Archie, whether he wants the laces on his bowling shoes tied over or under, he impatiently replies, "What's the difference?" Under de Man's gaze, Archie's question is fully explicable, first, as what its rhetoric suggests — a rhetorical question revealing Archie's belief that there is no difference — and, second, as what its grammar suggests, that is, a genuine question, asking for an explanation of difference. As a genuine question, it is a kind of challenge to Edith — if you're going to ask me such a question, I want you to explain the difference to me. It is worth noting that de Man's analysis includes the rhetorical situation but that he does not believe that an appeal to the situation can decide the case. Since the fault line between grammar and rhetoric is so wide, since the text finally does not contain sufficient evidence for its own interpretation, appealing to author, audience, occasion, or purpose for a resolution to the undecidability is not a valid move but instead an imposition of the interpreter's will on the text.

What deconstruction's attention to textual rhetoric means for narrative analysis is very nicely encapsulated in J. Hillis Miller's entry "Narrative" in *Critical Terms for Literary Study.* The "basic elements" of narrative, Miller declares, are three: plot, personification, and trope. Not surprisingly, he gives special emphasis to trope, arguing, in effect, that narrative inevitably tropes over itself. That is, narrative develops some pattern or repetition of trope, and this pat-

[7]Having offered these generalizations, I hasten to add some important qualifications. Barbara Johnson's work, especially in her recent book, *The Wake of Deconstruction* (1994), shows that deconstruction is neither passé nor incompatible with a politically engaged criticism. Furthermore, her statement — and demonstration — that "the point of a deconstructive analysis is not to treat intentionality as an 'on off' switch but to analyze the functioning of many different, sometimes incommensurable, *kinds* of intentionality" (18) moves deconstructive practice closer to the kind of rhetorical analysis I attempt here, just as, in ways I will discuss below, my shift away from emphasizing intention moves my rhetorical analysis in the direction of Johnson's. In other words, although Johnson remains more interested in incompatibilities among kinds of intentionality and I remain more interested in reconstructing coherences, I also find a greater overlap between the underlying conceptions of rhetorical reading in her work and mine than I do in the work of the earlier, more widely influential Anglo-American deconstructors such as Paul de Man and J. Hillis Miller, whose conceptions I focus on here. [Au.]

[8]Antifoundationalism: Philosophical position that would deny that truth is based on a "foundation" of self-evident propositions. While philosophers once prided themselves on the way their systems of thought could be rigorously derived from one or more apparently obvious axioms, in the way the theorems of plane geometry were derived from Euclid's definitions and axioms, most contemporary philosophers are antifoundationalists who would hold that alternative views of the world are merely alternative rhetorics or language games based on arbitrarily chosen terms and ideas. The deconstructionist Jacques Derrida (see pp. 877–89), the later Wittgenstein (of the *Philosophical Investigations),* and the American pragmatist Richard Rorty are, in different ways, examples of antifoundationalist thinkers. [Ed.]

terning invariably generates "fundamentally incongruous meanings" or "narrative disjunctions that can never be brought back to unity."[9]

Turning back to "Magic," then, we can see that a deconstructionist would be willing to accept much of the analysis I have presented so far but would go on to say that it stops too soon, that it does not do a sufficiently rigorous reading of the logic of Porter's narrative. The conclusion that the story demonstrates the magical power of narrative does not attend sufficiently to the first move of my analysis: the inference that Porter's story tells us that Ninette comes back not because of the cook's spell but because of the madam's power. Once we reexamine that inference, we can see that the powers of all the spells found through the analogies made in my analysis — between the cook's spell, the maid's story, and Porter's story — are built on an illusion. Consequently, Porter's story simultaneously demonstrates the power of narrative and exposes narrative as powerless. Everyone may be caught in the spell of narrative, but the spell is, finally, based on an illusion.

Furthermore, we can push the logic of Porter's technique of elision to its logical conclusion. The spell in Ninette's story that brings her back is cast by the cook, whereas the spell in the maid's story is cast by the maid's own telling. But it is just as much the spell cast by the maid's story that brings Ninette back, because there is no evidence other than the maid's word that Ninette came back in seven days. Indeed, there is no evidence that any of the events of the tale actually occurred or that Ninette is anything other than the maid's invention. Again, the effect is to demonstrate narrative's power and simultaneously to expose its powerlessness. The maid's narrative makes things happen — and makes them happen so vividly as to catch Madame Blanchard in its spell — but the things it makes happen may have happened only through the act of the maid's telling. If saying makes things so, then our sayings are powerful indeed; but if saying makes things so, then, to anyone's saying, we can say, "So what?" And of course, this same logic applies a fortiori to Porter's story.

Before discussing the relation of this deconstructive reading to the one I have offered, I would like to consider the pragmatist conception of rhetoric and its resultant claims for both readings. This conception, represented in the work of Richard Rorty, Stanley Fish, Steven Knapp and Walter Benn Michaels, and others, is well summarized in Fish's chapter entitled "Rhetoric" in *Doing What Comes Naturally*.[10] This view sees the world — especially that part of the world concerned with knowledge — as constituted by rhetoric. Our discourse about the world makes the world what we find it to be. In his essay, Fish points to two attitudes toward rhetoric that have been present in different forms throughout the history of Western thought: (1) the attitude that rhetoric is a means by which a truth independent of our discourse is folded, spindled, mutilated, or otherwise manipulated; and (2) the attitude that rhetoric is inescapable because truth is not independent of but rather constituted by our discourse about it. Fish emphasizes the point that the ancient quarrel can never be resolved, but upon reflection we can see that this emphasis itself indicates his preference for the second view. Someone committed to the position that truth is independent of our discourse would think that this truth could be demonstrated sufficiently for the quarrel to be resolved, whereas someone committed to the position that truth is constituted by our discourse about it can see both positions as consistent with the general principle — and therefore as engaged in a quarrel in which neither can win.

A pragmatist view of narrative as rhetoric would view narrative as inescapably bound up with its interpretation and its interpretation as endlessly malleable — according to the needs, interests, and values of the interpreter on any given occasion. Consequently, the pragmatist would regard both my analysis of "Magic" and that of the deconstructor as different instances of

[9]J. Hillis Miller, "Narrative," in *Critical Terms for Literary Study,* ed. Frank Lentricchla and Thomas McLaughlin (Chicago: University of Chicago Press, 1990), p. 77. [Ed.]

[10]Stanley Eugene Fish, "Rhetoric," in *Doing What Comes Naturally: Change, Rhetoric, and the Practice of Theory in Literary and Legal Studies* (Durham, NC: Duke University Press, 1984). [Ed.]

the same phenomenon: each is construing Porter's narrative in a particular way for its particular purposes. What neither view realizes, however, is how partial and particular it is, how much the questions it asks and the assumptions it makes — about language, the nature of narrative, readers, and many other things — participate in the construction not just of the interpretation but also of the text. And what each view needs to recognize is that no final resolution of disagreements is possible. There is no fixed ground, no foundation — either in the narrative text, in authorial agency, in reader response, or, indeed, in any general theory of interpretation — that would allow for any satisfactory adjudication. However, the pragmatist would also say that the difference between my analysis and the deconstructive one is the difference between a foundationalist and an antifoundationalist view of truth. From the pragmatist perspective, my analysis seems to assume Porter's narrative has some essential character that the interpretation seeks to describe, whereas the deconstructive analysis sees the textual rhetoric as frustrating any access to such an essential character. Although the pragmatist would want to qualify the deconstructor's claim for the necessity of the deconstructive reading, the pragmatist would also favor it over the one I have proposed.

Let me now reconsider my analysis in light of these critiques. As always, I find that the deconstructive analysis seems simultaneously counterintuitive and virtually irresistible: once the premises of deconstruction are granted, its logic is very persuasive. However, thinking about this logic from the pragmatist's antifoundational perspective clarifies the strength and weakness of deconstruction's appeal. From the pragmatist perspective, the logic is intriguing because it is an instance of what it describes, an enactment of the power and powerlessness of narrative. That is, the logic leads to a strong account of Porter's narrative, one capable of disrupting the analysis I proposed, but the logic also leaves us powerless to move beyond its contradictory assertions about power and powerlessness. To describe the logic this way is to make clear how deconstruction's claim to be reading the text more closely than anyone else can be legitimately questioned: the logic depends on two interpretive leaps. The first leap is to key terms — in this case, *magic* and *narrative,* as opposed, say, to *race* and *class;* the second is to a narrative about those terms in the text — in this case, the narrative about the power/powerlessness of narrative. In other words, the antifoundational perspective helps point out that although no narrative and no interpretation is deconstruction-proof, deconstruction's logic about textual logic is not as inevitable and necessary as its attention to textual rhetoric makes it appear. Laying bare the leaps that form the basis of the deconstructor's operation shows that deconstruction cannot really claim to be closer to the literal text than other approaches.

With this understanding in mind, we can return to the most important question that the deconstructive reading presents to the one I offered: what is the relation between the cook's magic spell and the maid's magic of narration? Does our awareness that the cook's magic is illusory make us suspect that the magic of narrative is similarly illusory? A closer look reveals that Porter's story, in effect, recognizes the deconstructive hypothesis but then sets out its affirmation of the power of narrative. That is, Porter's story indicates that the maid's narrative is more powerful than the cook's spell because the maid's narrative catches the powerful Madame Blanchard, whereas the cook's spell is not really responsible for Ninette's return and both that spell and the return may be a product of the maid's magic. Furthermore, the parallel between the maid and Ninette also works to point to the story's ultimate affirmation of narrative. Ninette, though sufficiently wily and resourceful to save enough money to leave the brothel, is not sufficiently wily and resourceful to construct a narrative for her madam that will allow her to keep the money and successfully escape. Regardless of whether the maid wants to ingratiate herself with Madame Blanchard, to scare her, or to warn her, the maid uses narrative in an effort to establish a different relationship with her employer than the one Ninette has with the madam. To be sure, Porter leaves open the question of whether the magic of the narrative will have any real effect. But in these situations "where it was almost always about the money" — situations faced by Ninette, the cook, and the maid — where the powerful have money and the powerless minorities and women have none, Porter's story suggests that the best weapon or best defense of the powerless is narrative. Porter's story, of course, does not offer any guarantee of the maid's success, but it certainly suggests that her odds are better than Ninette's.

Before turning from the deconstructionist to the pragmatist challenge, I would like to call attention to some other dimensions of the spell Porter casts in "Magic." To read the story is not only to inquire into the maid's motives but also to situate ourselves emotively and ethically in relationship to Ninette, the French cook, the two madams, the maid, and Porter herself. In Ninette's story, the emotive and ethical lines are clearly drawn: our sympathies are with Ninette in her nervy effort to escape the domineering, abusive madam (and her willing helper, the cook); we experience the madam's victory as a dispiriting defeat. In the maid's story, however, the emotive and ethical lines are blurry. Because we have no strong evidence of Madame Blanchard's ethical character, the maid's storytelling, in contrast to Ninette's efforts at escape, has the quality of a preemptive strike. Our inferences about Ninette's story and what it suggests about the plight of the powerless woman certainly make the maid's action understandable, and these inferences may incline us to sympathize with and even admire her ingenuity and resourcefulness. However, once we recall that the maid may have simply fabricated Ninette's story, the maid's character — and the ethical balance of her story — shift. If the maid has invented Ninette's story, then she is someone who aggressively manipulates her environment, someone who, above all, looks out for number one. Of course, with either construction of the maid's character, Madame Blanchard does not change. We never see her as a victim of the maid, and, indeed, she may remain ultimately unaffected by the maid's storytelling. Nevertheless, our reflections on the maid enable us to recognize more fully how charged this domestic scene of one woman brushing another's hair may be. It is certainly a subtle power struggle; it may also be one with an underlying threat of violence. If Ninette's story is dispiriting, the maid's is chilling: although its outcome is unknown, the story itself is full of ominous notes.

Moving to Porter's story, we can recognize that her technique of plunging us into this situation works not just to involve us cognitively but also to affect us emotionally and to challenge us ethically. Each inference we make about the maid's storytelling situation also leads us, first, to a tacit judgment of the maid's action, motives, and character, and second, to our sense of how powerfully the scene is charged. But virtually each new inference (the maid is telling a story from her past; the maid is making up this story) leads us to a reexamination of these same things, a reexamination that involves us in such ethical questions as how much we take the maid's side, regardless of her motives, how much we care about whether she is making up Ninette's story, how much we judge Madame Blanchard simply on the basis of her name and her class. In short, Porter's story so successfully casts its spell because it so efficiently arouses and so tightly interweaves the audience's cognitive, emotive, and ethical responses.

If, on the one hand, my effort to make space for my approach to narrative as rhetoric alongside the deconstructive one has been successful, it may, on the other, nevertheless serve to sharpen the pragmatist objection: the approach is based on a fundamental epistemological error, the notion that there are facts and truths outside of our discourse. Now note that the pragmatist, especially the pragmatist called Stanley Fish, works with a strict either/or logic: either language describes the world or language constructs the world; either there is transcendent Truth or there is no truth; either there are facts outside of discourse or discourse creates facts and truths. My response to the pragmatist objection is that this either/or logic inadequately captures the complexity of the relationship between facts, hypotheses, and theories, or in the realm of literary criticism, texts, interpretations, and approaches. I can better substantiate this claim after you read the following narrative, which I have entitled "Institutional Magic."

During a session at a conference I recently attended called "The Politics of Interpretation after Poststructuralism," I witnessed a disturbing event. A white middle-aged man was reading a paper arguing that the political consequences of much mainstream poststructuralist thought are inimical to the politics of multiculturalism and that this antithesis highlights some serious theoretical limitations of poststructuralism. His delivery indicated both that he felt very strongly about the political dimension of his argument and that he was very nervous about making this case at a conference where the reigning assumption seemed to be that the theoretical (non)foundations of poststructuralism were beyond question. After he had been talking for about ten minutes, a man in the audience began to hiss. At first the sound was barely audible, but the hisser gradually grew bolder and louder. Then the woman sitting next to him joined in. And then another person and another, until everyone in the room, including the speaker, could hear it. The speaker became increasingly flustered until, unable to stand it anymore, he looked up from his text and berated the audience: "You see, this is exactly the kind of negative political consequence I am talking about." But this chiding only incited the hissers to increase their volume. The speaker tried to return to his text but was now so distraught that he could not find his place. The hissing continued unabated, and the speaker's distress turned to panic: shouting, "The hell with it!" he threw his paper into the air and ran from the podium and out of the room. As he left, the hissing turned to applause.

Horrified by this event, I wrote two letters: one to the speaker to express some sympathy and support, and one to the conference organizer to complain about the behavior of the audience and to inquire whether any formal action was going to be taken. Within a few weeks I had two replies: a very brief thank-you from the speaker, and a longer letter from the conference organizer with a very surprising enclosure. Since an unsolicited apology had just arrived, he was not going to pursue any formal action; I would understand, he said, when I read the enclosed copy of the letter of apology. This letter, you see, was from the speaker. In addition to apologizing, the speaker detailed his conversion to a position much more sympathetic to poststructuralism, and he expressed gratitude for the audience's "creative resistance" to his earlier, erroneous argument. Finally, the speaker hoped that the organizer would be willing to consider the paper he wrote about his conversion experience for publication in the conference volume, adding as an aside that the acceptance of one more essay would clinch his pending tenure case.

Let us now consider the pragmatist question about the existence and force of the "facts" of this story and my use of it. There are, I maintain, numerous kinds of facts involved here: (1) Facts that will not be disputed — for example, that I asked you to read "Institutional Magic." (2) Facts that depend on the employment of our interpretive faculties — for example, that there are recognizable parallels between this story and Porter's "Magic," especially between Ninette's defeat and the conference speaker's change of heart. (3) Facts that depend on an even deeper excursion into the realm of interpretation so that the line between fact and interpretation is extremely blurry — for example, that the speaker's capitulation in "Institutional Magic" is different from Ninette's because he is more complicit in the oppressive system. Beyond this point, we get so deep into the territory of interpretation that rather than facts we have questions whose answers most will agree deserve the name "interpretations": How much is the "I" of "Institutional Magic" like the maid in "Magic"? How much is the "I" constructing you as a reader in a role like the one Madame Blanchard has in "Magic"? What is the relation between the "I" of "Institutional Magic" and the "I" of *Narrative as Rhetoric*? What is the veiled communication I want to make? Is "Institutional Magic" less open-ended than Porter's story? Given the context in which I have used it, how much is "Institutional Magic" thematizing narrative?

According to the pragmatist view, even this delineation of kinds of facts and this consideration of the interrelations between facts, interpretations, and questions needs to be seen as the product of a kind of discourse: everything I've said about "Magic" and "Institutional Magic" can be seen as arising from a set of beliefs and assumptions that in turn influence my way of talking about narrative, literary critical arguments, academic audiences, and other issues. Without those beliefs and assumptions and without that discursive framework, both "Institutional Magic" and the things I have said about it — indeed, perhaps most of the things you have thought about it — are not recognizable and therefore cannot be considered as facts of any kind. If we stepped out of the discursive framework provided by my beliefs and assumptions and moved into one that attended, say, only to the reproduction of the black marks on the white page, then even the data and the givens of my case apparently disappear.

With the point that there are no facts outside of some framework for describing them I am in complete agreement. It is the next step of the pragmatist logic, the conclusion that truth is constituted by our discourse about it, that gives me pause. That our facts change as our discursive frameworks change does not prove that there are no facts; it proves rather that there are multiple facts and multiple ways of construing facts. Thus the same phenomenon, for example, the phrase "happy to be here," may be, in one discursive frame, an ironic comment that reveals something about a character, while in another frame something that tells us about the importance of the letter *h*. In making this claim, I am not asserting that my rhetorical approach to "Magic" or "Institutional Magic" is the standard or foundation against which all other ways must be compared. But I am asserting that the approach makes a legitimate claim to propose one kind of truth about both stories: the way each functions as a communication from author to reader.

To put the point another way, to accept the pragmatist position would be to accept that your experience in reading "Institutional Magic" — its arousal of horror, pleasure, disgust, indifference, or anything else — is not primarily a function of textual phenomena and their shaping by me (under Porter's influence) but rather is rooted in something else — a set of beliefs about the academy, about stories, and about stories about the academy. My alternative view is quite simple: we should reject the institutional magic of pragmatism that makes the story and its techniques disappear, because those techniques and that shaped story do influence the experience. Indeed, I have told this story about the academy rather than a whole range of others precisely because I believe in its power to evoke a strong response from my expected audience. You will be willing to accept my alternative to the extent that you find yourself convinced that the shaped story is important to (though not necessarily determinative of) whatever response it evokes in you.

In countering the either/or logic of the pragmatist by arguing that there are multiple facts and multiple ways of construing them, I am proposing a different kind of antifoundationalism. The position is antifoundationalist because it insists on the incompatibility of the multiple facts, the impossibility of finding the one true account of them and their connection to each other. At the same time, my antifoundationalist position departs from Fish's version by insisting that although facts are always mediated, always seen from within the confines of a given perspective, the perspective does not create the facts. In doing interpretation, then, we will encounter narratives capable of providing recalcitrance to the rhetorical critic; furthermore, the perspectives of other approaches have the potential to complicate, revise, or even overturn the initial results of a rhetorical interpretation.

RHETORIC IN RELATION TO OTHER INTERESTS

As many readers will have already recognized, my approach is indebted to rhetorical theorists such as Kenneth Burke and Wayne C. Booth[11] who also emphasize narrative as a distinctive and powerful means for an author to communicate knowledge, feelings, values, and beliefs to an audience: indeed, viewing narrative as having the purpose of communicating knowledge, feelings, values, and beliefs is viewing narrative as rhetoric. There are various metaphors, all some-

[11]See Burke, p. 581, and Booth, p. 786. [Ed.]

what inadequate, that might be applied to this relationship between author, text, and audience: *interaction, exchange, transaction, intercourse. Interaction* is unexceptionable because unexceptional and bland. Both *exchange* and *transaction* carry connotations of buying and selling, and while these connotations are not entirely inappropriate, they are also reductive. *Gift exchange* is better, but it does not quite capture the effort frequently involved in the reader's half of the exchange. *Intercourse* is, well, sexy. Its calling attention to the play of desire and the erotic component in the writing and reading of narrative are genuine advantages, but again, it strikes me as too narrow. What I want is a shorthand term that might include all these things — interaction, transaction, (gift) exchange, intercourse. Rather than search for another metaphor, I propose to let *rhetoric* function as this shorthand. That is, in this book, when I talk about narrative as rhetoric or about a rhetorical relationship between author, text, and reader, I want to refer to the complex, multilayered processes of writing and reading, processes that call upon our cognition, emotions, desires, hopes, values, and beliefs.

Given this larger interest, I am more specifically interested in the elements of narrative (e.g., character, event, setting, narrative discourse) and in techniques, forms, structures, genres, and conventions of narrative for the ways in which they enable, enrich, interfere with, or otherwise complicate narrative as rhetoric. I am interested in the author in a way that parts company with Booth's highly influential rhetorical approach. Booth emphasizes the author as Constructor of the text, whose choices about the elements of narrative largely control the responses of the audience. As a result of this emphasis, Booth's work moves in the direction of defending the Author and the importance of authorial intention for determining the meaning of a text.[12] I do not see authorial intention as fully recoverable and as controlling response, even as I want to insist that when we read rhetorically we encounter something other than ourselves. The approach I am advocating shifts emphasis from author as controller to the recursive relationships among authorial agency, textual phenomena, and reader response, to the way in which our attention to each of these elements both influences and can be influenced by the other two. Shifting the emphasis this way also helps to open the rhetorical approach to the insights of many other approaches — from feminism to psychoanalysis, from Bakhtinian linguistics to cultural studies — about agency, response, and text. These insights, when integrated into the general approach, can complicate interpretations, even as the main concern with the rhetorical transaction of reading remains.[13]

In the case of "Magic," the rhetorical analysis I have presented so far benefits especially from being complicated by the insights of a feminist analysis. Attending more closely to issues of gender and especially to issues of gender and power in "Magic," several important points emerge or at least take on greater importance. First, although all the main actors and tellers in the story are women and, indeed, the maid's story occurs in a distinctly female space, there is a larger system of patriarchy controlling the events. The madam of the "fancy house" is, in one sense, not entirely successful in her battle with Ninette because she has to give in to the demands of the male customers and take steps to bring her back. Further-

[12]See especially *A Rhetoric of Irony* (1974), where Booth includes "intended" as one of the marks of stable irony and where he employs E. D. Hirsch Jr.'s distinction between meaning and significance throughout his argument; in addition, see the final — and longest — chapter of *Critical Understanding* (1979), where Booth employs different concepts of author as guides to rhetorical reading. In *The Company We Keep* (1988), Booth complicates his previous rhetorical model by introducing into it the concept of "coduction," the way in which readers' interactions with each other help modify their responses (especially their ethical responses) to narratives. With his sights set on the knotty problem of the "ethics of fiction," however, Booth does not directly address the question of how significant an adjustment he is making in his rhetorical model. [Au.]

[13]One recent strong example of the approach is Peter J. Rabinowitz's *Before Reading*, a study of the recursive relationships between interpretive conventions and textual details. Rabinowitz shows how these relations guide readers' efforts to fashion the text, which he metaphorically postulates as an unassembled swing set, into an intelligible whole. [Au.] See "From *Before Reading*," p. 998. [Ed.]

more, this development helps bring to the fore the way in which the brothel's existence depends upon the indulgence of the police and the larger patriarchal society. And why is Ninette unable to support herself except as a prostitute? This question is easily answered in light of the way the class-gender system worked in New Orleans of the 1920s (and still works in many places today) to prevent a poor woman from having any serious economic opportunity outside marriage. Ninette's parallel with the maid and the madam's with Madame Blanchard are also important in this connection. The maid's opportunities are severely limited by her gender, class, and race, and her effort to overcome these limitations through narrative becomes more important the more we attend to these limitations. If the madam of the brothel is dependent on a bargain she has made with patriarchal society, so, too, is Madame Blanchard. The difference, of course, is that her bargain seems to have left her better off. But Madame Blanchard's particular interest in Ninette's story may now appear as some kind of recognition, however unconscious, of some fundamental similarity among women that cuts across differences of class and race. Attending to these issues also suggests that we should not be too quick to move from the horror of Ninette's story to Porter's thematizing of the power of narrative: to do so is to blunt the narrative's genuine social critique. Indeed, it is the rhetorical power of the first-level story upon which all the effects of the narrative are built.

What is true of such a feminist approach is also true of other approaches: each of them is a potential source of complication for the rhetorical precisely because the rhetorical is interested in the multilayered relationships between authorial agency, textual phenomena, and reader response and because it believes that reading is endlessly recursive. Consequently, I could continue the analysis of "Magic" by bringing the conclusions reached so far into dialogue with some things I've barely touched on, such as the story's location in New Orleans in the 1920s. But rhetorical criticism must reach a (provisional) end, even if rhetorical reading, like relationships between people, stops nowhere.

2

STRUCTURALISM, SEMIOTICS, AND DECONSTRUCTION

No one disputes the principle of the arbitrary nature of the sign, but it is often easier to discover a truth than to assign to it its proper place. — FERDINAND DE SAUSSURE

What requires explanation is not the text itself so much as the possibility of reading and interpreting the text, the possibility of literary effects and literary communication.
— JONATHAN CULLER

The passage beyond philosophy does not consist in turning the page of philosophy (which usually comes down to philosophizing badly), but in continuing to read philosophers in a certain way. — JACQUES DERRIDA

The author has disappeared. . . . God and man have died a common death.
— MICHEL FOUCAULT

The special insight of the structuralist approach is that, though language may not be everything, practically everything we do that is specifically human is expressed in language. Most obviously we communicate with one another in hundreds of "natural" languages, whose conventions predate any human memory; and in recent decades we have become dependent upon computers, whose functioning is based on the creation of artificial languages for sorting and processing data, and for solving problems.

But most of the other activities of daily life, from the elegant to the homely, are equally dependent upon various codes. The performance of music requires a complex notation, as does the solution of mathematical problems. Our economic life rests upon the exchange of labor and goods for symbols, such as cash, checks, stock certificates, and various other documents that are more or less easily exchangeable for each other and for other people's labor and goods. The language of fashion is one we learn to speak with difficulty, and when we wonder if our tie is too loud or our dress too formal, we are considering whether our friends will be upset by the message our clothes convey. Social life depends on the meaningful gestures and signals of "body language" and revolves around the exchange of small, symbolic favors: drinks, parties, dinners. Family connections in patriarchal culture depend on the exchange — so momentous that it is difficult to think of it as symbolic — of a woman from one family group into another.

Merely noting that everything is language and cataloging the overwhelming variety of ways in which reality is structured in systems of signs and symbols does not get us very far. Structuralism required a method of analyzing systems of symbols, and this was provided by two developments. One was the theory of the nineteenth-century American philosopher Charles Sanders Peirce, which is termed *semiotics*. Peirce analyzed sign systems into three general types: (1) iconic signs, in which the signifier resembles the thing signified (such as the stick figures on washroom doors that signify "Men" or "Women"); (2) indexes, in which the signifier is a reliable indicator of the presence of the signified (like smoke and fire); and (3) true symbols, in which the signifier's relation to the thing signified is completely arbitrary and conventional (just as the sound /kat/ or the written word *cat* are conventional signs for the familiar feline).

The other development was the linguistic theory of Ferdinand de Saussure, who established that the special symbol systems of the natural languages are systems based on differences. In his lecture notes published posthumously as *Cours de linguistique générale* (1916), Saussure established the basic principles of structural linguistics and of structuralism more generally.[1] These principles rest on a number of technical distinctions:

1. *Langue* vs. *parole*. A language is a system of constitutive rules — that is, the rules *are* the language in the same way that the rules of chess constitute the game of chess. (If we break the rules of chess by, say, taking two moves at a time, there is no penalty as there is when we break traffic laws or other normative rules; we just aren't playing chess any longer.) But the system of the language (*langue*) appears only in the behavior of its individual speakers, who produce instances of speech (*parole*). Speakers may or may not be aware of the rules of the language, but they usually know whether an individual instance is correct or deviant. The activity of the linguist is to infer the rules of the *langue* from the evidence of *parole*. American linguist Noam Chomsky's distinction between *competence* (ideal language ability) and *performance* (individual activity) is similar to that of *langue* and *parole*.

2. *Synchronic* vs. *diachronic*. The system of a *langue* is complete at any one time, but languages, in their sound systems (phonology), their grammatical relationships (syntax), and their lexicons, change over time. In studying a language, one has to distinguish between a synchronic study, which attempts to display the *langue* at one particular time, and a *diachronic* investigation, which studies change.

[1] "Semiotics" and "structuralism" have been used here as though they were essentially similar terms, and certainly there was a great deal that connected the two movements. But semiotics takes off from Peirce — for whom language is one of numerous sign systems — and structuralism takes off from Saussure, for whom language was the sign system par excellence. As a result, semioticians discuss sign systems generically, while structuralists tend to use linguistic models exclusively — to speak of "the language of fashion" and so forth. A structuralist would compose a grammar of narrative, while a semiotician would analyze the multiple codes that relate expression to content, and so on.

3. *Paradigmata* and *syntagmata.* The two fundamental relationships of symbols are parataxis and syntaxis. An example of parataxis is the relationship of items in the same category on a menu: In ordering soup, one may choose the beef consommé *or* the lobster bisque *or* the clam chowder. The items are similar enough to belong to one category (soups) yet different (in their ingredients). In a language, the consonants and vowels are paradigms on the phonological level, nouns and verbs are paradigms on the grammatical level, and so on.

Syntaxis is the relationship of items from different categories in a meaningful structure. Back in the restaurant, when we choose a soup, an appetizer, a main course, and a dessert, we try to select a combination that will "go together" pleasantly. Or we try to pick items of clothing that will harmonize in color, texture, and social tone when worn together. The rules of syntax in a natural language are far more complex than the rules for wearing clothes or for ordering in a restaurant; it takes several years of hard work, from the ages of two to four, to learn the most basic relationships. But when we have succeeded, we comprehend subtle differences in the syntax of sentences, even some that traditional grammar textbooks ignore.

In Noam Chomsky's famous pair of sentences, "John is eager to please" and "John is easy to please," for example, the sentences appear to differ merely in one lexical item: for the third word of each sentence, a different member of the paradigm class of adjectives has been selected. But any native speaker also intuitively knows that the sentences also differ in their syntax. "John" is implicitly the "subject" of *please* in the first sentence and the "object" of *please* in the second, despite the fact that the sentences are apparently cut to the same pattern, and that "John" is by traditional standards the subject of the copula "is" in both.

4. The basic units, or *emes.* To return to paradigm classes, the problem is one of identifying the basic categories in an unfamiliar language, where the categories may not be the same as in one's native tongue. Saussure's basic principle was that distinctions within categories depend on differences; the practical difficulty is figuring out which differences, of all those we can learn to distinguish, really make a difference — which is not a simple matter.

Take the sound system of English. The letter *t* stands for the sound /t/ — but at various positions in words /t/ is not a single sound but several different sounds. The first sound in the word *tip* is not the same as the last sound in the word *pit.* The first *t* is *aspirated* — pronounced with an explosion of air — while the second is not. To complicate things further, the *t* sound in *bottle* is not the same as either of the other two. But in English, these differences *do not* make a difference. If you pronounce *pit* with an aspirated *t,* you have still said *pit;* no one will mistake which word you have pronounced. Aspiration is a feature that does not make a basic difference in English (though it does in Hindi and in several other languages). But voicing does make a difference in English. Words like *tip* and *dip,* or *pit* or *bit,* differ according to whether the initial consonant is *voiced* (pronounced with the vocal cords vibrating) or *unvoiced.* The point is that /t/ in all its various pronunciations (allophones) is a single *phoneme* in English, a basic and minimal unit of the sound system. And the phoneme /t/ differs from the phoneme /d/ because of the feature of voicing, and from all the other phonemes of English because of various other sorts of differences.

If the basic minimal unit of a sound system is the phoneme, the basic minimal unit of grammar is the *morpheme*. One example of a morpheme in English is the plural, which is formed in a number of different ways, usually by adding /s/ or /z/ or /iz/ to the singular noun (as in bat/bats, pin/pins, church/churches, respectively), but sometimes by changing the vowel (mouse/mice), or in other irregular ways. Languages other than English often have similar grammatical categories, but even languages with a common origin employ important variations (verbs in French have many more tenses, nouns in French always show gender). Some languages have grammatical categories and relationships that are totally distinct from those found in European languages. In each case it is important to locate the individual units of meaning as they occur, as spaces within a system made up of *differences*.

The impact of Saussure's general principles for discussing the structure of a language was felt first in linguistics. For several decades after Saussure's death, linguists and anthropologists trained in linguistics traveled to remote corners of the world, recording and analyzing the principles of hundreds of natural languages. But soon after the development of structural linguistics, the basic principles began to be generalized to other sorts of codes and structures, which could be analyzed in analogous fashion in terms of the combinations and permutations of various "emes," or basic elements. The smallest units or building blocks of stories were termed "mythemes" by Claude Lévi-Strauss; Julia Kristeva has called the irreducible atoms of social thought "ideologemes."

As Roland Barthes said in "The Structuralist Activity" (1964), structuralism is not a set of beliefs, but two complementary practices: analysis and synthesis. The structuralist analyzes the products of human making into their smallest significant component parts, then tries to discover the principles of their articulation — how the parts fit together and function.[2] In this very broad sense, the first structuralist was Aristotle, and the *Poetics* the first work of structuralist literary criticism. It would not be odd to consider formalist critics like R. S. Crane and Northrop Frye as structuralists. But today, the term is usually restricted to those whose practice of analysis and synthesis is performed using the tools, techniques, and terminology of linguistics.

Perhaps the chief human vector for the spread of structuralism was Roman Jakobson, one of the great linguists of the century. In his paper on "Linguistics and Poetics" (translated in 1960), Jakobson presented the following model of the act of communication: A *sender,* having made *contact* with a *receiver,* sends a *message* about some external *context* using a *code*. These six factors — sender, contact, receiver, message, context, and code — define the six functions of communication. Most normal communication is *referential:* It emphasizes the context, the content that is to be conveyed. The *emotive* function of communication emphasizes the

[2]Roland Barthes, "The Structuralist Activity," in *Critical Essays,* trans. Richard Howard (New York: Farrar, Straus and Giroux, 1972).

sender, while the *conative* emphasizes the receiver. The *phatic* function is that of establishing contact, like saying "hello" when we pick up the telephone. The *metalinguistic* function is to investigate the code that sender and receiver are both using to clear up disagreements or ambiguities. Finally, there is the linguistic function that centers on the message qua message. This Jakobson defines as the *poetic* function.

Jakobson began as an ally of the Russian Formalists in the 1920s, migrated to Czechoslovakia, where he joined the Prague Linguistic Circle in the 1930s, and then traveled to New York, where he exerted a wide influence on numerous intellectuals, including the ethnologist Claude Lévi-Strauss. They collaborated on literary essays, including an essay on Baudelaire's sonnet, "The Cats" (1962),[3] but the most important product was Lévi-Strauss's integration of linguistics and myth in his book *Structural Anthropology* (1958), which changed the theory and practice of cultural studies around the world.

MYTH AND LANGUAGE

Claude Lévi-Strauss began his career with a dissertation on *The Elementary Structures of Kinship* (1949), which was a synthesis of the available data on the rules by which a vast number of cultures regulated marriage and kinship ties. Lévi-Strauss's method was to use language-data to verify social rules (for example, if a culture has a word for "mother's brother" that is *also* its word for "father-in-law," this correspondence strongly suggests that a boy is supposed to marry his maternal cross-cousin). In the course of his research, Lévi-Strauss developed a general theory of the way in which the exchange and circulation of women between families is used to knit cultures together.

But in the course of that study he recognized that another aspect of culture is used for exchange and circulation: language. As Lévi-Strauss began to theorize about the homologies between languages and kinship systems, it occurred to him that cultures with complex kinship structures, which gave the individual a small number of marital choices, tended to speak languages with complex syntax and a small lexicon, while cultures (like our own) with simple kinship structures, which give the individual a vast number of marital choices, tended to speak languages with simple syntax and a large lexicon.[4] We can see here a key feature of Lévi-Strauss's method: to try to construct revealing analogies between very different aspects of life and society by seeing each as a structural system of symbols. While the surface structure of the symbols might be very different, the way in which they are combined (syntaxis) might point to a similar deep structure.

Given this interest, Lévi-Strauss was attracted to the study of the richest source of symbols in anthropology: mythology. His four volumes of *Mythologiques* (*The Raw and the Cooked* [1964]; *From Honey to Ashes* [1967]; *The Origin of Table Manners* [1968]; and *L'Homme Nu* [1971]) present an elaborate survey of world

[3]Roman Jakobson and Claude Lévi-Strauss, "Charles Baudelaire's 'The Cats' " (1962), in *Structuralism: A Reader,* ed. Michael Lane (London: Jonathan Cape, 1970).

[4]Claude Lévi-Strauss, "Language and the Analysis of Social Laws" (1951), in *Structural Anthropology* (New York: Basic Books, 1963), pp. 62–63.

myths to illustrate his basic thesis about mythic thinking: That myths are the way the "savage mind" — not the minds of savages, but the untamed mind within all of us — gives order to the world.

"The Structural Study of Myth" (1955), reprinted in part here, presents Lévi-Strauss's method in its purest form, as a way of reconstructing the *langue* of myth by the analysis of a particular *parole*. His analysis of the Oedipus myth demonstrates how he breaks down the chronological structure of the story in order to isolate the various elements (or *mythemes*) operating within the text. He next attempts to understand the relation between the mythemes as members of paradigm classes separated from one another by the way they embody concrete differences. He then finds a way of generalizing the concrete issues of the story as a system of abstract binary terms. Finally, he interprets the interaction of the mythemes as giving order and structure to a significant spiritual conflict. In the case of Oedipus, the myth mediates between conflicting theories: that humanity is born out of the earth (autochthonous) or of the sexual union between man and woman.[5] Lévi-Strauss's point is that as long as the spiritual conflict continues (and if it is a genuine conflict, it can never be fully resolved), the myth will continue to be told, elaborated, varied, and retold in other forms that — structurally, at least — address the same issue.

STRUCTURALIST POETICS

One of the central texts of high structuralism in its most confident phase was the collaborative essay of Roman Jakobson and Lévi-Strauss on Baudelaire's sonnet, "The Cats." Their elaborate analysis of the geometrical symmetry of the grammatical structures within the sonnet showed what structuralism could do. But their conclusion — that the cats symbolize love cleansed of feminine impurity and knowledge cleansed of the sages' austerity — has, despite the seemingly scientific method, not won universal assent. As Michael Riffaterre has said, "the poem has been rebuilt by the two critics into a 'superpoem' inaccessible to the normal reader, and yet the structures described do not explain what establishes contact between poetry and reader. No grammatical analysis of a poem can give us more than the grammar of the poem."[6]

The difficulty is not with grammatical analysis as such (in fact, Riffaterre presents his own grammatical analysis of "Les Chats"). Stylistics, the linguistic analysis of literary effects, is a venerable and useful tool of criticism, but most linguists would begin with an impression of the poem's effect and then seek something in the syntax that might have caused that effect.[7] The problem arises from the hypothesis that, by checking successively into every symmetry of every grammatical category, the critic will stumble onto the secret of the poem. As Jonathan Culler attempted to

[5]Two further examples of the interpretation of myth, dealing with relatively unfamiliar American Indian tales, have been omitted.

[6]Michael Riffaterre, "Describing Poetic Structures: Two Approaches to Baudelaire's *Les Chats*," in *Structuralism*, ed. Jacques Ehrmann (New York: Doubleday, 1970), pp. 201–02.

[7]As for example in David Richter, "Two Studies in Iconic Syntax: Alfred Lord Tennyson's 'Tears, Idle Tears' and William Carlos Williams's 'The Dance.'" *Language and Style* 18 (1985): 136–51.

show in the first half of *Structuralist Poetics* (1975), this hypothesis simply doesn't work: Structural analysis is not an effective discovery procedure. Or rather, it is too effective. Culler demonstrates that the elaborate syntactic symmetries that Jakobson and Lévi-Strauss found in the four strophes of "The Cats" can also be found in the first four prosy sentences of Jakobson's own "Postscriptum" to *Questions de poétique*.

As Culler suggests in the selection reprinted here, structuralist principles would be more fruitfully applied to literature, not in the search for new interpretations of texts or as an algorithm for generating interpretations, but in investigating how literary interpretation takes place. The title of Culler's chapter, "Literary Competence," is derived from Noam Chomsky's notion of linguistic competence — the ability of native speakers to create and understand sentences they have never heard before. In effect, Culler argues, structuralists should return to Saussure's original goal of understanding the rules of literary *langue* rather than investigate individual performances.[8]

In a long and useful pair of chapters, Culler goes on to discuss the poetics of the lyric poem in terms of the conventions through which we interpret its form and meaning and the operations we perform on the text in order to "naturalize" its language. (In effect, he suggests that to read a poem we have to *undo* the poet's defamiliarization of the material.) After giving a reading of a minimalist one-line poem by Apollinaire, Culler presents the universal principles underlying his performance:

> Such an interpretation depends upon three general conventions — that a poem should be unified, that it should be thematically significant, and that this significance can take the form of reflection on poetry — and four general interpretive operations: that one should try to establish binary relations of opposition or equivalence, that one should look for and integrate puns and ambiguities, that items may be read as synecdoches (or metaphors, etc.) in order to attain the level of generality required, and that what a poem says can be related to the fact that it is a poem.[9]

Culler's discussion of the poetics of fiction is less successful, partly because only a small fraction of novels depend for their effect, to the extent that modernist lyric poems do, upon peculiarities of language and thus upon the conventions and naturalization operations through which we read them. The lyric is typically a short and difficult utterance, but in scope it is often scarcely longer than a single speech by a character in a fictional work. The difficulty in analyzing fiction comes instead from the immense number of levels of plot, character, theme, and narrative structure that

[8]Culler's idea of literary competence is not precisely equivalent to Chomsky's notion of linguistic competence. Chomsky's notion of competence is constant throughout very different natural languages, and he has claimed that certain analytic and synthetic capacities are linguistic universals. Culler's notion of competence is restricted to a description of interpretive conventions in Western Europe and America during the late twentieth century. One of his notions, seemingly incontrovertible when the book appeared — that poems will be interpreted to maximize their unity — no longer seems so solid in the poststructuralist age.

[9]Jonathan Culler, "Poetics of the Lyric," in *Structuralist Poetics* (Ithaca: Cornell University Press, 1975), p. 177.

have to be integrated by the reader. Instead of presenting his own poetics of the novel, Culler presents elements from a variety of theories, including those of Northrop Frye, Tzvetan Todorov, and Roland Barthes.

THE POETICS OF FICTION: ECO AND GENETTE

When Culler wrote *Structuralist Poetics,* very little of the work of Umberto Eco had been translated from Italian; *The Role of the Reader* did not appear until 1979, although its constituent essays had been printed in various periodicals as early as 1962. The essay reprinted here, "The Myth of Superman" from *The Role of the Reader,* is typical in its combination of wit and intellectual rigor and in its immense range of reference, from revered texts like *Oedipus Rex* and *Finnegans Wake* to ephemera like Superman comics, Nero Wolfe detective stories, and the "Doctor Kildare" television series. Eco's essay takes up only one very limited question within narrative poetics: the way narrative time needs to be handled in fiction that belongs to a series, which must therefore be designed to have an indefinite number of sequels. It has been included as an example of what can be done practically, using a structuralist poetics of narrative. But *The Role of the Reader* as a whole has a much broader program: to understand the levels of discourse that occur within narratives (Eco's complex diagram lists ten such levels) and the interactions among them that give rise to interpretation. The result will be to reveal how each text produces the exact sort of Model Reader it needs to bring out its qualities — how "closed" texts elicit passively credulous and "open" texts actively suspicious readings.[10]

Perhaps the most influential theorist of narrative is Gérard Genette, whose trilogy *Figures* contains a series of arrestingly original and interconnected essays on the art of both fiction and poetry. As the overall title of the three volumes suggests, Genette's interest is in tropes, figures of speech; but he is far from being a naive grammarian, interested only in classifying and regulating the use of tropes. Figures of speech are important because they introduce into the usual system of signification a discontinuity requiring the reader's mediation. When we refer to "twenty sail of the line" instead of "twenty ships" we use the figure of *synecdoche* — the part for the whole. As we interpret the figure, we note the presence of one signifier (sail) and the absence of another (ship). Thus, the working of the figure depends on something it cannot contain: the reader's sense of the absent signifier. Or, as Genette put it, "A figure is a gap in relation to usage, but a gap that is nevertheless a part of usage: that is the paradox of rhetoric."

In "Frontiers of Narrative" Genette goes over some of the commonplace distinctions of narratology, such as the *diegetic* and the *mimetic,* or narration and description, always with a view toward shaking up the conventional distinctions and making the reader see the issues anew. In addition, Genette examines the distinctions between narrative (which presumes the existence of a narrator, a speaker, and

[10]These are not exhaustive categories. Eco finds a third sort of text, "an exclusive club whose chairman is probably *Tristam Shandy,*" which is neither open nor closed but operates as a trap. It lures the reader into "an excess of cooperation and then punishes him for having overdone it."

hence a point of view), and pure discourse (which has no speaker and seems to come from no subjective source). Stylisticians, like Émile Benveniste, had suggested that the distinction between narrative and discourse was essentially grammatical, that narrative could be defined in terms of certain words or usages — the first- and second-person pronouns, or adverbs like "here" or "then," which presuppose a spatial or temporal reference. Genette demonstrates to the contrary that the matter is far subtler and more complex and that apparently pure discourse often contains implicit appeals and judgments that make sense only in the context of a narrative. With both poetic figures and narrative techniques, Genette's version of the reader's necessary participation in the literary process links him, as it links the semiotician Umberto Eco, with the reader-response theorists in Chapter 3.

THE PASSING OF STRUCTURALISM

Structuralism had slowly grown in influence from just after World War II until the middle of the 1960s, spreading from the anthropological studies of Lévi-Strauss to affect the study of literature, philosophy, history, mathematics, politics, economics — all the human sciences. There was a palpable sense at the time that a new method for the synthesis of knowledge was at hand, a method more powerful than the synthesis provided by Platonic dialectic in the ancient world or by Thomistic logic in the Middle Ages. The notion, barely glimpsed, that by using the tools of semiotics and linguistics, structuralism might manage to reunite the branches of knowledge that post-Renaissance specialization had severed, gave its adherents a messianic sense of mission. But in the late 1960s, as radical politics came and went leaving disillusion in its wake, the confident, broadly humanistic, universalizing mission of structuralism foundered as well.

The primary problem was the irresponsible promise of a synthesis of all human knowledge, a promise that was slow in bearing fruit. Many adherents expounded the principles of structuralism and made claims for what structuralism would surely do for the study of literature, but few produced concrete achievements that justified those claims. The claims may in fact have been implausible. One question we have already raised is whether the enabling assumption of structuralism — that everything is a language — is adequate. As James Phelan has suggested, literature is a *second-order* sign system built upon the *first-order* sign system of language. In effect, structuralism stands or falls on its assumption that a second-order system must reproduce the categories and relations of the first-order system. But we have no evidence that this must be the case, and natural science suggests the contrary: Biology, built on biochemistry, does not imitate its organization; nor does chemistry, built on molecular physics, reproduce its lower-order system.

Structuralism may also have lost momentum because it had shifted the focus of the study of literature from the exegesis of individual texts to the exploration of general conditions of the act of interpretation. Ironically, deconstruction, despite its implicit attack on the traditional values and bases of humanistic study, proceeds according to the techniques of close reading in which literary critics throughout the English-speaking world had already been trained under the dominance of New

Criticism. In some ways, therefore, it was easier for American academics to follow deconstructionists such as Jacques Derrida and Paul de Man than to carry on the quest of Jakobson, Genette, and Eco.

But of course, in another sense, structuralism is not dead at all. Though it has had to relinquish its broadest assumptions together with its character as a world-historical movement, most of its original adherents — like Todorov and Eco, Genette and Riffaterre — have continued to pursue the study of systems of signs, and the results of their study have become, under the names semiotics, stylistics, and narratology, essential elements in the current battery of approaches to literature.

DERRIDA AND DECONSTRUCTION

One of the difficulties in reading Derrida is that there is no central document, no single, classic essay, like Sidney's *Apology for Poetry* or Kant's *Critique of Judgment,* that contains and expresses a body of systematic thought. In this, he is like some earlier philosophers, such as Hegel and Nietzsche, for whom no selection can give a sense of the whole. But what is unique to Derrida is that, while his rhetoric circles around the same themes, his terminology changes from essay to essay. (Even his principal term, "deconstruction," is not fully stable. At one point, Derrida wanted to replace it with "de-sedimentation," though that word never quite caught on.) This fluidity is entirely by design. Given his program, Derrida has tried to resist anything that would lead to setting up deconstruction as a *system of thought*.

Although it is risky to state that Derrida has a central issue, we can begin with his notion that all thought is necessarily inscribed in language, and that language itself is fraught with intractable paradoxes. We can repress or ignore these paradoxes, but we cannot escape from them or solve them. This is the burden of Derrida's most difficult work, *Of Grammatology*.

Derrida's basic concern is with how Western philosophy has built its metaphysics on a pervasive but fragile base, one that privileges the activity of *speech* over that of *writing*. Speech is opposed to writing and held to be logically prior as well as chronologically older. The valorization of speech begins in Plato's *Phaedrus,* in which Socrates condemns writing as a bastardized form of communication, separated from the Father (the moment of origin). Writing can easily mislead because the speaker is no longer there to explain what he had in mind. Socrates prefers speech because the speaker seems so immediately present in the voice. Meaning enters into sound, and sound as a real presence enters the listener and becomes meaning once more.

Derrida traces this position from Plato down through the centuries to philosophers such as Edmund Husserl and Martin Heidegger. Here we can discuss one classic example, that of the founder of structuralism. Ferdinand de Saussure treats writing as a means of representing speech; it remains an external accessory, however, a supplement that need not be fully taken into account in any philosophy of language. In fact, Saussure feels that writing is in a sense dangerous because it "disguises" language and "usurps" the role of speech (writing corrupts speech at times, as when people mispronounce words because of the way they are spelled). For all these reasons, writing is a *dangerous* supplement, which threatens the integrity of speech. The notion of the "dangerous supplement" is important to Derrida, for the very idea of a supplement challenges and calls into question the dichotomies and hierarchies on which philosophies are built. Like the appendix to a book, a supplement is part of and not part of the text at the same time: It seems to be adding something to what is already complete in itself, and the addition is thus implicitly a correction, even in a sense a recantation.

In Derrida's analysis of the writings of Jean-Jacques Rousseau, for example, he calls attention to Rousseau's characterization of education as a supplement to nature. As a supplement, education adds to something that is already supposedly complete in itself; at the same time, if education adds to nature, then nature must be somehow incomplete — at least to the extent that one must be educated to know what is natural and what is not. Nature is the prior term, a presence that is there at the start. Yet the "supplement" of education reveals an inherent absence or lack within nature — and also an essential condition of its being.

At another point in the *Confessions,* Rousseau himself speaks of masturbation as a "dangerous supplement" to coital sexuality: a perverse addiction that can substitute for and take the place of heterosexual intercourse. But paradoxically, the fact that masturbation can act as a supplement shows that it shares in the nature of sexuality. Furthermore, what characterizes masturbation — the focus on an imagined sexual object, the impossibility of genuinely possessing what one desires — also characterizes heterosexual intercourse. One could thus turn the dichotomy upside down and claim that heterosexual intercourse is a more generalized version of masturbation.

To generalize Derrida's method from the last example: a dominant entity is defined by a form of presence (heterosexual intercourse) next to its supplement (masturbation), which is defined by a corresponding absence as inferior and marginal. But the distinguishing qualities of the marginal entity are in fact the defining qualities of the dominant. The result is that the rigid hierarchy of the dichotomy dissolves: As we consider the matter, it is no longer clear which is dominant and which marginal.

To come back now to where we began, with Derrida's analysis of the dichotomy of speech and writing, we valorize speech over writing because there, signifier and signified, sound and meaning, seem to be given together, fused for the moment. Form and meaning are simultaneously present. Voice appears as the direct manifestation of thought. In contrast, written words lack this presence; they are physical marks a reader must interpret and animate to supply meanings that do not seem to be *given*.

But in fact, the kind of absence that distinguishes writing from speech is the very condition of the existence of signs in the first place. As we showed above, the structural model of language presupposes absence in the sense that it is an elaborate system of presences and absences that allows signifiers to operate. The letter or phoneme /t/ exists only as part of a system of differences that distinguish it from /d/ or /f/ or any of the other letters or phonemes. The phoneme /t/ differs from /d/ by the quality of voicing (vibration of the vocal cords), which is absent in the former and present in the latter. But /t/ is not a defective /d/; there is only a relational meaning here, not a real presence.

Furthermore, for a token to be a sign, it must be iterable — repeatable. We learn the meaning of a sign by hearing the same sound in similar contexts. The difference between a sign and a mere noise is that one cannot repeat the latter (even if one clap of thunder were exactly like another, it would make no difference). In the case of a language-sign, one must be able to repeat it back, to quote it; but to quote a sign is to produce it as an example, to reproduce it in the absence of the original communicative intention. For a signifier to have value as a sign, therefore, it must be possible to counterfeit it, and when a sign is counterfeited or cited or produced as an example, it is without its original meaning. But this is *always* possible for *any* sign. Therefore the notion that a sign depends upon the presence conferred by voice cannot be maintained, and we cannot hold that speech is logically prior to writing. (Derrida is not denying, of course, that speech preceded writing historically.)

If speech is not prior to writing, then it does not make sense to treat writing as an auxiliary form of speech; indeed, Derrida suggests, we should treat speech as a form of writing — and refer both to an *arché-écriture* (from the Greek and French: "original-writing"). Rather than achieving meaning through the presence of voice, language strives toward meaning through the play of signifiers. This play occurs through the mechanism of what Derrida calls *différance* (a coinage that blends the French words for "difference" and "deferral"). A word, a letter, or a sound is known not through what it is but through its differences relative to other possibilities — the other possibilities that are not present but absent, existing only through the transient traces they leave on memory. Ultimate meaning, genuine presence, is always deferred — just as looking one word up in a dictionary leads to another and so on indefinitely. Between signifier and signified, therefore, there is not the rigid relation of container and contained. Rather, there is always "freeplay" (*jeu*), which suggests that language can never be pinned down to meaning, that it is always already indeterminate.

It is hard to overestimate the furor Derrida's theory of language provoked. He was not merely saying, like the New Critic William Empson, that poetry depends on seven types of ambiguity. He was claiming in effect that everything in the human sciences — history, political philosophy, psychology, and so on — was a species of poetry, invariably based on a terminology that was necessarily as indeterminate as the language in which it was written. But the real target of his notion of language was the structuralist attempt to synthesize all humanistic knowledge by using the tools of linguistics, for if there was freeplay in the signifier-signified relationship, there was no guarantee of even making sense. In the 1920s, the German mathematician Kurt Gödel put an end to the massive Russell-Whitehead project for systematizing mathematics by proving conclusively that any mathematical system complicated enough to be useful had either to contain contradictions or to be incomplete. Derrida's *Grammatology* was in effect Gödel's *proof* for the human sciences in the late 1960s. It split the structuralist community down the middle, and even thirty years later, the debate continues between those who accept and those who dispute the validity and the motivation of the deconstructive turn.

But there is more at stake than the apparently abstract question of whether or not there is freeplay between the signifier and the signified. For, in its most general sense, the activity of deconstruction involves the skeptical re-examination, not just of speech and writing, but of *all* the dialectical polarities that have formed the basis of Western culture, a re-examination searching for the point of privilege upon which standard hierarchies rest. We are used to arguing about various other presences and absences: art vs. genius, culture vs. nature, transcendence vs. immanence, soul vs. body, divine vs. human, human vs. animal, man vs. woman, being vs. becoming, and so on. In each case, the first term denotes the presence and the second the absence of something. Derrida uses the paradoxes involved in the logic of "supplements" in an effort to decenter the first term of each pair, to remove it from its privileged position relative to the second. Against the dominant metaphysics of presence, Derrida sets the countermetaphysics of absence. To the extent that these polarities are at the heart of Western culture, deconstruction attempts to expose the illusions upon which authority in Western culture is established. Where the conservative W. B. Yeats complained that "Things fall apart. The center cannot hold," the anarchistic Derrida calls into question the very concept of a center. This is the argument of Derrida's most famous single essay, "Structure, Sign, and Play in the Discourse of the Human Sciences," reprinted here.

Invited to a conference on structuralism in 1966, Derrida proceeded to question the "whole history of the concept of structure" as the activity of naming and renaming in a succession of metaphors the center of the totality of existence: "the history of metaphysics, like the history of the West, is the history of these metaphors." Derrida then proceeded to deconstruct the concept of the center, beginning with the geometrical paradox that the center *defines* the circle but is not part of the line that *is* the circle. This center is, in effect, a transcendental point of absolute presence. So long as we can believe in a transcendental signified — a point of absolute meaning outside and above the world of discourse that gives significance to the whole — the center holds. But once we cease to have God and have only god-terms, once we accept that everything is a text and falls within the framework of discourse, then the very notion of a center must be challenged. And that, says Derrida, is where we currently stand: after the critiques of metaphysics by Nietzsche and Heidegger, after the critique of consciousness by Freud, the fundamental notions of being, truth, and self cannot be naively "centered" as they have been by the major philosophers from Plato through Hegel.

This brings Derrida to structuralism and its attempts to find a center through the science of signs. Most of "Structure, Sign, and Play" is devoted to a deconstruction of the opposition between nature and culture in the work of the founder of structuralism, Claude Lévi-Strauss. One must work out for oneself the chain of paradoxes, one within another, that Derrida finds in Lévi-Strauss's project in *Mythologiques* — for instance, that it is an empirical study that nevertheless rejects the principle of empiricism. Derrida concludes by exposing the ambivalence, the duality of Lévi-Strauss's attitudes. On the one hand, Lévi-Strauss accepts the presence of freeplay within the structure of myths and embraces the notion that mythography is itself a sort of mythical thinking; on the other hand, there is Lévi-Strauss's "ethic of presence, an ethic of nostalgia for origins, an ethic of archaic and natural innocence, of a purity of presence and self-presence in speech." Lévi-Strauss, and thus the structuralist activity in general, seems to be caught halfway between the old metaphysics, which "dreams of deciphering a truth or an origin," and the new revolutionary philosophy, like his own, that "tries to pass beyond man and humanism."

In his conclusion to "Structure, Sign, and Play," Derrida seems to be disclosing his attitudes toward the great precursors. In particular, he seems to be defining himself in opposition to Hegel and as a disciple of Nietzsche. Derrida circumvents Hegel's historical, progressive uses of dialectic; his oppositions always stay open, undecidable, untranscended. And like Nietzsche's philosophy, Derrida's attitudes toward political and social issues seem to be based on aesthetics rather than ethics; he revels in the sense of intellectual crisis and welcomes the coming transvaluation of all values.[11]

But what is more significant, Derrida's ironic gibe at "the nostalgia for the origin" is a slap directed at the existentialist philosopher Martin Heidegger, who influenced him deeply and against whom he reacted equally intensely. Although Heidegger, like Derrida, was an opponent of metaphysics, he did not go far enough for his disciple. As Christopher Norris has put it, Derrida questioned "Heidegger's own metaphysical motives, his quest for a grounding philosophy which would point the way back toward primordial Being. This nostalgic attachment to a lost or forgotten origin is, according to Derrida, the hallmark of all metaphysics."[12] Metaphysics, the abstract bugbear of twentieth-century philosophers from Wittgenstein onward, is like the "tar-baby" of the Uncle Remus stories: In combatting it one inevitably gets involved in it. As Derrida states in "Structure, Sign, and Play," "*there is no sense* in doing without the concepts of metaphysics in order to attack metaphysics. We . . . cannot utter a single destructive proposition which has not already slipped into the form, the logic, and the implicit postulations of precisely what it seeks to contest." Derrida's strategy is to disrupt systematic thought, to wage a guerrilla campaign against it in constantly shifting terms, to stay on the margins of philosophy and avoid its central castle. "The passage beyond philosophy does not consist in turning the page of philosophy . . . but in continuing to read philosophers *in a certain way*."

BARTHES AND FOUCAULT

As Derrida's message began its guerrilla war on the ends and assumptions of structuralism, a number of structuralism's leading figures became converts, including Roland Barthes, whose shifting aims and ideas are instructive. Barthes's interest, since his 1953 essay "Writing Degree Zero," has been in the immense tacit knowledge the reader must possess, over and above the syntax and basic semantics of a

[11]See the introductions to Hegel (p. 357), Nietzsche (p. 417), and Heidegger (p. 560).
[12]Christopher Norris, *The Deconstructive Turn* (London: Methuen, 1983), p. 24.

given language, to understand and interpret cultural systems of symbols. Barthes worked in *Mythologies* to demystify the complex languages spoken in wrestling matches, advertisements, and other maps of popular culture. The apex of this structuralist project appeared in the 1966 essay, "Introduction to the Structural Analysis of Narratives," a densely written attempt to do complete justice to the *langue* of fiction. Though he is normally a supple and witty stylist, Barthes's tone here was dry and abstract, as though he were somewhat daunted by the complex task of analyzing into their separate components the elements (the *emes*) in the interpretation of narrative, and he characterized his essay, which was based on the previous work of Vladimir Propp, Claude Bremond, A. J. Greimas, and Tzvetan Todorov, as a "tentative effort" rather than a triumphant success.

In *S/Z* (1970), Barthes simplified and reduced these multiple integrative dimensions into a skein of five *codes,* to which the individual bits of text (*lexies*) each make their contribution. Barthes distinguished a *hermeneutic* code of enigmas and their solutions; a *semic* code of characteristics that go into the description of characters and places; a *proairetic* code of actions; a *symbolic* code of themes; and a *referential* code comprising the historical and cultural allusions within the text. The elaborate result was a 220-page commentary on "Sarrasine" (a minor story by Balzac) that — since it remained on the levels of "functions" and "actions" and was incomplete even there — was clearly only a mere sketch toward a full interpretation. *S/Z* was simultaneously the masterpiece and the reductio ad absurdum of Barthes's holistic approach to fiction, because it made clear that any genuinely complete analysis of a fictional text would be so long and complex as to be nearly unreadable. It was widely admired but never imitated, even by Barthes himself.

By the next year, Barthes had produced "From Work to Text," an account of the difference in the way the object of literary study is perceived by formal and structural criticism on the one hand, and by poststructural criticism on the other. The essay is short, terse, informal, almost a set of jottings, but Barthes manages to characterize the stance of the deconstructive critic with lucidity and accuracy. Perhaps the most influential section of "From Work to Text" is the last, in which Barthes contrasts the emotional involvement of the reader before and after the deconstructive turn. The older, passive way of reading produced *plaisir* (pleasure), the consumer's enjoyment in being immersed in another's vision, actions, characters. The new way produces what Barthes terms *jouissance,* a nearly untranslatable word ("bliss" is the usual equivalent) that suggests both the joy and the sense of loss experienced in the sexual climax. Here and in later, more elaborate treatments of the phenomenology of reading, such as *The Pleasure of the Text,* Barthes's central contribution to Derrida's project was in clarifying its emotional as well as its intellectual appeal.

Whereas Barthes was a structuralist turned poststructuralist, Michel Foucault had never accepted the linguistic basis of structuralism. He had instead an independent poststructuralist framework of thought that is presented at greater length later in this book (see the introduction to New Historicism and Cultural Studies, p. 1204, and the introduction to Gender Studies and Queer Theory, p. 1431). Nevertheless, some of his influential essays contributed to the rejection of the structuralist model we have been exploring, and as an analyst of philosophical discourse he was as radical as Derrida. Like Derrida, Foucault was a disciple of the later Nietzsche and saw the will-to-power as dominant over any search for truth — as defining, in fact, the meaning and location of truth. As he puts it in his essay "Truth and Power":

> Truth isn't outside power, or lacking in power: contrary to a myth whose history and functions would repay further study, truth isn't the reward of free spirits, the child of protracted solitude, nor the privilege of those who have succeeded in liberating themselves. Truth is a thing of this world: it is produced only by virtue of multiple forms of constraint. And it induces regular effects of power. Each society has its regime of truth, its "general politics" of truth: that is, the types of discourse which it accepts and makes function as true; the mechanisms and instances which enable one to distinguish true and false statements, the means by which each is sanctioned; the techniques and procedures accorded value in the acquisition of truth, the status of those who are charged with saying what is true.[13]

Today, Foucault goes on, the general politics confers truth on the form of scientific discourse; statements are true if and only if they have been the object of well-financed studies, and capitalism not only creates the studies but devotes other massive institutions (education, the media, and so on) to the diffusion and consumption of this form of truth. But though this might be true today, Foucault, like Derrida, became convinced that Western civilization was moving toward a new moment of crisis, a change in the dominant *epistemé* (as Foucault called the historical modes of power/knowledge). His work is marked by an apocalyptic sense that it is in our interest — and our duty — to prepare the way for a new power and truth.

We can find some of these strains within Foucault's thought in his essay "What Is an Author?" included here. Foucault concentrates on the humanistic version of truth-power: authorship seen as a form of author-ity. Despite the apparent collapse of the Romantic conception of the author as incomprehensible genius and the advent of formalism and structuralism, which have successively substituted the central terms of *work* and of *écriture* (writing) for the romantic god-term of *author*, Foucault claims that authorship still remains its old power within advanced capitalism. While the author has been declared dead by some literary theorists, the author-function remains, "a certain functional principle by which, in our culture, one limits, excludes, and chooses; in short, by which one impedes the free circulation, the free manipulation, the free composition, decomposition, and recomposition of fiction. . . . The author is therefore the ideological figure by which one marks the manner in which we fear the proliferation of meaning." As long as literature belongs to the author, it cannot be truly ours. But Foucault looks forward to a moment of change in society when the "author-function will disappear." Foucault has no faith,

[13]Michel Foucault, "Truth and Power," in *The Foucault Reader*, ed. Paul Rabinow (New York: Pantheon Books, 1984), pp. 72–73.

however, that as author-ity fades, literature will belong to "us." He pessimistically foresees that it will instead be replaced by a new "system of constraint" yet to be understood or experienced. The old order changes, giving way to the new, but for Foucault, order is always a synonym for the prisons and asylums through which society controls thought. For Foucault, only a total breakdown of society could liberate us from the order of discourse.

DECONSTRUCTION AND CRITICISM

Like the structuralism it questions and attempts to supplant, deconstruction is not solely, or even primarily, a mode of literary criticism. As Derrida says in "Structure, Sign, and Play," he only wants "to read philosophers *in a certain way*." Indeed, deconstructionists like Rodolphe Gasché have suggested that the application of Derrida's methods to literary texts in search of new interpretations is paradoxical, almost perverse, since Derrida's revolutionary contribution was to treat philosophical texts as if they were bound by the same sorts of linguistic ambiguity and fluidity that had long been thought to characterize literature. (In effect Derrida constitutes the ultimate vindication of poetry against Plato's attack. For Derrida it is the poets, celebrating the freeplay of the signifier, who have had the right notion of language, and the philosophers, aiming for precision of terminology, who have been pursuing a will o' the wisp.)

Nevertheless, Derrida has had more impact in departments of English and French than in philosophy, as deconstruction has been applied less to Ayer or Sartre than to Yeats and Proust. To a large extent, the deconstruction of literature was made possible by the previous triumph of the New Criticism, which treated poetry as an especially complex mode of discourse, essentially dependent on tropes like irony or ambiguity, that led to the evocation of a set of propositions or attitudes toward the real world. If the ultimate purpose of poetry was to say something — in however complicated a form — then, like traditional philosophy and the other humane sciences, it was a discourse that sought "a truth and an origin." As such, it could also read "*in a certain way*." Furthermore, scholars trained in the New Criticism could easily adapt their methods to deconstruction; if once they sought paradox and ambiguity in pursuit of the meaning of texts, they could now seek it in the pursuit of the posited void at the center of meaning. In effect, the move from New Criticism to deconstruction principally involved abandoning the search for the balance and resolution that critics like Cleanth Brooks had sought behind the paradoxes and ambiguities of the text.

In America in the 1970s, the prime locus for this new mode of reading was Yale University, which had also become a haven for many of the New Critics in their last years. Professors Harold Bloom, Geoffrey Hartman, and J. Hillis Miller of the Yale English Department and the late Paul de Man of the Department of French and Comparative Literature became known collectively as the "Gang of Four," in ironic token of the radicalism of their readings and their coherence as a group. With the death of de Man in 1983 and the departure of Miller for California a few years later, the group broke up, but not before it had succeeded in bringing deconstruction to America.

Actually, Bloom (see Ch. 4, Psychoanalytic Theory) was never really a philosophically orthodox deconstructionist, though his notion that all reading was in fact creative misreading was not inconsistent with the Derridean notion of freeplay. With respect to the other three, it seems clear that the intellectual center and prime mover was de Man, whose "Semiology and Rhetoric" is reprinted here.

This essay is not only a defense of deconstruction but a brief and telling demonstration of its powers applied to three short texts, ranging from a trivial joke from the television comedy "All in the Family" to a moving passage from Proust's *Remembrance of Things Past.* The central argument of de Man's essay — that meaning is not a dependable function of syntax — challenges a form of structuralism that had long ceased to be current, but de Man's conclusion — that one does not deconstruct *texts* so much as show the means by which they deconstruct *themselves* — is crucially important. Or to use a metaphor derived from Roland Barthes, the deconstructionist finds the thread dangling from the sweater, pulls on it, and watches as the fabric of the garment unravels into the pile of yarn from which it was made.

If every text can be said to contain its own deconstruction, de Man's essay supplies most of the methods employed in the deconstructive act. What we find most often is not an overt contradiction within a single level of the structure of the text — a paradox of the sort Cleanth Brooks would have appreciated — but a demonstration of the inconsistency between a text's grammar and its rhetoric, between its message and its activity, between what a text means and the way it goes about meaning it. Thus de Man shows how Proust's passage evoking the power of metaphor operates less in terms of metaphor (substitution) than in terms of metonymy (association).

As a mode of literary criticism, deconstruction became extremely influential in the late 1970s and early 1980s, when a second generation of theorist-critics, disciples of de Man and Derrida, such as Barbara Johnson, Cynthia Chase, Timothy Bahti, and Carol Jacobs, produced their most influential work, rereading important texts by Herman Melville, George Eliot, William Wordsworth, and so on. Despite the inventiveness of these readings, it became clear that regardless of the text analyzed, the usual end product of deconstructive criticism was *aporia:* the intellectual vertigo caused by looking into an apparently endless hall of mirrors. This is an effect that, unfortunately, palls on repetition. Many scholars, initially struck by the power of deconstruction, found that, no matter how inventive the path, each venture led invariably to the same vista. Deconstruction nevertheless continued to be one of the most attractive modes of literary theory in the years following de Man's death from cancer in 1983.

But beginning in the summer of 1987, the news broke slowly over the literary world that Ortwin de Graef, a Belgian graduate student writing a thesis on de Man, had discovered over 100 articles by the critic published between 1940 and 1942 in Belgian newspapers sympathetic to the Nazi occupation, including essays espousing anti-Semitic and pro-Nazi sentiments. Even de Man's closest friends at Yale were clearly astonished to hear of this element from his past. De Man had not only kept silent about this episode but had actively misled acquaintances about where and how he had spent the wartime years. It was clear that de Man's posthumous reputation would be tarnished by his wartime collaboration, but it was not de Man's reputation alone that was at stake, but that of the theories of deconstruction with which he was indelibly associated.

When deconstruction began in France in the late 1960s, it had been associated with the leftist critical journal *Tel Quel,* and the politics of its founder, Jacques Derrida, which insofar as they were intelligible also leaned to the Left. But in the intense rivalry that developed in the 1970s between deconstruction and Marxist or New Historicist criticism, deconstruction was painted into the political right wing as a movement whose obsession with textuality blinded it to the significance of lived experience and historical change. American practitioners of deconstruction, in particular, feared that not only Marxists but liberals who (like the structuralist Tzvetan Todorov) had found de Man's theories antihumanistic might seek to find all deconstructionists guilty by association.

As journalists raked the scandal amid the atmosphere of a witch hunt, former students of de Man's, like Chase, colleagues like Hartman and Miller, and even Derrida himself, wrote elaborate and tormented defenses of de Man and, implicitly, of themselves. This still unresolved controversy, a Dreyfus case in reverse, is fraught with paradoxes of the sort de Man himself would have approved: that many of de Man's defenders are Jews (including Derrida himself); that the focus of the scandal has been dead for over a decade; and that de Man's offenses around 1942 predated his adoption of deconstruction by over 25 years. It is difficult to make out any strong connection between de Man's collaboration with Nazi sympathizers and his literary theories, but if there is one it is most likely to be negative. De Man's deconstructionist theories seem a more rigorous extension of his attacks in the 1950s on "salvational poetics" — of which Nazi cultural imperialism would be one crude version. If this is so, then de Man's life as a critic and theorist might be viewed as a long atonement for his juvenile sins.

The fate of deconstruction after the de Man scandal has been somewhat similar to the fall of structuralism: While its messianic atmosphere has dissipated, its utility has persisted. The primary use of deconstruction today is as a tool for breaking down binarisms and problematizing fields of discourse with seemingly fixed categories. Gender theorists such as Judith Butler and Lee Edelman (see Ch. 8, Gender Studies and Queer Theory) for example, value the deconstructive turn as a way of overturning essentialist views on sexual orientation and identity. As a tool of analysis and discursive rhetoric, deconstruction, like semiotics, is very much alive.

Selected Bibliography

Abrams, M. H. "The Deconstructive Angel." *Critical Inquiry* 3 (1977), 425–38.

Arac, Jonathan, Wlad Godzich, and Wallace Martin, eds. *The Yale Critics: Deconstruction in America.* Minneapolis: University of Minnesota Press, 1983.

Atkins, G. Douglas. "The Sign as a Structure of Difference: Derridean Deconstruction and Some of Its Implications." In *Semiotic Themes,* ed. Richard de George. Lawrence: University of Kansas, 1981, pp. 133–47.

Bal, Mieke. *Narratology*. Paris: Klincksieck, 1977.

Barthes, Roland. *Writing Degree Zero*. 1953; New York: Beacon, 1970.

———. *Critical Essays*. 1964; Evanston: Northwestern University Press, 1970.

———. *Mythologies*. 1957; New York: Hill and Wang, 1972.

———. *S/Z*. 1970; New York: Hill and Wang, 1974.

———. *The Pleasure of the Text*. New York: Hill and Wang, 1975.

———. *Sade, Fourier, Loyola*. New York: Hill and Wang, 1976.

———. *Image, Music, Text*. New York: Hill and Wang, 1977.

———. *A Barthes Reader*. New York: Hill and Wang, 1982.

———. *The Responsibility of Forms: New Critical Essays on Music, Art and Representation*. New York: Hill and Wang, 1984.

———. *The Rustle of Language*. New York: Hill and Wang, 1986.

Baudrillard, Jean. *Oublier Foucault*. Paris: Editions Galilee, 1977.

Benveniste, Émile. *Problems in General Linguistics*. Coral Gables, FL: University of Miami Press, 1971.

Bloom, Harold, et al. *Deconstruction and Criticism*. New York: Seabury, 1979.

Bové, Paul. *Deconstructive Poetics: Heidegger and Modern American Poetry*. New York: Columbia University Press, 1980.

Brooke-Rose, Christine. *A Grammar of Metaphor*. London: Secker and Warburg, 1958.

Cain, William E. "Deconstruction in America: The Recent Literary Criticism of J. Hillis Miller." *College English* 41 (1979), 367–82.

Cassirer, Ernst. "Structuralism in Modern Linguistics." *Word* 1 (1945): 99–120.

———. *Symbol, Myth and Culture*. New Haven: Yale University Press, 1979.

Caws, Peter. *Structuralism: The Art of the Intelligible*. Atlantic Highlands, NJ: Humanities, 1988.

Champagne, Roland A. *The Structuralists on Myth*. New York: Garland, 1992.

Chase, Cynthia. "The Decomposition of the Elephants: Double-Reading *Daniel Deronda*." *PMLA* 93 (1978): 215–27.

Chatman, Seymour, ed. *Essays on the Language of Literature*. Boston: Houghton Mifflin, 1967.

———. *Story and Discourse: Narrative Structure in Fiction and Film*. Ithaca: Cornell University Press, 1978.

Chomsky, Noam. *Syntactic Structures*. The Hague: Mouton, 1957.

———. *Aspects of the Theory of Syntax*. Cambridge: MIT Press, 1965.

Cohn, Dorrit. *Transparent Minds: Narrative Modes for Presenting Consciousness in Fiction*. Princeton: Princeton University Press, 1978.

Coward, Rosalind, and John Ellis. *Language and Materialism: Developments in Semiology and the Theory of the Subject*. London: Routledge and Kegan Paul, 1977.

Culler, Jonathan. *Structuralist Poetics*. Ithaca: Cornell University Press, 1975.

———. *The Pursuit of Signs: Semiotics, Literature, Deconstruction*. Ithaca: Cornell University Press, 1981.

———. *On Deconstruction: Theory and Criticism after Structuralism*. Ithaca: Cornell University Press, 1982.

———. *Roland Barthes*. New York: Oxford University Press, 1984.

———. *Ferdinand de Saussure*. Ithaca: Cornell University Press, 1986.

Deledalle, Gerard, ed. *Semiotics and Pragmatics*. Amsterdam: Benjamins, 1989.

de Man, Paul. *Blindness and Insight.* New York: Oxford University Press, 1971.
———. *Allegories of Reading: Figural Language in Rousseau, Nietzsche, Rilke, and Proust.* New Haven: Yale University Press, 1979.
———. *The Rhetoric of Romanticism.* New York: Columbia University Press, 1984.
———. *The Resistance to Theory.* Minneapolis: University of Minnesota Press, 1986.
Derrida, Jacques. *Of Grammatology.* 1967; Baltimore: Johns Hopkins University Press, 1976.
———. *Writing and Difference.* 1967; Chicago: University of Chicago Press, 1978.
———. *Margins of Philosophy.* 1972; Chicago: University of Chicago Press, 1982.
———. *Positions,* trans. Alan Bass. 1972; Chicago: University of Chicago Press, 1981.
———. *Dissemination.* 1972; Chicago: University of Chicago Press, 1982.
———. *Speech and Phenomena, and Other Essays on Husserl's Theory of Signs.* 1973; Evanston: Northwestern University Press, 1978.
———. *Glas.* 1974; Lincoln: University of Nebraska Press, 1986.
———. *The Post Card: From Socrates to Freud and Beyond.* 1980; Chicago: University of Chicago Press, 1987.
———. "Like the Sound of the Sea Deep within a Shell: Paul de Man's War," translated by Peggy Kamuf. In *Responses on Paul de Man's Wartime Journalism,* ed. Werner Hamacher, Neil Hertz, and Thomas Kennan. Lincoln: University of Nebraska Press, 1988, pp. 127–64.
———. "Given Time: The Time of the King," translated by Peggy Kamuf. *Critical Inquiry* 18 (1992): 161–87.
———. "Shibboleth: For Paul Célan," translated by Joshua Wilner. In *Wordtraces: Readings of Paul Celan,* ed. Aris Fioretos. Baltimore: Johns Hopkins University Press, 1994, pp. 3–72.
Donoghue, Denis. *Ferocious Alphabets.* Boston: Little, Brown, 1981.
Dreyfus, Hubert L., and Paul Rabinow. *Michel Foucault: Beyond Structuralism and Hermeneutics,* 2nd ed. Chicago: University of Chicago Press, 1983.
Eco, Umberto. *A Theory of Semiotics.* Bloomington: Indiana University Press, 1975.
———. *The Role of the Reader: Explorations in the Semiotics of Texts.* Bloomington: Indiana University Press, 1979.
———. *Semiotics and the Philosophy of Language.* London: Macmillan, 1984.
Foucault, Michel. *The Order of Things: An Archaeology of the Human Sciences.* 1966; London: Tavistock, 1970.
———. *The Archeology of Knowledge.* 1969; New York: Pantheon, 1972.
———. *Language, Counter-Memory, Practice.* Ithaca: Cornell University Press, 1977.
———. *The Foucault Reader.* New York: Pantheon, 1984.
Gasché, Rodolphe. "The Scene of Writing: A Deferred Outset." *Glyph* 1 (1977): 150–71.
———. "Deconstruction as Criticism." *Glyph* 6 (1979): 177–216.
———. *Inventions of Difference: On Jacques Derrida.* Cambridge: Harvard University Press, 1994.
Genette, Gérard. *Narrative Discourse: An Essay in Method.* Ithaca: Cornell University Press, 1980.
———. *Figures of Literary Discourse.* New York: Columbia University Press, 1982.
Girard, René. *Deceit, Desire, and the Novel: The Self and Other in Literary Structure.* Baltimore: Johns Hopkins University Press, 1965.
———. *Violence and the Sacred.* Baltimore: Johns Hopkins University Press, 1977.
Graef, Ortwin de. *Serenity in Crisis: A Preface to Paul de Man 1939–1960.* Lincoln: University of Nebraska Press, 1993.
Greimas, A. J. *Structural Semantics: An Attempt at a Method.* Lincoln: University of Nebraska Press, 1984.

Harari, Josué. *Structuralists and Structuralisms*. Ithaca: Cornell University Press, 1971.
———, ed. *Textual Strategies: Perspectives in Post-Structuralist Criticism*. Ithaca: Cornell University Press, 1979.
Harris, Zellig. *Methods in Structural Linguistics*. Chicago: University of Chicago Press, 1951.
Hartman, Geoffrey H. *Beyond Formalism*. New Haven: Yale University Press, 1970.
———. *The Fate of Reading and Other Essays*. Chicago: University of Chicago Press, 1975.
———. *Criticism in the Wilderness*. New Haven: Yale University Press, 1980.
———. *Saving the Text: Literature/Derrida/Philosophy*. Baltimore: Johns Hopkins University Press, 1981.
Hawkes, Terence. *Structuralism and Semiotics*. Berkeley: University of California Press, 1977.
Herman, Luc, Kris Humbeeck, and Geert Lernout, eds. *(Dis)continuities: Essays on Paul de Man*. Amsterdam: Rodopi, 1989.
Hjelmslev, Louis. *Prolegomena to a Theory of Language*. Madison: University of Wisconsin Press, 1961.
Holland, Norman N. *The Critical I*. New York: Columbia University Press, 1992.
Horton, Susan. *Interpreting Interpreting: Interpreting Dickens' Dombey*. Baltimore: Johns Hopkins University Press, 1979.
Husserl, Edmund. *The Idea of Phenomenology*. The Hague: M. Nijhoff, 1964.
Jacobs, Carol. *The Dissimulating Harmony: The Image of Interpretation in Nietzsche, Rilke, Artaud, and Benjamin*. Baltimore: Johns Hopkins University Press, 1978.
Jakobson, Roman. *Selected Writings*. 8 vols. The Hague: Mouton, 1962–.
——— and Lawrence Jones. *Shakespeare's Verbal Art in "Th' Expense of Spirit."* The Hague: Mouton, 1970.
Jameson, Fredric. *The Prison House of Language: A Critical Account of Structuralism and Russian Formalism*. Princeton: Princeton University Press, 1971.
Johnson, Barbara. *The Critical Difference: Essays in the Contemporary Rhetoric of Reading*. Baltimore: Johns Hopkins University Press, 1980.
———. *A World of Difference*. Baltimore: Johns Hopkins University Press, 1987.
Kofman, Sarah. *Nietzsche et la scène philosophique*. Paris Union generale d'editions, 1979.
———. *Lectures de Derrida*. Paris: Editions Galilee, 1984.
Kristeva, Julia. *Essays in Semiotics*. The Hague: Mouton, 1971.
Lane, Michael, ed. *Structuralism: A Reader*. London: Cape, 1970.
Leitch, Vincent. *Deconstructive Criticism: An Advanced Introduction*. New York: Columbia University Press, 1983.
Lévi-Strauss, Claude. *Structural Anthropology*. 1958; New York: Basic Books, 1963.
———. *The Savage Mind*. Chicago: University of Chicago Press, 1966.
———. *The Raw and the Cooked*. 1964; New York: Harper and Row, 1969.
———. *From Honey to Ashes*. 1966; London: Cape, 1973.
Lotman, Yuri. *Analysis of the Poetic Text*. Ann Arbor: Ardis, 1976.
Lyons, John. *Structural Semantics*. Oxford: Blackwell, 1973.
Lyotard, Jean-François. *The Post-Modern Condition: A Report on Knowledge*. 1979; Minneapolis: University of Minnesota Press, 1984.
Macksey, Richard, and Eugenio Donato, eds. *The Languages of Criticism and the Sciences of Man*. Baltimore: Johns Hopkins University Press, 1970.
———. *The Structuralist Controversy: The Languages of Criticism and the Sciences of Man*. Baltimore: Johns Hopkins University Press, 1970.
Martin, Bill. *Humanism and Its Aftermath: The Shared Fate of Deconstruction and Politics*. Atlantic Highlands, NJ: Humanities, 1995.

McDonald, Christie V. "Jacques Derrida's Reading of Rousseau." *The Eighteenth Century: Theory and Interpretation* 20 (1970): 82–95.
Miller, J. Hillis. "Ariadne's Thread: Repetition and the Narrative Line." *Critical Inquiry* 3 (1976): 57–78.
———. *Fiction and Repetition: Seven English Novels.* Cambridge: Harvard University Press, 1982.
———. *The Linguistic Moment: From Wordsworth to Stevens.* Princeton: Princeton University Press, 1985.
———. *The Ethics of Reading: Kant, de Man, Eliot, Trollope, James and Benjamin.* New York: Columbia University Press, 1987.
Nietzsche, Friedrich. *Complete Works.* 18 vols. Ed. Oscar Levy. New York: Russell and Russell, 1964.
Norris, Christopher. *The Deconstructive Turn: Essays in the Rhetoric of Philosophy.* New York: Methuen, 1984.
———. *The Contest of Faculties: Philosophy and Theory after Deconstruction.* New York: Methuen, 1985.
Piaget, Jean. *Structuralism.* New York: Basic Books, 1970.
Prince, Gerald. "Introduction à l'étude du narrataire." *Poétique* 14 (1963): 178–96.
Ricoeur, Paul. *The Conflict of Interpretations: Essays in Hermeneutics.* Evanston: Northwestern University Press, 1974.
———. *The Rule of Metaphor.* Toronto: University of Toronto Press, 1977.
———. *Time and Narrative.* Chicago: University of Chicago Press, 1984.
Riffaterre, Michael. *Semiotics of Poetry.* Bloomington: Indiana University Press, 1978.
———. *Text Production.* New York: Columbia University Press, 1983.
Robey, David, ed. *Structuralism: An Introduction.* London: Oxford University Press, 1973.
Rorty, Richard. "Philosophy as a Kind of Writing: An Essay on Derrida." *New Literary History* 10 (1978): 1411–60.
Royle, Nicholas. *After Derrida.* Manchester: Manchester University Press, 1995.
Ryan, Michael. *Marxism and Deconstruction.* Baltimore: Johns Hopkins University Press, 1982.
Saussure, Ferdinand de. *Course in General Linguistics.* 1923; New York: Philosophical Library, 1959.
Searle, John. *Speech Acts.* Cambridge: Cambridge University Press, 1969.
———. "Reiterating the Differences: A Reply to Derrida." *Glyph* 1 (1977): 198–208.
Sebeok, Thomas, ed. *Style in Language.* Cambridge: MIT Press, 1964.
———, ed. *Approaches to Semiotics.* The Hague: Mouton, 1964.
Silverman, Hugh J., and Gary E. Aylesworth, eds. *The Textual Sublime: Deconstruction and Its Differences.* Albany: State University of New York Press, 1990.
Smith, Barbara Herrnstein. *On the Margins of Discourse: The Relation of Literature to Language.* Chicago: University of Chicago Press, 1979.
Smith, Robert. *Derrida and Autobiography.* Cambridge: Cambridge University Press, 1995.
Sprinker, Michael. "Textual Politics: Foucault and Derrida." *Boundary* 28 (1980): 75–98.
Tejera, Victorino. *Literature, Criticism, and the Theory of Signs.* Amsterdam: Benjamins, 1995.
Todorov, Tzvetan. *The Poetics of Prose.* Ithaca: Cornell University Press, 1977.
———. *Introduction to Poetics.* Minneapolis: University of Minnesota Press, 1981.
———. *Symbolism and Interpretation.* Ithaca: Cornell University Press, 1982.
———. *Theories of the Symbol.* Ithaca: Cornell University Press, 1982.
Ullmann, Stephen. *Language and Style.* Oxford: Blackwell, 1964.
Waters, Lindsay, and Wlad Godzich, eds. *Reading de Man Reading.* Minneapolis: University of Minnesota Press, 1988.

Ferdinand de Saussure

1857–1913

Ferdinand de Saussure was born in Geneva and educated at the University of Geneva and the University of Berlin before taking his Ph.D. at the University of Leipzig in 1880. The linguist and philologist taught at the École Pratique des Hautes Études in Paris before returning to his birthplace and a professorship at the University of Geneva, where he taught from 1891 to 1912. Saussure published specialized monographs in linguistics during his lifetime, such as his Memoir on the Primitive System of Vowels in the Indo-European Languages *(1879). His current fame is based on the course in general linguistics that he gave in Geneva, which was posthumously recreated from lecture notes by his students and published in 1916 as* Cours de linguistique générale (The Course in General Linguistics), *from which the following selection is taken.*

Nature of the Linguistic Sign

1. SIGN, SIGNIFIED, SIGNIFIER

Some people regard language, when reduced to its elements, as a naming-process only — a list of words, each corresponding to the thing that it names. For example:

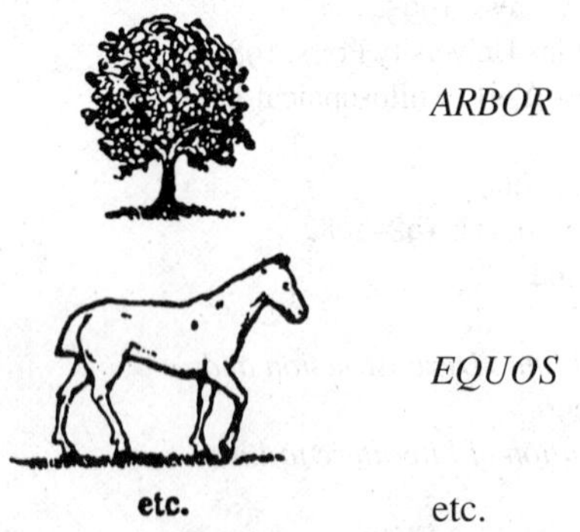

This conception is open to criticism at several points. It assumes that ready-made ideas exist before words; it does not tell us whether a name is vocal or psychological in nature (*arbor,* for instance, can be considered from either viewpoint); finally, it lets us assume that the linking of a name and a thing is a very simple operation — an assumption that is anything but true. But this rather naive approach can bring us near the truth by showing us that the linguistic unit is a double entity, one formed by the associating of two terms.

We have seen in considering the speaking-circuit that both terms involved in the linguistic sign are psychological and are united in the brain by an associative bond. This point must be emphasized.

The linguistic sign unites, not a thing and a name, but a concept and a sound-image.[1] The latter is not the material sound, a purely physical thing, but the psychological imprint of the sound, the impression that it makes on our senses. The sound-image is sensory, and if I happen to call it "material," it is only in that sense, and by way of

Translated by Wade Baskin.

[1]The term sound-image may seem to be too restricted inasmuch as beside the representation of the sounds of a word there is also that of its articulation, the muscular image of the phonational act. But for F. de Saussure language is essentially a depository, a thing received from without. The sound-image is par excellence the natural representation of the word as a fact of potential language, outside any actual use of it in speaking. The motor side is thus implied or, in any event, occupies only a subordinate role with respect to the sound-image. Bally and Sèchehaye. Bally and Sèchehaye redacted the lecture notes of Saussure's students into *Cours de linguistique générale.* [Ed.]

opposing it to the other term of the association, the concept, which is generally more abstract.

The psychological character of our sound-images becomes apparent when we observe our own speech. Without moving our lips or tongue, we can talk to ourselves or recite mentally a selection of verse. Because we regard the words of our language as sound-images, we must avoid speaking of the "phonemes" that make up the words. This term, which suggests vocal activity, is applicable to the spoken word only, to the realization of the inner image in discourse. We can avoid that misunderstanding by speaking of the *sounds* and *syllables* of a word provided we remember that the names refer to the sound-image.

The linguistic sign is then a two-sided psychological entity that can be represented by the drawing:

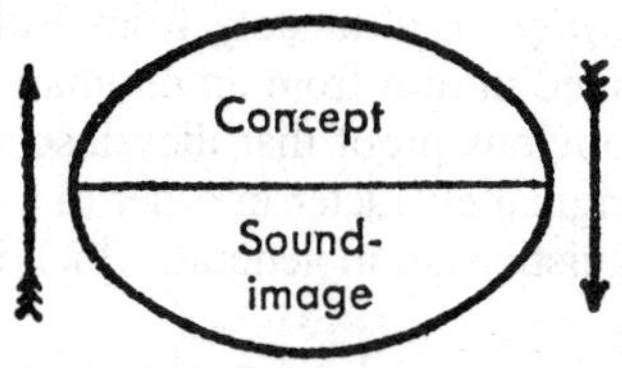

The two elements are intimately united, and each recalls the other. Whether we try to find the meaning of the Latin word *arbor* or the word that Latin uses to designate the concept "tree," it is clear that only the associations sanctioned by that language appear to us to conform to reality, and we disregard whatever others might be imagined.

Our definition of the linguistic sign poses an important question of terminology. I call the combination of a concept and a sound-image a *sign,* but in current usage the term generally designates only a sound-image, a word, for example (*arbor,* etc.). One tends to forget that *arbor* is called a sign only because it carries the concept "tree," with the result that the idea of the sensory part implies the idea of the whole.

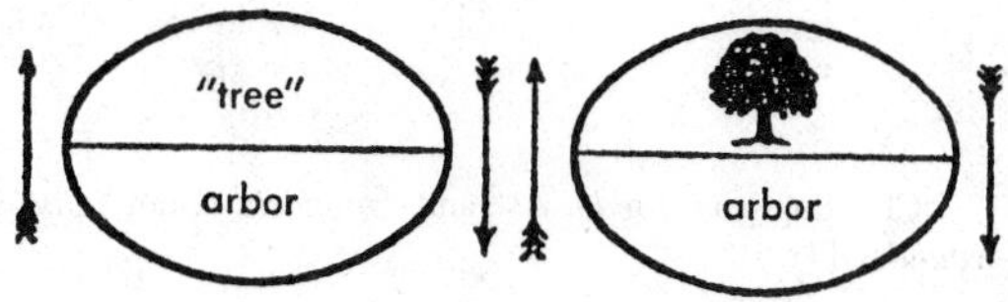

Ambiguity would disappear if the three notions involved here were designated by three names, each suggesting and opposing the others. I propose to retain the word *sign* [*signe*] to designate the whole and to replace *concept* and *sound-image* respectively by *signified* [*signifié*] and *signifier* [*signifiant*]; the last two terms have the advantage of indicating the opposition that separates them from each other and from the whole of which they are parts. As regards *sign,* if I am satisfied with it, this is simply because I do not know of any word to replace it, the ordinary language suggesting no other.

The linguistic sign, as defined, has two primordial characteristics. In enunciating them I am also positing the basic principles of any study of this type.

2. PRINCIPLE I: THE ARBITRARY NATURE OF THE SIGN

The bond between the signifier and the signified is arbitrary. Since I mean by sign the whole that results from the associating of the signifier with the signified, I can simply say: *the linguistic sign is arbitrary.*

The idea of "sister" is not linked by any inner relationship to the succession of sounds *s-ö-r* which serves as its signifier in French; that it could be represented equally by just any other sequence is proved by differences among languages and by the very existence of different languages: the signified "ox" has as its signifier *b-ö-f* on one side of the border and *o-k-s* (*Ochs*) on the other.

No one disputes the principle of the arbitrary nature of the sign, but it is often easier to discover a truth than to assign to it its proper place. Principle I dominates all the linguistics of language; its consequences are numberless. It is true that not all of them are equally obvious at first glance; only after many detours does one discover them, and with them the primordial importance of the principle.

One remark in passing: when semiology becomes organized as a science, the question will arise whether or not it properly includes modes of expression based on completely natural signs, such as pantomime. Supposing that the new science welcomes them, its main concern will still be the whole group of systems grounded on the arbitrariness of the sign. In fact, every means of expression used in society is based, in principle, on collective behavior or — what amounts to the same thing — on convention. Polite formulas, for instance, though often imbued with a certain natural expressiveness (as in the case of a Chinese who greets his emperor by bowing down to the ground nine times), are nonetheless fixed by rule; it is this rule and not the intrinsic value of the gestures that obliges one to use them. Signs that are wholly arbitrary realize better than the others the ideal of the semiological process; that is why language, the most complex and universal of all systems of expression, is also the most characteristic; in this sense linguistics can become the master-pattern for all branches of semiology although language is only one particular semiological system.

The word *symbol* has been used to designate the linguistic sign, or more specifically, what is here called the signifier. Principle I in particular weighs against the use of this term. One characteristic of the symbol is that it is never wholly arbitrary; it is not empty, for there is the rudiment of a natural bond between the signifier and the signified. The symbol of justice, a pair of scales, could not be replaced by just any other symbol, such as a chariot.

The word *arbitrary* also calls for comment. The term should not imply that the choice of the signifier is left entirely to the speaker (we shall see below that the individual does not have the power to change a sign in any way once it has become established in the linguistic community); I mean that it is unmotivated, i.e. arbitrary in that it actually has no natural connection with the signified.

In concluding let us consider two objections that might be raised to the establishment of Principle I:

1. *Onomatopoeia* might be used to prove that the choice of the signifier is not always arbitrary. But onomatopoeic formations are never organic elements of a linguistic system. Besides, their number is much smaller than is generally supposed. Words like French *fouet* "whip" or *glas* "knell" may strike certain ears with suggestive sonority, but to see that they have not always had this property we need only examine their Latin forms (*fouet* is derived from *fāgus* "beech-tree," *glas* from *classicum* "sound of a trumpet"). The quality of their present sounds, or rather the quality that is attributed to them, is a fortuitous result of phonetic evolution.

As for authentic onomatopoeic words (e.g. *glug-glug, tick-tock,* etc.), not only are they limited in number, but also they are chosen somewhat arbitrarily, for they are only approximate and more or less conventional imitations of certain sounds (cf. English *bow-bow* and French *ouaoua*). In addition, once these words have been introduced into the language, they are to a certain extent subjected to the same evolution — phonetic, morphological, etc. — that other words undergo (cf. *pigeon,* ultimately from Vulgar Latin *pīpiō,* derived in turn from an onomatopoeic formation): obvious proof that they lose something of their original character in order to assume that of the linguistic sign in general, which is unmotivated.

2. *Interjections,* closely related to onomatopoeia, can be attacked on the same grounds and come no closer to refuting our thesis. One is tempted to see in them spontaneous expressions of reality dictated, so to speak, by natural forces. But for most interjections we can show that there is no fixed bond between their signified and their signifier. We need only compare two languages on this point to see how much such expressions differ from one language to the next (e.g. the English equivalent of French *aïe!* is *ouch!*). We know, moreover, that many interjections were once words with specific meanings (cf. French *diable!* "darn!" *mordieu!* "golly!" from *mort Dieu* "God's death," etc.).[2]

Onomatopoeic formations and interjections are of secondary importance, and their symbolic origin is in part open to dispute.

[2]Cf. English *goodness!* and *zounds!* (from *God's wounds*). [Tr.]

3. PRINCIPLE II: THE LINEAR NATURE OF THE SIGNIFIER

The signifier, being auditory, is unfolded solely in time from which it gets the following characteristics: (a) it represents a span, and (b) the span is measurable in a single dimension; it is a line.

While Principle II is obvious, apparently linguists have always neglected to state it, doubtless because they found it too simple; nevertheless, it is fundamental, and its consequences are incalculable. Its importance equals that of Principle I; the whole mechanism of language depends upon it. In contrast to visual signifiers (nautical signals, etc.) which can offer simultaneous groupings in several dimensions, auditory signifiers have at their command only the dimension of time. Their elements are presented in succession; they form a chain. This feature becomes readily apparent when they are represented in writing and the spatial line of graphic marks is substituted for succession in time.

Sometimes the linear nature of the signifier is not obvious. When I accent a syllable, for instance, it seems that I am concentrating more than one significant element on the same point. But this is an illusion; the syllable and its accent constitute only one phonational act. There is no duality within the act but only different oppositions to what precedes and what follows.

Claude Lévi-Strauss

b. 1908

Claude Lévi-Strauss, one of the major figures of social anthropology and of twentieth-century intellectual life generally, was born in Brussels and took degrees in philosophy and law at the University of Paris (1927–32). From 1934 to 1937, Lévi-Strauss served as a professor of sociology at the University of São Paulo in Brazil; his research among the Brazilian Indians informs the heart of his intellectual autobiography, Tristes Tropiques *(1955). From 1941 to 1945 he was a visiting professor at the New School for Social Research in New York, where he came in contact with the ideas of Roman Jakobson. Made director of studies at the École Practique des Haute Études of the University of Paris in 1950, he was appointed in 1959 to the chair of social anthropology at the Collège de France. Lévi-Strauss's works include* The Elementary Structures of Kinship *(1949),* Structural Anthropology *(1958).* The Savage Mind *(1962), and the four volumes of* Mythologiques *(1964–71; translations 1969 ff.). "The Structural Study of Myth" first appeared in* Journal of American Folklore *78 (1955); this version is from the 1963 translation of* Structural Anthropology. *His latest books are* The Jealous Potter *(1988),* Regarder Ecouter Lire *(1993),* Saudades do Brasil *(1995), and* The Story of Lynx *(1995).*

The Structural Study of Myth

It would seem that mythological worlds have been built up only to be shattered again, and that new worlds were built from the fragments.

— FRANZ BOAS[1]

Despite some recent attempts to renew them, it seems that during the past twenty years anthropology has increasingly turned from studies in the field of religion. At the same time, and precisely because the interest of professional anthropologists has withdrawn from primitive religion, all kinds of amateurs who claim to belong to other disciplines have seized this opportunity to move in, thereby turning into their private playground what we had left as a wasteland. The prospects for the scientific study of religion have thus been undermined in two ways.

The explanation for this situation lies to some extent in the fact that the anthropological study of religion was started by men like Tylor, Frazer, and Durkheim, who were psychologically oriented although not in a position to keep up with the progress of psychological research and theory. Their interpretations, therefore, soon became vitiated by the outmoded psychological approach which they used as their basis. Although they were undoubtedly right in giving their attention to intellectual processes, the way they handled these remained so crude that it discredited them altogether. This is much to be regretted, since, as Hocart so profoundly noted in his introduction to a posthumous book recently published,[2] psychological interpretations were withdrawn from the intellectual field only to be introduced again in the field of affectivity, thus adding to "the inherent defects of the psychological school . . . the mistake of deriving clear-cut ideas . . . from vague emotions." Instead of trying to enlarge the framework of our logic to include processes which, whatever their apparent differences, belong to the same kind of intellectual operation, a naïve attempt was made to reduce them to inarticulate emotional drives, which resulted only in hampering our studies.

Of all the chapters of religious anthropology probably none has tarried to the same extent as studies in the field of mythology. From a theoretical point of view the situation remains very much the same as it was fifty years ago, namely, chaotic. Myths are still widely interpreted in conflicting ways: as collective dreams, as the outcome of a kind of esthetic play, or as the basis of ritual. Mythological figures are considered as personified abstractions, divinized heroes, or fallen gods. Whatever the hypothesis, the choice amounts to reducing mythology either to idle play or to a crude kind of philosophic speculation.

In order to understand what a myth really is, must we choose between platitude and sophism? Some claim that human societies merely express, through their mythology, fundamental feelings common to the whole of mankind, such as love, hate, or revenge or that they try to provide some kind of explanations for phenomena which they cannot otherwise understand — astronomical, meteorological, and the like. But why should these societies do it in such elaborate and devious ways, when all of them are also acquainted with empirical explanations? On the other hand, psychoanalysts and many anthropologists have shifted the problems away from the natural or cosmological toward the sociological and psychological fields. But then the interpretation becomes too easy: If a given mythology confers prominence on a certain figure, let us say an evil grandmother, it will be claimed that in such a society grandmothers are actually evil and that mythology reflects the social structure and the social relations; but should the actual data be conflicting, it would be as readily claimed that the purpose of mythology is to provide an outlet for repressed feelings. Whatever the situation, a

Translated by Claire Jacobson and Brooke Grundfest Schoepf.

[1]In Boas's Introduction to James Teit, "Traditions of the Thompson River Indians of British Columbia," *Memoirs of the American Folklore Society*, VI (1898), p. 18. [Au.]

[2]A. M. Hocart, *Social Origins* (London: 1954), p. 7. [Au.]

clever dialectic will always find a way to pretend that a meaning has been found.

Mythology confronts the student with a situation which at first sight appears contradictory. On the one hand it would seem that in the course of a myth anything is likely to happen. There is no logic, no continuity. Any characteristic can be attributed to any subject; every conceivable relation can be found. With myth, everything becomes possible. But on the other hand, this apparent arbitrariness is belied by the astounding similarity between myths collected in widely different regions. Therefore the problem: If the content of a myth is contingent, how are we going to explain the fact that myths throughout the world are so similar?

It is precisely this awareness of a basic antinomy pertaining to the nature of myth that may lead us toward its solution. For the contradiction which we face is very similar to that which in earlier times brought considerable worry to the first philosophers concerned with linguistic problems; linguistics could only begin to evolve as a science after this contradiction had been overcome. Ancient philosophers reasoned about language the way we do about mythology. On the one hand, they did notice that in a given language certain sequences of sounds were associated with definite meanings, and they earnestly aimed at discovering a reason for the linkage between those *sounds* and that *meaning*. Their attempt, however, was thwarted from the very beginning by the fact that the same sounds were equally present in other languages although the meaning they conveyed was entirely different. The contradiction was surmounted only by the discovery that it is the combination of sounds, not the sounds themselves, which provides the significant data.

It is easy to see, moreover, that some of the more recent interpretations of mythological thought originated from the same kind of misconception under which those early linguists were laboring. Let us consider, for instance, Jung's idea that a given mythological pattern — the so-called archetype — possesses a certain meaning. This is comparable to the long-supported error that a sound may possess a certain affinity with a meaning: for instance, the "liquid" semivowels with water, the open vowels with things that are big, large, loud, or heavy, etc., a theory which still has its supporters.[3] Whatever emendations the original formulation may now call for,[4] everybody will agree that the Saussurean principle of the *arbitrary character of linguistic signs* was a prerequisite for the accession of linguistics to the scientific level.

To invite the mythologist to compare his precarious situation with that of the linguist in the prescientific stage is not enough. As a matter of fact we may thus be led only from one difficulty to another. There is a very good reason why myth cannot simply be treated as language if its specific problems are to be solved; myth *is* language: to be known, myth has to be told; it is a part of human speech. In order to preserve its specificity we must be able to show that it is both the same thing as language, and also something different from it. Here, too, the past experience of linguists may help us. For language itself can be analyzed into things which are at the same time similar and yet different. This is precisely what is expressed in Saussure's distinction between *langue* and *parole,* one being the structural side of language, the other the statistical aspect of it, *langue* belonging to a reversible time, *parole* being nonreversible. If those two levels already exist in language, then a third one can conceivably be isolated.

We have distinguished *langue* and *parole* by the different time referents which they use. Keeping this in mind, we may notice that myth uses a third referent which combines the properties of the first two. On the one hand, a myth always refers to events alleged to have taken place long ago. But what gives the myth an operational value is that the specific pattern described is timeless; it explains the present and the past as well as the future. This can be made clear through a comparison between myth and what appears to have largely replaced it in modern societies, namely, politics. When the historian refers to the French Revolu-

[3]See, for instance, Sir R. A. Paget, "The Origin of Language," *Journal of World History,* I, No. 2 (UNESCO, 1953). [Au.]

[4]See Émile Benveniste, "Nature du signe linguistique," *Acta Linguistica,* I, No. 1 (1939); and Chapter V in *Structural Anthropology.* [Au.]

tion, it is always as a sequence of past happenings, a nonreversible series of events the remote consequences of which may still be felt at present. But to the French politician, as well as to his followers, the French Revolution is both a sequence belonging to the past — as to the historian — and a timeless pattern which can be detected in the contemporary French social structure and which provides a clue for its interpretation, a lead from which to infer future developments. Michelet, for instance, was a politically minded historian. He describes the French Revolution thus: "That day . . . everything was possible. . . . Future became present . . . that is, no more time, a glimpse of eternity."[5] It is that double structure, altogether historical and ahistorical, which explains how myth, while pertaining to the realm of *parole* and calling for an explanation as such, as well as to that of *langue* in which it is expressed, can also be an absolute entity on a third level which, though it remains linguistic by nature, is nevertheless distinct from the other two.

A remark can be introduced at this point which will help to show the originality of myth in relation to other linguistic phenomena. Myth is the part of language where the formula *traduttore, traditttore*[6] reaches its lowest truth value. From that point of view it should be placed in the gamut of linguistic expressions at the end opposite to that of poetry, in spite of all the claims which have been made to prove the contrary. Poetry is a kind of speech which cannot be translated except at the cost of serious distortions; whereas the mythical value of the myth is preserved even through the worst translation. Whatever our ignorance of the language and the culture of the people where it originated, a myth is still felt as a myth by any reader anywhere in the world. Its substance does not lie in its style, its original music, or its syntax, but in the *story* which it tells. Myth is language, functioning on an especially high level where meaning succeeds practically at "taking off" from the linguistic ground on which it keeps on rolling.

[5]Jules Michelet, *Histoire de la Révolution française,* IV, 1. I took this quotation from M. Merleau-Ponty, *Les Aventures de la dialectique* (Paris: 1955), p. 273. [Au.]

[6]To translate is to betray. [Ed.]

To sum up the discussion at this point, we have so far made the following claims: (1) If there is a meaning to be found in mythology, it cannot reside in the isolated elements which enter into the composition of a myth, but only in the way those elements are combined. (2) Although myth belongs to the same category as language, being, as a matter of fact, only part of it, language in myth exhibits specific properties. (3) Those properties are only to be found *above* the ordinary linguistic level, that is, they exhibit more complex features than those which are to be found in any other kind of linguistic expression.

If the above three points are granted, at least as a working hypothesis, two consequences will follow: (1) Myth, like the rest of language, is made up of constituent units. (2) These constituent units presuppose the constituent units present in language when analyzed on other levels — namely, phonemes, morphemes, and sememes — but they, nevertheless, differ from the latter in the same way as the latter differ among themselves; they belong to a higher and more complex order. For this reason, we shall call them *gross constituent units.*

How shall we proceed in order to identify and isolate these gross constituent units or mythemes? We know that they cannot be found among phonemes, morphemes, or sememes, but only on a higher level; otherwise myth would become confused with any other kind of speech. Therefore, we should look for them on the sentence level. The only method we can suggest at this stage is to proceed tentatively, by trial and error, using as a check the principles which serve as a basis for any kind of structural analysis: economy of explanation; unity of solution; and ability to reconstruct the whole from a fragment, as well as later stages from previous ones.

The technique which has been applied so far by this writer consists in analyzing each myth individually, breaking down its story into the shortest possible sentences, and writing each sentence on an index card bearing a number corresponding to the unfolding of the story.

Practically each card will thus show that a certain function is, at a given time, linked to a given subject. Or, to put it otherwise, each gross constituent unit will consist of a *relation.*

However, the above definition remains highly unsatisfactory for two different reasons. First, it is well known to structural linguists that constituent units on all levels are made up of relations, and the true difference between our *gross* units and the others remains unexplained; second, we still find ourselves in the realm of a nonreversible time, since the numbers of the cards correspond to the unfolding of the narrative. Thus the specific character of mythological time, which as we have seen is both reversible and nonreversible, synchronic and diachronic, remains unaccounted for. From this springs a new hypothesis, which constitutes the very core of our argument: The true constituent units of a myth are not the isolated relations but *bundles of such relations,* and it is only as bundles that these relations can be put to use and combined so as to produce a meaning. Relations pertaining to the same bundle may appear diachronically at remote intervals, but when we have succeeded in grouping them together we have reorganized our myth according to a time referent of a new nature, corresponding to the prerequisite of the initial hypothesis, namely a two-dimensional time referent which is simultaneously diachronic and synchronic, and which accordingly integrates the characteristics of *langue* on the one hand, and those of *parole* on the other. To put it in even more linguistic terms, it is as though a phoneme were always made up of all its variants.

Two comparisons may help to explain what we have in mind.

Let us first suppose that archaeologists of the future coming from another planet would one day, when all human life had disappeared from the earth, excavate one of our libraries. Even if they were at first ignorant of our writing, they might succeed in deciphering it — an undertaking which would require, at some early stage, the discovery that the alphabet, as we are in the habit of printing it, should be read from left to right and from top to bottom. However, they would soon discover that a whole category of books did not fit the usual pattern — these would be the orchestra scores on the shelves of the music division. But after trying, without success, to decipher staffs one after the other, from the upper down to the lower, they would probably notice that the same patterns of notes recurred at intervals, either in full or in part, or that some patterns were strongly reminiscent of earlier ones. Hence the hypothesis: What if patterns showing affinity, instead of being considered in succession, were to be treated as one complex pattern and read as a whole? By getting at what we call *harmony,* they would then see that an orchestra score, to be meaningful, must be read diachronically along one axis — that is, page after page, and from left to right — and synchronically along the other axis, all the notes written vertically making up one gross constituent unit, that is, one bundle of relations.

The other comparison is somewhat different. Let us take an observer ignorant of our playing cards, sitting for a long time with a fortune-teller. He would know something of the visitors: sex, age, physical appearance, social situation, etc., in the same way as we know something of the different cultures whose myths we try to study. He would also listen to the séances and record them so as to be able to go over them and make comparisons — as we do when we listen to myth-telling and record it. Mathematicians to whom I have put the problem agree that if the man is bright and if the material available to him is sufficient, he may be able to reconstruct the nature of the deck of cards being used, that is, fifty-two or thirty-two cards according to the case, made up of four homologous sets consisting of the same units (the individual cards) with only one varying feature, the suit.

Now for a concrete example of the method we propose. We shall use the Oedipus myth, which is well known to everyone. I am well aware that the Oedipus myth has only reached us under late forms and through literary transmutations concerned more with esthetic and moral preoccupations than with religious or ritual ones, whatever these may have been. But we shall not interpret the Oedipus myth in literal terms, much less offer an explanation acceptable to the specialist. We simply wish to illustrate — and without reaching any conclusions with respect to it — a certain technique, whose use is probably not legitimate in this particular instance, owing to the problematic elements indicated above. The "demonstration" should therefore be conceived, not in terms of what the scientist means by this term, but at best in terms of what is meant by the street peddler, whose aim is not to achieve a concrete result, but to explain, as succinctly as possible, the functioning of the mechanical toy which he is trying to sell to the onlookers.

The myth will be treated as an orchestra score would be if it were unwittingly considered as a unilinear series; our task is to re-establish the correct arrangement. Say, for instance, we were confronted with a sequence of the type: 1,2,4,7,8,2,3,4,6,8,1,4,5,7,8,1,2,5,7,3,4,5,6,8 . . . , the assignment being to put all the 1's together, all the 2's, the 3's, etc.; the result is a chart:

1	2		4			7	8
	2	3	4		6		8
1			4	5		7	8
1	2			5		7	
		3	4	5	6		8

We shall attempt to perform the same kind of operation on the Oedipus myth, trying out several arrangements of the mythemes until we find one which is in harmony with the principles enumerated above. Let us suppose, for the sake of argument, that the best arrangement is as shown in Table 1 (although it might certainly be improved with the help of a specialist in Greek mythology).

We thus find ourselves confronted with four vertical columns, each of which includes several relations belonging to the same bundle. Were we to *tell* the myth, we would disregard the columns and read the rows from left to right and from top to bottom. But if we want to *understand* the myth, then we will have to disregard one half of the diachronic dimension (top to bottom) and read from left to right, column after column, each one being considered as a unit.

All the relations belonging to the same column exhibit one common feature which it is our task to discover. For instance, all the events

Table 1

Cadmos seeks his sister Europa, ravished by Zeus			
		Cadmos kills the dragon	
	The Spartoi kill one another		
			Labdacos (Laios' father) = *lame (?)*
	Oedipus kills his father, Laios		Laios (Oedipus' father) = *left-sided (?)*
		Oedipus kills the Sphinx	
			Oedipus = *swollen-foot (?)*
Oedipus marries his mother, Jocasta			
	Eteocles kills his brother, Polynices		
Antigone buries her brother, Polynices, despite prohibition			

grouped in the first column on the left have something to do with blood relations which are overemphasized, that is, are more intimate than they should be. Let us say, then, that the first column has as its common feature the *overrating of blood relations.* It is obvious that the second column expresses the same thing, but inverted: *underrating of blood relations.* The third column refers to monsters being slain. As to the fourth, a few words of clarification are needed. The remarkable connotation of the surnames in Oedipus' father-line has often been noticed. However, linguists usually disregard it, since to them the only way to define the meaning of a term is to investigate all the contexts in which it appears, and personal names, precisely because they are used as such, are not accompanied by any context. With the method we propose to follow the objection disappears, since the myth itself provides its own context. The significance is no longer to be sought in the eventual meaning of each name, but in the fact that all the names have a common feature: All the hypothetical meanings (which may well remain hypothetical) refer to *difficulties in walking straight and standing upright.*

What then is the relationship between the two columns on the right? Column three refers to monsters. The dragon is a chthonian[7] being which has to be killed in order that mankind be born from the Earth; the Sphinx is a monster unwilling to permit men to live. The last unit reproduces the first one, which has to do with the *autochthonous*[8] *origin* of mankind. Since the monsters are overcome by men, we may thus say that the common feature of the third column is *denial of the autochthonous origin of man.*[9]

This immediately helps us to understand the meaning of the fourth column. In mythology it is a universal characteristic of men born from the Earth that at the moment they emerge from the depth they either cannot walk or they walk clumsily. This is the case of the chthonian beings in the mythology of the Pueblo: Muyingwu, who leads the emergence, and the chthonian Shumaikoli are lame ("bleeding-foot," "sore-foot"). The same happens to the Koskimo of the Kwakiutl after they have been swallowed by the chthonian monster, Tsiakish: When they returned to the surface of the earth "they limped forward or tripped sideways." Thus the common feature of the fourth column is *the persistence of the autochthonous origin of man.* It follows that column four is to column three as column one is to

[7]Living within or under the earth. [Ed.]

[8]Born or sprung from the earth. Lévi-Strauss uses the term in a sense in opposition to "born from the sexual union of man and woman." [Ed.]

[9]We are not trying to become involved with specialists in an argument; this would be presumptuous and even meaningless on our part. Since the Oedipus myth is taken here merely as an example treated in arbitrary fashion, the chthonian nature ascribed to the Sphinx might seem surprising; we shall refer to the testimony of Marie Delcourt: "In the archaic legends, [she is] certainly born of the Earth itself" (*Oedipe ou la légende du conquérant* [*Liège:* 1944], p. 108). No matter how remote from Delcourt's our method may be (and our conclusions would be, no doubt, if we were competent to deal with the problem in depth), it sees to us that she has convincingly established the nature of the Sphinx in the archaic tradition, namely, that of a female monster who attacks and rapes young men; in other words, the personification of a female being with an inversion of the sign. This explains why, in the handsome iconography compiled by Delcourt at the end of her work, men and women are always found in an inverted "sky/earth" relationship.

As we shall point out below, we selected the Oedipus myth as our first example because of the striking analogies that seem to exist between certain aspects of archaic Greek thought and that of the Pueblo Indians, from whom we have borrowed the examples that follow. In this respect it should be noted that the figure of the Sphinx, as reconstructed by Delcourt, coincides with two figures of North American mythology (who probably merge into one). We are referring, on the one hand, to "the old hag," a repulsive witch whose physical appearance presents a "problem" to the young hero. If he "solves" this problem — that is, if he responds to the advances of the abject creature — he will find in his bed, upon awakening, a beautiful young woman who will confer power upon him (this is also a Celtic theme). The Sphinx, on the other hand, recalls even more "the child-protruding woman" of the Hopi Indians, that is, a phallic mother par excellence. This young woman was abandoned by her group in the course of a difficult migration, just as she was about to give birth. Henceforth she wanders in the desert as the "Mother of Animals," which she withholds from hunters. He who meets her in her bloody clothes "is so frightened that he has an erection," of which she takes advantage to rape him, after which she rewards him with unfailing success in hunting. See H. R. Voth, "The Oraibi Summer Snake Ceremony," *Field Columbian Museum,* Publication No. 83, Anthropological Series, Vol. III, No. 4 (Chicago: 1903), pp. 352–53 and p. 353, *n* 1. [Au.]

column two. The inability to connect two kinds of relationships is overcome (or rather replaced) by the assertion that contradictory relationships are identical inasmuch as they are both self-contradictory in a similar way. Although this is still a provisional formulation of the structure of mythical thought, it is sufficient at this stage.

Turning back to the Oedipus myth, we may now see what it means. The myth has to do with the inability, for a culture which holds the belief that mankind is autochthonous (see, for instance, Pausanias, VIII, xxix, 4: plants provide a *model* for humans), to find a satisfactory transition between this theory and the knowledge that human beings are actually born from the union of man and woman. Although the problem obviously cannot be solved, the Oedipus myth provides a kind of logical tool which relates the original problem — born from one or born from two? — to the derivative problem: born from different or born from same? By a correlation of this type, the overrating of blood relations is to the underrating of blood relations as the attempt to escape autochthony is to the impossibility to succeed in it. Although experience contradicts theory, social life validates cosmology by its similarity of structure. Hence cosmology is true.

Two remarks should be made at this stage.

In order to interpret the myth, we left aside a point which has worried the specialists until now, namely, that in the earlier (Homeric) versions of the Oedipus myth, some basic elements are lacking, such as Jocasta killing herself and Oedipus piercing his own eyes. These events do not alter the substance of the myth although they can easily be integrated, the first one as a new case of autodestruction (column three) and the second as another case of crippledness (column four). At the same time there is something significant in these additions, since the shift from foot to head is to be correlated with the shift from autochthonous origin to self-destruction.

Our method thus eliminates a problem which has, so far, been one of the main obstacles to the progress of mythological studies, namely, the quest for the *true* version, or the *earlier* one. On the contrary, we define the myth as consisting of all its versions; or to put it otherwise, a myth remains the same as long as it is felt as such. A striking example is offered by the fact that our interpretation may take into account the Freudian use of the Oedipus myth and is certainly applicable to it. Although the Freudian problem has ceased to be that of autochthony *versus* bisexual reproduction, it is still the problem of understanding how *one* can be born from *two:* How is it that we do not have only one procreator, but a mother plus a father? Therefore, not only Sophocles, but Freud himself, should be included among the recorded versions of the Oedipus myth on a par with earlier or seemingly more "authentic" versions.

An important consequence follows. If a myth is made up of all its variants, structural analysis should take all of them into account. After analyzing all the known variants of the Theban version, we should thus treat the others in the same way: first, the tales about Labdacos' collateral line including Agave, Pentheus, and Jocasta herself; the Theban variant about Lycos with Amphion and Zetos as the city founders; more remote variants concerning Dionysus (Oedipus' matrilateral cousin); and Athenian legends where Cecrops take the place of Cadmos, etc. For each of them a similar chart should be drawn and then compared and reorganized according to the findings: Cecrops killing the serpent with the parallel episode of Cadmos; abandonment of Dionysus with abandonment of Oedipus; "Swollen Foot" with Dionysus' *loxias,* that is, walking obliquely; Europa's quest with Antiope's; the founding of Thebes by the Spartoi or by the brothers Amphion and Zetos; Zeus kidnapping Europa and Antiope and the same with Semele; the Theban Oedipus and the Argian Perseus, etc. We shall then have several two-dimensional charts, each dealing with a variant, to be organized in a three-dimensional order, as shown in Figure 1, so that three different readings become possible: left to right, top to bottom, front to back (or vice versa). All of these charts cannot be expected to be identical; but experience shows that any difference to be observed may be correlated with other differences, so that a logical treatment of the whole will allow simplifications, the final outcome being the structural law of the myth.

At this point the objection may be raised that the task is impossible to perform, since we can

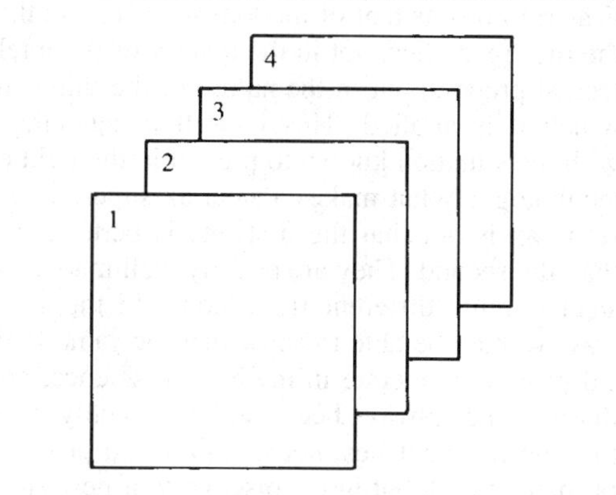

Figure 1

only work with known versions. Is it not possible that a new version might alter the picture? This is true enough if only one or two versions are available, but the objection becomes theoretical as soon as a reasonably large number have been recorded. Let us make this point clear by a comparison. If the furniture of a room and its arrangement were known to us only through its reflection in two mirrors placed on opposite walls, we should theoretically dispose of an almost infinite number of mirror images which would provide us with a complete knowledge. However, should the two mirrors be obliquely set, the number of mirror images would become very small; nevertheless, four or five such images would very likely give us, if not complete information, at least a sufficient coverage so that we would feel sure that no large piece of furniture is missing in our description.

On the other hand, it cannot be too strongly emphasized that all available variants should be taken into account. If Freudian comments on the Oedipus complex are a part of the Oedipus myth, then questions such as whether Cushing's version of the Zuni origin myth should be retained or discarded become irrelevant. There is no single "true" version of which all the others are but copies or distortions. Every version belongs to the myth.

The reason for the discouraging results in works on general mythology can finally be understood. They stem from two causes. First, comparative mythologists have selected preferred versions instead of using them all. Second, we have seen that the structural analysis of *one* variant of *one* myth belonging to *one* tribe (in some cases, even *one* village) already requires two dimensions. When we use several variants of the same myth for the same tribe or village, the frame of reference becomes three-dimensional, and as soon as we try to enlarge the comparison, the number of dimensions required increases until it appears quite impossible to handle them intuitively. The confusions and platitudes which are the outcome of comparative mythology can be explained by the fact that multidimensional frames of reference are often ignored or are naïvely replaced by two- or three-dimensional ones. Indeed, progress in comparative mythology depends largely on the cooperation of mathematicians who would undertake to express in symbols multidimensional relations which cannot be handled otherwise.

Three final remarks may serve as conclusion.

First, the question has often been raised why myths, and more generally oral literature, are so much addicted to duplication, triplication, or quadruplication of the same sequence. If our hypotheses are accepted, the answer is obvious: The function of repetition is to render the structure of the myth apparent. For we have seen that the synchronic-diachronic structure of the myth permits us to organize it into diachronic sequences (the rows in our tables) which should be read synchronically (the columns). Thus, a myth exhibits a "slated" structure, which comes to the surface, so to speak, through the process of repetition.

However, the slates are not absolutely identical. And since the purpose of myth is to provide a logical model capable of overcoming a contradiction (an impossible achievement if, as it happens, the contradiction is real), a theoretically infinite number of slates will be generated, each one slightly different from the others. Thus, myth grows spiral-wise until the intellectual impulse which has produced it is exhausted. Its *growth* is a continuous process, whereas its *structure* remains discontinuous. If this is the case, we should assume that it closely corresponds, in the realm of the spoken word, to a crystal in the realm of physical matter. This analogy may help us to better understand the relationship of myth to both *langue* on the one hand and *parole* on the other. Myth is an intermediary entity between a statistical aggregate of molecules and the molecular structure itself.

Prevalent attempts to explain alleged differences between the so-called primitive mind and scientific thought have resorted to qualitative differences between the working processes of the mind in both cases, while assuming that the entities which they were studying remained very much the same. If our interpretation is correct, we are led toward a completely different view — namely, that the kind of logic in mythical thought is as rigorous as that of modern science, and that the difference lies, not in the quality of the intellectual process, but in the nature of the things to which it is applied. This is well in agreement with the situation known to prevail in the field of technology: What makes a steel ax superior to a stone ax is not that the first one is better made than the second. They are equally well made, but steel is quite different from stone. In the same way we may be able to show that the same logical processes operate in myth as in science, and that man has always been thinking equally well; the improvement lies, not in an alleged progress of man's mind, but in the discovery of new areas to which it may apply its unchanged and unchanging powers.

Gérard Genette

b. 1930

Gérard Genette, one of the founders of the structuralist journal Poétique *(1970), was born in Paris in 1930 and educated at the École Normale Superiéure, where he took his Agrégé de lettres classiques in 1954; he received his Docteur ès lettres in 1972. After teaching for several years in provincial lycées, he was appointed to the Sorbonne in 1963 and taught there until 1967. Since 1967 Genette has been on the faculty at the École Practique des Hautes Études en sciences sociales in Paris, where he is one of the Directeurs d'études, combining this appointment with frequent visiting professorships at New York University. Genette's publications include the three volumes of essays published as* Figures *(1966, 1969, 1972); the long essay on Proust from* Figures III *was translated as* Narrative Discourse. *A selection of shorter essays, from which "Frontiers of Narrative" is taken, was translated as* Figures of Literary Discourse *in 1982. His other works include* Mimologiques *(1976),* Introduction à l'architexte *(1979),* Seuils *(1987),* Fiction et diction *(1991; translated as* Fiction and Diction, *1993),* L'Oeuvre de l'art: immanence et transcendence *(1994), and* Mimologiques *(1995).*

Frontiers of Narrative

If one agrees, following convention, to confine oneself to the domain of literary expression, one will define narrative without difficulty as the representation of an event or sequence of events, real or fictitious, by means of language and, more particularly, by means of written language. This positive (and current) definition has the merit of being simple and self-evident; its principal inconvenience may be precisely that it confines itself and confines us to self-evidence, that it conceals from us what specifically, in the very being of narrative, constitutes a problem and a diffi-

Translated by Alan Sheridan.

culty, by effacing as it were the frontiers of its operation, the conditions of its existence. To define the narrative positively is to give credence, perhaps dangerously, to the idea of feeling that narrative *tells itself,* that nothing is more natural than to tell a story or to put together a set of actions in a myth, a tale, an epic, or a novel. The evolution of literature and of literary consciousness in the last half century will have had, among other fortunate consequences, that of drawing our attention, on the contrary, to the singular, artificial, and problematic aspect of the narrative act. We must return once more to Valéry's amazement at a statement like "the marquise went out at five o'clock." We know how, in various and sometimes contradictory ways, modern literature has lived and illustrated this fruitful amazement, how it has striven and succeeded, in its very foundations, to be a questioning, a disturbance, a contestation of the notion of narrative. That falsely naïve question "why narrative?" could at least encourage us to seek, or more simply to recognize, what might be called the negative limits of narrative, to consider the principal sets of oppositions through which narrative is defined, and constitutes itself over against the various forms of the non-narrative.

DIEGESIS AND MIMESIS

The first opposition to occur to us is that indicated by Aristotle in a few brief sentences in the *Poetics*. For Aristotle, narrative (*diegesis*) is one of the two modes of poetic imitation (*mimesis*), the other being the direct representation of events by actors speaking and moving before the public.[1] It is here that the classic distinction between narrative poetry and dramatic poetry is established. This distinction was already suggested by Plato in the third book of the *Republic,* though with two differences: first, Socrates denied to narrative the quality (that is to say, for him, the defect) of imitation and, second, he took into account aspects of direct representation (dialogues) that can be included in a nondramatic poem like those of Homer. There are, therefore, at the origins of the classical tradition, two apparently contradictory divisions, in which narrative is opposed to imitation, either as its antithesis or as one of its modes.

For Plato, the domain of what he calls *lexis* (or way of saying, as opposed to *logos,* which designates what is said) is theoretically divided into imitation proper (*mimesis*) and simple narrative (*diegesis*). By simple narrative, Plato means whatever the poet relates "in his own person," without trying "to persuade us that the speaker is anyone but himself,"[2] as when Homer, in Book I of the *Iliad,* tells us of Chryses: "[He] had come to the Achaean ships to recover his captured daughter. He brought with him a generous ransom and carried the chaplet of the Archer God Apollo on a golden staff in his hand. He appealed to the whole Achaean army, and most of all to its two commanders, the sons of Atreus."[3] Imitation, on the other hand, begins with the next line, when Homer has Chryses himself say, or rather, according to Plato, when Homer speaks in the person of Chryses and "does his best to make us think that it is not Homer but an aging priest that is talking." This is the text of Chryses' speech: "My lords, and you Achaean men-at-arms; you hope to sack King Priam's city and get home in safety. May the gods that live on Olympus grant your wish — on this condition, that you show your reverence for the Archer-god Apollo Son of Zeus by accepting this ransom and releasing my daughter." Now, Plato adds, Homer could equally well have continued his narrative in a purely narrative form, *recounting* Chryses' words instead of quoting them, which, for the same passage, would have given, in indirect style and in prose: "The priest came and prayed that the gods would allow the Achaeans to capture Troy and return in safety, and begged the Achaeans to show their respect for the god by releasing his daughter in exchange for the ransom."[4] This theoretical division, which opposes, within poetic diction, the two pure, heterogeneous modes of narrative and imitation, brings

[1]Aristotle, *Poetics,* 1448a [Au.]; see pp. 43–44. [Ed.]

[2]Plato, *Republic,* 393a; *Republic,* D. Lee, tr. 2nd. rev. ed. (Harmondsworth: Penguin, 1974), p. 150. [Au.]

[3]Homer, *Iliad,* Book I, lines 12–16; *Iliad,* E. V. Rieu, tr. (Harmondsworth: Penguin, 1953), p. 23. [Au.]

[4]Plato, *Republic,* 393e; *Repub.,* p. 151. [Au.]

with it and establishes a practical classification of the genres, which comprises the two pure modes (narrative, represented by the ancient dithyramb, and mimetic, represented by the theater), plus a mixed or, to be more precise, alternate mode, which is that of the epic, as we have just seen with the example from the *Iliad*.

At first sight Aristotle's classification is quite different, since it reduces all poetry to imitation, distinguishing only two imitative modes, the direct, which is the one Plato calls strict imitation, and the narrative, which he calls, as does Plato, *diegesis*. On the other hand, Aristotle seems to fully identify not only, like Plato, the dramatic genre with the imitative mode, but also, without taking into account in principle its mixed character, the epic genre with the pure narrative mode. This reduction may derive from the fact that Aristotle defines the imitative mode, more strictly than Plato, by the scenic conditions of dramatic representation. It might also be justified by the fact that the epic work, however important a part is played in it by dialogues or discourse in the direct style, and even if this part exceeds that of the narrative, remains essentially narrative, in that the dialogues are necessarily framed in it and induced by narrative parts that constitute, in the strict sense, the *basis* or, to put it another way, the web of its discourse. In any case, Aristotle recognizes Homer's superiority over all other epic poets in that he intervenes personally as little as possible in his poem, usually dramatizing his characters directly, in accordance with the role of the poet, which is to imitate as much as possible.[5] This would suggest that he implicitly recognizes the imitative character of the Homeric dialogues and therefore the mixed character of epic diction, basically narrative, but dramatic in a wider sense.

The difference between Plato's and Aristotle's classifications amounts, then, to a simple variation of terms; these two classifications certainly agree on the main point, that is to say, the opposition between the dramatic and the narrative, the first being regarded by both philosophers as more fully imitative than the second: an agreement on facts that is in a sense brought out more by the disagreement on values, since Plato condemns poets as imitators, beginning with the dramatists, and not excepting Homer, who is regarded as still being too mimetic for a narrative poet, admitting into the City only some ideal poet whose austere diction would be as little mimetic as possible;[6] whereas Aristotle, symmetrically, places tragedy above epic, and praises in Homer whatever brings his writing closer to dramatic diction.[7] The two systems, then, are certainly identical, except for a reversal of values: for Plato as for Aristotle, narrative is the weakened, attenuated mode of literary representation — and it is difficult, at first sight, to see how one could come to a different conclusion.

However, we must introduce here an observation which does not seem to have concerned either Plato or Aristotle, and which will restore to the narrative all its value and all its importance. Direct imitation, as it functions on the stage, consists of gestures and speech. Insofar as it consists of gestures, it can obviously represent actions, but at this point it escapes from the linguistic plane, which is that in which the specific activity of the poet is practised. Insofar as it consists of words, discourse spoken by characters (and it goes without saying that in a narrative work the role of direct imitation is reduced to that), it is not strictly speaking representative, since it is confined to reproducing a real or fictitious discourse as such. It can be said that verses 12 to 16 of the *Iliad*, quoted above, give us a verbal representation of Chryses' actions, but the same cannot be said of the next five lines; they do not *represent* Chryses' speech: if this is a speech, actually spoken, they *repeat* it, literally, and if it is fictitious speech, they *constitute* it, just as literally. In both cases, the work of representation is nil; in both cases, Homer's five lines are strictly identical with Chryses' speech: this is obviously not so in the case of the five narrative lines preceding it, which are in no way identical with Chryses' actions: "The word 'dog' does not bite," William James remarked. If we call poetic imitation the fact of representing by verbal means a nonverbal reality and, in exceptional cir-

[5]Aristotle, *Poetics*, 1460a [Au.]; see p. 61. [Ed.]

[6]See Plato, *Republic*, Book X, pp. 28–29. [Ed.]

[7]See Aristotle, *Poetics*, p. 61. [Ed.]

cumstances, a verbal reality (as one calls pictorial imitation the fact of representing in pictorial means nonpictorial reality and, in exceptional circumstances, a pictorial reality), it must be admitted that imitation is to be found in the five narrative lines and not at all in the five dramatic lines, which consist simply in the interpolation, in the middle of a text representing events, of another text directly taken from those events: as if a seventeenth-century Dutch painter, anticipating certain modern methods, had placed in the middle of a still life, not the painting of an oyster shell, but a real oyster shell. I make this simplistic comparison in order to point out the profoundly heterogeneous character of a mode of expression to which we are so used that we do not perceive its most sudden changes of register. Plato's "mixed" narrative, that is to say, the most common and universal mode or relation, "imitates" alternately and in the same register ("without even seeing the difference," as Michaux would say), nonverbal material, which in fact it must represent as best it can, and verbal material that represents itself, and which it is usually content to quote. In the case of a strictly faithful historical account, the historian-narrator must certainly be aware of the change of manner when he passes from the narrative effort of relating completed actions to the mechanical transcription of spoken words, but in the case of a partially or totally fictitious narrative, fictional activity, which bears equally on the verbal and nonverbal contents, no doubt has the effect of concealing the difference that separates the two types of imitation, one of which involves, if I may so put it, direct contact, while the other introduces a rather more complex system of levels. Even if one admits (as is difficult enough) that imagining actions and imagining spoken words proceed from the same mental operation, "telling" these actions and telling these words constitute two very different verbal operations. Or rather, only the first constitutes a true operation, an act of *diction* in the Platonic sense, involving a series of transpositions and equivalences, and a series of inevitable choices between the elements of the *story* to be retained and the elements to be left out, between the various possible points of view, and so on — all of which are operations that are obviously absent when the poet or historian confines himself to transcribing a speech. One may certainly (indeed one must) challenge this distinction between the act of mental representation and the act of verbal representation, between the *logos* and the *lexis,* but it amounts to challenging the very theory of imitation, which conceives poetic fiction as a simulacrum of reality, as transcendent to the discourse that sustains it as the historical event is external to the discourse of the historian or the landscape represented to the picture that represents it: a theory that makes no distinction between fiction and representation, the object of fiction being reduced to a feigned reality that is simply awaiting representation. Now it appears that from this point of view the very notion of imitation on the level of the *lexis* is a pure mirage, which vanishes as one approaches it; the only thing that language can imitate perfectly is language, or, to be more precise, a discourse can imitate only itself. *Qua lexis,* direct imitation is simply a tautology.

So we are led to this unexpected conclusion, that the only mode that knows literature as representation is the narrative, the verbal equivalent of nonverbal events and also (as the example made up by Plato shows) of verbal events, unless it vanishes, as in the last case, before a direct quotation in which all representative function is abolished, rather as a speaker in a court of law may interrupt his speech to allow the court to scrutinize some exhibit. Literary representation, the *mimesis* of the ancients, is not, therefore, narrative plus "speeches": it is narrative, and only narrative. Plato opposed *mimesis* to *diegesis* as a perfect imitation to an imperfect imitation; but (as Plato himself showed in the *Cratylus*) perfect imitation is no longer an imitation, it is the thing itself, and, in the end, the only imitation is an imperfect one. *Mimesis* is *diegesis*.

NARRATION AND DESCRIPTION

But if literary representation defined in this way is identical with narrative (in the broad sense), it is not to be reduced to the purely narrative elements (in the narrow sense) of the narrative. We must now admit, within diegesis itself, a distinction that appears neither in Plato nor in Aristotle, and which will draw a new frontier within the domain of representation. Every narrative in fact comprises two kinds of representations, which however are closely intermingled and in variable proportions: on the one hand, those of actions and events, which constitute the narration in the strict sense and, on the other hand, those of objects or characters that are the result of what we now call *description.* The opposition between narration and description, which was so stressed by academic tradition, is one of the major features of our literary consciousness. Yet it is a relatively recent distinction, the birth and development of which in the theory and practice of literature should one day be studied. It does not seem, at first sight, that it enjoyed a very active existence before the nineteenth century, when the introduction of long descriptive passages in a typically narrative genre like the novel brought out the resources and the requirements of the method.[8]

This persistent confusion, or carelessness of distinction, which in Greek is shown very clearly by the use of the common term *diegesis,* derives perhaps above all from the very unequal literary status of the two types of representation. In principle, it is obviously possible to conceive of purely descriptive texts, the aim of which is to represent objects simply and solely in their spatial existence, outside any event and even outside any temporal dimension. It is even easier to conceive of a pure description of any narrative element than the reverse, for the most neutral designation of the elements and circumstances of a process can already be regarded as the beginnings of a description: a sentence like "The house is white, with a slate roof and green shutters," involves no element of narration, whereas a sentence like "The man went over to the table and picked up a knife," contains at least, apart from two verbs of action, three substantives which, however little qualified, can be regarded as descriptive by the very fact that they designate animate or inanimate beings; even a verb can be more or less descriptive, in the precision that it gives to the spectacle of the action (one has only to compare "grabbed a knife," for example, with "picked up a knife"), and consequently no verb is quite exempt from descriptive resonance. It may be said, then, that description is more indispensable than narration, since it is easier to describe without relating than it is to relate without describing (perhaps because objects can exist without movement, but not movement without objects). But this elementary situation already indicates, in fact, the nature of the relation that unites the two functions in the overwhelming majority of literary texts: description might be conceived independently of narration, but in fact it is never found in a so to speak free state; narration cannot exist without description, but this dependence does not prevent it from constantly playing the major role. Description is quite naturally *ancilla narrationis,*[9] the ever-necessary, ever-submissive, never-emancipated slave. There are narrative genres, such as the epic, the tale, the novella, the novel, in which description can occupy a very large place, even in terms of sheer quantity the larger place, without ceasing to be, by its very vocation, a mere auxiliary of the narrative. On the other hand, there are no descriptive genres, and one finds it difficult to imagine, outside the didactic domain (or semididactic fictions such as those of Jules Verne), a work in which narrative would serve as an auxiliary to description.

The study of the relations between the narrative and the descriptive amounts, then, in essence, to a consideration of the *diegetic functions* of description, that is to say, the role played by the descriptive passages or aspects in the general economy of narrative. Without attempting to go into the detail of such a study here, one could at least mention, in the "classical" literary tradition (from Homer to the end of the nineteenth century), two relatively distinct functions. The first is of what might be called a decorative kind. We know that traditional rhetoric places description, together with the other figures of style, among the ornaments of discourse: extended, detailed description appears here as a recreational pause

[8]It is to be found however in Boileau on the subject of the epic: "Soyez vif et pressé dans vos narations; / Soyez riche et pompeux dans vos descriptions." (*Art Poétique,* III, 257–58). [Au.]

[9]The servant of narration. [Ed.]

in the narrative, carrying out a purely esthetic role, like that of sculpture in a classical building. The most famous example is perhaps the description of Achilles' shield in Book XVIII of the *Iliad.*[10] It is no doubt this decorative role that Boileau has in mind when he recommends richness and splendor in this kind of piece. The Baroque epic was noted for a sort of proliferation of the descriptive excursus, very marked for example in Saint-Amant's *Moyse sauvé,* which finally destroyed the balance of the narrative poem in its decline.

The second major function of description, and the most obvious in our own day because it was imposed, with Balzac, on the tradition of the novel, is both explanatory and symbolic: physical portraits, descriptions of dress and furniture tend, in Balzac and his realist successors, to reveal and at the same time to justify the psychology of the characters, of which they are at once the sign, the cause, and the effect. Description becomes here a major element in the exposition, which it was not in the classical period: one has only to think of the houses of Mlle Cormon in *La Vieille fille* or of Balthazar Claës in *La Recherche de l'absolu.* But all this is too well known to be labored here. I would just like to remark that, in substituting significant description for ornamental description, the evolution of narrative form has tended (at least until the early twentieth century) to reinforce the domination of the narrative element: without the slightest doubt description has lost in terms of autonomy what it has gained in dramatic importance. As for certain forms of the contemporary novel that appeared initially as attempts to free the descriptive mode from the tyranny of the narrative, it is by no means certain that the question should really be interpreted in this way: if one considers it from this point of view, the work of Robbe-Grillet appears rather perhaps as an effort to constitute a narrative (a *story*) almost exclusively by means of descriptions imperceptibly modified from one page to the next, which can be regarded both as a spectacular promotion of the descriptive function and as a striking confirmation of its irreducible narrative finality.

Lastly, it should be noted that all the differences which separate description and narration are differences of content, which, strictly speaking, have no semiological existence: narration is concerned with actions or events considered as pure processes, and by that very fact it stresses the temporal, dramatic aspect of the narrative; description, on the other hand, because it lingers on objects and beings considered in their simultaneity, and because it considers the processes themselves as spectacles, seems to suspend the course of time and to contribute to spreading the narrative in space. These two types of discourse may, then, appear to express two antithetical attitudes to the world and to existence, one more active, the other more contemplative, and therefore, following a traditional equivalence, more "poetic." But from the point of view of modes of representation, to recount an event and to describe an object are two similar operations, which bring into play the same resources of language. The most significant difference might be that narration restores, in the temporal succession of its discourse, the equally temporal succession of events, whereas description must modulate, in discursive succession, the representation of objects that are simultaneous and juxtaposed in space: narrative language, then, would appear to be distinguished by a sort of temporal coincidence with its object, of which descriptive language would, on the contrary, be irremediably deprived. But this opposition loses much of its force in written literature, where nothing prevents the reader from going back and considering the text, in its spatial simultaneity, as an *analogon* of the spectacle that it describes: Apollinaire's calligrams or the graphic dispositions of Mallarmé's *coup de dés* simply push to the limit the exploitation of certain resources latent in written expression. Furthermore, no narration, not even that of broadcast reporting, is strictly synchronic with the events that it relates, and the variety of the relations which can exist between the time of the story and that of the narrative have the effect of reducing the specificity of narrative representation. Aristotle already observed that one of the advantages of narrative over the-

[10]At least as interpreted and imitated by the classical tradition. It should be noted however that description here tends to become animated and therefore to turn itself into narrative. [Au.]

atrical representation was that it could deal with several simultaneous actions;[11] but it has to deal with them successively, and from then on its situation, its resources, and its limits are similar to those of descriptive language.

It would appear then that description, as a mode of literary representation, does not distinguish itself sufficiently clearly from narration, either by the autonomy of its ends, or by the originality of its means, for it to be necessary to break the narrative-descriptive (chiefly narrative) unity that Plato and Aristotle have called narrative. If description marks one of the frontiers of narrative, it is certainly an internal frontier, and really a rather vague one: it will do no harm, therefore, if we embrace within the notion of narrative all forms of literary representation and consider description not as one of its modes (which would imply a specificity of language), but, more modestly, as one of its aspects — if, from a certain point of view, the most attractive.

NARRATIVE AND DISCOURSE

Reading the *Republic* and the *Poetics,* it would seem that, from the outset, Plato and Aristotle implicitly reduce the field of literature to the particular domain of representative literature: *poiesis = mimesis.* If one considers everything that is excluded from the poetic by this decision, we see the emergence of a last frontier of narrative that might be the most important and most significant. This frontier concerns nothing less than lyric, satirical, and didactic poetry: namely, to confine ourselves to a few of the names that would be known to a fifth- or fourth-century Greek, Pindar, Alcaeus, Sappho, Archilochos, and Hesiod. Thus, for Aristotle, Empedocles is not a poet, even though he uses the same meter as Homer: "Hence the proper term for the one is 'poet,' for the other 'science-writer' rather than 'poet.' "[12] But certainly Archilochos, Sappho, and Pindar cannot be called scientists: what all those excluded from the *Poetics* have in common is that their work does not consist in the imitation, by narrative or theatrical representation, of an action, real or pretended, external to the person and speech of the poet, but simply in a discourse spoken by him directly and in his own name. Pindar sings the merits of the winner at the Olympics, Archilochos inveighs against his political enemies, Hesiod gives advice to farmers, Empedocles or Parmenides expounds his theory of the universe: no representation, no fiction is involved here, simply speech that is invested directly in the discourse of the work. The same could be said of Latin elegiac poetry and of everything that makes use of eloquence, moral and philosophical reflection,[13] scientific or parascientific exposition, the essay, correspondence, the journal, etc. All this vast domain of direct expression, whatever the modes, peculiarities, forms, eludes the consideration of the *Poetics* in that it neglects the representative function of poetry. We have here a new division, of very wide scope, since it divides into two parts of roughly equal importance the whole of what we now call literature.

This division corresponds more or less to the distinction proposed by Émile Benveniste between *narrative* (or *story*) and *discourse,*[14] except that Benveniste includes in the category of discourse everything that Aristotle called direct imitation, and which actually consists, at least as far as its verbal part is concerned, of discourse attributed by the poet or narrator to one of his characters. Benveniste shows that certain grammatical forms, like the pronoun "I" (and its implicit reference "you"), the pronominal (certain demonstratives), or adverbial indicators (like "here," "now," "yesterday," "today," "tomorrow," etc.) and — at least in French — certain tenses of the verb, like the present, the present anterior, or the future, are confined to discourse, whereas narrative in its strict form is marked by the exclusive

[11]Aristotle, *Poetics,* 1459b; see p. 60. [Ed.]

[12]Aristotle, *Poetics,* 1447b; see p. 42. [Ed.]

[13]Since it is the diction that counts here, and not what is said, we will exclude from this list, as does Aristotle (*Poetics* 1447b), Plato's Socratic dialogues, and all expositions in dramatic form, which belong to imitation in prose. [Au.] See p. 42. [Ed.]

[14]Émile Benveniste, "Les relations de temps dans le verbe français," *Problèmes de linguistique générale,* pp. 237–50; "The Correlations of Tense in the French Verb," *Problems in General Linguistics,* M. E. Meek, tr. (Coral Cables, Florida: University of Miami Press, 1971), pp. 205–15. [Au.]

use of the third person and such forms as the aorist (past definite) and the pluperfect. Whatever the details and variations from one idiom to another, all these differences amount clearly to an opposition between the objectivity of narrative and the subjectivity of discourse; but it should be pointed out that such objectivity and subjectivity are defined by criteria of a strictly linguistic order: "subjective" discourse is that in which, explicitly or not, the presence of (or reference to) *I* is marked, but this is not defined in any other way except as the person who is speaking this discourse, just as the present, which is the tense *par excellence* of the discursive mode, is not defined other than as the moment when the discourse is being spoken, its use marking "the coincidence of the event described with the instance of discourse that describes it."[15] Conversely, the objectivity of narrative is defined by the absence of any reference to the narrator: "As a matter of fact, there is then no longer even a narrator. The events are set forth chronologically, as they occur. No one speaks here; the events seem to narrate themselves."[16]

We have here, no doubt, a perfect description of what is, in its essence and in its radical opposition to any form of personal expression on the part of the speaker, narrative in the pure state, as it may be conceived ideally and as it may in fact be grasped in a few privileged examples, like those borrowed by Benveniste himself from the historian Glotz and from Balzac. Let us reproduce here the extract from the latter's *Gambara,* which we will have to consider with some attention:

> After a walk round the gallery, the young man looked in turn at the sky and at his watch, made a gesture of impatience, entered a tobacconist's, lit a cigar, placed himself in front of a mirror, and examined his clothes, which were somewhat richer than the laws of taste allow in France. He adjusted his collar and black velvet waistcoat over which was crossed several times one of those thick gold chains made in Genoa; then, after flinging his velvet-lined overcoat over his left shoulder, draping it elegantly, in a single movement, he resumed his walk without allowing himself to be distracted by the bourgeois glances cast in his direction. When the shops began to light up and the night seemed dark enough, he walked towards the Place du Palais-Royal like a man who was fearful of being recognized, for he skirted the square as far as the fountain, before reaching, under cover of the cabs, the end of the Rue Froidmanteau.

At this degree of purity, the diction proper to the narrative is in some sense the absolute transitivity of the text, the complete absence (if we ignore a few exceptions to which we will return shortly), not only of the narrator, but also of the narration itself, by the rigorous expunging of any reference to the instance of discourse that constitutes it. The text is there, before our eyes, without being proffered by anyone, and none (or almost none) of the information it contains needs, in order to be understood or appreciated, to be related to its source, judged by its distance from or its relation to the speaker or to the utterance. If we compare such a statement to a sentence like "I was waiting to write to you that I had definitely decided to stay. At last I have made up my mind: I shall spend the winter here,"[17] one appreciates to what extent the autonomy of narrative is opposed to the dependence of discourse, the essential determinations of which (who is "I," who is "you," what place is referred to by "here"?) can be deciphered only in relation to the situation in which it was produced. In discourse, someone speaks, and his situation in the very act of speaking is the focus of the most important significations; in narrative, as Benveniste forcefully puts it, *no one speaks,* in the sense that at no moment do we ask ourselves *who is speaking, where, when,* and so forth, in order to receive the full signification of the text.

But it should be added at once that these essences of narrative and discourse so defined are almost never to be found in their pure state in any text: there is almost always a certain proportion of narrative in discourse, a certain amount of discourse in narrative. In fact, the symmetry stops

[15]Émile Benveniste, "De la subjectivité dans le langage" in *Problèmes,* p. 262; "Subjectivity in Language" in *Problems,* p. 227. [Au.]

[16]Benveniste, "Les relations des temps," p. 241; *Problems,* p. 208. [Au.]

[17]Senancour, *Obermann,* Lettre v. [Au.]

here, for it is as if both types of expression were very differently affected by the contamination: the insertion of narrative elements in the level of discourse is not enough to emancipate discourse, for they generally remain linked to the reference by the speaker, who remains implicitly present in the background, and who may intervene again at any moment without this return being experienced as an "intrusion." Thus, we read in Chateaubriand's *Mémoires d'outre-tombe* this apparently objective passage:

> When the sea was high and it was stormy, the waves, beating at the foot of the castle, along the great shore, spouted up as far as the great towers. Twenty feet above the base of one of these towers was a granite parapet, narrow and gleaming, sloping outwards, from which one communicated with the ravelin that defended the moat: we would seize the moment between two waves, and cross the perilous place before the flow broke again and covered the tower.[18]

But we know that the narrator, who has momentarily effaced himself during this passage, is not very far away, and we are neither surprised nor embarrassed when he speaks again, adding: "Not one of *us* refused the adventure, but *I* have seen children pale before attempting it." The narration had not really emerged from the order of discourse in the first person, which had absorbed it without effort or distortion, and without ceasing to be itself. On the contrary, any intervention of discursive elements within a narrative is felt as a relaxation of the rigor of the narrative part. The same goes for the brief reflection inserted by Balzac mentioned above: "his clothes, which were *somewhat richer than the laws of taste allow in France*." The same can be said for the demonstrative expression "*one of those thick gold chains made at Genoa,*" which obviously contains the beginnings of a passage ("made" corresponds not to *which were made,* but *which are made*) and of a direct address to the reader, who is implicitly taken as a witness. Again, the same could be said of the adjective in "*bourgeois* glances" and of the adverb "*elegantly,*" which imply a judgment the source of which is here quite obviously the narrator; the relative expression "*like a man who was fearful,*" which Latin would mark with a subjunctive for the personal appraisal that it involves; and lastly of the conjunction "*for* he skirted," which introduces an explanation offered by the narrator. It is obvious that narrative does not integrate these discursive enclaves, rightly called by Georges Blin "authorial intrusions," as easily as discourse receives the narrative enclaves: narrative inserted into discourse is transformed into an element of discourse, discourse inserted into narrative remains discourse and forms a sort of cyst that is very easy to recognize and to locate. The purity of narrative, one might say, is more manifest than that of discourse.

Though the reason for this dissymmetry is very simple, it indicates for us a decisive character of narrative: in fact, discourse has no purity to preserve, for it is the broadest and most universal "natural" mode of language, welcoming by definition all other forms; narrative, on the other hand, is a particular mode, marked, defined by a number of exclusions and restrictive conditions (refusal of the present, the first person, and so forth). Discourse can "recount" without ceasing to be discourse, narrative cannot "discourse" without emerging from itself. Nor can it abstain from it completely, however, without falling into aridity and poverty: this is why narrative exists nowhere, so to speak, in its strict form. The slightest general observation, the slightest adjective that is little more than descriptive, the most discreet comparison, the most modest "perhaps," the most inoffensive of logical articulations introduces into its web a type of speech that is alien to it, refractory as it were. In order to study the detail of these sometimes microscopic accidents, we would need innumerable, meticulous analyses of texts. One of the objects of this study would be to list and classify the means by which narrative literature (and in particular the novel) has tried to organize in an acceptable way, within its own *lexis,* the delicate relations maintained within it between the requirements of narrative and the needs of discourse.

We know in fact that the novel has never succeeded in resolving in a convincing and definitive way the problem posed by these relations.

[18]F. R. de Chateaubriand, *Mémoires d'outre-tombe,* Book I, ch. 5. [Au.]

Sometimes, as was the case in the classical period, with a Cervantes, a Scarron, a Fielding, the author-narrator, happily assuming his own discourse, intervenes in the narrative with ironically labored indiscretion, addressing his reader in a familiar, conversational tone; sometimes, on the other hand, as we also see in the same period, he transfers all responsibility for the discourse to a principal character who will *speak,* that is to say, both recount events and comment on them in the first person: this is the case of the picaresque novels, from *Lazarillo de Tormes* to *Gil Blas,* and other fictively autobiographical works, such as *Manon Lescaut* and *La Vie de Marianne;* sometimes, again, being unable to make up his mind whether to speak in his own name or to entrust this task to a single character, he distributes discourse between the various actors, either in the form of letters, as was often the case in the eighteenth-century novel (*La Nouvelle Héloïse, Les Liaisons dangereuses*) or, in the more supple and subtle manner of a Joyce or a Faulkner, by letting his principal characters assume the narrative successively through their interior discourse. The only moment when the balance between narrative and discourse seems to have been assumed with a perfectly good conscience, without either scruple or ostentation, is obviously in the nineteenth century, the classical age of objective narration, from Balzac to Tolstoy; we see, on the contrary, how the modern period has stressed awareness of difficulty to the extent of making certain types of elocution almost physically impossible for the most lucid and rigorous of writers.

We know, for example, how the effort to bring narrative to its highest degree of purity led certain American writers, such as Hammett or Hemingway, to exclude any exposition of psychological motives, which are always difficult to carry off without recourse to general considerations of a discursive kind, qualifications implying a personal judgment on the part of the narrator, logical links, and the like, to the point of reducing fictional diction to that jerky succession of short sentences without articulations, which Sartre recognized in 1943 in Camus' *L'Étranger,* and which were to turn up again ten years later in Robbe-Grillet. What has often been interpreted as an application to literature of behaviorist theories may have been no more than the effect of a particularly acute sensitivity to certain incompatibilities of language. All the fluctuations of contemporary fictional writing could no doubt be analyzed from this point of view, and particularly the tendency today, perhaps the reverse of the earlier one, and quite overt in a Phillipe Sollers of a Jean Thibaudeau, for example, to absorb the narrative in the present discourse of the writer in the process of writing, in what Michel Foucault calls "discourse bound up with the act of writing, contemporary with its unfolding and enclosed within it."[19] It is as if literature had exhausted or overflowed the resources of its representative mode, and wanted to fold back into the indefinite murmur of its own discourse. Perhaps the novel, after poetry, is about to emerge definitively from the age of representation. Perhaps narrative, in the negative singularity that we have just attributed to it, is already for us, as art was for Hegel, *a thing of the past,* which we must hurry to consider as it retreats, before it has completely disappeared from our horizon.

[19]"L'Arrière-fable," *L'Arc* (1965), 29:6. [Au.]

Jonathan Culler

b. 1944

To the extent that structuralism and poststructuralism have been well received in North America, much of the credit should be given to Jonathan Dwight Culler, whose lucid distillations of structuralist, semiotic, and deconstructivist theories have reached a wide audience. Culler was born in Cleveland, Ohio, but moved with his family to New Haven, Connecticut, in 1946, when his father,

A. Dwight Culler, accepted a position as professor of Victorian literature at Yale. Culler received a B.A. in history and literature (1966) at Harvard and a Rhodes scholarship to St. John's College at Oxford (1966–69), where he took a B.Phil. in comparative literature (1968) and a D.Phil. in modern languages (1972). Culler was a fellow of Selwyn College, Cambridge (1969–74), and of Brasenose College, Oxford (1974–77), and since 1977 he has been a professor of English and comparative literature at Cornell University. His list of publications is extensive — his books include Flaubert: The Uses of Uncertainty *(1974),* Saussure *(1976, 1977; revised 1986),* The Pursuit of Signs *(1981),* On Deconstruction *(1983), and* Framing the Sign: Criticism and Its Institutions *(1988). "Literary Competence" is the sixth chapter of* Structuralist Poetics *(1975), a revised version of his doctoral thesis, which won the Modern Language Association's prestigious James Russell Lowell Award.*

Literary Competence

> *To understand a sentence means to understand a language. To understand a language means to be master of a technique.*
> — WITTGENSTEIN[1]

When a speaker of a language hears a phonetic sequence, he is able to give it meaning because he brings to the act of communication an amazing repertoire of conscious and unconscious knowledge. Mastery of the phonological, syntactic and semantic systems of his language enables him to convert the sounds into discrete units, to recognize words, and to assign a structural description and interpretation to the resulting sentence, even though it be quite new to him. Without this implicit knowledge, this internalized grammar, the sequence of sounds does not speak to him. We are nevertheless inclined to say that the phonological and grammatical structure and the meaning are *properties* of the utterance, and there is no harm in that way of speaking so long as we remember that they are properties of the utterance only with respect to a particular grammar. Another grammar would assign different properties to the sequence (according to the grammar of a different language, for example, it would be nonsense). To speak of the structure of a sentence is necessarily to imply an internalized grammar that gives it that structure.

We also tend to think of meaning and structure as properties of literary works, and from one point of view this is perfectly correct: when the sequence of words is treated *as a literary work* it has these properties. But that qualification suggests the relevance and importance of the linguistic analogy. The work has structure and meaning because it is read in a particular way, because these potential properties, latent in the object itself, are actualized by the theory of discourse applied in the act of reading. "How can one discover structure without the help of a methodological model?" asks Barthes (*Critique et vérité*, p. 19).[2] To read a text as literature is not to make one's mind a *tabula rasa*[3] and approach it without preconceptions; one must bring to it an implicit understanding of the operations of literary discourse which tells one what to look for.

Anyone lacking this knowledge, anyone wholly unacquainted with literature and unfamiliar with the conventions by which fictions are read, would, for example, be quite baffled if presented with a poem. His knowledge of the language would enable him to understand phrases and sentences, but he would not know, quite literally, what to *make* of this strange concatenation of phrases. He would be unable to read it *as* literature — as we say with emphasis to those who would use literary works for other purposes — because he lacks the complex "literary compe-

[1]Ludwig Wittgenstein, *Philosophical Investigations*. [Ed.]

[2]See Roland Barthes, *Criticism and Truth* (London: Athlone, 1987). [Ed.]

[3]Blank slate. [Ed.]

tence" which enables others to proceed. He has not internalized the "grammar" of literature which would permit him to convert linguistic sequences into literary structures and meanings.

If the analogy seems less than exact it is because in the case of language it is much more obvious that understanding depends on mastery of a system. But the time and energy devoted to literary training in schools and universities indicate that the understanding of literature also depends on experience and mastery. Since literature is a second-order semiotic system which has language as its basis, a knowledge of language will take one a certain distance in one's encounter with literary texts, and it may be difficult to specify precisely where understanding comes to depend on one's supplementary knowledge of literature. But the difficulty of drawing a line does not obscure the palpable difference between understanding the language of a poem, in the sense that one could provide a rough translation into another language, and understanding the poem. If one knows French, one can translate Mallarmé's "Salut," but that translation is not a thematic synthesis — it is not what we would ordinarily call "understanding the poem" — and in order to identify various levels of coherence and set them in relation to one another under the synoptic heading or theme of the "literary quest" one must have considerable experience of the conventions for reading poetry.

The easiest way to grasp the importance of these conventions is to take a piece of journalistic prose or a sentence from a novel and set it down on the page as a poem. The properties assigned to the sentence by a grammar of English remain unchanged, and the different meanings which the text acquires cannot therefore be attributed to one's knowledge of the language but must be ascribed to the special conventions for reading poetry which lead one to look at the language in new ways, to make relevant properties of the language which were previously unexploited, to subject the text to a different series of interpretive operations. But one can also show the importance of these conventions by measuring the distance between the language of a poem and its critical interpretation — a distance bridged by the conventions of reading which comprise the institution of poetry.

Anyone who knows English understands the language of Blake's "Ah! Sun-flower":

> Ah, Sun-flower, weary of time,
> Who countest the steps of the Sun,
> Seeking after that sweet golden clime
> Where the traveller's journey is done:
>
> Where the Youth pined away with desire,
> And the pale Virgin shrouded in snow
> Arise from their graves, and aspire
> Where my Sun-flower wishes to go.

But there is some distance between an understanding of the language and the thematic statement with which a critic concludes his discussion of the poem: "Blake's dialectical thrust at asceticism is more than adroit. You do not surmount Nature by denying its prime claim of sexuality. Instead you fall utterly into the dull round of its cyclic aspirations."[4] How does one reach this reading? What are the operations which lead from the text to this representation of understanding? The primary convention is what might be called the rule of significance: read the poem as expressing a significant attitude to some problem concerning man and/or his relation to the universe. The sunflower is therefore given the value of an emblem and the metaphors of "counting" and "seeking" are taken not just as figurative indications of the flower's tendency to turn towards the sun but as metaphorical operators which make the sunflower an instance of the human aspirations compassed by these two lines. The conventions of metaphorical coherence — that one should attempt through semantic transformations to produce coherence on the levels of both tenor and vehicle — lead one to oppose time to eternity and to make "that sweet golden clime" both the sunset which marks the closure of the daily temporal cycle and the eternity of death when "the traveller's journey is done." The identification of sunset and death is further justified by the convention which allows one to inscribe the poem in a poetic tradition. More important, how-

[4]Harold Bloom, *The Visionary Company* (New York, 1961), p. 42. [Au.]

ever, is the convention of thematic unity, which forces one to give the youth and virgin of the second stanza a role which justifies choosing them as examples of aspiration; and since the semantic feature they share is a repression of sexuality, one must find a way of integrating that with the rest of the poem. The curious syntactic structure, with three clauses each depending on a "where," provides a way of doing this:

> The Youth and the Virgin have denied their sexuality to win the allegorical abode of the conventionally visualized heaven. Arriving there, they arise from their graves to be trapped in the same cruel cycle of longings; they are merely at the sunset and aspire to go where the Sun-flower seeks his rest, which is precisely where they already are.[5]

Such interpretations are not the result of subjective associations. They are public and can be discussed and justified with respect to the conventions of reading poetry — or, as English allows us to say, of *making* sense. Such conventions are the constituents of the institution of literature, and in this perspective one can see that it may well be misleading to speak of poems as harmonious totalities, autonomous natural organisms, complete in themselves and bearing a rich immanent meaning. The semiological approach suggests, rather, that the poem be thought of as an utterance that has meaning only with respect to a system of conventions which the reader has assimilated. If other conventions were operative its range of potential meanings would be different.

Literature, as Genette says, "like any other activity of the mind, is based on conventions of which, with some exceptions, it is not aware" (*Figures,* p. 258). One can think of these conventions not simply as the implicit knowledge of the reader but also as the implicit knowledge of authors. To write a poem or a novel is immediately to engage with a literary tradition or at the very least with a certain idea of the poem or the novel. The activity is made possible by the existence of genre, which the author can write against, certainly, whose conventions he may attempt to subvert, but which is none the less the context within which his activity takes place, as surely as the failure to keep a promise is made possible by the institution of promising. Choices between words, between sentences, between different modes of presentation, will be made on the basis of their effects; and the notion of effect presupposes modes of reading which are not random or haphazard. Even if the author does not think of readers, he is himself a reader of his own work and will not be satisfied with it unless he can read it as producing effects. One would find very strange the notion of a poet saying, "when I reflect on the sunflower I have a particular feeling, which I shall call '*p*' and which I think can be connected with another feeling which I shall call '*q*,'" and then writing "if *p* then *q*" as a poem on the sunflower. This would not be a poem because even the poet himself cannot read the meanings in that series of signs. He can take them as referring to the feelings in question, but that is very much another matter. His text does not explore, evoke or even make use of the feelings, and he will be unable to read it as if it did. To experience any of the satisfactions of having written a poem he must create an order of words which he can read according to the conventions of poetry: he cannot simply assign meaning but must make possible, for himself and for others, the production of meaning.

"Every work," wrote Valéry, "is the work of many things besides an author"; and he proposed that literary history be replaced by a poetics which would study "the conditions of the existence and development of literature." Among all the arts, it is "the one in which convention plays the greatest role," and even those authors who may have thought their works due only to personal inspiration and the application of genius

> had developed, without suspecting it, a whole system of habits and notions which were the fruit of their experience and indispensable to the process of production. However little they might have suspected all the definitions, all the conventions, the

[5]Ibid. [Au.] The syntax of Blake's "Sun-flower" is even more curious than Culler and Bloom acknowledge; it is a sentence fragment consisting of a series of adjectival and adverbial clauses, all linked to the opening vocative, or to each other, but lacking any usual predicate. Like the sunflower itself, Blake's sentence yearns after completeness. [Ed.]

logic and the system of combinations that composition presupposes, however much they believed that they owed nothing but to the instant itself, their work necessarily called into play all these procedures and these inevitable operations of the mind.[6]

The conventions of poetry, the logic of symbols, the operations for the production of poetic effects, are not simply the property of readers but the basis of literary forms. However, for a variety of reasons it is easier to study them as the operations performed by readers than as the institutional context taken for granted by authors. The statements authors make about the process of composition are notoriously problematic, and there are few ways of determining what they are taking for granted. Whereas the meanings readers give to literary works and the effects they experience are much more open to observation. Hypotheses about the conventions and operations which produce these effects can therefore be tested not only by their ability to account for the effects in question but by their ability, when applied to other poems, to account for the effects experienced in those cases. Moreover, when one is investigating the process of reading one can make alterations in the language of a text so as to see how this changes literary effects, whereas that kind of experimentation is not possible if one is investigating the conventions assumed by authors, who are not available to give their reactions to the effects of proposed alterations in their texts. As the example of transformational grammar suggests, the best way of producing a formal representation of the implicit knowledge of both speakers and hearers is to present sentences to oneself or to colleagues and then to formulate rules which account for the hearer's judgments about meaning, well-formedness, deviance, constituent structure, and ambiguity.

To speak, therefore, as I shall do, of literary competence as a set of conventions for reading literary texts is in no way to imply that authors are congenital idiots who simply produce strings of sentences, while all the truly creative work is done by readers who have artful ways of processing these sentences. Structuralist discussions may seem to promote such a view by their failure to isolate and praise an author's "conscious art," but the reason is simply that here, as in most other human activities of any complexity, the line between the conscious and the unconscious is highly variable, impossible to identify, and supremely uninteresting. "*When* do you know how to play chess? All the time? or just while you are making a move? And the *whole* of chess during each move?"[7] When driving a car is it consciously or unconsciously that you keep to the correct side of the road, change gears, apply the brakes, dip the headlights? To ask of what an author is conscious and of what unconscious is as fruitless as to ask which rules of English are consciously employed by speakers and which are followed unconsciously. Mastery may be largely unconscious or it may have reached a stage of highly self-conscious theoretical elaboration, but it is mastery in both cases. Nor does one in any way impugn the author's talent in speaking of his mastery as an ability to construct artefacts which prove extremely rich when subjected to the operations of reading.

The task of a structuralist poetics, as Barthes defines it, would be to make explicit the underlying system which makes literary effects possible. It would not be a "science of contents" which, in hermeneutic fashion, proposes interpretations for works,

> but a science of the conditions of content, that is to say of forms. What interests it will be the variations of meaning generated and, as it were, capable of being generated by works; it will not interpret symbols but describe their polyvalency. In short, its object will not be the full meanings of the work but on the contrary the empty meaning which supports them all. (*Critique et vérité*, p. 57)

In this sense structuralism effects an important reversal of perspective, granting precedence to the task of formulating a comprehensive theory of literary discourse and assigning a secondary place to the interpretation of individual texts. Whatever the benefits of interpretation to those

[6]P. Valéry, *Œuvres*, II, pp. 629 and I, pp. 1439–41. [Au.]

[7]Wittgenstein, p. 59. [Au.]

who engage in it, within the context of poetics it becomes an ancillary activity — a way of using literary works — as opposed to the study of literature itself as an institution. To say that is in no way to condemn interpretation, as the linguistic analogy should make perfectly evident. Most people are more interested in using language to communicate than in studying the complex linguistic system which underlies communication, and they need not feel that their interests are threatened by those who make the study of linguistic competence a coherent and autonomous discipline. Similarly, a structuralist poetics would claim that the study of literature involves only indirectly the critical act of placing a work in situation, reading it as a gesture of a particular kind, and thus giving it a meaning. The task is rather to construct a theory of literary discourse which would account for the possibilities of interpretation, the "empty meanings" which support a variety of full meanings but which do not permit the work to be given just any meaning.

This would not need to be said if interpretive criticism had not tried to persuade us that the study of literature means the elucidation of individual works. But in this cultural context it is important to reflect on what has been lost or obscured in the practice of an interpretive criticism which treats each work as an autonomous artefact, an organic whole whose parts all contribute to a complex thematic statement. The notion that the task of criticism is to reveal thematic unity is a post-Romantic concept, whose roots in the theory of organic form are, at the very least, ambiguous. The organic unity of a plant is not easily translated into thematic unity, and we are willing to admit that the botanical gaze be allowed to compare one plant with another, isolating similarities and differences, or to dwell on formal organization without immediately invoking some teleological purpose or thematic unity. Nor has discourse on literature always been so imperiously committed to interpretation. It used to be possible, in the days before the poem became pre-eminently the act of an individual and emotion recollected in tranquility, to study its interaction with norms of rhetoric and genre, the relation of its formal features to those of the tradition, without feeling immediately compelled to produce an interpretation which would demonstrate their thematic relevance. One did not need to move from poem to world but could explore it within the institution of literature, relating it to a tradition and identifying formal continuities and discontinuities. That this should have been possible may tell us something important about literature or at least lead us to reflect on the possibility of loosening interpretation's hold on critical discourse.

Such loosening is important because if the analyst aims at understanding how literature works he must, as Northrop Frye says, set about "formulating the broad laws of literary experience, and in short writing as though he believed that there is a totally intelligible structure of knowledge attainable about poetry, which is not poetry itself, or the experience of it, but poetics" (*Anatomy of Criticism,* p. 14).[8] Few have put the case for poetics more forcefully than Frye, but in his perspective, as this quotation shows, the relationship between poetry, the experience of poetry and poetics remains somewhat obscure, and that obscurity affects his later formulations. His discussions of modes, symbols, myths and genres lead to the production of taxonomies which capture something of the richness of literature, but the status of his taxonomic categories is curiously indeterminate. What is their relation to literary discourse and to the activity of reading? Are the four mythic categories of Spring, Summer, Autumn and Winter devices for classifying literary works or categories on which the experience of literature is based? As soon as one asks why these categories are to be preferred to those of other possible taxonomies it becomes evident that there must be something implicit in Frye's theoretical framework which needs to be made explicit.

The linguistic model provides a slight reorientation which makes apparent what is needed. Study of the linguistic system becomes theoretically coherent when we cease thinking that our goal is to specify the properties of objects in a corpus and concentrate instead on the task of formulating the internalized competence which enables objects to have the properties they do for those who have mastered the system. To discover

[8]For a similar statement, see Frye, p. 643. [Ed.]

and characterize structures one must analyse the system which assigns structural descriptions to the objects in question, and thus a literary taxonomy should be grounded on a theory of reading. The relevant categories are those which are required to account for the range of acceptable meanings which works can have for readers of literature.

The notion of literary competence or of a literary system is, of course, anathema to some critics, who see in it an attack on the spontaneous, creative and affective qualities of literature. Moreover, they might argue, the very concept of literary competence, which carries the presumption that we can distinguish between competent and incompetent readers, is objectionable for precisely those reasons which lead one to propose it: the postulation of a norm for "correct" reading. In other human activities where there are clear criteria for success and failure, such as playing chess or climbing mountains, we can speak of competence and incompetence, but the richness and power of literature depend, precisely, on the fact that it is not an activity of this kind and that appreciation is varied, personal, and not subject to the normative legislation of self-styled experts.

Such arguments, however, would seem to miss the point. None would deny that literary works, like most other objects of human attention, can be enjoyed for reasons that have little to do with understanding and mastery — that texts can be quite blatantly misunderstood and still be appreciated for a variety of personal reasons. But to reject the notion of misunderstanding as a legislative imposition is to leave unexplained the common experience of being shown where one went wrong, of grasping a mistake and seeing why it was a mistake. Though acquiescence may occasionally be disgruntled yielding to a higher authority, none would maintain that it was always thus; more often one feels that one has indeed been shown the way to a fuller understanding of literature and a better grasp of the procedures of reading. If the distinction between understanding and misunderstanding were irrelevant, if neither party to a discussion believed in the distinction, there would be little point to discussing and arguing about literary works and still less to writing about them.

Moreover, the claims of schools and universities to offer literary training cannot be lightly dismissed. To believe that the whole institution of literary education is but a gigantic confidence trick, would strain even a determined credulity, for it is, alas, only too clear that knowledge of a language and a certain experience of the world do not suffice to make someone a perceptive and competent reader. That achievement requires acquaintance with a range of literature and in many cases some form of guidance. The time and effort devoted to literacy education by generations of students and teachers creates a strong presumption that there is something to be learned, and teachers do not hesitate to judge their pupil's progress towards a general literary competence. Most would claim, no doubt with good reason, that their examinations are designed not simply to determine whether their students have read various set works but to test their acquisition of an ability.

"Everyone who has seriously studied literature," Northrop Frye maintains, "knows that the mental process involved is as coherent and progressive as the study of science. A precisely similar training of the mind takes place, and a similar sense of the unity of the subject is built up" (ibid., pp. 10–11). If that seems overstated it is no doubt because what is explicit in the teaching of science usually remains implicit in the teaching of literature. But it is clear that study of one poem or novel facilitates the study of the next: one gains not only points of comparison but a sense of how to read. One develops a set of questions which experience shows to be appropriate and productive and criteria for determining whether they are, in a given case, productive; one acquires a sense of the possibilities of literature and how these possibilities may be distinguished. We may speak, if we like, of extrapolating from one work to another, so long as we do not thereby obscure the fact that the process of extrapolation is precisely what requires explanation. To account for extrapolation, to explain what are the formal questions and distinctions whose relevance the student learns, would be to formulate a theory of literary competence. If we are to make any sense at all of the process of literary education and of criticism itself we must, as Frye argues, assume the possibility of "a coherent and comprehensive theory of literature, logically and scientifically organized, some of which the student unconsciously learns as he goes on, but the main principles of which are as yet unknown to us" (p. 11).

It is easy to see why, from this perspective, linguistics offers an attractive methodological analogy: a grammar, as Chomsky says, "can be regarded as a theory of a language," and the theory of literature of which Frye speaks can be regarded as the "grammar" of literary competence which readers have assimilated but of which they may not be consciously aware. To make the implicit explicit is the task of both linguistics and poetics, and generative grammar has placed renewed emphasis on two fundamental requirements for theories of this kind: that they state their rules as formal operations (since what they are investigating is a kind of intelligence, they cannot take for granted intelligence used in applying rules but must make them as explicit as possible) and that they be testable (they must reproduce, as it were, attested facts about semiotic competence).

Can this step be taken in literary criticism? The major obstacle would seem to be that of determining what will count as evidence about literary competence. In linguistics it is not difficult to identify facts that an adequate grammar must account for: though one may need to speak of "degrees of grammaticalness" one can produce lists of sentences which are incontestably well formed and sentences which are unquestionably deviant. Moreover, we have a sufficiently strong intuitive sense of paraphrase relations to be able to say roughly what a sentence means for speakers of a language. In the study of literature, however, the situation is considerably more complex. Notions of "well-formed" or "intelligible" literary works are notoriously problematic, and it may be difficult to secure agreement about what should count as a proper "understanding" of a text. That critics should differ so widely in their interpretations might seem to undermine any notion of a general literary competence.

But in order to overcome this apparent obstacle we have only to ask what we want a theory of literature to account for. We cannot ask it to account for the "correct" meaning of a work since we manifestly do not believe that for each work there is a single correct reading. We cannot ask it to draw a clear line between the well-formed and the deviant work if we believe that no such line exits. Indeed, the striking facts that do require explanation are how it is that a work can have a variety of meanings but not just any meaning whatsoever or how it is that some works give an impression of strangeness, incoherence, incomprehensibility. The model does not imply that there must be unanimity on any particular count. It suggests only that we must designate a set of facts, of whatever kind, which seem to require explanation and then try to construct a model of literary competence which would account for them.

The facts can be of many kinds: that a given prose sentence has different meanings if set down as a poem, that readers are able to recognize the plot of a novel, that some symbolic interpretations of a poem are more plausible than others, that two characters in a novel contrast with one another, that *The Waste Land* or *Ulysses* once seemed strange and now seems intelligible. Poetics bears, as Barthes says, not so much on the work itself as on its intelligibility (*Critique et vérité,* p. 62) and therefore problematic cases — the work which some find intelligible and others incoherent, or the work which is read differently in two different periods — furnish the most decisive evidence about the system of operative conventions. Any work can be made intelligible if one invents appropriate conventions: the most obscure poem could be interpreted if there were a convention which permitted us to replace every lexical item by a word beginning with the same letter of the alphabet and chosen according to the ordinary demands of coherence. There are numerous other bizarre conventions which might be operative if the institution of literature were different, and hence the difficulty of interpreting some works provides evidence of the restricted nature of the conventions actually in force in a culture. Moreover, if a difficult work later becomes intelligible it is because new ways of reading have been developed in order to meet what is the fundamental demand of the system: the demand for sense. A comparison of old and new readings will shed light on the change in the institution of literature.

As in linguistics, there is no automatic procedure for obtaining information about competence, but there is no dearth of facts to be explained.[9] To take surveys of the behaviour of readers would serve little purpose, since one is interested not in performance itself but in the tacit knowledge or competence which underlies it. Performance may not be a direct reflection of competence, for behaviour can be influenced by a host of irrelevant factors: I may not have been paying attention at a given moment, may have been led astray by purely personal associations, may have forgotten something important from an earlier part of the text, may have made what I would recognize as a mistake, if it were pointed out to me. One's concern is with the tacit knowledge that recognition of a mistake would show rather than with the mistake itself, and so even if one were to take surveys one would still have to judge whether particular reactions were in fact a direct reflection of competence. The question is not what actual readers happen to do but what an ideal reader must know implicitly in order to read and interpret works in ways which we consider acceptable, in accordance with the institution of literature.

The ideal reader is, of course, a theoretical construct, perhaps best thought of as representation of the central notion of acceptability. Poetics, Barthes writes, "will describe the logic according to which meanings are engendered in ways that can be *accepted* by man's logic of symbols, just as the sentences of French are *accepted* by the linguistic intuitions of Frenchmen" (*Critique et vérité,* p. 63). Though there is no automatic procedure for determining what is acceptable, that does not matter, for one's proposals will be sufficiently tested by one's readers' acceptance or rejection of them. If readers do not accept the facts one sets out to explain as bearing any relation to their knowledge and experience of literature, then one's theory will be of little interest; and therefore the analyst must convince his readers that meanings or effects which he is attempting to account for are indeed appropriate ones. The meaning of a poem within the institution of literature is not, one might say, the immediate and spontaneous reaction of individual readers but the meanings which they are willing to accept as both plausible and justifiable when they are explained. "Ask yourself: How does one *lead* anyone to comprehension of a poem or of a theme? The answer to this tells us how meaning is to be explained here."[10] The paths by which the reader is led to comprehension are precisely those of the logic of literature: the effects must be related to the poem in such a way that the reader sees the connection to be just in terms of his own knowledge of literature.

One cannot therefore emphasize too strongly that every critic, whatever his persuasion, encounters the problems of literary competence as soon as he begins to speak or write about literary works, and that he takes for granted notions of acceptability and common ways of reading. The critic would not write unless he thought he had something new to say about a text, yet he assumes that his reading is not a random and idiosyncratic phenomenon. Unless he thinks that he is merely recounting to others the adventures of his own subjectivity, he claims that his interpretation is related to the text in ways which he presumes his readers will accept once those relations are pointed out: either they will accept his interpretation as an explicit version of what they intuitively felt or they will recognize from their own knowledge of literature the justice of the operations that lead the critic from text to interpretation. Indeed, the possibility of critical argument depends on shared notions of the acceptable and the unacceptable, a common ground which is nothing other than the procedures of reading. The critic must invariably make decisions about what can in fact be taken for granted, what must be explicitly defended, and what constitutes an acceptable defence. He must show his readers that the effects he notices fall within the compass of an implicit logic which they are presumed to accept;

[9]See N[oam] Chomsky, *Aspects of the Theory of Syntax,* p. 19. [Au.]

[10]L[udwig] Wittgenstein, p. 144. [Au.]

and thus he deals in his own practice with the problems which a poetics would hope to make explicit.

William Empson's *Seven Types of Ambiguity* is a work from a nonstructuralist tradition which shows considerable awareness of the problems of literary competence and illustrates just how close one comes to a structuralist formulation if one begins to reflect on them. Even if Empson were content to present his work as a display of ingenuity in discovering ambiguities, his enterprise would still be governed by conceptions of plausibility. But of course he wants to make broader claims for his analysis and finds that to do so entails a position very like that recommended above:

> I have continually employed a method of analysis which jumps the gap between two ways of thinking; which produces a possible set of alternative meanings with some ingenuity, and then says it is grasped in the preconsciousness of the reader by a native effort of the mind. This must seem very dubious; but then the facts about the apprehension of poetry are in any case very extraordinary. Such an assumption is best judged by the way it works in detail.[11]

Poetry has complex effects which are extremely difficult to explain, and the analyst finds that his best strategy is to assume that the effects he sets out to account for have been conveyed to the reader and then to postulate certain general operations which might explain these effects and analogous effects in other poems. To those who protest against such assumptions one might reply, with Empson, that the test is whether one succeeds in accounting for effects which the reader accepts when they are pointed out to him. The assumption is in no way dangerous, for the analyst "must convince the reader that he knows what he is talking about" — make him see the appropriateness of the effects in question — and "must coax the reader into seeing that the cause he names does, in fact, produce the effect which is experienced; otherwise they will not seem to have anything to do with each other" (p. 249). If the reader is brought to accept both the effects in question and the explanation he will have helped to validate what is, in essence, a theory of reading. "I have claimed to show how a properly-qualified mind works when it reads the verses, how those properly-qualified minds have worked which have not at all understood their own working" (p. 248). Such claims about literary competence are not to be verified by surveys of readers' reactions to poems but by readers' assent to the effects which the analyst attempts to explain and the efficacy of his explanatory hypotheses in other cases.

It is Empson's self-awareness and outspokenness as much as his brilliance which make his work invaluable to students of poetics; he has little respect for the critical piety that meanings are always implicitly and objectively present in the language of the poem, and thus he can attend to the operations which produce meanings. Discussing the translation of a Chinese fragment,

> Swiftly the years, beyond recall.
> Solemn the stillness of this spring morning.

he notes that

> these lines are what we should normally call poetry only by virtue of their compactness; two statements are made as if they were connected, and the reader is forced to consider their relations for himself. The reason why these facts should have been selected for a poem is left for him to invent; he will invent a variety of reasons and order them in his own mind. This, I think, is the essential fact about the poetical use of language. (p. 25)

This is indeed an essential fact, and one should hasten to point out what it implies: reading poetry is a rule-governed process of producing meanings; the poem offers a structure which must be filled up and one therefore attempts to invent something, guided by a series of formal rules derived from one's experience of reading poetry, which both make possible invention and impose limits on it. In this case the most obvious feature of literary competence is the intent at totality of the interpretive process: poems are supposed to cohere, and one must therefore discover a semantic level at which the two lines can be related to one another. An obvious point of contact is the contrast between "swiftly" and "stillness,"

[11]See Empson, p. 739. [Ed.]

and there is thus a primary condition on "invention": any interpretation should succeed in making thematic capital out of this opposition. Moreover, "years" in the first sentence and "this morning" in the second, both located in the dimension of time, provide another opposition and point of contact. The reader might hope to find an interpretation which relates these two pairs of contrasts. If this is indeed what happens it is no doubt because the experience of reading poetry leads to implicit recognition of the importance of binary oppositions as thematic devices: in interpreting a poem one looks for terms which can be placed on a semantic or thematic axis and opposed to one another.

The resulting structure or "empty meaning" suggests that the reader try to relate the opposition between "swiftly" and "stillness" to two ways of thinking about time and draw some kind of thematic conclusion from the tension between the two sentences. It seems eminently possible to produce in this way a reading which is "acceptable" in terms of poetic logic. On the one hand, taking a large panoramic view, we can think of the human life-span as a unit of time and of the years as passing swiftly; on the other, taking the moment of consciousness as the unit, we can think of the difficulty of experiencing time except discontinuously, of the stillness of a clock's hand when one looks at it. "Swiftly the years" implies a vantage point from which one can consider the passage of time, and the swiftness of passage is compensated for by what Empson calls "the answering stability of self-knowledge" implicit in this view of life (p. 24). "This morning" implies other mornings — a discontinuity of experience reflected in the ability to separate and name — and hence an instability which makes "stillness" the more valued. This process of binary structuring, then, can lead one to find tension within each of the lines as well as between the two lines. And since thematic contrasts should be related to opposed values we are led to think about the advantages and disadvantages of these two ways of conceiving of time. A variety of conclusions are of course possible. The claim is not that competent readers would agree on an interpretation but only that certain expectations about poetry and ways of reading guide the interpretive process and impose severe limitations on the set of acceptable or plausible readings.

Empson's example indicates that as soon as one reflects seriously on the status of critical argument and the relation of interpretation to text one approaches the problems which confront poetics, in that one must justify one's reading by locating it within the conventions of plausibility defined by a generalized knowledge of literature. From the point of view of poetics, what requires explanation is not the text itself so much as the possibility of reading and interpreting the text, the possibility of literary effects and literary communication. To account for the notions of acceptability and plausibility on which criticism relies is, as J.-C. Gardin emphasizes, the primary task of the systematic study of literature.

> This is in any case the only sort of objective that a "science" may set for itself, even if it be a science of literature: the regularities unveiled by natural phenomena correspond, in the literary field, to certain convergences of perception for members of a given culture.[12]

But one should stress that even if the analyst showed little explicit interest in notions of acceptability and merely set out to explain in a systematic way his own reading of literature, the results would be of considerable moment for poetics. If he began by noting his own interpretations and reactions to literary works and succeeded in formulating a set of explicit rules which accounted for the fact that he produced these interpretations and not others, one would then possess the basis of an account of literary competence. Adjustments could be made to include other readings which seemed acceptable and to exclude any readings which seemed wholly personal and idiosyncratic, but there is every reason to expect that other readers would be able to recognize substantial portions of their own tacit knowledge in his account. To be an experienced reader of literature is, after all, to have gained a sense of what can be done with literary works and thus to have assimilated a system

[12]J.-C. Gardin, "Semantic Analysis Procedures in the Sciences of Man," *Social Science Information* 8 (1969): 33. [Au.]

which is largely interpersonal. There is little reason to worry initially about the validity of the facts which one sets out to explain; the only risk one runs is that of wasting one's time. The important thing is to start by isolating a set of facts and then to construct a model to account for them, and though structuralists have often failed to do this in their own practice, it is at least implicit in the linguistic model: "Linguistics can give literature the generative model which is the principle of all science, since it is a matter of making use of certain rules to explain particular results" (Barthes, *Critique et vérité,* p. 58).

Since poetics is essentially a theory of reading, critics of every persuasion who have tried to be explicit about what they are doing have made some contribution to it and indeed in many cases have more to offer than structuralists themselves. What structuralism does provide is a reversal of critical perspective and a theoretical framework within which the work of other critics can be organized and exploited. Granting precedence to the task of formulating a theory of literary competence and relegating critical interpretation to a secondary role, it leads one to reformulate as conventions of literature and operations of reading what others might think of facts about various literary texts. Rather than say, for example, that literary texts are fictional, we might cite this as a convention of literary interpretation and say that to read a text as literature is to read it as fiction. Such a reversal may, at first sight, seem trivial, but to restate propositions about poetic or novelistic discourse as procedures of reading is a crucial reorientation for a number of reasons, wherein lie the revitalizing powers of a structuralist poetics.

First of all, to stress literature's dependence on particular modes of reading is a firmer and more honest starting point than is customary in criticism. One need not struggle, as other theorists must, to find some objective property of language which distinguishes the literary from the non-literary but may simply start from the fact that we can read texts as literature and then inquire what operations that involves. The operations will, of course, be different for different genres, and here by the same model we can say that genres are not special varieties of language but sets of expectations which allow sentences of a language to become signs of different kinds in a second-order literary system. This same sentence can have a different meaning depending on the genre in which it appears. Nor is one upset, as a theorist working on the distinctive properties of literary language must be, by the fact that the boundaries between the literary and the non-literary or between one genre and another change from age to age. On the contrary, change in modes of reading offers some of the best evidence about the conventions operative in different periods.

Second, in attempting to make explicit what one does when reading or interpreting a poem one gains considerably in self-awareness and awareness of the nature of literature as an institution. As long as one assumes that what one does is natural it is difficult to gain any understanding of it and thus to define the differences between oneself and one's predecessors or successors. Reading is not an innocent activity. It is charged with artifice, and to refuse to study one's modes of reading is to neglect a principal source of information about literary activity. By seeing literature as something animated by special sets of conventions one can attain more easily a sense of its specificity, its peculiarity, its difference, shall we say, from other modes of discourse about the world. Those differences lie in the work of the literary sign: in the ways in which meaning is produced.

Third, a willingness to think of literature as an institution composed of a variety of interpretive operations makes one more open to the most challenging and innovatory texts, which are precisely those that are difficult to process according to received modes of understanding. An awareness of the assumptions on which one proceeds, an ability to make explicit what one is attempting to do, makes it easier to see where and how the text resists one's attempts to make sense of it and how, by its refusal to comply with one's expectations, it leads to that questioning of the self and of ordinary social modes of understanding which has always been the result of the greatest literature. My readers, says the narrator at the end of *A la recherche du temps perdu,* will become "les propres lecteurs d'eux-mêmes"[13]: in my book they will read themselves and their own limits. How better to facilitate a reading of oneself than by trying to make explicit one's sense of the comprehensible and the incomprehensible, the significant and the insignificant, the ordered and the inchoate. By offering sequences and combinations which escape our accustomed grasp, by subjecting language to a dislocation which fragments the ordinary signs of our world, literature challenges the limits we set to the self as a device or order and allows us, painfully or joyfully, to accede to an expansion of self. But that requires, if it is to be fully accomplished, a measure of awareness of the interpretive models which inform one's culture. Structuralism, because of its interest in the adventures of the sign, has been exceedingly open to the revolutionary work, finding in its resistance to the operations of reading confirmation of the fact that literary effects depend on these conventions and that literary evolution proceeds by displacement of old conventions of reading and the development of new.

And so, finally, structuralism's reversal of perspective can lead to a mode of interpretation based on poetics itself, where the work is read against the conventions of discourse and where one's interpretation is an account of the ways in which the work complies with or undermines our procedures for making sense of things. Though it does not, of course, replace ordinary thematic interpretations, it does avoid premature foreclosure — the unseemly rush from word to world — and stays within the literary system for as long as possible. Insisting that literature is something other than a statement about the world, it establishes, finally, an analogy between the production or reading of signs in literature and in other areas of experience and studies the ways in which the former explores and dramatizes the limitations of the latter. In this kind of interpretation the meaning of the work is what it shows the reader, by the acrobatics in which it involves him, about the problems of his condition as *homo significans*, maker and reader of signs. The notion of literary competence thus comes to serve as the basis of a reflexive interpretation.

[13]"Proper readers of themselves." [Ed.]

Umberto Eco

b. 1932

Although his surprise best-selling novel The Name of the Rose *(1980; tr. 1983) made him internationally famous, Umberto Eco has long been recognized in other circles as the leading contemporary theorist of semiotics. Born in Alessandria, Italy, Eco was educated at the University of Turin (Ph.D. 1954) and has taught at the universities of Turin, Florence, Milan, and Bologna, where he has been professor of semiotics since 1975. Eco has also been a visiting professor at universities the world over — in the United States alone he has taught at New York University, Yale, Columbia, and Northwestern. The sheer number of Eco's publications is daunting; those books that deal with semiotics and are available in English include* A Theory of Semiotics *(1975),* The Role of the Reader: Explorations in the Semiotics of Texts *(1979),* Semiotics and the Philosophy of Language *(1984),* The Open Work *(1989),* The Limits of Interpretation *(1990),* Interpretation and Overinterpretation *(1992), and* The Search for the Perfect Language *(1995). In addition, Eco has published two volumes of occasional essays,* Travels in Hyperreality *(1986) and* Apocalypse Postponed *(1994), and two more novels combining suspense with erudition,* Foucault's Pendulum *(1989) and* The Island of the Day Before *(1995). "The Myth of Superman," from* The Role of the Reader, *was first published in English in a 1972 issue of* Diacritics.

The Myth of Superman

The hero equipped with powers superior to those of the common man has been a constant of the popular imagination — from Hercules to Siegfried, from Roland to Pantagruel, all the way to Peter Pan. Often the hero's virtue is humanized, and his powers, rather than being supernatural, are the extreme realization of natural endowments such as astuteness, swiftness, fighting ability, or even the logical faculties and the pure spirit of observation found in Sherlock Holmes. In an industrial society, however, where man becomes a number in the realm of the organization which has usurped his decision-making role, he has no means of production and is thus deprived of his power to decide. Individual strength, if not exerted in sports activities, is left abased when confronted with the strength of machines which determine man's very movements. In such a society the positive hero must embody to an unthinkable degree the power demands that the average citizen nurtures but cannot satisfy.

Superman is not from Earth; he arrived here as a youth from the planet Krypton. Growing up on Earth, Superman finds he is gifted with superhuman powers. His strength is practically unlimited. He can fly through space at the speed of light, and, when he surpasses that speed, he breaks through the time barrier and can transfer himself to other epochs. With no more than the pressure of his hands, he can subject coal to the temperature required to change it into diamond; in a matter of seconds, at supersonic speed, he can fell an entire forest, make lumber from trees, and construct a ship or a town; he can bore through mountains, lift ocean liners, destroy or construct dams; his X-ray vision allows him to see through any object to almost unlimited distances and to melt metal objects at a glance; his superhearing puts him in extremely advantageous situations permitting him to tune in on conversations however far away. He is kind, handsome, modest, and helpful; his life is dedicated to the battle against the forces of evil; and the police find him an untiring collaborator.

Nevertheless, the image of Superman is not entirely beyond the reach of the reader's self-identification. In fact, Superman lives among men disguised as the journalist Clark Kent; as such, he appears fearful, timid, not overintelligent, awkward, nearsighted, and submissive to his matriarchal colleague, Lois Lane, who, in turn, despises him, since she is madly in love with Superman. In terms of narrative, Superman's double identity has a function, since it permits the suspense characteristic of a detective story and great variation in the mode of narrating our hero's adventures, his ambiguities, his histrionics. But, from a mythopoeic point of view, the device is even subtle: in fact, Clark Kent personifies fairly typically the average reader who is harassed by complexes and despised by his fellow men; through an obvious process of self-identification, any accountant in any American city secretly feeds the hope that one day, from the slough of his actual personality, there can spring forth a superman who is capable of redeeming years of mediocre existence.

THE STRUCTURE OF MYTH AND THE "CIVILIZATION" OF THE NOVEL

With the undeniable mythological connotation of our hero established, it is necessary to specify the narrative structure through which the myth is offered daily or weekly to the public. There is, in fact, a fundamental difference between the figure of Superman and the traditional heroic figures of classical and nordic mythology or the figures of Messianic religions.

The traditional figure of religion was a character of human or divine origin, whose image had immutable characteristics and an irreversible destiny. It was possible that a story, as well as a number of traits, backed up the character; but the story followed a line of development already established, and it filled in the character's features in a gradual, but definitive, manner.

Translated by Natalie Chilton.

In other words, a Greek statue could represent Hercules or a scene of Hercules' labors; in both cases, but more so in the latter, Hercules would be seen as someone who has a story, and this story would characterize his divine features. The story has taken place and can no longer be denied. Hercules has been made real through a development of temporal events. But once the development ended his image symbolized, along with the character, the story of his development, and it became the substance of the definitive record and judgments about him. Even the account greatly favored by antiquity was almost always the story of something which had already happened and of which the public was aware.

One could recount for the *n*th time the story of Roland the Paladin, but the public already knew what happened to the hero. New additions and romantic embellishments were not lacking, but neither would they have impaired the substance of the myth being narrated. A similar situation existed in the plastic arts and the paintings of Gothic cathedrals or of Counter-Reformation and Renaissance churches. What had already happened was often narrated in moving and dramatic ways.

The "civilization" of the modern novel offers a story in which the reader's main interest is transferred to the unpredictable nature of *what will happen* and, therefore, to the plot invention which now holds our attention. The event has not happened *before* the story; it happens *while* it is being told, and usually even the author does not know what will take place.

At the time of its origin, the *coup de théâtre*[1] where Oedipus finds himself guilty as a result of Tiresias' revelation "worked" for the public, not because it caught them unaware of the myth, but because the mechanism of the "plot," in accordance with Aristotelian rules, succeeded in making them once more co-participants through pity and terror. The reader is brought to identify both with the situation and with the character. In contrast, there is Julien Sorel shooting Madame de Rênal, or Poe's detective discovering the party guilty of the double crime in Rue de la Morgue, or Javert paying his debt of gratitude to Jean Valjean,[2] where we are spectators to a *coup de théâtre* whose unpredictable nature is part of the invention and, as such, takes on aesthetic value. This phenomenon becomes important in direct proportion to the popularity of the novel, and the *feuilleton,*[3] for the masses — the adventures of Rocambole and of Arsène Lupin[4] — have, as craft, no other value than the ingenious invention of unexpected events.

This new dimension of the story sacrifices for the most part the mythic potential of the character. The mythic character embodies a law, or a universal demand, and therefore must be in part *predictable* and cannot hold surprises for us; the character of a novel wants, rather, to be a man like anyone else, and what could befall him is as unforeseeable as what may happen to us. Such a character will take on what we will call an "aesthetic universality," a capacity to serve as a reference point for behavior and feelings which belong to us all. He does not contain the universality of myth, nor does he become an archetype, the emblem of a supernatural reality. He is the result of a universal rendering of a particular and eternal event. The character of a novel is a "historic type." Therefore, to accommodate this character, the aesthetics of the novel must revive an old category particularly necessary when art abandons the territory of myth; this we may term the "typical."

The mythological character of comic strips finds himself in this singular situation: he must be an archetype, the totality of certain collective aspirations, and therefore he must necessarily become immobilized in an emblematic and fixed nature which renders him easily recognizable (this is what happens to Superman); but, since he

[1]A sudden dramatic event that alters a situation, which Aristotle called a *peripeteia.* [Ed.]

[2]Eco refers to Stendhal's *The Red and the Black,* Poe's "Murders in the Rue Morgue," and Hugo's *Les Misérables.* [Ed.]

[3]Light, serialized fiction, such as that contained in those parts of a French newspaper also devoted to reviews and entertaining articles. [Ed.]

[4]*Rocambole, or The Knaves of Hearts and the Companions of Crime:* a romance by Pierre Alexis, Vicomte de Ponson du Terrail (1829–71). *Arsène Lupin, Gentleman-burglar,* a romance by Maurice Leblanc (1864–1941). [Ed.]

is marketed in the sphere of a "romantic" production for a public that consumes "romances," he must be subjected to a development which is typical, as we have seen, of novelistic characters.

THE PLOT AND THE "CONSUMPTION" OF THE CHARACTER

A tragic plot, according to Aristotle, involves the character in a series of events, reversals, recognitions, pitiful and terrifying cases that culminate in a catastrophe;[5] a novelistic plot, let us add, develops these dramatic units in a continuous and narrated series which, in the popular novel, becomes an end in itself. They must proliferate as much as possible *ad infinitum. The Three Musketeers,* whose adventures continue in *Twenty Years Later* and conclude finally in *The Vicomte de Bragelonne* (but here intervene parasitic narrators who continue to tell us about the adventures of the Musketeers' sons, or the clash between d'Artagnan and Cyrano de Bergerac, and so on), is an example of narrative plot which multiplies like a tapeworm; the greater its capacity to sustain itself through an indefinite series of contrasts, oppositions, crises, and solutions, the more vital it seems.

Superman, by definition the character whom nothing can impede, finds himself in the worrisome narrative situation of being a hero without an adversary and therefore without the possibility of any development. A further difficulty arises because his public, for precise psychological reasons, cannot keep together the various moments of a narrative process over the space of several days. Each story concludes within the limits of a few pages; or, rather, every weekly edition is composed of two or three complete stories in which a particular narrative episode is presented, developed, and resolved. Aesthetically and commercially deprived of the possibility of narrative development, Superman gives serious problems to his scriptwriters. Little by little, varying formulae are offered to provoke and justify a contrast; Superman, for example, does have a weakness. He is rendered almost helpless by the radiation of kryptonite, a metal of meteoric origin, which his adversaries naturally procure at any cost in order to neutralize their avenger. But a creature gifted with superhuman intellectual and physical powers easily finds a means to get out of such scrapes, and that is what Superman does. Furthermore, one must consider that as a narrative theme the attempt to weaken him through the employment of kryptonite does not offer a broad range of solutions, and it must be used sparingly.

There is nothing left to do except to put Superman to the test of several obstacles which are intriguing because they are unforeseen but which are, however, surmountable by the hero. In that case two effects are obtained. First, the reader is struck by the strangeness of the obstacles — diabolically conceived inventions, curiously equipped apparitions from outer space, machines that can transmit one through time, teratological results of new experiments, the cunning of evil scientists to overwhelm Superman with kryptonite, the hero's struggles with creatures endowed with powers equal to his, such as Mxyzptlk, the gnome, who comes from the fifth dimension and who can be countered only if Superman manages to make him pronounce his own name backwards (Kltpzyxm), and so on. Second, thanks to the hero's unquestionable superiority, the crisis is rapidly resolved and the account is maintained within the bounds of the short story.

But this resolves nothing. In fact, the obstacle once conquered (and within the space allotted by commercial requirements), Superman has still *accomplished something.* Consequently, the character has made a gesture which is inscribed in his past and which weighs on his future. He has taken a step toward death, he has gotten older, if only by an hour; his storehouse of personal experiences has irreversibly enlarged. *To act,* then, for Superman, as for any other character (or for each of us), means to "consume" himself.

Now, Superman cannot "consume" himself, since a myth is "inconsumable." The hero of the classical myth became "inconsumable" precisely because he was already "consumed" in some exemplary action. Or else he had the possibility of a

[5]See Aristotle, *Poetics,* p. 46ff. [Ed.]

continuing rebirth or of symbolizing some vegetative cycle — or at least a certain circularity of events or even of life itself. But Superman is myth on condition of being a creature immersed in everyday life, in the present, apparently tied to our own conditions of life and death, even if endowed with superior faculties. An immortal Superman would no longer be a man, but a god, and the public's identification with his double identity would fall by the wayside.

Superman, then, must remain "inconsumable" and at the same time be "consumed" according to the ways of everyday life. He possesses the characteristics of timeless myth, but is accepted only because his activities take place in our human and everyday world of time. The narrative paradox that Superman's scriptwriters must resolve somehow, even without being aware of it, demands a paradoxical solution with regard to time.

TEMPORALITY AND "CONSUMPTION"

The Aristotelian definition of time is "the amount of movement from before to after," and since antiquity time has implied the idea of *succession;* the Kantian analysis has established unequivocally that this idea must be associated with an idea of *causality:* "It is a necessary law of our sensibility and therefore a condition of all perception that preceding Time necessarily determines what follows."[6] This idea has been maintained even by relativistic physics, not in the study of the transcendental conditions of the perceptions, but in the definition of the nature of time in terms of cosmological objectivity, in such a way that time would appear as the *order of causal chains.* Reverting to these Einsteinian concepts, Reichenbach recently redefined the order of time as the order of causes, the order of open causal chains which we see verified in our universe, and the *direction* of time in terms of *growing entropy*[7] (taking up in terms even of information theory the thermodynamic concept which had recurrently interested philosophers and which they adopted as their own in speaking of the irreversibility of time.[8]

Before causally determines *after,* and the series of these determinations cannot be traced back, at least in our universe (according to the epistemological model that explains the world in which we live), but is irreversible. That other cosmological models can foresee other solutions to this problem is well known; but, in the sphere of our daily understanding of events (and, consequently, in the structural sphere of a narrative character), this concept of time is what permits us to move around and to recognize events and their directions.

Expressing themselves in other words, but always on the basis of the order of *before* and *after* and of the causality of the before on the after (emphasizing variously the determination of the before on the after), existentialism and phenomenology have shifted the problem of time into the sphere of the structures of subjectivity, and discussions about action, possibility, plan, and liberty have been based on time. Time as a *structure of possibility* is, in fact, the problem of our moving toward a future, having behind us a past, whether this past is seen as a block with respect to our freedom to plan (planning which forces us to choose necessarily what we have already been) or is understood as a basis of future possibilities and therefore possibilities of conserving or changing what has been, within certain limits of freedom, yet always within the terms of positive processes.

Sartre says that "the past is the ever-growing totality of the in-itself which we are." When I want to tend toward a possible future, I must be and cannot not be this past. My possibilities of choosing or not choosing a future depend upon acts already accomplished, and they constitute the point of departure for my possible decisions. And as soon as I make another decision, it, in turn, belongs to the past and modifies what I am and offers another platform for successive projects. If it is meaningful to put the problem of

[6]*Critique of Pure Reason,* "Analytic of Principles," Ch. 2, sec. 3. [Au.]

[7]Disorder. [Ed.]

[8]See in particular Hans Reichenbach, *The Direction of Time* (Berkeley and Los Angeles: University of California Press, 1956). [Au.]

freedom and of the responsibility of our decisions in philosophical terms, the basis of the discussion and the point of departure for a phenomenology of these acts is always the structure of temporality.[9]

For Husserl, the "I" is free inasmuch as it is in the past. In effect, the past determines me and therefore also determines my future, but the future, in turn, "frees" the past. My temporality is my freedom, and on my freedom depends my "Being-having-been" which determines me. But, in its continuous synthesis with the future, the content of my "Being-having-been" depends on the future. Now, if the "I" is free because it is already determined together with the "I-that-should-be," there exists within this freedom (so encumbered by conditions, so burdened with what was and is hence irreversible) a "sorrowfulness" (*Schmerzhaftigkeit*) which is none other than "facticity." (Compare with Sartre: "I am my future in the continuous prospective of the possibility of not being it. In this is the suffering which we described before and which gives sense to my present; I am a being whose sense is always problematic.")[10] Each time I plan I notice the tragic nature of the condition in which I find myself, without being able to avoid it. Nevertheless, I plan to oppose the tragic elements with the possibility of something positive, which is a change from that which is and which I put into effect as I direct myself toward the future. Plan, freedom, and condition are articulated while I observe this connection of structures in my actions, according to a dimension of *responsibility*. This is what Husserl observes when he says that, in this "directed" being of the "I" toward possible scopes, an ideal "teleology" is established and that the future as possible "having" with respect to the original futurity in which I already always *am* is the universal prefiguration of the aim of life.

In other words, the subject situated in a temporal dimension is aware of the gravity and difficulty of his decisions, but at the same time he is aware that he must decide, that it is he who must decide, and that this process is linked to an indefinite series of necessary decision making that involves all other men.

A PLOT WHICH DOES NOT "CONSUME" ITSELF

If contemporary discussions which involve man in meditation upon his destiny and his condition are based on this concept of time, the narrative structure of Superman certainly evades it in order to save the situation which we have already discussed. In Superman it is the concept of time that breaks down. The very structure of time falls apart, not in the time *about which,* but, rather, in the time *in which the story is told.*

In Superman stories the time that breaks down is the *time of the story,* that is, the notion of time which ties one episode to another. In the sphere of a story, Superman accomplishes a given job (he routs a band of gangsters); at this point the story ends. In the same comic book, or in the edition of the following week, a new story begins. If it took Superman up again at the point where he left off, he would have taken a step toward death. On the other hand, to begin a story without showing that another had preceded it would manage, momentarily, to remove Superman from the law that leads from life to death through time. In the end (Superman has been around since 1938), the public would realize the comicality of the situation — as happened in the case of Little Orphan Annie, who prolonged her disaster-ridden childhood for decades.

Superman's scriptwriters have devised a solution which is much shrewder and undoubtedly more original. The stories develop in a kind of oneiric climate — of which the reader is not aware at all — where what has happened before and what has happened after appear extremely hazy. The narrator picks up the strand of the event again and again, as if he had forgotten to say something and wanted to add details to what had already been said.

It occurs, then, that along with Superman stories, Superboy stories are told, that is, stories of Superman when he was a boy, or a tiny child

[9]For the Sartrian discussion, see *Being and Nothingness,* Ch. 2. [Au.]

[10]Ibid. [Au.]

under the name of Superbaby. At a certain point, Supergirl appears on the scene. She is Superman's cousin, and she, too, escaped from the destruction of Krypton. All of the events concerning Superman are retold in one way or another in order to account for the presence of this new character (who has hitherto not been mentioned, because, it is explained, she has lived in disguise in a girls' school, awaiting puberty, at which time she could come out into the world; the narrator goes back in time to tell in how many and in which cases she, of whom nothing was said, participated during those many adventures where we saw Superman alone involved). One imagines, using the solution of travel through time, that Supergirl, Superman's contemporary, can encounter Superboy in the past and be his playmate; and even Superboy, having broken the time barrier by sheer accident, can encounter Superman, his own self of many years later.

But, since such a fact could comprise the character in a series of developments capable of influencing his future actions, the story ends here and insinuates that Superboy has dreamed, and one's approval of what has been said is deferred. Along these lines the most original solution is undoubtedly that of the *Imaginary Tales*. It happens, in fact, that the public will often request delightful new developments of the scriptwriters; for example, why doesn't Superman marry Lois Lane, the journalist, who has loved him for so long? If Superman married Lois Lane, it would of course be another step toward his death, as it would lay down another irreversible premise; nevertheless, it is necessary to find continually new narrative stimuli and to satisfy the "romantic" demands of the public. And so it is told "what would have happened *if* Superman had married Lois." The premise is developed in all of its dramatic implications, and at the end is the warning: Remember, this is an "imaginary" story which in truth has not taken place. (In this respect, note Roberto Giammanco's remarks about the consistently homosexual nature of characters like Superman or Batman — another variation of the theme of "superpowers." This aspect undoubtedly exists, particularly in Batman, and Giammanco offers reasons for it which we refer to later; but, in the specific case of Superman, it seems that we must speak not so much of homosexuality as of "parsifalism."[11] In Superman the element of masculine societies is nearly absent, though it is quite evident in characters like Batman and Robin, Green Arrow and his partner, and so on. Even if he often collaborates with the Legion of Super Heroes of the Future — youngsters gifted with extraordinary powers, usually ephebic but of both sexes — Superman does not neglect working with his cousin, Supergirl, as well, nor can one say that Lois Lane's advances, or those of Lana Lang, an old schoolmate and rival of Lois, are received by Superman with the disgust of a misogynist. He shows, instead, the bashful embarrassment of an average young man in a matriarchal society. On the other hand, the most perceptive philologists have not overlooked his unhappy love for Lori Lemaris, who, being a mermaid, could offer him only an underwater *ménage*[12] corresponding to a paradisiacal exile which Superman must refuse because of his sense of duty and the indispensable nature of his mission. What characterizes Superman is, instead, the platonic dimension of his affections, the implicit vow of chastity which depends less on his will than on the state of things, and the singularity of his situation. If we have to look for a structural reason for this narrative fact, we cannot but go back to our preceding observations: the "parsifalism" of Superman is one of the conditions that prevents his slowly "consuming" himself, and it protects him from the events, and therefore from the passing of time, connected with erotic ventures.)

The *Imaginary Tales* are numerous, and so are the *Untold Tales* or those stories that concern events already told but in which "something was left out," so they are told again from another point of view, and in the process lateral aspects come to the fore. In this massive bombardment of events which are no longer tied together by any strand of logic, whose interaction is ruled no longer by any necessity, the reader, without real-

[11]In Wolfram von Eschenbach's medieval epic, *Parsifal*, the hero, of amazing powers, is a pure but utterly naive and foolish boy. [Ed.]

[12]Household. [Ed.]

izing it, of course, loses the notion of temporal progression. Superman happens to live in an imaginary universe in which, as opposed to ours, causal chains are not open (A provokes B, B provokes C, C provokes D, and so on, *ad infinitum*), but closed (A provokes B, B provokes C, C provokes D, and D provokes A), and it no longer makes sense to talk about temporal progression on the basis of which we usually describe the happenings of the macrocosm.

One could observe that, apart from the mythopoeic and commercial necessities which together force such a situation, a similar structural assessment of Superman stories reflects, even though at a low level, a series of diffuse persuasions in our culture about the problem of concepts of causality, temporality, and the irreversibility of events; and, in fact, a great deal of contemporary art, from Joyce to Robbe-Grillet, or a film such as *Last Year at Marienbad,* reflects paradoxical temporal situations, whose models, nevertheless, exist in the epistemological discussions of our times. But it is a fact that, in works such as *Finnegans Wake* or Robbe-Grillet's *In the Labyrinth,* the breakdown of familiar temporal relations happens in a conscious manner, on the part both of the writer and of the one who derives aesthetic satisfaction from the operation. The disintegration of temporality has the function both of quest and of denunciation and tends to furnish the reader with imaginative models capable of making him accept situations of the new science and of reconciling the activity of an imagination accustomed to old schemes with the activity of an intelligence which ventures to hypothesize or to describe universes that are not reducible to an image or a scheme. In consequence, these works (but here another problem opens up) carry out a mythopoeic function, offering the inhabitant of the contemporary world a kind of symbolic suggestion or allegorical diagram of that absolute which science has resolved, not so much in a metaphysical modality of the world, but in a possible way of establishing our relation with the world and, therefore, in a possible way of describing the world.

The adventures of Superman, however, do not have this critical intention, and the temporal paradox on which they are sustained should not be obvious to the reader (just as the authors themselves are probably unaware of it), since a confused notion of time is the only condition which makes the story credible. Superman comes off as a myth only if the reader loses control of the temporal relationships and renounces the need to reason on their basis, thereby giving himself up to the uncontrollable flux of the stories which are accessible to him and, at the same time, holding on to the illusion of a continuous present. Since the myth is not isolated exemplarily in a dimension of eternity, but, in order to be assimilated, must enter into the flux of the story in question, this same story is refuted as flux and seen instead as an immobile present.

In growing accustomed to the idea of events happening in an ever-continuing present, the reader loses track of the fact that they should develop according to the dictates of time. Losing consciousness of it, he forgets the problems which are at its base, that is, the existence of freedom, the possibility of planning, the necessity of carrying plans out, the sorrow that such planning entails, the responsibility that it implies, and, finally, the existence of an entire human community whose progressiveness is based on making plans.

SUPERMAN AS A MODEL OF "HETERODIRECTION"

The proposed analysis would be greatly abstracted and could appear apocalyptic if the man who reads Superman, and for whom Superman is produced, were not the selfsame man with whom several sociological reports have dealt and who has been defined as "other directed man."

In advertising, as in propaganda, and in the area of human relations, the absence of the dimension of "planning" is essential to establishing a paternalistic pedagogy, which requires the hidden persuasion that the subject is not responsible for his past, nor master of his future, not even subject to the laws of planning according to the three "ecstasies" of temporality (Heidegger). All of this would imply pain and labor, while society is capable of offering to the heterodirected man the results of projects already accomplished. Such are they as to respond to man's desires, which themselves have been introduced in man in order to make him recognize that what he is offered is precisely what he would have planned.

The analysis of temporal structures in Superman has offered us the image of a *way of telling stories* which would seem to be fundamentally tied to pedagogic principles that govern that type of society. Is it possible to establish connections between the two phenomena affirming that Superman is no other than one of the pedagogic instruments of this society and that the destruction of time that it pursues is part of a plan to make obsolete the idea of planning and of personal responsibility?

DEFENSE OF THE ITERATIVE SCHEME

A series of events repeated according to a set scheme (iteratively, in such a way that each event takes up again from a sort of virtual beginning, ignoring where the preceding event left off) is nothing new in popular narrative. In fact, this scheme constitutes one of its more characteristic forms.

The device of iteration is one on which certain escape mechanisms are founded, particularly the types realized in television commercials: one distractedly watches the playing out of a sketch, then focuses one's attention on the punch line that reappears at the end of the episode. It is precisely on this foreseen and awaited reappearance that our modest but irrefutable pleasure is based.

This attitude does not belong only to the television spectator. The reader of detective stories can easily make an honest self-analysis to establish the modalities that explain his "consuming" them. First, from the beginning the reading of a traditional detective story presumes the enjoyment of following a scheme: from the crime to the discovery and the resolution through a chain of deductions. The scheme is so important that the most famous authors have founded their fortune on its very immutability. Nor are we dealing only with a schematism in the order of a "plot," but with a fixed schematism involving the same sentiments and the same psychological attitudes: in Simenon's Maigret or in Agatha Christie's Poirot, there is a recurrent movement of compassion to which the detective is led by his discovery of the facts and which merges into an empathy with the motives of the guilty party, an act of *caritas* which is combined with, if not opposed to, the act of justice that unveils and condemns.

Furthermore, the writer of stories then introduces a continuous series of connotations (for example, the characteristics of the policeman and of his immediate "entourage") to such an extent that their reappearance in each story is an essential condition of its reading pleasure. And so we have the by now historical "tics" of Sherlock Holmes, the punctilious vanity of Hercule Poirot, the pipe and the familiar fixes of Maigret, on up to the daily idiosyncrasies of the most unabashed heroes of postwar detective stories, such as the cologne water and Player's #6 of Peter Cheyney's Slim Callaghan or the cognac with a glass of cold water of Brett Halliday's Michael Shayne. Vices, gestures, nervous tics permit us to find an old friend in the character portrayed, and they are the principal conditions which allow us to "enter into" the event. Proof of this is when our favorite author writes a story in which the usual character does not appear and we are not even aware that the fundamental scheme of the book is still like the others: we read the book with a certain detachment and are immediately prone to judge it a "minor" work, a momentary phenomenon, or an interlocutory remark.

All this becomes very clear if we take a famous character such as Nero Wolfe, immortalized by Rex Stout. For sheer preterition[13] and by way of caution, in the likelihood of one of our readers' being so "highbrow" as to have never encountered our character, let us briefly recall the elements which combine to form Nero Wolfe's "type" and his environment. Nero Wolfe, from Montenegro, a naturalized American from time immemorial, is outlandishly fat, so much so that his leather easy chair must be expressly designed for him. He is fearfully lazy. In fact, he never leaves the house and depends, for his investigations, on the open-minded Archie Goodwin, with whom he indulges in a continuous relationship of a sharp and tensely polemic nature, tempered somewhat by their mutual sense of humor. Nero

[13]There is a problem with the translation: preterition means an intentional act of omission. [Ed.]

Wolfe is an absolute glutton, and his cook, Fritz, is the vestal virgin in the pantry, devoted to the unending care of this highly cultivated palate and equally greedy stomach; but along with the pleasures of the table, Wolfe cultivates an all-absorbing and exclusive passion for orchids; he has a priceless collection of them in the greenhouse on the top floor of the villa where he lives. Quite possessed by gluttony and flowers, assailed by a series of accessory tics (love of scholarly literature, systematic misogyny, insatiable thirst for money), Nero Wolfe conducts his investigations, masterpieces of psychological penetration, sitting in his office, carefully weighing the information with which the enterprising Archie furnishes him, studying the protagonists of each event who are obliged to visit him in his office, arguing with Inspector Cramer (attention: he always holds a methodically extinguished cigar in his mouth), quarreling with the odious Sergeant Purley Stebbins; and, finally, in a fixed setting from which he never veers, he summons the protagonists of the case to a meeting in his studio, usually in the evening. There, with skillful dialectical subterfuges, almost always before he himself knows the truth, he drives the guilty one into a public demonstration of hysteria and thus into giving himself away.

Those who know Rex Stout's stories know that these details hardly scratch the surface of the repertoire of *topoi,* of recurrent stock situations which animate these stories. The gamut is much more ample: Archie's almost canonic arrest under suspicion of reticence and false testimony; the legal diatribes about the conditions on which Wolfe will take on a client; the hiring of part-time agents like Saul Panzer or Orrie Cather; the painting in the studio behind which Wolfe or Archie can watch, through a peephole, the behavior and reactions of a subject put to the test in the office itself; the scenes with Wolfe and an insincere client — one could go on forever; we realize, at the end, that the list of these *topoi* is such that it could exhaust almost every possibility of the events permitted within the number of pages allowed to each story. Nevertheless, there are infinite variations of the theme; each crime has new psychological and economic motivations, each time the author devises what appears as a new situation. We say "appear"; the fact is that the reader is never brought to verify the extent to which something new is told. The noteworthy moments are those when Wolfe repeats his usual gestures, when he goes up for the *n*th time to take care of his orchids while the case itself is reaching its dramatic climax, when Inspector Cramer threateningly enters with one foot between the door and the wall, pushing aside Goodwin and warning Wolfe with a shake of his finger that this time things will not go so smoothly. The attraction of the book, the sense of repose, of psychological extension which it is capable of conferring, lies in the fact that, plopped in an easy chair or in the seat of a train compartment, the reader continuously recovers, point by point, what he already knows, what he wants to know again: that is why he has purchased the book. He derives pleasure from the nonstory (if indeed a story is a development of events which should bring us from the point of departure to a point of arrival where we would never have dreamed of arriving); the distraction consists in the refutation of a development of events, in a withdrawal from the tension of past-present-future to the focus of an *instant,* which is loved because it is recurrent.

THE ITERATIVE SCHEME AS A REDUNDANT MESSAGE

It is certain that mechanisms of this kind proliferate more widely in the popular narrative of today than in the eighteenth-century romantic *feuilleton,* where, as we have seen, the event was founded upon a *development* and where the character was required to "consume" himself through to death. Perhaps one of the first inexhaustible characters during the decline of the *feuilleton* and bridging the two centuries at the close of *la belle époque*[14] is Fantomas.[15] (Each episode of *Fantomas* closes with a kind of "unsuccessful catharsis"; Juve and Fandor finally come to get their hands on the elusive one when he, with an unforeseeable move, foils the arrest. Another singu-

[14]The turn of the twentieth century. [Ed.]

[15]*Fantomas* (1911–13) was a serialized novel by Marcel Allain (1885–1969) and Pierre Souvestre (1874–1914) about an elusive criminal. [Ed.]

lar fact: Fantomas — responsible for blackmail and sensational kidnappings — at the beginning of each episode finds himself inexplicably poor and in need of money and, therefore, also of new "action." In this way the cycle can keep going.) With him the epoch ends. It remains to be asked if modern iterative mechanisms do not answer some profound need in contemporary man and, therefore, do not seem more justifiable and better motivated than we are inclined to admit at first glance.

If we examine the iterative scheme from a structural point of view, we realize that we are in the presence of a typical *high-redundance message*. A novel by Souvestre and Allain or by Rex Stout is a message which informs us very little and which, on the contrary, thanks to the use of redundant elements, keeps hammering away at the same meaning which we have peacefully acquired upon reading the first work of the series (in the case in point, the meaning is a certain mechanism of the action, due to the intervention of "topical" characters). The taste for the iterative scheme is presented then as a taste for redundance. The hunger for entertaining narrative based on these mechanisms is a *hunger for redundance*. From this viewpoint, the greater part of popular narrative is a narrative of redundance.

Paradoxically, the same detective story that one is tempted to ascribe to the products that satisfy the taste for the unforeseen or the sensational is, in fact, read for exactly the opposite reason, as an invitation to that which is taken for granted, familiar, expected. Not knowing who the guilty party is becomes an accessory element, almost a pretext; certainly, it is true that in the action detective story (where the iteration of the scheme triumphs as much as in the investigation detective story), the suspense surrounding the guilty one often does not even exist; it is not a matter of discovering who committed the crime, but, rather, of following certain "topical" gestures of "topical" characters whose stock behavior we already love. To explain this "hunger for redundance," extremely subtle hypotheses are not needed. The *feuilleton,* founded on the triumph of information, represented the preferred fare of a society that lived in the midst of messages loaded with redundance; the sense of tradition, the norms of associative living, moral principles, the valid rules of proper comportment in the environment of nineteenth-century bourgeois society, of the typical public which represented the consumers of the *feuilleton* — all this constituted a system of foreseeable communication that the social system provided for its members and which allowed life to flow smoothly without unexpected jolts and without upsets in its value system. In this sphere the "informative" shock of a short story by Poe or the *coup de théâtre* of Ponson du Terrail[16] acquired a precise meaning. In a contemporary industrial society, instead, the alternation of standards, the dissolution of tradition, social mobility, the fact that models and principles are "consumable" — everything can be summed up under the sign of a continuous load of information which proceeds by way of massive jolts, implying a continual reassessment of sensibilities, adaptation of psychological assumptions, and requalification of intelligence. Narrative of a redundant nature would appear in this panorama as an indulgent invitation to repose, the only occasion of true relaxation offered to the consumer. Conversely, "superior" art only proposes schemes in evolution, grammars which mutually eliminate each other, and codes of continuous alternations.

Is it not also natural that the cultural person who in moments of intellectual tension seeks a stimulus in an action painting or in a piece of serial music should in moments of relaxation and escape (healthy and indispensable) tend toward triumphant infantile laziness and turn to the consumer product for pacification in an orgy of redundance?

As soon as we consider the problem from this angle, we are tempted to show more indulgence toward escape entertainments (among which is included our myth of Superman), reproving ourselves for having exercised an acid moralism on what is innocuous and perhaps even beneficial.

The problem changes according to the degree to which pleasure in redundance breaks the convulsed rhythm of an intellectual existence based upon the reception of information and becomes the *norm* of every imaginative activity.

[16]Author of romances like *Rocambole* in n. 4. [Ed.]

The problem is not to ask ourselves if different ideological contents conveyed by the same narrative scheme can elicit different effects. Rather, an iterative scheme becomes and remains that *only* to the extent that the scheme sustains and expresses a world; we realize this even more, once we understand how the world has the same configuration as the structure which expressed it. The case of Superman reconfirms this hypothesis. If we examine the ideological contents of Superman stories, we realize that, on the one hand, that content sustains itself and functions communicatively thanks to the narrative structure; on the other hand, the stories help define their expressive structure as the circular, static conveyance of a pedagogic message which is substantially immobilistic.

CIVIC CONSCIOUSNESS AND POLITICAL CONSCIOUSNESS

Superman stories have a characteristic in common with a series of other adventures that hinge on heroes gifted with *superpowers*. In Superman the real elements blend into a more homogeneous totality, which justifies the fact that we have devoted special attention to him; and it is no accident that Superman is the most popular of the heroes we talk about: he not only represents the forerunner of the group (in 1938), but of all the characters he is still the one who is most carefully sketched, endowed with a recognizable personality, dug out of longstanding anecdote, and so he can be seen as the representative of all his similars. (In any case, the observation that follows can be applied to a whole series of superheroes, from Batman and Robin to Green Arrow, Flash, the Manhunter from Mars, Green Lantern, and Aquaman up to the more recent Fantastic Four, Devil, and Spider Man, where the literary "genre," however, has acquired a more sophisticated form of self-irony.)

Each of these heroes is gifted with such powers that he could actually take over the government, defeat the army, or alter the equilibrium of planetary politics. On the other hand, it is clear that each of these characters is profoundly kind, moral, faithful to human and natural laws, and therefore it is right (and it is nice) that he use his powers only to the end of good. In this sense the pedagogic message of these stories would be, at least on the plane of children's literature, highly acceptable, and the same episodes of violence with which the various stories are interspersed would appear directed toward this final indictment of evil and the triumph of honest people.

The ambiguity of the teaching appears when we ask ourselves, *What is Good?* It is enough to reexamine in depth the situation of Superman, who encompasses the others, at least in their fundamental structure.

Superman is practically omnipotent, as we have said, in his physical, mental, and technological capacities. His operative capacity extends to a cosmic scale. A being gifted with such capacities offered to the good of humanity (let us pose the problem with a maximum of candor and of responsibility, taking everything as probable) would have an enormous field of action in front of him. From a man who could produce work and wealth in astronomic dimensions in a few seconds, one could expect the most bewildering political, economic, and technological upheavals in the world. From the solution of hunger problems to the tilling of uninhabitable regions, from the destruction of inhuman systems (if we read Superman into the "spirit of Dallas," why does he not go to liberate six hundred million Chinese from the yoke of Mao?), Superman could exercise good on a cosmic level, or on a galactic level, and furnish us in the meantime with a definition that through fantastic amplification could clarify precise ethical lines everywhere.

Instead, Superman carries on his activity on the level of the small community where he lives (Smallville as a youth, Metropolis as an adult), and — as in the case of the medieval countryman who could have happened to visit the Sacred Land, but not the closed and separate community which flourished fifty kilometers from the center of his life — if he takes trips to other galaxies with ease, he practically ignores, not exactly the dimension of the "world," but that of the "United States" (only once, but in one of the *Imaginary Tales,* he becomes president of the United States).

In the sphere of his own little town, evil, the only evil to combat, is incarnate in species which adheres to the underworld, that of organized crime. He is busy by preference, not against blackmarket drugs, nor, obviously, against corrupt administrators or politicians, but against bank and mail-truck robbers. In other words, *the only visible form that evil assumes is an attempt on private property.* Outerspace evil is added spice; it is casual, and it always assumes unforeseeable and transitory forms; the underworld is an endemic evil, like some kind of impure stream that pervades the course of human history, clearly divided into zones of Manichaean incontrovertibility — where each authority is fundamentally pure and good and where each wicked man is rotten to the core without hope of redemption.

As others have said, in Superman we have a perfect example of civic consciousness, completely split from political consciousness. Superman's civic attitude is perfect, but it is exercised and structured in the sphere of a small, closed community (a "brother" of Superman — as a model of absolute fidelity to established values — might appear in someone such as the movie and television hero Dr. Kildare).

It is strange that Superman, devoting himself to good deeds, spends enormous amounts of energy organizing benefit performances in order to collect money for orphans and indigents. The paradoxical waste of means (the same energy could be employed to produce directly riches or to modify radically larger situations) never ceases to astound the reader who sees Superman forever employed in parochial performances. As evil assumes only the form of an offense to private property, *good is represented only as charity.* This simple equivalent is sufficient to characterize Superman's moral world. In fact, we realize that Superman is obliged to continue his activities in the sphere of small and infinitesimal modifications of the immediately visible for the same motives noted in regard to the static nature of his plots: each general modification would draw the world, and Superman with it, toward final consumption.

On the other hand, it would be inexact to say that Superman's judicious and measured virtue depends only on the structure of the plot, that is, on the need to forbid the release of excessive and irretrievable developments. The contrary is also true: the immobilizing metaphysics underlying this kind of conceptual plot is the direct, though not the desired, consequence of a total structural mechanism which seems to be the only one suited to communicate, through the themes discussed, a particular kind of teaching. The plot must be static and must evade any development, because Superman *must* make virtue consist of many little activities on a small scale, never achieving a total awareness. Conversely, virtue must be characterized in the accomplishment of only partial acts, so that the plot can remain static. Again, the discussion does not take on the features of the authors' preferences as much as their adaptation to a concept of "order" which pervades the cultural model in which the authors live and where they construct on a small scale "analogous" models which mirror the larger one.

Jacques Derrida

b. 1930

The prime mover of poststructuralism, Jacques Derrida was born in Algiers and educated in France. Trained as a philosopher — early in his career he published a study of Edmund Husserl, the founder of phenomenology — Derrida teaches the history of philosophy at the École des Hautes Études en Sciences Sociales while teaching from time to time at leading American universities. Derrida's fame — or notoriety — in America can be traced to a talk he delivered at a structuralist conference at Johns Hopkins University in 1966. "Structure, Sign, and Play in the Discourse of the Human Sciences" confounded the structuralist enterprise and many of its adherents and precipitated the rise of poststruc-

turalist theories. Derrida's publications are steadily being translated into English; among them are Speech and Phenomena *(1967),* Of Grammatology *(1967),* Writing and Difference *(1967),* Margins of Philosophy *(1972),* Positions *(1972),* Glas *(1974),* The Post Card *(1980),* Limited, Inc. *(1988),* Acts of Literature *(1991),* Cinders *(1991),* Memoirs of the Blind *(1993),* Aporias *(1993),* Specters of Marx *(1994),* On the Name *(1995),* The Gift of Death *(1995), and* Archive Fever: A Freudian Impression *(1996). This translation of "Structure, Sign, and Play in the Discourse of the Human Sciences" is from* The Structuralist Controversy *(1970), translated by Richard Macksey and Eugenio Donato; another version appears in* Writing and Difference *(1967; translated 1978 by Alan Bass).*

Structure, Sign, and Play in the Discourse of the Human Sciences

Perhaps something has occurred in the history of the concept of structure that could be called an "event," if this loaded word did not entail a meaning which it is precisely the function of structural — or structuralist — thought to reduce or to suspect. But let me use the term "event" anyway, employing it with caution and as if in quotation marks. In this sense, this event will have the exterior form of a *rupture* and a *redoubling*.

It would be easy enough to show that the concept of structure and even the word "structure" itself are as old as the *epistemé*[1] — that is to say, as old as western science and western philosophy — and that their roots thrust deep into the soil of ordinary language, into whose deepest recesses the *epistemé* plunges to gather them together once more, making them part of itself in a metaphorical displacement. Nevertheless, up until the event which I wish to mark out and define, structure — or rather the structurality of structure — although it has always been involved, has always been neutralized or reduced, and this by a process of giving it a center or referring it to a point of presence, a fixed origin. The function of this center was not only to orient, balance, and organize the structure — one cannot in fact conceive of an unorganized structure — but above all to make sure that the organizing principle of the structure would limit what we might call the *freeplay* of the structure. No doubt that by orienting and organizing the coherence of the system, the center of a structure permits the freeplay of its elements inside the total form. And even today the notion of a structure lacking any center represents the unthinkable itself.

Nevertheless, the center also closes off the freeplay it opens up and makes possible. *Qua* center, it is the point at which the substitution of contents, elements, or terms is no longer possible. At the center, the permutation or the transformation of elements (which may of course be structures enclosed within a structure) is forbidden. At least this permutation has always remained *interdicted*[2] (I use this word deliberately). Thus it has always been thought that the center, which is by definition unique, constituted that very thing within a structure which governs the structure, while escaping structurality. This is why classical thought concerning structure could say that the center is, paradoxically, *within* the structure and *outside* it. The center is at the center of the totality, and yet, since the center does not belong to the totality (is not part of the totality), the totality *has its center elsewhere.* The center is not the center. The concept of centered

Translated by Richard Macksey and Eugenio Donato.

[1]System of thought and knowledge of a culture. [Ed.]

[2]*Interdite:* "forbidden," "disconcerted," "confounded," "speechless." [Tr.]

structure — although it represents coherence itself, the condition of the *epistemé* as philosophy or science — is contradictorily coherent. And, as always, coherence in contradiction expresses the force of a desire. The concept of centered structure is in fact the concept of a freeplay based on a fundamental ground, a freeplay which is constituted upon a fundamental immobility and a reassuring certitude, which is itself beyond the reach of the freeplay. With this certitude anxiety can be mastered, for anxiety is invariably the result of a certain mode of being implicated in the game, of being caught by the game, of being as it were from the very beginning at stake in the game.[3] From the basis of what we therefore call the center (and which, because it can be either inside or outside, is as readily called the origin as the end, as readily *arché* as *telos*),[4] the repetitions, the substitutions, the transformations, and the permutations are always *taken* from a history of meaning [*sens*] — that is, a history, period — whose origin may always be revealed or whose end may always be anticipated in the form of presence. This is why one could perhaps say that the movement of any archeology, like that of any eschatology,[5] is an accomplice of this reduction of the structurality of structure and always attempts to conceive of structure from the basis of a full presence which is out of play.

If this is so, the whole history of the concept of structure, before the rupture I spoke of, must be thought of as a series of substitutions of center for center, as a linked chain of determinations of the center. Successively, and in a regulated fashion, the center receives different forms or names. The history of metaphysics, like the history of the West, is the history of these metaphors and metonymies. Its matrix — if you will pardon me for demonstrating so little and for being so elliptical in order to bring me more quickly to my principal theme — is the determination of being as *presence* in all the senses of this word. It would be possible to show that all the names related to fundamentals, to principles, or to the center have always designated the constant of a presence — *eidos, arché, telos, energeia, ousia* (essence, existence, substance, subject) *aletheia,*[6] transcendentality, consciousness, or conscience, God, man, and so forth.

The event I called a rupture, the disruption I alluded to at the beginning of this paper, would presumably have come about when the structurality of structure had to begin to be thought, that is to say, repeated, and this is why I said that this disruption was repetition in all of the senses of this word. From then on it became necessary to think the law which governed, as it were, the desire for the center in the constitution of structure and the process of signification prescribing its displacements and its substitutions for this law of the central presence — but a central presence which was never itself, which has always already been transported outside itself in its surrogate. The surrogate does not substitute itself for anything which has somehow pre-existed it. From then on it was probably necessary to begin to think that there was no center, that the center could not be thought in the form of a being-present, that the center had no natural locus, that it was not a fixed locus but a function, a sort of non-locus in which an infinite number of sign-substitutions came into play. This moment was that in which language invaded the universal problematic; that in which, in the absence of a center or origin, everything became discourse — provided we can agree on this word — that is to say, when everything became a system where the central signified, the original or transcendental signified, is never absolutely present outside a system of differences. The absence of the transcendental signified extends the domain and the interplay of signification *ad infinitum*.

Where and how does this decentering, this notion of the structurality of structure, occur? It would be somewhat naïve to refer to an event, a doctrine, or an author in order to designate this

[3]". . . qui naît toujours d'une certaine manière d'être impliqué dans le jeu, d'être pris au jeu, d'être comme être d'entreé de jeu dans le jeu." [Tr.]

[4]Beginning as end. *Telos* means "end" in the sense of "purpose." [Ed.]

[5]Study of last things. [Ed.]

[6]The six preceding Greek terms mean, respectively: form, origin, purpose, energy, being, and truth. [Ed.]

occurrence. It is no doubt part of the totality of an era, our own, but still it has already begun to proclaim itself and begun to *work*. Nevertheless, if I wished to give some sort of indication by choosing one or two "names," and by recalling those authors in whose discourses this occurrence has most nearly maintained its most radical formulation, I would probably cite the Nietzschean critique of metaphysics, the critique of the concepts of being and truth, for which were substituted the concepts of play, interpretation, and sign (sign without truth present); the Freudian critique of self-presence, that is, the critique of consciousness, of the subject, of self-identity and of self-proximity or self-possession; and, more radically, the Heideggerean destruction of metaphysics, of onto-theology, of the determination of being as presence. But all these destructive discourses and all their analogues are trapped in a sort of circle. This circle is unique. It describes the form of the relationship between the history of metaphysics and the destruction of the history of metaphysics. *There is no sense* in doing without the concepts of metaphysics in order to attack metaphysics. We have no language — no syntax and no lexicon — which is alien to this history; we cannot utter a single destructive proposition which has not already slipped into the form, the logic, and the implicit postulations of precisely what it seeks to contest. To pick out one example from many: the metaphysics of presence is attacked with the help of the concept of the *sign*. But from the moment anyone wishes this to show, as I suggested a moment ago, that there is no transcendental or privileged signified and that the domain or the interplay of signification has, henceforth, no limit, he ought to extend his refusal to the concept and to the word sign itself — which is precisely what cannot be done. For the signification "sign" has always been comprehended and determined, in its sense, as sign-of, signifier referring to a signified, signifier different from its signified. If one erases the radical difference between signifier and signified, it is the word signifier itself which ought to be abandoned as a metaphysical concept. When Lévi-Strauss says in the preface to *The Raw and the Cooked*[7] that he has "sought to transcend the opposition between the sensible and the intelligible by placing [himself] from the very beginning at the level of signs," the necessity, the force, and the legitimacy of his act cannot make us forget that the concept of the sign cannot in itself surpass or bypass this opposition between the sensible and the intelligible. The concept of the sign is determined by this opposition: through and throughout the totality of its history and by its system. But we cannot do without the concept of the sign, we cannot give up this metaphysical complicity without also giving up the critique we are directing against this complicity, without the risk of erasing difference [altogether] in the self-identity of a signified reducing into itself its signifier, or, what amounts to the same thing, simply expelling it outside itself. For there are two heterogeneous ways of erasing the difference between the signifier and the signified: one, the classic way, consists in reducing or deriving the signifier, that is to say, ultimately in *submitting* the sign to thought; the other, the one we are using here against the first one, consists in putting into question the system in which the preceding reduction functioned: first and foremost, the opposition between the sensible and the intelligible. The *paradox* is that the metaphysical reduction of the sign needed the opposition it was reducing. The opposition is part of the system, along with the reduction. And what I am saying here about the sign can be extended to all the concepts and all the sentences of metaphysics, in particular to the discourse on "structure." But there are many ways of being caught in this circle. They are all more or less naïve, more or less empirical, more or less systematic, more or less close to the formulation or even to the formalization of this circle. It is these differences which explain the multiplicity of destructive discourses and the disagreement between those who make them. It was within concepts inherited from metaphysics that Nietzsche, Freud, and Heidegger worked, for example. Since these concepts are not elements or atoms and since they are taken from a syntax and a system, every particular borrowing drags along with it the whole of metaphysics. This is what allows these destroyers to destroy each other reciprocally — for example, Heidegger considering Nietzsche, with as

[7]*Le cru et le cuit* (Paris: Plon, 1964). [Tr.]

much lucidity and rigor as bad faith and misconstruction, as the last metaphysician, the last "Platonist." One could do the same for Heidegger himself, for Freud, or for a number of others. And today no exercise is more widespread.

What is the relevance of this formal schema when we turn to what are called the "human sciences"? One of them perhaps occupies a privileged place — ethnology.[8] One can in fact assume that ethnology could have been born as a science only at the moment when a de-centering had come about: at the moment when European culture — and, in consequence, the history of metaphysics and of its concepts — had been *dislocated,* driven from its locus, and forced to stop considering itself as the culture of reference. This moment is not first and foremost a moment of philosophical or scientific discourse, it is also a moment which is political, economic, technical, and so forth. One can say in total assurance that there is nothing fortuitous about the fact that the critique of ethnocentrism — the very condition of ethnology — should be systematically and historically contemporaneous with the destruction of the history of metaphysics. Both belong to a single and same era.

Ethnology — like any science — comes about within the element of discourse. And it is primarily a European science employing traditional concepts, however much it may struggle against them. Consequently, whether he wants to or not — and this does not depend on a decision on his part — the ethnologist accepts into his discourse the premises of ethnocentrism at the very moment when he is employed in denouncing them. This necessity is irreducible; it is not a historical contingency. We ought to consider very carefully all its implications. But if nobody can escape this necessity, and if no one is therefore responsible for giving in to it, however little, this does not mean that all the ways of giving in to it are of an equal pertinence. The quality and the fecundity of a discourse are perhaps measured by the critical rigor with which this relationship to the history of metaphysics and to inherited concepts is thought. Here it is a question of a critical relationship to the language of the human sciences and a question of a critical responsibility of the discourse. It is a question of putting expressly and systematically the problem of the status of a discourse which borrows from a heritage the resources necessary for the deconstruction of that heritage itself. A problem of *economy* and *strategy.*

If I now go on to employ an examination of the texts of Lévi-Strauss as an example, it is not only because of the privilege accorded to ethnology among the human sciences, nor yet because the thought of Lévi-Strauss weighs heavily on the contemporary theoretical situation. It is above all because a certain choice has made itself evident in the work of Lévi-Strauss and because a certain doctrine has been elaborated there, and precisely in a *more or less explicit manner,* in relation to this critique of language and to this critical language in the human sciences.

In order to follow this movement in the text of Lévi-Strauss, let me choose as one guiding thread among others the opposition between nature and culture. In spite of all its rejuvenations and its disguises, this opposition is congenital to philosophy. It is even older than Plato. It is at least as old as the Sophists. Since the statement of the opposition — *physis/nomos, physis/techne*[9] — it has been passed on to us by a whole historical chain which opposes "nature" to the law, to education, to art, to technics — and also to liberty, to the arbitrary, to history, to society, to the mind, and so on. From the beginnings of his quest and from his first book, *The Elementary Structures of Kinship,*[10] Lévi-Strauss has felt at one and the same time the necessity of utilizing this opposition and the impossibility of making it acceptable. In the *Elementary Structures,* he begins from this axiom or definition: that belongs to nature which is *universal* and spontaneous, not depending on any particular culture or on any determinate norm. That belongs to culture, on the other hand, which depends on a system of *norms* regulating society and is therefore capable of *varying* from one social structure to another. These two definitions are of the traditional type.

[8]Cultural anthropology. [Ed.]

[9]Nature vs. culture; nature vs. art. [Ed.]

[10]*Les structures élémentaires de la parenté* (Paris: Presses Universitaires de France, 1949). [Tr.]

But, in the very first pages of the *Elementary Structures,* Lévi-Strauss, who has begun to give these concepts an acceptable standing, encounters what he calls a *scandal,* that is to say, something which no longer tolerates the nature/culture opposition he has accepted and which seems to require *at one and the same time* the predicates of nature and those of culture. This scandal is the *incest-prohibition.* The incest-prohibition is universal; in this sense one could call it natural. But it is also a prohibition, a system of norms and interdicts; in this sense one could call it cultural.

> Let us assume therefore that everything universal in man derives from the order of nature and is characterized by spontaneity, that everything which is subject to a norm belongs to culture and presents the attributes of the relative and the particular. We then find ourselves confronted by a fact, or rather an ensemble of facts, which, in the light of the preceding definitions, is not far from appearing as a scandal: the prohibition of incest presents without the least equivocation, and indissolubly linked together, the two characteristics in which we recognized the contradictory attributes of two exclusive orders. The prohibition of incest constitutes a rule, but a rule, alone of all the social rules, which possesses at the same time a universal character (p. 9).

Obviously there is no scandal except in the *interior* of a system of concepts sanctioning the difference between nature and culture. In beginning his work with the *factum*[11] of the incest-prohibition, Lévi-Strauss thus puts himself in a position entailing that this difference, which has always been assumed to be self-evident, becomes obliterated or disputed. For, from the moment that the incest-prohibition can no longer be conceived within the nature/culture opposition, it can no longer be said that it is a scandalous fact, a nucleus of opacity within a network of transparent significations. The incest-prohibition is no longer a scandal one meets with or comes up against in the domain of traditional concepts; it is something which escapes these concepts and certainly precedes them — probably as the condition of their possibility. It could perhaps be said that the whole of philosophical conceptualization, systematically relating itself to the nature/culture opposition, is designed to leave in the domain of the unthinkable the very thing that makes this conceptualization possible: the origin of the prohibition of incest.

I have dealt too cursorily with this example, only one among so many others, but the example nevertheless reveals that language bears within itself the necessity of its own critique. This critique may be undertaken along two tracks, in two "manners." Once the limit of nature/culture opposition makes itself felt, one might want to question systematically and rigorously the history of these concepts. This is a first action. Such a systematic and historic questioning would be neither a philological nor a philosophical action in the classic sense of these words. Concerning oneself with the founding concepts of the whole history of philosophy, de-constituting them, is not to undertake the task of the philologist or of the classic historian of philosophy. In spite of appearances, it is probably the most daring way of making the beginnings of a step outside of philosophy. The step "outside philosophy" is much more difficult to conceive than is generally imagined by those who think they made it long ago with cavalier ease, and who are in general swallowed up in metaphysics by the whole body of the discourse that they claim to have disengaged from it.

In order to avoid the possibly sterilizing effect of the first way, the other choice — which I feel corresponds more nearly to the way chosen by Lévi-Strauss — consists in conserving in the field of empirical discovery all these old concepts, while at the same time exposing here and there their limits, treating them as tools which can still be of use. No longer is any truth-value attributed to them; there is a readiness to abandon them if necessary if other instruments should appear more useful. In the meantime, their relative efficacy is exploited, and they are employed to destroy the old machinery to which they belong and of which they themselves are pieces. Thus it is that the language of the human sciences criticizes *itself.* Lévi-Strauss thinks that in this way he can separate *method* from *truth,* the instru-

[11]Given fact. [Ed.]

ments of the method and the objective significations aimed at by it. One could almost say that this is the primary affirmation of Lévi-Strauss; in any event, the first words of the *Elementary Structures* are: "One begins to understand that the distinction between state of nature and state of society (we would be more apt to say today: state of nature and state of culture), while lacking any acceptable historical signification, presents a value which fully justifies its use by modern sociology: its value as a methodological instrument."

Lévi-Strauss will always remain faithful to this double intention: to preserve as an instrument that whose truth-value he criticizes.

On the one hand, he will continue in effect to contest the value of the nature/culture opposition. More than thirteen years after the *Elementary Structures, The Savage Mind*[12] faithfully echoes the text I have just quoted: "The opposition between nature and culture which I have previously insisted on seems today to offer a value which is above all methodological." And this methodological value is not affected by its "ontological" non-value (as could be said, if this notion were not suspect here): "It would not be enough to have absorbed particular humanities into a general humanity; this first enterprise prepares the way for others . . . which belong to the natural and exact sciences: to reintegrate culture into nature, and finally, to reintegrate life into the totality of its physiochemical conditions" (p. 327).

On the other hand, still in *The Savage Mind,* he presents as what he calls *bricolage*[13] what might be called the discourse of this method. The *bricoleur,* says Lévi-Strauss, is someone who uses "the means at hand," that is, the instruments he finds at his disposition around him, those which are already there, which had not been especially conceived with an eye to the operation for which they are to be used and to which one tries by trial and error to adapt them, not hesitating to change them whenever it appears necessary, or to try several of them at once, even if their form and their origin are heterogeneous — and so forth. There is therefore a critique of language in the form of *bricolage,* and it has even been possible to say that *bricolage* is the critical language itself. I am thinking in particular of the article by G[érard] Genette, "Structuralisme et Critique littéraire," published in homage to Lévi-Strauss in a special issue of *L'Arc* (no. 26, 1965), where it is stated that the analysis of *bricolage* could "be applied almost word for word" to criticism, and especially to "literary criticism."[14]

If one calls *bricolage* the necessity of borrowing one's concept from the text of a heritage which is more or less coherent or ruined, it must be said that every discourse is *bricoleur.* The engineer, whom Lévi-Strauss opposes to the *bricoleur,* should be one to construct the totality of his language, syntax, and lexicon. In this sense the engineer is a myth. A subject who would supposedly be the absolute origin of his own discourse and would supposedly construct it "out of nothing," "out of whole cloth," would be the creator of the *verbe,* the *verbe* itself. The notion of the engineer who had supposedly broken with all forms of *bricolage* is therefore a theological idea; and since Lévi-Strauss tells us elsewhere that *bricolage* is mythopoetic, the odds are that the engineer is a myth produced by the *bricoleur.* From the moment that we cease to believe in such an engineer and in a discourse breaking with the received historical discourse, as soon as it is admitted that every finite discourse is bound by a certain *bricolage,* and that the engineer and the scientist are also species of *bricoleurs* then the very idea of *bricolage* is menaced and the difference in which it took on its meaning decomposes.

This brings out the second thread which might guide us in what is being unraveled here.

Lévi-Strauss describes *bricolage* not only as an intellectual activity but also as a mythopoetical activity. One reads in *The Savage Mind,* "Like *bricolage* on the technical level, mythical reflection can attain brilliant and unforeseen results on the intellectual level. Reciprocally, the

[12] *La pensée sauvage* (Paris: Plon, 1962). [Tr.]

[13] A *bricoleur* is a jack-of-all-trades, someone who potters about with odds-and-ends, who puts things together out of bits and pieces. [Tr.]

[14] Reprinted in: G. Genette, *Figures* (Paris: Editions du Seuil, 1966), p. 145. [Tr.]

mythopoetical character of *bricolage* has often been noted" (p. 26).

But the remarkable endeavor of Lévi-Strauss is not simply to put forward, notably in the most recent of his investigations, a structural science of knowledge of myths and of mythological activity. His endeavor also appears — I would say almost from the first — in the status which he accords to his own discourse on myths, to what he calls his "mythologicals." It is here that his discourse on the myth reflects on itself and criticizes itself. And this moment, this critical period, is evidently of concern to all the languages which share the field of the human sciences. What does Lévi-Strauss say of his "mythologicals"? It is here that we rediscover the mythopoetical virtue (power) of *bricolage*. In effect, what appears most fascinating in this critical search for a new status of the discourse is the stated abandonment of all reference to a *center,* to a *subject,* to a privileged *reference,* to an origin, or to an absolute *arché*. The theme of this decentering could be followed throughout the "Overture" to his last book, *The Raw and the Cooked*. I shall simply remark on a few key points.

1. From the very start, Lévi-Strauss recognizes that the Bororo myth which he employs in the book as the "reference-myth" does not merit this name and this treatment. The name is specious and the use of the myth improper. This myth deserves no more than any other its referential privilege:

> In fact the Bororo myth which will from now on be designated by the name *reference-myth* is, as I shall try to show, nothing other than a more or less forced transformation of other myths originating either in the same society or in societies more or less far removed. It would therefore have been legitimate to choose as my point of departure any representative of the group whatsoever. From this point of view, the interest of the reference-myth does not depend on its typical character, but rather on its irregular position in the midst of a group (p. 10).

2. There is no unity or absolute source of the myth. The focus or the source of the myth are always shadows and virtualities which are elusive, unactualizable, and nonexistent in the first place. Everything begins with the structure, the configuration, the relationship. The discourse on this acentric structure, the myth, that is, cannot itself have an absolute subject or an absolute center. In order not to shortchange the form and the movement of the myth, that violence which consists in centering a language which is describing an acentric structure must be avoided. In this context, therefore, it is necessary to forego scientific or philosophical discourse, to renounce the *epistemé* which absolutely requires, which is the absolute requirement that we go back to the source, to the center, to the founding basis, to the principle, and so on. In opposition to *epistémic* discourse, structural discourse on myths — *mythological* discourse — must itself be *mythomorphic*. It must have the form of that of which it speaks. This is what Lévi-Strauss says in *The Raw and the Cooked,* from which I would now like to quote a long and remarkable passage:

> In effect the study of myths poses a methodological problem by the fact that it cannot conform to the Cartesian principle of dividing the difficulty into as many parts as are necessary to resolve it. There exists no veritable end or term to mythical analysis, no secret unity which could be grasped at the end of the work of decomposition. The themes duplicate themselves to infinity. When we think we have disentangled them from each other and can hold them separate, it is only to realize that they are joining together again, in response to the attraction of unforeseen affinities. In consequence, the unity of the myth is only tendential and projective; it never reflects a state or a moment of the myth. An imaginary phenomenon implied by the endeavor to interpret, its role is to give a synthetic form to the myth and to impede its dissolution into the confusion of contraries. It could therefore be said that the science or knowledge of myths is an *anaclastic,* taking this ancient term in the widest sense authorized by its etymology, a science which admits into its definition the study of the reflected rays along with that of the broken ones. But, unlike philosophical reflection, which claims to go all the way back to its source, the reflections in question here concern rays without any other than a virtual focus. . . . In wanting to imitate the spontaneous movement of mythical thought, my enterprise, itself too brief and too long, has had to yield to its demands and respect its rhythm. Thus is this book on myths itself and in its own way a myth.

This statement is repeated a little farther on (p. 20): "Since myths themselves rest on second-order codes (the first-order codes being those in which language consists), this book thus offers the rough draft of a third-order code, destined to insure the reciprocal possibility of translation of several myths. This is why it would not be wrong to consider it a myth: the myth of mythology, as it were." It is by this absence of any real and fixed center of the mythical or mythological discourse that the musical model chosen by Lévi-Strauss for the composition of his book is apparently justified. The absence of a center is here the absence of a subject and the absence of an author: "The myth and the musical work thus appear as orchestra conductors whose listeners are the silent performers. If it be asked where the real focus of the work is to be found, it must be replied that its determination is impossible. Music and mythology bring man face to face with virtual objects whose shadow alone is actual. . . . Myths have no authors" (p. 25).

Thus it is at this point that ethnographic *bricolage* deliberately assumes its mythopoetic function. But by the same token, this function makes the philosophical or epistemological requirement of a center appear as mythological, that is to say, as a historical illusion.

Nevertheless, even if one yields to the necessity of what Lévi-Strauss has done, one cannot ignore its risks. If the mythological is mythomorphic, are all discourses on myths equivalent? Shall we have to abandon any epistemological requirement which permits us to distinguish between several qualities of discourse on the myth? A classic question, but inevitable. We cannot reply — and I do not believe Lévi-Strauss replies to it — as long as the problem of the relationships between the philosopheme or the theorem, on the one hand, and the mytheme or the mythopoem(e), on the other, has not been expressly posed. This is no small problem. For lack of expressly posing this problem, we condemn ourselves to transforming the claimed transgression of philosophy into an unperceived fault in the interior of the philosophical field. Empiricism would be the genus of which these faults would always be the species. Trans-philosophical concepts would be transformed into philosophical naïvetés. One could give many examples to demonstrate this risk: the concepts of sign, history, truth, and so forth. What I want to emphasize is simply that the passage beyond philosophy does not consist in turning the page of philosophy (which usually comes down to philosophizing badly), but in continuing to read philosophers *in a certain way*. The risk I am speaking of is always assumed by Lévi-Strauss and it is the very price of his endeavor. I have said that empiricism is the matrix of all the faults menacing a discourse which continues, as with Lévi-Strauss in particular, to elect to be scientific. If we wanted to pose the problem of empiricism and *bricolage* in depth, we would probably end up very quickly with a number of propositions absolutely contradictory in relation to the status of discourse in structural ethnography. On the one hand, structuralism justly claims to be the critique of empiricism.[15] But at the same time there is not a single book or study by Lévi-Strauss which does not offer itself as an empirical essay which can always be completed or invalidated by new information. The structural schemata are always proposed as hypotheses resulting from a finite quantity of information and which are subjected to the proof of experience. Numerous texts could be used to demonstrate this double postulation. Let us turn once again to the "Overture" of *The Raw and the Cooked,* where it seems clear that if this postulation is double, it is because it is a question here of a language on language:

> Critics who might take me to task for not having begun by making an exhaustive inventory of South American myths before analyzing them would be making a serious mistake about the nature and the role of these documents. The totality of the myths of a people is of the order of the discourse. Provided that this people does not become physically or morally extinct, this totality is never closed. Such a criticism would therefore be equivalent to reproaching a linguist with writing the grammar of a language without having recorded the totality of

[15] Because the aim of structuralism is to learn the constitutive rules of an activity, which are implicit in every instance of the activity, so that the massing of large quantities of data is unnecessary. [Ed.]

the words which have been uttered since that language came into existence and without knowing the verbal exchanges which will take place as long as the language continues to exist. Experience proves that an absurdly small number of sentences . . . allows the linguist to elaborate a grammar of the language he is studying. And even a partial grammar or an outline of a grammar represents valuable acquisitions in the case of unknown languages. Syntax does not wait until it has been possible to enumerate a theoretically unlimited series of events before becoming manifest, because syntax consists in the body of rules which presides over the generation of these events. And it is precisely a syntax of South American mythology that I wanted to outline. Should new texts appear to enrich the mythical discourse, then this will provide an opportunity to check or modify the way in which certain grammatical laws have been formulated, an opportunity to discard certain of them and an opportunity to discover new ones. But in no instance can the requirement of a total mythical discourse be raised as an objection. For we have just seen that such a requirement has no meaning (pp. 15–16).

Totalization is therefore defined at one time as *useless,* at another time as *impossible.* This is no doubt the result of the fact that there are two ways of conceiving the limit of totalization. And I assert once again that these two determinations coexist implicitly in the discourses of Lévi-Strauss. Totalization can be judged impossible in the classical style: one then refers to the empirical endeavor of a subject or of a finite discourse in a vain and breathless quest of an infinite richness which it can never master. There is too much, more than one can say. But nontotalization can also be determined in another way: not from the standpoint of the concept of finitude as assigning us to an empirical view, but from the standpoint of the concept of *freeplay.* If totalization no longer has any meaning, it is not because the infinity of a field cannot be covered by a finite glance or a finite discourse, but because the nature of the field — that is, language and a finite language — excludes totalization. This field is in fact that of *freeplay,* that is to say, a field of infinite substitutions in the closure of a finite ensemble. This field permits these infinite substitutions only because it is finite, that is to say, because instead of being an inexhaustible field, as in the classical hypothesis, instead of being too large, there is something missing from it: a center which arrests and grounds the freeplay of substitutions. One could say — rigorously using that word whose scandalous signification is always obliterated in French — that this movement of the freeplay, permitted by the lack, the absence of a center of origin, is the movement of *supplementarity.* One cannot determine the center, the sign which *supplements*[16] it, which takes its place in its absence — because this sign adds itself, occurs in addition, over and above, comes as a *supplement.*[17] The movement of signification adds something, which results in the fact that there is always more, but this addition is a floating one because it comes to perform a vicarious function, to supplement a lack on the part of the signified. Although Lévi-Strauss in his use of the word supplementary never emphasizes as I am doing here the two directions of meaning which are so strangely compounded within it, it is not by chance that he uses this word twice in his "Introduction to the Work of Marcel Mauss,"[18] at the point where he is speaking of the "superabundance of signifier, in relation to the signifieds to which this superabundance can refer":

> In his endeavor to understand the world, man therefore always has at his disposition a surplus of signification (which he portions out amongst things according to the laws of symbolic thought — which it is the task of ethnologists and linguists to study). This distribution of a *supplementary* allowance [*ration* supplémentaire] — if it is permissible to put it that way — is absolutely necessary in order that on the whole the available signifier and the signified it aims at may remain in the relationship of complementarity which is the very condition of the use of symbolic thought (p. xlix).

[16]The point being that the word, both in English and French, means "to supply a deficiency," on the one hand, and "to supply something additional," on the other. [Tr.] See the introduction, pp. 818–19, on Derrida's antinomy of the supplement. [Ed.]

[17]". . . ce signe s'ajoute, vient en sus, en *supplément.*" [Tr.]

[18]"Introduction à l'oeuvre de Marcel Mauss," in: Marcel Mauss, *Sociologie et anthropologie* (Paris: Presses Universitaires de France, 1950). [Tr.] Marcel Mauss (1872–1950) was the French social anthropologist who wrote *The Gift* (1925). [Ed.]

(It could no doubt be demonstrated that this *ration supplémentaire* of signification is the origin of the *ratio* itself.) The word reappears a little farther on, after Lévi-Strauss has mentioned "this floating signifier, which is the servitude of all finite thought":

> In other words — and taking as our guide Mauss's precept that all social phenomena can be assimilated to language — we see in *mana, Wakau, oranda* and other notions of the same type, the conscious expression of a semantic function, whose role it is to permit symbolic thought to operate in spite of the contradiction which is proper to it. In this way are explained the apparently insoluble antinomies attached to this notion. . . . At one and the same time force and action, quality and state, substantive and verb; abstract and concrete, omnipresent and localized — *mana* is in effect all these things. But is it not precisely because it is none of these things that *mana* is a simple form, or more exactly, a symbol in the pure state, and therefore capable of becoming charged with any sort of symbolic content whatever? In the system of symbols constituted by all cosmologies, *mana* would simply be a *valeur symbolique zéro,* that is to say, a sign marking the necessity of a symbolic content *supplementary* [my italics] to that with which the signified is already loaded, but which can take on any value required, provided only that this value still remains part of the available reserve and is not, as phonologists put it, a group-term.

Lévi-Strauss adds the note:

> Linguists have already been led to formulate hypotheses of this type. For example: "A zero phoneme is opposed to all the other phonemes in French in that it entails no differential characters and no constant phonetic value. On the contrary, the proper function of the zero phoneme is to be opposed to phoneme absence." (R. Jakobson and J. Lutz, "Notes on the French Phonemic Pattern," *Word,* vol. 5, no. 2 [August, 1949], p. 155). Similarly, if we schematize the conception I am proposing here, it could almost be said that the function of notions like *mana* is to be opposed to the absence of signification, without entailing by itself any particular signification (p. 1 and note).

The *superabundance* of the signifier, its *supplementary* character, is thus the result of a finitude, that is to say, the result of a lack which must be *supplemented.*

It can now be understood why the concept of freeplay is important in Lévi-Strauss. His references to all sorts of games, notably to roulette, are very frequent, especially in his *Conversations,*[19] in *Race and History,*[20] and in *The Savage Mind.* This reference to the game or free-play is always caught up in a tension.

It is in tension with history, first of all. This is a classical problem, objections to which are now well worn or used up. I shall simply indicate what seems to me the formality of the problem: by reducing history, Lévi-Strauss has treated as it deserves a concept which has always been in complicity with a teleological and eschatological metaphysics, in other words, paradoxically, in complicity with that philosophy of presence to which it was believed history could be opposed. The thematic of historicity, although it seems to be a somewhat late arrival in philosophy, has always been required by the determination of being as presence. With or without etymology, and in spite of the classic antagonism which opposes these significations throughout all of classical thought, it could be shown that the concept of *epistemé* has always called forth that of *historia,* if history is always the unity of a becoming, as tradition of truth or development of science or knowledge oriented toward the appropriation of truth in presence and self-presence, toward knowledge in consciousness-of-self.[21] History has always been conceived as the movement of a resumption of history, a diversion between two presences. But if it is legitimate to suspect this concept of history, there is a risk, if it is reduced without an express statement of the problem I am indicating here, of falling back into an ahistoricism of a classical type, that is to say, in a determinate moment of the history of metaphysics. Such is the algebraic formality of the problem as

[19]Presumably: G. Charbonnier, *Entretiens avec Claude Lévi-Strauss* (Paris: Plon-Julliard, 1961). [Tr.]

[20]*Race and History* (Paris: UNESCO Publications, 1958). [Tr.]

[21]". . . l'unité d'un devenir, comme tradition de la vérité dans la présence et la présence à soi, vers le savoir dans la conscience de soi." [Tr.]

I see it. More concretely, in the work of Lévi-Strauss it must be recognized that the respect for structurality, for the internal originality of the structure, compels a neutralization of time and history. For example, the appearance of a new structure, of an original system, always comes about — and this is the very condition of its structural specificity — by a rupture with its past, its origin, and its cause. One can therefore describe what is peculiar to the structural organization only by not taking into account, in the very moment of this description, its past conditions: by failing to pose the problem of the passage from one structure to another, by putting history into parentheses. In this "structuralist" moment, the concepts of chance and discontinuity are indispensable. And Lévi-Strauss does in fact often appeal to them as he does, for instance, for that structure of structures, language, of which he says in the "Introduction to the Work of Marcel Mauss" that it "could only have been born in one fell swoop":

> Whatever may have been the moment and the circumstances of its appearance in the scale of animal life, language could only have been born in one fell swoop. Things could not have set about signifying progressively. Following a transformation the study of which is not the concern of the social sciences, but rather of biology and psychology, a crossing over came about from a stage where nothing had a meaning to another where everything possessed it (p. xlvi).

This standpoint does not prevent Lévi-Strauss from recognizing the slowness, the process of maturing, the continuous toil of factual transformations, history (for example, in *Race and History*). But, in accordance with an act which was also Rousseau's and Husserl's, he must "brush aside all the facts" at the moment when he wishes to recapture the specificity of a structure. Like Rousseau, he must always conceive of the origin of a new structure on the model of catastrophe — an overturning of nature in nature, a natural interruption of the natural sequence, a brushing aside *of* nature.

Besides the tension of freeplay with history, there is also the tension of freeplay with presence. Freeplay is the disruption of presence. The presence of an element is always a signifying and substitutive reference inscribed in a system of differences and the movement of a chin. Freeplay is always an interplay of absence and presence, but if it is to be radically conceived, freeplay must be conceived of before the alternative of presence and absence; being must be conceived of as presence or absence beginning with the possibility of freeplay and not the other way around. If Lévi-Strauss, better than any other, has brought to light the freeplay of repetition and the repetition of freeplay, one no less perceives in his work a sort of ethic presence, an ethic of nostalgia for origins, an ethic of archaic and natural innocence, of a purity of presence and self-presence in speech[22] — an ethic, nostalgia, and even remorse which he often presents as the motivation of the ethnological project when he moves toward archaic societies — exemplary societies in his eyes. These texts are well known.

As a turning toward the presence, lost or impossible, of the absent origin, this structuralist thematic of broken immediateness is thus the sad, *negative,* nostalgic, guilty, Rousseauist facet of the thinking of freeplay of which the Nietzschean *affirmation* — the joyous affirmation of the freeplay of the world and of the innocence of becoming, the affirmation of a world of signs without fault, without truth, without origin, offered to an active interpretation — would be the other side. *This affirmation then determines the noncenter otherwise than as loss of the center.* And it plays the game without security. For there is a *sure* freeplay: that which is limited to the *substitution of given and existing, present,* pieces. In absolute chance, affirmation also surrenders itself to *genetic* indetermination, to the *seminal* adventure of the trace.[23]

[22]". . . de la présence à soi dans la parole." [Tr.]

[23]"Tournée vers la présence, perdue ou impossible, de l'origine absente, cette thématique structuraliste de l'immédiateté rompue est donc la face triste, *négative,* nostalgique, coupable, rousseauiste, de la pensée du jeu dont *l'affirmation* nietzschéenne, l'affirmation joyeuse du jeu du monde et de l'innocence du devenir, l'affirmation d'un monde de signes sans faute, sans vérité, sans origine, offert à une interprétation active, serait l'autre face. *Cette affirmation détermine alors le* non-centre *autrement que comme perte du centre.* Et elle joue sans sécurité. Car il y a un jeu *sûr:* celui qui se limite à la *substitution* de pièces *données et existantes, présentes.* Dans le

There are thus two interpretations of interpretation, of structure, of sign, of freeplay. The one seeks to decipher, dreams of deciphering, a truth or an origin which is free from freeplay and from the order of the sign, and lives like an exile the necessity of interpretation. The other, which is no longer turned toward the origin, affirms freeplay and tries to pass beyond man and humanism, the name man being the name of that being who, throughout the history of metaphysics or of ontotheology — in other words, through the history of all of his history — has dreamed of full presence, the reassuring foundation, the origin and the end of the game. The second interpretation of interpretation, to which Nietzsche showed us the way, does not seek in ethnography, as Lévi-Strauss wished, the "inspiration of a new humanism."

There are more than enough indications today to suggest we might perceive that these two interpretations of interpretation — which are absolutely irreconcilable even if we live them simultaneously and reconcile them in an obscure economy — together share the field which we call, in such a problematic fashion, the human sciences.

hasard absolu, l'affirmation se livre aussi à l'indétermination *génétique*, à l'aventure *séminale* de la trace." [Tr.] Derrida contrasts two methods of freeplay, Lévi-Strauss's and his own. The former is "sad" and "negative" in that it seeks a substitute for the absent center once provided by metaphysics; it is "nostalgic" for origins, "guilty" over European imperialism, "Rousseauist" in propounding a myth of the noble savage and privileging myth over rational thought. Its method of freeplay is "sure" in that its substitutions of one mytheme for another within the system of myths create a closed system. On the contrary, Derrida's system of freeplay, like the philosophy of Nietzsche, is "joyful" in its affirmation of the power of the will to assign and alter all values. For Derrida, the lack of a center betokens freedom, not the loss of security. The Derridean is an adventurer who must abandon certainty for chance in following the "trace" — the chain of signifiers — wherever it leads. [Ed.]

For my part, although these two interpretations must acknowledge and accentuate their difference and define their irreducibility, I do not believe that today there is any question of *choosing* — in the first place because here we are in a region (let's say, provisionally, a region of historicity) where the category of choice seems particularly trivial; and in the second, because we must first try to conceive of the common ground, and the *différance* of this irreducible difference.[24] Here there is a sort of question, call it historical, of which we are only glimpsing today the *conception, the formation, the gestation, the labor.* I employ these words, I admit, with a glance toward the business of childbearing — but also with a glance toward those who, in a company from which I do not exclude myself, turn their eyes away in the face of the as yet unnameable which is proclaiming itself and which can do so, as is necessary whenever a birth is in the offing, only under the species of the non-species, in the formless, mute, infant, and terrifying form of monstrosity.

[24]From *différer,* in the sense of "to postpone," "put off," "defer." Elsewhere Derrida uses the word as a synonym for the German *Aufschub:* "postponement," and relates it to the central Freudian concepts of *Verspätung, Nachträglichkeit,* and to the *"détours* to death" of *Beyond the Pleasure Principle* by Sigmund Freud (Standard Edition, ed. James Strachey, vol. XIX, London, 1961), Ch. V. [Tr.]

Michel Foucault

1926–1984

Michel Foucault, a major intellectual presence in France since the 1960s, was renowned for his writings, which attempted to erase the traditional boundaries between the disciplines of science, history, philosophy, and sociology. Born in Poitiers, the son of a doctor, Foucault was trained as a philosopher, but his earliest work, such as Madness and Civilization *(1961), dealt with history — specifically, the history of attitudes toward mental illness and its treatment. Foucault taught at the*

University of Clermont-Ferrand between 1960 and 1968, spent two years at the University of Paris-Vincennes, and in 1970 was elevated to a professorship at the Collège de France — the highest position in the French academic system. He was also a visiting professor at a host of universities worldwide. In addition to Madness and Civilization, *other works that have been translated into English include* The Birth of the Clinic *(1963),* The Order of Things *(1966),* The Archaeology of Knowledge *(1969),* Discipline and Punish *(1975), three volumes of* The History of Sexuality *(1976, 1985, 1986), and* Power/Knowledge *(1980). "What Is an Author?" originally appeared in the* Bulletin de la Société Française de Philosophie *in 1969.*

What Is an Author?

The coming into being of the notion of "author" constitutes the privileged moment of *individualization* in the history of ideas, knowledge, literature, philosophy, and the sciences. Even today, when we reconstruct the history of a concept, literary genre, or school of philosophy, such categories seem relatively weak, secondary, and superimposed scansions in comparison with the solid and fundamental unit of the author and the work.

I shall not offer here a sociohistorical analysis of the author's persona. Certainly it would be worth examining how the author became individualized in a culture like ours, what status he has been given, at what moment studies of authenticity and attribution began, in what kind of system of valorization the author was involved, at what point we began to recount the lives of authors rather than of heroes, and how this fundamental category of "the-man-and-his-work criticism" began. For the moment, however, I want to deal solely with the relationship between text and author and with the manner in which the text points to this "figure" that, at least in appearance, is outside it and antecedes it.

Beckett nicely formulates the theme with which I would like to begin: " 'What does it matter who is speaking,' someone said, 'what does it matter who is speaking.' " In this indifference appears one of the fundamental ethical principles of contemporary writing [*écriture*]. I say "ethical" because this indifference is not really a trait characterizing the manner in which one speaks and writes, but rather a kind of immanent rule, taken up over and over again, never fully applied, not designating writing as something completed, but dominating it as a practice. Since it is too familiar to require a lengthy analysis, this immanent rule can be adequately illustrated here by tracing two of its major themes.

First of all, we can say that today's writing has freed itself from the dimension of expression. Referring only to itself, but without being restricted to the confines of its interiority, writing is identified with its own unfolded exteriority. This means that it is an interplay of signs arranged less according to its signified content than according to the very nature of the signifier. Writing unfolds like a game [*jeu*] that invariably goes beyond its own rules and transgresses its limits. In writing, the point is not to manifest or exalt the act of writing, nor is it to pin a subject within language; it is rather a question of creating a space into which the writing subject constantly disappears.

The second theme, writing's relationship with death, is even more familiar. This link subverts an old tradition exemplified by the Greek epic, which was intended to perpetuate the immortality of the hero: if he was willing to die young, it was so that his life, consecrated and magnified by death, might pass into immortality; the narrative then redeemed this accepted death. In another way, the motivation, as well as the theme and the

Translated by Josué Harari.

pretext of Arabian narratives — such as *The Thousand and One Nights* — was also the eluding of death: one spoke, telling stories into the early morning, in order to forestall death, to postpone the day of reckoning that would silence the narrator. Scheherazade's narrative is an effort, renewed each night, to keep death outside the circle of life.

Our culture has metamorphosed this idea of narrative, or writing, as something designed to ward off death. Writing has become linked to sacrifice, even to the sacrifice of life: it is now a voluntary effacement which does not need to be represented in books, since it is brought about in the writer's very existence. The work, which once had the duty of providing immortality, now possesses the right to kill, to be its author's murderer, as in the cases of Flaubert, Proust, and Kafka. That is not all, however: this relationship between writing and death is also manifested in the effacement of the writing subject's individual characteristics. Using all the contrivances that he sets up between himself and what he writes, the writing subject cancels out the signs of his particular individuality. As a result, the mark of the writer is reduced to nothing more than the singularity of his absence; he must assume the role of the dead man in the game of writing.

None of this is recent; criticism and philosophy took note of the disappearance — or death — of the author some time ago. But the consequences of their discovery of it have not been sufficiently examined, nor has its import been accurately measured. A certain number of notions that are intended to replace the privileged position of the author actually seem to preserve that privilege and suppress the real meaning of his disappearance. I shall examine two of these notions, both of great importance today.

The first is the idea of the work. It is a very familiar thesis that the task of criticism is not to bring out the work's relationships with the author, not to reconstruct through the text a thought or experience, but rather, to analyze the work through its structure, its architecture, its intrinsic form, and the play of its internal relationships. At this point, however, a problem arises: "What is a work? What is this curious unity which we designate as a work? Of what elements is it composed? Is it not what an author has written?" Difficulties appear immediately. If an individual were not an author, could we say that what he wrote, said, left behind in his papers, or what has been collected of his remarks, could be called a "work"? When Sade was not considered an author, what was the status of his papers? Were they simply rolls of paper onto which he ceaselessly uncoiled his fantasies during his imprisonment?

Even when an individual has been accepted as an author, we must still ask whether everything that he wrote, said, or left behind is part of his work. The problem is both theoretical and technical. When undertaking the publication of Nietzsche's works, for example, where should one stop? Surely everything must be published, but what is "everything"? Everything that Nietzsche himself published, certainly. And what about the rough drafts for his works? Obviously. The plans for his aphorisms? Yes. The deleted passages and the notes at the bottom of the page? Yes. What if, within a workbook filled with aphorisms, one finds a reference, the notation of a meeting or of an address, or a laundry list: is it a work, or not? Why not? And so on, ad infinitum. How can one define a work amid the millions of traces left by someone after his death? A theory of the work does not exist, and the empirical task of those who naively undertake the editing of works often suffers in the absence of such a theory.

We could go even further: does *The Thousand and One Nights* constitute a work? What about Clement of Alexandria's *Miscellanies* or Diogenes Laertius' *Lives*? A multitude of questions arises with regard to this notion of the work. Consequently, it is not enough to declare that we should do without the writer (the author) and study the work in itself. The word "work" and the unity that it designates are probably as problematic as the status of the author's individuality.

Another notion which has hindered us from taking full measure of the author's disappearance, blurring and concealing the moment of this effacement and subtly preserving the author's existence, is the notion of writing [*écriture*]. When rigorously applied, this notion should allow us not only to circumvent references to the author, but also to situate his recent absence. The notion of writing, as currently employed, is concerned with neither the act of writing nor the indication — be it symptom or sign — of a meaning which someone might have wanted to express. We try, with great effort, to imagine the general condition of each text, the condition of both the space in which it is dispersed and the time in which it unfolds.

In current usage, however, the notion of writing seems to transpose the empirical characteristics of the author into a transcendental anonymity. We are content to efface the more visible marks of the author's empiricity by playing off, one against the other, two ways of characterizing writing, namely, the critical and the religious approaches. Giving writing a primal status seems to be a way of retranslating, in transcendental terms, both the theological affirmation of its sacred character and the critical affirmation of its creative character. To admit that writing is, because of the very history that it made possible, subject to the test of oblivion and repression, seems to represent, in transcendental terms, the religious principle of the hidden meaning (which requires interpretation) and the critical principle of implicit significations, silent determinations, and obscured contents (which gives rise to commentary). To imagine writing as absence seems to be a simple repetition, in transcendental terms, of both the religious principle of inalterable and yet never fulfilled tradition, and the aesthetic principle of the work's survival, its perpetuation beyond the author's death, and its enigmatic *excess* in relation to him.

This usage of the notion of writing runs the risk of maintaining the author's privileges under the protection of writing's a priori status: it keeps alive, in the grey light of neutralization, the interplay of those representations that formed a particular image of the author. The author's disappearance, which, since Mallarmé, has been a constantly recurring event, is subject to a series of transcendental barriers. There seems to be an important dividing line between those who believe that they can still locate today's discontinuities [*ruptures*] in the historico-transcendental tradition of the nineteenth century, and those who try to free themselves once and for all from that tradition.[1]

It is not enough, however, to repeat the empty affirmation that the author has disappeared. For the same reason, it is not enough to keep repeating (after Nietzsche) that God and man have died a common death. Instead, we must locate the space left empty by the author's disappearance, follow the distribution of gaps and breaches, and watch for the openings that this disappearance uncovers.

First, we need to clarify briefly the problems arising from the use of the author's name. What is an author's name? How does it function? Far from offering a solution, I shall only indicate some of the difficulties that it presents.

The author's name is a proper name, and therefore it raises the problems common to all proper names. (Here I refer to Searle's analyses, among others.[2]) Obviously, one cannot turn a proper name into a pure and simple reference. It has other than indicative functions: more than an indication, a gesture, a finger pointed at someone, it is the equivalent of a description. When one says "Aristotle," one employs a word that is the equivalent of one, or a series of, definite descriptions, such as "the author of the *Analytics,*" "the founder of ontology," and so forth. One cannot stop there, however, because a proper name does not have just one signification. When we discover that Rimbaud did not write *La Chasse spirituelle,* we cannot pretend that the meaning of this proper name, or that of the author, has been altered. The proper name and the author's name are situated between the two poles of description and designation: they must have a certain link with what they name, but one that is neither entirely in the mode of designation nor in that of description; it must be a *specific* link. However — and it is here that the particular difficulties of the author's name arise — the links between the proper name and the individual named and be-

[1]For a discussion of the notions of discontinuity and historical tradition see Foucault's *Les Mots et les choses* (Paris: Gallimard, 1966), translated as *The Order of Things* (New York: Pantheon, 1971). [Tr.]

[2]John Searle, *Speech Acts: An Essay in the Philosophy of Language* (Cambridge: Cambridge University Press, 1969), pp. 162–74. [Tr.]

tween the author's name and what it names are not isomorphic and do not function in the same way. There are several differences.

If, for example, Pierre Dupont does not have blue eyes, or was not born in Paris, or is not a doctor, the name Pierre Dupont will still always refer to the same person; such things do not modify the link of designation. The problems raised by the author's name are much more complex, however. If I discover that Shakespeare was not born in the house that we visit today, that is a modification which, obviously, will not alter the functioning of the author's name. But if we proved that Shakespeare did not write those sonnets which pass for his, that would constitute a significant change and affect the manner in which the author's name functions. If we proved that Shakespeare wrote Bacon's *Organon* by showing that the same author wrote both the works of Bacon and those of Shakespeare, that would be a third type of change which would entirely modify the functioning of the author's name. The author's name is not, therefore, just a proper name like the rest.

Many other facts point out the paradoxical singularity of the author's name. To say that Pierre Dupont does not exist is not at all the same as saying that Homer or Hermes Trismegistus did not exist. In the first case, it means that no one has the name Pierre Dupont; in the second, it means that several people were mixed together under one name, or that the true author had none of the traits traditionally ascribed to the personae of Homer or Hermes. To say that X's real name is actually Jacques Durand instead of Pierre Dupont is not the same as saying that Stendhal's name was Henri Beyle.[3] One could also question the meaning and functioning of propositions like "Bourbaki is so-and-so, so-and-so, etc."[4] and "Victor Eremita, Climacus, Anticlimacus, Frater Taciturnus, Constantine Constantius, all of these are Kierkegaard."

These differences may result from the fact that an author's name is not simply an element in a discourse (capable of being either subject or object, of being replaced by a pronoun, and the like); it performs a certain role with regard to narrative discourse, assuring a classificatory function. Such a name permits one to group together a certain number of texts, define them, differentiate them from and contrast them to others. In addition, it establishes a relationship among the texts. Hermes Trismegistus did not exist, nor did Hippocrates — in the sense that Balzac existed — but the fact that several texts have been placed under the same name indicates that there has been established among them a relationship of homogeneity, filiation,[5] authentification of some texts by the use of others, reciprocal explication, or concomitant utilization. The author's name serves to characterize a certain mode of being of discourse: the fact that the discourse has an author's name, that one can say "this was written by so-and-so" or "so-and-so is its author," shows that this discourse is not ordinary everyday speech that merely comes and goes, not something that is immediately consumable. On the contrary, it is a speech that must be received in a certain mode and that, in a given culture, must receive a certain status.

It would seem that the author's name, unlike other proper names, does not pass from the interior of a discourse to the real and exterior individual who produced it; instead, the name seems always to be present, marking off the edges of the text, revealing, or at least characterizing, its mode of being. The author's name manifests the appearance of a certain discursive set and indicates the status of this discourse within a society and a culture. It has no legal status, nor is it located in the fiction of the work; rather, it is located in the break that founds a certain discursive construct and its very particular mode of being. As a result, we could say that in a civilization like our own there are a certain number of discourses that are endowed with the "author-function," while others are deprived of it. A private letter may well have a signer — it does not have an author; a contract may well have a guarantor — it does not have an author. An anonymous text posted on a wall probably has a writer — but not

[3]Marie-Henri Beyle wrote under the name of Stendhal. [Ed.]

[4]Bourbaki was the collective name of a group of French mathematicians. [Ed.]

[5]Descent, derivation. [Ed.]

an author. The author-function is therefore characteristic of the mode of existence, circulation, and functioning of certain discourses within a society.

Let us analyze this "author-function" as we have just described it. In our culture, how does one characterize a discourse containing the author-function? In what way is this discourse different from other discourses? If we limit our remarks to the author of a book or a text, we can isolate four different characteristics.

First of all, discourses are objects of appropriation. The form of ownership from which they spring is of a rather particular type, one that has been codified for many years. We should note that, historically, this type of ownership has always been subsequent to what one might call penal appropriation. Texts, books, and discourses really began to have authors (other than mythical, "sacralized" and "sacralizing" figures) to the extent that authors became subject to punishment, that is, to the extent that discourses could be transgressive. In our culture (and doubtless in many others), discourse was not originally a product, a thing, a kind of goods; it was essentially an act — an act placed in the bipolar field of the sacred and the profane, the licit and the illicit, the religious and the blasphemous. Historically, it was a gesture fraught with risks before becoming goods caught up in a circuit of ownership.

Once a system of ownership for texts came into being, once strict rules concerning author's rights, author-publisher relations, rights of reproduction, and related matters were enacted — at the end of the eighteenth and the beginning of the nineteenth century — the possibility of transgression attached to the act of writing took on, more and more, the form of an imperative peculiar to literature. It is as if the author, beginning with the moment at which he was placed in the system of property that characterizes our society, compensated for the status that he thus acquired by rediscovering the old bipolar field of discourse, systematically practicing transgression and thereby restoring danger to a writing which was now guaranteed the benefits of ownership.

The author-function does not affect all discourses in a universal and constant way, however. This is its second characteristic. In our civilization, it has not always been the same types of texts which have required attribution to an author. There was a time when the texts that we today call "literary" (narratives, stories, epics, tragedies, comedies) were accepted, put into circulation, and valorized without any question about the identity of their author; their anonymity caused no difficulties since their ancientness, whether real or imagined, was regarded as a sufficient guarantee of their status. On the other hand, those texts that we now would call scientific — those dealing with cosmology and the heavens, medicine and illnesses, natural sciences and geography — were accepted in the Middle Ages, and accepted as "true," only when marked with the name of their author. "Hippocrates said," "Pliny recounts," were not really formulas of an argument based on authority; they were the markers inserted in discourses that were supposed to be received as statements of demonstrated truth.

A reversal occurred in the seventeenth or eighteenth century. Scientific discourses began to be received for themselves, in the anonymity of an established or always redemonstrable truth; their membership in a systematic ensemble, and not the reference to the individual who produced them, stood as their guarantee. The author-function faded away, and the inventor's name served only to christen a theorem, proposition, particular effect, property, body, group of elements, or pathological syndrome. By the same token, literary discourses come to be accepted only when endowed with the author-function. We now ask of each poetic or fictional text: from where does it come, who wrote it, when, under what circumstances, or beginning with what design? The meaning ascribed to it and the status or value accorded it depend upon the manner in which we answer these questions. And if a text should be discovered in a state of anonymity — whether as a consequence of an accident or the author's explicit wish — the game becomes one of rediscovering the author. Since literary anonymity is not tolerable, we can accept it only in the guise of an enigma. As a result, the author-function today plays an important role in our view of literary works. (These are obviously generalizations that would have to be refined insofar as recent critical practice is concerned.)

The third characteristic of this author-function is that it does not develop spontaneously as the attribution of a discourse to an individual. It is, rather, the result of a complex operation which constructs a certain rational being that we call "author." Critics doubtless try to give this intelligible being a realistic status, by discerning, in the individual, a "deep" motive, a "creative" power, or a "design," the milieu in which writing originates. Nevertheless, these aspects of an individual which we designate as making him an author are only a projection, in more or less psychologizing terms, of the operations that we force texts to undergo, the connections that we make, the traits that we establish as pertinent, the continuities that we recognize, or the exclusions that we practice. All these operations vary according to periods and types of discourse. We do not construct a "philosophical author" as we do a "poet," just as, in the eighteenth century, one did not construct a novelist as we do today. Still, we can find through the ages certain constants in the rules of author-construction.

It seems, for example, that the manner in which literary criticism once defined the author — or rather constructed the figure of the author beginning with existing texts and discourses — is directly derived from the manner in which Christian tradition authenticated (or rejected) the texts at its disposal. In order to "rediscover" an author in a work, modern criticism uses methods similar to those that Christian exegesis employed when trying to prove the value of a text by its author's saintliness. In *De viris illustribus,* Saint Jerome explains that homonymy is not sufficient to identify legitimately authors of more than one work: different individuals could have had the same name, or one man could have, illegitimately, borrowed another's patronymic. The name as an individual trademark is not enough when one works within a textual tradition.

How then can one attribute several discourses to one and the same author? How can one use the author-function to determine if one is dealing with one or several individuals? Saint Jerome proposes four criteria: (1) if among several books attributed to an author one is inferior to the others, it must be withdrawn from the list of the author's works (the author is therefore defined as a constant level of value); (2) the same should be done if certain texts contradict the doctrine expounded in the author's other works (the author is thus defined as a field of conceptual or theoretical coherence); (3) one must also exclude works that are written in a different style, containing words and expressions not ordinarily found in the writer's production (the author is here conceived as a stylistic unity); (4) finally, passages quoting statements that were made, or mentioning events that occurred after the author's death must be regarded as interpolated texts (the author is here seen as a historical figure at the crossroads of a certain number of events).

Modern literary criticism, even when — as is now customary — it is not concerned with questions of authentification, still defines the author the same way: the author provides the basis for explaining not only the presence of certain events in a work, but also their transformations, distortions, and diverse modifications (through his biography, the determination of his individual perspective, the analysis of his social position, and the revelation of his basic design). The author is also the principle of a certain unity of writing — all differences having to be resolved, at least in part, by the principles of evolution, maturation, or influence. The author also serves to neutralize the contradictions that may emerge in a series of texts: there must be — at a certain level of his thought or desire, of his consciousness or unconscious — a point where contradictions are resolved, where incompatible elements are at last tied together or organized around a fundamental or originating contradiction. Finally, the author is a particular source of expression that, in more or less completed forms, is manifested equally well, and with similar validity, in works, sketches, letters, fragments, and so on. Clearly, Saint Jerome's four criteria of authenticity (criteria which seem totally insufficient for today's exegetes) do define the four modalities according to which modern criticism brings the author-function into play.

But the author-function is not a pure and simple reconstruction made secondhand from a text given as passive material. The text always contains a certain number of signs referring to the author. These signs, well known to grammarians, are personal pronouns, adverbs of time and place, and verb conjugation. Such elements do not play the same role in discourses provided with the author-function as in those lacking it. In the latter, such "shifters" refer to the real speaker and to the spatio-temporal coordinates of his discourse (although certain modifications can occur, as in the operation of relating discourses in the first person). In the former, however, their role is more complex and variable. Everyone knows that, in a novel narrated in the first person, neither the first person pronoun, nor the present indicative refer exactly either to the writer or to the moment in which he writes, but rather to an alter ego whose distance from the author varies, often changing in the course of the work. It would be just as wrong to equate the author with the real writer as to equate him with the fictitious speaker; the author-function is carried out and operates in the scission itself, in this division and this distance.

One might object that this is a characteristic peculiar to novelistic or poetic discourse, a "game" in which only "quasi-discourses" participate. In fact, however, all discourses endowed with the author-function do possess this plurality of self. The self that speaks in the preface to a treatise on mathematics — and that indicates the circumstances of the treatise's composition — is identical neither in its position nor in its functioning to the self that speaks in the course of a demonstration, and that appears in the form of "I conclude" or "I suppose." In the first case, the "I" refers to an individual without an equivalent who, in a determined place and time, completed a certain task; in the second, the "I" indicates an instance and a level of demonstration which any individual could perform provided that he accept the same system of symbols, play of axioms, and set of previous demonstrations. We could also, in the same treatise, locate a third self, one that speaks to tell the work's meaning, the obstacles encountered, the results obtained, and the remaining problems; this self is situated in the field of already existing or yet-to-appear mathematical discourses. The author-function is not assumed by the first of these selves at the expense of the other two, which would then be nothing more than a fictitious splitting in two of the first one. On the contrary, in these discourses the author-function operates so as to effect the dispersion of these three simultaneous selves.

No doubt analysis could discover still more characteristic traits of the author-function. I will limit myself to these four, however, because they seem both the most visible and the most important. They can be summarized as follows: (1) the author-function is linked to the juridical and institutional system that encompasses, determines, and articulates the universe of discourses; (2) it does not affect all discourses in the same way at all times and in all types of civilization; (3) it is not defined by the spontaneous attribution of a discourse to its producer, but rather by a series of specific and complex operations; (4) it does not refer purely and simply to a real individual, since it can give rise simultaneously to several selves, to several subjects — positions that can be occupied by different classes of individuals.

Up to this point I have unjustifiably limited my subject. Certainly the author-function in painting, music, and other arts should have been discussed, but even supposing that we remain within the world of discourse, as I want to do, I seem to have given the term "author" much too narrow a meaning. I have discussed the author only in the limited sense of a person to whom the production of a text, a book, or a work can be legitimately attributed. It is easy to see that in the sphere of discourse one can be the author of much more than a book — one can be the author of a theory, tradition, or discipline in which other books and authors will in their turn find a place. These authors are in a position which we shall call "transdiscursive." This is a recurring phenomenon — certainly as old as our civilization. Homer, Aristotle, and the Church Fathers, as well as the first mathematicians and the originators of the Hippocratic tradition, all played this role.

Furthermore, in the course of the nineteenth century, there appeared in Europe another, more uncommon, kind of author, whom one should confuse with neither the "great" literary authors, nor the authors of religious texts, nor the founders of science. In a somewhat arbitrary way we shall call those who belong in this last group "founders of discursivity." They are unique in that they are not just the authors of their own works. They have produced something else: the possibilities and the rules for the formation of other texts. In this sense, they are very different, for example, from a novelist, who is, in fact, nothing more than the author of his own text. Freud is not just the author of *The Interpretation of Dreams* or *Jokes and Their Relation to the Unconscious;* Marx is not just the author of the *Communist Manifesto* or *Capital:* they both have established an endless possibility of discourse.

Obviously, it is easy to object. One might say that it is not true that the author of a novel is only the author of his own text; in a sense, he also, provided that he acquires some "importance," governs and commands more than that. To take a very simple example, one could say that Ann Radcliffe not only wrote *The Castles of Athlin and Dunbayne* and several other novels, but also made possible the appearance of the Gothic horror novel at the beginning of the nineteenth century; in that respect, her author-function exceeds her own work. But I think there is an answer to this objection. These founders of discursivity (I use Marx and Freud as examples, because I believe them to be both the first and the most important cases) make possible something altogether different from what a novelist makes possible. Ann Radcliffe's texts opened the way for a certain number of resemblances and analogies which have their model or principle in her work. The latter contains characteristic signs, figures, relationships, and structures which could be reused by others. In other words, to say that Ann Radcliffe founded the Gothic horror novel means that in the nineteenth-century gothic novel one will find, as in Ann Radcliffe's works, the theme of the heroine caught in the trap of her own innocence, the hidden castle, the character of the black, cursed hero devoted to making the world expiate the evil done to him, and all the rest of it.

On the other hand, when I speak of Marx or Freud as founders of discursivity, I mean that they made possible not only a certain number of analogies, but also (and equally important) a certain number of differences. They have created a possibility for something other than their discourse, yet something belonging to what they founded. To say that Freud founded psychoanalysis does not (simply) mean that we find the concept of the libido or the technique of dream analysis in the works of Karl Abraham or Melanie Klein; it means that Freud made possible a certain number of divergences — with respect to his own texts, concepts, and hypotheses — that all arise from the psychoanalytical discourse itself.

This would seem to present a new difficulty, however: is the above not true, after all, of any founder of a science, or of any author who has introduced some important transformation into a science? After all, Galileo made possible not only those discourses that repeated the laws that he had formulated, but also statements very different from what he himself had said. If Cuvier is the founder of biology or Saussure the founder of linguistics, it is not because they were imitated, nor because people have since taken up again the concept of organism or sign; it is because Cuvier made possible, to a certain extent, a theory of evolution diametrically opposed to his own fixism; it is because Saussure made possible a generative grammar radically different from his structural analyses. Superficially, then, the initiation of discursive practices appears similar to the founding of any scientific endeavor.

Still, there is a difference, and a notable one. In the case of a science, the act that founds it is on an equal footing with its future transformations; this act becomes in some respects part of the set of modifications that it makes possible. Of course, this belonging can take several forms. In the future development of a science, the founding act may appear as little more than a particular instance of a more general phenomenon which unveils itself in the process. It can also turn out to be marred by intuition and empirical bias; one must then reformulate it, making it the object of a certain number of supplementary theoretical operations which establish it more rigorously, etc. Finally, it can seem to be a hasty generalization which must be limited, and whose restricted domain of validity must be retraced. In other words, the founding act of a science can always be reintroduced within the machinery of those transformations that derive from it.

In contrast, the initiation of a discursive practice is heterogeneous to its subsequent transformations. To expand a type of discursivity, such as psychoanalysis as founded by Freud, is not to give it a formal generality that it would not have permitted at the outset, but rather to open it up to a certain number of possible applications. To limit psychoanalysis as a type of discursivity is, in reality, to try to isolate in the founding act an eventually restricted number of propositions or statements to which, alone, one grants a founding value, and in relation to which certain concepts or theories accepted by Freud might be considered as derived, secondary, and accessory. In addition, one does not declare certain propositions in the work of these founders to be false: instead, when trying to seize the act of founding, one sets aside those statements that are not pertinent, either because they are deemed inessential, or because they are considered "prehistoric" and derived from another type of discursivity. In other words, unlike the founding of a science, the initiation of a discursive practice does not participate in its later transformations.

As a result, one defines a proposition's theoretical validity in relation to the work of the founders — while, in the case of Galileo and Newton, it is in relation to what physics or cosmology *is* (in its intrinsic structure and "normativity") that one affirms the validity of any proposition that those men may have put forth. To phrase it very schematically: the work of initiators of discursivity is not situated in the space that science defines; rather, it is the science or the discursivity which refers back to their work as primary coordinates.

In this way we can understand the inevitable necessity, within these fields of discursivity, for a "return to the origin." This return, which is part of the discursive field itself, never stops modifying it. The return is not a historical supplement which would be added to the discursivity, or merely an ornament; on the contrary, it constitutes an effective and necessary task of transforming the discursive practice itself. Re-examination of Galileo's text may well change our knowledge of the history of mechanics, but it will never be able to change mechanics itself. On the other hand, re-examining Freud's texts modifies psychoanalysis itself just as a re-examination of Marx's would modify Marxism.[6]

What I have just outlined regarding the initiation of discursive practices is, of course, very schematic; this is true, in particular, of the opposition that I have tried to draw between discursive initiation and scientific founding. It is not always easy to distinguish between the two; moreover, nothing proves that they are two mutually exclusive procedures. I have attempted the distinction for only one reason: to show that the author-function, which is complex enough when one tries to situate it at the level of a book or a series of texts that carry a given signature, involves still more determining factors when one tries to analyze it in larger units, such as groups of works or entire disciplines.

To conclude, I would like to review the reasons why I attach a certain importance to what I have said.

First, there are theoretical reasons. On the one hand, an analysis in the direction that I have outlined might provide for an approach to a typology of discourse. It seems to me, at least at first glance, that such a typology cannot be constructed solely from the grammatical features, formal structures, and objects of discourse: more likely there exist properties or relationships peculiar to discourse (not reducible to the rules of

[6]To define these returns more clearly, one must also emphasize that they tend to reinforce the enigmatic link between an author and his works. A text has an inaugurative value precisely because it is the work of a particular author, and our returns are conditioned by this knowledge. As in the case of Galileo, there is no possibility that the rediscovery of an unknown text by Newton or Cantor will modify classical cosmology or set theory as we know them (at best, such an exhumation might modify our historical knowledge of their genesis). On the other hand, the discovery of a text like Freud's "Project for a Scientific Psychology" — insofar as it is a text by Freud — always threatens to modify not the historical knowledge of psychoanalysis, but its theoretical field, even if only by shifting the accentuation or the center of gravity. Through such returns, which are part of their make-up, these discursive practices maintain a relationship with regard to their "fundamental" and indirect author unlike that which an ordinary text entertains with its immediate author. [Tr.]

grammar and logic), and one must use these to distinguish the major categories of discourse. The relationship (or nonrelationship) with an author, and the different forms this relationship takes, constitutes — in a quite visible manner — one of these discursive properties.

On the other hand, I believe that one could find here an introduction to the historical analysis of discourse. Perhaps it is time to study discourses not only in terms of their expressive value or formal transformations, but according to their modes of existence. The modes of circulation, valorization, attribution, and appropriation of discourses vary with each culture and are modified within each. The manner in which they are articulated according to social relationships can be more readily understood. I believe, in the activity of the author-function and in its modifications, than in the themes or concepts that discourses set in motion.

It would seem that one could also, beginning with analyses of this type, re-examine the privileges of the subject. I realize that in undertaking the internal and architectonic analysis of a work (be it a literary text, philosophical system, or scientific work), in setting aside biographical and psychological references, one has already called back into question the absolute character and founding role of the subject. Still, perhaps one must return to this question, not in order to re-establish the theme of an originating subject, but to grasp the subject's points of insertion, modes of functioning, and system of dependencies. Doing so means overturning the traditional problem, no longer raising the questions "How can a free subject penetrate the substance of things and give it meaning? How can it activate the rules of a language from within and thus give rise to the designs which are properly its own?" Instead, these questions will be raised: "How, under what conditions, and in what forms can something like a subject appear in the order of discourse? What place can it occupy in each type of discourse, what functions can it assume, and by obeying what rules?" In short, it is a matter of depriving the subject (or its substitute) of its role as originator, and of analyzing the subject as a variable and complex function of discourse.

Second, there are reasons dealing with the "ideological" status of the author. The question then becomes: How can one reduce the great peril, the great danger with which fiction threatens our world? The answer is: One can reduce it with the author. The author allows a limitation of the cancerous and dangerous proliferation of significations within a world where one is thrifty not only with one's resources and riches, but also with one's discourses and their significations. The author is the principle of thrift in the proliferation of meaning. As a result, we must entirely reverse the traditional idea of the author. We are accustomed, as we have seen earlier, to saying that the author is the genial creator of a work in which he deposits, with infinite wealth and generosity, an inexhaustible world of significations. We are used to thinking that the author is so different from all other men, and so transcendent with regard to all languages that, as soon as he speaks, meaning begins to proliferate, to proliferate indefinitely.

The truth is quite the contrary: the author is not an indefinite source of significations which fill a work; the author does not precede the works, he is a certain functional principle by which, in our culture, one limits, excludes, and chooses; in short, by which one impedes the free circulation, the free manipulation, the free composition, decomposition, and recomposition of fiction. In fact, if we are accustomed to presenting the author as a genius, as a perpetual surging of invention, it is because, in reality, we make him function in exactly the opposite fashion. One can say that the author is an ideological product, since we represent him as the opposite of his historically real function. (When a historically given function is represented in a figure that inverts it, one has an ideological production.) The author is therefore the ideological figure by which one marks the manner in which we fear the proliferation of meaning.

In saying this, I seem to call for a form of culture in which fiction would not be limited by the figure of the author. It would be pure romanticism, however, to imagine a culture in which the fictive would operate in an absolutely free state, in which fiction would be put at the disposal of everyone and would develop without passing through something like a necessary or constraining figure. Although, since the eighteenth century, the author has played the role of the regulator of the fictive, a role quite characteristic of our era of industrial and bourgeois society, of individualism and private property, still, given the historical modifications that are taking place, it does not seem necessary that the author-function remain constant in form, complexity, and even in existence. I think that, as our society changes, at the very moment when it is in the process of changing, the author-function will disappear, and in such a manner that fiction and its polysemic texts will once again function according to another mode, but still with a system of constraint — one which will no longer be the author, but which will have to be determined or, perhaps, experienced.

All discourses, whatever their status, form, value, and whatever the treatment to which they will be subjected, would then develop in the anonymity of a murmur. We would no longer hear the questions that have been rehashed for so long: "Who really spoke? Is it really he and not someone else? With what authenticity or originality? And what part of his deepest self did he express in his discourse?" Instead, there would be other questions, like these: "What are the modes of existence of this discourse? Where has it been used, how can it circulate, and who can appropriate it for himself? What are the places in it where there is room for possible subjects? Who can assume these various subject-functions?" And behind all these questions, we would hear hardly anything but the stirring of an indifference: "What difference does it make who is speaking?"

Roland Barthes

1915–1980

*Before his untimely death in a traffic accident, the French critic and man of letters Roland Barthes was a prolific interpreter, disseminator, and reviser of most of the complex theoretical concepts that wound through his country's centers of learning from the 1950s on. Barthes's father, a naval officer, died in battle in the first year of his son's life. Barthes grew up in Bayonne, attended secondary school in Paris, and received degrees in classical letters (1939) and grammar and philosophy (1943) from the University of Paris. He taught French in Bucharest (1948–49) and Alexandria (1949–50). Although Barthes was director of the social sciences at the École Pratique des Hautes Études in Paris from 1960 to 1977, there is the sense that he was more comfortable intellectually on the margins of the academy, carrying on guerrilla conversation with it. (*On Racine *[1963], for example, caused a furor among institutional classicists because of its nontraditional approach to the canonical playwright.) Barthes was elected to the chair of literary semiology at the Collège de France in 1976 and acknowledged as the leading critic of his generation in 1978. Barthes's works, many of which have been translated since his death, include* Writing Degree Zero *(1953),* Mythologies *(1957),* Elements of Semiology *(1964),* Criticism and Truth *(1966),* S/Z *(1970),* Sade/Fourier/Loyola *(1971),* New Critical Essays *(1972),* The Pleasure of the Text *(1973),* A Lover's Discourse: Fragments *(1977),* The Grain of the Voice *(1981),* The Responsibilities of Forms *(1982), and* The Rustle of Language *(1984). "From Work to Text" is from* Image — Music — Text *(1977), and was originally published in French in 1971.*

Post structuralism

From Work to Text

It is a fact that over the last few years a certain change has taken place (or is taking place) in our conception of language and, consequently, of the literary work which owes at least its phenomenal existence to this same language. The change is clearly connected with the current development of (amongst other disciplines) linguistics, anthropology, Marxism and psychoanalysis (the term "connection" is used here in a deliberately neutral way: one does not decide a determination, be it multiple and dialectical). What is new and which affects the idea of the work comes not necessarily from the internal recasting of each of these disciplines, but rather from their encounter in relation to an object which traditionally is the province of none of them. It is indeed as though the *interdisciplinarity* which is today held up as a prime value in research cannot be accomplished by the simple confrontation of specialist branches of knowledge. Interdisciplinarity is not the calm of an easy security; it begins *effectively* (as opposed to the mere expression of a pious wish) when the solidarity of the old disciplines breaks down — perhaps even violently, via the jolts of fashion — in the interests of a new object and a new language neither of which has a place in the field of the sciences that were to be brought peacefully together, this unease in classification being precisely the point from which it is possible to diagnose a certain mutation. The mutation in which the idea of the work seems to be gripped must not, however, be over-estimated: it is more in the nature of an epistemological slide than of a real break. The break, as is frequently stressed, is seen to have taken place in the last century with the appearance of Marxism and Freudianism; since then there has been no further break, so that in a way it can be said that for the last hundred years we have been living in repetition. What History, our History, allows us today is merely to slide, to vary, to exceed, to repudiate. Just as Einsteinian science demands that *the relativity of the frames of reference* be included in the object studied, so the combined action of Marxism, Freudianism and structuralism demands, in literature, the relativization of the relations of writer, reader and observer (critic). Over against the traditional notion of the *work,* for long — and still — conceived of in a, so to speak, Newtonian way, there is now the requirement of a new object, obtained by the sliding or overturning of former categories. That object is the *Text.* I know the word is fashionable (I am myself often led to use it) and therefore regarded by some with suspicion, but that is exactly why I should like to remind myself of the principal propositions at the intersection of which I see the Text as standing. The word "proposition" is to be understood more in a grammatical than in a logical sense: the following are not argumentations but enunciations, "touches," approaches that consent to remain metaphorical. Here then are these propositions; they concern method, genres, signs, plurality, filiation, reading and pleasure.

1. The Text is not to be thought of as an object that can be computed. It would be futile to try to separate out materially works from texts. In particular, the tendency must be avoided to say that the work is classic, the text avant-garde; it is not a question of drawing up a crude honours list in the name of modernity and declaring certain literary productions "in" and others "out" by virtue of their chronological situation: there may be "text" in a very ancient work, while many products of contemporary literature are in no way texts. The difference is this: the work is a fragment of substance, occupying a part of the space of books (in a library for example), the Text is a methodological field. The opposition may recall (without at all reproducing term for term) Lacan's distinction between "reality" and "the real": the one is displayed, the other demonstrated; likewise, the work can be seen (in bookshops, in catalogues, in exam syllabi), the text is a process of demonstration, speaks according to certain rules (or against certain rules); the work can be held in the hand, the text is held in language, only exists in the movement of a dis-

Translated by Richard Howard.

course (or rather, it is Text for the very reason that it knows itself as text); the Text is not the decomposition of the work, it is the work that is the imaginary tail of the Text; or again, *the Text is experienced only in an activity of production.* It follows that the Text cannot stop (for example on a library shelf); its constitutive movement is that of cutting across (in particular, it can cut across the work, several works).

2. In the same way, the Text does not stop at (good) Literature; it cannot be contained in a hierarchy, even in a simple division of genres. What constitutes the Text is, on the contrary (or precisely), its subversive force in respect of the old classifications. How do you classify a writer like Georges Bataille? Novelist, poet, essayist, economist, philosopher, mystic? The answer is so difficult that the literary manuals generally prefer to forget about Bataille who, in fact, wrote texts, perhaps continuously one single text. If the Text poses problems of classification (which is furthermore one of its "social" functions), this is because it always involves a certain experience of limits (to take up an expression from Philippe Sollers). Thibaudet used already to talk — but in a very restricted sense — of limit-works (such as Chateaubriand's *Vie de Rancé,* which does indeed come through to us today as a "text"); the Text is that which goes to the limit of the rules of enunciation (rationality, readability, etc.). Nor is this a rhetorical idea, resorted to for some "heroic" effect: the Text tries to place itself very exactly *behind* the limit of the *doxa*[1] (is not general opinion — constitutive of our democratic societies and powerfully aided by mass communications — defined by its limits, the energy with which it excludes, its *censorship*?). Taking the word literally, it may be said that the Text is always *paradoxical.*

3. The Text can be approached, experienced, in reaction to the sign. The work closes on a signified. There are two modes of signification which can be attributed to this signified; either it is claimed to be evident and the work is then the object of a literal science, of philology, or else it is considered to be secret, ultimate, something to be sought out, and the work then falls under the scope of a hermeneutics, of an interpretation (Marxist, psychoanalytic, thematic, etc.); in short, the work itself functions as a general sign and it is normal that it should represent an institutional category of the civilization of the Sign. The Text, on the contrary, practices the infinite deferment of the signified, is dilatory; its field is that of the signifier and the signifier must not be conceived of as "the first stage of meaning," its material vestibule, but, in complete opposition to this, as its *deferred action.* Similarly, the *infinity* of the signifier refers not to some idea of the ineffable (the unnameable signified) but to that of a *playing;* the generation of the perpetual signifier (after the fashion of a perpetual calendar) in the field of the text (better, of which the text is the field) is realized not according to an organic progress of maturation or a hermeneutic course of deepening investigation, but, rather, according to a serial movement of disconnections, overlappings, variations. The logic regulating the Text is not comprehensive (define "what the work means") but metonymic; the activity of associations, contiguities, carryings-over coincides with a liberation of symbolic energy (lacking it, man would die); the work — in the best of cases — is *moderately* symbolic (its symbolic runs out, comes to a halt); the Text is *radically* symbolic: *a work conceived, perceived and received in its integrally symbolic nature is a text.* Thus is the Text restored to language; like language, it is structured but off-centred, without closure (note, in reply to the contemptuous suspicion of the "fashionable" sometimes directed at structuralism, that the epistemological privilege currently accorded to language stems precisely from the discovery there of a paradoxical idea of structure: a system with neither close nor centre).

4. The Text is plural. Which is not simply to say that it has several meanings, but that it accomplishes the very plural of meaning: an *irreducible* (and not merely an acceptable) plural. The Text is not a co-existence of meanings but a passage, an overcrossing; thus it answers not to an interpretation, even a liberal one, but to an explosion, a dissemination. The plural of the Text depends, that is, not on the ambiguity of its con-

[1]Opinion. [Ed.]

tents but on what might be called the *stereographic plurality* of its weave of signifiers (etymologically, the text is a tissue, a woven fabric). The reader of the Text may be compared to someone at a loose end (someone slackened off from any imaginary); this passably empty subject strolls — it is what happened to the author of these lines, then it was that he had a vivid idea of the Text — on the side of a valley, a *oued*[2] flowing down below (*oued* is there to bear witness to a certain feeling of unfamiliarity); what he perceives is multiple, irreducible, coming from a disconnected, heterogeneous variety of substances and perspectives: lights, colours, vegetation, heat, air, slender explosions of noises, scant cries of birds, children's voices from over on the other side, passages, gestures, clothes of inhabitants near or far away. All these *incidents* are half-identifiable: they come from codes which are known but their combination is unique, founds the stroll in a difference repeatable only as difference. So the Text: it can be it only in its difference (which does not mean its individuality), its reading is semelfactive[3] (this rendering illusory any inductive-deductive science of texts — no "grammar" of the text) and nevertheless woven entirely with citations, references, echoes, cultural languages (what language is not?), antecedent or contemporary, which cut across it through and through in a vast stereophony. The intertextual in which every text is held, it itself being the text-between of another text, is not to be confused with some origin of the text: to try to find the "sources," the "influences" of a work, is to fall in with the myth of filiation;[4] the citations which go to make up a text are anonymous, untraceable, and yet *already read:* they are quotations without inverted commas. The work has nothing disturbing for any monistic philosophy (we know that there are opposing examples of these); for such a philosophy, plural is the Evil. Against the work, therefore, the text could well take as its motto the words of the man possessed by demons *(Mark* 5:9): "My name is Legion: for we are many." The plural of demoniacal texture which opposes text to work can bring with it fundamental changes in reading, and precisely in areas where monologism appears to be the Law: certain of the "texts" of Holy Scripture traditionally recuperated by theological monism (historical or anagogical) will perhaps offer themselves to a diffraction of meanings (finally, that is to say, to a materialist reading), while the Marxist interpretation of works, so far resolutely monistic, will be able to materialize itself more by pluralizing itself (if, however, the Marxist "institutions" allow it).

5. The work is caught up in a process of filiation. Are postulated: a *determination* of the work by the world (by race, then by History), a *consecution* of works amongst themselves, and a *conformity* of the work to the author. The author is reputed the father and the owner of his work: literary science therefore teaches *respect* for the manuscript and the author's declared intentions, while society asserts the legality of the relation of author to work (the *"droit d'auteur"* or "copyright," in fact of recent date since it was only really legalized at the time of the French Revolution). As for the Text, it reads without the inscription of the Father. Here again, the metaphor of the Text separates from that of the work: the latter refers to the image of an *organism* which grows by vital expansion, by "development" (a word which is significantly ambiguous, at once biological and rhetorical); the metaphor of the Text is that of the *network;* if the Text extends itself, it is as a result of a combinatory systematic (an image, moreover, close to current biological conceptions of the living being). Hence no vital "respect" is due to the Text: it can be *broken* (which is just what the Middle Ages did with two nevertheless authoritative texts — Holy Scripture and Aristotle); it can be read without the guarantee of its father, the restitution of the inter-text paradoxically abolishing any legacy. It is not that the Author may not "come back" in the Text, in his text, but he then does so as a "guest." If he is a novelist, he is inscribed in the novel like one of his characters, figured in the carpet; no longer privileged, paternal, aletheolog-

[2]A North African watercourse; a wadi. [Ed.]

[3]A nonce word made up from the Latin roots "semel" (half) and "factive" (creative). [Ed.]

[4]Descent, derivation. [Ed.]

ical,[5] his inscription is ludic.[6] He becomes, as it were, a paper-author: his life is no longer the origin of his fictions but a fiction contributing to his work; there is a reversion of the work on to the life (and no longer the contrary); it is the work of Proust, of Genet which allows their lives to be read as a text. The word "bio-graphy" re-acquires a strong, etymological sense, at the same time as the sincerity of the enunciation — veritable "cross" borne by literary morality — becomes a false problem: the *I* which writes the text, it too, is never more than a paper-*I*.

6. The work is normally the object of a consumption; no demagogy is intended here in referring to the so-called consumer culture but it has to be recognized that today it is the "quality" of the work (which supposes finally an appreciation of "taste") and not the operation of reading itself which can differentiate between books: structurally, there is no difference between "cultured" reading and casual reading in trains. The Text (if only by its frequent "unreadability") decants the work (the work permitting) from its consumption and gathers it up as play, activity, production, practice. This means that the Text requires that one try to abolish (or at the very least to diminish) the distance between writing and reading, in no way by intensifying the projection of the reader into the work but by joining them in a single signifying practice. The distance separating reading from writing is historical. In the times of the greatest social division (before the setting up of democratic cultures), reading and writing were equally privileges of class. Rhetoric, the great literary code of those times, taught one to *write* (even if what was then normally produced were speeches, not texts). Significantly, the coming of democracy reversed the word of command: what the (secondary) School prides itself on is teaching to *read* (well) and no longer to write (consciousness of the deficiency is becoming fashionable again today: the teacher is called upon to teach pupils to "express themselves," which is a little like replacing a form of repression by a misconception). In fact, *reading,* in the sense of consuming, is far from *playing* with the text. "Playing" must be understood here in all its polysemy:[7] the text itself *plays* (like a door, like a machine with "play") and the reader plays twice over, playing the Text as one plays a game, looking for a practice which reproduces it, but, in order that that practice not be reduced to a passive, inner *mimesis* (the Text is precisely that which resists such a reduction), also playing the Text in the musical sense of the term. The history of music (as a practice, not as an "art") does indeed parallel that of the Text fairly closely: there was a period when practicing amateurs were numerous (at least within the confines of a certain class) and "playing" and "listening" formed a scarcely differentiated activity; then two roles appeared in succession, first that of the performer, the interpreter to whom the bourgeois public (though still itself able to play a little — the whole history of the piano) delegated its playing, then that of the (passive) amateur, who listens to music without being able to play (the gramophone record takes the place of the piano). We know that today post-serial music has radically altered the role of the "interpreter," who is called on to be in some sort the co-author of the score, completing it rather than giving it "expression." The Text is very much a score of this new kind: it asks of the reader a practical collaboration. Which is an important change, for who executes the work? (Mallarmé posed the question, wanting the audience to *produce* the book). Nowadays only the critic executes the work (accepting the play on words). The reduction of reading to a consumption is clearly responsible for the "boredom" experienced by many in the face of the modern ('unreadable') text, the avant-garde film or painting: to be bored means that one cannot produce the text, open it out, *set it going.*

7. This leads us to pose (to propose) a final approach to the Text, that of pleasure. I do not know whether there has ever been a hedonistic aesthetics (eudæmonist philosophies are themselves rare). Certainly there exists a pleasure of

[5]A portmanteau word composed of *aletheia,* "truth," and *theological.* [Ed.]

[6]Playful. [Ed.]

[7]Multiplicity of meaning. [Ed.]

the work (of certain works); I can delight in reading and re-reading Proust, Flaubert, Balzac, even — why not? — Alexandre Dumas. But this pleasure, no matter how keen and even when free from all prejudice, remains in part (unless by some exceptional critical effort) a pleasure of consumption; for if I can read these authors, I also know that I cannot *re-write* them (that it is impossible today to write "like that") and this knowledge, depressing enough, suffices to cut me off from the production of these works, in the very moment their remoteness establishes my modernity (is not to be modern to know clearly what cannot be started over again?). As for the Text, it is bound to *jouissance,*[8] that is to a pleasure without separation. Order of the signifier, the Text participates in its own way in a social utopia; before History (supposing the latter does not opt for barbarism), the Text achieves, if not the transparence of social relations, that at least of language relations: the Text is that space where no language has a hold over any other, where languages circulate (keeping the circular sense of the term).

These few propositions, inevitably, do not constitute the articulations of a Theory of the Text and this is not simply the result of the failings of the person here presenting them (who in many respects has anyway done no more than pick up what is being developed round about him). It stems from the fact that a Theory of the Text cannot be satisfied by a metalinguistic exposition: the destruction of metalanguage, or at least (since it may be necessary provisionally to resort to metalanguage) its calling into doubt, is part of the theory itself: the discourse on the Text should itself be nothing other than text, research, textual activity, since the Text is that *social* space which leaves no language safe, outside, nor any subject of the enunciation in position as judge, master, analyst, confessor, decoder. The theory of the Text can coincide only with a practice of writing.

[8]Joy, bliss. See the introduction, p. 823. [Ed.]

Paul de Man

1919–1983

At once the most suasive and reticent of deconstructive theorists, Paul de Man exerted a powerful influence on a generation of the most elite students of literature in the United States. Born in Antwerp to a prominent Belgian family, de Man studied science and philosophy at the University of Brussels from 1939 to 1942. In 1947 he moved to New York City and from 1949 to 1951 taught at Bard College. Starting in 1952 de Man attended Harvard University, earning a Ph.D. in comparative literature in 1960. From there he moved on to teach at Cornell (1960–67), Johns Hopkins (1967–70), and Yale (1970–83), where he taught until his death. For a theorist of his stature, de Man published little criticism, all of it in the form of essays: Blindness and Insight: Essays in the Rhetoric of Contemporary Criticism *(1971; revised 1983);* Allegories of Reading: Figural Language in Rousseau, Nietzsche, Rilke, and Proust *(1979);* The Rhetoric of Romanticism *(1984);* The Resistance to Theory *(1986; edited by Wlad Godzich). Since his death, de Man's reputation has been tarnished by the revelation that during World War II, when he was a student at the University of Brussels, he wrote anti-Semitic articles for a publication that sympathized with the Nazi regime (these columns and reviews are collected in* Wartime Journalism: 1940–1942, *1988). "Semiology and Rhetoric," originally published in* Diacritics *(1975), is reprinted from* Allegories of Reading.

Semiology and Rhetoric

To judge from various recent publications, the spirit of the times is not blowing in the direction of formalist and intrinsic criticism. We may no longer be hearing very much about relevance, but we do continue to hear a great deal about reference, about the nonverbal "outside" to which language refers, by which it is conditioned, and upon which it acts. The stress falls not so much on the fictional status of literature — a property now perhaps somewhat too easily taken for granted — but on the interplay between these fictions and categories that are said to partake of reality, such as the self, man, society, "the artist, his culture, and the human community," as one critic puts it. Hence the emphasis on hybrid texts considered to be partly literary and partly referential, on popular fictions deliberately aimed toward social and psychological gratification, on literary autobiography as a key to the understanding of the self, and so on. We speak as if, with the problems of literary form resolved once and forever, and with techniques of structural analysis refined to near-perfection, we could now move "beyond formalism" toward the questions that really interest us and reap, at last, the fruits of the ascetic concentration on techniques that prepared us for this decisive step. With the internal law and order of literature well policed, we can now confidently devote ourselves to the foreign affairs, the external politics of literature. Not only do we feel able to do so, but we also think we owe it to ourselves to take this step: our moral conscience would not allow us to do otherwise. Behind the assurance that valid interpretation is possible, behind the recent interest in writing and reading as potentially effective public speech acts, stands a highly respectable moral imperative that strives to reconcile the internal, formal, private structures of literary language with their external, referential, and public effects.

I want, for the moment, to consider briefly this tendency in itself, as an undeniable and recurrent historical fact, without regard for its truth or falseness or for its value as desirable or pernicious. It is a fact that this sort of thing happens again and again in literary studies. On the one hand, literature cannot merely be received as a definite unit of referential meaning that can be decoded without leaving a residue. The code is unusually conspicuous, complex, and enigmatic; it attracts an inordinate amount of attention to itself, and this attention has to acquire the rigor of a method. The structural moment of concentration on the code for its own sake cannot be avoided, and literature necessarily breeds its own formalism. Technical innovations in the methodological study of literature only occur when this kind of attention predominates. It can legitimately be said, for example, that, from a technical point of view, very little has happened in American criticism since the innovative works of the New Criticism. There certainly have been numerous excellent books of criticism since, but in none of them have the techniques of description and interpretation evolved beyond the techniques of close reading established in the forties. Formalism, it seems, is an all-absorbing and tyrannical muse; the hope that one can be at the same time technically original and discursively eloquent is not borne out by the history of literary criticism.

On the other hand — and this is the real mystery — no literary formalism, no matter how accurate and enriching in its analytic powers, is ever allowed to come into being without seeming reductive. When form is considered to be the external trappings of literary meaning or content, it seems superficial and expendable. The development of intrinsic, formalist criticism in the twentieth century has changed this model: form is now a solipsistic category of self-reflection, and the referential meaning is said to be extrinsic. The polarities of inside and outside have been reversed, but they are still the same polarities that are at play: internal meaning has become outside reference, and the outer form has become the intrinsic structure. A new version of reductiveness at once follows this reversal: formalism nowadays is mostly described in an imagery of imprisonment and claustrophobia: the "prison house of language," "the impasse of formalist criticism," and the like. Like the grandmother in Proust's novel, ceaselessly driving the young Marcel out into the garden, away from the unhealthy inwardness of his closeted reading, critics cry out for the fresh air of referential meaning. Thus, with the structure of the code so opaque, but with the meaning so anxious to blot out the obstacle of form, it is no wonder that the reconciliation of form and meaning seems so attractive. The attraction of reconciliation is the elective breeding-ground of false models and metaphors; it accounts for the metaphorical model of literature as a kind of box that separates an inside from an outside, with the reader or critic as the person who opens the lid in order to release into the open what was secreted but inaccessible inside. It matters little whether we call the inside of the box the content or the form and the outside the meaning or the appearance. The recurrent debate opposing intrinsic to extrinsic criticism stands under the aegis of an inside/outside metaphor that has never been seriously questioned.

Metaphors are much more tenacious than facts, and I certainly don't expect to dislodge this age-old model in one short expository essay. I merely wish to speculate on a different set of terms, perhaps less simple in their differential relationship than the strictly polar, binary opposition between inside and outside, and therefore less likely to enter into the easy play of chiasmic reversals. I derive these terms (which are as old as the hills) pragmatically from the observation of developments and debates in recent critical methodology.

One of the most controversial among these developments coincides with a new approach to poetics — or, as it is called in Germany, poetology — as a branch of general semiotics. In France, a semiology of literature was the outcome of the long-deferred but all the more explosive encounter of the nimble French literary mind with the category of form. Semiology, as opposed to semantics, is the science or study of signs as signifiers; it does not ask what words mean but how they mean. Unlike American New Criticism, which derived the internalization of form from the practice of highly self-conscious modern writers, French semiology turned to linguistics for its model and adopted Saussure and Jakobson rather than Valéry or Proust for its masters.[1] By an awareness of the arbitrariness of the sign (Saussure) and of literature as an autotelic statement "focused on the way it is expressed" (Jakobson), the entire question of meaning can be bracketed, thus freeing critical discourse from the debilitating burden of paraphrase. The demystifying power of semiology, within the context of French historical and thematic criticism, has been considerable. It demonstrated that the perception of the literary dimensions of language is largely obscured if one submits uncritically to the authority of reference. It also revealed how tenaciously this authority continues to assert itself in a variety of disguises, ranging from the crudest ideology to the most refined forms of aesthetic and ethical judgment. It especially exploded the myth of semantic correspondence between sign and referent, the wishful hope of having it both ways, of being, to paraphrase Marx, a formalist critic in the morning and a communal moralist in the afternoon, of serving both the technique of form and the substance of meaning. The results, in the practice of French criticism, have been as fruitful as they are irreversible. Perhaps for the first time since the late eighteenth century, French critics can come at least somewhat closer to the kind of linguistic awareness that never ceased to be operative in French poets and novelists, that forced all of them, including Sainte-Beuve, to write their main works "contre Sainte-Beuve."[2] The distance was never so considerable in England and the United States, which does not mean, however, that we may be able, in this country, to dispense with a preventative semiological hygiene altogether.

One of the most striking characteristics of literary semiology as it is practiced today, in France and elsewhere, is the use of grammatical (especially syntactical) structures conjointly with rhetorical structures, without apparent awareness of a possible discrepancy between them. In their literary analyses, Barthes, Genette, Todorov, Greimas, and their disciples all simplify and

[1]See the introduction, pp. 810–12. [Ed.]

[2]"Against Sainte-Beuve," the title of a book by Marcel Proust. [Ed.]

regress from Jakobson in letting grammar and rhetoric function in perfect continuity, and in passing from grammatical to rhetorical structures without difficulty or interruption. Indeed, as the study of grammatical structures is refined in contemporary theories of generative, transformational, and distributive grammar, the study of tropes and of figures (which is how the term rhetoric is used throughout this essay, not in the derived sense of comment, eloquence, or persuasion) becomes a mere extension of grammatical models, a particular subset of syntactical relations. In the recent *Dictionnaire encyclopédique des sciences du langage,* Ducrot and Todorov write: ". . . rhetoric has always been satisfied with a paradigmatic view over words (word substituting for each other), without questioning their syntagmatic relationship (the contiguity of words to each other). There ought to be another perspective, complementary to the first, in which metaphor, for example, would not be defined as a substitution but as a particular type of combination. Research inspired by linguistics or, more narrowly, by syntactical studies, has begun to reveal this possibility — but it remains to be explored."[3] Todorov, who calls one of his books a *Grammar of the Decameron,*[4] rightly thinks of his own work and that of his associates as first explorations in the elaboration of a systematic grammar of literary modes, genres, and also literary figures. Perhaps the most perceptive work to come out of this school, Genette's studies of figural modes, can be shown to be assimilations of rhetorical transformations or combinations to syntactical, grammatical patterns. Thus a recent study, now printed in *Figures III* and entitled "Métonymie chez Proust," shows the combined presence, in a wide and astute selection of passages, of paradigmatic, metaphorical figures with syntagmatic, metonymic structures.[5] The combination of both is treated descriptively and nondialectically without suggesting the possibility of logical tensions.

One can ask whether this reduction of figure to grammar is legitimate. The existence of grammatical structures within and beyond the unit of the sentence in literary texts is undeniable, and their description and classification are indispensable. The question remains if and how figures of rhetoric can be included in such a taxonomy. This question is at the core of the debate going on, in a wide variety of apparently unrelated forms, in contemporary poetics; but I do not plan to make clear the connection between this "real" problem and the countless pseudo-problems that agitate literary studies. This historical picture of contemporary criticism is too confused to make the mapping out of such a topography a useful exercise. Not only are these questions mixed in and mixed up within particular groups or local trends, but they are often co-present, without apparent contradiction, within the work of a single author.

Neither is the theory of the question suitable for quick expository treatment. To distinguish the epistemology of grammar from the epistemology of rhetoric is a redoubtable task. On an entirely naive level, we tend to conceive of grammatical systems as tending toward universality and as simply generative, that is, as capable of deriving an infinity of versions from a single model (that may govern transformations as well as derivations) without the intervention of another model that would upset the first. We therefore think of the relationship between grammar and logic, the passage from grammar to propositions, as being relatively unproblematic: no true propositions are conceivable in the absence of grammatical consistency or of controlled deviation from a system of consistency no matter how complex. Grammar and logic stand to each other in a dyadic relationship of unsubverted support. In a logic of acts rather than of statements, as in Austin's theory of speech acts,[6] which has had such a strong influence on recent American work in literary semiology, it is also possible to move between speech acts and grammar without difficulty. The performance of what are called illocutionary acts, such

[3]From the entry on rhetoric in Ducrot and Todorov, *Dictionnaire encyclopédique des sciences du langage* (Paris, Seuil, 1972), p. 352. [Au.]

[4]Tzvetan Todorov, *Grammaire du Décaméron* (The Hague: Mouton, 1969). [Ed.]

[5]Gérard Genette, *Figures III* (Paris: Seuil, 1972), pp. 41–63. [Au.]

[6]See J. L. Austin, *How to Do Things with Words.* [Ed.]

as ordering, questioning, denying, and assuming, within the language is congruent with the grammatical structures of syntax in the corresponding imperative, interrogative, negative, and optative sentences. "The rules of illocutionary acts," writes Richard Ohmann in a recent paper, "determine whether performance of a given act is well-executed, in just the same way as grammatical rules determine whether the product of a locutionary act — a sentence — is well formed. . . . But whereas the rules of grammar concern the relationships among sound, syntax, and meaning, the rules of illocutionary acts concern relationships among people."[7] And since rhetoric is then conceived exclusively as persuasion, as actual action upon others (and not as an intralinguistic figure or trope), the continuity between the illocutionary realm of grammar and the perlocutionary realm of rhetoric is self-evident. It becomes the basis for a new rhetoric that, exactly as is the case for Todorov and Genette, would also be a new grammar.

Without engaging the substance of the question, it can be pointed out, without having to go beyond recent and American examples, and without calling upon the strength of an age-old tradition, that the continuity here assumed between grammar and rhetoric is not borne out by theoretical and philosophical speculation. Kenneth Burke mentions *deflection* (which he compares structurally to Freudian displacement), defined as "any slight bias or even unintended error," as the rhetorical basis of language, and deflection is then conceived as a dialectical subversion of the consistent link between sign and meaning that operates within grammatical patterns;[8] hence Burke's well-known insistence on the distinction between grammar and rhetoric. Charles Sanders Peirce, who, with Nietzsche and Saussure, laid the philosophical foundation for modern semiology, stressed the distinction between grammar and rhetoric in his celebrated and so suggestively unfathomable definition of the sign. He insists, as is well known, on the necessary presence of a third element, called the interpretant, within any relationship that the sign entertains with its object. The sign must be interpreted if we are to understand the idea it is to convey, and this is so because the sign is not the thing but a meaning derived from the thing by a process — here called representation — that is not simply generative, that is, dependent on a univocal origin. The interpretation of the sign is not, for Peirce, a meaning but another sign; it is a reading, not a decodage, and this reading has, in its turn, to be interpreted into another sign, and so on, ad infinitum. Peirce calls this process by means of which "one sign gives birth to another" pure rhetoric, as distinguished from pure grammar, which postulates the possibility of unproblematic, dyadic meaning, and pure logic, which postulates the possibility of the universal truth of meanings. Only if the sign engendered meaning in the same way that the object engenders the sign — that is, by representation — would there be no need to distinguish between grammar and rhetoric.[9]

These remarks should indicate at least the existence and the difficulty of the question, a difficulty which puts its concise theoretical exposition beyond my powers. I must retreat therefore into a pragmatic discourse and try to illustrate the tension between grammar and rhetoric in a few specific textual examples. Let me begin by considering what is perhaps the most commonly known instance of an apparent symbiosis between a grammatical and a rhetorical structure, the so-called rhetorical question, in which the figure is conveyed directly by means of a syntactical device. I take the first example from the subliterature of the mass media: asked by his wife whether he wants to have his bowling shoes laced over or laced under, Archie Bunker[10] an-

[7]"Speech, Literature, and the Space in Between," *New Literary History* 4 (1971). [Au.]

[8]Kenneth Burke, "Rhetoric — Old and New," *Journal of General Education* 5 (1951), rpt. in *New Rhetorics*, ed. Martin Steinmann, Jr. (New York: Scribner, 1967), p. 75. [Au.]

[9]See Peirce, *Collected Papers*, ed. Charles Hartshorne and Paul Weiss (Cambridge, Mass.: Harvard University Press, 1960), II, 156–157: ". . . if a sunflower, in turning toward the sun, becomes by that very act fully capable, without further condition, of reproducing a sunflower which turns in precisely corresponding ways toward the sun, and of so doing with the same reproductive power, the sunflower would become a Representamen [and not a sign] of the sun." It seems, however, that thought-signs, or words, are in this respect precisely not heliotropic. [Au.]

[10]Irascible protagonist of the 1970s television comedy series *All in the Family*. [Ed.]

swers with a question. He asks, "What's the difference?" Being a reader of sublime simplicity, his wife replies by patiently explaining the difference between lacing over and lacing under, whatever this may be, but provokes only ire. "What's the difference?" did not ask for difference but meant instead "I don't give a damn what the difference is." The same grammatical pattern engenders two meanings that are mutually exclusive: the literal meaning asks for the concept (difference) whose existence is denied by the figurative meaning. As long as we are talking about bowling shoes, the consequences are relatively trivial; Archie Bunker, who is a great believer in the authority of origins (as long, of course, as they are the right origins), muddles along in a world where literal and figurative meanings get in each other's way, though not without discomforts. But if a *de*-Bunker rather than a Bunker, a de-bunker of the *arché* (origin), an "Archie De-Bunker" such as Nietzsche or Jacques Derrida, asks the question "What is the Difference?" we cannot even tell from his grammar whether he "really" wants to know "what" difference is or is merely telling us that we should not even try to find out. Confronted with the question of the difference between grammar and rhetoric, grammar allows us to ask the question, but the sentence by means of which we ask it may deny the very possibility of asking. For what is the use of asking, I ask, when we cannot even authoritatively decide whether a question asks or doesn't ask?

The point is as follows. A perfectly clear syntactical paradigm (the question) engenders a sentence that has at least two meanings, one which asserts and the other which denies its own illocutionary mode. It is not that there are simply two meanings, one literal and the other figural, and that we have to decide which one of these meanings is the right one in this particular situation. The confusion can only be cleared up by the intervention of an extratextual intention, such as Archie Bunker setting his wife straight; but the very anger he displays is indicative of more than impatience: it reveals his despair when confronted with a structure of linguistic meaning that he cannot control and that holds the discouraging prospect of an infinity of similar future confusions, all of them potentially catastrophic in their consequences. Nor is this intervention really a part of the minitext constituted by the figure, which holds our attention only as long as it remains suspended and unresolved. I follow the usage of common speech in calling this semiological enigma "rhetorical." The grammatical model of the question becomes rhetorical not when we have, on the one hand, a literal meaning and, on the other hand, a figural meaning, but when it is impossible to decide by grammatical or other linguistic devices which of the two meanings (that can be entirely contradictory) prevails. Rhetoric radically suspends logic and opens up vertiginous possibilities of referential aberration. And although it would perhaps be somewhat more remote from common usage, I would not hesitate to equate the rhetorical, figural potentiality of language with literature itself. I could point to a great number of antecedents to this equation of literature with figure; the most recent reference would be to Monroe Beardsley's insistence in his contribution to the essays in honor of William Wimsatt that literary language is characterized by being "distinctly above the norm in ratio of implicit (or, I would say rhetorical) to explicit meaning."[11]

Let me pursue the question of the rhetorical question through one more example. Yeats's "Among School Children" ends with the famous line: "How can we know the dancer from the dance?" Although there are some revealing inconsistencies within the commentaries, the line is usually interpreted as stating, with the increased emphasis of a rhetorical device, the potential unity between form and experience, between creator and creation. It could be said that it denies the discrepancy between the sign and the referent from which we started. Many elements in the imagery and the dramatic development of the poem strengthen this traditional reading; without having to look any further than the immediately preceding lines, one finds powerful consecrated images of the continuity from part to whole that

[11]Frank Brady, John Palmer, and Martin Price, eds., *Literary Theory and Structure: Essays in Honor of William K. Wimsatt* (New Haven: Yale University Press, 1973), p. 37. [Au.]

makes synecdoche into the most seductive of metaphors: the organic beauty of the tree, stated in the parallel syntax of a similar rhetorical question, or the convergence, in the dance, of erotic desire with musical form:

> O chestnut tree, great-rooted blossomer,
> Are you the leaf, the blossom or the bole?
> O body swayed to music, O brightening glance,
> How can we know the dancer from the dance?

A more extended reading, always assuming that the final line is to be read as a rhetorical question, reveals that the thematic and rhetorical grammar of the poem yields a consistent reading that extends from the first line to the last and that can account for all the details in the text. It is equally possible, however, to read the last line literally rather than figuratively, as asking with some urgency the question asked at the beginning of this essay within the context of contemporary criticism: it is *not* that sign and referent are so exquisitely fitted to each other that all difference between them is at times blotted out; but, rather, since the two essentially different elements, sign and meaning, are so intricately intertwined in the imagined "presence" which the poem addresses, how can we possibly make the distinctions that would shelter us from the error of identifying what cannot be identified? The clumsiness of the paraphrase reveals that it is not necessarily the literal reading which is simpler than the figurative one, as was the case in my first example; here the figural reading, which assumes the question to be rhetorical, is perhaps naive, whereas the literal reading leads to greater complications of theme and statement. For it turns out that the entire scheme set up by the first reading can be undermined, or deconstructed, in the terms of the second, in which the final line is read literally as meaning that, since the dancer and the dance are not the same, it might be useful, perhaps even desperately necessary — for the question can be given a ring of urgency: "Please tell me, how *can* I know the dancer from the dance?" — to tell them apart. But this will replace the reading of each symbolic detail by a divergent interpretation. The oneness of trunk, leaf, and blossom, for example, that would have appealed to Goethe, would find itself replaced by the much less reassuring Tree of Life from the Mabinogion[12] that appears in the poem "Vacillation," in which the fiery blossom and the earthly leaf are held together, as well as apart, by the crucified and castrated god Attis, of whose body it can hardly be said that it is "not bruised to pleasure soul." This hint should suffice to suggest that two entirely coherent but entirely incompatible readings can be made to hinge on one line whose grammatical structure is devoid of ambiguity but whose rhetorical mode turns the mood as well as the mode of the entire poem upside down. Neither can we say, as was already the case in the first example, that the poem simply has two meanings which exist side by side. The two readings have to engage each other in direct confrontation, for the one reading is precisely the error denounced by the other and has to be undone by it. Nor can we in any way make a valid decision as to which of the readings can be given priority over the other; neither can exist in the other's absence. There can be no dance without a dancer, no sign without a referent. On the other hand, the authority of the meaning engendered by the grammatical structure is fully obscured by the duplicity of a figure that cries out for the differentiation that it conceals.

Yeats's poem is not explicitly "about" rhetorical questions but about images or metaphors, and about the possibility of convergence between experiences of consciousness such as memory or emotions (what the poem calls passion, piety, and affection) and entities accessible to the senses, such as bodies, persons, or icons. We return to the inside/outside model from which we started and which the poem puts into question by means of a syntactical device (the question) made to operate on a grammatical as well as on a rhetorical level. The couple grammar/rhetoric, certainly not a binary opposition since they in no way exclude each other, disrupts and confuses the neat antithesis of the inside/outside pattern. We can transfer this scheme to the act of reading and interpretation. By reading we get, as we say, inside a text that was first something alien to us and which we now make our own by an act of

[12]Welsh Arthurian epic. [Ed.]

understanding. But this understanding becomes at once the representation of an extratextual meaning; in Austin's terms, the illocutionary speech act becomes a perlocutionary actual act; in Frege's terms, *Bedeutung* becomes *Sinn.*[13] Our recurrent question is whether this transformation is semantically controlled along grammatical or along rhetorical lines. Does the metaphor of reading really unite outer meaning and inner understanding, action and reflection, into one single totality? The assertion is powerfully and suggestively made in a passage from Proust that describes the experience of reading as such a union. It describes the young Marcel hiding in the closed space of his room in order to read. The example differs from the earlier ones in that we are not dealing with a grammatical structure which also functions rhetorically but have instead the representation, the dramatization, in terms of the experience of a subject, of a rhetorical structure — just as, in many other passages, Proust dramatizes tropes by means of landscapes or descriptions of objects. The figure here dramatized is that of metaphor, an inside/outside correspondence as represented by the act of reading. The reading scene is the culmination of a series of actions taking place in enclosed spaces and leading up to the "dark coolness" of Marcel's room.

> I had stretched out on my bed, with a book, in my room which sheltered, tremblingly, its transparent and fragile coolness against the afternoon sun, behind the almost closed blinds through which a glimmer of daylight had nevertheless managed to push its yellow wings, remaining motionless between the wood and the glass, in a corner, poised like a butterfly. It was hardly light enough to read, and the sensation of the light's splendor was given to me only by the noise of Camus . . . hammering dusty crates; resounding in the sonorous atmosphere that is peculiar to hot weather, they seemed to spark off scarlet stars; and also by the flies executing their little concert, the chamber music of summer: evocative not in the manner of a human tune that, heard perchance during the summer, afterwards reminds you of it; it is connected to summer by a more necessary link: born from beautiful days, resurrecting only when they return, containing some of their essence, it does not only awaken their image in our memory; it guarantees their return, their actual, persistent, unmediated presence.
>
> The dark coolness of my room related to the full sunlight of the street as the shadow relates to the ray of light, that is to say it was just as luminous and it gave my imagination the total spectacle of the summer, whereas my senses, if I had been on a walk, could only have enjoyed it by fragments; it matched my repose which (thanks to the adventures told by my book and stirring my tranquility) supported, like the quiet of a motionless hand in the middle of a running brook, the shock and the motion of a torrent of activity.[14]

From the beginning of the passage, inwardness is valorized positively as something desirable that has to protect itself against the intrusion of outside forces, but that nevertheless has to borrow, as it were, some of its constitutive properties from the outside. A chain of binary properties is set up and antithetically differentiated in terms of the inside/outside polarity: properties of coolness, darkness, repose, silence, imagination, and totality, associated with inwardness, contrast with the heat, the light, the activity, the sounds, the senses, and the fragmentation that govern the outside. By the act of reading, these static oppositions are put in motion, thus allowing for the play of substitutions by means of which the claim for totalization can be made. Thus, in a beautifully seductive effort of chiaroscuro,[15] mediated by the metaphor of light as a poised butterfly, the inner room is convincingly said to acquire the amount of light necessary to reading. In the wake of this light, warmth can also enter the room, incarnate in the auditive synaesthesia[16] of the various sounds. According to the narrator, these metaphorical substitutions and reversals render the presence of summer in the room more completely than the actual experience of summer in the outside world could have done. The text achieves this synthesis and comments on it in normative[17] terms, comparable to the manner in which treatises of practical rhetoric recommend

[13]Significance becomes meaning. [Ed.]

[14]*A la recherche du temps perdu* (Paris: Pléiade, 1954), I, 83. Translation by de Man. [Au.]

[15]Mixture of light and shadow. [Ed.]

[16]Sensual confusion, as when a sound strikes one as like a color. [Ed.]

[17]Evaluative. [Ed.]

the use of one figure in preference to another in a given situation: here it is the substitutive totalization by metaphor which is said to be more effective than the mere contiguity of metonymic association. As opposed to the random contingency of metonymy ("*par hasard*"),[18] the metaphor is linked to its proper meaning by, says Proust, the "necessary link" that leads to perfect synthesis. In the wake of this synthesis, the entire conceptual vocabulary of metaphysics enters the text: a terminology of generation, of transcendental necessity, of totality, of essence, of permanence, and of unmediated presence. The passage acts out and asserts the priority of metaphor over metonymy in terms of the categories of metaphysics and with reference to the act of reading.

The actual test of the truth of the assertion comes in the second paragraph when the absurd ratio set up at the beginning has to be verified by a further substitution. This time, what has to be exchanged are not only the properties of light and dark, warm and cool, fragment and totality (part and whole), but the properties of action and repose. The full seduction of the text can come into being only when the formal totalization of light and dark is completed by the transfer from rest to action that represents the extratextual, referential moment. The text asserts the transfer in the concluding sentence: "The dark coolness of my room . . . supported, like the quiet of a motionless hand in the middle of a running brook, the shock and the motion of a torrent of activity." The verb "to support" here carries the full weight of uniting rest and action (*repos et activité*), fiction and reality, as firmly as the base supports the column. The transfer, as is so often the case in Proust, is carried out by the liquid element of the running brook. The natural, representational connotation of the passage is with coolness, so particularly attractive within the predominant summer-mood of the entire *Recherche.* But coolness, it will be remembered, is one of the characteristic properties of the "inside" world. It cannot therefore by itself transfer us into the opposite world of activity. The movement of the water evokes a freshness which in the binary logic of the passage is associated with the inward, imaginary world of reading and fiction. In order to accede to action, it would be necessary to capture one of the properties belonging to the opposite chain, such as warmth. The mere "cool" action of fiction cannot suffice: it is necessary to reconcile the cool immobility of the hand with the heat of action if the claim made by the sentence is to stand up as true. This transfer is carried out, within the same sentence, when it is said that repose supports "a torrent of activity." The expression "torrent d'activité" is not, or is no longer, a metaphor in French: it is a cliché, a dead or sleeping metaphor that has lost the suggestive, connotative values contained in the word "torrent." It simply means "a great deal of activity," the amount of activity that is likely to agitate one to the point of getting hot. Heat is thus surreptitiously smuggled into the passage from a cold source, closing the ring of antithetical properties and allowing for their exchange and substitution: from the moment tranquility can be active and warm without losing its coolness and its distinctive quality of repose, the fragmented experience of reality can become whole without losing its quality of being real.

The transfer is made to seem convincing and seductive by the double play of the cliché "torrent of activity." The proximate, contiguous image of the brook awakens, as it were, the sleeping beauty of the dozing metaphor which, in its common use, had become the metonymic association of two words united by sheer habit and no longer by the inner necessity, the "necessary link," of a transcendental signification. "Torrent" functions in a double semantic register: in its reawakened literal meaning it relays the attribute of coolness that is actually part of the running water, whereas in its figural nonmeaning it designates the quantity of activity connotative of the contrary property of warmth.

The rhetorical structure of this sentence is therefore not simply metaphorical. It is at least doubly metonymic, first because the coupling of words in a cliché is governed not by the necessary link that reveals their potential identity but by the contingent habit of proximity; second, because the reawakening of the metaphorical term "torrent" is carried out by a statement that happens to be in the vicinity, but without there being any necessity for this proximity on the level of

[18]By chance. [Ed.]

the referential meaning. The most striking thing is that this doubly metonymic structure is found in a text that also contains highly seductive and successful metaphors (as in the chiaroscuro effect of the beginning, or in the condensation of light in the butterfly image) and that explicitly asserts the superiority of metaphor over metonymy in terms of metaphysical categories.

That these metaphysical categories do not remain unaffected by such a reading would become clear from an inclusive reading of Proust's novel and would become even more explicit in a language-conscious philosopher such as Nietzsche who, as a philosopher, has to be concerned with the epistemological consequences of the kind of rhetorical seductions exemplified by the Proust passage. It can be shown that the systematic critique of the main categories of metaphysics undertaken by Nietzsche in his late work, the critique of the concepts of causality, of the subject, of identity, of referential and revealed truth, and others, occurs along the same pattern of deconstruction that is operative in Proust's text; and it can also be shown that this pattern exactly corresponds to Nietzsche's description, in texts that precede *The Will to Power* by more than fifteen years, of the structure of the main rhetorical tropes. The key to this critique of metaphysics, which is itself a recurrent gesture throughout the history of thought, is the rhetorical model of the trope or, if one prefers to call it that, literature. It turns out that in these innocent-looking didactic exercises we are in fact playing for very sizable stakes.

It is therefore all the more necessary to know what is linguistically involved in a rhetorically conscious reading of the type here undertaken on a brief fragment from a novel and extended by Nietzsche to the entire text of post-Hellenic thought. Our first examples, which dealt with rhetorical questions, were rhetorizations of grammar, figures generated by syntactical paradigms, whereas the Proust example could be better described as a grammatization of rhetoric. The passage from a paradigmatic structure based on contingent association, such as metonymy, shows the mechanical, repetitive aspect of grammatical forms to be operative in a passage that seems at first sight to celebrate the self-willed and autonomous inventiveness of a subject. Figures are assumed to be inventions, the products of a highly particularized individual talent, whereas no one can claim credit for the programmed pattern of grammar. Yet our reading of the Proust passage shows that precisely when the highest claims are being made for the unifying power of metaphor, these very images rely in fact on the deceptive use of semi-automatic grammatical patterns. The deconstruction of metaphor and of all rhetorical patterns, such as mimesis, paronomasis,[19] or personification, that use resemblance as a way to disguise differences, takes us back to the impersonal precision of grammar and of a semiology derived from grammatical patterns. Such a deconstruction puts into question a whole series of concepts that underlie the value judgments of our critical discourse: the metaphors of primacy, of genetic history, and, most notably, of the autonomous power to will of the self.

There seems to be a difference, then, between what I called the rhetorization of grammar (as in the rhetorical question) and the grammatization of rhetoric, as in the deconstructive readings of the type sketched in the passage from Proust. The former ends up in indetermination, in a suspended uncertainty that was unable to choose between two modes of reading, whereas the latter seems to reach a truth, albeit by the negative road of exposing an error, a false pretense. After the deconstructive reading of the Proust passage we can no longer believe the assertion made in this passage about the intrinsic, metaphysical superiority of metaphor over metonymy. We seem to end up in a mood of negative assurance that is highly productive of critical discourse. The further text of Proust's novel, for example, responds perfectly to an extended application of this deconstructive pattern: not only can similar gestures be repeated throughout the novel, at all the crucial articulations or all passages where large aesthetic and metaphysical claims are being made (the scenes of involuntary memory, the workshop of Elstir, the septette of Vinteuil, the convergence of author and narrator at the end of

[19]Paronomasia: plays on words, puns. [Ed.]

the novel), but a vast thematic and semiotic network is revealed, a network that structures the entire narrative and that remains invisible to a reader caught in a naive metaphorical mystification. The whole of literature would respond in similar fashion, although the techniques and the patterns would have to vary considerably, of course, from author to author. But there is absolutely no reason why analyses of the kind here suggested for Proust would not be applicable, with proper modifications of technique, to Milton or to Dante or to Hölderlin. This will in fact be the task of literary criticism in the coming years.

It would seem that we are saying that criticism is the deconstruction of literature, the reduction to the rigors of grammar of rhetorical mystifications. And if we hold up Nietzsche as the philosopher of such a critical deconstruction, then the literary critic would become the philosopher's ally in his struggle with the poets. Criticism and literature would separate around the epistemological axis that distinguishes grammar from rhetoric. It is easy enough to see that this apparent glorification of the critic-philosopher in the name of truth is in fact a glorification of the poet as the primary source of this truth; if truth is the recognition of the systematic character of a certain kind of error, then it would be fully dependent on the prior existence of this error. Philosophers of science like Gaston Bachelard or Wittgenstein are notoriously dependent on the aberrations of the poets. We are back at our unanswered question: does the grammatization of rhetoric end up in the negative certainty, or does it, like the rhetorization of grammar, remain suspended in the ignorance of its own truth or falsehood?

Two concluding remarks should suffice to answer the question. First of all, it is not true that Proust's text can simply be reduced to the mystified assertion — the superiority of metaphor over metonymy — that our reading deconstructs. The reading is not "our" reading, since it uses only the linguistic elements provided by the text itself; the distinction between author and reader is one of the false distinctions that the deconstruction makes evident. The deconstruction is not something we have added to the text; it constituted the text in the first place. A literary text simultaneously asserts and denies the authority of its own rhetorical mode; and, by reading the text as we did, we were only trying to come closer to being as rigorous a reader as the author had to be in order to write the sentence in the first place. Poetic writing is the most advanced and refined mode of deconstruction; it may differ from critical or discursive writing in the economy of its articulation, but it is not different in kind.

But if we recognize the existence of the deconstructive moment as constitutive of all literary language, we have surreptitiously reintroduced the categories that this deconstruction was supposed to eliminate and that have merely been displaced. We have, for example, displaced the question of the self from the referent into the figure of the narrator, who then becomes the *signifié*[20] of the passage. It again becomes possible to ask such naive questions as what Proust's, or Marcel's, motives may have been in thus manipulating language: was he fooling himself, or was he represented as fooling himself and fooling us into believing that fiction and action are as easy to unite, by reading, as the passage asserts? The pathos of the entire section, which would have been more noticeable if the quotation had been a little more extended, the narrator's constant vacillation between guilt and well-being, invites such questions. They are absurd questions, of course, since the reconciliation of fact and fiction occurs itself as a mere assertion made in a text, and is thus productive of more text at the moment when it asserts its decision to escape from textual confinement. But even if we free ourselves of all false questions of intent and rightfully reduce the narrator to the status of a mere grammatical pronoun, without which the deconstructive narrative could not come into being, this subject remains endowed with a function that is not grammatical but rhetorical, in that it gives voice, so to speak, to a grammatical syntagm.[21] The term "voice," even when we speak of the passive or interrogative voice, is, of course, a metaphor inferring by analogy the intent of the subject from the struc-

[20]Signified; the thing represented by a sign. [Ed.]
[21]Linkage. [Ed.]

ture of the predicate. In the case of the deconstructive discourse that we call literary, or rhetorical, or poetic, this creates a distinctive complication illustrated by the Proust passage. The deconstructive reading revealed a first paradox: the passage valorizes metaphor as being the "right" literary figure, but then proceeds to constitute itself by means of the epistemologically incompatible figure of metonymy. The deconstructive critical discourse reveals the presence of this delusion and affirms it as the irreversible mode of its truth. It cannot pause there however. For if we then ask the obvious and simple next question, whether the rhetorical mode of the text in question is that of metaphor or metonymy, it is impossible to give an answer. Individual metaphors, such as the chiaroscuro effect or the butterfly, are shown to be subordinate figures in a general clause whose syntax is metonymic; from this point of view, it seems that the rhetoric is superseded by a grammar that deconstructs it. But this metonymic clause has as its subject a voice whose relationship to this clause is again metaphorical. The narrator who tells us about the impossibility of metaphor is himself, or itself, a metaphor, the metaphor of a grammatical syntagm whose meaning is the denial of metaphor stated, by antiphrasis, as its priority. And this subject-metaphor is, in its turn, open to the kind of deconstruction to the second degree, the rhetorical deconstruction of psycholinguistics, in which the more advanced investigations of literature are presently engaged, against considerable resistance.

We end up, therefore, in the case of the rhetorical grammatization of semiology, just as in the grammatical rhetorization of illocutionary phrases, in the same state of suspended ignorance. Any question about the rhetorical mode of a literary text is always a rhetorical question that does not even know whether it is really questioning. The resulting pathos is an anxiety (or bliss, depending on one's momentary mood or individual temperament) of ignorance, not an anxiety of reference — as becomes thematically clear in Proust's novel when reading is dramatized, in the relationship between Marcel and Albertine, not as an emotive reaction to what language does, but as an emotive reaction to the impossibility of knowing what it might be up to. Literature as well as criticism — the difference between them being delusive — is condemned (or privileged) to be forever the most rigorous and, consequently, the most unreliable language in terms of which man names and modifies himself.

3

READER-RESPONSE CRITICISM

The literary work cannot be completely identical with the text, or with the [reader's] realization of the text, but in fact must lie halfway between the two. — WOLFGANG ISER

Interpretive communities are made up of those who share interpretive strategies not for reading (in the conventional sense) but for writing texts, for constituting their properties and assigning their intentions. — STANLEY FISH

It is . . . impossible to say from a text alone how people will respond to it. Only after we have understood how some specific individual responds, how the different parts of his individual personality re-create the different details of the text, can we begin to formulate general hypotheses about the way many or all readers respond. Only then — if then.
— NORMAN N. HOLLAND

The critics grouped together here as reader-response theorists share a topic rather than a set of assumptions. They all have in common the conviction that the audience plays a vitally important role in shaping the literary experience and the desire to help to explain that role. But their interpretations of that role and their definitions of the literary experience vary enormously, in ways that dwarf the usual doctrinal distinctions even within diverse movements like formalism or semiotics.

Interest in the role of the reader goes back to the early classical period. Plato's Book X of *Republic* testifies to the philosopher's concern lest the audience be corrupted by texts that imitate falsely or concentrate the attention of the audience on unworthy matters; the *Ion,* while centrally involved with the question of creativity, suggests that the *enthousiasmós* the muse grants to the poet is transmitted, like magnetic force, through the performer to the spectator. In Aristotle's *Poetics,* tragedy is partially defined in terms of the emotional activity of the spectator, and the construction of the text is constantly subject to the question of how the audience will view the completed product. In Horace the audience becomes central. The chief criterion of excellence in *The Art of Poetry* is what will delight and instruct the reader or spectator, and the text is defined in operational terms as something whose language, incidents, and characters are to be judged as part of a literary (and in general, a cultural) scene. The legacy of Horace long endured; the rhetorical principle of criticism, based on an operational mode of thought, dominated Western literary criticism for nearly eighteen hundred years.

The displacement of the audience from the center of critical attention to its periphery is the result of Romanticism, which exalted the genius of the author at the expense of the critic (who might be considered the reader's better-paid persona). Most nineteenth- and early twentieth-century criticism centered on the author, and even the shift toward formalism at midcentury displaced the creator only to focus attention on the text itself. The New Critics may have paid greatest attention to the intentional fallacy, since the tendency of the historical scholars they had displaced was to read for authorial meaning. But Wimsatt and Beardsley also wrote a companion piece, "The Affective Fallacy," to defend the autonomous text against the encroachment of critics (primarily I. A. Richards) who might attempt to define the text in terms of the emotions it aroused in a real audience. The autonomous text of the New Criticism expressed feelings and attitudes to an ideal audience, and no evidence of how actual readers had reacted to it could possibly budge the critics' theory. While the once-controversial and experimental works of high modernism (the fiction of Joyce and Woolf, the poetry of Yeats and Eliot) were becoming canonical texts in the first two decades after World War II, the New Criticism was establishing theoretical strictures valorizing the objective textual surface and cultivating the tactic of ignoring the audience.

During the New Critical ascendancy works of audience-oriented theory, like Louise Rosenblatt's *Literature as Exploration* (1938), led a buried life, valued by the education establishment and used in pedagogy but ignored by literary theorists. But like Plato's banishment of the poets, the exile of the audience could not be enforced for long. The return of the reader to center stage was encouraged by one of the Chicago Aristotelians, Wayne C. Booth, with *The Rhetoric of Fiction* (1961). Booth's innovative ideas fit within the prevailing formalism (see p. 712), but in the following decades, other definably different modes of audience-centered criticism emerged. Within the structuralist movement, the audience became a central focus for theorists like Gerald Prince in addition to critics we have already discussed, like Gérard Genette, Jonathan Culler, and Umberto Eco (Ch. 2). A reader-oriented version of psychological criticism also developed, led by such theorists as David Bleich and Norman Holland. More recently, a phenomenological criticism of literature has arisen, which considers the reader as the performer of the text. And the reader has become a key topic in the feminist criticism of Judith Fetterley and Patrocinio Schweickart.

RHETORICAL CRITICISM

Probably the loosest of these groupings is the rhetorical approach, since it covers any perspective that treats the text as sending signals to the reader for interpretation. From Horace to Samuel Johnson, the principal variants in rhetorical theory have turned on two issues: the *object* communicated and the *character* of the audience addressed. On the first axis some critics, such as Dante, have emphasized the way literature communicates ethical and religious doctrine, while others, such as Horace, have concerned themselves chiefly with the pleasures enjoyed by the reader. On the other axis, critics such as Johnson have been concerned with what will be most generally pleasing to any audience, while others, such as Dryden, have assumed that texts are written to please and instruct a particular national group, or even a class within that group, and that the specific characteristics of the audience will dictate the rhetoric employed in the text. In a sense, the discrepancies in contemporary rhetorical criticism are most strongly marked along the axis of reader participation. The range runs from Wayne Booth, who emphasizes the way texts shape their audience into "proper" readers, through Susan Sontag, whose ideal condition would be the mutual transparency of text and reader, to Stanley Fish, who (in one phase of his work) views the text as being created by the reader's mental experience of it.

Booth's approach is both the most traditionally formalistic of the audience-centered modes and the one that has achieved the most widespread recognition. So thoroughly have its methods been embraced by contemporary practical critics that some textbook writers have taken it for a form of the New Criticism. In fact, Booth, like his mentor R. S. Crane, opposed New Critical doctrine on fiction and wrote *The Rhetoric of Fiction* partly to refute the ideas of New Critics like Allen Tate and Caroline Gordon. The prevailing doctrines, derived from the theory and practice of Henry James, valorized realistic stories told through a "natural," objective narrative technique that avoided authorial commentary and other overt signals of the creator behind the tale. Booth's book made it clear that such "natural" techniques of modernism were no less artificial, no less rhetorical, than the direct address to the reader practiced by Fielding and Sterne.

The real question was not *whether* the novelist should use rhetoric — it was impossible to avoid doing so — but what sort of rhetoric to use. Each of the author's technical decisions would shape in a particular way the reader's evaluation of the characters and the action, making some effects easy and others impossible. The axioms that arise from Booth's theory are less simple than those implicit in the New Criticism. They suggest that a reader's emotional distance from the characters in a narrative depends not only on the characters' values and beliefs but on the distance from the reader at which the narrative technique places them. Even relatively vicious characters can become sympathetic if readers are granted access to their consciousness and distanced from that of their victims.

The impact of *The Rhetoric of Fiction* was immense, not only in the development of theory but also in altering the canon of fiction. The popularity of eighteenth-century novelists like Defoe, Fielding, and Sterne, long muted by the disapproval of the New Critics, recovered, in part owing to Booth's debunking of modernist premises. In addition, Booth's terminology — such as "implied author" for the formal location of authorial values within a text, or "unreliable narrator" for a narrator (either personified or not within the text) whose values (intellectual, aesthetic, or ethical) depart from those of the implied author — has become the standard vocabulary in fiction courses.

Booth's concern with "implied authors" and "unreliable narrators," while presenting a view of literature as ineluctibly rhetorical, largely focuses on the ways in which authors make texts that will engage or persuade their audiences: The focus, in other words, remains on the writer more than the reader and largely takes for granted the ways in which readers decode the symbols on the page. Booth's former student, Peter Rabinowitz, has reversed the emphasis. While Rabinowitz still deals with the literary text as a formal object, he focuses on the tacit knowledge the reader must possess to re-create its form.

Rabinowitz's most essential distinction is between the "narrative audience" and the "authorial audience": personifications of the two aspects of reading that all of us perform. As part of the "narrative audience," we follow the events of the narrative as if they were really happening; at the same time, as members of the "authorial audience," we read the text knowing that it is just a story created by an author with some sort of effect in mind.[1] The emotional power of a text depends on the success of the pretense that the events it portrays are real. Our sense of the shape of the narrative, our ability to predict what is going to happen, and our need to sympathize with some characters more than with others depends on our communion with the values and plans of the creating author. Ideally, that is. Actual readers may find it impossible to believe in the reality of a given narrative and may fail to capture an author's signals about the plot and values of a story, either because of the author's lack of artistry or because of conflict with their own ideas, values, and preconceptions. For Rabinowitz both the "narrative audience" and the "authorial audience" are virtual beings, a product of the text and of the rules for reading texts, rules we generally absorb while we are still too young to read on our own.

The first part of Rabinowitz's *Before Reading* (part of which is reprinted in this chapter) consists of an analysis of some of the rules for reading texts that constitute the contemporary interpretive community: "rules of notice," which assign priority to certain kinds of details; "rules of signification," which help us interpret the meaning, symbolic and literal, of what we read; "rules of configuration," which give us a sense of completeness, closure and genre; and "rules of coherence" that allow us to harmonize and naturalize textual gaps or disjunctures. The second part, keyed to the book's subtitle, *Narrative Conventions and the Politics of Interpretation,* is an inquiry into the meaning of rules of reading as social texts, products of the ideology of the current age. Here Rabinowitz questions, for example, why we so often sympathize with irresponsible idealists when they are males (like Jay Gatsby) but find them lacking or contemptible when they are females (like Emma Bovary), and suggests that the rules of reading our society follows are implicitly sexist, racist, and bourgeois rather than working-class in bias. He suggests that the first steps toward the formation of a just society should include understanding the ways in which we have been molded by our culture's implicit rules of reading. In this way,

[1]For texts with narrators who present facts and values in a way so skewed that we need to allow for their distortions merely to reconstruct what is happening on the level of the text, Rabinowitz also distinguishes an "ideal narrative audience." This would contain the virtual audience for whom Jason Compson in Faulkner's *The Sound and the Fury,* or Whitey the Barber in Ring Lardner's "Haircut" is speaking.

Rabinowitz's rhetorical mode of audience-oriented criticism shows links with some of the Marxists discussed in Chapter 5.

Whereas Booth views readers as being constructed by authors, and Rabinowitz hopes that readers can become aware of the ways in which they are manipulated by their culture's rules of reading, Stanley Fish argues that the text is completely malleable and that the all-powerful reader can interrogate it as he or she wishes. Fish began his career by advocating a method of interpretation that he called "affective stylistics," which could be seen as a special mode of the New Criticism. According to this method, the reader reads the text slowly, word by word, alive at each moment to the shifts in apparent position and direction. Texts that seemed to lead first to one conclusion, then another, Fish termed "self-consuming artifacts." The following passage from Sir Thomas Browne is an example:

> That Judas perished by hanging himself, there is no certainty in Scripture: though in one place it seems to affirm it, and by a doubtful word hath given occasion to translate it; yet in another place, in a more punctual description, it maketh it improbable, and seems to overthrow it.

Fish argues that Browne seems to commit himself to Judas's death by hanging up to the first comma, then gradually and *almost* entirely takes it all back: "The prose is continually opening, but then closing, on the possibility of verification in one direction or another."[2] (In a sense, this a variation on New Critic William Empson's sixth type of ambiguity, ambiguity of syntax.) But gradually Fish moved away from the idea that these features belonged primarily to the text, and insisted on their location within the reader. In effect, the text is not the words on the page but the minutely detailed performance they elicit from the reader.

"Interpreting the *Variorum*" begins with the latter view of the text, but it also marks the transition to Fish's theory of interpretive communities. The essay opens with a demonstration of affective stylistics and spells out some of the implications of locating the text within the reader. In the first part of the essay, Fish examines three Milton sonnets and discovers three difficult interpretive tangles that the combined wisdom of decades of Milton scholarship has been unable to untie. His conclusion is that the tangles are not merely an ineluctible part of the poems. The reader's vacillation between one possibility and the next, the experience of the undecidability of the meaning of the sonnets, in fact constitutes their meaning.

Locating the text within the reader rather than in the words on the page is a bold procedure, since each reader is likely to come up with at least a slightly different "text." (Elsewhere, in *Self-Consuming Artifacts,* Fish blocks this objection by his appeal to the "informed reader.") Fish is willing to concede that the text-within-the-reader is unstable, but he attempts to demonstrate, as do Derrida and his followers, that the text-as-author's-words is equally unstable, although he does not base this radical skepticism about meaning on the Derridean metaphysics of absence. Instead,

[2] Stanley Fish, "Literature in the Reader," in *Is There a Text in This Class?* (Cambridge: Harvard University Press, 1980), p. 24.

for each posited location of meaning within the so-called hermeneutic circle, Fish casts doubt by pushing the point of anchor back, one step at a time — from the words to the conventions for reading the words to the linguistic rules themselves, and so forth. But Fish does not give the full proof, and his argument assumes that readers either can complete it for themselves or trust it can be done.[3]

Whether the reader is convinced is not important, however, since Fish finally accounts for the *relative* stability of readers' sense of canonical texts of literature by appealing to the idea of *interpretive communities*. Interpretive communities have tacitly agreed to certain principles of textual interpretation, which authors must recognize as they write their poems or plays or novels. (In legal circles Fish's theory is seen as one way of accounting for the relationship between statute law and the "community" of judges whose profession it is to interpret that law.) Fish does not attempt to describe in "*Variorum*" how an interpretive community is formed, or how, once constituted, its members change their minds and the way they read (and thereby create) texts. But he takes up these issues in the last four essays of *Is There a Text in This Class?* (1980), in which he develops the idea that the interpretive communities existing at any given time constitute systems of beliefs. New communities develop owing to gaps between existing systems (affective stylistics, for example, filled a gap produced by the New Critics' rejection of the audience), and they gain followers by appealing to the deeper, more fundamental beliefs of interpreters who previously were members of other communities. People change their interpretive communities as they discover conflicts between levels within their personal systems of belief. A conflict between a critic's formalist training and his or her social and historical interests, at a deeper level of belief, might be resolved, for example, by creating a new theory that would mediate between formalism and Marxism, or by joining a community based on a theorist (like Bakhtin) who had created such a mediating system.

THE STRUCTURALIST READER

The structuralist concern with the role of reader as the decoder of the text has already been discussed. In Chapter 2, Jonathan Culler's "Literary Competence" and Umberto Eco's "The Myth of Superman" present in theoretical and in practical terms how the central issues of semiotics have been applied to the audience. Culler argues that structuralism has been led astray by its long search for syntactic keys to authorial meaning and suggests that the movement would gain momentum if it concentrated its attention on the conventions that readers must learn and the procedures they must follow in interpreting the text. In a sense, this would dictate a search for rules and conventions. Eco's "The Myth of Superman" is a study of how certain of

[3]The "hermeneutic circle" (a vicious circle only when one is trying to think about it) refers to the difficulty of finding a stable point in the ascription of meaning to any text. Since any word has a large finite number of meanings, we are able to give a stable meaning to any word only from context, but the context itself consists of other words, with equally unstable meanings. Attempts to find a stable point by locating it in (for example) the speaker's intention, simply move the circularity elsewhere.

those conventions function in representing time within popular fiction — like comic books that must permit indefinite sequelae.

The most "rhetorical" structuralist analyst of the reader's role is Gerald Prince. In "Introduction to the Study of the Narratee," Prince, taking off from Wayne Booth's differentiation between *real* and *implied* authors, distinguishes between the *reader,* the human being who peruses the text, and the *narratee* (in French, *narrataire*), whom the narrator explicitly or implicitly addresses within the text.[4] The narratee also differs from the *ideal reader* ("one who would understand perfectly and would approve entirely the least of his words, the most subtle of his intentions") and from the *virtual reader,* "a certain type of reader" on whom the author bestows "certain qualities, faculties and inclinations according to his opinion of men in general . . . and according to the obligations he feels should be respected."[5]

Prince's narratee may be a very well-defined individual, like the "you" to whom Jean-Baptiste Clamence speaks in Albert Camus's *The Fall,* who is defined explicitly as a French lawyer on holiday in Amsterdam. Or the narratee may be defined only by class, like the middle-class lady or gentleman reading Balzac's *Père Goriot:* "You who hold this book with a white hand, you who settle back in a well-padded arm-chair." At other times, the narratee is defined by very subtle signals indeed, such as what has to be explained and what does not. (The narratee of Hemingway's *The Sun Also Rises* does not know what sort of drink Pernod is or the order of events in a bullfight.) The narratee's various functions are outlined by Prince:

> He constitutes a relay between the narrator and the reader, he helps establish the narrative framework, he serves to characterize the narrator, he emphasizes certain themes, he contributes to the development of the plot, he becomes the spokesman for the moral of the work.

What links Prince with Genette, Culler, and Eco, and with other semioticians like Michael Riffaterre, is his confidence that the parameters of reading can be specified and codified. But on this point, other structuralists, like Roland Barthes, have been less sure. In his late study, *The Pleasure of the Text* (1975), Barthes distinguishes between "*textes de plaisir,*" those readerly texts whose order can be uncovered, and "*textes de jouissance*" or texts of bliss, those writerly texts, like the novels of Alain Robbe-Grillet, whose indefinite ambiguity frustrates the structuralist design.

THE PSYCHOLOGY AND SOCIOLOGY OF THE AUDIENCE

In both the formalist-rhetorical and the semiotic-structuralist versions of reader-oriented criticism, the reader considered is generally the reader constructed within the tale: either the posited or implied reader for whom the rhetoric is contrived, or the narratee located explicitly, like a half-realized character, within the narrative

[4]In *Poétique,* no. 14 (1973): 177–96.

[5]See also Peter Rabinowitz, "Truth in Fiction: A Re-examination of Audiences," *Critical Inquiry* 4 (1977): 121–41.

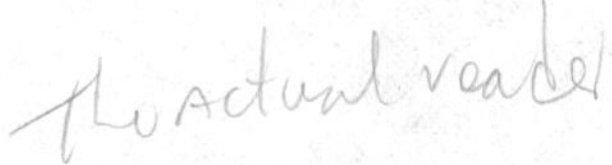

framework. The psychological and sociological versions of reader-oriented criticism introduce a different reader, the *actual* reader whom Prince distinguishes from the objects of his concern. Psychoanalytic critics like Norman Holland and social psychologists like David Bleich leave the ideal reader behind in favor of the quivering and unpredictable individual reader and his or her genuine but subjective response. Shared by these theories is a relaxed acceptance of a fact most of us have observed: There are so many idiosyncratic differences between the response of one reader and that of another that, after listening to a group of people discussing a text, we sometimes wonder if they have all read the same words.

One of the earliest of the psychological theorists was Louise Rosenblatt, whose *Literature as Exploration* (1938) pioneered the notion of reading as a *transaction* between text and reader. Rosenblatt conceived of the reading process in this way:

> Through the medium of words, the text brings into the reader's consciousness certain concepts, certain sensuous experiences, certain images of things, people, actions, and scenes. The special meanings and, more particularly, the submerged associations that these words and images have for the individual reader will largely determine what the work communicates to *him*. The reader brings to the work personality traits, memories of past events, present needs and preoccupations, a particular mood of the moment, and a particular physical condition. These and many other elements in a never-to-be-duplicated combination determine his response to the peculiar contribution of the text.[6]

For Rosenblatt, each reading of a given text, even by a single individual, will be different, not because the text is inexhaustible but because each time we read it we are at least slightly different people. Despite this seemingly free-wheeling attitude, Rosenblatt retains the sense that though our response to the work of art is inevitably subjective, some sorts of subjectivity are preferable to others. Minimally, a reader's response should be to what is in the text, not to what is projected onto the text. At one point Rosenblatt warns that "an undistorted vision of the work of art requires a consciousness of one's own preconceptions and prejudices concerning the situations presented in the work, in contrast to the basic attitudes toward life assumed in the text." While it is useful to know what sorts of distortions one is likely to perpetrate on situations in literature and in life (psychologists call this "reality-testing"), the implication of Rosenblatt's warning is that it is possible to achieve an "undistorted" view of a text — something equivalent to an objective interpretation.

Rosenblatt presents the reader's subjective response in terms of the commonsense psychology of prejudices and preoccupations; Norman Holland arrived at his reader-oriented criticism by way of orthodox Freudianism (see the introduction to Psychoanalytic Theory, p. 1018). His book *The Dynamics of Literary Response* (1968) presumed that the content of the text essentially determined the reader's response. Holland's text then had a manifest content (the story or poem, its events, its characters, its language, its form) and a latent content of primitive fantasy (oral aggression, anal withholding) hedged about and hidden by defenses (like symboliza-

[6] Louise Rosenblatt, *Literature as Exploration* (rev. ed.; London: Heinemann, 1968), pp. 30–31.

tion or sublimation). In the reading transaction, the audience, in absorbing consciously the manifest content, would also be stimulated, under the table as it were, by the latent content, and the reader's own orality or anality would be gratified by the experience. In effect, the reader's experience would mirror the text's central fantasy and modes of defense.

As Holland explains in his introduction to *5 Readers Reading* — "The Question: Who Reads What How?" — reprinted in this chapter, this model gradually began to seem less and less satisfactory as it became clearer that the actual responses of self-aware individuals differed a great deal more than this approach could explain. In Holland's new model, the text still possesses manifest and latent content, but instead of assuming that all individuals will react to this content in much the same way, Holland suggests not only that different types of readers will react in different ways, but that even people with similar obsessions may react differently according to their individual styles of coping. In "UNITY IDENTITY TEXT SELF," Holland claims that "any individual shapes the materials the literary work offers him . . . to give him what he characteristically both wishes and fears, and . . . he also constructs his characteristic way of achieving what he wishes and defeating what he fears."

As an example, Holland invites us to imagine three readers responding to *Hamlet,* all of whom share a love-hate relationship with authority figures. The one whose characteristic defense against authority figures is to establish "alternatives in response to their demands" might find in the play "dualisms, split characters, the interplay of multiple plots." The one who reacts by "establishing limits and qualifications on authority" might stress "irony and occasional farce, Osric, Polonius, the gravediggers." The one who reacts with total compliance would respond "by seeking out and accepting, totally, uncritically, with a gee-gosh, the authority of its author."[7]

Holland would reject Rosenblatt's notion that an "undistorted" view of a text is possible; for Holland the solid ground upon which interpretation may be based is that of the individual personality itself. Texts may come and go, but the self, the personality style, the *identity theme* that determines the individual's repertoire of fantasies and defense mechanisms remains remarkably constant over time. What Holland suggests is that to the extent that a work of art threatens the reader's identity theme, the reader recomposes the text so that it replicates this theme. In effect, Holland substitutes the unity of the self for the unity of art. He usually speaks of the self as though it were more objectively knowable than texts are. As Holland admits from time to time, however, we can know others' selves only through our own (and thus the issue of counter-transference between the reader of the text and the observer of that reader cannot be evaded). Furthermore, Holland's idea of the self — his notion that one's identity does not change as the result of life experience — is debatable. Whether the defensive reading of the text replicates precisely the self that

[7]Norman Holland, "UNITY IDENTITY TEXT SELF," *PMLA* 90 (1975): 817–18.

began to read or whether the self is not at least slightly altered by the experience are questions that cannot be defined out of existence.

David Bleich's theory of reading, as presented in *Readings and Feelings* (1975) and *Subjective Criticism* (1978), is closer to social psychology than to orthodox Freudianism. Bleich places the reading of texts in a social setting — the classroom — where knowledge about art and life is synthesized by a group. For Bleich, the text is a symbolic object upon which readers act, and the reader's initial and private response to a text is totally subjective, including all sorts of idiosyncratic associations and feelings. Within the social setting of the classroom, the private response is "negotiated" into meaningful knowledge via the individual's sense of the group's purposes. In the course of articulating a response to a text under the social pressure of the group, the reader prunes away, or at least brackets off as private or irrelevant, those aspects of the response that may not apply to others or that are inconsistent with the aim of the class. The response to the text is generalized, placed within a context determined by the ideology of the group. Bleich feels that within the pedagogical setting, knowledge does not move from teacher to student but is constructed by students in accord with a sense of the group aim, which may be initially defined and articulated by a teacher. But Bleich's notions of reading apply beyond his posited pedagogical setting, since people often read or experience works of art within a social setting, with friends or family, and try to communicate a sense of the experience to others.

Any study of this process inevitably leads to the sociology of literature, a field in which one might expect the Marxists to have done a great deal of work. In practice, however, Marxist theorists have tended to shy away from empirical studies of the literary marketplace and how individuals and groups within social settings actually read texts. Two fine studies in literary sociology are Jeffrey Sammons's *Literary Sociology and Practical Criticism* (1977) and Janice Radway's *Reading the Romance: Women, Patriarchy, and Popular Literature* (1984). The former is a lucid overview of the major issues of literary sociology; the latter, a practical demonstration of what can be done in the field. Radway examines why women read popular romances, but instead of merely theorizing about the repressed American housewife and her need for escape, she uses interviews and questionnaires to study the responses of a community of romance readers. Radway's study is well grounded in reader-response theory, and her initial chapter presents an overview of literary reception.

A feminist approach to the reading process that is related to the work of both Bleich and Radway is contained in Judith Fetterley's *The Resisting Reader,* the introduction to which is reprinted in this chapter. Fetterley argues that the socialization produced by reading literature carries a special burden for the female reader. Because most canonical authors are male, their subjects, styles, modes of symbolism, desires, and images for those desires all presume a masculine attitude toward the world, which the female reader is forced to adopt in the course of reception. Just as sexist language (such as the use of "man" to include both men and women) denigrates women by implying that they are not to be taken into account, Fetterley believes the shape of desire in narratives written by men "immasculates" women by forcing them to internalize the values of the other sex.

This is particularly true of American literature, according to Fetterley, who draws on Nina Baym's essay, "Melodramas of Beset Manhood" (see p. 1540), which argues that once the westward expansion of the frontier came to be defined as the central experience of American history, the crucial moments of American literature came to be seen as those that showed men encountering Mother Nature at the edge of civilization in the wilderness. Fetterley sharply suggests that if Baym is correct, then "America is female; to be American is to be male; and the quintessential American experience is betrayal by woman." Like Rabinowitz, Fetterley believes that the first step in contesting ideology is to make oneself aware of it, and she suggests that women become "resisting readers" of patriarchal texts, reading not passively with but actively against the grain of the masculine ideology that informs them.

While Fetterley argues cogently for the violence done to the female sensibility by the process of "immasculation," her own readings of male texts are sometimes not merely resistant but deeply obtuse. For example, her analysis reads Sherwood Anderson's "I Want To Know Why" as yet one more quintessential example of "betrayal by woman." In Fetterley's reading, the narrator, an adolescent boy mad for horses, feels the sting of disillusionment when he catches Jerry Tillford, a heroic jockey he idolizes, in the act of kissing a red-headed whore. What is lost in Fetterley's binary fixation on men and women is the polymorphous perversity of Anderson's tale: the way the narrator's libido attaches first to a powerful horse, and then to the rider who can successfully control it; the way the tale's climax speaks less of betrayed ideals than of sexual jealousy.

THE PHENOMENOLOGISTS

In effect, formalist/structuralist theories have staked out the reader within the text, while psycho/social theories have been based on the actual reader outside the text. To the extent that there can be a middle ground, it is occupied by the phenomenological approaches to literature, which focus on literature as it is experienced by the thinking subject, the "I" in the center of our conscious world. Two traditions occupy this territory — one represented by the French phenomenologists Jean-Paul Sartre and Georges Poulet, the other by the West German critics of the school of Constance, Wolfgang Iser and Hans Robert Jauss.

Although the late Jean-Paul Sartre has often been labeled a Marxist critic, his discussion of the role of the reader and the writer in *What Is Literature?* (1966) is thoroughly existentialist — and existentialism, as has often been observed, is the ethical and political branch of phenomenology. The reader of "Why Write?" (see p. 624) will find major similarities between it and the theories of Georges Poulet.

Poulet's discussion of the act of reading emphasizes the way reading transforms the book-as-object — the heavy, dead, material thing — into a subject, an intelligence, a mind to which we subordinate our own.

Whenever I read, I mentally pronounce an *I,* yet the *I* which I pronounce is not myself. This is true even when the hero of a novel is presented in the third person, and even when there is no hero and nothing but reflections or propositions. . . . Another *I,* who has replaced my own, and who will continue to do so as long as I read. . . . A second self takes over, a self which thinks and feels for me.

For Poulet, the purpose of this abdication of the self is, paradoxically, the further realization of the self:

The annexation of my consciousness by . . . the other which is the work . . . in no way implies that I am the victim of any deprivation of consciousness. Everything happens, on the contrary, as though, from the moment I become a prey to what I read, I begin to share the use of my consciousness with . . . the conscious subject ensconced at the heart of the work.[8]

Poulet's characteristic images are close to those of Plato. The subjective consciousness of the text is *inbreathed* by the reader in a sort of passive inspiration, like the *enthousiasmós* of the *Ion* or the *Phaedrus*. For Iser and Jauss the relationship of author and reader is less like that of the demon and the human being it has possessed than that of the composer and the performer of a piece of music, a metaphor that suggests a new kind of connection between writer and reader. For the formalists and structuralists, the reader is essentially determined by the text. Fish's interpretive communities create the text themselves; the author's words are an indeterminate framework to which the community brings the meaning. Psychological critics like Holland view the text as fantasy material with which the reader copes, as with a disturbing dream. But Iser and Jauss perceive in the text the mutual dependence — the creative collaboration — of composer and performer. Although the composer is clearly the primary genius whose intentions must be respected, without the performer the composer would remain mute. Following the terminology of Roman Ingarden, Iser and Jauss speak of the text as being *concretized* by the reader: The vague and ideal word is in the reading process made flesh. The difference between Iser and Jauss is primarily one of perspective: Iser's interest is in the *act* of reading as it happens for each of us; Jauss's concern has been with the *history* of reading and the contribution a history of reception can make to the broader concerns of literary history.

For Iser, the reader's performative activity is called into play by the gaps that every text contains, since no text can be fully explicit about everything. In the process of reading, for example, we imagine what the hero and heroine look like in ways consistent with the descriptions we are given in the text; nevertheless, two readers' mental pictures of Tom Jones would be vastly different. (This, Iser says, is why film realizations of novels invariably make us say to ourselves, "That's not the way I pictured him.") But beyond filling in descriptions the text leaves indeterminate, the reader also imagines scenes the text leaves tacit, dialogue that is left un-

[8]Georges Poulet, "Criticism and the Experience of Interiority," in Richard Macksey and Eugenio Donato, *The Structuralist Controversy: The Languages of Criticism and the Sciences of Man* (Baltimore: Johns Hopkins University Press, 1972), p. 56.

spoken, and so on. Furthermore, it is not just a matter of understanding and creating a full sense of illusion out of the words that are directly before the reader's eyes. In a novel, the reading process takes place within the flow of a narrative moving from a beginning through a middle to an end. As we read a given sentence, we may be forced to revise our understanding of what we have already read and processed, or to form expectations of what will happen in the future, expectations that may be fulfilled or shattered. Underlying this process, and guiding it, are "two main structural components within the text: first, a repertoire of familiar literary patterns and recurrent literary themes, together with allusions to familiar social and historical contexts; and second, techniques or strategies used to set the familiar against the unfamiliar." The text in any mature work of art, in other words, depends on the reader's prior understanding of the themes and conventions of story-telling, but it works *against* those conventions as much as it employs them in order to *defamiliarize* the reader, who would otherwise be bored by a predictable text.

During the last two hundred years, according to Iser's *The Implied Reader,* these general principles have been worked out in the English novel in very different ways. The reader in the eighteenth century was "guided — directly or indirectly, through affirmation or through negation — toward a conception of human nature and of reality." The nineteenth-century reader, by contrast, "was not told what part he was to play. Instead he had to discover the fact that society had imposed a part on him, the object being for him eventually to take up a critical attitude toward this imposition." Readers of the Victorian novel, therefore, were nudged into making the correct discoveries for themselves. Both of these modes depend upon the reader's capacity for subscribing to the illusion provoked by the text. The twentieth-century novel, in contrast, insists on rupturing these illusions and calling attention to its own use of technique — all this in order

> to provoke the reader into establishing for himself the connections between perception and thought. . . . In this way he may then be given the chance of discovering himself, both in and through his constant involvement in "home-made" illusions and fictions.[9]

For Iser, the history of the novel is the history of the ways in which writers created gaps for their readers to fill, and to an extent, his ideas are easily assimilated to those of rhetorical critics like Peter Rabinowitz. For Hans Robert Jauss, on the other hand, literary history is as much the history of the reader as of the canonized authors, or to be more accurate, of the relationship between writing and the reading public that consumes and stimulates its production. These ideas are based on the philosophy of Hans-Georg Gadamer (see p. 676), whose theories of interpretation turn on the positive contributions made by our prejudices. Normally, "prejudice" has a negative connotation when it refers to one cause of our injustice to others, but for Gadamer and his pupils, these prejudices (in German, *Vorurteilungen*) are what allow us to understand the changing world at all. Our preunderstandings give us a

[9]Wolfgang Iser, *The Implied Reader: Patterns of Communication in Prose Fiction from Bunyan to Beckett* (Baltimore: Johns Hopkins University Press, 1974), pp. xiii–xiv.

settled context, a *horizon of expectations,* against which we can place and evaluate the new. And our horizon of expectations is constantly changing as our life experience adds to and alters our framework of vision.

In literary terms, there is a dialogical relation between the text and the reading public. The public reads the text from within its current horizon of expectations — that set of cultural, ethical, and aesthetic norms current at any given moment — and attempts to bring the work within those horizons. For some works, like popular literature meant for instant consumption, there will be no problem in fitting the text into such a horizon, but other works may challenge the audience's horizon of expectations along one or more fronts. Such works may succeed in changing the preunderstanding of the reading public, or a substantial portion of it, as was the case with Flaubert's *Madame Bovary.* On the other hand, such works may fail to engage the audience entirely and may be forgotten; or, like Melville's *Moby-Dick,* they may be read, but their most individual qualities may be ignored because they cannot be assimilated to the preunderstanding of the day. Forgotten or misread works, however, may be rediscovered by a later audience, when the horizon of expectations has, so to speak, caught up with them. Change in the horizon is produced partly by literary texts themselves, whose success creates a market and stimulates imitation by other authors, and partly by changes in economic, social, and political conditions, which make ideas and relations within texts more or less attractive.

For Jauss the writing of literary history would require that we recreate the horizon of expectations of the reading public for any given period. This we can piece together, partly from the texts themselves, and partly from the public and private responses of various levels of the reading public: other authors, publishers, critics, and private consumers. Creating the materials out of which a literary history might be written would require both synchronic and diachronic studies. One might begin with a synchronic study, in effect taking a "snapshot" of the literary world at a given date (Jauss himself has done a study of the horizon of expectations in France in 1857, the year of *Madame Bovary* and of Baudelaire's *Fleurs du Mal*), and by comparing such "snapshots" at various dates, put together a sense of how these horizons changed over time. In addition, diachronic studies, like histories of the reception of a given text from its publication to the present day, would be a useful supplement to the snapshots.

These "time-lapse photos" would give a stronger sense of how literary opinion shifts over the centuries (Jauss has produced a study over time of the reception of Baudelaire's "Spleen" poems). The end product will take a long time to produce, given the sheer amount of research into the reception of texts the method requires. But the result proposed is a literary history that goes beyond the "scissors-and-paste" histories detailing the lives and works of those authors that are currently valued. The history Jauss envisions would allow us to understand the evolution of textual production in relation to changes in the cultural scene that generated that evolution, including many factors we currently ignore, such as those evanescent productions whose popularity in one age were a passport to obscurity in the next.

As one might expect, the Marxists were most offended by Jauss's insistence that literary history needed to be reformed in order to include the participation of the readers who made up the market for literature. One might have thought them the group most concerned with the influence of the individual in a mass society, yet Jauss's competition with them exposed their neglect of the group they theoretically most favored. In fact, the publication of "Literary History as a Challenge to Literary Theory" provoked a decade of quarreling between the reception theorists of Constance and the Marxists across what was then the border with East Germany. By the 1980s, however, both parties saw that what they had in common dwarfed their area of contention, and indeed, some post-Althusserian Marxists (like the British Tony Bennett) have proposed programs for revamping literary history using methods that closely resemble Jauss's proposals. In addition to these quarrels with the Marxists, Jauss's theories have also provoked a large number of scholars, not just in Germany but in England and North America as well, into undertaking reception studies, which are just beginning to produce the "snapshots" and "time-lapse photos" of the audience that will eventuate in the new literary history Jauss prophesied.

Interest in the reader is a late development in critical theory. As a topic for investigation, it has attracted each of the major schools of thought, from Marxism through structuralism and feminism to deconstruction. It is likely that, following its neglect in the wake of the "affective fallacy," critical understanding of the audience — in all its various manifestations — has changed more in the past twenty-five years than in the previous two thousand.

Selected Bibliography

Altick, Richard. *The English Common Reader: A Social History of the Mass Reading Public, 1800–1900*. Chicago: University of Chicago Press, 1957.

Appleyard, J. A. *Becoming a Reader: The Experience of Fiction from Childhood to Adulthood*. Cambridge: Cambridge University Press, 1990.

Barthes, Roland. *The Pleasure of the Text*. New York: Hill and Wang, 1975.

Bleich, David. *Readings and Feelings: An Introduction to Subjective Criticism*. Urbana, IL: National Council of Teachers of English, 1975.

———. *Subjective Criticism*. Baltimore: Johns Hopkins University Press, 1978.

Booth, Stephen. *An Essay on Shakespeare's Sonnets*. New Haven: Yale University Press, 1969.

Booth, Wayne C. *The Rhetoric of Fiction*. Chicago: University of Chicago Press, 1961; 2nd ed. 1983.

———. *A Rhetoric of Irony*. Chicago: University of Chicago Press, 1974.

———. *The Company We Keep: Ethical Criticism and the Ethics of Reading*. Berkeley: University of California Press, 1988.

Cruse, Amy. *The Englishman and His Books in the Early Nineteenth Century*. London: George G. Harrap, 1930.

Culler, Jonathan. *Structuralist Poetics*. Ithaca: Cornell University Press, 1975.

Eco, Umberto. *The Role of the Reader: Explorations in the Semiotics of Texts*. Bloomington: Indiana University Press, 1979.

Escarpit, Robert. *Sociology of Literature.* Painesville, OH: Lake Erie College Press, 1965.
———. "The Sociology of Literature." *International Encyclopaedia of Social Science.* Vol. 9. New York: Macmillan, 1968, pp. 417–25.
Fetterley, Judith. *The Resisting Reader: A Feminist Approach to American Fiction.* Bloomington: Indiana University Press, 1978.
———. "Reading about Reading: 'A Jury of Her Peers,' 'The Murders in the Rue Morgue,' and 'The Yellow Wallpaper.'" In *Gender and Reading: Essays on Readers, Texts, and Contexts,* ed. Elizabeth Flynn and Patrocinio Schweickart. Baltimore: Johns Hopkins University Press, 1986, pp. 147–64.
Fish, Stanley. *Self-Consuming Artifacts: The Experience of Seventeenth-Century Literature.* Berkeley: University of California Press, 1972.
———. *Is There a Text in This Class? The Authority of Interpretive Communities.* Cambridge: Harvard University Press, 1980.
———. *Doing What Comes Naturally: Change, Rhetoric, and the Practice of Theory in Literary and Legal Studies.* Durham: Duke University Press, 1989.
Flynn, Elizabeth A. "Gender and Reading." *College English* 45 (1983): 236–53.
Gadamer, Hans-Georg. *Truth and Method.* London: Sheed and Ward, 1975.
Hohendahl, Peter Uwe. "Introduction to Reception Aesthetics." *New German Critique* 10 (1977): 29–63.
Holland, Norman N. *The Dynamics of Literary Response.* New York: Oxford University Press, 1968.
———. *5 Readers Reading.* New Haven: Yale University Press, 1975.
———. "I-ing Film." *Critical Inquiry* 12 (1986): 654–71.
———. "I-ing Lacan." In *Criticism and Lacan: Essays and Dialogue on Language, Structure, and the Unconscious,* ed. Patrick C. Hogan and Lalita Pandit. Athens: University of Georgia Press, 1990, pp. 97–108.
———. *The Critical I.* New York: Columbia University Press, 1992.
Holub, Robert C. *Reception Theory: A Critical Introduction.* London: Methuen, 1984.
Ingarden, Roman. *The Cognition of the Literary Work of Art.* Evanston, IL: Northwestern University Press, 1973.
Iser, Wolfgang. *The Implied Reader: Patterns of Communication in Prose Fiction from Bunyan to Beckett.* Baltimore: Johns Hopkins University Press, 1974.
———. *The Act of Reading: A Theory of Aesthetic Response.* Baltimore: Johns Hopkins University Press, 1978.
———. "Towards a Literary Anthropology." In *The Future of Literary Theory,* ed. Ralph Cohen. New York: Routledge, 1989, pp. 208–28.
———. "Fictionalizing: The Anthropological Dimension of Literary Fictions." *New Literary History* 21 (1990): 939–55.
Jauss, Hans Robert. "Theses on the Transition from the Aesthetics of Literary Works to a Theory of Aesthetic Experience." In *Interpretation of Narrative,* ed. Mario J. Valdès and Owen J. Miller. Toronto: University of Toronto Press, 1978, pp. 138–46.
———. *Aesthetic Experience and Literary Hermeneutics.* Minneapolis: University of Minnesota Press, 1982.
———. "Literary History as a Challenge to Literary Theory." In *Toward an Aesthetics of Reception,* trans. Timothy Bahti. Minneapolis: University of Minnesota Press, 1982, pp. 3–46.
———. "The Book of Jonah: A Paradigm of the 'Hermeneutics of Strangeness'." In *Contexts of Pre-Novel Narrative: The European Tradition.* Berlin: Mouton de Gruyter, 1994, pp. 1–26.

Kavanagh, Thomas M., ed. *The Limits of Theory.* Stanford: Stanford University Press, 1989.

Koelb, Clayton. *The Incredulous Reader: Literature and the Function of Disbelief.* Ithaca: Cornell University Press, 1984.

Leavis, Q. D. *Fiction and the Reading Public.* London: Chatto and Windus, 1932.

Lesser, Simon O. *Fiction and the Unconscious.* Boston: Vintage, 1957.

Mailloux, Steven J. *Interpretive Conventions.* Ithaca: Cornell University Press, 1982.

Miles, David H. "Literary Sociology: Some Introductory Notes." *German Quarterly* 48 (1975): 20–45.

Miller, Owen J. "Reading as a Process of Reconstruction: A Critique of Recent Structuralist Formulations." In *Interpretation of Narrative,* ed. Mario J. Valdès and Owen J. Miller. Toronto: University of Toronto Press, 1978, pp. 19–27.

Morrison, Ronald D. "Reader Response Criticism in the Nineties." *Kentucky Philological Review* 8 (1993): 41–45.

Naumann, Manfred. "Literary Production and Reception." *New Literary History* 8 (1976): 107–26.

Nelson, Cary. "Reading Criticism." *PMLA* 91 (1976): 801–15.

Poulet, Georges. "Criticism and the Experience of Interiority." In *The Structuralist Controversy: The Languages of Criticism and the Sciences of Man,* ed. Richard Macksey and Eugenio Donato. Baltimore: Johns Hopkins University Press, 1972.

Preston, John. *The Created Self: The Reader's Role in Eighteenth-Century Fiction.* New York: Barnes and Noble, 1970.

Prince, Gerald. "Introduction to the Study of the Narratee." *Poétique* 14 (1973): 177–96.

Rabinowitz, Peter. "Truth in Fiction: A Reexamination of Audiences." *Critical Inquiry* 4 (1977): 121–41.

———. *Before Reading.* Ithaca: Cornell University Press, 1987.

———. "Readings of Narrative, 1937–1987." *PMLA* 108 (1993): 410–532.

———. "'Betraying the Sender': The Rhetoric and Ethics of Fragile Texts." *Narrative* 2 (1994): 201–13.

Radway, Janice A. *Reading the Romance: Women, Patriarchy, and Popular Literature.* Chapel Hill: University of North Carolina Press, 1984.

Reichert, John. *Making Sense of Literature.* Chicago: University of Chicago Press, 1977.

Richards, I. A. *Practical Criticism: A Study of Literary Judgment.* New York: Harcourt, Brace, 1935.

Richter, David. *The Reader, the Text, the Poem: The Transactional Theory of the Literary Work.* Carbondale: Southern Illinois University Press, 1978.

———. "The Reader as Ironic Victim." *Novel* 14 (1981): 135–51.

———. "The Reception of the Gothic Novel in the 1790's." In *The Idea of the Novel in the Eighteenth Century,* ed. Robert Uphaus. East Lansing, MI: Colleagues Press, 1988.

———. "The Unguarded Prison: Reception Theory, Structural Marxism, and the Structure of Literary History." *The Eighteenth Century: Theory and Interpretation* 30 (1989): 1–17.

Rosenblatt, Louise. *Literature as Exploration.* 1938; New York: Modern Language Association, 1983.

Sammons, Jeffrey. *Literary Sociology and Practical Criticism.* Bloomington: Indiana University Press, 1977.

Sartre, Jean-Paul. *What Is Literature?* New York: Philosophical Library, 1966.

Schücking, L. L. *The Sociology of Literary Taste,* 3rd ed. Chicago: University of Chicago Press, 1966.

Suleiman, Susan, and Inge Crosman, eds. *The Reader in the Text: Essays on Audience and Interpretation.* Princeton: Princeton University Press, 1980.

Tompkins, Jane P., ed. *Reader-Response Criticism: From Formalism to Post-Structuralism.* Baltimore: Johns Hopkins University Press, 1980.
Weimann, Robert. "'Reception Aesthetics' and the Crisis of Literary History." *Clio* 5 (1975): 3–33.
Wellek, René. "Zur methodischen Aporie einen Rezeptions-geschichte." In *Geschichte: Ereignis und Erzählung,* ed. Reinhart Koselleck and Wolf-Dieter Stempel. Munich: Wilhelm Fink Verlag, 1973.

Hans Robert Jauss

b. 1921

Hans Robert Jauss has been acknowledged the leader and principal theorist of the movement termed "reception aesthetics," which views literary history as formed, at least in part, by the readings and assessments that texts have received throughout the past. Jauss was born in 1921 and served on the Eastern front in the Waffen-*SS throughout World War II. He completed his Ph.D. at the University of Heidelberg and taught there, and at Münster and Giessen, before joining the faculty at Konstanz, where he has been professor of Romance languages and literature since 1967. He has held visiting professorships at the Sorbonne, Columbia, Yale, Berkeley, and UCLA. Jauss's prodigious scholarly output (which also comprises over 75 articles, in addition to editions and translations) includes* Erinnerung in Marcel Proust's *À la Recherche du temps perdue (Memory in Marcel Proust's* Remembrance of Things Past, *1955);* Untersuchungen zu mittelalterischen Tierdichtung *(Researches into Medieval Beast Literature, 1959);* La génèse de la poésie allegorique française au Moyen-Age *(The Origin of Medieval French Allegory, 1962);* Literaturgeschichte als Provokation der Literaturwissenschaft *(Literary History as a Challenge to Literary Theory, 1967);* Kleine Apologie der ästhetischen Erfahrung *(Short Defense of Aesthetic Experience, 1972);* Alternität und Modernität der mittelalterischen Literatur *(Ancientness and Modernity in Medieval Literature, 1977); and* Ästhetische Erfahrung und literarische Hermeneutik *(Aesthetic Experience and Literary Hermeneutics, 1977). Jauss's major essays have been translated into English and are collected in* Toward an Aesthetics of Reception *(1978),* Aesthetic Experience and Literary Hermeneutics *(1982), and* Question and Answer: Forms of Dialogic Understanding *(1989). "Literary History as a Challenge," excerpted here, was Jauss's inaugural lecture at Konstanz in 1967.*

From *Literary History as a Challenge to Literary Theory*

V[1]

In the question thus posed, I see the challenge to literary studies of taking up once again the problem of literary history, which was left unresolved in the dispute between Marxist and Formalist methods. My attempt to bridge the gap between literature and history between historical and aesthetic approaches, begins at the point at which both schools stop. Their methods conceive the *literary fact* within the closed circle of an aesthetics of production and of representation. In doing so, they deprive literature of a dimension that inalienably belongs to its aesthetic character as well as to its social function: the dimension of its reception and influence. Reader, listener, and spectator — in short, the factor of the audience — play an extremely limited role in both literary theories. Orthodox Marxist aesthetics treats the reader — if at all — no differently from the author: it inquires about his social position or seeks to recognize him in the structure of a represented society. The Formalist school needs the reader only as a perceiving subject who follows the directions in the text in order to distinguish the [literary] form or discover the [literary] procedure. It assumes that the reader has the theoretical understanding of the philologist who can reflect on the artistic devices, already knowing them; conversely, the Marxist school candidly equates the spontaneous experience of the reader with the scholarly interest of historical materialism, which would discover relationships between superstructure and basis in the literary work. However, as Walter Bulst has stated, "no text was ever written to be read and interpreted philologically by philologists,"[2] nor, may I add, historically by historians. Both methods lack the reader in his genuine role, a role as unalterable for aesthetic as for historical knowledge: as the addressee for whom the literary work is primarily destined.

For even the critic who judges a new work, the writer who conceives of his work in light of positive or negative norms of an earlier work, and the literary historian who classifies a work in its tradition and explains it historically are first simply readers before their reflexive relationship to literature can become productive again. In the triangle of author, work, and public the last is no passive part, no chain of mere reactions, but rather itself an energy formative of history. The historical life of a literary work is unthinkable without the active participation of its addressees. For it is only through the process of its mediation that the work enters into the changing horizon-of-experience of a continuity in which the perpetual inversion occurs from simple reception to critical understanding, from passive to active reception, from recognized aesthetic norms to a new production that surpasses them. The historicity of literature as well as its communicative character presupposes a dialogical and at once processlike relationship between work, audience,

Translated by Timothy Bahti.

[1]In the first third of his essay, Jauss attempts to explain why "literary history has increasingly fallen into disrepute": Most literary history as written is merely the compilation of the lives and works of famous authors; it is unworthy of the name of history because it attempts no causal explanations of how events occurred as they did. Two schools of literary theory which have attempted to write genuine literary history, the Marxists and the Russian Formalists, are each hamstrung by an inadequate conception of the literary work of art and a simplistic notion of how art operates within history. [Ed.]

[2]Bendenken eines Philologen," *Studium generale* 7 (1954): 321–23. The new approach to literary tradition that R. Guiette has sought in a series of pioneering essays (partly in *Questions de littérature* [Ghent, 1960]), using his own method of combining aesthetic criticism with historical knowledge, corresponds almost literally to his (unpublished) axiom, "The greatest error of philologists is to believe that literature has been made for philologists." See also his "Eloge de la lecture," *Revue générale belge* (January 1966): 3–14. [Au.]

and new work that can be conceived in the relations between message and receiver as well as between question and answer, problem and solution. The closed circle of production and of representation within which the methodology of literary studies has mainly moved in the past must therefore be opened to an aesthetics of reception and influence if the problem of comprehending the historical sequence of literary works as the coherence of literary history is to find a new solution.

The perspective of the aesthetics of reception mediates between passive reception and active understanding, experience formative of norms, and new production. If the history of literature is viewed in this way within the horizon of a dialogue between work and audience that forms a continuity, the opposition between its aesthetic and its historical aspects is also continually mediated. Thus the thread from the past appearance to the present experience of literature, which historicism had cut, is tied back together.

The relationship of literature and reader has aesthetic as well as historical implications. The aesthetic implication lies in the fact that the first reception of a work by the reader includes a test of its aesthetic value in comparison with works already read.[3] The obvious historical implication of this is that the understanding of the first reader will be sustained and enriched in a chain of receptions from generation to generation; in this way the historical significance of a work will be decided and its aesthetic value made evident. In this process of the history of reception, which the literary historian can only escape at the price of leaving unquestioned the presuppositions that guide his understanding and judgment, the reappropriation of past works occurs simultaneously with the perpetual mediation of past and present art and of traditional evaluation and current literary attempts. The merit of a literary history based on an aesthetics of reception will depend upon the extent to which it can take an active part in the ongoing totalization of the past through aesthetic experience. This demands on the one hand — in oppositon to the objectivism of positivist literary history — a conscious attempt at the formation of a canon, which, on the other hand — in opposition to the classicism of the study of traditions — presupposes a critical revision if not destruction of the received literary canon. The criterion for the formation of such a canon and the ever necessary retelling of literary history is clearly set out by the aesthetics of reception. The step from the history of the reception of the individual work to the history of literature has to lead to seeing and representing the historical sequence of works as they determine and clarify the coherence of literature, to the extent that it is meaningful for us, as the prehistory of its present experience.[4]

From this premise, the question as to how literary history can today be methodologically grounded and written anew will be addressed in the following seven theses.

VI

Thesis 1. A renewal of literary history demands the removal of the prejudices of historical objectivism and the grounding of the traditional aesthetics of production and representation in an aesthetics of reception and influence. The historicity of literature rests not on an organization of "literary facts" that is established *post factum,*[5] but rather on the preceding experience of the literary work by its readers.

R. G. Collingwood's postulate, posed in his critique of the prevailing ideology of objectivity in history — "History is nothing but the re-enactment of past thought in the historian's mind"[6] — is even more valid for literary history. For the positivistic view of history as the "objective" de-

[3]This thesis is one of the main points of the *Introduction à une esthétique de la littérature* by G. Picon (Paris, 1953); see esp. pp. 90 ff. [Au.]

[4]Correspondingly, Walter Benjamin (1931) formulated: "For it is not a question of representing the written works in relation to their time but of bringing to representation the time that knows them — that is our time — in the time when they originated. Thus literature becomes an organon of history and the task of literary history is to make it this — and not to make written works the material of history" (*Angelus Novus* [Frankfurt a.M., 1966], p. 456). [Au.]

[5]After the fact. [Ed.]

[6]*The Idea of History* (New York and Oxford, 1956), p. 228. [Au.]

scription of a series of events in an isolated past neglects the artistic character as well as the specific historicity of literature. A literary work is not an object that stands by itself and that offers the same view to each reader in each period.[7] It is not a monument that monologically reveals its timeless essence. It is much more like an orchestration that strikes ever new resonances among its readers and that frees the text from the material of the words and brings it to a contemporary existence: "words that must, at the same time that they speak to him, create an interlocutor capable of understanding them."[8] This dialogical character of the literary work also establishes why philological understanding can exist only in a perpetual confrontation with the text, and cannot be allowed to be reduced to a knowledge of facts.[9] Philological understanding always remains related to interpretation that must set as its goal, along with learning about the object, the reflection on and description of the completion of this knowledge as a moment of new understanding.

History of literature is a process of aesthetic reception and production that takes place in the realization of literary texts on the part of the receptive reader, the reflective critic, and the author in his continuing productivity. The endlessly growing sum of literary "facts" that winds up in the conventional literary histories is merely left over from this process; it is only the collected and classified past and therefore not history at all, but pseudo-history. Anyone who considers a series of such literary facts as a piece of the history of literature confuses the eventful character of a work of art with that of historical matter-of-factness. The *Perceval* of Chrétien de Troyes, as a literary event, is not "historical" in the same sense as, for example, the Third Crusade, which was occurring at about the same time.[10] It is not a "fact" that could be explained as caused by a series of situational preconditions and motives, by the intent of a historical action as it can be reconstructed, and by the necessary and secondary consequences of this deed. The historical context in which a literary work appears is not a factual, independent series of events that exists apart from an observer. *Perceval* becomes a literary event only for its reader, who reads this last work of Chrétien with a memory of his earlier works and who recognizes its individuality in comparison with these and other works that he already knows, so that he gains a new criterion for evaluating future works. In contrast to a political event, a literary event has no unavoidable consequences subsisting on their own that no succeeding generation can ever escape. A literary event can continue to have an effect only if those who come after it still or once again respond to it — if there are readers who again appropriate the past work of authors who want to imitate, outdo, or refute it. The coherence of literature as an event is primarily mediated in the horizon of expectations of the literary experience of contemporary and later readers, critics, and authors. Whether it is possible to comprehend and represent the history of literature in its unique historicity depends on whether this horizon of expectations can be objectified.

[7]Here I am following A. Nisin in his criticism of the latent Platonism of philological methods, that is, of their belief in the timeless substance of a literary work and in a timeless point of view of the reader: "For the work of art, if it cannot incarnate the essence of art, is also not an object which we can regard according to the Cartesian rule 'without putting anything of ourselves into it but what can apply indiscriminately to all objects' "; *La Littérature et le lecteur* (Paris, 1959), p. 57 (see also my review in *Archiv für das Studium der neueren Sprachen* 197 [1960]: 223–35). [Au.]

[8]Picon, *Introduction,* p. 34. This view of the dialogical mode of being of a literary work of art is found in Malraux (*Les voix du silence*) as well as in Picon, Nisin, and Guiette — a tradition of literary aesthetics which is still alive in France and to which I am especially indebted; it finally goes back to a famous sentence in Valéry's poetics, "It is the execution of the poem which is the poem." [Au.]

[9]Peter Szondi, "Über philologische Erkenntnis," *Hölderlin-Studien* (Frankfurt a.M., 1967), rightly sees in this the decisive difference between literary and historical studies, p. 11: "No commentary, no stylistic examination of a poem should aim to give a description of the poem that could be taken by itself. Even the least critical reader will want to confront it with the poem and will not understand it until he has traced the claim back to the acts of knowledge whence they originated." Guiette says something very similar in "Eloge de la lecture" (see note 2). [Au.]

[10]Note also J. Storost (1960), who simply equates the historical event with the literary event ("A work of art is first of all an artistic act and hence historical like the Battle of Isos"). [Au.]

VII

Thesis 2. The analysis of the literary experience of the reader avoids the threatening pitfalls of psychology if it describes the reception and the influence of a work within the objectifiable system of expectations that arises for each work in the historical moment of its appearance, from a pre-understanding of the genre, from the form and themes of already familiar works, and from the opposition between poetic and practical language.

My thesis opposes a widespread skepticism that doubts whether an analysis of aesthetic influence can approach the meaning of a work of art at all or can produce, at best, more than a simple sociology of taste. René Wellek in particular directs such doubts against the literary theory of I. A. Richards. Wellek argues that neither the individual state of consciousness, since it is momentary and only personal, nor a collective state of consciousness, as Jan Mukařovský assumes the effect of a work of art to be, can be determined by empirical means.[11] Roman Jakobson wanted to replace the "collective state of consciousness" by a "collective ideology" in the form of a system of norms that exists for each literary work as *langue* and that is actualized as *parole* by the receiver — although incompletely and never as a whole.[12] This theory, it is true, limits the subjectivity of the influence, but it stills leaves open the question of which data can be used to comprehend the influence of a particular work on a certain public and to incorporate it into a system of norms. In the meantime there are empirical means that had never been thought of before — literary data that allow one to ascertain a specific disposition of the audience for each work (a disposition that precedes the psychological reaction as well as the subjective understanding of the individual reader). As in the case of every actual experience, the first literary experience of a previously unknown work also demands a "foreknowledge which is an element of the experience itself, and on the basis of which anything new that we come across is available to experience at all, i.e., as it were readable in a context of experience."[13]

A literary work, even when it appears to be new, does not present itself as something absolutely new in an informational vacuum, but predisposes its audience to a very specific kind of reception by announcements, overt and covert signals, familiar characteristics, or implicit allusions. It awakens memories of that which was already read, brings the reader to a specific emotional attitude, and with its beginning arouses expectations for the "middle and end," which can then be maintained intact or altered, reoriented, or even fulfilled ironically in the course of the reading according to specific rules of the genre or type of text. The psychic process in the reception of a text is, in the primary horizon of aesthetic experience, by no means only an arbitrary series of merely subjective impressions, but rather the carrying out of specific instructions in a process of directed perception, which can be comprehended according to its constitutive motivations and triggering signals, and which also can be described by a textual linguistics. If, along with W. D. Stempel, one defines the initial horizon of expectations of a text as paradigmatic isotopy, which is transposed into an immanent syntagmatic horizon of expectations to the extent that the utterance grows, then the process of reception becomes describable in the expansion of a semiotic system that accomplishes itself between the development and the correction of a system.[14] A corresponding process of the continuous establishing and altering of horizons also determines the relationship of the individual text to the suc-

[11]René Wellek, "The Theory of Literary History," in *Études dédiées au quatrième Congrès de linguistes — Travaux du Cercle Linguistique de Prague* (1936), p. 179. [Au.]

[12]In *Slovo a slovenost,* I, p. 192, cited by Wellek (1936), pp. 179 ff. [Au.]

[13]G. Buck, *Lernen und Erfahrung* (Stuttgart, 1967), p. 56, who refers here to Husserl (*Erfahrung und Urteil,* esp. § 8) but who more broadly goes beyond Husserl in a determination of the negativity in the process of experience that is of significance for the horizontal structure of aesthetic experience (cf. note 56 below). [Au.]

[14]Wolf Dieter Stempel, "Pour une description des genres littéraires," in *Actes du XIIe congrès international de linguistique Romane* (Bucharest, 1968), also in *Beiträge zur Textlinguistik,* ed. W. D. Stempel (Munich, 1970). [Au.]

cession of texts that forms the genre. The new text evokes for the reader (listener) the horizon of expectations and rules familiar from earlier texts, which are then varied, corrected, altered, or even just reproduced. Variation and correction determine the scope, whereas alteration and reproduction determine the borders of a genre-structure.[15] The interpretative reception of a text always presupposes the context of experience of aesthetic perception: the question of the subjectivity of the interpretation and of the taste of different readers or levels of readers can be asked meaningfully only when one has first clarified which transsubjective horizon of understanding conditions the influence of the text.

The ideal cases of the objective capability of such literary-historical frames of reference are works that evoke the reader's horizon of expectations, formed by a convention of genre, style, or form, only in order to destroy it step by step — which by no means serves a critical purpose only, but can itself once again produce poetic effects. Thus Cervantes allows the horizon of expectations of the favorite old tales of knighthood to arise out of the reading of *Don Quixote,* which the adventure of his last knight then seriously parodies.[16] Thus Diderot, at the beginning of *Jacques le Fataliste,* evokes the horizon of expectations of the popular novelistic schema of the "journey" (with the fictive questions of the reader to the narrator) along with the (Aristotelian) convention of the romanesque fable and the providence unique to it, so that he can then provocatively oppose to the promised journey- and love-novel a completely unromanesque "vérité de l'histoire":[17] the bizarre reality and moral casuistry of the enclosed stories in which the truth of life continually denies the mendacious character of poetic fiction.[18] Thus Nerval in the *Chimères* cites, combines, and mixes a quintessence of well-known romantic and occult motifs to produce the horizon of expectations of a mythical metamorphosis of the world only in order to signify his renunciation of romantic poetry. The identifications and relationships of the mythic state that are familiar or disclosable to the reader dissolve into an unknown to the same degree as the attempted private myth of the lyrical "I" fails, the law of sufficient information is broken, and the obscurity that has become expressive itself gains a poetic function.[19]

There is also the possibility of objectifying the horizon of expectations in works that are historically less sharply delineated. For the specific disposition toward a particular work that the author anticipates from the audience can also be arrived at, even if explicit signals are lacking, through three generally presupposed factors: first, through familiar norms or the immanent poetics of the genre; second, through the implicit relationships to familiar works of the literary-historical surroundings; and third, through the opposition between fiction and reality, between the poetic and the practical function of language, which is always available to the reflective reader during the reading as a possibility of comparison. The third factor includes the possibility that the reader of a new work can perceive it within the narrower horizon of literary expectations, as well as within the wider horizon of experience of life. I shall return to this horizontal structure, and its ability to be objectified by means of the hermeneutics of question and answer, in the discussion of the relationship between literature and lived praxis (see XII).

VIII

Thesis 3. Reconstructed in this way, the horizon of expectations of a work allows one to determine its artistic character by the kind and the degree of its influence on a presupposed audience.

[15]Here I can refer to my study, "Theory of Genres and Medieval Literature," Ch. 3 in this volume. [Au.] "This volume" is *Toward an Aesthetic of Reception.* [Ed.]

[16]According to the interpretation of H. J. Neuschäfer, "Der Sinn der Parodie im Don Quijote," *Studia Romanica* 5 (Heidelberg, 1963). [Au.]

[17]Truth of history. [Ed.]

[18]According to the interpretation of Rainer Warning, "Illusion und Wirklichkeit in *Tristram Shandy* und *Jacques le Fataliste,*" *Theorie und Geschichte der Literature und der schönen Künste* 4 (Munich, 1965), esp. pp. 80 ff. [Au.]

[19]According to the interpretation of Karl Heinz Stierle, "Dunkelheit und Form in Gérard de Nervals 'Chimères,' " *Theorie und Geschichte der Literatur und der schönen Künste* 5 (Munich, 1967), esp. pp. 55 and 91. [Au.]

If one characterizes as aesthetic distance the disparity between the given horizon of expectations and the appearance of a new work, whose reception can result in a "change of horizons" through negation of familiar experiences or through raising newly articulated experiences to the level of consciousness, then this aesthetic distance can be objectified historically along the spectrum of the audience's reactions and criticism's judgment (spontaneous success, rejection or shock, scattered approval, gradual or belated understanding).

The way in which a literary work, at the historical moment of its appearance, satisfies, surpasses, disappoints, or refutes the expectations of its first audience obviously provides a criterion for the determination of its aesthetic value. The distance between the horizon of expectations and the work, between the familiarity of previous aesthetic experience and the "horizontal change"[20] demanded by the reception of the new work, determines the artistic character of a literary work, according to an aesthetics of reception: to the degree that this distance decreases, and no turn toward the horizon of yet-unknown experience is demanded of the receiving consciousness, the closer the work comes to the sphere of "culinary" or entertainment art [*Unterhaltungskunst*].[21] This latter work can be characterized by an aesthetics of reception as not demanding any horizontal change, but rather as precisely fulfilling the expectations prescribed by a ruling standard of taste, in that it satisfies the desire for the reproduction of the familiarly beautiful; confirms familiar sentiments; sanctions wishful notions; makes unusual experiences enjoyable as "sensations"; or even raises moral problems, but only to "solve" them in an edifying manner as predecided questions.[22] If, conversely, the artistic character of a work is to be measured by the aesthetic distance with which it opposes the expectations of its first audience, then it follows that this distance, at first experienced as a pleasing or alienating new perspective, can disappear for later readers, to the extent that the original negativity of the work has become self-evident and has itself entered into the horizon of future aesthetic experience, as a henceforth familiar expectation. The classical character of the so-called masterworks especially belongs to this second horizontal change;[23] their beautiful form that has become self-evident, and their seemingly unquestionable "eternal meaning" bring them, according to an aesthetics of reception, dangerously close to the irresistibly convincing and enjoyable "culinary" art, so that it requires a special effort to read them "against the grain" of the accustomed experience to catch sight of their artistic character once again (see section X).

The relationship between literature and audience includes more than the facts that every work has its own specific, historically and sociologically determinable audience, that every writer is dependent on the milieu, views, and ideology of his audience, and that literary success presupposes a book "which expresses what the group expects, a book which presents the group with its own image."[24] This objectivist determination of

[20]On this Husserlian concept, see Buck, *Lernen und Erfahrung*, pp. 64 ff. [Au.]

[21]"Culinary" art refers to popular literature that the public "eats up." [Ed.]

[22]Here I am incorporating results of the discussion of "kitsch," as a borderline phenomenon of the aesthetic, which took place during the third colloquium of the research group "Poetik und Hermeneutik" (now in the volume *Die nicht mehr schönen Künste — Grenzphänomene des Ästhetischen*, ed. H. R. Jauss [Munich, 1968]). For the "culinary" approach, which presupposes mere entertainment art, the same thing holds as for kitsch, namely, that here the "demands of the consumers are *a priori* satisfied" (P. Beylin), that "the fulfilled expectation becomes the norm of the product" (Wolfgang Iser), or that "its work, without having or solving a problem, presents the appearance of a solution to a problem" (M. Imdahl), pp. 651–67. [Au.]

[23]As also the epigonal; on this, see Boris Tomashevsky, in *Théorie de la littérature. Textes des formalistes russes*, ed. T. Todorov (Paris, 1965), p. 306, n. 53: "The appearance of a genius always equals a literary revolution which dethrones the dominant canon and gives power to processes subordinated until then. . . . The epigones repeat a worn-out combination of processes, and as original and revolutionary as it was, this combination becomes stereotypical and traditional. Thus the epigones kill, sometimes for a long time, the aptitude of their contemporaries to sense the aesthetic force of the examples they imitate: they discredit their masters." [Au.]

[24]R. Escarpit, *Das Buch und der Leser: Entwurf einer Literatursoziologie* (Cologne and Opladen, 1961; first, expanded German edition of *Sociologie de la littérature* [Paris, 1958]), p. 116. [Au.]

literary success according to the congruence of the work's intention with the expectations of a social group always leads literary sociology into a dilemma whenever later or ongoing influence is to be explained. Thus R. Escarpit wants to presuppose a "collective basis in space or time" for the "illusion of the lasting quality" of a writer, which in the case of Molière leads to an astonishing prognosis: "Molière is still young for the Frenchman of the twentieth century because his world still lives, and a sphere of culture, views, and language still binds us to him. . . . But the sphere becomes ever smaller, and Molière will age and die when the things which our culture still has in common with the France of Molière die" (p. 117). As if Molière had only mirrored the "mores of his time" and had only remained successful through this supposed intention! Where the congruence between work and social group does not exist, or no longer exists, as for example with the reception of a work in a foreign language, Escarpit is able to help himself by inserting a "myth" in between: "myths that are invented by a later world for which the reality that they substitute for has become alien" (p. 111). As if all reception beyond the first, socially determined audience for a work were only a "distorted echo," only a result of "subjective myths," and did not itself have its objective a priori once again in the received work as the limit and possibility of later understanding! The sociology of literature does not view its object dialectically enough when it determines the circle of author, work, and audience so one-sidedly.[25] The determination is reversible: there are works that at the moment of their appearance are not yet directed at any specific audience, but that break through the familiar horizon of literary expectations so completely that an audience can only gradually develop for them.[26] When, then, the new horizon of expectations has achieved more general currency, the power of the altered aesthetic norm can be demonstrated in that the audience experiences formerly successful works as outmoded, and withdraws its appreciation. Only in view of such horizontal change does the analysis of literary influence achieve the dimension of a literary history of readers,[27] and do the statistical curves of the best-sellers provide historical knowledge.

A literary sensation from the year 1857 may serve as an example. Alongside Flaubert's *Madame Bovary,* which has since become world-famous, appeared his friend Feydeau's *Fanny,* today forgotten. Although Flaubert's novel brought with it a trial for offending public morals, *Madame Bovary* was at first overshadowed by Feydeau's novel: *Fanny* went through thirteen editions in one year, achieving a success the likes of which Paris had not experienced since Chateaubriand's *Atala.* Thematically considered, both novels met the expectations of a new audience that — in Baudelaire's analysis — had foresworn all romanticism, and despised great as well as naive passions equally:[28] they treated a trivial subject, infidelity in a bourgeois and provincial milieu. Both authors understood how to give to the con-

[25]K. H. Bender, "König und Vasall: Untersuchungen zur Chanson de Geste des XII. Jahrhunderts," *Studia Romanica* 13 (Heidelberg, 1967), shows what step is necessary to get beyond this one-sided determination. In this history of the early French epic, the apparent congruence of feudal society and epic ideality is represented as a process that is maintained through a continually changing discrepancy between "reality" and "ideology," that is, between the historical constellations of feudal conflicts and the poetic responses of the epics. [Au.]

[26]The incomparably more promising literary sociology of Erich Auerbach brought these aspects to light in the variety of epoch-making breaks in the relationship between author and reader; for this see the evaluation of Fritz Schalk in his edition of Auerbach's *Gesammelte Aufsätze zur romanischen Philologie* (Bern and Munich, 1967), pp. 11 ff. [Au.]

[27]See Harald Weinrich, "Für eine Literaturgeschichte des Lesers," *Merkur* 21 (November, 1967), an attempt arising from the same intent as mine, which, analogously to the way that the linguistics of the speaker, customary earlier, has been replaced by the linguistics of the listener, argues for a methodological consideration of the perspective of the reader in literary history and thereby most happily supports my aims. Weinrich shows above all how the empirical methods of literary sociology can be supplemented by the linguistic and literary interpretation of the role of the reader implicit in the work. [Au.]

[28]In "*Madame Bovary* par Gustave Flaubert," Baudelaire, *Oeuvres complètes,* Pléiade ed. (Paris, 1951), p. 998: "The last years of Louise-Philippe witnessed the last explosions of a spirit still excitable by the play of the imagination; but the new novelist found himself faced with a completely worn-out society — worse than worn-out — stupefied and gluttonous, with a horror only of fiction, and love only for possession." [Au.]

ventional, ossified triangular relationship a sensational twist that went beyond the expected details of the erotic scenes. They put the worn-out theme of jealousy in a new light by reversing the expected relationship between the three classic roles: Feydeau has the youthful lover of the *femme de trente ans*[29] become jealous of his lover's husband despite his having already fulfilled his desires, and perishing over this agonizing situation; Flaubert gives the adulteries of the doctor's wife in the provinces — interpreted by Baudelaire as a sublime form of *dandysme* — the surprise ending that precisely the laughable figure of the cuckolded Charles Bovary takes on dignified traits at the end. In the official criticism of the time, one finds voices that reject *Fanny* as well as *Madame Bovary* as a product of the new school of *réalisme,* which they reproach for denying everything ideal and attacking the ideas on which the social order of the Second Empire was founded.[30] The audience's horizon of expectations in 1857, here only vaguely sketched in, which did not expect anything great from the novel after Balzac's death,[31] explains the different success of the two novels only when the question of the effect of their narrative form is posed. Flaubert's formal innovation, his principle of "impersonal narration" (*impassibilité*) — attacked by Barbey d'Aurevilly with the comparison that if a story-telling machine could be cast of English steel it would function no differently than Monsieur Flaubert[32] — must have shocked the same audience that was offered the provocative contents of *Fanny* in the inviting tone of a confessional novel. It could also find incorporated in Feydeau's descriptions the modish ideals and suppressed desires of a stylish level of society,[33] and could delight without restraint in the lascivious central scene in which Fanny (without suspecting that her lover is watching from the balcony) seduces her husband — for the moral indignation was already diminished for them through the reaction of the unhappy witness. As *Madame Bovary,* however, became a worldwide success, when at first it was understood and appreciated as a turning-point in the history of the novel by only a small circle of connoisseurs, the audience of novel-readers that was formed by it came to sanction the new canon of expectations; this canon made Feydeau's weaknesses — his flowery style, his modish effects, his lyrical-confessional cliches — unbearable, and allowed *Fanny* to fade into yesterday's bestseller.

IX

Thesis 4. The reconstruction of the horizon of expectations, in the face of which a work was created and received in the past, enables one on the other hand to pose questions that the text gave an answer to, and thereby to discover how the contemporary reader could have viewed and understood the work. This approach corrects the mostly unrecognized norms of a classicist or modernizing understanding of art, and avoids the circular recourse to a general "spirit of the age." It brings to view the hermeneutic difference between the former and the current understanding of a work; it raises to consciousness the history of its reception, which mediates both positions; and it thereby calls into question as a platonizing dogma of philological metaphysics the apparently self-evident claims that in the literary text, literature [*Dichtung*] is eternally present, and that

[29]Woman in her thirties. [Ed.]

[30]Cf. ibid., p. 999, as well as the accusation, speech for the defense, and verdict of the *Bovary* trial in Flaubert, *Oeuvres,* Pléiade ed. (Paris, 1951), I, pp. 649–717, esp. p. 717; also about *Fanny,* E. Montégut, "Le roman intime de la littérature réaliste," *Revue des deux mondes* 18 (1858), pp. 196–213, esp. pp. 201 and 209 ff. [Au.]

[31]As Baudelaire declares, *Oeuvres complètes,* p. 996: "for since the disappearance of Balzac . . . all curiosity relative to the novel has been pacified and put to rest." [Au.]

[32]For these and other contemporary verdicts see H. R. Jauss, "Die beiden Fassungen von Flauberts *Education sentimentale,*" *Heidelberger Jahrbücher* 2 (1958), pp. 96–116, esp. p. 97. [Au.]

[33]On this, see the excellent analysis by the contemporary critic E. Montégut (see note 30 above), who explains in detail why the dream-world and the figures in Feydeau's novel are typical for the audience in the neighborhoods "between the Bourse and the boulevard Montmartre" (p. 209) that needs an "alcool poétique," enjoys "seeing their vulgar adventures of yesterday and their vulgar projects of tomorrow poeticized" (p. 210), and subscribes to an "idolatry of the material," by which Montégut understands the ingredients of the "dream factory" of 1858 — "a sort of sanctimonious admiration, almost devout, for furniture, wallpaper, dress, escapes like a perfume of patchouli from each of its pages" (p. 201). [Au.]

its objective meaning, determined once and for all, is at all times immediately accessible to the interpreter.

The method of historical reception[34] is indispensable for the understanding of literature from the distant past. When the author of a work is unknown, his intent undeclared, and his relationship to sources and models only indirectly accessible, the philological question of how the text is "properly" — that is, "from its intention and time" — to be understood can best be answered if one foregrounds it against those works that the author explicitly or implicitly presupposed his contemporary audience to know. The creator of the oldest branches of the *Roman de Renart,*[35] for example, assumes — as his prologue testifies — that his listeners know romances like the story of Troy and *Tristan,* heroic epics (*chansons de geste*), and verse fables (*fabliaux*), and that they are therefore curious about the "unprecedented war between the two barons, Renart and Ysengrin," which is to overshadow everything already known. The works and genres that are evoked are then all ironically touched on in the course of the narrative. From this horizontal change one can probably also explain the public success, reaching far beyond France, of this rapidly famous work that for the first time took a position opposed to all the long-reigning heroic and courtly poetry.[36]

Philological research long misunderstood the originally satiric intention of the medieval *Reineke Fuchs* and, along with it, the ironic-didactic meaning of the analogy between animal and human natures, because ever since Jacob Grimm it had remained trapped within the romantic notion of pure nature poetry and naive animal tales. Thus, to give yet a second example of modernizing norms, one could also rightly reproach French research into the epic since Bédier for living — unconsciously — by the criteria of Boileau's poetics, and judging a nonclassical literature by the norms of simplicity, harmony of part and whole, probability, and still others.[37] The philological-critical method is obviously not protected by its historical objectivism from the interpreter who, supposedly bracketing himself, nonetheless raises his own aesthetic preconceptions to an unacknowledged norm and unreflectively modernizes the meaning of the past text. Whoever believes that the "timelessly true" meaning of a literary work must immediately, and simply through one's mere absorption in the text, disclose itself to the interpreter as if he had a standpoint outside of history and beyond all "errors" of his predecessors and of the historical reception — whoever believes this "conceals the involvement of the historical consciousness itself in the history of influence." He denies "those presuppositions — certainly not arbitrary but rather fundamental — that govern his own understanding," and can only feign an objectivity "that in truth depends upon the legitimacy of the questions asked."[38]

In *Truth and Method* Hans-Georg Gadamer, whose critique of historical objectivism I am assuming here, described the principle of the history of influence, which seeks to present the reality of history in understanding itself,[39] as an application of the logic of question and answer to the historical tradition. In a continuation of

[34]Examples of this method, which not only follow the success, fame, and influence of a writer through history but also examine the historical conditions and changes in understanding him, are rare. The following should be mentioned: G. F. Ford, *Dickens and His Readers* (Princeton, 1955); A. Nisin, *Les Oeuvres et les siècles* (Paris, 1960), which discusses "Virgile, Dante et nous," Ronsard, Corneille, Racine; E. Lämmert, "Zur Wirkungsgeschichte Eichendorffs in Deutschland," *Festschrift für Richard Alewyn,* ed. H. Singer and B. von Wiese (Cologne and Graz, 1967). The methodological problem of the step from the influence to the reception of a work was indicated most sharply by F. Vodička already in 1941 in his study "Die Problematik der Rezeption von Nerudas Werk" (now in *Struktur vývoje,* Prague, 1969) with the question of the changes in the work that are realized in its successive aesthetic perceptions. [Au.]

[35]Medieval French collection of beast-fables centering on Renart (the fox) and Ysengrin (the wolf). [Ed.]

[36]See H. R. Jauss, *Untersuchungen zur mittelalterlichen Tierdichtung* (Tübingen, 1959), esp. chap. IV A and D. [Au.]

[37]A. Vinaver, "A la recherche d'une poétique médiévale," *Cahiers de civilisation médiévale* 2 (1959), 1–16. [Au.]

[38]Hans-Georg Gadamer, *Wahrheit und Methode — Grundzüge einer philosophischen Hermeneutik* (Tübingen, 1960), pp. 284–85; English edition as *Truth and Method: Fundamentals of a Philosophical Hermeneutics* (New York, 1975), p. 268. [Au.] See Gadamer, p. 671. [Ed.]

[39]Ibid., p. 283; Eng., p. 267. [Au.]

Collingwood's thesis that "one can understand a text only when one has understood the question to which it is an answer,"[40] Gadamer demonstrates that the reconstructed question can no longer stand within its original horizon because this historical horizon is always already enveloped within the horizon of the present: "Understanding is always the process of the fusion of these horizons that we suppose to exist by themselves."[41] The historical question cannot exist for itself; it must merge with the question "that the tradition is for us."[42] One thereby solves the question with which René Wellek described the aporia[43] of literary judgment: should the philologist evaluate a literary work according to the perspective of the past, the standpoint of the present, or the "verdict of the ages"?[44] The actual standards of a past could be so narrow that their use would only make poorer a work that in the history of its influence had unfolded a rich semantic potential. The aesthetic judgment of the present would favor a canon of works that correspond to modern taste, but would unjustly evaluate all other works only because their function in their time is no longer evident. And the history of influence itself, as instructive as it might be, is an "authority open to the same objections as the authority of the author's contemporaries."[45] Wellek's conclusion — that there is no possibility of avoiding our own judgment; one must only make this judgment as objective as possible in that one does what every scholar does, namely, "isolate the object"[46] — is no solution to the aporia, but rather a relapse into objectivism. The "verdict of the ages" on a literary work is more than merely "the accumulated judgment of other readers, critics, viewers, and even professors";[47] it is the successive unfolding of the potential for meaning that is embedded in a work and actualized in the stages of its historical reception as it discloses itself to understanding judgment, so long as this faculty achieves in a controlled fashion the "fusion of horizons" in the encounter with the tradition.

The agreement between my attempt to establish a possible literary history on the basis of an aesthetics of reception and H.-G. Gadamer's principle of the history of influence nonetheless reaches its limit where Gadamer would like to elevate the concept of the classical to the status of prototype for all historical mediation of past with present. His definition, that "what we call 'classical' does not first require the overcoming of historical distance — for in its own constant mediation it achieves this overcoming,"[48] falls out of the relationship of question and answer that is constitutive of all historical tradition. If classical is "what says something to the present as if it were actually said to it,"[49] then for the classical text one would not first seek the question to which it gives an answer. Doesn't the classical, which "signifies itself and interprets itself,"[50] merely describe the result of what I called the "second horizontal change": the unquestioned, self-evident character of the so-called "masterwork," which conceals its original negativity within the retrospective horizon of an exemplary tradition, and which necessitates our regaining the "right horizon of questioning" once again in the face of the confirmed classicism? Even with the classical work, the receiving consciousness is not relieved of the task of recognizing the "tensional relationship between the text and the present."[51] The concept of the classical that interprets itself, taken over from Hegel, must lead to a reversal of the historical relationship of question and answer,[52] and contradicts the principle of the history of influence that understanding is "not merely a reproductive, but always a productive attitude as well."[53]

[40]Ibid., p. 352; Eng., p. 333. [Au.]
[41]Ibid., p. 289; Eng., p. 273. [Au.]
[42]Ibid., p. 356; Eng., p. 337. [Au.]
[43]Intractable paradox. [Ed.]
[44]Wellek, 1936, p. 184; ibid., 1963, pp. 17–20. [Au.]
[45]Ibid., p. 17. [Au.]
[46]Ibid. [Au.]
[47]Ibid. [Au.]

[48]*Wahrheit und Methode*, p. 274; Eng., p. 257. [Au.]
[49]Ibid. [Au.]
[50]Ibid. [Au.]
[51]Ibid., p. 290; Eng., p. 273. [Au.]
[52]This reversal becomes obvious in the chapter "Die Logik von Frage und Antwort" (ibid., pp. 351–60; Eng., pp. 333–41); see my "History of Art and Pragmatic History," § VII, included in this volume. [Au.]
[53]Ibid., p. 280; Eng., p. 264. [Au.] For another critique of Gadamer's valorization of the "classical," see Barbara Herrnstein Smith in Ch. 9. [Ed.]

This contradiction is evidently conditioned by Gadamer's holding fast to a concept of classical art that is not capable of serving as a general foundation for an aesthetics of reception beyond the period of its origination, namely, that of humanism. It is the concept of *mimesis,* understood as "recognition," as Gadamer demonstrates in his ontological explanation of the experience of art: "What one actually experiences in a work of art and what one is directed toward is rather how true it is, that is, to what extent one knows and recognizes something and oneself."[54] This concept of art can be validated for the humanist period of art, but not for its preceding medieval period and not at all for its succeeding period of our modernity, in which the aesthetics of mimesis has lost its obligatory character, along with the substantialist metaphysics ("knowledge of essence") that founded it. The epistemological significance of art does not, however, come to an end with this period-change, whence it becomes evident that art was in no way bound to the classical function of recognition.[55] The work of art can also mediate knowledge that does not fit into the Platonic schema if it anticipates paths of future experience, imagines as-yet-untested models of perception and behavior, or contains an answer to newly posed questions.[56] It is precisely concerning this virtual significance and productive function in the process of experience that the history of the influence of literature is abbreviated when one gathers the mediation of past art and the present under the concept of the *classical.* If, according to Gadamer, the classical *itself* is supposed to achieve the overcoming of historical distance through its constant mediation, it must, as a perspective of the hypostatized tradition, displace the insight that classical art at the time of its production did not yet appear "classical": rather, it could open up new ways of seeing things and perform new experiences that only in historical distance — in the recognition of what is now familiar — give rise to the appearance that a timeless truth expresses itself in the work of art.

The influence of even the great literary works of the past can be compared neither with a self-mediating event nor with an emanation: the tradition of art also presupposes a dialogical relationship of the present to the past, according to which the past work can answer and "say something" to us only when the present observer has posed the question that draws it back out of its seclusion. When, in *Truth and Method,* understanding is conceived — analogous to Heidegger's "event of being" [*Seinsgeschehen*] — as "the placing of oneself within a process of tradition in which past and present are constantly mediated,"[57] the "productive moment which lies in understanding"[58] must be shortchanged. This productive function of progressive understanding, which necessarily also includes criticizing the tradition and forgetting it, shall in the following sections establish the basis for the project of a literary history according to an aesthetics of reception. This project must consider the historicity of literature in a threefold manner: diachronically in the interrelationships of the reception of literary works (see X), synchronically in the frame of reference of literature of the same moment, as well as in the sequence of such frames (see XI), and finally in the relationship of the immanent literary development to the general process of history (see XII).

X

Thesis 5. The theory of the aesthetics of reception not only allows one to conceive the meaning and form of a literary work in the historical unfolding of its understanding. It also demands that one insert the individual work into its "literary series" to recognize its historical position and significance in the context of the experience of

[54]Ibid., p. 109; Eng., p. 102. [Au.]

[55]See ibid., p. 110; Eng., p. 103. [Au.]

[56]This also follows from Formalist aesthetics and especially from Viktor Shklovsky's theory of "deautomatization"; cf. Victor Erlich's summary, *Russian Formalism,* p. 76: "As the 'twisted, deliberately impeded form' interposes artificial obstacles between the perceiving subject and the object perceived, the chain of habitual association and of automatic responses is broken: thus, we become able to *see* things instead of merely *recognizing* them." [Au.] See Shklovsky in Ch. 1. [Ed.]

[57]*Wahrheit und Methode,* p. 275; Eng., p. 258. [Au.]

[58]Ibid., p. 280; Eng., p. 264. [Au.]

literature. In the step from a history of the reception of works to an eventful history of literature, the latter manifests itself as a process in which the passive reception is on the part of authors. Put another way, the next work can solve formal and moral problems left behind by the last work, and present new problems in turn.

How can the individual work, which positivistic literary history determined in a chronological series and thereby reduced to the status of a "fact," be brought back into its historical-sequential relationship and thereby once again be understood as an "event"? The theory of the Formalist school, as already mentioned, would solve this problem with its principle of "literary evolution," according to which the new work arises against the background of preceding or competing works, reaches the "high point" of a literary period as a successful form, is quickly reproduced and thereby increasingly automatized, until finally, when the next form has broken through, the former vegetates on as a used-up genre in the quotidian sphere of literature. If one were to analyze and describe a literary period according to this program — which to date has hardly been put into use[59] — one could expect a representation that would in various respects be superior to that of the conventional literary history. Instead of the works standing in closed series, themselves standing one after another and unconnected, at best framed by a sketch of general history — for example, the series of the works of an author, a particular school, or one kind of style, as well as the series of various genres — the Formalist method would relate the series to one another and *discover the evolutionary alternating relationship of functions and forms.*[60] The works that thereby stand out from, correspond to, or replace one another would appear as moments of a process that no longer needs to be construed as tending toward some end point, since as the *dialectical self-production of new forms* it requires no teleology. Seen in this way, the autonomous dynamics of literary evolution would furthermore eliminate the dilemma of the criteria of selection: the criterion here is the work as a new form in the literary series, and not the self-reproduction of worn-out forms, artistic devices, and genres, which pass into the background until at a new moment in the evolution they are made "perceptible" once again. Finally, in the Formalist project of a literary history that understands itself as "evolution" and — contrary to the usual sense of this term — excludes any directional course, the historical character of a work becomes synonymous with literature's historical character: the "evolutionary" significance and characteristics of a literary phenomenon presuppose innovation as the decisive feature, just as a work of art is perceived against the background of other works of art.[61]

The Formalist theory of "literary evolution" is certainly one of the most significant attempts at a renovation of literary history. The recognition that historical changes also occur within a system in the field of literature, the attempted functionalization of literary development, and, not least of all, the theory of automatization — these are achievements that are to be held onto, even if the one-sided canonization of change requires a correction. Criticism has already displayed the weaknesses of the Formalist theory of evolution: mere opposition or aesthetic variation does not suffice to explain the growth of literature; the question of the direction of change of literary forms remains unanswerable; innovation for itself does not alone make up artistic character;

[59]In the 1927 article, "Über literarische Evolution," by Yuri Tynyanov (in *Die literarischen Kunstmittel und die Evolution in der Literatur,* pp. 37–60), this program is most pregnantly presented. It was only partially fulfilled — as Yuri Striedter informed me — in the treatment of problems of structural change in the history of literary genres, as for example in the volume *Russkaja proza,* Voprosy poètiki 8 (Leningrad, 1926), or Y. Tynyanov, "Die Ode als rhetorische Gattung" (1922), now in *Texte der russischen Formalisten,* II, ed. J. Striedter (Munich, 1970). [Au.] See Tynyanov in Ch. 1. [Ed.]

[60]Y. Tynyanov, "Über literarische Evolution," p. 59. [Au.]

[61]"A work of art will appear as a positive value when it regroups the structure of the preceding period, it will appear as a negative value if it takes over the structure without changing it." (Jan Mukařovský, cited by R. Wellek, 1963, pp. 48, 49.) [Au.]

and the connection between literary evolution and social change does not vanish from the face of the earth through its mere negation.[62] My thesis XII responds to the last question; the problematic of the remaining questions demands that the descriptive literary theory of the Formalists be opened up, through an aesthetics of reception, to the dimension of historical experience that must also include the historical standpoint of the present observer, that is, the literary historian.

The description of literary evolution as a ceaseless struggle between the new and the old, or as the alternation of the canonization and automatization of forms reduces the historical character of literature to the one-dimensional actuality of its changes and limits historical understanding to their perception. The alterations in the literary series nonetheless only become a historical sequence when the opposition of the old and new form also allows one to recognize their specific mediation. This mediation, which includes the step from the old to the new form in the interaction of work and recipient (audience, critic, new producer) as well as that of past event and successive reception, can be methodologically grasped in the formal and substantial problem "that each work of art, as the horizon of the 'solutions' which are possible after it, poses and leaves behind."[63] The mere description of the altered structure and the new artistic devices of a work does not necessarily lead to this problem, nor, therefore, back to its function in the historical series. To determine this, that is, to recognize the problem left behind to which the new work in the historical series is the answer, the interpreter must bring his own experience into play, since the past horizon of old and new forms, problems and solutions, is only recognizable in its further mediation, within the present horizon of the received work. Literary history as "literary evolution" presupposes the historical process of aesthetic reception and production up to the observer's present as the condition for the mediation of all formal oppositions or "differential qualities" ["*Differenzqualitäten*"].[64]

Founding "literary evolution" on an aesthetics of reception thus not only returns its lost direction insofar as the standpoint of the literary historian becomes the vanishing point — but not the goal! — of the process. It also opens to view the temporal depths of literary experience, in that it allows one to recognize the variable distance between the actual and the virtual significance of a literary work. This means that the artistic character of a work, whose semantic potential Formalism reduces to innovation as the single criterion of value, must in no way always be immediately perceptible within the horizon of its first appearance, let alone that it could then also already be exhausted in the pure opposition between the old and the new form. The distance between the actual first perception of a work and its virtual significance, or, put another way, the resistance that the new work poses to the expectations of its first audience, can be so great that it requires a long process of reception to gather in that which was unexpected and unusable within the first horizon. It can thereby happen that a virtual significance of the work remains long unrecognized until the "literary evolution," through the actualization of a newer form, reaches the horizon that now for the first time allows one to find access to the understanding of the misunderstood older form. Thus the obscure lyrics of Mallarmé and his school prepared the ground for the return to baroque poetry, long since unappreciated and therefore forgotten, and in particular for the philological reinterpretation and "rebirth" of Góngora. One can line up the examples of how a new literary form can reopen access to forgotten literature. These include the so-called "renaissances" — so called, because the word's meaning gives rise to the appearance of an automatic return, and often prevents one from recognizing

[62]See. V. Erlich, *Russian Formalism*, pp. 254–57, R. Wellek, 1963, pp. 48 ff., and J. Striedter, *Texte der russischen Formalisten*, I, Introduction, § X. [Au.]

[63]Hans Blumenberg, in *Poetik und Hermeneutik* 3 (see note 22), p. 692. [Au.]

[64]According to V. Erlich, *Russian Formalism*, p. 252, this concept meant three things to the Formalists: "on the level of the representation of reality, *Differenzqualität* stood for the 'divergence' from the actual, i.e., for creative deformation. On the level of language it meant a departure from current linguistic usage. Finally, on the plane of literary dynamics, a . . . modification of the prevailing artistic norm." [Au.]

that literary tradition can not transmit itself alone. That is, a literary past can return only when a new reception draws it back into the present, whether an altered aesthetic attitude willfully reaches back to reappropriate the past, or an unexpected light falls back on forgotten literature from the new moment of literary evolution, allowing something to be found that one previously could not have sought in it.[65]

The new is thus not only an *aesthetic* category. It is not absorbed into the factors of innovation, surprise, surpassing, rearrangement, or alienation, to which the Formalist theory assigned exclusive importance. The new also becomes a *historical* category when the diachronic analysis of literature is pushed further to ask which historical moments are really the ones that first make new that which is new in a literary phenomenon; to what degree this new element is already perceptible in the historical instant of its emergence; which distance, path, or detour of understanding was required for its realization in content; and whether the moment of its full actualization was so influential that it could alter the perspective on the old, and thereby the canonization of the literary past.[66] How the relationship of poetic theory to aesthetically productive praxis is represented in this light has already been discussed in another context.[67] The possibilities of the interaction between production and reception in the historical change of aesthetic attitudes are admittedly far from exhausted by these remarks. Here they should above all illustrate the dimension into which a diachronic view of literature leads when it would no longer be satisfied to consider a chronological series of literary facts as already the historical appearance of literature.

XI

Thesis 6. The achievements made in linguistics through the distinction and methodological interrelation of diachronic and synchronic analysis are the occasion for overcoming the diachronic perspective — previously the only one practiced — in literary history as well. If the perspective of the history of reception always bumps up against the functional connections between the understanding of new works and the significance of older ones when changes in aesthetic attitudes are considered, it must also be possible to take a synchronic cross-section of a moment in the development, to arrange the heterogeneous multiplicity of contemporaneous works in equivalent, opposing, and hierarchical structures, and thereby to discover an overarching system of relationships in the literature of a historical moment. From this the principle of representation of a new literary history could be developed, if further cross-sections diachronically before and after were so arranged as to articulate historically the change in literary structures in its epochmaking moments.

Siegfried Kracauer has most decisively questioned the primacy of the diachronic perspective in historiography. His study "Time and History"[68] disputes the claim of "General History" to render comprehensible events from all spheres of life within a homogeneous medium of chronological time as a unified process, consistent in each historical moment. This understanding of history, still standing under the influence of Hegel's concept of the "objective spirit," presupposes that everything that happens contemporaneously is equally informed by the significance

[65]For the first possibility the (antiromantic) reevaluation of Boileau and of the classical *contrainte* poetics by Gide and Valéry can be introduced; for the second, the belated discovery of Hölderlin's hymns or Novalis's concept of future poetry (on the latter see H. R. Jauss in *Romanische Forschungen* 77 [1965], pp. 174–83). [Au.]

[66]Thus, since the reception of the "minor romantic" Nerval, whose *Chimères* only attracted attention under the influence of Mallarmé, the canonized "major romantics" Lamartine, Vigny, Musset, and a large part of the "rhetorical" lyrics of Victor Hugo have been increasingly forced into the background. [Au.]

[67]*Poetik und Hermeneutik* 2 (*Immanente Ästhetik — Ästhetische Reflexion*), ed. W. Iser (Munich, 1966), esp. pp. 395–418. [Au.]

[68]In *Zeugnisse — Theodor W. Adorno zum 60.* Geburtstag (Frankfurt a.M., 1963), pp. 50–64, and also in "General History and the Aesthetic Approach," *Poetik und Hermeneutik* 3. See also *History: The Last Things Before the Last* (New York, 1969), esp. chap. 6: "Ahasverus, or the Riddle of Time," pp. 139–63. [Au.]

of this moment, and it thereby conceals the actual noncontemporaneity of the contemporaneous.[69] For the multiplicity of events of one historical moment, which the universal historian believes can be understood as exponents of a unified content, are de facto moments of entirely different time-curves, conditioned by the laws of their "special history,"[70] as becomes immediately evident in the discrepancies of the various "histories" of the arts, law, economics, politics, and so forth: "The shaped times of the diverse areas overshadow the uniform flow of time. Any historical period must therefore be imagined as a mixture of events which emerge at different moments of their own time."[71]

It is not in question here whether this state of affairs presupposes a primary inconsistency to history, so that the consistency of general history always only arises retrospectively from the unifying viewpoint and representation of the historian; or whether the radical doubt concerning "historical reason," which Kracauer extends from the pluralism of chronological and morphological courses of time to the fundamental antinomy of the general and the particular in history, in fact proves that universal history is philosophically illegitimate today. For the sphere of literature in any case, one can say that Kracauer's insights into the "coexistence of the contemporaneous and non-contemporaneous,"[72] far from leading historical knowledge into an aporia, rather make apparent the necessity and possibility of discovering the historical dimension of literary phenomena in synchronic cross-sections. For it follows from these insights that the chronological fiction of the moment that informs all contemporaneous phenomena corresponds as little to the historicity of literature as does the morphological fiction of a homogeneous literary series, in which all phenomena in their sequential order only follow immanent laws. The purely diachronic perspective, however conclusively it might explain changes in, for example, the histories of genres according to the immanent logic of innovation and automatization, problem and solution, nonetheless only arrives at the properly historical dimension when it breaks through the morphological canon, to confront the work that is important in historical influence with the historically worn-out, conventional works of the genre, and at the same time does not ignore its relationship to the literary milieu in which it had to make its way alongside works of other genres.

The historicity of literature comes to light at the intersections of diachrony and synchrony. Thus it must also be possible to make the literary horizon of a specific historical moment comprehensible as that synchronic system in relation to which literature that appears contemporaneously could be received diachronically in relations of noncontemporaneity, and the work could be received as current or not, as modish, outdated, or perennial, as premature or belated.[73] For if, from the point of view of an aesthetics of production, literature that appears contemporaneously breaks down into a heterogeneous multiplicity of the noncontemporaneous, that is, of works informed by the various moments of the "shaped time" of their genre (as the seemingly present heavenly

[69]"First, in identifying history as a process in chronological time, we tacitly assume that our knowledge of the moment at which an event emerges from the flow of time will help us to account for its appearance. The date of the event is a value-laden fact. Accordingly, all events in the history of a people, a nation, or a civilization that take place at a given moment are supposed to occur then and there for reasons bound up, somehow, with that moment" (Kracauer, *History,* p. 141). [Au.]

[70]This concept goes back to H. Foccillon, *The Life of Forms in Art* (New York, 1948), and G. Kubler, *The Shape of Time: Remarks on the History of Things* (New Haven, 1962). [Au.]

[71]Kracauer, *History,* p. 53. [Au.]

[72]*Poetik und Hermeneutik* 3, p. 569. The formula of "the contemporaneity of the different," with which F. Sengle, "Aufgaben der heutigen Literaturgeschichtsschreibung," 1964, pp. 247 ff., refers to the same phenomenon, fails to grasp one dimension of the problem which becomes evident in his belief that this difficulty of literary history can be solved by simply combining comparative methods and modern interpretation ("that is, carrying out comparative interpretation on a broader basis," p. 249). [Au.]

[73]In 1960 Roman Jakobson also made this claim in a lecture that now constitutes chap. 11, "Linguistique et poétique," of his book, *Essais de linguistique générale* (Paris, 1963). Cf. p. 212: "Synchronic description envisages not only the literary production of a given period, but also that part of the literary tradition which has remained alive or been resuscitated in the period in question. . . . Historical poetics, exactly like the history of language, if it wants to be truly comprehensive, ought to be conceived as a superstructure built upon a series of successive synchronic descriptions." [Au.]

constellations move apart astronomically into points of the most different temporal distance), this multiplicity of literary phenomena nonetheless, when seen from the point of view of an aesthetics of reception, coalesces again for the audience that perceives them and relates them to one another as works of *its* present, in the unity of a common horizon of literary expectations, memories, and anticipations that establishes their significance.

Since each synchronic system must contain its past and its future as inseparable structural elements,[74] the synchronic cross-section of the literary production of a historical point in time necessarily implies further cross-sections that are diachronically before and after. Analogous to the history of language, constant and variable factors are thereby brought to light that can be localized as functions of a system. For literature as well is a kind of grammar or syntax, with relatively fixed relations of its own: the arrangement of the traditional and the uncanonized genres; modes of expression, kinds of style, and rhetorical figures; contrasted with this arrangement is the much more variable realm of a semantics: the literary subjects, archetypes, symbols, and metaphors. One can therefore seek to erect for literary history an analogy to that which Hans Blumenberg has postulated for the history of philosophy, elucidating it through examples of the change in periods and, in particular, the successional relationship of Christian theology and philosophy, and grounding it in his historical logic of question and answer: a "formal system of the explanation of the world . . . , within which structure the reshufflings can be localized which make up the process-like character of history up to the radicality of period-changes."[75] Once the substantialist notion of a self-reproducing literary tradition has been overcome through a functional explanation of the processlike relationships of production and reception, it must also be possible to recognize behind the *transformation* of literary forms and contents those *reshufflings* in a literary system of world-understanding that make the horizontal change in the process of aesthetic experience comprehensible.

From these premises one could develop the principle of representation of a literary history that would neither have to follow the all too familiar high road of the traditional great books, nor have to lose itself in the lowlands of the sumtotal of all texts that can no longer be historically articulated. The problem of selecting that which is important for a new history of literature can be solved with the help of the synchronic perspective in a manner that has not yet been attempted: a horizontal change in the historical process of "literary evolution" need not be pursued only throughout the web of all the diachronic facts and filiations, but can also be established in the altered remains of the synchronic literary system and read out of further cross-sectional analyses. In principle, a representation of literature in the historical succession of such systems would be possible through a series of arbitrary points of intersection between diachrony and synchrony. The historical dimension of literature, its eventful continuity that is lost in traditionalism as in positivism, can meanwhile be recovered only if the literary historian finds points of intersection and brings works to light that articulate the processlike character of "literary evolution" in its moments formative of history as well as its caesurae between periods. But neither statistics nor the subjective willfulness of the literary historian decides on this historical articulation, but rather the history of influence: that "which results from the event" and which from the perspective of the present constitutes the coherence of literature as the prehistory of its present manifestation.

XII

Thesis 7. The task of literary history is thus only completed when literary production is not only represented synchronically and diachronically in the succession of its systems, but also seen as

[74]Yuri Tynyanov and Roman Jakobson, "Probleme der Literatur- und Sprachforschung" (1928), now in *Kursbuch* 5 (Frankfurt a.M., 1966), p. 75: "The history of the system itself represents another system. Pure synchrony now proves to be illusory: each synchronic system has its past and its future as inseparable structural elements of this system." [Au.]

[75]First in "Epochenschwelle und Rezeption," *Philosophische Rundschau* 6 (1958), pp. 101 ff., most recently in *Die Legitimatät der Neuzeit* (Frankfurt a.M., 1966); see esp. pp. 41 ff. [Au.]

"special history" in its own unique relationship to "general history." This relationship does not end with the fact that a typified, idealized, satiric, or utopian image of social existence can be found in the literature of all times. The social function of literature manifests itself in its genuine possibility only where the literary experience of the reader enters into the horizon of expectations of his lived praxis, preforms his understanding of the world, and thereby also has an effect on his social behavior.

The functional connection between literature and society is for the most part demonstrated in traditional literary sociology within the narrow boundaries of a method that has only superficially replaced the classical principle of *imitatio naturae* with the determination that literature is the representation of a pregiven reality, which therefore must elevate a concept of style conditioned by a particular period — the "realism" of the nineteenth century — to the status of the literary category par excellence. But even the literary "structuralism" now fashionable,[76] which appeals, often with dubious justification, to the archetypal criticism of Northrop Frye or to the structural anthropology of Claude Lévi-Strauss,[77] still remains quite dependent on this basically classicist aesthetics of representation with its schematizations of "reflection" [*Wiederspiegelung*] and "typification." By interpreting the findings of linguistic and literary structuralism as archaic anthropological constants disguised in literary myths — which it not infrequently manages only with the help of an obvious allegorization of the text[78] — it reduces on the one hand historical existence to the structures of an original social nature, on the other hand literature to this nature's mythic or symbolic expression. But with this viewpoint, it is precisely the eminently social, i.e., socially *formative* function of literature that is missed. Literary structuralism — as little as the Marxist and Formalist literary studies that came before it — does not inquire as to how literature "itself turns around to help inform . . . the idea of society which it presupposes" and has helped to inform the processlike character of history. With these words, Gerhard Hess formulated in his lecture on "The Image of Society in French Literature" (1954) the unsolved problem of a union of literary history and sociology, and then explained to what extent French literature, in the course of its modern development, could claim for itself to have first discovered certain law-governed characteristics of social existence.[79] To answer the question of the socially formative function of literature according to an aesthetics of reception exceeds the competence of the traditional aesthetics of representation. The attempt to close the gap between literary-historical and sociological research through the methods of an aesthetics of reception is made easier because the concept of the *horizon of expectations* that I introduced into literary-historical interpretation[80] also has played a role in the axiomatics of the social sciences since Karl Mannheim.[81] It likewise stands in the center of a methodological essay on "Natural Laws and Theoretical Systems" by Karl R. Popper, who would anchor the scientific formation of theory in the prescientific experience of lived praxis. Popper here develops the problem of observation from out of the presupposition of a "horizon of expectations," thereby offering a basis of comparison for my attempt to determine the specific achievement of literature in the general process of the formation of experience, and to delimit it vis-à-vis other forms of social behavior.[82]

[76]N.B. This was composed in 1967. [Tr.]

[77]See Frye, p. 641 and Lévi-Strauss, p. 835. [Ed.]

[78]Lévi-Strauss himself testifies to this involuntarily but extremely impressively in his attempt to "interpret" with the help of his structural method a linguistic description of Baudelaire's poem "Les chats" provided by Roman Jakobson. See *L'Homme* 2 (1962), pp. 5–21; Eng. in *Structuralism,* ed. Jacques Ehrmann (Garden City, N.Y., 1971), a reprint of *Yale French Studies,* nos. 36–37 (1966). [Au.]

[79]Now in *Gesellschaft — Literatur — Wissenschaft: Gesammelte Schriften 1938*–1966. eds. H. R. Jauss and C. Müller-Daehn (Munich, 1967), pp. 1–13, esp. pp. 2 and 4. [Au.]

[80]First in *Untersuchungen zur mittelalterlichen Tierdichtung,* see pp. 153, 180, 225, 271; further in *Archiv für das Studium der neueren Sprachen* 197 (1961), pp. 223–25. [Au.]

[81]Karl Mannheim, *Mensch und Gesellschaft in Zeitalter des Umbaus* (Darmstadt, 1958), pp. 212 ff. [Au.]

[82]In *Theorie und Realität,* ed. H. Albert (Tübingen, 1964), pp. 87–102. [Au.]

According to Popper, progress in science has in common with prescientific experience the fact that each hypothesis, like each observation, always presupposes expectations, "namely those that constitute the horizon of expectations which first makes those observations significant and thereby grants them the status of observations."[83] For progress in science as for that in the experience of life, the most important moment is the "disappointment of expectations": "It resembles the experience of a blind person, who runs into an obstacle and thereby experiences its existence. Through the falsification of our assumptions we actually make contact with 'reality.' The refutation of our errors is the positive experience that we gain from reality."[84] This model certainly does not sufficiently explain the process of the scientific formation of theory,[85] and yet it can well illustrate the "productive meaning of negative experience" in lived praxis,[86] as well as shed a clearer light upon the specific function of literature in social existence. For the reader is privileged above the (hypothetical) nonreader because the reader — to stay with Popper's image — does not first have to bump into a new obstacle to gain a new experience of reality. The experience of reading can liberate one from adaptations, prejudices, and predicaments of a lived praxis in that it compels one to a new perception of things. The horizon of expectations of literature distinguishes itself before the horizon of expectations of historical lived praxis in that it not only preserves actual experiences, but also anticipates unrealized possibility, broadens the limited space of social behavior for new desires, claims, and goals, and thereby opens paths of future experience.

The pre-orientation of our experience through the creative capability of literature rests not only on its artistic character, which by virtue of a new form helps one to break through the automatism of everyday perception. The new form of art is not only "perceived against the background of other art works and through association with them." In this famous sentence, which belongs to the core of the Formalist credo,[87] Victor Shklovsky remains correct only insofar as he turns against the prejudice of classicist aesthetics that defines the beautiful as *harmony of form and content* and accordingly reduces the new form to the secondary function of giving shape to a pregiven content. The new form, however, does not appear just "in order to relieve the old form that already is no longer artistic." It also can make possible a new perception of things by preforming the content of a new experience first brought to light in the form of literature. The relationship between literature and reader can actualize itself in the sensorial realm as an incitement to aesthetic perception as well as in the ethical realm as

[83]Ibid., p. 91. [Au.]

[84]Ibid., p. 102. [Au.]

[85]Popper's example of the blind man does not distinguish between the two possibilities of a merely reactive behavior and an experimenting mode of action under specific hypotheses. If the second possibility characterizes reflected scientific behavior in distinction to the unreflected behavior in lived praxis, the researcher would be "creative" on his part, and thus to be placed above the "blind man" and more appropriately compared with the writer as a creator of new expectations. [Au.]

[86]G. Buck, *Lernen und Erfahrung,* pp. 70 ff. "[Negative experience] has its instructive effect not only by causing us to revise the context of our subsequent experience so that the new fits into the corrected unity of an objective meaning. . . . Not only is the object of the experience differently represented, but the experiencing consciousness itself reverses itself. The work of negative experience is one of becoming conscious of oneself. What one becomes conscious of are the motifs which have been guiding experience and which have remained unquestioned in this guiding function. Negative experience thus has primarily the character of self-experience, which frees one for a qualitatively new kind of experience." From these premises Buck developed the concept of a hermeneutics, which, as a "relationship of lived praxis that is guided by the highest interest of lived praxis — the agent's self-information," legitimizes the specific experience of the so-called humanities [*Geisteswissenschaften*] in contrast to the empiricism of the natural sciences. See his "Bildung durch Wissenschaft," in *Wissenschaft, Bildung und pädagogische Wirklichkeit* (Heidenheim, 1969), p. 24. [Au.]

[87]Yuri Striedter has pointed out that in the diaries and examples from the prose of Leo Tolstoy to which Shklovsky referred in his first explanation of the procedure of "alienation," the purely aesthetic aspect was still bound up with an epistemological and ethical aspect. "Shklovsky was interested — in contrast to Tolstoy — above all in the artistic 'procedure' and not in the question of its ethical presuppositions and effects." (*Poetik und Hermeneutik* 2 [see note 67], pp. 288 ff.) [Au.] See Shklovsky in Ch. 1. [Ed.]

a summons to moral reflection.[88] The new literary work is received and judged against the background of other works of art as well as against the background of the everyday experience of life. Its social function in the ethical realm is to be grasped according to an aesthetics of reception in the same modalities of question and answer, problem and solution, under which it enters into the horizon of its historical influence.

How a new aesthetic form can have moral consequences at the same time, or, put another way, how it can have the greatest conceivable impact on a moral question, is demonstrated in an impressive manner by the case of *Madame Bovary,* as reflected in the trial that was instituted against the author Flaubert after the prepublication of the work in the *Révue de Paris* in 1857. The new literary form that compelled Flaubert's audience to an unfamiliar perception of the "well-thumbed fable" was the principle of impersonal (or uninvolved) narration, in conjunction with the artistic device of the so-called *style indirect libre,*[89] handled by Flaubert like a virtuoso and in a perspectively consequential manner. What is meant by this can be made clear with a quotation from the book, a description that the prosecuting attorney Pinard accused in his indictment as being immoral in the highest degree. In the novel it follows upon Emma's first "false step" and relates how she catches sight of herself in the mirror after her adultery:

> Seeing herself in the mirror she wondered at her face. Never had her eyes been so large, so black, or so deep. Something subtle spread about her being transfigured her.
>
> She repeated: "I have a lover! a lover!", delighting at the idea as at that of a second puberty that had come to her. So at last she was going to possess those joys of love, that fever of happiness of which she had despaired. She was entering upon something marvelous where all would be passion, ecstasy, delirium.

The prosecuting attorney took the last sentences for an objective depiction that included the judgment of the narrator and was upset over the "glorification of adultery" which he held to be even much more dangerous and immoral than the false step itself.[90] Yet Flaubert's accuser thereby succumbed to an error, as the defense immediately demonstrated. For the incriminating sentences are not any objective statement of the narrator's to which the reader can attribute belief, but rather a subjective opinion of the character, who is thereby to be characterized in her feelings that are formed according to novels. The artistic device consists in bringing forth a mostly inward discourse of the represented character without the signals of direct discourse ("So I am at last going to possess") or indirect discourse ("She said to herself that she was therefore at last going to possess"), with the effect that the reader himself has to decide whether he should take the sentence for a true declaration or understand it as an opinion characteristic of this character. Indeed, Emma Bovary is "judged, simply through a plain description of her existence, out of her own feelings."[91] This result of a modern stylistic analysis agrees exactly with the counterargument of the defense attorney Sénard, who emphasized that the disillusion began for Emma already from the second day onward: "The dénouement for morality is found in each line of the book"[92] (only that Sénard himself could not yet name the artistic device that was not yet recorded at this time!). The consternating effect of the formal innovations of Flaubert's narrative style became evident in the trial: the impersonal form of narration not only compelled his readers to perceive things differently — "photographically exact," according to the judgment of the time — but at the same time thrust them into an alienating uncertainty of judgment. Since the new artistic device broke through an old novelistic convention — the moral judgment of the represented characters that

[88]Flaubert, *Oeuvres,* I, p. 657: "Thus, as early as this first mistake, as early as this first fall, she glorified adultery, its poetry, its voluptuousness. Voilà, gentlemen, that for me is much more dangerous, much more immoral than the fall itself!" [Au.]

[89]The English term is "free indirect discourse." [Ed.]

[90]Erich Auerbach, *Mimesis: Dargestellte Wirklichkeit in der abendländischen Literatur* (Bern, 1946), p. 430; Eng., *Mimesis: The Representation of Reality in Western Literature,* trans. Willard R. Trask (Princeton, 1953), p. 485. [Au.]

[91]Flaubert, *Oeuvres,* I, p. 673. [Au.]

[92]Ibid., p. 670. [Au.]

is always unequivocal and confirmed in the description — the novel was able to radicalize or to raise new questions of lived praxis, which during the proceedings caused the original occasion for the accusation — alleged lasciviousness — to recede wholly into the background. The question with which the defense went on its counterattack turned the reproach, that the novel provides nothing other than the "story of a provincial woman's adulteries," against the society: whether, then, the subtitle to *Madame Bovary* must not more properly read, "story of the education too often provided in the provinces."[93] But the question with which the prosecuting attorney's *réquisitoire* reaches its peak is nonetheless not yet thereby answered: "Who can condemn that woman in the book? No one. Such is the conclusion. In the book there is not a character who can condemn her. If you find a wise character there, if you find a single principle there by virtue of which the adultery might be stigmatized, I am in error."[94]

If in the novel none of the represented characters could break the staff across Emma Bovary, and if no moral principle can be found valid in whose name she would be condemnable, then is not the ruling "public opinion" and its basis in "religious feeling" at once called into question along with the "principle of marital fidelity"? Before what court could the case of *Madame Bovary* be brought if the formerly valid social norms — public opinion, religious sentiment, public morals, good manners — are no longer sufficient to reach a verdict in this case?[95] These open and implicit questions by no means indicate an aesthetic lack of understanding and moral philistinism on the part of the prosecuting attorney. Rather, it is much more that in them the unsuspected influence of a new art form comes to be expressed, which through a new *manière de voir les choses*[96] was able to jolt the reader of *Madame Bovary* out of the self-evident character of his moral judgment, and turned a predecided question of public morals back into an open problem. In the face of the vexation that Flaubert, thanks to the artistry of his impersonal style, did not offer any handhold with which to ban his novel on grounds of the author's immorality, the court to that extent acted consistently when it acquitted Flaubert as writer, but condemned the literary school that he was supposed to represent, but that in truth was the as yet unrecognized artistic device:

> Whereas it is not permitted, under the pretext of portraying character and local color, to reproduce in their errors the facts, utterances and gestures of the characters whom the author's mission it is to portray; that a like system, applied to works of the spirit as well as to productions of the fine arts, leads to a realism which would be the negation of the beautiful and the good, and which, giving birth to works equally offensive to the eye and to the spirit, would commit continual offences against public morals and good manners.[97]

Thus a literary work with an unfamiliar aesthetic form can break through the expectations of its readers and at the same time confront them with a question, the solution to which remains lacking for them in the religiously or officially sanctioned morals. Instead of further examples, let one only recall here that it was not first Bertolt Brecht, but rather already the Enlightenment that proclaimed the competitive relationship between literature and canonized morals, as Friedrich Schiller not least of all bears witness to when he expressly claims for the bourgeois drama: "The laws of the stage begin where the sphere of worldly laws end."[98] But the literary work can also — and in the history of literature this possibility characterizes the latest period of our modernity — reverse the relationship of question and answer and in the medium of art confront the reader with a new, "opaque" reality that no longer allows itself to be understood from a pregiven horizon of expectations. Thus, for ex-

[93]Ibid., p. 666. [Au.]
[94]Cf. ibid., pp. 666–67. [Au.]
[95]Ibid., p. 717. [Au.]
[96]Way of looking at things. [Ed.]

[97]Die Schaubühne als eine moralische Anstalt betrachtet," in *Schillers Sämtliche Werke,* Säkularausgabe, XI, p. 99. See also R. Koselleck, *Kritik und Krise* (Freiburg and Munich, 1959), pp. 82 ff. [Au.]
[98]"Zur Systematik der künstlerischen Probleme," *Jahrbuch für Ästhetik* (1925), p. 440; for the application of this principle to works of art of the present, see M. Imdahl, *Poetik und Hermeneutik* 3, pp. 493–505, 663–64. [Au.]

ample, the latest genre of novels, the much-discussed *nouveau roman,* presents itself as a form of modern art that according to Edgar Wind's formulation, represents the paradoxical case "that the solution is given, but the problem is given up, so that the solution might be understood as a problem." Here the reader is excluded from the situation of the immediate audience and put in the position of an uninitiated third party who in the face of a reality still without significance must himself find the questions that will decode for him the perception of the world and the interpersonal problem toward which the answer of the literature is directed.

It follows from all of this that the specific achievement of literature in social existence is to be sought exactly where literature is not absorbed into the function of a *representational* art. If one looks at the moments in history when literary works toppled the taboos of the ruling morals or offered the reader new solutions for the moral casuistry of his lived praxis, which thereafter could be sanctioned by the consensus of all readers in the society, then a still-little-studied area of research opens itself up to the literary historian. The gap between literature and history, between aesthetic and historical knowledge, can be bridged if literary history does not simply describe the process of general history in the reflection of its works one more time, but rather when it discovers in the course of "literary evolution" that properly *socially formative* function that belongs to literature as it competes with other arts and social forces in the emancipation of mankind from its natural, religious, and social bonds.

If it is worthwhile for the literary scholar to jump over his ahistorical shadow for the sake of this task, then it might well also provide an answer to the question: toward what end and with what right can one today still — or again — study literary history?

Wolfgang Iser

b. 1926

Partly because his method involves critical analysis rather than historical scholarship and partly because he works on well-known British fiction, Wolfgang Iser is more familiar to North American critics than his phenomenologist colleague, Hans Robert Jauss. Iser was born in Marienberg, Germany, in 1926, and received his Ph.D. from the University of Heidelberg in 1957. His published books include Die Weltanschauungs Henry Fieldings (Henry Fielding's World View, *1952),* Walter Pater — Die Autonomie des Ästhetischen *(1960; translated as* Walter Pater: The Aesthetic Moment), Die Appelstruktur der Texte *(*The Affective Structure of the Text, *1970), and* Spensers Arkadien: Fiktion und Geschichte in der Englische Renaissance *(*Spenser's Arcadia: Fiction and History in the English Renaissance, *1970). In North America, his most influential works are the two theoretical treatises based on the hermeneutics of Hans-Georg Gadamer and Roman Ingarden,* Der Implizite Leser *(1972; translated as* The Implied Reader) *and* Der Akte des Lesens *(1976; translated as* The Act of Reading). *Starting in the mid-1980s, Iser's work turned from purely phenomenological research to what he called "literary anthropology," a study of the cultural uses of literature. His recent work along that line is contained in* Prospecting: From Reader Response to Literary Anthropology *(1989);* The Fictive and the Imaginary: Charting Literary Anthropology *(1993); and* Staging Politics: The Lasting Impact of Shakespeare's Historical Plays *(1993). Iser is professor of English literature at the University of Konstanz in Germany and permanent visiting professor at the University of California at Irvine.*

The Reading Process: A Phenomenological Approach

I

The phenomenological theory of art lays full stress on the idea that, in considering a literary work, one must take into account not only the actual text but also, and in equal measure, the actions involved in responding to that text. Thus Roman Ingarden confronts the structure of the literary text with the ways in which it can be *konkretisiert* (realized).[1] The text as such offers different "schematised views"[2] through which the subject matter of the work can come to light, but the actual bringing to light is an action of *Konkretisation.* If this is so, then the literary work has two poles, which we might call the artistic and the esthetic: the artistic refers to the text created by the author, and the esthetic to the realization accomplished by the reader. From this polarity it follows that the literary work cannot be completely identical with the text, or with the realization of the text, but in fact must lie halfway between the two. The work is more than the text, for the text only takes on life when it is realized, and furthermore the realization is by no means independent of the individual disposition of the reader — though this in turn is acted upon by the different patterns of the text. The convergence of text and reader brings the literary work into existence, and this convergence can never be precisely pinpointed, but must always remain virtual, as it is not to be identified either with the reality of the text or with the individual disposition of the reader.

It is the virtuality of the work that gives rise to its dynamic nature, and this in turn is the precondition for the effects that the work calls forth. As the reader uses the various perspectives offered him by the text in order to relate the patterns and the "schematised views" to one another, he sets the work in motion, and this very process results ultimately in the awakening of responses within himself. Thus, reading causes the literary work to unfold its inherently dynamic character. That this is no new discovery is apparent from references made even in the early days of the novel. Laurence Sterne remarks in *Tristram Shandy:* ". . . no author, who understands the just boundaries of decorum and good-breeding, would presume to think all: The truest respect which you can pay to the reader's understanding, is to halve this matter amicably, and leave him something to imagine, in his turn, as well as yourself. For my own part, I am eternally paying him compliments of this kind, and do all that lies in my power to keep his imagination as busy as my own."[3] Sterne's conception of a literary text is that it is something like an arena in which reader and author participate in a game of the imagination. If the reader were given the whole story, and there were nothing left for him to do, then his imagination would never enter the field, the result would be the boredom which inevitably arises when everything is laid out cut and dried before us. A literary text must therefore be conceived in such a way that it will engage the reader's imagination in the task of working things out for himself, for reading is only a pleasure when it is active and creative. In this process of creativity, the text may either not go far enough, or may go too far, so we may say that boredom and overstrain form the boundaries beyond which the reader will leave the field of play.

The extent to which the "unwritten" part of a text stimulates the reader's creative participation is brought out by an observation of Virginia Woolf's in her study of *Jane Austen:*

> Jane Austen is thus a mistress of much deeper emotion than appears upon the surface. She stimulates

[1]Cf. Roman Ingarden, *Vom Erkennen des literarischen Kuntstwerks* (Tübingen, 1968), pp. 49 ff. [Au.]

[2]For a detailed discussion of this term see Roman Ingarden, *Das literarische Kunstwerk* (Tübingen, 1960), pp. 270 ff. [Au.]

[3]Laurence Sterne, *Tristram Shandy* (London, 1956), II, 11: 79. [Au.]

us to supply what is not there. What she offers is, apparently, a trifle, yet is composed of something that expands in the reader's mind and endows with the most enduring form of life scenes which are outwardly trivial. Always the stress is laid upon character. . . . The turns and twists of the dialogue keep us on the tenterhooks of suspense. Our attention is half upon the present moment, half upon the future. . . . Here, indeed, in this unfinished and in the main inferior story, are all the elements of Jane Austen's greatness.[4]

The unwritten aspects of apparently trivial scenes and the unspoken dialogue within the "turns and twists" not only draw the reader into the action but also lead him to shade in the many outlines suggested by the given situations, so that these take on a reality of their own. But as the reader's imagination animates these "outlines," they in turn will influence the effect of the written part of the text. Thus begins a whole dynamic process: the written text imposes certain limits on its unwritten implications in order to prevent these from becoming too blurred and hazy, but at the same time these implications, worked out by the reader's imagination, set the given situation against a background which endows it with far greater significance than it might have seemed to possess on its own. In this way, trivial scenes suddenly take on the shape of an "enduring form of life." What constitutes this form is never named, let alone explained in the text, although in fact it is the end product of the interaction between text and reader.

II

The question now arises as to how far such a process can be adequately described. For this purpose a phenomenological analysis recommends itself, especially since the somewhat sparse observations hitherto made of the psychology of reading tend mainly to be psychoanalytical, and so are restricted to the illustration of predetermined ideas concerning the unconscious. We shall, however, take a closer look later at some worthwhile psychological observations.

As a starting point for a phenomenological analysis we might examine the way in which sequent sentences act upon one another. This is of especial importance in literary texts in view of the fact that they do not correspond to any objective reality outside themselves. The world presented by literary texts is constructed out of what Ingarden has called *intentionale Satzkorrelate* (intentional sentence correlatives):

> Sentences link up in different ways to form more complex units of meaning that reveal a very varied structure giving rise to such entities as a short story, a novel, a dialogue, a drama, a scientific theory. . . . In the final analysis, there arises a particular world, with component parts determined in this way or that, and with all the variations that may occur within these parts — all this as a purely intentional correlative of a complex of sentences. If this complex finally forms a literary work, I call the whole sum of sequent intentional sentence correlatives the "world presented" in the work.[5]

This world, however, does not pass before the reader's eyes like a film. The sentences are "component parts" insofar as they make statements, claims, or observations, or convey information, and so establish various perspectives in the text. But they remain only "component parts" — they are not the sum total of the text itself. For the intentional correlatives disclose subtle connections which individually are less concrete than the statements, claims, and observations, even though these only take on their real meaningfulness through the interaction of their correlatives.

How is one to conceive the connection between the correlatives? It marks those points at which the reader is able to "climb aboard" the text. He has to accept certain given perspectives, but in doing so he inevitably causes them to interact. When Ingarden speaks of intentional sentence correlatives in literature, the statements made or information conveyed in the sentence is already in a certain sense qualified: the sentence does not consist solely of a statement — which, after all, would be absurd, as one can only make statements about things that exist — but aims at

[4]Virginia Woolf, *The Common Reader,* First Series (London, 1957), p. 174. [Au.]

[5]Ingarden, *Vom Erkennen des literarischen Kunstwerks,* p. 29. [Au.]

something beyond what it actually says. This is true of all sentences in literary works, and it is through the interaction of these sentences that their common aim is fulfilled. This is what gives them their own special quality in literary texts. In their capacity as statements, observations, purveyors of information, etc., they are always indications of something that is to come, the structure of which is foreshadowed by their specific content.

They set in motion a process out of which emerges the actual content of the text itself. In describing man's inner consciousness of time, Husserl once remarked: "Every originally constructive process is inspired by pre-intentions, which construct and collect the seed of what is to come, as such, and bring it to fruition."[6] For this bringing to fruition, the literary text needs the reader's imagination, which gives shape to the interaction of correlatives foreshadowed in structure by the sequence of the sentences. Husserl's observation draws our attention to a point that plays a not insignificant part in the process of reading. The individual sentences not only work together to shade in what is to come; they also form an expectation in this regard. Husserl calls this expectation "preintentions." As this structure is characteristic of *all* sentence correlatives, the interaction of these correlatives will not be a fulfillment of the expectation so much as a continual modification of it.

For this reason, expectations are scarcely ever fulfilled in truly literary texts. If they were, then such texts would be confined to the individualization of a given expectation, and one would inevitably ask what such an intention was supposed to achieve. Strangely enough, we feel that any confirmative effect — such as we implicitly demand of expository texts, as we refer to the objects they are meant to present — is a defect in a literary text. For the more a text individualizes or confirms an expectation it has initially aroused, the more aware we become of its didactic purpose, so that at best we can only accept or reject the thesis forced upon us. More often than not, the very clarity of such texts will make us want to free ourselves from their clutches. But generally the sentence correlatives of literary texts do not develop in this rigid way, for the expectations they evoke tend to encroach on one another in such a manner that they are continually modified as one reads. One might simplify by saying that each intentional sentence correlative opens up a particular horizon, which is modified, if not completely changed, by succeeding sentences. While these expectations arouse interest in what is to come, the subsequent modification of them will also have a retrospective effect on what has already been read. This may now take on a different significance from that which it had at the moment of reading.

Whatever we have read sinks into our memory and is foreshortened. It may later be evoked again and set against a different background with the result that the reader is enabled to develop hitherto unforeseeable connections. The memory evoked, however, can never reassume its original shape, for this would mean that memory and perception were identical, which is manifestly not so. The new background brings to light new aspects of what we had committed to memory; conversely these, in turn, shed their light on the new background, thus arousing more complex anticipations. Thus, the reader, in establishing these interrelationships between past, present and future, actually causes the text to reveal its potential multiplicity of connections. These connections are the product of the reader's mind working on the raw material of the text, though they are not the text itself — for this consists just of sentences, statements, information, etc.

This is why the reader often feels involved in events which, at the time of reading, seem real to him, even though in fact they are very far from his own reality. The fact that completely different readers can be differently affected by the "reality" of a particular text is ample evidence of the degree to which literary texts transform reading into a creative process that is far above mere perception of what is written. The literary text activates our own faculties, enabling us to recreate the world it presents. The product of this creative activity is what we might call the virtual dimension of the text, which endows it with its reality.

[6]Edmund Husserl, *Zur Phänomenologie des inneren Zeitbewusstseins, Gesammelte Werke* (The Hague, 1966), 10:52. [Au.]

This virtual dimension is not the text itself, nor is it the imagination of the reader: it is the coming together of text and imagination.

As we have seen, the activity of reading can be characterized as a sort of kaleidoscope of perspectives, preintentions, recollections. Every sentence contains a preview of the next and forms a kind of viewfinder for what is to come; and this in turn changes the "preview" and so becomes a "viewfinder" for what has been read. This whole process represents the fulfillment of the potential, unexpressed reality of the text, but it is to be seen only as a framework for a great variety of means by which the virtual dimension may be brought into being. The process of anticipation and retrospection itself does not by any means develop in a smooth flow. Ingarden has already drawn attention to this fact and ascribes a quite remarkable significance to it:

> Once we are immersed in the flow of *Satzdenken* (sentence-thought), we are ready, after completing the thought of one sentence, to think out the "continuation," also in the form of a sentence — and that is, in the form of a sentence that connects up with the sentence we have just thought through. In this way the process of reading goes effortlessly forward. But if by chance the following sentence has no tangible connection whatever with the sentence we have just thought through, there then comes a blockage in the stream of thought. This hiatus is linked with a more or less active surprise, or with indignation. This blockage must be overcome if the reading is to flow once more.[7]

The hiatus that blocks the flow of sentences is, in Ingarden's eyes, the product of chance, and is to be regarded as a flaw; this is typical of his adherence to the classical idea of art. If one regards the sentence sequence as a continual flow, this implies that the anticipation aroused by one sentence will generally be realized by the next, and the frustration of one's expectations will arouse feelings of exasperation. And yet literary texts are full of unexpected twists and turns, and frustration of expectations. Even in the simplest story there is bound to be some kind of blockage, if only because no tale can ever be told in its entirety. Indeed, it is only through inevitable omissions that a story gains its dynamism. Thus whenever the flow is interrupted and we are led off in unexpected directions, the opportunity is given to us to bring into play our own faculty for establishing connections — for filling in the gaps left by the text itself.[8]

These gaps have a different effect on the process of anticipation and retrospection, and thus on the "gestalt" of the virtual dimension, for they may be filled in different ways. For this reason, one text is potentially capable of several different realizations, and no reading can ever exhaust the full potential, for each individual reader will fill in the gaps in his own way, thereby excluding the various other possibilities; as he reads, he will make his own decision as to how the gap is to be filled. In this very act the dynamics of reading are revealed. By making his decision he implicitly acknowledges the inexhaustibility of the text; at the same time it is this very inexhaustibility that forces him to make his decision. With "traditional" texts this process was more or less unconscious, but modern texts frequently exploit it quite deliberately. They are often so fragmentary that one's attention is almost exclusively occupied with the search for connections between the fragments; the object of this is not to complicate the "spectrum" of connections, so much as to make us aware of the nature of our own capacity for providing links. In such cases, the text refers back directly to our own preconceptions — which are revealed by the act of interpretation that is a basic element of the reading process. With all literary texts, then, we may say that the reading process is selective, and the potential text is infinitely richer than any of its individual realizations. This is borne out by the fact that a second reading of a piece of literature often produces a different impression from the first. The reasons for this may lie in the reader's own change of circumstances, still, the text must be such as to allow this variation. On a

[7]Ingarden, *Vom Erkennen des literarischen Kunstwerks,* p. 32. [Au.]

[8]For a more detailed discussion of the function of "gaps" in literary texts see Wolfgang Iser, "Indeterminacy and the Reader's Response in Prose Fiction," *Aspects of Narrative* (English Institute Essays), ed. J. Hillis Miller (New York, 1971), pp. 1–45. [Au.]

second reading familiar occurrences now tend to appear in a new light and seem to be at times corrected, at times enriched.

In every text there is a potential time sequence which the reader must inevitably realize, as it is impossible to absorb even a short text in a single moment. Thus the reading process always involves viewing the text through a perspective that is continually on the move, linking up the different phases, and so constructing what we have called the virtual dimension. This dimension, of course, varies all the time we are reading. However, when we have finished the text, and read it again, clearly our extra knowledge will result in a different time sequence; we shall tend to establish connections by referring to our awareness of what is to come, and so certain aspects of the text will assume a significance we did not attach to them on a first reading, while others will recede into the background. It is a common enough experience for a person to say that on a second reading he noticed things he had missed when he read the book for the first time, but this is scarcely surprising in view of the fact that the second time he is looking at the text from a different perspective. The time sequence that he realized on his first reading cannot possibly be repeated on a second reading, and this unrepeatability is bound to result in modifications of his reading experience. This is not to say that the second reading is "truer" than the first — they are, quite simply, different: the reader establishes the virtual dimension of the text by realizing a new time sequence. Thus even on repeated viewings a text allows and, indeed, induces innovative reading.

In whatever way, and under whatever circumstances the reader may link the different phases of the text together, it will always be the process of anticipation and retrospection that leads to the formation of the virtual dimension, which in turn transforms the text into an experience for the reader. The way in which this experience comes about through a process of continual modification is closely akin to the way in which we gather experience in life. And thus the "reality" of the reading experience can illuminate basic patterns of real experience:

> We have the experience of a world, not understood as a system of relations which wholly determine each event, but as an open totality the synthesis of which is inexhaustible. . . . From the moment that experience — that is, the opening on to our *de facto* world — is recognized as the beginning of knowledge, there is no longer any way of distinguishing a level of *a priori* truths and one of factual ones, what the world must necessarily be and what it actually is.[9]

The manner in which the reader experiences the text will reflect his own disposition, and in this respect the literary text acts as a kind of mirror; but at the same time, the reality which this process helps to create is one that will be *different* from his own (since, normally, we tend to be bored by texts that present us with things we already know perfectly well ourselves). Thus we have the apparently paradoxical situation in which the reader is forced to reveal aspects of himself in order to experience a reality which is different from his own. The impact this reality makes on him will depend largely on the extent to which he himself actively provides the unwritten part of the text, and yet in supplying all the missing links, he must think in terms of experiences different from his own; indeed, it is only by leaving behind the familiar world of his own experience that the reader can truly participate in the adventure the literary text offers him.

III

We have seen that, during the process of reading, there is an active interweaving of anticipation and retrospection, which on a second reading may turn into a kind of advance retrospection. The impressions that arise as a result of this process will vary from individual to individual, but only within the limits imposed by the written as opposed to the unwritten text. In the same way, two people gazing at the night sky may both be looking at the same collection of stars, but one will see the image of a plough, and the other will make out a dipper. The "stars" in a literary text

[9] M. Merleau-Ponty, *Phenomenology of Perception,* trans. Colin Smith (New York, 1962), pp. 219, 221. [Au.]

are fixed; the lines that join them are variable. The author of the text may, of course, exert plenty of influence on the reader's imagination — he has the whole panoply of narrative techniques at his disposal — but no author worth his salt will ever attempt to set the *whole* picture before his reader's eyes. If he does, he will very quickly lose his reader, for it is only by activating the reader's imagination that the author can hope to involve him and so realize the intentions of his text.

Gilbert Ryle, in his analysis of imagination, asks: "How can a person fancy that he sees something, without realizing that he is not seeing it?" He answers as follows:

> Seeing Helvellyn [the name of a mountain] in one's mind's eye does not entail, what seeing Helvellyn and seeing snapshots of Helvellyn entail, the having of visual sensations. It does involve the thought of having a view of Helvellyn and it is therefore a more sophisticated operation than that of having a view of Helvellyn. It is one utilization among others of the knowledge of how Helvellyn should look, or, in one sense of the verb, it is thinking how it should look. The expectations which are fulfilled in the recognition at sight of Helvellyn are not indeed fulfilled in picturing it, but the picturing of it is something like a rehearsal of getting them fulfilled. So far from picturing involving the having of faint sensations, or wraiths of sensations, it involves missing just what one would be due to get, if one were seeing the mountain.[10]

If one sees the mountain, then of course one can no longer imagine it, and so the act of picturing the mountain presupposes its absence. Similarly, with a literary text we can only picture things which are not there; the written part of the text gives us the knowledge, but it is the unwritten part that gives us the opportunity to picture things; indeed without the elements of indeterminacy, the gaps in the text, we should not be able to use our imagination.[11]

The truth of this observation is borne out by the experience many people have on seeing, for instance, the film of a novel. While reading *Tom Jones*, they may never have had a clear conception of what the hero actually looks like, but on seeing the film, some may say, "That's not how I imagined him." The point here is that the reader of *Tom Jones* is able to visualize the hero virtually for himself, and so his imagination senses the vast number of possibilities; the moment these possibilities are narrowed down to one complete and immutable picture, the imagination is put out of action, and we feel we have somehow been cheated. This may perhaps be an oversimplification of the process, but it does illustrate plainly the vital richness of potential that arises out of the fact that the hero in the novel must be pictured and cannot be seen. With the novel the reader must use his imagination to synthesize the information given him, and so his perception is simultaneously richer and more private; with the film he is confined merely to physical perception, and so whatever he remembers of the world he had pictured is brutally cancelled out.

IV

The "picturing" that is done by our imagination is only one of the activities through which we form the "gestalt" of a literary text. We have already discussed the process of anticipation and retrospection, and to this we must add the process of grouping together all the different aspects of a text to form the consistency that the reader will always be in search of. While expectations may be continually modified, and images continually expanded, the reader will still strive, even if unconsciously, to fit everything together in a consistent pattern. "In the reading of images, as in the hearing of speech, it is always hard to distinguish what is given to us from what we supplement in the process of projection which is triggered off by recognition . . . it is the guess of the beholder that tests the medley of forms and colours for coherent meaning, crystallizing it into shape when a consistent interpretation has been found."[12] By grouping together the written parts

[10]Gilbert Ryle, *The Concept of Mind* (Harmondsworth, 1968), p. 255. [Au.]

[11]Cf. Iser, "Indeterminacy," pp. 11 ff., 42 ff. [Au.]

[12]E. H. Gombrich, *Art and Illusion* (London, 1962), p. 204. [Au.]

of the text, we enable them to interact, we observe the direction in which they are leading us, and we project onto them the consistency which we, as readers, require. This "gestalt" must inevitably be colored by our own characteristic selection process. For it is not given by the text itself; it arises from the meeting between the written text and the individual mind of the reader with its own particular history of experience, its own consciousness, its own outlook. The "gestalt" is not the true meaning of the text; at best it is a configurative meaning; ". . . comprehension is an individual act of seeing-things-together, and only that."[13] With a literary text such comprehension is inseparable from the reader's expectations, and where we have expectations, there too we have one of the most potent weapons in the writer's armory — illusion.

Whenever "consistent reading suggests itself . . . illusion takes over."[14] Illusion, says Northrop Frye, is "fixed or definable, and reality is best understood as its negation."[15] The "gestalt" of a text normally takes on (or, rather, is given) this fixed or definable outline, as this is essential to our own understanding, but on the other hand, if reading were to consist of nothing but an uninterrupted building up of illusions, it would be a suspect, if not downright dangerous, process: instead of bringing us into contact with reality, it would wean us away from realities. Of course, there is an element of "escapism" in all literature, resulting from this very creation of illusion, but there are some texts which offer nothing but a harmonious world, purified of all contradiction and deliberately excluding anything that might disturb the illusion once established, and these are the texts that we generally do not like to classify as literary. Women's magazines and the brasher forms of the detective story might be cited as examples.

However, even if an overdose of illusion may lead to triviality, this does not mean that the process of illusion-building should ideally be dispensed with altogether. On the contrary, even in texts that appear to resist the formation of illusion, thus drawing our attention to the cause of this resistance, we still need the abiding illusion that the resistance itself is the consistent pattern underlying the text. This is especially true of modern texts, in which it is the very precision of the written details which increases the proportion of indeterminacy; one detail appears to contradict another, and so simultaneously stimulates and frustrates our desire to "picture," thus continually causing our imposed "gestalt" of the test to disintegrate. Without the formation of illusions, the unfamiliar world of the text would remain unfamiliar; through the illusions, the experience offered by the text becomes accessible to us, for it is only the illusion, on its different levels of consistency, that makes the experience "readable." If we cannot find (or impose) this consistency, sooner or later we will put the text down. The process is virtually hermeneutic. The text provokes certain expectations which in turn we project onto the text in such a way that we reduce the polysemantic possibilities to a single interpretation in keeping with the expectations aroused, thus extracting an individual, configurative meaning. The polysemantic nature of the text and the illusion-making of the reader are opposed factors. If the illusion were complete, the polysemantic nature would vanish; if the polysemantic nature were all-powerful, the illusion would be totally destroyed. Both extremes are conceivable, but in the individual literary text we always find some form of balance between the two conflicting tendencies. The formation of illusions, therefore, can never be total, but it is this very incompleteness that in fact gives it its productive value.

With regard to the experience of reading, Walter Pater once observed: "For to the grave reader words too are grave; and the ornamental word, the figure, the accessory form or colour or reference, is rarely content to die to thought precisely at the right moment, but will inevitably linger awhile, stirring a long 'brainwave' behind it of perhaps quite alien associations."[16] Even

[13]Louis O. Mink, "History and Fiction as Modes of Comprehension," *New Literary History* I (1970): 553. [Au.]

[14]Gombrich, *Art and Illusion*, p. 278. [Au.]

[15]Northrop Frye, *Anatomy of Criticism* (New York, 1967), pp. 169 f. [Au.]

[16]Walter Pater, *Appreciations* (London, 1920), p. 18. [Au.]

while the reader is seeking a consistent pattern in the text, he is also uncovering other impulses which cannot be immediately integrated or will even resist final integration. Thus the semantic possibilities of the text will always remain far richer than any configurative meaning formed while reading. But this impression is, of course, only to be gained through reading the text. Thus the configurative meaning can be nothing but a *pars pro toto*[17] fulfillment of the text, and yet this fulfillment gives rise to the very richness which it seeks to restrict, and indeed in some modern texts, our awareness of this richness takes precedence over any configurative meaning.

This fact has several consequences which, for the purpose of analysis, may be dealt with separately, though in the reading process they will all be working together. As we have seen, a consistent, configurative meaning is essential for the apprehension of an unfamiliar experience, which through the process of illusion-building we can incorporate in our own imaginative world. At the same time, this consistency conflicts with the many other possibilities of fulfillment it seeks to exclude, with the result that the configurative meaning is always accompanied by "alien associations" that do not fit in with the illusions formed. The first consequence, then, is the fact that in forming our illusions, we also produce at the same time a latent disturbance of these illusions. Strangely enough, this also applies to texts in which our expectations are actually fulfilled — though one would have thought that the fulfillment of expectations would help to complete the illusion. "Illusion wears off once the expectation is stepped up; we take it for granted and want more."[18]

The experiments in gestalt psychology referred to by Gombrich in *Art and Illusion* make one thing clear: ". . . though we may be intellectually aware of the fact that any given experience *must* be an illusion, we cannot, strictly speaking, watch ourselves having an illusion."[19] Now, if illusion were not a transitory state, this would mean that we could be, as it were, permanently caught up in it. And if reading were exclusively a matter of producing illusion — necessary though this is for the understanding of an unfamiliar experience — we should run the risk of falling victim to a gross deception. But it is precisely during our reading that the transitory nature of the illusion is revealed to the full.

As the formation of illusions is constantly accompanied by "alien associations" which cannot be made consistent with the illusions, the reader constantly has to lift the restrictions he places on the "meaning" of the text. Since it is he who builds the illusions, he oscillates between involvement in and observation of those illusions; he opens himself to the unfamiliar world without being imprisoned in it. Through this process the reader moves into the presence of the fictional world and so experiences the realities of the text as they happen.

In the oscillation between consistency and "alien associations," between involvement in and observation of the illusion, the reader is bound to conduct his own balancing operation, and it is this that forms the esthetic experience offered by the literary text. However, if the reader were to achieve a balance, obviously he would then no longer be engaged in the process of establishing and disrupting consistency. And since it is this very process that gives rise to the balancing operation, we may say that the inherent nonachievement of balance is a prerequisite for the very dynamism of the operation. In seeking the balance we inevitably have to start out with certain expectations, the shattering of which is integral to the esthetic experience.

> Furthermore, to say merely that "our expectations are satisfied" is to be guilty of another serious ambiguity. At first sight such a statement seems to deny the obvious fact that much of our enjoyment is derived from surprises, from betrayals of our expectations. The solution to this paradox is to find some ground for a distinction between "surprise" and "frustration." Roughly, the distinction can be made in terms of the effects which the two kinds of experiences have upon us. Frustration blocks or checks activity. It necessitates new orientation for our activity, if we are to escape the *cul de sac*. Consequently, we abandon the frustrating object and return to blind impulse activity. On the other hand,

[17]Partial. [Ed.]
[18]Gombrich, *Art and Illusion*, p. 54. [Au.]
[19]Ibid., p. 5. [Au.]

surprise merely causes a temporary cessation of the exploratory phase of the experience, and a recourse to intense contemplation and scrutiny. In the latter phase the surprising elements are seen in their connection with what has gone before, with the whole drift of the experience, and the enjoyment of these values is then extremely intense. Finally, it appears that there must always be some degree of novelty or surprise in all these values if there is to be a progressive specification of the direction of the total act . . . and any aesthetic experience tends to exhibit a continuous interplay between "deductive" and "inductive" operations.[20]

It is this interplay between "deduction" and "induction" that gives rise to the configurative meaning of the text, and not the individual expectations, surprises, or frustrations arising from the different perspectives. Since this interplay obviously does not take place in the text itself, but can only come into being through the process of reading, we may conclude that this process formulates something that is unformulated in the text and yet represents its "intention." Thus, by reading we uncover the unformulated part of the text, and this very indeterminacy is the force that drives us to work out a configurative meaning while at the same time giving us the necessary degree of freedom to do so.

As we work out a consistent pattern in the text, we will find our "interpretation" threatened, as it were, by the presence of other possibilities of "interpretation," and so there arise new areas of indeterminacy (though we may only be dimly aware of them, if at all, as we are continually making "decisions" which will exclude them). In the course of a novel, for instance, we sometimes find that characters, events, and backgrounds seem to change their significance; what really happens is that the other "possibilities" begin to emerge more strongly, so that we become more directly aware of them. Indeed, it is this very shifting of perspectives that makes us feel that a novel is much more "true-to-life." Since it is we ourselves who establish the levels of interpretation and switch from one to another as we conduct our balancing operation, we ourselves impart to the text the dynamic lifelikeness which, in turn, enables us to absorb an unfamiliar experience into our personal world.

As we read, we oscillate to a greater or lesser degree between the building and the breaking of illusions. In a process of trial and error, we organize and reorganize the various data offered us by the text. These are the given factors, the fixed points on which we base our "interpretation," trying to fit them together in the way we think the author meant them to be fitted. "For to perceive, a beholder must *create* his own experience. And his creation must include relations comparable to those which the original producer underwent. They are not the same in any literal sense. But with the perceiver, as with the artist, there must be an ordering of the elements of the whole that is in form, although not in details, the same as the process of organization the creator of the work consciously experienced. Without an act of recreation the object is not perceived as a work of art."[21]

The act of recreation is not a smooth or continuous process, but one which, in its essence, relies on *interruptions* of the flow to render it efficacious. We look forward, we look back, we decide, we change our decisions, we form expectations, we are shocked by their nonfulfillment, we question, we muse, we accept, we reject; this is the dynamic process of recreation. This process is steered by two main structural components within the text: first, a repertoire of familiar literary patterns and recurrent literary themes, together with allusions to familiar social and historical contexts; second, techniques or strategies used to set the familiar against the unfamiliar. Elements of the repertoire are continually backgrounded or foregrounded with a resultant strategic overmagnification, trivialization, or even annihilation of the allusion. This defamiliarization of what the reader thought he recognized is bound to create a tension that will intensify his expectations as well as his distrust of those expectations. Similarly, we may be confronted by narrative techniques that establish links between things we find difficult to connect, so that we are

[20]B. Ritchie, "The Formal Structure of the Aesthetic Object," in *The Problems of Aesthetics*, ed. Eliseo Vivas and Murray Krieger (New York, 1965), pp. 230 f. [Au.]

[21]John Dewey, *Art as Experience* (New York, 1958), p. 54. [Au.]

forced to reconsider data we at first held to be perfectly straightforward. One need only mention the very simple trick, so often employed by novelists, whereby the author himself takes part in the narrative, thus establishing perspectives which would not have arisen out of the mere narration of the events described. Wayne Booth once called this the technique of the "unreliable narrator,"[22] to show the extent to which a literary device can counter expectations arising out of the literary text. The figure of the narrator may act in permanent opposition to the impressions we might otherwise form. The question then arises as to whether this strategy, opposing the formation of illusions, may be integrated into a consistent pattern, lying, as it were, a level deeper than our original impressions. We may find that our narrator, by opposing us, in fact turns us against him and thereby strengthens the illusion he appears to be out to destroy; alternatively, we may be so much in doubt that we begin to question all the processes that lead us to make interpretative decisions. Whatever the cause may be, we will find ourselves subjected to this same interplay of illusion-forming and illusion-breaking that makes reading essentially a recreative process.

We might take, as a simple illustration of this complex process, the incident in Joyce's *Ulysses* in which Bloom's cigar alludes to Ulysses's spear. The context (Bloom's cigar) summons up a particular element of the repertoire (Ulysses's spear); the narrative technique relates them to one another as if they were identical. How are we to "organize" these divergent elements, which, through the very fact that they are put together, separate one element so clearly from the other? What are the prospects here for a consistent pattern? We might say that it is ironic — at least that is how many renowned Joyce readers have understood it.[23] In this case, irony would be the form of organization that integrates the material. But if this is so, what is the object of the irony? Ulysses's spear, or Bloom's cigar? The uncertainty surrounding this simple question already puts a strain on the consistency we have established and, indeed, begins to puncture it, especially when other problems make themselves felt as regards the remarkable conjunction of spear and cigar. Various alternatives come to mind, but the variety alone is sufficient to leave one with the impression that the consistent pattern has been shattered. And even if, after all, one can still believe that irony holds the key to the mystery, this irony must be of a very strange nature; for the formulated text does not merely mean the opposite of what has been formulated. It may even mean something that cannot be formulated at all. The moment we try to impose a consistent pattern on the text, discrepancies are bound to arise. These are, as it were, the reverse side of the interpretative coin, an involuntary product of the process that creates discrepancies by trying to avoid them. And it is their very presence that draws us into the text, compelling us to conduct a creative examination not only of the text but also of ourselves.

This entanglement of the reader is, of course, vital to any kind of text, but in the literary text we have the strange situation that the reader cannot know what his participation actually entails. We know that we share in certain experiences, but we do not know what happens to us in the course of this process. This is why, when we have been particularly impressed by a book, we feel the need to talk about it; we do not want to get away from it by talking about it — we simply want to understand more clearly what it is in which we have been entangled. We have undergone an experience, and now we want to know consciously *what* we have experienced. Perhaps this is the prime usefulness of literary criticism — it helps to make conscious those aspects of the text which would otherwise remain concealed in the subconscious; it satisfies (or helps to satisfy) our desire to talk about what we have read.

The efficacy of a literary text is brought about by the apparent evocation and subsequent negation of the familiar. What at first seemed to be an affirmation of our assumptions leads to our own rejection of them, thus tending to prepare us for a re-orientation. And it is only when we have outstripped our preconceptions and left the shelter of

[22]Cf. Wayne C. Booth, *The Rhetoric of Fiction* (Chicago, 1961), pp. 211 ff., 339 ff. [Au.]

[23]Richard Ellmann, "Ulysses: The Divine Nobody," in *Twelve Original Essays on Great English Novels*, ed. Charles Shapiro (Detroit, 1960), p. 247, classified this particular allusion as "mock-heroic." [Au.]

the familiar that we are in a position to gather new experiences. As the literary text involves the reader in the formation of illusion and the simultaneous formation of the means whereby the illusion is punctured, reading reflects the process by which we gain experience. Once the reader is entangled, his own preconceptions are continually overtaken, so that the text becomes his "present" while his own ideas fade into the "past"; as soon as this happens he is open to the immediate experience of the text, which was impossible so long as his preconceptions were his "present."

V

In our analysis of the reading process so far, we have observed three important aspects that form the basis of the relationship between reader and text: the process of anticipation and retrospection, the consequent unfolding of the text as a living event, and the resultant impression of lifelikeness.

Any "living event" must, to a greater or lesser degree, remain open. In reading, this obliges the reader to seek continually for consistency, because only then can he close up situations and comprehend the unfamiliar. But consistency-building is itself a living process in which one is constantly forced to make selective decisions — and these decisions in their turn give a reality to the possibilities which they exclude, insofar as they may take effect as a latent disturbance of the consistency established. This is what causes the reader to be entangled in the text-"gestalt" that he himself has produced.

Through this entanglement the reader is bound to open himself up to the workings of the text and so leave behind his own preconceptions. This gives him the chance to have an experience in the way George Bernard Shaw once described it: "You have learnt something. That always feels at first as if you had lost something."[24] Reading reflects the structure of experience to the extent that we must suspend the ideas and attitudes that shape our own personality before we can experience the unfamiliar world of the literary text. But during this process, something happens to us.

This "something" needs to be looked at in detail, especially as the incorporation of the unfamiliar into our own range of experience has been to a certain extent obscured by an idea very common in literary discussion: namely, that the process of absorbing the unfamiliar is labeled as the *identification* of the reader with what he reads. Often the term "identification" is used as if it were an explanation, whereas in actual fact it is nothing more than a description. What is normally meant by "identification" is the establishment of affinities between oneself and someone outside oneself — a familiar ground on which we are able to experience the unfamiliar. The author's aim, though, is to convey the experience and, above all, an attitude toward that experience. Consequently, "identification" is not an end in itself, but a stratagem by means of which the author stimulates attitudes in the reader.

This of course is not to deny that there does arise a form of participation as one reads; one is certainly drawn into the text in such a way that one has the feeling that there is no distance between oneself and the events described. This involvement is well summed up by the reaction of a critic to reading Charlotte Brontë's *Jane Eyre:* "We took up *Jane Eyre* one writer's evening, somewhat piqued at the extravagant commendations we had heard, and sternly resolved to be as critical as Croker. But as we read on we forgot both commendations and criticism, identified ourselves with Jane in all her troubles, and finally married Mr. Rochester about four in the morning."[25] The question is how and why did the critic identify himself with Jane?

In order to understand this "experience," it is well worth considering Georges Poulet's observations on the reading process. He says that books only take on their full existence in the reader.[26] It is true that they consist of ideas thought out by someone else, but in reading the

[24]G. B. Shaw, *Major Barbara* (London, 1964), p. 316. [Au.]

[25]William George Clark, *Fraser's* (December, 1849): 692, quoted by Kathleen Tillotson, *Novels of the Eighteen-Forties* (Oxford, 1961), pp. 19 f. [Au.]

[26]Cf. Georges Poulet, "Phenomenology of Reading," *New Literary History* I (1969): 54. [Au.]

reader becomes the subject that does the thinking. Thus there disappears the subject-object division that otherwise is a prerequisite for all knowledge and all observation, and the removal of this division puts reading in an apparently unique position as regards the possible absorption of new experiences. This may well be the reason why relations with the world of the literary text have so often been misinterpreted as identification. From the idea that in reading we must think the thoughts of someone else, Poulet draws the following conclusion: "Whatever I think is a part of *my* mental world. And yet here I am thinking a thought which manifestly belongs to another mental world, which is being thought in me just as though I did not exist. Already the notion is inconceivable and seems even more so if I reflect that, since every thought must have a subject to think it, this *thought* which is alien to me and yet in me, must also have in me a *subject* which is alien to me. . . . Whenever I read, I mentally pronounce an *I*, and yet the *I* which I pronounce is not myself."[27]

But for Poulet this idea is only part of the story. The strange subject that thinks the strange thought in the reader indicates the potential presence of the author, whose ideas can be "internalized" by the reader: "Such is the characteristic condition of every work which I summon back into existence by placing my consciousness at its disposal. I give it not only existence, but awareness of existence."[28] This would mean that consciousness forms the point at which author and reader converge, and at the same time it would result in the cessation of the temporary self-alienation that occurs to the reader when his consciousness brings to life the ideas formulated by the author. This process gives rise to a form of communication which, however, according to Poulet, is dependent on two conditions: the life-story of the author must be shut out of the work and the individual disposition of the reader must be shut out of the act of reading. Only then can the thoughts of the author take place subjectively in the reader, who thinks what he is not. It follows that the work itself must be thought of as a consciousness, because only in this way is there an adequate basis for the author-reader relationship — a relationship that can only come about through the negation of the author's own life-story and the reader's own disposition. This conclusion is actually drawn by Poulet when he describes the work as the self-presentation or materialization of consciousness: "And so I ought not to hesitate to recognize that so long as it is animated by this vital inbreathing inspired by the act of reading, a work of literature becomes (at the expense of the reader whose own life it suspends) a sort of human being, that it is a mind conscious of itself and constituting itself in me as the subject of its own objects."[29] Even though it is difficult to follow such a substantialist conception of the consciousness that constitutes itself in the literary work, there are, nevertheless, certain points in Poulet's argument that are worth holding onto. But they should be developed along somewhat different lines.

[27]Ibid., p. 56. [Au.]
[28]Ibid., p. 59. [Au.]

If reading removes the subject-object division that constitutes all perception, it follows that the reader will be "occupied" by the thoughts of the author, and these in turn will cause the drawing of new "boundaries." Text and reader no longer confront each other as object and subject, but instead the "division" takes place within the reader himself. In thinking the thoughts of another, his own individuality temporarily recedes into the background, since it is supplanted by these alien thoughts, which now become the theme on which his attention is focused. As we read, there occurs an artificial division of our personality, because we take as a theme for ourselves something that we are not. Consequently when reading we operate on different levels. For although we may be thinking the thoughts of someone else, what we are will not disappear completely — it will merely remain a more or less powerful virtual force. Thus, in reading there are these two levels — the alien "me" and the real, virtual "me" — which are never completely cut off from each other. Indeed, we can only make someone else's thoughts into an absorbing theme for ourselves, provided the virtual background of our own per-

[29]Ibid. [Au.]

sonality can adapt to it. Every text we read draws a different boundary within our personality, so that the virtual background (the real "me") will take on a different form, according to the theme of the text concerned. This is inevitable, if only for the fact that the relationship between alien theme and virtual background is what makes it possible for the unfamiliar to be understood.

In this context there is a revealing remark made by D. W. Harding, arguing against the idea of identification with what is read: "What is sometimes called wish-fulfilment in novels and plays can . . . more plausibly be described as wish-formulation or the definition of desires. The cultural levels at which it works may vary widely; the process is the same. . . . It seems nearer the truth . . . to say that fictions contribute to defining the reader's or spectator's values, and perhaps stimulating his desires, rather than to suppose that they gratify desire by some mechanism of vicarious experience."[30] In the act of reading, having to think something that we have not yet experienced does not mean only being in a position to conceive or even understand it; it also means that such acts of conception are possible and successful to the degree that they lead to something being formulated in us. For someone else's thoughts can only take a form in our consciousness if, in the process, our unformulated faculty for deciphering those thoughts is brought into play — a faculty which, in the act of deciphering, also formulates itself. Now since this formulation is carried out on terms set by someone else, whose thoughts are the theme of our reading, it follows that the formulation of our faculty for deciphering cannot be along our own lines of orientation.

Herein lies the dialectical structure of reading. The need to decipher gives us the chance to formulate our own deciphering capacity — i.e., we bring to the fore an element of our being of which we are not directly conscious. The production of the meaning of literary texts — which we discussed in connection with forming the "gestalt" of the text — does not merely entail the discovery of the unformulated, which can then be taken over by the active imagination of the reader; it also entails the possibility that we may formulate ourselves and so discover what had previously seemed to elude our consciousness. These are the ways in which reading literature gives us the chance to formulate the unformulated.

[30]D. W. Harding, "Psychological Processes in the Reading of Fiction," in *Aesthetics in the Modern World,* ed. Harold Osborne (London, 1968), pp. 313 f. [Au.]

Norman N. Holland

b. 1927

An orthodox New Critic in his first book on Restoration comedy, Norman Holland is best known for his contributions to psychoanalytical and reader-response criticism. Holland was born in New York City and educated at the Massachusetts Institute of Technology (B.S., 1947) and at Harvard, where he received an LL.B. in 1950 and a Ph.D. in English in 1956. During the next ten years, Holland taught English at MIT while undergoing psychoanalytic training at the Boston Psychoanalytic Institute. One result of this dual endeavor was Psychoanalysis and Shakespeare *(1966). In 1966 Holland moved to the State University of New York at Buffalo as professor and chairman of the English department. There he analyzed the theory underlying the literary techniques of his Shakespeare book in writing* The Dynamics of Literary Response *(1968), which claims that meaning is produced in a transaction between text and reader: The text manages the reader's defensive transformation of its informing fantasy. In 1970 Holland founded the Center for the Psychological Study of the Arts and served as director until 1979. During that decade, Holland's interests shifted from the text to the reader, influenced by Heinz Lichtenstein's notion of the "identity theme" by which the individual ego styles its response to threatening stimuli. Holland's reader-response criticism appears in works such as* Poems in Persons *(1973),* 5 Readers Reading *(1975),* Laughing *(1982),* The I *(1985),* The Brain of Robert Frost: A Cognitive Approach to Literature *(1988), and* The Critical I *(1991). Since 1983, Holland has been Millbauer Eminent Scholar and professor of English at the University of Florida, Gainesville. "The Question: Who Reads What How?" is from* 5 Readers Reading.

The Question: Who Reads What How?

The story was William Faulkner's "A Rose for Emily," and its one description of Miss Emily as a young girl was as clear as a description could be. The narrator, apparently one of the townspeople, says: "We had long thought of them as a tableau, Miss Emily a slender figure in white in the background, her father a spraddled silhouette in the foreground, his back to her and clutching a horsewhip, the two of them framed by the back-flung front door." Faulkner has pictured the Griersons as exactly as a photographer would, but that precision quite disappears when the description passes over into the mind of a reader. It disappears even if the reader is as well trained and fairly experienced as the five students of English literature who are the subjects of this book. Sam, Saul, Shep, Sebastian, and Sandra (as I shall call them) all spoke about this "tableau."

Good-natured, easygoing, dapper Sam singled it out as virtually the first thing he wanted to talk about in the story: "The father was very domineering. One of the most striking [*sic*] images in the book is that of the townsfolk looking through the door as her father stands there with a horsewhip in his hands, feet spread apart and between or through him you see a picture of Emily standing in the background, and that pretty much sums up exactly the kind of relationship they had." Sam was stressing the father's dominance and, in doing so, was positioning the townspeople so that they could see Emily between her father's legs.

This was part of what he found highly romantic in the story. "The frailty and femininity that that evokes!" he sighed. "Just that one frail, 'slender figure in white,' just those words there really show us the Emily that was and the Emily that might have been." Yet, almost at the same moment he was responding to this lacy, feminine Emily, he could say, "The word 'tableau' is important. While they [the townspeople] may be envious and while they may be angry at the way that these people act, they yet need it, it seems, they in a way like to have it, much as one is terrified at the power of a god and yet needing him so much and, you know, sidling up to him and paying homage to him and in the same way I think Emily comes to function as this god symbol." A curious turnabout from frailty and femininity.

By contrast, Saul, a scholarly type, was circumspect. Sam, in his expansive way, trusted his memory, but Saul, when I asked him about that image, took out his copy of the story and read it over carefully to himself. "Ummm. I had remembered the word 'tableau,' and I had forgotten the rest of it. 'Horsewhip' there — rings — 'spraddled silhouette.' That seems right to me. That summarizes the relationship, I think. She's in the back in white, of course, I think of these white gowns in the plantation balls. The father a 'spraddled silhouette.' He's no longer stern and erect. He's spraddled across the door." Saul was seeing Emily's father exactly the opposite way from Sam, as a weakened, sprawled figure, at least until he read over to himself the sentence with the horsewhip in it again. "A horsewhip suggesting all sorts of nasty, sexual, sadistic overtones," but then he blurred that image. "Do they mean the horsewhip rather than his own stern demeanor? Or just the normal embodiment of his traditions suggests the decline like 'spraddled' does? And then 'framed by the back-flung front door' just completes the tableau. It's a nice device. Faulkner makes that one work, too. That's a nice emblem." Well, maybe so, but Saul had so divided it up and dissolved it into questions and alternatives as to leave me quite puzzled about what he thought the thrust of the image finally was.

Shep presented himself as a rebel and radical, but his reading of the tableau seemed to me no more original or idiosyncratic than Saul's or Sam's. I read the passage to him, and he commented simply. "O.K. Protective image. That he's defending Southern womanhood, perhaps, and defending it in that same sort of mindless way that says, 'Well, now, we've got to defend it.'" He went on to decide that Southern womanhood might well have defended itself and then to make a suggestion quite opposite to "protective image." "You could, I suppose, as an alternative interpretation say that the horsewhip is something which he's also adept with indoors as well as outdoors, but I don't think so. Maybe there's overtones that Daddy is sadistic enough — horsewhips being pretty sadistic things to carry around when you're greeting people, you know — that Daddy is sadistic enough where he wouldn't mind taking a belt at Emily once in a while, but I don't think they're much more than overtones." In talking about the tableau as such, he talked only about Emily's father, and in this curiously alternative or opposed way. Earlier he had recalled Emily as a young woman (and the tableau is the only place she is so described): "I can see her as a very good-looking, dark-haired girl who had a penchant for wearing dark clothes." Again, I sense in his substituting dark for white a will opposing the text, although at the same time, Shep said he liked this story very much.

Sophisticated, sardonic, somewhat cynical, a lapsed Catholic with aspirations toward aristocracy, Sebastian did not discuss the tableau as such, although he clearly remembered it in typing Emily as "the aristocrat of the Southern town, whose father is the original superego with a horsewhip, beating off suitors." "He's denying her access to suitable sexual partners." Often, Sebastian tended to distance and type the characters this way and to flirt with the actual, physical details. Here he saw Miss Emily as "the aristocrat," her father as "the original superego," but converted the "suitors" to "sexual partners."

Sandra, the fifth reader, was a tall, very attractive woman, gentle and subdued in her manner. She liked the story intensely, had read it several times, and had even, in her freshman year, written a term paper on it. Yet she recalled the tableau oddly: "They said they always had this picture of him standing, you know, sitting in the door with a whip in his hand." As for Emily, "I see her as very young and dressed in white and standing up, I guess she's supposed to be standing up behind her father, who would probably be looking *very* cross, say, if someone had come to call on her. No doubt, she would have a certain amount — Possibly fearful, but probably more regretful because she's being, they even say, robbed of something at that point. . . . There would be a great amount of strain on her face because of her inability to do anything except just watch." Sandra saw the emotional overtones in the tableau in a more subtle, emphatic way than the four male readers did, so that she, too, had her own version of the image.

Indeed, one can say that each of the readers had a different version of Emily and her father. He was standing, sitting; erect, sprawled; domineering, weakened; sadistic, protective, and so on — sometimes even to the same reader. Emily was dressed in white, as for a plantation ball, or black; frail, but godlike; fearful, but "the aristocrat." Some of these differences involve outright misreadings, but most do not. Conceivably, one could "teach" or coerce these five readers into consensus, but even so, whatever in each person's character originally colored his perception of the tableau would go on coloring his perception of every other element in the story. What is that something, that ineffable effect of personality on perception? That is the issue this book explores.

As the late Stanley Edgar Hyman once said, "Each reader poems his own poem." Yet we know very little — practically nothing — about such "poeming," about the way a reader recreates the literary experience in himself. Today's literary critics are expert in pointing out an essence for any literary work. Today's psychologists — particularly the psychoanalytic psychologists —

are equally adept at conceptualizing the essential dynamics of individuals. Yet we do not know how literature and readers interact.

We can find out, if you and I apply to what Sam and the other readers said, a combination of the close reading literary critics have so skillfully developed in the last decades and psychological methods of reading from language to personality. We shall move slowly — sometimes we shall seem to go word by word — but once we have put psychoanalytic interpretation together with the literary critic's, we shall have established four principles that account for the way readers read to fit their personalities.

As for now, however, in the words of a recent book on the problem of literary response, "We know almost nothing about the process of reading and the interaction of man and book."[1] In a manner all too common in the world of belles-lettres, however, the "almost nothing" we know tends to become complexity piled upon complexity, language explained by more language, authorities resting on other authorities — a splendid disguise of abstractions much like the emperor's new clothes. "Scholars and critics," Walter Slatoff writes, "who would distinguish carefully between various sorts of Neo-Platonism, or examine in minute detail the structure of a chapter or the transmutations of a prevailing metaphor, or trace the full nuances of a topical allusion, will settle happily for mere labels like distance, involvement, identification,"[2] labels that not only suffer from vagueness but deceive, creating the illusion that they refer to some real reaction people in fact shared and the critic in fact observed.

This tradition — assuming a uniform response on the part of readers and audiences that the critic somehow knows and understands — goes back to Aristotle's concept of catharsis, and his notions about people's apparently fixed responses to details of wording. Or this tradition might even have originated in Plato's assertion that poetry debilitates. Although the Greeks observed the phenomena that they ascribed to audiences better than later theorists, the tradition flourished after them, reaching a peak with the "rules" of the lesser neoclassical critics. Early psychoanalytic writers on literature followed, rather uncritically, this collectivist view from the litterateurs. Thus we find Otto Rank defending his oedipal interpretations of myths because, "The people imagine the hero in this manner, investing him with their own infantile fantasies."[3] Freud himself assumed a collective response to *Oedipus Rex* in the letter of October 15, 1897, in which he reported to his confidant Fliess, "I have found love of the mother and jealousy of the father in my own case too, and now believe it to be a general phenomenon of early childhood." "If that is the case, the gripping power of *Oedipus Rex,* in spite of all the rational objections to the inexorable fate that the story presupposes, becomes intelligible." "Every member of the audience was once a budding Oedipus in phantasy, and this dream-fulfillment played out in reality causes everyone to recoil in horror, with the full measure of repression which separates his infantile from his present state."[4]

Everyone recoils? Freud himself avoided this fallacy when he studied jokes as a kind of mini-literature; they have a "frame" and a text with especially sensitive formal balances and a response. What would one think of a theory of jokes that always concluded, "and so you laugh" or "and so you don't laugh," regardless of whether you did nor didn't in fact laugh? After all, someone might have heard the joke before; someone else might be depressed; a third person might have no sense of humor, and so on. Indeed, responses to jokes are so various that, for a time, researchers (at Yale) were exploring a "mirth response test," trying to sort personality types by observing which cartoons they found funny.[5] Should we then postulate that responses to tragedy, something so infinitely more subtle than

[1]Walter J. Slatoff, *With Respect to Readers: Dimensions of Literary Response* (Ithaca and London: Cornell University Press, 1970), p. 188. [Au.]

[2]Ibid., p. 35. [Au.]

[3]Otto Rank, *The Myth of the Birth of the Hero* (1914) (New York: Vintage Books, 1959), Chapter 3, p. 89n. [Au.]

[4]Marie Bonaparte, Anna Freud, Ernst Kris, eds., *The Origins of Psychoanalysis,* trans. Eric Mosbacher and James Strachey (New York: Basic Books, 1954), letter of October 15, 1897. [Au.]

[5]Jacob Levine, "Response to Humor," *Scientific American* 194 (1956): 31–35. [Au.]

a cartoon, are fixed? No, and for some decades now we have, in fact, known the contrary.

It was in the 1920s that I. A. Richards asked his Cambridge undergraduates for the protocols that led to his ground-breaking *Practical Criticism*.[6] He asked his students "to comment freely in writing on" a series of poems, their authorship undisclosed. Richards found that these supposedly well-educated young Englishmen were evaluating very strangely indeed, misreading the plain sense of the poems, imposing cranky sets of preconceptions, responding in terms of stock sentimentalities, cynicisms, and other doctrines, as well as (perhaps) irrelevant memories. Richards, let us notice, was exploring his readers' conscious, verbalized responses to literature. Interested in education, he tended to concentrate on those parts of literary response that could be taught, and indeed, his analysis of misreadings helped to reform, root and branch, the teaching of literature over the next four decades. Today, even among schoolchildren, one finds more sophisticated reading than Richards found among his jazz-age Cantabrigians.[7]

One would expect the giant entertainment corporations, with millions riding on each reel of celluloid, to have studied response far more carefully than impoverished English teachers could. But the published research in this field remains rather elementary.[8] There are many studies of effect, but they move casually back and forth between the transfer of information, the fulfillment of individuals' needs (for example, to escape), the impact on morality (typically delinquency), and immediate reactions of "like" and "dislike." Indeed, the industry has developed machines — the Lazarsfeld-Stanton program analyzer, the Cirlin Reactograph — with which an audience can indicate its fluctuating likes, dislikes, and indifferences. Of course, such a device cannot sort out variables — one cannot tell, for example, whether a member of the audience is disliking the whole movie or just the "bad guy" in it. In general, this one-dimensional quality carries over to the analysis of the content of films. The most sophisticated scheme I have seen only gets to issues like "Main story type," that is, "Is it a Western or a gangster movie?", "Marital status and changes of leads A, B, and C," "Sports (type and prominence)," or "Importance of part and characterization of unskilled labor." I understand that much research in this field is kept secret because of its commercial value. If what has been published is an accurate sample, there would seem to be little reason to do so.

Such simple categories show that a study of audience response demands at least one thing: some sensibly subtle way of analyzing the texts, both the text the artist creates and the text of what the audience says. I. A. Richards had that, with his marvelous sense of language, but his experience showed a second tool one must have to understand audiences. Without a psychology adequate to explain individual responses, one does not know what to do with them except pass judgment on them. "We rarely concern ourselves, for example," says Walter Slatoff, surveying the post-Richards critical scene, "with the problem of individual differences among readers. . . . On the few occasions we do entertain such questions we speak as though they were settled by reducing response to two categories — appropriate and inappropriate."[9] Thus, although Richards avowed a concern to maintain differences of opinion, he shifted the problem of evaluating poems to a much harsher dogmatism: passing judgment on "the relative values of different states of mind, about varying forms, and degrees, of order in the personality."[10]

[6]I. A. Richards, *Practical Criticism: A Study of Literary Judgment* (New York: Harcourt, Brace, 1951). [Au.]

[7]James R. Squire, *The Responses of Adolescents While Reading Four Short Stories,* NCTE Research Report No. 2, 1964. James R. Wilson, *Responses of College Freshmen to Three Novels,* NCTE Research Report No. 7, 1966. Alan C. Purves with Victoria Rippere, *Elements of Writing about a Literary Work: A Study of Response to Literature,* NCTE Research Report No. 9, 1968. All published by National Council of Teachers of English, 508 South Sixth Street, Champaign, Illinois 61820. [Au.]

[8]Leo A. Handel, *Hollywood Looks at Its Audience: A Report of Film Audience Research* (Urbana: University of Illinois Press, 1950), particularly Chapters 11 and 12, provides an accurate sample of what is being published currently, although the work is twenty years old. [Au.]

[9]Slatoff, *With Respect to Readers,* pp. 13–14. [Au.]

[10]Richards, *Practical Criticism,* pp. 347–49. [Au.]

Had Richards had a usable psychology of individuals, he would have been able, presumably, to see how his protocols were reflecting personality at all levels, not just the teachable surface of consciousness. Indeed, David Bleich has recently done just that: shown how some of Richard's protocols reveal the unconscious themes his Cantabrigians were projecting into the texts as part of their response.[11] "It has become a matter of course that any item of human behavior shows a continuum of dynamic meaning, reaching from the surface through many layers of crust to the 'core' " — thus, Erik Erikson,[12] articulating with his customary eloquence one of the most basic and widely confirmed of psychoanalytic discoveries. Freud's earliest case histories showed it and so did this morning's experience in hundreds of clinics and consulting-rooms. I know, for example, how the style and subject and method of this book stem from very early experiences of my own and my whole present character, including various half-conscious wishes and fears. Although these unconscious and infantile sources are by no means the only ones, if so conscious an act as writing an experimental and theoretical book has strong buried components, I find it hard to believe that responding to a play, a movie, or a poem does not. And, of course, it does.

As the remainder of this book will show, readers respond to literature in terms of their own "lifestyle" (or "character" or "personality" or "identity"). By such terms, psychoanalytic writers mean an individual's characteristic way of dealing with the demands of outer and inner reality. Such a style will have grown through time from earliest infancy. It will also be what the individual brings with him to any new experience, including the experience of literature. Each new experience develops the style, while the preexisting style shapes each new experience. And this style can be described quite accurately (but not, of course, impersonally).

[11]David Bleich, "The Determination of Literary Value," *Literature and Psychology* 17 (1967): 19–30. [Au.]

[12]Erik H. Erikson, "The Dream Specimen of Psychoanalysis," in Robert P. Knight and Cyrus R. Friedman, eds., *Psychoanalytic Psychiatry and Psychology,* Clinical and Theoretical Papers of the Austen Riggs Center, Vol. 1 (New York: Hallmark-Hubner Press, 1954), p. 140. [Au.]

In short, psychoanalysis offers a powerful theory of individual responses to literature, and it has done so ever since Freud's 1905 study of jokes. (Interestingly, in that very early study, he also showed how social and economic factors would affect the pattern of inhibitions an individual brought to a joke and so affect his responses, but *indirectly,* as they filtered through his personality.) Other writers have extended this first psychoanalytic aesthetics, Freud's theory of jokes, to other genres and to literature generally.[13]

For the most part, however, psychoanalytic students of literature, like conventional literary critics, have looked not at the actual individual reading but at the text, the words-on-the-page. Then they have posited a response on the basis of the text. Thus, paradoxically, the psychology that more than any other deals closely and intensely with individuals — psychoanalytic psychology — has in this instance retreated from the living human being, the spirit, if you will, to the letter.

By contrast, conventional psychological literature offers hundreds of studies that deal with actual readers but that suffer from a lack of theory.[14] For example, physiological studies tell how heart rate, the electrical resistance of the palm of the hand, or its sweat pattern, vary as subjects watch a movie. Indeed, an Italian experi-

[13]Norman N. Holland, *The Dynamics of Literary Response* (New York: Oxford University Press, 1968). Robert Waelder, *Psychoanalytic Avenues to Art* (New York: International Universities Press, 1965). Ernst Kris, *Psychoanalytic Explorations in Art* (New York: International Universities Press, 1952). Simon O. Lesser, *Fiction and the Unconscious* (Boston: Beacon Press, 1957). Philip Weissman, *Creativity in the Theater: A Psychoanalytic Study* (New York: Dell Publishing Co., 1965). In addition to Freud's essays on *Jokes* (1905) and "The 'Uncanny' " (1919), see my attempt at a synthesis: "Freud on the Response," in Holland, *Psychoanalysis and Shakespeare* (New York: McGraw-Hill Book Co., 1966). [Au.]

[14]I am exceedingly grateful to Ms. Betty Jane Saik, Ms. Mary Z. Bartlett, and Mr. Stephen Gormey for assembling and helping me punch-card as complete an index of studies of response to the arts as *Psychological Abstracts* affords. It was after our own work, in 1972, that an excellent survey appeared by Alan C. Purves and Richard Beach, *Literature and the Reader: Research in Response to Literature, Reading Interests, and the Teaching of Literature* (University of Illinois at Urbana-Champaign: National Council of Teachers of English, 1972). It supports our general conclusion that results are many but unsystematic. [Au.]

ment even investigated the differing ways identical and fraternal twins fidgeted![15] But I find it hard to believe a single variable such as pulse rate or fidget frequency could represent a complex, multivariant transaction like a response to a film.

Other studies resort to personality tests, but I think it is not much of an improvement over the physiological approach to be able to say that reading gruesome passages from Edgar Allan Poe increases the anxious and aggressive responses to inkblots. Much closer to the method of this book is the study in which judges were able to match viewers' open-ended comments on a movie to their Rorschach responses. Again, however, the experiment merely shows the correlation; it does not suggest an underlying mechanism, only that "individual differences in the perception of a motion picture are a function of global aspects of personality as elicited by the Rorschach."[16] Different personality tests lead to similarly vague conclusions: "Movie attendance is related in some instances to the central aspects of personality." A child's choices among stories "cohere with other observable characteristics of his personality."[17] Other studies claim to have shown that men watch the men in movies more than women do; that boys prefer adventure stories, while girls prefer stories about love, private life, and glamor; that children who are already pretty aggressive identify with different characters in a Western according to the degree of their pre-existing aggression, their sex, and the ending of the film.[18] No doubt, these studies (and hundreds more like them) follow out admirably the canons of experimental rigor. As a continuing line of research, however, they end most inconclusively, to judge, if nothing else, by the number of experimenters who turn to the same old issues over and over again. Instead of coherent research, one finds random observations. What these studies may have gained in rigor they certainly lack in theory.

One returns then to literary and psychoanalytic studies, weak in experiment but strong on theory. Not always, of course. I do not feel that my understanding of the differences in readers' responses is advanced by a literary critic's introducing an "*informed* reader" with (also italicized) "*literary* competence" or even a more generalized "reading self," who (or that) is roughly the critic's age, shares his ethnic background, "has experienced war, marriage, and the responsibility of children," and so on.[19] Some statements about response by literary and psychoanalytic folk do add more rigor and theory than sense; some do suggest pervasive links between, on the one hand, the reader's personality (in depth) and his conscious reading skill and, on the other, his response. I am thinking of Morse Peckham's explanation of the effect of one's past aesthetic experiences on response, a theory supported by very detailed analyses from a variety of arts and corresponding to psychoanalytic notions of the role of the ego in art.[20] Similarly, child therapists like Lilli Peller and Kate Friedlaender have shown how children's stories reflect at a conscious level the child's unconscious fantasies, and therefore how the age appropriate to the fantasy determines the age at which a child will like the story. They, too, are showing a theoretical basis for combining the detailed analysis of a story with the depth analysis of the response.[21]

[15]When I am not using these studies substantively, I shall simply list them by author and *Psychological Abstracts (PA)* reference. Edward Opton, Jr., *PA* (1967): 5663. Jack Block, *PA* (1963): 7682. Richard C. Pillard et al., *PA* (1967): 6610. Luigi Gedda et al., *PA* (1956): 443. [Au.]

[16]Lutz von Rosenstiel, *PA* (1967): 4630. Marvin Spiegelman, "Effect of Personality on the Perception of a Motion Picture," *Journal of Projective Techniques* 19 (1955): 461–464. [Au.]

[17]E. M. Scott, *PA* (1958): 4129. G. Foulds, *PA* (1943): 994. [Au.]

[18]Eleanor E. Maccoby et al., *PA* (1960): 4080. Paul I. Lyness, *PA* (1952): 7218. Robert S. Albert, *PA* (1959): 4603. [Au.]

[19]Stanley E. Fish, *Self-Consuming Artifacts: The Experience of Seventeenth-Century Literature* (Berkeley: University of California Press, 1972), p. 406. Slatoff, *With Respect to Readers,* pp. 55–56. [Au.]

[20]Morse Peckham, *Man's Rage for Chaos: Biology, Behavior, and the Arts* (New York: Chilton Books, 1965). See also my review article, "Psychoanalytic Criticism and Perceptual Psychology," *Literature and Psychology* 16 (1966): 81–92. [Au.]

[21]Lilli E. Peller, "Libidinal Phases, Ego Development, and Play," *The Psychoanalytic Study of the Child* 9 (1954): 178–98; "Reading and Daydreams in Latency; Boy-Girl Differences," *Journal of the American Psychoanalytic Association* 6 (1958): 57–70; "Daydreams and Children's Favorite

Such studies, in effect, deal with classes of readers. Psychoanalysis, however, is par excellence the science of human individuality (if there can be a "science" of uniqueness), and we would expect it to be most interesting about literary response when it speaks about individuals. However, it must then necessarily give up repeatable experiments. For example, a group of experimenters, in projecting films for hospitalized psychiatric patients, found that the viewers interposed their individual defensive patterns between themselves and the film to keep the affect something they could tolerate. Hence, one could not assume that any given film would necessarily arouse certain feelings. Similarly, in an example of "poetry therapy," David V. Forrest showed how disturbed patients responded to the well-known lyric, "Western wind, when wilt thou blow," in terms of their several personality types, paranoid, schizoid, hysteric, and so on.[22] These papers suggest structures relating personality to response (through defense mechanisms or diagnostic categories that combine defense and level of fixation). They do not, however, take the further step: going beyond types and categories to examine the work of art, the response, and the responder in detail.

One often finds analyses of the individual (but not the work) in case histories. Avery Weisman, for example, describes a rigid, obsessional man who could not face a sea captain's loss of authority in a movie and left the theater before the film's end. The whole setting — other patrons, streets, bodily sensations — seemed unreal to him: he had dealt with his guilt and anxiety by separating his intellectual processes of reality-testing from his conventional, pleasurable attachment to the dream world of the film. Edith Buxbaum, in a famous case, tells of a boy compulsively driven to read detective stories almost to the exclusion of any other activity. He was satisfying his aggressive wishes toward his mother by allying himself with the murderer. At the same time, he assuaged his guilt by feeling like the victim and also the detective. Thus his symptom served both defense and the gratification of instincts, and he became locked into it. Still more tragic was the patient of Gilbert J. Rose who committed suicide after witnessing a performance of Duerrenmatt's *The Visit:* he, like the hero of the play, felt himself the victim of a fantastically powerful bitch-goddess.[23]

Caroline Shrodes, however, has studied individual students' responses to particular literary works on the assumption that literary experience matches the therapeutic process: from identification and interaction with the work, to emotional catharsis, to insight into one's particular conflicts and relationships.[24] Less clinically, David Bleich in a growing series of moving and perceptive essays has analyzed the responses of ordinary readers, students usually, in order to elicit the unconscious themes of the text. In other words, he reverses the usual assumption of critics, that by analyzing the text one can understand the response; rather, he argues, by analyzing what readers find in it, one comes to understand the text.[25] And he is right to do so. To analyze the text in formal isolation as so many "words-on-a-

Books: Psychoanalytic Comments," *The Psychoanalytic Study of the Child* 14 (1959): 414–33. Kate Friedlaender, "Children's Books and Their Function in Latency and Prepuberty," *American Imago* 3 (1942): 129–50. [Au.]

[22]Gordon Globus and Roy Shulman, "Considerations on Affective Response to Motion Pictures" (unpublished paper, Department of Psychiatry, Boston University School of Medicine); also cited in Holland, *Dynamics* (see note 13), pp. 94–95. David V. Forrest, "The Patient's Sense of the Poem: Affinities and Ambiguities," in Jack J. Leedy, ed., *Poetry Therapy: The Use of Poetry in the Treatment of Emotional Disorders* (Philadelphia: J. B. Lippincott Co., 1969), Chapter 20, pp. 231–59. [Au.]

[23]Avery D. Weisman, "Reality Sense and Reality Testing," *Behavioral Science* 3 (1958): 228–61. Edith Buxbaum, "The Role of Detective Stories in a Child Analysis," *Psychoanalytic Quarterly* 10 (1941): 373–81. Gilbert J. Rose, "Creative Imagination in Terms of Ego 'Core' and Boundaries," *International Journal of Psycho-Analysis* 45 (1964): 75–85. [Au.]

[24]Caroline Shrodes, "Bibliotherapy: An Application of Psychoanalytic Theory," *American Imago* 17 (1960): 311–19; "The Dynamics of Reading: Implications for Bibliotherapy," *ETC.: A Review of General Semantics* 18 (1961): 21–33. Both articles are based on her "Bibliotherapy: A Theoretical and Clinical Experimental Study" (Ph.D. dissertation, University of California, Berkeley, 1949). [Au.]

[25]David Bleich, "The Determination of Literary Value," *Literature and Psychology* 17 (1967): 19–30; "Emotional Origins of Literary Meaning," *College English* 31 (1969): 30–40; "Psychological Bases of Learning from Literature," *College English* 33 (1971): 32–45. [Au.]

page" (in the old formula of the New Criticism) is a highly artificial procedure. A literary text, after all, in an objective sense consists only of a certain configuration of specks of carbon black on dried wood pulp. When these marks become words, when those words become images or metaphors or characters or events, they do so because the reader plays the part of a prince to the sleeping beauty. He gives them life out of his own desires. When he does so, he brings his lifestyle to bear on the work. He mingles his unconscious loves and fears and adaptations with the words and images he synthesizes at a conscious level.

It is, therefore, quite impossible to say from a text alone how people will respond to it. Only after we have understood how some specific individual responds, how the different parts of his individual personality recreate the different details of the text, can we begin to formulate general hypotheses about the way many or all readers respond. Only then — if then.

At the same time, however, the reader is surely responding to *something*. The literary text may be only so many marks on a page — at most a matrix of psychological possibilities for its readers. Nevertheless only some possibilities, we would say, truly fit the matrix. One would not say, for example, that a reader of that sentence from "A Rose for Emily" who thought the "tableau" described an Eskimo was really responding to the story at all — only pursuing some mysterious inner exploration. In the basic question of this book, "Who reads what how?", there must be a "what," and our next task is to find out what it is.

Stanley Fish

b. 1938

The agent provocateur of contemporary literary theory, Stanley Fish was born in Providence, Rhode Island, and raised in Philadelphia. He received his A.B. at Penn (1959) and his A.M. and Ph.D. (1962) at Yale, which published his dissertation on John Skelton. Fish taught at Berkeley, becoming a full professor in 1974. In that year, Fish moved to Johns Hopkins as Kenan professor, and in 1986, as both professor of law and as chairman of the English department, to Duke University, where he has attracted a stellar group of theorists, including Fredric Jameson (Ch. 5) and Barbara Herrnstein Smith (Ch. 9). In his most recent metatheoretical work, Fish has attacked theory as pointless, impotent to constrain the will-to-power of interpretation, whereas formerly, he had restricted his rhetorical assaults to individual theorists like Wolfgang Iser or to fields like linguistics and stylistics. Fish's career as a gadfly began with his second book, Surprised by Sin: The Reader in *Paradise Lost (1967), which transgressed with both feet the "affective fallacy" by which the New Criticism had eliminated the study of the audience. The object of Fish's concern has shifted from the implied reader immanent within the text in* Self-Consuming Artifacts: The Experience of Seventeenth-Century Literature *(1972), to the experience of actual readers and interpretive communities of readers in* Is There a Text in This Class? *(1980). Most recently, Fish has generalized his pragmatic approach to rhetoric and the reader beyond literary concerns; his social and political essays appear in* Doing What Comes Naturally: Change, Rhetoric, and the Practice of Theory in Literary and Legal Studies *(1989),* There's No Such Thing As Free Speech: and It's a Good Thing, Too *(1994), and* Professional Correctness: Literary Studies and Political Change *(1995). "Interpreting the* Variorum,*" the transitional essay in Fish's career, was included in a different form in* Is There a Text in This Class?; *the original version, reprinted here, is from* Critical Inquiry *3 (1977).*

Interpreting the Variorum

I

The first two volumes of the Milton *Variorum Commentary* have now appeared, and I find them endlessly fascinating. My interest, however, is not in the questions they manage to resolve (although these are many) but in the theoretical assumptions which are responsible for their occasional failures. These failures constitute a pattern, one in which a host of commentators — separated by as much as two hundred and seventy years but contemporaries in their shared concerns — are lined up on either side of an interpretive crux. Some of these are famous, even infamous: what is the two-handed engine in *Lycidas*? what is the meaning of Haemony in *Comus*? Others, like the identity of whoever or whatever comes to the window in *L'Allegro,* line 46, are only slightly less notorious. Still others are of interest largely to those who make editions: matters of pronoun referents, lexical ambiguities, punctuation. In each instance, however, the pattern is consistent: every position taken is supported by wholly convincing evidence — in the case of *L'Allegro* and the coming to the window there is a persuasive champion for every proper noun within a radius of ten lines — and the editorial procedure always ends either in the graceful throwing up of hands, or in the recording of a disagreement between the two editors themselves. In short, these are problems that apparently cannot be solved, at least not by the methods traditionally brought to bear on them. What I would like to argue is that they are not *meant* to be solved, but to be experienced (they signify), and that consequently any procedure that attempts to determine which of a number of readings is correct will necessarily fail. What this means is that the commentators and editors have been asking the wrong questions and that a new set of questions based on new assumptions must be formulated. I would like at least to make a beginning in that direction by examining some of the points in dispute in Milton's sonnets. I choose the sonnets because they are brief and because one can move easily from them to the theoretical issues with which this paper is finally concerned.

Milton's twentieth sonnet — "Lawrence of virtuous father virtuous son" — has been the subject of relatively little commentary. In it the poet invites a friend to join him in some distinctly Horatian pleasures — a neat repast intermixed with conversation, wine, and song; a respite from labor all the more enjoyable because outside the earth is frozen and the day sullen. The only controversy the sonnet has inspired concerns its final two lines:

> Lawrence of virtuous father virtuous son,
>   Now that the fields are dank, and ways are mire,
>   Where shall we sometimes meet, and by the fire
>   Help waste a sullen day; what may be won
> From the hard season gaining; time will run
>   On smoother, till Favonius reinspire
>   The frozen earth; and clothe in fresh attire
>   The lily and rose, that neither sowed nor spun.
> What neat repast shall feast us, light and choice,
>   Of Attic taste, with wine, whence we may rise
>   To hear the lute well touched, or artful voice
> Warble immortal notes and Tuscan air?
>   He who of those delights can judge, and spare
>   To interpose them oft, is not unwise.[1]

The focus of the controversy is the word "spare," for which two readings have been proposed: leave time for and refrain from. Obviously the point is crucial if one is to resolve the sense of the lines. In one reading "those delights" are being recommended — he who can leave time for them is not unwise; in the other, they are the subject of a warning — he who knows when to refrain from them is not unwise. The proponents of the two interpretations cite as evidence both English and Latin syntax, various sources and analogues, Milton's "known attitudes" as they are found in his other writings, and the unambiguously expressed sentiments of

[1]All references are to *The Poems of John Milton,* ed., John Carey and Alastair Fowler (London, 1968). [Au.]

the following sonnet on the same question. Surveying these arguments, A. S. P. Woodhouse roundly declares: "It is plain that all the honours rest with" the meaning "refrain from" or "forbear to." This declaration is followed immediately by a bracketed paragraph initialled D. B. for Douglas Bush, who, writing presumably after Woodhouse has died, begins "In spite of the array of scholarly names the case for 'forbear to' may be thought much weaker, and the case for 'spare time for' much stronger, than Woodhouse found them."[2] Bush then proceeds to review much of the evidence marshaled by Woodhouse and to draw from it exactly the opposite conclusion. If it does nothing else, this curious performance anticipates a point I shall make in a few moments: evidence brought to bear in the course of formalist analyses — that is, analyses generated by the assumption that meaning is embedded in the artifact — will always point in as many directions as there are interpreters; that is, not only will it prove something, it will prove anything.

It would appear then that we are back at square one, with a controversy that cannot be settled because the evidence is inconclusive. But what if that controversy is *itself* regarded as evidence, not of an ambiguity that must be removed, but of an ambiguity that readers have always experienced? What, in other words, if for the question "what does 'spare' mean?" we substitute the question "what does the fact that the meaning of 'spare' has always been an issue mean"? The advantage of this question is that it can be answered. Indeed it has already been answered by the readers who are cited in the *Variorum Commentary*. What the readers debate is the judgment the poem makes on the delights of recreation; what their debate indicates is that the judgment is blurred by a verb that can be made to participate in contradictory readings. (Thus the important thing about the evidence surveyed in the *Variorum* is not how it is marshaled, but that it could be marshaled at all, because it then becomes evidence of the equal availability of both interpretations.) In other words, the lines first generate a pressure for judgment — "he who of those delights can judge" — and then decline to deliver it; the pressure, however, still exists, and it is transferred from the words on the page to the reader (the reader is "he who"), who comes away from the poem not with a statement, but with a responsibility, the responsibility of deciding when and how often — if at all — to indulge in "those delights" (they remain delights in either case). This transferring of responsibility from the text to its readers is what the lines ask us to do — it is the essence of their experience — and in my terms it is therefore what the lines *mean*. It is a meaning the *Variorum* critics attest to even as they resist it, for what they are laboring so mightily to do by fixing the sense of the lines is to give the responsibility back. The text, however, will not accept it and remains determinedly evasive, even in its last two words, "not unwise." In their position these words confirm the impossibility of extracting from the poem a moral formula, for the assertion (certainly too strong a word) they complete is of the form, "He who does such and such, of him it cannot be said that he is unwise"; but of course neither can it be said that he is wise. Thus what Bush correctly terms the "defensive" "not unwise" operates to prevent us from attaching the label "wise" to any action, including *either* of the actions — leaving time for or refraining from — represented by the ambiguity of "spare." Not only is the pressure of judgment taken off the poem, it is taken off the activity the poem at first pretended to judge. The issue is finally not the moral status of "those delights" — they become in seventeenth-century terms "things indifferent" — but on the good or bad uses to which they can be put by readers who are left, as Milton always leaves them, to choose and manage by themselves.

Let us step back for a moment and see how far we've come. We began with an apparently insoluble problem and proceeded, not to solve it, but to make it signify; first by regarding it as evidence of an experience and then by specifying for that experience a meaning. Moreover, the

[2]*A Variorum Commentary on the Poems of John Milton*, vol. 2, pt. 2, ed. A. S. P. Woodhouse and Douglas Bush (New York, 1972), p. 475. [Au.]

configurations of that experience, when they are made available by a reader-oriented analysis, serve as a check against the endlessly inconclusive adducing of evidence which characterizes formalist analysis. That is to say, any determination of what "spare" means (in a positivist or literal sense) is liable to be upset by the bringing forward of another analogue, or by a more complete computation of statistical frequencies, or by the discovery of new biographical information, or by anything else; but if we first determine that everything in the line before "spare" creates the expectation of an imminent judgment, then the ambiguity of "spare" can be assigned a significance in the context of that expectation. (It disappoints it and transfers the pressure of judgment to us.) That context is experiential, and it is within its contours and constraints that significances are established (both in the act of reading and in the analysis of that act). In formalist analyses the only constraints are the notoriously open-ended possibilities and combination of possibilities that emerge when one begins to consult dictionaries and grammars and histories; to consult dictionaries, grammars, and histories is to assume that meanings can be specified independently of the activity of reading; what the example of "spare" shows is that it is in and by that activity that meanings — experiential, not positivist — are created.

In other words, it is the structure of the reader's experience rather than any structures available on the page that should be the object of description. In the case of Sonnet XX, that experiential structure was uncovered when an examination of formal structures led to an impasse; and the pressure to remove that impasse led to the substitution of one set of questions for another. It will more often be the case that the pressure of a spectacular failure will be absent. The sins of formalist-positivist analysis are primarily sins of omission, not an inability to explain phenomena, but an inability to see that they are there because its assumptions make it inevitable that they will be overlooked or suppressed. Consider, for example, the concluding lines of another of Milton's sonnets, "Avenge O Lord thy slaughtered saints."

Avenge O Lord thy slaughtered saints, whose
bones
Lie scattered on the Alpine mountains cold,
Even them who kept thy truth so pure of old
When all our fathers worshipped stocks and
stones,
Forget not: in thy book record their groans
Who were thy sheep and in their ancient fold
Slain by the bloody Piedmontese that rolled
Mother with infant down the rocks. Their
moans
The vales redoubled to the hills, and they
To heaven. Their martyred blood and ashes sow
O'er all the Italian fields where still doth sway
The triple Tyrant: that from these may grow
A hundredfold, who having learnt thy way
Early may fly the Babylonian woe.

In this sonnet, the poet simultaneously petitions God and wonders aloud about the justice of allowing the faithful — "Even them who kept thy truth" — to be so brutally slaughtered. The note struck is alternately one of plea and complaint, and there is more than a hint that God is being called to account for what has happened to the Waldensians. It is generally agreed, however, that the note of complaint is less and less sounded and that the poem ends with an affirmation of faith in the ultimate operation of God's justice. In this reading, the final lines are taken to be saying something like this: From the blood of these martyred, O God, raise up a new and more numerous people, who, by virtue of an early education in thy law, will escape destruction by fleeing the Babylonian woe. Babylonian woe has been variously glossed;[3] but whatever it is taken to mean it is always read as part of a statement that specifies a set of conditions for the escaping of destruction or punishment; it is a warning to the reader as well as a petition to God. As a warning, however, it is oddly situated since the conditions it seems to specify were in fact met by

[3]It is first of all a reference to the city of iniquity from which the Hebrews are urged to flee in Isaiah and Jeremiah. In Protestant polemics Babylon is identified with the Roman Church whose destruction is prophesied in the book of Revelation. And in some Puritan tracts, Babylon is the name for Augustine's earthly city, from which the faithful are to flee inwardly in order to escape the fate awaiting the unregenerate. See *Variorum Commentary,* pp. 440–41. [Au.]

the Waldensians, who of all men most followed God's laws. In other words, the details of their story would seem to undercut the affirmative moral the speaker proposes to draw from it. It is further undercut by a reading that is fleetingly available, although no one has acknowledged it because it is a function, not of the words on the page, but of the experience of the reader. In that experience, line 13 will for a moment be accepted as a complete sense unit and the emphasis of the line will fall on "thy way" (a phrase that has received absolutely no attention in the commentaries). At this point "thy way" can refer only to the way in which God has dealt with the Waldensians. That is, "thy way" seems to pick up the note of outrage with which the poem began, and if we continue to so interpret it, the conclusion of the poem will be a grim one indeed: since by this example it appears that God rains down punishment indiscriminately, it would be best perhaps to withdraw from the arena of his service, and thereby hope at least to be safely out of the line of fire. This is not the conclusion we carry away, because as line 14 unfolds, another reading of "thy way" becomes available, a reading in which "early" qualifies "learnt" and refers to something the faithful should do (learn thy way at an early age) rather than to something God has failed to do (save the Waldensians). These two readings are answerable to the pulls exerted by the beginning and ending of the poem: the outrage expressed in the opening lines generates a pressure for an explanation, and the grimmer reading is answerable to that pressure (even if it is also disturbing); the ending of the poem, the forward and upward movement of lines 10–14, creates the expectation of an affirmation, and the second reading fulfills that expectation. The criticism shows that in the end we settle on the more optimistic reading — it feels better — but even so the other has been a part of our experience, and because it has been a part of our experience, it *means*. What it means is that while we may be able to extract from the poem a statement affirming God's justice, we are not allowed to forget the evidence (of things seen) that makes the extraction so difficult (both for the speaker and for us). It is a difficulty we experience in the act of reading, even though a criticism which takes no account of that act has, as we have seen, suppressed it.

II

In each of the sonnets we have considered, the significant word or phrase occurs at a line break where a reader is invited to place it first in one and then in another structure of syntax and sense. This moment of hesitation, of semantic or syntactic slide, is crucial to the experience the verse provides, but, in a formalist analysis, that moment will disappear, either because it has been flattened out and made into an (insoluble) interpretive crux, or because it has been eliminated in the course of a procedure that is incapable of finding value in temporal phenomena. In the case of "When I consider how my light is spent," these two failures are combined.

When I consider how my light is spent,
  Ere half my days, in this dark world and wide,
  And that one talent which is death to hide,
  Lodged with me useless, though my soul more bent
To serve therewith my maker, and present
  My true account, lest he returning chide,
  Doth God exact day-labour, light denied,
  I fondly ask; but Patience to prevent
That murmur, soon replies, God doth not need
  Either man's work or his own gifts, who best
  Bear his mild yoke, they serve him best, his state
Is kingly. Thousands at his bidding speed
  And post o'er land and ocean without rest:
  They also serve who only stand and wait.

The interpretive crux once again concerns the final line: "They also serve who only stand and wait." For some this is an unqualified acceptance of God's will, while for others the note of affirmation is muted or even forced. The usual kinds of evidence are marshaled by the opposing parties, and the usual inconclusiveness is the result. There are some areas of agreement. "All the interpretations," Woodhouse remarks, "recognize that the sonnet commences from a mood of depression, frustration [and] impatience."[4] The ob-

[4]*Variorum Commentary,* p. 469. [Au.]

ject of impatience is a God who would first demand service and then take away the means of serving, and the oft noted allusion to the parable of the talents lends scriptural support to the accusation the poet is implicitly making: you have cast the wrong servant into unprofitable darkness. It has also been observed that the syntax and rhythm of these early lines, and especially of lines 6–8, are rough and uncertain; the speaker is struggling with his agitated thoughts and he changes directions abruptly, with no regard for the line as a unit of sense. The poem, says one critic, "seems almost out of control."[5]

The question I would ask is "whose control?"; for what these formal descriptions point to (but do not acknowledge) is the extraordinary number of adjustments required of readers who would negotiate these lines. The first adjustment is the result of the expectations created by the second half of line 6 — "lest he returning chide." Since there is no full stop after "chide," it is natural to assume that this will be an introduction to reported speech, and to assume further that what will be reported is the poet's anticipation of the voice of God as it calls him, to an unfair accounting. This assumption does not survive line 7 — "Doth God exact day-labour, light denied" — which rather than chiding the poet for his inactivity seems to rebuke him for having expected that chiding. The accents are precisely those heard so often in the Old Testament when God answers a reluctant Gideon, or a disputatious Moses, or a self-justifying Job: do you presume to judge my ways or to appoint my motives? Do you think I would exact day labor, light denied? In other words, the poem seems to turn at this point from a questioning of God to a questioning of that questioning; or, rather, the reader turns from the one to the other in the act of revising his projection of what line 7 will say and do. As it turns out, however, that revision must itself be revised because it had been made within the assumption that what we are hearing is the voice of God. This assumption falls before the very next phrase "I fondly ask," which requires not one, but two adjustments. Since the speaker of line 7 is firmly identified as the poet, the line must be reinterpreted as a continuation of his complaint — Is that the way you operate, God, denying light, but exacting labor? — but even as that interpretation emerges, the poet withdraws from it by inserting the adverb "fondly," and once again the line slips out of the reader's control.

In a matter of seconds, then, line 7 has led four experiential lives, one as we anticipate it, another as that anticipation is revised, a third when we retroactively identify its speaker, and a fourth when that speaker disclaims it. What changes in each of these lives is the status of the poet's murmurings — they are alternately expressed, rejected, reinstated, and qualified — and as the sequence ends, the reader is without a firm perspective on the question of record: does God deal justly with his servants?

A firm perspective appears to be provided by Patience, whose entrance into the poem, the critics tell us, gives it both argumentative and metrical stability. But in fact the presence of Patience in the poem finally assures its continuing instability by making it impossible to specify the degree to which the speaker approves, or even participates in, the affirmation of the final line: "They also serve who only stand and wait." We know that Patience to prevent the poet's murmur soon replies (not soon enough however to prevent the murmur from registering), but we do not know when that reply ends. Does Patience fall silent in line 12, after "kingly"? or at the conclusion of line 13? or not at all? Does the poet appropriate these lines or share them or simply listen to them, as we do? These questions are unanswerable, and it is because they remain unanswerable that the poem ends uncertainly. The uncertainty is not in the statement it makes — in isolation line 14 is unequivocal — but in our inability to assign that statement to either the poet or to Patience. Were the final line marked unambiguously for the poet, then we would receive it as a resolution of his earlier doubts; and were it marked for Patience, it would be a sign that those doubts were still very much in force. It is marked for neither, and therefore we are with-

[5] Ibid., p. 457. [Au.]

out the satisfaction that a firmly conclusive ending (in *any* direction) would have provided. In short, we leave the poem unsure, and our unsureness is the realization (in our experience) of the unsureness with which the affirmation of the final line is, or is not, made. (This unsureness also operates to actualize the two possible readings of "wait": wait in the sense of expecting, that is waiting for an opportunity to serve actively; or wait in the sense of waiting *in* service, a waiting that is itself fully satisfying because the impulse to self-glorifying action has been stilled.)

The question debated in the *Variorum Commentary* is, how far from the mood of frustration and impatience does the poem finally move? The answer given by an experiential analysis is that you can't tell, and the fact that you can't tell is responsible for the uneasiness the poem has always inspired. It is that uneasiness which the critics inadvertently acknowledge when they argue about the force of the last line, but they are unable to make analytical use of what they acknowledge because they have no way of dealing with or even recognizing experiential (that is, temporal) structures. In fact, more than one editor has eliminated those structures by punctuating them out of existence: first by putting a full stop at the end of line 6 and thereby making it unlikely that the reader will assign line 7 to God (there will no longer be an expectation of reported speech), and then by supplying quotation marks for the sestet in order to remove any doubts one might have as to who is speaking. There is of course no warrant for these emendations, and in 1791 Thomas Warton had the grace and honesty to admit as much. "I have," he said, "introduced the turned commas both in the question and answer, not from any authority, but because they seem absolutely necessary to the sense."[6]

III

Editorial practices like these are only the most obvious manifestations of the assumptions to which I stand opposed: the assumption that there *is* a sense, that it is embedded or encoded in the text, and that it can be taken in at a single glance. These assumptions are, in order, positivist, holistic, and spatial, and to have them is to be committed both to a goal and to a procedure. The goal is to settle on a meaning, and the procedure involves first stepping back from the text, and then putting together or otherwise calculating the discrete units of significance it contains. My quarrel with this procedure (and with the assumptions that generate it) is that in the course of following it through the reader's activities are at once ignored and devalued. They are ignored because the text is taken to be self-sufficient — everything is *in* it — and they are devalued because when they are thought of at all, they are thought of as the disposable machinery of extraction. In the procedures I would urge, the reader's activities are at the center of attention, where they are regarded, not as leading to meaning, but as *having* meaning. The meaning they have is a consequence of their not being empty; for they include the making and revising of assumptions, the rendering and regretting of judgments, the coming to and abandoning of conclusions, the giving and withdrawing of approval, the specifying of causes, the asking of questions, the supplying of answers, the solving of puzzles. In a word, these activities are interpretive — rather than being preliminary to questions of value they are at every moment settling and resettling questions of value — and because they are interpretive, a description of them will also be, and without any additional step, an interpretation, not after the fact, but of the fact (of experiencing). It will be a description of a moving field of concerns, at once wholly present (not waiting for meaning, but constituting meaning) and continually in the act of reconstituting itself.

As a project such a description presents enormous difficulties, and there is hardly time to consider them here;[7] but it should be obvious from

[6]*Poems Upon Several Occasions, English, Italian, And Latin, With Translations, By John Milton,* ed. Thomas Warton (London, 1791), p. 352. [Au.]

[7]See my *Surprised by Sin: The Reader in* Paradise Lost (London and New York, 1967); *Self-consuming Artifacts; The Experience of Seventeenth-Century Literature* (Berkeley, 1972); "What Is Stylistics and Why Are They Saying Such Terrible Things About It?" in *Approaches to Poetics*, ed. Seymour Chatman (New York, 1973), pp. 109–52; "How Ordinary Is Ordinary Language?" in *New Literary History* 5 (Au-

my brief examples how different it is from the positivist-formalist project. Everything depends on the temporal dimension, and as a consequence the notion of a mistake, at least as something to be avoided, disappears. In a sequence where a reader first structures the field he inhabits and then is asked to restructure it (by changing an assignment of speaker or realigning attitudes and positions) there is no question of priority among his structurings; no one of them, even if it is the last, has privilege; each is equally legitimate, each equally the proper object of analysis, because each is equally an event in his experience.

The firm assertiveness of this paragraph only calls attention to the questions it avoids. Who is this reader? How can I presume to describe his experiences, and what do I say to readers who report that they do not have the experiences I describe? Let me answer these questions or rather make a beginning at answering them in the context of another example, this time from Milton's *Comus*. In line 46 of *Comus* we are introduced to the villain by way of a genealogy:

Bacchus that first from out the purple grape,
Crushed the sweet poison of misused wine.

In almost any edition of this poem, a footnote will tell you that Bacchus is the god of wine. Of course most readers already know that, and because they know it, they will be anticipating the appearance of "wine" long before they come upon it in the final position. Moreover, they will also be anticipating a negative judgment on it, in part because of the association of Bacchus with revelry and excess, and especially because the phrase "sweet poison" suggests that the judgment has already been made. At an early point then, we will have both filled in the form of the assertion and made a decision about its moral content. That decision is upset by the word "misused": for what "misused" asks us to do is transfer the pressure of judgment from wine (where we have already placed it) to the abusers of wine, and therefore when "wine" finally appears, we must declare it innocent of the charges we have ourselves made.

tumn 1973): 41–54; "Facts and Fictions: A Reply to Ralph Rader," *Critical Inquiry* 1 (June 1975): 883–91. [Au.]

This, then, is the structure of the reader's experience — the transferring of a moral label from a thing to those who appropriate it. It is an experience that depends on a reader for whom the name Bacchus has precise and immediate associations; another reader, a reader for whom those associations are less precise will not have that experience because he will not have rushed to a conclusion in relation to which the word "misused" will stand as a challenge. Obviously I am discriminating between these two readers and between the two equally real experiences they will have. It is not a discrimination based simply on information, because what is important is not the information itself, but the action of the mind which its possession makes possible for one reader and impossible for the other. One might discriminate further between them by noting that the point at issue — whether value is a function of objects and actions or of intentions — is at the heart of the seventeenth-century debate over "things indifferent." A reader who is aware of that debate will not only *have* the experience I describe; he will recognize at the end of it that he has been asked to take a position on one side of a continuing controversy; and that recognition (also a part of his experience) will be part of the disposition with which he moves into the lines that follow.

It would be possible to continue with this profile of the optimal reader, but I would not get very far before someone would point out that what I am really describing is the intended reader, the reader whose education, opinions, concerns, linguistic competencies, etc. make him capable of having the experience the author wished to provide. I would not resist this characterization because it seems obvious that the efforts of readers are always efforts to discern and therefore to realize (in the sense of becoming) an author's intention. I would only object if that realization were conceived narrowly, as the single act of comprehending an author's purpose, rather than (as I would conceive it) as the succession of acts readers perform in the continuing assumption that they are dealing with intentional beings. In this view discerning an intention is no more or less than understanding, and understanding includes (is constituted by) all the activities which make up what I call the structure of the reader's experience. To describe that experience is therefore to describe the reader's efforts at understanding, and to describe the reader's efforts at understanding is to describe his realization (in two senses) of an author's intention. Or to put it another way, what my analyses amount to are descriptions of a succession of decisions made by readers about an author's intention; decisions that are not limited to the specifying of purpose but include the specifying of every aspect of successively intended words; decisions that are precisely the shape, because they are the content, of the reader's activities.

Having said this, however, it would appear that I am open to two objections. The first is that the procedure is a circular one. I describe the experience of a reader who in his strategies is answerable to an author's intention, and I specify the author's intention by pointing to the strategies employed by that same reader. But this objection would have force only if it were possible to specify one independently of the other. What is being specified from either perspective are the conditions of utterance, of what could have been understood to have been meant by what was said. That is, intention and understanding are two ends of a conventional act, each of which necessarily stipulates (includes, defines, specifies) the other. To construct the profile of the informed or at-home reader is at the same time to characterize the author's intention and vice versa, because to do either is to specify the *contemporary* conditions of utterance, to identify, by becoming a member of, a community made up of those who share interpretive strategies.

The second objection is another version of the first: if the content of the reader's experience is the succession of acts he performs in search of an author's intentions, and if he performs those acts at the bidding of the text, does not the text then produce or contain everything — intention *and* experience — and have I not compromised my antiformalist position? This objection will have force only if the formal patterns of the text are assumed to exist independently of the reader's experience, for only then can priority be claimed for them. Indeed, the claims of independence and priority are one and the same; when they are separated it is so that they can give circular and illegitimate support to each other. The question "do formal features exist independently?" is usually answered by pointing to their priority: they are "in" the text before the reader comes to it. The question "are formal features prior?" is usually answered by pointing to their independent status: they are "in" the text before the reader comes to it. What looks like a step in an argument is actually the spectacle of an assertion supporting itself. It follows then that an attack on the independence of formal features will also be an attack on their priority (and vice versa), and I would like to mount such an attack in the context of two short passages from *Lycidas*.

The first passage (actually the second in the poem's sequence) begins at line 42:

> The willows and the hazel copses green
> Shall now no more be seen,
> Fanning their joyous leaves to thy soft lays.
> (ll. 42–44)

It is my thesis that the reader is always making sense (I intend "making" to have its literal force), and in the case of these lines the sense he makes will involve the assumption (and therefore the creation) of a completed assertion after the word "seen," to wit, the death of Lycidas has so affected the willows and the hazel copses green that, in sympathy, they will wither and die (will no more be seen by *anyone*). In other words at the end of line 43 the reader will have hazarded an interpretation, or performed an act of perceptual closure, or made a decision as to what is being asserted. I do not mean that he has done four things, but that he has done one thing the description of which might take any one of four forms — making sense, interpreting, performing perceptual closure, deciding about what is intended. (The importance of this point will become clear later.) Whatever he has done (that is, however we characterize it) he will undo it in the act of reading the next line; for here he discovers that his closure, or making of sense, was premature and that he must make a new one in which the relationship between man and nature is exactly the reverse of what was first assumed. The willows and the hazel copses green will in fact be seen, but they will not be seen by Lycidas. It is he who will be no more, while they go on as before, fanning their joyous leaves to someone else's soft lays (the whole of line 44 is now perceived as modifying and removing the absoluteness of "seen"). Nature is not sympathetic, but indifferent, and the notion of her sympathy is one of those "false surmises" that the poem is continually encouraging and then disallowing.

The previous sentence shows how easy it is to surrender to the bias of our critical language and begin to talk as if poems, not readers or interpreters, did things. Words like "encourage" and "disallow" (and others I have used in this paper) imply agents, and it is only "natural" to assign agency first to an author's intentions and then to the forms that assumedly embody them. What really happens, I think, is something quite different: rather than intention and its formal realization producing interpretation (the "normal" picture), interpretation creates intention and its formal realization by creating the conditions in which it becomes possible to pick them out. In other words, in the analysis of these lines from *Lycidas* I did what critics always do: I "saw" what my interpretive principles permitted or directed me to see, and then I turned around and attributed what I had "seen" to a text and an intention. What my principles direct me to "see" are readers performing acts; the points at which I find (or to be more precise, declare) those acts to have been performed become (by a sleight of hand) demarcations *in* the text; those demarcations are then available for the designation "formal features," and as formal features they can be (illegitimately) assigned the responsibility for producing the interpretation which in fact produced them. In this case, the demarcation my interpretation calls into being is placed at the end of line 42; but of course the end of that (or any other) line is worth noticing or pointing out only because my model *demands* (the word is not too strong) perceptual closures and therefore locations at which they occur; in that model this point will be one of those locations, although (1) it needn't have been (not every line ending occasions a closure) and (2) in another model, one that does not give value to the activities of readers, the possibility of its being one would not have arisen.

What I am suggesting is that formal units are always a function of the interpretative model one brings to bear; they are not "in" the text, and I would make the same argument for intentions. That is, intention is no more embodied "in" the text than are formal units; rather an intention, like a formal unit, is made when perceptual or interpretive closure is hazarded; it is verified by an interpretive act, and I would add, it is not verifiable in any other way. This last assertion is too large to be fully considered here, but I can sketch out the argumentative sequence I would follow were I to consider it: intention is known when and only when it is recognized; it is recognized as soon as you decide about it; you decide about it as soon as you make a sense; and you make a sense (or so my model claims) as soon as you can.

Let me tie up the threads of my argument with a final example from *Lycidas:*

> He must not float upon his wat'ry bier
> Unwept . . . (ll. 13–14)

Here the reader's experience has much the same career as it does in lines 42–44: at the end of line 13 perceptual closure is hazarded, and a sense is made in which the line is taken to be a resolution bordering on a promise: that is, there is now an expectation that something will be done about this unfortunate situation, and the reader anticipates a call to action, perhaps even a program for the undertaking of a rescue mission. With "Unwept," however, that expectation and anticipation are disappointed, and the realization of that disappointment will be inseparable from the making of a new (and less comforting) sense: nothing will be done; Lycidas will continue to float upon his wat'ry bier, and the only action taken will be the lamenting of the fact that no action will be efficacious, including the actions of speaking and listening to this lament (which in line 15 will receive the meretricious and self-mocking designation "melodious tear"). Three "structures" come into view at precisely the same moment, the moment when the reader having resolved a sense unresolves it and makes a new one; that moment will also be the moment of picking out a formal pattern or unit, end of line/beginning of line, and it will also be the moment at which the reader having decided about the speaker's intention, about what is meant by what has been said, will make the decision again and in so doing will make another intention.

This, then, is my thesis: that the form of the reader's experience, formal units, and the structure of intention are one, that they come into view simultaneously, and that therefore the questions of priority and independence do not arise. What does arise is another question: what produces *them?* That is, if intention, form, and the shape of the reader's experience are simply different ways of referring to (different perspectives on) the same interpretive act, what is that act an interpretation *of?* I cannot answer that question, but neither, I would claim, can anyone else, although formalists try to answer it by pointing to patterns and claiming that they are available independently of (prior to) interpretation. These patterns vary according to the procedures that yield them: they may be statistical (number of two-syllable words per hundred words), grammatical (ratio of passive to active constructions, or of right-branching to left-branching sentences, or of anything else); but whatever they are I would argue that they do not lie innocently in the world but are themselves constituted by an interpretive act, even if, as is often the case, that act is unacknowledged. Of course, this is as true of my analyses as it is of anyone else's. In the examples offered here I appropriate the notion "line ending" and treat it as a fact of nature; and one might conclude that as a fact it is responsible for the reading experience I describe. The truth I think is exactly the reverse: line endings exist by virtue of perceptual strategies rather than the other way around. Historically, the strategy that we know as "reading (or hearing) poetry" has included paying attention to the line as a unit, but it is precisely that attention which has made the line as a unit (either of print or of aural duration) available. A reader so practiced in paying that attention that he regards the line as a brute fact rather than as a convention will have a great deal of difficulty with concrete poetry; if he overcomes that difficulty, it will not be because he has learned to ignore the line as a unit but because he will have acquired a new set of interpretive strategies (the strategies constitutive of "concrete poetry reading") in the context of which the line as a unit no longer exists. In short, what is noticed is what has been *made* noticeable, not by a clear and undistorting glass, but by an interpretive strategy.

This may be hard to see when the strategy has become so habitual that the forms it yields seem part of the world. We find it easy to assume that alliteration as an effect depends on a "fact" that exists independently of any interpretive "use" one might make of it, the fact that words in proximity begin with the same letter. But it takes only a moment's reflection to realize that the sameness, far from being natural, is enforced by an orthographic convention; that is to say, it is the product of an interpretation. Were we to substitute phonetic conventions for orthographic ones (a "reform" traditionally urged by purists), the supposedly "objective" basis for alliteration would disappear because a phonetic transcription would require that we distinguish between the initial sounds of those very words that enter into alliterative relationships; rather than conforming to those relationships the rules of spelling make them. One might reply that, since alliteration is an aural rather than a visual phenomenon when poetry is heard, we have unmediated access to the physical sounds themselves and hear "real" similarities. But phonological "facts" are no more uninterpreted (or less conventional) than the "facts" of orthography; the distinctive features that make articulation and reception possible are the product of a system of differences that must be *imposed* before it can be recognized; the patterns the ear hears (like the patterns the eye sees) are the patterns its perceptual habits make available.

One can extend this analysis forever, even to the "facts" of grammar. The history of linguistics is the history of competing paradigms each of which offers a different account of the constituents of language. Verbs, nouns, cleft sentences, transformations, deep and surface structures, semes, rhemes, tagmemes — now you see them, now you don't, depending on the descriptive apparatus you employ. The critic who confidently rests his analyses on the bedrock of syntactic descriptions is resting on an interpretation; the facts he points to are there, but only as a consequence of the interpretive (man-made) model that has called them into being.

The moral is clear: the choice is never between objectivity and interpretation but between an interpretation that is unacknowledged as such and an interpretation that is at least aware of itself. It is this awareness that I am claiming for myself, although in doing so I must give up the claims implicitly made in the first part of this paper. There I argue that a bad (because spatial) model has suppressed what was really happening, but by my own declared principles the notion "really happening" is just one more interpretation.

IV

It seems then that the price one pays for denying the priority of either forms or intentions is an inability to say how it is that one ever begins. Yet we do begin, and we continue, and because we do there arises an immediate counter-objection to the preceding pages. If interpretive acts are the source of forms rather than the other way around, why isn't it the case that readers are always performing the same acts or a random succession of forms? How, in short, does one explain these two "facts" of reading?: (1) the same reader will perform differently when reading two "different" (the word is in quotation marks because its status is precisely what is at issue) texts; and (2) different readers will perform similarly when reading the "same" (in quotes for the same reason) text. That is to say, both the stability of interpretation among readers and the variety of interpretation in the career of a single reader would seem to argue for the existence of something independent of and prior to interpretive acts, something which produces them. I will answer this challenge by asserting that both the stability and the variety are functions of interpretive strategies rather than of texts.

Let us suppose that I am reading *Lycidas*. What is it that I am doing? First of all, what I am not doing is "simply reading," an activity in which I do not believe because it implies the possibility of pure (that is, disinterested) perception. Rather, I am proceeding on the basis of (at least) two interpretive decisions: (1) that *Lycidas* is a pastoral and (2) that it was written by Milton. (I should add that the notions "pastoral" and "Milton" are also interpretations; that is they do not stand for a set of indisputable, objective facts; if they did, a great many books would not now be getting written.) Once these decisions have been made (and if I had not made these I would have made others, and they would be consequential in the same way), I am immediately predisposed to perform certain acts, to "find," by looking for, themes (the relationship between natural processes and the careers of men, the efficacy of poetry or of any other action), to confer significances (on flowers, streams, shepherds, pagan deities), to mark out "formal" units (the lament, the consolation, the turn, the affirmation of faith, etc.). My disposition to perform these acts (and others; the list is not meant to be exhaustive) constitutes a set of interpretive strategies, which, when they are put into execution, become the large act of reading. That is to say, interpretive strategies are not put into execution after reading (the pure act of perception in which I do not believe); they are the shape of reading, and because they are the shape of reading, they give texts their shape, making them rather than, as it is usually assumed, arising from them. Several important things follow from this account:

1. I did not have to execute this particular set of interpretive strategies because I did not have to make those particular interpretive (prereading) decisions. I could have decided, for example, that *Lycidas* was a text in which a set of fantasies and defenses find expression. These decisions would have entailed the assumption of another set of interpretive strategies (perhaps like that put forward by Norman Holland in *The Dynamics of Literary Response*) and the execution of that set would have made another text.

2. I could execute this same set of strategies when presented with texts that did not bear the title (again a notion which is itself an interpretation) *Lycidas, A Pastoral Monody*. . . . I could decide (it is a decision some have made) that *Adam Bede* is a pastoral written by an author who consciously modeled herself on Milton (still remembering that "pastoral" and "Milton" are interpretations, not facts in the public domain); or I could

decide, as Empson did, that a great many things not usually considered pastoral were in fact to be so read; and either decision would give rise to a set of interpretive strategies, which, when put into action, would *write* the text I write when reading *Lycidas.* (Are you with me?)

3. A reader other than myself who, when presented with *Lycidas,* proceeds to put into execution a set of interpretive strategies similar to mine (how he could do so is a question I will take up later), will perform the same (or at least a similar) succession of interpretive acts. He and I then might be tempted to say that we agree about the poem (thereby assuming that the poem exists independently of the acts either of us performs); but what we really would agree about is the way to write it.

4. A reader other than myself who, when presented with *Lycidas* (please keep in mind that the status of *Lycidas* is what is at issue), puts into execution a different set of interpretive strategies will perform a different succession of interpretive acts. (I am assuming, it is the article of my faith, that a reader will always execute some set of interpretive strategies and therefore perform some succession of interpretive acts.) One of us might then be tempted to complain to the other that we could not possibly be reading the same poem (literary criticism is full of such complaints) and he would be right; for each of us would be reading the poem he had made.

The large conclusion that follows from these four smaller ones is that the notions of the "same" or "different" texts are fictions. If I read *Lycidas* and *The Waste Land* differently (in fact I do not), it will not be because the formal structures of the two poems (to term them such is also an interpretive decision) call forth different interpretive strategies but because my predisposition to execute different interpretive strategies will *produce* different formal structures. That is, the two poems are different because I have decided that they will be. The proof of this is the possibility of doing the reverse (that is why point 2 is so important). That is to say, the answer to the question "why do different texts give rise to different sequences of interpretive acts?" is that *they don't have to,* an answer which implies strongly that "they" don't exist. Indeed it has always been possible to put into action interpretive strategies designed to make all texts one, or to put it more accurately, to be forever making the same text. Augustine urges just such a strategy, for example, in *On Christian Doctrine* where he delivers the "rule of faith" which is of course a rule of interpretation. It is dazzlingly simple: everything in the Scriptures, and indeed in the world when it is properly read, points to (bears the meaning of) God's love for us and our answering responsibility to love our fellow creatures for His sake. If only you should come upon something which does not at first seem to bear this meaning, that "does not literally pertain to virtuous behavior or to the truth of faith," you are then to take it "to be figurative" and proceed to scrutinize it "until an interpretation contributing to the reign of charity is produced." This then is both a stipulation of what meaning there is and a set of directions for finding it, which is of course a set of directions — of interpretive strategies — for making it, that is, for the endless reproduction of the same text. Whatever one may think of this interpretive program, its success and ease of execution are attested to by centuries of Christian exegesis. It is my contention that any interpretive program, any set of interpretive strategies, can have a similar success, although few have been as spectacularly successful as this one. (For some time now, for at least three hundred years, the most successful interpretive program has gone under the name "ordinary language.") In our own discipline programs with the same characteristic of always reproducing one text include psychoanalytic criticism, Robertsonianism (always threatening to extend its sway into later and later periods), numerology (a sameness based on the assumption of innumerable fixed differences).

The other challenging question — "why will different readers execute the same interpretive strategy when faced with the 'same' text?" — can be handled in the same way. The answer is again that *they don't have to,* and my evidence is the entire history of literary criticism. And again this answer implies that the notion "same text" is the product of the possession by two or more readers of similar interpretive strategies.

But why should this ever happen? Why should two or more readers ever agree, and why should regular, that is, habitual, differences in the career of a single reader ever occur? What is the explanation on the one hand of the stability of interpretation (at least among certain groups at certain times) and on the other of the orderly variety of interpretation if it is not the stability and variety of texts? The answer to all of these questions is to be found in a notion that has been implicit in my argument, the notion of *interpretive communities*. Interpretive communities are made up of those who share interpretive strategies not for reading (in the conventional sense) but for writing texts, for constituting their properties and assigning their intentions. In other words these strategies exist prior to the act of reading and therefore determine the shape of what is read rather than, as is usually assumed, the other way around. If it is an article of faith in a particular community that there are a variety of texts, its members will boast a repertoire of strategies for making them. And if a community believes in the existence of only one text, then the single strategy its members employ will be forever writing it. The first community will accuse the members of the second of being reductive, and they in turn will call their accusers superficial. The assumption in each community will be that the other is not correctly perceiving the "true text," but the truth will be that each perceives the text (or texts) its interpretive strategies demand and call into being. This, then, is the explanation both for the stability of interpretation among different readers (they belong to the same community) and for the regularity with which a single reader will employ different interpretive strategies and thus make different texts (he belongs to different communities). It also explains why there are disagreements and why they can be debated in a principled way: not because of a stability in texts, but because of a stability in the makeup of interpretive communities and therefore in the opposing positions they make possible. Of course this stability is always temporary (unlike the longed for and timeless stability of the text). Interpretive communities grow larger and decline, and individuals move from one to another; thus while the alignments are not permanent, they are always there, providing just enough stability for the interpretive battles to go on, and just enough shift and slippage so assure that they will never be settled. The notion of interpretive communities thus stands between an impossible ideal and the fear which leads so many to maintain it. The ideal is of perfect agreement and it would require texts to have a status independent of interpretation. The fear is of interpretive anarchy, but it would only be realized if interpretation (text making) were completely random. It is the fragile but real consolidation of interpretive communities that allows us to talk to one another, but with no hope or fear of ever being able to stop.

In other words interpretive communities are no more stable than texts because interpretive strategies are not natural or universal, but *learned*. This does not mean that there is a point at which an individual has not yet learned any. The ability to interpret is not acquired; it is constitutive of being human. What is acquired are the ways of interpreting and those same ways can also be forgotten or supplanted, or complicated or dropped from favor ("no one reads that way anymore"). When any of these things happens, there is a corresponding change in texts, not because they are being read differently, but because they are being written differently.

The only stability, then, inheres in the fact (at least in my model) that interpretive strategies are always being deployed, and this means that communication is a much more chancy affair than we are accustomed to think it. For if there are no fixed texts, but only interpretive strategies making them; and if interpretive strategies are not natural, but learned (and are therefore unavailable to a finite description), what is it that utterers (speakers, authors, critics, me, you) do? In the old model utterers are in the business of handing over ready made or prefabricated meanings. These meanings are said to be encoded, and the code is assumed to be in the world independently of the individuals who are obliged to attach themselves to it (if they do not they run the danger of being declared deviant). In my model, however, meanings are not extracted but made and made not by encoded forms but by interpretive strategies that call forms into being. It follows then that what utterers do is give hearers and readers the opportunity to make meanings (and texts) by inviting them to put into execution a set of strategies. It is presumed that the invitation will be recognized, and that presumption rests on a projection on the part of a speaker or author of the moves *he* would make if confronted by the sounds or marks he is uttering or setting down.

It would seem at first that this account of things simply reintroduces the old objection; for isn't this an admission that there is after all a formal encoding, not perhaps of meanings, but of the directions for making them, for executing interpretive strategies? The answer is that they will only *be* directions to those who already have the interpretive strategies in the first place. Rather than producing interpretive acts, they are the product of one. An author hazards his projection, not because of something "in" the marks, but because of something he assumes to be in his reader. The very existence of the "marks" is a function of an interpretive community, for they will be recognized (that is, made) only by its members. Those outside that community will be deploying a different set of interpretive strategies (interpretation cannot be withheld) and will therefore be making different marks.

So once again I have made the text disappear, but unfortunately the problems do not disappear with it. If everyone is continually executing interpretive strategies and in that act constituting texts, intentions, speakers, and authors, how can any one of us know whether or not he is a member of the same interpretive community as any other of us? The answer is that he can't, since any evidence brought forward to support the claim would itself be an interpretation (especially if the "other" were an author long dead). The only "proof" of membership is fellowship, the nod of recognition from someone in the same community, someone who says to you what neither of us could ever prove to a third party: "we know." I say it to you now, knowing full well that you will agree with me (that is, understand) only if you already agree with me.

Judith Fetterley

b. 1938

Judith Fetterley was born in New York City but was raised in Toronto until the age of ten, when her family moved to Franklin, Indiana. Fetterley's special interest and slant on U.S. culture comes from this complex position as both insider and outsider. Fetterley took her A.B. from Swarthmore in 1960, then worked for the Harvard Business School and the American Friends Service Committee before returning to graduate school at Indiana University, where she received her Ph.D. in 1969. Fetterley taught at the University of Pennsylvania from 1967 to 1973, then moved to the State University of New York at Albany, where she is currently professor of English and women's studies. Fetterley's scholarly and theoretical work includes The Resisting Reader: A Feminist Approach to American Fiction *(1978) along with numerous articles on nineteenth- and twentieth-century American writers. She also founded and is general editor for the Rutgers University Press American Women Writers reprint series. Fetterley has edited* Provisions: A Reader from Nineteenth-Century American Women Writers *(1985) and (with Marjorie Pryse) the* Norton Anthology of American Women Regionalists, 1850–1910 *(1995). Currently she is at work on a new book on nineteenth-century American women writers and the politics of recovery.*

Introduction to *The Resisting Reader*

I

Literature is political. It is painful to have to insist on this fact, but the necessity of such insistence indicates the dimensions of the problem. John Keats once objected to poetry "that has a palpable design upon us."[1] The major works of American fiction constitute a series of designs on the female reader, all the more potent in their effect because they are "impalpable." One of the main things that keeps the design of our literature unavailable to the consciousness of the woman reader, and hence impalpable, is the very posture of the apolitical, the pretense that literature speaks universal truths through forms from which all the merely personal, the purely subjective, has been burned away or at least transformed through the medium of art into the representative. When only one reality is encouraged, legitimized, and transmitted and when that limited vision endlessly insists on its comprehensiveness, then we have the conditions necessary for that confusion of consciousness in which impalpability flourishes. it is the purpose of this book to give voice to a different reality and different vision, to bring a different subjectivity to bear on the old "universality." To examine American fictions in light of how attitudes toward women shape their form and content is to make available to consciousness that which has been largely left unconscious and thus to change our understanding of these fictions, our relation to them, and their effect on us. It is to make palpable their designs.

American literature is male. To read the canon of what is currently considered classic American literature is perforce to identify as male. Though exceptions to this generalization can be found here and there — a Dickinson poem, a Wharton novel — these exceptions usually function to obscure the argument and confuse the issue: American literature is male. Our literature neither leaves women alone nor allows them to participate. It insists on its universality at the same time that it defines that universality in specifically male terms. "Rip Van Winkle" is paradigmatic of this phenomenon. While the desire to avoid work, escape authority, and sleep through the major decisions of one's life is obviously applicable to both men and women, in Irving's story this "universal" desire is made specifically male. Work, authority, and decision-making are symbolized by Dame Van Winkle, and the longing for flight is defined against her. She is what one must escape from, and the "one" is necessarily male. In Mailer's *An American Dream,* the fantasy of eliminating all one's ills through the ritual of scapegoating is equally male: the sacrificial scapegoat is the woman/wife and the cleansed survivor is the husband/male. In such fictions the female reader is co-opted into participation in an experience from which she is explicitly excluded; she is asked to identify with a selfhood that defines itself in opposition to her; she is required to identify against herself.

The woman reader's relation to American literature is made even more problematic by the fact that our literature is frequently dedicated to defining what is peculiarly American about experience and identity. Given the pervasive male bias of this literature, it is not surprising that in it the experience of being American is equated with the experience of being male. In Fitzgerald's *The Great Gatsby,* the background for the experience of disillusionment and betrayal revealed in the novel is the discovery of America, and Daisy's failure of Gatsby is symbolic of the failure of America to live up to the expectations in the imagination of the men who "discovered" it. America is female; to be American is male; and the quintessential American experience is betrayal by woman. Henry James certainly defined

[1]From Keats's letter to John Hamilton Reynolds of February 3, 1818. Keats goes on to say that "Poetry should be great & unobtrusive, a thing which enters into one's soul, and does not startle or amaze it with itself but with its subject." [Ed.]

our literature, if not our culture, when he picked the situation of women as the subject of *The Bostonians,* his very American tale.

Power is the issue in the politics of literature, as it is in the politics of anything else. To be excluded from a literature that claims to define one's identity is to experience a peculiar form of powerlessness — not simply the powerlessness which derives from not seeing one's experience articulated, clarified, and legitimized in art, but more significantly the powerlessness which results from the endless division of self against self, the consequence of the invocation to identify as male while being reminded that to be male — to be universal, to be American — is to be *not female*. Not only does powerlessness characterize woman's experience of reading, it also describes the content of what is read. Each of the works chosen for this study presents a version and an enactment of the drama of men's power over women. The final irony, and indignity, of the woman reader's relation to American literature, then, is that she is required to dissociate herself from the very experience the literature engenders. Powerlessness is the subject and powerlessness the experience, and the design insists that Rip Van Winkle/Frederic Henry/Nick Carraway/Stephen Rojack speak for us all.

The drama of power in our literature is often disguised. In "Rip Van Winkle," Rip poses as powerless, the hen-pecked husband cowering before his termagant Dame. Yet, when Rip returns from the mountains, armed by the drama of female deposition witnessed there, to discover that his wife is dead and he is free to enjoy what he has always wanted, the "Shucks, Ma'am, I don't mean no harm" posture dissolves. In Sherwood Anderson's "I Want to Know Why," the issue of power is refracted through the trauma of a young boy's discovery of what it means to be male in a culture that gives white men power over women, horses, and niggers. More sympathetic and honest than "Rip," Anderson's story nevertheless exposes both the imaginative limits of our literature and the reasons for those limits. Storytelling and art can do no more than lament the inevitable — boys must grow up to be men; it can provide no alternative vision of being male. Bathed in nostalgia, "I Want to Know Why" is infused with the perspective it abhors, because finally to disavow that perspective would be to relinquish power. The lament is self-indulgent; it offers the luxury of feeling bad without the responsibility of change. And it is completely male-centered, registering the tragedy of sexism through its cost to men. At the end we cry for the boy and not for the whores he will eventually make use of.

In Hawthorne's "The Birthmark," the subject of power is more explicit. The fact of men's power over women and the full implications of that fact are the crux of the story. Aylmer is free to experiment on Georgiana, to the point of death, because she is both woman and wife. Hawthorne indicates the attractiveness of the power that marriage puts in the hands of men through his description of Aylmer's reluctance to leave his laboratory and through his portrayal of Aylmer's inherent discomfort with women and sex. And why does Aylmer want this power badly enough to overcome his initial reluctance and resistance? Hitherto Aylmer has failed in all his efforts to achieve a power equal to that of "Mother" nature. Georgiana provides an opportunity for him to outdo nature by remaking her creation. And if he fails, he still will have won because he will have destroyed the earthly embodiment and representative of his adversary. Hawthorne intends his character to be seen as duplicitous, and he maneuvers Aylmer through the poses of lover, husband, and scientist to show us how Aylmer attempts to gain power and to use that power to salve his sense of inadequacy. But even so, Hawthorne, like Anderson, is unwilling to do more with the sickness than call it sick. He obscures the issue of sexual politics behind a haze of "universals" and clothes the murder of wife by husband in the language of idealism.

Though the grotesque may serve Faulkner as a disguise in the same way that the ideal serves Hawthorne, "A Rose for Emily" goes farther than "The Birthmark" in making the power of men over women an overt subject. Emily's life is shaped by her father's absolute control over her; her murder of Homer Barron is *re*action, not action. Though Emily exercises the power the myths of sexism make available to her, that power is minimal; her retaliation is no alternative to the patriarchy which oppresses her. Yet

Faulkner, like Anderson and Hawthorne, ultimately protects himself and short-circuits the implications of his analysis, not simply through the use of the grotesque, which makes Emily eccentric rather than central, but also through his choice of her victim. In having Emily murder Homer Barron, a northern day-laborer, rather than Judge Stevens, the southern patriarch, Faulkner indicates how far he is willing to go in imagining even the minimal reversal of power involved in retaliation. The elimination of Homer Barron is no real threat to the system Judge Stevens represents. Indeed, a few day-laborers may have to be sacrificed here and there to keep that system going.

In *A Farewell to Arms,* the issue of power is thoroughly obscured by the mythology, language, and structure of romantic love and by the invocation of an abstract, though spiteful, "they" whose goal it is to break the good, the beautiful, and the brave. Yet the brave who is broken is Catherine; at the end of the novel Catherine is dead, Frederic is alive, and the resemblance to "Rip Van Winkle" and "The Birthmark" is unmistakable. Though the scene in the hospital is reminiscent of Aylmer's last visit to Georgiana in her chambers, Hemingway, unlike Hawthorne, separates his protagonist from the source of his heroine's death, locating the agency of Catherine's demise not simply in "them" but in her biology. Frederic survives several years of war, massive injuries, the dangers of a desperate retreat, and the threat of execution by his own army; Catherine dies in her first pregnancy. Clearly, biology is destiny. Yet, Catherine is as much a scapegoat as Dame Van Winkle, Georgiana, Daisy Fay, and Deborah Rojack. For Frederic to survive, free of the intolerable burdens of marriage, family, and fatherhood, yet with his vision of himself as the heroic victim of cosmic antagonism intact, Catherine must die. Frederic's necessities determine Catherine's fate. He is, indeed, the agent of her death.

In its passionate attraction to the phenomenon of wealth, *The Great Gatsby* reveals its author's consuming interest in the issue of power. In the quintessentially male drama of poor boy's becoming rich boy, ownership of women is invoked as the index of power: he who possesses Daisy Fay is the most powerful boy. But when the rich boy, fearing finally for his territory, repossesses the girl and, by asking "Who is he," strips the poor boy of his presumed power, the resultant animus is directed not against the rich boy but against the girl, whose rejection of him exposes the poor boy's powerlessness. The struggle for power between men is deflected into safer and more certain channels, and the consequence is the familiar demonstration of male power over women. This demonstration, however, is not simply the result of a greater safety in directing anger at women than at men. It derives as well from the fact that even the poorest male gains something from a system in which all women are at some level his subjects. Rather than attack the men who represent and manifest that system, he identifies with them and acquires his sense of power through superiority to women. It is not surprising, therefore, that the drama of *The Great Gatsby* involves an attack on Daisy, whose systematic reduction from the glamorous object of Gatsby's romantic longings to the casual killer of Myrtle Wilson provides an accurate measure of the power available to the most "powerless" male.

By his choice of scene, context, and situation, Henry James in *The Bostonians* directly confronts the hostile nature of the relations between men and women and sees in that war the defining characteristics of American culture. His honesty provides the opportunity for a clarification rather than a confusion of consciousness and offers a welcome relief from the deceptions of other writers. Yet the drama, while correctly labeled, is still the same. *The Bostonians* is an unrelenting demonstration of the extent, and an incisive analysis of the sources, of the power of men as a class over women as a class. Yet, though James laments women's oppression, and laments it because of its effects *on women,* he nevertheless sees it as inevitable. *The Bostonians* represents a kind of end point in the literary exploration of sex/class power; it would be impossible to see more clearly and feel more deeply and still remain convinced that patriarchy is inevitable. Indeed, there is revolution latent in James's novel, and, while he would be articulating and romanticizing the tragic elements in women's powerlessness, *The Bostonians* provides the material for that analysis of American social reality which is the beginning of change.

Norman Mailer's *An American Dream* represents another kind of end point. Mailer is thoroughly enthralled by the possibility of power that sexism makes available to men, absolutely convinced that he is in danger of losing it, and completely dedicated to maintaining it, at whatever cost. It is impossible to imagine a more frenzied commitment to the maintenance of male power than Mailer's. In *An American Dream* all content has been reduced to the enactment of men's power over women, and to the development and legitimization of that act Mailer brings every strategy he can muster the least of which is an extended elaboration of the mythology of female power. In Mailer's work the effort to obscure the issue, disguise reality, and confuse consciousness is so frantic that the antitheses he provides to protect his thesis become in fact his message and his confusions shed a lurid illumination. If *The Bostonians* induces one to rearrange James's conceptual framework and so to make evitable his inevitable, *An American Dream* induces a desire to eliminate Mailer's conceptual framework altogether and start over. Beyond his frenzy is only utter nausea and weariness of spirit and a profound willingness to give up an exhausted, sick, and sickening struggle. In Mailer, the drama of power comes full circle; at once the most sexist writer, he is also the most freeing, and out of him it may be possible to create anew.

II

> But what have I to say of *Sexual Politics* itself? Millett has undertaken a task which I find particularly worthwhile: the consideration of certain events or works of literature from an unexpected, even startling point of view. Millett never suggests that hers is a sufficient analysis of any of the works she discusses. Her aim is to wrench the reader from the vantage point he has long occupied, and force him to look at life and letters from a new coign.[2] Hers is not meant to be the last word on any writer, but a wholly new word, little heard before and strange. For the first time we have been asked to look at literature as women; we, men, women and Ph.D.'s, have always read it as men. Who cannot point to a certain over-emphasis in the way Millett reads Lawrence or Stalin or Euripides. What matter? We are rooted in our vantage points and require transplanting which, always dangerous, involves violence and the possibility of death.
>
> — CAROLYN HEILBRUN[3]

> The method that is required is not one of correlation but of *liberation*. Even the term "method" must be reinterpreted and in fact wrenched out of its usual semantic field, for the emerging creativity in women is by no means a merely cerebral process. In order to understand the implications of this process it is necessary to grasp the fundamental fact that women have had the power of *naming* stolen from us. We have not been free to use our own power to name ourselves, the world, or God. The old naming was not the product of dialogue — a fact inadvertently admitted in the Genesis story of Adam's naming the animals and the woman. Women are now realizing that the universal imposing of names by men has been false because partial. That is, inadequate words have been taken as adequate. — MARY DALY[4]

> Re-vision — the act of looking back, of seeing with fresh eyes, of entering an old text from a new critical direction — is for us more than a chapter in cultural history: it is an act of survival. Until we can understand the assumptions in which we are drenched we cannot know ourselves. And this drive to self-knowledge, for woman, is more than a search for identity: it is part of her refusal of the self-destructiveness of male-dominated society. A radical critique of literature, feminist in its impulse, would take the work first of all as a clue to how we live, how we have been living, how we have been led to imagine ourselves, how our language has trapped as well as liberated us; and how we can begin to see — and therefore live — afresh.
>
> — ADRIENNE RICH[5]

> A culture which does not allow itself to look clearly at the obvious through the universal accessi-

[2]Vantage point. [Ed.]

[3]Carolyn Heilbrun, "Millett's *Sexual Politics:* A Year Later," *Aphra* 2 (Summer 1971), 39. [Au.]

[4]Mary Daly, *Beyond God the Father: Toward a Philosophy of Women's Liberation* (Boston: Beacon, 1973), p. 8. [Au.]

[5]Adrienne Rich, "When We Dead Awaken: Writing as Re-Vision," *College English* 34 (1972), 18. [Au.]

bility of art is a culture of tragic delusion, hardly viable. — CYNTHIA OZICK[6]

When a system of power is thoroughly in command, it has scarcely need to speak itself aloud; when its workings are exposed and questioned, it becomes not only subject to discussion, but even to change. — KATE MILLETT[7]

Consciousness is power. To create a new understanding of our literature is to make possible a new effect of that literature on us. And to make possible a new effect is in turn to provide the conditions for changing the culture that the literature reflects. To expose and question that complex of ideas and mythologies about women and men which exist in our society and are confirmed in our literature is to make the system of power embodied in the literature open not only to discussion but even to change. Such questioning and exposure can, of course, be carried on only by a consciousness radically different from the one that informs the literature. Such a closed system cannot be opened up from within but only from without. It must be entered into from a point of view which questions its values and assumptions and which has its investment in making available to consciousness precisely that which the literature wishes to keep hidden. Feminist criticism provides that point of view and embodies that consciousness.

In "A Woman's Map of Lyric Poetry," Elizabeth Hampsten, after quoting in full Thomas Campion's "My Sweetest Lesbia," asks, "And Lesbia, what's in it for her?"[8] The answer to this question is the subject of Hampsten's essay and the answer is, of course, nothing. But implicit in her question is another answer — a great deal, for someone. As Lillian Robinson reminds us, "and, always, *cui bono* — who profits?"[9] The questions of who profits, and how, are crucial because the attempt to answer them leads directly to an understanding of the function of literary sexual politics. Function is often best known by effect. Though one of the most persistent of literary stereotypes is the castrating bitch, the cultural reality is not the emasculation of men by women but the *immasculation* of women by men. As readers and teachers and scholars, women are taught to think as men, to identify with a male point of view, and to accept as normal and legitimate a male system of values, one of whose central principles is misogyny.

One of the earliest statements of the phenomenon of immasculation, serving indeed as a position paper, is Elaine Showalter's "Women and the Literary Curriculum." In the opening part of her article, Showalter imaginatively recreates the literary curriculum the average young woman entering college confronts:

> In her freshman year she would probably study literature and composition, and the texts in her course would be selected for their timeliness, or their relevance, or their power to involve the reader, rather than for their absolute standing in the literary canon. Thus she might be assigned any one of the texts which have recently been advertised for Freshman English: an anthology of essays, perhaps such as *The Responsible Man,* "for the student who wants literature relevant to the world in which he lives," or *Conditions of Men,* or *Man in Crisis: Perspectives on The Individual and His World,* or again, *Representative Men: Cult Heroes of Our Time,* in which thirty-three men represent such categories of heroism as the writer, the poet, the dramatist, the artist, and the guru, and the only two women included are the Actress Elizabeth Taylor and The Existential Heroine Jacqueline Onassis. . . . By the end of her freshman year, a woman student would have learned something about intellectual neutrality; she would be learning, in fact, how to think like a man.[10]

Showalter's analysis of the process of immasculation raises a central question: "What are the effects of this long apprenticeship in negative capability[11] on the self-image and the self-confidence

[6]Cynthia Ozick, "Women and Creativity: The Demise of the Dancing Dog," *Motive* 29 (1969); reprinted in *Woman in Sexist Society,* eds. Vivian Gornick and Barbara Moran (New York: Signet-New American Library, 1972), p. 450. [Au.]

[7]Kate Millett, *Sexual Politics* (Garden City: Doubleday, 1970), p. 58. [Au.]

[8]*College English* 34 (1973), 1075. [Au.]

[9]"Dwelling in Decencies: Radical Criticism and the Feminist Perspective," *College English* 32 (1971), 887; reprinted in *Sex, Class, and Culture* (Bloomington: Indiana University Press, 1978), p. 16. [Au.]

[10]*College English* 32 (1971), 855. [Au.]

[11]Showalter means something like "self-abnegation," not the prelude to creativity postulated by Keats; cf. p. 336. [Ed.]

of women students?" And the answer is self-hatred and self-doubt: "Women are estranged from their own experience and unable to perceive its shape and authenticity. . . . they are expected to identify as readers with a masculine experience and perspective, which is presented as the human one. . . . Since they have no faith in the validity of their own perceptions and experiences, rarely seeing them confirmed in literature, or accepted in criticism, can we wonder that women students are so often timid, cautious, and insecure when we exhort them to 'think for themselves'?"[12]

The experience of immasculation is also the focus of Lee Edwards' article, "Women, Energy, and *Middlemarch*." Summarizing her experience, Edwards concludes:

> Thus, like most women, I have gone through my entire education — as both student and teacher — as a schizophrenic, and I do not use this term lightly, for madness is the bizarre but logical conclusion of our education. Imagining myself male, I attempted to create myself male. Although I knew the case was otherwise, it seemed I could do nothing to make this other critically real.

Edwards extends her analysis by linking this condition to the effects of the stereotypical presentation of women in literature:

> I said simply, and for the most part silently that, since neither those women nor any women whose acquaintances I had made in fiction had much to do with the life I led or wanted to lead, I was not female. Alien from the women I saw most frequently imagined, I mentally arranged them in rows labelled respectively insipid heroines, sexy survivors, and demonic destroyers. As organizer I stood somewhere else, alone perhaps, but hopefully above them.[13]

Intellectually male, sexually female, one is in effect no one, nowhere, immasculated.

Clearly, then, the first act of the feminist critic must be to become a resisting rather than an assenting reader and, by this refusal to assent, to begin the process of exorcizing the male mind that has been implanted in us. The consequence of this exorcism is the capacity for what Adrienne Rich describes as re-vision — "the act of looking back, of seeing with fresh eyes, of entering an old text from a new critical direction." And the consequence, in turn, of this re-vision is that books will no longer be read as they have been read and thus will lose their power to bind us unknowingly to their designs. While women obviously cannot rewrite literary works so that they become ours by virtue of reflecting our reality, we can accurately name the reality they do reflect and so change literary criticism from a closed conversation to an active dialogue.

In making available to women this power of naming reality, feminist criticism is revolutionary. The significance of such power is evident if one considers the strength of the taboos against it:

> I permit no woman to teach . . . she is to keep silent.
>
> — ST. PAUL

> By Talmudic law a man could divorce a wife whose voice could be heard next door. From there to Shakespeare: "Her voice was ever soft, / Gentle, and low — an excellent thing in woman." And to Yeats: "The women that I picked spoke sweet and low / And yet gave tongue." And to Samuel Beckett, guessing at the last torture, The Worst: "a woman's voice perhaps, I hadn't thought of that, they might engage a soprano."
>
> — MARY ELLMANN[14]

> The experience of the class in which I voiced my discontent still haunts my nightmares. Until my face froze and my brain congealed, I was called prude and, worse yet, insensitive, since I willfully misread the play in the interest of proving a point false both to the work and in itself.
>
> — LEE EDWARDS[15]

The experience Edwards describes of attempting to communicate her reading of the character of Shakespeare's Cleopatra is a common memory for most of us who have become feminist critics. Many of us never spoke; those of us who did speak were usually quickly silenced. The need to keep certain things from being thought and said

[12]Ibid., 856–57. [Au.]

[13]*Massachusetts Review* 13 (1972), 226, 227. [Au.]

[14]*Thinking About Women* (New York: Harcourt Brace Jovanovich, 1968), pp. 149–50. [Au.]

[15]Edwards, p. 230. [Au.]

reveals to us their importance. Feminist criticism represents the discovery/recovery of a voice, a unique and uniquely powerful voice capable of canceling out those other voices, so movingly described in Sylvia Plath's *The Bell Jar,* which spoke about us and to us and at us but never for us.

III

The eight works analyzed in this book were chosen for their individual significance, their representative value, and their collective potential. They are interconnected in the ways that they comment on and illuminate each other, and they form a dramatic whole whose meaning transcends the mere sum of the parts. These eight are meant to stand for a much larger body of literature; their individual and collective designs can be found elsewhere repeatedly.

The four short stories form a unit, as do the four novels. These units are subdivided into pairs. "Rip Van Winkle" and "I Want to Know Why" are companion pieces whose focus is the fear of and resistance to growing up. The value of Anderson's story lies mainly in the light it sheds on Irving's, making explicit the fear of sexuality only implied in "Rip" and focusing attention on the strategy of deflecting hostility away from men and onto women. "The Birthmark" and "A Rose for Emily" are richly related studies of the consequences of growing up and, by implication, of the reasons for the resistance to it. In both stories sexual desire leads to death. More significantly, they are brilliant companion analyses of that sex/class hostility that is the essence of patriarchal culture and that underlies the adult identity Anderson's boy recoils from assuming. "The Birthmark" is the story of how to murder your wife and get away with it; "A Rose for Emily" is the story of how the system which allows you to murder your wife makes it possible for your wife to murder you.

Both *A Farewell to Arms* and *The Great Gatsby* are love stories; together they demonstrate the multiple uses of the mythology of romantic love in the maintenance of male power. In addition they elaborate on the function of scapegoating evident in "Rip Van Winkle" and "The Birthmark." In its more obvious connection of the themes of love and power, *The Great Gatsby* brings closer to consciousness the hostility which *A Farewell to Arms* seeks to disguise and bury. *The Bostonians* and *An American Dream* form the most unlikely and perhaps the most fascinating of the pairs. In both, the obfuscation of romantic love has been cleared away and the issue of power directly joined. James's novel describes a social reality — male power, female powerlessness — which Mailer's denies by creating a social mythology — female power, male powerlessness — that inverts that reality. Yet finally, the intention of Mailer's mythology is to maintain the reality it denies. *The Bostonians* forces the strategies of *An American Dream* into the open by its massive documentation of women's oppression, and *An American Dream* provides the political answer to *The Bostonians'* inevitability by its massive, though unintended, demonstration of the fact that women's oppression grows not out of biology but out of men's need to oppress.

The sequence of both the stories and the novels is generated by a scale of increasing complexity, increasing consciousness, and increasing "feminist" sympathy and insight. Thus, the movement of the stories is from the black and white of "Rip Van Winkle," with its postulation of good guy and villain and its formulation in terms of innocent fable, to the complexity of "A Rose for Emily," whose action forces sexual violence into consciousness and demands understanding for the erstwhile villain. The movement of the novels is similar. *A Farewell to Arms* is as simplistic and disguised and hostile as "Rip Van Winkle"; indeed, the two have many affinities, not the least of which is the similarity of their sleep-centered protagonists who believe that women are a bad dream that will go away if you just stay in bed long enough. The sympathy and complexity of consciousness in *The Bostonians* is even larger than that in "A Rose for Emily," and is exceeded only by the imagination of *An American Dream,* which is "feminist" not by design but by default. Yet the decision to end with *An American Dream* comes not simply from its position on the incremental scale. *An American Dream* is "Rip Van Winkle" one hundred and fifty years later, intensified to be sure, but *exactly the same story*. Thus, the complete trajectory of the immasculating imagination of American literature is described by the movement from "Rip Van Winkle" to *An American Dream,* and that movement is finally circular. This juxtaposition of beginning and end provides the sharpest possible exposure of that circular quality in the design of our literature, apparent in the movements within and between works, which defines its imaginative limits. Like the race horse so loved by Anderson's boy, the imagination which informs our "classic" American literature runs endlessly round a single track, unable because unwilling to get out of the race.

Peter Rabinowitz

b. 1944

Peter Rabinowitz was born and raised in New Rochelle, New York, and educated at the University of Chicago where he earned his doctorate in comparative literature. Since his undergraduate years, Rabinowitz has negotiated divided loyalties to music and literature, and to educational politics as well. In the summer of 1964 he taught at a Freedom School in Meridian, Mississippi. His next academic appointment was at Kirkland, an experimental women's college, where he and his wife, the former Nancy Sorkin, were one of the first couples in the country to share a single tenure-track job. When Kirkland merged with Hamilton College, the Rabinowitzes helped create the comparative literature program at the new institution, where they teach and where Peter is currently chair. Rabinowitz is the author of Before Reading: Narrative Conventions and the Politics of Interpretation *(1987) and academic articles on detective fiction, forgotten novels, theory, and the music of Mahler, Gottschalk, and Scott Joplin. He is the co-editor, with James Phelan, of* Understanding Narrative *(1994), and has co-authored a book,* Resistance and Respect in the Teaching of Literature *(1997), with education professor Michael W. Smith. Rabinowitz's current project is a book, with composer Jay Reise, on the act of listening. The following selection is taken from the first chapter of* Before Reading.

From *Before Reading*

WHO IS READING?

There can be no reading without a reader — but the term *reader* is slippery, not only because all individual readers read differently, but also because for almost all of them, there are several different ways of appropriating a text. This fact has been recognized, at least implicitly, by the large number of critics whose models of reading are multitiered. Usually, a two-leveled opposition is posited, although different critics use different terms. For Hirsch, it is "significance" and "meaning." For Wayne Booth, it is "understanding" and "overstanding." For Tzvetan Todorov, there are three terms: "interpretation," "description," and "reading."[1] Many other critics, despite the recent arguments of Fish, remain wedded, in one form or another, to the distinction between literal meaning and interpretation.

[1]E. D. Hirsch, Jr., *Validity in Interpretation* (New Haven: Yale University Press, 1967), esp. p. 8; Wayne C. Booth, *Critical Understanding* (Chicago: University of Chicago Press, 1979) passim; Tzvetan Todorov, *Poetics of Prose,* trans. Richard Howard (Ithaca: Cornell University Press), pp. 238–46. [Au.]

These distinctions all discriminate among activities that a reader can engage in under different circumstances or for different purposes. I would like to start with a different kind of distinction, one that discriminates among *simultaneous* roles that the audience of a text can play. There are three of these roles that will be central to my argument, but I will reserve the third for Chapter 3 and will only outline the first two here. First, there is the *actual audience*. This consists of the flesh-and-blood people who read the book. This is the audience that booksellers are most concerned with — but it happens to be the audience over which an author has no guaranteed control. Each member of the actual audience is different, and each reads in his or her own way, with a distance from other readers depending upon such variables as class, gender, race, personality, training, culture, and historical situation.

This difference among readers has always posed a problem for writers, one that has grown with increased literacy and the correspondingly increased heterogeneity of the reading public. An author has, in most cases, no firm knowledge of the actual readers who will pick up his or her book. Yet he or she cannot begin to fill up a blank page without making assumptions about the readers' beliefs, knowledge, and familiarity with conventions. As a result, authors are forced to guess; they design their books rhetorically for some more or less specific *hypothetical* audience, which I call the *authorial audience*. Artistic choices are based upon these assumptions — conscious or unconscious — about readers, and to a certain extent, artistic success depends on their shrewdness, on the degree to which actual and authorial audience overlap. Some assumptions are quite specific. William Demby's *Catacombs*, for instance, takes place in the early 1960s, and it achieves its sense of impending doom only if the reader already knows that John F. Kennedy will be assassinated when the events of the novel reach November 22, 1963. One of the Encyclopedia Brown mysteries is soluble only by the reader who knows that skydivers always wear two parachutes. Other assumptions are more general: "Rip van Winkle" assumes readers who know that during the Revolution, the American colonies became independent of England. Some assumptions are historical: Flaubert assumes considerable knowledge of the revolution of 1848 in *Sentimental Education*. Some are sociological: at least one critic has argued convincingly that *The Turn of the Screw* makes proper sense only to a reader who knows something about the conduct deemed proper to governesses in the nineteenth century.[2] Some authors rely on our precise knowledge of cultural fads (Peter Cameron, in "Fear of Math," assumes that his audience will draw the proper conclusions about a character when he tells us that she eats a "tabbouleh-and-pita bread sandwich"),[3] others on our knowledge of more widespread cultural conventions (in Nabokov's *Lolita*, the refusal of the Enchanted Hunters to accept Humbert Humbert as a guest when he first shows up makes sense only if readers recognize both that they have garbled his name so that it sounds Jewish, and that the phrase in their advertising, "Near Churches," is a code phrase for "No Jews").[4] Some authors presume that we have a knowledge of specific previous texts (Stoppard assumes that his readers know *Hamlet* before reading *Rosencrantz and Guildenstern Are Dead*). Sometimes authors assume that our higher motives will triumph (Dostoyevsky assumes that we are capable of sympathy for the sufferings of Raskolnikov in *Crime and Punishment* even though he is a murderer). Sometimes authors — even the same authors — assume that we will be influenced by our baser prejudices (in *The Idiot* we are expected to be distrustful of Ganya because his teeth are "altogether too dazzling and even").[5] The potential range of assumptions an author can make, in other words, is infinite.

[2]Elliott M. Schrero, "Exposure in *The Turn of the Screw*," *Modern Philology* 78 (February 1981): 261–74. [Au.]

[3]*New Yorker*, March 11, 1985, 42. [Au.]

[4]Although I have taught this novel several times, none of my students — coming as they do from a cultural context quite different from that of the authorial audience — has caught this, or any of the other references to anti-Semitism in the novel. [Au.]

[5]Fyodor Dostoyevsky, *The Idiot*, trans. David Magarshack (Baltimore: Penguin, 1955), p. 48 (pt. 1, chap. 2). In Dickens' *Dombey and Son*, we are expected to distrust Carker for the same reason. [Au.]

The notion of the authorial audience is clearly tied to authorial intention, but it gets around some of the problems that have traditionally hampered the discussion of intention by treating it as a matter of social convention rather than of individual psychology. In other words, my perspective allows us to treat the reader's attempt to read as the author intended, not as a search for the author's private psyche, but rather as the joining of a particular social/interpretive community; that is, the acceptance of the author's invitation to read in a particular socially constituted way that is shared by the author and his or her expected readers. Indeed, authorial reading is not only a way of reading but, perhaps equally important, a way of talking about how you read — that is, the result of a community agreement that allows discussion of a certain sort to take place by treating meanings in a particular way (as found rather than made). In this sense, what Susan R. Suleiman says about the notions of the implied author and the implied reader which are themselves only variant formulations of the notion of authorial intention) applies to the authorial audience as well: they are, she says, "necessary fictions, guaranteeing the consistency of a specific reading without guaranteeing its validity in any absolute sense."[6] But it is crucial to note that this is not just an arbitrary convention invented by academics for their own convenience — it is a broader social usage, one that is shared by authors as well as their readers, including their nonprofessional readers. My position here is thus very close to that of Foley, who rightly sees fiction "as a contract designed by an intending author who invites his or her audience to adopt certain paradigms for understanding reality."[7] In other words, as Terry Eagleton argues, intention is best seen not in terms of "essentially private 'mental acts,'" but rather in terms of social practice.[8]

By thinking in terms of the authorial audience rather than private intention, furthermore, we are reminded of the constraints within which writers write. For despite the theoretically infinite number of potential authorial audiences, it does not follow that authors have total control over the act of writing, any more than that readers have total control over the act of interpretation. In a trivial sense, of course, they do: authors can put down whatever marks they wish on the page; readers can construe them however they wish. But once authors and readers accept the communal nature of writing and reading, they give up some of that freedom. Specifically, once he or she has made certain initial decisions, any writer who wishes to communicate — even if he or she wishes to communicate ambiguity — has limited the range of subsequent choices.

Some of those limitations spring from what might be called brute facts. Writers of realistic historical novels, for instance, shackle themselves to events that are independent of their imaginations. As Suleiman has argued:

> The most obvious . . . difference between fictional and historical characters in a novel is that the latter impose greater constraints on the novelist who wants to be a "painter of his time." He cannot make

[6]Susan R. Suleiman, "Introduction," in *The Reader in the Text,* ed. Susan R. Suleiman and Inge Crossman (Princeton: Princeton University Press, 1980), p. 11. [Au.]

[7]Barbara Foley, *Telling the Truth* (Ithaca: Cornell University Press, 1986), p. 43. [Au.]

[8]Terry Eagleton, *Literary Theory* (Minneapolis: University of Minnesota Press, 1983), p. 114. See also Patrocinio P. Schweickart's claim that validity is not "a property inherent in an interpretation, but rather . . . a *claim* implicit in the *act* of propounding an interpretation" — that is, that validity is "contingent on the agreement of others" ("Reading Ourselves," in *Gender and Reading,* ed. Elizabeth A. Flynn and Patrocinio P. Schweickart [Baltimore: Johns Hopkins University Press, 1986], p. 56). Fish argues similarly that authorial intention "is not private but a form of conventional behavior" ("Working on the Chain Gang," *Critical Inquiry* 9 [September 1982]: 213); Hirsch, with less enthusiasm, notes that "we can circumvent the whole question of author psychology by adopting a semiotic account of interpretation. Instead of referring an interpretation back to an original author, we could . . . refer it back to an original code or convention system" ("Politics of Theories of Interpretation," *Critical Inquiry* 9 [September 1982]: 239). Hirsch insists that this would not really be an adequate account, but I suspect it is as adequate as any that relies on actual psychology. It is worth remembering that this is not simply a matter of arbitrary definitions; as Mailloux's arguments in "Rhetorical Hermeneutics" (*Critical Inquiry* 11 [June 1985]: 620–41) make clear, the very act of treating readings in this way has serious effects on the ways in which people subsequently *do* read — on what counts as evidence, for instance. [Au.]

Napoleon die — or win the battle — at Waterloo, just as he cannot make Hugo the court poet of Napoleon III. . . . And if the novelist chooses to place in the foreground events as well-known and public as the Boulanger affair or the Panama scandal, then he will have to bend to similar constraints even as far as the activities of the *fictional* characters are concerned.[9]

Thus, once Margaret Mitchell chose to write *Gone with the Wind* as a historical novel about the Civil War, she relinquished control over certain areas of her text. She could have saved Melanie had she wished, or killed off Rhett, but there was no way to give victory to the South or to preserve Atlanta from the flames.

More central to my argument, though, are *conventional* limitations on choice. There are no brute facts preventing an author from writing a religious parable in which a cross represented Judaism, but it would not communicate successfully. As Mary Pratt puts it, "Although the fictional discourse in a work of literature may in theory take any form at all, readers have certain expectations about what form it will take, and *they can be expected to decode the work according to those assumptions unless they are overtly invited or required to do otherwise*" (italics in original).[10] The writer who wishes to be understood — even to be understood by a small group of readers — has to work within such conventional restraints.

Despite these limitations, however, there are still an incalculable number of possible authorial audiences; and since the structure of a work is designed with the authorial audience in mind, actual readers must come to share its characteristics as they read if they are to experience the text as the author wished.[11] Reading as authorial audience therefore involves a kind of distancing from the actual audience, from one's own immediate needs and interests. This distancing, however, must be distinguished sharply from the apparently similar kind of objectivity, represented in its baldest form by Dr. Blimber, in Dickens' *Dombey and Son,* who claimed "that all the fancies of the poets, and lessons of the sages, were a mere collection of words and grammar, and had no other meaning in the world."[12] Of course, few critics subscribe to Blimberism in its purest form, yet many critical windows are draped with remnants from Blimber's school. Northrop Frye insists that "the fundamental act of criticism is a disinterested response to a work of literature in which all one's beliefs, engagements, commitments, prejudices, stampedings of pity and terror, are ordered to be quiet."[13] Similarly, the reader postulated by Stanley Fish's once-popular "Affective Stylistics" is psychologically blank and politically unaware, an automaton who approaches each new sentence with the same anesthetized mind.[14] In a radically different critical tradition, Gerald Prince's degree-zero narratee — whom he assumes to be the addressee of the text except where "an indication to the contrary is supplied in the narration intended for him" — has no "personality or social characteristics," and although he (apparently, the degree-zero narratee

[9]Susan Robin Suleiman, *Authoritarian Fictions* (New York: Columbia University Press, 1983), p. 120. [Au.]

[10]Mary Louise Pratt, *Toward a Speech Act Theory of Literary Discourse* (Bloomington: Indiana University Press, 1977), p. 204. Pratt's own strong critique of speech-act theory (including her own work) can be found in "The Ideology of Speech-Act Theory," *Centrum,* n.s. 1 (Spring 1981): 5–18. I think that my definition of fictionality (Chapter 3) solves some of the questions that Pratt raises; while my book tends to focus on a type of reading that includes an attempt at author-reader cooperation, I have accepted many of the arguments on which her critique is based, and have tried not to "normalize" this particular kind of reading, nor to define others as "deviant" (see "The Value[s] of Authorial Reading" below). Even if one accepts her new position, though, much of Pratt's earlier work remains useful as a description of certain kinds of reading. [Au.]

[11]See Booth's discussion of this process in *Rhetoric of Fiction,* 2nd ed. (Chicago: University of Chicago Press), pp. 138–41. [Au.]

[12]Charles Dickens, *Dombey and Son* (New York: Dutton/Everyman's Library, 1907), pp. 134–35 (chap. 11). [Au.]

[13]Northrop Frye, *Well-Tempered Critic* (Bloomington: Indiana University Press, 1963), p. 140. Frye backs off a bit from the implications of this statement by distinguishing later between the pure disinterested critical act and the act of ordinary reading. [Au.]

[14]Stanley Fish, "Literature in the Reader: Affective Stylistics," in *Is There a Text in This Class?* (Cambridge: Harvard University Press, 1980), pp. 21–67. Indeed, as Culler has pointed out, he or she does not even learn from reading; see *Pursuit of Signs* (Ithaca: Cornell University Press, 1982), p. 130. [Au.]

is male) knows grammar and the denotations of words, he knows neither connotations nor conventions. He is, in other words, capable of reading a text without any distorting presuppositions; neither his "character" nor his "position in society . . . colors his perception of the events described to him."[15]

Authorial reading, however, is quite different. It does *not* escape "distorting presuppositions." Rather, it recognizes that distorting presuppositions lie at the heart of the reading process. To read as authorial audience is to read in an impersonal way, but only in a special and limited sense. The authorial audience has knowledge and beliefs that may well be *extra*personal — that is, not shared by the actual individual reader (I, for instance, do not personally share the racist perspective of the authorial audience of Ian Fleming's *Live and Let Die*). The authorial audience's knowledge and beliefs may even be extracommunal — that is, not shared by any community (and we all belong to several) of which the actual reader is a member at the historical moment of reading (what current community shares the belief in Zeus characteristic of the authorial audience of the *Odyssey*?). But these authorial audiences, whatever their distance from actual readers, certainly have their own engagements and prejudices. To join the authorial audience, then, you should not ask what a *pure* reading of a given text would be. Rather, you need to ask what sort of *corrupted* reader this particular author wrote for: what were that reader's beliefs, engagements, commitments, prejudices, and stampedings of pity and terror?

The reader, in other words, can read as the author intended only by being in the right place to begin with — and that can come about only through an intuitive mix of experience and faith, knowledge and hunch — plus a certain amount of luck. There is consequently no ideal point of departure that will work for any and all books. And since each point of departure involves its own corruptions, commitments, and prejudices, every authorial reading has significant ideological strands. As I suggested earlier, my primary concern here is with a particular aspect of the authorial audience's corruptions: the literary conventions that it applies to the text in order to transform it. As such critics as Culler are now making clearer, reading (especially the reading of literature) is not only not a natural activity — it is not even a logical consequence of knowledge of the linguistic system and its written signs. It is, rather, a separately learned, *conventional* activity.

In other words, literary conventions are not in the text waiting to be uncovered, but in fact *precede* the text and make discovery possible in the first place.[16] Note, however, that I speak here of discovery, not creation. The notion of reading as authorial audience is closer to what Steven Mailloux calls "textual realism" (the belief that "meaning-full texts exist independent of interpretation") than to what he calls "readerly idealism" (the belief that "meaning is made, not found,"

[15]Gerald Prince, "Introduction," trans. Francis Mariner. In *Reader-Response Criticism,* ed. Jane Tompkins (Baltimore: Johns Hopkins University Press, 1980), pp. 10–11. But see also his claim, "There may frequently be points in my reading where . . . I have to rely not only on my linguistic knowledge and the textual information supplied but also on my mastery of logical operations, my familiarity with interpretive conventions and my knowledge of the world" (*Narratology* [Berlin: Mouton, 1982], p. 128). [Au.]

[16]As Culler argues, "The implication that the ideal reader is a *tabula rasa* on which the text inscribes itself not only makes nonsense of the whole process of literary education and conceals the conventions and norms which make possible the production of meaning but also insures the bankruptcy of literary theory, whose speculations on the properties of literary texts become ancillary and *ex post facto* generalizations which are explicitly denied any role in the activity of reading" (*Pursuit of Signs* [Ithaca: Cornell University Press, 1981], p. 121). See also Mailloux's claim that "a reader's understanding of authorial intention always depends on shared communicative conventions, but the success of the intention to achieve certain perlocutionary effects is not guaranteed by those conventions, only made possible by them" (*Interpretive Conventions* [Ithaca: Cornell University Press, 1982], p. 106). This notion of reading is confirmed by research into cognitive psychology. See, for instance, Mary Crawford and Roger Chaffin's claim that "understanding is a product of both the text and the prior knowledge and viewpoint that the reader brings to it" ("Reader's Construction of Meaning," in *Gender and Reading,* ed. Elizabeth A. Flynn and Patrocinio P. Schweickart [Baltimore: Johns Hopkins University Press, 1986], p. 3). [Au.]

since "textual facts are never prior to or independent of the hermeneutic activity of readers and critics").[17] True, I share the idealists' belief that texts are incomplete when we get them and must be put together according to the principles of the reader's interpretive community, but in the case of successful authorial reading, the author and readers are members of the same community, so while the reader does in fact engage in an act of production, he or she makes what the author intended to be found. Of course, as I will discuss in more detail in Chapters 6 and 7, not all attempts at authorial reading are successful. Even readers who try to find out what an author intends may thus in fact *make* something the author never expected; in such cases, though, the readers will still act as if they have in fact *found* the meaning of the text.

I am not arguing that we do not use logic to interpret literary texts. Given that Edna Losser is twenty in 1900 when Margaret Ayer Barnes' *Edna His Wife* opens, we can reasonably infer — as the author intended us to — that she is in her fifties when the novel ends, in the early 1930s. But such inferences are not sufficient for a complete authorial reading. Nor am I arguing that one cannot describe the features of literary artifacts or the rules that govern reading according to "logical" categories. Thus, for instance, Gerald Prince is quite correct when he claims, "Should an event A precede an event B in time, the two may be temporally adjacent, or proximate, or distant."[18] Similarly, we can claim, with some precision, that in any book, the rule that we should eliminate likely suspects either applies or does not apply. But providing a logical classification of all possibilities is quite different from providing a logical system that explains which of those possibilities will be actualized in a given novel. A reader who picks up Ellery Queen's *Tragedy of X* for the first time knows to eliminate obvious suspects, not because of some *systematic* understanding of possible literary types, but rather because it is the *conventional* thing to do in that kind of book. For this reason, discussions of the actual conventions of reading will always appear arbitrary and ad hoc compared to the classifications of structuralists.[19]

Knowledge of these conventions is a major part of what Culler calls "literary competence."[20] It is not simply that we need to know conventions in order to read Joyce; even the simplest literary artifact (say, a comic strip) calls nonlinguistic conventions (such as the left-to-right spatial representation of the passage of time) into play.[21] As Janice Radway puts it, "Comprehension is . . . a process of sign production where the reader actively attributes significance to signifiers on the basis of previously learned cultural codes."[22]

As I will demonstrate, the reliance of reading on conventions that precede the text has enormous consequences for the processes of interpre-

[17]Steven Mailloux, "Rhetorical Hermeneutics," *Critical Inquiry* 11 (June 1985): 622. Mailloux attacks both schools and argues against doing "Theory" at all. Although I do not follow this path, I find his alternative, — a study of the *institutional* politics of interpretation — a profitable one as well. [Au.]

[18]Gerald Prince, *Narratology* (Berlin: Mouton, 1982), p. 64. [Au.]

[19]For a different perspective, see Todorov's discussion of the difference between logical ("theoretical") and historical genres (*The Fantastic,* trans. Richard Howard [Ithaca: Cornell University Press, 1975], chap. 1). [Au.]

[20]Jonathan Culler, *Structuralist Poetics* (Ithaca: Cornell University Press, 1975), esp. chap. 6. Conventions are also one aspect of Hans Robert Jauss' notion of "horizon of expectations." See, for instance, *Toward an Aesthetic of Reception,* trans. Timothy Bahti (Minneapolis: University of Minnesota Press, 1982). For a strong critique of Culler's notion of competence, see Pratt, "Interpretive Strategies/Strategic Interpretations," *Boundary*2 11 (Fall–Winter 1981/82), esp. pp. 215–21. Pratt points out that, as Culler uses the concept, literary competence can end up as a theoretical justification for the mainstream practices of academic criticism. Literary competence, however, need not be restricted to what the academy believes it to be; as I hope will be clear in Chapters 6 and 7, my own stress on actual authorial intention, rather than on received opinion about the "right" way to read "good" books, helps avoid this problem. [Au.]

[21]For a good unpacking of the conventions of the comic strip, see Seymour Chatman, *Story and Discourse* (Ithaca: Cornell University Press, 1978), pp. 37–41. [Au.]

[22]Janice Radway, *Reading the Romance* (Chapel Hill: University of North Carolina Press, 1984), p. 7. Radway sees this as a process of "making" meaning, but as I have argued, reading as authorial audience at least attempts to "find" a meaning that is in some sense already there. [Au.]

tation and evaluation, in many ways the central activities of the academic literary community.

THE VALUE(S) OF AUTHORIAL READING

In this book, I will focus primarily on authorial reading. In so doing, I am not claiming that this is either the only or even the best way to read. I do not agree with Steven Knapp and Walter Benn Michaels that "the meaning of a text is simply identical to the author's intended meaning" or that "authorial intention is the necessary object of interpretation."[23] And I do not agree with Wayne Booth and E. D. Hirsch, Jr., who often suggest that there is a moral imperative to read as the author intended.[24] At the same time, I would argue that authorial reading is more than just another among a large set of equally valid and equally important ways of approaching a text. Authorial reading has a special status for at least two reasons.

First, while Knapp and Michaels are wrong that "the object of *all* reading is *always* the historical author's intention" (italics added),[25] it is true that most people actually do read — or attempt to read — this way most of the time. Of course, different individuals may disagree about what the author's intention is, just as they may react differently to it once they think they have found it. Nonetheless, the initial question most commonly asked of a literary text in our culture is, What is the author saying? The critical revolutions of the 1970s and 1980s may have deluded us, but the millions of readers of Len Deighton's *SS-GB* or Judith Krantz's *Scruples* were interested neither in deconstructing texts nor in discovering their underlying semiotic codes. In fact, even among the most jaded readers — academics — the majority still attempts to read as authorial audience. Authorial reading continues to provide the basis for most academic articles and papers — and, even more, for classroom teaching.

Second, and perhaps more important for critical theory, reading as authorial audience provides the foundation for many other types of reading. True, some approaches to texts skip over the authorial audience entirely: certain kinds of structuralist or stylistic studies, for instance, or the kind of subjective reading proposed by David Bleich in *Readings and Feelings*.[26] But then again, many types of reading depend for their power on a prior understanding of the authorial meaning.[27] The manifest/latent distinction of certain Freudian studies, for instance, collapses if we don't have a manifest meaning to begin with. Georg Lukács' Marxist analysis of Balzac depends on the distinction between what Balzac wanted to see and what he really did see.[28] Most important — if importance has any connection to the power of a critical movement to make us recognize the world with new eyes — we see the same dependence on authorial intention in much feminist criticism. Judith Fetterley's "resisting

[23]Steven Knapp and Walter Benn Michaels, "Against Theory," *Critical Inquiry* 8 (Summer 1982): 724, and "A Reply to Our Critics," *Critical Inquiry* 9 (Summer 1983): 796. For a series of incisive responses to Knapp and Michaels, see *Critical Inquiry* 9 (June 1983): 725–89. [Au.]

[24]See Booth: "It is simply self-maiming to pretend that any blissful improvisation on [Henry James'] words, sentences, or themes . . . can equal the value of his making" (*Critical Understanding*, p. 284). See also E. D. Hirsch, Jr., *The Aims of Interpretation* (Chicago: University of Chicago Press, 1976). For positions that oppose Booth's, see, for instance, Barbara Herrnstein Smith, *On the Margins of Discourse* (Chicago: University of Chicago Press, 1978), esp. chap. 6; and "English 692" [Joanna Brent, Rita Conley, et al.], "Poem Opening: An Invitation to Transactive Criticism," *College English* 40 (September 1978): 2–16. [Au.]

[25]Knapp and Michaels, "A Reply to Our Critics," p. 798.

[26]Urbana, IL: National Council of Teachers of English, 1975, esp. pp. 80–95. For a further development of Bleich's ideas, see also his *Subjective Criticism* (Baltimore: Johns Hopkins University Press, 1978). [Au.]

[27]Booth has called such readings "parasitical" ("M. H. Abrams," *Critical Inquiry* 2 [Spring 1976]: 441). See J. Hillis Miller's response, "Critic as Host," *Critical Inquiry* 3 (Spring 1977): 439–47. [Au.]

[28]Lukács claims, for instance, that Balzac was faced with a contradiction between the torments of "the transition to the capitalist system of production" and his awareness that this "transformation was not only socially inevitable, but at the same time progressive. This contradiction in his experience Balzac *attempted* to force into a system based on a Catholic legitimism and tricked out with Utopian conceptions of English Toryism. But this system was contradicted all the time by the social realities of his day and the Balzacian vision which mirrored them" (*Studies in European Realism* [New York: Grossett and Dunlap, 1964], pp. 12–13, emphasis added). [Au.]

reader" can come into being only if there is something to resist.[29]

Two examples may clarify how certain kinds of political criticism can be strengthened if they are built on a foundation of authorial reading. Imagine a critic who wanted to uncover Natasha's victimization in *War and Peace* — to show how Russian society restricts the development of her natural talents, how it curbs and punishes her spirit and individuality. Such a critic could well point out Natasha's unjust fate — even explain its social, psychological, and historical causes — without any reference to authorial intention. But if — and only if — the critic works through an authorial reading of the text, the scope of this political analysis can be enlarged to explore the *contradiction* between the authorial audience and the critic. For only by starting with an authorial reading could the critic analyze the social, historical, and biographical implications of the fact that from Tolstoy's point of view (and from the point of view of the authorial audience, as well as of millions of actual readers), Natasha does not suffer in the end. Indeed, her victimization is worse than invisible — it is construed as a reward.[30] Without this grounding in an authorial reading, Tolstoy's misogynist text is indistinguishable from feminist irony.

Similarly, reading *Jane Eyre* in the context of Jean Rhys' *Wide Sargasso Sea* — and Mary Wollstonecraft's *Maria* — provides a useful perspective that underscores the inhumanity of Rochester's — and Jane's — treatment of Bertha and suggests that we look behind her function as a convenient Gothic plot device to consider her as a significant character who has been driven mad by her social and economic conditions. But again, with authorial reading one can go further to explore the extent to which Brontë was herself unable to see the oppression behind that convention.[31]

Thus, in arguing for the importance of reading as authorial audience, I am not suggesting that it is either the final reading or the most important. Were I teaching either Tolstoy or Brontë, I would be disappointed in a student who could produce an authorial reading but who could not, in Terry Eagleton's phrase, "show the text as it cannot know itself"[32] — that is, move beyond that reading to look at the work critically from some perspective other than the one called for by the author. But while authorial reading without further critique is often incomplete, so is a critical reading without an understanding of the authorial audience as its base.

So far, I have argued the importance of authorial reading on the grounds that many readers try to engage in it, and that it is a necessary precondition for many other kinds of reading. But it does not logically follow that it is actually possible. Indeed, I would argue that in a sense it is not. I am not referring here to the problems of interpretation that arise because authors simply fail at the act of writing, or because, when editors are allowed to muddle with finished texts, authors, as Hershel Parker puts it, "very often lose authority, with the result that familiar literary texts at some points have no meaning, only partially authorial meaning, or quite adventitious meaning unintended by the author or anyone else."[33] Even beyond this, even among the most polished and accurately edited of texts, there are many (perhaps all) where neither scholarship nor imagination is sufficient to allow us to recover the text in the sense of experiencing the full response that the author intended us to have as we read. This im-

[29]See also Mailloux's claim that "every feminist and nonfeminist approach must posit some kind of reading experience upon which to base its interpretation. Only after a reader-response description is completed or assumed can a feminist critique begin" (*Interpretive Conventions* [Ithaca: Cornell University Press, 1982], p. 89). [Au.]

[30]See, in this regard, Eve Kosofsky Sedgwick's discussion of the " 'happy ending' " of *Our Mutual Friend* and what it really means for Lizzie (*Between Men: English Literature and Male Homosocial Desire* [New York: Columbia University Press, 1985], p. 178). [Au.]

[31]For a different perspective on this problem, considered in the context of European imperialism, see Gayatri Chakravorty Spivak, "Three Women's Texts and a Critique of Imperialism," *Critical Inquiry* 12 (Autumn 1985): 243–61. [Au.]

[32]Terry Eagleton, *Criticism and Ideology* (London: New Left Books, 1976), p. 43. [Au.]

[33]Hershel Parker, *Flawed Texts and Verbal Icons* (Evanston, IL: Northwestern University Press, 1984), p. 4. [Au.]

possibility stems directly from the actual/authorial split. These audiences differ in, among other things, the knowledge and belief they bring to a text. To the extent that the knowledge distinguishing the authorial from the actual audience is positive or additive (that is, to the extent that the authorial audience knows something that the actual audience does not), the gap can often be bridged through education. The reader of *The Catacombs* who does not know the date of Kennedy's assassination can be informed. But knowledge can also be negative. That is, sometimes actual readers can respond to a text as authorial audience only by *not* knowing something that they in fact know — not knowing, as they read John Steinbeck's *In Dubious Battle,* the actual (often unidealistic) course that the American labor movement would eventually follow; not knowing, as they read *U.S.A.,* that Dos Passos would later shift his political views. As for beliefs — they are usually neither additive nor negative, but substitutive: it was difficult for some college-age readers in the late 1960s to accept the passion with which Clarissa protected her virginity.[34]

The problems of recovery caused by the actual/authorial split have a musical equivalent: what I call the authentic-performance paradox. Many performing groups assume that by recreating the physical sounds that a composer had available, they come closer to recreating the intended musical experiences. But do contemporary listeners really move closer to Beethoven's intended experiences when they listen to his sonatas on a Conrad Graf fortepiano? In at least one way, they take a significant step *away* from Beethoven. I am not convinced by those structuralists who argue that binary oppositions underlie all of our perceptions of the world, but structuralists are surely right that we see things not in themselves but rather in terms of their relations, and specifically in terms of oppositions determined largely by culturally imposed categories that may change radically over time. Thus, when *I* hear Beethoven on an early-nineteenth-century fortepiano (and I think this experience is shared by many contemporary listeners), I hear it first and foremost *against* modern sounds. That is, the sound is defined by me (and hence experienced by me) partly in terms of its being not-that-of-a-modern-piano. That component of the listening experience was obviously not envisioned by Beethoven. Similarly, the range of choices that Mozart faced now seems restricted in ways that it did not in 1790, since we now know what Beethoven, Wagner, Schoenberg, and Jay Reise have added to available harmonic and formal vocabulary.[35]

In other words, we live in a world with a history and with traditions, and it is impossible to experience what an author wanted us to because it is impossible to forget all that has happened between the time when a text was written and the time when it is read. What reasonably educated member of our culture can read *Hamlet* — even for the first time — without being influenced by the traditions of interpretation encrusted on it? Of course, tradition is a factor in authorial reading as well; the tradition of literature out of which *Hamlet* grew is, to some extent, part of Shakespeare's assumed starting point. But the traditions coming *afterward* are assuredly not, and modern readers are more likely to be familiar with the latter (which cannot be erased) than with the former.

Thus, while books do sometimes have the power to take readers out of themselves, that power is limited. Nor is that limitation necessarily to be lamented. Despite romantic notions about the beneficial consequences of great art, books are in fact capable of moving readers in immoral as well as in moral directions. In the cli-

[34]John Steinbeck's novel *In Dubious Battle* (1936) concerns a strike of California fruit-pickers in violent conflict with labor goons; by the 1950s, some unions on both coasts were enmeshed with organized crime. John Dos Passos's trilogy *U.S.A.* (*The 42nd Parallel* [1930], *1919* [1932], and *The Big Money* [1936]) contained biting satire on American capitalism and patriotic hypocrisies, which made the author a darling of the Left, although he never joined the Communist Party. In Spain during the Civil War in 1938, Dos Passos became disenchanted with the Soviet Union and its supporters, and his later work reflected a sharp political turn to the Right. Samuel Richardson's *Clarissa, or the History of a Young Lady* (1747–48) concerns a young heiress who is raped after resisting repeated attempts at seduction. [Ed.]

[35]For a fuller discussion of this problem, see my "Circumstantial Evidence: Music Analysis and Theories of Reading," *Mosaic* 18 (Fall 1985): 159–73. [Au.]

mactic chapter of Thomas Dixon, Jr.'s once-popular *The Leopard's Spots,* for instance, our hero, entering a chaotic Democratic convention, makes a stunning speech that unites the party, gains him the nomination for the governorship, provides the first step toward the routing of the Republicans — and, happily, wins over the father of the woman he loves. Few of the readers who pick up this text have trouble recognizing that, for the authorial audience, this is an inspiring moment — especially since Dixon gives clear signals as to how we should react:

> Two thousand men went mad. With one common impulse they sprang to their feet, screaming, shouting, cheering, shaking each other's hands, crying and laughing. With the sullen roar of crashing thunder another whirlwind of cheers swept the crowd, shook the earth, and pierced the sky with its challenge. Wave after wave of applause swept the building and flung their rumbling echoes among the stars.[36]

But should the actual reader respond emotionally, as the author intended, to the *content* of the speech?

> "Shall we longer tolerate negro inspectors of white schools, and negroes in charge of white institutions? Shall we longer tolerate the arrest of white women by negro officers and their trial before negro magistrates?
>
> "Let the manhood of the Aryan race with its four thousand years of authentic history answer that question!" [436]

> "The African has held one fourth of this globe for 3000 years. He has never taken one step in progress or rescued one jungle from the ape and the adder, except as the slave of a superior race . . . and he has not produced one man who has added a feather's weight to the progress of humanity." [437]

The ability to "forget" the viciousness of this passage is not an ability to be nourished, even if it increases our aesthetic enjoyment of this text. And New Critical dogma to the contrary, it is not simply in works of lesser aesthetic quality that this problem emerges.[37] The ability to forget the ways that women have been abused is not a moral asset either, even if it increases our enjoyment of the way Don Giovanni makes a laughingstock of Donna Elvira, or our pleasure in Rochester's final release from the burden of a mad wife.

But while it is neither always possible nor always desirable to experience a text as an author intended, it does not follow that all interpretation need be subjective or idiosyncratic. We can, after all, describe what we cannot experience — and we can often determine what the authorial audience's response is without sharing it fully. A reader can, for instance, know that the authorial audience of *The Leopard's Spots* finds the speech gratifying, or that the authorial audience of *Jane Eyre* finds Bertha unsympathetic — even if, as actual audience, the gratification or the lack of sympathy are problematic. This is important because, as I have argued, authorial reading has a special status against which other readings can be measured (although not necessarily negatively); it is a kind of norm (although not necessarily a positive value), in that it serves as a point of orientation (although not necessarily as an ultimate destination). In short, authorial reading — in the sense of *understanding* the values of the authorial audience — has its own kind of validity, even if, in the end, actual readers share neither the experiences nor the values presumed by the author.

THE DIFFICULTIES OF AUTHORIAL READING

Any discussion of reading must eventually come to grips with a fundamental fact: texts are often ambiguous. This claim of ambiguity, of course, is

[36]Thomas Dixon, Jr., *The Leopard's Spots: A Romance of the White Man's Burden, 1865–1900* (New York: Doubleday, Page, 1902), p. 443 (bk. 3, chap. 13). Further references to this edition are made in the text. [Au.]

[37]Thus, for instance, Brooks and Warren admit that there are some works that "offend us at too deep a level" for us to accept them. "But always we should be careful that we have made the imaginative effort to understand what values may be there, and what common ground might, with more effort, be found." It is significant, though, that they hasten to add, "Furthermore, in the end, we may find that we have rejected the story not because of its theme as such, but because we have found the story unconvincing" (*Understanding Fiction,* 2nd ed. [New York: Appleton-Century-Crofts, 1959], p. 276). [Au.]

itself ambiguous, for it means several different things. It means, for instance, that readers from different interpretive communities — readers who are using the text for different ends — may well find different things in it, and may well call on different kinds of evidence to support their claims: Marxists and Freudians may well see *The Trial* as different texts that are both contained within the same marks on the page. It also means, as many deconstructionist readings have made clear, that the nature of our linguistic system is such that actual readers may find meanings in a text that subvert the meaning apparently intended by the author. It means, in addition, that authors often attempt to communicate ambiguity itself — thus, even readers in the same interpretive community may well see different things in *The Trial,* since Kafka was consciously trying to confuse.

The actual/authorial distinction, however, suggests yet another type of ambiguity. Even among readers attempting to read as authorial audience (whatever they may call it) — that is, even among readers who share ties to the same critical methodologies — there are bound to be disagreements that literary theory can explain but never erase. For even within a given interpretive community, interpretation depends radically on the reader's starting point, which will influence (although not necessarily determine) his or her reading experience. And the proper starting point is always, as I have suggested, presupposed by the text, not contained within it.

To be sure, it is often claimed that texts provide their own rules for unlocking their meanings. "What attitude are we to take toward Walter Mitty?" ask Brooks and Warren. "The reader will need no special help in deciding how to 'take' this story . . . The action of the story serves to suggest the proper blend of sympathy and amusement."[38] And it is true that we often apply rules of interpretation with so little thought that the act of literary perception appears to be automatic; furthermore, texts do, to some extent, give directions for their own decoding. But the phrase "give directions" is revealing. Every literary theoretician these days needs a governing metaphor about texts: text as seduction, text as fabric, text as abyss, text as system. I suppose that my metaphor would have to be text as unassembled swing set. It's a concrete thing that, when completed, offers opportunities (more or less restricted depending on the particular swing set involved) for free play, but you have to assemble it first. It comes with rudimentary directions, but you have to know what directions *are,* as well as how to perform basic tasks.[39] It comes with its own materials, but you must have certain tools of your own at hand. Most important, the instructions are virtually meaningless unless you know, beforehand, what sort of an object you are aiming at. If you have never seen a swing set before, your chances of riding on the trapeze without cracking open your head are slight.

The same is true of reading. You must be somewhere to begin with. Even when a text gives some fairly explicit guidance, you need to know how to recognize it and how to apply it. The moment I pick up Vanessa James' Harlequin romance, *The Fire and the Ice,* and find a story that

[38]Ibid., p. 63. [Au.]

[39]See Gerald Graff's comment that "the reason most students are baffled by what we ask them to do is that they do not know what kind of thing it is that they are supposed to *say* about literary works, and they can't infer those kinds of things from the literary works themselves, because literary works themselves don't tell one what it is one is supposed to say about them" ("The Joys of Not Reading," presented at the Conference on Narrative Poetics, Ohio State University, April 1986). See also Eagleton's remark, "The competent reader is the one who can apply to the text certain rules; but what are the rules for applying rules?" (*Literary Theory* [Minneapolis: University of Minnesota Press, 1983], p. 125). Wolfgang Iser also relies heavily on the notion of giving directions; see, in particular, *The Act of Reading* (Baltimore: Johns Hopkins University Press, 1978). Iser, however, stresses what the text offers, rather than what the reader is presumed to bring; that is, he starts with a reader who already incorporates all the rules I am discussing here. And by suggesting that all worthwhile texts develop their own codes (see, for instance, p. 21), he smudges the line between the text's directions and the readerly presuppositions that allow those directions to work. He thus minimizes the different types of presuppositions required by different texts. Despite his theoretical insistence that "the reader's role can be fulfilled in different ways, according to historical or individual circumstances" (p. 37), he rarely discusses different possible approaches to a text (for an exception, see his pp. 201–02). As a consequence, his analyses, and especially his view of the canon, differ radically from mine. [Au.]

begins with an erotically charged confrontation between a journalist heroine and her new boss (a wealthy playboy she had attacked in print two years earlier), I know a great deal about what to expect — but that is only because I have met the genre and its conventions before. One can well appreciate the kind of insensitive reading that led such critics as I. A. Richards to launch an attack on stock responses — but the fact remains that without some stock responses to begin with, reading is impossible.[40]

Now suppose you are given something to assemble and a set of directions. If you make a mistake in construction, you may eventually find yourself in a self-contradictory position, one where you cannot go further — where following the directions is made impossible by the material reality ("attach the dowel to the holes in posts A and B" — where the posts are six inches further apart than the dowel is long). At this point, you have to reconsider your whole "interpretation," often starting over again from scratch. So it is with reading. The reader of *Crime and Punishment* who assumed that the rule of the least likely suspect applied and that, as in Agatha Christie's *A.B.C. Murders,* our protagonist had been framed — such a reader would eventually reach an interpretive dead end. And unless the reader were exceptionally dull witted or strong willed, he or she would eventually have to rethink what had been done so far.[41]

But sometimes erroneous assembly produces something internally consistent: the swing set holds up, but the swings are three inches closer to the ground than the manufacturer had in mind. And that can happen in reading as well. That is, there is a significant number of texts (perhaps all texts) where two or more starting points can result in conflicting, but equally coherent and consistent, *meanings* — using the word broadly to include the step-by-step experience of tension and relaxation, surprise, confusion, and euphoria. Jane Austen fans will remember the scene in *Emma* where Emma and Harriet have a conversation in which neither understands the other — although both *think* they are communicating — because they are beginning with different assumptions about the referent of the pronoun "he." This kind of misunderstanding comes up in our conversations with authors, too — more often than we may believe.[42] An example may show more specifically what I mean.

On the surface, Agatha Christie's *Mystery of the Blue Train* is a commonplace member of the genre "classical British detective story." It has a murder; it has an adequate collection of readily identifiable cardboard characters, most with plausible motives and questionable alibis; it has trains and timetables, jewels and false jewels, accusations and false accusations, disguises and discrepancies; and, of course, it has an eccentric detective. A reader experienced in the genre will know fairly quickly what to fasten on to. Of particular importance will be such details as who has seen the victim after the train has left the Gare de Lyon. Such a reader, from his or her experience with other similar novels, will also know that in detective stories, "there must be no love interest."[43] He or she will therefore rightfully dismiss as window dressing the romantic story of the pure and simple Katherine Grey, who has just in-

[40]See, for instance, Richards, *Practical Criticism: A Study of Literary Judgment* (New York: Harcourt, Brace, and World/Harvest, 1964), pp. 223–40, esp. p. 232. See also Rosenblatt, *Literature as Exploration* (New York: Appleton-Century, 1938), pp. 113–23. [Au.]

[41]For an amusing exploration of this issue, see James Thurber's story about an attempt to read *Macbeth* as if it were a classical detective story: "The Macbeth Murder Mystery," in *The Thurber Carnival* (New York: Modern Library, 1957), pp. 60–63. [Au.]

[42]I thus disagree with Monroe C. Beardsley's claim that "the more complicated a text, the more difficult it becomes (in general) to devise two disparate and incompatible readings that are equally faithful to it" ("Textual Meaning and Authorial Meaning," *Genre* 1 [1968]: 171). One problem with Beardsley's position is that he does not take sufficient account of the differing conceptions of what it means to be "faithful" to a given text. In this regard, see Thomas S. Kuhn's observation that when philosophers and historians read the same texts, they read them differently. "Undoubtedly the two had looked at the same signs, but they had been trained (programmed if you will) to process them differently" (*The Essential Tension: Selected Studies in Scientific Tradition and Change* [Chicago: University of Chicago Press, 1977], p. 6). [Au.]

[43]S. S. Van Dine, "Twenty Rules for Writing Detective Stories," in *The Art of the Mystery Story: A Collection of Critical Essays,* ed. Howard Haycraft (New York: Grossett and Dunlap/Universal Library, 1947), p. 189. [Au.]

herited a fortune from the crotchety old woman to whom she was a companion.

Read in this way, the book works well. As we expect, some of the apparent clues turn out to be important, others to be red herrings, and there is the expected unexpected twist so that the average reader will, at the end, experience that very special emotion that only a good classical English detective story can offer: the rush of "Oh! I should have caught that!" I have taught the novel several times as a model of the genre, and most students have enjoyed it and been both surprised and pleased by the ending.

I had two students, however, who used a different point of departure. The rule that love interest is secondary, after all, is not *in* the text. Nor, for that matter, is it an article of faith of any regularly constituted interpretive community. Rather, it is brought to bear *on* the text from the outside. And without a prior decision to apply that rule, there is no textually imposed reason not to pay more attention to Katherine Grey, especially since her actions are given considerable prominence, as is her perspective on the events. In fact, it is possible to treat the novel as a kind of romance. From this standpoint, the timing of the trains becomes a secondary consideration, and a different stock pattern emerges: a sympathetic and lovely young woman is wooed by two apparently suitable suitors. From our knowledge of such texts as *Sense and Sensibility* and *War and Peace,* we expect that one of them will be eliminated. But we wouldn't be satisfied if one were simply bumped off (like Tolstoy's Andrei) or one were simply rejected, for we like them both, and this is not the sort of novel in which the tragedy of life or even the sadness of having to make difficult decisions seems a major theme. The best solution, therefore, is to have one of them lose our respect, like Austen's Willoughby; he must turn out to be a scoundrel beneath the surface. Given the subject matter of the story, the most appropriate resolution would be to have one of the suitors turn out to be the killer. The author, in fact, fulfills the expectations raised by this pattern; indeed, so that we can maintain our love and respect for Katherine, Christie goes so far as to assure us that she has known the truth for some time. When Knighton turns out to be the villain, then, the reader starting off from this romance premise experiences something quite different from the surprise that the detective reader experiences: a satisfying, Austenesque confirmation of expectations.

These two readings of the book — and given the radically different effects they produce, they have to be considered two distinct readings — do not stem from differences in critical methodology. And for this reason, they are (in contrast, say, to Freudian and Marxist readings of *The Trial*) irreconcilable. The argument that Joseph K.'s experiences represent his inner psychodrama does not necessarily contradict the claim that they reflect the irrationality of modern-day society; one can well believe both simultaneously. But one cannot simultaneously be surprised and not surprised by the ending of *The Mystery of the Blue Train.* Each reading confers a different meaning on the text, and each is consistent and coherent in itself.

How can we explain this double-barreled detective story? We could, perhaps, conclude that all texts are open, that they are all susceptible to multiple (even infinite) equally correct readings. Alternatively, we could claim that this novel plays on the conflict between knowledge and ignorance, and that it thus either speaks the truth through paradox or artfully deconstructs the genres to which it appears to belong. We might also conclude that it is a poor text. But there is another perfectly reasonable claim one could make: that it is a detective story that does not provide enough *internal* evidence for the actual reader to determine correctly the nature of the authorial audience. This does not make it any less of a mystery story — but to read it correctly (in the sense of successfully joining the authorial audience), you have to know what its genre is *before* you read it. In other words, it is a text that readily opens itself up to misreadings — a term that I use to refer not to readings that simply skirt the authorial audience, but rather to readings that *attempt* to incorporate the strategies of the authorial audience, but fail to do so. In this regard, as we shall see, it is far from an unusual case.

In Chapters 6 and 7, I have a great deal to say about the implications of such misreadings, especially about the ways in which they interact with ideology. But before doing so, I need to look more closely at the kinds of conversations on which competing authorial readings are apt to be based.

RULES OF READING

The term *convention* may appear, at first, somewhat restricted — for many people, when they think of literary conventions, think of formulas of plot and character. Conventions, however, inform our reading in far more complex ways. There are any number of ways of classifying them, and I would like to suggest now a four-part system. Let me make it clear from the outset that this framework is neither exhaustive nor privileged. That is, I intend neither to provide a complete taxonomy of interpretive conventions nor to oust other systems that have been offered (my scheme, for instance, complements, rather than replaces, the typology suggested by Steven Mailloux).[44] Rather, I am offering what I hope will be a useful if rough sorting out of an extremely thorny area — a system that is not only convenient for organizing the ways that we can think about narrative conventions, but that also serves to illuminate some of the relationships between them. Specifically, the system sets out four types of rules. These rules govern operations or activities that, from the author's perspective, it is appropriate for the reader to perform when transforming texts — and indeed, that it is even necessary for the reader to perform if he or she is to end up with the expected meaning. And they are, from the other end, what readers implicitly call upon when they argue for or against a particular paraphrase of a text. The rules, in other words, serve as a kind of assumed contract between author and reader — they specify the grounds on which the intended reading should take place. They are, of course, socially constructed — and they can vary with genre, culture, history, and text. And readers do not always apply them as authors hope they will — even if they are trying to do so, which they sometimes are not.[45] Indeed, as I will argue in Chapter 7, canonization is, in large part, a matter of misapplication. But even when readers do not apply the *specific* rules the author had in mind, in our culture virtually *all* readers apply *some* rules in each of the four categories whenever they approach a text.

First, there are what I call rules of notice. Despite repeated claims by critics that everything counts in literature (especially poetry), we know from experience that there are always more details in a text — particularly a novel — than we can ever hope to keep track of, much less account for. We have learned to tame this multiplicity with a number of implicit rules, shared by readers and writers alike, that give priority to certain kinds of details, and that thus help us sort out figures from ground by making a hierarchy of importance. Some rules of notice cover a wide spectrum of texts: for instance, there is the simple rule that titles are privileged. This may seem trivial, but it is a tremendous help for the first-time viewer of *Hamlet.* In the opening scenes, there are so many characters that he or she would not know where to focus attention without some cue. Similarly, the first and last sentences of most texts are privileged; that is, any interpretation of a text that cannot account for those sentences is generally deemed more defective than a reading that cannot account for some random sentence in the middle. Other rules of notice are specific to smaller groups of texts. For instance, when we

[44]See, for instance, the distinction Mailloux proposes among traditional, regulative, and constitutive conventions, as well as among social, linguistic, literary, and authorial conventions and conventions within individual works (*Interpretive Conventions* [Ithaca: Cornell University Press, 1982], esp. chap. 5). See also the distinction among linguistic, pragmatic, and literary conventions in Ellen Schauber and Ellen Spolsky, "Reader, Language, and Character," in *Theories of Reading, Looking, and Listening,* ed. Henry Garvin (Lewisburg, PA: Bucknell University Press, 1981); and the classification of codes in Barthes, *S/Z,* trans. Richard Miller (New York: Hill and Wang, 1974). [Au.]

[45]See, for instance, Umberto Eco's claim that "we must keep in mind a principle, characteristic of any examination of mass communication media . . . : the message which has been evolved by an educated elite (in a cultural group or a kind of communications headquarters, which takes its lead from the political or economic group in power) is expressed at the outset in terms of a fixed code, but it is caught by diverse groups of receivers and deciphered on the basis of other codes" (*Role of the Reader* [Bloomington: Indiana University Press, 1979], p. 141). [Au.]

are given some apparently obscure detail about a character's grandmother in a novel by Faulkner, we are supposed to pay more attention to it than we would in one by Dostoyevsky.

Second, there are rules of signification. These are the rules that tell us how to recast or symbolize or draw the significance from the elements that the first set of rules has brought to our attention. Included here are rules for determining symbolic meaning (the rules that tell us when to invoke the religious connotations of words, for instance); rules for distinguishing degrees of realism in fiction (the rules that allow us to discriminate, for instance, among the degrees and types of realism in the various representations of Napoleon in *War and Peace,* Anthony Burgess' *Napoleon Symphony,* and Woody Allen's *Love and Death*); the rule that allows us, in fiction, to assume that post hoc *is* propter hoc;[46] rules that permit us to assume that characters have psychologies and to draw conclusions about those psychologies from their actions.

Third, there are rules of configuration. Certain clumps of literary features tend to occur together; because of our familiarity with such groupings, we know how to assemble disparate elements in order to make patterns emerge. We can thus both develop expectations and experience a sense of completion. Our ability to perceive form — in Kenneth Burke's sense of the creation and satisfaction of appetites ("Psychology and Form") — involves applying rules of configuration. As Barbara Herrnstein Smith's *Poetic Closure* demonstrates, so does our ability to experience closure. And so does our recognition of the plot patterns and formulas so often illuminated in traditional genre studies. One need not get much further than the opening scenes of Philip Barry's *Holiday* to know how it is going to end. But that is not because it signals its own unique form; rather, it is because we know how to put together a few elements — a charming man, a rigid fiancée, an attractively zany fiancée's sister — and see an emerging pattern.[47]

Finally, there are rules of coherence. The most general rule here, familiar in part through such critics as Wayne Booth and Mary Louise Pratt,[48] states that we should read a text in such a way that it becomes the best text possible. Of course, as Pratt notes, "this is not to say . . . that we do or should assume all literary works to be somehow perfect. It means only that in literary works . . . the range of deviations which will be construed as intentional is much larger" than in "many other speech contexts."[49] From this follow more specific rules that deal with textual disjunctures, permitting us to repair apparent inconsistencies by transforming them into metaphors, subtleties, and ironies. Even deconstructive readings, which widen rather than bridge textual gaps, often find some overarching theme or philosophical point in terms of which the discontinuities make sense.[50]

Now while there is a certain logical order to these rules, I am not suggesting that we read a text by applying them one after another. Reading is a more complex holistic process in which various rules interact with one another in ways that we may never understand, even though we seem

[46]After this . . . because of this. [Ed.]

[47]In the film version, there is an added signal, since we assume that the characters played by Cary Grant and Katharine Hepburn will be the ones who get romantically entangled. [Au.]

[48]See, for instance, Booth, *Critical Understanding,* esp. chap. 7; Pratt, *Toward a Speech Act Theory of Literary Discourse* (Bloomington: Indiana University Press, 1977), esp. chap. 5. [Au.]

[49]Pratt, *Toward a Speech Act Theory of Literary Discourse,* p. 170. See also Ronald Dworkin's rather more extravagant claim that "an interpretation of a piece of literature attempts to show which way of reading (or speaking or directing or acting) the text reveals it as the best work of art. Different theories or schools or traditions of interpretation disagree . . . because they assume significantly different normative theories about what literature is and what it is for and about what makes one work of literature better than another" ("Law as Interpretation," *Critical Inquiry* 9 [September 1982]: 183). In subsuming *all* interpretation under rules of coherence, Dworkin is not the only critic to privilege this category of rules. [Au.]

[50]Thus, it is not surprising that Serge Doubrovsky, writing in 1966 of what was then "the new criticism" in France — and what now appears to have been the initial stage of what eventually grew into post-structuralism — argues as follows: "Unity, totality, coherence: I believe that to be a motto common to all the new critics or, if you prefer, their common postulate" (*New Criticism in France,* trans. Derek Coltman [Chicago: University of Chicago Press, 1973], p. 119). [Au.]

to have little difficulty putting them into practice intuitively. Thus, for instance, rules of notice would seem to precede rules of configuration, since we cannot perceive a pattern until we notice the elements out of which it is formed. But one of the ways elements become visible is that they form parts of a recognizable pattern. Thus, when Lisa is stabbed in the breast near the end of D. H. Thomas' *White Hotel,* the authorial audience notices that it is the left rather than the right breast in part because her left breast has been mentioned so many times in the novel (repetition is one of the basic means of attracting attention). But it is noticeable for another reason as well: the reference fills out a basic configurational pattern in the novel centering around the theme of clairvoyance.

In addition, a given convention may well be capable of reformulation so that it fits into more than one of the four categories. Take, for instance, the way we are expected to respond to the conventional use of literary parallels. It involves a rule of notice (it is appropriate to pay attention to textual elements that parallel one another), but it is also a rule of signification (parallel forms suggest parallel meanings), a rule of configuration (given an element A, there is a good chance that there will be an element A′ parallel to it), and a rule of coherence (given elements A and B, their mutual presence can be explained to the extent that we are able to interpret them as parallel to one another). The division of conventions into these four types, therefore, is intended neither as a descriptive model of the way the human mind actually reads nor as an absolute and exhaustive classification. It is, rather, a practical analytic device, of value to the extent that it is useful for answering particular questions.

4

PSYCHOANALYTIC THEORY

The Unconscious is structured like a language. — JACQUES LACAN

Oedipus, blind, was on the path to oracular godhood, and the strong poets have followed him by transforming their blindness towards their precursors into the revisionary insights of their own work. — HAROLD BLOOM

The analyst . . . accepts the text and puts all his effort and desire, his passion and personal virtuosity, into reciting it, while remaining indifferent to the events that he enacts. This "indifference," called "benevolent neutrality," is the modest toga with which we cover our interpretive desire. Yet by shedding it, by implicating ourselves, we bring to life, to meaning, the dead discourses . . . which summon us. — JULIA KRISTEVA

Because Sigmund Freud once acknowledged that most of his discoveries about the unconscious mind had been anticipated by the poets and artists of the past, it should not be surprising that the light of depth psychology has long been trained upon literature in an effort to explain its origins, character, and effects. While Freud's own reflections on literature are included in Part One of this book, this chapter contains essays by followers of Freud who, like Peter Brooks, have discovered new ways of using Freudian theory to understand the psychological significance of literary form, or who, like Harold Bloom, have used Freud's doctrines as an enabling metaphor for building a new theory of literature. It also contains essays by Jacques Lacan, the French psychoanalyst whose recasting of Freud's ideas in a new semiotic form has done so much to revitalize our thinking about language and the mind, and by followers and revisers of Lacan, like Jane Gallop and Julia Kristeva, who can help us to understand both the powers of Lacan's thought and its limitations.

Freud's ideas originated not in the ivory tower of theory but in his Vienna consulting room, where he practiced as a neurologist specializing in the treatment of hysteria. Only after experimenting with various physical cures did Freud come to believe that many of his patients' symptoms were caused by something less tangible. At first he hypothesized that hysteria was always a delayed psychosomatic reaction to a real trauma, like childhood rape or incest; eventually, however, he concluded that the cause was the patient's own incestuous desires, desires so unacceptable that they could not be admitted to consciousness but were instead repressed and held in the unconscious, emerging as symptoms in later life.

In Freud's original scheme, the unconscious was part of a system consisting of the conscious mind; the preconscious mind, which included anything on which attention was not currently focused, including forgotten memories and thoughts that could with effort be brought back up into consciousness; and the unconscious itself, whose workings were not directly available to consciousness. The evidence for the existence of the unconscious, as well as the sense of its contents, comes from dreams and fantasies and from *parapraxes* or meaningful mistakes — slips of the tongue, pen, or memory — that also reveal repressed desires and fears. In the original formulation, the unconscious was a realm of energies, generated by the instincts or drives, focusing and binding onto objects *(cathexis),* and being diverted from their goals. Two major drives function in the unconscious: the sexual drive *(libido),* which aims at pleasure, and the aggressive drive, which aims at destruction. These drives are generally fused, and often the term "libido" is used for both.

In the course of infancy and childhood, the libido is focused on different parts of the body *(erogenous zones),* starting with the mouth in early infancy and shifting to include the anus around the second year and the genitals in the third year. These are the oral, anal, and phallic phases of what is termed *infantile sexuality,* and whether or not it feels appropriate to use the term "sexual" for the pleasure infants get from sucking on their thumbs (or adults from smoking), it is clearly a drive, and one that has to do with pleasure rather than with nourishment or any other obviously physiological mechanism.

As Freud elaborated his notion of a mind within the mind, the unconscious was transformed from a simple, dark cave of repression into a complex transactional world. In his later, "topographical" formulation of the unconscious (1923), Freud theorized a polity inhabited in earliest infancy only by the *id* (the location of the drives). As the infant becomes socialized, however, the direct satisfaction of the drives is no longer possible. Most of us gradually learn to eat and eliminate wastes at socially appropriate times and to refrain from grabbing the man or woman we want and forcibly eliminating our rivals. Thus the unconscious develops as the battleground between the pleasure principle — the desire to gratify impulses immediately — and the reality principle, which controls these impulses for the sake of higher social values.

Part of this learning takes the form of the suppression or redirection of our unconscious drives: The libido is opposed by alternative energies or shifted to a more appropriate object or aim or occasion. These shiftings of the libido are called *defenses,* and their operation is the function of a differentiated part of the unconscious, the *ego.* One of the major defenses against the power of the drives is *repression,* which Freud discovered in his patients, but there are many others as well. Among those most often occurring in literature are *projection* (ascribing an impulse of one's own to someone else) and *symbolization* (shifting the object of a drive to something else that can stand as a metaphorical or metonymic substitute for it).

Freud used the term "primary process" to refer to the direct work of libido-energy within the unconscious — primary because it is how psychic energy functions before the development of the ego. It is characterized by the instantaneous gratification of impulses or their rapid rechanneling into other, similar activities. The person who cannot express anger at work but shouts at his or her spouse at home is engaging in "primary process thinking." The term "secondary process" denotes the working of the mature ego, which might channel the energy of inexpressible anger at the boss into doing a better job at work — or finding a more satisfying career.

The third part of the unconscious is called the *superego,* which begins to form during childhood as a result of the Oedipus complex, one of the most powerfully determinative elements in the growth of the child. The Oedipus complex begins in a late phase of infantile sexuality, between the child's third and sixth year, and it takes a different form in males than it does in females. Boys and girls together begin life relating more powerfully to the mother than to the father, and both sexes wish to possess the mother exclusively. They also begin to sense that their claim to exclusive attention is thwarted by the mother's attention to the father, and, already in the phallic stage in which the genitals have become an erogenous zone, they connect that attention to the sexual activities that mother and father participate in and from which they are excluded. The result is a murderous rage against the father (and any other siblings who may be potential competitors) and a desire to possess the mother. (There is also a rage against the mother for permitting the primacy of the father.) Many things keep this rage from being acted out, including feelings of love for the father, dependency on him, and fear of loss of approval or retaliation for aggressive behavior.

Where the Oedipus complex differs in boys and girls is in the functioning of the related *castration complex.* Boys know from observing their own bodies and those of their fathers that they have a penis but that some people (including their mother) do not. Freud theorized that during the Oedipal rivalry, boys fantasize that punishment for their rage will take the form of the loss of the penis. Fear of this leads the boy to repress his rage and desire. In a successful Oedipal outcome, the boy learns to identify with the father in the hope of someday possessing a woman like his mother. In girls, the castration complex does not take the form of *anxiety,* because their lack of a penis suggests that the dreaded castration has already occurred, as it has to the desired mother as well. The result is a frustrated rage in which the girl shifts her sexual desire from the mother to the father (who possesses the penis she wants), and then, when her sexual advances to the father are opposed, begins to identify with the mother in order eventually to possess another man like the father.

The process, as Freud theorized it, is like so many love affairs, long and painful; it involves not only frustration and repression of desires but the turning of desire against itself in the form of self-criticism, self-punishment, and even self-hatred. The conflict generates the moralist of the unconscious, the superego, which is itself divided into the ego-ideal, the repository of images of perfection against which the child (and later the adult) will unhappily compare him- or herself, and the conscience, where approval and disapproval of one's actions are registered. It must be remembered, of course, that Freud's conscience is part of the unconscious, and its work of judgment and self-punishment takes the form of irrational feelings of guilt and unworthiness, and neurotic behavior against which the ego must make defenses as surely as it does against the id.

The final topographical configuration of the unconscious as id, superego, and ego may seem rather like Plato's tripartite soul, mythologized in the *Phaedrus* as Evil Horse, Good Horse, and Charioteer, which may reflect Plato's intuitive sense of the unconscious as well as Freud's own classical education.

STYLES OF FREUDIAN CRITICISM

Traditionally, there have been three stages at which psychoanalysis may enter the study of the literary work: We can examine the mind of the author, the minds of the author's characters, and our own minds as we read the text. Though Freud concludes his essay on "Creative Writers and Daydreaming" (see p. 483) with the suggestion that artistic works allow the audience to revel in their own forbidden fantasies, his focus is primarily on the text as the fantasy-construct of the artist. And there is a long tradition of Freudian criticism that seeks in the text for the buried motives and hidden neurotic conflicts that generated the writer's art. One widely admired study of this sort is Frederick C. Crews's *The Sins of the Fathers: Hawthorne's Psychological Themes* (1966), which examines the tales of the 1840s for the different ways in which they embody the unresolved Oedipus complex suggested by what we know of Hawthorne's youth and manhood. Hawthorne provided a great deal of material for such a study in his private diaries, and biographers began their work soon after his death. The hazards of doing psychoanalytic criticism in this mode are inversely proportional to the amount of material available on the author's life and private thoughts. It is never completely safe to guess at the psychic significance of a work of art, even that of a candid living author, and for some major writers (like Chaucer and Shakespeare), we have only the most minimal sense of what their private lives may have been like, so that psychoanalytic criticism in this mode must be mere speculation.

After the author, we can analyze the characters. This has also been a popular mode of criticism, beginning with *Hamlet and Oedipus* by Freud's disciple and biographer, Ernest Jones, who interpreted Hamlet's problematic hesitation to slay Claudius as stemming from an identification with his uncle, since Hamlet, too, wished to kill the elder Hamlet and marry Gertrude. It is tempting to analyze characters whom we see rendered with telling truth both internally and externally, but, in fact, the hazards of speculation about characters are even greater than about authors. Although Hamlet's actions and language reveal a great deal about him, all we will ever know is contained in the four thousand lines of Shakespeare's play.

Another problem stems from the fact that characters are both more and less than real persons. While some aspects of characters have a *mimetic* function (the representation of human action and motivation), others have primarily *textual* functions (the revelation — or concealment — of information to an audience), which has no precise parallel in life.[1] The contradictions in Hamlet's character may result from the psychic complexities Shakespeare imagined, but they also result from the fact that Hamlet is an agent in a tragic drama with a highly developed system of conventions. An additional problem of psychoanalytic interpretation is whether a character's degree of self-awareness is to be seen as a psychological "fact" or an unintended consequence of the character's textual function. One might raise this question about James Bryan's discussion of J. D. Salinger's *The Catcher in the Rye* (1974), in which Holden Caulfield's maladjustment is ascribed to his repressed incestuous desires for his prepubescent sister Phoebe. The material on which Bryan bases his interpretation comes directly from Holden, whose only mildly embarrassed awareness of his sister's sexiness argues against rather than for Bryan's diagnosis of neurotic repression.[2]

It is tempting to seek in psychoanalysis the secret of a text, but it can be more illuminating to reverse the explanation and to look to literature, as Freud himself did, for clarifications of psychology. Such an approach is exemplified in Samuel Alexander's discussion (1939) of the *Henry IV* plays, which claims that they portray the growth of the ego (Prince Hal), resisting the id's blandishments of immediate gratification (Falstaff), rejecting also the superego's repression (the Chief Justice), mastering phallic desire (Hotspur), and reconciling his rivalry with the father (King Henry) before assuming the crown of adulthood.

Since authors may not provide much material for the would-be analyst and, since characters are not real persons, it would seem that the safest form of psychoanalytic criticism is the analysis of the audience. The readers' gaze into their own unconscious responses to literature is limited only by their insight into their own psychic processes. In the hands of Norman Holland and David Bleich this has produced a reader-response mode of analytic criticism (see the introduction to Reader-Response Criticism, pp. 923–26). The questions that tend to be raised about methods like those of Holland and Bleich have less to do with the tact and accuracy of their findings than with their subjectivity. If readers find anal imagery in a poem, are they revealing its author's fixations or only their own? Two possible answers result, depending on whether the analytic critic believes in the objective existence of a "text" to be analyzed. Those who do believe, like David Bleich or Norman Holland in his early phase, have replied that in the first place, *all* criticism is necessarily subjective, and the personal character of analytic criticism is only more honestly and explicitly so; and that in the second place, idiosyncratic readings can be identified and corrected by the usual forms of reality-testing, through self-examination and self-analysis and through exposure to debate with others. Those who do not, like Holland in his later phase (*5 Readers Reading* [1975] and thereafter), would reply that the question, in the form in which it was posed, is meaningless. The text has no meaning before it is read, and there can be no distinction between what is "in" the text and what is "in" the reader.

[1]One should remember that though literary characters are not the same as real persons, real persons in the masks they present to the world often resemble literary characters.

[2]James Bryan, "The Psychological Structure of *The Catcher in the Rye*," *PMLA* 89 (1974): 1065–74.

Author, character, and audience usually exhaust the spectrum of Freudian criticism. A fourth alternative has been proposed by Peter Brooks in *Reading for the Plot* (1984). In its central chapter, "Freud's Masterplot" reprinted in this chapter, Brooks discusses *Beyond the Pleasure Principle* (1920), that ambiguous late treatise in which Freud examines the *repetition-compulsion,* a neurotic form of behavior that substitutes repetition for remembrance when a memory is too distressing for repression to overcome. Freud finds that he cannot account for the excruciating manifestations of the repetition-compulsion on the basis of the pleasure principle. He is forced to theorize that it is the product of a death-drive, which balances the life-drive of libido. For Brooks, the repetition-compulsion is the central motif of literature. Repetition not only sets the conditions of narrative (one thinks of fairy tales, in which the same situation recurs three times), but it is also basic, through rhyme, refrains, and thematic devices, to poetry. Brooks reads *Beyond the Pleasure Principle* "as a text about textuality" in which "plot mediates meanings within the contradictory human world of the eternal and the mortal. Freud's masterplot speaks of the temporality of desire, and speaks to our very desire for fictional plots."

A more metaphorical variety of Freudian criticism is that of Harold Bloom, who begins with the notion that literary influence is analogous to paternity. Weak poets may merely copy their forebears, but for strong poets of the post-Romantic era, Bloom expects an Oedipal rivalry between the younger "ephebe" and the earlier strong poet he has chosen as his artistic "father." The "son" needs metaphorically to kill or castrate the "father" to make room for his own adult life, and he does so by creatively *misreading* his predecessor in ways that necessitate his own corrective labors. Bloom's theory is not simple, and he posits a vast repertoire of ways in which the younger "ephebe" can perform this liberating act of misprision. Bloom's work has not only proved influential in itself, it has also inspired imitation and challenge. In *The Madwoman in the Attic* (1979), Sandra Gilbert and Susan Gubar have appropriated Bloom's method for their feminist purposes. In effect, they discuss how Bloom's question must be adapted when talking of *women* writers and the Fathers who would seem to exclude them from the succession by reason of their sex, and the special anxiety of authorship women suffer, which can be overcome, at least in part, by participation in the powerful sisterhood of the female literary tradition (see Feminist Literary Criticism, p. 1353).

LACAN

The revisions to Freudian theory of Jacques Lacan, the French psychoanalyst whose thought has had such a broad influence on literary theory since the 1960s through seminars attended by Parisian intellectuals — including Louis Althusser, Michel Foucault, Paul Ricoeur, Roland Barthes, and Julia Kristeva — can only be discussed briefly. His ideas are still unfamiliar to many practicing American psychoanalysts, perhaps because Lacan largely jettisoned the therapeutic model of psychoanalysis leading to the cure of symptoms, considering it a branch more of philosophy than of medicine. Of course, while Lacan deviated from the mainstream of psychoanalytic thought and was expelled from the International Psychoanalytic Association, he believed himself to be returning to Freud rather than departing from him.

Where Freud views the mechanisms of the unconscious as generated by libido (sexual energy) in a transactional system resembling that of thermodynamics, Lacan centers the theory of the unconscious on the sense within us of something *absent*.[3] The sense of absence can take the form of mere lack *(manque)* or need *(besoin)*, which force the psyche to make demands, or it can take the higher form of desire *(désir)*. It is in the true desire — for an object that is itself conscious and can desire us in return — that the higher forms of self-consciousness arise. (This dialectic of desire Lacan took not from Freud but from Hegel's *Phenomenology of Spirit,* 1807.) Lacan's term for the universal symbol, or signifier of desire is the *Phallus*. It is important not to confuse the Phallus in this sense with the male sexual organ, the penis. *Both* sexes experience the absence of and desire for the Phallus — which may be one reason Lacan's restructuring of Freud has appealed to feminists like Hélène Cixous and Luce Irigaray.

This revision of Freud shifts the description of mental processes from a purely biological model to a semiotic one. Freud, for instance, discusses the first phase of childhood as the oral phase, in which the child's pleasure come largely from suckling; the anal phase follows, when the child learns to control and to enjoy controlling the elimination of feces. In Lacan, the analogue of the oral phase is the Mirror-Stage, from six to eighteen months, in which the child's image of its bodily self changes from mere formlessness and fragmentation to a jubilant identification with the unified shape it can see in the mirror. During this development, the child experiences itself as "le Désir de la Mère," the desire of the mother in both senses. The baby not only knows it needs its mother but also feels itself to be what completes and fulfills the mother (the Phallus). Within this phase of development there is no unconscious, because there is nothing to repress and no way to repress it. From this phase Lacan derives the psychic field of the Imaginary, which continues into adult life, where the sense of reality is grasped purely as images and fantasies of the fulfillment of desire.

Repression and the unconscious arrive together with the insertion of the child into language, around eighteen months, when Freud's anal stage begins. As the child learns the names of things, its desires are no longer met automatically; the child finds that it must ask for what it wants and that it can no longer ask for things that do not have names. As the child learns to ask for a signified by pronouncing a signifier, it learns that one thing can symbolize another. As Muller and Richardson have put it, "from this point on the child's desire, like an endless quest for a lost paradise, must be channelled like an underground river through the subterranean passageways of the symbolic order, which make it possible that things be present in their absence in some ways through words."[4] Now desires can be repressed, and the child can ask for something that metaphorically or metonymically replaces the de-

[3]Like the deconstructionist Jacques Derrida and the Marxist Louis Althusser, whom he influenced, Lacan subscribes to a metaphysic based on *absence* rather than one based on *presence*.

[4]John P. Muller and William J. Richardson, *Lacan and Language: A Reader's Guide to Écrits* (New York: International Universities Press, 1982), p. 23.

sired object. Lacan punningly called this stage of development "le Nom-du-Père": "the Name-of-the-Father," which, in French, is pronounced like "the no-of-the-Father"; for language is only the first of the negations and subjections to law that will now begin to affect the child. The child has entered what Lacan calls the field of the Symbolic.

A third Lacanian field, less discussed in his writings than the others, is that of the Real. By this Lacan seems to mean those incomprehensible aspects of experience that exist beyond the grasp of images and symbols through which we think and constitute our reality. The Real functions rather like the noumena in Kant (see pp. 316–17). Lacan recognizes that adult humans are always inscribed within language, but he does not suggest that language must thereby constitute the ultimate reality.

Since in Lacan's dialectic of desire one object may symbolize another, which is a substitute for still another, Lacan has said that "the unconscious is structured like a language." Lacan derives his ideas of language and the unconscious not from Freud but from one of the fathers of semiotics, Ferdinand de Saussure, as he was interpreted by the structuralist anthropologist Claude Lévi-Strauss. Lévi-Strauss considered the unconscious not as "the repository of a unique history which makes each of us an irreplacible being" but rather as "reducible to a function — the symbolic function," which in turn was merely "the aggregate of the laws" of language.[5]

The primary laws of language in structural linguistics are those of the selection and combination of primary basic elements.[6] Metaphor is a mode of symbolization in which one thing is signified by another that is like it, that is part of the same paradigmatic class. And Lacan saw metaphor as equivalent to the Freudian defense of condensation (in which one symbol becomes the substitute for a whole series of associations). Metonymy is a mode of symbolization in which one thing is signified by another that is associated with it but not of the same class — a syntagmatic relationship — which Lacan regarded as equivalent to Freudian displacement. Because most of the Freudian defenses could be read as versions either of condensation or displacement, it appears that unconscious psychic mechanisms operate like linguistic tropes. On the other hand, we should not look within Lacan's linguistic psychology for anything like the hierarchical structure imposed on the elements of language by a syntax.[7]

If the unconscious is like a language, it is one characterized as a foreign tongue: "the discourse of the Other." What Lacan means by this is not clear or simple. Since in Lacan's thought the original Other is the father, the unconscious is Other in its

[5]Claude Lévi-Strauss, "The Effectiveness of Symbols," in *Structural Anthropology* (New York: Anchor Books, 1967), p. 198.

[6]Technically these are called paradigmatic and syntagmatic relationships and are discussed at greater length in the introduction to Chapter 2, Structuralism, Semiotics, and Deconstruction.

[7]This gap may betoken a blind spot in Lacan's use of linguistics. Much of the French theory that is ultimately based on Saussure (Lacan, Derrida, Althusser), seems trapped in the limitations of structural linguistics, a rigid schema of polarized differences that was better able to explain the phonology and morphology of words than the hierarchical reorderings of grammar. If Lacan regretted that Freud's conception of language had been impoverished by the state of linguistics in his time, we may regret that Lacan was not exposed to the revolution in syntactic theory that began with Zellig Harris and Noam Chomsky.

origins — in the *Nom-du-Père.* But the unconscious is also the residence of alterity and alienation within ourselves, the Other to whom we must speak and whom we hear speaking in our internal dialogue. In treating the unconscious as a language rather than a polity, Lacan eliminates the notion of the ego as a homunculus inside ourselves, constantly defending itself against the depredations of the id. What he leaves in its place is far less solid and reified. The ego is an Imaginary construct, a false image of identity and wholeness; but the ego is less important to Lacan than the subject, and the subject is simply the fluid position from which an "I" speaks and the signification of desire takes place. The subject is not entirely effaced, but it is decentered from a privileged spot to that of a function of language.

Like Freud, Lacan approached literature primarily as material that, properly interpreted, illustrated the major concepts of his psychology. He gave seminars on "Desire and the Interpretation of Desire in *Hamlet*";[8] and the somewhat more accessible "Seminar on 'The Purloined Letter.' "[9] The latter essay takes off from a strictly Freudian account of Poe's "The Purloined Letter" by the analyst Marie Bonaparte, who, noting the resemblances between the detective Dupin and his quarry, the Minister D., suggested that the latter was a father figure and analyzed the story as an Oedipal triangle in which Dupin succeeds in destroying the father/minister for the sake of the mother/queen. Lacan finds that the resemblances and repetitions, once he starts to look, go much further than this, and involve the author — and the reader — in the Lacanian dialectic of desire.

Lacan's indirect influence on criticism has been considerable, primarily because his psychology has affected the philosophy and literary theory of the many French intellectuals who attended his seminars (and at a further remove, British and American scholars influenced by the French, as Fredric Jameson has been influenced by Althusser). But a strain of direct Lacanian criticism also began to appear in the 1980s, in separate essays and in collections such as those edited by Shoshana Felman (1981) and Robert Con Davis (1983). Many of these works have taken the form of interpenetrative readings of Lacan and a literary text, which inevitably find the basic themes of Lacan's psychology within the text. Perhaps this is a workable compromise while Lacan's ideas are still relatively unfamiliar, but one suspects that, like Lacanian analysis itself, Lacanian criticism will be centered intensively on the Word and the chains of association that are developed within the text.

The selection from Lacan reprinted in this chapter, "The Agency of the Letter in the Unconscious or Reason since Freud," presents his analysis of metaphor and metonymy as the tropes for the ego defenses Freud called displacement and condensation, and his discussion of the way in which language constructs the subject as a decentered focus of consciousness in dialogue with the unconscious as the voice of the Other. It is one of his most central essays, first presented as a lecture to students of literature at the Sorbonne rather than to a conclave of psychoanalysts, and it is no

[8]Published 1977 in *Yale French Studies* 55/56, and reprinted in Shoshana Felman's *Literature and Psychoanalysis: The Question of Reading: Otherwise* (Baltimore: Johns Hopkins University Press, 1981).

[9]Published in the French edition of *Écrits* and translated by Jeffrey Mehlman in *Yale French Studies* 47/48 (1966).

accident that it has become one of the most influential for Lacanian literary critics. And while *nothing* Lacan wrote would be called easy reading, this is one of his most difficult pieces.

For this reason Lacan's essay is followed by Jane Gallop's chapter on "Metaphor and Metonymy" from *Reading Lacan,* a full-length gloss on "The Agency of the Letter" that comes candidly to terms with the problems of understanding Lacan's bizarrely dissociative style, his semiotic terminology, and his use of "algorithms," pseudomathematical formulas that express complicated psychoanalytic relationships with a few symbols. By the middle of her essay, Gallop is confessedly "free-associating" in response to Lacan's text as much as she is explicating it as a logical structure. She is in effect recommending that readers do the same thing for themselves, since the connections between Lacan's isolated sentences and paragraphs need to be made by a sympathetic reader listening to Lacan as an analyst listens to her patient. In addition to Gallop's reading, extensive gloss notes to the Lacan selection have been included where the reader is likely to be led seriously astray.

JULIA KRISTEVA

The doyenne of psychoanalytic criticism, Julia Kristeva was born in Bulgaria and traveled to Paris in the cultural thaw of 1966, working first with her structuralist compatriot Tzvetan Todorov and with French-born semiotician Gérard Genette, but mentored by Roland Barthes. Kristeva's doctoral thesis, *La Révolution du langage poétique* (1974; about one third of the original was translated into English as *Revolution in Poetic Language,* 1984), marks a turning point between pure linguistics and psychoanalysis, for the book is an application of psychoanalytic theory to language and literature. Kristeva's point of departure is the psychoanalytic theory of Jacques Lacan. In Lacan's terms, the field of the "Imaginary" is the realm of the wordless image, informed by desire *(le désir de la mère),* and thus characterized by Lacan as feminine; whereas the field of the "Symbolic," the realm of the word informed by the *"nom-du-père,"* is characterized as masculine, although both are obviously operative in individuals of both sexes. Nevertheless, for Lacanians literature as a symbolic product is implicitly marked as a masculine domain.

Kristeva's feminist revision of Lacan involves substituting what she calls the "semiotic" for the Imaginary. She posits that prior to its insertion into language, the infant is the site of drives *(pulsions)* and primary processes: "discrete quantities of energy move through the body of the subject who is not yet constituted as such."[10] These quanta of energy operate according to regulated bodily rhythms whose articulations are, like language, a signifying process, though they do not constitute a symbol system. Kristeva calls the "nonexpressive totality formed by the drives and their stases" the *chora,* after Plato's term in the *Timaeus* for "an invisible and formless being which receives all things and mysteriously participates in the intelligible, and which is most incomprehensible."[11] For the child to learn language at all, the chora

[10]Julia Kristeva, *Revolution in Poetic Language* (New York: Columbia University Press, 1984), p. 25.

[11]Plato, *Timaeus* 51 a–b (Cornford translation), in *Plato: Collected Dialogues,* edited by Edith Hamilton and Huntington Cairns (New York: Pantheon Books, 1961), p. 1178.

must be repressed. But as Terry Eagleton has put it, "the repression . . . is not total: for the semiotic can still be discerned as a kind of pulsional pressure within language itself, in tone, rhythm, the bodily and material qualities of language, but also in contradiction, meaninglessness, disruption, silence and absence."[12]

In all language, but particularly within poetic language (with its emphasis on sonority and on tropes), one may discern the irruption of the chora: Like all productions of the subject, poetic discourse is split between the pre-Oedipal semiotic and the Oedipal symbolic: "The very practice of art necessitates reinvesting the maternal *chora* so that it transgresses the symbolic order."[13] The "revolution" to which Kristeva's title refers has to do with this "transgression": The semiotic is always subversive of the symbolic and sometimes, especially in poetic discourse, the semiotic manages to overrun the symbolic and to rule the signifying process.

The important difference between Kristeva and Lacan is that Lacan imagines the Imaginary and the Symbolic as exclusive binaries, the former non-linguistic and feminine, the product of the "désir de la mère"; the latter linguistic and masculine, the product of the "nom-du-père." Kristeva's binaries are opened up: Her semiotic field is not mute image but operates as a continual pressure upon language, and it is not gendered specifically as feminine either. As Toril Moi puts it, the image of the pre-Oedipal mother, with whom Kristeva locates the semiotic field, "looms as large for baby boys as for baby girls" and thus "cannot be reduced to an example of 'femininity' for the simple reason that the opposition between feminine and masculine does not exist in pre-Oedipality."[14] Indeed, Kristeva's textual criticism of the literary operations of the "semiotic" in *La Révolution du langage poétique* is applied primarily to texts by male poets, such as Lautréamont, Mallarmé, and Artaud.

Kristeva's later monograph, *Pouvoirs de l'horreur* (1980; translated as *Powers of Horror: An Essay on Abjection,* 1982), centers on the concept of abjection, an affect that includes physical disgust, spiritual repulsion, and religious renunciation. For Kristeva, the origin of abjection is coterminous with the origin of the self when the infant separates as an individual from the pre-Oedipal mother. It is the obverse side of the pleasure the infant takes in fusion with the mother's body; in this moment of abjection Kristeva discovers the sources of fetish and taboo, and, more generally, of language and culture. She explores the social ramifications of abjection in Eastern and Western societies, but her primary interest is the place of women — as objects of disgust and of religious taboo.

"Psychoanalysis and the Polis" (1982), reprinted in this chapter, emerged from Kristeva's work on *Powers of Horror.* Written in response to a collection of Marxist and deconstructionist essays on the general topic "The Politics of Interpretation," Kristeva's essay asserts the utility of psychoanalytic thought and interpretive technique. Psychoanalysis, with its presumption of overdetermination, of "both/and" structures of thought rather than "either/or," becomes a way of countering the totalizing force of contemporary political theory, whose ideology, whether on the Left

[12]Terry Eagleton, *Literary Theory: An Introduction* (Minneapolis: University of Minnesota Press, 1983), p. 188.

[13]Kristeva, *Revolution in Poetic Language,* p. 102.

[14]Toril Moi, *Sexual/Textual Politics* (New York: Methuen, 1985), p. 165.

or the Right, makes the interpreter deaf to the object of study. For Kristeva, psychoanalysis is uniquely able to let the object of interpretation become a speaking subject, enter into a dialogue with the analyst, and even influence decisively the theory by which he or she is understood.

Kristeva demonstrates the way psychoanalysis enters politics with her approach to the brilliant, ferociously anti-Semitic writer Louis-Ferdinand Céline, and what can be discovered about his paradoxical talent not merely from exterior issues like "monotheism . . . and the history of France and the reality of the Second World War" but from more generalizable issues including "the psychic instability of the writer and the speaking subject in general." Kristeva's approach involves understanding the deep connections between anti-Semitism and misogyny, how the Jew became for Céline what Woman was for many other French writers, and how this Othered "abject" is invested with qualities "both feminine and phallic, miserable and all-powerful, victim and satrap, idiot and genius, bestial and wily." Neo-Freudian psychoanalysis had been criticized from the Left as a quietist evasion of politics — which may not be altogether unfair as far as Lacan himself was concerned — but it is aptly defended by Kristeva as the most incisive way of understanding political discourse in contemporary life.

Selected Bibliography

Alexander, Samuel. *Philosophic and Literary Pieces*. London: Macmillan, 1939.

Benjamin, Jessica. *Like Subjects, Love Objects: Essays on Recognition and Sexual Difference*. New Haven: Yale University Press, 1995.

Bersani, Leo. *The Freudian Body: Psychoanalysis and Art*. New York: Columbia University Press, 1985.

Bleich, David. *Readings and Feelings: An Introduction to Subjective Criticism*. Urbana, IL: National Council of Teachers of English, 1975.

———. *Subjective Criticism*. Baltimore: Johns Hopkins University Press, 1978.

Bloom, Harold. *The Anxiety of Influence*. New York: Oxford University Press, 1975.

———. *A Map of Misreading*. Oxford and New York: Oxford University Press, 1980.

———. *Agon: Toward a Theory of Revisionism*. Oxford and New York: Oxford University Press, 1982.

Bonaparte, Marie. *The Life and Works of Edgar Allan Poe*. 1933; London: Imago, 1949.

Boothby, Richard. *Death and Desire: Psychoanalytic Theory in Lacan's Return to Freud*. New York: Routledge, 1991.

Bowie, Malcolm. *Freud, Proust, and Lacan: Theory as Fiction*. New York: Cambridge University Press, 1987.

———. *Lacan*. Cambridge: Harvard University Press, 1991.

Brennan, Teresa. *History after Lacan*. New York: Routledge, 1991.

———. *The Interpretation of the Flesh: Freud and Femininity*. New York: Routledge, 1994.

Brenner, Charles. *An Elementary Textbook of Psychoanalysis*. New York: Anchor Books, 1974.

Brooks, Peter. *Reading for the Plot*. New York: Knopf, 1984.

Clément, Catherine. *The Lives and Legends of Jacques Lacan*. New York: Columbia University Press, 1983.

Crews, Frederick. *The Sins of the Fathers: Hawthorne's Psychological Themes*. New York: Oxford University Press, 1966.

———. *Out of My System: Psychology, Ideology and Critical Method.* New York: Oxford University Press, 1976.
Davis, Robert Con, ed. *Lacan and Narration: The Psychoanalytic Difference in Narrative Theory.* Baltimore: Johns Hopkins University Press, 1983.
Deleuze, Gilles, and Félix Guattari. *Anti-Oedipus: Capitalism and Schizophrenia,* trans. Robert Hurley, Mark Seem, and Helen R. Lane. Preface by Michel Foucault. Minneapolis: University of Minnesota Press, 1983.
———. *Kafka: Towards a Minor Literature.* Minneapolis: University of Minnesota Press, 1985.
Derrida, Jacques. "The Purveyor of Truth." *Yale French Studies* 52 (1975): 31–113.
Elliott, Anthony, and Stephen Frosh, eds. *Psychoanalysis in Contexts: Paths between Theory and Modern Culture.* New York: Routledge, 1995.
Felman, Shoshana. "Turning the Screw of Interpretation." *Yale French Studies* 55/56 (1977): 94–207.
———, ed. *Literature and Psychoanalysis: The Question of Reading: Otherwise.* Baltimore, Johns Hopkins University Press, 1981.
———. "Rereading Femininity." *Yale French Studies* 62 (1981): 19–44.
Freud, Anna. *The Ego and the Mechanisms of Defense.* 1936; New York: International Universities Press, 1966.
Freud, Sigmund. *The Standard Edition of the Complete Psychological Works.* 24 vols. 1940–68; London: Hogarth Press and the Institute of Psychoanalysis, 1953.
Gallop, Jane. *The Daughter's Seduction: Feminism and Psychoanalysis.* Ithaca: Cornell University Press, 1982.
———. *Reading Lacan.* Ithaca: Cornell University Press, 1984.
Gilbert, Sandra, and Susan Gubar. *The Madwoman in the Attic.* New Haven: Yale University Press, 1979.
Gilman, Sander L., ed. *Introducing Psychoanalytic Theory.* New York: Brunner/Mazel, 1982.
Grosz, Elizabeth. *Jacques Lacan: A Feminist Introduction.* New York: Routledge, 1990.
Hartman, Geoffrey H., ed. *Psychoanalysis and the Question of the Text: Selected Papers from the English Institute.* Baltimore: Johns Hopkins University Press, 1979.
Hertz, Neil. "Freud and the Sandman." In *Textual Strategies: Perspectives in Post-Structural Criticism,* ed. Josué V. Harari. Ithaca: Cornell University Press, 1979.
Holland, Norman N. *The Dynamics of Literary Response.* New York: Oxford University Press, 1968.
———. *Poems in Persons.* New York: Norton, 1975.
———. *5 Readers Reading.* New Haven: Yale University Press, 1975.
Johnson, Barbara. "The Frame of Reference: Poe, Lacan, Derrida." *Yale French Studies* 55/56 (1977): 457–505.
Jones, Ernest. *Hamlet and Oedipus.* New York: Doubleday, 1949.
Jung, Carl Gustav. *Complete Works.* 17 vols. Ed. Herbert Read, Michael Fordham, and Gerhard Adler. New York: Pantheon, 1953–.
Kris, Ernst. *Psychoanalytic Explorations in Art.* 1952; New York: Schocken Books, 1964.
Kristeva, Julia. *Desire in Language.* New York: Columbia University Press, 1980.
Kurzweil, Edith, and William Phillips, eds. *Literature and Psychoanalysis.* New York: Columbia University Press, 1983.
Lacan, Jacques. "The Seminar on 'The Purloined Letter.'" *Yale French Studies* 48 (1972): 39–72.

———. *Écrits: A Selection.* New York: Norton, 1977.
———. *The Seminar of Jacques Lacan,* ed. Jacques-Alain Miller. *Book I: Freud's Papers on Technique 1953–1954,* trans. John Forrester. New York and London: Norton, 1988.
———. *The Seminar of Jacques Lacan,* ed. Jacques-Alain Miller. *Book II: The Ego in Freud's Theory and in the Technique of Psychoanalysis 1954–1955,* trans. Sylvana Tomaselli. New York and London: Norton, 1988.
———. *The Seminar of Jacques Lacan,* ed. Jacques-Alain Miller. *Book III: The Psychoses 1955–1956,* trans. Russell Grigg. New York and London: Norton, 1993.
Laplanche, Jean, and Jean-Baptiste Pontalis. *The Language of Psychoanalysis.* London: Hogarth Press, 1973.
Lawrence, D. H. *Studies in Classical American Literature.* New York: Penguin, 1977.
Lesser, Simon O. *Fiction and the Unconscious.* Chicago: University of Chicago Press, 1957.
MacCannell, Juliet Flower. *Figuring Lacan: Criticism and the Cultural Unconscious.* Beckenham: Croon Helm, 1986.
Muller, John P., and William J. Richardson. *Lacan and Language: A Reader's Guide to Écrits.* New York: International Universities Press, 1982.
Nancy, J.-L., and P. Lacoue-Labarthe (1973). *The Title of the Letter: A Reading of Lacan,* trans. F. Raffoul and D. Pettigrew. Albany, NY: State University of New York Press, 1992.
Samuels, Andrew. *The Political Psyche.* New York: Routledge, 1993.
Shamdasani, Sonu, and Michael Munchow, eds. *Speculations after Freud: Psychoanalysis, Philosophy and Culture.* New York: Routledge, 1994.
Skura, Meredith Anne. *The Literary Use of the Psychoanalytic Process.* New Haven: Yale University Press, 1981.
Smith, Joseph H., and William Kerrigan, eds. *Interpreting Lacan.* New Haven and London: Yale University Press, 1983.
Trilling, Lionel. "Art and Neurosis" and "Freud and Literature." *The Liberal Imagination.* New York: Doubleday, 1947.
Turkle, Sherry. *Psychoanalytic Politics: Freud's French Revolution.* New York: Basic Books, 1978.
Wilden, Anthony. *The Language of the Self: The Function of Language in Psychoanalysis.* New York: Dell, 1968.
Wright, Elizabeth. *Psychoanalytic Criticism: Theory in Practice.* New York and London: Methuen, 1984.
Zizek, Slavoj. *Looking Awry: An Introduction to Jacques Lacan through Popular Culture.* Cambridge: MIT Press, 1991.
———. *Enjoy Your Symptom! Jacques Lacan in Hollywood and Out.* New York: Routledge, 1992.

Harold Bloom

b. 1930

Harold Bloom's theories of poetic misprision and anxiety have changed how critics think about literary tradition. Bloom was born in New York City, took his B.A. at Cornell, and received his Ph.D. from Yale in 1955. He has been a member of the Yale faculty since then and is at present Sterling Professor of the Humanities. Bloom's brilliance is fabled; he possesses an eidetic memory and is said to have read English before he spoke it. In 1985 he received one of the so-called genius awards from the MacArthur Foundation. His studies of Romantic poets include Shelley's Mythmaking *(1959),* The Visionary Company: A Reading of English Romantic Poetry *(1961),* Blake's Apocalypse: A Study in Poetic Argument *(1963), and* The Ringers in the Tower: Studies in Romantic Tradition *(1971). His theories about creative misreading in the poetic tradition are unfolded — recursively — through several books, including* The Anxiety of Influence: A Theory of Poetry *(1973) excerpted here,* A Map of Misreading *(1975),* Kabbalah and Criticism *(1975),* Poetry and Repression: Revisionism from Blake to Stevens *(1976), and* Agon: Towards a Theory of Revisionism *(1982). After shaking up traditional notions of literary history in his "revision" tetralogy, Bloom defended the objects of traditional history in* The Western Canon: The Books and School of the Ages *(1994). He seems to have turned for a long-term project, however, to the Bible and religion. In* The Book of J *(1990), Bloom identifies the author of the J-text, the oldest strand of narrative in Genesis, Exodus, and Numbers, as a woman, specifically a princess of the line of David writing in the reigns of Solomon and Rehoboam; the book has sold millions of copies but has been scorned by biblical scholars, less for its wild speculations than its defective understanding of the Hebrew text. Bloom's latest pronouncements on religion are contained in* The American Religion: The Emergence of the Post-Christian Nation *(1992) and* Omens of Millennium: The Gnosis of Angels, Dreams, and Resurrection *(1996).*

A Meditation upon Priority

This short book offers a theory of poetry by way of a description of poetic influence, or the story of intrapoetic relationships. One aim of this theory is corrective: to deidealize our accepted accounts of how one poet helps to form another. Another aim, also corrective, is to try to provide a poetics that will foster a more adequate practical criticism.

Poetic history, in this book's argument, is held to be indistinguishable from poetic influence, since strong poets make that history by misreading one another, so as to clear imaginative space for themselves.

My concern is only with strong poets, major figures with the persistence to wrestle with their strong precursors, even to the death. Weaker talents idealize; figures of capable imagination appropriate for themselves. But nothing is got for nothing, and self-appropriation involves the immense anxieties of indebtedness, for what strong maker desires the realization that he has failed to create himself? Oscar Wilde, who knew he had failed as a poet because he lacked strength to overcome his anxiety of influence, knew also the darker truths concerning influence. *The Ballad of Reading Gaol* becomes an embarrassment to read, directly one recognizes that every lustre it exhibits is reflected from *The Rime of the Ancient Mariner;* and Wilde's lyrics anthologize the whole of English High Romanticism. Knowing this, and armed with his customary intelligence, Wilde bitterly remarks in *The Portrait of Mr. W. H.* that: "Influence is simply a transference of personality, a mode of giving away what is most precious to one's self, and its exercise produces a sense, and, it may be, a reality of loss. Every disciple takes away something from his master." This is the anxiety of influencing, yet no reversal in this area is a true reversal. Two years later, Wilde refined this bitterness in one of Lord Henry Wotton's elegant observations in *The Picture of Dorian Gray,* where he tells Dorian that all influence is immoral:

> Because to influence a person is to give him one's own soul. He does not think his natural thoughts, or burn with his natural passions. His virtues are not real to him. His sins, if there are such things as sins, are borrowed. He becomes an echo of someone else's music, an actor of a part that has not been written for him.

To apply Lord Henry's insight to Wilde, we need only read Wilde's review of Pater's *Appreciations,* with its splendidly self-deceptive closing observation that Pater "has escaped disciples." Every major aesthetic consciousness seems peculiarly more gifted at denying obligation as the hungry generations go on treading one another down. Stevens, a stronger heir of Pater than even Wilde was, is revealingly vehement in his letters:

> While, of course, I come down from the past, the past is my own and not something marked Coleridge, Wordsworth, etc. I know of no one who has been particularly important to me. My reality-imagination complex is entirely my own even though I see it in others.

He might have said: "particularly because I see it in others," but poetic influence was hardly a subject where Stevens's insights could center. Towards the end, his denials became rather violent, and oddly humored. Writing to the poet Richard Eberhart, he extends a sympathy all the stronger for being self-sympathy:

> I sympathize with your denial of any influence on my part. This sort of thing always jars me because, in my own case, I am not conscious of having been influenced by anybody and have purposely held off from reading highly mannered people like Eliot and Pound so that I should not absorb anything, even unconsciously. But there is a kind of critic who spends his time dissecting what he reads for echoes, imitations, influences, as if no one was ever simply himself but is always compounded of a lot of other people. As for W. Blake, I think that this means Wilhelm Blake.

This view, that poetic influence scarcely exists, except in furiously active pedants, is itself an illustration of one way in which poetic influence is a variety of melancholy or an anxiety-principle. Stevens was, as he insisted, a highly individual poet, as much an American original as Whitman or Dickinson, or his own contemporaries: Pound, Williams, Moore. But poetic influence need not make poets less original; as often it makes them more original, though not therefore necessarily better. The profundities of poetic influence cannot be reduced to source-study, to the history of ideas, to the patterning of images. Poetic influence, or as I shall more frequently term it, poetic misprision, is necessarily the study of the life-cycle of the poet-as-poet. When such study considers the context in which that life-cycle is enacted, it will be compelled to examine simultaneously the relations between poets as cases akin to what Freud called the family romance, and as chapters in the history of modern revisionism, "modern" meaning here post-Enlightenment. The modern poet, as W. J. Bate shows in *The Burden of the Past and the English Poet,* is the inheritor of a melancholy engendered in the mind of the Enlightenment by its skepticism of its own double heritage of imaginative wealth, from the ancients and from the Renaissance masters. In this book I largely neglect the area Bate has explored with great skill, in order to center upon intrapoetic relationships as parallels of family romance. Though I employ these parallels, I do so as a deliberate revisionist of some of the Freudian emphases.

Nietzsche and Freud are, so far as I can tell, the prime influences upon the theory of influence presented in this book. Nietzsche is the prophet of the antithetical, and his *Genealogy of Morals* is the profoundest study available to me of the revisionary and ascetic strains in the aesthetic temperament. Freud's investigations of the mechanisms of defense and their ambivalent functionings provide the clearest analogues I have found for the revisionary ratios that govern intrapoetic relations. Yet, the theory of influence expounded here is un-Nietzschean in its deliberate literalism, and in its Viconian insistence that priority in divination is crucial for every strong poet, lest he dwindle merely into a latecomer. My theory rejects also the qualified Freudian optimism that happy substitution is possible, that a second chance can save us from the repetitive quest for our earliest attachments. Poets as poets cannot accept substitutions, and fight to the end to have their initial chance alone. Both Nietzsche and Freud underestimated poets and poetry, yet each yielded more power to phantasmagoria than it truly possesses. They too, despite their moral realism, overidealized the imagination. Nietzsche's disciple, Yeats, and Freud's disciple, Otto Rank, show a greater awareness of the artist's fight against art, and of the relation of this struggle to the artist's antithetical battle against nature.

Freud recognized sublimation as the highest human achievement, a recognition that allies him to Plato and to the entire moral traditions of both Judaism and Christianity. If Wordsworth's *Ode: Intimations of Immortality from Recollections of Early Childhood* possessed only the wisdom found also in Freud, then we could cease calling it "the Great Ode." Wordsworth too saw repetition or second chance as essential for development, and his ode admits that we can redirect our needs by substitution or sublimation. But the ode plangently also awakens into failure, and into the creative mind's protest against time's tyranny. A Wordsworthian critic, even one as loyal to Wordsworth as Geoffrey Hartman, can insist upon clearly distinguishing between *priority,* as a concept from the natural order, and *authority,* from the spiritual order, but Wordsworth's ode declines to make this distinction. "By seeking to overcome priority," Hartman wisely says, "art fights nature on nature's own ground, and is bound to lose." The argument of this book is that strong poets are condemned to just this unwisdom; Wordsworth's Great Ode fights nature on nature's own ground, and suffers a great defeat, even as it retains its greater dream. That dream, in Wordsworth's ode, is shadowed by the anxiety of influence, due to the greatness of the precursor-poem, Milton's *Lycidas,* where the human refusal wholly to sublimate is even more rugged, despite the ostensible yielding to Christian teachings of sublimation.

For every poet begins (however "unconsciously") by rebelling more strongly against the consciousness of death's necessity than all other men and women do. The young citizen of poetry, or ephebe as Athens would have called him, is already the antinatural or antithetical man, and from his start as a poet he quests for an impossible object, as his precursor quested before him. That this quest encompasses necessarily the diminishment of poetry seems to me an inevitable realization, one that accurate literary history must sustain. The great poets of the English Renaissance are not matched by their Enlightened descendants, and the whole tradition of the post-Enlightenment, which is Romanticism, shows a further decline in its Modernist and post-Modernist heirs. The death of poetry will not be hastened by any reader's broodings, yet it seems just to assume that poetry in our tradition, when it dies, will be self-slain, murdered by its own past strength. An implied anguish throughout this book is that Romanticism, for all its glories, may have been a vast visionary tragedy, the self-baffled enterprise not of Prometheus but of blinded Oedipus, who did not know that the Sphinx was his Muse.

Oedipus, blind, was on the path to oracular godhood, and the strong poets have followed him by transforming their blindness towards their precursors into the revisionary insights of their own work. The six revisionary movements that I will trace in the strong poet's life-cycle could as well be more, and could take quite different names than those I have employed. I have kept them to six, because these seem to be minimal and essential to my understanding of how one poet deviates from another. The names, though arbitrary, carry on from various traditions that have been central in Western imaginative life, and I hope can be useful.

The greatest poet in our language is excluded from the argument of this book for several reasons. One is necessarily historical; Shakespeare belongs to the giant age before the flood, before the anxiety of influence became central to poetic consciousness. Another has to do with the contrast between dramatic and lyric form. As poetry has become more subjective, the shadow cast by the precursors has become more dominant. The main cause, though, is that Shakespeare's prime precursor was Marlowe, a poet very much smaller than his inheritor. Milton, with all his strength, yet had to struggle, subtly and crucially, with a major precursor in Spenser, and this struggle both formed and malformed Milton. Coleridge, ephebe of Milton and later of Wordsworth, would have been glad to find his Marlowe in Cowper (or in the much weaker Bowles), but influence cannot be willed. Shakespeare is the largest instance in the language of a phenomenon that stands outside the concern of this book: the absolute absorption of the precursor. Battle between strong equals, father and son as mighty opposites, Laius and Oedipus at the crossroads; only this is my subject here, though some of the fathers, as will be seen, are composite figures. That even the strongest poets are subject to influences not poetical is obvious even to me, but again my concern is only with *the poet in a poet,* or the aboriginal poetic self.

A change like the one I propose in our ideas of influence should help us read more accurately any group of past poets who were contemporary with one another. To give one example, as misinterpreters of Keats, *in their poems,* the Victorian disciples of Keats most notably include Tennyson, Arnold, Hopkins, and Rossetti. That Tennyson triumphed in his long, hidden contest with Keats, no one can assert absolutely, but his clear superiority over Arnold, Hopkins, and Rossetti is due to his relative victory or at least holding of his own in contrast to their partial defeats. Arnold's elegiac poetry uneasily blends Keatsian style with anti-Romantic sentiment, while Hopkins's strained intensities and convolutions of diction and Rossetti's densely inlaid art are also at variance with the burdens they seek to alleviate in their own poetic selves. Similarly, in our time we need to look again at Pound's unending match with Browning, as at Stevens's long and largely hidden civil war with the major poets of English and American Romanticism — Wordsworth, Keats, Shelley, Emerson, and Whitman. As with the Victorian Keatsians, these are instances among many, if a more accurate story is to be told about poetic history.

This book's main purpose is necessarily to present one reader's critical vision, in the context both of the criticism and poetry of his own generation, where their current crises most touch him, and in the context of his own anxieties of influence. In the contemporary poems that most move me, like the *Corsons Inlet* and *Saliences* of A. R. Ammons and the *Fragment* and *Soonest Mended* of John Ashbery, I can recognize a strength that battles against the death of poetry, yet also the exhaustions of being a latecomer. Similarly, in the contemporary criticism that clarifies for me my own evasions, in books like *Allegory* by Angus Fletcher, *Beyond Formalism* by Geoffrey Hartman, and *Blindness and Insight* by Paul de Man, I am made aware of the mind's effort to overcome the impasse of Formalist criticism, the barren moralizing that Archetypal criticism has come to be, and the antihumanistic plain dreariness of all those developments in European criticism that have yet to demonstrate that they can aid in reading any one poem by any poet whatsoever. My Interchapter, proposing a more antithetical practical criticism than any we now have, is my response in this area of the contemporary.

A theory of poetry that presents itself as a severe poem, reliant upon aphorism, apothegm, and a quite personal (though thoroughly traditional) mythic pattern, still may be judged, and may ask to be judged, as argument. Everything that makes up this book — parables, definitions, the working-through of the revisionary ratios as mechanisms of defense — intends to be part of a unified meditation on the melancholy of the creative mind's desperate insistence upon priority. Vico,[1] who read all creation as a severe poem, understood that priority in the natural order and authority in the spiritual order had been one and had to remain one, *for poets,* because only this harshness constituted Poetic Wisdom. Vico reduced both natural priority and spiritual authority to property, a Hermetic reduction that I recognize as the *Ananke,* the dreadful necessity still governing the Western imagination.

Valentinus,[2] second-century Gnostic speculator, came out of Alexandria to teach the Pleroma, the Fullness of thirty Aeons, manifold of Divin-

[1]Giambattista Vico (1668–1744), author of the *Scienza Nuova* (1725). [Ed.]

[2]Second-century Egyptian religious philosopher, founder of the Roman and Alexandrian Gnostics, author of *The Gospel of Truth.* [Ed.]

ity: "It was a great marvel that they were in the Father without knowing Him." To search for where you already are is the most benighted of quests, and the most fated. Each strong poet's Muse, his Sophia, leaps as far out and down as can be, in a solipsistic passion of quest. Valentinus posited a Limit, at which quest ends, but no quest ends, if its context is Unconditioned Mind, the cosmos of the greatest post-Miltonic poets. The Sophia of Valentinus recovered, wed again within the Pleroma, and only her Passion or Dark Intention was separated out into our world, beyond the Limit. Into this Passion, the Dark Intention that Valentinus called "strengthless and female fruit, " the ephebe must fall. If he emerges from it, however crippled and blinded, he will be among the strong poets.

SYNOPSIS: SIX REVISIONARY RATIOS

1. *Clinamen,* which is poetic misreading or misprision proper; I take the word from Lucretius,[3] where it means a "swerve" of the atoms so as to make change possible in the universe. A poet swerves away from his precursor, by so reading his precursor's poem as to execute a *clinamen* in relation to it. This appears as a corrective movement in his own poem, which implies that the precursor poem went accurately up to a certain point, but then should have swerved, precisely in the direction that the new poem moves.

2. *Tessera,* which is completion and antithesis; I take the word not from mosaic-making, where it is still used, but from the ancient mystery cults, where it meant a token of recognition, the fragment say of a small pot which with the other fragments would reconstitute the vessel. A poet antithetically "completes" his precursor, by so reading the parent-poem as to retain its terms but to mean them in another sense, as though the precursor had failed to go far enough.

3. *Kenosis,* which is a breaking-device similar to the defense mechanisms our psyches employ against repetition compulsions; *kenosis* then is a movement towards discontinuity with the precursor. I take the word from St. Paul, where it means the humbling or emptying-out of Jesus by himself, when he accepts reduction from divine to human status. The later poet, apparently emptying himself of his own afflatus, his imaginative godhood, seems to humble himself as though he were ceasing to be a poet, but this ebbing is so performed in relation to a precursor's poem-of-ebbing that the precursor is emptied out also, and so the later poem of deflation is not as absolute as it seems.

4. *Daemonization,* or a movement towards a personalized Counter-Sublime, in reaction to the precursor's Sublime; I take the term from general Neo-Platonic usage, where an intermediary being, neither divine nor human, enters into the adept to aid him. The later poet opens himself to what he believes to be a power in the parent-poem that does not belong to the parent proper, but to a range of being just beyond that precursor. He does this, in his poem, by so stationing its relation to the parent-poem as to generalize away the uniqueness of the earlier work.

5. *Askesis,* or a movement of self-purgation which intends the attainment of a state of solitude; I take the term, general as it is, particularly from the practice of pre-Socratic shamans like Empedocles. The later poet does not, as in *kenosis,* undergo a revisionary movement of emptying, but of curtailing; he yields up part of his own human and imaginative endowment, so as to separate himself from others, including the precursor, and he does this in his poem by so stationing it in regard to the parent-poem as to make that poem undergo an *askesis* too; the precursor's endowment is also truncated.

6. *Apophrades,* or the return of the dead; I take the word from the Athenian dismal or unlucky days upon which the dead returned to reinhabit the houses in which they had lived. The later poet, in his own final phase, already burdened by an imaginative solitude that is almost a solipsism, holds his own poem so open again to the precursor's work that at first we might believe the wheel has come full circle, and that we are back in the later poet's flooded apprenticeship, before his strength began to assert itself in the revisionary ratios. But the poem is now *held*

[3]In his cosmogony, *De rerum natura.* [Ed.]

open to the precursor, where once it *was* open, and the uncanny effect is that the new poem's achievement makes it seem to us, not as though the precursor were writing it, but as though the later poet himself had written the precursor's characteristic work.

Peter Brooks

b. 1938

Peter Preston Brooks was born in New York City and educated at Harvard University, where he received his Ph.D. in French in 1965. Since 1965 he has been professor of French and comparative literature at Yale. Brooks was a Guggenheim Fellow in 1973 and became Chester D. Tripp Professor of Humanities at Yale in 1980. His publications include The Novel of Worldliness *(1969),* The Child's Part *(1972), and* The Melodramatic Imagination *(1975). Recent essays have analyzed works by Balzac, Flaubert, Maupassant, Zola, and Henry James. His most influential book, a classic manifesto on the relationship between literature and modern French psychoanalysis is* Reading for the Plot: Design and Intention in Narrative *(1984; second edition 1990), from which the following selection is excerpted. His most recent books are* Body Work: Objects of Desire in Modern Narrative *(1993),* Psychoanalysis and Storytelling *(1994), and* Law's Stories: Narrative and Rhetoric in the Law *(1996).*

Freud's Masterplot

As if they would confine th' Interminable,
And tie him to his own prescript.[1]

In one of his best essays in "narratology," where he is working toward a greater formalization of principles advanced by Vladimir Propp and Viktor Shklovsky,[2] Tzvetan Todorov elaborates a model of narrative transformation whereby narrative plot *(le récit)* is constituted in the tension of two formal categories, difference and resemblance.[3] Transformation — a change in a predicate term common to beginning and end — represents a synthesis of difference and resemblance; it is, we might say, the same-but-different. Now "the same-but-different" is a common (and if inadequate, not altogether false) definition of metaphor. If Aristotle affirmed that the master of metaphor must have an eye for resemblances,[4] modern treatments of the subject

I wish at the outset of this essay to express my debt to two colleagues whose thinking has helped to clarify my own: Andrea Bertolini and David A. Miller. It is to the latter that I owe the term "the narratable." [Au.]

[1]From Milton, *Samson Agonistes,* lines 307–08. [Ed.]

[2]See the introduction to Formalism. [Ed.]

[3]Tzvetan Todorov, "Les Transformations narratives," in *Poétique de la prose* (Paris: Seuil, 1971), p. 240. Todorov's terms *récit* and *histoire* correspond to the Russian Formalist distinction between *sjužet* and *fabula.* In English, we might use with the same sense of distinctions: narrative *plot* and *story.* [Au.]

[4]See Aristotle, *Poetics,* p. 58. [Ed.]

have affirmed equally the importance of difference included within the operation of resemblance, the chief value of the metaphor residing in its "tension." Narrative operates as metaphor in its affirmation of resemblance, in that it brings into relation different actions, combines them through perceived similarities (Todorov's common predicate term), appropriates them to a common plot, which implies the rejection of merely contingent (or unassimilable) incident or action. The plotting of meaning cannot do without metaphor, for meaning in plot is the structure of action in closed and legible wholes. Metaphor is in this sense totalizing. Yet it is equally apparent that the key figure of narrative must in some sense be not metaphor but metonymy: the figure of contiguity and combination, the figure of syntagmatic relations.[5] The description of narrative needs metonymy as the figure of movement, of linkage in the signifying chain, of the slippage of the signified under the signifier. That Jacques Lacan has equated metonymy and desire[6] is of the utmost pertinence, since desire must be considered the very motor of narrative, its dynamic principle.

The problem with "the same-but-different" as a definition of narrative would be the implication of simultaneity and stasis in the formulation. The postulation of a static model indeed is the central deficiency of most formalist and structuralist work on narrative, which has sought to make manifest the structures of narrative in spatial and atemporal terms, as versions of Lévi-Strauss's "atemporal matrix structure."[7] Todorov is an exception in that, faithful to Propp, he recognizes the need to consider sequence and succession as well as the paradigmatic matrix. He supplements his definition with the remark: "Rather than a 'coin with two faces,' [transformation] is an operation in two directions: it affirms at once resemblance and difference; it puts time into motion and suspends it, in a single movement; it allows discourse to acquire a meaning without this meaning becoming pure information; in a word, it makes narrative possible and reveals its very definition."[8] The image of a double operation upon time has the value of returning us to the evident but frequently eluded fact that narrative meanings are developed in time, that any narrative partakes more or less of what Proust called "un jeu formidable . . . avec le Temps," and that this game of time is not merely in the world of reference (or in the *fabula*) but as well in the narrative, in the *sjužet,* be it only that the meanings developed by narrative *take time:* the time of reading.[9] If at the end of a narrative we can suspend time in a moment where past and present hold together in a metaphor which may be the very recognition which, said Aristotle, every good plot should bring,[10] that moment does not abolish the movement, the slidings, the errors and partial recognitions of the middle. As Roland Barthes points out, in what so far must be counted our most satisfactory dynamic analysis of plot, the proairetic and hermeneutic codes — code of actions, code of enigmas and answers — are irreversible: their interpretation is determined linearly, in sequence, in one direction.[11]

[5]See Roman Jakobson, "Two Types of Language and Two Types of Aphasic Disturbances," in Jakobson and Halle, *Fundamentals of Language* (The Hague: Mouton, 1956). Todorov in a later article adds to "transformation" the term "succession," and sees the pair as definitional of narrative. He discusses the possible equation of these terms with Jakobson's "metaphor" and "metonymy," to conclude that "the connection is possible but does not seem necessary." (Todorov, "The Two Principles of Narrative," *Diacritics,* Fall, 1971, p. 42.) But there seem to be good reasons to maintain Jakobson's terms as "master tropes" referring to two aspects of virtually any text. [Au.]

[6]See Jacques Lacan, "The Mirror Stage," in *Écrits: A Selection* (1977). [Ed.]

[7]See Claude Lévi-Strauss, "La Structure et la forme," *Cahiers de l'Institut de science économique appliquée,* 99, série M, no. 7 (1960), p. 29. This term is cited with approval by A. J. Greimas in *Sémantique structurale* (Paris: Larousse, 1966) and Roland Barthes, in "Introduction à l'analyse structurale des récits," *Communications* 8 (1966). [Au.]

[8]Todorov, "Les Transformations narratives," *Poétique de la prose,* p. 240. Translations from the French, here and elsewhere, are my own. [Au.]

[9]Proust's phrase is cited by Gérard Genette in "Discours du récit," *Figures III* (Paris: Seuil, 1972), p. 182. Whereas Barthes maintains in "Introduction à l'analyse structurale des récits" that time belongs only to the referent of narrative, Genette gives attention to the time of reading and its necessary linearity. See pp. 77–78. [Au.]

[10]See Aristotle, *Poetics,* p. 53. [Ed.]

[11]See Roland Barthes, *S/Z* (Paris: Seuil, 1970), p. 37. [Au.]

Ultimately — Barthes writes elsewhere — the passion that animates us as readers of narrative is the passion for (of) meaning.[12] Since for Barthes meaning (in the "classical" or "readable" text) resides in full predication, completion of the codes in a "plenitude" of signification, this passion appears to be finally a desire for the end. It is at the end — for Barthes as for Aristotle — that recognition brings its illumination, which then can shed retrospective light. The function of the end, whether considered syntactically (as in Todorov and Barthes) or ethically (as in Aristotle) or as formal or cosmological closure (as in Barbara H. Smith or Frank Kermode)[13] continues to fascinate and to baffle. One of the strongest statements of its determinative position in narrative plots comes in a passage from Sartre's *La Nausée* which bears quotation once again. Roquentin is reflecting on the meaning of "adventure" and the difference between living and narrating. When you narrate, you appear to start with a beginning. You say, "It was a fine autumn evening in 1922. I was a notary's clerk in Marommes." But, says Roquentin:

> In reality you have started at the end. It was there, invisible and present, it is what gives these few words the pomp and value of a beginning. "I was out walking, I had left the town without realizing it, I was thinking about my money troubles." This sentence, taken simply for what it is, means that the man was absorbed, morose, a hundred miles from an adventure, exactly in a mood to let things happen without noticing them. But the end is there, transforming everything. For us, the man is already the hero of the story. His moroseness, his money troubles are much more precious than ours, they are all gilded by the light of future passions. And the story goes on in the reverse: instants have stopped piling themselves up in a haphazard way one on another, they are caught up by the end of the story which draws them and each one in its turn draws the instant preceding it: "It was night, the street was deserted." The sentence is thrown out negligently, it seems superfluous; but we don't let ourselves be duped, we put it aside: this is a piece of information whose value we will understand later on. And we feel that the hero has lived all the details of this night as annunciations, as promises, or even that he has lived only those that were promises, blind and deaf to all that did not herald adventure. We forget that the future wasn't yet there; the man was walking in a night without premonitions, which offered him in disorderly fashion its monotonous riches, and he did not choose.[14]

The beginning in fact presupposes the end. The very possibility of meaning plotted through time depends on the anticipated structuring force of the ending: the interminable would be the meaningless. We read the incidents of narration as "promises and annunciations" of final coherence: the metaphor reached through the chain of metonymies. As Roquentin further suggests, we read only those incidents and signs which can be construed as promise and annunciation, enchained toward a construction of significance — those signs which, as in the detective story, appear to be *clues* to the underlying intentionality of event.

The sense of beginning, then, is determined by the sense of an ending. And if we inquire further into the nature of the ending, we no doubt find that it eventually has to do with the human end, with death. In *Les Mots,* Sartre pushes further his reflection on ends. He describes how in order to escape contingency and the sense of being unjustified he had to imagine himself as one of the children in *L'Enfance des hommes illustrés,* determined, as promise and annunciation, by what he would become for posterity. He began to live his life retrospectively, in terms of the death that alone would confer meaning and necessity on existence. As he succinctly puts it, "I became my own obituary."[15] All narration is obituary in that life acquires definable meaning only at, and through, death. In an independent but convergent argument, Walter Benjamin has

[12]"Introduction à l'analyse structurale des récits," p. 27. [Au.]

[13]Barbara Herrnstein Smith's *Poetic Closure* (1968) analyzed "formal closure"; Frank Kermode's *The Sense of an Ending* (1967) invoked the concept of cosmological closure. [Ed.]

[14]Jean-Paul Sartre, *La Nausée* (Paris: Livre de Poche, 1957), pp. 62–63. [Au.]

[15]Sartre, *Les Mots* (Paris: Gallimard, 1968), p. 171. [Au.]

claimed that life assumes transmissible form only at the moment of death. For Benjamin, this death is the very "authority" of narrative: we seek in fictions the knowledge of death, which in our own lives is denied to us. Death — which may be figural but in the classic instances of the genre is so often literal — quickens meaning: it is the "flame," says Benjamin, at which we warm our "shivering" lives.[16]

We need to know more about this deathlike ending which is nonetheless animating of meaning in relation to initiatory desire, and about how the interrelationship of the two determines, shapes, necessitates the middle — Barthes's "dilatory space" of retard, postponement — and the kinds of vacillation between illumination and blindness that we find there. If the end is recognition which retrospectively illuminates beginning and middle, it is not the exclusive truth of the text, which must include the processes along the way — the processes of "transformation" — in their metonymical complexity. If beginning is desire, and is ultimately desire for the end, between lies a process we feel to be necessary (plots, Aristotle tells us, must be of "a certain length")[17] but whose relation to originating desire and to end remains problematic. It is here that Freud's most ambitious investigation of ends in relation to beginnings may be of help — and may suggest a contribution to a properly dynamic model of plot.

We undertake, then, to read *Beyond the Pleasure Principle* as an essay about the dynamic interrelationship of ends and beginnings, and the kind of processes that constitute the middle. The enterprise may find a general sort of legitimation in the fact that *Beyond the Pleasure Principle* is in some sense Freud's own masterplot, the text in which he most fully lays out a total scheme of how life proceeds from beginning to end, and how each individual life in its own way repeats the masterplot. Of Freud's various intentions in this text, the boldest — and most mysterious — may be to provide a theory of comprehension of the dynamic of the life-span, its necessary duration and its necessary end, hence, implicitly, a theory of the very narratability of life. In his pursuit of his "beyond," Freud is forced to follow the implications of argument — "to throw oneself into a line of thought and follow it wherever it leads," as he says late in the essay — to ends that he had not originally or consciously conceived.[18] *Beyond the Pleasure Principle* shows the very plotting of a masterplot made necessary by the structural demands of Freud's thought, and it is in this sense that we shall attempt to read it as a model for narrative plot.

Narrative always makes the implicit claim to be in a state of repetition, as a going over again of a ground already covered: a *sjužet* repeating the *fabula,* as the detective retraces the tracks of the criminal.[19] This claim to an act of repetition — "I sing," "I tell" — appears to be initiatory of narrative. It is equally initiatory of *Beyond the Pleasure Principle;* it is the first problem and clue that Freud confronts. Evidence of a "beyond" that does not fit neatly into the functioning of the pleasure principle comes first in the dreams of patients suffering from war neuroses, or from the traumatic neuroses of peace: dreams which return to the moment of trauma, to relive its pain in apparent contradiction of the wish-fulfillment theory of dreams. This "dark and dismal" example is superseded by an example from "normal" life, and we have the celebrated moment of child's play: the toy thrown away, the reel on the string thrown out of the crib and pulled back, to the alternate exclamation of *fort* and *da.*[20] When he has established the equivalence between making the toy disappear and the child's mother's disappearance, Freud is faced with a set of possible interpretations. Why does the child repeat an unpleasurable experience? It

[16]Walter Benjamin, "The Storyteller," in *Illuminations,* translated by Harry Zohn (New York: Schocken Books, 1969), p. 101. [Au.]

[17]See Aristotle, *Poetics,* p. 48. [Ed.]

[18]Sigmund Freud, "Beyond the Pleasure Principle" (1920), in *The Standard Edition of the Complete Psychological Works of Sigmund Freud,* ed. James Strachey (London: Hogarth Press, 1955), 18, 59. Subsequent page references will be given between parentheses in the text. [Au.]

[19]J. Hillis Miller, in "Ariadne's Web" (unpublished manuscript), notes that the term *diegesis* suggests that narrative is a retracing of a journey already made. On the detective story, see Tzvetan Todorov, "Typologie du roman policier," *Poétique de la prose,* pp. 58–59. [Au.]

[20]"Gone" and "here." [Ed.]

may be answered that by staging his mother's disappearance and return, the child is compensating for his instinctual renunciation. Yet the child has also staged disappearance alone, without reappearance, as a game. This may make one want to argue that the essential experience involved is the movement from a passive to an active role in regard to his mother's disappearance, claiming mastery in a situation which he has been compelled to submit to.

Repetition as the movement from passivity to mastery reminds us of "The Theme of the Three Caskets," where Freud, considering Bassanio's choice of the lead casket in *The Merchant of Venice* — the correct choice in the suit of Portia — decides that the choice of the right maiden in man's literary play is also the choice of death; by this choice, he asserts an active mastery of what he must in fact endure. "Choice stands in the place of necessity, of destiny. In this way man overcomes death, which he has recognized intellectually."[21] If repetition is mastery, movement from the passive to the active; and if mastery is an assertion of control over what man must in fact submit to — choice, we might say, of an imposed end — we have already a suggestive comment on the grammar of plot, where repetition, taking us back again over the same ground, could have to do with the choice of ends.

But other possibilities suggest themselves to Freud at this point. The repetition of unpleasant experience — the mother's disappearance — might be explained by the motive of revenge, which would yield its own pleasure. The uncertainty which Freud faces here is whether repetition can be considered a primary event, independent of the pleasure principle, or whether there is always some direct yield of pleasure of another sort involved. The pursuit of this doubt takes Freud into the analytic experience, to his discovery of patients' need to repeat, rather than simply remember, repressed material: the need to reproduce and to "work through" painful material from the past as if it were present. The analyst can detect a "compulsion to repeat," ascribed to the unconscious repressed, particularly discernible in the transference, where it can take "ingenious" forms. The compulsion to repeat gives patients a sense of being fatefully subject to a "perpetual recurrence of the same thing"; it suggests to them pursuit by a daemonic power. We know also, from Freud's essay on "The Uncanny," that this feeling of the daemonic, arising from involuntary repetition, is a particular attribute of the literature of the uncanny.[22]

Thus in analytic work (as also in literary texts) there is slim but real evidence of a compulsion to repeat which can override the pleasure principle, and which seems "more primitive, more elementary, more instinctual than the pleasure principle which it overrides" (23). We might note at this point that the transference itself is a metaphor, a substitutive relationship for the patient's infantile experiences, and thus approximates the status of a text. Now repetition is so basic to our experience of literary texts that one is simultaneously tempted to say all and to say nothing on the subject. To state the matter baldly: rhyme, alliteration, assonance, meter, refrain, all the mnemonic elements of fictions and indeed most of its tropes are in some manner repetitions which take us back in the text, which allow the ear, the eye, the mind to make connections between different textual moments, to see past and present as related and as establishing a future which will be noticeable as some variation in the pattern. Todorov's "same but different" depends on repetition. If we think of the trebling characteristic of the folk tale, and of all formulaic literature, we may consider that the repetition by three constitutes the minimal repetition to the perception of series, which would make it the minimal intentional structure of action, the minimum plot. Narrative must ever present itself as a repetition of events that have already happened, and within this postulate of a generalized repetition it must make use of specific, perceptible repetitions in order to create plot, that is, to show us a significant interconnection of events. Event gains meaning by repeating (with variation) other events. Repetition is a *return* in the text, a dou-

[21]Freud, "The Theme of the Three Caskets" (1913), *Standard Edition,* 12, 299. [Au.] See pp. 492–93. [Ed.]

[22]See Freud, "The Uncanny" *(Das Unheimliche)* (1919), in *Standard Edition,* 17, 219–52. [Au.]

bling back. We cannot say whether this return is a return *to* or a return *of:* for instance, a return to origins or a return of the repressed. Repetition through this ambiguity appears to suspend temporal process, or rather, to subject it to an indeterminate shuttling or oscillation which binds different moments together as a middle which might turn forward or back. This inescapable middle is suggestive of the daemonic. The relation of narrative plot to story may indeed appear to partake of the daemonic, as a kind of tantalizing play with the primitive and the instinctual, the magic and the curse of reproduction or "representation." But in order to know more precisely the operations of repetition, we need to read further in Freud's text.

"What follows is speculation" (24). With this gesture, Freud, in the manner of Rousseau's dismissal of the facts in the *Discourse on the Origins of Inequality,* begins the fourth chapter and his sketch of the economic and energetic model of the mental apparatus: the system Pcpt-Cs and Ucs,[23] the role of the outer layer as shield against excitations, and the definition of trauma as the breaching of the shield, producing a flood of stimuli which knocks the pleasure principle out of operation. Given this situation, the repetition of traumatic experiences in the dreams of neurotics can be seen to have the function of seeking retrospectively to master the flood of stimuli, to perform a mastery or binding of mobile energy through developing the anxiety whose omission was the cause of the traumatic neurosis. Thus the repetition compulsion is carrying out a task that must be accomplished *before* the dominance of the pleasure principle can begin. Repetition is hence a primary event, independent of the pleasure principle and more primitive. Freud now moves into an exploration of the theory of the instincts.[24] The instinctual is the realm of freely mobile, "unbound" energy: the "primary process," where energy seeks immediate discharge, where no postponement of gratification is tolerated. It appears that it must be "the task of the higher strata of the mental apparatus to bind the instinctual excitation reaching the primary process" before the pleasure principle can assert its dominance over the psychic economy (34–35). We may say that at this point in the essay we have moved from a postulate of repetition as the assertion of mastery (as in the passage from passivity to activity in the child's game) to a conception whereby repetition works as a process of *binding* toward the creation of an energetic constant-state situation which will permit the emergence of mastery, and the possibility of postponement.

That Freud at this point evokes once again the daemonic and the uncanny nature of repetition, and refers us not only to children's play but as well to their demand for exact repetition in storytelling, points our way back to literature. Repetition in all its literary manifestations may in fact work as a "binding," a binding of textual energies that allows them to be mastered by putting them into serviceable form within the energetic economy of the narrative. Serviceable form must in this case mean perceptible form: repetition, repeat, recall, symmetry, all these journeys back in the text, returns to and returns of, that allow us to bind one textual moment to another in terms of similarity or substitution rather than mere contiguity. Textual energy, all that is aroused into expectancy and possibility in a text — the term will need more definition, but corresponds well enough to our experience of reading — can become usable by plot only when it has been bound or formalized. It cannot otherwise be plotted in a course to significant discharge, which is what the pleasure principle is charged with doing. To speak of "binding" in a literary text is thus to speak of any of the formalizations (which, like binding, may be painful, retarding) that force us to recognize sameness within difference, or the very emergence of a *sjužet* from the material of *fabula.*

We need at present to follow Freud into his closer inquiry concerning the relation between

[23]Standard abbreviations for "perceptual-conscious" and "unconscious." [Ed.]

[24]I shall use the term "instinct" since it is the translation of *Trieb* given throughout the Standard Edition. But we should realize that "instinct" is inadequate and somewhat misleading, since it loses the sense of "drive" associated with the word *Trieb.* The currently accepted French translation, *pulsion,* is more to our purposes: the model that interests me here might indeed be called "pulsional." [Au.]

the compulsion to repeat and the instinctual. The answer lies in "a universal attribute of instincts and perhaps of organic life in general," that *"an instinct is an urge inherent in organic life to restore an earlier state of things"* (36). Instincts, which we tend to think of as a drive toward change, may rather be an expression of "the conservative nature of living things." The organism has no wish to change; if its conditions remained the same, it would constantly repeat the very same course of life. Modifications are the effect of external stimuli, and these modifications are in turn stored up for further repetition, so that, while the instincts may give the appearance of tending toward change, they "are merely seeking to reach an ancient goal by paths alike old and new" (38). Hence Freud is able to proffer, with a certain bravado, the formulation: *"the aim of all life is death."* We are given an evolutionary image of the organism in which the tension created by external influences has forced living substance to "diverge ever more widely from its original course of life and to make ever more complicated *détours* before reaching its aim of death" (38–39). In this view, the self-preservative instincts function to assure that the organism shall follow its own path to death, to ward off any ways of returning to the inorganic which are not immanent to the organism itself. In other words, "the organism wishes to die only in its own fashion." It must struggle against events (dangers) which would help it to achieve its goal too rapidly — by a kind of short-circuit.

We are here somewhere near the heart of Freud's masterplot for organic life, and it generates a certain analytic force in its superimposition on fictional plots. What operates in the text through repetition is the death instinct, the drive toward the end. Beyond and under the domination of the pleasure principle is this baseline of plot, its basic "pulsation," sensible or audible through the repetitions which take us back in the text. Repetition can take us both backwards and forwards because these terms have become reversible: the end is a time before the beginning. Between these two moments of quiescence, plot itself stands as a kind of divergence or deviance, a postponement in the discharge which leads back to the inanimate. For plot starts (must give the illusion of starting) from that moment at which story, or "life," is stimulated from quiescence into a state of narratability, into a tension, a kind of irritation, which demands narration. Any reflection on novelistic beginnings shows the beginning as an awakening, an arousal, the birth of an appetency, ambition, desire or intention.[25] To say this is of course to say — perhaps more pertinently — that beginnings are the arousal of an intention in reading, stimulation into a tension. (The specifically erotic nature of the tension of writing and its rehearsal in reading could be demonstrated through a number of exemplary texts, notably Rousseau's account, in *The Confessions,* of how his novel *La Nouvelle Héloïse* was born of a masturbatory reverie and its necessary fictions, or the very similar opening of Jean Genet's *Notre-Dame des fleurs;* but of course the sublimated forms of the tension are just as pertinent.) The ensuing narrative — the Aristotelean "middle" — is maintained in a state of tension, as a prolonged deviance from the quiescence of the "normal" — which is to say, the unnarratable — until it reaches the terminal quiescence of the end. The development of a narrative shows that the tension is maintained as an ever more complicated postponement or *détour* leading back to the goal of quiescence. As Sartre and Benjamin compellingly argued, the narrative must tend toward its end, seek illumination in its own death. Yet this must be the right death, the correct end. The complication of the *détour* is related to the danger of short-circuit: the danger of reaching the end too quickly, of achieving the improper death. The improper end indeed lurks throughout narrative, frequently as the wrong choice: choice of the wrong casket, misapprehension of the magical agent, false erotic object-choice. The development of the subplot in the classical novel usually suggests (as William Empson has intimated) a different solution to the problems worked

[25]On the beginning as intention, see Edward Said, *Beginnings: Intention and Method* (New York: Basic Books, 1975). It occurs to me that the exemplary narrative beginning might be that of Kafka's *Metamorphosis:* waking up to find oneself transformed into a monstrous vermin. [Au.]

through by the main plot, and often illustrates the danger of short-circuit.[26] The subplot stands as one means of warding off the danger of short-circuit, assuring that the main plot will continue through to the right end. The desire of the text (the desire of reading) is hence desire for the end, but desire for the end reached only through the at least minimally complicated *détour,* the intentional deviance, in tension, which is the plot of narrative.

Deviance, *détour,* an intention which is irritation: these are characteristics of the narratable, of "life" as it is the material of narrative, of *fabula* become *sjužet.* Plot is a kind of arabesque or squiggle toward the end. It is like Corporal Trim's arabesque with his stick, in *Tristram Shandy,* retraced by Balzac at the start of *La Peau de chagrin* to indicate the arbitrary, transgressive, gratuitous line of narrative, its deviance from the straight line, the shortest distance between beginning and end — which would be the collapse of one into the other, of life into immediate death. Freud's text will in a moment take us closer to understanding of the formal organization of this deviance toward the end. But it also at this point offers further suggestions about the beginning. For when he has identified both the death instincts and the life (sexual) instincts as conservative, tending toward the restoration of an earlier state of things, Freud feels obliged to deconstruct the will to believe in a human drive toward perfection, an impulsion forward and upward: a force which — he here quotes *Faust* as the classic text of man's forward striving — "*ungebändigt immer vorwärts dringt.*"[27] The illusion of the striving toward perfection is to be explained by instinctual repression and the persisting tension of the repressed instinct, and the resulting difference between the pleasure of satisfaction *demanded* and that which is *achieved,* a difference which "provides the driving factor which will permit of no halting at any position attained" (36). This process of subtraction reappears in modified form in the work of Lacan, where it is the difference between *need* (the infant's need for the breast) and *demand* (which is always demand for recognition) that gives as its result *desire,* which is precisely the driving power, of plot certainly, since desire for Lacan is a metonymy, the forward movement of the signifying chain. If Roman Jakobson is able, in his celebrated essay, to associate the metonymic pole with prose fiction (particularly the nineteenth-century novel) — as the metaphoric pole is associated with lyric poetry — it would seem to be because the meanings peculiar to narrative inhere (or, as Lacan would say, "insist") in the metonymic chain, in the drive of desire toward meaning in time.[28]

The next-to-last chapter of *Beyond the Pleasure Principle* cannot here be rehearsed in detail. In brief, it leads Freud twice into the findings of biology, first on the track of the origins of death, to find out whether it is a necessary or merely a contingent alternative to interminability, then in pursuit of the origins of sexuality, to see whether it satisfies the description of the instinctual as conservative. Biology can offer no sure answer to either investigation, but it offers at least metaphorical confirmation of the necessary dualism of Freud's thought, and encouragement to reformulate his earlier opposition of ego instincts to sexual instincts as one between life instincts and death instincts, a shift in the grouping of oppositional forces which then allows him to reformulate the libidinal instincts themselves as the Eros "of the poets and philosophers" which holds all living things together, and which seeks to combine things in ever greater living wholes. Desire would then seem to be totalizing in intent, a process tending toward combination in new unities: metonymy in the search to become metaphor. But for the symmetry of Freud's opposition to be complete, he needs to be able to ascribe to

[26]See William Empson, "Double Plots," in *Some Versions of Pastoral* (New York: New Directions, 1960), pp. 25–84. [Au.]

[27]"Unhampered always moves forwards." [Ed.]

[28]See Jakobson, "Two Types of Language . . .". See, in Lacan's work, especially "Le Stade du miroir" and "L'Instance de la lettre dans l'inconscient," in *Écrits* (Paris: Seuil, 1966). [Au.] For Lacan's "L'Instance," see p. 1045. [Ed.]

Eros, as to the death instinct, the characteristic of a need to restore an earlier state of things. Since biology will not answer, Freud, in a remarkable gesture, turns toward myth, to come up with Plato's Androgyne, which precisely ascribes Eros to a search to recover a lost primal unity which was split asunder.[29] Freud's apologetic tone in this last twist to his argument is partly disingenuous, for we detect a contentment to have formulated the forces of the human masterplot as "philosopher and poet." The apology is coupled with a reflection that much of the obscurity of the processes Freud has been considering "is merely due to our being obliged to operate with the scientific terms, that is to say with the figurative language, peculiar to psychology" (60). *Beyond the Pleasure Principle,* we are to understand, is not merely metapsychology, it is also mythopoesis, necessarily resembling "an equation with two unknown quantities" (57), or, we might say, a formal dynamic the terms of which are not substantial but purely relational. We perceive that *Beyond the Pleasure Principle* is itself a plot which has formulated that dynamic necessary to its own *détour.*

The last chapter of Freud's text recapitulates, but not without difference. He returns to the problem of the relationship between the instinctual processes of repetition and the dominance of the pleasure principle. One of the earliest and most important functions of the mental apparatus is to bind the instinctual impulses which impinge upon it, to convert freely mobile energy into a quiescent cathexis. This is a preparatory act on behalf of the pleasure principle, which permits its dominance. Sharpening his distinction between a *function* and a *tendency,* Freud argues that the pleasure principle is a "tendency operating in the service of a function whose business it is to free mental apparatus from excitation or to keep the amount of excitation in it constant or to keep it as low as possible" (62). This function is concerned "with the most universal endeavour of all living substance — namely to return to the quiescence of the inorganic world." Hence one can consider "binding" to be a preliminary function which prepares the excitation for its final elimination in the pleasure of discharge. In this manner, we could say that the repetition compulsion and the death instinct serve the pleasure principle; in a larger sense, the pleasure principle, keeping watch on the invasion of stimuli from without and especially from within, seeking their discharge, serves the death instinct, making sure that the organism is permitted to return to quiescence. The whole evolution of the mental apparatus appears as a taming of the instincts so that the pleasure principle — itself tamed, displaced — can appear to dominate in the complicated *détour* called life which leads back to death. In fact, Freud seems here at the very end to imply that the two antagonistic instincts serve one another in a dynamic interaction which is a perfect and self-regulatory economy which makes both end and *détour* perfectly necessary and interdependent. The organism must live in order to die in the proper manner, to die the right death. We must have the arabesque of plot in order to reach the end. We must have metonymy in order to reach metaphor.

We emerge from reading *Beyond the Pleasure Principle* with a dynamic model which effectively structures ends (death, quiescence, nonnarratability) against beginnings (Eros, stimulation into tension, the desire of narrative) in a manner that necessitates the middle as *détour,* as struggle toward the end under the compulsion of imposed delay, as arabesque in the dilatory space of the text. We detect some illumination of the necessary distance between beginning and end, the drives which connect them but which prevent the one collapsing back into the other: the way in which metonymy and metaphor serve one another, the necessary temporality of the same-but-different which to Todorov constitutes the narrative transformation. The model suggests further that along the way of the path from beginning to end — in the middle — we have repetitions serving to bind the energy of the text in order to make its final discharge more effective. In fictional

[29]In Plato's *Symposium,* Aristophanes explains the nature of love in the form of a fable. Humanity was originally designed to be androgynous, but a mischievous demiurge split the double-sexed creature in half. The result is that we are all incomplete, seeking in Eros for our missing halves. [Ed.]

plots, these bindings are a system of repetitions which are returns to and returns of, confounding the movement forward to the end with a movement back to origins, reversing meaning within forward-moving time, serving to formalize the system of textual energies, offering the possibility (or the illusion) of "meaning" wrested from "life."

As a dynamic-energetic model of narrative plot, then, *Beyond the Pleasure Principle* gives an image of how "life," or the *fabula,* is stimulated into the condition of narrative, becomes *sjužet:* enters into a state of deviance and *détour* (ambition, quest, the pose of a mask) in which it is maintained for a certain time, through an at least minimally complex extravagance, before returning to the quiescence of the non-narratable. The energy generated by deviance, extravagance, excess — an energy which belongs to the textual hero's career and to the reader's expectation, his desire of and for the text — maintains the plot in its movement through the vacillating play of the middle, where repetition as binding works toward the generation of significance, toward recognition and the retrospective illumination which will allow us to grasp the text as total metaphor, but not therefore to discount the metonymies that have led to it. The desire of the text is ultimately the desire for the end, for that recognition which is the moment of the death of the reader in the text. Yet recognition cannot abolish textuality, does not annul the middle which, in its oscillation between blindness and recognition, between origin and endings, is the truth of the narrative text.

It is characteristic of textual energy in narrative that it should always be on the verge of premature discharge, of short-circuit. The reader experiences the fear — and excitation — of the improper end, which is symmetrical to — but far more immediate and present than — the fear of endlessness. The possibility of short-circuit can of course be represented in all manner of threats to the protagonist or to any of the functional logics which demand completion; it most commonly takes the form of temptation to the mistaken erotic object choice, who may be of the "Belle Dame sans merci" variety, or may be the too-perfect and hence annihilatory bride. Throughout the Romantic tradition, it is perhaps most notably the image of incest (of the fraternal-sororal variety) which hovers as the sign of a passion interdicted because its fulfillment would be too perfect, a discharge indistinguishable from death, the very cessation of narrative movement. Narrative is in a state of temptation to oversameness, and where we have no literal threat of incest (as in Chateaubriand, or Faulkner), lovers choose to turn the beloved into a soul-sister so that possession will be either impossible or mortal: Werther and Lotte, for instance, or, at the inception of the tradition, Rousseau's *La Nouvelle Héloïse,* where Saint-Preux's letter to Julie following their night of love begins: "Mourons, ô ma douce amie." Incest is only the exemplary version of a temptation of short-circuit from which the protagonist and the text must be led away, into *détour,* into the cure which prolongs narrative.

It may finally be in the logic of our argument that repetition speaks in the text of a return which ultimately subverts the very notion of beginning and end, suggesting that the idea of beginning presupposes the end, that the end is a time before the beginning, and hence that the interminable never can be finally bound in a plot. Analysis, Freud would eventually discover, is inherently interminable, since the dynamics of resistance and the transference can always generate new beginnings in relation to any possible end.[30] It is the role of fictional plots to impose an end which yet suggests a return, a new beginning: a rereading. A narrative, that is, wants at its end to refer us back to its middle, to the web of the text: to recapture us in its doomed energies.

One ought at this point to make a new beginning, and to sketch the possible operation of the model in the study of the plot of a fiction. One could, for instance, take Dickens's *Great Expectations.* One would have to show how the energy released in the text by its liminary "primal scene" — Pip's terrifying meeting with Magwitch in the graveyard — is subsequently bound in a number of desired but unsatisfactory ways (including

[30]See Freud, "Analysis Terminable and Interminable" (1937), in *Standard Edition,* 23, 216–53. [Au.]

Pip's "being bound" as apprentice, the "dream" plot of Satis House, the apparent intent of the "expectations"), and simultaneously in censored but ultimately more satisfying ways (through all the returns of the repressed identification of Pip and his convict). The most salient device of this novel's "middle" is literally the journey back — from London to Pip's home town — a repeated return to apparent origins which is also a return of the repressed, of what Pip calls "that old spell of my childhood." It would be interesting to demonstrate that each of Pip's choices in the novel, while consciously life-furthering, forward oriented, in fact leads back, to the insoluble question of origins, to the palindrome of his name, so that the end of the narrative — its "discharge" — appears as the image of a "life" cured of "plot," as celibate clerk for Clarrikers.

Pip's story, while ostensibly the search for progress, ascension, and metamorphosis, may after all be the narrative of an attempted homecoming: of the effort to reach an assertion of origin through ending, to find the same in the different, the time before in the time after. Most of the great nineteenth-century novels tell this same tale. Georg Lukács has called the novel "the literary form of the transcendent homelessness of the idea," and argued that it is in the discrepancy between idea and the organic that time, the process of duration, becomes constitutive of the novel as of no other genre:

> Only in the novel, whose very matter is seeking and failing to find the essence, is time posited together with the form: time is the resistance of the organic — which possesses a mere semblance of life — to the present meaning, the will of life to remain within its own completely enclosed immanence. . . . In the novel, meaning is separated from life, and hence the essential from the temporal; we might almost say that the entire inner action of the novel is nothing but a struggle against the power of time.[31]

The understanding of time, says Lukács, the transformation of the struggle against time into a process full of interest, is the work of memory — or more precisely, we could say with Freud, of "remembering, repeating, working through." Repetition, remembering, reenactment are the ways in which we replay time, so that it may not be lost. We are thus always trying to work back through time to that transcendent home, knowing of course that we cannot. All we can do is subvert or, perhaps better, pervert time: which is what narrative does.[32]

To forgo any true demonstration on a novel, and to bring a semblance of conclusion, we may return to the assertion, by Barthes and Todorov, that narrative is essentially the articulation of a set of verbs. These verbs are no doubt ultimately all versions of desire. Desire is the wish for the end, for fulfillment, but fulfillment delayed so that we can understand it in relation to origin, and to desire itself. The story of Scheherezade is doubtless the story of stories. This suggests that the tale as read is inhabited by the reader's desire, and that further analysis should be directed to that desire, not (in the manner of Norman Holland) his individual desire and its origins in his own personality,[33] but his transindividual and intertextually determined desire as a reader. Because it concerns ends in relation to beginnings and the forces that animate the middle in between, Freud's model is suggestive of what a reader engages when he responds to plot. It images that engagement as essentially dynamic, an interaction with a system of energy which the reader activates. This in turn suggests why we can read *Beyond the Pleasure Principle* as a text concerning textuality, and conceive that there can be psychoanalytic criticism of the text itself that does not become — as has usually been the case — a study of the psychogenesis of the text (the author's unconscious), the dynamics of literary response (the reader's unconscious), or the occult motivations of the characters (postulating an "unconscious" for them). It is rather the superimpo-

[31]Georg Lukács, *The Theory of the Novel,* trans. Anna Bostock (Cambridge, Mass.: MIT Press, 1971), p. 122. [Au.]

[32]Genette discusses Proust's "perversion" of time in "Discours du récit," p. 182. "Remembering, Repeating, and Working Through" *(Erinnern, Wiederholen und Durcharbeiten,* 1914) is the subject of one of Freud's papers on technique. See *Standard Edition,* 12, 145–56. [Au.]

[33]See Holland, "The Question: Who Reads What How?" in Ch. 3. [Ed.]

sition of the model of the functioning of the mental apparatus on the functioning of the text that offers the possibility of a psychoanalytic criticism. And here the superimposition of Freud's psychic masterplot on the plots of fiction seems a valid and useful maneuver. Plot mediates meanings with the contradictory human world of the eternal and the mortal. Freud's masterplot speaks of the temporality of desire, and speaks to our very desire for fictional plots.

Jacques Lacan

1901–1981

Probably the most controversial figure in French psychiatry, Jacques Marie Émile Lacan dedicated himself to getting strictly back to Freud by way of structural linguistics. An admirer of the surrealists, Lacan published his doctoral thesis on paranoid psychosis (1932). Expelled in 1953 from the International Psychoanalytic Association for unorthodox analytical practices, Lacan with Daniel Lagache, another analyst, created the Société Française de Psychoanalyse. As his theoretical positions continued to develop, Lacan and his followers went on to found the École Freudienne in Paris in 1964. The publication of his Écrits *(1966) gained Lacan international attention. Leading intellectuals flocked to his seminars, and he exercised a cryptic but powerful influence on the French cultural scene of the 1970s. Concerned that the École was losing its integrity, Lacan unilaterally dissolved it in 1980. His intention to begin a new one was unfulfilled at the time of his death from cancer the next year. Editions of Lacan available in English include selections from* Écrits *(1977);* The Language of the Self *(1968, translated and with a commentary by Anthony Wilden);* The Four Fundamental Concepts of Psychoanalysis *(1977);* Feminine Sexuality *(1982); and three volumes of* The Seminar of Jacques Lacan, *edited by Jacques-Alain Miller:* Freud's Writings on Technique 1953–1954 *(1988),* The Ego in Freud's Theory and in the Technique of Psychoanalysis 1954–55 *(1988), and* The Psychoses 1955–1956 *(1993). "The Agency of the Letter in the Unconscious or Reason Since Freud," translated by Alan Sheridan, is from* Écrits: A Selection. *An earlier version of this piece was delivered as a lecture by Lacan at the Sorbonne on May 9, 1957.*

The Agency of the Letter in the Unconscious or Reason since Freud[1]

Of Children in Swaddling Clothes

O cities of the sea, I behold in you your citizens, women as well as men tightly bound with stout bonds around their arms and legs by folk who will not understand your language; and you will only be able to give vent to your griefs and sense of loss of liberty by making tearful complaints, and sighs, and lamentations one to another; for those who bind you will not understand your language nor will you understand them.

— LEONARDO DA VINCI[2]

Although the nature of this contribution was determined by the theme of the third volume of *La Psychanalyse,*[3] I owe to what will be found there to insert it at a point somewhere between writing *(l'écrit)* and speech — it will be half-way between the two.

Writing is distinguished by a prevalence of the *text* in the sense that this factor of discourse will assume in this essay a factor that makes possible the kind of tightening up that I like in order to leave the reader no other way out than the way in, which I prefer to be difficult. In that sense, then, this will not be writing.

Because I always try to provide my seminars each time with something new, I have refrained so far from giving such a text, with one exception, which is not particularly outstanding in the context of the series, and which I refer to at all only for the general level of its argument.

For the urgency that I now take as a pretext for leaving aside such an aim only masks the difficulty that, in trying to maintain it at the level at which I ought to present my teaching here, I might push it too far from speech, whose very different techniques are essential to the formative effect I seek.

That is why I have taken the expedient offered me by the invitation to lecture to the philosophy group of the Fédération des étudiants ès lettres[4] to produce an adaptation suitable to what I have to say: its necessary generality matches the exceptional character of the audience, but its sole object encounters the collusion of their common training, a literary one, to which my title pays homage.

Indeed, how could we forget that to the end of his days Freud constantly maintained that such a training was the prime requisite in the formation of analysts, and that he designated the eternal *universitas litterarum* as the ideal place for its institution.[5]

Thus my recourse (in rewriting) to the movement of the (spoken) discourse, restored to its vitality, by showing whom I meant it for, marks even more clearly those for whom it is not intended.

I mean that it is not intended for those who, for any reason whatever, in psychoanalysis, allow their discipline to avail itself of some false identity — a fault of habit, but its effect on the mind is such that the true identity may appear as simply one alibi among others, a sort of refined reduplication whose implications will not be lost on the most subtle minds.

So one observes with a certain curiosity the beginnings of a new direction concerning symbolization and language in the *International Journal of Psychoanalysis,* with a great many sticky fingers leafing through the pages of Sapir

Translated by Alan Sheridan.

[1]Even the translation of Lacan's title is controversial. The French word "instance," here translated "agency," also means "urgency," "insistence," and "authority." [Ed.]

[2]*Codice Atlantico* 145. [Au.]

[3]*Psychanalyse et sciences de l'homme.* [Au.]

[4]The lecture took place on 9 May, 1957, in the Amphithéâtre Descartes of the Sorbonne, and the discussion was continued afterwards over drinks. [Au.] The audience was the "Federation of Students of Language and Literature." [Ed.]

[5]*Die Frage der Laienanalyse, G.W.*, XIV: 281–83. [Au.]

and Jespersen.[6] These exercises are still somewhat unpracticed, but it is above all the tone that is lacking. A certain "seriousness" as one enters the domain of veracity cannot fail to raise a smile.

And how could a psychoanalyst of today not realize that speech is the key to that truth, when his whole experience must find in speech alone its instrument, its context, its material, and even the background noise of its uncertainties.

I. THE MEANING OF THE LETTER

As my title suggests, beyond this "speech," what the psychoanalytic experience discovers in the unconscious is the whole structure of language. Thus from the outset I have alerted informed minds to the extent to which the notion that the unconscious is merely the seat of the instincts will have to be rethought.

But how are we to take this "letter" here? Quite simply, literally.[7]

By "letter" I designate that material support that concrete discourse borrows from language.

This simple definition assumes that language is not to be confused with the various psychical and somatic functions that serve it in the speaking subject — primarily because language and its structure exist prior to the moment at which each subject at a certain point in his mental development makes his entry into it.

Let us note, then, that aphasias, although caused by purely anatomical lesions in the cerebral apparatus that supplies the mental center for these functions, prove, on the whole, to distribute their deficits between the two sides of the signifying effect of what we call here "the letter" in the creation of signification.[8] A point that will be clarified later.

Thus the subject, too, if he can appear to be the slave of language is all the more so of a discourse in the universal movement in which his place is already inscribed at birth, if only by virtue of his proper name.

Reference to the experience of the community, or to the substance of this discourse, settles nothing. For this experience assumes its essential dimension in the tradition that this discourse itself establishes. This tradition, long before the drama of history is inscribed in it, lays down the elementary structures of culture. And these very structures reveal an ordering of possible exchanges which, even if unconscious, is inconceivable outside the permutations authorized by language.

With the result that the ethnographic duality of nature and culture is giving way to a ternary conception of the human condition — nature, society, and culture — the last term of which could well be reduced to language, or that which essentially distinguishes human society from natural societies.

But I shall not make of this distinction either a point or a point of departure, leaving to its own obscurity the question of the original relations between the signifier and labor. I shall be content, for my little jab at the general function of *praxis* in the genesis of history, to point out that the very society that wished to restore, along with the privileges of the producer, the causal hierarchy of the relations between production and the ideological superstructure to their full political rights, has none the less failed to give birth to an esperanto in which the relations of language to socialist realities would have rendered any literary formalism radically impossible.[9]

[6]Edward Sapir and Otto Jespersen are well-known traditional linguists. [Ed.]

[7]"*À la lettre*." [Tr.]

[8]This aspect of aphasia, so useful in overthrowing the concept of "psychological function," which only obscures every aspect of the question, becomes quite clear in the purely linguistic analysis of the two major forms of aphasia worked out by one of the leaders of modern linguistics, Roman Jakobson. See the most accessible of his works, the *Fundamentals of Language* (with Morris Halle), Mouton, 's Gravenhage, part II, Chapters 1 to 4. [Au.] Lacan's point is that while language pre-exists any individual, certain aspects of language are imprinted on the physical structure of the brain, as is shown by Jakobson's discovery that certain brain lesions make it impossible for an individual to understand the trope of metaphor, while others make it impossible to understand the trope of metonymy. [Ed.]

[9]We may recall that the discussion of the need for a new language in communist society did in fact take place, and Stalin, much to the relief of those who adhered to his philosophy, put an end to it with the following formulation: language is not a superstructure. [Au.]

For my part, I shall trust only those assumptions that have already proven their value by virtue of the fact that language through them has attained the status of an object of scientific investigation.

For it is by virtue of this fact that linguistics[10] is seen to occupy the key position in this domain, and the reclassification of the sciences and a regrouping of them around it signals, as is usually the case, a revolution in knowledge; only the necessities of communication made me inscribe it at the head of this volume under the title "the sciences of man" — despite the confusion that is thereby covered over.[11]

To pinpoint the emergence of linguistic science we may say that, as in the case of all sciences in the modern sense, it is contained in the constitutive moment of an algorithm that is its foundation. This algorithm is the following:

$$\frac{S}{s}$$

which is read as: the signifier over the signified, "over" corresponding to the bar separating the two stages.

This sign should be attributed to Ferdinand de Saussure although it is not found in exactly this form in any of the numerous schemas, which none the less express it, to be found in the printed version of his lectures of the years 1906–7, 1908–9, and 1910–11, which the piety of a group of his disciples caused to be published under the title, *Cours de linguistique générale,* a work of prime importance for the transmission of a teaching worthy of the name, that is, that one can come to terms with only in its own terms.[12]

That is why it is legitimate for us to give him credit for the formulation S/*s* by which, in spite of the differences among schools, the beginning of modern linguistics can be recognized.

The thematics of this science is henceforth suspended, in effect, at the primordial position of the signifier and the signified as being distinct orders separated initially by a barrier resisting signification. And that is what was to make possible an exact study of the connections proper to the signifier, and of the extent of their function in the genesis of the signified.

For this primordial distinction goes well beyond the discussion concerning the arbitrariness of the sign, as it has been elaborated since the earliest reflections of the ancients, and even beyond the impasse which, through the same period, has been encountered in every discussion of the bi-univocal correspondence between the word and the thing, if only in the mere act of naming. All this, of course, is quite contrary to the appearances suggested by the importance often imputed to the role of the index finger pointing to an object in the learning process of the *infans* subject learning his mother tongue, or the use in foreign language teaching of so-called "concrete" methods.

One cannot go further along this line of thought than to demonstrate that no signification can be sustained other than by reference to another signification[13]: in its extreme form this amounts to the proposition that there is no language *(langue)* in existence for which there is any question of its inability to cover the whole field of the signified, it being an effect of its existence as a language *(langue)* that it necessarily answers all needs. If we try to grasp in language the constitution of the object, we cannot fail to notice that this constitution is to be found only at the level of concept, a very different thing from a simple nominative, and that the *thing,* when reduced to the noun, breaks up into the double, divergent beam of the "cause" *(causa)* in which it has taken shelter in the French word *chose,* and the nothing *(rien)* to which it has abandoned its Latin dress *(rem).*

[10]By "linguistics" I mean the study of existing languages *(langues)* in their structure and in the laws revealed therein; this excludes any theory of abstract codes sometimes included under the heading of communication theory, as well as the theory, originating in the physical sciences, called information theory, or any semiology more or less hypothetically generalized. [Au.]

[11]*Psychanalyse et sciences de l'homme.* [Au.]

[12]As the reader will see from the selection in Ch. 2 (see p. 833), Saussure writes the signifier/signified relationship differently than Lacan: in Saussure's version the signified is placed over the signifier rather than under it and the *s*/*S* relation is circled, indicating its stability, with arrows moving up and down, indicating the move that can be made from word to thing and from thing to word. [Ed.]

[13]Cf. the *De Magistro* of St. Augustine, especially the chapter "De significatione locutionis" which I analyzed in my seminar of 23 June, 1954. [Au.]

These considerations, important as their existence is for the philosopher, turn us away from the locus in which language questions us as to its very nature. And we will fail to pursue the question further as long as we cling to the illusion that the signifier answers to the function of representing the signified, or better, that the signifier has to answer for its existence in the name of any signification whatever.

For even reduced to this latter formulation, the heresy is the same — the heresy that leads logical positivism in search of the "meaning of meaning,"[14] as its objective is called in the language of its devotees. As a result, we can observe that even a text highly charged with meaning can be reduced, through this sort of analysis, to insignificant bagatelles, all that survives being mathematical algorithms that are, of course, without any meaning.[15]

To return to our formula S/*s*: if we could infer nothing from it but the notion of the parallelism of its upper and lower terms, each one taken in its globality, it would remain the enigmatic sign of a total mystery. Which of course is not the case.

In order to grasp its function I shall begin by reproducing the classic, yet faulty illustration (see top of next column) by which its usage is normally introduced, and one can see how it opens the way to the kind of error referred to above.

In my lecture, I replaced this illustration with another, which has no greater claim to correctness than that it has been transplanted into that incongruous dimension that the psychoanalyst has not yet altogether renounced because of his quite justified feeling that his conformism takes its value entirely from it. Here is the other diagram:

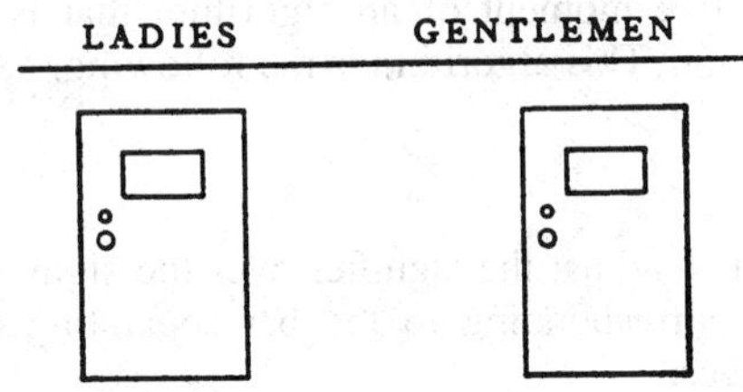

where we see that, without greatly extending the scope of the signifier concerned in the experiment, that is, by doubling a noun through the mere juxtaposition of two terms whose complementary meanings ought apparently to reinforce each other, a surprise is produced by an unexpected precipitation of an unexpected meaning: the image of twin doors symbolizing, through the solitary confinement offered Western Man for the satisfaction of his natural needs away from home, the imperative that he seems to share with the great majority of primitive communities by which his public life is subjected to the laws of urinary segregation.

It is not only with the idea of silencing the nominalist debate with a low blow that I use this example, but rather to show how in fact the signifier enters the signified, namely, in a form which, not being immaterial, raises the question of its place in reality. For the blinking gaze of a short sighted person might be justified in wondering whether this was indeed the signifier as he peered closely at the little enamel signs that bore it, a signifier whose signified would in this call re-

[14]English in the original. [Tr.] *The Meaning of Meaning* is the title of a 1923 book by I. A. Richards and C. K. Ogden on the relationship between language and thought. [Ed.]

[15]So, Mr. I. A. Richards, author of a work precisely in accord with such an objective, has in another work shown us its application. He took for his purposes a page from Mong-tse (Mencius, to the Jesuits) and called the piece, *Mencius on the Mind*. The guarantees of the purity of the experiment are nothing to the luxury of the approaches. And our expert on the traditional Canon that contains the text is found right on the spot in Peking where our demonstration-model mangle has been transported regardless of cost.

But we shall be no less transported, if less expensively, to see a bronze that gives out bell-tones at the slightest contact with thought, transformed into a rag to wipe the blackboard of the most dismaying British psychologism. And not without eventually being identified with the meninx of the author himself — all that remains of him or his object after having exhausted the meaning of the latter and the good sense of the former. [Au.]

ceive its final honors from the double and solemn procession from the upper nave.[16]

But no contrived example can be as telling as the actual experience of truth. So I am happy to have invented the above, since it awoke in the person whose word I most trust a memory of childhood, which having thus happily come to my attention is best placed here.

A train arrives at a station. A little boy and a little girl, brother and sister, are seated in a compartment face to face next to the window through which the buildings along the station platform can be seen passing as the train pulls to a stop. "Look," says the brother, "we're at Ladies!"; "Idiot!" replies his sister, "Can't you see we're at Gentlemen."

Besides the fact that the rails in this story materialize the bar in the Saussurian algorithm (and in a form designed to suggest that its resistance may be other than dialectical), we should add that only someone who didn't have his eyes in front of the holes (it's the appropriate image here) could possibly confuse the place of the signifier and the signified in this story, or not see from what radiating center the signifier sends forth its light into the shadow of incomplete significations.

For this signifier will now carry a purely animal Dissension, destined for the usual oblivion of natural mists, to the unbridled power of ideological warfare, relentless for families, a torment to the Gods. For these children, Ladies and Gentlemen will be henceforth two countries towards which each of their souls will strive on divergent wings, and between which a truce will be the more impossible since they are actually the same country and neither can compromise on its own superiority without detracting from the glory of the other.

But enough. It is beginning to sound like the history of France. Which it is more human, as it ought to be, to evoke here than that of England, destined to tumble from the Large to the Small End of Dean Swift's egg.[17]

It remains to be conceived what steps, what corridor, the S of the signifier, visible here in the plurals[18] in which it focuses its welcome beyond the window, must take in order to rest its elbows on the ventilators through which, like warm and cold air, indignation and scorn come hissing out below.

One thing is certain: if the algorithm S/*s* with its bar is appropriate, access from one to the other cannot in any case have a signification. For in so far as it is itself only pure function of the signifier, the algorithm can reveal only the structure of a signifier in this transfer.

Now the structure of the signifier is, as it is commonly said of language itself, that it should be articulated.

This means that no matter where one starts to designate their reciprocal encroachments and increasing inclusions, these units are subjected to the double condition of being reducible to ultimate differential elements and of combining them according to the laws of a closed order.[19]

These elements, one of the decisive discoveries of linguistics, are *phonemes;* but we must not expect to find any *phonetic* constancy in the modulatory variability to which this term applies, but rather the synchronic system of differential couplings necessary for the discernment of sounds in a given language. Through this, one sees that an essential element of the spoken word itself was predestined to flow into the mobile characters which, in a jumble of lower-case Didots or Garamonds,[20] render validly present what we call the "letter," namely, the essentially localized structure of the signifier.

With the second property of the signifier, that of combining according to the laws of a closed order, is affirmed the necessity of the topological substratum of which the term I ordinarily use, namely, the signifying chain, gives an approximate idea: rings of a necklace that is a ring in another necklace made of rings.

[16]Lacan's point is that the bar dividing the signifier from the signified cannot really separate the two here, since the two signifieds are apparently the same, except for the different signifiers that appropriate them as women's and men's toilets. [Ed.]

[17]In *Gulliver's Travels,* Book I, Swift symbolized the strife between Catholics and Protestants as that between the natives of Blefuscu, who break their eggs at the Big End, and those of Lilliput, who break them at the Small End. [Ed.]

[18]Not, unfortunately, the case in the English here — the plural of "gentleman" being indicated other than by the addition of an "s." [Tr.]

[19]Lacan alludes to the principles of structural linguistics; see the introduction to Structuralism, Semiotics, and Deconstruction, p. 809. [Ed.]

[20]Names of different type-faces. [Tr.]

Such are the structural conditions that define grammar as the order of constitutive encroachments of the signifier up to the level of the unit immediately superior to the sentence, and lexicology as the order of constitutive inclusions of the signifier to the level of the verbal locution.

In examining the limits by which these two exercises in the understanding of linguistic usage are determined, it is easy to see that only the correlations between signifier and signifier provide the standard for all research into signification, as is indicated by the notion of "usage" of a taxeme or semanteme which in fact refers to the context just above that of the units concerned.[21]

But it is not because the undertakings of grammar and lexicology are exhausted within certain limits that we must think that beyond those limits signification reigns supreme. That would be an error.

For the signifier, by its very nature, always anticipates meaning by unfolding its dimension before it. As is seen at the level of the sentence when it is interrupted before the significant term: "I shall never . . . ," "All the same it is . . . ," "And yet there may be . . ." Such sentences are not without meaning, a meaning all the more oppressive in that it is content to make us wait for it.[22]

But the phenomenon is no different which by the mere recoil of a "but" brings to the light, comely as the Shulamite, honest as the dew, the negress adorned for the wedding and the poor woman ready for the auction-block.[23]

From which we can say that it is in the chain of the signifier that the meaning "insists" but that none of its elements "consists" in the signification of which it is at the moment capable.

We are forced, then, to accept the notion of an incessant sliding of the signified under the signifier[24] which Ferdinand de Saussure illustrates with an image resembling the wavy lines of the upper and lower Waters in miniatures from manuscripts of *Genesis;* a double flux marked by fine streaks of rain, vertical dotted lines supposedly confining segments of correspondence.

All our experience runs counter to this linearity, which made me speak once, in one of my seminars on psychosis, of something more like "anchoring points" *("points de capiton")* as a schema for taking into account the dominance of the letter in the dramatic transformation that dialogue can effect in the subject.[25]

The linearity that Saussure holds to be constitutive of the chain of discourse, in conformity with its emission by a single voice and with its horizontal position in our writing — if this linearity is necessary, in fact, it is not sufficient. It applies to the chain of discourse only in the direction in which it is orientated in time, being taken as a signifying factor in all languages in which 'Peter hits Paul' reverses its time when the terms are inverted.

But one has only to listen to poetry, which Saussure was no doubt in the habit of doing,[26] for a polyphony to be heard, for it to become clear that all discourse is aligned along the several staves of a score.

There is in effect no signifying chain that does not have, as if attached to the punctuation of each

[21]Lacan's point is that the organization of most basic elements into a structure operates at the phonological level of the word (where the units are phonemes), the syntactic level of the sentence (where the units are words, or morphemes at least), and the semantic level of the utterance. "Taxeme" and "semanteme" signify atomistic units of grammar and meaning. [Ed.]

[22]To which verbal hallucination, when it takes this form, opens a communicating door with the Freudian structure of psychosis — a door until now unnoticed (cf. "On a Question Preliminary to any Possible Treatment of Psychosis," pp. 179–225). [Au.]

[23]The allusions are to the "I am black, but comely . . ." of the *Song of Solomon,* and to the nineteenth-century cliché of the "poor, but honest" woman. [Tr.]

[24]Compare Jacques Derrida's (somewhat later) notion of *jeu,* the free play between the signifier and the signified; see the introduction to Structuralism, Semiotics, and Deconstruction, p. 820. [Ed.]

[25]I spoke in my seminar of 6 June, 1956, of the first scene of *Athalie,* incited by an allusion — tossed off by a highbrow critic in the *New Statesman and Nation* — to the "high whoredom" of Racine's heroines, to renounce reference to the savage dramas of Shakespeare, which have become compulsional in analytic circles where they play the role of status-symbol for the Philistines. [Au.]

[26]The publication by Jean Starobinski, in *Le Mercure de France* (February 1964) of Saussure's notes on anagrams and their hypogrammatical use, from the Saturnine verses to the writings of Cicero, provide the corroboration that I then lacked (note 1966). [Au.]

of its units, a whole articulation of relevant contexts suspended "vertically," as it were, from that point.

Let us take our word "tree" again, this time not as an isolated noun, but at the point of one of these punctuations, and see how it crosses the bar of the Saussurian algorithm. (The anagram of *"arbre"* and *"barre"* should be noted.)[27]

For even broken down into the double specter of its vowels and consonants, it can still call up with the robur and the plane tree the significations it takes on, in the context of our flora, of strength and majesty. Drawing on all the symbolic contexts suggested in the Hebrew of the Bible, it erects on a barren hill the shadow of the cross. Then reduces to the capital Y, the sign of dichotomy which, except for the illustration used by heraldry, would owe nothing to the tree however genealogical we may think it. Circulatory tree, tree of life of the cerebellum, tree of Saturn, tree of Diana, crystals formed in a tree struck by lightning, is it your figure that traces our destiny for us in the tortoise-shell cracked by the fire, or your lightning that causes that slow shift in the axis of being to surge up from an unnamable night into the *῞Εν πάντα*[28] of language:

> No! says the Tree, it says No! in the shower of
> sparks
> Of its superb head

lines that require the harmonics of the tree just as much as their continuation:

> Which the storm treats as universally
> As it does a blade of grass.[29]

[27]The anagram works only in French, and Saussure had used the Latin signifier for tree, "*arbor*," which is not an anagram for anything. [Ed.]

[28]Greek for "all-in one." Here Lacan delineates what Derrida later calls the "trace": the way signifiers build up layers of meaning from the different ways they are used. [Ed.]

[29]

"Non! dit l'Arbre, il dit: Non! dans l'étincellement
De sa tête superbe
Que la tempête traite universellement
Comme elle fait une herbe."
(Paul Valéry, "Au Platane," *Les Charmes*) [Au.]

For this modern verse is ordered according to the same law of the parallelism of the signifier that creates the harmony governing the primitive Slavic epic or the most refined Chinese poetry.

As is seen in the fact that the tree and the blade of grass are chosen from the same mode of the existent in order for the signs of contradiction — saying "No!" and "treat as" — to affect them, and also so as to bring about, through the categorical contrast of the particularity of "superb" with the "universally" that reduces it, in the condensation of the "head" *(tête)* and the "storm" *(tempête)*, the indiscernible shower of sparks of the eternal instant.

But this whole signifier can only operate, it may be said, if it is present in the subject. It is this objection that I answer by supposing that it has passed over to the level of the signified.

For what is important is not that the subject know anything whatsoever. (If LADIES and GENTLEMEN were written in a language unknown to the little boy and girl, their quarrel would simply be the more exclusively a quarrel over words, but no less ready to take on signification.)

What this structure of the signifying chain discloses is the possibility I have, precisely in so far as I have this language in common with other subjects, that is to say, in so far as it exists as a language, to use it in order to signify *something quite other* than what it says. This function of speech is more worth pointing out than that of "disguising the thought" (more often than not indefinable) of the subject; it is no less than the function of indicating the place of this subject in the search for the true.

I have only to plant my tree in a locution; climb the tree, even project on to it the cunning illumination a descriptive context gives to a word; raise it *(arborer)* so as not to let myself be imprisoned in some sort of *communiqué* of the facts, however official, and if I know the truth, make it heard, in spite of all the *between-the-lines* censures by the only signifier my acrobatics through the branches of the tree can constitute, provocative to the point of burlesque, or perceptible only to the practiced eye, according to whether I wish to be heard by the mob or by the few.

The properly signifying function thus depicted in language has a name. We learned this name in some grammar of our childhood, on the last page, where the shade of Quintilian, relegated to some phantom chapter concerning "final considerations on style," seemed suddenly to speed up his voice in an attempt to get in all he had to say before the end.

It is among the figures of style, or tropes — from which the verb "to find" *(trouver)* comes to us — that this name is found. This name is *metonymy*.

I shall refer only to the example given there: "thirty sails." For the disquietude I felt over the fact that the word "ship," concealed in this expression, seemed, by taking on its figurative sense, through the endless repetition of the same old example, only to increase its presence, obscured *(voilait)* not so much those illustrious sails *(voiles)* as the definition they were supposed to illustrate.

The part taken for the whole, we said to ourselves, and if the thing is to be taken seriously, we are left with very little idea of the importance of this fleet, which "thirty sails" is precisely supposed to give us: for each ship to have just one sail is in fact the least likely possibility.

By which we see that the connection between ship and sail is nowhere but in the signifier, and that it is in the *word-to-word* connection that metonymy is based.[30]

I shall designate as metonymy, then, the one side *(versant)* of the effective field constituted by the signifier, so that meaning can emerge there.

The other side is *metaphor*. Let us immediately find an illustration; Quillet's dictionary seemed an appropriate place to find a sample that would not seem to be chosen for my own purposes, and I didn't have to go any further than the well known line of Victor Hugo:

> His sheaf was neither miserly nor spiteful . . .[31]

under which aspect I presented metaphor in my seminar on the psychoses.

It should be said that modern poetry and especially the Surrealist school have taken us a long way in this direction by showing that any conjunction of two signifiers would be equally sufficient to constitute a metaphor, except for the additional requirement of the greatest possible disparity of the images signified, needed for the production of the poetic spark, or in other words for metaphoric creation to take place.

It is true this radical position is based on the experiment known as automatic writing, which would not have been attempted if its pioneers had not been reassured by the Freudian discovery. But it remains a confused position because the doctrine behind it is false.

The creative spark of the metaphor does not spring from the presentation of two images, that is, of two signifiers equally actualized. It flashes between two signifiers one of which has taken

[30]I pay homage here to the works of Roman Jakobson — to which I owe much of this formulation; works to which a psychoanalyst can constantly refer in order to structure his own experience, and which render superfluous the "personal communications" of which I could boast as much as the next fellow.

Indeed, one recognizes in this oblique form of allegiance the style of that immortal couple, Rosencrantz and Guildenstern, who are virtually indistinguishable, even in the imperfection of their destiny, for it survives by the same method as Jeannot's knife, and for the same reason for which Goethe praised Shakespeare for presenting the character in double form: they represent, in themselves alone, the whole *Gesellschaft*, the Association itself (*Wilhelm Meisters Lehrjahre*, ed. Trunz, Christian Wegner Verlag, Hamburg, V (5): 299) — I mean the International Psychoanalytical Association.

We should savour the passage from Goethe as a whole: "*Dieses leise Auftreten dieses Schmiegen und Biegen, dies Jasagen, Streicheln und Schmeicheln, dieses Behendigkeit, dies Schwänzein, diese Allheit und Leerheit, diese rechtliche Schurkerei, diese Unfähigkeit, wie kann sie durch einen Menschen ausgedruckt werden? Es sollten ihrer wenigstens ein Dutzend sein, wenn man sie haben könnte; denn sie bloss in Gesellschaft etwas, sie sind die Gesellschaft . . .*"

Let us thank also, in this context, the author R. M. Loewenstein of "Some Remarks on the Role of Speech in Psychoanalytic Technique" (*I.J.P.*, Nov.–Dec., 1956, XXXVII (6): 467) for taking the trouble to point out that his remarks are "based on" work dating from 1952. This is no doubt the explanation for the fact that he has learned nothing from work done since then, yet which he is not ignorant of, as he cites me as their "editor" (sic). [Au.]

[31]"Sa gerbe n'était pas avare ni haineuse," a line from "Booz endormi." [Tr.]

the place of the other in the signifying chain, the occulted signifier remaining present through its (metonymic) connection with the rest of the chain.

One word for another: that is the formula for the metaphor and if you are a poet you will produce for your own delight a continuous stream, a dazzling tissue of metaphors. If the result is the sort of intoxication of the dialogue that Jean Tardieu wrote under this title, that is only because he was giving us a demonstration of the radical superfluousness of all signification in a perfectly convincing representation of a bourgeois comedy.

It is obvious that in the line of Hugo cited above, not the slightest spark of light springs from the proposition that the sheaf was neither miserly nor spiteful, for the reason that there is no question of the sheaf's having either the merit or demerit of these attributes, since the attributes, like the sheaf, belong to Booz, who exercises the former in disposing of the latter and without informing the latter of his sentiments in the case.

If, however, his sheaf does refer us to Booz, and this is indeed the case, it is because it has replaced him in the signifying chain at the very place where he was to be exalted by the sweeping away of greed and spite. But now Booz himself has been swept away by the sheaf, and hurled into the outer darkness where greed and spite harbor him in the hollow of their negation.

But once *his* sheaf has thus usurped his place, Booz can no longer return there; the slender thread of the little word *his* that binds him to it is only one more obstacle to his return in that it links him to the notion of possession that retains him at the heart of greed and spite. So *his* generosity, affirmed in the passage, is yet reduced to *less than nothing* by the munificence of the sheaf which, coming from nature, knows neither our reserve nor our rejections, and even in its accumulation remains prodigal by our standards.

But if in this profusion the giver has disappeared along with his gift, it is only in order to rise again in what surrounds the figure of speech in which he was annihilated. For it is the figure of the burgeoning of fecundity, and it is this that announces the surprise that the poem celebrates, namely, the promise that the old man will receive in the sacred context of his accession to paternity.

So, it is between the signifier in the form of the proper name of a man and the signifier that metaphorically abolishes him that the poetic spark is produced, and it is in this case all the more effective in realizing the signification of paternity in that it reproduces the mythical event in terms of which Freud reconstructed the progress, in the unconscious of all men, of the paternal mystery.

Modern metaphor has the same structure. So the line *Love is a pebble laughing in the sunlight*, recreates love in a dimension that seems to me most tenable in the face of its imminent lapse into the mirage of narcissistic altruism.

We see, then that, metaphor occurs at the precise point at which sense emerges from nonsense, that is, at that frontier which, as Freud discovered, when crossed the other way produces the word that in French is *the* word *par excellence,* the word that is simply the signifier *"esprit"*;[32] it is at this frontier that we realize that man defies his very destiny when he derides the signifier.

But to come back to our subject, what does man find in metonymy if not the power to circumvent the obstacles of social censure? Does not this form, which gives its field to truth in its very oppression, manifest a certain servitude inherent in its presentation?

One may read with profit a book by Leo Strauss, from the land that traditionally offers asylum to those who choose freedom, in which the author reflects on the relation between the art of writing and persecution.[33] By pushing to its

[32] *"Mot,"* in the broad sense means, "word." In the narrower sense, however, it means "a witticism." The French *"esprit"* is translated, in this context, as "wit," the equivalent of Freud's *Witz.* [Tr.]

"Esprit" is certainly the equivalent of the German *Witz* with which Freud marked the approach of his third fundamental work on the unconscious. The much greater difficulty of finding this equivalent in English is instructive: "wit," burdened with all the discussion of which it was the object from Davenant and Hobbes to Pope and Addison, abandoned its essential virtues to "humor," which is something else. There only remains the "pun," but this word is too narrow in its connotation. [Au.] The other meaning for *"esprit"* is "spirit"—the mind or soul. [Ed.]

[33] Leo Strauss, *Persecution and the Art of Writing,* The Free Press, Glencoe, Illinois. [Au.]

limits the sort of connaturality that links this art to that condition, he lets us glimpse a certain something which in this matter imposes its form, in the effect of truth on desire.

But haven't we felt for some time now that, having followed the ways of the letter in search of Freudian truth, we are getting very warm indeed, that it is burning all about us?

Of course, as it is said, the letter killeth while the spirit giveth life. We can't help but agree, having had to pay homage elsewhere to a noble victim of the error of seeking the spirit in the letter; but we should also like to know how the spirit could live without the letter. Even so, the pretentions of the spirit would remain unassailable if the letter had not shown us that it produces all the effects of truth in man without involving the spirit at all.

It is none other than Freud who had this revelation, and he called his discovery the unconscious.

II. THE LETTER IN THE UNCONSCIOUS

In the complete works of Freud, one out of every three pages is devoted to philological references, one out of every two pages to logical inferences, everywhere a dialectical apprehension of experience, the proportion of analysis of language increasing to the extent that the unconscious is directly concerned.

Thus in "The Interpretation of Dreams" every page deals with what I call the letter of the discourse, in its texture, its usage, its immanence in the matter in question. For it is with this work that the work of Freud begins to open the royal road to the unconscious. And Freud gave us notice of this; his confidence at the time of launching this book in the early days of this century[34] only confirms what he continued to proclaim to the end: that he had staked the whole of his discovery on this essential expression of his message.

The first sentence of the opening chapter announces what for the sake of the exposition could not be postponed: that the dream is a rebus. And Freud goes on to stipulate what I have said from the start, that it must be understood quite literally. This derives from the agency in the dream of that same literal (or phonematic) structure in which the signifier is articulated and analyzed in discourse. So the unnatural images of the boat on the roof, or the man with a comma for a head, which are specifically mentioned by Freud, are examples of dream-images that are to be taken only for their value as signifiers, that is to say, in so far as they allow us to spell out the "proverb" presented by the rebus of the dream. The linguistic structure that enables us to read dreams is the very principle of the "significance of the dream," the *Traumdeutung*.

Freud shows us in every possible way that the value of the image as signifier has nothing whatever to do with its signification, giving as an example Egyptian hieroglyphics in which it would be sheer buffoonery to pretend that in a given text the frequency of a vulture, which is an *aleph,* or of a chick, which is a *vau,* indicating a form of the verb "to be" or a plural, prove that the text has anything at all to do with these ornithological specimens. Freud finds in this writing certain uses of the signifier that are lost in ours, such as the use of determinatives, where a categorical figure is added to the literal figuration of a verbal term; but this is only to show us that even in this writing, the so-called "ideogram" is a letter.

But it does not require the current confusion on this last term for there to prevail in the minds of psychoanalysts lacking linguistic training the prejudice in favor of a symbolism deriving from natural analogy, or even of the image as appropriate to the instinct. And to such an extent that, outside the French school, which has been alerted, a distinction must be drawn between reading coffee grounds and reading hieroglyphics, by recalling to its own principles a technique that could not be justified were it not directed towards the unconscious.

It must be said that this is admitted only with difficulty and that the mental vice denounced above enjoys such favor that today's psychoanalyst can be expected to say that he decodes before he will come around to taking the necessary tour

[34] Cf. the correspondence, namely letters 107 and 109. [Au.]

with Freud (turn at the statute of Champollion,[35] says the guide) that will make him understand that what he does is decipher; the distinction is that a cryptogram takes on its full dimension only when it is in a lost language.

Taking the tour is simply continuing in the *Traumdeutung.*

Entstellung, translated as "distortion" or "transposition," is what Freud shows to be the general precondition for the functioning of the dream, and it is what I designated above, following Saussure, as the sliding of the signified under the signifier, which is always active in discourse (its action, let us note, is unconscious).

But what we call the two "sides" of the effect of the signifier on the signified are also found here.

Verdichtung, or "condensation," is the structure of the superimposition of the signifiers, which metaphor takes as its field, and whose name, condensing in itself the word *Dichtung,*[36] shows how the mechanism is connatural with poetry to the point that it envelops the traditional function proper to poetry.

In the case of *Verschiebung,* "displacement," the German term is closer to the idea of that veering off of signification that we see in metonymy, and which from its first appearance in Freud is represented as the most appropriate means used by the unconscious to foil censorship.

What distinguishes these two mechanisms, which play such a privileged role in the dream-work (*Traumarbeit*), from their homologous function in discourse? Nothing, except a condition imposed upon the signifying material, called *Rücksicht auf Darstellbarkeit,* which must be translated by "consideration of the means of representation." (The translation by "role of the possibility of figurative expression" being too approximative here.) But this condition constitutes a limitation operating *within* the system of writing; this is a long way from dissolving the system into a figurative semiology on a level with phenomena of natural expression. This fact could perhaps shed light on the problems involved in certain modes of pictography which, simply because they have been abandoned in writing as imperfect, are not therefore to be regarded as mere evolutionary stages. Let us say, then, that the dream is like the parlor-game in which one is supposed to get the spectators to guess some well known saying or variant of it solely by dumb-show. That the dream uses speech makes no difference since for the unconscious it is only one among several elements of the representation. It is precisely the fact that both the game and the dream run up against a lack of taxematic material for the representation of such logical articulations as causality, contradiction, hypothesis, etc., that proves they are a form of writing rather than of mime. The subtle processes that the dream is seen to use to represent these logical articulations, in a much less artificial way than games usually employ, are the object of a special study in Freud in which we see once more confirmed that the dream-work follows the laws of the signifier.

The rest of the dream-elaboration is designated as secondary by Freud, the nature of which indicates its value: they are fantasies or day-dreams *(Tagtraum)* to use the term Freud prefers in order to emphasize their function of wish-fulfillment *(Wunscherfüllung).* Given the fact that these fantasies may remain unconscious, their distinctive feature is in this case their signification. Now, concerning these fantasies, Freud tells us that their place in the dream is either to be taken up and used as signifying elements for the statement of the unconscious thoughts *(Traumgedanke),* or to be used in the secondary elaboration just mentioned, that is to say, in a function not to be distinguished from our waking thought *(von unserem wachen Denken nicht zu unterschieden).* No better idea of the effects of this function can be given than by comparing it to areas of color which, when applied here and there to a stencil-plate, can make the stencilled figures, rather forbidding in themselves, more reminiscent of hieroglyphics or of a rebus, look like a figurative painting.

[35]Jean-François Champollion (1790–1832), the first scholar to decipher the Ancient Egyptian hieroglyphics. [Tr.]

[36]German for "literature," or more specifically "poetry." [Ed.]

Forgive me if I seem to have to spell out Freud's text; I do so not only to show how much is to be gained by not cutting it about, but also in order to situate the development of psychoanalysis according to its first guide-lines, which were fundamental and never revoked.

Yet from the beginning there was a general *méconnnaissance*[37] of the constitutive role of the signifier in the status that Freud from the first assigned to the unconscious and in the most precise formal manner.

There are two reasons for this, of which the least obvious, of course, is that this formalization was not sufficient in itself to bring about a recognition of the agency of the signifier because the *Traumdeutung* appeared long before the formalizations of linguistics for which one could no doubt show that it paved the way by the sheer weight of its truth.

The second reason, which is after all only the reverse side of the first, is that if psychoanalysts were fascinated exclusively by the significations revealed in the unconscious, it is because these significations derived their secret attraction from the dialectic that seemed to be immanent in them.

I have shown in my seminars that it is the need to counteract the continuously accelerating effects of this bias that alone explains the apparent changes of direction or rather changes of tack, which Freud, through his primary concern to preserve for posterity both his discovery and the fundamental revisions it effected in our knowledge, felt it necessary to apply to his doctrine.

For, I repeat, in the situation in which he found himself, having nothing that corresponded to the object of his discovery that was at the same level of scientific development — in this situation, at least he never failed to maintain this object on the level of its ontological dignity.

The rest was the work of the gods and took such a course that analysis today takes its bearings in those imaginary forms that I have just shown to be drawn "resist-style" *(en reserve)* on the text they mutilate — and the analyst tries to accommodate his direction to them, confusing them, in the interpretation of the dream, with the visionary liberation of the hieroglyphic aviary, and seeking generally the control of the exhaustion of the analysis in a sort of "scanning"[38] of these forms whenever they appear, in the idea that they are witnesses of the exhaustion of the regressions and of the remodelling of the object relation from which the subject is supposed to derive his "character-type."[39]

The technique that is based on such positions can be fertile in its various effects, and under the aegis of therapy, difficult to criticize. But an internal criticism must none the less arise from the flagrant disparity between the mode of operation by which the technique is justified — namely the analytic rule, all the instruments of which, beginning with "free association," depend on the conception of the unconscious of its inventor — and, on the other hand, the general *méconnaissance* that reigns regarding this conception of the unconscious. The most ardent adherents of this technique believe themselves to be freed of any need to reconcile the two by the merest pirouette: the analytic rule (they say) must be all the more religiously observed since it is only the result of a lucky accident. In other words, Freud never knew what he was doing.

A return to Freud's text shows on the contrary the absolute coherence between his technique and his discovery, and at the same time this coherence allows us to put all his procedures in their proper place.

That is why any rectification of psychoanalysis must inevitably involve a return to the truth of that discovery, which, taken in its original moment, is impossible to obscure.

For in the analysis of dreams, Freud intends only to give us the laws of the unconscious in their most general extension. One of the reasons why dreams were most propitious for this dem-

[37]French for "misunderstanding" or "failure of recognition." [Ed.]

[38]That is the process by which the results of a piece of research are assured through a mechanical exploration of the entire extent of the field of its object. [Au.]

[39]By referring only to the development of the organism, the typology fails to recognize *(méconnaît)* the structure in which the subject is caught up respectively in fantasy, in drive, in sublimation. I am at present developing the theory of this structure (note 1966). [Au.]

onstration is exactly, Freud tells us, that they reveal the same laws whether in the normal person or in the neurotic.

But in either case, the efficacy of the unconscious does not cease in the waking state. The psychoanalytic experience does nothing other than establish that the unconscious leaves none of our actions outside its field. The presence of the unconscious in the psychological order, in other words in the relation-functions of the individual, should, however, be more precisely defined: it is not coextensive with that order, for we know that if unconscious motivation is manifest in conscious psychical effects, as well as in unconscious ones, conversely it is only elementary to recall to mind that a large number of psychical effects that are quite legitimately designated as unconscious, in the sense of excluding the characteristic of consciousness, are nonetheless without any relation whatever to the unconscious in the Freudian sense. So it is only by an abuse of the term that unconscious in that sense is confused with psychical, and that one may thus designate as psychical what is in fact an effect of the unconscious, as on the somatic for instance.

It is a matter, therefore, of defining the topography of this unconscious. I say that it is the very topography defined by the algorithm:

$$\frac{S}{s}$$

What we have been able to develop concerning the effects of the signifier on the signified suggests its transformation into:[40]

$$f(S)\frac{I}{s}$$

We have shown the effects not only of the elements of the horizontal signifying chain, but also of its vertical dependencies in the signified, divided into two fundamental structures called metonymy and metaphor. We can symbolize them by, first:[41]

$$f(S \ldots S')S \cong S(-)s$$

that is to say, the metonymic structure, indicating that it is the connection between signifier and signifier that permits the elision in which the signifier installs the lack-of-being in the object relation, using the value of "reference back" possessed by signification in order to invest it with the desire aimed at the very lack it supports. The sign – placed between () represents here the maintenance of the bar — which, in the original algorithm, marked the irreducibility in which, in the relations between signifier and signified, the resistance of signification is constituted.[42]

Secondly,

$$f\left(\frac{S'}{S}\right)S \cong S(+)s$$

the metaphoric structure indicating that it is in the substitution of signifier for signifier that an effect of signification is produced that is creative or poetic, in other words, which is the advent of the signification in question.[43] The sign + between () represents here the crossing of the bar — and the constitutive value of this crossing for the emergence of signification.

This crossing expresses the condition of passage of the signifier into the signified that I pointed out above, although provisionally confusing it with the place of the subject.

It is the function of the subject, thus introduced, that we must now turn to since it lies at the crucial point of our problem.

"I think, therefore I am" *(cogito ergo sum)* is not merely the formula in which is constituted, with the historical high point of reflection on the conditions of science, the link between the transparency of the transcendental subject and his existential affirmation.

Perhaps I am only object and mechanism (and so nothing more than phenomenon), but as-

[40]Perhaps to be read: "The function of the signifier in the unconscious as related to the signified meaning." [Ed.]

[41]Perhaps to be read: "The function of a chain of signifiers connected with a particular signifier is congruent to the signifier's relation to its signified." The metonymic chain, in other words, is to its signifier what the signifier is to its signified. [Ed.]

[42]The sign ≅ here designates congruence. [Au.]

[43]S′ designating here the term productive of the signifying effect (or significance); one can see that the term is latent in metonymy, patent in metaphor. [Au.]

suredly in so far as I think so, I am — absolutely. No doubt philosophers have brought important corrections to this formulation, notably that in that which thinks *(cogitans)*, I can never constitute myself as anything but object *(cogitatum)*. Nonetheless it remains true that by way of this extreme purification of the transcendental subject, my existential link to its project seems irrefutable, at least in its present form, and that: *"cogito ergo sum" ubi cogito, ibi sum,*[44] overcomes this objection.

Of course, this limits me to being there in my being only in so far as I think that I am in my thought; just how far I actually think this concerns only myself and if I say it, interests no one.[45]

Yet to elude this problem on the pretext of its philosophical pretensions is simply to admit one's inhibition. For the notion of subject is indispensable even to the operation of a science such as strategy (in the modern sense) whose calculations exclude all "subjectivism."

It is also to deny oneself access to what might be called the Freudian universe — in the way that we speak of the Copernican universe. It was in fact the so-called Copernican revolution to which Freud himself compared his discovery, emphasizing that it was once again a question of the place man assigns to himself at the center of a universe.

Is the place that I occupy as the subject of a signifier concentric or excentric, in relation to the place I occupy as subject of the signified? — that is the question.

It is not a question of knowing whether I speak of myself in a way that conforms to what I am, but rather of knowing whether I am the same as that of which I speak. And it is not at all inappropriate to use the word "thought" here. For Freud uses the term to designate the elements involved in the unconscious, that is the signifying mechanisms that we now recognize as being there.

It is nonetheless true that the philosophical *cogito* is at the center of the mirage that renders modern man so sure of being himself even in his uncertainties about himself, and even in the mistrust he has learned to practice against the traps of self-love.

Furthermore, if, turning the weapon of metonymy against the nostalgia that it serves, I refuse to seek any meaning beyond tautology, if in the name of "war is war" and "a penny's a penny" I decide to be only what I am, how even here can I elude the obvious fact that I am in that very act?

And it is no less true if I take myself to the other, metaphoric pole of the signifying quest, and if I dedicate myself to becoming what I am, to coming into being, I cannot doubt that even if I lose myself in the process, I am in that process.

Now it is on these very points, where evidence will be subverted by the empirical, that the trick of the Freudian conversion lies.

This signifying game between metonymy and metaphor, up to and including the active edge that splits my desire between a refusal of the signifier and a lack of being, and links my fate to the question of my destiny, this game, in all its inexorable subtlety, is played until the match is called, there where I am not, because I cannot situate myself there.

That is to say, what is needed is more than these words with which, for a brief moment I disconcerted my audience: I think where I am not, therefore I am where I do not think. Words that render sensible to an ear properly attuned with what elusive ambiguity[46] the ring of meaning flees from our grasp along the verbal thread.

What one ought to say is: I am not wherever I am the plaything of my thought; I think of what I am where I do not think to think.

This two-sided mystery is linked to the fact that the truth can be evoked only in that dimen-

[44]"Wherever I think 'I think therefore I am,' there I am." [Ed.]

[45]It is quite otherwise if by posing a question such as "Why philosophers?" I become more candid than nature, for then I am asking not only the question that philosophers have been asking themselves for all time, but also the one in which they are perhaps most interested. [Au.]

[46]*"Ambiguité de furet"* — literally, "ferret-like ambiguity." This is one of a number of references in Lacan to the game "hunt-the-slipper" *(jeu du furet)*. [Tr.]

sion of alibi in which all "realism" in creative works takes its virtue from metonymy; it is likewise linked to this other fact that we accede to meaning only through the double twist of metaphor when we have the one and only key: the S and the *s* of the Saussurian algorithm are not on the same level, and man only deludes himself when he believes his true place is at their axis, which is nowhere.

Was nowhere, that is, until Freud discovered it; for if what Freud discovered isn't that, it isn't anything.

The contents of the unconscious with all their disappointing ambiguities give us no reality in the subject more consistent than the immediate; their virtue derives from the truth and in the dimension of being: *Kern unseres Wesen*[47] are Freud's own terms.

The double-triggered mechanism of metaphor is the very mechanism by which the symptom, in the analytic sense, is determined. Between the enigmatic signifier of the sexual trauma and the term that is substituted for it in an actual signifying chain there passes the spark that fixes in a symptom the signification inaccessible to the conscious subject in which that symptom may be resolved — a symptom being a metaphor in which flesh or function is taken as a signifying element.

And the enigmas that desire seems to pose for a "natural philosophy" — its frenzy mocking the abyss of the infinite, the secret collusion with which it envelops the pleasure of knowing and of dominating with *jouissance,* these amount to no other derangement of instinct than that of being caught in the rails — eternally stretching forth towards the *desire for something else* — of metonymy. Hence its "perverse" fixation at the very suspension-point of the signifying chain where the memory-screen is immobilized and the fascinating image of the fetish is petrified.

There is no other way of conceiving the indestructibility of unconscious desire — in the absence of a need which, when forbidden satisfaction, does not sicken and die, even if it means the destruction of the organism itself. It is in a memory, comparable to what is called by that name in our modern thinking-machines (which are in turn based on an electronic realization of the composition of signification), it is in this sort of memory that is found the chain that *insists* on reproducing itself in the transference, and which is the chain of dead desire.

[47]"The nucleus of our being." [Tr.]

It is the truth of what this desire has been in his history that the patient cries out through his symptom, as Christ said that the stones themselves would have cried out if the children of Israel had not lent them their voice.

And that is why only psychoanalysis allows us to differentiate within memory the function of recollection. Rooted in the signifier, it resolves the Platonic aporias of reminiscence through the ascendancy of history in man.

One has only to read the "Three Essays on Sexuality" to observe, in spite of the pseudo-biological glosses with which it is decked out for popular consumption, that Freud there derives all accession to the object from a dialectic of return.

Starting from Hölderlin's υοστος,[48] Freud arrives less than twenty years later at Kierkegaard's repetition; that is, in submitting his thought solely to the humble but inflexible consequences of the "talking cure,"[49] he was unable ever to escape the living servitudes that led him from the sovereign principle of the Logos to re-thinking the Empedoclean antinomies of death.[50]

And how else are we to conceive the recourse of a man of science to a *Deus ex machina* than on that "other scene" he speaks of as the locus of the dream, a *Deus ex machina* only less derisory for the fact that it is revealed to the spectator that the machine directs the director? How else can we imagine that a scientist of the nineteenth century, unless we realize that he had to bow before the force of evidence that went well beyond his prejudices, valued more highly than all his other

[48]Greek for "return (to the homeland)." See the introduction to Heidegger, p. 562. [Ed.]

[49]English in the original. [Tr.]

[50]Empedocles denied the human experience of death: "When I am, Death is not; when Death is, I am not." [Ed.]

works his *Totem and Taboo,* with its obscene, ferocious figure of the primordial father, not to be exhausted in the expiation of Oedipus' blindness, and before which the ethnologists of today bow as before the growth of an authentic myth?[51]

So that imperious proliferation of particular symbolic creations, such as what are called the sexual theories of the child, which supply the motivation down to the smallest detail of neurotic compulsions, these reply to the same necessities as do myths.

Thus, to speak of the precise point we are treating in my seminars on Freud, little Hans, left in the lurch at the age of five by his symbolic environment, and suddenly forced to face the enigma of his sex and his existence, developed, under the direction of Freud and of his father, Freud's disciple, in mythic form, around the signifying crystal of his phobia, all the permutations possible on a limited number of signifiers.

The operation shows that even on the individual level the solution of the impossible is brought within man's reach by the exhaustion of all possible forms of the impossibilities encountered in solution by recourse to the signifying equation. It is a striking demonstration that illuminates the labyrinth of a case which so far has only been used as a source of demolished fragments. We should be struck, too, by the fact that it is in the coextensivity of the development of the symptom and of its curative resolution that the nature of the neurosis is revealed: whether phobic, hysterical, or obsessive, the neurosis is a question that being poses for the subject "from where it was before the subject came into the world" (Freud's phrase, which he used in explaining the Oedipal complex to little Hans).

The "being" referred to is that which appears in a lightning moment in the void of the verb "to be" and I said that it poses its question for the subject. What does that mean? It does not pose it *before* the subject, since the subject cannot come to the place where it is posed, but it poses it *in place* of the subject, that is to say, in that place it poses the question *with* the subject, as one poses a problem *with* a pen, or as Aristotle's man thought *with* his soul.

Thus Freud introduced the ego into his doctrine,[52] by defining it according to the resistances that are proper to it. What I have tried to convey is that these resistances are of an imaginary nature much in the same sense as those coaptative lures that the ethology of animal behavior shows us in display or combat, and that these lures are reduced in man to the narcissistic relation introduced by Freud, which I have elaborated in my essay on the mirror stage. I have tried to show that by situating in this ego the synthesis of the perceptual functions in which the sensori-motor selections are integrated, Freud seems to abound in that delegation that is traditionally supposed to represent reality for the ego, and that this reality is all the more included in the suspension of the ego.

For this ego, which is notable in the first instance for the imaginary inertias that it concentrates against the message of the unconscious, operates solely with a view to covering the displacement constituted by the subject with a resistance that is essential to the discourse as such.

That is why an exhaustion of the mechanisms of defense, which Fenichel the practitioner shows us so well in his studies of analytic technique (while his whole reduction on the theoretical level of neuroses and psychoses to genetic anomalies in libidinal development is pure platitude), manifests itself, without Fenichel's accounting for it or realizing it himself, as simply the reverse side of the mechanisms of the unconscious. Periphrasis, hyperbaton, ellipsis, suspension, anticipation, retraction, negation, digression, irony, these are the figures of style (Quintilian's *figurae sententiarum*); as catachresis, litotes, antonomasia, hypotyposis are the tropes, whose terms suggest themselves as the most proper for the labeling of these mechanisms. Can one really see these as mere figures of speech when it is the fig-

[51]In *Totem and Taboo,* Freud posits that the incest taboo arose in reaction to a primordial family struggle, in which the Father takes all the women for himself until the Sons, rising against him, kill him and eat his flesh. Lacan ironically alludes to the anthropologists who have taken Freud's fantasy as "authentic myth." [Ed.]

[52]This and the next paragraph were rewritten solely with a view to greater clarity of expression (note 1968). [Au.]

ures themselves that are the active principle of the rhetoric of the discourse that the analysand in fact utters?[53]

By persisting in describing the nature of resistance as a permanent emotional state, thus making it alien to the discourse, today's psychoanalysts have simply shown that they have fallen under the blow of one of the fundamental truths that Freud rediscovered through psychoanalysis. One is never happy making way for a new truth, for it always means making our way into it: the truth is always disturbing. We cannot even manage to get used to it. We are used to the real. The truth we repress.

Now it is quite specially necessary to the scientist, to the seer, even to the quack, that he should be the only one to *know*. The idea that deep in the simplest (and even sickest) of souls there is something ready to blossom is bad enough! But if someone seems to know as much as they about what we ought to make of it . . . then the categories of primitive, prelogical, archaic, or even magical thought, so easy to impute to others, rush to our aid! It is not right that these nonentities keep us breathless with enigmas that prove to be only too unreliable.

To interpret the unconscious as Freud did, one would have to be as he was, an encyclopedia of the arts and muses, as well as an assiduous reader of the *Fliegende Blätter*.[54] And the task is made no easier by the fact that we are at the mercy of a thread woven with allusions, quotations, puns, and equivocations. And is that our profession, to be antidotes to trifles?

Yet that is what we must resign ourselves to. The unconscious is neither primordial nor instinctual; what it knows about the elementary is no more than the elements of the signifier.

The three books that one might call canonical with regard to the unconscious — "The Interpretation of Dreams," "The Psychopathology of Everyday Life," and "Jokes and their Relation to the Unconscious" — are simply a web of examples whose development is inscribed in the formulas of connection and substitution (though carried to the tenth degree by their particular complexity — diagrams of them are sometimes provided by Freud by way of illustration); these are the formulas we give to the signifier in its *transference*-function. For in "The Interpretation of Dreams" it is in the sense of such a function that the term *Übertragung*, or transference, is introduced, which later gave its name to the mainspring of the intersubjective link between analyst and analysand.

Such diagrams are not only constitutive of each of the symptoms in a neurosis, but they alone make possible the understanding of the thematic of its course and resolution. The great case-histories provided by Freud demonstrate this admirably.

To fall back on a more limited incident, but one more likely to provide us with the final seal on our proposition, let me cite the article on fetishism of 1927,[55] and the case Freud reports there of a patient who, to achieve sexual satisfaction, needed a certain shine on the nose (*Glanz auf der Nase*); analysis showed that his early, English-speaking years had seen the displacement of the burning curiosity that he felt for the phallus of his mother, that is to say, for that eminent *manque-à-être*, for that want-to-be, whose privileged signifier Freud revealed to us, into a *glance at the nose*[56] in the forgotten language of his childhood, rather than a *shine on the nose*.[57]

It is the abyss opened up at the thought that a thought should make itself heard in the abyss that provoked resistance to psychoanalysis from the outset. And not, as is commonly said, the emphasis on man's sexuality. This latter has after all been the dominant object in literature throughout the ages. And in fact the more recent evolution of psychoanalysis has succeeded by a bit of comical legerdemain in turning it into a quite moral affair, the cradle and trysting-place of oblativity and attraction. The Platonic setting of the soul,

[53]Lacan lists some of Quintilian's obscurer figures of speech and thought as equivalents to the ego-defenses of repression, reversal, undoing, and so on, just as metaphor and metonymy have already been viewed as the symbolic equivalents of displacement and condensation. [Ed.]

[54]A German comic newspaper of the late nineteenth and early twentieth centuries. [Tr.]

[55]*Fetischismus, G.W.* XIV: 311; "Fetishism," *Collected Papers*, V: 198; *Standard Edition* XXI: 149. [Au.]

[56]English in the original. [Tr.]

[57]English in the original. [Tr.]

blessed and illuminated, rises straight to paradise.

The intolerable scandal in the time before Freudian sexuality was sanctified was that it was so "intellectual." It was precisely in that that it showed itself to be the worthy ally of all those terrorists whose plottings were going to ruin society.

At a time when psychoanalysts are busy remodeling psychoanalysis into a right-thinking movement whose crowning expression is the sociological poem of the *autonomous ego,* I would like to say, to all those who are listening to me, how they can recognize bad psychoanalysts; this is by the word they use to deprecate all technical or theoretical research that carries forward the Freudian experience along its authentic lines. That word is *"intellectualization"* — execrable to all those who, living in fear of being tried and found wanting by the wine of truth, spit on the bread of men, although their slaver can no longer have any effect other than that of leavening.

III. THE LETTER, BEING AND THE OTHER[58]

Is what thinks in my place, then, another I? Does Freud's discovery represent the confirmation, on the level of psychological experience, of Manicheism?[59]

In fact, there is no confusion on this point: what Freud's researches led us to is not a few more or less curious cases of split personality. Even at the heroic epoch I have been describing, when, like the animals in fairy stories, sexuality talked, the demonic atmosphere that such an orientation might have given rise to never materialized.[60]

[58]*La lettre, l'être et l'autre.* [Au.]

[59]One of my colleagues went so far in this direction as to wonder if the id *(Es)* of the last phase wasn't in fact the "bad ego." (It should now be obvious whom I am referring to — 1966.) [Au.]

[60]Note, nonetheless, the tone with which one spoke in that period of the "elfin pranks" of the unconscious; a work of Silberer's is called *Der Zufall und die Koboldstreiche des Unbewussten* (Chance and the Elfin Tricks of the Unconscious) — completely anachronistic in the context of our present soul-managers. [Au.]

The end that Freud's discovery proposes for man was defined by him at the apex of his thought in these moving terms: *Wo es war, soll Ich werden.* I must come to the place where that was.[61]

This is one of reintegration and harmony, I could even say of reconciliation *(Versöhnung).*

But if we ignore the self's radical ex-centricity to itself with which man is confronted, in other words, the truth discovered by Freud, we shall falsify both the order and methods of psychoanalytic mediation; we shall make of it nothing more than the compromise operation that it has, in effect, become, namely, just what the letter as well as the spirit of Freud's work most repudiates. For since he constantly invoked the notion of compromise as supporting all the miseries that his analysis is supposed to assuage, we can say that any recourse to compromise, explicit or implicit, will necessarily disorient psychoanalytic action and plunge it into darkness.

But neither does it suffice to associate oneself with the moralistic tartufferies of our time or to be forever spouting something about the "total personality" in order to have said anything articulate about the possibility of mediation.

The radical heteronomy that Freud's discovery shows gaping within man can never again be covered over without whatever is used to hide it being profoundly dishonest.

Who, then, is this other to whom I am more attached than to myself, since, at the heart of my assent to my own identity it is still he who agitates me?

His presence can be understood only as a second degree of otherness, which already places him in the position of mediating between me and the double of myself, as it were with my counterpart.

If I have said that the unconscious is the discourse of the Other (with a capital O), it is in order to indicate the beyond in which the recog-

[61]"Where Id was, there shall Ego be," is the usual English translation, suggesting the triumph of the autonomous ego in analytic ideology. But since "ego" and "id" are Latin for "I" and "it" (Freud had used the common German pronouns "ich" and "es"), Lacan's "I must come to the place where that was" is equally correct and holds very different connotations. [Ed.]

nition of desire is bound up with the desire for recognition.

In other words this other is the Other that even my lie invokes as a guarantor of the truth in which it subsists.

By which we can also see that it is with the appearance of language that the dimension of truth emerges.

Prior to this point, we can recognize in the psychological relation, which can be easily isolated in the observation of animal behavior, the existence of subjects, not by means of some projective mirage, the phantom of which a certain type of psychologist delights in hacking to pieces, but simply on account of the manifested presence of intersubjectivity. In the animal hidden in his lookout, in the well-laid trap of certain others, in the feint by which an apparent straggler leads a predator away from the flock, something more emerges than in the fascinating display of mating or combat ritual. Yet there is nothing even there that transcends the function of lure in the service of a need, or which affirms a presence in that beyond-the-veil where the whole of Nature can be questioned about its design.

For there even to be a question (and we know that it is one Freud himself posed in "Beyond the Pleasure Principle"), there must be language.

For I can lure my adversary by means of a movement contrary to my actual plan of battle, and this movement will have its deceiving effect only in so far as I produce it in reality and for my adversary.

But in the propositions with which I open peace negotiations with him, what my negotiations propose to him is situated in a third locus which is neither my speech nor my interlocutor.

This locus is none other than the locus of signifying convention, of the sort revealed in the comedy of the sad plaint of the Jew to his crony: "Why do you tell me you are going to Cracow so I'll believe you are going to Lvov, when you really are going to Cracow?"[62]

[62]Freud analyzes this feeble wheeze in *Jokes and Their Relation to the Unconscious.* His point, there, is the way the truth of the speaker (who says, rightly, that he is going to Cracow) is the lie of the listener (who assumes that the speaker's words are going to misdirect him, and so is *actually* misdirected by the truth). [Ed.]

Of course the flock-movement I just spoke of could be understood in the conventional context of game-strategy, where it is a rule that I deceive my adversary, but in that case my success is evaluated within the connotation of betrayal, that is to say, in relation to the Other who is the guarantor of Good Faith.

Here the problems are of an order the heteronomy of which is completely misconstrued *(méconnue)* if reduced to an "awareness of others," or whatever we choose to call it. For the "existence of the other" having once upon a time reached the ears of the Midas of psychoanalysis through the partition that separates him from the secret meetings of the phenomenologists, the news is now being whispered through the reeds: "Midas, King Midas, is the other of his patient. He himself has said it."

What sort of breakthrough is that? The other, what other?

The young André Gide, defying the landlady to whom his mother had confided him to treat him as a responsible person, opening with a key (false only in that it opened all locks of the same make) the lock that this lady took to be a worthy signifier of her educational intentions, and doing it quite obviously for her benefit — what "other" was he aiming at? She who was supposed to intervene and to whom he would then say: "Do you think my obedience can be secured with a ridiculous lock?" But by remaining out of sight and holding her peace until that evening in order, after primly greeting his return, to lecture him like a child, she showed him not just another with the face of anger, but another André Gide who is no longer sure, either then or later in thinking back on it, of just what he really meant to do — whose own truth has been changed by the doubt thrown on his good faith.

Perhaps it would be worth our while pausing a moment over this empire of confusion which is none other than that in which the whole human opera-buffa plays itself out, in order to understand the ways in which analysis can proceed not just to restore an order but to found the conditions for the possibility of its restoration.

Kern unseres Wesen, the nucleus of our being, but it is not so much that Freud commands us to seek it as so many others before him have with the empty adage "Know thyself" — as to reconsider the ways that lead to it, and which he shows us.

Or rather that which he proposes for us to attain is not that which can be the object of knowledge, but that (doesn't he tell us as much?) which creates our being and about which he teaches us that we bear witness to it as much and more in our whims, our aberrations, our phobias and fetishes, as in our more or less civilized personalities.

Madness, you are no longer the object of the ambiguous praise with which the sage decorated the impregnable burrow of his fear; and if after all he finds himself tolerably at home there, it is only because the supreme agent forever at work digging its tunnels is none other than reason, the very Logos that he serves.

So how do you imagine that a scholar with so little talent for the "commitments" that solicited him in his age (as they do in all ages), that a scholar such as Erasmus held such an eminent place in the revolution of a Reformation in which man has as much of a stake in each man as in all men?

The answer is that the slightest alteration in the relation between man and the signifier, in this case in the procedures of exegesis, changes the whole course of history by modifying the moorings that anchor his being.

It is precisely in this that Freudianism, however misunderstood it has been, and however confused its consequences have been, to anyone capable of perceiving the changes we have lived through in our own lives, is seen to have founded an intangible but radical revolution. There is no point in collecting witnesses to the fact:[63] everything involving not just the human sciences, but the destiny of man, politics, metaphysics, literature, the arts, advertising, propaganda, and through these even economics, everything has been affected.

Is all this anything more than the discordant effects of an immense truth in which Freud traced for us a clear path? What must be said, however, is that any technique that bases its claim on the mere psychological categorization of its object is not following this path, and this is the case of psychoanalysis today except in so far as we return to the Freudian discovery.

Furthermore, the vulgarity of the concepts by which it recommends itself to us, the embroidery of pseudo-Freudianism *(frofreudisme)* which is no longer anything but decoration, as well as the bad repute in which it seems to prosper, all bear witness to its fundamental betrayal of its founder.

By his discovery, Freud brought within the circle of science the boundary between the object and being that seemed to mark its outer limit.

That this is the symptom and the prelude of a re-examination of the situation of man in the existent such as has been assumed up to the present by all our postulates of knowledge — don't be content, I beg of you, to write this off as another case of Heideggerianism, even prefixed by a neo- that adds nothing to the dustbin style in which currently, by the use of his ready-made mental jetsam, one excuses oneself from any real thought.

When I speak of Heidegger, or rather when I translate him, I at least make the effort to leave the speech he proffers us its sovereign significance.

If I speak of being and the letter, if I distinguish the other and the Other,[64] it is because Freud shows me that they are the terms to which must be referred the effects of resistance and transference against which, in the twenty years I have engaged in what we all call after him the impossible practice of psychoanalysis, I have

[63]To pick the most recent in date, François Mauriac, in the *Figaro Littéraire* of 25 May, apologizes for refusing "to tell the story of his life." If no one these days can undertake to do that with the old enthusiasm, the reason is that, "a half century since, Freud, whatever we think of him" has already passed that way. And after being briefly tempted by the old saw that this is only the "history of our body," Mauriac returns to the truth that his sensitivity as a writer makes him face: to write the history of oneself is to write the confession of the deepest part of our neighbors' souls as well. [Au.]

[64]The "other" *(objet petit a)* is the "object" with which the ego interacts, any object of desire or its fetishistic equivalents; the "Other" is the unconscious, the decentered location of the subject that is brought into being by the fall into language. [Ed.]

done unequal battle. And it is also because I must help others not to lose their way there.

It is to prevent the field of which they are the inheritors from becoming barren, and for that reason to make it understood that if the symptom is a metaphor, it is not a metaphor to say so, any more than to say that man's desire is a metonymy. For the symptom *is* a metaphor whether one likes it or not, as desire *is* a metonymy, however funny people may find the idea.

Finally, if I am to rouse you to indignation over the fact that, after so many centuries of religious hypocrisy and philosophical bravado, nothing has yet been validly articulated as to what links metaphor to the question of being and metonymy to its lack, there must be an object there to answer to that indignation both as its instigator and its victim: that object is humanistic man and the credit, hopelessly affirmed, which he has drawn over his intentions.

Jane Gallop

b. 1952

The density of Jacques Lacan's ideas and the difficulties of his expression have created a minor industry in explicating Lacan to students of literature who want to understand and use his work. Jane Gallop has been among the most productive and original of those who have pointed the way for the appropriation of Lacan's revisions of Freud for feminist projects. Gallop was born in Duluth, Minnesota, and attended Cornell University, where she received her B.A. in 1972 and her Ph.D. in French in 1976. She taught for many years in the French department at Miami University but is now Professor of English and Comparative Literature at the University of Wisconsin at Milwaukee. Gallop's books include Intersection: A Reading of Sade with Bataille, Blanchot and Klossowski *(1981),* The Daughter's Seduction: Feminism and Psychoanalysis *(1982),* Reading Lacan *(1985),* Around 1981: American Feminist Literary Theory *(1991), and* Pedagogy: The Question of Impersonation *(1995).*

From *Reading Lacan*

On May 9, 1957, Lacan delivered a lecture at the Sorbonne. This lecture, which appears in slightly revised form in *Écrits,* is entitled "L'Instance de la lettre dans l'inconscient ou la raison depuis Freud" (The Agency of the Letter in the Unconscious or Reason since Freud). Jean-Luc Nancy and Philippe Lacoue-Labarthe, in their reading of this text, mention that it is "the first real intervention by Lacan in the University."[1] The capital "U" in their comment reminds us that the Sorbonne is, in France, *the* University, that it is, in some way, the very symbol of the academic institution at its most traditional. Lacan is thus intervening in the reigning order of knowledge, not simply in the university as a place but in the University as a symbolic structure. This same text also becomes (perhaps not coincidentally) Lacan's "first real intervention" in the American academy. Appearing in 1966 in the *Yale French Studies* issue on structuralism (under the title "The Insistence of the Letter in the Unconscious"), it is the first of the *Écrits* to be translated into English.

[1]Jean-Luc Nancy and Philippe Lacoue-Labarthe, *Le Titre de la lettre* (Paris: Galilée, 1973), p. 19. Henceforth referred to as "Titre." [Au.]

It is worth noting that the lecture was given at the request of the Philosophy Group of the Fédération des Étudiants ès Lettres. "Étudiantes ès Lettres" corresponds roughly to what we could call "Students in the Humanities." However, let us not translate too quickly this phrase that Sheridan leaves in the original French. In this context "Humanities" and "Letters" have quite different associations. Whereas Lacan ends his lecture by pointing to "humanistic man" as the "object" of our "indignation" (*E,* 528; *S,* 175),[2] throughout the lecture he is promulgating the power of the "letter" and establishing something Nancy and Lacoue-Labarthe call the "science of the letter." The phrase "Students in the Humanities" translates the spirit of "Étudiants ès Lettres" but not the letter. Yet the difference between the spirit and the letter, the question of the preeminence of one over the other, may be precisely what is at stake in the difference between "Humanities" and "Letters."

Lacan, at the beginning of the lecture, poses the question of how to take the "letter" in his title. He answers, "quite simply, *à la lettre*" (*E,* 405; *S,* 147). *À la lettre:* that is, literally, "to the letter"; figuratively, "literally." Sheridan translates with "literally," but adds a footnote that supplies the French. This problem of a translation of "à la lettre," of a translation *à la lettre,* marks with an efflorescence of bad jokes the point where a conflict between the spirit and the letter becomes telling.

The very first page of Lacan's *Écrits* begins with the Buffon quote "Le style est l'homme même," another locution that is difficult to translate. I would render it with something like "Style is [the] man himself [or itself]" or "Style is the essence of [the] man" or "Style makes the man." I can probably convey the spirit, but what gets lost in my translation is precisely the style.

In a first approximation I might line up the object of study of the Humanities with *l'homme,* whereas the object of study of Letters would be *le style.* Lacan's monumental book begins with what would seem to be the very assertion of identity between style and man. However, the balance between the two is upset precisely by that which literally appears on the side of *l'homme,* but which as we try to translate seems to have more to do with style; that is, the balance is upset by the word "même." That word is identity itself *(l'identité même),* capable of expressing both identity with something else and self-identity. Yet "même," there to underline the identity between the object of the Humanities and the object of the Letters, in this case impedes smooth translation, causes a disjunction between spirit and letter to appear.

The disjunction which translation imposes upon us is not immediately available in French. Buffon and his statement are "classics": nothing here that could constitute a disruptive intervention in the Sorbonne. But Lacan goes on to produce his own version of Buffon's formula: "Style is the man to whom one addresses oneself" ("Le style c'est l'homme à qui l'on s'adresse"). In the place of the "même," the translation's stumbling block, we find the interlocutor. The substitution of the interlocutor for the "même" — for the identical, for identity or self — is highly resonant with Lacan's notion of the ego as constituted through an identification with the other. We could here recall "The Mirror Stage." In the context of the present chapter, however, let us note that Lacan addresses himself to the Fédération des étudiants ès lettres.

Lacan has found his principal American audience among literary academics, and so this text addressed to those in Letters rather than to psychoanalysts is particularly appropriate for American readers of Lacan. Possibly this text was the first to be translated for that reason. I recently taught a seminar on psychoanalysis and literature for students of literature and chose "The Agency of the Letter" as the sole Lacan text in the syllabus. The aptness of this text for students *ès lettres* is not that it aids us in applying psychoanalysis to literature, nor even that it talks about literature proper at all. It has fewer literary allusions than many of Lacan's works. In his addresses to the students *ès lettres,* Lacan asserts that "Freud constantly maintained . . . [literary] training as the prime requisite for the formation

[2] *E* refers to *Écrits* (Paris: Seuil, 1966); *S* refers to *Écrits: A Selection,* trans. Alan Sheridan (New York: Norton, 1977). [Ed.]

of analysts, and . . . he designated the eternal *universitas litterarum* as the ideal place for its institution" (*E,* 494; *S,* 147). Rather than teach psychoanalysis as a basis for understanding literature, "The Agency of the Letter" implies that psychoanalysis itself be a regional branch of literary studies.

The object of psychoanalytic knowledge is traditionally considered to be man (object of the Humanities): psychoanalysis is a branch of psychology. Through his emphasis on the intersubjective dialogue of the analytic experience as well as his discovery that the ego itself is constituted in an intersubjective relation, Lacan has shifted the object of psychoanalysis from the individual person taken as separate monad to the intersubjective dialectic. One might now say that the object of psychoanalysis, what it as science and practice seeks to discern, is "the man to whom one addresses oneself." In other words, words from the second chapter of the present book, "the man to whom one addresses oneself" is the imago projected onto the neutral screen of the analyst. But as we read on the first page of *Écrits* "the man to whom one addresses oneself" is "style." The imago is carried in the style of address. The object of psychoanalytic study reveals itself as "style."

One might expect literary students to be at home in understanding Lacan. They have an apprenticeship in "style," have learned how to appreciate it, how to analyze it, and, in the best of cases, how to produce it. Yet my students had tremendous difficulty reading "The Agency of the Letter." (Admittedly, this was no surprise.) They came to class frustrated, disgruntled, feeling inadequate or outraged. Despite all their literary training, the major obstacle was precisely Lacan's style.

Now, if Lacan's style is the major obstacle to reading Lacan, and if style for Lacan is the interlocutor, then perhaps the block to reading Lacan is the reader herself. Or rather, since Lacan cannot address himself to the real reader but only to an imagined reader, perhaps the great difficulty in reading Lacan, the great *malaise* produced by his style, resides in the discrepancy the reader feels between her-self and the text's interlocutor, whose place she occupies but does not fill. The violence of Lacan's style is its capacity to make the reader feel nonidentical with herself as reader, or, in other more psychological terms, to make the reader feel inadequate to her role as "the man to whom Lacan addresses himself," that is, inadequate to Lacan's style.

In an attempt to induce the students to participate in reading Lacan, I began class by attempting to delineate some of the features of his style. One of these is the peculiar quality of his paragraphing. Lacan's paragraphs tend to be brief and choppy. A great number of them consist of only one sentence. Some of these sentences are actually sentence fragments. Conventionally, a paragraph has unity and there is continuity between the sentences within it. In Lacan's prose the sentences tend towards isolation and discontinuity. For this reason, rather than flowing discursivity, rather than a continuous progression of ideas, we find a series of discontinuous elements.

Lacan reminds us that Freud compares the dream to a rebus.[3] A rebus is a picture-puzzle in which the elements do not belong together, have no representational unity. The only way to understand a rebus, to interpret it, is to consider the elements one at a time. Thus Freud formulates a basic rule of dream interpretation: one must separate each element for consideration. As we saw in Chapter 1, Muller and Richardson call Lacan's writings a rebus.[4] Lacan's text in its discontinuity seems to break apart into distinct elements. One cannot follow the argument, but if the reader is willing to concentrate on one sentence or fragment at a time, much can be understood. It is our habit of discursive reading, our assumption that each sentence flows out of the preceding one that undoes us in the face of Lacan's rebuslike text. When we consider one sentence at a time, many sentences make sense and some do not but, just as with a dream, an interpretation can be quite

[3] *Écrits,* p. 510; *Écrits: A Selection,* p. 159. Freud says this in *The Interpretation of Dreams, S.E.* IV, 277–78. [Au.] *S.E.* is the Standard Edition of *The Complete Psychological Works of Sigmund Freud,* ed. James Strachey (London: Hogarth Press, 1953–74). [Ed.]

[4] John P. Muller and William J. Richardson, *Lacan and Language: A Reader's Guide to Écrits* (New York: International Universities Press, 1982), p. 3. [Au.]

valuable even though some elements remain mysterious.

Having established the principle that the text could be approached like a dream, that we could interpret one element at a time rather than feel responsible for understanding the totality, I suggested that we turn to one of the most enigmatic and frustrating parts of the text — the "algorithms" for metonymy and metaphor — and try our hand at interpreting them. These formulas are particularly intimidating to the literary student (Lacan's addressee). The assumption is that there is some logico-mathematical operation here that the reader cannot understand. But in fact these algorithms are absurd. As Nancy and Lacoue-Labarthe remark, these formulas "cannot in fact be read as real logical formulas (they neither suppose nor authorize, here, any calculation)" (*Titre,* 99). This realization releases us literary types from the obligation to master the operations and allows us to read.

An entire section of Chapter VI of Freud's *Interpretation of Dreams* is devoted to calculations in dreams. Freud writes there that "we may safely say that the dream-work does not in fact carry out any calculations at all, whether correctly or incorrectly; it merely throws into the *form* of a calculation numbers which are present in the dream-thoughts and can serve as allusions to matter that cannot be represented in any other way."[5] In Lacan's case the calculations consist of letters and not numbers, which not only heightens Lacan's insistence on the letter, but beckons a reading from the *étudiants ès lettres.*

Although they tend to dismiss the algorithms as a joke, Lacoue-Labarthe and Nancy do interpret one element of them in a footnote. The formula for metaphor contains an addition sign: + . Lacan writes of this: "the + sign . . . here manifesting the crossing of the bar" (*E,* 515; *S,* 164). The "bar" is always represented in Lacan's notations as a horizontal line; it is therefore "crossed" by the vertical line in the + sign. In their footnote, Nancy and Lacoue-Labarthe note that the "ideographic skewing" of the "usual symbol of addition . . . has all the airs of a *Witz* on the logico-mathematical notation" (*Titre,* 100n). Lacan treats the addition sign as an ideogram; such treatment is a *Witz,* a joke, a visual pun. The pun is more blatant in the English translation where "franchissement de la barre" is rendered by "*cross*ing of the bar." "Witz" is an allusion to the German title of *Jokes and Their Relation to the Unconscious,* in which Freud propounds the idea that the mechanisms of jokes are the same as the mechanisms of dreams. The visual pun on the addition sign as a cross is a familiar mechanism of the rebus.

Lacoue-Labarthe and Nancy present no further deciphering of this rebus. Thanks to the obviousness of the pun in English, their reading of the + sign corresponds to what was the point of departure for me and my class. For the remainder of this chapter I will present my associations with the various elements in the two algorithms. In the spirit of a Freudian dream-interpretation, I will give not the "meaning" of the algorithms, but the necessarily contradictory and errant process of reading the following formulas:

METONYMY $f(S \ldots S')S \cong S(-)s$

METAPHOR $f\left(\dfrac{S'}{S}\right) S \cong S(+)s$

[*E,* 515; *S,* 164]

Both of these are based on an earlier algorithm, one which, according to Lacan, founds modern linguistics: S/*s*. Although Lacan attributes this formula to Saussure, it differs in several significant ways from any of Saussure's formulations,[6] and so is actually, in letter if not in spirit, Lacan's creation. Lacan states that it should be read as "the signifier over the signified, 'over' corresponding to the bar separating the two stages" (*E,* 497; *S,* 149). At first this seems a "straight" formula, but even here there is an ideographic dimension. The signifier (S) is *over* the signified (*s*). Lacan will talk about the sovereignty or the rule of the signifier over signification. If "over correspond[s] to the bar [*barre*]," we might want to recall the French idiomatic expression "avoir barre sur" (literally, to have bar over), meaning to have the advantage over. The signifier is capital, and it is on top.

[5]Freud, *The Interpretation of Dreams, S.E.* V, 418. [Au.]

[6]See *Titre,* pp. 38–40. [Au.]

Lacoue-Labarthe and Nancy point out that in Saussure's formulations the signified is always on top (*Titre,* 38–39). Lacan's revision of Saussure is to put the signifier on top — that is, I would say, to give it preeminence. We could say that the signifier is the letter, the signified the spirit, and Lacan's gesture gives *instance* (that is — in a criticized neologistic but commonly used meaning — authority) to the letter.

In a psychoanalytic context, the notion of an above and a below can also remind us of depth psychology. The signified is here repressed into the depths of the unconscious. Its letter is not only small but in italic, as if it were more removed, foreign perhaps, from another realm.

And speaking of the letter, there is *the* letter, the only actual letter in the algorithms. The proliferation of S's creates a certain "insistence of the letter" (title of the *Yale French Studies* translation). The S insists and in its insistence, recalls the German *Es,* name of the id. (In *La Chose freudienne,* Lacan points out the homonymy between "Es" and "the initial letter of the word 'subject' " — *E,* 417; *S,* 129; see my preceding chapter). Finally, not unworthy of notice is the homonym "ès," that strange, archaic word retained only in academic usage. The phrase "ès lettres" might then be read S-letters, a description of our algorithms. Transferentially, I might add that my choice of *E* to refer to *Écrits* and *S* to refer to Sheridan's translation produces an *ES* in my text whenever I quote Lacan. Postscripturally, I must add that as I was doing the final revisions on this chapter the S on my typewriter suddenly stopped working.

"*f*" represents function. The metaphoric function (S′/S) is simple to understand. Lacan defines metaphor as "one word for another" (*E,* 507; *S,* 158). The replaced word (old signifier) becomes the signified of the new word (signifier). But the metonymic function (S . . . S′) is more difficult to grasp. It is more allusive, more — dare I say? — elliptical. Lacan defines metonymy as the relation word by word (*mot à mot* — *E,* 506; *S,* 156), which Roman Jakobson calls the relation of contiguity. It is the relation between two signifiers along the line of any concrete discourse (linear because only one word is pronounced or written at a time). For example, it can be the relation between two words in the same sentence or paragraph. In the metonymic dimension, the signifier can receive its complete signification only *après-coup* (by deferred action, after the fact).

I associate the ellipsis between S and S′ with the following paragraph, which appears earlier in the text: "For the signifier by its nature always anticipates meaning by unfolding in some way its dimension before it. As is seen at the level of the sentence when it is interrupted before the significative term: 'I shall never . . .', 'All the same it is . . .', 'And yet there may be . . .'. Such sentences are not without meaning, a meaning all the more oppressive in that it is content to make us wait for it" (*E,* 502; *S,* 153). For the moment, let us just note that the ellipsis, and therefore, perhaps, metonymy, is considered "oppressive."

One might say that the signifier for the metaphoric function in these algorithms itself functions as a metaphor and thus is easy to explain, since explanation demands only that we supply the old, replaced signifier (S/*s* has been replaced by S′/S). Likewise one could say that the signifier for the metonymic function (S . . . S′) is itself a metonymy and therefore demands an entire context to be understood. More ideograms.

Each algorithm contains two parentheses, one on either side of the congruence sign (≅). (As to what "congruence" means here, I haven't a clue.) In the metonymy formula we find a minus sign — that is, a horizontal "bar" — on the right and a horizontal configuration of S and S′ on the left. The left parenthesis of the second formula is a vertical configuration of S and S′. The terms "horizontal" and "vertical" actually appear in the sentence introducing the two formulas: "horizontal signifying chain" and "vertical dependencies." The distinction between horizontal and vertical in language corresponds to Lacan's use of Jakobson's alignment of metonymy with the horizontal dimension of language (the line of Western writing, the syntagmatic) and metaphor with the vertical dimension (the paradigmatic stack of possible selections for any point along the line).

Lacoue-Labarthe and Nancy consider that the opposition between horizontal and vertical is not value-free in Lacan's text, but that horizontality is linked to insufficiency. They cite the following passage from "The Agency of the Letter": "But the linearity that F. de Saussure holds as constitutive of the chain of discourse, in conformity with its emission by a single voice and with its *horizontal* inscription in our writing, if it is in fact necessary, *is not sufficient*" (*E,* 503; *S,* 154; emphasis mine). This sentence would not in itself constitute a link between horizontality and insufficiency, but they find that the idea of sufficiency insists since the next paragraph begins: "But *it suffices* [*il suffit*] to listen to poetry . . . for a polyphony to be heard, for it to become clear that all discourse is aligned along the several staves of a score" (*Titre*'s emphasis). The horizontal is insufficient; the nonlinear musical score (several staves) presents a sufficiency. Nancy and Lacoue-Labarthe then comment: "As much as linearity causes problems, so verticality (promised land . . .) goes without saying. And it is no coincidence if the latter is introduced here by a metaphor — and by a metaphor (the analogy of music) that is perhaps the metaphor of metaphor" (*Titre,* 58). The musical score is nonlinear — that is, both horizontal and vertical — but Nancy and Lacoue-Labarthe seem to think that Lacan is not simply asserting the insufficiency of linearity, of any one dimension. The ironic parenthesis "(promised land . . .)" suggests that for Lacan verticality promises sufficiency, wholeness, abundance. The remark "it is no coincidence" implies that the valorizing of verticality is complicitous with a privileging of metaphor over metonymy.

Although the authors of *Titre* seem to confuse verticality and nonlinearity in their interpretation of the image of the musical score, a similar confusion can be seen at work in the algorithm for metaphor. As I mentioned above, Lacan uses "horizontal" and "vertical" in his introduction to the algorithms, suggesting that one is horizontal and the other vertical. And in the metonymy formula, a horizontal configuration of S and S′ is paired with a horizontal line (the bar, the minus sign). But in the algorithm for metaphor, a vertical disposition of S and S′ is paired, not with a vertical line, but with a cross composed of a vertical and a horizontal line. The setup of the algorithms encourages the reader to see only the vertical line, which "crosses the bar," as representing metaphor. But what is actually in the right hand parenthesis is not the vertical crossing line, but the cross itself, two dimensional, nonlinear.

The text seems to supply two contradictory readings, a first, easier one that privileges the vertical, and another that shows that the privilege of the vertical is actually a confusion of the vertical with a nonlinear configuration that is both vertical and horizontal. And if the privilege of the vertical is wedded to the preference for metaphor, then a recognition of the two dimensions of the + suggests that metonymy is necessary for metaphor. Exactly one year before the lecture to the *étudiants ès lettres,* in his seminar of May 9, 1956, Lacan insists that "metonymy is there from the beginning, and it is what makes metaphor possible."[7]

Although our starting point in reading these algorithms was metaphor's cross as ideogram, the neat polarity of horizontal versus vertical made it very easy and gratifying to be taken in by metaphor's supposed verticality. Lacoue-Labarthe and Nancy's reading of metaphor's vertical promise is most tempting, and we will pursue this reading, the most obvious one, as a misreading invited by the text, all the while trying to remember that something else is also going on.

In the sentence following the metonymy algorithm, there are two occurrences of the words "manque" (lack). "Lack" has affinities to the minus sign of the right-hand parenthesis in the formula for metonymy as well as to the ellipsis of the left (S . . . S′). Where there is an ellipsis, something is missing. If the difference between metaphor and metonymy is that between a plus and a minus sign, between a more and a less, then metonymy bodies forth some lack. This lack, this minus might correspond to the "insufficiency" of horizontality.

In a psychoanalytic context, this binary opposition between a plus and a minus, between a lack and a nonlack, has resonances with sexual

[7]Lacan, *Le Seminaire* III: *Les psychoses* (Paris: Seuil, 1981), p. 259. Henceforth referred to as *S* III. [Au.]

difference, or more specifically with a certain binary misreading of sexual difference, the opposition phallic/castrated. This opposition characterizes what Freud calls the phallic phase, the last phase of infantile sexuality.[8] If we associate metonymy's horizontal insufficiency with this phallic lack, then the misreading of vertical privilege can be seen as the insistence of phallic phase reasoning, which is incorrect yet powerfully difficult to avoid.

In the sentence following the metaphor formula, Lacan says that in this vertical substitution "is produced an effect of signification which is that of poetry or of creation." Metonymy, that sad structure, horizontally laid out, offers up only lack; but metaphor reaches the heights of poetry or creation. Earlier in his lecture, Lacan talks about "the creative spark of metaphor" (*E,* 507; *S,* 157). A page later the expression "poetic spark" is found in close proximity with "paternal mystery." This word "creation," linked to metaphor and poetry, is not without its sexual, reproductive connotations. Yet once one is talking about reproduction, one is, supposedly, beyond the phallic phase and into adult sexuality.

In a footnote, Lacan comments on the algorithms: "S′ designating . . . the term productive of the signifying effect . . . one can see that this term is latent in metonymy, patent in metaphor" (*E,* 515n; *S,* 178n.29). Whereas in metonymy S is separated from S′ by an ellipsis (S′ is latent, it is only anticipatory), in metaphor S′ is on top (patent, if we remember the vertical resonance with depth psychology, the upper term is on the surface). If S′ designates the "term productive of the signifying effect" and if that effect is somehow linked to sexual creation, then we might associate a "latent" S′ with the internal, "hidden" female genitalia, whereas the male genitalia are "patent."[9]

[8]See Freud, "The Infantile Genital Organization," *S.E.* XIX. [Au.]

[9]In "Some Psychical Consequences of the Anatomical Distinction between the Sexes," Freud, in explaining the castration complex in girls (penis envy), calls the penis "strikingly visible" (*S.E.* XIX, 252). In the phallic phase, according to Freud, the female genitals are unknown, "latent" (*S.E.* XIX, 142). [Au.]

For us "Students in the Letters," another association is tempting. Jakobson links metaphor to poetry (particularly to romantic and symbolist poetry) and metonymy to the realist novel.[10] Lacan, as we have seen, explicitly links metaphor to poetry and also makes allusion to metonymy's tie to realism ("all 'realism' in creative work takes its virtue from metonymy"—*E,* 517–18; *S,* 166). The examples of realist metonymy Jakobson gives are both from Tolstoy: Anna Karenina's handbag and the synechdochic depiction of female characters in *War and Peace.* Lacan's seminar on May 9, 1956, devoted to metaphor and metonymy, likewise refers to Tolstoy in order to exemplify metonymy. "Metonymy is . . . appreciable in certain passages of Tolstoy's work; where each time it is a matter of the approach of a woman, you see emerging in her place, in a grand-style metonymic process, the shadow of a beauty mark, a spot on the upper lip, etc." (*S* III, 266). Lacan then goes on explicitly to link realism and metonymy: "In a general manner, metonymy animates this style of creation which we call, in opposition to symbolic style and poetic language, the so-called realist style." In both Jakobson and Lacan, a shadow of femininity haunts the juncture of metonymy and realism. It is not that either of them defines realism or metonymy as feminine (that would be a metaphoric, symbolic gesture), but that by contiguity, by metonymy, a certain femininity is suggested.

At the end of his article on the two types of aphasia, Jakobson complains that "nothing comparable to the rich literature on metaphor can be cited for the theory of metonymy" (p. 258). In his seminar of May 9, 1956, Lacan likewise finds a prejudice operating in favor of metaphor, and at the expense of metonymy: "the eternal temptation . . . is to consider that what is most apparent in a phenomenon is what explains everything . . . linguists have been victims of this illusion. The accent they place for example on metaphor, always given much more study than metonymy,

[10]Roman Jakobson, "Two Aspects of Language and Two Types of Aphasic Disturbances," in *Selected Writings,* II (Hague: Mouton, 1971), pp. 255–56. [Au.]

bears witness to it. . . . it is certainly what is most captivating" (*S* III, 255). Metaphor is more apparent than metonymy, and so it has been given greater consideration. But its importance participates in an illusion, a "captivating" illusion. Something that might belong to Lacan's imaginary order, the order of captivating illusions, beginning with the mirror image. More apparent or, as Lacan says in commentary on the algorithms, "patent." Metaphor is patent; metonymy is latent. The latency, the hiddenness of metonymy, like that of the female genitalia, lends it an appearance of naturalness or passivity so that "realism" — "which we call . . . the so-called realistic style," (*S* III, 260) — appears either as the lack of tropes, or as somehow mysterious, the "dark continent" of rhetoric.[11]

Luce Irigaray, the feminist psychoanalyst who has taken most articulate and interesting exception to the phallocentrism of psychoanalytic theory, also "accuses the privilege of metaphor (quasi solid) over metonymy (which has much more to do with fluids)."[12] This accusation is made in an article called "The 'Mechanics' of Fluids," in which she complains that science has studied solids and neglected fluids. She then links this to the neglect of feminine sexuality in psychoanalysis, by means of assertions that the feminine is fluid. Whatever doubts one might have about her assertion of feminine fluidity, it is interesting to note that Irigaray connects the privilege of metaphor over metonymy with the phallocentric neglect of femininity.

Irigaray's article is a critique of Lacan, whom she accuses of neglecting fluids, and thus women, in favor of the solidity of the phallus. She does not explicitly say that he privileges metaphor over metonymy, but Nancy and Lacoue-Labarthe do. As we have seen, their accusation of prejudice against metonymy is accompanied by a misreading of two dimensions in the musical score as simple verticality. That misreading is another example of what, in 1956, Lacan calls the "eternal temptation to consider that what is most apparent in a phenomenon is what explains everything." Metaphor's vertical privilege is "what is most apparent" in "The Agency of the Letter." Lacan sees that "eternal temptation" as responsible for linguists' prejudice in favor of metaphor. But it is equally involved in our reading of Lacan's prejudice in favor of metaphor. As if, whatever side one were on, this temptation was intimately tied to the privilege of metaphor.

Lacan's preference for metaphor and verticality may be an "illusion," but it is one to which we all fall "victim." It is an "eternal temptation," which is to say, we cannot ever be safe from its lures. If this temptation, with its "captivating" illusions, belongs to the imaginary order, then we cannot get beyond it by refusing it but must, as I suggested in Chapter 2 above, fall for and contemplate these illusions so as to get at what is structuring them.

The most extreme and explicit form of metaphor's privilege in Lacan's text inhabits its association with liberation, which contrasts with metonymy's link to servitude. As we noted above, metonymy's ellipsis can be considered "oppressive" (*E*, 502; *S*, 153). Metaphor, on the other hand, is "the crossing of the bar." The word for "crossing" — "franchissement" — has an older meaning of liberation from slavery, enfranchisement. The "bar" is an obstacle; metaphor unblocks us. Let us recall the association between the bar and repression mentioned briefly above. Michèle Montrelay, a Lacanian analyst, writes that the analyst's discourse is "a *metaphor* of the patient's discourse."[13] The analyst's intervention frees the patient from his suffering by allowing him to metaphorize.

In a passage that occurs some pages before the algorithms, "metaphor" again appears in proximity to "franchi" (crossed, but also enfranchised). Then, in the next paragraph, the question is posed as to whether metonymy "does not manifest

[11]"Dark continent" is a term Freud used for female sexuality, a term frequently quoted in French psychoanalytic works ("continent noir"). I have not yet succeeded in locating this term in Freud's text, but that may be my blind spot. [Au.]

[12]Luce Irigaray, "La 'Mécanique' des fluides" in *Ce Sexe qui n'en est pas un*, p. 108. For a discussion of this article in relation to Lacan see chap. 3 of Gallop, *The Daughter's Seduction*. [Au.]

[13]Michèle Montrelay, "Inquiry into Femininity," trans. Parveen Adams, *m/f* I (1978), 86; her emphasis. Originally published as "Recherches sur la féminité," *Critique* 278 (1970), 670. [Au.]

some servitude inherent in its presentation" (*E,* 508; *S,* 158). This paragraph where we find "metonymy" and "servitude" also includes "obstacle," "social censorship," and "oppression." My reading of links such as that between "metaphor" and "franchi" when they occur in the same sentence or between "metonymy" and other words in the same paragraph might be called a metonymic reading. Whereas a metaphoric interpretation would consist in supplying another signifier which the signifier in the text stands for (a means b; the tie represents a phallus), a metonymic interpretation supplies a whole context of associations. Perhaps this metonymic interpretation might be called feminine reading.

Metonymy is servitude; the subject bows under the oppressive weight of the bar. Metaphor is a liberation from that weight. Yet, as Nancy and Lacoue-Labarthe remind us, metaphor "must borrow the tricks and detours" of metonymy "in order to produce itself" (*Titre,* 58). Feminine metonymy has tricks and detours that, according to Lacan, allow it to "get around the obstacles of social censorship" (*E,* 508; *S,* 158). Masculine metaphor may be frank (*franc, franchi*), may be free of the obstacles shackling femininity, but it is dependent on feminine metonymy to "[re]produce itself." As Lacan puts it a year earlier in his seminar, "Metonymy is there from the beginning, and it is what makes metaphor possible" (*S* III, 259). The linearity of language may not be "sufficient," but it is "necessary" (*E,* 503; *S,* 154 — see discussion above). The phallic phase model of thinking (binary opposition between phallus and lack, vertical and horizontal) can applaud metaphor's freedom and demean metonymy's servitude. But the adult sexual model sees the masculine dependency on the feminine, sees the horizontal bar in metaphor's cross.

Something like a reading of Lacan's phallocentrism has begun to manifest itself in this study of the privilege of metaphor.[14] Nonetheless, such a reading necessitates attention to the signification of the phallus in Lacan's work. "The Signification of the Phallus" is, of course, the title of another essay in *Écrits,* the subject, in fact, of my next chapter. But I find a certain anticipation unavoidable.

Anticipation seems more and more to be the key notion for my reading of Lacan — one that returns, although differently, in every chapter. In "The Agency of the Letter," "anticipation" occurs in the context of incomplete sentences, in the paragraph we associated with the metonymic ellipsis. This anticipation, Lacan tells us, can be "seen . . . when [the sentence] is interrupted before the significative term" (*E,* 502; *S,* 153). The term "phallus" never appears in "The Agency of the Letter." I find myself compelled to read this text as if it were one of those sentences "interrupted before the significative term," and so this chapter will anticipate the Signification of the Phallus.

In that essay we find the assertion that the phallus "can play its role only when veiled" (*E,* 692; *S,* 288; *FS,* 82).[15] This veiled phallus has associations with Freud's notion of the maternal phallus (phallic mother), to which Lacan explicitly refers (*E,* 686; *S,* 282; *FS,* 76). Returning to our algorithms where Lacan designates the significative term by S′, we could here consider S′ as designating the phallus ("latent" in metonymy/mother, "patent" in metaphor/father). This reading ultimately suggests that metonymy is more truly phallic than metaphor and that it is in "The Agency of the Letter," rather than in "The Signification of the Phallus," that the phallus plays its role.

Lacan's complete sentence from "The Signification of the Phallus" reads: "All these propositions do nothing yet but veil [*voiler*] the fact that it can play its role only when veiled [*voilé*], that is to say, as itself a sign of the *latency* with which every signifiable is struck, as soon as it is raised to the function of the signifier" (my italics). This mention of "latency" recalls metonymy, and it turns out there is an even more insistent link be-

[14]Lacoue-Labarthe and Nancy come close to such a critique in one footnote. But they end the footnote by saying "It would thus remain — but this surpasses our intentions here — to tie all this to the motif that seems to dominate . . . a text like 'The Signification of the Phallus' " (*Titre,* 95n). [Au.]

[15]*FS* refers to *Feminine Sexuality and the École Freudienne,* ed. Juliet Mitchell and Jacqueline Rose (New York: Norton, 1982). [Ed.]

tween this passage with its two "veils" and metonymy. In "The Agency," Lacan's example of metonymy is: thirty sails [*voiles*] for thirty ships. Lacan comments that the malaise created by this classic example "veiled [*voilait*] less these illustrious sails [*voiles*] than the definition they were supposed to illustrate" (*E,* 505; *S,* 156). The "voile" in "Agency" (sail) is feminine, whereas "voile" meaning "veil" is masculine. But "voile" for "sail" is derived from "voile" for "veil," and it may be just this sort of slippage between a masculine and a feminine term that is at play in Lacan's notion of the phallus, which is a latent phallus, a metonymic, maternal, feminine phallus.

If metonymy in "Agency" thus anticipates the phallus in the later text, then, retrospectively, our earlier association of metonymy with lack and metaphor with phallus becomes problematic. Of course, both readings must be taken into account. Our first reading, which replaces metonymy by castration, must be here termed a metaphoric reading in that, by use of similarity (Jakobson's metaphoric relation), it replaces one term by another. Our second reading, the one which anticipates the latent context of "The Signification of the Phallus," would be more properly a metonymic reading of metonymy.

A metonymic reading construes metonymy as phallic whereas a metaphoric interpretation attributes the phallus to metaphor. Either sort of reading inevitably locates the phallus in its own narcissistic reflection in the text. What we may be approaching here is some sort of pathology of interpretation, and as I struggle with this portion of my reading/writing, struggle with my own narcissistic investment in my own phallus (femininely latent of course), a nausea, a paralysis creeps over me, a difficulty in going further, an aphasia on the level of metalanguage.

In Jakobson's article on the two types of aphasic disturbances, we read (p. 248) that the "loss of metalanguage" is characteristic of "similarity disorder." "Similarity disorder" means a speaker can operate quite well in the metonymic dimension, but experiences a breakdown in the metaphoric dimension. As I have progressively moved into and privileged a metonymic reading, I have suffered greater and greater difficulty in maintaining metalanguage.

Jakobson, as I mentioned earlier, points out a tendency in literary scholarship to privilege metaphor. His article concludes with the following statement (pointing toward a pathology of interpretation): "The actual bipolarity has been artificially replaced in these studies by an amputated, unipolar schema which, strikingly enough, coincides with one of the two aphasic patterns, namely with the contiguity disorder" (p. 259). Our mistaking the metaphoric formula as vertical (unipolar) rather than vertical *and* horizontal (bipolar) might be an example of the interpretive pathology Jakobson diagnoses. A unipolar schema in place of a bipolar one resembles the thinking characteristic of Freud's phallic phase. In the phallic phase, only one kind of genital organ comes into account — the male; the real female genitals are unknown.[16]

I have suggested links between what Jakobson calls the traditional "amputated, unipolar schema" and phallocentrism. Celebrating a new, feminine metonymic reading (which, as opposed to the metaphoric, I have *not* called interpretation), I have sought to go beyond that phallocentric interpretive tradition. But my metonymic reading has led me to the notion of the latent phallus, and I have come to see that, in its own way, metonymic interpretation can be phallocentric too. I realize that it would be yielding to simply another "amputated, unipolar schema" to choose the metonymic dimension and neglect the metaphoric. Any polar opposition between metaphor and metonymy (vertical versus horizontal, masculine versus feminine) is trapped in the imaginary order, subject to the play of identification and rivalry. One antidote to the "eternal temptation" to privilege metaphor might be, however, to recognize the horizontal line in metaphor's cross, the bar of metonymy, which is fundamentally intricated in metaphor, just as Lacan has taught us to see the rival other that is there "from the beginning" in the constitution of identity. . . .

[16]See Freud, "The Infantile Genital Organization," *S.E.* XIX, 142. [Au.]

Julia Kristeva

b. 1941

Born in Bulgaria, Julia Kristeva took a degree from the Literary Institute of Sofia before going to Paris in 1966 and submitting a troisième cycle *doctoral thesis and then a thesis for the* Doctorat d'État. *A tenured professor at the University of Paris, she was an early contributor to the influential avant-garde journal* Tel Quel, *an officer of the International Association of Semiotics, and an editor of the review* Sémiotica. *She is also a "Lacanian" psychoanalyst, which is not to suggest that Kristeva is merely an epigone or follower of Jacques Lacan or of the other imposing figures she has studied under, such as Lucien Goldmann and Claude Lévi-Strauss. Rather, Kristeva has persistently contributed to the development of structuralist and poststructuralist thought, at once helping shape emerging ideas and incorporating them as they emerge into her own eclectic, ever-evolving body of thought. Her* Σημειωτιχὴ *(1969), for example, is a critique of structuralism that pointed in the direction of the notion of "semanalysis" — a semiotic/psychoanalytical approach to texts for which Kristeva is perhaps best known. Her other works include* The Text of the Novel *(1970),* About Chinese Women *(1974),* Revolution in Poetic Language *(1974),* Powers of Horror: An Essay on Abjection *(1980),* Desire in Language: A Semiotic Approach to Literature and Art *(1980),* In the Beginning Was Love: Psychoanalysis and Faith *(1985),* Black Sun: Depression and Melancholia *(1987),* Language: The Unknown *(1989),* Nations without Nationalism *(1993),* Proust and the Sense of Time *(1993), and* Time and Sense: Proust and the Experience of Literature *(1996). "Psychoanalysis and the Polis" (1982) is from a special issue of* Critical Inquiry *entitled "The Politics of Interpretation."*

Psychoanalysis and the Polis

Up until now philosophers have only interpreted the world. The point now is to change it.
— KARL MARX and FRIEDRICH ENGELS, *Theses on Feuerbach*

*The delusions [*Wahnbildungen*] of patients appear to me to be the equivalents of the [interpretive] constructions which we build up in the course of an analytic treatment — attempts at explanation and cure.*
— SIGMUND FREUD, "Constructions in Analysis"

The essays in this volume convince me of something which, until now, was only a hypothesis of mine. Academic discourse, and perhaps American university discourse in particular, possesses an extraordinary ability to absorb, digest, and neutralize all of the key, radical, or dramatic moments of thought, particularly, a fortiori, of contemporary thought. Marxism in the United States, though marginalized, remains deafly dominant and exercises a fascination that we have not seen in Europe since the Russian *Proletkult* of the 1930s.[1] Post-Heideggerian "deconstructivism," though esoteric, is welcomed in the United States as an antidote to analytic philosophy or, rather, as a way to valorize, through contrast, that

Translated by Margaret Waller. I would like to thank Domna Stanton and Alice Jardine for their help on an earlier version of this translation. [Tr.]

[1]Art that supposedly reflects or encourages a proletarian ethos. [Ed.]

philosophy. Only one theoretical breakthrough seems consistently to *mobilize* resistances, rejections, and deafness: psychoanalysis — not as the "plague" allowed by Freud to implant itself in America as a "commerce in couches" but rather as that which, with Freud and after him, has led the psychoanalytic decentering of the speaking subject to the very foundations of language. It is this latter direction that I will be exploring here, with no other hope than to awaken the resistances and, perhaps, the attention of a concerned few, after the event *(après coup)*.

For I have the impression that the "professionalism" discussed throughout the "Politics of Interpretation" conference is never as strong as when professionals denounce it.[2] In fact, the same preanalytic rationality unites them all, "conservatives" and "revolutionaries" — in all cases, jealous guardians of their academic "chairs" whose very existence, I am sure, is thrown into question and put into jeopardy by psychoanalytic discourse. I would therefore schematically summarize what is to follow in this way:

1. There are political implications inherent in the act of interpretation itself, whatever meaning that interpretation bestows. What is the meaning, interest, and benefit of the interpretive position itself, a position from which I wish to give meaning to an enigma? To give a political meaning to something is perhaps only the ultimate consequence of the epistemological attitude which consists, simply, of the desire *to give meaning*. This attitude is not innocent but, rather, is rooted in the speaking subject's need to reassure himself of his image and his identity faced with an object. Political interpretation is thus the apogee of the obsessive quest for A Meaning.

2. The psychoanalytic intervention within Western knowledge has a fundamentally deceptive effect. Psychoanalysis, critical and dissolvant, cuts through political illusions, fantasies, and beliefs to the extent that they consist in providing only one meaning, an uncriticizable ultimate Meaning, to human behavior. If such a situation can lead to despair within the polis, we must not forget that it is also a source of lucidity and ethics. The psychoanalytic intervention is, from this point of view, a counterweight, an antidote, to political discourse which, without it, is free to become our modern religion: the final explanation.

3. The political interpretations of our century have produced two powerful and totalitarian results: fascism and Stalinism. Parallel to the socioeconomic reasons for these phenomena, there exists as well another, more intrinsic reason: the simple desire to give a meaning, to explain, to provide the answer, to interpret. In that context I will briefly discuss Louis Ferdinand Céline's texts insofar as the ideological interpretations given by him are an example of political delirium in avant-garde writing.[3]

I would say that interpretation as an epistemological and ethical attitude began with the Stoics. In other words, it should not be confused with *theory* in the Platonic sense, which assumes a prior knowledge of the ideal Forms to which all action or creation is subordinate. Man, says Epictetus,[4] is "born to contemplate God and his works, and not only to contemplate them but also to interpret them [*kai ou monon teatin, ala kai exegetin auton*]." "To interpret" in this context, and I think always, means "to make a connection." Thus the birth of interpretation is considered the birth of semiology, since the semiological sciences relate a sign (an event-sign) to a signified in order to *act* accordingly, consistently, consequently.[5]

Much has been made of the circularity of this connection which, throughout the history of interpretive disciplines up to hermeneutics, consists in enclosing the enigmatic (interpretable) object within the interpretive theory's preexistent system. Instead of creating an object, however,

[2]The Conference on the Politics of Interpretation took place at the Center for Continuing Education at the University of Chicago, October 30 to November 1, 1981. Other participants included Edward Said, Wayne Booth, Stanley Fish, and Gayatri Spivak. [Ed.]

[3]See the introduction, p. 1075. [Ed.]

[4]A Stoic philosopher of the first century A.D. [Ed.]

[5]See Victor Goldschmidt, *Le Système stoïcien et l'idée de temps* (Paris, 1953). [Au.]

this process merely produces what the interpretive theory had preselected as an object within the enclosure of its own system. Thus it seems that one does not interpret something outside theory but rather that theory harbors its object within its own logic. Theory merely projects that object onto a theoretical place at a distance, outside its grasp, thereby eliciting the very possibility of interrogation (Heidegger's *Sachverhalt*).[6]

We could argue at length about whether interpretation is a circle or a spiral: in other words, whether the interpretable object it assigns itself is simply constituted by the interpretation's own logic or whether it is recreated, enriched, and thus raised to a higher level of knowledge through the unfolding of interpretive discourse. Prestigious work in philosophy and logic is engaged in this investigation. I will not pursue it here. Such a question, finally, seems to me closer to a Platonic idea of interpretation (i.e., theorization) than it does to the true innovation of the Stoics' undertaking. This innovation is the reduction, indeed the elimination, of the distance between theory and action as well as between model and copy. What permits this elimination of the distance between nature (which the Stoics considered interpretable) and the interpreter is the extraordinary opening of the field of subjectivity. The person who does the interpretation, the subject who makes the connection between the sign and the signified, is the Stoic sage displaying, on the one hand, the extraordinary architectonics of his *will* and, on the other, his mastery of *time* (both momentary and infinite).

I merely want to allude to this Stoic notion of the primordial interdependence of *interpretation,* subjective *will,* and mastery of *time*. For my own interest is in contemporary thought which has rediscovered, in its own way, that even if interpretation does no more than establish a simple logical connection, it is nevertheless played out on the scene of speaking subjectivity and the moment of speech. Two great intellectual ventures of our time, those of Marx and Freud, have broken through the hermeneutic tautology to make of it a *revolution* in one instance and, in the other, a *cure*. We must recognize that all contemporary political thought which does not deal with technocratic administration — although technocratic purity is perhaps only a dream — uses interpretation in Marx's and Freud's sense: as transformation and as cure. Whatever *object* one selects (a patient's discourse, a literary or journalistic text, or certain sociopolitical behavior), its interpretation reaches its full power, so as to tip the object toward the *unknown* of the interpretive theory or, more simply, toward the theory's *intentions,* only when the interpreter *confronts* the interpretable object.

It is within this field of confrontation between the object and the subject of interpretation that I want to pursue my investigation. I assume that at its resolution there are two major outcomes. First, the object may succumb to the interpretive intentions of the interpreter, and then we have the whole range of domination from suggestion to propaganda to revolution. Or second, the object may reveal to the interpreter the unknown of his theory and permit the constitution of a new theory. Discourse in this case is renewed; it can begin again: it forms a new object and a new interpretation in this reciprocal transference.

Before going any further, however, I would like to suggest that another path, posthermeneutic and perhaps even postinterpretive, opens up for us within the lucidity of contemporary discourse. Not satisfied to stay within the interpretive place which is, essentially, that of the Stoic sage, the contemporary interpreter renounces the game of *indebtedness, proximity,* and *presence* hidden within the connotations of the concept of interpretation. (*Interpretare* means "to be mutually indebted"; *prêt:* from popular Latin *praestus,* from the classical adverb *praesto,* meaning "close at hand," "nearby"; *praesto esse:* "to be present, attend"; *praestare:* "to furnish, to pre-

[6]*Sachverhalt* is German for "circumstance," or in the plural, "state of affairs." Heidegger seems to use the term to denote the interpretandum, the object in the outside world that the subject must make sense of, in the tradition of his teacher, the phenomenologist Edmund Husserl, for whom the act of apprehension constitutes objects of perception into special forms *(Sachverhälte)* generating belief in the subject that they are the case. The *Sachverhalt* is thus the link between belief and assertion. In Heidegger's contemporary Wittgenstein, the term *Sachverhalt* denotes an "atomic fact," any state of affairs of which a proposition may or may not be true. [Ed.]

sent [as an object, e.g., money].") The modern interpreter avoids the presentness of subjects to themselves and to things. For in this presentness a strange object appears to speaking subjects, a kind of currency that they grant themselves — interpretation — to make certain that they are really there, close by, within reach. Breaking out of the enclosure of the presentness of meaning, the *new* "interpreter" no longer interprets: he speaks, he "associates," because there is no longer an object to interpret; there is, instead, the setting off of semantic, logical, phantasmatic, and indeterminable sequences. As a result, a fiction, an uncentered discourse, a subjective polytopia come about, canceling the metalinguistic status of the discourses currently governing the postanalytic fate of interpretation.

The Freudian position on interpretation has the immense advantage of being midway between a classic interpretive attitude — that of providing meaning through the connection of two terms from a stable place and theory — and the questioning of the subjective and theoretical stability of the interpretant which, in the act of interpretation itself, establishes the theory and the interpreter himself as interpretable objects. The dimension of *desire,* appearing for the first time in the citadel of interpretive will, steals the platform from the Stoic sage, but at the same time it opens up time, suspends Stoic suicide, and confers not only an interpretive power but also a transforming power to these new, unpredictable signifying effects which must be called *an imaginary.* I would suggest that the wise interpreter give way to delirium so that, out of his desire, the imaginary may join interpretive closure, thus producing a perpetual interpretive creative force.

I. WHAT IS DELIRIUM?

Delirium is a discourse which has supposedly strayed from a presumed reality. The speaking subject is presumed to have known an object, a relationship, an experience that he is henceforth incapable of reconstituting accurately. Why? Because the knowing subject is also a *desiring* subject, and the paths of desire ensnarl the paths of knowledge.

Repressed desire pushes against the repression barrier in order to impose its contents on consciousness. Yet the resistance offered by consciousness, on the one hand, and the pressure of desire, on the other, leads to a displacement and deformation of that which otherwise could be reconstituted unaltered. This dynamic of delirium recalls the constitution of the dream or the phantasm. Two of its most important moments are especially noteworthy here.

First, we normally assume the opposite of delirium to be an objective reality, objectively perceptible and objectively knowable, as if the speaking subject were only a simple knowing subject. Yet we must admit that, given the cleavage of the subject (conscious/unconscious) and given that the subject is also a subject of desire, perceptual and knowing apprehension of the original object is only a theoretical, albeit undoubtedly indispensable, hypothesis. More importantly, the system Freud calls perception-knowledge (subsequently an object of interpretation or delirium) is always already marked by a *lack:* for it shelters within its very being the nonsignifiable, the nonsymbolized. This "minus factor," by which, even in perception-knowledge, the subject signifies himself as subject of the desire of the Other, is what provokes, through its insistence on acceding to further significations, those deformations and displacements which characterize delirium. Within the nucleus of delirious construction, we must retain this hollow, this void, this "minus I," as the instinctual drive's insistence, as the unsymbolizable condition of the desire to speak and to know.

Yet delirium holds; it asserts itself to the point of procuring for the subject both *jouissance* and stability which, without that adhesive of delirium, would disintegrate rapidly into a somatic symptom, indeed, into the unleashing of the death drive. It can do so, however, only because the discourse of delirium "owes its convincing power to the element of historical truth which it inserts in the place of the rejected reality."[7] In

[7]Sigmund Freud, "Constructions in Analysis," *The Standard Edition of the Complete Psychological Works of Sigmund Freud,* trans. and ed. James Strachey, 24 vols. (London, 1953–74), 23:268. [Au.]

other words, delirium masks reality or spares itself from a reality while at the same time saying a truth about it. More true? Less true? Does delirium know a truth which is true in a different way than objective reality because it speaks a certain subjective truth, instead of a presumed objective truth? Because it presents the state of the subject's desire? This "mad truth" *(folle vérité)* of delirium is not evoked here to introduce some kind of relativism or epistemological skepticism.[8] I am insisting on the part played by truth in delirium to indicate, rather, that since the displacement and deformation peculiar to delirium are moved by desire, they are not foreign to the passion for knowledge, that is, the subject's subjugation to the desire to know. Desire and the desire to know are not strangers to each other, up to a certain point. What is that point?

Desire, the discourse of desire, moves toward its object through a connection, by displacement and deformation. The discourse of desire becomes a discourse of delirium when it forecloses its object, which is always already marked by that "minus factor" mentioned earlier, and when it establishes itself as the complete locus of *jouissance* (full and without exteriority). In other words, no other exists, no object survives in its irreducible alterity. On the contrary, he who speaks, Daniel Schreber, for example,[9] identifies himself with the very place of alterity, he merges with the Other, experiencing *jouissance* in and through the place of otherness. Thus in delirium the subject himself is so to speak the Phallus, which implies that he has obliterated the primordial object of desire — the mother — either because he has foreclosed the mother, whom he finds lacking, or because he has submerged himself in her, exaggerating the totality thus formed, as if it were the Phallus. Delirium's structure thus constitutes the foreclosure of the paternal function because of the place it reserves for the maternal — but also feminine — object which serves to exclude, moreover, any other consideration of objectality.

By contrast, if it is true that the discourse of knowledge leads its enigmatic preobject, that which solicits interpretation — its *Sachverhalt* — inside its own circle and as such brings about a certain hesitation of objectness, it does not take itself for the Phallus but rather places the Phallus outside itself in what is to be known: object, nature, destiny. That is why the person through whom knowledge comes about is not mad, but (as the Stoics have indicated) he is (subject to) death. The time of accurate interpretation, that is, an interpretation in accordance with destiny (or the Other's Phallus), is a moment that includes and completes eternity; interpretation is consequently both happiness and death of time and of the subject: suicide. The transformation of sexual desire into the desire to know an object deprives the subject of this desire and abandons him or reveals him as subject to death. Interpretation, in its felicitous accuracy, expurgating passion and desire, reveals the interpreter as master of his will but at the same time as slave of death. Stoicism is, and I'll return to this point, the last great pagan ideology, tributary of nature as mother, raised to the phallic rank of Destiny to be interpreted.

2. ANALYTIC INTERPRETATION

Like the delirious subject, the psychoanalyst builds, by way of interpretation, a construction which is true only if it triggers other associations on the part of the analysand, thus expanding the boundaries of the analyzable. In other words, this analytic interpretation is only, in the best of cases, *partially true,* and its truth, even though it operates with the past, is demonstrable only by its *effects in the present.*

In a strictly Stoic sense, analytic interpretation aims to correspond to a (repressed) event or sign in order to *act.* In the same sense, it is a *connection* between disparate terms of the patient's dis-

[8]See in my *Folle vérité* (Paris, 1979) the texts presented in my seminar at l'Hôpital de la Cité Universitaire, Service de psychiatrie. [Au.]

[9]The case of Daniel Paul Schreber can be found in the Standard Edition of the works of Sigmund Freud under "Psycho-Analytic Notes on an Autobiographical Account of a Case of Paranoia (Dementia Paranoides)." *Standard Edition.* Vol. 12. Ed. James Strachey (London: Hogarth, 1954–73), pp. 3–82. The Schreber case is interesting not only in itself but because Schreber was one of very few patients of Freud's to write up the history of his psychoanalysis from his own perspective. [Ed.]

course, thereby reestablishing the causes and effects of desire; but it is especially a connection of the signifiers peculiar to the analyst with those of the analysand. This second circulation, dependent on the analyst's desire and operative only with him, departs from interpretive mastery and opens the field to suggestion as well as to projection and indeterminable drifts. In this way, the analyst approaches the vertigo of delirium and, with it, the phallic *jouissance* of a subject subsumed in the dyadic, narcissistic construction of a discourse in which the *Same* mistakes itself for the *Other*. It is, however, only by detaching himself from such a vertigo that the analyst derives both his *jouissance* and his efficacy.

Thus far, we have seen that analytic interpretation resembles delirium in that it introduces desire into discourse. It does so by giving narcissistic satisfaction to the subject (the analyst or the analysand), who, at the risk of foreclosing any true object, derives phallic jubilation from being the author/actor of a connection that leaves room for desire or for death in discourse.

Yet the analytic position also has counterweights that make delirium work on behalf of analytic truth. The most obvious, the most often cited, of these is the *suspension* of interpretation: silence as frustration of meaning reveals the excentricity of desire with regard to meaning. Madness/meaninglessness *exists* — this is what interpretive silence suggests. Second, the analyst, constantly tracking his own desire, never stops analyzing not only his patient's discourse but also his own attitude toward it which is his own countertransference. He is not fixed in the position of the classical interpreter, who interprets by virtue of stable meanings derived from a solid system or morality or who at least tries to restrict the range of his delirium through a stable theoretical counterweight. That is not to say that analytic theory does not exist but rather that, all things considered, its consistency is rudimentary when compared to the countertransferential operation which is always specific and which sets the interpretive machine in motion differently every time. If I know that my desire can make me delirious in my interpretive constructions, my return to this delirium allows me to dissolve its meaning, to displace by one or more notches the quest for meaning which I suppose to be *one* and *one only* but which I can *only* indefinitely approach. *There is meaning, and I am supposed to know it to the extent that it escapes me.*

Finally, there is what I will call the *unnameable:* that which is necessarily enclosed in every questionable, interpretable, enigmatic object. The analyst does not exclude the unnameable. He knows that every interpretation will float over that shadowy point which Freud in *The Interpretation of Dreams* calls the dreams' "umbilical." The analyst knows that delirium, in its phallic ambition, consists precisely in the belief that light can rule everywhere, without a shadow. Yet the analyst can sight and hear the unnameable, which he preserves as the condition of interpretation, *only if he sees it as a phantasm.* As origin and condition of the interpretable, the unnameable is, perhaps, the primordial phantasm. What analysis reveals is that the human being does not speak and that, a fortiori, he does not interpret *without* the phantasm of a return to the origin, without the hypothesis of an unnameable, of a *Sachverhalt*.

Furthermore, analysis reveals that interpretive speech, like all speech which is concerned with an object, is acted upon by the desire to return to the archaic mother who is resistant to meaning. Interpretive speech does this so as to place the archaic mother within the order of language — where the subject of desire, insofar as he is a speaking subject, is immediately displaced and yet, henceforth, situated. The return to the unnameable mother may take the form of narcissistic and masochistic delirium, in which the subject merely confronts an idealized petrificaction of himself in the form of an interpretive Verb, interpretation becoming, in this case, Everything, subject and object. This is what analytic interpretation confronts, undergoes, and, also, displaces.

For, in short, the analyst-interpreter or the interpreter turned analyst derives the originality of his position from his capacity for displacement, from his mobility, from his polytopia. From past to present, from frustration to desire, from the parameter of pleasure to the parameter of death, and so on — he dazes the analysand with the unexpectedness of his interpretation; even so, however, the unexpectedness of the analysis is in any case sustained by a constant: the desire for the Other. ("If you want me to interpret, you are bound in my desire.")

Since Edward Glover's *Technique of Psychoanalysis* (1928), a highly regarded work in its time, analytic theory has appreciably refined its notion of interpretation.[10] The criteria for sound interpretation may undoubtedly vary: "good adaptation" of the analysand, "progress," appearance of remote childhood memories, encounter with the analyst's transference, and so on. Or criteria for a sound interpretation may even disappear, leaving only the need for a temporary sanction (which may be on the order of the parameters already outlined) within an essentially open interpretive process. In this process, *one* meaning and *one meaning alone* is always specifiable for a particular moment of transference; but, given the vast storehouse of the unknown from which analytic interpretation proceeds, this meaning must be transformed.

If it seems that analytic interpretation, like all interpretation in the strong sense of the word, is therefore an action, can we say that this interpretation aims to change the analysand? Two extreme practices exist. In one, the analysis suggests interpretations; in the other, it assumes a purist attitude: by refusing to interpret, the analysis leaves the patient, faced with the absolute silence of the interpreter, dependent on his own capacity for listening, interpreting, and eventually changing. Faced with these excesses, one could argue that in the vast majority of analyses a psychotherapeutic moment occurs which consists in compensating for previous traumatic situations and allowing the analysand to construct another transference, another meaning of his relationship to the Other, the analyst. In the analytic interpretation, however, such a therapeutic moment has, ultimately, no other function than to effect a transference which would otherwise remain doubtful. Only from that moment does true analytic work (i.e., *dissolving*) begin. Basically, this work involves removing obvious, immediate, realistic meaning from discourse so that the meaninglessness/madness of desire may appear and, beyond that, so that every phantasm is revealed as an attempt to return to the unnameable.

I interpret, the analyst seems to say, because Meaning exists. But my interpretation is infinite because Meaning is made infinite by desire. I am not therefore a dead subject, a wise interpreter, happy and self-annihilated in a uniform totality. I am subject to Meaning, a non-Total Meaning, which escapes me.

Analytic interpretation finally leads the analyst to a fundamental problem which I believe underlies all theory and practice of interpretation: the heterogeneous in meaning, the limitation of meaning, its incompleteness. Psychoanalysis, the only modern interpretive theory to hypothesize the heterogeneous in meaning, nevertheless makes that heterogeneity so interdependent with language and thought as to be its very condition, indeed, its driving force. Furthermore, psychoanalysis gives heterogeneity an operative and analyzable status by designating it as sexual desire and/or as death wish.

3. CAN POLITICAL INTERPRETATION BE TRUE?

The efficacy of interpretation is a function of its transferential truth: this is what political man learns from the analyst, or in any case shares with him. Consider, for example, those political discourses which are said to reflect the desires of a social group or even of large masses. There is always a moment in history when those discourses obtain a general consensus not so much because they interpret the situation correctly (i.e., in accordance with the exigencies of the moment and developments dictated by the needs of the majority) but rather because they correspond to the essentially utopian desires of that majority. Such political interpretation interprets *desires;* even if it lacks reality, it contains the truth of desires. It is, for that very reason, utopian and ideological.

Yet, as in analysis, such an interpretation can be a powerful factor in the mobilization of energies that can lead social groups and masses be-

[10]See esp. Jacques Lacan, "De l'interpretation au transfert," *Le Séminaire de Jacques Lacan,* vol. II, *Les Quatre Concepts fondamentaux de la psychanalyse* (Paris, 1973), pp. 221 ff. [Au.]

yond a sadomasochistic ascesis to change real conditions. Such a mobilizing interpretation can be called revolution or demagogy. By contrast, a more objective, neutral, and technocratic interpretation would only solidify or very slowly modify the real conditions.

All political discourse that wants to be and is efficacious shares that dynamic. Unlike the analytic dynamic, however, the dynamic of political interpretation does not lead its subjects to an elucidation of their own (and its own) truth. For, as I pointed out earlier, analytic interpretation uses desire and transference, but only to lead the subject, faced with the erosion of meaning, to the economy of his own speaking. It does so by deflating the subject's phantasms and by showing that all phantasms, like any attempt to give meaning, come from the phallic *jouissance* obtained by usurping that unnameable object, that *Sachverhalt,* which is the archaic mother.

Of course, no political discourse can pass into nonmeaning. Its goal, Marx stated explicitly, is to reach the goal of interpretation: interpreting the world in order to transform it according to our needs and desires. Now, from the position of the post-Freudian, post-phenomenological analyst — a position which is really an untenable locus of rationality, a close proximity of meaning and nonmeaning — it is clear that there is no World (or that the World is not all there is) and that *to transform* it is only one of the circles of the interpretation — be it Marxist — which refuses to perceive that it winds around a *void.*

Given this constant factor of the human psyche confirmed by the semiotician and the psychoanalyst when they analyze that ordeal of discourse which is the discourse of delirium, what becomes of interpretive discourse? Indeed, what happens to interpretive discourse in view of the void which is integral to meaning and which we find, for example, in the "arbitrariness of the sign" (the unmotivated relation between signifier and signified in Saussure),[11] in the "mirror stage" (where the subject perceives his own image as essentially split, foreign, other), or in the various forms of psychic alienation? Clearly, interpretive discourse cannot be merely a hermeneutics or a politics. Different variants of sacred discourse assume the function of interpretation at this point.

Our cultural orb is centered around the axiom that "the Word became flesh." Two thousand years after a tireless exploration of the comings and goings between discourse and the object to be named or interpreted, an object which is the solicitor of interrogation, we have finally achieved a discourse on discourse, an interpretation of interpretation. For the psychoanalyst, this vertigo in abstraction is, nevertheless, a means of protecting us from a masochistic and jubilatory fall into nature, into the full and pagan mother, a fall which is a tempting and crushing enigma for anyone who has not gained some distance from it with the help of an interpretive device. However, and this is the second step post-phenomenological analytic rationality has taken, we have also perceived the incompleteness of interpretation itself, the incompleteness characteristic of all language, sign, discourse. This perception prevents the closure of our interpretation as a self-sufficient totality, which resembles delirium, and at the same time this perception of interpretation constitutes the true life of interpretations (in the plural).

4. LITERATURE AS INTERPRETATION: THE TEXT

Philosophical interpretation as well as literary criticism therefore and henceforth both have a tendency to be written as *texts.* They openly assume their status as fiction without, however, abandoning their goal of stating One meaning, The True Meaning, of the discourse they interpret.

The fate of interpretation has allowed it to leave behind the protective enclosure of a metalanguage and to approach the imaginary, without necessarily confusing the two. I would now like to evoke some specifics and some dangers of openly fictional interpretation in literary discourse itself. So as not to simplify the task, I will take as my example a modern French novelist, Louis Ferdinand Céline (1894–1961), whose popular and musical style represents the height of twentieth-century French literature and whose

[11] See Saussure, p. 833. [Ed.]

anti-Semitic and para-Nazi pamphlets reveal one of the blackest aspects of contemporary history.

I consider all fiction (poetic language or narrative) already an interpretation in the broad sense of the speaking subject's implication in a transposition (connection) of a presupposed object. If it is impossible to assign to a literary text a preexisting "objective reality," the critic (the interpreter) can nevertheless find the mark of the interpretive function of writing in the transformation which that writing inflicts on the language of everyday communication. In other words, *style* is the mark of interpretation in literature. To quote Céline, "I am not a man of ideas. I am a man of style. . . . This involves taking sentences, I was telling you, and unhinging them."[12] Such an interpretive strategy is clearly an enunciative strategy, and, in Célinian language, it uses two fundamental techniques: *segmentation* of the sentence, characteristic of the first novels; and the more or less recuperable *syntactical ellipses* which appear in the late novels.

The peculiar segmentation of the Célinian phrase, which is considered colloquial, is a cutting up of the syntactic unit by the projected or rejected displacement of one of its components. As a result, the normally descending modulation of the phrasal melody becomes an intonation with two centers. Thus: "I had just discovered war in its entirety. . . . Have to be almost in front of it, like I was then, to really see it, the bitch, face on and in profile."[13]

An analysis of this utterance, not as a syntactic structure but as a *message* in the process of enunciation between a speaking subject and his addressee, would show that the aim of this ejection is to *thematize* the displaced element, which then acquires the status not merely of a theme but of an emphatic theme. "La vache" ("the bitch") is the vehicle for the primary information, the essential message which the speaker emphasizes. From this perspective, the ejected element is desyntacticized, but it is charged with supplementary semantic value, bearing the speaker's emotive attitude and his moral judgment. Thus, the ejection emphasizes the informative kernel at the expense of the syntactic structure and makes the logic of the message (theme/rheme,[14] support/apport, topic/comment, presupposed/posed) dominate over the logic of syntax (verb-object); in other words, the logic of enunciation dominates over that of the enunciated. In fact, the terminal intonational contour of the rheme (along two modalities: assertive and interrogative) indicates the very point at which the modality of enunciation is most profoundly revealed. The notable preponderance of this contour with the bipartition theme/rheme in children's acquisition of syntax or in the emotive or relaxed speech of popular or everyday discourse is added proof that it is a *deeper* organizer of the utterance than syntactic structures.

This "binary shape" in Céline's first novels has been interpreted as an indication of his uncertainty about self-narration in front of the Other. Awareness of the Other's existence would be what determines the phenomena of recall and excessive clarity, which then produces segmentation. In this type of sentence, then, the speaking subject would occupy two places: that of his own identity (when he goes straight to the information, to the rheme) and that of objective expression, for the Other (when he goes back, recalls, clarifies). Given the prevalence of this type of construction in the first phases of children's acquisition of syntax, we can state that this binomial, which is both intonational and logical, coincides with a fundamental stage in the constitution of the speaking subject: his autonomization with respect to the Other, the constitution of his own identity.

To Freud's and René Spitz's insistence that "no" is the mark of man's access to the symbolic and the founding of a distinction between the pleasure principle and the reality principle, one could add that the "binarism" of the message (theme/rheme and vice versa) is another step, a

[12]Louis Ferdinand Céline, "Louis Ferdinand Céline vous parle," *Oeuvres complètes,* 2 vols. (Paris, 1966–69), 2:934. [Au.]

[13]"Je venais de découvrir la guerre toute entière. . . . Faut être à peu près devant elle comme je l'étais à ce moment-là pour bien la voir, *la vache,* en face et de profil" (Céline, *Voyage au bout de la nuit, Oeuvres complètes,* 1:8). [Au.]

[14]In linguistics, the rheme is the part of a sentence giving new information about the theme. [Ed.]

fundamental step, in the symbolic integration of negativism, rejection, and the death drive. It is even a decisive step: with the binarism of the message and before the constitution of syntax, the subject not only differentiates pleasure from reality — a painful and ultimately impossible distinction — but he also distinguishes between the statements: "I say by presupposing" and "I say by making explicit," that is "I say what matters to me" versus "I say to be clear" or even "I say what I like" versus "I say for you, for us, so that we can understand each other." In this way, the binary message effects a slippage from the *I* as the pole of pleasure to the *you* as addressee and to the impersonal *one,* he, which is necessary to establish a true universal syntax. This is how the subject of enunciation is born. And it is in remembering this path that the subject rediscovers, if not his origin, at least his originality. The "spoken" writing of Céline achieves just such a remembering.

In addition, in Céline's last novels, *D'un château l'autre, Nord,* and *Rigodon,* he repeatedly uses the famous "three dots" (suspension points) and the exclamations which sometimes indicate an ellipsis in the clause but serve more fundamentally to make the clause overflow into the larger whole of the message. This technique produces a kind of long syntactic period, covering a half-page, a full page, or more. In contrast to Proustian fluctuation, it avoids subordinations, is not given as a logical-syntactical unit, and proceeds by brief utterances: clauses pronounceable in one breath which cut, chop, and give rhythm. Laconism (nominal sentences), exclamations, and the predominance of intonation over syntax reecho (like segmentation but in another way) the archaic phases of the subject of enunciation. On the one hand, these techniques, because of the influx of nonmeaning, arouse the nonsemanticized emotion of the reader. On the other hand, they give an infrasyntactical, intonational inscription of that same emotion which transverses syntax but integrates the message (theme/rheme and subject-addressee).[15]

From this brief linguistico-stylistic discussion, I would like to stress the following: style is interpretation in the sense that it is a connection between the logic of utterance and the logic of enunciation, between syntax and message and their two corresponding subjective structures. The unobjectifiable, unnameable "object" which is thereby caught in the text is what Céline calls an *emotion.* "Drive," and its most radical component, the death drive, is perhaps an even better term for it. "You know, in Scriptures, it is written: 'In the beginning was the Word.' No! In the beginning was emotion. The Word came afterwards to replace emotion as the trot replaced the gallop."[16] And again: "Slang is a language of hatred that knocks the reader over for you . . . annihilates him! . . . at your mercy! . . . he sits there like an ass."[17]

It is as if Céline's stylistic adventure were an aspect of the eternal return to a place which escapes naming and which can be named only if one plays on the whole register of language (syntax, but also message, intonation, etc.). This locus of emotion, of instinctual drive, of nonsemanticized hatred, resistant to logico-syntactic naming, appears in Céline's work, as in other great literary texts, as a locus of the ab-ject. The abject, not yet object, is anterior to the distinction between subject and object in normative language. But the abject is also the nonobjectality of the archaic mother, the locus of needs, of attraction and repulsion, from which an object of forbidden desire arises. And finally, abject can be understood in the sense of the horrible and fascinating abomination which is connoted in all cultures by the feminine or, more indirectly, by every partial object which is related to the state of abjection (in the sense of the nonseparation subject/object). It becomes what culture, the *sacred,* must purge, separate, and banish so that it may establish itself as such in the universal logic of catharsis.

Is the abject, the ultimate object of style, the archetype of the *Sachverhalt,* of what solicits interpretation? Is it the arche-interpretable? This is,

[15]For a lengthier discussion of Céline's style and its interpretation, see my *Pouvoirs de l'horreur: Essai sur l'abjection* (Paris, 1980). [Au.]

[16]Céline, "Céline vous parle," p. 933. [Au.]

[17]Céline, *Entretiens avec le professeur Y* (1955; Paris, 1976), p. 72. [Au.]

as I said earlier, something analytic interpretation can argue. Meaning, and the interpretation which both posits and lives off meaning, are sustained by that *elsewhere* which goes beyond them and which fiction, style (other variants of interpretation), never stops approaching — and dissolving.

For this is in fact the central issue in Céline as in the great writers of all times. By their themes (evil, idiocy, infamy, the feminine, etc.) and their styles, they immerse us in the ab-ject (the unnameable, the *Sachverhalt*), not in order to name, reify, or objectify them once and for all but to dissolve them and to displace us. In what direction? Into the harmony of the Word and into the fundamental incompleteness of discourse constituted by a cleavage, a void: an effervescent and dangerous beauty, the fragile obverse of a radical nihilism that can only fade away in "those sparkling depths which [say] that nothing exists any more."[18]

Yet this pulverization of the abject, the ultimate case of interpretation by style, remains fragile. Because it does not always satisfy desire, the writer is tempted to give one interpretation and one only to the outer limit of the nameable. The *Sachverhalt,* the abject, is then embodied in the figure of a maleficent agent, both feminine and phallic, miserable and all-powerful, victim and satrap, idiot and genius, bestial and wily. What once defied discourse now becomes the ultimate object of one and only one interpretation, the source and acme of a polymorphous *jouissance* in which the interpreter, this time in his delirium, is finally reunited with what denies, exceeds, and excites him. He blends into this abject and its feminine-maternal resonance which threatens identity itself. This interpretive delirium — writing's weak moment — found in Céline the Jew as its privileged object in the context of Hitlerism. The historical and social causes of Céline's anti-Semitism can be sought in monotheism, or, rather, in its denials, and in the history of France and the reality of the Second World War. His anti-Semitism also has a more subtle foundation, more intrinsically linked to the psychic instability of the writer and the speaking subject in general: it is the fascination with the wandering and elusive other, who attracts, repels, puts one literally beside oneself. This other, before being another subject, is an object of discourse, a nonobject, an abject. This abject awakens in the one who speaks archaic conflicts with his own improper objects, his ab-jects, at the edge of meaning, at the limits of the interpretable. And it arouses the paranoid rage to dominate those objects, to transform them, to exterminate them.

I do not presume to elucidate in this brief presentation the many causes and aspects of Céline's anti-Semitism. A lengthier consideration of the subject can be found in my *Pouvoirs de l'horreur.* I have broached this difficult and complex subject here to indicate by a *paroxysm,* which we could take as a *hyperbole,* the dangerous paths of interpretive passion, fascinated by an enigma that is beyond discourse. For the psychoanalyst, it recalls a desiring indebtedness to the maternal continent.

I would like the above remarks to be taken both as a "free association" and as the consequence of a certain position. I would want them to be considered not only an epistemological discussion but also a personal involvement (need I say one of desire?) in the dramas of thought, personality, and contemporary politics. Such a vast theme ("the politics of interpretation") cannot help but involve a multiplicity of questions. If their conjunction in my paper seems chaotic, inelegant, and nonscientific to a positivist rationality, this conjunction is precisely what defines for me the originality and the difficulty of psychoanalytic interpretation. The task is not to make an interpretive summa in the name of a system of truths — for that attitude has always made interpretation a rather poor cousin of theology. The task is, instead, to record the *crisis* of modern interpretive systems without smoothing it over, to affirm that this crisis is inherent in the symbolic function itself, and to perceive as symptoms all constructions, including totalizing interpretation, which try to deny this crisis: to dissolve, to displace indefinitely, in Kafka's words, "temporarily and for a lifetime."

Perhaps nothing of the wise Stoic interpreter remains in the analyst except his function as *actor:* he accepts the text and puts all his effort

[18]Céline, *Rigodon, Oeuvres complètes,* 2:927. [Au.]

and desire, his passion and personal virtuosity, into reciting it, while remaining indifferent to the events that he enacts. This "indifference," called "benevolent neutrality," is the modest toga with which we cover our interpretive desire. Yet by shedding it, by implicating ourselves, we bring to life, to meaning, the dead discourses of patients which summon us. The ambiguity of such an interpretive position is both untenable and pleasurable. Knowing this, knowing that he is constantly in abjection and in neutrality, in desire and in indifference, the analyst builds a strong ethics, not normative but directed, which no transcendence guarantees. That is where, it seems to me, the modern version of liberty is being played out, threatened as much by a single, total, and totalitarian Meaning as it is by delirium.

5

MARXIST CRITICISM

Not least among the tasks now confronting thought is that of placing all the reactionary arguments against Western culture in the service of progressive enlightenment.

— THEODOR W. ADORNO

It is the view of the world, the ideology or weltanschauung *underlying a writer's work, that counts. And it is the writer's attempt to reproduce this view of the world which constitutes his "intention" and is the formative principle underlying the style of a given piece of writing.*

— GEORG LUKÁCS

The socialist critic does not see literature in terms of ideology and class-struggle because they happen to be his or her political interests, arbitrarily projected onto literary works. Such matters are the very stuff of history, and in so far as literature is a historical phenomenon, they are the very stuff of literature too.

— TERRY EAGLETON

Always historicize!

— FREDRIC JAMESON

Like Sigmund Freud, Karl Marx not only created an immense, subtle and complex body of research but inspired an entire discourse written by his followers, a world of diverse social theory that speaks for itself but speaks, at the same time, in Marx's name. American philosophy and literary criticism have only recently become leavened by Marxist social theory, for reasons that have to do with the gyrations of twentieth-century history and politics. For American workers in the 1920s and 1930s, Marx was a hero who had proclaimed a new world of equality and meaningful work, whose followers set up schools to educate the proletariat of the future. But for many of those who grew up in the 1950s and 1960s, a world dominated by a Cold War between the Marxist-Leninist Soviet Union and the capitalist United States, Marxism carried a whiff of sulphur with it, as a dangerous and unpatriotic credo, a philosophy of the Other. After the purges and show trials of the 1930s, after the Hitler-Stalin pact, after the revelations of the Gulag, Marx became the "God that failed" even to many former socialists who had believed. It is no accident that so many of the important works of British and American historical scholarship written from the 1940s to the 1970s (with notable exceptions, like Christopher Hill's *Milton and the English Revolution*) proceeded in deliberate disregard of Marx and his theories of history and culture. During the 1960s European Marxists like Herbert Marcuse were read and discussed widely, at least within the counterculture. Today, with the Soviet Union no longer standing as a grim parody of the workers' state Marx had envisioned, it is possible for those of all political stripes to view Marx and the richly complex European traditions that he spawned as the key tools for viewing literature as a social text and as the product of history.

Marx's historicism was a product of the later Enlightenment, when historical change first began to be viewed as a source of explanation of changing social and cultural moves. While Philip Sidney viewed history as a source of ethical exempla, Samuel Johnson's criticism marks the beginnings of literature seen as a social text; he treated Shakespeare and the major English authors of the seventeenth century as men who must be judged (where morals were not concerned) by the standards of their own day rather than by those of his. Johnson's friend, Thomas Warton, was to write the first *History of English Poetry* (1774–81), operating on the then-novel assumption that an appreciation of the classics of one's own language had to be mediated by an understanding of the manners and concerns of earlier times. Their Scottish contemporary Adam Smith authored not only the great apologia for capitalism, *The Wealth of Nations* (1776), but a treatise on moral philosophy that presented human societies as advancing unevenly through successive stages of social and political development driven by the motor of economic change. Walter Scott, who absorbed Smith's lessons at the University of Edinburgh, used them to construct in *Waverley* (1814) and *Old Mortality* (1816) fables of the Jacobite risings where a still feudal Scotland, savage and hierarchical, bravely confronts at a hopeless disadvantage the more advanced commercial nation of England. And Marx may have derived his sense of how history works in practice as much from Scott, the novelist he most loved, as from his teacher, the philosopher Hegel.

Marx's social theories are more fully explicated in the introduction to Marx (see p. 385), and they are reviewed in Raymond Williams's discussion of "Base and Superstructure" (see p. 1154). Briefly, however, Marx was a dialectical materialist. He was a materialist in the sense that he believed, unlike Hegel, that what drives historical change are the material realities of the economic base of society *(Grundlage)*, rather than the ideological superstructure *(Überbau)* of politics, law, philosophy, religion, and art that is built upon that economic base. Like Hegel, Marx believed that change comes about through dialectical oppositions within a given state of society. Apparently stable societies develop sites of resistance: contradictions built into the social system that ultimately lead to social revolution and the development of a new society upon the ruins of the old. These contradictions are resolved by the structural shift to a new level of operation that in turn generates other contradictions, new tensions, further revolutions.

Beyond these basic assumptions, however, Marxist theory and the application of Marxist theory to literature have taken a dizzying variety of forms, depending, among other things, on how the literary text is positioned relative to material reality and to ideology.[1] Wide discrepancies were inevitable in part because Marxism is primarily a political and economic philosophy rather than a guide to the explication of literary texts. The few comments Marx and Engels addressed to matters of art and literature left many of the most important questions of method open. Differences also arise because Marxism is, as we have hinted, not only a philosophy but a movement with a conflicted history of its own where ideas, including ideas about art, have had fateful political consequences. For example, Georg Lukács's attack on Naturalism was also a covert attack on Soviet Realist art, which used naturalist premises, and therefore on its political sponsor, Joseph Stalin. Because of this conflicted history, there are many Marxist critics but no single Marxist school of criticism in the usual sense, and we will have to mention many more representatives of the tradition Marx began than we can include in this chapter.

THE AMERICAN LIBERALS

Largely because of the long-standing fear of the Soviet Union, there has been no strong American tradition of socialism since the Bolshevik revolution, and only the briefest of periods — in the mid-1930s — when the Communist party attracted any share of intellectuals. To the extent that American criticism was touched directly by this movement (as in the writings of Granville Hicks), it was of a form usually termed (not without reason) "vulgar Marxism," which featured the adulation of the proletariat: works written by proletarians themselves and works celebrating proletarian characters, denouncing capitalism, and forecasting the revolution. Leon

[1]The Marxist term "ideology" is an essentially contested concept. The notion of ideology presented in the introduction to Marx (see p. 386), as "a culture's collective consciousness of its own being," is one of several currently used in Marxist circles, but there are many others, often in direct contradiction to it. My definition is close to a sense in which Marx uses the term in the following famous passage from *A Contribution to a Critique of Political Economy* (1859): "A distinction should always be made between the material transformation of the economic conditions of production . . . and the legal, political, religious, aesthetic, or philosophic — in short, ideological — forms in which men become conscious of this conflict and fight it out" (see p. 392). But if here "ideology" means any representation of consciousness, the most common use of "ideology" in Marx and Engels is the pejorative one of "false consciousness," a set of illusions fostered by the dominant class in order to assure social stability — and its own continued dominance (Letter to Mehring, 1893). Ideology in this sense is expected to wither away and vanish in the Marxist utopia of the dictatorship of the proletariat. Louis Althusser's often quoted dictum, "Ideology has no history," would seem to contradict this view, since it implies that ideology will retain a function forever — and thus even in the workers' state. But Althusser's definition of ideology ("the 'lived' relation between men and their world, or a reflected form of this unconscious relation") is closer to the unpejorative usage of Marx in the *Critique of Political Economy.* See Raymond Williams, *Keywords: A Vocabulary of Culture and Society* (London: Oxford University Press, 1976), pp. 126–30; and Louis Althusser, *For Marx* (New York: Pantheon, 1969), p. 252.

Another worrisome ambiguity lurking in the word "ideology" arises from the relative concreteness with which it is represented to the consciousness. While most Marxist thinkers view "ideology" as something explicit and official, like a body of laws, a political doctrine, or a philosophy, other Marxists (or the same ones, in other circumstances) use the term to denote something more vague and implicit, even unconscious: a way of understanding, a worldview.

Trotsky had himself written with contempt (in *Literature and Revolution,* 1923) of such efforts to force literature to serve politics directly. Yet Raymond Williams has conceded that, although such a position is "crude and reductionist . . . no Marxist . . . can wholly give it up without abandoning the Marxist tradition."[2]

"Vulgar Marxism" as such did not become an important American tradition, but a group of New York intellectuals, associated with the Left magazine *Partisan Review,* had flirted with Communism during the Spanish Civil War and had become disillusioned with Stalinist Russia but not with the utopian ideals that Marxism represented. The most broadly learned among them was Edmund Wilson, whose journalistic essays and books introduced European writers and ideas to what even in the 1930s and 1940s was a largely provincial America. Their leading literary critic, Lionel Trilling, was instrumental in turning the college of Columbia University into a training camp for ideas on culture and society (see pp. 571 and 608). Important followers and contemporaries included Philip Rahv, Alfred Kazin, and Irving Howe. Neither Wilson nor Trilling should be credited with fashioning a significant critical methodology or a doctrinally pure way of reading Marx. Indeed, it may be going too far to call them Marxists, since both were influenced almost as heavily by Freud, and they avoided using most conventional Marxist terminology. They wrote, instead, in an Arnoldian tradition of cultural commentary, committed to literature as an expression of culture, and concerned primarily with expressing in their writings both the tension within their own responses to literature and the broadest and most complex views of life.

REFLECTION THEORIES: TROTSKY AND LUKÁCS

At least two major theories derive from the notion that literature consists of an imitation of social reality. The first, which can be traced to Marx but is best expressed by Leon Trotsky, Georgii Plekhanov, and other writers of the Third International (an organization founded in Moscow in 1919 to support the Bolshevik revolution), equates mimesis with a pure "slice of life" and considers it unimportant that writers take a radical stance toward the reality they portray. The royalist reactionary Balzac is thus a more valuable writer in his accurate portraits of society than a less perceptive writer of doctrinally correct (i.e., socialist) tendencies.

A second, more complex version of reflection theory is found in the criticism of Georg Lukács. Lukács held that writers must do more than reflect the mere surface features of their society: They must also portray the various forces acting on that society that eventuate in social change. Lukács despised the naturalists (like Émile Zola and Theodore Dreiser) who were satisfied to present characters typical of the social order. In "The Ideology of Modernism" (1956), reprinted here, Lukács pours equal scorn on the modernists' exaltation of the subjective and the psychological at

[2]Raymond Williams, "Marxism, Structuralism, and Literary Analysis" in *New Left Review* 129 (1981): 51–66.

the expense of any portrayal of the dynamic movements underlying social change. To either naturalism or modernism, Lukács prefers the realism — less sophisticated though it be — of Walter Scott. Scott's Edward Waverley is not the typical English gentleman of his time, nor is he invested with much psychological depth; nevertheless, in Waverley, whose relationships and loyalties position him between the mercantile English and the still feudal Highland Scots on the eve of the 1745 rebellion, Scott created a character who embodies the social and political conflicts of his epoch.

FORMS OF MEDIATION THEORY: BENJAMIN AND ADORNO

Just as there have been various forms of Marxian "reflection" so have there also been different versions of the principle of "mediation" — the notion that ideology establishes relationships between the two levels of Marxist dialectic, between the base and the superstructure, between the relations of production and the work of art. These versions arose in part because of the aesthetic inadequacy of the concept of reflection. "Reflection" was a useful term for discussing the novel, but most other modes of literature and art could not incorporate, as a novel could, a view of an entire society. At times the term "mediation" has been used merely to denote the more subtle versions of mimesis — like that of Lukács — but it more properly describes theories like Walter Benjamin's notion of correspondences.

One would not say that, for example, the poetry of Baudelaire reflects his society, in the sense that it depicts an image of it. But as Benjamin noted, industrialization had produced changes in the city and its crowds that resulted in a new version of both the individual and the individual's attitude toward himself, which connected with aspects of Baudelaire's poetry. Benjamin describes Baudelaire's notion of the *correspondance* as "an experience which seeks to establish itself in crisis-proof form." It is the artist's reaction to the impermanence of post-industrial urban life, typified in the shock and abrasion of the crowded streets. Benjamin viewed Baudelaire as nostalgic about the decline of that mystical quality of art Benjamin called "aura" — that spiritual quality, a relic of the human attachment to ritual and magic, which gives a work of art an almost animate sensibility: "To perceive the aura of an object means to invest it with the ability to look at us in return."

In "The Work of Art in the Age of Mechanical Reproduction" (1936), reprinted below, Benjamin examines the central fact of industrialism's relation to art in the twentieth century: that, for the first time, a painting or sculpture can be infinitely replicated. On the one hand there is the genuine possibility of art for the masses, not simply because anyone can possess a copy of Botticelli's *Birth of Venus* but also because of the evolution of film, a medium intended for mass audiences. On the other hand, the mystical aura, the cult value of the art object, is simultaneously beginning to disappear. As a socialist, Benjamin ought to be applauding this trend, but the essay is caught up in emotional ambiguity because of his own nostalgia for the cult of memory. Although the preface bravely declares that his theses "brush aside a number of outmoded concepts, such as creativity and genius, eternal value and mystery," the tone of the later sections seems at odds with this intent. When Benjamin contrasts the stage actor, engaged both in acting as an art and in a particular role, with the alienated film actor, who is at best an "exile" and at worst a "stage prop," or when he notes that aura survives in film in the obscene adulation paid to film stars, or when he observes that film is the art uniquely suited to the "distracted" and "absent-minded" spectator, a reader may infer that the proletarianization of art progressively dehumanizes both participants and spectators. Reading Benjamin, one may feel trapped within his ironies, but perhaps Benjamin was trapped in them himself. Although he knew well that socialism meant industrialization, mechanical reproduction, and the death of the cult value of art, he nevertheless felt intensely the loss of that value.

Benjamin was willing to allow for Baudelairean correspondences, for the mediation of ideology, at the level of content. Other members of the so-called Frankfurt school, like Theodor W. Adorno, were not so willing. For Adorno, the Frankfurt school's principal aesthetician, the relationship between art and society operated on the formal level and could easily be located even in nonreferential art such as music. Thus, in *Philosophy of Modern Music* (1949), Adorno suggested that the rootless chaos and tragic ambiguity of Arnold Schönberg's musical harmonies, together with his drive to mechanize and systematize composition, served as a correspondence with the dominant ideology of the early twentieth century. (Adorno judged Schönberg to be a more authentic artist than Igor Stravinsky, whose shifting formal allegiances — from neoclassicism to primitivism — were either ideologically reactionary or attempts to evade history altogether.)

As one might expect, Adorno took the opposite position from Lukács on the issue of modernism in literature and defended the bleak vision of novelists like Kafka. While Adorno agrees with Lukács that modern fiction is morbidly subjective and obsessed with the torture of the individual consciousness, he claimed that the modern novel took "a critical posture towards social reality by means of its style . . . not by its 'content' or view of the world."[3] In a sense, modernist fiction exemplifies "negative dialectic" — Adorno's term for criticism that operates without reproducing the conceptual features of what it criticizes — a necessary feature in capitalist society, where, according to Adorno, concepts distort and mask social realities.

The passages from Adorno's *Minima Moralia* (1951) reproduced below suggest in small compass the gnarled complexity of Adorno's thought and the jeweled paradoxes to which that complexity gave rise. These brief essays were, like Auerbach's *Mimesis,* the product of exile, and Adorno's exile was bitterer than most. He spent the war years in the safety of the United States, but unlike fellow Germans such as Thomas Mann who flourished during such exile in the paradise of southern California, Adorno was in a constant state of outrage against the politics of America, whose New Deal seemed a pale travesty of the just society for which he longed. "Bequest" presents in the briefest form the program of the "critical theory" es-

[3]Gillian Rose, *The "Melancholy Science": An Introduction to the Thought of Theodor W. Adorno* (London: Macmillan, 1978), p. 124.

poused by him and his fellow exile Max Horkheimer, who rejected the quietist notion that history, through its dialectical process of thesis and antithesis, would bring man to Utopia automatically. Adorno also asserts the need to broaden the Marxist vision of history to include not only the world historical forces that have been victorious and the opponents who have been defeated but the "cross-grained, opaque, unassimilated" aspects of history and culture that have fallen by the wayside.

Adorno was in rebellion against America's culture industry, his firsthand experience of which intensified his rejection of Benjamin's dreams of a mass culture derived from mass production. This is clear enough in "Late Extra," with its rough handling of Benjamin's theories about Poe and Baudelaire, and their valorization of the shock of the new. Nevertheless, the last paragraphs predict — long before the term came into existence — the premises of postmodernism, of a literary, musical, or film culture that makes us aware, by its style of representation, of the flimsy social relations of late capitalism. As Adorno says in "Baby with the Bathwater," "the notion of culture as ideology," as representations of soothing fantasies about a society worthy of man that stand in opposition to the real truths about that society, "like all expostulations about lies, has a tendency to become itself ideology" (*Minima Moralia* 43). The Marxist analysis of content alone can be patly self-congratulatory. There is the need to analyze form and the subjective effects of form as well. These elements in Adorno were not lost, as we shall see, on Fredric Jameson.

GENETIC STRUCTURALISM: LUCIEN GOLDMANN AND RAYMOND WILLIAMS

Between the mediation theories of the Frankfurt school and the structural Marxism of the Althusserians, there are transitional modes of Marxist criticism. One of the most important was that practiced by Lucien Goldmann, who called himself a "genetic" structuralist because the structures he was concerned about were derived from the work's genesis in the ideology of its times. Like Adorno, Goldmann believed that the correspondences between a work and an age would be correspondences of form rather than content. But unlike most Marxist critics, who would claim that the ideology of an age is invariably present in all of its products, Goldmann felt that only the greatest works of an age contain its deepest consciousness.

Goldmann's analysis of seventeenth-century France in *The Hidden God* (1955) presents *homologies* — analogies of function rather than content — between literary and ideological structures, which during that period take the form of tragic dilemmas. The seventeenth-century Jansenists were torn between obedience to a silent God and participation in the new rationalism; the "nobility of the robe" (the gentry deriving from the legal profession) were torn between the authority of the king and the new spirit of commercial enterprise. Similarly, in the plays of Racine, who was both a Jansenist and a scion of the *noblesse de robe,* the protagonists (such as Hippolytus and Andromache) must choose between service to a hidden God and the pleasures and duties of the world — and are damned no matter which they choose.

The most distinguished English practitioner of genetic structuralism was probably Raymond Williams. The son of working-class parents from the border country of Wales, Williams brought to his readings of literature a proletarian background highly unusual in a Marxist critic, few of whom have had any close acquaintance with hard manual labor. Instead of Benjamin's more abstract and aestheticized term "correspondences," Williams spoke of the "complex forms of feeling" within which literature and ideology find common ground. In Williams's *The Country and the City* (1973), for example, his thought about the industrial revolution is filtered through his personal sense of what alienation from the countryside might have meant to the poets of the eighteenth and early nineteenth centuries. As with Goldmann, the structures of feeling Williams found in poetry exhibit homologies with elements in the nonaesthetic segments of the superstructure or the relations of production in the base.

In fact, Williams talks of seeking "structures of feeling" in art instead of "ideology" as such; the novel phrase differentiates the concrete, lived experience represented in art ("social experiences *in solution*" as he calls it) from the "precipitated" manner in which social relationships are likely to be characterized in an expository text, a treatise, or a newspaper article.

It would be misleading to characterize Williams as merely a follower of Goldmann, however. Williams was a rather protean social and historical critic whose work shifted rapidly through a number of phases. He began his career rejecting the revolutionary doctrines of Marxism, particularly its concept of the masses, and went through a left-Leavisite phase of cultural criticism that kept what Williams himself termed "a certain conscious distance" from Marxism. After *Culture and Society* (1958), however, Williams converged with Marxist thought. Following his "genetic structuralist" phase, Williams became what he called a "cultural materialist," influenced primarily by the Italian Marxist Antonio Gramsci and his concept of *hegemony*.

To Gramsci, power is expressed partly through the direct means of control (*dominio:* rule) and partly through something at once less formal and conscious and yet more total (*egemonia:* hegemony). As Williams says in *Marxism and Literature* (1977), from which the selection in this chapter is taken:

> Hegemony is . . . a lived system of meanings and values — constitutive and constituting — which, as they are experienced as practices appear as reciprocally confirming. It thus constitutes a sense of reality for most people in the society . . . beyond which it is very difficult for most members of the society to move. . . . It is . . . in the strongest sense a "culture" but a culture which has also to be seen as the lived dominance and subordination of particular classes. (See p. 1159)

Williams finds this conception attractive because it allows for the notion of *alternative* hegemonies centered in the working class and for revolutionary activity in the shape of cultural rather than political action. The implication is that hegemonies may be relatively successful, but they are never complete. Instead of a single ruling class, there are interpenetrating hegemonic groups; and instead of a single catastrophic revolution, there are dominant, emergent, and residual elements of culture belonging to classes whose power has peaked or is increasing or declining. This concept of hegemony modifies the rigid base/superstructure formula of Marxist thought, a modification Williams had already sought in the homologies of Goldmann. In general, Williams seems to have sought a more fluid and responsive Marxism — also an aim of Louis Althusser.

LOUIS ALTHUSSER AND STRUCTURAL MARXISM

The newest development of Marxist thought — post-Althusserian Marxism — originates in the structural thought of the mature Marx as interpreted by Louis Althusser and in the theories of the signifier developed by Jacques Lacan (see Ch. 4), which were later to influence Jacques Derrida (Ch. 2). In *Reading Capital,* Althusser questions the traditional portrait of Marx as a Hegelian humanist; for Althusser there were two Marxes, a young Marx (up to the year 1845), whose ideas roughly corresponded with the usual view of dialectical materialism, and a mature Marx (from 1857 onward), whose way of thinking was radically different. For Althusser, the older Marx, author of *Capital,* had evolved a form of dialectic that was different from Hegel's — not just an inversion of it — and no longer held to the simple deterministic relation of base and superstructure. Economics is determinative but only *"in the last instance."*[4] But Althusser's most important shift is in his vision of history. Earlier writers on Marx had assumed that history is a real force, concrete, univocal, and ineluctable. In Althusser's reading of Marx, history has become a myth, or perhaps more properly, a text, in that it is a symbolic structure, produced by discourse. We cannot evade history any more than we can think without our faculty for symbolization, but neither can we view history from outside that subjective faculty.

In Althusser's interpretation, Marx becomes a canny reader of his own chosen texts, those of his predecessors, the classical economists; in quoting Marx, Althusser presents him as aware of their oversights, their subtle shifts in point of view. Althusser's point is that these writers' areas of blindness are as significant as their areas of insight, for the gaps and incoherencies that a critical reading of the texts reveals are the signs of what the writers are unconsciously hiding from themselves. This is not the personal, Freudian repression of individuals, but blind spots left by what the ideology of their age is unable to talk about.

Pierre Macherey's *A Theory of Literary Production* (1966) presents a literary-critical version of these ideas. In "Jules Verne: The Faulty Narrative," Macherey shows how Verne's plans for his novels went awry. *The Mysterious Island,* for example, originated in Verne's wish to rewrite *Robinson Crusoe* more rigorously. Unlike Defoe, who had provided Crusoe with a shipload of modern equipment and tools, Verne would demonstrate how castaways with a knowledge of science manage to recreate modern technology out of nothing on an empty island. The novel begins thus, but halfway along Verne reveals that the castaways are not alone on the island; he introduces Captain Nemo and his crew, who give the castaways a crate of

[4]Louis Althusser, "Contradiction and Overdetermination," in *For Marx,* trans. Ben Brewster (New York: Pantheon, 1969), pp. 84–114.

tools. Most readers would interpret this as a mere lapse on Verne's part, a melodramatic corruption of his plan. For Macherey, there are no mistakes, and Verne's introduction of Nemo betokens his attempt to *evade* what he knows: That science cannot be pure knowledge, as he would wish, but relies on the technological capacity of a capitalistic society to bring it into being. Furthermore, Verne's book implicitly acknowledges that there are no empty lands, only those whose aborigines are rendered invisible by imperialist ideology, just as technology cannot arise purely from scientific knowledge but must in fact emerge from a technological social organization. Macherey argues that the rifts in Verne's plot are there because of preexisting rifts in the ideology of bourgeois capitalism and that the novel itself, as an aesthetic practice whose raw materials are ideology, tends to widen these rifts as it foregrounds them, making them visible to the reader.

By reifying the flat notions of ideology in the roundness of a narrative, the artist unwittingly exposes their incoherencies to the view of a critical reader. This version of Marxism is practiced by Raymond Williams's disciple, Terry Eagleton, and by Althusser's most important American disciple, Fredric Jameson. Jameson's highly acclaimed *The Political Unconscious* (1981) presents a theory of interpretation in which Althusser's politics and Lacan's theory of the unconscious intersect.

EAGLETON

Terry Eagleton did not begin as a post-Althusserian Marxist but as a Christian humanist of working-class origins, studying literature at Cambridge under Raymond Williams. His post-Althusserian phase began in the mid-1970s, when he broke decisively with the humanist-socialist position he had inherited from Williams, just as Williams himself was refashioning a rigorous and dialectical Marxism based on the ideas of the Italian thinker Antonio Gramsci. In *Marxism and Literary Criticism* (1976), Eagleton surveys Marxist aesthetics from Marx's and Engels's own essays and letters to the continental neo-Marxists of the 1960s, portraying this history as a long decline from the insights of the original master until its post-Althusserian renaissance in his own day. He attacked not only the antiartistic repressions of Stalin and Zhdanov but also the British Marxists of the 1930s, like Christopher Caudwell and Arnold Kettle, and contrasted the broad world-historical issues favored by Georg Lukács (for Eagleton a "stiff-necked Stalinist") with the more subtle questions about the social determinants of art which post-Althusserian Marxists like Pierre Macherey were able to ask.

Eagleton went on in *Criticism and Ideology* (1976) to provide a fuller explanation of post-Althusserian literary theory as well as some practical criticism based on that theory. This work contains Eagleton's declaration of independence from Raymond Williams, whose shifting allegiances Eagleton subjects to the same sort of sharp but ultimately generous scrutiny that many well-adjusted post-adolescents apply to their fathers. For readers trying to learn how to read or write neo-Marxist criticism, the most important sections, however, are the second and third chapters. Here Eagleton presents the literary work as determined not solely by the "economic base," as in classical Marxism, but by a large number of interrelated factors, including the "literary mode of production" — whether the text is transmitted orally, through handwritten manuscripts, printed books, periodicals, etc. —, the "general ideology," the "aesthetic ideology" of the time, and the "authorial ideology" — the writer's particular slant on the social conflicts of his or her day. In addition, Eagleton presents the Althusserian thesis that ideology, far from being a coherent and unified mode of social consciousness (as Lukács, for example, had conceived of it), is actually fragmented and inconsistent. The artistic work, as a production of ideology, foregrounds such incoherencies and makes them visible to the reader. Thus, art can have revolutionary effects, regardless of the social views of the artist.

Ultimately, Eagleton came to see his attempt to create a "science of the text" as too sterile. During the Thatcher years, when the gains of the workers under the Labour Party quickly evaporated, this working-class theorist decided that criticism would have to do more than analyze literature. He espoused what he called a "revolutionary criticism," for which he claimed practical as well as intellectual aims:

> What seemed important when I wrote [*Criticism and Ideology*], at a time when "Marxist criticism" had little anchorage in Britain, was to examine its prehistory and to systematize the categories essential for a "science of the text." [This] is perhaps no longer the focal concern of Marxist cultural studies. Partly under the pressure of global capitalist crisis, partly under the influence of new themes and forces within socialism, the centre of such studies is shifting from narrowly textual or conceptual analysis to problems of cultural production and the political use of artefacts. . . . This shift in direction was in turn obscurely related to certain deep-seated changes in my own personal and political life. . . .[5]

One index to these "deep-seated changes" may be Eagleton's dedication of his book on Walter Benjamin to the poststructuralist feminist critic Toril Moi, whose intellectual influence he gratefully acknowledges. Moi's influence may be seen in Eagleton's vision of a "revolutionary criticism" based primarily on the "paradigm" of "feminist criticism." Like those contemporary feminist critics who attempt to make patriarchy visible in order to dismantle it, Eagleton proposes to "dismantle the ruling concepts of 'literature,' reinserting 'literary' texts into the whole field of cultural practices." He proposes further to "deconstruct the received hierarchies of 'literature,' " to reevaluate the canon, and to reveal the role of literature "in the ideological construction of the subject."[6] In effect, Eagleton is calling for a new political criticism that would apply to class issues the lessons that feminists have learned in their approach to gender. His books on subjects from Shakespeare to Richardson to Brontë to Wilde have come out at a rate of nearly one per year, but it remains an open question whether Eagleton has succeeded in fulfilling the promise of his theoretical manifesto.

[5]Terry Eagleton, *Walter Benjamin, or Towards a Revolutionary Criticism* (London: Verso, 1981), p. xii.

[6]Ibid., p. 98.

JAMESON AND THE POLITICAL UNCONSCIOUS

Fredric Jameson came to Marxism through his dissertation on Sartre, and his position as the foremost American Marxist critic solidified after the publication of *Marxism and Form* (1971). Like Eagleton, Jameson was at pains to jettison the tedious and tendentious forms of Russian Marxism, and he championed the more Hegelian Marxism of Lukács, Benjamin, and Adorno. What was most original in *Marxism and Form* was Jameson's final chapter, "Towards Dialectical Criticism," in which he sets forth his own ideas of what a genuine dialectical-materialist criticism would be like. The most important of these is his notion of criticism as "metacommentary" that must always "include a commentary on its own intellectual instruments as part of its own working structure."[7] Jameson would argue that while for a formalist like Wayne Booth the concept of "point of view" is a neutral tool of analysis without historical content — after all, any narrative, whenever written, must be told from some point of view — in fact, the notion of "point of view" is not timeless at all; it reflects the specific historical situation of Henry James (who invented the term) and the "lived experience" of the middle class in the late nineteenth century: "seeing life from the relatively restricted vision of our own monad."[8] For Jameson, a genuinely dialectical criticism would be self-conscious about the terms and structures that it assumes and would attempt to understand these tools in their historical contexts.

The last part of "Towards Dialectical Criticism" presents a complex "allegorical" vision of literary interpretation based on Jameson's notion of the interconvertability of form and content. For Jameson, in addition to the usual "form" and "content" of any literary text, there is the "form of the content" and the "content of the form." Jameson claims that the "content" of a literary work "never really is initially formless . . . but is rather already meaningful from the outset, being . . . the very components of our concrete social life itself: words, thoughts, objects, desires, people, places, activities."[9] It is the lived experience of the social world. On the other side "form" itself has its "content": styles and plots encode ideas about the material world. One obvious example would be the love sonnet of the Rennaissance, whose importance underscores the dynastic or commercial character of the marital bond in that era. (In our own era, men and women who can marry for love as a matter of course do not need to create such formal objectifications of feeling.) Sometimes the "content of the form" operates in surprising ways. For example, Jameson views the surface violence and anxiety of science fiction movies of the 1950s not merely as a covert reference to the terror of nuclear annihilation during a period of escalation in the Cold War, but as also encoding a collective wish-fulfillment fantasy on the part of postwar society, a utopian fantasy about genuinely gratifying work that is personified in the ubiquitous scientist hero whose activity — empowering, untrammeled by routine, rewarded by deep self-satisfactions rather

[7]Fredric Jameson, *Marxism and Form: Twentieth-Century Dialectical Theories of Literature* (Princeton, NJ: Princeton University Press, 1971), p. 336.

[8]Ibid., p. 355.

[9]Ibid., pp. 402–03.

than by cash — suggests "a return to older modes of work organization, the more personal and psychologically satisfying world of the guilds."[10] In *Marxism and Form* Jameson presents his vision of a new dialectical criticism that would interpret literature in such a way as to penetrate to the repressed collective political desires of the society in which it was produced: He would show that criticism in action ten years later in *The Political Unconscious* (1981).

The title of *The Political Unconscious* refers to the ideas of Althusser and Macherey discussed previously: that society represses its internal contradictions by means of ideology but that by carefully reading literary texts we are often able to witness the "return of the repressed," the surfacing of the fissures in the ideology of a society. For Jameson, literary texts are allegorical, encoding both the "false consciousness" of their age and its "utopian" dreams. This encoding takes place within the three "concentric frameworks" of *politics* (the plotting of particular events), *society* (the tensions operating between groups), and *history* (the succession of social formations within the larger vision of social change). For Jameson, these three frameworks point also to three moments in the act of interpretation that he calls the three "horizons" of the text. In the first horizon, it is within the boundaries of the text itself that the symbolic tensions of the political unconscious are set forth; in the second, the text is seen as an ideological utterance within a system of discourse, an example of *parole* within a *langue*. Finally the text is viewed as a field of force within which artifacts deriving from sign-systems dominant in successive social formations can be simultaneously viewed. Jameson aligns these three horizons with "phases" in Northrop Frye's *Anatomy of Criticism* that themselves derive roughly from the literal, the allegorical, and the anagogical modes of medieval interpretation.

In addition, Jameson employs two other methodological tropes. One is the "rectangle" of the structural linguist A. J. Greimas, which structures the themes of a narrative text into a synchronic system through various modes of equivalence and opposition. The other is what he calls the "molecular" and "molar" aspects of the allegorical representation of ideology in narrative. Generally, Marxist critics have dealt with the large-scale features of a text, its plot and themes, to the exclusion of its fine structure. Jameson calls this the "molar" level (in chemistry, a "mole" is 6.2×10^{19} molecules of a substance). But Jameson believes that the political thematics of narratives can also be found at the "molecular" level of the structure of individual sentences, and demonstrates, in passages from Balzac's "La Vieille Fille," Dreiser's *Sister Carrie,* and Conrad's *Lord Jim* and *Nostromo,* how the political unconscious operates at the stylistic level of the text.

It was *The Political Unconscious* that made Jameson one of the critics most frequently quoted in literary circles. However, some Marxists were less enthusiastic about this text. Terry Eagleton, already in his "revolutionary" phase, suggested that Jameson's subtle analyses of the "utopian moment" in various nineteenth century texts, while transcending the tendentious arguments of "vulgar Marxism," seemed also to have transcended its revolutionary spirit and its identification with the op-

[10]Ibid., p. 405.

pressed: "The question irresistibly raised for the Marxist reader of Jameson is simply this: how is a Marxist-Structuralist critique of a minor novel of Balzac to help shake the foundations of capitalism?"[11]

It is hard to know whether or not Jameson was stung by Eagleton's imputation of right-wing deviationism, but in the years since the publication of *The Political Unconscious,* Jameson has become more a cultural than a literary critic, and the "texts" upon which he works are much more likely to be films or buildings than novels or stories. His magisterial book on postmodernism depicts our contemporary world as suffering from a continuous and unresolved crisis in which our cultural representations parody and subvert themselves. The ultimate cause of these cultural and psychological phenomena is what Jameson calls "late capitalism," with its unfathomable bureaucratic web and fragmented social system. The individual today is even more alienated from any vision of supportive community and rewarding work than the nineteenth-century wage-slave of the industrial revolution. In the postindustrial West, factories themselves have often been moved by multinational corporations to developing countries, where wages are low, leaving behind the service industries and the large-scale corporate activities of finance and marketing. At the same time, the traditional Marxist distinction between economic base and cultural superstructure begins to dissolve in late capitalism, as the primary business of the developed world becomes the creation of culture for everyone, via designs for manufactured objects, architectural planning, media programming, and the computer and information systems. In general, Jameson's cultural criticism has continued to explore the political unconscious of artistic representations: the truth behind the false consciousness of ideology that is allegorically expressed in these fictions, and their utopian fantasy rooted in eternal human desire.

JÜRGEN HABERMAS AND PUBLIC DISCOURSE

Unlike Eagleton and Jameson, but like Marx himself, Jürgen Habermas is primarily a social philosopher rather than a literary and cultural critic. He is usually considered the premier thinker of the second generation of the Frankfurt school, whose first generation included Herbert Marcuse, Walter Benjamin, Max Horkheimer, and Habermas's teacher and chief influence, Theodor W. Adorno. Like any good Marxist, however, Habermas's goal has been not merely to extend the cultural critique of the Frankfurt school but to transcend it.

The Frankfurt school had itself been a continuation and transcendence of Marx's philosophy. Whereas Marx had embraced scientific rationalism as an antidote to the religious idealism of Hegel and his followers, by the 1930s capitalism had advanced to the point where science and technology appeared to be simultaneously the means of creating a just society and a major obstacle to social equality. The bureaucratic organizations that needed to produce scientific knowledge and use it for practical ends were producing a society organized from the top down, destructive of all dialogue, while the cult of scientific fact and the notion of a split between "hard" facts

[11]Terry Eagleton, "The Idealism of American Criticism." Review of *The Political Unconscious,* by Fredric Jameson. *New Left Review* 127 (1981): 65.

and "soft" values stifled any communal discussion of social justice. The Frankfurt school rejected the scientistic Marxism coming out of the Soviet Union in favor of an analysis of the social formation and mentalities produced by capitalism, eventuating in, as one can see in the work of Adorno, a grimly pessimistic critique in which artists like Kafka and Schönberg were seen as protesting — by means of literary or musical form — the inhuman societies developing around them.

Habermas saw Adorno's critique of culture as a blind alley leading only to alienation and quietism. He framed the need to heal the split between socioeconomic study and cultural critique, between fact and value, as a problem of the breakdown of public discourse, seeking a way to recuperate the Enlightenment ideal of a just and rational society within the context of late capitalism. For Habermas, the aim of society must be "the end of coercion and the attainment of autonomy through reason, the end of alienation through a consensual harmony of interests, and the end of injustice and poverty through the rational administration of justice."[12] As one might expect given his historical position as a philosopher, writing at a time when rhetoric and discourse are seen as the constituents of reality rather than as verbal veils of deeper material or spiritual truths, Habermas envisions progress as coming not just from material and organizational reform, but from a purification of public discourse.

Habermas's analysis of discourse owes a great deal to Wittgenstein, to Gadamer, and to the speech-act theorists,[13] whose ideas he adopted and against whom he reacted. His theory presumes that social dialogue occurs within a framework that makes certain idealizing assumptions (he calls them "validity claims") about real-life utterances: that what we say is understandable, that its objective propositional content is true, that the speaker is sincere, and that it is appropriate for the speaker to be performing the speech-act. Obviously these assumptions do not hold for all, or even most, real-life utterances, so that we often need to problematize one or another of these validity claims, questioning the speaker's truth or sincerity, say, and rising to a meta-level of discourse in our critique. Nonetheless, conversation and dialogue and the attainment of any consensus needed for action depend on these validity claims.[14] Genuine consensus can be built provided all the participants in a dialogue

[12]Jane Braaten, *Habermas's Critical Theory of Society* (Albany: State University of New York Press, 1991), p. 111.

[13]Speech-act theory relates to the branch of linguistics called "pragmatics," which operates above the level of the sentence to analyze the ways sentences are construed as part of a social situation. One pioneering volume is that of philosopher of language J. L. Austin (1921–60), whose *How to Do Things with Words* (Cambridge: Harvard University Press, 1962) contrasts "constative" language, which states facts (e.g., "The distance between New York and Chicago is 713 miles"), with "performative" language by which people promise, or threaten, or perform other acts (e.g., "I sentence you to be hanged by the neck until you are dead"). Austin suggests that "felicity conditions" need to be observed for performatives: The last example will not "work" as a performative unless the speaker is a judge, the recipient of the utterance is a person who has been found guilty of a capital crime, the scene is a courtroom, and so on. Ultimately Austin was dissatisfied with the distinction between constatives and performatives, and speech-act theory gradually shifted to distinguishing between "locutionary," "illocutionary," and "perlocutionary" speech-acts (in the first one would "say" something; in the second "argue" something to someone; in the third "convince" someone of something). See also John R. Searle, *Speech Acts* (Cambridge, Cambridge University Press, 1969).

[14]Thomas McCarthy, Translator's Introduction to Jürgen Habermas, *Legitimation Crisis* (Boston: Beacon, 1975), p. xiv.

have a fair share in the discourse, are allowed freely to assert or question any claim that is made, and are able to express attitudes, feelings, and intentions, without being dominated, materially or ideologically, by another speaker. In such a dialogue people attempt to persuade one another not by authority or by false claims of scientific rationality but by the force of the better argument. Habermas knows that such a situation is counterfactual, that contemporary society throws up hundreds of barriers to the production of what he calls "legitimate" consensus, but he holds up the ideal of a society in which the actors attempt to persuade each other on rational grounds. The conditions he envisions as a prerequisite for the attainment of such a consensus of intersubjective truth are the conditions of the just society of which Marx and Adorno dreamed.

Given his melioristic general program for social discourse and social organization, it is clear that neither postmodernism nor poststructural thought has any positive place in Habermas's thought. The fragmented bricolage of postmodernism implicitly presumes that what successive generations each in turn called the "modern" project of progress and enlightenment is over, that the fragmentation of an instrumentalist social system has left modern humanity in an alienation beyond remedy. And the anarchistic rhetoric of Jacques Derrida and Michel Foucault, derived from Heidegger and the later Nietzsche, is equally poisonous to Habermas's project, as it denies both the "validity claims" needed for communicative competence and the possibility of the social conditions needed for legitimate consensus. The selection from Habermas's *The Philosophical Discourse of Modernity* (1985) reprinted here, "Excursus on Leveling the Genre Distinction between Philosophy and Literature," argues that the poststructuralist versions of rhetoric held by Richard Rorty and Derrida essentially cheat, in that they employ logic and reason against the values of logic and reason, use the terms of metaphysics in order to destroy metaphysics, and require our consent to reasoned argument without recuperating any new mode of consensus discourse at some meta-level of reason. In a later chapter of the book, Habermas explores equally basic contradictions within the thought of Foucault, a philosopher whose empirical investigations of madness, disease, and criminal behavior operate within a system that denies empiricism, whose rebarbative truths operate within a system that portrays truth as merely a function of power. Habermas's ultimate point is that "the radical critique of reason exacts a high price for taking leave of modernity" (336). It leaves us with a hopeless solipsism, when what is needed for taking on the alienating conditions of late capitalism and the power of the interventionist state is a discourse that can build toward legitimate consensus, not to "pass beyond man and humanism" as Derrida put it (see p. 889), but to redeem the as-yet unrealized ideal of a liberal society.

Selected Bibliography

Adorno, Theodor. *Prisms: Cultural Criticism and Society.* 1955; London: Neville Spearman, 1967.

———. *Minima Moralia: Reflections from Damaged Life,* trans. E. F. Jephcott. New York: Norton, 1985.

———. *Notes to Literature,* trans. Shierry W. Nicholsen. New York: Columbia University Press, 1991.
———. *Aesthetic Theory,* trans. Rolf Tiedemann. Minneapolis: University of Minnesota Press, 1996.
Althusser, Louis. *For Marx.* New York: Pantheon, 1969.
———. *Lenin and Philosophy and Other Essays.* London: New Left Books, 1971.
———, and Etienne Balibar. *Reading Capital.* New York: Pantheon, 1970.
Bakhtin, Mikhail. *Between Phenomenology and Marxism.* New York: Cambridge University Press, 1995.
Barker, Francis, Peter Hulme, and Margaret Iverson, eds. *The Uses of History: Marxism, Postmodernism and the Renaissance.* New York: St. Martin's Press, 1991.
Benjamin, Walter. *Illuminations.* New York: Harcourt Brace & World, 1968.
———. *Charles Baudelaire: A Lyric Poet in the Era of High Capitalism.* London: New Left Books, 1973.
———. *Reflections: Essays, Aphorisms, Autobiographical Writings,* ed. Peter Demetz. New York: Harcourt Brace Jovanovich, 1978.
———. *Correspondence of Walter Benjamin.* Chicago: University of Chicago Press, 1994.
Bennett, Tony. *Formalism and Marxism.* London: Methuen, 1979.
Caudwell, Christopher. *Illusion and Reality: A Study of the Sources of Poetry.* New York: International Publishers, 1963.
Cohen, Naomi. *Feminism and Marxism in the Nineties: A Revolutionary Women's Agenda.* New York: World View Forum, 1993.
Coward, Rosemary, and John Ellis. *Language and Materialism: Developments in Semiology and the Theory of the Subject.* London: Routledge and Kegan Paul, 1977.
Demetz, Peter. *Marx, Engels and the Poets: Origins of Marxist Literary Criticism.* Chicago: University of Chicago Press, 1967.
Dowling, William. *Jameson, Althusser, Marx: An Introduction to the Political Unconscious.* Ithaca: Cornell University Press, 1984.
Eagleton, Terry. *Criticism and Ideology: A Study in Marxist Literary Theory.* London: New Left Books, 1976.
———. *Marxism and Literary Criticism.* Berkeley: University of California Press, 1976.
———. *Criticism and Ideology: A Study in Marxist Theory.* New York: Norton, 1978.
———. *Saint Oscar.* London: Faber and Faber, 1990.
———. *The Ideology of the Aesthetic.* London: Blackwell, 1994.
———. *Ideology.* White Plains: Longman Publishing Group, 1995.
———. *Heathcliff and the Great Hunger.* New York: Norton, 1995.
———. *The Illusions of Postmodernism.* London: Blackwell, 1996.
Fekete, John. *The Critical Twilight.* Boston: Routledge and Kegan Paul, 1976.
Fokkema, Douwe W., and Elrud Ibsch. *Theories of Literature in the Twentieth Century: Structuralism, Marxism, Aesthetics of Reception, Semiotics,* 2nd ed. New York: St. Martin's Press, 1995.
Foley, Barbara. *Telling the Truth: The Theory and Practice of Documentary Fiction.* Ithaca: Cornell University Press, 1986.
Frow, John. *Marxism and Literary History.* Ithaca: Cornell University Press, 1986.
Goldmann, Lucien. *The Hidden God: A Study of the Tragic Vision in the Pensées of Pascal and the Tragedies of Racine.* 1955; London: Routledge and Kegan Paul, 1964.
———. "Marxist Criticism." In *The Philosophy of the Enlightenment.* Cambridge: MIT Press, 1973, pp. 86–97.
Gramsci, Antonio. *The Modern Prince and Other Writings.* London: Lawrence and Wishart, 1957.

———. *Selections from the Prison Notebooks.* London: Lawrence and Wishart, 1971.
Habermas, Jürgen. *The Philosophical Discourse of Modernity: Twelve Lectures,* trans. Frederick G. Lawrence. Cambridge: MIT Press, 1990.
———. *Jürgen Habermas on Society and Politics: A Reader,* trans. Steven Seidman. Boston: Beacon Press, 1989.
———. *The Structural Transformation of the Public Sphere: An Inquiry into a Category of Bourgeois Society.* Cambridge: MIT Press, 1989.
———. *The Theory of Communicative Action, Vol. I: Reason and the Rationalization of Society,* trans. Thomas McCarthy. Boston: Beacon Press, 1985.
———. *The Theory of Communicative Action, Vol. II: Lifeworld and System: A Critique of Functionalist Reason,* trans. Thomas McCarthy. Boston: Beacon Press, 1989.
Hawthorn, Jeremy. *Cunning Passages: New Historicism, Cultural Materialism, and Marxism in the Contemporary Literary Debate.* New York: Routledge, 1996.
Hicks, Granville. *The Great Tradition: An Interpretation of American Literature Since the Civil War.* 1933; Chicago: Quadrangle Books, 1969.
Hohendahl, Peter Uwe. "Prolegomena to a History of Literary Criticism." *New German Critique* 11 (1977): 151–63.
Jameson, Fredric. *Marxism and Form: Twentieth Century Dialectical Theories of Literature.* Princeton: Princeton University Press, 1971.
———. *The Prison-House of Language: A Critical Account of Structuralism and Russian Formalism.* Princeton: Princeton University Press, 1972.
———. *The Political Unconscious: Studies in the Ideology of Form.* Ithaca: Cornell University Press, 1981.
———. *Late Marxism: Adorno or the Persistence of the Dialectic.* New York: Norton, 1990.
———. *Postmodernism, or, the Cultural Logic of Late Capitalism.* Durham, NC: Duke University Press, 1991.
———. *The Seeds of Time.* New York: Columbia University Press, 1996.
Kellner, Douglas. *Critical Theory, Marxism, and Modernity.* Baltimore: Johns Hopkins University Press, 1989.
Kettle, Arnold. *Introduction to the English Novel.* 2 vols. 1951; New York: Harper and Row, 1960.
Lifshitz, Mikail. *The Philosophy of Art of Karl Marx.* 1933; London: Pluto Press, 1973.
Lukács, Georg. *Realism in Our Time: Literature and the Class Struggle.* 1957; New York: Harper and Row, 1964.
———. *The Historical Novel.* London: Merlin Press, 1962.
———. *The Theory of the Novel: A Historico-Philosophical Essay on the Forms of Great Epic Literature.* 1920; London, Merlin Press, 1971.
Macherey, Pierre. *A Theory of Literary Production.* 1966; Boston: Routledge and Kegan Paul, 1978.
Marcuse, Herbert. *The Aesthetic Dimension: Toward a Critique of Marxist Aesthetics.* Boston: Beacon Press, 1978.
Marx, Karl, and Friedrich Engels. *Marx and Engels on Literature and Art.* St. Louis: Telos Press, 1973.
Morris, William. *On Art and Socialism.* London: Lehmann, 1947.
Ohmann, Richard. *English in America: A Radical View of the Profession.* New York: Oxford University Press, 1976.
Orwell, George. *Critical Essays.* London: Secker and Warberg, 1946.
Robinson, Lillian S. *Sex, Class, and Culture.* Bloomington: Indiana University Press, 1978.

Rose, Gillian. *The "Melancholy Science": An Introduction to the Thought of Theodor W. Adorno.* London: Macmillan, 1978.
Sartre, Jean-Paul. *What Is Literature?* New York: Harper and Row, 1965.
———. *Between Existentialism and Marxism.* New York: Pantheon, 1974.
Sherman, Howard J. *Reinventing Marxism.* Baltimore: Johns Hopkins University Press, 1995.
Smith, Steven B. *Reading Althusser.* Ithaca: Cornell University Press, 1984.
Trotsky, Leon. *Literature and Revolution.* 1924; Ann Arbor: University of Michigan Press, 1960.
Weimann, Robert. *Structure and Society in Literary History.* Charlottesville: University Press of Virginia, 1976.
Williams, Raymond. *Culture and Society, 1780–1950.* London: Chatto and Windus, 1958.
———. *The Country and the City.* New York: Oxford University Press, 1973.
———. *Marxism and Literature.* New York: Oxford University Press, 1977.
———. *The Sociology of Culture.* Chicago: University of Chicago Press, 1995.
Wilson, Edmund. *Axel's Castle.* 1931; New York: Scribner's, 1961.
———. *The Triple Thinkers.* 1938; New York: Oxford University Press, 1948.

Walter Benjamin

1892–1940

It is said that Walter Benjamin, one of the most influential cultural theorists in the Marxist tradition, did not look into Marx's writings until the final decade of his tragically abbreviated life. Benjamin was born in Berlin to a wealthy Jewish family. His studies at Freiburg, Munich, Berlin, and Berne resulted in a doctorate in 1919, but his dissertation on German tragic drama — a brilliant but unorthodox performance completed when he was thirty-three — was rejected by the University of Frankfurt. With a university career closed to him, Benjamin appears to have turned to journalism. From 1925 to 1933 Benjamin made his living mainly with his pen and became friendly with a number of left-wing intellectuals, including Bertolt Brecht. His visit to Moscow in the winter of 1926–27 affirmed his sympathy with the Soviet state, although he never joined the Communist party. When the Nazi seizure of power drove him from Berlin — he emigrated to Paris in 1933 — commissions from the Frankfurt Institute for Social Research enabled him to eke out a living. During these years of exile, he wrote some of his most admired work, including "The Work of Art in the Age of Mechanical Reproduction" (1936). In 1940, Benjamin committed suicide in Port Bou, Spain, in the mistaken belief that his plan to emigrate to America had been thwarted and that he would have to return to Nazi-occupied France. The translation of "The Work of Art in the Age of Mechanical Reproduction" is from the collection Illuminations *(1969).*

The Work of Art in the Age of Mechanical Reproduction

Our fine arts were developed, their types and uses were established, in times very different from the present, by men whose power of action upon things was insignificant in comparison with ours. But the amazing growth of our techniques, the adaptability and precision they have attained, the ideas and habits they are creating, make it a certainty that profound changes are impending in the ancient craft of the Beautiful. In all the arts there is a physical component which can no longer be considered or treated as it used to be, which cannot remain unaffected by our modern knowledge and power. For the last twenty years neither matter nor space nor time has been what it was from time immemorial. We must expect great innovations to transform the entire technique of the arts, thereby affecting artistic invention itself and perhaps even bringing about an amazing change in our very notion of art.[1]

— PAUL VALÉRY, *Pièces sur l'art*, "La Conquète de l'ubiquité," Paris

PREFACE

When Marx undertook his critique of the capitalistic mode of production, this mode was in its infancy. Marx directed his efforts in such a way as to give them prognostic value. He went back to the basic conditions underlying capitalistic production and through his presentation showed what could be expected of capitalism in the future. The result was that one could expect it not only to exploit the proletariat with increasing intensity, but ultimately to create conditions which would make it possible to abolish capitalism itself.

The transformation of the superstructure, which takes place far more slowly than that of the substructure, has taken more than half a century to manifest in all areas of culture the change in the conditions of production. Only today can it be indicated what form this has taken. Certain prognostic requirements should be met by these statements. However, theses about the art of the proletariat after its assumption of power or about the art of a classless society would have less bearing on these demands than theses about the developmental tendencies of art under present conditions of production. Their dialectic is no less noticeable in the superstructure than in the economy. It would therefore be wrong to underestimate the value of such theses as a weapon. They brush aside a number of outmoded concepts, such as creativity and genius, eternal value and mystery — concepts whose uncontrolled (and at present almost uncontrollable) application would lead to a processing of data in the Fascist sense. The concepts which are introduced into the theory of art in what follows differ from the more familiar terms in that they are completely useless for the purposes of Fascism. They are, on the other hand, useful for the formulation of revolutionary demands in the politics of art.

I

In principle a work of art has always been reproducible. Manmade artifacts could always be imitated by men. Replicas were made by pupils in practice of their craft, by masters for diffusing their works, and, finally, by third parties in the pursuit of gain. Mechanical reproduction of a work of art, however, represents something new. Historically, it advanced intermittently and in leaps at long intervals, but with accelerated intensity. The Greeks knew only two procedures of technically reproducing works of art: founding and stamping. Bronzes, terra cottas, and coins were the only art works which they could produce in quantity. All others were unique and could not be mechanically reproduced. With the woodcut, graphic art became mechanically reproducible for the first time, long before script became reproducible by print. The enormous changes which printing, the mechanical repro-

Translated by Harry Zohn.

[1]Quoted from Paul Valéry, "The Conquest of Ubiquity," *Aesthetics*, trans. Ralph Manheim (New York: Pantheon Books, Bollingen Series, 1964), p. 225. [Tr.]

duction of writing, has brought about in literature are a familiar story. However, within the phenomenon which we are here examining from the perspective of world history, print is merely a special, though particularly important, case. During the Middle Ages engraving and etching were added to the woodcut; at the beginning of the nineteenth century lithography made its appearance.

With lithography the technique of reproduction reached an essentially new stage. This much more direct process was distinguished by the tracing of the design of a stone rather than its incision on a block of wood or its etching on a copperplate and permitted graphic art for the first time to put its products on the market, not only in large numbers as hitherto, but also in daily changing forms. Lithography enabled graphic art to illustrate everyday life, and it began to keep pace with printing. But only a few decades after its invention, lithography was surpassed by photography. For the first time in the process of pictorial reproduction, photography freed the hand of the most important artistic functions which henceforth devolved only upon the eye looking into a lens. Since the eye perceives more swiftly than the hand can draw, the process of pictorial reproduction was accelerated so enormously that it could keep pace with speech. A film operator shooting a scene in the studio captures the images at the speed of an actor's speech. Just as lithography virtually implied the illustrated newspaper, so did photography foreshadow the sound film. The technical reproduction of sound was tackled at the end of the last century. These convergent endeavors made predictable a situation which Paul Valéry pointed up in this sentence: "Just as water, gas, and electricity are brought into our houses from far off to satisfy our needs in response to a minimal effort, so we shall be supplied with visual or auditory images, which will appear and disappear at a simple movement of the hand, hardly more than a sign." Around 1900 technical reproduction had reached a standard that not only permitted it to reproduce all transmitted works of art and thus to cause the most profound change in their impact upon the public; it also had captured a place of its own among the artistic processes. For the study of this standard nothing is more revealing than the nature of the repercussions that these two different manifestations — the reproduction of works of art and the art of the film — have had on art in its traditional form.

II

Even the most perfect reproduction of a work of art is lacking in one element: its presence in time and space, its unique existence at the place where it happens to be. This unique existence of the work of art determined the history to which it was subject throughout the time of its existence. This includes the changes which it may have suffered in physical condition over the years as well as the various changes in its ownership.[2] The traces of the first can be revealed only by chemical or physical analyses which it is impossible to perform on a reproduction; changes of ownership are subject to a tradition which must be traced from the situation of the original.

The presence of the original is the prerequisite of the concept of authenticity. Chemical analyses of the patina of a bronze can help to establish this, as does the proof that a given manuscript of the Middle Ages stems from an archive of the fifteenth century. The whole sphere of authenticity is outside technical — and, of course, not only technical — reproducibility.[3] Confronted with its manual reproduction, which was usually branded as a forgery, the original preserved all its authority; not so *vis à vis* technical reproduction. The reason is twofold. First, process reproduction is more independent of the original than manual re-

[2]Of course, the history of a work of art encompasses more than this. The history of the Mona Lisa, for instance, encompasses the kind and number of its copies made in the seventeenth, eighteenth, and nineteenth centuries. [Au.]

[3]Precisely because authenticity is not reproducible, the intensive penetration of certain (mechanical) processes of reproduction was instrumental in differentiating and grading authenticity. To develop such differentiations was an important function to the trade in works of art. The invention of the woodcut may be said to have struck at the root of the quality of authenticity even before its late flowering. To be sure, at the time of its origin a medieval picture of the Madonna could not yet be said to be "authentic." It became "authentic" only during the succeeding centuries and perhaps most strikingly so during the last one. [Au.]

production. For example, in photography, process reproduction can bring out those aspects of the original that are unattainable to the naked eye yet accessible to the lens, which is adjustable and chooses its angle at will. And photographic reproduction, with the aid of certain processes, such as enlargement or slow motion, can capture images which escape natural vision. Secondly, technical reproduction can put the copy of the original into situations which would be out of reach for the original itself. Above all, it enables the original to meet the beholder halfway, be it in the form of a photograph or a phonograph record. The cathedral leaves its locale to be received in the studio of a lover of art; the choral production, performed in an auditorium or in the open air, resounds in the drawing room.

The situations into which the product of mechanical reproduction can be brought may not touch the actual work of art, yet the quality of its presence is always depreciated. This holds not only for the art work but also, for instance, for a landscape which passes in review before the spectator in a movie. In the case of the art object, a most sensitive nucleus — namely, its authenticity — is interfered with whereas no natural object is vulnerable on that score. The authenticity of a thing is the essence of all that is transmissible from its beginning, ranging from its substantive duration to its testimony to the history which it has experienced. Since the historical testimony rests on the authenticity, the former too, is jeopardized by reproduction when substantive duration ceases to matter. And what is really jeopardized when the historical testimony is affected is the authority of the object.[4]

One might subsume the eliminated element in the term "aura" and go on to say: that which withers in the age of mechanical reproduction is the aura of the work of art. This is a symptomatic process whose significance points beyond the realm of art. One might generalize by saying: the technique of reproduction detaches the reproduced object from the domain of tradition. By making many reproductions it substitutes a plurality of copies for a unique existence. And in permitting the reproduction to meet the beholder or listener in his own particular situation, it reactivates the object reproduced. These two processes lead to a tremendous shattering of tradition which is the obverse of the contemporary crisis and renewal of mankind. Both processes are intimately connected with the contemporary mass movements. Their most powerful agent is the film. Its social significance, particularly in its most positive form, is inconceivable without its destructive, cathartic aspect, that is, the liquidation of the traditional value of the cultural heritage. This phenomenon is most palpable in the great historical films. It extends to ever new positions. In 1927 Abel Gance exclaimed enthusiastically: "Shakespeare, Rembrandt, Beethoven will make films . . . all legends, all mythologies and all myths, all founders of religion, and the very religions . . . await their exposed resurrection, and the heroes crowd each other at the gate."[5] Presumably without intending it, he issued an invitation to a far-reaching liquidation.

III

During long periods of history, the mode of human sense perception changes with humanity's entire mode of existence. The manner in which human sense perception is organized, the medium in which it is accomplished, is determined not only by nature but by historical circumstances as well. The fifth century, with its great shifts of population, saw the birth of the late Roman art industry and the Vienna Genesis, and there developed not only an art different from that of antiquity but also a new kind of perception. The scholars of the Viennese school, Riegl and Wickhoff, who resisted the weight of classical tradition under which these later art forms had been buried, were the first to draw conclusions from them concerning the organization of perception at the time. However far-reaching their insight, these scholars limited them-

[4]The poorest provincial staging of *Faust* is superior to a Faust film in that, ideally, it competes with the first performance at Weimar. Before the screen it is unprofitable to remember traditional contents which might come to mind before the stage — for instance, that Goethe's friend Johann Heinrich Merck is hidden in Mephisto, and the like. [Au.]

[5]Abel Gance, "Le Temps de l'image est venu," *L'Art Cinématographique* 2 (Paris, 1927): 94–95. [Tr.] Gance was the director of the epic film *Napoleon* (1927). [Ed.]

selves to showing the significant, formal hallmark which characterized perception in late Roman times. They did not attempt — and, perhaps, saw no way — to show the social transformations expressed by these changes of perception. The conditions for an analogous insight are more favorable in the present. And if changes in the medium of contemporary perception can be comprehended as decay of the aura, it is possible to show its social causes.

The concept of aura which was proposed above with reference to historical objects may usefully be illustrated with reference to the aura of natural ones. We define the aura of the latter as the unique phenomenon of a distance, however close it may be. If, while resting on a summer afternoon, you follow with your eyes a mountain range on the horizon or a branch which casts its shadows over you, you experience the aura of those mountains, of that branch. This image makes it easy to comprehend the social bases of the contemporary decay of the aura. It rests on two circumstances, both of which are related to the increasing significance of the masses in contemporary life. Namely, the desire of contemporary masses to bring things "closer" spatially and humanly, which is just as ardent as their bent toward overcoming the uniqueness of every reality by accepting its reproduction.[6] Every day the urge grows stronger to get hold of an object at very close range by way of its likeness, its reproduction. Unmistakably, reproduction as offered by picture magazines and newsreels differs from the image seen by the unarmed eye. Uniqueness and permanence are as closely linked in the latter as are transitoriness and reproducibility in the former. To pry an object from its shell, to destroy its aura, is the mark of a perception whose "sense of the universal equality of things" has increased to such a degree that it extracts it even from a unique object by means of reproduction. Thus is manifested in the field of perception what in the theoretical sphere is noticeable in the increasing importance of statistics. The adjustment of reality to the masses and of the masses to reality is a process of unlimited scope, as much for thinking as for perception.

[6]To satisfy the human interest of the masses may mean to have one's social function removed from the field of vision. Nothing guarantees that a portraitist of today, when painting a famous surgeon at the breakfast table in the midst of his family, depicts his social function more precisely than a painter of the seventeenth century who portrayed his medical doctors as representing this profession, like Rembrandt in his *Anatomy Lesson.* [Au.]

IV

The uniqueness of a work of art is inseparable from its being imbedded in the fabric of tradition. This tradition itself is thoroughly alive and extremely changeable. An ancient statue of Venus, for example, stood in a different traditional context with the Greeks, who made it an object of veneration, than with the clerics of the Middle Ages, who viewed it as an ominous idol. Both of them, however, were equally confronted with its uniqueness, that is, its aura. Originally the contextual integration of art in tradition found its expression in the cult. We know that the earliest art works originated in the service of a ritual — first the magical, then the religious kind. It is significant that the existence of the work of art with reference to its aura is never entirely separated from its ritual function.[7] In other words, the unique value of the "authentic" work of art has its basis in ritual, the location of its original use value. This ritualistic basis, however remote, is still recognizable as secularized ritual even in the most profane forms of the cult of beauty.[8] The secular

[7]The definition of the aura as a "unique phenomenon of a distance however close it may be" represents nothing but the formulation of the cult value of the work of art in categories of space and time perception. Distance is the opposite of closeness. The essentially distant object is the unapproachable one. Unapproachability is indeed a major quality of the cult image. True to its nature, it remains "distant, however close it may be." The closeness which one may gain from its subject matter does not impair the distance which it retains in its appearance. [Au.]

[8]To the extent to which the cult value of the painting is secularized, the ideas of its fundamental uniqueness lose distinctness. In the imagination of the beholder the uniqueness of the phenomena which hold sway in the cult image is more and more displaced by the empirical uniqueness of the creator or of his creative achievement. To be sure, never completely so; the concept of authenticity always transcends mere genuineness. (This is particularly apparent in the collector who always retains some traces of the fetishist and who, by owning the work of art, shares in its ritual power.) Nevertheless,

cult of beauty, developed during the Renaissance and prevailing for three centuries, clearly showed that ritualistic basis in its decline and the first deep crisis which befell it. With the advent of the first truly revolutionary means of reproduction, photography, simultaneously with the rise of socialism, art sensed the approaching crisis which has become evident a century later. At the time, art reacted with the doctrine of *l'art pour l'art,*[9] that is, with a theology of art. This gave rise to what might be called a negative theology in the form of the idea of "pure" art, which not only denied any social function of art but also any categorizing by subject matter. (In poetry, Mallarmé was the first to take this position.)

An analysis of art in the age of mechanical reproduction must do justice to these relationships, for they lead us to an all-important insight: for the first time in world history, mechanical reproduction emancipates the work of art from its parasitical dependence on ritual. To an ever greater degree the work of art reproduced becomes the work of art designed for reproducibility.[10] From a photographic negative, for example, one can make any number of prints; to ask for the "authentic" print makes no sense. But the instant the criterion of authenticity ceases to be applicable to artistic production, the total function of art is reversed. Instead of being based on ritual, it begins to be based on another practice — politics.

V

Works of art are received and valued on different planes. Two polar types stand out: with one, the accent is on the cult value; with the other, on the exhibition value of the work.[11] Artistic produc-

---

the function of the concept of authenticity remains determinate in the evaluation of art; with the secularization of art, authenticity displaces the cult value of the work. [Au.]

[9]Art for art's sake. [Ed.]

[10]In the case of films, mechanical reproduction is not, as with literature and painting, an external condition for mass distribution. Mechanical reproduction is inherent in the very technique of film production. This technique not only permits in the most direct way but virtually causes mass distribution. It enforces distribution because the production of a film is so expensive that an individual who, for instance, might afford to buy a painting no longer can afford to buy a film. In 1927 it was calculated that a major film, in order to pay its way, had to reach an audience of nine million. With the sound film, to be sure, a setback in its international distribution occurred at first: audiences became limited by language barriers. This coincided with the Fascist emphasis on national interests. It is more important to focus on this connection with Fascism than on this setback, which was soon minimized by synchronization. The simultaneity of both phenomena is attributable to the depression. The same disturbances which, on a larger scale, led to an attempt to maintain the existing property structure by sheer force led the endangered film capital to speed up the development of the sound film. The introduction of the sound film brought about a temporary relief, not only because it again brought the masses into the theaters but also because it merged new capital from the electrical industry with that of the film industry. Thus, viewed from the outside, the sound film promoted national interests, but seen from the inside it helped to internationalize film production even more than previously. [Au.]

[11]This polarity cannot come into its own in the aesthetics of Idealism. Its idea of beauty comprises these polar opposites without differentiating between them and consequently excludes their polarity. Yet in Hegel this polarity announces itself as clearly as possible within the limits of Idealism. We quote from his *Philosophy of History:*

> Images were known of old. Piety at an early time required them for worship, but it could do without *beautiful* images. These might even be disturbing. In every beautiful painting there is also something nonspiritual, merely external, but its spirit speaks to man through its beauty. Worshipping, conversely, is concerned with the work as an object, for it is but a spiritless stupor of the soul. . . . Fine art has arisen . . . in the church . . . , although it has already gone beyond its principle as art.

Likewise, the following passage from *The Philosophy of Fine Art* indicates that Hegel sensed a problem here.

> We are beyond the stage of reverence for works of art as divine and objects deserving our worship. The impression they produce is one of a more reflective kind, and the emotions they arouse require a higher test. . . . — G. W. F. Hegel, *The Philosophy of Fine Arts,* trans., with notes, by F. P. B. Osmaston, vol. I (London, 1920), p. 12.

The transition from the first kind of artistic reception to the second characterizes the history of artistic reception in general. Apart from that, a certain oscillation between these two polar modes of reception can be demonstrated for each work of art. Take the Sistine Madonna. Since Hubert Grimme's research it has been known that the Madonna originally was painted for the purpose of exhibition. Grimme's research was inspired by the question: What is the purpose of the molding in the foreground of the painting which the two cupids lean upon? How, Grimme asked further, did Raphael come to furnish the sky with two draperies? Research proved that the Madonna had been commissioned for the public tion begins with ceremonial objects destined to serve in a cult. One may assume that what mattered was their existence, not their being on view. The elk portrayed by the man of the Stone Age on the walls of his cave was an instrument of magic. He did expose it to his fellow men, but in the main it was meant for the spirits. Today the cult value would seem to demand that the work of art remain hidden. Certain statues of gods are accessible only to the priest in the cella;[12] certain Madonnas remain covered nearly all year round; certain sculptures on medieval cathedrals are invisible to the spectator on ground level. With the emancipation of the various art practices from ritual go increasing opportunities for the exhibition of their products. It is easier to exhibit a portrait bust that can be sent here and there than to exhibit the statue of divinity that has its fixed place in the interior of a temple. The same holds for the painting as against the mosaic or fresco that preceded it. And even though the public presentability of a mass originally may have been just as great as that of a symphony, the latter originated at the moment when its public presentability promised to surpass that of the mass.

With the different methods of technical reproduction of a work of art, its fitness for exhibition increased to such an extent that the quantitative shift between its two poles turned into a qualitative transformation of its nature. This is comparable to the situation of the work of art in prehistoric times when, by the absolute emphasis on its cult value, it was, first and foremost, an instrument of magic. Only later did it come to be recognized as a work of art. In the same way today, by the absolute emphasis on its exhibition value the work of art becomes a creation with entirely new functions, among which the one we are conscious of, the artistic function, later may be recognized as incidental.[13] This much is certain: today photography and the film are the most serviceable exemplifications of this new function.

VI

In photography, exhibition value begins to displace cult value all along the line. But cult value does not give way without resistance. It retires into an ultimate retrenchment: the human countenance. It is no accident that the portrait was the focal point of early photography. The cult of remembrance of loved ones, absent or dead, offers a last refuge for the cult value of the picture. For the last time the aura emanates from the early photographs in the fleeting expression of a human face. This is what constitutes their melancholy, incomparable beauty. But as man withdraws from the photographic image, the exhibition value for the first time shows its superiority to the ritual value. To have pinpointed this new stage constitutes the incomparable significance of Atget,[14] who, around 1900, took photographs of deserted Paris streets. It has quite justly been said of him that he photographed them like scenes of

lying-in-state of Pope Sixtus. The Popes lay in state in a certain side chapel of St. Peter's. On that occasion Raphael's picture had been fastened in a nichelike background of the chapel, supported by the coffin. In this picture Raphael portrays the Madonna approaching the papal coffin in clouds from the background of the niche, which was demarcated by green drapes. At the obsequies of Sixtus a preeminent exhibition value of Raphael's picture was taken advantage of. Some time later it was placed on the high altar in the church of the Black Friars at Piacenza. The reason for this exile is to be found in the Roman rites which forbid the use of paintings exhibited at obsequies as cult objects on the high altar. This regulation devalued Raphael's picture to some degree. In order to obtain an adequate price nevertheless, the Papal See resolved to add to the bargain the tacit toleration of the picture above the high altar. To avoid attention the picture was given to the monks of the far-off provincial town. [Au.]

[12]Cell (prison or monastic). [Ed.]

[13]Bertolt Brecht, on a different level, engaged in analogous reflections: "If the concept of 'work of art' can no longer be applied to the thing that emerges once the work is transformed into a commodity, we have to eliminate this concept with cautious care but without fear, lest we liquidate the function of the very thing as well. For it has to go through this phase without mental reservation, and not as noncommittal deviation from the straight path; rather, what happens here with the work of art will change it fundamentally and erase its past to such an extent that should the old concept be taken up again — and it will, why not? — it will no longer stir any memory of the thing it once designated." [Au.]

[14]Jean-Eugène-August Atget (1857–1927), Parisian photographer. [Ed.]

crime. The scene of a crime, too, is deserted; it is photographed for the purpose of establishing evidence. With Atget, photographs become standard evidence for historical occurrences, and acquire a hidden political significance. They demand a specific kind of approach; free-floating contemplation is not appropriate to them. They stir the viewer; he feels challenged by them in a new way. At the same time picture magazines begin to put up signposts for him, right ones or wrong ones, no matter. For the first time, captions have become obligatory. And it is clear that they have an altogether different character than the title of a painting. The directives which the captions give to those looking at pictures in illustrated magazines soon become even more explicit and more imperative in the film where the meaning of each single picture appears to be prescribed by the sequence of all preceding ones.

VII

The nineteenth-century dispute as to the artistic value of painting versus photography today seems devious and confused. This does not diminish its importance, however; if anything, it underlines it. The dispute was, in fact, the symptom of a historical transformation the universal impact of which was not realized by either of the rivals. When the age of mechanical reproduction separated art from its basis in cult, the semblance of its autonomy disappeared forever. The resulting change in the function of art transcended the perspective of the century; for a long time it even escaped that of the twentieth century, which experienced the development of the film.

Earlier much futile thought had been devoted to the question of whether photography is an art. The primary question — whether the very invention of photograph had not transformed the entire nature of art — was not raised. Soon the film theoreticians asked the same ill-considered question with regard to the film. But the difficulties which photography caused traditional aesthetics were mere child's play as compared to those raised by the film. Whence the insensitive and forced character of early theories of the film. Abel Gance, for instance, compares the film with hieroglyphs: "Here, by a remarkable regression, we have come back to the level of expression of the Egyptians. . . . Pictorial language has not yet matured because our eyes have not yet adjusted to it. There is as yet insufficient respect for, insufficient cult of, what it expresses."[15] Or, in the words of Séverin-Mars: "What art has been granted a dream more poetical and more real at the same time! Approached in this fashion the film might represent an incomparable means of expression. Only the most high-minded persons, in the most perfect and mysterious moments of their lives, should be allowed to enter its ambience."[16] Alexandre Arnoux concludes his fantasy about the silent film with the question: "Do not all the bold descriptions we have given amount to the definition of prayer?"[17] It is instructive to note how their desire to class the film among the "arts" forces these theoreticians to read ritual elements into it — with a striking lack of discretion. Yet when these speculations were published, films like *L'Opinion publique* and *The Gold Rush* had already appeared. This, however, did not keep Abel Gance from adducing hieroglyphs for purposes of comparison, nor Séverin-Mars from speaking of the film as one might speak of paintings by Fra Angelico. Characteristically, even today ultrareactionary authors give the film a similar contextual significance — if not an outright sacred one, then at least a supernatural one. Commenting on Max Reinhardt's film version of *A Midsummer Night's Dream,* Werfel states that undoubtedly it was the sterile copying of the exterior world with its streets, interiors, railroad stations, restaurants, motorcars, and beaches which until now had obstructed the elevation of the film to the realm of art. "The film has not yet realized its true meaning, its real possibilities . . . these consist in its unique faculty to express by natural means and with incomparable persuasiveness all that is fairylike, marvelous, supernatural."[18]

[15]Abel Gance, pp. 100–101. [Tr.]

[16]Séverin-Mars, quoted by Abel Gance, p. 100. [Tr.]

[17]Alexandre Arnoux, *Cinéma pris* (1929), p. 28. [Tr.]

[18]Franz Werfel, "Einsommersnachtstraum, Ein Film von Shakespeare und Reinhardt," *Neues Wiener Journal,* cited in *Lu* (November 1935). [Tr.]

VIII

The artistic performance of a stage actor is definitely presented to the public by the actor in person; that of the screen actor, however, is presented by a camera, with a twofold consequence. The camera that presents the performance of the film actor to the public need not respect the performance as an integral whole. Guided by the cameraman, the camera continually changes its position with respect to the performance. The sequence of positional views which the editor composes from the material supplied him constitutes the completed film. It comprises certain factors of movement which are in reality those of the camera, not to mention special camera angles, close-ups, etc. Hence, the performance of the actor is subjected to a series of optical tests. This is the first consequence of the fact that the actor's performance is presented by means of a camera. Also, the film actor lacks the opportunity of the stage actor to adjust to the audience during his performance, since he does not present his performance to the audience in person. This permits the audience to take the position of a critic, without experiencing any personal contact with the actor. The audience's identification with the actor is really an identification with the camera. Consequently the audience takes the position of the camera; its approach is that of testing.[19] This is not the approach to which cult values may be exposed.

[19]"The film . . . provides — or could provide — useful insight into the details of human actions. . . . Character is never used as a source of motivation; the inner life of the persons never supplies the principal cause of the plot and seldom is its main result." (Bertolt Brecht, "Der Dreigroschenprozess," *Versuche*, p. 268.) The expansion of the field of the testable which mechanical equipment brings about for the actor corresponds to the extraordinary expansion of the field of the testable brought about for the individual through economic conditions. Thus, vocational aptitude tests become constantly more important. What matters in these tests are segmental performances of the individual. The film shot and the vocational aptitude test are taken before a committee of experts. The camera director in the studio occupies a place identical with that of the examiner during aptitude tests. [Au.]

IX

For the film, what matters primarily is that the actor represents himself to the public before the camera, rather than representing someone else. One of the first to sense the actor's metamorphosis by this form of testing was Pirandello. Though his remarks on the subject in his novel *Si Gira* were limited to the negative aspects of the question and to the silent film only, this hardly impairs their validity. For in this respect, the sound film did not change anything essential. What matters is that the part is acted not for an audience but for a mechanical contrivance — in the case of the sound film, for two of them. "The film actor," wrote Pirandello, "feels as if in exile — exiled not only from the stage but also from himself. With a vague sense of discomfort he feels inexplicable emptiness: his body loses its corporeality, it evaporates, it is deprived of reality, life, voice, and the noises caused by his moving about, in order to be changed into a mute image, flickering an instant on the screen, then vanishing into silence. . . . The projector will play with his shadow before the public, and he himself must be content to play before the camera."[20] This situation might also be characterized as follows: for the first time — and this is the effect of the film — man has to operate with his whole living person, yet forgoing its aura. For aura is tied to his presence; there can be no replica of it. The aura which, on the stage, emanates from Macbeth, cannot be separated for the spectators from that of the actor. However, the singularity of the shot in the studio is that the camera is substituted for the public. Consequently, the aura that envelops the actor vanishes, and with it the aura of the figure he portrays.

It is not surprising that it should be a dramatist such as Pirandello who, in characterizing the film, inadvertently touches on the very crisis in

[20]Luigi Pirandello, *Si Gira,* quoted by Léon Pierre-Quint, "Signification du cinéma," *L'Art cinématographique,* pp. 14–15. [Tr.]

which we see the theater. Any thorough study proves that there is indeed no greater contrast than that of the stage play to a work of art that is completely subject to or, like the film, founded in, mechanical reproduction. Experts have long recognized that in the film "the greatest effects are almost always obtained by 'acting' as little as possible. . . ." In 1932 Rudolf Arnheim saw "the latest trend . . . in treating the actor as a stage prop chosen for its characteristics and . . . inserted at the proper place."[21] With this idea something else is closely connected. The stage actor identifies himself with the character of his role. The film actor very often is denied this opportunity. His creation is by no means all of a piece; it is composed of many separate performances. Besides certain fortuitous considerations, such as cost of studio, availability of fellow players, décor, etc., there are elementary necessities of equipment that split the actor's work into a series of mountable episodes. In particular, lighting and its installation require the presentation of an event that, on the screen, unfolds as a rapid and unified scene, in a sequence of separate shootings which may take hours at the studio; not to mention more obvious montage. Thus a jump from the window can be shot in the studio as a jump from a scaffold, and the ensuing flight, if need be, can be shot weeks later when outdoor scenes are taken. Far more paradoxical cases can easily be construed. Let us assume that an actor is supposed to be startled by a knock at the door. If his reaction is not satisfactory, the director can resort to an expedient: when the actor happens to be at the studio again he has a shot fired behind him without his being forewarned of it. The frightened reaction can be shot now and be cut into the screen version. Nothing more strikingly shows that art has left the realm of the "beautiful semblance" which, so far, had been taken to be the only sphere where art could thrive.

[21]Rudolf Arnheim, *Film als Kunst* (Berlin, 1932), pp. 176 f. In this context certain seemingly unimportant details in which the film director deviates from stage practices gain in interest. Such is the attempt to let the actor play without makeup, as made among others by Dreyer in his *Jeanne d'Arc*. Dreyer spent months seeking the forty actors who constitute the Inquisitors' tribunal. The search for these actors resembled that for stage properties that are hard to come by. Dreyer made every effort to avoid resemblances of age, build, and physiognomy. If the actor thus becomes a stage property, this latter, on the other hand, frequently functions as actor. At least it is not unusual for the film to assign a role to the stage property. Instead of choosing at random from a great wealth of examples, let us concentrate on a particularly convincing one. A clock that is working will always be a disturbance on the stage. There it cannot be permitted its function of measuring time. Even in a naturalistic play, astronomical time would clash with theatrical time. Under these circumstances, it is highly revealing that the film can, whenever appropriate, use time as measured by a clock. From this more than from many other touches it may clearly be recognized that under certain circumstances each and every prop in a film may assume important functions. From here it is but one step to Pudovkin's statement that "the playing of an actor which is connected with an object and is built around it . . . is always one of the strongest methods of cinematic construction." (W. Pudovkin, *Filmregie und Filmmanuskript* [Berlin, 1928], p. 126.) The film is the first art form capable of demonstrating how matter plays tricks on man. Hence, films can be an excellent means of materialistic representation. [Au.]

X

The feeling of strangeness that overcomes the actor before the camera, as Pirandello describes it, is basically of the same kind as the estrangement felt before one's own image in the mirror. But now the reflected image has become separable, transportable. And where is it transported? Before the public.[22] Never for a moment does the

[22]The change noted here in the method of exhibition caused by mechanical reproduction applies to politics as well. The present crisis of the bourgeois democracies comprises a crisis of the conditions which determine the public presentation of the rulers. Democracies exhibit a member of government directly and personally before the nation's representatives. Parliament is his public. Since the innovations of camera and recording equipment make it possible for the orator to become audible and visible to an unlimited number of persons, the presentation of the man of politics before camera and recording equipment becomes paramount. Parliaments, as much as theaters, are deserted. Radio and film not only affect the function of the professional actor but likewise the function of those who also exhibit themselves before this mechanical equipment, those who govern. Though their tasks may be

screen actor cease to be conscious of this fact. While facing the camera he knows that ultimately he will face the public, the consumers who constitute the market. This market, where he offers not only his labor but also his whole self, his heart and soul, is beyond his reach. During the shooting he has as little contact with it as any article made in a factory. This may contribute to that oppression, that new anxiety which, according to Pirandello, grips the actor before the camera. The film responds to the shriveling of the aura with an artificial build-up of the "personality" outside the studio. The cult of the movie star, fostered by the money of the film industry, preserves not the unique aura of the person but the "spell of the personality," the phony spell of a commodity. So long as the movie-makers' capital sets the fashion, as a rule no other revolutionary merit can be accredited to today's film than the promotion of a revolutionary criticism of traditional concepts of art. We do not deny that in some cases today's films can also promote revolutionary criticism of social conditions, even of the distribution of property. However, our present study is no more specifically concerned with this than is the film production of Western Europe.

It is inherent in the technique of the film as well as that of sports that everybody who witnesses its accomplishments is somewhat of an expert. This is obvious to anyone listening to a group of newspaper boys leaning on their bicycles and discussing the outcome of a bicycle race. It is not for nothing that newspaper publishers arrange races for their delivery boys. These arouse great interest among the participants, for the victor has an opportunity to rise from delivery boy to professional racer. Similarly, the newsreel offers everyone the opportunity to rise from passer-by to movie extra. In this way any man might even find himself part of a work of art, as witness Vertoff's *Three Songs About Lenin* or Ivens's *Borinage*. Any man today can lay claim to being filmed. This claim can best be elucidated by a comparative look at the historical situation of contemporary literature.

For centuries a small number of writers were confronted by many thousands of readers. This changed toward the end of the last century. With the increasing extension of the press, which kept placing new political, religious, scientific, professional, and local organs before the readers, an increasing number of readers became writers — at first, occasional ones. It began with the daily press opening to its readers space for "letters to the editor." And today there is hardly a gainfully employed European who could not, in principle, find an opportunity to publish somewhere or other comments on his work, grievances, documentary reports, or that sort of thing. Thus, the distinction between author and public is about to lose its basic character. The difference becomes merely functional; it may vary from case to case. At any moment the reader is ready to turn into a writer. As expert, which he had to become willy-nilly in an extremely specialized work process, even if only in some minor respect, the reader gains access to authorship. In the Soviet Union work itself is given a voice. To present it verbally is part of a man's ability to perform the work. Literary license is now founded on polytechnic rather than specialized training and thus becomes common property.[23]

different, the change affects equally the actor and the ruler. The trend is toward establishing controllable and transferrable skills under certain social conditions. This results in a new selection, a selection before the equipment from which the star and the dictator emerge victorious. [Au.]

[23]The privileged character of the respective techniques is lost. Aldous Huxley writes:

> Advances in technology have led . . . to vulgarity. . . . Process reproduction and the rotary press have made possible the indefinite multiplication of writing and pictures. Universal education and relatively high wages have created an enormous public who know how to read and can afford to buy reading and pictorial matter. A great industry has been called into existence in order to supply these commodities. Now, artistic talent is a very rare phenomenon; whence it follows . . . that, at every epoch and in all countries, most art has been bad. But the proportion of trash in the total artistic output is greater now than at any other period. That it must be so is a matter of simple arithmetic. The population of Western Europe has a little more than doubled during the last century. But the amount of reading — and seeing — matter has increased, I should

All this can easily be applied to the film, where transitions that in literature took centuries have come about in a decade. In cinematic practice, particularly in Russia, this changeover has partially become established reality. Some of the players whom we meet in Russian films are not actors in our sense but people who portray *themselves* — and primarily in their own work process. In Western Europe the capitalistic exploitation of the film denies consideration to modern man's legitimate claim to being reproduced. Under these circumstances the film industry is trying hard to spur the interest of the masses through illusion-promoting spectacles and dubious speculations.

XI

The shooting of a film, especially of a sound film, affords a spectacle unimaginable anywhere at any time before this. It presents as process in which it is impossible to assign to a spectator a viewpoint which would exclude from the actual scene such extraneous accessories as camera equipment, lighting machinery, staff assistants, etc. — unless his eye were on a line parallel with the lens. This circumstance, more than any other, renders superficial and insignificant any possible similarity between a scene in the studio and one on the stage. In the theater one is well aware of the place from which the play cannot immediately be detected as illusionary. There is no such place for the movie scene that is being shot. Its illusionary nature is that of the second degree, the result of cutting. That is to say, in the studio the mechanical equipment has penetrated so deeply into reality that its pure aspect freed from the foreign substance of equipment is the result of a special procedure, namely, the shooting by the specially adjusted camera and the mounting of the shot together with other similar ones. The equipment-free aspect of reality here has become the height of artifice; the sight of immediate reality has become an orchid in the land of technology.

Even more revealing is the comparison of these circumstances, which differ so much from those of the theater, with the situation in painting. Here the question is: How does the cameraman compare with the painter? To answer this we take recourse to an analogy with a surgical operation. The surgeon represents the polar opposite of the magician. The magician heals a sick person by the laying on of hands; the surgeon cuts into the patient's body. The magician maintains the natural distance between the patient and himself; though he reduces it very slightly by the laying on of hands, he greatly increases it by virtue of his authority. The surgeon does exactly the reverse; he greatly diminishes the distance between himself and the patient by penetrating into the patient's body, and increases it but little by the caution with which his hand moves among the organs. In short, in contrast to the magician — who is still hidden in the medical practitioner — the surgeon at the decisive moment abstains from facing the patient man to man; rather, it is through the operation that he penetrates into him.

Magician and surgeon compare to painter and cameraman. The painter maintains in his work a

---

imagine, at least twenty and possibly fifty or even a hundred times. If there were n men of talent in a population of x millions, there will presumably be 2n men of talent among 2x millions. The situation may be summed up thus. For every page of print and pictures published a century ago, twenty or perhaps even a hundred pages are published today. But for every man of talent then living, there are now only two men of talent. It may be of course that, thanks to universal education, many potential talents which in the past would have been stillborn are now enabled to realize themselves. Let us assume, then, that there are now three or even four men of talent to every one of earlier times. It still remains true to say that the consumption of reading — and seeing—matter has far outstripped the natural production of gifted writers and draughtsmen. It is the same with hearing-matter. Prosperity, the gramophone and the radio have created an audience of hearers who consume an amount of hearing-matter that has increased out of all proportion to the increase of population and the consequent natural increase of talented musicians. It follows from all this that in all the arts the output of trash is both absolutely and relatively greater than it was in the past; and that it must remain greater for just so long as the world continues to consume the present inordinate quantities of reading-matter, seeing-matter, and hearing-matter. — Aldous Huxley, *Beyond the Mexique Bay. A Traveller's Journal* (London, 1949), pp. 274 ff. First published in 1934.

This mode of observation is obviously not progressive. [Au.]

natural distance from reality, the cameraman penetrates deeply into its web.[24] There is a tremendous difference between the pictures they obtain. That of the painter is a total one, that of the cameraman consists of multiple fragments which are assembled under a new law. Thus, for contemporary man the representation of reality by the film is incomparably more significant than that of the painter, since it offers, precisely because of the thoroughgoing permeation of reality with mechanical equipment, as aspect of reality which is free of all equipment. And that is what one is entitled to ask from a work of art.

XII

Mechanical reproduction of art changes the reaction of the masses toward art. The reactionary attitude toward a Picasso painting changes into the progressive reaction toward a Chaplin movie. The progressive reaction is characterized by the direct, intimate fusion of visual and emotional enjoyment with the orientation of the expert. Such fusion is of great social significance. The greater the decrease in the social significance of an art form, the sharper the distinction between criticism and enjoyment by the public. The conventional is uncritically enjoyed, and the truly new is criticized with aversion. With regard to the screen, the critical and the receptive attitudes of the public coincide. The decisive reason for this is that individual reactions are predetermined by the mass audience response they are about to produce, and this is nowhere more pronounced than in the film. The moment these responses become manifest they control each other. Again, the comparison with painting is fruitful. A painting has always had an excellent chance to be viewed by one person or by a few. The simultaneous contemplation of paintings by a large public, such as developed in the nineteenth century, is an early symptom of the crisis of painting, a crisis which was by no means occasioned exclusively by photography but rather in a relatively independent manner by the appeal of art works to the masses.

Painting simply is in no position to present an object for simultaneous collective experience, as it was possible for architecture at all times, for the epic poem in the past, and for the movie today. Although this circumstance in itself should not lead one to conclusions about the social role of painting, it does constitute a serious threat as soon as painting, under special conditions and, as it were, against its nature, is confronted directly by the masses. In the churches and monasteries of the Middle Ages and at the princely courts up to the end of the eighteenth century, a collective reception of paintings did not occur simultaneously, but by graduated and hierarchized mediation. The change that has come about is an expression of the particular conflict in which painting was implicated by the mechanical reproducibility of paintings. Although paintings began to be publicly exhibited in galleries and salons, there was no way for the masses to organize and control themselves in their reception.[25] Thus the same public which responds in a progressive manner toward a grotesque film is bound to respond in a reactionary manner to surrealism.

XIII

The characteristics of the film lie not only in the manner in which man presents himself to mechanical equipment but also in the manner in

[24]The boldness of the cameraman is indeed comparable to that of the surgeon. Luc Durtain lists among specific technical sleights of hand those "which are required in surgery in the case of certain difficult operations. I choose as an example a case from oto-rhino-laryngology; . . . the so-called endonasal perspective procedure; or I refer to the acrobatic tricks of larynx surgery which have to be performed following the reversed picture in the laryngoscope. I might also speak of ear surgery which suggests the precision work of watchmakers. What range of the most subtle muscular acrobatics is required from the man who wants to repair or save the human body! We have only to think of the couching of a cataract where there is virtually a debate of steel with nearly fluid tissue, or of the major abdominal operations (laparotomy)." — Luc Durtain. [Au.]

[25]This mode of observation may seem crude, but as the great theoretician Leonardo has shown, crude modes of observation may at times be usefully adduced. Leonardo compares painting and music as follows: "Painting is superior to music because, unlike unfortunate music, it does not have to die as soon as it is born. . . . Music which is consumed in the very act of its birth is inferior to painting which the use of varnish has rendered eternal." (Trattato I, 29.) [Au.]

which, by means of this apparatus, man can represent his environment. A glance at occupational psychology illustrates the testing capacity of the equipment. Psychoanalysis illustrates it in a different perspective. The film has enriched our field of perception with methods which can be illustrated by those of Freudian theory. Fifty years ago, a slip of the tongue passed more or less unnoticed. Only exceptionally may such a slip have revealed dimensions of depth in a conversation which had seemed to be taking its course on the surface. Since the *Psychopathology of Everyday Life* things have changed. This book isolated and made analyzable things which had heretofore floated along unnoticed in the broad stream of perception. For the entire spectrum of optical, and now also acoustical, perception the film has brought about a similar deepening of apperception. It is only an obverse of this fact that behavior items shown in a movie can be analyzed much more precisely and from more points of view than those presented on paintings or on the stage. As compared with painting, filmed behavior lends itself more readily to analysis because of its incomparably more precise statements of the situation. In comparison with the stage scene, the filmed behavior item lends itself more readily to analysis because it can be isolated more easily. This circumstance derives its chief importance from its tendency to promote the mutual penetration of art and science. Actually, of a screened behavior item which is neatly brought out in a certain situation, like a muscle of a body, it is difficult to say which is more fascinating, its artistic value or its value for science. To demonstrate the identity of the artistic and scientific uses of photography which heretofore usually were separated will be one of the revolutionary functions of the film.[26]

By close-ups of the things around us, by focusing on hidden details of familiar objects, by exploring commonplace milieus under the ingenious guidance of the camera, the film, on the one hand, extends our comprehension of the necessities which rule our lives; on the other hand, it manages to assure us of an immense and unexpected field of action. Our taverns and our metropolitan streets, our offices and furnished rooms, our railroad stations and our factories appeared to have us locked up hopelessly. Then came the film and burst this prison-world asunder by the dynamite of the tenth of a second, so that now, in the midst of its far-flung ruins and debris, we calmly and adventurously go traveling. With the close-up, space expands; with slow motion, movement is extended. The enlargement of a snapshot does not simply render more precise what in any case was visible, though unclear: it reveals entirely new structural formations of the subject. So, too, slow motion not only presents familiar qualities of movement but reveals in them entirely unknown ones "which, far from looking like retarded rapid movements, give the effect of singularly gliding, floating, supernatural motions."[27] Evidently a different nature opens itself to the camera than opens to the naked eye — if only because an unconsciously penetrated space is substituted for a space consciously explored by man. Even if one has a general knowledge of the way people walk, one knows nothing of a person's posture during the fractional second of a stride. The act of reaching for a lighter or a spoon is familiar routine, yet we hardly know what really goes on between hand and metal, not to mention how this fluctuates with our moods. Here the camera intervenes with the resources of its lowerings and liftings, its interruptions and isolations, its extensions and accelerations, its enlargements and reductions. The camera introduces us to unconscious optics as does psychoanalysis to unconscious impulses.

[26]Renaissance painting offers a revealing analogy to this situation. The incomparable development of this art and its significance rested not least on the integration of a number of new sciences, or at least of new scientific data. Renaissance painting made use of anatomy and perspective, of mathematics, meteorology, and chromatology. Valéry writes: "What could be further from us than the strange claim of a Leonardo to whom painting was a supreme goal and the ultimate demonstration of knowledge? Leonardo was convinced that painting demanded universal knowledge, and he did not even shrink from a theoretical analysis which to us is stunning because of its very depth and precision. . . ." — Paul Valéry, "Autour de Corot," *Pièces sur l'art* (Paris), p. 191. [Au.]

[27]Rudolf Arnheim, p. 138. [Tr.]

XIV

One of the foremost tasks of art has always been the creation of a demand which could be fully satisfied only later.[28] The history of every art form shows critical epochs in which a certain art form aspires to effects which could be fully obtained only with a changed technical standard, that is to say, in a new art form. The extravagances and crudities of art which thus appear, particularly in the so-called decadent epochs, actually arise from the nucleus of its richest historical energies. In recent years, such barbarisms were abundant in Dadaism.[29] It is only now that its impulse becomes discernible: Dadaism attempted to create by pictorial — and literary — means the effects which the public today seeks in the film.

Every fundamentally new, pioneering creation of demands will carry beyond its goal. Dadaism did so to the extent that it sacrificed the market values which are so characteristic of the film in favor of higher ambitions — though of course it was not conscious of such intentions as here described. The Dadaists attached much less importance to the sales value of their work than to its uselessness for contemplative immersion. The studied degradation of their material was not the least of their means to achieve this uselessness. Their poems are "word salad" containing obscenities and every imaginable waste product of language. The same is true of their paintings, on which they mounted buttons and tickets. What they intended and achieved was a relentless destruction of the aura of their creations, which they branded as reproductions with the very means of production. Before a painting of Arp's or a poem by August Stramm it is impossible to take time for contemplation and evaluation as one would like before a canvas of Derain's or a poem by Rilke. In the decline of middle-class society, contemplation became a school for asocial behavior; it was countered by distraction as a variant of social conduct.[30] Dadaistic activities actually assured a rather vehement distraction by making works of art the center of scandal. One requirement was foremost: to outrage the public.

From an alluring appearance or persuasive structure of sound the work of art of the Dadaists became an instrument of ballistics. It hit the spectator like a bullet, it happened to him, thus acquiring a tactile quality. It promoted a demand for the film, the distracting element of which is also primarily tactile, being based on changes of place and focus which periodically assail the spectator. Let us compare the screen on which a film unfolds with the canvas of a painting. The

[28]"The work of art," says André Breton, "is valuable only insofar as it is vibrated by the reflexes of the future." Indeed, every developed art form intersects three lines of development. Technology works toward a certain form of art. Before the advent of the film there were photo booklets with pictures which flitted by the onlooker upon pressure of the thumb, thus portraying a boxing bout or a tennis match. Then there were the slot machines in bazaars; their picture sequences were produced by the turning of a crank.

Secondly, the traditional art forms in certain phases of their development strenuously work toward effects which later are effortlessly attained by the new ones. Before the rise of the movie the Dadaists' performances tried to create an audience reaction which Chaplin later evoked in a more natural way.

Thirdly, unspectacular social changes often promote a change in receptivity which will benefit the new art form. Before the movie had begun to create its public, pictures that were no longer immobile captivated an assembled audience in the so-called *Kaiserpanorama*. Here the public assembled before a screen into which stereoscopes were mounted, one to each beholder. By a mechanical process individual pictures appeared briefly before the stereoscopes, then made way for others. Edison still had to use similar devices in presenting the first movie strip before the film screen and projection were known. This strip was presented to a small public which stared into the apparatus in which the succession of pictures was reeling off. Incidentally, the institution of the *Kaiserpanorama* shows very clearly a dialectic of the development. Shortly before the movie turned the reception of pictures into a collective one, the individual viewing of pictures in these swiftly outmoded establishments came into play once more with an intensity comparable to that of the ancient priest beholding the statue of a divinity in the cella. [Au.]

[29]Movement in the 1920s in both poetry and graphic art characterized by a parodistic treatment of mechanized society and an outrageous assault on the viewer. Major works of Dada include the Buñuel-Dali film *Un Chien Andalou* and Alfred Jarry's play *Ubu roi;* its principal theorist was André Breton. [Ed.]

[30]The theological archetype of this contemplation is the awareness of being alone with one's God. Such awareness, in the heyday of the bourgeoisie, went to strengthen the freedom to shake off clerical tutelage. During the decline of the bourgeoisie this awareness had to take into account the hidden tendency to withdraw from public affairs those forces which the individual draws upon in his communion with God. [Au.]

painting invites the spectator to contemplation; before it the spectator can abandon himself to his associations. Before the movie frame he cannot do so. No sooner has his eye grasped a scene than it is already changed. It cannot be arrested. Duhamel, who detests the film and knows nothing of its significance, though something of its structure, notes this circumstance as follows: "I can no longer think what I want to think. My thoughts have been replaced by moving images."[31] The spectator's process of association in view of these images is indeed interrupted by their constant, sudden change. This constitutes the shock effect of the film, which, like all shocks, should be cushioned by heightened presence of mind.[32] By means of its technical structure, the film has taken the physical shock effect out of the wrappers in which Dadaism had, as it were, kept it inside the moral shock effect.[33]

XV

The mass is a matrix from which all traditional behavior toward works of art issues today in a new form. Quantity has been transmuted into quality. The greatly increased mass of participants has produced a change in the mode of participation. The fact that the new mode of participation first appeared in a disreputable form must not confuse the spectator. Yet some people have launched spirited attacks against precisely this superficial aspect. Among these, Duhamel has expressed himself in the most radical manner. What he objects to most is the kind of participation which the movie elicits from the masses. Duhamel calls the movie "a pastime for helots,[34] a diversion for uneducated, wretched, worn-out creatures who are consumed by their worries . . . , a spectacle which requires no concentration and presupposes no intelligence . . . , which kindles no light in the heart and awakens no hope other than the ridiculous one of somebody becoming a 'star' in Los Angeles."[35] Clearly, this is at bottom the same ancient lament that the masses seek distraction whereas art demands concentration from the spectator. That is a commonplace. The question remains whether it provides a platform for the analysis of the film. A closer look is needed here. Distraction and concentration form polar opposites which may be stated as follows: A man who concentrates before a work of art is absorbed by it. He enters into this work of art the way legend tells of the Chinese painter when he viewed his finished painting. In contrast, the distracted mass absorbs the work of art. This is most obvious with regard to buildings. Architecture has always represented the prototype of a work of art the reception of which is consummated by a collectivity in a state of distraction. The laws of its reception are most instructive.

Buildings have been man's companions since primeval times. Many art forms have developed and perished. Tragedy begins with the Greeks, is extinguished with them, and after centuries its "rules" only are revived. The epic poem, which had its origin in the youth of nations, expires in Europe at the end of the Renaissance. Panel painting is a creation of the Middle Ages, and nothing guarantees its uninterrupted existence. But the human need for shelter is lasting. Architecture has never been idle. Its history is more ancient than that of any other art, and its claim to being a living force has significance in every attempt to comprehend the relationship of the masses to art. Buildings are appropriated in a twofold manner: by use and by perception — or

[31]Georges Duhamel, *Scènes de la vie future* (Paris, 1930), p. 52. [Tr.]

[32]The film is the art form that is in keeping with the increased threat to his life which modern man has to face. Man's need to expose himself to shock effects is his adjustment to the dangers threatening him. The film corresponds to profound changes in the apperceptive apparatus — changes that are experienced on an individual scale by the man in the street in big-city traffic, on a historical scale by every present-day citizen. [Au.]

[33]As for Dadaism, insights important for Cubism and Futurism are to be gained from the movie. Both appear as deficient attempts of art to accommodate the pervasion of reality by the apparatus. In contrast to the film, these schools did not try to use the apparatus as such for the artistic presentation of reality, but aimed at some sort of alloy in the joint presentation of reality and apparatus. In Cubism, the premonition that this apparatus will be structurally based on optics plays a dominant part; in Futurism, it is the premonition of the effects of this apparatus which are brought out by the rapid sequence of the film strip. [Au.]

[34]Slaves. [Ed.]

[35]Duhamel, p. 58. [Tr.]

rather, by touch and sight. Such appropriation cannot be understood in terms of the attentive concentration of a tourist before a famous building. On the tactile side there is no counterpart to contemplation on the optical side. Tactile appropriation is accomplished not so much by attention as by habit. As regards architecture, habit determines to a large extent even optical reception. The latter, too, occurs much less through rapt attention than by noticing the object in incidental fashion. This mode of appropriation, developed with reference to architecture, in certain circumstances acquires canonical value. For the tasks which face the human apparatus of perception at the turning points of history cannot be solved by optical means, that is, by contemplation, alone. They are mastered gradually by habit, under the guidance of tactile appropriation.

The distracted person, too, can form habits. More, the ability to master certain tasks in a state of distraction proves that their solution has become a matter of habit. Distraction as provided by art presents a covert control of the extent to which new tasks have become soluble by apperception. Since, moreover, individuals are tempted to avoid such tasks, art will tackle the most difficult and most important ones where it is able to mobilize the masses. Today it does so in the film. Reception in a state of distraction, which is increasing noticeably in all fields of art and is symptomatic of profound changes in apperception, finds in the film its true means of exercise. The film with its shock effect meets this mode of reception halfway. The film makes the cult value recede into the background not only by putting the public in the position of the critic, but also by the fact that at the movies this position requires no attention. The public is an examiner, but an absent-minded one.

EPILOGUE

The growing proletarianization of modern man and the increasing formation of masses are two aspects of the same process. Fascism attempts to organize the newly created proletarian masses without affecting the property structure which the masses strive to eliminate. Fascism sees its salvation in giving these masses not their right, but instead a chance to express themselves.[36] The masses have a right to change property relations; Fascism seeks to give them an expression while preserving property. The logical result of Fascism is the introduction of aesthetics into political life. The violation of the masses, whom Fascism, with its *Führer* cult, forces to their knees, has its counterpart in the violation of an apparatus which is pressed into the production of ritual values.

All efforts to render politics aesthetic culminate in one thing: war. War and war only can set a goal for mass movements on the largest scale while respecting the traditional property system. This is the political formula for the situation. The technological formula may be stated as follows: Only war makes it possible to mobilize all of today's technical resources while maintaining the property system. It goes without saying that the Fascist apotheosis of war does not employ such arguments. Still, Marinetti[37] says in his manifesto on the Ethiopian colonial war: "For twenty-seven years we Futurists have rebelled against the branding of war as antiaesthetic. . . . Accordingly we state: . . . War is beautiful because it establishes man's dominion over the subjugated machinery by means of gas masks, terrifying megaphones, flame throwers, and small tanks. War is beautiful because it initiates the dreamt-of metalization of the human body. War is beautiful be-

[36]One technical feature is significant here, especially with regard to newsreels, the propagandist importance of which can hardly be overestimated. Mass reproduction is aided especially by the reproduction of masses. In big parades and monster rallies, in sports events, and in war, all of which nowadays are captured by camera and sound recording, the masses are brought face to face with themselves. This process, whose significance need not be stressed, is intimately connected with the development of the techniques of reproduction and photography. Mass movements are usually discerned more clearly by a camera than by the naked eye. A bird's-eye view best captures gatherings of hundreds of thousands. And even though such a view may be as accessible to the human eye as it is to the camera, the image received by the eye cannot be enlarged the way a negative is enlarged. This means that mass movements, including war, constitute a form of human behavior which particularly favors mechanical equipment. [Au.]

[37]Italian-French futurist writer and enthusiastic backer of Mussolini (1876–1944), author of *Guerra sola igiene del mundo* (*War — Sole Hygiene of the World,* 1915). [Ed.]

cause it enriches a flowering meadow with the fiery orchids of machine guns. War is beautiful because it combines the gunfire, the cannonades, the cease-fire, the scents, and the stench of putrefaction into a symphony. War is beautiful because it creates new architecture, like that of the big tanks, the geometrical formation flights, the smoke spirals from burning villages, and many others. . . . Poets and artists of Futurism! . . . remember these principles of an aesthetics of war so that your struggle for a new literature and a new graphic art . . . may be illumined by them!"

This manifesto has the virtue of clarity. Its formulations deserve to be accepted by dialecticians. To the latter, the aesthetics of today's war appears as follows: If the natural utilization of productive forces is impeded by the property system, the increase in technical devices, in speed, and in the sources of energy will press for an unnatural utilization, and this is found in war. The destructiveness of war furnishes proof that society has been mature enough to incorporate technology as its organ, that technology has not been sufficiently developed to cope with the elemental forces of society. The horrible features of imperialistic warfare are attributable to the discrepancy between the tremendous means of production and their inadequate utilization in the process of production — in other words, to unemployment and the lack of markets. Imperialistic war is a rebellion of technology which collects, in the form of "human material," the claims to which society has denied its natural material. Instead of draining rivers, society directs a human stream into a bed of trenches; instead of dropping seeds from airplanes, it drops incendiary bombs over cities; and through gas warfare the aura is abolished in a new way.

"Fiat ars — pereat mundus,"[38] says Fascism, and, as Marinetti admits, expect war to supply the artistic gratification of a sense perception that has been changed by technology. This is evidently the consummation of *"l'art pour l'art."* Mankind, which in Homer's time was an object of contemplation for the Olympian gods, now is one for itself. Its self-alienation has reached such a degree that it can experience its own destruction as an aesthetic pleasure of the first order. This is the situation of politics which Fascism is rendering aesthetic. Communism responds by politicizing art.

[38]Let art exist, let the world perish. [Ed.]

Theodor W. Adorno

1903–1969

Theodor Wiesengrund Adorno was born to middle-class parents in Frankfurt, Germany, where he studied psychology, sociology, and music, and took his Ph.D. in philosophy in 1924. He went to Vienna to study composition with the serial composer Alban Berg in 1925, then came back to Frankfurt for postdoctoral study in 1928. Strongly influenced by the Hegelian Marxism of Georg Lukács, he founded with Max Horkheimer the Institute for Social Research that was the nucleus of what became known as the Frankfurt school, a group that also included Herbert Marcuse, Walter Benjamin, and, in the next generation, Jürgen Habermas. In the waning days of the Weimar Republic, Adorno left for England, then spent the war years in America, settling in Princeton, New Jersey, where he wrote the essays for Minima Moralia *from which the following selections are taken. In 1949 he returned to the University of Frankfurt, where he served as professor of sociology and philosophy, and where he became assistant director of the Institute in 1949, and sole director from 1958 until his death. Adorno's works include* The Dialectic of Enlightenment *(1944, with Max Horkheimer; translated 1972);* The Philosophy of Modern Music *(1949; translated 1973);* Minima Moralia: Reflections from Damaged Life *(1951; translated 1974);* Prisms *(1955; translated 1967);* Introduction to the Sociology of Music

(1962; translated 1976); Negative Dialectics *(1966; translated 1973); and the posthumous* Aesthetic Theory *(1970; translated 1996).*

From *Minima Moralia*

BEQUEST

Dialectical thought is an attempt to break through the coercion of logic by its own means. But since it must use these means, it is at every moment in danger of itself acquiring a coercive character: the ruse of reason would like to hold sway over the dialectic too. The existing cannot be overstepped except by means of a universal derived from the existing order itself. The universal triumphs over the existing through the latter's own concept, and therefore, in its triumph, the power of mere existence constantly threatens to reassert itself by the same violence that broke it. Through the absolute rule of negation, the movement of thought as of history becomes, in accordance with the pattern of immanent antithesis, unambiguously, exclusively, implacably positive. Everything is subsumed under the principal economic phases and their development, which each in turn historically shape the whole of society; thought in its entirety has something of what Parisian artists call *le genre chef d'oeuvre.*[1] That calamity is brought about precisely by the stringency of such development; that this stringency is itself linked to domination, is, at the least, not made explicit in critical theory, which, like traditional theory, awaits salvation from stage-by-stage progression. Stringency and totality, the bourgeois intellectual ideals of necessity and generality, do indeed circumscribe the formula of history, but for just this reason the constitution of society finds its precipitate in those great, immovable, lordly concepts against which dialectical criticism and practice are directed. If Benjamin said that history had hitherto been written from the standpoint of the victor, and needed to be written from that of the vanquished,[2] we might add that knowledge must indeed present the fatally rectilinear succession of victory and defeat, but should also address itself to those things which were not embraced by this dynamic, which fell by the wayside — what might be called the waste products and blind spots that have escaped the dialectic. It is in the nature of the defeated to appear, in their impotence, irrelevant, eccentric, derisory. What transcends the ruling society is not only the potentiality it develops but also all that which did not fit properly into the laws of historical movement. Theory must needs deal with cross-grained, opaque, unassimilated material, which as such admittedly has from the start an anachronistic quality, but is not wholly obsolete since it has outwitted the historical dynamic. This can most readily be seen in art. Children's books like *Alice in Wonderland* or *Struwwelpeter,*[3] of which it would be absurd to ask whether they are progressive or reactionary, contain incomparably more eloquent ciphers even of history than the high drama of Hebbel,[4] concerned though it is with the official themes of tragic guilt, turning points of history, the course of the world and the individual, and in Satie's pert and puerile piano pieces there are flashes of

Translated by E. F. N. Jephcott.

[1]Class of works intended as masterpieces. [Ed.]

[2]Walter Benjamin, *Illuminations,* London 1973, pp. 258–9. [Tr.]

[3]*Shock-Headed Peter* (1847), world-famous children's book written by German novelist Heinrich Hoffmann (1809–1874). [Ed.]

[4]Christian Friedrich Hebbel (1813–1868) was a lyric dramatist of the mid-nineteenth century who had an extravagant melodramatic style. [Ed.]

experience undreamed of by the school of Schönberg, with all its rigor and all the pathos of musical development behind it. The very grandeur of logical deductions may inadvertently take on a provincial quality. Benjamin's writings are an attempt in ever new ways to make philosophically fruitful what has not yet been foreclosed by great intentions. The task he bequeathed was not to abandon such an attempt to the estranging enigmas of thought alone, but to bring the intentionless within the realm of concepts: the obligation to think at the same time dialectically and undialectically.

LATE EXTRA

In central passages of Poe and Baudelaire the concept of newness emerges. In the former,[5] in the description of the maelstrom and the shudder it inspires — equated with "the novel" — of which none of the traditional reports is said to give an adequate idea; in the latter, in the last line of the cycle *La Mort,* which chooses the plunge into the abyss, no matter whether hell or heaven, *"au fond de l'inconnu pour trouver du nouveau"* [in the depths of the unknown to find the new]. In both cases it is an unknown threat that the subject embraces and which, in a dizzy reversal, promises joy. The new, a blank place in consciousness, awaited as if with shut eyes, seems the formula by means of which a stimulus is extracted from dread and despair. It makes evil flower. But its bare contour is a cryptogram for the most unequivocal reaction. It circumscribes the precise reply given by the subject to a world that has turned abstract, the industrial age. The cult of the new, and thus the idea of modernity, is a rebellion against the fact that there is no longer anything new. The never-changing quality of machine-produced goods, the lattice of socialization that enmeshes and assimilates equally objects and the view of them, converts everything encountered into what always was, a fortuitous specimen of a species, the *doppel-gänger*[6] of a model. The layer of unpremeditatedness, freedom from intentions, on which alone intentions flourish, seems consumed. Of it the idea of newness dreams. Itself unattainable, newness installs itself in the place of overthrown divinity amidst the first consciousness of the decay of experience. But its concept remains chained to that sickness, as its abstraction attests, impotently reaching for a receding concreteness. For a "prehistory of modernity"[7] it would be instructive to analyze the change in the meaning of the word sensation, the exoteric synonym for the Baudelairian *nouveau.* The word became familiar to the educated European through epistemology. In Locke it means simple, direct perception, the opposite of reflection. It then became the great Unknown, and finally the arouser of masses, the destructive intoxicant, shock as a consumer commodity. To be still able to perceive anything at all, regardless of its quality, replaces happiness, since omnipotent quantification has taken away the possibility of perception itself. In place of the fulfilled relation of experience to its subject-matter, we find something merely subjective, physically isolated, feeling that is exhausted in the reading on the pressure-gauge. Thus the historical emancipation from being-in-itself is converted into the form of perception, a process that nineteenth-century sense-psychology accommodated by reducing the underlying level of experience to a mere "basic stimulus," of whose particular constitution the specific sense-energies were independent. Baudelaire's poetry, however, is full of those lightning flashes seen by a closed eye that has received a blow. As phantasmagoric as these lights is the idea of newness itself. What flashes thus, while serene contemplation now attains merely the socially pre-formed plaster-casts of things, is itself repetition. The new, sought for its own sake, a kind of laboratory product, petrified into a conceptual scheme, becomes in its sudden apparition a compulsive return of the old,

[5]Poe's story, "Descent into the Maelstrom" (1841). [Ed.]
[6]Monstrous double. [Ed.]

[7]Notion of Walter Benjamin: the whole passage here on Baudelaire and the concept of the "new" is constructed in implicit contrast to Benjamin's interpretation of them in *Charles Baudelaire — A Lyric Poet in the Era of High Capitalism* (London 1973). For an English translation of Adorno's famous critique of Benjamin's views, see "Letters to Walter Benjamin," *New Left Review* 81, September–October 1973. [Tr.]

not unlike that in traumatic neuroses. To the dazzled vision the veil of temporal succession is rent to reveal the archetypes of perpetual sameness: this is why the discovery of the new is satanic, an eternal recurrence of damnation. Poe's allegory of the "novel" is that of the breathlessly spinning yet in a sense stationary movement of the helpless boat in the eye of the maelstrom. The sensations in which the masochist abandons himself to the new are as many regressions. So much is true in psycho-analysis that the ontology of Baudelairian modernity, like all those that followed it, answers the description of infantile partial-instincts. Its pluralism is the many-colored *fata morgana*[8] in which the monism of bourgeois reason sees its self-destruction glitter deceptively as hope. This false promise makes up the idea of modernity, and everything modern, because of its never-changing core, has scarcely aged than it takes on a look of the archaic. The *Tristan* which rises in the middle of the nineteenth century as an obelisk of modernity is at the same time a soaring monument to the compulsion to repeat.[9] The new is ambivalent in its enthronement. While it embraces everything that strives beyond the oneness of an ever rigid established order, it is at the same time absorption by newness which, under the weight of that oneness, decisively furthers the decomposition of the subject into convulsive moments of illusory living, and so also furthers total society, which modishly ousts the new. Baudelaire's poem about the martyr of sex, the murder victim, allegorically celebrates the sanctity of pleasure in the fearsomely liberating still-life of crime,[10] but his intoxication before the naked headless body already resembles that which drove the prospective victims of Hitler's régime to buy, in paralyzed greed, the newspapers in which stood the measures announcing their own doom. Fascism was the absolute sensation: in a statement at the time of the first pogroms, Goebbels boasted that at least the National Socialists were not boring. In the Third Reich the abstract horror of news and rumor was enjoyed as the only stimulus sufficient to incite a momentary glow in the weakened sensorium of the masses. Without the almost irresistible force of the craving for headlines, in which the strangled heart convulsively sought a primeval world, the unspeakable could not have been endured by the spectators or even by the perpetrators. In the course of the war, even news of calamity was finally given full publicity in Germany, and the slow military collapse was not hushed up. Concepts like sadism and masochism no longer suffice. In the mass-society of technical dissemination they are mediated by sensationalism, by comet-like, remote, ultimate newness. It overwhelms a public writhing under shock and oblivious of who has suffered the outrage, itself or others. Compared to its stimulus-value, the content of the shock becomes really irrelevant, as it was ideally in its invocation by poets; it is even possible that the horror savored by Poe and Baudelaire, when realized by dictators, loses its quality as sensation, burns out. The violent rescuing of all qualities in the new was devoid of quality. Everything can, as the new, divested of itself, become pleasure, just as desensitized morphine addicts finally grab indiscriminately at any drug, including atropine. Sensation has submerged, together with differentiation between qualities, all judgment: it is really this that makes it an agent of catastrophic degeneration. In the terror of regressive dictatorship, modernity, the dialectical image of progress, has culminated in explosion. Newness in collective form, of which there was already a hint in Baudelaire's journalistic streak as in Wagner's drum-beating, is in fact a stimulating and paralyzing narcotic extract boiled out of external life: not for nothing were Poe, Baudelaire, Wagner addictive types. Newness only becomes mere evil in its totalitarian format, where all the tension between individual and society, that once gave rise to the category of the new, is dissipated. Today the appeal to newness, of no matter what kind, provided only that it is archaic enough, has become universal, the omnipresent medium of false mimesis. The decomposition of

[8]Literally Morgan Le Fay of the Arthurian stories; it means any illusion or will-of-the-wisp. [Ed.]

[9]Referring to the 1865 opera by Richard Wagner, *Tristan and Isolde,* which ushered in modernity in music; here the "new" depends upon endless repetitions of thematic melodies (*leitmotiven*). [Ed.]

[10]Adorno refers to Baudelaire's "Une Martyre" from *Fleurs du Mal* (1861). [Ed.]

the subject is consummated in his self-abandonment to an ever-changing sameness. This drains all firmness from characters. What Baudelaire commanded through the power of images, comes unbid to will-less fascination. Faithlessness and lack of identity, pathic subservience to situations, are induced by the stimulus of newness, which, as a mere stimulus, no longer stimulates. Perhaps in this lassitude mankind's renunciation of the wish for children is declared, because it is open to everyone to prophesy the worst: the new is the secret figure of all those unborn. Malthus is one of the forefathers of the nineteenth century,[11] and Baudelaire had reason to extol infertile beauty. Mankind, despairing of its reproduction, unconsciously projects its wish for survival into the chimera of the thing never known, but this resembles death. Such a chimera points to the downfall of an all-embracing constitution which virtually no longer needs its members.

[11]Thomas Robert Malthus (1766–1834), English clergyman who wrote *Essay on the Principle of Population* (1798), which advocated the control of population growth through the regulation of sexual activity. [Ed.]

Georg Lukács

1885–1971

The most influential Marxist aesthetician of the first half of this century, Georg Lukács was the son of a wealthy Hungarian family. He attended the University of Heidelberg and the University of Berlin, and received a Ph.D. from the University of Budapest in 1906. Lukács wrote several essays on aesthetic and literary theory (including Soul and Form *[1910],* Aesthetic Culture *[1913], and his influential* Theory of the Novel *[written 1916, published 1920] in a Hegelian phase before joining the Hungarian Communist Party in 1918. In 1919 he began a stint as commissar for culture and education in the regime of Bela Kun, an appointment that ended with the fall of Kun. Lukács left Hungary and settled in Vienna, where he produced* History and Class Consciousness *(1923), his most influential work of political theory. Driven by waves of political controversy, Lukács spent 1929–31 in Moscow, then moved to Berlin. When the Nazis came to power in 1933, he returned to Moscow, taking a post at the Soviet Academy of Sciences (1933–44). He managed, as a great many Central European intellectuals did not, to survive the Stalinist purges of 1937–38; it was in this dark time that he wrote* The Historical Novel *(published in English in 1962). Lukács did not return to Hungary until the more receptive political climate of 1945, when he was made a parliamentary minister and professor of aesthetics and cultural philosophy at the University of Budapest. In 1956, the year he wrote "The Ideology of Modernism," Lukács was again unseated by a political uprising. Deported in 1956 to Romania, Lukács worked on two major theoretical tomes, neither of which was complete at his death; neither has yet been translated:* Die Eigenart des Ästhetischen *("The Particularity of the Aesthetic," 1963), and the two-volume* Zur Ontologie der gesellschaftlisches Seins *("Toward an Ontology of Social Being," 1973).*

The Ideology of Modernism

It is in no way surprising that the most influential contemporary school of writing should still be committed to the dogmas of "modernist" anti-realism. It is here that we must begin our investigation if we are to chart the possibilities of a bourgeois realism. We must compare the two main trends in contemporary bourgeois literature, and look at the answers they give to the major ideological and artistic questions of our time.

We shall concentrate on the underlying ideological basis of these trends (ideological in the above-defined, not in the strictly philosophical, sense). What must be avoided at all costs is the approach generally adopted by bourgeois-modernist critics themselves: that exaggerated concern with formal criteria, with questions of style and literary technique. This approach may appear to distinguish sharply between "modern" and "traditional" writing (i.e., contemporary writers who adhere to the styles of the last century). In fact, it fails to locate the decisive formal problems and turns a blind eye to their inherent dialectic. We are presented with a false polarization which, by exaggerating the importance of stylistic differences, conceals the opposing principles actually underlying and determining contrasting styles.

To take an example: the *monologue intérieur*. Compare, for instance, Bloom's monologue in the lavatory or Molly's monologue in bed, at the beginning and at the end of *Ulysses,* with Goethe's early-morning monologue as conceived by Thomas Mann in his *Lotte in Weimar*. Plainly, the same stylistic technique is being employed. And certain of Thomas Mann's remarks about Joyce and his methods would appear to confirm this.

Yet it is not easy to think of any two novels more basically dissimilar than *Ulysses* and *Lotte in Weimar*. This is true even of the superficially rather similar scenes I have indicated. I am not referring to the — to my mind — striking difference in intellectual quality. I refer to the fact that with Joyce the stream-of-consciousness technique is no mere stylistic device; it is itself the formative principle governing the narrative pattern and the presentation of character. Technique here is something absolute; it is part and parcel of the aesthetic ambition informing *Ulysses*. With Thomas Mann, on the other hand, the *monologue intérieur* is simply a technical device, allowing the author to explore aspects of Goethe's world which would not have been otherwise available. Goethe's experience is not presented as confined to momentary sense-impressions. The artist reaches down to the core of Goethe's personality, to the complexity of his relations with his own past, present, and even future experience. The stream of association is only apparently free. The monologue is composed with the utmost artistic rigor: it is a carefully plotted sequence gradually piercing to the core of Goethe's personality. Every person or event, emerging momentarily from the stream and vanishing again, is given a specific weight, a definite position, in the pattern of the whole. However unconventional the presentation, the compositional principle is that of the traditional epic; in the way the pace is controlled, and the transitions and climaxes are organized, the ancient rules of epic narration are faithfully observed.

It would be absurd, in view of Joyce's artistic ambitions and his manifest abilities, to qualify the exaggerated attention he gives to the detailed recording of sense-data, and his comparative neglect of ideas and emotions, as artistic failure. All this was in conformity with Joyce's artistic intentions; and, by use of such techniques, he may be said to have achieved them satisfactorily. But between Joyce's intentions and those of Thomas Mann there is a total opposition. The perpetually oscillating patterns of sense- and memory-data, their powerfully charged — but aimless and directionless — fields of force, give rise to an epic structure which is *static,* reflecting a belief in the basically static character of events.

These opposed views of the world — dynamic and developmental on the one hand, static and sen-

Translated by John and Necke Mander.

sational on the other — are of crucial importance in examining the two schools of literature I have mentioned. I shall return to the opposition later. Here, I want only to point out that an exclusive emphasis on formal matters can lead to serious misunderstanding of the character of an artist's work.

What determines the style of a given work of art? How does the intention determine the form? (We are concerned here, of course, with the intention realized in the work; it need not coincide with the writer's conscious intention.) The distinctions that concern us are not those between stylistic "techniques" in the formalistic sense. It is the view of the world, the ideology or *weltanschauung*[1] underlying a writer's work, that counts. And it is the writer's attempt to reproduce this view of the world which constitutes his "intention" and is the formative principle underlying the style of a given piece of writing. Looked at in this way, style ceases to be a formalistic category. Rather, it is rooted in content; it is the specific form of a specific content.

Content determines form. But there is no content of which Man himself is not the focal point. However various the *données*[2] of literature (a particular experience, a didactic purpose), the basic question is, and will remain: what is Man?

Here is a point of division: if we put the question in abstract, philosophical terms, leaving aside all formal considerations, we arrive — for the realist school — at the traditional Aristotelian dictum (which was also reached by other than purely aesthetic considerations): Man is *zoon politikon,* a social animal. The Aristotelian dictum is applicable to all great realistic literature. Achilles and Werther, Oedipus and Tom Jones, Antigone, and Anna Karenina: their individual existence — their *Sein an sich,*[3] in the Hegelian terminology; their "ontological being," as a more fashionable terminology has it — cannot be distinguished from their social and historical environment. Their human significance, their specific individuality cannot be separated from the context in which they were created.

[1]World-picture. [Ed.]

[2]What is given: the subject matter chosen by the author. [Ed.]

[3]Being in itself. [Ed.]

The ontological view governing the image of man in the work of leading modernist writers is the exact opposite of this. Man, for these writers, is by nature solitary, asocial, unable to enter into relationships with other human beings. Thomas Wolfe once wrote: "My view of the world is based on the firm conviction that solitariness is by no means a rare condition, something peculiar to myself or to a few specially solitary human beings, but the inescapable, central fact of human existence." Man, thus imagined, may establish contact with other individuals, but only in a superficial, accidental manner; only, ontologically speaking, by retrospective reflection. For "the others," too, are basically solitary, beyond significant human relationship.

This basic solitariness of man must not be confused with that individual solitariness to be found in the literature of traditional realism. In the latter case, we are dealing with a particular situation in which a human being may be placed, due either to his character or to the circumstances of his life. Solitariness may be objectively conditioned, as with Sophocles' Philoctetes, put ashore on the bleak island of Lemnos. Or it may be subjective, the product of inner necessity, as with Tolstoy's Ivan Ilych or Flaubert's Frédéric Moreau in the *Education Sentimentale.* But it is always merely a fragment, a phase, a climax, or anticlimax, in the life of the community as a whole. The fate of such individuals is characteristic of certain human types in specific social or historical circumstances. Beside and beyond their solitariness, the common life, the strife and togetherness of other human beings, goes on as before. In a word, their solitariness is a specific social fate, not a universal *condition humaine.*

The latter, of course, is characteristic of the theory and practice of modernism. I would like, in the present study, to spare the reader tedious excursions into philosophy. But I cannot refrain from drawing the reader's attention to Heidegger's description of human existence as a "thrownness-into-being" *(Geworfenheit ins Dasein).* A more graphic evocation of the ontological solitariness of the individual would be hard to imagine. Man is "thrown-into-being." This implies, not merely that man is constitutionally unable to establish relationships with things or persons outside himself; but also that it is impossible to determine theoretically the origin and goal of human existence.

Man, thus conceived, is an ahistorical being. (The fact that Heidegger does admit a form of "authentic" historicity in his system is not really relevant. I have shown elsewhere that Heidegger tends to belittle historicity as "vulgar"; and his "authentic" historicity is not distinguishable from ahistoricity). This negation of history takes two different forms in modernist literature. First, the hero is strictly confined within the limits of his own experience. There is not for him — and apparently not for his creator — any preexistent reality beyond his own self, acting upon him or being acted upon by him. Secondly, the hero himself is without personal history. He is "thrown-into-the-world": meaninglessly, unfathomably. He does not develop through contact with the world; he neither forms nor is formed by it. The only "development" in this literature is the gradual revelation of the human condition. Man is now what he has always been and always will be. The narrator, the examining subject, is in motion; the examined reality is static.

Of course, dogmas of this kind are only really viable in philosophical abstraction, and then only with a measure of sophistry. A gifted writer, however extreme his theoretical modernism, will in practice have to compromise with the demands of historicity and of social environment. Joyce uses Dublin, Kafka and Musil the Hapsburg Monarchy, as the locus of their masterpieces.[4] But the locus they lovingly depict is little more than a backcloth; it is not basic to their artistic intention.

This view of human existence has specific literary consequences. Particularly in one category, of primary theoretical and practical importance, to which we must now give our attention: that of *potentiality*. Philosophy distinguishes between *abstract* and *concrete* (in Hegel, "real") *potentiality*. These two categories, their interrelation and opposition, are rooted in life itself. *Potentiality* — seen abstractly or subjectively — is richer than actual life. Innumerable possibilities for man's development are imaginable, only a small percentage of which will be realized. Modern subjectivism, taking these imagined possibilities for actual complexity of life, oscillates between melancholy and fascination. When the world declines to realize these possibilities, this melancholy becomes tinged with contempt. Hofmannsthal's Sobeide expressed the reaction of the generation first exposed to this experience:

> The burden of those endlessly pored-over
> And now forever perished possibilities . . .[5]

How far were those possibilities even concrete or "real"? Plainly, they existed only in the imagination of the subject, as dreams or daydreams. Faulkner, in whose work this subjective potentiality plays an important part, was evidently aware that reality must thereby be subjectivized and made to appear arbitrary. Consider this comment of his: "They were all talking simultaneously, getting flushed and excited, quarrelling, making the unreal into a possibility, then into a probability, then into an irrefutable fact, as human beings do when they put their wishes into words." The possibilities in a man's mind, the particular pattern, intensity and suggestiveness they assume, will of course be characteristic of that individual. In practice, their number will border on the infinite, even with the most unimaginative individual. It is thus a hopeless undertaking to define the contours of individuality, let alone to come to grips with a man's actual fate, by means of potentiality. The *abstract* character of potentiality is clear from the fact that it cannot determine development — subjective mental states, however permanent or profound, cannot here be decisive. Rather, the development of personality is determined by inherited gifts and qualities; by the factors, external or internal, which further or inhibit their growth.

But in life potentiality can, of course, become reality. Situations arise in which a man is confronted with a choice; and in the act of choice a man's character may reveal itself in a light that surprises even himself. In literature — and particularly in dramatic literature — the denouement often consists in the realization of just such a po-

[4]*Ulysses, The Castle,* and *The Man without Qualities,* respectively. [Ed.]

[5]*Die Hochzeit von Sobeide* (1899), a drama by Hugo von Hofmannsthal (1874–1929). [Ed.]

tentiality, which circumstances have kept from coming to the fore. These potentialities are, then, "real" or concrete potentialities. The fate of the character depends upon the potentiality in question, even if it should condemn him to a tragic end. In advance, while still a subjective potentiality in the character's mind, there is no way of distinguishing it from the innumerable abstract potentialities in his mind. It may even be buried away so completely that, before the moment of decision, it has never entered his mind even as an abstract potentiality. The subject, after taking his decision, may be unconscious of his own motives. Thus Richard Dudgeon, Shaw's Devil's Disciple, having sacrificed himself as Pastor Anderson, confesses: "I have often asked myself for the motive, but I find no good reason to explain why I acted as I did."

Yet it is a decision which has altered the direction of his life. Of course, this is an extreme case. But the qualitative leap of the denouement, cancelling and at the same time renewing the continuity of individual consciousness, can never be predicted. The concrete potentiality cannot be isolated from the myriad abstract potentialities. Only actual decision reveals the distinction.

The literature of realism, aiming at a truthful reflection of reality, must demonstrate both the concrete and abstract potentialities of human beings in extreme situations of this kind. A character's concrete potentiality once revealed, his abstract potentialities will appear essentially inauthentic. Moravia, for instance, in his novel *The Indifferent Ones,* describes the young son of a decadent bourgeois family, Michel, who makes up his mind to kill his sister's seducer. While Michel, having made his decision, is planning the murder, a large number of abstract — but highly suggestive — possibilities are laid before us. Unfortunately for Michel the murder is actually carried out; and, from the sordid details of the action, Michel's character emerges as what it is — representative of that background from which, in subjective fantasy, he had imagined he could escape.

Abstract potentiality belongs wholly to the realm of subjectivity; whereas concrete potentiality is concerned with the dialectic between the individual's subjectivity and objective reality. The literary presentation of the latter thus implies a description of actual persons inhabiting a palpable, identifiable world. Only in the interaction of character and environment can the concrete potentiality of a particular individual be singled out from the "bad infinity" of purely abstract potentialities, and emerge as the determining potentiality of just this individual at just this phase of his development. This principle alone enables the artist to distinguish concrete potentiality from a myriad abstractions.

But the ontology on which the image of man in modernist literature is based invalidates this principle. If the "human condition" — man as a solitary being, incapable of meaningful relationships — is identified with reality itself, the distinction between abstract and concrete potentiality becomes null and void. The categories tend to merge. Thus Cesare Pavese notes with John Dos Passos, and his German contemporary, Alfred Döblin, a sharp oscillation between "superficial *verisme*"[6] and "abstract Expressionist schematism." Criticizing Dos Passos, Pavese writes that fictional characters "ought to be created by deliberate selection and description of individual features" — implying that Dos Passos's characterizations are transferable from one individual to another. He describes the artistic consequences: by exalting man's subjectivity, at the expense of the objective reality of his environment, man's subjectivity itself is impoverished.

The problem, once again, is ideological. This is not to say that the ideology underlying modernist writings is identical in all cases. On the contrary: the ideology exists in extremely various, even contradictory forms. The rejection of narrative objectivity, the surrender to subjectivity, may take the form of Joyce's stream of consciousness, or of Musil's "active passivity," his "existence without quality," or of Gide's *"action gratuite,"*[7] where abstract potentiality achieves pseudo-realization. As individual character manifests itself in life's moments of decision, so too

[6]A crudely realistic style akin to newspaper reportage. [Ed.]

[7]"Gratuitous act": a crime committed to prove one's freedom. [Ed.]

in literature. If the distinction between abstract and concrete potentiality vanishes, if man's inwardness is identified with an abstract subjectivity, human personality must necessarily disintegrate.

T. S. Eliot described this phenomenon, this mode of portraying human personality, as

> Shape without form, shade without colour,
> Paralysed force, gesture without motion.[8]

The disintegration of personality is matched by a disintegration of the outer world. In one sense, this is simply a further consequence of our argument. For the identification of abstract and concrete human potentiality rests on the assumption that the objective world is inherently inexplicable. Certain leading modernist writers, attempting a theoretical apology, have admitted this quite frankly. Often this theoretical impossibility of understanding reality is the point of departure, rather than the exaltation of subjectivity. But in any case the connection between the two is plain. The German poet Gottfried Benn, for instance, informs us that "there is no outer reality, there is only human consciousness, constantly building, modifying, rebuilding new worlds out of its own creativity." Musil, as always, gives a moral twist to this line of thought. Ulrich, the hero of his *The Man without Qualities,* when asked what he would do if he were in God's place, replies: "I should be compelled to abolish reality." Subjective existence "without qualities" is the complement of the negation of outward reality.

The negation of outward reality is not always demanded with such theoretical rigor. But it is present in almost all modernist literature. In conversation, Musil once gave as the period of his great novel, "between 1912 and 1914." But he was quick to modify this statement by adding: "I have not, I must insist, written a historical novel. I am not concerned with actual events. . . . Events, anyhow, are interchangeable. I am interested in what is typical, in what one might call the ghostly aspect of reality." The word "ghostly" is interesting. It points to a major tendency in modernist literature: the attenuation of actuality. In Kafka, the descriptive detail is of an extraordinary immediacy and authenticity. But Kafka's artistic ingenuity is really directed towards substituting his *angst*-ridden vision of the world for objective reality. The realistic detail is the expression of a ghostly un-reality, of a nightmare world, whose function is to evoke *angst.* The same phenomenon can be seen in writers who attempt to combine Kafka's techniques with a critique of society — like the German writer, Wolfgang Koeppen, in his satirical novel about Bonn, *Das Treibhaus.* A similar attenuation of reality underlies Joyce's stream of consciousness. It is, of course, intensified where the stream of consciousness is itself the medium through which reality is presented. And it is carried *ad absurdum* where the stream of consciousness is that of an abnormal subject or of an idiot — consider the first part of Faulkner's *Sound and Fury* or, a still more extreme case, Beckett's *Molloy.*

Attentuation of reality and dissolution of personality are thus interdependent: the stronger the one, the stronger the other. Underlying both is the lack of a consistent view of human nature. Man is reduced to a sequence of unrelated experiential fragments; he is as inexplicable to others as to himself. In Eliot's *Cocktail Party* the psychiatrist, who voices the opinions of the author, describes the phenomenon:

> Ah, but we die to each other daily
> What we know of other people
> Is only our memory of the moments
> During which we knew them. And they have changed since then.
> To pretend that they and we are the same
> Is a useful and convenient social convention
> Which must sometimes be broken. We must also remember
> That at every meeting we are meeting a stranger.

The dissolution of personality, originally the unconscious product of the identification of concrete and abstract potentiality, is elevated to a deliberate principle in the light of consciousness. It is no accident that Gottfried Benn called one of his theoretical tracts *"Doppelleben."*[9] For Benn, this dissolution of personality took the form of a schizophrenic dichotomy. According to him,

[8]"The Hollow Men" (1925). [Ed.]

[9]Double life. [Ed.]

there was in man's personality no coherent pattern of motivation or behavior. Man's animal nature is opposed to his denaturized, sublimated thought processes. The unity of thought and action is "backwoods philosophy"; thought and being are "quite separate entities." Man must be either a moral or a thinking being — he cannot be both at once.

These are not, I think, purely private, eccentric speculations. Of course, they are derived from Benn's specific experience. But there is an inner connection between these ideas and a certain tradition of bourgeois thought. It is more than a hundred years since Kierkegaard first attacked the Hegelian view that the inner and outer world form an objective dialectical unity, that they are indissolubly married in spite of their apparent opposition. Kierkegaard denied any such unity. According to Kierkegaard, the individual exists within an opaque, impenetrable "incognito."

This philosophy attained remarkable popularity after the Second World War — proof that even the most abstruse theories may reflect social reality. Men like Martin Heidegger, Ernst Jünger, the lawyer Carl Schmitt, Gottfried Benn and others passionately embraced this doctrine of the eternal incognito which implies that a man's external deeds are no guide to his motives. In this case, the deeds obscured behind the mysterious incognito were, needless to say, these intellectuals' participation in Nazism: Heidegger, as Rector of Freiburg University, had glorified Hitler's seizure of power at his Inauguration; Carl Schmitt had put his great legal gifts at Hitler's disposal. The facts were too well known to be simply denied. But, if this impenetrable incognito were the true *"condition humaine,"*[10] might not — concealed within their incognito — Heidegger or Schmitt have been secret opponents of Hitler all the time, only supporting him in the world of appearances? Ernst von Salomon's cynical frankness about his opportunism in *The Questionnaire* (keeping his reservations to himself or declaring them only in the presence of intimate friends) may be read as an ironic commentary on this ideology of the incognito as we find it, say, in the writings of Ernst Jünger.

This digression may serve to show, taking an extreme example, what the social implications of such an ontology may be. In the literary field, this particular ideology was of cardinal importance; by destroying the complex tissue of man's relations with his environment, it furthered the dissolution of personality. For it is just the opposition between a man and his environment that determines the development of his personality. There is no great hero of fiction — from Homer's Achilles to Mann's Adrian Leverkühn or Sholochov's Grigory Melyekov[11] — whose personality is not the product of such an opposition. I have shown how disastrous the denial of the distinction between abstract and concrete potentiality must be for the presentation of character. The destruction of the complex tissue of man's interaction with his environment likewise saps the vitality of this opposition. Certainly, some writers who adhere to this ideology have attempted, not unsuccessfully, to portray this opposition in concrete terms. But the underlying ideology deprives these contradictions of their dynamic, developmental significance. The contradictions coexist, unresolved, contributing to the further dissolution of the personality in question.

It is to the credit of Robert Musil that he was quite conscious of the implications of his method. Of his hero Ulrich he remarked: "One is faced with a simple choice: either one must run with the pack (when in Rome, do as the Romans do); or one becomes a neurotic." Musil here introduces the problem, central to all modernist literature, of the significance of psychopathology.

This problem was first widely discussed in the Naturalist period. More than fifty years ago, that doyen of Berlin dramatic critics, Alfred Kerr, was writing: "Morbidity is the legitimate poetry of Naturalism. For what is poetic in everyday life? Neurotic aberration, escape from life's dreary routine. Only in this way can a character be translated to a rarer clime and yet retain an air of reality." Interesting, here, is the notion that the

[10]Human condition. Lukács's use of the French alludes to the Marxist novel about opposition to Fascism, *La Condition Humaine (Man's Fate)* by André Malraux. [Ed.]

[11]Heroes of the *Iliad, Doctor Faustus,* and *Quiet Flows the Don.* [Ed.]

poetic necessity of the pathological derives from the prosaic quality of life under capitalism. I would maintain — we shall return to this point — that in modern writing there is a continuity from Naturalism to the Modernism of our day — a continuity restricted, admittedly, to underlying ideological principles. What at first was no more than dim anticipation of approaching catastrophe developed, after 1914, into an all-pervading obsession. And I would suggest that the ever-increasing part played by psychopathology was one of the main features of the continuity. At each period — depending on the prevailing social and historical conditions — psychopathology was given a new emphasis, a different significance and artistic function. Kerr's description suggests that in naturalism the interest in psychopathology sprang from an aesthetic need; it was an attempt to escape from the dreariness of life under capitalism. The quotation from Musil shows that some years later the opposition acquired a moral slant. The obsession with morbidity had ceased to have a merely decorative function, bringing color into the greyness of reality, and become a moral protest against capitalism.

With Musil — and with many other modernist writers — psychopathology became the goal, the *terminus ad quem,*[12] of their artistic intention. But there is a double difficulty inherent in their intention, which follows from its underlying ideology. There is, first, a lack of definition. The protest expressed by this flight into psychopathology is an abstract gesture; its rejection of reality is wholesale and summary, containing no concrete criticism. It is a gesture, moreover, that is destined to lead nowhere; it is an escape into nothingness. Thus the propagators of this ideology are mistaken in thinking that such a protest could ever be fruitful in literature. In any protest against particular social conditions, these conditions themselves must have the central place. The bourgeois protest against feudal society, the proletarian against bourgeois society, made their point of departure a criticism of the old order. In both cases the protest — reaching out beyond the point of departure — was based on a concrete *terminus ad quem:* the establishment of a new order. However indefinite the structure and content of this new order, the will towards its more exact definition was not lacking.

How different the protest of writers like Musil! The *terminus a quo*[13] (the corrupt society of our time) is inevitably the main source of energy, since the *terminus ad quem* (the escape into psychopathology) is a mere abstraction. The rejection of modern reality is purely subjective. Considered in terms of man's relation with his environment, it lacks both content and direction. And this lack is exaggerated still further by the character of the *terminus ad quem.* For the protest is an empty gesture, expressing nausea, or discomfort, or longing. Its content — or rather lack of content — derives from the fact that such a view of life cannot impact a sense of direction. These writers are not wholly wrong in believing that psychopathology is their surest refuge; it is the ideological complement of their historical position.

This obsession with the pathological is not only to be found in literature. Freudian psychoanalysis is its most obvious expression. The treatment of the subject is only superficially different from that in modern literature. As everybody knows, Freud's starting point was "everyday life." In order to explain "slips" and daydreams, however, he had to have recourse to psychopathology. In his lectures, speaking of resistance and repression, he says: "Our interest in the general psychology of symptom-formation increases as we understand to what extent the study of pathological conditions can shed light on the workings of the normal mind." Freud believed he had found the key to the understanding of the normal personality in the psychology of the abnormal. This belief is still more evident in the typology of Kretschmer, which also assumes that psychological abnormalities can explain normal psychology. It is only when we compare Freud's psychology with that of Pavlov, who takes the Hippocratic view that mental abnormality is a deviation from a norm, that we see it in its true light.

Clearly, this is not strictly a scientific or literary-critical problem. It is an ideological

[12]End point. [Ed.]

[13]Starting point. [Ed.]

problem, deriving from the ontological dogma of the solitariness of man. The literature of realism, based on the Aristotelian concept of man as *zoon politikon,*[14] is entitled to develop a new typology for each new phase in the evolution of a society. It displays the contradictions within society and within the individual in the context of a dialectical unity. Here, individuals embodying violent and extraordinary passions are still within the range of a socially normal typology (Shakespeare, Balzac, Stendhal). For, in this literature, the average man is simply a dimmer reflection of the contradictions always existing in man and society; eccentricity is a socially-conditioned distortion. Obviously, the passions of the great heroes must not be confused with "eccentricity" in the colloquial sense: Christian Buddenbrook is an "eccentric"; Adrian Leverkühn is not.

The ontology of *Geworfenheit* makes a true typology impossible; it is replaced by an abstract polarity of the eccentric and the socially average. We have seen why this polarity — which in traditional realism serves to increase our understanding of social normality — leads in modernism to a fascination with morbid eccentricity. Eccentricity becomes the necessary complement of the average; and this polarity is held to exhaust human potentiality. The implications of this ideology are shown in another remark of Musil's: "If humanity dreamt collectively, it would dream Moosbrugger." Moosbrugger, you will remember, was a mentally retarded sexual pervert with homicidal tendencies.

What served, with Musil, as the ideological basis of a new typology — escape into neurosis as a protest against the evils of society — becomes with other modernist writers an immutable *condition humaine.* Musil's statement loses its conditional "if" and becomes a simple description of reality. Lack of objectivity in the description of the outer world finds its complement in the reduction of reality to a nightmare. Beckett's *Molloy* is perhaps the *ne plus ultra*[15] of this development, although Joyce's vision of reality as an incoherent stream of consciousness had already assumed in Faulkner a nightmare quality. In Beckett's novel we have the same vision twice over. He presents us with an image of the utmost human degradation — an idiot's vegetative existence. Then, as help is imminent from a mysterious unspecified source, the rescuer himself sinks into idiocy. The story is told through the parallel streams of consciousness of the idiot and of his rescuer.

Along with the adoption of perversity and idiocy as types of the *condition humaine,* we find what amounts to frank glorification. Take Montherlant's *Pasiphae,* where sexual perversity — the heroine's infatuation with a bull — is presented as a triumphant return to nature, as the liberation of impulse from the slavery of convention. The chorus — i.e., the author — puts the following question (which, though rhetorical, clearly expects an affirmative reply): "Si l'absence de pensée et l'absence de morale ne contribuent pas beaucoup à la dignité des bêtes, des plantes et des eaux . . . ?"[16] Montherlant expresses as plainly as Musil, though with different moral and emotional emphasis, the hidden — one might say repressed — social character of the protest underlying this obsession with psychopathology, its perverted Rousseauism,[17] its anarchism. There are many illustrations of this in modernist writing. A poem of Benn's will serve to make the point:

> O that we were our primal ancestors,
> Small lumps of plasma in hot, sultry swamps;
> Life, death, conception, parturition
> Emerging from those juices soundlessly.
>
> A frond of seaweed or a dune of sand,
> Formed by the wind and heavy at the base;
> A dragonfly or gull's wing — already, these
> Would signify excessive suffering.

This is not overtly perverse in the manner of Beckett or Montherlant. Yet, in his primitivism, Benn is at one with them. The opposition of man as animal to man as social being (for instance, Heidegger's devaluation of the social as *"das Man,"*[18] Klages's assertion of the incompatibility

[14]Political animal. [Ed.]

[15]Ultimate point. [Ed.]

[16]"If the absence of thought and the absence of morality do not contribute a good deal to the dignity of animals, plants, and bodies of water. . . ." [Ed.]

[17]Here, adulation of the primitive as noble. [Ed.]

[18]An untranslatable phrase signifying vague personhood. The German word *man* is the indefinite pronoun equivalent to the English "one." [Ed.]

of *Geist* and *Seele*,[19] or Rosenberg's racial mythology)[20] leads straight to a glorification of the abnormal and to an undisguised antihumanism.

A typology limited in this way to the *homme moyen sensuel* and the idiot also opens the door to "experimental" stylistic distortion. Distortion becomes as inseparable a part of the portrayal of reality as the recourse to the pathological. But literature must have a concept of the normal if it is to "place" distortion correctly; that is to say, to see it *as* distortion. With such a typology this placing is impossible, since the normal is no longer a proper object of literary interest. Life under capitalism is, often rightly, presented as a distortion (a petrification or paralysis) of the human substance. But to present psychopathology as a way of escape from this distortion is itself a distortion. We are invited to measure one type of distortion against another and arrive, necessarily, at universal distortion. There is no principle to set against the general pattern, no standard by which the petty-bourgeois and the pathological can be seen in their social context. And these tendencies, far from being relativized with time, become ever more absolute. Distortion becomes the normal condition of human existence; the proper study, the formative principle, of art and literature.

I have demonstrated some of the literary implications of this ideology. Let us now pursue the argument further. It is clear, I think, that modernism must deprive literature of a sense of *perspective*. This would not be surprising; rigorous modernists such as Kafka, Benn, and Musil have always indignantly refused to provide their readers with any such thing. I will return to the ideological implications of the idea of perspective later. Let me say here that, in any work of art, perspective is of overriding importance. It determines the course and content; it draws together the threads of the narration; it enables the artist to choose between the important and the superficial, the crucial and the episodic. The direction in which characters develop is determined by perspective, only those features being described which are material to their development. The more lucid the perspective — as in Molière or the Greeks — the more economical and striking the selection.

Modernism drops this selective principle. It asserts that it can dispense with it, or can replace it with its dogma of the *condition humaine*. A naturalistic style is bound to be the result. This state of affairs — which to my mind characterizes all modernist art of the past fifty years — is disguised by critics who systematically glorify the modernist movement. By concentrating on formal criteria, by isolating technique from content and exaggerating its importance, these critics refrain from judgment on the social or artistic significance of subject matter. They are unable, in consequence, to make the aesthetic distinction between *realism* and *naturalism*. This distinction depends on the presence or absence in a work of art of "hierarchy of significance" in the situations and characters presented. Compared with this, formal categories are of secondary importance. That is why it is possible to speak of the basically *naturalistic* character of modernist literature — and to see here the literary expression of an ideological continuity. This is not to deny that variations in style reflect changes in society. But the particular form this principle of naturalistic arbitrariness, this lack of hierarchic structure, may take is not decisive. We encounter it in the all-determining "social conditions" of Naturalism, in Symbolism's impressionist methods and its cultivation of the exotic, in the fragmentation of objective reality in Futurism and Constructivism and the German *Neue Sachlichkeit*,[21] or, again, in Surrealism's stream of consciousness.

These schools have in common a basically static approach to reality. This is closely related to their lack of perspective. Characteristically, Gottfried Benn actually incorporated this in his artistic program. One of his volumes bears the title, *Static Poems*. The denial of history, of development, and thus of perspective, becomes the mark of true insight into the nature of reality.

> The wise man is ignorant
> of change and development

[19]Spirit and soul. [Ed.]

[20]Alfred Rosenberg (1893–1946), a Nazi ideologist of anti-Semitism, author of *The Myth of the Twentieth Century* (1934). [Ed.]

[21]New objectivity or impersonality. [Ed.]

his children and children's children
are no part of his world.

The rejection of any concept of the future is for Benn the criterion of wisdom. But even those modernist writers who are less extreme in their rejection of history tend to present social and historical phenomena as static. It is, then, of small importance whether this condition is "eternal," or only a transitional stage punctuated by sudden catastrophes (even in early Naturalism the static presentation was often broken up by these catastrophes, without altering its basic character). Musil, for instance, writes in his essay, *The Writer in our Age:* "One knows just as little about the present. Partly, this is because we are, as always, too close to the present. But it is also because the present into which we were plunged some two decades ago is of a particularly all-embracing and inescapable character." Whether or not Musil knew of Heidegger's philosophy, the idea of *Geworfenheit* is clearly at work here. And the following reveals plainly how, for Musil, this static state was upset by the catastrophe of 1914: "All of a sudden, the world was full of violence. . . . In European civilization, there was a sudden rift. . . ." In short: this static apprehension of reality in modernist literature is no passing fashion; it is rooted in the ideology of modernism.

To establish the basic distinction between modernism and that realism which, from Homer to Thomas Mann and Gorky, has assumed change and development to be the proper subject of literature, we must go deeper into the underlying ideological problem. In *The House of the Dead* Dostoevsky gave an interesting account of the convict's attitude to work. He described how the prisoners, in spite of brutal discipline, loafed about, working badly or merely going through the motions of work until a new overseer arrived and allotted them a new project, after which they were allowed to go home. "The work was hard," Dostoevsky continues, "but, Christ, with what energy they threw themselves into it! Gone was all their former indolence and pretended incompetence." Later in the book Dostoevsky sums up his experiences: "If a man loses hope and has no aim in view, sheer boredom can turn him into a beast. . . ." I have said that the problem of perspective in literature is directly related to the principle of selection. Let me go further: underlying the problem is a profound ethical complex, reflected in the composition of the work itself. Every human action is based on a presupposition of its inherent meaningfulness, at least to the subject. Absence of meaning makes a mockery of action and reduces art to naturalistic description.

Clearly, there can be no literature without at least the appearance of change or development. This conclusion should not be interpreted in a narrowly metaphysical sense. We have already diagnosed the obsession with psychopathology in modernist literature as a desire to escape from the reality of capitalism. But this implies the absolute primacy of the *terminus a quo,* the condition from which it is desired to escape. Any movement towards a *terminus ad quem* is condemned to impotence. As the ideology of most modernist writers asserts the unalterability of outward reality (even if this is reduced to a mere state of consciousness) human activity is, *a priori,* rendered impotent and robbed of meaning.

The apprehension of reality to which this leads is most consistently and convincingly realized in the work of Kafka. Kafka remarks of Josef K., as he is being led to execution: "He thought of flies, their tiny limbs breaking as they struggle away from the fly-paper." This mood of total impotence, of paralysis in the face of the unintelligible power of circumstances, informs all his work. Though the action of *The Castle* takes a different, even an opposite, direction to that of *The Trial,* this view of the world, from the perspective of a trapped and struggling fly, is all-pervasive. This experience, this vision of a world dominated by *angst* and of man at the mercy of incomprehensible terrors, makes Kafka's work the very type of modernist art. Techniques, elsewhere of merely formal significance, are used here to evoke a primitive awe in the presence of an utterly strange and hostile reality. Kafka's *angst* is the experience *par excellence* of modernism.

Two instances from musical criticism — which can afford to be both franker and more theoretical than literary criticism — show that it is indeed a universal experience with which we are dealing. The composer, Hanns Eisler, says of Schönberg: "Long before the invention of the bomber, he expressed what people were to feel in the air raid shelters." Even more characteristic — though seen from a modernist point of view — is Theodor W. Adorno's analysis (in *The Aging of Modern Music*) of symptoms of decadence in modernist music: "The sounds are still the same. But the experience of *angst,* which made their originals great, has vanished." Modernist music, he continues, has lost touch with the truth that was its *raison d'être*. Composers are no longer equal to the emotional presuppositions of their modernism. And that is why modernist music has failed. The diminution of the original *angst*-obsessed vision of life (whether due, as Adorno thinks, to inability to respond to the magnitude of the horror or, as I believe, to the fact that this obsession with *angst* among bourgeois intellectuals has already begun to recede) has brought about a loss of substance in modern music, and destroyed its authenticity as a modernist art form.

This is a shrewd analysis of the paradoxical situation of the modernist artist, particularly where he is trying to express deep and genuine experience. The deeper the experience, the greater the damage to the artistic whole. But this tendency towards disintegration, this loss of artistic unity, cannot be written off as a mere fashion, the product of experimental gimmicks. Modern philosophy, after all, encountered these problems long before modern literature, painting or music. A case in point is the problem of *time*. Subjective Idealism had already separated time, abstractly conceived, from historical change and particularity of place. As if this separation were insufficient for the new age of imperialism, Bergson widened it further. Experienced time, subjective time, now became identical with real time; the rift between this time and that of the objective world was complete. Bergson and other philosophers, who took up and varied this theme claimed that their concept of time alone afforded insight into authentic, i.e., subjective, reality. The same tendency soon made its appearance in literature.

The German left-wing critic and essayist of the twenties, Walter Benjamin, has well described Proust's vision and the techniques he uses to present it in his great novel: "We all know that Proust does not describe a man's life as it actually happens, but as it is remembered by a man who has lived through it. Yet this puts it far too crudely. For it is not actual experience that is important, but the texture of reminiscence, the Penelope's tapestry of a man's memory." The connection with Bergson's theories of time is obvious. But whereas with Bergson, in the abstraction of philosophy, the unity of perception is preserved, Benjamin shows that with Proust, as a result of the radical disintegration of the time sequence, objectivity is eliminated: "A lived event is finite, concluded at least on the level of experience. But a remembered event is infinite, a possible key to everything that preceded it and to everything that will follow it."

It is the distinction between a philosophical and an artistic vision of the world. However hard philosophy, under the influence of Idealism, tries to liberate the concepts of space and time from temporal and spatial particularity, literature continues to assume their unity. The fact that, nevertheless, the concept of subjective time cropped up in literature only shows how deeply subjectivism is rooted in the experience of the modern bourgeois intellectual. The individual, retreating into himself in despair at the cruelty of the age, may experience an intoxicated fascination with his forlorn condition. But then a new horror breaks through. If reality cannot be understood (or no effort is made to understand it), then the individual's subjectivity — alone in the universe, reflecting only itself — takes on an equally incomprehensible and horrific character. Hugo von Hofmannsthal was to experience this condition very early in his poetic career:

> It is a thing that no man cares to think on,
> And far too terrible for mere complaint,
> That all things slip from us and pass away,
>
> And that my ego, bound by no outward force —
> Once a small child's before it became mine —
> Should now be strange to me, like a strange dog.

By separating time from the outer world of objective reality, the inner world of the subject is transformed into a sinister, inexplicable flux and acquires — paradoxically, as it may seem — a static character.

On literature this tendency towards disintegration, of course, will have an even greater impact than on philosophy. When time is isolated in this way, the artist's world disintegrates into a multiplicity of partial worlds. The static view of the world, now combined with diminished objectivity, here rules unchallenged. The world of man — the only subject matter of literature — is shattered if a single component is removed. I have shown the consequences of isolating time and reducing it to a subjective category. But time is by no means the only component whose removal can lead to such disintegration. Here, again, Hofmannsthal anticipated later developments. His imaginary "Lord Chandos" reflects: "I have lost the ability to concentrate my thoughts or set them out coherently." The result is a condition of apathy, punctuated by manic fits. The development towards a definitely pathological protest is here anticipated — admittedly in glamorous, romantic guise. But it is the same disintegration that is at work.

Previous realistic literature, however violent its criticism of reality, had always assumed the unity of the world it described and seen it as a living whole inseparable from man himself. But the major realists of our time deliberately introduce elements of disintegration into their work — for instance, the subjectivizing of time — and use them to portray the contemporary world more exactly. In this way, the once natural unity becomes a conscious, constructed unity (I have shown elsewhere that the device of the two temporal planes in Thomas Mann's *Doctor Faustus* serves to emphasize its historicity). But in modernist literature the disintegration of the world of man — and consequently the disintegration of personality — coincides with the ideological intention. Thus *angst,* this basic modern experience, this by-product of *Geworfenheit,* has its emotional origin in the experience of a disintegrating society. But it attains its effects by evoking the disintegration of the world of man.

To complete our examination of modernist literature, we must consider for a moment the question of allegory. Allegory is that aesthetic genre which lends itself *par excellence* to a description of man's alienation from objective reality. Allegory is a problematic genre because it rejects that assumption of an immanent meaning to human existence which — however unconscious, however combined with religious concepts of transcendence — is the basis of traditional art. Thus in medieval art we observe a new secularity (in spite of the continued use of religious subjects) triumphing more and more, from the time of Giotto, over the allegorizing of an earlier period.

Certain reservations should be made at this point. First, we must distinguish between literature and the visual arts. In the latter, the limitations of allegory can be the more easily overcome in that transcendental, allegorical subjects can be clothed in an aesthetic immanence (even if of a merely decorative kind) and the rift in reality in some sense be eliminated — we have only to think of Byzantine mosaic art. This decorative element has no real equivalent in literature; it exists only in a figurative sense, and then only as a secondary component. Allegorical art of the quality of Byzantine mosaic is only rarely possible in literature. Secondly, we must bear in mind in examining allegory — and this is of great importance for our argument — a historical distinction: does the concept of transcendence in question contain within itself tendencies towards immanence (as in Byzantine art or Giotto), or is it the product precisely of a rejection of these tendencies?

Allegory, in modernist literature, is clearly of the latter kind. Transcendence implies here, more or less consciously, the negation of any meaning immanent in the world or the life of man. We have already examined the underlying ideological basis of this view and its stylistic consequences. To conclude our analysis, and to establish the allegorical character of modernist literature, I must refer again to the work of one of the finest theoreticians of modernism — to Walter Benjamin. Benjamin's examination of allegory was a product of his researches into German Baroque drama. Benjamin made his analysis of these relatively minor plays the occasion for a general discussion of the aesthetics of allegory. He was asking, in effect, why it is that transcendence, which is the essence of allegory, cannot but destroy aesthetics itself.

Benjamin gives a very contemporary definition of allegory. He does not labor the analogies between modern art and the Baroque (such analogies are tenuous at best, and were much overdone by the fashionable criticism of the time). Rather, he uses the Baroque drama to criticize modernism, imputing the characteristics of the latter to the former. In so doing, Benjamin became the first critic to attempt a philosophical analysis of the aesthetic paradox underlying modernist art. He writes:

> In Allegory, the *facies hippocratica* of history looks to the observer like a petrified primeval landscape. History, all the suffering and failure it contains, finds expression in the human face — or, rather, in the human skull. No sense of freedom, no classical proportion, no human emotion lives in its features — not only human existence in general, but the fate of every individual human being is symbolized in this most palpable token of mortality. This is the core of the allegorical vision, of the Baroque idea of history as the passion of the world; History is significant only in the stations of its corruption. Significance is a function of mortality — because it is death that marks the passage from corruptibility to meaningfulness.

Benjamin returns again and again to this link between allegory and the annihilation of history:

> In the light of this vision history appears, not as the gradual realization of the eternal, but as a process of inevitable decay. Allegory thus goes beyond beauty. What ruins are in the physical world, allegories are in the world of the mind.

Benjamin points here to the aesthetic consequences of modernism — though projected into the Baroque drama — more shrewdly and consistently than any of his contemporaries. He sees that the notion of objective time is essential to any understanding of history, and that the notion of subjective time is a product of a period of decline. "A thorough knowledge of the problematic nature of art" thus becomes for him — correctly, from his point of view — one of the hallmarks of allegory in Baroque drama. It is problematic, on the one hand, because it is an art intent on expressing absolute transcendence that fails to do so because of the means at its disposal. It is also problematic because it is an art reflecting the corruption of the world and bringing about its own dissolution in the process. Benjamin discovers "an immense, anti-aesthetic subjectivity" in Baroque literature, associated with "a theologically-determined subjectivity." (We shall presently show — a point I have discussed elsewhere in relation to Heidegger's philosophy — how in literature a "religious atheism" of this kind can acquire a theological character.) Romantic — and, on a higher plane, Baroque — writers were well aware of this problem, and gave their understanding, not only theoretical, but artistic — that is to say allegorical — expression. "The image," Benjamin remarks, "becomes a rune in the sphere of allegorical intuition. When touched by the light of theology, its symbolic beauty is gone. The false appearance of totality vanishes. The image dies; the parable no longer holds true; the world it once contained disappears."

The consequences for art are far-reaching, and Benjamin does not hesitate to point them out: "Every person, every object, every relationship can stand for something else. This transferability constitutes a devastating, though just, judgment on the profane world — which is thereby branded as a world where such things are of small importance." Benjamin knows, of course, that although details are "transferable," and thus insignificant, they are not banished from art altogether. On the contrary. Precisely in modern art, with which he is ultimately concerned, descriptive detail is often of an extraordinary sensuous, suggestive power — we think again of Kafka. But this, as we showed in the case of Musil (a writer who does not consciously aim at allegory) does not prevent the materiality of the world from undergoing permanent alteration, from becoming transferable and arbitrary. Just this, modernist writers maintain, is typical of their own apprehension of reality. Yet presented in this way, the world becomes, as Benjamin puts it, "exalted and depreciated at the same time." For the conviction that phenomena are *not* ultimately transferable is rooted in a belief in the world's rationality and in man's ability to penetrate its secrets. In realistic literature each descriptive detail is both *individual* and *typical*. Modern allegory, and modernist ideology, however, deny the *typical*. By destroying the coherence of the world, they reduce detail to the level of mere particularity (once again, the connection between modernism and naturalism is plain). Detail, in its allegorical transferability, though brought into a direct, if paradoxical connection with transcendence, becomes an abstract function of the transcendence to which it points. Modernist literature thus replaces concrete typicality with abstract particularity.

We are here applying Benjamin's paradox directly to aesthetics and criticism, and particularly to the aesthetics of modernism. And, though we have reversed his scale of values, we have not deviated from the course of his argument. Elsewhere, he speaks out even more plainly — as though the Baroque mask had fallen, revealing the modernist skull underneath:

> Allegory is left empty-handed. The forces of evil, lurking in its depths, owe their very existence to allegory. Evil is, precisely, the non-existence of that which allegory purports to represent.

The paradox Benjamin arrives at — his investigation of the aesthetics of Baroque tragedy has culminated in a negation of aesthetics — sheds a good deal of light on modernist literature, and particularly on Kafka. In interpreting his writings allegorically I am not, of course, following Max Brod, who finds a specifically religious allegory in Kafka's works. Kafka refuted any such interpretation in a remark he is said to have made to Brod himself: "We are nihilistic figments, all of us; suicidal notions forming in God's mind." Kafka rejected, too, the gnostic concept of God as an evil demiurge: "The world is a cruel whim of God, an evil day's work." When Brod attempted to give this an optimistic slant, Kafka shrugged off the attempt ironically: "Oh, hope enough, hope without end — but not, alas, for us." These remarks, quoted by Benjamin in his brilliant essay on Kafka, point to the general spiritual climate of his work: "His profoundest experience is of the hopelessness, the utter meaninglessness of man's world, and particularly that of present day bourgeois man." Kafka, whether he says so openly or not, is an atheist. An atheist, though, of that modern species who regard God's removal from the scene not as a liberation — as did Epicurus and the Encyclopedists — but as a token of the "God-forsakenness" of the world, its utter desolation of futility. Jacobsen's *Niels Lyhne* was the first novel to describe this state of mind of the atheistic bourgeois intelligentsia. Modern religious atheism is characterized, on the one hand, by the fact that unbelief has lost its revolutionary *élan* — the empty heavens are the projection of a world beyond hope of redemption. On the other hand, religious atheism shows that the desire for salvation lives on with undiminished force in a world without God, worshipping the voice created by God's absence.

The supreme judges in *The Trial,* the castle administration in *The Castle,* represent transcendence in Kafka's allegories: the transcendence of Nothingness. Everything points to them, and they could give meaning to everything. Everybody believes in their existence and omnipotence; but nobody knows them, nobody knows how they can be reached. If there is a God here, it can only be the God of religious atheism: *atheos absconditus.*[22] We become acquainted with a repellent host of subordinate authorities; brutal, corrupt, pedantic — and, at the same time, unreliable and irresponsible. It is a portrait of the bourgeois society Kafka knew, with a dash of Prague local coloring. But it is also allegorical in that the doings of this bureaucracy and of those dependent on it, its impotent victims, are not concrete and realistic, but a reflection of that Nothingness which governs existence. The hidden, nonexistent God of Kafka's world derives his spectral character from the fact that his own non-existence is the ground of all existence; and the portrayed reality, uncannily accurate as it is, is spectral in the shadow of that dependence. The only purpose of transcendence — the intangible *nichtendes Nichts*[23] — is to reveal the *facies hippocratica*[24] of the world.

That abstract particularity which we saw to be the aesthetic consequence of allegory reaches its high mark in Kafka. He is a marvelous observer; the spectral character of reality affects him so deeply that the simplest episodes have an oppressive, nightmarish immediacy. As an artist, he is not content to evoke the surface of life. He is aware that individual detail must point to general significance. But how does he go about the business of abstraction? He has emptied everyday life of meaning by using the allegorical method; he has allowed detail to be annihilated by his transcendental Nothingness. This allegorical transcendence bars Kafka's way to realism, prevents him from investing observed detail with typical

[22]The departed no-God. [Ed.]
[23]Annihilating nothingness. [Ed.]
[24]Skull beneath the skin. [Ed.]

significance. Kafka is not able, in spite of his extraordinary evocative power, in spite of his unique sensibility, to achieve that fusion of the particular and the general which is the essence of realistic art. His aim is to raise the individual detail in its immediate particularity (without generalizing its content) to the level of abstraction. Kafka's method is typical, here, of modernism's allegorical approach. Specific subject matter and stylistic variation do not matter; what matters is the basic ideological determination of form and content. The particularity we find in Beckett and Joyce, in Musil and Benn, various as the treatment of it may be, is essentially of the same kind.

If we combine what we have up to now discussed separately we arrive at a consistent pattern. We see that modernism leads not only to the destruction of traditional literary forms; it leads to the destruction of literature as such. And this is true not only of Joyce, or of the literature of Expressionism and Surrealism. It was not André Gide's ambition, for instance, to bring about a revolution in literary style; it was his philosophy that compelled him to abandon conventional forms. He planned his *Faux-Monnayeurs*[25] as a novel. But its structure suffered from a characteristically modernist schizophrenia: it was supposed to be written by the man who was also the hero of the novel. And, in practice, Gide was forced to admit that no novel, no work of literature could be constructed in that way. We have here a practical demonstration that — as Benjamin showed in another context — modernism means not the enrichment, but the negation of art.

[25]André Gide, *The Counterfeiters* (1949). [Ed.]

Terry Eagleton

b. 1943

Terence Francis Eagleton was born in 1943 in Salford, England, and educated at Trinity College, Cambridge, where he became the student and disciple of Marxist literary critic Raymond Williams, who, like Eagleton, came from a rural working-class family of Celtic origin. Eagleton took his doctoral degree at Trinity and became a fellow of Jesus College, Cambridge, at the age of 21. In 1969, Eagleton moved as fellow to Wadham College, Oxford, where he is now tutor in English. Since the death of Williams in 1988, Eagleton has been regarded as the premier British Marxist literary critic. Eagleton's Marxism has gone through three distinct phases. In the first phase (1966–70), Eagleton wrote four books, including Shakespeare and Society: Critical Studies in Shakespearean Drama *(1967) and* Exiles and Emigres: Studies in Modern Literature *(1970). In these works Eagleton seems to be trying to reconcile Williams's humanist Marxism with the values of his own Roman Catholic upbringing. After a five-year hiatus, Eagleton rapidly published three books that rejected the humanist Marxism of Williams in favor of a post-Althusserian "science of the text":* Myths of Power: A Marxist Study of the Brontës *(1975);* Marxism and Literary Criticism *(1976); and* Criticism and Ideology: A Study in Marxist Literary Theory *(1976). After another five year hiatus (1976–81), Eagleton's position shifted once more. Though he has not explicitly repudiated the "scientific" theorizing of* Criticism and Ideology, *his books since* Walter Benjamin *(1981) have called for a "revolutionary criticism" that explicitly seeks practical social goals as the end of literary study rather than mere knowledge of the text. His latest works include* The Rape of Clarissa: Writing, Sexuality, and Class Struggle in Richardson *(1982),* Literary Theory: An Introduction *(1983; second edition 1997),* The Function of Criticism: From the Spectator to Post-Structuralism *(1984),* William Shakespeare *(1986),* Against the Grain: Selected Essays 1975–85 *(1986),* The Ideology of the Aesthetic *(1990),* Ideology: An Introduction *(1991),* The Significance of Theory *(1990), and* Heathcliff and the Great Hunger

(1995). He has also published a novel, Saints and Scholars *(1987). The following selection is the second chapter of* Criticism and Ideology.

Categories for a Materialist Criticism

Every work is the work of many things besides an author.
— VALÉRY

The work of Raymond Williams, flawed as it has been by "humanism" and idealism, represents one of the most significant sources from which a materialist aesthetics might be derived. Refusing that pervasive form of critical idealism which would repress the whole material infrastructure of artistic production, Williams has properly insisted on the reality of art as "material practice." Yet it is not only that his conception of art as "practice" retains strong residual elements of humanism; it is also that, to date at least, the constituent structures of that practice have received little systematic analysis in his work. It is necessary, then, to develop a method whereby those structures can be rigorously specified, and their precise articulations examined.

It is possible to set out in schematic form the major constituents of a Marxist theory of literature. They can be listed as follows:

(i) General Mode of Production (GMP)
(ii) Literary Mode of Production (LMP)
(iii) General Ideology (GI)
(iv) Authorial Ideology (AuI)
(v) Aesthetic Ideology (AI)
(vi) Text

The text, strictly speaking, is hardly a *constituent* of literary theory; it is, rather, its object. But in so far as it must be examined in its relations with the other elements set out, it can be regarded methodologically as a particular "level." The task of criticism is to analyse the complex historical *articulations* of these structures which produce the text.

(i) GENERAL MODE OF PRODUCTION (GMP)

A mode of production may be characterised as a unity of certain forces and social relations of material production. Each social formation is characterised by a combination of such modes of production, one of which will normally be dominant. By "General Mode of Production" I designate that dominant mode; I use the term "general," not because economic production is ever anything other than historically specific, but to distinguish economic production from:

(ii) LITERARY MODE OF PRODUCTION (LMP)

A unity of certain forces and social relations of literary production in a particular social formation. In any literate society there will normally exist a number of distinct modes of literary production, one of which will normally be dominant. These distinct LMPs will be mutually articulated in varying relations of homology, conflict and contradiction: they will constitute an "asymmetrical" totality, since the dominance of a particular LMP will force other modes into positions of subordination and partial exclusion. Structurally conflictual LMPs may thus coexist within a particular social formation: if it is possible in Western societies to produce fiction for the capitalist market, it is also possible to distribute one's handwritten poetry on the streets. Coexistent LMPs, however, need not be historically synchronous with one another. An LMP produced by an historically previous social formation may survive within and interpenetrate later modes: the co-presence of the "patronage" system and capitalist literary production in eighteenth-century England, the persistence of "artisanal" literary production within the capitalist LMP.[1] A classical instance of such survivals is typically to be found in the historical mutation from "oral" to "written" LMPs, where the social relations and kinds of literary product appropriate to the "oral" LMP normally persist as significant constituents of the "written" LMP itself, both interactive with and relatively autonomous of it. In medieval England, for example, "reading" continues to mean, almost invariably, reading aloud in public; and much of the "written" LMP consists in committing to manuscript form products of the "oral" mode. Conversely, the emergence of the "written" LMP perpetuates certain more complex and extensive oral products, developing that LMP as it is itself developed by it. With the development of a "written" LMP in sixth-century Ireland, the druidic "oral" mode, nurtured by the powerful intellectual caste of the *filí*,[2] continues its own separate existence independent of (although not uninfluenced by) written literary production. The Irish "oral" LMP is thus for some considerable time peculiarly unsubordinated to the written mode, even though in passing into that mode it undergoes certain mutations as a literary product, modified in such predominantly oral traits as alliteration and repetition. The significant moment in the mutual articulation of two such distinct LMPs occurs when the act of composition and writing become more or less simultaneous — when the "written" LMP assumes a certain autonomy of the "oral" rather than consigning its products to manuscript. This unity of writing and composition is exemplified by a number of early Irish texts which recreate the oral tradition — a *genre* closely associated with the scribal activities of the early monastic schools, who as "amateur" producers synthesising native and Latin literary elements (and so producing new literary *forms*) emerge in seventh-century Ireland as a distinct LMP in conflict with the dominant LMP of the professional, legally privileged, ideologically hegemonic *filí*.

The disjunction between historically coexistent LMPs, then, may be synchronic — determined by the structural distribution of possible modes of literary production enabled by the social formation — or diachronic (determined by historical survivals). There is also the case of diachronic disjunction which arises not from survival but from "prefigurement": LMPs which enter into contradiction with the dominant LMP by "anticipating" the productive forms and social relations of a future social formation (the revolutionary artists' commune, "epic theatre"[3] and so on). A particular LMP, then, may combine elements or structures of other past, contemporary or "future" modes. The "little magazine,"[4] for example, characteristically combines structures of the dominant capitalist LMP with elements of collaborative production, "informal" distribution mechanisms and "consumer-participation" untypical of the dominant productive mode. An LMP may constitute a complex unity in itself, as well as forming a complex contradictory unity with other LMPs; its internal complexity will be a function of its modes of articulation with those other LMPs.

Every LMP is constituted by structures of production, distribution, exchange and consumption. Production presupposes a producer or set of producers, materials, instruments and techniques of

[1]In the eighteenth century, most authors lived by making bargains with "booksellers" (publishers), selling outright for a fixed fee the copyright to their work. This mode of production Eagleton refers to as "artisanal," like that of other skilled craftsmen, such as cabinet-makers, rugweavers, musical instrument makers, and so on, who sell their work, rather than their time. Only a very few authors were capitalists who, like the novelist Samuel Richardson, were successful publishers of their own work. Meanwhile some writers still attempted, as authors had since the Middle Ages, to subsist on the payments of wealthy noblemen awarded for faithful attendance and flattery. In the 1740s, Samuel Johnson unsuccessfully attempted to court the patronage of Philip Dormer Stanhope, Lord Chesterfield, to finance the long labor on his dictionary. Johnson eventually was awarded a royal pension, another form of patronage enjoyed by politically well-connected authors. [Ed.]

[2]The *filí* or *fileadh* was an ancient Irish order of poets. [Ed.]

[3]Drama, strictly speaking, belongs to a distinct mode of production from literature, characterised by its own relatively autonomous forces and relations. Dramatic *texts* may belong to the LMP, depending upon the historical character of the theatrical mode of production; but the assimilation of drama to literature is an ideologically significant appropriation. [Au.]

[4]Any periodical devoted to serious artistic or literary interests. [Ed.]

production, and the product itself. In developed social formations, an initial private stage of production may be transmuted by a subsequent social mode of production (printing and publishing) to convert the original product ("manuscript") into a new one ("book"). The forces of literary production consist in the application of labour-power organised in certain "relations of production" (scribes, collaborative producers, printing and publishing organisations) to certain materials of production by means of certain determinate productive instruments. These forces of literary production determine and are overdetermined by the modes of literary distribution, exchange and consumption. The handwritten manuscript can only be distributed and consumed on a hand-to-hand basis, within, let us say, a courtly caste; the multiply dictated work (one copied simultaneously by several scribes) is able to achieve wider social consumption; the ballads peddled by a chapman may be consumed by an even wider audience; the "yellowback" railway novel[5] is available to a mass public.

Unified with these productive forces, then, are specific social relations of literary production. The tribal bard professionally authorised to produce for his king or chieftain; the "amateur" medieval poet presenting to his patron a personally requested product for private remuneration; the peripatetic minstrel housed and fed by his peasant audience; the ecclesiastically or royally patronised producer, or the author who sells his product to an aristocratic patron for a dedication fee; the "independent" author who sells his commodity to a bookseller-publisher or to a capitalist publishing firm; the state-patronised producer: all of these forms are familiar enough to the "sociology of literature." The point is to analyse the complex articulations of these various LMPs with the "general" mode of production of a social formation.

Before considering that question, however, it is important to note that the character of an LMP is a significant constituent of the literary product itself. We are not merely concerned here with the sociological outworks of the text; we are concerned rather with how the text comes to be what it is because of the specific determinations of its mode of production. If LMPs are historically extrinsic to particular texts, they are equally internal to them: the literary text bears the impress of its historical mode of production as surely as any product secretes in its form and materials the fashion of its making. The product of an "oral" LMP is typically more socially stylised, "anonymous," shorn of idiosyncratic introspectiveness than the product of a private printing press; the ecclesiastically patronised work is characteristically more devout and didactic than the fiction produced for the markets of monopoly capitalism. The work which survives solely by word of mouth from region to region is constrained to deploy conventions of "impersonality" inimical to the confessional forms of a producer whose relatively "privatised" LMP is under severe pressure from more public modes which threaten to dislodge it. A poet whose professional function is to recount heroic, mythological tales of military victory before kings and noblemen preparing for war will perpetuate *genres* superfluous to an author whose LMP constrains him to woo a Whig aristocrat dedicated to international capitalist "peace." One might add, too, that every literary text in some sense internalises its social relations of production — that every text intimates by its very conventions the way it is to be consumed, encodes within itself its own ideology of how, by whom and for whom it was produced. Every text obliquely posits a putative reader, defining its producibility in terms of a certain capacity for consumption. These, however, are questions of ideology which are properly postponable to a later point; it is enough to assert for the moment that the character of an LMP is an internal constituent rather than merely an extrinsic limit of the character of the text.

(iii) RELATIONS OF LMP AND GMP

The forces of production of the LMP are naturally provided by the GMP itself, of which the LMP is a particular substructure. In the case of literary production, the materials and instruments employed normally perform a common function within the GMP itself. This is less true of certain

[5]Paperback novels sold in railway stations in the 1870s as light reading while traveling. [Ed.]

other modes of artistic production, many of whose materials and instruments, though of course produced by the GMP, perform no significant function within it. (Trombones and greasepaint play no world-historical part within general production.) The relations between LMP and GMP, however, are dialectical, in that new productive forces developed for purposes specific to the LMP may enter into the field of general production. The extent to which the LMP contributes to the expansion of general production is historically variable. The role of pre-printing LMPs within general production is historically negligible; in such situations, the LMP operates with a high degree of autonomy of the GMP from the viewpoint of its contribution to the development of the productive forces. With the growth of printing, however, extensive speculative book production and marketing finally integrate the dominant LMP into the GMP as a specific branch of general commodity production. (This integration, in which literature becomes merely another aspect of commodity production, is typically coupled with significant mutations within the aesthetic region of ideology, and a subordination of that region within the dominant ideological formation.) In developed capitalist social formations, then, the most significant relation of LMP to GMP is that of the LMP's function in the reproduction and expansion of the GMP.

The LMP represents a specific division of labour determined by the character and stage of development of the GMP, becoming more specialised and diverse as the GMP develops. Only with a certain stage of development of the GMP is the relatively autonomous existence of an LMP possible. Literary production and consumption presuppose certain levels of literacy, physical and mental well-being, leisure and material affluence: the material conditions for writing and reading include economic resources, shelter, lighting, and privacy. The capitalist mode of production develops its dominant LMP by increasing the population, concentrating it in urban centres where it is within reach of the mechanisms of literary distribution, and permitting it limited degrees of literacy, affluence, leisure, shelter and privacy. At the same time it increasingly specialises and extends its modes of literary production and distribution to sell literary commodities on this market, and produces the material and cultural conditions essential for professional literary production within it. In such phenomena as poverty, physical and mental debility consequent on prolonged and intensive labour, illiteracy or partial literacy, lack of sufficient shelter, privacy and lighting (Charles Dickens described the window-tax as "a tax upon knowledge"), the GMP bears upon the LMP to exclude or partially exclude certain social groups and classes from literary production and consumption — a factor which, as we shall see, is also of ideological significance.

The social relations of the LMP are in general determined by the social relations of the GMP. The literary producer stands in a certain social relation to his consumers which is mediated by his social relations to the patrons, publishers and distributors of his product. These social relations are themselves materially embodied in the character of the product itself. The *filí* of early Ireland may again provide a convenient example. Before the emergence of a "written" LMP, the *filí* caste formed the dominant group of a *mélange* of literary entertainers, musicians, lampooners and others (generically categorised as "bards"), controlling the ideological apparatuses of learning and literature as advisers to kings, preservers of oral literary traditions and composers of heroic, panegyric and elegiac verse. They were social functionaries occupying a legally enshrined, privileged status within the social formation, exercising extensive ideological influence over it, and handsomely remunerated by their patrons. These social relations embodied themselves in the character of their literary products: as a secular, traditionalist caste, the *filí* preserved the Gaelic despised for its "pagan" elements by the higher, Latin-oriented clergy; the poetic *genres* they worked were the "privileged," heroic, genealogical and mythological modes of the literature of the Gaelic aristocracy. In this case, then, a peculiarly visible homology between the social relations of LMP and GMP is to be observed: the *filí's* function as literary producers is effectively coterminous with their function within the social relations of Irish society as a whole. By contrast, the individual class-position of a literary producer in certain other LMPs may be in contradiction with his mode of insertion into the class-structure *as an author*. A producer who is himself a member of the dominant social class may, as occasionally in Elizabethan England, be selected for literary patronage in preference to one from a subordinate social class; yet the aristocratic poet or haut-bourgeois novelist becomes, within the capitalist LMP, a petty-bourgeois producer.[6] (This, indeed, is a contradiction which may enter into "aesthetic ideology" itself, as in the case of bourgeois Romanticism.) The social relations of the LMP, then, while in general determined by the social relations of the GMP, are not necessarily homologous with them. In developed capitalist social formations, the dominant LMP of large-scale capitalist printing, publishing and distributing reproduces the dominant GMP, but incorporates as a crucial constituent a *subordinate* mode of production: the artisanal mode of the literary producer himself, who typically sells his product (manuscript) rather than his labour-power to the publisher in exchange for a fee.

The social classes into which the productive agents of a social formation are distributed may also exert a determination on the character of the LMPs. Coexistent LMPs may be mutually "disjunct" because each stands in distinct and particular relation to a specific social class. Thus, a dominant courtly class may operate an LMP constituted by the "amateur" production of texts for "informal," "coterie" distribution and consumption; an LMP based upon the professional producer and the capitalist mode of production, distribution, exchange and consumption (into which such "amateur" texts may enter) may simultaneously exist to supply literary commodities to a wider, aristocratic and bourgeois readership, while a complex combination of "oral" LMPs may persist within the most subordinate social classes. Such a schema naturally elides the degree of interdetermination which one would expect concretely to exist between such class-structured LMPs. In medieval England, for example, publicly-performed vernacular literature was consumed by all social classes, and the text produced by the "amateur" author at the request of his patron might be gradually disseminated until a stationer would undertake simultaneous duplication of the original, privately-owned manuscript for profit. Granted such interdeterminations, however, the class-determinations of literary consumption are a significant constituent of an LMP. In developed capitalist formations, for example, the distribution of income and high price of literary products determined by the GMP produces the social relation of "borrowing" rather than exchange between the mass of proletarian and petty-bourgeois consumers and the LMP; the purchase of books is increasingly confined to members of the dominant classes. Indeed the growth of the circulating libraries in nineteenth-century England is a classic instance of a major mutation in the dominant LMP, a radical reconstitution of the structures of production, distribution and consumption. The privileged status of the "three-decker" (three-volume) novel within the aesthetic ideology of Victorian England is a function of the economic power within the LMP of the circulating libraries, for whom such commodities were especially profitable since three subscribers could thus read a novel simultaneously. The libraries and publishers cartelised to keep the market price of such commodities prohibitively high, hence establishing the libraries as effectively the sole structure of literary distribution and consumption. The dominant social relation of consumption in the dominant LMP of Victorian England was the three guineas subscription of a consumer to Mudie's circulating library of New Oxford Street.[7] The libraries, moreover, reconstituted the structures of literary production: they were powerful determi-

[6]Eagleton's point is that even novelists from the landed aristocracy or from the "haut-bourgeoisie," the class of financiers and rentier capitalists, would *as novelists* become petty-bourgeois producers because their income from fiction depended, like any shopkeeper's, on the volume of their trade and the demand for their goods. [Ed.]

[7]The point of the three-decker novel as far as Mudie's circulating library was concerned was not to allow three subscribers to read the book simultaneously. It was rather to necessitate the purchase of three one-guinea subscriptions by the reader who wished to obtain all three volumes of the novel at once, so as not to have to wait for missing volumes to come in. Because the publication of novels in one volume threatened this way of mulcting the clientele, Mudie's Library boycotted such "subversive" literature. [Ed.]

nants in the *selection* of producers (if an author failed to get into Mudie's advertising list, he or she was effectively finished), of the *pace* of literary production (an author would need to produce one three-decker a year to scrape a modest living), and of the literary *product* itself. The multiple complicated plots, elaborate digressions and gratuitous interludes of such works were the effect of producers ingeniously elongating their material to meet the requirements of the form. Parallel modifications were produced in the printing process itself, where margins were widened and type enlarged to achieve the prerequisite bulk. Coupled with these material and textual factors was the hegemony exercised by the libraries in the region of aesthetic ideology: what was produced and consumed was regulated by their severely censorious owners in accordance with the demands of "general" ideology. In the Victorian circulating libraries, then, we observe at work a peculiarly close, complex conjuncture of GMP, LMP, "general" and "aesthetic" ideology, and text. The struggle of a producer like Thomas Hardy against elements of Victorian bourgeois ideology is intimately related to his scathing assaults on this particular LMP.

The extent to which the social relations of literary production reproduce the social relations of "general" production, then, is historically variable and determinate. In the case of the tribal bardic system, the two sets of relations are identical: the literary social relations between chief or king, bard and listeners are themselves "general" social relations, the bard himself is professional ideologue of the social formation. The literary social relations of the medieval era preserve elements of this structure: the medieval author is typically a cleric, part of an ideological apparatus. But his literary production is an aspect of this function rather than identical with it, a voluntary and "amateur" mode of exercising his priesthood; literary relations assume a certain relative autonomy of "general" ones. The same is true of the patronised medieval producer, whose literary relations to his patron and consumers is a specific articulation of the "general" social relations which hold between them. Capitalist formations differ from all of these modes. The specificity of the articulation between "general" and literary social relations in capitalist formations is to be found in the fact that although the literary social relations in general reproduce the social relations of the GMP, they do not necessarily reproduce these social relations as they hold between the *particular individual agents of the literary productive process.* In both tribalist and feudalist formations, the social relations in which the agents of literary production (patrons, authors, consumers, etc.) stand are determined by or effectively identical with the social relations in which these individual agents stand outside the LMP, in relation to the GMP. The individual functions within "general" social relations fulfilled by the LMP agents in capitalism, however, are autonomous of the functions they fulfil within the social relations of literary production. An aristocratic novelist may be consumed by proletarian readers, or *vice versa,* but these "general" social relations of the particular agents are "cancelled" by the market relations of literary commodity production. It is this unique and peculiar feature of the capitalist LMP which differentiates it markedly from other LMPs whose social relations depend upon certain "general" relations between the particular agents — relations which pre-exist the act of literary production. The capitalist LMP produces its own social relations between the particular agents independently of their pre-existent social functions — social relations which in general reproduce the "general" social relations appropriate to general commodity production.

(iv) GENERAL IDEOLOGY (GI)

As well as giving rise at a certain historical stage to a series of LMPs, a GMP also always produces a dominant ideological formation — a formation I provisionally term "general" to distinguish it from that specific region within it known as the aesthetic region, or, more summarily, as "aesthetic ideology." A dominant ideological formation is constituted by a relatively coherent set of "discourses" of values, representations and beliefs which, realised in certain material apparatuses and related to the structures of material production, so reflect the experiential relations of individual subjects to their social conditions as to guarantee those misperceptions of the "real" which contribute to the reproduction of the dominant social relations.

It is important to stress here that GI denotes, not some abstraction or "ideal type" or "ideology in general," but that particular dominated ensemble of ideologies to be found in any social formation. In speaking of the "relations" or conjunctures between GI and aesthetic or authorial ideologies, then, one is speaking not of certain extrinsically related "sets," but of the mode of insertion of authorial and aesthetic formations into the hegemonic ideology as a whole. I stress this point to avoid that hypostatisation of GI, AI and AuI which might follow from designating them thus for the purposes of analysis.

(v) RELATIONS OF GI AND LMP

GI typically contains certain general elements or structures, all or some of which may at a particular historical stage bear significantly on the character of the LMP. These general structures can be distinguished in the main as the linguistic, the political, and the "cultural." A set of complex interdeterminations will normally hold between them, which demand historical specification.

A literary text is related to GI not only by how it deploys language but by the particular language it deploys. Language, that most innocent and spontaneous of common currencies, is in reality a terrain scarred, fissured and divided by the cataclysms of political history, strewn with the relics of imperialist, nationalist, regionalist and class combat. The linguistic is always at base the *politico*-linguistic,[8] a sphere within which the struggles of imperial conqueror with subjugated state, nation-state with nation-state, region with nation, class with class are fought out. Literature is an agent as well as effect of such struggles, a crucial mechanism by which the language and ideology of an imperialist class establishes its hegemony, or by which a subordinated state, class or region preserves and perpetuates at the ideological level an historical identity shattered or eroded at the political. It is also a zone in which such struggles achieve stabilisation — in which the contradictory political unity of imperial and indigenous, dominant and subordinate social classes is articulated and reproduced in the contradictory unity of a "common language" itself. The moment of consolidation of the "nation-state" is of paradigmatic significance here — a moment in which the hegemony of a "national" class reflects itself in the linguistic coherence essential to its integrative, centralising state apparatuses. The history of the genesis of English as a "national" language is the history of imperialism and its aftermath — the linguistic class-division between Norman French and English, the development of Anglo-Norman French after the loss of Normandy, the mutations of Old English under Norman French influence, the gradual development from these sources of a distinctive English language legally recognised in 1362, the selection of the old East Midland dialect (embracing the political and ideological power-centres of London, Oxford and Cambridge) as the basis of the hegemonic language. Parallel interactions between the LMP and the linguistic, ideological and political structures of state power can be found by turning once more to the instance of Ireland. Towards the end of the twelfth century in Ireland there arose a cultural apparatus based upon the hereditary custody of native learning and literature by certain families within the hegemonic class — an apparatus which is shattered by the English subjugation of Ireland in the seventeenth century. Bereft of social institutions within which to perpetuate itself, indigenous literary culture passes from the possession of the extirpated native ruling class and is forced down to the level of the Gaelic-speaking peasantry, with resultant changes in aesthetic form and developments in dialectal and provincial literary production. The traditional LMP based on tales of the *Fíanna*[9] recounted by peripatetic or

[8] I do not mean to imply that language is merely "superstructural." Without language, there could be no material production in the sense characteristic of the human animal. Language is first of all a physical, material reality, and as such is part of the forces of material production. The specific historical forms of this general human reality are then constituted at the social, political and ideological levels. [Au.]

[9] An Irish band of warriors, soldiers of the legendary Fionn Mac Cumhail. [Ed.]

home-based bards is also effectively destroyed by English imperialism: few such tales pass over into the alien language of the imperial class.

The interdeterminations of the linguistic and the political, and their effect on the constitution of an LMP and the character of its products, are thus of central significance to a materialist criticism. No more graphic example of this conjuncture in English literary history can be found than in John Milton's decision to write *Paradise Lost* in his native tongue.[10] Milton's decision was a radically political act — an assertion of bourgeois Protestant nationalism over classical and aristocratic culture, or rather an assertive appropriation of those classical modes for historically progressive ends. The very forms and textures of his poem are a product of this linguistic, political and religious conjuncture within ideology. All literary production, in fact, belongs to that ideological apparatus which can be provisionally termed the "cultural." What is in question is not simply the process of production and consumption of literary texts, but the function of such production within the cultural ideological apparatus. That apparatus includes the specific institutions of literary production and distribution (publishing houses, bookshops, libraries and so on), but it also encompasses a range of "secondary," supportive institutions whose function is more directly ideological, concerned with the definition and dissemination of literary "standards" and assumptions. Among these are literary academies, societies and book-clubs, associations of literary producers, distributors and consumers, censoring bodies, and literary journals and reviews. In developed social formations, the literary substructure of the cultural apparatus interacts more or less intensively with the ideological apparatus of "communications"; but its real power lies in its articulation with the *educational* apparatus. It is within this apparatus that the ideological function of literature — its function, that is to say, in reproducing the social relations of the mode of production — is most apparent. From the infant school to the University faculty, literature is a vital instrument for the insertion of individuals into the perceptual and symbolic forms of the dominant ideological formation, able to accomplish this function with a "naturalness," spontaneity and experiential immediacy possible to no other ideological practice. But it is not only a question of the ideological use of particular literary works; it is, more fundamentally, a question of the ideological significance of the cultural and academic institutionalisation of literature as such. What is finally at stake is not literary texts but Literature — the ideological significance of that process whereby certain historical texts are severed from their social formations, defined as "literary," bound and ranked together to constitute a series of "literary traditions" and interrogated to yield a set of ideologically presupposed responses. The precise ideological function of this process is historically variable. It is determined in general by the internal structures of the educational apparatus, which are themselves determined in the last instance by the GMP; but it may present itself ideologically in the form of a conservative academicism, related to GI in its literary *positivism,* or (say) in the form of a liberal humanism which preserves a besieged enclave of idealist values supposedly incarnate in Literature from the invasions of a real history now moving beyond its liberal humanist phase. In any case, it is important to emphasise that the cultural ideological apparatus contains a dual set of literary institutions: "primary" institutions of production such as publishing houses, which exist both as elements of the GMP and as parts of the ideological apparatus of "culture," and "secondary" institutions, including the educational ones with which the cultural apparatus interacts, whose relation to the GMP is the more indirect one of contributing to its reproduction by aiding in the reproduction of its social relations through ideology.

A discussion of the specific relations between GI and the literary text belongs to the next chapter; but since the text is, after all, the product of the LMP, it is worth noting here one or two incidental points about the GI–LMP relation as it affects the literary text. The first point is that different LMPs may, in terms of the ideological character of their textual products, reproduce the

[10]In 1627 Milton seems to have contemplated writing a biblical epic in Latin. [Ed.]

same ideological formation. There is no necessary homology between GI and LMP: a serialised and directly published Victorian novel, despite belonging to alternative modes of production, may inhibit the same ideology. Conversely, the same LMP may reproduce mutually antagonistic ideological formations: the fiction of Defoe and Fielding. An LMP which reproduces the social relations of the GMP may conflict with some of its dominant ideological modes: the Romantic dissent from bourgeois values and relations is in part determined by the very integration of the LMP into general commodity production. Conversely, an LMP in conflict with GMP social relations may nevertheless reproduce its dominant ideological forms.

The second point concerns that direct bearing of GI on the literary text which is censorship. Such modes of direct ideological control over the text may take the form of simple repression at the point of production, distribution or consumption, or may be effected more obliquely: licensing, politically select patronage and so on. The most efficient form of censorship is, of course, the perpetuation of mass illiteracy. The factor of literacy represents a peculiarly complex conjuncture of GMP, LMP, GI and aesthetic ideology. The degree and social distribution of literacy are determined in the last instance by the GMP, but literacy is clearly in turn a significant determinant of the LMP, affecting the size and social composition not only of readers but of producers. The degree of literacy of producers and consumers may also influence the character of the literary product — whether, for instance, it is distributed orally, as well as its length and elaborateness (for there is a limit to the memorising capacity of the non- or semi-literate producer). Illiteracy may be effected by the exclusion of certain social groups and classes from the educational apparatus for political reasons; but there is a possibility of conflict here between those reasons and competing ideological imperatives. In nineteenth-century England, for example, there were sound political reasons why the proletariat should be excluded from literacy, but sound religious reasons why it should not be. Literacy is also determined by aesthetic ideology, which in ratifying (in conjuncture with GI) certain languages (French, Latin), or certain uses of language as appropriate to literature, determines the degree of its general availability. There is a practical, as well as theoretical, literacy.

(vi) AUTHORIAL IDEOLOGY (AuI)

I mean by "authorial ideology" the effect of the author's specific mode of biographical insertion into GI, a mode of insertion overdetermined by a series of distinct factors: social class, sex, nationality, religion, geographical region and so on. This formation is never to be treated in isolation from GI, but must be studied in its articulation with it. Between the two formations of GI and AuI, relations of effective homology, partial disjunction and severe contradiction are possible. The producer's biographical (as opposed to "aesthetic" or "textual") ideology may be effectively homologous with the dominant ideology of his or her historical moment, but not necessarily because the producer lives the social conditions of *class* most appropriate for such harmonious insertion into it. The producer may in terms of (say) class-position inhabit an ideological subensemble with conflictual relations to the dominant ideology, but by an overdetermination of other biographical factors (sex, religion, region) may be rendered homologous with it. The converse situation is equally possible. The degree of conjuncture or disjuncture between AuI and GI may also be "diachronically" determined: an author may relate to his or her contemporary GI by virtue of "belonging" to an historically previous GI, or (as with the case of the revolutionary author) to a putatively future one.[11] As GI mutates, an AuI which was at one point homologous with it may enter into conflict with it, and *vice versa.* It is not, in short, always a simple matter to specify the historical period to which a writer be-

[11]There is also the case of the insertion of an author into the GI of *another* society, whether contemporaneous or not: the problem of "cosmopolitanism." Such insertion is always in the last instance a question of the determination of the "native" GI. [Au.]

longs; nor does a writer necessarily belong only to one "history." It is significant in this respect that the two generally acknowledged major authors of Restoration England — John Milton and John Bunyan — do not in fact "belong" to "Restoration ideology" at all.[12] It is equally true, however, that their modes of ideological disinheritance from their contemporary historical moment are determined, in the last instance, by the nature of that moment itself.

AuI is not to be conflated with GI; nor is it to be identified with the "ideology of the text." The ideology of the text is not an "expression" of authorial ideology: it is the product of an aesthetic working of "general" ideology as that ideology is itself worked and "produced" by an overdetermination of authorial-biographical factors. AuI, then, is always GI as lived, worked and represented from a particular overdetermined standpoint within it. There is no question here of "centring" the literary text on the individual subject who produces it; but neither is it a matter of liquidating that subject into "general" aesthetic and ideological forms. It is a question of specifying the ideological determinations of the text — determinations which include the effect of the author's mode of insertion into GI.

(vii) AESTHETIC IDEOLOGY (AI)

I denote by this the specific aesthetic region of GI, articulated with other such regions — the ethical, religious, etc. — in relations of dominance and subordination determined in the last instance by the GMP. AI is an internally complex formation, including a number of sub-sectors, of which the *literary* is one. This literary sub-sector is itself internally complex, constituted by a number of "levels": theories of literature, critical practices, literary traditions, *genres,* conventions, devices and discourses. AI also includes what may be termed an "ideology of the aesthetic" — a signification of the function, meaning and value of the aesthetic itself within a particular social formation, which is in turn part of an "ideology of culture" included within GI.

(viii) RELATIONS OF AI, GI AND LMP

A GMP produces a GI which contributes to reproducing it; it also produces a (dominant) LMP which in general reproduces and is reproduced by the GMP, but which also reproduces and is reproduced by the GI. We may speak of the "ideology of the LMP" to designate the mutually reproductive relation which holds between GI and LMP — a relation which produces within the LMP an ideology of producer, product and consumer, as well as of the activities of production, exchange and consumption. This ideology is itself encoded within AI; more precisely, it is the effect of a conjuncture between AI and GI. The literary producer may be viewed as the privileged servant of a social order symbolised by his royal, ecclesial or aristocratic patron, as the inspired articulator of the collective values of his community, as an "independent" producer freely offering his private product to an amenable audience, as the prophetic or bohemian rebel dissidently marginal to "conventional" society, as a "worker" or "engineer" on a fraternal footing with his readership, and so on. Literary production itself may be ideologically encoded as revelation, inspiration, labour, play, reflection, fantasy, reproduction; the literary product as process, practice, medium, symbol, object, epiphany, gesture; literary consumption as magical influence, arcane ritual, participatory dialogue, passive reception, didactic instruction, spiritual encounter. Each of these ideologies will be determined by a specific conjuncture of LMP/GI/AI, on the basis of the final determination of the GMP. There is, however, no question of a necessarily *symmetrical* relation here between the various formations involved. Each of these formations is internally complex, and a series of internally and mutually conflictual relations may hold between them. An LMP which is itself an amalgam of historically

[12]Both Milton and Bunyan were Puritans whose political and religious ideas jibed better with the commonwealth period than with the secular, royalist era when their major works (*Paradise Lost,* 1667; *Pilgrim's Progress,* 1678) were published. [Ed.]

disparate elements may thus combine in contradictory unity disparate ideological elements of both GI and AI. A double-articulation GMP/GI–GI/AI/LMP is, for example, possible, whereby a GI category, when transformed by AI into an ideological component of an LMP, may then enter into conflict with the GMP social relations it exists to reproduce. The bourgeois-Romantic category of the producer as "individual creator," for example, reproduces but also conflicts with the bourgeois conception of the human subject as nuclear individual. Or again, the Romantic and symbolist ideology of the literary product as mysteriously autotelic object at once reproduces and represses its real status as commodity. Similarly, the ideology of "instant" or "disposable" literary art reproduces the consumer ideologies of advanced capitalism at the same time as it conflicts with certain imperatives of deferred fulfilment integral to that ideological formation.

The forces and relations of literary production, on the basis of their determination by the GMP, produce the possibility of certain distinct literary *genres.* The novel, for example, can be produced only at a certain stage of development of an LMP; but whether this potential is historically activated is determined not by the LMP alone, but by its conjuncture with GI and AI. What forms and *genres* are actually selected for development may be dictated by what exists already — dictated, that is, by AI on the basis of GI. Conversely, the concept of and "need for" a new form may develop relatively autonomously within aesthetic ideology, and an LMP modified or transformed to produce it. GI may occasionally impress itself directly upon the LMP to produce a particular form (say, "socialist realism") which is then encoded and elaborated by AI; but such unilateral action is historically untypical. GI more usually appears within the LMP in its particular aesthetic articulation; literary practices are typically the product of a complex conjuncture of LMP/GI/AI, with one or another of these elements assuming dominance.

GI and AI determine not only the process of production but also the process of consumption. The literary text is a text (as opposed to "book") because it is read; with it as with any other social product, the act of consumption is itself constitutive of its existence. Reading is an ideological decipherment of an ideological product; and the history of literary criticism is the history of the possible conjunctures between the ideologies of the text's productive and consumptive moments. Between those two ideological moments there will be relations of effective homology, conflict or contradiction, determined in part by the history of ideological receptions of the text which has intervened between them. The text is consumed within an aesthetic ideology constituted in part by a set of conjunctures between GI and AI which is the history of the text's production and consumption as constructed by the GI/AI conjuncture of the particular moment of consumption. GI may act as a dominant element within the ideology of consumption (witness the eccentric instance of the considerable increase in Trollope readers during the period of the Second World War),[13] but more commonly operates in the high degree of relative autonomy it ascribes to the aesthetic region. As well as an ideology of particular consumption, there will also be one of general consumption within which the former operates — an ideology of *the act of reading itself,* which may be encoded as religious ceremony, socially privileged compact, moral instruction and so on. Any particular act of reading is conducted within a general set of assumptions as to the ideological signification of reading itself within a social formation — assumptions which, as part of AI, belong also to the general "ideology of culture" of GI.

(ix) RELATIONS OF GI, AI AND AuI

The complexity of relations between GI and AI as constitutive of the literary text is properly the subject of the next chapter. It is enough to say

[13]The Victorian novels of Anthony Trollope collectively present a portrait of England as by far the most prosperous and most powerful nation on earth; Eagleton seems to be suggesting that British men and women eagerly consumed these novels as comfortable "false consciousness" at a time when England had been nearly defeated by Germany and was being overshadowed by the United States, when its overseas empire was clearly about to crumble, and when it was strictly rationing food and all other consumer goods. [Ed.]

here that as an aesthetic product the text is a multiply articulated structure, determined only in the last instance by the moment of its contemporary GI. Its various aesthetic elements may be the product of distinct ideological formations, may belong to disparate "histories," so that it is not necessarily identical, ideologically speaking, with itself. Nor need the "ideology of the text" be consonant with the historical progressiveness or obsolecence of the LMP within which it is produced. An author may produce progressive texts using outmoded forms within an obsolescent or partly obsolescent LMP (William Morris), or may produce ideologically conservative texts within an historically progressive LMP (Henry Fielding). It is a question in each case of specifying the precise relations between LMP, "ideology of LMP," GI and AI.

Authorial ideology may be an important determinant of both the type of LMP and the aesthetic ideology within which an author works. As with Alexander Pope's "choice" of satire, elegy and the mock-heroic, a certain AuI will exclude certain modes of literary production and license others. At certain levels of production, AuI may be so subordinated to AI that the question of differential relations between them does not arise. In such a situation, to be a literary producer at all is inevitably to work within a particular set of ideological representations of the character and significance of literary production. The relations between AuI and GI may be transformed by their mediation in terms of AI: within the text itself (Balzac is the classical example), the production of GI by means of certain aesthetic forms may "cancel" and contradict that production of GI which is authorial ideology. The methodological significance of AuI in the analysis of the text is therefore variable: it may be effectively homologous with GI/AI, or it may be "cancelled" as a specific factor by their distinct or conjoint effects. In either of these cases, AuI as a particular "level" effectively disappears.

(x) TEXT

The literary text is the product of a specific overdetermined conjuncture of the elements or formations set out schematically above. It is not, however, a merely passive product. The text is so constituted by this conjuncture as to actively determine its own determinants — an activity which is most apparent in its relations to ideology. It is those relations which we must now go on to examine.

Raymond Williams

1921–1988

Born to working-class parents in a Welsh border village, Raymond Williams was that rare creature, a Marxist intellectual with genuine proletarian roots. After serving in the British army from 1941 until the close of the war, Williams earned his M.A. from Trinity College, Cambridge, in 1946, and then attended Oxford, where he worked his way up the ladder of appointments. A professor of drama at Jesus College, Cambridge, until 1983, he was considered by many to be the preeminent Marxist literary critic and theorist of postwar Britain. In addition to his landmark study Culture and Society, 1780–1950 *(1958) and his masterpiece* The Country and the City *(1973), Williams wrote more than a dozen other books, including* The Long Revolution *(1961),* Drama from Ibsen to Brecht *(1969),* The English Novel from Dickens to Lawrence *(1970),* Keywords: A Vocabulary of Culture and Society *(1976),* The Sociology of Culture *(1982),* Writing in Society *(1983), and the posthumous* Politics of Modernism *(1989). The following selection is from Williams's primer on Marxist concepts,* Marxism and Literature *(1977).*

From *Marxism and Literature*

1. BASE AND SUPERSTRUCTURE

Any modern approach to a Marxist theory of culture must begin by considering the proposition of a determining base and a determined superstructure. From a strictly theoretical point of view this is not, in fact, where we might choose to begin. It would be in many ways preferable if we could begin from a proposition which originally was equally central, equally authentic: namely the proposition that social being determines consciousness. It is not that the two propositions necessarily deny each other or are in contradiction. But the proposition of base and superstructure, with its figurative element and with its suggestion of a fixed and definite spatial relationship, constitutes, at least in certain hands, a very specialized and at times unacceptable version of the other proposition. Yet in the transition from Marx to Marxism, and in the development of mainstream Marxism itself, the proposition of the determining base and the determined superstructure has been commonly held to be the key to Marxist cultural analysis.

The source of this proposition is commonly taken to be a well-known passage in Marx's 1859 Preface to *A Contribution to the Critique of Political Economy:*

> In the social production of their life, men enter into definite relations that are indispensable and independent of their will, relations of production which correspond to a definite stage of development of their material productive forces. The sum total of these relations of production constitutes the economic structure of society, the real foundation, on which rises a legal and political superstructure and to which correspond definite forms of social consciousness. The mode of production of material life conditions the social, political and intellectual life process in general. It is not the consciousness of men that determines their being, but, on the contrary, their social being that determines their consciousness. At a certain stage of their development, the material productive forces of society come in conflict with the existing relations of production or — what is but a legal expression for the same thing — with the property relations within which they have been at work hitherto. From forms of development of the productive forces these relations turn into their fetters. Then begins an epoch of social revolution. With the change of the economic foundation the entire immense superstructure is more or less rapidly transformed. In considering such transformations a distinction should always be made between the material transformation of the economic conditions of production, which can be determined with the precision of natural science, and the legal, political, religious, aesthetic or philosophic — in short, ideological — forms in which men become conscious of this conflict and fight it out.[1]

This is hardly an obvious starting-point for any cultural theory. It is part of an exposition of historical materialist method in the understanding of legal relations and forms of state. The first use of the term "superstructure" is explicitly qualified as "legal and political." (It should incidentally be noted that the English translation in most common use has a plural — "legal and political superstructures" — for Marx's singular "juristicher und politischer Überbau.") "Definite forms of social consciousness" are further said to "correspond" to it *(entsprechen).* Transformation of the "entire immense superstructure," in the social revolution which begins from the altered relations of productive forces and relations of production, is a process in which "men become conscious of this conflict and fight it out" in "ideological forms" which now include the "religious, aesthetic, or philosophic" as well as the legal and political. Much has been deduced from this formulation, but the real context is inevitably limited. Thus it would be possible, simply from this passage, to define "cultural" ("religious, aesthetic or philosophic") forms in which "men become conscious of this conflict," without necessarily supposing that these specific forms are the whole of "cultural" activity.

There is at least one earlier use, by Marx, of the term "superstructure." It is in *The Eighteenth Brumaire of Louis Napoleon,* 1851–2:

[1]Karl Marx and Friedrich Engels, *Selected Works,* vol. 1 (London, 1962), pp. 362–64. (See also Marx, p. 392.) [Ed.]

> Upon the several forms of property, upon the social conditions of existence, a whole superstructure is reared of various and peculiarly shaped feelings *(empfindungen),* illusions, habits of thought and conceptions of life. The whole class produces and shapes these out of its material foundation and out of the corresponding social conditions. The individual unit to whom they flow through tradition and education may fancy that they constitute the true reasons for and premises of his conduct.[2]

This is an evidently different use. The "superstructure" is here the whole "ideology" of the class: its "form of consciousness"; its constitutive ways of seeing itself in the world. It would be possible, from this and the later use, to see three senses of "superstructure" emerging: (a) legal and political forms which express existing real relations of production; (b) forms of consciousness which express a particular class view of the world; (c) a process in which, over a whole range of activities, men become conscious of a fundamental economic conflict and fight it out. These three senses would direct our attention, respectively, to (a) institutions; (b) forms of consciousness; (c) political and cultural practices.

It is clear that these three areas are related and must, in analysis, be interrelated. But on just this crucial question of interrelation the term itself is of little assistance, just because it is variably applied to each area in turn. Nor is this at all surprising, since the use is not primarily conceptual, in any precise way, but metaphorical. What it primarily expresses is the important sense of a visible and formal "superstructure" which might be analysed on its own but which cannot be understood without seeing that it rests on a "foundation." The same point must be made of the corresponding metaphorical term. In the use of 1851–2 it is absent, and the origins of a particular form of class consciousness are specified as "forms of property" and "social conditions of existence." In the use of 1859 it appears in almost conscious metaphor: "the economic structure of society — the real foundation *(die reale Basis),* on which rises *(erhebt)* a legal and political superstructure *(Überbau).*" It is replaced, later in the argument, by "the economic foundation" *(ökonomische Grundlage).* The continuity of meaning is relatively clear, but the variation of terms for one part of the relationship ("forms of property, social conditions of existence"; "economic structure of society"; "real basis"; "real foundation"; *Basis; Grundlage*) is not matched by explicit variation of the other term of the relationship, though the actual signification of this term (*Überbau;* superstructure) is, as we have seen, variable. It is part of the complexity of the subsequent argument that the term rendered in English explication (probably first by Engels) as "base" is rendered in other languages in significant variations (in French usually as *infrastructure,* in Italian as *struttura,* and so on, with some complicating effects on the substance of the argument).

In the transition from Marx to Marxism, and then in the development of expository and didactic formulations, the words used in the original arguments were projected, first, as if they were precise concepts, and second, as if they were descriptive terms for observable "areas" of social life. The main sense of the words in the original arguments had been relational, but the popularity of the terms tended to indicate either (a) relatively enclosed categories or (b) relatively enclosed areas of activity. These were then correlated either temporally (first material production, then consciousness, then politics and culture), or in effect, forcing the metaphor, spatially (visible and distinguishable "levels" or "layers" — politics and culture, then forms of consciousness, and so on down to "the base"). The serious practical problems of method, which the original words had indicated, were then usually in effect bypassed by methods derived from a confidence, rooted in the popularity of the terms, in the relative enclosure of categories or areas expressed as "the base," "the superstructure."

It is then ironic to remember that the force of Marx's original criticism had been mainly directed against the *separation* of "areas" of thought and activity (as in the separation of consciousness from material production) and against the related evacuation of specific content — real human activities — by the imposition of abstract categories. The common abstraction of "the base" and "the superstructure" is thus a radical

[2]Ibid., pp. 272–73. [Ed.]

persistence of the modes of thought which he attacked. That in the course of other arguments he gave some warrant for this, within the intrinsic difficulties of any such formulation, is certainly true. But it is significant that when he came to any sustained analysis, or to a realization of the need for such analysis, he was at once specific and flexible in his use of his own terms. He had already observed, in the formulation of 1859, a distinction between analysing "the economic conditions of production, which can be determined with the precision of natural science" and the analysis of "ideological forms," for which methods were evidently less precise. In 1857 he had noted:

> As regards art, it is well known that some of its peaks by no means correspond to the general development of society; nor do they therefore to the material substructure, the skeleton as it were of its organization.

His solution of the problem he then discusses, that of Greek art, is hardly convincing, but the "by no means correspond" is a characteristic practical recognition of the complexity of real relations. Engels, in his essay *Feuerbach and the End of Classical German Philosophy,* still argued specifically, showing how the "economic basis" of a political struggle could be dulled in consciousness or altogether lost sight of, and how a legal system could be projected as independent of its economic content, in the course of its professional development. Then:

> Still higher ideologies, that is, such as are still further removed from the material, economic basis, take the form of philosophy and religion. Hence the interconnection between conceptions and their material conditions of existence becomes more and more complicated, more and more obscured by intermediate links. But the interconnection exists.

This relational emphasis, including not only complexity but recognition of the ways in which some connections are lost to consciousness, is of course very far from the abstract categories (though it supports the implication of separate areas) of "superstructure" and "base."

In all serious Marxist analysis the categories are of course not used abstractly. But they may have their effect none the less. It is significant that the first phase of the recognition of practical complexities stressed what are really *quantitative* relations. By the end of the nineteenth century it was common to recognize what can best be described as disturbances, or special difficulties, of an otherwise regular relationship. This is true of the idea of "lags" in time, which had been developed from Marx's observation that some of the "peaks" of art "by no means correspond to the general development of society." This could be expressed (though Marx's own "solution" to this problem had not been of this kind) as a matter of *temporal* "delay" or "unevenness." The same basic model is evident in Engels's notion of the relative *distance* ("still further removed") of the "higher ideologies." Or consider Engels's letter to Bloch of September 1890:

> According to the materialist conception of history, the *ultimately* determining element in history is the production and reproduction of real life. More than this neither Marx nor I have ever asserted. Hence if somebody twists this into saying that the economic element is the *only* determining one, he transforms that proposition into a meaningless, abstract, senseless phrase. The economic situation is the basis, but the various elements of the superstructure — political forms of the class struggle and its results, to wit: constitutions established by the victorious class after a successful battle, etc., juridical forms, and even the reflexes of all these actual struggles in the brains of the participants, political, juristic, philosophical theories, religious views and their further development into systems of dogma — also exercise their influence upon the course of the historical struggles and in many cases preponderate in determining their *form.* There is an interaction of all these elements in which, amid all the endless host of accidents (that is, of things and events whose inner interconnection is so remote or so impossible of proof that we can regard it as non-existent, as negligible), the economic movement finally asserts itself as necessary. Otherwise the application of the theory to any period of history would be easier than the solution of a simple equation of the first degree.

This is a vital acknowledgement of real and methodological complexities. It is particularly relevant to the idea of "determination," which will be separately discussed, and to the decisive problem of consciousness as "reflexes" or "reflection." But within the vigour of his contrast between real history and a "meaningless, abstract, senseless phrase," and alongside his recognition of a new (and theoretically significant) exception — "the endless host of accidents" — Engels does not so much revise the enclosed categories — "the basis" ("the economic element," "the economic situation," "the economic movement") and "the various elements" (political, juridical, theoretical) of "the superstructure" — as reiterate the categories and instance certain exceptions, indirectnesses, and irregularities which obscure their otherwise regular relation. What is fundamentally lacking, in the theoretical formulations of this important period, is any adequate recognition of the indissoluble connections between material production, political and cultural institutions and activity, and consciousness. The classic summary of "the relationship between the base and the superstructure" is Plekhanov's[3] distinction of "five sequential elements: (i) the state of productive forces; (ii) the economic conditions; (iii) the socio-political regime; (iv) the psyche of social man; (v) various ideologies reflecting the properties of this psyche" (*Fundamental Problems of Marxism,* Moscow, 1922, 76). This is better than the bare projection of "a base" and "a superstructure," which has been so common. But what is wrong with it is its description of these "elements" as "sequential," when they are in practice indissoluble: not in the sense that they cannot be distinguished for purposes of analysis, but in the decisive sense that these are not separate "areas" or "elements" but the whole, specific activities and products of real men. That is to say, the analytic categories, as so often in idealist thought, have, almost unnoticed, become substantive descriptions, which then take habitual priority over the whole social process to which, as analytic categories, they are attempting to speak. Orthodox analysts began to think of "the base" and "the superstructure" as if they were separable concrete entities. In doing so they lost sight of the very processes — not abstract relations but constitutive processes — which it should have been the special function of historical materialism to emphasize. I shall be discussing later the major theoretical response to this loss: the attempt to reconstitute such processes by the idea of "mediation."

A persistent dissatisfaction, within Marxism, about the proposition of "base and superstructure," has been most often expressed by an attempted refinement and revaluation of "the superstructure." Apologists have emphasized its complexity, substance, and "autonomy" or autonomous value. Yet most of the difficulty still lies in the original extension of metaphorical terms for a relationship into abstract categories or concrete areas *between* which connections are looked for and complexities or relative autonomies emphasized. It is actually more important to observe the character of this extension in the case of "the base" than in the case of the always more varied and variable "superstructure." By extension and by habit, "the base" has come to be considered virtually as an object (a particular and reductive version of "material existence"). Or, in specification, "the base" is given very general and apparently uniform properties. "The base" is the real social existence of man. "The base" is the real relations of production corresponding to a stage of the development of material productive forces. "The base" is a mode of production at a particular stage of its development. Of course these are, in practice, different propositions. Yet each is also very different from Marx's central emphasis on productive *activities.* He had himself made the point against reduction of "the base" to a category:

> In order to study the connexion between intellectual and material production it is above all essential to conceive the latter in its determined historical form and not as a general category. For example, there corresponds to the capitalist mode of production a type of intellectual production quite different from that which corresponded to the medieval mode of production. Unless material production itself is understood in its specific historical form, it is impossible to grasp the characteristics of the intellectual production which corresponds to it or the reciprocal action between the two. (*Theorien über den Mehrwert,* cit. Bottomore and Rubel, 96–97.)

We can add that while a particular stage of "real social existence," or of "relations of production,"

[3]Gyorgi Valentinovich Plekhanov (1857–1918), Russian revolutionary and political philosopher. [Ed.]

or of a "mode of production," can be discovered and made precise by analysis, it is never, as a body of activities, either uniform or static. It is one of the central propositions of Marx's sense of history, for example, that in actual development there are deep contradictions in the relationships of production and in the consequent social relationships. There is therefore the continual possibility of the dynamic variation of these forces. The "variations" of the superstructure might be deduced from this fact alone, were it not that the "objective" implications of "the base" reduce all such variations to secondary consequences. It is only when we realize that "the base," to which it is habitual to *refer* variations, is itself a dynamic and internally contradictory process — the specific activities and modes of activity, over a range from association to antagonism, of real men and classes of men — that we can begin to free ourselves from the notion of an "area" or a "category" with certain fixed properties for deduction to the variable processes of a "superstructure." The physical fixity of the terms exerts a constant pressure against just this realization.

Thus, contrary to a development in Marxism, it is not "the base" and "the superstructure" that need to be studied, but specific and indissoluble real processes, within which the decisive relationship, from a Marxist point of view, is that expressed by the complex idea of "determination."

6. HEGEMONY

The traditional definition of "hegemony" is political rule or domination, especially in relations between states. Marxism extended the definition of rule or domination to relations between social classes, and especially to definitions of a *ruling class.* "Hegemony" then acquired a further significant sense in the work of Antonio Gramsci, carried out under great difficulties in a Fascist prison between 1927 and 1935. Much is still uncertain in Gramsci's use of the concept, but his work is one of the major turning-points in Marxist cultural theory.

Gramsci made a distinction between "rule" *(dominio)* and "hegemony." "Rule" is expressed in directly political forms and in times of crisis by direct or effective coercion. But the more normal situation is a complex interlocking of political, social, and cultural forces, and "hegemony," according to different interpretations, is either this or the active social and cultural forces which are its necessary elements. Whatever the implications of the concept for Marxist political theory (which has still to recognize many kinds of direct political control, social class control, and economic control, as well as this more general formation), the effects on cultural theory are immediate. For "hegemony" is a concept which at once includes and goes beyond two powerful earlier concepts: that of "culture" as a "whole social process," in which men define and shape their whole lives; and that of "ideology," in any of its Marxist senses, in which a system of meanings and values is the expression or projection of a particular class interest.

"Hegemony" goes beyond "culture," as previously defined, in its insistence on relating the "whole social process" to specific distributions of power and influence. To say that "men" define and shape their whole lives is true only in abstraction. In any actual society there are specific inequalities in means and therefore in capacity to realize this process. In a class society these are primarily inequalities between classes. Gramsci therefore introduced the necessary recognition of dominance and subordination in what has still, however, to be recognized as a whole process.

It is in just this recognition of the *wholeness* of the process that the concept of "hegemony" goes beyond "ideology." What is decisive is not only the conscious system of ideas and beliefs, but the whole lived social process as practically organized by specific and dominant meanings and values. Ideology, in its normal senses, is a relatively formal and articulated system of meanings, values, and beliefs, of a kind that can be abstracted as a "world-view" or a "class outlook." This explains its popularity as a concept in retrospective analysis (in base–superstructure models or in homology), since a *system* of ideas can be abstracted from that once living social process and represented, usually by the selection of "leading" or typical "ideologists" or "ideological features," as the decisive form in which consciousness was at once expressed and controlled (or, as in Althusser, was in effect unconscious, as an imposed structure). The relatively mixed, confused, incomplete, or inarticulate consciousness of actual men in that period and society is thus overridden in the name of this decisive generalized system, and indeed in structural homology is procedurally excluded as peripheral or ephemeral. It is the fully articulate and systematic forms which are recognizable as ideology, and there is a corresponding tendency in the analysis of art to look only for similarly fully articulate and systematic expressions of this ideology in the content (base–superstructure) or form (homology) of actual works. In less selective procedures, less dependent on the inherent classicism of the definition of form as fully articulate and systematic, the tendency is to consider works as variants of, or as variably affected by, the decisive abstracted ideology.

More generally, this sense of "an ideology" is applied in abstract ways to the actual consciousness of both dominant and subordinated classes. A dominant class "has" this ideology in relatively pure and simple forms. A subordinate class has, in one version, *nothing but* this ideology as its consciousness (since the production of all ideas is, by axiomatic definition, in the hands of those who control the primary means of production) or, in another version, has this ideology imposed on its otherwise different consciousness, which it must struggle to sustain or develop against "ruling-class ideology."

The concept of hegemony often, in practice, resembles these definitions, but it is distinct in its refusal to equate consciousness with the articulate formal system which can be and ordinarily is abstracted as "ideology." It of course does not exclude the articulate and formal meanings, values and beliefs which a dominant class develops and propagates. But it does not equate these with consciousness, or rather it does not reduce consciousness to them. Instead it sees the relations of domination and subordination, in their forms as practical consciousness, as in effect a saturation of the whole process of living — not only of political and economic activity, nor only of manifest social activity, but of the whole substance of lived identities and relationships, to such a depth that the pressures and limits of what can ultimately be seen as a specific economic, political, and cultural system seem to most of us the pressures and limits of simple experience and common sense. Hegemony is then not only the articulate upper level of "ideology," nor are its forms of control only those ordinarily seen as "manipulation" or "indoctrination." It is a whole body of practices and expectations, over the whole of living: our senses and assignments of energy, our shaping perceptions of ourselves and our world. It is a lived system of meanings and values — constitutive and constituting — which as they are experienced as practices appear as reciprocally confirming. It thus constitutes a sense of reality for most people in the society, a sense of absolute because experienced reality beyond which it is very difficult for most members of the society to move, in most areas of their lives. It is, that is to say, in the strongest sense a "culture," but a culture which has also to be seen as the lived dominance and subordination of particular classes.

There are two immediate advantages in this concept of hegemony. First, its forms of domination and subordination correspond much more closely to the normal processes of social organization and control in developed societies than the more familiar projections from the idea of a ruling class, which are usually based on much earlier and simpler historical phases. It can speak, for example, to the realities of electoral democracy, and to the significant modern areas of "leisure" and "private life," more specifically and more actively than older ideas of domination, with their trivializing explanations of simple "manipulation," "corruption," and "betrayal." If the pressures and limits of a given form of domination are to this extent experienced *and in practice internalized,* the whole question of class rule, and of opposition to it, is transformed. Gramsci's emphasis on the creation of an alternative hegemony, by the practical connection of many different forms of struggle, including those not easily recognizable as and indeed not primarily "political" and "economic," thus leads to a much more profound and more active sense of revolutionary activity in a highly developed society than the persistently abstract models derived from very different historical situations. The sources of any alternative hegemony are indeed difficult to define. For Gramsci they spring from the working class, but not this class as an ideal or abstract construction. What he sees, rather, is a working people which has, precisely, to become a class, and a potentially hegemonic class, against the pressures and limits of an existing and powerful hegemony.

Second, and more immediately in this context, there is a whole different way of seeing cultural activity, both as tradition and as practice. Cultural work and activity are not now, in any ordinary sense, a superstructure: not only because of the depth and thoroughness at which any cultural hegemony is lived, but because cultural tradition and practice are seen as much more than superstructural expressions — reflections, mediations, or typifications — of a formed social and economic structure. On the contrary, they are among the basic processes of the formation itself and, further, related to a much wider area of reality than the abstractions of "social" and "economic" experience. People seeing themselves and each other in directly personal relationships; people seeing the natural world and themselves in it; people using their physical and material resources for what one kind of society specializes to "leisure" and "entertainment" and "art": all these active experiences and practices, which make up so much of the reality of a culture and its cultural production can be seen as they are, without reduction to other categories of content, and without the characteristic straining to fit them (directly as reflection, indirectly as mediation or typification or analogy) to other and determining manifest economic and political relationships. Yet they can still be seen as elements of a hegemony: an inclusive social and cultural formation which indeed to be effective has to extend to and include, indeed to form and be formed from, this whole area of lived experience.

Many difficulties then arise, both theoretically and practically, but it is important to recognize how many blind alleys we may now be saved from entering. If any lived culture is necessarily so extensive, the problems of domination and subordination on the one hand, and of the extraordinary complexity of any actual cultural tradition and practice on the other, can at last be directly approached.

There is of course the difficulty that domination and subordination, as effective descriptions of cultural formation, will, by many, be refused; that the alternative language of co-operative shaping, of common contribution, which the traditional concept of "culture" so notably expressed, will be found preferable. In this fundamental choice there is no alternative, from any socialist position, to recognition and emphasis of the massive historical and immediate experience of class domination and subordination, in all their different forms. This becomes, very quickly, a matter of specific experience and argument. But there is a closely related problem within the concept of "hegemony" itself. In some uses, though not I think in Gramsci, the totalizing tendency of the concept, which is significant and indeed crucial, is converted into an abstract totalization, and in this form it is readily compatible with sophisticated senses of "the superstructure" or even "ideology." The hegemony, that is, can be seen as more uniform, more static, and more abstract than in practice, if it is really understood, it can ever actually be. Like any other Marxist concept it is particularly susceptible to epochal as distinct from historical definition, and to categorical as distinct from substantial description. Any isolation of its "organizing principles," or of its "determining features," which have indeed to be grasped in experience and by analysis, can lead very quickly to a totalizing abstraction. And then the problems of the reality of domination and subordination, and of their relations to co-operative shaping and common contribution, can be quite falsely posed.

A lived hegemony is always a process. It is not, except analytically, a system or a structure. It is a realized complex of experiences, relationships, and activities, with specific and changing pressures and limits. In practice, that is, hegemony can never be singular. Its internal structures are highly complex, as can readily be seen in any concrete analysis. Moreover (and this is crucial, reminding us of the necessary thrust of the concept), it does not just passively exist as a form of dominance. It has continually to be renewed, recreated, defended, and modified. It is also continually resisted, limited, altered, challenged by pressures not at all its own. We have then to add to the concept of hegemony the concepts of counter-hegemony and alternative hegemony, which are real and persistent elements of practice.

One way of expressing the necessary distinction between practical and abstract senses within the concept is to speak of "the hegemonic" rather than the "hegemony," and of "the dominant" rather than simple "domination." The reality of any hegemony, in the extended political and cultural sense, is that, while by definition it is always dominant, it is never either total or exclusive. At any time, forms of alternative or directly oppositional politics and culture exist as significant elements in the society. We shall need to explore their conditions and their limits, but their active presence is decisive, not only because they have to be included in any historical (as distinct from epochal) analysis, but as forms which have had significant effect on the hegemonic process itself. That is to say, alternative political and cultural emphases, and the many forms of opposition and struggle, are important not only in themselves but as indicative features of what the hegemonic process has in practice had to work to control. A static hegemony, of the kind which is indicated by abstract totalizing definitions of a dominant "ideology" or "world-view," can ignore or isolate such alternatives and opposition, but to the extent that they are significant the decisive hegemonic function is to control or transform or even incorporate them. In this active process the hegemonic has to be seen as more than the simple transmission of an (unchanging) dominance. On the contrary, any hegemonic process must be especially alert and responsible to the alternatives and opposition which question or threaten its dominance. The reality of cultural process must then always include the efforts and contributions of those who are in one way or another outside or at the edge of the terms of the specific hegemony.

Thus it is misleading, as a general method, to reduce all political and cultural initiatives and contributions to the terms of the hegemony. That is the reductive consequence of the radically different concept of "superstructure." The specific functions of "the hegemonic," "the dominant," have always to be stressed, but not in ways which suggest any *a priori* totality. The most interesting and difficult part of any cultural analysis, in complex societies, is that which seeks to grasp the hegemonic in its active and formative but also its transformational processes. Works of art, by their substantial and general character, are often especially important as sources of this complex evidence.

The major theoretical problem, with immediate effect on methods of analysis, is to distinguish between alternative and oppositional initiatives and contributions which are made within or against a specific hegemony (which then sets certain limits to them or which can succeed in neutralizing, changing or actually incorporating them) and other kinds of initiative and contribution which are irreducible to the terms of the original or the adaptive hegemony, and are in that sense independent. It can be persuasively argued that all or nearly all initiatives and contributions, even when they take on manifestly alternative or oppositional forms, are in practice tied to the hegemonic: that the dominant culture, so to say, at once produces and limits its own forms of counter-culture. There is more evidence for this view (for example in the case of the Romantic critique of industrial civilization) than we usually admit. But there is evident variation in specific kinds of social order and in the character of the consequent alternative and oppositional formations. It would be wrong to overlook the importance of works and ideas which, while clearly affected by hegemonic limits and pressures, are at least in part significant breaks beyond them, which may again in part be neutralized, reduced, or incorporated, but which in their most active elements nevertheless come through as independent and original.

Thus cultural process must not be assumed to be merely adaptive, extensive, and incorporative. Authentic breaks within and beyond it, in specific social conditions which can vary from extreme isolation to pre-revolutionary breakdowns and actual revolutionary activity, have often in fact occurred. And we are better able to see this, alongside more general recognition of the insistent pressures and limits of the hegemonic, if we develop modes of analysis which instead of reducing works to finished products, and activities to fixed positions, are capable of discerning, in good faith, the finite but significant openness of many actual initiatives and contributions. The finite but significant openness of many works of art, as signifying forms making possible but also requiring persistent and variable signifying responses, is then especially relevant.

7. TRADITIONS, INSTITUTIONS, AND FORMATIONS

Hegemony is always an active process, but this does not mean that it is simply a complex of dominant features and elements. On the contrary, it is always a more or less adequate organization and interconnection of otherwise separated and even disparate meanings, values, and practices, which it specifically incorporates in a significant culture and an effective social order. These are themselves living resolutions — in the broadest sense, political resolutions — of specific economic realities. This process of incorporation is of major cultural importance. To understand it, but also to understand the material on which it must work, we need to distinguish three aspects of any cultural process, which we can call traditions, institutions, and formations.

The concept of tradition has been radically neglected in Marxist cultural thought. It is usually seen as at best a secondary factor, which may at most modify other and more decisive historical processes. This is not only because it is ordinarily diagnosed as superstructure, but also because "tradition" has been commonly understood as a relatively inert, historicized segment of a social structure: tradition as the surviving past. But this version of tradition is weak at the very point where the incorporating sense of tradition is strong: where it is seen, in fact, as an actively shaping force. For tradition is in practice the most evident expression of the dominant and hegemonic pressures and limits. It is always more than an inert historicized segment; indeed it is the most powerful practical means of incorporation. What we have to see is not just "a tradition" but a *selective tradition:* an intentionally selective version of a shaping past and pre-shaped present, which is then powerfully operative in the process of social and cultural definition and identification.

It is usually not difficult to show this empirically. Most versions of "tradition" can be quickly shown to be radically selective. From a whole possible area of past and present, in a particular culture, certain meanings and practices are selected for emphasis and certain other meanings and practices are neglected or excluded. Yet, within a particular hegemony, and as one of its decisive processes, this selection is presented and usually successfully passed off as "the tradition," "the significant past." What has then to be said about any tradition is that it is in this sense an aspect of *contemporary* social and cultural organization, in the interest of the dominance of a specific class. It is a version of the past which is intended to connect with and ratify the present. What it offers in practice is a sense of *predisposed continuity*.

There are, it is true, weaker senses of "tradition," in explicit contrast to "innovation" and "the contemporary." These are often points of retreat for groups in the society which have been left stranded by some particular hegemonic development. All that is now left to them is the retrospective affirmation of "traditional values." Or, from an opposite position, "traditional habits" are isolated, by some current hegemonic development, as elements of the past which have now to be discarded. Much of the overt argument about tradition is conducted between representatives of these two positions. But at a deeper level the hegemonic sense of tradition is always the most active: a deliberately selective and connecting process which offers a historical and cultural ratification of a contemporary order.

It is a very powerful process, since it is tied to many practical continuities — families, places, institutions, a language — which are indeed directly experienced. It is also, at any time, a vulnerable process, since it has in practice to discard whole areas of significance, or reinterpret or dilute them, or convert them into forms which support or at least do not contradict the really important elements of the current hegemony. It is significant that much of the most accessible and influential work of the counter-hegemony is historical: the recovery of discarded areas, or the redress of selective and reductive interpretations. But this in turn has little effect unless the lines to the present, in the actual process of the selective tradition, are clearly and actively traced. Otherwise any recovery can be simply residual or marginal. It is at the vital points of *connection*, where a version of the past is used to ratify the present and to indicate directions for the future, that a selective tradition is at once powerful and vulnerable. Powerful because it is so skilled in making active selective connections, dismissing those it does not want as "out of date" or "nostalgic," attacking those it cannot incorporate as "unprecedented" or "alien." Vulnerable because the real record is effectively recoverable, and many of the alternative or opposing practical continuities are still available. Vulnerable also because the selective version of "a living tradition" is always tied, though often in complex and hidden ways, to explicit contemporary pressures and limits. Its practical inclusions and exclusions are selectively encouraged or discouraged, often so effectively that the deliberate selection is made to verify itself in practice. Yet its selective privileges and interests, material in substance but often ideal in form, including complex elements of style and tone and of basic method, can still be recognized, demonstrated, and broken. This struggle for and against selective traditions is understandably a major part of all contemporary cultural activity.

It is true that the effective establishment of a selective tradition can be said to depend on identifiable institutions. But it is an underestimate of the process to suppose that it depends on institutions alone. The relations between cultural, political, and economic institutions are themselves very complex, and the substance of these relations is a direct indication of the character of the culture in the wider sense. But it is never only a question of formally identifiable institutions. It is also a question of *formations;* those effective movements and tendencies, in intellectual and artistic life, which have significant and sometimes decisive influence on the active development of a culture, and which have a variable and often oblique relation to formal institutions.

Formal institutions, evidently, have a profound influence on the active social process. What is abstracted in orthodox sociology as "socialization" is in practice, in any actual society, a specific kind of incorporation. Its description as "socialization," the universal abstract process on which all human beings can be said to depend, is a way of avoiding or hiding this specific content and intention. Any process of socialization of course includes things that all human beings have to learn, but any specific process ties this necessary learning to a selected range of meanings, values, and practices which, in the very closeness of their association with necessary learning, constitute the real foundations of the hegemonic. In a family children are cared for and taught to care for themselves, but within this necessary process fundamental and selective attitudes to self, to others, to a social order, and to the material world are both consciously and unconsciously taught. Education transmits necessary knowledge and skills, but always by a particular selection from the whole available range, and with intrinsic attitudes, both to learning and social relations, which are in practice virtually inextricable. Institutions such as churches are explicitly incorporative. Specific communities and specific places of work, exerting powerful and immediate pressures on the conditions of living and of making a living, teach, confirm, and in most cases finally enforce selected meanings, values, and activities. To describe the effect of all institutions of these kinds is to arrive at an important but still incomplete understanding of incorporation. In modern societies we have to add the major communications systems. These materialize selected news and opinion, and a wide range of selected perceptions and attitudes.

Yet it can still not be supposed that the sum of all these institutions is an organic hegemony. On the contrary, just because it is not "socialization" but a specific and complex hegemonic process, it is in practice full of contradictions and of unresolved conflicts. This is why it must not be reduced to the activities of an "ideological state apparatus." Such apparatus exists, although variably, but the whole process is much wider, and is in some important respects self-generating. By selection it is possible to identify common features in family, school, community, work, and communications, and these are important. But just because they are specific processes, with variable particular purposes, and with variable but always effective relations with what must in any case, in the short term, be done, the practical consequence is as often confusion and conflict between what are experienced as different purposes and different values, as it is crude incorporation of a theoretical kind. An effective incorporation is usually in practice achieved; indeed to establish and maintain a class society it must be achieved. But no mere training or pressure is truly hegemonic. The true condition of hegemony is effective *self-identification* with the hegemonic forms: a specific and internalized "socialization" which is expected to be positive but which, if that is not possible, will rest on a (resigned) recognition of the inevitable and the necessary. An effective culture, in this sense, is always more than the sum of its institutions: not only because these can be seen, in analysis, to derive much of their character from it, but mainly because it is at the level of a whole culture that the crucial *interrelations,* including confusions and conflicts, are really negotiated.

This is why, in any analysis, we have also to include *formations.* These are most recognizable as conscious movements and tendencies (literary, artistic, philosophical or scientific) which can usually be readily discerned after their formative productions. Often, when we look further, we find that these are articulations of much wider effective formations, which can by no means be wholly identified with formal institutions, or their formal meanings and values, and which can sometimes even be positively contrasted with them. This factor is of the greatest importance for the understanding of what is habitually specialized as intellectual and artistic life. In this fundamental relation between the institutions and formations of a culture there is great historical variability, but it is generally characteristic of developed complex societies that formations, as distinct from institutions, play an increasingly important role. Moreover, since such formations relate, inevitably, to real social structures, and yet have highly variable and often oblique relations with formally discernible social institutions, any social and cultural analysis of them requires procedures radically different from those developed for institutions. What is really being analysed, in each case, is a mode of specialized practice. Moreover, within an apparent hegemony, which can be readily described in generalizing ways, there are not only alternative and oppositional formations (some of them, at certain historical stages, having become or in the process of becoming alternative and oppositional institutions) but, within what can be recognized as the dominant, effectively varying formations which resist any simple reduction to some generalized hegemonic function.

It is at this point, normally, that many of those in real contact with such formations and their work retreat to an indifferent emphasis on the complexity of cultural activity. Others altogether deny (even theoretically) the relation of such formations and such work to the social process and especially the material social process. Others again, when the historical reality of the formations is grasped, render this back to ideal constructions — national traditions, literary and artistic traditions, histories of ideas, psychological types, spiritual archetypes — which indeed acknowledge and define formations, often much more substantially than the usual generalizing accounts of explicit social derivation or superstructural function, but only by radically displacing them from the immediate cultural process. As a result of this displacement, the formations and their work are not seen as the active social and cultural substance that they quite invariably are. In our own culture, this form of displacement, made temporarily or comparatively convincing by the failures of derivative and superstructural interpretation, is itself, and quite centrally, hegemonic.

8. DOMINANT, RESIDUAL, AND EMERGENT

The complexity of a culture is to be found not only in its variable processes and their social definitions — traditions, institutions, and formations — but also in the dynamic interrelations, at every point in the process, of historically varied and variable elements. In what I have called "epochal" analysis, a cultural process is seized as a cultural system, with determinate dominant features: feudal culture or bourgeois culture or a transition from one to the other. This emphasis on dominant and definitive lineaments and features is important and often, in practice, effective. But it then often happens that its methodology is preserved for the very different function of historical analysis, in which a sense of movement within what is ordinarily abstracted as a system is crucially necessary, especially if it is to connect with the future as well as with the past. In authentic historical analysis it is necessary at every point to recognize the complex interrelations between movements and tendencies both within and beyond a specific and effective dominance. It is necessary to examine how these relate to the whole cultural process rather than only to the selected and abstracted dominant system. Thus "bourgeois culture" is a significant generalizing description and hypothesis, expressed within epochal analysis by fundamental comparisons with "feudal culture" or "socialist culture." However, as a description of cultural process, over four or five centuries and in scores of different societies, it requires immediate historical and internally comparative differentiation. Moreover, even if this is acknowledged or practically carried out, the "epochal" definition can exert its pressure as a static type against which all real cultural process is measured, either to show "stages" or "variations" of the type (which is still historical analysis) or, at its worst, to select supporting and exclude "marginal" or "incidental" or "secondary" evidence.

Such errors are avoidable if, while retaining the epochal hypothesis, we can find terms which recognize not only "stages" and "variations" but the internal dynamic relations of any actual process. We have certainly still to speak of the "dominant" and the "effective," and in these senses of the hegemonic. But we find that we have also to speak, and indeed with further differentiation of each, of the "residual" and the "emergent," which in any real process, and at any moment in the process, are significant both in themselves and in what they reveal of the characteristics of the "dominant."

By "residual" I mean something different from the "archaic," though in practice these are often very difficult to distinguish. Any culture includes available elements of its past, but their place in the contemporary cultural process is profoundly variable. I would call the "archaic" that which is wholly recognized as an element of the past, to be observed, to be examined, or even on occasion to be consciously "revived," in a deliberately specializing way. What I mean by the "residual" is very different. The residual, by definition, has been effectively formed in the past, but it is still active in the cultural process, not only and often not at all as an element of the past, but as an effective element of the present. Thus certain experiences, meanings, and values which cannot be expressed or substantially verified in terms of the dominant culture, are nevertheless lived and practised on the basis of the residue — cultural as well as social — of some previous social and cultural institution or formation. It is crucial to distinguish this aspect of the residual, which may have an alternative or even oppositional relation to the dominant culture, from that active manifestation of the residual (this being its distinction from the archaic) which has been wholly or largely incorporated into the dominant culture. In three characteristic cases in contemporary English culture this distinction can become a precise term of analysis. Thus organized religion is predominantly residual, but within this there is a significant difference between some practically alternative and oppositional meanings and values (absolute brotherhood, service to others without reward) and a larger body of incorporated meanings and values (official morality, or the social order of which the other-worldly is a separated neutralizing or ratifying component). Again, the idea of rural community is predominantly residual, but is in some limited respects alternative or oppositional to urban industrial capitalism, though for the most part it is incorporated, as idealization or fantasy, or as an exotic — residential or escape — leisure function of the dominant order itself. Again, in monarchy, there is virtually nothing that is actively residual (alternative or oppositional), but, with a heavy and deliberate additional use of the archaic, a residual function has been wholly incorporated as a specific political and cultural function — marking the limits as well as the methods — of a form of capitalist democracy.

A residual cultural element is usually at some distance from the effective dominant culture, but some part of it, some version of it — and especially if the residue is from some major area of the past — will in most cases have had to be incorporated if the effective dominant culture is to make sense in these areas. Moreover, at certain points the dominant culture cannot allow too much residual experience and practice outside itself, at least without risk. It is in the incorporation of the actively residual — by reinterpretation, dilution, projection, discriminating inclusion and exclusion — that the work of the selective tradition is especially evident. This is very notable in the case of versions of "the literary tradition," passing through selective versions of the character of literature to connecting and incorporated definitions of what literature now is and should be. This is one among several crucial areas, since it is in some alternative or even oppositional versions of what literature is (has been) and what literary experience (and in one common derivation, other significant experience) is and must be, that, against the pressures of incorporation, actively residual meanings and values are sustained.

By "emergent" I mean, first, that new meanings and values, new practices, new relationships and kinds of relationship are continually being created. But it is exceptionally difficult to distinguish between those which are really elements of some new phase of the dominant culture (and in this sense "species-specific") and those which are substantially alternative or oppositional to it: emergent in the strict sense, rather than merely novel. Since we are always considering relations within a cultural process, definitions of the emergent, as of the residual, can be made only in relation to a full sense of the dominant. Yet the social location of the residual is always easier to understand, since a large part of it (though not all) relates to earlier social formations and phases of the cultural process, in which certain real meanings and values were generated. In the subsequent default of a particular phase of a dominant culture there is then a reaching back to those meanings and values which were created in actual societies and actual situations in the past, and which still seem to have significance because they represent areas of human experience, aspiration, and achievement which the dominant culture neglects, undervalues, opposes, represses, or even cannot recognize.

The case of the emergent is radically different. It is true that in the structure of any actual society, and especially in its class structure, there is always a social basis for elements of the cultural process that are alternative or oppositional to the dominant elements. One kind of basis has been valuably described in the central body of Marxist theory: the formation of a new class, the coming to consciousness of a new class, and within this, in actual process, the (often uneven) emergence of elements of a new cultural formation. Thus the emergence of the working class as a class was immediately evident (for example, in nineteenth-century England) in the cultural process. But there was extreme unevenness of contribution in different parts of the process. The making of new social values and institutions far outpaced the making of strictly cultural institutions, while specific cultural contributions, though significant, were less vigorous and autonomous than either general or institutional innovation. A new class is always a source of emergent cultural practice, but while it is still, as a class, relatively subordinate, this is always likely to be uneven and is certain to be incomplete. For new practice is not, of course, an isolated process. To the degree that it emerges, and especially to the degree that it is oppositional rather than alternative, the process of attempted incorporation significantly begins. This can be seen, in the same period in England, in the emergence and then the effective incorporation of a radical popular press. It can be seen in the emergence and incorporation of working-class writing, where the fundamental problem of emergence is clearly revealed, since the basis of incorporation, in such cases, is the effective predominance of received literary forms — an incorporation, so to say, which already conditions and limits the emergence. But the development is always uneven. Straight incorporation is most directly attempted against the visibly alternative and oppositional class elements: trade unions, working-class political parties, working-class life styles (as incorporated into "popular" journalism, advertising, and commercial entertainment). The process of emergence, in such conditions, is then a constantly repeated, an always renewable, move beyond a phase of practical incorporation: usually made much more difficult by the fact that much incorporation looks like recognition, acknowledgement, and thus a form of *acceptance*. In this complex process there is indeed regular confusion between the locally residual (as a form of resistance to incorporation) and the generally emergent.

Cultural emergence in relation to the emergence and growing strength of a class is then always of major importance, and always complex. But we have also to see that it is not the only kind of emergence. This recognition is very difficult, theoretically, though the practical evidence is abundant. What has really to be said, as a way of defining important elements of both the residual and the emergent, and as a way of understanding the character of the dominant, is that *no mode of production and therefore no dominant social order and therefore no dominant culture ever in reality includes or exhausts all human practice, human energy, and human intention.* This is not merely a negative proposition, allowing us to account for significant things which happen outside or against the dominant mode. On the contrary it is a fact about the modes of domination, that they select from and consequently exclude the full range of human practice. What they exclude may often be seen as the personal or the private, or as the natural or even the metaphysical. Indeed it is usually in one or other of these terms that the excluded area is expressed, since what the dominant has effectively seized is indeed the ruling definition of the social.

It is this seizure that has especially to be resisted. For there is always, though in varying degrees, practical consciousness, in specific relationships, specific skills, specific perceptions, that is unquestionably social and that a specifically dominant social order neglects, excludes, represses, or simply fails to recognize. A distinctive and comparative feature of any dominant social order is how far it reaches into the whole range of practices and experiences in an attempt at incorporation. There can be areas of experience it is willing to ignore or dispense with: to assign as private or to specialize as aesthetic or to generalize as natural. Moreover, as a social order changes, in terms of its own developing needs, these relations are variable. Thus in advanced capitalism, because of changes in the social character of labour, in the social character of communications, and in the social character of decision-making, the dominant culture reaches much further than ever before in capitalist society into hitherto "reserved" or "resigned" areas of experience and practice and meaning. The area of effective penetration of the dominant order into the whole social and cultural process is thus now significantly greater. This in turn makes the problem of emergence especially acute, and narrows the gap between alternative and oppositional elements. The alternative, especially in areas that impinge on significant areas of the dominant, is often seen as oppositional and, by pressure, often converted into it. Yet even here there can be spheres of practice and meaning which, almost by definition from its own limited character, or in its profound deformation, the dominant culture is unable in any real terms to recognize. Elements of emergence may indeed be incorporated, but just as often the incorporated forms are merely facsimiles of the genuinely emergent cultural practice. Any significant emergence, beyond or against a dominant mode, is very difficult under these conditions; in itself and in its repeated confusion with the facsimiles and novelties of the incorporated phase. Yet, in our own period as in others, the fact of emergent cultural practice is still undeniable, and together with the fact of actively residual practice is a necessary complication of the would-be dominant culture.

This complex process can still in part be described in class terms. But there is always other social being and consciousness which is neglected and excluded: alternative perceptions of others, in immediate relationships; new perceptions and practices of the material world. In practice these are different in quality from the developing and articulated interests of a rising class. The relations between these two sources of the emergent — the class and the excluded social (human) area — are by no means necessarily contradictory. At times they can be very close and on the relations between them much in political practice depends. But culturally and as a matter of theory the areas can be seen as distinct.

What matters, finally, in understanding emergent culture, as distinct from both the dominant and the residual, is that it is never only a matter of immediate practice; indeed it depends crucially on finding new forms or adaptations of form. Again and again what we have to observe is in effect a *pre-emergence,* active and pressing but not yet fully articulated, rather than the evident emergence which could be more confidently named. It is to understand more closely this condition of pre-emergence, as well as the more evident forms of the emergent, the residual, and the dominant, that we need to explore the concept of structures of feeling.

9. STRUCTURES OF FEELING

In most description and analysis, culture and society are expressed in an habitual past tense. The strongest barrier to the recognition of human cultural activity is this immediate and regular conversion of experience into finished products. What is defensible as a procedure in conscious history, where on certain assumptions many actions can be definitively taken as having ended, is habitually projected, not only into the always moving substance of the past, but into contemporary life, in which relationships, institutions and formations in which we are still actively involved are converted, by this procedural mode, into formed wholes rather than forming and formative processes. Analysis is then centred on relations between these produced institutions, formations, and experiences, so that now, as in that produced past, only the fixed explicit forms exist, and living presence is always, by definition, receding.

When we begin to grasp the dominance of this procedure, to look into its centre and if possible past its edges, we can understand, in new ways, that separation of the social from the personal which is so powerful and directive a cultural mode. If the social is always past, in the sense that it is always formed, we have indeed to find other terms for the undeniable experience of the present: not only the temporal present, the realization of this and this instant, but the specificity of present being, the inalienably physical, within which we may indeed discern and acknowledge institutions, formations, positions, but not always as fixed products, defining products. And then if the social is the fixed and explicit — the known relationships, institutions, formations, positions — all that is present and moving, all that escapes or seems to escape from the fixed and the explicit and the known, is grasped and defined as the personal: this, here, now, alive, active, "subjective."

There is another related distinction. As thought is described, in the same habitual past tense, it is indeed so different, in its explicit and finished forms, from much or even anything that we can presently recognize as thinking, that we set against it more active, more flexible, less singular terms — consciousness, experience, feeling — and then watch even these drawn towards fixed, finite, receding forms. The point is especially relevant to works of art, which really are, in one sense, explicit and finished forms — actual objects in the visual arts, objectified conventions and notations (semantic figures) in literature. But it is not only that, to complete their inherent process, we have to make them present, in specifically active "readings." It is also that the making of art is never itself in the past tense. It is always a formative process, within a specific present. At different moments in history, and significantly different ways, the reality and even the primacy of such presences and such processes, such diverse and yet specific actualities, have been powerfully asserted and reclaimed, as in practice of course they are all the time lived. But they are then often asserted as forms themselves, in contention with other known forms: the subjective as distinct from the objective; experience from belief; feeling from thought; the immediate from the general; the personal from the social. The undeniable power of two great modern ideological systems — the "aesthetic" and the "psychological" — is, ironically, systematically derived from these senses of instance and process, where experience, immediate feeling, and then subjectivity and personality are newly generalized and assembled. Against these "personal" forms, the ideological systems of fixed social generality, of categorical products, of absolute formations, are relatively powerless, within their specific dimension. Of one dominant strain in Marxism, with its habitual abuse of the "subjective" and the "personal," this is especially true.

Yet it is the reduction of the social to fixed forms that remains the basic error. Marx often said this, and some Marxists quote him, in fixed ways, before returning to fixed forms. The mistake, as so often, is in taking terms of analysis as terms of substance. Thus we speak of a world-view or of a prevailing ideology or of a class outlook, often with adequate evidence, but in this regular slide towards a past tense and a fixed form suppose, or even do not know that we have to suppose, that these exist and are lived specifically and definitively, in singular and developing forms. Perhaps the dead can be reduced to fixed forms, though their surviving records are against it. But the living will not be reduced, at least in the first person; living third persons may be different. All the known complexities, the experienced tensions, shifts, and uncertainties, the intricate forms of unevenness and confusion, are against the terms of the reduction and soon, by extension, against social analysis itself. Social forms are then often admitted for generalities but debarred, contemptuously, from any possible relevance to this immediate and actual significance of being. And from the abstractions formed in their turn by this act of debarring — the "human imagination," the "human psyche," the "unconscious," with their "functions" in art and in myth and in dream — new and displaced forms of social analysis and categorization, overriding all specific social conditions, are then more or less rapidly developed.

Social forms are evidently more recognizable when they are articulate and explicit. We have seen this in the range from institutions to formations and traditions. We can see it again in the range from dominant systems of belief and education to influential systems of explanation and argument. All these have effective presence. Many are formed and deliberate, and some are quite fixed. But when they have all been identified they are not a whole inventory even of social consciousness in its simplest sense. For they become social consciousness only when they are lived, actively, in real relationships, and moreover in relationships which are more than systematic exchanges between fixed units. Indeed just because all consciousness is social, its processes occur not only between but within the relationship and the related. And this practical consciousness is always more than a handling of fixed forms and units. There is frequent tension between the received interpretation and practical experience. Where this tension can be made direct and explicit, or where some alternative interpretation is available, we are still within a dimension of relatively fixed forms. But the tension is as often an unease, a stress, a displacement, a latency: the moment of conscious comparison not yet come, often not even coming. And comparison is by no means the only process, though it is powerful and important. There are the experiences to which the fixed forms do not speak at all, which indeed they do not recognize. There are important mixed experiences, where the available meaning would convert part to all, or all to part. And even where form and response can be found to agree, without apparent difficulty, there can be qualifications, reservations, indications elsewhere: what the agreement seemed to settle but still sounding elsewhere. Practical consciousness is almost always different from official consciousness, and this is not only a matter of relative freedom or control. For practical consciousness is what is actually being lived, and not only what it is thought is being lived. Yet the actual alternative to the received and produced fixed forms is not silence: not the absence, the unconscious, which bourgeois culture has mythicized. It is a kind of feeling and thinking which is indeed social and material, but each in an embryonic phase before it can become fully articulate and defined exchange. Its relations with the already articulate and defined are then exceptionally complex.

This process can be directly observed in the history of a language. In spite of substantial and at some levels decisive continuities in grammar and vocabulary, no generation speaks quite the same language as its predecessors. The difference can be defined in terms of additions, deletions, and modifications, but these do not exhaust it. What really changes is something quite general, over a wide range, and the description that often fits the change best is the literary term "style." It is a general change, rather than a set of deliberate choices, yet choices can be deduced from it, as well as effects. Similar kinds of change can be observed in manners, dress, building, and other similar forms of social life. It is an open question — that is to say, a set of specific historical questions — whether in any of these changes this or that group has been dominant or influential, or whether they are the result of much more general interaction. For what we are defining is a particular quality of social experience and relationship, historically distinct from other particular qualities, which gives the sense of a generation or of a period. The relations between this quality and the other specifying historical marks of changing institutions, formations, and beliefs, and beyond these the changing social and economic relations between and within classes, are again an open question: that is to say, a set of specific historical questions. The methodological consequence of such a definition, however, is that the specific qualitative changes are not *assumed* to be epiphenomena of changed institutions, formations, and beliefs, or merely secondary evidence of changed social and economic relations between and within classes. At the same time they are from the beginning taken as *social* experience, rather than as "personal" experience or as the merely superficial or incidental "small change" of society. They are social in two ways that distinguish them from reduced senses of the social as the institutional and the formal: first, in that they are *changes of presence* (while they are being lived this is obvious; when they have been lived it is still their substantial characteristic); second, in that although they are emergent or pre-emergent, they do not have to await definition, classification, or rationalization before they exert palpable pressures and set effective limits on experience and on action.

Such changes can be defined as changes in *structures of feeling*. The term is difficult, but "feeling" is chosen to emphasize a distinction from more formal concepts of "world-view" or "ideology." It is not only that we must go beyond formally held and systematic beliefs, though of course we have always to include them. It is that we are concerned with meanings and values as they are actively lived and felt, and the relations between these and formal or systematic beliefs are in practice variable (including historically variable), over a range from formal assent with private dissent to the more nuanced interaction between selected and interpreted beliefs and acted and justified experiences. An alternative definition would be structures of *experience:* in one sense the better and wider word, but with the difficulty that one of its senses has that past tense which is the most important obstacle to recognition of the area of social experience which is being defined. We are talking about characteristic elements of impulse, restraint, and tone; specifically affective elements of consciousness and relationships: not feeling against thought, but thought as felt and feeling as thought: practical consciousness of a present kind, in a living and interrelating continuity. We are then defining these elements as a "structure": as a set, with specific internal relations, at once interlocking and in tension. Yet we are also defining a social experience which is still *in process,* often indeed not yet recognized as social but taken to be private, idiosyncratic, and even isolating, but which in analysis (though rarely otherwise) has its emergent, connecting, and dominant characteristics, indeed its specific hierarchies. These are often more recognizable at a later stage, when they have been (as often happens) formalized, classified, and in many cases built into institutions and formations. By that time the case is different; a new structure of feeling will usually already have begun to form, in the true social present.

Methodologically, then, a "structure of feeling" is a cultural hypothesis, actually derived from attempts to understand such elements and their connections in a generation or period, and needing always to be returned, interactively, to such evidence. It is initially less simple than more formally structured hypotheses of the social, but it is more adequate to the actual range of cultural evidence: historically certainly, but even more (where it matters more) in our present cultural process. The hypothesis has a special relevance to art and literature, where the true social content is in a significant number of cases of this present and affective kind, which cannot without loss be reduced to belief-systems, institutions, or explicit general relationships, though it may include all these as lived and experienced, with or without tension, as it also evidently includes elements of social and material (physical or natural) experience which may lie beyond, or be uncovered or imperfectly covered by, the elsewhere recognizable systematic elements. The unmistakable presence of certain elements in art which are not covered by (though in one mode they may be reduced to) other formal systems is the true source of the specializing categories of "the aesthetic," "the arts," and "imaginative literature." We need, on the one hand, to acknowledge (and welcome) the specificity of these elements — specific feelings, specific rhythms — and yet to find ways of recognizing their specific kinds of sociality, thus preventing that extraction from social experience which is conceivable only when social experience itself has been categorically (and at root historically) reduced. We are then not only concerned with the restoration of social content in its full sense, that of a generative immediacy. The idea of a structure of feeling can be specifically related to the evidence of forms and conventions — semantic figures — which, in art and literature, are often among the very first indications that such a new structure is forming. These relations will be discussed in more detail in subsequent chapters, but as a matter of cultural theory this is a way of defining forms and conventions in art and literature as inalienable elements of a social material process: not by derivation from other social forms and pre-forms, but as social formation of a specific kind which may in turn be seen as the articulation (often the only fully available articulation) of structures of feeling which as living processes are much more widely experienced.

For structures of feeling can be defined as social experiences *in solution,* as distinct from other social semantic formations which have been *precipitated* and are more evidently and more immediately available. Not all art, by any means, relates to a contemporary structure of feeling. The effective formations of most actual art relate to already manifest social formations, dominant or residual, and it is primarily to emergent formations (though often in the form of modification or disturbance in older forms) that the structure of feeling, *as solution,* relates. Yet this specific solution is never mere flux. It is a structured formation which, because it is at the very edge of semantic availability, has many of the characteristics of a pre-formation, until specific articulations — new semantic figures — are discovered in material practice: often, as it happens, in relatively isolated ways, which are only later seen to compose a significant (often in fact minority) generation; this often, in turn, the generation that substantially connects to its successors. It is thus a specific structure of particular linkages, particular emphases and suppressions, and, in what are often its most recognizable forms, particular deep starting-points and conclusions. Early Victorian ideology, for example, specified the exposure caused by poverty or by debt or by illegitimacy as social failure or deviation; the contemporary structure of feeling, meanwhile, in the new semantic figures of Dickens, of Emily Brontë, and others, specified exposure and isolation as a *general* condition, and poverty, debt, or illegitimacy as its connecting instances. An alternative ideology, relating such exposure to the nature of the social order, was only later generally formed: offering explanations but now at a reduced tension: the social explanation fully admitted, the intensity of experienced fear and shame now dispersed and generalized.

The example reminds us, finally, of the complex relation of differentiated structures of feeling to differentiated classes. This is historically very variable. In England between 1660 and 1690, for example, two structures of feeling (among the defeated Puritans and in the restored Court) can be readily distinguished, though neither, in its literature and elsewhere, is reducible to the ideologies of these groups or to their formal (in fact complex) class relations. At times the emergence of a new structure of feeling is best related to the rise of a class (England, 1700–60); at other times to contradiction, fracture, or mutation within a class (England, 1780–1830 or 1890–1930), when a formation appears to break away from its class norms, though it retains its substantial affiliation, and the tension is at once lived and articulated in radically new semantic figures. Any of these examples requires detailed substantiation, but what is now in question, theoretically, is the hypothesis of a mode of social formation, explicit and recognizable in specific kinds of art, which is distinguishable from other social and semantic formations by its articulation of *presence*.

Fredric Jameson

b. 1934

Without doubt the foremost Marxist literary critic in America today, Fredric R. Jameson was born in Cleveland, Ohio, raised in New Jersey, and educated at Haverford College and Yale University, where he received his Ph.D. in 1960. He has taught at Harvard University (1959–67), the University of California at San Diego (1967–76), Yale University (1976–83), and the University of California at Santa Cruz (1983–85), and since 1986 he has been Lane Professor of Comparative Literature at Duke University. In addition to studies of Jean-Paul Sartre (1961) and Wyndham Lewis (1979), his major works include Marxism and Form: Twentieth Century Dialectical Theories of Literature *(1971),* The Prison-House of Language: A Critical Account of Russian Formalism and Structuralism *(1972), and* The Political Unconscious: Narrative as a Socially Symbolic Act *(1981); two volumes of collected essays entitled* The Ideologies of Theory *(1988) and* Modernism and Imperialism *(1988); a book of film criticism entitled* Signatures of the Visible *(1990); and* Late Marxism: Adorno or the Persistence of the Dialectic *(1990),* Postmodernism, or, The Cultural Logic of Late Capitalism *(1991),* The Geopolitical Aesthetic: Cinema and Space in the World System *(1992), and the Wellek lecture series published as* The Seeds of Time *(1994). The following selection is from the introductory chapter of* The Political Unconscious.

From *The Political Unconscious*

III

At this point it might seem appropriate to juxtapose a Marxist method of literary and cultural interpretation with those just outlined,[1] and to document its claims to greater adequacy and validity. For better or for worse, however, as I warned in the Preface, this obvious next step is not the strategy projected by the present book, which rather seeks to argue the perspectives of Marxism as necessary preconditions for adequate literary comprehension. Marxist critical insights will therefore here be defended as something like an ultimate *semantic* precondition for the intelligibility of literary and cultural texts. Even this argument, however, needs a certain specification: in particular we will suggest that such semantic enrichment and enlargement of the inert givens and materials of a particular text must take place within three concentric frameworks, which mark a widening out of the sense of the social ground of a text through the notions, first, of political history, in the narrow sense of punctual event

[1]Jameson has just discussed psychoanalytic criticism and the myth criticism of Northrop Frye (see p. 641). [Ed.]

and a chroniclelike sequence of happenings in time; then of society, in the now already less diachronic and time-bound sense of a constitutive tension and struggle between social classes; and, ultimately, of history now conceived in its vastest sense of the sequence of modes of production and the succession and destiny of the various human social formations, from prehistoric life to whatever far future history has in store for us.[2]

These distinct semantic horizons are, to be sure, also distinct moments of the process of interpretation, and may in that sense be understood as dialectical equivalents of what Frye has called the successive "phases" in our reinterpretation — our rereading and rewriting — of the literary text. What we must also note, however, is that each phase or horizon governs a distinct reconstruction of its object, and construes the very structure of what can now only in a general sense be called "the text" in a different way.

Thus, within the narrower limits of our first, narrowly political or historical, horizon, the "text," the object of study, is still more or less construed as coinciding with the individual literary work or utterance. The difference between the perspective enforced and enabled by this horizon, however, and that of ordinary *explication de texte,* or individual exegesis, is that here the individual work is grasped essentially as a *symbolic act.*

When we pass into the second phase, and find that the semantic horizon within which we grasp a cultural object has widened to include the social order, we will find that the very object of our analysis has itself been thereby dialectically transformed, and that it is no longer construed as an individual "text" or work in the narrow sense, but has been reconstituted in the form of the great collective and class discourses of which a text is little more than an individual *parole* or utterance. Within this new horizon, then, our object of study will prove to be the *ideologeme,* that is, the smallest intelligible unit of the essentially antagonistic collective discourses of social classes.

When finally, even the passions and values of a particular social formation find themselves placed in a new and seemingly relativized perspective by the ultimate horizon of human history as a whole, and by their respective positions in the whole complex sequence of the modes of production, both the individual text and its ideologemes know a final transformation, and must be read in terms of what I will call the *ideology of form,* that is, the symbolic messages transmitted to us by the coexistence of various sign systems which are themselves traces or anticipations of modes of production.

The general movement through these three progressively wider horizons will largely coincide with the shifts in focus of the final chapters in this book, and will be felt, although not narrowly and programmatically underscored, in the methodological transformations determined by the historical transformations of their textual objects, from Balzac to Gissing to Conrad.[3]

We must now briefly characterize each of these semantic or interpretive horizons. We have suggested that it is only in the first narrowly political horizon — in which history is reduced to a series of punctual events and crises in time, to the diachronic agitation of the year-to-year, the

[2]A useful discussion of the phenomenological concept of "horizon" may be found in Hans-Georg Gadamer, *Truth and Method,* trans. G. Barden and J. Cumming (New York: Seabury, 1975), pp. 216–20, 267–74. It will become clear in the course of my subsequent discussion that a Marxian conception of our relationship to the past requires a sense of our radical difference from earlier cultures which is not adequately allowed for in Gadamer's influential notion of *Horizontverschmelzung* (fusion of horizons). This is perhaps also the moment to add that from the perspective of Marxism as an "absolute historicism," the stark antithesis proposed by E. D. Hirsch, Jr., between Gadamer's historicist "relativism" and Hirsch's own conception of a more absolute interpretive validity, will no longer seem particularly irreconcilable. Hirsch's distinction between *Sinn* and *Bedeutung,* between the scientific analysis of a text's intrinsic "meaning" and what he is pleased to call our "ethical" evaluation of its "significance" for us (see, for example, *The Aims of Interpretation* [Chicago: University of Chicago Press, 1976]), corresponds to the traditional Marxist distinction between science and ideology, particularly as it has been retheorized by the Althusserians. It is surely a useful working distinction, although in the light of current revisions of the idea of science one should probably make no larger theoretical claims for it than this operative one. [Au.] See the introduction to Gadamer, p. 668. [Ed.]

[3]In later chapters of *The Political Unconscious,* Jameson analyzes texts by these three authors, viewed as typical of realist, naturalist, and modernist eras in fiction. [Ed.]

chroniclelike annals of the rise and fall of political regimes and social fashions, and the passionate immediacy of struggles between historical individuals — that the "text" or object of study will tend to coincide with the individual literary work or cultural artifact. Yet to specify this individual text as a symbolic act is already fundamentally to transform the categories with which traditional *explication de texte* (whether narrative or poetic) operated and largely still operates.

The model for such an interpretive operation remains the readings of myth and aesthetic structure of Claude Lévi-Strauss as they are codified in his fundamental essay "The Structural Study of Myth."[4] These suggestive, often sheerly occasional, readings and speculative glosses immediately impose a basic analytical or interpretive principle: the individual narrative, or the individual formal structure is to be grasped as the imaginary resolution of a real contradiction. Thus, to take only the most dramatic of Lévi-Strauss's analyses — the "interpretation" of the unique facial decorations of the Caduveo Indians — the starting point will be an immanent description of the formal and structural peculiarities of this body art; yet it must be a description already preprepared and oriented toward transcending the purely formalistic, a movement which is achieved not by abandoning the formal level for something extrinsic to it — such as some inertly social "content" — but rather immanently, by construing purely formal patterns as a symbolic enactment of the social within the formal and the aesthetic. Such symbolic functions are, however, rarely found by an aimless enumeration of random formal and stylistic features; our discovery of a text's symbolic efficacity must be oriented by a formal description which seeks to grasp it as a determinate structure of still properly formal *contradictions.* Thus, Lévi-Strauss orients his still purely visual analysis of Caduveo facial decorations toward this climactic account of their contradictory dynamic: "the use of a design which is symmetrical but yet lies across an oblique axis . . . a complicated situation based upon two contradictory forms of duality, and resulting in a compromise brought about by a secondary opposition between the ideal axis of the object itself [the human face] and the ideal axis of the figure which it represents."[5] Already on the purely formal level, then, this visual text has been grasped as a contradiction by way of the curiously provisional and asymmetrical resolution it proposes for that contradiction.

Lévi-Strauss's "interpretation" of this formal phenomenon may now, perhaps overhastily, be specified. Caduveo are a hierarchical society, organized in three endogamous groups or castes. In their social development, as in that of their neighbors, this nascent hierarchy is already the place of the emergence, if not of political power in the strict sense, then at least of relations of domination: the inferior status of women, the subordination of youth to elders, and the development of a hereditary aristocracy. Yet whereas this latent power structure is, among the neighboring Guana and Bororo, masked by a division into moieties which cuts across the three castes, and whose exogamous exchange appears to function in a nonhierarchical, essentially egalitarian way, it is openly present in Caduveo life, as surface inequality and conflict. The social institutions of the Guana and Bororo, on the other hand, provide a realm of appearance, in which real hierarchy and inequality are dissimulated by the reciprocity of the moieties, and in which, therefore, "asymmetry of class is balanced . . . by symmetry of 'moieties.'"

As for the Caduveo,

> they were never lucky enough to resolve their contradictions, or to disguise them with the help of institutions artfully devised for that purpose. On the

[4]Claude Lévi-Strauss, *Structural Anthropology,* trans. C. Jacobson and B. G. Schoepf (New York: Basic, 1963), pp. 206–31. The later four-volume *Mythologiques* reverses the perspective of this analysis: where the earlier essay focused on the individual mythic *parole* or utterance, the later series models the entire system or *langue* in terms of which the various individual myths are related to each other. *Mythologiques* should therefore rather be used as suggestive material on the historical difference between the narrative mode of production of primitive societies and that of our own: in this sense, the later work would find its place in the third and final horizon of interpretation. [Au.] See p. 835. [Ed.]

[5]Claude Lévi-Strauss, *Tristes Tropiques,* trans. John Russell (New York: Atheneum, 1971), p. 176. [Au.]

social level, the remedy was lacking . . . but it was never completely out of their grasp. It was within them, never objectively formulated, but present as a source of confusion and disquiet. Yet since they were unable to conceptualize or to live this solution directly, they began to dream it, to project it into the imaginary. . . . We must therefore interpret the graphic art of Caduveo women, and explain its mysterious charm as well as its apparently gratuitous complication, as the fantasy production of a society seeking passionately to give symbolic expression to the institutions it might have had in reality, had not interest and superstition stood in the way.[6]

In this fashion, then, the visual text of Caduveo facial art constitutes a symbolic act, whereby real social contradictions, insurmountable in their own terms, find a purely formal resolution in the aesthetic realm.

This interpretive model thus allows us a first specification of the relationship between ideology and cultural texts or artifacts: a specification still conditioned by the limits of the first, narrowly historical or political horizon in which it is made. We may suggest that from this perspective, ideology is not something which informs or invests symbolic production; rather the aesthetic act is itself ideological, and the production of aesthetic or narrative form is to be seen as an ideological act in its own right, with the function of inventing imaginary or formal "solutions" to unresolvable social contradictions.

Lévi-Strauss's work also suggests a more general defense of the proposition of a political unconscious than we have hitherto been able to present, insofar as it offers the spectacle of so-called primitive peoples perplexed enough by the dynamics and contradictions of their still relatively simple forms of tribal organization to project decorative or mythic resolutions of issues that they are unable to articulate conceptually. But if this is the case for precapitalist and even pre-political societies, then how much more must it be true for the citizen of the modern *Gesellschaft*,[7] faced with the great constitutional options of the revolutionary period, and with the corrosive and tradition-annihilating effects of the spread of a money and market economy, with the changing cast of collective characters which oppose the bourgeoisie, now to an embattled aristocracy, now to an urban proletariat, with the great fantasms of the various nationalisms, now themselves virtual "subjects of history" of a rather different kind, with the social homogenization and psychic constriction of the rise of the industrial city and its "masses," the sudden appearance of the great transnational forces of communism and fascism, followed by the advent of the superstates and the onset of that great ideological rivalry between capitalism and communism, which, no less passionate and obsessive than that which, at the dawn of modern times, seethed through the wars of religion, marks the final tension of our now global village? It does not, indeed, seem particularly farfetched to suggest that these texts of history, with their fantasmatic collective "actants," their narrative organization, and their immense charge of anxiety and libidinal investment, are lived by the contemporary subject as a genuine politico-historical *pensée sauvage*[8] which necessarily informs all of our cultural artifacts, from the literary institutions of high modernism all the way to the products of mass culture. Under these circumstances, Lévi-Strauss's work suggests that the proposition whereby all cultural artifacts are to be read as symbolic resolutions of real political and social contradictions deserves serious exploration and systematic experimental verification. It will become clear in later chapters of this book that the most readily accessible formal articulation of the operations of a political *pensée sauvage* of this kind will be found in what we will call the structure of a properly political *allegory*, as it develops from networks of topical allusion in Spenser or Milton or Swift to the symbolic narratives of class representatives or "types" in novels like those of Balzac. With political allegory, then, a sometimes repressed ur-narrative[9] or master fantasy about the interaction of collective subjects, we have moved to the very borders of our second

[6]Ibid., pp. 179–80. [Au.]

[7]Community. [Ed.]

[8]Literally "savage mind"; Lévi-Strauss's term for the part of the mind that thinks using myth. [Ed.]

[9]Original narrative. [Ed.]

horizon, in which what we formerly regarded as individual texts are grasped as "utterances" in an essentially collective or class discourse.

We cannot cross those borders, however, without some final account of the critical operations involved in our first interpretive phase. We have implied that in order to be consequent, the will to read literary or cultural texts as symbolic acts must necessarily grasp them as resolutions of determinate contradictions; and it is clear that the notion of contradiction is central to any Marxist cultural analysis, just as it will remain central in our two subsequent horizons, although it will there take rather different forms. The methodological requirement to articulate a text's fundamental contradiction may then be seen as a test of the completeness of the analysis: this is why, for example, the conventional sociology of literature or culture, which modestly limits itself to the identification of class motifs or values in a given text, and feels that its work is done when it shows how a given artifact "reflects" its social background, is utterly unacceptable. Meanwhile, Kenneth Burke's play of emphases, in which a symbolic act is on the one hand affirmed as a genuine *act,* albeit on the symbolic level, while on the other it is registered as an act which is "merely" symbolic, its resolutions imaginary ones that leave the real untouched, suitably dramatizes the ambiguous status of art and culture.[10]

Still, we need to say a little more about the status of this external reality, of which it will otherwise be thought that it is little more than the traditional notion of "context" familiar in older social or historical criticism. The type of interpretation here proposed is more satisfactorily grasped as the rewriting of the literary text in such a way that the latter may itself be seen as the rewriting or restructuration of a prior historical or ideological *subtext,* it being always understood that that "subtext" is not immediately present as such, not some common-sense external reality, nor even the conventional narratives of history manuals, but rather must itself always be (re)constructed after the fact. The literary or aesthetic act therefore always entertains some active relationship with the Real;[11] yet in order to do so, it cannot simply allow "reality" to persevere inertly in its own being, outside the text and at distance. It must rather draw the Real into its own texture, and the ultimate paradoxes and false problems of linguistics, and most notably of semantics, are to be traced back to this process, whereby language manages to carry the Real within itself as its own intrinsic or immanent subtext. Insofar, in other words, as symbolic action — what Burke will map as "dream," "prayer," or "chart"[12] — is a way of doing something to the world, to that degree what we are calling "world" must inhere within it, as the content it has to take up into itself in order to submit it to the transformations of form. The symbolic act therefore begins by generating and producing its own context in the same moment of emergence in which it steps back from it, taking its measure with a view toward its own projects of transformation. The whole paradox of what we have here called the subtext may be summed up in this, that the literary work or cultural object, as though for the first time, brings into being that very situation to which it is also, at one and the same time, a reaction. It articulates its own situation and textualizes it, thereby encouraging and perpetuating the illusion that the situation itself did not exist before it, that there is nothing but a text, that there never was any extra- or con-textual reality before the text itself generated it in the form of a mirage. One does not have to argue the reality of history: necessity, like Dr. Johnson's stone, does that for us.[13] That history — Althusser's "absent cause," Lacan's "Real" — is *not* a text, for it is fundamentally non-narrative and nonrepresentational; what can be added, however, is the proviso that history is inaccessible to us except in textual form, or in other words, that it can be approached

[10]See the introduction to Burke, p. 581. [Ed.]

[11]Jameson is alluding to the Lacanian field of the Real; see the introduction to Psychoanalytic Theory, p. 1021. [Ed.]

[12]Kenneth Burke, *The Philosophy of Literary Form* (Berkeley: University of California Press, 1973), pp. 5–6; and see also my "Symbolic Inference; or Kenneth Burke and Ideological Analysis," *Critical Inquiry,* 4 (Spring, 1978), 507–23. [Au.]

[13]Samuel Johnson, when told that Bishop George Berkeley denied the existence of corporeal reality, kicked a stone, saying, "Thus I refute Berkeley." [Ed.]

only by way of prior (re)textualization. Thus, to insist on either of the two inseparable yet incommensurable dimensions of the symbolic act without the other: to overemphasize the active way in which the text reorganizes its subtext (in order, presumably, to reach the triumphant conclusion that the "referent" does not exist); or on the other hand to stress the imaginary status of the symbolic act so completely as to reify its social ground, now no longer understood as a subtext but merely as some inert given that the text passively or fantasmatically "reflects" — to overstress either of these functions of the symbolic act at the expense of the other is surely to produce sheer ideology, whether it be, as in the first alternative, the ideology of structuralism, or, in the second, that of vulgar materialism.

Still, this view of the place of the "referent" will be neither complete nor methodologically usable unless we specify a supplementary distinction between several types of subtext to be (re)constructed. We have implied, indeed, that the social contradiction addressed and "resolved" by the formal prestidigitation of narrative must, however reconstructed, remain an absent cause, which cannot be directly or immediately conceptualized by the text. It seems useful, therefore, to distinguish, from this ultimate subtext which is the place of social *contradiction,* a secondary one, which is more properly the place of ideology, and which takes the form of the *aporia* or the *antinomy:* what can in the former be resolved only through the intervention of praxis here comes before the purely contemplative mind as logical scandal or double bind, the unthinkable and the conceptually paradoxical, that which cannot be unknotted by the operation of pure thought, and which must therefore generate a whole more properly narrative apparatus — the text itself — to square its circles and to dispel, through narrative movement, its intolerable closure. Such a distinction, positing a system of antinomies as the symptomatic expression and conceptual reflex of something quite different, namely a social contradiction, will now allow us to reformulate that coordination between a semiotic and a dialectical method, which was evoked in the preceding section. The operational validity of semiotic analysis, and in particular of the Greimassian semiotic rectangle,[14] derives, as was suggested there, not from its adequacy to nature or being, nor even from its capacity to map all forms of thinking or language, but rather from its vocation specifically to model ideological closure and to articulate the workings of binary oppositions, here the privileged form of what we have called the antinomy. A dialectical reevaluation of the findings of semiotics intervenes, however, at the moment in which this entire system of ideological closure is taken as the symptomatic projection of something quite different, namely of social contradiction.

We may now leave this first textual or interpretive model behind, and pass over into the second horizon, that of the social. The latter becomes visible, and individual phenomena are revealed as social facts and institutions, only at the moment in which the organizing categories of analysis become those of social class. I have in another place described the dynamics of ideology in its constituted form as a function of social class:[15] suffice it only to recall here that for

[14]Jameson explains later that Greimas's "semiotic rectangle . . . is the representation of a binary opposition of two contraries (S and –S) along with the simple negations or contradictories of both terms (the so-called subcontraries –S̄ and S̄): significant slots are constituted by the various possible combinations of these terms, most notably the 'complex' term (or ideal synthesis of the two contraries) and the 'neutral' term (or ideal synthesis of the two subcontraries). See A. J. Greimas and François Rastier, 'The Interaction of Semiotic Constraints,' *Yale French Studies* No. 41 (1968), pp. 86–105" (*The Political Unconscious,* p. 166). For Jameson, the fascination of the "semiotic rectangle" is that a "static analytical scheme" can work in his dialectical criticism "as the very locus and model of ideological closure" (p. 47).

For example, Jameson analyzes the ideology of the "character system" of Conrad's *Lord Jim* in terms of the expansion of a binary opposition between activity and value. The "semiotic rectangle" presents four points (activity, value, not-activity, not-value) which then define the position of the various agents. Lord Jim himself represents the synthesis of activity and value; Gentleman Brown, of activity and not-value; the pilgrims on the Patna, of value and not-activity; the "desk-chair sailors" of not-value and not-activity (p. 256). This arrangement, for Jameson, represents the deep structure of the ideological work Conrad's novel was expected to perform. [Ed.]

[15]*Marxism and Form,* pp. 376–82; and see below, pp. 288–91. The most authoritative contemporary Marxist statement of this view of social class is to be found in E. P. Thompson, *The Making of the English Working Classes*

Marxism classes must always be apprehended relationally, and that the ultimate (or ideal) form of class relationship and class struggle is always dichotomous. The constitutive form of class relationships is always that between a dominant and a laboring class: and it is only in terms of this axis that class fractions (for example, the petty bourgeoisie) or ec-centric or dependent classes (such as the peasantry) are positioned. To define class in this way is sharply to differentiate the Marxian model of classes from the conventional sociological analysis of society into strata, subgroups, professional elites and the like, each of which can presumably be studied in isolation from one another in such a way that the analysis of their "values" or their "cultural space" folds back into separate and independent *Weltanschauungen,*[16] each of which inertly reflects its particular "stratum." For Marxism, however, the very content of a class ideology is relational, in the sense that its "values" are always actively in situation with respect to the opposing class, and defined against the latter: normally, a ruling class ideology will explore various strategies of the *legitimation* of its own power position, while an oppositional culture or ideology will, often in covert and disguised strategies, seek to contest and to undermine the dominant "value system."

This is the sense in which we will say, following Mikhail Bakhtin, that within this horizon class discourse — the categories in terms of which individual texts and cultural phenomena are now rewritten — is essentially *dialogical* in its structure.[17] As Bakhtin's (and Voloshinov's) own work in this field is relatively specialized, focusing primarily on the heterogeneous and explosive pluralism of moments of carnival or festival (moments, for example, such as the immense resurfacing of the whole spectrum of the religious or political sects in the English 1640s or the Soviet 1920s) it will be necessary to add the qualification that the normal form of the dialogical is essentially an *antagonistic* one, and that the dialogue of class struggle is one in which two opposing discourses fight it out within the general unity of a shared code. Thus, for instance, the shared master code of religion becomes in the 1640s in England the place in which the dominant formulations of a hegemonic theology are reappropriated and polemically modified.[18]

Within this new horizon, then, the basic formal requirement of dialectical analysis is maintained, and its elements are still restructured in terms of *contradiction* (this is essentially, as we have said, what distinguishes the relationality of a Marxist class analysis from static analysis of the sociological type). Where the contradiction of the earlier horizon was univocal, however, and limited to the situation of the individual text, to the place of a purely individual symbolic resolution, contradiction here appears in the form of the dialogical as the irreconcilable demands and positions of antagonistic classes. Here again, then, the requirement to prolong interpretation to the point at which this ultimate contradiction begins to appear offers a criterion for the completeness or insufficiency of the analysis.

Yet to rewrite the individual text, the individual cultural artifact, in terms of the antagonistic dialogue of class voices is to perform a rather different operation from the one we have ascribed to our first horizon. Now the individual text will be refocused as a *parole,* or individual utterance, of that vaster system, or *langue,* of class discourse. The individual text retains its formal structure as a symbolic act: yet the value and character of such symbolic action are now significantly modified and enlarged. On this rewriting, the individual utterance or text is grasped as a symbolic move in an essentially polemic and strategic ide-

(New York: Vintage, 1966), pp. 9–11; in *The Poverty of Theory,* Thompson has argued that his view of classes is incompatible with "structural" Marxism, for which classes are not "subjects" but rather "positions" within the social totality (see, for the Althusserian position, Nicos Poulantzas, *Political Power and Social Classes*). [Au.]

[16]World-pictures. [Ed.]

[17]Mikhail Bakhtin, *Problems of Dostoyevsky's Poetics,* trans. R. W. Rotsel (Ann Arbor: Ardis, 1973), pp. 153–69. See also Bakhtin's important book on linguistics, written under the name of V. N. Voloshinov, *Marxism and the Philosophy of Language,* trans. L. Matejka and I. R. Titunik (New York: Seminar Press, 1973), pp. 83–98; and Bakhtin's posthumous collection, *Esthétique et théorie du roman,* trans. Daria Olivier (Paris: Gallimard, 1978), esp. pp. 152–82. [Au.] See the introduction to Bakhtin, p. 527. [Ed.]

[18]See Christopher Hill, *The World Turned Upside Down* (London: Temple Smith, 1972). [Au.]

ological confrontation between the classes, and to describe it in these terms (or to reveal it in this form) demands a whole set of different instruments.

For one thing, the illusion or appearance of isolation or autonomy which a printed text projects must now be systematically undermined. Indeed, since by definition the cultural monuments and masterworks that have survived tend necessarily to perpetuate only a single voice in this class dialogue, the voice of a hegemonic class, they cannot be properly assigned their relational place in a dialogical system without the restoration or artificial reconstruction of the voice to which they were initially opposed, a voice for the most part stifled and reduced to silence, marginalized, its own utterances scattered to the winds, or reappropriated in their turn by the hegemonic culture.

This is the framework in which the reconstruction of so-called popular cultures must properly take place — most notably, from the fragments of essentially peasant cultures: folk songs, fairy tales, popular festivals, occult or oppositional systems of belief such as magic and witchcraft. Such reconstruction is of a piece with the reaffirmation of the existence of marginalized or oppositional cultures in our own time, and the reaudition of the oppositional voices of black or ethnic cultures, women's and gay literature, "naive" or marginalized folk art, and the like. But once again, the affirmation of such nonhegemonic cultural voices remains ineffective if it is limited to the merely "sociological" perspective of the pluralistic rediscovery of other isolated social groups: only an ultimate rewriting of these utterances in terms of their essentially polemic and subversive strategies restores them to their proper place in the dialogical system of the social classes. Thus, for instance, Bloch's reading of the fairy tale, with its magical wish-fulfillments and its Utopian fantasies of plenty and the *pays de Cocagne,*[19] restores the dialogical and antagonistic content of this "form" by exhibiting it as a systematic deconstruction and undermining of the hegemonic aristocratic form of the epic, with its somber ideology of heroism and baleful destiny; thus also the work of Eugene Genovese on black religion restores the vitality of these utterances by reading them, not as the replication of imposed beliefs, but rather as a process whereby the hegemonic Christianity of the slave-owners is appropriated, secretly emptied of its content and subverted to the transmission of quite different oppositional and coded messages.[20]

Moreover, the stress on the dialogical then allows us to reread or rewrite the hegemonic forms themselves; they also can be grasped as a process of the reappropriation and neutralization, the cooptation and class transformation, the cultural universalization, of forms which originally expressed the situation of "popular," subordinate, or dominated groups. So the slave religion of Christianity is transformed into the hegemonic ideological apparatus of the medieval system; while folk music and peasant dance find themselves transmuted into the forms of aristocratic or court festivity and into the cultural visions of the pastoral; and popular narrative from time immemorial — romance, adventure story, melodrama, and the like — is ceaselessly drawn on to restore vitality to an enfeebled and asphyxiating "high culture." Just so, in our own time, the vernacular and its still vital sources of production (as in black language) are reappropriated by the exhausted and media-standardized speech of a hegemonic middle class. In the aesthetic realm, indeed, the process of cultural "universalization" (which implies the repression of the oppositional voice, and the illusion that there is only one genuine "culture") is the specific form taken by what can be called the process of legitimation in the realm of ideology and conceptual systems.

Still, this operation of rewriting and of the restoration of an essentially dialogical or class horizon will not be complete until we specify the "units" of this larger system. The linguistic metaphor (rewriting texts in terms of the opposition of a *parole* to a *langue*) cannot, in other words, be particularly fruitful until we are able to convey something of the dynamics proper to a

[19]Ernst Bloch, "Zerstörung, Rettung des Mythos durch Licht," in *Verfremdungen* I (Frankfurt: Suhrkamp, 1963), pp. 152–62. [Au.]

[20]Eugene Genovese, *Roll Jordan Roll* (New York: Vintage, 1976), pp. 161–284. [Au.]

class *langue* itself, which is evidently, in Saussure's sense, something like an ideal construct that is never wholly visible and never fully present in any one of its individual utterances. This larger class discourse can be said to be organized around minimal "units" which we will call *ideologemes*. The advantage of this formulation lies in its capacity to mediate between conceptions of ideology as abstract opinion, class value, and the like, and the narrative materials with which we will be working here. The ideologeme is an amphibious formation, whose essential structural characteristic may be described as its possibility to manifest itself either as a pseudoidea — a conceptual or belief system, an abstract value, an opinion or prejudice — or as a protonarrative, a kind of ultimate class fantasy about the "collective characters" which are the classes in opposition. This duality means that the basic requirement for the full description of the ideologeme is already given in advance: as a construct it must be susceptible to both a conceptual description and a narrative manifestation all at once. The ideologeme can of course be elaborated in either of these directions, taking on the finished appearance of a philosophical system on the one hand, or that of a cultural text on the other; but the ideological analysis of these finished cultural products requires us to demonstrate each one as a complex work of transformation on that ultimate raw material which is the ideologeme in question. The analyst's work is thus first that of the identification of the ideologeme, and, in many cases, of its initial naming in instances where for whatever reason it had not yet been registered as such. The immense preparatory task of identifying and inventorying such ideologemes has scarcely even begun, and to it the present book will make but the most modest contribution: most notably in its isolation of that fundamental nineteenth-century ideologeme which is the "theory" of *ressentiment*,[21] and in its "unmasking" of ethics and the ethical binary opposition of good and evil as one of the fundamental forms of ideological thought in Western culture. However, our stress here and throughout on the fundamentally narrative character of such ideologemes (even where they seem to be articulated only as abstract conceptual beliefs or values) will offer the advantage of restoring the complexity of the transactions between opinion and protonarrative or libidinal fantasy. Thus we will observe, in the case of Balzac, the generation of an overt and constituted ideological and political "value system" out of the operation of an essentially narrative and fantasy dynamic; the chapter on Gissing, on the other hand, will show how an already constituted "narrative paradigm" emits an ideological message in its own right without the mediation of authorial intervention.

[21]Literally, rancor; Nietzsche's term for the hatred felt by the weak for the strong. [Ed.]

This focus or horizon, that of class struggle and its antagonistic discourses, is, as we have already suggested, not the ultimate form a Marxist analysis of culture can take. The example just alluded to — that of the seventeenth-century English revolution, in which the various classes and class fractions found themselves obliged to articulate their ideological struggles through the shared medium of a religious master code — can serve to dramatize the shift whereby these objects of study are reconstituted into a structurally distinct "text" specific to this final enlargement of the analytical frame. For the possibility of a displacement in emphasis is already given in this example: we have suggested that within the apparent unity of the theological code, the fundamental difference of antagonistic class positions can be made to emerge. In that case, the inverse move is also possible, and such concrete semantic differences can on the contrary be focused in such a way that what emerges is rather the all-embracing unity of a single code which they must share and which thus characterizes the larger unity of the social system. This new object — code, sign system, or system of the production of signs and codes — thus becomes an index of an entity of study which greatly transcends those earlier ones of the narrowly political (the symbolic act), and the social (class discourse and the ideologeme), and which we have proposed to term the historical in the larger sense of this word. Here the organizing unity will be what the

Marxian tradition designates as a *mode of production.*

I have already observed that the "problematic" of modes of production is the most vital new area of Marxist theory in all the disciplines today; not paradoxically, it is also one of the most traditional, and we must therefore, in a brief preliminary way, sketch in the "sequence" of modes of production as classical Marxism, from Marx and Engels to Stalin, tended to enumerate them.[22] These modes, or "stages" of human society, have traditionally included the following: primitive communism or tribal society (the horde), the *gens* or hierarchical kinship societies (neolithic society), the Asiatic mode of production (so-called Oriental despotism), the *polis* or an oligarchical slaveholding society (the ancient mode of production), feudalism, capitalism, and communism (with a good deal of debate as to whether the "transitional" stage between these last — sometimes called "socialism" — is a genuine mode of production in its own right or not). What is more significant in the present context is that even this schematic or mechanical conception of historical "stages" (what the Althusserians have systematically criticized under the term "historicism") includes the notion of a cultural dominant or form of ideological coding specific to each mode of production. Following the same order these have generally been conceived as magic and mythic narrative, kinship, religion or the sacred, "politics" according to the narrower category of citizenship in the ancient city state, relations of personal domination, commodity reification, and (presumably) original and as yet nowhere fully developed forms of collective or communal association.

Before we can determine the cultural "text" or object of study specific to the horizon of modes of production, however, we must make two preliminary remarks about the methodological problems it raises. The first will bear on whether the concept of "mode of production" is a synchronic one, while the second will address the temptation to use the various modes of production for a classifying or typologizing operation, in which cultural texts are simply dropped into so many separate compartments.

Indeed, a number of theorists have been disturbed by the apparent convergence between the properly Marxian notion of an all-embracing and all-structuring mode of production (which assigns everything within itself — culture, ideological production, class articulation, technology — a specific and unique place), and non-Marxist visions of a "total system" in which the various elements or levels of social life are programmed in some increasingly constricting way. Weber's dramatic notion of the "iron cage" of an increasingly bureaucratic society,[23] Foucault's image of the gridwork of an ever more pervasive "political technology of the body,"[24] but also more traditional "synchronic" accounts of the cultural programming of a given historical "moment," such as those that have variously been proposed from

[22]The "classical" texts on modes of production, besides Lewis Henry Morgan's *Ancient Society* (1877), are Karl Marx, *Pre-Capitalist Economic Formations,* a section of the *Grundrisse* (1857–58) published separately by Eric Hobsbawm (New York: International, 1965), and Friedrich Engels, *The Family, Private Property, and the State* (1884). Important recent contributions to the mode of production "debate" include Etienne Balibar's contribution to Althusser's collective volume, *Reading Capital;* Emmanuel Terray, *Marxism and "Primitive" Societies,* trans. M. Klopper (New York: Monthly Review, 1972); Maurice Godelier, *Horizon: trajets marxistes en anthropologie* (Paris: Maspéro, 1973); J. Chesneaux, ed., *Sur le "mode de production asiatique"* (Paris: Editions Sociales, 1969); and Barry Hindess and Paul Hirst, *Pre-Capitalist Modes of Production* (London: Routledge & Kegan Paul, 1975). [Au.]

[23]"The Puritan wanted to work in a calling; we are forced to do so. For when asceticism was carried out of monastic cells into everyday life, and began to dominate worldly morality, it did its part in building the tremendous cosmos of the modern economic order. This order is now bound to the technical and economic conditions of machine production which today determine the lives of all the individuals who are born into this mechanism, not only those directly concerned with economic acquisition, with irresistible force. Perhaps it will so determine them until the last ton of fossilized coal is burnt. In Baxter's view the care for external goods should only lie on the shoulders of the saint 'like a light cloak, which can be thrown aside at any moment,' But fate decreed that the cloak should become an iron cage." *The Protestant Ethic and the Spirit of Capitalism,* trans. T. Parsons (New York: Scribners, 1958), p. 181. [Au.]

[24]Michel Foucault, *Surveiller et punir* (Paris: Gallimard, 1975), pp. 27–28 and passim. [Au.]

Vico and Hegel to Spengler and Deleuze — all such monolithic models of the cultural unity of a given historical period have tended to confirm the suspicions of a dialectical tradition about the dangers of an emergent "synchronic" thought, in which change and development are relegated to the marginalized category of the merely "diachronic," the contingent or the rigorously nonmeaningful (and this, even where, as with Althusser, such models of cultural unity are attacked as forms of a more properly Hegelian and idealistic "expressive causality"). This theoretical foreboding about the limits of synchronic thought can perhaps be most immediately grasped in the political area, where the model of the "total system" would seem slowly and inexorably to eliminate any possibility of the *negative* as such, and to reintegrate the place of an oppositional or even merely "critical" practice and resistance back into the system as the latter's mere inversion. In particular, everything about class struggle that was anticipatory in the older dialectical framework, and seen as an emergent space for radically new social relations, would seem, in the synchronic model, to reduce itself to practices that in fact tend to reinforce the very system that foresaw and dictated their specific limits. This is the sense in which Jean Baudrillard has suggested that the "total-system" view of contemporary society reduces the options of resistance to anarchist gestures, to the sole remaining ultimate protests of the wildcat strike, terrorism, and death. Meanwhile, in the framework of the analysis of culture also, the latter's integration into a synchronic model would seem to empty cultural production of all its antisystemic capacities, and to "unmask" even the works of an overtly oppositional or political stance as instruments ultimately programmed by the system itself.

It is, however, precisely the notion of a series of enlarging theoretical horizons proposed here that can assign these disturbing synchronic frameworks their appropriate analytical places and dictate their proper use. This notion projects a long view of history which is inconsistent with concrete political action and class struggle only if the specificity of the horizons is not respected; thus, even if the concept of a mode of production is to be considered a synchronic one (and we will see in a moment that things are somewhat more complicated than this), at the level of historical abstraction at which such a concept is properly to be used, the lesson of the "vision" of a total system is for the short run one of the structural limits imposed on praxis rather than the latter's impossibility.

The theoretical problem with the synchronic systems enumerated above lies elsewhere, and less in their analytical framework than in what in a Marxist perspective might be called their infrastructural regrounding. Historically, such systems have tended to fall into two general groups, which one might term respectively the hard and soft visions of the total system. The first group projects a fantasy future of a "totalitarian" type in which the mechanisms of domination — whether these are understood as part of the more general process of bureaucratization, or on the other hand derive more immediately from the deployment of physical and ideological force — are grasped as irrevocable and increasingly pervasive tendencies whose mission is to colonize the last remnants and survivals of human freedom — to occupy and organize, in other words, what still persists of Nature objectively and subjectively (very schematically, the Third World and the Unconscious).

This group of theories can perhaps hastily be associated with the central names of Weber and Foucault; the second group may then be associated with names such as those of Jean Baudrillard and the American theorists of a "postindustrial society."[25] For this second group, the characteristics of the total system of contemporary world society are less those of political domination than those of cultural programming and penetration: not the iron cage, but rather the *société de consommation*[26] with its consumption of images and simulacra, its free-floating signifiers

[25]Jean Baudrillard, *Le Système des objets* (Paris: Gallimard, 1968); *La Société de consommation* (Paris: Denöel, 1970); *Pour une économie politique du signe* (Paris: Gallimard, 1972). The most influential statement of the American version of this "end of ideology"/consumer society position is, of course, that of Daniel Bell: see his *Coming of Post-Industrial Society* (New York: Basic, 1973) and *The Cultural Contradictions of Capitalism* (New York: Basic, 1976). [Au.]

[26]Consumer society typical of late capitalism. [Ed.]

and its effacement of the older structures of social class and traditional ideological hegemony. For both groups, world capitalism is in evolution toward a system which is not socialist in any classical sense, on the one hand the nightmare of total control and on the other the polymorphous or schizophrenic intensities of some ultimate counterculture (which may be no less disturbing for some than the overtly threatening characteristics of the first vision). What one must add is that neither kind of analysis respects the Marxian injunction of the "ultimately determining instance" of economic organization and tendencies: for both, indeed, economics (or political economy) of that type is in the new total system of the contemporary world at an end, and the economic finds itself in both reassigned to a secondary and nondeterminant position beneath the new dominant of political power or of cultural production, respectively.

There exist, however, within Marxism itself precise equivalents to these two non-Marxian visions of the contemporary total system: rewritings, if one likes, of both in specifically Marxian and "economic" terms. These are the analyses of late capitalism in terms of *capitalogic*[27] and of *disaccumulation*,[28] respectively; and while this book is clearly not the place to discuss such theories at any length, it must be observed here that both, seeing the originality of the contemporary situation in terms of systemic tendencies *within* capitalism, reassert the theoretical priority of the organizing concept of the mode of production which we have been concerned to argue.

We must therefore now turn to the second related problem about this third and ultimate horizon, and deal briefly with the objection that cultural analysis pursued within it will tend toward a purely typological or classificatory operation, in which we are called upon to "decide" such issues as whether Milton is to be read within a "precapitalist" or a nascent capitalist context, and so forth. I have insisted elsewhere on the sterility of such classificatory procedures, which may always, it seems to me, be taken as symptoms and indices of the repression of a more genuinely dialectical or historical practice of cultural analysis. This diagnosis may now be expanded to cover all three horizons at issue here, where the practice of homology, that of a merely "sociological" search for some social or class equivalent, and that, finally, of the use of some typology of social and cultural systems, respectively, may stand as examples of the misuse of these three frameworks. Furthermore, just as in our discussion of the first two we have stressed the centrality of the category of contradiction for any Marxist analysis (seen, within the first horizon, as that which the cultural and ideological artifact tries to "resolve," and in the second as the nature of the social and class conflict within which a given work is one act or gesture), so too here we can effectively validate the horizon of the mode of production by showing the form contradiction takes on this level, and the relationship of the cultural object to it.

Before we do so, we must take note of more recent objections to the very concept of the mode of production. The traditional schema of the various modes of production as so many historical "stages" has generally been felt to be unsatisfactory, not least because it encourages the kind of typologizing criticized above, in political quite as

[27]See, for a review and critique of the basic literature, Stanley Aronowitz, "Marx, Braverman, and the Logic of Capital," *Insurgent Sociologist,* VIII, No. 2/3 (Fall, 1978), pp. 126–46; and see also Hans-George Backhaus, "Zur Dialektik der Wertform," in A. Schmidt, ed., *Beiträge zur marxistischen Erkenntnistheorie* (Frankfurt: Suhrkamp, 1969), pp. 128–52; and Helmut Reichelt, *Zur logischen Struktur des Kapitalbegriffs bei Karl Marx* (Frankfurt: Europäische Verlagsanstalt, 1970). For the Capitalogicians, the "materialist kernel" of Hegel is revealed by grasping the concrete or objective reality of Absolute Spirit (the Notion in-and-for-itself) as none other than capital (Reichelt, pp. 77–78). This tends, however, to force them into the post-Marxist position for which the dialectic is seen as the thought-mode proper only to capitalism (Backhaus, pp. 140–41): in that case, of course, the dialectic would become unnecessary and anachronistic in a society that had abolished the commodity form. [Au.]

[28]The basic texts on "disaccumulation theory" are Martin J. Sklar, "On the Proletarian Revolution and the End of Political-Economic Society," *Radical America,* III, No. 3 (May–June, 1969), pp. 1–41; Jim O'Connor, "Productive and Unproductive Labor," *Politics and Society,* 5 (1975), pp. 297–336; Fred Block and Larry Hirschhorn, "New Productive Forces and the Contradictions of Contemporary Capitalism," *Theory and Society,* 7 (1979), 363–95; and Stanley Aronowitz, "The End of Political Economy," *Social Text,* No. 2 (1980), pp. 3–52. [Au.]

much as in cultural analysis. (The form taken in political analysis is evidently the procedure which consists in "deciding" whether a given conjuncture is to be assigned to a moment within feudalism — the result being a demand for bourgeois and parliamentary rights — or within capitalism — with the accompanying "reformist" strategy — or, on the contrary, a genuine "revolutionary" moment — in which case the appropriate revolutionary strategy is then deduced.)

On the other hand, it has become increasingly clear to a number of contemporary theorists that such classification of "empirical" materials within this or that abstract category is impermissible in large part because of the level of abstraction of the concept of a mode of production: no historical society has ever "embodied" a mode of production in any pure state (nor is *Capital* the description of a historical society, but rather the construction of the abstract concept of capitalism). This has led certain contemporary theorists, most notably Nicos Poulantzas,[29] to insist on the distinction between a "mode of production" as a purely theoretical construction and a "social formation" that would involve the description of some historical society at a certain moment of its development. This distinction seems inadequate and even misleading, to the degree that it encourages the very empirical thinking which it was concerned to denounce, in other words, subsuming a particular or an empirical "fact" under this or that corresponding "abstraction." Yet one feature of Poulantzas' discussion of the "social formation" may be retained: his suggestion that every social formation or historically existing society has in fact consisted in the overlay and structural coexistence of *several* modes of production all at once, including vestiges and survivals of older modes of production, now relegated to structurally dependent positions within the new, as well as anticipatory tendencies which are potentially inconsistent with the existing system but have not yet generated an autonomous space of their own.

But if this suggestion is valid, then the problems of the "synchronic" system and of the typological temptation are both solved at one stroke. What is synchronic is the "concept" of the mode of production; the moment of the historical coexistence of several modes of production is not synchronic in this sense, but open to history in a dialectical way. The temptation to classify texts according to the appropriate mode of production is thereby removed, since the texts emerge in a space in which we may expect them to be crisscrossed and intersected by a variety of impulses from contradictory modes of cultural production all at once.

Yet we have still not characterized the specific object of study which is constructed by this new and final horizon. It cannot, as we have shown, consist in the concept of an individual mode of production (any more than, in our second horizon, the specific object of study could consist in a particular social class in isolation from the others). We will therefore suggest that this new and ultimate object may be designated, drawing on recent historical experience, as *cultural revolution,* that moment in which the coexistence of various modes of production becomes visibly antagonistic, their contradictions moving to the very center of political, social, and historical life. The incomplete Chinese experiment with a "proletarian" cultural revolution may be invoked in support of the proposition that previous history has known a whole range of equivalents for similar processes to which the term may legitimately be extended. So the Western Enlightenment may be grasped as part of a properly bourgeois cultural revolution, in which the values and the discourses, the habits and the daily space, of the *ancien régime* were systematically dismantled so that in their place could be set the new conceptualities, habits and life forms, and value systems of a capitalist market society. This process clearly involved a vaster historical rhythm than such punctual historical events as the French Revolution or the Industrial Revolution, and includes in its *longue durée* such phenomena as those described by Weber in *The Protestant Ethic and the Spirit of Capitalism* — a work that can now in its turn be read as a contribution to the study of the bourgeois cultural revolution, just as the corpus of work on romanticism is now repositioned as the study of a significant and am-

[29]Poulantzas, *Political Power and Social Classes,* pp. 13–16. [Au.]

biguous moment in the resistance to this particular "great transformation," alongside the more specifically "popular" (precapitalist as well as working-class) forms of cultural resistance.

But if this is the case, then we must go further and suggest that all previous modes of production have been accompanied by cultural revolutions specific to them of which the neolithic "cultural revolution," say, the triumph of patriarchy over the older matriarchal or tribal forms, or the victory of Hellenic "justice" and the new legality of the *polis* over the vendetta system are only the most dramatic manifestations. The concept of cultural revolution, then — or more precisely, the reconstruction of the materials of cultural and literary history in the form of this new "text" or object of study which is cultural revolution — may be expected to project a whole new framework for the humanities, in which the study of culture in the widest sense could be placed on a materialist basis.

This description is, however, misleading to the degree to which it suggests that "cultural revolution" is a phenomenon limited to so-called "transitional" periods, during which social formations dominated by one mode of production undergo a radical restructuration in the course of which a different "dominant" emerges. The problem of such "transitions" is a traditional crux of the Marxian problematic of modes of production, nor can it be said that any of the solutions proposed, from Marx's own fragmentary discussions to the recent model of Etienne Balibar, are altogether satisfactory, since in all of them the inconsistency between a "synchronic" description of a given system and a "diachronic" account of the passage from one system to another seems to return with undiminished intensity. But our own discussion began with the idea that a given social formation consisted in the coexistence of various synchronic systems or modes of production, each with its own dynamic or time scheme — a kind of metasynchronicity, if one likes — while we have now shifted to a description of cultural revolution which has been couched in the more diachronic language of systemic transformation. I will therefore suggest that these two apparently inconsistent accounts are simply the twin perspectives which our thinking (and our presentation or *Darstellung* of that thinking) can take on this same vast historical object. Just as overt revolution is no punctual event either, but brings to the surface the innumerable daily struggles and forms of class polarization which are at work in the whole course of social life that precedes it, and which are therefore latent and implicit in "prerevolutionary" social experience, made visible as the latter's deep structure only in such "moments of truth" — so also the overtly "transitional" moments of cultural revolution are themselves but the passage to the surface of a permanent process in human societies, of a permanent struggle between the various coexisting modes of production. The triumphant moment in which a new systemic dominant gains ascendency is therefore only the diachronic manifestation of a constant struggle for the perpetuation and reproduction of its dominance, a struggle which must continue throughout its life course, accompanied at all moments by the systemic or structural antagonism of those older and newer modes of production that resist assimilation or seek deliverance from it. The task of cultural and social analysis thus construed within this final horizon will then clearly be the rewriting of its materials in such a way that this perpetual cultural revolution can be apprehended and read as the deeper and more permanent constitutive structure in which the empirical textual objects know intelligibility.

Cultural revolution thus conceived may be said to be beyond the opposition between synchrony and diachrony, and to correspond roughly to what Ernst Bloch has called the *Ungleichzeitigkeit* (or "nonsynchronous development") of cultural and social life.[30] Such a view imposes a

[30]Ernst Bloch, "Nonsynchronism and Dialectics," *New German Critique*, No. 11 (Spring, 1977), pp. 22–38; or *Erbschaft dieser Zeit* (Frankfurt: Suhrkamp, 1973). The "nonsynchronous" use of the concept of mode of production outlined above is in my opinion the only way to fulfill Marx's well-known program for dialectical knowledge "of rising from the abstract to the concrete" (1857 Introduction, *Grundrisse*, p. 101). Marx there distinguished three stages of knowledge: (1) the notation of the particular (this would correspond to something like empirical history, the collection of data and descriptive materials on the variety of human societies); (2) the conquest of abstraction, the coming into being of a properly "bourgeois" science or of what Hegel called the cate-

new use of concepts of periodization, and in particular of that older schema of the "linear" stages which is here preserved and canceled all at once. We will deal more fully with the specific problems of periodization in the next chapter: suffice it to say at this point that such categories are produced within an initial diachronic or narrative framework, but become usable only when that initial framework has been annulled, allowing us now to coordinate or articulate categories of diachronic origin (the various distinct modes of production) in what is now a synchronic or metasynchronic way.

We have, however, not yet specified the nature of the textual object which is constructed by this third horizon of cultural revolution, and which would be the equivalent within this dialectically new framework of the objects of our first two horizons — the symbolic act, and the ideologeme or dialogical organization of class discourse. I will suggest that within this final horizon the individual text or cultural artifact (with its appearance of autonomy which was dissolved in specific and original ways within the first two horizons as well) is here restructured as a field of force in which the dynamics of sign systems of several distinct modes of production can be registered and apprehended. These dynamics — the newly constituted "text" of our third horizon — make up what can be termed *the ideology of form,* that is, the determinate contradiction of the specific messages emitted by the varied sign systems which coexist in a given artistic process as well as in its general social formation.

gories of the Understanding (this moment, that of the construction of a static and purely classificatory concept of "modes of production," is what Hindess and Hirst quite properly criticize in *Precapitalist Modes of Production*); (3) the transcendence of abstraction by the dialectic, the "rise to the concrete," the setting in motion of hitherto static and typologizing categories by their reinsertion in a concrete historical situation (in the present context, this is achieved by moving from a classificatory use of the categories of modes of production to a perception of their dynamic and contradictory coexistence in a given cultural moment). Althusser's own epistemology, incidentally — Generalities I, II, and III (*Pour Marx* [Paris: Maspéro, 1965], pp. 187–90) — is a gloss on this same fundamental passage of the 1857 Introduction, but one which succeeds only too well in eliminating its dialectical spirit. [Au.]

What must now be stressed is that at this level "form" is apprehended as content. The study of the ideology of form is no doubt grounded on a technical and formalistic analysis in the narrower sense, even though, unlike much traditional formal analysis, it seeks to reveal the active presence within the text of a number of discontinuous and heterogeneous formal processes. But at the level of analysis in question here, a dialectical reversal has taken place in which it has become possible to grasp such formal processes as sedimented content in their own right, as carrying ideological messages of their own, distinct from the ostensible or manifest content of the works; it has become possible, in other words, to display such formal operations from the standpoint of what Louis Hjelmslev[31] will call the "content of form" rather than the latter's "expression," which is generally the object of the various more narrowly formalizing approaches. The simplest and most accessible demonstration of this reversal may be found in the area of literary genre. Our next chapter, indeed, will model the process whereby generic specification and description can, in a given historical text, be transformed into the detection of a host of distinct generic messages — some of them objectified survivals from older modes of cultural production, some anticipatory, but all together projecting a formal conjuncture through which the "conjuncture" of coexisting modes of production at a given historical moment can be detected and allegorically articulated.

Meanwhile, that what we have called the ideology of form is something other than a retreat from social and historical questions into the more narrowly formal may be suggested by the relevance of this final perspective to more overtly political and theoretical concerns; we may take the much debated relation of Marxism to feminism as a particularly revealing illustration. The notion of overlapping modes of production outlined above has indeed the advantage of allowing us to short-circuit the false problem of the prior-

[31]Danish linguist, author of *Prolegomena to a Theory of Language* (Ann Arbor: University of Wisconsin Press, 1961). [Ed.]

ity of the economic over the sexual, or of sexual oppression over that of social class. In our present perspective, it becomes clear that sexism and the patriarchal are to be grasped as the sedimentation and the virulent survival of forms of alienation specific to the oldest mode of production of human history, with its division of labor between men and women, and its division of power between youth and elder. The analysis of the ideology of form, properly completed, should reveal the formal persistence of such archaic structures of alienation — and the sign systems specific to them — beneath the overlay of all the more recent and historically original types of alienation — such as political domination and commodity reification — which have become the dominants of that most complex of all cultural revolutions, late capitalism, in which all the earlier modes of production in one way or another structurally coexist. The affirmation of radical feminism, therefore, that to annul the patriarchal is the most *radical* political act — insofar as it includes and subsumes more partial demands, such as the liberation from the commodity form — is thus perfectly consistent with an expanded Marxian framework, for which the transformation of our own dominant mode of production must be accompanied and completed by an equally radical restructuration of all the more archaic modes of production with which it structurally coexists.

With this final horizon, then, we emerge into a space in which History itself becomes the ultimate ground as well as the untranscendable limit of our understanding in general and our textual interpretations in particular. This is, of course, also the moment in which the whole problem of interpretive priorities returns with a vengeance, and in which the practitioners of alternate or rival interpretive codes — far from having been persuaded that History is an interpretive code that includes and transcends all the others — will again assert "History" as simply one more code among others, with no particularly privileged status. This is most succinctly achieved when the critics of Marxist interpretation, borrowing its own traditional terminology, suggest that the Marxian interpretive operation involves a thematization and a reification of "History" which is not markedly different from the process whereby the other interpretive codes produce their own forms of thematic closure and offer themselves as absolute methods.

It should by now be clear that nothing is to be gained by opposing one reified theme — History — by another — Language — in a polemic debate as to ultimate priority of one over the other. The influential forms this debate has taken in recent years — as in Jürgen Habermas' attempt to subsume the "Marxist" model of production beneath a more all-embracing model of "communication" or intersubjectivity,[32] or in Umberto Eco's assertion of the priority of the Symbolic in general over the technological and productive systems which it must organize as *signs* before they can be used as *tools*[33] — are based on the misconception that the Marxian category of a "mode of production" is a form of technological or "productionist" determinism.

It would seem therefore more useful to ask ourselves, in conclusion, how History as a ground and as an absent cause can be conceived in such a way as to resist such thematization or reification, such transformation back into one optional code among others. We may suggest such a possibility obliquely by attention to what the Aristotelians would call the generic satisfaction specific to the form of the great monuments of historiography, or what the semioticians might call the "history-effect" of such narrative texts. Whatever the raw material on which historiographic form works (and we will here only touch on that most widespread type of material which is the sheer chronology of fact as it is produced by the rote-drill of the history manual), the "emotion" of great historiographic form can then always be seen as the radical restructuration of that inert material, in this instance the powerful reorganization of otherwise inert chronological and "linear" data in the form of Necessity: why what happened (at first received as "empirical" fact) had to happen the way it did. From this perspective, then, causality is only one

[32]See Jürgen Habermas, *Knowledge and Human Interests*, trans, J. Shapiro (Boston: Beacon, 1971), esp. Part I. [Au.]

[33]Umberto Eco, *A Theory of Semiotics* (Bloomington: Indiana University Press, 1976), pp. 21–26. [Au.]

of the possible tropes by which this formal restructuration can be achieved, although it has obviously been a privileged and historically significant one. Meanwhile, should it be objected that Marxism is rather a "comic" or "romance" paradigm, one which sees history in the salvational perspective of some ultimate liberation, we must observe that the most powerful realizations of a Marxist historiography — from Marx's own narratives of the 1848 revolution through the rich and varied canonical studies of the dynamics of the Revolution of 1789 all the way to Charles Bettelheim's study of the Soviet revolutionary experience — remain visions of historical Necessity in the sense evoked above. But Necessity is here represented in the form of the inexorable logic involved in the determinate failure of all the revolutions that have taken place in human history: the ultimate Marxian presupposition — that socialist revolution can only be a total and worldwide process (and that this in turn presupposes the completion of the capitalist "revolution" and of the process of commodification on a global scale) — is the perspective in which the failure or the blockage, the contradictory reversal or functional inversion, of this or that local revolutionary process is grasped as "inevitable," and as the operation of objective limits.

History is therefore the experience of Necessity, and it is this alone which can forestall its thematization or reification as a mere object of representation or as one master code among many others. Necessity is not in that sense a type of content, but rather the inexorable *form* of events; it is therefore a narrative category in the enlarged sense of some properly narrative political unconscious which has been argued here, a retextualization of History which does not propose the latter as some new representation or "vision," some new content, but as the formal effects of what Althusser, following Spinoza, calls an "absent cause." Conceived in this sense, History is what hurts, it is what refuses desire and sets inexorable limits to individual as well as collective praxis, which its "ruses" turn into grisly and ironic reversals of their overt intention. But this History can be apprehended only through its effects, and never directly as some reified force. This is indeed the ultimate sense in which History as ground and untranscendable horizon needs no particular theoretical justification: we may be sure that its alienating necessities will not forget us, however much we might prefer to ignore them.

Jürgen Habermas

b. 1929

Jürgen Habermas, the most significant social philosopher in Germany and the Marxist most quoted by liberal humanists, was born in Düsseldorf and educated at the Universities of Göttingen and Zurich before taking his Ph.D. at Bonn in 1954. He taught at the University of Marburg and at Heidelberg before moving in 1964 to the Institute for Social Research at Frankfurt, where, as professor of philosophy, he was Theodor Adorno's assistant at the end of Adorno's career. Since 1981, Habermas has been director of the Max Planck Institute for Social Science at Starnberg. He has been an enormously prolific writer; and his books include Knowledge and Human Interests *(1968),* Toward a Rational Society *(1971),* Legitimation Crisis *(1971),* Communication and the Evolution of Society *(1979),* Autonomy and Solidarity *(1986),* On the Logic of the Social Sciences *(1988),* The New Conservatism: Cultural Criticism and the Historians' Debate *(1989),* Moral Consciousness and Communicative Action *(1990),* The Structural Transformation of the Public Sphere: An Inquiry into a Category of Bourgeois Society *(1991),* Remarks on Discourse Ethics *(1993), and* Between Facts and Norms: Contributions to a Discourse Theory of Law and Democracy *(1996). The following selection is from* The Philosophical Discourse of Modernity *(1985).*

From *The Philosophical Discourse of Modernity*

I

Adorno's "negative dialectics" and Derrida's "deconstruction" can be seen as different answers to the same problem. The totalizing self-critique of reason gets caught in a performative contradiction since subject-centered reason can be convicted of being authoritarian in nature only by having recourse to its own tools. The tools of thought, which miss the "dimension of nonidentity" and are imbued with the "metaphysics of presence," are nevertheless the only available means for uncovering their own insufficiency. Heidegger flees from this paradox to the luminous heights of an esoteric, special discourse, which absolves itself of the restrictions of discursive speech generally and is immunized by vagueness against any specific objections. He makes use of metaphysical concepts for purposes of a critique of metaphysics, as a ladder he casts away once he has mounted the rungs.[1] Once on the heights, however, the late Heidegger does not, as did the early Wittgenstein, withdraw into the mystic's silent intuition; instead, with the gestures of the seer and an abundance of words, he lays claim to the authority of the initiate.

Adorno operates differently. He does not slip out of the paradoxes of the self-referential critique of reason; he makes the performative contradiction within which this line of thought has moved since Nietzsche, and which he acknowledges to be unavoidable, into the organizational form of indirect communication. Identity thinking turned against itself becomes pressed into continual self-denial and allows the wounds it inflicts on itself and its objects to be seen. This exercise quite rightly bears the name negative dialectics because Adorno practices determinate negation unremittingly, even though it has lost any foothold in the categorial network of Hegelian Logic — as a fetishism of demystification, so to speak. This fastening upon a critical procedure that can no longer be sure of its foundations is explained by the fact that Adorno (in contrast to Heidegger) bears no elitist contempt for discursive thought. Like exiles, we wander about lost in the discursive zone; and yet it is only the insistent force of a groundless reflection turned against itself that preserves our connection with the utopia of a long since lost, uncoerced and intuitive knowledge belonging to the primal past.[2] Discursive thought cannot identify itself as the decadent form of this knowledge by means of its own resources; for this purpose, the aesthetic experience gained in contact with avant-garde art is needed. The promise for which the surviving philosophic tradition is no longer a match has withdrawn into the mirror-writing of the esoteric work of art and requires a negativistic deciphering. From this labor of deciphering, philosophy sucks the residue of that paradoxical trust in reason with which negative dialectics executes (in the double sense of this word) its performative contradiction.

Derrida cannot share Adorno's aesthetically certified, residual faith in a de-ranged reason that has been expelled from the domains of philosophy and become, literally, utopian [having no place]. He is just as little convinced that Heidegger actually escaped the conceptual constraints of the philosophy of the subject by using metaphysical concepts in order to "cancel them out." Derrida does, to be sure, want to advance the already forged path of the critique of metaphysics; he, too, would just as soon break out of the paradox

Translated by Frederick Lawrence.

[1]This metaphor was used by the philosopher Ludwig Wittgenstein in his early work, *Tractatus Logico-Philosophicus* (1922). [Ed.]

[2]H. Schnädelbach, "Dialektik als Vernunftkritik," in L. von Friedeburg and J. Habermas, eds., *Adorno-Konferenz 1983* (Frankfurt, 1983), pp. 66 ff. [Au.]

as broodingly encircle it. But like Adorno, he guards against the gestures of profundity that Heidegger unhesitatingly imitates from his opposite number, the philosophy of origins. And so there are also parallels between Derrida and Adorno.

This affinity in regard to their thought gestures calls for a more precise analysis. Adorno and Derrida are sensitized in the same way against definitive, totalizing, all-incorporating models, especially against the organic dimension in works of art. Thus, both stress the primacy of the allegorical over the symbolic, of metonymy over metaphor, of the Romantic over the Classical. Both use the fragment as an expository form; they place any system under suspicion. Both are abundantly insightful in decoding the normal case from the point of view of its limit cases; they meet in a negative extremism, finding the essential in the marginal and incidental, the right on the side of the subversive and the outcast, and the truth in the peripheral and the inauthentic. A distrust of everything direct and substantial goes along with an intransigent tracing of mediations, of hidden presuppositions and dependencies. The critique of origins, of anything original, of first principles, goes together with a certain fanaticism about showing what is merely produced, imitated, and secondary in everything. What pervades Adorno's work as a materialist motif — his unmasking of idealist positings, his reversal of false constitutive connections, his thesis about the primacy of the object — even for this there is a parallel in Derrida's logic of the supplement.[3] The rebellious labor of deconstruction aims indeed at dismantling smuggled-in basic conceptual hierarchies, at overthrowing foundational relationships and conceptual relations of domination, such as those between speech and writing, the intelligible and sensible, nature and culture, inner and outer, mind and matter, male and female. Logic and rhetoric constitute one of these conceptual pairs. Derrida is particularly interested in standing the primacy of logic over rhetoric, canonized since Aristotle, on its head.

[3]See the introduction to Structuralism, Semiotics, and Deconstruction, p. 819. [Ed.]

It is not as though Derrida concerned himself with these controversial questions in terms of viewpoints familiar from the history of philosophy. If he had done so, he would have had to relativize the status of his own project in relation to the tradition that was shaped from Dante to Vico, and kept alive through Hamann, Humboldt, and Droysen, down to Dilthey and Gadamer. For the protest against the Platonic-Aristotelian primacy of the logical over the rhetorical that is raised anew by Derrida was articulated in this tradition. Derrida wants to expand the sovereignty of rhetoric over the realm of the logical in order to solve the problem confronting the totalizing critique of reason. As I have indicated, he is satisfied neither with Adorno's negative dialectics nor with Heidegger's critique of metaphysics — the one remaining tied to the rational bliss of the dialectic, the other to the elevation of origins proper to metaphysics, all protestations to the contrary notwithstanding. Heidegger only escapes the paradoxes of a self-referential critique of reason by claiming a special status for *Andenken*,[4] that is, its release from discursive obligations. He remains completely silent about the privileged access to truth. Derrida strives to arrive at the same esoteric access to truth, but he does not want to admit it as a privilege — no matter for what or for whom. He does not place himself in lordly fashion above the objection of pragmatic inconsistency, but renders it *objectless*.

There can only be talk about "contradiction" in the light of consistency requirements, which lose their authority or are at least subordinated to other demands — of an aesthetic nature, for example — if logic loses its conventional primacy over rhetoric. Then the deconstructionist can deal with the works of philosophy as works of literature and adapt the critique of metaphysics to the standards of a literary criticism that does not misunderstand itself in a scientistic way. As soon as we take the *literary* character of Nietzsche's writings seriously, the suitableness of his critique of reason has to be assessed in accord with the standards of rhetorical success and not those of logical consistency. Such a critique (which is

[4]Speculations. [Ed.]

more adequate to its object) is not immediately directed toward the network of discursive relationships of which arguments are built, but toward the figures that shape style and are decisive for the literary and rhetorical power of a text. A literary criticism that in a certain sense merely *continues* the literary process of its objects cannot end up in science. Similarly, the deconstruction of great philosophical texts, carried out as literary criticism in this broader sense, is not subject to the criteria of problem-solving, purely cognitive undertakings.

Hence, Derrida *undercuts* the very problem that Adorno acknowledged as unavoidable and turned into the starting point of his reflectively self-transcending identity-thinking. For Derrida, this problem has no object since the deconstructive enterprise cannot be pinned down to the discursive obligations of philosophy and science. He calls his procedure deconstruction because it is supposed to *clear away* the ontological *scaffolding* erected by philosophy in the course of its subject-centered history of reason. However, in his business of deconstruction, Derrida does not proceed analytically, in the sense of identifying hidden presuppositions or implications. This is just the way in which each successive generation has critically reviewed the works of the preceding ones. Instead, Derrida proceeds by a critique of style, in that he finds something like indirect communications, by which the text itself denies its manifest content, in the rhetorical surplus of meaning inherent in the literary strata of texts that present themselves as nonliterary. In this way, he compels texts by Husserl, Saussure, or Rousseau to confess their guilt, against the explicit interpretation of their authors. Thanks to their rhetorical content, texts combed against the grain contradict what they state, such as the explicitly asserted primacy of signification over the sign, of the voice in relation to writing, of the intuitively given and immediately present over the representative and the postponed-postponing. In a philosophical text, the blind spot cannot be identified on the level of manifest content any more than it can in a literary text. "Blindness and insight" are rhetorically interwoven with one another. Thus, the constraints constitutive for knowledge of a philosophical text only become accessible when the text is handled as what it would not like to be — as a literary text.

If, however, the philosophical (or scholarly) text were thereby only *extraneously turned* into an apparently literary one, deconstruction would still be an arbitrary act. Derrida can only attain Heidegger's goal of bursting metaphysical thought-forms from the inside by means of his essentially rhetorical procedure if the philosophical text is *in truth* a literary one — if one can *demonstrate* that the genre distinction between philosophy and literature dissolves upon closer examination. This demonstration is supposed to be carried out by way of deconstruction itself; in every single case we see anew the impossibility of so specializing the language of philosophy and science for cognitive purposes that they are cleansed of everything metaphorical and merely rhetorical, and kept free of literary admixtures. The frailty of the genre distinction between philosophy and literature is evidenced in the practice of deconstruction; in the end, *all* genre distinctions are submerged in one comprehensive, all-embracing context of texts — Derrida talks in a hypostatizing manner about a "universal text." What remains is self-inscribing writing as the medium in which each text is woven together with everything else. Even before it makes its appearance, every text and every particular genre has already lost its autonomy to an all-devouring context and an uncontrollable happening of spontaneous text production. This is the ground of the primacy of rhetoric, which is concerned with the qualities of texts in general, over logic, as a system of rules to which only certain types of discourse are subjected in an exclusive manner — those bound to argumentation.

II

This — at first glance inconspicuous — transformation of the "destruction"[5] into the "deconstruction" of the philosophical tradition transposes the radical critique of reason into the domain of rhetoric and thereby shows it a way

[5]"Destruction" is Heidegger's term, "deconstruction" Derrida's. [Ed.]

out of the aporia of self-referentiality: Anyone who still wanted to attribute paradoxes to the critique of metaphysics after this transformation would have misunderstood it in a scientistic manner. This argument holds good only if the following propositions are true:

1. Literary criticism is not primarily a scientific (or scholarly: *wissenschaftliches*) enterprise but observes the same rhetorical criteria as its literary objects.
2. Far from there being a genre distinction between philosophy and literature, philosophical texts can be rendered accessible in their essential contents by literary criticism.
3. The primacy of rhetoric over logic means the overall responsibility of rhetoric for the general qualities of an all-embracing context of texts, within which all genre distinctions are ultimately dissolved; philosophy and science no more constitute their own proper universes than art and literature constitute a realm of fiction that could assert its autonomy vis-à-vis the universal text.

Proposition 3 explicates propositions 2 and 1 by despecializing the meaning of "literary criticism." Literary criticism does serve as a model that clarifies itself through a long tradition; but it is considered precisely as a model case of something more universal, namely, a criticism suited to the rhetorical qualities of everyday discourse as well as of discourse outside the everyday. The procedure of deconstruction deploys this generalized criticism to bring to light the suppressed surpluses of rhetorical meaning in philosophical and scientific texts — against their manifest sense. Derrida's claim that "deconstruction" is an instrument for bringing Nietzsche's radical critique of reason out of the dead end of its paradoxical self-referentiality therefore stands — or falls — along with thesis number 3.

Just this thesis has been the centerpoint of the lively reception Derrida's work has enjoyed in the literature faculties of prominent American universities.[6] In the United States, literary criticism has for a long time been institutionalized as an academic discipline, that is, within the scholarly-scientific enterprise. From the very start, the self-tormenting question about the scholarly-scientific character of literary criticism was institutionalized along with it. This endemic self-doubt forms the background for the reception of Derrida, along with the dissolution of the decades-long domination of the New Criticism, which was convinced of the autonomy of the literary work of art and drew nourishment from the scientific pathos of structuralism. The idea of "deconstruction" could catch on in this constellation because it opened up to literary criticism a task of undoubted significance, under exactly the opposite premises: Derrida disputes the autonomy of the linguistic work of art and the independent meaning of the aesthetic illusion no less energetically than he does the possibility of criticism's ever being able to attain scientific status. At the same time, literary criticism serves him as the model for a procedure that takes on an almost world-historical mission with its overcoming of the thinking of the metaphysics of presence and of the age of logocentrism.[7]

The leveling of the genre distinction between literary criticism and literature frees the critical enterprise from the unfortunate compulsion to submit to pseudo-scientific standards; it simultaneously lifts it above science to the level of creative activity. Criticism does not need to consider itself as something secondary; it gains literary status. In the texts of Hillis Miller, Geoffrey Hartman, and Paul de Man we can find the new self-awareness: "that critics are no more parasites than the texts they interpret, since both inhabit a host-text of pre-existing language which itself parasitically feeds on their host-like willingness to receive it." Deconstructionists break with the traditional Arnoldian conception of criticism's function as a mere servant: "Criticism is now

[6]This is especially true of the Yale Critics, Paul de Man, Geoffrey Hartman, J. Hillis Miller, and Harold Bloom. See J. Arac, W. Godzich, and W. Martin, eds., *The Yale Critics: Deconstruction in America* (Minneapolis, 1983). In addition to Yale, important centers of deconstructionism are located at Johns Hopkins and Cornell Universities. [Au.]

[7]See the introduction to Structuralism, Semiotics, and Deconstruction, p. 820. [Ed.]

crossing over into literature, rejecting its subservient, Arnoldian stance and taking on the freedom of interpretive style with a matchless gusto."[8] Thus, in perhaps his most brilliant book, Paul de Man deals with critical texts by Lukács, Barthes, Blanchot, and Jakobson with a method and finesse that are usually reserved only for literary texts: "Since they are not scientific, critical texts have to be read with the same awareness of ambivalence that is brought to the study of non-critical literary texts."[9]

Just as important as the equation of literary criticism with creative literary production is the increase in significance enjoyed by literary criticism as sharing in the business of the critique of metaphysics. This upgrading to the critique of metaphysics requires a counterbalancing supplement to Derrida's interpretation of the leveling of the genre distinction between philosophy and literature. Jonathan Culler recalls the strategic meaning of Derrida's treatment of philosophical texts through literary criticism in order to suggest that, in turn, literary criticism treat literary texts also as philosophical texts. Simultaneously maintaining and relativizing the distinction between the two genres "is essential to the demonstration that the most truly philosophical reading of a philosophical text . . . is one that treats the work as literature, as a fictive, rhetorical construct whose elements and order are determined by various textual exigencies." Then he continues: "Conversely, the most powerful and opposite readings of literary works may be those that treat them as philosophical gestures by teasing out the implications of their dealings with the philosophical oppositions that support them."[10] Proposition 2 is thus varied in the following sense:

2′. Far from there being a genre distinction between philosophy and literature, literary texts can be rendered accessible in their essential contents by a critique of metaphysics.

Of course, the two propositions, 2 and 2′, point in the direction of the primacy of rhetoric over logic, which is asserted in proposition 3. Consequently, American literary critics are concerned to develop a concept of *general* literature, equal in overall scope to rhetoric, which would correspond to Derrida's "universal text." The notion of literature as confined to the realm of the fictive is deconstructed at the same time as the conventional notion of philosophy that denies the metaphorical basis of philosophical thought: "The notion of literature or literary discourse is involved in several of the hierarchical oppositions on which deconstruction has focussed: serious/non-serious, literal/metaphorical, truth/fiction. . . . Deconstruction's demonstration that these hierarchies are undone by the working of the texts that propose them alters the standing of literary language." There now follows, in the form of a conditional statement, the thesis on which everything depends — both the self-understanding of a literary criticism upgraded to the critique of metaphysics and the deconstructionist dissolution of the performative contradiction of a self-referential critique of reason: "If serious language is a special case of non-serious, if truths are fictions whose fictionality has been forgotten, then literature is not a deviant, parasitical instance of language. On the contrary, other discourses can be seen as cases of a generalized literature, or archi-literature."[11] Since Derrida does not belong to those philosophers who like to argue, it is expedient to take a closer look at his disciples in literary criticism within the Anglo-Saxon climate of argument in order to see whether this thesis really can be held.

Jonathan Culler reconstructs in a very clear way the somewhat impenetrable discussion between Derrida and Searle in order to show by the example of Austin's speech-act theory that any attempt to demarcate the ordinary domain of normal speech from an "unusual" use of language, "deviating" from the standard cases, is doomed to failure. Culler's thesis is expanded and indirectly confirmed in a study of speech-act theory by Mary Louise Pratt, who wants to prove, by the

[8]Christopher Norris, *Deconstruction: Theory and Practice* (New York and London, 1982), pp. 93, 98. [Au.]

[9]Paul de Man, *Blindness and Insight*, 2d ed. (Minneapolis, 1983), p. 110. [Au.]

[10]Jonathan Culler, *On Deconstruction* (London, 1983), p. 150. [Au.]

[11]Ibid., p. 181. [Au.]

example of the structuralist theory of poetics, that even the attempt to delimit the extraordinary domain of fictive discourse from everyday discourse fails (see section III below). But first let us take a look at the debate between Derrida and Searle.[12]

From this complex discussion, Culler selects as the central issue the question of whether Austin does in fact, as it seems he does, make a totally unprejudiced, provisory, and purely methodical move. Austin wants to analyze the rules intuitively mastered by competent speakers, in accordance with which typical speech acts can be successfully executed. He undertakes this analysis with respect to sentences from *normal* everyday practice that are uttered *seriously* and used as *simply* and *literally* as possible. Thus, the unit of analysis, the standard speech act, is the result of certain abstractions. The theoretician of speech acts directs his attention to a sample of normal linguistic utterances from which all complex, derivative, parasitic, and deviant cases have been filtered out. A concept of "usual" or normal linguistic practice underpins this isolation, a concept of "ordinary language" whose harmlessness and consistency Derrida puts in doubt. Austin's intention is clear: He wants to analyze the universal properties of "promises," for example, with respect to cases in which the utterance of corresponding sentences actually *functions* as a promise. Now there are contexts in which the same sentences lose the illocutionary[13] force of a promise. Spoken by an actor on the stage, as part of a poem, or even in a monologue, a promise, according to Austin, becomes "null and void in a unique manner." The same holds true for a promise that comes up in a quotation, or one merely mentioned. In these contexts, there is no *serious* or *binding* use, and sometimes not even a *literal* use, of the respective performative sentence, but a derivative or parasitic use instead. As Searle constantly repeats, these fictive or simulated or indirect modes of use are "parasitic" in the sense that logically they presuppose the possibility of a serious, literal, and binding use of sentences grammatically appropriate for making promises. Culler extracts what are in essence three objections from Derrida's texts; they point toward the impossibility of such an operation and are meant to show that the common distinctions between serious and simulated, literal and metaphorical, everyday and fictional, usual and parasitic modes of speech break down.

(a) In his initial argument, Derrida posits a not very clear link between quotability and repeatability on the one hand, and fictionality on the other. The quotation of a promise is only apparently something secondary in comparison to the directly made promise, for the indirect rendition of a performative utterance in a quote is a form of repetition, and as quotability presupposes the possibility of repetition in accord with a rule, that is, conventionality, it belongs to the nature of any conventionally generated utterance (including performative ones) that it can be quoted — and fictively imitated, in a broader sense: "If it were not possible for a character in a play to make a promise, there could be no promise in real life, for what makes it possible to promise, as Austin tells us, is the existence of a conventional procedure, of formulas one can repeat. For me to be able to make a promise in real life, there must be iterable procedures or formulas such as are used on stage. Serious behavior is a case of role-playing."[14]

In this argument, Derrida obviously already presupposes what he wants to prove: that any convention which permits the repetition of exemplary actions possesses from the outset not only a symbolic, but also a fictional character. But it must first be shown that the conventions of a game are ultimately indistinguishable from norms of action. Austin introduces the quotation of a promise as an example of a derivative or parasitic form because the illocutionary force is removed from the quoted promise by the form of indirect rendition; it is thereby taken out of the context in which it "functions," that is, in which it coordinates the actions of the different partici-

[12]In his essay "Signature Event Context," in *Margins of Philosophy* (Chicago, 1982), pp. 307–30, Derrida devotes the last section to a discussion of Austin's theory. Searle refers to this in "Reiterating the Differences: A Reply to Derrida," *Glyph* 1 (1977): 198 ff. Derrida's response appeared in *Glyph* 12(1977):202ff. under the title "Limited, Inc." [Au.]

[13]See p. 1101, n. 13. [Ed.]

[14]Culler, *On Deconstruction*, p. 119. [Au.]

pants in interaction and has consequences relevant to action. Only the actually performed speech act is *effective as action;* the promise mentioned or reported in a quote depends grammatically upon this. A setting that deprives it of its illocutionary force constitutes the bridge between quotation and fictional representation. Even action on the stage rests on a basis of everyday action (on the part of the actors, director, stage-workers, and theater people); and in the context of this framework, promises can function *in another mode* than they do "on stage," that is, with obligations and consequences relevant for action. Derrida makes no attempt to "deconstruct" this distinctive functional mode of ordinary speech within communicative action. In the illocutionary binding force of linguistic utterances Austin discovered a mechanism for coordinating action that places normal speech, as part of everyday practice, under constraints different from those of fictional discourse, simulation, and interior monologue. The constraints under which illocutionary acts develop a force for coordinating action and have consequences relevant to action define the domain of "normal" language. They can be analyzed as the kinds of idealizing suppositions we have to make in communicative action.

(b) The second argument brought forward by Culler, with Derrida, against Austin and Searle relates to just such idealizations. Any generalizing analysis of speech acts has to be able to specify general contextual conditions for the illocutionary success of standardized speech acts. Searle has been especially occupied with this task.[15] Linguistic expressions, however, change their meanings depending on shifting contexts; moreover, contexts are so constituted as to be open to ever wider-reaching specification. It is one of the peculiarities of our language that we can separate utterances from their original contexts and transplant them into different ones — Derrida speaks of "grafting." In this manner, we can think of a speech act, such as a "marriage vow," in ever new and more improbable contexts; the specification of universal contextual conditions does not run into any natural limits: "Suppose that the requirements for a marriage ceremony were met but that one of the parties were under hypnosis, or that the ceremony were impeccable in all respects but had been called a 'rehearsal,' or finally, that while the speaker was a minister licensed to perform weddings and the couple had obtained a license, that three of them were on this occasion acting in a play that, coincidentally, included a wedding ceremony."[16] These variations of context that change meaning cannot in principle be arrested or controlled, because contexts cannot be exhausted, that is, they cannot be theoretically mastered once and for all. Culler shows clearly that Austin cannot escape this difficulty by taking refuge in the intentions of speakers and listeners. It is not the thoughts of bride, bridegroom, or priest that decide the validity of the ceremony, but their actions and the circumstances under which they are carried out: "What counts is the plausibility of the description: whether or not the features of the context adduced create a frame that alters the illocutionary force of the utterances."[17]

Searle reacted to this difficulty by introducing a qualification to the effect that the literal meaning of a sentence does not completely fix the validity conditions of the speech act in which it is employed; it depends, rather, on tacit supplementation by a system of background assumptions regarding the normality of general world conditions. These parareflective background certainties have a holistic nature; they cannot be exhausted by a countably finite set of specifications. Meanings of sentences, however well analyzed, are thus valid only relative to a shared background knowledge that is constitutive of the lifeworld of a linguistic community. But Searle makes clear that the addition of this relational moment does not bring with it the relativism of meaning that Derrida is after. As long as language games are functioning and the preunderstanding constitutive of the lifeworld has not broken down, participants rightly count on world conditions being what is understood in their linguistic community as "normal." And in cases

[15]John Searle, *Speech Acts* (Cambridge, 1969), and *Expression and Meaning* (Cambridge, 1979). [Au.]

[16]Culler, *On Deconstruction,* pp. 121 ff. [Au.]

[17]Ibid., p. 123. [Au.]

where individual background convictions do become problematic, they assume that they could reach a rationally motivated agreement. Both are strong, that is to say idealizing, suppositions; but these idealizations are not arbitrary, logocentric acts brought to bear by theoreticians on unmanageable contexts in order to give the illusion of mastery; rather, they are presuppositions that the participants themselves have to make if communicative action is to be at all possible.

(c) The role of idealizing suppositions can also be clarified in connection with some other consequences of this same state of affairs. Because contexts are changeable and can be expanded in any desired direction, the same text can be open to different readings; it is the text itself that makes possible its uncontrollable effective history. Still, Derrida's purposely paradoxical statement that any interpretation is inevitably a false interpretation, and any understanding a misunderstanding, does not follow from this venerable hermeneutic insight. Culler justifies the statement "Every reading is a misreading" as follows: "If a text can be understood, it can in principle be understood repeatedly, by different readers in different circumstances. These acts of reading or understanding are not, of course, identical. They involve modifications and differences, but differences which are deemed not to matter. We can thus say that understanding is a special case of misunderstanding, a particular deviation or determination of misunderstanding. It is a misunderstanding whose misses do not matter."[18] Yet Culler leaves one thing out of consideration. The productivity of the process of understanding remains unproblematic only so long as all participants stick to the reference point of possibly achieving a mutual understanding in which the *same* utterances are assigned the same meaning. As Gadamer has shown, the hermeneutic effort that would bridge over temporal and cultural distances remains oriented toward the idea of a possible consensus being brought about in the present.

Under the pressure for decisions proper to the communicative practice of everyday life, participants are dependent upon agreements that coordinate their actions. The more removed interpretations are from the "seriousness of this type of situation," the more they can prescind[19] from the idealizing supposition of an achievable consensus. But they can never be wholly absolved of the idea that wrong interpretations must in principle be criticizable in terms of consensus to be aimed for ideally. The interpreter does not impose this idea on his object; rather, with the performative attitude of a participant observer, he takes it over from the direct participants, *who can act communicatively only under the presupposition of intersubjectively identical ascriptions of meaning.* I do not mean to marshal a Wittgensteinian positivism of language games against Derrida's thesis. It is not habitual linguistic practice that determines just what meaning is attributed to a text or an utterance.[20] Rather, language games only work because they presuppose idealizations that transcend any particular language game; as a necessary condition of possibly reaching understanding, these idealizations give rise to the perspective of an agreement that is open to criticism on the basis of validity claims. A language operating under these kinds of constraints is subject to an ongoing test. Everyday communicative practice, in which agents have to reach an understanding about something in the world, stands under the need to prove its worth, and it is the idealizing suppositions that make such testing possible in the first place. It is in relation to this need for standing the test within ordinary practice that one may distinguish, with Austin and Searle, between "usual" and "parasitic" uses of language.

III

Up to this point, I have criticized Derrida's third and fundamental assumption only to the extent that (against Culler's reconstruction of Derrida's arguments) I have defended the possibility of demarcating normal speech from *derivative* forms. I have not yet shown how fictional discourse can be separated from the normal (everyday) use of language. This aspect is the most important for

[18]Ibid., p. 176. [Au.]

[19]Diverge. [Ed.]

[20]Compare ibid., pp. 130 ff. [Au.]

Derrida. If "literature" and "writing" constitute the model for a universal context of texts, which cannot be surpassed and within which all genre distinctions are ultimately dissolved, they cannot be separated from other discourses as an autonomous realm of fiction. For the literary critics who follow Derrida in the United States, the thesis of the autonomy of the linguistic work of art is, as I mentioned, also unacceptable, because they want to set themselves off from the formalism of the New Criticism and from structuralist aesthetics.

The Prague Structuralists originally tried to distinguish poetic from ordinary language in view of their relations to extralinguistic reality. Insofar as language occurs in *communicative functions*, it has to produce relations between linguistic expression and speaker, hearer, and the state of affairs represented. Bühler articulated this in his semiotic scheme as the sign-functions of expression, appeal, and representation.[21] However, when language fulfills a poetic function, it does so in virtue of a reflexive relation of the linguistic expression to itself. Consequently, reference to an object, informational content, and truth-value — conditions of validity in general — are extrinsic to poetic speech; an utterance can be poetic to the extent that it is directed to the linguistic medium itself, to its own linguistic form. Roman Jakobson integrated this characterization into an expanded scheme of functions; in addition to the basic functions — expressing the speaker's intentions, establishing interpersonal relations, and representing states of affairs — which go back to Bühler, and two more functions related to making contact and to the code, he ascribes to linguistic utterances a poetic function, which directs our attention to "the message as such."[22] We are less concerned here with a closer characterization of the poetic function (in accord with which the principle of equivalence is projected from the axis of selection to the axis of combination) than with an interesting consequence that is important for our problem of delimiting normal from other instances of speech: "Any attempt to reduce the sphere of the poetic function would be a deceptive oversimplification. The poetic function is not the only function of verbal artistry, merely a *predominant* and *structurally determinative* one, whereas in all other linguistic activities it plays a subordinate and supplementary role. Inasmuch as it *directs our attention to the sign's perceptibility*, this function deepens the fundamental dichotomy between signs and objects. For this reason, linguistics should not, when it studies the poetic function, restrict itself solely to the field of poetry."[23] Poetic speech, therefore, is to be distinguished only in virtue of the primacy and structure-forming force of a certain function that is always fulfilled together with other linguistic functions.

Richard Ohmann makes use of Austin's approach to specify poetic language in this sense. For him, the phenomenon in need of clarification is the fictionality of the linguistic work of art, that is, the generation of aesthetic illusion by which a second, specifically de-realized arena is opened up on the basis of a continued everyday practice. What distinguishes poetic language is its "world-generating" capacity: "A literary work creates a world . . . by providing the reader with *impaired* and incomplete speech acts which he completes by supplying the appropriate circumstances."[24] The unique *impairment* of speech acts that generates fictions arises when they are robbed of their illocutionary force, or maintain their illocutionary meanings only as in the refraction of indirect repetition or quotation: "A literary work is a discourse whose sentences lack the illocutionary forces that would normally attach to them. Its illocutionary force is mimetic. . . . Specifically, a literary work puportedly imitates a series of speech acts, which in fact have no other existence. By doing so, it leads the reader to imagine a speaker, a situation, a set of ancillary events, and so on."[25] The bracketing of illocutionary force virtualizes the relations to the world in which the speech acts are involved

[21]Karl Bühler, *Semiotic Foundations of Language Theory* (New York, 1982). [Au.]

[22]Roman Jakobson, "Linguistics and Poetics," in Thomas A. Sebeok, editor, *Style in Language* (Cambridge, MA, 1960), pp. 350–58. [Au.] See pp. 812–13. [Ed].

[23]Ibid. [Au.]

[24]R. Ohmann, "Speech-Acts and the Definition of Literature," *Philosophy and Rhetoric* 4 (1971): 17. [Au.]

[25]Ibid., p. 14. [Au.]

due to their illocutionary force, and releases the participants in interaction from reaching agreement about something in the world on the basis of idealizing understandings in such a way that they coordinate their plans of action and thus enter into obligations relevant to the outcomes of action: "Since the quasi-speech acts of literature are not *carrying on the world's business* — describing, urging, contradicting, etc. — the reader may well attend to them in a non-pragmatic way."[26] Neutralizing their binding force releases the disempowered illocutionary acts from the pressure to decide proper to everyday communicative practice, removes them from the sphere of usual discourse, and thereby empowers them for the playful creation of new worlds — or, rather, for the pure demonstration of the world-disclosing force of innovative linguistic expressions. This specialization in the world-disclosive function of speech explains the unique self-reflexivity of poetic language to which Jakobson refers and which leads Geoffrey Hartman to pose the rhetorical question: "Is not literary language the name we give to a diction whose frame of reference is such that the words stand out as words (even as sounds) rather than being, at once, assimilable meanings?"[27]

Mary L. Pratt makes use of Ohmann's studies[28] to refute, by means of speech-act theory, the thesis of the independence of the literary work of art in Derrida's sense. She does not consider fictionality, the bracketing of illocutionary force, and the disengagement of poetic language from everyday communicative practice to be adequate selective criteria, because fictional speech elements such as jokes, irony, wish-fantasies, stories, and parables pervade our everyday discourse and by no means constitute an autonomous universe apart from "the world's business." Conversely, nonfiction works, memoirs, travel reports, historical romances, even *romans à clef* or thrillers that, like Truman Capote's *In Cold Blood*, adapt a factually documented case, by no means create an unambiguously fictional world, even though we often relegate these productions, for the most part at least, to "literature." Pratt uses the results of studies in sociolinguistics by W. Labov[29] to prove that natural narratives, that is, the "stories" told spontaneously or upon request in everyday life, follow the same rhetorical laws of construction as and exhibit structural characteristics similar to literary narratives: "Labov's data make it necessary to account for narrative rhetoric in terms that are not exclusively literary; the fact that fictive or mimetically organized utterances can occur in almost any realm of extraliterary discourse requires that we do the same for fictivity or mimesis. In other words, the relation between a work's fictivity and its literariness is indirect."[30]

Nonetheless, the fact that normal language is permeated with fictional, narrative, metaphorical, and, in general, with rhetorical elements does not yet speak against the attempt to explain the autonomy of the linguistic work of art by the bracketing of illocutionary forces, for, according to Jakobson, the mark of fictionality is suited for demarcating literature from everyday discourses only to the degree that the world-disclosing function of language predominates over the other linguistic functions and determines the structure of the linguistic artifact. In a certain respect, it is the refraction and partial elimination of illocutionary validity claims that distinguishes the story from the statement of the eyewitness, teasing from insulting, being ironic from misleading, the hypothesis from the assertion, wish-fantasy from perception, a training maneuver from an act of warfare, and a scenario from a report of an actual catastrophe. But in none of these cases do the illocutionary acts lose their binding force for coordinating action. Even in the cases adduced for the sake of comparison, the communicative functions of the speech acts remain intact insofar as the fictive elements cannot be separated from contexts of life practice. The world-disclosive

[26]Ibid., p. 17. [Au.]

[27]Geoffrey Hartman, *Saving the Text* (Baltimore, 1981), p. xxi. [Au.]

[28]See also "Speech, Literature, and the Space Between," *New Literary History* 5 (1974): 34 ff. [Au.]

[29]William Labov, *Language in the Inner City* (Philadelphia, 1972). [Au.]

[30]Mary Louise Pratt, *A Speech-Act Theory of Literary Discourse* (Bloomington, 1977), p. 92; I am grateful to Jonathan Culler for his reference to this interesting book. [Au.]

function of language does not gain independence over against the expressive, regulative, and informative functions. By contrast, in Truman Capote's literary elaboration of a notorious and carefully researched incident, precisely this may be the case. That is to say, what grounds the *primacy* and the structuring force of the poetic function is not the deviation of a fictional representation from the documentary report of an incident, but the exemplary elaboration that takes the case out of its context and makes it the occasion for an innovative, world-disclosive, and eye-opening representation in which the rhetorical means of representation depart from communicative routines and take on a life of their own.

It is interesting to see how Pratt is compelled to work out this poetic function against her will. Her sociolinguistic counterproposal begins with the analysis of a speech situation that poetic discourse shares with other discourses — the kind of arrangement in which a narrator or lecturer turns to a public and calls its attention to a text. The text undergoes certain procedures of preparation and selection before it is ready for delivery. Before a text can lay claim to the patience and discretion of the audience, it has also to satisfy certain criteria of relevance: it *has to be worth telling*. The tellability is to be assessed in terms of the manifestation of some significant exemplary experience. In its content, a tellable text reaches beyond the local context of the immediate speech situation and is open to further elaboration: "As might be expected, these two features — contextual detachability and susceptibility to elaboration — are equally important characteristics of literature." Of course, literary texts share these characteristics with "display texts" in general. The latter are characterized by their special communicative functions: "They are designed to serve a purpose I have described as that of verbally representing states of affairs and experiences which are held to be *unusual* or *problematic* in such a way that the addressee will respond affectively in the intended way, adopt the intended evaluation and interpretation, take pleasure in doing so, and *generally find the whole undertaking worth it*."[31] One sees how the pragmatic linguistic analyst creeps up on literary texts from outside, as it were. The latter have still to satisfy a final condition; in the case of literary texts, tellability must gain a preponderance over other functional characteristics: "In the end, tellability can take precedence over assertability itself."[32] Only in this case do the functional demands and structural constraints of everyday communicative practice (which Pratt defines by means of Grice's conversation postulates[33]) lose their force. The concern to give one's contribution an informative shape, to say what is relevant, to be straightforward and to avoid obscure, ambiguous, and prolix utterances are idealizing presuppositions of the communicative action *of normal speech*, but not of poetic discourse: "Our tolerance, indeed propensity, for elaboration when dealing with the tellable suggests that, in Gricean terms, the standards of quantity, quality and manner for display texts differ from those Grice suggests for declarative speech in his maxims."

In the end, the analysis leads to a confirmation of the thesis it would like to refute. To the degree that the poetic, world-disclosing function of language gains primacy and structuring force, language escapes the structural constraints and communicative functions of everyday life. The space of fiction that is opened up when linguistic forms of expression become reflexive results from suspending illocutionary binding forces and those idealizations that make possible a use of language oriented toward mutual understanding — and hence make possible a coordination of plans of action that operates via the intersubjective recognition of criticizable validity claims. One can read Derrida's debate with Austin also as a denial of this independently structured domain of everyday communicative practice; it corresponds to the denial of an autonomous realm of fiction.

[31]Ibid., p. 148. [Au.]

[32]Ibid., p. 147. [Au.]

[33]H. Paul Grice's "conversation postulates" assume that speakers are rational and cooperative and therefore provide information that is truthful, relevant to their purposes, and perspicuous (both necessary and sufficient to their purposes). Given these idealizing assumptions, Grice is able to account for how speakers are able to convey meanings to listeners without actually voicing them. See H. Paul Grice, "Logic and Conversation" in *Speech Acts* (1975). [Ed.]

IV

Because Derrida denies both, he can analyze any given discourse in accord with the model of poetic language, and do so as if language generally were determined by the poetic use of language specialized in world-disclosure. From this viewpoint, language as such converges with literature or indeed with "writing." This *aestheticizing of language, which is purchased with the twofold denial of the proper senses of normal and poetic discourse*, also explains Derrida's insensitivity toward the tension-filled polarity between the poetic-world-disclosive function of language and its prosaic, innerworldly functions, which a modified version of Bühler's functional scheme takes into consideration.[34]

Linguistically mediated processes such as the acquisition of knowledge, the transmission of culture, the formation of personal identity, and socialization and social integration involve mastering problems posed by the world; the independence of learning processes that Derrida cannot acknowledge is due to the independent logics of these problems and the linguistic medium tailored to deal with them. For Derrida, linguistically mediated processes within the world are embedded in a *world-constituting* context that prejudices everything; they are fatalistically delivered up to the unmanageable happening of text production, overwhelmed by the poetic-creative transformation of a background designed by archewriting,[35] and condemned to be provincial. An aesthetic contextualism blinds him to the fact that everyday communicative practice makes learning processes possible (thanks to built-in idealizations) in relation to which the world-disclosive force of interpreting language has in turn to prove its worth. These learning processes unfold an independent logic that transcends all local constraints, because experiences and judgments are formed only in the light of criticizable validity claims. Derrida neglects the potential for negation inherent in the validity basis of action oriented toward reaching understanding; he permits the capacity to solve problems to disappear behind the world-creating capacity of language; the former capacity is possessed by language as the medium through which those acting communicatively get involved in relations to the world whenever they agree with one another about something in the objective world, in their common social world, or in the subjective worlds to which each has privileged access.

Richard Rorty proposes a similar leveling; unlike Derrida, however, he does not remain idealistically fixated upon the history of metaphysics as a transcendent happening that determines everything intramundane. According to Rorty, science and morality, economics and politics, are delivered up to a process of language-creating protuberances *in just the same way* as art and philosophy. Like Kuhnian history of science,[36] the flux of interpretations beats rhythmically between revolutions and normalizations of language. He observes this back-and-forth between two situations in all fields of cultural life: "One is the sort of situation encountered when people pretty much agree on what is wanted, and are talking about how best to get it. In such a situation there is no need to say anything terribly unfamiliar, for argument is typically about the truth of assertions rather than about the utility of vocabularies. The contrasting situation is one in which everything is up for grabs at once — in which the motives and terms of discussions are a central subject of argument. . . . In such periods people begin to toss around old words in new senses, to throw in the occasional neologism, and thus to hammer out a new idiom which initially attracts attention to itself and only later gets put to work."[37] One notices how the Nietzschean pathos of *Lebensphilosophie*[38] that has made the linguistic turn beclouds the sober insights of

[34]See Jürgen Habermas, *Theory of Communicative Action*, volume 1 (Boston, 1984), pp. 273 ff. [Au.]

[35]See the introduction to Structuralism, Semiotics, and Deconstruction, p. 820. [Ed.]

[36]Habermas refers to Thomas Kuhn and his work *The Structure of Scientific Revolutions* (Chicago: University of Chicago Press, 1960). [Ed.]

[37]Richard Rorty, "Deconstruction and Circumvention" (manuscript, 1983); and *Consequences of Pragmatism* (Minneapolis, 1982), especially the introduction and chapters 6, 7, and 9. [Au.]

[38]Philosophy of life. [Ed.]

pragmatism; in the picture painted by Rorty, the renovative process of linguistic world-disclosure no longer has a *counterpoise* in the testing processes of intramundane practice. The "Yes" and "No" of communicatively acting agents is so prejudiced and rhetorically overdetermined by their linguistic contexts that the anomalies that start to arise during the phases of exhaustion are taken to represent only symptoms of waning vitality, or aging processes analogous to processes of nature — and are not seen as the result of *deficient* solutions to problems and *invalid* answers.

Intramundane linguistic practice draws its power of negation from validity claims that go beyond the horizons of any currently given context. But the contextualist concept of language, laden as it is with *Lebensphilosophie*, is impervious to the very real force of the counterfactual, which makes itself felt in the idealizing presuppositions of communicative action. Hence Derrida and Rorty are also mistaken about the unique status of discourses differentiated from ordinary communication and tailored to a single validity dimension (truth or normative rightness), or to a single complex of problems (questions of truth or justice). In modern societies, the spheres of science, morality, and law have crystallized around these forms of argumentation. The corresponding cultural systems of action administer *problem-solving capacities* in a way similar to that in which the enterprises of art and literature administer *capacities for world-disclosure*. Because Derrida overgeneralizes this one linguistic function — namely, the poetic — he can no longer see the complex relationship of the ordinary practice of normal speech to the two extraordinary spheres, differentiated, as it were, in opposite directions. The polar tension between world-disclosure and problem-solving is held together within the functional matrix of ordinary language; but art and literature on the one side, and science, morality, and law on the other, are specialized for experiences and modes of knowledge that can be shaped and worked out within the compass of *one* linguistic function and *one* dimension of validity at a time. Derrida holistically levels these complicated relationships in order to equate philosophy with literature and criticism. He fails to recognize the special status that both philosophy and literary criticism, each in its own way, assume as mediators between expert cultures and the everyday world.

Literary criticism, institutionalized in Europe since the eighteenth century, has contributed to the differentiation of art. It has responded to the increasing autonomy of linguistic works of art by means of a discourse specialized for questions of taste. In it, the claims with which literary texts appear are submitted to examination — claims to "artistic truth," aesthetic harmony, exemplary validity, innovative force, and authenticity. In this respect, aesthetic criticism is similar to argumentative forms specialized for propositional truth and the rightness of norms, that is, to theoretical and practical discourse. It is, however, not merely an esoteric component of expert culture but, beyond this, has the job of mediating between expert culture and everyday world.

This *bridging function* of art criticism is more obvious in the cases of music and the plastic arts than in that of literary works, which are already formulated in the medium of language, even if it is a poetic, self-referential language. From this second, exoteric standpoint, criticism performs a translating activity of a unique kind. It brings the experiential content of the work of art into normal language; the innovative potential of art and literature for the lifeworlds and life histories that reproduce themselves through everyday communicative practice can only be unleashed in this maieutic[39] way. This is then deposited in the changed configuration of the evaluative vocabulary, in a renovation of value orientations and need interpretations, which alters the color of modes of life by way of altering modes of perception.

Philosophy also occupies a position with two fronts similar to that of literary criticism — or at least this is true of modern philosophy, which no longer promises to redeem the claims of religion in the name of theory. On the one hand, it directs its interest to the foundations of science, morality, and law and attaches theoretical claims to its statements. Characterized by universalist problematics

[39]Teaching by bringing out knowledge already latent in the mind of the learner. [Ed.]

and strong theoretical strategies, it maintains an intimate relationship with the sciences. And yet philosophy is not simply an esoteric component of an expert culture. It maintains just as intimate a relationship with the totality of the lifeworld and with sound common sense, even if in a subversive way it relentlessly shakes up the certainties of everyday practice. Philosophical thinking represents the lifeworld's interest in the whole complex of functions and structures connected and combined in communicative action, and it does so in the face of knowledge systems differentiated out in accord with particular dimensions of validity. Of course, it maintains this relationship to totality with a reflectiveness lacking in the intuitively present background proper to the lifeworld.

If one takes into consideration the two-front position of criticism and philosophy that I have only sketched here — toward the everyday world on the one side, and on the other toward the specialized cultures of art and literature, science and morality — it becomes clear what the leveling of the genre distinction between philosophy and literature, and the assimilation of philosophy to literature and of literature to philosophy, as affirmed in propositions 2 and 2′, mean. This leveling and this assimilation confusedly jumble the constellations in which the rhetorical elements of language assume *entirely different* roles. The rhetorical element occurs in its *pure form* only in the self-referentiality of the poetic expression, that is, in the language of fiction specialized for world-disclosure. Even the normal language of everyday life is ineradicably rhetorical; but within the matrix of different linguistic functions, the rhetorical elements recede here. The world-disclosive linguistic framework is almost at a standstill in the routines of everyday practice. The same holds true of the specialized languages of science and technology, law and morality, economics, political science, etc. They, too, live off of the illuminating power of metaphorical tropes; but the rhetorical elements, which are by no means expunged, are tamed, as it were, and enlisted for special purposes of problem-solving.

The rhetorical dimension plays a different and far more important role in the language of literary criticism and philosophy. They are both faced with tasks that are paradoxical in similar ways. They are supposed to feed the contents of expert cultures, in which knowledge is accumulated under one aspect of validity at a time, into an everyday practice in which all linguistic functions and aspects of validity are intermeshed to form one syndrome. And yet literary criticism and philosophy are supposed to accomplish this task of mediation with means of expression taken from languages specialized in questions of taste or of truth. They can only resolve this paradox by rhetorically expanding and enriching their special languages to the extent that is required to link up indirect communications with the manifest contents of statements, and to do so in a deliberate way. That explains the strong rhetorical strain characteristic of studies by literary critics and philosophers alike. Significant critics and great philosophers are also noted writers. Literary criticism and philosophy have a family resemblance to literature — and to this extent to one another as well — in their rhetorical achievements. But their family relationship stops right there, for in each of these enterprises the tools of rhetoric are subordinated to the discipline of a *distinct* form of argumentation.

If, following Derrida's recommendation, philosophical thinking were to be relieved of the duty of solving problems and shifted over to the function of literary criticism, it would be robbed not merely of its seriousness, but of its productivity. Conversely, the literary-critical power of judgment loses its potency when, as is happening among Derrida's disciples in literature departments, it gets displaced from appropriating aesthetic experiential contents into the critique of metaphysics. The false assimilation of one enterprise to the other robs both of their substance. And so we return to the issue with which we started. Whoever transposes the radical critique of reason into the domain of rhetoric in order to blunt the paradox of self-referentiality, also dulls the sword of the critique of reason itself. The false pretense of eliminating the genre distinction between philosophy and literature cannot lead us out of this aporia.[40]

[40]Our reflections have brought us to a point from which we can see why Heidegger, Adorno, and Derrida get into this

aporia at all. They all still defend themselves as if they were living in the shadow of the "last" philosopher, as did the first generation of Hegelian disciples. They are still battling against the "strong" concepts of theory, truth, and system that have actually belonged to the past for over a century and a half. They still think they have to arouse philosophy from what Derrida calls "the dream of its heart." They believe they have to tear philosophy away from the madness of expounding a theory that has the last word. Such a comprehensive, closed, and definitive system of propositions would have to be formulated in a language that is self-explanatory, that neither needs nor permits commentary, and thus that brings to a standstill the effective history in which interpretations are heaped upon interpretations without end. In this connection, Rorty speaks about the demand for a language "which can receive no gloss, requires no interpretation, cannot be distanced, cannot be sneered at by later generations. It is the hope for a vocabulary which is intrinsically and self-evidently final, not only the most comprehensive and fruitful vocabulary we have come up with so far" (Rorty, *Consequences of Pragmatism*, pp. 93 ff.).

If reason were bound, under penalty of demise, to hold on to these goals of metaphysics classically pursued from Parmenides to Hegel, if reason as such (even after Hegel) stood before the alternative of either maintaining the strong concepts of theory, truth, and system that were common in the great tradition or of throwing in the sponge, then an *adequate* critique of reason would really have to grasp the roots at such a depth that it could scarcely avoid the paradoxes of self-referentiality. Nietzsche viewed the matter in this way. And, unfortunately, Heidegger, Adorno, and Derrida all still seem to confuse the universalist *problematics still maintained* in philosophy with the long since *abandoned status claims* that philosophy once alleged its answers to have. Today, however, it is clear that the scope of universalist questions — for instance, questions of the necessary conditions for the rationality of utterances, or of the universal pragmatic presuppositions of communicative action and argumentation — does indeed have to be reflected in the grammatical form of universal propositions — but not in any unconditional validity or "ultimate foundations" claimed for themselves or their theoretical framework. The fallibilist consciousness of the sciences caught up with philosophy, too, a long time ago.

With this kind of fallibilism, we, philosophers and nonphilosophers alike, do not by any means eschew truth claims. Such claims cannot be raised in the performative attitude of the first person other than as transcending space and time — precisely as claims. But we are also aware that there is no zero-context for truth claims. They are raised here and now and are open to criticism. Hence we reckon upon the trivial *possibility* that they will be revised tomorrow or someplace else. Just as it always has, philosophy understands itself as the defender of rationality in the sense of the claim of reason endogenous to our form of life. In its work, however, it prefers a combination of strong propositions with weak status claims; so little is this totalitarian, that there is no call for a totalizing critique of reason against it. On this point, see my "Die Philosophie als Platzhalter und Interpret," in *Moralbewusstsein und kommunikatives Handeln* (Frankfurt, 1983), pp. 7 ff. (English translation: *Moral Consciousness and Communicative Action* [1990]). [Au.]

6

NEW HISTORICISM AND CULTURAL STUDIES

To understand the practices of writers and artists, and not least their products, entails understanding that they are the result of the meeting of two histories: the history of the positions they occupy and the history of their dispositions. — PIERRE BOURDIEU

As in more familiar exercises in close reading, one can start anywhere in a culture's repertoire of forms and end up anywhere else. . . . But whatever the level at which one operates, and however intricately, the guiding principle is the same: societies, like lives, contain their own interpretations. One has only to learn how to gain access to them.

— CLIFFORD GEERTZ

Modern thought and experience have taught us to be sensitive to what is involved in representation, in studying the Other, in racial thinking, in unthinking and uncritical acceptance of authority and authoritative ideas, in the sociopolitical role of intellectuals, in the great value of a skeptical critical consciousness. Perhaps if we remember that the study of human experience usually has an ethical, to say nothing of a political, consequence . . . we will not be indifferent to what we do as scholars. — EDWARD W. SAID

THE NEW HISTORICISM: THEORIES AND PRACTICES

Born around 1982, the new historicism quickly became one of the most vital modes of literary study in the 1980s. The name the brilliant young Renaissance scholar Stephen Greenblatt gave to the approach he pioneered was conferred in haste. Asked for a title for a special issue of the journal *Genre* in which his own essays and those of colleagues were appearing, Greenblatt carelessly threw out the title "New Historicism." Greenblatt has tried ever since to rename what he does "cultural poetics," in order to avoid the connotations of historical inevitability implicit in the word "historicism" and to more clearly label his practice as a literary version of cultural anthropology. But, alas, in vain: The name has stuck fast.

Greenblatt correctly insists that new historicism is not a theory or a set of doctrines but a practice.[1] However, it is a practice that has developed out of contemporary theory, particularly the structuralist realization that all human systems are symbolic and subject to the rules of language, and the deconstructive realization that there is no way of positioning oneself as an observer outside the closed circle of textuality. What sort of practice new historicism is and what its motives are is suggested by Michael Warner's fast-and-dirty positioning of it in relation to other critical practices current in the mid-1980s:

> New Historicism is a label that historians don't like much because they understand something different by historicism. But nobody's asking historians; the people the New Historicists are reacting against are the New Critics, and historicism seems an important term for that purpose because it emphasizes that meaning is established in concrete historical situations. . . . If the "Historicism" in the New Historicism is to distinguish it from the New Critics and their idea that a text means what it means regardless of what your cultural situation is, the "New" in New Historicism is to distinguish it from the somewhat dreary and encyclopedic historical work that the philologists used to do. . . . While critics have realized on the one hand that language and the symbolic are never essential and timeless but always contingent on cultural politics, on the other hand they have realized that cultural politics is always symbolic. New Historicism has a motto: "The text is historical, and history is textual." The first part means that meaning does not transcend context but is produced within it; the second part means that human actions and institutions and relations, while certainly hard facts, are not hard facts as distinguished from language. They are themselves symbolic representations, though this is not to say, as so many old historicists might conclude, that they are not real.[2]

Warner's characterization seems reasonably fair to the New Critics, who were deeply uncomfortable with the notion that the author's and reader's ways of construing a text might diverge with the passage of time. It is less fair to the philologists and historians, whose "dreary" labors give us what we picture we possess of past ages, and who were far less naive about the way language is used in writing history than Warner suggests. The philosopher of history R. G. Collingwood made it clear several decades before the advent of the new historicism that historians are politically and culturally implicated in the history they write, that their work tells us as much about them as the period they investigate and explore.[3]

What is new about the new historicism might be seen in Stephen Greenblatt's "*King Lear* and Harsnett's 'Devil-Fiction,'" reprinted below. Samuel Harsnett's *Declaration of Egregious Popish Impostures* (printed in 1603), exposes the impostures of Catholic exorcists, who would pretend to drive out devils from "possessed" individuals, shills of theirs, as a way of demonstrating their power and that of the Roman Catholic Church. Greenblatt did not discover Harsnett's text, which had long been recognized as one of the books Shakespeare must have read while composing *King Lear* since it contains names of the devils Edgar cites in the "Poor Tom" scenes on the heath. However, Greenblatt's essay is not a conventional

[1]See Stephen Greenblatt, "Toward a Poetics of Culture," in *The New Historicism*, ed. H. Aram Veeser (New York: Routledge, 1989), p. 1.

[2]Michael Warner, "Literary Studies and the History of the Book," *The Book* 12 (1987): 5.

[3]See, for example, Collingwood's *Essays in the Philosophy of History*, ed. William Debbins (New York and London: Garland, 1985).

source study; his take on the two texts is to compare the unlicensed, forbidden theatrical performances of the Catholic exorcists in Protestant England with the licensed, permitted theatrical performances conducted on the stage of Shakespeare's Globe, in order to view Shakespeare's play as "a secular version of the ritual of exorcism" and to show how the state benefits from a transgression that can be represented but contained within the wooden "O" of the theater.

While the new historicists are not, by and large, theorists, their work grew out of three or four advances in theory in radically disconnected fields. From Michel Foucault, the historical philosopher, the new historicists developed the notion that texts within a particular period are linked by a broad totalizing culture formation (the *épistème*), in which the workings of power and knowledge and their interrelationships can be defined. From Clifford Geertz, the cultural anthropologist, they absorbed a sense of how both primitive and advanced cultures operate through symbolic representation and ritual enactment of conflict, and they incorporated Geertz's ideal of the "thick description" of a culture that can come only from genuine immersion in its ways. From Hayden White, the philosopher of history, they took the notion that figural relationships — the tropes, or figures of speech used by a writer — can be clues to the way historians think and the way their representations of the past are filtered and shifted through the language of history. Finally, from French philosophical sociologists like Pierre Bourdieu and Michel de Certeau, new historical practice appropriated theories of intellectual practice aimed at understanding how the structure of learned professions alters the way knowledge and the power associated with it are originated and distributed.

CULTURAL STUDIES: THE WORLD AS SOCIAL TEXT

All five of the theorists just mentioned have been appropriated equally by the allied practice of cultural studies.[4] Cultural studies, though, is much harder to pin down than the new historicism. It is not even clear whether cultural studies is older as a practice than the new historicism or younger, since it depends on what one wants to count as examples of cultural studies. Books addressing cultural studies by name did not begin to appear until the early 1990s. Nevertheless, Simon During, the British editor of *The Cultural Studies Reader* (1993), views the key player as Richard Hoggart, who began the Center for Cultural Studies at the University of Birmingham in the 1950s, and who inspired, along with Raymond Williams, the

[4]There is no consensus concerning the intellectual substructures of new historicism and cultural studies. Other historians of criticism have portrayed new historicism as being influenced by the work of Karl Marx, Raymond Williams, the Italian Marxist Antonio Gramsci, Mikhail Bakhtin, philosopher of science Thomas Kuhn, Walter Benjamin, and dozens of others, including American Marxists such as Fredric Jameson and Frank Lentricchia who have ferociously attacked the new historicists. The variety of influence on cultural studies is literally unbounded, given the wide range of subject matter analyzed. My principle for choosing exemplars in this chapter has been to avoid duplication while focusing on those influences that seem widest and most significant.

media studies work of Stuart Hall.[5] In addition to the cultural materialism of British working-class Marxism, During locates an alternate, "structuralist" side to cultural studies arising from Althusserian Marxism and Lacanian psychoanalysis (for a description of these schools see the introductions to Chs. 5 and 4, respectively). The story is probably even more complicated than this, however. Many contemporary scholars would agree that continental criticism such as Theodor Adorno's *Philosophy of Modern Music* (1949), which compares the compositional practices of Schönberg and Stravinsky in terms of their responses to modernity, and Roland Barthes's essays on fashion, restaurant menus, and wrestling matches in *Mythologies* (1957) were engaged in practices not much different from Meaghan Morris's brilliant study of shopping centers or Ien Ang's approach to watching television, which date from the late 1980s and early 1990s.[6] Given its inchoate nature, trying to date cultural studies precisely is impossible, but it would be fair to claim that its origins long preceded its current vogue, which started in the late 1980s.

Cultural studies involves viewing and analyzing practically any recorded phenomenon, present or past, as a social text. The "texts" analyzed include such evanescent events as music videos, comic books, letters from summer camp, and radio talk shows: Madonna Studies at one point threatened to become a major subfield. In addition, they include phenomena that are not usually thought of as texts at all, such as government regulations, embroidery, surgical operations, meatpacking, and mapmaking. Since canonical literary works and their formal elements are also viewed as social texts, one could in theory write "cultural studies" about Alexander Pope's pastorals. But, in practice, the tendency has been to seek out subjects disdained by the traditional hierarchies of aesthetic value, or ones that in their exoticism stand outside the older canon.

To some extent, the new historicism has also focused on nonliterary texts. For example, Richard McCoy has written about the ritual order and physical arrangements of Elizabeth Tudor's coronation, which, as he demonstrates, were composed with as assiduous an eye to metaphor and symbol as any epic poem; he has also studied Henrician and Elizabethan tournaments as performance art, as ritual, and as political act.[7] But McCoy also discusses Sidney and Spenser in the light of the rituals of chivalry, so, in his work, there is certainly nothing like the absolute breach with literary texts and the literary canon that one finds in much of cultural studies.[8]

[5]See *The Cultural Studies Reader*, ed. Simon During (London: Routledge, 1993); Richard Hoggart, *The Uses of Literacy* (London: Penguin 1957); and Stuart Hall and Paddy Whannel, *The Popular Arts* (London: Hutchinson, 1964).

[6]See Meaghan Morris, "Things to Do with Shopping Centres," in *Grafts* (London: Verso, 1988); and Ien Ang, *Watching Television* (London: Routledge, 1991).

[7]See Richard McCoy, *The Rites of Knighthood: The Literature and Politics of Elizabethan Chivalry* (New York: Cambridge University Press, 1989).

[8]I am not sure precisely how to characterize my own work in progress, which includes a reading of the idea of "identity" (the concept of a sense of self that might be discarded, refashioned, stolen, or feigned) as a cultural phenomenon of England in the 1860s. This *mentalité* was stimulated by Wilkie Collins's sensational novel *The Woman in White* (1860), which sensitized English readers to the idea that one's identity might be stolen by a clever criminal, and clearly had taken hold ten years later, as is shown by the real-life case of the Titchborne claimant, an Australian rogue falsely claiming to be an English baronet, whose struggle in court to get his "rights" absorbed aristocrat and commoner alike for several

Like the new historicism, cultural studies is not a theory as such or even a combination of theories; it is not even a single coherent practice, but rather a disparate set of related practices. Some practitioners of cultural studies relate easily to Gramscian or Althusserian Marxism, while others like Michel Foucault himself and his numerous fellow travelers are loath to situate cultural power principally as a by-product of economics. Even if they do not present a single, consistent social philosophy,[9] essays in cultural studies must situate themselves in relation to *some* literary and social theory to make the questions they raise, the texts they choose, and the methods they follow comprehensible. More eclectic even than new historicism, cultural studies draws on structuralism, deconstruction, Lacanian psychology, post-Althusserian Marxism, reception theory, feminism, and gender studies; to fully understand its intellectual basis would require reading virtually this entire book. The placement of cultural studies in the same chapter as the new historicism marks the fact that they share many key influences, including Foucault's social and sexual theories, Geertz's ideal of "thick description," and Bourdieu's analysis of cultural power and capital.

FOUCAULT: ARCHAEOLOGIES AND GENEALOGIES, POWER AND KNOWLEDGE

It is hard to know how to characterize Foucault. He refused to be termed a philosopher, though for a time he held the chair in philosophy at the Collège de France. He was certainly not a literary critic. Most of his works are in the field of social history. *Folie et déraison: Histoire de la folie à l'âge classique* (1961; translated as *Madness and Civilization*, 1973) is a history of the forms of treatment for insanity since the Renaissance. *Surveillir et punir: Naissance de la prison* (1975; translated as *Discipline and Punish*, 1977) deals with the treatment of crime and delinquency over the same period. *The History of Sexuality* (1976), a projected six-volume treatise left unfinished at Foucault's death in 1984, examines moral attitudes towards sexual desire beginning with the ancient Greeks (see the introduction to Gender Studies and Queer Theory, p. 1431). Nevertheless, Foucault stood aloof from the social historians of the *Annales* school (including Fernand Braudel, Phillipe Ariès, and Emmanuel Leroi-Ladurie) who were working on the sort of "local knowledge" prized by Clifford Geertz, and Foucault was pilloried by social historians both in France and abroad for his cavalier use of facts and documents, and for his tendency to create universal generalizations based on slim and sometimes unrepresentative bits of evidence.

It was as a philosopher of history that Foucault was most influential, both on the new historicists and on the larger and more diverse group of cultural studies schol-

---

years. Is the analysis of how England developed a fixation on identity a form of new historicism or cultural studies? The reviewers will have to tell me. See *Crimes of the Century: The Ideology of True Crime Fiction*, forthcoming.

[9]It is probably a safe guess that most practitioners of both the new historicism and cultural studies would locate themselves well to the left of both the Labour Party of British Prime Minister Tony Blair and the Democratic Party of U.S. President Bill Clinton.

ars. But he was a philosopher of history who preached the obsolescence of history as it had been practiced. For Foucault, history was certainly not the working out of a single plotted idea, as it was for Hegel or Marx. Foucault believed that not only are there no ideas governing reality but that we cannot even know the reality of the past, as we have access only to representations purporting to map the real. Nor is there a unitary self doing this mapping, only a subject constituted by society as an effect of its repressive social and economic structures.

Furthermore, in addition to viewing history as a mode of knowledge that is obsolescent, tied to the modern *épistème* that he felt was on its way out, Foucault believed history constitutes a method of repression. For Foucault, history embodies

> the various . . . aspects of the will to knowledge [*vouloir-savoir*]: instinct, passion, the inquisitor's devotion, cruel subtlety, and malice. It discovers the violence of a position that sides with those who are happy in their ignorance, against the effective illusions by which humanity protects itself, a position that encourages the dangers of research and delights in disturbing discoveries. The historical analysis of the rancorous will to knowledge reveals that all knowledge rests upon injustice (that there is no right, not even in the act of knowing, to truth or a foundation for truth) and that the instinct for knowledge is malicious.[10]

For obsolescent history, Foucault wishes to substitute "genealogy" in Nietzsche's sense of a study of "emergences" that "rejects the metahistorical deployment of ideal significations and indefinite teleologies," that "opposes itself to the search for 'origins'" (140).

The key text for Foucault's vision of history is *Les mots et les choses* (1966; translated as *The Order of Things: An Archaeology of the Human Sciences*, 1970). The initial chapter of this work, in which Foucault treats Velázquez's masterpiece, *Las Meninas*, as a text of history, is reprinted below. Though Foucault is a philosophical nominalist, no Platonist could be more rigidly totalizing in his periodization. The four epochs into which Foucault divides Western history — conventionally called the Renaissance, the Enlightenment, the modern age, and the postmodern future — are each separated by what he refers to as a *coupure*, or rupture, that forces a complete break with the mode of thought of the past. For Foucault, these epochs are entirely discontinuous, like an archeological dig in which the culture of one era is separated by a fault line from what precedes and follows it. Each band of culture is integrated by what Foucault calls an *épistème*, a mode of power/knowledge with its own discursive practices: methods of expression that are also methods of oppression.

In the Renaissance, the connections between facts, their ordering and hierarchies, were expressed in terms of similitudes and sympathies, natural metaphors and metonymies that anyone could read in God's creation. In the Enlightenment, such connections were based on classifications, types and their tokens, ordered like grammars or taxonomies. In the modern age, history itself, with its emphasis on the

[10]Michel Foucault, "Nietzsche, Genealogy, History," in *Language, Counter-memory, Practice* (Oxford: Basil Blackwell, 1977), pp. 162–63.

narrative, has become the master mode of organization. For example Marx presents his ideas about economics and the social and political relations that emerge from economics not in the form of charts and tables but as a master narrative of humanity's history from the Bronze Age through the Industrial Revolution that culminates in his prophecy of the decline and violent overthrow of capitalism and the creation of a worker's state. Similarly, Freud presents his idea of the drives and defenses that make people so complex in terms of a developmental narrative in which the individual passes through oral, anal, and phallic phases of pregenital sexuality and emerges from the Oedipal crisis of adolescence before attaining adulthood. To argue against Marx and Freud, one has to attack not just their principles but their narratives — as their revisers have in fact done. This mode of argumentation belongs to the modern age, which in Foucault's view is passing with the coming of postmodernism, which will engender some new *épistème*, or way of organizing knowledge, that will make the historical, or narrative mode obsolete.

Foucault's "archaeological" method, as presented in *The Order of Things*, is essentially synchronic, presenting history as a series of sedimentary layers separated by fault lines. In contrast, his separate studies of madness, illness, crime, and sex are "genealogical," diachronic studies that link various discursive practices with one another — often through similitudes and catachreses — "in order to establish those diverse converging, and sometimes divergent, but never autonomous series that enable us to circumscribe the 'locus' of an event, the limits to its fluidity and the conditions of its emergence."[11] Within each of Foucault's genealogies — his stories of the emergence of new methods of punishment, new modes of treatment for mental illness, or new attitudes toward the body and sexuality — his treatment of historical change is more or less coherent.

A self-contradiction appears, however, when one places the various genealogies against one another. Then it becomes evident that although changes in each of the discursive formations are supposed to occur within a *coupure*, a fissure between *épistèmes*, the changes in one area of social regulation do not occur simultaneously with changes in other areas, as one would think they should. The beginning of the regulation of the lives of imprisoned criminals by timetables and rules, for example, starts about a century after one might expect, given Foucault's general vision of the Enlightenment with its fascination with types and taxonomies. Foucault does not attempt to disguise this fact. As he says in *The Archaeology of Knowledge,* "We must not imagine that rupture is a sort of great drift that carries with it all discursive formations at once. . . . The idea of a single break suddenly, at a given moment, dividing all discursive formations, interrupting them in a single moment and reconstituting them in accordance with the same rules — such an idea cannot be sustained. The contemporaneity of several transformations does not mean their exact chronological coincidence: each transformation may have its own particular index of temporal 'viscosity'" (175). But if discursive formations may linger for more than a

[11]Michel Foucault, "The Discourse on Language," in *The Archaeology of Knowledge and the Discourse on Language* (New York: Pantheon, 1971), p. 230.

century because of their "temporal viscosity," the notion of an *épistème* as a coherent historical formation begins to seem empty.

Another hollowness is Foucault's notion of causality. Unlike most social historians, Foucault has no interest in what made things happen, in baring the nexus of conditionality and contingency, of what is necessary and what sufficient for one state of affairs to transmute itself into another. As he says,

> The old questions of the traditional analysis (What link should be made between disparate events? How can a causal succession be established between them? What continuity or overall significance do they possess? Is it possible to define a totality, or must one be content with reconstitution of connexions?) are now being replaced by questions of another type: which strata should be isolated from others? What types of series should be established? What system of relations . . . may be established between them? What series of series may be established? And in what large-scale chronological table may distinct series of events be determined?[12]

For many a historian, such questions represent an evasion of history rather than its fulfillment. Nevertheless, the influence of Foucault's notions of historical periodization and of discursive practices of power/knowledge have been highly influential both on new historicists and practitioners of cultural studies.

For example, Stephen Greenblatt's discussion of the relationship between the bounded (and thereby licensed) representation of transgression within the theater of the English Renaissance and the remorseless persecution of similar transgressors (Catholics, witches, transvestites) in the society at large derives straight from Foucault, who uses it, among other places, in his *History of Sexuality*. Greenblatt also explicitly rejects the notion of causality as a principal focus of genealogical investigation. In the course of relating Shakespeare's theatrical representations of women who dress up as boys (like Viola in *Twelfth Night*) to a story of cross-dressing by Marin le Marcis in Montaigne's *Travel Journal,* to Jacques Duval's story of a woman married to a hermaphrodite (*De Hermaphroditis,* 1603), and to Galen's and Paré's various misconceptions about the male and female sexual organs (ca. 130 and 1510–90, respectively), Greenblatt hastens to assure us that he realizes that it is unlikely that Shakespeare had studied Galen and Paré, and almost inconceivable that he had heard about the cases of cross-dressing and hermaphroditism mentioned by Montaigne and Duval. These are not sources or even intertexts. "The relation I wish to establish between medical and theatrical practice is not one of cause and effect or source and literary realization. We are dealing rather with a shared code, a set of interlocking tropes and similitudes that function not only as the objects but as the conditions of the representation."[13] There is nothing dishonest at all going on here, but Greenblatt appears less defensive when the cultural text against which he reads Shakespeare is, like Samuel Harsnett's *Declaration of Egregious Popish Impostures,* a book Shakespeare is likely to have read while writing *King Lear,* or like

[12]Ibid., pp. 3–4.

[13]Stephen Greenblatt, *Shakespearean Negotiations: The Circulation of Social Energy in Renaissance England* (Oxford: Clarendon Press, 1988), p. 86.

William Strachey's account of storm and shipwreck near Bermuda, a text Shakespeare probably saw in manuscript while working on *The Tempest.*

GENDER AND THEORY

What Foucault shares with the practitioners of the *Annales* school in France and the various "history from the bottom up" movements in English-speaking countries is a central focus on social history rather than political history: history "without the king," centering on institutions like the family, the trades, and professions, as well as the ways in which societies deal with individuals and groups that are transgressive (heretics, criminals, sexual deviates) or "other" in less obvious ways, such as infants and the aged. Ironically, one charge leveled against the new historicism in the late 1980s was that it had ignored issues of sex and gender. Judith Lowder Newton complained in "History as Usual? Feminism and the 'New Historicism'" (1988) that while the king had been gotten rid of, the patriarch seemed to hold full sway. Newton argued that while many of her female colleagues were engaged with the new historicism, histories of the critical practice tended to ignore their work on changing gender roles. In particular, she wanted these histories to take account of such feminist scholarship as Catherine Gallagher's *The Industrial Reformation of English Fiction: Social Discourse and Narrative Form, 1832–1867* (1985), Mary Poovey's *Uneven Developments: The Ideological Work of Gender in Mid-Victorian England* (1988), and Nancy Armstrong's *Desire and Domestic Fiction: A Political History of the Novel* (1987).

Armstrong, influenced by the cultural materialism of Raymond Williams as well as by Foucault, has researched the ways in which institutions like the domestic household were created and reshaped by texts of domesticity — courtesy manuals, cookery books, and the domestic novel — written about and often by women with a conscious eye toward the changing structure of the family. Armstrong's notions that changes in society and the role of women are not on the fringes of politics but at its center, expressed in "Some Call It Fiction: On the Politics of Domesticity" (reprinted here), would find an echo in other feminist thinkers and gender theorists. Her placement in this chapter reminds us that both the new historicism and cultural studies have begun to move gender roles and the changes they have undergone to the center of the agenda.

WHITE: HISTORY AS DISCOURSE

Greenblatt's sense that common "tropes and similitudes" of representation are key indications of historical linkage is indebted to Foucault but also to Hayden White's study of histriography. White's first book, *Metahistory* (1974), was in effect an inside-out version of new historicism, a demonstration of the textuality of history centering on the ways in which various Enlightenment and post-Romantic historians (including Gibbon, Macaulay, and Burkhardt) were "literary" in the strongest sense of the word. White argued that these historians' imaginative conceptions of the Roman Empire, or the Glorious Revolution, or the Civilization of the Renaissance in Italy were shaped in accordance with the four primary literary genres (tragedy, comedy, romance, and satire) and conveyed their visions of truth through language mediated by the four "master tropes" of metaphor (analogy), metonymy (association), synecdoche (the part for the whole), and irony (reversal).

In analyzing the rhetoric of a particular historian, White sometimes finds that a sequence of tropes works to signify the development of consciousness. In his analysis of E. P. Thompson's classic history, *The Making of an English Working Class* (1963), White argues that Thompson's rhetoric presents the "awakening" of working-class consciousness in the eighteenth century in an analogical, or "metaphorical" mode of thought. White categorizes Thompson's later account of labor in the early nineteenth century as "metonymic," because Thompson emphasizes the ways in which working-class consciousness became defined in terms of the "distinctive kinds" of work into which labor was transformed. White views Thompson's description of laborers after the Peterloo Massacre of 1819 as "synecdochic," since Thompson presents the workers as viewing themselves as parts of one whole. Finally, White argues that Thompson's presentation of the class-consciousness of the workers as developing, around 1835, into a form of *self*-consciousness falls into the mode of irony, from which we would correctly predict "the fatal fracturing of the working-class movement itself."[14]

In "The Politics of Historical Interpretation: Discipline and De-Sublimation" (1982), reprinted here, White sets up a relationship between aesthetics, politics, and history different from that outlined in *Metahistory*. It presents the eighteenth-century distinction between the Beautiful and the Sublime[15] as a trope for the distinction between history viewed as a *discipline* pretending to genuine *knowledge* of a past that makes coherent sense, and history viewed as an attempt to understand "a spectacle of crimes, superstitions, errors, duplicities and terrorisms." For White, both "bourgeois" and Marxist historiographers have taken the former view, and, with their aesthetic of the Beautiful, have written histories that offer little in the way of surprise (since humanity seems merely to be following the laws of its own social nature) and nothing in the way of genuine political impetus. The history that leads to genuine utopian aspiration, White thinks, is one that can oppose to the sublime Gothic chaos of the past a coherent and beneficent future worth living and dying for. Though he does not explicitly acknowledge this as his intention, White is, in effect, presenting a defense of the fragmentary and grotesque visions of history that the new historicism has been generating since its inception.

GEERTZ: LOCAL KNOWLEDGE AND THICK DESCRIPTION

Clifford Geertz is no more a literary critic than Foucault or White; he is a cultural anthropologist, and his immense influence on both the new historicism and cultural studies stems from his "semiotic" view of culture. Like Claude Lévi-Strauss, Geertz

[14]Hayden White, *Tropics of Discourse: Essays in Cultural Criticism* (Baltimore: Johns Hopkins University Press, 1978), pp. 16–20.

[15]See Kant, p. 269.

reads cultures as systems of signs in which relationships in one social arena stand in for others, but unlike Lévi-Strauss, who argues that kinship patterns within a culture can always be extracted from the interrelationships of myth, Geertz carries no metaphysical baggage and has no preconceived sense of the way in which cultures are constructed. He stands in the central tradition of the field anthropologists who, from the time of Bronislaw Malinowski (1884–1942), went out to see exotic peoples for themselves. However, in contrast to the positivistic ethos of classical anthropology, Geertz displays the postmodern sense that the observer cannot be detached from what is observed.

Geertz insists that, to understand a society, one cannot stand aloof from it, observing behaviors and gleaning information from informants; instead, one needs to be immersed in a culture's relationships to bring out a credible report of what events mean to their participants. Such a credible report Geertz calls a "thick description," borrowing a term from the English philosopher Gilbert Ryle, who contrasted "thin" descriptions of external behavior (which are unable to distinguish a wink from a facial tic) with the "thick" descriptions that include the significance of events. A tic is an involuntary behavior, whereas a wink is a message, one that, as Geertz puts it, communicates "(1) deliberately, (2) to someone in particular, (3) to impart a particular message, (4) according to a socially established code, (5) without the cognizance of the rest of the company."[16] And of course things can get even more complicated: Winks can be feigned, or parodied, or performed to show how one winks.

Different observers of a culture will bring back different reports, of course, particularly because of their individual preconceptions and partly because of the different ways in which each individual will relate to an exotic culture (and will be related to the culture's members). This means that anthropology cannot be a precise science, any more than history can, because the meaning found in cultural activities is ultimately constructed by the anthropologist. The inevitable contradictions between anthropologists' reports cannot be mediated by any "objective" observer (since no observer can be objective), and in the last analysis the proof of an anthropologist's account rests on the conviction that the rhetoric of "thick description" can convey.

Geertz's most influential single article is "Deep Play: Notes on the Balinese Cockfight" (1992), reproduced here, which presents a concrete example of "thick description" focused on an aspect of Balinese society that other observers had ignored as trivial. Geertz's theoretical coda modestly insists that no "close reading" of the sort he has performed can reveal more than a single facet of a complete culture. But if "the culture of a people is an ensemble of texts," then each "reading" of social semiotics brings us closer to an understanding of a society. Cultural theorists have read our own contemporary society through the semiotics of the texts of television series and the layout of shopping centers, just as new historicists have produced "readings" of Henrician and Elizabethan jousting scorecards, and enriched our sense of the literature as well as the life of the times.

[16]Clifford Geertz, "Local Knowledge," in *The Interpretation of Cultures* (New York: Basic Books, 1973), p. 6.

BOURDIEU: CULTURAL POWER

A fourth major influence on both new historicism and cultural studies has been the neo-Marxist sociology of Pierre Bourdieu.[17] Beginning in the early 1970s, Bourdieu attempted to construct a new way of looking at practices and power relationships. First of all, he divided society into a series of fields (such as the economic, the political, the cultural, and the educational) within which relationships occur. Although he did not want to reinstate the romantic notion of the "self," Bourdieu also rejected the poststructuralist "subject position," with its vision of actions without agents. Instead, he put forward the notion of a "habitus," which he defined as a "system of dispositions," the social equivalent of "linguistic competence" (Noam Chomsky's term for the sum of all the tacit knowledge one has to possess to speak a language with native fluency; see p. 810). Randal Johnson defines "habitus" not as a set of rules but rather as "the feel for the game" that one possesses for life, that one passes on to other players in the course of playing.[18] Bourdieu viewed "habitus" as class related: Persons of the same class were likely, he found, to adopt a similar habitus across different social fields.

For the new historicism and cultural studies, the main contribution of Bourdieu has been his provision of a way of thinking about culture that complicates the Marxist notion of superstructure (see the introduction to Marx, p. 385). For Bourdieu the field of cultural production depends in part on the fields of political power and large-scale economic production, but it also obeys rules of its own that are dictated by its relation to other fields such as education. "The Market in Symbolic Goods" (1971), reproduced here, starts out with the notion that what Bourdieu calls "goods of restricted production" (objects of art and highly skilled craft) were for much of human history financed by the patronage of the aristocracy and the church. A shift toward relative autonomy occurred with the development of mercantile capitalism during the Renaissance, as cultural production came to be regulated primarily by the market, as opposed to the patronage system. The cultural market operates not only on goods being produced at any given moment (contemporary paintings, music, literature, fine porcelains, and such) but on the goods of the past which are simultaneously in circulation. Bourdieu points out that the social value of such symbolic goods, their worth in the cultural field, rests not merely in their rarity (as with gold and gemstones) but in the cultural "capital" derived from the education that needs to be invested to appreciate them. What this means is that the popular art of one era (Elizabethan drama, for example) may subsequently become the highly valued masterpiece of another.

Like any form of securities in a market, the value of certain forms of cultural capital can be disconcertingly variable. At the end of the last century, when the newly rich were vying for prestige with an established aristocracy, certain forms of

[17]In this context, see also the somewhat later ideas of Michel de Certeau, especially in *The Practice of Everyday Life* (1985).

[18]Randal Johnson, "Introduction" to Pierre Bourdieu, *The Field of Cultural Production* (New York: Columbia University Press, 1993), p. 6.

symbolic goods, and the connoisseurship required for their appreciation, were valued highly because such cultural capital was a way of asserting the status of the traditional ruling class. Today, with different social structures and habitus among the rich, such knowledge is much less valuable than it used to be. As John Guillory points out in *Cultural Capital* (see Ch. 9), the fury of the current quarrels over the literary canon may reflect what happens when academics in the humanities — guardians of a certain store of cultural capital — find their trust fund vastly devalued, and begin to search for new stocks in which to invest.

POST-COLONIAL CULTURAL THEORY: SAID AND BHABHA

Many of the primary issues of cultural studies, including gender and class, the problems of signification and the process of canonization, are treated elsewhere in this text; one that is not is the issue of nationality and relations between Europe and the United States and those countries that used to be lumped together as the Third World. (The old distinction between "industrialized" countries and "developing" nations is no longer applicable, as there are fewer and fewer industrial jobs in Europe and America now that more and more goods are being manufactured, using capital supplied by global corporations, in countries like Kenya and Pakistan.) The term *post-colonial studies* is applied primarily to analyses of the relations of power and knowledge, politics and aesthetics, in countries that in the nineteenth and earlier twentieth centuries were administered by England, France, and the United States, particularly the Indian subcontinent, northern and central Africa, and southeast Asia. *Post-colonial criticism* has focused on both the literatures developed by these new nations, which are often — as in the case of the works of Chinua Achebe, Salman Rushdie, and Naguib Mahfouz — written in European languages, and on European responses to colonialism in familiar texts by such authors as Joseph Conrad, E. M. Forster, George Orwell, and Albert Camus. However, like other cultural critics, post-colonial theorists enjoy examining texts outside the standard genres, and frequently examine phenomena that are only analogically related to those encountered in former European colonies. These include the writings and cultural productions of aboriginal groups (like Native Americans or Maoris in New Zealand), marginalized groups that have been included within a nation as the result of its border wars (such as Latinos who became citizens of the United States as a result of its treaties with Mexico), and immigrant groups, willing and otherwise (including African American descendants of slaves in the Unites States and "guest-workers" in Europe). It should go without saying that the histories, legal status, and cultural relations of these groups with the dominant culture differ from one another, and that it is dangerous to import ideas taken from a cultural study of one group into that of another without critically examining their applicability.[19]

[19]Toni Morrison's notion of "Africanism" as an American counterpart of European Orientalism is an example of an analogy that raises as many questions as it answers. See Morrison, "Black Matter(s)," in *Falling into Theory*, ed. David Richter (Boston: Bedford Books, 1994), pp. 255–68; and Edward Said, "Introduction to *Orientalism*," p. 1279 in this text.

In this growing field, Edward Said's *Orientalism* (1978) is a key text, one that for two decades has inspired both imitation and refutation. Itself influenced significantly by Foucault, Said's study is of the relationship between power and knowledge in the domination of the East by the West. In particular, Said witheringly critiques the Western image of the Oriental as "irrational, depraved (fallen), childlike, 'different,'" which has allowed the West to define itself as "rational, virtuous, mature, 'normal.'" (40). Western students of Oriental literature and culture, from artists to professors of language and history, have helped to create this self-affirming vision, which in turn has been used to justify the domination of the Arab and Asian peoples by European governments, the marginalization of their languages and cultures, and the uprooting of their institutions. For Said, the cultural practices and forms of knowledge typical of Orientalism have not vanished with the official colonial regimes. As a Palestinian theorist, Said views his own attempt to understand the cultural work of Orientalism as a site of resistance to the hegemony of Western values and ideas.

The notion of post-colonial studies as constituting a site of resistance appears as well in theorists who are less taken with Foucault's methodology of cultural study than Said is. Gayatri Chakravorti Spivak, born in Calcutta, began her career as the first English translator of Derrida's *Of Grammatology* (1967), and Spivak's version of post-colonialism prefers the deconstructive mode as a way of questioning the binarisms and exposing the misunderstandings of language and signification set up within colonial discourse. Spivak's feminist version of what she terms "subaltern studies" is often devoted to showing how the female subject is silenced by the dialogue between (male-dominated) Western and (male-dominated) Asian characterizations of social institutions. Bombay-born Homi Bhabha, like Spivak, is interested in probing and problematizing Said's binaries of East/West. For Bhabha, the problem with Said's analysis is the way in which it restricts itself to analyzing the consciousness of Europeans vis-à-vis the Orient, with little attention to the way in which colonized peoples are implicated in this relationship. Bhabha sees the experience of colonial peoples as creating a "hybridity" of perspective, a split consciousness in which the individual identifies simultaneously with his or her own people and with the colonial power. This hybridity or "liminality" (existing on the borderline) is not necessarily an undesirable state: It is, as Bhabha sees it, part of the postmodern condition. It is the situation not only of the colonial subject but of minority groups like African Americans and, to one extent or another, of every inhabitant of the globe. Bhabha's "Locations of Culture," reproduced here, presents his view of the connections between minority and post-colonial literature as sites of resistance. While W. E. B. Du Bois a century ago had understood "double consciousness" to be an inevitable condition of the souls of black folk, Bhabha understands it as inevitable for us all.

THE INEVITABILITY OF CULTURAL STUDIES

Cultural studies is the "hegemonic" critical discourse at the moment, one that contains the humanities and social sciences' collective response to what we might call the Era of Grand Theory, the two decades beginning with the structuralist revolution in the 1960s. The Era of Grand Theory produced a vital set of competing ideas about literature, society, and the mind but failed to coalesce in any single new rationale for textual and literary study. The New Criticism had been displaced and decentered, but nothing had taken its place. In its enormous variety and eclecticism, cultural studies is not a new paradigm of knowledge so much as a way of making do temporarily without a paradigm. Or as Vincent Leitch puts it, cultural studies "aspired to be a new discipline but served as an unstable meeting point for various interdisciplinary feminists, Marxists, literary and media critics, postmodern theorists, social semioticians, rhetoricians, fine arts specialists, and sociologists and historians of culture."[20]

The eclecticism of Leitch's list is not an anomaly. As of this writing, the "Cultural Studies" page of the Internet "Voice of the Shuttle" resource file describes itself as including "resources in cultural criticism and theory, Marxist and later Marxist critique, popular culture studies, post-colonial theory, and sociology." It also includes resources on select special topics in the field such as "body theory, censorship, culture/canon wars, the Sokal controversy."[21] Other topics with separate pages of their own not listed in the summary include "cyberculture," "generation studies," "Millennial Studies (the Year 2000 Fetish)," and "post-industrial business theory."

Besides its eclecticism, what is most obvious about this list of topics is its topicality: Cultural studies is about whatever is happening at the moment, rather than about a body of texts created in the past. "Happening" topics, generally speaking, are the mass media themselves, which, in a postmodern culture, dominates the cultural lives of its inhabitants, or topics that have been valorized by the mass media. One of the great virtues of cultural studies is in fact its relentlessly critical attitude towards journalism, publishing, cinema, television, and other forms of mass media, whose seemingly transparent windows through which we view "reality" probably constitute the most blatant and pervasive mode of false consciousness of our era. But though some cultural critics would deny it, their bias toward what is "happening" tends to valorize mass culture at the expense of the more local, private, and reclusive formations whose study would require the rigorous methods of field anthropology. In a sense this is as much a bias toward an easier object of study as was the restriction of literary "history," in the era before the new historicism, to the relations among a small body of canonical texts.

[20]See Vincent Leitch, "Cultural Studies," in *The Johns Hopkins Guide to Literary Criticism and Theory,* ed. Michael Grodin and Michael Kreiswirth (Baltimore: Johns Hopkins University Press, 1994), p. 188.

[21]Recently, much ink was lavished on the "Sokal Affair," the publication in the journal *Social Text* of an essay by New York University physicist Alan Sokal claiming that poststructuralist theory forced scientists to recognize the fact that there was no external world beyond their construction of it, that given different societies' mathematics and ways of measuring, pi (the ratio between the circumference and diameter of a circle) should be viewed as a social construct rather than a mathematical constant. The essay was a hoax attempting to demonstrate that the most prestigious journal in cultural studies would publish something patently absurd because the views expressed were those the editors wanted to hear.

Cultural studies is willing to question the cultural significance of the canon wars discussed in Chapter 9, in the sense of analyzing what might be at stake for partisans on both sides. However, rather than entering the fray, it has questioned all attempts at canon formation, particularly attempts to valorize the classic Western canon. This negative bias of cultural studies toward canonical literature can be seen as an inevitable result of what Pierre Bourdieu calls the devaluation of canonical literature as part of the cultural capital needed for membership in the ruling class of late capitalist society. Investment bankers were once expected to read Jane Austen and be able to quote Shakespeare; today's managers of mutual funds need only know whether revenues from Kenneth Branagh's *Hamlet* surpassed Mel Gibson's at the box office. Writing still holds a key to power, but not critically acclaimed writing. Even those who still aspire to write canonical literature, to become the next Faulkner, are aware that writing the Great American Novel can guarantee one a living only if the novel gets optioned as the basis for a movie or turned into a successful television series.[22] Young theorists are trained in the doctrine that everything is some sort of text, analyzable through the structuralist principles that underlie most contemporary theory. It isn't strange that they should find it hard to resist the urge to study the objects and practices contemporary culture actually values rather than those it merely enshrines. The oppositional stance of cultural studies toward the methods and products of contemporary corporate America thus veils what might otherwise be taken as worship of its success. Madonna Studies, anyone?

Selected Bibliography

Ang, Ien. *Watching Television.* New York: Routledge, 1991.

Armstrong, Nancy. *Desire and Domestic Fiction.* New York: Oxford University Press, 1987.

Ashcroft, Bill, GaBreth Griffiths, and Helen Tiffin, eds. *The Post-Colonial Studies Reader.* New York: Routledge, 1995.

Barthes, Roland. *Mythologies.* 1957; New York: Farrar, Straus and Giroux, 1972.

Belsey, Catherine. *Critical Practice.* New York: Methuen, 1980.

Bhabha, Homi K. *Nation and Narration.* New York: Routledge, 1990.

———. *The Location of Culture.* New York: Routledge, 1994.

Bourdieu, Pierre. *Outline of a Theory of Practice.* Cambridge: Cambridge University Press, 1977.

———. *Homo Academicus.* 1984; Stanford: Stanford University Press, 1988.

———. *The Field of Cultural Production.* New York: Columbia University Press, 1993.

Brantlinger, Patrick. *Crusoe's Footprints: Cultural Studies in Britain and America.* New York: Routledge, 1990.

de Certeau, Michel. *The Practice of Everyday Life.* Berkeley: University of California Press, 1984.

Clifford, James. *The Predicament of Culture.* Cambridge: Harvard University Press, 1988.

Dollimore, Jonathan. *Radical Tragedy: Religion, Ideology and Power in the Drama of Shakespeare and His Contemporaries.* Brighton, Eng.: Harvester, 1984.

[22]Even half a century ago, Faulkner wrote screenplays in Hollywood for projects like *Land of the Pharaohs* to finance the whiskey he needed to write *Absalom, Absalom!*

During, Simon, ed. *The Cultural Studies Reader*. New York: Routledge, 1993.
Foucault, Michel. *Madness and Civilization: A History of Insanity in the Age of Reason*. 1961; New York: Pantheon, 1973.
———. *The Birth of the Clinic: An Archaeology of Medical Perception*. 1963; New York: Pantheon, 1973.
———. *The Order of Things: An Archaeology of the Human Sciences*. 1966; New York: Vintage, 1973.
———. *The Archaeology of Knowledge and the Discourse on Language*. 1969; New York: Pantheon, 1972.
———. *Discipline and Punish: The Birth of the Prison*. 1975; New York: Pantheon, 1977.
———. *Language, Counter-Memory, Practice*. Ithaca: Cornell University Press, 1977.
———. *The Foucault Reader*. New York: Pantheon, 1984.
Gallagher, Catherine. *The Industrial Reformation of English Fiction: Social Discourse and Narrative Form, 1832–1867*. Chicago: University of Chicago Press, 1985.
Geertz, Clifford. *The Interpretation of Cultures: Selected Essays*. New York: Basic Books, 1973.
———. *Local Knowledge*. New York: Basic Books, 1985.
———. *Works and Lives: The Anthropologist as Author*. Stanford: Stanford University Press, 1988.
Goldberg, Jonathan. *James I and the Politics of Literature*. Baltimore: Johns Hopkins University Press, 1983.
Gramsci, Antonio. *Selections from Cultural Writings*. London: Lawrence and Wishart, 1985.
Greenblatt, Stephen. *Renaissance Self-Fashioning: From More to Shakespeare*. Chicago: University of Chicago Press, 1980.
———. *Shakespearean Negotiations*. Berkeley: University of California Press, 1988.
Greenblatt, Stephen, ed. *Representing the English Renaissance*. Berkeley: University of California Press, 1988.
Grossberg, Lawrence, Cary Nelson, and Paula Treichler, eds. *Cultural Studies*. New York: Routledge, 1992.
Guillory, John. *Cultural Capital*. Chicago: University of Chicago Press, 1993.
Hall, Stuart, and Paddy Whannel. *The Popular Arts*. London: Hutchinson, 1964.
Hoggart, Richard. *The Uses of Literacy: Changing Patterns in English Mass Culture*. Harmondsworth: Penguin, 1957.
Howard, Jean E., and Marion F. O'Connor, eds. *Shakespeare Reproduced: The Text in History and Ideology*. New York: Methuen, 1987.
Hutcheon, Linda. *The Politics of Postmodernism*. London: Routledge, 1989.
JanMohammed, Abdul, and David Lloyd. "Introduction: Toward a Theory of Minority Discourse." *Cultural Critique* 6 (1987): 5–12.
LaCapra, Dominick. *History and Criticism*. Ithaca: Cornell University Press, 1985.
Laclau, Ernesto, and Chantal Mouffe. "Postmarxism without Apologies." *New Left Review* 166 (1987): 79–106.
Lindenberger, Herbert. *Historical Drama: The Relation of Literature and Reality*. Chicago: University of Chicago Press, 1975.
Lindenberger, Herbert, ed. *History in Literature: On Value, Genre, Institutions*. New York: Columbia University Press, 1990.
Lyotard, Jean-François. *The Post-Modern Condition: A Report on Knowledge*. Minneapolis: University of Minnesota Press, 1984.
McCoy, Richard. *The Rites of Knighthood: The Literature and Politics of Elizabethan Chivalry*. Berkeley: University of California Press, 1989.

McGann, Jerome. *The Beauty of Inflections: Literary Investigations in Historical Method and Theory.* Oxford: Clarendon Press, 1985.

McGann, Jerome, ed. *Historical Studies and Literary Criticism.* Madison: University of Wisconsin Press, 1985.

Michaels, Walter Benn. *The Gold Standard and the Logic of Naturalism.* Berkeley: University of California Press, 1987.

Minh-ha, Trinh T. *Woman/Native/Other: Writing Postcoloniality and Feminism.* Bloomington: Indiana University Press, 1989.

Montrose, Louis. "Renaissance Literary Studies and the Subject of History." *English Literary Renaissance* 16 (1986): 3–21.

Morris, Meaghan. "Things to Do with Shopping Centres." In *Grafts: Feminist Cultural Criticism*, ed. Susan Sheridan. London: Verso, 1988.

Newton, Judith. "History as Usual?: Feminism and the 'New Historicism.'" *Cultural Critique* 8 (1988): 87–121.

Poovey, Mary. *Uneven Developments: The Ideological Work of Gender in Mid-Victorian England.* Chicago: University of Chicago Press, 1988.

Richter, David H. *The Progress of Romance: Literary Historiography and the Gothic Novel.* Columbus: Ohio State University Press, 1996.

Ricoeur, Paul. *Time and Narrative.* Chicago: University of Chicago Press, 1984.

Said, Edward W. *Orientalism.* New York: Random House, 1978.

———. *The World, the Text, and the Critic.* Cambridge: Harvard University Press, 1983.

———. *Culture and Imperialism.* New York: Alfred A. Knopf, 1993.

Spivak, Gayatri Chakravorty. *In Other Worlds: Essays in Cultural Politics.* New York: Routledge, 1987.

———. "Can the Subaltern Speak?" In *Marxism and the Interpretation of Culture*, ed. Cary Nelson and Lawrence Grossberg. Urbana: University of Illinois Press, 1988.

Storey, John, ed. *What Is Cultural Studies?* New York: St. Martin's Press, 1996.

Tennenhouse, Leonard. *Power on Display: The Politics of Shakespeare's Genres.* New York: Methuen, 1986.

Thomas, Brook. *The New Historicism and Other Old-Fashioned Topics.* Princeton: Princeton University Press, 1991.

Veeser, H. Aram., ed. *The New Historicism.* New York: Routledge, 1989.

White, Hayden. *Metahistory: The Historical Imagination in Nineteenth-Century Europe.* Baltimore: Johns Hopkins University Press, 1974.

———. *Tropics of Discourse: Essays in Cultural Criticism.* Baltimore: Johns Hopkins University Press, 1978.

———. *The Content of the Form.* Baltimore: Johns Hopkins University Press, 1988.

Williams, Raymond. *The Country and the City.* New York: Oxford University Press, 1973.

Michel Foucault

1926–1984

The following selection is the initial chapter of Foucault's Les mots et les choses *(1966; translated as* The Order of Things: An Archaeology of the Human Sciences, *1970).* Las Meninas *("The Maids of Honor") is the title of the Spanish painter Velázquez's 1656 masterpiece* *(see p. 1223)**. (For biographical information on Foucault,* *see the introduction on p. 889.)*

Las Meninas

I

The painter is standing a little back from his canvas. He is glancing at his model; perhaps he is considering whether to add some finishing touch, though it is also possible that the first stroke has not yet been made. The arm holding the brush is bent to the left, towards the palette; it is motionless, for an instant, between canvas and paints. The skilled hand is suspended in mid-air, arrested in rapt attention on the painter's gaze; and the gaze, in return, waits upon the arrested gesture. Between the fine point of the brush and the steely gaze, the scene is about to yield up its volume.

But not without a subtle system of feints. By standing back a little, the painter has placed himself to one side of the painting on which he is working. That is, for the spectator at present observing him he is to the right of his canvas, while the latter, the canvas, takes up the whole of the extreme left. And the canvas has its back turned to that spectator: he can see nothing of it but the reverse side, together with the huge frame on which it is stretched. The painter, on the other hand, is perfectly visible in his full height; or at any rate, he is not masked by the tall canvas which may soon absorb him, when, taking a step towards it again, he returns to his task; he has no doubt just appeared, at this very instant, before the eyes of the spectator, emerging from what is virtually a sort of vast cage projected backwards by the surface he is painting. Now he can be seen, caught in a moment of stillness, at the neutral center of this oscillation. His dark torso and bright face are half-way between the visible and the invisible: emerging from that canvas beyond our view, he moves into our gaze; but when, in a moment, he makes a step to the right, removing himself from our gaze, he will be standing exactly in front of the canvas he is painting; he will enter that region where his painting, neglected for an instant, will, for him, become visible once more, free of shadow and free of reticence. As though the painter could not at the same time be seen on the picture where he is represented and also see that upon which he is representing something. He rules at the threshold of those two incompatible visibilities.

The painter is looking, his face turned slightly and his head leaning towards one shoulder. He is staring at a point to which, even though it is invisible, we, the spectators, can easily assign an object, since it is we, ourselves, who are that point: our bodies, our faces, our eyes. The spectacle he is observing is thus doubly invisible: first, because it is not represented within the space of the painting, and, second, because it is situated precisely in that blind point, in that essential hiding-place into which our gaze disappears from ourselves at the moment of our actual looking. And yet, how could we fail to see that invisibility, there in front of our eyes, since it has its own perceptible equivalent, its sealed-in figure, in the painting itself? We could, in effect, guess what it is the painter is looking at if it were possible for us to glance for a moment at the canvas he is working on; but all we can see of that canvas is its texture, the horizontal and vertical

Diego Rodriguez Velázquez, *Las Meninas,* 1656. Museo del Prado, Madrid, Spain. Erich Lessing/Art Resources, N. Y.

bars of the stretcher, and the obliquely rising foot of the easel. The tall, monotonous rectangle occupying the whole left portion of the real picture, and representing the back of the canvas within the picture, reconstitutes in the form of a surface the invisibility in depth of what the artist is observing: that space in which we are, and which we are. From the eyes of the painter to what he is observing there runs a compelling line that we, the onlookers, have no power of evading: it runs through the real picture and emerges from its surface to join the place from which we see the painter observing us; this dotted line reaches out to us ineluctably, and links us to the representation of the picture.

In appearance, this locus is a simple one; a matter of pure reciprocity: we are looking at a picture in which the painter is in turn looking out at us. A mere confrontation, eyes catching one another's glance, direct looks superimposing themselves upon one another as they cross. And yet this slender line of reciprocal visibility embraces a whole complex network of uncertainties, exchanges, and feints. The painter is turning his eyes towards us only in so far as we happen to occupy the same position as his subject. We, the spectators, are an additional factor. Though greeted by that gaze, we are also dismissed by it, replaced by that which was always there before we were: the model itself. But, inversely, the painter's gaze, addressed to the void confronting him outside the picture, accepts as many models as there are spectators; in this precise but neutral place, the observer and the observed take part in a ceaseless exchange. No gaze is stable, or rather, in the neutral furrow of the gaze piercing at a right angle through the canvas, subject and object, the spectator and the model, reverse their roles to infinity. And here the great canvas with its back to us on the extreme left of the picture exercises its second function: stubbornly invisible, it prevents the relation of these gazes from ever being discoverable or definitely established. The opaque fixity that it establishes on one side renders forever unstable the play of metamorphoses established in the center between spectator and model. Because we can see only that reverse side, we do not know who we are, or what we are doing. Seen or seeing? The painter is observing a place which, from moment to moment, never ceases to change its content, its form, its face, its identity. But the attentive immobility of his eyes refers us back to another direction which they have often followed already, and which soon, there can be no doubt, they will take again: that of the motionless canvas upon which is being traced, has already been traced perhaps, for a long time and forever, a portrait that will never again be erased. So that the painter's sovereign gaze commands a virtual triangle whose outline defines this picture of a picture: at the top — the only visible corner — the painter's eyes; at one of the base angles, the invisible place occupied by the model; at the other base angle, the figure probably sketched out on the invisible surface of the canvas.

As soon as they place the spectator in the field of their gaze, the painter's eyes seize hold of him, force him to enter the picture, assign him a place at once privileged and inescapable, levy their luminous and visible tribute from him, and project it upon the inaccessible surface of the canvas within the picture. He sees his invisibility made visible to the painter and transposed into an image forever invisible to himself. A shock that is augmented and made more inevitable still by a marginal trap. At the extreme right, the picture is lit by a window represented in very sharp perspective; so sharp that we can see scarcely more than the embrasure; so that the flood of light streaming through it bathes at the same time, and with equal generosity, two neighbouring spaces, overlapping but irreducible: the surface of the painting, together with the volume it represents (which is to say, the painter's studio, or the salon in which his easel is now set up), and, in front of that surface, the real volume occupied by the spectator (or again, the unreal site of the model). And as it passes through the room from right to left, this vast flood of golden light carries both the spectator towards the painter and the model towards the canvas; it is this light too, which, washing over the painter, makes him visible to the spectator and turns into golden lines, in the model's eyes, the frame of that enigmatic canvas on which his image, once transported there, is to be imprisoned. This extreme, partial, scarcely indicated window frees a whole flow of daylight which serves as the common locus of the representation. It balances the invisible canvas on the other side of the picture: just as that canvas, by turning its back to the spectators, folds itself in against the picture representing it, and forms, by the superimposition of its reverse and visible side upon the surface of the picture depicting it, the ground, inaccessible to us, on which there shimmers the Image *par excellence,* so does the window, a pure aperture, establish a space as manifest as the other is hidden; as much the common ground of painter, figures, models, and spectators, as the other is solitary (for no one is looking at it, not even the painter). From the right, there streams in through an invisible window the pure volume of a light that renders all representation visible; to the left extends the surface that conceals, on the other side of its all too visible woven texture, the representation it bears. The light, by flooding the scene (I mean the room as well as the canvas, the room represented on the canvas, and the room in which the canvas stands), envelops the figures and the spectators and carries them with it, under the painter's gaze, towards the place where his brush will represent them. But that place is concealed from us. We are observing ourselves being observed by the painter, and made visible to his eyes by the same light that enables us to see him. And just as we are about to apprehend ourselves, transcribed by his hand as though in a mirror, we find that we can in fact apprehend nothing of that mirror but its lusterless back. The other side of a psyche.

Now, as it happens, exactly opposite the spectators — ourselves — on the wall forming the far end of the room, Velázquez has represented a series of pictures; and we see that among all those hanging canvases there is one that shines with particular brightness. Its frame is wider and darker than those of the others; yet there is a fine white line around its inner edge diffusing over its whole surface a light whose source is not easy to determine; for it comes from nowhere, unless it be from a space within itself. In this strange light, two silhouettes are apparent, while above them, and a little behind them, is a heavy purple curtain. The other pictures reveal little more than a few paler patches buried in a darkness without depth. This particular one, on the other hand, opens onto a perspective of space in which recognizable forms recede from us in a light that belongs only to itself. Among all these elements intended to provide representations, while impeding them, hiding them, concealing them because of their position or their distance from us, this is the only one that fulfills its function in all honesty and enables us to see what it is supposed to show. Despite its distance from us, despite the shadows all around it. But it isn't a picture: it is a mirror. It offers us at last that enchantment of the double that until now has been denied us, not only by the distant paintings but also by the light in the foreground with its ironic canvas.

Of all the representations represented in the picture this is the only one visible; but no one is looking at it. Upright beside his canvas, his attention entirely taken up by his model, the painter is unable to see this looking-glass shining so softly behind him. The other figures in the picture are also, for the most part, turned to face what must be taking place in front — towards the bright invisibility bordering the canvas, towards that balcony of light where their eyes can gaze at those who are gazing back at them, and not towards that dark recess which marks the far end of the room in which they are represented. There are, it is true, some heads turned away from us in profile: but not one of them is turned far enough to see, at the back of the room, that solitary mirror, that tiny glowing rectangle which is nothing other than visibility, yet without any gaze able to grasp it, to render it actual, and to enjoy the suddenly ripe fruit of the spectacle it offers.

It must be admitted that this indifference is equaled only by the mirror's own. It is reflecting nothing, in fact, of all that is there in the same space as itself: neither the painter with his back to it, nor the figures in the center of the room. It is not the visible it reflects, in those bright depths. In Dutch painting it was traditional for mirrors to play a duplicating role: they repeated the original contents of the picture, only inside an unreal, modified, contracted, concave space. One saw in them the same things as one saw in the first instance in the painting, but decomposed and recomposed according to a different law. Here, the mirror is saying nothing that has already been said before. Yet its position is more or less completely central: its upper edge is exactly on an imaginary line running half-way between the top and the bottom of the painting, its hands right in the middle of the far wall (or at least in the middle of the portion we can see); it ought, therefore, to be governed by the same lines of perspective as the picture itself; we might well expect the same studio, the same painter, the same canvas to be arranged within it according to an identical space: it could be the perfect duplication.

In fact, it shows us nothing of what is represented in the picture itself. Its motionless gaze extends out in front of the picture, into that necessarily invisible region which forms its exterior face, to apprehend the figures arranged in that space. Instead of surrounding visible objects, this mirror cuts straight through the whole field of the representation, ignoring all it might apprehend within that field, and restores visibility to that which resides outside all view. But the invisibility that it overcomes in this way is not the invisibility of what is hidden: it does not make its way around any obstacle, it is not distorting any perspective, it is addressing itself to what is invisible both because of the picture's structure and because of its existence as painting. What it is reflecting is that which all the figures within the painting are looking at so fixedly, or at least those who are looking straight ahead; it is therefore what the spectator would be able to see if the painting extended further forward, if its bottom edge were brought lower until it included the figures the painter is using as models. But it is also, since the picture does stop there, displaying only the painter and his studio, what is exterior to the picture, in so far as it is a picture — in other words, a rectangular fragment of lines and colors intended to represent something to the eyes of any possible spectator. At the far end of the room, ignored by all, the unexpected mirror holds in its glow the figures that the painter is looking at (the painter in his represented, objective reality, the reality of the painter at his work); but also the figures that are looking at the painter (in that material reality which the lines and the colors have laid out upon the canvas). These two groups of figures are both equally inaccessible, but in different ways: the first because of an effect of composition peculiar to the painting; the second because of the law that presides over the very existence of all pictures in general. Here, the action of representation consists in bringing one of these two forms of invisibility into the place of the other, in an unstable superimposition — and in rendering them both, at the same moment, at the other extremity of the picture — at that pole which is the very height of its representation: that of a reflected depth in the far recess of the painting's depth. The mirror provides a metathesis of visibility that affects both the space represented in the picture and its nature as representation; it allows us to see, in the center of the canvas, what in the painting is of necessity doubly invisible.

A strangely literal, though inverted, application of the advice given, so it is said, to his pupil by the old Pacheco[1] when the former was working in his studio in Seville: "The image should stand out from the frame."

[1]Francesco Pacheco (1564–1644), minor painter of Seville, Velázquez's teacher and later his father-in-law, author of *Arte de la pintura* (1649). [Ed.]

II

But perhaps it is time to give a name at last to that image which appears in the depths of the mirror, and which the painter is contemplating in front of the picture. Perhaps it would be better, once and for all, to determine the identities of all the figures presented or indicated here, so as to avoid embroiling ourselves forever in those vague, rather abstract designations, so constantly prone to misunderstanding and duplication, "the painter," "the characters," "the models," "the spectators," "the images." Rather than pursue to infinity a language inevitably inadequate to the visible fact, it would be better to say that Velázquez composed a picture; that in this picture he represented himself, in his studio or in a room of the Escurial,[2] in the act of painting two figures whom the Infanta Margarita[3] has come there to watch, together with an entourage of duennas, maids of honor, courtiers, and dwarfs; that we can attribute names to this group of people with great precision: tradition recognizes that here we have Doña Maria Augustina Sarmiento, over there Nieto, in the foreground Nicolaso Pertusato, an Italian jester.[4] We could then add that the two personages serving as models to the painter are not visible, at least directly; but that we can see them in a mirror; and that they are, without any doubt, King Philip IV and his wife, Mariana.[5]

These proper names would form useful landmarks and avoid ambiguous designations; they would tell us in any case what the painter is looking at, and the majority of the characters in the picture along with him. But the relation of language to painting is an infinite relation. It is not that words are imperfect, or that, when con-

[2]Royal palace in Madrid. [Ed.]

[3]"Infanta" designates the crown princess, eldest daughter of the king of Spain. Margherita was the daughter of Philip IV's first wife, Isabella of Bourbon. [Ed.]

[4]Doña Maria was one of the royal maids of honor, on the left of the Infanta. Don José Nieto is the back-lit gentleman standing on the staircase in the background. Pertusato is the youth prodding the royal mastiff. [Ed.]

[5]Philip IV (1605–1665) ruled Spain from 1621–65. Mariana, Archduchess of Austria, became his second wife in 1649. [Ed.]

fronted by the visible, they prove insuperably inadequate. Neither can be reduced to the other's terms: it is in vain that we say what we see; what we see never resides in what we say. And it is in vain that we attempt to show, by the use of images, metaphors, or similes, what we are saying; the space where they achieve their splendour is not that deployed by our eyes but that defined by the sequential elements of syntax. And the proper name, in this particular context, is merely an artifice: it gives us a finger to point with, in other words, to pass surreptitiously from the space where one speaks to the space where one looks; in other words, to fold one over the other as though they were equivalents. But if one wishes to keep the relation of language to vision open, if one wishes to treat their incompatibility as a starting-point for speech instead of as an obstacle to be avoided, so as to stay as close as possible to both, then one must erase those proper names and preserve the infinity of the task. It is perhaps through the medium of this grey, anonymous language, always over-meticulous and repetitive because too broad, that the painting may, little by little, release its illuminations.

We must therefore pretend not to know who is to be reflected in the depths of that mirror, and interrogate that reflection in its own terms.

First, it is the reverse of the great canvas represented on the left. The reverse, or rather the right side, since it displays in full face what the canvas, by its position, is hiding from us. Furthermore, it is both in opposition to the window and a reinforcement of it. Like the window, it provides a ground which is common to the painting and to what lies outside it. But the window operates by the continuous movement of an effusion which, flowing from right to left, unites the attentive figures, the painter, and the canvas, with the spectacle they are observing; whereas the mirror, on the other hand, by means of a violent, instantaneous movement, a movement of pure surprise, leaps out from the picture in order to reach that which is observed yet invisible in front of it, and then, at the far end of its fictitious depth, to render it visible yet indifferent to every gaze. The compelling tracer line, joining the reflection to that which it is reflecting, cuts perpendicularly through the lateral flood of light. Lastly — and this is the mirror's third function — it stands adjacent to a doorway which forms an opening, like the mirror itself, in the far wall of the room. This doorway too forms a bright and sharply defined rectangle whose soft light does not shine through into the room. It would be nothing but a gilded panel if it were not recessed out from the room by means of one leaf of a carved door, the curve of a curtain, and the shadows of several steps. Beyond the steps, a corridor begins; but instead of losing itself in obscurity, it is dissipated in a yellow dazzle where the light, without coming in, whirls around on itself in dynamic repose. Against this background, at once near and limitless, a man stands out in full-length silhouette; he is seen in profile; with one hand he is holding back the weight of a curtain; his feet are placed on different steps; one knee is bent. He may be about to enter the room; or he may be merely observing what is going on inside it, content to surprise those within without being seen himself. Like the mirror, his eyes are directed towards the other side of the scene; nor is anyone paying any more attention to him than to the mirror. We do not know where he has come from: it could be that by following uncertain corridors he has just made his way around the outside of the room in which these characters are collected and the painter is at work; perhaps he too, a short while ago, was there in the forefront of the scene, in the invisible region still being contemplated by all those eyes in the picture. Like the images perceived in the looking-glass, it is possible that he too is an emissary from that evident yet hidden space. Even so, there is a difference: he is there in flesh and blood; he has appeared from the outside, on the threshold of the area represented; he is indubitable — not a probable reflection but an irruption. The mirror, by making visible, beyond even the walls of the studio itself, what is happening in front of the picture, creates in its sagittal[6] dimension, an oscillation between the interior and the exterior. One foot only on the lower step, his body entirely in profile, the ambiguous visitor

[6]In optics, "sagittal" designates a plane intersecting the rays from an off-center light source. [Ed.]

is coming in and going out at the same time, like a pendulum caught at the bottom of its swing. He repeats on the spot, but in the dark reality of his body, the instantaneous movement of those images flashing across the room, plunging into the mirror, being reflected there, and springing out from it again like visible, new, and identical species. Pale, minuscule, those silhouetted figures in the mirror are challenged by the tall, solid stature of the man appearing in the doorway.

But we must move down again from the back of the picture towards the front of the stage; we must leave that periphery whose volute[7] we have just been following. Starting from the painter's gaze, which constitutes an off-center center to the left, we perceive first of all the back of the canvas, then the paintings hung on the wall, with the mirror in their center, then the open doorway, then more pictures, of which, because of the sharpness of the perspective, we can see no more than the edges of the frames, and finally, at the extreme right, the window, or rather the groove in the wall from which the light is pouring. This spiral shell presents us with the entire cycle of representation: the gaze, the palette and brush, the canvas innocent of signs (these are the material tools of representation), the paintings, the reflections, the real man (the completed representation, but as it were freed from its illusory or truthful contents, which are juxtaposed to it); then the representation dissolves again: we can see only the frames, and the light that is flooding the pictures from outside, but that they, in return, must reconstitute in their own kind, as though it were coming from elsewhere, passing through their dark wooden frames. And we do, in fact, see this light on the painting, apparently welling out from the crack of the frame; and from there it moves over to touch the brow, the cheekbones, the eyes, the gaze of the painter, who is holding a palette in one hand and in the other a fine brush . . . And so the spiral is closed, or rather, by means of that light, is opened.

This opening is not, like the one in the back wall, made by pulling back a door; it is the whole breadth of the picture itself, and the looks that pass across it are not those of a distant visitor. The frieze that occupies the foreground and the middle ground of the picture represents — if we include the painter — eight characters. Five of these, their heads more or less bent, turned or inclined, are looking straight out at right angles to the surface of the picture. The center of the group is occupied by the little Infanta, with her flared pink and grey dress. The princess is turning her head towards the right side of the picture, while her torso and the big panniers of her dress slant away slightly towards the left; but her gaze is directed absolutely straight towards the spectator standing in front of the painting. A vertical line dividing the canvas into two equal halves would pass between the child's eyes. Her face is a third of the total height of the picture above the lower frame. So that here, beyond all question, resides the principal theme of the composition; this is the very object of this painting. As though to prove this and to emphasize it even more, Velázquez has made use of a traditional visual device: beside the principal figure he has placed a secondary one, kneeling and looking in towards the central one. Like a donor in prayer, like an angel greeting the Virgin, a maid of honor on her knees is stretching out her hands towards the princess. Her face stands out in perfect profile against the background. It is at the same height as that of the child. This attendant is looking at the princess and only at the princess. A little to the right, there stands another maid of honor, also turned towards the Infanta, leaning slightly over her, but with her eyes clearly directed towards the front, towards the same spot already being gazed at by the painter and the princess. Lastly, two other groups made up of two figures each: one of these groups is further away; the other, made up of the two dwarfs, is right in the foreground. One character in each of these pairs is looking straight out, the other to the left or the right. Because of their positions and their size, these two groups correspond and themselves form a pair: behind, the courtiers (the woman, to the left, looks to the right); in front, the dwarfs (the boy, who is at the extreme right, looks in towards the center of the picture). This group of characters, arranged in this manner, can be taken to constitute, according to the way one looks at the picture and the center of reference chosen, two different figures. The

[7]Spiral. [Ed.]

first would be a large X: the top left-hand point of this X would be the painter's eyes; the top right-hand one, the male courtier's eyes; at the bottom left-hand corner there is the corner of the canvas represented with its back towards us (or, more exactly, the foot of the easel); at the bottom right-hand corner, the dwarf (his foot on the dog's back). Where these two lines intersect, at the center of the X, are the eyes of the Infanta. The second figure would be more that of a vast curve, its two ends determined by the painter on the left and the male courtier on the right — both these extremities occurring high up in the picture and set back from its surface; the center of the curve, much nearer to us, would coincide with the princess's face and the look her maid of honor is directing towards her. This curve describes a shallow hollow across the center of the picture which at once contains and sets off the position of the mirror at the back.

There are thus two centers around which the picture may be organized, according to whether the fluttering attention of the spectator decides to settle in this place or in that. The princess is standing upright in the center of a St. Andrew's cross,[8] which is revolving around her with its eddies of courtiers, maids of honor, animals, and fools. But this pivoting movement is frozen. Frozen by a spectacle that would be absolutely invisible if those same characters, suddenly motionless, were not offering us, as though in the hollow of a goblet, the possibility of seeing in the depths of a mirror the unforeseen double of what they are observing. In depth, it is the princess who is superimposed on the mirror; vertically, it is the reflection that is superimposed on the face. But, because of the perspective, they are very close to one another. Moreover, from each of them there springs an ineluctable line: the line issuing from the mirror crosses the whole of the depth represented (and even more, since the mirror forms a hole in the back wall and brings a further space into being behind it); the other line is shorter: it comes from the child's eyes and crosses only the foreground. These two sagittal lines converge at a very sharp angle, and the point where they meet, springing out from the painted surface, occurs in front of the picture, more or less exactly at the spot from which we are observing it. It is an uncertain point because we cannot see it; yet it is an inevitable and perfectly defined point too, since it is determined by those two dominating figures and confirmed further by other, adjacent dotted lines which also have their origin inside the picture and emerge from it in a similar fashion.

What is there, then, we ask at last, in that place which is completely inaccessible because it is exterior to the picture, yet is prescribed by all the lines of its composition? What is the spectacle, what are the faces that are reflected first of all in the depths of the Infanta's eyes, then in the courtiers' and the painter's, and finally in the distant glow of the mirror? But the question immediately becomes a double one: the face reflected in the mirror is also the face that is contemplating it; what all the figures in the picture are looking at are the two figures to whose eyes they too present a scene to be observed. The entire picture is looking out at a scene for which it is itself a scene. A condition of pure reciprocity manifested by the observing and observed mirror, the two stages of which are uncoupled at the two lower corners of the picture: on the left the canvas with its back to us, by means of which the exterior point is made into pure spectacle; to the right the dog lying on the floor, the only element in the picture that is neither looking at anything nor moving, because it is not intended, with its deep reliefs and the light playing on its silky hair, to be anything but an object to be seen.

Our first glance at the painting told us what it is that creates this spectacle-as-observation. It is the two sovereigns. One can sense their presence already in the respectful gaze of the figures in the picture, in the astonishment of the child and the dwarfs. We recognize them, at the far end of the picture, in the two tiny silhouettes gleaming out from the looking-glass. In the midst of all those attentive faces, all those richly dressed bodies, they are the palest, the most unreal, the most compromised of all the painting's images: a movement, a little light, would be sufficient to eclipse them. Of all these figures represented before us, they are also the most ignored, since no one is paying the slightest attention to that reflec-

[8]A St. Andrew's Cross is an X. [Ed.]

tion which has slipped into the room behind them all, silently occupying its unsuspected space; in so far as they are visible, they are the frailest and the most distant form of all reality. Inversely, in so far as they stand outside the picture and are therefore withdrawn from it in an essential invisibility, they provide the center around which the entire representation is ordered: it is they who are being faced, it is towards them that everyone is turned, it is to their eyes that the princess is being presented in her holiday clothes; from the canvas with its back to us to the Infanta, and from the Infanta to the dwarf playing on the extreme right, there runs a curve (or again, the lower fork of the X opens) that orders the whole arrangement of the picture to their gaze and thus makes apparent the true center of the composition, to which the Infanta's gaze and the image in the mirror are both finally subject.

In the realm of the anecdote, this center is symbolically sovereign, since it is occupied by King Philip IV and his wife. But it is so above all because of the triple function it fulfills in relation to the picture. For in it there occurs an exact superimposition of the model's gaze as it is being painted, of the spectator's as he contemplates the painting, and of the painter's as he is composing his picture (not the one represented, but the one in front of us which we are discussing). These three "observing" functions come together in a point exterior to the picture: that is, an ideal point in relation to what is represented, but a perfectly real one too, since it is also the starting-point that makes the representation possible. Within that reality itself, it cannot not be invisible. And yet, that reality is projected within the picture — projected and diffracted in three forms which correspond to the three functions of that ideal and real point. They are: on the left, the painter with his palette in his hand (a self-portrait of Velázquez); to the right, the visitor, one foot on the step, ready to enter the room; he is taking in the scene from the back, but he can see the royal couple, who are the spectacle itself, from the front; and lastly, in the center, the reflection of the king and queen, richly dressed, motionless, in the attitude of patient models.

A reflection that shows us quite simply, and in shadow, what all those in the foreground are looking at. It restores, as if by magic, what is lacking in every gaze: in the painter's, the model, which his represented double is duplicating over there in the picture; in the king's, his portrait, which is being finished off on that slope of the canvas that he cannot perceive from where he stands; in that of the spectator, the real center of the scene, whose place he himself has taken as though by usurpation. But perhaps this generosity on the part of the mirror is feigned; perhaps it is hiding as much as and even more than it reveals. That space where the king and his wife hold sway belongs equally well to the artist and to the spectator: in the depths of the mirror there could also appear — there ought to appear — the anonymous face of the passer-by and that of Velázquez. For the function of that reflection is to draw into the interior of the picture what is intimately foreign to it: the gaze which has organized it and the gaze for which it is displayed. But because they are present within the picture, to the right and to the left, the artist and the visitor cannot be given a place in the mirror: just as the king appears in the depths of the looking-glass precisely because he does not belong to the picture.

In the great volute that runs around the perimeter of the studio, from the gaze of the painter, with his motionless hand and palette, right around to the finished paintings, representation came into being, reached completion, only to dissolve once more into the light; the cycle was complete. The lines that run through the depth of the picture, on the other hand, are not complete; they all lack a segment of their trajectories. This gap is caused by the absence of the king — an absence that is an artifice on the part of the painter. But this artifice both conceals and indicates another vacancy which is, on the contrary, immediate: that of the painter and the spectator when they are looking at or composing the picture. It may be that, in this picture, as in all the representations of which it is, as it were, the manifest essence, the profound invisibility of what one sees is inseparable from the invisibility of the person seeing — despite all mirrors, reflections, imitations, and portraits. Around the scene are arranged all the signs and successive forms of representation; but the double relation of the representation to its model and to its sovereign, to its author as well as to the person to whom it is being offered, this relation is necessarily interrupted. It can never be present without some residuum, even in a representation that offers itself as a spectacle. In the depth that traverses the picture, hollowing it into a fictitious recess and projecting it forward in front of itself, it is not possible for the pure felicity of the image ever to present in a full light both the master who is representing and the sovereign who is being represented.

Perhaps there exists, in this painting by Velázquez, the representation as it were, of Classical[9] representation, and the definition of the space it opens up to us. And, indeed, representation undertakes to represent itself here in all its elements, with its images, the eyes to which it is offered, the faces it makes visible, the gestures that call it into being. But there, in the midst of this dispersion which it is simultaneously grouping together and spreading out before us, indicated compellingly from every side, is an essential void: the necessary disappearance of that which is its foundation — of the person it resembles and the person in whose eyes it is only a resemblance. This very subject — which is the same — has been elided. And representation, freed finally from the relation that was impeding it, can offer itself as representation in its pure form.

[9]*Classical* is Foucault's term for the *épistème* associated with the early modern period. [Ed.]

Pierre Bourdieu

b. 1930

It is no surprise that academics should find interesting the man who attempted to demystify their own mysterious behaviors and affiliations, applying a mordant Marxist sociology to the culture of culture. Pierre Bourdieu was born in Denguin, France, and educated at the elite École Normale Superieure where he took his Agrégé in philosophy in 1954. Bourdieu taught philosophy in the provincial lycée at Moulins, then accepted a position at the University of Algiers in the closing days of French colonial possession. He moved back to Paris in 1960, becoming director of studies at the École des Hautes Études in 1964 and professor of sociology at the Collège de France in 1982. Bourdieu's many works include Outline of a Theory of Practice *(1977),* Reproduction in Education, Society and Culture *(1977; revised 1990),* Distinction: A Social Critique of the Judgement of Taste *(1987),* Homo Academicus *(1988),* The Logic of Practice *(1990),* Language and Symbolic Power *(1991),* The Field of Cultural Production: Essays on Art and Literature *(1993),* Free Exchange *(1995), and* The Rules of Art: Genesis and Structure of the Literary Field *(1995). Bourdieu has himself been analyzed in* Bourdieu: Critical Perspectives, *edited by Craig Calhoun, Edward LiPuma, and Moishe Postone (1993). "The Market of Symbolic Goods" was originally published in French as "Le Marché des biens symboliques" in* L'Année sociologique *22 (1971): 49–126. The present translation first appeared in* Poetics *14 (1985): 13–44.*

The Market of Symbolic Goods

Theories and schools, like microbes and globules, devour each other and, through their struggle, ensure the continuity of life.

— M. PROUST, *Sodom and Gomorrah*

1. THE LOGIC OF THE PROCESS OF AUTONOMIZATION

Intellectual and artistic life was dominated by external sources of legitimacy throughout the Middle Ages. For part of the Renaissance and, in the case of French court-life, throughout the classical age, it has progressively freed itself from aristocratic and ecclesiastical tutelage.

This process is correlated with the constant growth of a public of potential consumers, of increasing social diversity, which guarantee the producers of symbolic goods minimal conditions of economic independence and, also, a competing principle of legitimacy. It is also correlated with the constitution of an ever growing, ever more diversified corps of producers and purveyors of symbolic goods, who tend to reject all constraints apart from technical imperatives and credentials. Finally, it is correlated with the multiplication of authorities having the power to consecrate but placed in a situation of competition for cultural legitimacy: Not only academies and salons, but also institutions for diffusion, such as publishers and theatrical impresarios, whose selective operations are invested with a truly cultural legitimacy even if they are subordinated to economic and social constraints.[1]

The autonomization of intellectual and artistic production is thus correlative with the constitution of a socially distinguishable category of professional artists or intellectuals. They are less inclined to recognize rules other than the specifically intellectual or artistic traditions handed down by their predecessors. They are increasingly in a position to liberate their products from all social servitude, whether the moral censure and aesthetic programs of a proselytizing church, or the academic controls of directives of political power, inclined to regard art as an instrument of propaganda. This process of autonomization is comparable to those in other realms. Thus, as Engels wrote to Conrad Schmidt, the appearance of law as such, i.e., as an "autonomous field," is correlated with a division of labor that led to the constitution of a body of professional jurists. Max Weber similarly notes in *Wirtschaft und Gesellschaft*,[2] the "rationalization" of religion owes its own "auto-normativity" — relatively independent of economic factors — to the fact that it rests on the development of a priestly corps with its own interests.

The process leading to the development of art *as art* is also correlated with the transformed relations between artists and non-artists and hence, with other artists. This transformation leads to the establishment of a relatively autonomous artistic field and to a fresh definition of the artist's function as well as that of his art. Artistic development toward autonomy progressed at different rates, according to the society and field of artistic life in question. It began in quattrocento Florence, with the affirmation of a truly artistic legitimacy, i.e. the right of artists to legislate within their own sphere — that of form and style

Translated by Rupert Swyer.

[1]"Historically regarded," observes Schücking, "the publisher begins to play a part at the stage at which the patron disappears, in the eighteenth century." (L. L. Schücking, *The Sociology of Literary Taste,* trans. E. W. Dickes [London: Routledge and Kegan Paul, 1966], pp. 50–51.) (With a transition period, in which the publisher was dependent on subscriptions, which in turn largely depended on relations between authors and their patrons.) There is no uncertainty about this among the poets. And indeed such publishing firms such as Dodsley in England or Cotta in Germany gradually become a source of authority. Schücking shows, similarly, that the influence of theater managers *(Dramaturgs)* can be even greater where, as in the case of Otto Brahm, "an individual may help to determine the general trend of taste" of an entire epoch through his choices (Schücking, p. 52). [Au.]

[2]*Economy and Society* (1921); also known as "A Theory of Social and Economic Behavior" in the translation by Talcott Parsons. [Ed.]

— free from subordination to religious or political interests. It was interrupted for two centuries under the influence of absolute monarchy and — with the Counter Reformation — of the Church; both were eager to procure artists a social position and function distinct from the manual labourers, yet not integrated into the ruling class.

This movement toward artistic autonomy accelerated abruptly with the industrial revolution and the Romantic reaction. The development of a veritable cultural industry and, in particular, the relationship which grew up between the daily press and literature, encouraging the mass production of works produced by quasi-industrial methods — such as the serialized story (or, in other fields, melodrama and vaudeville) — coincides with the extension of the public, resulting from the expansion of primary education, which turned new classes (including women) into consumers of culture.[3] The development of the system of cultural production is accompanied by a process of differentiation generated by the diversity of the publics at which the different categories of producers aim their products. Symbolic goods are a two-faced reality, a commodity and a symbolic object: Their specifically cultural value and their commercial value remain relatively independent although the economic sanction may come to reinforce their cultural consecration.[4]

By an apparent paradox, as the art market began to develop, writers and artists found themselves able to affirm the irreducibility of the work of art to the status of a simple article of merchandise and, at the same time, the singularity of the intellectual and artistic condition. The process of differentiation among fields of practice produces conditions favorable to the construction of "pure" theories (of economics, politics, law, art, etc.) which reproduce the prior differentiation of the social structures in the initial abstraction by which they are constituted.[5] The emergence of the work of art as a commodity, and the appearance of a distinct category of producers of symbolic goods specifically destined for the market, to some extent prepared the ground for a pure theory of art, that is, of art as art. It did so by dissociating art-as-commodity from art-as-pure-symbolism and intended for purely symbolic appropriation.

The end of dependence on a patron or collector and, more generally, the ending of the dependence upon direct commissions, with the development of an impersonal market, tend to increase the liberty of writers and artists. They can hardly fail to notice, however, that this liberty is purely formal; it constitutes no more than the condition of their submission to the laws of the market of symbolic goods, that is, to a form of demand which necessarily lags behind the supply of the commodity (in this case, the work of art). They are reminded of this demand through the sales figures and other forms of pressure, explicit or diffuse, exercised by publishers, theater managers, art-dealers. It follows that those "inventions" of Romanticism — the representation of culture as a kind of superior reality, irreducible to the vulgar demands of economics, and the ideology of free, disinterested "creation" founded on the spontaneity of innate inspiration — appear to be just so many reactions to the pressures of an anonymous market. It is significant that the appearance of an anonymous "bourgeois" public, and the irruption of methods borrowed from the economic order coincide with the rejection of bourgeois aesthetics and with the methodical at-

[3]Thus, Ian Watt, in *The Rise of the Novel* (Harmondsworth: Penguin Books, 1957), gives a good description of the correlative transformation of the modes of literary reception and production respectively, conferring its most specific characteristics on the novel and in particular the appearance of rapid, superficial, easily forgotten reading, as well as rapid and prolix writing, linked with the extension of the public. [Au.]

[4]The adjective "cultural" will be used from now on, as shorthand for "intellectual, artistic and scientific" (e.g. cultural consecration, legitimacy, production, value, etc.). [Au.]

[5]At a time when the influence of linguistic structuralism is leading some sociologists towards a pure theory of sociology, it would undoubtedly be useful to enrich the *sociology of pure theory,* sketched here, and to analyze the social conditions of the appearance of theories such as those of Kelsen, de Saussure or Walras, and of the formal and immanent science of art such as that proposed by Wölfflin. In this last case, one can see clearly that the intention itself of extracting the formal properties of all possible artistic expression assumed that the process of autonomization and purification of the work of art and of artistic perception had already been effected. [Au.]

tempt to distinguish the artist and the intellectual from other commoners by positing the unique products of "creative genius" against interchangeable products, utterly and completely reducible to their commodity value. Concomitantly, the absolute autonomy of the "creator" is affirmed, as is his claim to recognize as recipient of his art none but an *alter ego* — another "creator" — whose understanding of works of art presupposes an identical "creative" disposition.

2. THE STRUCTURE AND FUNCTIONING OF THE FIELD OF RESTRICTED PRODUCTION

The system of production and circulation of symbolic goods is defined as the system of objective relations among different institutions, functionally defined by their role in the division of labor of production, reproduction and diffusion of symbolic goods. The field of production per se owes its own structure to the opposition between the *field of restricted production* as a system producing cultural goods objectively destined for a public of producers of cultural goods, and the *field of large-scale cultural production,* specifically organized with a view to the production of cultural goods destined for non-producers of cultural goods, "the public at large."

In contrast to the field of large-scale cultural production, which submits to the laws of competition for the conquest of the largest possible market, the field of restricted production tends to develop its own criteria for the evaluation of its products, thus achieving the truly cultural recognition accorded by the peer group whose members are both privileged clients and competitors. The field of restricted production can only become a system objectively producing for producers by breaking with non-culture-producing sections of the dominant class. This rupture could only be the inverse image, in the cultural sphere, of the relations that develop between the intellectual and the dominating sections of the dominant class in the economic and political sphere. From 1830 literary society isolated itself in an aura of indifference and rejection towards the buying and reading public, i.e. towards the "bourgeois." By an effect of circular causality, separation and isolation engender further separation and isolation, and cultural production develops a dynamic autonomy.

Freed from the censorship and auto-censorship consequent on direct confrontation with a public foreign to the profession, and encountering within the corps of producers itself a public at once of critics and accomplices, it tends to obey its own logic, that of the continual outbidding inherent to the dialectic of cultural distinction.

The autonomy of a field of restricted production can be measured by its power to define its own criteria for the production and evaluation of its products. This implies translation of all external determinations in conformity with its own principles of functioning. Thus, the more cultural producers form a closed field of competition for cultural legitimacy, the more the internal demarcations appear irreducible to any external factors of economic, political or social differentiation.[6]

It is significant that the progress of the field of restricted production towards autonomy is marked by an increasingly distinct tendency of criticism to devote itself to the task, not of producing the instruments of appropriation — the more imperatively demanded by a work the further it separates itself from the public — but to provide a "creative" interpretation for the benefit of the "creators." And so, tiny "mutual admiration societies" grew up, closed in upon their own esotericism, as, simultaneously, signs of a new solidarity between artist and critic emerged. This

[6]Here, as elsewhere, the laws objectively governing social relations tend to constitute themselves as norms that are explicitly professed and assumed. In this way, as the field's autonomy grows, or as one moves towards the most autonomous sectors of the field, the direct introduction of external powers increasingly attracts disapproval; as the members of autonomous sectors consider such an introduction as a dereliction, they tend to sanction it by the symbolic exclusion of the guilty. This is shown, for instance, by the discredit attaching to any mode of thought which is suspected of reintroducing the total, brutal classificatory principles of a political order into intellectual life; and it is as if the field exercised its autonomy to the maximum, in order to render unknowable the external principles of opposition (especially the political ones) or, at least intellectually to "overdetermine" them by subordinating them to specifically intellectual principles. [Au.]

new criticism, no longer feeling itself qualified to formulate peremptory verdicts, placed itself unconditionally at the service of the artist. It attempted scrupulously to decipher his intentions, while excluding the public of non-producers from the entire business, by attesting, through its "inspired" readings, the intelligibility of works which were bound to remain unintelligible to those not sufficiently integrated into the producers' field.[7] Intellectuals and artists always look suspiciously — though not without a certain fascination — at dazzlingly successful works and authors, sometimes to the extent of seeing worldly failure as a guarantee of salvation in the hereafter: Among other reasons the interference of the "general public" is such that it threatens the field's claims to a monopoly of cultural consecration. It follows that the gulf between the hierarchy of producers dependent on "public success" (measured by volume of sales or fame outside the body of producers) and the hierarchy dependent upon recognition within the peer competitor group undoubtedly constitute the best indicator of the autonomy of the field of restricted production.

No one has ever completely extracted all the implications of the fact that the writer, the artist, or even the scientist writes not only for a public, but for a public of equals who are also competitors. Few people depend, as much as artists and intellectuals do, for their self image upon the image others, and particularly other writers and artists, have of them.

"There are," writes Jean-Paul Sartre, "qualities that we acquire uniquely through the judgments of others."[8] This is especially so for the quality of a writer, artist or scientist, which is so difficult to define because it exists only in, and through, the circular relations of reciprocal recognition among peers.[9] Any act of cultural production implies an affirmation of its claim to cultural legitimacy:[10] When different producers confront each other, it is still in the name of their claims to orthodoxy or, in Max Weber's terms, to the legitimate and monopolized use of a certain class of symbolic goods; when they are recognized, it is their claim to orthodoxy that is being recognized. As witnessed by the fact that oppositions express themselves in terms of reciprocal excommunication, the field of restricted production can never be dominated by one orthodoxy without continuously being dominated by the general question of orthodoxy itself, that is by the question of the criteria defining the legitimate exertion of a certain type of cultural practice. It follows that the degree of autonomy enjoyed by a field of restricted production is measurable by the degree to which it is capable of functioning as a specific market, generating a specifically cultural type of scarcity and value irreducible to the economic scarcity and value of the goods in question. To put it another way, the more the field is capable of functioning as a field of competition for cultural legitimacy, the more individual production must be orientated toward the search for culturally pertinent features endowed with value in the field's own economy. This confers properly cultural value on the producers by endowing them with marks of distinction (a specialty, a manner, a style) liable to be recognized as such within the historically available cultural taxonomies.

Consequently, it is a structural law, and not a fault in nature, that draws intellectuals and artists into the dialectic of cultural distinction — often confused with an all-out quest for any difference

[7]"As for criticism, it hides under big words the explanations it no longer knows how to furnish. Remembering Albert Wolff, Bourde, Brunetière or France, the critic, for fear of failing, like his predecessors, to recognize artists of genius, no longer judges at all" (J. Lethève, *Impressionistes et symbolistes devant la presse* [Paris: Armand Colin, 1959], p. 276.) [Au.]

[8]Jean-Paul Sartre, *Qu'est-ce que la littérature?* (Paris: Gallimard, 1948), p. 98. [Au.]

[9]In this sense, the intellectual field represents the almost complete model of a social universe knowing no principles of differentiation or hierarchization other than specifically symbolic distinctions. [Au.]

[10]It is the same, at least objectively (in the sense that no one is supposed to be ignorant of the cultural law), with any act of consumption which finds itself objectively within the field of application of the rules governing cultural practices with claims to legitimacy. [Au.]

that might raise them out of anonymity and insignificance.[11] The same law also imposes limits within which the quest may be carried on legitimately. The brutality with which a strongly integrated intellectual or artistic community condemns any unorthodox attempt at distinction bears witness to the fact that the community can affirm the autonomy of the specifically cultural order only if it controls the dialectic of cultural distinction, continually liable to degenerate into an anomic quest for difference at any price.

It follows from all that has just been said, that the principles of differentiation regarded as most legitimate by an autonomous field are those which most completely express the specificity of a determinate type of practice. In the field of art, for example, stylistic and technical principles tend to become the privileged subject of debate among producers (or their interpreters). Apart from laying bare the desire to exclude those artists suspected of submitting to external demands, the affirmation of the primacy of the mode of representation over the object of representation is the most specific expression of the field's claim to wield and to impose the principles of a properly cultural legitimacy regarding both the production and the reception of an artwork.[12] Affirming the primacy of the saying over the thing said, sacrificing the "subject" to the manner in which it is treated, constraining language in order to draw attention to language, all this comes down to an affirmation of the specificity and the irreplaceability of the product and producer. Delacroix said, aptly, "All subjects become good through the merits of their author. Oh! young artist, do you seek a subject? Everything is a subject; the subject is you yourself, your impression, your emotions before nature. You must look within yourself, and not around you."[13] The true subject of the work of art is nothing other than the specifically artistic manner in which the artist grasps the world, those infallible signs of his mastery of his art. Stylistic principles, in becoming the dominant subject of controversy among producers, are ever more rigorously perfected and fulfilled in works of art. At the same time, they are ever more systematically affirmed in the theoretical discourse, accompanying confrontation. Because the logic of cultural distinction leads producers to develop original modes of expression, the different types of restricted production (painting, music, novels, theater, poetry, etc.) are destined to fulfill themselves in their most specific aspects — those least reducible to any other form of expression.

The circularity of the relations of cultural production and consumption resulting from the objectively closed nature of the field of restricted production, enables the development of symbolic

[11]Thus Proudhon, all of whose aesthetic writings clearly express the petit-bourgeois representation of art and the artist, imputes the process of differentiation generated from the intellectual field's internal logic to a cynical choice on the part of artists: "On the one hand, artists will do anything, because everything is indifferent to them; on the other, they become infinitely specialized. Delivered up to themselves, without a guiding light, without compass, obedient to an inappropriately applied industrial law, they class themselves into genera and species, firstly according to the nature of commissions, and subsequently according to the method distinguishing them. Thus, there are church painters, historical painters, painters of battles, genre painters — that is, of anecdotes and comedy, portrait painters, landscape painters, animal painters, marine artists, painters of Venus, fantasy painters. This one cultivates the nude, another cloth. Then, each of them labors to distinguish himself by one of the competing methods of execution. One of them applies himself to drawing, the other to color; this one cares for composition, that one for perspective, yet another for costume or local color; this one shines through sentiment, another through the idealism or the realism of his figures; still another makes up for the nullity of his subjects by the finesse of his details. Each one labors to develop his trick, his style, his manner and, with the help of fashion, reputations are made and unmade." Proudhon, *Contradictions économiques* (Paris: Rivière, 1846), p. 271. [Au.] Pierre-Joseph Proudhon (1809–1865) was a French utopian socialist. [Ed.]

[12]The emergence of the theory of art which, rejecting the classical conception of artistic production as the simple execution of a pre-existent internal model, turns artistic "creation" into a sort of apparition that was unforeseeable for the artist himself — inspiration, genius, etc. — undoubtedly assumed the completion of the transformation of the social relations of production which, liberating artistic production from the directly and explicitly formulated order, permitted the conception of artistic labor as autonomous "creation," and no longer as mere execution. [Au.]

[13]Eugène Delacroix, *Oeuvres littéraires,* Vol. 1 (Paris: Crès, 1923), p. 76. [Au.] Delacroix (1798–1863) was a French painter and exponent of Romanticism. [Ed.]

production to take on the form of an almost reflexive history: The incessant clarification of the foundations of his work provoked by criticism or the work of others determines a decisive transformation of the relation between the producer and his work, which reacts, in turn, on the work itself.

Few works do not bear within them the imprint of the system of positions in relation to which their originality is defined; few works do not contain indications of the manner in which the author conceived the novelty of his undertaking or of what, in his own eyes, distinguished it from his contemporaries and competitors. The objectification achieved by criticism which elucidates the meaning inscribed in a work, instead of subjecting it to normative judgments, tends to play a determining role in this process by stressing the efforts of artists and writers to realize their idiosyncrasy. The parallel variations in critical interpretation, in the producer's discourse, and even in the structure of the work itself, bear witness to the recognition of critical discourse by the producer — both because he feels himself to be recognized through it, and because he recognizes himself within it. The public meaning of a work in relation to which the author must define himself, originates in the process of circulation and consumption, dominated by the objective relations between the institutions and agents implicated in the process. The social relations which produce this public meaning are determined by the relative position these agents occupy in the structure of the field of restricted production. These relations, e.g. between author and publisher, publisher and critic, author and critic, are revealed as the ensemble of relations attendant on the "publication" of the work, that is, its becoming a public object. In each of these relations, each of these agents engages not only his own image of other factors in the relationship (consecrated or exorcised author, avant-garde or traditional publisher, etc.) which depends on his relative position within the field, but also his image of the other factor's image of himself, i.e. of the social definition of his objective position in the field.

To appreciate the gulf separating experimental art, which originates in the field's own internal dialectic, from popular art forms, one might consider the evolutionary logic of literary language use. As this restricted language is produced in accordance with social relations, whose dominant feature is the quest for distinction, its use obeys what one might term "the gratuitousness principle." Its manipulation demands the almost reflexive knowledge of schemes of expression which are transmitted by an education explicitly aimed at inculcating the allegedly appropriate categories.

"Pure" poetry appears as the methodical application of a system of explicit principles which were at work, though only in a diffuse manner, in earlier writings. Its most specific effects, for example, derive from games of suspense and surprise, from the concerted betrayal of expectations, and from the gratifying frustration provoked by archaism, preciosity, lexicological or syntactic dissonances, the destruction of stereotyped sounds or meaning sequences, ready-made formulae, *idées reçues*[14] and commonplaces. The recent history of music, whose evolution consists in the increasingly professionalized search for technical solutions to fundamentally technical problems, appears to be the culmination of a process of refinement which began the moment popular music became subject to the learned manipulation of professionals. But probably nowhere is this dynamic model of a field tending to closure more completely fulfilled than in the history of painting. Having banished all narrative content with impressionism and recognizing only specifically pictorial principles, painting progressively repudiated all traces of naturalism and sensual hedonism. Painting was thus set on the road to an explicit employment of the most characteristically pictorial principles of painting, which was tantamount to the questioning of these principles and, hence, of painting itself.[15]

One needs only compare the functional logic of the field of restricted production with the laws

[14]Generally accepted opinions. [Ed.]

[15]It can be seen that the history leading up to what has been called a "denovelization" of the novel obeys the same type of logic. [Au.]

governing both the circulation of symbolic goods and the production of the consumers to perceive that such an autonomously developing field, making no reference to external demands, tends to nullify the conditions for its acceptance outside the field. To the extent that its products require extremely scarce instruments of appropriation, they are bound to precede their market or to have no clients at all, apart from producers themselves. Consequently they tend to fulfill socially distinctive functions, at first, in conflicts between sections of the dominant class, and, eventually, in relations among social classes. By an effect of circular causality, the structural gap between supply and demand contributes to the artists' determination to steep themselves in the search for "originality" (with its concomitant ideology of the misunderstood genius). This comes about, as Arnold Hauser has suggested,[16] by placing them in difficult economic circumstances, and, above all, by effectively ensuring the incommensurability of the specifically cultural value and economic value in a work.

3. THE FIELD OF INSTITUTIONS OF REPRODUCTION AND CONSECRATION

Works produced by the field of restricted production are "pure," "abstract" and "esoteric." They are "pure" because they demand of the receiver a specifically aesthetic disposition in conformity with the principles of their production. They are "abstract" because they call for a multiplicity of specific approaches, in contrast with the undifferentiated art of primitive societies which is unified within an immediately accessible spectacle involving music, dance, theater, and song.[17] They are "esoteric" for all the above reasons and because their complex structure continually implies tacit reference to the entire history of previous structures. This is only accessible to those who possess practical or theoretical mastery of a refined code, of successive codes, and of the code of these codes.

So, while consumption in the field of large-scale cultural production is more or less independent of the educational level of consumers (which is quite understandable since this system tends to adjust to the level of demand), works of restricted art owe their specifically cultural rarity to the rarity of the instruments with which they may be deciphered. This rarity is a function of the unequal distribution of the conditions underlying the acquisition of the specifically aesthetic disposition and of the codes indispensable to the deciphering of works belonging to the field of restricted production.[18]

It follows that a complete definition of the mode of restricted production must include not only those institutions which ensure the production of competent consumers, but also those which produce agents capable of renewing it. Consequently, one cannot fully comprehend the functioning of the field of restricted production as a scene of competition for properly cultural consecration — i.e. legitimacy — and for the power to grant it unless one analyzes the relationships between the various institutions. These consist, on the one hand, of institutions which conserve the capital of symbolic goods, such as museums, for example; and, on the other hand, of institutions (such as the educational system)

[16]"As long as the opportunities on the art market remain favorable for the artist, the cultivation of individuality does not develop into a mania for originality — this does not happen until the age of mannerism, when new conditions on the art market create painful economic disturbances for the artist." (A. Hauser, *The Social History of Art,* Vol. II, trans. S. Godman [New York: Vintage, 1951], p. 71.) [Au.]

[17]Cf. J. Greenway, *Literature Among the Primitives* (Hartboro: Folklore Associates, 1964), p. 37. On primitive art as a total and multiple art, produced by the group as a whole and addressed to the group as a whole, see also Firth (R. Firth, *Elements of Social Organization* [Boston: Beacon Press, 1963], p. 155 ff.); Junod (H. Junod, *The Life of a South African Tribe* [London: Macmillan, 1927], p. 215); and Malinowski (B. Malinowski, *Myth in Primitive Psychology* [New York: W. W. Norton and Co., 1926], p. 31). On the transformation of the function and signification of the dance and festivals see Caro Baroja (1964). [Au.]

[18]For an analysis of the function of the educational system in the production of consumers endowed with a propensity and aptitude to consume learned works and in the reproduction of the unequal distribution of this propensity and this aptitude, and, hence, of the *differential rarity* and of the *distinctive value* of these works, see Bourdieu and Darbel (P. Bourdieu and A. Darbel, *L'amour de l'art: Les musées d'art européens et leur public* [Paris: Minuit, 1969]). [Au.]

which ensure the reproduction of agents imbued with the categories of action, expression, conception, imagination, perception, specific to the "cultivated disposition."[19]

Just as in the case of the system of reproduction, in particular the educational system, so the field of production and diffusion can only fully be understood if one treats it as a field of competition for the monopoly of the legitimate exercise of symbolic violence. Such a construction allows us to define the field of restricted production as the scene of competition for the power to grant cultural consecration. But we also see it as the system specifically designed to fulfill a consecration function as well as a system for reproducing producers of a determinate type of cultural goods, and the consumers capable of consuming them. All internal and external relations (including relations with their own work) that agents of production, reproduction and diffusion manage to establish are mediated by the structure of relations between members of various institutions claiming to exercise a specifically cultural authority. In a given space of time a hierarchy of relations is establishing itself between the different domains, the works and the agents having a varying amount of legitimizing authority. This hierarchy, which is in fact dynamic, expresses the objective relations between the producers of symbolic goods who work for either a restricted or unrestricted public and are consequently consecrated by differentially legitimized and legitimizing institutions. Thus it also includes the objective relations between producers and different agents of consecration authorities belonging to specific institutions such as academies, museums, learned societies and the educational system; by their symbolic sanctions, especially by practising a form of cooptation,[20] these authorities are consecrating a certain type of work and a certain type of cultivated man. These agents of consecration moreover belong to organisations which may not be fully institutionalized: Literary cenacles,[21] critical circles, salons, and small groups surrounding a famous author or associating with a publisher, a review or a literary or artistic magazine. Lastly, this hierarchy includes, of course, the objective relations between the various agents of legitimation. Both the function and the mode of functioning of the latter depend upon their position in the hierarchic structure of the system they constitute; that is, they depend on the scope and kind of authority — conservative or challenging — these agents exercise or pretend to exercise over the bulk of cultural producers and, via their critical judgments, over the public at large.

By defending the sphere of legitimate culture against competing, schismatic or heretical messages, which may provoke radical demands and heterodox practices among various publics, the system of conservation and cultural consecration fulfills a function homologous to that of the church. Sainte-Beuve, together with Auger, whom he quotes, quite naturally turns to religious metaphor to express the structurally determined logic of that legitimizing institution *par excellence,* the Académie Française:

> Once it comes to think of itself as an orthodox sanctuary (and it easily does so), the Académie needs some external heresy to combat. At that time, in 1817, in default of any other heresy, and the Romantics either not yet born or not having reached manhood, they attacked the followers and imitators of Abbé Delille (. . .). [Auger, in 1824] opened the

[19]The education system fulfills a culturally legitimizing function by reproducing, via the delimitation of what deserves to be conserved, transmitted and acquired, the distinction between the legitimate and the illegitimate way of dealing with legitimate works. The different sectors of the field of restricted production are very markedly distinguished by the degree to which they depend, for their reproduction, on generic institutions (such as the educational system), or on specific ones (such as the École des Beaux Arts, or the Conservatoire de Musique). Everything points to the fact that the proportion of contemporary producers having received an academic education is far smaller among painters (especially among the more avant-garde currents) than among musicians. [Au.]

[20]All forms of recognition, prizes, rewards and honors, election to an Academy, a university, a scientific committee, invitation to a congress or to a university, publication in a scientific review or by a consecrated publishing house, in anthologies, mentions in the work of contemporaries, in works on art history or the history of science, in encyclopedias and dictionaries, etc., are just so many forms of *cooptation,* whose value depends on the very position of the cooptants in the hierarchy of consecration. [Au.]

[21]Cliques. [Ed.]

session with a speech amounting to a declaration of war, and a formal denunciation of Romanticism: "A new literary schism," he said, "is appearing today." "Many men, brought up with a religious respect for ancient teachings, consecrated by countless masterpieces, are worried by and nervous of the projects of this emergent sect, and seem to wish to be reassured (. . .)." This speech had a great effect: it brought happiness and jubilation to the adversaries. That witty swashbuckler, Henri Beyle (Stendhal) in his pamphlets, was to repeat it gaily: "M. Auger said it, I'm a sectarian!" Obliged to receive M. Soumet that same year (25th November), M. Auger redoubled his anathemas against the Romantic dramatic form, "against that barabarian poetic they wish to praise," he said, and which violated, in every way, literary orthodoxy. Every sacramental word, *orthodoxy, sect, schism* was uttered, and he could not blame himself if the Académie did not transform itself into a synod or a council.[22]

The functions of reproduction and legitimization may, in accord with historical traditions, either be concentrated into a single institution, as was the case in the 17th century with the French Académie Royale de Peinture,[23] or divided among different institutions such as the educational system, the Académies, and official and semi-official institutions of diffusion (museums, theaters, operas, concert halls, etc.). To these may be added certain institutions which, though less widely recognized, are more narrowly expressive of the cultural producers, such as learned societies, literary circles, reviews or galleries; these are more inclined to reject the judgments of the canonical institutions the more intensely the cultural field asserts its autonomy.

However varied the relations among agents of preservation and consecration may be, the length of "the process of canonization," culminating in consecration, appears to vary in proportion to the degree that their authority is widely recognized and can be durably imposed. Competition for consecration, which is assumed and conferred by the power to consecrate, condemns those agents whose province is most limited to a state of perpetual emergency. Avant-garde critics fall into this category, haunted by the fear of compromising their authority as discoverers by overlooking some discovery, and thus obliged to enter into mutual attestations of charisma, making them into spokesmen and theoreticians and sometimes even publicists and impresarios for artists. Academies, and the corps of museum curators, both institutions claiming a monopoly over the consecration of contemporary producers, are obliged to combine tradition and tempered innovation. And the educational system, claiming a monopoly over the consecration of the past and over the production and consecration of cultural consumers, only posthumously accords that infallible mark of consecration, the elevation of works into "classics" by their inclusion in curricula.

Among those characteristics of the educational system liable to affect the structure of its relations with other elements of the system of production and circulation of symbolic goods, the most important is surely its extremely slow rate of evolution. This inertia, deriving from its function of cultural conservation, is pushed to the limit by the logic which allows it to wield a monopoly over its own reproduction. Thus, the educational system contributes to the maintenance of a disjunction between intellectual culture (involving categories of perception related to new cultural products), and scholastic culture: the lat-

[22]Saint-Beuve, "L'Académie Française," in *Paris-Guide, par les principaux écrivains et artistes de la France* (Paris: A. Lacroix, Verboeckhoven et Cie. T. I., 1867), pp. 96–97. [Au.]

[23]This Academy, which accumulated the monopoly of the consecration of creators, of the transmission of consecrated works and traditions and even of production and the control of production, wielded, at the time of Le Brun, "a sovereign and universal supremacy over the world of art. For him [Le Brun], everything stopped at these two points: prohibition from teaching elsewhere than in the Academy, prohibition from practicing without being of the Academy." (L. Vitet, *L'académie royal de peinture et de sculpture, étude historique.* [Paris: Michel Lévy, 1861], p. 134.) Thus, "this sovereign company (. . .) possessed, during a quarter of a century, the exclusive privilege of carrying out all painting and sculpture ordered by the state and alone to direct, from one end of the kingdom to the other, the teaching of drawing: in Paris, in its own schools, outside of Paris, in subordinate schools, branch academies founded by it, placed under its direction, subject to its surveillance. Never had such a unified and concentrated system been applied, anywhere, to the production of the beautiful" (Vitet, p. 176). [Au.] Charles le Brun (1619–1690), a French painter, organized the Académie in 1648 with the backing of the finance minister Colbert, and in 1660 founded the Gobelins as a site for the exclusive manufacture of all decorative works (furniture and porcelains as well as tapestries) intended for the royal palaces. [Ed.]

ter is "routinized" and rationalized by — and in view of — its being inculcated. This disjunction manifests itself notably in the distinct schemes of perception and appreciation involved by the two kinds of culture: The fact is that products emanating from the field of restricted production require other schemes than those already mastered by the "cultivated public."

As indicated, it is impossible to understand the peculiar characteristics of restricted culture without appreciating its profound dependence on the educational system, the indispensable means of its reproduction and growth. Among the transformations which occur, the quasi-systematization and theorizing imposed on the inculcated content are rather less evident than their concomitant effects, such as "routinization," and "neutralization."

The time-lag between cultural production and scholastic consecration is not the only opposition between the field of restricted production and the system of institutions burdened with cultural conservation and production of consumers. As the field of restricted production gains in autonomy, producers tend, as we have seen, to think of themselves as intellectuals or artists by divine right, as "creators," that is as *auctors*[24] "claiming authority by virtue of their charisma." They cannot but resist, moreover, the institutional authority which the educational system, as a consecratory institution, opposes to their competing claims. They feel exacerbated by that type of teacher, the *lector,*[25] who elucidates the works of others (as Gilbert de la Porrée had already pointed out), and whose own production owes much to the professional practice of its author and to the position he occupies within the system of production and circulation of symbolic goods. We are thus brought to the principle underlying the ambivalent relations between producers and scholastic authority.

If the denunciation of professional routine is to some extent consubstantial with prophetic ambition, even to the point where this may amount to official proof of one's charismatic qualifications, it is nonetheless true that producers cannot fail to pay attention to the judgments of university institutions. They cannot ignore the fact that it is these who will have the last word, and that ultimate consecration can only be accorded them by an authority whose legitimacy is challenged by their entire practice, their entire professional ideology. There are plenty of attacks upon the university which bear witness to the fact that their authors recognize the legitimacy of its verdicts sufficiently to reproach it for not having recognized them.

The relationship between the field of production and the educational system is both strengthened, in one sense, and undermined in another, by the action of social mechanisms tending to ensure a sort of pre-established harmony between positions and their occupants. These mechanisms orient very diverse personnel toward the obscure security of an intellectual functionary's career or toward the prestigious vicissitudes of independent artistic or intellectual enterprise. Their social origins, predominantly petit-bourgeois in the former case and bourgeois in the latter, dispose them to import very divergent ambitions into their activities, as though they were measured in advance for the available positions.[26] Before oversimplifying the opposition between petit-bourgeois institutional servants and the bohemians of the upper-bourgeoisie, two points should be made. First, whether they be free entrepreneurs or state employees, intellectuals and artists occupy a subservient position in the field of power. And second, while the rebellious audacity of the *auctor* may find its limits within the inherited ethics and politics of a bourgeois primary education, artists and especially professors coming from the "petite bourgeoisie" are most directly under the control of the state. The state, after all, has the power to orient intellectual production by means of subsidies, commissions, promotion, honorific posts, even decorations, all of which are for speaking or keeping silent, for compromise or abstention.

[24]Authors. [Ed.]

[25]Reader. [Ed.]

[26]The same systematic opposition can be seen in very different fields of artistic and intellectual activity; between researchers and teachers, for example, or between writers and teachers in higher education and, above all, between painters and musicians on the one hand, and teachers of drawing and music on the other. [Au.]

4. RELATIONS BETWEEN THE FIELD OF RESTRICTED PRODUCTION AND THE FIELD OF LARGE-SCALE PRODUCTION

Without analyzing the connections uniting the system of consecratory institutions with the producers for producers, a full definition of the relationship between the field of restricted production and the field of large-scale production would have been impossible. The field of large-scale production, whose submission to external demand is characterized by the subordinate position of cultural producers in relation to the controllers of production and diffusion media, principally obeys the imperatives of competition for conquest of the market. The structure of its socially neutralized product is the result of the economic and social conditions surrounding its production. *Middle-brow art* is aimed at a public frequently referred to as "average." Even when it is more specifically aimed at a determinate category of non-producers, it may nonetheless eventually reach a socially heterogeneous public. Such is the case with the bourgeois theater of the *belle-époque*,[27] which is nowadays broadcast on television.

It is legitimate to define middle-brow culture as the product of the system of large-scale production, because these works are entirely defined by their public. Thus, the very ambiguity of any definition of the "average public" or the "average viewer" very realistically designates the field of potential action which producers of this type of art and culture *explicitly* assign themselves, and which determines their technical and aesthetic choices.

The following remarks by a French television-writer, author of some twenty novels, recipient of the *Prix Interallié* and the *Grand prix du roman de l'Académie Française*, bears this out: "My sole ambition is *to be easily read by the widest possible public*. I never attempt a 'masterpiece,' and *I do not write for intellectuals;* I leave that to others. For me, a good book is one that grips you within the first three pages."[28] It follows that the most specific characteristics of middle-brow art, such as reliance on immediately accessible technical processes and aesthetic effects, or the systematic exclusion of all potentially controversial themes, or those liable to shock this or that section of the public, derive from the social conditions in which it is produced.

Middle-brow art is the product of a productive system dominated by the quest for investment profitability; this creates the need for the widest possible public. It cannot, moreover, content itself with seeking to intensify consumption within a determinate social class; it is obliged to orient itself toward a generalization of the social and cultural composition of this public. This means that the production of goods, even when they are aimed at a specific *statistical category* (the young, women, football fans, stamp collectors, etc.), must represent a kind of highest social denominator.[29] On the other hand, middle-brow art is most often the culmination of transactions and compromises among various categories of agents. These transactions occur not only between controllers of the means of production and cultural producers — who are more or less locked into the role of pure technicians — but also between different categories of producers themselves. The latter come to use their specific competences to guarantee a wide variety of cultural interests while simultaneously reactivating the self-censorship engendered by the vast industrial and bureaucratic organizations of cultural production through invocation of the "average spectator." In all fields of artistic life the same opposition between the two modes of production is to be observed, separated alike by the nature of the works produced as by the social composition of the publics to which they are offered. As Bertrand Poirot-Delpech (1970) observes, "Apart from drama critics, hardly anyone believes — or seems to believe — that the various spectacles demanding qualification by the word 'theater' still belong to a single and identical art form (. . .).

[27]France in the last third of the nineteenth century. [Ed.]

[28]Cf. *Télé-Sept-Jours*, nr. 547, October 1970, p. 45. [Au.]

[29]In this, the strategy of producers of average art is radically opposed to the spontaneous strategy of the institutions for the diffusion of restricted art who, as we can see in the case of museums, aim at intensifying the practice of the classes from whence consumers are recruited rather than at attracting new classes. [Au.]

The potential publics are so distinct; ideologies, modes of functioning, styles and actors on offer are so opposed, inimical even, that professional rules and solidarity have practically disappeared."[30]

> Consigned by the laws of profitability to "concentration" and to integration into world-wide "show-business" production circuits, the commercial theater in France survives today in three forms: "French (or English, etc.) versions of foreign shows supervised, distributed and, to some extent, organized by those responsible for the original show"; repeats of the most successful works for the traditional commercial theater and, finally, "intelligent comedy for the enlightened bourgeoisie." The same dualism, taking the form of downright cultural schism, exists, in Western Europe at least, in the musical sphere. Here the opposition between the artificially supported market for works of restricted scope and the market for commercial work, produced and distributed by the music-hall and recording industry, is far more brutal than elsewhere.

One should beware of seeing anything more than limiting parameter construction in the opposition between the two modes of production of symbolic goods, which can only be defined in terms of their relations with each other. Within a single universe one always finds the entire range of intermediaries between works produced with reference to the restricted market on the one hand, and works determined by a representation of the expectations of the widest possible public. The range might include avant-garde works reserved for a few initiates within the peer-group, avant-garde works on the road to consecration, works of "bourgeois art" aimed at the non-intellectual sections of the dominant class and often already consecrated by the most official of legitimizing institutions (the Academies), works of middle-brow art aimed at various "target publics" and involving, besides brand-name culture (with, for example, works crowned by the big literary prizes), imitation culture aimed at the rising petite bourgeoisie (popularizing literary or scientific works, for example), and mass-culture, that is, the ensemble of socially neutralized works.

In fact, the professional ideology of producers-for-producers establishes an opposition between creative liberty and the laws of the market, between works which create their public and works created by their public. This is undoubtedly a defense against the *disenchantment* produced by the progress of the division of labor, the establishment of various fields of action — each involving the explicitation of its peculiar functions — and the rational organization of technical means appertaining to these functions.

It is no mere chance that middle-brow art and art for art's sake are both produced by highly professionalized intellectuals and artists, and are both characterized by the same valorization of technique. In the one case this orients production toward the search for effect (understood both as effect produced on the public and as ingenious construction) and, in the other, it orients production toward the cult of form for its own sake. The latter orientation is an unprecedented affirmation of the most characteristic aspect of professionalism and thus an affirmation of the specificity and irreducibility of producers.

> This explains why certain works of middle-brow art may present formal characteristics predisposing them to enter into legitimate culture. The fact that producers of Westerns have to work within the very strict conventions of a heavily stereotyped genre leads them to demonstrate their highly professionalized technical virtuosity by continually referring back to previous solutions — assumed to be known — in the solutions they provide to canonical problems, and they are continually bordering on pastiche or parody of previous authors, against whom they measure themselves. A genre containing ever more references to the history of that genre calls for a second-degree reading, reserved for the initiate, who can only grasp the work's nuances and subtleties by relating it back to previous works. By introducing subtle breaks and fine variations, with regard to assumed expectations, the play of internal allusions (the same one that has always been practiced by lettered traditions) authorizes detached and distanced perception, quite as much as first-degree adherence, and calls for either erudite analysis or

[30]B. Poirot-Delpech, *Le Monde*, July 22nd, 1970. [Au.]

the aesthete's wink. "Intellectual" Westerns are the logical conclusion of these pure cinematographic language games which assume, among their authors, as much the cinephile's as the cineast's inclinations.[31]

More profoundly, middle-brow art, which is characterized by tried and proven techniques and an oscillation between plagiarism and parody most often linked with either indifference or conservatism, displays one of the great covert truths underlying the aestheticism of art for art's sake. The fact is that its fixation on technique draws pure art into a covenant with the dominant sections of the bourgeoisie. The latter hereby recognize the intellectual's and the artist's monopoly on the production of the work of art as an instrument of pleasure (and, secondarily as an instrument for the symbolic legitimization of economic or political power); in return, the artist is expected to avoid serious matters, namely social and political questions. The opposition between art for art's sake and middle-brow art which, on the ideological plane, becomes transmitted into an opposition between the idealism of devotion to art and the cynicism of submission to the market, should not hide the fact that the desire to oppose a specifically cultural legitimacy to the prerogatives of power and money, constitutes one more way of recognizing that business is business.

What is most important is that these two fields of production, as opposed as they are, coexist and that their products owe their very unequal symbolic and material values on the market to their unequal consecration which, in turn, stems from their very unequal power of distinction.[32] The various kinds of cultural competence encountered in a class-divided society derive their social value from the power of social discrimination, and from the specifically cultural rarity conferred on them by their position in the system of cultural competences; this system is more or less integrated according to the social formation in question, but it is always hierarchized. To be unaware of the fact that a dominant culture owes its main features and social functions — especially that of symbolically legitimizing a form of domination — to the fact that it is not perceived as such, in short, to ignore the *fact* of legitimacy is either to condemn oneself to a class-based ethnocentrism: This drives the defenders of restricted culture to ignore the material foundations of the symbolic domination of one culture by another. Or this ignorance implies a commitment to a populism which betrays a shameful recognition of the legitimacy of the dominant culture in an effort to rehabilitate middle-brow culture. This cultural relativism is accomplished by treating distinct but *objectively* hierarchized cultures in a class-divided society as if they were the cultures of such perfectly independent social formations as the Eskimos and the Fuegians.[33]

Fundamentally heteronomous, middle-brow culture is objectively condemned to define itself in relation to legitimate culture; this is so in the field of production as well as of consumption. Original experimentation entering the field of large-scale production almost always comes up against the breakdown in communication liable to arise from the use of codes inaccessible to the "mass public." Moreover, middle-brow art can-

[31]Bourdieu apparently distinguishes between the mere "cinephile," or lover of the movies as entertainment, and the true "cineast," a cultivated expert in film history, technique, and theory. [Ed.]

[32]The educational system very heavily contributes to the unification of the market in symbolic goods, and to the generalized imposition of the legitimacy of the dominant culture, not only by legitimizing the goods consumed by the dominant class, but by devaluing those transmitted by the dominated classes (and, also, regional traditions) and by tending, in consequence, to prohibit the constitution of cultural counter-legitimacies. [Au.]

[33]The attempt to gain rehabilitation leads those at the forefront of the revolt against the university's conservative traditions (as well as those of the Academies) to betray their recognition of academic legitimacy in the very discourse attempting to challenge it. One sociologist, for instance, argues that the leisure practices he intends to rehabilitate are genuinely cultural because they are "disinterested," hence reintroducing an academic, and mundane, definition of the cultivated relationship to culture and writes: "We think that certain works said, today, to be minor, in fact reveal qualities of the first order; it seems barely acceptable to place the entire repertoire of French songs on a low level, as does Shils with American songs. The works of Brassens, Jacques Brel and Léo Ferré, all of which are highly successful, are not just songs from a variety show. All three are also, quite rightly, considered as poets." [Au.]

not renew its techniques and themes without borrowing from high-brow art or, more frequently still, from the "bourgeois art" of a generation or so earlier. This includes "adopting" the more venerable themes or subjects, or those most amenable to the traditional laws of composition in the popular arts (the Manichean division of roles, for example). In this sense, the history of middle-brow art amounts to no more than that imposed by technical changes and the laws of competition.

But, however agents may dissimulate this, the hierarchical difference between the two productive systems is continually imposing itself. Indeed, the practices and ideologies of consumers are largely determined by the level of the goods they produce or consume in this hierarchy. The connoisseur can immediately discern, from such reference points as the work's genre, the radio station, the name of the theater, gallery or director, the order of legitimacy and the appropriate posture to be adopted in each case.

The opposition between legitimate and illegitimate, imposing itself in the field of symbolic goods with the same arbitrary necessity as the distinction between the sacred and the profane elsewhere, expresses the different social and cultural valuation of two modes of production: The one a field that is its own market, allied with an educational system which legitimizes it; the other a field of production organized as a function of external demand.

This opposition between the two markets, between producers-for-producers and producers-for-non-producers, entirely determines the representation writers and artists have of their profession and constitutes the taxonomic principle according to which they classify and hierarchize works (beginning with their own). Producers-for-producers have to overcome the contradiction in their relationship with their (limited) public through a transfigured representation of their social function. Whereas in the case of producers-for-non-producers the quasi-coincidence of their authentic representation and the objective truth of the writer's profession is either a fairly inevitable effect or a prior condition of the success with their specific public. Nothing could be further, for example, from the charismatic vision of the writer's "mission" than the image proposed by the successful writer previously cited: "Writing is a job like any other. Talent and imagination are not enough. Above all, discipline is required. It is better to force oneself to write two pages a day than ten pages once a week. There is one essential condition for this: One has to be in form, as a sportsman has to be in form to run a hundred meters or to play a football match."

It is unlikely that all writers and artists whose works are objectively addressed to the "mass public" have, at least at the outset of their career, quite so realistic and "disenchanted" an image of their function. Nonetheless, they can hardly avoid applying to themselves the objective image of their work received from the field. This image expresses the opposition between the two modes of production as objectively revealed in the social quality of their public ("intellectual" or "bourgeois," for example). The more a certain class of writers and artists are defined as beyond the bounds of the universe of legitimate art, the more they are inclined to defend the professional qualities of the worthy, entertaining technician, complete master of his technique and metier against the uncontrolled, disconcerting experiments of "intellectual" art.

There is no doubt, moreover, that the emergence of large collective production units in the fields of radio, television, cinema and journalism as well as in scientific research, and the concomitant decline of the intellectual artisan in favor of the salaried worker, entail a transformation of the relationship between the producer and his work. This will be reflected in his own representation of his position and function in the social structure, and, consequently, of the political and aesthetic ideologies he professes. Intellectual labor carried out collectively, within technically and socially differentiated production units, can no longer surround itself with the charismatic aura attaching to traditional independent production. The traditional cultural producer was a master of his means of production and invested only his *cultural* capital, which was likely to be perceived as a gift of grace. The demystification of intellectual and artistic activity consequent on the transformation of the social conditions of production particularly affects intellectuals and artists engaged in large units of cultural production (radio, television, journalism). These constitute a proletaroid intelligentsia forced to experience the contradiction between aesthetic and political standpoints stemming from its inferior position in the field of production and the objectively conservative functions of its activity.

5. POSITIONS AND POSITION-TAKINGS

The relationship maintained by producers of symbolic goods with other producers, with the significations available within the cultural field and, consequently, with their own work, depends very directly upon the position they occupy within the field of production and circulation of symbolic goods. This, in turn, is related to the specifically cultural hierarchy of degrees of consecration. Such a position implies an objective definition of their practice and of the products resulting from it. Whether they like it or not, whether they know it or not, this definition imposes itself on them as a fact, determining their ideology and their practice, and its potency manifests itself never so clearly as in conduct aimed at transgressing it. For example, it is the ensemble of determinations inscribed in their position which inclines professional jazz or film critics to issue very divergent and incompatible judgments destined to reach only restricted cliques of producers and little sects of devotees. These critics tend to ape the learned, sententious tone, and the cult of erudition characterizing academic criticism, and to seek theoretical, political or aesthetic security in the obscurity of a borrowed language.[34]

As distinct from a solidly legitimate activity, an activity on the way to legitimization continually confronts its practitioners with the question of its own legitimacy. In this way, photography — that middle-brow art — condemns its practitioners to create a substitute for the sense of cultural legitimacy which is given to the priests of all the legitimate arts. More generally, all those marginal cultural producers whose position obliges them to conquer the cultural legitimacy unquestioningly accorded to the consecrated professions expose themselves to redoubled suspicion by the efforts they can hardly avoid making to challenge its principles. The ambivalent aggression they frequently display toward consecratory institutions, especially the educational system, without being able to offer a counter-legitimacy, bears witness to their desire for recognition and, consequently, to the recognition they accord to the educational system.

All relations that a determinate category of intellectuals or artists may establish with any and all external social factors — whether economic (e.g. publishers, dealers), political or cultural (consecrating authorities such as Academies) — are mediated by the structure of the field. Thus, they depend upon the position occupied by the category in question within the hierarchy of cultural legitimacy.

The sociology of intellectual and artistic production thus acquires its specific object in constructing the relatively autonomous system of relations of production and circulation of symbolic goods. In doing this, it acquires the possibility of grasping the positional properties that any category of agents of cultural production or diffusion owes to its place within the structure of the field. Consequently, it acquires the capacity to explain those characteristics which products, as position-takings, owe to the *position* of their producers within the system of social relations of production and circulation and to the corresponding position which they occupy within the system of *cultural positions objectively possible* within a given state of the field of production and circulation.

The position-takings constitutive of the cultural field do not all suggest themselves with the same probability to those occupying at a given moment a determinate position in this field. Conversely, a particular class of cultural position-takings is attached as a potentiality to each of the positions in the field of production and circula-

[34]If these analyses can equally obviously be applied to certain categories of avant-garde art critics, this is because the position of the least consecrated agents of a more consecrated field may present certain analogies with the position of the most consecrated agents of a less consecrated field. [Au.]

tion (that is, a particular bundle of problems and structures of resolution, themes and procedures, aesthetic and political positions, etc.). These can only be defined differentially, that is, in relation to the other constitutive cultural positions in the cultural field under consideration. "Were I as glorious as Paul Bourget," Arthur Craven used to say, "I'd present myself nightly in music-hall revues in nothing but a G-string, and I guarantee you I'd make a bundle."[35] This attempt to turn literary glory into a profitable undertaking only appears at first sight to be self-destructive and comical because it assumes a desacralized and desacralizing relationship with literary authority. And such a stance would be inconceivable for anyone other than a marginal artist, knowing and recognizing the principles of cultural legitimacy well enough to be able to place himself outside of the cultural law.[36] There is no position within the field of cultural production that does not call for a determinate type of position-taking *(prise de position)* and which does not exclude, simultaneously, an entire gamut of abstractly possible position-takings. This does not require that possible or excluded position-takings be explicitly prescribed or prohibited. But one should beware of taking as the basis of all practice the strategies half-consciously elaborated in reference to a never more than partial consciousness of structures. In this connection one might think, for example, of the knowledge of the present and future structure of the labor market that is mobilized at the moment of a change in orientation.

All relations among agents and institutions of diffusion or consecration are mediated by the field's structure. To the extent that the ever-ambiguous marks of recognition owe their specific form to the objective relations (perceived and interpreted as they are in accordance with the unconscious schemes of the habitus) they contribute to form the *subjective* representation which agents have of the *social* representation of their position within the hierarchy of consecrations. And this semi-conscious representation itself constitutes one of the mediations through which, by reference to the social representation of possible, probable or impossible position-takings the system of relatively unconscious strategies of the occupants of a given class of positions is defined.

It would be vain to claim to assess from among the determinants of practices, the impact of durable, generalized and transposable dispositions, the impact of the perception of this situation and of the intentional or semi-intentional strategies which arise in response to it. The least conscious dispositions, such as those constituting the primary class habitus, are themselves constituted through the internalization of an objectively selected system of signs, indices and sanctions. And these are nothing but the materialization, within objects, words or conducts, of a particular kind of objective structure. Such dispositions remain the basis upon which all the signs and indices characterizing very varied situations are selected and interpreted.

In order to gain some idea of the complex relations between unconscious dispositions and the experiences which they structure or, what amounts to the same, between the unconscious strategies engendered by habitus and strategies consciously produced in response to a situation designed in accordance with the schemes of the habitus, it will be necessary to analyze an example.

The manuscripts a publisher receives are the product of a kind of pre-selection by the authors themselves according to their representation of the publisher who is occupying a specific posi-

[35]Arthur Craven, quoted by A. Breton in *Anthologie de l'humour noir* (Paris: J. J. Pauvert, 1966), p. 324. [Au.]

[36]More generally, if the occupants of a determinate position in the social structure only rarely do what the occupants of a different position think they ought to do ("if I was in his place . . ."), it is because the latter project the position-takings inscribed into their own position into a position which excludes them. The theory of relations between positions and position-takings reveals the basis of all those errors of perspective, to which all attempts at abolishing the differences associated with differences in position by means of a simple imaginary projection, or by an effort of "comprehension" (at the back of which always lies the principle of "putting oneself in someone else's place"), or again, attempts at transforming the objective relations between agents by transforming the representations they have of these relations, are inevitably exposed. [Au.]

tion within the space of publishers. The authors' representation of their publisher which may have oriented their production is itself a function of the objective relationship between the positions authors and publishers occupy in the field. The manuscripts are, moreover, colored from the first by a series of determinations (e.g. "interesting, but not very commercial," or "not very commercial, but interesting"), stemming quasi-mechanically from the relationship between the author's position in the field of production (unknown young author, consecrated author, house author, etc.) and the publisher's position within the system of production and circulation ("commercial" publisher, consecrated or avant-garde). They usually bear the marks of the intermediary whereby they came to the publisher (editor of a series, reader, "house author," etc.) and whose authority, once again, is a function of respective positions in the field. Because subjective intentions and unconscious dispositions contribute to the effectiveness of the objective structures to which they are adjusted, their interlacing tends to guide each agent to his "natural niche" in the structure of the field. It will be understood, moreover, that publisher and author can only experience and interpret the pre-established harmony achieved and revealed by their meeting as a miracle of predestination: "Are you happy to be published by Editions de Minuit?"[37] "If I had followed my instincts, I would have gone there straight away but . . . I didn't dare; I thought they were too good for me . . . So I first sent my manuscript to Publisher *X*. What I just said about *X* isn't very kind! They refused my book, and so I took it to Minuit anyway." "How do you get on with the publisher?" "He began by telling me a lot of things I hoped had not shown, everything concerning time, coincidences."[38]

The publisher's image of his "vocation" combines the aesthetic relativism of the discoverer, conscious of having no other principle than that of defiance of all canonic principles, with the most complete faith in an absolute kind of "flair." This ultimate and often indefinable principle behind his choices finds itself continually strengthened and confirmed by his perception of the selective choices of authors and by the representations authors, critics, the public and other publishers have of his function within the division of intellectual labor.

The critic's situation is hardly any different: The works which he receives have undergone a process of pre-selection. They bear a supplementary mark, that of the publisher (and, sometimes, that of the author of a preface, an author or another critic). The value of this mark is a function, once more, of the structure of objective relations between the respective positions of author, publisher and critic. It is also affected by the relationship of the critic to the predominant taxonomies in the critical world or in the field of restricted production (for example, the *nouveau roman,*[39] "objectal literature," etc.).

> Apart from the opening pages, which seem to be a more or less voluntary pastiche of the *nouveau roman, L'Auberge espagnole* tells a fantastic, though perfectly clear, story, whose development obeys the logic of dreams rather than reality.[40]

So the critic, suspecting the young novelist of having entered the hall of mirrors, enters there himself by describing what he takes for a reflection of the *nouveau roman.* Schönberg describes the same type of effect: "On the occasion of a concert given by my pupils, a critic with a particularly fine ear defined a piece for string quartet whose harmony — as can be proved — was only a very slight development of Schubert's, as a product bearing signs of my influence." Even if such errors of identification are not rare especially among the conservative critics, they may also bring profit to the "innovators": On account of his position, a critic may find himself predisposed in favor of all kinds of avant-garde; accordingly he may act as an initiate, communicat-

[37]Popular publishing series of some prestige, equivalent to Penguin in Great Britain and Vintage in the United States. [Ed.]

[38]*La Quinzaine Littéraire,* September 15, 1966. [Au.]

[39]Term for difficult, self-reflexive postmodern fiction by writers that included Michel Butor, Marguerite Duras, and Alain Robbe-Grillet. [Ed.]

[40]E. Lalou, *L'Express,* October 26, 1966. [Au.]

ing the deciphered revelation back to the artist from whom he received it. The artist, in return, confirms the critic in his vocation, that of privileged interpreter, by confirming the accuracy of his decipherment.[41]

On account of the specific nature of his interests, and of the structural ambiguity of his position as a trader objectively invested with some power of cultural consecration, the publisher is more strongly inclined than the other agents of production and diffusion to take the regularities objectively governing relations between agents into account in his conscious strategies. The selective discourse which he engages with the critic, who has been selected not merely because of his influence but also because of the affinities he may have with the work, and which may even go to the length of declared allegiance to the publisher and his entire list of publications, or to a certain category of authors, is an extremely subtle mixture, in which his own idea of the work combines with his idea of the idea the critic is likely to have, given the representation he has of the house's publications.

Hence, it is quite logical, and highly significant that what has become the name of a literary school (the *"nouveau roman"*), adopted by the authors themselves, should have begun as a pejorative label, accorded by a traditionalist critic to novels published by Editions de Minuit. Just as critics and public found themselves invited to seek the links that might unite works published under the same imprint, so authors were defined by this public definition of their works to the extent that they had to define themselves in relation to it. Moreover, confronted with the public's and the critics' image of them, they were encouraged to think of themselves as constituting more than simply a chance grouping. They became a school endowed with its own aesthetic program, its eponymous ancestors, its accredited critics and spokesmen.

In short, the most personal judgments it is possible to make of a work, even of one's own work, are always collective judgments in the sense of position-takings referring to other position-takings through the intermediary of the objective relations between the positions of their authors within the field. Through the public meaning of the work, through the objective sanctions imposed by the symbolic market upon the producer's "aspirations" and "ambitions" and, in particular, through the degree of recognition and consecration it accords him, the entire structure of the field interposes itself between the producer and his work. This imposes a definition of his ambitions as either legitimate or illegitimate according to whether his position objectively implies, or denies, their fulfillment.

Because the very logic of the field condemns them to risk their cultural salvation in even the least of their position-takings and to watch, uncertainly, for the ever-ambiguous signs of an ever-suspended election, intellectuals and artists may experience a failure as a sign of election, or over-rapid or too brilliant success as a threat of damnation. They cannot ignore the value attributed to them, that is the position they are entitled to within the hierarchy of cultural legitimacy, as it is continually brought home by the signs of recognition or exclusion appearing in their relations with peers or with institutions of consecration.

For each position in the hierarchy of consecration there is a corresponding relationship — more or less ambitious or resigned — to the field of cultural practices which is, itself, hierarchized. An analysis of artistic or intellectual trajectories attests that those "choices" most commonly imputed to "vocation," such as choice of intellectual or artistic specialization — author rather than critic, poet rather than novelist — and, more profoundly, everything defining the manner in which one fulfills oneself in that "chosen" speciality depend on the actual and potential position that the field attributes to the different categories of agents notably through the intermediary of the institutions of cultural consecration. It might be

[41]Bourdieu's point is that middle-brow critics often identify a relatively unadventurous work of art with a voguish avant-garde movement, thus enhancing both the artist's prestige and their own. Similarly, reviewers from the popular press two decades ago routinely identified any difficult work of literary theory as "deconstruction." [Ed.]

supposed that the laws governing intellectual or artistic "vocations" are similar in principle to those governing scholastic "choices," such as the "choice" of faculty or discipline. Such a supposition would imply, for example, that the "choice" of discipline be increasingly "ambitious" (with respect to the reigning hierarchy in the university field) as one ascends towards those categories of students or teachers most highly consecrated, scholastically, and most favored in terms of social origin. Again, it might be supposed that the greater the scholastic consecration, mediated by social origin, of a determinate category of teachers and researchers, the more abundant and ambitious would be their production.

Among the social factors determining the functional laws of any field of cultural production (literary, artistic or scientific), undoubtedly the most important is the hierarchic position of each discipline or specialization and the position of the different producers in the hierarchy peculiar to each subfield. The migrations of labor power which drive large sections of producers towards the currently most consecrated scientific discipline (or, elsewhere, artistic genre), and which are experienced as though "inspired" by vocation or determined by some intellectual itinerary and often imputed to the effects of fashion, could be merely reconversions aimed at ensuring the best possible economic or symbolic return on a determinate kind of cultural capital. And the sensitivity necessary to sniff out these movements of the cultural value stock-exchange, the audacity requisite to abandoning well-worn paths for the most opportune-seeming future once more depend on social factors, such as the nature of the capital possessed and scholastic and social origins with their attendant objective chances and aspirations.[42] Similarly, the interest which different categories of researchers manifest in different types of practice (for example, empirical research or theory) is also a composite function. It is dependent, first, on the ambitions which their formation and their scholastic success and, thus, their position in the discipline's hierarchy allow them to form by assuring them of reasonable chances of success. Secondly, it is a function of the objectively recognized hierarchy of the very different material and symbolic profits which particular practices or objects of study are in a position to procure.[43]

If the relations which make the cultural field into a field of (intellectual, artistic or scientific) position-takings only reveal their meaning and function in the light of the relations among cultural subjects who are holding specific positions in this field, it is because intellectual or artistic position-takings are also always semi-conscious strategies in a game in which the conquest of cultural legitimacy and of the concomitant power of legitimate symbolic violence is at stake. To claim to be able to discover the entire truth of the cultural field within that field is to transfer the objective relations between different positions in the field of cultural production into the heaven of logical and semiologic relations of opposition and homology. Moreover, it is to do away with the question of the relationship between this "positional" field and the cultural field; in other words, it is to ignore the question of the dependence of the different systems of cultural position-takings constituting a given state of the cultural field upon the specifically cultural interests of different groups competing for cultural legitimacy. It is also to deprive oneself of the possibility of determining what particular cultural position-takings owe to the social functions they fulfill in these groups' strategies.

Consequently, we can postulate that there is no cultural position-taking that cannot be submitted to a *double interpretation:* It can be related, on the one hand, to the realm of cultural position-takings constituent of the specifically cultural

[42]The development of psychology in Germany, at the end of the 19th century, can be explained by the state of the university market, favoring the movement of physiology students and teachers towards other fields, and by the relatively lowly position occupied by philosophy in the academic field, which made it a dream ground for the innovative enterprises of deserters from the higher disciplines (cf. J. Ben-David and R. Collins, "Social factors in the origins of a new science: The case of psychology," *American Sociological Review* 31 [1966]: 451–65). [Au.]

[43]Short-term movements in the cultural value stock market ought not to obscure the constants, such as the domination of the most theoretical discipline over those more practically orientated. [Au.]

field; on the other hand, it can be interpreted as a consciously or unconsciously orientated strategy elaborated in regard to the field of allied or hostile positions.[44] Research starting from this hypothesis would doubtless find its surest landmarks in a methodical analysis of *privileged references.* These would be conceived, not as simple indices of information exchanges (in particular, implicit or explicit borrowings of words or ideas), but as so many landmarks circumscribing, within the common battlefield, the small network of privileged allies and adversaries proper to each category of producer.

"Citatology"[45] nearly always ignores this question, implicitly treating references to an author as an index of recognition (of indebtedness or legitimacy). In point of fact this apparent function may nearly always be associated with such diverse functions as the manifestation of relations of allegiance or dependence, of strategies of affiliation, of annexation or of defense (this is the role, for example, of guarantee references, ostentatious references or alibi-references). We should mention, here, two "citatologists" who have the merit of having posed a question systematically ignored: "People quote another author for complex reasons — to confer meaning, authority or depth upon a statement, to demonstrate familiarity with other work in the same field and to avoid the appearance of plagiarizing even ideas conceived independently. The quotation is aimed at readers of whom some, at least, are supposed to have some knowledge of the work quoted (there would be no point in quoting if this were not so) and to adhere to the norms concerning what may, and what may not, be attributed to it."[46] When it is not immediately explicit and direct (as in the case of polemical or deforming references), the strategic function of a reference may be apprehended in its modality — humble or sovereign, impeccably academic or sloppy, explicit or implicit and, in this case, unconscious, repressed (and betraying a strong relationship of ambivalence) or knowingly dissimulated (whether through tactical prudence, through a more or less visible and naive will to annexation — plagiarism — or through disdain). Strategic considerations may also stalk those quotations most directly orientated towards the functions commonly recognized as theirs by "citatology." One just has to think of what might be termed an *a minima* reference, which consists in recognizing a precise and clearly specified debt (by the full-length quotation of a sentence or an expression) in order to hide a far more global and more diffuse debt. (We should note, in passing, the existence of *a maxima* references, whose functions may vary from grateful homage to autovalorizing annexation — when the contribution of the quoter to the thought quoted, which, in this case, must be prestigious, is fairly important and obvious.)

The construction of the system of relations between each of the categories of producers and competing, hostile, allied or neutral powers, which are to be destroyed, intimidated, cajoled, annexed or won over presumes a decisive rupture, first, with naive citatology as this does not go beyond any but the most phenomenal relationships; furthermore — and in particular — with that supremely naive representation of cultural production which takes only *explicit references* into account. How can we reduce Plato's presence in Aristole's texts to explicit references alone, or that of Descartes in Leibniz's writings, of Hegel in those of Marx? We speak here more generally of those *privileged interlocutors,* implicit in the writings of every producer, those masters whose thought structures he has internalized to the point where he no longer thinks except in them and through them, to the point where they have become intimate adversaries de-

[44]We should pay particular attention to the strategies employed in relation with groups occupying a neighboring position in the field. The law of the quest for distinction explains the apparent paradox which has it that the fiercest and most fundamental conflicts oppose each group to its immediate neighbors, for it is these who most directly threaten its identity, hence its distinction and even its specifically cultural existence. [Au.]

[45]Bourdieu's coinage for the sociological analysis of references to one researcher in the works of another. The usual assumption, which Bourdieu wishes to correct, is that the cited author has inspired or enabled the work of the citer. [Ed.]

[46]J. S. Cloyd and A. P. Bates, "George Homans in Footnotes: The Fate of Ideas in Scholarly Communication," *Sociological Inquiry* 34 (1964): 115–28. [Au.]

termining his thinking and imposing on him both the shape and the substance of conflict. Manifest conflicts dissimulate the *consensus* within the *dissensus* which defines the field of cultural battle in a given epoch, and which the educational system contributes to produce, by inculcating an uncontested hierarchy of themes and problems worthy of discussion. Given this, implicit references allow also to construct that intellectual space defined by a system of common references appearing so natural, so incontestable that they are never the object of conscious position-takings at all. However, it is in relation to this referential space that all the standpoints of the different categories of producers are differentially defined.

In addition to other possible functions, theories, methods and concepts in whatever realm are to be considered as strategies aimed at installing, restoring, strengthening, safe-guarding or upsetting a determinate structure of relationships of symbolic domination; that is, they constitute the means for obtaining or safe-guarding the monopoly of the legitimate mode of practicing a — literary, artistic or scientific — activity.

> How, for example, could one fail to see that "epistemological couples" are nearly always covers for oppositions between different groups within the field? Such groups are led to transform interests associated with possession of a determinate type of scientific capital and with a determinate position within the scientific field, into epistemological choices. Is it not legitimate to suppose that there is a strategic intention (which may remain perfectly unconscious) lurking behind a theory of theory such as Merton's? Does one not better understand the *raison d'être* of works by the "high methodologists," such as Lazarsfeld,[47] as one realizes that these scholastic codifications of the rules of scientific practice are inseparable from the project of building a kind of intellectual papacy, replete with its international corps of vicars, regularly visited or gathered together in *concilium* and charged with the exercise of rigorous and constant control over common practice?

By ignoring the systems of social relations within which symbolic systems are produced and utilized, the strictly internal interpretation most frequently condemns itself to the gratuitousness of an arbitrary formalism: In point of fact, an appropriate construction of the object of analysis presupposes a sociological analysis of the social functions at the basis of the structure and functioning of any symbolic system. The semiologist, who claims to reveal the structure of a literary or artistic work through so-called strictly internal analysis, exposes himself to a theoretical error by disregarding the social conditions underlying the production of the work and those determining its functioning.

A field of cultural production may have achieved virtually complete autonomy in relation to external forces and demands (as in the case of the purest sciences), while still remaining amenable to specifically sociological analysis. It is the job of sociology to establish the external conditions for a system of social relations of production, circulation and consumption necessary to the autonomous development of science or art; its task, moreover, is to determine those functional laws which characterize such a relatively autonomous field of social relations and which can also account for the structure of corresponding symbolic productions and its transformations. The principles of "selection," objectively employed by the different groups of producers competing for cultural legitimacy are always defined within a system of social relations obedient to a specific logic. The symbolic standpoints are, moreover, functions of the interest-systems objectively attached to the position producers occupy in *special power relations*. These are the social relations of symbolic production, circulation and consumption.

As the field of restricted production closes in upon itself, and confirms itself as capable of organizing its production by reference to its own internal norms of perfection — excluding all social, or socially marked content from the work — the dynamic of competition for specifically

[47]Robert K. Merton (b. 1910) and Paul F. Lazarsfeld (1901–1976) were both professors of sociology at Columbia University and allied as associate director and director, respectively, of the Bureau of Applied Social Research. Both were involved in the use of mathematics and statistics in sociological research. The scathing tone of Bourdieu's reference to them may perhaps be explained by the overlap of Merton's and Lazarsfeld's topics of interest (including mass media and the sociology of science) with Bourdieu's and the disparity in their ideas about method. [Ed.]

cultural consecration becomes the exclusive principle of the production of works. Especially since the middle of the 19th century, the principle of change in art has come from within art itself, as though history were internal to the system and as if the development of forms of representation and expression were merely the product of the logical development of axiomatic systems specific to the various arts. To explain this, there is no need to hypostatize the laws of this evolution: If a relatively autonomous history of art and literature (or of science) exists, it is because the "action of works upon works," of which Brunetière spoke,[48] explains an ever increasing proportion of artistic or literary production. At the same time, the field as such explicates and systematizes specifically artistic principles of the production and the evaluation of the work of art. The relationship, moreover, which each category of producer enjoys with its own production is more and more exclusively determined by its relationship with the specifically artistic traditions and norms inherited from the past. The exact nature of the latter relationship is, again, a function of its position in the structure of the field of production.

True, cultural legitimacy appears to be the "fundamental norm," to employ the language of Kelsen, of the field of restricted production. But this "fundamental norm,"[49] as Jean Piaget has noted, "is nothing other than the abstract expression of the fact that society 'recognizes' the normative value of this order." It does this in such a way that it "corresponds to the social reality of the exercise of some power and of the 'recognition' of this power or of the system of rules emanating from it." Thus, the relative autonomy of the field of restricted production authorizes the attempt to construct a "pure" model of the objective relations defining it, and the interactions which develop within it. But one must remember that this formal construction is the product of the temporary bracketing-off of the field of restricted production (as a system of specific power relations) from the surrounding field of the power relations between classes. It would be futile to search for the ultimate foundation of this "fundamental norm" within the field itself, since it resides in structures governed by powers other than the culturally legitimate; consequently, the functions objectively assigned to each category of producer and its products by its position in the field are always duplicated by the external functions objectively fulfilled through the accomplishment of its internal functions.

[48]Ferdinand Brunetière, *L'evolution des genres dans l'histoire de la littérature: Leçons professées à l'Ecole normale supérieure* (Paris: Hachette, 1890). [Ed.]

[49]Jean Piaget, *Introduction à l'épistémologie génétique*, Vol. III (Paris: P.U.F., 1950), p. 239. [Au.]

Clifford Geertz

b. 1926

The notion that culture is a language that can be learned by studying social practices with the same attention to nuance, motif, and transformational tropes that literary critics apply to difficult poetry is one which seems familiar today, owing to Clifford Geertz's many years of labor combating the once dominant "functionalist" approach. Geertz was born in San Francisco and served in the navy during World War II before resuming his education at Antioch College. He took his Ph.D. at Harvard University in 1956. Geertz combined field work in Bali and Morocco with academic appointments at Harvard, MIT, Stanford, and Berkeley, becoming professor of anthropology at the University of Chicago in 1964. In 1972 he moved to Princeton University, where he spent the rest of his career as a professor of social science at the Institute for Advanced Study. His voluminous publications include Islam

Observed: Religious Development in Morocco and Indonesia *(1968),* The Interpretation of Cultures *(1973),* Myth, Symbol and Culture *(1974),* Local Knowledge *(1983),* Works and Lives *(1988), and* After the Fact: Two Countries, Four Decades, One Anthropologist *(1995). Geertz's insistence that the anthropologist cannot be a pure observer but inevitably affects the social practices he or she studies is apparent in the following selection, "Deep Play: Notes on the Balinese Cockfight," originally published in* Daedalus *in 1972. This version is from* The Interpretation of Cultures.

Deep Play: Notes on the Balinese Cockfight

THE RAID

Early in April of 1958 my wife and I arrived, malarial and diffident, in a Balinese village we intended, as anthropologists, to study. A small place, about five hundred people, and relatively remote, it was its own world. We were intruders, professional ones, and the villagers dealt with us as Balinese seem always to deal with people not part of their life who yet press themselves upon them: as though we were not there. For them, and to a degree for ourselves, we were nonpersons, specters, invisible men.

We moved into an extended family compound (that had been arranged before through the provincial government) belonging to one of the four major factions in village life. But except for our landlord and the village chief, whose cousin and brother-in-law he was, everyone ignored us in a way only a Balinese can do. As we wandered around, uncertain, wistful, eager to please, people seemed to look right through us with a gaze focused several yards behind us on some more actual stone or tree. Almost nobody greeted us; but nobody scowled or said anything unpleasant to us either, which would have been almost as satisfactory. If we ventured to approach someone (something one is powerfully inhibited from doing in such an atmosphere), he moved, negligently but definitely, away. If, seated or leaning against a wall, we had him trapped, he said nothing at all, or mumbled what for the Balinese is the ultimate nonword — "yes." The indifference, of course, was studied; the villagers were watching every move we made, and they had an enormous amount of quite accurate information about who we were and what we were going to be doing. But they acted as if we simply did not exist, which, in fact, as this behavior was designed to inform us, we did not, or anyway not yet.

This is, as I say, general in Bali. Everywhere else I have been in Indonesia, and more latterly in Morocco, when I have gone into a new village, people have poured out from all sides to take a very close look at me, and, often an all-too-probing feel as well. In Balinese villages, at least those away from the tourist circuit, nothing happens at all. People go on pounding, chatting, making offerings, staring into space, carrying baskets about while one drifts around feeling vaguely disembodied. And the same thing is true on the individual level. When you first meet a Balinese, he seems virtually not to relate to you at all; he is, in the term Gregory Bateson and Margaret Mead made famous, "away."[1] Then — in a day, a week, a month (with some people the magic moment never comes) — he decides, for reasons I have never quite been able to fathom, that you *are* real, and then he becomes a warm, gay, sensitive, sympathetic, though, being Balinese, always precisely controlled, person. You have crossed, somehow, some moral or metaphysical shadow line. Though you are not exactly taken as a Balinese (one has to be born to that), you are at least regarded as a human being rather than a cloud or a gust of wind. The whole com-

[1]G. Bateson and M. Mead, *Balinese Character: A Photographic Analysis* (New York: New York Academy of Sciences, 1942), p. 68. [Au.]

plexion of your relationship dramatically changes to, in the majority of cases, a gentle, almost affectionate one — a low-keyed, rather playful, rather mannered, rather bemused geniality.

My wife and I were still very much in the gust-of-wind stage, a most frustrating, and even, as you soon begin to doubt whether you are really real after all, unnerving one, when, ten days or so after our arrival, a large cockfight was held in the public square to raise money for a new school.

Now, a few special occasions aside, cockfights are illegal in Bali under the Republic (as, for not altogether unrelated reasons, they were under the Dutch), largely as a result of the pretensions to puritanism radical nationalism tends to bring with it. The elite, which is not itself so very puritan, worries about the poor, ignorant peasant gambling all his money away, about what foreigners will think, about the waste of time better devoted to building up the country. It sees cockfighting as "primitive," "backward," "unprogressive," and generally unbecoming an ambitious nation. And, as with those other embarrassments — opium smoking, begging, or uncovered breasts — it seeks, rather unsystematically, to put a stop to it.

Of course, like drinking during Prohibition or, today, smoking marihuana, cockfights, being a part of "The Balinese Way of Life," nonetheless go on happening, and with extraordinary frequency. And, as with Prohibition or marihuana, from time to time the police (who, in 1958 at least, were almost all not Balinese but Javanese) feel called upon to make a raid, confiscate the cocks and spurs, fine a few people, and even now and then expose some of them in the tropical sun for a day as object lessons which never, somehow, get learned, even though occasionally, quite occasionally, the object dies.

As a result, the fights are usually held in a secluded corner of a village in semisecrecy, a fact which tends to slow the action a little — not very much, but the Balinese do not care to have it slowed at all. In this case, however, perhaps because they were raising money for a school that the government was unable to give them, perhaps because raids had been few recently, perhaps, as I gathered from subsequent discussion, there was a notion that the necessary bribes had been paid, they thought they could take a chance on the central square and draw a larger and more enthusiastic crowd without attracting the attention of the law.

They were wrong. In the midst of the third match, with hundreds of people, including, still transparent, myself and my wife, fused into a single body around the ring, a superorganism in the literal sense, a truck full of policemen armed with machine guns roared up. Amid great screeching cries of "pulisi! pulisi!" from the crowd, the policemen jumped out, and, springing into the center of the ring, began to swing their guns around like gangsters in a motion picture, though not going so far as actually to fire them. The superorganism came instantly apart as its components scattered in all directions. People raced down the road, disappeared headfirst over walls, scrambled under platforms, folded themselves behind wicker screens, scuttled up coconut trees. Cocks armed with steel spurs sharp enough to cut off a finger or run a hole through a foot were running wildly around. Everything was dust and panic.

On the established anthropological principle, "When in Rome," my wife and I decided, only slightly less instantaneously than everyone else, that the thing to do was run too. We ran down the main village street, northward, away from where we were living, for we were on that side of the ring. About halfway down another fugitive ducked suddenly into a compound — his own, it turned out — and we, seeing nothing ahead of us but rice fields, open country, and a very high volcano,[2] followed him. As the three of us came tumbling into the courtyard, his wife, who had apparently been through this sort of thing before, whipped out a table, a tablecloth, three chairs, and three cups of tea, and we all, without any explicit communication whatsoever, sat down, commenced to sip tea, and sought to compose ourselves.

A few moments later, one of the policemen marched importantly into the yard, looking for

[2]Mt. Agung, which erupted in 1963. [Ed.]

the village chief. (The chief had not only been at the fight, he had arranged it. When the truck drove up he ran to the river, stripped off his sarong, and plunged in so he could say, when at length they found him sitting there pouring water over his head, that he had been away bathing when the whole affair had occurred and was ignorant of it. They did not believe him and fined him three hundred rupiah, which the village raised collectively.) Seeing me and my wife, "White Men," there in the yard, the policeman performed a classic double take. When he found his voice again he asked, approximately, what in the devil did we think we were doing there. Our host of five minutes leaped instantly to our defense, producing an impassioned description of who and what we were, so detailed and so accurate that it was my turn, having barely communicated with a living human being save my landlord and the village chief for more than a week, to be astonished. We had a perfect right to be there, he said, looking the Javanese upstart in the eye. We were American professors; the government had cleared us; we were there to study culture; we were going to write a book to tell Americans about Bali. And we had all been there drinking tea and talking about cultural matters all afternoon and did not know anything about any cockfight. Moreover, we had not seen the village chief all day; he must have gone to town. The policeman retreated in rather total disarray. And, after a decent interval, bewildered but relieved to have survived and stayed out of jail, so did we.

The next morning the village was a completely different world for us. Not only were we no longer invisible, we were suddenly the center of all attention, the object of a great outpouring of warmth, interest, and most especially, amusement. Everyone in the village knew we had fled like everyone else. They asked us about it again and again (I must have told the story, small detail by small detail, fifty times by the end of the day), gently, affectionately, but quite insistently teasing us: "Why didn't you just stand there and tell the police who you were?" "Why didn't you just say you were only watching and not betting?" "Were you really afraid of those little guns?" As always, kinesthetically minded and, even when fleeing for their lives (or, as happened eight years later, surrendering them),[3] the world's most poised people, they gleefully mimicked, also over and over again, our graceless style of running and what they claimed were our panic-stricken facial expressions. But above all, everyone was extremely pleased and even more surprised that we had not simply "pulled out our papers" (they knew about those too) and asserted our Distinguished Visitor status, but had instead demonstrated our solidarity with what were now our covillagers. (What we had actually demonstrated was our cowardice, but there is fellowship in that too.) Even the Brahmana priest, an old, grave, halfway-to-heaven type who because of its associations with the underworld would never be involved, even distantly, in a cockfight, and was difficult to approach even to other Balinese, had us called into his courtyard to ask us about what had happened, chuckling happily at the sheer extraordinariness of it all.

In Bali, to be teased is to be accepted. It was the turning point so far as our relationship to the community was concerned, and we were quite literally "in." The whole village opened up to us, probably more than it ever would have otherwise (I might actually never have gotten to that priest, and our accidental host became one of my best informants), and certainly very much faster. Getting caught, or almost caught, in a vice raid is perhaps not a very generalizable recipe for achieving that mysterious necessity of anthropological field work, rapport, but for me it worked very well. It led to a sudden and unusually complete acceptance into a society extremely difficult for outsiders to penetrate. It gave me the kind of immediate, inside-view grasp of an aspect of "peasant mentality" that anthropologists not fortunate enough to flee headlong with their subjects from armed authorities normally do not get. And, perhaps most important of all, for the other things might have come in other ways, it put me very quickly on to a combination emotional explosion, status war, and philosophical drama of central significance to the society whose inner

[3]Geertz alludes to the massacres of leftists and intellectuals used as the occasion for thousands of random murders following the unsuccessful coup against General Suharto in 1965. See p. 1278, n. 49. [Ed.]

nature I desired to understand. By the time I left I had spent about as much time looking into cockfights as into witchcraft, irrigation, caste, or marriage.

OF COCKS AND MEN

Bali, mainly because it is Bali, is a well-studied place. Its mythology, art, ritual, social organization, patterns of child rearing, forms of law, even styles of trance, have all been microscopically examined for traces of that elusive substance Jane Belo called "The Balinese Temper."[4] But, aside from a few passing remarks, the cockfight has barely been noticed, although as a popular obsession of consuming power it is at least as important a revelation of what being a Balinese "is really like" as these more celebrated phenomena.[5] As much of America surfaces in a ball park, on a golf links, at a race track, or around a poker table, much of Bali surfaces in a cock ring. For it is only apparently cocks that are fighting there. Actually, it is men.

To anyone who has been in Bali any length of time, the deep psychological identification of Balinese men with their cocks is unmistakable. The double entendre here is deliberate. It works in exactly the same way in Balinese as it does in English, even to producing the same tired jokes, strained puns, and uninventive obscenities. Bateson and Mead have even suggested that, in line with the Balinese conception of the body as a set of separately animated parts, cocks are viewed as detachable, self-operating penises, ambulant genitals with a life of their own.[6] And while I do not have the kind of unconscious material either to confirm or disconfirm this intriguing notion, the fact that they are masculine symbols par excellence is about as indubitable, and to the Balinese about as evident, as the fact that water runs downhill.

The language of everyday moralism is shot through, on the male side of it, with roosterish imagery. *Sabung*, the word for cock (and one which appears in inscriptions as early as A.D. 922), is used metaphorically to mean "hero," "warrior," "champion," "man of parts," "political candidate," "bachelor," "dandy," "lady-killer," or "tough guy." A pompous man whose behavior presumes above his station is compared to a tailless cock who struts about as though he had a large, spectacular one. A desperate man who makes a last, irrational effort to extricate himself from an impossible situation is likened to a dying cock who makes one final lunge at his tormentor to drag him along to a common destruction. A stingy man, who promises much, gives little, and begrudges that, is compared to a cock which, held by the tail, leaps at another without in fact engaging him. A marriageable young man still shy with the opposite sex or someone in a new job anxious to make a good impression is called "a fighting cock caged for the first time."[7] Court trials, wars, political contests, inheritance disputes, and street arguments are all compared to cockfights.[8] Even the very island itself is perceived from its shape as a small, proud cock, poised, neck extended, back taut, tail raised, in

[4]J. Belo, "The Balinese Temper," in *Traditional Balinese Culture,* ed. J. Belo (New York, 1970) (originally published in 1935), pp. 85–110. [Au.]

[5]The best discussion of cockfighting is again Bateson and Mead's *Balinese Character*, pp. 24–25, 140; but it, too, is general and abbreviated. [Au.]

[6]Ibid., pp. 25–26. The cockfight is unusual within Balinese culture in being a single-sex public activity from which the other sex is totally and expressly excluded. Sexual differentiation is culturally extremely played down in Bali and most activities, formal and informal, involve the participation of men and women on equal ground, commonly as linked couples. From religion, to politics, to economics, to kinship, to dress, Bali is a rather "unisex" society, a fact both its customs and its symbolism clearly express. Even in contexts where women do not in fact play much of a role — music, painting, certain agricultural activities — their absence, which is only relative in any case, is more a mere matter of fact than socially enforced. To this general pattern, the cockfight, entirely of, by, and for men (women — at least *Balinese* women — do not even watch), is the most striking exception. [Au.]

[7]C. Hooykaas, *The Lay of the Jaya Prana* (London, 1958), p. 39. The lay has a stanza (no. 17) with the reluctant bridegroom use. Jaya Prana, the subject of a Balinese Uriah myth, responds to the lord who has offered him the loveliest of six hundred servant girls: "Godly King, my Lord and Master / I beg you, give me leave to go / such things are not yet in my mind; / like a fighting cock encaged / indeed I am on my mettle / I am alone / as yet the flame has not been fanned." [Au.]

[8]For these, see V. E. Korn, *Het Adatrecht van Bali*, 2d ed. (The Hague, 1932), index under *toh*. [Au.]

eternal challenge to large, feckless, shapeless Java.[9]

But the intimacy of men with their cocks is more than metaphorical. Balinese men, or anyway a large majority of Balinese men, spend an enormous amount of time with their favorites, grooming them, feeding them, discussing them, trying them out against one another, or just gazing at them with a mixture of rapt admiration and dreamy self-absorption. Whenever you see a group of Balinese men squatting idly in the council shed or along the road in their hips down, shoulders forward, knees up fashion, half or more of them will have a rooster in his hands, holding it between his thighs, bouncing it gently up and down to strengthen its legs, ruffling its feathers with abstract sensuality, pushing it out against a neighbor's rooster to rouse its spirit, withdrawing it toward his loins to calm it again. Now and then, to get a feel for another bird, a man will fiddle this way with someone else's cock for a while, but usually by moving around to squat in place behind it, rather than just having it passed across to him as though it were merely an animal.

In the houseyard, the high-walled enclosures where the people live, fighting cocks are kept in wicker cages, moved frequently about so as to maintain the optimum balance of sun and shade. They are fed a special diet, which varies somewhat according to individual theories but which is mostly maize, sifted for impurities with far more care than it is when mere humans are going to eat it, and offered to the animal kernel by kernel. Red pepper is stuffed down their beaks and up their anuses to give them spirit. They are bathed in the same ceremonial preparation of tepid water, medicinal herbs, flowers, and onions in which infants are bathed, and for a prize cock just about as often. Their combs are cropped, their plumage dressed, their spurs trimmed, and their legs massaged, and they are inspected for flaws with the squinted concentration of a diamond merchant. A man who has a passion for cocks, an enthusiast in the literal sense of the term, can spend most of his life with them, and even those, the overwhelming majority, whose passion though intense has not entirely run away with them, can and do spend what seems not only to an outsider, but also to themselves, an inordinate amount of time with them. "I am cock crazy," my landlord, a quite ordinary *aficionado* by Balinese standards, used to moan as he went to move another cage, give another bath, or conduct another feeding. "We're all cock crazy."

The madness has some less visible dimensions, however, because although it is true that cocks are symbolic expressions or magnifications of their owner's self, the narcissistic male ego writ out in Aesopian terms, they are also expressions — and rather more immediate ones — of what the Balinese regard as the direct inversion, aesthetically, morally, and metaphysically, of human status: animality.

The Balinese revulsion against any behavior regarded as animal-like can hardly be overstressed. Babies are not allowed to crawl for that reason. Incest, though hardly approved, is a much less horrifying crime than bestiality. (The appropriate punishment for the second is death by drowning, for the first being forced to live like an animal.)[10] Most demons are represented — in sculpture, dance, ritual, myth — in some real or fantastic animal form. The main puberty rite consists in filing the child's teeth so they will not look like animal fangs. Not only defecation but eating is regarded as a disgusting, almost obscene activity, to be conducted hurriedly and privately, because of its association with animality. Even falling down or any form of clumsiness is considered to be bad for these reasons. Aside from cocks and a few domestic animals — oxen,

[9]There is indeed a legend to the effect that the separation of Java and Bali is due to the action of a powerful Javanese religious figure who wished to protect himself against a Balinese culture hero (the ancestor of two Ksatria castes) who was a passionate cockfighting gambler. See C. Hooykaas, *Agama Tirtha* (Amsterdam, 1964), p. 184. [Au.]

[10]An incestuous couple is forced to wear pig yokes over their necks and crawl to a pig trough and eat with their mouths there. On this, see J. Belo, "Customs Pertaining to Twins in Bali," in *Traditional Balinese Culture*, ed. J. Belo, p. 49; on the abhorrence of animality generally, Bateson and Mead, *Balinese Character*, p. 22. [Au.]

ducks — of no emotional significance, the Balinese are aversive to animals and treat their large number of dogs not merely callously but with a phobic cruelty. In identifying with his cock, the Balinese man is identifying not just with his ideal self, or even his penis, but also, and at the same time, with what he most fears, hates, and ambivalence being what it is, is fascinated by — "The Powers of Darkness."

The connection of cocks and cockfighting with such Powers, with the animalistic demons that threaten constantly to invade the small, cleared-off space in which the Balinese have so carefully built their lives and devour its inhabitants, is quite explicit. A cockfight, any cockfight, is in the first instance a blood sacrifice offered, with the appropriate chants and oblations, to the demons in order to pacify their ravenous, cannibal hunger. No temple festival should be conducted until one is made. (If it is omitted, someone will inevitably fall into a trance and command with the voice of an angered spirit that the oversight be immediately corrected.) Collective responses to natural evils — illness, crop failure, volcanic eruptions — almost always involve them. And that famous holiday in Bali, "The Day of Silence" *(Njepi),* when everyone sits silent and immobile all day long in order to avoid contact with a sudden influx of demons chased momentarily out of hell, is preceded the previous day by large-scale cockfights (in this case legal) in almost every village on the island.

In the cockfight, man and beast, good and evil, ego and id, the creative power of aroused masculinity and the destructive power of loosened animality fuse in a bloody drama of hatred, cruelty, violence, and death. It is little wonder that when, as is the invariable rule, the owner of the winning cock takes the carcass of the loser — often torn limb from limb by its enraged owner — home to eat, he does so with a mixture of social embarrassment, moral satisfaction, aesthetic disgust, and cannibal joy. Or that a man who has lost an important fight is sometimes driven to wreck his family shrines and curse the gods, an act of metaphysical (and social) suicide. Or that in seeking earthly analogues for heaven and hell the Balinese compare the former to the mood of a man whose cock has just won, the latter to that of a man whose cock has just lost.

THE FIGHT

Cockfights *(tetadjen; sabungan)* are held in a ring about fifty feet square. Usually they begin toward late afternoon and run three or four hours until sunset. About nine or ten separate matches *(sehet)* comprise a program. Each match is precisely like the others in general pattern: there is no main match, no connection between individual matches, no variation in their format, and each is arranged on a completely ad hoc basis. After a fight has ended and the emotional debris is cleaned away — the bets have been paid, the curses cursed, the carcasses possessed — seven, eight, perhaps even a dozen men slip negligently into the ring with a cock and seek to find there a logical opponent for it. This process, which rarely takes less than ten minutes, and often a good deal longer, is conducted in a very subdued, oblique, even dissembling manner. Those not immediately involved give it at best but disguised, sidelong attention; those who, embarrassedly, are, attempt to pretend somehow that the whole thing is not really happening.

A match made, the other hopefuls retire with the same deliberate indifference, and the selected cocks have their spurs *(tadji)* affixed — razor-sharp, pointed steel swords, four or five inches long. This is a delicate job which only a small proportion of men, a half-dozen or so in most villages, know how to do properly. The man who attaches the spurs also provides them, and if the rooster he assists wins, its owner awards him the spur-leg of the victim. The spurs are affixed by winding a long length of string around the foot of the spur and the leg of the cock. For reasons I shall come to presently, it is done somewhat differently from case to case, and is an obsessively deliberate affair. The lore about spurs is extensive — they are sharpened only at eclipses and the dark of the moon, should be kept out of the sight of women, and so forth. And they are handled, both in use and out, with the same curious combination of fussiness and sensuality the Balinese direct toward ritual objects generally.

The spurs affixed, the two cocks are placed by their handlers (who may or may not be their owners) facing one another in the center of the ring.[11] A coconut pierced with a small hole is placed in a pail of water, in which it takes about twenty-one seconds to sink, a period known as a *tjeng* and marked at beginning and end by the beating of a slit gong. During these twenty-one seconds the handlers *(pengangkeb)* are not permitted to touch their roosters. If, as sometimes happens, the animals have not fought during this time, they are picked up, fluffed, pulled, prodded, and otherwise insulted, and put back in the center of the ring and the process begins again. Sometimes they refuse to fight at all, or one keeps running away, in which case they are imprisoned together under a wicker cage, which usually gets them engaged.

Most of the time, in any case, the cocks fly almost immediately at one another in a wing-beating, head-thrusting, leg-kicking explosion of animal fury so pure, so absolute, and in its own way so beautiful, as to be almost abstract, a Platonic concept of hate. Within moments one or the other drives home a solid blow with his spur. The handler whose cock has delivered the blow immediately picks it up so that it will not get a return blow, for if he does not the match is likely to end in a mutually mortal tie as the two birds wildly hack each other to pieces. This is particularly true if, as often happens, the spur sticks in its victim's body, for then the aggressor is at the mercy of his wounded foe.

With the birds again in the hands of their handlers, the coconut is now sunk three times after which the cock which has landed the blow must be set down to show that he is firm, a fact he demonstrates by wandering idly around the ring for a coconut sink. The coconut is then sunk twice more and the fight must recommence.

During this interval, slightly over two minutes, the handler of the wounded cock has been working frantically over it, like a trainer patching a mauled boxer between rounds, to get in shape for a last, desperate try for victory. He blows in its mouth, putting the whole chicken head in his own mouth and sucking and blowing, fluffs it, stuffs its wounds with various sorts of medicines, and generally tries anything he can think of to arouse the last ounce of spirit which may be hidden somewhere within it. By the time he is forced to put it back down he is usually drenched in chicken blood, but, as in prize fighting, a good handler is worth his weight in gold. Some of them can virtually make the dead walk, at least long enough for the second and final round.

In the climactic battle (if there is one; sometimes the wounded cock simply expires in the handler's hands or immediately as it is placed down again), the cock who landed the first blow usually proceeds to finish off his weakened opponent. But this is far from an inevitable outcome, for if a cock can walk, he can fight, and if he can fight, he can kill, and what counts is which cock expires first. If the wounded one can get a stab in and stagger on until the other drops, he is the official winner, even if he himself topples over an instant later.

Surrounding all this melodrama — which the crowd packed tight around the ring follows in near silence, moving their bodies in kinesthetic sympathy with the movement of the animals, cheering their champions on with wordless hand motions, shiftings of the shoulders, turnings of the head, falling back en masse as the cock with the murderous spurs careens toward one side of the ring (it is said that spectators sometimes lose eyes and fingers from being too attentive), surging forward again as they glance off toward another — is a vast body of extraordinarily elaborate and precisely detailed rules.

These rules, together with the developed lore of cocks and cockfighting which accompanies them, are written down in palm-leaf manuscripts *(lontar; rontal)* passed on from generation to

[11]Except for unimportant, small-bet fights (on the question of fight "importance," see below) spur affixing is usually done by someone other than the owner. Whether the owner handles his own cock or not more or less depends on how skilled he is at it, a consideration whose importance is again relative to the importance of the fight. When spur affixers and cock handlers are someone other than the owner, they are almost always a quite close relative — a brother or cousin — or a very intimate friend of his. They are thus almost extensions of his personality, as the fact that all three will refer to the cock as "mine," say "I" fought So-and-So, and so on, demonstrates. Also, owner-handler-affixer triads tend to be fairly fixed, though individuals may participate in several and often exchange roles within a given one. [Au.]

generation as part of the general legal and cultural tradition of the villages. At a fight, the umpire *(saja komong; djuru kembar)* — the man who manages the coconut — is in charge of their application and his authority is absolute. I have never seen an umpire's judgment questioned on any subject, even by the more despondent losers, nor have I ever heard, even in private, a charge of unfairness directed against one, or, for that matter, complaints about umpires in general. Only exceptionally well trusted, solid, and, given the complexity of the code, knowledgeable citizens perform this job, and in fact men will bring their cocks only to fights presided over by such men. It is also the umpire to whom accusations of cheating, which, though rare in the extreme, occasionally arise, are referred; and it is he who in the not infrequent cases where the cocks expire virtually together decides which (if either, for, though the Balinese do not care for such an outcome, there can be ties) went first. Likened to a judge, a king, a priest, and a policeman, he is all of these, and under his assured direction the animal passion of the fight proceeds within the civic certainty of the law. In the dozens of cockfights I saw in Bali, I never once saw an altercation about rules. Indeed, I never saw an open altercation, other than those between cocks, at all.

This crosswise doubleness of an event which, taken as a fact of nature, is rage untrammeled and, taken as a fact of culture, is form perfected, defines the cockfight as a sociological entity. A cockfight is what, searching for a name for something not vertebrate enough to be called a group and not structureless enough to be called a crowd, Erving Goffman has called a "focused gathering" — a set of persons engrossed in a common flow of activity and relating to one another in terms of that flow.[12] Such gatherings meet and disperse; the participants in them fluctuate; the activity that focuses them is discrete — a particulate process that reoccurs rather than a continuous one that endures. They take their form from the situation that evokes them, the floor on which they are placed, as Goffman puts it; but it is a form, and an articulate one, nonetheless. For the situation, the floor is itself created, in jury deliberations, surgical operations, block meetings, sit-ins, cockfights, by the cultural preoccupations — here, as we shall see, the celebration of status rivalry — which not only specify the focus but, assembling actors and arranging scenery, bring it actually into being.

In classical times (that is to say, prior to the Dutch invasion of 1908), when there were no bureaucrats around to improve popular morality, the staging of a cockfight was an explicitly societal matter. Bringing a cock to an important fight was, for an adult male, a compulsory duty of citizenship; taxation of fights, which were usually held on market day, was a major source of public revenue; patronage of the art was a stated responsibility of princes; and the cock ring, or *wantilan,* stood in the center of the village near those other monuments of Balinese civility — the council house, the origin temple, the marketplace, the signal tower, and the banyan tree. Today, a few special occasions aside, the newer rectitude makes so open a statement of the connection between the excitements of collective life and those of blood sport impossible, but, less directly expressed, the connection itself remains intimate and intact. To expose it, however, it is necessary to turn to the aspect of cockfighting around which all the others pivot, and through which they exercise their force, an aspect I have thus far studiously ignored. I mean, of course, the gambling.

ODDS AND EVEN MONEY

The Balinese never do anything in a simple way that they can contrive to do in a complicated one, and to this generalization cockfight wagering is no exception.

In the first place, there are two sorts of bets, or *toh.*[13] There is the single axial bet in the center

[12]E. Goffman, *Encounters: Two Studies in the Sociology of Interaction* (Indianapolis, 1961), pp. 9–10. [Au.]

[13]This word, which literally means an indelible stain or mark, as in a birthmark or a vein in a stone, is used as well for a deposit in a court case, for a pawn, for security offered in a loan, for a stand-in for someone else in a legal or ceremonial context, for an earnest advanced in a business deal, for a sign placed in a field to indicate its ownership is in dispute, and for the status of an unfaithful wife from whose lover her husband must gain satisfaction or surrender her to him. See Korn, *Het*

between the principals *(toh ketengah),* and there is the cloud of peripheral ones around the ring between members of the audience *(toh kesasi).* The first is typically large; the second typically small. The first is collective, involving coalitions of bettors clustering around the owner; the second is individual, man to man. The first is a matter of deliberate, very quiet, almost furtive arrangement by the coalition members and the umpire huddled like conspirators in the center of the ring; the second is a matter of impulsive shouting, public offers, and public acceptances by the excited throng around its edges. And most curiously, and as we shall see most revealingly, *where the first is always, without exception, even money, the second, equally without exception, is never such.* What is a fair coin in the center is a biased one on the side.

The center bet is the official one, hedged in again with a webwork of rules, and is made between the two cock owners, with the umpire as overseer and public witness.[14] This bet, which, as I say, is always relatively and sometimes very large, is never raised simply by the owner in whose name it is made, but by him together with four or five, sometimes seven or eight, allies — kin, village mates, neighbors, close friends. He may, if he is not especially well-to-do, not even be the major contributor; though, if only to show that he is not involved in any chicanery, he must be a significant one.

Of the fifty-seven matches for which I have exact and reliable data on the center bet, the range is from fifteen ringgits to five hundred, with a mean at eighty-five and with the distribution being rather noticeably trimodal: small fights (15 ringgits either side of 35) accounting for about 45 percent of the total number; medium ones (20 ringgits either side of 70) for about 25 percent; and large (75 ringgits either side of 175) for about 20 percent, with a few very small and very large ones out at the extremes. In a society where the normal daily wage of a manual laborer — a brickmaker, an ordinary farmworker, a market porter — was about three ringgits a day, and considering the fact that fights were held on the average about every two-and-a-half days in the immediate area I studied, this is clearly serious gambling, even if the bets are pooled rather than individual efforts.

The side bets are, however, something else altogether. Rather than the solemn, legalistic pact-making of the center, wagering takes place rather in the fashion in which the stock exchange used to work when it was out on the curb. There is a fixed and known odds paradigm which runs in a continuous series from ten-to-nine at the short end to two-to-one at the long: 10–9, 9–8, 8–7, 7–6, 6–5, 5–4, 4–3, 3–2, 2–1. The man who wishes to back the *underdog cock* (leaving aside how favorites, *kebut*, and underdogs, *ngai*, are established for the moment) shouts the short-side number indicating the odds he wants *to be given.* That is, if he shouts *gasal*, "five," he wants the underdog at five-to-four (or, for him, four-to-five); if he shouts "four," he wants it at four-to-three (again, he putting up the "three"); if "nine," at nine-to-eight, and so on. A man backing the favorite, and thus considering giving odds if he can get them short enough, indicates the fact by crying out the color-type of that cock — "brown," "speckled," or whatever.[15]

Adatrecht van Bali; Th. Pigeaud, *Javaans-Nederlands Handwoordenboek* (Groningen, 1938); H. H. Juynboll, *Oudjavaansche-Nederlandsche Woordenlijst* (Leiden, 1923). [Au.]

[14]The center bet must be advanced in cash by both parties prior to the actual fight. The umpire holds the stakes until the decision is rendered and then awards them to the winner, avoiding, among other things, the intense embarrassment both winner and loser would feel if the latter had to pay off personally following his defeat. About 10 percent of the winner's receipts are subtracted for the umpire's share and that of the fight sponsors. [Au.]

[15]Actually, the typing of cocks, which is extremely elaborate (I have collected more than twenty classes, certainly not a complete list), is not based on color alone, but on a series of independent, interacting, dimensions, which include — besides color — size, bone thickness, plumage, and temperament. (But *not* pedigree. The Balinese do not breed cocks to any significant extent, nor, so far as I have been able to discover, have they ever done so. The *asil*, or jungle cock, which is the basic fighting strain everywhere the sport is found, is native to southern Asia, and one can buy a good example in the chicken section of almost any Balinese market for anywhere from four or five ringgits up to fifty or more.) The color element is merely the one normally used as the type name, except when the two cocks of different types — as on principle they must be — have the same color, in which case a secondary indication from one of the other dimensions ("large speckled" v. "small speckled," etc.) is added. The

As odds-takers (backers of the underdog) and odds-givers (backers of the favorite) sweep the crowd with their shouts, they begin to focus in on one another as potential betting pairs, often from far across the ring. The taker tries to shout the giver into longer odds, the giver to shout the taker into shorter ones.[16] The taker, who is the wooer in this situation, will signal how large a bet he wishes to make at the odds he is shouting by holding a number of fingers up in front of his face and vigorously waving them. If the giver, the wooed, replies in kind, the bet is made; if he does not, they unlock gazes and the search goes on.

The side betting, which takes place after the center bet has been made and its size announced, consists then in a rising crescendo of shouts as backers of the underdog offer their propositions to anyone who will accept them, while those who are backing the favorite but do not like the price being offered, shout equally frenetically the color of the cock to show they too are desperate to bet but want shorter odds.

Almost always odds-calling, which tends to be very consensual in that at any one time almost all callers are calling the same thing, starts off toward the long end of the range — five-to-four or four-to-three — and then moves, also consensually, toward the short end with greater or lesser speed and to a greater or lesser degree. Men crying "five" and finding themselves answered only with cries of "brown" start crying "six," either drawing the other callers fairly quickly with them or retiring from the scene as their too-generous offers are snapped up. If the change is made and partners are still scarce, the procedure is repeated in a move to "seven," and so on, only rarely, and in the very largest fights, reaching the ultimate "nine" or "ten" levels. Occasionally, if the cocks are clearly mismatched, there may be no upward movement at all, or even a movement down the scale to four-to-three, three-to-two, very, very rarely two-to-one, a shift which is accompanied by a declining number of bets as a shift upward is accompanied by an increasing number. But the general pattern is for the betting to move a shorter or longer distance up the scale toward the, for sidebets, nonexistent pole of even money, with the overwhelming majority of bets falling in the four-to-three to eight-to-seven range.[17]

As the moment for the release of the cocks by the handlers approaches, the screaming, at least in a match where the center bet is large, reaches almost frenzied proportions as the remaining unfulfilled bettors try desperately to find a last-minute partner at a price they can live with. (Where the center bet is small, the opposite tends

types are coordinated with various cosmological ideas which help shape the making of matches, so that, for example, you fight a small, headstrong, speckled brown-on-white cock with flat-lying feathers and thin legs from the east side of the ring on a certain day of the complex Balinese calendar, and a large, cautious, all-black cock with tufted feathers and stubby legs from the north side on another day, and so on. All this is again recorded in palm-leaf manuscripts and endlessly discussed by the Balinese (who do not all have identical systems), and a full-scale componential-cum-symbolic analysis of cock classifications would be extremely valuable both as an adjunct to the description of the cockfight and in itself. But my data on the subject, though extensive and varied, do not seem to be complete and systematic enough to attempt such an analysis here. For Balinese cosmological ideas more generally see Belo, ed., *Traditional Balinese Culture*, and J. L. Swellengrebel, ed., *Bali: Studies in Life, Thought, and Ritual* (The Hague, 1960). [Au.]

[16]For purposes of ethnographic completeness, it should be noted that it is possible for the man backing the favorite — the odds-giver — to make a bet in which he wins if his cock wins or there is a tie, a slight shortening of the odds (I do not have enough cases to be exact, but ties seem to occur about once every fifteen or twenty matches). He indicates his wish to do this by shouting *sapih* ("tie") rather than the cock-type, but such bets are in fact infrequent. [Au.]

[17]The precise dynamics of the movement of the betting is one of the most intriguing, most complicated, and, given the hectic conditions under which it occurs, most difficult to study, aspects of the fight. Motion picture recording plus multiple observers would probably be necessary to deal with it effectively. Even impressionistically — the only approach open to a lone ethnographer caught in the middle of all this — it is clear that certain men lead both in determining the favorite (that is, making the opening cock-type calls which always initiate the process) and in directing the movement of the odds, these "opinion leaders" being the more accomplished cockfighters-cum-solid-citizens to be discussed below. If these men begin to change their calls, others follow; if they begin to make bets, so do others and — though there are always a large number of frustrated bettors crying for shorter or longer odds to the end — the movement more or less ceases. But a detailed understanding of the whole process awaits what, alas, it is not very likely ever to get: a decision theorist armed with precise observations of individual behavior. [Au.]

to occur: betting dies off, trailing into silence, as odds lengthen and people lose interest.) In a large-bet, well-made match — the kind of match the Balinese regard as "real cockfighting" — the mob scene quality, the sense that sheer chaos is about to break loose, with all those waving, shouting, pushing, clambering men is quite strong, an effect which is only heightened by the intense stillness that falls with instant suddenness, rather as if someone had turned off the current, when the slit gong sounds, the cocks are put down, and the battle begins.

When it ends, anywhere from fifteen seconds to five minutes later, *all bets are immediately paid*. There are absolutely no IOUs, at least to a betting opponent. One may, of course, borrow from a friend before offering or accepting a wager, but to offer or accept it you must have the money already in hand and, if you lose, you must pay it on the spot, before the next match begins. This is an iron rule, and as I have never heard of a disputed umpire's decision (though doubtless there must sometimes be some), I have also never heard of a welshed bet, perhaps because in a worked-up cockfight crowd the consequences might be, as they are reported to be sometimes for cheaters, drastic and immediate.

It is, in any case, this formal asymmetry between balanced center bets and unbalanced side ones that poses the critical analytical problem for a theory which sees cockfight wagering as the link connecting the fight to the wider world of Balinese culture. It also suggests the way to go about solving it and demonstrating the link.

The first point that needs to be made in this connection is that the higher the center bet, the more likely the match will in actual fact be an even one. Simple considerations of rationality suggest that. If you are betting fifteen ringgits on a cock, you might be willing to go along with even money even if you feel your animal somewhat the less promising. But if you are betting five hundred you are very, very likely to be loathe to do so. Thus, in large-bet fights, which of course involve the better animals, tremendous care is taken to see that the cocks are about as evenly matched as to size, general condition, pugnacity, and so on as is humanly possible. The different ways of adjusting the spurs of the animals are often employed to secure this. If one cock seems stronger, an agreement will be made to position his spur at a slightly less advantageous angle — a kind of handicapping, at which spur affixers are, so it is said, extremely skilled. More care will be taken, too, to employ skillful handlers and to match them exactly as to abilities.

In short, in a large-bet fight the pressure to make the match a genuinely fifty-fifty proposition is enormous, and is consciously felt as such. For medium fights the pressure is somewhat less, and for small ones less yet, though there is always an effort to make things at least approximately equal, for even at fifteen ringgits (five days' work) no one wants to make an even money bet in a clearly unfavorable situation. And, again, what statistics I have tend to bear this out. In my fifty-seven matches, the favorite won thirty-three times overall, the underdog twenty-four, a 1.4 : 1 ratio. But if one splits the figures at sixty ringgits center bets, the ratios turn out to be 1.1 : 1 (twelve favorites, eleven underdogs) for those above this line, and 1.6 : 1 (twenty-one and thirteen) for those below it. Or, if you take the extremes, for very large fights, those with center bets over a hundred ringgits the ratio is 1 : 1 (seven and seven); for very small fights, those under forty ringgits, it is 1.9 : 1 (nineteen and ten).[18]

Now, from this proposition — that the higher the center bet the more exactly a fifty-fifty proposition the cockfight is — two things more or less immediately follow: (1) the higher the center bet is, the greater the pull on the side betting toward the short-odds end of the wagering spectrum, and vice versa; (2) the higher the center bet is, the

[18]Assuming only binomial variability, the departure from a fifty-fifty expectation in the sixty-ringgits-and-below case is 1.38 standard deviations, or (in a one direction test) an eight in one hundred possibility by chance alone; for the below-forty-ringgits case it is 1.65 standard deviations, or about five in one hundred. The fact that these departures though real are not extreme merely indicates, again, that even in the smaller fights the tendency to match cocks at least reasonably evenly persists. It is a matter of relative relaxation of the pressures toward equalization, not their elimination. The tendency for high-bet contests to be coin-flip propositions is, of course, even more striking, and suggests the Balinese know quite well what they are about. [Au.]

greater the volume of side betting, and vice versa.

The logic is similar in both cases. The closer the fight is in fact to even money, the less attractive the long end of the odds will appear and, therefore, the shorter it must be if there are to be takers. That this is the case is apparent from mere inspection, from the Balinese's own analysis of the matter, and from what more systematic observations I was able to collect. Given the difficulty of making precise and complete recordings of side betting, this argument is hard to cast in numerical form, but in all my cases the odds-giver, odds-taker consensual point, a quite pronounced mini-max saddle where the bulk (at a guess, two-thirds to three-quarters in most cases) of the bets are actually made, was three or four points further along the scale toward the shorter end for the large-center-bet fights than for the small ones, with medium ones generally in between. In detail, the fit is not, of course, exact, but the general pattern is quite consistent: the power of the center bet to pull the side bets toward its own even-money pattern is directly proportional to its size, because its size is directly proportional to the degree to which the cocks are in fact evenly matched. As for the volume question, total wagering is greater in large-center-bet fights because such fights are considered more "interesting," not only in the sense that they are less predictable, but, more crucially, that more is at stake in them — in terms of money, in terms of the quality of the cocks, and consequently, as we shall see, in terms of social prestige.[19]

The paradox of fair coin in the middle, biased coin on the outside is thus a merely apparent one. The two betting systems, though formally incongruent, are not really contradictory to one another, but are part of a single larger system in which the center bet is, so to speak, the "center of gravity," drawing, the larger it is the more so, the outside bets toward the short-odds end of the scale. The center bet thus "makes the game," or perhaps better, defines it, signals what, following a notion of Jeremy Bentham's,[20] I am going to call its "depth."

The Balinese attempt to create an interesting, if you will, "deep," match by making the center bet as large as possible so that the cocks matched will be as equal and as fine as possible, and the outcome, thus, as unpredictable as possible. They do not always succeed. Nearly half the matches are relatively trivial, relatively uninteresting — in my borrowed terminology, "shallow" — affairs. But that fact no more argues against my interpretation than the fact that most painters, poets, and playwrights are mediocre argues against the view that artistic effort is directed toward profundity and, with a certain frequency, approximates it. The image of artistic technique is indeed exact: the center bet is a means, a device, for creating "interesting," "deep" matches, *not* the reason, or at least not the main reason, *why* they are interesting, the source of their fascination, the substance of their depth. The question of why such matches are interesting — indeed, for the Balinese, exquisitely absorbing — takes us out of the realm of formal concerns into more broadly sociological and social-psychological ones, and to a less purely economic idea of what "depth" in gaming amounts to.[21]

[19]The reduction in wagering in smaller fights (which, of course, feeds on itself; one of the reasons people find small fights uninteresting is that there is less wagering in them, and contrariwise for large ones) takes place in three mutually reinforcing ways. First, there is a simple withdrawal of interest as people wander off to have a cup of coffee or chat with a friend. Second, the Balinese do not mathematically reduce odds, but bet directly in terms of stated odds as such. Thus, for a nine-to-eight bet, one man wagers nine ringgits, the other eight; for five-to-four, one wagers five, the other four. For any given currency unit, like the ringgit, therefore, 6.3 times as much money is involved in a ten-to-nine bet as in a two-to-one bet, for example, and, as noted, in small fights betting settles toward the longer end. Finally, the bets which are made tend to be one- rather than two-, three-, or in some of the very largest fights, four- or five-finger ones. (The fingers indicate the *multiples* of the stated bet odds at issue, not absolute figures. Two fingers in a six-to-five situation means a man wants to wager ten ringgits on the underdog against twelve, three in an eight-to-seven situation, twenty-one against twenty-four, and so on.) [Au.]

[20]Jeremy Bentham (1748–1832) was an English philosopher and the father of Utilitarianism. His *Principles of Morals and Legislation* (1780) advocated a "felicific calculus" that based ethics on the achievement of the greatest good for the greatest number. [Ed.]

[21]Besides wagering there are other economic aspects of the cockfight, especially its very close connection with the local market system which, though secondary both to its motivation and to its function, are not without importance. Cock-

Bentham's concept of "deep play" is found in his *The Theory of Legislation.*[22] By it he means play in which the stakes are so high that it is, from his utilitarian standpoint, irrational for men to engage in it at all. If a man whose fortune is a thousand pounds (or ringgits) wagers five hundred of it on an even bet, the marginal utility of the pound he stands to win is clearly less than the marginal disutility of the one he stands to lose. In genuine deep play, this is the case for both parties. They are both in over their heads. Having come together in search of pleasure they have entered into a relationship which will bring the participants, considered collectively, net pain rather than net pleasure. Bentham's conclusion was, therefore, that deep play was immoral from first principles and, a typical step for him, should be prevented legally.

But more interesting than the ethical problem, at least for our concerns here, is that despite the logical force of Bentham's analysis men do engage in such play, both passionately and often, and even in the face of law's revenge. For Bentham and those who think as he does (nowadays mainly lawyers, economists, and a few psychiatrists), the explanation is, as I have said, that such men are irrational — addicts, fetishists, children, fools, savages, who need only to be protected against themselves. But for the Balinese, though naturally they do not formulate it in so many words, the explanation lies in the fact that in such play, money is less a measure of utility, had or expected, than it is a symbol of moral import, perceived or imposed.

It is, in fact, in shallow games, ones in which smaller amounts of money are involved, that increments and decrements of cash are more nearly synonyms for utility and disutility, in the ordinary, unexpanded sense — for pleasure and pain, happiness and unhappiness. In deep ones, where the amounts of money are great, much more is at stake than material gain: namely, esteem, honor, dignity, respect — in a word, though in Bali a profoundly freighted word, status.[23] It is at stake symbolically, for (a few cases of ruined addict gamblers aside) no one's status is actually altered by the outcome of a cockfight; it is only, and that momentarily, affirmed or insulted. But for the Balinese, for whom nothing is more pleasurable than an affront obliquely delivered or more painful than one obliquely received — particularly when mutual acquaintances, undeceived by surfaces, are watching — such appraisive drama is deep indeed.

This, I must stress immediately, is *not* to say that the money does not matter, or that the Balinese are no more concerned about losing five hundred ringgits than fifteen. Such a conclusion would be absurd. It is because money *does,* in this hardly unmaterialistic society, matter and matter very much that the more of it one risks, the more of a lot of other things, such as one's pride, one's poise, one's dispassion, one's mas-

fights are open events to which anyone who wishes may come, sometimes from quite distant areas, but well over 90 percent, probably over 95, are very local affairs, and the locality concerned is defined not by the village, nor even by the administrative district, but by the rural market system. Bali has a three-day market week with the familiar "solar-system"-type rotation. Though the markets themselves have never been very highly developed, small morning affairs in a village square, it is the microregion such rotation rather generally marks out — ten or twenty square miles, seven or eight neighboring villages (which in contemporary Bali is usually going to mean anywhere from five to ten or eleven thousand people) from which the core of any cockfight audience, indeed virtually all of it, will come. Most of the fights are in fact organized and sponsored by small combines of petty rural merchants under the general premise, very strongly held by them and indeed by all Balinese, that cockfights are good for trade because "they get money out of the house, they make it circulate." Stalls selling various sorts of things as well as assorted sheer-chance gambling games (see below) are set up around the edge of the area so that this even takes on the quality of a small fair. This connection of cockfighting with markets and market sellers is very old, as, among other things, their conjunction in inscriptions [R. Goris, *Prasasti Bali,* 2 vols. (Bandung, 1954)] indicates. Trade has followed the cock for centuries in rural Bali, and the sport has been one of the main agencies of the island's monetization. [Au.]

[22]The phrase is found in the Hildreth translation, International Library of Psychology (1931), note to p. 106; see L. L. Fuller, *The Morality of Law* (New Haven, 1964), p. 6 ff. [Au.]

[23]Of course, even in Bentham, utility is not normally confined as a concept to monetary losses and gains, and my argument here might be more carefully put in terms of a denial that for the Balinese, as for any people, utility (pleasure, happiness . . .) is merely identifiable with wealth. But such terminological problems are in any case secondary to the essential point: the cockfight is not roulette. [Au.]

culinity, one also risks, again only momentarily but again very publicly as well. In deep cockfights an owner and his collaborators, and, as we shall see, to a lesser but still quite real extent also their backers on the outside, put their money where their status is.

It is in large part *because* the marginal disutility of loss is so great at the higher levels of betting that to engage in such betting is to lay one's public self, allusively and metaphorically, through the medium of one's cock, on the line. And though to a Benthamite this might seem merely to increase the irrationality of the enterprise that much further, to the Balinese what it mainly increases is the meaningfulness of it all. And as (to follow Weber rather than Bentham) the imposition of meaning on life is the major end and primary condition of human existence, that access of significance more than compensates for the economic costs involved.[24] Actually, given the even-money quality of the larger matches, important changes in material fortune among those who regularly participate in them seem virtually nonexistent, because matters more or less even out over the long run. It is, actually, in the smaller, shallow fights, where one finds the handful of more pure, addict-type gamblers involved — those who *are* in it mainly for the money — that "real" changes in social position, largely downward, are affected. Men of this sort, plungers, are highly dispraised by "true cockfighters" as fools who do not understand what the sport is all about, vulgarians who simply miss the point of it all. They are, these addicts, regarded as fair game for the genuine enthusiasts, those who do understand, to take a little money away from — something that is easy enough to do by luring them, through the force of their greed, into irrational bets on mismatched cocks. Most of them do indeed manage to ruin themselves in a remarkably short time, but there always seems to be one or two of them around, pawning their land and selling their clothes in order to bet, at any particular time.[25]

This graduated correlation of "status gambling" with deeper fights and, inversely, "money gambling" with shallower ones is in fact quite general. Bettors themselves form a sociomoral hierarchy in these terms. As noted earlier, at most cockfights there are, around the very edges of the cockfight area, a large number of mindless, sheer-chance-type gambling games (roulette, dice throw, coin-spin, pea-under-the-shell) operated by concessionaires. Only women, children, adolescents, and various other sorts of people who do not (or not yet) fight cocks — the extremely poor, the socially despised, the personally idiosyncratic — play at these games, at, of course, penny ante levels. Cockfighting men would be ashamed to go anywhere near them. Slightly above these people in standing are those who though they do not themselves fight cocks, bet on the smaller matches around the edges. Next, there are those who fight cocks in small, or occasionally medium matches, but have not the status to join the large ones, though they may bet from time to time on the side in those. And fi-

[24]M. Weber, *The Sociology of Religion* (Boston, 1963). There is nothing specifically Balinese, of course, about deepening significance with money, as Whyte's description of corner boys in a working-class district of Boston demonstrates: "Gambling plays an important role in the lives of Cornerville people. Whatever game the corner boys play, they nearly always bet on the outcome. When there is nothing at stake, the game is not considered a real contest. This does not mean that the financial element is all-important. I have frequently heard men say that the honor of winning was much more important than the money at stake. The corner boys consider playing for money the real test of skill and, unless a man performs well when money is at stake, he is not considered a good competitor." W. F. Whyte, *Street Corner Society*, 2d ed. (Chicago, 1955), p. 140. [Au.]

[25]The extremes to which this madness is conceived on occasion to go — and the fact that it is considered madness — is demonstrated by the Balinese folk tale *I Tuhung Kuning*. A gambler becomes so deranged by his passion that, leaving on a trip, he orders his pregnant wife to take care of the prospective newborn if it is a boy but to feed it as meat to his fighting cocks if it is a girl. The mother gives birth to a girl, but rather than giving the child to the cocks she gives them a large rat and conceals the girl with her own mother. When the husband returns, the cocks, crowing a jingle, inform him of the deception and, furious, he sets out to kill the child. A goddess descends from heaven and takes the girl up to the skies with her. The cocks die from the food given them, the owner's sanity is restored, the goddess brings the girl back to the father, who reunites him with his wife. The story is given as "Geel Komkommertje" in J. Hooykaas-van Leeuwen Boomkamp, *Sprookjes en Verhalen van Bali* (The Hague, 1956), pp. 19–25. [Au.]

nally, there are those, the really substantial members of the community, the solid citizenry around whom local life revolves, who fight in the larger fights and bet on them around the side. The focusing element in these focused gatherings, these men generally dominate and define the sport as they dominate and define the society. When a Balinese male talks, in that almost venerative way, about "the true cockfighter," the *bebatoh* ("bettor") or *djuru kurung* ("cage keeper"), it is this sort of person, not those who bring the mentality of the pea-and-shell game into the quite different, inappropriate context of the cockfight, the driven gambler (*potét*, a word which has the secondary meaning of thief or reprobate), and the wistful hanger-on, that they mean. For such a man, what is really going on in a match is something rather closer to an *affaire d'honneur* (though, with the Balinese talent for practical fantasy, the blood that is spilled is only figuratively human) than to the stupid, mechanical crank of a slot machine.

What makes Balinese cockfighting deep is thus not money itself, but what, the more of it that is involved the more so, money causes to happen: the migration of the Balinese status hierarchy into the body of the cockfight. Psychologically an Aesopian representation of the ideal/demonic, rather narcissistic, male self, sociologically it is an equally Aesopian representation of the complex fields of tension set up by the controlled, muted, ceremonial, but for all that deeply felt, interaction of those selves in the context of everyday life. The cocks may be surrogates for their owners' personalities, animal mirrors of psychic form, but the cockfight is — or more exactly, deliberately is made to be — a simulation of the social matrix, the involved system of cross-cutting, overlapping, highly corporate groups — villages, kingroups, irrigation societies, temple congregations, "castes" — in which its devotees live.[26] And as prestige, the necessity to affirm it, defend it, celebrate it, justify it, and just plain bask in it (but not, given the strongly ascriptive character of Balinese stratification, to seek it), is perhaps the central driving force in the society, so also — ambulant penises, blood sacrifices, and monetary exchanges aside — is it of the cockfight. This apparent amusement and seeming sport is, to take another phrase from Erving Goffman, "a status bloodbath."[27]

The easiest way to make this clear, and at least to some degree to demonstrate it, is to invoke the village whose cockfighting activities I observed the closest — the one in which the raid occurred and from which my statistical data are taken.

Like all Balinese villages, this one — Tihingan, in the Klungkung region of southeast Bali — is intricately organized, a labyrinth of alliances and oppositions. But, unlike many, two sorts of corporate groups, which are also status groups, particularly stand out, and we may concentrate on them, in a part-for-whole way, without undue distortion.

First, the village is dominated by four large, patrilineal, partly endogamous[28] descent groups which are constantly vying with one another and form the major factions in the village. Sometimes they group two and two, or rather the two larger ones versus the two smaller ones plus all the unaffiliated people; sometimes they operate independently. There are also subfactions within them, subfactions within the subfactions, and so on to rather fine levels of distinction. And second, there is the village itself, almost entirely endogamous, which is opposed to all the other villages round about in its cockfight circuit (which, as explained, is the market region), but which also forms alliances with certain of these neighbors against certain others in various supravillage political and social contexts. The exact situation

[26]For a fuller description of Balinese rural social structure, see C. Geertz, "Form and Variation in Balinese Village Structure," *American Anthropologist* 61 (1959): pp. 94–108; "Tihingan, A Balinese Village," in R. M. Koentjaraningrat, *Villages in Indonesia* (Ithaca, 1967), pp. 210–43; and, though it is a bit off the norm as Balinese villages go, V. E. Korn, *De Dorpsrepubliek tnganan Pagringsingan* (Santpoort, Netherlands, 1933). [Au.]

[27]Goffman, *Encounters*, p. 78. [Au.]

[28]A *patrilineal* society traces descent through the father's line; an *endogamous* society requires its members to marry within their kinship group. [Ed.]

is thus, as everywhere in Bali, quite distinctive; but the general pattern of a tiered hierarchy of status rivalries between highly corporate but various based groupings (and, thus, between the members of them) is entirely general.

Consider, then, as support of the general thesis that the cockfight, and especially the deep cockfight, is fundamentally a dramatization of status concerns, the following facts, which to avoid extended ethnographic description I shall simply pronounce to be facts — though the concrete evidence, examples, statements, and numbers that could be brought to bear in support of them, is both extensive and unmistakable:

1. A man virtually never bets against a cock owned by a member of his own kingroup. Usually he will feel obliged to bet for it, the more so the closer the kin tie and the deeper the fight. If he is certain in his mind that it will not win, he may just not bet at all, particularly if it is only a second cousin's bird or if the fight is a shallow one. But as a rule he will feel he must support it and, in deep games, nearly always does. Thus the great majority of the people calling "five" or "speckled" so demonstratively are expressing their allegiance to their kinsman, not their evaluation of his bird, their understanding of probability theory, or even their hopes of unearned income.

2. This principle is extended logically. If your kingroup is not involved you will support an allied kingroup against an unallied one in the same way, and so on through the very involved networks of alliances which, as I say, make up this, as any other, Balinese village.

3. So, too, for the village as a whole. If an outsider cock is fighting any cock from your village, you will tend to support the local one. If, what is a rarer circumstance but occurs every now and then, a cock from outside your cockfight circuit is fighting one inside it, you will also tend to support the "home bird."

4. Cocks which come from any distance are almost always favorites, for the theory is the man would not have dared to bring it if it was not a good cock, the more so the further he has come. His followers are, of course, obliged to support him, and when the more grand-scale legal cockfights are held (on holidays, and so on) the people of the village take what they regard to be the best cocks in the village, regardless of ownership, and go off to support them, although they will almost certainly have to give odds on them and to make large bets to show that they are not a cheapskate village. Actually, such "away games," though infrequent, tend to mend the ruptures between village members that the constantly occurring "home games," where village factions are opposed rather than united, exacerbate.

5. Almost all matches are sociologically relevant. You seldom get two outsider cocks fighting, or two cocks with no particular group backing, or with group backing which is mutually unrelated in any clear way. When you do get them, the game is very shallow, betting very slow, and the whole thing very dull, with no one save the immediate principals and an addict gambler or two at all interested.

6. By the same token, you rarely get two cocks from the same group, even more rarely from the same subfaction, and virtually never from the same sub-subfaction (which would be in most cases one extended family) fighting. Similarly, in outside village fights two members of the village will rarely fight against one another, even though, as bitter rivals, they would do so with enthusiasm on their home grounds.

7. On the individual level, people involved in an institutionalized hostility relationship, called *puik,* in which they do not speak or otherwise have anything to do with each other (the causes of this formal breaking of relations are many: wife-capture, inheritance arguments, political differences) will bet very heavily, sometimes almost maniacally, against one another in what is a frank and direct attack on the very masculinity, the ultimate ground of his status, of the opponent.

8. The center bet coalition is, in all but the shallowest games, *always* made up by structural allies — no "outside money" is involved. What is "outside" depends upon the context, of course, but given it, no outside money is mixed in with

the main bet; if the principals cannot raise it, it is not made. The center bet, again especially in deeper games, is thus the most direct and open expression of social opposition, which is one of the reasons why both it and matchmaking are surrounded by such an air of unease, furtiveness, embarrassment, and so on.

9. The rule about borrowing money — that you may borrow *for* a bet but not *in* one — stems (and the Balinese are quite conscious of this) from similar considerations: you are never at the *economic* mercy of your enemy that way. Gambling debts, which can get quite large on a rather short-term basis, are always to friends, never to enemies, structurally speaking.

10. When two cocks are structurally irrelevant or neutral so far as *you* are concerned (though, as mentioned, they almost never are to each other) you do not even ask a relative or a friend whom he is betting on, because if you know how he is betting and he knows you know, and you go the other way, it will lead to strain. This rule is explicit and rigid; fairly elaborate, even rather artificial precautions are taken to avoid breaking it. At the very least you must pretend not to notice what he is doing, and he what you are doing.

11. There is a special word for betting against the grain, which is also the word for "pardon me" *(mpura)*. It is considered a bad thing to do, though if the center bet is small it is sometimes all right as long as you do not do it too often. But the larger the bet and the more frequently you do it, the more the "pardon me" tack will lead to social disruption.

12. In fact, the institutionalized hostility relation, *puik*, is often formally initiated (though its causes always lie elsewhere) by such a "pardon me" bet in a deep fight, putting the symbolic fat in the fire. Similarly, the end of such a relationship and resumption of normal social intercourse is often signalized (but, again, not actually brought about) by one or the other of the enemies supporting the other's bird.

13. In sticky, cross-loyalty situations, of which in this extraordinarily complex social system there are of course many, where a man is caught between two more or less equally balanced loyalties, he tends to wander off for a cup of coffee or something to avoid having to bet, a form of behavior reminiscent of that of American voters in similar situations.[29]

14. The people involved in the center bet are, especially in deep fights, virtually always leading members of their group — kinship, village, or whatever. Further, those who bet on the side (including these people) are, as I have already remarked, the more established members of the village — the solid citizens. Cockfighting is for those who are involved in the everyday politics of prestige as well, not for youth, women, subordinates, and so forth.

15. So far as money is concerned, the explicitly expressed attitude toward it is that it is a secondary matter. It is not, as I have said, of no importance; Balinese are no happier to lose several weeks' income than anyone else. But they mainly look on the monetary aspects of the cockfight as self-balancing, a matter of just moving money around, circulating it among a fairly well-defined group of serious cockfighters. The really important wins and losses are seen mostly in other terms, and the general attitude toward wagering is not any hope of cleaning up, of making a killing (addict gamblers again excepted), but that of the horseplayer's prayer: "Oh, God, please let me break even." In prestige terms, however, you do not want to break even, but, in a momentary, punctuate sort of way, win utterly. The talk (which goes on all the time) is about fights against such-and-such a cock of So-and-So which your cock demolished, not on how much you won, a fact people, even for large bets, rarely remember for any length of time, though they will remember the day they did in Pan Loh's finest cock for years.

16. You must bet on cocks of your own group aside from mere loyalty considerations, for if you do not people generally will say, "What! Is he too proud for the likes of us? Does he have to go to Java or Den Pasar [the capital town] to bet, he is such an important man?" Thus there is a gen-

[29]B. R. Berelson, P. F. Lazersfeld, and W. N. McPhee, *Voting: A Study of Opinion Formation in a Presidential Campaign* (Chicago, 1954). [Au.]

eral pressure to bet not only to show that you are important locally, but that you are not so important that you look down on everyone else as unfit even to be rivals. Similarly, home team people must bet against outside cocks or the outsiders will accuse them — a serious charge — of just collecting entry fees and not really being interested in cockfighting, as well as again being arrogant and insulting.

17. Finally, the Balinese peasants themselves are quite aware of all this and can and, at least to an ethnographer, do state most of it in approximately the same terms as I have. Fighting cocks, almost every Balinese I have ever discussed the subject with has said, is like playing with fire only not getting burned. You activate village and kingroup rivalries and hostilities, but in "play" form, coming dangerously and entrancingly close to the expression of open and direct interpersonal and intergroup aggression (something which, again, almost never happens in the normal course of ordinary life), but not quite, because, after all, it is "only a cockfight."

More observations of this sort could be advanced, but perhaps the general point is, if not made, at least well-delineated, and the whole argument thus far can be usefully summarized in a formal paradigm:

THE MORE A MATCH IS . . .

1. Between near status equals (and/or personal enemies)
2. Between high status individuals

THE DEEPER THE MATCH.

THE DEEPER THE MATCH . . .

1. The closer the identification of cock and man (or, more properly, the deeper the match the more the man will advance his best, most closely-identified-with cock).
2. The finer the cocks involved and the more exactly they will be matched.
3. The greater the emotion that will be involved and the more the general absorption in the match.
4. The higher the individual bets center and outside, the shorter the outside bet odds will tend to be, and the more betting there will be overall.
5. The less an "economic" and the more a "status" view of gaming will be involved, and the "solider" the citizens who will be gaming.[30]

Inverse arguments hold for the shallower fight, culminating, in a reversed-signs sense, in the coin-spinning and dice-throwing amusements. For deep fights there are no absolute upper limits, though there are of course practical ones, and there are a great many legendlike tales of great Duel-in-the-Sun combats between lords and princes in classical times (for cockfighting has always been as much an elite concern as a popular one), far deeper than anything anyone, even aristocrats, could produce today anywhere in Bali.

Indeed, one of the great culture heroes of Bali is a prince, called after his passion for the sport, "The Cockfighter," who happened to be away at a very deep cockfight with a neighboring prince when the whole of his family — father, brothers, wives, sisters — were assassinated by commoner usurpers. Thus spared, he returned to dispatch the upstart, regain the throne, reconstitute the Balinese high tradition, and build its most powerful, glorious, and prosperous state. Along with everything else that the Balinese see in fighting cocks — themselves, their social order, abstract hatred, masculinity, demonic power — they also see the archetype of status virtue, the arrogant, resolute, honor-mad player with real fire, the ksatria prince.[31]

[30]As this is a formal paradigm, it is intended to display the logical, not the causal, structure of cockfighting. Just which of these considerations leads to which, in what order, and by what mechanisms, is another matter — one I have attempted to shed some light on in the general discussion. [Au.]

[31]In another of Hooykaas-van Leeuwen Boomkamp's folk tales ("De Gast," *Sprookjes en Verhalen van Bali*, pp. 172–180), a low caste *Sudra*, a generous, pious, and carefree man who is also an accomplished cockfighter, loses, despite his accomplishment, fight after fight until he is not only out of money but down to his last cock. He does not despair, however — "I bet," he says, "upon the unseen World."

His wife, a good and hard-working woman, knowing how much he enjoys cockfighting, gives him her last "rainy day" money to go and bet. But, filled with misgivings due to his run of ill luck, he leaves his own cock at home and bets merely on the side. He soon loses all but a coin or two and re-

FEATHERS, BLOOD, CROWDS, AND MONEY

"Poetry makes nothing happen," Auden says in his elegy of Yeats, "it survives in the valley of its saying . . . a way of happening, a mouth." The cockfight too, in this colloquial sense, makes nothing happen. Men go on allegorically humiliating one another and being allegorically humiliated by one another, day after day, glorying quietly in the experience if they have triumphed, crushed only slightly more openly by it if they have not. *But no one's status really changes.* You cannot ascend the status ladder by winning cockfights; you cannot, as an individual, really ascend it at all. Nor can you descend it that way.[32] All you can do is enjoy and savor, or suffer and withstand, the concocted sensation of drastic and momentary movement along an aesthetic semblance of that ladder, a kind of behind-the-mirror status jump which has the look of mobility without its actuality.

Like any art form — for that, finally, is what we are dealing with — the cockfight renders ordinary, everyday experience comprehensible by presenting it in terms of acts and objects which have had their practical consequences removed and been reduced (or, if you prefer, raised) to the level of sheer appearances, where their meaning can be more powerfully articulated and more exactly perceived. The cockfight is "really real" only to the cocks — it does not kill anyone, castrate anyone, reduce anyone to animal status, alter the hierarchical relations among people, or refashion the hierarchy; it does not even redistribute income in any significant way. What it does is what, for other peoples with other temperaments and other conventions, *Lear* and *Crime and Punishment* do; it catches up these themes — death, masculinity, rage, pride, loss, beneficence, chance — and, ordering them into an encompassing structure, presents them in such a way as to throw into relief a particular view of their essential nature. It puts a construction on them, makes them, to those historically positioned to appreciate the construction, meaningful — visible, tangible, graspable — "real," in an

pairs to a food stand for a snack, where he meets a decrepit, odorous, and generally unappetizing old beggar leaning on a staff. The old man asks for food, and the hero spends his last coins to buy him some. The old man then asks to pass the night with the hero, which the hero gladly invites him to do. As there is no food in the house, however, the hero tells his wife to kill the last cock for dinner. When the old man discovers this fact, he tells the hero he has three cocks in his own mountain hut and says the hero may have one of them for fighting. He also asks for the hero's son to accompany him as a servant, and, after the son agrees, this is done.

The old man turns out to be Siva and, thus, to live in a great palace in the sky, though the hero does not know this. In time, the hero decides to visit his son and collect the promised cock. Lifted up into Siva's presence, he is given the choice of three cocks. The first crows: "I have beaten fifteen opponents." The second crows, "I have beaten twenty-five opponents." The third crows, "I have beaten the king." "That one, the third, is my choice," says the hero, and returns with it to earth.

When he arrives at the cockfight, he is asked for any entry fee and replies, "I have no money; I will pay after my cock has won." As he is known never to win, he is let in because the king, who is there fighting, dislikes him and hopes to enslave him when he loses and cannot pay off. In order to insure that this happens, the king matches his finest cock against the hero's. When the cocks are placed down, the hero's flees, and the crowd, led by the arrogant king, hoots in laughter. The hero's cock then flies at the king himself, killing him with a spur stab in the throat. The hero flees. His house is encircled by the king's men. The cock changes into a Garuda, the great mythic bird of Indic legend, and carries the hero and his wife to safety in the heavens.

When the people see this, they make the hero king and his wife queen and they return as such to earth. Later their son, released by Siva, also returns and the hero-king announces his intention to enter a hermitage. ("I will fight no more cockfights. I have bet on the Unseen and won.") He enters the hermitage and his son becomes king. [Au.] Ksatria is a Hindu warrior caste; Siva is a Hindu god, the third of the high trinity of Brahma, Vishna, and Siva. [Ed.]

[32]Addict gamblers are really less declassed (for their status is, as everyone else's, inherited) than merely impoverished and personally disgraced. The most prominent addict gambler in my cockfight circuit was actually a very high caste *satria* who sold off most of his considerable lands to support his habit. Though everyone privately regarded him as a fool and worse (some, more charitable, regarded him as sick), he was publicly treated with the elaborate deference and politeness due his rank. On the independence of personal reputation and public status in Bali, see above, Chapter 14. [Au.] See "Person, Time, and Combat in Bali," in C. Geertz, *The Interpretation of Cultures*, pp. 360–411. [Ed.]

ideational sense. An image, fiction, a model, a metaphor, the cockfight is a means of expression; its function is neither to assuage social passions nor to heighten them (though, in its playing-with-fire way it does a bit of both), but, in a medium of feathers, blood, crowds, and money, to display them.

The question of how it is that we perceive qualities in things — paintings, books, melodies, plays — that we do not feel we can assert literally to be there has come, in recent years, into the very center of aesthetic theory.[33] Neither the sentiments of the artist, which remain his, nor those of the audience, which remain theirs, can account for the agitation of one painting or the serenity of another. We attribute grandeur, wit, despair, exuberance to strings of sounds; lightness, energy, violence, fluidity to blocks of stone. Novels are said to have strength, buildings eloquence, plays momentum, ballets repose. In this realm of eccentric predicates, to say that the cockfight, in its perfected cases at least, is "disquietful" does not seem at all unnatural, merely as I have just denied it practical consequence, somewhat puzzling.

The disquietfulness arises, "somehow," out of a conjunction of three attributes of the fight: its immediate dramatic shape; its metaphoric content; and its social context. A cultural figure against a social ground, the fight is at once a convulsive surge of animal hatred, a mock war of symbolical selves, and a formal simulation of status tensions, and its aesthetic power derives from its capacity to force together these diverse realities. The reason it is disquietful is not that it has material effects (it has some, but they are minor); the reason that it is disquietful is that, joining pride to selfhood, selfhood to cocks, and cocks to destruction, it brings to imaginative realization a dimension of Balinese experience normally well-obscured from view. The transfer of a sense of gravity into what is in itself a rather blank and unvarious spectacle, a commotion of beating wings and throbbing legs, is effected by interpreting it as expressive of something unsettling in the way its authors and audience live, or, even more ominously, what they are.

As a dramatic shape, the fight displays a characteristic that does not seem so remarkable until one realizes that it does not have to be there: a radically atomistical structure.[34] Each match is a world unto itself, a particulate burst of form. There is the matchmaking, there is the betting, there is the fight, there is the result — utter triumph and utter defeat — and there is the hurried, embarrassed passing of money. The loser is not consoled. People drift away from him, look around him, leave him to assimilate his momentary descent into nonbeing, reset his face, and return, scarless and intact, to the fray. Nor are winners congratulated, or events rehashed; once a match is ended the crowd's attention turns totally to the next, with no looking back. A shadow of the experience no doubt remains with the principals, perhaps even with some of the witnesses of a deep fight, as it remains with us when we leave the theater after seeing a powerful play well-performed; but it quite soon fades to become at most a schematic memory — a diffuse glow or an abstract shudder — and usually not even that. Any expressive form lives only in its own present — the one it itself creates. But, here, that present

[33]For four, somewhat variant, treatments, see S. Langer, *Feeling and Form* (New York, 1953); R. Wollheim, *Art and Its Objects* (New York, 1968); N. Goodman, *Languages of Art* (Indianapolis, 1968); M. Merleau-Ponty, "The Eye and the Mind," in his *The Primacy of Perception* (Evanston, Ill., 1964), pp. 159–90. [Au.]

[34]British cockfights (the sport was banned there in 1840) indeed seem to have lacked it, and to have generated, therefore, a quite different family of shapes. Most British fights were "mains," in which a preagreed number of cocks were aligned into two teams and fought serially. Score was kept and wagering took place both on the individual matches and on the main as a whole. There were also "battle Royales," both in England and on the Continent, in which a large number of cocks were let loose at once with the one left standing at the end the victor. And in Wales, the so-called Welsh main followed an elimination pattern, along the lines of a present-day tennis tournament, winners proceeding to the next round. As a genre, the cock fight has perhaps less compositional flexibility than, say, Latin comedy, but it is not entirely without any. On cockfighting more generally, see A. Ruport, *The Art of Cockfighting* (New York, 1949); G. R. Scott, *History of Cockfighting* (London, 1957); and I Fitz-Barnard, *Fighting Sports* (London, 1921). [Au.]

is severed into a string of flashes, some more bright than others, but all of them disconnected, aesthetic quanta. Whatever the cockfight says, it says in spurts.

But, as I have argued lengthily elsewhere, the Balinese live in spurts.[35] Their life, as they arrange it and perceive it, is less a flow, a directional movement out of the past, through the present, toward the future than an on-off pulsation of meaning and vacuity, and arrhythmic alternation of short periods when "something" (that is, something significant) is happening, and equally short ones where "nothing" (that is, nothing much) is — between what they themselves call "full" and "empty" times, or, in another idiom, "junctures" and "holes." In focusing activity down to a burning-glass dot, the cockfight is merely being Balinese in the same way in which everything from the monadic encounters of everyday life, through the clanging pointillism of *gamelan*[36] music, to the visiting-day-of-the-gods temple celebrations are. It is not an imitation of the punctuateness of Balinese social life, nor a depiction of it, nor even an expression of it; it is an example of it, carefully prepared.[37]

If one dimension of the cockfight's structure, its lack of temporal directionality, makes it seem a typical segment of the general social life, however, the other, its flat-out, head-to-head (or spur-to-spur) aggressiveness, makes it seem a contradiction, a reversal, even a subversion of it. In the normal course of things, the Balinese are shy to the point of obsessiveness of open conflict. Oblique, cautious, subdued, controlled, masters of indirection and dissimulation — what they call *alus,* "polished," "smooth" — they rarely face what they can turn away from, rarely resist what they can evade. But here they portray themselves as wild and murderous, with manic explosions of instinctual cruelty. A powerful rendering of life as the Balinese most deeply do not want it (to adapt a phrase Frye has used of Gloucester's blinding) is set in the context of a sample of it as they do in fact have it.[38] And, because the context suggests that the rendering, if less than a straightforward description, is nonetheless more than an idle fancy; it is here that the disquietfulness — the disquietfulness of the *fight,* not (or, anyway, not necessarily) its patrons, who seem in fact rather thoroughly to enjoy it — emerges. The slaughter in the cock ring is not a depiction of how things literally are among men, but, what is almost worse, of how, from a particular angle, they imaginatively are.[39]

The angle, of course, is stratificatory. What, as we have already seen, the cockfight talks most forcibly about is status relationships, and what it says about them is that they are matters of life and death. That prestige is a profoundly serious business is apparent everywhere one looks in Bali — in the village, the family, the economy, the state. A peculiar fusion of Polynesian title ranks and Hindu castes, the hierarchy of pride is the moral backbone of the society. But only in the cockfight are the sentiments upon which that hierarchy rests revealed in their natural colors. Enveloped elsewhere in a haze of etiquette, a

[35]See "Person, Time and Combat in Bali," in C. Geertz, *The Interpretation of Cultures*, pp. 391–98. [Ed.]

[36]An Indonesian percussion band which includes instruments like xylophones. [Ed.]

[37]For the necessity of distinguishing among "description," "representation," "exemplification," and "expression" (and the irrelevance of "imitation" to all of them) as modes of symbolic reference, see Goodman, *Languages of Art*, pp. 61–110, 45–91, 225–41. [Au.]

[38]N. Frye, *The Educated Imagination* (Bloomington, Ind., 1964), p. 99. [Au.] The reference to Gloucester's blinding is to a scene in Shakespeare's *King Lear*. [Ed.]

[39]There are two other Balinese values and disvalues which, connected with punctuate temporality on the one hand and unbridled aggressiveness on the other, reinforce the sense that the cockfight is at once continuous with ordinary social life and a direct negation of it: what the Balinese call *ramé*, and what they call *paling*. *Ramé* means crowded, noisy, and active, and is a highly sought-after social state: crowded markets, mass festivals, busy streets are all *ramé*, as, of course, is, in the extreme, a cockfight. *Ramé* is what happens in the "full" times (its opposite, *sepi,* "quiet," is what happens in the "empty" ones). *Paling* is social vertigo, the dizzy, disoriented, lost, turned-around feeling one gets when one's place in the coordinates of social space is not clear, and it is a tremendously disfavored, immensely anxiety-producing state. Balinese regard the exact maintenance of spatial orientation ("not to know where north is" is to be crazy), balance, decorum, status relationships, and so forth, as fundamental to ordered life *(krama)* and *paling,* the sort of whirling confusion of position the scrambling cocks exemplify as its profoundest enemy and contradiction. On *ramé,* see Bateson and Mead, *Balinese Character,* pp. 3, 64; on *paling,* ibid., p. 11, and Belo, ed., *Traditional Balinese Culture,* p. 90 ff. [Au.]

thick cloud of euphemism and ceremony, gesture and allusion, they are here expressed in only the thinnest disguise of an animal mask, a mask which in fact demonstrates them far more effectively than it conceals them. Jealousy is as much a part of Bali as poise, envy as grace, brutality as charm; but without the cockfight the Balinese would have a much less certain understanding of them, which is, presumably, why they value it so highly.

Any expressive form works (when it works) by disarranging semantic contexts in such a way that properties conventionally ascribed to certain things are unconventionally ascribed to others, which are then seen actually to possess them. To call the wind a cripple, as Steven does, to fix tone and manipulate timbre, as Schoenberg does, or, closer to our case, to picture an art critic as a dissolute bear, as Hogarth does, is to cross conceptual wires; the established conjunctions between objects and their qualities are altered, and phenomena — fall weather, melodic shape, or cultural journalism — are clothed in signifiers which normally point to other referents.[40] Similarly, to connect — and connect, and connect — the collision of roosters with the divisiveness of status is to invite a transfer of perceptions from the former to the latter, a transfer which is at once a description and a judgment. (Logically, the transfer could, of course, as well go the other way; but, like most of the rest of us, the Balinese are a great deal morc interested in understanding men than they are in understanding cocks.)

What sets the cockfight apart from the ordinary course of life, lifts it from the realm of everyday practical affairs, and surrounds it with an aura of enlarged importance is not, as functionalist sociology[41] would have it, that it reinforces status discriminations (such reinforcement is hardly necessary in a society where every act proclaims them), but that it provides a metasocial commentary upon the whole matter of assorting human beings into fixed hierarchical ranks and then organizing the major part of collective existence around that assortment. Its function, if you want to call it that, is interpretive: it is a Balinese reading of Balinese experience, a story they tell themselves about themselves.

SAYING SOMETHING OF SOMETHING

To put the matter this way is to engage in a bit of metaphorical refocusing of one's own, for it shifts the analysis of cultural forms from an endeavor in general parallel to dissecting an organism, diagnosing a symptom, deciphering a code, or ordering a system — the dominant analogies in contemporary anthropology — to one in general parallel with penetrating a literary text. If one takes the cockfight, or any other collectively sustained symbolic structure, as a means of "saying something of something" (to invoke a famous Aristotelian tag), then one is faced with a problem not in social mechanics but social semantics.[42] For the anthropologist, whose concern is with formulating sociological principles, not with promoting or appreciating cockfights, the question is, what does one learn about such

[40]The Stevens reference is to his "The Motive for Metaphor" ("You like it under the trees in autumn, / Because everything is half dead. / The wind moves like a cripple among the leaves / And repeats words without meaning") [Copyright 1947 by Wallace Stevens, reprinted from *The Collected Poems of Wallace Stevens* by permission of Alfred A. Knopf, Inc., and Faber and Faber Ltd.]; the Schoenberg reference is to the third of his *Five Orchestral Pieces* (Opus 16), and is borrowed from H. H. Drager, "The Concept of 'Tonal Body.'" in *Reflections on Art*, ed. S. Langer (New York, 1961), p. 174. On Hogarth, and on this whole problem — there called "multiple matrix matching" — see E. H. Gombrich, "The Use of Art for the Study of Symbols," in *Psychology and the Visual Arts*, ed. J. Hogg (Baltimore, 1969), pp. 149–170. The more usual term for this sort of semantic alchemy is "metaphorical transfer," and good technical discussions of it can be found in M. Black, *Models and Metaphors* (Ithaca, N.Y., 1962), p. 25 ff; Goodman, *Language as Art*, p. 44 ff; and W. Percy, "Metaphor as Mistake," *Sewanee Review* 66 (1958): 78–99. [Au.]

[41]As the name implies, "functionalist" sociology views social rituals in terms of the performance of social "work": moving individuals from one age-group to another, from one kin-group to another, asserting or claiming social status, and so on. Geertz, to the contrary, sees them as making meanings and interpretations. [Ed.]

[42]The tag is from the second book of the *Organon, On Interpretation*. For a discussion of it, and for the whole argument for freeing "the notion of text . . . from the notion of scripture or writing" and constructing, thus, a general hermeneutics, see P. Ricoeur, *Freud and Philosophy* (New Haven, 1970), p. 20 ff. [Au.]

principles from examining culture as an assemblage of texts?

Such an extension of the notion of a text beyond written material, and even beyond verbal, is, though metaphorical, not, of course, all that novel. The *interpretatio naturae* tradition of the middle ages, which, culminating in Spinoza, attempted to read nature as Scripture, the Nietzschean effort to treat value systems as glosses on the will to power (or the Marxian one to treat them as glosses on property relations), and the Freudian replacement of the enigmatic text of the manifest dream with the plain one of the latent, all offer precedents, if not equally recommendable ones.[43] But the idea remains theoretically undeveloped; and the more profound corollary, so far as anthropology is concerned, that cultural forms can be treated as texts, as imaginative works built out of social materials, has yet to be systematically exploited.[44]

In the case at hand, to treat the cockfight as a text is to bring out a feature of it (in my opinion, the central feature of it) that treating it as a rite or a pastime, the two most obvious alternatives, would tend to obscure: its use of emotion for cognitive ends. What the cockfight says it says in a vocabulary of sentiment — the thrill of risk, the despair of loss, the pleasure of triumph. Yet what it says is not merely that risk is exciting, loss depressing, or triumph gratifying, banal tautologies of affect, but that it is of these emotions, thus exampled, that society is built and individuals are put together. Attending cockfights and participating in them is, for the Balinese, a kind of sentimental education. What he learns there is what his culture's ethos and his private sensibility (or, anyway, certain aspects of them) look like when spelled out externally in a collective text; that the two are near enough alike to be articulated in the symbolics of a single such text; and — the disquieting part — that the text in which this revelation is accomplished consists of a chicken hacking another mindlessly to bits.

Every people, the proverb has it, loves its own form of violence. The cockfight is the Balinese reflection on theirs: on its look, its uses, its force, its fascination. Drawing on almost every level of Balinese experience, it brings together themes — animal savagery, male narcissism, opponent gambling, status rivalry, mass excitement, blood sacrifice — whose main connection is their involvement with rage and the fear of rage, and, binding them into a set of rules which at once contains them and allows them play, builds a symbolic structure in which, over and over again, the reality of their inner affiliation can be intelligibly felt. If, to quote Northrop Frye again, we go to see *Macbeth* to learn what a man feels like after he has gained a kingdom and lost his soul, Balinese go to cockfights to find out what a man, usually composed, aloof, almost obsessively self-absorbed, a kind of moral autocosm, feels like when, attacked, tormented, challenged, insulted, and driven in result to the extremes of fury, he has totally triumphed or been brought totally low. The whole passage, as it takes us back to Aristotle (though to the *Poetics* rather than the *Hermeneutics*), is worth quotation:

> But the poet [as opposed to the historian], Aristotle says, never makes any real statements at all, certainly no particular or specific ones. The poet's job is not to tell you what happened, but what happens: not what did take place, but the kind of thing that always does take place. He gives you the typical, recurring, or what Aristotle calls universal event. You wouldn't go to *Macbeth* to learn about the history of Scotland — you go to it to learn what a man feels like after he's gained a kingdom and lost his soul. When you meet such a character as Micawber in Dickens, you don't feel that there must have been a man Dickens knew who was exactly like this: you feel that there's a bit of Micawber in almost everybody you know, including yourself. Our impressions of human life are picked up one by one, and remain for most of us loose and disorganized. But we constantly find things in literature that suddenly coordinate and bring into focus a

[43]Ibid. [Au.]

[44]Lévi-Strauss' "structuralism" might seem an exception. But it is only an apparent one, for, rather than taking myths, totem rites, marriage rules, or whatever as texts to interpret, Lévi-Strauss takes them as ciphers to solve, which is very much not the same thing. He does not seek to understand symbolic forms in terms of how they function in concrete situations to organize perceptions (meanings, emotions, concepts, attitudes); he seeks to understand them entirely in terms of their internal structure, *independent de tout sujet, de tout objet, et de toute contexte*. [Au.] See "The Cerebral Savage: On the Work of Claude Lévi-Strauss," in C. Geertz, *The Interpretation of Cultures*, pp. 345–59. [Ed.]

great many such impressions, and this is part of what Aristotle means by the typical or universal human event.[45]

It is the kind of bringing of assorted experiences of everyday life to focus that the cockfight, set aside from that life as "only a game" and reconnected to it as "more than a game," accomplishes, and so creates what, better than typical or universal, could be called a paradigmatic human event — that is, one that tells us less what happens than the kind of thing that would happen if, as is not the case, life were art and could be as freely shaped by styles of feeling as *Macbeth* and *David Copperfield* are.

Enacted and re-enacted, so far without end, the cockfight enables the Balinese, as, read and reread, *Macbeth* enables us, to see a dimension of his own subjectivity. As he watches fight after fight, with the active watching of an owner and a bettor (for cockfighting has no more interest as a pure spectator sport than does croquet or dog racing), he grows familiar with it and what it has to say to him, much as the attentive listener to string quartets or the absorbed viewer of still life grows slowly more familiar with them in a way which opens his subjectivity to himself.[46]

Yet, because — in another of those paradoxes, along with painted feelings and unconsequenced acts, which haunt aesthetics — that subjectivity does not properly exist until it is thus organized, art forms generate and regenerate the very subjectivity they pretend only to display. Quartets, still lifes, and cockfights are not merely reflections of a pre-existing sensibility analogically represented; they are positive agents in the creation and maintenance of such a sensibility. If we see ourselves as a pack of Micawbers, it is from reading too much Dickens (if we see ourselves as unillusioned realists, it is from reading too little); and similarly for Balinese, cocks, and cockfights. It is in such a way, coloring experience with the light they cast it in, rather than through whatever material effects they may have, that the arts play their role, as arts, in social life.[47]

In the cockfight, then, the Balinese forms and discovers his temperament and his society's temper at the same time. Or, more exactly, he forms and discovers a particular facet of them. Not only are there a great many other cultural texts providing commentaries on status hierarchy and self-regard in Bali, but there are a great many other critical sectors of Balinese life besides the stratificatory and the agonistic that receive such commentary. The ceremony consecrating a Brahmana priest, a matter of breath control, postural immobility, and vacant concentration upon the depths of being, displays a radically different, but to the Balinese equally real, property of social hierarchy — its reach toward the numinous transcendent. Set not in the matrix of the kinetic emotionality of animals, but in that of the static passionlessness of divine mentality, it expresses tranquillity not disquiet. The mass festivals at the village temples, which mobilize the whole local population in elaborate hostings of visiting gods — songs, dances, compliments, gifts — assert

[45]Frye, *The Educated Imagination*, pp. 63–64. [Au.] See Aristotle, p. 48. [Ed.]

[46]The use of the, to Europeans, "natural" visual idiom for perception — "see," "watches," and so forth — is more than usually misleading here, for the fact that, as mentioned earlier, Balinese follow the progress of the fight as much (perhaps, as fighting cocks are actually rather hard to see except as blurs of motion, more) with their bodies as with their eyes, moving their limbs, heads, and trunks in gestural mimicry of the cocks' maneuvers, means that much of the individual's experience of the fight is kinesthetic rather than visual. If ever there was an example of Kenneth Burke's definition of a symbolic act as "the dancing of an attitude" [*The Philosophy of Literary Form*, rev. ed. (New York, 1957), p. 9] the cockfight is it. On the enormous role of kinesthetic perception in Balinese life, Bateson and Mead, *Balinese Character*, pp. 84–88; on the active nature of aesthetic perception in general, Goodman, *Language of Art*, pp. 241–44. [Au.] For Burke, see p. 581. [Ed.]

[47]All this coupling of the occidental great with the oriental lowly will doubtless disturb certain sorts of aestheticians as the earlier efforts of anthropologists to speak of Christianity and totemism in the same breath disturbed certain sorts of theologians. But as ontological questions are (or should be) bracketed in the sociology of religion, judgmental ones are (or should be) bracketed in the sociology of art. In any case, the attempt to deprovincialize the concept of art is but part of the general anthropological conspiracy to deprovincialize all important social concepts — marriage, religion, law, rationality — and though this is a threat to aesthetic theories which regard certain works of art as beyond the reach of sociological analysis, it is no threat to the conviction, for which Robert Graves claims to have been reprimanded at his Cambridge tripos, that some poems are better than others. [Au.]

the spiritual unity of village mates against their status inequality and project a mood of amity and trust.[48] The cockfight is not the master key to Balinese life, any more than bullfighting is to Spanish. What it says about that life is not unqualified nor even unchallenged by what other equally eloquent cultural statements say about it. But there is nothing more surprising in this than in the fact that Racine and Molière were contemporaries, or that the same people who arrange chrysanthemums cast swords.[49]

The culture of a people is an ensemble of texts, themselves ensembles, which the anthropologist strains to read over the shoulders of those to whom they properly belong. There are enormous difficulties in such an enterprise, methodological pitfalls to make a Freudian quake, and some moral perplexities as well. Nor is it the only way that symbolic forms can be sociologically handled. Functionalism lives, and so does psychologism. But to regard such forms as "saying something of something," and saying it to somebody, is at least to open up the possibility of an analysis which attends to their substance rather than to reductive formulas professing to account for them.

As in more familiar exercises in close reading, one can start anywhere in a culture's repertoire of forms and end up anywhere else. One can stay, as I have here, within a single, more or less bounded form, and circle steadily within it. One can move between forms in search of broader unities or informing contrasts. One can even compare forms from different cultures to define their character in reciprocal relief. But whatever the level at which one operates, and however intricately, the guiding principle is the same: societies, like lives, contain their own interpretations. One has only to learn how to gain access to them.

[48]For the consecration ceremony, see V. E. Korn, "The Consecration of the Priest," in Swellengrebel, ed., *Bali: Studies*, pp. 131–154; for (somewhat exaggerated) village communion, R. Goris, "The Religious Character of the Balinese Village," ibid., pp. 79–100. [Au.]

[49]That what the cockfight has to say about Bali is not altogether without perception and the disquiet it expresses about the general pattern of Balinese life is not wholly without reason is attested by the fact that in two weeks of December 1965, during the upheavals following the unsuccessful coup in Djakarta, between forty and eighty thousand Balinese (in a population of about two million) were killed, largely by one another — the worst outburst in the country. [J. Hughes, *Indonesian Upheaval* (New York, 1967), pp. 173–83. Hughes' figures are, of course, rather casual estimates, but they are not the most extreme.] This is not to say, of course, that the killings were caused by the cockfight, could have been predicted on the basis of it, or were some sort of enlarged version of it with real people in the place of the cocks — all of which is nonsense. It is merely to say that if one looks at Bali not just through the medium of its dances, its shadow-plays, its sculpture, and its girls, but — as the Balinese themselves do — also through the medium of its cockfight, the fact that the massacre occurred seems, if no less appalling, less like a contradiction to the laws of nature. As more than one real Gloucester has discovered, sometimes people actually get life precisely as they most deeply do not want it. [Au.]

Edward W. Said

b. 1935

Although his early writings tended to focus on the usefulness of Continental philosophy and interdisciplinary approaches to literary studies, Edward W. Said's work has increasingly come to deal with questions of the relation of literary criticism to politics. Said was born in Jerusalem, and attended Western schools in Jerusalem, Cairo, and Massachusetts; he went on to take his B.A. at Princeton University (1960) and his Ph.D. at Harvard (1964). Since 1963 he has been a professor of English and comparative literature at Columbia University and a visiting professor at Yale, Stanford, Har-

vard, and Johns Hopkins. Said's professional awards are legion, including a Guggenheim fellowship (1972); his book Orientalism *(1978) was a runner up for a National Book Award for criticism. His other work includes* Joseph Conrad and the Fiction of Autobiography *(1966),* Beginnings: Intention and Method *(1975),* The Question of Palestine *(1979),* The World, the Text, and the Critic *(1983),* After the Last Sky: Palestinian Lives *(1986),* Musical Elaborations *(1991),* Culture and Imperialism *(1993), and* The Politics of Dispossession: The Struggle for Palestinian Self-Determination *(1994). The following selection is taken from the Introduction to* Orientalism.

From the Introduction to *Orientalism*

II

I have begun with the assumption that the Orient is not an inert fact of nature. It is not merely *there,* just as the Occident itself is not just *there* either. We must take seriously Vico's[1] great observation that men make their own history, that what they can know is what they have made, and extend it to geography: as both geographical and cultural entities — to say nothing of historical entities — such locales, regions, geographical sectors as "Orient" and "Occident" are man-made. Therefore as much as the West itself, the Orient is an idea that has a history and a tradition of thought, imagery, and vocabulary that have given it reality and presence in and for the West. The two geographical entities thus support and to an extent reflect each other.

Having said that, one must go on to state a number of reasonable qualifications. In the first place, it would be wrong to conclude that the Orient was *essentially* an idea, or a creation with no corresponding reality. When Disraeli said in his novel *Tancred* that the East was a career,[2] he meant that to be interested in the East was something bright young Westerners would find to be an all-consuming passion; he should not be interpreted as saying that the East was *only* a career for Westerners. There were — and are — cultures and nations whose location is in the East, and their lives, histories, and customs have a brute reality obviously greater than anything that could be said about them in the West. About that fact this study of Orientalism has very little to contribute, except to acknowledge it tacitly. But the phenomenon of Orientalism as I study it here deals principally, not with a correspondence between Orientalism and Orient, but with the internal consistency of Orientalism and its ideas about the Orient (the East as career) despite or beyond any correspondence, or lack thereof, with a "real" Orient. My point is that Disraeli's statement about the East refers mainly to that created consistency, that regular constellation of ideas as that pre-eminent thing about the Orient, and not to its mere being, as Wallace Stevens's phrase has it.[3]

A second qualification is that ideas, cultures, and histories cannot seriously be understood or studied without their force, or more precisely their configurations of power, also being studied. To believe that the Orient was created — or, as I call it, "Orientalized" — and to believe that such things happen simply as a necessity of the imagination, is to be disingenuous. The relationship between Occident and Orient is a relationship of power, of domination, of varying degrees of a complex hegemony, and is quite accurately indicated in the title of K. M. Panikkar's classic *Asia and Western Dominance*.[4] The Orient was Orien-

[1]The *Scienza nuova* (1725) of Italian philosopher Giambattista Vico (1668–1744) presented a theory of historical evolution of cultures. [Ed.]

[2]British prime minister and novelist Benjamin Disraeli (1804–1871) wrote *Tancred* as part of his Condition of England trilogy in 1847. [Ed.]

[3]The author is referring to Wallace Stevens's poem "Of Mere Being" (1955). [Ed.]

[4]K. M. Panikkar, *Asia and Western Dominance* (London: George Allen & Unwin, 1959). [Au.]

talized not only because it was discovered to be "Oriental" in all those ways considered commonplace by an average nineteenth-century European, but also because it *could be* — that is, submitted to being — *made* Oriental. There is very little consent to be found, for example, in the fact that Flaubert's encounter with an Egyptian courtesan produced a widely influential model of the Oriental woman; she never spoke of herself, she never represented her emotions, presence, or history. *He* spoke for and represented her. He was foreign, comparatively wealthy, male, and these were historical facts of domination that allowed him not only to possess Kuchuk Hanem physically but to speak for her and tell his readers in what way she was "typically Oriental." My argument is that Flaubert's situation of strength in relation to Kuchuk Hanem was not an isolated instance. It fairly stands for the pattern of relative strength between East and West, and the discourse about the Orient that it enabled.[5]

This brings us to a third qualification. One ought never to assume that the structure of Orientalism is nothing more than a structure of lies or of myths which, were the truth about them to be told, would simply blow away. I myself believe that Orientalism is more particularly valuable as a sign of European-Atlantic power over the Orient than it is as a veridic discourse about the Orient (which is what, in its academic or scholarly form, it claims to be). Nevertheless, what we must respect and try to grasp is the sheer knitted-together strength of Orientalist discourse, its very close ties to the enabling socio-economic and political institutions, and its redoubtable durability. After all, any system of ideas that can remain unchanged as teachable wisdom (in academies, books, congresses, universities, foreign-service institutes) from the period of Ernest Renan[6] in the late 1840s until the present in the United States must be something more formidable than a mere collection of lies. Orientalism, therefore, is not an airy European fantasy about the Orient, but a created body of theory and practice in which, for many generations, there has been a considerable material investment. Continued investment made Orientalism, as a system of knowledge about the Orient, an accepted grid for filtering through the Orient into Western consciousness, just as that same investment multiplied — indeed, made truly productive — the statements proliferating out from Orientalism into the general culture.

Gramsci[7] has made the useful analytic distinction between civil and political society in which the former is made up of voluntary (or at least rational and noncoercive) affiliations like schools, families, and unions, the latter of state institutions (the army, the police, the central bureaucracy) whose role in the polity is direct domination. Culture, of course, is to be found operating within civil society, where the influence of ideas, of institutions, and of other persons works not through domination but by what Gramsci calls consent. In any society not totalitarian, then, certain cultural forms predominate over others, just as certain ideas are more influential than others; the form of this cultural leadership is what Gramsci has identified as *hegemony,* an indispensable concept for any understanding of cultural life in the industrial West. It is hegemony, or rather the result of cultural hegemony at work, that gives Orientalism the durability and the strength I have been speaking about so far. Orientalism is never far from what Denys Hay has called the idea of Europe,[8] a collective notion identifying "us" Europeans as against all "those" non-Europeans, and indeed it can be argued that the major component in European culture is precisely what made that culture hegemonic both in and outside Europe: the idea of European identity as a superior one in comparison with all the non-European peoples and cultures. There is in addition the hegemony of European ideas about the Orient, themselves reiterating European superiority over

[5]As Said explains later, Kutchuk Hanem was an Egyptian dancer and courtesan with whom Gustave Flaubert slept during his 1859 tour of Greece and the Middle East. Said argues that the experience influenced Flaubert's portraits of oriental women like Salammbô and Salomé as visions of escapist sexual fantasy. [Ed.]

[6]Ernest Renan (1823–1892) won the Prix Volney for his 1847 *General History of the Semitic Languages,* a work Said characterizes as racist and reductive. [Ed.]

[7]See the introduction to Marxist Criticism, p. 1094. [Ed.]

[8]Denys Hay, *Europe: The Emergence of an Idea,* 2nd ed. (Edinburgh: Edinburgh University Press, 1968). [Au.]

Oriental backwardness, usually overriding the possibility that a more independent, or more skeptical, thinker might have had different views on the matter.

In a quite constant way, Orientalism depends for its strategy on this flexible *positional* superiority, which puts the Westerner in a whole series of possible relationships with the Orient without ever losing him the relative upper hand. And why should it have been otherwise, especially during the period of extraordinary European ascendancy from the late Renaissance to the present? The scientist, the scholar, the missionary, the trader, or the soldier was in, or thought about, the Orient because he *could be there,* or could think about it, with very little resistance on the Orient's part. Under the general heading of knowledge of the Orient, and within the umbrella of Western hegemony over the Orient during the period from the end of the eighteenth century, there emerged a complex Orient suitable for study in the academy, for display in the museum, for reconstruction in the colonial office, for theoretical illustration in anthropological, biological, linguistic, racial, and historical theses about mankind and the universe, for instances of economic and sociological theories of development, revolution, cultural personality, national or religious character. Additionally, the imaginative examination of things Oriental was based more or less exclusively upon a sovereign Western consciousness out of whose unchallenged centrality an Oriental world emerged, first according to general ideas about who or what was an Oriental, then according to a detailed logic governed not simply by empirical reality but by a battery of desires, repressions, investments, and projections. If we can point to great Orientalist works of genuine scholarship like Silvestre de Sacy's *Chrestomathie arabe* or Edward William Lane's *Account of the Manners and Customs of the Modern Egyptians,*[9] we need also to note that Renan's and Gobineau's[10] racial ideas came out of the same impulse, as did a great many Victorian pornographic novels (see the analysis by Steven Marcus of "The Lustful Turk"[11]).

And yet, one must repeatedly ask oneself whether what matters in Orientalism is the general group of ideas overriding the mass of material — about which who could deny that they were shot through with doctrines of European superiority, various kinds of racism, imperialism, and the like, dogmatic views of "the Oriental" as a kind of ideal and unchanging abstraction? — or the much more varied work produced by almost uncountable individual writers, whom one would take up as individual instances of authors dealing with the Orient. In a sense the two alternatives, general and particular, are really two perspectives on the same material: in both instances one would have to deal with pioneers in the field like William Jones, with great artists like Nerval or Flaubert.[12] And why would it not be possible to employ both perspectives together, or one after the other? Isn't there an obvious danger of distortion (of precisely the kind that academic Orientalism has always been prone to) if either too general or too specific a level of description is maintained systematically?

My two fears are distortion and inaccuracy, or rather the kind of inaccuracy produced by too dogmatic a generality and too positivistic a localized focus. In trying to deal with these problems I have tried to deal with three main aspects of my own contemporary reality that seem to me to point the way out of the methodological or perspectival difficulties I have been discussing, difficulties that might force one, in the first instance, into writing a coarse polemic on so unacceptably

[9]Baron Antoine Isaac Silvestre de Sacy (1758–1838), French Arabist, published his influential anthology *Chrestomathie Arabe* (3 Vols.) in 1806. Edward William Lane (1801–1876), scholar of oriental languages, published his *Account of the Manners and Customs of the Modern Egyptians* in 1836. [Ed.]

[10]Joseph Arthur, comte de Gobineau (1816–1882), was a French sociologist, whose most important work, *The Moral and Intellectual Diversity of Races* (1854), stated the thesis of Nordic racial superiority espoused by composer Richard Wagner and adopted by Adolf Hitler. [Ed.]

[11]Steven Marcus, *The Other Victorians: A Study of Sexuality and Pornography in Mid-Nineteenth Century England* (1966; reprint ed., New York: Bantam Books, 1967), pp. 200–19. [Au.]

[12]Sir William Jones (1746–1794) translated Arabic and Sanskrit poetry in the 1780s and 1790s. Gérard de Nerval (1808–1855) was a French symbolist poet who wrote *Le Voyage en orient* in 1851. [Ed.]

general a level of description as not to be worth the effort, or in the second instance, into writing so detailed and atomistic a series of analyses as to lose all track of the general lines of force informing the field, giving it its special cogency. How then to recognize individuality and to reconcile it with its intelligent, and by no means passive or merely dictatorial, general and hegemonic context?

III

I mentioned three aspects of my contemporary reality: I must explain and briefly discuss them now, so that it can be seen how I was led to a particular course of research and writing.

1. *The distinction between pure and political knowledge.* It is very easy to argue that knowledge about Shakespeare or Wordsworth is not political whereas knowledge about contemporary China or the Soviet Union is. My own formal and professional designation is that of "humanist," a title which indicates the humanities as my field and therefore the unlikely eventuality that there might be anything political about what I do in that field. Of course, all these labels and terms are quite unnuanced as I use them here, but the general truth of what I am pointing to is, I think, widely held. One reason for saying that a humanist who writes about Wordsworth, or an editor whose specialty is Keats, is not involved in anything political is that what he does seems to have no direct political effect upon reality in the everyday sense. A scholar whose field is Soviet economics works in a highly charged area where there is much government interest, and what he might produce in the way of studies or proposals will be taken up by policymakers, government officials, institutional economists, intelligence experts. The distinction between "humanists" and persons whose work has policy implications, or political significance, can be broadened further by saying that the former's ideological color is a matter of incidental importance to politics (although possibly of great moment to his colleagues in the field, who may object to his Stalinism or fascism or too easy liberalism), whereas the ideology of the latter is woven directly into his material — indeed, economics, politics, and sociology in the modern academy are ideological sciences — and therefore taken for granted as being "political."

Nevertheless the determining impingement on most knowledge produced in the contemporary West (and here I speak mainly about the United States) is that it be nonpolitical, that is, scholarly, academic, impartial, above partisan or small-minded doctrinal belief. One can have no quarrel with such an ambition in theory, perhaps, but in practice the reality is much more problematic. No one has ever devised a method for detaching the scholar from the circumstances of life, from the fact of his involvement (conscious or unconscious) with a class, a set of beliefs, a social position, or from the mere activity of being a member of a society. These continue to bear on what he does professionally, even though naturally enough his research and its fruits do attempt to reach a level of relative freedom from the inhibitions and the restrictions of brute, everyday reality. For there is such a thing as knowledge that is less, rather than more, partial than the individual (with his entangling and distracting life circumstances) who produces it. Yet this knowledge is not therefore automatically nonpolitical.

Whether discussions of literature or of classical philology are fraught with — or have unmediated — political significance is a very large question that I have tried to treat in some detail elsewhere.[13] What I am interested in doing now is suggesting how the general liberal consensus that "true" knowledge is fundamentally nonpolitical (and conversely, that overtly political knowledge is not "true" knowledge) obscures the highly if obscurely organized political circumstances obtaining when knowledge is produced. No one is helped in understanding this today when the adjective "political" is used as a label to discredit any work for daring to violate the protocol of pretended suprapolitical objectivity. We may say, first, that civil society recognizes a gradation of political importance in the various fields of knowledge. To some extent the political importance given a field comes from the possibility of its direct translation into economic terms;

[13]See my book *The World, the Text, and the Critic* (Cambridge, Mass.: Harvard University Press, 1983). [Au.]

but to a greater extent political importance comes from the closeness of a field to ascertainable sources of power in political society. Thus an economic study of long-term Soviet energy potential and its effect on military capability is likely to be commissioned by the Defense Department, and thereafter to acquire a kind of political status impossible for a study of Tolstoi's early fiction financed in part by a foundation. Yet both works belong in what civil society acknowledges to be a similar field, Russian studies, even though one work may be done by a very conservative economist, the other by a radical literary historian. My point here is that "Russia" as a general subject matter has political priority over nicer distinctions such as "economics" and "literary history," because political society in Gramsci's sense reaches into such realms of civil society as the academy and saturates them with significance of direct concern to it.

I do not want to press all this any further on general theoretical grounds: it seems to me that the value and credibility of my case can be demonstrated by being much more specific, in the way, for example, Noam Chomsky has studied the instrumental connection between the Vietnam War and the notion of objective scholarship as it was applied to cover state-sponsored military research.[14] Now because Britain, France, and recently the United States are imperial powers, their political societies impart to their civil societies a sense of urgency, a direct political infusion as it were, where and whenever matters pertaining to their imperial interests abroad are concerned. I doubt that it is controversial, for example, to say that an Englishman in India or Egypt in the later nineteenth century took an interest in those countries that was never far from their status in his mind as British colonies. To say this may seem quite different from saying that all academic knowledge about India and Egypt is somehow tinged and impressed with, violated by, the gross political fact — and yet *that is what I am saying* in this study of Orientalism. For if it is true that no production of knowledge in the human sciences can ever ignore or disclaim its author's involvement as a human subject in his own circumstances, then it must also be true that for a European or American studying the Orient there can be no disclaiming the main circumstances of *his* actuality: that he comes up against the Orient as a European or American first, as an individual second. And to be a European or an American in such a situation is by no means an inert fact. It meant and means being aware, however dimly, that one belongs to a power with definite interests in the Orient, and more important, that one belongs to a part of the earth with a definite history of involvement in the Orient almost since the time of Homer.

Put in this way, these political actualities are still too undefined and general to be really interesting. Anyone would agree to them without necessarily agreeing also that they mattered very much, for instance, to Flaubert as he wrote *Salammbô*, or to H. A. R. Gibb as he wrote *Modern Trends in Islam*.[15] The trouble is that there is too great a distance between the big dominating fact, as I have described it, and the details of everyday life that govern the minute discipline of a novel or a scholarly text as each is being written. Yet if we eliminate from the start any notion that "big" facts like imperial domination can be applied mechanically and deterministically to such complex matters as culture and ideas, then we will begin to approach an interesting kind of study. My idea is that European and then American interest in the Orient was political according to some of the obvious historical accounts of it that I have given here, but that it was the culture that created that interest, that acted dynamically along with brute political, economic, and military rationales to make the Orient the varied and complicated place that it obviously was in the field I call Orientalism.

Therefore, Orientalism is not a mere political subject matter or field that is reflected passively by culture, scholarship, or institutions; nor is it a large and diffuse collection of texts about the Orient; nor is it representative and expressive of

[14]Principally in his *American Power and the New Mandarins: Historical and Political Essays* (New York: Pantheon Books, 1969) and *For Reasons of State* (New York: Pantheon Books, 1973). [Au.]

[15]In this 1947 text Sir Hamilton Gibb wrote of the Muslim "rejection of rationalist modes of thought." [Ed.]

some nefarious "Western" imperialist plot to hold down the "Oriental" world. It is rather a *distribution* of geopolitical awareness into aesthetic, scholarly, economic, sociological, historical, and philological texts; it is an *elaboration* not only of a basic geographical distinction (the world is made up of two unequal halves, Orient and Occident) but also of a whole series of "interests" which, by such means as scholarly discovery, philological reconstruction, psychological analysis, landscape and sociological description, it not only creates but also maintains; it *is,* rather than expresses, a certain *will* or *intention* to understand, in some cases to control, manipulate, even to incorporate, what is a mainfestly different (or alternative and novel) world; it is, above all, a discourse that is by no means in direct, corresponding relationship with political power in the raw, but rather is produced and exists in an uneven exchange with various kinds of power, shaped to a degree by the exchange with power political (as with a colonial or imperial establishment), power intellectual (as with reigning sciences like comparative linguistics or anatomy, or any of the modern policy sciences), power cultural (as with orthodoxies and canons of taste, texts, values), power moral (as with ideas about what "we" do and what "they" cannot do or understand as "we" do). Indeed, my real argument is that Orientalism is — and does not simply represent — a considerable dimension of modern political-intellectual culture, and as such has less to do with the Orient than it does with "our" world.

Because Orientalism is a cultural and a political fact, then, it does not exist in some archival vacuum; quite the contrary, I think it can be shown that what is thought, said, or even done about the Orient follows (perhaps occurs within) certain distinct and intellectually knowable lines. Here too a considerable degree of nuance and elaboration can be seen working as between the broad superstructural pressures and the details of composition, the facts of texuality. Most humanistic scholars are, I think, perfectly happy with the notion that texts exist in contexts, that there is such a thing as intertextuality, that the pressures of conventions, predecessors, and rhetorical styles limit what Walter Benjamin once called the "overtaxing of the productive person in the name of . . . the principle of 'creativity,'" in which the poet is believed on his own, and out of his pure mind, to have brought forth his work.[16] Yet there is a reluctance to allow that political, institutional, and ideological constraints act in the same manner on the individual author. A humanist will believe it to be an interesting fact to any interpreter of Balzac that he was influenced in the *Comédie humaine* by the conflict between Geoffroy Saint-Hilaire and Cuvier,[17] but the same sort of pressure on Balzac of deeply reactionary monarchism is felt in some vague way to demean his literary "genius" and therefore to be less worth serious study. Similarly — as Harry Bracken has been tirelessly showing — philosophers will conduct their discussions of Locke, Hume, and empiricism without ever taking into account that there is an explicit connection in these classic writers between their "philosophic" doctrines and racial theory, justifications of slavery, or arguments for colonial exploitation.[18] These are common enough ways by which contemporary scholarship keeps itself pure.

Perhaps it is true that most attempts to rub culture's nose in the mud of politics have been crudely iconoclastic; perhaps also the social interpretation of literature in my own field has simply not kept up with the enormous technical advances in detailed textual analysis. But there is no getting away from the fact that literary studies in general, and American Marxist theorists in

[16]Walter Benjamin, *Charles Baudelaire: A Lyric Poet in the Era of High Capitalism,* trans. Harry Zohn (London: New Left Books, 1973), p. 71. [Au.]

[17]Étienne Geoffroy Saint-Hilaire (1772–1844), French naturalist, collaborated with paleontologist Baron Georges Cuvier (1769–1832) on five works of natural history published in the first decade of the nineteenth century. The two later quarrelled furiously over biological principle. Cuvier was a functionalist who believed that invariant species were specialized by nature for their ecological niches. Saint-Hilaire, on the contrary, thought that all organisms stemmed from one original structure, and that there were many rudimentary organs that betrayed a long-term evolution of organisms from one mode of functioning to another. [Ed.]

[18]Harry Bracken, "Essence, Accident and Race," *Hermathena* 116 (Winter 1973): 81–96. [Au.]

particular, have avoided the effort of seriously bridging the gap between the superstructural and the base levels in textual, historical scholarship;[19] on another occasion I have gone so far as to say that the literary-cultural establishment as a whole has declared the serious study of imperialism and culture off limits.[20] For Orientalism brings one up directly against that question — that is, to realizing that political imperialism governs an entire field of study, imagination, and scholarly institutions — in such a way as to make its avoidance an intellectual and historical impossibility. Yet there will always remain the perennial escape mechanism of saying that a literary scholar and a philosopher, for example, are trained in literature and philosophy respectively, not in politics or ideological analysis. In other words, the specialist argument can work quite effectively to block the larger and, in my opinion, the more intellectually serious perspective.

Here it seems to me there is a simple two-part answer to be given, at least so far as the study of imperialism and culture (or Orientalism) is concerned. In the first place, nearly every nineteenth-century writer (and the same is true enough of writers in earlier periods) was extraordinarily well aware of the fact of empire: this is a subject not very well studied, but it will not take a modern Victorian specialist long to admit that liberal cultural heroes like John Stuart Mill, Arnold, Carlyle, Newman, Macaulay, Ruskin, George Eliot, and even Dickens had definite views on race and imperialism, which are quite easily to be found at work in their writing. So even a specialist must deal with the knowledge that Mill, for example, made it clear in *On Liberty* and *Representative Government* that his views there could not be applied to India (he was an India Office functionary for a good deal of his life, after all) because the Indians were civilizationally, if not racially, inferior. The same kind of paradox is to be found in Marx, as I try to show in this book. In the second place, to believe that politics in the form of imperialism bears upon the production of literature, scholarship, social theory, and history writing is by no means equivalent to saying that culture is therefore a demeaned or denigrated thing. Quite the contrary: my whole point is to say that we can better understand the persistence and the durability of saturating hegemonic systems like culture when we realize that their internal constraints upon writers and thinkers were *productive,* not unilaterally inhibiting. It is this idea that Gramsci, certainly, and Foucault and Raymond Williams in their very different ways have been trying to illustrate. Even one or two pages by Williams on "the uses of the Empire" in *The Long Revolution* tell us more about nineteenth-century cultural richness than many volumes of hermetic textual analyses.[21]

Therefore I study Orientalism as a dynamic exchange between individual authors and the large political concerns shaped by the three great empires — British, French, American — in whose intellectual and imaginative territory the writing was produced. What interests me most as a scholar is not the gross political verity but the detail, as indeed what interests us in someone like Lane or Flaubert or Renan is not the (to him) indisputable truth that Occidentals are superior to Orientals, but the profoundly worked over and modulated evidence of his detailed work within the very wide space opened up by that truth. One need only remember that Lane's *Manners and Customs of the Modern Egyptians* is a classic of historical and anthropological observation because of its style, its enormously intelligent and brilliant details, not because of its simple reflection of racial superiority, to understand what I am saying here.

The kind of political questions raised by Orientalism, then, are as follows: What other sorts of intellectual, aesthetic, scholarly, and cultural energies went into the making of an imperialist tradition like the Orientalist one? How did philology, lexicography, history, biology, political and economic theory, novel-writing, and lyric poetry come to the service of Orientalism's broadly imperialist view of the world? What changes, mod-

[19]See Raymond Williams on base and superstructure, pp. 1154. [Ed.]

[20]In an interview published in *Diacritics* 6, no. 3 (Fall 1976): 38. [Au.]

[21]Raymond Williams, *The Long Revolution* (London: Chatto & Windus, 1961), pp. 66–7. [Au.]

ulations, refinements, even revolutions take place within Orientalism? What is the meaning of originality, of continuity, of individuality, in this context? How does Orientalism transmit or reproduce itself from one epoch to another? In fine, how can we treat the cultural, historical phenomenon of Orientalism as a kind of *willed human work* — not of mere unconditioned ratiocination — in all its historical complexity, detail, and worth without at the same time losing sight of the alliance between cultural work, political tendencies, the state, and the specific realities of domination? Governed by such concerns a humanistic study can responsibly address itself to politics *and* culture. But this is not to say that such a study establishes a hard-and-fast rule about the relationship between knowledge and politics. My argument is that each humanistic investigation must formulate the nature of that connection in the specific context of the study, the subject matter, and its historical circumstances.

2. *The methodological question.* In a previous book I gave a good deal of thought and analysis to the methodological importance for work in the human sciences of finding and formulating a first step, a point of departure, a beginning principle.[22] A major lesson I learned and tried to present was that there is no such thing as a merely given, or simply available, starting point: beginnings have to be made for each project in such a way as to *enable* what follows from them. Nowhere in my experience has the difficulty of this lesson been more consciously lived (with what success — or failure — I cannot really say) than in this study of Orientalism. The idea of beginning, indeed the act of beginning, necessarily involves an act of delimitation by which something is cut out of a great mass of material, separated from the mass, and made to stand for, as well as be, a starting point, a beginning; for the student of texts one such notion of inaugural delimitation is Louis Althusser's idea of the *problematic,* a specific determinate unity of a text, or group of texts, which is something given rise to by analysis.[23] Yet in the case of Orientalism (as opposed to the case of Marx's texts, which is what Althusser studies) there is not simply the problem of finding a point of departure, or problematic, but also the question of designating which texts, authors, and periods are the ones best suited for study.

It has seemed to me foolish to attempt an encyclopedic narrative history of Orientalism, first of all because if my guiding principle was to be "the European idea of the Orient" there would be virtually no limit to the material I would have had to deal with; second, because the narrative model itself did not suit my descriptive and political interests; third, because in such books as Raymond Schwab's *La Renaissance orientale,* Johann Fück's *Die Arabischen Studien in Europa bis in den Anfang des 20. Jahrhunderts,* and more recently, Dorothee Metlitzki's *The Matter of Araby in Medieval England*[24] there already exist encyclopedic works on certain aspects of the European-Oriental encounter such as make the critic's job, in the general political and intellectual context I sketched above, a different one.

There still remained the problem of cutting down a very fat archive to manageable dimensions, and more important, outlining something in the nature of an intellectual order within that group of texts without at the same time following a mindlessly chronological order. My starting point therefore has been the British, French, and American experience of the Orient taken as a unit, what made that experience possible by way of historical and intellectual background, what the quality and character of the experience has been. For reasons I shall discuss presently I limited that already limited (but still inordinately large) set of questions to the Anglo-French-American experience of the Arabs and Islam, which for almost a thousand years together stood for the Orient. Immediately upon doing that, a large part of the Orient seemed to have been eliminated — India, Japan, China, and other sections of the Far East — not because these regions

[22]In my *Beginnings: Intention and Method* (New York: Basic Books, 1975). [Au.]

[23]Louis Althusser, *For Marx,* trans. Ben Brewster (New York: Pantheon Books, 1969), pp. 65–7. [Au.]

[24]Raymond Schwab, *La Renaissance orientale* (Paris: Payot, 1950); Johann W. Fück, *Die Arabischen Studien in Europa bis in den Anfang des 20. Jahrhunderts* (Leipzig: Otto Harrassowitz, 1955); Dorothee Metlitzki, *The Matter of Araby in Medieval England* (New Haven, Conn.: Yale University Press, 1977). [Au.]

were not important (they obviously have been) but because one could discuss Europe's experience of the Near Orient, or of Islam, apart from its experience of the Far Orient. Yet at certain moments of that general European history of interest in the East, particular parts of the Orient like Egypt, Syria, and Arabia cannot be discussed without also studying Europe's involvement in the more distant parts, of which Persia and India are the most important; a notable case in point is the connection between Egypt and India so far as eighteenth- and nineteenth-century Britain was concerned. Similarly the French role in deciphering the Zend-Avesta,[25] the pre-eminence of Paris as a center of Sanskrit studies during the first decade of the nineteenth century, the fact that Napoleon's interest in the Orient was contingent upon his sense of the British role in India: all these Far Eastern interests directly influenced French interest in the Near East, Islam, and the Arabs.

Britain and France dominated the Eastern Mediterranean from about the end of the seventeenth century on. Yet my discussion of that domination and systematic interest does not do justice to *(a)* the important contributions to Orientalism of Germany, Italy, Russia, Spain, and Portugal and *(b)* the fact that one of the important impulses toward the study of the Orient in the eighteenth century was the revolution in Biblical studies[26] stimulated by such variously interesting pioneers as Bishop Lowth, Eichhorn, Herder, and Michaelis. In the first place, I had to focus rigorously upon the British-French and later the American material because it seemed inescapably true not only that Britain and France were the pioneer nations in the Orient and in Oriental studies, but that these vanguard positions were held by virtue of the two greatest colonial networks in pre-twentieth-century history; the American Oriental position since World War II has fit — I think, quite self-consciously — in the places excavated by the two earlier European powers. Then, too, I believe that the sheer quality, consistency, and mass of British, French, and American writing on the Orient lifts it above the doubtless crucial work done in Germany, Italy, Russia, and elsewhere. But I think it is also true that the major steps in Oriental scholarship were first taken in either Britain and France, then elaborated upon by Germans. Silvestre de Sacy, for example, was not only the first modern and institutional European Orientalist, who worked on Islam, Arabic literature, the Druze religion, and Sassanid Persia; he was also the teacher of Champollion[27] and of Franz Bopp, the founder of German comparative linguistics. A similar claim of priority and subsequent pre-eminence can be made for William Jones and Edward William Lane.

In the second place — and here the failings of my study of Orientalism are amply made up for — there has been some important recent work on the background in Biblical scholarship to the rise of what I have called modern Orientalism. The best and the most illuminatingly relevant is E. S. Shaffer's impressive *"Kubla Khan" and The Fall of Jersualem,*[28] an indispensable study of the origins of Romanticism, and of the intellectual activity underpinning a great deal of what goes on in Coleridge, Browning, and George Eliot. To some degree Shaffer's work refines upon the outlines provided in Schwab, by articulating the material of relevance to be found in the German Biblical scholars and using that material to read, in an intelligent and always interesting way, the

[25]The "bible" of the Zoroastrian religion, sacred to the Parsees. [Ed.]

[26]Said alludes to the "higher criticism" of the late eighteenth and nineteenth centuries which, taking the Bible as created by men (however inspired) rather than by God, sought to understand the biblical texts as products of the near eastern societies of the first millenium B.C. and the two subsequent centuries. This in turn led to intense study of near eastern languages, customs, geography, and history as a means of illuminating the chief documents of Western European religion. [Ed.]

[27]Jean François Champollion (1790–1832) was a French archaeologist who worked out the grammar and lexicon of the ancient Egyptian hieroglyphic language by deciphering the Rosetta Stone. The stone is a black basalt slab discovered by Napoleon's troops in 1799; about two thousand years earlier, it had been inscribed with a royal decree in three scripts: hieroglyphic and demotic Egyptian and Greek. [Ed.]

[28]E. S. Shaffer, *"Kubla Khan" and The Fall of Jerusalem: The Mythological School in Biblical Criticism and Secular Literature, 1770–1880* (Cambridge: Cambridge University Press, 1975). [Au.]

work of three major British writers. Yet what is missing in the book is some sense of the political as well as ideological edge given the Oriental material by the British and French writers I am principally concerned with; in addition, unlike Shaffer I attempt to elucidate subsequent developments in academic as well as literary Orientalism that bear on the connection between British and French Orientalism on the one hand and the rise of an explicitly colonial-minded imperialism on the other. Then too, I wish to show how all these earlier matters are reproduced more or less in American Orientalism after the Second World War.

Nevertheless there is a possibly misleading aspect to my study, where, aside from an occasional reference, I do not exhaustively discuss the German developments after the inaugural period dominated by Sacy. Any work that seeks to provide an understanding of academic Orientalism and pays little attention to scholars like Steinthal, Müller, Becker, Goldziher, Brockelmann, Nöldeke — to mention only a handful — needs to be reproached, and I freely reproach myself. I particularly regret not taking more account of the great scientific prestige that accrued to German scholarship by the middle of the nineteenth century, whose neglect was made into a denunciation of insular British scholars by George Eliot. I have in mind Eliot's unforgettable portrait of Mr. Casaubon in *Middlemarch.* One reason Casaubon cannot finish his Key to All Mythologies is, according to his young cousin Will Ladislaw, that he is unacquainted with German scholarship. For not only has Casaubon chosen a subject "as changing as chemistry: new discoveries are constantly making new points of view": he is undertaking a job similar to a refutation of Paracelsus because "he is not an Orientalist, you know."[29]

Eliot was not wrong in implying that by about 1830, which is when *Middlemarch* is set, German scholarship had fully attained its European pre-eminence. Yet at no time in German scholarship during the first two-thirds of the nineteenth century could a close partnership have developed between Orientalists and a protracted, sustained *national* interest in the Orient. There was nothing in Germany to correspond to the Anglo-French presence in India, the Levant, North Africa. Moreover, the German Orient was almost exclusively a scholarly, or at least a classical, Orient: it was made the subject of lyrics, fantasies, and even novels, but it was never actual, the way Egypt and Syria were actual for Chauteaubriand, Lane, Lamartine, Burton, Disraeli, or Nerval. There is some significance in the fact that the two most renowned German works on the Orient, Goethe's *Westöstlicher Diwan* and Friedrich Schlegel's *Über die Sprache und Weisheit der Indier,*[30] were based respectively on a Rhine journey and on hours spent in Paris libraries. What German Oriental scholarship did was to refine and elaborate techniques whose application was to texts, myths, ideas, and languages almost literally gathered from the Orient by imperial Britain and France.

Yet what German Orientalism had in common with Anglo-French and later American Orientalism was a kind of intellectual *authority* over the Orient within Western culture. This authority must in large part be the subject of any description of Orientalism, and it is so in this study. Even the name *Orientalism* suggests a serious, perhaps ponderous style of expertise; when I apply it to modern American social scientists (since they do not call themselves Orientalists, my use of the word is anomalous), it is to draw attention to the way Middle East experts can still draw on the vestiges of Orientalism's intellectual position in nineteenth-century Europe.

There is nothing mysterious or natural about authority. It is formed, irradiated, disseminated; it is instrumental, it is persuasive; it has status, it establishes canons of taste and value; it is virtually indistinguishable from certain ideas it dignifies as true, and from traditions, perceptions, and judgments it forms, transmits, reproduces. Above

[29]George Eliot, *Middlemarch: A Study of Provincial Life* (1872; reprint ed., Boston: Houghton Mifflin Co., 1956), p. 164. [Au.]

[30]Goethe's *West-östliche Diwan* (1819; the title is untranslatable: the first word is German for "Western/Eastern," the second is Persian for the audience-chamber where the Sultan meets with his court) consists of lyrics imitated from the fourteenth-century Persian poet Hafiz; it is not a scientific treatise like the younger Schlegel's *On the Languages and Learning of India* (1808). [Ed.]

all, authority can, indeed must, be analyzed. All these attributes of authority apply to Orientalism, and much of what I do in this study is to describe both the historical authority in and the personal authorities of Orientalism.

My principal methodological devices for studying authority here are what can be called *strategic location,* which is a way of describing the author's position in a text with regard to the Oriental material he writes about, and *strategic formation,* which is a way of analyzing the relationship between texts and the way in which groups of texts, types of texts, even textual genres, acquire mass, density, and referential power among themselves and thereafter in the culture at large. I use the notion of strategy simply to identify the problem every writer on the Orient has faced: how to get hold of it, how to approach it, how not to be defeated or overwhelmed by its sublimity, its scope, its awful dimensions. Everyone who writes about the Orient must locate himself vis-à-vis the Orient; translated into his text, this location includes the kind of narrative voice he adopts, the type of structure he builds, the kinds of images, themes, motifs that circulate in his text — all of which add up to deliberate ways of addressing the reader, containing the Orient, and finally, representing it or speaking in its behalf. None of this takes place in the abstract, however. Every writer on the Orient (and this is true even of Homer) assumes some Oriental precedent, some previous knowledge of the Orient, to which he refers and on which he relies. Additionally, each work on the Orient *affiliates* itself with other works, with audiences, with institutions, with the Orient itself. The ensemble of relationships between works, audiences, and some particular aspects of the Orient therefore constitutes an analyzable formation — for example, that of philological studies, of anthologies of extracts from Oriental literature, of travel books, of Oriental fantasies — whose presence in time, in discourse, in institutions (schools, libraries, foreign services) gives it strength and authority.

It is clear, I hope, that my concern with authority does not entail analysis of what lies hidden in the Orientalist text, but analysis rather of the text's surface, its exteriority to what it describes. I do not think that this idea can be overemphasized. Orientalism is premised upon exteriority, that is, on the fact that the Orientalist, poet or scholar, makes the Orient speak, describes the Orient, renders its mysteries plain for and to the West. He is never concerned with the Orient except as the first cause of what he says. What he says and writes, by virtue of the fact that it is said or written, is meant to indicate that the Orientalist is outside the Orient, both as an existential and as a moral fact. The principal product of this exteriority is of course representation: as early as Aeschylus's play *The Persians* the Orient is transformed from a very far distant and often threatening Otherness into figures that are relatively familiar (in Aeschylus's case, grieving Asiatic women). The dramatic immediacy of representation in *The Persians* obscures the fact that the audience is watching a highly artificial enactment of what a non-Oriental has made into a symbol for the whole Orient. My analysis of the Orientalist text therefore places emphasis on the evidence, which is by no means invisible, for such representations *as representations,* not as "natural" depictions of the Orient. This evidence is found just as prominently in the so-called truthful text (histories, philological analyses, political treatises) as in the avowedly artistic (i.e., openly imaginative) text. The things to look at are style, figures of speech, setting, narrative devices, historical and social circumstances, *not* the correctness of the representation nor its fidelity to some great original. The exteriority of the representation is always governed by some version of the truism that if the Orient could represent itself, it would; since it cannot, the representation does the job, for the West, and *faute de mieux,*[31] for the poor Orient. "Sie können sich nicht vertreten, sie müssen vertreten werden," as Marx wrote in *The Eighteenth Brumaire of Louis Bonaparte.*[32]

Another reason for insisting upon exteriority is that I believe it needs to be made clear about cultural discourse and exchange within a culture that what is commonly circulated by it is not

[31]For want of better. [Ed.]

[32]"They cannot represent themselves: they must be represented." Marx's statement about the class of small peasant proprietors in *The Eighteenth Brumaire of Louis Bonaparte.* [Ed.]

"truth" but representations. It hardly needs to be demonstrated again that language itself is a highly organized and encoded system, which employs many devices to express, indicate, exchange messages and information, represent, and so forth. In any instance of at least written language, there is no such thing as a delivered presence, but a *re-presence,* or a representation. The value, efficacy, strength, apparent veracity of a written statement about the Orient therefore relies very little, and cannot instrumentally depend, on the Orient as such. On the contrary, the written statement is a presence to the reader by virtue of its having excluded, displaced, made supererogatory any such *real thing* as "the Orient." Thus all of Orientalism stands forth and away from the Orient: that Orientalism makes sense at all depends more on the West than on the Orient, and this sense is directly indebted to various Western techniques of representation that make the Orient visible, clear, "there" in discourse about it. And these representations rely upon institutions, traditions, conventions, agreed-upon codes of understanding for their effects, not upon a distant and amorphous Orient.

The difference between representations of the Orient before the last third of the eighteenth century and those after it (that is, those belonging to what I call modern Orientalism) is that the range of representation expanded enormously in the later period. It is true that after William Jones and Anquetil-Duperron,[33] and after Napoleon's Egyptian expedition, Europe came to know the Orient more scientifically, to live in it with greater authority and discipline than ever before. But what mattered to Europe was the expanded scope and the much greater refinement given its techniques for receiving the Orient. When around the turn of the eighteenth century the Orient definitively revealed the age of its languages — thus outdating Hebrew's divine pedigree — it was a group of Europeans who made the discovery, passed it on to other scholars, and preserved the discovery in the new science of Indo-European philology. A new powerful science for viewing the linguistic Orient was born, and with it, as Foucault has shown in *The Order of Things,* a whole web of related scientific interests. Similarly William Beckford,[34] Byron, Goethe, and Hugo restructured the Orient by their art and made its colors, lights, and people visible through their images, rhythms, and motifs. At most, the "real" Orient provoked a writer to his vision; it very rarely guided it.

Orientalism responded more to the culture that produced it than to its putative object, which was also produced by the West. Thus the history of Orientalism has both an internal consistency and a highly articulated set of relationships to the dominant culture surrounding it. My analyses consequently try to show the field's shape and internal organization, its pioneers, patriarchal authorities, canonical texts, doxological ideas, exemplary figures, its followers, elaborators, and new authorities; I try also to explain how Orientalism borrowed and was frequently informed by "strong" ideas, doctrines, and trends ruling the culture. Thus there was (and is) a linguistic Orient, a Freudian Orient, a Spenglerian Orient, a Darwinian Orient, a racist Orient — and so on. Yet never has there been such a thing as a pure, or unconditional, Orient; similarly, never has there been a nonmaterial form of Orientalism, much less something so innocent as an "idea" of the Orient. In this underlying conviction and in its ensuing methodological consequences do I differ from scholars who study the history of ideas. For the emphases and the executive form, above all the material effectiveness, of statements made by Orientalist discourse are possible in ways that any hermetic history of ideas tends completely to scant. Without those emphases and that material effectiveness Orientalism would be just another idea, whereas it is and was much more than that. Therefore I set out to examine not only scholarly works but also works of literature, political tracts, journalistic texts, travel books, re-

[33]Abraham Hyacinthe Anquetil-Duperron (1731–1805), French orientalist, author of *Zend-Avesta* (1771, 3 vols.), a life of Zoroaster and a collection of Zoroastrisan writings. [Ed.]

[34]William Beckford (1760–1844), English author of *The History of the Caliph Vathek* (1782 in French, translated in 1786), an oriental Gothic tale. [Ed.]

ligious and philological studies. In other words, my hybrid perspective is broadly historical and "anthropological," given that I believe all texts to be worldly and circumstantial in (of course) ways that vary from genre to genre, and from historical period to historical period.

Yet unlike Michel Foucault, to whose work I am greatly indebted, I do believe in the determining imprint of individual writers upon the otherwise anonymous collective body of texts constituting a discursive formation like Orientalism. The unity of the large ensemble of texts I analyze is due in part to the fact that they frequently refer to each other: Orientalism is after all a system for citing works and authors. Edward William Lane's *Manners and Customs of the Modern Egyptians* was read and cited by such diverse figures as Nerval, Flaubert, and Richard Burton.[35] He was an authority whose use was an imperative for anyone writing or thinking about the Orient, not just about Egypt: when Nerval borrows passages verbatim from *Modern Egyptians* it is to use Lane's authority to assist him in describing village scenes in Syria, not Egypt. Lane's authority and the opportunities provided for citing him discriminately as well as indiscriminately were there because Orientalism could give his text the kind of distributive currency that he acquired. There is no way, however, of understanding Lane's currency without also understanding the peculiar features of *his* text; this is equally true of Renan, Sacy, Lamartine, Schlegel, and a group of other influential writers. Foucault believes that in general the individual text or author counts for very little; empirically, in the case of Orientalism (and perhaps nowhere else) I find this not to be so. Accordingly my analyses employ close textual readings whose goal is to reveal the dialectic between individual text or writer and the complex collective formation to which his work is a contribution.

Yet even though it includes an ample selection of writers, this book is still far from a complete history or general account of Orientalism. Of this failing I am very conscious. The fabric of as thick a discourse as Orientalism has survived and functioned in Western society because of its richness: all I have done is to describe parts of that fabric at certain moments, and merely to suggest the existence of a larger whole, detailed, interesting, dotted with fascinating figures, texts, and events. I have consoled myself with believing that this book is one installment of several, and hope there are scholars and critics who might want to write others. There is still a general essay to be written on imperialism and culture; other studies would go more deeply into the connection between Orientalism and pedagogy, or into Italian, Dutch, German, and Swiss Orientalism, or into the dynamic between scholarship and imaginative writing, or into the relationship between administrative ideas and intellectual discipline. Perhaps the most important task of all would be to undertake studies in contemporary alternatives to Orientalism, to ask how one can study other cultures and peoples from a libertarian, or a nonrepressive and nonmanipulative, perspective. But then one would have to rethink the whole complex problem of knowledge and power. These are all tasks left embarrassingly incomplete in this study.

The last, perhaps self-flattering, observation on method that I want to make here is that I have written this study with several audiences in mind. For students of literature and criticism, Orientalism offers a marvelous instance of the interrelations between society, history, and textuality; moreover, the cultural role played by the Orient in the West connects Orientalism with ideology, politics, and the logic of power, matters of relevance, I think, to the literary community. For contemporary students of the Orient, from university scholars to policymakers, I have written with two ends in mind: one, to present their intellectual genealogy to them in a way that has not been done; two, to criticize — with the hope of stirring discussion — the often unquestioned assumptions on which their work for the most part depends. For the general reader, this study deals with matters that always compel attention, all of them connected not only with Western conceptions and treatments of the Other but also with

[35]Sir Richard Francis Burton (1821–1890), known for his African explorations as well as his sixteen-volume translation of *The Arabian Nights* (1885–88). [Ed.]

the singularly important role played by Western culture in what Vico called the world of nations. Lastly, for readers in the so-called Third World, this study proposes itself as a step towards an understanding not so much of Western politics and of the non-Western world in those politics as of the *strength* of Western cultural discourse, a strength too often mistaken as merely decorative or "superstructural." My hope is to illustrate the formidable structure of cultural domination and, specifically for formerly colonized peoples, the dangers and temptations of employing this structure upon themselves or upon others.[36]

[36]Said's third aspect "of my contemporary reality" (see p. 1282), omitted in this selection, is "the personal dimension," his own experience as "a child growing up in two British colonies." [Ed.]

Stephen Greenblatt

b. 1943

Renaissance scholar Stephen Jay Greenblatt is in the vanguard of academics responsible for the rise of New Historicist studies in the United States. Greenblatt was born in Cambridge, Massachusetts; he took a B.A. (1964), an M.Phil. (1968), and a Ph.D. (1969) in English at Yale, and an A.B. (1966) and M.A. (1968) at Pembroke College, Cambridge University. Since 1969 Greenblatt has taught at the University of California at Berkeley, becoming a full professor in 1980. Among Greenblatt's honors are a Fulbright scholarship (1964–66), a Guggenheim fellowship (1975), and a visiting professorship at the University of Peking (1982). His books include Sir Walter Raleigh: The Renaissance Man and His Roles *(1973),* Allegory and Representation *(1979),* Renaissance Self-Fashioning: From More to Shakespeare *(1980),* Representing the English Renaissance *(1988),* Shakespearean Negotiations: The Circulation of Social Energy in Renaissance England *(1988),* Learning to Curse: Essays in Early Modern Culture *(1990),* Marvelous Possessions: The Wonder of the New World *(1991),* Re-Drawing the Boundaries: The Transformation of English and American Literary Studies *(1992, ed., with Giles Gunn), and* New World Encounters *(1992). Greenblatt is also the editor of* Representations, *a Berkeley-based journal in which New Historicist articles regularly appear. The selections here are from a special issue of* Genre *(Spring/Summer 1982), titled* The Power of Forms in the English Renaissance. *In the Introduction, Greenblatt makes reference to some of the other essays in the volume but not to his own* "King Lear *and Harsnett's 'Devil-Fiction.'"*

Introduction to *The Power of Forms in the English Renaissance*

"I am Richard II. Know ye not that?" exclaimed Queen Elizabeth on August 4, 1601, in the wake of the abortive Essex rising. On the day before the rising, someone had paid the Lord Chamberlain's Men forty shillings to revive their old play about the deposing and killing of Richard II. As far as we know, the play — almost certainly Shakespeare's — was performed only once at the Globe, but in Elizabeth's bitter recollection the performance has metastasized: "this tragedy was played 40tie times in open streets and houses."[1]

The Queen enjoyed and protected the theater; against moralists who charged that it was a corrupting and seditious force, she evidently sided with those who replied that it released social tensions, inculcated valuable moral lessons, and occupied with harmless diversion those who might otherwise conspire against legitimate authority. But there were some in the Essex faction who saw in the theater the power to subvert, or rather the power to wrest legitimation from the established ruler and confer it on another. This power, notwithstanding royal protection, censorship, and the players' professions of unswerving loyalty, could be purchased for forty shillings.

The story of Richard II was obviously a highly charged one in a society where political discussion was conducted, as in parts of the world today, with Aesopian indirection. Clearly it is not the text alone — over which the censor had some control — that bears the full significance of Shakespeare's play, or of any version of the story. It is rather the story's full situation — the genre it is thought to embody, the circumstances of its performance, the imaginings of its audience — that governs its shifting meanings. "40tie times in open streets and houses": for the Queen the repeatability of the tragedy, and hence the numbers of people who have been exposed to its infection, is part of the danger, along with the fact (or rather her conviction) that the play had broken out of the boundaries of the playhouse, where such stories are clearly marked as powerful illusions, and moved into the more volatile zone — the zone she calls "open" — of the streets. In the streets the story begins to lose the conventional containment of the playhouse, where audiences are kept at a safe distance both from the action on stage and from the world beyond the walls. And in the wake of this subversive deregulation, the terms that mark the distinction between the lucid and the real become themselves problematic: are the "houses" to which Elizabeth refers public theaters or private dwellings where her enemies plot her overthrow? can "tragedy" be a strictly literary term when the Queen's own life is endangered by the play?[2]

Modern historical scholarship has assured Elizabeth that she had nothing to worry about: *Richard II* is not at all subversive but rather a hymn to Tudor order. The play, far from encouraging thoughts of rebellion, regards the deposition of the legitimate king as a "sacrilegious" act that drags the country down into "the abyss of chaos"; "that Shakespeare and his audience regarded Bolingbroke as a usurper," declares J. Dover Wilson, "is incontestable."[3] But in 1601 neither Queen Elizabeth nor the Earl of Essex were so sure: after all, someone on the eve of a

[1]Elizabeth was speaking to William Lambarde the antiquary; see the Arden edition of Shakespeare's *King Richard II,* ed. Peter Ure (Cambridge: Harvard University Press, 1956), pp. lvii–lxii. [Au.]

[2]The ambiguity is intensified by the Queen's preceding comment, according to Lambarde: "*Her Majestie.* 'He that will forget God, will also forget his benefactors; this tragedy was played 40tie times in open streets and houses'" (Ure, p. lix). [Au.]

[3]John Dover Wilson, "The Political Background of Shakespeare's *Richard II* and *Henry IV,*" *Shakespeare-Jahrbuch,* 75 (1939), 47. The condemnation of Bolingbroke is "evident," we are told, "from the whole tone and emphasis of *Richard II*" (p. 48). I am grateful to Patricia Allen for the reference to this essay. [Au.]

rebellion thought the play sufficiently seditious to warrant squandering two pounds on the players, and the Queen understood the performance as a threat. Moreover, even before the Essex rising, the actual deposition scene (IV.i.154–318 in the Arden edition) was carefully omitted from the first three quartos of Shakespeare's play and appears for the first time only after Elizabeth's death.

How can we account for the discrepancy between Dover Wilson's historical reconstruction and the anxious response of the figures whose history he purports to have accurately reconstructed? The answer lies at least in part in the difference between a conception of art that has no respect whatsoever for the integrity of the text ("I am Richard II. Know ye not that?") and one that hopes to find, through historical research, a stable core of meaning within the text, a core that united disparate and even contradictory parts into an organic whole. That whole may provide a perfectly orthodox celebration of legitimacy and order, as measured by homilies, royal pronouncements, and official propaganda, but the Queen is clearly responding to something else: to the presence of *any* representation of deposition, whether regarded as sacrilegious or not; to the choice of this particular story at this particular time; to the place of the performance; to her own identity as it is present in the public sphere and as it fuses with the figure of the murdered king. Dover Wilson is not a New Critic: he does not conceive of the text as an iconic object whose meaning is perfectly contained within its own formal structure. Yet for him historical research has the effect of conferring autonomy and fixity upon the text, and it is precisely this fixity that is denied by Elizabeth's response.

Dover Wilson's work is a distinguished example of the characteristic assumptions and methods of the mainstream literary history practiced in the first half of our century, and a further glance at these may help us to bring into focus the distinctive assumptions and methods exemplified in the essays collected in this volume. To be sure, these essays are quite diverse in their concerns and represent no single critical practice; a comparative glance, for example, at the brilliant pieces by Franco Moretti and John Traugott will suggest at once how various this work is. Yet diverse as they are, many of the present essays give voice, I think, to what we may call the new historicism, set apart from both the dominant historical scholarship of the past and the formalist criticism that partially displaced this scholarship in the decades after World War Two. The earlier historicism tends to be monological; that is, it is concerned with discovering a single political vision, usually identical to that said to be held by the entire literate class or indeed the entire population ("In the eyes of the later middle ages," writes Dover Wilson, Richard II "represented the type and exemplar of royal martyrdom" [p. 50]). This vision, most often presumed to be internally coherent and consistent, though occasionally analyzed as the fusion of two or more elements, has the status of an historical fact. It is not thought to be the product of the historian's interpretation, nor even of the particular interests of a given social group in conflict with other groups. Protected then from interpretation and conflict, this vision can serve as a stable point of reference, beyond contingency, to which literary interpretation can securely refer. Literature is conceived to mirror the period's beliefs, but to mirror them, as it were, from a safe distance.

The new historicism erodes the firm ground of both criticism and literature. It tends to ask questions about its own methodological assumptions and those of others: in the present case, for example, it might encourage us to examine the ideological situation not only of *Richard II* but of Dover Wilson on *Richard II*. The lecture from which I have quoted — "The Political Background of Shakespeare's *Richard II* and *Henry IV*" — was delivered before the German Shakespearean Society, at Weimar, in 1939. We might, in a full discussion of the critical issues at stake here, look closely at the relation between Dover Wilson's reading of *Richard II* — a reading that discovers Shakespeare's fears of chaos and his consequent support for legitimate if weak authority over the claims of ruthless usurpers — and the eerie occasion of his lecture ("these plays," he concludes, "should be of particular interest to German students at this moment of that everlasting adventure which we call history" [p. 51]).

Moreover, recent criticism has been less concerned to establish the organic unity of literary works and more open to such works as fields of force, places of dissension and shifting interests, occasions for the jostling of orthodox and subversive impulses. "The Elizabeth playhouse, playwright, and player," writes Louis Adrian Montrose in a brilliant recent essay, "exemplify the contradictions of Elizabethan society and make those contradictions their subject. If the world is a theatre and the theatre is an image of the world, then by reflecting upon its own artifice, the drama is holding the mirror up to nature."[4] As the problematizing of the mirror metaphor suggests, Renaissance literary works are no longer regarded either as a fixed set of texts that are set apart from all other forms of expression and that contain their own determinate meanings or as a stable set of reflections of historical facts that lie beyond them. The critical practice represented in [*The Power of Forms in the English Renaissance*] challenges the assumptions that guarantee a secure distinction between "literary foreground" and "political background" or, more generally, between artistic production and other kinds of social production. Such distinctions do in fact exist, but they are not intrinsic to the texts; rather they are made up and constantly redrawn by artists, audiences, and readers. These collective social constructions on the one hand define the range of aesthetic possibilities within a given representational mode and, on the other, link that mode to the complex network of institutions, practices, and beliefs that constitute the culture as a whole. In this light, the study of genre is an exploration of the poetics of culture.

[4]"The Purpose of Playing: Reflections on a Shakespearean Anthropology," *Helios*, n.s. 7 (1980), 57. [Au.]

King Lear *and Harsnett's "Devil-Fiction"*

Modern critics tend to assume that Shakespearean self-consciousness and irony lead to a radical transcendence of the network of social conditions, paradigms, and practices in the plays. I would submit, by contrast, that Renaissance theatrical representation itself is fully implicated in this network and that Shakespeare's self-consciousness is in significant ways bound up with the institutions and the symbology of power it anatomizes.

To grasp this wc might consider *King Lear*. We happen to know one of the books that Shakespeare had been reading and seems indeed to have had open before him as he revised the old play of *King Leir*. The book, printed in 1603, is by Samuel Harsnett, then chaplain to the Bishop of London, and is entitled *A Declaration of Egregious Popish Impostures, to with-draw the harts of her Majesties Subjects from their allegeance, and from the truth of Christian Religion professed in England, under the pretense of casting out devils. Practised by Edmunds, alias Weston a Jesuit, and divers Romish Priests his wicked associates. Where-unto are annexed the Copies of the Confessions and Examinations of the parties themselves, which were pretended to be possessed, and dispossessed, taken upon oath before her Majesties Commissioners for Causes Ecclesiasticall.*[1] From this remarkable book — a scathing account of a series of spectacular exor-

[1]On Harsnett, see D. P. Walker, *Unclean Spirits: Possession and Exorcism in France and England in the Late Sixteenth and Early Seventeenth Centuries* (Philadelphia: University of Pennsylvania Press, 1981), pp. 43–49; Keith Thomas, *Religion and the Decline of Magic* (Longon: Weidenfeld and Nicolson, 1971), pp. 477–92. On Harsnett and *Lear*, see Kenneth Muir, "Samuel Harsnett and *King Lear*," *RES*, New Series 2 (1951), 11–21; William Elton, *King Lear and the Gods* (San Marino, CA: Huntington Library, 1966). [Au.]

cisms conducted between the spring of 1585 and the summer of 1586 principally in the house of a recusant gentleman, Sir George Peckham of Denham, Buckinghamshire — Shakespeare took many small details, especially for the demonology Edgar exhibits in his disguise as the possessed Poor Tom. My interest here is not in these details which have been noted since the eighteenth century, but in the broader institutional implications of Harsnett's text and of the uses to which Shakespeare puts it.

The *Declaration* is a semi-official attack on exorcism as practiced by Jesuits secretly residing in England (and under constant threat of capture and execution), but the charges are not limited to Catholicism, since Harsnett had earlier written against the Puritan exorcist John Darrell. Like other spokesmen for the Anglican establishment, Harsnett concedes that at some distant time exorcism was a legitimate practice (as, of course, it is in the Bible), but miracles have ceased and corporeal possession by demons is no longer possible. What has taken its place, he writes, is fraud, and, more precisely, theater: exorcisms are stage plays written by cunning clerical dramatists and performed by skilled actors. To be sure, not all the participants are professionals, but the priests, as Harsnett depicts them, run what is in effect an acting school. They begin by talking about the way successful exorcisms abroad had taken place and describe in lurid detail the precise symptoms of the possessed; then the young "schollers," as Harsnett calls those whom the priests have chosen to manipulate, "*frame* themselves jumpe and fit unto the Priests humors, to mop, mow, jest, raile, rave, roare, commend & discommend, and as the priest would have them, upon fitting occasions (according to the difference of times, places, and commers in) in all things to play the devils accordinglie" (p. 38).

Harsnett's *Declaration* then is a massive document of disenchantment; the solemn ceremony of exorcism is, as the attack on Darrell puts it, "now discovered to be but a pure play," and the reverence and fear that the performance inspires are nothing but "miserable shiftes to helpe [the exorcist] off the stage, that he might not be hissed at of all the world."[2] The Jesuits and their retinue are not a holy band driven by religious persecution to move from place to place but closely resemble "vagabond players, that coast from Towne to Towne with a trusse and a cast of fiddles, to carry in theyr consort, broken queanes, and *Ganimedes,* as well for their night pleasance, as their dayes pastime" (p. 149). The power this sleazy crew possesses is the power of the theater. If the end of a comedy, Harsnett notes, is applause for the author and actors, while the end of a tragedy is the "moving of affection, and passion in the spectators," our "*Daemonopoiia,* or devil-fiction, is *Tragico-commaedia,*" for it elicits both exclamations of admiration — "*O that all the Protestans* (sic) *in England did see the power of the Catholick Church*" — and tears (p. 50).

The spectators, of course, do not know that they are merely responding to an effective if tawdry play; they believe that they are celebrants at a moving and sanctified communal ritual. "The devil speakes treason . . . so aptly, distinctly, and elegantly on the stage, that it enchaunted the harts, and affections of the poore bewitched people, and chained them to the Pope" (p. 154); the lowest estimate of the conversions achieved "by this well acted tragedie" is five hundred, and Harsnett states that "devil-tragedians" themselves claim four to five thousand converts. To impress these large crowds, the exorcists, led by Father Edmunds, invoke the vast forces of heaven and hell, call forth by name whole legions of devils, and drive them from the bodies of the possessed by means of powerful amulets and charms. The performance is spectacular, with the writhing demoniac bound in a chair and tortured until the devils are compelled to depart. But the devils, says Harsnett, are tattered figures from the old Church plays, their names grotesque forgeries, and the hallowed vestments and holy objects contemptible stage properties. As for the possessed themselves, they are either histrionic scoundrels like Robert Maynie or servant girls like the sisters Sara and Friswood Williams,

[2]Samuel Harsnett, *A Discovery of the Fraudulent Practices of John Darrel* (London, 1599), p. A3^r. [Au.]

whose position of social dependency made them susceptible to the powers of suggestion, intimidation, and torture.

Harsnett's detailed identification of exorcism as theater, a conception that is elaborated through almost three hundred pages, is more than a satirical analogy; it is a polemical institutional analysis whose purpose is not only to expose the fraudulence of exorcism but to link that practice to the pervasive theatricality of the Catholic Church (or, as Harsnett elsewhere terms it, "the Pope's playhouse").[3] Priests do not actually believe in their "charmes, and consecrate attire," but only "act, fashion, and play them" in order to gull the ignorant (p. 88); the Mass itself is nothing but "a pageant of moppes, mowes, elevations, crouches, and ridiculous gesticulations" (p. 158). Theatricality here is not so much the consequence of the Church's deviation from the truth as the very essence of that deviation and hence the explanatory key to the entire institution: Catholicism is a "Mimick superstition (it being the onely religion to catch fooles, children, and women, by reason it is naught else, save a conceited pageant of Puppits, and gaudes" (p. 20).

Now *King Lear* at once stages a version of these disenchanted perceptions — most notably in the representation of Edgar's histrionic and fraudulent demonic possession, complete with names drawn directly from the *Declaration* — and insinuates itself paradoxically into the place made vacant by Harsnett's attack: that is, where Harsnett had condemned exorcism as a stage play, Shakespeare's play is itself a secular version of the ritual of exorcism. What exactly is being exorcised? Harsnett would say, in effect, that the question is misguided: what matters is the theatrical experience, the power of the performance to persuade the audience that it has heard the voices of radical evil and witnessed the violent expulsion of the agents of Darkness.

The ritual in this staged form is acceptable because the institution it serves is not a theatrical church but a public, state-supervised theater, and the on-lookers are induced to pay homage (and the price of admission) not to a competing religious authority but to professional entertainers safely circumscribed by the wooden walls of the playhouse. Within these walls, the force of Shakespeare's theatrical improvisation is to appropriate the power of the traditional, quasi-magical practice and of the newer, rationalized analysis and then, with this convergent power, to raise questions about the production of the enabling distinctions between supernatural and secular evil, real and theatrical ritual, authority and madness, belief and illusion. Such disturbing questions are at once licensed and contained by the aesthetic, economic, and physical demarcation of playing companies in a play space. Hence the ideological and historical situation of *King Lear* produces the oscillation, the simultaneous affirmation and negation, the constant undermining of its own assertions and questioning of its own practices — in short, the supreme aesthetic self-consciousness — that lead us to celebrate its universality, its literariness, and its transcendence of all ideology.

[3]Harsnett, *Discovery*, p. A3^{r}. [Au.]

Hayden White

b. 1928

While many of us had long suspected that our history books were fiction, it took Hayden White to demonstrate that they were actually poetry, imbued with metaphor, metonymy, and irony. White was born in Martin, Tennessee, and attended Wayne State University before taking his masters and doctoral degrees at the University of Michigan. He began teaching at Wayne State but soon moved to the University of Rochester, where he rose to full professor and chair of the department. From 1973 to

1977 he directed the Center for the Humanities at Wesleyan University and from 1976–78 was Kenan Professor of History there. In 1978 he moved to the University of California at Santa Cruz, where he was Professor of the History of Consciousness. White has published almost a dozen books, but it was Metahistory: The Historical Imagination in Nineteenth-Century Europe *(1973) that established his indispensability to the New Historicism, with its readings of history as both rhetoric and poetry. His other major books are* Tropics of Discourse: Essays in Cultural Criticism *(1978), and* The Content of the Form: Narrative Discourse and Historical Representation *(1987). "The Politics of Historical Interpretation: Discipline and De-Sublimation" was originally published in* Critical Inquiry, *volume 9 (1982). The following version is from* The Content of the Form.

The Politics of Historical Interpretation: Discipline and De-Sublimation

The politics of interpretation should not be confused with interpretative practices that have politics itself as a specific object of interest — political theory, political commentary, or histories of political institutions, parties, conflicts, and so on. For in these interpretative practices, the politics that informs or motivates them — politics in the sense of political values or ideology — is relatively easily perceived, and no particular metainterpretative analysis is required for its identification. The politics of interpretation, on the other hand, arises in those interpretative practices that are ostensibly most remote from overtly political concerns, practices carried out under the aegis of a purely disinterested search for the truth or inquiry into the natures of things that appear to have no political relevance at all. This politics has to do with the kind of authority the interpreter claims vis-à-vis the established political authorities of the society of which he is a member, on the one side, and vis-à-vis other interpreters in his own field of study or investigation, on the other, as the basis of whatever rights he conceives himself to possess and whatever duties he feels himself obligated to discharge in his status as a professional seeker of truth. This politics that presides over interpretative conflicts is difficult to identify, because traditionally, in our culture at least, interpretation is conceived to operate properly only as long as the interpreter does not have recourse to the one instrumentality that the politician *per vocationem*[1] utilizes as a matter of course in his practice, the appeal to force as a means of resolving disputes and conflicts.[2]

[1]Professional politician. [Ed.]

[2]I have followed the lead of Max Weber in my construction of the meaning of the phrase "politics of interpretation." In "Politics as a Vocation," Weber wrote that "'politics' means for us striving to share power or striving to influence the distribution of power, either among states or among groups within a state" (*From Max Weber: Essays in Sociology,* ed. H. H. Gerth and C. Wright Mills [New York, 1958], 78). Rather than discuss the age-old problem of the professional interpreter's political responsibilities, a problem already raised and rendered virtually irresolvable by Socrates' insistence that the pursuit of truth must take precedence over political exigencies, that, indeed, the pursuit of truth was the highest political good, I shall consider the politics that is endemic to the pursuit of truth itself — the striving to share power amongst interpreters themselves. The activity of interpreting becomes political when a given interpreter claims authority over rival interpreters. As long as this claim remains unreinforced by appeal to the power of the state to compel conformity of belief or conviction, it is political only in a metaphorical sense. The state is the one institution of society that claims the right to use force to compel conformity to the law. Properly speaking, interpretation becomes political only when its products appear to conduce to the breaking of a law or result in a stand for or against specific laws. Of course, interpretation becomes political when a given point of view or finding is taken as orthodoxy of belief by those holding political power, as in the Soviet Union, Germany under Hitler, or any number of religiously puritanical regimes. But these are the easy cases. It is much more difficult to determine the po-

Interpretative conflicts reach a limit as specifically interpretative ones when political power or authority is invoked in order to resolve them. This suggests that interpretation is an activity that, in principle, stands over against political activity in much the same way that contemplation is seen to stand over against action, or theory over against practice.[3] But in the same way that contemplation presupposes action and theory presupposes practice, so, too, interpretation presupposes politics as one of the conditions of its possibility as a social activity. "Pure" interpretation, the disinterested inquiry into anything whatsoever, is unthinkable as an ideal without the presupposition of the kind of activity that politics represents. The purity of any interpretation can be measured only by the extent to which it succeeds in repressing any impulse to appeal to political authority in the course of earning its understanding or explanation of its object of interest. This means that the politics of interpretation must find the means either to effect this repression or to so sublimate the impulse to appeal to political authority as to transform it into an instrument of interpretation itself.[4]

litical nature of interpretive practices that, as in literary criticism or antiquarian scholarship, appear to have no bearing upon political policies or practices. [Au.]

[3]In modern Western culture, the relation between the activity of interpretation and politics has been construed in four ways: Hobbes insisted on the absolute subordination of interpretation to the demands of the state; Kant viewed the interpreter's social function as that of mediator between the people and the sovereign; Nietzsche subordinated politics to interpretation, conceived as the form that the will to power took in its intellectual or artistic manifestation; and Weber held that interpretation and politics occupied different and essentially mutually exclusive domains of culture — science for him was a "vocation" with aims and values quite other than those of "politics" (see Thomas Hobbes, *Leviathan* [Oxford, 1929], pt. 2, chaps. 26, and 29; Immanuel Kant, "The Strife of the Faculties" [pt. 2], trans. Robert E. Anchor, in *Kant on History,* ed. Lewis White Beck [New York, 1963], sec. 8, pp. 148–50; Friedrich Nietzsche, *The Genealogy of Morals,* trans. Francis Golffing [New York, 1956], preface, "First Essay," and "Second Essay," secs. 1–3; and Max Weber, "Science as a Vocation," *From Max Weber,* 145–56). [Au.]

[4]Here I am extending René Girard's notion of "the sacrificial crisis" to include the kinds of crises that arise in situations of radical doubt as to the kind of science that should be used for interpreting social and cultural phenomena (see Girard's remarks about "impartiality" in *Violence and the Sacred,* trans. Patrick Gregory [Baltimore, 1977], chap. 2). [Au.]

This may seem an inordinately circuitous and abstract entry into our subject, but it is necessary for my purpose, which is to consider the question of the politics of interpretation within the context of the disciplinization of fields of study in the human and social sciences. The question is, What is involved in the transformation of a field of studies into a discipline, especially in the context of modern social institutions designed for the regulation of knowledge production, in which the physical sciences function as a paradigm for all cognitive disciplines? The question has special importance for any understanding of the social function of the institutionalized forms of study in the human and social sciences, for all of them have been promoted to the status of disciplines without having attained to the theoretical and methodological regimentation that characterizes the physical sciences.[5]

It is often argued that the human and social sciences are precluded from developing into true sciences by virtue of the nature of their objects of study (man, society, culture), which differ from natural objects in their interiority, an autonomy vis-à-vis their environments, and their capacity to change social processes through the exercise of a certain freedom of will. For some theorists, the human possession of this interiority, autonomy, and freedom of will makes it not only impossible but also undesirable even to aspire to the creation of full-blown sciences of man, culture, and society.[6] In fact, one tradition of theory and philoso-

[5]See Michel Foucault, *The Order of Things: An Archaeology of the Human Sciences* (New York, 1910), chap. 10. Cf. Thomas S. Kuhn, *The Structure of Scientific Revolutions,* 2d ed. (Chicago, 1970), a work that, on its appearance in 1962, effectively defined the terms within which the whole question of the difference between "professionalization" in the physical sciences and in the social sciences would be debated for the next twenty years. On the debate itself see Imre Lakatos and Alan Musgrave, eds., *Criticism and the Growth of Knowledge* (Cambridge, 1970); and J. P. Nettl, "Ideas, Intellectuals, and Structures of Dissent," in *On Intellectuals: Theoretical and Case Studies,* ed. Philip Rieff (New York, 1969), 53–122. [Au.]

[6]This is the neoidealist tradition deriving from Hegel by way of Wilhelm Dilthey and Wilhelm Windelband and any

phy of science has it that such an aspiration is politically undesirable. For this tradition, if man, society, and culture are to be objects of disciplined inquiry, the disciplines in question should aim at understanding these objects, not at explaining them, as in the physical sciences.[7]

The field of historical studies may be taken as exemplary of those disciplines in the human and social sciences that rest content with the understanding of the matters with which they deal in place of aspiring to explain them. This is not to say that historians do not purport to explain certain aspects either of the past or of the historical process. It is rather that in general they do not claim to have discovered the kinds of causal laws that would permit them to explain phenomena by viewing them as instantiations of the operations of such laws, in the way that physical scientists do in their explanations. Historians also often claim to explain the matters of which they treat by providing a proper understanding of them. The means by which this understanding is provided is *interpretation*. *Narration* is both the way in which a historical interpretation is achieved and the mode of discourse in which a successful understanding of matters historical is represented.[8]

number of "vitalists" and humanists in the twentieth century. On Dilthey see Michael Earmarth, *Wilhelm Dilthey: The Critique of Historical Reason* (Chicago, 1978), esp. 95–108; and for a survey of the modern development of the question of a specifically human science see Lucien Goldmann, *The Human Sciences and Philosophy,* trans. Hayden White and Robert E. Anchor (London, 1969). [Au.]

[7]This is the position represented by Karl R. Popper on the neopositivist side of the question and Hannah Arendt on the more humanistic side. Both thought that pretentions to the scientific in the human and social sciences contributed to the creation of totalitarian political philosophies. For their positions on social and political philosophy in general and their relation to philosophy of history in the "scientistic" vein see Popper, *The Poverty of Historicism* (London, 1957); and Arendt, *Between Past and Future* (London, 1961). [Au.]

[8]On the problem of narration and its relation to historical understanding see Hayden White, "The Value of Narrativity in the Representation of Reality," chap. 1 in this volume; see also Paul Ricoeur, "Narrative Time," *Critical Inquiry* 7, no. 1 (1980): 169–90. For a consideration of recent philosophers' handling of the question see Hayden White, "The Politics of Contemporary Philosophy of History," *Clio* 3, no. 1 (October 1973): 35–53; and idem, "Historicism, History, and the Figurative Imagination," *History and Theory* 14 (1975): 48–67. [Au.]

The connection between interpretation, narration, and understanding provides the theoretical rationale for considering historical studies as a special kind of discipline and for resisting the demand (made by positivists and Marxists) for the transformation of historical studies into a science. The ideological nature of both is indicated by the politics that each is seen to be able to serve. In general, the demand that historical studies be transformed into a science is advanced in the interest of promoting a politics thought to be progressive — liberal in the case of positivists, radical in the case of Marxists. The resistance to this demand, per contra, is usually justified by appeal to political or ethical values that are manifestly conservative or reactionary.[9] Since the constitution of historical studies as a discipline was carried out in the modern period in the service of political values and regimes that were in general antirevolutionary and conservative, the burden for establishing the feasibility and desirability of treating history as the object of a possible science falls upon those who would so treat it. This means that the politics of interpretation in modern historical studies turns upon the question of the political uses to which a knowledge thought to be specifically historical can or ought conceivably to be put.

My approach here requires that I attempt to specify what was involved in the transformation of historical studies into a discipline that applied rules for construing and studying their objects of interest that were different from the rules of scientific investigation prevailing in the physical sciences. The social function of a properly disciplined study of history and the political interests it served at its inception in the early nineteenth century, the period of the consolidation of the (bourgeois) nation-state, are well-known and

[9]This kind of division over the political implications of any attempt to transform historical studies into a science is as old as the debate between Edmund Burke and Thomas Paine over the possibilities of a rationalist approach to the study of society. And it appears even within Marxism from time to time (see, for example, Perry Anderson, *Arguments within English Marxism* [London, 1980] 194–207; see also *History and Theory* 17, no. 4 [1978], a special edition on *Historical Consciousness and Political Action*). [Au.]

hardly in need of documentation. We do not have to impute dark ideological motives to those who endowed history with the authority of a discipline in order to recognize the ideological benefits to new social classes and political constituencies that professional, academic historiography served and, *mutatis mutandis,*[10] continues to serve down to our own time.

The desirability of transforming historical studies into a discipline could be urged on grounds more purely theoretical and epistemological. In an age characterized by conflicts between representatives of a host of political positions, each of which came attended by a "philosophy of history" or master narrative of the historical process, on the basis of which their claims to "realism" were in part authorized, it made eminently good sense to constitute a specifically historical discipline. The purpose of such a discipline would be simply to determine the "facts" of history, by which to assess the objectivity, veridicality, and realism of the philosophies of history that authorized the different political programs. Under the auspices of the philosophy of history, programs of social and political reconstruction shared an ideology with utopian visions of man, culture, and society. This linkage justified both and made a study of history, considered as a recovery of the facts of the past, a social desideratum at once epistemologically necessary and politically relevant. To analyze the elements of this linkage, the epistemological criticism proceeded by opposing a properly disciplined historical method conceived as empirical to a philosophy of history conceived as inherently metaphysical. The political aspect of this analytical effort consisted in opposing a properly disciplined historical consciousness to utopian thinking in all its forms (religious, social, and above all political). The combination of these two aspects of history's disciplinization had the effect of permitting the kind of historical knowledge produced by professional historians to serve as the standard of realism in political thought and action in general.[11]

[10]With necessary changes. [Ed.]

[11]On historical knowledge as a basis for political realism see Hayden White, *Metahistory: The Historical Imagination in Nineteenth-Century Europe* (Baltimore, 1973), pt. 2. [Au.]

What politics of interpretation is involved in this transformation of historical studies into a discipline that purports to serve as custodian of realism in political and social thinking? I take issue with a view of the relation between historical and political thinking that has become a commonplace of modern theories of totalitarian ideologies. This view has been forcefully represented by the late Hannah Arendt, and it is shared by many, especially humanistically oriented theorists of totalitarianism who attribute the degeneration of classical politics and its attendant theory to the rise of modern philosophy of history of the sort associated with Hegel, Marx, Nietzsche, Spengler, and so forth. In "The Concept of History," Arendt put the matter in the following terms: "In any consideration of the modern concept of history one of the crucial problems is to explain its sudden rise during the last third of the eighteenth century *and the concomitant decrease* of interest in purely political thinking" (my emphasis).[12]

Leaving aside the question of whether there has actually been a general "decrease of interest in purely political thinking" (not to mention the difficulty of distinguishing between a thinking that is purely political and one that is not), we may accept as generally valid Arendt's linkage of history and politics in those ideologies that took shape in the wake of the French Revolution and continue, in one form or another, to contaminate even the most chaste efforts to contrive a theory of politics free of the charge of being ideological in either motivation or effect. But Arendt leads us astray, I think, in identifying "the modern concept of history" with those philosophies of history that take their rise in Hegel's effort to use historical knowledge as a basis for a metaphysics adequate to the aims and interests of the modern secular state. For while it is true that, as Arendt says, Marx went even further than Hegel and sought to give direction to "the aims of political action," it was not his "influence" alone (or even primarily) that "politicized" both "the historian and the philosopher of history," thereby causing the "decrease in purely political thinking" that

[12]Arendt, *Between Past and Future,* 77. [Au.]

she laments.[13] The politicalization of historical thinking was a virtual precondition of its own professionalization, the basis of its promotion to the status of a discipline worthy of being taught in the universities, and a prerequisite of whatever "constructive" social function historical knowledge was thought to serve. This was true especially of professional, academic, institutionalized (or to use Nietzsche's term, "incorporated") historical studies, that approach to the study of history that defined its aims in opposition to those of philosophy of history, that limited itself to the unearthing of the facts relevant to finite domains of the past, contented itself with the narration of "true stories," and eschewed any temptation to construct grandiose "metahistorical" theories, to find the key to the secret of the whole historical process, to prophesy the future, and to dictate what was both best and necessary for the present.

The "politics" of this disciplinization, conceived, as all disciplinization must be, as a set of negations, consists of what it marks out for repression for those who wish to claim the authority of discipline itself for their learning. What it marks out for repression in general is utopian thinking — the kind of thinking without which revolutionary politics, whether of the Left or the Right, becomes unthinkable (insofar, of course, as such thinking is based on a claim to authority by virtue of the knowledge of history that informs it). To be sure, positivists and Marxists claimed to transcend the opposition of historical thinking and utopian thinking by virtue of their claims to have provided the basis of a genuinely scientific study of history capable of revealing the laws of historical process. From the standpoint of a properly disciplined historical consciousness, however, such claims simply evidenced the presence in positivism and Marxism of the philosophy of history which a properly disciplined historical consciousness was supposed to guard against. The fact that Marxism especially claimed to be a science of history that both justified the hope for and would help to bring about the revolution of bourgeois society only attested to the utopian nature of Marxism and its putative science of history.

Now I am against revolutions, whether launched from "above" or "below" in the social hierarchy and whether directed by leaders who profess to possess a science of society and history or be celebrators of political "spontaneity."[14] Like Arendt, I would wish that in political and social matters both politicians and political thinkers were guided by the kind of realism to which a disciplined historical knowledge conduces. But on the level of interpretative theory, where the matter under contention is the politics inherent in alternative conceptions of what historical discipline itself consists of, one cannot seek to resolve differences of opinion by an appeal either to political values or to some criterion of what a properly disciplined historical knowledge consists of. For it is political values and what constitutes historical discipline that are at issue. The problem lies, however, not with philosophy of history, which is at least openly political, but with a conception of historical studies that purports to be above politics and at the same time rules out as unrealistic any political program or thought in the least tinged with utopianism. And it does so, moreover, by so disciplining historical consciousness as to make realism effectively identical with antiutopianism. One is at least obliged to try to clarify the nature of the politics implicit in the disciplinization of a field of studies undertaken with the express purpose of recuperating its objects of study from the "distortions" of political ideology in general.

It may seem perverse, however, to characterize as a politics of interpretation the disengagement of historical thought from utopian thinking, the de-

[13]Ibid., 77–78. [Au.]

[14]It seems necessary to register this item of personal belief because the relativism with which I am usually charged is conceived by many theorists to imply the kind of nihilism that invites revolutionary activism of a particularly irresponsible sort. In my view, relativism is the moral equivalent of epistemological skepticism; moreover, I conceive relativism to be the basis of social tolerance, not a license to "do as you please." As for revolution, it always misfires. In any event, political revolution, in advanced industrial states at least, is likely to result in the further consolidation of oppressive powers rather than the dissolution thereof. After all, those who control the military-industrial-economic complex hold all the cards. In such a situation, the socially responsible interpreter can do two things: (1) expose the fictitious nature of any political program based on an appeal to what "history" supposedly teaches and (2) remain adamantly "utopian" in any criticism of political "realism." [Au.]

ideologization of its discipline which modern historical studies values most highly. Those who value the kinds of works that professional historians typically produce must regard the philosophy of history (à la Hegel, Marx, and so on) as a pernicious, when not deluded, activity — even if, unlike many modern humanists, they do not regard it as a mainstay of totalitarian ideologies. But the fight between historians and philosophers of history is really more in the nature of a family feud than a conflict between practitioners of different disciplines or between a discipline properly practiced and one improperly practiced. For historians and philosophers of history do have the same objects of study in common, and the fight between them is over what a properly disciplined study of those objects should consist of. Since this dispute cannot be arbitrated on the grounds of any appeal to "what history teaches" (since this is what is at issue), it becomes incumbent upon us to attempt to characterize what constitutes the notion of disciplined historical reflection itself, the general belief in the possibility of which both parties share. The problem can be narrowed to that of characterizing the positive content of the historical object for which philosophy of history is conceived to be the "undisciplined" (or what amounts to the same thing, the "overdisciplined") counterpart. And this problem can be approached by asking, What is ruled out by conceiving the historical object in such a way that *not* to conceive it in that way would constitute prima facie evidence of want of "discipline"?

In order to get a handle on this question, we must recall what was considered "undisciplined" about historical studies prior to the nineteenth century. Throughout the eighteenth century, historical studies had no discipline proper to itself alone. It was for the most part an activity of amateurs. Scholars *per vocationem* were trained in ancient and modern languages, in how to study different kinds of documents (a discipline known as diplomatic), and in mastering the techniques of rhetorical composition. Historical writing, in fact, was regarded as a branch of the art of rhetoric. These constituted the methods of the historian.[15]

The eighteenth-century historian's field of phenomena was simply "the past," conceived as the source and repository of tradition, moral exemplars, and admonitory lessons to be investigated by one of the modes of interpretation into which Aristotle divided the kinds of rhetorical discourse: ceremonial, forensic, and political.[16] The preliminary ordering of this field of phenomena was consigned to the "disciplines" of chronology and the techniques of ordering documents for study in the form of "annals." As for the uses to which historical reflection was to be put, these were as wide as rhetorical practice, political partisanship, and confessional variation admitted. And as for what history, considered as a record of human development, told about human society, this either fell under the charge of Christian myth or its secular, Enlightenment counterpart, the myth of Progress, or displayed a panorama of failure, duplicity, fraud, deceit, and stupidity.

When Kant turned to the consideration of what could be known from the study of history, so as to be able to determine what mankind could legitimately hope on the basis of that knowledge, he identified three kinds of equally pertinent conclusions. These were that (1) the human race was progressing continually; (2) the human race was degenerating continually; and (3) the human race remained at the same general level of development continually. He called these three notions of historical development "eudaemonism," "terrorism," and "farce," respectively; they might just as well be called comedy, tragedy, and irony (if considered from the standpoint of the plot structures they impose upon the historical panorama) or idealism, cynicism, and skepticism (if considered from the standpoint of the world-views they authorize).[17]

[15]On the relation between rhetoric and history see Hayden White, with Frank E. Manuel, "Rhetoric and History," in *Theories of History: Papers of the Clark Library Seminar,* ed. Peter Reill (Los Angeles, 1978), 1–25. See also Lionel Gossman, "History and Literature," in *The Writing of History: Literary Form and Historical Understanding,* ed. Robert H. Canary and Henry Kozicki (Madison, Wis., 1978). [Au.]

[16]See Aristotle, *Rhetoric* 1.3. [Au.]

[17]Kant, "Strife of the Faculties," 139. Actually, Kant calls the third type of historical conceptualization "Abderitism," after the city of Abdera, where the Atomic School of Philosophy was centered in the ancient world. I have substituted

Whatever names we attach to them, Kant's three conceptualizations of the process of historical development indicate that all of the types of philosophy of history subsequently developed in the nineteenth century were not distinctively "modern" (as Arendt argues) but were already conceptually present in historical thinking of the premodern period. Moreover, far from being a modern innovation, the "politicalization" of the historian and philosopher of history was the rule rather than the exception. The important point is that the variety of uses to which written history's subordination to rhetoric permitted it to be put exposed historical thinking to the threat of being conceived solely in terms of Kant's third type, the farce: as long as history was subordinated to rhetoric, the historical field itself (that is, the past or the historical process) had to be viewed as a chaos that made no sense at all or one that could be made to bear as many senses as wit and rhetorical talent could impose upon it. Accordingly, the disciplining of historical thinking that had to be undertaken if history considered as a kind of knowledge was to be established as arbitrator of the realism of contending political programs, each attended by its own philosophy of history, had first of all to consist of a rigorous de-rhetoricization.

The de-rhetoricization of historical thinking was an effort to distinguish history from fiction, especially from the kind of prose fiction represented by the romance and the novel. This effort was, of course, a rhetorical move in its own right, the kind of rhetorical move that Paolo Valesio calls "the rhetoric of anti-rhetoric."[18] It consisted of little more than a reaffirmation of the Aristotelian distinction between history and poetry — between the study of events that had actually occurred and the imagining of events that might have occurred, or could possibly occur — and the affirmation of the fiction that the "stories" historians tell are found in the evidence rather than invented.[19] Thus the whole question of the composition of the historian's discourse was moot: it appeared to be solely a function of the rigorous application of "rules of evidence" to the examination of the "historical record." In point of fact, the narratives produced by historians lend themselves to analysis in terms of their rhetorical *topoi,* which in general have been canonized in the classical notion of the so-called middle style of declamation.[20]

The subordination of historical narrative to the deliberative mode of the middle style entails stylistic exclusions, and this has implications for the kinds of events that can be represented in a narrative. Excluded are the kinds of events traditionally conceived to be the stuff of religious belief and ritual (miracles, magical events, godly events), on the one side, and the kinds of "grotesque" events that are the stuff of farce, satire, and calumny, on the other. Above all, these two orders of exclusion consign to historical thinking the kinds of events that lend themselves to the understanding of whatever currently passes for educated common sense. They effect a disciplining of the imagination, in this case the historical imagination, and they set limits on what constitutes a specifically historical event. Moreover, since these exclusions effectively set limits on rules of description (or descriptive protocols), and since a "fact" must be regarded as "an event under a description," it follows that they constitute what can count as a specifically historical fact.[21]

---

farce because, as Beck indicates in a note, *Abderitism* was generally regarded as a synonym for *silliness;* moreover, Kant says: "It is a vain affair to have good so alternate with evil that the whole traffic of our species with itself on this globe would have to be considered as a mere farcical comedy [*als ein blosses Possenspiel*]" (141). Cr. *Immanuel Kants Werke,* ed. Ernst Cassirer, vol. 7, *Der Streit der Fakultäten* (Berlin, 1916), 395. [Au.]

[18]Paolo Valesio, *Novantiqua: Rhetorics as a Contemporary Theory* (Bloomington, Ind., 1980), 41–60. [Au.]

[19]See Aristotle, *Poetics,* p. 48. [Ed.]

[20]Aristotle's *topoi* (in the *Topika*) classifies rhetorical commonplaces, like arguing from the general to the particular, or vice versa. The "middle style" is that which avoids either high-flown diction or mean expression. The "deliberative" mode of rhetoric is the mode suited to politics, in that it is a discourse with the goal of determining what is fit to be said or done. [Ed.]

[21]See Louis O. Mink, "Narrative Form as a Cognitive Instrument," in Canary and Kozicki, *The Writing of History,* 132. [Au.]

The imagination was discussed in the late eighteenth century in terms of the notions of taste and sensibility and the question, addressed by the newly constituted field of aesthetics, of the difference between the ideas of "the beautiful and the sublime."[22] If, as Arendt suggested, the disciplinization of historical studies must be considered in terms of its relation to political thinking, then it must also be considered in terms of its relation to aesthetic theory and especially to the notions of "the beautiful and the sublime." For insofar as the disciplinization of history entailed regulation, not only of what could count as a proper object of historical study but also of what could count as a proper representation of that object in a discourse, discipline consisted in subordinating written history to the categories of the "beautiful" and suppressing those of the "sublime."

Because history, unlike fiction, is supposed to represent real events and therefore contribute to knowledge of the real world, imagination (or "fancy") is a faculty particularly in need of disciplinization in historical studies. Political partisanship and moral prejudice may lead the historian to misread or misrepresent documents and thus to construct events that never took place. On the conscious level, the historian can, in his investigative operations, guard against such errors by the judicious employment of "the rules of evidence." The imagination, however, operates on a different level of the historian's consciousness. It is present above all in the effort, peculiar to the modern conceptualization of the historian's task, to enter sympathetically into the minds or consciousnesses of human agents long dead, to empathize with the intentions and motivations of actors impelled by beliefs and values that may differ totally from anything the historian might himself honor in his own life, and to understand, even when he cannot condone, the most bizarre social and cultural practices. This is often described as putting oneself in the place of past agents, seeing things from their point of view, and so forth, all of which leads to a notion of objectivity that is quite different from anything that might be meant by that term in the physical sciences.[23]

This notion is quite specific to modern historical theory, and it is typically thought to be imaginative rather than rational. For it is one thing to try to be rational, in the sense of being on guard against unwarranted inferences or one's own prejudices, and quite another to think one's way into the minds and consciousnesses of past actors whose "historicity" consists in part in the fact that they acted under the impulsion of beliefs and values peculiar to their own time, place, and cultural presuppositions. But imagination is dangerous for the historian, because he cannot know that what he has "imagined" was actually the case, that it is not a product of his "imagination" in the sense in which that term is used to characterize the activity of the poet or writer of fiction. Here, of course, the imagination is disciplined by its subordination to the rules of evidence which require that whatever is imagined be consistent with what the evidence permits one to assert as a "matter of fact." Yet "imagination," precisely in the sense in which it is used to characterize the activity of the poet or novelist, is operative in the work of the historian at the last stage of his labors, when it becomes necessary to compose a discourse or narrative in which to represent his findings, that is, his notion of "what really happened" in the past. It is at this point that what some theorists call the style of the historian, considered now as a writer of prose, takes over and an operation considered to be exactly like that of the novelist, an operation that is openly admitted to be literary, supervenes.[24] And since it is liter-

[22]See Kant, *Critique of Judgment,* p. 269. [Ed.]

[23]This position found its most forceful representation in the work of R. G. Collingwood, *The Idea of History* (Oxford and New York, 1956), pt. 5, secs. 2 and 4. See also Louis O. Mink, *Mind, History, and Dialectic: The Philosophy of R. G. Collingwood* (Bloomington, Ind., 1969), 162ff. [Au.]

[24]No more vexed — and mystifying — notion appears in the theory of historical writing than that of the historian's "style." It is a problem because insofar as the historian's discourse is conceived to have style, it is also conceived to be literary. But insofar as a historian's discourse is literary, it seems to *be* rhetorical, which is anathema for those who wish to claim for historical discourse the status of objective representation. On the whole question see Roland Barthes, "His-

ary, the disciplinization of this aspect of the historian's work entailed an aesthetic regulation. What is the nature of a disciplined historical style?

Here again we must recall that discipline consists less of prescriptions of what must be done than of exclusions or proscriptions of certain ways of imaging historical reality. And this is where the late-nineteenth-century debate over what Edmund Burke[25] called "our ideas of the sublime and the beautiful" becomes relevant to our understanding of what was involved in the disciplinization of historical sensibility.[26] This debate, as it extends into the nineteenth century, is complex and was rendered more so by the particular obsessions the Romantics brought to their considerations of issues considered relevant to it. For our purposes, however, the crucial turn in this discussion has to do with the progressive demotion of the sublime in favor of the beautiful as a solution to the problems of taste and imagination. For the most part, these problems were construed in terms of the imagination's response to different kinds of natural phenomena: those that possessed the capacity to "charm," and those that "terrified" (by their grandeur, extent, awesomeness, and so forth).[27] While he likened the feeling of the sublime to what the subject must feel in the presence of political majesty, Burke did not explicitly address the question of the sublime and the beautiful with respect to historical or social phenomena.[28] Indeed, he condemned the French Revolution as a "strange chaos of levity and ferocity" and a "monstrous tragi-comic scene" that could only fill its observers with "disgust and horror" rather than with that feeling of "astonishment" that the sublime in nature inspired or that feeling of respect for sheer "power" that he took to be the essence of religious awe.[29] Viewed as a

torical Discourse," in *Structuralism: A Reader*, ed. Michael Lane (London, 1970), 145–55; Peter Gay, *Style in History* (New York, 1974); and Stephen Bann, "Towards a Critical Historiography: Recent Work in Philosophy of History," *Philosophy* 56 (1981): 365–85. [Au.]

[25]Edmund Burke (1729–1797), Irish statesman and political writer, published *A Philosophical Inquiry into the Origin of Our Ideas on the Sublime and Beautiful* in 1756; his *Reflections on the Revolution in France* was published in 1790. [Ed.]

[26]See Thomas Weiskel, *The Romantic Sublime: Studies in the Structure and Psychology of Transcendence* (Baltimore, 1976), 78–103. [Au.]

[27]See Edmund Burke, *A Philosophical Inquiry into the Origin of Our Ideas of the Sublime and Beautiful* (New York, 1909), pt. 1, sec. 8, p. 36 and sec. 10, p. 39. I exclude from this discussion certain rhetoricians who continued to invoke the notion of the sublime to designate a specific style of oratory or poetic mode. [Au.]

[28]"Thus we are affected by strength, which is *natural* power. The power which arises from institution in kings and commanders, has the same connexion with terror. Sovereigns are frequently addressed with the title of *dread majesty*" (ibid., pt. 2, sec. 5, p. 59). [Au.]

[29]Burke dilates on religious awe in a passage immediately following that which describes kingly dread:

> And though a consideration of [God's] other attributes may relieve, in some measure, our apprehensions; yet no conviction of the justice with which it is exercised, nor the mercy with which it is tempered, can wholly remove the terror that naturally arises from a force which nothing can withstand. If we rejoice, we rejoice with trembling; and even whilst we are receiving benefits, we cannot but shudder at a power which can confer benefits of such mighty importance. . . . In the Scripture, wherever God is represented as appearing or speaking, everything terrible in nature is called up to heighten the awe and solemnity of the Divine presence. (ibid., 61)

Later, speaking of a kind of "pain" and "terror" that are "capable of producing delight; . . . a sort of delightful horror . . . which . . . is one of the strongest of all the passions," Burke stipulates as the object of this horror "the sublime." And he adds: "Its highest degree I call *astonishment;* the subordinate degrees are awe, reverence, and respect, which . . . stand distinguished from positive pleasure" (ibid., pt. 4, sec. 8, p. 114).

Then, in his *Reflections on the Revolution in France*, when he turns to a general description of this phenomenon, he writes:

> All circumstances taken together, the French revolution is the most astonishing that has hitherto happened in the world. The most wonderful things are brought about in many instances by means the most absurd and ridiculous; in the most ridiculous modes; and apparently, by the most contemptible instruments. Every thing seems out of nature in this strange chaos of levity and ferocity, and of all sorts of crimes jumbled together with all sorts of follies. In viewing this monstrous tragi-comic scene, the most opposite passions necessarily succeed, and sometimes mix with each other in the mind; alternate contempt and indignation; alternate laughter and tears; alternate scorn and horror. (Edmund Burke, *Reflections on the Revolution in France*, and Thomas Paine, *The Rights of Man*, together in one volume [New York: 1961], 21–22)

Later, Burke writes that "the very idea of the fabrication

contribution to the aesthetics (or what amounts to the same thing, the psychology) of historical consciousness, Burke's *Reflections on the Revolution in France* can be seen as one of many efforts to exorcise the notion of the sublime from any apprehension of the historical process, so that the "beauty" of its "proper" development, which for him was given in the example of the "English constitution," could be adequately comprehended.[30]

It was quite otherwise with Schiller,[31] who, in his theory of the imagination, equated the "attraction" of the "bizarre savagery in physical nature" to the "delight" one might feel in contemplating "the uncertain anarchy of the moral world."[32] Meditation on the "confusion" that the "spectacle" of history displayed could produce a sense of a specifically human "freedom," and insofar as it did, "world history" appeared to him "a sublime object" (204–5). The feeling of the sublime, Schiller believed, could transform the "pure daemon" in humankind into grounds for belief in a "dignity" unique to man. The sublime, then, was a necessary "complement" to the beautiful if "aesthetic education" were to be made into a "complete whole" (210). Because the beautiful ruled over the "ceaseless quarrel between our natural and rational vocations, it took precedence over the sublime in this education, constantly returning us to "our *spiritual* mission" which has its sphere in "the world of sense" and "action to which we are after all committed" (210–11).

Schiller's linkage of the beautiful with the sphere of "sense" and "action" anticipated what was to become a commonplace of nineteenth-century aesthetics and had important consequences for both historical thought and political theory, radical as well as conservative. The gradual displacement of the sublime by the beautiful in a generally accredited aesthetic theory, as uncritically accepted by Marxists as by their conservative and liberal opponents, had the effect of restricting speculation on any ideal social order to some variant in which freedom was apprehended less as an exercise of individual will than as a release of beautiful "feelings." Yet Schiller himself joined the notion of the historical sublime to the kind of response to it that would authorize a totally different politics:

> Away then with falsely construed forbearance and vapidly effeminate taste which cast a veil over the solemn face of necessity and, in order to curry favor with the senses, *counterfeit* a harmony between good fortune and good behavior of which not a trace is to be found in the actual world. . . . We are aided [in the attainment of this point of view] by the terrifying spectacle of change which destroys everything and creates it anew, and destroys again. . . . We are aided by the pathetic spectacle of mankind wrestling with fate, the irresistible elusiveness of happiness, confidence betrayed, unrighteousness triumphant and innocence laid low; of these history supplies ample instances, and tragic art imitates them before our eyes. (209–10)

This could have been written by Nietzsche.

Hegel saw the dangers in such a conception of history, and in the introduction to his *Philosophy of History* he subjects it to scathing criticism on both cognitive and moral grounds.[33] Cognitively, such a conception remains on the level of appearances and fails to subject the phenomena to the critical analysis that would reveal the laws governing their articulation. Morally, such a conception could lead, not to the apprehension of human

of a new government, is enough to fill us with disgust and horror" (ibid., 43). [Au.]

[30]See ibid., 43–47. [Au.]

[31]See the introduction to Schiller, p. 294. [Ed.]

[32]*Two Essays by Friedrich von Schiller: "Naive and Sentimental Poetry" and "On the Sublime,"* trans. Julius A. Elias (New York, 1966), 205; further references to this work are cited parenthetically in the text. [Au.]

[33]According to Hegel, any merely "objective" view of historical phenomena would suggest that "the most effective springs of human action" are nothing other than "passions, private aims, and the satisfaction of selfish desires." Any "simply truthful combination of the miseries that have overwhelmed the noblest of nations and polities and the finest exemplars of human virtue" forms a "picture of such a horrifying aspect [*furchtbarsten Gemälde*]" that we are inclined to take refuge in fatalism and to withdraw in disgust "into the more agreeable environment of our individual life, the present formed by our private aims and interests" (G. W. F. Hegel, *The Philosophy of History,* trans. J. Sibree [New York, 1956], 20–21). [Au.]

freedom and dignity, but to pessimism, lassitude, and submission to fate. The sublimity of the spectacle of history had to be transcended if it was to serve as an object of knowledge and deprived of the terror it induced as a "panorama of sin and suffering."[34]

Kant's "analytic of the sublime," in the *Critique of Judgment,* relates the apprehension of anything merely "powerful" (which belonged to what he called "the dynamical sublime") to our feeling of possessing a freedom and dignity uniquely human, but he grounds this feeling in the faculty of the reason alone.[35] Thus envisaged, the sublime is effectively cut free from the aesthetic faculty, which remains under the sway of judgments appropriate to the "beautiful," in order to be relegated to the rule of the cognitive and moral faculties.[36] And this for obvious reasons: Kant had no faith in the capacity of reflection on history to teach anything that could not be learned — and learned better — from reflection on present human existence or, indeed, on the experience of a single socialized individual.

Although Hegel took up the question of the sublime, both explicitly in his *Aesthetics* and implicitly in the *Philosophy of History,* he subordinated it to the notion of the beautiful in the former and to the notion of the rational in the latter. It was this demotion of the sublime in favor of the beautiful that constituted the heritage from German idealism to both radical and conservative thought about the kind of utopian existence mankind could justifiably envisage as the ideal aim or goal of any putatively progressive historical process. Here is a prime example of a certain kind of "politics of interpretation" which produces an "interpretation of politics" with distinct ideological implications. It is the aesthetics of the beautiful that, as Thomas Weiskel suggests, undercuts the radical impulse of this tradition.[37] This undercutting may account in part for the weak psychological appeal of the "beautiful life" as a project to be realized in political struggles and, what is more important, for the apparent incapacity of political regimes founded on Marxist principles to sustain their professed programs for the radical transformation of society in anything but the most banal ways.

What must be recognized, however, is that for both the Left and the Right, this same aesthetics of the beautiful presides over the process in which historical studies are constituted as an autonomous scholarly discipline. It takes little reflection to perceive that aestheticism is endemic to what is regarded as a proper attitude towards objects of historical study in a certain tradition, deriving from Leopold von Ranke and his epigones,[38] which represents the nearest thing to an orthodoxy that the profession possesses. For this tradition, whatever "confusion" is displayed by the historical record is only a surface phenomenon: a product of lacunae in the documentary sources, of mistakes in ordering the archives, or of previous inattention or scholarly errors. If this confusion is not reducible to the kind of order that a science of laws might impose upon it, it can still be dispelled by historians endowed with the proper kind of understanding. And when this understanding is subjected to analysis, it is always revealed to be of an essentially aesthetic nature.

This aestheticism underwrites the conviction (periodically reaffirmed when history fails to

[34]Ibid., 21. I analyze this passage in *Metahistory,* 105–8. [Au.]

[35]See Immanuel Kant, *Critique of Judgment,* trans. J. H. Bernard (New York, 1951), bk. 2, "Analytic of the Sublime": "Now we may see from this that, in general, we express ourselves incorrectly if we call any *object of nature* sublime, although we can quite correctly call many objects of nature beautiful" (83). [Au.]

[36]"Sublimity, therefore, does not reside in anything of nature, but only in our mind, in so far as we can become conscious that we are superior to nature within, and therefore also to nature without us (so far as it influences us)." And again: "Properly speaking, the word [*sublime*] should only be applied to a state of mind, or rather to its foundation in human nature" (ibid., 104, 121). [Au.]

[37]Weiskel, *The Romantic Sublime,* 48. [Au.]

[38]Leopold von Ranke (1795–1886) was a German historian who pioneered an "objective" method of producing history through documents and other primary sources: His goal was to present the past *wie es eigenlich gewesen* (as it really was). His "epigones" would be the following generations of scholars who shared his faith in the objectivity of primary sources. [Ed.]

provide a knowledge that can legitimately claim the title "scientific") that historical studies are, after all, a branch of belles-lettres, a calling suitable for a kind of gentleman-scholar for whom "taste" serves as a guide to comprehension, and "style" as an index of achievement. When the notions of taste and style are given a specifically moral connotation, as they inevitably are when they serve as the basis of a professional ethics, they authorize the attitudes that the socially responsible historian properly assumes before his designated objects of study. These attitudes include respect for the "individuality," "uniqueness," and "ineffability" of historical entities, sensitivity to the "richness" and "variety" of the historical field, and a faith in the "unity" that makes of finite sets of historical particulars comprehensible wholes. All this permits the historian to see some beauty, if not good, in everything human and to assume an Olympian calm in the face of any current social situation, however terrifying it may appear to anyone who lacks historical perspective. It renders him receptive to a genial pluralism in matters epistemological, suspicious of anything smacking of reductionism, irritated with theory, disdainful of technical terminology or jargon, and contemptuous of any effort to discern the direction that the future development of his own society might take.

Viewed as the positive content of a program for transforming history into a discipline, these attitudes and the values they imply are undeniably attractive; they possess all the "charm" that an aesthetics of the beautiful might prescribe for a scholarly discipline. And they were undeniably effective in blocking any impulse to use history as the basis for a science or as a basis for justifying a visionary politics. At the same time, the establishment of these attitudes and values as an orthodoxy for professional historical studies made of history (conceived as a body of established learning) a repository of the kinds of facts that could serve as the subject matter of those human and social sciences called into existence to de-ideologize thought about man, society, and culture in the late nineteenth century. Historical facts are politically domesticated precisely insofar as they are effectively removed from displaying any aspect of the sublime that Schiller attributed to them in his essay of 1801. By this I mean nothing more than the following: insofar as historical events and processes become understandable, as conservatives maintain, or explainable, as radicals believe them to be, they can never serve as a basis for a visionary politics more concerned to endow social life with meaning than with beauty. In my view, the theorists of the sublime had correctly divined that whatever dignity and freedom human beings could lay claim to could come only by way of what Freud called a "reaction-formation" to an apperception of history's meaninglessness.

Let me try to put this somewhat more clearly. It seems to me that the kind of politics that is based on a vision of a perfected society can compel devotion to it only by virtue of the contrast it offers to a past that is understood in the way that Schiller conceived it, that is, as a "spectacle" of "confusion," "uncertainty," and "moral anarchy." Surely this is the appeal of those eschatological religions[39] that envision a "rule of the saints" that is the very antithesis of the spectacle of sin and corruption that the history of a fallen humanity displays to the eye of the faithful. But the appeal of these religions must be quite different from that of secular ideologies, radical and reactionary alike, which seek to justify the obligations they lay upon their devotees by virtue of their claim to have divined the pattern, plan, or meaning of the historical process for which a humanity that is neither inherently corrupt nor fallen from an originally Edenic condition, but simply "unenlightened," is responsible. But modern ideologies seem to me to differ crucially from eschatological religious myths in that they impute a meaning to history that renders its manifest confusion comprehensible to either reason, understanding, or aesthetic sensibility. To the extent that they succeed in doing so, these ideologies deprive history of the kind of meaninglessness that alone

[39]Eschatology is the study of the "four last things": death, judgment, heaven, and hell. Eschatological religions are those whose emphasis is on the coming end of the world and the New Jerusalem promised in Revelations. [Ed.]

can goad living human beings to make their lives different for themselves and their children, which is to say, to endow their lives with a meaning for which they alone are fully responsible. One can never move with any politically effective confidence from an apprehension of "the way things actually are or have been" to the kind of moral insistence that they "should be otherwise" without passing through a feeling of repugnance for and negative judgment of the condition that is to be superseded. And precisely insofar as historical reflection is disciplined to understand history in such a way that it can forgive everything or at best to practice a kind of "disinterested interest" of the sort that Kant imagined to inform every properly aesthetic perception, it is removed from any connection with a visionary politics and consigned to a service that will always be antiutopian in nature. Indeed, this is as true of a Marxist view of the way things are or have been in the past as it is of the bourgeois historians' concern with the study of the past "for itself alone."

It is bound to seem paradoxical to suggest that Marxism is inherently antiutopian as a philosophy of history, especially inasmuch as professional academic historiography in the West derives much of its political prestige from its proven capacity to counter the kind of utopian thinking that Marxism is supposed to exemplify. But Marxism is antiutopian insofar as it shares with its bourgeois counterpart the conviction that history is not a sublime spectacle but a comprehensible process the various parts, stages, epochs, and even individual events of which are transparent to a consciousness endowed with the means to make sense of it in one way or another.

I am not suggesting that Marxists have got history wrong and their bourgeois opponents have it right, or vice versa. Nor am I suggesting that the claim merely to understand history rather than to explain it, which non-Marxist humanist historians make, is a more appropriate way to approach the study of history than that recommended by Marxists and that therefore Marxism can be dismissed as either tactless or arrogant. Everyone recognizes that the way one makes sense of history is important in determining what politics one will credit as realistic, practicable, and socially responsible. But it is often overlooked that the conviction that one can make sense of history stands on the same level of epistemic plausibility as the conviction that it makes no sense whatsoever. My point is that the kind of politics that one can justify by an appeal to history will differ according to whether one proceeds on the basis of the former or the latter conviction. I am inclined to think that a visionary politics can proceed only on the latter conviction. And I conclude that however radical Marxism may be as a social philosophy and especially as a critique of capitalism, in its aspect as a philosophy of history it is no more visionary than its bourgeois counterpart.

Prior to the nineteenth century, history had been conceived as a spectacle of crimes, superstitions, errors, duplicities, and terrorisms that justified visionary recommendations for a politics that would place social processes on a new ground. Philosophies of history such as Voltaire's and Condorcet's constituted the basis of the Enlightenment's contribution to a progressive political theory. Schiller caught the spirit of this conception when he wrote:

> For where is the man whose moral disposition is not wholly degenerate who can read about the determined yet vain struggle of Mithradates, of the collapse of Syracuse and Carthage, or in the presence of like events can refrain from paying homage with a shudder to the grim law of necessity, or from instantly curbing his desires and, shaken by the perpetual infidelity of all sensuous objects, can avoid fastening upon the eternal in his breast?[40]

But this "shudder," occasioned by reflection on this historical spectacle, and the "fastening upon the eternal" that it was supposed instinctively to call up were progressively cosigned to the class of errors to which the Romantics in general and Romanticist historians in particular — Michelet and Carlyle above all — were singularly prone.[41] In fact, the extent to which histori-

[40]Schiller, "On the Sublime," in Schiller, *Two Essays*, 210. [Au.]

[41]In his essay "On History" Carlyle wrote: "It is not in acted, as it is in written History: actual events are nowise so simply related to each other as parent and offspring are; every single event is an offspring not of one, but of all other events, prior or contemporaneous, and it will in its turn combine with

cal studies were disciplinized can be measured by the extent to which professional practitioners on both sides of the political barricades succeeded in identifying as errors the attitudes with which the Romantics approached history. The domestication of historical thinking required that Romanticism be consigned to the category of well-meaning but ultimately irresponsible cultural movements which used history for only literary or poetic purposes. Michelet and Carlyle looked to history for neither understanding nor explanation but rather for inspiration — the kind of inspiration, moreover, that an older aesthetics called sublime. Their demotion by professional historians to the status of thinkers who should be read for their literary style rather than for any insight that they might have had into history and its processes is the measure of the price paid in utopian aspiration for the transformation of history into a discipline.[42]

In the politics of contemporary discussions of historical interpretation, the kind of perspective on history that I have been implicitly praising is conventionally associated with the ideologies of fascist regimes. Something like Schiller's notion of the historical sublime or Nietzsche's version of it is certainly present in the thought of such philosophers as Heidegger and Gentile and in the intuitions of Hitler and Mussolini. But having granted as much, we must guard against a sentimentalism that would lead us to write off such a conception of history simply because it has been associated with fascist ideologies. One must face the fact that when it comes to apprehending the historical record, there are no grounds to be found in the historical record itself for preferring one way of construing its meaning over another. Nor can such grounds be found in any putative science of man, society, or culture, because such sciences are compelled simply to presuppose some conception of historical reality in order to get on with their program of constituting themselves as sciences. Far from providing us with grounds for choosing among different conceptions of history, the human and social sciences merely beg the question of history's meaning, which, in one sense, they were created to resolve. Therefore, to appeal to sociology, anthropology, or psychology for some basis for determining an appropriate perspective on history is rather like basing one's notion of the soundness of a building's foundations on the structural properties of its second or third story. The human and social sciences, insofar as they are based on or presuppose a specific conception of historical reality, are as blind to the sublimity of the historical process and to the visionary politics it authorizes as is the disciplinized historical consciousness that informs their investigative procedures.

The domestication of history effected by the suppression of the historical sublime may well be the sole basis for the proud claim to social responsibility in modern capitalist as well as in communist societies. While this pride derives in part from the claim to see through the distortions and duplicities of fascist ideologies, it is possible that fascist politics is in part the price paid for the very domestication of historical consciousness that is supposed to stand against it. Fascist social and political policies are undeniably horrible, and they may well be a function of a vision of history that sees no meaning in it and therefore imposes a meaning where none is to be found. But the appeal of fascism not only to the masses but to any number of intellectuals who had certainly been exposed to a culture of history that explained and understood the past to the very depths of all possibility leaves us with the necessity of trying to understand why this culture provided so weak an impediment to fascism's appeal.

The problem of fascism's appeal to modern political constituencies is certainly not to be solved by intellectual historical inquiry, by the

others to give birth to new: it is an ever-living, ever-working Chaos of Being, wherein shape after shape bodies itself forth from innumerable elements" (Thomas Carlyle, "On History," in *A Carlyle Reader: Selections from the Writings of Thomas Carlyle*, ed. G. B. Tennyson [New York, 1969], 59–60; cf. White, *Metahistory*, 144–49. On Michelet see ibid., 149–62). [Au.]

[42]I have in mind such judgments as that of Hugh Trevor-Roper, who in a recent essay remarks of Carlyle: "Perhaps it is the surest sign of Carlyle's genius that we read him still, and are interested in him still, although his ideas are totally discredited" ("Thomas Carlyle's Historical Philosophy," *Times Literary Supplement* 26 June 1981, 734). [Au.]

history of ideas, or, if what I have suggested thus far regarding the politics of interpretation in the human and social sciences is correct, by historical inquiry in general. The events that make up fascism's history occupy a domain of human experience far removed from the kinds of theoretical questions addressed here. But fascism in its Nazi incarnation and especially in its aspect as a politics of genocide constitutes a crucial test case for determining the ways in which any human or social science may construe its "social responsibilities" as a discipline productive of a certain kind of knowledge.

It is often alleged that "formalists" such as myself, who hold that any historical object can sustain a number of equally plausible descriptions or narratives of its processes, effectively deny the reality of the referent, promote a debilitating relativism that permits any manipulation of the evidence as long as the account produced is structurally coherent, and thereby allow the kind of perspectivism that permits even a Nazi version of Nazism's history to claim a certain minimal credibility. Such formalists are typically confronted with questions such as the following: Do you mean to say that the occurrence and nature of the Holocaust is only a matter of opinion and that one can write its history in whatever way one pleases? Do you imply that any account of that event is as valid as any other account so long as it meets certain formal requirements of discursive practices and that one has no responsibility to the victims to tell the truth about the indignities and cruelties they suffered? Are there not certain historical events that tolerate none of that mere cleverness that allows criminals or their admirers to feign accounts of their crimes that effectively relieve them of their guilt or responsibility or even, in the worst instances, allows them to maintain that the crimes they committed never happened? In such questions we come to the bottom line of the politics of interpretation which informs not only historical studies but the human and social sciences in general.

These questions have been given a new urgency by the appearance in recent years of a group of "revisionist" historians of the Holocaust who indeed argue that this event never occurred.[43] The claim is as morally offensive as it is intellectually bewildering. It is not, of course, bewildering to most Jews, who have no difficulty recognizing in it another instance of the kind of thinking that led to the implementation of the "final solution" in Germany in the first place. But it has proven bewildering to some Jewish scholars who had thought that fidelity to a rigorous "historical method" could not possibly result in a conclusion so monstrous. For, indeed, as Pierre Vidal-Naquet has recently written, the revisionist case features as an important element of its brief that massive research in the archives and pursuit of documentary and oral testimony that are the mainstays of this "method."[44]

[43]On the "revisionist" group of historians of the Holocaust see Lucy S. Dawidowicz, "Lies about the Holocaust," *Commentary* 70, no. 6 (December 1980): 31–37. Dawidowicz surveys the entire literature on the Holocaust in *The Holocaust and the Historians* (Cambridge, Mass., 1981), an invaluable work for anyone interested in the ethics of historical interpretation. Arno J. Mayer summarizes the issues of "revisionism" in "A Note on Vidal-Naquet," his introduction to the English translation of Pierre Vidal-Naquet's "A Paper Eichmann?" *Democracy,* April 1981, 67–95. [Au.]

[44]It is precisely the issue of historical method that I wish to examine in this essay. Vidal-Naquet views this method as the best insurance against the kind of ideological distortion of which the "revisionists" are justly accused (see Vidal-Naquet, "A Paper Eichmann?" 74; further references to this work are cited parenthetically in the text). So, too, Dawidowicz conflates the problem of that "fairness and objectivity" for which historians strive with adherence "to methodological rules concerning the use of historical evidence" (*The Holocaust and the Historians,* 26). She remarks that "in our time, distance in writing the history of the Holocaust can be achieved by an act of will, by the imposition of discipline itself" (130). And she ends her book by citing G. J. Renier's dictum that "the morality of history-writing is exclusively methodological" (146). Yet, in her survey of the work of professional historians who have dealt with the Holocaust since World War II, she finds them all wanting in the kind of "conscientious" approach to history commended by Lord Acton as the sole possible basis of a genuinely "objective history" (144). It does not occur to her, it seems, that her study indicts the very "professionalism" that she prescribes as the necessary precondition of objectivity (133). Indeed, one could conclude from her study that the failure of historians to come to terms with the Holocaust in a morally responsible way is a result of this professionalism.

As for the question of "historical method," one can legitimately and responsibly ask what it consists of. It is a commonplace of current social scientific theory that there is no

Vidal-Naquet takes it as a matter requiring nothing more than its assertion that the "research" that has gone into the putative search for anyone or anything that could "prove" that the Holocaust actually "happened" is not genuinely "historical" but rather "ideological." The aim of this research "is to deprive a community of what is represented by its historic memory." But he is confident that "on the terrain of positive history . . . true opposes false quite simply, independent of any kind of interpretation," and that when it is a matter of the occurrence of events (he cites the taking of the Bastille on 14 July 1789 as an example), there is no question of alternative interpretations or "revisionist" hypotheses. Such an occurrence is simply a matter of fact, and therefore a positive historiography can always set a limit on its interpretation that permits of no transgression and distinguishes well enough between a genuinely historical account and a fictive or mythic deformation of "reality." Vidal-Naquet extends his criticism of such deformations to include a Zionism that "exploits this terrible massacre in a way that is at times quite scandalous." "Finally," he writes, "it is the duty of historians to take historical facts out of the hands of ideologists who exploit them" and set limits on "this permanent rewriting of history that characterizes ideological speech." For him, these limits are approached when one encounters the kind of manifest "total lie" produced by the revisionists (75, 90–91).

This is clear enough, although the distinction between a lie and an error or a mistake in interpretation may be more difficult to draw with respect to historical events less amply documented than the Holocaust. What is less clear is the relative validity of an interpretation of the Holocaust that, according to Vidal-Naquet, has been produced by "the Israelis, or rather their ideologists," for whom "Auschwitz was the ineluctable, logical outcome of life lived in the Diaspora, and all the victims of the death camps were destined to become Israeli citizens," which he labels less a lie than an "untruth" (90). Here the distinction seems to turn, for Vidal-Naquet at least, on the difference between an interpretation that would "have profoundly transformed the *reality* of the massacre" and one that would not. The Israeli interpretation leaves the "reality" of the event intact, whereas the revisionist interpretation derealizes it by redescribing it in such a way as to make it something other than what the victims know the Holocaust to have been. The phenomenon in question is rather like that met with in A. J. P. Taylor's controversial interpretation of Hitler as a run-of-the-mill European statesman whose methods were a bit excessive but whose ends were respectable enough, given the conventions of European politics in his time.[45] The theoretical point to be taken, however, is that an interpretation falls into the category of a lie when it denies the reality of the events of which it treats, and into the category of an untruth when it draws false conclusions from reflection on events whose reality remains attestable on the level of "positive" historical inquiry.

There is a question of interpretative tact that should be raised at this point. It must seem unconscionably pedantic, arguably eristic, and conceivably tasteless to be fiddling with what appear to be points of method in the context of a question having to do with an event so horrendous that those who experienced it, as well as their rel-

"method" specific to historical research. Claude Lévi-Strauss is only the most prominent of social theorists holding this view. In "History and Dialectic," his famous conclusion to *The Savage Mind* (London, 1966), he denies that history is either object- or method-specific. The whole issue was debated in a conference organized by Alan Bullock and Raymond Aron, held in Venice in 1971, on the relation between historical, sociological, and anthropological inquiry. Here Peter Wiles pilloried "historical method" by dismissing it as simply "measurement without theory" and stating bluntly: "There is no such thing as a historical explanation." See the account of the proceedings of the conference, *The Historian between the Ethnologist and the Futurologist,* ed. Jerome Dumoulin and Dominique Moisi (Paris and The Hague, 1973), 89–90 and passim; and my review of this book, "The Historian at the Bridge of Sighs," *Reviews in European History* 1, no. 4 (March 1975): 437–45. [Au.]

45 A. J. P. Taylor, *The Origins of the Second World War* (New York, 1964). See also William H. Dray, "Concepts of Causation in A. J. P. Taylor's *The Origins of the Second World War,*" *History and Theory* 17, no. 2 (1978): 149–74. [Au.]

atives and descendants, can hardly bear to hear it spoken of, much less turned into an occasion for a purely scholarly discussion of the politics of interpretation. But if this question is not a crucial example of how the politics of interpretation arises from an interpretation of politics, especially in matters historical, how could we imagine a better one? The cause of taste and sensitivity to the feelings of those who have a living investment in the memory of this event could be served by taking an example more remote in time — the French Revolution, the American Civil War, the Wars of Religion, the Crusades, the Inquisition — events remote enough in time to permit us to disengage whatever emotional weight they might have had for the people who experienced them from our purely intellectual "interest" in what they were or how they happened. But this very temptation to discuss the problem of the politics of interpretation in historical studies in the context of a consideration of events remote in time should itself enliven us to the morally domesticating effects of consigning an event definitively to "history."

Vidal-Naquet eloquently dilates on the poignant moment at which a people or group is forced, by the death of its members, to transfer an experience, existentially determinative of its own image of the nature of its existence as a historical entity, from the domain of memory to that of history. The resolution of the Holocaust question, he says, does not lie in the direction of simply exposing the "fraudulence" of the revisionists' "version" of history.

> For whatever the circumstances, today we are witnessing the transformation of memory into history. . . . My generation, people of about fifty, is probably the last one for whom Hitler's crimes are still a memory. That both disappearance and, worse still, depreciation of this memory must be combated seems to me obvious. Neither prescription nor pardon seems conceivable. . . . But what are we going to do with this memory that, while it is our memory, is not that of everybody? (93–94)

What indeed? In the answer that a historian gives to that question is contained an entire politics of interpretation — and not only for historical studies. Vidal-Naquet's own efforts to answer it are instructive and illuminate some of the points I have been trying to make here. His remarks warrant full quotation, for they return us to the relevance of the historical sublime to the larger questions of historical interpretation:

> It is hard for me to explain myself on this point. I was brought up with an elevated — some might say megalomaniacal — conception of the task of the historian, and it was during the war that my father made me read Chateaubriand's famous article in the *Mercure* of July 4, 1807:
>
>> In the silence of abjection, when the only sounds to be heard are the chains of the slave and the voice of the informer; when everything trembles before the tyrant and it is as dangerous to incur his favor as to deserve his disfavor, this is when the historian appears, charged with avenging the people.
>
> I still believe in the need to remember and, in my way, I try to be a man of memory; but I no longer believe that historians are "charged with avenging the people." We must accept the fact that "the war is over," that the tragedy has become, in a way secularized, even if this carries with it for us, I mean for we who are Jewish, the loss of a certain privilege of speech that has largely been ours since Europe discovered the great massacre. And this, in itself, is not a bad thing; for what can be more intolerable than the pose of certain personages draped in the sash of the Order of Extermination, who believe that in this way they can avoid the everyday pettiness and baseness that are our human lot? (94)

I find these words moving, not least because over and above the humaneness to which they attest, they attest to the politically domesticating effects of a historical attitude that is always much too prone to equate the consignment of an event to history with the end of a war. In point of fact, for French anti-Semites the war was far from over, as the attack on the synagogue in the rue Copernic in October 1980 (which postdated the composition of Vidal-Naquet's article) amply indicated. It is less easy than Vidal-Naquet suggests to neutralize human memory by the consignment of an event or experience of it to history. What he condemns as ideology may be nothing other than the treatment of a historical event as if it were still a memory of living men; but a memory, whether real or only felt to be so, cannot be deprived of the emotional charge and the action it seems to justify by presenting a historical-real that has remembrance as its only purpose.

Vidal-Naquet is inclined — too hastily, I think — to consign the Zionist interpretation of the Holocaust (or his version of that interpretation) to the category of untruth. In fact, its truth, as a historical interpretation, consists precisely of its effectiveness in justifying a wide range of current Israeli political policies that, from the standpoint of those who articulate them, are crucial to the security and indeed the very existence of the Jewish people. Whether one supports these policies or condemns them, they are undeniably a product, at least in part, of a conception of Jewish history that is conceived to be meaningless to Jews insofar as this history was dominated by agencies, processes, and groups who encouraged or permitted policies that led to the "final solution" of "the Jewish Question." The totalitarian, not to say fascist, aspects of Israeli treatment of the Palestinians on the West Bank may be attributable primarily to a Zionist ideology that is detestable to anti-Zionists, Jews and non-Jews alike. But who is to say that this ideology is a product of a distorted conception of history in general and of the history of Jews in the Diaspora specifically? It is, in fact, fully comprehensible as a morally responsible response to the meaninglessness of a certain history, that spectacle of "moral anarchy" that Schiller perceived in "world history" and specified as a "sublime object." The Israeli political response to this spectacle is fully consonant with the aspiration to human freedom and dignity that Schiller took to be the necessary consequence of sustained reflection on it. So far as I can see, the effort of the Palestinian people to mount a politically effective response to Israeli policies entails the production of a similarly effective ideology, complete with an interpretation of their history capable of endowing it with a meaning that it has hitherto lacked (a project to which Edward Said wishes to contribute).

Does this imply that historical knowledge, or, rather, the kind of discourses produced by historians, finds the measure of its validity in its status as an instrument of a political program or of an ideology that rationalizes, when it does not inspire, such a program? And if so, what does this tell us about the kind of historical knowledge that comes attended by a claim to have forgone service to any specific political cause and simply purports to tell the truth about the past as an end in itself and *sine ira et studio,*[46] to provide "understanding" of what cannot be perfectly "explained," and to lead to tolerance and forbearance rather than reverence or a spirit of vengefulness?

In answer to the first question, one must grant that while it is possible to produce a kind of knowledge that is not explicitly linked to any specific political program, all knowledge produced in the human and social sciences lends itself to use by a given ideology better than it does to others. This is especially true of historical knowledge of the conceptually underdetermined sort that appears in the form of a conventional narrative. Which brings us back to the question of the political or ideological implications of narrativity itself as a modality of historical representation of the sort that Barthes associates with nineteenth-century bourgeois notions of realism.[47] Is narrativity itself an ideological instrument? It is sufficient here to indicate the extent to which a number of contemporary analysts of narratology, among whom must be numbered Julia Kristeva, think it to be so.[48] If, by contrast, it is possible to imagine a conception of history that would signal its resistance to the bourgeois ideology of realism by its refusal to attempt a narrativist mode for the representation of its truth, is it possible that this refusal itself signals a recovery of the historical sublime that bourgeois historiography repressed in the process of its disciplinization? And if this is or might be the case, is this recovery of the historical sublime a necessary

[46]Without anger or zeal. [Ed.]

[47]See Barthes, "Historical Discourse." A new translation with an introduction by Stephen Bann appears in *Comparative Criticism: A Year Book,* vol. 3, ed. E. S. Shaffer (Cambridge, 1981), 3–19. [Au.]

[48]Julia Kristeva, "The Novel as Polylogue," in Kristeva, *Desire in Language: A Semiotic Approach to Literature and Art,* ed. Leon S. Roudiez (New York, 1980), esp. 201–8. [Au.] See Kristeva, p. 1075. [Ed.]

precondition for the production of a historiography of the sort that Chateaubriand conceived to be desirable in times of "abjection"? a historiography "charged with avenging the people"? This seems plausible to me.

As for the second question, namely, what all of this might imply for any effort to comprehend that politics of interpretation in historical studies that instructs us to recognize that "the war is over" and to forgo the attractions of a desire for revenge, it seems obvious to me that such instruction is the kind that always emanates from centers of established political power and social authority and that this kind of tolerance is a luxury only devotees of dominant groups can afford. For subordinant, emergent, or resisting social groups, this recommendation — that they view history with the kind of "objectivity," "modesty," "realism," and "social responsibility" that has characterized historical studies since their establishment as a professional discipline — can only appear as another aspect of the ideology they are indentured to oppose. They cannot effectively oppose such an ideology while only offering their own versions, Marxist or otherwise, of this "objectivity" and so forth that the established discipline claims. This opposition can be carried forward only on the basis of a conception of the historical record as being not a window through which the past "as it really was" can be apprehended but rather a wall that must be broken through if the "terror of history" is to be directly confronted and the fear it induces dispelled.

Santayana said that "those who neglect the study of the past are condemned to repeat it." It is not so much the study of the past itself that assures against its repetition as it is how one studies it, to what aim, interest, or purpose. Nothing is better suited to lead to a repetition of the past than a study of it that is either reverential or convincingly objective in the way that conventional historical studies tend to be. Hegel opined that "the only thing anyone ever learned from the study of the study of history is that no one ever learned anything from the study of history." But he was convinced, and demonstrated to the satisfaction of a number of students of history more sapient than I, that one could learn a great deal, of both practical and theoretical worth, from the study of the study of history. And one of the things one learns from the study of history is that such study is never innocent, ideologically or otherwise, whether launched from the political perspective of the Left, the Right, or the Center. This is because our very notion of the possibility of discriminating between the Left, the Right, and the Center is in part a function of the disciplinization of historical studies which ruled out the possibility — a possibility that should never be ruled out of any area of inquiry — that history may be as meaningless "in itself" as the theorists of the historical sublime thought it to be.

Nancy Armstrong

b. 1938

The American scholar who has perhaps done the most to breach the barrier between feminism and cultural studies, Nancy Armstrong attended Wellesley College for two years, had three children in rapid succession, completed her B.A. at the State University of New York at Buffalo, and left, children in tow, for the Ph.D. program at the University of Wisconsin–Madison in 1967. Before receiving her doctorate in 1977, she taught on a Fulbright Fellowship in Portugal at the University of Coimbra, where she tries to return every two or three years. Since then, she has taught at Wayne State University, the State University of New York at Buffalo, the University of Minnesota, and Yale, Wesleyan, and Brown Universities. She is currently Nancy Duke Lewis Professor of Comparative Literature, Modern Culture and Media, English, and Women's Studies at Brown. Her books include two collec-

tions of essays edited with Leonard Tennenhouse: The Ideology of Conduct: Essays on Literature and the History of Sexuality *(1986) and* The Violence of Representation *(1989);* Desire and Domestic Fiction: A Political History of the Novel *(1987),* The Imaginary Puritan: Literature, Intellectual Labor, and the Origins of Personal Life *(with Leonard Tennenhouse, 1992); and* Fiction in the Age of Photography *(1997). "Some Call It Fiction" was originally presented to the Focused Research Program in Gender and Women's Studies at the University of California at Irvine during 1985–88, before being published in Juliet Flower MacCannell's collection of papers from that program,* The Other Perspective in Gender and Culture *(1990).*

Some Call It Fiction: On the Politics of Domesticity

It is queer how out of touch with truth women are. They live in a world of their own, and there has never been anything like it, and never can be.

— JOSEPH CONRAD, *Heart of Darkness*

For some years now, American scholars have been puzzling out the relationship between literature and history. Apparently the right connections were not made when literary histories were first compiled. Yet in turning to the question of how some of the most famous British novelists were linked to their moment in time, I have found I must begin at step one, with extremely powerful conventions of representation. Though old and utterly familiar, nothing new has taken their place. Their potency has not diminished in this country despite the theory revolution and the calls for a new literary history that came in its wake. The conventions to which I refer are many and various indeed, but all reinforce the assumption that history consists of economic or political events, as if these were essentially different from other cultural events. Some of us — a distinct minority, to be sure — feel that to proceed on this assumption is to brush aside most of the activities composing everyday life and so shrink the category of "the political" down to a very limited set of cultural practices. And then, having classified most of our symbolic activities as "personal," "social," or "cultural" (it is all much the same), traditional histories would have us place them in a secondary relationship either to the economy or to the official institutions of state. This essay is written in opposition to models of history that confine political practices to activities directly concerned with the marketplace, the official institutions of the state, or else resistance to these. I write as one who feels that such models have not provided an adequate basis for understanding the formation of a modern bureaucratic culture or for our place, as intellectuals, within it. More than that, I regard any model that places personal life in a separate sphere and that grants literature a secondary and passive role in political history as unconsciously sexist. I believe such models necessarily fail to account for the formation of a modern bureaucratic culture because they fail to account for the place of women within it.

Some of our best theorizers of fiction's relationship to history — Raymond Williams in England and Edward Said[1] in the United States — have done much to tear down the barrier between culture and state. They demonstrate that the middle-class hegemony succeeded in part because it constructed separate historical narratives for self and society, family and factory, literature and history. They suggest that by maintaining these divisions within culture, liberal intellectu-

[1]See Williams, p. 1153, and Said, p. 1278. [Ed.]

als continue to sanitize certain areas of culture — namely, the personal, domestic, and literary. The practices that go by these names consequently appear to be benignly progressive, in their analyses, to provide a place of escape from the political world, and even to offer forms of resistance. Still, I would argue, such efforts as those of Williams and Said will be only partially successful so long as they continue to ignore *the sexual division of labor* that underwrites and naturalizes the difference between culture and politics.

THE LIMITS OF POLITICAL HISTORY

To put some life into all these abstractions, let me now turn to domestic fiction and the difficulties that scholars encounter when they try to place writing of this kind in history. Ian Watt convincingly describes the socioeconomic character of the new readership for whom Defoe, Richardson, and Fielding wrote, a readership whose rise in turn gave rise to the novel. But Watt has no similar explanation for Austen. Her popularity he ascribes to her talent, and her talent, to nature. And so he concludes that nature must have given Austen a good eye for details.[2] Although Williams moves well beyond such reflection theories in his ground-breaking account of the information revolution, his model of history ultimately serves us no better than Watt's when it comes to explaining domestic fiction. His *Long Revolution* regards intellectual labor as a political force in its own right without which capitalism could not have unfolded as smoothly and completely as it appears to have done. But however much power Williams grants this domain, it belongs to culture and, as such, exists in a secondary relationship with political history. To historicize writing, he feels compelled to give it a source in events outside of and prior to writing. He does not entertain the possibility that the classic unfolding of capitalism was predicated on writing, much less on writing by women or writing that appealed to the interests of a female readership.[3] For Williams as for Watt, historical events take place in the official institutions of state or else through resistance to these institutions, and both forms of power are exercised primarily through men.

I have found Watt and Williams especially helpful for establishing links between the history of fiction and the rise of the new middle classes in England. At the same time, I am perplexed to find that, in establishing a relationship between writing and political history, these otherwise conscientious scholars completely neglect to account for the most obvious fact of all, namely, that sometime during the eighteenth century, in the words of Virginia Woolf, "the middle class woman began to write."[4] If, as Watt and Williams say, the rise of the novel was directly related to the rise of the new middle classes, then

[2]Ian Watt, *The Rise of the Novel* (Berkeley: University of California Press, 1957), p. 57. [Au.]

[3]In *The Long Revolution* (New York: Columbia University Press, 1961), Williams sets out to show how the "creative" or cultural dimension of social experience opposed existing forms of political authority during the seventeenth and eighteenth centuries and won. Part one of his book indeed gives culture priority over the official institutions of state (as it must during the eighteenth century), claiming that cultural history "is more than a department, a special area of change. In this creative area the changes and conflicts of the whole way of life are necessarily involved" (p. 122). But latent in this promise to extend the category of "the political" broadly to include "the whole way of life" is the contradictory suggestion that political practices are also a special category of "the whole." The second notion of politics emerges in part two, where Williams describes such historical processes as the growth of the reading public, of the popular press, and of standard English through which the new middle classes converted the power of language into economic power. Here the narrow definition of political events, as those which take place in the houses of government, the courts, and the marketplace, assumes control over the "creative" cultural dimension of social experience. For example, Williams writes, "as 1688 is a significant political date, so 1695 is significant in the history of the press. For in that year Parliament declined to renew the 1662 Licensing Act, and the stage for expansion was now fully set" (p. 180). Had Williams actually gathered data that would compose the record of "the whole" of life, he might have broken out of this circle. But, in producing cultural histories, he invariably bows to tradition and stops before entering into the female domain. [Au.]

[4]Virginia Woolf, *A Room of One's Own* (New York: Harcourt, Brace and World, 1975), p. 69. [Au.] See Woolf in this text, p. 548. [Ed.]

which rest upon preserving the line that divvies up cultural information according to gender. This is the line between inside and outside that is implanted in his metaphor from the beginning to distinguish personal from political life. This is the first division of the conceptual zygote, the line without which the fantasy of an entire political world cannot develop its inexorable symmetry, a symmetry that cuts beneath and through particular features that culture manifests at one site rather than another. While he opens the category of political power considerably by including institutions other than those officially charged to distribute wealth and power, Foucault extends the cultural scope of discipline only so far as institutions that, in becoming institutions, came to be dominated by men. Thus if power does not originate in the minds of individual men or in the bodies of men collectively, it arises from the cultural patterns that make men think of themselves as certain kinds of men and exercise power accordingly.

But if one pursues the implications of Foucault's chosen metaphor for modern power, his city under plague, in contrast with a Boccaccian remedy, contains a certain form of household that is the perfect and obvious answer to the indiscriminate mingling of bodies spreading the infection. When we expand our concept of the political further even than Foucault's, we discover grounds on which to argue that the modern household rather than the clinic provided the proto-institutional setting where government through relentless supervision first appeared, and appeared in its most benevolent guise. Foucault never takes note of these continuities between home and state even though they are as plain as the words on his page. More curious still is his failure to acknowledge the fact that a home espoused by various subgroups aspiring for the status of "respectability," a home overseen by a woman, actually preceded the formation of other social institutions by at least fifty years. There is little to suggest this household took root in practice much before the beginning of the nineteenth century, even though it frequently appeared in the literature and political argumentation of the previous century. From writing, it can be argued, the new family passed into the realm of common sense, where it came to justify the distribution of national wealth through wages paid to men. Indeed, it remains extremely powerful to this day as both metaphor and metonymy, the unacknowledged model and source of middle-class power.[14]

THE POWER OF DOMESTICITY

It is at this point in my argument that a feminist perspective must be invoked, but it cannot be a feminism that sinks comfortably into the rhetoric of victimization. It has to be thoroughly politicized. By this I mean we must be willing to accept the idea that, as middle-class women, we are empowered, although we are not empowered in traditionally masculine ways. We have to acknowledge that as middle-class intellectuals we are not critical mirrors of a separate and more primary process orchestrated by others — be they politicians, bureaucrats, captains of industry, or simply men. As women intellectuals we are doubly implicated in the process of reproducing the state of mind upon which other openly and avowedly political institutions depend. It is on this basis that I reject the notion that women's writing exists in a domain of experience outside of political history. I can no longer accept what conventional histories assume — that such writing occupies the secondary status of a "reflection" or "consequence" of changes within more primary social institutions — the army, hospital, prison, or factory. To the contrary, my evidence reveals domestic fiction actively disentangled the language of sexual relations from that of political economy. The rhetoric of this fiction (in Wayne Booth's sense of the term[15]) laid out a new cultural logic that would eventually become com-

[14]I have argued this at length in *Desire and Domestic Fiction.* This essay began as an early version of the introduction and later developed into a theoretical investigation of my argument with literature, history, and academic feminism. I refer readers to the book for evidence supporting the necessarily brief outline of the events in the history of modern sexuality which composes part of this essay. [Au.]

[15]See the introduction to Reader-Response Criticism, p. 919. [Ed.]

mon sense, sensibility, and public opinion. In this way, female knowledge successfully combatted one kind of power, based on title, wealth, and physical force, with another, based on the control of literacy. By equating good reading with what was good for women readers, a new standard for reading laid down the semantic ground for common sense and established the narrative conventions structuring public opinion. The new standard of literacy helped to bring a new class of people into existence. This class laid claim to the right to privacy on behalf of each individual. Yet this class set in motion the systematic invasion of private life by surveillance, observation, evaluation, and remediation. In a word, it ruled, still rules, through countless microtechniques of socialization, all of which may be lumped together under the heading of education.[16] During the second half of the nineteenth century, institutions were created to perform these operations upon masses of people in much the same way as domestic fiction did upon characters.

Those of us who have grown up within an institutional culture consequently carry around a voice much like that of a fictional narrator in his or her head. Sensitive to the least sign of disorder — a foul word, a piece of clothing undone, some food sliding off one's fork, or, worse still, some loss of control over bodily functions — the presence of this voice, now nearly two hundred years old, more surely keeps us in line than fear of the police or the military. For the unofficial forms of power have a terrible advantage over those which are openly and avowedly regulatory. They make us afraid of ourselves. They operate on the supposition that we harbor desires dangerous to the general good. Believing in the presence of a self that is essentially subversive, we keep watch over ourselves — in mirrors, on clocks, on scales, through medical exams, and by means of any number of other such practices. Thus we internalize a state that is founded on the conflict between self and state interests, and we feel perfectly justified in enacting its power — which is, after all, only good for oneself — upon others.

Convinced that power exerted in and through the female domain is at least as powerful as the more conventional forms of power associated with the male, I want to sketch out the relationship between the two during the modern period. I will suggest that modern institutional cultures depend upon the separation of "the political" from "the personal" and that they produce and maintain this separation on the basis of gender — the formation of masculine and feminine domains of culture. For, I will argue, even as certain forms of cultural information were separated into these two opposing fields, they were brought together as an intricate set of pressures that operated on the subject's body and mind to induce self-regulation. We can observe this peculiarly effective collaboration of the official and unofficial forms of power perhaps most clearly in the formation of a national education system during the Victorian period and in the whole constellation of efforts that went on simultaneously to appropriate leisure time.[17] British fiction participates in both efforts and therefore demonstrates the modes of collaboration between them.

To introduce their highly influential *Practical Education* in 1801, Maria Edgeworth and her father announce their break with the curriculum that reinforced traditional political distinctions: "On religion and politics we have been silent because we have no ambition to gain partisans, or to make proselytes, and because we do not address ourselves to any sect or party."[18] In virtu-

[16]In "'The Mother Made Conscious': The Historical Development of a Primary School Pedagogy," *History Workshop* (1985), vol. 20, Carolyn Steedman has researched the rationale and analyzed the process by which the techniques of mothering were extended beyond the household and, through the establishment of a national educational system, became the gentle but unyielding girders of a new institutional culture. [Au.]

[17]See, for example, Peter Stallybrass and Allon White, *The Politics and Poetics of Transgression* (London: Methuen, 1986); Peter Clark, *The English Alehouse: A Social History, 1200–1830* (London: Longman, 1983); Thomas Walter Laqueur, *Religion and Respectability: Sunday Schools and Working Class Culture, 1780–1850* (New Haven: Yale University Press, 1976). [Au.]

[18]Maria Edgeworth and Robert L. Edgeworth, *Practical Education* (London, 1801), 2: ix. Citations in the text are to this edition. [Au.]

ally the same breath, they assure readers, "With respect to what is commonly called the education of the heart, we have endeavored to suggest the easiest means of inducing useful and agreeable habits, well regulated sympathy and benevolent affections" (p. viii). Their program substitutes abstract terms of emotion and behavior for those of one's specific socioeconomic identity. Rooting identity in the very subjective qualities that earlier curricula had sought to inculcate in young women alone, the Edgeworths' program gives priority to the schoolroom and parlor over the church and courts for purposes of regulating human behavior. In doing this, their educational program promises to suppress the political signs of human identity (which is of course a powerful political gesture in its own right). Perfectly aware of the power to be exercised through education, the Edgeworths justify their curriculum for cultivating the heart on grounds that it offered a new and more effective method of policing. In their words, "It is the business of education to prevent crimes, and to prevent all those habitual propensities which necessarily lead to their commission" (p. 354).

To accomplish their ambitious political goal, the Edgeworths invoke an economy of pleasure which cannot in fact be understood apart from the novel and the criticism that was produced both to censor and to foster it. First, the Edgeworths accept the view prevailing during the eighteenth century which said that fiction was sure to mislead female desire:

> With respect to sentimental stories, and books of mere entertainment, we must remark, that they should be sparingly used, especially in the education of girls. This species of reading cultivates what is called the heart prematurely, lowers the tone of the mind, and induces indifference for those common pleasures and occupations which . . . constitute by far the greatest portion of our daily happiness. (p. 105)

But the same turn of mind could as easily recognize the practical value of pleasure when it is harnessed and aimed at the right goals. Convinced that "the pleasures of literature" acted upon the reader in much the same way as a child's "taste for sugar-plums" (p. 80), forward-thinking educators began to endorse the reading of fiction, so long as it was governed by principles that made conformity seem desirable.

In formulating a theory of mass education in which fiction had a deceptively marginal role to play, the Edgeworths and their colleagues were adopting a rhetoric which earlier reformers had used to level charges of violence and corruption against the old aristocracy. They placed themselves in the tradition of radical Protestant dissent going back to the sixteenth century, a tradition which had always argued that political authority should be based on moral superiority. Sexual relations so often provided the terms for making this claim that no representation of the household could be considered politically neutral. To contest that notion of the state which depended upon inherited power, puritan treatises on marriage and household governance represented the family as a self-enclosed social unit into whose affairs the state had no right to intervene. Against genealogy they posited domesticity. But in claiming sovereignty for the natural father over his household, these treatises were not proposing a new distribution of political power. They were simply trying to limit the monarch's power. To understand the social transformation that was achieved by the English Revolution (according to Christopher Hill, not achieved until more than a century later), we have to turn away from what we consider to be the political themes of the puritan argument and consider instead what happens to gender.[19]

[19]For a discussion of the paternalism that emerged in opposition to patriarchy in seventeenth-century puritan writing, see Leonard Tennenhouse, *Power on Display: the Politics of Shakespeare's Genres* (New York: Methuen, 1986), especially the chapter entitled "Family Rites." In describing the alternative to patriarchy that arose at the end of the seventeenth and beginning of the eighteenth century in aristocratic families, Randolph Trumbach opposes the term "patriarchal" to the term "domesticity," by which he refers to the modern household. This social formation is authorized by internal relations of gender and generation rather than by way of analogy to external power relations between monarch and subject or between God and man, *The Rise of the Egalitarian Family* (New York: Academic Press, 1978), pp. 119–63. [Au.]

According to Kathleen M. Davis, the puritan doctrine of equality insisted upon the difference of sexual roles, in which the female was certainly subordinate to the male, and not upon the equality of the woman in kind. "The result of this partnership," she explains, "was a definition of mutual and complementary duties and characteristics." Gender was so clearly understood in these oppositional terms that it could be graphically represented:[20]

Husband	Wife
Get goods	Gather them together and save them
Travel, seek a living	Keep the house
Get money and provisions	Do not vainly spend it
Deal with many men	Talk with few
Be "entertaining"	Be solitary and withdrawn
Be skillful in talk	Boast of silence
Be a giver	Be a saver
Apparel yourself as you may	Apparel yourself as it becomes you
Dispatch all things outdoors	Oversee and give order within

In so representing the household as the opposition of complementary genders, the authors of countless puritan tracts asked readers to imagine the household as a self-enclosed social unit. But if these authors wanted to define the family as an independent source of authority, their moment did not arrive. The puritan household consisted of a male and a female who were structurally identical, positive and negative versions of the same thing. The authority of the housewife described above could not yet be imagined as a positive thing in its own right. Until she took up her vigil and began to order personal life, a single understanding of power reigned, and men fought to determine the balance among its various parts.

[20]Kathleen M. Davis, "The Sacred Condition of Equality — How Original Were Puritan Doctrines of Marriage?" *Social History* (1977), 5: 570. Davis quotes this list from John Dod and Robert Cleaver, *A Godly Forme of Householde Gouernment* (London, 1614). [Au.]

Unlike the authors of seventeenth-century marriage manuals and domestic economies, the educational reformers of nineteenth-century England could look back on a substantial body of writing whose main purpose was to produce a historically new woman. During the centuries between the English Revolution and the present day, this woman was inscribed with values which appealed to a whole range of competing interest groups, and, through her, these groups seized authority over domestic relations and personal life. In this way, I believe, they created a need for the kind of surveillance which modern institutions provide. Indeed, the last two decades of the seventeenth century saw an explosion of writing aimed at educating the daughters of the numerous aspiring social groups. The new curriculum promised to educate these women in such a way as to make them more desirable than women who had only their own rank and fortune to recommend them. This curriculum exalted a woman whose value resided chiefly in her femaleness rather than in the traditional signs of status, a woman who possessed emotional depth rather than a physically stimulating surface, one who, in other words, excelled in the very qualities that differentiated her from the male. As gender was redefined in these terms, the woman exalted by an aristocratic tradition of letters ceased to appear so desirable. In becoming the other side of this new sexual coin, she represented surface rather than depth, embodied material as opposed to moral value, and displayed idle sensuality instead of unflagging concern for the well-being of others. So conceived, the aristocratic woman no longer defined what was truly and most desirably female.

But it was not until the mid-nineteenth century that the project of defining people on the basis of gender began to acquire some of the immense political influence it still exercises today. Around the 1830s, one can see the discourse of sexuality relax its critical gaze on the aristocracy as the newly forming working classes became a more obvious target of moral reform. Authors suddenly took notice of social elements who had hardly mattered before. These reformers and men of letters discovered that rebellious artisans and urban laborers, for example, lacked the kind of motivation that supposedly characterized normal individuals. Numerous writers sought out the source of poverty, illiteracy, and demographic change in these underdeveloped individuals, whose behavior was generally found to be not only promiscuous but also ambiguously gendered. Once they succeeded in translating an overwhelming economic problem into a sexual scandal, middle-class intellectuals could step forward and offer themselves, their technology, their supervisory skills, and their institutions of education and social welfare as the appropriate remedy for growing political resistance.

In all fairness, as Foucault notes, the middle classes rarely applied institutional procedures to others without first trying them out on themselves. When putting together a national curriculum, the government officials and educators in charge adopted one modeled on the educational theory that grew up around the Edgeworths and their intellectual circle, the heirs of the dissenting tradition.[21] This was basically the same as the curriculum proposed by eighteenth-century pedagogues and reformers as the best way of producing a marriageable daughter. By the end of the eighteenth century, the Edgeworths were among those who had already determined that the program aimed at producing the ideal woman could be applied to boys just as well as to girls. And by the mid-nineteenth century, one can see the government figuring out how to administer much the same program on a mass basis. In providing the conceptual foundation for a national curriculum, a particular idea of the self thus became commonplace, and as gendered forms of identity determined how people thought of themselves as well as others, that self became the dominant social reality.

Such an abbreviated history cannot do justice to the fierce controversies punctuating the institution of a national education system in England. I simply call attention to this material as a site where political history obviously converged with the history of sexuality as well as with that of the novel to produce a specific kind of individual. I do this to suggest the political implications of representing these as separate narratives. As it began to deny its political and religious bias and to present itself instead as a moral and psychological truth, the rhetoric of reform obviously severed its ties with an aristocratic past and took up a new role in history. It no longer constituted a form of resistance but enclosed a specialized domain of culture apart from political relations where apolitical truths could be told. The novel's literary status hinged upon this event. Henceforth fiction would deny the political basis for its meaning and refer instead to the private regions of the self or to the specialized world of art but never to the use of words that created and still maintains these distinctions so basic to our culture. Favored among kinds of fiction were novels that best performed the rhetorical operations of division and self-containment and thus turned existing political information into the discourse of sexuality. These works of fiction gave novels a good name, a name free of politics, and often the name of a woman such as Pamela, Evelina, Emma, or Jane Eyre.[22] Then, with the translation of human identity into sexual identity came widespread repression of the political literacy characterizing an earlier culture, and with it, too, mass forgetting that there was a history of sexuality to tell.

THE POLITICS OF DOMESTIC FICTION

Let me offer a detailed example of the exchange between reader and literary text to provide a sense of how the power of domesticity works through such an exchange. Charlotte Brontë flaunted this very power in writing her novel *Shirley*.[23] The novel contains an otherwise gratuitous scene where Shakespeare's *Coriolanus* is read aloud and critiqued, as if to give the reader

[21]See Brian Simon, *Studies in the History of Education, 1780–1870* (London: Lawrence and Wishart, 1960), pp. 1–62. [Au.]

[22]Eponymous heroines of novels by Samuel Richardson (1740), Fanny Burney (1778), Jane Austen (1816), and Charlotte Brontë (1847). [Ed.]

[23]Published in 1849. [Ed.]

precise rules for reading, rules that should fascinate literary historians. They are not Brontë's own but rules developed during the preceding century by countless authors of ladies' conduct books and educational treatises. These authors proposed the first curriculum to include native British literature. Around the time Brontë sat down to write *Shirley,* a new generation of writers had taken up the question of how to distinguish good reading from bad. Their efforts swelled the growing number of Victorian magazines. Whether or not girls should read novels was the concern that shaped the debates over a curriculum for women during the eighteenth century, then nineteenth-century pedagogical theory developed around the question of how to make fiction useful for teaching foreigners and working-class people as well as women and children. Rules for reading developed along with the national standard curriculum that extended a curriculum originally meant only for girls of the literate classes to young Englishmen and women at various levels and their counterparts throughout the colonies. It is much the same theory of education that informs our educational system today. By using this example from *Shirley* to illustrate the rationale and procedures by which Victorian intellectuals extended what had been regarded as a female form of literacy to male education, I also want to mark an important difference between Charlotte Brontë's understanding of this process and our own. She was, I believe, far more aware of the politics of literary interpretation than we are.

One of her least colorful heroines, Carolyn Helstone, uses Shakespeare to while away an evening of leisure with her beloved cousin and future husband Robert Moore, a surly manufacturer, whose authoritarian way of dealing with factory hands is earning him threats of Luddite[24] reprisals. During this, their one intimate moment together until the end of the novel, they reject all the pastimes available to lovers in an Austen novel in favor of reading Shakespeare's *Coriolanus.* Far more detailed than any such exchange in earlier fiction, this act of reading spells out the procedures by which reading literature was thought to produce a form of knowledge that was also a form of social control. Robert Moore is half Belgian, half English. It is through reading Shakespeare that, according to Carolyn, he "shall be entirely English."[25] For, as she patiently explains to him, "Your French forefathers don't speak so sweetly, not so solemnly, nor so impressively as your English ancestors, Robert." But being English does not identify a set of political affiliations — as it would in Shakespeare's time. It refers instead to essential qualities of human mind. Caroline has selected a part for Robert to read aloud that, in her words, "is toned with something in you. It shall waken your nature, fill your mind with music, it shall pass like a skillful hand over your heart. . . . Let glorious William come near and touch it; you will see how he will draw the English power and melody out of its chords."

I have called this relationship between reader and text an exchange in order to stress the fact that writing cannot be turned to the task of constituting readers without giving up old features and acquiring new ones of its own; to dwell on the reader is to explain but one half of the transformational logic of this exchange. Just as Robert, the rude Belgian, becomes a gentle Englishman by reading Shakespeare, so, too, the Jacobean playwright is transformed by the domestic setting in which he is read. Carolyn urges Robert to receive the English of another historical moment as the voice of an ancestor speaking to him across time and cultural boundaries. To no one's surprise, the written Shakespeare, thus resurrected, has acquired the yearnings and anxieties of an early nineteenth-century factory owner. And as we observe the Bard becoming the nineteenth-century man, we also witness an early version of our own literary training. Here, extending through the educated middle-class female to the male and, through him, acquiring uni-

[24]Named after the semilegendary Ned Lud, who in a fit had smashed stocking frames in 1779, the Luddites were organized groups of laborers who destroyed industrial machinery in the British midlands and northern counties during the years 1811–16. [Ed.]

[25]Charlotte Brontë, *Shirley,* Andrew and Judith Hock, eds. (Harmondsworth: Penguin, 1974), p. 114. Citations of the text are to this edition. [Au.]

versal application, we can see how voices that speak from positions vastly different in social space and time quickly translate into aspects of modern consciousness.

Thus Shakespeare becomes the means of reproducing specifically modern states of mind within the reader. Reading Shakespeare is supposed "to stir you," Carolyn explains, "to give you new sensations. It is to make you feel your life strongly, not only your virtues, but your vicious, perverse points. Discover by the feeling the reading will give you at once how high and how low you are" (p. 115). If Shakespeare loses the very turns of mind that would identify him with his moment in history, then Robert loses features of a similar kind in Brontë's representation of the scene of reading. And this, of course, is the point. Reading Shakespeare translates Robert's political attitudes into essential features of mind. It simultaneously objectifies those features and subjects them to evaluation. The "English power" that Robert acquires by reading literature is simply the power of observing himself through the lens of liberal humanism — as a self flushed with the grandiosity of an ordinariness that has been totally liberated from historical bias and political commitment. For it is through this lens that the novel has us perceive the transformations that come over Robert as he reads *Coriolanus* under the gentle tutelage of Carolyn Helstone: "stepping out of the narrow line of private prejudices, he began to revel in the large picture of human nature, to feel the reality stamped upon the characters who were speaking from that page before him" (p. 116).

Her tutoring induces Robert to renounce one mode of power — which Carolyn associates with the imperiously patriarchal nature of *Coriolanus* — and to adopt another — which she identifies as a benevolent form of paternalism. As it is administered by a woman and used to mediate a sexual exchange, *Coriolanus* becomes the means for effecting historical change: *Coriolanus* becomes Carolyn. Performed as writing and reading, that is, the play becomes the means of internalizing a form of authority identified with the female. The political implications of feminizing the reader are clear as Carolyn gives Robert a moral to "tack to the play: . . . you must not be proud to your workpeople; you must not neglect chances of soothing them, and you must not be of an inflexible nature, uttering a request as austerely as if it were a command" (p. 114). Brontë is less than subtle in dramatizing the process by which reading rids Robert of the foreign devil. She seems to know exactly what political objective is fulfilled as he fills the mold of the Englishman and benevolent father. Brontë also puts the woman in charge of this process even though she gives her heroine the less imperious passages to read. Retiring, feminine, and thoroughly benign, Carolyn's power is hardly visible as such. Yet she is clearly the one who declares that reading has the power "to stir you; to give you new sensations. It is to make you feel your life strongly, not only your virtues, but your vicious, perverse points" (p. 115). And when Robert has finished reading, she is the one to ask, "Now, have you felt Shakespeare?" (p. 117). She suppresses all that belongs to the past as so much noise in her effort to being under examination the grand currents of emotion that run straight from Shakespeare to the modern day reader, a reader who is thoroughly English. In thus guiding his reading with her smiles and admonitions, Caroline executes a set of delicate procedures capable of translating any and all cultural information into shades of modern middle-class consciousness and the substance of a literary text. Although its setting — during the Luddite rebellions — makes *Shirley* anachronistic by about thirty years, the solution it proposes for the problem of political resistance, through the production of a new ruling-class mentality, marks this novel as utterly Victorian — perhaps even ahead of its time.

As similar textualizing strategies were deployed here and elsewhere throughout Victorian culture, an intricate system of psychological differences completely triumphed over a long-standing tradition of overtly political signs to usher in a new form of state power. This power — the power of representation over the thing represented — wrested authority from the old aristocracy on grounds that a government was morally obliged to rehabilitate deviant individuals rather than subdue them by force. The Peterloo Massacre of 1819 made it clear that the state's capacity for violence had become a source of embarrassment to the state. Overt displays of force worked against legitimate authority just as they did against subversive factions.[26] If acts of open rebellion had justified intervention in areas of society that government had not had to deal with before, then the government's use of force gave credence to the workers' charges of government oppression. The power of surveillance came into dominance at precisely this moment in English history, displacing traditional displays of violence. Remarkably like the form of vigilance that insured an orderly household, this power did not create equality so much as trivialize the material signs of difference by translating all such signs into differences in the quality, intensity, direction, and self-regulatory capability of an individual's desire.

In saying this, I am not suggesting that we should use British fiction to identify forms of repression or to perform acts of liberation, although my project has a definite political goal. I simply want to represent the discourse of sexuality as deeply implicated in — if not directly responsible for — the shape of the novel, and to show the novel's implication, at the same time, in producing a subject who knew herself and saw that self in relation to others according to the same feminizing strategies that had shaped fiction. I regard fiction, in other words, both as a document and as an agency of cultural history. I believe it helped to formulate the ordered space we now recognize as the household, that it made that space totally functional and used it as the context for representing normal behavior. In doing all this, fiction contested alternative bases for human relationships. As the history of this female domain is figured into political history, then, it will outline boldly the telling cultural move upon which, I believe, the supremacy of middle-class culture ultimately hinged. That is, it will reenact the moment when writing invaded, revised, and contained the household according to strategies that distinguished private from social life and thus detached sexuality from political history.

Where others have isolated rhetorical strategies that naturalize the subordination of female to male, no one has thoroughly examined the figure that differentiates the sexes as it links them together by sexual desire. And if no one asks why, how, and when gender differentiation became the root of human identity, no degree of theoretical sophistication can help us understand the totalizing power of this figure and the very real interests such power inevitably serves. So basic are the terms "male" and "female" to the semiotics of modern life that no one can use them without to some degree performing the very reifying gesture whose operations we need to understand and whose power we want to historicize. Whenever we cast our political lot in the dyadic formation of gender, we place ourselves in a classic double bind, which confines us to alternatives that are not really alternatives at all. That is to say, any political position founded primarily on sexual identity ultimately confirms the limited choices offered by such a dyadic model. Once one thinks within such a structure, sexual relationships appear as the model for all power relationships. This makes it possible to see the female as representative of all subjection and to use her subjectivity as if it were a form of resistance. Having inscribed social conflict within a domestic configuration, however, one loses sight of all the various and contrary political affiliations for which any given individual provides the site. This power of sexuality to appropriate the voice of the victim works as surely through inversion, of course, as by strict adherence to the internal organization of the model.

Still, there is a way in which I owe everything to the very academic feminism I seem to critique, for unless it were now acceptable to read women's texts as women's texts, there would be no call to historicize this area of culture. In view of the fact that women writers have been taken up by the Norton Anthology as part of the standard survey of British literature and also as a collection all of their own, and in view of the fact that we now have male feminists straining to hop

[26]E. P. Thompson, pp. 680–85. [Au.] What became known as the "Peterloo Massacre" was the Fifteenth Hussars' attack on a peaceful and well-organized demonstration of over sixty thousand workers massed at St. Peter's Fields outside Manchester, England, in 1819; they had been protesting against the Corn Laws and in favor of Parliamentary reform. Eleven workers were killed and many hundreds seriously injured by sabre cuts and flying hooves. [Ed.]

on the bandwagon, I feel it is simply time to take stock. It is time to consider why literary criticism presently feels so comfortable with a kind of criticism that began as a critique both of the traditional canon and of the interpretive procedures the canon called forth. This should tell us that by carving out a separate domain for women within literary criticism, feminist criticism has yet to destabilize the reigning metaphysics of sexuality. Literary historians continue to remain aloof from but still firmly anchored in a narrow masculinist notion of politics as more and more areas within literary studies have given ground to the thematics of sexuality promoted by academic feminism. Indeed, a sexual division of labor threatens to reproduce itself within the academy whereby women scholars interpret literature as the expression of the sexual subject while male scholars attend to matters of history and politics. To subvert this process, I believe we must read fiction not as literature but as the history of gender differences and a means by which we have reproduced a class and culture specific form of consciousness.

Homi K. Bhabha

b. 1949

Homi Bhabha was born into the Parsi community of Bombay and grew up in the shade of the Fire Temple. Bhabha received a B.A. from Bombay University, and an M.A., M.Phil., and D.Phil. from Christ Church, Oxford University. Bhabha has been a Reader in English Literature at the University of Sussex. He has also been Senior Fellow and Old Dominion Visiting Professor at Princeton University, Steinberg Visiting Professor at the University of Pennsylvania, where he delivered the Richard Wright Lecture Series, and a Faculty Fellow in the School of Criticism and Theory, Dartmouth College. He is currently Chester D. Tripp Professor in the Humanities at the University of Chicago, where he teaches in the Departments of English and Art. Bhabha will be delivering the Du Bois Lectures at Harvard University in the fall of 1997 and will be Beckman Professor of English at the University of California, Berkeley in 1998. He has edited the essay collection Nation and Narration *(1990) and is the author of* The Location of Culture *(1994). He is currently working on* A Measure of Dwelling, *a history of cosmopolitanism. The following selection is the Introduction to* The Location of Culture.

Locations of Culture

> *A boundary is not that at which something stops but, as the Greeks recognized, the boundary is that from which* something begins its presencing.
>
> — Martin Heidegger

BORDER LIVES: THE ART OF THE PRESENT

It is the trope of our times to locate the question of culture in the realm of the *beyond*. At the century's edge, we are less exercised by annihilation — the death of the author — or epiphany — the birth of the "subject."[1] Our existence today is marked by a tenebrous sense of survival, living on the borderlines of the "present," for which there seems to be no proper name other than the

[1]Bhabha alludes to "The Death of the Author," a 1968 essay by Roland Barthes raising issues similar to those discussed in Michel Foucault's "What Is an Author?" (see p. 889. *Epiphany* refers here to a sudden appearance. By *subject,* Bhabha refers to the Lacanian *I* (see the introduction to Psychoanalytic Theory, p. 1022). [Ed.]

current and controversial shiftiness of the prefix "post": *postmodernism, postcolonialism, postfeminism*. . . .

The "beyond" is neither a new horizon, nor a leaving behind of the past. . . . Beginnings and endings may be the sustaining myths of the middle years; but in the *fin de siècle*,[2] we find ourselves in the moment of transit where space and time cross to produce complex figures of difference and identity, past and present, inside and outside, inclusion and exclusion. For there is a sense of disorientation, a disturbance of direction, in the "beyond": an exploratory, restless movement caught so well in the French rendition of the words *au-delà* — here and there, on all sides, *fort/da,* hither and thither, back and forth.[3]

The move away from the singularities of "class" or "gender" as primary conceptual and organizational categories, has resulted in an awareness of the subject positions — of race, gender, generation, institutional location, geopolitical locale, sexual orientation — that inhabit any claim to identity in the modern world. What is theoretically innovative, and politically crucial, is the need to think beyond narratives of originary and initial subjectivities and to focus on those moments or processes that are produced in the articulation of cultural differences. These "in-between" spaces provide the terrain for elaborating strategies of selfhood — singular or communal — that initiate new signs of identity, and innovative sites of collaboration, and contestation, in the act of defining the idea of society itself.

It is in the emergence of the interstices — the overlap and displacement of domains of difference — that the intersubjective and collective experiences of *nationness,* community interest, or cultural value are negotiated. How are subjects formed "in-between," or in excess of, the sum of the "parts" of difference (usually intoned as race/class/gender, etc.)? How do strategies of representation or empowerment come to be formulated in the competing claims of communities where, despite shared histories of deprivation and discrimination, the exchange of values, meanings and priorities may not always be collaborative and dialogical, but may be profoundly antagonistic, conflictual and even incommensurable?

The force of these questions is borne out by the "language" of recent social crises sparked off by histories of cultural difference. Conflicts in South Central Los Angeles between Koreans, Mexican-Americans and African-Americans focus on the concept of "disrespect" — a term forged on the borderlines of ethnic deprivation that is, at once, the sign of racialized violence and the symptom of social victimage. In the aftermath of the *The Satanic Verses* affair[4] in Great Britain, Black and Irish feminists, despite their different constituencies, have made common cause against the "racialization of religion"[5] as the dominant discourse through which the State represents their conflicts and struggles, however secular or even "sexual" they may be.

Terms of cultural engagement, whether antagonistic or affiliative, are produced performatively. The representation of difference must not be hastily read as the reflection of *pre-given* ethnic or cultural traits set in the fixed tablet of tradition. The social articulation of difference, from the minority perspective, is a complex, on-going negotiation that seeks to authorize cultural hybridities that emerge in moments of historical transformation. The "right" to signify from the periphery of authorized power and privilege does not depend on the persistence of tradition; it is resourced by the power of tradition to be reinscribed through the conditions of contingency and contradictoriness that attend upon the lives of those who are "in the minority." The recognition that tradition bestows is a partial form of

[2]Literally, end of the era; usually used to refer to the close of the nineteenth century, as in n. 3. [Ed.]

[3]For an interesting discussion of gender boundaries in the *fin de siècle,* see E. Showalter, *Sexual Anarchy: Gender and Culture in the Fin de Siècle* (London: Bloomsbury, 1990), especially "Borderlines," pp. 1–18. [Au.] *Au-delà:* yonder; *fort/da:* gone/here (see Peter Brooks, p. 1036). [Ed.]

[4]"*The Satanic Verses* affair" refers to the fatwa pronounced by Islamic mullahs authorizing any of the faithful to take vengeance against Pakistani-born novelist Salman Rushdie, author of a 1988 novel of that name thought to ridicule Mohammed and Islam. Rushdie lived in hiding for years following the pronouncement of the fatwa. [Ed.]

[5]Bhabha is referring to groups like "Women Against Fundamentalism." [Ed.]

identification. In restaging the past it introduces other, incommensurable cultural temporalities into the invention of tradition. This process estranges any immediate access to an originary identity or a "received" tradition. The borderline engagements of cultural difference may as often be consensual as conflictual; they may confound our definitions of tradition and modernity; realign the customary boundaries between the private and the public, high and low; and challenge normative expectations of development and progress.

> I wanted to make shapes or set up situations that are kind of open. . . . My work has a lot to do with a kind of fluidity, a movement back and forth, not making a claim to any specific or essential way of being.[6]

Thus writes Renée Green, the African-American artist. She reflects on the need to understand cultural difference as the production of minority identities that "split" — are estranged unto themselves — in the act of being articulated into a collective body:

> Multiculturalism doesn't reflect the complexity of the situation as I face it daily. . . . It requires a person to step outside of him/herself to actually see what he/she is doing. I don't want to condemn well-meaning people and say (like those T-shirts you can buy on the street) "It's a black thing, you wouldn't understand." To me that's essentialising blackness.[7]

Political empowerment, and the enlargement of the multiculturalist cause, come from posing questions of solidarity and community from the interstitial perspective. Social differences are not simply given to experience through an already authenticated cultural tradition; they are the signs of the emergence of community envisaged as a project — at once a vision and a construction — that takes you "beyond" yourself in order to return, in a spirit of revision and reconstruction, to the political *conditions* of the present:

> Even then, it's still a struggle for power between various groups within ethnic groups about what's being said and who's saying what, who's representing who? What is a community anyway? What is a black community? What is a Latino community? I have trouble with thinking of all these things as monolithic fixed categories.[8]

If Renée Green's questions open up an interrogatory, interstitial space between the act of representation — who? what? where? — and the presence of community itself, then consider her own creative intervention within this in-between moment. Green's "architectural" site-specific work, *Sites of Genealogy* (Out of Site, The Institute of Contemporary Art, Long Island City, New York), displays and displaces the binary logic through which identities of difference are often constructed — Black/White, Self/Other. Green makes a metaphor of the museum building itself, rather than simply using the gallery space:

> I used architecture literally as a reference, using the attic, the boiler room, and the stairwell to make associations between certain binary divisions such as higher and lower and heaven and hell. The stairwell became a liminal space, a pathway between the upper and lower areas, each of which was annotated with plaques referring to blackness and whiteness.[9]

The stairwell as liminal space, in-between the designations of identity, becomes the process of symbolic interaction, the connective tissue that constructs the difference between upper and lower, black and white. The hither and thither of the stairwell, the temporal movement and passage that it allows, prevents identities at either end of it from settling into primordial polarities. This interstitial passage between fixed identifications opens up the possibility of a cultural hybridity that entertains difference without an assumed or imposed hierarchy:

> I always went back and forth between racial designations and designations from physics or other symbolic designations. All these things blur in some way. . . . To develop a genealogy of the way

[6]Renée Green interviewed by Elizabeth Brown, from catalogue published by Allen Memorial Art Museum, Oberlin College, Ohio. [Au.]

[7]Interview conducted by Miwon Kwon for the exhibition "Emerging New York Artists," Sala Mendonza, Caracas, Venezuela (xeroxed manuscript copy). [Au.]

[8]Ibid., p. 6. [Au.]

[9]Renée Green in conversation with Donna Harkavy, Curator of Contemporary Art at the Worcester Museum. [Au.]

colours and noncolours function is interesting to me.[10]

"Beyond" signifies spatial distance, marks progress, promises the future; but our intimations of exceeding the barrier or boundary — the very act of going *beyond* — are unknowable, unrepresentable, without a return to the "present" which, in the process of repetition, becomes disjunct and displaced. The imaginary of spatial distance — to live somehow beyond the border of our times — throws into relief the temporal, social differences that interrupt our collusive sense of cultural contemporaneity. The present can no longer be simply envisaged as a break or a bonding with the past and the future, no longer a synchronic presence: our proximate self-presence, our public image, comes to be revealed for its discontinuities, its inequalities, its minorities. Unlike the dead hand of history that tells the beads of sequential time like a rosary, seeking to establish serial, causal connections, we are now confronted with what Walter Benjamin describes as the blasting of a monadic moment from the homogenous course of history, "establishing a conception of the present at the 'time of the now.'"[11]

If the jargon of our times — postmodernity, postcoloniality, postfeminism — has any meaning at all, it does not lie in the popular use of the "post" to indicate sequentiality — *after*-feminism; or polarity — *anti*-modernism. These terms that insistently gesture to the beyond, only embody its restless and revisionary energy if they transform the present into an expanded and ex-centric site of experience and empowerment. For instance, if the interest in postmodernism is limited to a celebration of the fragmentation of the "grand narratives" of postenlightenment rationalism then, for all its intellectual excitement, it remains a profoundly parochial enterprise.

The wider significance of the postmodern condition lies in the awareness that the epistemological "limits" of those ethnocentric ideas[12] are also the enunciative boundaries of a range of other dissonant, even dissident histories and voices — women, the colonized, minority groups, the bearers of policed sexualities. For the demography of the new internationalism is the history of postcolonial migration, the narratives of cultural and political diaspora, the major social displacements of peasant and aboriginal communities, the poetics of exile, the grim prose of political and economic refugees. It is in this sense that the boundary becomes the place from which *something begins its presencing* in a movement not dissimilar to the ambulant, ambivalent articulation of the beyond that I have drawn out: "Always and ever differently the bridge escorts the lingering and hastening ways of men to and fro, so that they may get to other banks. . . . The bridge *gathers* as a passage that crosses."[13]

The very concepts of homogeneous national cultures, the consensual or contiguous transmission of historical traditions, or "organic" ethnic communities — *as the grounds of cultural comparativism* — are in a profound process of redefinition. The hideous extremity of Serbian nationalism proves that the very idea of a pure, "ethnically cleansed" national identity can only be achieved through the death, literal and figurative, of the complex interweavings of history, and the culturally contingent borderlines of modern nationhood. This side of the psychosis of patriotic fervour, I like to think, there is overwhelming evidence of a more transnational and translational sense of the hybridity of imagined communities. Contemporary Sri Lankan theatre represents the deadly conflict between the Tamils and the Sinhalese through allegorical references to State brutality in South Africa and Latin America; the Anglo-Celtic canon of Australian literature and cinema is being rewritten from the perspective of Aboriginal political and cultural imperatives; the South African novels of Richard Rive, Bessie Head, Nadine Gordimer, John Coetzee, are documents of a society divided by the effects of apartheid that enjoin the international in-

[10]Ibid. [Au.]

[11]W. Benjamin, "Theses on the philosophy of history," in *Illuminations* (London: Jonathan Cape, 1970), p. 265. [Au.]

[12]The reference here is to "the 'grand narratives' of postenlightenment rationalism" in the previous paragraph. Bhabha is referring to "grand narratives" such as Marx's history of the past development and future fall of capitalism. [Ed.]

[13]M. Heidegger, "Building, dwelling, thinking," in *Poetry, Language, Thought* (New York: Harper & Row, 1971), pp. 152–53. [Au.]

tellectual community to meditate on the unequal, asymmetrical worlds that exist elsewhere; Salman Rushdie writes the fabulist historiography of post-Independence India and Pakistan in *Midnight's Children* and *Shame,* only to remind us in *The Satanic Verses* that the truest eye may now belong to the migrant's double vision; Toni Morrison's *Beloved* revives the past of slavery and its murderous rituals of possession and self-possession, in order to project a contemporary fable of a woman's history that is at the same time the narrative of an affective, historic memory of an emergent public sphere of men and women alike.

What is striking about the "new" internationalism is that the move from the specific to the general, from the material to the metaphoric, is not a smooth passage of transition and transcendence. The "middle passage"[14] of contemporary culture, as with slavery itself, is a process of displacement and disjunction that does not totalize experience. Increasingly, "national" cultures are being produced from the perspective of disenfranchised minorities. The most significant effect of this process is not the proliferation of "alternative histories of the excluded" producing, as some would have it, a pluralist anarchy. What my examples show is the changed basis for making international connections. The currency of critical comparativism, or aesthetic judgement, is no longer the sovereignty of the national culture conceived as Benedict Anderson proposes as an "imagined community" rooted in a "homogeneous empty time" of modernity and progress.[15] The great connective narratives of capitalism and class drive the engines of social reproduction, but do not, in themselves, provide a foundational frame for those modes of cultural identification and political affect that form around issues of sexuality, race, feminism, the lifeworld of refugees or migrants, or the deathly social destiny of AIDS.

The testimony of my examples represents a radical revision in the concept of human community itself. What this geopolitical space may be, as a local or transnational reality, is being both interrogated and reinitiated. Feminism, in the 1990s, finds its solidarity as much in liberatory narratives as in the painful ethical position of a slavewoman, Morrison's Sethe, in *Beloved,* who is pushed to infanticide. The body politic can no longer contemplate the nation's health as simply a civic virtue; it must rethink the question of rights for the entire national, and international, community, from the AIDS perspective. The Western metropole must confront its postcolonial history, told by its influx of postwar migrants and refugees, as an indigenous or native narrative *internal to its national identity;* and the reason for this is made clear in the stammering, drunken words of Mr "Whisky" Sisodia from *The Satanic Verses:* "The trouble with the Engenglish is that their hiss hiss history happened overseas, so they dodo don't know what it means."[16]

Postcoloniality, for its part, is a salutary reminder of the persistent "neo-colonial" relations within the "new" world order and the multinational division of labour. Such a perspective enables the authentication of histories of exploitation and the evolution of strategies of resistance. Beyond this, however, postcolonial critique bears witness to those countries and communities — in the North and the South, urban and rural — constituted, if I may coin a phrase, "otherwise than modernity." Such cultures of a postcolonial *contra-modernity* may be contingent to modernity, discontinuous or in contention with it, resistant to its oppressive, assimilationist technologies; but they also deploy the cultural hybridity of their borderline conditions to "translate," and therefore reinscribe, the social imaginary of both metropolis and modernity. Listen to Guillermo Gomez-Peña, the performance artist who lives, amongst other times and places, on the Mexico/US border:

[14]The "middle passage" refers to the transportation of black slaves from Africa to the sugar islands of the Caribbean in the eighteenth and nineteenth centuries; it was a "middle" in that it was preceded by the shipping of rum from New England to Africa, where the rum was traded for slaves, and it was followed by the shipping of raw sugar to New England, where it was made into rum. [Ed.]

[15]Bhabha alludes to *Imagined Communities: Reflections on the Origin and Spread of Nationalism* (1983) by Benedict O'Gorman Anderson (b. 1936). [Ed.]

[16]S. Rushdie, *The Satanic Verses* (London: Viking, 1988), p. 343. [Au.]

hello America
this is the voice of *Gran Vato Charollero*
broadcasting from the hot deserts of Nogales, Arizona
zona de libre cogercio
2000 megaherz en todas direciones
you are celebrating Labor Day in Seattle
while the Klan demonstrates
against Mexicans in Georgia
ironia, 100% ironia[17]

Being in the "beyond," then, is to inhabit an intervening space, as any dictionary will tell you. But to dwell "in the beyond" is also, as I have shown, to be part of a revisionary time, a return to the present to redescribe our cultural contemporaneity; to reinscribe our human, historic commonality; *to touch the future on its hither side*. In that sense, then, the intervening space "beyond," becomes a space of intervention in the here and now. To engage with such invention, and intervention, as Green and Gomez-Peña enact in their distinctive work, requires a sense of the new that resonates with the hybrid chicano aesthetic of "*rasquachismo*" as Tomas Ybarra-Frausto describes it:

> the utilization of available resources for syncretism, juxtaposition, and integration. *Rasquachismo* is a sensibility attuned to mixtures and confluence . . . a delight in texture and sensuous surfaces . . . self-conscious manipulation of materials or iconography . . . the combination of found material and satiric wit . . . the manipulation of *rasquache* artifacts, code and sensibilities from both sides of the border.[18]

The borderline work of culture demands an encounter with "newness" that is not part of the continuum of past and present. It creates a sense of the new as an insurgent act of cultural translation. Such art does not merely recall the past as social cause or aesthetic precedent; it renews the past, refiguring it as a contingent "in-between" space, that innovates and interrupts the performance of the present. The "past–present" becomes part of the necessity, not the nostalgia, of living.

Pepon Osorio's *objets trouvés*[19] of the Nuyorican (New York/Puerto Rican) community — the statistics of infant mortality, or the silent (and silenced) spread of AIDS in the Hispanic community — are elaborated into baroque allegories of social alienation. But it is not the high drama of birth and death that captures Osorio's spectacular imagination. He is the great celebrant of the migrant act of survival, using his mixed-media works to make a hybrid cultural space that forms contingently, disjunctively, in the inscription of signs of cultural memory and sites of political agency. *La Cama (The Bed)* turns the highly decorated four-poster into the primal scene of lost-and-found childhood memories, the memorial to a dead nanny Juana, the *mise-en-scène* of the eroticism of the "emigrant" everyday. Survival, for Osorio, is working in the interstices of a range of practices: the "space" of installation, the spectacle of the social statistic, the transitive time of the body in performance.

Finally, it is the photographic art of Alan Sekula that takes the borderline condition of cultural translation to its global limit in *Fish Story*, his photographic project on harbours: "the harbour is the site in which material goods appear in bulk, in the very flux of exchange."[20] The harbour and the stockmarket become the *paysage moralisé*[21] of a containerized, computerized world of global trade. Yet, the non-synchronous time–space of transnational "exchange," and exploitation, is embodied in a navigational allegory:

> Things are more confused now. A scratchy recording of the Norwegian national anthem blares out from a loudspeaker at the Sailor's Home on the bluff above the channel. The container ship being greeted flies a Bahamian flag of convenience. It was built by Koreans working long hours in the giant shipyards of Ulsan. The underpaid and the understaffed crew could be Salvadorean or Filipino. Only the Captain hears a familiar melody.[22]

[17]G. Gomez-Peña, *American Theatre*, vol. 8, no. 7, October 1991. [Au.]

[18]T. Ybarra-Frausto, "Chicano movement/chicano art" in I. Karp and S. D. Lavine (eds.) *Exhibiting Cultures: The Poetics and Politics of Museum Display* (Washington and London: Smithsonian Institution Press, 1991), pp. 133–34. [Au.]

[19]"Found objects," such as those used by Dadaist artists in creating sculptures out of toilets, telescopes, and such. [Ed.]

[20]A. Sekula, *Fish Story*, manuscript, p. 2. [Au.]

[21]Moralized landscape. [Ed.]

[22]Ibid., p. 3. [Au.]

Norway's nationalist nostalgia cannot drown out the babel on the bluff. Transnational capitalism and the impoverishment of the Third World certainly create the chains of circumstance that incarcerate the Salvadorean or the Filipino/a. In their cultural passage, hither and thither, as migrant workers, part of the massive economic and political diaspora of the modern world, they embody the Benjaminian "present": that moment blasted out of the continuum of history. Such conditions of cultural displacement and social discrimination — where political survivors become the best historical witnesses — are the grounds on which Frantz Fanon, the Martinican psychoanalyst and participant in the Algerian revolution, locates an agency of empowerment:

> As soon as I *desire* I am asking to be considered. I am not merely here-and-now, sealed into thingness. I am for somewhere else and for something else. I demand that notice be taken of my *negating activity* [my emphasis] insofar as I pursue something other than life; insofar as I do battle for the creation of a human world — that is a world of reciprocal recognitions.

I should constantly remind myself that the real *leap* consists in introducing invention into existence.

> In the world in which I travel, I am endlessly creating myself. And it is by going beyond the historical, instrumental hypothesis that I will initiate my cycle of freedom.[23]

Once more it is the desire for recognition, "for somewhere else and for something else" that takes the experience of history *beyond* the instrumental hypothesis. Once again, it is the space of intervention emerging in the cultural interstices that introduces creative invention into existence. And one last time, there is a return to the performance of identity as iteration, the re-creation of the self in the world of travel, the resettlement of the borderline community of migration. Fanon's desire for the recognition of cultural presence as "negating activity" resonates with my breaking of the time-barrier of a culturally collusive "present."

[23]F. Fanon, *Black Skin, White Masks,* Introduction by H. K. Bhabha (London: Pluto, 1986), pp. 218, 229, 231. [Au.]

UNHOMELY LIVES: THE LITERATURE OF RECOGNITION

Fanon recognizes the crucial importance, for subordinated peoples, of asserting their indigenous cultural traditions and retrieving their repressed histories. But he is far too aware of the dangers of the fixity and fetishism of identities within the calcification of colonial cultures to recommend that "roots" be struck in the celebratory romance of the past or by homogenizing the history of the present. The negating activity is, indeed, the intervention of the "beyond" that establishes a boundary: a bridge, where "presencing" begins because it captures something of the estranging sense of the relocation of the home and the world[24] — the unhomeliness — that is the condition of extra-territorial and cross-cultural initiations. To be unhomed is not to be homeless, nor can the "unhomely" be easily accommodated in that familiar division of social life into private and public spheres. The unhomely moment creeps up on you stealthily as your own shadow and suddenly you find yourself with Henry James's Isabel Archer, in *The Portrait of a Lady,* taking the measure of your dwelling in a state of "incredulous terror."[25] And it is at this point that the world first shrinks for Isabel and then expands enormously. As she struggles to survive the fathomless waters, the rushing torrents, James introduces us to the "unhomeliness" inherent in that rite of extra-territorial and cross-cultural initiation. The recesses of the domestic space become sites for history's most intricate invasions. In that displacement, the borders between home and world become confused; and, uncannily, the private and the public become part of each other, forcing upon us a vision that is as divided as it is disorienting.

Although the "unhomely"[26] is a paradigmatic colonial and post-colonial condition, it has a resonance that can be heard distinctly, if erratically,

[24]Bhabha is alluding to the 1919 novel *The Home and the World,* by Rabindranath Tagore, filmed by Satyajit Ray. [Ed.]

[25]H. James, *The Portrait of a Lady* (New York: Norton, 1975), p. 360. [Au.]

[26]As becomes clearer in the next paragraph, Bhabha is playing on the connection between "unhomely" and the Ger-

in fictions that negotiate the powers of cultural difference in a range of transhistorical sites. You have already heard the shrill alarm of the unhomely in that moment when Isabel Archer realizes that her world has been reduced to one high, mean window, as her house of fiction becomes "the house of darkness, the house of dumbness, the house of suffocation."[27] If you hear it thus at the Palazzo Roccanera in the late 1870s, then a little earlier in 1873 on the outskirts of Cincinnati, in mumbling houses like 124 Bluestone Road, you hear the undecipherable language of the black and angry dead; the voice of Toni Morrison's *Beloved,* "the thoughts of the women of 124, unspeakable thoughts, unspoken."[28] More than a quarter of a century later in 1905, Bengal is ablaze with the Swadeshi or Home Rule movement[29] when "home-made Bimala, the product of the confined space," as Tagore describes her in *The Home and the World,* is aroused by "a running undertone of melody, low down in the bass . . . the true manly note, the note of power." Bimala is possessed and drawn forever from the zenana, the secluded women's quarters, as she crosses that fated verandah into the world of public affairs — "over to another shore and the ferry had ceased to ply."[30] Much closer to our own times in contemporary South Africa, Nadine Gordimer's heroine Aila in *My Son's Story* emanates a stilling atmosphere as she makes her diminished domesticity into the perfect cover for gun-running: suddenly the home turns into another world, and the narrator notices that "It was as if everyone found that he had unnoticingly entered a strange house, *and it was hers. . . .*"[31]

The historical specificities and cultural diversities that inform each of these texts would make a global argument purely gestural; in any case, I shall only be dealing with Morrison and Gordimer in any detail. But the "unhomely" does provide a "non-continuist" problematic that dramatizes — in the figure of woman — the ambivalent structure of the civil State as it draws its rather paradoxical boundary between the private and the public spheres. If, for Freud, the *unheimlich* is "the name for everything that ought to have remained . . . secret and hidden but has come to light," then Hannah Arendt's description of the public and private realms is a profoundly unhomely one: "it is the distinction between things that should be hidden and things that should be shown," she writes, which through their inversion in the modern age "discovers how rich and manifold the hidden can be under conditions of intimacy."[32]

This logic of reversal, that turns on a disavowal, informs the profound revelations and reinscriptions of the unhomely moment. For what was "hidden from sight" for Arendt, becomes in Carole Pateman's *The Disorder of Women* the "ascriptive domestic sphere" that is *forgotten* in the theoretical distinctions of the private and public spheres of civil society. Such a forgetting — or disavowal — creates an uncertainty at the heart of the generalizing subject of civil society, compromising the "individual" that is the support for its universalist aspiration. By making visible the forgetting of the "unhomely" moment in civil society, feminism specifies the patriarchal, gendered nature of civil society and disturbs the symmetry of private and public which is now shadowed, or uncannily doubled, by the difference of genders which does not neatly map on to the private and the public, but becomes disturbingly supplementary to them. This results in redrawing the domestic space as the space of the normalizing, pastoralizing, and individuating techniques of modern power and police: the personal-*is*-the political; the world-*in*-the home.

man cognate "*unheimlich,*" which is more usually rendered as "uncanny." [Ed.]

[27]Ibid., p. 361. [Au.]

[28]T. Morrison, *Beloved* (London: Chatto & Windus, 1987), pp. 198–99. [Au.]

[29]The Swadeshi movement was a boycott of British goods in support of national liberation; demonstrations included arson and assassinations. The movement was at first savagely suppressed by the Viceroy, Lord Minto, but by 1909 the British were offering seats on governing councils to Hindus and Muslims. [Ed.]

[30]R. Tagore, *The Home and the World* (Harmondsworth: Penguin, 1985), pp. 70–71. [Au.]

[31]N. Gordimer, *My Son's Story* (London: Bloomsbury, 1990), p. 249. [Au.]

[32]S. Freud, "The uncanny," Standard Edition XVII, p. 225; H. Arendt, *The Human Condition* (Chicago: Chicago University Press, 1958), p. 72. [Au.]

The unhomely moment relates the traumatic ambivalences of a personal, psychic history to the wider disjunctions of political existence. Beloved, the child murdered by her own mother, Sethe, is a daemonic, belated repetition of the violent history of black infant deaths, during slavery, in many parts of the South, less than a decade after the haunting of 124 Bluestone Road.[33] (Between 1882 and 1895 from one-third to a half of the annual black mortality rate was accounted for by children under five years of age.[34]) But the memory of Sethe's act of infanticide emerges through "the holes — the things the fugitives did not say; the questions they did not ask . . . the unnamed, the unmentioned."[35] As we reconstruct the narrative of child murder through Sethe, the slave mother, who is herself the victim of social death, the very historical basis of our ethical judgement undergoes a radical revision.

Such forms of social and psychic existence can best be represented in that tenuous survival of literary language itself, which allows memory to speak:

> while knowing Speech can (be) at best, a shadow
> echoing the silent light, bear witness
> To the truth, it is not. . . .

W. H. Auden wrote those lines on the powers of *poesis* in *The Cave of Making,* aspiring to be, as he put it, "a minor Atlantic Goethe."[36] And it is to an intriguing suggestion in Goethe's final "Note on world literature" (1830) that I now turn to find a comparative method that would speak to the "unhomely" condition of the modern world.

Goethe suggests that the possibility of a world literature arises from the cultural confusion wrought by terrible wars and mutual conflicts. Nations

> could not return to their settled and independent life again without noticing that they had learned many foreign ideas and ways, which they had unconsciously adopted, and come to feel here and there previously unrecognized spiritual and intellectual needs.[37]

Goethe's immediate reference is, of course, to the Napoleonic wars and his concept of "the feeling of neighbourly relations" is profoundly Eurocentric, extending as far as England and France. However, as an Orientalist who read Shakuntala[38] at seventeen years of age, and who writes in his autobiography of the "unformed and overformed"[39] monkey god Hanuman,[40] Goethe's speculations are open to another line of thought.

What of the more complex cultural situation where "previously unrecognized spiritual and intellectual needs" emerge from the imposition of "foreign" ideas, cultural representations, and structures of power? Goethe suggests that the "inner nature of the whole nation as well as the individual man works all unconsciously."[41] When this is placed alongside his idea that the cultural life of the nation is "unconsciously" lived, then there may be a sense in which world literature could be an emergent, prefigurative category that is concerned with a form of cultural dissensus and alterity, where non-consensual terms of affiliation may be established on the grounds of historical trauma. The study of world literature might be the study of the way in which cultures recognize themselves through their projections of "otherness." Where, once, the transmission of national traditions was the major theme of a world literature, perhaps we can now suggest that transnational histories of migrants,

[33]In the somewhat inconsistent chronology of Morrison's novel, Sethe kills her infant daughter, Beloved, in 1855 (the same year of the real-life event that provided the germ of the story, Margaret Garner's murder of her infant daughter), ten years before slavery was ended by the Civil War. The "haunting of 124 Bluestone Road" by what may be the ghost of Beloved takes place about eighteen years later, in 1873–74. [Ed.]

[34]Bhabha is suggesting quite generally that children were the subjects and the focus — highly disproportionately — of black mortality. [Ed.]

[35]Morrison, *Beloved,* p. 170. [Au.]

[36]W. H. Auden, "The cave of making," in *About the House* (London: Faber, 1959), p. 20. [Au.]

[37]*Goethe's Literary Essays,* J. E. Spingarn (ed.) (New York: Harcourt, Brace, 1921), pp. 98–99. [Au.]

[38]Celebrated Sanskrit drama written around the third century A.D. by Kalidasa. [Ed.]

[39]*The Autobiographigraphy of Goethe,* J. Oxenford (ed.) (London: Henry G. Bohn, 1948), p. 467. [Au.]

[40]The monkey-god in Valmiki's Sanskrit epic, the *Ramayana.* [Ed.]

[41]Goethe, "Note on world literature," p. 96. [Au.]

the colonized, or political refugees — these border and frontier conditions — may be the terrains of world literature. The centre of such a study would neither be the "sovereignty" of national cultures, nor the universalism of human culture, but a focus on those "freak social and cultural displacements" that Morrison and Gordimer represent in their "unhomely" fictions. Which leads us to ask: can the perplexity of the unhomely, intrapersonal world lead to an international theme?

If we are seeking a "worlding" of literature, then perhaps it lies in a critical act that attempts to grasp the sleight of hand with which literature conjures with historical specificity, using the medium of psychic uncertainty, aesthetic distancing, or the obscure signs of the spirity-world, the sublime and the subliminal. As literary creatures and political animals we ought to concern ourselves with the understanding of human action and the social world as a moment when *something is beyond control, but it is not beyond accommodation.* This act of writing the world, of taking the measure of its dwelling, is magically caught in Morrison's description of her house of fiction — art as "the fully realized presence of a haunting"[42] of history. Read as an image that describes the relation of art to social reality, my translation of Morrison's phrase becomes a statement on the political responsibility of the critic. For the critic must attempt to fully realize, and take responsibility for, the unspoken, unrepresented pasts that haunt the historical present.

Our task remains, however, to show how historical agency is transformed through the signifying process; how the historical event is represented in a discourse that is *somehow beyond control.* This is in keeping with Hannah Arendt's suggestion that the author of social action may be the initiator of its unique meaning, but as agent he or she cannot control its outcome. It is not simply what the house of fiction contains or "controls" *as content.* What is just as important is the metaphoricity of the houses of racial memory that both Morrison and Gordimer construct — those subjects of the narrative that mutter or mumble like 124 Bluestone Road, or keep a still silence in a "grey" Cape Town suburb.

Each of the houses in Gordimer's *My Son's Story* is invested with a specific secret or a conspiracy, an unhomely stirring. The house in the ghetto is the house of the collusiveness of the coloureds in their antagonistic relations to the blacks; the lying house is the house of Sonny's adultery; then there is the silent house of Aila's revolutionary camouflage; there is also the nocturnal house of Will, the narrator, writing of the narrative that charts the phoenix rising in his home, while the words must turn to ashes in his mouth. But each "unhomely" house marks a deeper historical displacement. And that is the condition of being "coloured" in South Africa, or as Will describes it, "halfway between . . . being not defined — and it was this lack of definition in itself that was never to be questioned, but observed like a taboo, something which no one, while following, could ever admit to."[43]

This halfway house of racial and cultural origins bridges the "in-between" diasporic origins of the coloured South African and turns it into the symbol for the disjunctive, displaced everyday life of the liberation struggle: "like so many others of this kind, whose families are fragmented in the diaspora of exile, code names, underground activity, people for whom a real home and attachments are something for others who will come after."[44]

Private and public, past and present, the psyche and the social develop an interstitial intimacy. It is an intimacy that questions binary divisions through which such spheres of social experience are often spatially opposed. These spheres of life are linked through an "in-between" temporality that takes the measure of dwelling at home, while producing an image of the world of history. This is the moment of aesthetic distance that provides the narrative with a double edge, which like the coloured South African subject represents a hybridity, a difference "within," a subject that inhabits the rim of an "in-between" reality. And the inscription of this borderline existence inhabits a stillness of time and a strangeness of framing that creates the discursive "image" at the crossroads of

[42]T. Morrison, *Honey and Rue* programme notes, Carnegie Hall Concert, January 1991. [Au.]

[43]Gordimer, *My Son's Story,* pp. 20–21. [Au.]

[44]Ibid., p. 21. [Au.]

history and literature, bridging the home and the world.

Such a strange stillness is visible in the portrait of Aila. Her husband Sonny, now past his political prime, his affair with his white revolutionary lover in abeyance, makes his first prison visit to see his wife. The wardress stands back, the policeman fades, and Aila emerges as an unhomely presence, on the opposite side from her husband and son:

> but through the familiar beauty there was a vivid strangeness. . . . It was as if some chosen experience had seen in her, as a painter will in his subject, what she was, what was there to be discovered. In Lusaka, in secret, in prison — who knows where — she had sat for her hidden face. *They had to recognise her.*[45]

Through this painterly distance a vivid strangeness emerges; a partial or double "self" is framed in a climactic political moment that is also a contingent historical event — "some chosen experience . . . who knows where . . . or what there was to be discovered."[46] They had to recognize her, but *what* do they recognize in her?

Words will not speak and the silence freezes into the images of apartheid: identity cards, police frame-ups, prison mug-shots, the grainy press pictures of terrorists. Of course, Aila is not judged, nor is she judgemental. Her revenge is much wiser and more complete. In her silence she becomes the unspoken "totem" of the taboo of the coloured South African. She displays the unhomely world, "the halfway between . . . not defined" world of the coloured as the "distorted place and time in which they — all of them — Sonny, Aila, Hannah — lived."[47] The silence that doggedly follows Aila's dwelling now turns into an image of the "interstices," the in-between hybridity of the history of sexuality and race.

> The necessity for what I've done — She placed the outer edge of each hand, fingers extended and close together, as a frame on either sides of the sheets of testimony in front of her. And she placed herself before him, to be judged by him.[48]

Aila's hidden face, the outer edge of each hand, these small gestures through which she speaks describe another dimension of "dwelling" in the social world. Aila as coloured woman defines a boundary that is at once inside and outside, the insider's outsideness. The stillness that surrounds her, the gaps in her story, her hesitation and passion that speak between the self and its acts — these are moments where the private and public touch in contingency. They do not simply transform the content of political ideas; the very "place" from which the political is spoken — the public sphere itself, becomes an experience of liminality which questions, in Sonny's words, what it means to speak "from the centre of life."[49]

The central political preoccupation of the novel — till Aila's emergence — focuses on the "loss of absolutes," the meltdown of the cold war, the fear "that if we can't offer the old socialist paradise in exchange for the capitalist hell here, we'll have turned traitor to our brothers."[50] The lesson Aila teaches requires a movement away from a world conceived in binary terms, away from a notion of the people's aspirations sketched in simple black and white. It also requires a shift of attention from the political as a pedagogical, ideological practice to politics as the stressed necessity of everyday life — politics as a performativity. Aila leads us to the unhomely world where, Gordimer writes, the banalities are enacted — the fuss over births, marriages, family affairs with their survival rituals of food and clothing.[51] But is it precisely in these banalities that the unhomely stirs, as the violence of a racialized society falls most enduringly on the details of life: where you can sit, or not; how you can live, or not; what you can learn, or not; who you can love, or not. Between the banal act of freedom and its historic denial rises the silence: "Aila emanated a stilling atmosphere; the parting jabber stopped. It was as if everyone

[45]Ibid., p. 230. [Au.]
[46]Ibid. [Au.]
[47]Ibid., p. 241. [Au.]
[48]Ibid. [Au.]
[49]Ibid. [Au.]
[50]Ibid. p. 214. [Au.]
[51]Ibid. p. 243. [Au.]

found he had unnoticingly entered a strange house, and it was hers; she stood there."[52]

In Aila's stillness, its obscure necessity, we glimpse what Emmanuel Levinas has magically described as the twilight existence of the aesthetic image — art's image as "the very event of obscuring, a descent into night, an invasion of the shadow."[53] The "completion" of the aesthetic, the distancing of the world in the image, is precisely not a transcendental activity. The image — or the metaphoric, "fictional" activity of discourse — makes visible "an interruption of time by a movement going on on the hither side of time, in its interstices."[54] The complexity of this statement will become clearer when I remind you of the stillness of time through which Aila surreptitiously and subversively interrupts the ongoing presence of political activity, using her interstitial role, her domestic world to both "obscure" her political role and to articulate it the better. Or, as *Beloved,* the continual eruption of "undecipherable languages" of slave memory obscures the historical narrative of infanticide only to articulate the unspoken: that ghostly discourse that enters the world of 124 "from the outside" in order to reveal the transitional world of the aftermath of slavery in the 1870s, its private and public faces, its historical past and its narrative present.

The aesthetic image discloses an ethical time of narration because, Levinas writes "the real world appears in the image as it were between parentheses."[55] Like the outer edges of Aila's hands holding her enigmatic testimony, like 124 Bluestone Road which is a fully realized presence haunted by undecipherable languages, Levinas's parenthetical perspective is also an ethical view. It effects an "externality of the inward" as the very enunciative position of the historical and narrative subject, "introducing into the heart of subjectivity a radical and anarchical reference to the other which in fact constitutes the inwardness of the subject."[56] Is it not uncanny that Levinas's metaphors for this unique "obscurity" of the image should come from those Dickensian unhomely places — those dusty boarding schools, the pale light of London offices, the dark, dank second-hand clothes shops?

For Levinas the "art-magic" of the contemporary novel lies in its way of "seeing inwardness from the outside," and it is this ethical–aesthetic positioning that returns us, finally, to the community of the unhomely, to the famous opening lines of *Beloved:* "124 was spiteful. The women in the house knew it and so did the children."

It is Toni Morrison who takes this ethical and aesthetic project of "seeing inwardness from the outside" furthest or deepest — right into Beloved's naming of her desire for identity: "I want you to touch me on my inside part and call me my name."[57] There is an obvious reason why a ghost should want to be so realized. What is more obscure — and to the point — is how such an inward and intimate desire would provide an "inscape" of the memory of slavery. For Morrison, it is precisely the signification of the historical and discursive boundaries of slavery that are the issue.

Racial violence is invoked by historical dates — 1876, for instance — but Morrison is just a little hasty with the events "in-themselves," as she rushes past "the true meaning of the Fugitive Bill, the Settlement Fee, God's Ways, antislavery, manumission, skin voting."[58] What has to be

[52]Ibid. p. 249. [Au.]

[53]E. Levinas, "Reality and its shadow," in *Collected Philosophical Papers* (Dordrecht: Martinus Nijhoff, 1987), pp. 1–13. [Au.]

[54]Ibid. [Au.]

[55]Ibid., pp. 6–7. [Au.]

[56]Robert Bernasconi quoted in "Levinas's ethical discourse, between individuation and universality," in *Re-Reading Levinas,* R. Bernasconi and S. Critchley (eds.) (Bloomington: Indiana University Press, 1991), p. 90. [Au.]

[57]Morrison, *Beloved,* p. 116. [Au.]

[58]Ibid., p. 173. [Au.] The quotation from Morrison alludes to a number of historical events that shaped interracial attitudes, starting with the Fugitive Slave Laws which (beginning around 1850) made it criminal to assist slaves to escape to freedom, and ending with "skin voting," which refers to the tendency of Southern blacks to vote Republican (for Lincoln's party) and Southern whites to vote Democrat between the end of the Civil War and the Great Depression. The significance of 1876 was the contested Tilden-Hayes election, which resulted in the removal of Federal troops from the South, and consequently the legal return of white supremacy to that region for nearly a century. [Ed.]

endured is the knowledge of doubt that comes from Sethe's eighteen years of disapproval and a solitary life, her banishment in the unhomely world of 124 Bluestone Road, as the pariah of her postslavery community. What finally causes the thoughts of the women of 124 "unspeakable thoughts to be unspoken" is the understanding that the victims of violence are themselves "signified upon": they are the victims of projected fears, anxieties and dominations that do not originate within the oppressed and will not fix them in the circle of pain. The stirring of emancipation comes with the knowledge that the racially supremacist belief "that under every dark skin there was a jungle" was a belief that grew, spread, touched every perpetrator of the racist myth, turned them mad from their own untruths, and was then expelled from 124 Bluestone Road.

But before such an emancipation from the ideologies of the master, Morrison insists on the harrowing ethical repositioning of the slave mother, who must be the enunciatory site for seeing the inwardness of the slave world from the outside — when the "outside" is the ghostly return of the child she murdered; the double of herself, for "she is the laugh I am the laugher I see her face which is mine."[59] What could be the ethics of child murder? What historical knowledge returns to Sethe, through the aesthetic distance or "obscuring" of the event, in the phantom shape of her dead daughter Beloved?

In her fine account of forms of slave resistance in *Within the Plantation Household,* Elizabeth Fox-Genovese considers murder, self-mutilation and infanticide to be the core psychological dynamic of all resistance. It is her view that "these extreme forms captured the essence of the slave woman's self-definition."[60] Again we see how this most tragic and intimate act of violence is performed in a struggle to push back the boundaries of the slave world. Unlike acts of confrontation against the master or the overseer which were resolved within the household context, infanticide was recognized as an act against the system and at least acknowledged the slavewoman's legal standing in the public sphere. Infanticide was seen to be an act against the master's property — against his surplus profits — and perhaps that, Fox-Genovese concludes, "led some of the more desperate to feel that, by killing an infant they loved, they would be in some way reclaiming it as their own."[61]

Through the death and the return of Beloved, precisely such a reclamation takes place: the slave mother regaining through the presence of the child, the property of her own person. This knowledge comes as a kind of self-love that is also the love of the "other": Eros and Agape[62] together. It is an ethical love in the Levinasian sense in which the "inwardness" of the subject is inhabited by the "radical and anarchical reference to the other." This knowledge is visible in those intriguing chapters[63] which lay over each other, where Sethe, Beloved and Denver perform a fugue-like ceremony of claiming and naming through intersecting and interstitial subjectivities: "Beloved, she my daughter"; "Beloved is my sister"; "I am Beloved and she is mine." The women speak in tongues, from a space "in-between each other" which is a communal space. They explore an "interpersonal" reality: a social reality that appears within the poetic image as if it were in parentheses — aesthetically distanced, held back, and yet historically framed. It is difficult to convey the rhythm and the improvization of those chapters, but it is impossible not to see in them the healing of history, a community reclaimed in the making of a name. We can finally ask ourselves:

> Who is Beloved?

Now we understand: she is the daughter that returns to Sethe so that her mind will be homeless no more.

> Who is Beloved?

[59]Ibid., p. 213. [Au.]

[60]E. Fox-Genovese, *Within the Plantation Household* (Chapel Hill, NC: University of North Carolina Press, 1988), p. 329. [Au.]

[61]Ibid., p. 324. [Au.]

[62]Two Greek words for *love* — the first associated with sexual desire, the second with spirituality. [Ed.]

[63]Morrison, *Beloved,* Pt II, pp. 200–17. [Au.]

Now we may say: she is the sister that returns to Denver, and brings hope of her father's return, the fugitive who died in his escape.

> Who is Beloved?

Now we know: she is the daughter made of murderous love who returns to love and hate and free herself. Her words are broken, like the lynched people with broken necks; disembodied, like the dead children who lost their ribbons. But there is no mistaking what her live words say as they rise from the dead despite their lost syntax and their fragmented presence.

> My face is coming   I have to have it   I am looking for the join   I am loving my face so much   I want to join   I am loving my face so much   my dark face is close to me   I want to join.[64]

LOOKING FOR THE JOIN

To end, as I have done, with the nest of the phoenix, not its pyre is, in another way, to return to my beginning in the *beyond.* If Gordimer and Morrison describe the historical world, forcibly entering the house of art and fiction in order to invade, alarm, divide and dispossesses, they also demonstrate the contemporary compulsion to move beyond; to turn the present into the "post"; or, as I said earlier, to touch the future on its hither side. Aila's in-between identity and Beloved's double lives both affirm the borders of culture's insurgent and interstitial existence. In that sense, they take their stand with Renée Green's pathway between racial polarities; or Rushdie's migrant history of the English written in the margins of satanic verses; or Osorio's bed — *La Cama* — a place of dwelling, located between the unhomeliness of migrancy and the baroque belonging of the metropolitan, New York/Puerto-Rican artist.

When the public nature of the social event encounters the silence of the word it may lose its historical composure and closure. At this point we would do well to recall Walter Benjamin's insight on the disrupted dialectic of modernity: "Ambiguity is the figurative appearance of the dialectic, the law of the dialectic at a standstill."[65] For Benjamin that stillness is Utopia; for those who live, as I described it, "otherwise" than modernity but not outside it, the Utopian moment is not the necessary horizon of hope. I have ended this argument with the woman framed — Gordimer's Aila — and the woman renamed — Morrison's Beloved — because in both their houses great world events erupted — slavery and apartheid — and their happening was turned, through that peculiar obscurity of art, into a second coming.

Although Morrison insistently repeats at the close of *Beloved,* "This is not a story to pass on," she does this only in order to engrave the event in the deepest resources of our amnesia, of our unconsciousness. When historical visibility has faded, when the present tense of testimony loses its power to arrest, then the displacements of memory and the indirections of art offer us the image of our psychic survival. To live in the unhomely world, to find its ambivalencies and ambiguities enacted in the house of fiction, or its sundering and splitting performed in the work of art, is also to affirm a profound desire for social solidarity: "I am looking for the join . . . I want to join . . . I want to join."

[64]Ibid., p. 213. [Au.]

[65]W. Benjamin, *Charles Baudelaire: A Lyric Poet in the Era of High Capitalism* (London: NLB, 1973), p. 171. [Au.]

7

FEMINIST LITERARY CRITICISM

The madwoman in literature by women is not, as she might be in male literature, an antagonist or foil to the heroine. Rather she is usually in some sense the author's double, an image of her own anxiety and rage.
— SANDRA GILBERT AND SUSAN GUBAR

To write chapters decrying the sexual stereotyping of women in our literature while closing our eyes to the sexual harassment of our women students and colleagues . . . destroys both the spirit and meaning of what we are about.
— ANNETTE KOLODNY

Not only have Black women writers been "disenfranchised" . . . by white women scholars on the "female tradition," but they have also been frequently excised from . . . the Afro-American literary tradition by Black scholars, most of whom are males.
— DEBORAH E. MCDOWELL

What is feminist criticism and what is not? To begin, feminist criticism does not include all literary criticism written by women, since some commentators on literature, from Anna Laetitia Barbauld to Camille Paglia, do not seem to meet their own era's definition of feminism or ours. Nor does it include all criticism written by feminists. Julia Kristeva has written eloquently on feminist subjects in such classic essays as "Women's Time," but her "Psychoanalysis and the Polis" (see Ch. 4) explores subjects whose relation to feminism is decidedly tangential. The characteristic common to the six essays grouped together here (all by women, as it happens, though that need not have been the case) is their concern for how being a woman affects both reading and writing: How men write about women; how women read both men's and women's writing; how the sexes differ in their use of language and the roots of their creativity.

Very specifically, this chapter centers on a particular tradition of Anglo-American feminist literary criticism, a particular set of stages in the evolution of thinking about sex and writing. Histories of feminist criticism, such as those of Kenneth Ruthven and Toril Moi, or that implicit in the selection by Elaine Showalter reprinted here, usually present an evolutionary sequence. It begins with a critique of patriarchal culture. In the field of literary criticism, this critique strives to expose the explicit and implicit misogyny in male writing about women. This phase would also include, as a corrective, a presentation of the very different ways in which women read male writers — and each other. The second phase might be characterized by a concern about the place of female writers within a canon largely shaped by male publishers, reviewers, and academic critics. The third phase (to which Showalter has given the term "gynocritics," as a translation of the French *gynocritique*) consists of a search for the conditions of women's language and creativity, for modes of textuality based in gender.

This is the evolutionary history, or a part of it, of feminist literary criticism in England and America in the 1970s and 1980s, although it should be remembered that each "phase" previously described continues to inspire significant work. None of the successive stages of feminist criticism has been ousted from its evolutionary niche by its successors. Both the evolutionary history and the issues of concern to successive stages of feminist criticism look different when one turns to France, where patriarchy has taken a different form than in Anglophone cultures. In "Women's Time" (1979),[1] Julia Kristeva distinguishes between three "generations" of feminists. The first, which she identifies with women who came to feminism before the radicalizing moment of May 1968 (when students and workers united in a strike intended to bring on a new French revolution), is concerned to reform patriarchy and to achieve liberal political goals: "abortion, contraception, equal pay, professional recognition, etc." This process of reform, Kristeva states, is transforming the world but does represent a revolution in values, for women are only attempting to appropriate the things men had formerly kept for themselves. The second, post-1968 generation, that of Hélène Cixous (see Ch. 8), proposes a radical shift in values: the valorization of "feminine" over "masculine" characteristics, a revaluation Kristeva rejects as a mere inversion of the dialectic of patriarchy. The third generation, according to Kristeva, is in formation as she writes, wherein "the very dichotomy man/woman as an opposition between two rival entities" is coming to be understood as "belonging to metaphysics." In effect Kristeva heralds the deconstruction of the premises of both patriarchy and feminism in a move that prophecies the work of Judith Butler and other gender theorists we shall meet in Chapter 8, Gender Studies and Queer Theory.

Patriarchal misogyny, the canon, and women's writing are key issues for the critics represented in this chapter, but it is important to note that the feminist criticism of the 1970s and 1980s had important forbears whose representatives appear in Part One of this book. Christine de Pisan in the Middle Ages and Aphra Behn in the Restoration were concerned to counter misogyny and the claim that women could not be effective and creative writers. Germaine de Staël in eighteenth-century France had a strong sense of what literary tasks women writers could perform more effectively than men. Simone de Beauvoir explicated the ways in which Woman becomes the site of Alterity for men — always an Object, never allowed to attain the status of Subject on her own. And many of the concerns addressed in this chapter

[1]Julia Kristeva, "Le Temps des femmes" (1979), translated by Alice Jardine and Harry Blake as "Women's Time," *Signs* 7 (1981): 13–35.

were raised as long ago as 1929 in Virginia Woolf's *A Room of One's Own.* Woolf's ironic commentary, set in the British Museum and one of the new women's colleges at Oxford, on how women have been traditionally denigrated by male scholars and teachers, long predates the work of both de Beauvoir and images-of-women critics such as Kate Millett and Mary Ellmann. Woolf's analysis of the women novelists of the nineteenth century — how Austen succeeded in devising a "feminine" sentence that allowed her to say just what she needed to, while the adoption of a "masculine" prose by Charlotte Brontë and George Eliot hampered their expressiveness — anticipates more recent research on women's language and writing. And Woolf's emphatic endorsement of Coleridge's claim that a great mind is naturally androgynous takes a stand on an issue that moves us beyond the concerns of the current chapter into those of the next.

WOMEN READING MEN READING WOMEN

Woolf's groundbreaking exploration of the major issues precipitated no immediate outpouring of feminist studies. Feminist criticism is a cultural outgrowth of the women's movement in general, and the 1930s and 1940s, owing to the Depression, the rise of fascism, and World War II, were not favorable times for feminist politics. After the war, however, feminist criticism revived and focused on the ways in which male authors present women — distorted by their own masculine prejudices and needs. The precursor text here is Simone de Beauvoir's *The Second Sex* (1949), in which Beauvoir analyzes sexism in most of its cultural forms (see p. 635 for a detailed discussion). De Beauvoir recognizes that even the greatest poets and writers, and even those who were most favorably disposed toward women, like Stendhal, created Women either subtly or grossly as the Other they required.

Although *The Second Sex* was published in North America in 1953, Beauvoir did not become an iconic figure here until the 1970s, when the American feminist movement began to gather steam. By that time, two other important American works, Mary Ellmann's *Thinking about Women* (1968) and Kate Millett's *Sexual Politics* (1970), had launched the feminist critique of male writing. Ellmann's *Thinking about Women* is an ironic work, concerned less about the way male writers talk about women than about the way male reviewers talk about women *writers;* the result is a "phallic criticism" that emphasizes the writers' figurative "bust, waist, and hip measurements" rather than their literary qualities. Kate Millett's book proclaimed the general thesis that, if the century from 1830 to 1930 had been one of sexual revolution, the succeeding three decades had been years of counterrevolution. In the earlier period, women gained the right to education, the right to work, and the right to vote, and generally achieved the capacity for political existence independent of men; in the more recent period, ideologies from Freudian psychology to Marxism to fascism had conspired to keep women in their place. In literary terms, Millett's critique of the new patriarchy operates through readings of Henry Miller, Norman Mailer, and D. H. Lawrence. By the standards of today's feminist writers, Millett's readings of texts can often seem simplistic and reductive; her passages for analysis, however, are aptly chosen for the polemical points she makes.

WOMEN READING

In the 1960s Millett and Ellmann were primarily concerned with how men read women; in the 1970s women began to read men — and each other — in new and theoretically interesting ways. Perhaps the most sophisticated of the reader-response feminist critics is Annette Kolodny, whose "Some Notes on Defining a 'Feminist Literary Criticism'" (1975), explored problems of methodology, aiming to prove to prejudiced males that feminist questions required serious thought. Kolodny's position was empiricist. While women's experience in the past and present differed from men's, it would be unsafe to claim that women's literature was distinctive until this could be demonstrated directly. Kolodny appears to be skeptical about contemporary claims, like those of Showalter, for a distinctively female kind of writing. The case she makes out is that women read differently from men; they read both life and literature from the perspective of a disparate personal experience.[2] Kolodny's "A Map for Rereading" (1980) discusses two issues: how the differing interpretive modes of men and women appear *within* two stories (Charlotte Perkins Gilman's "The Yellow Wallpaper" and Susan Keating Glaspell's "A Jury of Her Peers"); and how the discrepancy between male and female ways of apprehending the world was mirrored in the fate of these two stories in the male-dominated literary marketplace. Kolodny has been more concerned than most feminist critics with finding a rhetoric to counter male opposition to feminism. In "Dancing Through the Minefield" (reprinted in this chapter), Kolodny presents her feminist theses so "that current hostilities might be transformed into a true dialogue with our critics."

Kolodny's theoretical perspective on the differences between male and female ways of reading the codes of literature and life is echoed in the practical criticism of Judith Fetterley. Fetterley's book, *The Resisting Reader* (1978; see p. 990), begins by dismantling the assumption that texts — in her case, the primary texts of American fiction — are written for a universal audience. In fact, Fetterley states, "to read the canon of what is currently considered classic American literature is perforce to identify as male. . . . It insists on its universality at the same time that it defines that universality in specifically male terms" (p. xii). Traditionally, women have allowed themselves to be "immasculated" — inscribed within masculinity — in reading these texts, but they do so at the heavy price of internalizing self-hatred or at least self-doubt. Today, that price is too high: "The first act of the feminist critic must be to become a resisting rather than an assenting reader, to begin the process of exorcising the male mind that has been implanted in us" (p. xxii).

WOMEN TALKING

One of the more intriguing questions feminist criticism has broached is whether there is a special "women's language" that is different from that spoken by men. One would expect that inscription within patriarchy would have its effects on the way women speak, and this notion has been firmly endorsed by the pioneering stud-

[2] "Some Notes on Defining a 'Feminist Literary Criticism,'" *Critical Inquiry* 2 (1975): 75–92.

ies of linguist Robin Lakoff in *Language and Woman's Place* (1975). Lakoff suggests that more is involved in "talking like a lady" than mere vocabulary (e.g., the use of adjectives like "adorable" or "divine" and of color-words like "mauve"; the avoidance of scatological terms). Lakoff considers some syntactic constructions as typically female, like the "tag-question," which seeks agreement rather than aggressively taking a stand (e.g., "Mozart is a wonderful composer, isn't he?"). She suggests that women's traditional powerlessness is reflected in their greater use of indirect utterances but that such usages also reinforce current sex roles.

While Lakoff was developing the concept of "genderlect" — dialectical differences owing to gender — she tended to believe that sexist usages were unalterably fixed in language. She doubted that it was possible to dislodge the generic use of "man" to include women or of "he" as the neutral pronoun; but she was equally uncertain that these forms were seriously sexist and was inclined to consider them innocuous asymmetries. But are they innocuous? In an empirical study (1980), Jeanette Silveira found that respondents often did not understand that females were included in the generic "man" or "he," and that this was true of female as well as male subjects.[3] On the issue of change, Lakoff's conservatism seemed justified at the time by the long and futile history — going back to 1850 — of attempts at pronoun reform (the use of constructed neuter pronouns like "thon" or "hiser"). But since 1975 an effective series of guidelines for using sex-neutral language has been adopted by most publishers. Not only has the generic masculine been dropped but also phrases suggesting that certain jobs are gender-oriented, either by direct implication ("fireman" or "policeman") or by marking the less-common gender (e.g., "lady lawyer" or "male nurse"). Another sexist practice noted by Lakoff, that of referring to a female author by both first and last names (Jane Austen, Emily Dickinson) but to a male author by last name alone (Dickens, Lawrence), seems to be passing. Similarly "Ms." as the marriage-neutral form of address for women has become common if not universal. In effect, Lakoff's work has dated because society has become sensitive to sexist language and has made some significant attempts at reform.

Lakoff's work has dated in another sense, too: Some of its assertions have been questioned by later empirical studies. For example, her claim that women use tag questions more often than men do was supported by two experiments and refuted by three others. It now appears that social setting may be more important than gender in determining whether speakers produce tag questions; even powerful males tend to use many tag questions when they are running meetings. In general, theories of "genderlect" are less popular than they were in the 1970s, as researchers recognize that the variations in speech patterns *within* each gender are greater than the differences *between* genders.

Feminist linguists have focused instead on sociolinguistic issues, such as the frequency with which women are addressed in familiar terms ("dear" or "honey") by people they do not know, the relative frequency with which women and men inter-

[3]Jeanette Silveira, "Generic Masculine Words and Thinking," in *The Voices and Words of Women and Men*, ed. Cheris Kramarae (Oxford: Pergamon Press, 1980), pp. 165–78.

rupt each other and allow themselves to be interrupted,[4] the large number of pejorative terms for women as opposed to those for men,[5] and the unexamined assumptions that women will take their father's name at birth and their husband's name upon marriage. (Feminist linguists sensitive to this issue have changed or reinvented their names: e.g., Cheris Kramarae previously published as Chris Kramer, Julia Penelope Stanley is now Julia Penelope.)

More recently, the work of Deborah Tannen, another sociolinguist and a former collaborator of Robin Lakoff, has enjoyed extraordinary popular success. Tannen's *You Just Don't Understand: Women and Men in Conversation* (1990) explicates the mutual misprisions of men and women in terms of the differences between their customary purposes of dialogue: Males make "report talk" presenting facts evaluable with hierarchal logic, while females make "rapport talk" to create alliances and cement relationships. Whether these generalizations are any more defensible than Lakoff's, the success of *You Just Don't Understand,* which stayed on the *New York Times* bestseller list for over four years, was immense, partly because the book was interpreted as an important tool for corporate management techniques. Tannen has followed up *You Just Don't Understand* with further discussions of gender styles, including *That's Not What I Meant* (1992) and *Talking Nine to Five: Men and Women in the Workplace: Language Sex and Power* (1995). Her earlier scholarly articles on such psycholinguistic issues as interruption, origination of topics, and ethnic styles of conversation are collected in *Gender and Discourse* (1994).

WOMEN WRITING

Perhaps the least controversial aspect of recent feminist studies has been its attempt to locate and expand a female tradition of writing. Some authors (from Christine de Pisan to Kate Chopin) have been exhumed from near-oblivion and raised to the status of classics; others (like Anne Bradstreet and Mary Shelley), never really lost to sight, have been reinterpreted as central to the literary canon rather than as marginal, if well-known, figures. As in all efforts to expand the canon, more candidates will inevitably be proposed than will eventually find a place within. And if some writers now receiving general attention are those like Charlotte Perkins Gilman, who enrich and deepen feminists' sense of their own history, others, like Mary Shelley and Anna Laetitia Barbauld, espoused conservative attitudes toward "woman's place," which their present-day readers would be loath to adopt.

If the criterion is whether literature by women is taught in colleges and universities, the effort to expand the canon has been successful. But much of this success has occurred within special "women's studies" programs and in special courses within traditional programs, so that one may wonder whether women have truly been in-

[4]Candice West and Don H. Zimmerman, "Small Insults: A Study of Interruptions in Cross-sex Conversations between Unacquainted Persons," in *Language, Gender, and Society,* ed. Barrie Thorne et al. (Rowley, Mass.: Newbury House, 1983), pp. 103–18.

[5]Julia Penelope Stanley found 220 terms for a sexually promiscuous woman, only 22 for a man. See "Paradigmatic Woman: The Prostitute," in *Papers in Language Variation,* ed. David Shores (Birmingham: University of Alabama Press, 1977).

cluded within the traditional canon or whether a counter-canon of literature by women has been advanced to parallel the former canon defined primarily by men. And feminist critics like Nina Baym have questioned whether the canon has been created in a gender-neutral fashion or whether the books have been cooked. When literary theorists define the archetypal American novel in such a way as to privilege male experience, women writers are automatically relegated to the sidelines. This is the argument Baym advances in "Melodramas of Beset Manhood," reprinted in Chapter 9.

Lillian Robinson's classic essay on the female canon, "Treason Our Text" reprinted here, takes a rather different tack from Baym's. While Baym sees the canon of American literature as having been defined for everybody by a small number of prestigious Americanists, Robinson, whose work is primarily in English literature, is not clear that the dirty work was done by a few magisterial critics. For Robinson, the existence of the literary canon as a cultural monument in which women are seriously underrepresented creates a series of dilemmas. Should feminist scholars accept the canon as it is, but work to get this or that writer into the canon or promoted from minor to major status? Or should they reject the established canon, proclaiming (as the French Impressionists did in their Salon des Refusées) an alternative "counter-canon" of texts by women? This isn't an easy choice: The latter practice implicitly accepts the ghettoization of the "minority" text; the former implicitly concedes the validity of the master's rules. And what about the criteria for excellence themselves? Robinson argues that the dominant culture's supposedly neutral aesthetic values are framed in ways that make it difficult or impossible for women to enter the canon. She nevertheless recognizes that trying to define alternative aesthetic criteria may lead to similar pitfalls. One may create a new Great Tradition that includes some of the authors disenfranchised by the old one but systematically excludes members of other disenfranchised groups. Robinson's solution to these dilemmas is to work toward getting literature by women and minorities admitted into "the" canon by systematically contesting the cultural biases of the values on which the current canon rests. Not everyone is going to agree with this solution, but even those who do not can appreciate Robinson's cogent and candid overview of the interlocking dilemmas that make evaluative issues the agony they are.

One question that remains is how to understand the body of literature by women, and whether it forms a tradition on its own that can be understood apart from the body of literature by men. Most critics are likely to identify the three major texts of the second phase of feminist criticism, the analysis of women's writing, as Ellen Moers's *Literary Women* (1976), Elaine Showalter's *A Literature of Their Own* (1977), and Sandra Gilbert and Susan Gubar's *The Madwoman in the Attic* (1979). As Toril Moi's survey of feminist criticism puts it, "Taken together, these three books represent the coming-of-age of Anglo-American feminist criticism."[6]

Moers's *Literary Women* is subtitled *"The Great Writers,"* as if to establish its relationship to F. R. Leavis's *The Great Tradition* (1948; see p. 599), and there is indeed something Leavisite about its socially oriented survey of centuries of female creativity. Moers focuses on those aspects of women writers that derive from the

[6]Toril Moi, *Sexual/Textual Politics: Feminist Literary Theory* (New York: Methuen, 1985), p. 52.

central fact of their being women and ignores the rest as far as possible. Thus, Moers interprets Mary Shelley's *Frankenstein* as a myth of birth, in which the newborn is "at once monstrous agent of destruction and piteous victim of parental abandonment," a myth she sees as the product of Shelley's personal history — as an unwed mother at the time of its writing and as an infant whose birth occasioned her mother's death. Moers's method, if it can be called that, is impressionistic and biographical; in calling up her most admired heroine, George Sand, she asks the reader to picture "her typical country evening at Nohant. At the center sits Madame Sand with the needle work she loved in her hands, surrounded by a houseful of friends, children, lovers, guests, neighbors. Nohant was a messy household, full of laughter and games and theatricals and family arguments and good intellectual talk and tobacco smoke and music — just like yours and mine." Later critics were to avoid her chattiness and decry her insistence on biographical explanations, but feminist criticism was advanced by her wide-ranging discussion of the canon of women's literature and the central place of women's experience in forming that canon.

Elaine Showalter's book, *A Literature of Their Own,* has been more influential than Moers's. In addition to establishing a complex relationship to Woolf's *A Room of One's Own,* Showalter's title alludes ironically to John Stuart Mill, who in *The Subjection of Women* (1869) stated that "if women lived in a different country from men and had never read any of their writings, they would have a literature of their own." As things stood, Mill thought, they did not: "[A] much longer time is necessary . . . before [women's literature] can emancipate itself from the influence of accepted models, and guide itself by its own impulses." Showalter would not claim that the body of texts produced by women has the coherent character of a national literature that can be studied entirely apart from the texts produced by men, and she suspects that the hypothesis of a distinctive "female imagination" will encourage the stereotyped images of women that feminists have been so eager to dispel. Nevertheless, Showalter claims that women, as a subculture within English society, have produced something definable as a "female literary tradition" in the English novel from the generation of the Brontës to the present.

Showalter's analysis of nineteenth-century English fiction by women presents an evolutionary theory of the development of women's writing, which she argues ran parallel to that by blacks, Jews, and other groups outside the white Christian male power elite:

> In looking at literary subcultures . . . we can see that they all go through three major phases. First, there is a prolonged phase of *imitation* of the prevailing modes of the dominant tradition, and *internalization* of its standards of art and its views on social roles. Second, there is a phase of *protest* against these standards and values, and *advocacy* of minority rights and values, including a demand for autonomy. Finally, there is a phase of *self-discovery,* a turning inward freed from some of the dependency of opposition, a search for identity. An appropriate terminology for women writers is to call these stages *Feminine, Feminist,* and *Female.* These are obviously not rigid categories. . . . The phases overlap. . . . One might . . . find all three phases in the career of a single novelist. Nonetheless, it seems useful to point to periods of crisis when a shift of literary values occurred. In this book I identify the Feminine phase as the period from the appearance of the male pseudonym in the 1840s to the death of George Eliot in 1880; the Feminist phase as

1880 to 1920, or the winning of the vote; and the Female phase as 1920 to the present, but entering a new stage of self-awareness about 1960 (p. 13).

Obviously in Showalter's program there is some danger of overestimating the extent to which the female tradition and the male tradition are separable and (as Kenneth Ruthven has put it) of feminist critics "repeating exactly the same mistake for which they take male critics to task, namely an exclusive preoccupation with the writings of one sex."[7] This is a problem, however, of which Showalter is well aware. What seems less guarded is her bias against that version of feminism represented by Virginia Woolf — a foremother whom she attacks with what may seem an Electra's fury. Showalter considers Woolf's idealization of androgyny a mere flight from any genuine femininity and terms her vision of womanhood "as deadly as it is disembodied" (p. 289). Showalter's arguments against an androgynous ideal seem *ad feminam* (so to speak), and she does not understand the appeal of androgyny even to women (like Mary Shelley) who loved men and were devoted to their children.

Whatever the controversies surrounding Showalter's attitudes toward nineteenth- and twentieth-century fiction by women, her methodology is simple and straightforward. *The Madwoman in the Attic,* by Sandra Gilbert and Susan Gubar, brought to the female tradition some less traditional ways of reading, similar to those we associate with Yale (which eventually published their study). In particular, Gilbert and Gubar take off from the poetics of Harold Bloom's *Anxiety of Influence* (see Ch. 4). But where Bloom was concerned with the Oedipal relation between the "strong" poet and the forebear he has chosen as his ghostly "father," whose works he must misread to make room for his own, Gilbert and Gubar are concerned with the female half of the equation, with the woman writer who, defined always by men, is uncomfortable defining herself, who, lacking a pen/penis, is anxious about whether she can create at all. Whatever women's lesser disabilities today, women writers in the nineteenth century eventually "overcame their 'anxiety of authorship,' repudiated debilitating patriarchal prescriptions, and recovered or remembered the lost foremothers who could help them find their distinctive female power" (p. 59).

But within a partriarchy, women's writing cannot fully express itself; as a result, women writers (consciously or unconsciously) revised their own meanings to make them acceptable to their culture. "Women from Jane Austen and Mary Shelley to Emily Brontë and Emily Dickinson produced literary works . . . whose surface designs conceal or obscure deeper, less accessible (and less socially acceptable) levels of meaning" (p. 73). Women authors used a "cover story" — coded messages disguising their intent. They often created villainesses, in Gilbert and Gubar's readings of the novels, who speak powerfully for the values they were forced to repress. Under the surface, Bertha Mason Rochester, the titular Madwoman in the Attic, is the true heroine of *Jane Eyre.* Her frank impulsiveness and sensuality underlie what the reader values in Jane herself.

The Madwoman in the Attic gave an enormous new impetus to feminist criticism, yet there were skeptics, largely among Gilbert and Gubar's fellow feminists. In her re-

[7]K. K. Ruthven, *Feminist Literary Studies: An Introduction* (Cambridge: Cambridge University Press, 1984), p. 125.

view of *Madwoman* in *Signs,* Mary Jacobus attacked the book's "unstated complicity with the autobiographical 'phallacy,' whereby male critics hold that women's writing is somehow closer to their own experience than men's, that the female text *is* the author."[8] From her own poststructuralist perspective, Toril Moi has a rather different problem with *Madwoman,* in fact, a set of problems.[9] In the first place, Moi is unhappy with the implication of the "cover story," because the result is that everywhere in literature by women one can find nothing but overt or disguised versions of the author's "constant, never-changing *feminist rage*. This position . . . manages to transform *all* texts written by women into feminist texts." Moi also worries about the Gilbert and Gubar notion of patriarchy as a relentless and all-pervasive force, and wonders how, if this were so, women learned to write at all. Moi thinks that Gilbert and Gubar need to learn the Althusserian lesson: that patriarchal ideology is actually contradictory and fragmentary, rather than coherent and irresistible.

ON THE MARGINS

In *A Literature of Their Own,* Elaine Showalter's attempt to describe female writing as a variant of the experience of minority cultures searching for a place within the mainstream implicitly suggests that women's writing belongs to the white, male, Protestant, and British or American traditions with one exception: that of gender. While this was true of the British writers Showalter discussed, obviously some women may be multiply marginalized, not only as women but as African Americans, Chicanos, Asian Americans, Caribbean Islanders, or as lesbians on the margin of the heterosexual majority.

The marginalization of the African American female writer has become a significant issue as writers such as Phillis Wheatley and Zora Neale Hurston, Alice Walker and Toni Morrison, Gwendolyn Brooks and Nikki Giovanni are entering the canon, either in courses in American literature or through their success as popular best-sellers. In a number of ways, the issues of black feminist criticism overlap with those of white feminism. But African American women have long felt excluded from white feminist politics, and some of the central texts of women's studies ignore women who are not white. In her manifesto, "Toward a Black Feminist Criticism," Barbara Smith expresses outrage at this failure to recognize that "Black and female identity ever co-exist, specifically in a group of Black women writers." Smith attacks as "barely disguised cultural imperialism" Showalter's proposal to build a feminist scholarship on the model of "black American novelists." Smith also notes that most studies of women writers written by white women tend to ignore African Americans and other minorities — Moers's *Literary Women* "includes the names of four Black and one Puertoriqueña writer in her seventy pages of bibliographical notes" — and that other feminist writers show a "suspiciously selective" ignorance of the existence of black women writers. The feminists are not the only target here, however, for Smith sees both black and white male scholars of black writing as even more distortive of the creative achievements of black women. The essay by Deborah McDowell, "New Direc-

[8]*Signs* 6 (1981): 520.
[9]Moi, pp. 57–69.

tions for Black Feminist Criticism," while entirely sympathetic to the sense of marginality against which earlier black feminists reacted, seeks to escape the divisiveness of black vs. white, women vs. men, lesbian vs. heterosexual, that organizes Smith's manifesto. For McDowell black feminist criticism is less a cause than a task, for which one must go beyond politics and slogans. Whereas earlier black feminists had simply equated their race and sex with a special use of language, McDowell calls instead for concrete investigations into the content of black female poetics using contemporary methodologies. Like Kolodny, McDowell considers the walls of separation between male and female, black and white, at best a mixed blessing. She quotes the Nigerian playwright Wole Soyinka on the creative asphyxiation that accompanies too exclusive an attention to ideology, fearing that a separatist black feminist criticism could become a narrower and less vital enterprise than it has the potential to be.

Lesbian feminist literary criticism centers on a different sort of marginality. Just as black women writers and critics have felt excluded from white feminist studies, so lesbian writers and critics have been excluded by feminist attempts to seek a specifically heterosexual female identity. Bonnie Zimmerman points out the homophobia of both Moers's *Literary Women* and Patricia Meyer Spacks's *The Female Imagination:* "Spacks claims that Gertrude Stein, 'whose life lack[ed] real attachments' (a surprise to Alice B. Toklas) also 'denied whatever is special to women' (which lesbianism is not?)"[10] Lesbian feminist criticism confronts some of the same difficulties as heterosexual feminism, such as whether lesbian writing has a historical continuity apart from the writing of women and, indeed, of men, and whether it encounters unique difficulties of its own. For example, establishing the canon of lesbian writers involves first establishing writers' sexual orientation, which may be ambiguous or simply indecipherable owing to lack of evidence. Lesbian literature itself is difficult to define: Adrienne Rich defines lesbianism so inclusively as to embrace all female bonding and most female creativity, yet the lesbian canon might also be restricted to texts by exclusively homosexual women.

The expansion of the feminist dialogue to take into account various groups previously marginalized within the women's movement is only one version, perhaps, of the tendency of women's studies to expand its boundaries and to address areas traditionally dominated by men. It is impossible to do justice to the breadth of the movement here, but no study of feminist criticism can be complete without at least mentioning the connections between feminism and psychoanalysis (drawn by writers such as Jane Gallop and Mary Jacobus), between feminism and deconstruction (Peggy Kamuf and Nancy K. Miller), and between feminism and Marxism (Juliet Mitchell and Michèle Barrett).

Like Marxism, feminism was a social and political movement long before it was a mode of literary criticism, but, also like Marxism, the cultural wing of the ideology has naturally attracted many of the brightest and most energetic minds. This poses a problem to the movement as a whole. Just as Terry Eagleton scoffed at the idea that Jameson's analyses of Balzac were going to shake the foundations of capi-

[10]Bonnie Zimmerman, "What Has Never Been: An Overview of Lesbian Feminist Literary Criticism," in *The New Feminist Criticism,* ed. Elaine Showalter (New York: Pantheon, 1985), p. 203.

talism, so some feminists have wondered how analyzing Charlotte Brontë would alter the fact that women's pay is only seventy-one percent of men's.

It is obviously necessary for women to understand their past and the accomplishments that their forebears have achieved against heavy odds. But there is at least a slight edge of irony about the success of feminist criticism as an academic career choice. Lillian Robinson has been concerned that feminist critics be feminists first and critics second. "Some people are trying to make an honest woman out of the feminist critic, to claim that every 'worthwhile' department should stock one. I am not terribly interested in whether feminism becomes a respectable part of academic criticism. I am very much concerned that feminist critics become a useful part of the women's movement. . . . Marx's note about philosophers may apply to cultural critics as well: that up to now they have interpreted the world and the real point is to change it."[11]

THE FATE OF ANGLO-AMERICAN FEMINISM

Most scholars would agree that the essays reproduced in this chapter represent a particular phase of Anglo-American feminism, one whose theoretical constitution was essentially complete before 1985. This does not mean that the movement has died out or even lost its steam. On the contrary, all the projects promoted by that constitution are continuing with great vigor. For example, Showalter's argument, elaborated in *A Literature of Their Own,* that there was a long and healthy tradition of women's writing all through the nineteenth century, has been extended backwards by many other hands, and extraordinary efforts are under way to rediscover women's writing from all periods and to make it available to readers. The advent of computers and the internet has assisted enormously in this endeavor, because poetry and fiction by women that commercial publishers might deem too marginal in popular interest to warrant republication in book form can now be circulated as text files or hard copy to interested readers using electronic media. Thus the Women's Collective at Brown University, to take only one example, has made available to scholars literally hundreds of seventeenth- and eighteenth-century British novels by women that would otherwise have to be sought in rare book collections.[12] While scholars of my generation merely learned of the existence of popular women novelists at the time of Defoe, such as Eliza Haywood and Delariviere Manley, scholars today can read their works and come directly to terms with their concerns and those of their readership. Similar efforts are under way to unearth unsung and underappreciated American women writers, and, as Deborah McDowell predicted, women writers of color are reaping gains as well. Where a dozen years ago college reading

[11]Lillian S. Robinson, *Sex, Class, and Culture* (Bloomington: Indiana University Press, 1978), pp. 19–20.

[12]When I was a young scholar, for example, the major poetical romance by Lady Mary Wroth, *The Countess of Montgomery's Urania* (1621), was an obscure work mentioned in literary histories and available only in one of the rare copies held at the North Library of the British Museum. About a decade ago, with the rapid growth of Wroth's reputation as one of the major poets of the seventeenth century, it became possible to read the *Urania* using the computer text version made available by the Women's Collective. Today it is possible to consult a hardbound scholarly edition edited by the late Josephine Roberts.

lists were incomplete without Kate Chopin's *The Awakening* (1899), today the most assigned novels by women writers are probably Toni Morrison's *Beloved* (1987) and Zora Neale Hurston's *Their Eyes Were Watching God* (1937). And while Judith Fetterley recommended "resistant reading" to women threatened with "immasculation" by canonical male texts (see p. 990), a good deal of interesting research has gone on, in ways hinted at by Annette Kolodny in "Dancing through the Minefield," into how women actually read. Both Susan Sniader Lanser and Peter Rabinowitz have suggested that women may be decoding texts in ways that men would not.[13]

But while the projects of Anglo-American feminism continue, the 1980s saw the development of a rift in American feminist criticism between adherents of the Anglo-American tradition and a new generation of feminist theorists interested both in considering the implications of deconstructivist, psychoanalytic, Marxist, and new historical theory for their studies of gender difference and in opening up such originally androcentric movements to a consideration of gender.[14] There was a reluctance on the part of some of the most important Anglo-American feminists to problematize the concept of gender and to theorize about the relationship between femaleness and femininity. Showalter's edited collection, *The New Feminist Criticism,* published in 1985, was designed to showcase the best that had been known and thought in the feminist world, but it pointedly sidelined the theorizing about gender that had been going on in France for at least a decade. A single short and rather lukewarm essay by Ann Rosalind Jones, positioned at the end of the volume, briefly summarized some of the positions of Julia Kristeva, Hélène Cixous, Luce Irigaray, and Monique Wittig, without presenting the Lacanian psychoanalytic theory that would have allowed the reader to make sense of them.[15] Showalter's own treatment of the French feminists in her introduction was less than lukewarm, dourly arguing that "Anglo-American feminist poetics must insist on an analysis of specific cultural contexts rather than merely relying on an idealized and abstract view of the feminine" (p. 15).

It is not clear exactly what motivated the refusal to admit theorizing about gender into the big tent of Anglo-American feminism, but the reason may have been academic politics. The world of literary scholarship was deeply split in the early 1980s between traditional scholars who could make no sense of the theoretical revolution that had been building for at least a decade and theorists who were using the new Marxism, psychoanalysis, semiotics, and deconstruction to produce radically new work, who saw no sense at all in continuing the old practices. Showalter's stand in favor of "specific cultural contexts" may have been a way of stationing feminism as a mode of traditional criticism that should be supported by old-style

[13]See Susan Sniader Lanser, *Fictions of Authority: Women Writers and Narrative Voice* (Ithaca: Cornell University Press, 1992); and Peter Rabinowitz, "End Sinister: Neat Closure as Disruptive Force," in *Reading Narrative: Form, Ethics, Ideology* (Columbus: Ohio State University Press, 1989).

[14]See, for example, the work of Nancy Armstrong, p. 1316. For feminist reworkings of Lacanian psychoanalytic thought, see Jane Gallop, p. 1065.

[15]Ann Rosalind Jones, "Writing the Body: Toward an Understanding of *l'Écriture Féminine,*" in *The New Feminist Criticism: Women, Literature, Theory,* ed. Elaine Showalter (New York: Pantheon, 1985), pp. 361–77. Showalter's volume also sidelines reader-response feminist theory, presenting the central strand as what she calls "gynocritics," the analysis of female creativity.

scholars for its conservative methodology as well as by radical theorists taken with its political program. But the genie of gender theory was already out of the bottle, and the ideas and movements that are currently reshaping our understanding of the relationship between sex, gender, and literature are considered in Chapter 8.

Selected Bibliography

Abel, Elizabeth, ed. *Writing and Sexual Difference*. Chicago: University of Chicago Press, 1982.

Auerbach, Nina. *Woman and the Demon: The Life of a Victorian Myth*. Cambridge: Harvard University Press, 1982.

Barrett, Michèle. *Women's Oppression Today: Problems in Marxist Feminist Analysis*. New York: Schocken, 1980.

Baym, Nina. *Woman's Fiction: A Guide to Novels by and about Women in America*. Ithaca: Cornell University Press, 1978.

———. *Feminism and American Literary History*. New Brunswick: Rutgers University Press, 1992.

Beauvoir, Simone de. *Le deuxième sexe*. Paris: Gallimard, 1949. Trans. H. M. Parshley as *The Second Sex*. New York: Knopf, 1972.

Belsey, Catherine. *Critical Practice*. London: Methuen, 1980.

Blau Duplessis, Rachel. *Writing Beyond the Ending: Narrative Strategies of Twentieth-Century Women Writers*. Bloomington: Indiana University Press, 1985.

Brownstein, Rachel. *Becoming a Heroine: Reading about Women in Novels*. New York: Viking, 1982.

Cameron, Deborah. *Feminism in Linguistic Theory*. London: Macmillan, 1992.

Chodorow, Nancy. *The Reproduction of Mothering: Psychoanalysis and the Sociology of Gender*. Berkeley: University of California Press, 1978.

———. *Feminism and Psychoanalytic Theory*. New Haven: Yale University Press, 1989.

Christian, Barbara. *Black Women Novelists: The Development of a Tradition*. Westport, CT: Greenwood Press, 1980.

Delany, Sheila. *Writing Women: Women Writers and Women in Literature, Medieval to Modern*. New York: Schocken, 1984.

Donovan, Josephine, ed. *Feminist Literary Criticism: Explorations in Theory*. Lexington: University Press of Kentucky, 1975.

Douglas, Ann. *The Feminization of American Culture*. New York: Knopf, 1978.

Eisenstein, Hester. *Contemporary Feminist Thought*. Boston: G. K. Hall, 1983.

Ellmann, Mary. *Thinking about Women*. New York: Harcourt Brace Jovanovich, 1968.

Faderman, Lillian. *Surpassing the Love of Men: Romantic Friendship and Love Between Women from the Renaissance to the Present*. New York: William Morrow, 1981.

Felman, Shoshana. "Rereading Femininity." *Yale French Studies* 62 (1981): 19–44.

Fetterley, Judith. *The Resisting Reader: A Feminist Approach to American Fiction*. Bloomington: Indiana University Press, 1978.

Firestone, Shulamith. *The Dialectic of Sex: The Case for Feminist Revolution*. London: Women's Press, 1979.

Flynn, Elizabeth A., and Patrocinio P. Schweickart. *Gender and Reading: Essays on Readers, Texts and Contexts*. Baltimore: Johns Hopkins University Press, 1986.

Gallop, Jane. *The Daughter's Seduction: Feminism and Psychoanalysis*. Ithaca: Cornell University Press, 1982.

Gilbert, Sandra M., and Susan Gubar. *The Madwoman in the Attic: The Woman Writer and the Nineteenth-Century Literary Imagination*. New Haven: Yale University Press, 1979.

Griffin, Susan. *Woman and Nature: The Roaring Inside Her*. New York: Harper and Row, 1978.

Greer, Germaine. *The Female Eunuch*. London: McGibbon and Kee, 1970.

hooks, bell [Gloria Watkins]. *Ain't I a Woman? Black Women and Feminism*. Boston: South End Press, 1981.

Jacobus, Mary. *Women's Writing and Writing about Women*. New York: Barnes and Noble, 1979.

Jehlen, Myra. "Archimedes and the Paradox of Feminist Criticism." *Signs* 6 (1981): 575–601.

Kahn, Coppélia, and Gayle Greene, eds. *Making a Difference: Feminist Literary Criticism*. New York: Methuen, 1985.

Kamuf, Peggy. "Replacing Feminist Criticism." *Diacritics* 12 (1982): 42–47.

Kennard, Jean. "Ourself Behind Ourself: A Theory for Lesbian Readers." *Signs* 9 (1984): 647–62.

Kolodny, Annette. "Some Notes on Defining a 'Feminist Literary Criticism.'" *Critical Inquiry* 2 (1975): 75–92.

———. "Dancing Through the Minefield: Some Observations on the Theory, Practice and Politics of a Feminist Literary Criticism." *Feminist Studies* 6 (1980): 1–25.

———. *The Land Before Her: Fantasy and Experience of the American Frontiers, 1630–1860*. Chapel Hill: University of North Carolina Press, 1984.

Kramarae, Cheris. *Women and Men Speaking: Frameworks for Analysis*. Rowley, MA: Newbury House, 1981.

Kristeva, Julia. *About Chinese Women*. New York: Urizen Books, 1977.

———. "Women's Time." *Signs* 7 (1981): 13–35.

Lakoff, Robin. *Language and Women's Place*. New York: Harper and Row, 1975.

Leavy, Barbara. *In Search of the Swan Maiden: A Narrative on Folklore and Gender*. New York: New York University Press, 1994.

McConnell-Ginet, Sally, Ruth Borker, and Nelly Furman, eds. *Women and Language in Literature and Society*. New York: Praeger, 1980.

Marks, Elaine, and Isabelle de Courtrivon, eds. *New French Feminisms: An Anthology*. Amherst: University of Massachusetts Press, 1980.

Martin, Wendy. *An American Triptych: Anne Bradstreet, Emily Dickinson, and Adrienne Rich*. Chapel Hill: University of North Carolina Press, 1984.

Miller, Nancy K. "The Text's Heroine: A Feminist Critic and Her Fictions." *Diacritics* 12 (1982): 48–53.

Millett, Kate. *Sexual Politics*. New York: Avon Books, 1970.

Mitchell, Juliet. *Psychoanalysis and Feminism*. New York: Pantheon, 1974.

———. *Women's Estate*. New York: Vintage Books, 1971.

———. *The Longest Revolution*. New York: Pantheon, 1984.

Moers, Ellen. *Literary Women*. New York: Doubleday, 1976.

Moi, Toril. *Sexual/Textual Politics: Feminist Literary Theory*. New York: Methuen, 1985.

Newton, Judith Lowder. *Women, Power, and Subversion: Social Strategies in British Fiction, 1778–1860*. Athens: University of Georgia Press, 1981.

———, and Deborah Rosenfelt, eds. *Feminist Criticism and Social Change*. New York: Methuen, 1985.

Poovey, Mary. *The Proper Lady and the Woman Writer: Ideology as Style in the Works of Mary Wollstonecraft, Mary Shelley, and Jane Austen*. Chicago: University of Chicago Press, 1984.

Rich, Adrienne. *On Lies, Secrets and Silence*. New York: Norton, 1979.
Robinson, Lillian. *Sex, Class and Culture*. Bloomington: Indiana University Press, 1978.
Rogers, Katherine M. *The Troublesome Helpmate: A History of Misogyny in Literature*. Seattle: University of Washington Press, 1966.
Ruthven, Kenneth K. *Feminist Literary Studies: An Introduction*. Cambridge: Cambridge University Press, 1984.
Showalter, Elaine. *A Literature of Their Own: British Women Novelists from Brontë to Lessing*. Princeton: Princeton University Press, 1977.
———, ed. *The New Feminist Criticism: Essays on Women, Literature, Theory*. New York: Pantheon, 1985.
———. *Sexual Anarchy: Gender and Culture at the Fin de Siècle*. New York: Viking, 1990.
Spacks, Patricia Meyer. *The Female Imagination*. New York: Knopf, 1975.
Spender, Dale. *Man Made Language*. London: Routledge and Kegan Paul, 1980.
Spivak, Gayatri Chakravorty. *In Other Worlds: Essays in Cultural Politics*. New York: Methuen, 1987.
Thorne, Barrie, Cheris Kramarae, and Nancy Henley, eds. *Language, Gender, and Society*. Rowley, MA: Newbury House, 1983.
Walker, Alice. *In Search of Our Mother's Gardens*. New York: Harcourt Brace Jovanovich, 1983.
Washington, Mary Helen. *Midnight Birds: Stories of Contemporary Black Women Writers*. Garden City, NY: Anchor Books, 1980.
Zimmerman, Bonnie. "What Has Never Been: An Overview of Lesbian Feminist Literary Criticism." *Feminist Studies* 7 (1981): 451–75.

Sandra M. Gilbert and

b. 1936

Susan Gubar

b. 1944

Sandra M. Gilbert and Susan Gubar are best known for their collaborative explorations of women's literary tradition. They have co-authored The Madwoman in the Attic: The Woman Writer and the Nineteenth-Century Literary Imagination *(1979) and have extended their tracing of the special characteristics of women's writing into the twentieth century in a three-volume sequel collectively entitled* No Man's Land, *the volumes of which are separately titled* The War of the Words *(1988),* Sexchanges *(1991), and* Letters from the Front *(1994). They have also coedited* Shakespeare's Sisters: Feminist Essays on Women Poets *(1979) and* The Norton Anthology of Literature by Women, *second edition (1996), which provides canonical treatment of literature by women in English for college courses and have coauthored* Masterpiece Theatre: An Academic Melodrama *(1995). Both Gilbert and Gubar were born in New York City. Sandra Mortola Gilbert took a B.A. at Cornell (1957), an M.A. at New York University (1961), and a Ph.D. at Columbia (1968). After appointments at Indiana University and Princeton, she is now professor of English at the University of California at Davis. In addition to a scholarly study of D. H. Lawrence's poetry, Gilbert has written poetry of her own, some of which is collected in* The Summer Kitchen *(1983),* Emily's Bread *(1984), and* Ghost Volcano *(1995). Susan David Gubar, professor of English at Indiana University at Bloomington, received her B.A. from City College of New York (1965), her M.A. from the University of Michigan (1968), and her Ph.D. from the University of Iowa (1972). Gubar's career includes a Guggenheim Fellowship (1983–84) and teaching at the University of Illinois and at Tufts. Gubar has written numerous essays on eighteenth-century literature, science fiction and fantasy, and contemporary women's writing. "Infection in the Sentence" is the second chapter of* The Madwoman in the Attic.

From *Infection in the Sentence: The Woman Writer and the Anxiety of Authorship*

The man who does not know sick women does not know women.

— S. WEIR MITCHELL

I try to describe this long limitation, hoping that with such power as is now mine, and such use of language as is within that power, this will convince any one who cares about it that this "living" of mine had been done under a heavy handicap. . . .

— CHARLOTTE PERKINS GILMAN

A Word dropped careless on a Page
May stimulate an eye
When folded in perpetual seam
The Wrinkled Maker lie
Infection in the sentence breeds
We may inhale Despair
At distances of Centuries
From the Malaria —

— EMILY DICKINSON

I stand in the ring
in the dead city
and tie on the red shoes
. . . .
They are not mine,
they are my mother's,
her mother's before,
handed down like an heirloom
but hidden like shameful letters.

— ANNE SEXTON

What does it mean to be a woman writer in a culture whose fundamental definitions of literary authority are, as we have seen, both overtly and covertly patriarchal? If the vexed and vexing polarities of angel and monster, sweet dumb Snow White and fierce mad Queen, are major images literary tradition offers women, how does such imagery influence the ways in which women attempt the pen? If the Queen's looking glass speaks with the King's voice, how do its perpetual kingly admonitions affect the Queen's own voice? Since his is the chief voice she hears, does the Queen try to sound like the King, imitating his tone, his inflections, his phrasing, his point of view? Or does she "talk back" to him in her own vocabulary, her own timbre, insisting on her own viewpoint? We believe these are basic questions feminist literary criticism — both theoretical and practical — must answer, and consequently they are questions to which we shall turn again and again, not only in this chapter but in all our readings of nineteenth-century literature by women.

Dis-eased and infected by the sentences of patriarchy, yet unable to deny the urgency of that "poet-fire"[1] she felt within herself, what strategies did the woman writer develop for overcoming her anxiety of authorship? How did she dance

[1]Gilbert and Gubar allude to Elizabeth Barrett Browning's sonnet to George Sand. [Ed.]

out of the looking glass of the male text into a tradition that enabled her to create her own authority? Denied the economic, social, and psychological status ordinarily essential to creativity; denied the right, skill, and education to tell their own stories with confidence, women who did not retreat into angelic silence seem at first to have had very limited opinions. On the one hand, they could accept the "parsley wreath"[2] of self-denial, writing in "lesser" genres — children's books, letters, diaries — or limiting their readership to "mere" women like themselves and producing what George Eliot called "Silly Novels by Lady Novelists."[3] On the other hand, they could become males *manqués,* mimics who disguised their identities and, denying themselves, produced most frequently a literature of bad faith and inauthenticity. Given such weak solutions to what appears to have been an overwhelming problem, how could there be a great tradition of literature by women? Yet, as we shall show, there is just such a tradition, a tradition especially encompassing the works of nineteenth-century women writers who found viable ways of circumventing the problematic strategies we have just outlined.

Inappropriate as male-devised genres must always have seemed, some women have always managed to work seriously in them. Indeed, when we examine the great works written by nineteenth-century women poets and novelists, we soon notice two striking facts. First, an extraordinary number of literary women either eschewed or grew beyond both female "modesty" and male mimicry. From Austen to Dickinson, these female artists all dealt with central female experiences from a specifically female perspective. But this distinctively feminine aspect of their art has been generally ignored by critics because the most successful women writers often seem to have channeled their female concerns into secret or at least obscure corners. In effect, such women have created submerged meanings, meanings hidden within or behind the more accessible, "public" content of their works, so that their literature could be read and appreciated even when its vital concern with female dispossession and disease was ignored. Second, the writing of these women often seems "odd" in relation to the predominantly male literary history defined by the standards of what we have called patriarchal poetics. Neither Augustans nor Romantics, neither Victorian sages nor Pre-Raphaelite sensualists, many of the most distinguished late eighteenth-century and nineteenth-century English and American women writers do not seem to "fit" into any of those categories to which our literary historians have accustomed us. Indeed, to many critics and scholars, some of these literary women look like isolated eccentrics.

We may legitimately wonder, however, if the second striking fact about nineteenth-century literature by women may not in some sense be a function of the first. Could the "oddity" of this work be associated with women's secret but insistent struggle to transcend their anxiety of authorship? Could the "isolation" and apparent "eccentricity" of these women really represent their common female struggle to solve the problem of what Anne Finch[4] called the literary woman's "fall," as well as their common female search for an aesthetic that would yield a healthy space in an overwhelmingly male "Palace of Art"? Certainly when we consider the "oddity" of women's writing in relation to its submerged content, it begins to seem that when women did not turn into male mimics or accept the "parsley wreath" they may have attempted to transcend their anxiety of authorship by *revising* male genres, using them to record their own dreams and their own stories *in disguise.* Such writers, therefore, both participated in and — to use one of Harold Bloom's key terms[5] — "swerved" from the central sequences of male literary history, enacting a uniquely female process of revision and redefinition that necessarily caused them to seem "odd." At the same time, while they achieved essential authority by telling their own stories,

[2]As opposed to the laurel wreath traditionally given to (male) poets of distinction. [Ed.]

[3]See George Eliot, "Silly Novels by Lady Novelists," *Westminster Review* 64 (1856):442–61. [Au.]

[4]The Countess of Winchilsea (1661–1720), a poet whose *Miscellanies* was published in 1713. [Ed.]

[5]See Bloom, p. 1033. [Ed.]

these writers allayed their distinctively female anxieties of authorship by following Emily Dickinson's famous (and characteristically female) advice to "Tell all the Truth but tell it slant — ."[6] In short, like the twentieth-century American poet H. D., who declared her aesthetic strategy by entitling one of her novels *Palimpsest,*[7] women from Jane Austen and Mary Shelley to Emily Brontë and Emily Dickinson produced literary works that are in some sense palimpsestic, works whose surface designs conceal or obscure deeper, less accessible (and less socially acceptable) levels of meaning. Thus these authors managed the difficult task of achieving true female literary authority by simultaneously conforming to and subverting patriarchal literary standards.

Of course, as the allegorical figure of Duessa[8] suggests, men have always accused women of the duplicity that is essential to the literary strategies we are describing here. In part, at least, such accusations are well founded, both in life and in art. As in the white-black relationship, the dominant group in the male-female relationship rightly fears and suspects that the docility of the subordinate caste masks rebellious passions. Moreover, just as blacks did in the master-slave relationships of the American South, women in patriarchy have traditionally cultivated accents of acquiescence in order to gain freedom to live their lives on their own terms, if only in the privacy of their own thoughts. Interestingly, indeed, several feminist critics have recently used Frantz Fanon's model of colonialism to describe the relationship between male (parent) culture and female (colonized) literature.[9] But with only one language at their disposal, women writers in England and America had to be even more adept at doubletalk than their colonized counterparts. We shall see, therefore, that in publicly presenting acceptable facades for private and dangerous visions women writers have long used a wide range of tactics to obscure but not obliterate their most subversive impulses. Along with the twentieth-century American painter Judy Chicago, any one of these artists might have noted that "formal issues" were often "something that my content had to be hidden behind in order for my work to be taken seriously." And with Judy Chicago, too, any one of these women might have confessed that "Because of this duplicity, there always appeared to be something 'not quite right' about my pieces according to the prevailing aesthetic."[10]

To be sure, male writers also "swerve" from their predecessors, and they too produce literary texts whose revolutionary messages are concealed behind stylized facades. The most original male writers, moreover, sometimes seem "not quite right" to those readers we have recently come to call "establishment" critics. As Bloom's theory of the anxiety of influence implies, however, and as our analysis of the metaphor of literary paternity also suggests, there are powerful paradigms of male intellectual struggle which enable the male writer to explain his rebelliousness, his "swerving," and his "originality" both to himself and to the world, no matter how many readers think him "not quite right." In a sense, therefore, he conceals his revolutionary energies only so that he may more powerfully reveal them, and swerves or rebels so that he may triumph by founding a new order, since his struggle against his precursor is a "battle of strong equals."

For the woman writer, however, concealment is not a military gesture but a strategy born of fear and dis-ease. Similarly, a literary "swerve" is not a motion by which the writer prepares for a victorious accession to power but a necessary evasion. Locked into structures created by and for men, eighteenth- and nineteenth-century women writers did not so much rebel against the prevailing aesthetic as feel guilty about their inability to conform to it. With little sense of a viable female culture, such women were plainly much troubled by the fact that they needed to communicate truths which other (i.e. male) writ-

[6]J. 1129, *The Complete Poems of Emily Dickinson,* 3 vols., ed. Thomas H. Johnson (Cambridge, MA: The Belknap Press of Harvard University Press, 1955). [Au.]

[7]A palimpsest is a manuscript that has been erased and written over. [Ed.]

[8]In Spenser's *Faerie Queene,* Duessa is the daughter of Falsehood and Shame. [Ed.]

[9]See, for instance, Barbara Charlesworth Gelpi, "A Common Language: The American Woman Poet," in *Shakespeare's Sisters,* ed. Gilbert and Gubar, pp. 269–79. [Au.]

[10]Judy Chicago, *Through the Flower: My Struggle as a Woman Artist* (New York: Doubleday, 1977), p. 40. [Au.]

ers apparently never felt or expressed. Conditioned to doubt their own authority anyway, women writers who wanted to describe what, in Dickinson's phrase, is "not brayed of tongue"[11] would find it easier to doubt themselves than the censorious voices of society. The evasions and concealments of their art are therefore far more elaborate than those of most male writers. For, given the patriarchal biases of nineteenth-century literary culture, the literary woman did have something crucial to hide.

Because so many of the lost or concealed truths of female culture have recently been retrieved by feminist scholars, women readers in particular have lately become aware that nineteenth-century literary women felt they had things to hide. Many feminist critics, therefore, have begun to write about these phenomena of evasion and concealment in women's writing. In *The Female Imagination,* for instance, Patricia Meyer Spacks repeatedly describes the ways in which women's novels are marked by "subterranean challenges" to truths that the writers of such works appear on the surface to accept. Similarly, Carolyn Heilbrun and Catharine Stimpson discuss "the presence of absence" in literature by women, the "hollows, centers, caverns within the work — places where activity that one might expect is missing . . . or deceptively coded." Perhaps most trenchantly, Elaine Showalter has recently pointed out that feminist criticism, with its emphasis on the woman writer's inevitable consciousness of her own gender, has allowed us to "see meaning in what has previously been empty space. The orthodox plot recedes, and another plot, hitherto submerged in the anonymity of the background, stands out in bold relief like a thumbprint."[12]

But what is this other plot? Is there any *one* other plot? What is the secret message of literature by women, if there is a single secret message? What, in other words, have women got to hide? Most obviously, of course, if we return to the angelic figure of Makarie[13] — that ideal of "contemplative purity" who no doubt had headaches precisely because her author inflicted upon her a life that seemed to have "no story" — what literary women have hidden or disguised is what each writer knows is in some sense her own story. Because, as Simone de Beauvoir puts it, women "still dream through the dreams of men," internalizing the strictures that the Queen's looking glass utters in its kingly voice, the message or story that has been hidden is "merely," in Carolyn Kizer's bitter words, "the private lives of one half of humanity."[14] More specifically, however, the one plot that seems to be concealed in most of the nineteenth-century literature by women which will concern us here is in some sense a story of the woman writer's quest for her own story; it is the story, in other words, of the woman's quest for self-definition. Like the speaker of Mary Elizabeth Coleridge's[15] "The Other Side of a Mirror," the literary woman frequently finds herself staring with horror at a fear-

[11]Dickinson, *Poems,* J. 512 ("The Soul has Bandaged moments —"). [Au.]

[12]Patricia Meyer Spacks, *The Female Imagination* (New York: Knopf, 1975), p. 317; Carolyn Heilbrun and Catharine Stimpson, "Theories of Feminist Criticism: A Dialogue," in Josephine Donovan, ed., *Feminist Literary Criticism* (Lexington: The University Press of Kentucky, 1975), p. 62; Elaine Showalter, "Review Essay," *Signs* 1, no. 2 (Winter 1975): 435. See also Annis V. Pratt, "The New Feminist Criticism: Exploring the History of the New Space," in *Beyond Intellectual Sexism: A New Woman, A New Reality,* ed. Joan I. Roberts (New York: David McKay, 1976). On p. 183 Pratt describes what she calls her "drowning theory," which "comes from a phenomenon in black culture: You have a little black church back in the marsh and you're going to sing 'Go Down Moses' [but] Every now and then the members of the congregation want to break loose and sing 'Oh Freedom' . . . Whenever they sing that, they've got this big old black pot in the vestibule, and as they sing they pound the pot. That way, no white folks are going to hear. The drowning effect, this banging on the pot to drown out what they are actually saying about feminism, came in with the first woman's novel and hasn't gone out yet. Many women novelists have even succeeded in hiding the covert or implicit feminism in their books from themselves. . . . As a result we get explicit cultural norms superimposed upon an authentic creative mind in the form of all kinds of feints, ploys, masks and disguises embedded in the plot structure and characterization." [Au.]

[13]Makarie is a character in *Wilhelm Meisters Wanderjahre* (1821–29) by Johann Wolfgang von Goethe (1749–1832). [Ed.]

[14]De Beauvoir, *The Second Sex* (New York: Knopf, 1973), p. 132; Kizer, "Three," from "Pro Femina," in *No More Masks!,* ed. Florence Howe and Ellen Bass (New York: Doubleday, 1973), p. 175. [Au.]

[15]English poet (1861–1907), author of *Fancy's Following* (1896) and *Fancy's Guerdon* (1897). [Ed.]

ful image of herself that has been mysteriously inscribed on the surface of the glass, and she tries to guess the truth that cannot be uttered by the wounded and bleeding mouth, the truth behind the "leaping fire / Of jealousy and fierce revenge," the truth "of hard unsanctified distress." Uneasily aware that, like Sylvia Plath, she is "inhabited by a cry," she secretly seeks to unify herself by coming to terms with her own fragmentation. Yet even though, with Mary Elizabeth Coleridge, she strives to "set the crystal surface" of the mirror free from frightful images, she continually feels, as May Sarton puts it, that she has been "broken in two / By sheer definition."[16] The story "no man may guess," therefore, is the story of her attempt to make herself whole by healing her own infections and diseases.

To heal herself, however, the woman writer must exorcise the sentences which bred her infection in the first place; she must overtly or covertly free herself of the despair she inhaled from some "Wrinkled Maker," and she can only do this by revising the Maker's texts. Or, to put the matter in terms of a different metaphor, to "set the crystal surface free" a literary woman must shatter the mirror that has so long reflected what every woman was supposed to be. For these reasons, then, women writers in England and America, throughout the nineteenth century and on into the twentieth, have been especially concerned with assaulting and revising, deconstructing and reconstructing those images of women inherited from male literature, especially, as we noted in our discussion of the Queen's looking glass, the paradigmatic polarities of angel and monster. Examining and attacking such images, however, literary women have inevitably had consciously or unconsciously to reject the values and assumptions of the society that created these fearsome paradigms. Thus, even when they do not overtly criticize patriarchal institutions or conventions (and most of the nineteenth-century women we shall be studying do *not* overtly do so), these writers almost obsessively create characters who enact their own, covert authorial anger. With Charlotte Brontë, they may feel that there are "evils" of which it is advisable "not too often to think." With George Eliot, they may declare that the "woman question" seems "to overhang abysses, of which even prostitution is not the worst."[17] But over and over again they project what seems to be the energy of their own despair into passionate, even melodramatic characters who act out the subversive impulses every woman inevitably feels when she contemplates the "deep-rooted" evils of patriarchy.

It is significant, then, that when the speaker of "The Other Side of a Mirror" looks into her glass the woman that she sees is a madwoman, "wild / With more than womanly despair," the monster that she fears she really is rather than the angel she has pretended to be. What the heroine of George Eliot's verse-drama *Armgart* calls "basely feigned content, the placid mask / Of woman's misery" *is* merely a mask, and Mary Elizabeth Coleridge, like so many of her contemporaries, records the emergence from behind the mask of a figure whose rage "once no man on earth could guess."[18] Repudiating "basely feigned content," this figure arises like a bad dream, bloody, envious, enraged, as if the very process of writing had itself liberated a madwoman, a crazy and angry woman, from a silence in which neither she nor her author can continue to acquiesce. Thus although Coleridge's mirrored madwoman is an emblem of "speechless woe" because she has "no voice to speak her dread," the poet ultimately speaks *for* her when she whispers "I am she!" More, she speaks for her in writing the poem that narrates her emergence from behind the placid mask, "the aspects glad and gay, / That erst were found reflected there."

As we explore nineteenth-century literature, we will find that this madwoman emerges over and over again from the mirrors women writers hold up both to their own natures and to their own visions of nature. Even the most apparently conservative and decorous women writers obsessively create fiercely independent characters who

[16]Plath, "Elm," *Ariel* (New York: Harper & Row, 1966), p. 16; Sarton, "Birthday on the Acropolis," *A Private Mythology* (New York: Norton, 1966), p. 48. [Au.]

[17]*The George Eliot Letters,* 7 vols., ed. Gordon S. Haight (New Haven: Yale University Press, 1954–55), 5:58. [Au.]

[18]Eliot, *Poems,* 2 vols. (New York: Croscup, 1896), p. 124. [Au.]

seek to destroy all the patriarchal structures which both their authors and their authors' submissive heroines seem to accept as inevitable. Of course, by projecting their rebellious impulses not into their heroines but into mad or monstrous women (who are suitably punished in the course of the novel or poem), female authors dramatize their own self-division, their desire both to accept the strictures of patriarchal society and to reject them. What this means, however, is that the madwoman in literature by women is not merely, as she might be in male literature, an antagonist or foil to the heroine. Rather, she is usually in some sense the *author's* double, an image of her own anxiety and rage. Indeed, much of the poetry and fiction written by women conjures up this mad creature so that female authors can come to terms with their own uniquely female feelings of fragmentation, their own keen sense of the discrepancies between what they are and what they are supposed to be.

We shall see, then, that the mad double is as crucial to the aggressively sane novels of Jane Austen and George Eliot as she is in the more obviously rebellious stories told by Charlotte and Emily Brontë. Both gothic and anti-gothic writers represent themselves as split like Emily Dickinson between the elected nun and the damned witch, or like Mary Shelley between the noble, censorious scientist and his enraged, childish monster. In fact, so important is this female schizophrenia of authorship that, as we hope to show, it links these nineteenth-century writers with such twentieth-century descendants as Virginia Woolf (who projects herself into both ladylike Mrs. Dalloway and crazed Septimus Warren Smith), Doris Lessing (who divides herself between sane Martha Hesse and mad Lynda Coldridge), and Sylvia Plath (who sees herself as both a plaster saint and a dangerous "old yellow" monster).

To be sure, in the works of all these artists — both nineteenth- and twentieth-century — the mad character is sometimes created only to be destroyed: Septimus Warren Smith and Bertha Mason Rochester are both good examples of such characters, as is Victor Frankenstein's monster. Yet even when a figure of rage seems to function only as a monitory image, her (or his) fury must be acknowledged not only by the angelic protagonist to whom s/he is opposed, but, significantly, *by the reader as well.* With his usual perceptiveness, Geoffrey Chaucer anticipated the dynamics of this situation in the *Canterbury Tales.* When he gave the Wife of Bath a tale of her own, he portrayed her projecting her subversive vision of patriarchal institutions into the story of a furious hag who demands supreme power over her own life and that of her husband: only when she gains his complete acceptance of her authority does this witch transform herself into a modest and docile beauty. Five centuries later, the threat of the hag, the monster, the witch, the madwoman, still lurks behind the compliant paragon of women's stories.

To mention witches, however, is to be reminded once again of the traditional (patriarchally defined) association between creative women and monsters. In projecting their anger and dis-ease into dreadful figures, creating dark doubles for themselves and their heroines, women writers are both identifying with and revising the self-definitions patriarchal culture has imposed on them. All the nineteenth- and twentieth-century literary women who evoke the female monster in their novels and poems alter her meaning by virtue of their own identification with her. For it is usually because she is in some sense imbued with interiority that the witch-monster-madwoman becomes so crucial an avatar of the writer's own self. From a male point of view, women who reject the submissive silences of domesticity have been seen as terrible objects — Gorgons, Sirens, Scyllas, serpent-Lamias, Mothers of Death or Goddesses of Night. But from a female point of view the monster woman is simply a woman who seeks the power of self-articulation, and therefore, like Mary Shelley giving the first-person story of a monster who seemed to his creator to be merely a "filthy mass that moves and talks," she presents this figure for the first time from the inside out. Such a radical misreading of patriarchal poetics frees the woman artist to imply her criticism of the literary conventions she has inherited even as it allows her to express her ambiguous relationship to a culture that has not only defined her gender but shaped her mind. In a sense, as a famous poem by Muriel Rukeyser implies, all these women ultimately embrace the role of that most mythic of female monsters, the Sphinx, whose indecipherable message is the key to existence, because they know that the secret wisdom so long hidden from men is precisely *their* point of view.[19]

There is a sense, then, in which the female literary tradition we have been defining participates on all levels in the same duality or duplicity that necessitates the generation of such doubles as monster characters who shadow angelic authors and mad anti-heroines who complicate the lives of sane heroines. Parody, for instance, is another one of the key strategies through which this female duplicity reveals itself. As we have noted, nineteenth-century women writers frequently both use and misuse (or subvert) a common male tradition or genre. Consequently, we shall see over and over again that a "complex vibration" occurs between stylized generic gestures and unexpected deviations from such obvious gestures, a vibration that undercuts and ridicules the genre being employed. Some of the best-known recent poetry by women openly uses such parody in the cause of feminism: traditional figures of patriarchal mythology like Circe, Leda, Cassandra, Medusa, Helen, and Persephone have all lately been reinvented in the images of their female creators, and each poem devoted to one of these figures is a reading that reinvents her original story.[20] But though nineteenth-century women did not employ this kind of parody so openly and angrily, they too deployed it to give contextual force to their revisionary attempts at self-definition. Jane Austen's novels of sense and sensibility, for instance, suggest a revolt against both those standards of female excellence. Similarly, Charlotte Brontë's critical revision of *Pilgrim's Progress* questions the patriarchal ideal of female submissiveness by substituting a questing Everywoman for Bunyan's questing Christian. In addition, as we shall show in detail in later chapters, Mary Shelley, Emily Brontë, and George Eliot covertly reappraise and repudiate the misogyny implicit in Milton's mythology by misreading and revising Milton's story of woman's fall. Parodic, duplicitous, extraordinarily sophisticated, all this female writing is both revisionary and revolutionary, even when it is produced by writers we usually think of as models of angelic resignation.

To summarize this point, it is helpful to examine a work by the woman who seems to be the most modest and gentle of the three Brontë sisters. Anne Brontë's *The Tenant of Wildfell Hall* (1848) is generally considered conservative in its espousal of Christian values, but it tells what is in fact a story of woman's liberation. Specifically, it describes a woman's escape from the prison-house of a bad marriage, and her subsequent attempts to achieve independence by establishing herself in a career as an artist. Since Helen Graham, the novel's protagonist, must remain incognito in order to elude her husband, she signs with false initials the landscapes she produces when she becomes a professional artist, and she titles the works in such a way as to hide her whereabouts. In short, she uses her art both to express and to camouflage herself. But this functionally ambiguous aesthetic is not merely a result of her flight from home and husband. For even earlier in the novel, when we encounter Helen before her marriage, her use of art is duplicitous. Her painting and drawing seem at first simply to be genteel social accomplishments, but when she shows one of her paintings to her future husband, he discovers a pencil sketch of his own face on the back of the canvas. Helen has been using the reverse side of her paintings to express her secret desires, and although she has remembered to rub out all the other sketches, this one remains, eventually calling his attention to the dim traces on the backs of all the others.

In the figure of Helen Graham, Anne Brontë has given us a wonderfully useful paradigm of the female artist. Whether Helen covertly uses a supposedly modest young lady's "accomplish-

[19]Rukeyser, "Myth," *Breaking Open* (New York: Random House, 1973), p. 20. [Au.]

[20]For "complex vibration," see Elaine Showalter, "Review Essay," p. 435. For reinventions of mythology, see Mona Van Duyn, "Leda" and "Leda Reconsidered," in *No More Masks!*, pp. 129–32, and Margaret Atwood, "Circe/Mud Poems," in *You Are Happy* (New York: Harper & Row, 1974), pp. 71–94. A poet like H. D. continually reinvents Persephone, Medusa, and Helen in her uniquely female epics, for example in *Helen in Egypt* (New York: New Directions, 1961). [Au.]

ments" for unladylike self-expression or publicly flaunts her professionalism and independence, she must in some sense deny or conceal her own art, or at least deny the self-assertion implicit in her art. In other words, there is an essential ambiguity involved in her career as an artist. When, as a girl, she draws on the backs of her paintings, she must make the paintings themselves work as public masks to hide her private dreams, and only behind such masks does she feel free to choose her own subjects. Thus she produces a public art which she herself rejects as inadequate but which she secretly uses to discover a new aesthetic space for herself. In addition, she subverts her genteelly "feminine" works with personal representations which endure only in tracings, since her guilt about the impropriety of self-expression has caused her to efface her private drawings just as it has led her to efface herself.

It is significant, moreover, that the sketch on the other side of Helen's canvas depicts the face of the Byronically brooding, sensual Arthur Huntingdon, the man she finally decides to marry. Fatally attracted by the energy and freedom that she desires as an escape from the constraints of her own life, Helen pays for her initial attraction by watching her husband metamorphose from a fallen angel into a fiend, as he relentlessly and self-destructively pursues a diabolical career of gaming, whoring, and drinking. In this respect, too, Helen is prototypical, since we shall see that women artists are repeatedly attracted to the Satanic/Byronic hero even while they try to resist the sexual submission exacted by this oppressive younger son who seems, at first, so like a brother or a double. From Jane Austen, who almost obsessively rejected this figure, to Mary Shelley, the Brontës, and George Eliot, all of whom identified with his fierce presumption, women writers develop a subversive tradition that has a unique relationship to the Romantic ethos of revolt.

What distinguishes Helen Graham (and all the women authors who resemble her) from male Romantics, however, is precisely her anxiety about her own artistry, together with the duplicity that anxiety necessitates. Even when she becomes a professional artist, Helen continues to fear the social implications of her vocation. Associating female creativity with freedom from male domination, and dreading the misogynistic censure of her community, she produces art that at least partly hides her experience of her actual place in the world. Because her audience potentially includes the man from whom she is trying to escape, she must balance her need to paint her own condition against her need to circumvent detection. Her strained relationship to her art is thus determined almost entirely by her gender, so that from both her anxieties and her strategies for overcoming them we can extrapolate a number of the crucial ways in which women's art has been radically qualified by their femaleness.

As we shall see, Anne Brontë's sister Charlotte depicts similar anxieties and similar strategies for overcoming anxiety in the careers of all the female artists who appear in her novels. From timid Frances Henri to demure Jane Eyre, from mysterious Lucia to flamboyant Vashti, Brontë's women artists withdraw behind their art even while they assert themselves through it, as if deliberately adopting Helen Graham's duplicitous techniques of self-expression. For the great women writers of the past two centuries are linked by the ingenuity with which all, while no one was really looking, danced out of the debilitating looking glass of the male text into the health of female authority. Tracing subversive pictures behind socially acceptable facades, they managed to appear to dissociate themselves from their own revolutionary impulses even while passionately enacting such impulses. Articulating the "private lives of one half of humanity," their fiction and poetry both records and transcends the struggle of what Marge Piercy has called "Unlearning to not speak."[21]

We must not forget, however, that to hide behind the facade of art, even for so crucial a process as "Unlearning to not speak," is still to be hidden, to be confined: to be secret is to be secreted. In a poignant and perceptive poem to Emily Dickinson, Adrienne Rich has noted that in her "half-cracked way" Dickinson chose "silence for enter-

[21]Marge Piercy, "Unlearning to not speak," *To Be Of Use* (New York: Doubleday, 1973), p. 38. [Au.]

tainment, / chose to have it out at last / on [her] own premises."[22] This is what Jane Austen, too, chose to do when she ironically defined her workspace as two inches of ivory, what Emily Brontë chose to do when she hid her poems in kitchen cabinets (and perhaps destroyed her Gondal stories), what Christina Rossetti chose when she elected an art that glorified the religious constrictions of the "convent threshold." Rich's crucial pun on the word *premises* returns us, therefore, to the confinement of these women, a confinement that was inescapable for them even at their moments of greatest triumph, a confinement that was implicit in their secretness. This confinement was both literal and figurative. Literally, women like Dickinson, Brontë, and Rossetti were imprisoned in their homes, their father's houses; indeed, almost all nineteenth-century women were in some sense imprisoned in men's houses. Figuratively, such women were, as we have seen, locked into male texts, texts from which they could escape only through ingenuity and indirection. It is not surprising, then, that spatial imagery of enclosure and escape, elaborated with what frequently becomes obsessive intensity, characterizes much of their writing.

In fact, anxieties about space sometimes seem to dominate the literature of both nineteenth-century women and their twentieth-century descendants. In the genre Ellen Moers has recently called "female Gothic,"[23] for instance, heroines who characteristically inhabit mysteriously intricate or uncomfortably stifling houses are often seen as captured, fettered, trapped, even buried alive. But other kinds of works by women — novels of manners, domestic tales, lyric poems — also show the same concern with spatial constrictions. From Ann Radcliffe's melodramatic dungeons to Jane Austen's mirrored parlors, from Charlotte Brontë's haunted garrets to Emily Brontë's coffin-shaped beds, imagery of enclosure reflects the woman writer's own discomfort, her sense of powerlessness, her fear that she inhabits alien and incomprehensible places. Indeed, it reflects her growing suspicion that what the nineteenth century called "woman's place" is itself irrational and strange. Moreover, from Emily Dickinson's haunted chambers to H. D.'s tightly shut sea-shells and Sylvia Plath's grave-caves, imagery of entrapment expresses the woman writer's sense that she has been dispossessed precisely because she is so thoroughly possessed — and possessed in every sense of the word.

The opening stanzas of Charlotte Perkins Gilman's punningly titled "In Duty Bound" show how inevitable it was for a female artist to translate into spatial terms her despair at the spiritual constrictions of what Gilman ironically called "home comfort."

In duty bound, a life hemmed in,
  Whichever way the spirit turns to look;
No chance of breaking out, except by sin;
  Not even room to shirk —
  Simply to live, and work.

An obligation preimposed, unsought,
  Yet binding with the force of natural law;
The pressure of antagonistic thought;
  Aching within, each hour,
  A sense of wasting power.

A house with roof so darkly low
  The heavy rafters shut the sunlight out;
One cannot stand erect without a blow;
  Until the soul inside
  Cries for a grave — more wide.[24]

Literally confined to the house, figuratively confined to a single "place," enclosed in parlors and encased in texts, imprisoned in kitchens and enshrined in stanzas, women artists naturally found themselves describing dark interiors and confusing their sense that they were house-bound with their rebellion against being duty bound. The same connections Gilman's poem made in the nineteenth century had after all been made by Anne Finch in the eighteenth, when she complained that women who wanted to write poetry were scornfully told that "the dull mannage of a servile house" was their "outmost art and use." Inevitably, then, since they were trapped in so many ways in the architecture — both the houses

[22]"I am in danger — sir — ," *Adrienne Rich's Poetry,* ed. Barbara Charlesworth Gelpi and Albert Gelpi (New York: Norton, 1975), pp. 30–31. [Au.]

[23]Ellen Moers, *Literary Women* (New York: Doubleday, 1976), pp. 90–112. [Au.]

[24]*The Living of Charlotte Perkins Gilman* (1935; New York: Harper & Row, 1975), p. 77. [Au.]

and the institutions — of patriarchy, women expressed their anxiety of authorship by comparing their "presumptuous" literary ambitions with the domestic accomplishments that had been prescribed for them. Inevitably, too, they expressed their claustrophobic rage by enacting rebellious escapes.

Dramatizations of imprisonment and escape are so all-pervasive in nineteenth-century literature by women that we believe they represent a uniquely female tradition in this period. Interestingly, though works in this tradition generally begin by using houses as primary symbols of female imprisonment, they also use much of the other paraphernalia of "woman's place" to enact their central symbolic drama of enclosure and escape. Ladylike veils and costumes, mirrors, paintings, statues, locked cabinets, drawers, trunks, strongboxes, and other domestic furnishings appear and reappear in female novels and poems throughout the nineteenth century and on into the twentieth to signify the woman writer's sense that, as Emily Dickinson put it, her "life" has been "shaven and fitted to a frame," a confinement she can only tolerate by believing that "the soul has moments of escape / When bursting all the doors / She dances like a bomb abroad."[25] Significantly, too, the explosive violence of these "moments of escape" that women writers continually imagine for themselves returns us to the phenomenon of the mad double so many of these women have projected into their works. For it is, after all, through the violence of the double that the female author enacts her own raging desire to escape male houses and male texts, while at the same time it is through the double's violence that this anxious author articulates for herself the costly destructiveness of anger repressed until it can no longer be contained.

As we shall see, therefore, infection continually breeds in the sentences of women whose writing obsessively enacts this drama of enclosure and escape. Specifically, what we have called the distinctively female diseases of anorexia and agoraphobia are closely associated with this dramatic/thematic pattern. Defining themselves as prisoners of their own gender, for instance, women frequently create characters who attempt to escape, if only into nothingness, through the suicidal self-starvation of anorexia. Similarly, in a metaphorical elaboration of bulimia, the disease of overeating which is anorexia's complement and mirror-image (as Marlene Boskind-Lodahl has recently shown),[26] women writers often envision an "outbreak" that transforms their characters into huge and powerful monsters. More obviously, agoraphobia and its complementary opposite, claustrophobia, are by definition associated with the spatial imagery through which these poets and novelists express their feelings of social confinement and their yearning for spiritual escape. The paradigmatic female story, therefore — the story such angels in the house of literature as Goethe's Makarie and Patmore's Honoria[27] were in effect "forbidden" to tell — is frequently an arrangement of the elements most readers will readily remember from Charlotte Brontë's *Jane Eyre*. Examining the psychosocial implications of a "haunted" ancestral mansion, such a tale explores the tension between parlor and attic, the psychic split between the lady who submits to male dicta and the lunatic who rebels. But in examining these matters the paradigmatic female story inevitably considers also the equally uncomfortable spatial options of expulsion into the cold outside or suffocation in the hot indoors, and in addition it often embodies an obsessive anxiety both about starvation to the point of disappearance and about monstrous inhabitation.

Many nineteenth-century male writers also, of course, used imagery of enclosure and escape to make deeply felt points about the relationship of the individual and society. Dickens and Poe, for instance, on opposite sides of the Atlantic, wrote of prisons, cages, tombs, and cellars in similar ways and for similar reasons. Still, the male writer is so much more comfortable with his literary role that he can usually elaborate upon his visionary

[25]Dickinson, *Poems*, J. 512 ("The Soul has Bandaged moments — "). [Au.]

[26]Boskind-Lodahl, "Cinderella's Step-Sisters: A Feminist Perspective on Anorexia Nervosa and Bulimia," *Signs* 2, no. 2 (1976): 342–56. [Au.]

[27]*The Angel in the House* (1854–63) was the lyric sequence by Coventry Patmore (1823–90) extolling his own marriage. [Ed.]

theme more consciously and objectively than the female writer can. The distinction between male and female images of imprisonment is — and always has been — a distinction between, on the one hand, that which is both metaphysical and metaphorical, and on the other hand, that which is social and actual. Sleeping in his coffin, the seventeenth-century poet John Donne was piously rehearsing the constraints of the grave in advance, but the nineteenth-century poet Emily Dickinson, in purdah in her white dress, was anxiously living those constraints in the present. Imagining himself buried alive in tombs and cellars, Edgar Allan Poe was letting his mind poetically wander into the deepest recesses of his own psyche, but Dickinson, reporting that "I do not cross my Father's ground to any house in town," was recording a real, self-willed, self-burial. Similarly, when Byron's Prisoner of Chillon notes that "my very chains and I grew friends," the poet himself is making an epistemological point about the nature of the human mind, as well as a political point about the tyranny of the state. But when Rose Yorke in *Shirley* describes Caroline Helstone as living the life of a toad enclosed in a block of marble, Charlotte Brontë is speaking through her about her own deprived and constricted life, and its real conditions.[28]

Thus, though most male metaphors of imprisonment have obvious implications in common (and many can be traced back to traditional images used by, say, Shakespeare and Plato), such metaphors may have very different aesthetic functions and philosophical messages in different male literary works. Wordsworth's prison-house in the "Intimations" ode serves a purpose quite unlike that served by the jails in Dickens's novels. Coleridge's twice-five miles of visionary greenery ought not to be confused with Keats's vale of soul-making, and the escape of Tennyson's Art from her Palace should not be identified with the resurrection of Poe's Ligeia. Women authors, however, reflect the literal reality of their own confinement in the constraints they depict, and so all at least begin with the same unconscious or conscious purpose in employing such spatial imagery. Recording their own distinctively female experience, they are secretly working through and within the conventions of literary texts to define their own lives.

While some male authors also use such imagery for implicity or explicitly confessional projects, women seem forced to live more intimately with the metaphors they have created to solve the "problem" of their fall. At least one critic does deal not only with such images but with their psychological meaning as they accrue around houses. Noting in *The Poetics of Space* that "the house image would appear to have become the topography of our inmost being," Gaston Bachelard shows the ways in which houses, nests, shells, and wardrobes are in us as much as we are in them.[29] What is significant from our point of view, however, is the extraordinary discrepancy between the almost consistently "felicitous space" he discusses and the negative space we have found. Clearly, for Bachelard the protective asylum of the house is closely associated with its maternal features, and to this extent he is following the work done on dream symbolism by Freud and on female inner space by Erikson. It seems clear too, however, that such symbolism must inevitably have very different implications for male critics and for female authors.

Women themselves have often, of course, been described or imagined as houses. Most recently Erik Erikson advanced his controversial theory of female "inner space" in an effort to account for little girls' interest in domestic enclosures. But in medieval times, as if to anticipate Erikson, statues of the Madonna were made to open up and reveal the holy family hidden in the Virgin's inner space. The female womb has certainly, always and everywhere, been a child's first and most satisfying house, a source of food and dark security, and therefore a mythic paradise imaged over and over again in sacred caves, secret shrines, consecrated huts. Yet for many a woman writer these ancient associations

[28]Dickinson, *The Letters of Emily Dickinson,* 3 vols., ed. Thomas H. Johnson (Cambridge, MA: The Belknap Press of Harvard University Press, 1958), 2:460; Byron, "The Prisoner of Chillon," lines 389–92; Brontë, *Shirley* (New York: Dutton, 1970), p. 316; see also Brontë to W. S. Williams, 26 July 1849. [Au.]

[29]Gaston Bachelard, *The Poetics of Space,* trans. Maria Jolas (Boston: Beacon, 1970), p. xxxii. [Au.]

of house and self seem mainly to have strengthened the anxiety about enclosure which she projected into her art. Disturbed by the real physiological prospect of enclosing an unknown part of herself that is somehow also not herself, the female artist may, like Mary Shelley, conflate anxieties about maternity with anxieties about literary creativity. Alternatively, troubled by the anatomical "emptiness" of spinsterhood, she may, like Emily Dickinson, fear the inhabitations of nothingness and death, the transformation of womb into tomb. Moreover, conditioned to believe that as a house she is herself owned (and ought to be inhabited) by a man, she may once again but for yet another reason see herself as inescapably an object. In other words, even if she does not experience her womb as a kind of tomb or perceive her child's occupation of her house/body as depersonalizing, she may recognize that in an essential way she has been defined simply by her purely biological usefulness to her species.

To become literally a house, after all, is to be denied the hope of that spiritual transcendence of the body which, as Simone de Beauvoir has argued, is what makes humanity distinctively human. Thus, to be confined in childbirth (and significantly "confinement" was the key nineteenth-century term for what we would now, just as significantly, call "delivery") is in a way just as problematical as to be confined in a house or prison. Indeed, it might well seem to the literary woman that, just as ontogeny may be said to recapitulate phylogeny, the confinement of pregnancy replicates the confinement of society. For even if she is only metaphorically denied transcendence, the woman writer who perceives the implications of the house/body equation must unconsciously realize that such a trope does not just "place" her in a glass coffin, it transforms her into a version of the glass coffin herself. There is a sense, therefore, in which, confined in such a network of metaphors, what Adrienne Rich has called a "thinking woman" might inevitably feel that now she has been imprisoned within her own alien and loathsome body.[30] Once again, in other words, she has become not only a prisoner but a monster.

As if to comment on the unity of all these points — on, that is, the anxiety-inducing connections between what women writers tend to see as their parallel confinements in texts, houses, and maternal female bodies — Charlotte Perkins Gilman brought them all together in 1890 in a striking story of female confinement and escape, a paradigmatic tale which (like *Jane Eyre*) seems to tell *the* story that all literary women would tell if they could speak their "speechless woe." "The Yellow Wallpaper," which Gilman herself called "a description of a case of nervous breakdown," recounts in the first person the experiences of a woman who is evidently suffering from a severe postpartum psychosis.[31] Her husband, a censorious and paternalistic physician, is treating her according to methods by which S. Weir Mitchell, a famous "nerve specialist," treated Gilman herself for a similar problem. He has confined her to a large garret room in an "ancestral hall" he has rented, and he has forbidden her to touch pen to paper until she is well again, for he feels, says the narrator, "that with my imaginative power and habit of story-making, a nervous weakness like mine is sure to lead to all manner of excited fancies, and that I ought to use my will and good sense to check the tendency" (15–16).

The cure, of course, is worse than the disease, for the sick woman's mental condition deteriorates rapidly. "I think sometimes that if I were only well enough to write a little it would relieve the press of ideas and rest me," she remarks, but literally confined in a room she thinks is a one-time nursery because it has "rings and things" in the walls, she is literally locked away from creativity. The "rings and things," although reminiscent of children's gymnastic equipment, are really the paraphernalia of confinement, like the gate at the head of the stairs, instruments that definitively indicate her imprisonment. Even more tormenting, however, is the room's wallpaper: a sulphurous yellow paper, torn off in spots, and

[30] *Adrienne Rich's Poetry,* p. 12: "A thinking woman sleeps with monsters. / The beak that grips her, she becomes" ("Snapshots of a Daughter-in-Law," #3). [Au.]

[31] Charlotte Perkins Gilman, *The Yellow Wallpaper* (Old Westbury: The Feminist Press, 1973). All references in the text will be to page numbers in this edition. [Au.]

patterned with "lame uncertain curves" that "plunge off at outrageous angles" and "destroy themselves in unheard of contradictions." Ancient, smoldering, "unclean" as the oppressive structures of the society in which she finds herself, this paper surrounds the narrator like an inexplicable text, censorious and overwhelming as her physician husband, haunting as the "hereditary estate" in which she is trying to survive. Inevitably she studies its suicidal implications — and inevitably, because of her "imaginative power and habit of story-making," she revises it, projecting her own passion for escape into its otherwise incomprehensible hieroglyphics. "This wall-paper," she decides, at a key point in her story,

> has a kind of sub-pattern in a different shade, a particularly irritating one, for you can only see it in certain lights, and not clearly then.
>
> But in the places where it isn't faded and where the sun is just so — I can see a strange, provoking, formless sort of figure, that seems to skulk about behind that silly and conspicuous front design. [18]

As time passes, this figure concealed behind what corresponds (in terms of what we have been discussing) to the facade of the patriarchal text becomes clearer and clearer. By moonlight the pattern of the wallpaper "becomes bars! The outside pattern I mean, and the woman behind it is as plain as can be." And eventually, as the narrator sinks more deeply into what the world calls madness, the terrifying implications of both the paper and the figure imprisoned behind the paper begin to permeate — that is, to *haunt* — the rented ancestral mansion in which she and her husband are immured. The "yellow smell" of the paper "creeps all over the house," drenching every room in its subtle aroma of decay. And the woman creeps too — through the house, in the house, and out of the house, in the garden and "on that long road under the trees." Sometimes, indeed, the narrator confesses, "I think there are a great many women" both behind the paper and creeping in the garden,

> and sometimes only one, and she crawls around fast, and her crawling shakes [the paper] all over. . . . And she is all the time trying to climb through. But nobody could climb through that pattern — it strangles so; I think that is why it has so many heads. [30]

Eventually it becomes obvious to both reader and narrator that the figure creeping through and behind the wallpaper is both the narrator and the narrator's double. By the end of the story, moreover, the narrator has enabled this double to escape from her textual/architectural confinement: "I pulled and she shook, I shook and she pulled, and before morning we had peeled off yards of that paper." Is the message of the tale's conclusion mere madness? Certainly the righteous Doctor John — whose name links him to the antihero of Charlotte Brontë's *Villette*[32] — has been temporarily defeated, or at least momentarily stunned. "Now why should that man have fainted?" the narrator ironically asks as she creeps around her attic. But John's unmasculine swoon of surprise is the least of the triumphs Gilman imagines for her madwoman. More significant are the madwoman's own imaginings and creations, mirages of health and freedom with which her author endows her like a fairy godmother showering gold on a sleeping heroine. The woman from behind the wallpaper creeps away, for instance, creeps fast and far on the long road, in broad daylight. "I have watched her sometimes away off in the open country," says the narrator, "creeping as fast as a cloud shadow in a high wind."

Indistinct and yet rapid, barely perceptible but inexorable, the progress of that cloud shadow is not unlike the progress of nineteenth-century literary women out of the texts defined by patriarchal poetics into the open spaces of their own authority. That such an escape from the numb world behind the patterned walls of the text was a flight from dis-ease into health was quite clear to Gilman herself. When "The Yellow Wallpaper" was published she sent it to Weir Mitchell, whose strictures had kept her from attempting the pen during her own breakdown, thereby aggravating her illness, and she was delighted to learn, years later, that "he had changed his treatment of

[32]John Bretton is the doctor for the school where Lucy Snowe works in Charlotte Brontë's *Villette*. [Ed.]

nervous prostration since reading" her story. "If that is a fact," she declared, "I have not lived in vain."[33] Because she was a rebellious feminist besides being a medical iconoclast, we can be sure that Gilman did not think of this triumph of hers in narrowly therapeutic terms. Because she knew, with Emily Dickinson, that "Infection in the sentence breeds," she knew that the cure for female despair must be spiritual as well as physical, aesthetic as well as social. What "The Yellow Wallpaper" shows she knew, too, is that even when a supposedly "mad" woman has been sentenced to imprisonment in the "infected" house of her own body, she may discover that, as Sylvia Plath was to put it seventy years later, she has "a self to recover, a queen."[34]

[33]*The Living of Charlotte Perkins Gilman*, p. 121. [Au.]

[34]"Stings," *Ariel*, p. 62. [Au.]

Elaine Showalter

b. 1941

A founder of feminist criticism in the United States, Elaine Showalter remains one of its most creative and influential proponents. Showalter developed the concept and practice of gynocriticism. Showalter was born Elaine Cottler in Cambridge, Massachusetts. Against the wishes of her parents, she pursued an intellectual career, taking degrees in English at Bryn Mawr College (B.A., 1962), at Brandeis University (M.A., 1964), and at the University of California at Davis (Ph.D., 1970). She has taught at Davis, at the University of Delaware, and at the Douglass College of Rutgers University, and she is now a professor of English at Princeton University. Her academic honors include a Guggenheim fellowship (1977–78) and a Rockefeller Humanities fellowship (1981–82). Author of the pioneering A Literature of Their Own: British Women Novelists from Brontë to Lessing *(1977), Showalter has also published* The Female Malady: Women, Madness, and English Culture (1830–1980) *(1986). She has written dozens of articles and essays on feminist topics and has edited* Women's Liberation and Literature *(1971), the first textbook on women in literature;* These Modern Women: Autobiographies of American Women in the 1920s *(1978); and* The New Feminist Criticism *(1985). Showalter's recent work includes* Sexual Anarchy: Gender and Culture at the Fin de Siècle *(1990),* Sister's Choice: Traditions and Change in American Women's Writing *(1991), and* Daughters of Decadence: Women Writers of the Fin-de-Siècle *(1993). "Toward a Feminist Poetics" was originally published in* Women's Writing and Writing About Women, *edited by Mary Jacobus (London: Croom Helm, 1979). The version reprinted here is from* The New Feminist Criticism.

Toward a Feminist Poetics

In 1977, Leon Edel, the distinguished biographer of Henry James, contributed to a London symposium of essays by six male critics called *Contemporary Approaches to English Studies.* Professor Edel presented his essay as a dramatized discussion between three literary scholars who stand arguing about art on the steps of the British Museum:

> There was Criticus, a short, thick-bodied intellectual with spectacles, who clung to a pipe in his right hand. There was Poeticus, who cultivated a Yeatsian forelock, but without the eyeglasses and the ribbon. He made his living by reviewing and had come to the B.M. to look up something or other. Then there was Plutarchus, a lean and lanky biographer wearing a corduroy jacket.

As these three gentlemen are warming to their important subject, a taxi pulls up in front of them and releases "an auburn-haired young woman, obviously American, who wore ear-rings and carried an armful of folders and an attaché case." Into the museum she dashes, leaving the trio momentarily wondering why femininity requires brainwork. They are still arguing when she comes out, twenty-one pages later.[1]

I suppose we should be grateful that at least one woman — let us call her Critica — makes an appearance in this gathering, even if she is not invited to join the debate. I imagine that she is a feminist critic — in fact, if I could afford to take taxis to the British Museum, I would think they had perhaps seen me — and it is pleasing to think that while the men stand gossiping in the sun, she is inside hard at work. But these are scant satisfactions when we realize that of all the approaches to English studies current in the 1970s, feminist criticism is the most isolated and the least understood. Members of English departments who can remember what Harold Bloom means by *clinamen,* and who know the difference between Tartu and Barthian semiotics, will remark that they are against feminist criticism and consequently have never read any.[2] Those who have read it, often seem to have read through a glass darkly, superimposing their stereotypes on the critical texts. In his introduction to Nina Auerbach's subtle feminist analysis of *Dombey and Son* in the *Dickens Studies Annual,* for example, Robert Partlow discusses the deplorable but nonexistent essay of his own imagining:

> At first glance, Nina Auerbach's essay . . . might seem to be a case of special pleading, another piece of women's lib propaganda masquerading as literary criticism, but it is not quite that . . . such an essay could have been . . . ludicrous . . . it could have seen dark phallic significance in curving railroad tracks and upright church pews — but it does not.[3]

In contrast to Partlow's caricature (feminist criticism will naturally be obsessed with the phallus), there are the belligerent assumptions of Robert Boyers, in the Winter 1977 issue of *Partisan Review,* that it will be obsessed with destroying great male artists. In "A Case Against Feminist Criticism," Boyers used a single work, Joan Mellen's *Women and Their Sexuality in the New Film* (1973), as an example of feminist deficiency in "intellectual honesty" and "rigor." He defines feminist criticism as the "insistence on asking the same questions of every work and de-

[1]Leon Edel, "The Poetics of Biography," in *Contemporary Approaches to English Studies,* ed. Hilda Schiff (New York: Barnes & Noble, 1977), p. 38. The other contributors to the symposium are George Steiner, Raymond Williams, Christopher Butler, Jonathan Culler, and Terry Eagleton. [Au.]

[2]See p. 1032 for Bloom's definition of *clinamen.* "Tartu semiotics" alludes to a group of contemporary theorists based in Moscow beginning in the 1960s whose literary analysis is based on the semiotic theories of Charles Sanders Peirce (see p. 810), the Russian Formalists (see p. 700), and Mikhail Bakhtin (see p. 527). Their most prominent representative is Yuri Lotman. For Roland Barthes, see the introduction to Structuralism, Semiotics, and Deconstruction, p. 822. [Ed.]

[3]Robert Partlow, Introduction to *Dickens Studies Annual,* vol. 5 (Carbondale: Southern Illinois University Press, 1976), pp. xiv–xv. Nina Auerbach's essay is called "Dickens and Dombey: A Daughter After All." [Au.]

manding ideologically satisfactory answers to those questions as a means of evaluating it," and concludes his diatribe thus:

> Though I do not think anyone has made a credible case for feminist criticism as a viable alternative to any other mode, no one can seriously object to feminists continuing to try. We ought to demand that such efforts be minimally distinguished by intellectual candor and some degree of precision. This I have failed to discover in most feminist criticism.[4]

Since his article makes its "case" so recklessly that Joan Mellen brought charges for libel, and the *Partisan Review* was obliged to print a retraction in the following issue, Boyers hardly seems the ideal champion to enter the critical lists under the twin banners of honesty and rigor. Indeed, his terminology is best understood as a form of intimidation, intended to force women into using a discourse more acceptable to the academy, characterized by the "rigor" which my dictionary defines as strictness, a severe or cruel act, or a "state of rigidity in living tissues or organs that prevents response to stimuli." In formulating a feminist literary theory, one ought never to expect to appease a Robert Boyers. And yet these "cases" cannot continue to be settled, one by one, out of court. The absence of a clearly articulated theory makes feminist criticism perpetually vulnerable to such attacks, and not even feminist critics seem to agree what it is that they mean to profess and defend.

A second obstacle to the articulation of a feminist critical practice is the activist's suspicion of theory, especially when the demand for clarification comes from sources as patently sexist as the egregiously named Boyerses and Mailers of the literary quarterlies. Too many literary abstractions which claim to be universal have in fact described only male perceptions, experiences, and options, and have falsified the social and personal contexts in which literature is produced and consumed. In women's fiction, the complacently precise and systematizing male has often been the target of satire, especially when his subject is Woman. George Eliot's impotent structuralist Casaubon is a classic instance, as is Mr. Ramsay, the self-pitying philosopher in Virginia Woolf's *To the Lighthouse*. More recently Doris Lessing's Professor Bloodrot in *The Golden Notebook* lectures confidently on orgasm in the female swan; as Bloodrot proceeds, the women in the audience rise one by one and leave. What women have found hard to take in such male characters is their self-deception, their pretense to objectivity, their emotion parading as reason. As Adrienne Rich comments in *Of Woman Born*, "the term 'rational' relegates to its opposite term all that it refuses to deal with, and thus ends by assuming itself to be purified of the nonrational, rather than searching to identify and assimilate its own surreal or nonlinear elements."[5] For some radical feminists, methodology itself is an intellectual instrument of patriarchy, a tyrannical methodolatry which sets implicit limits to what can be questioned and discussed. "The God Method," writes Mary Daly,

> is in fact a subordinate deity, serving higher powers. These are social and cultural institutions whose survival depends upon the classification of disruptive and disturbing information as nondata. Under patriarchy, Method has wiped out women's questions so totally that even women have not been able to hear and formulate our own questions, to meet our own experiences.[6]

From this perspective, the academic demand for theory can only be heard as a threat to the feminist need for authenticity, and the visitor looking for a formula he or she can take away without personal encounter is not welcome. In the United States, where women's-studies programs offer degree options in nearly three hundred colleges and universities, there are fears that feminist analysis has been coopted by academia, and counterdemands that we resist the pressure to assimilate. Some believe that the activism and empiricism of feminist criticism is its greatest strength, and point to the flourishing international

[4]Robert Boyers, "A Case Against Feminist Criticism," *Partisan Review* 44 (Winter 1977): 602, 610. [Au.]

[5]Adrienne Rich, *Of Woman Born: Motherhood as Experience and Institution* (New York: W. W. Norton, 1977), p. 62. [Au.]

[6]Mary Daly, *Beyond God the Father: Towards a Philosophy of Women's Liberation* (Boston: Beacon Press, 1973), pp. 12–13. [Au.]

women's press, to new feminist publishing houses, and to writing collectives and manifestos. They are afraid that if the theory is perfected, the movement will be dead. But these defensive responses may also be rationalizations of the psychic barriers to women's participation in theoretical discourse. Traditionally women have been cast in the supporting rather than the starring roles of literary scholarship. Whereas male critics in the twentieth century have moved to center stage, openly contesting for primacy with writers, establishing coteries and schools, speaking unabashedly (to quote Geoffrey Hartman) of their "pen-envy,"[7] women are still too often translators, editors, hostesses at the conference and the Festschrift,[8] interpreters; to congratulate ourselves for working patiently and anonymously for the coming of Shakespeare's sister, as Virginia Woolf exhorted us to do in 1928,[9] is in a sense to make a virtue of necessity. In this essay, therefore, I would like to outline a brief taxonomy, if not a poetics, of feminist criticism, in the hope that it will serve as an introduction to a body of work which needs to be considered both as a major contribution to English studies and as part of an interdisciplinary effort to reconstruct the social, political, and cultural experience of women.

Feminist criticism can be divided into two distinct varieties. The first type is concerned with *woman as reader* — with woman as the consumer of male-produced literature, and with the way in which the hypothesis of a female reader changes our apprehension of a given text, awakening us to the significance of its sexual codes. I shall call this kind of analysis the *feminist critique,* and like other kinds of critique it is a historically grounded inquiry which probes the ideological assumptions of literary phenomena. Its subjects include the images and stereotypes of women in literature, the omissions of and misconceptions about women in criticism, and the fissures in male-constructed literary history. It is also concerned with the exploitation and manipulation of the female audience, especially in popular culture and film; and with the analysis of woman-as-sign in semiotic systems. The second type of feminist criticism is concerned with *woman as writer* — with woman as the producer of textual meaning, with the history, themes, genres, and structures of literature by women. Its subjects include the psychodynamics of female creativity; linguistics and the problem of a female language; the trajectory of the individual or collective female literary career; literary history; and, of course, studies of particular writers and works. No term exists in English for such a specialized discourse, and so I have adapted the French term *la gynocritique:* "gynocritics" (although the significance of the male pseudonym in the history of women's writing also suggested the term "georgics").[10]

The feminist critique is essentially political and polemical, with theoretical affiliations to Marxist sociology and aesthetics; gynocritics is more self-contained and experimental, with connections to other modes of new feminist research. In a dialogue between these two positions, Carolyn Heilbrun, the writer, and Catharine Stimpson, editor of the journal *Signs: Women in Culture and Society,* compare the feminist critique to the Old Testament, "looking for the sins and errors of the past," and gynocritics to the New Testament, seeking "the grace of imagination." Both kinds are necessary, they explain, for only the Jeremiahs of the feminist critique can lead us out of the "Egypt of female servitude" to the promised land of the feminist vision. That the discussion makes use of these Biblical metaphors points to the connections between feminist consciousness and conversion narratives which often appear in women's literature; Carolyn Heilbrun comments on her own text, "When I talk about feminist criticism, I am amazed at how high a moral tone I take."[11]

[7]Geoffrey H. Hartman, *The Fate of Reading* (Chicago: University of Chicago Press, 1975), p. 3. [Au.]

[8]A book collecting essays published in honor of a famous scholar. [Ed.]

[9]See Woolf, p. 551. [Ed.]

[10]Virgil's *Georgics* celebrates the rural life. George was the pseudonym taken by both Mary Ann Evans (George Eliot) and Amandine-Aurore Dupin (George Sand). [Ed.]

[11]Carolyn G. Heilbrun and Catharine R. Stimpson, "Theories of Feminist Criticism," in *Feminist Literary Criticism: Explorations in Theory,* ed. Josephine Donovan (Lexington: University Press of Kentucky, 1976), pp. 64, 68, 72. [Au.]

THE FEMINIST CRITIQUE: HARDY

Let us take briefly as an example of the way a feminist critique might proceed, Thomas Hardy's *The Mayor of Casterbridge,* which begins with the famous scene of the drunken Michael Henchard selling his wife and infant daughter for five guineas at a country fair. In his study of Hardy, Irving Howe has praised the brilliance and power of this opening scene:

> To shake loose from one's wife; to discard that drooping rag of a woman, with her mute complaints and maddening passivity; to escape not by a slinking abandonment but through the public sale of her body to a stranger, as horses are sold at a fair; and thus to wrest, through sheer amoral wilfulness, a second chance out of life — it is with this stroke, so insidiously attractive to male fantasy, that *The Mayor of Casterbridge* begins.[12]

It is obvious that a woman, unless she has been indoctrinated into being very deeply identified indeed with male culture, will have a different experience of this scene. I quote Howe first to indicate how the fantasies of the male critic distort the text; for Hardy tells us very little about the relationship of Michael and Susan Henchard, and what we see in the early scenes does not suggest that she is drooping, complaining, or passive. Her role, however, is a passive one; severely constrained by her womanhood, and further burdened by her child, there is no way that *she* can wrest a second chance out of life. She cannot master events, but only accommodate herself to them.

What Howe, like other male critics of Hardy, conveniently overlooks about the novel is that Henchard sells not only his wife but his child, a child who can only be female. Patriarchal societies do not readily sell their sons, but their daughters are all for sale sooner or later. Hardy wished to make the sale of the daughter emphatic and central; in early drafts of the novel Henchard has two daughters and sells only one, but Hardy revised to make it clearer that Henchard is symbolically selling his entire share in the world of women. Having severed his bonds with this female community of love and loyalty, Henchard has chosen to live in the male community, to define his human relationships by the male code of paternity, money, and legal contract. His tragedy lies in realizing the inadequacy of this system, and in his inability to repossess the loving bonds he comes desperately to need.

The emotional center of *The Mayor of Casterbridge* is neither Henchard's relationship to his wife nor his superficial romance with Lucetta Templeman, but his slow appreciation of the strength and dignity of his wife's daughter, Elizabeth-Jane. Like the other women in the book, she is governed by her own heart — man-made laws are not important to her until she is taught by Henchard himself to value legality, paternity, external definitions, and thus in the end to reject him. A self-proclaimed "woman-hater," a man who has felt at best a "supercilious pity" for womankind, Henchard is humbled and "unmanned" by the collapse of his own virile façade, the loss of his mayor's chain, his master's authority, his father's rights. But in Henchard's alleged weakness and "womanishness," breaking through in moments of tenderness, Hardy is really showing us the man at his best. Thus Hardy's female characters in *The Mayor of Casterbridge,* as in his other novels, are somewhat idealized and melancholy projections of a repressed male self.

As we see in this analysis, one of the problems of the feminist critique is that it is male-oriented. If we study stereotypes of women, the sexism of male critics, and the limited roles women play in literary history, we are not learning what women have felt and experienced, but only what men have thought women should be. In some fields of specialization, this may require a long apprenticeship to the male theoretician, whether he be Althusser, Barthes, Macherey, or Lacan; and then an application of the theory of signs or myths or the unconscious to male texts or films. The temporal and intellectual investment one makes in such a process increases resistance to questioning it, and to seeing its historical and

[12]Irving Howe, *Thomas Hardy* (London: Weidenfeld & Nicolson, 1968), p. 84. For a more detailed discussion of this problem, see my essay "The Unmanning of the Mayor of Casterbridge," in *Critical Approaches to the Fiction of Hardy,* ed. Dale Kramer (New York: Barnes & Noble, 1979), pp. 99–115. [Au.]

ideological boundaries. The critique also has a tendency to naturalize women's victimization by making it the inevitable and obsessive topic of discussion. One sees, moreover, in works like Elizabeth Hardwick's *Seduction and Betrayal,* the bittersweet moral distinctions the critic makes between women merely betrayed by men, like Hetty in *Adam Bede,* and the heroines who make careers out of betrayal, like Hester Prynne in *The Scarlet Letter*. This comes dangerously close to a celebration of the opportunities of victimization, the seduction *of* betrayal.[13]

GYNOCRITICS AND FEMALE CULTURE

In contrast to this angry or loving fixation on male literature, the program of gynocritics is to construct a female framework for the analysis of women's literature, to develop new models based on the study of female experience, rather than to adapt male models and theories. Gynocritics begins at the point when we free ourselves from the linear absolutes of male literary history, stop trying to fit women between the lines of the male tradition, and focus instead on the newly visible world of female culture. This is comparable to the ethnographer's effort to render the experience of the "muted" female half of a society, which is described in Shirley Ardener's collection *Perceiving Women.*[14] Gynocritics is related to feminist research in history, anthropology, psychology, and sociology, all of which have developed hypotheses of a female subculture including not only the ascribed status, and the internalized constructs of feminity, but also the occupations, interactions, and consciousness of women. Anthropologists study the female subculture in the relationships between women, as mothers, daughters, sisters, and friends; in sexuality, reproduction, and ideas about the body; and in rites of initiation and passage, purification ceremonies, myths, and taboos. Michelle Rosaldo writes in *Woman, Culture, and Society:*

> The very symbolic and social conceptions that appear to set women apart and to circumscribe their activities may be used by women as a basis for female solidarity and worth. When men live apart from women, they in fact cannot control them, and unwittingly they may provide them with the symbols and social resources on which to build a society of their own.[15]

Thus in some women's literature, feminine values penetrate and undermine the masculine systems that contain them; and women have imaginatively engaged the myths of the Amazons, and the fantasies of a separate female society, in genres from Victorian poetry to contemporary science fiction.

In recent years, pioneering work by four young American feminist scholars has given us some new ways to interpret the culture of nineteenth-century American women and the literature that was its primary expressive form. Carroll Smith-Rosenberg's essay "The Female World of Love and Ritual" examines several archives of letters between women, and outlines the homosocial emotional world of the nineteenth century. Nancy Cott's *The Bonds of Womanhood: Woman's Sphere in New England, 1780–1835* explores the paradox of a cultural bondage, a legacy of pain and submission, which nonetheless generates a sisterly solidarity, a bond of shared experience, loyalty, and compassion. Ann Douglas's ambitious book, *The Feminization of American Culture,* boldly locates the genesis of American mass culture in the sentimental literature of women and clergymen, two allied and "disestablished" postindustrial groups. These three are social historians; but Nina Auerbach's *Communities of Women: An Idea in Fiction* seeks the bonds of womanhood in women's literature, ranging from the matriarchal households of Louisa May Alcott and Mrs. Gaskell to the women's schools and colleges of Dorothy Sayers, Sylvia Plath, and Muriel Spark. Historical and literary studies like these, based on English

[13]Elizabeth Hardwick, *Seduction and Betrayal: Women and Literature* (New York: Random House, 1974). [Au.]

[14]Shirley Ardener, ed., *Perceiving Women* (New York: Halsted Press, 1975). [Au.]

[15]Michelle Z. Rosaldo, "Women, Culture, and Society: A Theoretical Overview," in *Women, Culture, and Society,* ed. Michelle Z. Rosaldo and Louise Lamphere (Stanford, Calif.: Stanford University Press, 1974), p. 39. [Au.]

women, are badly needed; and the manuscript and archival sources for them are both abundant and untouched.[16]

GYNOCRITICS: ELIZABETH BARRETT BROWNING AND MURIEL SPARK

Gynocritics must also take into account the different velocities and curves of political, social, and personal histories in determining women's literary choices and careers. "In dealing with women as writers," Virginia Woolf wrote in her 1929 essay, "Women and Fiction," "as much elasticity as possible is desirable; it is necessary to leave oneself room to deal with other things besides their work, so much has that work been influenced by conditions that have nothing whatever to do with art."[17] We might illustrate the need for this completeness by looking at Elizabeth Barrett Browning, whose verse novel *Aurora Leigh* (1856) has recently been handsomely reprinted by the Women's Press. In her excellent introduction Cora Kaplan defines Barrett Browning's feminism as romantic and bourgeois, placing its faith in the transforming powers of love, art, and Christian charity. Kaplan reviews Barrett Browning's dialogue with the artists and radicals of her time; with Tennyson and Clough, who had also written poems on the "woman question"; with the Christian Socialism of Fourier, Owen, Kingsley, and Maurice; and with such female predecessors as Madame de Staël and George Sand. But in this exploration of Barrett Browning's intellectual milieu, Kaplan omits discussion of the male poet whose influence on her work in the 1850s would have been most pervasive: Robert Browning. When we understand how susceptible women writers have always been to the aesthetic standards and values of the male tradition, and to male approval and validation, we can appreciate the complexity of a marriage between artists. Such a union has almost invariably meant internal conflicts, self-effacement, and finally obliteration for the woman, except in the rare cases — Eliot and Lewes, the Woolfs — where the husband accepted a managerial rather than a competitive role. We can see in Barrett Browning's letters of the 1850s the painful, halting, familiar struggle between her womanly love and ambition for her husband and her conflicting commitment to her own work. There is a sense in which she *wants* him to be the better artist. At the beginning of the decade she was more famous than he; then she notes with pride a review in France which praises him more; his work on *Men and Women* goes well; her work on *Aurora Leigh* goes badly (she had a young child and was recovering from the most serious of her four miscarriages). In 1854 she writes to a woman friend:

> I am behind hand with my poem. . . . Robert swears he shall have his book ready in spite of everything for print when we shall be in London for the purpose, but, as for mine, it must wait for the next spring I begin to see clearly. Also it may be better not to bring out the two works together.

And she adds wryly, "If mine were ready I might not say so perhaps."[18]

Without an understanding of the framework of the female subculture, we can miss or misinterpret the themes and structures of women's literature, fail to make necessary connections within a tradition. In 1852, in an eloquent passage from her autobiographical essay "Cassandra," Florence Nightingale identified the pain of feminist awakening as its essence, as the guarantee of progress and free will. Protesting against the protected unconscious lives of middle-class Victorian women, Nightingale demanded the restoration of their suffering:

> Give us back our suffering, we cry to Heaven in our hearts — suffering rather than indifferentism —

[16]Carroll Smith-Rosenberg, "The Female World of Love and Ritual: Relations Between Women in Nineteenth-Century America," *Signs* 1 (Fall 1975): 1–30; Nancy F. Cott, *The Bonds of Womanhood: "Woman's Sphere" in New England, 1780–1835* (New Haven, Conn.: Yale University Press, 1977); Ann Douglas, *The Feminization of American Culture* (New York: Alfred A. Knopf, 1977); Nina Auerbach, *Communities of Women: An Idea in Fiction* (Cambridge, Mass.: Harvard University Press, 1978). [Au.]

[17]Virginia Woolf, "Women and Fiction," *Collected Essays*, vol. 2 (London: Chatto & Windus, 1967), p. 141. [Au.]

[18]Peter N. Heydon and Philip Kelley, eds., *Elizabeth Barrett Browning's Letters to Mrs. David Ogilvy* (New York: Quadrangle Books, 1973), p. 115. [Au.]

> for out of suffering may come the cure. Better to have pain than paralysis: A hundred struggle and drown in the breakers. One discovers a new world.[19]

It is fascinating to see how Nightingale's metaphors anticipate not only her own medical career but also the fate of the heroines of women's novels in the nineteenth and twentieth centuries. To waken from the drugged, pleasant sleep of Victorian womanhood was agonizing; in fiction it is much more likely to end in drowning than in discovery. It is usually associated with what George Eliot in *Middlemarch* calls "the chill hours of a morning twilight," and the sudden appalled confrontation with the contingencies of adulthood. Eliot's Maggie Tulliver, Edith Wharton's Lily Bart, Olive Schreiner's Lyndall, Kate Chopin's Edna Pontellier wake to worlds which offer no places for the women they wish to become; and rather than struggling they die. Female suffering thus becomes a kind of literary commodity which both men and women consume. Even in these important women's novels — *The Mill on the Floss, The Story of an African Farm, The House of Mirth* — the fulfillment of the plot is a visit to the heroine's grave by a male mourner.

According to Dame Rebecca West, unhappiness is still the keynote of contemporary fiction by English women.[20] Certainly the literary landscape is strewn with dead female bodies. In Fay Weldon's *Down Among the Women and Female Friends,* suicide has come to be a kind of domestic accomplishment, carried out after the shopping and the washing-up. When Weldon's heroine turns on the gas, "she feels that she has been half-dead for so long that the difference in state will not be very great." In Muriel Spark's stunning short novel of 1970, *The Driver's Seat,* another half-dead and desperate heroine gathers all her force to hunt down a woman-hating psychopath and persuade him to murder her. Garishly dressed in a purposely bought outfit of clashing purple, green, and white — the colors of the suffragettes (and the colors of the school uniform in *The Prime of Miss Jean Brodie*) — Lise goes in search of her killer, lures him to a park, gives him the knife. But in Lise's careful selection of her death-dress, her patient pursuit of her assassin, Spark has given us the devastated postulates of feminine wisdom: that a woman creates her identity by choosing her clothes, that she creates her history by choosing her man. That, in the 1970s, Mr. Right turns out to be Mr. Goodbar[21] is not the sudden product of urban violence but a latent truth fiction exposes. Spark asks whether men or women are in the driver's seat and whether the power to choose one's destroyer is women's only form of self-assertion. To label the violence or self-destructiveness of these painful novels as neurotic expressions of a personal pathology, as many reviewers have done, is to ignore, Annette Kolodny suggests,

> the possibility that the worlds they inhabit may in fact be real, or true, and for them the only worlds available, and further, to deny the possibility that their apparently "odd" or unusual responses may in fact be justifiable or even necessary.[22]

But women's literature must go beyond these scenarios of compromise, madness, and death. Although the reclamation of suffering is the beginning, its purpose is to discover the new world. Happily, some recent women's literature, especially in the United States, where novelists and poets have become vigorously involved in the women's liberation movement, has gone beyond reclaiming suffering to its reinvestment. This newer writing relates the pain of transformation to history. "If I'm lonely," writes Adrienne Rich in "Song,"

> it must be the loneliness
> of waking first, of breathing

[19]Florence Nightingale, "Cassandra," in *The Cause: A History of the Women's Movement in Great Britain,* ed. Ray Strachey (1928; reprint ed., Port Washington, N.Y.: Kennikat Press, 1969), p. 398. [Au.]

[20]Rebecca West, "And They All Lived Unhappily Ever After," *Times Literary Supplement,* July 26, 1974, p. 779. [Au.]

[21]Showalter alludes to a popular 1975 novel by Judith Rossner, *Looking for Mr. Goodbar,* whose heroine, looking for liberation from a repressive family, discovers the dating bar scene where she picks up a psychopathic murderer. [Ed.]

[22]Annette Kolodny, "Some Notes on Defining a 'Feminist Literary Criticism,'" *Critical Inquiry* 2 (Fall 1975): 84. For an illuminating discussion of *The Driver's Seat,* see Auerbach, *Communities of Women,* p. 181. [Au.]

dawn's first cold breath on the city
of being the one awake
in a house wrapped in sleep[23]

Rich is one of the spokeswomen for a new women's writing which explores the will to change. In her recent book, *Of Woman Born: Motherhood as Experience and Institution,* Rich challenges the alienation from and rejection of the mother that daughters have learned under patriarchy. Much women's literature in the past has dealt with "matrophobia" or the fear of becoming one's mother.[24] In Sylvia Plath's *The Bell Jar,* for example, the heroine's mother is the target for the novel's most punishing contempt. When Esther announces to her therapist that she hates her mother, she is on the road to recovery. Hating one's mother was the feminist enlightenment of the fifties and sixties; but it is only a metaphor for hating oneself. Female literature of the 1970s goes beyond matrophobia to a courageously sustained quest for the mother, in such books as Margaret Atwood's *Surfacing,* and Lisa Alther's recent *Kinflicks.* As the death of the father has always been an archetypal rite of passage for the Western hero, now the death of the mother as witnessed and transcended by the daughter has become one of the most profound occasions of female literature. In analyzing these purposeful awakenings, these reinvigorated mythologies of female culture, feminist criticism finds its most challenging, inspiriting, and appropriate task.

WOMEN AND THE NOVEL: THE "PRECIOUS SPECIALTY"

The most consistent assumption of feminist reading has been the belief that women's special experience would assume and determine distinctive forms in art. In the nineteenth century, such a contribution was ambivalently valued. When Victorian reviewers like G. H. Lewes, Richard Hutton, and Richard Simpson began to ask what the literature of women might mean and what it might become, they focused on the educational, experiential, and biological handicaps of the woman novelist, and this was also how most women conceptualized their situation. Some reviewers, granting women's sympathy, sentiment, and powers of observation, thought that the novel would provide an appropriate, even a happy, outlet for female emotion and fantasy. In the United States, the popular novelist Fanny Fern understood that women had been granted access to the novel as a sort of repressive desublimation, a harmless channel for frustrations and drives that might otherwise threaten the family, the church, and the state. Fern recommended that women write as therapy, as a release from the stifling silence of the drawing room, and as a rebellion against the indifference and insensitivity of the men closest to them:

> Look around, and see innumerable women, to whose barren and loveless lives this would be improvement and solace, and I say to them, write! write! It will be a safe outlet for thoughts and feelings that maybe the nearest friend you have has never dreamed had place in your heart and brain. . . . It is not *safe* for the women of 1867 to shut down so much that cries out for sympathy and expression, because life is such a maelstrom of business or folly or both that those to whom they have bound themselves, body and soul, recognize only the needs of the former. . . . One of these days, when that diary is found, when the hand that penned it shall be dust, with what amazement and remorse will many a husband or father exclaim, I never knew my wife or my child until this moment.[25]

Fern's scribbling woman spoke with fierce indirectness to the male audience, to the imagined husband or father; her purpose was to shock rather than to please, but the need to provoke masculine response was the controlling factor in her writing. At the turn of the century, members of the Women Writers Suffrage League, an important organization of English novelists and journalists, began to explore the psychological bondage of women's literature and its relationships to a male-dominated publishing industry. Elizabeth Robins, the first president of the

[23]Adrienne Rich, *Diving into the Wreck* (New York: W. W. Norton, 1973), p. 20. [Au.]

[24]The term "matrophobia" was coined by Lynn Sukenick; see Rich, *Of Woman Born,* pp. 235 ff. [Au.]

[25]Quoted in Ann Douglas Wood, "The 'Scribbling Women' and Fanny Fern: Why Women Wrote," *American Quarterly* 23 (Spring 1971): 3–24. [Au.]

league, a novelist and actress who had starred in early English productions of Ibsen, argued in 1908 that no woman writer had ever been free to explore female consciousness:

> The realization that she had access to a rich and as yet unrifled storehouse may have crossed her mind, but there were cogent reasons for concealing her knowledge. With that wariness of ages which has come to be instinct, she contented herself with echoing the old fables, presenting to a man-governed world puppets as nearly as possible like those that had from the beginning found such favour in men's sight.
>
> Contrary to the popular impression, to say in print what she thinks is the last thing the woman-novelist or journalist is so rash as to attempt. There even more than elsewhere (unless she is reckless) she must wear the aspect that shall have the best chance of pleasing her brothers. Her publishers are not women.[26]

It was to combat this inhibiting commercial monopoly that nineteenth-century women began to organize their own publishing houses, beginning with Emily Faithfull's Victoria Press in the 1870s, and reaching a peak with the flourishing suffrage presses at the beginning of this century. One of the most fervent beliefs of the Women Writers Suffrage League was that the *terra incognita* of the female psyche would find unique literary expression once women had overthrown male domination. In *A Room of One's Own,* Virginia Woolf argued that economic independence was the essential precondition of an autonomous women's art. Like George Eliot before her, Woolf also believed that women's literature held the promise of a "precious speciality," a distinctly female vision.

FEMININE, FEMINIST, FEMALE

All of these themes have been important to feminist literary criticism in the 1960s and 1970s, but we have approached them with more historical awareness. Before we can even begin to ask how the literature of women would be different and special, we need to reconstruct its past, to rediscover the scores of women novelists, poets, and dramatists whose work has been obscured by time, and to establish the continuity of the female tradition from decade to decade, rather than from Great Woman to Great Woman. As we re-create the chain of writers in this tradition, the patterns of influence and response from one generation to the next, we can also begin to challenge the periodicity of orthodox literary history and its enshrined canons of achievement. It is because we have studied women writers in isolation that we have never grasped the connections between them. When we go beyond Austen, the Brontës, and Eliot, say, to look at a hundred and fifty or more of their sister novelists, we can see patterns and phases in the evolution of a female tradition which correspond to the developmental phases of any subcultural art. In my book on English women writers, *A Literature of Their Own,* I have called these the Feminine, Feminist, and Female stages.[27] During the Feminine phase, dating from about 1840 to 1880, women wrote in an effort to equal the intellectual achievements of the male culture, and internalized its assumptions about female nature. The distinguishing sign of this period is the male pseudonym, introduced in England in the 1840s, and a national characteristic of English women writers. In addition to the famous names we all know — George Eliot, Currer, Ellis, and Acton Bell — dozens of other women chose male pseudonyms as a way of coping with a double literary standard. This masculine disguise goes well beyond the title page; it exerts an irregular pressure on the narrative, affecting tone, diction, structure, and characterization. In contrast to the English male pseudonym, which signals such clear self-awareness of the liabilities of female authorship, American women during the same period adopted superfeminine, little-me pseudonyms (Fanny Fern, Grace Greenwood, Fanny Forester), disguising behind these nominal bouquets their boundless energy, powerful economic motives, and keen professional skills. It is pleasing to discover the occasional Englishwoman who com-

[26]Elizabeth Robins, *Woman's Secret,* WSPU pamphlet in the collection of the Museum of London, p. 6. Jane Marcus is preparing a full-length study of Elizabeth Robins. [Au.]

[27]Elaine Showalter, *A Literature of Their Own: British Women Novelists from Brontë to Lessing* (Princeton, N.J.: Princeton University Press, 1977). [Au.]

bines both these techniques, and creates the illusion of male authorship with a name that contains the encoded domestic message of femininity — such as Harriet Parr who wrote under the pen name "Holme Lee." The feminist content of feminine art is typically oblique, displaced, ironic, and subversive; one has to read it between the lines, in the missed possibilities of the text.

In the Feminist phase, from about 1880 to 1920, or the winning of the vote, women are historically enabled to reject the accommodating postures of femininity and to use literature to dramatize the ordeals of wronged womanhood. The personal sense of injustice which feminine novelists such as Elizabeth Gaskell and Frances Trollope expressed in their novels of class struggle and factory life become increasingly and explicitly feminist in the 1880s, when a generation of New Women redefined the woman artist's role in terms of responsibility to suffering sisters. The purest examples of this phase are the Amazon utopias of the 1890s, fantasies of perfected female societies set in an England or an America of the future, which were also protests against male government, male laws, and male medicine. One author of Amazon utopias, the American Charlotte Perkins Gilman, also analyzed the preoccupations of masculine literature with sex and war, and the alternative possibilities of an emancipated feminist literature. Gilman's utopian feminism carried George Eliot's idea of the "precious speciality" to its matriarchal extremes. Comparing her view of sisterly collectivity to the beehive, she writes that

> the bee's fiction would be rich and broad, full of the complex tasks of comb-building and filling, the care and feeding of the young. . . . It would treat of the vast fecundity of motherhood, the educative and selective processes of the group-mothers, and the passion of loyalty, of social service, which holds the hives together.[28]

This is Feminist Socialist Realism with a vengeance, but women novelists of the period — even Gilman, in her short stories — could not be limited to such didactic formulas, or such maternal topics.

In the Female phase, ongoing since 1920, women reject both imitation and protest — two forms of dependency — and turn instead to female experience as the source of an autonomous art, extending the feminist analysis of culture to the forms and techniques of literature. Representatives of the formal Female Aesthetic, such as Dorothy Richardson and Virginia Woolf, begin to think in terms of male and female sentences, and divide their work into "masculine" journalism and "feminine" fictions, redefining and sexualizing external and internal experience. Their experiments were both enriching and imprisoning retreats into the celebration of consciousness; even in Woolf's famous definition of life: "a luminous halo, a semi-transparent envelope surrounding us from the beginning of consciousness to the end,"[29] there is a submerged metaphor of uterine withdrawal and containment. In this sense, the Room of One's Own becomes a kind of Amazon utopia, population 1.

FEMINIST CRITICISM, MARXISM, AND STRUCTURALISM

In trying to account for these complex permutations of the female tradition, feminist criticism has tried a variety of theoretical approaches. The most natural direction for feminist criticism to take has been the revision and even the subversion of related ideologies, especially Marxist aesthetics and structuralism, altering their vocabularies and methods to include the variable of gender. I believe, however, that this thrifty feminine making-do is ultimately unsatisfactory. Feminist criticism cannot go around forever in men's ill-fitting hand-me-downs, the Annie Hall[30] of English studies; but must, as John Stuart Mill wrote about women's literature in 1869, "emancipate itself from the influence of accepted models, and guide itself by its own impulses"[31] — as, I think, gynocritics is beginning to do. This is

[28]Charlotte Perkins Gilman, *The Man-made World: or, Our Androcentric Culture* (1911; reprint ed., New York: Johnson Reprints, 1971), pp. 101–2. [Au.]

[29]Virginia Woolf, "Modern Fiction," *Collected Essays*, vol. 2, p. 106. [Au.]

[30]Heroine of a 1977 Woody Allen film of that name, whose wardrobe features second-hand men's clothing. [Ed.]

[31]John Stuart Mill, *The Subjection of Women* (London, 1969), p. 133. [Au.]

not to deny the necessity of using the terminology and techniques of our profession. But when we consider the historical conditions in which critical ideologies are produced, we see why feminist adaptations seem to have reached an impasse.

Both Marxism and structuralism see themselves as privileged critical discourse, and preempt the claim to superior places in the hierarchy of critical approaches. A key word in each system is "science"; both claim to be sciences of literature, and repudiate the personal, fallible, interpretative reading. Marxist aesthetics offers a "science of the text,"[32] in which the author becomes not the creator but the producer of a text whose components are historically and economically determined. Structuralism presents linguistically based models of textual permutations and combinations, offering a "science of literary meaning," a grammar of genre. The assimilation of these positivist and evangelical literary criticisms by Anglo-American scholarship in the 1960s and 1970s is not, I would argue, a spontaneous or accidental cultural phenomenon. In the Cold War atmosphere of the late 1950s, when European structuralism began to develop, the morale of the Anglo-American male academic humanist was at its nadir. This was the era of Sputnik, of scientific competition with the Soviet Union, of government money flowing to the laboratories and research centers. Northrop Frye has written about the plight of the male intellectual confronting

> the dismal sexist symbology surrounding the humanities which he meets everywhere, even in the university itself, from freshman classes to the president's office. This symbology, or whatever one should call it, says that the sciences, especially the physical sciences, are rugged, aggressive, out in the world doing things, and so symbolically male, whereas the literatures are narcissistic, intuitive, fanciful, staying at home and making the home more beautiful but not doing anything serious and are therefore symbolically female.[33]

Frye's own *Anatomy of Criticism,* published in 1957, presented the first postulates of a systematic critical theory, and the "possibility of literary study's attaining the progressive, cumulative qualities of science."[34]

The new sciences of the text based on linguistics, computers, genetic structuralism, deconstructionism, neoformalism and deformalism, affective stylistics, and psychoaesthetics, have offered literary critics the opportunity to demonstrate that the work they do is as manly and aggressive as nuclear physics — not intuitive, expressive, and feminine, but strenuous, rigorous, impersonal, and virile. In a shrinking job market, these new levels of professionalization also function as discriminators between the marketable and the marginal lecturer. Literary science, in its manic generation of difficult terminology, its establishment of seminars and institutes of postgraduate study, creates an elite corps of specialists who spend more and more time mastering the theory, less and less time reading the books. We are moving towards a two-tiered system of "higher" and "lower" criticism, the higher concerned with the "scientific" problems of form and structure, the "lower" concerned with the "humanistic" problems of content and interpretation. And these levels, it seems to me, are now taking on subtle gender identities and assuming a sexual polarity — hermeneutics and hismeneutics. Ironically, the existence of a new criticism practiced by women has made it even more possible for structuralism and Marxism to strive, Henchard-like, for systems of formal obligation and determination. Feminists writing in these modes, such as Hélène Cixous[35] and the women contributors to *Diacritics,* risk being allotted the symbolic ghettos of the special issue or the back of the book for their essays.

It is not only because the exchange between feminism, Marxism, and structuralism has hitherto been so one-sided, however, that I think attempts at syntheses have so far been unsuccessful. While scientific criticism struggles to purge

[32]Terry Eagleton's post-Althusserian phrase; see p. 1097. [Ed.]

[33]Northrop Frye, "Expanding Eyes," *Critical Inquiry* 2 (1975): 201–02. [Au.]

[34]Robert Scholes, *Structuralism in Literature: An Introduction* (New Haven, Conn.: Yale University Press, 1974), p. 118. [Au.]

[35]See p. 1453. [Ed.]

itself of the subjective, feminist criticism is willing to assert (in the title of a recent anthology) *The Authority of Experience*.[36] The experience of women can easily disappear, become mute, invalid, and invisible, lost in the diagrams of the structuralist or the class conflict of the Marxists. Experience is not emotion; we must protest now as in the nineteenth century against the equation of the feminine with the irrational. But we must also recognize that the questions we most need to ask go beyond those that science can answer. We must seek the repressed messages of women in history, in anthropology, in psychology, and in ourselves, before we can locate the feminine not-said, in the manner of Pierre Macherey, by probing the fissures of the female text.[37]

Thus the current theoretical impasse in feminist criticism, I believe, is more than a problem of finding "exacting definitions and a suitable terminology," or "theorizing in the midst of a struggle." It comes from our own divided consciousness, the split in each of us. We are both the daughters of the male tradition, of our teachers, our professors, our dissertation advisers, and our publishers — a tradition which asks us to be rational, marginal, and grateful; and sisters in a new women's movement which engenders another kind of awareness and commitment, which demands that we renounce the pseudo-success of token womanhood and the ironic masks of academic debate. How much easier, how less lonely it is, not to awaken — to continue to be critics and teachers of male literature, anthropologists of male culture, and psychologists of male literary response, claiming all the while to be universal. Yet we cannot will ourselves to go back to sleep. As women scholars in the 1970s we have been given a great opportunity, a great intellectual challenge. The anatomy, the rhetoric, the poetics, the history, await our writing.

I am sure that this divided consciousness is sometimes experienced by men, but I think it unlikely that many male academics would have had the division in themselves as succinctly and publicly labeled as they were for me in 1976 when my official title at the University of Delaware was Visiting Minority Professor. I am deeply aware of the struggle in myself between the professor, who wants to study major works by major writers and to mediate impersonally between these works and the readings of other professors, and the minority, the woman who wants connections between my life and my work and who is committed to a revolution of consciousness that would make my concerns those of the majority. There have been times when the Minority wishes to betray the Professor by isolating herself in a female ghetto; or when the Professor wishes to betray the Minority by denying the troubling voice of difference and dissent. What I hope is that neither will betray the other, because neither can exist by itself. The task of feminist critics is to find a new language, a new way of reading that can integrate our intelligence and our experience, our reason and our suffering, our skepticism and our vision. This enterprise should not be confined to women. I invite Criticus, Poeticus, and Plutarchus to share it with us. One thing is certain: feminist criticism is not visiting. It is here to stay, and we must make it a permanent home.

[36]Lee R. Edwards and Arlyn Diamond, eds., *The Authority of Experience: Essays in Feminist Criticism* (Amherst: University of Massachusetts Press, 1977). [Au.]

[37]See the introduction to Marxist Criticism, p. 1095. [Ed.]

Annette Kolodny

b. 1941

Annette Kolodny's career is an exemplary combination of feminist scholarship and political activism. Born in New York City, Kolodny was briefly on the editorial staff of Newsweek *before attending the University of California at Berkeley, where she received her M.A. and Ph.D. In 1969–70, she taught at Yale before removing to Canada with her husband, who had been denied conscientious objector status and faced conscription into the military. At the University of British Columbia in 1970–74,*

Kolodny designed Western Canada's first accredited, multidisciplinary women's studies program. On her return to the United States in 1974, Kolodny organized a women's studies program at the University of New Hampshire. Her first book, The Lay of the Land, *appeared in 1975. When Kolodny was denied promotion and tenure, she filed an anti-Semitism and sexism suit against the University and in 1980 was awarded a landmark out-of-court settlement, a portion of which she used to set up a legal fund and a task force against discrimination. Kolodny stayed in New Hampshire to complete* The Land Before Her *(1984) before joining the faculty at Rensselaer Polytechnic Institute. She is currently a professor of literature at the University of Arizona. The third volume of her projected "Land" trilogy, titled* Dancing Through the Minefield, *is forthcoming. The following selection is excerpted from her well-known article of the same title, which was originally published in* Feminist Studies *6 (1980).*

Dancing Through the Minefield: Some Observations on the Theory, Practice, and Politics of a Feminist Literary Criticism

Had anyone the prescience, ten years ago, to pose the question of defining a "feminist" literary criticism, she might have been told, in the wake of Mary Ellmann's *Thinking About Women,*[1] that it involved exposing the sexual stereotyping of women in both our literature and our literary criticism and, as well, demonstrating the inadequacy of established critical schools and methods to deal fairly or sensitively with works written by women. In broad outline, such a prediction would have stood well the test of time, and, in fact, Ellmann's book continues to be widely read and to point us in useful directions. What could not have been anticipated in 1969, however, was the catalyzing force of an ideology that, for many of us, helped to bridge the gap between the world as we found it and the world as we wanted it to be. For those of us who studied literature, a previously unspoken sense of exclusion from authorship, and a painfully personal distress at discovering whores, bitches, muses, and heroines dead in childbirth where we had once hoped to discover ourselves, could — for the first time — begin to be understood as more than "a set of disconnected, unrealized private emotions."[2] With a renewed courage to make public our otherwise private discontents, what had once been "felt individually as personal insecurity" came at last to be "viewed collectively as structural inconsistency"[3] within the very disciplines we studied. Following unflinchingly the full implications of Ellmann's percipient observations, and emboldened by the liberating energy of feminist ideology — in all its various forms and guises — feminist criticism very quickly moved beyond merely "expos[ing] sexism in one work of literature after another,"[4] and promised, instead, that we might at last "begin to record new choices in a new literary history."[5] So powerful was that

[1]Mary Ellmann, *Thinking About Women* (New York: Harcourt Brace Jovanovich, Harvest, 1968). [Au.]

[2]See Clifford Geertz, "Ideology as a Cultural System," in his *The Interpretation of Cultures: Selected Essays* (New York: Basic Books, 1973), p. 232. [Au.]

[3]Ibid., p. 204. [Au.]

[4]Lillian S. Robinson, "Cultural Criticism and the *Horror Vacui," College English* 33, no. 1 (1972); reprinted as "The Critical Task" in her *Sex, Class, and Culture* (Bloomington: Indiana University Press, 1978), p. 51. [Au.]

[5]Elaine Showalter, *A Literature of Their Own: British Women Novelists from Brontë to Lessing* (Princeton: Princeton University Press, 1977), p. 36. [Au.]

impulse that we experienced it, along with Adrienne Rich, as much "more than a chapter in cultural history": it became, rather, "an act of survival."[6] What was at stake was not so much literature or criticism as such, but the historical, social, and ethical consequences of women's participation in, or exclusion from, either enterprise.

The pace of inquiry these last ten years has been fast and furious—especially after Kate Millett's 1970 analysis of the sexual politics of literature[7] added a note of urgency to what had earlier been Ellmann's sardonic anger — while the diversity of that inquiry easily outstripped all efforts to define feminist literary criticism as either a coherent system or a unified set of methodologies. Under its wide umbrella, everything has been thrown into question: our established canons, our aesthetic criteria, our interpretative strategies, our reading habits, and, most of all, ourselves as critics and as teachers. To delineate its full scope would require nothing less than a book — a book that would be outdated even as it was being composed.

To have attempted so many difficult questions and to have accomplished so much — even acknowledging the inevitable false starts, overlapping, and repetition — in so short a time, should certainly have secured feminist literary criticism an honored berth on that ongoing intellectual journey which we loosely term in academia, "critical analysis." Instead of being welcomed onto the train, however, we've been forced to negotiate a minefield. The very energy and diversity of our enterprise have rendered us vulnerable to attack on the grounds that we lack both definition and coherence; while our particular attentiveness to the ways in which literature encodes and disseminates cultural value systems calls down upon us imprecations echoing those heaped upon the Marxist critics of an earlier generation. If we are scholars dedicated to rediscovering a lost body of writings by women, then our finds are questioned on aesthetic grounds. And if we are critics, determined to practice revisionist readings, it is claimed that our focus is too narrow, and our results are only distortions or, worse still, polemical misreadings.

The very vehemence of the outcry, coupled with our total dismissal in some quarters,[8] suggests not our deficiencies, however, but the potential magnitude of our challenge. For what we are asking be scrutinized are nothing less than shared cultural assumptions so deeply rooted and so long ingrained that, for the most part, our critical colleagues have ceased to recognize them as such. In other words, what is really being bewailed in the claims that we distort texts or threaten the disappearance of the great Western literary tradition itself[9] is not so much the disappearance of either text or tradition but, instead, the eclipse of that particular *form* of the text, and that particular *shape* of the canon, which previously reified male readers' sense of power and significance in the world. Analogously, by asking whether, as readers, we ought to be "really satisfied by the marriage of Dorothea Brooke to Will Ladislaw? of Shirley Keeldar to Louis Moore?"[10]

[6]Adrienne Rich, "When We Dead Awaken: Writing as Re-Vision," *College English* 34, no. 1 (October 1972); reprinted in *Adrienne Rich's Poetry,* ed. Barbara Charlesworth Gelpi and Albert Gelpi (New York: W. W. Norton Co., 1975), p. 90. [Au.]

[7]Kate Millett, *Sexual Politics* (Garden City, N.Y.: Doubleday and Co., 1970). [Au.]

[8]Consider, for example, Robert Boyers's reductive and inaccurate generalization that "what distinguishes ordinary books and articles about women from feminist writing is the feminist insistence on asking the same questions of every work and demanding ideologically satisfactory answers to those questions as a means of evaluating it," in his "A Case Against Feminist Criticism," *Partisan Review* 43, no. 4 (1976): 602. It is partly as a result of such misconceptions, that we have the paucity of feminist critics who are granted a place in English departments which otherwise pride themselves on the variety of their critical orientations. [Au.]

[9]Ambivalent though he is about the literary continuity that begins with Homer, Harold Bloom nonetheless somewhat ominously prophesies "that the first true break . . . will be brought about in generations to come, if the burgeoning religion of Liberated Woman spreads from its clusters of enthusiasts to dominate the West," in his *A Map of Misreading* (New York: Oxford University Press, 1975), p. 33. On p. 36, he acknowledges that while something "as violent [as] a quarrel would ensue if I expressed my judgment" on Robert Lowell and Norman Mailer, "it would lead to something more intense than quarrels if I expressed my judgment upon . . . the 'literature of Women's Liberation.'" [Au.]

[10]Dorothea Brooke and Will Ladislaw marry in the denouement of George Eliot's novel, *Middlemarch* (1871–72), Shirley Keeldar and Louis Moore in that of Charlotte Brontë's *Shirley* (1849). [Ed.]

or whether, as Jean Kennard suggests, we must reckon with the ways in which "the qualities we have been invited to admire in these heroines [have] been sacrificed to structural neatness,"[11] is to raise difficult and profoundly perplexing questions about the ethical implications of our otherwise unquestioned aesthetic pleasures. It is, after all, an imposition of high order to ask the viewer to attend to Ophelia's sufferings in a scene where, before, he'd always so comfortably kept his eye fixed firmly on Hamlet. To understand all this, then, as the real nature of the challenge we have offered and, in consequence, as the motivation for the often overt hostility we've aroused, should help us learn to negotiate the minefield, if not with grace, then with at least a clearer comprehension of its underlying patterns.

The ways in which objections to our work are usually posed, of course, serve to obscure their deeper motivations. But this may, in part, be due to our own reticence at taking full responsibility for the truly radicalizing premises that lie at the theoretical core of all we have so far accomplished. It may be time, therefore, to redirect discussion, forcing our adversaries to deal with the substantive issues and pushing ourselves into a clearer articulation of what, in fact, we are about. Up until now, I fear, we have only piecemeal dealt with the difficulties inherent in challenging the authority of established canons and then justifying the excellence of women's traditions, sometimes in accord with standards to which they have no intrinsic relation.

At the very point at which we must perforce enter the discourse — that is, claiming excellence or importance for our "finds" — all discussion has already, we discover, long ago been closed. "If Kate Chopin were *really* worth reading," an Oxford-trained colleague once assured me, "she'd have lasted — like Shakespeare"; and he then proceeded to vote against the English department's crediting a women's studies seminar I was offering in American women writers. The canon, for him, conferred excellence; Chopin's exclusion demonstrated only her lesser worth. As far as he was concerned, I could no more justify giving English department credit for the study of Chopin than I could dare publicly to question Shakespeare's genius. Through hindsight, I've now come to view that discussion as not only having posed fruitless oppositions, but also as having entirely evaded the much more profound problem lurking just beneath the surface of our disagreement. That is, that the fact of canonization puts any work beyond questions of establishing its merit and, instead, invites students to offer only increasingly more ingenious readings and interpretations, the purpose of which is to validate the greatness already imputed by canonization.

Had I only understood it for what it was then, into this circular and self-serving set of assumptions I might have interjected some statement of my right to question why *any* text is revered and my need to know what it tells us about "how we live, how we have been living, how we have been led to imagine ourselves, [and] how our language has trapped as well as liberated us."[12] The very fact of our critical training within the strictures imposed by an established canon of major works and authors, however, repeatedly deflects us from such questions. Instead, we find ourselves endlessly responding to the *riposte* that the overwhelmingly male presence among canonical authors was only an accident of history — and never intentionally sexist — coupled with claims to the "obvious" aesthetic merit of those canonized texts. It is, as I say, a fruitless exchange, serving more to obscure than to expose the territory being protected and dragging us, again and again, through the minefield.

It is my contention that current hostilities might be transformed into a true dialogue with our critics if we at last make explicit what appear, to this observer, to constitute the three crucial propositions to which our special interests inevitably give rise. They are, moreover, propositions which, if handled with care and intelligence, could breathe new life into now moribund areas of our profession: (1) Literary history (and with that, the historicity of literature) is a fiction; (2) insofar as we are taught how to read, what we

[11]Jean E. Kennard, *Victims of Convention* (Hamden, Conn.: Archon Books, 1978), p. 14. [Au.]

[12]Rich, "When We Dead Awaken," p. 90. [Au.]

engage are not texts but paradigms; and, finally, (3) that since the grounds upon which we assign aesthetic value to texts are never infallible, unchangeable, or universal, we must reexamine not only our aesthetics but, as well, the inherent biases and assumptions informing the critical methods which (in part) shape our aesthetic responses. For the sake of brevity, I won't attempt to offer the full arguments for each but, rather, only sufficient elaboration to demonstrate what I see as their intrinsic relation to the potential scope of and present challenge implied by feminist literary study.

1. *Literary history (and, with that, the historicity of literature) is a fiction.* To begin with, an established canon functions as a model by which to chart the continuities and discontinuities, as well as the influences upon and the interconnections between works, genres, and authors. That model we tend to forget, however, is of our own making. It will take a very different shape, and explain its inclusions and exclusions in very different ways, if the reigning critical ideology believes that new literary forms result from some kind of ongoing internal dialectic within preexisting styles and traditions or if, by contrast, the ideology declares that literary change is dependent upon societal development and thereby determined by upheavals in the social and economic organization of the culture at large.[13] Indeed, whenever in the previous century of English and American literary scholarship one alternative replaced the other, we saw dramatic alterations in canonical "wisdom."

This suggests, then, that our sense of a "literary history" and, by extension, our confidence in a "historical" canon, is rooted not so much in any definitive understanding of the past, as it is in our need to call up and utilize the past on behalf of a better understanding of the present. Thus, to paraphrase David Couzens Hoy, it becomes "necessary to point out that the understanding of art and literature is such an essential aspect of the present's self-understanding that this self-understanding conditions what even gets taken" as comprising that artistic and literary past. To quote Hoy fully, "this continual reinterpretation of the past goes hand in hand with the continual reinterpretation by the present of itself."[14] In our own time, uncertain as to which, if any, model truly accounts for our canonical choices or accurately explains literary history, and pressured further by the feminists' call for some justification of the criteria by which women's writings were largely excluded from both that canon and history, we suffer what Harold Bloom has called "a remarkable dimming" of "our mutual sense of canonical standards."[15]

Into this apparent impasse, feminist literary theorists implicitly introduce the observation that our choices and evaluations of current literature have the effect either of solidifying or of reshaping our sense of the past. The authority of any established canon, after all, is reified by our perception that current work seems to grow, almost inevitably, out of it (even in opposition or rebellion), and is called into question when what we read appears to have little or no relation to what we recognize as coming before. So, were the larger critical community to begin to seriously attend to the recent outpouring of fine literature by women, this would surely be accompanied by a concomitant researching of the past, by literary historians, in order to account for the present phenomenon. In that process, literary history would itself be altered: works by seventeenth-, eighteenth-, or nineteenth-century women, to which we had not previously attended, might be given new importance as "precursors" or as prior influences upon present-day authors; while selected male writers might also be granted new prominence as figures whom the women today, or even yesterday, needed to reject. I am arguing, in other words, that the choices we make in the present inevitably alter our sense of the past that led to them.

Related to this is the feminist challenge to that patently mendacious critical fallacy that we read

[13]The first is a proposition currently expressed by some structuralists and formalist critics; the best statement of the second probably appears in Georg Lukács, *Writer and Critic* (New York: Grosset and Dunlap, 1970), p. 119. [Au.]

[14]David Couzens Hoy, "Hermeneutic Circularity, Indeterminacy, and Incommensurability," *New Literary History* 10, no. 1 (Autumn 1978): 166–67. [Au.]

[15]Bloom, *Map of Misreading*, p. 36. [Au.]

the "classics" in order to reconstruct the past "the way it really was," and that we read Shakespeare and Milton in order to apprehend the meanings that they intended. Short of time machines or miraculous resurrections, there is simply no way to know, precisely or surely, what "really was," what Homer intended when he sang, or Milton when he dictated. Critics more acute than I have already pointed out the impossibility of grounding a reading in the imputation of authorial intention because the further removed the author is from us, so too must be her or his systems of knowledge and belief, points of view, and structures of vision (artistic and otherwise).[16] (I omit here the difficulty of finally either proving or disproving the imputation of intentionality because, inescapably, the only appropriate authority is unavailable: deceased.) What we have really come to mean when we speak of competence in reading historical texts, therefore, is the ability to recognize literary conventions which have survived through time — so as to remain operational in the mind of the reader — and, where these are lacking, the ability to translate (or perhaps transform?) the text's ciphers into more current and recognizable shapes. But we never really reconstruct the past in its own terms. What we gain when we read the "classics," then, is neither Homer's Greece nor George Eliot's England *as they knew it* but, rather, an approximation of an already fictively imputed past made available, through our interpretive strategies, for present concerns. Only by understanding this can we put to rest that recurrent delusion that the "continuing relevance" of the classics serves as "testimony to perennial features of human experience."[17] The only "perennial feature" to which our ability to read and reread texts written in previous centuries testifies is our inventiveness — in the sense that all of literary history is a fiction which we daily recreate as we reread it. What distinguishes feminists in this regard is their desire to alter and extend what we take as historically relevant from out of that vast storehouse of our literary inheritance and, further, feminists' recognition of the storehouse for what it really is: a resource for remodeling our literary history, past, present, and future.

2. *Insofar as we are taught how to read, what we engage are not texts but paradigms*. To pursue the logical consequences of the first proposition leads, however uncomfortably, to the conclusion that we appropriate meaning from a text according to what we need (or desire) or, in other words, according to the critical assumptions or predispositions (conscious or not) that we bring to it. And we appropriate different meanings, or report different gleanings, at different times — even from the same text — according to our changed assumptions, circumstances, and requirements. This, in essence, constitutes the heart of the second proposition. For insofar as literature is itself a social institution, so, too, reading is a highly socialized — or learned — activity. What makes it so exciting, of course, is that it can be constantly relearned and refined, so as to provide either an individual or an entire reading community, over time, with infinite variations of the same text. It *can* provide that, but, I must add, too often it does not. Frequently our reading habits become fixed, so that each successive reading experience functions, in effect, normatively, with one particular kind of novel stylizing our expectations of those to follow, the stylistic devices of any favorite author (or group of authors) alerting us to the presence or absence of those devices in the works of others, and so on. "Once one has read his first poem," Murray Krieger has observed, "he turns to his second and to the others that will follow thereafter with an increasing series of preconceptions about the sort

[16]John Dewey offered precisely this argument in 1934 when he insisted that a work of art "is recreated every time it is esthetically experienced. . . . It is absurd to ask what an artist 'really' meant by his product: he himself would find different meanings in it at different days and hours and in different stages of his own development." Further, he explained, "It is simply an impossibility that any one today should experience the Parthenon as the devout Athenian contemporary citizen experienced it, any more than the religious statuary of the twelfth century can mean, esthetically, even to a good Catholic today just what it meant to the worshipers of the old period," in *Art as Experience* (New York: Capricorn Books, 1958), pp. 108–09. [Au.]

[17]Charles Altieri, "The Hermeneutics of Literary Indeterminacy: A Dissent from the New Orthodoxy," *New Literary History* 10, no. 1 (Autumn 1978): 90. [Au.]

of activity in which he is indulging. In matters of literary experience, as in other experiences," Krieger concludes, "one is a virgin but once."[18]

For most readers, this is a fairly unconscious process, and not unnaturally, what we are taught to read well and with pleasure, when we are young, predisposes us to certain specific kinds of adult reading tastes. For the professional literary critic, the process may be no different, but it is at least more conscious. Graduate schools, at their best, are training grounds for competing interpretive paradigms or reading techniques: affective stylistics, structuralism, and semiotic analysis, to name only a few of the more recent entries. The delight we learn to take in the mastery of these interpretive strategies is then often mistakenly construed as our delight in reading specific texts, especially in the case of works that would otherwise be unavailable or even offensive to us. In my own graduate career, for example, with superb teachers to guide me, I learned to take great pleasure in *Paradise Lost*, even though as both a Jew and a feminist, I can subscribe neither to its theology nor to its hierarchy of sexual valuation. If, within its own terms (as I have been taught to understand them), the text manipulates my sensibilities and moves me to pleasure — as I will affirm it does — then, at least in part, that must be because, in spite of my real-world alienation from many of its basic tenets, I have been able to enter that text through interpretive strategies which allow me to displace less comfortable observations with others to which I have been taught pleasurably to attend. Though some of my teachers may have called this process "learning to read the text properly," I have now come to see it as learning to effectively manipulate the critical strategies which they taught me so well. Knowing, for example, the poem's debt to epic conventions, I am able to discover in it echoes and reworkings of both lines and situations from Virgil and Homer; placing it within the ongoing Christian debate between Good and Evil, I comprehend both the philosophic and the stylistic significance of Satan's ornate rhetoric as compared to God's majestic simplicity in Book III. But, in each case, an interpretative model, already assumed, had guided my discovery of the evidence for it.[19]

When we consider the implications of these observations for the processes of canon formation and for the assignment of aesthetic value, we find ourselves locked in a chicken-and-egg dilemma, unable easily to distinguish as primary the importance of *what* we read as opposed to *how* we have learned to read it. For, simply put, we read well, and with pleasure, what we already know how to read; and what we know how to read is to a large extent dependent upon what we have already read (works from which we've developed our expectations and learned our interpretive strategies). What we then choose to read — and, by extension, teach and thereby "canonize" — usually follows upon our previous reading. Radical breaks are tiring, demanding, uncomfortable, and sometimes wholly beyond our comprehension.

Though the argument is not usually couched in precisely these terms, a considerable segment of the most recent feminist rereadings of women writers allows the conclusion that, where those authors have dropped out of sight, the reason may be due not to any lack of merit in the work but, instead, to an incapacity of predominantly male readers to properly interpret and appreciate women's texts — due, in large part, to a lack of prior acquaintance. The fictions which women compose about the worlds they inhabit may owe a debt to prior, influential works by other women or, simply enough, to the daily experience of the writer herself or, more usually, to some combination of the two. The reader coming upon such fiction, with knowledge of neither its informing literary traditions nor its real-world contexts, will thereby find himself hard-pressed, though he may recognize the words on the page, to competently decipher its intended meanings. And this is what makes the recent studies by Patricia Meyer

[18]Murray Krieger, *Theory of Criticism: A Tradition and Its System* (Baltimore: The Johns Hopkins University Press, 1976), p. 6. [Au.]

[19]See Stanley E. Fish, "Normal Circumstances, Literal Language, Direct Speech Acts, the Ordinary, the Everyday, the Obvious, What Goes without Saying, and Other Special Cases," *Critical Inquiry* 4, no. 4 (Summer 1978): 627–28. [Au.]

Spacks, Ellen Moers, Elaine Showalter, Sandra Gilbert and Susan Gubar, and others so crucial. For, by attempting to delineate the connections and interrelations that make for a female literary tradition, they provide us invaluable aids for recognizing and understanding the unique literary traditions and sex-related contexts out of which women write.

The (usually male) reader who, both by experience and by reading, has never made acquaintance with those contexts — historically, the lying-in room, the parlor, the nursery, the kitchen, the laundry, and so on — will necessarily lack the capacity to fully interpret the dialogue or action embedded therein; for, as every good novelist knows, the meaning of any character's action or statement is inescapably a function of the specific situation in which it is embedded.[20] Virginia Woolf therefore quite properly anticipated the male reader's disposition to write off what he could not understand, abandoning women's writings as offering "not merely a difference of view, but a view that is weak, or trivial, or sentimental because it differs from his own." In her 1929 essay, "Women and Fiction," Woolf grappled most obviously with the ways in which male writers and male subject matter had already preempted the language of literature. Yet she was also tacitly commenting on the problem of (male) audience and conventional reading expectations when she speculated that the woman writer might well "find that she is perpetually wishing to alter the established values [in literature] — to make serious what appears insignificant to a man, and trivial what is to him important."[21] "The 'competence' necessary for understanding [a] literary message . . . depends upon a great number of codices," after all; as Cesare Segre has pointed out, to be competent, a reader must either share or at least be familiar with, "in addition to the code language . . . the codes of custom, of society, and of conceptions of the world"[22] (what Woolf meant by "values"). Males ignorant of women's "values" or conceptions of the world will necessarily, thereby, be poor readers of works that in any sense recapitulate their codes.

The problem is further exacerbated when the language of the literary text is largely dependent upon figuration. For it can be argued, as Ted Cohen has shown, that while "in general, and with some obvious qualifications . . . all literal use of language is accessible to all whose language it is . . . figurative use can be inaccessible to all but those who share information about one another's knowledge, beliefs, intentions, and attitudes."[23] There was nothing fortuitous, for example, in Charlotte Perkins Gilman's decision to situate the progressive mental breakdown and increasing incapacity of the protagonist of *The Yellow Wallpaper* in an upstairs room that had once served as a nursery (with barred windows, no less). But the reader unacquainted with the ways in which women traditionally inhabited a household might not have taken the initial description of the setting as semantically relevant; and the progressive infantilization of the adult protagonist would thereby lose some of its symbolic implications. Analogously, the contemporary poet who declares, along with Adrienne Rich, the need for "a whole new poetry beginning here" is acknowledging that the materials available for symbolization and figuration from women's contexts will necessarily differ from those that men have traditionally utilized:

> Vision begins to happen in such a life
> as if a woman quietly walked away
> from the argument and jargon in a room
> and sitting down in the kitchen, began turning in
> her lap
> bits of yarn, calico and velvet scraps,
> . . . .
> pulling the tenets of a life together
> with no mere will to mastery,
> only care for the many-lived, unending
> forms in which she finds herself.[24]

[20]Ibid., p. 643. [Au.]

[21]Virginia Woolf, "Women and Fiction," *Granite and Rainbow: Essays* (London: Hogarth, 1958), p. 81. [Au.]

[22]Cesare Segre, "Narrative Structures and Literary History," *Critical Inquiry* 3, no. 2 (Winter 1976): 272–73. [Au.]

[23]Ted Cohen, "Metaphor and the Cultivation of Intimacy," *Critical Inquiry* 5, no. 1 (Autumn 1978): 9. [Au.]

[24]From Adrienne Rich's "Transcendental Etude" in her *The Dream of a Common Language: Poems 1974–1977* (New York: W. W. Norton and Co., 1978), pp. 76–77. [Au.]

What, then, is the fate of the woman writer whose competent reading community is composed only of members of her own sex? And what, then, the response of the male critic who, on first looking into Virginia Woolf or Doris Lessing, finds all of the interpretative strategies at his command inadequate to a full and pleasurable deciphering of their pages? Historically, the result has been the diminished status of women's products and their consequent absence from major canons. Nowadays, however, by pointing out that the act of "interpreting language is no more sexually neutral than language use or the language system itself," feminist students of language, like Nelly Furman, help us better understand the crucial linkage between our gender and our interpretive, or reading, strategies. Insisting upon "the contribution of the . . . reader [in] the active attribution of significance to formal signifiers,"[25] Furman and others promise to shake us all — female and male alike — out of our canonized and conventional aesthetic assumptions.

3. *Since the grounds upon which we assign aesthetic value to texts are never infallible, unchangeable, or universal, we must reexamine not only our aesthetics but, as well, the inherent biases and assumptions informing the critical methods which (in part) shape our aesthetic responses.* I am, on the one hand, arguing that men will be better readers, or appreciators, of women's books when they have read more of them (as women have always been taught to become astute readers of men's texts). On the other hand, it will be noted, the emphasis of my remarks shifts the act of critical judgment from assigning aesthetic valuations to texts and directs it, instead, to ascertaining the adequacy of any interpretive paradigm to a full reading of both female and male writing. My third proposition — and, I admit, perhaps the most controversial — thus calls into question that recurrent tendency in criticism to establish norms for the evaluation of literary works when we might better serve the cause of literature by developing standards for evaluating the adequacy of our critical methods.[26] This does not mean that I wish to discard aesthetic valuation. The choice, as I see it, is not between retaining or discarding aesthetic values; rather, the choice is between having some awareness of what constitutes (at least in part) the bases of our aesthetic responses and going without such an awareness. For it is my view that insofar as aesthetic responsiveness continues to be an integral aspect of our human response system — in part spontaneous, in part learned and educated — we will inevitably develop theories to help explain, formalize, or even initiate those responses.

In challenging the adequacy of received critical opinion or the imputed excellence of established canons, feminist literary critics are essentially seeking to discover how aesthetic value is assigned in the first place, where it resides (in the text or in the reader), and, most importantly, what validity may really be claimed by our aesthetic "judgments." What ends do those judgments serve, the feminist asks; and what conceptions of the world or ideological stances do they (even if unwittingly) help to perpetuate? In so doing, she points out, among other things, that any response labeled "aesthetic" may as easily designate some immediately experienced moment or event as it may designate a species of nostalgia, a yearning for the components of a simpler past, when the world seemed known or at least understandable. Thus the value accorded an opera or a Shakespeare play may well reside in the viewer's immediate viewing pleasure, or it may reside in the play's nostalgic evocation of a once-comprehensible and ordered world. At the same time, the feminist confronts, for example, the reader who simply cannot entertain the possibility that women's worlds are symbolically rich, the reader who, like the male characters in Susan Glaspell's 1917 short story, "A Jury of Her Peers," has already assumed the innate "insignificance of kitchen things."[27] Such a reader, she

[25]Furman, "The Study of Women and Language, Nelly: Comment on Vol. 3, no. 3" in *Signs* 4, no. 1 (Autumn 1978), p. 184. [Au.]

[26]"A recurrent tendency in criticism is the establishment of false norms for the evaluation of literary works," notes Robert Scholes in his *Structuralism in Literature: An Introduction* (New Haven: Yale University Press, 1974), p. 131. [Au.]

[27]For a full discussion of the Glaspell short story which takes this problem into account, please see my "A Map for

knows, will prove himself unable to assign significance to fictions that attend to "kitchen things" and will, instead, judge such fictions as trivial and as aesthetically wanting. For her to take useful issue with such a reader, she must make clear that what appears to be a dispute about aesthetic merit is, in reality, a dispute about the *contexts of judgment;* and what is at issue, then, is the adequacy of the prior assumptions and reading habits brought to bear on the text. To put it bluntly: we have had enough pronouncements of aesthetic valuation for a time; it is now our task to evaluate the imputed norms and normative reading patterns that, in part, led to those pronouncements.

By and large, I think I've made my point. Only to clarify it do I add this coda: when feminists turn their attention to the works of male authors which have traditionally been accorded high aesthetic value and, where warranted, follow Tillie Olsen's advice that we assert our "right to say: this is surface, this falsifies reality, this degrades,"[28] such statements do not necessarily mean that we will end up with a diminished canon. To question the source of the aesthetic pleasures we've gained from reading Spenser, Shakespeare, Milton, and so on, does not imply that we must deny those pleasures. It means only that aesthetic response is once more invested with epistemological, ethical, and moral concerns. It means, in other words, that readings of *Paradise Lost* which analyze its complex hierarchal structures but fail to note the implications of gender within that hierarchy; or which insist upon the inherent (or even inspired) perfection of Milton's figurative language but fail to note the consequences, for Eve, of her specifically gender-marked weakness, which, like the flowers to which she attends, requires "propping up"; or which concentrate on the poem's thematic reworking of classical notions of martial and epic prowess into Christian (moral) heroism but fail to note that Eve is stylistically edited out of that process — all such readings, however useful, will no longer be deemed wholly adequate. The pleasures we had earlier learned to take in the poem will not be diminished thereby, but they will become part of an altered reading attentiveness.

These three propositions I believe to be at the theoretical core of most current feminist literary criticism, whether acknowledged as such or not. If I am correct in this, then that criticism represents more than a profoundly skeptical stance toward all other preexisting and contemporaneous schools and methods, and more than an impassioned demand that the variety and variability of women's literary expression be taken into full account, rather than written off as caprice and exception, the irregularity in an otherwise regular design. It represents that locus in literary study where, in unceasing effort, female self-consciousness turns in upon itself, attempting to grasp the deepest conditions of its own unique and multiplicitous realities, in the hope, eventually, of altering the very forms through which the culture perceives, expresses, and knows itself. For, if what the larger women's movement looks for in the future is a transformation of the structures of primarily male power which now order our society, then the feminist literary critic demands that we understand the ways in which those structures have been — and continue to be — reified by our literature and by our literary criticism. Thus, along with other "radical" critics and critical schools, though our focus remains the power of the word to both structure and mirror human experience, our overriding commitment is to a radical alteration — an improvement, we hope — in the nature of that experience.

What distinguishes our work from those similarly oriented "social consciousness" critiques, it is said, is its lack of systematic coherence. Pitted against, for example, psychoanalytic or Marxist readings, which owe a decisive share of their persuasiveness to their apparent internal consistency as a system, the aggregate of feminist literary criticism appears woefully deficient in system, and painfully lacking in program. It is, in fact, from all quarters, the most telling defect alleged against us, the most explosive threat in the mine-

Re-Reading: Or, Gender and the Interpretation of Literary Texts," forthcoming in a Special Issue on Narrative, *New Literary History* (1980). [Au.]

[28]Tillie Olsen, *Silences* (New York: Delacorte Press/ Seymour Lawrence, 1978), p. 45. [Au.]

field. And my own earlier observation that, as of 1976, feminist literary criticism appeared "more like a set of interchangeable strategies than any coherent school or shared goal orientation," has been taken by some as an indictment, by others as a statement of impatience. Neither was intended. I felt then, as I do now, that this would "prove both its strength *and* its weakness,"[29] in the sense that the apparent disarray would leave us vulnerable to the kind of objection I've just alluded to; while the fact of our diversity would finally place us securely where, all along, we should have been: camped out, on the far side of the minefield, with the other pluralists and pluralisms.

In our heart of hearts, of course, most critics are really structuralists (whether or not they accept the label) because what we are seeking are patterns (or structures) that can order and explain the otherwise inchoate; thus, we invent, or believe we discover, relational patternings in the texts we read which promise transcendence from difficulty and perplexity to clarity and coherence. But, as I've tried to argue in these pages, to the imputed "truth" or "accuracy" of these findings, the feminist must oppose the painfully obvious truism that what is attended to in a literary work, and hence what is reported about it, is often determined not so much by the work itself as by the critical technique or aesthetic criteria through which it is filtered or, rather, read and decoded. All the feminist is asserting, then, is her own equivalent right to liberate new (and perhaps different) significances from these same texts; and, at the same time, her right to choose which features of a text she takes as relevant because she is, after all, asking new and different questions of it. In the process, she claims neither definitiveness nor structural completeness for her different readings and reading systems, but only their usefulness in recognizing the particular achievements of woman-as-author and their applicability in conscientiously decoding woman-as-sign.

That these alternate foci of critical attentiveness will result in alternate readings or interpretations of the same text — even among feminists — should be no cause for alarm. Such developments illustrate only the pluralist contention that, "in approaching a text of any complexity . . . the reader must choose to emphasize certain aspects which seem to him crucial" and that, "in fact, the variety of readings which we have for many works is a function of the selection of crucial aspects made by the variety of readers." Robert Scholes, from whom I've been quoting, goes so far as to assert that "there is no single 'right' reading for any complex literary work," and, following the Russian formalist school, he observes that "we do not speak of readings that are simply true or false, but of readings that are more or less rich, strategies that are more or less appropriate."[30] Because those who share the term "feminist" nonetheless practice a diversity of critical strategies, leading, in some cases, to quite different readings, we must acknowledge among ourselves that sister critics, "having chosen to tell a different story, may in their interpretation identify different aspects of the meanings conveyed by the same passage."[31]

Adopting a "pluralist" label does not mean, however, that we cease to disagree; it means only that we entertain the possibility that different readings, even of the same text, may be differently useful, even illuminating, within different contexts of inquiry. It means, in effect, that we enter a dialectical process of examining, testing, even trying out the contexts — be they prior critical assumptions or explicitly stated ideological stances (or some combination of the two) — that led to the disparate readings. Not all will be equally acceptable to every one of us, of course, and even those prior assumptions or ideologies that are acceptable may call for further refinement and/or clarification. But, at the very least,

[29]Annette Kolodny, "Literary Criticism," Review Essay in *Signs* 2, no. 2 (Winter 1976): 420. [Au.]

[30]Scholes, *Structuralism in Literature,* pp. 144–45. These comments appear within his explication of Tzvetan Todorov's theory of reading. [Au.]

[31]I borrow this concise phrasing of pluralistic modesty from M. H. Abrams's "The Deconstructive Angel," *Critical Inquiry* 3, no. 3 (Spring 1977): 427. Indications of the pluralism that was to mark feminist inquiry were to be found in the diversity of essays collected by Susan Koppelman Cornillon for her early and ground-breaking anthology, *Images of Women in Fiction: Feminist Perspectives* (Bowling Green, Ohio: Bowling Green University Popular Press, 1972). [Au.]

because we will have grappled with the assumptions that led to it, we will be better able to articulate *why* we find a particular reading or interpretation adequate or inadequate. This kind of dialectical process, moreover, not only makes us more fully aware of what criticism is, and how it functions; it also gives us access to its future possibilities, making us conscious, as R. P. Blackmur put it, "of what we have done," "of what can be done next, or done again,"[32] or, I would add, of what can be done differently. To put it still another way: just because we will no longer tolerate the specifically sexist omissions and oversights of earlier critical schools and methods does not mean that, in their stead, we must establish our own "party line."

In my view, our purpose is not and should not be the formulation of any single reading method or potentially procrustean set of critical procedures nor, even less, the generation of prescriptive categories for some dreamed-of nonsexist literary canon.[33] Instead, as I see it, our task is to initiate nothing less than a playful pluralism, responsive to the possibilities of multiple critical schools and methods, but captive of none, recognizing that the many tools needed for our analysis will necessarily be largely inherited and only partly of our own making. Only by employing a plurality of methods will we protect ourselves from the temptation of so oversimplifying any text — and especially those particularly offensive to us — that we render ourselves unresponsive to what Scholes has called "its various systems of meaning and their interaction."[34] Any text we deem worthy of our critical attention is usually, after all, a locus of many and varied kinds of (personal, thematic, stylistic, structural, rhetorical, etc.) relationships. So, whether we tend to treat a text as a *mimesis,* in which words are taken to be recreating or representing viable worlds; or whether we prefer to treat a text as a kind of equation of communication, in which decipherable messages are passed from writers to readers; and whether we locate meaning as inherent in the text, the act of reading, or in some collaboration between reader and text — whatever our predilection, let us not generate from it a straitjacket that limits the scope of possible analysis. Rather, let us generate an ongoing dialogue of competing potential possibilities — among feminists and, as well, between feminist and nonfeminist critics.

The difficulty of what I describe does not escape me. The very idea of pluralism seems to threaten a kind of chaos for the future of literary inquiry while, at the same time, it seems to deny the hope of establishing some basic conceptual model which can organize all data — the hope which always begins any analytical exercise. My effort here, however, has been to demonstrate the essential delusions that inform such objections: If literary inquiry has historically escaped chaos by establishing canons, then it has only substituted one mode of arbitrary action for another — and, in this case, at the expense of half the population. And if feminists openly acknowledge ourselves as pluralists, then we do not give up the search for patterns of opposition and connection — probably the basis of thinking itself; what we give up is simply the arrogance of claiming that our work is either exhaustive or definitive. (It is, after all, the identical arrogance we are asking our nonfeminist colleagues to abandon.) If this kind of pluralism appears to threaten both the present coherence of and the inherited aesthetic criteria for a canon of "greats," then, as I have earlier argued, it is precisely that threat which, alone, can free us from the prejudices, the strictures, and the blind spots of the past. In feminist hands, I would add, it is less a threat than a promise.

What unites and repeatedly invigorates feminist literary criticism, then, is neither dogma nor method but, as I have indicated earlier, an acute and impassioned *attentiveness* to the ways in which primarily male structures of power are inscribed (or encoded) within our literary inheri-

[32]R. P. Blackmur, "A Burden for Critics," *The Hudson Review* 1 (1948): 171. Blackmur, of course, was referring to the way in which criticism makes us unconscious of how art functions; I use his wording here because I am arguing that that same awareness must also be focused on the critical act itself. "Consciousness," he avers, "is the way we feel the critic's burden." [Au.]

[33]I have earlier elaborated my objection to prescriptive categories for literature in "The Feminist as Literary Critic," Critical Response in *Critical Inquiry* 2, no. 4 (Summer 1976): 827–28. [Au.]

[34]Scholes, *Structuralism in Literature,* pp. 151–52. [Au.]

tance; the consequences of that encoding for women — as characters, as readers, and as writers; and, with that, a shared analytic *concern* for the implications of that encoding not only for a better understanding of the past, but also for an improved reordering of the present and future as well. If that *concern* identifies feminist literary criticism as one of the many academic arms of the larger women's movement, then that *attentiveness,* within the halls of academe, poses no less a challenge for change, generating, as it does, the three propositions explored here. The critical pluralism that inevitably follows upon those three propositions, however, bears little resemblance to what Lillian Robinson has called "the greatest bourgeois theme of all, the myth of pluralism, with its consequent rejection of ideological commitment as 'too simple' to embrace the (necessarily complex) truth."[35] Only ideological commitment could have gotten us to enter the minefield, putting in jeopardy our careers and our livelihood. Only the power of ideology to transform our conceptual worlds, and the inspiration of that ideology to liberate long-suppressed energies and emotions, can account for our willingness to take on critical tasks that, in an earlier decade, would have been "abandoned in despair or apathy."[36] The fact of differences among us proves only that, despite our shared commitments, we have nonetheless refused to shy away from complexity, preferring rather to openly disagree than to give up either intellectual honesty or hard-won insights.

Finally, I would argue, pluralism informs feminist literary inquiry not simply as a description of what already exists but, more importantly, as the only critical stance consistent with the current status of the larger women's movement. Segmented and variously focused, the different women's organizations neither espouse any single system of analysis nor, as a result, express any wholly shared, consistently articulated ideology. The ensuing loss in effective organization and political clout is a serious one, but it has not been paralyzing; in spite of our differences, we have united to *act* in areas of clear mutual concern (the push for the Equal Rights Amendment is probably the most obvious example). The trade-off, as I see it, has made possible an ongoing and educative dialectic of analysis and profferred solutions, protecting us thereby from the inviting traps of reductionism and dogma. And so long as this dialogue remains active, both our politics and our criticism will be free of dogma — but never, I hope, of feminist ideology, in all its variety. For, "whatever else ideologies may be — projections of unacknowledged fears, disguises for ulterior motives, phatic expressions of group solidarity" (and the women's movement, to date, has certainly been all of these, and more) — whatever ideologies express, they are, as Clifford Geertz astutely observes, "most distinctively, maps of problematic social reality and matrices for the creation of collective conscience." And despite the fact that "ideological advocates . . . tend as much to obscure as to clarify the true nature of the problems involved," as Geertz notes, "they at least call attention to their existence and, by polarizing issues, make continued neglect more difficult. Without Marxist attack, there would have been no labor reform; without Black Nationalists, no deliberate speed."[37] Without Seneca Falls, I would add, no enfranchisement of women, and without "consciousness raising," no feminist literary criticism nor, even less, women's studies.

Ideology, however, only truly manifests its power by ordering the *sum* of our actions.[38] If feminist criticism calls anything into question, it must be that dog-eared myth of intellectual neutrality. For, what I take to be the underlying spirit, or message, of any consciously ideologically premised criticism — that is, that ideas are

[35]Lillian Robinson, "Dwelling in Decencies: Radical Criticism and the Feminist Perspective," *College English* 32, no. 8 (May 1971); reprinted in *Sex, Class, and Culture,* p. 11. [Au.]

[36]"Ideology bridges the emotional gap between things as they are and as one would have them be, thus insuring the performance of roles that might otherwise be abandoned in despair or apathy," comments Geertz in "Ideology as a Cultural System," p. 205. [Au.]

[37]Ibid., p. 220, 205. [Au.]

[38]I here follow Fredric Jameson's view in *The Prison-House of Language: A Critical Account of Structuralism and Russian Formalism* (Princeton: Princeton University Press, 1974), p. 107, that: "Ideology would seem to be that grillwork of form, convention, and belief which orders our actions." [Au.]

important *because* they determine the ways we live, or want to live, in the world — is vitiated by confining those ideas to the study, the classroom, or the pages of our books. To write chapters decrying the sexual stereotyping of women in our literature, while closing our eyes to the sexual harassment of our women students and colleagues; to display Katherine Hepburn and Rosalind Russell in our courses on "The Image of the Independent Career Women in Film," while managing not to notice the paucity of female administrators on our own campus; to study the women who helped make universal enfranchisement a political reality, while keeping silent about our activist colleagues who are denied promotion or tenure; to include segments on "Women in the Labor Movement" in our American studies or women's studies courses, while remaining willfully ignorant of the department secretary fired for her efforts to organize a clerical workers' union; to glory in the delusions of "merit," "privilege," and "status" which accompany campus life in order to insulate ourselves from the millions of women who labor in poverty — all this is not merely hypocritical; it destroys both the spirit and the meaning of what we are about. It puts us, however unwittingly, in the service of those who laid the minefield in the first place. In my view, it is a fine thing for many of us, individually, to have traversed the minefield; but that happy circumstance will only prove of lasting importance if, together, we expose it for what it is (the male fear of sharing power and significance with women) and deactivate its components, so that others, after us, may literally dance through the minefield.

Lillian S. Robinson

b. 1941

Lillian S. Robinson was born in New York City and educated at Brown, New York University, and Columbia, where she received her Ph.D. in comparative literature in 1974. Her dissertation, Monstrous Regiment: The Lady Knight in Sixteenth-Century Epic, *was published in 1985. Robinson taught American studies and women's studies at the State University of New York at Buffalo, but since the late 1970s she has been an academic vagabond, teaching as visiting professor for a semester or two at colleges like Albright, Scripps, San Diego State, the University of Hawaii, the University of Tulsa, and the University of Texas, and eking out a living on fellowships, writing and lecture fees, and unemployment insurance and food stamps in the intervening times. Robinson's rootlessness has a great deal to do with the fact that her radical social critique is her life, not merely her ideology; she wants not just to study the world, but to change it. Robinson was jailed for her protest activities during the late 1960s. As her radicalism moved into feminist themes, she became outraged at the way that women's studies tended to leave out poor women, minority women, and working-class women and to concentrate on more genteel modes of oppression. And she was scandalized by the fact that academic feminist theory had become an attractive option with a quick route to the top at the same time that women's income remained 71 percent of men's. Her early essays, collected in* Sex, Class, and Culture *(1978), insist that the preference for masculine values and male authors over feminine and female ones is only one of a series of preordained imbalances in Western society, and that working-class texts and "low-brow" forms of entertainment are marginalized as entirely as those by women. Robinson's more recent work has appeared in* Feminist Scholarship: Kindling in the Groves of Academe *(1985) and* In the Canon's Mouth *(1997) and* Women and Fictions *(forthcoming). Robinson is currently professor of English at East Carolina University at Greenville. The following essay was originally published in* Tulsa Studies in Women's Literature *2 (1983).*

Treason Our Text: *Feminist Challenges to the Literary Canon*

Successful plots have often had gunpowder in them. Feminist critics have gone so far as to take treason to the canon as our text.[1]

— JANE MARCUS

THE LOFTY SEAT OF CANONIZED BARDS (Pollok, 1827)

As with many other restrictive institutions, we are hardly aware of it until we come into conflict with it; the elements of the literary canon are simply absorbed by the apprentice scholar and critic in the normal course of graduate education, without anyone's ever seeming to inculcate or defend them. Appeal, were any necessary, would be to the other meaning of "canon," that is, to established standards of judgment and of taste. Not that either definition is presented as rigid and immutable — far from it, for lectures in literary history are full of wry references to a benighted though hardly distant past when, say, the metaphysical poets were insufficiently appreciated or Vachel Lindsay[2] was the most modern poet recognized in American literature. Whence the acknowledgment of a subjective dimension, sometimes generalized as "sensibility," to the category of taste. Sweeping modifications in the canon are said to occur because of changes in collective sensibility, but individual admissions and elevations from "minor" to "major" status tend to be achieved by successful critical promotion, which is to say, demonstration that a particular author does meet generally accepted criteria of excellence.

The results, moreover, are nowhere codified: they are neither set down in a single place, nor are they absolutely uniform. In the visual arts and in music, the cold realities of patronage, purchase, presentation in private and public collections, or performance on concert programs create the conditions for a work's canonical status or lack of it. No equivalent set of institutional arrangements exists for literature, however. The fact of publication and even the feat of remaining in print for generations, which are at least analogous to the ways in which pictures and music are displayed, are not the same sort of indicators; they represent less of an investment and hence less general acceptance of their canonicity. In the circumstances, it may seem somewhat of an exaggeration to speak of "the" literary canon, almost paranoid to call it an institution, downright hysterical to characterize that institution as restrictive. The whole business is so much more informal, after all, than any of these terms implies, the concomitant processes so much more gentlemanly. Surely, it is more like a gentlemen's agreement than a repressive instrument — isn't it?

But a gentleman is inescapably — that is, by definition — a member of a privileged class and of the male sex. From this perspective, it is probably quite accurate to think of the canon as an entirely gentlemanly artifact, considering how few works by nonmembers of that class and sex make it into the informal agglomeration of course syllabi, anthologies, and widely commented-upon "standard authors" that constitutes the canon as it is generally understood. For, beyond their availability on bookshelves, it is through the teaching and study — one might even say the habitual teaching and study — of certain works that they become institutionalized as canonical literature. Within that broad canon, moreover, those admitted but read only in advanced courses, com-

[1]Jane Marcus, "Gunpowder Treason and Plot," talk delivered at the School of Criticism and Theory, Northwestern University, colloquium "The Challenge of Feminist Criticism," November 1981. Seeking authority for the sort of creature a literary canon might be, I turned, like many another, to the *Oxford English Dictionary*. The tags that head up the several sections of this essay are a by-product of that effort rather than of any more exact and laborious scholarship. [Au.]

[2]Nicholas Vachel Lindsay (1879–1931), an American poet best known for "General William Booth Enters into Heaven" (1913) and "The Congo" (1914). [Ed.

mented upon only by more or less narrow specialists, are subjected to the further tyranny of "major" versus "minor."

For more than a decade now, feminist scholars have been protesting the apparently systematic neglect of women's experience in the literary canon, neglect that takes the form of distorting and misreading the few recognized female writers and excluding the others. Moreover, the argument runs, the predominantly male authors in the canon show us the female character and relations between the sexes in a way that both reflects and contributes to sexist ideology — an aspect of these classic works about which the critical tradition remained silent for generations. The feminist challenge, although intrinsically (and, to my mind, refreshingly) polemical, has not been simply a reiterated attack, but a series of suggested alternatives to the male-dominated membership and attitudes of the accepted canon. In this essay, I propose to examine these feminist alternatives, assess their impact on the standard canon, and propose some directions for further work. Although my emphasis in each section is on the substance of the challenge, the underlying polemic is, I believe, abundantly clear.

THE PRESENCE OF CANONIZED FOREFATHERS (Burke, 1790)

Start with the Great Books, the traditional desert-island ones, the foundation of courses in the Western humanistic tradition. No women authors, of course, at all, but within the works thus canonized, certain monumental female images:[3] Helen, Penelope, and Clytemnestra, Beatrice and the Dark Lady of the Sonnets, Bérénice, Cunégonde, and Margarete. The list of interesting female characters is enlarged if we shift to the Survey of English Literature and its classic texts; here, moreover, there is the possible inclusion of a female author or even several, at least as the course's implicit "historical background" ticks through and past the Industrial Revolution. It is a possibility that is not always honored in the observance. "*Beowulf* to Virginia Woolf" is a pleasant enough joke, but though lots of surveys begin with the Anglo-Saxon epic, not all that many conclude with *Mrs. Dalloway*. Even in the nineteenth century, the pace and the necessity of mass omissions may mean leaving out Austen, one of the Brontës, or Eliot. The analogous overview of American literary masterpieces, despite the relative brevity and modernity of the period considered, is likely to yield a similarly all-male pantheon; Emily Dickinson may be admitted — but not necessarily — and no one else even comes close.[4] Here again, the male-authored canon contributes to the body of infor-

[3]Helen and Penelope are the principal female characters in the *Iliad* and the *Odyssey*, respectively; Clytemnestra is the wife of Agamemnon and mistress of Aegisthus in Aeschylus's *Oresteia*. Beatrice is Beatrice Portinari, Dante's muse in the *Vita Nuova* and his guide through the *Paradiso;* the "Dark Lady of the Sonnets" is the addressee of Shakespeare's Sonnets 127–152. Bérénice, Cunégonde, and Margarete are the heroines, respectively, of Racine's tragedy *Bérénice* (1670), Voltaire's satire *Candide, or Optimism* (1759), and Goethe's verse drama *Faust*, Part One (1808). [Ed.]

[4]In a survey of 50 introductory courses in American literature offered at 25 U.S. colleges and universities, Emily Dickinson's name appeared more often than that of any other woman writer: 20 times. This frequency puts her in a fairly respectable twelfth place. Among the 61 most frequently taught authors, only 7 others are women; Edith Wharton and Kate Chopin are each mentioned 8 times, Sarah Orne Jewett and Anne Bradstreet 6 each, Flannery O'Connor 4 times, Willa Cather and Mary Wilkins Freeman each 3 times. The same list includes 5 black authors, all of them male. Responses from other institutions received too late for compilation only confirmed these findings. See Paul Lauter, "A Small Survey of Introductory Courses in American Literature," *Women's Studies Quarterly* 9 (Winter 1981): 12. In another study, 99 professors of English responded to a survey asking which works of American literature published since 1941 they thought should be considered classics and which books should be taught to college students. The work mentioned by the most respondents (59 citations) was Ralph Ellison's *Invisible Man*. No other work by a black appears among the top 20 that constitute the published list of results. Number 19, *The Complete Stories of Flannery O'Connor*, is the only work on this list by a woman. (*Chronicle of Higher Education*, September 29, 1982.) For British literature, the feminist claim is not that Austen, the Brontës, Eliot, and Woolf are habitually omitted, but rather that they are by no means always included in courses that, like the survey I taught at Columbia some years ago, had room for a single nineteenth-century novel. I know, however, of no systematic study of course offerings in this area more recent than Elaine Showalter's "Women in the Literary Curriculum," *College English* 32 (May 1971): 855–62. [Au.]

mation, stereotype, inference, and surmise about the female sex that is generally in the culture.

Once this state of affairs has been exposed, there are two possible approaches for feminist criticism. It can emphasize alternative readings of the tradition, readings that reinterpret women's character, motivations, and actions and that identify and challenge sexist ideology. Or it can concentrate on gaining admission to the canon for literature by women writers. Both sorts of work are being pursued, although, to the extent that feminist criticism has defined itself as a subfield of literary studies — as distinguished from an approach or method — it has tended to concentrate on writing by women.

In fact, however, the current wave of feminist theory began as criticism of certain key texts, both literary and paraliterary, in the dominant culture. Kate Millett, Eva Figes, Elizabeth Janeway, Germaine Greer, and Carolyn Heilbrun all use the techniques of essentially literary analysis on the social forms and forces surrounding those texts.[5] The texts themselves may be regarded as "canonical" in the sense that all have had significant impact on the culture as a whole, although the target being addressed is not literature or its canon.

In criticism that is more strictly literary in its scope, much attention has been concentrated on male writers in the American tradition. Books like Annette Kolodny's *The Lay of the Land* and Judith Fetterley's *The Resisting Reader* have no systematic, comprehensive equivalent in the criticism of British or European literature.[6] Both of these studies identify masculine values and imagery in a wide range of writings, as well as the alienation that is their consequence for women, men, and society as a whole. In a similar vein, Mary Ellmann's *Thinking About Women* examines ramifications of the tradition of "phallic criticism" as applied to writers of both sexes.[7] These books have in common with one another and with overarching theoretical manifestos like *Sexual Politics* a sense of having been betrayed by a culture that was supposed to be elevating, liberating, and one's own.

By contrast, feminist work devoted to that part of the Western tradition which is neither American nor contemporary is likelier to be more evenhanded. "Feminist critics," declare Lenz, Greene, and Neely in introducing their collection of essays on Shakespeare, "recognize that the greatest artists do not necessarily duplicate in their art the orthodoxies of their culture; they may exploit them to create character or intensify conflict, they may struggle with, criticize, or transcend them."[8] From this perspective, Milton may come in for some censure, Shakespeare and Chaucer for both praise and blame, but the clear intention of a feminist approach to these classic authors is to enrich our understanding of what is going on in the texts, as well as how — for better, for worse, or for both — they have shaped our own literary and social ideas.[9] At its angriest, none of this reinterpretation offers a fundamental challenge to the canon *as canon;* although it posits new values, it never suggests that, in the light of those

[5]Kate Millett, *Sexual Politics* (Garden City, N.Y.: Doubleday, 1970): Eva Figes, *Patriarchal Attitudes* (New York: Stein & Day, 1970); Elizabeth Janeway, *Man's World, Woman's Place: A Study in Social Mythology* (New York: William Morrow, 1971); Germaine Greer, *The Female Eunuch* (New York: McGraw-Hill, 1971): Carolyn G. Heilbrun, *Toward a Recognition of Androgyny* (New York: Harper & Row, 1974). The phenomenon these studies represent is discussed at greater length in a study of which I am a co-author; see Ellen Carol DuBois, Gail Paradise Kelly, Elizabeth Lapovsky Kennedy, Carolyn W. Korsmeyer, and Lillian S. Robinson, *Feminist Scholarship: Kindling in the Groves of Academe* (Urbana: University of Illinois Press, 1985). [Au.]

[6]Annette Kolodny, *The Lay of the Land: Metaphor as Experience and History in American Life and Letters* (Chapel Hill: University of North Carolina Press, 1975); Judith Fetterley, *The Resisting Reader: A Feminist Approach to American Fiction* (Bloomington: Indiana University Press, 1978). [Au.]

[7]Mary Ellmann, *Thinking About Women* (New York: Harcourt, Brace & World, 1968). [Au.]

[8]Carolyn Ruth Swift Lenz, Gayle Greene, and Carol Thomas Neely, eds. *The Woman's Part: Feminist Criticism of Shakespeare* (Urbana: University of Illinois Press, 1980), p. 4. In this vein, see also Juliet Dusinberre, *Shakespeare and the Nature of Woman* (London: Macmillan, 1975); Irene G. Dash, *Wooing, Wedding, and Power: Women in Shakespeare's Plays* (New York: Columbia University Press, 1981). [Au.]

[9]Sandra M. Gilbert, "Patriarchal Poetics and the Woman Reader: Reflections on Milton's Bogey," *PMLA* 93 (May 1978): 368–82. The articles on Chaucer and Shakespeare in *The Authority of Experience: Essays in Feminist Criticism*, ed. Arlyn Diamond and Lee R. Edwards (Amherst: University of Massachusetts Press, 1977), reflect the complementary tendency. [Au.]

values, we ought to reconsider whether the great monuments are really so great, after all.

SUCHE AS ALL THE WORLDE HATHE CONFIRMED AND AGREED UPON, THAT IT IS AUTHENTIQUE AND CANONICAL. (T. Wilson, 1553)

In an evolutionary model of feminist studies in literature, work on male authors is often characterized as "early," implicitly primitive, whereas scholarship on female authors is the later development, enabling us to see women — the writers themselves and the women they write about — as active agents rather than passive images or victims. This implicit characterization of studies addressed to male writers is as inaccurate as the notion of an inexorable evolution. In fact, as the very definition of feminist criticism has come increasingly to mean scholarship and criticism devoted to women writers, work on the male tradition has continued. By this point, there has been a study of the female characters or the views on the woman question of every major — perhaps every known — author in Anglo-American, French, Russian, Spanish, Italian, German, and Scandinavian literature.[10]

Nonetheless, is it an undeniable fact that most feminist criticism focuses on women writers, so that the feminist efforts to humanize the canon have usually meant bringing a woman's point of view to bear by incorporating works by women into the established canon. The least threatening way to do so is to follow the accustomed pattern of making the case for individual writers one by one. The case here consists in showing that an already recognized woman author has been denied her rightful place, presumably because of the general devaluation of female efforts and subjects. More often than not, such work involves showing that a woman already securely established in the canon belongs in the first rather than the second rank. The biographical and critical efforts of R.W.B. Lewis and Cynthia Griffin Wolff, for example, have attempted to enhance Edith Wharton's reputation in this way.[11] Obviously, no challenge is presented to the particular notions of literary quality, timelessness, universality, and other qualities that constitute the rationale for canonicity. The underlying argument, rather, is that consistency, fidelity to those values, requires recognition of at least the few best and best-known women writers. Equally obviously, this approach does not call the notion of the canon itself into question.

WE ACKNOWLEDGE IT CANONLIKE, BUT NOT CANONICALL. (Bishop Barlow, 1601)

Many feminist critics reject the method of case-by-case demonstration. The wholesale consignment of women's concerns and productions to a grim area bounded by triviality and obscurity cannot be compensated for by tokenism. True equity can be attained, they argue, only by opening up the canon to a much larger number of female voices. This is an endeavor that eventually brings basic aesthetic questions to the fore.

Initially, however, the demand for wider representation of female authors is substantiated by an extraordinary effort of intellectual reappropriation. The emergence of feminist literary study has been characterized, at the base, by scholarship devoted to the discovery, republication, and reappraisal of "lost" or undervalued writers and their work. From Rebecca Harding Davis and Kate Chopin through Zora Neale Hurston and Mina Loy to Meridel LeSueur and Rebecca West, reputations have been reborn or remade and a female countercanon has come into being, out of components that were largely unavailable even a dozen years ago.[12]

[10]As I learned when surveying fifteen years' worth of *Dissertation Abstracts* and MLA programs, much of this work has taken the form of theses or conference papers rather than books and journal articles. [Au.]

[11]See R. W. B. Lewis, *Edith Wharton: A Biography* (New York: Harper & Row, 1975); Cynthia Griffin Wolff, *A Feast of Words: The Triumph of Edith Wharton* (New York: Oxford University Press, 1977); see also Marlene Springer, *Edith Wharton and Kate Chopin: A Reference Guide* (Boston: G. K. Hall, 1976). [Au.]

[12]See, for instance, Rebecca Harding Davis, *Life in the Iron Mills* (Old Westbury, N.Y.: Feminist Press, 1972), with

In addition to constituting a feminist alternative to the male-dominated tradition, these authors also have a claim to representation in "the" canon. From this perspective, the work of recovery itself makes one sort of prima facie case, giving the lie to the assumption, where it has existed, that aside from a few names that are household words — differentially appreciated, but certainly well known — there simply has not been much serious literature by women. Before any aesthetic arguments have been advanced either for or against the admission of such works to the general canon, the new literary scholarship on women has demonstrated that the pool of potential applicants is far larger than anyone has hitherto suspected.

WOULD AUGUSTINE, IF HE HELD ALL THE BOOKS TO HAVE AN EQUAL RIGHT TO CANONICITY . . . HAVE PREFERRED SOME TO OTHERS? (W. Fitzgerald, trans. Whitaker, 1849)

But the aesthetic issues cannot be forestalled for very long. We need to understand whether the claim is being made that many of the newly recovered or validated texts by women meet existing criteria or, on the other hand, that those criteria themselves intrinsically exclude or tend to exclude women and hence should be modified or replaced. If this polarity is not, in fact, applicable to the process, what are the grounds for presenting a large number of new female candidates for (as it were) canonization?

The problem is epitomized in Nina Baym's introduction to her study of American women's fiction between 1820 and 1870:

> Reexamination of this fiction may well show it to lack the esthetic, intellectual, and moral complexity and artistry that we demand of great literature. I confess frankly that, although I have found much to interest me in these books, I have not unearthed a forgotten Jane Austen or George Eliot or hit upon the one novel that I would propose to set alongside *The Scarlet Letter*. Yet I cannot avoid the belief that "purely" literary criteria, as they have been employed to identify the best American works, have inevitably had a bias in favor of things male — in favor of, say, a whaling ship, rather than a sewing circle as a symbol of the human community. . . . While not claiming any literary greatness for any of the novels . . . in this study, I would like at least to begin to correct such a bias by taking their content seriously. And it is time, perhaps — though this task lies outside my scope here — to reexamine the grounds upon which certain hallowed American classics have been called great.[13]

Now, if students of literature may be allowed to confess to one Great Unreadable among the Great Books, my own *bête noire* has always been the white whale; I have always felt I was missing something in *Moby-Dick* that is clearly there for many readers and that is there for me when I read, say, Aeschylus or Austen. So I find Baym's strictures congenial, at first reading. Yet the contradictory nature of the position is also evident on the face of it. Am I or am I not being invited to construct a (feminist) aesthetic rationale for my impatience with *Moby-Dick?* Do Baym and the current of thought she represents accept "esthetic, intellectual, and moral complexity and

a biographical and critical Afterword by Tillie Olsen; Kate Chopin, *The Complete Works,* ed. Per Seyersted (Baton Rouge: Louisiana State University Press, 1969); Alice Walker, "In Search of Zora Neale Hurston," *Ms.,* March 1975, pp. 74–75; Robert Hemenway, *Zora Neale Hurston* (Urbana: University of Illinois Press, 1978); Zora Neale Hurston, *I Love Myself When I Am Laughing and Also When I Am Looking Mean and Impressive* (Old Westbury: Feminist Press, 1979), with introductory material by Alice Walker and Mary Helen Washington; Carolyn G. Burke, "Becoming Mina Loy," *Women's Studies* 7 (1979): 136–50; Meridel LeSueur, *Ripening* (Old Westbury: Feminist Press, 1981); on LeSueur, see also Mary McAnally, ed., *We Sing Our Struggle: A Tribute to Us All* (Tulsa, Okla.: Cardinal Press, 1982); *The Young Rebecca: Writings of Rebecca West, 1911–1917,* selected and introduced by Jane Marcus (New York: Viking Press, 1982).

The examples cited are all from the nineteenth and twentieth centuries. Valuable work has also been done on women writers before the Industrial Revolution. See Joan Goulianos, ed., *By a Woman Writt: Literature from Six Centuries by and about Women* (Indianapolis: Bobbs-Merrill, 1973); Mary R. Mahl and Helene Koon, eds., *The Female Spectator: English Women Writers before 1800* (Bloomington: Indiana University Press, 1977). [Au.]

[13]Nina Baym, *Women's Fiction: A Guide to Novels by and about Women in America, 1820–70* (Ithaca: Cornell University Press, 1978), pp. 14–15. [Au.]

artistry" as the grounds of greatness, or are they challenging those values as well?

As Myra Jehlen points out most lucidly, this attractive position will not bear close analysis: "[Baym] is having it both ways, admitting the artistic limitations of the women's fiction . . . and at the same time denying the validity of the rulers that measure these limitations, disdaining any ambition to reorder the literary canon and, on second thought, challenging the canon after all, or rather challenging not the canon itself but the grounds for its selection."[14] Jehlen understates the case, however, in calling the duality a paradox, which is, after all, an intentionally created and essentially rhetorical phenomenon. What is involved here is more like the *agony* of feminist criticism, for it is the champions of women's literature who are torn between defending the quality of their discoveries and radically redefining literary quality itself.

Those who are concerned with the canon as a pragmatic instrument rather than a powerful abstraction — the compilers of more equitable anthologies or course syllabi, for example — have opted for an uneasy compromise. The literature by women that they seek — as well as that by members of excluded racial and ethnic groups and by working people in general — conforms as closely as possible to the traditional canons of taste and judgment. Not that it reads like such literature as far as content and viewpoint are concerned, but the same words about artistic intent and achievement may be applied without absurdity. At the same time, the rationale for a new syllabus or anthology relies on a very different criterion: that of truth to the culture being represented, the *whole* culture and not the creation of an almost entirely male white elite. Again, no one seems to be proposing — aloud — the elimination of *Moby-Dick* or *The Scarlet Letter,* just squeezing them over somewhat to make room for another literary reality, which, joined with the existing canon, will come closer to telling the (poetic) truth.

The effect is pluralist, at best, and the epistemological assumptions underlying the search for a more fully representative literature are strictly empiricist: by including the perspective of women (who are, after all, half-the-population), we will know more about the culture as it actually was. No one suggests that there might be something in this literature itself that challenges the values and even the validity of the previously all-male tradition. There is no reason why the canon need speak with one voice or as one man on the fundamental questions of human experience. Indeed, even as an elite white male voice, it can hardly be said to do so. Yet a commentator like Baym has only to say "it is time, perhaps . . . to reexamine the grounds," *while not proceeding to do so,* for feminists to be accused of wishing to throw out the entire received culture. The argument could be more usefully joined, perhaps, if there *were* a current within feminist criticism that went beyond insistence on representation to consideration of precisely how inclusion of women's writing alters our view of the tradition. Or even one that suggested some radical surgery on the list of male authors usually represented.

After all, when we turn from the construction of pantheons, which have no *prescribed* number of places, to the construction of course syllabi, then something does have to be eliminated each time something else is added, and here ideologies, aesthetic and extra-aesthetic, do necessarily come into play. Is the canon and hence the syllabus based on it to be regarded as the compendium of excellence or as the record of cultural history? For there comes a point when the proponent of making the canon recognize the achievement of both sexes has to put up or shut up; either a given woman writer is good enough to replace some male writer on the prescribed reading list or she is not. If she is not, then either she should replace him anyway, in the name of telling the truth about the culture, or she should not, in the (unexamined) name of excellence. This is the debate that will have to be engaged and that has so far been broached only in the most "inclusionary" of terms. It is ironic that in American literature, where attacks on the male tradition have been most bitter and the reclamation of women writers so spectacular, the appeal has still been only to pluralism, generosity, and guilt. It is populism without the politics of populism.

[14]Myra Jehlen, "Archimedes and the Paradox of Feminist Criticism," *Signs* 6 (Summer 1981): 592. [Au.]

TO CANONIZE YOUR OWNE WRITERS (Polimanteria, 1595)

Although I referred earlier to a feminist counter-canon, it is only in certain rather restricted contexts that literature by women has in fact been explicitly placed "counter" to the dominant canon. Generally speaking, feminist scholars have been more concerned with establishing the existence, power, and significance of a specifically female tradition. Such a possibility is adumbrated in the title of Patricia Meyer Spacks's *The Female Imagination;* however, this book's overview of selected themes and stages in the female life-cycle as treated by some women writers neither broaches nor (obviously) suggests an answer to the question whether there is a female imagination and what characterizes it.[15]

Somewhat earlier, in her anthology of British and American women poets, Louise Bernikow had made a more positive assertion of a continuity and connection subsisting among them.[16] She leaves it to the poems, however, to forge their own links, and, in a collection that boldly and incisively crosses boundaries between published and unpublished writing, literary and anonymous authorship, "high" art, folk art, and music, it is not easy for the reader to identify what the editor believes it is that makes women's poetry specifically *"women's."*

Ellen Moers centers her argument for a (trans-historical) female tradition upon the concept of "heroinism," a quality shared by women writers over time with the female characters they created.[17] Moers also points out another kind of continuity, documenting the way that women writers have read, commented on, and been influenced by the writings of other women who were their predecessors or contemporaries. There is also an unacknowledged continuity between the writer and her female reader. Elaine Showalter conceives the female tradition, embodied particularly in the domestic and sensational fiction of the nineteenth century, as being carried out through a kind of subversive conspiracy between author and audience.[18] Showalter is at her best in discussing this minor "women's fiction." Indeed, without ever making a case for popular genres as serious literature, she bases her arguments about a tradition more solidly on them than on acknowledged major figures like Virginia Woolf. By contrast, Sandra Gilbert and Susan Gubar focus almost exclusively on key literary figures, bringing women writers and their subjects together through the theme of perceived female aberration — in the act of literary creation itself, as well as in the behavior of the created persons or personae.[19]

Moers's vision of a continuity based on "heroinism" finds an echo in later feminist criticism that posits a discrete, perhaps even autonomous "women's culture." The idea of such a culture has been developed by social historians studying the "homosocial" world of nineteenth-century women.[20] It is a view that underlies, for example, Nina Auerbach's study of relationships among women in selected novels, where strong, supportive ties among mothers, daughters, sisters, and female friends not only constitute the real history in which certain women are conceived as living but function as a normative element as well.[21]

[15]Patricia Meyer Spacks, *The Female Imagination* (New York: Alfred A. Knopf, 1975). [Au.]

[16]*The World Split Open: Four Centuries of Women Poets in England and America, 1552–1950*, ed. and intro. Louise Bernikow (New York: Vintage Books, 1974). [Au.]

[17]Ellen Moers, *Literary Women: The Great Writers* (Garden City, N.Y.: Doubleday, 1976). [Au.]

[18]Elaine Showalter, *A Literature of Their Own: British Women Novelists from Brontë to Lessing* (Princeton, N.J.: Princeton University Press, 1977). [Au.]

[19]Sandra M. Gilbert and Susan Gubar, *The Madwoman in the Attic: The Woman Writer and the Nineteenth-Century Literary Imagination* (New Haven, Conn.: Yale University Press, 1979). [Au.]

[20]Carroll-Smith Rosenberg, "The Female World of Love and Ritual: Relations Between Women in Nineteenth-Century America," *Signs* 1 (Fall 1975): 1–30; Nancy F. Cott, *The Bonds of Womanhood: "Woman's Sphere" in New England, 1780–1830* (New Haven, Conn.: Yale University Press, 1977). [Au.]

[21]Nina Auerbach, *Communities of Women: An Idea in Fiction* (Cambridge, Mass.: Harvard University Press, 1979). See also Janet M. Todd, *Women's Friendship in Literature* (New York: Columbia University Press, 1980); Louise Bernikow, *Among Women* (New York: Crown, 1980). [Au.]

That is, fiction in which positive relations subsist to nourish the heroine comes off much better, from Auerbach's point of view, than fiction in which such relations do not exist.

In contrast, Judith Lowder Newton sees the heroines of women's fiction as active, rather than passive, precisely because they do live in a man's world, not an autonomous female one.[22] Defining their power as "ability" rather than "control," she perceives "both a preoccupation with power and subtle power strategies" being exercised by the women in novels by Fanny Burney, Jane Austen, Charlotte Brontë, and George Eliot. Understood in this way, the female tradition, whether or not it in fact reflects and fosters a "culture" of its own, provides an alternative complex of possibilities for women, to be set beside the pits and pedestals offered by all too much of the Great Tradition.

CANONIZE SUCH A MULTIFARIOUS GENEALOGIE OF COMMENTS. (Nashe, 1593)

Historians like Smith-Rosenberg and Cott are careful to specify that their generalizations extend only to white middle- and upper-class women of the nineteenth century. Although literary scholars are equally scrupulous about the national and temporal boundaries of their subject, they tend to use the gender term comprehensively. In this way, conclusions about "women's fiction" or "female consciousness" have been drawn or jumped to from considering a body of work whose authors are all white and comparatively privileged. Of the critical studies I have mentioned, only Bernikow's anthology, *The World Split Open,* brings labor songs, black women's blues lyrics, and anonymous ballads into conjunction with poems that were written for publication by professional writers, both black and white. The other books, which build an extensive case for a female tradition that Bernikow only suggests, delineate their subject in such a way as to exclude not only black and working-class authors but any notion that race and class might be relevant categories in the definition and apprehension of "women's literature." Similarly, even for discussions of writers who were known to be lesbians, this aspect of the female tradition often remains unacknowledged; worse yet, some of the books that develop the idea of a female tradition are openly homophobic, employing the word "lesbian" only pejoratively.[23]

Black and lesbian scholars, however, have directed much less energy to polemics against the feminist "mainstream" than to concrete, positive work on the literature itself. Recovery and reinterpretation of a wealth of unknown or undervalued texts has suggested the existence of both a black women's tradition and a lesbian tradition. In a clear parallel with the relationship between women's literature in general and the male-dominated tradition, both are by definition part of women's literature, but they are also distinct from and independent of it.

There are important differences, however, between these two traditions and the critical effort surrounding them. Black feminist criticism has the task of demonstrating that, in the face of all the obstacles a racist and sexist society has been able to erect, there is a continuity of black women who have written and written well. It is a matter of gaining recognition for the quality of the writing itself and respect for its principal subject, the lives and consciousness of black women. Black women's literature is also an element of black literature as a whole, where the recognized voices have usually been male. A triple imperative is therefore at work: establishing a discrete and significant black female tradition, then situating it within black literature and (along with the rest of that literature) within the common Ameri-

[22]Judith Lowder Newton, *Women, Power, and Subversion: Social Strategies in British Fiction* (Athens: University of Georgia Press, 1981). [Au.]

[23]On the failings of feminist criticism with respect to black and/or lesbian writers, see Barbara Smith, "Toward a Black Feminist Criticism," *Conditions,* 2 (1977); Mary Helen Washington, "New Lives and New Letters: Black Women Writers at the End of the Seventies," *College English,* 43 (1981); Bonnie Zimmerman, "What Has Never Been: An Overview of Lesbian Feminist Literary Criticism," *Feminist Studies,* 7 (1981). [Au.]

can literary heritage.[24] So far, unfortunately, each step toward integration has met with continuing exclusion. A black women's tradition has been recovered and reevaluated chiefly through the efforts of black feminist scholars. Only some of that work has been accepted as part of either a racially mixed women's literature or a two-sex black literature. As for the gatekeepers of American literature in general, how many of them are willing to swing open the portals even for Zora Neale Hurston or Paule Marshall? How many have heard of them?

The issues of "inclusion," moreover, brings up questions that echo those raised by opening the male-dominated canon to women. How do generalizations about women's literature "as a whole" change when the work of black women is not merely added to but fully incorporated into that tradition? How does our sense of black literary history change? And what implications do these changes have for reconsideration of the American canon?

Whereas many white literary scholars continue to behave as if there were no major black women writers, most are prepared to admit that certain well-known white writers were lesbians for all or part of their lives. The problem is getting beyond a position that says either "so *that's* what was wrong with her!" or, alternatively, "it doesn't matter who she slept with — we're talking about literature." Much lesbian feminist criticism has addressed theoretical questions about *which* literature is actually part of the lesbian tradition, all writing by lesbians, for example, or all writing by women about women's relations with one another. Questions of class and race enter here as well, both in their own guise and in the by now familiar form of "aesthetic standards." Who speaks for the lesbian community: the highly educated experimentalist with an unearned income or the naturalistic working-class autobiographer? Or are both the *same kind* of foremother, reflecting the community's range of cultural identities and resistance?[25]

A CHEAPER WAY OF CANON-MAKING IN A CORNER (Baxter, 1639)

It is not only members of excluded social groups, however, who have challenged the fundamentally elite nature of the existing canon. "Elite" is a literary as well as a social category. It is possible to argue for taking all texts seriously as texts without arguments based on social oppression or cultural exclusion, and popular genres have therefore been studied as part of the female literary tradition. Feminists are not in agreement as to whether domestic and sentimental fiction, the female Gothic, the women's sensational novel functioned as instruments of expression, repression, or subversion, but they have successfully revived interest in the question as a legitimate cultural issue.[26] It is no longer automatically as-

[24]See, e.g., Smith, "Toward a Black Feminist Criticism"; Barbara Christian, *Black Women Novelists: The Development of a Tradition, 1892–1976* (Westport, Conn.: Greenwood Press, 1980); Erlene Stetson, ed., *Black Sister: Poetry by Black American Women, 1764–1980* (Bloomington: Indiana University Press, 1981) and its forthcoming sequel; Gloria Hull, "Black Women Poets from Wheatley to Walker," in *Sturdy Black Bridges: Visions of Black Women in Literature*, ed. Roseann P. Bell et al. (Garden City, N.Y.: Anchor Books, 1979); Mary Helen Washington, "Introduction: In Pursuit of Our Own History," *Midnight Birds: Stories of Contemporary Black Women Writers* (Garden City, N.Y.: Anchor Books, 1980); the essays and bibliographies in *But Some of Us Are Brave: Black Women's Studies*, ed. Gloria Hull, Patricia Bell Scott, and Barbara Smith (Old Westbury: Feminist Press, 1982). [Au.]

[25]See Zimmerman, "What Has Never Been"; Adrienne Rich, "Jane Eyre: Trials of a Motherless Girl," *Lies, Secrets, and Silence: Selected Prose, 1966–1978* (New York: W. W. Norton, 1979); Lillian Faderman, *Surpassing the Love of Men: Romantic Friendship and Love Between Women from the Renaissance to the Present* (New York: William Morrow, 1981); the literary essays in *Lesbian Studies*, ed. Margaret Cruikshank (Old Westbury, N.Y.: Feminist Press, 1982). [Au.]

[26]Some examples on different sides of the question are: Ann Douglas, *The Feminization of American Culture* (New York: Alfred A. Knopf, 1976); Elaine Showalter, *A Literature of Their Own* and her article "Dinah Mulock Craik and the Tactics of Sentiment: A Case Study in Victorian Female Authorship," *Feminist Studies* 2 (May 1975): 5–23; Katherine Ellis, "Paradise Lost: The Limits of Domesticity in the Nineteenth-Century Novel," *Feminist Studies* 2 (May 1975): 55–65. [Au.]

sumed that literature addressed to the mass female audience is necessarily bad because it is sentimental, or for that matter, sentimental because it is addressed to that audience. Feminist criticism has examined without embarrassment an entire literature that was previously dismissed solely because it was popular with women and affirmed standards and values associated with femininity. And proponents of the "continuous tradition" and "women's culture" positions have insisted that this material be placed beside women's "high" art as part of the articulated and organic female tradition.

This point of view remains controversial within the orbit of women's studies, but the real problems start when it comes into contact with the universe of canon formation. Permission may have been given the contemporary critic to approach a wide range of texts, transcending and even ignoring the traditional canon. But in a context where the ground of struggle — highly contested, moreover — concerns Edith Wharton's advancement to somewhat more major status, fundamental assumptions have changed very little. Can Hawthorne's "d———d mob of scribbling women" *really* be invading the realms so long sanctified by Hawthorne himself and his brother geniuses? Is this what feminist criticism or even feminist cultural history means? Is it — to apply some outmoded and deceptively simple categories — a good development or a bad one? If these questions have not been raised, it is because women's literature and the female tradition tend to be evoked as an autonomous cultural experience, not impinging on the rest of literary history.

WISDOME UNDER A RAGGED COATE IS SELDOME CANONICALL. (Crosse, 1603)

Whether dealing with popular genres or high art, commentary on the female tradition usually has been based on work that was published at some time and was produced by professional writers. But feminist scholarship has also pushed back the boundaries of literature in other directions, considering a wide range of forms and styles in which women's writing — especially that of women who did not perceive themselves as writers — appears. In this way, women's letters, diaries, journals, autobiographies, oral histories, and private poetry have come under critical scrutiny as evidence of women's consciousness *and expression.*

Generally speaking, feminist criticism has been quite open to such material, recognizing that the very conditions that gave many women the impetus to write made it impossible for their culture to define them as writers. This acceptance has expanded our sense of possible forms and voices, but it has not challenged our received sense of appropriate style. What it amounts to is that if a woman writing in isolation and with no public audience in view nonetheless has "good" — that is, canonical — models, we are impressed with the strength of her text when she applies what she has assimilated about writing to her own experiences as a woman. If, however, her literary models were chosen from the same popular literature that some critics are now beginning to recognize as part of the female tradition, then she has not got hold of an expressive instrument that empowers her.

At the Modern Language Association meeting in 1976, I included in my paper the entire two-page autobiography of a participant in the Summer Schools for Women Workers held at Bryn Mawr in the first decades of the century. It is a circumstantial narrative in which events from the melancholy to the melodramatic are accumulated in a serviceable, somewhat hackneyed style. The anonymous "Seamer on Men's Underwear" had a unique sense of herself both as an individual and as a member of the working class. But was she a writer? Part of the audience was as moved as I was by the narrative, but the majority was outraged at the piece's failure to meet the criteria — particularly, the "complexity" criteria — of good art.

When I developed my remarks for publication, I wrote about the problems of dealing with an author who is trying too hard to write elegantly, and attempted to make the case that clichés or sentimentality need not be signals of meretricious prose and that ultimately it is honest writing for which criticism should be looking.[27]

[27]Lillian S. Robinson, "Working/Women/Writing," *Sex, Class, and Culture* (Bloomington: Indiana University Press, 1978), p. 252. [Au.]

Nowadays, I would also address the question of the female tradition, the role of popular fiction within it, and the influence of that fiction on its audience. It seems to me that, if we accept the work of the professional "scribbling woman," we have also to accept its literary consequences, not drawing the line at the place where that literature may have been the force that enabled an otherwise inarticulate segment of the population to grasp a means of expression and communication.

Once again, the arena is the female tradition itself. If we are thinking in terms of canon formation, it is the alternative canon. Until the aesthetic arguments can be fully worked out in the feminist context, it will be impossible to argue, in the general marketplace of literary ideas, that the novels of Henry James ought to give place — a *little* place, even — to the diaries of his sister Alice. At this point, I suspect most of our male colleagues would consider such a request, even in the name of Alice James, much less the Seamer on Men's Underwear, little more than a form of "reverse discrimination" — a concept to which some of them are already overly attached. It is up to feminist scholars, when we determine that this is indeed the right course to pursue, to demonstrate that such an inclusion would constitute a genuinely affirmative action for all of us.

The development of feminist literary criticism and scholarship has already proceeded through a number of identifiable stages. Its pace is more reminiscent of the survey course than of the slow processes of canon formation and revision, and it has been more successful in defining and sticking to its own intellectual turf, the female countercanon, than in gaining general canonical recognition for Edith Wharton, Fanny Fern, or the female diarists of the Westward Expansion. In one sense, the more coherent our sense of the female tradition is, the stronger will be our eventual case. Yet the longer we wait, the more comfortable the women's literature ghetto — separate, apparently autonomous, and far from equal — may begin to feel.

At the same time, I believe the challenge cannot come only by means of the patent value of the work of women. We must pursue the questions certain of us have raised and retreated from as to the eternal verity of the received standards of greatness or even goodness. And, while not abandoning our newfound female tradition, we have to return to confrontation with "the" canon, examining it as a source of ideas, themes, motifs, and myths about the two sexes. The point in so doing is not to label and hence dismiss even the most sexist literary classics, but to enable all of us to apprehend them, finally, in all their human dimensions.

Barbara Smith

b. 1946

For at least twenty years, Barbara Smith has been a writer, a teacher, and a black feminist leader. Born in Cleveland, Smith was educated at Mount Holyoke College and at the University of Pittsburgh. She has taught English and women's studies at the University of Massachusetts, Barnard College, and New York University, and has been a visiting professor at the University of Minnesota and at Hobart and William Smith colleges. In 1974, she was cofounder of the Combahee River Collective, a black feminist group in Boston, which she helped direct until 1980. In 1982 she coedited All the Women Are White, All the Blacks Are Men, but Some of Us Are Brave, *the title of which reflects Smith's feeling that black women have frequently been excluded from both feminist and African American studies. In 1983 Smith edited* Home Girls, *a black feminist anthology highlighting the rela-*

tionships between race, gender, sexual orientation, and class that became a major influence on the current renaissance of African American women writers. A short story writer as well as a feminist theorist, Smith has been artist-in-residence at the Hambridge Center for the Arts, the Millay Colony, Yaddo, and the Blue Mountain Center. As a result of her many activities, Smith was presented with the Outstanding Woman of Color award for 1982 and the Women Educator's Curriculum Award for 1983. She is currently the publisher of the Kitchen Table/Women of Color Press. The following piece was published as a pamphlet in 1977, and reprinted in Some of Us Are Brave.

Toward a Black Feminist Criticism

For all my sisters, especially Beverly and Demita

I do not know where to begin. Long before I tried to write this I realized that I was attempting something unprecedented, something dangerous merely by writing about Black women writers from a feminist perspective and about Black lesbian writers from any perspective at all. These things have not been done. Not by white male critics, expectedly. Not by Black male critics. Not by white women critics who think of themselves as feminists. And most crucially not by Black women critics who, although they pay the most attention to Black women writers as a group, seldom use a consistent feminist analysis or write about Black lesbian literature. All segments of the literary world — whether establishment, progressive, Black, female, or lesbian — do not know, or at least act as if they do not know, that Black women writers and Black lesbian writers exist.

For whites, this specialized lack of knowledge is inextricably connected to their not knowing in any concrete or politically transforming way that Black women of any description dwell in this place. Black women's existence, experience, and culture and the brutally complex systems of oppression which shape these are in the "real world" of white and/or male consciousness beneath consideration, invisible, unknown.

This invisibility, which goes beyond anything that either Black men or white women experience and tell about in their writing, is one reason it is so difficult for me to know where to start. It seems overwhelming to break such a massive silence. Even more numbing, however, is the realization that so many of the women who will read this have not yet noticed us missing either from their reading matter, their politics, or their lives. It is galling that ostensible feminists and acknowledged lesbians have been so blinded to the implications of any womanhood that is not white womanhood and that they have yet to struggle with the deep racism in themselves that is at the source of this blindness.

I think of the thousands and thousands of books, magazines, and articles which have been devoted, by this time, to the subject of women's writing and I am filled with rage at the fraction of those pages that mention Black and other Third World women. I finally do not know how to begin because in 1977 I want to be writing this for a Black feminist publication, for Black women who know and love these writers as I do and who, if they do not yet know their names, have at least profoundly felt the pain of their absence.

The conditions that coalesce into the impossibilities of this essay have as much to do with politics as with the practice of literature. Any discussion of Afro-American writers can rightfully begin with the fact that for most of the time we have been in this country we have been categorically denied not only literacy, but the most minimal possibility of a decent human life. In her landmark essay, "In Search of Our Mothers' Gardens," Alice Walker discloses how the political, economic, and social restrictions of slavery and racism have historically stunted the creative lives of Black women.[1]

At the present time I feel that the politics of feminism have a direct relationship to the state of Black women's literature. A viable, autonomous Black feminist movement in this country would open up the space needed for the exploration of Black women's lives and the creation of consciously Black woman-identified art. At the same time a redefinition of the goals and strategies of the white feminist movement would lead to much needed change in the focus and content of what is now generally accepted as women's culture.

I want to make in this essay some connections between the politics of Black women's lives, what we write about, and our situation as artists. In order to do this I will look at how Black women have been viewed critically by outsiders, demonstrate the necessity for Black feminist criticism, and try to understand what the existence or nonexistence of Black lesbian writing reveals about the state of Black women's culture and the intensity of *all* Black women's oppression.

The role that criticism plays in making a body of literature recognizable and real hardly needs to be explained here. The necessity for nonhostile and perceptive analysis of works written by persons outside the "mainstream" of white/male cultural rule has been proven by the Black cultural resurgence of the 1960s and '70s and by the even more recent growth of feminist literary scholarship. For books to be read and remembered they have to be talked about. For books to be understood they must be examined in such a way that the basic intentions of the writers are at least considered. Because of racism Black literature has usually been viewed as a discrete subcategory of American literature and there have been Black critics of Black literature who did much to keep it alive long before it caught the attention of whites. Before the advent of specifically feminist criticism in this decade, books by white women, on the other hand, were not clearly perceived as the cultural manifestation of an oppressed people. It took the surfacing of the second wave of the North American feminist movement to expose the fact that these works contain a stunningly accurate record of the impact of patriarchal values and practice upon the lives of women and more significantly that literature by women provides essential insights into female experience.

In speaking about the current situation of Black women writers, it is important to remember that the existence of a feminist movement was an essential precondition to the growth of feminist literature, criticism, and women's studies, which focused at the beginning almost entirely upon investigations of literature. The fact that a parallel Black feminist movement has been much slower in evolving cannot help but have impact upon the situation of Black women writers and artists and explains in part why during this very same period we have been so ignored.

There is no political movement to give power or support to those who want to examine Black women's experience through studying our history, literature, and culture. There is no political presence that demands a minimal level of consciousness and respect from those who write or talk about our lives. Finally, there is not a developed body of Black feminist political theory whose assumptions could be used in the study of Black women's art. When Black women's books are dealt with at all, it is usually in the context of Black literature which largely ignores the implications of sexual politics. When white women look at Black women's works they are of course ill-equipped to deal with the subtleties of racial politics. A Black feminist approach to literature that embodies the realization that the politics of sex as well as the politics of race and class are crucially interlocking factors in the works of Black women writers is an absolute necessity. Until a Black feminist criticism exists we will not even know what these writers mean. The citations from a variety of critics which follow prove that without a Black feminist critical perspective not only are books by Black women misunderstood, they are destroyed in the process.

Jerry H. Bryant, the *Nation's* white male reviewer of Alice Walker's *In Love & Trouble: Stories of Black Women,* wrote in 1973:

[1]Alice Walker, "In Search of Our Mothers' Gardens," in *Ms.* (May 1974) and in *Southern Exposure* 4: 4, *Generations: Women in the South* (Winter 1977): 60–64. [Au.]

The subtitle of the collection, "Stories of Black Women," is probably an attempt by the publisher to exploit not only black subjects but feminine ones. There is nothing feminist but these stories, however.[2]

Blackness and feminism are to his mind mutually exclusive and peripheral to the act of writing fiction. Bryant of course does not consider that Walker might have titled the work herself, nor did he apparently read the book which unequivocally reveals the author's feminist consciousness.

In *The Negro Novel in America,* a book that Black critics recognize as one of the worst examples of white racist pseudoscholarship, Robert Bone cavalierly dismisses Ann Petry's classic, *The Street.* He perceives it to be ". . . a superficial social analysis" of how slums victimize their Black inhabitants.[3] He further objects that:

> It is an attempt to interpret slum life in terms of *Negro* experience, when a larger frame of reference is required. As Alain Locke has observed, "*Knock on Any Door* is superior to *The Street* because it designates class and environment, rather than mere race and environment, as its antagonist."[4]

Neither Robert Bone nor Alain Locke, the Black male critic he cites, can recognize that *The Street* is one of the best delineations in literature of how sex, race, *and* class interact to oppress Black women.

In her review of Toni Morrison's *Sula* for *The New York Times Book Review* in 1973, putative feminist Sara Blackburn makes similarly racist comments. She writes:

> . . . Toni Morrison is far too talented to remain only a marvelous recorder of the black side of provincial American life. If she is to maintain the large and serious audience she deserves, she is going to have to address a riskier contemporary reality than this beautiful but nevertheless distanced novel. *And if she does this, it seems to me that she might easily transcend that early and unintentionally limiting classification "black woman writer" and take her place among the most serious, important and talented American novelists now working.*[5] [Italics mine.]

Recognizing Morrison's exquisite gift, Blackburn unashamedly asserts that Morrison is "too talented" to deal with mere Black folk, particularly those double nonentities, Black women. In order to be accepted as "serious," "important," "talented," and "American," she must obviously focus her efforts upon chronicling the doings of white men.

The mishandling of Black women writers by whites is paralleled more often by their not being handled at all, particularly in feminist criticism. Although Elaine Showalter in her review essay on literary criticism for *Signs* states that: "The best work being produced today [in feminist criticism] is exacting and cosmopolitan," her essay is neither.[6] If it were, she would not have failed to mention a single Black or Third World woman writer, whether "major" or "minor," to cite her questionable categories. That she also does not even hint that lesbian writers of any color exist renders her purported overview virtually meaningless. Showalter obviously thinks that the identities of being Black and female are mutually exclusive, as this statement illustrates:

> Furthermore, there are other literary subcultures (black American novelists, for example) whose history offers a precedent for feminist scholarship to use.[7]

The idea of critics like Showalter *using* Black literature is chilling, a case of barely disguised cultural imperialism. The final insult is that she footnotes the preceding remark by pointing readers to works on Black literature by white males Robert Bone and Roger Rosenblatt!

Two recent works by white women, Ellen Moers's *Literary Women: The Great Writers* and Patricia Meyer Spacks's *The Female Imagina-*

[2]Jerry H. Bryant, "The Outskirts of a New City," in the *Nation* 12 (November 1973): 502. [Au.]

[3]Robert Bone, *The Negro Novel in America* (New Haven: Yale University Press, 1958), p. 180. [Au.]

[4]Idem. (*Knock on Any Door* is a novel by Black writer Willard Motley.) [Au.]

[5]Sara Blackburn, "You Still Can't Go Home Again," in *The New York Times Book Review,* 30 December 1973, p. 3. [Au.]

[6]Elaine Showalter, "Review Essay: Literary Criticism," *Signs* 2 (Winter 1975): 460. [Au.]

[7]Ibid., p. 445. [Au.]

tion, evidence the same racist flaw.[8] Moers includes the names of four Black and one Puertorriqueña writer in her seventy pages of bibliographical notes and does not deal at all with Third World women in the body of her book. Spacks refers to a comparison between Negroes (sic) and women in Mary Ellmann's *Thinking About Women* under the index entry, "blacks, women and." "*Black Boy* (Wright)" is the preceding entry. Nothing follows. Again there is absolutely no recognition that Black and female identity ever coexist, specifically in a group of Black women writers. Perhaps one can assume that these women do not know who Black women writers are, that they have little opportunity like most Americans to learn about them. Perhaps. Their ignorance seems suspiciously selective, however, particularly in the light of the dozens of truly obscure white women writers they are able to unearth. Spacks was herself employed at Wellesley College at the same time that Alice Walker was there teaching one of the first courses on Black women writers in the country.

I am not trying to encourage racist criticism of Black women writers like that of Sara Blackburn, to cite only one example. As a beginning I would at least like to see in print white women's acknowledgment of the contradictions of who and what are being left out of their research and writing.[9]

Black male critics can also *act* as if they do not know that Black women writers exist and are, of course, hampered by an inability to comprehend Black women's experience in sexual as well as racial terms. Unfortunately there are also those who are as virulently sexist in their treatment of Black women writers as their white male counterparts. Darwin Turner's discussion of Zora Neale Hurston in his *In a Minor Chord: Three Afro-American Writers and Their Search for Identity* is a frightening example of the near assassination of a great Black woman writer.[10] His descriptions of her and her work as "artful," "coy," "irrational," "superficial," and "shallow" bear no relationship to the actual quality of her achievements. Turner is completely insensitive to the sexual political dynamics of Hurston's life and writing.

In a recent interview the notoriously misogynist writer, Ishmael Reed, comments in this way upon the low sales of his newest novel:

> . . . but the book only sold 8000 copies. I don't mind giving out the figure: 8000. Maybe if I was one of those young *female* Afro-American writers that are so hot now, I'd sell more. You know, fill my books with ghetto women who can *do no wrong*. . . . But come on, I think I could have sold 8000 copies by myself.[11]

The politics of the situation of Black women are glaringly illuminated by this statement. Neither Reed nor his white male interviewer has the slightest compunction about attacking Black women in print. They need not fear widespread public denunciation since Reed's statement is in perfect agreement with the values of a society that hates Black people, women, and Black women. Finally the two of them feel free to base their actions on the premise that Black women are powerless to alter either their political or cultural oppression.

In her introduction to "A Bibliography of Works Written by American Black Women" Ora Williams quotes some of the reactions of her colleagues toward her efforts to do research on Black women. She writes:

> Others have reacted negatively with such statements as, "I really don't think you are going to find very much written," "Have 'they' written anything that is any good?" and, "I wouldn't go overboard with this woman's lib thing." When discussions touched on the possibility of teaching a course in

[8]Ellen Moers, *Literary Women: The Great Writers* (Garden City, N.Y.: Anchor Books, 1977); Patricia Meyer Spacks, *The Female Imagination* (New York: Avon Books, 1976). [Au.]

[9]An article by Nancy Hoffman, "White Women, Black Women: Inventing an Adequate Pedagogy," in the *Women's Studies Newsletter* 5: 1 & 2 (Spring 1977): 21–24, gives valuable insights into how white women can approach the writing of Black women. [Au.]

[10]Darwin T. Turner, *In a Minor Chord: Three Afro-American Writers and Their Search for Identity* (Carbondale and Edwardsville: Southern Illinois University Press, 1971). [Au.]

[11]John Domini, "Roots and Racism: An Interview with Ishmael Reed," in *The Boston Phoenix*, 5 April 1977, p. 20. [Au.]

which emphasis would be on the literature by Black women, one response was, "Ha, ha. That will certainly be the most nothing course ever offered!"[12]

A remark by Alice Walker capsulizes what all the preceding examples indicate about the position of Black women writers and the reasons for the damaging criticism about them. She responds to her interviewer's question, "Why do you think that the black woman writer has been so ignored in America? Does she have even more difficulty than the black male writer, who perhaps has just begun to gain recognition?" Walker replies:

> There are two reasons why the black woman writer is not taken as seriously as the black male writer. One is that she's a woman. Critics seem unusually ill-equipped to intelligently discuss and analyze the works of black women. Generally, they do not even make the attempt; they prefer, rather, to talk about the lives of black women writers, not about what they write. And, since black women writers are not — it would seem — very likable — until recently they were the least willing worshippers of male supremacy — comments about them tend to be cruel.[13]

A convincing case for Black feminist criticism can obviously be built solely upon the basis of the negativity of what already exists. It is far more gratifying, however, to demonstrate its necessity by showing how it can serve to reveal for the first time the profound subtleties of this particular body of literature.

Before suggesting how a Black feminist approach might be used to examine a specific work I will outline some of the principles that I think a Black feminist critic could use. Beginning with a primary commitment to exploring how both sexual and racial politics and Black and female identity are inextricable elements in Black women's writings, she would also work from the assumption that Black women writers constitute an identifiable literary tradition. The breadth of her familiarity with these writers would have shown her that not only is theirs a verifiable historical tradition that parallels in time the tradition of Black men and white women writing in this country, but that thematically, stylistically, aesthetically, and conceptually Black women writers manifest common approaches to the act of creating literature as a direct result of the specific political, social, and economic experience they have been obliged to share. The way, for example, that Zora Neale Hurston, Margaret Walker, Toni Morrison, and Alice Walker incorporate the traditional Black female activities of rootworking, herbal medicine, conjure, and midwifery into the fabric of their stories is not mere coincidence, nor is their use of specifically Black female language to express their own and their characters' thoughts accidental. The use of Black women's language and cultural experience in books *by* Black women *about* Black women results in a miraculously rich coalescing of form and content and also takes their writing far beyond the confines of white/male literary structures. The Black feminist critic would find innumerable commonalities in works by Black women.

Another principle which grows out of the concept of a tradition and which would also help to strengthen this tradition would be for the critic to look first for precedents and insights in interpretation within the works of other Black women. In other words she would think and write out of her own identity and not try to graft the ideas or methodology of white/male literary thought upon the precious materials of Black women's art. Black feminist criticism would by definition be highly innovative, embodying the daring spirit of the works themselves. The Black feminist critic would be constantly aware of the political implications of her work and would assert the connections between it and the political situation of all Black women. Logically developed, Black feminist criticism would owe its existence to a Black feminist movement while at the same time contributing ideas that women in the movement could use.

Black feminist criticism applied to a particular work can overturn previous assumptions about it

[12]Ora Williams, "A Bibliography of Works Written by American Black Women," in *College Language Association Journal* 15:3 (March 1972): 355. There is an expanded book-length version of this bibliography: *American Black Women in the Arts and Social Sciences: A Bibliographic Survey* (Metuchen, N.J.: The Scarecrow Press, 1973; rev. and expanded ed., 1978). [Au.]

[13]John O'Brien, ed., *Interviews with Black Writers* (New York: Liveright, 1973), p. 201. [Au.]

and expose for the first time its actual dimensions. At the "Lesbians and Literature" discussion at the 1976 Modern Language Association convention Bertha Harris suggested that if in a woman writer's work a sentence refuses to do what it is supposed to do, if there are strong images of women and if there is a refusal to be linear, the result is innately lesbian literature. As usual, I wanted to see if these ideas might be applied to the Black women writers that I know and quickly realized that many of their works were, in Harris's sense, lesbian. Not because women are "lovers," but because they are the central figures, are positively portrayed and have pivotal relationships with one another. The form and language of these works are also nothing like what white patriarchal culture requires or expects.

I was particularly struck by the way in which Toni Morrison's novels *The Bluest Eye* and *Sula* could be explored from this new perspective.[14] In both works the relationships between girls and women are essential, yet at the same time physical sexuality is overtly expressed only between men and women. Despite the apparent heterosexuality of the female characters I discovered in re-reading *Sula* that it works as a lesbian novel not only because of the passionate friendship between Sula and Nel, but because of Morrison's consistently critical stance toward the heterosexual institutions of male/female relationships, marriage, and the family. Consciously or not, Morrison's work poses both lesbian and feminist questions about Black women's autonomy and their impact upon each other's lives.

Sula and Nel find each other in 1922 when each of them is twelve, on the brink of puberty and the discovery of boys. Even as awakening sexuality "clotted their dreams," each girl desires "a someone" obviously female with whom to share her feelings. Morrison writes:

> . . . for it was in dreams that the two girls had met. Long before Edna Finch's Mellow House opened, even before they marched through the chocolate halls of Garfield Primary School . . . they had already made each other's acquaintance in the delirium of their noon dreams. They were solitary little girls whose loneliness was so profound it intoxicated them and sent them stumbling into Technicolored visions that always included a presence, a someone who, quite like the dreamer, shared the delight of the dream. When Nel, an only child, sat on the steps of her back porch surrounded by the high silence of her mother's incredibly orderly house, feeling the neatness pointing at her back, she studied the poplars and fell easily into a picture of herself lying on a flower bed, tangled in her own hair, waiting for some fiery prince. He approached but never quite arrived. But always, watching the dream along with her, were some smiling sympathetic eyes. Someone as interested as she herself in the flow of her imagined hair, the thickness of the mattress of flowers, the voile sleeves that closed below her elbows in gold-threaded cuffs.
>
> Similarly, Sula, also an only child, but wedged into a household of throbbing disorder constantly awry with things, people, voices and the slamming of doors, spent hours in the attic behind a roll of linoleum galloping through her own mind on a gray-and-white horse tasting sugar and smelling roses in full view of someone who shared both the taste and the speed.
>
> So when they met, first in those chocolate halls and next through the ropes of the swing, they felt the ease and comfort of old friends. Because each had discovered years before that they were neither white nor male, and that all freedom and triumph was forbidden to them, they had set about creating something else to be. Their meeting was fortunate, for it let them use each other to grow on. Daughters of distant mothers and incomprehensible fathers (Sula's because he was dead; Nel's because he wasn't), they found in each other's eyes the intimacy they were looking for. (51–52)

As this beautiful passage shows, their relationship, from the very beginning, is suffused with an erotic romanticism. The dreams in which they are initially drawn to each other are actually complementary aspects of the same sensuous fairytale. Nel imagines a "fiery prince" who never quite arrives while Sula gallops like a prince "on a gray-and-white horse."[15] The "real world" of patriarchy requires, however, that they channel this

[14]Toni Morrison, *The Bluest Eye* (New York: Pocket Books, 1972, 1976, orig. 1970) and *Sula* (New York: Alfred A. Knopf, 1974). All subsequent references to this work will be designated in the text. [Au.]

[15]My sister, Beverly Smith, pointed out this connection to me. [Au.]

energy away from each other to the opposite sex. Lorraine Bethel explains this dynamic in her essay "Conversations With Ourselves: Black Female Relationships in Toni Cade Bambara's *Gorilla, My Love* and Toni Morrison's *Sula*." She writes:

> I am not suggesting that Sula and Nel are being consciously sexual, or that their relationship has an overt lesbian nature. I am suggesting, however, that there is a certain sensuality in their interactions that is reinforced by the mirror-like nature of their relationship. Sexual exploration and coming of age is a natural part of adolescence. Sula and Nel discover men together, and though their flirtations with males are an important part of their sexual exploration, the sensuality that they experience in each other's company is equally important.[16]

Sula and Nel must also struggle with the constrictions of racism upon their lives. The knowledge that "they were neither white nor male" is the inherent explanation of their need for each other. Morrison depicts in literature the necessary bonding that has always taken place between Black women for the sake of barest survival. Together the two girls can find the courage to create themselves.

Their relationship is severed only when Nel marries Jude, an unexceptional young man who thinks of her as "the hem — the tuck and fold that hid his raveling edges" (83). Sula's inventive wildness cannot overcome social pressure or the influence of Nel's parents who "had succeeded in rubbing down to a dull glow any sparkle or splutter she had" (83). Nel falls prey to convention while Sula escapes it. Yet at the wedding which ends the first phase of their relationship, Nel's final action is to look past her husband toward Sula:

> . . . a slim figure in blue, gliding, with just a hint of a strut, down the path towards the road. . . . Even from the rear Nel could tell that it was Sula and that she was smiling; that something deep down in that litheness was amused. (85)

When Sula returns ten years later, her rebelliousness full-blown, a major source of the town's suspicions stems from the fact that although she is almost thirty, she is still unmarried. Sula's grandmother, Eva, does not hesitate to bring up the matter as soon as she arrives. She asks:

> "When you gone to get married? You need to have some babies. It'll settle you. . . . Ain't no woman got no business floatin' around without no man." (92)

Sula replies: "I don't want to make somebody else. I want to make myself" (92). Self-definition is a dangerous activity for any woman to engage in, especially a Black one, and it expectedly earns Sula pariah status in Medallion.

Morrison clearly points out that it is the fact that Sula has not been tamed or broken by the exigencies of heterosexual family life which most galls the others. She writes:

> Among the weighty evidence piling up was the fact that Sula did not look her age. She was near thirty and, unlike them, had lost no teeth, suffered no bruises, developed no ring of fat at the waist or pocket at the back of her neck. (115)

In other words she is not a domestic serf, a woman run down by obligatory childbearing or a victim of battering. Sula also sleeps with the husbands of the town once and then discards them, needing them even less than her own mother did, for sexual gratification and affection. The town reacts to her disavowal of patriarchal values by becoming fanatically serious about their own family obligations, as if in this way they might counteract Sula's radical criticism of their lives.

Sula's presence in her community functions much like the presence of lesbians everywhere to expose the contradictions of supposedly "normal" life. The opening paragraph of the essay "Woman Identified Woman" has amazing relevance as an explanation of Sula's position and character in the novel. It asks:

> What is a lesbian? A lesbian is the rage of all women condensed to the point of explosion. She is

[16]Lorraine Bethel, "Conversations With Ourselves: Black Female Relationships in Toni Cade Bambara's *Gorilla, My Love* and Toni Morrison's *Sula*," unpublished paper written at Yale, 1976, 47 pp. (Bethel has worked from a premise similar to mine in a much more developed treatment of the novel.) [Au.]

the woman who, often beginning at an extremely early age, acts in accordance with her inner compulsion to be a more complete and freer human being than her society — perhaps then, but certainly later — cares to allow her. These needs and actions, over a period of years, bring her into painful conflict with people, situations, the accepted ways of thinking, feeling and behaving, until she is in a state of continual war with everything around her, and usually with herself. She may not be fully conscious of the political implications of what for her began as personal necessity, but on some level she has not been able to accept the limitations and oppression laid on her by the most basic role of her society — the female role.[17]

The limitations of the *Black* female role are even greater in a racist and sexist society as is the amount of courage it takes to challenge them. It is no wonder that the townspeople see Sula's independence as imminently dangerous.

Morrison is also careful to show the reader that despite their years of separation and their opposing paths, Nel and Sula's relationship retains its primacy for each of them. Nell feels transformed when Sula returns and thinks:

> It was like getting the use of an eye back, having a cataract removed. Her old friend had come home. Sula. Who made her laugh, who made her see old things with new eyes, in whose presence she felt clever, gentle and a little raunchy. (95)

Laughing together in the familiar "rib-scraping" way, Nel feels "new, soft and new" (98). Morrison uses here the visual imagery which symbolizes the women's closeness throughout the novel.

Sula fractures this closeness, however, by sleeping with Nel's husband, an act of little import according to her system of values. Nel, of course, cannot understand. Sula thinks ruefully:

> Nel was the one person who had wanted nothing from her, who had accepted all aspects of her. Now she wanted everything, and all because of *that.* Nel was the first person who had been real to her, whose name she knew, who had seen as she had the slant of life that made it possible to stretch it to its limits. Now Nel was one of *them.* (119–20)

Sula also thinks at the realization of losing Nel about how unsatisfactory her relationships with men have been and admits:

> She had been looking all along for a friend, and it took her a while to discover that a lover was not a comrade and could never be — for a woman. (121)

The nearest that Sula comes to actually loving a man is in a brief affair with Ajax and what she values most about him is the intellectual companionship he provides, the brilliance he "allows" her to show.

Sula's feelings about sex with men are also consistent with a lesbian interpretation of the novel. Morrison writes:

> She went to bed with men as frequently as she could. It was the only place where she could find what she was looking for: *misery and the ability to feel deep sorrow.* . . . During the lovemaking she found and needed to find the cutting edge. When she left off cooperating with her body and began to assert herself in the act, particles of strength gathered in her like steel shavings drawn to a spacious magnetic center, forming a tight cluster that nothing, it seemed, could break. *And there was utmost irony and outrage in lying under someone, in a position of surrender, feeling her own abiding strength and limitless power.* . . . When her partner disengaged himself, she looked up at him in wonder trying to recall his name. . . . waiting impatiently for him to turn away. . . . *leaving her to the postcoital privateness in which she met herself, welcomed herself, and joined herself in matchless harmony.* (122–23) [Italics mine.]

Sula uses men for sex which results not in communion with them, but in her further delving into self.

Ultimately the deepest communion and communication in the novel occurs between two women who love each other. After their last painful meeting, which does not bring reconciliation, Sula thinks as Nel leaves her:

> "So she will walk on down that road, her back so straight in that old green coat . . . thinking how much I have cost her and never remember the days

[17]New York Radicalesbians, "Woman Identified Woman," in *Lesbians Speak Out* (Oakland: Women's Press Collective, 1974), p. 87. [Au.]

when we were two throats and one eye and we had no price." (147)

It is difficult to imagine a more evocative metaphor for what women can be to each other, the "pricelessness" they achieve in refusing to sell themselves for male approval, the total worth that they can only find in each other's eyes.

Decades later the novel concludes with Nel's final comprehension of the source of the grief that has plagued her from the time her husband walked out. Morrison writes:

> "All that time, all that time, I thought I was missing Jude." And the loss pressed down on her chest and came up into her throat. "We was girls together," she said as though explaining something. "O Lord, Sula," she cried, "girl, girl, girlgirlgirl."
>
> It was a fine cry — loud and long — but it had no bottom and it had no top, just circles and circles of sorrow. (174)

Again Morrison exquisitely conveys what women, Black women, mean to each other. This final passage verifies the depth of Sula and Nel's relationship and its centrality to an accurate interpretation of the work.

Sula is an exceedingly lesbian novel in the emotions expressed, in the definition of female character, and in the way that the politics of heterosexuality are portrayed. The very meaning of lesbianism is being expanded in literature, just as it is being redefined through politics. The confusion that many readers have felt about *Sula* may well have a lesbian explanation. If one sees Sula's inexplicable "evil" and nonconformity as the evil of not being male-identified, many elements in the novel become clear. The work might be clearer still if Morrison had approached her subject with the consciousness that a lesbian relationship was at least a possibility for her characters. Obviously Morrison did not *intend* the reader to perceive Sula and Nel's relationship as inherently lesbian. However, this lack of intention only shows the way in which heterosexist assumptions can veil what may logically be expected to occur in a work. What I have tried to do here is not to prove that Morrison wrote something that she did not, but to point out how a Black feminist critical perspective at least allows consideration of this level of the novel's meaning.

In her interview in *Conditions: One* Adrienne Rich talks about unconsummated relationships and the need to re-evaluate the meaning of intense yet supposedly non-erotic connections between women. She asserts:

> We need a lot more documentation about what actually happened: I think we can also imagine it, because we know it happened — we know it out of our own lives.[18]

Black women are still in the position of having to "imagine," discover, and verify Black lesbian literature because so little has been written from an avowedly lesbian perspective. The near nonexistence of Black lesbian literature which other Black lesbians and I so deeply feel has everything to do with the politics of our lives, the total suppression of identity that all Black women, lesbian or not, must face. This literary silence is again intensified by the unavailability of an autonomous Black feminist movement through which we could fight our oppression and also begin to name ourselves.

In a speech, "The Autonomy of Black Lesbian Women," Wilmette Brown comments upon the connection between our political reality and the literature we must invent:

> Because the isolation of Black lesbian women, given that we are superfreaks, given that our lesbianism defies both the sexual identity that capital gives us and the racial identity that capital gives us, the isolation of Black lesbian women from heterosexual Black women is very profound. Very profound. I have searched throughout Black history, Black literature, whatever, looking for some women that I could see were somehow lesbian. Now I know that in a certain sense they were all lesbian. But that was a very painful search.[19]

Heterosexual privilege is usually the only privilege that Black women have. None of us have racial or sexual privilege, almost none of us have

[18]Elly Bulkin, "An Interview With Adrienne Rich: Part I," in *Conditions: One*, Vol. 1, no. 1 (April 1977), p. 62. [Au.]

[19]Wilmette Brown, "The Autonomy of Black Lesbian Women," ms. of speech delivered July 24, 1976, Toronto, Canada, p. 7. [Au.]

class privilege, maintaining "straightness" is our last resort. Being out, particularly out in print, is the final renunciation of any claim to the crumbs of "tolerance" that nonthreatening "ladylike" Black women are sometimes fed. I am convinced that it is our lack of privilege and power in every other sphere that allows so few Black women to make the leap that many white women, particularly writers, have been able to make in this decade, not merely because they are white or have economic leverage, but because they have had the strength and support of a movement behind them.

As Black lesbians we must be out not only in white society, but in the Black community as well, which is at least as homophobic. That the sanctions against Black lesbians are extremely high is well illustrated in this comment by Black male writer Ishmael Reed. Speaking about the inroads that whites make into Black culture, he asserts:

> In Manhattan you find people actively trying to impede intellectual debate among Afro-Americans. The powerful "liberal/radical/existentialist" influences of the Manhattan literary and drama establishment speak through tokens, like for example that ancient notion of the *one* black ideologue (who's usually a Communist), the *one* black poetess (who's usually a feminist lesbian).[20]

To Reed, "feminist" and "lesbian" are the most pejorative terms he can hurl at a Black woman and totally invalidate anything she might say, regardless of her actual politics or sexual identity. Such accusations are quite effective for keeping Black women writers who are writing with integrity and strength from any conceivable perspective in line, but especially ones who are actually feminist and lesbian. Unfortunately Reed's reactionary attitude is all too typical. A community which has not confronted sexism, because a widespread Black feminist movement has not required it to, has likewise not been challenged to examine its heterosexism. Even at this moment I am not convinced that one can write explicitly as a Black lesbian and live to tell about it.

[20]Domini, op. cit., p. 18. [Au.]

Yet there are a handful of Black women who have risked everything for truth. Audre Lorde, Pat Parker, and Ann Allen Shockley have at least broken ground in the vast wilderness of works that do not exist.[21] Black feminist criticism will again have an essential role not only in creating a climate in which Black lesbian writers can survive, but in undertaking the total reassessment of Black literature and literary history needed to reveal the Black woman-identified-women that Wilmette Brown and so many of us are looking for.

Although I have concentrated here upon what does not exist and what needs to be done, a few Black feminist critics have already begun this work. Gloria T. Hull at the University of Delaware has discovered in her research on Black women poets of the Harlem Renaissance that many of the women who are considered "minor" writers of the period were in constant contact with each other and provided both intellectual stimulation and psychological support for each other's work. At least one of these writers, Angelina Weld Grimké, wrote many unpublished love poems to women. Lorraine Bethel, a recent graduate of Yale College, has done substantial work on Black women writers, particularly in her senior essay. "This Infinity of Conscious Pain: Blues Lyricism and Hurston's Black Female Folk Aesthetic and Cultural Sensibility in *Their Eyes Were Watching God,*" in which she brilliantly defines and uses the principles of Black feminist criticism. Elaine Scott at the State University of New York at Old Westbury is also involved in highly creative and politically resonant research on Hurston and other writers.

[21]Audre Lorde, *New York Head Shop and Museum* (Detroit: Broadside, 1974); *Coal* (New York: W. W. Norton, 1976); *Between Our Selves* (Point Reyes, Calif.: Eidolon Editions, 1976); *The Black Unicorn* (New York: W. W. Norton, 1978). Pat Parker, *Child of Myself* (Oakland: Women's Press Collective, 1972 and 1974); *Pit Stop* (Oakland: Women's Press Collective, 1973); *Womanslaughter* (Oakland: Diana Press, 1978); *Movement in Black* (Oakland: Diana Press, 1978). Ann Allen Shockley, *Loving Her* (Indianapolis: Bobbs-Merrill, 1974).

There is at least one Black lesbian writers' collective, Jemima, in New York. They do public readings and have available a collection of their poems. They can be contacted c/o Boyce, 41–11 Parsons Blvd., Flushing, NY 11355. [Au.]

The fact that these critics are young and, except for Hull, unpublished merely indicates the impediments we face. Undoubtedly there are other women working and writing whom I do not even know, simply because there is no place to read them. As Michele Wallace states in her article, "A Black Feminist's Search for Sisterhood":

> We exist as women who are Black who are feminists, each stranded for the moment, working independently because there is not yet an environment in this society remotely congenial to our struggle — [or our thoughts].[22]

I only hope that this essay is one way of breaking our silence and our isolation, of helping us to know each other.

Just as I did not know where to start I am not sure how to end. I feel that I have tried to say too much and at the same time have left too much unsaid. What I want this essay to do is lead everyone who reads it to examine *everything* that they have ever thought and believed about feminist culture and to ask themselves how their thoughts connect to the reality of Black women's writing and lives. I want to encourage in white women, as a first step, a sane accountability to all the women who write and live on this soil. I want most of all for Black women and Black lesbians somehow not to be so alone. This last will require the most expansive of revolutions as well as many new words to tell us how to make this revolution real. I finally want to express how much easier both my waking and my sleeping hours would be if there were one book in existence that would tell me something specific about my life. One book based in Black feminist and Black lesbian experience, fiction or nonfiction. Just one work to reflect the reality that I and the Black women whom I love are trying to create. When such a book exists then each of us will not only know better how to live, but how to dream.

[22]Michele Wallace, "A Black Feminist's Search for Sisterhood," in *The Village Voice*, 28 July 1975, p. 7. [Au.]

Deborah E. McDowell

b. 1951

Deborah E. McDowell is one of the leading voices of African American literature and women's studies. Born in Birmingham, Alabama, McDowell received her B.A. from Tuskegee Institute (1972) and her M.A. (1974) and Ph.D. (1979) in American and Afro-American literature from Purdue University. She has taught at Colby College (1979–87), where she was tenured as associate professor of English. Since 1987, she has been a professor of English at the University of Virginia. McDowell's publications include studies of the work of Alice Walker, Toni Morrison, Dorothy West, and Jesse Redmon Fauset, and she is the general editor of the Black Women Writers Series. Her recent publications include Slavery and the Literary Imagination *(ed., with Arnold Rampersad, 1989), and* The Changing Same *(1995), a study of generational connections among black women novelists. "New Directions for Black Feminist Criticism" is reprinted from* Black American Literature Forum *14 (1980).*

New Directions for Black Feminist Criticism

"What is commonly called literary history," writes Louise Bernikow, "is actually a record of choices. Which writers have survived their times and which have not depends upon who noticed them and chose to record their notice."[1] Women writers have fallen victim to arbitrary selection. Their writings have been "patronized, slighted, and misunderstood by a cultural establishment operating according to male norms out of male perceptions."[2] Both literary history's "sins of omission" and literary criticism's inaccurate and partisan judgments of women writers have come under attack since the early 1970s by feminist critics.[3] To date, no one has formulated a precise or complete definition of feminist criticism, but since its inception, its theorists and practitioners have agreed that it is a "corrective, unmasking the omissions and distortions of the past — the errors of a literary critical tradition that arise from and reflect a culture created, perpetuated, and dominated by men."[4]

These early theorists and practitioners of feminist literary criticism were largely white females who, wittingly or not, perpetrated against the Black woman writer the same exclusive practices they so vehemently decried in white male scholars. Seeing the experiences of white women, particularly white middle-class women, as normative, white female scholars proceeded blindly to exclude the work of Black women writers from literary anthologies and critical studies. Among the most flagrant examples of this chauvinism is Patricia Meyer Spacks's *The Female Imagination*. In a weak defense of her book's exclusive focus on women in the Anglo-American literary tradition, Spacks quotes Phyllis Chesler (a white female psychologist): "I have no theory to offer of Third World female psychology in America. . . . As a white woman, I'm reluctant and unable to construct theories about experiences I haven't had."[5] But, as Alice Walker observes, "Spacks never lived in nineteenth-century Yorkshire, so why theorize about the Brontës?"[6]

Not only have Black women writers been "disenfranchised" from critical works by white women scholars on the "female traditions," but they have also been frequently excised from those on the Afro-American literary tradition by Black scholars, most of whom are males. For example, Robert Stepto's *From Behind the Veil: A Study of Afro-American Narrative* purports to be "a history . . . of the historical consciousness of an Afro-American art form — namely, the Afro-American written narrative."[7] Yet, Black women writers are conspicuously absent from the table of contents. Though Stepto does have a token two-page discussion of Zora Neale Hurston's *Their Eyes Were Watching God* in which he refers to it as a "seminal narrative in Afro-American letters,"[8] he did

[1]Louise Bernikow, *The World Split Open: Four Centuries of Women Poets in England and America, 1552–1950* (New York: Vintage Books, 1974), p. 3. [Au.]

[2]William Morgan, "Feminism and Literary Study: A Reply to Annette Kolodny," *Critical Inquiry* 2 (Summer 1976): B11. [Au.]

[3]The year 1970 was the beginning of the Modern Language Association's Commission on the Status of Women, which offered panels and workshops that were feminist in approach. [Au.]

[4]Statement by Barbara Desmarais quoted in Annis Pratt, "The New Feminist Criticisms: Exploring the History of the New Space," in *Beyond Intellectual Sexism: A New Woman, A New Reality*, ed. Joan I. Roberts (New York: David McKay, 1976), p. 176. [Au.]

[5]Patricia Meyer Spacks, *The Female Imagination* (New York: Avon Books, 1976), p. 5. Ellen Moers, *Literary Women: The Great Writers* (Garden City, N.Y.: Anchor Books, 1977) is another example of what Alice Walker terms "white female chauvinism." [Au.]

[6]Alice Walker, "One Child of One's Own — An Essay on Creativity," *Ms.*, August 1979, p. 50. [Au.]

[7]Robert Stepto, *From Behind the Veil: A Study of Afro-American Narrative* (Urbana: University of Illinois Press, 1979), p. x. Other sexist critical works include Donald B. Gibson, ed., *Five Black Writers* (New York: New York University Press, 1970), a collection of essays on Wright, Ellison, Baldwin, Hughes, and Leroi Jones, and Jean Wagner, *Black Poets of the United States: From Paul Laurence Dunbar to Langston Hughes*, trans. Kenneth Douglas (Urbana: University of Illinois Press, 1973). [Au.]

[8]Stepto, *From Behind the Veil*, p. 166. [Au.]

not feel that the novel merited its own chapter or the thorough analysis accorded the other works he discusses.

When Black women writers are neither ignored altogether nor merely given honorable mention, they are critically misunderstood and summarily dismissed. In *The Negro Novel in America,* for example, Robert Bone's reading of Jessie Fauset's novels is both partisan and superficial and might explain the reasons Fauset remains obscure. Bone argues that Fauset is the foremost member of the "Rear Guard" of writers "who lagged behind," clinging to established literary traditions. The "Rear Guard" drew their source material from the Negro middle class in their efforts "to orient Negro art toward white opinion," and "to apprise educated whites of the existence of respectable Negroes." Bone adds that Fauset's emphasis on the Black middle class results in novels that are "uniformly sophomoric, trivial and dull."[9]

While David Littlejohn praises Black fiction since 1940, he denigrates the work of Fauset and Nella Larsen. He maintains that "the newer writers are obviously writing as men, for men," and are avoiding the "very close and steamy" writing that is the result of "any subculture's taking itself too seriously, defining the world and its values exclusively in the terms of its own restrictive norms and concerns."[10] This "phallic criticism,"[11] to use Mary Ellmann's term, is based on masculine-centered values and definitions. It has dominated the criticism of Black women writers and has done much to guarantee that most would be, in Alice Walker's words, "casually pilloried and consigned to a sneering oblivion."[12]

Suffice it to say that the critical community has not favored Black women writers. The recognition among Black female critics and writers that white women, white men, and Black men consider their experiences as normative and Black women's experiences as deviant has given rise to Black feminist criticism. Much as in white feminist criticism, the critical postulates of Black women's literature are only skeletally defined. Although there is no concrete definition of Black feminist criticism, a handful of Black female scholars have begun the necessary enterprise of resurrecting forgotten Black women writers and revising misinformed critical opinions of them. Justifiably enraged by the critical establishment's neglect and mishandling of Black women writers, these critics are calling for, in the words of Barbara Smith, "nonhostile and perceptive analysis of works written by persons outside the 'mainstream' of white/male cultural rule."[13]

Despite the urgency and timeliness of the enterprise, however, no substantial body of Black feminist criticism — either in theory or practice — exists, a fact which might be explained partially by our limited access to and control of the media.[14] Another explanation for the paucity of Black feminist criticism, notes Barbara Smith, is the lack of a "developed body of Black feminist political theory whose assumptions could be used in the study of Black women's art."

Despite the strained circumstances under which Black feminist critics labor, a few committed Black female scholars have broken necessary ground. For the remainder of this essay I would like to focus on selected writings of Black feminist critics, discussing their strengths and weaknesses and suggesting new directions toward which the criticism might move and pitfalls that it might avoid.

[9]Robert Bone, *The Negro Novel in America* (1958; reprint ed., New Haven, Conn.: Yale University Press, 1972), pp. 97, 101. [Au.]

[10]David Littlejohn, *Black on White: A Critical Survey of Writing by American Negroes* (New York: Viking Press, 1966), pp. 48–49. [Au.]

[11]Ellmann's concept of "phallic criticism" is discussed in a chapter of the same name in her *Thinking about Women* (New York: Harcourt, Brace & World, 1968), pp. 28–54. [Au.]

[12]Introduction to *Zora Neale Hurston: A Literary Biography* by Robert Hemenway (Urbana: University of Illinois Press, 1976), p. xiv. Although Walker makes this observation specifically about Hurston, it is one that can apply to a number of Black women writers. [Au.]

[13]Barbara Smith, "Toward a Black Feminist Criticism," pp. 168–85. [Au.] See Smith, p. 1411. [Ed.]

[14]See Evelyn Hammonds, "Toward a Black Feminist Aesthetic," *Sojourner,* October 1980, p. 7, for a discussion of the limitations on Black feminist critics. She correctly points out that Black feminist critics "have no newspapers, no mass-marketed magazines or journals that are explicitly oriented toward the involvement of women of color in the feminist movement." [Au.]

Unfortunately, Black feminist scholarship has been decidedly more practical than theoretical, and the theories developed thus far have often lacked sophistication and have been marred by slogans, rhetoric, and idealism. The articles that attempt to apply these theoretical tenets often lack precision and detail. These limitations are not without reason. As Dorin Schumacher observes, "the feminist critic has few philosophical shelters, pillars, or guideposts," and thus "feminist criticism is fraught with intellectual and professional risks, offering more opportunity for creativity, yet greater possibility of errors."[15]

The earliest theoretical statement on Black feminist criticism is Barbara Smith's "Toward a Black Feminist Criticism." Though its importance as a groundbreaking piece of scholarship cannot be denied, it suffers from lack of precision and detail. In justifying the need for a Black feminist aesthetic, Smith argues that "a Black feminist approach to literature that embodies the realization that the politics of sex as well as the politics of race and class are crucially interlocking factors in the works of Black women writers is an absolute necessity." Until such an approach exists, she continues, "we will not even know what these writers mean."

Smith points out that "thematically, stylistically, aesthetically, and conceptually Black women writers manifest common approaches to the act of creating literature as a direct result of the specific political, social, and economic experience they have been obliged to share." She offers, as an example, the incorporation of rootworking, herbal medicine, conjure, and midwifery in the stories of Zora Neale Hurston, Margaret Walker, Toni Morrison, and Alice Walker. While these folk elements certainly do appear in the work of these writers, they also appear in the works of certain Black male writers, a fact that Smith omits. If Black women writers use these elements differently from Black male writers, such a distinction must be made before one can effectively articulate the basis of a Black feminist aesthetic.

Smith maintains further that Zora Neale Hurston, Margaret Walker, Toni Morrison, and Alice Walker use a "specifically black female language to express their own and their characters' thoughts," but she fails to describe or to provide examples of this unique language. Of course, we have come recently to acknowledge that "many of our habits of language usage are sex-derived, sex-associated, and/or sex-distinctive," that "the ways in which men and women internalize and manipulate language" are undeniably sex-related.[16] But this realization in itself simply paves the way for further investigation that can begin by exploring some critical questions. For example, is there a monolithic Black female language? Do Black female high school dropouts, welfare mothers, college graduates, and Ph.D.s share a common language? Are there regional variations in this common language? Further, some Black male critics have tried to describe the uniquely "Black linguistic elegance"[17] that characterizes Black poetry. Are there noticeable differences between the languages of Black females and Black males? These and other questions must be addressed with precision if current feminist terminology is to function beyond mere critical jargon.

Smith turns from her discussion of the commonalities among Black women writers to describe the nature of her critical enterprise. "Black feminist criticism would by definition be highly innovative," she maintains. "Applied to a particular work [it] can overturn previous assumptions about [the work] and expose for the first time its actual dimensions." Smith then proceeds to demonstrate this critical postulate by interpreting Toni Morrison's *Sula* as a lesbian novel, an interpretation she believes is maintained in "the emotions expressed, in the definition of female char-

[15]Dorin Schumacher, "Subjectivities: A Theory of the Critical Process," in *Feminist Literary Criticism: Explorations in Theory,* ed. Josephine Donovan (Lexington: University Press of Kentucky, 1975), p. 34. [Au.]

[16]Annette Kolodny, "The Feminist as Literary Critic," Critical Response, *Critical Inquiry* 2 (Summer 1976): 824–25. See also Cheris Kramer, Barrie Thorne, and Henley, "Perspectives on Language and Communication," *Signs* 3 (Spring 1978): 638–51, and Nelly Furman, "The Study of Women and Language: Comment on Vol. 3, no. 3," *Signs* 4 (Fall 1978): 152–85. [Au.]

[17]Stephen Henderson, *Understanding the New Black Poetry: Black Speech and Black Music as Poetic References* (New York: William Morrow, 1973), pp. 31–46. [Au.]

acter and in the way that the politics of heterosexuality are portrayed." Smith vacillates between arguing forthrightly for the validity of her interpretation and recanting or overqualifying it in a way that undercuts her own credibility.

According to Smith, "if in a woman writer's work a sentence refuses to do what it is supposed to do, if there are strong images of women and if there is a refusal to be linear, the result is innately lesbian literature." She adds, "because of Morrison's consistently critical stance toward the heterosexual institutions of male-female relationships, marriage, and the family," *Sula* works as a lesbian novel. This definition of lesbianism is vague and imprecise; it subsumes far more Black women writers, particularly contemporary ones, than not into the canon of Lesbian writers. For example, Jessie Fauset, Nella Larsen, and Zora Neale Hurston all criticize major socializing institutions, as do Gwendolyn Brooks, Alice Walker, and Toni Cade Bambara. Further, if we apply Smith's definition of lesbianism, there are probably a few Black male writers who qualify as well. As of this is to say that Smith has simultaneously oversimplified and obscured the issue of lesbianism. Obviously aware of the delicacy of her position, she interjects that "the very meaning of lesbianism is being expanded in literature." Unfortunately, her qualification does not strengthen her argument. One of the major tasks ahead of Black feminist critics who write from a lesbian perspective, then, is to define lesbianism and lesbian literature precisely. Until they can offer a definition which is not vacuous, their attempts to distinguish Black lesbian writers from those who are not will be hindered.[18]

Even as I call for firmer definitions of lesbianism and lesbian literature, I question whether a lesbian aesthetic is not finally a reductive approach to the study of Black women's literature which possibly ignores other equally important aspects of the literature. For example, reading *Sula* solely from a lesbian perspective overlooks the novel's density and complexity, its skillful blend of folklore, omens, and dreams, its metaphorical and symbolic richness. Although I do not quarrel with Smith's appeal for fresher, more innovative approaches to Black women's literature, I suspect that "innovative" analysis is pressed to the service of an individual political persuasion. One's personal and political presuppositions enter into one's critical judgments. Nevertheless, we should heed Annette Kolodny's warning for feminist critics to

> be wary of reading literature as though it were polemic. . . . If when using literary materials to make what is essentially a political point, we find ourselves virtually rewriting a text, ignoring certain aspects of plot or characterization, or over-simplifying the action to fit our "political" thesis, then we are neither practicing an honest criticism nor saying anything useful about the nature of art (or about the art of political persuasion, for that matter).[19]

Alerting feminist critics to the dangers of political ideology yoked with aesthetic judgment is not synonymous with denying that feminist criticism is a valid and necessary cultural and political enterprise. Indeed, it is both possible and useful to translate ideological positions into aesthetic ones, but if the criticism is to be responsible, the two must be balanced.

Because it is a cultural and political enterprise, feminist critics, in the main, believe that their criticism can effect social change. Smith certainly argues for socially relevant criticism in her conclusion that "Black feminist criticism would owe its existence to a Black feminist movement while at the same time contributing ideas that women in the movement could use." This is an exciting idea in itself, but we should ask: What ideas, specifically, would Black feminist criticism contribute to the movement? Fur-

[18]Some attempts have been made to define or at least discuss lesbianism. See Adrienne Rich's two essays, "It Is the Lesbian in Us . . ." and "The Meaning of Our Love for Woman Is What We Have," in *On Lies, Secrets and Silence* (New York: W. W. Norton, 1979), pp. 199–202 and 223–30, respectively. See also Bertha Harris's "*What We Mean to Say:* Notes Toward Defining the Nature of Lesbian Literature," *Heresies* 1 (Fall 1977): 5–8, and Blanche Cook's "'Women Alone Stir My Imagination': Lesbianism and the Cultural Tradition," *Signs* 4 (Summer 1979): 718–39. Also, at least one bibliography of Black lesbian writers has been compiled. See Ann Allen Shockley's "The Black Lesbian in American Literature: An Overview," *Conditions: Five* 2 (Fall 1979): 133–42. [Au.]

[19]Annette Kolodny, "Some Notes on Defining a 'Feminist Literary Criticism,' " *Critical Inquiry* 2 (Fall 1975): 90. [Au.]

ther, even though the proposition of a fruitful relationship between political activism and the academy is an interesting (and necessary) one, I doubt its feasibility. I am not sure that either in theory or in practice Black feminist criticism will be able to alter significantly circumstances that have led to the oppression of Black women. Moreover, as Lillian Robinson pointedly remarks, there is no assurance that feminist aesthetics "will be productive of a vision of art or of social relations that is of the slightest use to the masses of women, or even one that acknowledges the existence and struggle of such women."[20] I agree with Robinson that "ideological criticism must take place in the context of a political movement that can put it to work. The revolution is simply not going to be made by literary journals."[21] I should say that I am not arguing a defeatist position with respect to the social and political uses to which feminist criticism can be put. Just as it is both possible and useful to translate ideological positions into aesthetic ones, it must likewise be possible and useful to translate aesthetic positions into the machinery for social change.

Despite the shortcomings of Smith's article, she raises critical issues on which Black feminist critics can build. There are many tasks ahead of these critics, not the least of which is to attempt to formulate some clear definitions of what Black feminist criticism is. I use the term here simply to refer to Black female critics who analyze the works of Black female writers from a feminist or political perspective. But the term can also apply to any criticism written by a Black woman regardless of her subject or perspective — a book written by a male from a feminist or political perspective, a book written by a Black woman or about Black women authors in general, or any writings by women.[22]

[20]Lillian S. Robinson, "Working Women Writing," *Sex, Class, and Culture* (Bloomington: Indiana University Press, 1978), p. 226. [Au.]

[21]Robinson, "The Critical Task," *Sex, Class, and Culture,* p. 52. [Au.]

[22]I am borrowing here from Kolodny, who makes similar statements in "Some Notes on Defining a 'Feminist Literary Criticism,' " p. 75. [Au.]

In addition to defining the methodology, Black feminist critics need to determine the extent to which their criticism intersects with that of white feminist critics. Barbara Smith and others have rightfully challenged white women scholars to become more accountable to Black and Third World women writers, but will that require white women to use a different set of critical tools when studying Black women writers? Are white women's theories predicated upon culturally specific values and assumptions? Andrea Benton Rushing has attempted to answer these questions in her series of articles on images of Black women in literature. She maintains, for example, that critical categories of women, based on analyses of white women characters, are Euro-American in derivation and hence inappropriate to a consideration of Black women characters.[23] Such distinctions are necessary and, if held uniformly, can materially alter the shape of Black feminist scholarship.

Regardless of which theoretical framework Black feminist critics choose, they must have an informed handle on Black literature and Black culture in general. Such a grounding can give this scholarship more texture and completeness and perhaps prevent some of the problems that have had a vitiating effect on the criticism.

This footing in Black history and culture serves as a basis for the study of the literature. Termed "contextual" by theoreticians, this approach is often frowned upon if not dismissed entirely by critics who insist exclusively upon

[23]Andrea Benton Rushing, "Images of Black Women in Afro-American Poetry," in *The Afro-American Woman: Struggles and Images,* ed. Sharon Harley and Rosalyn Terborg-Penn (Port Washington, N.Y.: Kennikat Press, 1978), pp. 74–84. She argues that few of the stereotypic traits which Mary Ellmann described in *Thinking about Women* "seem appropriate to Afro-American images of black women." See also her "Images of Black Women in Modern African Poetry: An Overview," in *Sturdy Black Bridges: Visions of Black Women in Literature,* ed. Roseann P. Bell et al. (New York: Anchor Books, 1979), pp. 18–24. Rushing argues similarly that Mary Ann Ferguson's categories of women (the submissive wife, the mother angel or "mom," the woman on a pedestal, for example) cannot be applied to Black women characters, whose cultural imperatives are different from white women's. [Au.]

textual and linguistic analysis. Its limitations notwithstanding, I firmly believe that the contextual approach to Black women's literature exposes the conditions under which literature is produced, published, and reviewed. This approach is not only useful but necessary to Black feminist critics.

To those working with Black women writers prior to 1940, the contextual approach is especially useful. In researching Jessie Fauset, Nella Larsen, and Zora Neale Hurston, for example, it is useful to determine what the prevalent attitudes about Black women were during the time that they wrote. There is much information in the Black "little" magazines published during the Harlem Renaissance. An examination of *The Messenger,* for instance, reveals that the dominant social attitudes about Black women were strikingly consistent with traditional middle-class expectations of women. *The Messenger* ran a monthly symposium for some time entitled "Negro Womanhood's Greatest Needs." While a few female contributors stressed the importance of women being equal to men socially, professionally, and economically, the majority emphasized that a woman's place was in the home. It was her duty "to cling to the home [since] great men and women evolve from the environment of the hearthstone."[24]

One of the most startling entries came from a woman who wrote:

> The New Negro Woman, with her head erect and spirit undaunted, is resolutely marching forward, ever conscious of her historic and noble mission of doing her bit toward the liberation of her people in particular and the human race in general. Upon her shoulders rests the big task to create and keep alive, in the breast of black men, a holy and consuming passion to break with the slave traditions of the past; to spurn and overcome the fatal, insidious inferiority complex of the present, which . . . bobs up ever and anon, to arrest the progress of the New Negro Manhood Movement; and to fight with increasing vigor, with dauntless courage, unrelenting zeal and intelligent vision for the attainment of the stature of a full man, a free race and a new world.[25]

Not only does the contributor charge the Black woman with a formidable task, but she also sees her solely in relation to Black men.

This information enhances our understanding of what Fauset, Larsen, and Hurston confronted in attempting to offer alternative images of Black women. Moreover, it helps to clarify certain textual problems and ambiguities of their work. Though Fauset and Hurston, for example, explored feminist concerns, they leaned toward ambivalence. Fauset especially is alternately forthright and cagey, radical and traditional, on issues that confront women. Her first novel, *There Is Confusion* (1924), is flawed by an unanticipated and abrupt reversal in characterization that brings the central female character more in line with a feminine norm. Similarly, in her last novel, *Seraph on the Swanee* (1948), Zora Neale Hurston depicts a female character who shows promise for growth and change, for a departure from the conventional expectations of womanhood, but who in the end apotheosizes marriage, motherhood, and domestic servitude.

These two examples alone clearly capture the tension between social pressure and artistic integrity which is felt, to some extent, by all women writers. As Tillie Olsen points out, the fear of reprisal from the publishing and critical arenas is a looming obstacle to the woman writer's coming into her own authentic voice. "Fear — the need to please, to be safe — in the literary realm too. Founded fear. Power is still in the hands of men. Power of validation, publication, approval, reputation. . . ."[26]

While insisting on the validity, usefulness, and necessity of contextual approaches to Black women's literature, the Black feminist critic must not ignore the importance of rigorous textual analysis. I am aware of many feminist critics' stubborn resistance to the critical methodology handed down by white men. Although the resistance is certainly politically consistent and logical, I agree with Annette Kolodny that feminist criticism would be "shortsighted if it summarily

[24]*The Messenger* 9 (April 1927): 109. [Au.]
[25]*The Messenger* 5 (July 1923): 757. [Au.]

[26]Tillie Olsen, *Silences* (New York: Delacorte Press, 1978), p. 257. [Au.]

rejected all the inherited tools of critical analysis simply because they are male and western." We should, rather, salvage what we find useful in past methodologies, reject what we do not, and, where necessary, move toward "inventing new methods of analysis."[27] Particularly useful is Lillian Robinson's suggestion that "a radical kind of textual criticism . . . could usefully study the way the texture of sentences, choice of metaphors, patterns of exposition and narrative relate to [feminist] ideology."[28]

This rigorous textual analysis involves, as Barbara Smith recommends, isolating as many thematic, stylistic, and linguistic commonalities among Black women writers as possible. Among contemporary Black female novelists, the thematic parallels are legion. In Alice Walker and Toni Morrison, for example, the theme of the thwarted female artist figures prominently.[29] Pauline Breedlove in Morrison's *The Bluest Eye*, for example, is obsessed with ordering things:

> Jars on shelves at canning, peach pits on the step, sticks, stones, leaves. . . . Whatever portable plurality she found, she organized into neat lines, according to their size, shape or gradations of color. . . . She missed without knowing what she missed — paints and crayons.[30]

Similarly, Eva Peace in *Sula* is forever ordering the pleats in her dress. And Sula's strange and destructive behavior is explained as "the consequence of an idle imagination."

> Had she paints, clay, or knew the discipline of the dance, or strings; had she anything to engage her tremendous curiosity and her gift for metaphor, she might have exchanged the restlessness and preoccupation with whim for an activity that provided her with all she yearned for. And like any artist with no form, she became dangerous.[31]

Likewise, Meridian's mother in Alice Walker's novel *Meridian* makes artificial flowers and prayer pillows too small for kneeling.

The use of "clothing as iconography"[32] is central to writings by Black women. For example, in one of Jessie Fauset's early short stories, "The Sleeper Wakes" (1920), Amy, the protagonist, is associated with pink clothing (suggesting innocence and immaturity) while she is blinded by fairy-tale notions of love and marriage. However, after she declares her independence from her racist and sexist husband, Amy no longer wears pink. The imagery of clothing is abundant in Zora Neale Hurston's *Their Eyes Were Watching God* (1937). Janie's apron, her silks and satins, her head scarves, and finally her overalls all symbolize various stages of her journey from captivity to liberation. Finally, in Alice Walker's *Meridian*, Meridian's railroad cap and dungarees are emblems of her rejection of conventional images and expectations of womanhood.

A final theme that recurs in the novels of Black women writers is the motif of the journey. Though one can also find this same motif in the works of Black male writers, they do not use it in the same way as do Black female writers.[33] For example, the journey of the Black male character in works by Black men takes him underground. It is a "descent into the underworld,"[34] and is primarily political and social in its implications. Ralph Ellison's *Invisible Man*, Imamu Amiri Baraka's *The System of Dante's Hell*, and Richard Wright's "The Man Who Lived Underground" exemplify this quest. The Black female's journey, on the other hand, though at times touching the political and social, is basi-

[27]Kolodny, "Some Notes on Defining a 'Feminist Literary Criticism,' " p. 89. [Au.]

[28]Lillian S. Robinson, "Dwelling in Decencies: Radical Criticism and Feminist Perspectives," in *Feminist Criticism*, ed. Cheryl Brown and Karen Olsen (Metuchen, N.J.: Scarecrow Press, 1978), p. 34. [Au.]

[29]For a discussion of Toni Morrison's frustrated female artists see Renita Weems, "Artists Without Art Form: A Look at One Black Woman's World of Unrevered Black Women," *Conditions: Five* 2 (Fall 1979): 48–58. See also Alice Walker's classic essay, "In Search of Our Mothers' Gardens," *Ms.*, May 1974, for a discussion of Black women's creativity in general. [Au.]

[30]Toni Morrison, *The Bluest Eye* (New York: Pocket Books, 1970), pp. 88–89. [Au.]

[31]Toni Morrison, *Sula* (New York: Bantam Books, 1980), p. 105. [Au.]

[32]Kolodny, "Some Notes on Defining a 'Feminist Literary Criticism,' " p. 86. [Au.]

[33]In an NEH Summer Seminar at Yale University in the summer of 1980, Carolyn Naylor of Santa Clara University suggested this to me. [Au.]

[34]For a discussion of this idea see Michael G. Cooke, "The Descent into the Underworld and Modern Black Fiction," *Iowa Review* 5 (Fall 1974): 72–90. [Au.]

cally a personal and psychological journey. The female character in the works of Black women is in a state of becoming "part of an evolutionary spiral, moving from victimization to consciousness."[35] The heroines in Zora Neale Hurston's *Their Eyes Were Watching God,* in Alice Walker's *Meridian,* and in Toni Cade Bambara's *The Salt Eaters,* are emblematic of this distinction.

Even though isolating such thematic and imagistic commonalities should continue to be one of the Black feminist critic's most urgent tasks, she should beware of generalizing on the basis of too few examples. If one argues authoritatively for the existence of a Black female "conciousness" or "vision" or "literary tradition," one must be sure that the parallels found recur with enough consistency to support these generalizations. Further, Black feminist critics should not become obsessed in searching for common themes and images in Black women's works. As I pointed out earlier, investigating the question of "female" language is critical and may well be among the most challenging jobs awaiting the Black feminist critic. The growing body of research on gender-specific uses of language might aid these critics. In fact, wherever possible, feminist critics should draw on the scholarship of feminists in other disciplines.

An equally challenging and necessary task ahead of the Black feminist critic is a thoroughgoing examination of the works of Black male writers. In her introduction to *Midnight Birds,* Mary Helen Washington argues for the importance of giving Black women writers their due first:

> Black women are searching for a specific language, specific symbols, specific images with which to record their lives, and, even though they can claim a rightful place in the Afro-American tradition and the feminist tradition of women writers, it is also clear that, for purposes of liberation, black women writers will first insist on their own name, their own space.[36]

I likewise believe that the immediate concern of Black feminist critics must be to develop a fuller understanding of Black women writers who have not received the critical attention Black male writers have. Yet, I cannot advocate indefinitely such a separatist position, for the countless thematic, stylistic, and imagistic parallels between Black male and female writers must be examined. Black feminist critics should explore these parallels in an effort to determine the ways in which these commonalities are manifested differently in Black women's writing and the ways in which they coincide with writings by Black men.

Of course, there are feminist critics who are already examining Black male writers, but much of the scholarship has been limited to discussions of the negative images of Black women found in the works of these authors.[37] Although this scholarship served an important function in pioneering Black feminist critics, it has virtually run its course. Feminist critics run the risk of plunging their work into cliché and triviality if they continue merely to focus on how Black men treat Black women in literature. Hortense Spillers offers a more sophisticated approach to this issue in her discussion of the power of language and myth in female relations in James Baldwin's *If Beale Street Could Talk.* One of Spillers's most cogent points is that "woman-freedom, or its negation, is tied to the assertions of myth, or ways of saying things."[38]

Black feminist criticism is a knotty issue, and while I have attempted to describe it, to call for clearer definitions of its methodology, to offer warnings of its limitations, I await the day when Black feminist criticism will expand to embrace other modes of critical inquiry. In other words, I am philosophically opposed to what Annis Pratt calls "methodolatry." Wole Soyinka has offered one of the most cogent defenses against critical absolutism. He explains:

[35]Mary Helen Washington, *Midnight Birds: Stories of Contemporary Black Women Writers* (Garden City, N.Y.: Anchor Books, 1980), p. 43. [Au.]

[36]Ibid., p. xvii. [Au.]

[37]See Saundra Towns, "The Black Woman as Whore: Genesis of the Myth," *The Black Position* 3 (1974): 39–59, and Sylvia Keady, "Richard Wright's Women Characters and Inequality," *Black American Literature Forum* 10 (1976): 124–28, for example. [Au.]

[38]Hortense Spillers, "The Politics of Intimacy: A Discussion," in Bell et al., eds., *Sturdy Black Bridges,* p. 88. [Au.]

The danger which a literary ideology poses is the act of consecration — and of course excommunication. Thanks to the tendency of the modern consumer-mind to facilitate digestion by putting in strict categories what are essentially fluid operations of the creative mind upon social and natural phenomena, the formulation of a literary ideology tends to congeal sooner or later into instant capsules which, administered also to the writer, may end by asphyxiating the creative process.[39]

[39]Wole Soyinka, *Myth, Literature and the African World* (London: Cambridge University Press, 1976), p. 61. [Au.]

Whether Black feminist criticism will or should remain a separatist enterprise is a debatable point. Black feminist critics ought to move from this issue to consider the specific language of Black women's literature, to describe the ways Black women writers employ literary devices in a distinct way, and to compare the way Black women writers create their own mythic structures. If they focus on these and other pertinent issues, Black feminist critics will have laid the cornerstone for a sound, thorough articulation of the Black feminist aesthetic.

8

GENDER STUDIES AND QUEER THEORY[1]

It is the nature of power — particularly the kind of power that operates in our society — to be repressive, and to be especially careful in repressing useless energies, the intensity of pleasures, and irregular modes of behavior. — MICHEL FOUCAULT

Woman . . . is only a more or less complacent facilitator for the working out of man's fantasies. It is possible, and even certain, that she experiences vicarious pleasure there, but this pleasure is above all a masochistic prostitution of her body to a desire that is not her own. . . . — LUCE IRIGARAY

Gender is not a performance that a prior subject elects to do, but gender is performative. . . . *It is a* compulsory *performance in the sense that acting out of line with heterosexual norms brings with it ostracism, punishment, and violence, not to mention the transgressive pleasures produced by those very prohibitions.* — JUDITH BUTLER

GENDER STUDIES AND FEMINISM

From the words themselves one might expect that "feminism" is a political movement and "gender studies" a research project. There is some truth to this, but in a more important sense it was the ease with which certain forms of feminism within the academy had become co-opted politically into a series of research projects in women's studies, with the usual rewards for the top players, that gave rise to the new field of gender studies. Much of the most praised feminist research in the 1980s

[1]The term "queer theory" was popularized by Teresa de Lauretis in a special "Queer Theory" issue of the journal *Differences* (vol. 3, no. 2, 1992). One of de Lauretis's motives was to link up the theoretical activities of academics with the activist politics of the gay and lesbian rights group Queer Nation. The "in your face" quality of the term "queer" appeals to such groups because it forces straight people using or hearing the term to confront their own feelings about homosexuals and homosexuality. De Lauretis's other motive was to distinguish the theorists presented in her special issue, who were questioning and problematizing issues of gender identity and sexual orientation, from other researchers in gay and lesbian studies who were happy with the notion of stable gender identity. In the five years since the publication of the "Queer Theory" issue of *Differences,* that distinction has muddied. While some gay and lesbian gender theorists may still resist the term "queer theory," most on both sides of the gender identity issue have embraced it because of its defiant political implications.

took the form of new editions of women writers, proposals to add such writers to the existing literary canon, and analyses of the work of patriarchy in keeping males in the front ranks. Effective as this work was in changing what teachers taught and what students read, there was a sense on the part of some feminist critics that though the expansion team was successfully playing the game, it was still the old game that was being played, when what was needed was a new game entirely. The argument posed was that in order to counter patriarchy, it was necessary not merely to think about new texts, but to think about them in radically new ways.

The problem was not that male chauvinists held the named chairs at Princeton — feminists of stature would in their turn be appointed to those professorships — or that males got most of the pages in the Norton Anthologies, but that academic discourse about gender and the gender system was being conducted within a language and a logic, a discursive system, that had been fashioned by male supremacy and reproduced that unconscious ideology at every step. Contemporary feminists might note the prevalence of that ideology in my own figure of speech in the previous paragraph, where male team sports (only the all-male professional leagues have expansion teams) are used as a metaphor for gender politics. But how does one change a discursive system from within, when we can only speak with words that have already been tainted by ideology?

The first step is to recognize the need for a change. The work of Gilbert and Gubar, in revising for the female tradition Bloom's crypto-Freudian analysis of the male poet's impetus to originality, had obviously not gone far enough. Freud viewed women as inherently lacking, warped by the sense that they had already been castrated. In representing this metaphoric wound as the site of female creativity and resistance, Gilbert and Gubar had in effect reinforced Freud's demeaning psychological discourse. For the pioneers of what has come to be known as gender studies, a way to avoid this double bind was to recuperate Freud with a difference, to find a way of reading psychology that could turn the tables on patriarchy. The key to doing this was the work of French psychologist Jacques Lacan.[2] Lacan's postmodern reading of Freud replaced the Viennese doctor's thermodynamic metaphors (about energies, drives, and transferences) with linguistic metaphors: The unconscious was structured not like an infernal machine but like a language. Although Lacan was often given to misogynistic remarks, his recasting of Freud's conception of the physical penis (a fleshly organ for women to envy) into the privileged signifier of the Phallus, a symbol with which both sexes identify as *le désir de la Mère* and from which both sexes feel alienated after the fall into language, was a major step toward feminist revisions of Freud.

THE FEMALE (AS) TEXT: IRIGARAY AND CIXOUS

One of the most influential of the French theorists, Luce Irigaray, is a disciple of Lacan. Irigaray's difficult, learned, ironically allusive thesis, *Speculum of the Other Woman* (1974), undertakes a re-examination of Plato, Freud, and a dozen thinkers

[2]See the introduction to Psychoanalytic Theory, p. 1019, and readings by both Lacan and Gallop, pp. 1044 and 1065, respectively.

in between. Like Simone de Beauvoir, Irigaray is outraged about the way women have been seen as an Other by men, spoken about and spoken for, but never allowed to speak themselves.[3] Her critique of Freud is largely of his theories of sexual differences (like the notions of penis envy and the castration complex), theories that falter, according to Irigaray, on Freud's failure to perceive that men and women actually *are* different, rather than more or less adequate versions of the same (male) norm. Quoting Freud against himself, Irigaray demonstrates the incoherence of his theories of femininity.

Despite Irigaray's training as a Lacanian psychoanalyst, her own version of femininity seems to have a biological basis that harks back to the source of the errors she exposes in Freud. In her most famous essay, "This Sex Which Is Not One" (1977), she characterizes both males and females as essentially like their primary genitalia: men, like the phallus, are single (-minded), hard, simple, direct; women, like the two lips of the vulva and their sensations, are multiple, diffuse, soft, indirect. Similarly, Irigaray's notion of women's writing takes off from this genital analogy of the labia, which always touch each other:

> This "style" or "writing" of women tends to put the torch to fetish words, proper terms, well-constructed forms. This "style" does not privilege sight; instead, it takes each figure back to its source, which is among other things *tactile*. It comes back in touch with itself in that origin without ever constituting in it, constituting itself in it, as some sort of unity. *Simultaneity* is its "proper" aspect — a proper(ty) that is never fixed in the possible identity-to-self of some form or other. It is always *fluid,* without neglecting the characteristics of fluids that are difficult to idealize: those rubbings between two infinitely near neighbors that create a dynamics. Its "style" resists and explodes every firmly established form, figure, idea, or concept. Which does not mean that it lacks style . . . but its "style" cannot be upheld as a thesis, cannot be the object of a position.[4]

Despite the abstract tenor of this characterization, the general traits Irigaray posits for women's discourse — inconsistency, fluidity, incoherence, tactility — are the very ones men have used to denigrate the female intellect. Irigaray's position seems a jumping-off point for a separatist feminism that renounces for women whatever has been tainted by masculinity — logic, coherence, power.

Hélène Cixous is a more difficult writer than Irigaray, but the problems of reading her are somewhat different. Where Irigaray is learned, detached, abstract, and so ambiguously ironical that her meaning is often in danger of being misunderstood, Cixous speaks primarily through images and metaphors. The intense poetic quality of her prose is part of what has caused her essay "The Laugh of the Medusa" to become the central manifesto of French feminism. Cixous's difficulty is intentional and programmatic: Feeling that the major modes of conceptual analysis themselves are anti-female, she writes in a way that resists dialectic. To show this, Cixous (following Derrida in *Of Grammatology*) sets up a series of binary oppositions (active/passive, sun/moon, culture/nature, day/night, father/mother, logos/pathos).

[3]See de Beauvoir, p. 635.

[4]Luce Irigaray, "The Power of Discourse," in *This Sex Which Is Not One* (Ithaca: Cornell University Press, 1985), p. 79.

Each pair can be analyzed as a hierarchy in which the former term represents the positive and masculine and the latter the negative and feminine principle. Nor can the terms live in harmony: Cixous suggests that, in each case, the masculine term is forced to "kill" the feminine one. This for her is the deadly "phallocentric" principle that she derives from Derrida's critique of logocentrism. Cixous rejects the idea of "feminine writing," as "a dangerous and stylish expression full of traps. . . . My work in fact aims at getting rid of words like 'feminine and masculine,' even 'man' and 'woman.'. . ."[5]

One might think Cixous, like Virginia Woolf, would be an exponent of androgyny; in fact Cixous attacks androgyny as an annulment of differences, and supports instead what she calls "the *other bisexuality,*" which involves the "multiplication of the effects of the inscription of desire, over all parts of my body and the other body, indeed, this *other bisexuality* doesn't annul differences, but stirs them up, pursues them, increases them" ("The Laugh of the Medusa"). For Cixous, woman is bisexual; man, unwilling to give up the phallus, is monosexual. This is the point at which the binary polarities, having been kicked out the door, creep back in through the window, and they return upside down, with the female terms on top. At one point Cixous speaks "of a decipherable libidinal femininity which can be read in a writing produced by a male or a female." But as she later explains "libidinal femininity," she ends up attributing it almost exclusively to biological females. She finds its essential, moist, life-giving properties, for example, in the work of women writers like Clarice Lispector, while the work of a male writer like Maurice Blanchot is "a text that goes toward the drying up." (She finds a feminine sensibility in one male writer, Heinrich von Kleist, but that, as she says, is "highly exceptional.") Female sexuality is "giving," where the male is retentive, avaricious; female sexuality achieves full genitality, while male sexuality is fixated in oral dominance or anal "exchange."[6] Where Derrida presented the standard polarities of Western culture in order to dismantle and discredit dialectical thinking, it seems that Cixous has adopted Derridean terminology for a philosophically different program that simply inverts the standard pairings.

GENDERING THE LOOK

Around the same time Cixous and Irigaray were theorizing about how to write the female body, the British film scholar Laura Mulvey was analyzing the inscription of the male gaze in film. Written from the same Lacanian perspective used by the French feminists, Mulvey's essay "Visual Pleasure and Narrative Cinema" (1975), reprinted here, has inspired not only an entire school of film theory, but an approach to literature in which narrative point of view, the seeing eye of the text and its reader, is substituted for the gaze of the camera and the spectator. In a sense the issues raised by such reader-oriented feminists as Judith Fetterley and Patrocinio Schweickart connect with Mulvey's analysis of the psychology of the reader as split

[5]Interview with Cixous in Verena Andermatt Conley, *Hélène Cixous: Writing the Feminine* (Lincoln and London: University of Nebraska Press, 1984), p. 129.

[6]Conley, 129–33.

between identification with the (usually female) object of the gaze of desire and identification with the (usually male) subject who functions as the protagonist of the narrative.[7]

Mulvey believes that the split psychodynamics between the male subject and female object is intractable within narrative film, whose drive from beginning through middle to end must turn on an erotics of desire and frustration.[8] She recommends as the only envisageable feminist solution the rejection of narrative itself. Her feminist heroes, like Chantal Akerman, are independent filmmakers who follow an aesthetic — pioneered by Bertolt Brecht in the theater and Jean-Luc Godard in film — of breaking the spectator's engagement with protagonists within plots and making discovery rather than pleasure the object of the film experience. Such an asceticism inevitably leads to a division between the commercial movies that define contemporary culture and an avant-garde cinema of ideas whose major audience, ironically, comprises the academics and intellectuals already converted to those ideas. Teresa de Lauretis, in *Alice Doesn't* (1984), rejects the hopelessness of Mulvey's conclusion, and explicates how women might "construct the terms of reference of another measure of desire and the conditions of visibility for another social subject" (155). Mulvey, too, has had second thoughts about the use being made of her work.

One also wonders, with a distance of more than twenty years from Mulvey's groundbreaking essay, whether her distinction between male as subject and female as passive object of the gaze may have been based too exclusively on the "classic cinema" of directors like Hitchcock and von Sternberg, who were notoriously obsessed with their leading ladies. The blockbuster films of the 1990s continue to show objects of voyeurism, but our gaze is often focused on male actors such as Arnold Schwartzenegger and Bruce Willis rather than on female icons comparable to Marlene Dietrich and Kim Novak. Have the post-feminist nineties created a new female-oriented cinema, where the erotic gaze of desire has shifted to sweaty leading men? Or has popular culture merely found new female objects of the gaze such as the supermodel, who can inspire desire without narrative? Minimally, it would seem that the classic split between the male subject and female object of the gaze has broken down within contemporary popular film, and that now *either* a Demi Moore *or* a Bruce Willis can be either the *subject* or the *object* of the gaze. The Oedipal agon continues to be the basic fantasy underlying film plots, but the male version of the conflict is featured less exclusively than it used to be, and where it is present, it can often operate unencumbered by obsessive heterosexual erotics.[9]

[7]Judith Fetterley has given the name "immasculation" to the process whereby female readers are forced to identify with male authors and characters, and thus with patriarchal ideology; she suggests that one answer is to become a "resisting reader": to read against the grain of the text when it asks one to reject one's own femininity (see p. 995). Patrocinio Schweickart in "Reading Ourselves" gives some support to this strategy but argues that it may go too far, since at least some androcentric texts contain what Fredric Jameson calls a "utopian moment" that can be recuperated for women by (mentally) reversing the sexes, giving the role of Subject to the female. See "Reading Ourselves: Toward a Feminist Theory of Reading," in *Gender and Reading: Essays on Readers Texts and Contexts,* ed. Elizabeth Flynn and Patrocinio P. Schweickart (Baltimore: Johns Hopkins University Press, 1986), pp. 1–62.

[8]For a fuller explanation of this erotics of plot, see Peter Brooks's "Freud's Masterplot," p. 1033.

[9]More is going on here than the traditional split between subject and object of the gaze. The close relationships between oddly matched "buddies" in contemporary action films (such as Bruce Willis and

BINARIES AND TALK ABOUT BINARIES

It is difficult to talk about "heterosexuality," as I just did, without raising the question of its binary opposite, "homosexuality." And just as the impulse of gender theory began with an effort to destabilize the customary boundaries of "masculinity" and "femininity," to clear the way for a different sort of discourse that could subvert the entrenched language of patriarchy, the next stage for gender theory was to take on the issues of sexual orientation and sexual identity.

While our society portrays binary oppositions like "masculine" and "feminine" or "straight" and "gay" as elementary "natural" categories, the rules have little to do with nature and everything to do with culture. The word "homosexual" has an astonishingly short history, dating from the last quarter of the nineteenth century, and "heterosexual" is an even newer term, apparently coined in opposition to "homosexual." It is not clear that "sexual identity" had the binary structure it does today much before the coining of these terms, and even today many people perform sexual acts that do not accord with the label they would apply to themselves. Precisely which sexual acts are "normal" and accepted and for whom depends upon the society in which one lives. For example, among the upper classes in Periclean Athens, it was considered normal for mature men to play the active sexual role with women, with both male and female slaves, and with male adolescents of their own class; and it was normal for male adolescents to take the passive sexual role with an adult mentor. But Athenian society thought it abnormal for men to continue to prefer the passive sexual role after coming to mature years and shameful to be the slave of sexual desire at any age.

Nor do the various binary oppositions hold their shape under close inspection. "Homosexuality" and "heterosexuality" cover not two but many forms of identity and map an enormous range of overlapping behaviors. The readers of Dr. Alfred Kinsey's pioneering surveys of sexual behavior in American men and women (1948 and 1953) were shocked to learn that men and women who considered themselves heterosexual had, more often than not, a history of experimentation with homosexual activities, and that it was unusual for homosexuals not to have tried heterosexual acts. Today we are no longer shocked: Indeed, we tend to think that every man, however masculine, has his feminine side (and vice versa), and that being too "manly" to stay in touch with one's inner woman is a defect rather than a virtue. In this sense we are all bisexual, to one degree or another: Our "sexual orientation" is merely a bias to one side or the other. Adrienne Rich speaks of the "lesbian continuum" as a way of suggesting the range of activities by which women bond to each other, not confined to "consciously desired genital sexual experience with another woman," activities including "the sharing of a rich inner life, the bonding against male tyranny, the giving and receiving of practical and political support."[10]

Danny Glover in *Die Hard with a Vengeance* or Sean Connery and Nicolas Cage in *The Rock*) are often triangulated through their mutual concern about one or both men's relationships with a woman (wife, girlfriend, daughter) who is either kept offscreen or relegated to a bit part. Eve Kosofsky Sedgwick's discussion of male homosocial desire and how it can be handled so as to defuse its erotic potential clearly applies to more than the nineteenth-century narratives she treats in *Between Men.* See the discussion of Sedgwick, p. 1440.

[10]Adrienne Rich, "Compulsory Heterosexuality" (1980), in *The Lesbian and Gay Studies Reader,* ed. Henry Abelove et al. (New York: Routledge, 1993), p. 227.

Similarly, the distinction between "masculine" and "feminine" activities and behaviors is constantly changing, so that women who wear baseball caps and fatigues, pump iron, and smoke cigars (at the appropriate times and seasons) can be perceived as more piquantly sexy by some heterosexual men than those women who wear white frocks and gloves and look down demurely. (Needless to say, the sexual orientation of the observer makes a difference: What most lesbians find appealing in a woman may differ from what attracts most heterosexual men.) One needs to question, too, whether such change simply involves crossing borders: Is the drag queen appropriating onto his male body the signifiers of feminine gender (makeup, wigs, gowns, high heels), or does the drag queen represent a separate form of sexuality? Even the physical dualism of sexual genetic structures and bodily parts breaks down when one considers those instances — the XXY syndromes, natural sexual bimorphisms, as well as surgical transsexuals — that defy attempts at binary classification. However, the real question for all the theorists represented in this chapter is not about the physical signifiers of sexuality but about its psychology and its discourse.

SEX AND POLITICS

If none of this is late-breaking news, much of the credit goes to contemporary gender theorists, who have been researching the historical parameters of sex and gender for the past twenty years. But while theirs is a research project, mostly financed by the universities, it is a politically committed research project, more an Arnoldian "criticism of life" than a disinterested investigation of literary texts. Toward the end of his essay "Homographesis," Lee Edelman becomes momentarily defensive about drawing conclusions that could be seen as leading merely to newer and more subtle readings of literary texts, and feels compelled to insist that his analysis of the rhetoric of gender is not "an apolitical formalism" but the grounding of an effective political critique of the patriarchal, homophobic ideology of gender.

The political movement, comparable to suffragist feminism, that aims to overturn the homophobic constructions of contemporary American discourse and the legal penalties gay men and lesbians endure was given a powerful impetus nearly thirty years ago with the legendary Stonewall rebellion of 1969 in New York City, which occurred in reaction to an illegal police raid on a gay bar. A more militant "gay liberation" program has been the unspoken motivation of much of gender studies since that time. The force, even stridency, of such political critique has much to do with conditions in contemporary America, where gays and lesbians are among the few minorities still suffering under *legal* discrimination, discrimination that is not merely a threat to dignity and peace of mind but which can have serious, even lethal, consequences.

While some European countries, notably England and Germany, have decriminalized all sexual activities between consenting adults, in many (perhaps most) American jurisdictions consensual homosexual activity is still a felony carrying a prison term, with longer terms for repeat offenders. Although many gays have served with conspicuous bravery in the U.S. military, admitting one's homosexual orientation constitutes sufficient grounds for dishonorable discharge from the armed services. For more than a decade, AIDS research was limited and underfinanced, at least partly because almost all of those dying at the outset were gay males. (AIDS was popularly called "the gay plague," as though the viral disease were a punishment from Jehovah.) Homosexuality is often considered just grounds for denying a parent custody and visitation rights, and millions of gay men and women have children they love dearly. One's estate descends without a will and untaxed to one's spouse of the opposite sex but not to a long-term companion of the same sex, and few employers extend the fringe benefits of employment — insurance, medical coverage, and so on — to anyone except a husband or wife.

Those who are outraged that Jews, women, and blacks still often suffer from illegal discrimination should find even more unspeakable the *legal* burdens under which gays and lesbians live. It is no wonder that so many are reluctant to come "out of the closet" and announce their preference for fear of the hundreds of legal penalties and the thousands of extralegal modes of retaliation. Homophobic prejudices are all the more irrational since homosexuality is neither a disease nor a lifestyle decision one intentionally makes. Recent biological research has begun to suggest that attraction to one's own or the opposite sex is governed, at least in part, by complex genetic codes. However, gay liberationists are not entirely happy about the prospect of isolating a "gay gene." While it might help dissolve some people's prejudices to think of homosexuality as a genetically determined trait, it could also encourage homophobic parents to abort fetuses carrying the gene and would allow societies more repressive than ours to discover gays in even the darkest closet. More important to the issues raised by the theorists collected here, the notion of biological determinism reifies and essentializes homosexuality as a genetic outcome rather than encouraging us to understand it as a social practice or a discourse.

FOUCAULT AND THE HISTORICIZATION OF SEXUALITY

That homosexuality should be thought of preeminently as a "discourse" rather than as an action that can be studied by positivistic scientific method, or thoughts and feelings that can be analyzed by the polls of social science, is a sign of the pervasive influence on gay studies of Michel Foucault.[11] When it appeared in 1976, Foucault's *Le Volonté de savoir* (*The Will to Knowledge*), Volume I of *The History of Sexuality,* seemed to promise an appropriate sequel to his historical studies of madhouses (*Folie et Deraison* [*Madness and Civilization*], 1961), hospitals (*Le Naissance du Clinique* [*The Birth of the Clinic*], 1963), and prisons (*Surveillir et Punir* [*Discipline and Punish*], 1975) as the sites in which society isolates and punishes deviation.

While the popular view of the Victorian era is that it was a unique period of sexual repression preceded and followed by eras of greater personal liberty and sexual

[11]For more on Foucault, see the introductions to Structuralism, Semiotics, and Deconstruction and New Historicism and Cultural Studies, pp. 823 and 1208, respectively, and the Foucault texts in those chapters.

candor, Foucault suggests that in fact a variety of different forms of repression had succeeded one another in the centuries before, during, and after the nineteenth century. Though Foucault was gay, the gay male is not the sole or even the principal focus of *The History of Sexuality,* but only one of four categories he suggests as sites of study. (The others are the hysterical female, the masturbating child, and the Malthusian couple.) Foucault planned to analyze the transformations of power and knowledge from the early modern era to the present in relation to each of these categories.

Foucault's first volume is an extended meditation, without very much in the way of specific data, on the way he intends to approach sexuality as a site of what he had come to call *pouvoir/savoir* ("power/knowledge"). For Foucault, knowledge confers power, while having power allows one to define what counts as knowledge. But, for Foucault, power is not necessarily the centralized power of the monarch or the ruling class; it is not a system imposed from above, like the juridical system of law; Foucault conceives of power as a field of forces operating in all directions in private as well as public life. Foucault uses this conception of power to analyze the different ways in which the human body, conceived as a type of machine from the seventeenth century onward, was "improved" in its operation by what he calls a "technology" of sex that was directed by experts of various sorts — priests, lawyers, doctors, scientists, educators, therapists — and operated both through and outside the family structure. The specific forms of repression, prohibition, and blockage of sexual desires operate differently in different areas and at different times (genuine liberation for the individual being a hopeless ideal beyond the reach of any social system Foucault is capable of envisioning). In the early twentieth century, for example, an unhappy and rebellious adolescent might have been diagnosed by educators as suffering from excessive masturbation, which was presumed to cause insanity; today, however, he or she might be treated by therapists who would interview the parents about their own sexual problems, which would be presumed to be responsible for those of their children.

Foucault had apparently prepared to spend the rest of what promised to be a long life researching the changing social practices and discourses of various forms of sexuality. But during a stay at the University of California at Berkeley, he decided to shift his project from exterior questions concerning the impact of power and knowledge on the individual to the more psychological issue of how individuals come "to recognize themselves as subjects of a 'sexuality'" through the "hermeneutics of desire" (*Uses of Pleasure,* 4–6). Foucault, in other words, shifted his study towards the production of a history of sexual identity rather than a history of sexual practices. The second volume of the *History of Sexuality, The Uses of Pleasure* (1984; translated 1985), which takes up the place of sexuality and desire in ancient Greece, and the third volume, *The Care of the Self* (1984; translated 1986) which covers the first two centuries of the Roman empire, bear the marks of this shift in Foucault's program. These volumes, obviously meant to be continued, were also written under the pressure of time, as Foucault was diagnosed with AIDS in the early 1980s. Both volumes were published after Foucault's death in 1984.

QUEER THEORY AND HOMOSEXUAL PANIC

The history of sexuality has continued to be a subject of theorizing and research since Foucault, and perhaps the most celebrated American contributor to this field has been Eve Kosofsky Sedgwick. Her groundbreaking *Between Men: English Literature and Male Homosocial Desire* (1985) theorized that the strong and close personal relationships between men needed for success in nineteenth-century Britain placed Victorian males in a state of continual homosexual panic, a panic that was often assuaged by triangulating the relationship through a woman. David Copperfield's relation to Steerforth via Little Em'ly is an obvious fictional representation of this, but such triangulated relationships also appear, as one might expect, in literary biography and other non-fiction narratives of the age. One recalls, for example, that Arthur Henry Hallam was not only Tennyson's closest friend at the time of his death, but had become his sister's fiancé. Sedgwick's *Epistemology of the Closet* (1990) advances her study to the end of World War I, with discussions of Melville, Wilde, James, and Proust. It also makes explicit the antihomophobic politics on which it is founded. Indeed, Sedgwick insists that homosexuality is everyone's issue, as heterosexual males define their own identity in opposition to — and thus in terms of — that of the gay Other, and maneuver in significant ways to obscure their own objects of desire.

The issue of gay identity as such dominates the work of both Lee Edelman and Judith Butler. Butler's book *Gender Trouble* (1990) uses a deconstructive rhetoric to subvert the binarisms of male/female, masculine/feminine, and gay/straight. While many gay liberationists have attempted to construct positive models of gay identity as a way of resisting a homophobic society, to Butler the entire issue of gender identity is political poison. The essentialization of categories like "gay" and "straight" or "female" and "male," is inherently restrictive. Just as the 1970s feminist project of creating a positive image of Woman implicitly defined an ideal for every woman to live up to, depriving each individual of the right to be whoever and whatever she was, the creation of fixed images of gay and lesbian identity can result in the "regulatory imperative" to be a "proper" gay or lesbian individual.

In "Imitation and Gender Insubordination" (1991), Butler confesses that she "suffered for a long time . . . from being told that what I 'am' is a copy, an imitation, a derivative example, a shadow of the real." For those who essentialize sexuality, biological sex defines one's gender, and gender defines one's sexual orientation. Heterosexuals define themselves by oppressing those who transgress, whose signifiers don't line up. And just as the notion of a platonic ideal of Woman has been used to oppress lesbians, the image of an ideal Lesbian can be used to oppress those who do not come up to whatever mark the politics of the group has set forth. In good Derridean fashion, Butler deconstructs the binary of original vs. copy, questioning not merely which is the real and which the imitation, but whether our entire concept of gender is not in fact based on imitations for which no real essences exist. Both homosexuals and heterosexuals seem to want to buy into this destructive mythic logic, in which gender is "an imitation that performatively constitutes itself as the original." But to perform something is to play at something; to *play* something as opposed to *being* something. Just as Derrida insisted on recognizing language as a freeplay of signifiers lacking a stable center, Butler suggests that we would spare ourselves a great deal of misery by recognizing that there are no fixed sexual identities that shape our actions and thoughts, that gender is something we "put on" or perform. What we do, our performances from moment to moment, driven by strong inner imperatives, are all we are or can be.

Lee Edelman, in "Homographesis" (1989), also uses deconstruction to displace and call into question the notion of "gay identity." For Edelman, homosexuality has a complex relation to writing. Sodomy was notoriously the "sin that dare not speak its name," the capital crime that British law found so "unspeakable" that a description of what constituted it was not even written down in the statute books. At the same time, homosexual desire was represented as being inscribed on the bodies of its participants, who were supposed to bear some mark like that of Cain upon their faces, like the portrait (as opposed to the visage) of Wilde's Dorian Gray. Edelman's title is a verbal play upon the opposition between the unwritable and the already-written. A *homograph* is one word that can represent two signifieds, such as *last,* which can signify both the ultimate in a series and the wooden mold for a leather shoe. The word "homographesis" can signify both the practice of such a doubled writing (homograph/esis) and the act of inscribing, or putting into writing, homosexuality (homo/graphesis). *Homographesis* is thus itself a homograph.

Edelman discusses a wide variety of literary texts, including works by Milton, Stevens, and Proust, analyzing in each case the way in which sameness and difference in sexuality are articulated into the rhetorical structure of the text as metaphorical or metonymic tropes. He thus expands the range of texts on which queer theory operates from works by gay writers and works with gay characters to all of literature, since practically every literary text bears witness to the "textual articulations and cultural constructions of sexuality." In doing so, his aim is to deconstruct not merely literature, but the concept of gay identity itself.

ESCAPING THE FREUDIAN MATRIX

Butler and Edelman are engaged in one side of the theoretical task of gay liberation, that of liberating the movement from its recapitulation of the same binarism and exclusionary politics that characterize patriarchal ideology, and that, as we have seen, continue to characterize some schools of feminist thought. The other side of the theoretical task is that of accomplishing for gays what Cixous and Irigaray have achieved for women in their rereadings of Freud and Lacan: the recuperation of the psychoanalytical discourse of gender as a language that heals rather than wounds the spirit. This is not an easy task, as Freud's view of homosexuality is that it stems from a wrong turning, a regression to an earlier stage of development caused by failure to make a necessary leap. According to Freud, the individual progresses through a series of stages, from early infantile sexuality, an autoeroticism that seeks pleasure purely in the self, to a primary narcissism in which one loves oneself in undifferentiated unity with the parent, to the conflicts of the Oedipal crisis, in which genuine object relations develop that lead to desire for the opposite sex. In the case of the homosexual, Freud argues that some crushing of the self-image occurs in the course of development that leads the child to choose as a sexual object a figure of the same sex, embodying the ideal elements the child feels to be missing from himself.

Freud's gendering of the subject of this analysis as male is not an accident, of course. In "Homo-Narcissism, or, Heterosexuality" (1990), Michael Warner analyzes Freud's various modelings of heterosexual and homosexual development at different stages of his analytic theories. Warner notes the arbitrariness of Freud's assumptions about both the gender of the subject and the gender of the parent with whom the subject identifies, and points to Freud's own recognition of this arbitrariness and his strange neglect of this recognition. Warner shows that Freud's analysis of the development of adult love and sexuality — and Lacan's as well — is warped by what Simone de Beauvoir, in *The Second Sex,* viewed as the ideological basis of patriarchy: the constitution of man as subject and woman as Other.[12] For Freud and Lacan, the "other" marked in the term *hetero*-sexuality can only mean Other in gender: The Subject must be a man, the Object must be a woman. But Warner argues that surely there are many markers of sameness and difference between the self and the nonself. Warner's claim is that, freed of the patriarchal bias that sees gender as our only access to alterity, or otherness, homosexual love (which loves in the Other the ego ideal, what it would like to be) is no more regressive than heterosexual love (which loves in the Other the reflection of its own ego on the imaginary level). Indeed, Warner suggests that heterosexual love would be more deeply fulfilling to the extent that it too engaged that utopian longing for the ego ideal. Apart from a brief reference to Charles Brockden Brown's novel *Arthur Mervyn,* Warner does not bring literature into his analysis, but it is clear how productive the application of this sort of theorizing about homosexual and homosocial relations to a variety of literary texts could be. In addition to deepening the analysis Sedgwick has made of the close triangulated relationships between male characters in much of nineteenth-century literature, Warner's ideas help to illuminate the bonding that occurs in apparently nonerotic relationships between male and female characters (such as that between Lydgate and Dorothea in Eliot's *Middlemarch*).

While queer theory and gender studies have become areas of theory that are distinct from feminist criticism and women's studies, it would be misleading to ignore the connections between these schools. Gender studies became possible as a result of the projects of feminist criticism, and queer theory has drawn both energies and insights from feminist thinkers. In their first books, both Butler and Sedgwick defined their work as feminist, and Butler, especially, is still very sensitive to the connections between gender theory and feminism. Which is more important: likeness or difference? The contradictions inherent in identity politics inevitably generate dual impulses to split off and to merge, as gay males, lesbians, bisexuals, and cross-dressers sense how different their cultural situations and concerns are from those of

[12]See the introduction to de Beauvoir, p. 635.

"mainstream" feminists but simultaneously understand the political consequences of isolation and the advantages of a combined resistance to normative patriarchy.

Selected Bibliography

Abelove, Henry, Michèle Aina Barale, and David M. Halperin, eds. *The Lesbian and Gay Studies Reader.* New York: Routledge, 1993.

Belsey, Catherine. *Critical Practice.* New York: Methuen, 1980.

Bersani, Leo. "Is the Rectum a Grave?" *October* 43 (1987): 197–222.

Boone, Joseph Allen. *Tradition Counter Tradition: Love and the Form of Fiction.* Chicago: University of Chicago Press, 1987.

Boone, Joseph Allen, and Michael Caddon, eds. *Engendering Men: The Question of Male Feminist Criticism.* New York: Routledge, 1990.

Boswell, John. *Christianity, Social Tolerance, and Homosexuality: Gay People in Western Europe from the Beginning of the Christian Era to the Fourteenth Century.* Chicago: University of Chicago Press, 1980.

Bray, Alan. *Homosexuality in Renaissance England.* London: Gay Men's Press, 1982.

Butler, Judith. *Gender Trouble: Feminism and the Subversion of Identity.* New York and London: Routledge, 1990.

Butters, Ronald R., John M. Clum, and Michael Mood, eds. *Displacing Homophobia: Gay Male Perspectives in Literature and Culture.* Durham, NC: Duke University Press, 1989.

Cixous, Hélène. "Le Rire de la Méduse." *L'Arc* 61 (1975): 39–54. Trans. Keith and Paula Cohen as "The Laugh of the Medusa," *Signs* 1 (1976): 875–99.

———. *La Jeune née* (with Catherine Clément). Paris: UGE Press, 1975. Trans. Betsy Wing as *The Newly Born Woman.* Minneapolis: University of Minnesota Press, 1986.

Crompton, Louis. *Byron and Greek Love: Homophobia in Nineteenth-Century England.* Berkeley and Los Angeles: University of California Press, 1985.

De Lauretis, Teresa. *Alice Doesn't: Feminism, Semiotics, Cinema.* Bloomington: Indiana University Press, 1984.

———, ed. *The Practice of Love: Lesbian Sexualities and Perverse Desire.* Bloomington: Indiana University Press, 1994.

Edelman, Lee. *Homographesis: Essays in Gay Literary and Cultural Theory.* New York and London: Routledge, 1994.

Foucault, Michel. *The History of Sexuality,* Volume I: *The Will to Knowledge,* trans. Robert Hurley. New York: Random House, 1980.

———. Volume II: *The Uses of Pleasure,* trans. Robert Hurley. New York: Pantheon, 1985.

———. Volume III: *The Care of the Self,* trans. Robert Hurley. New York: Pantheon, 1986.

Fuss, Diana, ed. *Inside/Out: Lesbian Theories, Gay Theories.* New York: Routledge, 1991.

Gallop, Jane. *The Daugher's Seduction: Feminism and Psychoanalysis.* Ithaca: Cornell University Press, 1982.

Halperin, David. *One Hundred Years of Homosexuality and Other Essays on Greek Love.* New York: Routledge, 1990.

Irigaray, Luce. *Spéculum de l'autre femme.* Paris: Minuit, 1974. Trans. Gillian C. Gill as *The Speculum of the Other Woman.* Ithaca: Cornell University Press, 1985.

———. *Ce sexe qui n'en est pas un.* Paris: Minuit, 1977. Trans. Catharine Porter with Carolyn Burke as *This Sex Which is Not One.* Ithaca: Cornell University Press, 1985.

Jagose, Annamarie. *Queer Theory.* Victoria: Melbourne University Press, 1996.

Jardine, Alice. *Gynesis: Configurations of Woman and Modernity.* Ithaca: Cornell University Press, 1985.

Kauffman, Linda, ed. *Gender and Theory: Dialogues on Feminist Criticism.* New York: Blackwell, 1985.
Keohane, Nannerl, Michelle Z. Rosaldo, and Barbara C. Gelpi, eds. *Feminist Theory: A Critique of Ideology.* Chicago: University of Chicago Press, 1982.
Koestenbaum, Wayne. *The Queen's Throat: Opera, Homosexuality and the Mystery of Desire.* New York: Poseidon Press, 1993.
Kruger, Steven. *AIDS Narratives.* New York: Garland, 1996.
Marks, Elaine, and Isabelle de Courtivron, eds. *New French Feminisms: An Anthology.* Amherst: University of Massachusetts Press, 1980.
Miller, D. A. *The Novel and the Police.* Berkeley: University of California Press, 1988.
Miller, Nancy K., ed. *The Poetics of Gender.* New York: Columbia University Press, 1986.
Morton, Donald, ed. *The Material Queer.* Boulder, CO: Westview Press, 1996.
Mulvey, Laura. *Visual and Other Pleasures.* Basingstoke: Macmillan, 1989.
Rich, Adrienne. "Compulsory Heterosexuality and Lesbian Existence." In *Women, Sex and Sexuality,* ed. Catharine Stimpson and Ethel Spector Person. Chicago: University of Chicago Press, 1980, pp. 62–91.
Rosario, Vernon A., ed. *Science and Homosexualities.* New York: Routledge, 1997.
Rubin, Gayle. "Thinking Sex: Notes for a Radical Theory of the Politics of Sexuality." In *Pleasure and Danger: Exploring Female Sexuality,* ed. Carol A. Vance. New York: Routledge, 1984, pp. 267–319.
Sedgwick, Eve Kosofsky. *Between Men: English Literature and Male Homosocial Desire.* New York: Columbia University Press, 1985.
———. *Epistemology of the Closet.* Berkeley: University of California Press, 1990.
Seidman, Steven. *Queer Theory/Sociology.* Cambridge: Blackwell, 1996.
Watney, Simon. *Policing Desire: Pornography, AIDS and the Media.* Minneapolis: University of Minnesota Press, 1987.
Weeks, Jeffrey. *Sex, Politics and Society: The Regulation of Sexuality Since 1800.* New York: Longman, 1981.
———. *Sexuality and Its Discontents: Meanings, Myths and Modern Sexualities.* London: Routledge, 1985.
Wittreich, Joseph. *Feminist Milton.* Ithaca: Cornell University Press, 1987.

Laura Mulvey

b. 1941

Laura Mulvey is a British filmmaker and director who teaches cinema studies at the University of East Anglia and the London College of Printing. Her films include Penthesilea *(1974),* Riddles of the Sphinx *(1978),* Amyl *(1980),* Crystal Gazing *(1981), and* The Bad Sister *(1983). Her books on the gaze in cinema and photography include* Visual and Other Pleasures *(1989),* Citizen Kane *(1993),* Jimmie Durham *(1995), and* Fetishism and Curiosity *(1996). "Visual Pleasure and Narrative Cinema," written originally in 1973, appeared in* Screen *in 1975. In a piece entitled "Afterthoughts on Visual Pleasure and Narrative Cinema," published in* Framework *in 1981, Mulvey reflects on her famous essay.*

Visual Pleasure and Narrative Cinema

I. INTRODUCTION

(a) A Political Use of Psychoanalysis

This paper intends to use psychoanalysis to discover where and how the fascination of film is reinforced by pre-existing patterns of fascination already at work within the individual subject and the social formations that have moulded him. It takes as its starting-point the way film reflects, reveals and even plays on the straight, socially established interpretation of sexual difference which controls images, erotic ways of looking and spectacle. It is helpful to understand what the cinema has been, how its magic has worked in the past, while attempting a theory and a practice which will challenge this cinema of the past. Psychoanalytic theory is thus appropriated here as a political weapon, demonstrating the way the unconscious of patriarchal society has structured film form.

The paradox of phallocentrism[1] in all its manifestations is that it depends on the image of the castrated woman to give order and meaning to its world. An idea of woman stands as linchpin to the system: it is her lack that produces the phallus as a symbolic presence, it is her desire to make good the lack that the phallus signifies. Recent writing in *Screen* about psychoanalysis and the cinema has not sufficiently brought out the importance of the representation of the female form in a symbolic order in which, in the last resort, it speaks castration and nothing else. To summarise briefly: the function of woman in forming the patriarchal unconscious is twofold: she firstly symbolises the castration threat by her real lack of a penis and secondly thereby raises her child into the symbolic. Once this has been achieved, her meaning in the process is at an end. It does not last into the world of law and language except as a memory, which oscillates between memory of maternal plentitude and memory of lack. Both are posited on nature (or on anatomy in Freud's famous phrase).[2] Woman's desire is subjugated to her image as bearer of the bleeding wound; she can exist only in relation to castration and cannot transcend it. She turns her child into the signifier of her own desire to possess a penis (the condition, she imagines, of entry into the symbolic). Either she must gracefully give way to the word, the name of the father and the law, or else struggle to keep her child down with her in the half-light of the imaginary. Woman then stands in patriarchal culture as a signifier for the male other, bound by a symbolic order in which man can live out his fantasies and obsessions through linguistic command by imposing them on the silent image of woman still tied to her place as bearer, not maker, of meaning.

There is an obvious interest in this analysis for feminists, a beauty in its exact rendering of the frustration experienced under the phallocentric order. It gets us nearer to the roots of our oppression, it brings closer an articulation of the problem, it faces us with the ultimate challenge: how to fight the unconscious structured like a language (formed critically at the moment of arrival of language) while still caught within the language of the patriarchy? There is no way in which we can produce an alternative out of the blue, but we can begin to make a break by examining patriarchy with the tools it provides, of which psychoanalysis is not the only but an important one. We are still separated by a great gap from important issues for the female unconscious which are scarcely relevant to phallocentric theory: the sexing of the female infant and her relationship to the symbolic, the sexually mature woman as non-mother, maternity outside the sig-

[1]*Phallocentrism* refers to the organization of the symbolic order, specifically, the binary opposition in which the phallus represents the positive principle of presence as a masculine entity, as opposed to a "castrated" feminine entity (see the introduction, p. 1434). Mulvey's terminology here — the *phallus* as the signifier of desire, the *imaginary* and *symbolic* orders as the sites of image and word, the dialectical relation between *lack, need,* and *desire* — derives from Jacques Lacan; see the introduction to Psychoanalytic Theory, p. 1019. [Ed.]

[2]Freud's famous phrase is "Anatomy is destiny." [Ed.]

nification of the phallus, the vagina. But, at this point, psychoanalytic theory as it now stands can at least advance our understanding of the *status quo,* of the patriarchal order in which we are caught.

(b) Destruction of Pleasure as a Radical Weapon

As an advanced representation system, the cinema poses questions about the ways the unconscious (formed by the dominant order) structures ways of seeing and pleasure in looking. Cinema has changed over the last few decades. It is no longer the monolithic system based on large capital investment exemplified at its best by Hollywood in the 1930s, 1940s and 1950s. Technological advances (16mm and so on) have changed the economic conditions of cinematic production, which can now be artisanal as well as capitalist.[3] Thus it has been possible for an alternative cinema to develop. However self-conscious and ironic Hollywood managed to be, it always restricted itself to a formal *mise en scène*[4] reflecting the dominant ideological concept of the cinema. The alternative cinema provides a space for the birth of a cinema which is radical in both a political and an aesthetic sense and challenges the basic assumptions of the mainstream film. This is not to reject the latter moralistically, but to highlight the ways in which its formal preoccupations reflect the psychical obsessions of the society which produced it and, further, to stress that the alternative cinema must start specifically by reacting against these obsessions and assumptions. A politically and aesthetically avant-garde cinema is now possible, but it can still only exist as a counterpoint.

The magic of the Hollywood style at its best (and of all the cinema which fell within its sphere of influence) arose, not exclusively, but in one important aspect, from its skilled and satisfying manipulation of visual pleasure. Unchallenged, mainstream film coded the erotic into the language of the dominant patriarchal order. In the highly developed Hollywood cinema it was only through these codes that the alienated subject, torn in his imaginary memory by a sense of loss, by the terror of potential lack in fantasy, came near to finding a glimpse of satisfaction: through its formal beauty and its play on his own formative obsessions. This article will discuss the interweaving of that erotic pleasure in film, its meaning and, in particular, the central place of the image of woman. It is said that analysing pleasure, or beauty, destroys it. That is the intention of this article. The satisfaction and reinforcement of the ego that represent the high point of film history hitherto must be attacked. Not in favour of a reconstructed new pleasure, which cannot exist in the abstract, nor of intellectualised unpleasure, but to make way for a total negation of the ease and plenitude of the narrative fiction film. The alternative is the thrill that comes from leaving the past behind without simply rejecting it, transcending outworn or oppressive forms, and daring to break with normal pleasurable expectations in order to conceive a new language of desire.

II. PLEASURE IN LOOKING/ FASCINATION WITH THE HUMAN FORM

A. The cinema offers a number of possible pleasures. One is scopophilia (pleasure in looking). There are circumstances in which looking itself is a source of pleasure, just as, in the reverse formation, there is pleasure in being looked at. Originally, in his *Three Essays on Sexuality,*[5] Freud isolated scopophilia as one of the component instincts of sexuality which exist as drives quite independently of the erotogenic zones. At this point he associated scopophilia with taking other people as objects, subjecting them to a controlling and curious gaze. His particular examples centre on the voyeuristic activities of children,

[3]The 35mm film used by Hollywood was too expensive to permit very extensive use by those outside the studios; the advent of 16mm film in the 1960s allowed an alternative cinema to develop and proliferate. [Ed.]

[4]Staging. [Ed.]

[5]Sigmund Freud published *Three Essays on the Theory of Sexuality* in 1905, "Instincts and Their Vicissitudes" in 1915. [Ed.]

their desire to see and make sure of the private and forbidden (curiosity about other people's genital and bodily functions, about the presence or absence of the penis and, retrospectively, about the primal scene). In this analysis scopophilia is essentially active. (Later, in "Instincts and Their Vicissitudes," Freud developed his theory of scopophilia further, attaching it initially to pregenital auto-eroticism, after which, by analogy, the pleasure of the look is transferred to others. There is a close working here of the relationship between the active instinct and its further development in a narcissistic form.) Although the instinct is modified by other factors, in particular the constitution of the ego, it continues to exist as the erotic basis for pleasure in looking at another person as object. At the extreme, it can become fixated into a perversion, producing obsessive voyeurs and Peeping Toms whose only sexual satisfaction can come from watching, in an active controlling sense, an objectified other.

At first glance, the cinema would seem to be remote from the undercover world of the surreptitious observation of an unknowing and unwilling victim. What is seen on the screen is so manifestly shown. But the mass of mainstream film, and the conventions within which it has consciously evolved, portray a hermetically sealed world which unwinds magically, indifferent to the presence of the audience, producing for them a sense of separation and playing on their voyeuristic fantasy. Moreover the extreme contrast between the darkness in the auditorium (which also isolates the spectators from one another) and the brilliance of the shifting patterns of light and shade on the screen helps to promote the illusion of voyeuristic separation. Although the film is really being shown, is there to be seen, conditions of screening and narrative conventions give the spectator an illusion of looking in on a private world. Among other things, the position of the spectators in the cinema is blatantly one of repression of their exhibitionism and projection of the repressed desire onto the performer.

B. The cinema satisfies a primordial wish for pleasurable looking, but it also goes further, developing scopophilia in its narcissistic aspect. The conventions of mainstream film focus attention on the human form. Scale, space, stories are all anthropomorphic. Here, curiosity and the wish to look intermingle with a fascination with likeness and recognition: the human face, the human body, the relationship between the human form and its surroundings, the visible presence of the person in the world. Jacques Lacan has described how the moment when a child recognises its own image in the mirror is crucial for the constitution of the ego. Several aspects of this analysis are relevant here. The mirror phase occurs at a time when children's physical ambitions outstrip their motor capacity, with the result that their recognition of themselves is joyous in that they imagine their mirror image to be more complete, more perfect than they experience in their own body. Recognition is thus overlaid with misrecognition: the image recognised is conceived as the reflected body of the self, but its misrecognition as superior projects this body outside itself as an ideal ego, the alienated subject which, reintrojected as an ego ideal, prepares the way for identification with others in the future. This mirror moment predates language for the child.[6]

Important for this article is the fact that it is an image that constitutes the matrix of the imaginary, of recognition/misrecognition and identification, and hence of the first articulation of the I, of subjectivity. This is a moment when an older fascination with looking (at the mother's face, for an obvious example) collides with the initial inklings of self-awareness. Hence it is the birth of the long love affair/despair between image and self-image which has found such intensity of expression in film and such joyous recognition in the cinema audience. Quite apart from the extraneous similarities between screen and mirror (the framing of the human form in its surroundings, for instance), the cinema has structures of fascination strong enough to allow temporary loss of ego while simultaneously reinforcing it. The sense of forgetting the world as the ego has come to perceive it (I

[6]See Jacques Lacan, "The Mirror Stage as Formative of the Function of the I as Revealed in Psychoanalytic Experience" (1949), in *Écrits: A Selection,* trans. Alan Sheridan (New York: Norton, 1977), pp. 1–7. [Ed.]

forgot who I am and where I was) is nostalgically reminiscent of that pre-subjective moment of image recognition. While at the same time, the cinema has distinguished itself in the production of ego ideals, through the star system for instance. Stars provide a focus or centre both to screen space and screen story where they act out a complex process of likeness and difference (the glamorous impersonates the ordinary).

C. Sections A and B have set out two contradictory aspects of the pleasurable structures of looking in the conventional cinematic situation. The first, scopophilic, arises from pleasure in using another person as an object of sexual stimulation through sight. The second, developed through narcissism and the constitution of the ego, comes from identification with the image seen. Thus, in film terms, one implies a separation of the erotic identity of the subject from the object on the screen (active scopophilia), the other demands identification of the ego with the object on the screen through the spectator's fascination with and recognition of his like. The first is a function of the sexual instincts, the second of ego libido. This dichotomy was crucial for Freud. Although he saw the two as interacting and overlaying each other, the tension between instinctual drives and self-preservation polarises in terms of pleasure. But both are formative structures, mechanisms without intrinsic meaning. In themselves they have no signification, unless attached to an idealisation. Both pursue aims in indifference to perceptual reality, and motivate eroticised phantasmagoria that affect the subject's perception of the world to make a mockery of empirical objectivity.

During its history, the cinema seems to have evolved a particular illusion of reality in which this contradiction between libido and ego has found a beautifully complementary fantasy world. In *reality* the fantasy world of the screen is subject to the law which produces it. Sexual instincts and identification processes have a meaning within the symbolic order which articulates desire. Desire, born with language, allows the possibility of transcending the instinctual and the imaginary, but its point of reference continually returns to the traumatic moment of its birth: the castration complex. Hence the look, pleasurable in form, can be threatening in content, and it is woman as representation/image that crystallises this paradox.

III. WOMAN AS IMAGE, MAN AS BEARER OF THE LOOK

A. In a world ordered by sexual imbalance, pleasure in looking has been split between active/male and passive/female. The determining male gaze projects its fantasy onto the female figure, which is styled accordingly. In their traditional exhibitionist role women are simultaneously looked at and displayed, with their appearance coded for strong visual and erotic impact so that they can be said to connote *to-be-looked-at-ness*. Woman displayed as sexual object is the *leitmotif*[7] of erotic spectacle: from pin-ups to strip-tease, from Ziegfeld to Busby Berkeley,[8] she holds the look, and plays to and signifies male desire. Mainstream film neatly combines spectacle and narrative. (Note, however, how, in the musical, song-and-dance numbers interrupt the flow of the diegesis.[9]) The presence of woman is an indispensable element of spectacle in normal narrative film, yet her visual presence tends to work against the development of a story-line, to freeze the flow of action in moments of erotic contemplation. This alien presence then has to be integrated into cohesion with the narrative. As Budd Boetticher has put it:

> What counts is what the heroine provokes, or rather what she represents. She is the one, or rather the love or fear she inspires in the hero, or else the concern he feels for her, who makes him act the way he does. In herself the woman has not the slightest importance.

(A recent tendency in narrative film has been to dispense with this problem altogether; hence the

[7]Recurring theme. [Ed.]

[8]Florenz Ziegfeld (1867–1932) was the producer, from 1907, of the *Ziegfeld Follies*, an annual musical revue staged in New York, featuring beautiful, often scantily clad, chorus girls. Busby Berkeley (1895–1976) was the director and choreographer of numerous films, beginning with *42nd Street* (1933); he created geometrically elaborate dance numbers featuring hundreds of nearly identical starlets. [Ed.]

[9]The act of telling a story (as opposed to the story that is told). See Genette, p. 844. [Ed.]

development of what Molly Haskell has called the "buddy movie," in which the active homosexual eroticism of the central male figures can carry the story without distraction.) Traditionally, the woman displayed has functioned on two levels: as erotic object for the characters within the screen story, and as erotic object for the spectator within the auditorium, with a shifting tension between the looks on either side of the screen. For instance, the device of the show-girl allows the two looks to be unified technically without any apparent break in the diegesis. A woman performs within the narrative; the gaze of the spectator and that of the male characters in the film are neatly combined without breaking narrative verisimilitude. For a moment the sexual impact of the performing woman takes the film into a no man's land outside its own time and space. Thus Marilyn Monroe's first appearance in *The River of No Return* and Lauren Bacall's songs in *To Have and Have Not.* Similarly, conventional close-ups of legs (Dietrich, for instance) or a face (Garbo) integrate into the narrative a different mode of eroticism. One part of a fragmented body destroys the Renaissance space, the illusion of depth demanded by the narrative; it gives flatness, the quality of a cut-out or icon, rather than verisimilitude, to the screen.

B. An active/passive heterosexual division of labour has similarly controlled narrative structure. According to the principles of the ruling ideology and the psychical structures that back it up, the male figure cannot bear the burden of sexual objectification. Man is reluctant to gaze at his exhibitionist like. Hence the split between spectacle and narrative supports the man's role as the active one of advancing the story, making things happen. The man controls the film fantasy and also emerges as the representative of power in a further sense: as the bearer of the look of the spectator, transferring it behind the screen to neutralise the extradiegetic tendencies represented by woman as spectacle. This is made possible through the processes set in motion by structuring the film around a main controlling figure with whom the spectator can identify. As the spectator identifies with the main male protagonist, he projects his look onto that of his like, his screen surrogate, so that the power of the male protagonist as he controls events coincides with the active power of the erotic look, both giving a satisfying sense of omnipotence. A male movie star's glamorous characteristics are thus not those of the erotic object of the gaze, but those of the more perfect, more complete, more powerful ideal ego conceived in the original moment of recognition in front of the mirror. The character in the story can make things happen and control events better than the subjects/spectator, just as the image in the mirror was more in control of motor co-ordination.

In contrast to woman as icon, the active male figure (the ego ideal of the identification process) demands a three-dimensional space corresponding to that of the mirror recognition, in which the alienated subject internalised his own representation of his imaginary existence. He is a figure in a landscape. Here the function of film is to reproduce as accurately as possible the so-called natural conditions of human perception. Camera technology (as exemplified by deep focus in particular) and camera movements (determined by the action of the protagonist), combined with invisible editing (demanded by realism), all tend to blur the limits of screen space. The male protagonist is free to command the stage, a stage of spatial illusion in which he articulates the look and creates the action. (There are films with a woman as main protagonist, of course. To analyse this phenomenon seriously here would take me too far afield. Pam Cook and Claire Johnston's study of *The Revolt of Mamie Stover* in Phil Hardy [ed.], *Raoul Walsh* [Edinburgh, 1974], shows in a striking case how the strength of this female protagonist is more apparent than real.)

C1. Sections III A and B have set out a tension between a mode of representation of woman in film and conventions surrounding the diegesis. Each is associated with a look: that of the spectator in direct scopophilic contact with the female form displayed for his enjoyment (connoting male fantasy) and that of the spectator fascinated with the image of his like set in an illusion of natural space, and through him gaining control and possession of the woman within the diegesis. (This tension and the shift from one pole to the other can structure a single text. Thus both in *Only Angels Have Wings* and in *To Have and Have Not,* the film opens with the woman as object of the combined gaze of spectator and all the male protagonists in the film. She is isolated, glamorous, on display, sexualised. But as the narrative progresses she falls in love with the main male protagonist and becomes his property, losing her outward glamorous characteristics, her generalised sexuality, her show-girl connotations; her eroticism is subjected to the male star alone. By means of identification with him, through participation in his power, the spectator can indirectly possess her too.)

But in psychoanalytic terms, the female figure poses a deeper problem. She also connotes something that the look continually circles around but disavows: her lack of a penis, implying a threat of castration and hence unpleasure. Ultimately, the meaning of woman is sexual difference, the visually ascertainable absence of the penis, the material evidence on which is based the castration complex essential for the organisation of entrance to the symbolic order and the law of the father. Thus the woman as icon, displayed for the gaze and enjoyment of men, the active controllers of the look, always threatens to evoke the anxiety it originally signified. The male unconscious has two avenues of escape from this castration anxiety: preoccupation with the re-enactment of the original trauma (investigating the woman, demystifying her mystery), counterbalanced by the devaluation, punishment or saving of the guilty object (an avenue typified by the concerns of the *film noir*[10]); or else complete disavowal of castration by the substitution of a fetish object or turning the represented figure itself into a fetish so that it becomes reassuring rather than dangerous (hence overvaluation, the cult of the female star).

This second avenue, fetishistic scopophilia, builds up the physical beauty of the object, transforming it into something satisfying in itself. The first avenue, voyeurism, on the contrary, has associations with sadism: pleasure lies in ascertaining guilt (immediately associated with castration), asserting control and subjugating the guilty person through punishment or forgiveness. This sadistic side fits in well with narrative. Sadism demands a story, depends on making something happen, forcing a change in another person, a battle of will and strength, victory/defeat, all occurring in a linear time with a beginning and an end. Fetishistic scopophilia, on the other hand, can exist outside linear time as the erotic instinct is focused on the look alone. These contradictions and ambiguities can be illustrated more simply by using works by Hitchcock and Sternberg, both of whom take the look almost as the content or subject matter of many of their films. Hitchcock is the more complex, as he uses both mechanisms. Sternberg's work, on the other hand, provides many pure examples of fetishistic scopophilia.

C2. Sternberg once said he would welcome his films being projected upside-down so that the story and character involvement would not interfere with the spectator's undiluted appreciation of the screen image. This statement is revealing but ingenuous: ingenuous in that his films do demand that the figure of the woman (Dietrich, in the cycle of films with her, as the ultimate example) should be identifiable; but revealing in that it emphasises the fact that for him the pictorial space enclosed by the frame is paramount, rather than narrative or identification processes. While Hitchcock goes into the investigative side of voyeurism, Sternberg produces the ultimate fetish, taking it to the point where the powerful look of the male protagonist (characteristic of traditional narrative film) is broken in favour of the image in direct erotic rapport with the spectator. The beauty of the woman as object and the screen space coalesce; she is no longer the bearer of guilt but a perfect product, whose body, stylised and fragmented by close-ups, is the content of the film and the direct recipient of the spectator's look.

Sternberg plays down the illusion of screen depth; his screen tends to be one-dimensional, as light and shade, lace, steam, foliage, net, streamers and so on reduce the visual field. There is little or no mediation of the look through the eyes of the main male protagonist. On the contrary, shadowy presences like La Bessière in *Morocco* act as sur-

[10]The term *film noir*, literally "black cinema," refers to genre movies of the 1940s and early 1950s portraying the underside of a corrupt society with seductive female villains and cynical heroes. Well-known examples include Michael Curtiz's *Casablanca*, Howard Hawks's *The Big Sleep*, and Billy Wilder's *Sunset Boulevard*. [Ed.]

rogates for the director, detached as they are from audience identification. Despite Sternberg's insistence that his stories are irrelevant, it is significant that they are concerned with situation, not suspense, and cyclical rather than linear time, while plot complications revolve around misunderstanding rather than conflict. The most important absence is that of the controlling male gaze within the screen scene. The high point of emotional drama in the most typical Dietrich films, her supreme moments of erotic meaning, take place in the absence of the man she loves in the fiction. There are other witnesses, other spectators watching her on the screen, their gaze is one with, not standing in for, that of the audience. At the end of *Morocco,* Tom Brown has already disappeared into the desert when Amy Jolly kicks off her gold sandals and walks after him. At the end of *Dishonoured,* Kranau is indifferent to the fate of Magda. In both cases, the erotic impact, sanctified by death, is displayed as a spectacle for the audience. The male hero misunderstands and, above all, does not see.

In Hitchcock, by contrast, the male hero does see precisely what the audience sees. However, although fascination with an image through scopophilic eroticism can be the subject of the film, it is the role of the hero to portray the contradictions and tensions experienced by the spectator. In *Vertigo* in particular, but also in *Marnie* and *Rear Window,* the look is central to the plot, oscillating between voyeurism and fetishistic fascination. Hitchcock has never concealed his interest in voyeurism, cinematic and non-cinematic. His heroes are exemplary of the symbolic order and the law — a policeman *(Vertigo),* a dominant male possessing money and power *(Marnie)* — but their erotic drives lead them into compromised situations. The power to subject another person to the will sadistically or to the gaze voyeuristically is turned onto the woman as the object of both. Power is backed by a certainty of legal right and the established guilt of the woman (evoking castration, psychoanalytically speaking). True perversion is barely concealed under a shallow mask of ideological correctness — the man is on the right side of the law, the woman on the wrong. Hitchcock's skilful use of identification processes and liberal use of subjective camera from the point of view of the male protagonist draw the spectators deeply into his position, making them share his uneasy gaze. The spectator is absorbed into a voyeuristic situation within the screen scene and diegesis, which parodies his own in the cinema.

In an analysis of *Rear Window,* Douchet takes the film as a metaphor for the cinema. Jeffries is the audience, the events in the apartment block opposite correspond to the screen. As he watches, an erotic dimension is added to his look, a central image to the drama. His girlfriend Lisa had been of little sexual interest to him, more or less a drag, so long as she remained on the spectator side. When she crosses the barrier between his room and the block opposite, their relationship is reborn erotically. He does not merely watch her through his lens, as a distant meaningful image, he also sees her as a guilty intruder exposed by a dangerous man threatening her with punishment, and thus finally giving him the opportunity to save her. Lisa's exhibitionism has already been established by her obsessive interest in dress and style, in being a passive image of visual perfection; Jeffries's voyeurism and activity have also been established through his work as a photojournalist, a maker of stories and captor of images. However, his enforced inactivity,[11] binding him to his seat as a spectator, puts him squarely in the fantasy position of the cinema audience.

In *Vertigo,* subjective camera predominates. Apart from one flashback from Judy's point of view, the narrative is woven around what Scottie sees or fails to see. The audience follows the growth of his erotic obsession and subsequent despair precisely from his point of view. Scottie's voyeurism is blatant: he falls in love with a woman he follows and spies on without speaking to. Its sadistic side is equally blatant: he has chosen (and freely chosen, for he had been a successful lawyer) to be a policeman, with all the attendant possibilities of pursuit and investigation. As a result, he follows, watches and falls in love with a perfect image of female beauty and mystery. Once he actually confronts

[11]The hero of *Rear Window* is housebound with a broken leg as the story begins. [Ed.]

her, his erotic drive is to break her down and force her *to tell* by persistent cross-questioning.

In the second part of the film, he re-enacts his obsessive involvement with the image he loved to watch secretly. He reconstructs Judy as Madeleine, forces her to conform in every detail to the actual physical appearance of his fetish. Her exhibitionism, her masochism, make her an ideal passive counterpart to Scottie's active sadistic voyeurism. She knows her part is to perform, and only by playing it through and then replaying it can she keep Scottie's erotic interest. But in the repetition he does break her down and succeeds in exposing her guilt. His curiosity wins through; she is punished.

Thus, in *Vertigo,* erotic involvement with the look boomerangs: the spectator's own fascination is revealed as illicit voyeurism as the narrative content enacts the processes and pleasures that he is himself exercising and enjoying. The Hitchcock hero here is firmly placed within the symbolic order, in narrative terms. He has all the attributes of the patriarchal superego. Hence the spectator, lulled into a false sense of security by the apparent legality of his surrogate, sees through his look and finds himself exposed as complicit, caught in the moral ambiguity of looking. Far from being simply an aside on the perversion of the police, *Vertigo* focuses on the implications of the active/looking, passive/looked-at split in terms of sexual difference and the power of the male symbolic encapsulated in the hero. Marnie, too, performs for Mark Rutland's gaze and masquerades as the perfect to-be-looked-at image. He, too, is on the side of the law until, drawn in by obsession with her guilt, her secret, he longs to see her in the act of committing a crime, make her confess and thus save her. So he, too, becomes complicit as he acts out the implications of his power. He controls money and words; he can have his cake and eat it.

IV. SUMMARY

The psychoanalytic background that has been discussed in this article is relevant to the pleasure and unpleasure offered by traditional narrative film. The scopophilic instinct (pleasure in looking at another person as an erotic object) and, in contradistinction, ego libido (forming identification processes) act as formations, mechanisms, which mould this cinema's formal attributes. The actual image of woman as (passive) raw material for the (active) gaze of man takes the argument a step further into the content and structure of representation, adding a further layer of ideological significance demanded by the patriarchal order in its favourite cinematic form — illusionistic narrative film. The argument must return again to the psychoanalytic background: women in representation can signify castration, and activate voyeuristic or fetishistic mechanisms to circumvent this threat. Although none of these interacting layers is intrinsic to film, it is only in the film form that they can reach a perfect and beautiful contradiction, thanks to the possibility in the cinema of shifting the emphasis of the look. The place of the look defines cinema, the possibility of varying it and exposing it. This is what makes cinema quite different in its voyeuristic potential from, say, strip-tease, theatre, shows and so on. Going far beyond highlighting a woman's to-be-looked-at-ness, cinema builds the way she is to be looked at into the spectacle itself. Playing on the tension between film as controlling the dimension of time (editing, narrative) and film as controlling the dimension of space (changes in distance, editing), cinematic codes create a gaze, a world and an object, thereby producing an illusion cut to the measure of desire. It is these cinematic codes and their relationship to formative external structures that must be broken down before mainstream film and the pleasure it provides can be challenged.

To begin with (as an ending), the voyeuristic — scopophilic look that is a crucial part of traditional filmic pleasure can itself be broken down. There are three different looks associated with cinema: that of the camera as it records the profilmic event, that of the audience as it watches the final product, and that of the characters at each other within the screen illusion. The conventions of narrative film deny the first two and subordinate them to the third, the conscious aim being always to eliminate intrusive camera presence and prevent a distancing awareness in the audience. Without these two absences (the material existence of the recording process, the critical reading of the spectator), fictional drama cannot achieve reality, obviousness and truth. Nevertheless, as this article has argued, the structure of looking in narrative fiction film contains a contradiction in its own premises: the female image as a castration threat constantly endangers the unity of the diegesis and bursts through the world of illusion as an intrusive, static, one-dimensional fetish. Thus the two looks materially present in time and space are obsessively subordinated to the neurotic needs of the male ego. The camera becomes the mechanism for producing an illusion of Renaissance space, flowing movements compatible with the human eye, an ideology of representation that revolves around the perception of the subject; the camera's look is disavowed in order to create a convincing world in which the spectator's surrogate can perform with verisimilitude. Simultaneously, the look of the audience is denied an intrinsic force: as soon as fetishistic representation of the female image threatens to break the spell of illusion, and the erotic image on the screen appears directly (without mediation) to the spectator, the fact of fetishisation, concealing as it does castration fear, freezes the look, fixates the spectator and prevents him from achieving any distance from the image in front of him.

This complex interaction of looks is specific to film. The first blow against the monolithic accumulation of traditional film conventions (already undertaken by radical film-makers) is to free the look of the camera into its materiality in time and space and the look of the audience into dialectics and passionate detachment. There is no doubt that this destroys the satisfaction, pleasure and privilege of the "invisible guest," and highlights the way film has depended on voyeuristic active/passive mechanisms. Women, whose image has continually been stolen and used for this end, cannot view the decline of the traditional film form with anything much more than sentimental regret.

Hélène Cixous

b. 1937

Hélène Cixous, one of the most versatile and radical voices in contemporary French feminism, was born in Oran, Algeria. A brilliant student, she received her agrégation *in English in 1959 and her Docteur en lettres in 1968, the year that also saw her participation in the May student uprisings. Cixous taught at the University of Bordeaux (1962), the Sorbonne (1965–67), Nanterre (1967), and the University of Paris VIII-Vincennes (now at Saint-Denis), where she is a professor of English literature. In 1970 with Gérard Genette and Tzvetan Todorov she founded the structuralist journal* Poétique, *and in 1974 established a center for women's studies at the University of Paris VIII. The work of Shakespeare and James Joyce (about whom she wrote her doctoral thesis), Heinrich von Kleist and Franz Kafka, Arthur Rimbaud and the Brazilian writer Clarice Lispector, Jacques Derrida and Jacques Lacan, has been particularly important to her. Cixous has written short stories (*Le Prénom de Dieu, *1966), novels (*Dédans, *1969, which won the Prix Médicis), and a great deal of literary and cultural criticism. Some of her other writings are* Portrait of Dora *(1976),* The Newly Born Woman *(1975; with Catherine Clément), and* La Venue à l'écriture *(1977; with Annie LeClerc and Madeleine Gagnon). Cixous's most recent fiction includes* L'Ange au secret *(1991),* La Fiancée juive *(1995), and* Messie *(1996). Her most recent criticism and theory in English include* Writing Differences: Readings from the Seminar of Hélène Cixous *(1988),* Readings: The Poetics of Blanchot, Joyce, Kafka, Kleist, Lispector and Tsvetayeva *(1991),* Coming to Writing and Other Essays *(1991),* The Hélène Cixous Reader *(1994), and* Manna *(1994). "The Laugh of the Medusa," first published in* L'Arc *in 1975, was translated for the first volume of the feminist journal* Signs *(1976).*

The Laugh of the Medusa

I shall speak about women's writing: about *what it will do*. Woman must write her self: must write about women and bring women to writing, from which they have been driven away as violently as from their bodies — for the same reasons, by the same law, with the same fatal goal. Woman must put herself into the text — as into the world and into history — by her own movement.

The future must no longer be determined by the past. I do not deny that the effects of the past are still with us. But I refuse to strengthen them by repeating them, to confer upon them an irremovability the equivalent of destiny, to confuse the biological and the cultural. Anticipation is imperative.

Since these reflections are taking shape in an area just on the point of being discovered, they necessarily bear the mark of our time — a time during which the new breaks away from the old, and, more precisely, the (feminine) new from the old *(la nouvelle de l'ancien)*. Thus, as there are no grounds for establishing a discourse, but rather an arid millennial ground to break, what I say has at least two sides and two aims: to break up, to destroy; and to foresee the unforeseeable, to project.

I write this as a woman, toward women. When I say "woman," I'm speaking of woman in her inevitable struggle against conventional man; and of a universal woman subject who must bring women to their senses and to their meaning in history. But first it must be said that in spite of the enormity of the repression that has kept them in the "dark" — that dark which people have been trying to make them accept as their attribute — there is, at this time, no general woman, no one typical woman. What they have *in common* I will say. But what strikes me is the infinite richness of their individual constitutions: you can't talk about *a* female sexuality, uniform, homogeneous, classifiable into codes — any more than you can talk about one unconscious resembling another. Women's imaginary[1] is inexhaustible, like music, painting, writing: their stream of phantasms is incredible.

I have been amazed more than once by a description a woman gave me of a world all her own which she had been secretly haunting since early childhood. A world of searching, the elaboration of a knowledge, on the basis of a systematic experimentation with the bodily functions, a passionate and precise interrogation of her erotogeneity. This practice, extraordinarily rich and inventive, in particular as concerns masturbation, is prolonged or accompanied by a production of forms, a veritable aesthetic activity, each stage of rapture inscribing a resonant vision, a composition, something beautiful. Beauty will no longer be forbidden.

I wished that that woman would write and proclaim this unique empire so that other women, other unacknowledged sovereigns, might exclaim: I, too, overflow; my desires have invented new desires, my body knows unheard-of songs. Time and again, I, too, have felt so full of luminous torrents that I could burst — burst with forms much more beautiful than those which are put up in frames and sold for a stinking fortune. And I, too, said nothing, showed nothing; I didn't open my mouth, I didn't repaint my half of the world. I was ashamed. I was afraid, and I swallowed my shame and my fear. I said to myself: You are mad! What's the meaning of these waves, these floods, these outbursts? Where is the ebullient, infinite woman who, immersed as she was in her naiveté, kept in the dark about herself, led into self-disdain by the great arm of parental-conjugal phallocentrism, hasn't been ashamed of her strength? Who, surprised and horrified by the fantastic tumult of her drives (for she was made to believe that a well-adjusted nor-

Translated by Keith Cohen and Paula Cohen.

[1]The imaginary is a "field" in the psychology of Jacques Lacan. Cixous refers later to the other Lacanian field, the symbolic, and to Lack (*manque*), the sense of absence that is the basis of unconscious desire. See the introduction to Psychoanalytic Theory, p. 1019. [Ed.]

for a moment thrown off balance and an ephemeral wildness sweeps order away, that the poet slips something by, for a brief span, of woman. Thus did Kleist expend himself in his yearning for the existence of sister-lovers, maternal daughters, mother-sisters, who never hung their heads in shame. Once the palace of magistrates is restored, it's time to pay: immediate bloody death to the uncontrollable elements.

But only the poets — not the novelists, allies of representationalism. Because poetry involves gaining strength through the unconscious and because the unconscious, that other limitless country, is the place where the repressed manage to survive: women, or as Hoffmann would say, fairies.

She must write her self, because this is the invention of a *new insurgent* writing which, when the moment of her liberation has come, will allow her to carry out the indispensable ruptures and transformations in her history, first at two levels that cannot be separated.

1. Individually. By writing her self, woman will return to the body which has been more than confiscated from her, which has been turned into the uncanny stranger on display — the ailing or dead figure, which so often turns out to be the nasty companion, the cause and location of inhibitions. Censor the body and you censor breath and speech at the same time.

Write your self. Your body must be heard. Only then will the immense resources of the unconscious spring forth. Our naphtha will spread, throughout the world, without dollars — black or gold — nonassessed values that will change the rules of the old game.

To write. An act which will not only "realize" the decensored relation of woman to her sexuality, to her womanly being, giving her access to her native strength; it will give her back her goods, her pleasures, her organs, her immense bodily territories which have been kept under seal; it will tear her away from the superegoized structure in which she has always occupied the place reserved for the guilty (guilty of everything, guilty at every turn: for having desires, for not having any; for being frigid, for being "too hot"; for not being both at once; for being too motherly and not enough; for having children and for not having any; for nursing and for not nursing . . .) — tear her away by means of this research, this job of analysis and illumination, this emancipation of the marvelous text of her self that she must urgently learn to speak. A woman without a body, dumb, blind, can't possibly be a good fighter. She is reduced to being the servant of the militant male, his shadow. We must kill the false woman who is preventing the live one from breathing. Inscribe the breath of the whole woman.

2. An act that will also be marked by woman's *seizing* the occasion to *speak,* hence her shattering entry into history, which has always been based *on her suppression.* To write and thus to forge for herself the antilogos weapon. To become *at will* the taker and initiator, for her own right, in every symbolic system, in every political process.

It is time for women to start scoring their feats in written and oral language.

Every woman has known the torment of getting up to speak. Her heart racing, at times entirely lost for words, ground and language slipping away — that's how daring a feat, how great a transgression it is for a woman to speak — even just open her mouth — in public. A double distress, for even if she transgresses, her words fall almost always upon the deaf male ear, which hears in language only that which speaks in the masculine.

It is by writing, from and toward women, and by taking up the challenge of speech which has been governed by the phallus, that women will confirm women in a place other than that which is reserved in and by the symbolic, that is, in a place other than silence. Women should break out of the snare of silence. They shouldn't be conned into accepting a domain which is the margin or the harem.

Listen to a woman speak at a public gathering (if she hasn't painfully lost her wind). She doesn't "speak," she throws her trembling body forward; she lets go of herself, she flies; all of her passes into her voice, and it's with her body that she vitally supports the "logic" of her speech. Her flesh speaks true. She lays herself bare. In fact, she physically materializes what she's thinking; she signifies it with her body. In a certain way she *inscribes* what she's saying, because she doesn't deny her drives the intractable and impassioned part they have in speaking. Her speech, even when "theoretical" or political, is never simple or linear or "objectified," generalized: she draws her story into history.

There is not that scission, that division made by the common man between the logic of oral speech and the logic of the text, bound as he is by his antiquated relation — servile, calculating — to mastery. From which proceeds the niggardly lip service which engages only the tiniest part of the body, plus the mask.

In women's speech, as in their writing, that element which never stops resonating, which, once we've been permeated by it, profoundly and imperceptibly touched by it, retains the power of moving us — that element is the song: first music from the first voice of love which is alive in every woman. Why this privileged relationship with the voice? Because no woman stockpiles as many defenses for countering the drives as does a man. You don't build walls around yourself, you don't forego pleasure as "wisely" as he. Even if phallic mystification has generally contaminated good relationships, a woman is never far from "mother" (I mean outside her role functions: the "mother" as nonname and as source of goods). There is always within her at least a little of that good mother's milk. She writes in white ink.

Woman for women. — There always remains in woman that force which produces/is produced by the other — in particular, the other woman. *In* her, matrix, cradler; herself giver as her mother and child; she is her own sister-daughter. You might object, "What about she who is the hysterical offspring of a bad mother?" Everything will be changed once woman gives woman to the other woman. There is hidden and always ready in woman the source; the locus for the other. The mother, too, is a metaphor. It is necessary and sufficient that the best of herself be given to woman by another woman for her to be able to love herself and return in love the body that was "born" to her. Touch me, caress me, you the living no-name, give me my self as myself. The relation to the "mother," in terms of intense pleasure and violence, is curtailed no more than the relation to childhood (the child that she was, that she is, that she makes, remakes, undoes, there at the point where, the same, she others herself). Text: my body — shot through with streams of song; I don't mean the overbearing, clutchy "mother" but, rather, what touches you, the equivoice that affects you, fills your breast with an urge to come to language and launches your force; the rhythm that laughs you; the intimate recipient who makes all metaphors possible and desirable; body (body? bodies?), no more describable than god, the soul, or the Other; that part of you that leaves a space between yourself and urges you to inscribe in language your woman's style. In women there is always more or less of the mother who makes everything all right, who nourishes, and who stands up against separation; a force that will not be cut off but will knock the wind out of the codes. We will rethink womankind beginning with every form and every period of her body. The Americans remind us, "We are all Lesbians"; that is, don't denigrate woman, don't make of her what men have made of you.

Because the "economy" of her drives is prodigious, she cannot fail, in seizing the occasion to speak, to transform directly and indirectly *all* systems of exchange based on masculine thrift. Her libido will produce far more radical effects of political and social change than some might like to think.

Because she arrives, vibrant, over and again, we are at the beginning of a new history, or rather of a process of becoming in which several histories intersect with one another. As subject for history, woman always occurs simultaneously in several places. Woman un-thinks[5] the unifying, regulating history that homogenizes and channels forces, herding contradictions into a single battlefield. In woman, personal history blends together with the history of all women, as well as national and world history. As a militant, she is an integral part of all liberations. She must be farsighted, not limited to a blow-by-blow interaction. She foresees that her liberation will do

[5]"*Dé-pense*," a neologism formed on the verb *penser*, hence "unthinks," but also "spends" (from *dépenser*). [Tr.]

more than modify power relations or toss the ball over to the other camp; she will bring about a mutation in human relations, in thought, in all praxis: hers is not simply a class struggle, which she carries forward into a much vaster movement. Not that in order to be a woman-in-struggle(s) you have to leave the class struggle or repudiate it; but you have to split it open, spread it out, push it forward, fill it with the fundamental struggle so as to prevent the class struggle, or any other struggle for the liberation of a class or people, from operating as a form of repression, pretext for postponing the inevitable, the staggering alteration in power relations and in the production of individualities. This alteration is already upon us — in the United States, for example, where millions of night crawlers are in the process of undermining the family and disintegrating the whole of American sociality.

The new history is coming; it's not a dream, though it does extend beyond men's imagination, and for good reason. It's going to deprive them of their conceptual orthopedics, beginning with the destruction of their enticement machine.

It is impossible to *define* a feminine practice of writing, and this is an impossibility that will remain, for this practice can never be theorized, enclosed, coded — which doesn't mean that it doesn't exist. But it will always surpass the discourse that regulates the phallocentric system; it does and will take place in areas other than those subordinated to philosophico-theoretical domination. It will be conceived of only by subjects who are breakers of automatisms, by peripheral figures that no authority can ever subjugate.

Hence the necessity to affirm the flourishes of this writing, to give form to its movement, its near and distant byways. Bear in mind to begin with (1) that sexual opposition, which has always worked for man's profit to the point of reducing writing, too, to his laws, is only a historico-cultural limit. There is, there will be more and more rapidly pervasive now, a fiction that produces irreducible effects of femininity. (2) That it is through ignorance that most readers, critics, and writers of both sexes hesitate to admit or deny outright the possibility or the pertinence of a distinction between feminine and masculine writing. It will usually be said, thus disposing of sexual difference: either that all writing, to the extent that it materializes, is feminine; or, inversely — but it comes to the same thing — that the act of writing is equivalent to masculine masturbation (and so the woman who writes cuts herself out a paper penis); or that writing is bisexual, hence neuter, which again does away with differentiation. To admit that writing is precisely working (in) the in-between, inspecting the process of the same and of the other without which nothing can live, undoing the work of death — to admit this is first to want the two, as well as both, the ensemble of the one and the other, not fixed in sequences of struggle and expulsion or some other form of death but infinitely dynamized by an incessant process of exchange from one subject to another. A process of different subjects knowing one another and beginning one another anew only from the living boundaries of the other: a multiple and inexhaustible course with millions of encounters and transformations of the same into the other and into the in-between, from which woman takes her forms (and man, in his turn; but that's his other history).

In saying "bisexual, hence neuter," I am referring to the classic conception of bisexuality, which, squashed under the emblem of castration fear and along with the fantasy of a "total" being (though composed of two halves), would do away with the difference experienced as an operation incurring loss, as the mark of dreaded sectility.

To this self-effacing, merger-type bisexuality, which would conjure away castration (the writer who puts up his sign: "bisexual written here, come and see," when the odds are good that it's neither one nor the other), I oppose the *other bisexuality* on which every subject not enclosed in the false theater of phallocentric representationalism has founded his/her erotic universe. Bisexuality: that is, each one's location in self *(répérage en soi)* of the presence — variously manifest and insistent according to each person, male or female — of both sexes, nonexclusion either of the difference or of one sex, and, from this "self-permission," multiplication of the effects of the inscription of desire, over all parts of my body and the other body.

Now it happens that at present, for historico-cultural reasons, it is women who are opening up to and benefiting from this vatic bisexuality which doesn't annul differences but stirs them up, pursues them, increases their number. In a certain way, "woman is bisexual"; man — it's a secret to no one — being poised to keep glorious phallic monosexuality in view. By virtue of affirming the primacy of the phallus and of bringing it into play, phallocratic ideology has claimed more than one victim. As a woman, I've been clouded over by the great shadow of the scepter and been told: idolize it, that which you cannot brandish. But at the same time, man has been handed that grotesque and scarcely enviable destiny (just imagine) of being reduced to a single idol with clay balls. And consumed, as Freud and his followers note, by a fear of being a woman! For, if psychoanalysis was constituted from woman, to repress femininity (and not so successful a repression at that — men have made it clear), its account of masculine sexuality is now hardly refutable; as with all the "human" sciences, it reproduces the masculine view, of which it is one of the effects.

Here we encounter the inevitable man-with-rock, standing erect in his old Freudian realm, in the way that, to take the figure back to the point where linguistics is conceptualizing it "anew," Lacan preserves it in the sanctuary of the phallos (ϕ) "sheltered" from *castration's lack!* Their "symbolic" exists, it holds power — we, the sowers of disorder, know it only too well. But we are in no way obliged to deposit our lives in their banks of lack, to consider the constitution of the subject in terms of a drama manglingly restaged, to reinstate again and again the religion of the father. Because we don't want that. We don't fawn around the supreme hole. We have no womanly reason to pledge allegiance to the negative. The feminine (as the poets suspected) affirms: ". . . And yes," says Molly, carrying *Ulysses* off beyond any book and toward the new writing; "I said yes, I will Yes."

The Dark Continent is neither dark nor unexplorable. — It is still unexplored only because we've been made to believe that it was too dark to be explorable. And because they want to make us believe that what interests us is the white continent, with its monuments to Lack. And we believed. They riveted us between two horrifying myths: between the Medusa and the abyss. That would be enough to set half the world laughing, except that it's still going on. For the phallologocentric sublation[6] is with us, and it's militant, regenerating the old patterns, anchored in the dogma of castration. They haven't changed a thing: they've theorized their desire for reality! Let the priests tremble, we're going to show them our sexts!

Too bad for them if they fall apart upon discovering that women aren't men, or that the mother doesn't have one. But isn't this fear convenient for them? Wouldn't the worst be, isn't the worst, in truth, that women aren't castrated, that they have only to stop listening to the Sirens (for the Sirens were men) for history to change its meaning? You only have to look at the Medusa straight on to see her. And she's not deadly. She's beautiful and she's laughing.

Men say that there are two unrepresentable things: death and the feminine sex. That's because they need femininity to be associated with death; it's the jitters that gives them a hard-on! for themselves! They need to be afraid of us. Look at the trembling Perseuses moving backward toward us, clad in apotropes.[7] What lovely backs! Not another minute to lose. Let's get out of here.

Let's hurry: the continent is not impenetrably dark. I've been there often. I was overjoyed one day to run into Jean Genêt. It was in *Pompes funèbres*.[8] He had come there led by his Jean. There are some men (all too few) who aren't afraid of femininity.

Almost everything is yet to be written by women about femininity: about their sexuality, that is, its infinite and mobile complexity, about their eroticization, sudden turn-ons of a certain minuscule-immense area of their bodies; not about destiny, but about the adventure of such and such a drive, about trips, crossings, trudges,

[6]Standard English term for the Hegelian *Aufhebung*, the French *la relève*. [Tr.]

[7]A coinage from two Greek roots meaning "to turn away." [Ed.]

[8]Jean Genêt, *Pompes funèbres* (Paris, 1948), p. 185. [Au.]

abrupt and gradual awakenings, discoveries of a zone at one time timorous and soon to be forthright. A woman's body, with its thousand and one thresholds of ardor — once, by smashing yokes and censors, she lets it articulate the profusion of meanings that run through it in every direction — will make the old single-grooved mother tongue reverberate with more than one language.

We've been turned away from our bodies, shamefully taught to ignore them, to strike them with that stupid sexual modesty; we've been made victims of the old fool's game: each one will love the other sex. I'll give you your body and you'll give me mine. But who are the men who give women the body that women blindly yield to them? Why so few texts? Because so few women have as yet won back their body. Women must write through their bodies, they must invent the impregnable language that will wreck partitions, classes, and rhetorics, regulations and codes, they must submerge, cut through, get beyond the ultimate reserve-discourse, including the one that laughs at the very idea of pronouncing the word "silence," the one that, aiming for the impossible, stops short before the word "impossible" and writes it as "the end."

Such is the strength of women that, sweeping away syntax, breaking that famous thread (just a tiny little thread, they say) which acts for men as a surrogate umbilical cord, assuring them — otherwise they couldn't come — that the old lady is always right behind them, watching them make phallus, women will go right up to the impossible.

When the "repressed" of their culture and their society returns, it's an explosive, *utterly* destructive, staggering return, with a force never yet unleashed and equal to the most forbidding of suppressions. For when the Phallic period comes to an end, women will have been either annihilated or borne up to the highest and most violent incandescence. Muffled throughout their history, they have lived in dreams, in bodies (though muted), in silences, in aphonic revolts.

And with such force in their fragility; a fragility, a vulnerability, equal to their incomparable intensity. Fortunately, they haven't sublimated; they've saved their skin, their energy. They haven't worked at liquidating the impasse of lives without futures. They have furiously inhabited these sumptuous bodies: admirable hysterics who made Freud succumb to many voluptuous moments impossible to confess, bombarding his Mosaic statue with their carnal and passionate body words, haunting him with their unaudible and thundering denunciations, dazzling, more than naked underneath the seven veils of modesty. Those who, with a single word of the body, have inscribed the vertiginous immensity of a history which is sprung like an arrow from the whole history of men and from biblico-capitalist society, are the women, the supplicants of yesterday, who come as forebears of the new women, after whom no intersubjective relation will ever be the same. You, Dora,[9] you the indomitable, the poetic body, you are the true "mistress" of the Signifier. Before long your efficacity will be seen at work when your speech is no longer suppressed, its point turned in against your breast, but written out over against the other.

In body. — More so than men who are coaxed toward social success, toward sublimation, women are body. More body, hence more writing. For a long time it has been in body that women have responded to persecution, to the familial-conjugal enterprise of domestication, to the repeated attempts at castrating them. Those who have turned their tongues 10,000 times seven times before not speaking are either dead from it or more familiar with their tongues and their mouths than anyone else. Now, I-woman am going to blow up the Law: an explosion henceforth possible and ineluctable; let it be done, right now, *in* language.

Let us not be trapped by an analysis still encumbered with the old automatisms. It's not to be feared that language conceals an invincible adversary, because it's the language of men and their grammar. We mustn't leave them a single place that's any more theirs alone than we are.

If woman has always functioned "within" the discourse of man, a signifier that has always referred back to the opposite signifier which anni-

[9]The female subject of Freud's first case study in hysteria. [Ed.]

hilates its specific energy and diminishes or stifles its very different sounds, it is time for her to dislocate this "within," to explode it, turn it around, and seize it; to make it hers, containing it, taking it in her own mouth, biting that tongue with her very own teeth to invent for herself a language to get inside of. And you'll see with what ease she will spring forth from that "within" — the "within" where once she so drowsily crouched — to overflow at the lips she will cover the foam.

Nor is the point to appropriate their instruments, their concepts, their places, or to begrudge them their position of mastery. Just because there's a risk of identification doesn't mean that we'll succumb. Let's leave it to the worriers, to masculine anxiety and its obsession with how to dominate the way things work — knowing "how it works" in order to "make it work." For us the point is not to take possession in order to internalize or manipulate, but rather to dash through and to "fly."[10]

Flying is woman's gesture — flying in language and making it fly. We have all learned the art of flying and its numerous techniques; for centuries we've been able to possess anything only by flying; we've lived in flight, stealing away, finding, when desired, narrow passageways, hidden crossovers. It's no accident that *voler* has a double meaning, that it plays on each of them and thus throws off the agents of sense. It's no accident: women take after birds and robbers just as robbers take after women and birds. They *(illes)*[11] go by, fly the coop, take pleasure in jumbling the order of space, in disorienting it, in changing around the furniture, dislocating things and values, breaking them all up, emptying structures, and turning propriety upside down.

What woman hasn't flown/stolen? Who hasn't felt, dreamt, performed the gesture that jams sociality? Who hasn't crumbled, held up to ridicule, the bar of separation? Who hasn't inscribed with her body the differential, punctured the system of couples and opposition? Who, by some act of transgression, hasn't overthrown successiveness, connection, the wall of circumfusion?

A feminine text cannot fail to be more than subversive. It is volcanic; as it is written it brings about an upheaval of the old property crust, carrier of masculine investments; there's no other way. There's no room for her if she's not a he. If she's a her-she, it's in order to smash everything, to shatter the framework of institutions, to blow up the law, to break up the "truth" with laughter.

For once she blazes *her* trail in the symbolic, she cannot fail to make of it the chaosmos of the "personal" — in her pronouns, her nouns, and her clique of referents. And for good reason. There will have been the long history of gynocide. This is known by the colonized peoples of yesterday, the workers, the nations, the species off whose backs the history of men has made its gold; those who have known the ignominy of persecution derive from it an obstinate future desire for grandeur; those who are locked up know better than their jailers the taste of free air. Thanks to their history, women today know (how to do and want) what men will be able to conceive of only much later. I say woman overturns the "personal," for if, by means of laws, lies, blackmail, and marriage, her right to herself has been extorted at the same time as her name, she has been able, through the very movement of mortal alienation, to see more closely the inanity of "propriety," the reductive stinginess of the masculine-conjugal subjective economy, which she doubly resists. On the one hand she has constituted herself necessarily as that "person" capable of losing a part of herself without losing her integrity. But secretly, silently, deep down inside, she grows and multiplies, for, on the other hand, she knows far more about living and about the relation between the economy of the drives and the management of the ego than any man. Unlike man, who holds so dearly to his title and his titles, his pouches of value, his cap, crown, and everything connected with his head, woman couldn't care less about the fear of decapitation (or castration), adventuring, without the masculine temerity, into anonymity, which she can

[10]Also, "to steal." Both meanings of the verb *voler* are played on, as the text itself explains in the following paragraph. [Tr.]

[11]*Illes* is a fusion of the masculine pronoun *ils*, which refers back to birds and robbers, with the feminine pronoun *elles*, which refers to women. [Tr.]

merge with without annihilating herself: because she's a giver.

I shall have a great deal to say about the whole deceptive problematic of the gift. Woman is obviously not that woman Nietzsche dreamed of who gives only in order to.[12] Who could ever think of the gift as a gift-that-takes? Who else but man, precisely the one who would like to take everything?

If there is a "propriety of woman," it is paradoxically her capacity to depropriate unselfishly: body without end, without appendage, without principal "parts." If she is a whole, it's a whole composed of parts that are wholes, not simple partial objects but a moving, limitlessly changing ensemble, a cosmos tirelessly traversed by Eros, an immense astral space not organized around any one sun that's any more of a star than the others.

This doesn't mean that she's an undifferentiated magma, but that she doesn't lord it over her body or her desire. Though masculine sexuality gravitates around the penis, engendering that centralized body (in political anatomy) under the dictatorship of its parts, woman does not bring about the same regionalization which serves the couple head/genitals and which is inscribed only within boundaries. Her libido is cosmic, just as her unconscious is worldwide. Her writing can only keep going, without ever inscribing or discerning contours, daring to make these vertiginous crossing of the other(s) ephemeral and passionate sojourns in him, her, them, whom she inhabits long enough to look at from the point closest to their unconscious from the moment they awaken, to love them at the point closest to their drives; and then further, impregnated through and through with these brief, identificatory embraces, she goes and passes into infinity. She alone dares and wishes to know from within, where she, the outcast, has never ceased to hear the resonance of fore-language. She lets the other language speak — the language of 1,000 tongues which knows neither enclosure nor death. To life she refuses nothing. Her language does not contain, it carries; it does not hold back, it makes possible. When id is ambiguously uttered — the wonder of being several — she doesn't defend herself against these unknown women whom she's surprised at becoming, but derives pleasure from this gift of alterability. I am spacious, singing flesh, on which is grafted no one knows which I, more or less human, but alive because of transformation.

Write! and your self-seeking text will know itself better than flesh and blood, rising, insurrectionary dough kneading itself, with sonorous, perfumed ingredients, a lively combination of flying colors, leaves, and rivers plunging into the sea we feed. "Ah, there's her sea," he will say as he holds out to me a basin full of water from the little phallic mother from whom he's inseparable. But look, our seas are what we make of them, full of fish or not, opaque or transparent, red or black, high or smooth, narrow or bankless; and we are ourselves sea, sand, coral, seaweed, beaches, tides, swimmers, children, waves. . . . More or less wavily sea, earth, sky — what matter would rebuff us? We know how to speak them all.

Heterogeneous, yes. For her joyous benefit she is erogenous; she is the erotogeneity of the heterogeneous: airborne swimmer, in flight, she does not cling to herself; she is dispersible, prodigious, stunning, desirous and capable of others, of the other woman that she will be, of the other woman she isn't, of him, of you.

Woman be unafraid of any other place, of any same, or any other. My eyes, my tongue, my ears, my nose, my skin, my mouth, my body-for-(the)-other — not that I long for it in order to fill up a hole, to provide against some defect of mine, or because, as fate would have it, I'm spurred on by feminine "jealousy"; not because I've been dragged into the whole chain of substitutions that brings that which is substituted back to its ultimate object. That sort of thing you would expect to come straight out of "Tom Thumb," out of the *Penisneid* whispered to us by old grandmother ogresses, servants to their father-sons. If they be-

[12]Reread Derrida's text, "Le Style de la femme," in *Nietzsche aujourd'hui* (Paris: Union Générale d'Editions, Coll. 10/18), where the philosopher can be seen operating an *Aufhebung* of all philosophy in its systematic reducing of woman to the place of seduction: she appears as the one who is taken for; the bait in person, all veils unfurled, the one who doesn't give but who gives only in order to (take). [Au.]

lieve, in order to muster up some self-importance, if they really need to believe that we're dying of desire, that we are this hole fringed with desire for their penis — that's their immemorial business. Undeniably (we verify it at our own expense — but also to our amusement), it's their business to let us know they're getting a hard-on, so that we'll assure them (we the maternal mistresses of their little pocket signifier) that they still can, that it's still there — that men structure themselves only by being fitted with a feather. In the child it's not the penis that the woman desires, it's not that famous bit of skin around which every man gravitates. Pregnancy cannot be traced back, except within the historical limits of the ancients, to some form of fate, to those mechanical substitutions brought about by the unconscious of some eternal "jealous woman"; not to penis envies; and not to narcissism or to some sort of homosexuality linked to the everpresent mother! Begetting a child doesn't mean that the woman or the man must fall ineluctably into patterns or must recharge the circuit of reproduction. If there's a risk there's not an inevitable trap: may women be spared the pressure, under the guise of consciousness-raising, of a supplement of interdictions. Either you want a kid or you don't — *that's your business*. Let nobody threaten you; in satisfying your desire, let not the fear of becoming the accomplice to a sociality succeed the old-time fear of being "taken." And man, are you still going to bank on everyone's blindness and passivity, afraid lest the child make a father and, consequently, that in having a kid the woman land herself more than one bad deal by engendering all at once child — mother — father — family? No; it's up to you to break the old circuits. It will be up to man and woman to render obsolete the former relationship and all its consequences, to consider the launching of a brand-new subject, alive, with defamilialization. Let us demater-paternalize rather than deny woman, in an effort to avoid the co-optation of procreation, a thrilling era of the body. Let us defetishize. Let's get away from the dialectic which has it that the only good father is a dead one, or that the child is the death of his parents. The child is the other, but the other without violence, bypassing loss, struggle. We're fed up with the reuniting of bonds forever to be severed, with the litany of castration that's handed down and genealogized. We won't advance backward anymore; we're not going to repress something so simple as the desire for life. Oral drive, anal drive, vocal drive — all these drives are our strengths, and among them is the gestation drive — just like the desire to write: a desire to live self from within, a desire for the swollen belly, for language, for blood. We are not going to refuse, if it should happen to strike our fancy, the unsurpassed pleasures of pregnancy which have actually been always exaggerated or conjured away — or cursed — in the classic texts. For if there's one thing that's been repressed here's just the place to find it: in the taboo of the pregnant woman. This says a lot about the power she seems invested with at the time, because it has always been suspected, that, when pregnant, the woman not only doubles her market value, but — what's more important — takes on intrinsic value as a woman in her own eyes and, undeniably, acquires body and sex.

There are thousands of ways of living one's pregnancy; to have or not to have with that still invisible other a relationship of another intensity. And if you don't have that particular yearning, it doesn't mean that you're in any way lacking. Each body distributes in its own special way, without model or norm, the nonfinite and changing totality of its desires. Decide for yourself on your position in the arena of contradictions, where pleasure and reality embrace. Bring the other to life. Women know how to live detachment; giving birth is neither losing nor increasing. It's adding to life an other. Am I dreaming? Am I mis-recognizing? You, the defenders of "theory," the sacrosanct yes-men of Concept, enthroners of the phallus (but not of the penis):

Once more you'll say that all this smacks of "idealism," or what's worse, you'll splutter that I'm a "mystic."

And what about the libido? Haven't I read the "Signification of the Phallus"? And what about separation, what about that bit of self for which, to be born, you undergo an ablation — an ablation, so they say, to be forever commemorated by your desire?

Besides, isn't it evident that the penis gets around in my texts, that I give it a place and appeal? Of course I do. I want all. I want all of me with all of him. Why should I deprive myself of a part of us? I want all of us. Woman of course has a desire for a "loving desire" and not a jealous one. But not because she is gelded; not because she's deprived and needs to be filled out, like some wounded person who wants to console herself or seek vengeance: I don't want a penis to decorate my body with. But I do desire the other for the other, whole and entire, male or female; because living means wanting everything that is, everything that lives, and wanting it alive. Castration? Let others toy with it. What's a desire originating from a lack? A pretty meager desire.

The woman who still allows herself to be threatened by the big dick, who's still impressed by the commotion of the phallic stance, who still leads a loyal master to the beat of the drum: that's the woman of yesterday. They still exist, easy and numerous victims of the oldest of farces: either they're cast in the original silent version in which, as titanesses lying under the mountains they make with their quivering, they never see erected that theoretic monument to the golden phallus looming, in the old manner, over their bodies. Or, coming today out of their *infans*[13] period and into the second, "enlightened" version of their virtuous debasement, they see themselves suddenly assaulted by the builders of the analytic empire and, as soon as they've begun to formulate the new desire, naked, nameless, so happy at making an appearance, they're taken in their bath by the new old men, and then, whoops! Luring them with flashy signifiers, the demon of interpretation — oblique, decked out in modernity — sells them the same old handcuffs, baubles, and chains. Which castration do you prefer? Whose degrading do you like better, the father's or the mother's? Oh, what pwetty eyes, you pwetty little girl. Here, buy my glasses and you'll see the Truth-Me-Myself tell you everything you should know. Put them on your nose and take a fetishist's look (you are me, the other analyst — that's what I'm telling you) at your body and the body of the other. You see? No? Wait, you'll have everything explained to you, and you'll know at last which sort of neurosis you're related to. Hold still, we're going to do your portrait, so that you can begin looking like it right away.

Yes, the naives to the first and second degree are still legion. If the New Women, arriving now, dare to create outside the theoretical, they're called in by the cops of the signifier, fingerprinted, remonstrated, and brought into the line of order that they are supposed to know; assigned by force of trickery to a precise place in the chain that's always formed for the benefit of a privileged signifier. We are pieced back to the string which leads back, if not to the Name-of-the-Father, then, for a new twist, to the place of the phallic-mother.

Beware, my friend, of the signifier that would take you back to the authority of a signified! Beware of diagnoses that would reduce your generative powers. "Common" nouns are also proper nouns that disparage your singularity by classifying it into species. Break out of the circles; don't remain within the psychoanalytic closure. Take a look around, then cut through!

And if we are legion, it's because the war of liberation has only made as yet a tiny breakthrough. But women are thronging to it. I've seen them, those who will be neither dupe nor domestic, those who will not fear the risk of being a woman; will not fear any risk, any desire, any space still explored in themselves, among themselves and others or anywhere else. They do not fetishize, they do not deny, they do not hate. They observe, they approach, they try to see the other woman, the child, the lover — not to strengthen their own narcissism or verify the solidity or weakness of the master, but to make love better, to invent.

Other love. — In the beginning are our differences. The new love dares for the other, wants the other, makes dizzying, precipitous flights between knowledge and invention. The woman arriving over and over again does not stand still; she's everywhere, she exchanges, she is the desire-that-gives. (Not enclosed in the paradox of the gift that takes nor under the illusion of unitary fusion. We're past that.) She comes in, comes-in-between herself me and you, between the other me where one is always infinitely more than one and more than me, without the fear of ever reach-

[13]Mute. [Ed.]

ing a limit; she thrills in our becoming. And we'll keep on becoming! She cuts through defensive loves, motherages, and devourations: beyond selfish narcissism, in the moving, open, transitional space, she runs her risks. Beyond the struggle-to-the-death that's been removed to the bed, beyond the love-battle that claims to represent exchange, she scorns at an Eros dynamic that would be fed by hatred. Hatred: a heritage, again, a remainder, a duping subservience to the phallus. To love, to watch-think-seek the other in the other, to despecularize, to unhoard. Does this seem difficult? It's not impossible, and this is what nourishes life — a love that has no commerce with the apprehensive desire that provides against the lack and stultifies the strange; a love that rejoices in the exchange that multiplies. Wherever history still unfolds as the history of death, she does not tread. Opposition, hierarchizing exchange, the struggle for mastery which can end only in at least one death (one master — one slave, or two nonmasters ≠ two dead) — all that comes from a period in time governed by phallocentric values. The fact that this period extends into the present doesn't prevent woman from starting the history of life somewhere else. Elsewhere, she gives. She doesn't "know" what she's giving, she doesn't measure it; she gives, though, neither a counterfeit impression nor something she hasn't got. She gives more, with no assurance that she'll get back even some unexpected profit from what she puts out. She gives that there may be life, thought, transformation. This is an "economy" that can no longer be put in economic terms. Wherever she loves, all the old concepts of management are left behind. At the end of a more or less conscious computation, she finds not her sum but her differences. I am for you what you want me to be at the moment you look at me in a way you've never seen me before: at every instant. When I write, it's everything that we don't know we can be that is written out of me, without exclusions, without stipulation, and everything we will be calls us to the unflagging, intoxicating, unappeasable search for love. In one another we will never be lacking.

Luce Irigaray

b. 1930

Luce Irigaray was born in Belgium and took her master's degree in philosophy in 1955 with a thesis on Paul Valéry. After teaching in a lycée in Brussels for four years until 1959, she went to Paris, taking a doctorat de troisieme cycle *in linguistics at the University of Paris at Nanterre in 1968 and a* doctorat d'état *in philosophy at the University of Paris at Vincennes in 1974. She also did psychoanalytic training at the Freudian School, directed by Jacques Lacan. Her dissertation,* Speculum d' l'autre femme *(1974; translated in 1985 as* Speculum of the Other Woman*) is a feminist interrogation of philosophical psychology from Plato through Freud, and it so outraged the Lacanian establishment that upon its paperback publication Irigaray was barred from teaching at Vincennes and expelled from the Freudian School, which blacklisted her from teaching in Paris for over ten years. Nevertheless, Irigaray continued to produce her radical feminist essays including* Ce Sexe qui n'en est pas un *(1977; translated in 1985 as* This Sex Which Is Not One*),* Amante marine *(1980), and* Passions elementaires *(1982; translated in 1992 as* Elemental Passions*). Irigaray's reputation developed abroad through translations of her work, including the title essay of* This Sex Which Is Not One, *which began to appear in English as early as 1978. In the early 1980s, she taught at Erasmus University at Rotterdam and at the University of Bologna. By 1985 it was clear that Irigaray had become an international luminary and had to be recognized as such even in Paris. She was given a seminar at the École des Hautes Études en Sciences Sociales that year and she has taught there ever since, at the*

College International de Philosophie, and at the Centre Americain d'Études Critiques. Irigaray's other works include I You We: Towards a Culture of Difference *(1992),* Sexes and Genealogies *(1992),* An Ethics of Sexual Difference *(1993), and* Thinking the Difference: For a Peaceful Revolution *(1994). The Claudia Reeder translation of "This Sex Which Is Not One," reprinted here, first appeared in* New French Feminisms, *edited by Elaine Marks and Isabelle de Courtivron (Amherst: University of Massachusetts Press, 1980).*

This Sex Which Is Not One

Female sexuality has always been theorized within masculine parameters. Thus, the opposition "viril" clitoral activity/"feminine" vaginal passivity which Freud — and many others — claims are alternative behaviors or steps in the process of becoming a sexually normal woman, seems prescribed more by the practice of masculine sexuality than by anything else. For the clitoris is thought of as a little penis which is pleasurable to masturbate, as long as the anxiety of castration does not exist (for the little boy), while the vagina derives its value from the "home" it offers the male penis when the now forbidden hand must find a substitute to take its place in giving pleasure.

According to these theorists, woman's erogenous zones are no more than a clitoris-sex, which cannot stand up in comparison with the valued phallic organ; or a hole-envelope, a sheath which surrounds and rubs the penis during coition; a nonsex organ or a masculine sex organ turned inside out in order to caress itself.

Woman and her pleasure are not mentioned in this conception of the sexual relationship. Her fate is one of "lack," "atrophy" (of her genitals), and "penis envy," since the penis is the only recognized sex organ of any worth. Therefore she tries to appropriate it for herself, by all the means at her disposal: by her somewhat servile love of the father-husband capable of giving it to her; by her desire of a penis-child, preferably male; by gaining access to those cultural values which are still "by right" reserved for males alone and are therefore always masculine, etc. Woman lives her desire only as an attempt to possess at long last the equivalent of the male sex organ.

Translated by Claudia Reeder.

All of that seems rather foreign to her pleasure however, unless she remains within the dominant phallic economy. Thus, for example, woman's autoeroticism is very different from man's. He needs an instrument in order to touch himself: his hand, woman's genitals, language — And this self-stimulation requires a minimum of activity. But a woman touches herself by and within herself directly, without mediation, and before any distinction between activity and passivity is possible. A woman "touches herself" constantly without anyone being able to forbid her to do so, for her sex is composed of two lips which embrace continually. Thus, within herself she is already two — but not divisible into ones — who stimulate each other.

This autoeroticism, which she needs in order not to risk the disappearance of her pleasure in the sex act, is interrupted by a violent intrusion: the brutal spreading of these two lips by a violating penis. If, in order to assure an articulation between autoeroticism and heteroeroticism in coition (the encounter with the absolute other which always signifies death), the vagina must also, but not only, substitute for the little boy's hand, how can woman's autoeroticism possibly be perpetuated in the classic representation of sexuality? Will she not indeed be left the impossible choice between defensive virginity, fiercely turned back upon itself, or a body open for penetration, which no longer recognizes in its "hole" of a sex organ the pleasure of retouching itself? The almost exclusive, and ever so anxious, attention accorded the erection in Occidental sexuality proves to what extent the imaginary that commands it is foreign to everything female. For the most part, one finds in Occidental sexuality nothing more than imperatives dictated by rivalry among males: the "strongest" being the one who "gets it up the most," who has the longest, thickest, hardest penis or indeed the one who "pisses the farthest" (cf. little boys' games). These imperatives can also be dictated by sadomasochist fantasies, which in turn are ordered by the relationship between man and mother: his desire to force open, to penetrate, to appropriate for himself the mystery of the stomach in which he was conceived, the secret of his conception, of his "origin." Desire-need, also, once again, to make blood flow in order to revive a very ancient — intrauterine, undoubtedly, but also prehistoric — relation to the maternal.

Woman, in this sexual imaginary, is only a more or less complacent facilitator for the working out of man's fantasies. It is possible, and even certain, that she experiences vicarious pleasure there, but this pleasure is above all a masochistic prostitution of her body to a desire that is not her own and that leaves her in her well-known state of dependency. Not knowing what she wants, ready for anything, even asking for more, if only he will "take" her as the "object" of *his* pleasure, she will not say what *she* wants. Moreover, she does not know, or no longer knows, what she wants. As Freud admits, the beginnings of the sexual life of the little girl are so "obscure," so "faded by the years," that one would have to dig very deep in order to find, behind the traces of this civilization, this history, the vestiges of a more archaic civilization which could give some indication as to what woman's sexuality is all about. This very ancient civilization undoubtedly would not have the same language, the same alphabet — Woman's desire most likely does not speak the same language as man's desire, and it probably has been covered over by the logic that has dominated the West since the Greeks.

In this logic, the prevalence of the gaze, discrimination of form, and individualization of form is particularly foreign to female eroticism. Woman finds pleasure more in touch than in sight and her entrance into a dominant scopic economy[1] signifies, once again, her relegation to passivity: she will be the beautiful object. Although her body is in this way eroticized and solicited to a double movement between exhibition and pudic retreat in order to excite the instincts of the "subject," her sex organ represents the horror of having nothing to see. In this system of representation and desire, the vagina is a flaw, a hole in the representation's scoptophilic objective. It was admitted already in Greek statuary that this "nothing to be seen" must be excluded, rejected, from such a scene of representation. Woman's sexual organs are simply absent from this scene: they are masked and her "slit" is sewn up.

In addition, this sex organ which offers nothing to the view has no distinctive form of its own. Although woman finds pleasure precisely in this incompleteness of the form of her sex organ, which is why it retouches itself indefinitely, her pleasure is denied by a civilization that privileges phallomorphism. The value accorded to the only definable form excludes the form involved in female autoeroticism. The *one* of form, the individual sex, proper name, literal meaning — supersedes, by spreading apart and dividing, this touching of *at least two* (lips) which keeps woman in contact with herself, although it would be impossible to distinguish exactly what "parts" are touching each other.

Whence the mystery that she represents in a culture that claims to enumerate everything, cipher everything by units, inventory everything by individualities. *She is neither one nor two*. She cannot, strictly speaking, be determined either as one person or as two. She renders any definition inadequate. Moreover she has no "proper" name. And her sex organ, which is not *a* sex organ, is counted as *no* sex organ. It is the negative, the opposite, the reverse, the counterpart, of the only visible and morphologically designatable sex organ (even if it does pose a few problems in its passage from erection to detumescence): the penis.

But woman holds the secret of the "thickness" of this "form," its many-layered volume, its metamorphosis from smaller to larger and vice

[1]See Mulvey, p. 1446. [Ed.]

versa, and even the intervals at which this change takes place. Without even knowing it. When she is asked to maintain, to revive, man's desire, what this means in terms of the value of her own desire is neglected. Moreover, she is not aware of her desire, at least not explicitly. But the force and continuity of her desire are capable of nurturing all the "feminine" masquerades that are expected of her for a long time.

It is true that she still has the child, with whom her appetite for touching, for contact, is given free reign, unless this appetite is already lost, or alienated by the taboo placed upon touching in a largely obsessional civilization. In her relation to the child she finds compensatory pleasure for the frustrations she encounters all too often in sexual relations proper. Thus maternity supplants the deficiencies of repressed female sexuality. Is it possible that man and woman no longer even caress each other except indirectly through the mediation between them represented by the child? Preferably male. Man, identified with his son, rediscovers the pleasure of maternal coddling; woman retouches herself in fondling that part of her body: her baby-penis-clitoris.

What that entails for the amorous trio has been clearly spelled out. The Oedipal interdict seems, however, a rather artificial and imprecise law — even though it is the very means of perpetuating the authoritarian discourse of fathers — when it is decreed in a culture where sexual relations are impracticable, since the desire of man and the desire of woman are so foreign to each other. Each of them is forced to search for some common meeting ground by indirect means: either an archaic, sensory relation to the mother's body, or a current, active or passive prolongation of the law of the father. Their attempts are characterized by regressive emotional behavior and the exchange of words so far from the realm of the sexual that they are completely exiled from it. "Mother" and "father" dominate the couple's functioning, but only as social roles. The division of labor prevents them from making love. They produce or reproduce. Not knowing too well how to use their leisure. If indeed they have any, if moreover they want to have any leisure. For what can be done with leisure? What substitute for amorous invention can be created?

We could go on and on — but perhaps we should return to the repressed female imaginary? Thus woman does not have a sex. She has at least two of them, but they cannot be identified as ones. Indeed she has many more of them than that. Her sexuality, always at least double, is in fact *plural*. Plural as culture now wishes to be plural? Plural as the manner in which current texts are written, with very little knowledge of the censorship from which they arise? Indeed, woman's pleasure does not have to choose between clitoral activity and vaginal passivity, for example. The pleasure of the vaginal caress does not have to substitute itself for the pleasure of the clitoral caress. Both contribute irreplaceably to woman's pleasure but they are only two caresses among many to do so. Caressing the breasts, touching the vulva, opening the lips, gently stroking the posterior wall of the vagina, lightly massaging the cervix, etc., evoke a few of the most specifically female pleasures. They remain rather unfamiliar pleasures in the sexual difference as it is currently imagined, or rather as it is currently ignored: the other sex being only the indispensable complement of the only sex.

But *woman has sex organs just about everywhere*. She experiences pleasure almost everywhere. Even without speaking of the hysterization of her entire body,[2] one can say that the geography of her pleasure is much more diversified, more multiple in its differences, more complex, more subtle, than is imagined — in an imaginary centered a bit too much on one and the same.

"She" is indefinitely other in herself. That is undoubtedly the reason she is called temperamental, incomprehensible, perturbed, capricious — not to mention her language in which "she" goes off in all directions and in which "he" is unable to discern the coherence of any meaning. Contradictory words seem a little crazy to the logic of reason, and inaudible for him who listens with ready-made grids, a code prepared in advance. In her statements — at least when she dares to speak out — woman retouches herself

[2]See Foucault, p. 1478. [Ed.]

constantly. She just barely separates from herself some chatter, an exclamation, a half-secret, a sentence left in suspense — When she returns to it, it is only to set out again from another point of pleasure or pain. One must listen to her differently in order to hear an *"other meaning" which is constantly in the process of weaving itself, at the same time ceaselessly embracing words and yet casting them off to avoid becoming fixed, immobilized.* For when "she" says something, it is already no longer identical to what she means. Moreover, her statements are never identical to anything. Their distinguishing feature is one of contiguity. They touch *(upon).* And when they wander too far from this nearness, she stops and begins again from "zero": her body-sex organ.

It is therefore useless to trap women into giving an exact definition of what they mean, to make them repeat (themselves) so the meaning will be clear. They are already elsewhere than in this discursive machinery where you claim to take them by surprise. They have turned back within themselves, which does not mean the same thing as "within yourself." They do not experience the same interiority that you do and which perhaps you mistakenly presume they share. "Within themselves" means *in the privacy of this silent, multiple, diffuse tact.* If you ask them insistently what they are thinking about, they can only reply: nothing. Everything.

Thus they desire at the same time nothing and everything. It is always more and other than this *one* — of sex, for example — that you give them, that you attributed to them and which is often interpreted, and feared, as a sort of insatiable hunger, a voracity which will engulf you entirely. While in fact it is really a question of another economy which diverts the linearity of a project, undermines the target-object of a desire, explodes the polarization of desire on only one pleasure, and disconcerts fidelity to only one discourse —

Must the multiple nature of female desire and language be understood as the fragmentary, scattered remains of a raped or denied sexuality? This is not an easy question to answer. The rejection, the exclusion of a female imaginary undoubtedly places woman in a position where she can experience herself only fragmentarily as waste or as excess in the little structured margins of a dominant ideology, this mirror entrusted by the (masculine) "subject" with the task of reflecting and redoubling himself. The role of "femininity" is prescribed moreover by this masculine specula(riza)tion and corresponds only slightly to woman's desire, which is recuperated only secretly, in hiding, and in a disturbing and unpardonable manner.

But if the female imaginary happened to unfold, if it happened to come into play other than as pieces, scraps, deprived of their assemblage, would it present itself for all that as *a* universe? Would it indeed be volume rather than surface? No. Unless female imaginary is taken to mean, once again, the prerogative of the maternal over the female. This maternal would be phallic in nature however, closed in upon the jealous possession of its valuable product, and competing with man in his esteem for surplus. In this race for power, woman loses the uniqueness of her pleasure. By diminishing herself in volume, she renounces the pleasure derived from the nonsuture of her lips: she is a mother certainly, but she is a virgin mother. Mythology long ago assigned this role to her in which she is allowed a certain social power as long as she is reduced, with her own complicity, to sexual impotence.

Thus a woman's (re)discovery of herself can only signify the possibility of not sacrificing any of her pleasures to another, of not identifying with anyone in particular, of never being simply one. It is a sort of universe in expansion for which no limits could be fixed and which, for all that, would not be incoherency. Nor would it be the polymorphic perversion of the infant during which its erogenous zones await their consolidation under the primacy of the phallus.

Woman would always remain multiple, but she would be protected from dispersion because the other is a part of her, and is autoerotically familiar to her. That does not mean that she would appropriate the other for herself, that she would make it her property. Property and propriety are undoubtedly rather foreign to all that is female. At least sexually. *Nearness,* however, is not foreign to woman, a nearness so close that any identification of one or the other, and therefore any form of property, is impossible. Woman enjoys a closeness with the other that is *so near she cannot possess it, any more than she can possess herself.* She constantly trades herself for the other without any possible identification of either one of them. Woman's pleasure, which grows indefinitely from its passage in/through the other, poses a problem for any current economy in that all computations that attempt to account for woman's incalculable pleasure are irremediably destined to fail.

However, in order for woman to arrive at the point where she can enjoy her pleasure as a woman, a long detour by the analysis of the various systems of oppression which affect her is certainly necessary. By claiming to resort to pleasure alone as the solution to her problem, she runs the risk of missing the reconsideration of a social practice upon which *her* pleasure depends.

For woman is traditionally use-value for man, exchange-value among men. Merchandise, then. This makes her the guardian of matter whose price will be determined by "subjects": workers, tradesmen, consumers, according to the standard of their work and their need-desire. Women are marked phallically by their fathers, husbands, procurers. This stamp(ing) determines their value in sexual commerce. Woman is never anything more than the scene of more or less rival exchange between two men, even when they are competing for the possession of mother-earth.

How can this object of transaction assert a right to pleasure without extricating itself from the established commercial system? How can this merchandise relate to other goods on the market other than with aggressive jealousy? How can raw materials possess themselves without provoking in the consumer fear of the disappearance of his nourishing soil? How can this exchange in nothingness that can be defined in "proper" terms of woman's desire not seem to be pure enticement, fool, all too quickly covered over by a more sensible discourse and an apparently more tangible system of values?

A woman's evolution, however radical it might seek to be, would not suffice then to liberate woman's desire. Neither political theory nor political practice have yet resolved nor sufficiently taken into account this historical problem, although Marxism has announced its importance. But women are not, strictly speaking, a class and their dispersion in several classes makes their political struggle complex and their demands sometimes contradictory.

Their underdeveloped condition stemming from their submission by/to a culture which oppresses them, uses them, cashes in on them, still remains. Women reap no advantage from this situation except that of their quasi-monopoly of masochistic pleasure, housework, and reproduction. The power of slaves? It is considerable since the master is not necessarily well served in matters of pleasure. Therefore, the inversion of the relationship, especially in sexual economy, does not seem to be an enviable objective.

But if women are to preserve their auto-eroticism, their homo-sexuality, and let it flourish, would not the renunciation of heterosexual pleasure simply be another form of this amputation of power that is traditionally associated with women? Would this renunciation not be a new incarceration, a new cloister that women would willingly build? Let women tacitly go on strike, avoid men long enough to learn to defend their desire notably by their speech, let them discover the love of other women protected from that imperious choice of men which puts them in a position of rival goods, let them forge a social status which demands recognition, let them earn their living in order to leave behind their condition of prostitute — These are certainly indispensable steps in their effort to escape their proletarization on the trade market. But, if their goal is to reverse the existing order — even if that were possible — history would simply repeat itself and return to phallocratism, where neither women's sex, their imaginary, nor their language can exist.

Michel Foucault

1926–1984

The following selection is taken from Robert Hurley's translation of Le Volonté de savoir *(*The Will to Knowledge*), Volume I of Foucault's* History of Sexuality *(1980). (For biographical information, see the introduction to Foucault, p. 889.)*

From *The History of Sexuality*

1. OBJECTIVE

. . . This history of sexuality, or rather this series of studies concerning the historical relationships of power and the discourse on sex, is, I realize, a circular project in the sense that it involves two endeavors that refer back to one another. We shall try to rid ourselves of a juridical and negative representation of power, and cease to conceive of it in terms of law, prohibition, liberty, and sovereignty. But how then do we analyze what has occurred in recent history with regard to this thing — seemingly one of the most forbidden areas of our lives and bodies — that is sex? How, if not by way of prohibition and blockage, does power gain access to it? Through which mechanisms, or tactics, or devices? But let us assume in turn that a somewhat careful scrutiny will show that power in modern societies has not in fact governed sexuality through law and sovereignty; let us suppose that historical analysis has revealed the presence of a veritable "technology" of sex, one that is much more complex and above all much more positive than the mere effect of a "defense" could be; this being the case, does this example — which can only be considered a privileged one, since power seemed in this instance, more than anywhere else, to function as prohibition — not compel one to discover principles for analyzing power which do not derive from the system of right and the form of law? Hence it is a question of forming a different grid of historical decipherment by starting from a different theory of power; and, at the same time, of advancing little by little toward a different conception of power through a closer examination of an entire historical material. We must at the same time conceive of sex without the law, and power without the king.

Translated by Robert Hurley.

2. METHOD

Hence the objective is to analyze a certain form of knowledge regarding sex, not in terms of repression or law, but in terms of power. But the word *power* is apt to lead to a number of misunderstandings — misunderstandings with respect to its nature, its form, and its unity. By power, I do not mean "Power" as a group of institutions and mechanisms that ensure the subservience of the citizens of a given state. By power, I do not mean, either, a mode of subjugation which, in contrast to violence, has the form of the rule. Finally, I do not have in mind a general system of domination exerted by one group over another, a system whose effects, through successive derivations, pervade the entire social body. The analysis, made in terms of power, must not assume that the sovereignty of the state, the form of the law, or the over-all unity of a domination are given at the outset; rather, these are only the terminal forms power takes. It seems to me that power must be understood in the first instance as the multiplicity of force relations immanent in the sphere in which they operate and which constitute their own organization; as the process which, through ceaseless struggles and confrontations, transforms, strengthens, or reverses them; as the support which these force relations find in one another, thus forming a chain or a system, or on the contrary, the disjunctions and contradictions which isolate them from one another; and lastly, as the strategies in which they take effect, whose general design or institutional crystallization is embodied in the state apparatus, in the formulation of the law, in the various social hegemonies. Power's condition of possibility, or in any case the viewpoint which permits one to understand its exercise, even in its more "peripheral" effects, and which also makes it possible to use its mechanisms as a grid of intelligibility of the social order, must not be sought in the primary existence of a central point, in a unique source of sovereignty from which secondary and descendent forms would emanate; it is the moving substrate of force relations which, by virtue of their inequality, constantly engender states of power, but the latter are always local and unstable. The omnipresence of power: not because it has the privilege of consolidating everything under its invincible unity, but because it is produced from one moment to the next, at every point, or rather in every relation from one point to another. Power is everywhere; not because it embraces everything, but because it comes from everywhere. And "Power," insofar as it is permanent, repetitious, inert, and self-reproducing, is simply the over-all effect that emerges from all these mobilities, the concatenation that rests on each of them and seeks in turn to arrest their movement. One needs to be nominalistic, no doubt: power is not an institution, and not a structure; neither is it a certain strength we are endowed with; it is the name that one attributes to a complex strategical situation in a particular society.

Should we turn the expression around, then, and say that politics is war pursued by other means?[1] If we still wish to maintain a separation between war and politics, perhaps we should postulate rather that this multiplicity of force relations can be coded — in part but never totally — either in the form of "war," or in the form of "politics"; this would imply two different strategies (but the one always liable to switch into the other) for integrating these unbalanced, heterogeneous, unstable, and tense force relations.

Continuing this line of discussion, we can advance a certain number of propositions:

Power is not something that is acquired, seized, or shared, something that one holds on to or allows to slip away; power is exercised from innumerable points, in the inter-play of nonegalitarian and mobile relations.

Relations of power are not in a position of exteriority with respect to other types of relationships (economic processes, knowledge relationships, sexual relations), but are immanent in the latter; they are the immediate effects of the divisions, inequalities, and disequilibriums which occur in the latter, and conversely they are the internal conditions of these differentiations; relations of power are not in the superstructural[2] positions, with merely a role of prohibition or accompaniment; they have a directly productive role, wherever they come into play.

Power comes from below; that is, there is no binary and all-encompassing opposition between rulers and ruled at the root of power relations, and serving as a general matrix — no such duality extending from the top down and reacting on more and more limited groups to the very depths of the social body. One must suppose rather that the manifold relationships of force that take shape and come into play in the machinery of production, in families, limited groups, and institutions, are the basis for wide-ranging effects of cleavage that run through the social body as a whole. These then form a general line of force that traverses the local oppositions and links them together; to be sure, they also bring about redistributions, realignments, homogenizations, serial arrangements, and convergences of the force relations. Major dominations are the hege-

[1]Foucault is alluding to the famous definition of Prussian General Karl von Clausewitz (1780–1831) in *On War* (1832): "War is the continuation of politics by other means." [Ed.]

[2]Although no Marxist, Foucault is here making use of Marx's distinction between base and superstructure. In the two paragraphs following this one, he refers to Gramsci's notion of hegemony and Althusser's notion of "ideological state apparatuses." See the introduction to Marxist Criticism, p. 1095. [Ed.]

monic effects that are sustained by all these confrontations.

Power relations are both intentional and nonsubjective. If in fact they are intelligible, this is not because they are the effect of another instance that "explains" them, but rather because they are imbued, through and through, with calculation: there is no power that is exercised without a series of aims and objectives. But this does not mean that it results from the choice or decision of an individual subject; let us not look for the headquarters that presides over its rationality; neither the caste which governs, nor the groups which control the state apparatus, nor those who make the most important economic decisions direct the entire network of power that functions in a society (and makes *it* function); the rationality of power is characterized by tactics that are often quite explicit at the restricted level where they are inscribed (the local cynicism of power), tactics which, becoming connected to one another, attracting and propagating one another, but finding their base of support and their condition elsewhere, end by forming comprehensive systems: the logic is perfectly clear, the aims decipherable, and yet it is often the case that no one is there to have invented them, and few who can be said to have formulated them: an implicit characteristic of the great anonymous, almost unspoken strategies which coordinate the loquacious tactics whose "inventors" or decisionmakers are often without hypocrisy.

Where there is power, there is resistance, and yet, or rather consequently, this resistance is never in a position of exteriority in relation to power. Should it be said that one is always "inside" power, there is no "escaping" it, there is no absolute outside where it is concerned, because one is subject to the law in any case? Or that, history being the ruse of reason, power is the ruse of history, always emerging the winner? This would be to misunderstand the strictly relational character of power relationships. Their existence depends on a multiplicity of points of resistance: these play the role of adversary, target, support, or handle in power relations. These points of resistance are present everywhere in the power network. Hence there is no single locus of great Refusal, no soul of revolt, source of all rebellions, or pure law of the revolutionary. Instead there is a plurality of resistances, each of them a special case: resistances that are possible, necessary, improbable; others that are spontaneous, savage, solitary, concerted, rampant, or violent; still others that are quick to compromise, interested, or sacrificial; by definition, they can only exist in the strategic field of power relations. But this does not mean that they are only a reaction or rebound, forming with respect to the basic domination an underside that is in the end always passive, doomed to perpetual defeat. Resistances do not derive from a few heterogeneous principles; but neither are they a lure or a promise that is of necessity betrayed. They are the odd term in relations of power; they are inscribed in the latter as an irreducible opposite. Hence they too are distributed in irregular fashion: the points, knots, or focuses of resistance are spread over time and space at varying densities, at times mobilizing groups or individuals in a definitive way, inflaming certain points of the body, certain moments in life, certain types of behavior. Are there no great radical ruptures, massive binary divisions, then? Occasionally, yes. But more often one is dealing with mobile and transitory points of resistance, producing cleavages in a society that shift about, fracturing unities and effecting regroupings, furrowing across individuals themselves, cutting them up and remolding them, marking off irreducible regions in them, in their bodies and minds. Just as the network of power relations ends by forming a dense web that passes through apparatuses and institutions, without being exactly localized in them, so too the swarm of points of resistance traverses social stratifications and individual unities. And it is doubtless the strategic codification of these points of resistance that makes a revolution possible, somewhat similar to the way in which the state relies on the institutional integration of power relationships.

It is in this sphere of force relations that we must try to analyze the mechanisms of power.

In this way we will escape from the system of Law-and-Sovereign which has captivated political thought for such a long time. And if it is true that Machiavelli was among the few — and this no doubt was the scandal of his "cynicism" — who conceived the power of the Prince in terms of force relationships, perhaps we need to go one step further, do without the persona of the Prince, and decipher power mechanisms on the basis of a strategy that is immanent in force relationships.

To return to sex and the discourses of truth that have taken charge of it, the question that we must address, then, is not: Given a specific state structure, how and why is it that power needs to establish a knowledge of sex? Neither is the question: What over-all domination was served by the concern, evidenced since the eighteenth century, to produce true discourses on sex? Nor is it: What law presided over both the regularity of sexual behavior and the conformity of what was said about it? It is rather: In a specific type of discourse on sex, in a specific form of extortion of truth, appearing historically and in specific places (around the child's body, apropos of women's sex, in connection with practices restricting births, and so on), what were the most immediate, the most local power relations at work? How did they make possible these kinds of discourses, and conversely, how were these discourses used to support power relations? How was the action of these power relations modified by their very exercise, entailing a strengthening of some terms and a weakening of others, with effects of resistance and counterinvestments, so that there has never existed one type of stable subjugation, given once and for all? How were these power relations linked to one another according to the logic of a great strategy, which in retrospect takes on the aspect of a unitary and voluntarist politics of sex? In general terms: rather than referring all the infinitesimal violences that are exerted on sex, all the anxious gazes that are directed at it, and all the hiding places whose discovery is made into an impossible task, to the unique form of a great Power, we must immerse the expanding production of discourses on sex in the field of multiple and mobile power relations.

Which leads us to advance, in a preliminary way, four rules to follow. But these are not intended as methodological imperatives; at most they are cautionary prescriptions.

1. *Rule of Immanence*

One must not suppose that there exists a certain sphere of sexuality that would be the legitimate concern of a free and disinterested scientific inquiry were it not the object of mechanisms of prohibition brought to bear by the economic or ideological requirements of power. If sexuality was constituted as an area of investigation, this was only because relations of power had established it as a possible object; and conversely, if power was able to take it as a target, this was because techniques of knowledge and procedures of discourse were capable of investing it. Between techniques of knowledge and strategies of power, there is no exteriority, even if they have specific roles and are linked together on the basis of their difference. We will start, therefore, from what might be called "local centers" of power-knowledge: for example, the relations that obtain between penitents and confessors, or the faithful and their directors of conscience. Here, guided by the theme of the "flesh" that must be mastered, different forms of discourse — self-examination, questionings, admissions, interpretations, interviews — were the vehicle of a kind of incessant back-and-forth movement of forms of subjugation and schemas of knowledge. Similarly, the body of the child, under surveillance, surrounded in his cradle, his bed, or his room by an entire watch-crew of parents, nurses, servants, educators, and doctors, all attentive to the least manifestations of his sex, has constituted, particularly since the eighteenth century, another "local center" of power-knowledge.

2. *Rules of Continual Variations*

We must not look for who has the power in the order of sexuality (men, adults, parents, doctors) and who is deprived of it (women, adolescents, children, patients); nor for who has the right to know and who is forced to remain ignorant. We must seek rather the pattern of the modifications which the relationships of force imply by the very nature of their process. The "distributions of power" and the "appropriations of knowledge" never represent only instantaneous slices taken from processes involving, for example, a cumulative reinforcement of the strongest factor, or a reversal of relationship, or again, a simultaneous increase of two terms. Relations of power-knowledge are not static forms of distribution, they are "matrices of transformations." The nineteenth-century grouping made up of the father, the mother, the educator, and the doctor, around the child and his sex, was subjected to constant modifications, continual shifts. One of the more spectacular results of the latter was a strange reversal: whereas to begin with the child's sexuality had been problematized within the relationship established between doctor and parents (in the form of advice, or recommendations to keep the child under observation, or warnings of future dangers), ultimately it was in the relationship of the psychiatrist to the child that the sexuality of adults themselves was called into question.

3. *Rule of Double Conditioning*

No "local center," no "pattern of transformation" could function if, through a series of sequences, it did not eventually enter into an over-all strategy. And inversely, no strategy could achieve comprehensive effects if it did not gain support from precise and tenuous relations serving, not as its point of application or final outcome, but as its prop and anchor point. There is no discontinuity between them, as if one were dealing with two different levels (one microscopic and the other macroscopic); but neither is there homogeneity (as if the one were only the enlarged projection or the miniaturization of the other); rather, one must conceive of the double conditioning of a strategy by the specificity of possible tactics, and of tactics by the strategic envelope that makes them work. Thus the father in the family is not the "representative" of the sovereign or the state; and the latter are not projections of the father on a different scale. The family does not duplicate society, just as society does not imitate the family. But the family organization, precisely to the extent that it was insular and heteromorphous with respect to the other power mechanisms, was used to support the great "maneuvers" employed for the Malthusian control of the birthrate,[3] for the populationist incitements, for the medicalization of sex and the psychiatrization of its nongenital forms.

4. *Rule of the Tactical Polyvalence of Discourses*

What is said about sex must not be analyzed simply as the surface of projection of these power mechanisms. Indeed, it is in discourse that power and knowledge are joined together. And for this very reason, we must conceive discourse as a series of discontinuous segments whose tactical function is neither uniform nor stable. To be more precise, we must not imagine a world of discourse divided between accepted discourse and excluded discourse, or between the dominant discourse and the dominated one; but as a multiplicity of discursive elements that can come into play in various strategies. It is this distribution that we must reconstruct, with the things said and those concealed, the enunciations required and those forbidden, that it comprises; with the variants and different effects — according to who is speaking, his position of power, the institutional context in which he happens to be situated — that it implies; and with the shifts and reutilizations of identical formulas for contrary objectives that it also includes. Discourses are not once and for all subservient to power or raised up against it, any more than silences are. We must make allowance for the complex and unstable process whereby discourse can be both an instrument and an effect of power, but also a hindrance, a stum-

[3]In *An Essay on the Principle of Population* (1798), British economist Thomas Robert Malthus (1766–1834), observing that population increased geometrically while consumer goods increased arithmetically, recommended sexual restraint as an alternative to the otherwise inevitable consequences of poverty and starvation. [Ed.]

bling-block, a point of resistance and a starting point for an opposing strategy. Discourse transmits and produces power; it reinforces it, but also undermines and exposes it, renders it fragile and makes it possible to thwart it. In like manner, silence and secrecy are a shelter for power, anchoring its prohibitions; but they also loosen its holds and provide for relatively obscure areas of tolerance. Consider for example the history of what was once "the" great sin against nature. The extreme discretion of the texts dealing with sodomy — that utterly confused category — and the nearly universal reticence in talking about it made possible a twofold operation: on the one hand, there was an extreme severity (punishment by fire was meted out well into the eighteenth century, without there being any substantial protest expressed before the middle of the century), and on the other hand, a tolerance that must have been widespread (which one can deduce indirectly from the infrequency of judicial sentences, and which one glimpses more directly through certain statements concerning societies of men that were thought to exist in the army or in the courts). There is no question that the appearance in nineteenth-century psychiatry, jurisprudence, and literature of a whole series of discourses on the species and subspecies of homosexuality, inversion, pederasty, and "psychic hermaphrodism" made possible a strong advance of social controls into this area of "perversity"; but it also made possible the formation of a "reverse" discourse: homosexuality began to speak in its own behalf, to demand that its legitimacy or "naturality" be acknowledged, often in the same vocabulary, using the same categories by which it was medically disqualified. There is not, on the one side, a discourse of power, and opposite it, another discourse that runs counter to it. Discourses are tactical elements or blocks operating in the field of force relations; there can exist different and even contradictory discourses within the same strategy; they can, on the contrary, circulate without changing their form from one strategy to another, opposing strategy. We must not expect the discourses on sex to tell us, above all, what strategy they derive from, or what moral divisions they accompany, or what ideology — dominant or dominated — they represent; rather we must question them on the two levels of their tactical productivity (what reciprocal effects of power and knowledge they ensure) and their strategical integration (what conjunction and what force relationship make their utilization necessary in a given episode of the various confrontations that occur).

In short, it is a question of orienting ourselves to a conception of power which replaces the privilege of the law with the viewpoint of the objective, the privilege of prohibition with the viewpoint of tactical efficacy, the privilege of sovereignty with the analysis of a multiple and mobile field of force relations, wherein far-reaching, but never completely stable, effects of domination are produced. The strategical model, rather than the model based on law. And this, not out of a speculative choice or theoretical preference, but because in fact it is one of the essential traits of Western societies that the force relationships which for a long time had found expression in war, in every form of warfare, gradually became invested in the order of political power.

3. DOMAIN

Sexuality must not be described as a stubborn drive, by nature alien and of necessity disobedient to a power which exhausts itself trying to subdue it and often fails to control it entirely. It appears rather as an especially dense transfer point for relations of power: between men and women, young people and old people, parents and offspring, teachers and students, priests and laity, an administration and a population. Sexuality is not the most intractable element in power relations, but rather one of those endowed with the greatest instrumentality: useful for the greatest number of maneuvers and capable of serving as a point of support, as a linchpin, for the most varied strategies.

There is no single, all-encompassing strategy, valid for all of society and uniformly bearing on all the manifestations of sex. For example, the idea that there have been repeated attempts, by various means, to reduce all of sex to its reproductive function, its heterosexual and adult form, and its matrimonial legitimacy fails to take into account the manifold objectives aimed for, the manifold means employed in the different sexual politics concerned with the two sexes, the different age groups and social classes.

In a first approach to the problem, it seems that we can distinguish four great strategic unities which, beginning in the eighteenth century, formed specific mechanisms of knowledge and power centering on sex. These did not come into being fully developed at that time; but it was then that they took on a consistency and gained an effectiveness in the order of power, as well as a productivity in the order of knowledge, so that it is possible to describe them in their relative autonomy.

1. *A hysterization of women's bodies:* a threefold process whereby the feminine body was analyzed — qualified and disqualified — as being thoroughly saturated with sexuality; whereby it was integrated into the sphere of medical practices, by reason of a pathology intrinsic to it; whereby, finally, it was placed in organic communication with the social body (whose regulated fecundity it was supposed to ensure), the family space (of which it had to be a substantial and functional element), and the life of children (which it produced and had to guarantee, by virtue of a biologico-moral responsibility lasting through the entire period of the children's education): the Mother, with her negative image of "nervous woman," constituted the most visible form of this hysterization.

2. *A pedagogization of children's sex:* a double assertion that practically all children indulge or are prone to indulge in sexual activity; and that, being unwarranted, at the same time "natural" and "contrary to nature," this sexual activity posed physical and moral, individual and collective dangers; children were defined as "preliminary" sexual beings, on this side of sex, yet within it, astride a dangerous dividing line. Parents, families, educators, doctors, and eventually psychologists would have to take charge, in a continuous way, of this precious and perilous, dangerous and endangered sexual potential: this pedagogization was especially evident in the war against onanism, which in the West lasted nearly two centuries.

3. *A socialization of procreative behavior:* an economic socialization via all the incitements and restrictions, the "social" and fiscal measures brought to bear on the fertility of couples; a political socialization achieved through the "responsibilization" of couples with regard to the social body as a whole (which had to be limited or on the contrary reinvigorated), and a medical socialization carried out by attributing a pathogenic value — for the individual and the species — to birth-control practices.

4. *A psychiatrization of perverse pleasure:* the sexual instinct was isolated as a separate biological and psychical instinct; a clinical analysis was made of all the forms of anomalies by which it could be afflicted; it was assigned a role of normalization or pathologization with respect to all behavior; and finally, a corrective technology was sought for these anomalies.

Four figures emerged from this preoccupation with sex, which mounted throughout the nineteenth century — four privileged objects of knowledge, which were also targets and anchorage points for the ventures of knowledge: the hysterical woman, the masturbating child, the Malthusian couple, and the perverse adult. Each of them corresponded to one of these strategies which, each in its own way, invested and made use of the sex of women, children, and men.

What was at issue in these strategies? A struggle against sexuality? Or were they part of an effort to gain control of it? An attempt to regulate it more effectively and mask its more indiscreet, conspicuous, and intractable aspects? A way of formulating only that measure of knowledge about it that was acceptable or useful? In actual fact, what was involved, rather, was the very production of sexuality. Sexuality must not be thought of as a kind of natural given which power tries to hold in check, or as an obscure domain which knowledge tries gradually to uncover. It is the name that can be given to a historical construct: not a furtive reality that is difficult to grasp, but a great surface network in which the stimulation of bodies, the intensification of pleasures, the incitement to discourse, the formation of special knowledges, the strengthening of controls and resistances, are linked to one another, in accordance with a few major strategies of knowledge and power.

It will be granted no doubt that relations of sex gave rise, in every society, to a *deployment of alliance:* a system of marriage, of fixation and development of kinship ties, of transmission of names and possessions. This deployment of alliance, with the mechanisms of constraint that ensured its existence and the complex knowledge it often required, lost some of its importance as economic processes and political structures could no longer rely on it as an adequate instrument or sufficient support. Particularly from the eighteenth century onward, Western societies created and deployed a new apparatus which was superimposed on the previous one, and which, without completely supplanting the latter, helped to reduce its importance. I am speaking of the *deployment of sexuality:* like the *deployment of alliance,* it connects up with the circuit of sexual partners, but in a completely different way. The two systems can be contrasted term by term. The deployment of alliance is built around a system of rules defining the permitted and the forbidden, the licit and the illicit, whereas the deployment of sexuality operates according to mobile, polymorphous, and contingent techniques of power. The deployment of alliance has as one of its chief objectives to reproduce the interplay of relations and maintain the law that governs them; the deployment of sexuality, on the other hand, engenders a continual extension of areas and forms of control. For the first, what is pertinent is the link between partners and definite statutes; the second is concerned with the sensations of the body, the quality of pleasures, and the nature of impressions, however tenuous or imperceptible these may be. Lastly, if the deployment of alliance is firmly tied to the economy due to the role it can play in the transmission or circulation of wealth, the deployment of sexuality is linked to the economy through numerous and subtle relays, the main one of which, however, is the body — the body that produces and consumes. In a word, the deployment of alliance is attuned to a homeostasis of the social body, which it has the function of maintaining; whence its privileged link with the law; whence too the fact that the important phase for it is "reproduction." The deployment of sexuality has its reason for being, not in reproducing itself, but in proliferating, innovating, annexing, creating, and penetrating bodies in an increasingly detailed way, and in controlling populations in an increasingly comprehensive way. We are compelled, then, to accept three or four hypotheses which run counter to the one on which the theme of a sexuality repressed by the modern forms of society is based: sexuality is tied to recent devices of power; it has been expanding at an increasing rate since the seventeenth century; the arrangement that has sustained it is not governed by reproduction; it has been linked from the outset with an intensification of the body — with its exploitation as an object of knowledge and an element in relations of power.

It is not exact to say that the deployment of sexuality supplanted the deployment of alliance. One can imagine that one day it will have replaced it. But as things stand at present, while it does tend to cover up the deployment of alliance, it has neither obliterated the latter nor rendered it useless. Moreover, historically it was around and on the basis of the deployment of alliance that the deployment of sexuality was constructed. First the practice of penance, then that of the examination of conscience and spiritual direction, was the formative nucleus: as we have seen, what was at issue to begin with at the tribunal of penance was sex insofar as it was the basis of relations; the questions posed had to do with the commerce allowed or forbidden (adultery, extramarital relations, relations with a person prohibited by blood or statute, the legitimate or illegitimate character of the act of sexual congress); then, coinciding with the new pastoral[4] and its application in seminaries, secondary schools, and convents, there was a gradual progression away from the problematic of relations toward a problematic of the "flesh," that is, of the body, sensation, the nature of pleasure, the more secret forms of enjoyment or acquiescence. "Sexuality" was taking shape, born of a technology of power that was originally

[4]Pastoral refers to the duties of priests. [Ed.]

focused on alliance. Since then, it has not ceased to operate in conjunction with a system of alliance on which it has depended for support. The family cell, in the form in which it came to be valued in the course of the eighteenth century, made it possible for the main elements of the deployment of sexuality (the feminine body, infantile precocity, the regulation of births, and to a lesser extent no doubt, the specification of the perverted) to develop along its two primary dimensions: the husband-wife axis and the parents-children axis. The family, in its contemporary form, must not be understood as a social, economic, and political structure of alliance that excludes or at least restrains sexuality, that diminishes it as much as possible, preserving only its useful functions. On the contrary, its role is to anchor sexuality and provide it with a permanent support. It ensures the production of a sexuality that is not homogeneous with the privileges of alliance, while making it possible for the systems of alliance to be imbued with a new tactic of power which they would otherwise be impervious to. The family is the interchange of sexuality and alliance: it conveys the law and the juridical dimension in the deployment of sexuality; and it conveys the economy of pleasure and the intensity of sensations in the regime of alliance.

This interpenetration of the deployment of alliance and that of sexuality in the form of the family allows us to understand a number of facts: that since the eighteenth century the family has become an obligatory locus of affects, feelings, love; that sexuality has its privileged point of development in the family; that for this reason sexuality is "incestuous" from the start. It may be that in societies where the mechanisms of alliance predominate, prohibition of incest is a functionally indispensable rule. But in a society such as ours, where the family is the most active site of sexuality, and where it is doubtless the exigencies of the latter which maintain and prolong its existence, incest — for different reasons altogether and in a completely different way — occupies a central place; it is constantly being solicited and refused; it is an object of obsession and attraction, a dreadful secret and an indispensable pivot. It is manifested as a thing that is strictly forbidden in the family insofar as the latter functions as a deployment of alliance; but it is also a thing that is continuously demanded in order for the family to be a hotbed of constant sexual incitement. If for more than a century the West has displayed such a strong interest in the prohibition of incest, if more or less by common accord it has been seen as a social universal and one of the points through which every society is obliged to pass on the way to becoming a culture, perhaps this is because it was found to be a means of self-defense, not against an incestuous desire, but against the expansion and the implications of this deployment of sexuality which had been set up, but which, among its many benefits, had the disadvantage of ignoring the laws and juridical forms of alliance. By asserting that all societies without exception, and consequently our own, were subject to this rule of rules, one guaranteed that this deployment of sexuality, whose strange effects were beginning to be felt — among them, the affective intensification of the family space — would not be able to escape from the grand and ancient system of alliance.[5] Thus the law would be secure, even in the new mechanics of power. For this is the paradox of a society which, from the eighteenth century to the present, has created so many technologies of power that are foreign to the concept of law: it fears the effects and proliferations of those technologies and attempts to recode them in forms of law. If one considers the threshold of all culture to be prohibited incest, then sexuality has been, from the dawn of time, under the sway of law and right. By devoting so much effort to an endless reworking of the transcultural theory of the incest taboo, anthropology has proved worthy of the whole modern deployment of sexuality and the theoretical discourses it generates.

What has taken place since the seventeenth century can be interpreted in the following manner: the deployment of sexuality which first developed on the fringes of familial institutions (in the direction of conscience and pedagogy, for example) gradually became focused on the family: the

[5]Foucault refers to the theory of anthropologist Claude Lévi-Strauss that the incest-taboo is universal within human cultures, indeed defines human culture. See Lévi-Strauss, p. 882. [Ed.]

alien, irreducible, and even perilous effects it held in store for the deployment of alliance (an awareness of this danger was evidenced in the criticism often directed at the indiscretion of the directors, and in the entire controversy, which occurred somewhat later, over the private or public, institutional or familial education of children[6]) were absorbed by the family, a family that was reorganized, restricted no doubt, and in any case intensified in comparison with the functions it formerly exercised in the deployment of alliance. In the family, parents and relatives became the chief agents of a deployment of sexuality which drew its outside support from doctors, educators, and later psychiatrists, and which began by competing with the relations of alliance but soon "psychologized" or "psychiatrized" the latter. Then these new personages made their appearance: the nervous woman, the frigid wife, the indifferent mother — or worse, the mother beset by murderous obsessions — the impotent, sadistic, perverse husband, the hysterical or neurasthenic girl, the precocious and already exhausted child, and the young homosexual who rejects marriage or neglects his wife. These were the combined figures of an alliance gone bad and an abnormal sexuality; they were the means by which the disturbing factors of the latter were brought into the former; and yet they also provided an opportunity for the alliance system to assert its prerogatives in the order of sexuality. Then a pressing demand emanated from the family: a plea for help in reconciling these unfortunate conflicts between sexuality and alliance; and, caught in the grip of this deployment of sexuality which had invested it from without, contributing to its solidification into its modern form, the family broadcast the long complaint of its sexual suffering to doctors, educators, psychiatrists, priests, and pastors, to all the "experts" who would listen. It was as if it had suddenly discovered the dreadful secret of what had always been hinted at and inculcated in it: the family, the keystone of alliance, was the germ of all the misfortunes of sex. And lo and behold, from the mid-nineteenth century onward, the family engaged in searching out the slightest traces of sexuality in its midst, wrenching from itself the most difficult confessions, soliciting an audience with everyone who might know something about the matter, and opening itself unreservedly to endless examination. The family was the crystal in the deployment of sexuality: it seemed to be the source of a sexuality which it actually only reflected and diffracted. By virtue of its permeability, and through that process of reflections to the outside, it became one of the most valuable tactical components of the deployment.

[6]Molière's *Tartuffe* and Jakob Michael Lenz's *Tutor*, separated by more than a century, both depict the interference of the deployment of sexuality in the family organization, apropos of spiritual direction in *Tartuffe* and education in *The Tutor*. [Au.]

Eve Kosofsky Sedgwick

b. 1950

Few would have guessed from Eve Kosofsky Sedgwick's 1975 doctoral dissertation, published as The Coherence of Gothic Conventions *in 1980, that she was to be one of the founders of gay and lesbian studies in America, nor that her 1989 MLA talk "Jane Austen and the Masturbating Girl" (published in 1991 in* Critical Inquiry*) would be singled out for attack by right-wing columnist Roger Kimball as a prime example of "tenured radicalism." Eve Sedgwick was born in Dayton, Ohio, and educated at Cornell and Yale. Her strikingly original work on homosocial desire began from lectures she gave while teaching women's studies at Boston University. Sedgwick writes: "When I began work on* Between Men: English Literature and Male Homosocial Desire *(1986), I saw myself as working mainly in the context of feminist literary criticism and theory. By the time I published* Epistemology of the Closet *in 1990, it was unmistakably clear that lesbian/gay criticism was a going concern in its own* *right. I see my work as being strongly marked by a queer politics that is at once antiseparatist and antiassimilationist; by a methodology that draws on deconstruction among other techniques; and by writerly experimentation." A poet as well as a critic, Sedgwick has taught writing and literature at Hamilton College, Boston University, and Amherst College; she is currently Newman Ivey White Professor of English at Duke University. Her most recent books are* Tendencies *(1993) and* Fat Art, Thin Art *(1994). The following selection is from the "Introduction: Axiomatic" to* Epistemology of the Closet.

From *Epistemology of the Closet*

AXIOM 6: THE RELATION OF GAY STUDIES TO DEBATES ON THE LITERARY CANON IS, AND HAD BEST BE, TORTUOUS.

Early on in the work on *Epistemology of the Closet,* in trying to settle on a literary text that would provide a first example for the kind of argument I meant the book to enable, I found myself circling around a text of 1891, a narrative that in spite of its relative brevity has proved a durable and potent centerpiece of gay male intertexuality and indeed has provided a durable and potent physical icon for gay male desire. It tells the story of a young Englishman famous for an extreme beauty of face and figure that seems to betray his aristocratic origin — an origin marked, however, also by mystery and class misalliance. If the gorgeous youth gives his name to the book and stamps his bodily image on it, the narrative is nonetheless more properly the story of a male triangle: a second, older man is tortured by a desire for the youth for which he can find no direct mode of expression, and a third man, emblem of suavity and the world, presides over the dispensation of discursive authority as the beautiful youth murders the tortured lover and is himself, in turn, by the novel's end ritually killed.

But maybe, I thought, one such text would offer an insufficient basis for cultural hypothesis. Might I pick two? It isn't yet commonplace to read *Dorian Gray* and *Billy Budd* by one another's light, but that can only be a testimony to the power of accepted English and American literary canons to insulate and deform the reading of politically important texts. In any gay male canon the two contemporaneous experimental works must be yoked together as overarching gateway texts of our modern period, and the conventionally obvious differences between them of style, literary positioning, national origin, class ethos, structure, and the thematics must cease to be taken for granted and must instead become newly salient in the context of their startling erotic congruence. The book of the beautiful male English body foregrounded on an international canvas; the book of its inscription and evocation through a trio of male figures — the lovely boy, the tormented desirer, the deft master of the rules of their discourse; the story in which the lover is murdered by the boy and the boy is himself sacrificed; the deftly magisterial recounting that finally frames, preserves, exploits, and desublimates the male bodily image: *Dorian Gray* and *Billy Budd* are both that book.

The year 1891 is a good moment to which to look for a cross section of the inaugural discourses of modern homo/heterosexuality — in medicine and psychiatry, in language and law, in the crisis of female status, in the career of imperialism. *Billy Budd* and *Dorian Gray* are among the texts that have set the terms for a modern homosexual identity. And in the Euro-American culture of this past century it has been notable that foundational texts of modern gay culture — *A la recherche du temps perdu* and *Death in Venice,* for instance, along with *Dorian Gray* and *Billy Budd* — have often been the identical texts that mobilized and promulgated the most potent images and categories for (what is now visible as) the canon of homophobic mastery.

Neither *Dorian Gray* nor *Billy Budd* is in the least an obscure text. Both are available in numerous paperback editions, for instance; and, both conveniently short, each differently canonical within a different national narrative, both are taught regularly in academic curricula. As what they are taught, however, and as what canonized, comes so close to disciplining the reading permitted of each that even the contemporaneity of the two texts (*Dorian Gray* was published as a book the year *Billy Budd* was written) may startle. That every major character in the archetypal American "allegory of good and evil" is English; that the archetypal English fin-de-siècle "allegory of art and life" was a sufficiently American event to appear in a Philadelphia publisher's magazine nine months before it became a London book — the canonic regimentation that effaces these international bonds has how much the more scope to efface the intertext and the intersexed. How may the strategy of a new canon operate in this space?

Contemporary discussions of the question of the literary canon tend to be structured either around the possibility of change, of rearrangement and reassignment of texts, within one overarching master-canon of literature — the strategy of adding Mary Shelley to the Norton Anthology — or, more theoretically defensible at the moment, around a vision of an exploding master-canon whose fracture would produce, or at least leave room for, a potentially infinite plurality of mini-canons, each specified as to its thematic or structural or authorial coverage: francophone Canadian or Inuit canons, for instance; clusters of magical realism or national allegory; the blues tradition; working-class narrative; canons of the sublime or the self-reflexive; Afro-Caribbean canons; canons of Anglo-American women's writing.

In fact, though, the most productive canon effects that have been taking place in recent literary studies have occurred, not from within the mechanism either of the master-canon or of a postfractural plurality of canons, but through an interaction between these two models of the canon. In this interaction the new pluralized mini-canons have largely failed to dislodge the master-canon from its empirical centrality in such institutional practices as publishing and teaching, although they have made certain specific works and authors newly available for inclusion in the master-canon. Their more important effect, however, has been to challenge, if not the empirical centrality, then the conceptual anonymity of the master-canon. The most notorious instance of this has occurred with feminist studies in literature, which by on the one hand confronting the master-canon with alternative canons of women's literature, and on the other hand reading rebelliously within the master-canon, has not only somewhat rearranged the table of contents for the master-canon but, more important, given it a title. If it is still in important respects *the* master-canon it nevertheless cannot now escape naming itself with every syllable also *a* particular canon, a canon of mastery, in this case of men's mastery over, and over against, women. Perhaps never again need women — need, one hopes, anybody — feel greeted by the Norton Anthology of mostly white men's Literature with the implied insolent salutation, "I'm nobody. Who are you?"

This is an encouraging story of female canon-formation, working in a sort of pincers movement with a process of feminist canon-*naming*, that has been in various forms a good deal told by now. How much the cheering clarity of this story is indebted, however, to the scarifying coarseness and visibility with which women and men are, in most if not all societies, distinguished publicly and once and for all from one another emerges only when attempts are made to apply the same model to that very differently structured though closely related form of oppression, modern homophobia. It is, as we have seen, only recently — and, I am arguing, only very incompletely and raggedly, although to that extent violently and brutally — that a combination of discursive forces have carved out, for women and for men, a possible though intensively proscribed homosexual identity in Euro-American culture. To the extent that such an identity is traceable, there is clearly the possibility, now being realized within literary criticism, for assembling alternative canons of lesbian and gay male writing *as* minority canons, as a literature of oppression and resistance and survival and heroic making. This modern view of lesbians and gay men as a distinctive minority population is of course importantly anachronistic in relation to earlier writing, however; and even in relation to modern writing it seems to falter in important ways in the implicit analysis it offers of the mechanisms of homophobia and of same-sex desire. It is with these complications that the relation between lesbian and gay literature as a minority canon, and the process of making salient the homosocial, homosexual, and homophobic strains and torsions in the already existing master-canon, becomes especially revealing.

It's revealing only, however, for those of us for whom relations within and among canons are active relations of thought. From the keepers of a dead canon we hear a rhetorical question — that is to say, a question posed with the arrogant intent of maintaining ignorance. Is there, as Saul Bellow put it, a Tolstoi of the Zulus? Has there been, ask the defenders of a monocultural curriculum, not intending to stay for an answer, has there ever yet been a Socrates of the Orient, an African American Proust, a female Shakespeare? However assaultive or fatuous, in the context of the current debate the question has not been unproductive. To answer it in good faith has been to broach inquiries across a variety of critical fronts: into the canonical or indeed world-historic texts of non–Euro-American cultures, to begin with, but also into the nonuniversal functions of literacy and the literary, into the contingent and uneven secularization and sacralization of an aesthetic realm, into the relations of public to private in the ranking of genres, into the cult of the individual author and the organization of liberal arts education as an expensive form of masterpiece theatre.

Moreover, the flat insolent question teases by the very difference of its resonance with different projects of inquiry: it stimulates or irritates or reveals differently in the context of oral or written cultures; of the colonized or the colonizing, or cultures that have had both experiences; of peoples concentrated or in diaspora; of traditions partially internal or largely external to a dominant culture of the latter twentieth century.

From the point of view of this relatively new and inchoate academic presence, then, the gay studies movement, what distinctive soundings are to be reached by posing the question our way — and staying for an answer? Let's see how it sounds.

> Has there ever been a gay Socrates?
> Has there ever been a gay Shakespeare?
> Has there ever been a gay Proust?

Does the Pope wear a dress? If these questions startle, it is not least as tautologies. A short answer, though a very incomplete one, might be that not only have there been a gay Socrates, Shakespeare, and Proust but that their names are Socrates, Shakespeare, Proust; and, beyond that, legion — dozens or hundreds of the most centrally canonic figures in what the monoculturalists are pleased to consider "our" culture, as indeed, always in different forms and senses, in every other.

What's now in place, in contrast, in most scholarship and most curricula is an even briefer response to questions like these: Don't ask. Or, less laconically: You shouldn't know. The vast preponderance of scholarship and teaching, accordingly, even among liberal academics, does simply neither ask nor know. At the most expansive, there is a series of dismissals of such questions on the grounds that:

1. Passionate language of same-sex attraction was extremely common during whatever period is under discussion — and therefore must have been completely meaningless. Or
2. Same-sex genital relations may have been perfectly common during the period under discussion — but since there was no language about them, *they* must have been completely meaningless. Or
3. Attitudes about homosexuality were intolerant back then, unlike now — so people probably didn't do anything. Or
4. Prohibitions against homosexuality didn't exist back then, unlike now — so if people did anything, it was completely meaningless. Or
5. The word "homosexuality" wasn't coined until 1869 — so everyone before then was heterosexual. (Of course, heterosexuality has always existed.) Or

6. The author under discussion is certified or rumored to have had an attachment to someone of the other sex — so their feelings about people of their own sex must have been completely meaningless. Or (under a perhaps somewhat different rule of admissible evidence)
7. There is no actual proof of homosexuality, such as sperm taken from the body of another man or a nude photograph with another woman — so the author may be assumed to have been ardently and exclusively heterosexual. Or (as a last resort)
8. The author or the author's important attachments may very well have been homosexual — but it would be provincial to let so insignificant a fact make any difference at all to our understanding of any serious project of life, writing, or thought.

These responses reflect, as we have already seen, some real questions of sexual definition and historicity. But they only reflect them and don't reflect *on* them: the family resemblance among this group of extremely common responses comes from their closeness to the core grammar of *Don't ask; You shouldn't know*. It didn't happen; it doesn't make any difference; it didn't mean anything; it doesn't have interpretive consequences. Stop asking just here; stop asking just now; we know in advance the kind of difference that would be made by the invocation of *this* difference; it makes no difference; it doesn't mean. The most openly repressive project of censorship, such as William Bennett's[1] literally murderous opposition to serious AIDS education in schools on the grounds that it would communicate a tolerance for the lives of homosexuals, are, through this mobilization of the powerful mechanism of the open secret, made perfectly congruent with the smooth, dismissive knowingness of the urbane and the pseudo-urbane.

And yet the absolute canonical centrality of the list of authors about whom one might think to ask these questions — What was the structure, function, historical surround of same-sex love in and for Homer or Plato or Sappho? What, then, about Euripides or Virgil? If a gay Marlowe, what about Spenser or Milton? Shakespeare? Byron? But what about Shelley? Montaigne, Leopardi . . . ? Leonardo, Michelangelo, but . . . ? Beethoven? Whitman, Thoreau, Dickinson (Dickinson?), Tennyson, Wilde, Woolf, Hopkins, but Brontë? Wittgenstein, but . . . Nietzsche? Proust, Musil, Kafka, Cather, but . . . Mann? James, but . . . Lawrence? Eliot? but . . . Joyce? The very centrality of this list and its seemingly almost infinite elasticity suggest that no one *can* know *in advance* where the limits of a gay-centered inquiry are to be drawn, or where a gay theorizing of and through even the hegemonic high culture of the Euro-American tradition may need or be able to lead. The emergence, even within the last year or two, of nascent but ambitious programs and courses in gay and lesbian studies, at schools including those of the Ivy League, may now make it possible for the first time to ask these difficult questions from within the very heart of the empowered cultural institutions to which they pertain, as well as from the marginal and endangered institutional positions from which, for so long, the most courageous work in this area has emanated.

Furthermore, as I have been suggesting, the violently contradictory and volatile energies that every morning's newspaper proves to us are circulating even at this moment, in our society, around the issues of homo/heterosexual definition show over and over again how preposterous is anybody's urbane pretense at having a clear, simple story to tell about the outlines and meanings of what and who are homosexual and heterosexual. To be gay, or to be potentially classifiable as gay — that is to say, *to be sexed or gendered* — in this system is to come under the radically overlapping aegises of a universalizing discourse of acts or bonds and at the same time of a minoritizing discourse of kinds of persons. Because of the double binds implicit in the space overlapped by universalizing and minoritizing models, the stakes in matters of definitional control are extremely high.

[1]William Bennett was Secretary of Education in the Bush administration (1988–1992). [Ed.]

Obviously, this analysis suggests as one indispensable approach to the traditional Euro-American canon a pedagogy that could treat it neither as something quite exploded nor as something quite stable. A canon seen to be genuinely unified by the maintenance of a particular tension of homo/heterosexual definition can scarcely be dismantled; but neither can it ever be treated as the repository of reassuring "traditional" truths that could be made matter for any settled consolidation or congratulation. Insofar as the problematics of homo-heterosexual definition, in an intensely homophobic culture, are seen to be precisely internal to the central nexuses of that culture, this canon must always be treated as a loaded one. Considerations of the canon, it becomes clear, while vital in themselves cannot take the place of questions of pedagogic relations within and around the canon. Canonicity itself then seems the necessary wadding of pious obliviousness that allows for the transmission from one generation to another of texts that have the potential to dismantle the impacted foundations upon which a given culture rests.

Lee Edelman

b. 1953

Lee Edelman was born in Middletown, New York, and raised in Poughkeepsie. After completing his B.A. at Northwestern University in 1975, he went on to graduate study in English at Yale, from which he received his doctorate in 1981. He is currently professor of English at Tufts University, where he has taught since 1979. Trained as a scholar of modern American poetry, his first book was Transmemberment of Song: Hart Crane's Anatomies of Rhetoric and Desire *(1987). Strongly influenced by the points of contact among poststructural investigations of tropology, psychoanalytic accounts of sexual difference, and feminist responses to masculinist cultural assumptions, he began to explore the possible grounds for theorizing the figural logics within which modern Euro-American cultures conceptualize gay male sexuality. The result was* Homographesis: Essays in Gay Literary and Cultural Theory *(1994), a volume that reads the implications of dominant sexual ideologies through texts that range from eighteenth-century broadsides to twentieth-century film. His forthcoming book,* Hollywood's Anal Compulsion, *reads film against Freud in examining the links among visualization, rhetoric, and the fantasmatics of the male body. "Homographesis," reprinted here, was first published in 1989 in the* Yale Journal of Criticism.

Homographesis

When I was invited to participate in the conference that inaugurated the Center for Lesbian and Gay Studies at Yale, the organizers asked me to join other gay scholars in a panel that would offer some answers to the questions "What's Gay about Gay Literature? What's Lesbian about Lesbian Literature?"[1] Although the rubric for our session was substantially different by the time

[1]This essay is a slightly modified version of a lecture presented at a conference, "Lesbian/Gay Studies '87: Definitions and Explorations," sponsored by the Center for Lesbian and

the conference program appeared, the mode of its title remained pointedly — and almost aggressively — interrogative; now, though, the question it posed was if anything more blunt: "Can There Be a Gay Criticism?" All of these questions implicitly presupposed that our interest and energy as gay literary critics is, or should be, focused on determining the specificity of a gay or lesbian critical procedure. They seemed to call upon those of us who work from explicitly nonheterosexual or anti-homophobic perspectives not only to confront the inscriptions of sexuality within the texts about which we write, but also to make legible within our own criticism some distinctively gay theoretical enterprise. The questions, in short, demanded of us a willingness to assert and affirm a singular, recognizable, and therefore reproducible critical identity: to commodify lesbian and gay criticism by packaging it as a distinctive flavor of literary theory that might find its appropriate market share in the upscale economy of literary production. In the process these questions directed us to locate "homosexual difference" as a determinate entity rather than as an unstable differential relation, and they invited us to provide some general guidelines by which to define what constitutes the homosexual itself. How, they seemed to ask, can literary criticism "see" the homosexual? How can homosexuality find a place in the arena of contemporary critical discourse so that it will no longer be unmarked or invisible or perceptible only when tricked out in the most blatant thematic or referential drag?

This imperative to produce homosexual difference as an object of cognitive and perceptual scrutiny remains, of course, deeply embedded within the ideology of a liberationist politics committed to the necessity of opening the closet door. It partakes of the desire to bring into focus the historical, political and representational differences that are inscribed in our culture's various readings of sexual variation and it impels us to recognize sexual difference where it manages still to pass unobserved. But at just this point the liberationist project can too easily echo, though in a different key, the homophobic insistence upon the social importance of codifying and registering sexual identities. Both the homosexual advocate and the enforcer of homophobic norms inflect the issue of gay legibility with a sense of painful urgency — an urgency that reflects, at least in part, their differing anxieties in response to the enormous social and political stakes involved both in the culture's reading of homosexuality and in its ability to read *as* homosexual any given individual.

That such readings, or even the possibility of such readings, should be weighted with so much anxiety on either side, points to the critical, indeed the *diacritical* significance placed by our culture on the definition of the homosexual; at the same time it underscores the historical relationship between gay sexuality and figures of nomination or inscription as demonstrated for at least the past three centuries in the West. As recently as 1986, for example, Chief Justice Burger, in a concurring opinion filed in the case of Bowers v. Hardwick, went out of his way to remind the court that "Blackstone described 'the infamous crime against nature' as an offense of 'deeper malignity' than rape, an heinous act 'the very mention of which is a disgrace to human nature.' "[2] So conscious was Blackstone of the impropriety inherent in "the very mention" of this crime that he went on to observe, in a passage not cited by Burger, that "it will be more eligible to imitate in this respect the delicacy of our English law, which treats it, in its very indictments, as a crime not fit to be named: '*peccatum illud horribile, inter christianos non nominandum.*' "[3] In his history of British criminal law, Sir Leon Rad-

Gay Studies at Yale and by the Whitney Humanities Center. I would like to thank all those who helped organize the conference for making possible a valuable and impressive exchange of ideas; in particular I would like to thank Professor Ralph Hexter for inviting me to participate in it. [Au.]

[2]"The Supreme Court Opinion: Michael J. Bowers, Attorney General of Georgia, Petition v. Michael Hardwick and John and Mary Doe, Respondents," *The New York Native*, July 14, 1986: 13. [Au.]

[3]Sir William Blackstone, *Commentaries on the Laws of England*, ed. James DeWitt Andrews, vol. 2, bk. 4 (Chicago: 1899), 1377. [Au.] *Peccatum . . . nominandum* is translated as "A sin so horrible that it must not be named among Christians." [Ed.]

zinowicz suggests that a similar concern about the subversive relationship of homosexual practice to linguistic propriety may have influenced the report of the Criminal Law Commissioners when they undertook in 1836 to recommend reform in the legislative designation of capital offenses: "Sodomy, which they referred to as 'a nameless offense of great enormity,' they excluded for the time being from consideration, perhaps with the same feelings that influenced Edward Livingston when he omitted it altogether from the penal code for the state of Louisiana, lest its very definition should 'inflict a lasting wound on the morals of the people.' "[4]

If homosexual practices were placed in so powerful, and so powerfully proscriptive, a relation to language, homosexuals themselves were seen as producing — and, by some medical "experts," as being produced by — bodies that bore a distinct and legible code. Cesare Lombroso and A. Tardieu, for instance, both claimed to have developed physiological profiles that made it possible to identify "sexual deviants," thus allowing the medicalization of sexual discourse in the nineteenth century to serve more efficiently the purposes of criminology and the law. Consequently, John Addington Symonds could evoke the received idea of the homosexual as a man with "lusts written on his face";[5] the narrator of *Teleny* (1893),[6] offering a strikingly similar pronouncement, could express his very real concern that his outlawed sexuality might be marked upon his flesh: "Like Cain," he says, "it seemed as if I carried my crime written upon my brow."[7] By the second decade of the twentieth century such notions were less readily acceptable as scientific fact, but they were still available for appropriation as metaphors that could effectively reinforce the ideological construction of homosexual difference. Thus Lord Sumner could assert in 1918 that sodomites bore "the hallmark of a specialised and extraordinary class as much as if they had carried on their bodies some physical peculiarities" (cited in Weeks, 100). Homosexuals, in other words, were not only conceptualized in terms of a radically potent, if negatively charged, relation to the signifying ability of language, they were also conceptualized as inherently textual — as bodies that might well bear a "hallmark" that could, and must, be read. Indeed, in one of the most explicit instances of this perception of the gay body as inescapably textual, Proust observed the way in which "upon the smooth surface of an individual indistinguishable from everyone else, there suddenly appears, traced in an ink hitherto invisible, the characters that compose the word dear to the ancient Greeks."[8] That this topos still effectively expresses a pervasive (and ideologically manipulable) imperative to read the gay body as text is evidenced by its rearticulation some forty years later in James Baldwin's *Another Country:* "How could Eric have known that his fantasies, however unreadable they were for him, were inscribed in every one of his gestures, were betrayed in every inflection of his voice, and lived in his eyes with all the brilliance and beauty and terror of desire?"[9]

The textual significance thus attributed to homosexuality is dauntingly overdetermined. If homosexuality was designated as a crime not fit to be named among Christians, and if it was long understood, and represented, as the love that dared not speak its name, Judeo-Christian culture has been intent, nonetheless, on reading a vast array of signifiers as evidence of what we now designate as homosexual desire. Alan Bray has discussed the historical transition in Britain from

[4]Sir Leon Radzinowicz, *A History of the English Criminal Law*, vol. 4, *Grappling for Control* (London: Stevens and Sons, 1968), 316. [Au.]

[5]Cited in Jeffrey Weeks, "The Construction of Homosexuality," *Sex, Politics and Society: The Regulation of Sexuality Since 1800* (New York: Longman, 1981), 111. [Au.]

[6]Anonymous homoerotic novel. [Ed.]

[7]Oscar Wilde and Others, *Teleny*, ed. John McRae (London: Gay Men's Press, 1986), 134. [Au.]

[8]Marcel Proust, *Remembrance of Things Past*, vol. 2, *Cities of the Plain*, trans. C. K. Scott Moncrieff and Terence Kilmartin (New York: Random House, 1981), 636. The original reads, "sur la surface unie de l'individu pareil aux autres sont venues apparaître, tracés en une encre jusque-là invisible, les caractères qui composent le mot cher aux anciens Grecs." *A la recherche du temps perdu*. II (Paris: Pléiade, 1954), 614. [Au.]

[9]James Baldwin, *Another Country* (New York: Dell, 1988), 170. [Au.]

the "socially diffused homosexuality of the early seventeenth century," a homosexuality whose signifying potential lay in its mythic association with sorcerers and heretics, werewolves and basilisks, to the emergence in the following century of a "continuing culture . . . in which homosexuality could be expressed and therefore recognized; clothes, gestures, language, particular buildings and particular public places — all could be identified as having specifically homosexual connotations."[10] With this transition we enter an era in which homosexuality becomes socially constituted in ways that not only make it available to signification, but also cede to it the power to signify the instability of the signifying function *per se,* the arbitrary and tenuous nature of the relationship between any signified and signifier. It comes to figure, and to be figured in terms of, subversion of the theological order through heresy, of the legitimate political order through treason, and of the social order through disturbance of codified gender roles and stereotypes. As soon as homosexuality is localized and consequently can be read within the social landscape it becomes subject to a metonymic dispersal that allows it to be read *into* almost anything. The field of sexuality — which is always, under patriarchy, implicated in and productive of, though not identical with, the field of power relations — is not, then, merely bifurcated by the awareness of homosexual possibilities; it is not simply divided into separate but unequal realms of hetero- and homosexual relations. Rather, homosexuality comes to signify the potential permeability of every sexual signifier — and finally, by extension, of every signifier as such — by an "alien" signification. Once sexuality can be read and interpreted in the light of homosexuality, all sexuality is subject to a hermeneutics of suspicion.

Yet if the cultural enterprise of reading homosexuality would affirm that the homosexual is distinctively and *legibly* marked, it must also recognize that those markings have been, can be, or can pass as, unremarked and unremarkable. One historically specifiable ramification of this awareness is the interimplication of homophobia and paranoia as brilliantly mapped by Eve Kosofsky Sedgwick, who observes that "it is the paranoid insistence with which the definitional barriers between 'the homosexual' (minority) and 'the heterosexual' (majority) are charged up, in this century, by nonhomosexuals, and especially by men against men, that most saps one's ability to believe in 'the homosexual' as an unproblematically discrete category of persons."[11] As Sedgwick notes elsewhere, these "definitional barriers" are the defensively erected sites of an anxious and brutally enforced will to power over the interpretation of (primarily male) selfhood that "acts out the structure of a much more specific erotic/erotophobic project as well: the project of paranoia. In the ultimate phrase of knowingness, 'It takes one to know one.'" Interpretive access to the code that renders homosexuality legible may carry with it, in consequence, the stigma of a suspect relation to the code and its production, potentially situating the too savvy reader of homosexual signs in the context, as Sedgwick puts it, "of fearful, projective mirroring recognition."[12]

Underwriting all of these versions of the graphic inscriptions of homosexuality, and making possible the culture of paranoia that Sedgwick so deftly anatomizes, is, as Foucault famously argues in his *History of Sexuality,* a transformation in the discursive practices governing the modern articulation of sexuality itself.

[10]Alan Bray, *Homosexuality in Renaissance England* (London: Gay Men's Press, 1982), 92. Randolph Trumbach, following the lead of Mary McIntosh, has also come to a similar conclusion: "I would now agree with Mary McIntosh that a profound shift occurred in the conceptualization and practice of male homosexual behavior in the late seventeenth and early eighteenth centuries. It was a shift caused by the reorganization of gender identity that was occurring as part of the emergence of a modern Western culture" ("Sodomitical Subcultures, Sodomitical Roles, and the Gender Revolution of the Eighteenth Century: The Recent Historiography," *'Tis Nature's Fault: Unauthorized Sexuality During the Enlightenment,* ed. Robert P. Maccubbin [New York: Cambridge Univ. Press, 1987], 118). [Au.]

[11]Eve Kosofsky Sedgwick, "The Epistemology of the Closet (I)," *Raritan* 7 (Spring 1988): 55. For a fuller working out of Sedgwick's argument, see her ground-breaking study *Between Men: English Literature and Male Homosocial Desire* (New York: Columbia Univ. Press, 1985). [Au.]

[12]Eve Kosofsky Sedgwick, "Comments on Swann," *Berkshire Review* 21 (1986): 107. [Au.]

Noting that sodomy was a category of "forbidden acts" in the "ancient civil or canonical codes," Foucault argues that in the nineteenth century the "homosexual became a personage, a past, a case history, and a childhood, in addition to being a type of life, a life form, and a morphology, with an indiscreet anatomy and possibly a mysterious physiology. Nothing that went into his total composition was unaffected by his sexuality. It was everywhere present in him: at the root of all his actions because it was their insidious and indefinitely active principle; written immodestly on his face and body because it was a secret that always gave itself away. It was consubstantial with him, less as a habitual sin than as a singular nature."[13] Homosexuality becomes visible as that which is "written immodestly" on the "indiscreet anatomy" of the homosexual body only when it ceases to be viewed in terms of a specific set of actions or practices situated among an array of actions, none of which has a privileged relation to the identity of the subject, and becomes instead, in Foucault's words, "the root of all . . . actions" and thus a defining characteristic of the actor, the subject, with whom it is "consubstantial."

One way of reformulating this discursive shift is to see it as a transformation in the rhetorical or tropological framework through which the concept of the sexual is produced: a transformation from a reading of the subject's relation to sexuality as contingent or metonymic to a reading in which sexuality is reinterpreted as essential or metaphoric. When homosexuality is no longer conceived of as a discrete set of acts but as an "indiscreet anatomy," we are in the presence of a powerful tropological imperative that needs to produce a visible emblem or metaphor for the "singular nature" that now defines or identifies a specifically homosexual person. That legible marking or emblem, however, must be recognized as a figure for the now metaphorical conceptualization of sexuality itself — a figure for the privileged relationship to identity with which the sexual now will be charged.

Thus sexuality, as we use the word to designate a systematic organization and orientation of desire, comes into existence when desire — which Lacan, unfolding the implications of Freud's earlier pronouncements, explicitly defines as a metonymy — is misrecognized or tropologically misinterpreted as a metaphor.[14] Yet if we view this misrecognition as an "error," it is an error that is inseparable from sexuality as we know it, for sexuality cannot in any simple way be identified with the metonymic without acknowledging that the very act of identification through which it is constituted *as* sexuality is itself a positing of its meaning in terms of a metaphoric necessity. As Lacan writes in a different context, "metonymy is there from the beginning and is what makes metaphor possible."[15] Given this investiture of sexuality with a metaphoric rather than a metonymic significance, it becomes possible historically to search for signifiers that will figure this newly posited sexual "essence." And so, reinforcing Foucault's assertion, and pointing once more to the convergence of medical and juridical interest upon the ques-

[13]Michel Foucault, *The History of Sexuality*, vol. 1, *An Introduction*, trans. Robert Hurley (New York: Vintage, 1980), 43. [Au.]

[14]See Jacques Lacan, "Sexuality in the Defiles of the Signifier," *The Four Fundamental Concepts of Psychoanalysis*, ed. Jacques-Alain Miller, trans. Alan Sheridan (New York: Norton, 1981), 149–60, esp. 154. [Au.] See the discussion of Lacan in the introduction to Psychoanalytic Theory, p. 1021. [Ed.]

[15]Cited in Jane Gallop, *Reading Lacan* (Ithaca: Cornell Univ. Press, 1985), 124. We can reinterpret Lacan's words to suggest that metaphor imposes meaning upon a prior metonymic relationship that can only be *recognized* as meaningful by virtue of its being read as metaphorical. This pattern, of course, will recall the process of deferred or retroactive meaning that Freud sees as crucially operative in the constitution of sexuality itself. Jean Laplanche articulates the intimate connection between sexuality and deferred meaning as follows: "*Why sexuality?* Freud's answer is that sexuality alone is available for that action in two phases which is also an action 'after the event.' It is there and there alone that we find that complex and endlessly repeated interplay — midst a temporal succession of missed occasions — of 'too early' and 'too late.' " (Jean Laplanche, *Life and Death in Psychoanalysis*, trans. Jeffrey Mehlman [Baltimore: Johns Hopkins Univ. Press, 1976]), 43. What follows in this essay will, I hope, give retroactive significance to this notion of retroactive meaning. Note for now Lacan's formulation: "The legibility of sex in the interpretation of the unconscious mechanisms is always retroactive" (Jacques Lacan, "The Partial Drive and Its Circuit," *The Four Fundamental Concepts of Psychoanalysis*, 176). [Au.] See Gallop, p. 1070. [Ed.]

tion of sexual taxonomy in the nineteenth century, Arno Karlen notes that the "two most widely quoted writers" on homosexuality "after the mid-century were the leading medico-legal experts in Germany and France, the doctors Casper and Tardieu. Both were chiefly concerned with whether the disgusting breed of pederasts could be physically identified for courts."[16]

I want in particular to call attention here to the historical formation of a category of homosexual person whose very condition of possibility — both cognitively and anatomically — is a determining relationship to writing or textuality. This inscription of the homosexual within a tropology that produces him in constitutive relation to inscription is the first of the things that I intend "homographesis" to denote.[17] This neologism literally incorporates within its structure — and figuratively incorporates by referring back to the body — the notion of "graphesis," which I appropriate from the title of an issue of *Yale French Studies*. In her introduction to that issue, Marie-Rose Logan defined graphesis as "the nodal point of the articulation of a text" since it "de-limits the locus where the question of writing is raised" and "de-scribes the action of writing as it actualizes itself in the text independently of the notion of intentionality."[18] Homographesis, then, would refer to the process by which homosexuality is put into writing through a rhetorical or tropological articulation that raises the question of writing as difference by constituting the homosexual as text.[19] The process whereby homosexuality becomes a subject of discourse, and therefore a subject on which one may write, coincides with the process whereby the homosexual as subject is conceived of as being, even more than as inhabiting, a body on which his sexuality is written.

Just as the superimposition of metaphoric significance upon the metonymic category of desire makes possible conventional figurations, like those cited earlier, of the legibility of homosexuality in the literal figure — the "morphology" — of the homosexual, so it produces the *need* to construe an emblem of homosexual difference that will securely situate that difference within the register of visibility. This reference to a visible analogue of difference draws, of course, upon cultural associations that joined sodomy with effeminacy in the European mind long before the so-called "invention" of the homosexual.[20] As Randolph Trumbach has recently noted, between the twelfth and the eighteenth centuries men engaging in sodomy with other men were already likely to be characterized as effeminate; but since sexual relations between men were not viewed as expressions of sexual "orientation," those associations with effeminacy were largely metonymic, focusing on aspects of behavior that were defined as affectation or mimicry.[21] Trumbach goes on to suggest that it is "very likely that in early seven-

[16]Arno Karlen, *Sexuality and Homosexuality: A New View* (New York: Norton, 1971), 185. [Au.]

[17]This essay focuses exclusively on issues of male homosexuality not because the issues of lesbian inscription are not of interest or do not warrant attention, but because the issues involved are, in my opinion, very differently constituted. Although lesbianism, when it finally achieves a public articulation, comes to be read in terms of male homosexuality, that reading is itself a masculinist appropriation of a relationship with a distinct history and sociology. While lesbians and gay men often have been, and for the most part remain, allies in struggling for their civil rights, the fact of their common participation in same-gender relationships should not obscure the differences of experience, power and ideology that invariably derive from the differences of their genders. [Au.]

[18]Marie-Rose Logan, "Graphesis . . . ," *Graphesis: Perspectives in Literature and Philosophy, Yale French Studies*, no. 52 (1975): 12. [Au.]

[19]This should be considered in relation to Alice Jardine's notion of "gynesis," which she defines as "the putting into discourse of 'woman' as that *process* diagnosed in France as intrinsic to the condition of modernity; indeed the valorization of the feminine, woman, and her obligatory, that is, historical, connotations, as somehow intrinsic to new and necessary modes of thinking, writing, speaking" (*Gynesis: Configurations of Woman and Modernity* [Ithaca: Cornell Univ. Press, 1985], 25). [Au.]

[20]See Randolph Trumbach, "London's Sodomites: Homosexual Behavior and Western Culture in the Eighteenth Century," *Journal of Social History* 11, no 1: 1–33. [Au.]

[21]See Randolph Trumbach, "Sodomitical Subcultures, Sodomitical Roles, and the Gender Revolution of the Eighteenth Century: The Recent Historiography," esp. 117. See also the description by Ned Ward (1709) of the behavior of homosexual men gathered together in the molly houses: "They fancy themselves women, . . . affecting to speak, walk, tattle, curtsy, cry, scold, and mimick all manner of effeminacy" (cited in Trumbach, "London's Sodomites," 12–13). [Au.]

teenth-century London there was a sodomitical network or subculture that perhaps, because it was not as large as it later became, because policing was not as effective as the Societies for the Reformation of Manners later made it,[22] and, most of all, because sodomy with men was not yet conceived of as excluding sex with women, was not attacked in the early seventeenth century in the way it occasionally was in the eighteenth."[23]

In the discursive transformation toward which Foucault's work gestures, these contingent connections between sodomy and effeminacy undergo translation into essential or metaphorical equivalences as soon as sexuality itself is metaphorized as essential and largely exclusive. "In this culture," Trumbach writes, "the sodomite became an individual interested exclusively in his own gender and inveterately effeminate and passive. A man interested in women never risked becoming effeminate as he had once done, since there was never a chance that he might passively submit to another male. In this world it was no slander to say that a man was debauched or a whoremonger — it was a proof of his masculinity — and such cases disappeared from the courts, but adult men could not tolerate a charge that they were sodomites."[24] Once sexuality becomes so intimately bound up with a strict ideology of gender binarism, and once male sexuality in particular becomes susceptible to (mis)reading in relation to absolutely discontinuous heterosexual and homosexual identities, it becomes both possible and necessary to posit the homosexual difference in terms of visual representation — the very terms that psychoanalysis posits as central to the process whereby gender distinctions become meaningful in the symbolic order of sexuality. Unlike gender difference, however, which many feminist and psychoanalytic critics see as grounding the notion of difference itself, the homosexual difference produces the imperative to recognize and expose it precisely to the extent that it threatens to remain unmarked and undetected, and thereby to disturb the stability of the paradigms through which sexual difference can be interpreted and gender difference can be enforced.

Thus while homographesis signifies the act of putting homosexuality into writing under the aegis of writing itself, it also suggests the putting into writing — and therefore the putting into the realm of difference — of the sameness, the similitude, or the metaphors of identity that the graphesis of homosexuality historically deconstructs. For the insistent tropology of the inscribed gay body testifies to a deep-seated heterosexual concern that a widely available conceptualization of homosexual personhood might subvert the cognitive security that the categories of sameness and difference serve to anchor; it indicates, by its defensive assertion of a visible marker of sexual otherness, a fear that the categorical institutionalization of homosexual difference may challenge the integrity and reliability of sameness as the guarantor of identity, that this hypostatized difference between socially constructed and biologically determined understandings of maleness can vitiate the certainty by which one's own self-identity can be known.

To frame this in another way, homographesis can be unpacked not only as the graphesis of the homosexual, but also as the inscription of the homosexual within the purview of the homograph. As an explicitly graphemic structure, the homograph provides a useful point of reference for the consideration of a gay graphesis. A homograph, after all, refers to a "word of the same written form as another but of different origin and meaning"; it posits, therefore, the necessity of reading difference within graphemes that appear to be the same. The OED,[25] for instance, cites a definition from 1873 that describes homographs as "identical to the eye," and another that refers to "groups of words identical in spelling, but perhaps really

[22]The Societies for the Reformation of Manners were founded in England around 1699 with the aim of controlling vice, especially prostitution and sodomy. They grew up in reaction to the sexual license of the Restoration court that had spread into the byways of London and other major English cities. Their operations, which included hounding female and male whores off the streets, were widely resented for their invasion of private life, and by the 1740s these societies were in decline. [Ed.]

[23]Trumbach, "Sodomitical Subcultures," 119. [Au.]

[24]Trumbach, "Sodomitical Subcultures," 118. [Au.]

[25]*Oxford English Dictionary*. [Ed.]

consisting of several distinct parts of speech, or even of words having no connexion." The homographic nature of homographesis would thus point to the potential for misreading inherent in the graphesis of homosexuality to the extent that such a graphesis exposes the non-coincidence of what appears to be identical or what passes for identity. Recalling in this context metaphor's appeal to the idea of essence or totalizable identity,[26] we can say that the homographic element in the notion of homographesis reinterprets what seems to be a mirroring or a (re)production of identity — which is to say, a structure of metaphoric correspondence — as a relation of contiguity, of items so close in the graphic register that they share a single signifier though they may be radically different in meaning and derivation.

Now the usefulness of this homographic implication to the concept of homographesis may become clearer if we return to the original question of defining the homosexual difference. For the literature in which homosexuality enters the Western field of vision characteristically arrives at what passes for a moment of sexual revelation or recognition; but that moment, on closer inspection, can be seen as the point at which what is "recognized" is also constituted and produced, the point at which a crisis of retroactive interpretation finds expression as a crisis of representation. Since I have room for only two brief examples I have chosen to discuss passages from two canonical works that definitively, in their very different ways, engage a graphesis of homosexuality.

The first instance that I wish to adduce is a moment of recognition from *The Picture of Dorian Gray* — or, rather, it is the temporal juxtaposition of two separate but apparently analogous moments in the text. The earlier of the two begins with Dorian listening to Lord Henry Wotton's diatribe against belatedness and influence, his call for the realization of one's intrinsic identity or nature:

> But the bravest man amongst us is afraid of himself. The mutilation of the savage has its tragic survival in the self-denial that mars our lives. . . . The only way to get rid of a temptation is to yield to it. Resist it, and your soul grows sick with longing for the things it has forbidden itself, with desire for what its monstrous laws have made monstrous and unlawful.
>
> . . . You, Mr. Gray, you yourself, with your rose-red youth and your rose-white boyhood, you have had passions that have made you afraid, thoughts that have filled you with terror, day-dreams and sleeping dreams whose mere memory might stain your cheek with shame —[27]

Though Dorian interrupts Lord Henry here, the sinuous and insinuating logic of these words produces an epiphany that dazzles the younger man: "Yes, there had been things in his boyhood that he had not understood. He understood them now. Life suddenly had become fiery-colored to him. It seemed to him that he had been walking in fire. Why had he not known it?" (19).

If Dorian's life blazes out with fiery colors just as he seems to realize that he "had been walking in fire" all along, it is because his perception has been influenced by the tropological construction, the rhetorical coloring, so effectively deployed in Lord Henry's speech. And since that rhetoric insists upon the need to "realize one's nature perfectly" (17) it is inscribed within the ideology of identity and essence that characterizes metaphor. The effect of Lord Henry's seductive oration in opposition to influence — which, as he argues, transforms the person influenced into "an actor of a part that has not been written for him" (17) — shows itself as Dorian becomes "dimly conscious that entirely fresh influences were at work within him. Yet they seemed to him to have come really from himself" (18).

In a moment fraught with irony, the metaphoric ideology implicit in Lord Henry's discourse — the ideology that insists upon "realiz[ing] one's nature perfectly" — produces

[26]See, for instance, Paul de Man's observation that "the inference of identity and totality . . . is constitutive of metaphor" ("Semiology and Rhetoric," *Allegories of Reading: Figural Language in Rousseau, Nietzsche, Rilke, and Proust* [New Haven: Yale Univ. Press, 1979], 14). [Au.] See de Man, p. 905. [Ed.]

[27]Oscar Wilde, *The Picture of Dorian Gray* (New York: Oxford Univ. Press, 1987), 18. All subsequent citations will be to this edition and will be indicated in the text. [Au.]

the very "nature" or self that it seems only to reveal. Dorian appears to recognize as much when he muses upon Lord Henry's eloquence just prior to his moment of sudden illumination: "Words! Mere words! How terrible they were! How clear, and vivid, and cruel. One could not escape from them. And yet what a subtle magic there was in them! They seemed to be able to give a plastic form to formless things, and to have a music of their own . . . Was there anything so real as words?" (19). It is, of course, to Dorian himself that Lord Henry's words have given "plastic form" by making possible this revelation of the meaning of his experience; indeed, their informing power is not least to be observed in the way they make possible Dorian's retroactive understanding of his earlier state as one of "formless" or uncomprehending boyhood.

Ed Cohen, in a noteworthy recent essay on *The Picture of Dorian Gray,* points to this process by which, as he puts it, "Lord Henry's language creates a new reality for Dorian" so that "the young man's concept of his own material being is transformed — he is 'revealed to himself.'"[28] Where Cohen's focus falls primarily upon the constitution of Dorian's "material being," or what he calls elsewhere the "representations of his identity,"[29] I am more interested in the way in which identity turns out to be a trope of representation — specifically a trope of metaphoric correspondence that asserts its dominance over the metonymic contingency that it seizes upon and vivifies with meaning.

Cohen quite rightly juxtaposes the effect produced upon Dorian by Lord Henry's speech with the effect produced upon the young man by his viewing of Basil Hallward's painting: "Dorian made no answer, but passed listlessly in front of his picture and turned towards it. When he saw it he drew back, and his cheeks flushed for a moment with pleasure. A look of joy came into his eyes, as if he had recognized himself for the first time" (24). Implicitly bringing into play Lacan's theorization of the mirror stage, Cohen writes of Dorian's response: "The image organizes the disparate perceptions of his body into an apparently self-contained whole and reorients Dorian in relation both to his own identity and his social context. . . . Dorian's identification with the painted image constitutes a misrecognition as much as a recognition, leading him to confuse an overdetermined set of representations with the 'truth' of his experience."[30] One might reposition this Lacanian interpretation of Dorian's moment of self-interpretation by conceiving of Dorian as occupying a homographic relation to his painted image — a relation, that is, of apparent identity in which signifiers are perceived as mirroring one another even though the metaphoric privileging of the image misrecognizes the very contingency that produced it. After all, as Hallward explains to Lord Henry, "every portrait that is painted with feeling is a portrait of the artist, not of the sitter. The sitter is merely the accident, the occasion. It is not he who is revealed by the painter; it is rather the painter who, on the coloured canvas, reveals himself" (5). And when Dorian finds himself swayed by Lord Henry's words so that they "seemed to him to have come really from himself," the words that produce this effect of self-discovery — and that allow Hallward to finish the painting by catching "just the effect [he] want[s] — the half-parted lips, and the bright look in the eyes" (19) — are explicitly located in the register of chance: "The few words that Basil's friend had said to him — words spoken by chance, no doubt, and with willful paradox in them — had touched some secret chord that had never been touched before, but that he felt was now vibrating and throbbing to curious pulses" (18). The accident of Lord Henry's speech, with its arbitrary subject matter, defines the constitution of Dorian's subjectivity as a metaphoric identification with, and appropriation of, a relationship that is, in the first place, one of contiguity. Though Lord Henry, in his call for "self-development," castigated those who submitted to being influenced, declaring them no better than "an echo of some one else's music," the "secret chord" that Dorian misrecognizes as the realiza-

[28]Ed Cohen, "Writing Gone Wilde: Homoerotic Desire in the Closet of Representation," *PMLA* 102 (October 1987): 808. [Au.]

[29]Cohen, 806. [Au.]

[30]Cohen, 808. [Au.]

tion of his nature vibrates with an energy not its own, an energy borrowed from the "touch," the random contact, that is the hallmark of metonymy.[31]

Ironically, after this crystallization of his identity through the misrecognition of his homograph, after this metaphoric naturalization of the contiguous, Dorian goes on to repudiate the very register of metaphoric identity through which his own self-(mis)recognition is produced. For the identity that he comes to fix as his own is one that refuses the concept of fixed identity — as Wilde observes of him later in the text: "He used to wonder at the shallow psychology of those who conceive the Ego in man as a thing simple, permanent, reliable, and of one essence" (202). Dorian thus arrives at a homographic reading of identity — a reading of essence and Ego in terms of difference and divisions brought together only by metonymic contact; but the logic of homographesis that allows such differences to become visible decrees that Dorian's reading remain bound to imaginary or metaphoric identifications. The very denial of fixed identity is thus itself to be seen as an effect of Dorian's identification with the picture of himself — an identification posited through and across the differences the picture opens up.

Prominent among those differences, of course, is the question of sexual difference — a question that led to an intriguing line of questioning during the trial of the Marquess of Queensberry for libel.[32] Cross-examining Wilde, Edward Carson, the counsel for the defendant, read into the record a passage from *Dorian Gray* in which Hallward warns Dorian of the "dreadful things" that are being said about him in London:

> You don't want people to talk of you as something vile and degraded. Of course you have your position, and your wealth, and all that kind of thing. But position and wealth are not everything. Mind you, I don't believe these rumors at all. At least, I can't believe them when I see you. Sin is a thing that writes itself across a man's face. It cannot be concealed. People talk of secret vices. There are no such things as secret vices. If a wretched man has a vice, it shows itself in the lines of his mouth, the droop of his eyelids, the moulding of his hands even.[33]

Cutting through these elaborate figural evasions, Carson followed the citation of this passage by bluntly and literal-mindedly (though not erroneously) inquiring: "Does not this passage suggest a charge of unnatural vice?"[34] Though Wilde avoided a direct answer to the question, his deployment of the trope of legibility here calls attention to a feature of his novel that may well have contributed to the disturbing effect it had on its contemporary readers: Dorian's implication in a world of "unnatural vice" fails to produce the "appropriate" inscription of difference upon his body; that inscription, instead, is displaced onto the picture to which he stood at first in a relation of self-evident similarity or metaphoric identity. That sameness or identity is both reinforced and subverted as the painting alone, that "most magical of mirrors" (106), is written over with the markings of difference generated by Dorian's illicit actions, making it "the visible emblem of conscience" (91–92) and the "visible symbol of

[31]At this point one might want to think about Freud's discussions of the development of the ego — especially as they are reformulated by Jean Laplanche in *Life and Death in Psychoanalysis*. As Laplanche implies, the ego is an organization that reads its own metonymic relation to the living organism in metaphorical terms so that it comes to name not only the part, but the whole, through that act of misrecognition. [Au.]

[32]See the introduction to Wilde, p. 448. [Ed.]

[33]*The Three Trials of Oscar Wilde*, ed. H. Montgomery Hyde (New York: University Books, 1956), 131. [Au.]

[34]*The Three Trials*, 132. It is worth noting that the difference metaphorically appropriated as identity by Dorian when he "recognizes" himself in the painting is informed by that of the artist, Hallward, whose own sexual identity is inscribed in the work of art. *Dorian Gray*, in this respect, articulates the circulation of homosexual desire in relation to the notion of "influence." Significantly, that notion also played an important role in Wilde's trials. Denying that the passage cited earlier in the text suggests "unnatural vice," Wilde declared that it "describes Dorian as a man of very corrupt influence, though there is no statement as to the nature of the influence." Moments later, denying that a man could ever corrupt a youth, Wilde asserted, "I do not think one person influences another" (132). But when Wilde himself was put on trial, Alfred Wood testified against him, insisting that Wilde and he "went up to a bedroom where [they] had hock and seltzer. Here an act of the grossest indecency occurred. Mr. Wilde used his influence to induce me to consent" (202). [Au.]

the degradation of sin" (95). As the picture's initial similitude concealed its homographic otherness, so Dorian himself, as an embodiment of undifferentiated sexual difference, threatens to confound the security with which the sameness of (heterosexual) identity can be known. Even the moralizing conclusion of the novel, in which the "proper" attributes of portrait and person are reassuringly restored and Hallward's certainty that "sin . . . writes itself across a man's face" is justified by the image of Dorian's corpse lying "withered, wrinkled, and loathsome of visage" (224), even this cannot fully compensate for the unsettling possibility raised throughout the text: the possibility that the sameness on which identity is predicated can prove to be a homograph that masks a difference as bafflingly unreadable as that between Dorian Gray and his picture at the decisive moment of self-(mis)recognition.

I want briefly to place the issues of recognition and inscription raised in *Dorian Gray* beside a passage from the overture to Proust's *Cities of the Plain*, a text that focuses much of its energy upon the visualization of the homosexual, literalizing that purpose in the narrator's observation of a flirtatious encounter between M. Jupien and the Baron de Charlus. In language that recalls the moment of Dorian's access to understanding, the narrator declares, after watching the ritual of desire enacted by these two men: "From the beginning of this scene my eyes had been opened by a transformation in M. de Charlus as complete and immediate as if he had been touched by a magician's wand. Until then, because I had not understood, I had not seen."[35] At this moment it is Charlus who is said to undergo a transformation, but that claim displaces the transformation that the narrator himself experiences as he discovers, in the course of this scene, the importance of reading homographically — as he learns that the appearance of similitude can conceal a startling divergence of meaning.

[35]Proust, 635. The original reads: "Dès le début de cette scène, une révolution, pour mes yeux dessillés, s'était opérée en M. de Charlus, aussi complète, aussi immédiate que s'il avait été touché par une baguette magique. Jusque-là, parce que je n'avais pas compris, je n'avais pas vu" (613). [Au.]

As with Dorian Gray, however, this moment of recognition retroactively produces the vast array of "meanings" that it claims to disclose. Thus the "truth" of Charlus' sexuality, when read as the metaphor or essence of his identity, invests with meaningfulness all of his actions that were hitherto understood as contingent; but this reading of Charlus as homograph — as a signifier whose apparent self-identity occludes internal difference — dismantles the notion of identity only to refigure the difference that splinters identity as a graphesis of his identity as a homosexual. And in the passage with which I want to conclude these glancing remarks on Proust, the narrator expresses that homographesis in terms that place the issue of gay visibility in explicit relation to the realm of the graphemic:

> Although in the person of M. de Charlus another creature was coupled, as the horse in the centaur, which made him different from other men, although this creature was one with the Baron, I had never perceived it. Now the abstraction had become materialised, the creature at last discerned had lost its power of remaining invisible, and the transformation of M. de Charlus into a new person was so complete that not only the contrasts of his face and of his voice, but, in retrospect, the very ups and downs of his relations with myself, everything that hitherto had seemed to my mind incoherent, became intelligible, appeared self-evident, just as a sentence which presents no meaning so long as it remains broken up in letters arranged at random expresses, if those letters be rearranged in the proper order, a thought that one can never afterwards forget.[36]

[36]Proust, trans. Moncrieff and Kilmartin, 635. The original reads: "En M. de Charlus un autre être avait beau s'accoupler, qui le différenciait des autres homme, comme dans le centaure le cheval, cet être avait beau faire corps avec le baron, je ne l'avais jamais aperçu. Maintenant l'abstrait s'était matérialisé, l'être enfin compris avait aussitôt perdu son pouvoir de rester invisible, et la transmutation de M. de Charlus en une personne nouvelle était si complète que non seulement les contrasts de son visage, de sa voix, mais rétrospectivement les hauts et les bas eux-mêmes de ses relations avec moi, tout ce qui avait paru jusque-là incohérent à mon esprit, devenait intelligible, se montrait évident, comme une phrase, n'offrant aucun sens tant qu'elle reste décomposée en lettres disposées au hasard, exprime, si les caractères se trouvent replacés dans l'ordre qu'il faut, une pensée que l'on ne pourra plus oublier" (614). [Au.]

Here we have the unfolding of a homographesis fully cognizant of the retrospective act of interpretation that produces meaning from phenomena understood at first to be arbitrary and inconsequential. The model for this homographesis comes, explicitly, from the legibility of writing itself — from the "proper" ordering ("*l'ordre qu'il faut*") that allows us to make sense of what otherwise presents itself unintelligibly as "letters arranged at random." The ascription of propriety and necessity to this ordering invokes the governing logic of metaphor, but the "meaning" that becomes "self-evident" through the proper arrangement of these random letters remains rooted in the metonymic contiguity of the graphemes through which the sentence they form takes shape. Thus this metaphor for the legibility of Charlus as homosexual, this metaphor for the graphesis of homosexuality itself, gestures toward the meaningfulness of a proper, that is to say, a *metaphoric* identity that can only be produced through the syntagmatic relation characteristic of metonymy.[37]

How, one might ask, does this rhetorical analysis of the figurations of homosexual legibility offer us any purchase on the original question of an emergent gay critical procedure? On one level it suggests that a significant project for gay critics must be the study of the historically variable rhetorics, the discursive strategies and tropological formations, in which sexuality is not only embedded but conceived; it suggests that the differing psychologies of figuration in different places and at different times bear crucially on the textual articulations of homosexuality; and it suggests that the sphere of lesbian and gay criticism need not be restricted to the examination of texts that thematize gay sexuality or dramatize homosocial desire. Appropriating for ideological purposes the historical construction of homosexuality in an entrenched relation to questions of social power and the constitution of identity, the project of homographesis would reposition homosexuality at the nodal point of the very discrimination of sameness and difference as cognitive landmarks that govern our rhetorical field of operations. Not only the logic of sexual identity, but the logic of the tropology through which identity and difference themselves are constructed and registered, thereby becomes susceptible to homographic analysis.

But no sooner do I make this claim than I am mindful of a criticism the preceding paragraph may provoke: for to place the study of rhetoric and tropology at the center of a lesbian and gay criticism risks the charge of seeming to advocate or condone an apolitical formalism. It is, however, precisely the inescapable politics of any formalism, the insistence of ideology in any and every graphesis of gay sexuality, that the study of homographesis takes as its point of departure. To do otherwise, to remain enchanted by the phantom of a political engagement outside and above an engagement with issues of rhetoric, is to ignore the historical conceptualization of homosexuality in a distinctive relation to language and to endorse an ideology of textual interpretation that is, as Paul de Man writes in another context, "the elective breeding ground of false models and metaphors; it accounts for the metaphorical model of literature as a kind of box that separates an inside from an outside, and the reader or critic as the person who opens the lid in order to release in the open what was secreted but inaccessible inside."[38]

As this language implies, metaphor can be seen as the "breeding ground" in which a heterosexual poetics (re)produces the ideology of identity by prescriptively articulating a hierarchical relation between categories conceived in terms of polar opposition. The heterosexual valence of metaphor is particularly significant in the passage cited above because this "breeding ground of false models and metaphors" generates a paradigm of reading or interpretation as the opening of a box to reveal a truth that was "secreted but inaccessible inside." If it is difficult, in the context of this essay, not to read that box as an uncanny refiguration of the closet (especially since de Man illustrates his remarks by reference to a passage from *Swann's Way* in which the narra-

[37]See the introduction to Structuralism, Semiotics, and Deconstruction, p. 811. [Ed.]

[38]Paul de Man, "Semiology and Rhetoric," 5. [Au.]

tor's grandmother urges him to abandon what de Man describes as the "unhealthy inwardness of his closeted reading"), it is also difficult not to see it as a figure for the gay body as indecipherable homograph, concealing a difference that always threatens to remain "secreted but inaccessible inside." The "metaphorical model" of reading as "release," as revelation or disclosure of the truth of identity, responds defensively to that threat, and in the process suggests the implicit heterosexuality informing the belief that some interpretive privilege inheres in "the inside/outside metaphor."[39] Thus the logic subtending the charge of apolitical formalism, the totalizing logic of binary opposition, reasserts the ideological structure centrally at work in metaphor, which we now can identify, in the sense suggested above, as the hallmark of a heterosexual poetics.

But this inside/outside metaphor governs both the homophobic and the antihomophobic insistence upon the essential division between gay and straight. Such an institutionalization of difference, as I have argued, serves the purpose of reinforcing the possibility of belief in the sameness of the self; and by asserting the legibility of sexual difference, it can bestow a significant degree of social power. That power, however, may be purchased at the expense of rigorous examination of what is differently at stake for gay and straight readers in this insistence upon the reading (which is at the same time the inscribing) of difference. Rather than reengage in our critical practice this heterosexually inflected inside/outside, either/or model of sexual discriminations, lesbian and gay critics might do well to consider Barbara Johnson's description of a criticism informed by deconstructive insights in order "to elaborate a discourse that says *neither* 'either/or,' *nor* 'both/and' nor even 'neither/nor,' while at the same time not totally abandoning these logics either."[40] For however politically enabling the metonymic and the metaphoric conceptualizations of sexuality have been for particular groups or on particular occasions, we must bear in mind, as Jane Gallop writes with reference to the reading of gender, that "any polar opposition between metaphor and metonymy (vertical versus horizontal, masculine versus feminine) is trapped in the imaginary order, subject to the play of identification and rivalry,"[41] — in other words, that it reproduces the very binarism informing the logic of metaphoric identity.

The tropological analysis called for in the practice of homographesis refuses, therefore, to define itself over and against the politically engaged; to the contrary, its mode of analysis suggests immediate political implications. The historical siting of homosexuality at the ambiguous intersection of the metaphorical and the metonymic may help to account for such current phenomena as the brutal insistence upon homosexual legibility as evinced in the escalating violence of gay-bashing and the hysterical response to the AIDS epidemic through persistent, though counterfactual, belief in the metonymically contagious dissemination of the disease. Much to the sorrow of the intellectual life, it is true that accounting for phenomena such as these will not, in itself, put an end to them; but it can allow us to formulate strategies through which to confront our oppressive historical moment more effectively than by responding in an *ad hoc* fashion to the festering symptoms of homophobia alone.

Moreover, the study of homographesis is an *instance* of homographesis; to write about the putting into writing of homosexuality is to produce yet another moment within the field that one is studying. In this sense too its project is something other than a "sterile" formalism; to the contrary, it would intervene to make a *critical* difference by reading the ideological implications of the cultural markings of *sexual* difference. For to escape both the constrictions of a sexuality that is unmarked and the dangers of a sexuality that is inscribed as essential identity, we must make or construct retroactively out of the accidents of our history a difference from the logic of sexual difference with which to deconstruct the repressive ideology of similitude or identity itself.

[39]De Man, "Semiology and Rhetoric," 5. [Au.]

[40]Barbara Johnson, *A World of Difference* (Baltimore: Johns Hopkins Univ. Press, 1987), 12. [Au.]

[41]Jane Gallop, *Reading Lacan*, 132. [Au.]

Michael Warner

b. 1958

One of the few queer theorists to graduate from Oral Roberts University, Michael Warner survived to take his M.A. at the University of Wisconsin and his doctorate at Johns Hopkins. After teaching at Northwestern University, Warner moved on to Rutgers, where he is now professor of English. His interests are split between social theory and queer culture, and the institutional history of literature and criticism in America. Warner has written The Letters of the Republic: Publication and the Public Sphere in Eighteenth-Century America *(1990) and has edited* Fear of a Queer Planet: Queer Politics and Social Theory *(1993). Warner's other works include* The Origins of Literary Studies in America *(ed., with Gerald Graff, 1988) and* The English Literatures of America, 1500 to 1800 *(ed., with Myra Jehlen, 1997). He writes on AIDS and queer theory for both* The Village Voice *and academic journals. The following essay "Homo-Narcissism; or, Heterosexuality," originally appeared in the anthology* Engendering Men: The Question of Male Feminist Criticism *(ed. Joseph Boone and Michael Cadden, 1990); it was followed by a companion essay, "Thoreau's Bottom," in* Raritan *(Winter 1992).*

Homo-Narcissism; or, Heterosexuality

The modern system of sex and gender would not be possible without a disposition to interpret the difference between genders as the difference between self and Other. This elementary structure has been a subject for feminist theory at least since 1949, when Simone de Beauvoir posed it as the central problem of *The Second Sex:* how does it happen that man is constituted as the subject, and woman is constituted as the Other? For de Beauvoir, this is not just what men would like to believe, but the psychic structure of gender. Femininity is learned as a way of constructing oneself as object, a way of attributing full subjectivity only to the masculine. This identification of the male as subject and the female as Other, she argues, underwrites all the asymmetries of gender throughout history.

But the same insidious identification also has a more specially modern variant.[1] In the modern West, having a sexual object of the opposite gender is taken to be the normal and paradigmatic form of an interest either in the Other or, more generally, in others. That is why in our own century it has acquired the name *heterosexuality* — a sexuality of otherness. In this organization of

[1]The question of what is "modern" can here get a bit tricky. At this point, I mean only the broadest extension of the term: heterosexuality as a cultural system does not date from prehistory, nor is it universally the same. Later on, however, I shall be speaking of links between the sex/gender system of heterosexuality and "modern society." The task then will be to describe the relation of that sex/gender system not simply to a recent period of history, but to the set of social forms and normative principles that are programmatically linked together as "modernity." Included under this heading are the imperatives of universal law and morality, rationalized social life, autonomous discipline of art, and objective science. And although this development in social organization has sources in the Renaissance, its full and classic expression comes with the height of the Enlightenment and its liberal aftermath. The key descriptions of this term and its history are by Jürgen Habermas: although his defense of modernity is highly controversial, his exposition of its meaning remains unmatched. See, for a brief version, "Modernity — An Incomplete Project," in Hal Foster, ed., *The Anti-Aesthetic* (Seattle: The Bay Press, 1983), 3–15. The much more developed version is in Jürgen Habermas, *The Philosophical Discourse of Modernity*, trans. Frederick Lawrence (Cambridge: MIT Press, 1987), esp. chapters 1 and 2. For the debate about the ongoing value of modernity and Habermas' use of the notion, see the essays in Richard Bernstein, ed., *Habermas and Modernity* (Cambridge: MIT Press, 1985). [Au.] See Habermas, p. 1188. [Ed.]

sexuality, heteroerotics can be understood as the opposite *either* of homoerotics *or*, in the more general extension, of autoerotics. Indeed, according to this logic homoerotics is an unrecognized version of autoerotics, or more precisely of narcissism; both are seen as essentially an interest in self rather than in the other. The perverse options are therefore the exceptions that prove the rule, since both are overcome in the otherness of heterosexuality. The very categories of hetero-, homo-, and auto-erotics are jointly defined by the same understanding of gender as simple alterity.[2]

In *The Second Sex*, for instance, de Beauvoir herself writes a sentence that is both bland and startling: "When the boy reaches the genital phase, his evolution is completed, though he must pass from the autoerotic inclination, in which pleasure is subjective, to the heteroerotic inclination, in which pleasure is bound up with an object, normally woman."[3] As a summary of Freud, this is quite bland. But in the context of de Beauvoir's argument, this way of opposing interest in others simultaneously to autoerotics and to homoerotics is startling. As she shows so eloquently, there is nothing innocent about the slippage from interest in "an object" to the assumption that such an interest is "normally" in woman. Nothing guarantees such an outcome other than the boy's discovery that women are defined as objects to him in a way that other men are not. And since the girl discovers at the same time that her destiny is to be an object of desire, her encounter with alterity is very different from the boy's. She is not offered the same simple distinction between her own subjectivity and the other's objectivity. The discovery of otherness in the other gender, therefore, is neither neutral nor symmetrical. In de Beauvoir's argument, as in the work of other feminists who continue her Hegelian tradition, this construction of gendered otherness is seen as the structure of domination.[4]

[2]Otherness. [Ed.]

[3]Simone de Beauvoir, *The Second Sex*, trans. H. M. Parshley (1952; rpt. New York: Vintage, 1974), 44. [Au.] See de Beauvoir, p. 635. [Ed.]

[4]The best recent example of this tradition is Jessica Benjamin's *The Bonds of Love: Psychoanalysis, Feminism, and the Problem of Domination* (New York: Pantheon, 1988). [Au.]

If the scenario of gender difference is difficult to imagine without the asymmetries of domination, it is also true that all of our accounts of this scenario bear the stamp of the modern organization of sexuality. Every description of the subject's access to gender and alterity, beginning with Freud's account of the Oedipus complex, seems already to be oriented by the poles of hetero- and homosexuality. Could the modern system of hetero- and homosexualities be imagined without this ideological core, or vice versa? By shifting the question in this way, I mean to indicate how difficult it is to analyze a discourse of sexuality, when our own tools of analysis already *are* that discourse. But I also mean to indicate ways in which gender domination presents problems besides the obvious one that it poses for women.

Where women are "normally" defined by otherness, the transition from autoerotics to heteroerotics entails a peculiar problem for men. To cite de Beauvoir once more, a key feature of male subjectivity comes about as a corollary of the subjugation of women: "For the male it is always another male who is the fellow being, the other who is also the same, with whom reciprocal relations are established."[5] The point of this for feminism is clear: insofar as woman is Other, she stands outside of reciprocity. But an important question for the male subject is less clear. Since sexual desire is directed toward an object, male desire will be directed only toward women, rather than toward the men who are fellow beings, subjects, the same. But what if this does not take place? And well it might not: for the man values other men as fellow beings and will accordingly seek their recognition and desire. At the same time, no matter how much he wants to think of the Other as woman, it remains true that men are others to him as well, just as women are fellow beings. When another man, this "other who is also the same," becomes the object of desire, has the male subject failed to distinguish self and other?

It may sound absurd, but that is just what psychoanalysis classically concludes. Psychoana-

[5]De Beauvoir, *The Second Sex*, 79. [Au.]

lytic theory has from the beginning described homosexuality — especially among men — as a version of narcissism. Freud, for example, declares that the homosexual chooses "not another of the same sex, but himself in the guise of another."[6] This is not a simple judgment. And it would certainly not hold much intuitive force outside of the modern West, where erotic relations either among men or among women are imagined by most cultures as something other than relations of mere sameness.[7] But there has never been a sustained critique of the premises behind Freud's judgment, on this issue so widely taken as common sense. The gay movement has either ignored it or tried to reject it out of hand, no doubt because its invidious consequences are so easy to apprehend. Yet we need not wave away this powerful tradition, nor even deny that one kind of homoerotics in the modern West has the logic of a relation to self. It is imperative, though immensely difficult, for us to retheorize that relation.

The first difficulty lies in appropriating psychoanalysis. Although it is uniquely equipped to analyze the slippage in our culture between understandings of gender and understandings of self and other, traditionally psychoanalysis has been the principal site of that slippage. "Psychoanalysis," de Beauvoir concludes, "fails to explain why woman is the *Other*."[8] Of course, different directions have been taken by psychoanalytic theory since 1949, and one would not offer so simple a conclusion today. But the related problems of heterosexuality remain as unclear — indeed, ideologically clouded — as they were then. What guarantees that a transition from autoerotics will or should lead to heteroerotics? How does it come to be taken as self-evident that homoerotics is really an arrested form of interest in oneself? Why do we find it so difficult to think about sex and gender without these ideological categories and their teleological narratives? And why do these questions seem linked to the structure of modern liberal society? Only modern liberal society, after all, understands sexuality as a choice between hetero- and homosexualities, conceiving them as sexualities of difference and sameness. The only way to pose such large questions is by examining the theory of narcissism, where the issue of gender and alterity arises with peculiar insistence.

Freud postulated a connection between homosexuality and narcissism before the notion of narcissism was even fully developed. He went so far as to argue that the existence of the link between the two is "the strongest of the reasons which have led us to adopt the hypothesis of narcissism."[9] In the same essay, "On Narcissism," Freud argues that homosexuals express something different from what he calls primary narcissism. In primary narcissism, a child cathects[10] itself in a unity with its parent, without differentiation, without a developed ego. This narcissistic love of the parent-child dyad is what the later love of the parent as a separate person will be propped on. Homosexuality, by contrast, is described by Freud as coming about in the later stage, when the subject's original narcissism encounters "the admonitions of others" and the awakening of his [sic] own critical judgment."[11] The subject's primary attachment to itself, suddenly broken and troubled by criticism, is recu-

[6]Juliet Mitchell, *Psychoanalysis and Feminism* (New York: Random House, 1974), 34 (summarizing Freud). [Au.]

[7]This appears in a voluminous literature on sexuality in other cultures. For a general survey of the problem of "homo" and "hetero" sexualities, along with the projection of these categories onto cultures that order sexuality differently, see David Greenberg, *The Construction of Homosexuality* (Chicago: University of Chicago Press, 1988). [Au.]

[8]De Beauvoir, *The Second Sex*, 55 (italics in original). In *Psychoanalysis and Feminism*, Juliet Mitchell offers a critical but, in my reading, not entirely fair account of de Beauvoir's rejection of Freud. See pp. 305–18. [Au.]

[9]Sigmund Freud, "On Narcissism," in James Strachey, ed., *The Standard Edition of the Complete Psychological Works of Sigmund Freud*, 24 vols. (London: Hogarth, 1953–1974), 14:88. [Au.]

[10]*Cathexis* refers to the investment of libido in an object. [Ed.]

[11]"As always where the libido is concerned, man has here again shown himself incapable of giving up a satisfaction he had once enjoyed. He is not willing to forgo the narcissistic perfection of his childhood; and when, as he grows up, he is disturbed by the admonitions of others and by the awakening of his own critical judgement, so that he can not longer retain that perfection, he seeks to recover it in the new form of an ego ideal" ("On Narcissism," 94). [Au.]

perated in the development of the ego ideals. It then happens, says Freud, that the individual seeks in another some ideal excellence missing from his own ego. And this is the type of narcissistic choice made by the homosexual, by which Freud generally means the male homosexual: the choice of what he himself would like to be.

Without reconstructing any more of the difficulties raised by Freud's problematic essay, I would like to make two observations about his argument. The first is that the two kinds of narcissism are very different. One is residual, an effect of infancy that lingers into later life. The other is proleptic[12] and utopian. The homosexual (male), according to Freud, develops his narcissism not simply because of the residual attachment to the parent-child dyad, but because of a developmentally advanced ego ideal that is difficult to realize. I will return to this point later; it is important because Freud's thinking here leads him close to breaking his usual frame of reference. Indeed, by foregrounding the development of critical judgment and the admonitions of others, Freud places the subject in a context much larger than that of the restricted family. And by indicating the relation between narcissism and ideals, Freud works no longer in the realm of simple pathology. What is puzzling, then, is that Freud continues to treat homosexuality as regressive. Although one important criticism of Freud's account is that his narrative is rather arbitrarily committed to a hypotactic[13] logic of linear development, an equally important one is that his own analysis, in this essay, does not necessarily show the homosexual's narcissism as a developmental regression.

A second observation then follows: Freud cannot account for the normative implications of his analysis. It is not a neutral analysis. He speaks with an unmistakable tone of condescension toward the homosexuals who are really seeking themselves. He does not imagine that one might speak of narcissism other than pejoratively in this context, though he does in others.[14] Nor does he acknowledge that to describe homosexuality as *merely* a version of narcissism is counterintuitive. The homosexual, after all, is by definition interested in others in a way that is not true of the narcissist in general. Ovid tells us that Narcissus rejects not just the girls who love him, but also the boys. Those boys, then, have an interest in other persons, if not in the other gender, and the myth of Narcissus does not collapse the two. What warrants the forgetting of this difference, which becomes a nondifference, sameness? Why should gender amount to alterity *tout court?*[15]

Freud's secondary narcissism does not preclude a recognition of alterity. Everyone undergoes — and indeed requires — the kind of narcissism Freud describes. Everyone makes identifications with others on the basis of ego ideals. But we call them ideals only insofar as identification is accompanied by alienation and longing. The act of taking up ego ideals therefore does not foreclose a sense of the other's otherness, no matter how much we might like to eliminate that otherness. Indeed, in the last section of "On Narcissism" Freud suggests that this double movement of identification and desire is what makes the subject truly social. In the very action of taking an ideal, the subject apprehends a difference between the ideal and the actual ego. And that difference is just what produces our sense of longing and our search for the recognition of others. Because the ideals remain alien, insofar as they are ideals at all, they drive the subject to the pursuit of the other.

Identification in this sense is not a satisfactory unity; Freud shows that the ideals of identification have a critical relation to the self that the ego will continue to feel as dissonance, especially in the form of guilt.[16] It follows — though this does

[12]Forward looking, anticipatory. [Ed.]

[13]Subordinating. [Ed.]

[14]Several commentators have noted the evaluative instability of the term, usefully surveyed by Arnold Cooper, "Narcissism," in an excellent collection edited by Andrew Morrison: *Essential Papers on Narcissism* (New York: New York University Press, 1986), 112–43. [Au.]

[15]Alterity, or otherness, in and of itself. [Ed.]

[16]In *The Ego and the Id*, trans. Joan Riviere (New York: Norton, 1962), by which time Freud has begun to treat the ego ideals as the superego, he writes that "the super-ego manifests itself essentially as a sense of guilt (or rather, as criticism — for the sense of guilt is the perception in the ego answering to this criticism)" (43). This narrowing of the dissonance of the ego ideals is, in my view, too simple and in-

not always remain clear in Freud — that they are both identifications and objects of longing. And that can be true even of the ideals that are most critical and guilt-inducing. As Kaja Silverman points out, the most normally Oedipal boy in the world is placed in a relation of longing with the image of the father; insofar as the father's image is taken as an ideal, or superego, it remains "susceptible to sexualization."[17] Identification, in short, does not result in a relation of identity, and this is especially the case where another subject is involved. The difference that is therefore inevitably involved in taking the other as a sexual object, an other, cannot entirely be elided — even where the desire is founded on an identification. But that is what Freud does when he claims that homosexuals "are plainly seeking *themselves* as a love object."

Freud here imagines, in effect, that the dialectic of desire could not continue beyond the first moment of alienated identification. The figure of Narcissus represents that blockage; in Jacqueline Rose's phrase, Narcissus shows how "an apparent reciprocity reveals itself as *no more than* the return of an image to itself."[18] But it is not so easy to explain any erotic attachment as merely the reflexive attachment of a self to itself. Even the apparent return of an image reveals also some forms of reciprocity. When the subject chooses another on the basis of a desired ego ideal, he or she is already engaged in dialogue with others and in multiple perspectives on self. In Freud's account, the individual is encountering the admonitions of others and the development of his or her own critical judgment. As a result, the subject adopts the position of the other toward him- or herself. This kind of narcissism, therefore, already involves the subject in the negativity of speech.[19] If desire arises in these alienated identifications, it by the same token must always reactivate the potential for mutual recognition. Freud does not imagine this possibility long enough to argue against it. He concludes that homosexual desire *reduces* to narcissism without significant remainder and hence is a developmental misdirection.

Freud's conclusion here has hardly proven to be idiosyncratic. It remains the most powerful way of treating homoerotics as a symptomology, and some version of it still dominates every major branch of psychoanalytic theory.[20] Though the DSM III[21] no longer lists homosexuality as a disease, the theoretical tradition continues to reveal it in the light of pathology. Professional psychology and psychoanalysis continue to understand themselves as explaining homosexuality, as giving its causes. But the entire discourse is possible at all only if the pathological status of the homosexual is assumed from the outset. If homosexuality is taken to be a symptom, then etiology[22] provides a logic for saying that it reduces to narcissism. But if the symptomatic character of homosexuality is not simply taken for granted, then it would be necessary to theorize its dialectical and interactive character — precisely that which would prevent a reductive etiology. It is not surprising to find such ideological effects in the medical and scientific institutions that

dicates a symbolic valence that has since eroded. For describing the dissonance between ego and its ideals in modernity, "criticism" is probably more accurate. [Au.]

[17]Kaja Silverman, "Masochism and Male Subjectivity," *Camera Obscura* 17 (1988):41. [Au.]

[18]Jacqueline Rose, *Sexuality in the Field of Vision* (London: Verso, 1986), 170 (emphasis added). [Au.]

[19]For a much fuller version of this argument, see John Brenkman, *Culture and Domination* (Ithaca: Cornell University Press, 1987), especially chapter 5, "The Social Constitution of Subjectivity." Explicating the *fort-da* game, Brenkman writes: "It is essential not to collapse the distinctive moments of the dialectic of desire and interaction; the child's mirror play is already marked with the liberating negativity of speech" (165). [Au.] In his reference to the *fort-da:* [gone-here] game, Warner alludes to Freud's story, in *Beyond the Pleasure Principle*, of a small child throwing a toy on a string out of its cradle with the cry of *"Fort!"* and reeling it back in with the cry of *"Da."* Freud analyzes the child's repetitious play as being a way of relieving anxiety about the absence of the parent, and links this mastery-through-repetition to the analysis of the significance of recurrent dreams and nightmares. Peter Brooks uses this notion as a way to explain aspects of literary form (see p. 1019). [Ed.]

[20]There are a number of general surveys on this subject. None, as far as I know, is really satisfactory. The most recent is Kenneth Lewes, *The Psychoanalytic Theory of Male Homosexuality* (New York: Simon and Schuster, 1988). [Au.]

[21]DSM III refers to the third edition of the *Diagnostic and Statistical Manual of Mental Disorders* used by psychologists to catalog psychiatric conditions. [Ed.]

[22]Causal structure, especially of a disease. [Ed.]

have, after all, generated the modern discourse of hetero- and homosexualities. It is more surprising to find the normalizing conclusion in Freud, since his own account demonstrates the dialectical and interactive movement that leads from the ego to homoerotics. (And back: one more reason Freud might have avoided his normalizing conclusion is that he was intermittently conscious of his own investment in homoerotics, particularly with Josef Breuer and Wilhelm Fliess. After his break with Fliess, Freud wrote to Sandor Ferenczi about his "overcoming" the trauma of the break: "A part of homosexual cathexis has been withdrawn and made use of to enlarge my own ego.")[23]

My point, however, is not simply that we should depathologize the homosexual. There is also a further, equally unremarked problem in the argument. If normal development leads from autoerotics to narcissism to heterosexuality, how would heterosexuality transcend its sources in narcissism more than homosexuality does? Freud assumes, as does psychoanalytic discourse generally, that the heterosexual (male) is a better realist than the homosexual (male). The heterosexual male chooses the Other — woman — but the homosexual male only *thinks* he chooses another. Yet it is not difficult to read Freud's essay as showing that all erotic life — not just the pathology of homosexuals — takes its form from the search for the ego ideal in the position of the other. (This of course is the direction in which Jacques Lacan will push the inquiry.) When Freud initially describes how the investment of the ego ideal can be transferred into a sexual desire for another, he is describing the pathology of homosexuals. By the end of the essay, he is using the same language to interpret a form of heterosexual romance. The lover, says Freud, overvalues the other in whose eyes he sees *himself* ideally desired. Yet Freud does not draw the obvious inference that it might not be so easy as first appeared to construct a normative hierarchy of hetero- and homosexuality by showing the function of the ego ideal in generating desire.

What, then, is developmental in the development from narcissism to heterosexuality? Or at least, what is developmental here that is not equally characteristic of homosexuality? Freud's various solutions to this problem come to grief because they are in the last analysis based on an *a priori* opposition of the genders as subject and Other. Nowhere are the difficulties of the project more clear than in *The Ego and the Id*, a text in which Freud returns to the unstable problems of the narcissism essay. In the earlier essay, identification and the ego ideals stemmed from the admonitions of others and the development of the subject's critical judgment. Now, in the later work, Freud writes that the "origin of the ego-ideal" lies in "an individual's first and most important identification, his [sic] identification with the father in his own personal prehistory."[24] The difference is that Freud has now introduced the Oedipus complex in an attempt to explain the developmental path that leads to heterosexuality. But why have the male subject and the male parent been singled out as the primary axis of identification?

In an astonishing footnote to this sentence, Freud acknowledges that there is no good reason at all: "Perhaps it would be safer to say 'with the parents'; for before a child has arrived at definite knowledge of the difference between the sexes, the lack of a penis, it does not distinguish in value between its father and its mother. . . . In order to simplify my presentation I shall discuss only identification with the father." According to the footnote, identification with the father has been emphasized only arbitrarily, for convenience. But the text that it glosses shows that the father must not be just any identification, but "the first and most important" one. That is what guarantees the Oedipalized heterosexual outcome. If nothing naturally makes this axis of identification the primary one, then the heterosexual resolution will be no more of a development than a homosexual one. Without this ideological support, Freud's derivation of heterosexual norms is subject to narrative incoherence.

[23]Freud to Sandor Ferenczi, 6 October 1910, quoted in Ernest Jones, *The Life and Work of Sigmund Freud*, 3 vols. (New York: Basic Books, 1953), 2:83. On the erotics of Freud's collaborative friendships, see Wayne Koestenbaum, *Double Talk: The Erotics of Male Literary Collaboration* (New York: Routledge, 1989), 17–42. [Au.]

[24]Freud, *The Ego and the Id*, 21. [Au.]

The footnote admits, in effect, that the father has primacy only in his symbolic cultural value, which is learned later; he has no primacy in the simple development of the child's identification. Both parents are subjects of identification, and both are objects of attachment. This leads Freud to postulate both "positive" and "negative" forms of the Oedipal situation. Again, however, he presupposes the chiastic[25] axes of heterosexuality that the model is designed to derive. Freud assumes that an identification with the mother will retain an attachment to the father and vice versa. He does not imagine that one might identify with the mother and yet have an attachment to other women or identity with the father and yet have an attachment to other men. Nor can he justify the primacy of one axis over another. In an especially striking moment of circularity, Freud writes that only the child's "sexual disposition" — i.e., its "masculine" or "feminine" bent — will determine the relative weight of these identification axes.[26] At this point, nothing establishes which axis — if indeed we can assume their constitution as axes — will be primary, or "positive" rather than "negative."

Freud maintains the normative character of Oedipal resolution only by ignoring these qualifications in a rather blunt declaration that the male child identifies with the father and takes the mother as object. In *Group Psychology and the Analysis of the Ego,* published two years before *The Ego and the Id,* Freud presents this declaration in its most normalized form:

> A little boy will exhibit a special interest in his father; he would like to grow like him and be like him, and take his place everywhere. We may say simply that he takes his father as his ideal. This behaviour has nothing to do with a passive or feminine attitude toward his father (and towards males in general); it is on the contrary typically masculine. It fits very well with the Oedipus complex, for which it helps to prepare the way.
>
> At the same time as this identification with his father, or a little later, the boy has begun to develop a true object cathexis towards his mother according to the attachment [anaclitic] type.[27]

As we know from Freud's qualifications in *The Ego and the Id,* nothing in this narrative can be assumed. The child takes both parents as ideals and has object attachments to both parents. Why does Freud so insist, despite his own observations, on the primacy of this "positive" form of what has already been assumed as a chiastic structure? Both the supremacy of the father and the goal of heterosexuality seem to derive from the Oedipal scene as it is summarized here. If this is the moment when de Beauvoir's mastery relation has been established, it is also the moment when the available object choices have been resolved into hetero- and homosexualities. The father's supremacy is assured since, for children of both sexes, he will be identified with as subject, while the mother's nurturing role will result in an object attachment to her.

But what is easier to miss is that Freud has presupposed that the child's identification and its object attachment will be assigned to different genders. Hence Freud's anxious haste to deny that identification with the father results in a "passive or feminine" attitude toward him. Freud consistently supposes that identification desexualizes the parental image, that the positive Oedipus complex cancels out the object choice of the negative complex and vice versa.[28] This is partly because he presupposes that the parents' heterosexual choices will be internalized along with their images, so that identification with the father will simply transfer the father's gendered desire to the boy. (To explain himself in this way, however, would amount to an admission that heterosexual desire is only a status quo.) But it is also partly because Freud's entire account is based on the exclusiveness of identification and attachment.

Identification and attachment are the structuring moments in psychoanalysis that correspond

[25]Crossed, shaped like the letter X (chi in Greek). [Ed.]
[26]Freud, *The Ego and the Id,* 23–24. [Au.]

[27]Sigmund Freud, *Group Psychology and the Analysis of the Ego*, trans. James Strachey (New York: Norton, 1959), 37. [Au.]
[28]See Silverman, "Masochism and Male Subjectivity," 39ff., for a discussion of the implications of this scenario. [Au.]

to subject and object. Identification constructs a feature of the world as a feature of the subject; attachment constructs its features as objects. But the opposition is unstable. As Mikkel Borch-Jacobsen shows, the two operations can be read as mutual forms of denial. If identification denies the radical alterity of the other, attachment-desire "is organized as a vehement rejection of all resemblance, all mimesis."[29] Freud's deepest commitment, throughout the changes in his position on the subject, is that these two operations will be exclusive, and one will be reserved for each gender. An admission that it would be possible both to identify with *and* to desire a gendered image would be the most troubling of all. If Freud implies in "On Narcissism" that the homosexual narcissist does just that, he has a very different account in the later works.

Here it is striking that Freud has two entirely different pathologies for homosexuality, and they accompany entirely different accounts of the ego ideal. Both *Group Psychology* and *The Ego and the Id* attempt to explain the homosexual by means of the chiasmus of gender identification and desire. The ego ideal with which the child identifies is a gendered parental image, and the child's sexual object will accordingly be the parental image of the opposite sex. In both of these later texts, the homosexual is said simply to choose the "negative" axis — for the male child, identifying with the mother and taking on her desire for the father. But in the earliest essay, the sources of the ego ideals had been much more general. They had not necessarily entailed the gendered parental images, with the chiastic Oedipal teleology of those images.

What if it is possible, as Freud implied in the earlier essay, that the boy might both identify with the father and yet desire his image? This possibility is implied insofar as the boy's identification would still not close the gap between himself and the gendered ideal. Indeed, identification could result in a longing because of that gap between actual and ideal. But subject and object would not be distributed to different genders. Freud is therefore obliged in this essay to regard the relation as one of mere sameness. Freud explains homosexuality alternately as sameness (in the earlier essay) or as inverted difference (in the later works). No matter which route of explanation Freud takes, he does not infer from his own insights that difference and sameness might coexist, in both desire and identification, without being reducible to the difference or sameness of gender.

It is only the more striking that Lacan never makes this inference either, since it is he who radicalizes the function of the ego ideal in a way only suggested by Freud. Lacan's analysis of the *imago* of the ego shows it to be *both* the site of identification *and* the source of desire. "We call libidinal investment," he says, "that which makes an object desirable, that is to say, the way it becomes confused with the image we carry within us."[30] Where Freud initially argued that an intricate confusion of the desired object with the image of what one would like to be is just the pathological derivation of homosexuality, Lacan shows that such an investment always structures the erotic. Lacan cites Goethe's Werther as an example of the way heterosexual investment is based not only on anaclitic[31] parental cathexis but also on the reflective function of the ego ideal. When Werther first sees Lotte, he writes,

> No, I do not deceive myself! In her dark eyes I have read a genuine sympathy for me and my destiny. Yes, I feel . . . that she loves me! Loves me! — And how precious I become in my own eyes, how I — to you as an understanding person I may say it — how I admire myself since she loves me.

With this passage in mind, Lacan says, "That's what love is. It's one's own ego that one loves in love, one's own ego made real on the imaginary

[29]Mikkel Borch-Jacobsen, *The Freudian Subject*, trans. Catherine Porter (Stanford: Stanford University Press, 1988), 93. The passage continues: "To recognize that I resemble the other, that I resemble myself in him even in my own desire, would be tantamount to admitting the inadmissible: that I am not myself and that my most proper being is over there, in that double who enrages me." [Au.]

[30]Jacques Lacan, *Seminaire* I (Paris: Seuil, 1975), 162. Translation modified from the English version: *The Seminar of Jacques Lacan: Book I*, trans. John Forrester (New York: Norton, 1988), 141. [Au.]

[31]Choosing a love object because of resemblance to a parent. [Ed.]

level."[32] Of course, there are other things that one could say about Werther; his is not the only form of "what love is." My point is simply that Lacan made it one of the central projects of his career to critique our elementary assumptions about the difference between identification and desire, subject and object. In so doing, he definitively removed any possibility of making narcissism a basis for a normative hierarchy between hetero- and homosexuality. Homosexuality may indeed be a way of loving one's own ego, but so is heterosexual romance.

Yet however radical and subtle Lacan's analysis of the imaginary might be, it seems never to have occurred to him that it might now be unnecessary to pathologize the homosexual's relation to narcissism. Quite the contrary. In a passage from the seminars of the very same year (1954), Lacan takes it on himself to describe homosexuality as a perversion, not because of the contingency of morals, nor because of the supposed needs of biology, but because of the narcissistic structure of homosexual desire. "It is himself," Lacan says of the homosexual, "whom he pursues." What I find especially incomprehensible about this classical assertion is that it appears as a gloss on one of Lacan's most Hegelian formulations: "the [homosexual] subject exhausts himself in pursuing the desire of the other, which he will never be able to grasp as his own desire, because his own desire is the desire of the other."[33] This, as Lacan notes, is the form of "the imaginary intersubjective relation." Nothing about it is peculiar to homosexuality. Moreover, when he is pursuing the Hegelian logic of his analysis, Lacan is capable of treating this same imaginary intersubjectivity as opening onto a dialectic of recognition.[34] In this case, he does not do so.

Compare the tone of his account with the tone of the equally Hegelian description that de Beauvoir had given five years earlier of the logic of lesbianism:

> To be willing to be changed into a passive object is not to renounce all claim to subjectivity: woman hopes in this way to find self-realization under the aspect of herself as a thing; but then she will be trying to find herself in her otherness, her alterity. When alone she does not succeed in really creating her double; if she caresses her own bosom, she still does not know how her breasts seem to a strange hand, nor how they are felt to react under a strange hand; a man can reveal to her the existence of her flesh *for herself*— that is to say, as she herself perceives it, but not what it is *to others*. It is only when her fingers trace the body of a woman whose fingers in turn trace her body that the miracle of the mirror is accomplished.

But de Beauvoir does not mean, by "the miracle of the mirror," an entrapment in a circuit of sameness. Far from it. Because she understands the problem of alterity sketched here as one taking place in a setting of domination, the dialectic of lesbianism is a model of how the imaginary transcends its limitations: "in exact reciprocity each is at once subject and object, sovereign and slave; duality becomes mutuality."[35] This is exactly what Lacan denies. Though he offers no reason for this belief, he asserts that the homosexual is perverse because the recognition of the other's desire remains closed to him. Lacan goes so far as to say that it is "not without reason" that homosexuality is called "a desire which dare not speak its name." (Of course, however, Lacan like Freud assumes that only male homosexuality is in question. If the lesbian dialectic allows women access to their subjectivity in addition to their normal objectivity, we might say the reverse for male homosexuals: they seek access to their objectivity in addition to their normal subjectivity. And because that means that would imply a compromise of privilege, a feminization, it is more unthinkable.)

Lacan's position in this respect is not as different as one would like to think from that of the reactionary Christopher Lasch. Lasch's writings on the subject have infinitely less subtlety and intelligence than Lacan's. But partly for that reason they lay bare the politics of the analytic tradition from which Lacan, less understandably, could

[32]Lacan, *Seminar*, 1:142. [Au.]

[33]Ibid., 1:221. [Au.]

[34]There is an excellent article by Wilfried Ver Eecke on this subject: "Hegel as Lacan's Source for Necessity in Psychoanalytic Theory," in Joseph Smith and William Kerrigan, eds., *Interpreting Lacan* (New Haven: Yale University Press, 1983), 113–38. [Au.]

[35]De Beauvoir, *Second Sex*, 464–65. [Au.]

not free himself. In a complimentary preface to a book by Chasseguet-Smirgel, Lasch claims that by eradicating differences of gender, the homosexual pervert "erases the more fundamental distinction between the self and the not-self, the source of every other distinction."[36] One hardly knows where to begin with this kind of comment. In the first place, it would simply be absurd to think that homosexuals eradicate gender; the very logic of homosexuality as a category is impossible without gender and its utopian identifications. Equally foolish is the rather crude form of heterosexist ideology in which it is supposed that people who have homosexual relations do not also have other kinds.

More deceptive, however, is the assumption that gender is the phenomenology of difference itself. This is the core of the psychoanalytic tradition I am trying to map. It is a staggeringly primitive confusion. Can it actually be imagined that people in homosexual relations have no other way of distinguishing between self and not-self? That no other marker of difference, such as race, could intervene; or that the pragmatics of dialogue would not render alterity meaningful, even in the minimal imaginary intersubjectivity of cruising? Why is gender assumed to be our only access to alterity? It is not even the only line of sameness and difference that structures erotic images. Race, age, and class are capable of doing that as well. Sexuality has any number of forms of the dialectic between identification and desire. But we do not say of people whose erotic objects are chosen partly on the basis of racial identity or of generation or of class that they have eradicated the distinction between self and not-self. We say that only of gender. The difference between hetero- and homosexualities is not, in fact, a difference between sexualities of otherness and sameness. It is an allegory about gender.

We have only to consider the breathtaking simplicity of the premises for the whole argument to dissolve. But let me emphasize that I am not making a point about Lasch's blindness. He merely reproduces an ideological confusion that is axiomatic for the modern sex/gender system. Even Lacan ascribes to what he calls "the cosmic polarity of male and female"[37] nothing less than the transition from ego-identification to dialogue:

> For it is a truth of experience for analysis that the subject is presented with the question of his [*sic*] existence, not in terms of the anxiety that it arouses at the level of the ego, and which is only one element in the series, but as an articulated question: "What am I there?", concerning his sex and his contingency in being, namely, that, on the one hand, he is a man or a woman, and, on the other, that he might not be, the two conjugating their mystery, and binding it in the symbols of procreation and death.[38]

This passage appears exactly as an explanation of how alterity can be grasped within the narcissistic structure of subjectivity. Lacan is explaining the so-called "schema L," which describes the mediations between the subject and the Other, by which Lacan means "the locus from which the question of his existence may be presented to him." He here proposes that it is the otherness of gender that allows the subject to apprehend his or her own ego as an other. If we are to read Lacan generously here, we will emphasize the qualifier, "it is a truth *of experience for analysis*" as meaning that the situation he depicts is only a nonnormative description of how gender operates in the present culture. We could then make these assumptions the subject of critique, as does de Beauvoir. But Lacan does not take that step, and it is just as possible to read the emphasis differently: "it is a *truth* of experience for analysis."

The passage is not without a sentimental and mystifying element. Lacan implies that the realization "I am this individual and not that one" not only does but *should* come in the form "I am this gender and not that one." He further assumes that a recognition of gender implicitly contains the particular form of mortality-transcendence found in the myths and rituals of heterosexual conjugal-

[36]Christopher Lasch, Introduction to Janine Chasseguet-Smirgel, *The Ego Ideal*, trans. Paul Barrows (New York: Norton, 1984), xiii-xiv. [Au.]

[37]Jacques Lacan, "Aggressivity in Psychoanalysis," *Écrits*, trans. Alan Sheridan (New York: Norton, 1977), 27. [Au.]

[38]Jacques Lacan, "On a Question Preliminary to Any Possible Treatment of Psychosis," *Écrits*, 194. [Au.]

ity. But the dialectic of identification does not lead without mediation to procreative, genital sexuality. Indeed, Lacan often paints a very different picture himself:

> What is my desire? What is my position in the imaginary structuration? This position is only conceivable in so far as one finds a guide beyond the imaginary, on the level of the symbolic plane, of the legal exchange which can only be embodied in the verbal exchange between human beings. This guide governing the subject is the ego-ideal.[39]

Here, as elsewhere, Lacan argues that the narcissism of desire is transcended only by the rule-governed multiple perspectives of symbolic interaction. Language in general brings about forms of difference and norms of reciprocity and thus allows the subject the negativity with which to consider his or her identity in the role of another. Yet no absolute break with narcissistic identification has occurred, since the subject's ability to do this continues to be regulated by the ego ideals. As a picture of the development of subjectivity, Lacan's scene here resembles the "admonitions" and "critical judgment" referred to by Freud as the origin of the ego ideals in "On Narcissism." The subject has encountered the Other, "the locus from which the question of his existence may be presented to him." But significantly, that locus and its questioning do not imply the gender of an object choice.

Lacan moves between this account, in which the decisive factor is symbolic interaction, and another account, closer to the so-called second topography of Freud's later work, in which the ego ideal is specifically the paternal image. Again, the generous reading is that Lacan's analysis is descriptive of the way the father's authority stands for the subjective function he describes in our culture. But again, Lacan is not critical of that cultural equation, and he does not analyze the ways in which it is possible for subjects to interact without the prescribed relation to the paternal image. Instead, as we have seen, he adheres to models of pathology that incorporate and presuppose the normative role of gender defined as the simple apprehension of alterity. Because of this elision, the fundamental phenomenology of gender in Lacan's account often has an ideological character, though his most radical (and most Hegelian) arguments work in another direction. Indeed, if the equation between homosexuality and narcissism in psychoanalysis tells us anything, it is that the central premises and vocabulary of psychoanalysis have been designed for a heterosexist self-understanding. They have totalized gender as an allegory of difference, leaving little analytic space between the development of subjectivity and the production of heterosexual norms.

How does this mystification get sustained? When Lasch declares homosexuality perverse because it eradicates the distinction between self and not-self, does he not realize that many of his readers will come to the passage with the experience that must inevitably disclose its falseness? In fact, I think he does not. The entire psychoanalytic heritage on this subject does not imagine itself in dialogue with those it describes.[40] If I have taken some pains to show this, it is because I consider it a *tactical* necessity to have a better understanding of what the sources of this discourse's power are. If the tradition I have described simply reflects the illiberal intolerance of a few homophobic theorists, then we need not sweat it any more. If it is structural to the premises of psychoanalysis, then we need more of an attack on modern psychoanalysis. If it lies in the heart of modern social organization, then we should consider how, and in what institutions, and where a more organized resistance should begin.

That is not to say that we need a theory of homosexuality in the usual sense. There may be any number of logics lumped together under this heading, from the "lesbian continuum" theorized by Adrienne Rich to the more recent phenomenon of gay communities organized through a discourse of rights. Both for women and for men in our culture there are probably as many ways of

[39]Lacan, *Seminar*, 1:141. [Au.]

[40]In this way the discourse on narcissism and homosexuality bears an important resemblance to the psychoanalytic discourse on femininity. See Shoshana Felman, "Rereading Femininity," *Yale French Studies* 62 (1981):19–44. [Au.]

cathecting other women or men as there are ways in other cultures, where the discourse of homosexuality remains so foreign. Indeed, part of the oppressiveness of the modern formation is that all forms of erotics among men or among women get classified by the same logic. We might begin to clarify the question by saying that the theorization of homosexuality as narcissism is itself a form of narcissism peculiar to modern heterosexuality. The central imperative of heterosexist ideology is that the homosexual be supposed to be out of dialogue on the subject of his being. Imagining that the homosexual is narcissistically contained in an unbreakable fixation on himself serves two functions at once: it allows a self-confirming pathology by declaring homosexuals' speech, their interrelations, to be an illusion; *and more fundamentally it allows the constitution of heterosexuality as such.*

If that sounds like a strong claim, let me repeat that by heterosexuality I mean the modern discursive organization of sex that treats gender difference as difference in general. It is a sexuality organized by its self-understanding as *hetero*-sexuality and therefore also includes the categories of homo- and autoerotics against which it defines itself. What I would like to suggest is that it is possible to read this historically recent discourse as, in part, a reaction formation. The allegory of gender protects against a recognition of the role of the imaginary in the formation of the erotic. It provides reassurance that imaginary intersubjectivity has been transcended. To the extent that our culture relies on the allegorization of gender to disguise from itself its own ego erotics, it will recognize those ego erotics only in the person of the homosexual, apparently bereft of the master trope of difference. If it were possible to admit that any relevant forms of otherness operate in homosexuality, then the main feature of heterosexual self-understanding would be lost. The heterosexual would no longer be able to interpret the gendered, binary form of his or her own captation[41] in desire as already being the transcendence of that captation.

[41]Endeavoring to get what one desires through appeals. [Ed.]

But there is a broader issue at stake here, and one that could be raised as an objection. What if we are to return to the more generous reading of Lacan, seeing the psychoanalytic account not only as an ideological rationalization, but as an essentially accurate description of the *cultural* mechanisms whereby gender and alterity are equated? For surely Lacan is correct to point out that the equation takes place not just in psychoanalytic theory, but on very elementary levels of subjective experience. It *is* a truth of experience for analysis, in our society, that the subject is presented with the question of his or her existence through the problematic alterity of gender. That is why the *psychoanalytic* tradition of linking narcissism and homosexuality has been so easy to confirm. And although the categories and norms of that tradition can be shown to be ideological and incoherent, they are the categories and norms of subjective experience in our culture, rather than simply the prejudices of a few theorists. The argument that I have made here therefore raises a whole new problem: what is the social and historical character of this organization of sexuality and gender?

This issue challenges us to separate the two problematics that I have brought together in this essay: on the one hand the problem of women's construction as the Other, with its prehistoric sources in phallocentrism; on the other hand, a sex/gender system in which object choice is posed as an apprehension of alterity *tout court.* These two structures of power are currently co-articulated as a unity of experience, but they have different histories. The system of hetero- and homosexualities is a much more recent phenomenon, codified in discourse only for the past century. Through most of Western history erotics among men in particular have been understood precisely along axes of difference: the active/passive difference in the discourse of sodomy, for instance, or the pedagogic difference of generations in the classical discourse of pederasty. If suddenly it has become necessary and commonsensical to imagine erotics among men or among women as homosexuality, a sexuality of sameness, we might ask how that has come about. We might also ask what relation there might be between this recent organization of sexuality and the longer history of phallocentrism that constructs woman as Other. Indeed, one reason it is so hard for us to imagine hetero- and homosexualities as recent developments is that they have been articulated so closely with that phallocentric construction of Otherness.

Unfortunately, if the organization of sexuality around the axis of the hetero and the homo is the result of historical change, we have virtually no social theory of why its organization in this form should have been so recent or what kind of historical narrative it would call for. The account typically given in the wake of Michel Foucault has been to attribute the system of heterosexuality to its discourse, beginning roughly with the naming of *homosexuality* in the late nineteenth century.[42] The Foucauldian account has an undeniable force in showing that the discourse of sexuality is a form of biotechnical power, not a superstructural effect. Nevertheless, I think my argument suggests, in effect, a different strategy of historicizing the whole organization of sexuality. If I am correct that the ideology of gender as alterity is a special way of not recognizing the imaginary sources of desire, then why should Western society have developed that need for misrecognition so recently? Why should there have been an imperative for such a massive displacement of ego erotics?

To pose the question in this way is to link the problem of heterosexuality not simply to modern society in the sense of recent society, but to the force of modernity. A full critique of heterosexism would involve questions about the role of the ego in post-Enlightenment capitalist society. That debate is a complex one, but I can at least indicate its relevance here. On one side Christopher Lasch, in *The Culture of Narcissism*, laments the ego orientation of consumer society as producing debased forms of individualism and symptomatic perversions such as the gay rights movement.[43] On the other side, Jürgen Habermas can argue that the self-reflection of the autonomous ego is the source of a still progressive modernity. And he can show in a fairly nuanced way that ego-identity becomes both necessary and problematic in a whole new range of social contexts.[44] Both sides agree that a tension between the ego and its ideals has become newly important in post-Enlightenment Western capitalism. In response to that debate, could we speculate that the ego erotics coded in homosexuality is a special feature of this social history?

Obviously, that subject is too large to be treated here. But I should note that the possibility of such an account is already implicit in the way Freud imagines an erotics of the ego ideal. In the essay on narcissism, Freud takes a broad social view. Having once stated that secondary narcissism is possible only after the development of critical judgment and the encountering of the admonitions of others, he returns with an even more general description:

> For what prompted the subject to form an ego ideal, on whose behalf his conscience acts as watchman, arose from the critical influence of his parents (con-

[42]Michel Foucault, *The History of Sexuality, Vol. 1: An Introduction* (New York: Pantheon, 1978). I have no interest in minimizing the value of work that has followed in the same general direction, especially in its value as a critique of the liberal-essentialist discourse of sexuality. For versions that specifically treat the question of homosexuality, see especially Jeffrey Weeks, *Sexuality and Its Discontents: Meanings, Myths, and Modern Sexualities* (London: Routledge, Kegan, Paul, 1985); or the work of Eve Sedgwick, most recently exemplified in "Across Gender, Across Sexuality: Willa Cather and Others," *South Atlantic Quarterly* 88 (Winter 1989):53–72; or David M. Halperin, *One Hundred Years of Homosexuality and Other Essays on Greek Love* (New York: Routledge, 1990). [Au.]

[43]Christopher Lasch, *The Culture of Narcissism* (New York: Norton, 1979). [Au.]

[44]See especially Jürgen Habermas, "Moral Development and Ego Identity," in *Communication and the Evolution of Society*, trans. Thomas McCarthy (Boston: Beacon Press, 1979), 69–94. Habermas argues, for instance, that the subject of modernity "takes into account that traditionally settled forms of life can prove to be mere conventions, to be irrational. Thus he has to retract his ego behind the line of all particular roles and norms and stabilize it only through the abstract ability to present himself credibly in any situation as someone who can satisfy the requirements of consistency even in the face of incompatible role expectations and in the passage through a sequence of contradictory periods of life. Role identity is replaced by ego identity; actors meet as individuals across, so to speak, the objective contexts of their lives" (85–86). [Au.]

veyed to him by the medium of the voice), to whom were added, as time went on, those who trained and taught him and the innumerable and indefinable host of all the other people in his environment — his fellow men — and public opinion.

In this way large amounts of libido of an essentially homosexual kind are drawn into the formation of the narcissistic ego ideal and find outlet and satisfaction in maintaining it.

Here Freud advances a notion to which he returned often, especially in the *Group Psychology* — the notion that sociality itself is in some essential way a desexualized homosexuality. But when Freud describes the environment to which the subject must relate in such a homosexual way, he depicts an essentially modern society. It is defined by the critical force of training and teaching. It is made up of an "innumerable and indefinable host" of people. And at its limits it finds expression in a highly generalized perspective of criticism: public opinion. This set of social pressures on the ego may also be what Freud has in mind when he links his developmental narrative with the historical transition from traditional to modern. He claims, for instance, that "primitive peoples," like children, orient themselves to the world through primary narcissism rather than secondary.[45] One doesn't have to be uncritical of Freud's ethnocentrism here to imagine that a special role for critical judgment in modern Western societies might also mean that the subject of these societies might be structured by a correspondingly special ego erotics.

Lacan's account also suggests as much, and Lacan in fact often asserts that social modernity has brought about a general pathology of ego erotics.[46] His example of Werther's narcissistic love, we might note, is already articulated within the normative subjectivity of modernity. We can see how that articulated relation works by taking a strikingly similar example from an American admirer and contemporary of Goethe, Charles Brockden Brown, also writing in the context of the late Enlightenment:

Good God! You say, she loves; loves *me!* me, a boy in age; bred in clownish ignorance; scarcely ushered into the world; more than childishly unlearned and raw; a barn-door simpleton; a plow-tail, kitchen-hearth, turnip-hoeing novice![47]

Arthur Mervyn here encounters his heterosexual love as a relation between his ego ideals and his actual ego. Several things follow. First, it is a moment of narcissistic ego erotics ("loves *me!* me . . ."), but the affective charge is attached to what seems like an unbridgable gulf of difference ("Good God!"). The extravagant otherness of his beloved — she is, in fact, older, foreign, and Jewish — allows her to be the fulcrum of Mervyn's desire-laden self-relation. The passage therefore marks the mutual involvement of a conspicuous *hetero*sexuality with a potentially homoerotic fixation on a reflexive ego erotics. And in fact, its usual charge, both in this novel and in Brown's work generally, is decisively, even sensationally homoerotic. Mervyn's awakening here might be constructed as the origin of heterosexuality, but that only shows how closely linked heterosexuality and homosexuality are in the erotics of the ego.

Mervyn's desirous self-relation, however, is also a moment of critical self-consciousness. In the very act of focusing on himself as a possible object of desire, he confronts the difference between his ideals and his actual ego. He occupies the vantage of a critical public opinion, defining an image of himself there: "a boy in age; bred in clownish ignorance; scarcely ushered into the world; more than childishly unlearned and raw; a barn-door simpleton; a plow-tail, kitchen-hearth, turnip-hoeing novice!" This is exactly the sort of role-detached, posttraditional self-consciousness that Habermas identifies with the normative content of modernity. If this sort of ego erotics seems to bear the stamp of the special social contexts of modernity, with its norm of critical self-consciousness in an environment of equals, then both hetero- and homosexuality share its essential structure.

But I do not wish to emphasize only the normative, critical content of modernity. It should also be possible to specify a whole range of so-

[45]Freud, "On Narcissism," 75. [Au.]

[46]See, for instance, Lacan, "Aggressivity," 27. [Au.]

[47]Charles Brockden Brown, *Arthur Mervyn* (1799–1800), ed. Sydney Krause et al. (Kent, Ohio: Kent State University Press, 1980), p. 434. [Au.]

cial and historical institutions in which the subject is called on to take an evaluative/desirous posture toward his or her ego ideal. The imaginary register will be important, albeit in different ways, for the discourse of rights, the forms of exchange in capitalism, the role-detachment that comes with a system-differentiated society, the mass imaginary of video capitalism, rituals and markets of adolescence, and the like. The work of analyzing the subjectivity of these interarticulated contexts has only begun.

The possibility I'm trying to indicate is that homosexuality, encoded as such, takes these multiple sites of ego-reflection in modern liberal capitalism as multiple sites of erotic play and interaction. Heterosexuality deploys an understanding of gender as alterity in order to mobilize, but also to obscure, a self-reflexive erotics of the actual ego measured against its ideals. In a modernity constituted by multiple sites of ego erotics, sex ceases to be complacently patriarchal and becomes heterosexual, mystifying its own imaginary register with its liberal logic of difference. Homosexuality, however, engages the same self-reflexive erotics, without the mechanism of obscuring it. The homosexual who makes the choice of "what he himself would like to be" expresses the utopian erotics of modern subjectivity. This utopian self-relation, far from being the pathology of the homosexual, could instead be seen as a historical condition and, in the perverse and unrecuperated mode of homosexual subjectivity, the source of a critical potential. This is why modern heterosexuality needs a discourse about homosexuality as a displacement of its own narcissistic sources. The psychoanalytic tradition enacts and justifies that displacement.

Judith Butler

b. 1956

Judith Butler's first training in philosophy took place at the synagogue in her hometown of Cleveland, Ohio. She attended Bennington College and then Yale University, where she received her B.A. in philosophy in 1978 and her Ph.D. in 1984. She taught at Wesleyan and at Johns Hopkins Universities before becoming Chancellor Professor of rhetoric and comparative literature at the University of California at Berkeley. Butler has written extensively on questions of identity politics, gender, and sexuality. Her books include Subjects of Desire *(1987),* Gender Trouble: Feminism and the Subversion of Identity *(1989), and* Bodies That Matter: On the Discursive Limits of "Sex" *(1993). Her most recent work includes* The Psychic Life of Power: Theories in Subjection *(1997), which concerns the double meaning of "subjection" (to be subordinated to another and to become a subject) and* Excitable Speech: Politics of the Performance *(1997), published within one month of* The Psychic Life of Power, *which analyzes name-calling as both a social injury and the way in which individuals are "interpellated" or called into action for political purposes. Originally given as a lecture in 1989 at a conference on homosexuality at Yale, "Imitation and Gender Insubordination" is reprinted from* Inside/Out: Lesbian Theories, Gay Theories, *edited by Diana Fuss (New York: Routledge, 1991).*

mimicry

Imitation and Gender Insubordination

So what is this divided being introduced into language through gender? It is an impossible being, it is a being that does not exist, an ontological joke.

— MONIQUE WITTIG[1]

Beyond physical repetition and the psychical or metaphysical repetition, is there an ontological *repetition? . . . This ultimate repetition, this ultimate theatre, gathers everything in a certain way; and in another way, it destroys everything; and in yet another way, it selects from everything.*

— GILLES DELEUZE[2]

TO THEORIZE AS A LESBIAN?

At first I considered writing a different sort of essay, one with a philosophical tone: the "being" of being homosexual. The prospect of *being* anything, even for pay, has always produced in me a certain anxiety, for "to be" gay, "to be" lesbian seems to be more than a simple injunction to become who or what I already am. And in no way does it settle the anxiety for me to say that this is "part" of what I am. To write or speak *as a lesbian* appears a paradoxical appearance of this "I," one which feels neither true nor false. For it is a production, usually in response to a request, to come out or write in the name of an identity which, once produced, sometimes functions as a politically efficacious phantasm. I'm not at ease with "lesbian theories, gay theories," for as I've argued elsewhere,[3] identity categories tend to be instruments of regulatory regimes, whether as the normalizing categories of oppressive structures or as the rallying points for a liberatory contestation of that very oppression. This is not to say that I will not appear at political occasions under the sign of lesbian, but that I would like to have it permanently unclear what precisely that sign signifies. So it is unclear how it is that I can contribute to this book and appear under its title, for it announces a set of terms that I propose to contest. One risk I take is to be recolonized by the sign under which I write, and so it is this risk that I seek to thematize. To propose that the invocation of identity is always a risk does not imply that resistance to it is always or only symptomatic of a self-inflicted homophobia. Indeed, a Foucaultian perspective might argue that the affirmation of "homosexuality" is itself an extension of a homophobic discourse. And yet "discourse," he writes on the same page, "can be both an instrument and an effect of power, but also a hindrance, a stumbling-block, a point of resistance and a starting point for an opposing strategy."[4]

So I am skeptical about how the "I" is determined as it operates under the title of the lesbian sign, and I am no more comfortable with its homophobic determination than with those normative definitions offered by other members of the "gay or lesbian community." I'm permanently troubled by identity categories, consider them to be invariable stumbling-blocks, and understand them, even promote them, as sites of necessary trouble. In fact, if the category were to offer no trouble, it would cease to be interesting to me: it is precisely the *pleasure* produced by the instability of those categories which sustains the various erotic practices that make me a candidate for the category to begin with. To install myself within the terms of an identity category would be to turn against the sexuality that the category purports to describe; and this might be true for any identity category which seeks to control the very eroticism that it claims to describe and authorize, much less "liberate."

And what's worse, I do not understand the notion of "theory," and am hardly interested in being cast as its defender, much less in being signified as part of an elite gay/lesbian theory crowd that seeks to establish the legitimacy and domestication of gay/lesbian studies within the academy. Is there a pregiven distinction between theory, politics, culture, media? How do those

[1]"The Mark of Gender," *Feminist Issues* 5 no. 2 (1985): 6. [Au.]

[2]*Différence et répétition* (Paris: PUF, 1968), 374; my translation. [Au.]

[3]*Gender Trouble: Feminism and the Subversion of Identity* (New York and London: Routledge, 1990). [Au.]

[4]Michel Foucault, *The History of Sexuality, Vol. I,* trans. Robert Hurley (New York: Random House, 1980), 101. [Au.]

divisions operate to quell a certain intertextual writing that might well generate wholly different epistemic maps? But I am writing here now: is it too late? Can this writing, can any writing, refuse the terms by which it is appropriated even as, to some extent, that very colonizing discourse enables or produces this stumbling block, this resistance? How do I relate the paradoxical situation of this dependency and refusal?

If the political task is to show that theory is never merely *theoria,* in the sense of disengaged contemplation, and to insist that it is fully political (*phronesis*[5] or even *praxis*), then why not simply call this operation *politics,* or some necessary permutation of it?

I have begun with confessions of trepidation and a series of disclaimers, but perhaps it will become clear that *disclaiming,* which is no simple activity, will be what I have to offer as a form of affirmative resistance to a certain regulatory operation of homophobia. The discourse of "coming out" has clearly served its purposes, but what are its risks? And here I am not speaking of unemployment or public attack or violence, which are quite clearly and widely on the increase against those who are perceived as "out" whether or not of their own design. Is the "subject" who is "out" free of its subjection and finally in the clear? Or could it be that the subjection that subjectivates the gay or lesbian subject in some ways continues to oppress, or oppresses most insidiously, once "outness" is claimed? What or who is it that is "out," made manifest and fully disclosed, when and if I reveal myself as lesbian? What is it that is now known, anything? What remains permanently concealed by the very linguistic act that offers up the promise of a transparent revelation of sexuality? Can sexuality even remain sexuality once it submits to a criterion of transparency and disclosure, or does it perhaps cease to be sexuality precisely when the semblance of full explicitness is achieved?[6] Is sexuality of any kind even possible without that opacity designated by the unconscious, which means simply that the conscious "I" who would reveal its sexuality is perhaps the last to know the meaning of what it says?

To claim that this is what I *am* is to suggest a provisional totalization of this "I." But if the I can so determine itself, then that which it excludes in order to make that determination remains constitutive of the determination itself. In other words, such a statement presupposes that the "I" exceeds its determination, and even produces that very excess in and by the act which seeks to exhaust the semantic field of that "I." In the act which would disclose the true and full content of that "I," a certain radical *concealment* is thereby produced. For it is always finally unclear what is meant by invoking the lesbian-signifier, since its signification is always to some degree out of one's control, but also because its *specificity* can only be demarcated by exclusions that return to disrupt its claim to coherence. What, if anything, can lesbians be said to share? And who will decide this question, and in the name of whom? If I claim to be a lesbian, I "come out" only to produce a new and different "closet." The "you" to whom I come out now has access to a different region of opacity. Indeed, the locus of opacity has simply shifted: before, you did not know whether I "am," but now you do not know what that means, which is to say that the copula[7] is empty, that it cannot be substituted for with a set of descriptions.[8] And perhaps that is a situation to be valued. Conventionally, one comes out *of* the closet (and yet, how often is it the case that we are "outted" when we are young and without resources?); so we are out of the closet, but into what? what new unbounded spatiality? the room, the den, the attic, the basement, the house, the bar, the university, some new enclosure whose door, like Kafka's door,[9]

[5]Practical understanding. [Ed.]

[6]Here I would doubtless differ from the very fine analysis of Hitchcock's *Rope* offered by D. A. Miller in this volume. [Au.] See D. A. Miller, "Anal Rope." *Inside/Out: Lesbian Theories, Gay Theories,* ed. Diana Fuss (New York: Routledge, 1991), pp. 119–41. [Ed.]

[7]Refers to the verb "to be," used with a predicate noun or adjective. [Ed.]

[8]For an example of "coming out" that is strictly unconfessional and which, finally, offers no content for the category of lesbian, see Barbara Johnson's deftly constructed "Sula Passing: No Passing" presentation at UCLA, May 1990. [Au.]

[9]Butler refers to the parable of the law in *The Trial* by Franz Kafka [Ed.]

produces the expectation of a fresh air and a light of illumination that never arrives? Curiously, it is the figure of the closet that produces this expectation, and which guarantees its dissatisfaction. For being "out" always depends to some extent on being "in"; it gains its meaning only within that polarity. Hence, being "out" must produce the closet again and again in order to maintain itself as "out." In this sense, *outness* can only produce a new opacity; and *the closet* produces the promise of a disclosure that can, by definition, never come. Is this infinite postponement of the disclosure of "gayness," produced by the very act of "coming out," to be lamented? Or is this very deferral of the signified *to be valued,* a site for the production of values, precisely because the term now takes on a life that cannot be, can never be, permanently controlled?

It is possible to argue that whereas no transparent or full revelation is afforded by "lesbian" and "gay," there remains a political imperative to use these necessary errors or category mistakes, as it were (what Gayatri Spivak might call "catachrestic"[10] operations: to use a proper name improperly[11]), to rally and represent an oppressed political constituency. Clearly, I am not legislating against the use of the term. My question is simply: which use will be legislated, and what play will there be between legislation and use such that the instrumental uses of "identity" do not become regulatory imperatives? If it is already true that "lesbians" and "gay men" have been traditionally designated as impossible identities, errors of classification, unnatural disasters within juridico-medical discourses, or, what perhaps amounts to the same, the very paradigm of what calls to be classified, regulated, and controlled, then perhaps these sites of disruption, error, confusion, and trouble can be the very rallying points for a certain resistance to classification and to identity as such.

The question is not one of *avowing* or *disavowing* the category of lesbian or gay, but, rather, why it is that the category becomes the site of this "ethical" choice? What does it mean to *avow* a category that can only maintain its specificity and coherence by performing a prior set of *disavowals?* Does this make "coming out" into the avowal of disavowal, that is, a return to the closet under the guise of an escape? And it is not something like heterosexuality or bisexuality that is disavowed by the category, but a set of identificatory and practical crossings between these categories that renders the discreteness of each equally suspect. Is it not possible to maintain and pursue heterosexual identifications and aims within homosexual practice, and homosexual identifications and aims within heterosexual practices? If a sexuality is to be disclosed, what will be taken as the true determinant of its meaning: the phantasy structure, the act, the orifice, the gender, the anatomy? And if the practice engages a complex interplay of all of those, which one of these erotic dimensions will come to stand for the sexuality that requires them all? Is it the *specificity* of a lesbian experience or lesbian desire or lesbian sexuality that lesbian theory needs to elucidate? Those efforts have only and always produced a set of contests and refusals which should by now make it clear that there is no necessarily common element among lesbians, except perhaps that we all know something about how homophobia works against women — although, even then, the language and the analysis we use will differ.

To argue that there might be a *specificity* to lesbian sexuality has seemed a necessary counterpoint to the claim that lesbian sexuality is just heterosexuality once removed, or that it is derived, or that it does not exist. But perhaps the claim of specificity, on the one hand, and the claim of derivativeness or non-existence, on the other, are not as contradictory as they seem. Is it not possible that lesbian sexuality is a process that reinscribes the power domains that it resists, that it is constituted in part from the very heterosexual matrix that it seeks to displace, and that its specificity is to be established, not *outside* or *beyond* that reinscription or reiteration, but in the very modality and effects of that reinscription. In other words, the negative constructions of lesbianism as a fake or a bad copy can be occupied

[10]*Catachresis:* Rhetorical term for an outrageous play on words. [Ed.]

[11]Gayatri Chakravorty Spivak, "Displacement and the Discourse of Woman." In *Displacement: Derrida and After,* ed. Mark Krupnick (Bloomington: Indiana University Press, 1983). [Au.]

and reworked to call into question the claims of heterosexual priority. In a sense I hope to make clear in what follows, lesbian sexuality can be understood to redeploy its "derivativeness" in the service of displacing hegemonic heterosexual norms. Understood in this way, the political problem is not to establish the specificity of lesbian sexuality over and against its derivativeness, but to turn the homophobic construction of the bad copy against the framework that privileges heterosexuality as origin, and so "derive" the former from the latter. This description requires a reconsideration of imitation, drag, and other forms of sexual crossing that affirm the internal complexity of a lesbian sexuality constituted in part within the very matrix of power that it is compelled both to reiterate and to oppose.

ON THE BEING OF GAYNESS AS NECESSARY DRAG

The professionalization of gayness requires a certain performance and production of a "self" which is the *constituted effect* of a discourse that nevertheless claims to "represent" that self as a prior truth. When I spoke at the conference on homosexuality in 1989,[12] I found myself telling my friends beforehand that I was off to Yale to be a lesbian, which of course didn't mean that I wasn't one before, but that somehow then, as I spoke in that context, I *was* one in some more thorough and totalizing way, at least for the time being. So I *am* one, and my qualifications are even fairly unambiguous. Since I was sixteen, being a lesbian is what I've been. So what's the anxiety, the discomfort? Well, it has something to do with that redoubling, the way I can say, I'm going to Yale to be a lesbian; a lesbian is what I've been being for so long. How is it that I can both "be" one, and yet endeavor to be one at the same time? When and where does my being a lesbian come into play, when and where does this playing a lesbian constitute something like what I am? To say that I "play" at being one is not to say that I am not one "really"; rather, how and where I play at being one is the way in which that "being" gets established, instituted, circulated, and confirmed. This is not a performance from which I can take radical distance, for this is deep-seated play, psychically entrenched play, *and this "I" does not play its lesbianism as a role.* Rather, it is through the repeated play of this sexuality that the "I" is insistently reconstituted as a lesbian "I"; paradoxically, it is precisely the *repetition* of that play that establishes as well the *instability* of the very category that it constitutes. For if the "I" is a site of repetition, that is, if the "I" only achieves the semblance of identity

[12]The conference on homosexuality at Yale, at which this essay was given as an oral presentation in somewhat different form. [Ed.] Let me take this occasion to apologize to the social worker at that conference who asked a question about how to deal with those clients with AIDS who turned to Bernie Segal and others for the purposes of psychic healing. At the time, I understood this questioner to be suggesting that such clients were full of self-hatred because they were trying to find the causes of AIDS in their own selves. The questioner and I appear to agree that any effort to locate the responsibility for AIDS in those who suffer from it is politically and ethically wrong. I thought the questioner, however, was prepared to tell his clients that they were self-hating, and I reacted strongly (too strongly) to the paternalistic prospect that this person was going to pass judgment on someone who was clearly not only suffering, but already passing judgment on him or herself. To call another person self-hating is itself an act of power that calls for some kind of scrutiny, and I think in response to someone who is already dealing with AIDS, that is perhaps the last thing one needs to hear. I also happened to have a friend who sought out advice from Bernie Segal, not with the belief that there is an exclusive or even primary psychic cause or solution for AIDS, but that there might be a psychic contribution to be made to surviving with AIDS. Unfortunately, I reacted quickly to this questioner, and with some anger. And I regret now that I didn't have my wits about me to discuss the distinctions with him that I have just laid out.

Curiously, this incident was invoked at a CLAGS (Center for Lesbian and Gay Studies) meeting at CUNY sometime in December of 1989 and, according to those who told me about it, my angry denunciation of the social worker was taken to be symptomatic of the political insensitivity of a "theorist" in dealing with someone who is actively engaged in AIDS work. That attribution implies that I do not do AIDS work, that I am not politically engaged, and that the social worker in question does not read theory. Needless to say, I was reacting angrily on behalf of an absent friend with AIDS who sought out Bernie Segal and company. So as I offer this apology to the social worker, I wait expectantly that the CLAGS member who misunderstood me will offer me one in turn. [Au.]

through a certain repetition of itself, then the I is always displaced by the very repetition that sustains it. In other words, does or can the "I" ever repeat itself, cite itself, faithfully, or is there always a displacement from its former moment that establishes the permanently non-self-identical status of that "I" or its "being lesbian"? What "performs" does not exhaust the "I"; it does not lay out in visible terms the comprehensive content of that "I," for if the performance is "repeated," there is always the question of what differentiates from each other the moments of identity that are repeated. And if the "I" is the effect of a certain repetition, one which produces the semblance of a continuity or coherence, then there is no "I" that precedes the gender that it is said to perform; the repetition, and the failure to repeat, produce a string of performances that constitute and contest the coherence of that "I."

But *politically,* we might argue, isn't it quite crucial to insist on lesbian and gay identities precisely because they are being threatened with erasure and obliteration from homophobic quarters? Isn't the above theory *complicitous* with those political forces that would obliterate the possibility of gay and lesbian identity? Isn't it "no accident" that such theoretical contestations of identity emerge within a political climate that is performing a set of similar obliterations of homosexual identities through legal and political means?

The question I want to raise in return is this: ought such threats of obliteration dictate the terms of the political resistance to them, and if they do, do such homophobic efforts to that extent win the battle from the start? There is no question that gays and lesbians are threatened by the violence of public erasure, but the decision to counter that violence must be careful not to reinstall another in its place. Which version of lesbian or gay ought to be rendered visible, and which internal exclusions will that rendering visible institute? Can the visibility of identity *suffice* as a political strategy, or can it only be the starting point for a strategic intervention which calls for a transformation of policy? Is it not a sign of despair over public politics when identity becomes its own policy, bringing with it those who would "police" it from various sides? And this is not a call to return to silence or invisibility, but, rather, to make use of a category that can be called into question, made to account for what it excludes. That any consolidation of identity requires some set of differentiations and exclusions seems clear. But which ones ought to be valorized? That the identity-sign I use now has its purposes seems right, but there is no way to predict or control the political uses to which that sign will be put in the future. And perhaps this is a kind of openness, regardless of its risks, that ought to be safeguarded for political reasons. If the rendering visible of lesbian/gay identity now presupposes a set of exclusions, then perhaps part of what is necessarily excluded is *the future uses of the sign.* There is a political necessity to use some sign now, and we do, but how to use it in such a way that its futural significations are not *foreclosed?* How to use the sign and avow its temporal contingency at once?

In avowing the sign's strategic provisionality (rather than its strategic essentialism), that identity can become a site of contest and revision, indeed, take on a future set of significations that those of us who use it now may not be able to foresee. It is in the safeguarding of the future of the political signifiers — preserving the signifier as a site of rearticulation — that Laclau and Mouffe discern its democratic promise.

Within contemporary U.S. politics, there are a vast number of ways in which lesbianism in particular is understood as precisely that which cannot or dare not *be.* In a sense, Jesse Helms's attack on the NEA for sanctioning representations of "homoeroticism" focuses various homophobic fantasies of what gay men are and do on the work of Robert Mapplethorpe.[13] In a sense, for Helms, gay men exist as objects of prohibition; they are, in his twisted fantasy, sadomasochistic exploiters of children, the paradigmatic exemplars of "obscenity"; in a sense, the lesbian is not even produced within this discourse as a prohibited object. Here it becomes important to recognize that oppression works not merely through acts of

[13]See my "The Force of Fantasy: Feminism, Mapplethorpe, and Discursive Excess," *differences* 2, no. 2 (Summer 1990). Since the writing of this essay, lesbian artists and representations have also come under attack. [Au.]

overt prohibition, but covertly, through the constitution of viable subjects and through the corollary constitution of a domain of unviable (un)subjects — *abjects,* we might call them — who are neither named nor prohibited within the economy of the law. Here oppression works through the production of a domain of unthinkability and unnameability. Lesbianism is not explicitly prohibited in part because it has not even made its way into the thinkable, the imaginable, that grid of cultural intelligibility that regulates the real and the nameable. How, then, to "be" a lesbian in a political context in which the lesbian does not exist? That is, in a political discourse that wages its violence against lesbianism in part by excluding lesbianism from discourse itself? To be prohibited explicitly is to occupy a discursive site from which something like a reverse-discourse can be articulated; to be implicitly proscribed is not even to qualify as an object of prohibition.[14] And though homosexualities of all kinds in this present climate are being erased, reduced, and (then) reconstituted as sites of radical homophobic fantasy, it is important to retrace the different routes by which the unthinkability of homosexuality is being constituted time and again.

It is one thing to be erased from discourse, and yet another to be present within discourse as an abiding falsehood. Hence, there is a political imperative to render lesbianism visible, but how is that to be done outside or through existing regulatory regimes? Can the exclusion from ontology itself become a rallying point for resistance?

Here is something like a confession which is meant merely to thematize the impossibility of confession: As a young person, I suffered for a long time, and I suspect many people have, from being told, explicitly or implicitly, that what I "am" is a copy, an imitation, a derivative example, a shadow of the real. Compulsory heterosexuality sets itself up as the original, the true, the authentic; the norm that determines the real implies that "being" lesbian is always a kind of miming, a vain effort to participate in the phantasmatic plenitude of naturalized heterosexuality which will always and only fail.[15] And yet, I remember quite distinctly when I first read in Esther Newton's *Mother Camp: Female Impersonators in America*[16] that drag is not an imitation or a copy of some prior and true gender; according to Newton, drag enacts the very structure of impersonation by which *any gender* is assumed. Drag is not the putting on of a gender that belongs properly to some other group, i.e. an act of *ex*propriation or *ap*propriation that assumes that gender is the rightful property of sex, that "masculine" belongs to "male" and "feminine" belongs to "female." There is no "proper" gender, a gender proper to one sex rather than another, which is in some sense that sex's cultural prop-

[14]It is this particular ruse of erasure which Foucault for the most part fails to take account of in his analysis of power. He almost always presumes that power takes place through discourse as its instrument, and that oppression is linked with subjection and subjectivation, that is, that it is installed as the formative principle of the identity of subjects. [Au.]

[15]Although miming suggests that there is a prior model which is being copied, it can have the effect of exposing that prior model as purely phantasmatic. In Jacques Derrida's "The Double Session" in *Dissemination,* trans. Barbara Johnson (Chicago: University of Chicago Press, 1981), he considers the textual effect of the mime in Mallarmé's "Mimique." There Derrida argues that the mime does not imitate or copy some prior phenomenon, idea, or figure, but constitutes — some might say *performatively* — the phantasm of the original in and through the mime:

> He represents nothing, imitates nothing, does not have to conform to any prior referent with the aim of achieving adequation or verisimilitude. One can here foresee an objection: since the mime imitates nothing, reproduces nothing, opens up in its origin the very thing he is tracing out, presenting, or producing, he must be the very movement of truth. Not, of course, truth in the form of adequation between the representation and the present of the thing itself, or between the imitator and the imitated, but truth as the present unveiling of the present. . . . But this is not the case. . . . We are faced then with mimicry imitating nothing: faced, so to speak, with a double that couples no simple, a double that nothing anticipates, nothing at least that is not itself already double. There is no simple reference. . . . This speculum reflects no reality: it produces mere "reality-effects." . . . In this speculum with no reality, in this mirror of a mirror, a difference or dyad does exist, since there are mimes and phantoms. But it is a difference without reference, or rather reference without a referent, without any first or last unit, a ghost that is the phantom of no flesh . . . (206). [Au.]

[16]Esther Newton, *Mother Camp: Female Impersonators in America* (Chicago: University of Chicago Press, 1972). [Au.]

erty. Where that notion of the "proper" operates, it is always and only *improperly* installed as the effect of a compulsory system. Drag constitutes the mundane way in which genders are appropriated, theatricalized, worn, and done; it implies that all gendering is a kind of impersonation and approximation. If this is true, it seems, there is no original or primary gender that drag imitates, but *gender is a kind of imitation for which there is no original;* in fact, it is a kind of imitation that produces the very notion of the original as an *effect* and consequence of the imitation itself. In other words, the naturalistic effects of heterosexualized genders are produced through imitative strategies; what they imitate is a phantasmatic ideal of heterosexual identity, one that is produced by the imitation as its effect. In this sense, the "reality" of heterosexual identities is performatively constituted through an imitation that sets itself up as the origin and the ground of all imitations. In other words, heterosexuality is always in the process of imitating and approximating its own phantasmatic idealization of itself — *and failing.* Precisely because it is bound to fail, and yet endeavors to succeed, the project of heterosexual identity is propelled into an endless repetition of itself. Indeed, in its efforts to naturalize itself as the original, heterosexuality must be understood as a compulsive and compulsory repetition that can only produce the *effect* of its own originality; in other words, compulsory heterosexual identities, those ontologically consolidated phantasms of "man" and "woman," are theatrically produced effects that posture as grounds, origins, the normative measure of the real.[17]

[17]In a sense, one might offer a redescription of the above in Lacanian terms. The sexual "positions" of heterosexually differentiated "man" and "woman" are part of the *Symbolic,* that is, an ideal embodiment of the Law of sexual difference which constitutes the object of imaginary pursuits, but which is always thwarted by the "real." These symbolic positions for Lacan are by definition impossible to occupy even as they are impossible to resist as the structuring telos of desire. I accept the former point, and reject the latter one. The imputation of universal necessity to such positions simply encodes compulsory heterosexuality at the level of the Symbolic, and the "failure" to achieve it is implicitly lamented as a source of heterosexual pathos. [Au.] See the introduction to Psychoanalytic Theory, p. 1019. [Ed.]

Reconsider then the homophobic charge that queens and butches and femmes are imitations of the heterosexual real. Here "imitation" carries the meaning of "derivative" or "secondary," a copy of an origin which is itself the ground of all copies, but which is itself a copy of nothing. Logically, this notion of an "origin" is suspect, for how can something operate as an origin if there are no secondary consequences which retrospectively confirm the originality of that origin? The origin requires its derivations in order to affirm itself as an origin, for origins only make sense to the extent that they are differentiated from that which they produce as derivatives. Hence, if it were not for the notion of the homosexual *as* copy, there would be no construct of heterosexuality *as* origin. Heterosexuality here presupposes homosexuality. And if the homosexual *as* copy *precedes* the heterosexual as *origin,* then it seems only fair to concede that the copy comes before the origin, and that homosexuality is thus the origin, and heterosexuality the copy.

But simple inversions are not really possible. For it is only *as* a copy that homosexuality can be argued to *precede* heterosexuality as the origin. In other words, the entire framework of copy and origin proves radically unstable as each position inverts into the other and confounds the possibility of any stable way to locate the temporal or logical priority of either term.

But let us then consider this problematic inversion from a psychic/political perspective. If the structure of gender imitation is such that the imitat*ed* is to some degree produced — or, rather, *re*produced — by imitation (see again Derrida's inversion and displacement of mimesis in "The Double Session"), then to claim that gay and lesbian identities are implicated in heterosexual norms or in hegemonic culture generally is not to *derive* gayness from straightness. On the contrary, *imitation* does not copy that which is prior, but produces and *inverts* the very terms of priority and derivativeness. Hence, if gay identities are implicated in heterosexuality, that is not the same as claiming that they are determined or derived from heterosexuality, and it is not the same as claiming that that heterosexuality is the only cultural network in which they are implicated. These are, quite literally, *inverted* imitations, ones which invert the order of imitated and imitation, and which, in the process, expose the fundamental dependency of "the origin" on that which it claims to produce as its secondary effect.

What follows if we concede from the start that gay identities as derivative inversions are in part defined in terms of the very heterosexual identities from which they are differentiated? If heterosexuality is an impossible imitation of itself, an imitation that performatively constitutes itself as the original, then the imitative parody of "heterosexuality" — when and where it exists in gay cultures — is always and only an imitation of an imitation, a copy of a copy, for which there is no original. Put in yet a different way, the parodic or imitative effect of gay identities works neither to copy nor to emulate heterosexuality, but rather, to expose heterosexuality as an incessant and *panicked* imitation of its own naturalized idealization. That heterosexuality is always in the act of elaborating itself is evidence that it is perpetually at risk, that is, that it "knows" its own possibility of becoming undone: hence, its compulsion to repeat which is at once a foreclosure of that which threatens its coherence. That it can never eradicate that risk attests to its profound dependency upon the homosexuality that it seeks fully to eradicate and never can or that it seeks to make second, but which is always already there as a prior possibility.[18] Although this failure of naturalized heterosexuality might constitute a source of pathos for heterosexuality itself — what its theorists often refer to as its constitutive malaise — it can become an occasion for a subversive and proliferating parody of gender norms in which the very claim to originality and to the real is shown to be the effect of a certain kind of naturalized gender mime.

It is important to recognize the ways in which heterosexual norms reappear within gay identities, to affirm that gay and lesbian identities are not only structured in part by dominant heterosexual frames, but that they are *not* for that reason *determined* by them. They are running commentaries on those naturalized positions as well, parodic replays and resignifications of precisely those heterosexual structures that would consign gay life to discursive domains of unreality and unthinkability. But to be constituted or structured in part by the very heterosexual norms by which gay people are oppressed is not, I repeat, to be claimed or determined by those structures. And it is not necessary to think of such heterosexual constructs as the pernicious intrusion of "the straight mind," one that must be rooted out in its entirety. In a way, the presence of heterosexual constructs and positionalities in whatever form in gay and lesbian identities presupposes that there is a gay and lesbian repetition of straightness, a racapitulation of straightness — which is itself a repetition and recapitulation of its own ideality — within its own terms, a site in which all sorts of resignifying and parodic repetitions become possible. The parodic replication and resignification of heterosexual constructs within non-heterosexual frames brings into relief the utterly constructed status of the so-called original, but it shows that heterosexuality only constitutes itself as the original through a convincing act of repetition. The more that "act" is expropriated, the more the heterosexual claim to originality is exposed as illusory.

Although I have concentrated in the above on the reality-effects of gender practices, performances, repetitions, and mimes, I do not mean to suggest that drag is a "role" that can be taken on or taken off at will. There is no volitional subject behind the mime who decides, as it were, which gender it will be today. On the contrary, the very possibility of becoming a viable subject requires that a certain gender mime be already under way. The "being" of the subject is no more self-identical than the "being" of any gender; in fact, coherent gender, achieved through an apparent repetition of the same, produces as its *effect* the illusion of a prior and volitional subject. In this sense, gender is not a performance that a prior subject elects to do, but gender is *performative* in the sense that it constitutes as an effect the very subject it appears to express. It is a *compulsory* performance in the sense that acting out of line with heterosexual norms brings with it ostracism, punishment, and violence, not to mention the

[18]Of course, it is Eve Kosofsky Sedgwick's *Epistemology of the Closet* (Berkeley: University of California Press, 1990) which traces the subtleties of this kind of panic in Western heterosexual epistemes. [Au.]

transgressive pleasures produced by those very prohibitions.

To claim that there is no performer prior to the performed, that the performance is performative, that the performance constitutes the appearance of a "subject" as its effect is difficult to accept. This difficulty is the result of a predisposition to think of sexuality and gender as "expressing" in some indirect or direct way a psychic reality that precedes it. The denial of the *priority* of the subject, however, is not the denial of the subject; in fact, the refusal to conflate the subject with the psyche marks the psychic as that which exceeds the domain of the conscious subject. This psychic excess is precisely what is being systematically denied by the notion of a volitional "subject" who elects at will which gender and/or sexuality to be at any given time and place. It is this excess which erupts within the intervals of those repeated gestures and acts that construct the apparent uniformity of heterosexual positionalities, indeed which compels the repetition itself, and which guarantees its perpetual failure. In this sense, it is this excess which, within the heterosexual economy, implicitly includes homosexuality, that perpetual threat of a disruption which is quelled through a reenforced repetition of the same. And yet, if repetition is the way in which power works to construct the illusion of a seamless heterosexual identity, if heterosexuality is compelled to *repeat itself* in order to establish the illusion of its own uniformity and identity, then this is an identity permanently at risk, for what if it fails to repeat, or if the very exercise of repetition is redeployed for a very different performative purpose? If there is, as it were, always a compulsion to repeat, repetition never fully accomplishes identity. That there is a need for a repetition at all is a sign that identity is not self-identical. It requires to be instituted again and again, which is to say that it runs the risk of becoming *de*-instituted at every interval.

So what is this psychic excess, and what will constitute a subversive or *de*-instituting repetition? First, it is necessary to consider that sexuality always exceeds any given performance, presentation, or narrative which is why it is not possible to derive or read off a sexuality from any given gender presentation. And sexuality may be said to exceed any definitive narrativization. Sexuality is never fully "expressed" in a performance or practice; there will be passive and butchy femmes, femmy and aggressive butches, and both of those, and more, will turn out to describe more or less anatomically stable "males" and "females." There are no direct expressive or causal lines between sex, gender, gender presentation, sexual practice, fantasy and sexuality. None of those terms captures or determines the rest. Part of what constitutes sexuality is precisely that which does not appear and that which, to some degree, can never appear. This is perhaps the most fundamental reason why sexuality is to some degree always closeted, especially to the one who would express it through acts of self-disclosure. That which is excluded for a given gender presentation to "succeed" may be precisely what is played out sexually, that is, an "inverted" relation, as it were, between gender and gender presentation, and gender presentation and sexuality. On the other hand, both gender presentation and sexual practices may corollate such that it appears that the former "expresses" the latter, and yet both are jointly constituted by the very sexual possibilities that they exclude.

This logic of inversion gets played out interestingly in versions of lesbian butch and femme gender stylization. For a butch can present herself as capable, forceful, and all-providing, and a stone butch may well seek to constitute her lover as the exclusive site of erotic attention and pleasure. And yet, this "providing" butch who seems *at first* to replicate a certain husband-like role, can find herself caught in a logic of inversion whereby that "providingness" turns to a self-sacrifice, which implicates her in the most ancient trap of feminine self-abnegation. She may well find herself in a situation of radical need, which is precisely what she sought to locate, find, and fulfill in her femme lover. In effect, the butch inverts into the femme or remains caught up in the specter of that inversion, or takes pleasure in it.[19] On the other hand, the femme who, as Amber Hollibaugh has argued, "orchestrates"

[19]Butler's argument here recapitulates Hegel's paradox of the master and the slave, in which the master, in his dependency, becomes in effect the slave to his slaves. [Ed.]

sexual exchange,[20] may well eroticize a certain dependency only to learn that the very power to orchestrate that dependency exposes her own incontrovertible power, at which point she inverts into a butch or becomes caught up in the specter of that inversion, or perhaps delights in it.

PSYCHIC MIMESIS

What stylizes or forms an erotic style and/or a gender presentation — and that which makes such categories inherently unstable — is a set of *psychic identifications* that are not simple to describe. Some psychoanalytic theories tend to construe identification and desire as two mutually exclusive relations to love objects that have been lost through prohibition and/or separation. Any intense emotional attachment thus divides into either wanting to have someone or wanting to be that someone, but never both at once. It is important to consider that identification and desire can coexist, and that their formulation in terms of mutually exclusive oppositions serves a heterosexual matrix. But I would like to focus attention on yet a different construal of that scenario, namely, that "wanting to be" and "wanting to have" can operate to differentiate mutually exclusive positionalities internal to lesbian erotic exchange. Consider that identifications are always made in response to loss of some kind, and that they involve a certain *mimetic practice* that seeks to incorporate the lost love within the very "identity" of the one who remains. This was Freud's thesis in "Mourning and Melancholia" in 1917 and continues to inform contemporary psychoanalytic discussions of identification.[21]

For psychoanalytic theorists Mikkel Borch-Jacobsen and Ruth Leys, however, identification and, in particular, identificatory mimetism, *precedes* "identity" and constitutes identity as that which is fundamentally "other to itself." The notion of this Other *in* the self, as it were, implies that the self/Other distinction is *not* primarily external (a powerful critique of ego psychology follows from this); the self is from the start radically implicated in the "Other." This theory of primary mimetism differs from Freud's account of melancholic incorporation. In Freud's view, which I continue to find useful, incorporation — a kind of psychic miming — is a response to, and refusal of, *loss*. Gender as the site of such psychic mimes is thus constituted by the variously gendered Others who have been loved and lost, where the loss is suspended through a melancholic and imaginary incorporation (and preservation) of those Others into the psyche. Over and against this account of psychic mimesis by way of incorporation and melancholy, the theory of primary mimetism argues an even stronger position in favor of the non-self-identity of the psychic subject. Mimetism is not motivated by a drama of loss and wishful recovery, but appears to precede and constitute desire (and motivation) itself; in this sense, mimetism would be prior to the possibility of loss and the disappointments of love.

Whether loss or mimetism is primary (perhaps an undecidable problem), the psychic subject is nevertheless constituted internally by differentially gendered Others and is, therefore, never, as a gender, self-identical.

In my view, the self only becomes a self on the condition that it has suffered a separation (grammar fails us here, for the "it" only becomes differentiated through that separation), a loss which is suspended and provisionally resolved through a melancholic incorporation of some "Other." That "Other" installed in the self thus establishes the permanent incapacity of that "self" to achieve self-identity; it is as it were always already disrupted by that Other; the disruption of the Other at the heart of the self is the very condition of that self's possibility.[22]

[20]Amber Hollibaugh and Cherríe Moraga, "What We're Rollin Around in Bed With: Sexual Silences in Feminism," in *Powers of Desire: The Politics of Sexuality,* ed. Ann Snitow, Christine Stansell, and Sharon Thompson (New York: Monthly Review Press, 1983), 394–405. [Au.]

[21]Mikkel Borch-Jacobsen, *The Freudian Subject* (Stanford: Stanford University Press, 1988); for citations of Ruth Leys's work, see the following two notes. [Au.]

[22]For a very fine analysis of primary mimetism with direct implications for gender formation, see Ruth Leys, "The Real Miss Beauchamp: The History and Sexual Politics of the Multiple Personality Concept," in *Feminists Theorize the Political,* eds. Judith Butler and Joan W. Scott (New York and London: Routledge, 1992). For Leys, a primary mimetism or suggestibility requires that the "self" from the start is consti-

Such a consideration of psychic identification would vitiate the possibility of any stable set of typologies that explain or describe something like gay or lesbian identities. And any effort to supply one — as evidenced in Kaja Silverman's recent inquiries into male homosexuality — suffer from simplification, and conform, with alarming ease, to the regulatory requirements of diagnostic epistemic regimes. If incorporation in Freud's sense in 1914 is an effort to *preserve* a lost and loved object and to refuse or postpone the recognition of loss and, hence, of grief, then to become *like* one's mother or father or sibling or other early "lovers" may be an act of love and/or a hateful effort to replace or displace. How would we "typologize" the ambivalence at the heart of mimetic incorporations such as these?[23]

How does this consideration of psychic identification return us to the question, what constitutes a subversive repetition? How are troublesome identifications apparent in cultural practices? Well, consider the way in which heterosexuality naturalizes itself through setting up certain illusions of continuity between sex, gender, and desire. When Aretha Franklin sings, "you make me feel like a natural woman," she seems at first to suggest that some natural potential of her biological sex is actualized by her participation in the cultural position of "woman" as object of heterosexual recognition. Something in her "sex" is thus expressed by her "gender" which is then fully known and consecrated within the heterosexual scene. There is no breakage, no discontinuity between "sex" as biological facticity and essence, or between gender and sexuality. Although Aretha appears to be all too glad to have her naturalness confirmed, she also seems fully and paradoxically mindful that that confirmation is never guaranteed, that the effect of naturalness is only achieved as a consequence of that moment of heterosexual recognition. After all, Aretha sings, you make me feel *like* a natural woman, suggesting that this is a kind of metaphorical substitution, an act of imposture, a kind of sublime and momentary participation in an ontological illusion produced by the mundane operation of heterosexual drag.

But what if Aretha were singing to me? Or what if she were singing to a drag queen whose performance somehow confirmed her own?

How do we take account of these kinds of identifications? It's not that there is some kind of *sex* that exists in hazy biological form that is somehow *expressed* in the gait, the posture, the gesture; and that some sexuality then expresses both that apparent gender or that more or less magical sex. If gender is drag, and if it is an imitation that regularly produces the ideal it attempts to approximate, then gender is a performance that *produces* the illusion of an inner sex or essence or psychic gender core; it *produces* on the skin, through the gesture, the move, the gait (that array of corporeal theatrics understood as gender presentation), the illusion of an inner depth. In effect, one way that gender gets naturalized is through being constructed as an inner psychic or physical *necessity*. And yet, it is always a surface sign, a signification on and with the public body that produces this illusion of an inner depth, necessity or essence that is somehow magically, causally expressed.

To dispute the psyche as *inner depth,* however, is not to refuse the psyche altogether. On the contrary, the psyche calls to be rethought precisely as a compulsive repetition, as that which conditions and disables the repetitive performance of identity. If every performance repeats itself to institute the effect of identity, then every repetition requires an interval between the acts, as it were, in which risk and excess threaten to

---

tuted by its incorporations; the effort to differentiate oneself from that by which one is constituted is, of course, impossible, but it does entail a certain "incorporative violence," to use her term. The violence of identification is in this way in the service of an effort at differentiation, to take the place of the Other who is, as it were, installed at the foundation of the self. That this replacement, which seeks to be a displacement, fails, and must repeat itself endlessly, becomes the trajectory of one's psychic career. [Au.]

[23]Here again, I think it is the work of Ruth Leys which will clarify some of the complex questions of gender constitution that emerge from a close psychoanalytic consideration of imitation and identification. Her forthcoming book manuscript will doubtless galvanize this field: *The Subject of Imitation.* [Au.]

disrupt the identity being constituted. The unconscious is this excess that enables and contests every performance, and which never fully appears within the performance itself. The psyche is not "in" the body, but in the very signifying process through which that body comes to appear; it is the lapse in repetition as well as its compulsion, precisely what the performance seeks to deny, and that which compels it from the start.

To locate the psyche within this signifying chain as the instability of all iterability[24] is not the same as claiming that it is inner core that is awaiting its full and liberatory expression. On the contrary, the psyche is the permanent failure of expression, a failure that has its values, for it impels repetition and so reinstates the possibility of disruption. What then does it mean to pursue disruptive repetition within compulsory heterosexuality?

Although compulsory heterosexuality often presumes that there is first a sex that is expressed through a gender and then through a sexuality, it may now be necessary fully to invert and displace that operation of thought. If a regime of sexuality mandates a compulsory performance of sex, then it may be only through that performance that the binary system of gender and the binary system of sex come to have intelligibility at all. It may be that the very categories of sex, of sexual identity, of gender are produced or maintained in the *effects* of this compulsory performance, effects which are disingenuously renamed as causes, origins, disingenuously lined up within a causal or expressive sequence that the heterosexual norm produces to legitimate itself as the origin of all sex. How then to expose the causal lines as retrospectively and performatively produced fabrications, and to engage gender itself as an inevitable fabrication, to fabricate gender in terms which reveal every claim to the origin, the inner, the true, and the real as nothing other than the effects of *drag,* whose subversive possibilities ought to be played and replayed to make the "sex" of gender into a site of insistent political play? Perhaps this will be a matter of working sexuality *against* identity, even against gender, and of letting that which cannot fully appear in any performance persist in its disruptive promise.

[24]See the introduction to Structuralism, Semiotics, and Deconstruction, p. 820. [Ed.]

9

MULTICULTURALISM AND THE CANON WARS: THE POLITICS OF LITERATURE

The reverence due to writings that have long subsisted arises therefore not from any credulous confidence in the superior wisdom of past ages. . . . but is the consequence of acknowledged and indubitable positions, that what has been longest known has been most considered, and what is most considered is best understood.
— SAMUEL JOHNSON

The endurance of a classic canonical author such as Homer . . . owes not to the alleged transcultural or universal value of his works but, on the contrary, to the continuity of their circulation in a particular culture.
— BARBARA HERRNSTEIN SMITH

The category of "literature" names the cultural capital of the old bourgeoisie, a form of capital increasingly marginal to the functioning of the present educational system.
— JOHN GUILLORY

THEORY OF THE CANON

What is a canon? The Greek word κανον literally denotes a straight rod or pole; figuratively, it is whatever keeps something straight: a rule. In a further figurative interpretation, the canon became the list of texts containing the rules that mattered — the books that held full religious authority. The establishment of this canon was the duty of the compilers of the Masoretic text of the Old Testament in the second century A.D. and of the patristic fathers establishing the New Testament in the third century. At that time the scrolls of Daniel and Esther were accepted into the canon, while the prophecies of Baruch ben Sirach and the chronicles of the Maccabees were relegated to apocryphal status; the gospels according to Matthew and Luke were given canonical authority, while the gospel of Nicodemus was discarded. In a third and far more recent figurative move, the word canon was applied to secular texts believed to embody the highest standards of literary culture. This chapter focuses on the questionings of the literary canon that have erupted in the last quarter century, as critics have debated the politics of canon formation and the question of how traditional definitions of the Western literary canon can be justified in a multicultural society. Also of concern is the issue of precisely what is at stake in the current canon wars.

To begin, any list of required reading a culture prescribes for its educated elite has to be tailored to fit the short span of a human life. Literature, therefore, has an ecology that forbids unlimited expansion: When something is added, something else must go. The debate over the literary canon began when poets realized that they were competing for fame, not merely with their coevals but with all their predecessors. Hence the Roman satirist Horace's remark, "I hate it when a book is condemned, not for being bad but for being new," which has been echoed by poet-critics for centuries thereafter.[1] But the contemporary debate over the canon is not entirely parallel with the poets' long-standing complaint that there cannot be room in Parnassus for everyone. The new focus in not so much on the *facts* of literary ecology, as on the *process* by which certain texts achieve canonical status, particularly the relationship between literary value and the more sordid matters of literary economics and politics.

Debate over the canon is something that has evolved, like the canon itself. For over a millennium, from the philosophers of classical times to the medieval and Renaissance followers of Plato, literary excellence was an objective predicate. Quality was defined as a measure of a poem's participation in the eternal forms of Truth, Goodness, and Beauty — ideas that were more truly real than the mutable material universe itself. Disagreements over taste were considered reflections of the defective nature of human perception and intelligence, its cloudy understanding of the eternal forms. The true canon — however mistily it might be revealed to us — was thought to be a canon for all time.

In the mid-eighteenth century Enlightenment, the notion of quality as an objective predicate was replaced (in the writings of philosophers such as David Hume and Immanuel Kant) by the notion of taste as a subjective universal. The idea that tastes are universal may seem ridiculous at first, as it is difficult to find even two people who share a majority of the same tastes. However, such diversity appears only when we compare things on roughly the same level of quality, where the distinctions are fine and the arguments subtle. We could argue for centuries whether Rembrandt or Michelangelo is the greater painter, but we do not often argue whether a Rembrandt is more or less beautiful than a lump of mud. Our agreement here need not depend on the existence of an objective Idea of the Beautiful: In fact there is no *objective* reason why a Rembrandt should be considered more beautiful than a lump of mud. Hume could account for the fact that over centuries and in various cultures 99.9999 percent of human beings have aesthetically preferred a paint-

[1]Horace, *Epistles* II. I. 76–77.

ing by Rembrandt to a lump of mud only by assuming that there exists something invariant over time and space that one might call "common human nature."[2]

As late as the mid-nineteenth century, in essays like Charles Augustin Sainte-Beuve's "What Is a Classic" (1850) or Matthew Arnold's "The Study of Poetry" (1888; see p. 411), literary value was assumed to be based upon human nature. Sainte-Beuve believes

> A true classic is an author who has enriched the human spirit, who has truly increased its treasure, who has caused it to take a step forward, who has discovered some unequivocal moral truth or laid fresh hold on some eternal passion in that heart where all seemed known and explored; who has conveyed his thought, his observation, or his discovery in whatever form, only let it be liberal and grand, choice and judicious, intrinsically wholesome and seemly; who has spoken to all men in a style of his own which at the same time turns out to be every man's style, a style which is new without neologism, at once new and old, easily contemporaneous with every age.[3]

Arnold appeals to "the best that has been known and thought in the world," as though that would be true for all time.

By the twentieth century the canon was seen as operating less throughout history than outside it altogether. In "Tradition and the Individual Talent" (1917), T. S. Eliot speaks of the literary "tradition" as an "ideal order" — a club to which new members, agreeable to the charter founders, are always welcome (see Eliot's essay, p. 499). Some philosophers still view canonical texts as operating outside history. In *Truth and Method* (1960), Hans-Georg Gadamer, mentor of the reception-theorists Wolfgang Iser and Hans Robert Jauss, defends the classic as "a truly historical category, a consciousness of something enduring, of significance that cannot be lost and is independent of all the circumstances of time." Like Hegel, who (in *Introduction to the Philosophy of Art*) understood the classic as "that which signifies itself and hence also interprets itself," Gadamer believes that the timelessness of the classic is in itself "a mode of historical being."[4]

[2]Hume's actual aesthetic comparison is between the puritan novelist John Bunyan and the elegant belletrist Joseph Addison, both of whom, in the mid-eighteenth century, had diametrically opposed reputations. The passing of two centuries has narrowed the perceived aesthetic gap between Bunyan and Addison considerably, so that a recasting of Hume's argument seems necessary to make its force felt. One can ask, but unfortunately not predict, whether the passage of another two centuries will narrow the aesthetic gap between a Rembrandt and a lump of mud. See Hume, p. 244.

[3]Charles Augustin de Sainte-Beuve, *Essays on Literature,* tr. Elizabeth Lee (London: Walter Scott Ltd., n.d.), pp. 14–15.

[4]See Gadamer, p. 677. In this sense, many old and respected works would not necessarily be classics. Trevor Ross argues, in *The Making of the English Literary Canon: From the Middle Ages to the Late Eighteenth Century* (Montreal: Queens-McGill University Press, 1997), that the Renaissance idea of a canon is one of texts whose excellence transcends time; it presumes, as Gadamer does, that such texts are unmediatedly available to the contemporary reader. By the eighteenth century, it began to be clear that even educated audiences could no longer un–self-consciously enjoy some of the finest specimens of, for example, Old English and Middle English poetry, and that the long tradition of English literature was in danger of being cut off from its roots. Around the 1760s, the genre of "literary history" arose (in major books like Thomas Warton's *History of English Poetry* [1774–81]) to help explain and contextualize texts which no longer were "classic" in Gadamer's sense: They did not "interpret themselves" any longer. For Ross, the idea of a "canon" and the idea of "literary history" are thus complementary. Prior to

ANTIFOUNDATIONALISM AND CANONICAL CHANGE

While all of these thinkers from Plato to Gadamer may disagree about whether beauty is an objective property of texts or a function of a common human nature, they all consider literary quality as a universal, and they all share a "foundationalist" discourse. That is, they all make strong, essentially unprovable assumptions about the nature of reality or society or human psychological processes that, if contested, leave their theories without explanatory power. In Western philosophy today, foundationalism is very much out of fashion, and most current theories on the canon avoid appealing to principles whose validity can be questioned.

One of the strongest antifoundationalist theories of canon-formation and change is that of Barbara Herrnstein Smith. In her essay, "Contingencies of Value" (1983), reprinted below, Smith argues that the public's initial estimation of a literary work's quality is the result of happenstance, rather than the work's possession of any absolute quality. Some works happen to meet the cultural and aesthetic needs of a particular reading public. As a society changes, such works take one of two trajectories: downward, to oblivion, or upward, toward canonical status; most do the former. Smith recognizes that even works that have achieved canonical status can, under unfavorable circumstances, drift into a "trajectory of extinction" — as the works of American poets Henry Wadsworth Longfellow and John Greenleaf Whittier seem to be doing. However, she argues that, once achieved, canonical status works to protect a text from this path, because "features that would, in a noncanonical work, be found alienating — ... technically crude, philosophically naive, or narrowly topical — will be glozed over[5] or backgrounded. . . ." Even when works are racially bigoted or chauvinistic, Smith believes "there will be a tendency among humanistic scholars and academic critics to 'save the text' by transferring the locus of its interest to more formal or structural features."

How do works get into the canon? It has been widely assumed that respected, magisterial critics like Samuel Johnson, Matthew Arnold, T. S. Eliot, and F. R. Leavis had a great deal to do with forming the canons of their day. According to Smith, though, social factors are usually more important than individual agents. For example, the politics of feminism during the past twenty years has sparked a growing interest in previously neglected female authors. However, the canon has not altered as much as one might expect given the rapid changes in society that have occurred over the past half-century. Strong conservative forces — including the very *idea* of a canon — operate to keep the canon constant. Institutional education may be the strongest of these. The literary texts most widely read today are those read in schools, and teachers are likely to teach texts that were valued when they were students. Furthermore, some texts may survive precisely because they are useful to

---

the eighteenth century, the canon was conceived in terms of production: literature as a way of circulating symbolic capital, or performing through rhetoric the instrumental functions of prompting readers into moral or other productive acts. By the late eighteenth century, the emphasis within canon-making shifted toward consumption, toward reading literature as a mode of self-enrichment or as a way of acquiring prestige for taste or scholarly expertise.

[5]Subjected to explanation and commentary; explained away.

educators: Xenophon's *Epigrapha* (4th century B.C.) may have survived into the nineteenth century not because of its literary quality but because it was a perfect vehicle for teaching children the principles of Greek syntax. Similarly, some poems may be surviving primarily because they are perfect examples of alliteration, symbolism, or some other prosodic or tropological feature that today's teachers like to explain.

In addition to educators, many other groups are responsible for preserving and altering the literary canon. Since education is an important conservative force, those who compile textbooks and anthologies function — more and more self-consciously these days — as both the preservers and reshapers of a tradition.[6] Henry Louis Gates, Jr., the editor of *The Norton Anthology of African American Literature,* and Sandra M. Gilbert and Susan Gubar, editors of *The Norton Anthology of Literature by Women,* are explicitly aware of their responsibilities as canon-makers. Yet, while editors of anthologies are indeed tastemakers, their tastes as individuals are seldom given free rein. Whatever an editor's ideas, a publisher has suggestions for inclusion and exclusion, and, after these are assimilated, the table of contents is sent to a long list of expert reviewers, who have their own notions of the canon. Editors themselves have reasons for repressing their personal tastes: Most want their books to sell, and that will happen only if the books provide what the teachers who assign textbooks want.

In this process, we find initiators (the authors of texts), mediators (editors, publishers, marketers, teachers), and ultimately consumers. The same structure exists for new works of fiction, though here book reviewers (and the editors and publishers who choose to promote certain titles more aggressively than others) have an important mediating role. In the nineteenth century, the editors of magazines determined which novels would be serialized — an important determinant of sales and reputation. The governing boards of circulating libraries (and some of these, like Mudie's, were large and influential) could often make or break reputations. All these mediators between author and reader are subject to the rigors of capitalism. They may indulge their personal tastes, but in doing so take an enormous risk: that the market may disagree and put them out of business.

None of these "accidental" factors in literary reputation stems from either a platonic Idea of the Beautiful or the notion of a common human nature. Literary quality is thus simply a function of the current interests of the reading public; each public revises the short lists drawn up by publics of the past in accordance with its own cultural needs. In effect, Smith's analysis leads to the conclusion that a text's

[6]While Alexander Pope wondered just when "British bards began t'immortalize," it seems that the process, in contemporary America at least, begins with the bards being Nortonized. *The Norton Anthology of English Literature,* with its near monopoly as a text for the standard "Beowulf to Virginia Woolf" British survey course, seems to be the established mirror of "the best that has been known and thought in the world," and canonization for poets once thought to be of merely historical interest, such as Lady Mary Wroth and Amelia Lanyer, begins when the poets find a spot, experimentally perhaps, in a new edition of the *Norton Anthology*. The logic of commerce, however, dictates that W. W. Norton also try to corner the market on African American and women's studies courses, both of which implicitly reject the notion of a single central canon.

acceptance into the canon is and always has been a political decision that can be influenced by interest groups with social and cultural agendas. The Western canon is (consciously or otherwise) a product of Eurocentrism and patriarchy, and deserves no particular respect for its antiquity; furthermore, Smith's analysis suggests that the works the old canon enshrines can be decanonized by a new politics operating within and outside academia.

Smith's article has been enormously controversial. While most of its detractors have been adherents of foundationalist arguments who have challenged her perspective on the relative and contingent nature of literary quality, some have argued that it is possible to find value and meaning in the old literary canon from an explicitly antifoundationalist perspective. The most interesting of these antifoundationalist challenges is that made by Charles Altieri in "The Idea and Ideal of Literary Canon." Altieri argues that Smith is correct in claiming that the literary canon reflects nothing more or less than a society's "interests" but wrong to jump to the conclusion that the current canon therefore has no legitimate authority. The question is how one defines "interest." Altieri insists that societies' interests are broader than "the desire for power over others" and "the pursuit of self-representations that satisfy narcissistic demands." In any heterogeneous society, Altieri argues, the literary canon is more expansive than any individual or group would wish and thereby exerts pressure on each reader to "undergo through imagination protean changes of identity and sympathy." This evolution gives readers access to other "possible worlds," other visions, and other values. According to Altieri, acceptance of a traditional canon leads to a pluralistic society, with individuals' egoism and group interests tempered by their having walked (as readers) in the shoes of various Others, whereas rejection of the ideal of a literary canon and promotion of counter-canons by special interest groups engaged in "identity politics" can lead only to a splintering of society into ever-narrower interest groups engaged in a war of each against all.[7]

MYTH AMERICA

Of course, some would argue that the traditional Western canon is itself the product of the ideology of a narrow interest group. Nina Baym's essay, "Melodramas of Beset Manhood" (1981), reprinted below, explicates the patriarchal ideology at the core of the traditional canon of American literature. Baym's historical research has revealed that women authors such as Susannah Rowson dominated the American fiction market in the decades before 1800, and that many women, including Harriet Beecher Stowe and Emma D. E. N. Southworth, were among the most widely read novelists in the nineteenth century. How did it happen, Baym asks, that by 1977 the canon "did not contain any women novelists"? Bracketing the overly simplistic hypotheses that women wrote nothing but sensational trash and that American literary historians were simply misogynistic bigots hostile to women's writing, Baym ex-

[7]Charles Altieri, "The Idea and Ideal of a Literary Canon," in *Canons and Consequences: Reflections on the Ethical Force of Imaginative Ideals* (Evanston, IL: Northwestern University Press, 1990), pp. 21–47.

plores the way the formation of an American canon was influenced by an emerging Idea of America. Texts were not evaluated according to an ostensibly pure aesthetic: Instead, the best American literature was believed to be that which most clearly reflected the current consensus as to what was quintessentially American. Various formulations of the essence of American culture were in competition in the early years of the twentieth century, but eventually a consensus formed around the myth "that in this new land, untrammeled by history and social accident, a person will be able to achieve complete self-definition. . . . Society exerts an unmitigatedly destructive pressure on individuality. . . . Thus . . . the essential quality of America comes to reside in its unsettled wilderness and the opportunities that such a wilderness offers to the individual as the medium on which he may inscribe, unhindered, his own destiny and his own nature."

A likely foundation for this vision of the essence of American culture is Frederick Jackson Turner's enormously influential historical study, *The Frontier in American History* (1920), with its nostalgic vision of the uniqueness of the American experiment until the closing of the Western frontier at the end of the nineteenth century. Although Baym does not specifically mention Turner's book, it was republished in 1947, and the books she accuses of peddling the American myth of the individual versus society (by Lionel Trilling, Henry Nash Smith, Charles Feidelson, R. W. B. Lewis, Richard Chase, and Daniel Hoffman) all appeared within the following decade. Whether the origin of the myth is Turner or, as Baym seems to think, Trilling, is immaterial: The result was that works in touch with this myth, like James Fenimore Cooper's *Leatherstocking Tales* (1823–41) and Nathaniel Hawthorne's *The Scarlet Letter* (1850), or ones that operated in some ironic relation to it, like Mark Twain's *Huckleberry Finn* (1885) and F. Scott Fitzgerald's *The Great Gatsby* (1925), were canonized at the expense of works, many of them by women, that centered on the discontents of civilization rather than the romance of the wilderness. But the issue is not purely a feminist one: Baym argues that writers like William Dean Howells and Henry James also posed a "continual challenge to the masculinist bias of American critical theory."

The opening chapter of Jane Tompkins's *Sensational Designs: The Cultural Work of American Fiction 1790–1860* (1985) examines a specific case which illustrates the effects of the cultural bias Baym discusses. Tompkins advocates the recanonization of Susan Warner's *The Wide, Wide World* (1855), a sentimental melodrama that was immensely popular in the mid–nineteenth century because it defined cultural stereotypes in an intelligible way for a public set adrift by the rapidity of social change. Tompkins argues that when we read pre-Civil War novelists like Hawthorne and Melville, we should recognize that it was not they but writers like Warner or Stowe who most closely defined the interests and tastes of the American public. After the Civil War, Warner's reputation declined, and might be entirely extinct except for her revival by recent literary historians and scholars of women's studies. As for Hawthorne, according to Tompkins, good fortune worked in his favor. His early survival was primarily due to his connections among the New England editorial and publishing circle, which kept his works alive through biographies and new editions for the twenty years after his death. After that, Hawthorne's balloon ascended, largely because his interest in colonial America melded with America's growing fascination with its past in the era of the 1876 centennial. More recently, his tortured heroes and heroines have found eager explicators among psychoanalytic critics of both Freudian and Jungian persuasions.

A dozen years after Tompkins's analysis there is as yet no evidence that *The Wide, Wide World* has entered the canon of American literature or that *The House of the Seven Gables* (1851) will be displaced. It is significant that for all the feminist interest in Warner and her mid-century sisters, Hawthorne's popularity continues unabated. Perhaps Hawthorne's own highly charged representations of women in the grip of patriarchy (in *The Scarlet Letter* and elsewhere) have found enough attackers and defenders among feminist readers to keep him in the forefront of critical attention — yet one more lucky break for the sage of Salem. Meanwhile, *The Wide, Wide World,* like many other once-forgotten works by women, is in print for the first time since the nineteenth century and available as a textbook for university courses.

COUNTER-CANONS AND IDENTITY POLITICS

Consolation prizes are notorious for not providing consolation, and the difference between a Nathaniel Hawthorne in every student's syllabus and a Susan Warner finally available in print is the difference between the canon and the penumbral fringe. And of course women writers are not the only group to have been marginalized by the Western literary canon. African Americans, Latinos/as, Asians, Native Americans, and many other groups have also been excluded or underrepresented.[8] Practically every reader is likely to identify with one or more of these interest groups, since apart from a relatively few native-born white male Christian heterosexuals of Western European descent, we all belong to at least one group engaged in "identity politics." The existence of the canon as a cultural monument from which writers of our own group (or groups) are either totally excluded or underrepresented creates a series of dilemmas. Should we accept the traditional Western canon while working to get this or that writer included, or promoted from minor to major status? Or should we reject the traditional canon, proclaiming an alternative "counter-canon" of texts by women, African Americans, Latinos, working-class writers, and others? This is not an easy choice, for the latter practice implicitly accepts the ghettoization of "minority" texts, while the former implicitly concedes the validity of the master's rules.

Current trends seem to favor the creation of "counter-canons." Many schools have founded special area studies programs devoted to texts by women, African Americans, Latinos and Latinas, Asian Americans, and Native Americans. While such programs have the benefit of giving students the opportunity of exposure to these areas, there may be a down side. Robert Hemenway argues that the current trend toward multiculturalism has resulted in "ghettoizing" African American writ-

[8]As Eve Kosofsky Sedgwick stresses in *Epistemology of the Closet* (see Ch. 8), gays and bisexuals are well represented in the canon, certainly in proportion to their presence in society at large. The problem is not neglect as such, but the homophobic "don't ask, don't tell" attitude of teachers and scholars toward the sexuality of gay writers.

ers into specific Black Literature courses, thereby leaving the required American literature survey course as lily-white as ever.[9] As the author of a prize-winning biography of Zora Neale Hurston, the latest African American writer to be adopted into the heart of the American canon, Hemenway may have reason to feel sanguine about the prospects for expanding the canon through integration, rather than through the formation of counter-canons. In contrast, Henry Louis Gates, Jr., whose first book came out of his discovery and republication of the first novel by a black woman (Harriet Wilson's *Our Nig* [1859]) and who is still series editor of the *Schomberg Library of Nineteenth-Century Black Women's Writing*, has opted for the creation of a counter-canon and has taken on the responsibility of defining an African American canon in the *Norton Anthology of African American Literature*, for which he is general editor.

In "Writing, 'Race,' and the Difference It Makes," reprinted in this chapter, Gates makes a strong case for the creation of a counter-canon by examining the history of doubt, expressed by freeborn Englishmen and slaveowners, as to whether people of African origin were truly human (that is, possessed of reason, the Enlightenment criterion of humanity) and able to be subjects as well as objects of discourse. Some seventeenth-century philosophers held that the "Negro" was not human at all, while Hume and Kant placed the African at the bottom of the human scale on the Great Chain of Being. The poems of Phillis Wheatley, a young African girl whose master had taught her to read and write both English and Latin, offended Thomas Jefferson's prejudice that blacks should be unable to write poetry, though it is not clear whether his contemptuous opinion — "the compositions published under her name are below the dignity of criticism" — was meant to dismiss the poems on the ground of quality, Wheatley's authorship, or both. To keep them from establishing their humanity through participation in the world of letters, slaves were forbidden to learn to write or read. Thus the slave narratives of African Americans, such as Frederick Douglass, William Wells Brown, and dozens of others, were assertions of their transgressive existence as subjects. But Gates argues that "black people . . . have not been 'liberated' from racism by their writings. . . . Black writing . . . served not to obliterate the difference of 'race,' . . . rather, the inscription of the black voice in Western literatures has preserved those very cultural differences to be imitated and revised in a separate Western literary tradition, a tradition of black difference."

For Gates, the African American writer is torn between two traditions: the written tradition of Western European culture into which African slaves were forcibly transplanted, and what he calls the "talking book" or the "speakerly text," the oral tradition of Africa that survives in the songs, legends, and stories of the people. In

[9]See Robert Hemenway, "In the American Canon," Reprinted in *Narrative/Theory*, ed. David Richter (White Plains: Longman, 1996), pp. 249–59. Collections like the *Heath Anthology of American Literature*, edited by Paul Lauter et al., seem to be motivated by a desire to radically reshape the American Literature survey course, by providing extensive materials written by previously ignored individuals and groups. But the *Heath* consists of six thousand pages of small print, only a small fraction of which can be visited during even a year's course of study. Many instructors who are in fullest sympathy with the anthology's motives tell me that they are still trying to figure out how to use it.

creating his prestigious *Norton Anthology of African American Literature*, Gates has not only included work songs and blues, legends and stories, but a cassette tape as well so that the "reader" can listen to the texts as performed. One might ask, though, whether Gates may be unfairly slanting the African American canon by privileging texts with the strongest oral roots at the expense of those that, written in an English indistinguishable from that of the oppressor, exploit the "double consciousness" W.E.B. Du Bois felt was the inevitable lot of the African American. For Gates, it would be Paul Laurence Dunbar's dialect poems, such as "Little Brown Baby" and "When Malindy Sings," rather than his poems written in standard English, like "We Wear the Mask" that would most fully express the African American tradition.[10]

There are dangers inherent in the attempt to essentialize some particular version of "blackness" as the core of the African American tradition. As Nina Baym complains in relation to the essentialization of "Americanness" as a mythic melodrama of beset manhood, every construction of an "essence" defines some writers as part of a tradition while excluding others. While there is no danger of his excluding African American women from his canon, it seems clear that Gates values the oral tradition descending from Esu-Elegbara, the African trickster figure, over a dense and "writerly" tradition of African American literature that pays allegiance to the white Master Henry James.[11] Such an identification of an oppressed minority with a particular mode of writing inevitably marginalizes those who write otherwise. Louis Owens once pronounced criteria for the Great Native American Novel, complete with requisite plot lines, themes, and narrative techniques — which, fortunately, his fellow novelists ignored. Such counter-canons come to inspire endless counter–counter-canons of the texts and writers they themselves have marginalized.

CAPITULATING CULTS AND CULTURAL CAPITAL

The "canon wars," as the media have dubbed the contemporary controversy to which the essays in this chapter refer, are generally characterized as a battle between cultural conservatives who defend a literary tradition of texts written by "dead white European males" and radicals who attack the conservative ideal of the Western literary canon as a way of espousing writers who have been ignored or rejected by that canon. At this point in the hostilities, the battle lines have long been drawn and the action has quieted down to a bit of sniping from the trenches. For both sides, the battle has, in effect, been lost and won.

[10]Gates extends his embrace of the counter-canon to literary theory as well, when he argues that "we must turn to the black tradition itself to arrive at theories of criticism indigenous to our literatures." There are ironies here, for, as is well known, Gates's national reputation exploded when he became the first African American critic to adopt poststructuralist theory in analyzing the oral traditions of African American literature. (See *The Signifying Monkey* [Chicago: University of Chicago Press, 1988].) Gates seems to be trying to insist that his acceptance of continental ideas and frames of reference is not innocent but "critical."

[11]Both James Baldwin and Ralph Ellison considered themselves heirs of James.

Harold Bloom's *The Western Canon: The Books and School of the Ages* opens and closes with two elegies for the canon, prophesying in the canonical voice of Jeremiah that

> what are now called "Departments of English" will be renamed departments of "Cultural Studies" where Batman comics, Mormon theme parks, television, movies and rock will replace Chaucer, Shakespeare, Milton, Wordsworth and Wallace Stevens. . . . This development hardly need be deplored; only a few handfuls of students now enter Yale with an authentic passion for reading. You cannot teach such love. How can you teach solitude?[12]

The publication of Bloom's book by Harcourt Brace, rather than a university press, and its immediate best-sellerhood, suggests that the American public, or that part of it that still buys trade hardbacks, is still firm in its commitment to a canon based on Homer, Dante, Shakespeare, and all the rest, and is happy to read *about* those texts as a preface to, or a substitute for, actually reading them. But Bloom's weary tone and flabby prose suggest that he has tired himself out preaching to the unconvertible, and that the students at Yale, New York University, and all the other schools where this indefatigable shaman teaches are considerably more eager to read Bloom the untraditional theorist than the texts of the tradition that made Bloom the reader he is.

The moral would seem to be that the canon of Western literature is secure except at the universities where it is supposed to be taught, studied, researched, and understood, and that what the world has witnessed on a large scale is a *trahison des clercs*, a betrayal on the part of the clerisy, a desertion of their post. If this is true, then there can be nothing very much at stake in the canon wars, since the books and their defenders remain at the center of Western culture no matter whether that center holds for the academic institutions at its periphery. If John Guillory is correct, however, the canon wars have been already decided, and the *status quo post bellum* is very different. Indeed it may be that much more is at stake even than the Western canon itself.

Based on Pierre Bourdieu's post-Marxist analysis of culture and class (see Ch. 6), John Guillory's *Cultural Capital: The Problem of Literary Canon Formation* (1993), reprinted in part below, interprets the canon wars as a symptom of a slow but massive shift in the class structure of the Western democracies. Guillory insists, in the first place, that the function of the school as institution is not peripheral but central to the class structure of capitalist society. Schools not only train the young in the specific information and skills they need to operate in a utilitarian society under capitalism, they also reproduce the structure of that society by creating young heirs to take their places within the social hierarchy. The class basis of culture requires the reproduction of "cultural capital" from one generation to the next, and in a society based on inequalities the distribution of such capital must be unequal: Some people must get more than others. The acquisition of a certain quantity of cultural capital is needed to produce the vision and discourse of a member of the ruling class

[12]Harold Bloom, *The Western Canon: The Books and School of the Ages* (New York: Harcourt Brace, 1994), p. 519.

and to distinguish him or her from social inferiors. There is no rule that allows one to predict precisely which forms of cultural capital will be valued in a particular time and place: The mandarins of the Ming Dynasty were required to know literary classics from the previous millennium, the aristocrats of the Enlightenment were required to be able to compose Latin and Greek verses, and the upper bourgeoisie of the nineteenth century were required to know and revere the classics of Western literature from Homer and Virgil through the early modern period. Needless to say, things are different now. Guillory writes that

> At the present moment, the nation-state still requires a relatively homogeneous language to administer its citizenry, but it no longer requires that a distinctive practice of that language identify a culturally homogeneous bourgeoisie. That class has long since been replaced by a culturally heterogeneous New Class, which has in turn been fully integrated into mass culture, a media culture mediating the desires of every class and group. In this "new phase of civilization" the historical function of the literary curriculum — to produce at the lower levels of the educational system a practice of Standard English and at the higher levels a more refined bourgeois language, a "literary" English — is no longer important to the social order. (p. 263)

The "crisis of the humanities," which is the name journalism has given to the flight of young men and women in the universities away from specializing in literature, history, and other traditional liberal arts subjects, is thus a purely utilitarian reaction. Students' future employers will want them to calculate market shares and perform multiple regressions, so the less time they spend developing an expertise in the liberal arts, the better. Guillory argues that professors of literature experience themselves as powerless precisely because they have become functionless. The allusive literary language that was once the possession of every successful businessman and bureaucrat is no longer a prerequisite for success. The one thing English departments do that still has genuine value for contemporary capitalism is training the university's students in composition and rhetoric. The art of incisive expository writing with "proper" diction and syntax, almost universally neglected at the primary and secondary levels of schooling, is still a necessary component of the education of the professional-managerial elite, one that in fact differentiates those who will rise to executive management positions from those who will stay at the lower sales and technical levels of the corporate structure. One irony is that, in the last two decades, composition training has itself become a specialization within the English faculty, rather than a natural and unspoken part of the expertise of any teacher of literature. Another is that most of the composition training at universities in the 1990s is done by underpaid graduate assistants serving apprenticeships to become professors of literature, who hope, if they are successful in their pursuit, to do less and less of what their society actually values.

The warfare over the canon represents, for Guillory, the thrashing about of a profession whose central preoccupation, literature, no longer has the significance for society that it once did. The humanities professoriate imagines that it could reclaim its usefulness within the educational system if it could only redefine the canon, or replace it with other objects of study. The problem, Guillory argues, is that the noncanonical texts that multiculturalists want to substitute for the Western canon do *not* in fact constitute a different form of cultural capital.

Meanwhile the revolution in the social order has made theory itself, rather than the canon, the center of the study of the humanities. Literary study, in order to be viewed as equivalent in value to the scientific and economic studies that are actually useful within the technical and bureaucratic culture of the current ruling class, had to be made more difficult and technical than heretofore, more rigorous, less a matter of genteel improvisation than the close readings that characterized the New Criticism. Just as the discipline of economics has become ever more pervasively mathematical, providing a factitious precision to its descriptions of the workings of society, literary studies has become wed to the technical rigor of rhetoric and philosophy. At the same time, theory itself has been routinized. As Guillory notes in *Cultural Capital,*

> Those authors or texts designated as "theoretical" are now increasingly capable of being introduced to students in traditional routinized forms, even by anthologies. It is difficult to imagine how graduate education could proceed at the present moment without recourse to a relatively standardized set of theoretical texts, which are employed not only in the context of "application" to works of literature but also in the seminar on theory. (p. 260)

The logic of the structural shift of the ruling class in capitalism has driven the task of the humanities from the comprehension and reproduction of the canon of Western literature to the understanding and reproduction of the canon of literary theory, of what one might call the critical tradition. The book you hold in your hands is evidence of this sea-change in the structure of the class system, the school, and the humanities, and we are all, I am afraid — students and teachers alike — in on this together. *Adieu, hypocrite lecteur: mon semblable, mon frère.*[13]

Selected Bibliography

Adams, Hazard. "Canons: Literary Criteria/Power Criteria." *Critical Inquiry* 14 (1988): 748–64.

Atlas, James. *Battle of the Books: The Curriculum Debate in America*. New York: Norton, 1990.

Baker, Houston A., Jr. "The Promised Body: Reflections on Canon in an Afro-American Context." *Poetics Today* 9 (1988): 339–55.

Baraka, Amiri. "Cultural Revolution and the Literary Canon." *Callaloo* 14 (1991): 150–56.

Berman, Paul, ed. *Debating P.C.: The Controversy over Political Correctness on College Campuses*. New York: Laurel, 1992.

Ezell, Margaret J. M. "The Myth of Judith Shakespeare: Creating the Canon of Women's Literature." *New Literary History* 21 (1990): 579–92.

Foley, Barbara. "What's at Stake in the Culture Wars." *New England Quarterly* 68 (1995): 458–79.

[13]"Farewell, hypocritical reader: my likeness, my brother." From Charles Baudelaire's preface to *Les Fleurs du mal* (1857).

Garber, Marjorie. "'Greatness': Philology and the Politics of Mimesis." *Boundary2* 19 (1992): 233–59.

Gates, Henry Louis, Jr. "Canon Formation, Literary History, and the Afro-American Tradition: From the Seen to the Told." In *Afro-American Literary Study in the 1990s*, ed. Houston Baker and Patricia Redmond. Chicago: University of Chicago Press, 1989, pp. 14–50.

Gilbert, Sandra M., and Susan Gubar. *Masterpiece Theatre: An Academic Melodrama.* New Brunswick: Rutgers University Press, 1995.

Gless, Darryl J., and Barbara Herrnstein Smith, eds. *The Politics of Liberal Education.* Durham, NC: Duke University Press, 1990.

Guillory, John. *Cultural Capital: The Problem of Literary Canon Formation.* Chicago: University of Chicago Press, 1993.

Harris, Wendell V. "Canonicity." *PMLA* 106 (1991): 110–21.

Hemenway, Robert. "In the American Canon." In *Redefining American Literary History*, ed. A. Lavonne Ruoff and Jerry Ward. New York: MLA Press, 1990, pp. 62–72.

Hirsch, E. D., Jr. "Cultural Literacy." In *Literacy: Language and Power*, ed. Dianne L. Vipond and Ronald Strahl. Long Beach: University Press of California State, 1994, pp. 104–14.

Hutcheon, Linda. "Loading the Canon." *University of Toronto Quarterly* 63 (1993): pp. 369–74.

Jameson, Fredric. "Third World Literature in the Era of Multinational Capitalism." *Pretexts* 3 (1991): 82–104.

Jay, Gregory S. "The Discipline of the Syllabus." In *Reconceptualizing American Literary/Cultural Studies: Rhetoric, History, and Politics in the Humanities*, ed. William E. Cain. New York: Garland, 1996, pp. 101–16.

Kermode, Frank. "Canons." *Dutch Quarterly Review* 18 (1988): 258–70.

Kimball, Roger. "The Academy Debates the Canon." *The New Criterion* 6 (1987): 31–43.

Lauter, Paul. "Canon Theory and Emergent Practice." In *Left Politics and the Literary Profession*, ed. Lennard Davis and Bella Mirabella. New York: Columbia University Press, 1990, pp. 127–46.

Lawrence, Karen R., ed. *Decolonizing Tradition: New Views of Twentieth-Century "British" Literary Canon.* Urbana: University of Illinois Press, 1992.

Lerner, Laurence. "Subverting the Canon." *British Journal of Aesthetics* 32 (1992): 347–58.

McCrea, Brian. *Addison and Steele Are Dead: The English Department, Its Canon, and the Professionalization of Literary Criticism.* Newark: University of Delaware Press, 1990.

McGann, Jerome. "Canonade." *New Literary History* 25 (1994): 487–504.

Nemoianu, Virgil, and Robert Royal, eds. *The Hospitable Canon: Essays on Literary Play, Scholarly Choice, and Popular Pressures.* Philadelphia: Benjamins, 1991.

Palumbo-Liu, David, ed. *The Ethnic Canon: Histories, Institutions, and Interventions.* Minneapolis: University of Minnesota Press, 1995.

Peer, Willie van. "Canon Formation: Ideology or Aesthetic Quality?" *British Journal of Aesthetics* 36 (1996): 97–108.

Robinson, Lillian S. "Canon Fathers and Myth Universe." In *Left Politics and the Literary Profession*, ed. Lennard Davis and Bella Mirabella. New York: Columbia University Press, 1990, pp. 147–61.

Ross, Trevor. "Just When Did 'British Bards Begin t'Immortalize'?" *Studies in Eighteenth Century Culture* 19 (1989): 383–98.

———. "The Emergence of 'Literature': Making and Reading the English Canon in the Eighteenth Century." *ELH* 63 (1996): 397–422.

Scholes, Robert. "Canonicity and Textuality." In *Introduction to Scholarship in Modern Languages and Literatures*. New York: MLA Press, 1992, pp. 138–58.

Spivak, Gayatri Chakravorty. "How To Read a 'Culturally Different' Book." In *Colonial Discourse/Postcolonial Theory*, ed. Francis Barker et al. Manchester: Manchester University Press, 1994, pp. 126–50.

Verhoeven, W. M., ed. *Rewriting the Dream: Reflections on the Changing American Literary Canon*. Amsterdam: Rodopi, 1992.

West, Cornel. "Minority Discourse and the Pitfalls of Canon Formation." *Yale Journal of Criticism* 1 (1987): 193–201.

Nina Baym

b. 1936

Nina Baym's work has been instrumental in bringing about academic recognition of women's studies across the United States. Born in Princeton, New Jersey, Baym received her B.A. from Cornell University (1957) and her M.A. (1958) and Ph.D. (1963) in English from Harvard University. Since receiving her doctorate, Baym has taught English and American literature at the University of Illinois at Urbana-Champaign, where she became a full professor in 1972 and Director of the School of Humanities in 1976. Baym has been a Guggenheim fellow (1975–76) and a fellow of the National Endowment for the Humanities (1982–83). She has served on the editorial boards of several major journals, including American Quarterly, New England Quarterly, *and* American Literature, *and is an editor of* The Norton Anthology of American Literature. *Her publications include* The Shape of Hawthorne's Career *(1976),* Woman's Fiction: A Guide to Novels by and about Women in America (1820–1870) *(1978),* Nathaniel Hawthorne and His Mother *(1982),* Novels, Readers, and Reviewers: Responses to Fiction in Antebellum America *(1984), and* Feminism and American Literary History *(1992). "Melodramas of Beset Manhood" is reprinted from* American Quarterly *33 (1981).*

Melodramas of Beset Manhood

How Theories of American Fiction Exclude Women Authors

This paper is about American literary criticism rather than American literature. It proceeds from the assumption that we never read American literature directly or freely, but always through the perspective allowed by theories. Theories account for the inclusion and exclusion of texts in anthologies, and theories account for the way we read them. My concern is with the fact that the theories controlling our reading of American literature have led to the exclusion of women authors from the canon.

Let me use my own practice as a case in point. In 1977 there was published a collection of essays on images of women in major British and American literature, to which I contributed.[1] The American field was divided chronologically

[1]Marlene Springer, ed., *What Manner of Woman: Essays on English and American Life and Literature* (New York: New York University Press, 1977). [Au.]

among six critics, with four essays covering literature written prior to World War II. Taking seriously the charge that we were to focus only on the major figures, the four of us — working quite independently of each other — selected altogether only four women writers. Three of these were from the earliest period, a period which predates the novel: the poet Anne Bradstreet and the two diarists Mary Rowlandson and Sarah Kemble Knight. The fourth was Emily Dickinson. For the period between 1865 and 1940 no women were cited at all. The message that we — who were taking women as our subject — conveyed was clear: there have been almost no major women writers in America; the major novelists have all been men.

Now, when we wrote our essays we were not undertaking to reread all American literature and make our own decisions as to who the major authors were. That is the point: we accepted the going canon of major authors. As late as 1977, that canon did not include any women novelists. Yet, the critic who goes beyond what is accepted and tries to look at the totality of literary production in America quickly discovers that women authors have been active since the earliest days of settlement. Commercially and numerically they have probably dominated American literature since the middle of the nineteenth century. As long ago as 1854, Nathaniel Hawthorne complained to his publisher about the "damned mob of scribbling women" whose writings — he fondly imagined — were diverting the public from his own.

Names and figures help make this dominance clear. In the years between 1774 and 1799 — from the calling of the First Continental Congress to the close of the eighteenth century — a total of thirty-eight original works of fiction were published in this country.[2] Nine of these, appearing pseudonymously or anonymously, have not yet been attributed to any author. The remaining twenty-nine are the work of eighteen individuals, of whom four are women. One of these women, Susannah Rowson, wrote six of them, or more than a fifth of the total. Her most popular work, *Charlotte* (also known as *Charlotte Temple*), was printed three times in the decade it was published, nineteen times between 1800 and 1810, and eighty times by the middle of the nineteenth century. A novel by a second of the four women, Hannah Foster, was called *The Coquette* and had thirty editions by mid-nineteenth century. *Uncle Tom's Cabin*, by a woman, is probably the all-time biggest seller in American history. A woman, Mrs. E.D.E.N. Southworth, was probably the most widely read novelist in the nineteenth century. How is it possible for a critic or historian of American literature to leave these books, and these authors, out of the picture?

I see three partial explanations for the critical invisibility of the many active women authors in America. The first is simple bias. The critic does not like the idea of women as writers, does not believe that women can be writers, and hence does not see them even when they are right before his eyes. His theory or his standards may well be nonsexist but his practice is not. Certainly, an *a priori* resistance to recognizing women authors as serious writers has functioned powerfully in the mind-set of a number of influential critics. One can amusingly demonstrate the inconsistencies between standard and practice in such critics, show how their minds slip out of gear when they are confronted with a woman author. But this is only a partial explanation.

A second possibility is that, in fact, women have not written the kind of work that we call "excellent," for reasons that are connected with their gender although separable from it. This is a serious possibility. For example, suppose we required a dense texture of classical allusion in all works that we called excellent. Then, the restriction of a formal classical education to men would have the effect of restricting authorship of excellent literature to men. Women would not have written excellent literature because social conditions hindered them. The reason, though gender-connected, would not be gender per se.

The point here is that the notion of the artist, or of excellence, has efficacy in a given time and reflects social realities. The idea of "good" literature is not only a personal preference, it is also a cultural preference. We can all think of species

[2]See Lyle H. Wright, *American Fiction: A Contribution Towards a Bibliography*, vol. 1, *1774–1850*, 2d ed. (San Marino, Calif.: Huntington Library Press, 1969). [Au.]

of women's literature that do not aim in any way to achieve literary excellence as society defines it: for example, the "Harlequin Romances." Until recently, only a tiny proportion of literary women aspired to artistry and literary excellence in the terms defined by their own culture. There tended to be a sort of immediacy in the ambitions of literary women leading them to professionalism rather than artistry, by choice as well as by social pressure and opportunity. The gender-related restrictions were really operative, and the responsible critic cannot ignore them. But again, these restrictions are only partly explanatory.

There are, finally, I believe, gender-related restrictions that do not arise out of cultural realities contemporary with the writing woman, but out of later critical theories. These theories may follow naturally from cultural realities pertinent to their own time, but they impose their concerns anachronistically, after the fact, on an earlier period. If one accepts current theories of American literature, one accepts as a consequence — perhaps not deliberately but nevertheless inevitably — a literature that is essentially male. This is the partial explanation that I shall now develop.

Let us begin where the earliest theories of American literature begin, with the hypothesis that American literature is to be judged less by its form than by its content. Traditionally, one ascertains literary excellence by comparing a writer's work with standards of performance that have been established by earlier authors, where formal mastery and innovation are paramount. But from its historical beginnings, American literary criticism has assumed that literature produced in this nation would have to be ground-breaking, equal to the challenge of the new nation, and completely original. Therefore, it could not be judged by referring it back to earlier achievements. The earliest American literary critics began to talk about the "most American" work rather than the "best" work because they knew no way to find out the best other than by comparing American with British writing. Such a criticism struck them as both unfair and unpatriotic. We had thrown off the political shackles of England; it would not do for us to be servile in our literature. Until a tradition of American literature developed its own inherent forms, the early critic looked for a standard of Americanness rather than a standard of excellence. Inevitably, perhaps, it came to seem that the quality of "Americanness," whatever it might be, *constituted* literary excellence for American authors. Beginning as a nationalistic enterprise, American literary criticism and theory has retained a nationalist orientation to this day.

Of course, the idea of Americanness is even more vulnerable to subjectivity than the idea of the best. When they speak of "most American," critics seldom mean the statistically most representative or most typical, the most read or the most sold. They have some qualitative essence in mind, and frequently their work develops as an explanation of this idea of "American" rather than a description and evaluation of selected authors. The predictable recurrence of the term "America" or "American" in works of literary criticism treating a dozen or fewer authors indicates that the critic has chosen his authors on the basis of their conformity to his idea of what is truly American. For examples: *American Renaissance, The Romance in America, Symbolism and American Literature, Form and Fable in American Fiction, The American Adam, The American Novel and Its Tradition, The Place of Style in American Literature* (a subtitle), *The Poetics of American Fiction* (another subtitle). But an idea of what is American is no more than an idea, needing demonstration. The critic all too frequently ends up using his chosen authors as demonstrations of Americanness, arguing through them to his definition.

So Marius Bewley explains in *The Eccentric Design* that "for the American artist there was no social surface responsive to his touch. The scene was crude, even beyond successful satire," but later, in a concluding chapter titled "The Americanness of the American Novel," he agrees that "this 'tradition' as I have set it up here has no room for the so-called realists and naturalists."[3] F. O. Matthiessen, whose *American Renaissance*

[3]Marius Bewley, *The Eccentric Design: Form in the Classic American Novel* (New York: Columbia University Press, 1963), pp. 15, 291. [Au.]

enshrines five authors, explains that "the one common denominator of my five writers, uniting even Hawthorne and Whitman, was their devotion to the possibilities of democracy."[4] The jointly written *Literary History of the United States* proclaims in its "address to the reader" that American literary history "will be a history of the books of the great and the near-great writers in a literature which is most revealing when studied as a by-product of American experience."[5] And Joel Porte announces confidently in *The Romance in America* that "students of American literature . . . have provided a solid theoretical basis for establishing that the rise and growth of fiction in this country is dominated by our authors' conscious adherence to a tradition of nonrealistic romance sharply at variance with the broadly novelistic mainstream of English writing. When there has been disagreement among recent critics as to the contours of American fiction, it has usually disputed, not the existence per se of a romance tradition, but rather the question of which authors, themes, and stylistic strategies *deserve* to be placed with certainty at the heart of that tradition" (emphasis added).[6]

Before he is through, the critic has had to insist that some works in America are much more American than others, and he is as busy excluding certain writers as "un-American" as he is including others. Such a proceeding in the political arena would be extremely suspect, but in criticism it has been the method of choice. Its final result goes far beyond the conclusion that only a handful of American works are very good. *That* statement is one we could agree with, since very good work is rare in any field. But it is odd indeed to argue that only a handful of American works are really American.[7]

[4]F. O. Matthiessen, *American Renaissance* (New York: Oxford University Press, 1941), p. ix. [Au.]

[5]Robert E. Spiller et al., eds., *Literary History of the United States* (New York: Macmillan, 1959), p. xix. [Au.]

[6]Joel Porte, *The Romance in America: Studies in Cooper, Poe, Hawthorne, Melville, and James* (Middletown, Conn.: Wesleyan University Press, 1969), p. ix. [Au.]

[7]A good essay on this topic is William C. Spengemann's "What Is American Literature?" *Centennial Review* 22 (Spring 1978): 119–38. [Au.]

Despite the theoretical room for an infinite number of definitions of Americanness, critics have generally agreed on it — although the shifting canon suggests that agreement may be a matter of fad rather than fixed objective qualities.[8] First, America as a nation must be the ultimate subject of the work. The author must be writing about aspects of experience and character that are American only, setting Americans off from other people and the country from other nations. The author must be writing his story specifically to display these aspects, to meditate on them, and to derive from them some generalizations and conclusions about "the" American experience. To Matthiessen the topic is the possibilities of democracy; Sacvan Bercovitch (in *The Puritan Origins of the American Self*) finds it in American identity. Such content excludes, at one extreme, stories about universals, aspects of experience common to people in a variety of times and places — mutability, mortality, love, childhood, family, betrayal, loss. Innocence versus experience is an admissible theme *only* if innocence is the essence of the American character, for example.

But at the other extreme, the call for an overview of America means that detailed, circumstantial portrayals of some aspect of American life are also, peculiarly, inappropriate: stories of wealthy New Yorkers, Yugoslavian immigrants, Southern rustics. Jay B. Hubbell rather ingratiatingly admits as much when he writes, "in both my teaching and my research I had a special interest in literature as a reflection of American life and thought. This circumstance may explain in part why I found it difficult to appreciate the merits of the expatriates and why I was slow in doing justice to some of the New Critics. I was repelled by the sordid subject matter found in some of the novels written by Dreiser, Dos Passos, Faulkner, and some others."[9] Richard Poirier writes that "the books which in my view constitute a distinctive American tradition . . . resist within their pages forces of environment that oth-

[8]See Jay B. Hubbell, *Who Are the Major American Authors?* (Durham, N.C.: Duke University Press, 1972). [Au.]

[9]Ibid., pp. 335–36. [Au.]

erwise dominate the world," and he distinguishes this kind from "the fiction of Mrs. Wharton, Dreiser, or Howells."[10] The *Literary History of the United States* explains that "historically, [Edith Wharton] is likely to survive as the memorialist of a dying aristocracy."[11] And so on. These exclusions abound in all the works which form the stable core of American literary criticism at this time.

Along with Matthiessen, the most influential exponent of this exclusive Americanness is Lionel Trilling, and his work has particular applicability because it concentrates on the novel form. Here is a famous passage from his 1940 essay, "Reality in America," in which Trilling is criticizing Vernon Parrington's selection of authors in *Main Currents in American Thought:*

> A culture is not a flow, nor even a confluence: the form of its existence is struggle — or at least debate — it is nothing if not a dialectic. And in any culture there are likely to be certain artists who contain a large part of the dialectic within themselves, their meaning and power lying in their contradictions: they contain within themselves, it may be said, the very essence of the culture. To throw out Poe because he cannot be conveniently fitted into a theory of American culture . . . to find his gloom to be merely personal and eccentric . . . as Hawthorne's was . . . to judge Melville's response to American life to be less noble than that of Bryant or of Greeley, to speak of Henry James as an escapist . . . this is not merely to be mistaken in aesthetic judgment. Rather it is to examine without attention and from the point of view of a limited and essentially arrogant conception of reality the documents which are in some respects the most suggestive testimony to what America was and is, and of course to get no answer from them.[12]

Trilling's immediate purpose is to exclude Greeley and Bryant from the list of major authors and to include Poe, Melville, Hawthorne, and James. We probably share Trilling's aesthetic judgment. But note that he does not base his judgment on aesthetic grounds; indeed, he dismisses aesthetic judgment with the word "merely." He argues that Parrington has picked the wrong artists because he doesn't understand the culture. Culture is his real concern.

But what makes Trilling's notion of culture more valid than Parrington's? Trilling really has no argument; he resorts to such value-laden rhetoric as "a limited and essentially arrogant conception of reality" precisely because he cannot objectively establish his version of culture over Parrington's. For the moment, there are two significant conclusions to draw from this quotation. First, the disagreement is over the nature of our culture. Second, there is no disagreement over the value of literature — it is valued as a set of "documents" which provide "suggestive testimony to what America was and is."

One might think that an approach like this which is subjective, circular, and in some sense nonliterary or even antiliterary would not have had much effect. But clearly Trilling was simply carrying on a longstanding tradition of searching for cultural essence, and his essays gave the search a decided and influential direction toward the notion of cultural essence as some sort of tension. Trilling succeeded in getting rid of Bryant and Greeley, and his choice of authors is still dominant. They all turn out — and not by accident — to be white, middle-class, male, of Anglo-Saxon derivation or at least from an ancestry which had settled in this country before the big waves of immigration which began around the middle of the nineteenth century. In every case, however, the decision made by these men to become professional authors pushed them slightly to one side of the group to which they belonged. This slight alienation permitted them to belong, and yet not to belong, to the so-called "mainstream." These two aspects of their situation — their membership in the dominant middle-class white Anglo-Saxon group, and their modest alienation from it — defined their boundaries, enabling them to "contain within themselves" the "contradictions" that, in Trilling's view, constitute the "very essence of the culture." I will call the literature they pro-

[10]Richard Poirier, *A World Elsewhere: The Place of Style in American Literature* (New York: Oxford University Press, 1966), p. 5. [Au.]

[11]Spiller et al., *Literary History of the United States*, p. 1211. [Au.]

[12]Lionel Trilling, *The Liberal Imagination* (Garden City, N.Y.: Anchor Books, 1950), pp. 7–9. [Au.]

duced, which Trilling assesses so highly, a "consensus criticism of the consensus."

This idea plainly excludes many groups but it might not seem necessarily to exclude women. In fact, nineteenth-century women authors were overwhelmingly white, middle-class, and Anglo-Saxon in origin. Something more than what is overtly stated by Trilling (and others cited below) is added to exclude them. What critics have done is to assume, for reasons shortly to be expounded, that the women writers invariably represented the consensus, rather than the criticism of it; to assume that their gender made them part of the consensus in a way that prevented them from partaking in the criticism. The presence of these women and their works is acknowledged in literary theory and history as an impediment and obstacle, that which the essential American literature had to criticize as its chief task.

So, in his lively and influential book of 1960, *Love and Death in the American Novel*, Leslie Fiedler describes women authors as creators of the "flagrantly bad best-seller" against which "our best fictionists" — all male — have had to struggle for "their integrity and their livelihoods."[13] And, in a 1978 reader's introduction to an edition of Charles Brockden Brown's *Wieland*, Sydney J. Krause and S. W. Reid write as follows:

> What it meant for Brown personally, and belles lettres in America historically, that he should have decided to write professionally is a story unto itself. Americans simply had no great appetite for serious literature in the early decades of the Republic — certainly nothing of the sort with which they devoured . . . the ubiquitous melodramas of beset womanhood, "tales of truth," like Susanna Rowson's *Charlotte Temple* and Hannah Foster's *The Coquette*.[14]

There you see what has happened to the woman writer. She has entered literary history as the enemy. The phrase "tales of truth" is put in quotes by the critics, as though to cast doubt on the very notion that a "melodrama of beset womanhood" could be either true or important. At the same time, ironically, they are proposing for our serious consideration, as a candidate for intellectually engaging literature, a highly melodramatic novel with an improbable plot, inconsistent characterizations, and excesses of style that have posed tremendous problems for all students of Charles Brockden Brown. But by this strategy it becomes possible to begin major American fiction historically with male rather than female authors. The certainty here that stories about women could not contain the essence of American culture means that the matter of American experience is inherently male. And this makes it highly unlikely that American women would write fiction encompassing such experience. I would suggest that the theoretical model of a story which may become the vehicle of cultural essence is: "a melodrama of beset manhood." This melodrama is presented in a fiction which, as we will later see, can be taken as representative of the author's literary experience, his struggle for integrity and livelihood against flagrantly bad best-sellers written by women. Personally beset in a way that epitomizes the tensions of our culture, the male author produces his melodramatic testimony to our culture's essence — so the theory goes.

Remember that the search for cultural essence demands a relatively uncircumstantial kind of fiction, one which concentrates on national universals (if I may be pardoned the paradox). This search has identified a sort of nonrealistic narrative, a romance, a story free to catch an essential, idealized American character, to intensify his essence and convey his experience in a way that ignores details of an actual social milieu. This nonrealistic or antisocial aspect of American fiction is noted — as a fault — by Trilling in a 1947 essay, "Manners, Morals, and the Novel." Curiously, Trilling here attacks the same group of writers he had rescued from Parrington in "Reality in America." But, never doubting that his selection represents "the" American authors, he goes ahead with the task that really interests him

[13]Leslie Fiedler, *Love and Death in the American Novel* (New York: Criterion Books, 1960), p. 93. [Au.]

[14]Charles Brockden Brown, *Wieland*, ed. Sydney J. Krause and S. W. Reid (Kent, Ohio: Kent State University Press, 1978), p. xii. [Au.]

— criticizing the culture through its representative authors:

> The novel in America diverges from its classic [i.e., British] intention which . . . is the investigation of the problem of reality beginning in the social field. The fact is that American writers of genius have not turned their minds to society. Poe and Melville were quite apart from it; the reality they sought was only tangential to society. Hawthorne was acute when he insisted that he did not write novels but romances — he thus expressed his awareness of the lack of social texture in his work. . . . In America in the nineteenth century, Henry James was alone in knowing that to scale the moral and aesthetic heights in the novel one had to use the ladder of social observation.[15]

Within a few years after publication of Trilling's essay, a group of Americanists took its rather disapproving description of American novelists and found in this nonrealism or romanticism the essentially American quality they had been seeking. The idea of essential Americanness then developed in such influential works of criticism as *Virgin Land* by Henry Nash Smith (1950), *Symbolism and American Literature* by Charles Feidelson (1953), *The American Adam* by R. W. B. Lewis (1955), *The American Novel and Its Tradition* by Richard Chase (1957), and *Form and Fable in American Fiction* by Daniel G. Hoffman (1961). These works, and others like them, were of sufficiently high critical quality, and sufficiently like each other, to compel assent to the picture of American literature that they presented. They used sophisticated New Critical close-reading techniques to identify a myth of America which had nothing to do with the classical fictionist's task of chronicling probable people in recognizable social situations.

The myth narrates a confrontation of the American individual, the pure American self divorced from specific social circumstances, with the promise offered by the idea of America. This promise is the deeply romantic one that in this new land, untrammeled by history and social accident, a person will be able to achieve complete self-definition. Behind this promise is the assurance that individuals come before society, that they exist in some meaningful sense prior to, and apart from, societies in which they happen to find themselves. The myth also holds that, as something artificial and secondary to human nature, society exerts an unmitigatedly destructive pressure on individuality. To depict it at any length would be a waste of artistic time; and there is only one way to relate it to the individual — as an adversary.

One may believe all this and yet look in vain for a way to tell a believable story that could free the protagonist from society or offer the promise of such freedom, because nowhere on earth do individuals live apart from social groups. But in America, given the original reality of large tracts of wilderness, the idea seems less a fantasy, more possible in reality or at least more believable in literary treatment. Thus it is that the essential quality of America comes to reside in its unsettled wilderness and the opportunities that such a wilderness offers to the individual as the medium on which he may inscribe, unhindered, his own destiny and his own nature.

As the nineteenth century wore on, and settlements spread across the wilderness, the struggle of the individual against society became more and more central to the myth; where, let's say, Thoreau could leave in chapter 1 of *Walden*, Huckleberry Finn has still not made his break by the end of chapter 42 (the conclusion) of the book that bears his name. Yet one finds a struggle against society as early as the earliest Leatherstocking tale (*The Pioneers*, 1823). In a sense, this supposed promise of America has always been known to be delusory. Certainly by the twentieth century the myth has been transmuted into an avowedly hopeless quest for unencumbered space *(On the Road)*, or the evocation of flight for its own sake (*Rabbit, Run* and *Henderson the Rain King*), or as pathetic acknowledgment of loss — for example, the close of *The Great Gatsby* where the narrator Nick Carraway summons up "the old island here that flowered once for Dutch sailors' eyes — a fresh, green breast of the new world . . . the last and greatest of all human dreams" where man is "face to face for the last time in history with something commensurate to his capacity for wonder."

[15]Trilling, *The Liberal Imagination*, p. 206. [Au.]

We are all very familiar with this myth of America in its various fashionings, and owing to the selective vision that has presented this myth to us as the whole story, many of us are unaware of how much besides it has been created by literary Americans. Keeping our eyes on this myth, we need to ask whether anything about it puts it outside women's reach. In one sense, and on one level, the answer is no. The subject of this myth is supposed to stand for human nature, and if men and women share a common human nature, then all can respond to its values, its promises, and its frustrations. And in fact, as a teacher I find women students responsive to the myth insofar as its protagonist is concerned. It is true, of course, that in order to represent some kind of believable flight into the wilderness, one must select a protagonist with a certain believable mobility, and mobility has until recently been a male prerogative in our society. Nevertheless, relatively few men are actually mobile to the extent demanded by the story, and hence the story is really not much more vicarious, in this regard, for women than for men. The problem is thus not to be located in the protagonist or his gender per se; the problem is with the other participants in his story — the entrammeling society and the promising landscape. For both of these are depicted in unmistakably feminine terms, and this gives a sexual character to the protagonist's story which does, indeed, limit its applicability to women. And this sexual definition has melodramatic, misogynist implications.

In these stories, the encroaching, constricting, destroying society is represented with particular urgency in the figure of one or more women. There are several possible reasons why this might be so. It seems to be a fact of life that we all — women and men alike — experience social conventions and responsibilities and obligations first in the persons of women, since women are entrusted by society with the task of rearing young children. Not until he reaches mid-adolescence does the male connect up with other males whose primary task is socialization; but at about this time — if he is heterosexual — his lovers and spouses become the agents of a permanent socialization and domestication. Thus, although women are not the source of social power, they are experienced as such. And although not all women are engaged in socializing the young, the young do not encounter women who are not. So from the point of view of the young man, the only kind of women who exist are entrappers and domesticators.

For heterosexual man, these socializing women are also the locus of powerful attraction. First, because everybody has social and conventional instincts: second, because his deepest emotional attachments are to women. This attraction gives urgency and depth to the protagonist's rejection of society. To do it, he must project onto the woman those attractions that he feels, and cast her in the melodramatic role of temptress, antagonist, obstacle — a character whose mission in life seems to be to ensnare him and deflect him from life's important purposes of self-discovery and self-assertion. (A Puritan would have said: from communion with Divinity.) As Richard Chase writes in *The American Novel and Its Tradition,* "The myth requires celibacy." It is partly against his own sexual urges that the male must struggle, and so he perceives the socializing and domesticating woman as a doubly powerful threat; for this reason, Chase goes on to state, neither Cooper nor "any other American novelist until the age of James and Edith Wharton" could imagine "a fully developed woman of sexual age."[16] Yet in making this statement, Chase is talking about his myth rather than Cooper's. (One should add that, for a homosexual male, the demands of society that he link himself for life to a woman make for a particularly misogynist version of this aspect of the American myth, for the hero is propelled not by a rejected attraction but by true revulsion.) Both heterosexual and homosexual versions of the myth cooperate with the hero's perceptions and validate the notion of woman as threat.

Such a portrayal of women is likely to be uncongenial, if not basically incomprehensible, to a woman. It is not likely that women will write books in which women play this part; and it is by no means the case that most novels by American men reproduce such a scheme. Even major male

[16]Richard Chase, *The American Novel and Its Tradition* (Garden City, N.Y.: Anchor Books, 1957), pp. 55, 64. [Au.]

authors prominent in the canon have other ways of depicting women: for example, Cooper's *Pathfinder* and *The Pioneers,* Hemingway's *For Whom the Bell Tolls,* Fitzgerald's *The Beautiful and Damned.* The novels of Henry James and William Dean Howells pose a continual challenge to the masculinist bias of American critical theory. And in one work — *The Scarlet Letter* — a "fully developed woman of sexual age" who is the novel's protagonist has been admitted into the canon, but only by virtue of strenuous critical revisions of the text that remove Hester Prynne from the center of the novel and make her subordinate to Arthur Dimmesdale.

So Leslie Fiedler, in *Love and Death in the American Novel,* writes this of *The Scarlet Letter:*

> It is certainly true, in terms of the plot, that Chillingworth drives the minister toward confession and penance, while Hester would have lured him to evasion and flight. But this means, for all of Hawthorne's equivocations, that the eternal feminine does not draw us on toward grace, rather that the woman promises only madness and damnation. . . . [Hester] is the female temptress of Puritan mythology, but also, though sullied, the secular madonna of sentimental Protestantism.[17]

In the rhetorical "us" Fiedler presumes that all readers are men, that the novel is an act of communication among and about males. His characterization of Hester as one or another myth or image makes it impossible for the novel to be in any way about Hester as a human being. Giving the novel so highly specific a gender reference, Fiedler makes it inaccessible to women and limits its reference to men in comparison to the issues that Hawthorne was treating in the story. Not the least of these issues was, precisely, the human reference of a woman's tale.

Amusingly, then, since he has produced this warped reading, Fiedler goes on to condemn the novel for its sexual immaturity. *The Scarlet Letter* is integrated into Fiedler's general exposure of the inadequacies of the American male — inadequacies which, as his treatment of Hester shows, he holds women responsible for. The melodrama here is not Hawthorne's but Fiedler's — the American critic's melodrama of beset manhood. Of course, women authors as major writers are notable and inevitably absent from Fiedler's chronicle.

In fact, many books by women — including such major authors as Edith Wharton, Ellen Glasgow, and Willa Cather — project a version of the particular myth we are speaking of but cast the main character as a woman. When a woman takes the central role, it follows naturally that the socializer and domesticator will be a man. This is the situation in *The Scarlet Letter*. Hester is beset by the male reigning oligarchy and by Dimmesdale, who passively tempts her and is responsible for fathering her child. Thereafter, Hester (as the myth requires) elects celibacy, as do many heroines in versions of this myth by women: Thea in Cather's *The Song of the Lark,* Dorinda in Glasgow's *Barren Ground,* Anna Leath in Wharton's *The Reef.* But what is written in the criticism about these celibate women? They are said to be untrue to the imperatives of their gender, which require marriage, childbearing, domesticity. Instead of being read as a woman's version of the myth, such novels are read as stories of the frustration of female nature. Stories of female frustration are not perceived as commenting on, or containing, the essence of our culture, and so we do not find them in the canon.

So the role of entrapper and impediment in the melodrama of beset manhood is reserved for women. Also, the role of the beckoning wilderness, the attractive landscape, is given a deeply feminine quality. Landscape is deeply imbued with female qualities, as society is; but where society is menacing and destructive, landscape is compliant and supportive. It has the attributes simultaneously of a virginal bride and a nonthreatening mother; its female qualities are articulated with respect to a male angle of vision: what can nature do for me, asks the hero, what can it give me?

Of course, nature has been feminine and maternal from time immemorial, and Henry Nash Smith's *Virgin Land* picks up a timeless archetype in its title. The basic nature of the image leads one to forget about its potential for imbuing

[17]Fiedler, *Love and Death in the American Novel,* p. 236. [Au.]

with sexual meanings any story in which it is used, and the gender implications of a female landscape have only recently begun to be studied. Recently, Annette Kolodny has studied the traditional canon from this approach.[18] She theorizes that the hero, fleeing a society that has been imagined as feminine, then imposes on nature some ideas of women which, no longer subject to the correcting influence of real-life experience, become more and more fantastic. The fantasies are infantile, concerned with power, mastery, and total gratification: the all-nurturing mother, the all-passive bride. Whether one accepts all the Freudian or Jungian implications of her argument, one cannot deny the way in which heroes of American myth turn to nature as sweetheart and nurture, anticipating the satisfaction of all desires through her and including among these the desires for mastery and power. A familiar passage that captures these ideas is one already quoted: Carraway's evocation of the "fresh green breast" of the New World. The fresh greenness is the virginity that offers itself to the sailors, but the breast promises maternal solace and delight. *The Great Gatsby* contains our two images of women: while Carraway evokes the impossible dream of a maternal landscape, he blames a non-maternal woman, the socialite Daisy, for her failure to satisfy Gatsby's desires. The true adversary, of course, is Tom Buchanan, but he is hidden, as it were, behind Daisy's skirts.

I have said that women are not likely to cast themselves as antagonists in a man's story; they are even less likely, I suggest, to cast themselves as virgin land. The lack of fit between their own experience and the fictional role assigned to them is even greater in the second instance than in the first. If women portray themselves as brides or mothers it will not be in terms of the mythic landscape. If a woman puts a female construction on nature — as she certainly must from time to time, given the archetypal female resonance of the image — she is likely to write of it as more active, or to stress its destruction or violation. On the other hand, she might adjust the heroic myth to her own psyche by making nature out to be male — as, for example, Willa Cather seems to do in *O Pioneers!* But a violated landscape or a male nature does not fit the essential American pattern as critics have defined it, and hence these literary images occur in an obscurity that criticism cannot see. Thus, one has an almost classic example of the double bind. When the woman writer creates a story that conforms to the expected myth, it is not recognized for what it is because of a superfluous sexual specialization in the myth as it is entertained in the critics' minds. (Needless to say, many male novelists also entertain this version of the myth, and do not find the masculinist bias with which they imbue it to be superfluous. It is possible that some of these novelists, especially those who write in an era in which literary criticism is a powerful influence, have formed their ideas from their reading in criticism.) But if she does not conform to the myth, she is understood to be writing minor or trivial literature.

Two remaining points can be treated much more briefly. The description of the artist and of the act of writing which emerges when the critic uses the basic American story as his starting point contains many attributes of the basic story itself. This description raises the exclusion of women to a more abstract, theoretical — and perhaps more pernicious — level. Fundamentally, the idea is that the artist writing a story of this essential American kind is engaging in a task very much like the one performed by his mythic hero. In effect, the artist writing his narrative is imitating the mythic encounter of hero and possibility in the safe confines of his study; or, reversing the temporal order, one might see the mythic encounter of hero and possibility as a projection of the artist's situation.

Although this idea is greatly in vogue at the moment, it has a history. Here, for example, is Richard Chase representing the activity of writing in metaphors of discovery and exploration, as though the writer were a hero in the landscape: "The American novel has usually seemed content to explore . . . the remarkable and in some ways unexampled territories of life in the New World and to reflect its anomalies and dilemmas. It has . . . wanted . . . to discover a new place and a new

[18]Annette Kolodny, *The Lay of the Land: Metaphor As Experience and History in American Life and Letters* (Chapel Hill: University of North Carolina Press, 1975). [Au.]

state of mind."[19] Richard Poirier takes the idea further:

> The most interesting American books are an image of the creation of America itself. . . . They carry the metaphoric burden of a great dream of freedom — of the expansion of national consciousness into the vast spaces of a continent and the absorption of those spaces into ourselves. . . . The classic American writers try through style temporarily to free the hero (and the reader) from systems, to free them from the pressures of time, biology, economics, and from the social forces which are ultimately the undoing of American heroes and quite often of their creators. . . . The strangeness of American fiction has . . . to do . . . with the environment [the novelist] tries to create for his hero, usually his surrogate.[20]

The implicit union of creator and protagonist is made specific and overt at the end of Poirier's passage here. The ideas of Poirier and Chase, and others like them, are summed up in an anthology called *Theories of American Literature*, edited by Donald M. Kartiganer and Malcolm A. Griffith. The editors write, "It is as if with each new work our writers feel they must invent again the complete world of a literary form." (Yet, the true subject is not what the writers feel, but what the critics think they feel.) "Such a condition of nearly absolute freedom to create has appeared to our authors both as possibility and liability, an utter openness suggesting limitless opportunity for the imagination, or an enormous vacancy in which they create from nothing. For some it has meant an opportunity to play Adam, to assume the role of an original namer of experience.[21] One can see in this passage the transference of the American myth from the Adamic hero *in* the story to the Adamic creator *of* the story, and the reinterpretation of the American myth as a metaphor for the American artist's situation.

This myth of artistic creation, assimilating the act of writing novels to the Adamic myth, imposes on artistic creation all the gender-based restrictions that we have already examined in that myth. The key to identifying an "Adamic writer" is the formal appearance, or, more precisely, the *informal* appearance, of his novel. The unconventionality is interpreted as a direct representation of the open-ended experience of exploring and taming the wilderness, as well as a rejection of "society" as it is incorporated in conventional literary forms. There is no place for a woman author in this scheme. Her roles in the drama of creation are those allotted to her in a male melodrama: either she is to be silent, like nature, or she is the creator of conventional works, the spokesperson of society. What she might do as an innovator in her own right is not to be perceived.

In recent years, some refinements of critical theory coming from the Yale and Johns Hopkins and Columbia schools have added a new variant to the idea of creation as a male province. I quote from a 1979 book entitled *Home as Found* by Eric Sundquist. The author takes the idea that in writing a novel the artist is really writing a narrative about himself and proposes this addition:

> Writing a narrative about oneself may represent an extremity of Oedipal usurpation or identification, a bizarre act of self fathering. . . . American authors have been particularly obsessed with *fathering* a tradition of their own, with becoming their "own sires." . . . The struggle . . . is central to the crisis of representation, and hence of style, that allows American authors to find in their own fantasies those of a nation and to make of those fantasies a compelling and instructive literature.[22]

These remarks derive clearly from the work of such critics as Harold Bloom, as any reader of recent critical theory will note. The point for our purpose is the facile translation of the verb "to author" into the verb "to father," with the profound gender restrictions of that translation unacknowledged. According to this formulation, insofar as the author writes about a character who is his surrogate — which, apparently, he always does — he is trying to become his own father.

[19]Chase, *American Novel*, p. 5. [Au.]

[20]Poirier, *A World Elsewhere*, pp. 3, 5, 9. [Au.]

[21]Donald M. Kartiganer and Malcolm A. Griffith, eds., *Theories of American Literature: The Critical Perspective* (New York: Macmillan, 1962), pp. 4–5. [Au.]

[22]Eric J. Sundquist, *Home as Found: Authority and Genealogy in Nineteenth-Century American Literature* (Baltimore: Johns Hopkins University Press, 1979), pp. xviii–xix. [Au.]

We can scarcely deny that men think a good deal about, and are profoundly affected by, relations with their fathers. The theme of fathers and sons is perennial in world literature. Somewhat more spaciously, we recognize that intergenerational conflict, usually perceived from the point of view of the young, is a recurrent literary theme, especially in egalitarian cultures. Certainly, this idea involves the question of authority, and "authority" is a notion related to that of "the author." And there is some gender-specific significance involved since authority in most cultures that we know tends to be invested in adult males. But the theory has built from these useful and true observations to a restriction of literary creation to a sort of therapeutic act that can only be performed by men. If literature is the attempt to *father* oneself by the author, then every act of writing by a woman is both perverse and absurd. And, of course, it is bound to fail.

Since this particular theory of the act of writing is drawn from psychological assumptions that are not specific to American literature, it may be argued that there is no need to confine it to American authors. In fact, Harold Bloom's *Anxiety of Influence,* defining literature as a struggle between fathers and sons, or the struggle of sons to escape from their fathers, is about British literature.[23] And so is Edward Said's book *Beginnings,* which chronicles the history of the nineteenth-century British novel as exemplification of what he calls "filiation." His discussion omits Jane Austen, George Eliot, all three Brontë sisters, Mrs. Gaskell, Mrs. Humphrey Ward — not a sign of a woman author is found in his treatment of Victorian fiction. The result is a revisionist approach to British fiction that recasts it in the accepted image of the American myth. Ironically, just at the time that feminist critics are discovering more and more important women, the critical theorists have seized upon a theory that allows the women less and less presence. This observation points up just how significantly the critic is engaged in the act of *creating* literature.

Ironically, then, one concludes that in pushing the theory of American fiction to this extreme, critics have "deconstructed" it by creating a tool with no particular American reference. In pursuit of the uniquely American, they have arrived at a place where Americanness has vanished into the depths of what is alleged to be the universal male psyche. The theory of American fiction has boiled down to the phrase in my title: a melodrama of beset manhood. What a reduction this is of the enormous variety of fiction written in this country, by both women and men! And, ironically, nothing could be further removed from Trilling's idea of the artist as embodiment of a culture. As in the working out of all theories, its weakest link has found it out and broken the chain.

[23]See Bloom, p. 1027. [Ed.]

Barbara Herrnstein Smith

b. 1932

Barbara Herrnstein Smith is a scholar of aesthetics, literary theory, and linguistic theory. Born in New York City, Smith took her B.A. (1954), M.A. (1955), and Ph.D. (1965) in English and American literature at Brandeis University in Massachusetts. She has been an instructor at the Sanz School of Languages in Washington, D.C. (1956–57), a member of the literature faculty at Bennington College (1962–74), and a professor at the University of Pennsylvania (1974–87), where in 1979 she was named director of the Center for the Study of Art and Symbolic Behavior, and in 1980 University Professor of English and communications. Smith has been a fellow of (1970–71) and a consultant for (1974) the National Endowment of the Humanities as well as a Guggenheim fellow (1977–78) and a chair of the Modern Language Association (1987–88). Currently she is a professor at Duke University in a department that includes other renowned literary theorists, such as Stanley Fish (Ch. 3) and Fredric Jameson (Ch. 5). Most of Smith's publications have been academic articles. Her books include Poetic Closure: A Study of How Poems End, *which won the Christian Gauss Award and the Explicator Award for 1968,* On the Margins of Discourse: The Relation of Literature to Language *(1978),* Contingencies of Value: Alternative Perspectives for Critical Theory *(1988), and* The Politics of Liberal Education *(ed., with Darryl Gless, 1991). "Contingencies of Value" is from* Critical Inquiry *10 (1983).*

Contingencies of Value

1. THE EXILE OF EVALUATION

It is a curious feature of literary studies in America that one of the most venerable, central, theoretically significant, and pragmatically inescapable set of problems relating to literature has not been a subject of serious inquiry for the past fifty years. I refer here to the fact not merely that the study of literary evaluation has been, as we might say, "neglected," but that the entire problematic of value and evaluation has been evaded and explicitly exiled by the literary academy. It is clear, for example, that there has been no broad and sustained investigation of literary evaluation that could compare to the constant and recently intensified attention devoted to every aspect of literary *interpretation*. The past decades have witnessed an extraordinary proliferation of theories, approaches, movements, and entire disciplines focused on interpretive criticism, among them (to recite a familiar litany) New Criticism, structuralism, psychoanalytic criticism, reader-response criticism, reception aesthetics, speech-act theory, deconstructionism, communications theory, semiotics, and hermeneutics. At the same time, however, aside from a number of scattered and secondary essays by theorists and critics who are usually otherwise occupied,[1] no one in particular has been concerned with questions of literary value and evaluation, and such questions regularly go begging — and, of course, begged — even among those whose inquiries into other matters are most rigorous, substantial, and sophisticated.

Reasons for the specific disparity of attention are not hard to locate. One is the obvious attachment of problems of interpretation and meaning to the more general preoccupation with language that has dominated the entire century and probably, as well, the fact that disciplines such as linguistics and the philosophy of language are more accessible to literary scholars than the corresponding disciplines, especially economics and sociology, that are more broadly concerned with the nature of value and evaluative behavior. The reasons for the general neglect and exile, however, are more complex, reflecting, among other things, the fact that literary studies in America, from the time of its inception as an institutionalized academic discipline, has been shaped by two conflicting and mutually compromising intellectual traditions and ideologies, namely — or

[1]The most recent of these include E. D. Hirsch, Jr., *The Aims of Interpretation* (Chicago, 1976), esp. the essays "Evaluation as Knowledge" (1968) and "Privileged Criteria in Evaluation" (1969); Murray Krieger, "Literary Analysis and Evaluation — and the Ambidextrous Critic," in *Criticism: Speculative and Analytic Essays,* ed. L. S. Dembo (Madison, Wis., 1968); a number of brief essays by Anglo-American as well as continental European theorists in *Problems of Literary Evaluation,* ed. Joseph Strelka (University Park, Pa., and London, 1969); and the chapters on value and evaluation in John Ellis, *The Theory of Literary Criticism* (Berkeley and Los Angeles, 1974), John Reichert, *Making Sense of Literature* (Chicago, 1977), and Jeffrey Sammons, *Literary Sociology and Practical Criticism* (Bloomington, Ind., and London, 1977). All of them either participate directly in the self-justifying academic debates outlined below or are haunted by them into equivocation. [Au.]

roughly namely — positivistic philological scholarship and humanistic pedagogy. That is, while professors of literature have sought to claim for their activities the rigor, objectivity, cognitive substantiality, and progress associated with science and the empirical disciplines, they have also attempted to remain faithful to the essentially conservative and didactic mission of humanistic studies: to honor and preserve the culture's traditionally esteemed objects — in this case, its canonized texts — and to illuminate and transmit the traditional cultural values presumably embodied in them. One consequence or manifestation of this conflict has been the continuous absorption of "literary theory" in America with institutional debates over the proper methods and objectives of the academic *study* of literature and, with respect to the topic at hand, the drastic confinement of its concern with literary evaluation to debates over the cognitive status of evaluative criticism and its proper place, if any, in the discipline.

A bit of history will be helpful here. In accord with the traditional empiricist doctrine of a fundamental split or discontinuity between fact and value (or description and evaluation, or knowledge and judgment), it was possible to regard the emerging distinction within literary studies between "scholarship" and "criticism" as a reasonable division of labor. Thus, the scholar who devoted himself to locating and assembling the historical and philological facts necessary to edit and annotate the works of, say, Bartholomew Griffin might remark that, although Griffin was no doubt a less fashionable poet than such contemporaries as Spenser and Shakespeare, the serious and responsible scholar must go about his work in a serious and responsible manner, leaving questions of literary merit "to the critics." The gesture that accompanied the remark, however, was likely to signal not professional deference but intellectual condescension; for the presumably evenhanded distribution of the intellectual responsibilities of literary study — the determination of facts to the scholar and value to the critic — depended on an always questionable and increasingly questioned set of assumptions: namely, that literary value was a determinate property of texts and that the critic, by virtue of certain innate and acquired capacities (taste, sensibility, etc., which could be seen as counterparts to the scholar's industry and erudition), was someone specifically equipped to discriminate it.

The magisterial mode of literary evaluation that issued from this set of assumptions (and which, in Anglo-American criticism, characteristically reproduced itself after the image — and in the voice — of Dr. Johnson and also of such latter-day "master-critics" as Matthew Arnold and T. S. Eliot) was practiced most notably by F. R. Leavis in England and, in America, perhaps most egregiously, by Yvor Winters.[2] Its reaches and a taste of its once familiar flavor can be recalled in this passage from Leavis' *Revaluation:*

> There are, of course, discriminations to be made: Tennyson, for instance, is a much better poet than any of the pre-Raphaelites. And Christina Rossetti deserves to be set apart from them and credited with her own thin and limited but very notable distinction. . . . There is, too, Emily Brontë, who has hardly yet had full justice as a poet. I will record, without offering it as a checked and deliberated judgment, the remembered impression that her *Cold in the earth* is the finest poem in the nineteenth-century part of *The Oxford Book of English Verse.*[3]

Such unabashed "debaucheries of judiciousness" (as Northrop Frye would later characterize them)[4] were, however, increasingly seen as embarrassments to the discipline, and the practice of evaluative criticism became more defensive, at least partly in response to the renewed and updated authority given to axiological skepticism.

In the thirties and forties, a number of prominent philosophers, among them A. J. Ayer and Rudolph Carnap, began to argue that value judgments are not merely distinct from empirically verifiable statements of fact but vacuous pseudostatements, at best suasive and commendatory, at worst simply the emotive expressions of per-

[2]See Johnson, "Preface to Shakespeare," p. 224; Arnold, "The Study of Poetry," p. 411; Eliot, "Tradition and the Individual Talent," p. 497; Leavis, *The Great Tradition,* p. 599. [Ed.]

[3]F. R. Leavis, *Revaluation: Tradition and Development in English Poetry* (London, 1936; New York, 1963), pp. 5–6. [Au.]

[4]See Frye, "The Archetypes of Literature," p. 641. [Ed.]

sonal sentiment, and in any case neither reflecting nor producing genuine knowledge.[5] For the positivistic literary scholar, such arguments reinforced his impression that the work of his critical colleague was the intellectually insubstantial activity of a dilettante, while the true discipline of literary studies was exhibited in his own labors, in which he had always sought to achieve a rigor and objectivity as free as possible from the contamination of value ascription. In the institutional struggles that ensued, various maneuvers were developed to secure for "criticism" not only a central place in the discipline but also an intellectual status equal in respectability to that of empirical science and what was commonly referred to as "serious scholarship."

One obvious tactic, still favored in many quarters of the literary academy, was to invoke the humanistic mission of literary studies and turn the fact-value split against the scholars' claim of centrality. Thus Winters would maintain that while science was value-neutral — or, as he put it, "amoral" — literary studies had moral responsibilities. The function of historical scholarship and philology was, accordingly, ancillary: specifically, it was "to lay the groundwork for criticism," while the important job was, precisely, to evaluate literature.[6] For Winters, this meant to declare, forthrightly and unequivocally, what was good and bad literature (which was to say, "moral" or "decadent" literature), and he did not hesitate, himself, to rank-order not only poets and poems but also literary genres, verse forms, and entire centuries.

Winters had a genius for unequivocality that was imitated but never matched by his numerous followers. In any case, a more common tactic, exemplified by a number of the New Critics, was to devise some formulation of critical activity that bridged the fact-value split or at least unobtrusively edged the two sides together. Thus, in 1951, W. K. Wimsatt, Jr., in an important essay titled "Explication as Criticism," observed that it was necessary to find "an escape between the two extremes of sheer affectivism and sheer scientific neutralism" and attempted to demonstrate how evaluation could be assimilated into the typical New Critical production of increasingly exquisite explications and fine-grained analyses: "But then, finally, it is possible to conceive and produce instances where explication in the neutral sense is so integrated with special and local value intimations that it rises from neutrality gradually and convincingly to the point of total judgment."[7]

It may be recalled here that Wimsatt's attempt to expose "the affective fallacy" was directed largely at the "psychological theory of value" developed by I. A. Richards in the twenties, which Wimsatt charged with amounting to subjectivism and leading to impressionism and relativism. Richards' theory was, however, in effect an updated rehearsal of the eighteenth-century empiricist-normative account and, like the latter, designed to *rebut* axiological skepticism.[8] An adequate theory of criticism, Richards wrote, must be able to answer such questions as "What gives the experience of reading a certain poem its value?" and "Why is one opinion about works of art not as good as another?",[9] and while the first of these questions no doubt seemed to Wimsatt altogether different from what, for him, would have been the more proper question of what gives *the poem itself* its value, the second of them makes Richards' normative objectives quite clear. Indeed, he consistently put his psychoneurological account of value in the service of canonical judgments and repeatedly translated it into versions of evaluative absolutism and objectivism. Thus, the remarkable chapter on "Badness in Poetry" in *Principles of Literary Criticism* concludes its excruciating examination of the failure of a sonnet by Ella Wheeler Wilcox to

[5]See esp. A. J. Ayer, *Language, Truth, and Logic* (London, 1936). [Au.]

[6]Yvor Winters, *The Function of Criticism* (Denver, 1957), p. 17 [Au.]

[7]W. K. Wimsatt, Jr., *The Verbal Icon* (Louisville, Ky., 1954), p. 250. [Au.]

[8]See the discussion of David Hume below, p. 1563 [Au]. See Hume, p. 242. Axiology is the study of norms or values. [Ed.]

[9]I. A. Richards, *Principles of Literary Criticism* (1924; London, 1960), pp. 5–6. "The two pillars upon which a theory of criticism must rest," Richards declared, "are an account of value and an account of communication" (p. 25). It was, of course, the latter that subsequently became the overriding concern of critical theory. [Au.]

produce a "high level of organization" of "adequate [neural] impulses" with Richards' observation that, although "those who enjoy [the sonnet] certainly seem to enjoy it to a high degree," nevertheless, with good and bad poetry, as with brandy and beer, the "actual universal preference of those who have tried both fairly is the same as superiority in value of one over the other. Keats, by universal qualified opinion, is a more efficient poet than Wilcox, and that is the same as saying his works are more valuable."[10] The invocation of an "actual" universality coupled with such question-begging hedges as "fairly" and "qualified" is, as we shall see, characteristic of traditional empiricist-normative accounts. It was not, one suspects, its alleged relativism that made Richards' theory so unabsorbable by the literary academy but rather the raw jargon and unedifying physiology that attended it.

The boldest move in the midcentury effort to give disciplinary respectability and cognitive substance to criticism was, of course, Frye's call upon it to redefine itself as a project that banished evaluation altogether. In his "Polemical Introduction" to the *Anatomy of Criticism,* Frye insisted that, if criticism was ever to become a "field of genuine learning" (significantly exemplified by "chemistry or philology"), it would have to "snip . . . off and throw . . . away" that part that had "no organic connection with [it]," — namely, evaluation.[11] For Frye, the shifting assessments and rank-orderings made by critics were not only a noncumulative accumulation of subjective judgments but also irrelevant to "real criticism," since he believed, echoing and endorsing Eliot, that "the existing monuments of literature form an ideal order among themselves." "This," Frye commented, "is criticism, and very fundamental criticism. Much of this book attempts to annotate it" (*AC,* p. 18).

In what proved to be a memorable passage, he derided "all the literary chit-chat which makes the reputations of poets boom and crash in an imaginary stock-exchange," and observed:

> This sort of thing cannot be part of any systematic study, for a systematic study can only progress: whatever dithers or vacillates or reacts is merely leisure-class gossip. The history of taste is no more a part of the *structure* of criticism than the Huxley-Wilberforce debate[12] is a part of the structure of biological science. (*AC,* p. 18)

In view of Frye's Platonic conception of literature and positivistic conception of science, it is not surprising that he failed to recognize that his analogy here cuts both ways. For not only could the Huxley-Wilberforce debate be seen as very much a part of the "structure" of biological science (which, like that of any other science, including any science of literature, is by no means independent of its own intellectual, social, and institutional history), but, since the "order" of "the existing monuments of literature" is the distinctly sublunary product of, among other things, evaluative practices, any truly systematic study of literature would sooner or later have to include a study of *those practices*. In other words, the structure of criticism cannot be so readily disengaged from the history of taste because they are mutually implicating and incorporating.

Joining as it did both an appeal to scientific objectivity and a humanistic conception of literature, while at the same time extending the promise of a high calling and bright future to a project pursued in the name of "criticism," Frye's effort to banish evaluation from literary study was remarkably effective — at least to the extent

[10]Ibid., p. 206. [Au.]

[11]Northrop Frye, *Anatomy of Criticism: Four Essays* (Princeton, N.J., 1957), pp. 18, 19; all further references to this work, abbreviated *AC,* will be included in the text. [Au.]

[12]Strictly speaking, there was never a formal debate between biologist Thomas Henry Huxley (1825–1895), a well-known defender of the theories of Charles Darwin, and Samuel Wilberforce (1805–1873), Bishop of Oxford and a fellow of the Royal Society. On June 30, 1860, after a lecture at Oxford on Darwin's *Origin of Species* (1859) presented by an American biologist named Draper, the audience of about seven hundred asked Wilberforce, who had already attempted to refute Darwin in print, to respond. Wilberforce spoke against Darwin for half an hour, concluding his remarks with a flippant attack on Huxley, who was sitting in the audience: "Is it on your grandmother's or grandfather's side, Mr. Huxley, that you claim descent from a monkey?" Huxley's sententious reply, which won the crowd's approval, was that he would prefer to "have a miserable ape for a grandfather" than a man like Wilberforce, "highly endowed by nature and possessed of great means and influence and yet who employs those faculties and that influence for the mere purpose of introducing ridicule into a grave scientific discussion." [Ed.]

of haunting a generation of literary scholars, critics, and teachers, many of whom are still inclined to apologize for making overt value judgments, as if for some temporary intellectual or moral lapse.[13] It was hardly the last word on the subject, however, and as late as 1968 we find E. D. Hirsch, Jr., attempting to rehabilitate the cognitive status of evaluative criticism in an essay significantly titled "Evaluation as Knowledge." In the essay, Hirsch argues that the value judgment of a literary work, when properly directed to the work itself and not to a "distorted version of it," closely coordinated with a correct interpretation of its objective meaning and rationally justified with reference to a specific criteria, *does* constitute a genuine proposition and, therefore, like a "pure description," does "qualify as objective knowledge."[14] Since just about every concept engaged by Hirsch's argument is at issue in contemporary epistemology and critical theory, it is not surprising that it did not settle the question of the intellectual status of evaluative criticism — for Hirsch or anyone else.[15]

The debate over the proper place of evaluation in literary studies remains unresolved and is, I believe, unresolvable in the terms in which it has been formulated. Meanwhile, although evaluative criticism remains intellectually suspect, it certainly continues to be practiced as a magisterial privilege in the classrooms of the literary academy and granted admission to its journals as long as it comes under cover of other presumably more objective types of literary study, such as historical description, textual analysis, or explication. At the same time, however, the fact that literary evaluation is not merely an aspect of formal academic criticism but a complex set of social and cultural activities central to the very nature of literature has been obscured, and an entire domain that is properly the object of theoretical, historical, and empirical exploration has been lost to serious inquiry.

Although I confine my comments here primarily to the American literary academy and to Anglo-American critical theory, the situation — and its intellectual and institutional history — has not been altogether different in continental Europe. The dominance of language- and interpretation-centered theories, movements, and approaches, for example, is clearly international, and versions of the positivist/humanist conflict have shaped the development of literary studies in Europe as well. Certain exceptions are, however, instructive. When, in the twenties and thirties, East European theorists also sought to transform literary studies into a progressive, systematic science, the problematic of value and evaluation was not excluded from the project. For example, the historically variable functions of texts and the interrelations among canonical and noncanonical works and other cultural products and activities were recognized and documented by, among others, Jurij Tynjanov and Mikhail Bakhtin; and Jan Mukařovský's explorations of the general question of aesthetic value were both original and substantial.[16] Also, studies in the sociology of literature, especially in France and Germany, and the project of reception aesthetics have concerned themselves with as-

[13]It should be recalled that, like many others (e.g., Hirsch [see n. 15]), Frye continued to maintain that *interpretive* criticism could lay claim to objectivity. See his remarks in a paper delivered in 1967: "The fundamental critical act . . . is the act of recognition, seeing what is there, as distinguished from merely seeing in a Narcissus mirror of our own experience and social and moral prejudice. . . . When a critic interprets, he is talking about his poet; when he evaluates, he is talking about himself" ("Value Judgements," in *Criticism: Speculative and Analytic Essays*, p. 39). [Au.]

[14]Hirsch, *The Aims of Interpretation*, p. 108. See also n. 44 below, for Hirsch's neo-Kantian formulation. [Au.]

[15]In a recent unpublished essay, "Literary Value: The Short History of a Modern Confusion" (1980), Hirsch argues that, although literary *meaning* is determinate, literary value is not. With respect to the latter, however, he concludes that "there are some stable principles" — namely, ethical ones — "that escape the chaos of purely personal relativity" (p. 22). As will be seen in the analysis below, "personal relativity" neither produces chaos nor is in itself chaotic. The escape route of ethical principles and other appeals to higher goods are discussed below. [Au.]

[16]See Jurij Tynjanov, "On Literary Evolution" (Moscow, 1927), trans. Ladislav Matejka and Krystyna Pomorska, in *Readings in Russian Poetics*, ed. Matejka and Pomorska (Cambridge, Mass., 1971); Mikhail Bakhtin, *Rabelais and His World* (Moscow, 1965), trans. Helene Iswolsky (Cambridge, Mass., 1968); and Jan Mukařovský, *Aesthetic Norm, Function, and Value as Social Facts* (Prague, 1934), trans. Mark E. Suino (Ann Arbor, Mich., 1970). [Au.] See Tynyanov, p. 727. [Ed.]

pects of literary evaluation.[17] It should also be noted, however, that the study of value and evaluation remained relatively undeveloped in the later work of formalists and structuralists,[18] while Marxist literary theory has only recently begun to move from minimal revisions of orthodox aesthetic axiology toward a radical reformulation.[19] It may be added that, although the theoretical perspective, conceptual structures, and analytic techniques developed by Jacques Derrida are potentially of great interest here (especially in conjunction with the renewed attention to Nietzsche), their radical axiological implications remain largely unexplored,[20] and, insofar as it has been appropriated by American critical theory, deconstruction has been put almost entirely in the service of antihermeneutics, which is to say that it has been absorbed by our preemptive occupation with interpretive criticism. Recent moves toward opening the question of value and evaluation in the American literary academy have come primarily from those who have sought to subject its canon to dramatic revaluation, notably feminist critics. Although their efforts have been significant to that end, they have not, however, amounted as yet to the articulation of a well-developed noncanonical theory of value and evaluation.

One of the major effects of prohibiting or inhibiting explicit evaluation is to forestall the exhibition and obviate the possible acknowledgment of divergent systems of value and thus to ratify, by default, established evaluative authority. It is worth noting that in none of the debates of the forties and fifties was the traditional academic canon itself questioned, and that where evaluative authority was not ringingly affirmed, asserted, or self-justified, it was simply assumed. Thus Frye himself could speak almost in one breath of the need to "get rid of . . . all casual, sentimental, and prejudiced value-judgments" as "the first step in developing a genuine poetics" and of "the masterpieces of literature" which are "the materials of literary criticism" (*AC*, pp. 18, 15). The identity of those masterpieces, it seemed, could be taken for granted or followed more or less automatically from the "direct value-judgement of informed good taste" or "certain literary values . . . fully established by critical experience" (*AC*, pp. 27, 20).

In a passage of particular interest, Frye wrote:

> Comparative estimates of value are really inferences, most valid when silent ones, from critical practice. . . . The critic will find soon, and constantly, that Milton is a more rewarding and suggestive poet to work with than Blackmore. But the more obvious this becomes, the less time he will want to waste belaboring the point. (*AC*, p. 25)

In addition to the noteworthy correlation of validity with silence (comparable, to some extent, to Wimsatt's discreet "intimations" of value), two other aspects of Frye's remarks here repay some attention. First, in claiming that it is altogether obvious that Milton, rather than Blackmore, is "a more rewarding and suggestive poet [for the critic] to work with," Frye begged the question of *what kind of work* the critic would be doing. For surely if one were concerned with a question such as the relation of canonical and noncanonical texts in the system of literary value in eighteenth-

[17] For surveys and discussions, see Sammons, *Literary Sociology and Practical Criticism,* and Rien T. Segers, *The Evaluation of Literary Texts: An Experimental Investigation into the Rationalization of Value Judgments with Reference to Semiotics and Esthetics of Reception* (Lisse, 1978). For a recent study of considerable interest, see Jacques Leenhardt and Pierre Jozsa, *Lire la lecture: Essai du sociologie de la lecture* (Paris, 1982). [Au.]

[18] It is not mentioned as such, e.g., in Jonathan Culler's *Structuralist Poetics: Structuralism, Linguistics, and the Study of Literature* (Ithaca, N.Y., 1975). [Au.]

[19] See, e.g., the thoroughly equivocal discussions of "objective value" in Stefan Morawski, *Inquiries into Fundamentals of Aesthetics* (Cambridge, Mass., and London, 1974), and the revalorization of the standard Eng. Lit. canon in Althusserian terms in Terry Eagleton, *Criticism and Ideology: A Study in Marxist Literary Theory* (London, 1976), pp. 162–87. For other discussions of this point, see Hans Robert Jauss, "The Idealist Embarrassment: Observations on Marxist Aesthetics," *New Literary History* 7 (Autumn 1975): 191–208; Raymond Williams, *Marxism and Literature* (Oxford, 1977), esp. pp. 45–54 and 151–57; Tony Bennett, *Formalism and Marxism* (London, 1979), esp. pp. 172–75; and Peter Widowson, " 'Literary Value' and the Reconstruction of Criticism," *Literature and History* 6 (1980): 138–50. See also n. 36 below. [Au.] See Jauss, p. 934. [Ed.]

[20] See, however, Arkady Plotnitsky, "Constraints of the Unbound: Transformation, Value, and Literary Interpretation" (Ph.D. diss., University of Pennsylvania, 1982), for an extensive and sophisticated effort along such lines. [Au.]

century England, one would find Blackmore just as rewarding and suggestive *to work with* as Milton. Both here and in his repeated insistence that the "material" of criticism must be "the masterpieces of literature" (he refers also to "a feeling we have all had: that the study of mediocre works of art remains a random and peripheral form of critical experience" [*AC*, p. 17], Frye exhibits a severely limited conception of the potential domain of literary study and of the sort of problems and phenomena with which it could or should deal. In this conceptual and methodological confinement, however (which betrays the conservative force of the ideology of traditional humanism even in the laboratories of the new progressive poetics), he has been joined by just about every other member of the Anglo-American literary academy during the past fifty years.

The second point of interest in Frye's remarks is his significant conjoining of Milton with Blackmore as an illustration of the sort of comparative estimate that is so obvious as not to need belaboring. Blackmore, we recall, was the author of an ambitious epic poem, *The Creation,* notable in literary history primarily as the occasion of some faint praise from Dr. Johnson and otherwise as a topos of literary disvalue; its function — indeed, one might say, its *value* — has been to stand as an instance of bad poetry. This handy conjunction, however (and similar ones, such as Shakespeare and Edgar Guest, John Keats and Joyce Kilmer, T. S. Eliot and Ella Wheeler Wilcox, that occur repeatedly in the debates outlined above), evades the more difficult and consequential questions of judgment posed by genuine evaluative diversity and conflict: questions that are posed, for example, by specific claims of value made for noncanonical works (such as modern texts, especially highly innovative ones, and such culturally exotic works as oral or tribal literature, popular literature, and "ethnic" literature) and also by judgments of literary value made by or on behalf of what might be called noncanonical or culturally exotic audiences (such as all those readers who are not now students, critics, or professors of literature and perhaps never were and never will be within the academy or on its outskirts).

The evasion is dramatized when conflicts of judgment arising from fundamental and perhaps irreconcilable diversity of interest are exhibited in currently charged political contexts. A specific example will illustrate my point here. In 1977 a study of Langston Hughes's poetry was published by Onwuchekwa Jemie, a Nigerian-born, American-educated poet and critic, at that time associate professor of English and Afro-American literature at the University of Minnesota. In one section of his study, Jemie discusses Hughes's poetic cycle, "Madame," in relation to Eliot's "The Love Song of J. Alfred Prufrock" and Ezra Pound's "Hugh Selwyn Mauberley," comparing various formal and thematic aspects of the three works. He observes, for example, that each of them is "consistent in language, tone and attitude with the socio-psychological milieu which it explores: the ghetto dialect and sassy humor [in Hughes's work], the cynical polished talk of literary London [in Pound's], and the bookish ruminations of Prufrock's active mind in inactive body"; he then concludes pointedly: "In short, to fault one poem for not being more like the other, for not dealing with the matter and in the manner of the other, is to err in judgment."[21] Soon after its publication, a reviewer of Jemie's book in the London *Times Literary Supplement* took it very much to task for, among other things, its "painfully irrelevant comparisons," citing the passage quoted above.[22] And, a few weeks later, there appeared in *TLS* an extraordinary letter to the editor from Chinweizu, himself a Nigerian-born, American-educated writer and critic. Responding to the review and particularly to the phrase, "painfully irrelevant comparisons," he shot back:

> Painful to whom? Irrelevant to whom? To idolators of white genius? Who says that Shakespeare, Aristophanes, Dante, Milton, Dostoevsky, Joyce, Pound, Sartre, Eliot, etc. are the last word in literary achievement, unequalled anywhere? . . . The point of these comparisons is not to thrust a black

[21]Onwuchekwa Jemie, *Langston Hughes: An Introduction to the Poetry* (New York, 1976), p. 184. [Au.]

[22]C. W. B. Bigsby, "Hand in Hand with the Blues," *Times Literary Supplement,* 17 June 1977, p. 734. [Au.]

face among these local idols of Europe which, to our grave injury, have been bloated into "universality"; rather it is to help heave them out of our way, clear them from our skies by making clear . . . that we have, among our own, the equals and betters of these chaps. . . . In this day and age, British preferences do not count in the Black World. As Langston Hughes himself put it half a century ago: "If white people are pleased, we are glad. If they are not, it doesn't matter."[23]

This brief case history in the problem of literary evaluation illustrates, among other things, what genuine evaluative conflict sounds like. (It also illustrates that, contrary to Frye's assertion, the history of taste is not "a history where there are no facts" [*AC*, p. 18], though we have barely begun to recognize either how to chronicle its episodes and shape its narrative or its significance not only for "the structure of criticism" but also for the structure of "literature.") I would suggest that it is, also among other things, the very possibility of that sound that is being evaded in Anglo-American literary studies and, furthermore, that when the sound reaches the intensity that we hear in Chinweizu's letter, the literary academy has no way to acknowledge it except, perhaps, in the language of counteroutrage.[24]

It is clear that, with respect to the central pragmatic issues as well as theoretical problems of literary value and evaluation, American critical theory has simply painted itself out of the picture. Beguiled by the humanist's fantasy of transcendence, endurance, and universality, it has been unable to acknowledge the most fundamental character of literary value, which is its mutability and diversity. And, at the same time, magnetized by the goals and ideology of a naive scientism, distracted by the arid concerns of philosophic axiology, obsessed by a misplaced quest for "objectivity," and confined in its very conception of literary studies by the narrow intellectual traditions and professional allegiances of the literary academy, it has foreclosed from its own domain the possibility of investigating the dynamics of that mutability and understanding the nature of that diversity.

The type of investigation I have in mind here would seek neither to establish normative "criteria," devise presumptively objective evaluative procedures, nor discover grounds for the "justification" of critical judgments or practices. It would not, in short, be a literary axiology or, in effect, the counterpart for evaluative criticism of what a literary hermeneutics offers to be for interpretive criticism. It would seek, rather, to clarify the nature of literary — and, more broadly, aesthetic — value in conjunction with a more general rethinking of the concept of value; to explore the multiple forms and functions of literary evaluation, institutional as well as individual, in relation to the circumstantial constraints and conditions to which they are responsive; to chronicle "the history of taste" in relation to a general model of historical evaluative dynamics and specific local conditions; and to describe and account for the various phenomena and activities that appear to be involved in literary and aesthetic evaluation in relation to our more general understanding — as it is and as it develops — of human culture and behavior.

The sort of inquiry suggested here (which obviously could not be pursued within the confines of literary study or critical theory as they are presently conceived and demarcated) might be expected to make its accounts internally consistent, externally connectable, and amenable to continuous extension and refinement; for it is thus that the theoretical power and productivity of those accounts would be served and secured. This is not, however, to imagine a monolithic intellectual project that would offer to yield an ultimately comprehensive, unified, and objective ac-

[23]Chinweizu, letter to the editor, *Times Literary Supplement,* 15 July 1977, p. 871. [Au.] The reader who examines the full text of both Bigsby's review and Chinweizu's letter will wonder whether this is a quarrel over "literary evaluation" or over turf between black and white literary critics. In a sentence omitted by Smith, for example, Chinweizu says, "Any *bête blanche* intruder into the affairs of a "Burnt Cork" is free to submit his preferences, but he is not likely to get them filled." [Ed.]

[24]Thus Sammons, in his embattled book, writes of "the elements . . . in the canon of great literature" to which we should be attentive so that, faced with charges of elitism, "we will not have to stand mute before claims that inarticulateness, ignorance, occult mumbling, and loutishness are just as good as fine literature" (*Literary Sociology and Practical Criticism,* p. 134). [Au.]

count of its subject; for to imagine it thus would, of course, be to repeat, only on a grander scale, elements of the raw positivism and naive scientism that were, in part, responsible for both the exile of evaluation and the confinements of modern critical theory. What is desirable, rather, is an inquiry pursued with the recognition that, like any other intellectual enterprise, it would consist, at any given time, of a set of heterogeneous projects; that the conceptual structures and methodological practices adopted in those projects would themselves be historically and otherwise contingent (reflecting, among other things, prevailing or currently interesting conceptual structures and methods in related areas of inquiry); that whatever other value the descriptions and accounts produced by any of those projects might and undoubtedly would have (as indices of twentieth-century thought, for example, to future historians), their specific value as descriptions and accounts would be a function of how well they made intelligible the phenomena within their domain to whoever, at whatever time and from whatever perspective, had an interest in them; and that its pursuit would be shaped by — that is, energized and transformed in response to — those interests, and its descriptions and accounts continuously and variously interpreted and employed in accord with them.[25]

The discussion that follows is designed to suggest a theoretical framework for such an inquiry.[26]

2. THE ECONOMICS OF LITERARY AND AESTHETIC VALUE

All value is radically contingent, being neither an inherent property of objects nor an arbitrary projection of subjects but, rather, the product of the dynamics of an economic system. It is readily granted, of course, that it is in relation to a system of that sort that commodities such as gold, bread, and paperback editions of *Moby-Dick* acquire the value indicated by their market prices. It is traditional, however, both in economic and aesthetic theory as well as in informal discourse, to distinguish sharply between the value of an entity in that sense (that is, its "exchange-value") and some other type of value that may be referred to as its utility (or "use-value") or, especially with respect to so-called "nonutilitarian" objects such as artworks or works of literature, as its "intrinsic value." Thus, it might be said that whereas the fluctuating price of a particular paperback edition of *Moby-Dick* is a function of such variables as supply and demand, production and distribution costs, and the publisher's calculation of corporate profits, these factors do not affect the value of *Moby-Dick* as experienced by an individual reader or its intrinsic value as a work of literature. These distinctions, however, are not as clear-cut as may appear.

Like its price in the marketplace, the value of an entity to an individual subject is *also* the product of the dynamics of an economic system, specifically the personal economy constituted by the subject's needs, interests, and resources — biological, psychological, material, and experiential. Like any other economy, moreover, this too is a continuously fluctuating or shifting system, for our individual needs, interests, and resources are themselves functions of our continuously changing states in relation to an environment that may be relatively stable but is never absolutely fixed. The two systems are, it may be noted, not only analogous but also interactive and interdependent; for part of our environment *is* the market economy, and, conversely, the market economy is comprised, in part, of the diverse personal economies of individual producers, distributors, consumers, and so forth.

The traditional discourse of value — including a number of terms I have used here, such as "subject," "object," "needs," "interests," and, indeed, "value" itself — reflects an arbitrary arresting, segmentation, and hypostasization of the continuous process of our interactions with our environments — or what could also be described as the continuous interplay among multiple configurable systems. It is difficult to devise (and would be, perhaps, impossible to sustain) a truly

[25]See Gonzalo Munévar, *Radical Knowledge: A Philosophical Inquiry into the Nature and Limits of Science* (Indianapolis, 1981), for an elaboration of a "performance model" of scientific activity along the lines implied here. [Au.]

[26]For a companion piece to the present essay, see my "Fixed Marks and Variable Constancies: A Parable of Literary Value," *Poetics Today* 1 (Autumn 1979): 7–31. [Au.]

Heraclitean discourse that did not reflect such conceptual operations, but we may recognize that, insofar as such terms project images of discrete acts, agents, and entities, fixed attributes, unidirectional forces, and simple causal and temporal relationships, they obscure the dynamics of value and reinforce dubious concepts of noncontingency — that is, concepts such as "intrinsic," "objective," "absolute," "universal," and "transcendent." It is necessary, therefore, to emphasize a number of other interactive relationships and forms of interdependence that are fragmented by our language and commonly ignored in critical theory and aesthetic axiology.

First, as I have already suggested, a subject's experience of an entity is always a function of his or her personal economy: that is, the specific "existence" of an object or event, its integrity, coherence, and boundaries, the category of entities to which it "belongs" and its specific "features," "qualities," or "properties" are all the variable products of the subject's engagement with his or her environment under a particular set of conditions. Not only is an entity always experienced under more or less different conditions, but the various experiences do not yield a simple cumulative (corrected, improved, deeper, more thorough, or complete) knowledge of the entity because they are not additive. Rather, each experience of an entity frames it in a different role and constitutes it as a different configuration, with different "properties" foregrounded and repressed. Moreover, the subject's experiences of an entity are not discrete or, strictly speaking, successive, because recollection and anticipation always overlay perception and the units of what we call "experience" themselves vary and overlap.

Second, what we speak of as a subject's "needs," "interests," and "purposes" are not only always changing (and it may be noted here that a subject's "self" — or that on behalf of which s/he may be said to act with "self-interest" — is also variable, being multiply reconstituted in terms of different roles and relationships), but they are also not altogether independent of or prior to the entities that satisfy or implement them; that is, entities also produce the needs and interests they satisfy and evoke the purposes they implement. Moreover, because our purposes are continuously transformed and redirected by the objects we produce in the very process of implementing them, and because of the complex interrelations among human needs, technological production, and cultural practices, there is a continuous process of mutual modification between our desires and our universe.[27]

Of particular significance for the value of "works of art" and "literature" is the interactive relation between the *classification* of an entity and the functions it is expected or desired to perform. In perceiving an object or artifact in terms of some category — *as,* for example, "a clock," "a dictionary," "a doorstop," "a curio" — we implicitly isolate and foreground certain of its possible functions and typically refer its value to the extent to which it performs those functions more or less effectively. But the relation between function and classification also operates in reverse: thus, under conditions that produce the "need" for a door-stopping object or an "interest" in Victorian artifacts, certain properties and possible functions of various objects in the neighborhood will be foregrounded, and both the classification and value of those objects will follow accordingly. As we commonly put it, one will "realize" the value of the dictionary *as* a doorstop or "appreciate" the value of the clock *as* a curio.[28] (The

[27]Some aspects of this process are discussed by Pierre Bourdieu in "La Métamorphose des goûts," *Questions de sociologie* (Paris, 1980), pp. 161–72. The more general interrelations among human "needs and wants," cultural practices, and economic production have been examined by Marshall Sahlins in *Culture and Practical Reason* (Chicago, 1976), Mary Douglas in *The World of Goods* (New York, 1979), and Jean Baudrillard in *For a Critique of the Political Economy of the Sign* (Paris, 1972), trans. Charles Levin (St. Louis, 1981). Although Baudrillard's critical analysis of the concept of "use-value" — and, with it, of "sign value" — is of considerable interest for a semiotics of the marketplace, his effort to develop, "as a basis for the practical overthrow of political economy" (p. 122), a theory of a value "beyond value" (created out of what he calls "symbolic exchange") is less successful, partly because of its utopian anthropology and partly because the value in question does not escape economic accounting. [Au.]

[28]For an excellent analysis of the relation between classification and value, see Michael Thompson, *Rubbish Theory: The Creation and Destruction of Value* (Oxford, 1979), esp. pp. 13–56. [Au.]

mutually defining relations among classification, function, and value are nicely exhibited in the *OED*'s definition of "curio" as "an object of art, piece of bric-à-brac, etc., valued as a curiosity," which is, of course, something like — and no less accurate than — defining "clock" as "an object valued as a clock.") It may be noted here that human beings have evolved as distinctly opportunistic creatures and that our survival, both as individuals and as a species, continues to be enhanced by our ability and inclination to reclassify objects and to "realize" and "appreciate" novel and alternate functions for them — which is also to "misuse" them and to fail to respect their presumed purposes and conventional generic classifications.

The various forms of interdependence emphasized here have considerable bearing on what may be recognized as the economics of literary and aesthetic value. The traditional — idealist, humanist, genteel — tendency to isolate or protect certain aspects of life and culture, among them works of art and literature, from consideration in economic terms has had the effect of mystifying the nature — or, more accurately, the dynamics — of their value. In view of the arbitrariness of the exclusion, it is not surprising that the languages of aesthetics and economics nevertheless tend to drift toward each other and that their segregation must be constantly patrolled.[29] (Thus, an aesthetician deplores a pun on "appreciation" appearing in an article on art investment and warns of the dangers of confusing "the uniqueness of a painting that gives it scarcity value . . . with its unique value as a work of art.")[30] To those for whom terms such as "utility," "effectiveness," and "function" suggest gross pragmatic instrumentality, crass material desires, and the satisfaction of animal needs, a concept such as use-value will be seen as irrelevant to or clearly to be distinguished from aesthetic value. There is, however, no good reason to confine the domain of the utilitarian to objects that serve only immediate, specific, and unexalted ends or, for that matter, to assume that the value of artworks has altogether nothing to do with pragmatic instrumentality or animal needs.[31] The recurrent impulse or effort to define aesthetic value by contradistinction to all forms of utility or as the negation of all other nameable sources of interest or forms of value — hedonic, practical, sentimental, ornamental, historical, ideological, and so forth — is, in effect, to define it out of existence; for when all such particular utilities, interests, and sources of value have been subtracted, nothing remains. Or, to put this in other terms: the "essential value" of an artwork consists of everything from which it is usually distinguished.

To be sure, various candidates have been proposed for a pure, nonutilitarian, interest-free, and, in effect, value-free source of aesthetic value, such as the eliciting of "intrinsically rewarding" intellectual, sensory, or perceptual activities, or Kant's "free play of the cognitive faculties." A strict accounting of any of these seemingly gratuitous activities, however, would bring us sooner or later to their biological utility and/or survival value (and indeed to something very much like "animal needs"). For although we may be individually motivated to engage in them "for their own sake" (which is to say, for the sake of the gratifications they provide), our doing so apparently yields a long-term profit in enhanced cognitive development, behavioral flexibility, and thus biological fitness, and our general tendency to do so is in all likelihood the product of

[29]The magnetism or recurrent mutually metaphoric relation between economic and aesthetic — especially literary — discourse is documented and discussed by Marc Shell in *The Economy of Literature* (Baltimore, 1978) and Kurt Heinzelman in *The Economics of the Imagination* (Amherst, Mass., 1980). [Au.]

[30]Andrew Harrison, *Making and Thinking* (Indianapolis, 1978), p. 100. [Au.]

[31]See George J. Stigler and Gary S. Becker, "De gustibus non est disputandum," *American Economics Review* 67 (March 1977): 76–90, for an ingenious and influential attempt (at the opposite extreme, perhaps, of Baudrillard's [see n. 27 above]) to demonstrate that differences and changes of behavior (including aesthetic behavior) that appear to be matters of "taste" and, as such, beyond explanation in economic terms can be accounted for (*a*) as functions of subtle forms of "price" and "income" and (*b*) on the usual (utilitarian) assumption that we always behave, all things considered, so as to maximize utility. As Stigler and Becker acknowledge, recent experimental studies of "choice behavior" in human (and other) subjects suggest that this latter assumption itself requires modification. [Au.]

evolutionary mechanisms.[32] Moreover, as I have pointed out elsewhere, the occasioning of such activities (or "experiences") is not confined to "works of art" and therefore cannot, without circularity, be said to constitute the defining "aesthetic function" of the objects so labeled.[33] More generally, it may be observed that since there are no functions performed by artworks that may be specified as unique to them and also no way to distinguish the "rewards" provided by the art-related experiences or behavior from those provided by innumerable other kinds of experience and behavior, any distinctions drawn between "aesthetic" and "non- (or "extra-) aesthetic" value are fundamentally problematic.[34]

Suggestions of the radically contingent nature of aesthetic value are commonly countered by evidence of apparent noncontingent value: for example, the endurance of certain classic canonical works (the invocation of Homer being a topos of the critical tradition) and, if not quite Pope's "gen'ral chorus of mankind," then at least the convergent sentiments of people of education and discrimination. Certainly any theory of aesthetic value must be able to account for continuity, stability, and apparent consensus as well as for drift, shift, and diversity. The tendency throughout formal aesthetic axiology has been to explain the constancies and convergences by the inherent qualities of the objects and/or some set of presumed human universals and to explain the variabilities and divergences by the errors, defects, and biases of individual subjects. The classic development of this account is found in Hume's essay, *Of the Standard of Taste,* where the "catholic and universal beauty" is seen to be the result of

> [t]he relation which nature has placed between the form and the sentiment. . . . We shall be able to ascertain its influence . . . from the durable admiration which attends those works that have survived all the caprices of mode and fashion, all the mistakes of ignorance and envy.
>
> The same Homer who pleased at Athens two thousand years ago, is still admired at Paris and London. All the changes of climate, government, religion and language have not been able to obscure his glory. . . .
>
> It appears then, that amidst all the variety and caprice of taste, there are certain general principles of approbation and blame, whose influence a careful eye may trace in all the operations of the mind. Some particular forms or qualities, from the original structure of the internal fabric are calculated to please, and others to displease; and if they fail of their effect in any particular instance, it is from some apparent defect or imperfection in the organ.
>
> Many and frequent are the defects . . . which prevent or weaken the influence of those general principles.[35]

The essay continues by enumerating and elaborating these defects, introducing the familiar catalog (already given vivid expression in, among other places, Pope's *Essay on Criticism:* "Of all the causes which conspire to blind / Man's erring judgment and misguide the mind") with an analogy, also a commonplace of the tradition, between "the perfect beauty," as agreed upon by men "in a sound state of the organ," and "the true and real colors" of objects as they appear "in daylight to the eye of a man in health."[36]

[32]See Robert Fagen, *Animal Play Behavior* (Oxford, 1981), pp. 248–358, for an extensive analysis of "intrinsically rewarding" physical activities and an account of the evolutionary mechanisms that apparently produce and sustain them. [Au.]

[33]See the related discussion of "cognitive play" in my *On the Margins of Discourse: The Relation of Literature to Language* (Chicago, 1978), pp. 116–24. [Au.]

[34]Monroe Beardsley's "instrumentalist" (that is, utilitarian) theory of aesthetic value (*Aesthetics: Problems in the Philosophy of Criticism* [New York, 1958], pp. 524–76) and Mukařovský's otherwise quite subtle exploration of these questions (see n. 16, above) do not altogether escape the confinements and circularities of formalist conceptions of, respectively, "aesthetic experience" and "aesthetic function." [Au.]

[35]David Hume, *"Of the Standard of Taste" and Other Essays,* ed. John W. Lenz (Indianapolis, 1965), pp. 8–10. [Au.] See Hume, p. 242. [Ed.]

[36]Ibid., p. 10. At the conclusion of the essay, Hume almost — but not quite — reinstalls the very *de gustibus* argument that the standard of taste was presumably designed to answer: "But where there is such a diversity in the internal frame or external situation as is entirely blameless on both sides, . . . a certain degree of diversity of judgment is unavoidable and we seek in vain a standard by which we can reconcile the contrary sentiments" (pp. 19–20). Of course, the qualification ("as is entirely blameless on both sides") that keeps this from being a total turnabout also introduces a new

The following is a more recent statement of the traditional view:

> False judgments and intuitions of an object can only be corrected if there is a correct and permanently valid intuition of an object. . . . The relativity of value judgments merely proves that subjective judgments are conjoined with the person, that mistaken judgments — of which there is no dearth in the history of literature — are always the fault of the person.
>
> . . . Just as the universal validity of a mathematical proposition does not necessarily imply that everyone can understand it, "but merely that everyone who understands it must agree with it," so the universal validity of aesthetic value does not necessarily mean that evidence of it is felt by everyone. Aesthetic values demand an adequate attitude, a trained or reliably functioning organ. Moreover, the fact that the history of literature contains, albeit tacitly, a firm gradation of valuable works of art is an indication that values transcend historicity.
>
> . . . The value-feeling organ must not be encumbered with prejudgments, pre-feelings, or arbitrarily formed opinions if it wishes to address itself adequately to the object, a process that is by no means always easy, . . . for the human being is in part — an external but not uninfluential part — a historical creature, embedded in a whole cluster of behavior compulsions that stem from his environment.[37]

This conflation of, among others, Hume, Kant, Nicolai Hartmann, and Roman Ingarden is remarkable only in making particularly flagrant the logical incoherence of the standard account, whether in its empiricist, idealist, or phenomenological guise.

Given a more sophisticated formulation, Hume's belief that the individual experience of "beauty" can be related to "forms" and "qualities" that gratify human beings "naturally" by virtue of certain physiological structures and psychological mechanisms is probably not altogether without foundation.[38] Taken as a ground for the justification of normative claims, however, and transformed accordingly into a model of standards-and-deviations, it obliged him (as it did and does many others) to interpret as so many instances of individual pathology what are, rather, the variable products of the interaction between, on the one hand, certain *relatively* uniform innate structures, mechanisms, and tendencies and, on the other, innumerable cultural and contextual variables as well as other individual variables — the latter including particulars of personal history, temperament, age, and so forth. What produces evaluative consensus, such as it is, is not the healthy functioning of universal organs but the playing out of the *same* dynamics and variable contingencies that produce evaluative divergences.

Although value is always subject-relative, not all value is equally subject-variable. Within a particular community, the tastes and preferences of subjects — that is, their tendency to find more satisfaction of a particular kind in one rather than another of some array of comparable items and to select among them accordingly — will be conspicuously *divergent* (or indeed idiosyncratic) to the extent that the satisfactions in question are themselves functions of types of needs, interests, and resources that (*a*) vary individually along a wide spectrum, (*b*) are especially resistant, if not altogether intractable, to cultural channeling, and/or (*c*) are especially responsive to circumstantial context. Conversely, their tastes and preferences will tend to be similar to the extent that the satisfactions in question are functions of types of needs, interests, and resources that (*a*) vary individually within a narrow spectrum, (*b*) are especially tractable to cultural channeling, and (*c*) remain fairly stable under a variety of conditions.

Insofar as satisfactions ("aesthetic" or any other: erotic, for example) with regard to some array of objects are functions of needs, interests,

normative consideration (how to determine whether or not — or to what extent — something "in the internal frame or external situation" is *blamable*) and thus moves again toward the type of potentially infinite regress into which all axiologies typically tumble. [Au.]

[37]Walter Hinderer, "Literary Value Judgments and Value Cognition," trans. Leila Vannewitz, in *Problems of Literary Evaluation*, pp. 58–59. [Au.]

[38]The discipline of "empirical aesthetics" has been developed out of precisely such a belief. For a recent survey and discussion of its findings, see Hans and Shulamith Kreitler, *Psychology of the Arts* (Durham, N.C., 1972). See also n. 52 below. [Au.]

and resources of the first kind, preferences for those objects will appear "subjective," "eccentric," "stubborn," and "capricious." Insofar as they are functions of the second, preferences will seem so obvious, "natural," and "rational" as not to appear to be matters of taste at all. Indeed, it is precisely under the latter conditions that the value of particular objects will appear to be inherent, that distinctions or gradations of value among them will appear to reduce to differences in the properties or qualities of the objects themselves, and that explicit judgments of their value will appear to be objective. In short, here as elsewhere, a coincidence of contingencies among individual subjects will be interpreted by those subjects as noncontingency.

Because we are dealing here not with two opposed sets of discrete determinants but with the possibility of widely differing specifications for a large number of complexly interacting variables, we may expect to find a continuous exhibition of every degree of divergence and convergence among the subjects in a particular community over the course of its history, depending in each instance on the extent of the disparity and uniformity of each of the relevant contingencies *and* on the strength of various social practices and cultural institutions that control the exhibition of extreme "deviance."[39] It may be noted that the latter — that is, the normative mechanisms within a community that suppress divergence and tend to obscure as well as deny the contingency of value — will always have, as their counterpart, a *counter*mechanism that permits a recognition of that contingency and a more or less genial acknowledgement of the inevitability of divergence: hence the ineradicability, in spite of the efforts of establishment axiology, of what might be called folk-relativism: "Chacun à son goût"; "De gustibus . . ."[40] "One man's meat is another's poison"; and so forth.

[39]See Morse Peckham, *Explanation and Power: The Control of Human Behavior* (New York, 1979), for an account of deviance (or what he calls "the delta effect") as the product of the relation between cultural practices and the randomness of behavior and, more generally, for a highly original discussion of the processes and institutions of cultural channeling. [Au.]

[40]Each to his own taste; about tastes [there is no disputing]. . . . [Ed.]

The prevailing structure of tastes and preferences (and the consequent illusion of a consensus based on objective value) will always be implicitly threatened or directly challenged by the divergent tastes and preferences of some subjects within the community (for example, those not yet adequately acculturated, such as the young, and others with "uncultivated" tastes, such as provincials and social upstarts) as well as by most subjects outside it or, more significantly, on its *periphery* and who thus have occasion to interact with its members (for example, exotic visitors, immigrants, colonials, and members of various minority or marginalized groups). Consequently, institutions of evaluative authority will be called upon repeatedly to devise arguments and procedures that validate the community's established tastes and preferences, thereby warding off barbarism and the constant apparition of an imminent collapse of standards and also justifying the exercise of their own normative authority. In Hume's words, "It is natural to seek a Standard of Taste; a rule by which the various sentiments of men may be reconciled; at least a decision afforded confirming one sentiment and denying another" — the usefulness of such a rule to the latter end being illustrated in the essay by that memorable vignette of the barbarian in the drawing room who "would assert an equality of genius and elegance between Ogilby and Milton or Bunyan and Addison" and what ensues: "Though there may be found *persons* who give preference to the former authors, *no one* pays attention to such taste; and *we* pronounce without scruple the sentiment of these pretended critics to be absurd and ridiculous."[41] The sequence emphasized here is no less telling than the embarrassment of the argument by the examples.

Both informally, as in the drawing rooms of men of cultivation and discrimination or the classrooms of the literary academy, and formally, as in Hume's essay and throughout the central tradition of Western critical theory, the validation commonly takes the form of privileging absolutely — that is, "standard"-izing — the particular contingencies that govern the preferences of

[41]Hume, *"Of the Standard of Taste,"* pp. 5, 7. [Au.]

the members of the group and discounting or, as suggested above, pathologizing all other contingencies.[42] Thus it will be assumed or maintained: (*a*) that the particular *functions* they expect and desire the class of objects in question (for example, "works of art" or "literature") to perform are their intrinsic or proper functions, all other expected, desired, or emergent functions being inappropriate, irrelevant, extrinsic, abuses of the true nature of those objects or violations of their authorially intended or generically intrinsic purposes; (*b*) that the particular *conditions* (circumstantial, technological, institutional, and so forth) under which the members of the group typically interact with those objects are suitable, standard, or necessary for their proper appreciation, all other conditions being irregular, unsuitable, substandard, or outlandish; and, perhaps most significantly, (*c*) that the particular *subjects* who compose the members of the group are of sound mind and body, duly trained and informed, and generally competent, all other subjects being defective, deficient, or deprived — suffering from crudenesses of sensibility, diseases and distortions of perception, weaknesses of character, impoverishment of background-and-education, cultural or historical biases, ideological or personal prejudices, and/or undeveloped, corrupted, or jaded tastes.

With regard to this last point (*c*), we may recall here the familiar specifications of the "ideal critic" as one who, in addition to possessing various exemplary natural endowments and cultural competencies, has, through exacting feats of self-liberation, freed himself of all forms of particularity and individuality, all special interests (or, as in Kant, all interests whatsoever), and thus of all bias — which is to say, one who is "free" of everything in relation to which any experience or judgment of value occurs. (In these respects, the ideal critic of aesthetic axiology is the exact counterpart of the "ideal reader" of literary hermeneutics.)

We may also note, with regard to the first point (*a*), that the privileging of a particular set of functions for artworks or works of literature may be (and often is) itself justified on the grounds that the performance of such functions serves some higher individual, social, or transcendent good, such as the psychic health of the reader, the brotherhood of mankind, the glorification of God, the project of human emancipation, or the survival of Western civilization. Any selection from among these alternate and to some extent mutually exclusive higher goods, however, would itself require justification in terms of some yet *higher* good, and there is no absolute stopping point for this theoretically infinite regress of judgments and justifications. This is not to say that certain functions of artworks do not serve higher — or at least more general comprehensive, or longer-range — goods better than others. It is to say, however, that our selection among higher goods, like our selection among any array of goods, will always be contingent.

3. THE MULTIPLE FORMS, FUNCTIONS, AND CONTEXTS OF EVALUATIVE BEHAVIOR

It follows from the conception of value outlined here that evaluations are not discrete acts or episodes punctuating experience but indistinguishable from the very processes of acting and experiencing themselves. In other words, for a responsive creature, to exist is to evaluate. We are always calculating how things "figure" for us — always pricing them, so to speak, in relation to the total economy of our personal universe. Throughout our lives, we perform a continuous succession of rapid-fire cost-benefit analyses, estimating the probable "worthwhileness" of alternate courses of action in relation to our always limited resources of time and energy, assessing, reassessing, and classifying entities with respect to their probable capacity to satisfy our current needs and desires and to serve our emergent interests and long-range plans and purposes. We tend to become most conscious of our own evaluative behavior when the need to select among an

[42]Communities are of all sizes and so are drawing rooms; the provincials, colonials, and marginalized groups mentioned above (including the young), insofar as they constitute social communities, may also be expected to have prevailing structures of tastes and preferences and to control them in the same ways as do more obviously "establishment" groups. Folk-relativism is neither confined to the folk nor always exhibited by them. [Au.]

array of alternate "goods" and/or to resolve an internal "contest of sentiments" moves us to specifically verbal or other symbolic forms of cost accounting: thus we draw up our lists of pros and cons, lose sleep, and bore our friends by overtly rehearsing our options, estimating the risks and probable outcomes of various actions, and so forth. Most of these calculations, however, are performed intuitively and inarticulately, and many of them are so recurrent that the habitual arithmetic becomes part of our personality and comprises the very style of our being and behavior, forming what we may call our principles or tastes — and what others may call our biases and prejudices.

I have been speaking up to this point of the evaluations we make for ourselves. As social creatures, however, we also evaluate for one another through various kinds of individual acts and also through various institutional practices. The long-standing preoccupation of aesthetic axiology with the logical form and cognitive substance of verbal "value judgments" and, in particular, with debates over their "validity," "truth-value," and "verifiability," has obscured the operation and significance of institutional and other less overt forms of evaluation. It has also deflected attention from the social contexts, functions, and consequences of all forms of aesthetic and literary evaluation, including their complex productive relation to literary and aesthetic value. Although I am more concerned here with the latter questions and shall return to them below, some comments on *explicit* aesthetic judgments (and on certain familiar axiological perplexities regarding them) are in order.

Evaluations are among the most fundamental forms of social communication and probably among the most primitive benefits of social interaction. (Animals — insects and birds as well as mammals — evaluate *for* one another, that is, signal to other members of their group the "quality" of a food supply or territory by some form of specialized overt behavior.)[43] We not only produce but also solicit and seek out both "expressions of personal sentiment" and "objective judgments of value" because, although neither will (for nothing can) give us "knowledge" of *the* value of an object, both may let us know other things we could find useful. For example, other people's reports of how well certain objects have gratified them, though "mere expressions of subjective likes and dislikes," may nevertheless be useful to us if we ourselves have produced those objects or if — as lovers, say, or parents or potential associates — we have an independently motivated interest in the current states, specific responses, or general structure of tastes and preferences of those people. Also, an assertion that some object (for example, some artwork) is good, great, bad, or middling can, no matter how magisterially delivered or with what attendant claims or convictions of absoluteness, usually be unpacked as a judgment of its *contingent* value: specifically, as the evaluator's observation and/or estimate of how well that object, relative to others of the same implied category, has performed and/or is likely to perform certain particular (though taken-for-granted) functions for some particular (though only implicitly defined) set of subjects under some particular (unspecified but assumed) set or range of conditions. Any evaluation, therefore, is "cognitively substantial" in the sense of being potentially informative about *something.* The actual interest of that information, however, and hence the value of that evaluation to *us* (and "we" are always heterogeneous) will vary, depending on, among other things, the extent to which we have any interest in the object evaluated, believe that we take for granted the same taken-for-granted functions and assume the same assumed conditions, and also think that we (or others whose interests are of interest to us) are among that implicitly defined set of subjects — or, of course, the extent to which we have an interest in the evaluator's sentiments by reason of our independently motivated interest in him or her.

In view of the centrality of the question in post-Kantian aesthetic axiology, it may be noted

[43]To the extent that such forms of behavior are under the control of innate mechanisms that respond directly to — or, in effect, "register" — the conditions in question, they are not, strictly speaking, verbal or symbolic. For this reason, such evaluations may be "objective" in a way that, for better or worse, no human value judgment can be. [Au.]

that if the set of relevant subjects implied by an evaluation is not contextually defined or otherwise indicated, it will usually be appropriately taken to consist of the evaluator himself and all others whom s/he believes are *like* himself or herself in the pertinent respects. Of course, some evaluators believe that *all* other people are — or should be — like themselves in the pertinent respects: hence, apparently, the curious and distracting notion that every aesthetic judgment "claims universal subjective validity."[44] The familiar subjectivist/objectivist controversy is commonly seen to turn on whether, in making an aesthetic judgment, I speak "for myself *alone*" or "for *everyone*." A consideration of the social functions of such judgments, however, suggests that, if such a formulation is wanted at all, it should be that, in making aesthetic judgments, I tend to speak "for myself *and some others*."

We may also consider here what is thought to be the suspect propositional status of value judgments as distinguished from and compared to that of so-called factual statements and the consequent demotion of the former to the status of "pseudostatements." There is, of course, no way for us to be certain that someone's reports of his or her personal likes or dislikes are sincere, or that the estimates and observations offered are the estimates and observations actually made. Like all other utterances, value judgments are context-dependent and shaped by the relation of the speaker to his or her audience and by the structure of interests that sustains the verbal transaction between them. (In effect, there is no such thing as an honest opinion.) For this reason, we will always interpret (supplement and discount) evaluations in the light of other knowledge we have of the evaluator (or think we have: there is no absolute end to this regress, though in practice we do the best we can), including our sense — on whatever grounds — of the possibility of flattery or other kinds of deception: the evaluator may be the author's personal friend or professional rival, s/he may not want to hurt the cook's feelings, s/he may want to recommend himself or herself by creating the impression that s/he shares our tastes, and so forth. In all these respects, however, value judgments are no different from any other kind of utterance, and neither their reliability nor their "validity" as "propositions" is any more (or any less) compromised by these possibilities than that of any other type of verbal behavior, from someone's saying (or otherwise implying) that s/he has a headache to his or her solemn report of the measurement of a scientific instrument.

There is a tenacious conviction among those who argue these questions that unless one judgment can be said or shown to be more "valid" than another, then all judgments must be "equal" or "equally valid." Indeed, it is the horror or apparent absurdity of such egalitarianism that commonly gives force to the charge that "relativism" produces social chaos or is a logically untenable position. While the radical contingency of all value certainly does imply that no value judgment can be more valid than another in the sense of being a more accurate statement of *the* value of an object (for the latter concept then becomes vacuous), it does not follow that all value judgments are equal or equally valid. On the contrary, what does follow is that the concept of "validity" is *inappropriate* with regard to evaluations and that there is no nontrivial parameter with respect to which they *could* be "equal." This is not to say that no evaluations can be better or worse than others. What must be emphasized, however, is that the value — the "goodness" or "badness" — of an evaluation, like that of anything else (including any other type of utterance), is *itself* con-

[44]Kant's tortured attempt, which occupies most of *The Critique of Judgment,* to ground such a claim on the possibility of a cognition of pure aesthetic value (that is, "beauty") produced by nothing but the free operation of universal cognitive faculties has been recently revived and supplemented by Hirsch's attempt to ground it on the possibility of "correct interpretation," specifically the "re-cognition" of that "universally valid cognition of a work . . . constituted by the kind of subjective stance adopted in its creation" *(The Aims of Interpretation,* pp. 105–6). For a recent and very thorough examination of *The Critique of Judgment,* see Paul Guyer, *Kant and the Claims of Taste* (Cambridge, Mass., and London, 1979); for a thoroughly irreverent examination of it, see Jacques Derrida, "Economimesis," trans. Richard Klein, *Diacritics* 2 (Summer 1981): 3–25. [Au.] See Kant, p. 262. Smith apparently understands Kant as claiming that the judgment of taste is universal in fact rather than in its subjective aspect. See the introduction to Kant, p. 254. [Ed.]

tingent, and thus a matter not of its abstract "truth-value" but of how well it performs various desired/able functions for the various people who may at any time be concretely involved with it. In the case of an aesthetic evaluation, these people will always include the evaluator, who will have his or her own particular interest in the various effects of the judgments s/he produces, and may also include anyone from the artist to a potential publisher or patron, various current or future audiences of the work, and perhaps someone who just likes to know what's going on and what other people think is going on. Each of them will have his or her own interest in the evaluation, and it will be better or worse for each of them in relation to a different set of desired/able functions. What all this suggests is that the obsessive debates over the cognitive substance, logical status, and "truth-value" of aesthetic judgments are not only unresolvable in the terms given but, strictly speaking, pointless.

As was indicated above, the value of an explicit verbal evaluation — that is, its utility to those who produce and receive it — will, like that of any other type of utterance, always be a function of specific features of the various transactions of which it may be a part, including the relevant interests of the speaker and any of those who, at any time, become members of his or her de facto audience. It follows that the value of a value judgment may also be quite minimal or negative. For example, depending on specific (and readily imaginable) contextual features, an aesthetic judgment may be excruciatingly *un*interesting to the listener or elicited from the speaker at considerable expense to himself or herself. Also, aesthetic judgments, like any other use of language, may be intimidating, coercive, and otherwise socially and politically oppressive. If they are so, however, it is not because of any characteristic frailty of their propositional status (and "justifying" them — that is, giving a show of justice to their claims of objectivity or universal validity — will not eliminate the oppression) but, once again, because of the nature of the transactions of which they are a part, particularly the social or political relationship between the evaluator and his or her audience (professor and student, for example, or censor and citizen) and the structure of power that governs that relationship.[45] We may return now from the discussion of individual overt value judgments to the more general consideration of evaluative behavior, normative institutions, and the social mechanisms by which literary and aesthetic value are produced.

4. THE CULTURAL RE-PRODUCTION OF VALUE

We do not move about in a raw universe. Not only are the objects we encounter always to some extent pre-interpreted and preclassified for us by our particular cultures and languages, but also pre-evaluated, bearing the marks and signs of their prior valuings and evaluations by our fellow creatures. Indeed, preclassification is itself a form of pre-evaluation, for the labels or category names under which we encounter objects not only, as we suggested earlier, foreground certain of their possible functions but also operate as signs — in effect, as culturally certified endorsements — of their more or less effective performance of those functions.

Like all other objects, works of art and literature bear the marks of their own evaluational history, signs of value that acquire their force by virtue of various social and cultural practices and, in this case, certain highly specialized and elaborated institutions. The labels "art" and "literature" are, of course, commonly signs of membership in distinctly honorific categories. The particular functions that may be endorsed by these labels, however, are, unlike those of "doorstops" and "clocks," neither narrowly confined nor readily specifiable but, on the contrary, exceptionally heterogeneous, mutable, and elusive. To the extent — always limited — that the relation between these labels and a particular set of expected and desired functions is stabilized within a community, it is largely through the nor-

[45]I discuss these and related aspects of verbal transactions in *On the Margins of Discourse,* pp. 15–24 and 82–106, and in "Narrative Versions, Narrative Theories," *Critical Inquiry* 7 (Autumn 1980): 225–26 and 231–36. [Au.]

mative activities of various institutions: most significantly, the literary and aesthetic academy which, among other things, develops pedagogic and other acculturative mechanisms directed at maintaining at least (and, commonly, at most) a *sub*population of the community whose members "appreciate the value" of works of art and literature "as such." That is, by providing them with "necessary backgrounds," teaching them "appropriate skills," "cultivating their interests," and, generally, "developing their tastes," the academy produces generation after generation of subjects for whom the objects and texts thus labeled do indeed perform the functions thus privileged, thereby insuring the continuity of mutually defining canonical works, canonical functions, and canonical audiences.[46]

It will be instructive at this point to consider the very beginning of a work's valuational history, namely, its initial evaluation by the artist (here, the author); for it is not only a prefiguration of all the subsequent acts of evaluation of which the work will become the subject but also a model or paradigm of all evaluative activity generally. I refer here not merely to that ultimate gesture of authorial judgment that must exhibit itself negatively — that is, in the author's either letting the work stand or ripping it up — but to the thousand individual acts of approval and rejection, preference and assessment, trial and revision that constitute the entire process of literary composition. The work we receive is not so much the achieved consummation of that process as its enforced abandonment: "abandonment" not because the author's techniques are inadequate to his or her goals but because the goals themselves are inevitably multiple, mixed, mutually competing, and thus mutually constraining, and also because they are inevitably unstable, changing their nature and relative potency and priority during the very course of composition. The completed work is thus always, in a sense, a temporary truce among contending forces, achieved at the point of exhaustion, that is, the literal depletion of the author's current resources or, given the most fundamental principle of the economics of existence, at the point when the author simply has something else — more worthwhile — to do: when, in other words, the time and energy s/he would have to give to further tinkering, testing, and adjustment are no longer compensated for by an adequately rewarding sense of continuing interest in the process or increased satisfaction in the product.

It is for comparable reasons that we, as readers of the work, will later let our own experience of it stand: not because we have fully "appreciated" the work, not because we have exhausted all its possible sources of interest and hence of value, but because we, too, ultimately have something else — more worthwhile — to do. The reader's experience of the work is prefigured — that is, both calculated and preenacted — by the author in other ways as well: for, in selecting this word, adjusting that turn of phrase, preferring this rhyme to that, the author is all the while testing the local and global effectiveness of each decision by impersonating in advance his or her various presumptive audiences, who thereby themselves participate in shaping the work they will later read. Every literary work — and, more generally, artwork — is thus the product of a complex evaluative feedback loop that embraces not only the ever-shifting economy of the artist's own interests and resources as they evolve during and in reaction to the process of composition, but also all the shifting economies of his or her assumed and imagined audiences, including those who do not yet exist but whose emergent interests, variable conditions of encounter, and rival sources of gratification the artist will attempt to predict — or will intuitively surmise — and to which, among other things, his or her own sense of the fittingness of each decision will be responsive.[47]

But this also describes all the other diverse forms of evaluation by which the work will be

[46]Pierre Macherey and Etienne Balibar analyze some aspects of this process in "Literature as an Ideological Form: Some Marxist Propositions," trans. James Kavanagh, *Praxis* 6 (1981): 43–58. [Au.]

[47]See Howard Becker, *Art Worlds* (Berkeley, Los Angeles, and London, 1982), pp. 198–209, for a description of some of the specific constraints that shape both the process and its termination and, more generally, for a useful account of the ways in which artworks are produced by "social networks." [Au.]

subsequently marked and its value reproduced and transmitted: that is, the innumerable implicit acts of evaluation performed by those who, as may happen, publish the work, purchase, preserve, display, quote, cite, translate, perform, allude to, and imitate it; the more explicit but casual judgments made, debated, negotiated in informal contexts by readers and by all those others in whose personal economies the work, in some way, "figures"; and the highly specialized institutionalized forms of evaluation exhibited in the more or less professional activities of scholars, teachers, and academic or journalistic critics — not only their full-dress reviews and explicit rank-orderings, evaluations, and revaluations, but also such activities as the awarding of literary prizes, the commissioning and publishing of articles about certain works, the compiling of anthologies, the writing of introductions, the construction of department curricula, and the drawing up of class reading lists. All of these forms of evaluation, whether overt or covert, verbal or inarticulate, and whether performed by the common reader, professional reviewer, big-time bookseller, or small-town librarian, have functions and effects that are significant in the production and maintenance or destruction of literary value, both reflecting and contributing to the various economies in relation to which a work acquires value. And each of the evaluative acts mentioned, like those of the author, represents a set of individual economic decisions, an ajudication among competing claims for limited resources of time, space, energy, attention — or, of course, money — and also, insofar as the evaluation is a socially responsive act or part of a social transaction, a set of surmises, assumptions, or predictions regarding the personal economies of other people.

Although, as I have emphasized, the evaluation of texts is not confined to the formal critical judgments issued within the rooms of the literary academy or upon the pages of its associated publications, the activities of the academy certainly figure significantly in the production of literary value. For example, the repeated inclusion of a particular work in literary anthologies not only promotes the value of that work but goes some distance toward creating its value, as does also its repeated appearance on reading lists or its frequent citation or quotation by professors, scholars, and academic critics. For all these acts, at the least, have the effect of drawing the work into the orbit of attention of a population of potential readers; and, by making it more accessible to the interests of those readers (while, as indicated above, at the same time shaping and supplying the very interests in relation to which they will experience the work), they make it more likely both that the work will be experienced at all and also that it will be experienced as valuable.

The converse side to this process is well known. Those who are in positions to edit anthologies and prepare reading lists are obviously those who occupy positions of some cultural power; and their acts of evaluation — represented in what they exclude as well as in what they include — constitute not merely recommendations of value but, for the reasons just mentioned, also determinants of value. Moreover, since they will usually exclude not only what they take to be inferior literature but also what they take to be nonliterary, subliterary, or paraliterary, their selections not only imply certain "criteria" of literary value, which may in fact be made explicit, but, more significantly, they produce and maintain certain definitions of "literature" and, thereby, certain assumptions about the desired and expected functions of the texts so classified and about the interests of their appropriate audiences, all of which are usually not explicit and, for that reason, less likely to be questioned, challenged, or even noticed. Thus the privileging power of evaluative authority may be very great, even when it is manifested inarticulately.[48] The academic activities described here, however, are only a small part of the complex process of literary canonization.

When we consider the cultural re-production of value on a larger time scale, the model of eval-

[48]For a well-documented illustration of the point, see Nina Baym, "Melodramas of Beset Manhood: How Theories of American Fiction Exclude Women Authors," *American Quarterly* 33 (Summer 1981): 125–39. In addition to anthologies, Baym mentions historical studies, psychological and sociological theories of literary production, and particular methods of literary interpretation. [Au.] See Baym, p. 1540. [Ed.]

uative dynamics outlined above suggests that the "survival" or "endurance" of a text — and, it may be, its achievement of high canonical status not only as a "work of literature" but as a "classic" — is the product neither of the objectively (in the Marxist sense) conspiratorial force of establishment institutions nor of the continuous appreciation of the timeless virtues of a fixed object by succeeding generations of isolated readers, but, rather, of a series of continuous interactions among a variably constituted object, emergent conditions, and mechanisms of cultural selection and transmission. These interactions are, in certain respects, analogous to those by virtue of which biological species evolve and survive and also analogous to those through which artistic choices evolve and are found fit or fitting by the individual artist. The operation of these cultural-historical dynamics may be briefly indicated here in quite general terms.

At a given time and under the contemporary conditions of available materials, technology, and techniques, a particular object — let us say a verbal artifact or text — may perform certain desired/able functions quite well for some set of subjects. It will do so by virtue of certain of its "properties" as they have been specifically constituted — framed, foregrounded, and configured — by those subjects under those conditions and in accord with their particular needs, interests, and resources — and also perhaps largely as prefigured by the artist who, as described earlier, in the very process of producing the work and continuously evaluating its fitness and adjusting it accordingly, will have multiply and variably constituted it. Two points implied by this description need emphasis here. One is that the value of a work — that is, its effectiveness in performing desired/able functions for some set of subjects — is not independent of authorial design, labor, and skill. The second, however, is that what may be spoken of as the "properties" of the work — its "structure," "features," "qualities," and, of course, its "meanings" — are not fixed, given or inherent in the work "itself" but are at every point the variable products of some subject's interaction with it. (It is thus never "the *same* Homer.") To the extent that any aspect of a work is recurrently constituted in similar ways by various subjects at various times, it will be because the subjects who do the constituting, *including the author,* are themselves similar, not only in being human creatures and in occupying a particular universe that may be, for them, in many respects recurrent or relatively continuous and stable, but also in inheriting from one another, through mechanisms of cultural transmission, certain ways of interacting with that universe, including certain ways of interacting with texts and "works of literature."

An object or artifact that performs certain desired/able functions particularly well at a given time for some community of subjects, being perhaps not only "fit" but exemplary — that is, "the best of its kind" — under those conditions, will have an immediate survival advantage; for, relative to (or in competition with) other comparable objects or artifacts available at that time, it will not only be better protected from physical deterioration but will also be more frequently used or widely exhibited and, if it is a text or verbal artifact, more frequently read or recited, copied or reprinted, translated, imitated, cited, and commented upon — in short, culturally reproduced — and thus will be more readily available to perform those or other functions for other subjects at a subsequent time.

Two possible trajectories ensue:

1. If, on the one hand, under the changing and emergent conditions of that subsequent time, the functions for which the text was earlier valued are no longer desired/able or if, in competition with comparable works (including, now, those newly produced with newly available materials and techniques), it no longer performs those original functions particularly well, it will, accordingly, be less well maintained and less frequently cited and recited so that its visibility as well as interest will fade, and it will survive, if at all, simply as a physical relic. It may, of course, be subsequently valued specifically *as* a relic (for its archeological or "historical" interest), in which case it *will* be performing desired/able functions and pursue the trajectory described below. It may also be subsequently "rediscovered" as an "unjustly neglected masterpiece," either when the functions it had originally performed are again

desired/able or, what is more likely, when different of its properties and possible functions become foregrounded by a new set of subjects with emergent interests and purposes.

2. If, on the other hand, under changing conditions and in competition with newly produced and other re-produced works, it continues to perform *some* desired/able functions particularly well, even if not the same ones for which it was initially valued (and, accordingly, by virtue of *other* newly foregrounded or differently framed or configured properties — including, once again, emergent "meanings"), it will continue to be cited and recited, continue to be visible and available to succeeding generations of subjects, and thus continue to be culturally re-produced. A work that has in this way survived for some time can always move into a trajectory of extinction through the sudden emergence or gradual conjunction of unfavorable conditions of the kind described above under (1). There are, however, a number of reasons why, once it has achieved canonical status, it will be more secured from that risk.

First, when the value of a work is seen as unquestionable, those of its features that would, in a noncanonical work, be found alienating — for example, technically crude, philosophically naive, or narrowly topical — will be glozed over[49] or backgrounded. In particular, features that conflict intolerably with the interests and ideologies of subsequent subjects (and, in the West, with those generally benign "humanistic" values for which canonical works are commonly celebrated) — for example, incidents or sentiments of brutality, bigotry, and racial, sexual, or national chauvinism — will be repressed or rationalized, and there will be a tendency among humanistic scholars and academic critics to "save the text" by transferring the locus of its interest to more formal or structural features and/or allegorizing its potentially alienating ideology to some more general ("universal") level where it becomes more tolerable and also more readily interpretable in terms of contemporary ideologies. Thus we make texts timeless by suppressing their temporality. (It may be added that to those scholars and critics for whom those features are not only palatable but for whom the value of the canonical works consist precisely in their "embodying" and "preserving" such "traditional values," the transfer of the locus of value to formal properties will be seen as a descent into formalism and "aestheticism," and the tendency to allegorize it too generally or to interpret it too readily in terms of "modern values" will be seen not as saving the text but as betraying it.)

Second, in addition to whatever various and perhaps continuously differing functions a work performs for succeeding generations of individual subjects, it will also begin to perform certain characteristic cultural functions by virtue of the very fact that it *has* endured — that is, the functions of a canonical work as such — and will be valued and preserved accordingly: as a witness to lost innocence, former glory, and/or apparently persistent communal interests and "values" and thus a banner of communal identity; as a reservoir of images, archetypes, and topoi — characters and episodes, passages and verbal tags — repeatedly invoked and recurrently applied to new situations and circumstances; and as a stylistic and generic exemplar that will energize the production of subsequent works and texts (upon which the latter will be modeled and by which, as a normative "touchstone," they will be measured). It these ways, the canonical work begins increasingly not merely to survive within but to shape and create the culture in which its value is produced and transmitted and, for that very reason, to perpetuate the conditions of its own flourishing. Nothing endures like endurance.

To the extent that we develop within and are formed by a culture that is itself constituted in part *by* canonical texts, it is not surprising that those texts seem, as Hans-Georg Gadamer puts it, to "speak" to us "directly" and even "specially":

> The classical is what is preserved precisely because it signifies and interprets itself; [that is,] that which speaks in such a way that it is not a statement about what is past, as mere testimony to something that needs to be interpreted, but says something to the present as if it were said specially to us. . . . This is just what the word "classical" means, that the dura-

[49]Explained away. [Ed.]

tion of the power of a work to speak directly is fundamentally unlimited.[50]

It is hardly, however, as Gadamer implies here, because such texts are uniquely self-mediated or unmediated and hence not needful of interpretation but, rather, because they have already been so thoroughly mediated — evaluated as well as interpreted — for us by the very culture and cultural institutions through which they have been preserved and by which we ourselves have been formed.

What is commonly referred to as "the test of time" (Gadamer, for example, characterizes "the classical" as "a notable mode of 'being historical,' that historical process of preservation that through the constant proving of itself sets before us something that is true")[51] is not, as the figure implies, an impersonal and impartial mechanism; for the cultural institutions through which it operates (schools, libraries, theaters, museums, publishing and printing houses, editorial boards, prize-awarding commissions, state censors, etc.) are, of course, all managed by persons (who, by definition, are those with cultural power and commonly other forms of power as well), and, since the texts that are selected and preserved by "time" will always tend to be those which "fit" (and, indeed, have often been *designed* to "fit") their characteristic needs, interests, resources, and purposes, that testing mechanism has its own built-in partialities accumulated in and thus *intensified by* time. For example, the characteristic resources of the culturally dominant members of a community include access to specific training and the opportunity and occasion to develop not only competence in a large number of cultural codes but also a large number of diverse (or "cosmopolitan") interests. The works that are differentially re-produced, therefore, will often be those that gratify the exercise of such competencies and engage interests of that kind: specifically, works that are structurally complex and, in the technical sense, information-rich — and which, by virtue of those very qualities, are especially amenable to multiple reconfiguration, more likely to enter into relation with the emergent interests of various subjects, and thus more readily adaptable to emergent conditions.[52] Also, as is often remarked, since those with cultural power tend to be members of socially, economically, and politically established classes (or to serve them and identify their own interests with theirs), the texts that survive will tend to be those that appear to reflect and reinforce establishment ideologies. However much canonical works may be seen to "question" secular vanities such as wealth, social position, and political power, "remind" their readers of more elevated values and virtues, and oblige them to "confront" such hard truths and harsh realities as their own mortality and the hidden griefs of obscure people, they would not be found to please long and well if they were seen to undercut establishment interests *radically* or to subvert the ideologies that support them *effectively*. (Construing them to the latter ends, of course, is one of the characteristic ways in which those with antiestablishment interests participate in the cultural re-production of canonical texts and thus in their endurance as well.)

It is clear that the needs, interests, and purposes of culturally and otherwise dominant members of a community do not exclusively or totally determine which works survive. The antiquity and longevity of domestic proverbs, popular tales, children's verbal games, and the entire phenomenon of what we call "folklore," which occurs through the same or corresponding mecha-

[50]Hans-Georg Gadamer, *Truth and Method,* trans. Barden Cumming: Sheed and Ward, Ltd. (New York, 1982), pp. 257–58. [Au.] For a very different refutation of Gadamer, see Jauss, p. 944; for Gadamer, see p. 677. [Ed.]

[51]Ibid., p. 255. [Au.]

[52]Structural complexity and information-richness are, of course, subject-relative as "qualities" and also experientially subject-variable; that is, we apparently differ individually in our tolerance for complexity in various sensory/perceptual modes and in our competence in processing information in different codes, so that what is interestingly complex and engagingly information-rich to one subject may be intolerably chaotic to another. See Gerda Smets, *Aesthetic Judgment and Arousal* (Louvain, 1973), and Sven Sandström, *A Common Taste in Art: An Experimental Attempt* (Lund, 1977), for two recent studies relevant to the point. Its relation to the general problem of aesthetic and literary value, itself a very complex matter, cannot be pursued here but is discussed briefly in *On the Margins of Discourse,* pp. 116–24. [Au.]

nisms of cultural selection and re-production as those described above specifically for "texts," demonstrate that the "endurance" of a verbal artifact (if not its achievement of *academic* canonical status as a "work of literature" — many folkloric works do, however, perform all the functions described above as characteristic of canonical works *as such*) may be more or less independent of institutions controlled by those with political power. Moreover, the interests and purposes of the latter must always operate in interaction with non- or antiestablishment interests and purposes as well as with various other contingencies and "accidents of time" over which they have limited, if any, control, from the burning of libraries to political and social revolutions, religious iconoclasms, and shifts of dominance among entire languages and cultures.

As the preceding discussion suggests, the value of a literary work is continuously produced and re-produced by the very acts of implicit and explicit evaluation that are frequently invoked as "reflecting" its value and therefore as being evidence of it. In other words, what are commonly taken to be the *signs* of literary value are, in effect, also its *springs*. The endurance of a classic canonical author such as Homer, then, owes not to the alleged transcultural or universal value of his works but, on the contrary, to the continuity of their circulation in a particular culture. Repeatedly cited and recited, translated, taught and imitated, and thoroughly enmeshed in the network of intertextuality that continuously *constitutes* the high culture of the orthodoxly educated population of the West (and the Western-educated population of the rest of the world), that highly variable entity we refer to as "Homer" recurrently enters our experience in relation to a large number and variety of our interests and thus can perform a large number of various functions for us and obviously has performed them for many of us over a good bit of the history of our culture. It is well to recall, however, that there are many people in the world who are not — or are not yet, or choose not to be — among the orthodoxly educated population of the West: people who do not encounter Western classics at all or who encounter them under cultural and institutional conditions very different from those of American and European college professors and their students. The fact that Homer, Dante, and Shakespeare do not figure significantly in the personal economies of these people, do not perform individual or social functions that gratify their interests, *do not have value for them,* might properly be taken as qualifying the claims of transcendent universal value made for such works. As we know, however, it is routinely taken instead as evidence or confirmation of the cultural deficiency — or, more piously, "deprivation" — of such people. The fact that other verbal artifacts (not necessarily "works of literature" or even "texts") and other objects and events (not necessarily "works of art" or even artifacts) have performed and do perform for them the various functions that Homer, Dante, and Shakespeare perform for us and, moreover, that the possibility of performing the totality of such functions is always distributed over the totality of texts, artifacts, objects, and events — a possibility continuously realized and thus a value continuously "appreciated" — commonly cannot be grasped or acknowledged by the custodians of the Western canon.

Henry Louis Gates, Jr.

b. 1950

Henry Louis Gates, Jr., was born in Keyser, West Virginia, and received his bachelor's degree in history from Yale University. At 20, he hitchhiked through Africa on a Carnegie Foundation fellowship. In 1973, Gates studied at Clare College, Cambridge University, where his tutor, the African writer Wole Soyinka, shifted Gates's interests from history to literature, particularly to the ways in which

African mythology and folktales inform the literature of Africa and the African diaspora. Upon completing his Ph.D. in English literature at Cambridge in 1979, Gates was appointed to a professorship at Yale, where he had been teaching since 1976. Gates's initial groundbreaking publication was the reprinting in 1983 of the first novel by a black woman, Harriet Wilson's Our Nig *(1859). Gates has continued his recovery of "lost" texts by black Americans in the* Schomberg Library of Nineteenth-Century Black Women's Writings, *of which he is series editor. In 1987 he published two books,* Figures in Black: Words, Signs, and the Racial Self, *and* The Signifying Monkey: Towards a Theory of Afro-American Literature, *which together established his reputation as one of the premier black theorists at work in the world today. Drawing on his work with Soyinka in African mythology, Gates's poststructuralist approach to African American literature defines its particular way of "signifying" as being based on an inherited oral tradition. His work is equally concerned with the continuities between African and African American modes of reader-response and interpretation. Gates has taught at Yale, Cornell, and Duke Universities, and is currently W. E. B. Du Bois Professor of the Humanities and Chairman of the Afro-American Studies Department at Harvard University. His most recent books are* Loose Canons: Notes on the Culture Wars *(1992),* Speaking of Race, Speaking of Sex: Hate Speech, Civil Rights, and Civil Liberties *(1994),* The Future of the Race *(with Cornel West, 1996), and* The Norton Anthology of African American Literature *(general editor, with Nelly Y. McKay, 1996). The present selection, which was first published in* Critical Inquiry *in 1985, is reprinted from* Loose Canons.

Writing, "Race," and the Difference It Makes

The truth is that, with the fading of the Renaissance ideal through progressive stages of specialism, leading to intellectual emptiness, we are left with a potentially suicidal movement among "leaders of the profession," while, at the same time, the profession sprawls, without its old center, in helpless disarray.

One quickly cited example is the professional organization, the Modern Language Association. . . . A glance at its thick program for its last meeting shows a massive increase and fragmentation into more than 500 categories! I cite a few examples: . . . "The Trickster Figure in Chicano and Black Literature." . . . Naturally, the progressive trivialization of topics has made these meetings a laughingstock in the national press.

— W. JACKSON BATE

. . . language, for the individual consciousness, lies on the borderline between oneself and the other. The word in language is half someone else's. It becomes "one's own" only when the speaker populates it with his own intention, his own accent, when he appropriates the word, adapting it to his own semantic and expressive intention. Prior to this moment of appropriation, the word does not exist in a neutral and impersonal language (it is not, after all, out of a dictionary that the speaker gets his words!), but rather it exists in other people's mouths, in other people's contexts, serving other people's intentions: it is from there that one must take the word, and make it "one's own."

— MIKHAIL BAKHTIN

They cannot represent themselves; they must be represented.

— MARX

I

Of what import is "race" as a meaningful category in the study of literature and the shaping of critical theory? If we attempt to answer this question by examining the history of Western literature and its criticism, our initial response would ostensibly be "nothing," or at the very least, "nothing explicitly." Indeed, until the past decade or so, even the most subtle and sensitive literary critics would most probably have argued that, except for aberrant moments in the history of criticism, "race" has been brought to bear upon the study of literature in no apparent way. The Western literary tradition, after all, and the canonical texts that comprise this splendid tradition, has been defined since Eliot as a more-or-less closed set of works that somehow speak to, or respond to, the "human condition" and to each other in formal patterns of repetition and revision.[1] And while judgment is subject to the moment and indeed does reflect temporal-specific presuppositions, certain works seem to transcend value judgments of the moment, speaking irresistibly to the "human condition." The question of the place of texts written by "the Other" (be that odd metaphor defined as African, Arabic, Chinese, Latin American, female, or Yiddish authors) in the proper study of "literature," "Western literature," or "comparative literature" has, until recently, remained an unasked question, suspended or silenced by a discourse in which the "canonical" and the "noncanonical" stand as the ultimate opposition. "Race," in much of the thinking about the proper study of literature in this century, has been an invisible quality, present implicitly at best.

This was not always the case, of course. By the middle of the nineteenth century, "national spirit" and "historical period" had become widely accepted metaphors within theories of the nature and function of literature which argued that the principal value in a "great" work of literary art resided in the extent to which these categories were *reflected* in that work of art. Montesquieu's *Esprit des lois* had made a culture's formal social institution the repository of its "guiding spirit," while Vico's *Principii d'una scienza nuova* had read literature against a complex pattern of historical cycles.[2] The two Schlegels managed rather deftly to bring to bear upon the interpretation of literature "both national spirit and historical period," as Walter Jackson Bate has shown.[3] But it was Taine who made the implicit explicit by postulating "race, moment, and *milieu*" as positivistic criteria through which any work could be read, and which, by definition, any work reflected. Taine's *History of English Literature* is the great foundation upon which subsequent nineteenth-century notions of "national literatures" would be constructed.[4]

What Taine called "race" was the source of all structures of feeling. To "track the root of man," he wrote, "is to consider the race itself, . . . the structure of his character and mind, his general processes of thought and feeling, . . . the irregularity and revolutions of his conception, which arrest in him the birth of fair dispositions and harmonious forms, the disdain of appearances, the desire for truth, the attachment for bare and abstract ideas, which develop in him conscience, at the expense of all else." In "race," Taine concluded, was predetermined "a particularity inseparable from all the motions of his intellect and his heart. Here lie the grand causes, for they are the universal and permanent causes, . . . indestructible, and finally infallibly supreme." "Poetries," as Taine put it, and all other forms of social expression, "are in fact only the imprints stamped by their seal."

"Race," for Taine was "the first and richest source of these master faculties from which historical events take their rise"; it was a "community of blood and intellect which to this day binds its off-shoots together." Lest we misunderstand the *naturally* determining role of "race," Taine

[1]Gates alludes to T. S. Eliot's "Tradition and the Individual Talent"; see p. 498. [Ed.]

[2]Charles-Louis de Secondat Montesquieu (1689–1755), a French philosopher, wrote *De l'esprit des lois (On the Spirit of the Laws)* in 1749. Giambattista Vico (1668–1744), an Italian philosopher, wrote *Principii d'una scienza nuova intorno alla natura delle nazioni (Principles of a New Science of Nations)*, proposing a cyclical theory of history in 1725; the work is generally referred to as the *Scienza nuova*. [Ed.]

[3]August Wilhelm (1767–1845) and Friedrich von Schlegel (1772–1829) were German philologists, theorists of the Romantic movement. [Ed.]

[4]The *Histoire de la littérature anglaise* (1863) of Hippolyte Taine (1828–1893) accounted for national literatures in terms of a scheme involving ethnicity, environment, and history: *race, milieu, moment*. [Ed.]

concluded that it "is no simple spring but a kind of lake, a deep reservoir wherein other springs have, for a multitude of centuries, discharged their several streams."

Taine's originality lay not in these ideas about the nature and role of race, but in their almost "scientific" application to the history of literature. These ideas about race were received from the Enlightenment, if not from the Renaissance. By midpoint in the nineteenth century, ideas of irresistible racial differences were commonly held: when Abraham Lincoln invited a small group of black leaders to the White House in 1862 to share with them his ideas about returning all blacks in America to Africa, his argument turned upon these "natural" differences. "You and we are different races," he said. "We have between us a broader difference than exists between any other two races." Since this sense of difference was never to be bridged, Lincoln concluded, the slaves and the ex-slaves should be returned to their own. The growth of canonical "national" literatures was coterminous with the shared assumption among intellectuals that "race" was a "thing," an ineffaceable quantity, which irresistibly determined the shape and contour of thought and feelings as surely as it did the shape and contour of human anatomy.

How did the great movement away from "race, moment, and *milieu*" and toward the language of the text in the 1920s and 1930s in the Practical Criticism movement at Cambridge[5] and the New Criticism movement at Yale affect this category of "race" in the reading of literature? Race, along with all sorts of other unseemly or untoward notions about the composition of the literary work of art, was bracketed or suspended. Race, within these theories of literature to which we are all heir, was rendered *implicit* in the elevation of ideas of canonical *cultural* texts that comprise the Western tradition in Eliot's simultaneous order, with a simultaneous existence. History, *milieu*, and even moment were brought to bear upon the interpretation of literature through philology and etymology: the dictionary — in the Anglo-American tradition, the *Oxford English Dictionary* — was the castle in which Taine's criteria took refuge. Once the concept of value became encased in the belief in a canon of texts whose authors purportedly shared a "common culture" inherited from *both* the Greco-Roman and the Judeo-Christian traditions, no one need speak of matters of "race" since "the race" of these authors was "the same." One not heir to these traditions was, by definition, of another "race." This logic was impenetrable.

Despite their beliefs in the unassailable primacy of language in the estimation of a work of literature, however, both I. A. Richards and Allen Tate,[6] in separate prefaces to books of poems by black authors, paused to wonder aloud about the black faces of the authors, and the import this had upon the reading of their texts. The often claimed "racism" of the Southern Agrarians,[7] while an easily identifiable target, was only an explicit manifestation of presuppositions that formed a large segment of the foundation upon which formalism was built. The citizens of the republic of literature, in other words, were all white, and mostly male. Difference, if difference obtained at all, was a difference obliterated by the "simultaneity" of Eliot's "tradition." Eliot's fiction of tradition, for the writer of a culture of color, was the literary equivalent of the "grandfather clause." So, in response to Robert Penn Warren's statement in "Pondy Woods" — "Nigger, your breed ain't metaphysical" — Sterling A. Brown wrote, "Cracker, your breed ain't exegetical." The Signifyin(g) pun deconstructed the "racialism" inherent in these claims of tradition.

[5]The "Practical Criticism movement at Cambridge" refers to the British branch of New Criticism pioneered by I. A. Richards and William Empson. See the introduction to Formalisms, p. 704. [Ed.]

[6]John Orley Allen Tate (1899–1979) was a Kentucky-born poet and critic whose *Reason in Madness* (1941) allied him with the group of other Southern critics (including Cleanth Brooks, Robert Penn Warren, John Crowe Ransom) who led the American wing of "New Criticism." See the introduction to Ch. 1, p. 703. [Ed.]

[7]Social philosophy of the 1930s, hostile to both Marxism and corporate capitalism, espoused primarily by Southern intellectuals. Tate contributed an essay, "Remarks on the Southern Religion" to *I'll Take My Stand: The South and the Agrarian Tradition by Twelve Southerners* (1930). [Ed.]

II

"Race" as a meaningful criterion within the biological sciences has long been recognized to be a fiction. When we speak of the "white race" or the "black race," the "Jewish race" or the "Aryan race," we speak in misnomers, biologically, and in metaphors, more generally. Nevertheless, our conversations are replete with usages of *race* which have their sources in the dubious pseudoscience of the eighteenth and nineteenth centuries. One need only flip through the pages of the *New York Times* to find headlines such as "Brown University President Sees School Racial Problems," or "Sensing Racism, Thousands March in Paris." In a lead editorial of its March 29, 1985, number, "The Lost White Tribe," the *Times* notes that while "racism is not unique to South Africa," we must condemn that society because "Betraying the religious tenets underlying Western culture, it has made race the touchstone of political rights." Eliot's "dissociation of sensibility," caused in large part by the "fraternal" atrocities of World War I, and then by the inexplicable and insane murder of European Jews two decades later, the *Times* editorial echoes. (For millions of people who originated outside Europe, however, this dissociation of sensibility had its origins in colonialism and human slavery.) *Race,* in these usages, pretends to be an objective term of classification, when in fact it is a trope.[8]

The sense of difference defined in popular usages of the term *race* has been used both to describe and *inscribe* differences of language, belief system, artistic tradition, "gene pool," and all sorts of supposedly "natural" attributes such as rhythm, athletic ability, cerebration, usury, and fidelity. The relation between "racial character" and these sorts of "characteristics" has been inscribed through tropes of race, lending to even supposedly "innocent" descriptions of cultural tendencies and differences the sanction of God, biology, or the natural order. "Race consciousness," Zora Neale Hurston wrote, "is a deadly explosive on the tongues of men." I even heard a member of the House of Lords in 1973 describe the differences between Irish Protestants and Catholics in terms of their "distinct and clearly definable differences of race."

"You mean to say that you can tell them apart?" I asked incredulously.

"Of course," responded the lord. "Any Englishman can."

Race has become a trope of ultimate, irreducible difference between cultures, linguistic groups, or practitioners of specific belief systems, who more often than not have fundamentally opposed economic interests. Race is the ultimate trope of difference because it is so very arbitrary in its application. The sanction of biology contained in sexual difference, simply put, does not and can never obtain when one is speaking of "racial difference." Yet, we carelessly use language in such a way as to *will* this sense of *natural* difference into our formulations. To do so is to engage in a pernicious act of language, one which exacerbates the complex problem of cultural or "ethnic" difference, rather than assuages or redresses it. This is especially the case at a time when racism has become fashionable, once again. That, literally every day, scores of people are killed in the name of differences ascribed to "race" only makes even more imperative this gesture to "deconstruct," if you will, the ideas of difference inscribed in the trope of race, to take discourse itself as our common subject to be explicated to reveal the latent relations of power and knowledge inherent in popular and academic usages of "race." When twenty-five thousand people feel compelled to gather on the Rue de Rivoli in support of the antiracist "Ne touche pas à mon pote" movement,[9] when thousands of people willingly accept arrest to protest apartheid, when Iran and Iraq feel justified in murdering the other's citizens because of their "race," when Beirut stands as a museum of shards and pieces reflecting degrees of horror impossible to comprehend, the gesture that we make here seems local and tiny.

There is a curious dialectic between formal language use and the inscription of metaphorical

[8]Gates may be alluding to the fact that the word "race" originates with the Latin *radix*, "root." [Ed.]

[9]The slogan of an antiracist movement founded in Paris in the 1980s by Harlem Désir was "Touche pas mon pote," colloquial French for "Don't touch my pal." [Ed.]

"racial" differences. At times, as Nancy Stepan expertly shows in *The Idea of Race in Science,* these metaphors have sought a universal and transcendent sanction in biological science. Western writers in French, Spanish, German, Portuguese, and English have sought to make literal these rhetorical figures of "race," to make them natural, absolute, essential. In doing so, they have *inscribed* these differences as fixed and finite categories which they merely report or draw upon for authority. But it takes little reflection to recognize that these pseudoscientific categories are themselves figures of thought. Who has seen a black or red person, a white, yellow, or brown? These terms are arbitrary constructs, not reports of reality. But language is not only the medium of this often pernicious tendency, it is its *sign*. Language use signifies the difference between cultures and their possession of power, spelling the difference between subordinate and superordinate, between bondsman and lord. Its call into use is simultaneous with the shaping of an economic order in which the cultures of color have been dominated in several important senses by Western Judeo-Christian, Greco-Hellenic cultures and their traditions. To use contemporary theories of criticism to explicate these modes of inscription is to demystify large and obscure ideological relations and indeed theory itself. It would be useful here to consider a signal example of the black tradition's confinement and delimitation by the commodity of writing. For literacy, as I hope to demonstrate, could be the most pervasive emblem of capitalist commodity functions.

III

Where better to test this thesis than in the example of the black tradition's first poet in English, the African slave girl Phillis Wheatley. Let us imagine a scene:

One bright morning in the spring of 1772, a young African girl walked demurely into the courthouse at Boston, to undergo an oral examination, the results of which would determine the direction of her life and work. Perhaps she was shocked upon entering the appointed room. For there, gathered in a semicircle, sat eighteen of Boston's most notable citizens. Among them was John Erving, a prominent Boston merchant; the Reverend Charles Chauncey, pastor of the Tenth Congregational Church and a son of Cotton Mather; and John Hancock, who would later gain fame for his signature on the Declaration of Independence. At the center of this group would have sat His Excellency, Thomas Hutchinson, governor of the colony, with Andrew Oliver, his lieutenant governor, close by his side.

Why had this august group been assembled? Why had it seen fit to summon this young African girl, scarcely eighteen years old, before it? This group of "the most respectable characters in *Boston*," as it would later define itself, had assembled to question the African adolescent closely on the slender sheaf of poems that the young woman claimed to have written by herself. We can only speculate on the nature of the questions posed to the fledgling poet. Perhaps they asked her to explain for all to hear exactly who were the Greek and Latin gods and poets alluded to so frequently in her work. Or perhaps they asked her to conjugate a verb in Latin, or even to translate randomly selected passages from the Latin, which she and her master, John Wheatley, claimed that she "had made some progress in." Or perhaps they asked her to recite from memory key passages from the texts of Milton and Pope, the two poets by whom the African claimed to be most directly influenced. We do not know.

We do know, however, that the African poet's responses were more than sufficient to prompt the eighteen august gentlemen to compose, sign, and publish a two-paragraph "Attestation," an open letter "To the Publick" that prefaces Phillis Wheatley's book, and which reads in part:

> We whose Names are underwritten, do assure the World, that the poems specified in the following Page, were (as we veribly believe) written by Phillis, a young Negro Girl, who was but a few Years since, brought an uncultivated Barbarian from *Africa,* and has ever since been, and now is, under the Disadvantage of serving as a Slave in a Family in this Town. She has been examined by some of the best judges, and is thought qualified to write them.

So important was this document in securing a publisher for Phillis's poems that it forms the signal element in the prefatory matter printed in the opening pages of her *Poems on Various Subjects, Religious and Moral,* published at London in 1773.

Without the published "Attestation," Wheatley's publisher claimed, few would believe that an African could possibly have written poetry all by herself. As the eighteen put the matter clearly in their letter, "Numbers would be ready to suspect they were not really the Writings of Phillis." Phillis's master, John Wheatley, and Phillis had attempted to publish a similar volume in 1770 at Boston, but Boston publishers had been incredulous. Three years later, "Attestation" in hand, Phillis and her mistress's son, Nathaniel Wheatley, sailed for England, where they completed arrangements for the publication of a volume of her poems, with the aid of the Countess of Huntington and the Earl of Dartmouth.

This curious anecdote, surely one of the oddest oral examinations on record, is only a tiny part of a larger, and even more curious, episode in the eighteenth century's Enlightenment. At least since 1600, Europeans had wondered aloud whether or not the African "species of men," as they most commonly put it, *could* ever create formal literature, could ever master the "arts and sciences." If they could, the argument ran, then the African variety of humanity and the European variety were fundamentally related. If not, then it seemed clear that the African was destined by nature to be a slave.

Determined to discover the answer to this crucial quandary, several Europeans and Americans undertook experiments in which young African slaves were tutored and trained along with white children. Phillis Wheatley was merely one result of such an experiment. Francis Williams, a Jamaican who took the B.A. at the University of Cambridge before 1730; Jacobus Capitein, who earned several degrees in Holland; Wilheim Amo, who took the doctorate degree in philosophy at Halle; and Ignatius Sancho, who became a friend of Sterne's and who published a volume of letters in 1782 — these were just a few of the black subjects of such "experiments." The published writings of these black men and one woman, who wrote in Latin, Dutch, German, and English, were seized upon both by pro- and antislavery proponents as proof that their arguments were sound.

So widespread was the debate over "the nature of the African" between 1730 and 1830 that not until the Harlem Renaissance would the work of black writers be as extensively reviewed as it was in the eighteenth century. Phillis Wheatley's list of reviewers includes Voltaire, Thomas Jefferson, George Washington, Samuel Rush, and James Beatty, to name only a few.[10] Francis Williams's work was analyzed by no less than David Hume and Immanuel Kant. Hegel, writing in the *Philosophy of History* in 1813, used the writings of these Africans as the sign of their innate inferiority. The list of commentators is extensive, amounting to a "Who's Who" of the French, English, and American Enlightenment.

Why was the *creative writing* of the African of such importance to the eighteenth century's debate over slavery? I can briefly outline one thesis: After Descartes, *reason* was privileged, or valorized, among all other human characteristics. Writing, especially after the printing press became so widespread, was taken to be the *visible* sign of reason. Blacks were "reasonable," and hence "men," if — and only if — they demonstrated mastery of the "arts and sciences," the eighteenth century's formula for writing. So, while the Enlightenment is famous for establishing its existence upon the human ability to reason, it simultaneously used the absence and presence of "reason" to delimit and circumscribe the very humanity of the cultures and people of color which Europeans had been "discovering" since the Renaissance. The urge toward the systematization of all human knowledge, by which we characterize the Enlightenment, led directly to the relegation of black people to a lower rung on the Great Chain of Being, an eighteenth-century construct that arranged all of creation on a vertical scale from animals and plants and insects through humans to the angels and God himself.

By 1750, the chain had become individualized; the human scale slid from "the lowliest

[10]"Samuel Rush" may be Benjamin Rush (1745–1813), Pennsylvania-born scientist and abolitionist; "James Beatty" may be James Beattie (1735–1803), Scottish poet and philosopher. [Ed.]

Hottentot" (black south Africans) to "glorious Milton and Newton." If blacks could write and publish imaginative literature, then they could, in effect, take a few Giant Steps up the Chain of Being, in a pernicious game of "Mother, May I?" As the Reverend James W. C. Pennington, an ex-slave who wrote a slave narrative and who was a prominent black abolitionist, summarized this curious idea in his prefatory note "To the Reader" that authorized Ann Plato's 1841 book of essays, biographies, and poems: "The history of the arts and sciences is the history of individuals, of individual nations." Only by publishing books such as Plato's, he argued, could blacks demonstrate "the fallacy of that stupid theory, *that nature has done nothing but fit us for slaves, and that art cannot unfit us for slavery!*"

IV

The relation between what, for lack of a better term, I shall call the "nonwhite" writer and the French, Portuguese, Spanish, and English languages and literatures manifests itself in at least two ways of interest to theorists of literature and literary history. I am thinking here of what in psychoanalytic criticism is sometimes called "the other," and more especially of this "other" as the subject and object in literature. What I mean by citing these two overworked terms is precisely this: how blacks are figures in literature, and also how blacks *figure,* as it were, literature of their own making.

These two poles of a received opposition have been formed, at least since the early seventeenth century, by an extraordinary *subdiscourse* of the European philosophies of aesthetic theory and language. The two subjects, often in marginal ways, have addressed directly the supposed relation among "race," defined variously as language use and "place in nature." Human beings wrote books. Beautiful books were reflections of sublime genius. Sublime genius was the province of the European.

Blacks, and other people of color, could not "write." "Writing," these writers argued, stood alone among the fine arts as the most salient repository of "genius," the visible sign of reason itself. In this subordinate role, however, "writing," although secondary to "reason," was nevertheless the *medium* of reason's expression. They *knew* reason by its writing, by its representations. This representation could assume the spoken or the written form. And while several superb scholars gave priority to the *spoken* as the privileged of the pair, in their writings about blacks, at least, Europeans privileged *writing* as the principal measure of Africans' "humanity," their "capacity for progress," their very place in "the great chain of being."

This system of signs is arbitrary. Key words, such as *capacity,* which became a metaphor for cranial size, reflect the predominance of "scientific" discourse in metaphysics. That "reason," moreover, could be seen to be "natural" was the key third term of a homology which, in practice, was put to pernicious uses. The transformation of writing from an activity of mind into a commodity not only reflects larger mercantile relations between Africa and Europe but is also the subject I wish to explore here. Let me retrace, in brief, the history of this idea, of the relationship of the absence of "writing" and the absence of "humanity" in European letters of 1600.

We must understand this correlation of use and *presence* in language if we are to begin to learn how to read, for example, the slave's narrative within what Geoffrey H. Hartman calls its "text-milieu." The slave narratives, taken together, represent the attempt of blacks to *write themselves into being.* What a curious idea: Through the mastery of formal Western languages, the presupposition went, a black person could posit a full and sufficient self, as an act of self-creation through the medium of language. Accused of having no collective history by Hegel, blacks effectively responded by publishing hundreds of individual histories which functioned as the part standing for the whole. As Ralph Ellison defined this relation, "We tell ourselves our individual stories so as to become aware of our *general* story."

Writing as the visible sign of Reason, at least since the Renaissance in Europe, had been consistently invoked in Western aesthetic theory in the discussion of the enslavement and status of the black. The origin of this received association of political salvation and artistic genius can be traced at least to the seventeenth century. What we arrive at by extracting a rather black and slender thread from among the philosophical discourses of the Enlightenment is a reading of another side of the philosophy of enlightenment, indeed its nether side. Writing in *The New Organon* in 1620, Sir Francis Bacon, confronted with the problem of classifying the people of color which a seafaring Renaissance Europe had "discovered," turned to the arts as the ultimate measure of a race's place in nature. "Again," he wrote, "let a man only consider what a difference there is between the life of men in the most civilized province of Europe, and in the wildest and most barbarous districts of New India; he will feel it be great enough to justify the saying that 'man is a god to man,' not only in regard to aid and benefit, but also by comparison of condition. And this difference comes not from soil, not from climate, not from race, but from the arts." Eleven years later, Peter Heylyn, in his *Little Description of the Great World*, used Bacon's formulation to relegate the blacks to a subhuman status: Black Africans, he wrote, lacked completely "the use of Reason which is peculiar unto man; [they are] of little Wit; and destitute of all arts and sciences; prone to luxury, and for the greatest part Idolators." All subsequent commentaries on the matter were elaborations upon Heylyn's position.

By 1680, Heylyn's key words, *reason* and *wit*, had been reduced to "reading and writing," as Morgan Godwyn's summary of received opinion attests:

> [A] disingenuous and unmanly *Position* had been formed; and privately (and as it were *in the dark*) handed to and again, which is this, That the Negro's though in their figure they carry some resemblances of manhood, yet are indeed *no* men. . . . the consideration of the shape and figure of our Negro's Bodies, their Limbs and members; their Voice and Countenance, in all things according with other mens; together with their *Risibility* and *Discourse* (man's Peculiar Faculties) should be sufficient Conviction. How should they otherwise be capable of *Trades*, and other no less manly imployments; as also of *Reading and Writing*, or show so much Discretion in management of Business; . . . but wherein (we know) that many of our own People are *deficient*, were they not truly Men?

Such a direct correlation of political rights and literacy helps us to understand both the transformation of writing into a commodity and the sheer burden of received opinion that motivated the black slave to seek his or her text. As well, it defined the "frame" against which each black text would be read. The following 1740 South Carolina statute was concerned to make it impossible for black literacy mastery even to occur:

> *And whereas* the having of slaves taught to write, or suffering them to be employed in writing, may be attending with great inconveniences;
>
> *Be it enacted*, that all and every person and persons whatsoever, who shall hereafter teach, or cause any slave or slaves to be taught to write, or shall use or employ any slave as a scribe in any manner of writing whatsoever, hereafter taught to write; every such person or persons shall, for every offense, forfeit the sum of one hundred pounds current money.

Learning to read and to write, then, was not only difficult, it was a violation of a law. That Frederick Douglass, Thomas Smallwood, William Wells Brown, Moses Grandy, James Pennington, and John Thompson, among numerous others,[11] all rendered statements about the direct relation between freedom and discourse not only as central scenes of instruction but also as repeated fundamental structures of their very rhetorical strategies only emphasizes the dialectical relation of black texts to a "context," defined here as *"other,"* racist texts, against which the slave's narrative, by definition, was forced to react.

By 1705, a Dutch explorer, William Bosman, had encased Peter Heylyn's bias into a myth which the Africans he had "discovered" had purportedly related to him. It is curious insofar as it justifies human slavery. According to Bosman, the blacks "tell us that in the beginning God created Black as well as White men; thereby giving the Blacks the first Election, who chose Gold, and left the Knowledge of Letters to the White. God granted their request, but being incensed at their Avarice, resolved that the Whites should ever be their masters, and they obliged to wait on

[11]Frederick Douglass and the rest were authors of slave narratives. [Ed.]

them as their slaves." Bosman's fabrication, of course, was a myth of origins designed to sanction through mythology a political order created by Europeans. It was David Hume, writing at midpoint in the eighteenth century, who gave to Bosman's myth the sanction of Enlightenment philosophical reasoning.

In a major essay, "Of National Characters" (1748), Hume discussed the "characteristics" of the world's major division of human beings. In a footnote added to his original text in 1753 (the margins of his discourse), Hume posited with all of the authority of philosophy the fundamental identity of complexion, character, and intellectual capacity. "I am apt to suspect the negroes," he wrote,

> and in general all the other species of men (for there are four or five different kinds) to be naturally inferior to the whites. There never was a civilized nation of any other complexion than white, nor even any individual eminent either in action or speculation. No ingenious manufacturers amongst them, *no arts, no sciences*. . . . Such a uniform and constant difference could not happen, in so many countries and ages, if *nature* had not made our original distinction betwixt these breeds of men. Not to mention our colonies, there are Negroe slaves dispersed all over Europe, of which none ever discovered any symptoms of ingenuity; . . . In Jamaica, indeed they talk of one negroe as a man of parts and learning [Francis Williams, the Cambridge-educated poet who wrote verse in Latin]; but 'tis likely he is admired for very slender accomplishments, like a parrot who speaks a few words plainly.

Hume's opinion on the subject, as we might expect, became prescriptive.

Writing in 1764, in his *Observations on the Feelings of the Beautiful and the Sublime,* Immanuel Kant elaborated upon Hume's essay in a fourth section entitled "Of National Characteristics, as far as They Depend upon the Distinct Feeling of the Beautiful and the Sublime." Kant first claimed that "So fundamental is the difference between [the black and white] races of man, and it appears to be as great in regard to mental capacities as in color." Kant, moreover, was one of the earliest major European philosophers to conflate "color" with "intelligence," a determining relation he posited with dictatorial surety. The excerpt bears citation:

> . . . Father Labat reports that a Negro carpenter, whom he reproached for haughty treatment toward his wives, answered: "You whites are indeed fools, for first you make great concessions to your wives, and afterward you complain when they drive you mad." And it might be that there were something in this which perhaps deserved to be considered; but in short, this fellow was *quite black* from head to foot, a clear proof that what he said was stupid. (emphasis added)

The correlation of "blackness" and "stupidity" Kant posited as if self-evident.

Writing in "Query XIV" of *Notes on the State of Virginia,* Thomas Jefferson maintained that "Never yet could I find that a black had uttered a thought above the level of plain narration, never see even an elementary trait of painting or sculpture." Of Wheatley, the first black person to publish a book of poetry in England, Jefferson the critic wrote, "Misery is often the parent of the most affecting touches in poetry. Among the blacks is misery enough, God knows, but not poetry. . . . The compositions published under her name are below the dignity of criticism."

In that same year (1785), Kant, basing his observations on the absence of published writing among blacks, noted as if simply obvious that "Americans [Indians] and blacks are lower in their mental capacities than all other races." Again, Hegel, echoing Hume and Kant, noted the absence of history among black people and derided them for failing to develop indigenous African scripts, or even to master the art of writing in modern languages.

Hegel's strictures on the African about the absence of "history" presume a crucial role of *memory* — a collective, cultural memory — in the estimation of civilization. Metaphors of the "childlike" nature of the slaves, of the masked, puppetlike "personality" of the black, all share this assumption about the absence of memory. Mary Langdon, in her 1855 novel *Ida May: A Story of Things Actual and Possible,* wrote that "but then they *are* mere children. . . . You seldom hear them say much about anything that's past, if they only get enough to eat and drink at the present moment." Without writing, there could exist no *repeatable* sign of the workings of reason, of mind. Without memory or mind, there could exist no history. Without history, there could exist no "humanity," as defined consistently from Vico to Hegel. As William Gilmore Simms[12] argued at the middle of the nineteenth century:

> [If one can establish] that the negro intellect is fully equal to that of the white race . . . you not only take away the best argument for keeping him in subjection, but you take away the possibility of doing so. *Prima facie*, however, the fact that he *is* a slave, is conclusive against the argument for his freedom, as it is against his equality of claim in respect of intellect. . . . Whenever the negro shall be fully fit for freedom, he will make himself free, and no power on earth can prevent him.

V

Ironically, Anglo-African writing arose as a response to allegations of its absence. Black people responded to these profoundly serious allegations about their "nature" as directly as they could: they wrote books, poetry, autobiographical narratives. Political and philosophical discourse were the predominant forms of writing. Among these, autobiographical "deliverance" narratives were the most common, and the most accomplished. Accused of lacking a formal and collective history, blacks published individual histories which, taken together, were intended to narrate, in segments, the larger yet fragmented history of blacks in Africa, now dispersed throughout a cold New World. The narrated, descriptive "eye" was put into service as a literary form to posit both the individual "I" of the black author and the collective "I" of the race. Text created author, and black authors, it was hoped, would create, or re-create, the image of the race in European discourse. The very *face* of the race, representations of the features of which are common in all sorts of writings about blacks at this time, was contingent upon the recording of the black *voice*. Voice presupposes a face but also seems to have been thought to determine the contours of the black face.

The recording of an "authentic" black voice, a voice of deliverance from the deafening discursive silence which an enlightened Europe cited as proof of the absence of the African's humanity, was the millennial instrument of transformation through which the African would become the European, the slave become the ex-slave, the brute animal become the human being. So central was this idea to the birth of the black literary tradition in the eighteenth century that five of the earliest slave narratives draw upon the figure of the voice in the text as crucial "scenes of instruction" in the development of the slave on the road to freedom. James Gronniosaw in 1770, John Marrant in 1785, Ottobah Cugoano in 1787, Olaudah Equiano in 1789, and John Jea in 1815 — all drew upon the trope of the talking book. Gronniosaw's usage bears citing here especially because it repeats Kant's correlation of physical — and, as it were, metaphysical — characteristics:

> My master used to read prayers in public to the ship's crew every Sabbath day; and when I first saw him read, I was never so surprised in my life, as when I saw the book talk to my master, for I thought it did, as I observed him to look upon it, and move his lips. I wished it would do so with me. As soon as my master had done reading, I followed him to the place where he put the book, being mightily delighted with it, and when nobody saw me, I opened it, and put my ear down close upon it, in great hope that it would say something to me; but I was very sorry, and greatly disappointed, when I found that it would not speak. This thought immediately presented itself to me, that every body and every thing despised me because I was black.

Even for this black author, his own mask of black humanity was a negation, a sign of absence. Gronniosaw accepted his role as a nonspeaking would-be subject and the absence of his common humanity with the European.

That the figure of the talking book recurs in these five black eighteenth-century texts says much about the degree of presupposition and intertextuality in early black letters, more than we heretofore thought. Equally important, however, this figure itself underscores the received correlation between silence and blackness which we

[12]Gilmore Simms (1806–1870) is best known as the author of *The Yemasee* (1835), a romance influenced by Walter Scott about the conflict between the Carolina colonists and the native Yemasee tribe. [Ed.]

have been tracing, as well as the urgent need to make the text speak, the process by which the slave marked his distance from the master. The voice in the text was truly a millennial voice for the African person of letters in the eighteenth century, for it was that very voice of deliverance and of redemption which would signify a new order for the black.

These narrators, linked by revision of a trope into the very first black chain of signifiers, implicitly signify upon another "chain," the metaphorical Great Chain of Being. Blacks were most commonly represented on the chain either as the "lowest" of the human races, or as first cousin to the ape. Since writing, according to Hume, was the ultimate sign of difference between animal and human, these writers implicitly were Signifyin(g) upon the figure of the chain itself, simply by publishing autobiographies that were indictments of the received order of Western culture, of which slavery, to them, by definition stood as the most salient sign. The writings of Gronniosaw, Marrant, Equiano, Cugoano, and Jea served as a critique of the sign of the Chain of Being and the black person's figurative "place" on the chain. This chain of black signifiers, regardless of their intent or desire, made the first political gesture in the Anglo-African literary tradition "simply" by the act of writing, a collective act that gave birth to the black literary tradition and defined it as the "other's chain," the chain of black being as black people themselves would have it. Making the book speak, then, constituted a motivated, and political, engagement with and condemnation of Europe's fundamental figure of domination, the Great Chain of Being.

The trope of the talking book is not a trope of the presence of voice at all, but of its absence. To speak of a "silent voice" is to speak in an oxymoron. There is no such thing as a silent voice. Furthermore, as Juliet Mitchell has put the matter, there is something untenable about the attempt to represent what is not there, to represent that which is *missing* or absent. Given that this is what these five black authors sought to do, we are justified in wondering aloud if the sort of subjectivity that they sought could be realized through a process that was so very ironic from the outset. Indeed, how can the black subject posit a full and sufficient self in a language in which blackness is a sign of absence? Can writing, the very "difference" it makes and marks, mask the blackness of the black face that addresses the text of Western letters, in a voice that "speaks English" in an idiom that contains the irreducible element of cultural difference that shall always separate the white voice from the black? Black people, we know, have not been "liberated" from racism by their writings, and they accepted a false premise by assuming that racism would be destroyed once white racists became convinced that we were human, too. Writing stood as a complex "certificate of humanity," as Paulin J. Hountondji put it. Black writing, and especially the literature of the slave, served not to obliterate the difference of "race," as a would-be white man such as Gronniosaw so ardently desired; rather, the inscription of the black voice in Western literatures has preserved those very cultural differences to be imitated and revised in a separate Western literary tradition, a tradition of black difference.

Blacks, as we have seen, tried to write themselves out of slavery, a slavery even more profound than mere physical bondage. Accepting the challenge of the great white Western tradition, black writers wrote as if their lives depended upon it — and, in a curious sense, their lives did, the "life" of "the race" in Western discourse. But if blacks accepted this challenge, we also accepted its premises, premises in which perhaps lay concealed a trap. What trap might this be? Let us recall the curious case of M. Edmond Laforest.

In 1915, Edmond Laforest, a prominent member of the Haitian literary movement called La Ronde, made of his death a symbolic, if ironic, statement of the curious relation of the "non-Western" writer to the act of writing in a modern language. M. Laforest, with an inimitable, if fatal, flair for the grand gesture, stood upon a bridge, calmly tied a Larousse dictionary[13] around his neck, then proceeded to leap to his

[13]The Larousse is the standard French dictionary-encyclopedia. [Ed.]

death by drowning. While other black writers, before and after M. Laforest, have suffocated as artists beneath the weight of various modern languages, Laforest chose to make his death an emblem of this relation of indenture.

It is the challenge of the black tradition to critique this relation of indenture, an indenture that obtains for our writers and for our critics. We must master, as Derrida wrote, "how to speak the other's language without renouncing (our) own." When we attempt to appropriate, by inversion, *race* as a term for an essence, as did the Negritude movement, for example ("We feel, therefore we are," as Senghor argued of the African), we yield too much, such as the basis of a shared humanity. Such gestures, as Anthony Appiah has observed, are futile and dangerous because of their further inscription of new and bizarre stereotypes. How do we meet Derrida's challenge in the discourse of criticism? The Western critical tradition has a canon, just as does the Western literary tradition. Whereas I once thought it our most important gesture to *master* the canon of criticism, to *imitate* and *apply* it, I now believe that we must turn to the black tradition itself to arrive at theories of criticism indigenous to our literatures. Alice Walker's revision of a parable of white interpretation written in 1836 by Rebecca Cox Jackson, a Shaker eldress and black visionary, makes this point most tellingly. Jackson, who like John Jea claimed to have been taught to read by the Lord, wrote in her autobiography that she dreamed that a "white man" came to her house to teach her how to *interpret* and "understand" the word of God, now that God had taught her to read:

> A white man took me by my right hand and led me on the north side of the room, where sat a square table. On it lay a book open. And he said to me, "Thou shall be instructed in this book, from Genesis to Revelations." And then he took me on the west side, where stood a table. And it looked like the first. And said, "Yea, thou shall be instructed from the beginning of creation to the end of time." And then he took me on the east side of the room also, where stood a table and book like the two first, and said, "I will instruct thee — yea, thou shall be instructed from the beginning of all things to the end of all things. Yea, thou shall be well instructed. I will instruct."
>
> And then I awoke, and I saw him as plain as I did in my dream. And after that he taught me daily. And when I would be reading and come to a hard word, I would see him standing by my side and he would teach me the word right. And often, when I would be in meditation and looking into things which was hard to understand, I would find him by me, teaching and giving me understanding. And oh, his labor and care which he had with me often caused me to weep bitterly, when I would see my great ignorance and the great trouble he had to make me understand eternal things. For I was so buried in the depth of the tradition of my forefathers, that it did seem as if I never could be dug up.

In response to Jackson's relation of interpretive indenture to a "white man," Alice Walker, writing in *The Color Purple,* records an exchange between Celie and Shug about turning away from "the old white man," which soon turns into a conversation about the elimination of "man" as a mediator between a woman and "everything":

> . . . You have to git man off your eyeball, before you can see anything a'tall.
>
> Man corrupt everything, say Shug. He on your box of grits, in your head, and all over the radio. He try to make you think he everywhere. Soon as you think he everywhere, you think he God. But he ain't. Whenever you trying to pray, and man plot himself on the other end of it, tell him to git lost, say Shug.

Celie and Shug's omnipresent "man," of course, echoes the black tradition's epithet for the white power structure, "the man."

For non-Western, so-called noncanonical critics, getting the "man off your eyeball" means using the most sophisticated critical theories and methods generated by the Western tradition to reappropriate and to define our own "colonial" discourses. We must use these theories and methods insofar as these are relevant and applicable to the study of our own literatures. The danger in doing so, however, is best put, again by Anthony Appiah in his definition of what he calls the "Naipaul fallacy"[14]: "It is not necessary to show

[14]V[idiadhar] S[urajprasad] Naipaul (b. 1932), a Trinidad-

that African literature is fundamentally the same as European literature in order to show that it can be treated with the same tools. . . . Nor should we endorse a more sinister line . . . : the post-colonial legacy which requires us to show that African literature is worthy of study precisely (but only) because it is fundamentally the same as European literature." We *must* not, Appiah concludes, "ask the reader to understand Africa by embedding it in European culture."

We must, of course, analyze the ways in which writing relates to "race," how attitudes toward racial differences generate and structure literary texts by us *and* about us; we must determine how critical methods can effectively disclose the traces of racial difference in literature; but we must also understand how certain forms of difference and the *languages* we employ to define those supposed "differences" not only reinforce each other but tend to create and maintain each other. Similarly, and as importantly, we must analyze the language of contemporary criticism itself, recognizing that hermeneutical systems, especially, are not "universal," "color-blind," or "apolitical," or "neutral." Whereas some critics wonder aloud, as Appiah notes, about such matters as whether or not "a structuralist poetics is inapplicable in Africa because structuralism is European," the concern of the "Third World" critic should properly be to understand the ideological subtext which any critical theory reflects and embodies, and what relation this subtext bears to the production of meaning. No critical theory — be that Marxism, feminism, poststructuralism, Nkrumah's consciencism, or whatever — escapes the specificity of value and ideology, no matter how mediated these may be. To attempt to appropriate our own discourses using Western critical theory "uncritically" is to substitute one mode of neocolonialism for another. To begin to do this in my own tradition, theorists have turned to the black vernacular tradition — to paraphrase Rebecca Cox Jackson, to dig into the depths of the tradition of our foreparents — to isolate the signifying black difference through which to theorize about the so-called Discourse of the Other.

born, Oxford-educated novelist and journalist whose works chronicle racism, corruption, and violence in the new nations of Africa and the Caribbean ruled by blacks, is a favorite object of odium to Africanist cultural critics such as Gates and Appiah. [Ed.]

John Guillory

b. 1952

John Guillory was born in New Orleans, Louisiana, and was educated there until 1974, when he graduated with a B.A. from Tulane University. In the same year he entered graduate school at Yale University, where he received his Ph.D in 1979. He taught at Yale until 1989, and since 1989 has been a professor at Johns Hopkins University. His first book, Poetic Authority: Spenser, Milton, and Literary History, *was published by Columbia University Press in 1983. He has since published a number of essays on Milton concerning issues of gender, Protestant vocation, and the relationship between theology and science. His second book,* Cultural Capital: The Problem of Literary Canon Formation, *was published by the University of Chicago Press in 1993 and won the René Wellek Prize of the American Comparative Literature Association. Guillory is currently studying the relationship between the development of literary study in the modern university and the development of a professional-managerial class. Guillory's work may be described broadly as an attempt to understand the history and future of literary study in the context of the emergence of the modern constellation of disciplines. The following selection is from* Cultural Capital.

From *Cultural Capital: The Problem of Literary Canon Formation*

MULTICULTURAL INTERLUDE: THE QUESTION OF A CORE CURRICULUM

Every relationship of "hegemony" is an educational relationship. — GRAMSCI, *Prison Notebooks*

While the debate over the canon concerns what texts should be taught in the schools, what remains invisible within this debate — too large to be seen at all — is the school itself. The absence of reflection on the school as an institution is the condition for the most deluded assumption of the debate, that the school is the vehicle of transmission for something like a national culture. What is transmitted by the school is, to be sure, a kind of culture; but it is the *culture of the school.* School culture does not unify the nation culturally so much as it projects out of a curriculum of artifact-based knowledge an imaginary cultural unity never actually coincident with the culture of the nation-state. In this way the left hand of the educational system — the dissemination of a supposedly national culture — remains ignorant of what the right hand is doing — the differential tracking of students according to class or the possession of cultural capital. If the structure of the system, its multiple levels and its division between public and private institutions, divides the population in this way, the culture the *university* produces (as opposed to other kinds or levels of school), can only be "national" for that plurality which acquires this level of education. What this group may learn to think of as a national culture is always a specific *relation* to the knowledge defined by the university curriculum.[1]

The extraordinary effects of confusing school culture with national culture are most conspicuous when the national culture is made to swallow whole the even larger fish called "Western culture," and in such a way as to produce an image of the American nation as the telos[2] of Western cultural evolution. Here we may adduce William Bennett's complacent version of this narrative in "To Reclaim a Legacy":

> We are a part and a product of Western civilization. That our society was founded upon such principles as justice, liberty, government with the consent of the governed, and equality under the law is the result of ideas descended directly from great epochs of Western civilization — Enlightenment England and France, Renaissance Florence, and Periclean Athens. These ideas, so revolutionary in their times yet so taken for granted now, are the glue that binds together our pluralistic nation. The fact that we as Americans — whether black or white, Asian or Hispanic, rich or poor — share these beliefs aligns us with other cultures of the Western tradition.[3]

The interesting point about this argument is not the typically American chauvinism Bennett immediately denies ("It is not ethnocentric or chauvinistic to acknowledge this"), or the dubious assimilation of Western thinkers to democratic political principles many or even most of them would not in fact have endorsed. What remains interesting and consequential in Bennett's statement is a confusion which, as we shall see, characterizes both Bennett and his opponents in the canon debate: the slippage between *culture* and *civilization.* The semantic burden of the latter term obliquely recognizes what the concept of the national culture denies — the necessity of defining that culture largely by reference to the

[1]Bourdieu makes this point in his essay "Systems of Education and Systems of Thought," *International Social Science Journal* 19 (1967), 349: "An individual's contact with his culture depends basically on the circumstances in which he has acquired it, among other things because the act whereby culture is communicated is, as such, the exemplary expression of a certain type of relation to the culture." [Au.] See Bourdieu, p. 1231. [Ed.]

[2]End product. [Ed.]

[3]William Bennett, "To Reclaim a Legacy," 21. [Au.]

High Cultural artifacts to which access is provided in the schools. Bennett admits as much, without drawing any adverse conclusion from this point: "No student of our civilization should be denied access to the best that tradition has to offer." Is "our civilization," then, the same as "our culture"? One may reasonably question what necessary *cultural* relation a university-trained suburban manager or technocrat has to Plato or Homer by virtue of his or her American citizenship — no more, in fact, than an educationally disadvantaged dweller in the most impoverished urban ghetto. The suburban technocrat and the ghetto dweller on the other hand have very much more in common culturally with each other than either of them ever need have with the great writers of Western civilization. If "Western" civilization — defined by a collection of cultural artifacts — can imaginarily displace the real cultural continuities that obtain at the national level, such an exemplary expression of the social imaginary is the effect of a crucial ambiguity in the concept of culture itself, an ambiguity familiar enough in the history of the concept as the distinction between culture in the sense of refinement — in this case, familiarity with the great works of "civilization" — and in the ethnographic sense of common beliefs, behaviors, attitudes — what a "national culture" would really have to mean.[4] The attempt to make the first sense of culture *stand for* the second names a certain project for the university, but one which it seems less well suited to undertake than ever (for reasons I will consider presently). The apparent failure of the university's cultural project of constituting a national culture elicits from the New Right the clamorous demand for a return to what was after all the *bourgeois* school, the institution enabling the old bourgeoisie to identify itself culturally by acquiring the cultural capital formerly restricted to the aristocratic or clerical estates. This capital consisted of nothing other than the "great works" of Western civilization.

If the national cultural project of the school is no longer a real possibility (it was always a class project anyway), the canon debate has nevertheless decisively problematized the notion of culture in its controversial language. The absence, however, of any concept of a specific *school* culture in the debate has meant that the perceived monolith of Western culture has had to be contested by the assertion of an antithetical "multiculturalism" as the basis of a politically progressive curriculum. Multiculturalism defines Western culture as its political antagonist, and vice versa. Yet the rather too neat polarization of these terms elides the question of what school culture really is, that is, what *relation to culture* is produced by the formal study of cultural artifacts. Whatever other effects the introduction of multicultural curricula may have, the *theory* of multiculturalism perpetuates the confusion of culture as the study of preserved artifacts with the sense of culture as common beliefs, behaviors, attitudes. It is by no means the case that the study of cultural works simply operates as the agency of cultural transmission in the second sense — although school culture, as Bourdieu has shown, does its part to install a *class* habitus[5] in the subjects of its pedagogy. This habitus is defined not by the content of cultural works (Plato is not really part of "our culture"), but by the relation to culture inculcated by the school, the relation named precisely by Bennett's "legacy" — a relation of *ownership.* It is not the ideas expressed in the great works that account for their status in arguments such as Bennett's, but the fact that these works are appropriated as the cultural capital of a dominant fraction. That appropriation is in turn justified by representing the ideational content of the great works as an ex-

[4]See the entry for "culture" in Raymond Williams's *Keywords: A Vocabulary of Culture and Society,* revised edition (New York: Oxford University Press, 1976, 1983), 87–93, for a lucid account of what is at stake in the different meanings of "culture" historically. We might sum up the difference between our national culture and our school culture by acknowledging that for national culture "Nike" is the name of an athletic shoe, for school culture a Greek goddess. [Au.]

[5]Bourdieu defines *habitus* as a "system of dispositions," the social equivalent of "linguistic competence" (Noam Chomsky's term for the sum of all the tacit knowledge one has to possess to speak a natural language), or the feel a skilled player has for a game. Bourdieu viewed *habitus* as class-related: Persons of the same class were likely, he found, to adopt a similar habitus across different social fields. [Ed.]

pression of the same ideas which are realized in the current social order, with its current distribution of cultural goods.

In order to accomplish the cultural task of appropriation, however, the school must traverse the heavily mined terrain of a certain alienation produced by the formal study of cultural works. We should not forget that the effects of this alienation are sometimes permanent, and that it is precisely "one's own" culture which sometimes fails to survive the culture of the school (that is to say, the school sometimes produces, despite its acculturative function, dissident intellectuals). Similarly the formal study of cultural works produced within minority cultures is not a means of reproducing minority culture (in the ethnographic sense). If the formal study of Latin-American novels in the university does not really transmit or reproduce Latino culture, it follows that the relation of even Latino students to these artifacts will not be entirely unlike the relation of "American" students to the works of "Western" (American or European) culture. The question is what this relation is, or what it should be.

One conclusion to be drawn immediately from this argument is that there is no ground of commensuration between Western cultural artifacts on the one hand, if examples of these are the *Odyssey* or the Parthenon; and Latino culture on the other, if the latter means the totality of a living culture, and not just its artifacts. Insofar as it is only the *works* of Western or Latino culture to which one has direct access in the school, these works will ultimately be constructed and legitimated as objects of study *in the same way,* by a process of deracination from the actual cultural circumstances of their production and consumption.[6] If works by Afro-American, Latin-American, or postcolonial writers are read now in formal programs of university study, this fact may be the immediate result of a political project of inclusion, or the affirmation of cultural diversity. But the survival of these works in future school curricula will be seen otherwise, as a consequence of their status as interesting and important cultural works that no intellectually responsible program of study can ignore. The current project of affirming *cultures themselves* through the legitimation of cultural works in university curricula is enabled by the very conflation between the senses of culture to which I have drawn attention. The very intensity of our "symbolic struggle" reduces cultural conditions of extreme complexity to an allegorical conflict between a Western cultural Goliath and its Davidic multicultural antagonists. Hence it is never really Greek culture, or French culture, or Roman culture, that is compared with Latino culture or Afro-American culture, but always "Western" culture. Multiculturalism finds itself in the position of having to credit both the reality and the homogeneity of that fictional cultural entity, which achieves its spurious self-identity only by consisting of *nothing but* cultural artifacts.[7]

---

[6]Bourdieu, "Systems of Education and Systems of Thought," *International Social Science Journal* 19 (1967), 351, points to an analogous confusion when the concept of culture is made to refer indifferently both to popular culture and to school culture: "Just as Basil Bernstein contrasts the 'public language' of the working classes, employing descriptive rather than analytical concepts, with a more complex 'formal language,' more conducive to verbal elaboration and abstract thought, we might contrast an academic culture, confined to those who have been long subjected to the disciplines of the school, with a 'popular' culture, peculiar to those who have been excluded from it, were it not that, by using the same concept of culture in both cases, we should be in danger of concealing that these two systems of patterns of perception, language, thought, action and appreciation are separated by an essential difference. This is that only the system of patterns cultivated by the school, i.e. academic culture (in the subjective sense of personal cultivation or *Bildung* in German), is organized primarily by reference to a system of works embodying that culture, by which it is both supported and expressed." [Au.]

[7]This argument should not be taken to deny the fact that the "West" is a real politico-economic entity, even though its cultural homogeneity lags far behind the unity of its politico-economic system. The *image* of that cultural unity remains the ideological support for the real unity of the West in its imperial relations with the Third World, or in its militarist competition with what was formerly the Eastern Bloc. The collapse of the Soviet Union as a result of that competition, and the consolidation of a Western alliance in the Persian Gulf War are sufficient evidence of what was and is at stake in maintaining the fiction of the cultural unity of the West. Finally, do we need to be reminded that it is Coca-Cola and not Plato which signifies Western culture in the realm of what Immanuel Wallerstein calls "geo-culture"? On this subject, see John Tomlinson, *Cultural Imperialism: A Critical Intro-*

If the fiction of the cultural homogeneity of the West is nevertheless a very powerful one (because it is ideological), perhaps the better strategy for resisting its domination-effect may be to expose the relation between the "culture" it pretends to embody and the institution which is its support in reality. It is just by suppressing culture in the ethnographic sense — or reserving that sense of culture for non-"Western" artifacts — that the traditional curriculum can appropriate the "great works" of Western civilization for the purpose of constituting an imaginary cultural unity such as Bennett or Hirsch[8] envisions. The deracination of the text tradition thus forces us to define the intertextual relation, say, between Aquinas and Aristotle as evidence of the continuity of Western culture, but it allows us to set aside the fact that Aristotle and Aquinas have almost nothing in common *culturally*. It should be remarked here also that the construction of Western culture depends more upon a body of philosophical than literary texts. If the canon debate originated in university literature departments, the defenders of the canon extended the debate to the question of the humanities curriculum as a whole — the "core" curriculum — by resurrecting the philosophical text tradition as the basis for that core curriculum. This text tradition can be invoked more easily than national vernacular literatures to maintain the fiction of a profound evolution or destiny of Western thought extending from the pre-Socratics to the present.[9] Yet the fact remains that this continuity was always the historical support for *nationalist* agendas. The schools in the early modern nation-states provided an instrument by means of which the state could dissolve the residually feudal bonds of local sovereignty and reattach personal loyalty to itself. Nationalism is, as we have seen, entirely on the surface in Bennett's document. In the early modern period, the great vernacular literary works of the nation-states were taught in such a way as to constitute retroactively a pre-national "West" (usually classical rather than medieval), a continuity intended to cover over the traumatic break of early modern societies with traditional feudal cultures. The "West" was always the creation of nationalism, and that is why one observes that the assertion of the continuity of Western tradition exactly corresponds in its intensity to the assertion of nationalism itself.[10]

The homogenizing textual effects of deracination are even more obvious when we consider the fact that, for us, Plato and Aristotle, Virgil and Dante, are great works of literature *in English*. The translation of the "classics" into one's own vernacular is a powerful institutional buttress of imaginary cultural continuities; it confirms the nationalist agenda by permitting the easy appropriation of texts in foreign languages. Yet the device of translation should not be regarded as extraordinary or atypical of school culture, for translation is only a more explicit version of the same technique of deracination by which all cultural works are constructed as objects of study. This point may clarify the otherwise confusing status of "oral literature," which has become a favored site for the contestation of Western culture's hegemony. It is not a mere contingency that oral works must become "written" in order

---

duction (Baltimore: Johns Hopkins University Press, 1991). [Au.]

[8]Eric Donald Hirsch (b. 1928), formerly professor of English at the University of Virginia, argued in his best-selling book, *Cultural Literacy: What Every American Needs to Know* (1987), that the deficiencies of American primary and secondary education were owing partly to the systematic neglect of geographical, historical, and scientific facts, without which students were unable to make sense of political and cultural ideas. Hirsch's book concluded with a list of facts with which he thought every citizen ought to be familiar. While Guillory admits that Hirsch's agenda is not quite so simplistic as those of right-wing pundits like Bennett, he argues elsewhere that the "handy finiteness" of Hirsch's list of significant facts conferring cultural literacy "is the ideological denial of the heterogeneity" of Western culture (p. 354). [Ed.]

[9]This is the argument of Joan Shelley Rubin, *The Making of Middlebrow Culture* (Chapel Hill: University of North Carolina Press, 1992). Discussing John Erskine's original idea for a "great books" program at Columbia University, Rubin notes: "[B]y contending that 'great books' portrayed timeless, universal human situations [Erskine] permitted the conclusion that the classics of Western literature *were* the American heritage" (173). [Au.]

[10]The example of Heidegger almost goes without saying, but not quite. Heidegger's belief in the deep affinity between the Greek and German languages, supposedly the only truly philosophical languages, forces us to recall that the text tradition which is the support of the notion of the West is itself supported in modern European thought both by philological and racial concepts of continuity. [Au.]

to be brought into the arena of curricular conflict as "noncanonical" works, excluded or devalued by the Western text tradition. In fact, oral works *cannot* otherwise enter the institutional field, since orality as a cultural condition can only be studied at all ethnographically, as the "writing of culture." When the condition of oral production is on the other hand ignored in the context of interpreting or evaluating these works (by treating oral works as though they were other written works), the real difference between school culture and the culture which gives rise to works disappears from view. By suppressing the context of a cultural work's production and consumption, the school produces the illusion that "our" culture (or the culture of the "other") is transmitted simply by contact with the works themselves. But a text tradition is not sufficient in itself either to constitute or to transmit a culture, and thus school culture can never be more than a part of a total process of acculturation which, for societies with schools, is always complex and has many other institutional sites.

The function imposed upon schools of acculturating students in "our" culture often thus requires that texts be read "out of context," as signs of cultural continuity, or cultural unity. We need not deny that the text tradition can sustain intertextual dialogue over centuries and millennia, however, in order to insist that what is revealed by the historical context of this dialogue is cultural discontinuity and heterogeneity.[11] A rather different pedagogy, one that emphasizes historical contextualization, would at the very least inhibit the assimilation of cultural works to the agenda of constituting a national culture, or the Western culture which is its ideological support.[12] For the very same reason, only the simplest countercultural pedagogy can make the works of the multicultural curriculum stand in a "subversive" relation to Western culture. The historicization of these works too will have to confront the mutual influence and interrelation between dominant Western and dominated non-Western cultures (in the case of postcolonial works, for example, the fact that "Western culture" appears as a cultural unity *only* through the lens of the colonial educational system, and that postcolonial literatures are in constant dialogue with the works taught in that system). While there exists a multiplicity of sites of cultural production, then, this multiplicity can never really be equated with the multiplicity of cultures, as though every cultural work were only the organic expression of a discrete and autonomous culture.[13] The fact that we now expect the curriculum to reflect as a principle of its organization the

[11]Bourdieu, "Systems of Education and Systems of Thought": "Because of its own inertia, the school carries along categories and patterns of thought belonging to different ages. In the observance of the rules of the dissertation in three points, for example, French schoolchildren are still contemporaries of Saint Thomas. The feeling of the 'unity of European culture' is probably due to the fact that the school brings together and reconciles — as it must for the purposes of teaching — types of thought belonging to very different periods" (352). What I have been calling a "text tradition" is obviously the site of critical judgment, in the sense that the entire domain of intertextuality, or response to earlier by later writers, is a powerful agency for the preservation of these writers. Nevertheless I have consistently argued for locating the site of canon formation in the school, for the reason implied by Bourdieu in the passage just quoted. The point of the sociological argument, for both Bourdieu and myself, is that authors learn whom to read and how to judge in the schools, and that even the judgment of recent but uncanonized work must eventually be validated in the passage of writers into school curricula in order for one to speak of canonicity. One should not forget that literary history is filled with the names of writers whose high standing with other, more famous authors was still insufficient to insure their canonicity. [Au.]

[12]Schools do not always have to acknowledge the fact of deracination, nor do they necessarily have to employ historicizing strategies of recontextualization in classroom practice. Precisely to the extent that they deny the former and decline the latter, they can realize the objective of merely reproducing culture as dogma, as in the case of religious schools. The operation of culture as dogma will be taken up in Chapter 3, Ideology and Canonical Form. [Au.]

[13]This point has been eloquently argued by Kwame Anthony Appiah in the context of the production and consumption of African cultural works: "If there is a lesson in the broad shape of this circulation of cultures, it is surely that we are all already contaminated by each other, that there is no longer a fully autochthonous *echt*-African culture awaiting salvage by our artists (just as there is, of course, no American culture without African roots). And there is a clear sense in some postcolonial writing that the postulation of a unitary Africa over against a monolithic West — the binarism of Self and Other — is the last of the shibboleths of the modernizers that we must learn to live without." "Is the Post- in Postmodernism the Post- in Postcolonial?" *Critical Inquiry* 17 (1991), 354. [Au.]

very distinctness of cultures, Western or non-Western, canonical or noncanonical, points to a certain insistent error of culturalist politics, its elision of the difference the school itself makes in the supposed transmission of culture.

From the perspective of long-term developments in the educational system, the canon debate itself may seem oddly beside the point. Bennett and his associates already acknowledged in their 1984 document that the "crisis of the humanities" refers to the fact that fewer undergraduates choose to major in traditional humanities than in the past. One has the impression in surveying the musings of the right-wing pundits that this fact is the result of nothing less than abdication by the professors of their duty to teach the traditional texts.[14] Nothing could be further from the truth — these texts still constitute the vastly greater part of the humanities curriculum — and in that sense the complaint of the New Right is simply fraudulent. A welcome reality check is provided by Patrick Brantlinger in his analysis of the "crisis":

> Tradition gives the humanities an importance that current funding and research priorities belie. At giant public "multiversities" like the Big Ten schools, humanities courses are taken by many students only as requirements — a sort of force-feeding in writing skills, history, great books, and appropriate "values" before they select the chutes labeled "pre-professional" — pre-med, pre-law, and so forth. . . . Clearly, one doesn't need to blame the radical sixties for the current marginalization and sense of irrelevance that pervades the humanities today.[15]

The crisis of the humanities is the result not of university professors' unwillingness to teach great works (the idea is an insult especially to those teachers and graduate students who could not find employment in the recessions of the 70s and 80s) but of the decisions students themselves make in the face of economic realities. Granted the fact that the crisis is not the result of curricular decisions by humanities teachers, why is the content of the curriculum the site of such controversy? The canon debate will not go away, and it is likely to intensify as the positions of the right and of the multiculturalists are further polarized. The very strength of the reactionary backlash, its success in acquiring access to the national media and funding for its agitprop, suggests that the symptomatic importance of the debate is related in some as yet obscurely discerned way to the failure of the contestants to give an account of the general decline in the significance of the humanities in the educational system. It has proven to be much easier to quarrel about the content of the curriculum than to confront the implications of a fully emergent professional-managerial class which no longer requires the cultural capital of the old bourgeoisie. The decline of the humanities was never the result of newer noncanonical courses or texts, but of a large-scale "capital flight" in the domain of culture. The debate over what amounts to the supplementation (or modernization) of the traditional curriculum is thus a misplaced response to that capital flight, and as such the debate has been conducted largely in the realm of the pedagogic imaginary. I would propose, then, that the division now characterizing the humanities syllabus — between Western and multicultural, canonical and noncanonical, hegemonic and nonhegemonic works — is the symptom of a more historically significant split between two kinds of cultural capital, one of which is "traditional," the other organic to the constitution of the professional-managerial class.

In this larger socioeconomic context, the polarization of the debate into a conflict between Western culture and multiculturalism has proven to be a political misstep for the left. For both the reactionary scapegoating of the noncanonical syllabus as the cause of the crisis of the humanities, and multiculturalism's reduction of canonical works to the ideology of a monolithic Western culture fail to recognize the real relations between the humanities curriculum and the social forces which operate on it. If the debate is ever to acknowledge the presence of these forces, it will have to move beyond the curricular distinction

[14]See Allan Bloom, *The Closing of the American Mind* (New York: Simon and Schuster, 1987), p. 352. [Au.]

[15]Patrick Brantlinger, *Crusoe's Footprints: Cultural Studies in Britain and America* (New York: Routledge, 1990), p. 7. [Au.]

between the canonical and the noncanonical; it will have to raise the much larger question of what is at stake in the relation between the kinds of cultural capital. Since both canonical and noncanonical works constitute at base, despite their apparent conflict, the same *kind* of cultural capital, the social forces displacing this kind of capital will sooner or later strand the participants in the canon debate on an ever shrinking island within the university itself.

What needs urgently to be recognized now is that the polarization of the curriculum into canonical and noncanonical works is very much more in the interest of the right than of the left. The investment of the right in the great works of Western civilization — a "core" curriculum — is in extreme bad faith. For Bennett has already decided that what Bloom calls the "big questions" have been given definitive answers in the American social and political system, which rests on the unshakeable foundation of the *free market.* Yet it is the market itself which produces the effect of cultural capital flight. The professional-managerial class has made the correct assessment that, so far as its future profit is concerned, the reading of great works is not worth the investment of very much time or money. The perceived devaluation of the humanities curriculum is in reality a decline in its *market* value. If the liberal arts curriculum still survives as the preferred course of study in some elite institutions, this fact has everything to do with the class constituency of these institutions. With few exceptions, it is only those students who belong to the financially secure upper classes who do not feel compelled to acquire professional or technical knowledge as undergraduates. The professional-managerial class, on the other hand, many of whose members have only recently attained to middle and upper middle-class status, depends entirely on the acquisition of technical knowledge in order to maintain its status, or to become upwardly mobile. The challenge posed to a class analysis of culture by the professional-managerial class has been well described by Gouldner in his *The Future of Intellectuals and the Rise of the New Class:* "What is needed for the systematic analysis of the old and new class is a *general theory of capital* in which moneyed capital is seen as part of the whole, as a special case of capital. Conversely, what is required for the understanding of culture as capital is nothing less than a political economy of culture."[16] Whether such a political economy of culture has been successfully elaborated in the work of Gouldner or Bourdieu, it is entirely indicative of the conceptual limits of the curriculum debate that it could be carried on for over a decade virtually without reference to either figure.

In this context the right-wing design of purging noncanonical works from the curriculum has as one of its evident objectives the revaluation of the cultural capital of canonical works by associating them with currently popular nationalist and xenophobic sentiments. Mary Louise Pratt is surely correct in identifying the aim of this polemic as the creation of "a narrowly specific cultural capital that will be the normative *referent* for everyone, but will remain the *property* of a small and powerful caste that is linguistically and ethnically unified."[17] The crucial question, however, is not how "narrowly specific" this cultural capital is to be, but how it is to produce the effect of unifying a "caste." Because this unity is not preexistent in American society — capital itself is dispersed now among a number of ethnicities, genders, and even linguistic groups — it

[16]Alvin W. Gouldner, *The Future of Intellectuals and the Rise of the New Class* (New York: Oxford University Press, 1979), p. 21. Gouldner argues persuasively that "An investment in education is not simply a consumable. Something is left over, which produces a subsequent flow of income. It is *cultural capital,* the economic basis of the New Class" (27). On the other hand, I am not convinced that the problem-solving orientation of the New Class constitutes what Gouldner calls a "culture of critical discourse." This is not to say that the professional-managerial class has not produced some forms of social criticism — it has — but that this criticism is seldom systemic (it is usually anti-state but not anti-capital). I am also aware that arguments *against* systemic critique have been made on certain "post-Marxist" grounds. Foucault's concept of the "specific intellectual" might in this context be compared to Gouldner's concept of the New Class intellectual. My own argument follows Bourdieu, however, in his version of systemic critique. [Au.]

[17]Pratt, "Humanities for the Future: Reflections on the Western Culture Debate at Stanford," *South Atlantic Quarterly* 89 (1990): 9. [Au.]

must be constituted in the university *after the fact,* as a new project for that institution. This circumstance explains why the right's agenda for the university always makes room for *some* members of minority groups, because the right believes these self-made individuals can be assimilated to the "caste" of all those with an interest in preserving the rights and privileges of their acquired capital. Such assimilation will leave (and has left) the grossly inequitable social structure more or less unchallenged. It is not quite the case, then, that the New Right wishes to purge the university of all linguistic or ethnic others, but that it sets the university the project of unifying the new possessors of cultural capital by cultural means, by means of a "common" curriculum which will identify them as (justly) privileged. In this way Bennett's "legacy" can be reclaimed for its proper inheritors, those who leave the university possessed of capital, of whatever kind. The cultural legacy so probated will present an image to a somewhat more ethnically heterogeneous propertied class of its unified cultural identity as the inheritors of cultural capital.

If this analysis is correct it does not seem the most effective strategy for the left to cede to the right the *definition* of cultural capital; but this is exactly what a multiculturalism does when it yields canonical works to the right, when it accepts the right's characterization of the canonical syllabus as constitutive of a unified and monolithic Western culture. Basing its agenda upon such assumptions, a left politics of representation seems to have no other choice than to institutionalize alternative syllabi as representative images of non-Western or "counter"-cultures. This is finally why the project of legitimizing noncanonical works in the university produces an irresolvable contradiction between the presentation of these works as equal in cultural value to canonical works, and at the same time as the embodiment of countercultural values which by their very definition are intended to delegitimize the cultural values embodied in canonical works. The polarization of the debate into Western culturalism versus multiculturalism must then be seen not as a simple conflict between regressive and progressive pedagogies but as the symptom of the transformation of cultural capital in response to social conditions not yet recognized as the real and ultimately determining context of the canon debate. Both the right-wing attempt to shore up the cultural capital of the "great works" by advocating a return to a core curriculum, and the pluralist advocacy of multiculturalism respond to the same demographic circumstances, the heterogeneous constituency of the university. But neither version of culturalist politics responds to the heterogenous constitution of cultural capital, and hence both movements are condemned to register this condition symptomatically, as a false perception of the mutual (cultural) exclusivity of canonical and noncanonical works.

It is chastening to recall that a leftist analysis of the heterogeneity of cultural capital was available long before Bourdieu or Gouldner, in the work of Antonio Gramsci. In his prescient notes on the subject of education, Gramsci recognized that the displacement of the classical curriculum by professional and technical knowledge would have the effect of precipitating the "humanist" curriculum into what seems to be a permanent state of crisis:

> The basic division of schools into classical (i.e. grammar) and trade schools was a rational scheme: trade schools for the instrumental classes, classical schools for the ruling classes and intellectuals. The development of the industrial base in both town and country led to a growing need for a new type of urban intellectual: alongside the classical school there developed the technical school (professional but not manual), and this brought into question the very principle of the concrete orientation of general culture based on the Greco-Roman tradition. This orientation, once brought into question was in fact doomed, since its formative capacity was largely based on the general and traditionally indisputable prestige of a particular form of civilization.[18]

Gramsci expresses in his notes what may seem to the present liberal academy a surprising conservatism on curricular issues. Without arguing for the retention of the classical curriculum —

[18]Antonio Gramsci, *The Modern Prince and Other Writings* (New York: International Publishers, 1957), 126. [Au.]

Gramsci allows that it had to be replaced — he was concerned to point out the paradoxical social effects of the "new type of school" which, while it "appears and is advocated as being democratic" is actually "destined not merely to perpetuate social differences but to crystallize them in Chinese complexities."[19] The apparently conservative tenor of his remarks should not be confused, then, with the usual complaint about "specialization," which expresses nostalgia for the even less democratic educational system of the past (Gramsci insists that the older system was always "intended for the new generation of the ruling class"). The question is not whether technical or professional knowledges will or should be taught, but whether there exists a body of knowledge to which *everyone* should have access in the schools. Gramsci's solution to the emergence of a "crisis of the humanities" was to propose the formation of a "single, humanistic, formative, primary school of general culture which will correctly balance the development of ability for manual (technical, industrial) work with the development of ability for intellectual work."[20] Gramsci's proposal may seem, at this date, uncritical of the content of such a curriculum, since he did not have to consider his own society as in our sense "pluralist"; but we should remember that his sense of a politically strategic educational practice is supported by what is perhaps the most powerful theory of intellectual labor in the Marxist tradition, as well as by the very concept of hegemony that is invoked in virtually all forms of current cultural criticism. For these reasons a serious consideration of Gramsci's analysis may be in order.

What Gramsci called the "unitary school" was supposed to "break [the] pattern" of the traditional educational system, in which "each group has its own type of school, intended to perpetuate a specific traditional function, ruling or subordinate."[21] The new technical and professional schools reinstated the division of society "into juridically fixed and crystallized estates rather than moving towards the transcendence of class divisions." The issue here is not only class division but the conditions of possibility for democratic self-government, since Gramsci rightly sees the schools as providing the means for participating in government: "But democracy, by definition, cannot mean merely that an unskilled worker can become skilled. It must mean that every 'citizen' can 'govern' and that society places him, even if only abstractly, in a general condition to achieve this" (318). This is of course an old theme, but the simultaneous and not unrelated decline of both public education and participatory democracy in the United States should confirm its continued pertinence. For reasons too obvious to belabor, Gramsci's "unitary school" was never a goal in this country; but since our concern is with the American educational system, we can at least note that the very limited "democratization" of that system has been accompanied by the gradual displacement upwards to the university level of the curriculum Gramsci conceived as the basis of a "unitary school." This arrangement accomplishes the effect of class fractioning by tracking most students into the work force at the end of their primary or secondary schooling (an effect reinforced also by the distinction between public and private schools). Given the social pressure to enforce vocational tracking at the lower levels of the educational system, and to dispense more highly valued professional and technical knowledge at the university level, the slot into which the humanities curriculum is confined is very small — as we know, the first two years of college study. In the absence of a "unitary school" at the primary or secondary levels, the possibility of installing a core curriculum of philosophical or literary works exists only during this brief period. Many colleges, of course, have always had some form of a core curriculum, but the important point is that the formal study of a set list of "great works" is condemned to have something of a remedial status for those students who have not read literary or philosophical works, either historical or contemporary, at the lower levels of the system, and who will not continue to study them

[19]Antonio Gramsci, *The Antonio Gramsci Reader: Selected Writings 1916–1935*, ed. David Forgacs (New York: Schocken Books, 1988), 317. [Au.]

[20]Gramsci, *The Modern Prince*, 127. [Au.]

[21]Gramsci, *The Antonio Gramsci Reader*, 318. [Au.]

after their sophomore year. It is only by first recognizing the remedial status of the first two years of college study that we can then pose the question of what Gramsci's analysis may have to offer the present debate.

It will first be necessary to exit the social imaginary by acknowledging that there is no question of producing a *national* culture by means of a *university* curriculum. Or conversely of producing a national multiculturalist ethos by the same means. The question is rather what social effects are produced by the knowledges disseminated in the university, and by the manner of their dissemination. It should not be the business of the university to produce a "common culture" even if the educational system inevitably produces a school culture, a specific relation to knowledge among its subjects. The objective of political integration is not to be confused with the altogether questionable objective of cultural assimilation. Gramsci's analysis suggests that a necessary social condition of democracy is the general exercise of a certain kind of intellectual labor, and that a specific body of knowledge (by which is meant neither *information* in Hirsch's sense, nor *culture* in Bennett's) is the necessary medium in the schools for the exercise of this intellectual labor. The point of the unitary school is that it is a school for everyone; by definition it is not the university. A necessary objective of a Gramscian reconsideration of the curriculum debate would thus be the rearticulation of that debate in the context of the educational system *as* a system. In this context, we can recognize that the constraints upon the university curriculum at its present moment and in its present form account for the fact that the project of a core curriculum is so easily annexed to a socially regressive agenda. Time is one such constraint, since it intensifies the effect of deracination to the point of reducing the study of "great works" to a shallow rehearsal of contextless ideas; such "ideas" turn out unsurprisingly to be nothing more than the clichés of right-wing ideology.[22] It has been all too easy as a consequence for the left/liberal professoriate to identify the only respectable adversarial stance with opposition to a core curriculum. The institutionalization of the distinction between canonical and noncanonical works thus emerges as the necessary response to any attempt to reinstitute an exclusively traditional curriculum. As an expression of the same culturalist politics which confuses school culture with culture in general, this adversarial position unfortunately also deprives the teaching of canonical works of an adequate progressive rationale.

It is perhaps time for progressive teachers to take back the humanities curriculum — all of it — as an integrated program of study. Such a program will be severely limited by the narrow stratum of the educational system which it is forced to inhabit, but until we can begin to think and speak about education as a system of interrelated levels, these limits will continue to function subliminally, beyond analysis or intervention. In the meantime, we can imagine that an integrated curriculum would supersede the distinction between canonical and noncanonical works in the recognition that a syllabus of study always enacts a negotiation between *historical* works and *modern* works. There is no question now, nor has there

[22]There is reason to believe that the inevitable brevity and shallowness of the great-books tour are not so undesirable to the New Right. For they are less interested finally in inquiring closely into historical complexities or discursive ambiguities than in making sure that students come away from their experience of reading great works with the *right ideas*. This objective is quite openly acknowledged by the classicist Donald Kagan, who has been celebrated in the right-wing media for using his position as the dean of Yale College as a bully pulpit for what he calls "common studies." Mindful of the liberal persuasion of many of his faculty, however, the dean has expressed some doubt about their suitability to teach these works in the *right way:* "Consider what a core constructed by the current faculty would look like, and the consequences that would ensue if they also had the responsibility of teaching it." See Donald Kagan, "Yale University: Testing the Limits," *Academic Questions* 4 (1991), 33. On the historical origins of the idea of "great books" in American society, and the tendency toward the "superficial" assimilation of the books, see Rubin, *The Making of Middlebrow Culture,* 192ff. Rubin demonstrates persuasively that Mortimer Adler's transformation of John Erskine's notion of a great-books program into the Encyclopaedia Britannica's *Great Books of the Western World* produced nothing less than a monument of middlebrow culture. The almost exclusive emphasis on philosophical rather than literary works in the Britannica project called forth the famous "Syntopicon" of "Great Ideas," which virtually assured that no one would ever have to read the books themselves. [Au.]

even been, of the inevitability of curricular change: the latter-day curriculum is the archaeological evidence of its own sedimented history. When we read Plato or Homer or Virgil in a humanities course, then, we are reading what *remains* of the classical curriculum after the vernacular revolutions of the early modern period. The fact that we no longer read these works in Greek or Latin, or that we read far fewer classical Greek or Latin works than students of premodern school systems, represents a real loss; but this loss must be reckoned as the price of the *integration* of these works into a modern curriculum. The inevitable loss of older works in any humanities curriculum, even one hypothetically much larger than current programs tend to be, is the result, as we have observed, of the *absolute* accumulation of cultural works. The reactionary defense of the traditional "canon" thus betrays itself as ignorant of the cultural history sedimented in the very syllabus it desires to fix. On the other hand it should no longer be necessary to present certain other works, "noncanonical" works, as intrinsically opposed to a hegemonic principle of canonicity, as this is likewise to forget the history sedimented in any syllabus of study.

An alternative theoretical formulation of the curriculum problem will thus have to repudiate the practice of fetishizing the curriculum, of locating the politics of pedagogy in the anxious drawing up of a list of representative names. The *particular* names matter even less at the university level, since the number of historical and modern works worth studying is vastly greater than any (remedial) course of study could begin to consider. The syllabus should rather be conceived as the means of providing *access* to cultural works, both historical and modern (the contrary assumption — that works not on the syllabus will never be read — is an entirely disreputable assumption for teachers to make). Since noncanonical works are in every case either historical works (the objects of research or revaluation) or modern works (the objects of legitimation for the first time as cultural capital), they are in fact what all canonical works once were. To contend otherwise is to commit oneself to the notion that some works are intrinsically canonical, simply expressive of the dominant ideology, and other works intrinsically noncanonical, utterly unassimilable to hegemonic culture. If that were true, what would the struggle to legitimize new works as objects of study be *for?* Hegemony, in Gramsci's sense, is to be fought for; it is something that is continually won and lost by struggles which take place at the specific sites of social practice.

What difference would such a reformulation of terms make? First, that current research programs such as women's studies, or Afro-American studies be recognized as such, as research programs and not as the institution of separate curricula for separate constituencies. But even more important, the humanities curriculum should be presented as an integrated program of study in which the written works studied constitute a certain kind of cultural capital, and in which works therefore cannot be allegorized as intrinsically canonical or intrinsically noncanonical, intrinsically hegemonic or intrinsically antihegemonic. No cultural work of any interest at all is simple enough to be credibly allegorized in this way, because any cultural work will *objectify* in its very form and content the same social conflicts that the canon debate allegorizes by means of a divided curriculum. Further, a conception of an integrated curriculum would make it impossible to forget that what one internalizes in the school is not one's own culture but the culture of the school (which has in turn a certain relation, but not a relation of identity, to culture in the ethnographic sense). The school produces a culture, then, neither unambiguously good or bad, but it does not simply reproduce a given culture, hegemonic or antihegemonic, through the *content* of the curriculum. If it is a defensible objective of the school to disseminate knowledge about the "multicultural" diversity of the nation (defensible because the nation *is* so diverse), it follows from this very objective that it is just as important for majority students to study the cultural products of minority cultures as it is for minority students to be able to study the cultural works of their own cultures. Hence when works by minority writers are legitimized as cultural capital by becoming objects of study in the university, it will follow that everyone will have a right of access to them.

Especially in the wake of a reactionary backlash which indicts the liberal critique of the canon for the abandonment of all standards of judgment, it is no longer politically strategic to argue for the necessity of teaching certain "noncanonical" works solely on the grounds that these works represent social minorities. It is on the contrary much more strategic to argue that the school has the social obligation of providing access to these works, *because they are important and significant cultural works*. In this way we will disabuse ourselves and our students of the idea that canonical or noncanonical syllabi have natural constituencies, the members of dominant or subordinate cultures respectively. The latter notion operates tacitly in the canon debate as the illegitimate displacement of liberal concepts of representation to a site — the school — where democratic objectives are better served by the modestly coercive structure of (in Gramsci's terms) a "unitary" curriculum. Extrapolating from Gramsci's analysis of the relation between the school and democracy, we can predict that different curricula for different constituencies will produce the same effects of social stratification as different schools for different classes. There is not, and should not be, one national culture, but there is, and there should be, one educational system.

But here we return to the fundamental point: pluralism has been able to affirm different cultures but not the fact that cultures are inescapably interdependent both at the moment of a cultural work's production and at that of its consumption. The question is whether or not the school is to acknowledge this "postmodern" condition. It is certainly acknowledged in the domain of mass culture, where cultural products are very often produced for particular constituencies, but where their circulation "interculturally" is virtually assured by the restless promiscuity of commodity exchange. These conditions need not be denied in the university but rather made the occasion of what Christopher Miller, in responding to Hirsch's notion of a national culture, has called "intercultural literacy": "Intercultural literacy would consist of a mode of inquiry that respects the accumulation of shared symbols (thus the term *literacy*) but also invites research into the processes by which cultures are formed and particularly encourages analysis of how cultures constitute themselves *by reference to each other*."[23]

An integrated curriculum would imply a second, pragmatic assumption: It is just as important for both minority and nonminority students to study historical works as it is for both groups to study modern works. The study of historical works need not be justified as an apotropaic[24] exercise — because these works are supposed to embody hegemonic values — but because they *are* historical works. The cultures which give rise to them are as other to all of us as minority cultures are to some of us. Here we can take leave of another fetish of the canon debate, namely, the exclusive emphasis on cultural artifacts as representative of cultures, in the absence of real knowledge about the history of these cultures. The relative lack of reference to history in the curriculum debate is symptomatic of how the concept of culture is deformed in the mirror of the pedagogic imaginary, all the more so since this deformation fails to account for the immanent historicity of even the most recent works. No program of multiculturalism will succeed in producing more than a kind of favorable media-image of minority cultures if it is not supported at every point by an understanding of the historical relations between cultures. At the same time one must insist that it is no longer intellectually defensible to equate historical knowledge with "Western history." It has always been the case (if not always acknowledged) that Western history is the history of the *global* relations of Western states, societies, and cultures; and even more that it is only as a consequence of its global relations that the "West" could conceive or write its own history. If the curriculum is to produce intercultural literacy, in recognition of the imbricated[25] sites of cultural production, we must assume that the context of cultural production is nothing *less* than global.

[23]Christopher L. Miller, "Literary Studies and African Literature: The Challenge of Intercultural Literacy," in *Africa and the Disciplines: Contributions of Research in Africa to the Social Sciences and Humanities*, ed. Robert H. Bates et al. (Chicago: University of Chicago Press, 1983). [Au.]

[24]Intended to avert evil. [Ed.]

[25]Composed of overlapping parts. [Ed.]

Were the left/liberal academy to reappropriate the "humanities," that is, to take back the authority to define the cultural capital embodied in its curriculum of study, it would have to devise a rationale for an integrated curriculum of textual/historical study exceeding the laudable objective of affirming cultural diversity. A left rationale for an integrated curriculum would have to present all of the cultural works in that curriculum, whatever their provenance, as a species of cultural capital constitutively different from the capital embodied in technical and professional knowledge. This difference can be defined by the proposition that *everyone* has a right of access to cultural works, to the means of both their production and their consumption. The dissemination of these means produces at every level of the educational system a form of "literacy," or what we would otherwise recognize as the practices of *reading* and *writing*. It would make an immense social difference if the knowledge designated by the latter terms were the property of everyone; but we are speaking here of what may be called "socialized" education, that is, of something that does not exist in this country. If the current educational institution does indeed (like every other social institution) reproduce social inequities, it achieves this effect by the unequal distribution of cultural capital, or by presenting cultural works in the classroom as the organic expression of the dominant classes' entitlement to those works. This effect cannot be undone by changing the university curriculum alone, because it is an effect of the educational *system,* of which the university is only a part. Does this mean that curricular reform is pointless, or that it has no social consequences? On the contrary, the university curriculum is at this moment a privileged site for raising questions about the educational system as a whole, just because it is the site at which a "crisis" of cultural capital (or the "humanities") has occurred. The claim of the present argument is that an analysis of this crisis in terms of the distribution of cultural capital will produce a more strategic theory of curricular reform than will a pluralist critique.

If progressive teachers have a considerable stake in disseminating the kind of knowledge (the study of cultural works as a practice of reading and writing) that is the vehicle for critical thinking, this knowledge is nevertheless only the vehicle for critical thought, not its realization. As cultural capital it is always also the object of appropriation by the dominant classes. The pluralist strategy of institutionalizing the category of the noncanonical is incapable of grasping this essential ambiguity of the school as an institution. For the same reason that a syllabus of canonical works cannot reproduce a culture of the dominant outside a certain total structuration of the educational system, no syllabus of noncanonical works can function ipso facto as the embodiment of that system's critique. To demand that critical thinking be institutionalized entails an obvious contradiction, but the desire for the institutionalization of a pluralist critique is what drives the current form of curricular revision. We can at most, however, institutionalize the *conditions* of critical thought, in this case a curriculum that makes possible the maximum dissemination of the practices of reading and writing. Inasmuch as the study of cultural works in historical context constitutes a good condition for these practices, no curricular intervention which does not *reaffirm* the cultural capital of these works can ensure the viability of that condition. In the present regime of capital distribution, the school will remain both the agency for the reproduction of unequal social relations and a necessary site for the critique of that system.

LITERATURE AS CULTURAL CAPITAL: AN ALTERNATIVE ANALYSIS

What need for purists when the demotic is built to last,
To outlast us, and no dialect hears us?

— JOHN ASHBERY, "Purists Will Object"

The School and the Reproduction of Social Relations

The defense of the noncanonical may justly take as its epigraph Walter Benjamin's remark that "there is no document of civilization which is not at the same time a document of barbarism."[26]

[26]Walter Benjamin, *Illuminations,* trans. Henry Zohn (New York: Schocken Books, 1969), 256. [Au.]

Benjamin offers no unequivocal response to the fact of barbarism, rather a certain "cautious detachment"; but what is the barbarism congealed in the work such that one can remove oneself to a distance from it? This question is further complicated by the continuation of Benjamin's thought: "And just as it [the document of civilization] is itself not free of barbarism, neither is the process of transmission [*Überlieferung*] by which it descends from one to another." The latter statement suggests how one might begin to conceptualize the social effects of the canonical form. Canonicity is not a property of the work itself but of its transmission, its relation to other works in a collocation of works — the syllabus in its institutional locus, the school. Is the barbarism of transmission, then, the same barbarism we find in the "document of civilization"? Ultimately no doubt, but not immediately. Whatever the relation of the work to its initial audience, it must certainly have other relations as a canonical work. The failure to make this distinction is the premise of every ideology of "tradition," if tradition implies the supposed reproduction of cultural values by the monuments of culture themselves. Yet if canonical works do not all by themselves reproduce cultural values, it is significant — even integral — to the real social process of reproduction that they are thought to do so. The real social process is the reproduction not of values but of *social relations*. These relations consist of much more than a relation of text to reader.

The form of the canon belongs to the process of the reproduction of social relations, but it does not enter this process immediately. The canon does not accrete over time like a pyramid built by invisible hands, nor does it act directly and irresistibly on social relations, like a chemical reagent; in its concrete form as a syllabus or curriculum, the canon is a discursive instrument of "transmission" situated historically within a specific institution of reproduction: the school. We may define the latter institution as a more or less formal arrangement for undertaking intensively educational functions also distributed extensively across the institutional breadth of any social formation. The system of educational institutions reproduces social relations by distributing, and where necessary redistributing, knowledges. The canon is thus not grounded in an "institution of criticism," as is sometimes said. Criticism is not an institution but a disciplinary discourse inhabiting a historically specific educational institution.

The instrumentality of the canon within this system is a function of its status as an objectification of the reproduction process, Benjamin's "cultural treasure," or Bennett's "legacy," which is inexhaustible because it appears to reproduce itself — it is wealth never consumed by consumption. The educational apparatus regulates, because it makes possible, access to this inheritable treasure. Individual works are taken up into this system (preserved, disseminated, taught) and confront their receptors first as canonical, as cultural capital. There is no other access to works: they must be confronted as the cultural capital of educational institutions, a circumstance proven rather than disproven by the exceptional case of the autodidact. The question of access, however, is far from simple. The school does not exist merely to lift a veil of ignorance, or to set one at the threshold of the temple. The school functions as a system of credentialization by which it produces a specific *relation* to culture. That relation is different for different people, which is to say that it reproduces social relations.

To give an account of the exact constitution of these relations is to index the "barbarism" of which Benjamin writes: the social relations of domination and exploitation. But to foreground the particular barbarities of the historical record, as though mere exposure to canonical works were the same as exposure to these barbarities, is to misrecognize certain recurrent structural features of the institutions which constitute the mechanism of social reproduction. The implications of this fact are immensely significant if the duration of educational institutions can be shown to be (in part) an effect of formal objectifications of reproduction, such as canons of texts. The institution elicits out of its very structure a demand for the subordination of the historical specificity of individual works to the ideology of the canonical form (tradition), and this subordination is recognizable in pedagogic practice as a homogenizing of dogmatic content, the positing of universal truths discovered and rediscovered in the great works. Against this inert narrative one can respond with Benjamin's determination to "brush history against the grain"; but this is never a simple act, for reasons Bourdieu persuasively argues. Institutions of reproduction succeed by taking as their first object not the reproduction of social relations but the reproduction of the institution itself.[27] No institution is in that sense reducible to its social function. Only by reason of its relative autonomy does an institution succeed in the remote function of reproducing social relations. Autonomy in no way transcends social formations but rather takes the form of a structural atavism[28] existing in complex relation to the motors of social change. Hence major reorganizations of social relations alter only very slowly the larger structural features that allow the school historically "to occupy homologous positions in the system of relations which link it to the dominant classes" (129). Elsewhere Bourdieu draws a stark conclusion from such facts: "it is no doubt in the area of education and culture that the members of the dominated classes have least chance of discovering their objective interest and of producing and imposing the problematic most consistent with their interests."[29] This conclusion might be qualified, but not until the full measure of its force is acknowledged.

Bourdieu's argument will seem most surprising to those critics who would like to represent education as a means of directly effecting social change. Schools have seldom conceived of themselves in this way, and in fact it is only at certain privileged moments of crisis that consistently adversarial pedagogic practices have been cultivated. From the perspective of the present analysis, we can say that strategies such as the "opening of the canon," or the institution of noncanonical syllabi, repress the fact of reproduction through institutional forms in the belief that social relations are directly acted upon in the classroom. To insist again on what may now seem an obvious point, the apparatus of stratification by which knowledge is socially distributed — the educational system itself, with its multiple levels of access and procedures of credentialization — remains largely untouched by such programs; and it is unfortunately also a fact that adversarial pedagogies are largely restricted to elite institutions. More important, only a very impoverished notion of reproduction represents it as incompatible with social change. In the present socioeconomic order the reproduction of the system as a whole demands rapid transformations in social relations in response to rapid changes in the relations of production and consumption. In this context, the very success, for example, of feminist revisions of the literary canon must be read not simply as the victory of an oppositional culture but as a systemic feature of the reproduction of the sexual division of labor, the most recent form of which is manifested by the entrance (not without struggle) of middle-class women into expanded professional and managerial fields. Educational institutions facilitate the production of new relations (in necessary conflict with other institutions of reproduction, such as the family) and thus facilitate the reproduction of the system as a whole. This is to say nothing, of course, about the desirability of these new relations, or about the possibility of their use as a staging ground for more systemic strategies of resistance. Progressive teachers must first intervene, however, at the site of reproduction, *and even as one of its agents,* in order to put into circulation any critique of the system as a whole.

To repress the fact of the school's institutional structure, as though the classroom had no walls, does not mean that the social effectivity of such strategies as curricular revision is merely illusory, but rather that it will never be quite what is intended, that pedagogy is never wholly within the control of pedagogues. But it is better to be aware of this fact than not, particularly in the case of the canonical/noncanonical distinction, which, as we have seen, has effects which exceed the immediate intention of affirming the cultural products of minority cultures. The crucial point in extending and qualifying Bourdieu's account of an apparently homeostatic system of reproduction is the question of institutional atavism, Bour-

[27]On this thesis, see Pierre Bourdieu and Jean-Claude Passeron, *Reproduction in Education, Society and Culture,* trans. Richard Nice (London: Sage Publications, 1977), p. 32. [Au.]

[28]Primitive tendency. [Ed.]

[29]Pierre Bourdieu, *Distinction: A Social Critique of the Judgment of Taste,* trans. Richard Nice (Cambridge: Harvard University Press, 1984), p. 387. [Au.]

dieu's insistence that "by ignoring all demands other than that of its own reproduction, the school most effectively contributes to the reproduction of the social order."[30] Such a condition certainly obtains in the short run (even countercultural movements, once institutionalized, direct a good deal of their energy to ensuring the reproduction of their institutional forms); but Bourdieu's analysis seems to beg the question of very large systemic transformations.[31] Any given social formation constructs itself out of much older apparatuses of reproduction that must be adapted to new social relations. These older apparatuses coexist with and complicate the social space of recent, perhaps more organic institutions (the capitalist corporation, for example). In the face of inevitable struggles within and at the juncture of institutional ensembles, the most atavistic features of older institutional structures serve to legitimate and stabilize what is always illegitimate and unstable — the momentary conjunctural order.[32] But let us name this situation exactly: it is contradiction. John B. Thompson draws a similar conclusion to the one implied here in his critique of Bourdieu, when he argues that social reproduction is not so much "a concert performed without a conductor" (Bourdieu's phrase) as it is a "cacaphony of divergent and discordant notes." Reproduction succeeds in late capitalist society as the effect of the proliferation of difference itself, the extreme divergence of interests resulting in "a lack of consensus at the very point where oppositional attitudes could be translated into political action."[33] This observation stops short of theorizing a mechanism of systemic transformation, displacing it to the effects of extremely dispersed struggles upon the social totality. But no such theorization is necessary to advance the present argument, only a recognition of the exponentially increasing complexity of reproduction in the context of a historical *durée*[34] in which many institutions survive long after the conditions of their emergence have disappeared.

Canons of texts belong to the *durée* of the school as both an objectification of "tradition" and as a list of texts (syllabus, curriculum) continuously changing in response to the frictional relations between institutional and social reproduction. Yet the significance of this tension between the two sites of reproduction is concealed from revisionists of the canon, who see a direct relation between the canon and social struggle but misrecognize the institution mediating this relation as a mythical "interpretive community," or as an autonomous "profession." The profession is not an institution any more than criticism is: it is the self-representation in the "pedagogic imaginary" through which teachers misrecognize their relation both to their discursive practices and to the institution of the school. The objective history of canon formation, if the latter is an effect of syllabus construction and revision, exhibits enormous variation, but this history can be recovered only in the context of the history of the school, whose invariant social function is the distribution of knowledge by means of techniques of dissemination and rituals of credentialization. The invariant function of credentialization, however, does not determine what constitutes credentials in a given social order, the certifiable possession of skill, knowledge, judgment, taste, genius, or whatever. The forms of cultural capital are rather determined within the whole social order as arenas of both certification and contestation, because the social totality is structured by the multiple and relatively incommensurable dis-

[30]Bourdieu and Passeron, *Reproduction,* 98. [Au.]

[31]Perhaps only "seems": For Bourdieu's response to the question about long-term historical transformation, see his *In Other Words: Essays towards a Reflexive Sociology,* trans. Matthew Adamson (Stanford: Stanford University Press, 1990), pp. 41–46. [Au.]

[32]An example: If the sheer formal atavism of an institution such as the church suits the function of social reproduction, the prestige deriving from its atavistic features can as well become the ground of resistance in a complex agonistic game requiring the expenditure of that prestige as cultural capital. Consider the fate of the Sanctuary movement in the mid-1980s: This movement staged the literalization of the church's institutional autonomy as the autonomy of its physical space, the imaginary "sanctuary" within which political refugees from the right-wing Latin American dictatorships could take sanctuary. Before such an elegant atavism, even our authoritarian state paused, though not for long. [Au.]

[33]John B. Thompson, *Studies in the Theory of Ideology* (Berkeley: University of California Press, 1984), 24. [Au.]

[34]Literally "duration," the time span of an institution. [Ed.]

tinctions of class, sex, race, national status (to name only the crudest of many), distinctions produced and reproduced in a system that never closes upon its objective of homeostasis.[35]

If the critique of the canon posited a direct relation of "representation" between social identity and the canonicity of certain texts, the effect of that correlation was to dehistoricize the forms of cultural capital, as well as the forms of social identity. This fact can be demonstrated by raising the specific question of what historical forms of cultural capital are embodied in *literary* texts. The answer to this question will of course entail recognizing the historicity of the category of literature itself, the recognition that its history cannot be dissociated from the history of the school. Let us begin with an example drawn from R. R. Bolgar's authoritative study, *The Classical Heritage and Its Beneficiaries,* an encyclopedic account of the transmission of classical literature from late antiquity through the end of the Renaissance. The example concerns the teaching of Graeco-Roman literature in the provinces of imperial Rome, and it is chosen both because it is an extreme case, and because its extremity disturbs Bolgar's narrative of transmission in instructive ways:

> As the protective might of the legions weakened, so the imperial government came to rely to an ever greater extent on its intangible assets; and the excellence of Graeco-Roman culture was turned into useful bait for retaining the loyalty of uncertain provincials. Steel was in short supply. So the provinces were to be grappled to the soul of Rome by hoops of a different make. Literature was taught with great zeal as an introduction to the Roman way of life; but what it introduced men to was in the last analysis the old life of the city-states.[36]

When Bolgar reaches this point in his account, his prose is excited into an unusual state of figurative radiation by the spectacle of what Bourdieu calls "symbolic violence," "the imposition of a cultural arbitrary *(arbitraire)* by an arbitrary power."[37] The legions withdraw and are replaced by schools. But for Bolgar this fact in no way compromises the excellence of Graeco-Roman literature. On the contrary, the reproduction of the Roman system in the provinces comes to rely in part upon the very quality of its literature, which for Bolgar remains uncontaminated by the business of imperial administration. It would seem that the original context of a work's production becomes simply irrelevant when individual works are appropriated by the empire's ideological machinery, which flattens local cultures in its path. Bolgar is struck by this discrepancy and cannot refrain from noting and even belaboring the bewildering circumstance that the literature read in the provincial curriculum seemed to reflect favorably the "old life of the city-states" rather than the contemporary norms of the imperium.

There is indeed a real and irresolvable discrepancy in the relation between the historical specificity of works and the factitious universality of the canonical form, which aspires to transhistorical validity by masking the pedagogic function of disseminating this year's orthodoxy. But the puzzle of why this discrepancy does not seem obvious to everyone is not nearly so inexplicable in the context of Bourdieu's point that social reproduction is not effected directly through the contents of the curriculum. At the moment when the spectacle of symbolic violence begins to play on the stage of empire, it becomes easy to forget what is elsewhere for Bolgar merely given, that the first objective of the educational system in the provinces was to teach future colonial subalterns the Latin language. As students of Roman education, these administrators had a different relation to Latin than native speakers, as well as a different relation to their own languages. If the primary objective of education in the provinces was to produce this linguistic differentiation of the subject populace as a technical means of administration — government by symbolic rather than by physical violence — then the signifying effects of Latin literature, its ideological "contents," were necessarily mediated, diffused, or even contained by the ef-

[35]Equilibrium. [Ed.]

[36]R. R. Bolgar, *The Classical Heritage and Its Beneficiaries* (Cambridge: Cambridge University Press, 1954), 24. [Au.]

[37]Bourdieu and Passeron, *Reproduction,* 30. [Au.]

fects of this superimposed social stratification. The primary fact about the teaching of Latin literature was thus not that it conveyed Roman cultural values but that it was the vehicle for the teaching of the Latin language. This goal was important enough to overwhelm any objection that might have been raised to particular Latin works whose contents may not have been wholly compatible with the norms of the imperium. As carriers first and foremost of *linguistic capital* these works could then become the vector of ideological motifs not necessarily expressed within the works themselves.

The example of imperial education is not exceptional. The situation of provincial administrators was not markedly different from that of the educated citizenry of Rome itself, where the Roman way of life also had to be reproduced. This fact is quite apparent in Bolgar's discussion of the "well organized educational system of the Empire," which had for its main aim not so much to teach the Roman way of life as to teach the two literary languages of Latin and Greek. These were not, of course, the languages learned by Roman infants; they were languages "remote from ordinary speech" (22), second languages learned in the formal context of an institutional relation between teacher and student, and by means of that abstract alienation of language known in the classical world as "grammar." At this point the question of literacy may be taken up again, in recognition of the fact that the systematic regulation of reading and writing belongs to the project of social reproduction. What one learns to read is always another language, and because that language is unequally distributed, it is a form of capital. The internal differentiation of language produced by the classical educational system as the distinction between a credentialed and a noncredentialed speech reproduces social stratification on the model of the distinction between the tribe or nation and its sociolinguistic other, the "barbarian." Incorrect speech is marked from the first appearance of Alexandrian grammars as "barbarism," a characterization persisting into the present as a strategy for mobilizing xenophobia in the service of an internal linguistic stratification constructed upon and reproducing internal social distinctions. The barbarism about which Benjamin writes is nothing other than the ironic inversion of that ideological representation of the dominated lower classes as the barbarians *within the walls*.

It has long been known that the appearance of literature as a collection of canonical texts was from the first a scholarly pedagogic device of the classical grammarians. Thus E. R. Curtius, in his *European Literature and the Latin Middle Ages:* "In antiquity, the concept of the model author was oriented upon a grammatical criterion, the criterion of correct speech."[38] Quintilian writes of the classical world's primary educators, the *grammatici,* that they were concerned to teach "the art of speaking correctly" and "the interpretation of the poets," the one by means of the other.[39] They developed procedures for the selection of texts that sometimes constituted the sole means of their preservation (for example, the anthological handbooks within which many classical authors survive as exemplary fragments). Nor is the formation of textual canons merely accidentally allied to the emergence of grammatical speech as socially marked. The constitutive link in classical education between the selection of texts and the distribution of cultural capital in linguistic form is remarked by Curtius in connection with Aulus Gellius's extension of the term *classicus,* one of Rome's five propertied classes, to the best of the poets, "a first class and taxpaying author, not a proletarian" — about which Curtius comments, "What a tidbit for Marxist sociology of literature" (250). But this genealogy of the classics has remained merely an etymological joke (and Curtius himself is seldom cited in the canon debate) because selections of texts historically have the appearance of having selected themselves. This is certainly the case in any very complex social conditions of literary production, where the literary tradition is generalized as the heritage of homogeneous literary culture, whose text tradition is curiously independent of the institutions transmitting that tradition. It is by no

[38]Ernst Robert Curtius, *European Literature and the Latin Middle Ages,* trans. Willard R. Trask (New York: Harper and Row, 1953), 250. [Au.]

[39]Quintilian, *Institutio Oratoria,* 4 vols., trans H. E. Butler (Cambridge: Harvard University Press, 1969), 1:63. [Au.]

means necessary to reduce the former to the latter in order to see what lies plainly before us: a process of unnatural selection, a social history. The literary canon has always functioned in the schools as a pedagogic device for producing an effect of linguistic distinction, of "literacy." The production of this effect does not depend upon the biasing of judgment — the educational system works better with better works — nor is it a question of insuring the ideological orthodoxy of texts by extraordinary procedures of exclusion and censorship (these measures have for the most part been imposed from above, by church or state). Literary curricula, historically the substance of most educational programs, are capable of assimilating the otherwise dangerous heterodoxies expressed in some works by means of homogenizing methods of textual appropriation exercised within institutional structures of symbolic violence. The ideological effect rides on the back of the effect of sociolinguistic differentiation produced by access to the literary language, which is therefore its vector. Only in this way can one explain the use of the *same* canonical works to inculcate in different generations of students many different and even incompatible ideologies.

Authors themselves do not produce the effect of linguistic differentiation, any more than their works can produce for later generations of readers the same effects of persuasion they may have intended for readers of their own time, and which, when we set out to critique these effects, we call "ideological." Authors cannot be said to write *for* the educational system but in a determinate relation to it, *as the subjects it produces*. The history of canon formation belongs to the history of literary production, therefore, as a condition of production; in the same way, literary production is a condition of reproduction, of the history of canon formation. Hence the production of literary texts cannot be reduced to a specific and unique social function, not even the ideological one. Authors confront a monumentalized textual tradition already immersed as speakers and writers in the social condition of linguistic stratification that betrays at every level the struggle among social groups over the resources of language, over cultural capital in its linguistic form. When these authors are joined to the frieze upon which they formerly gazed, the record of struggle seems to pass into oblivion as the unwritten. Yet that record is immediately available in works themselves as the *language of literature,* out of which literature is made, and in the process of canon formation as the institutional intervention by which the literary curriculum becomes the pedagogic vehicle for producing the distinction between credentialed and uncredentialed speech.

Alternative Contents

1. AXIOLOGY AND CANONICAL STUDIES

2. CULTURAL STUDIES

3. DECONSTRUCTION

4. FEMINIST CRITICISM AND GENDER STUDIES

5. FORMALISM

6. HERMENEUTICS

7. MARXIST APPROACHES TO LITERATURE

8. PHENOMENOLOGICAL CRITICISM

9. PSYCHOANALYTIC APPROACHES TO LITERATURE

10. QUEER THEORY

11. READER-RESPONSE CRITICISM

12. RHETORICAL THEORY

13. STRUCTURALISM AND SEMIOTICS

Acknowledgments *(continued from page iv)*

Nina Baym, "Melodramas of Beset Manhood: How Theories of American Fiction Exclude Women Authors," from *American Quarterly* vol. 33.2 (1981): 123–39. Copyright © 1981, American Studies Association.

Simone de Beauvoir, "Myths: Of Women in Five Authors." From *The Second Sex* by Simone de Beauvoir, trans. H. M. Parshley. Copyright 1952 and renewed 1980 by Alfred A. Knopf, Inc. Reprinted by permission of the publisher.

Walter Benjamin, "The Work of Art in the Age of Mechanical Reproduction" from *Illuminations* by Walter Benjamin, copyright © 1995 Suhrkamp Verlag, Frankfurt a.M.; English translation by Harry Zohn copyright © 1968 and renewed 1996 by Harcourt Brace & Company, reprinted by permission of Harcourt Brace & Company.

Homi K. Bhabha, "Locations of Culture," from *The Location of Culture* by Homi K. Bhabha. Reprinted by permission of the publisher, Routledge (UK).

Harold Bloom, "A Meditation upon Priority," from *The Anxiety of Influence: A Theory of Poetry* by Harold Bloom. Copyright © 1973 by Oxford University Press, Inc. Reprinted by permission of the publisher.

Wayne C. Booth, "Pluralism and Its Rivals," from *Don't Try to Reason with Me: Essays and Ironies for a Credulous Age.* Copyright © 1970 by the University of Chicago. Reprinted by permission of the author and the University of Chicago Press.

Pierre Bourdieu, "The Market of Symbolic Goods." Reprinted from *Poetics,* Vol. 15. Pierre Bourdieu, "The market of symbolic goods," pages 13–44, copyright © 1985 with permission from Elsevier Science-NL, Sara Burgerhartstraat 25, 1055 KV Amsterdam, The Netherlands.

Cleanth Brooks, "Irony as a Principle of Structure," from *Literary Opinion in America,* edited by Morton Dauwen Zobel. Reprinted by permission of the author.

Peter Brooks, "Freud's Masterplot: Questions of Narrative," from *Yale French Studies* 55/56 (1977). Copyright © 1977 by Yale University Press. Reprinted by permission of the publisher.

Kenneth Burke, "Literature as Equipment for Living," from *The Philosophy of Literary Form,* 3rd ed. rev., by Kenneth Burke. Copyright © 1973 by the Regents of the University of California. Reprinted by permission of the University of California Press. "Symbolic Action in a Poem by Keats," from *A Grammar of Motives* by Kenneth Burke. Copyright © 1969 Kenneth Burke. Reprinted by permission of the University of California Press.

Judith Butler, "Imitation and Gender Subordination," from *Inside/Out: Lesbian Theories, Gay Theories,* edited by Diana Fuss. Reprinted by permission of the publisher, Routledge (NY).

Hélène Cixous, "The Laugh of the Medusa," translated by Keith Cohen and Paula Cohen, reprinted from *Signs* I (1976) by permission of the translators and the University of Chicago Press.

R. S. Crane, "Toward a More Adequate Criticism of Poetic Structure," from *The Language of Criticism and the Structure of Poetry* by R. S. Crane. Copyright © 1953 by the University of Toronto Press. Reprinted by permission of the University of Chicago Press.

Jonathan Culler, "Literary Competence," reprinted from *Structuralist Poetics: Structuralism, Linguistics, and the Study of Literature,* copyright © Jonathan Culler 1975. Used by permission of the publishers, Cornell University Press and Routledge & Kegan Paul.

Paul de Man, "Semiology and Rhetoric," from *Diacritics* 3:3 (Fall 1973). Reprinted by permission of The Johns Hopkins University Press.

Jacques Derrida, "Structure, Sign, and Play in the Discourse of the Human Sciences," from *The Structuralist Controversy: The Languages of Criticism and the Science of Man,* edited by Richard Macksey and Eugenio Donato, published by the Johns Hopkins University Press. Reprinted by permission of the publisher.

Terry Eagleton, "Categories for a Materialist Criticism," from *Criticism and Ideology: A Study in Marxist Literary Theory.* Copyright © 1976 Verso / NLB. Reprinted by permission of the publisher.

Umberto Eco, "The Myth of Superman," translated by Natalie Chilton from *The Role of the Reader: Explorations in the Semiotics of Texts* by Umberto Eco. Reprinted by permission of Indiana University Press.

Lee Edelman, "Homographesis," from *Yale Journal of Criticism,* vol. 3.1 (1989): 189–207. Copyright © The Johns Hopkins University Press. Reprinted by permission of The Johns Hopkins University Press.

T. S. Eliot, "Tradition and the Individual Talent." From *Selected Works* by T. S. Eliot. Published by Faber and Faber Ltd. (UK) and Harcourt Brace & Company (USA). Reprinted for distribution in Canada by permission of Faber and Faber Ltd.

William Empson, Epilogue to *Seven Types of Ambiguity.* Reprinted with permission of Curtis Brown, Ltd., London, on behalf of The Estate of William Empson. Copyright © The Estate of William Empson 1930.

Judith Fetterley, "Introduction: On the Politics of Literature" from *The Resisting Reader: A Feminist Approach to American Fiction* by Judith Fetterley. Copyright © by Judith Fetterley. Published by Indiana University Press. Reprinted by permission of Indiana University Press.

Stanley Fish, "Interpreting the *Variorum,*" from *Critical Inquiry* 2. Copyright © 1976 by the University of Chicago. Reprinted by permission of the author and the University of Chicago Press.

Michel Foucault, "What Is an Author?" Reprinted from Michel Foucault, "What Is an Author?" Translated from the French by the editor, Josué V. Harari, in *Textual Strategies: Perspectives in Post-Structuralist Criticism.* Copyright © 1979 by Cornell University. Used by permission of the publisher, Cornell University Press. "Las Meninas," pp. 3–10 from *The Order of Things: An Archaeology of the Human Sciences* by Michel Foucault (New York: Random House, Inc., 1970). Copyright © 1966 by Éditions Gallímard. Reprinted by permission of Georges Borchardt, Inc. Pp. 90–111 from *The History of*

Sexuality, Volume I. An Introduction by Michel Foucault, translated by Robert Hurley (New York: Random House, Inc., 1978). Copyright © 1976 Éditions Gallímard. Reprinted by permission of Georges Borchardt, Inc.

Sigmund Freud, "The Relation of the Poet to Daydreaming" and "The Theme of the Three Caskets" from *The Collected Papers,* Volume 4, by Sigmund Freud. Authorized translation under the supervision of Joan Riviere. Published by Basic Books, Inc. by arrangement with The Hogarth Press Ltd. and the Institute of Psycho-Analysis, London. Reprinted by permission of BasicBooks, a division of HarperCollins Publishers, Inc., and by permission of The Hogarth Press.

Northrop Frye, "The Archetypes of Literature," from *Fables of Identity* by Northrop Frye. Copyright © 1951 (renewed 1978) by Kenyon College; copyright © 1963 by Harcourt Brace & Company and renewed 1991 Jane Widdicombe. Reprinted by permission of Kenyon College, Harcourt Brace & Company, and the author.

Hans Georg Gadamer, "The Elevation of the Historicality of Understanding to the Status of Hermeneutical Principle," from *Truth and Method* by Hans Georg Gadamer. Copyright © 1975 by Sheed & Ward Ltd. Reprinted with the permission of The Continuum Publishing Group, 370 Lexington Avenue, New York NY 10017.

Henry Louis Gates, Jr., "Writing, 'Race,' and the Difference It Makes," from *Loose Canons: Notes on the Culture Wars* by Henry Louis Gates, Jr. Copyright © 1992 by Henry Louis Gates, Jr. Reprinted by permission of Oxford University Press.

Jane Gallop, excerpt from *Reading Lacan* by Jane Gallop. Copyright © 1985 by Cornell University Press. Used by permission of the publisher.

Clifford Geertz, "Deep Play: Notes on the Balinese Cockfight," reprinted by permission of *Daedalus,* Journal of the American Academy of Arts and Sciences, from the issue entitled "Myth, Symbol, and Culture," Winter 1972, Vol. 101, No. 1.

Gérard Genette, "Frontiers of Narrative," from *Figures of Literary Discourse* by Gérard Genette, translated by Alan Sheridan. Copyright © 1982 by Columbia University Press. Reprinted with permission of the publisher.

Sandra M. Gilbert and Susan Gubar, "Infection in the Sentence: The Woman Writer and the Anxiety of Authorship," from *The Madwoman in the Attic: The Woman Writer and the Nineteenth-Century Literary Imagination* by Sandra Gilbert and Susan Gubar, published by Yale University Press. Copyright © 1979 Yale University Press. Reprinted by permission of Yale University Press.

Stephen Greenblatt, Introduction and "*King Lear* and Harsnett's 'Devil Fiction,'" from the special issue of *Genre: The Power of Forms in the English Renaissance,* edited by Stephen Greenblatt. Copyright © 1982 by the University of Oklahoma. Reprinted by permission.

John Guillory, excerpt from *Cultural Capital: The Problem of Literary Canon Formation.* Copyright © 1993 by the University of Chicago. Reprinted by permission of the author and the University of Chicago Press.

Jürgen Habermas, "Excursus on Leveling the Genre Distinction between Philosophy and Literature," translated by Fred Lawrence, from *The Philosophical Discourse of Modernity.* Copyright © 1987 by MIT Press. Reprinted by permission of MIT Press.

Georg Wilhelm Friedrich Hegel, "Introduction to the Philosophy of Fine Art." Reprinted with the permission of Scribner, a division of Simon & Schuster, from *Hegel: Selections,* translated and edited by J. Loewenberg. Copyright © 1929 by Charles Scribner's Sons; copyright renewed © 1957.

Martin Heidegger, "Hölderlin and the Essence of Poetry." Reprinted from *Existence and Being* by Martin Heidegger, translated by Douglas Scott, introduction by Werner Brock, published by Henry Regnery, 1949.

Norman N. Holland, "The Question: Who Reads What How?" from *5 Readers Reading* by Norman N. Holland, published by Yale University Press. Copyright © 1975 by Yale University. Reprinted by permission of Yale University Press.

Horace, *The Art of Poetry,* from *Satires and Epistles of Horace,* edited and translated by Smith Palmer Bovie. Copyright © 1959 by the University of Chicago. Reprinted by permission of the author and the University of Chicago Press.

Luce Irigaray, "This Sex Which Is Not One," translated by Claudia Reeder in *New French Feminisms,* edited by Elaine Marks and Isabelle de Courtivron, copyright © 1980 by the University of Massachusetts Press. Originally published as "Ce sexe qui n'en est pas un," by Luce Irigaray in *Ce sexe qui n'en est pas un* by Luce Irigaray, Éditions de Minuit, 1977. Reprinted by permission of Éditions de Minuit and the University of Massachusetts Press.

Wolfgang Iser, "The Reading Process: A Phenomenological Approach," from *The Implied Reader,* published by The Johns Hopkins University Press. Reprinted by permission of the publisher.

Fredric Jameson, excerpt from *The Political Unconscious.* Reprinted from Fredric Jameson, *The Political Unconscious: Narrative as a Socially Symbolic Act.* Copyright © 1981 by Cornell University Press. Used by permission of the publisher.

Randall Jarrell, lines from "Eighth Air Force" (in "Irony as a Principle of Structure" by Cleanth Brooks), reprinted from *The Complete Poems* by Randall Jarrell. Copyright © 1945, 1951, 1955, by Randall Jarrell. Copyright renewed 1968, 1969 by Mrs. Randall Jarrell. Reprinted by permission of Farrar, Straus and Giroux, Inc.

Hans Robert Jauss, "Literary History as a Challenge to Literary Theory," from *Toward an Aesthetic of Reception* by Hans Robert Jauss, translated by Timothy Bahti, published by the University of Minnesota Press. Copyright © 1970 Suhrkamp Verlag; English translation copyright © 1982 by the University of Minnesota. Reprinted by permission of Suhrkamp Verlag, Frankfurt a.M. and the University of Minnesota Press.

Carl Gustav Jung, "On the Relation of Analytical Psychology to Poetry," from *The Collected Works of G. G. Jung,* translated by R. F. C. Hull, Bollingen Series XX, vol. 15,

The Spirit in Man, Art, and Literature, pp. 65–83. Copyright © 1966 Princeton University Press. Reprinted with permission of Princeton University Press. "The Principal Archetypes," from *The Collected Works of C. G. Jung*, translated by R. F. C. Hull, Bollingen Series XX, vol. 9, *Aion: Researches into the Phenomenology of the Self*, pp. 3–22. Copyright © 1959 by Princeton University Press. Reprinted with permission of Princeton University Press.

Immanuel Kant, excerpt from *Critique of Judgment*. Reprinted with permission of The Free Press, an imprint of Simon & Schuster, from *Critique of Judgment* by Immanuel Kant. Translated by J. H. Bernard. Copyright © 1951 by Hafner Press.

Annette Kolodny, "Dancing through the Minefield: Some Observations on the Theory, Practice, and Politics of a Feminist Literary Criticism." Copyright © 1979 by Annette Kolodny; all rights reserved. Reprinted by permission of the author.

Julia Kristeva, "Psychoanalysis and the Polis," translated by Margaret Waller, in *Critical Inquiry* 9 (1982): pp. 77–92. Copyright © 1982 by the University of Chicago. Reprinted by permission of the author and the University of Chicago Press.

Jacques Lacan, "The Agency of the Letter in the Unconscious or Reason Since Freud," from *Écrits: A Selection* by Jacques Lacan, translated by Alan Sheridan. Copyright © 1966 by Editions de Seuil. English translation copyright © 1977 by Tavistock Publications. Reprinted by permission of W. W. Norton & Company, Inc.

F. R. Leavis, excerpt from *The Great Tradition* by F. R. Leavis. Copyright © 1969 by F. R. Leavis. Reprinted by permission of New York University Press.

Claude Lévi-Strauss, "The Structural Study of Myth," pages 202–215, 226–228 from *Structural Anthropology, Volume I* by Claude Lévi-Strauss. English translation copyright © by Basic Books, Inc. Reprinted by permission of BasicBooks, a division of HarperCollins Publishers, Inc.

Georg Lukács, "The Ideology of Modernism," from *Realism in Our Time: Literature and the Class Struggle* by Georg Lukács, translated from the German by John and Necke Mander. Copyright © 1962 by Merlin Press Ltd. Introduction copyright © 1964 by George Steiner. Reprinted by permission of The Merlin Press, Ltd., and by permission of HarperCollins Publishers, Inc.

Karl Marx, "Consciousness Derived from Material Conditions," from *The German Ideology* by Karl Marx. Reprinted by permission of International Publishers Co., New York.

Deborah E. McDowell, "New Directions for Black Feminist Criticism," reprinted from *Black American Literature Forum* 14:4 (Winter 1980). Copyright © 1980 by Indiana State University. Reprinted by permission.

Laura Mulvey, "Visual Pleasure and Narrative Cinema," from *Screen* 16:3 (1975): pp. 6–18. Copyright © The Society for Education in Film and Television. Used by permission.

Friedrich Nietzsche, excerpt from *The Birth of Tragedy from the Spirit of Music*, translated by Francis Golffing, in *The Birth of Tragedy and The Genealogy of Morals* by Friedrich Nietzsche. Copyright © 1956 by Doubleday, a division of Bantam Doubleday Dell Publishing Group, Inc. Used by permission of Doubleday, a division of Bantam Doubleday Dell Publishing Group, Inc.

James Phelan, "Narrative as Rhetoric: Reading the Spells of Porter's 'Magic.'" From *Narrative as Rhetoric: Technique, Audiences, Ethics, Ideology* by James Phelan. Copyright © 1996 Ohio State University Press. Reprinted by permission of the publisher.

Christine de Pisan, "Response to Jean de Montreuil's Treatise on the *Roman de la Rose*." From *La Querelle de la Rose*, translated by Joseph L. Baird and John R. Kane. Published for the North Carolina Studies in the Romance Languages and Literatures (no. 199), 1973. Used by permission of the publisher.

Plato, *Ion*. Reprinted from *Plato: "Phaedrus," "Ion," "Georgias," and "Symposium," with passages from the "Republic" and "Laws,"* translated by Lane Cooper. Copyright © 1938 by Lane Cooper. Used by permission of the publisher, Cornell University Press.

Plotinus, "On the Intellectual Beauty," from *Plotinus: The Enneads*, edited by B. S. Page, translation by Stephen Mackenna. Published by Faber and Faber Ltd. Reprinted with permission of the publisher.

Katherine Anne Porter, "Magic" (in "Narrative as Rhetoric: Reading the Spells of Porter's 'Magic,'" by James Phelan). From *Flowering Judas and Other Stories* by Katherine Anne Porter. Copyright © 1930 and renewed 1958 by Katherine Anne Porter, reprinted by permission of Harcourt Brace & Company.

Peter Rabinowitz, "Who Is Reading?" and "Rules of Reading," pages 20–46 from *Before Reading: Narrative Conventions and the Politics of Interpretation* by Peter J. Rabinowitz. Copyright © 1986 by Peter J. Rabinowitz. Used by permission of the author.

Lillian S. Robinson, "Treason Our Text: Feminist Challenges to the Literary Canon," from *Tulsa Studies in Women's Literature*, Vol. 2, No. 1 (Spring 1983). Copyright © 1983 by the University of Tulsa. Reprinted by permission of the publisher.

Edward W. Said, Introduction to *Orientalism*. From *Orientalism* by Edward W. Said. Copyright © 1978 by Edward W. Said. Reprinted by permission of Pantheon Books, a division of Random House, Inc.

Jean Paul Sartre, "Why Write?" from *What Is Literature?* by Jean-Paul Sartre, translated by Bernard Frechtman. Reprinted by permission of The Philosophical Library, New York.

Ferdinand de Saussure, "Nature of the Linguistic Sign," pages 65–70 from *Course in General Linguistics* by Ferdinand de Saussure. Reprinted by permission of The Philosophical Library, New York.

Friedrich von Schiller, from "On Naïve and Sentimental Poetry," from *Two Essays by Friedrich von Schiller*, translated by Julius A. Elias. Copyright © 1966 by Frederick Ungar Publishing Company. Reprinted by permission of the publisher.

Eve Kosofsky Sedgwick, excerpt from *Epistemology of the Closet*, pages 48 to 54. Copyright © 1990 The Regents of the University of California. Reprinted by permission of the University of California Press.

Victor Shklovsky, "Art as Technique," reprinted from *Russian Formalist Criticism: Four Essays,* translated and with an introduction by Lee T. Lemon and Marion J. Reis by permission of the University of Nebraska Press. Copyright © 1965 by the University of Nebraska Press. Copyright © renewed 1993 by the University of Nebraska Press.

Elaine Showalter, "Toward a Feminist Poetics." From *The New Feminist Criticism,* edited by Elaine Showalter. Copyright © 1985 Elaine Showalter. Reprinted by permission of Pantheon Books, a division of Random House, Inc.

Barbara Smith, "Toward a Black Feminist Criticism." Originally published in *Conditions: Two,* Vol. 1, No. 2, 1977. Reprinted in *All the Women are White, All the Blacks Are Men, But Some of Us Are Brave,* edited by Gloria T. Hull, Patricia Bell Scott, and Barbara Smith. Copyright © 1982 Barbara Smith.

Barbara Herrnstein Smith, "Contingencies of Value," from *Critical Inquiry* 10 (1984): 1–31. Copyright © 1984 by the University of Chicago. Reprinted by permission of the author and the University of Chicago Press.

Susan Sontag, "Against Interpretation," from *A Susan Sontag Reader* by Susan Sontag. Copyright © 1963, 1964, 1966, 1967, 1968, 1969, 1973, 1974, 1975, 1977, 1978, 1980, 1982 by Susan Sontag. Reprinted by permission of Farrar, Straus and Giroux, Inc.

Germaine de Staël, "Essay on Fiction" and "On Women Writers," from *An Extraordinary Woman: Selected Writings of Germaine de Staël,* edited and translated by Vivian Folkenflik. Copyright © 1987 Columbia University Press. Reprinted by permission of the publisher.

Leo Tolstoy, Chapter 16 from *What Is Art?* by Leo Tolstoy, translated by Aylmer Maude (1930) by permission of Oxford University Press.

Lionel Trilling, "The Meaning of a Literary Idea," from *The Liberal Imagination* by Lionel Trilling. Reproduced by permission of the Estate of Lionel Trilling.

Yuri Tynyanov, "On Literary Evolution," from *Readings in Russian Poetics* (Michigan Slavic Contributions 8), edited and translated by Ladislaw Matejka and Krystyna Pomorska, published by MIT Press. Copyright © 1978. Reprinted by permission.

Michael Warner, "Homo-Narcissism; or, Heterosexuality," from *Engendering Men,* edited by Joseph Boone and Michael Cadden. Reprinted by permission of the author and Routledge (NY).

Hayden White, "The Politics of Historical Interpretation: Discipline and De-Sublimation." From *The Content of the Form: Narrative Discourse and Historical Representation,* pages 58–82. Copyright © 1987 The Johns Hopkins University Press. Used by permission of the author and The Johns Hopkins University Press.

Raymond Williams, excerpt from *Marxism and Literature.* Copyright © Oxford University Press 1977. Reprinted from *Marxism and Literature* by Raymond Williams (1977) by permission of Oxford University Press.

Edmund Wilson, "The Historical Interpretation of Literature," from *The Triple Thinkers* by Edmund Wilson. Copyright © 1938, 1948 by Edmund Wilson. Copyright renewed 1956, 1971 by Edmund Wilson and 1976 by Elena Wilson, executrix of the Estate of Edmund Wilson. Reprinted by permission of Farrar, Straus and Giroux, Inc.

W. K. Wimsatt and Monroe C. Beardsley, "The Intentional Fallacy," from *The Verbal Icon* by William K. Wimsatt and Monroe Beardsley. Copyright © 1954 by the University Press of Kentucky. Copyright renewed 1982 by Margaret H. Wimsatt. Reprinted by permission.

Virginia Woolf, "Shakespeare's Sister" and "Austen–Brontë–Eliot," from *A Room of One's Own* by Virginia Woolf. Copyright © 1929 by Harcourt Brace & Company and renewed 1957 by Leonard Woolf, reprinted by permission of the publisher.

Figure 3, page 11: Paul Hernadi, Map 4 from "Literary Theory: A Compass for Critics," from *Critical Inquiry* 3 (1976), p. 382. Copyright © 1976 by the University of Chicago. Reprinted by permission of the University of Chicago Press.

Index

Page numbers in bold type refer to the reprinted selections.

Kundera male author - female reader p926